A Practical Dictionary of

German Usage

A Practical Dictionary of

German Usage

K. B. Beaton

CLARENDON PRESS · OXFORD
1996

Oxford University Press, Walton Street, Oxford OX2 6DP

Oxford New York
Athens Auckland Bangkok Bombay
Calcutta Cape Town Dar es Salaam Delhi
Florence Hong Kong Istanbul Karachi
Kuala Lumpur Madras Madrid Melbourne
Mexico City Nairobi Paris Singapore
Taipei Tokyo Toronto
and associated companies in
Berlin Ibadan

Oxford is a trade mark of Oxford University Press

Published in the United States
by Oxford University Press Inc., New York

British Library Cataloguing in Publication Data
Data available

Library of Congress Cataloging-in-Publication Data
A practical dictionary of German usage / K.B. Beaton.
Includes bibliographical references.
1. German language—Usage—Dictionaries.   2. German language—
Idioms—Dictionaries.   3. German language—Dictionaries—English.
4. English language—Dictionaries—German.   I. Title.
PF3460.B35   1996   438'.003—dc20   95–40022
ISBN 0–19–824002–3

1 3 5 7 9 10 8 6 4 2

Printed in Great Britain
on acid-free paper by
St. Edmundsbury Press, Bury St. Edmunds

Publisher's Note

Sadly, Bruce Beaton died on 1 August 1994 just before putting the final touches to this book. The main text is reproduced exactly as he wrote it. At the time of his death he was revising his Preface and Introduction in response to advice from readers appointed by the Press. Some of the readers' suggestions have been incorporated by the Press in the versions that appear here.

Preface

GERMAN vocabulary presents considerable difficulties to English speakers who have progressed beyond the initial stages of learning the language. In a brief introduction to a chapter in his book that elucidates some of the most confusing cases in which an English word covers a wider area than any single German equivalent, Martin Durrell points out that more than two-thirds of errors made by advanced English-speaking learners of German involve matters of vocabulary (1992: 41). He attributes the underlying difficulty to the fact that each language divides up things, ideas, events, and so on from a different viewpoint. As a result there are few one-to-one correspondences between English and German items of vocabulary. Learning German, or any other foreign language for that matter, therefore involves learning to break out of the framework and structure of meaning characteristic of English and acquiring the knowledge to operate in the framework peculiar to the second language. Durrell also explains that there are no rules because we are dealing with individual words, each of which has to be taken on its own terms. Farrell's (1953) *A Dictionary of German Synonyms*, and Eggeling's (1961) *Dictionary of Modern German Prose Usage* were both written to address this problem. Although many of the examples in Eggeling's text were already fifty or more years old in 1961, his information is by and large more accurate than Farrell's. But despite its weaknesses Farrell's book has been a useful guide for many students including the writer, and he deserves the credit due to a pioneer in the field of comparative German–English lexicography. What is presented in the following pages began as an attempt to work through the material covered in these two books. This task was carried out without any sense of obligation to either of the authors, and I have dealt with every word in the way I thought appropriate. This has led to a new text which owes to its predecessors little more than the selection of words treated. The German equivalents are, inevitably, in many cases the same, but the explanations have been completely rewritten, and additional equivalents suggested. Less significant words have been omitted partly in favour of a fuller treatment of ones considered important, partly to add new ones which seem to be of greater use. The illustrative examples are new.

Although working in the written and spoken language, not reproduction of English texts in German, may now be the main teaching method, an explanatory dictionary such as this one still has much to offer. Even at a relatively early stage learners come across cases in which two, three, or more German words correspond to one English one. The more German they hear and read, the more frequently this will happen and the greater the likelihood that they will seek an explanation. It could be argued that what one needs to know to master these difficulties is to be found in a conventional bilingual dictionary. The information the latest dictionaries offer is certainly not incorrect, but it is very brief, and most provide little guidance on how to use the equivalents that they list. What is given here is a much more detailed explanation of a limited number of points designed to meet the special difficulties of English speakers. These difficulties are often so complex that only a thorough study of the use of several related words will enable the learner to find the correct German expression.

Monolingual German dictionaries may also be seen as a solution to the problems of English-speaking learners, but a monolingual dictionary seldom gives the basic information the non-native speaker requires. Information that is so obvious to the native speaker that it need not be mentioned is often precisely the kind of information that the learner needs. Thus considerable experience with the language is necessary before monolingual dictionaries can be used effectively. Words are often defined in terms of synonyms, without the relation between them being explained. It is often assumed that the constructions and contexts in which words can occur are known. If a monolingual dictionary gives a number of examples, the native speaker knows immediately which are unusual and which are not. One of the aims of the present work is to supply the information which is not needed by the native speaker but is essential for learners who speak another language.

Whether a student translates into German or only writes and speaks it, English word usage is likely to intrude into his or her German. To overcome this at least in part, some understanding of how English works is necessary. One well-known source of difficulty is the large number of meanings certain English words have. Irrespective of the method by which they are taught, learners must understand what the consequences are for their acquisition of another language. One difference in method between this and the earlier books is the attempt to make the English meaning as clear as possible, often by giving examples as well as a definition. (Farrell gave more definitions in the new articles in his second edition than in the original text.) Words are also often distinguished purely in terms of syntax and context where Farrell, for example, sought differences in meaning. Besides this, many articles include advice about the syntactic patterns in which the words occur.

Among the reference works I have consulted, special mention is due to Klappenbach and Steinitz, *Wörterbuch der deutschen Gegenwartssprache* (1964–77), and to Duden: *Das große Wörterbuch der deutschen Sprache* (1976–81), to both of which I owe numerous examples and much information. I have also used the *Oxford–Harrap Standard German Dictionary* extensively, particularly for English translations. For the English definitions I have used the *OED* and *Webster* throughout. Some definitions are also taken from the *Oxford Advanced Learners' Dictionary of Current English*. When about half-way through the text I came across the *Collins Cobuild Dictionary* and have drawn on it for some of the later articles. A number of the German sentences are translations of examples in these dictionaries and in Friedrich and Canavan's (1979) *Dictionary of English Words in Context*. In his 'German Synonyms: A Bibliography' (1989), W. A. Benware lists numerous contributions in German popular language periodicals. These led me to information in *Sprachdienst* (Gesellschaft für deutsche Sprache, Wiesbaden) and *Sprachpflege: Zeitschrift für gutes Deutsch* (Leipzig), which I have incorporated in some articles.

Such a project as this would not have been possible without considerable help from a number of sources. I am grateful for the generous support of the Research Grants Committee of the University of Sydney, which has enabled me to pursue this work over a period of several years, for assistance from the DAAD during sojourns in Germany, and to my two referees Len McGlashan (formerly Macquarie University, Sydney) and the late Leslie Seiffert (Oxford). The greater part of the work has been done with a group of Göttingen students, partly while I was there, partly by mail from Australia. In discussions with Regina Bank (Göttingen), Thomas Grüneklee (Göttingen), Erika Wagner (Göttingen), Uwe Isreal (Homburg/Saar), Manfred Kaluza (Göttingen), Tanya Kuchenbecker (Lüneburg), Birgit Südbeck (Cloppenburg), Alexandra Rehfeld (Göttingen), and Jan Schnittker (Göttingen) I have worked out a large number of examples and explanations. Friends in Germany have helped considerably. I should like to thank Karl-Ludwig and Elisabeth Barkhausen (Soltau), Till Büthe (Hanover), Fritz Dette (Göttingen), Peter and Sabine Marburger (Trier), August Ohage (Göttingen), and Udo and Roswitha Waßmann (Hanover). On several occasions Alois Allkemper, Stefan Greif, and Brigitte Weber (all of Paderborn) gave me advice. I am indebted to my colleague Gero von Wilpert (Sydney) for sustained assistance. Udo Borgert (Sydney) was always ready to answer questions. Manfred Pienemann (Sydney) cleared up a few difficulties when the opinions of other informants conflicted. Helen Simic (Sydney) often told me whether a German version of an English sentence was idiomatic or not. I also received help from Elmar Wolters, Ulrich Ammon (Duisburg), and Eva Wagner (Oxford) while they were in Sydney. With Michael Nelson and Brian Taylor (both Sydney) and the late John Fletcher I have discussed the meanings of English words. Bruce Bolin and Mandy Hume helped with English examples. Jan Gibson-Egert typed the manuscript on to disks.

Contents

Abbreviations

acc.	accusative
act.	active
adj., adjs.	adjective, adjectives
adv., advs.	adverb, adverbs
AV	Authorized or King James Version of the Bible of 1611
cf.	*confer*, compare
conj., conjs.	conjunction, conjunctions
constr., constrs.	construction, constructions
dat.	dative
E.	English
etw.	*etwas*
exp., exps.	expression, expressions
fig.	figurative, figuratively
G.	German
gen.	genitive
imp.	imperative
infin., infins.	infinitive, infinitives
insep.	inseparable
intr.	intransitive
jmd.	*jemand*
jmdm.	*jemandem*
jmdn.	*jemanden*
jmds.	*jemandes*
lang., langs.	language, languages
lit.	literal, literally
n., ns.	noun, nouns
neg.	negative
obj., objs.	(grammatical) object, objects
OED	*Oxford English Dictionary*
part., parts.	participle, participles
pass.	passive
perf.	perfect
pers.	person or persons
phr., phrs.	phrase, phrases
pl.	plural
pos.	positive
prep., preps.	preposition, prepositions
pres.	present
refl.	reflexive
sent., sents.	sentence, sentences
sing.	singular
s.o.	someone
sth.	something
subj.	subject
syn., syns.	synonym, synonyms
thg., thgs.	thing, things

trans.	transitive
transl., transls.	translation, translations
v., vs.	verb, verbs

Words enclosed in round brackets (. . .) give additional information.

Words enclosed in square brackets [. . .] are optional. The sentence is correct and makes good sense if they are omitted.

Underlined words or syllables are stressed.

Words in SMALL CAPITALS indicate cross-references to headwords in this dictionary.

Introduction

Advice to the User

Tʜɪs dictionary has two main aims, both of which are directed to helping English speakers who are learning German to master the use of certain important German words. If you look up one of the common simple English words like *cover* in an English–German dictionary, you will find a host of equivalents, each usually indicated by a separate number. How does this bewildering complexity come about? The first thing to realize is that common English words tend to have several meanings. We use them so frequently and are so familiar with what they mean in different contexts that we often overlook this fact. The first step towards finding the appropriate German equivalent of an English word is to ask which meaning of the English word you are dealing with in a particular instance. Different German words translate *cover* in the following sentences. *The mother covered the child with a blanket, The valley was covered in snow, We covered twenty miles a day, Are the goods covered for loss through fire? The price we got only just covers our costs.* To take another example: In *The baby put out its hand and touched the balloon* and *We put out the fire*, *put out* clearly has different meanings. In the first it is a synonym of *stretch out*, in the second of *extinguish*. If you look up *put out* in a bilingual dictionary and get the wrong word, you might end up saying that the baby extinguished its hand. *Put out* has other meanings, for example 'to issue' (*Someone put out a scare story*), 'to move out of a place or one's house' (*Have you put out the rubbish?*), and 'to upset' (*He looked put out when the audience began to laugh*). There is likely to be a different German word for each of these meanings. Many mistakes in the use of German vocabulary by English speakers arise because a German word which corresponds to one meaning of a particular English word is simply transferred to another meaning of the same English word.

One of the principal aims of this dictionary, therefore, is to make the various meanings of the English words clear before the German equivalents are discussed. The meanings are defined and are often illustrated with examples. Longer articles have introductions in which arabic numbers correspond to the main section numbers of the article (see e.g. ᴀᴠᴏɪᴅ). In the articles that follow, each of the different English meanings is the subject of a section headed by an arabic number. Each meaning of the English word may be connected to several German synonyms, and in such cases the main sections are further subdivided by the use of roman numerals. As roman numerals in introductions to articles do not correspond to these German synonym subsections, they are distinguished by being placed in parentheses (see e.g. ᴀᴘᴘʀᴇᴄɪᴀᴛᴇ).

While the understanding of the precise meaning of an English word is an important step towards finding the appropriate German expression, it is not the only one. When a bilingual dictionary gives the equivalents of a particular meaning of an English word, it often lists more than one word. These words are likely to be synonyms to a greater or lesser degree, and the other main task of the present work is to explain the use of such synonyms or near-synonyms. If you look at the article on ᴄʜᴀɴɢᴇ, you will find that four German verbs, *ändern, wechseln, wandeln* (mostly in the forms with the prefixes *um-* and *ver-*), and *tauschen*, express the four basic meanings which are listed in a monolingual English dictionary. These

are 'to make or become different', 'to substitute one thing for another', 'to transform or convert into something else', and 'to give and receive reciprocally, to
exchange'. Closely connected with *ändern* are its derivatives *verändern* and *umändern*, with *wechseln* its derivative *auswechseln*, with *wandeln* its derivatives *umwandeln* and *verwandeln*, and with *tauschen* its derivatives *vertauschen, umtauschen,* and
austauschen. The English equivalents of these are often, though not always, *change*.
The words in this and every group of synonyms relate to one another in a way
that is peculiar to German. Similarly, as synonyms of *change* in the sense of *ändern*
English has *alter* and *modify*, and in the sense of *wandeln* it has *convert* and *transform*, but again the way in which these resemble each other and differ from each
other is peculiar to English, and it may or may not correspond to the distinctions
drawn in German. (Synonyms in German are not always prefixed forms of a base
verb but often completely different verbs, like *fallen* and *stürzen*, which are discussed under FALL.) Related groups of synonyms in English or German may or may
not contain the same number of words, and distinctions made in the one language may or may not be made in the other.

Synonyms may relate to each other in a number of ways. The relationship may
be semantic in that they express variations on a single underlying idea, as in the
way English *hurl* and *fling* vary the meaning of *throw*. Another possible distinction
is that of context. *Anordnen* and *anweisen* express one meaning of *to order*, but
while *anweisen* takes a person as an object, *anordnen* needs a non-personal object
such as an action. Thus *Der Richter ordnete die Räumung des Saales an*, but *Er wies die
Anwesenden an, den Saal zu verlassen*. Differences between synonyms may be purely
syntactic, in that the meaning of two words may be the same, but each is appropriate for particular grammatical constructions. You may say *Man hinderte die Leute
am Abflug* or *Man hinderte die daran, abzufliegen*, but when *der Abflug* is the object it
is necessary to use *verhindern*, as in *Die Behörden verhinderten den Abflug vieler Leute,
die das Land verlassen wollten*. The meaning of *hindern an* and *verhindern* is the same.
They simply require different constructions.

The words in a set of synonyms may also be differentiated stylistically. For
example, English *chuck* is a colloquial variant on *throw*. By contrast, when used as
a synonym of *throw*, as in *He was cast into prison* or *She cast the stone into the water*,
cast is somewhat old-fashioned, only found in formal or perhaps literary language.
In certain contexts such as *to cast a shadow* or *to cast a glance* it is, however, still the
standard expression. The present dictionary concentrates on what is called the
neutral or unmarked level of style. Above the neutral level is the formal level on
which, for instance, *request* is used instead of *ask* and *inform* instead of *tell*. This is
appropriate for reports, essays, business letters or for formal situations such as a
meeting or a speech, though some speakers may use it in other situations as well.
It should not be assumed that because there is a specifically formal or colloquial
variant in the one language there will necessarily be one in the other. Above the
formal level in German there is one that German dictionaries call *gehoben* ('elevated'). It consists to a large extent of usages which, as they drop out of general
use, take on a poetical or high-sounding aura. In a speech, the former German
President Richard von Weizsäcker once said, '*Das können und wollen wir nicht hindern*.' As the normal verb with a non-personal object is now *verhindern*, most native
speakers find this unusual. Although not all elevated terms are as uncommon as
this, non-native speakers should nevertheless be wary of them. In the articles in
this dictionary colloquial words and phrases are often suggested; for example,
under ANGRY you will find *Ich bin sauer auf ihn*. Anyone who goes to Germany will
hear such expressions. Whether the learner uses them or not is a matter of

choice, as it is with colloquialisms in English. They should not, of course, be used when the situation calls for more formal style.

This dictionary concentrates on common words which cause difficulties for English speakers. The articles are longer than the corresponding ones in a bilingual dictionary, but the number of words treated is much more limited. Some articles discuss only a few meanings of an English word, many cover all the important meanings, but even these are not exhaustive. If you understand what a particular article has to say, you will easily find your way through the corresponding entry in a bilingual dictionary and quickly locate any senses not dealt with here.

This book, therefore, gives you, the learner, a method of approaching English words, together with a set of German words which express the same concepts. The differences between the two languages arise because each divides up the field of meaning in its own way. Mastering German vocabulary may seem like a laborious process of picking out the appropriate equivalent to an English word. For anyone who learns a language other than by continuous contact with its speakers, this is probably an unavoidable stage in its acquisition. But with practice learning quickly becomes less difficult. You begin to become accustomed to the way in which German structures and organizes meaning, and this book will help you in that learning process in a way that no bilingual dictionary can. The ultimate aim, then, is to enable you to use and understand German without reference to English.

accept *v.*

1. The first meaning of **accept** is 'to take or receive sth. when offered'. The obj. can be something tangible, a gift, money, etc., a job, a scholarship, a position, help, an invitation, or something intangible like hospitality.

i. Annehmen is the usual equivalent. The obj. can be something concrete like *ein Geschenk, etw. zu essen oder zu trinken, ein Trinkgeld, Bezahlung, eine Stelle* or something less tangible like *ein Angebot, eine Einladung, jmds. Hilfe*, etc. The obj. can also be a means of payment such as *ein Scheck* or *eine Kreditkarte*. The E. and G. vs. are also used without an obj. *He has accepted* becomes *Er hat angenommen*.

Als man ihr ein Stipendium anbot, hat sie es sofort angenommen.
Das Geschenk wurde dankend angenommen.   *Die meisten Geschäfte nehmen Kreditkarten an.*
Erst der vierte Verlag, dem er das Manuskript anbot, hat es angenommen.
Wir haben sie eingeladen, und sie haben sofort angenommen.
Alle Hotels nehmen einen Scheck an, wenn man eine Scheckkarte hat.

ii. Accept and RECEIVE are interchangeable in some contexts. *Applications will be accepted/received until 31 October.* The equivalent is **entgegennehmen**, a partial syn. of *annehmen*. *Entgegennehmen* needs an obj. In one use it occurs with ns. such as *eine Postsendung* or *ein Brief* which in everyday language are found with *annehmen*. In such a context the only difference is that *entgegennehmen* is more formal. It is sometimes met with in official, legal, and commercial language. The second use arises from the fact that as *entgegennehmen* does not imply willingness to follow a suggestion, advice, etc., it does not express sense 2 of **accept**. Because *annehmen* means 'to accept' in both sense 1 and sense 2, *entgegennehmen* is used to avoid ambiguity. *Der Lehrer nahm den Vorschlag der Schüler entgegen*, 'he received/was given it'; *er nahm ihren Vorschlag an*, 'he accepted their suggestion', i.e. 'was ready to follow it'. An organization which calls for tenders or bids *nimmt Angebote entgegen*, receives or accepts them up to a certain time, but eventually *nimmt das Angebot einer Firma an*, accepts one firm's tender/bid and awards it the contract.

Zweckdienliche Auskunft (z. B. über ein Verbrechen) nimmt jede Polizeidienststelle entgegen.
Auf der Messe finden Sie in unserem Ausstellungstand Mitarbeiter der Firma, die jederzeit bereit sind, Bestellungen entgegenzunehmen.
Die Bank nimmt Bewerbungen bis zum 31. Oktober entgegen.
Nimmt ein Beamter Zuwendungen entgegen, um dafür von seinem Dienstwege abzuweichen, liegt ein besonders schweres Dienstvergehen vor.
Die Frau des Preisträgers nahm den Preis für ihn entgegen. (At the ceremony it was handed over to her. *Er nahm den Preis an*, said he was willing to be awarded it.)
Der Jubilar nahm die Glückwünsche freudig entgegen.

2. Accept also means 'to agree to and act upon' a suggestion, plan, proposal, etc.

i. Annehmen is used with objs. like *ein Vorschlag, ein Heiratsantrag, eine Bedingung, eine Forderung, die Wahl zum Vorsitzenden*, etc., and *der Antrag*, 'motion' (at a meeting), so that it also translates *carry* or *pass* in such a context. *Jmds./Diesen Rat annehmen* means 'to accept, take, or follow s.o.'s/this advice'.

Die Gewerkschaft hat schließlich die von den Unternehmern gestellten Bedingungen angenommen.
Er bat sie, ihn zu heiraten, und sie nahm seinen Antrag an.

ii. Besides meaning 'to go into' a question, details, etc., **eingehen auf** means 'to accept' with some objs. such as *eine Bedingung, eine Forderung, ein Kompromiß, ein Vergleich,* 'legal settlement', or *eine Bitte.*

Obwohl es zuerst so aussah, als wollte er die von ihm vorgeschlagene Lösung um jeden Preis durch-setzen, ist er dennoch auf unseren Plan eingegangen.
Um einen Streik zu vermeiden, ging der Unternehmer auf die Forderung der Gewerkschaft ein.
Der Kläger wollte auf keinen Vergleich eingehen.

3. With an obj. which denotes something disadvantageous, such as *bad working conditions, one's lot, the inevitable,* **accept** means 'to take with patience or resigna-tion, to put up with or endure without complaint' and is translated by **hin-nehmen**. Cf. TAKE 5. vi.

Er nahm sein Schicksal, so schwer es auch war, gelassen hin.
Die Arbeiter sind nicht bereit, Lohnkürzungen hinzunehmen.
Obwohl der Schüler heftig protestierte, mußte er die für ihn schlechte Note hinnehmen.
Obwohl man sie schlecht behandelte, hat sie alles ohne Klage hingenommen.
Die Partei mußte in diesem Wahlkreis eine vollkommene Niederlage hinnehmen.
Diese Beleidigung kann ich einfach nicht hinnehmen.

Hinnehmen is also used with a *daß*-clause, usually preceded by *es. Da er keine kon-struktiven Verbesserungsvorschläge machen konnte, mußte er [es] hinnehmen, daß man seine Kritik abwies.*

Wir können oder wollen [es] nicht hinnehmen, daß so mit Menschen umgegangen wird.

4. In a sent. like *I accept responsibility for [the] carrying out [of] the plan,* **accept** means 'to take an obligation or work upon oneself with the awareness of the conse-quences'.

i. This meaning is expressed by **übernehmen**. Whereas *annehmen* means little more than 'to say yes', *übernehmen* implies that one is ready to take on or take upon oneself the work a task entails or the burden it involves. It is used with ns. such as *die Verantwortung, die Haftung, die Garantie, eine Arbeit, eine Aufgabe, die Verteidigung eines Angeklagten, eine Rolle (in einem Stück), die Betreuung der Kinder, Schulden, die Kosten für etw.,* etc. (The E. equivalent is not always **accept**.) Cf. TAKE 5. viii.

Nur widerstrebend übernahm sie die Rolle der Vermittlerin zwischen den Interessengruppen.
Man bot dem Künstler zwar viel Geld an, aber er hat den Auftrag doch nicht übernommen.

Übernehmen also takes an infin. and *es. Würden Sie es übernehmen, die Eintrittskarten zu besorgen?*

ii. While *übernehmen* is neutral, **auf sich nehmen** has a negative tone, as it stresses the onerous nature of what one takes on. With this difference in implication it is combined with some of the same ns. as *übernehmen* and, like it, is often translated by words other than **accept**, such as *to take upon oneself*. Sometimes it occurs in a context which stresses that a burdensome task is accepted voluntarily.

Man nimmt Gefahren/Opfer/Entbehrungen/Schwierigkeiten/eine Arbeit/eine Aufgabe/die Folgen einer Handlung [bereitwillig] auf sich.
Die große Mehrheit der Bevölkerung scheint bereit zu sein, zur Sicherung unserer wirtschaftlichen Zukunft Einschränkungen auf sich zu nehmen.
Aus reinem Idealismus hat er diese schwere Aufgabe auf sich genommen.
Sie nahm die Schuld an dem Verkehrsunfall auf sich.
Er nahm die Schuld daran, daß er an der Universität versagt hatte, voll und ganz auf sich.

With *Verantwortung* as obj., *übernehmen* would be the appropriate v. for accepting responsibility when something is planned, i.e. beforehand, *Er übernahm die Verantwortung für die Durchführung des Projekts,* and *auf sich nehmen* for taking the blame for failures and mistakes while something is being carried out, *Er nimmt die Verantwortung für den Mißerfolg auf sich.* The distinction is, however, not always observed, and the two vs. are found in both circumstances. Either could be used in the above sents.

5. In contexts such as *to accept refugees* or *an applicant (for membership)* or *The children readily accepted their new classmate*, **accept** means 'to receive people into a group, country, organization, etc.'

i. The general equivalent is **aufnehmen**, which may be followed by *in*.
Mehrere europäische Länder haben vietnamesische Flüchtlinge aufgenommen.
Wir haben alle drei Bewerber als Mitglieder in den Verein/in die Partei aufgenommen.

ii. When, however, no more than a vague general tolerance or treatment as equals by a group or society is meant, only **akzeptieren** is used.
Die Schüler haben den neuen Klassenkameraden akzeptiert. Alternative: *. . . haben ihn/sie wohlwollend in ihren Kreis aufgenommen.*   *Solche Minderheiten sind jetzt akzeptiert.*

6. In the sense 'to recognize as true', as in *I accept this argument/this criticism*, **accept** corresponds to **gelten lassen**. This may imply that what was done or said, although not perfect, can be allowed to pass.
Der Quizmaster sagte: 'Diese Antwort entspricht nicht genau dem, was ich hier als richtige Antwort habe, aber wir können sie doch gelten lassen.'
Similarly if someone said, *'Ich lasse diese Entschuldigung gelten'*, he/she would be prepared to accept the excuse given, though not fully convinced of its validity. Otherwise it would be usual to say, *'Ich nehme diese Entschuldigung an.'* However, with words as obj. like *ein Argument, eine Theorie, ein Grund, eine Meinung, ein Vorwurf, Kritik*, etc., *gelten lassen* means 'to recognize as true or valid'.
Sogar seine besten Freunde wollten die Gründe nicht gelten lassen, mit denen Friedrich ihnen seine Ablehnung der angebotenen Stelle erklärte.
Ich kann dieses Argument nicht gelten lassen.   *Ich lasse diesen Einwand gelten.*

7. Anerkennen sometimes means 'accept', particularly *einen Grundsatz/ein Prinzip anerkennen*, to acknowledge a principle. Cf. REALIZE. The idea that a theory, innovation, new method, explanation, etc. is accepted, in the sense that it is adopted or believed by most people, is expressed by **sich durchsetzen**.
Es wird wohl lange dauern, bis sich diese Neuerung [allgemein] durchsetzt.
Diese Theorie, die jetzt als richtig gilt, hat sich erst allmählich durchgesetzt.
The meaning of the past part. *accepted* in *an accepted opinion/custom/theory*, etc. is expressed by **geltend**, considered as true, prevailing. *Diese Auffassung stimmt mit den geltenden Meinungen/Ansichten überein.*

8. Akzeptieren has spread from commercial and legal language without, however, displacing any of the vs. of G. origin. It can be used in senses 1 and 2, instead of *hinnehmen* (sense 3) but usually qualified, *Sie akzeptierten notgedrungen/widerstrebend/unter Druck, daß unter den Umständen nichts mehr unternommen werden konnte*, as described in 5, and in place of *gelten lassen* (sense 6).
Glaubst du, daß sie unser Angebot/meinen Vorschlag/diese Bedingung akzeptieren werden?
Dieses Argument erscheint mir nicht stichhaltig. Ich kann es nicht akzeptieren/gelten lassen.

accident, mishap, disaster *ns.*

1. In the sense 'an unforeseen event which causes damage, injury, or death', **accident** covers a broad range of consequences. The result can be slight or serious damage or minor or major injury as well as death. A **mishap** is 'a slight accident', and a **disaster** in one sense is 'a severe or terrible accident', e.g. *a mine disaster*.

i. The most common and broadest term is **der Unfall**, which extends from accidents involving minor damage to ones causing injuries or death, but it is not as broad as **accident**.

Der Unfall ging noch glimpflich mit Blechschäden ab.

Zwei Arbeiter wurden in einem Betriebsunfall verletzt.

Ein Reiter hatte einen Unfall. Er ist vom Pferd gefallen und hat sich den Arm gebrochen.

Vorige Woche ereigneten sich auf den vereisten Straßen mehrere Unfälle, darunter einer mit tödlichem Ausgang. Wir sind gegen Unfälle versichert.

Wir wurden in einen Unfall verwickelt, sind aber ohne Verletzungen davongekommen.

ii. Das Malheur and **das Mißgeschick**, which differ only in that *Malheur* is colloquial and *Mißgeschick* stylistically higher, are applied to a **mishap** or piece of bad luck which results in no serious damage and causes at the most embarrassment or disappointment.

Mir ist ein Malheur passiert. Ich habe das Buch ausgeliehen, und nun habe ich Kaffee darüber geschüttet.

Mir ist ein Mißgeschick passiert. Ich habe die Teekanne von meinem neuen Service fallengelassen.

Das Malheur bestand darin, daß ihr nicht nur eine Flasche Cola aus den Händen gerutscht und am Boden zerbrochen war, sondern daß sie sich beim Aufsammeln der Scherben auch noch in die Hand geschnitten hatte.

iii. Das Unglück denotes an accident caused either by human error or by natural forces. It is of greater proportions than *ein Unfall* and usually, though not always, involves loss of life.

Ein Flugzeugunglück hat mehrere Todesopfer gefordert.

Gestern ist in einem russischen Bergwerk ein schweres Unglück geschehen.

Bei dem Eisenbahnunglück gab es mehr als hundert zum Teil schwer Verletzte.

(*Unglück* also means 'distress or misery'. *Der Krieg hat das Land ins Unglück gestürzt. Der Preissturz brachte Unglück über das kleine Land.* Another sense is 'bad luck, ill fortune'. *Ich hatte das Unglück, meine Fahrkarte zu verlieren. Eine schwarze Katze bedeutet Unglück.*)

iv. Die Katastrophe describes major disasters in nature and in the economic and political spheres.

Der Verlust dieses Marktes war für das kleine Land eine wirtschaftliche Katastrophe.

Voriges Jahr ereignete sich wieder ein Erdbeben, und wie die früheren Naturkatastrophen verwüstete es einen Teil des Landes.

Katastrophe is also often used colloquially to denote something bad or chaotic. *Die Organisation in diesem Betrieb ist eine Katastrophe! Nichts klappt*, it is an absolute disaster.

v. Das Unheil means 'deep distress', 'a calamitous situation', a sense *das Unglück* can also have. *Unheil* is vaguer and stronger than the more precise *Unglück* and refers to the consequences of an event or of a person's actions which inflict suffering or hardship on one or many people.

Er brachte großes Unheil über die Familie, und am Ende war sie vollkommen ruiniert.

Die Wahrsagerin prophezeite, daß großes Unheil über sie hereinbrechen würde.

Jahrelang hatten die Menschen in dieser Region alle Wälder abgeholzt und weder die Warnungen der Experten noch die bereits erkennbaren Vorzeichen einer herannahenden Katastrophe beachtet. Nun brach das Unheil über sie herein. Die Ernte fiel schlecht aus, da die Erosion den Boden abgetragen hatte, und es kam zu einer Hungerkatastrophe.

2. i. The idea that a decision, action, etc. is a disaster or disastrous for s.o./sth., i.e. it has extremely bad consequences, can be expressed by **verhängnisvoll**. Cf. FATAL.

Die Wahl dieses Vorsitzenden war für die Partei verhängnisvoll.

ii. Disaster = 'a complete failure', as in *The new production (of the play) was a disaster,* can be expressed in several ways. **Der Mißerfolg** and **der Fehlschlag** mean 'failure'. *Die Neuinszenierung des Stückes war ein vollkommener Mißerfolg oder ein*

Fehlschlag in jeder Beziehung; also sometimes **ein Desaster** or colloquially **eine Katastrophe.**

3. Accident also means 'chance'. *We met by accident.* **Der Zufall** expresses this sense. **Durch Zufall** means 'by chance'. **Zufällig**, 'accidental, happening by chance', can express the meaning of *durch Zufall.*

> *Das habe ich durch Zufall erfahren. Also Das habe ich zufällig erfahren.*
> *Das Bild kam mir durch Zufall wieder in die Hände.*
> *Es war reiner Zufall, daß ich hier vorbeigekommen bin.*

The usual way of translating *It was an accident (that I kicked him)* meaning 'I did not do it deliberately/on purpose' is to express the meaning. *Das habe ich* **nicht mit Absicht/nicht absichtlich/ohne Absicht** *gemacht/getan* or *Das ist* **aus Versehen** *passiert.* For *Versehen* cf. MISTAKE.

> *Der Junge beteuerte immer wieder, seinen Mitspieler aus Versehen und völlig ohne böse Absicht getreten zu haben.   Glaub mir doch! Es war ein Versehen und keine Absicht.*

accuse, charge (with an offence) *vs.*

1. Legal uses. **Charge** someone with [having committed] an offence means 'to institute a criminal prosecution against a person believed to have committed a crime'. **Accuse** is a syn. *S.o. is accused of stealing/murder,* etc. The legal term meaning 'to charge or accuse' is **anklagen**. *Die Staatsanwaltschaft klagt jmdn. an* or *erhebt Anklage gegen jmdn.* Hence *der Angeklagte.* Although **beschuldigen, anlasten, zur Last legen,** and **vorwerfen** all imply laying blame on someone for a wrong or bad action rather than a formal charge (cf. 2), they are used as syns. of *anklagen,* and are all translated as **accuse** in such contexts. (In legal usage *beschuldigen* has a special meaning. Someone suspected of theft *wird des Diebstahls verdächtigt.* If the evidence seems conclusive, he/she is called *der/die Beschuldigte* and only when charged *der/die Angeklagte.*) *Anklagen* and *beschuldigen* are used with a n. in the gen. stating the crime, *anlasten, zur Last legen,* and *vorwerfen* with an acc.; all can be used with an infin., and all except *anklagen* occur with a *daß*-clause. *Anklagen* also takes *wegen* + a crime. The past parts. of *anklagen* and *beschuldigen* can only be applied to a person. *Der des Diebstahls angeklagte/beschuldigte Arbeiter leugnete seine Schuld.* The past parts. of the other vs. describe a crime. *Er leugnete den ihm angelasteten/zur Last gelegten/vorgeworfenen Diebstahl.* (This must be a clause in E., e.g. *the theft of which he was accused.*)

> *Die Spione wurden des Hochverrats angeklagt.   Er wurde wegen Diebstahls angeklagt.*
> *Er wurde angeklagt, einen Mord begangen zu haben.*
> *Diesem Mitarbeiter hat man Betrug vorgeworfen. Or Man hat diesen Mitarbeiter des Betrugs beschuldigt.   Er wurde beschuldigt, eine falsche Aussage gemacht zu haben.*
> *Man hat sie beschuldigt, daß sie dem Täter bei der Flucht geholfen hätte.*
> *Dem Mechaniker wurde zur Last gelegt, er habe sich vom Materiallager einen Elektromotor angeeignet.*
> *Ihm wurde ein Verbrechen angelastet, das er nicht begangen hatte.*

2. Non-legal uses. **Accuse** is used in non-legal situations when one person attributes to another qualities or actions regarded as wrong or undesirable. *She accused me of lying. He was accused of incompetence.* The sense is often 'to criticize'. *The French accuse the English of being extremely reserved.* **Charge** also means 'to assert as an accusation or criticism'. *Critics charge that video-games are violent, sexist, and racist.* **Beschuldigen** is the most common equivalent of **accuse** in a non-legal situation when one person ascribes guilt or blame to another for (alleged) wrongdoing or unacceptable behaviour. In this sense a clause or infin. mostly states what the person is accused of, although a gen. is possible. *Sie beschuldigte mich, gelogen zu haben,* or *Sie beschuldigte mich, ich hätte sie belogen. Beschuldigen* is also used without the accusation being specified. *Alle beschuldigen mich* or *Sie haben mich fälschlich beschuldigt.* **Anschuldigen** has the same meaning but is fairly uncommon. However, the n. *die Anschuldigung* occurs frequently but does not differ in sense from *die Beschuldigung.* **Bezichtigen** is found only in elevated language. **Anlasten** and **zur Last legen** mean either 'to accuse of' or 'to blame or criticize for'. Both take the person accused in the dat. and an obj. or clause. *Man legt mir diese Versäumnisse zur Last. Mir können Sie nicht anlasten, daß die Firma diesen Auftrag verloren hat.* **Anklagen** is also possible in non-legal contexts but has a dramatic tone, and in a sent. like *Der Roman klagt die Urheber der sozialen Mißstände an, anklagt* could be translated as *indicts* or *attacks.* **Vorwerfen**, which can translate *to reproach*, is an appropriate equivalent particularly when **accuse** means 'to criticize'. *Die Franzosen werfen den Engländern vor, sie seien äußerst zugeknöpft. Man hat ihm/Ihm wurde Unfähigkeit vorgeworfen.* All these vs. need a personal obj. The sent. *Critics charge that video-games . . .* could become *Man kritisiert an den Videospielen, daß sie viele gewalttätige Handlungen zeigen und rassistischen und sexistischen Einstellungen Vorschub leisten.* Cf. BLAME 5. ii.

> *Die Opposition beschuldigte den Minister, Aufträge an seine Freunde vergeben zu haben.*
> *Der Junge beschuldigte seinen Kameraden, daß er ihm den Ball weggenommen hätte.*
> *Weil ihr jüngerer Bruder mit dem Fahrrad hingefallen war, beschuldigte die Mutter die Tochter, nicht richtig auf ihn aufgepaßt zu haben.*
> *Die Nachbarn bezichtigten/beschuldigten den Vater, seine Kinder wiederholt brutal geschlagen zu haben.*
> *Die Anschuldigungen, die gegen mich erhoben worden sind, sind vollkommen grundlos.*
> *Die Dienstvergehen, die man dem Polizisten angelastet hat, sind völlig aus der Luft gegriffen.*
> *Die Rezession legt man dem Finanzminister und seiner angeblich verfehlten Politik zur Last.*
> *Durch zahlreiche Episoden klagt Tolstoi in diesem Roman die Ungerechtigkeit der Rechtssprechung und die Unmenschlichkeit des Strafvollzugs im damaligen Rußland an.*

3. Sue. For civil cases, i.e. when one person, firm, etc. sues another, **verklagen** and **klagen** (both + *auf* = 'for' and *wegen*) are used and differ only syntactically. *Verklagen* always needs an obj. *Mein Vater verklagte den Fahrer, der bei Rot über die Kreuzung gefahren und mit seinem Wagen zusammengestoßen war, auf Schadensersatz. Der Anwalt riet seinem Mandanten, die Firma zu verklagen, falls der Defekt im Motor nicht sofort behoben würde. Klagen* is used alone, *Die Firma wollte klagen, weil der Vertragspartner den Liefertermin nicht eingehalten hatte,* and with *auf*, but without the person sued as obj., *Weil er durch einen Betriebsunfall arbeitsunfähig geworden war, klagte er auf eine Abfindung. Der Anwalt hatte ihm geraten, auf Schmerzensgeld zu klagen. Klagen* can be used with *gegen* + a person, firm, etc. instead of *verklagen* but is less common. Thus *Die Firma klagte gegen den Vertragspartner auf Entschädigung wegen Nichteinhaltung der Lieferbedingungen* and *Die Firma verklagte den Partner auf Entschädigung wegen Nichteinhaltung . . .* both occur. In civil cases the plaintiff is *der Kläger*, the defendant *der Beklagte.*

accustom or get s.o. used to *vs.* get used or accustom oneself to *vs.* accustomed or used to *parts.*

1. i. Jmdn. an etw. gewöhnen means 'to accustom a pers. or get a pers. used to sth. or to doing sth.' **Sich an jmdn./etw. gewöhnen** or **sich daran gewöhnen, etw. zu tun** means 'to get used to s.o., sth., or doing sth.' People, [new] conditions, or actions follow *an*.

> *Die Armee will die Rekruten so bald wie möglich an strenge Disziplin gewöhnen.*
> *Er konnte sich nur langsam an die militärische Disziplin gewöhnen.*

Man muß Kinder an Ordnung und Sauberkeit gewöhnen.

Wir haben uns bemüht, den Hund an Lärm zu gewöhnen.

Es dauerte einige Zeit, bis sich das Kind an die Adoptiveltern gewöhnte.

Wer in den Tropen aufgewachsen ist, gewöhnt sich nicht leicht an ein kaltes Klima.

Unsere Augen hatten sich schon an die Dunkelheit gewöhnt.

Der junge Soldat hat sich noch nicht an das Frühaufstehen gewöhnt. Or . . . *hat sich noch nicht daran gewöhnt, früh aufzustehen.*

ii. Ich gewöhne mir etw. an means that I take on something as a customary way of acting or accustom myself to doing something. The obj. is usually a manner of behaving or speaking but cannot be people or conditions. An infin. is also used. The transl. varies.

Als ich bei der Bundeswehr war, gewöhnte ich mir einen ziemlichen rauhen Umgangston an.

Du mußt dir Pünktlichkeit/Ordnung angewöhnen.

Gewöhne dir endlich an, deutlich zu sprechen!

Der Junge hat sich verschiedene üble Ausdrücke angewöhnt.

Seitdem er das Mädchen kennt, hat er sich bessere Manieren angewöhnt.

2. Both **gewohnt** and **gewöhnt** mean 'accustomed, used to'. Only *gewohnt* is used attributively. *Sie hat die Aufgabe mit der gewohnten Sorgfalt/Gründlichkeit erledigt. Sie fühlte sich nur in ihrer gewohnten Umgebung wohl.* Both occur after *sein* but differ syntactically. *Gewohnt* is used with an acc., *Er ist schwere Arbeit gewohnt*, *gewöhnt* with *an*, *Er ist an schwere Arbeit gewöhnt.* Both take an infin., but *gewöhnt* needs *daran. Dem Ton seiner Stimme war anzumerken, daß er zu befehlen gewohnt war. Ich bin gewohnt, früh aufzustehen. Ich bin daran gewöhnt, zeitig aufzustehen. Gewohnt*, usually preceded by *es*, is used with a *daß*-clause, *Die Kinder waren es gewohnt, daß alle sie verwöhnten*, and with *es* in a clause introduced by *wie, wie ihr es gewohnt seid.* On receiving an order from a known customer a shopkeeper might say, '*Ich mach' es, wie Sie es gewohnt sind*', in the way you are accustomed to having such orders carried out. There is also a slight difference in meaning. *Gewöhnt* implies as a result of usually conscious habituation which has changed the person's behaviour, *gewohnt* that something is what someone normally does or experiences and that this is due to circumstances or character, not to habituation.

Der Minister war gewohnt, in Sitzungen seine Ansichten rücksichtslos zu äußern.

Schillers Vater wurde vom Herzog Karl-Eugen aufgefordert, seinen Sohn zur kostenfreien Erziehung in die vom Herzog gegründete Schule zu geben. Da Schiller Theologie studieren wollte, antwortete der Vater ausweichend. Der Herzog aber, gewohnt, seinen Willen bedingungslos durchzusetzen, verlangte kurzerhand, der Sohn solle ein anderes Studium wählen. Schließlich konnte der ohnedies an soldatischen Gehorsam gewöhnte Vater nichts anderes tun, als sich dem Wunsch seines Herrn zu fügen. (K. Berger, *Schiller*)

Ich bin es so gewohnt. (That's what I'm used to.)

3. Pflegen + *zu* + infin. expresses the idea that someone does something as a matter of custom or habit, i.e. is accustomed to or in the habit of doing something, or, with an action as subj., that it repeatedly happens. It is, however, not an everyday expression, belonging higher up the stylistic scale. With a personal subj., it is used only for those habitual actions which possess a certain dignity, are not e.g. brutal. It is only used in the pres. and past, *ich pflege, pflegte.* In speech the idea is usually expressed by *gewöhnlich* or *normalerweise* or by the words in 2.

Er pflegt nach dem Mittagessen eine Stunde zu schlafen. Or *Gewöhnlich schläft er . . .*

Seit sie von dem tödlichen Absturz gelesen hatte, pflegte sie sich stets zu vergewissern, daß der Aufzug auch angekommen war, bevor sie durch die offene Tür einstieg.

Sie pflegt die Mahlzeiten im Restaurant einzunehmen/jeden Tag spazieren zu gehen.

Solche Meinungsverschiedenheiten pflegten von Zeit zu Zeit zwischen ihnen aufzutreten.

Du weißt ja, wie es so zu gehen pflegt.

achieve, accomplish *vs.* achievement *n.*

1. Achieve and **accomplish** are syns. in the meaning 'to bring about a [desired] result'. The obj. is frequently an indefinite expression like *much, a lot, little,* etc. *Because of his efforts much has been achieved. If you attempt nothing, you will achieve nothing. She works hard but accomplishes nothing. I've only achieved half of what I hoped to do. You won't achieve anything with these children if you're too strict.* In comparison with *She did a lot, She has achieved/accomplished a lot/a great deal* suggests continued effort and stresses the result.

i. Leisten has two related senses, the first being 'to do or get through work'. In this sense it is a syn. of *machen* and normally has *Arbeit* as obj. *Arbeit* is, however, optional with *viel* and *wenig. Sie leistet viel. Er leistet wenig.* In extended use, *was ein Motor leistet* and *die Leistung eines Motors* mean 'its power, the work it is capable of doing'. When *Arbeit* is the stated or implied obj., *leisten* is often translated as *do.* In contrast to *machen* and *tun, leisten* is more formal and suggests sustained effort and work demanding all the person's strength and ability. When no judgement on the quality of the work is involved, the main difference is that *leisten* is stylistically higher, which excludes it from a context like *Die Gastarbeiter müssen die dreckigsten Arbeiten machen.* Elsewhere all three are possible, but *leisten* belongs more to the written language. *Alle bewundern die Arbeit, die sie macht/leistet. Er leistet/macht schwere Arbeit. Als er das Projekt übernahm, hatten andere schon einen beträchtlichen Teil der Arbeit geleistet* is written style. A speaker would say of him- or herself, '*Ich habe die Hälfte der Arbeit gemacht/getan.*' Only a zealous employee who is praising himself might use *geleistet. Leisten* is the usual v. when making a judgement on someone's work. *Was für Arbeit macht sie?* asks about the nature of the work, the occupation. *Was für Arbeit leistet er?* asks about the quality. The answer to the second question might be *Er leistet gute/ordentliche Arbeit* or *mäßige/schlechte Arbeit. Gut, schwach,* and other adjs. can describe e.g. *die Leistungen eines Schülers,* the pupil's work or performance. *Was dieser Schüler geleistet hat, ist erstaunlich* expresses praise. *Leisten* in this sense translates **achieve** and **accomplish** only when they mean 'to do the amount of work specified'. The E. intr. use *S.o. must achieve* can be expressed as *Jmd. muß gute Arbeit/etw. leisten.*

In its second sense *leisten* implies attaining a result which requires skill and efficiency and is mostly translated as **achieve**. It has an obj. which suggests an impressive result. *Sie hat in ihrem Fach Hervorragendes/Großes geleistet. Er glaubt, auf diesem Gebiet etw. leisten zu können (etw. Wertvolles* is implied). Although in pos. sents. both senses of *leisten* imply that the effort has some result, this result may not always be what is intended or hoped for. If *leisten* is to be translated as **achieve** or **accomplish**, it must be clear from the context that the desired result was achieved. **Erreichen**, on the other hand, implies that the effort expended accomplishes what is being aimed at or, in the neg., does not have the result to be expected. Thus *Sie hat viel Arbeit geleistet, aber wenig erreicht* or *Er hat für das Projekt eine enorme Leistung erbracht, konnte es aber nicht zu einem befriedigenden Ergebnis führen.* Because it always points to a result, *erreichen* is often the best equivalent of **achieve**. *Er hat nichts geleistet* would usually mean he did nothing or expended no effort, while *Er hat nichts erreicht* means he achieved nothing. Thus *Wir sind mit dem Erreichten zufrieden,* satisfied with what has been achieved. **Ausrichten** implies achieving something by changing a situation. *Erreichen* can replace *ausrichten* in the sents. below but does not convey the implication of changing the situation.

Die Entwicklungshelfer haben in kurzer Zeit sehr viel geleistet (suggests both effort and a result).
Er hat gründliche (colloquially *ganze) Arbeit geleistet* (did a thorough job).

Nicht nur durch seine Taten als Feldherr, sondern auch durch seinen Einfluß auf Kunst und
*   Wissenschaft hat Karl der Große Überragendes geleistet.*
Wir haben sehr viel Mühe aufgewendet. Was haben wir erreicht?
Alle bewundern, was wir erreicht haben/geleistet haben.
Bei diesen Kindern wirst du mit Strenge nichts ausrichten.
Mit Freundlichkeit kannst du mehr ausrichten als mit bösen Worten.
Ich habe in der Sache wenig ausgerichtet.
Allein und ohne Helfer konnte er gegen die Epidemie kaum etw. ausrichten.

ii. Achieve used with words denoting an aim or goal such as an objective, success, independence, or a victory means 'to succeed in gaining or bringing about
as a result of exertion'. *To achieve a purpose, goal, aim, objective,* or *end* is *ein/sein/das*
Ziel **erreichen**. *Sie haben endlich das Ziel erreicht, das sie sich gesetzt hatten.* **Erzielen**, 'to
aim for and reach as a result of one's efforts', is used with *das Ergebnis* and *das*
Resultat, ein Erfolg, der Durchbruch, 'breakthrough', *eine Einigung,* and *eine*
Übereinkunft (with the last two it means 'to reach an agreement', 'to achieve una-
nimity'). **Erringen** implies gaining something by great effort. It is broader than
achieve, but, used with *Sieg, Erfolg,* and *Unabhängigkeit,* is sometimes the equivalent. **Zustandebringen** suggests overcoming difficulties and bringing something
about and is sometimes translated as **achieve**. *Es gelang der Parteiführung, eine*
Einigung/eine Koalition zustandezubringen.

Das Land kann die Unabhängigkeit nur dann erringen, wenn alle bereit sind, Opfer zu bringen.
Nach hartem Kampf gelang es der australischen Hockeymannschaft, einen Sieg zu erringen.
Anfangs waren die Meinungen sehr verschieden. Aber nach gründlicher Diskussion wurde zwischen
*   den Gesprächspartnern eine Einigung/Übereinkunft erzielt.*

2. Accomplish has two further nuances. Firstly, with *task* as obj., it means 'to
carry out', the equivalent of which is **ausführen**. *Er hatte die Aufgabe, die man ihm*
übertragen hatte, ausgeführt. In some contexts it is interchangeable with **achieve**. *I*
have accomplished/achieved what I set out to do would become *Ich habe alles ausgeführt,*
was ich mir vorgenommen hatte, if carrying out work is implied, or *alles erreicht* if
attaining an objective is meant. Secondly, **accomplish** sometimes means 'to complete', a sense expressed by **abschließen** or **vollenden**. *Solange es noch etw. zu*
reformieren gab, war die Arbeit des Reformators nicht abgeschlossen/vollendet, his work
was not accomplished. Cf. END.

3. Achievement. Die Leistung is occasionally found in formal language as a verbal n. meaning 'the carrying out' of work, etc. *Die Leistung dieser Arbeit hat längere*
Zeit gedauert, als wir erwarteten. In relation to people it translates both **achievement** and *performance,* the latter denoting the quality of someone's work. The
context usually makes it clear that *Leistung* implies a specially good result and
means 'achievement'. *Das war eine hervorragende Leistung. Die Besteigung von Mount*
Everest war eine große Leistung. Die Erfindung der Dampfmaschine war eine bahn-
brechende/ großartige Leistung. Eine gute Leistung means 'a good performance', and
Leistung always has the sense of 'performance' with adjs. meaning 'poor' or
'bad'. *Dieser Aufsatz ist eine schwache/schlechte Leistung.* A n. which always implies a
pos. result is **die Errungenschaft**, an achievement requiring effort. It is
restricted to what a group of people achieves, e.g. a country, political system,
branch of scholarship, historical period, etc. *Die Errungenschaften der*
Naturwissenschaften/der Technik/der Forschung. Thus *die Errungenschaften der*
Archäologie but *die Leistung eines Archäologen.* Although the pl. is usual, the sing.
does occur. *Die Freiheit der Forschung ist eine Errungenschaft, auf die wir nicht leicht*
verzichten sollten. (*Errungenschaft* occurs frequently in the jocular use *unsere neueste*
Errungenschaft, our latest acquisition.)

act, action, deed *ns.*

1. Both an **act** and an **action** denote a single thing done, the result of the carrying out by an intelligent being of an intention, wish, etc. A **deed** is also 'what is done or performed by an intelligent or responsible agent', but except in the expression *a good deed*, or when contrasted with words, *What we now need is deeds, not words,* **deed** usually has the connotation of out of the ordinary either in badness, *an evil deed*, or goodness or bravery, *brave deeds* or *great and wonderful deeds.*

i. The G. equivalents are *die Handlung* and *die Tat*. **Die Handlung** is the general term which is used whenever human actions of an unspecified kind are being discussed. It is not restricted by any implications. *Eine Handlung* can be of an everyday nature, even trivial and insignificant. Thus *bewußte und unbewußte Handlungen.* Even what someone neglects to do is called *eine Handlung. Das Unterlassen, wie z. B. das Verhungernlassen eines Kleinkindes, kann eine strafbare Handlung sein.* Except in *eine gute Tat,* and when contrasted to words etc. (cf. 2. i), and in the meaning 'crime' (cf. 1. iii), **die Tat** is applied only to an action of considerable strength and power, one in some way out of the ordinary. *Tat* is still often encountered and does not have the old-fashioned ring **deed** sometimes has. In translating *His only action on hearing the bad news was to put his hand to his head, Handlung* is used because the action is trivial, *Als er die schlechte Nachricht hörte, war seine einzige Handlung, den Kopf mit der Hand zu stützen,* whereas *The rescue of the shipwrecked crew was a heroic action/act* can be *Die Rettung der Schiffbrüchigen war eine heroische Tat.* Similarly, telling a lie could only be called a *Handlung. Er hatte den Freund belogen, aber bald sollte er diese Handlung bitter bereuen. Tat* contains a judgement on an action which is mostly made when it is looked at in retrospect. Thus *eine große/tapfere/verwegene/edle Tat* or *eine böse/grauenvolle Tat* are judgements made after the event. In some contexts both words could occur. *Man beurteilt Menschen nach ihren Taten* or *nach ihren Handlungen,* but *Taten* suggests major, significant actions, while *Handlungen* is quite general and includes small, everyday acts. Likewise *Man steht für eine Tat ein* or *steht für seine Handlungen ein. Handlung* should be used unless a significant action is implied. Some compounds of *Handlung* are *Affekthandlung,* 'action committed under the influence of strong emotion', *Amtshandlung,* 'action taken in an official position or capacity', *Instinkthandlung, Kurzschlußhandlung,* 'irrational act committed in a moment of extreme strain or tension', *Notwehrhandlung,* 'action in self-defence', *Triebhandlung,* 'action resulting from physical urges', *Zwangshandlung,* 'compulsive act[ion]'. Some compounds of *Tat* are *Bluttat,* 'bloody deed', *Gewalttat,* 'act of violence', *Greueltat,* 'atrocious or horrifying deed', *Heldentat,* 'heroic deed', *Ruhmestat,* 'glorious deed', *Schandtat,* 'infamous act[ion]'.

Jeder muß handeln, aber niemand weiß, was für Folgen seine Handlungen haben werden.

Deine Handlungen sind nicht gerade wohl durchdacht.   Sie mußte ihre Handlung rechtfertigen.

Er ließ sich zu einer unüberlegten Handlung hinreißen.

Eine Rechtsordnung befaßt sich mit menschlichen Handlungen, aber Probleme entstehen bei der Bestimmung dessen, was das Recht, und insbesondere das Strafrecht, unter Handlung verstehen soll.

Der Abschluß eines Handelsvertrages war die letzte Amtshandlung des Ministers.

Die Taten Friedrichs der Großen sprechen für seinen Machtwillen und seine eiserne Disziplin.

Das Überfliegen des Atlantischen Ozeans wurde seinerzeit (at that time) als heldenhafte Tat angesehen.

ii. Der Akt is used as a syn. of *Handlung* in formal, particularly official, language *Ein freundlicher* or *feindseliger Akt* would in normal language be *eine freundliche* or *feindselige Handlung. Akt* is, however, usual with a following gen. stating that a certain state or quality is manifested in the action, as with *act of folly, mercy*, etc. *Tat* is also possible, but less common. *Der Selbstmordversuch war ein Akt der Verzweiflung* or *eine Verzweiflungstat*. Some common compounds are *Racheakt, Sabotageakt, Terrorakt*, and *Verwaltungsakt*, administrative action. *Der Gewaltakt* is mostly used in the political sphere, *Gewalttat* in non-political cases. (*Akt* also means 'ceremony'. *Die Königin wohnte dem feierlichen Akt der Einweihung bei*.)

> *Die Rehabilitierung des zu Unrecht zu einer Gefängnisstrafe verurteilten Polizisten war ein Akt der Gerechtigkeit.   Der Mord war die Tat eines Wahnsinnigen.*
> *Die Erschießung der Geiseln war ein brutaler Akt der Willkür.*
> *Es war ein Akt des Wahnsinns/eine Wahnsinnstat, mit diesem Lieferanten zu brechen.*
> *Während der Herrschaft dieses Diktators fanden Gewaltakte regelmäßig statt.*

iii. Die Tat also means 'crime'. It is a shortened form of **die Straftat**, 'criminal offence or act', for which *eine strafbare* or *verbrecherische Handlung* is also used in formal language. Hence, *der Tatort*, 'scene of a crime', and *der Täter*, 'the person who has committed the crime'.

> *Der Angeklagte hat die Tat gestanden.*
> *Er stand unter Anklage, die Tat geplant und ausgeführt/begangen zu haben.*

iv. If **in the act** refers to wrongdoing, the equivalent is **auf frischer Tat**. *Der Dieb wurde auf frischer Tat ertappt/erwischt*, caught in the act or red-handed. Cf. CATCH 2. ii. If a gerund is added, e.g. *caught in the act of stealing [money]*, the *act of* is omitted, and the gerund either becomes a n., *Er wurde beim Diebstahl ertappt*, or is turned into a clause, *Er wurde dabei ertappt, wie er Geld gestohlen hat*. When **in the act** means 'in the process of carrying out an action', **gerade dabei sein, etw. zu tun**, 'to be just doing sth.', is used. *Das Bild stellt einen Bogenschützen dar, der gerade dabei ist, einen Pfeil abzuschießen*.

2. Action, used mostly without an article, denotes a series of acts rather than a single one, the steps taken to bring about a result. *Quick action is called for. It's time to take action. We will accomplish more by joint action. That was a sensible/honourable course of action.*

i. Die Tat is used in combination with *Wort* and in contrast to just talking, thinking, or doing nothing. *Sie stand ihm mit Wort und Tat bei. Jetzt sind Taten nötig, nicht Worte. Tat* also has this sense in the expression *ein Mann der Tat*, 'man of action', and in the phr. *einen Plan/ein Vorhaben in die Tat umsetzen*, put into action, carry out.

> *Laßt Taten sprechen, denn große Worte können dem Elend der Flüchtlinge nicht abhelfen!*
> *Ihre Taten stimmten mit ihren Worten nicht überein.*

ii. The sense conveyed by *Tat* can be expressed by the v. **handeln**. *Wir haben lange genug geredet, jetzt muß gehandelt werden*, we must act/take action/do sth. *Handeln* may be able to express the meaning of 'action' in other contexts. *Wenn es darauf ankommt zu handeln, dann versagt er immer* is a possible transl. of *when action is called for*. As **das Handeln** is a verbal n. meaning 'the process of acting', it denotes more than one action. It is used for the actions of both individuals and institutions and may be contrasted to thought, words, or inaction. Both v. and n. are used when talking about human action or behaviour in a general way. *Unterliegt unser Handeln gewissen Gesetzen?* With *gegen*, *handeln* means 'to act contrary to'. *Ich darf nicht gegen die Vorschrift handeln*. When **take action against** means 'to act to curb or stamp out', **vorgehen gegen** is a common equivalent. *Gegen solche Verbrecher muß man mit allen Mitteln/mit aller Schärfe vorgehen*. In this sense *vorgehen* means 'to proceed or act in a certain way in a particular matter' and refers either to steps taken by governments etc. or to personal action. *Wie will Indien in dieser Angelegenheit vorgehen? Er ist rücksichtslos/energisch/geschickt vorgegangen*. **Das Vorgehen** also denotes a sequence of actions in either the official or private spheres. It takes *gegen*. *Viele mißbilligten das harte Vorgehen der Polizei gegen die Demonstranten*. **Die Handlungsweise** and **die Vorgehensweise**, 'manner or way of acting', are the appropriate transls. if **action** refers to the manner of proceeding. They imply more than one action, but possibly only in a single matter.

> *Wir haben zu lange gefackelt, wir müssen handeln.*
> *Sein Handeln kam mir höchst verdächtig vor.*
> *Unüberlegtes Handeln/zu rasches Handeln könnte in einer Katastrophe enden.*
> *Schnelles Handeln seitens der Gesundheitsbehörde verhinderte den Ausbruch einer Epidemie.*
> *Der Augenblick des Handelns war gekommen. Also Der Augenblick war gekommen, wo wir handeln*
>   *mußten.*   *Sie entschlossen sich zu gemeinsamem Handeln/Vorgehen.*
> *Das Vorgehen der Regierung gegen den pensionierten Abwehroffizier, der seine Memoiren veröf-*
>   *fentlichen wollte, ließ den Verdacht aufkommen, sie wollte gesetzwidrige Handlungen des*
>   *Abwehrdienstes vertuschen.*   *Wir kritisierten sein rücksichtsloses/übereiltes Vorgehen.*
> *Bundeskanzler und Bundespräsident forderten ein schärferes Vorgehen gegen rechte Krawalle.*
> *Die Handlungsweise/Vorgehensweise der Direktion erschien mir unklug.*
> *Die Vorgehensweise des Anwalts in dem Prozeß war ungewöhnlich.*

iii. Der Schritt, 'step', is often found, particularly in the pl., meaning 'action or steps to achieve a specific end'. **Die Maßnahme**, 'administrative measure', is used with *ergreifen* or *treffen* in the same sense. Both are common in the official sphere, and *Schritt* is also used for personal action.

> *Die von der Regierung unternommenen Schritte haben den erwünschten Erfolg gehabt.*
> *Ich werde sofort die nötigen Schritte tun* (take the necessary action).
> *Du hättest diesen Schritt nicht tun sollen.*
> *Die Maßnahmen, die die Regierung zur Ankurbelung der Wirtschaft ergriffen hatte, erwiesen sich als*
>   *ziemlich wirkungslos.*   *Diese Maßnahme kommt viel zu spät.*

iv. The idea of taking action against something objectionable is also conveyed by **einschreiten**, 'to intervene', which presupposes an actual occasion on which the police etc. proceed physically against people to curb infringements of the law, illegal behaviour, etc., and **durchgreifen**, 'to take strong or decisive action', which need not suggest direct intervention but strong measures over a longer period to check abuses, corruption, bad behaviour, etc. It implies that threatened penalties are strictly enforced. Both are used alone if it is clear what must be curbed, *Die Polizei müßte hier einschreiten*, otherwise with *gegen*.

> *Die Gewerkschaft wollte gegen diesen Übelstand einschreiten.*
> *Die Polizei schritt gegen die Randalierer ein.*
> *In letzter Zeit greift die Verkehrspolizei energischer gegen die Verkehrssünder durch.*
> *Wegen mangelnder Disziplin einiger Schüler mußte der Lehrer streng durchgreifen.*

v. Take action, meaning 'to do something about', can be expressed by **etw. unternehmen**, and **take no action** by **nichts unternehmen**. Both are common in the personal sphere but can refer to government action, although they are not official expressions. *Etw. gegen etw. unternehmen* does not presuppose violations, unlike *einschreiten* and *durchgreifen*.

> *Wir müssen etw. unternehmen, um ihn zur Vernunft zu bringen.*
> *A. Was wollen Sie in dieser Angelegenheit unternehmen?* (What do you want to do? What action
>   do you want to take?) *B. Ich halte es für ratsam, im Augenblick nichts zu unternehmen.*

vi. Action followed by *in* + gerund, as in *The government's action in closing the banks*, can be translated by *Vorgehen* and an *als*-clause, *Das Vorgehen der Regierung, als sie die Banken schließen ließ, führte zu ihrem Sturz*, but the simplest way to deal with it is to omit *action* and translate *the government's closing of the banks* as *Die Schließung der Banken durch die Regierung/auf Anordnung der Regierung führte* . . . Similarly *the American action in bombing Tripoli* could become *die Bombadierung von Tripolis durch die Amerikaner*.

3. Die Aktion denotes an undertaking which, although it may be initiated by one person, is carried out by a number of people together and often extends over a period of time. The equivalents are mostly *operation, campaign,* or sometimes *scheme.* However, in *eine militärische Aktion* it could also be translated as **action**. *Aktion* occurs in many areas and forms compounds. *Eine Hilfsaktion,* a relief scheme or operation, *Rettungsaktion,* a rescue operation, *Bergungsaktion,* a rescue operation for survivors or a salvage operation for a ship, *die Suchaktion,* search, *die Sparaktion,* savings campaign or economy drive, *Sammelaktion, Protestaktion, Polizeiaktion.*

> *Die Wiederansiedlung der Millionen von Menschen, die durch den zweiten Weltkrieg heimatlos geworden waren, war eine riesenhafte Aktion.*
>
> *Hitler benutzte den Röhm-Putsch, bei dem mindestens 83 Menschen ermordet wurden, um sich einer Reihe politischer Gegner zu entledigen. Ein Reichsgesetz vom 3.7.1934 erklärte diese Mordaktion als 'Staatsnotwehr' für rechtens.*
>
> *Umfangreiche Aktionen wurden in Ländern der dritten Welt unternommen, um die Erzeugung von Nahrungsmitteln zu steigern.   Die Polizei hat die Suchaktion eingestellt.*

4. The **action** or *plot* of a novel, play, film, etc. is **die Handlung.**

> *Die Handlung von Goethes Egmont spielt in den Niederlanden.*
> *Neben der Haupthandlung hat der Roman zwei Nebenhandlungen.*
> *Die Handlung des Films setzt mitten in einer Kampfszene ein.*
> *Dieses Stück ist arm an Handlung.*
> *Die Handlung ist gut motiviert/historisch treu/frei erfunden/hält den Leser in Spannung.*

5. i. Military action. Die Kampfhandlungen, which is used only in the pl., implies military action on a broad scale. *Nur Kampfhandlungen defensiver Art haben stattgefunden. Die Kampfhandlungen eröffnen, abbrechen,* and *einstellen* mean 'to open, break off, and stop the action'. An **action** meaning 'an engagement or fight' is **das Gefecht.** *Das Gefecht dauerte 20 Minuten. Durch ein kurzes Gefecht eroberte man den Hügel. Das Schiff ist klar zum Gefecht,* ready for action. *Ein Schiff/Einen Panzer außer Gefecht setzen* is 'to put a ship/tank out of action'.

ii. One sense of **einsetzen** is 'to use, bring, or send into action' troops, ships, aircraft, police, etc. *Der General setzte Panzer ein. Das Bataillon wurde gegen die Guerillaverbände eingesetzt.* The corresponding n. is **der Einsatz.** *Zum Einsatz bringen* means 'to bring or put into action'. *Man brachte alle verfügbaren Truppen zum Einsatz.* The pass. can also be expressed by *zum Einsatz kommen. Truppen/Bomber kamen zum Einsatz* or *wurden zum Einsatz gebracht. Im Einsatz sein* means 'to be in action', and *zum Einsatz bereit* or *einsatzbereit* 'ready for action'. In non-military contexts *der Einsatz* means 'using or putting into operation'. *Durch den Einsatz der modernsten Maschinen verdoppelte man den Ausstoß.*

> *Durch den Einsatz von Panzern und der ganzen Infanterie warf die Armee den Feind zurück.*
> *Wegen des schweren Gewitters waren alle Polizisten vierzehn Stunden lang in pausenlosem Einsatz.*

6. Take legal action. General expressions are **gerichtliche Schritte** *gegen jmdn./etw.* **unternehmen, einen Prozeß** *gegen jmdn.* **anstrengen,** 'to start or bring an action', or *jmdn.* *gerichtlich* **belangen,** 'to take to court or bring an action against'. *Einen Politiker, der ihn verleumdet hatte, hat er gerichtlich belangt.* When **action** means 'a civil suit', **die Klage** is the usual word. *Seine Klage gegen den Nachbarn auf Schadensersatz wird morgen vor dem Gericht verhandelt. Das Gericht hat seine Klage abgewiesen,* 'dismissed his action', can also be expressed as *Er wurde mit seiner Klage abgewiesen.* Cf. SUE under ACCUSE 3.

add *v.*

1. Add figures, amounts, etc., frequently **add up** or **add together**. The interchangeable terms of G. origin are **zusammenzählen, zusammenrechnen,** and less commonly **zusammenziehen**. All need an obj. **Addieren** is a syn. but is used both with and without an obj.

> *Um all diese Zahlen im Kopf addieren/zusammenzählen/zusammenrechnen/zusammenziehen zu kön-*
> *nen, müßte man ein guter Rechner sein.*   *Er kann schnell [im Kopf] addieren.*
> *Wenn wir alle Beträge zusammenzählen, ergibt sich eine Gesamtsumme von DM 560.*
> *Wenn man alle Ausgaben zusammenrechnet, so war die Reise doch sehr teuer.*
> *Sie hat alles/die einzelnen Posten zusammengezählt/zusammengerechnet.*
> *Der Lehrer zog die einzelnen Noten zusammen, um den Durchschnitt der Klasse zu errechnen.*

2. Add one number, amount, etc. **to** another/others is **rechnen zu** when both numbers etc. are stated. *Wenn ich diesen Betrag zu den übrigen rechne, ergibt sich die Gesamtsumme. Ich rechne diese Note zu den anderen und nehme den Mittelwert. Man muß das Porto zu dem Preis rechnen.* If only one number etc. is stated, i.e. when E. uses **add on**, **dazurechnen** is used. *Du mußt das Porto dazurechnen. Wir haben den Gesamtpreis, wenn wir die Versicherung dazurechnen. Du mußt diese Summe noch dazurechnen.*

3. Add a charge, fee, additional cost, etc. [**to** sth.]. **Aufschlagen** + *auf* + acc. and **zuschlagen** + dat. both express this idea, but whereas *aufschlagen* is more common as a v., **der Zuschlag**, 'additional charge or cost', is more common than **der Aufschlag**.

> *Die Transportkosten werden auf den Preis aufgeschlagen.* Or . . . *werden dem Preis zugeschlagen.*
> *Der Verkäufer schlug auch gleich die Mehrwertsteuer auf den Preis auf.*
> *Wenn man mit ICE-Zügen fährt, muß man einen Zuschlag von 15 Mark zahlen.*

4. In *I'll add [another] $50 (to what you've got)*, **add** means 'to contribute a further amount'. The main equivalent is **dazugeben**. *Wenn die Gemeinde 100 000 Mark zusammenbringt, gibt die Landesregierung 50 000 Mark dazu.* An alternative is **dazulegen**. *Wenn du das teurere Fahrrad haben willst, lege ich 100 Mark dazu.* More colloquial is **drauflegen**. *Ich lege 50 Mark drauf, wenn du dieses Fahrrad kaufen willst.*

5. Add up [to] is also intr. When the resulting figure is stated, it means 'to amount to'. *My debts add up to £3,000.* A common equivalent is **sich belaufen auf**, to amount to. *Meine Schulden belaufen sich auf 3 000 Pfund. Ende 1991 wird sich die Verschuldung aller öffentlichen Haushalte in der Bundesrepublik auf gut 1,3 Billionen Mark belaufen. Die in diesem Jahr fertiggestellten Autobahnstrecken belaufen sich auf 760 Kilometer.* A more formal alternative is **sich addieren auf**. *Die Forderungen der Rohstofflieferanten addieren sich auf fünf Millionen Dollar.* With *Zahlen* as subj., **ergeben**, 'to yield', is used. *Diese Zahlen ergeben zusammengerechnet 99.* In *These small expenses soon add up*, **add up** means 'to yield a larger or large amount'. Here G. uses **sich summieren**. *Die täglichen kleinen Ausgaben summieren sich. Sich summieren* is sometimes found with *auf* or *zu*. *Die Entschädigungen für enteignetes Eigentum in der Ex-DDR, das nicht zurückgegeben werden kann, summieren sich schnell auf zweistellige Milliardenbeträge.*

6. Add up is used in idioms. One meaning is 'to cause s.o. to understand the true nature of a situation'. *It all added up* can be *Dann wurde [mir] alles klar—der Gärtner war der Dieb. It just doesn't add up* can be *Ich verstehe nicht/Mir ist nicht klar, was dahinter steckt.* Another sense is 'to mean, amount to'. Besides *auf etw. hinauslaufen*, 'to amount to sth.', *bedeuten* or *heißen*', 'to MEAN', can be used. *All this adds up to is that you don't want to help: Das läuft alles darauf hinaus, daß du nicht helfen willst. Das alles heißt/bedeutet, daß wir wieder von vorn anfangen müssen. Das alles ergibt eine sehr gefährliche Lage* can translate *That all adds up to a very dangerous situation (ergeben, to result in).* *Bedeuten* is also possible.

7. Add something in speech or writing **to** what has already been said or written. **i.** The most common word is **hinzufügen**. **Hinzusetzen** is possible but now unusual. *Hinzufügen* is used alone in reporting direct speech or with an obj. like *nichts, etw., ein paar Worte, einige Bemerkungen,* or a *daß*-clause, to which a dat. may be added. *'Aber es gibt Ausnahmen,' fügte er hinzu. Dem habe ich nichts hinzuzufügen.*

> *Der Richter fragte den Angeklagten: 'Haben Sie den Plädoyers des Staatsanwalts und des Verteidigers etw. hinzuzufügen?'*
>
> *Der Äußerung meines Kollegen möchte ich hinzufügen, daß wir alle mit der Änderung einverstanden sind.*
>
> *Der Vortragende setzte/fügte seinen Erläuterungen noch einige Beispiele hinzu.*

ii. Ergänzen means 'to make complete by adding the missing component[s]'. It is translated as *complement, supplement,* or *complete,* but also sometimes as **add**. It is not confined to what is spoken or written. *Der Archäologe ergänzte die abgebrochene Nase der ausgegrabenen Marmorstatue in Gips.*

> *Die fehlenden Wörter im Text sind zu ergänzen. Also . . . hinzuzufügen.*
>
> *Zu der Rede meines Kollegen möchte ich noch etwas ergänzen.*

iii. Anfügen means 'to attach, append, or add' and is a formal syn. of *hinzufügen*. *Eine Liste der benutzten Literatur wird dem Referat angefügt. Sie fügte dem Brief eine Nachschrift/einige Zeilen an.*

8. Hinzufügen also expresses the sense 'to add sth. concrete to sth.' *Der Sammler wollte seiner Sammlung dieses prächtige Stück hinzufügen. Er fügte dem Geschenk eine Schachtel Pralinen hinzu.*

9. Hinzukommen, hinzutreten, and **dazukommen** convey the idea that a further factor is added or has arisen in addition to those already existing. *Andere Erfolge/Rückschläge kamen noch hinzu/dazu. Ein erschwerender Umstand trat hinzu.* When a phr. with *zu* is present, *hinzu* is optional, but it must be used when there is no *zu* phr. *Hinzu/Dazu kommt noch [der Umstand], daß . . .* means 'to this is added the fact that', and is often simply rendered as *in addition.* When a shop assistant asks, *'Kommt noch etw. hinzu?'* he or she means 'Is anything to be added to what you have already asked for?', i.e. 'Would you like anything else?' (Note: *Später kamen/traten andere Gäste hinzu,* others joined those already mentioned.)

> *Der übermäßige Alkoholgenuß kommt als erschwerender Umstand hinzu.*
>
> *In der Tombola ist zu dem Fernsehapparat noch eine Waschmaschine hinzugekommen.*
>
> *Zu seinen Geschäftssorgen kam noch die Erkrankung seiner Frau [hinzu].*
>
> *Hinzu kommt noch der Umstand, daß das Wetter ohnehin nicht warm genug ist, um baden zu gehen.*
>
> *Er war schon immer kränklich, nun aber traten Atembeschwerden hinzu.*
>
> *Wenn keine Komplikationen hinzutreten, so ist er in zehn Tagen wieder zu Hause.*
>
> *Hinzu kommt noch, daß du dich für dein taktloses Benehmen vorige Woche noch nicht entschuldigt hast.*

10. Add something solid or liquid. In writing it is possible to use **hinzufügen** in a context like *Man fügt dann das Fleisch, die Gewürze, das Wasser und den Wein hinzu,* but this would sound strange in the spoken language. The simplest way to convey the idea in speech is to use **etw. in etw. geben**, 'to put in', or the syn. **etw. in etw. tun**. *Hinein,* modified in speech to *rein,* must be added if there is no phr. with *in* but is optional if this is present. *Der Koch wollte noch etwas Gewürz in die Suppe [hinein]geben. Ich habe vergessen, Salz hineinzugeben. Tun Sie noch etwas Zucker hinein! Tun Sie noch Zucker in den Tee [hinein]!* **Geben zu** means 'to add one thing to another'. Both things must be stated. *Gib noch etwas Wein zu der Soße!* **Zugeben** + dat. is used in formal language. *Man braucht dem Eintopf keine Gewürze zuzugeben. Zugeben* can also be used if only the thing added is stated. *Man muß jetzt das Gemüse in Öl anbraten, das Wasser und das Salz zugeben und alles zum Kochen bringen.* When only the thing added is stated, the usual v. in speech is **dazugeben** + acc., 'to add one thing to something else previously mentioned'. *Du kannst ruhig etwas Gewürz dazugeben.*

Hinzugeben and **hinzutun** are more formal vs. meaning 'to add' something liquid or solid. They need an acc. *Ich gebe noch etwas Gewürz hinzu. Die Kartoffeln schmecken zu fade, du mußt Salz hinzutun.* A dat. can state to what thing something is added. *Gib der Soße noch etwas Tabasco hinzu! Man gibt/tut dem Mehl die Eier hinzu.* **Hinein-, hinzu-, zu-,** and **dazugießen** are used in the same way for liquids. *Wenn Ihnen der Tee zu stark ist, gieße ich noch etwas Wasser hinein* or sometimes *hinzu.* (With a phr. with *in, hinein* is optional and best omitted. *Ich gieße noch etwas Wasser in die Vase [hinein].*) *Ich gieße noch etwas kaltes Wasser zu. Man schneidet den Schmelzkäse in kleine Stückchen und gießt einen Löffel von der heißen Fleischbrühe dazu.* **Nachgießen** is 'to fill again what has become partly or completely empty'. *Darf ich Ihnen Kaffee nachgießen?* For chemicals *geben zu* is usual when one thing is added to another, e.g. to produce a reaction. *Zu einer Lösung von Magnesiumchlorid gebe man etwas festes Ammoniumchlorid und verdünntes Ammoniak.* **Zusetzen** does not imply producing a reaction but mixing one thing with another, often to enrich it. *Dem Futter müssen Vitamine zugesetzt werden, damit die Tiere im Winter gesund bleiben.*

> *Erhebliche Mengen an künstlichem Dünger müssen dem Boden zugesetzt werden, damit er fruchtbar bleibt.*
>
> *Wenn man [dem] Wein Zucker zusetzt, wird der natürliche Geschmack verdorben.*

11. Add = 'to attach or enclose'. The usual word for enclosing something with a letter etc. is **beilegen**. However, in commercial and official style **beifügen** is also common. It means 'to enclose' as well as 'to attach or add' something like photographs or a map to something in writing (at the back of it, not in the text). *To be enclosed* is **beiliegen**. *Ein Scheck liegt dem Brief bei.*

> *Ich habe dem Brief einen Scheck und einen frankierten Umschlag beigelegt.*
>
> *Der Sachbearbeiter war sich noch darüber im Unklaren, ob er dem Bericht nicht noch ein paar Abbildungen beifügen sollte.   Der Reisebeschreibung ist eine Landkarte beigefügt.*
>
> *Wir fügen ein Anmeldeformular bei und bitten um Rücksendung.*

12. Add [on] by building. **Anbauen** is 'to build on'. *Sie haben zwei Zimmer und eine Garage [an das Haus] angebaut.* **Einbauen** means 'to build into'. *In die Maschine ist ein Frühwarnsystem eingebaut worden. Bei der geringsten Störung schaltet sie sich automatisch ab.*

> *Ich möchte ein zusätzliches Fach in den Schrank einbauen.*

13. Add to in a sent. like *That only added to our difficulties* means 'to INCREASE'.

advertise *v.* **advertisement** *n.* **Advertise** means either 'to make generally known', 'to call attention to by a published notice', *to advertise a position,* or 'to arouse a desire to buy or patronize by emphasizing desirable qualities'. *The new product was widely advertised. Die Anzeige, die Annonce,* and *das Inserat* are confined to advertising in newspapers and periodicals and cover both meanings, while *die Werbung* and *die Reklame* are applied only to promoting goods, services, entertainment, etc. in all media.

1. Print media.

i. Eine Anzeige is the general term for a newspaper advertisement. *Anzeigen* means 'to make known'. The section of a newspaper containing advertisements is usually called *der Anzeigenteil,* though *Annoncen-* and *Inseratenteil* also exist. Advertising material in a newspaper which might be mistaken for an article is marked *Anzeige.* **Die Annonce** and **das Inserat** tend to be used when someone is trying to sell something, but they may also denote advertisements seeking to fill positions or to buy something. *Anzeige* is possible in all three cases. The choice of word depends on personal preference. *Positions vacant* are *Stellenanzeigen* or *Stellenangebote.*

Tageszeitungen veröffentlichen verschiedene Arten von Anzeigen.
Tageszeitungen und Zeitschriften gewinnen einen grossen Teil ihrer Einnahmen aus Anzeigen.
Die Anzeigenabteilung der Zeitung nimmt die Anzeigen/Annoncen/Inserate der Kunden an.
Um mein Fahrrad zu verkaufen, habe ich eine Annonce/Inserat/Anzeige aufgegeben.
Da die Häuser der neuen Wohnsiedlung verkauft werden sollen, hat der Makler ein Inserat aufgegeben.
Der Supermarkt hat heute ein mehrseitiges Inserat in der Zeitung.
Ich meldete mich auf die heutige Anzeige/Annonce einer Sekretärinnenstelle der Firma Lohmann hin.
Sie blätterte den Anzeigenteil der Stadtzeitung durch und kreuzte die entsprechenden Annoncen/Inserate/Anzeigen an.

ii. Die Anzeige is also the usual word for the notices in newspapers giving information about private, official, or business happenings: *die Heiratsanzeige, die Todesanzeige. Als die Firma ihre Geschäftsräume verlegte, setzte sie zwei Wochen lang eine Anzeige in die Zeitung.* Hence the use of the v. *Sie haben die Geburt des Kindes/ihre Verlobung in der Zeitung angezeigt.* In the sense 'to advertise' **anzeigen** occurs with ns. that suggest making something known. *Die Kinoprogramme werden dreimal in der Woche in der Zeitung angezeigt. Der Verlag zeigt die Neuerscheinungen an.*

iii. Inserieren means 'to put an advertisement in a newspaper etc.' With *wegen* it implies the desire to find something and corresponds to *advertise for sth. Er inserierte wegen einer Wohnung in der Lokalzeitung.* With an obj. it implies wanting to sell or let something. *Ich habe das Auto [zum Verkauf] inseriert. Die Wohnung wird Ende des Monats frei—wir haben sie gerade inseriert.* It is also used without a phr. or obj. *Wir müssen inserieren.* **Annoncieren** means 'to make known by an advertisement'. It is used with and without an obj. *Die Computerfirma annoncierte die neuen Modelle gestern. Wir wollen annoncieren.* It is also used with *wegen* in the same meaning as *inserieren. Annoncieren* is often used in connection with filling positions. *Wir annoncieren heute in der Zeitung, um die vakante Stelle zu besetzen.* Or *Wir annoncieren die Stelle.*

iv. Ausschreiben, 'to make known in writing', can be translated as *to advertise* when the obj. is a position or something someone wants to sell or let. It seems to be the preferred v. in official language but is not confined to it. *Einen Auftrag ausschreiben* is 'to call for tenders or bids'.

Mit sechzehn beschloß er, seine elektrische Eisenbahn für 200 Mark auszuschreiben, weil er sich nicht mehr dafür interessierte.   Die Firma hat zwei Stellen heute ausgeschrieben.
Die Universität schreibt alle zu besetzenden Stellen aus.
Da die Wohnung am Ende des Monats leer wird, haben wir sie zum Vermieten ausgeschrieben.

2. Words meaning 'to arouse a desire to buy or patronize'. **Die Reklame** can refer to handbills, placards on hoardings or billboards, advertisements on the sides of buses and on *Litfaßsäulen* (pillars for advertising material on streets), newspaper advertisements, and advertising on radio, television, and in the cinema, all of which involve the wish to promote sales or gain patronage. The word can denote a single advertisement but is also a collective n. meaning 'advertising'. Thus *Nur im Vorabendprogramm zwischen 18 und 20 Uhr wird im deutschen Fernsehen Reklame gesendet.* The pl. of *Reklame* is rare. **Reklame machen für** is a common expression meaning 'to advertise or promote s.o./sth.' A single advertisement on radio and television is now called **der Werbespot**. The pl. is *Werbespots.* **Die Werbung** is also a collective n. meaning 'advertising and could replace *Reklame* in the sent. above. *Der Handel kommt ohne Werbung/Reklame nicht aus.* **Werben** with a personal obj. means 'to seek to gain'. *Die Zeitung wirbt Abonnenten* or *Der Verein/Die Partei wirbt Mitglieder.* With *für*, *werben* has the general sense of making propaganda for and can mean 'to promote or to advertise' a product or person. *Das Plakat wirbt für eine neue Zahnpasta.*

Die Reklame/Werbung für Coca-Cola spricht besonders das jüngere Publikum an.

Die reißerisch aufgemachte Werbung erhöhte nicht die Nachfrage und führte somit nicht zum gewünschten Erfolg.

Für den neuen Film wurde viel Reklame gemacht, und bald war er in aller Munde.

Auf den großen Reklamewänden/Werbeflächen wie Bushaltestellen, Häuserwänden und ähnlichem wurde das Produkt in den grellsten Farben angepriesen.

Diese Werbespots dauern nur dreißig Sekunden. Was wird ein [Werbe]spot wohl kosten?

Mit ihrer Kampagne wirbt die Werbefirma für ein angeblich verbessertes Waschmittel.

In den Reklamesendungen des Fernsehens wird für die verschiedensten Produkte geworben.

affect, have an effect. Some senses of **act [on]** and **influence** *vs.* Affect has several meanings. (i) The first is 'to produce a change or have an effect, sometimes a detrimental one'. *The climate affected his health. Does this change affect your plans? The drought has affected the harvest. The recession has affected many firms. How many factories are affected by the strike? The change in the law affects our civil rights.* In a related sense it is much the same as *concern*, but may imply a change. *The new regulations [do not] affect groceries/first-year students.* (ii) In reference to a disease, **affect** means 'to attack or produce an effect' on people or part of the body. *Half the village was affected by the illness. The swelling in her foot affected the whole leg. Whooping-cough mainly affects children under five. The disease affected his lungs.* (iii) **Affect** also means 'to make an impression on the mind or feelings and arouse sadness, pity, love, etc.' *This letter/S.o.'s fate affected us all profoundly. The news of Jim's death affected him deeply.* (iv) For **affect** meaning 'to pretend' as in *They affected indifference,* see PRETEND. This article is divided into three sections. 1 discusses *wirken,* its derivatives, and related words, 2 deals with *treffen, betreffen,* and words applied to illnesses, and 3 treats *berühren* and a syn. The three sections correspond only partly to the first three E. senses as vs. in all three sections express parts of the first E. sense.

1. i. Applied to a force or something like a drug or poison which, because of its nature, produces an effect, **wirken** means 'to act'. *Eine Kraft wirkt. Die Naturgesetze wirken unabhängig vom Tun oder Wollen der Menschen. Die Spritze wirkt schnell.* Cf. WORK 1 and 2. With *auf,* it means 'to act on' or 'affect'. *Die Arznei wirkt auf die Nerven/die Verdauung.* With a pres. part. it states that something has the effect specified. *Der Sturm wirkte verheerend,* had a devastating effect.

Der richtige Luftdruck wirkt reifenschonend.   *Kaffee wirkt anregend.*

Diese Nachricht wirkte niederschmetternd auf uns.   *Alkohol wirkt berauschend.*

Applied to works of art, performances, speeches, etc., *wirken* means 'to have an effect', normally the one intended. An effect of a specific kind is not implied as both *eine Tragödie* and *eine Komödie wirkt.* Cf. 3. iv.

Die Inszenierung eines klassischen Stückes muß modern sein, wenn sie wirken soll.

Das Theaterstück hat stark auf mich gewirkt.

Diese Art Musik wirkt stark auf meine Gefühle.   *Ich lasse die Musik auf mich wirken.*

ii. Whereas *wirken* suggests an immediate reaction, **sich auswirken** implies an indirect effect, one that spreads, often slowly, from one thing to others. Transls. are **affect** or **have an/its effect**. It is used with and without an adv. stating the nature of the effect. *Dieses Klima wirkte sich günstig/positiv auf ihre Gesundheit aus. Die Krise in der Autoindustrie wirkte sich auf die übrige Wirtschaft aus.* As *sich auswirken* implies neither a good nor a bad effect, an adv. like *ungünstig* or *nachteilig* must be added if **affect** implies a detrimental effect, as in *The heavy rain affected the harvest. Die schweren Regenfälle wirkten sich ungünstig/katastrophal auf die Ernte aus.* Sich auswirken cannot be applied to an effect intentionally brought about.

Lohnerhöhungen ohne Produktionsanstieg wirken sich über kurz oder lang auf die Preise aus.

Die Veränderungen in der Wirtschaftspolitik wirkten sich negativ auf die Beziehungen der beiden Staaten zueinander aus.

Die veränderte Zusammensetzung der Luft wirkt sich langsam auf das Klima aus.

Der Protektionismus wirkte sich nachteilig/verhängnisvoll auf den Welthandel aus.

To express the idea of an adverse effect more forcibly the vs. in 2. i or **schaden**, 'to harm', and **beeinträchtigen**, 'to be detrimental to or to impair', may be more appropriate. Cf. DAMAGE 2 and 4.

iii. With a person as subj. **einwirken** means 'to attempt to bring about an effect or to exert an influence on a pers. or thg.' Depending on the context, it is translated as **influence** or **affect**. Nowadays when a person is the subj., *einwirken* is used only when the effect or influence is intended. *Kannst du nicht auf sie einwirken, daß sie zustimmt?* Where there is no question of a deliberate influence, **beeinflussen** is normal, as it leaves the question of intention open. *Ohne es zu wollen, hatte er seinen Bruder erheblich beeinflußt.* This restriction on the use of *einwirken* does not apply where no intention can be present, as in *Schlechte Filme haben auf seinen Charakter/seine Gesinnung eingewirkt* or *Dieses Buch wirkte auf die Geisteshaltung einer ganzen Epoche ein.* *Einwirken* can also be used for the influence exerted by literary figures no longer living, as in *Shakespeare hat auf Goethe stark eingewirkt* or *hat Goethe stark beeinflußt.*

Die Regierung versuchte, auf die Preisentwicklung einzuwirken.

Vergeblich versuchte der Trainer, durch Zurufen positiv auf den Matchverlauf einzuwirken.

Kannst du versuchen, mit Vernunftgründen auf ihn einzuwirken?

Er hatte keine Nachricht von Luise erhalten. Viel zu stolz, den Versuch zu machen, auf ihre Entschlüsse einzuwirken, hatte er es vorgezogen, nichts zu tun.

Ich möchte Sie in keiner Weise beeinflussen.

Jmd. läßt sich leicht beeinflussen/ist leicht zu beeinflussen.

Seine Gefühle scheinen sein Urteil in dieser Sache beeinflußt zu haben.

Einwirken also means 'to act on' or 'affect' in reference to a chemical change or one brought about by wind, heat, water, etc. *Salzsäure wirkt auf Metalle ein. Regen, Frost und Hitze haben auf die Gesteine eingewirkt.*

iv. If **affect** means 'to bring about an alteration or change', it can be rendered by **ändern an** with *etw., viel*, or *nichts* as obj. *Das ändert viel/nichts/etw. an einer Sache.* The pass. is translated by **sich ändern an** with *nichts, viel*, or *etw.* as subj. Cf. CHANGE 1.

Auch wenn Sie ein paar Sätze umschreiben, ändert das nichts an der eigentlichen Aussage des Artikels. Or . . . ändert sich dadurch nichts an . . .

Ändert dieser mißliche Umstand vielleicht etw. an unserer Abmachung/an Ihren Plänen?

Die Regierung hat gewechselt, doch dadurch hat sich an der Lage der armen Landbevölkerung nicht viel/nichts geändert.

2. i. With a subj. denoting an evil or something unpleasant **treffen** means that the obj. was directly affected, i.e. HIT or struck by a calamity, disaster, hurricane, etc. *Hart* or *schwer* is often added, as *hard* frequently is to *hit. Die Rezession hat viele Firmen schwer getroffen. Das Küstengebiet wurde vom Orkan hart getroffen.* **Betreffen** expresses a similar sense, but implies an indirect, though immediate, effect. It means 'not to suffer the full force of the evil but some adverse consequences' and resembles **affect** in denoting a less severe harmful effect than *hit. Das Unglück hat mehrere Familien hart getroffen/ . . . hat auch unsere Familie betroffen.* The effect is usually bad, but may occasionally be otherwise, provided this is stated. *Wenn der Handelskrieg zwischen den USA und der EU plötzlich aufhören sollte, wäre Australien davon betroffen, und zwar in positiver Weise.* In this sense *betreffen* is only used in the perf. or pass. In the pres. and past tenses it is taken to mean 'to CONCERN'. The E. past tense can be translated by *treffen, Der Preisrückgang traf die Zuckerindustrie schwer*, 'affected it badly', or by the perf. or pass. of *betreffen, Die gesamte Landwirtschaft war* *vom Preisrückgang betroffen.* The past part. is applied, like **affected**, to all those suffering directly or indirectly from the consequences of flood, famine, etc. It often occurs in the form *die Betroffenen.*

> *Sechs Dörfer wurden von dem Vulkanausbruch hart/schwer getroffen, aber der ganze Landstrich war davon betroffen.*
>
> *Die Seminarbibliothek im Erdgeschoß war auch vom Brand im dritten Stock betroffen—einige Bücher wurden beschädigt.*   *Nicht alle Fabriken waren von dem Streik betroffen.*
>
> *Mit Ausnahme der Wohlhabenden waren alle Bevölkerungsschichten von der Hungersnot betroffen.*
>
> *Man hat Lebensmittel an alle von der Überschwemmung Betroffenen verteilt.*

ii. Betreffen is also used with a subj. like a law, regulation, change of rules, etc. where E. sometimes uses **affect**, sometimes *concern.*

> *Lebensmittel sind von dieser Anordnung nicht betroffen.*
>
> *Das neue Gesetz betrifft nur die größeren Bauern.*
>
> *Die geänderten Bestimmungen betreffen etwa 50 000 Rentner/nur Studenten im ersten Jahr/Semester.*

iii. Applied to illness, exertion, climatic and other conditions, **angreifen** means 'to have an injurious effect on' a person, someone's health, or parts of the body, and sometimes corresponds to **affect**. *Unterernährung griff die Gesundheit der Kinder an.* With illnesses it implies a weaker adverse effect than *befallen.* Cf. ATTACK 3. **Befallen** needs to be used when **affect** means 'to attack'. *Keuchhusten befällt gewöhnlich Kinder unter fünf Jahren. Das halbe Dorf wurde von der Krankheit befallen.*

> *Die fortgesetzte Überanstrengung/Das heiße, feuchte Klima hat ihre Gesundheit angegriffen.*
>
> *Dieses Waschmittel greift die Hände nicht an.*   *Die ständige Aufregung greift die Nerven an.*
>
> *Die Krankheit könnte auch die Lunge angreifen, was der Arzt unter allen Umständen zu verhindern suchte.*
>
> *Der dreißigstündige Flug hat mich sehr angegriffen.*

Angreifen also means 'to attack, eat away, or corrode' metal etc., and is applied fig. to savings, reserves, stores, supplies of money, etc. In some cases it can translate or be translated by **affect**.

> *Alle Metallteile müssen durch Schmiere oder Farbe geschützt werden, sonst greift sie die Feuchtigkeit an.*
>
> *Die eiserne Ration darf nur im Notfall angegriffen werden.*
>
> *Er mußte seine Ersparnisse angreifen, um die hohen Reparaturkosten zu bezahlen.*
>
> *Der Urlaub hat meine Kasse stark angegriffen.*

iv. In Mitleidenschaft ziehen means that the harmful effect of an ailment etc. located in one part of the body spreads to another part, or that something unpleasant centred on one place, institution, etc. causes others to suffer adverse effects.

> *Bei der Leberoperation wurde auch sein Magen in Mitleidenschaft gezogen.*
>
> *Der Bankrott des großen Unternehmens zog mehrere kleine Firmen in Mitleidenschaft.*
>
> *Bei dem Fabrikbrand wurden auch die umliegenden Häuser in Mitleidenschaft gezogen.*

3. Berühren, the basic meaning of which is 'to TOUCH', is close in some of its senses to the following meanings of **affect**.

i. 'To have a bearing or effect on' when the obj. relates to interests, rights, power, or relations, particularly in the legal and political spheres. **Berühren** says nothing about whether the effect is good or bad, although this may be clear from the context. In *Diese Maßnahmen berühren die Kleinbauern, berühren* is neutral and suggests an indirect effect. *Alle Kleinbauern wurden von den Maßnahmen betroffen* implies a stronger immediate effect, but one not as severe as [*schwer/hart*] *getroffen.*

> *Der Zwischenfall an der Grenze berührte die chinesisch-russischen Beziehungen.*
>
> *Der Abbau des Zollschutzes berührt die Interessen sowohl der Unternehmer als auch der Arbeiter.*
>
> *Diese Entscheidung des Obersten Gerichtshofes berührt die Rechte der Bundesstaaten.*
>
> *Die Veränderungen in der Organisation des Betriebes berühren unsere Abteilung nicht.*

ii. 'To have an effect on', with people or an area as obj. Like *touch* and **affect**, berühren implies a change, in the case of people a mental one, but again leaves open the question as to whether this is favourable or not, although the context may make it clear. A speaker who talks of *ein von der modernen Zivilisation unberührtes Land* could be praising or censuring the country, depending on his or her attitude. In a context like *Die Verderbtheit ihrer Umgebung hatte sie nicht berührt*, the attitude to the surroundings is clear.

Dieses ländliche Gebiet ist von den Ausläufern der Industriestadt noch nicht berührt.

iii. With advs. like *unangenehm, peinlich, schmerzlich, seltsam, sympathisch*, etc., berühren means 'to create a certain kind of impression on the mind'. This sense mostly requires a transl. other than **affect**.

Sein bescheidenes Auftreten und seine intelligenten Bemerkungen haben mich sympathisch berührt.
Sie war von dem ihr überreichten Blumenstrauß angenehm berührt.
Die Taktlosigkeiten der beiden Gäste gegenüber dem Gast aus dem Ausland berührten die Gastgeber peinlich (caused them embarrassment).
Die Heiterkeit Karls bei der Erkrankung seines Vaters hat mich seltsam berührt.

iv. With *tief*, berühren means 'to affect deeply' or 'move', and suggests the arousing of feelings related to sadness. Cf. MOVE 5. *Das Theaterstück hat uns alle tief berührt.* With *nur wenig*, or in the neg., to which *sonderlich* or *sichtlich* are often added, it suggests that someone was only slightly or not affected, moved, or touched by something.

Die Not der armen Menschen hat die reichen Touristen nicht sonderlich berührt.
Die Beschuldigungen des Kollegen haben sie nicht berührt.

v. Nahegehen means 'to affect deeply either with grief or mental pain'.

Der Tod ihres Mannes ist ihr sehr nahegegangen.
Die völlig ungerechtfertigten Vorwürfe ihres Kollegen gingen ihr sehr nahe.

after *prep.* and *adv.* **afterwards** *adv.* **after all** phr. used as *adv.*

1. After, afterwards.

i. The equivalent of the prep. **after** when this refers to a sequence in importance, in order, or in place, and especially to one in time, is **nach**. A sequence in order of importance: *Nach Hamburg ist München die größte Stadt der Bundesrepublik. Nach dem Hauptmann kommt der Major. Nach Monika ist Ulrich der beste Schüler in der Klasse. Nach mir bist du an der Reihe.* A sequence of places: *Oldenburg ist die nächste Station nach Delmenhorst.* Time: *Nach dem Essen gehen wir spazieren. Drei Monate nach der Wahl. Nach einer zweijährigen Abwesenheit kehrte Richard nach England zurück.* The idea of a sequence in time and a logical consequence is also expressed by both **after** and *nach*. The sense is 'in view of', 'as a consequence of'. *Ich werde nie mehr mit ihm reden, nach dem, was er über mich gesagt hat. Nach dem, was wir schon über die beiden wissen, hättest du etw. anderes erwartet?* Sometimes **after** and *nach* express logical opposition. *Es wundert mich, daß er nach einer so schroffen Abweisung seine Besuche überhaupt fortsetzt.*

ii. The adv. **after** in *three months after* is usually **danach** meaning 'after this', i.e. some specific event. *Drei Monate danach. Am 15. März war er abgereist, und eine Woche danach erhielt sie schon den ersten Brief. Bald danach. Kurz danach. Gleich danach. Ein Jahr danach. Zu den Zeiten Chaucers und lange danach.* When **afterwards** and **after** are syns., as in *What'll we do afterwards?* or *I was never so badly treated either before or after*, the equivalent can be either *danach*, **nachher**, or **hinterher**. *Nachher* is combined with *vorher, Ich bin weder vorher noch nachher so schlecht behandelt worden wie damals*, but elsewhere it is interchangeable with *hinterher*. They are somewhat less precise than *danach*, which means, as already mentioned, 'after this/that (event, etc.)', 'after doing sth.', but all three are often possible.

Sie ging an die frische Luft. Danach fühlte sie sich besser.

Mach' erst einmal deine Hausaufgaben fertig! Nachher kannst du Fußball spielen.
Wir sind ins Kino gegangen. Nachher haben wir uns in ein Café gesetzt und haben Kaffee und Kuchen gegessen. *Sie aßen zu Mittag und gingen hinterher spazieren.*
Man kann erst nachher feststellen, ob eine Entscheidung richtig oder falsch war.
Es hat sich erst hinterher herausgestellt, daß er sich verrechnet hatte.
Die Bedeutung dieser Worte wurde mir erst hinterher/nachher klar.

iii. The original sense of **after** was 'behind', but this survives only in a few expressions which must all be translated by **hinter**. *Shut the door after you!* is *Mach' die Tür hinter dir zu! Hinter dem Gouverneur kam der oberste Richter,* after/behind. **After** is also found as an adv. in the same sense, but is no longer in common use. The line from the nursery rhyme *Jill came tumbling after* would now be *after him,* in G. *Jill purzelte hinter ihm her.* Used with some vs. of motion, the single word **hinterher** is the exact equivalent of **after** in the old sense and is now usually translated as *along behind.* It is used when the n. is understood, not stated. *Die Kinder radelten durch den Wald, und der Hund lief hinterher,* along behind or along after them. **Hinter jmdm. her** has the same meaning. *Der Hund lief hinter ihnen her.* With *to be* or vs. of motion, **after** suggests at least trying to overtake, catch [up with], or reach s.o./sth. *The police are after the thief. Run after her and tell her to come back! Hinter jmdm. her* and *hinterher* with a v. of motion mostly mean 'to go/run, etc. along behind s.o.' and do not imply overtaking. However, in some cases, especially with *sein*, they do imply trying to get or getting what one is after. *Die Polizei ist hinter einem Mann her, den sie für den Täter hält.* Which sense is intended depends on the context. *Hinter jmdm./etw. her sein* is restricted to money and people. *Er ist hinter jedem Rock her.*

Ich ging/lief/rannte/fuhr hinter ihm her. *Sie riefen hinter ihnen her, 'Kommt bald wieder!'*
Ein Stein flog hinter ihm her (was thrown in his direction).
Er schickte einen Boten hinter uns her.
Sie sind hinter dem Geld her wie der Teufel hinter der armen Seele.

Other equivalents of **be after**. *Er hat es auf ihr Geld/eine Spitzenposition abgesehen.* Cf. AIM 2. iv. *Er war auf Beförderung/eine leitende Stelle aus.* **Be after** can mean 'to be looking for'. *They are after gold, Sie suchen Gold.*

iv. Vs. of motion with the prefix *nach* imply at least trying or wanting to reach what one is after. **Nachgehen** and **nachfahren** are exceptions because in certain contexts they may only mean 'to follow', though in others they also imply the wish to overtake. *Der Polizist ging/fuhr dem Verdächtigen nach, um festzustellen, wo er hinging. Sie will uns mit dem Rad in einer Stunde nachfahren.*

Wir sind der Spur nachgegangen. *Die Polizei setzte dem Flüchtigen nach.*
Das Auto fuhr dem Zug nach. *Die Polizisten jagten den Verbrechern nach.*
Sie hat ihren Regenschirm liegenlassen/liegengelassen. Lauf ihr schnell nach!

2. After all.

i. One function of **doch** is to contradict neg. and some pos. statements. In some cases this is the equivalent of **after all**. Let us assume that A says to B, *'Es wird heute regnen.'* If B does not believe this, he would say, *'Nein, es wird nicht regnen.'* If A wishes to dispute this, he could say either, *'Doch, es wird regnen'*, which is a firm way of restating his position and putting an end to the discussion, or less firmly, *'Es wird doch regnen.'* (Underlining denotes stress.) *Doch* could in both these cases be translated as *No,* and *will* would be stressed. [No,] it will rain. If it then does rain, so that A is proved right, he could say to B later, *'Es hat doch geregnet'*, it did rain/rained after all. (*Do* and *did* give increased emphasis, but have no equivalents in G.) If no rain falls so that B is right, he could say, *'Es hat doch nicht geregnet'*, it didn't rain after all. *Es hat doch geregnet* thus corrects the neg. statement *es wird nicht regnen* when it turns out to have been wrong, while *Es hat doch nicht geregnet* corrects the pos. utterance *Es wird regnen* when it has proved to be inaccurate. Not all these steps need be present. C might say, *'Ich glaube, daß Becker gewinnen wird.'* Doubts may or may not be expressed. If Becker loses, C would admit his mistake by saying, *'Er hat <u>doch</u> nicht gewonnen'*, he didn't win after all.

> *Monika bot Andrea Kuchen an. Zunächst sagte Andrea: 'Nein, ich habe keinen Hunger', aß aber dann drei Stück. Lächelnd sagte Monika: 'Siehst du, du hattest doch Hunger.'*

ii. Nun doch implies that the person concerned has already said that something will not happen. *Der Spieler Y, der vorige Woche verletzt wurde, wird am kommenden Samstag nun doch spielen* implies that he had said he would not be playing but will now be playing after all. *Das Seminar morgen wird nun doch stattfinden—dem Professor geht es wieder besser.*

iii. Also doch is similar but presupposes the verification, by what is heard or observed, of a surmise which has been disputed. It expresses surprise because the rejection of the surmise has been accepted. *Also doch!* can be used as an exclamation, meaning that what was once believed but then was disputed or denied is right after all. Suppose you had heard or thought that someone was going to get married but had been told when you mentioned it to the person concerned that this was not correct. Later, however, it turns out to be correct after all, and you could say, *'Du wirst also doch heiraten'*, you are getting married after all.

> *Vor kurzem hast du gesagt, du würdest einen so dicken Roman wie* Die Blechtrommel *nie lesen. Du hast aber in den letzten Tagen mehrere Male davon gesprochen. Du hast ihn also doch gelesen.*

iv. Doch noch means 'contrary to expectations' or 'although this outcome seemed very unlikely at one stage'. *Er hat doch noch reisen können* implies that, although he had originally intended to go, something happened which seemed to make this impossible, but that the difficulty was overcome. Similarly *Die Mannschaft Z war bei der Halbzeit mit 0 : 2 im Rückstand, konnte aber aufholen, und hat doch noch gewonnen*, won after all. Under other circumstances someone can say, *'Die Mannschaft Y hat doch noch verloren.'*

> *Obwohl niemand glaubte, es würde ihnen gelingen, haben sie es doch noch geschafft.*

v. Immerhin points to some good feature which should not be ignored or which offers some consolation in an otherwise bad situation. In statements, sometimes strengthened by *doch*, it means '[well,] after all/at any rate/at least' (we have achieved sth.). It occurs as an exclamation in the form *Na, immerhin*, well, after all, that's sth. or better than nothing.

> *Peter erzählt Ursula vom Urlaub: 'Das Hotel war nicht gerade komfortabel, und das Essen war auch nicht besonders, aber das Wetter war ganz gut.' 'Na, immerhin!' antwortet Ursula.*
>
> *Immerhin, den ersten Teil der Aufgabe hätten wir gelöst!*
>
> *Auch wenn sie sich nicht oft hat blicken lassen, sie hat doch immerhin oft angerufen.*
>
> *Auch wenn der neue Umweltminister die Umweltverschmutzung von heute auf morgen nicht beseitigen kann, so ist seine Ernennung [doch] immerhin ein Fortschritt.*

vi. After all can give a reason or opinion relating to a previous statement. *They did not expect heavy losses in the air—they had, after all, excellent aircraft. I couldn't be expected to follow his reasoning—I was, after all, only a schoolboy.* While *schließlich*, which is discussed in the next paragraph, is the general equivalent, **immerhin** can have this sense, though only in pos. sents.

> *So schlecht kann er nicht sein. Er hat dir immerhin oft geholfen* (after all, he has often . . .).
>
> *In diesem Ton kannst du nicht zu ihm reden. Er ist immerhin dein Vater* (he is after all . . .).
>
> *Der Marsch ging immerhin über dreißig Kilometer* (explains or justifies a previous statement).

In this sense **schließlich** refers to a fact which gives a reason for doing something or behaving in a particular way, or points to a truth which explains something and must not be overlooked. It is often strengthened by *doch* when not at the beginning of the sent. At the beginning it functions like *Well, after all*. *Schließlich hast du es so gewollt.*

Ich will dir keine Vorschriften machen. Du bist [doch] schließlich kein Kind mehr.

Seiner komplizierten Beweisführung konnte ich nicht folgen. Ich war doch schließlich nur Schüler.

Mit hohen Verlusten im Luftkrieg hatten sie nicht gerechnet. Sie hatten schließlich gute Flugzeuge.

Sprich nicht in diesem Ton zu ihm! Er ist doch schließlich dein Chef.

Jetzt muß gearbeitet werden. Wir sind schließlich nicht zu unserem Vergnügen hier.

Sie nahm die Schuld daran, daß er sich verspätet hatte, auf sich. Schließlich war sie es, die auf dem Umweg bestanden hatte.

again *adv.* **once more, once again** phrs. used as *advs.* The equivalents are *wieder, nochmal, noch einmal, nochmals,* and *wiederum.* In the spoken language, *wieder* and *nochmal* are probably used most frequently to denote the repetition of an action or state. *Noch einmal,* 'once again', is also common. *Nochmals* is a more formal expression, and *wiederum* an emphatic syn. of *wieder.* In many cases they are interchangeable, but in some only one is usual.

1. Again = 'a second or further time'.

i. Wieder, nochmal, and **noch einmal** are interchangeable in many pos. sents. *Wir mußten nochmal/wieder/noch einmal von vorn anfangen.*

Wann kommst du wieder mal/nochmal/noch einmal nach Hannover? (In the spoken language *mal* is often added to *wieder,* but it does not change the meaning.)

Ich mußte die ganze Geschichte nochmal/noch einmal/wieder erzählen.

Er hat mit 70 Jahren nochmal/noch einmal/wieder geheiratet.

Da haben Sie aber nochmal Glück gehabt, daß Sie sich nichts gebrochen haben.

Keiner schien ihn gehört zu haben. Da rief er noch einmal, nur lauter.

Wir waren zwar beim ersten Versuch gescheitert, aber es war keine Frage, daß wir es nochmal versuchen würden.   Spiel es nochmal, Sam!

Da bin ich wieder/nochmal/noch einmal. (Here I am again.)

Ich bin es wieder/nochmal/noch einmal. (It's me again.)

ii. Wieder, nochmal, and **noch einmal** are all used after *nicht.*

Ein so teures Geschenk sollst du mir nicht noch einmal geben.

Der soll bloß warten! Das sagt der nicht noch einmal ungestraft zu mir.

Tu' das nicht noch einmal!   Komm' nicht wieder zu spät nach Hause!

Laß dich nicht noch einmal/nochmal/wieder reinlegen!   Ich geh' nicht nochmal hin.

2. Only **wieder** is used:

i. After *nie. Nie wieder, schwor er sich, würde er einen Tropfen Alkohol anrühren.*

Nie wieder Krieg!   Das darfst du nie wieder tun.

ii. In *immer wieder,* again and again, over and over again. *Wieder und wieder* is a stylistically higher syn. *Wiederholt,* 'repeatedly', expresses a similar meaning.

Was man immer wieder hört, behält man endlich.

Er macht immer wieder/wiederholt denselben Fehler.

Er mußte sich ihre Rolle wieder und wieder anhören, bis sie glaubte, daß nichts mehr schief gehen würde.

Ich habe wiederholt bei ihr angerufen, aber niemand meldet sich.

iii. After *schon. Was gibt's schon wieder?*

Seid ihr schon wieder da? (Could express annoyance or surprise.)

Gehst du schon wieder weg? Du bist doch eben erst angekommen.

Es wird schon wieder werden. (Things will turn out all right again.)

iv. In the meaning 'back' or 'back again'.

Du wirst doch fünf Minuten warten können. Ich bin gleich wieder da/Ich komme sofort wieder.

Sie legte das Buch wieder an die richtige Stelle.   Der Taucher kam wieder an die Oberfläche.

v. In the meaning **again** = 'once more as before', i.e. when a state which once existed, but was interrupted or disturbed, is restored. Thus *Sie ist wieder gesund. Er ist wieder frei. Man hat ihn wieder freigelassen.*

Sie fiel hin, aber stand sofort wieder auf.   *Alles ist wieder beim Alten.*
Bruno mußte erst einen Augenblick warten, bis das Herzklopfen wieder nachließ.
Du mußt dein Zimmer erst wieder aufräumen, bevor du spielen gehen darfst.

vi. To state that something is another or an additional point or fact. *Das ist wieder was anderes,* sth. else again.

Einige sind dafür, andere dagegen, und wieder andere haben keine Meinung.

3. Nochmals is a formal and emphatic syn. of *wieder, nochmal,* and *noch einmal.*

Ich bitte nochmals um Verzeihung.   *Nochmals vielen Dank für Ihre Hilfe!*
Ich möchte mich nochmals für Ihre Hilfe bedanken.
Ich muß nochmals darauf hinweisen, daß die Sache streng geheim ist.

4. Wiederum differs from *wieder* in being more emphatic. Because of this it tends to be used when feelings are involved in order to stress them. *Wieder* can always be substituted for it, but lacks the emphasis and emotion. Sometimes *wiederum* corresponds to *all over again.*

Wiederum richtete er seinen Blick auf das Bild.
Und wiederum war alle Mühe umsonst gewesen.
Wiederum hatte er unglaubliches Glück gehabt.   *Der Versuch ist wiederum fehlgeschlagen.*
Geduldig beschrieb er ihnen den Weg nochmals, und als er erkannte, daß es auch diesmal ohne Erfolg geschehen war, tat er es wiederum.

5. In one of its many uses, **noch** indicates that an action will take place in the future. It either denotes an unspecified time in the future and can be translated as *sometime, Das werde ich euch noch erzählen,* or it refers to the intervening period between the present and a specified occurrence in the fairly near future. In the latter situation it corresponds to **again**. *Wir sehen uns noch* is only used when a clause or phr. meaning 'before sth. happens' follows or is implied, e.g. *Sehen wir uns noch, bevor du abfährst?* Thus *Kommst du vor der Prüfung noch vorbei?* It is the only equivalent of **again** in this context.

ago *adv.* The equivalent in a sent. with a v. in the past tense is **vor** preceding an expression of time. *Ich habe sie zuletzt vor zwei Wochen gesehen. Er wurde vor zwei Jahren gewählt. Das ist vor langer Zeit geschehen.* With the pres. tense of *sein* **her** is used. *Das ist lange her. Das ist/sind zwei Jahre her.* When narrating from the point of view of the past, *her* is possible with the past tense of *sein. Das war[en] zwei Jahre her.*

agree *v.*

1. Agree or **agree on** means that at least two people, countries, organizations, etc. come to a harmonious understanding regarding a course of action to be taken either together or with the approval of both. *They have agreed on a price/[on] what action they should take. They have finally agreed.* Note that the equivalent of *unanimously, einstimmig,* is not used with any of the vs. discussed in 1. *The jury agreed unanimously that X should be acquitted, Die Geschworenen beschlossen einstimmig, X freizusprechen.* Cf. DECIDE 1. ii.

i. Sich einigen implies that the parties were initially in disagreement and that, as a result of discussions, negotiations, or mutual concessions, they reach [an] agreement. Only if used with *mit* can it take a sing. subj. Thus *A und B haben sich geeinigt,* or *A hat sich mit B geeinigt.* It is used alone, with *auf* which gives the result of the agreement, with *über* or *in* which state the area in which agreement is sought, and with *darauf* or *darüber* + infin. or clause giving the contents of the agreement. In formal language *dahingehend,* 'to the effect', can replace *darauf.* A person can follow *auf*. *Als* states his or her function. *Die SPD einigte sich schnell auf den Ministerpräsidenten von Rheinland-Pfalz als Kanzlerkandidat.*

Es dauerte einige Zeit, bis sich die beiden Seiten geeinigt hatten.   *Habt ihr euch geeinigt?*

Nachdem alle Meinungen angehört worden waren, einigte man sich auf einen Kompromiß.

Sie haben sich auf den Preis/auf die zu unternehmenden Schritte geeinigt.

Erst nach einiger Diskussion einigten sich die Mitglieder auf die Farben für die Clubräume.

Ich habe mich mit ihm über die Aufteilung der Arbeit geeinigt.

Sie einigten sich in der Frage der Finanzierung.

Die Kommission konnte sich nur in einem Punkt einigen.

Die Anwesenden einigten sich darauf, die Abstimmung auf die nächste Sitzung zu verschieben. Or *Sie einigten sich darauf, daß die Abstimmung . . . verschoben wurde/werden sollte.*

Die Firmen einigten sich darauf, die Zusammenarbeit fortzusetzen. Or *Sie einigten sich dahingehend, daß sie die Zusammenarbeit nur in bestimmten Bereichen fortsetzen würden.*

Die Erben konnten sich nicht darüber einigen, wie der Besitz aufzuteilen war.

Bei der Suche nach einer Sprecherin einigte sich der Ausschuß auf eine unbekannte Person.

The pass. is not possible. The E. pass. is expressed by the act. with *man* or a person as subj. *Terms of reconciliation were quickly agreed on* is *Man einigte sich schnell auf die Bedingungen der Aussöhnung.*

ii. Sich einig werden has the same meaning as *sich einigen*, but it is less common. **Handelseinig werden** means 'to reach agreement on a business matter'.

Es hängt von der Kompromißbereitschaft der Mitglieder ab, ob wir uns einig werden.

Wann werdet ihr euch endlich einig?

Erst nach langen Verhandlungen wurden wir mit unserem Geschäftspartner handelseinig.

iii. Übereinkommen implies that two or more people have come to an understanding about a course of action etc. It emphasizes more the decision to act in a certain way than the resolving of differences, although it does not exclude some initial disagreement. It needs to be followed by an infin. or a *daß*-clause.

Beide Vertragspartner kamen überein, die Zusammenarbeit fortzusetzen.

Die Deutschlehrer sind übereingekommen, daß sie ein neues Lehrbuch so bald wie möglich einführen werden. Or *Sie sind übereingekommen, ein neues Lehrbuch . . . einzuführen.*

iv. Sich verständigen, 'to come to an understanding about sth.', also implies deciding on action by discussion between at least two people etc. It takes either *über* or *auf*, or *darüber* or *darauf* or *dahingehend* in formal language + infin. or clause. Unlike *sich einigen*, which stresses the difficulties to be overcome, it suggests that the agreement or understanding is reached without much trouble.

Wir haben uns mit unseren Vertragspartnern über die Bedingungen für weitere Zusammenarbeit verständigt.   *Die Parteien verständigten sich auf ein einheitliches Vorgehen.*

Wir haben uns darauf verständigt, in dieser Angelegenheit gemeinsam vorzugehen. Or *Wir haben uns darauf verständigt, daß wir gemeinsam vorgehen [werden].*

Wir müssen uns darüber verständigen, wie wir vorgehen werden.

Die Firmen verständigten sich darauf, ein neues Automodell gemeinsam zu entwickeln.

v. Vereinbaren means 'to reach an understanding', 'to agree [on]', or 'to arrange'. It is used with an infin. or a clause and is the only word so far discussed which takes an obj., so that it alone is used in the pass. and its past part. as an adj. *Es wurde vereinbart, daß wir uns regelmäßig treffen. Die Waren wurden zum vereinbarten Preis geliefert.* It is only slightly formal in tone and also stresses the result, rather than the resolving of differences.

Obwohl die Minister keine Einigung erzielt hatten, vereinbarten sie eine weitere Zusammenkunft. Or *. . . vereinbarten sie, sich wieder zu treffen.*

Haben Sie schon ein Honorar für die Übersetzung vereinbart?

Wir vereinbarten, die Kosten zu teilen.

Haben Sie vereinbart, wieviel jeder zahlen soll?   *Das war so aber nicht vereinbart.*

Zur vereinbarten Zeit erschienen die Vertreter der Gewerkschaft.
Sie gaben das vereinbarte Zeichen.

vi. While the words previously discussed are fairly formal expressions mostly restricted to important areas of life, **ausmachen** or **abmachen** and **verabreden** are not formal, are used in everyday situations, and are often translated by *arrange*. They are appropriate when *arrange* and **agree** are synonymous. *Have you arranged/agreed where to go? We have arranged/agreed on a time.* For their use see ARRANGE 2.

vii. Absprechen implies discussing something and reaching agreement but sometimes suggests secrecy and intrigue. *Eine geheime Absprache* is a fixed expression.

Die Redner hatten sich miteinander abgesprochen, so daß in ihrem Argumentationsgang keine Lücke zu finden war.
Die beiden Zeugen haben ihre Aussagen offensichtlich miteinander abgesprochen.

2. Agree [to] = 'say yes to', 'consent or assent to', 'approve of' a proposal, request, idea, etc.

i. Eingehen auf means 'to agree to' a request, demand, conditions, etc. See ACCEPT 2. ii.

ii. Einwilligen is used when a person in a position of authority gives his or her approval, and also when someone agrees to something concerning him/herself. It is used alone, with *in*, and *darin, daß*.

Wenn Schüler an einem Klassenausflug teilnehmen, müssen die Eltern oder Erziehungsberechtigten [darin] einwilligen. *Der alte Mann willigte in die Operation ein.*
Die Frau bat ihren Mann, nun doch endlich in die Scheidung einzuwilligen.
Man bat mich, die Redaktion einer Zeitschrift zu übernehmen. Mit trüben Ahnungen willigte ich ein.
Er hatte sie gebeten, darin einzuwilligen, daß sie sich einige Wochen nicht sehen.

iii. Zustimmen means 'to state one's acceptance or approval' of a proposal etc. It is used with a dat., *Ich stimme dem zu, was du vorgeschlagen hast*, or alone if it is clear what is being agreed to, *Wir stimmen zu*.

Die Arbeiter wollten dem von der Gewerkschaft ausgehandelten Lohnabschluß nicht zustimmen.
Die Mehrheit der Mitglieder stimmten dem Vorschlag/dem Plan zu.
Nachdem er den Plan erklärt hatte, stimmten alle zu.

iv. Einverstanden sein in *Sie ist mit einem Vorschlag einverstanden* means 'to be in agreement with or approve of'. *Einverstanden* is used alone, with *mit*, or with a *daß*-clause or infin. after *damit*. *Ich bin [damit] einverstanden*, I agree or approve. People often simply say, *Einverstanden!* It is also used with *mit* + a person and *als*. *Wir sind mit ihm als Sprecher der Gruppe nicht einverstanden*. **Sich einverstanden erklären** conveys the idea of expressing agreement. *Sie erklärten sich mit der vorgeschlagenen Lösung einverstanden.*

Alle Familienmitglieder waren mit dem Umbau der Wohnung einverstanden.
Sie ist damit einverstanden, daß die Buchhandlung ihr die noch fehlenden Bücher nachschickt.
Sie erklärte sich damit einverstanden, alle Kosten zu übernehmen.
Der Graf erklärte sich damit einverstanden, daß Fontane Ereignisse und Gestalten aus der Geschichte der gräflichen Familie in seinen Werken behandelte.

v. The main expression conveying the idea that someone, when asked, agrees to do something is **sich bereit erklären zu**. An infin. may follow or a n. after *zu*. *Sie erklärte sich bereit, die unliebsame Aufgabe zu übernehmen*. Or *Sie erklärte sich zur Übernahme der unliebsamen Aufgabe bereit*.

Wer erklärt sich bereit, heute das Protokoll für die Sitzung des Seminars zu übernehmen?
Sobald er sich dazu bereit erklärt hatte mitzuhelfen, fingen sie mit der Arbeit an.

3. In *The two accounts of the wreck do not agree*, **agree** means 'to tally', 'to be the same', a sense which **übereinstimmen** expresses. The subj. can also be a report, opinion, evidence, estimate, calculation, etc.

Wir haben beide, aber getrennt von einander, die Ausgaben zusammengerechnet, und die Ergebnisse stimmen überein.

Ihr Bericht stimmt mit dem überein, was ich bereits gelesen habe.

Die Aussage des ersten Zeugen stimmt mit der des zweiten überein. Or Die Aussagen der beiden Zeugen stimmen überein.

Meine Meinung in dieser Frage stimmt mit der meiner Frau nicht überein.

Ihre Ansichten stimmten in allen wichtigen Angelegenheiten weitgehend überein.

4. Agree [with] = 'to be of the same mind or opinion'. *I agree [with you] [on that point].*

i. Übereinstimmen is used with a person as subj. but is formal in tone. With a sing. subj. it needs *mit. In dieser Frage stimme ich mit Ihnen vollkommen überein. Mit* also expresses agreement with an opinion etc. *Ich stimme mit dieser Ansicht überein.* Thus *Ich stimme damit überein* can translate *I agree.*

> *Ich stimme mit Ihnen darin/dahingehend überein, daß wir unsere Anstrengungen auf dieses Gebiet konzentrieren müssen. (Dahingehend is very formal.)*
> *In der Gesamtbeurteilung der Lage stimmten sie überein.*

ii. [Sich] einig sein also expresses agreement in opinion, although it does not exclude the process of reaching this. It usually has a pl. subj. and the refl. dat., *Wir sind uns einig,* but can have a sing. subj. and *mit, Ich bin [mir] mit ihm einig. Mir* is usually omitted in speech. **Einig** takes *in* or *über. In der Beurteilung des Romans sind wir uns einig. Über die Nutzlosigkeit weiterer Versuche waren sie sich einig.* It is also used with *darin* or *darüber* + *daß*-clause.

> *Sobald wir uns einig sind, werden wir es ihn wissen lassen.*
> *In einem Punkt waren sie sich noch nicht ganz einig.*
> *Die Antragsteller waren sich über die Höhe der Schadensersatzforderung nicht einig.*
> *Alle Pädagogen sind sich darin/darüber einig, daß man Kinder mit Liebe erziehen muß.*

iii. The usual v. in this sense is **zustimmen**. Sents. containing it can usually also be formulated with *[sich] einig sein. In dieser Frage stimme ich dir zu/sind wir uns einig/bin ich [mir] mit dir einig. Wir sind uns darin einig/Ich stimme dir zu, daß dieser Plan der beste ist.*

> *Viele stimmten dem Redner zu und gaben ihre Zustimmung durch Beifall zu erkennen.*
> *Du wirst mir sicher zustimmen, wenn ich dir die eigentlichen Beweggründe erkläre.*
> *Ich stimme dir [in deiner Beurteilung der Lage] zu.*

iv. Expressions related to *zustimmen* are **jmds. Meinung teilen** and **der[selben] Meinung/Ansicht sein**. *I agree*, when the person agreed with is not stated, can be *Ich bin derselben Ansicht* or *Der Meinung bin ich auch*, or if the person is mentioned *Ich teile deine/seine/ihre Meinung. I agree that . . .* is *Ich bin auch der Ansicht, daß wir keine andere Wahl haben.* **Einverstanden sein** is used when someone finds an interpretation of a text, law, etc., an argument, an explanation, etc. acceptable. When agreement with someone's opinion is implied, a phr. like *in dieser Frage* or *in diesem Punkt* is added to *einverstanden*, but it is very formal in this use and suggests giving approval. *In dieser Frage bin ich mit Ihnen/Ihrem Standpunkt einverstanden. Ich gebe dir recht* is an admission that what another has said is correct. If a spontaneous response to a remark, it is like *I agree. In dem ersten Punkt gebe ich dir recht, in dem zweiten aber nicht.* **Jmdm. rechtgeben** is also used when, after disagreement or dispute, one person concedes that the other's point of view is right. Then it is usual to say, *'Da muß ich dir recht geben.'*

> *In dieser Frage teile ich Ihre Meinung/sind wir derselben Meinung/Ansicht.*
> *Mit dieser Auslegung der unklaren Textstelle waren alle einverstanden.*

5. Agree = 'to live or act together harmoniously'. **Sich vertragen** (+ **gut** or **einigermaßen** in pos. sents.) or **gut mit jmdm. auskommen**, both = 'to get on with', express this now dated use of **agree**.

Die Kinder streiten dauernd. Sie vertragen sich nicht. Or Sie kommen nicht gut miteinander aus.
Wolfgang hat sich immer gut mit Heinz vertragen.
Sie vertragen sich einigermaßen, so daß wir keine Streitigkeiten zu befürchten brauchen.

6. Agree in *Food* or *climate agrees with a pers.* **Vertragen** is used with the person or thing affected as subj. Cf. BEAR 4. iii. **Jmdm. gut/schlecht bekommen** expresses the same idea, but needs food etc. as subj.

Ich kann das heiße, feuchte Klima gut/schlecht/nicht vertragen. (The hot, humid climate agrees/doesn't agree with me.)   *Das Essen ist mir gut bekommen.*
Austern hätte ich zum Mittagessen nicht essen sollen. Ich vertrage sie nicht. Or Sie bekommen mir nicht.   *Hat es dir gut bekommen?* (Refers to food or drink.)
Meine Haut verträgt diese Salbe nicht.   *Mein Magen verträgt den starken Kaffee nicht.*

aim [at] *v.*

1. Aim a weapon.

i. The usual word for aiming a gun etc. is **zielen**. It implies using *das Visier*, 'sights', to take careful aim. It is used alone or with *auf* = 'at', but does not take a gun etc. as obj. The E. *to aim a gun* becomes *mit dem Gewehr [auf jmdn./etw.] zielen.* **Anvisieren**, a formal syn., takes as acc. what is aimed at.

Er hielt die Pistole in Augenhöhe und zielte.   *Er visierte die Zielscheibe an und drückte ab.*
Er zielte auf die [Ziel]scheibe, schoß und traf ins Schwarze.
Die Jungen zielten mit ihren Zwillen auf Vögel, trafen sie aber nie.
Er zielte mit einem Schneeball auf den Lehrer, traf ihn aber nicht.
Die Luftraumüberwachung zielte mit Boden–Luft-Raketen auf die feindlichen Flugzeuge.

ii. Richten has as its first general sense 'to direct or turn in a certain direction'. It is applied to guns as well as to things like *ein Fernrohr, ein Scheinwerfer, eine Antenne, die Augen, eine Kamera*, etc. With guns it does not necessarily imply a precise aim but simply being directed to a general area, so that it translates both **aim** and *point at*. When a gun is used for deterrence or as a threat, *richten* is the usual v. as *zielen* mostly implies that the person will also fire the weapon. *Richten* is the technical term for aiming *Geschütze* (large guns used by the artillery) and translates the military expressions *to lay* or *train a (large) gun on sth. Der Richtschütze* or *Richtkanonier* is the gunner who aims the artillery piece.

Vermummt drangen drei Räuber in den Schalterraum ein und richteten je einen Revolver auf Kassierer und Kunden.   *Alle Scheinwerfer waren auf den Star des Abends gerichtet.*
Zur Sicherheit blieb ein Posten zurück, der seine Maschinenpistole auf die Kreuzung richtete, um im Notfall nachfolgende Fahrzeuge aufzuhalten.

iii. One sense of **anlegen** is a syn. of *zielen. Ein Gewehr anlegen* means 'to bring a gun to the shoulder'. *Er legte an* can, but need not, imply taking aim. Followed by *auf jmdn./etw.* either with or without *Gewehr* as obj., it means 'to aim at'. *Der Wachsoldat legte [sein Gewehr] auf den Flüchtenden an.* Anlegen is only used with guns one holds to the shoulder.

Er legte an und schoß. (Leaves the question of aiming open, but it makes it appear likely.)
Er legte auf den Hasen an, drückte aber nicht ab.

2. Fig. uses. The obj. of **aim** can be remarks, criticism, etc., *The judge aimed his remarks at the journalists in the court,* and the subj. a person pursuing a certain goal, *He's aiming at a leading position,* or actions, laws, etc. directed to a certain objective, *The law aims at a reduction in the road-toll.*

i. Zielen auf is found in such contexts, but the usual vs. are now **abzielen auf** and **hinzielen auf**. They are interchangeable as far as meaning is concerned, but *abzielen* is more often heard. They are used either with a person as subj. and *mit, Ich weiß nicht, auf wen/worauf du [mit dieser Bemerkung] abzielst/hinzielst,* or with the remark or action as subj., *Ich weiß nicht, auf wen/worauf diese Bemerkung abzielt/hinzielt.*

> *Seine Kritik zielte darauf hin/ab, daß der Autor als Dilettant entlarvt und sein Buch der Lächerlichkeit preisgegeben werden sollte.*
>
> *Ich habe keine Ahnung, worauf ihre Anspielungen hinzielen.*
>
> *Er zielte auf einen möglichst raschen Aufstieg/auf einen hohen Posten/auf den Ruin seines Konkurrenten ab.   Der Vorwurf zielte auf seine Geldgier hin/ab.*
>
> *Die neuen Maßnahmen zielen auf die Beseitigung der Mißstände/auf eine Verringerung der Zahl der Verkehrsunfälle ab.*
>
> *Es war leicht zu durchschauen, daß er auf die Verunsicherung der Zuhörer abzielte.*
>
> *Die Zwischenrufe zielten weniger darauf ab, Heiterkeit auszulösen, als die Zuhörer zu schockieren.*
>
> *Er zielte mit dieser Bemerkung auf dich ab. Or Seine Bemerkung zielte auf dich ab.*

ii. Anvisieren also means 'to pursue' an objective. An alternative is **anstreben**, to strive for.

> *Die Firma visierte eine Ausweitung des Produktionsvolumens an.*
>
> *Die Autoindustrie visiert die Entwicklung eines, wenn auch nicht schadstofffreien, so doch zumindest wesentlich schadstoffärmeren Autos an.*
>
> *In der Beschreibung der Ereignisse ist Vollständigkeit anzustreben.*
>
> *Wir streben eine schnelle Lösung des Konfliktes an.*

iii. Sich richten an means 'to be aimed or directed at' a particular group. *Die Werbekampagne gegen das Rauchen richtet sich vor allem an Jugendliche. Der Appell richtet sich an alle.* When criticism, spoken or written critical remarks, suspicion, etc. are the subj., the prep. is **gegen**. *Seine Kritik richtet sich gegen die Wirtschaftspolitik der Regierung. Der Autor richtet sich in seinem Roman gegen soziale Mißstände. Gegen wen richtet sich Ihr Verdacht?*

iv. Close in meaning to the vs. discussed in 2. i are **es auf jmdn./etw. absehen** and **es auf jmdn./etw. anlegen** followed by a person or thing. While *absehen* needs a personal subj., *anlegen* can also have a person's actions as subj. but must remain directly connected with people. Both take *darauf* and an infin. Both present the aim or the underlying attitude as questionable, if not bad. *Er hat es darauf abgesehen, möglichst schnell reich zu werden* suggests he is unscrupulous in the methods he employs. If A says that something has happened, B might reply, *'Darauf habe ich es abgesehen.'* From B's point of view this is neutral (unless he is praising his ability to manipulate events), but when it refers to a third person, *absehen* is usually pejorative and would not be used if someone's aim were to be, for example, *ein Wohltäter der Menschheit.* Such an aim is expressed as *Es war sein Ziel/Er hatte sich das Ziel gesetzt, Wohltäter der Menschheit zu werden.* A special use of *absehen* is *Der Chef hat es heute auf dich abgesehen*, which means 'to criticize continually', 'to get at'.

> *Er hat es mit dieser Bemerkung/dieser Kritik/diesem Vorwurf auf dich abgesehen.*
>
> *Mit dieser Heirat könnte er es bloß auf ihr Geld abgesehen haben.*
>
> *Sie haben es darauf abgesehen/es darauf angelegt, uns zu ärgern.*
>
> *Alles schien darauf angelegt zu sein, den Hauptkonkurrenten zu ruinieren.*
>
> *Sie hatten alles darauf angelegt, ihn zu täuschen.*

Es absehen auf also means 'to be bent on having or getting sth.' *Er hätte das bestellte Auto in grauer oder grüner Farbe sofort haben können, er hatte es aber auf einen roten Wagen abgesehen.*

3. Aim to do something can be expressed by **beabsichtigen**, 'to intend', or **wollen**, 'to want'. *Wir beabsichtigen, bis Ende des Monats fertig zu sein. Wir wollen den Wünschen unserer Kinder nachkommen.*

all, each, every, whole *adjs.* Some uses.

1. All + sing. ns.

i. E. **all** is used with sing. ns. meaning 'the whole amount, extent, or the entire number of'. In cases in which **all** is interchangeable with **whole**, only **ganz** is used in G. *All day, all the week, all his life, all the time, all the family, all the class, all the army,* or *all the country* can be expressed as *the whole day, his whole life, the whole class, country,* etc. and become *der ganze Tag, die ganze Woche, sein ganzes Leben, die ganze Zeit, die ganze Familie, die ganze Klasse, die ganze Armee,* and *das ganze Land. Ganz* translates *all* and *whole* as well as *all of* or *the whole of. Ganz* is also used where only **all** (not **whole**) is possible in E., as in *mein ganzes Geld, die ganze Arbeit, das ganze Wasser, das ganze Obst, das ganze Brot,* etc. An expression like *all sein Leben* may occur in the written language, but it does not belong to ordinary speech, which uses *sein ganzes Leben.* In *all die Zeit* or *all das Wasser, die* and *das* are stressed demonstratives corresponding to *that,* not to *the. All das Geld* = 'all that money'. Cf. 2. i. *Ganz* is used with geographical names without an article or inflection and means 'the whole population or area'. *Ganz Schottland, ganz Berlin, ganz Afrika,* and *die schönste Stadt in ganz Europa.*

> *Wir haben den ganzen Sommer/das ganze Jahr in Indien verbracht.*
> *Das ganze Land war besetzt/lag unter einer tiefen Schneedecke.*
> *Sie sind die ganze Nacht aufgeblieben.*   *Sie haben den ganzen Kuchen gegessen.*
> *Obwohl es erst der 18. ist, habe ich mein ganzes Gehalt für diesen Monat schon ausgegeben.*
> *Wir waren drei Stunden weg, und sie hat die ganze Zeit ohne Pause gearbeitet.*

ii. Alle does occur with sing. ns. With ns. which denote something immeasurable or uncountable, *alle* and *ganz* are interchangeable. *Alle* is either declined and the article omitted, *alles Wissen,* or it appears as *all* before a possessive, *all sein Geld.* Except in fixed phrs., however, **ganz** is the everyday form, and *alle* belongs to the written language. Many people would say, for instance, *'Alle Mühe war vergebens',* because this is a fixed expression, but *die ganze Mühe* is possible.

> *Alles Unglück kommt von seiner Unentschlossenheit.* Or *Das ganze Unglück kommt von . . .*
> *Er hat die ganze Schuld/alle Schuld auf sich genommen.*
> *Ihr habt allen Spaß gehabt, und wir alle schwere Arbeit.* (More commonly: *Ihr habt den ganzen Spaß gehabt, und wir die ganze schwere Arbeit.*)   *Sie bot ihre ganze Energie/all ihre Energie auf.*
> *Meine ganze Kraft/All meine Kraft ist verbraucht.*
> *Und wiederum war alles Lernen umsonst gewesen.*

2. Uses of **alle** and syns.

i. Alle is used with pl. ns. with the article omitted, whether the article is included in E. or not. *Alle Pferde haben vier Beine. Alle Studenten sind schon da. Wir haben alle Vorbereitungen schon getroffen. All die* means 'all those'. *Sieh dir all die Studenten an! Alle die* also means 'all those', but it is usual only with a following relative clause, though this may be implied. *Alle die Studenten, die an dem Ausflug teilgenommen haben, haben viel Neues gelernt. Alle die Leute wollen mit dem Zug mit* implies something like *Alle die Leute, die hier auf dem Bahnsteig stehen . . .* In speech, *die ganzen* is often used for *alle,* but many people regard its use as substandard. *Wo gehen die ganzen Leute hin?*

ii. Ganze following a number means 'whole'. *Wir mußten drei ganze Stunden warten.* Preceding a number it means 'only' or colloquially 'all of'. *Das Buch hat ganze zwei Mark gekostet. Ganze elf Studenten waren da.*

> *Mit ganzen zwei Mann kann ich so viel Arbeit an einem Tag nicht schaffen.*

iii. Sämtlich and **gesamt**, 'all without exception, total', are formal syns. of *alle* or of *ganz,* 'whole'. The main difference is that *sämtlich* is usual with pl. ns., *gesamt* with sing. ones. *Sämtliche Kinder der Familie. Man hat uns durch sämtliche Räume des*

Schlosses geführt. Die gesamte Bevölkerung. Die gesamte Belegschaft. Das gesamte Vermögen. Another distinction is that *gesamt* needs an article while *sämtlich* does not take one. With pl. ns. requiring an article or possessive *gesamt* is used. *Die gesamten Länder der EU. Meine gesamten Ersparnisse.* Thus *die gesamten Räume* expresses the same meaning as *sämtliche Räume. Sämtlich* is sometimes found with sing. ns. without an article. *Sämtlicher abgelieferte Schrott. Sämtliches gesammelte Material.* It is also an adv. *Wir haben Ihre Aufträge sämtlich erledigt. Die Lehrkräfte waren sämtlich erschienen.*

3. Every expressing a distribution over time or space, as in *A train leaves every five minutes* or *We stopped and rested every three miles*, is **jeder** when a sing. n. follows and **alle** with a pl. one.

> *Busse fahren alle zehn Minuten zum Opernhaus.*   *Jede Stunde fliegt ein Flugzeug nach Berlin.*
> *Alle 100 Meter hielten sie Bekannte an, die ihr gratulieren wollten.* Also *Alle paar Meter.*
> *Alle vier Jahre wird der Präsident gewählt.*   *Er ruft jeden dritten Tag an.*
> *Alle fünf Kilometer/Jede halbe Stunde/Alle fünfzig Minuten machten wir für zehn Minuten halt.*
> *Schreiben Sie in jeder zweiten Zeile!* (on every other line)

4. Every emphasizes the speaker's confidence that a feeling, quality, or action is correct or will happen. *They have every reason to be pleased. There is every prospect of success.* In translating *I have every reason to believe he is innocent* both **alle** and **jeder** can be used. *Ich habe allen/jeden Grund anzunehmen, daß er unschuldig ist. Es besteht alle/jede Aussicht auf Erfolg.* Both *alle* and *jeder* occur in other expressions which have different E. equivalents. *Die Wahrheit dieser Aussage war über jeden/allen Zweifel/ Verdacht erhaben.* Both occur with Art. *Boote aller/jeder Art.* After *ohne*, E. requires *any. Ohne jeden/allen Grund* or *ohne jede/alle Provokation.* **Every** is more frequently used than the G. equivalents, so that E. expressions containing it may need to be translated as the idea they express. *I have every confidence in her* is *Ich habe volles Vertrauen zu ihr.*

5. Each emphasizes that every individual person or thing in a group is referred to. *She gave me five wads of fifty notes each.* This sense is expressed by **je**. *Sie gab mir fünf Bündel von je fünfzig Scheinen. Die Teilnehmer zahlten je zehn Mark.* An alternative is *Jeder Teilnehmer* or *Jeder der Teilnehmer zahlte zehn Mark. Je* also states how much each one of a group of things costs, but **das Stück** or **pro Stück** are also common. *Die Äpfel kosten je fünfzig Pfennig,* or *Die Äpfel kosten fünfzig Pfennig das Stück/pro Stück.*

amount *n.*

1. Amount and **quantity** can state how much there is of something concrete. *A small amount/quantity of salt. The same amount/quantity of gravel.* **Quantity** is usual with pl. ns., *the quantity of goods*, while **amount** alone is used for money and with abstracts, *Only few people possess that amount of patience.*

i. Die Menge means 'a definite quantity or amount of' a substance other than money and is used with both sing. and pl. ns. *Die Nachbarn haben eine Tonne Sand bestellt; wir brauchen die gleiche Menge/die dreifache Menge,* three times that amount. *Die Menge der beschädigten Waren ist unbedeutend.* Note that when a sing. n. follows *Menge*, neither *von* nor the gen. is needed. *Diese Menge Brot.*

> *Beim Einnehmen dieser Arznei muß man die vorgeschriebene Menge genau beachten.*
> *Von den Vorräten ist nur noch eine kleine Menge übrig.*
> *Wir haben eine enorme Menge Material gesammelt.*

ii. In everyday speech **die Menge** also denotes a large but unspecified amount or number, a lot of all kinds of things including money. *Ganz* makes it stronger. *Das hat eine Menge [Geld] gekostet. Wir haben eine ganze Menge [Geld] ausgegeben. Das hat eine Menge Arbeit verursacht. Sie haben eine Menge Bücher.*

iii. Der Betrag, sometimes **der Geldbetrag**, is 'an amount of money'. An alternative is **die Summe**. Some compounds are *die Gesamtsumme* and *der Gesamtbetrag, die Endsumme*, 'final amount', *der Restbetrag*, 'amount left or balance', *die Versicherungssumme*, 'sum insured'. *To pay off sth. in small amounts, Er zahlte die Schulden in kleinen Beträgen/in Raten ab.*

> *Das Buch kostet 25 Mark mit Porto. Ich überweise diesen Betrag auf Ihr Postscheckkonto.*
> *Der Rechnungsbetrag ist bis zum 31. Oktober zu zahlen.*
> *Ich habe die ganze Summe aufgebracht.   Diese Summe muß bar bezahlt werden.*
> *Die Eltern des entführten Kindes haben die von den Kidnappern geforderte Summe bezahlt.*

iv. With abstracts the main equivalent is **das Maß**, a measure (of something). *Die Arbeit mit diesen Kindern erfordert ein erstaunliches Maß an Geduld.* For further examples see *Maß* under EXTENT 3. In relation to knowledge and things to be learned **die Menge** is used. *Ein Student oder ein Schüler kann an einem Tag nur eine bestimmte Menge Wissensstoff bewältigen.*

2. Amount followed by a non-numerical n., *the amount of the bill/fine/subscription*, is **die Höhe**, the primary meaning of which is 'height'. *Alle staunten über die Höhe der Rechnung. In Höhe von* states what something amounts to. *Sie erhielt ein Stipendium in Höhe von 700 Mark im Monat.*

> *Die Höhe des Bußgeldes ist für jeden Verstoß gegen die Straßenverkehrsordnung gesetzlich festgelegt.*
> *Man ist sich über die Höhe des Zuschusses noch nicht einig.*

3. A great/large/small amount of sth. is often best translated by **viel** and **wenig**. *A large amount of prejudice* is *viele Vorurteile; a small amount of trouble* is *wenig[e] Schwierigkeiten; a large amount of evidence* is *viele Beweise*. **Half that amount** is simply *die Hälfte. Er schuldete mir 1 000 Mark, konnte aber nur die Hälfte [davon] zahlen.*

4. Any amount of work means 'a lot of it' and can always be translated by **viel**. Closer to the E. expression is **jede Menge**, 'any amount or number', which can be followed by a sing. or pl. n. *Es gibt viel/jede Menge Arbeit, die du erledigen kannst. Wir hatten viel/jede Menge Schwierigkeiten.*

5. No amount of talking will do any good. One equivalent is *kein* + a verbal n. *Oil and water do not mix—no amount of stirring and shaking will produce a solution, Öl und Wasser vermischen sich nicht—kein Rühren und kein Schütteln erzeugen eine Lösung.* Thus *Kein Wunschdenken wird die Lage ändern.* An alternative to *Kein Zureden hat geholfen* is *Alles Zureden half nichts* or *war umsonst*, no amount of persuasion/persuading did any good. Likewise *Kein Schreien nutzte etw.* and *Alles Schreien nutzte nichts. No amount of* is a variant on a concessive clause. A general transl. is to formulate the part of the sent. it introduces as such a clause. *No amount of stirring* could be expressed as *however much one stirs (them). Wie sehr man Öl und Wasser auch rührt und schüttelt, es entsteht keine Lösung* or *Man kann Öl und Wasser auch noch so sehr rühren und schütteln, es entsteht keine Lösung.*

angry *adj.* annoy *v.* be annoyed *v.*

1. Words denoting annoyance and a moderate degree of anger.

i. One of the most frequently encountered words is **böse**, which covers displeasure, annoyance, and mild anger. It is mostly applied to people, but only when a fairly close relationship exists between the person whose displeasure is aroused and the one who arouses it. It suggests a hostile attitude or resentment felt by someone who feels hurt or offended by another's behaviour or does not approve of what the other person is doing. In this sense it is only used predicatively or as an adv. *Er wird immer gleich böse. Sie sah mich böse an.* If used attributively as in *ein böser Mensch*, it would mean 'evil' or 'BAD'. However, with ns. like *Worte* or *Blick, böse* means 'angry'. Likewise, *böses Blut* denotes anger and ill-feeling. The most common construction is *böse auf jmdn.*, *Sie war einige Zeit böse auf ihn*, but it also occurs frequently with *mit*, *Sie war einige Zeit böse mit mir*, and with the dat. without a prep., *Ich hoffe, du bist mir wegen dieser Sache nicht mehr böse*. About is *über* or *wegen*. If I were annoyed about the way a shop assistant I did not know had treated me, I would say *Ich habe mich über den Verkäufer geärgert*. *Böse* would only be used for people I know fairly well. If, however, I were voicing criticism to a person I did not know about something for which he or she might feel responsible but for which I do not wish to attribute any blame to him or her, I might begin with a request not to take offence at my remarks by saying, '*Seien Sie mir nicht böse!*', which creates the close relationship that *böse* presupposes.

> *Ich bin auf Kai böse. Er hat mir versprochen, einen kleinen Lastwagen für den Umzug zu besorgen, aber sich nicht darum gekümmert. Nun melde ich mich erstmal nicht mehr bei ihm.*
>
> *Sie war wegen der zerbrochenen Vase ziemlich böse auf ihn.*
>
> *Sie ist böse mit ihrem Vater über die Ereignisse vom letzten Wochenende. Er hat sie ausgescholten, als sie um zwei Uhr morgens nach Hause kam.*
>
> *Wir hatten uns über Politik gestritten. Es waren zuletzt böse Worte gefallen, und wir waren nicht als gute Freunde auseinandergegangen.*

ii. Ärgerlich implies temporary displeasure, irritatation, or annoyance because of dissatisfaction with some matter or someone's behaviour. *Der arme Jan wurde richtig ärgerlich*. It takes *auf* and *über* with people and *über* with things. *Er ist auf/über seine Kollegen ärgerlich. Sie ist ärgerlich über diese Klatschgeschichten*. *Ärgerlich* can also be applied to what gives rise to irritation, i.e. is annoying or irritating. *Ein ärgerlicher Vorfall. Ein ärgerliches Erlebnis*. In reference to looks, speech, etc. it means 'showing annoyance'. *Sie machte ein ärgerliches Gesicht. Ein ärgerlicher Blick/Zuruf. Sie antwortete ärgerlich*.

> *Sie reagierte ärgerlich auf die Kritik ihrer beiden Brüder an dem Essen, das sie gekocht hatte.*
>
> *Eine ärgerliche Bemerkung.*   *Er machte eine ärgerliche Handbewegung.*

iii. Ärgern is a trans. v. meaning 'to annoy, irritate, or make angry' when the anger is relatively mild. The refl. form **sich ärgern** means 'to be annoyed, irritated, or mildly angry' and is used alone or with *über*.

> *Ihre Unpünktlichkeit ärgert mich sehr.* Or *Ich ärgere mich sehr über ihre Unpünktlichkeit.*
>
> *Was er über mich sagte, war so ungerecht, daß ich mich noch über ihn/darüber ärgere.*
>
> *Nur um mich zu ärgern, sehen sich Rolf und Dietmar den Krimi im Fernsehen an. Sie interessieren sich nicht dafür und wissen doch, daß ich was anderes sehen will.*
>
> *Er wird rot im Gesicht, wenn er sich ärgert.*

iv. Verärgern suggests a higher degree of annoyance than *ärgern*, a state that lasts longer and has more consequences. *Sein Verhalten hat mich verärgert*. It is most frequently found as a past part. *Ich bin über seine Handlungsweise verärgert*.

> *Sie hat heute ihren schlechten Tag. Verärgert ist sie, übel gelaunt.*
>
> *Er war so verärgert, daß er niemand sehen wollte; sogar gute Freunde mied er.*

v. In everyday speech **sauer** is often heard in the sense 'annoyed, mildly angry', but it should not be used in a situation requiring formal language. It suggests that someone is so annoyed at another's behaviour that for a time he or she can only speak ill of the other. It takes *auf*. **Grantig** means 'ill-humoured, bad-tempered, and likely to give vent to this at every opportunity'. It belongs to familiar speech, used in talking with family or friends. *Grantig* suggests weaker irritation than *sich ärgern* but implies disapproval of the ill-humour.

> *Er ist jetzt ziemlich sauer auf seinen Chef/Kollegen.*
>
> *Ich bin ganz schön sauer auf dich, weil du nicht zur Verabredung erschienen bist.*
>
> *Er wird immer grantig, wenn man ihn auf seine Fehler anspricht, und antwortet kurz angebunden.*
>
> *Ich würde ihn heute nicht fragen, er scheint sehr grantig zu sein.*

Jmdm. auf die Nerven gehen and **jmdn. nerven** mean 'to get on s.o.'s nerves, to irritate', often by repeated questions or requests. *Die ewige Streiterei geht mir auf die Nerven. Die laute Musik nervt mich—stell' sie bitte leiser! Allmählich nervt er mich mit seinen endlosen Bitten und Fragen.*

vi. Der Unwille and **unwillig** suggest displeasure and indignation, but they are not commonly used.

Mit unwilligen Worten machte er seinem Ärger Luft.

Die Lehrerin schüttelte unwillig den Kopf über den Witz, den sich der Schüler erlaubt hatte.

Ihr Unwille darüber, daß man ihr zumutete, mit Hand anzulegen, war ihr deutlich anzusehen.

vii. Gereizt describes more a potential state in which someone can easily burst into anger. It is similar to *irritable*, which means 'readily excited to anger, easily ruffled or annoyed'. The cause need not be latent aggressiveness, but something which might appear justified like tiredness or over-exertion.

Die Mutter sagte zu den Kindern: 'Vater ist heute abend gereizt. Treibt es nicht so wild, sonst explodiert er.'

viii. Ungehalten means 'moderately angry' but is a formal and refined word.

Nachdem sie eine halbe Stunde auf ihn gewartet hatte, war sie sichtlich ungehalten.

Der Tennisspieler war recht ungehalten über die Entscheidung des Linienrichters.

ix. One sense of **aufbringen** is 'to anger or make angry'. It suggests a moderate degree of anger which is always apparent in the appearance of those concerned. It occurs most frequently in the past part. *aufgebracht*, angry, incensed. It suggests only a temporary state, in contrast to *zornig*, which is applied to anger which continues for a longer period or is permanent. *Die zornigen jungen Männer.* Cf. 2. ii.

Die aufgebrachte Menge durchbrach die Polizeiabsperrungen.

Die Bewohner aller umliegenden Dörfer waren über den Beschluß der Landesregierung aufgebracht, den zwischen den Dörfern liegenden Wald zu roden.

2. Words denoting a higher degree of anger.

i. The most common words in the spoken language are **wütend** and **die Wut**. *Wut* really means 'fury'. It still has this sense, but the range of meaning has been extended to include less strong states of anger in much the same way as that of *furious* has been in E. **Jmdn. in Harnisch bringen** and colloquially **jmdn. auf die Palme bringen** mean 'to make s.o. angry/furious'. **Jmd. gerät in Wut** or **in Harnisch** or **geht auf die Palme**, gets angry or in a rage.

Ich war so wütend, daß ich hätte zuhauen können.

Er äußerte sich wütend über den Dorfklatsch. Es wurde behauptet, seine Ehe sei zerrüttet.

Die Wut des Volkes richtete sich gegen den Diktator.

Daß man diesem unzuverläßigen Kerl einen Vertrauensposten gegeben hat, kann auch den ruhigsten Menschen in Harnisch bringen.

Der kann einen wirklich auf die Palme bringen mit seinem dauernden Dazwischengerede. Sag' ihm doch endlich mal, daß er sich zu Wort melden soll!

ii. Der Zorn and **zornig** suggest strong anger, sometimes justified anger about an injustice, but, although not completely literary words like *ire* or *wrath*, they are confined to educated speech. This applies even more to **zürnen** + dat., 'to be angry', and **erzürnen**, 'to make angry'.

Sie hatten sich gestritten und gingen im Zorn auseinander.

Ihr Zorn richtete sich gegen die Parteibonzen.

In seinem Zorn hätte er seine Frau beinahe erschlagen.

Er wurde rot vor Zorn, als er diese Beleidigung hörte.

Früher dachten die Menschen, die Götter zürnten ihnen, wenn sie ihnen keine Opfer brachten. Aus Angst, die Götter zu erzürnen, opferten sie regelmäßig.

Tagelang hat sie ihm gezürnt.   Seine Frechheit hat mich sehr erzürnt.

iii. Der Jähzorn denotes a sudden and violent outburst of anger which is set off by a particular incident but which arises from a tendency in the person's character. *In seinem Jähzorn schlug er auf den Jungen ein.*

announce *v.* **announcement** *n.* **proclaim** *v.* **report** *n.* and *v.* Order of treatment: 1. Mostly equivalents of **announce** and related ns. 2. Senses of **report** carried by *melden*. 3. Vs. for media reporting. 4. Other equivalents of the n. **report**.

1. The chief sense of **announce** is 'to make known publicly, usually for the first time and by word of mouth, sth. regarded as news or of interest either of an official or private nature or related to one's area of responsibility'.

i. Bekanntgeben and bekanntmachen both express this meaning and differ only in that the latter tends to be used for official announcements (although it is not restricted to them), whereas *bekanntgeben* is more common in the private and non-governmental spheres, though not unknown in official announcements. They refer to announcements in both speech and writing. (For *jmdn. mit jmdm./etw. bekanntmachen* see INTRODUCE.)

> *Der Bundestrainer hat die Aufstellung der Fußball-Nationalmannschaft bekanntgegeben.*
> *Daß die Straße wegen Bauarbeiten am Wochenende gesperrt wird, wurde gestern in der Zeitung bekanntgemacht/bekanntgegeben.*
> *Die Gewinner des Wettbewerbs wurden im Rundfunk bekanntgegeben/bekanntgemacht.*
> *Der Schuldirektor machte den Inhalt des Schreibens bekannt, das er vom Kultusministerium erhalten hatte.*   *Im Laufe des Abends haben sie ihre Verlobung bekanntgegeben.*

ii. The ns. are **die Bekanntmachung** and **die Bekanntgabe**. The former is an official announcement or a public notice. *Während ich im Rathaus wartete, las ich die behördlichen Bekanntmachungen, die dort aushingen.* Both also mean 'the action of announcing sth.', but *Bekanntgabe* is more usual with a following gen. *Die Bekanntgabe der Ergebnisse der Tarifverhandlungen erfolgte durch Anschlag/Aushang in allen Betrieben.* (*Die Bekanntmachung* is possible, but less common.)

iii. Bekanntmachen and bekanntgeben are the equivalents of **report** and **announce** when they mean 'to give a formal or official account of sth.' *The company reported/announced an increased profit/the discovery of a uranium deposit. The treasurer reported a balance of £100.*

> *Der Schatzmeister des Vereins gab bekannt, daß der Überschuß der Einnahmen über die Ausgaben 500 Mark betrug.*   *Die Gesellschaft gab einen erhöhten Gewinn bekannt.*
> *Die Gesellschaft gab bekannt, daß sie ein Uranvorkommen entdeckt hatte/gab die Entdeckung eines Uranvorkommens bekannt.*

iv. Durchsagen means 'to announce information by loudspeaker' and is also applied to the announcement by radio of information useful to the public. *Der Wetterbericht wird um Mittag im Radio durchgesagt.* The corresponding n. is **die Durchsage**. *Ich habe die Durchsage nicht verstanden.*

> *Es wurde durchgesagt, daß der Intercity-Zug nach Köln sich um zehn Minuten verspätet hat.*
> *Wir müssen uns beeilen. Man hat gerade die Ankunft deines Zuges durchgesagt.*
> *Es wurde im Radio durchgesagt, daß ein langer Stau sich auf der Autobahn wegen eines schweren Unfalls in der Nähe von Kassel gebildet hatte.*

v. Ansagen means 'to announce programmes or items on radio and television'. *Die Ansagerin im Fernsehen/Radio sagt die Sendungen an.* It is also used for announcing matters which will take place or come into effect in the future. It usually implies that the information is made known orally.

> *Ich weiß nicht, von wem das Musikstück ist. Ich habe nicht aufgepaßt, als es angesagt wurde.*
> *Der Direktor hat eine Kollegiumssitzung für Donnerstag nachmittag angesagt.*
> *Der Seminarleiter sagte: 'Ich möchte zuerst etw. Geschäftliches ansagen.'*
> *Sie hat ihre Ankunft/ihre Rückkehr für nächsten Monat angesagt.*
> *Der neue Premierminister hat der Korruption den Kampf angesagt* (announced that he will fight it, declared war on it).

vi. Ankündigen means 'to announce' action, steps, or measures to be undertaken by governments etc., or organized events which are planned for the future.

Die Direktion hat eine Neuorganisation des Betriebes angekündigt.
Die Regierung kündigte verschärfte Maßnahmen gegen die Steuerhinterziehung an.
Man kündigte das Konzert durch Plakate und Zeitungsanzeigen an.
Man hat eine Reform des Schulwesens angekündigt.

vii. Announce a visit is einen Besuch ansagen or ankündigen. Sich ansagen expresses the same meaning, but is not formal, so that *Franz hat sich angesagt* is often best translated as *He said he would come to see us*. Sich [zu Besuch] anmelden is more formal and usually implies that the person will arrive as announced or expected. *Sich ansagen* does not suggest such a firm arrangement, so that the person may not turn up.

Mein Bruder hat sich mit seiner Familie zu Besuch angemeldet.
Sie hatte sich bei ihrer Freundin angesagt/angemeldet.

viii. In the public sphere **verkünden** is used for the announcement of court judgments, resolutions (*Beschlüsse*), the results of elections, etc. though *bekanntgeben* is not unusual. *Ein Gesetz verkünden* is 'to proclaim or promulgate a law'. In the private sphere *verkünden* implies announcing something of importance to the subj. with great emphasis and with ceremony.

Das Gericht wird morgen sein Urteil/seine Entscheidung in dem Prozeß Schmidt gegen Witte verkünden.
Die neue Regierung verkündete eine Amnestie für alle politischen Gefangenen.
Sobald man die abgegebenen Stimmen ausgezählt hatte, hat man das Ergebnis verkündet.
Freudestrahlend verkündete sie ihre Verlobung.   *Er verkündete stolz, daß er gewonnen habe.*
Nach dem Essen verkündete er seinen Entschluß, Missionar zu werden. (Here bekanntgeben would
    be unemotional in tone.)

ix. Verkündigen is now used only in religious contexts.

Die Apostel haben das Evangelium verkündigt.
Es ist die Aufgabe eines Pfarrers, das Wort Gottes im Gottesdienst zu verkündigen.

x. Melden means 'to announce the names of guests arriving at a reception etc. or coming to see s.o. on business etc.' *Eine Sekretärin meldet Besucher. Die Hausangestellte trat ins Zimmer und meldete Herrn Hoffmann.* If I have an appointment with the headmaster at eleven, the secretary might say, *'Ich melde Sie kurz vor elf.'* However, in the construction with *sich lassen* **anmelden** is used. *Ich lasse mich durch die Sekretärin beim Direktor anmelden.* Although the action expressed by both vs. is identical, *sich anmelden lassen* is preferred when the person is not expected.

2. Melden corresponds to four senses of **report**.

i. 'To notify' meaning 'to make known to the relevant authority or to a superior sth. that has happened, an accident, fire, crime, case of infectious disease, etc., or s.o. who has offended in some way'.

Jeder Fall von Typhus muß der Gesundheitsbehörde gemeldet werden.
Ich muß den Wasserrohrbruch vor dem Haus melden.
Der Lehrer meldete den Schüler, der ihn beschimpft und bedroht hatte, dem Direktor.
Nach der Explosion wurden keine Toten und Verwundeten gemeldet (no casualties were reported).
Wir haben den Unfall/den Einbruch/den Vorfall usw. bei der Polizei gemeldet.

If a crime is the obj., **anzeigen**, 'to report to the police', is used, but is less common than *melden*. If a person is the obj., *melden* is possible, but *anzeigen* is the usual word. *Anzeigen* also translates *to denounce*. While *to report s.o. to the police* suggests that the action is justified, *to denounce s.o.* implies that it is not. *Anzeigen* covers both these situations as it does not have any particular implication. *Denunzieren* exists, but is a fairly learned word. *Ein Spitzel muß ihn angezeigt/denunziert haben.*

Sie haben den Verbrecher angezeigt. Or Sie haben ihn wegen des Verbrechens angezeigt.
Ein Zeuge des Unfalls zeigte den Fahrer, der Fahrerflucht begangen hatte, bei der Polizei an.

(In *Man meldet die Geburt eines Kindes beim Standesamt, melden* means 'to register'. *Die Geburt eines Kindes anzeigen* is 'to put a birth notice in the newspaper'.)

ii. Report meaning 'inform s.o. in charge what one has seen, heard, or done'. **Melden** is used with the police and military, in the official sphere, and where someone has to report something to a superior. Because of the connotation of official duty, it is not common in the private sphere. Cf. *Vorkommnis* under EVENT 1. iv.

Melden Sie dem Kompanieführer, wann Sie den Auftrag ausgeführt haben!
Der Abschluß der Arbeit ist dem Werkleiter zu melden.
Der Spähtrupp meldete Truppenbewegungen des Gegners.

Berichten is used for highly placed people like ambassadors. *Der Botschafter berichtete die Antwort des Präsidenten an seine Regierung.* It is also used in connection with spies. *Der Spion berichtete regelmäßig über alles, was im Kanzleramt geschah.* Berichten needs an obj. or *über*. On his return from the Summit the Chancellor reported to cabinet becomes *Nach seiner Rückkehr vom Gipfeltreffen berichtete der Kanzler dem Kabinett über dessen Verlauf.* An alternative which may or may not have a phr. with *über* is *Er erstattete dem Kabinett Bericht [über den Verlauf des Wirtschaftsgipfels].*

For **report** in the sense 'to convey information or repeat sth. heard or observed to another when this is not one's official duty', **mitteilen** or **benachrichtigen**, 'to inform', or **weitergeben**, 'to pass on information', can be used. **Erzählen** expresses the same idea, but belongs more to familiar language and implies a fairly close relationship between the person passing on the information and the one receiving it.

Er teilte seinem Freund alles mit, was er über die Pläne von dessen Konkurrenten erfahren hatte.
Ich habe euch eine wichtige Neuigkeit mitzuteilen/zu erzählen.
Günter erzählt mir alles, was er erfährt.

iii. Sich melden means 'to report or to present oneself for duty or work, make known to s.o. who is often, but not necessarily, a superior, that one has arrived or is present at a certain place'. *Bei seiner Ankunft muß sich jeder Offizier beim Kommandanten melden.* **Sich zurückmelden** is 'to report back' or 'report one's return'. Neither is confined to military-type situations. *Sich krank melden*, to report sick. (*Sich für eine Arbeit melden* means 'to volunteer for a job'. *Viele haben sich [freiwillig] zur Bekämpfung der Waldbrände gemeldet.*)

Teilnehmer an der Konferenz werden gebeten, sich im Sekretariat zu melden.
Nach Ausführung der Befehle haben sich die Soldaten bei ihrem Vorgesetzten zu melden/zurückzumelden.
Vom Urlaub zurückgekehrt, meldeten sich alle Soldaten gesund zum Dienst [zurück].
Der Chef hat nach Ihnen gefragt. Melden Sie sich bitte bei ihm!

iv. Sich melden is used of expeditions, ships, etc. which report their progress etc. regularly. It also occurs frequently in private life in the meaning 'to contact s.o. and make one's whereabouts and activities known'. *Ich melde mich* is thus like *I'll get in touch with you*. In school, *sich melden* means 'to put up one's hand to make known that one wants to say sth.' *Sich zu Wort melden* is 'to ask leave to speak' in a meeting etc.

Die Expedition meldete sich per Funk alle zwölf Stunden.
Sie versprach, sich während der Reise regelmäßig brieflich zu melden.

3. With regard to reporting for newspapers, radio, and television, both *melden* and *berichten* are used. **Melden** and **die Meldung** are applied to a brief report which gives only the barest facts, while **berichten** and **der Bericht** imply a fuller account. *Am Dienstag meldeten die Zeitungen ein schweres Erdbeben in Peru. Am Freitag berichteten sie [ausführlich] über die angerichtete Verwüstung.* Although it often makes little difference which v. is used, only *berichten* is combined with a word implying detail, such as *ausführlich*. *Berichten* + acc. means 'to report in full', *Er berichtete die Ergebnisse seiner Untersuchung*, but it is normally found with *über* meaning 'to report (less than fully) on'. *Berichten über* is the usual expression for newspaper etc. reporting, and also translates 'to cover events, a meeting, etc.' *Wilfried Schirlau berichtet für den Norddeutschen Rundfunk über Ereignisse in Australien und Neuseeland. Hunderte von Reportern/Berichterstattern berichteten über die Olympischen Spiele.* The E. construction *A coup is reported to have taken place* or *The president is reported to have fled from the capital* is expressed impersonally by *es wird gemeldet/berichtet* or *man meldet/berichtet* + clause. *Es wird [aus einem Land oder einer Stadt] gemeldet/berichtet, daß ein Staatsstreich stattgefunden habe/daß der Präsident aus der Hauptstadt geflüchtet sei.* The idea can also be expressed as *Nach einer [bisher unbestätigten] Meldung aus . . . hat ein Staatsstreich stattgefunden. Berichten* is also applied to private and public accounts of a wide range of activities, journeys, debates, speeches, meetings, scientific and other research, carrying out of projects, etc. *Sie hat uns ein bißchen über ihre Reise berichtet.*

4. Other equivalents of **report**.

i. If a parliamentary or similar committee investigates something and prepares a report, the appropriate n. is **der Bericht** and the v. **berichten über** if the matter concerns existing conditions or occurrences in the past. **Das Gutachten**, originally a legal term, is applied to a report on someone/something when this means 'an expert opinion', e.g. *ein ärztliches oder psychiatrisches Gutachten* in a court case or a report by an engineer on a bridge, etc. It is also the appropriate word if the report is an expert prediction or a recommendation by specialists on any kind of matter, say the sugar industry in the next ten years. *Gutachten* is also used for reports on people applying for positions. The v. **begutachten**, which needs an obj., means 'to write or prepare a report on'. The v. **gutachten** is occasionally found as a pres. part. or infin. *Der gutachtende Arzt,* the doctor preparing a/the report. *Wer kann in diesem Fall gutachten?*

> *Der Untersuchungsausschuß legt nächste Woche seinen Bericht dem Bundestag vor* (it will report).
> *Der Bericht der Enquêtekommission umfaßt fünf Bände.*
> *Der Richter forderte ein medizinisches Gutachten an.*
> *Das Gutachten/Der Bericht der Behörde über den Zustand des Bergwerks ist noch nicht abgeschlossen.*
> *Das Gutachten des Dozenten über die beiden Studenten, die sich um Aufnahme in den diplomatischen Dienst beworben hatten, war sehr positiv.*
> *Zwei Sachverständige/Experten begutachteten die Konstruktionsteile des Flugzeuges.*

ii. Das Zeugnis is 'a school report'. *Deutsche Schüler bekommen Zeugnisse zweimal im Jahr.*

iii. Report also means 'the sound of an explosion'. *There was a loud report: Dann gab es einen lauten* **Knall**.

answer, reply, rejoin, retort, respond *vs.*

1. The main equivalents of to **answer** or **reply to** a question, letter, remark, or any expression of desire or opinion in speech or writing, *antworten* and *beantworten*, differ in the main syntactically.

i. Antworten is used alone, *Er antwortete sofort,* and may take a dat. and/or a clause. *Sie antwortete mir, daß sie mit dem Ergebnis zufrieden sei. Er antwortete, alles sei in Ordnung/daß er das Gerücht schon gehört habe.* A n. stating what is being answered must follow *auf. Sie antwortete [mir] auf meine Frage.* The only possible objs. are words like *[k]ein Wort, Er antwortete kein Wort, Sie antwortete nur zwei Sätze,* or indefinite expressions, *Er hat nichts geantwortet.* Cf. 3.

> *Denk doch gut darüber nach, bevor du antwortest!*   *Antworte mir doch, wenn ich mit dir rede!*
> *Er hat einsilbig/kühl/klipp und klar/zerstreut geantwortet.*
> *Ich habe noch nicht auf seinen Brief geantwortet.*

'Wann hast du ihn zuletzt gesehen?' fragte er. 'Gestern', antwortete sie.

Auf die Bitte um weitere Auskunft antworteten sie nicht.   *Was hat sie geantwortet?*

ii. Beantworten needs an obj. which is frequently *Frage* or *Brief*, but can be other words like *die Einladung* or *der Zwischenruf*. The person answered is in the dat. Thus both *Beantworte [mir] diese Frage!* and *Antworte mir auf diese Frage!* are possible. *Antworten* is more common in the spoken language. In contexts in which either word is possible, *beantworten* usually implies that the answer is adequate and complete, whereas *antworten auf* leaves this open and means no more than that some answer is given. *Er beantwortete die Frage mit 'Ja'* implies that this is an adequate response. *Beantworten* is also used for answering questions in examinations. Note that only *antworten*, not *beantworten*, is followed by a *daß*-clause.

> *Ich werde mich bemühen, Ihre Frage sachlich zu beantworten.*
>
> *Auf die Frage seiner Mutter hat er nur mit 'Mmm' geantwortet.*
>
> *Der Minister hat auf die Frage nach den Folgen der Wirtschaftspolitik der Regierung ausweichend geantwortet.*   *Alle Prüfungsaufgaben sind zu beantworten.*
>
> *Der Prüfling/Der Examenskandidat hat die Fragen der Prüfungskommission vollständig beantwortet.*

2. Special cases.

i. Bejahen and **verneinen** mean 'to say yes or no' to a question etc. and translate *answer*, *reply*, or *respond in the affirmative* or *negative/affirmatively/negatively*. *Sie bejahte/verneinte die Frage.*

ii. Answer is also applied to a knock on the door or the ringing of a (telephone) bell. G. does not use *antworten*. *Answer the door!* is *Geh' bitte mal zur Tür!* or, if it is clear that it is necessary to go to the door, *Geh' bitte mal hin!* The question is *Gehst du zur Tür?* The imp. *Answer the phone!* is *Geh' [du] mal ran! Ich gehe mal ran* means that I am going to the ringing phone. When stating who answers or that someone or no one answered, the usual terms are **sich melden** and **abnehmen**, to take off the receiver. *Das Telefon klingelte, und Steiner meldete sich/nahm ab.* (Note that *Ich melde mich telefonisch* means that I will get in touch with you by phone. Cf. ANNOUNCE 2. iv.)

> *Ich habe angerufen, aber es hat sich niemand gemeldet.* Or . . . *aber niemand hat abgenommen.*
>
> *Wenn Sie anrufen, wird sich die Sekretärin melden.*

iii. Sich melden is used for answering advertisements, though **antworten** also occurs. *Ich habe mich auf die Anzeige der Firma Hennig und Co. gemeldet. Ich habe auf die Stellenanzeige geantwortet.*

> *Zwanzig Bewerber meldeten sich auf die Anzeige einer Sekretärenstelle [hin].*

3. Syns. of *antworten*.

i. Erwidern means firstly 'to react to another's feeling, greeting, smile, etc. in a similar way', i.e. 'to answer or reciprocate'. It occurs with ns. like *Liebe, ein Dienst, ein Blick, ein Besuch, jmds. Zuneigung, Abneigung*, etc. as obj. *Sie hat seine Liebe nicht erwidert. Er erwiderte ihr freundliches Lächeln mit einem Gruß. Das Feuer des Feindes erwidern*, to return or answer the enemy's fire. *Erwidern* is secondly a refined syn. of *antworten*. It is used with and without *auf*, with a dat., a clause, or an obj. such as *nichts. 'Ja', erwiderte sie. Er erwiderte nach einiger Überlegung, daß er es nicht wisse. Auf diese Frage erwiderte sie [mir] nichts.* It stresses the emotional involvement of the person answering and is often modified by an adv. With advs. like *scharf* or *schlagfertig*, it is similar to **retort**, which suggests either a reply in kind to a jest, sarcasm, criticism, etc. or simply a sharp or aggressive reply. *'Das wird bei mir nicht so sein', erwiderte er scharf.*

> *Auf seine Frage erwiderte sie freundlich, sie finde die Aufführung ausgezeichnet.*

ii. Entgegnen means 'to counter sth. just said with an objection or with the opposite opinion' and is similar to **retort** or **rejoin**. It is used in the same constructions as *erwidern*.

Auf meine Behauptung, alles sei in bester Ordnung, entgegnete sie, genau das Gegenteil treffe zu.
Auf diese Beschuldigung wußte er nichts zu entgegnen.

iii. Versetzen is now used only in the written language. It implies an energetic reply which often takes up the words just used. Unlike *erwidern* and *entgegnen*, it does not take a dat.

'Vorteile', versetzte er nicht ohne Bitterkeit, 'die du dir nicht entgehen lassen willst.'

4. Answer a charge, answer for.

i. Answer is also used with *a charge* as obj. *He was released on bail to answer a charge of embezzlement at the next sitting of the court.* One equivalent is **sich verteidigen**, to defend oneself. *Er mußte sich gegen die Anklage von Veruntreuung verteidigen.* **Sich verantworten** expresses a similar idea, but is used without *Anklage* and with *wegen. Er muß sich wegen Diebstahls/Mordes [vor Gericht] verantworten. Charge* is understood.

ii. Sich verantworten müßen also occurs in situations in which people are known to have acted in a certain way and have to defend themselves against criticism of what they have done, i.e. answer for their actions. The defence is an explanation of the reasons why they have acted in this way. *Du mußt dich beim Chef wegen der Art und Weise verantworten, wie du den Auftrag ausgeführt hast.*

iii. Answer for also means 'to accept responsibility for' or 'guarantee'. **Verantworten** + acc. means 'to take responsibility for' and may correspond to *answer for. Ich verantworte diese Maßnahme/Handlung.* To **answer for** *people* or *s.o.'s behaviour* is translated by **bürgen, gutsagen,** or **einstehen,** 'to vouch for, guarantee', or **die Verantwortung übernehmen.** *Ich bürge für jmd[n.], dem eine Geldsumme anvertraut wird,* means that I declare the person reliable and honest and make myself liable for any loss that may occur.

Eine so hohe Ausgabe kann ich nicht verantworten.   *Ich bürge für die Wahrheit des Berichts.*

Du kannst ihm das Geld ruhig anvertrauen. Ich bürge für ihn/seine Ehrlichkeit. Or Ich verantworte es.

Er sagte für die Summe gut.   *Sie sagte für ihre Kollegin gut.*

Wenn wir nicht sofort Reformen durchführen, kann ich für die Folgen nicht einstehen.

Wenn sie mitkommt, übernehme ich die Verantwortung für ihre Sicherheit (answer/be responsible for).

iv. Answer for occasionally means 'atone or pay the penalty for sth.' The equivalent is **büßen.** *Irgendwann wirst du für dieses Unrecht büßen. Er hat meine Familie betrogen—das soll er mir büßen.*

5. Answer or meet requirement, wishes, hopes, expectations, etc. *Sth. answers the purpose, Es* **erfüllt** *den Zweck.* Cf. MEET 7.

6. Answer *a description* is either **der Beschreibung genau entsprechen** or **genau auf die Beschreibung passen.**

Ich mußte gestern eine Freundin meiner Mutter, die ich nie gesehen hatte, die meine Mutter aber beschrieben hatte, vom Bahnhof abholen. Erst nach einiger Zeit bemerkte ich eine Frau, die den Bahnsteig langsam entlang ging, und die genau auf die Beschreibung paßte.

Ein Mann, der der von der Polizei verbreiteten Beschreibung genau entsprach, wurde in einer Stadt auf dem Lande gesehen.

7. Answer = 'to act in or by way of response', or **respond [to]** = 'to answer by some responsive act' or 'to act in response to an influence', are applied both to people, *Thousands responded to/answered the appeal for the famine victims, He responded to the treatment,* and to things, *The ship was listing heavily and would not answer/respond to the helm.*

i. With *der Aufruf* and *der Appell*, both = 'appeal or call' for support etc., **folgen** is the usual word.

Millionen sind dem Spendenaufruf gefolgt. Or . . . *sind dem Aufruf gefolgt, für die von der Hungersnot Betroffenen zu spenden.*

ii. Applied to mechanical devices, **ansprechen auf** means 'to respond to'. It is also applied to people and to parts of the body which respond to treatment. It implies a pos. or beneficial response.

Der Thermostat spricht auf Temperaturänderungen bis zu 0,5 °C an.
Das Schiff hatte starke Schlagseite und sprach nicht mehr auf das Steuer an.
Der Patient/Das verletzte Bein sprach gut auf die Behandlung an.

iii. Reagieren auf, 'to react to', is the commonest equivalent of **respond** in situations other than the ones described in i and ii. *Reagieren* normally has an adv. or phr. with *mit* showing how the person etc. responded. *Auf* + n. can be understood. *Er hat sauer [auf den Vorschlag] reagiert. Sie reagierte [auf diese Anspielung] mit einem Lächeln.* As in *The horse responded to the kindly treatment,* **respond** implies a pos. or good response, this idea needs to be added in G. *Das Pferd reagierte positiv auf die freundliche Behandlung.* (Here also *ansprechen auf* without *positiv.*) The adv. or *mit* phr. can be omitted, as in the first two sents. below, if the context makes the nature of the response clear. A question is formed with *wie. Wie hat er [auf die Frage] reagiert?* Two alternatives are **beantworten** and **quittieren**, which need an obj. and a phr with *mit.* Both state how individuals respond to or meet remarks or actions. *Sie beantwortete den Gruß mit einem Lächeln. Die Zurechtweisung quittierte er mit Spott. Beantworten* is used with weightier matters. *Die Regierung beschloß, weitere Provokationen des Feindes mit Waffengewalt zu beantworten.*

Die Pupillen der Augen reagieren auf die Intensität des Lichts, indem sie sich weiten und verengen.
Die Regierung reagierte auf den Druck der öffentlichen Meinung.
Er reagierte mit Wut auf die Kritik.
Die Arbeiter beantworteten die Lohnkürzung mit einem Streik.
Die Studenten quittierten diese Ansage mit Pfiffen.   *Er quittierte meine Frage mit Achselzucken.*

As the pass. of *reagieren* is not usual, the E. pass., as in *Every word of protest would be answered by a blow,* can be expressed by *reagieren* in the act., *Auf jedes Wort des Protestes reagierte der Wärter mit einem Schlag,* or by the other two vs. in the pass., *Jedes Wort des Protestes wurde mit einem Schlag beantwortet/quittiert.*

apparent *adj.* In the sense dealt with here, **apparent** means 'seeming to be the case even though there is no definite proof that it really is so'. It may be contrasted with what is real, but it does not always imply that what is apparent is not in reality as it seems. If we talk of *the apparent size of the sun,* we know from our knowledge of astronomy that this is not in reality as small as it seems. However, *an apparent contradiction* may or may not be a real one, and someone talking of another's apparent fidelity may consider that person really faithful although he or she may not be certain. The G. equivalents. are *scheinbar* and *anscheinend.* **Scheinbar** means that what seems to be the case is in reality *not* so, whereas **anscheinend** leaves the question open. *Was nur scheinbar der Fall ist* involves an illusion or deception, *nur* being often added to *scheinbar* to strengthen the meaning. If someone uses *anscheinend,* e.g. *Sie haben anscheinend nichts dagegen,* then he or she is not sure whether the observation and the conclusions drawn from it correspond to reality. However, the probability that they do is assumed to be high. There is also a syntactic difference. Only *scheinbar* is commonly used as an adj., as in *die scheinbare Bahn der Sonne um die Erde.* Both are used as advs. (The distinction given above is sometimes not observed, although the use of *scheinbar* as an exact syn. of *anscheinend* is decried in the Duden *Zweifelsfälle der deutschen Sprache,* a guide to good usage. An example of the use of *scheinbar* in the sense of *anscheinend* is *Der Redner wurde scheinbar nicht verstanden. Anscheinend* is, of course, just as acceptable, and the non-native speaker is well-advised to use it. Many people consider *scheinbar* wrong here.)

Die Oase lag scheinbar zum Greifen nahe, aber es dauerte noch Stunden, bis er sie erreicht hatte.
Ihre scheinbaren Einwände dienten nur dazu, die Entscheidung hinauszuschieben.
Das Wasser ist scheinbar ruhig, doch nehmt euch in Acht vor den starken Strömungen!
Er sprach mit scheinbarer Begeisterung von dem Plan, aber er konnte uns nicht täuschen.
Es ist anscheinend gestern nacht sehr kalt gewesen, denn auf allen Pfützen ist noch Eis.
Sie ist anscheinend nicht sehr gut informiert. Andernfalls hätte sie uns auf unsere Fragen umfassendere Antworten gegeben.
Deine Theorie trifft scheinbar zu, doch du hast bei deinen Überlegungen einen entscheidenden Punkt nicht berücksichtigt.

appear, seem *vs.*

1. This section is chiefly concerned with **appear** and **seem** in the meaning 'to give an impression'.

i. Seem and **appear** differ as little in meaning as do the equivalents **scheinen** and **erscheinen**, which differ mainly syntactically. In strict use, *scheinen* alone is followed by an infin., and *erscheinen* by an adj. Hence the transformation: *Der Vorschlag scheint mir gut zu sein*, and *Der Vorschlag erscheint mir gut.*

Seine Aussage erscheint mir nicht ganz glaubhaft.
Seine Aussage scheint mir nicht ganz glaubhaft zu sein.

Thus, whenever an infin. is present, *scheinen* is used. *Er schien nicht zu merken, daß jmd. ihm folgte.*

Ihnen schien mein Besuch eine Abwechselung zu bedeuten.

In some cases, *erscheinen* seems to be used with an infin., but this is dependent on an adj.

Es erschien ihr ratsam, sich nicht in diese Angelegenheit einzumischen.

Particularly in the spoken language, however, *scheinen* occurs with an adj. without an infin., though the infin. can be regarded as *sein* understood.

Das scheint mir falsch.   *Weitere Schritte schienen nötig/unumgänglich.*
Ein Zusammenstoß schien unvermeidlich.

Scheinen only is used in three expressions: *es scheint* with and without a dat. + *daß* or *als ob*, *so scheint es*, which in speech can be shortened to *scheint's*, and *wie es scheint*.

Es scheint [uns], daß du helfen kannst/könntest.   *Sie sind reicher, als es scheint.*
Es schien [mir], als ob die Stunde nie enden wollte.
Es war, scheint's, eine gute Fete.   *Er hat, so scheint es, kein Geld bei sich.*
Uns scheint [es], daß es eine andere Möglichkeit gibt.

However, if an adj. is present, *erscheinen* is used. It is also used with *wie* = 'like'.

Es erschien uns allen merkwürdig, daß er nichts über den Vorfall sagen wollte.
Was passiert war, erschien ihm wie ein Rätsel.

ii. Closely related to *erscheinen* is **vorkommen**, which suggests a subjective, and usually spontaneous, impression based more on feeling than on rational considerations. It occurs frequently, though not exclusively, with adjs. denoting something strange, such as *seltsam, sonderbar, merkwürdig, verdächtig, komisch*, etc. It must have a dat. of the person. *Erscheinen* is also possible in these contexts.

Diese Frau kommt mir irgendwie bekannt vor, aber ich weiß nicht, wo ich sie getroffen habe.
Sein Verhalten kam mir gleich verdächtig vor. Später habe ich erfahren, daß jmd. versucht hat, ein Auto aufzubrechen.
Die Sache kommt uns seltsam/sonderbar/lächerlich vor.
Was du mir da erzählt hast, kommt mir komisch vor.

If the impression is about oneself, i.e. about the person speaking or spoken about, only *vorkommen* is used. *Er kam sich unverstanden/vollkommen verlassen vor.*

Bei ihnen komme ich mir wie ein dummer Junge vor.

Du kommst dir wohl sehr wichtig vor. An alternative: *Du scheinst dich wohl sehr wichtig zu nehmen.*

It is used with *wie* = '[to be] like'.

Nach der langen Trennung kam ihr der Bruder wie ein Fremder vor.

Das wäre mir wie Verrat vorgekommen.

Vorkommen is also used impersonally. *Es kommt einem [so] vor, als ob . . .*

Es ist mir gleich vorgekommen, als ob etw. nicht in Ordnung wäre.

Es kam ihm so vor, als hätte er sie schon einmal gesehen.

Manchmal kommt es einem vor, als ob die Zeit stillstände.

iii. In one sense **wirken** denotes the total impression someone or his/her behaviour makes. It does not take a dat. *Neben seinem besonders großen Bruder wirkte er wie ein Zwerg.*

Der Vortragende wirkte nervös und zerfahren.   *Um alles in der Welt wollte er männlich wirken.*

Das Dorf mit seinen leeren trostlosen Straßen wirkte ausgestorben.

iv. If one is quite certain that the impression corresponds to reality, E. uses *look* (*tired, excited,* etc.), which is in G. **aussehen.** Cf. LOOK 8.

2. Erscheinen covers most other senses of **appear**.

i. 'To come into view, become visible'. *Das Schiff erschien am Horizont. Am Fenster erschienen lachende Kindergesichter.*

ii. 'To be found, occur'. *Der Name des Dorfes erscheint in einer Urkunde des 12. Jahrhunderts.*

iii. 'To present oneself' before a tribunal etc. *Sie mußten vor Gericht erscheinen.* In other contexts it means 'to come, go, arrive'. *Bitte erscheinen Sie heute abend pünktlich zur Versammlung! Er ist heute nicht zum Frühstück erschienen.*

iv. Hence of actors etc. *Er erschien 1955 zum ersten Mal auf der Bühne.* A syn. in this context is **auftreten.** *Er trat letztes Jahr als Hamlet auf. Als die Sängerin auftrat, begrüßte man sie mit lautem Beifall.*

v. Of books and periodicals. *Die erste Auflage ist 1978 erschienen. Die Zeitschrift erscheint wöchentlich.*

appearance, semblance *ns.*

1. The first meaning of **appearance** is 'the way people, animals, and thgs. look or seem to be'. *He doesn't care about his appearance. She has a well-cared-for appearance.*

i. The usual expression for people is **das Äußere, sein/ihr Äußeres,** which refers to the total appearance, i.e. the impression a person's bodily features and clothing make together. As *das Äußere* also means 'the exterior or outside', *Das Äußere des Hauses ist sehr schön,* the meaning of 'appearance' is confined to people.

Sie hat ein angenehmes/gepflegtes/ansprechendes/vornehmes/anziehendes Äußeres.

Er hält auf/legt Wert auf sein Äußeres.   *Seit einiger Zeit vernachlässigt er sein Äußeres.*

Sie sollte sich nicht so gehen lassen. Ihr Äußeres läßt in letzter Zeit sehr zu wünschen übrig. Also Ihr Aussehen . . . Cf. 1. iii.   *Er kümmert sich nicht um sein Äußeres.*

Seinem Äußeren nach zu urteilen, muß er ungefähr die Hälfte seines Verdienstes für Kleidung ausgeben.

ii. Die äußere Erscheinung is a syn. of *das Äußere,* and both are sometimes contrasted with the inner qualities or feelings and character.

Ihre äußere Erscheinung entsprach in ihrer Korrektheit und Eleganz ihrer beruflichen Stellung.

Von dem Äußeren/der äußeren Erscheinung eines Menschen auf sein Inneres zu schließen hieße oft, voreilige Schlüsse ziehen.

Sein Äußeres war, wie immer, gepflegt, obwohl er im Inneren gegen eine schwere Enttäuschung anzukämpfen hatte.

Erscheinung, used after *sein,* is not restricted to looks and clothes but includes a person's bearing, the way he/she moves and behaves towards others. The usual transl. is *figure. Er/Sie ist eine Erscheinung* implies in some way out of the ordinary, impressive, dignified, or stately. It usually occurs with an adj. such as *imposant, anziehend, angenehm,* or *sympathisch.*

Sie war eine elegante Erscheinung und erregte einiges Aufsehen, als sie den Saal betrat.

Er war eine finstere/düstere Erscheinung mit einem dichten, schwarzen Bart und buschigen Augenbrauen.

iii. Das Aussehen is strictly what remains constant about a person's appearance despite changes of clothes. It may refer to the total appearance, but it is the only word possible when just the facial expression is meant. *Sein Aussehen veränderte sich plötzlich* means *Sein Gesicht[sausdruck] veränderte sich. Das Aussehen* (but not *das Äußere*) is used with *gut* and *schlecht* to refer both to the general appearance and to the facial expression as an indication of health. *Ich erschrak über sein schlechtes Aussehen. Das Aussehen* only is possible with words which indicate qualities of character or states of mind. *Sie hat ein kluges, zufriedenes Aussehen.*

Bei ihren Angestellten legt das Hotel großen Wert auf gutes Aussehen und Benehmen/ . . . auf ein gepflegtes Äußeres und gutes Benehmen. *Seinem Aussehen nach ist er Araber.*

Sie hat ein gutes, gepflegtes Aussehen. *Ein Mann finsteren Aussehens kam auf ihn zu.*

Nach langer Krankheit kehrte der Lehrer an die Schule zurück, doch sein schlechtes Aussehen entsetzte die Schüler. Er sah aus wie ein alter Mann.

Aussehen can be applied to things, *Das Aussehen der Stadt hat sich verändert,* but for reasons of simplicity of style, such ideas are best formulated with the v. *aussehen.* Cf. LOOK 8.

Das Dorf hat in den letzten zehn Jahren ein ganz anderes Aussehen bekommen. (. . . sieht anders aus als vor zehn Jahren.)

Die alten, baufälligen Häuser zeigen ein ärmliches, verwahrlostes Aussehen. (. . . sehen ärmlich und verwahrlost aus.)

2. When someone's **appearance** means that he or she appeared in a place, it must be rendered by **das Erscheinen**, or with reference to appearing as an actor on the stage or as a speaker etc. by **das Auftreten** or **der Auftritt**. The latter is restricted to the stage and also translates *s.o.'s entry. Das Erscheinen* is also used for the appearance of books etc. in the sense 'coming on to the market'.

Das Erscheinen feindlicher Truppen in der Nähe der Hauptstadt verbreitete Schrecken unter der Bevölkerung. *Sein Erscheinen vor dem Gericht wurde verlangt.*

Bis zum Erscheinen der neuen verbesserten Auflage des Lehrbuches müssen wir eben die alte benutzen.

Niemand rechnete noch mit dem Erscheinen dieses Kollegen in der Sitzung, als die Tür aufging und er eintrat. *Der Schauspieler wartete auf seinen Auftritt.*

Durch wiederholtes Auftreten in diesem Stück konnte sie nicht nur ihre Rolle, sondern fast den ganzen Text auswendig. *Beim Auftreten des Clowns fingen die Kinder an zu klatschen.*

3. Appearance = 'an outward state of appearing which may or may not be the actual state', as in *They wanted to maintain/keep up/preserve an appearance of neutrality.* It is frequently found in the pl. **appearances** meaning 'outward show or indications'. *Appearances are deceptive. To all appearances he works very hard* means that he seems to, but this may not be true. A meaning related to that of **appearance[s]** is expressed by **semblance**. If there is a semblance of a condition or quality, this appears to exist, even though this impression may be false. *The trial was conducted without even a semblance of justice.*

i. Der Schein denotes an appearance which does not correspond to reality. *Der Schein trügt,* appearances are deceptive. *Das ist alles nur Schein,* outward show. It is linked with *das Sein* or *die Wirklichkeit. Das ist mehr Schein als Sein,* it is only outward show, things are not what they seem to be. *Der Schein blendet/täuscht jmdn.;* thus *sich vom Schein blenden/täuschen lassen. Etw. zum Schein tun* is 'to pretend to be doing or make a pretence of doing sth.' *Man wahrt* (sometimes *bewahrt*) *den Schein,* maintains/keeps up a certain impression or appearance. Unlike *Anschein*, *Schein* forms compounds: *der Scheinangriff, das Scheinargument, die Scheinlösung, die Scheinopposition, das Scheinmanöver*, etc. All imply that the action is not what it seems to be. In the expressions *den Anschein erwecken* and *sich den Anschein geben* + gen., infin., or *als ob*, **der Anschein** also denotes a false impression, but one which is deliberately created. *Er gab sich den Anschein, als ob er etw. davon verstände* (or *verstünde*). *They wanted to maintain an appearance of neutrality* can only be translated as *Sie wollten den Schein der Neutralität wahren* if it is clear that the impression is false. *Sie wollten den Anschein erwecken, als wären sie neutral* also implies that the impression is false. If the people are really neutral or if their real attitude is unclear, the transl. should be *Sie wollten neutral erscheinen*. In another use *Anschein* leaves the question open as to whether what appears to be the case also conforms to reality. *Dem/Allem Anschein nach*, 'to all appearances, apparently', and *den Anschein haben*, 'to appear, seem', give an impression of what one observes and state that this, in the opinion of the speaker, could well, but may not, correspond with reality. *Dem Anschein nach ist das eine wohlhabende Familie*, it seems to be and probably is.

> *Er beschäftigte sich nur zum Schein mit der Mathematikaufgabe und las unter der Bank ein Buch.*
> *In der Gerichtsverhandlung bemühte man sich nicht einmal darum, den Schein der Gerechtigkeit zu wahren.*
> *Alles sah friedlich aus, doch der Schein trog/täuschte.*
> *Der Schein ist gegen mich, doch darf ich hoffen, daß ich nicht nach dem Schein gerichtet werde.* (Schiller, *Maria Stuart*) *Dem Anschein nach sind sie zu Konzessionen bereit.*
> *Nach außen hin wirken sie wie eine glückliche Familie, doch das ist alles nur [schöner] Schein.*
> *Nur notdürftig wahrte er den Schein der Höflichkeit. Nur seine Vertrauten ahnten seinen Ärger und seine Enttäuschung. Er gab sich den Anschein, als könne er alles.*
> *Die Schwierigkeiten sind größer, als es den Anschein hat.*
> *Er gab sich den Anschein eines Lebemannes, doch seine Freunde wußten, daß er es sich eigentlich gar nicht leisten konnte und daß eine solche Lebensweise ihm gar nicht lag.*
> *Es hatte wirklich den Anschein, als hätte ich das Geld gestohlen.*

ii. Der Augenschein is 'what the eye sees when looking at sth.' and leaves the question open as to whether what is seen corresponds to reality. It occurs mostly in fixed expressions. *Dem Augenschein nach kommen sie gut miteinander aus*, 'according to what our eyes tell us', i.e. 'from what we can see'. *Etw. in Augenschein nehmen* means 'to look at sth. carefully' and is translated as *inspect* or *examine*. *Jmd. läßt sich vom Augenschein überzeugen* suggests looking closely to find out just what has happened.

> *Dem Augenschein nach kreist die Sonne um die Erde, aber der Augenschein trügt.*
> *Nach dem ersten Augenschein war der Wagen in bester Ordnung, aber es stellte sich heraus, daß er an einigen Stellen durchgerostet war.*
> *Um uns ein besseres Bild von dem entstandenen Schaden machen zu können, sollten wir das Haus vor Ort in Augenschein nehmen.*
> *Dem Augenschein nach zu urteilen, müssen es harte Verhandlungen gewesen sein, denn alle Verhandlungsteilnehmer verließen sichtlich erschöpft den Saal.*

apply *v.*

1. The original sense of **apply** is 'to bring or place in contact with sth. for a particular purpose' as in *to apply a foot-rule* or *heat to sth.* **Anlegen**, the basic meaning of which is 'to put or lay on or against', is used in the lit. sense with *ein Lineal*, 'ruler', and *der Winkel*, 'square', and fig., like **apply**, with *der Maßstab*, 'criterion, yardstick'. *Bei dieser Prüfung muß man strengere Maßstäbe anlegen. Welchen Maßstab legen wir hier an?* Other uses of **apply** are often circumlocutions for which there is a simple v. in one or both languages. *To apply the brakes* is *die Bremsen betätigen*

(*betätigen* = 'to bring or put into operation'), but *bremsen*, 'to brake', means the same. *To apply heat* is *erwärmen* or *erhitzen*. Cf. WARM and HEAT. With ointments, lotions, (sticking) plaster, make-up, etc., **apply** means 'to bring into contact with the body to serve a purpose' and with paint, polish, etc. 'to bring into contact with any surface'. **Auftragen**, 'to spread or put on a surface', is used with ointments, paint, etc.

Die Farbe/Das Bohnerwachs darf man nicht zu dick auftragen.
Man trägt die Schminke/das Rouge/den Puder leicht auf das Gesicht auf.
Tragen Sie die Salbe regelmäßig auf die Wunde auf!

Auflegen expresses the idea of placing on or over. Thus *Man legt ein Pflaster auf* (but *Man legt ein Pflaster auf eine Wunde*). *Auflegen* can also be used with *die Schminke*.

2. Apply also means 'to make use of' or 'to employ for some purpose'. *S.o. applies an idea/a process/a remedy/another method/his or her knowledge and skill/his or her findings in new developments.* **Anwenden** and **verwenden**, which both have the general sense 'to use for a purpose', differ mainly in the contexts in which they occur, despite some overlapping. *Anwenden* is used like **apply** in the sense of administering a remedy. *Der Facharzt beschloß, ein anderes Heilmittel anzuwenden.* (*Verwenden* is possible, but less common.) It is usual with *die Methode* and *das Verfahren*, 'process', although *verwenden* is sometimes found. The E. equivalent is not always **apply**. *Eine Kraft anwenden*, 'to apply a force', *seine Kräfte anwenden*, 'to use one's strength', and *Gewalt anwenden*, 'to use or employ force'. *Anwenden* is used with *das Mittel*, 'a means of doing sth.', *eine List*, 'ruse or trick', *ein Kunstgriff*, 'trick, dodge', and *ein Trick*. *Applied science* is *angewandte Naturwissenschaften*. Thus *die angewandte Mathematik*. *Verwenden* is used when talking of applying or using money for a certain purpose. Both express the sense of applying knowledge to a specific task. Cf. USE.

Diese Arznei darf nur äußerlich angewandt/angewendet werden.
Bei der Analyse dieser Stoffe wenden wir eine neue Technik/ein vereinfachtes Verfahren an.
Er scheute nicht davor zurück, unerlaubte Mittel und eine gemeine List anzuwenden.
Die Summe, die der reiche Unternehmer der Stadt hinterlassen hatte, wurde für die Ausbildung verwaister Kinder verwendet.   *Die Polizei mußte Gewalt anwenden.*
In der neuen Arbeit können Sie Ihre Erfahrung anwenden.
Was du in der Schule gelernt hast, mußt du nun in deinem Beruf anwenden.
In dieser Stelle kannst du deine Deutschkenntnisse gut verwenden.

3. Anwenden also corresponds to **apply** when it means 'to bring a rule, law, test, principle to bear on or into contact with certain facts', but it is less broad. *Anwenden* implies bringing something of a general nature to bear on a specific case. It is used with *ein Gesetz, ein Paragraph (eines Gesetzes), eine Regel, eine Verfügung, eine Wahrheit, ein Sprichwort*, etc. *Der Richter wandte ein neues Gesetz auf den Fall an.* It cannot be used when something which is asserted about one specific case is simply transferred to another, as in *You can apply this criticism (of New Zealand novelists) to Australian novelists*. The only G. word possible here is **beziehen**, to REFER.

Diese Regel kann man nicht auf alle Fälle anwenden, aber auf die meisten.
Diese Regel läßt sich auf die meisten Fälle anwenden.
Dieser Begriff/Dieses Wort kann auf viele Dinge angewendet werden.
Diese Kritik, die an neuseeländischen Romanciers geübt wurde, kann man auch auf australische beziehen.   *Soll ich diesen Vorwurf auf mich beziehen?*

4. Apply is also intr. With and without *to* it means 'to be relevant' and 'to have a bearing on', 'to be true of'. *That rule does not apply in this case. This criticism applies to us all.* The main equivalents are **gelten**, 'to be valid [for], be true of, hold for, apply to', and **zutreffen**, 'to be true [of]'. *Gelten* is used with and without *für* for laws, regulations, agreements, etc., as well as for truths, assertions, criticisms, etc. *In diesem Fall gilt diese Regel nicht. Diese Kritik gilt für alle.* *Zutreffen* occurs only with an assertion, truth, etc. as subj. It can be used alone: *Was Sie sagen, trifft genau zu;* with *für* or *auf*, it is translated as *to apply to* or *to hold for. Das trifft für viele Studenten zu.*

Diese Anordnung gilt für alle Betriebsangehörigen.
Beim Fußball gelten ähnliche Regeln wie beim Hockey.
Diese grammatikalische Regel gilt für alle Fälle, in denen ein Relativpronomen gebraucht wird.
Diese Bemerkung gilt auch für die Regierungszeit Friedrichs des Großen.
Was der Vorredner behauptet hat, trifft nicht zu.
Der Vergleich trifft nicht auf diesen Fall zu.   Das trifft für die meisten Abiturienten zu.
Diese Personalbeschreibung trifft auf viele Jugendliche zu.

5. Apply as a refl. v., *I applied myself [to my work]*, or in the expressions *to apply one's mind* or *energies to a task* or *to doing sth.* means 'to give or devote one's attention assiduously to some pursuit'. **Sich widmen** + dat., 'to devote oneself to', expresses the idea, but more common, especially in the spoken language, is **sich konzentrieren auf**, 'to concentrate on', or **konzentrieren** + acc.

Ich brach sofort mein eben begonnenes Studium ab, um mich anderen Plänen zu widmen. (Böll)
Sie widmete sich dem Studium/dem Beruf.
Ich muß mich jetzt konzentrieren und brauche Ruhe.
Er konzentriert sich seit einiger Zeit auf diese Aufgabe/auf seine Arbeit.
Der Detektiv konzentrierte seine Energie auf die Aufklärung des Verbrechens.

6. In the sense 'to address oneself to s.o. for information, aid, etc.', as in *Apply to the secretary for further information/particulars!* or *Apply at the booking office!*, **apply** is like *approach*. **Sich wenden an**, discussed under APPROACH 4. ii, is the usual equivalent of both words. *Um Näheres [zu erfahren,] wende man sich an die Sekretärin.* If an enquiry is meant, **anfragen** can be used. Cf. ASK 4. i. *Apply within!* can be *Anfragen im Geschäft/Büro* (here *Anfragen* is the pl. of *die Anfrage,* enquiry).

7. Apply = 'to ask for formally and in writing'. **Beantragen** means 'to put sth. to s.o. for approval'. It is used for applications for something like *eine Einreisegenehmigung* which require an administrative decision, when one section of an organization or a person in a firm requests something from a controlling administration, for applying for something to which a citizen has a right like *ein Paß* or *eine Rente* but which requires checking and approval, and can be used for applying to join a club, in which case it is more formal than *sich bewerben.* **Sich bewerben um** is used for employment or for things for which there is open competition. *Man bewirbt sich bei einer Firma um eine Stelle, die ausgeschrieben worden ist,* implies competition and selection. Like **apply**, it is also used if someone writes asking for employment without an advertisement appearing. *Bei dieser Firma kann man sich jederzeit bewerben.* With *als* it means 'to apply for a job as sth.' *Nach einigem Zögern hat sie sich als Stewardeß beworben.*

Ich fliege in zwei Monaten nach Amerika und muß einen Reisepaß und ein Visum beantragen.
Für die neue Zweigstelle beantragte der Geschäftsführer einen Computer und einen zusätzlichen
*   Mitarbeiter.   Der Abteilungsleiter beantragte eine Gehaltserhöhung für zwei Angestellte.*
Aufgrund ihrer guten Leistungen bewarb sie sich um ein Stipendium. Also . . . beantragte es.
Er hat sich leider erfolglos um die Stelle des Geschäftsführers beworben.
Sie bewarb sich um Aufnahme in den Tennisclub. Also Sie bewarb sich um Mitgliedschaft in dem . . .
*   Or Sie beantragte die Aufnahme . . .*

appoint, employ, engage, take on, sign on *vs.* employees *n.*

1. Employ or **take on** = 'to provide with paid work'.
i. Einstellen means 'to give s.o. paid work' and denotes, like **take on**, only the beginning of employment. It is therefore often used in advertisements offering work. Notice-boards in front of industrial establishments read *Wir stellen ein* and

list the positions vacant. *Einstellen* is used for positions up to the middle level, but not for the highest positions. Unlike **take on** and **employ**, it can be used without an obj. *Das Eisenwerk stellt wieder ein/will wieder einstellen.*

Das Werk, das nächsten Monat in Betrieb genommen wird, stellt jetzt Putzfrauen, Schreibkräfte, Facharbeiter und Ingenieure ein.   *Diese Fabrik stellt jederzeit junge Fachkräfte ein.*

Sie ist gerade als Geschichtslehrerin am Theodor-Heuß-Gymnasium eingestellt worden.

Die Post stellt neue Briefträger ein.

ii. Anstellen also means 'to take into one's employ'. Unless otherwise stated, it implies permanent employment at all but the highest levels. *Fest* may be added to make the meaning clear. *Bei einer Firma* etc. *angestellt sein* can simply mean 'to work for a firm etc.' without any further implication, but it often denotes permanent employment with the status of *der/die Angestellte* under G. labour law.

Seit nunmehr zwanzig Jahren bin ich bei diesem Verlag angestellt.

Nach der Probezeit hat man sie fest angestellt.

Die Schule muß zwei Mathematiklehrer anstellen.

Alle Bewerberinnen sind für die Sekretärinnenstelle gut geeignet, aber wir können leider nur eine anstellen.   *Er ist aushilfsweise/vorübergehend/nur halbtags angestellt.*

Sie ist bei einer großen Bank/bei der Stadt[verwaltung] angestellt.

iii. Anstellen can also mean 'to employ or use' for a special purpose.

Man hat ihn angestellt, um den Garten umzugraben.

Man kann ihn überall/zu allen Arbeiten anstellen.

Die beiden wurden für ein Jahr angestellt, um eine Untersuchung durchzuführen.

Er wurde zum Kartoffelschälen/zum Schuhputzen angestellt.

2. i. Beschäftigen is the equivalent of **employ** when this means 'to have in one's employment', not when **employ** can be replaced by **take on.** It is thus common in statements about the number of people employed somewhere or, in the case of individuals, about where they are employed and with *weiter* about continuing to employ someone. *Die Universität will die in diesem Jahr eingestellten Tutoren im nächsten weiter beschäftigen.* (*Beschäftigen* also means 'to keep occupied'. *Die Klasse muß während der Abwesenheit des Lehrers [sinnvoll] beschäftigt werden.*)

Diese Fabrik beschäftigt mehr als tausend Arbeiter.

Mein Vater ist bei der Bundesbahn beschäftigt.

Die Firma plant in Zukunft ein Drittel weniger Arbeiter zu beschäftigen.

ii. Employees. Die Beschäftigten is a general term for the employees of a particular organization. *Die Firma hat 4 250 Beschäftigte.* **Employees** meaning 'those who work for others' as a group is **die Arbeitnehmer** in contrast to **die Arbeitgeber**, those who provide employment. *Wenn es um das Überleben eines Betriebs geht, decken sich die Interessen von Arbeitnehmern und Arbeitgebern. Arbeitnehmer* can be a syn. of *Beschäftigte* in connection with whole industries, but not in relation to one particular firm. *Die Industriegewerkschaft Metall fordert Lohn- und Gehaltserhöhungen von 9,5% für die rund eine Million Arbeitnehmer/Beschäftigten der nordrheinisch-westfälischen Metallindustrie.* **Die Belegschaft** denotes those employed at an industrial plant. *Anfang 1992 hielten die Belegschaften mehrerer Betriebe an der Ostsee besetzt, um deren Schließung zu verhindern.* Cf. STAFF.

Die Beschäftigten des öffentlichen Dienstes fordern eine dreiprozentige Lohn- und Gehaltserhöhung.

In Ostdeutschland weiten sich Protestaktionen von Beschäftigten gegen den Abbau von Arbeitsplätzen aus.

Beschäftigte der Eko Stahl AG, Eisenhüttenstadt, äußerten sich auf einer Belegschaftsversammlung besorgt über einen drohenden Arbeitsplatzabbau.   *Die Belegschaft besteht aus 120 Personen.*

3. Appoint s.o. to a position.

i. Ernennen and **bestellen**, being restricted to higher positions, correspond to **appoint** in this sense. They are used both for appointments to full-time positions and for appointing someone for a special task, e.g. appointing someone guardian or executor or to a commission or board. The only difference between them is that *ernennen* tends to be used for government appointments, and *bestellen* for those in the private sector of the economy. In other areas, such as the private legal sphere, both occur. Both take as obj. either a n. denoting a position, *Sie hat ihren Vertreter ernannt/bestellt*, or a person with the position given after *zu* or *als*, *Man ernannte/bestellte Dr. Steffens zum Vorsitzenden des Ausschusses. Wenn jmd. zu einer Stellung ernannt wird*, the appointment is definite and not subject to ratification.

> *Vor dreißig Jahren wurde er als Aushilfe eingestellt, und heute hat man ihn zum Direktor ernannt.*
> *Das Gericht hat einen Sachverständigen zum/als Gutachter bestellt. Or . . . hat zwei Gutachter bestellt.*
> *Ein Staatssekretär im Auswärtigen Amt wurde zum Botschafter in Paris ernannt.*
> *Bankkaufmann Wolfgang Faßbender ist zum Vorstandsmitglied der Bank bestellt worden.*

ii. Ernennen is used with all types of work when the position is reached by way of promotion.

> *Als erfahrenster Mann in diesem Teil der Fabrik wurde er zum Werkmeister ernannt.*
> *Das Ministerium hat zwei Studienräte zu Oberstudienräten ernannt. Or befördert (promoted).*

4. i. When **appoint to** is followed not by the name of the position but by the place where the work will be pursued, or by *der Posten* or *der Lehrstuhl*, 'a university chair', only **berufen** is possible. It is also used only for higher positions. In G. university parlance, *einen Ruf erhalten/bekommen* means 'to receive an offer of a position'. If the offer is accepted, the person is then *berufen*.

> *Er wurde auf den frei gewordenen Lehrstuhl für Geschichte an der Universität Edinburg berufen.* But
>   *Er wurde zum Professor ernannt.*
> *In die Untersuchungskommission wurden zwei erfahrene Ingenieure berufen.*
> *Sie wurde auf einen neu geschaffenen Posten berufen.*
> *Man hat einen der leitenden Angestellten in den Aufsichtsrat berufen.*

ii. Zuweisen, 'to appoint to an institution', is used for middle order and lower positions.

> *In England wählen die Schuldirektoren ihre Lehrkräfte aus. In Australien werden alle fest angestellten Lehrer den Schulen vom Ministerium für das Bildungswesen des betreffenden Landes zugewiesen.*
> *Er wurde als Arzt einem Zerstörer der Bundesmarine zugewiesen.*
> *Sie ist einer höheren Schule in einer Kleinstadt zugewiesen worden. Or Sie hat eine Anstellung an einer höheren Schule in einer Kleinstadt erhalten.*

5. Einsetzen, which can mean 'to use or employ for a special purpose', is applied to people and things. It translates **appoint** when its obj. is a commission or committee set up for a particular purpose. *Das Parlament hat einen Ausschuß eingesetzt, um Parteispenden zu untersuchen.* It is also used with *Erben*, to name or appoint s.o. [as] heir. *In ihrem Testament hatte sie ihre Neffen und Nichten zu/als Erben eingesetzt.* (It also means 'to put or bring into action' (cf. ACT. 5. ii). *Soldaten wurden eingesetzt, um Dämme aus Sandsäcken an beiden Ufern des Flusses zu bauen.*)

> *Man hat sie zu einer Aufgabe eingesetzt, die ihr wenig lag.*
> *Er hatte seinen Sohn zum Testamentsvollstrecker eingesetzt/bestellt/ernannt.*
> *Da er als Polizist sehr flexibel ist, kann er in vielen Aufgabenbereichen eingesetzt werden.*

6. Heranziehen means 'to employ, call in, or consult s.o.', usually an expert or specialist, and 'to draw on' someone's services or labour or on specialist literature.

> *Ein Betriebsberater wurde herangezogen, um den Betriebsleiter über die Möglichkeiten der Verringerung der Verwaltungs- und Produktionskosten zu beraten.*
> *Da der Hausarzt die Krankheit nicht genau diagnostizieren konnte, hat er einen Facharzt herangezogen.*
> *Für diese Forschungsaufgaben müssen wir einige Fachleute heranziehen.*

7. Dingen, 'to take on domestic servants and farm labourers', has gone out of general use.

8. Sign on.

i. Anheuern is used for merchant seamen. It translates **sign on** both when trans., *S.o. signs seamen on*, and intr., *A seaman signs on*, i.e. accepts employment. *Die Reederei hat zehn Matrosen angeheuert. Er heuerte als Smutje* (ship's cook) *auf einem Frachter an, der nach Neuseeland bestimmt war.*

ii. Verpflichten was originally applied to the engaging of actors, singers, musicians, etc. and has been extended to sportsmen, for whom the E. v. is to **sign on/up**. An alternative for performing artists is **engagieren**. If the actor etc. is the subj., i.e. if **sign on** is intr., it is necessary to use the refl., **sich verpflichten**, 'to accept an engagement or sign up/on', or the pass. of *engagieren. Sie verpflichtete sich für zwei Jahre/wurde für zwei Jahre engagiert. Sich verpflichten* is also used for the armed forces. *Er hat sich für drei Jahre bei der Bundeswehr verpflichtet.*

> *Für das Symphonieorchester werden nur die besten Spieler verpflichtet/engagiert.*
> *Das Stadttheater hat fünf Nachwuchsschauspieler für die nächste Spielzeit verpflichtet/engagiert.*
> *Der Fußballverein hat einen Spieler aus Spanien verpflichtet.*
> *In dem Vertrag verpflichtet sich der Spieler/Schauspieler für drei Jahre.*
> *Der Spieler, der aus dem aktiven Sport ausgeschieden war, wurde als Trainer verpflichtet.*

appointment, engagement *ns.* The sense of **appointment** dealt with here is 'an arrangement one person makes to see another at a specified time for the purpose of consultation, treatment, or the discussion of matters in the area of responsibility or experience of the person giving the appointment'. The meaning of **engagement** treated is less specific. In *I have another engagement* or *business engagements,* it denotes an obligation to meet others for any purpose.

1. Der Termin has become the usual equivalent of **appointment**. It has developed from legal language in which it designates either the time set down for a case or hearing, or, in the expression *Jmd. hat Termin*, means that someone has to appear in court whether as witness, accused, plaintiff, or defendant. It was then applied to a specific time at which something like a visit to a doctor, lawyer, etc. takes place. Cf. TIME.

> *Ich habe einen Termin beim Arzt/beim Zahnarzt/beim Friseur etc.*
> *Ich lasse mir einen Termin beim Rechtsanwalt geben* (make an appointment).
> *Er hat schon viele Termine in der übernächsten Woche.*
> *Morgen um zehn habe ich einen anderen Termin.*

2. Alternatives. In *Ich habe dich beim Zahnarzt angemeldet,* **anmelden** means 'to make an appointment for'. Hence *Ich bin morgen um fünfzehn Uhr beim Arzt angemeldet,* I have an appointment. *Obwohl er nicht angemeldet war, wurde er vorgelassen.* **Bestellt sein** is similar, but implies that the desire for a meeting comes from the person giving the appointment. *A bestellt B zu sich* may imply a relationship in which a subordinate has to obey a superior and correspond to *summon. Beim Arzt bestellt sein* usually means no more than that an appointment has been made for a certain time. In *Sie hatte ihn um sieben Uhr in ein Café in der Hauptstraße bestellt,* bestellt is probably used ironically, implying that the person was summoned there.

3. Die Verpflichtung is 'engagement' in the sense defined above, and also means 'the engagement' of an actor, singer, etc., for which **das Engagement** is also used. Cf. APPOINT 8. ii.

> *Dienstliche Verpflichtungen hinderten mich daran, zu dem Vortrag zu gehen.*
> *Um elf Uhr/Morgen nachmittag habe ich eine andere Verpflichtung.*

Der Vertrag sieht die Verpflichtung des Spielers für drei Jahre und eine Verlängerung um zwei Jahre vor.

appreciate *v.* E. senses: (i) 'To have a proper estimation of the worth, merit, quality, or significance of s.o./sth., to understand with judgement and discrimination'. *This writer was not appreciated in his lifetime. We all appreciate his achievements. Nuclear weapons have made us appreciate the horrors of war. I appreciate the fact that we cannot turn back the clock. Napoleon instantly appreciated how great the danger was.* (ii) 'To judge and be aware of', especially aesthetic and artistic values. *They could not appreciate artistic quality/music/the beauty of the landscape.* (iii) 'To be grateful for'. *I appreciate your kindness/help. I should/would appreciate it, if you could help me.* (iv) 'To approve warmly of' (people). *To be loved, to be appreciated and admired, that is what everyone desires.* (v) Although **appreciate** usually implies wise judgement, keen perception, and insight, it is sometimes used in the sense of *enjoy. A hungry man appreciates a good meal. You appreciate a holiday after a year's hard work.* Cf. ENJOY. In *I don't appreciate being kept waiting,* it means 'to like'. Cf. LIKE 2. (vi) 'To increase in value'. *Land has appreciated considerably in the last two years.* This is **an Wert zunehmen** or **gewinnen** or **im Wert steigen**.

1. Equivalents of E. senses i and iv.
i. Würdigen originally meant 'to assess' the monetary value of an object, but this sense is now obsolete. The idea survives, however, in the application to less tangible values in the sense 'to recognize the true worth or quality of s.o./sth.' Two senses have developed depending on whether someone's personal judgement is paramount or whether expressing this in a speech etc. is the main idea. *Würdigen* occurs in the sense 'to have in one's mind a correct estimate of the worth or quality of s.o./sth.', but the idea of purely mental appreciation is usually conveyed by **zu würdigen wissen**.

Der Dichter ist zu seinen Lebzeiten nicht voll gewürdigt worden.
Vor dem ersten Weltkrieg hat man das Werk dieses Malers nicht genügend gewürdigt.
Ich weiß die Gründe für die Entscheidung zu würdigen, bin aber nicht damit einverstanden.
Ich weiß seine Leistungen/deine Mitarbeit/deine Hilfe zu würdigen.

If expressing what one understands as the real worth of s.o./sth. is the dominant idea, *würdigen* means 'to pay tribute to' or 'to praise'. It is an elevated word restricted to solemn occasions. In a speech or article outlining the work or achievements of e.g. a *Preisträger* or *Jubilar* or someone retiring, moving, or deceased, *der Redner/Autor würdigt dessen/deren Leistungen und Verdienste.*

Die Verdienste des betagten Jubilars würdigte er in wohlgesetzten Worten.
In einer kurzen Rede würdigte der Leiter der Forschungsanstalt die Arbeit, die eine kleine Gruppe soeben erfolgreich abgeschlossen hatte.
Der Redner würdigte das Leben des Verstorbenen.

ii. Schätzen in the sense concerning us here means 'to have a high opinion of'. Applied to people, it ranges from esteeming to liking and covers E. meaning iv and parts of i. Applied to personal qualities or people's characters or work, it means 'to value' or 'to have a high estimation of its/their worth'.

Die Studenten schätzen den Professor/die Vorlesungen des Professors.
Viele Bürger schätzen die Offenheit und die natürliche Art dieses Politikers.
Erst als er in Schwierigkeiten geriet und der Freund ihm half, ohne an sich selbst zu denken, lernte er ihn wirklich schätzen.
Ich schätze ihre Zuverlässigkeit/Pünktlichkeit/präzise Formulierungen.

iii. Zu schätzen wissen implies having a correct recognition of the worth of s.o./sth. and is very like *zu würdigen wissen,* though less formal.

Alle wußten seine Aufrichtigkeit/seine Leistung zu schätzen/würdigen.
Sie hatte ihn nie so recht zu schätzen gewußt.

iv. Sich (dat.) **bewußt sein** + gen., 'to be aware of', has a sense like 'to appreciate' when it implies a proper estimation or understanding, as in *I appreciate that the expedition involves certain dangers.*

Ich bin mir der Gefahr durchaus/vollauf bewußt.
Ich bin mir dessen bewußt, daß die Expedition nicht ungefährlich ist.
Sie war sich offenbar der Tragweite ihrer Handlung nicht bewußt.

v. In some cases **verstehen**, 'to UNDERSTAND', and **erkennen**, 'to REALIZE', may be appropriate.

Napoleon erkannte sofort, wie groß die Gefahr sei, die seiner Armee drohte.
Ich verstehe/habe Verständnis dafür, daß man die Uhr nicht zurückstellen kann/daß ein neues Zeitalter angebrochen ist.

2. Equivalents of E. sense ii.

i. Sinn haben für, to have a feeling and understanding for, a developed mental faculty for, the power of appreciating. *Sinn für Humor* is 'sense of humour'.

Hast du denn gar keinen Sinn für die Schönheiten der Natur?
Sinn für Stil lag ihr offenbar im Blut.
Sein Sinn für die altgriechische Kultur begann sich schon in der Schulzeit zu entwickeln.

ii. Ein Verhältnis haben/finden zu. *Das Verhältnis* means 'relation[ship]'. It is applied to an understanding of or feeling for literature, art, music, etc. *Finden* denotes the beginning of such an understanding. An alternative is the syn. of *Verhältnis* = 'RELATION[SHIP]', **die Beziehung.** *Eine [innere] Beziehung zur Musik* etc. *haben.* *Innere* is often added to both words. **Verständnis haben für**, 'to have an understanding of', is used in similar contexts, but is broader in application. Although from its derivation it means 'understanding', it is more like *appreciation* and *sympathy.* Cf. UNDERSTANDING 4. It translates uses like *I appreciate your difficulties/anxiety* and *The author appreciates the differences between these cultures.*

Ich finde trotz aller Bemühungen kein Verhältnis zur modernen Musik.
Ich verstehe gar nicht, warum Anna Deutsch studiert. Ich finde, sie hat gar kein Verhältnis zur Literatur.   Er hatte ein inneres Verhältnis zur Musik/zur Malerei/zur Literatur.
Er sagte, er habe Verständnis für meine Schwierigkeiten, weil er selbst in derselben Lage gewesen sei.
Ich habe volles Verständnis für deine Sorgen.
Sie hat wenig Verständnis für die Malerei, aber zeigt viel/ein feines Verständnis für die Literatur.

3. The usual equivalent of E. sense iii of **appreciate** is **dankbar sein für.**

Für Ihre Hilfsbereitschaft/Freundlichkeit bin ich sehr dankbar.
Ich wäre Ihnen sehr dankbar, wenn Sie mir bei der Übersetzung des Briefes helfen könnten.
Wir sind Ihnen dankbar dafür, daß Sie uns bei der Überwindung dieser Schwierigkeiten helfen wollen (appreciate your wanting to help us).

approach, come/go/move close[r] to, come/go up to *vs.*

1. Approach in space. The main v. expressing the concept of coming near in space is **sich nähern**. It is used with a dat. or alone. People, animals, and things can be the subj. It implies that they are closer than they were before, but says nothing about the distance separating them. As it is refl., a sent. like *They slowly approached each other* is *Langsam näherten sie sich einander.* (An alternative: *Sie gingen langsam aufeinander zu.* Cf. 2. ii.)

Wir nähern uns der Stadt.   *Wir näherten uns dem verletzten Tier mit aller Vorsicht.*
Leise Schritte/Stimmen näherten sich.   *Eine Kaltfront nähert sich der Küste Westaustraliens.*
Nach einer vierstündigen Wanderung näherten wir uns dem Gipfel des Berges.
Sobald er sich dem Bauernhof näherte, fing der Hund an zu bellen.
Die Rehe waren so zahm, daß sie sich uns näherten und uns aus der Hand fraßen.

Die Temperatur nähert sich dem Gefrierpunkt.

Sich nähern also means 'to approach a pers.' when this implies an attempt to take up some kind of contact.

Er hat sich dem Mädchen in plumper Weise genähert.

Er näherte sich der Dame in einer Weise, die auf kultivierte Manieren schließen ließ.

Sie näherte sich dem Sänger schüchtern und bat um ein Autogramm.

S.o. is difficult to approach is expressed as *An ihn ist nur schwer/nicht heranzukommen.* Cf. 2. v.

2. Words with a related meaning.

i. Herangehen an, to go [up] close to. It implies that only a very short distance separates the people etc. *Dicht* or *nahe*, 'NEAR', may be added to emphasize the idea of closeness. *Er ging dicht an das Aquarium heran, um die Fische zu beobachten.*

Sie ging ohne Furcht an die beiden kämpfenden Hunde heran.

Er ging nahe an das Gemälde heran, um sich die Technik genau anzusehen.

Both sents. *He approached to within two metres of the fence* and *He approached the fence to within a distance of two metres* can be translated as *Er ging bis auf zwei Meter an den Zaun heran* or with *sich nähern, Er näherte sich dem Zaun bis auf zwei Meter,* or ... *bis auf eine Entfernung von zwei Metern.* A transl. with a changed construction is *Er näherte sich der Schlange soweit, daß er nur noch zwei Meter davon entfernt war.*

ii. Auf jmdn./etw. zugehen is 'to go towards s.o./sth.' The person or thing approached must be visible to the person approaching so that it is possible for them to meet. It may, but need not, imply going right up to the other person or thing. *Sie gingen aufeinander zu und schüttelten sich die Hand.*

Sie ging langsam auf den Zaun zu.

Er ging auf die Tür zu, blieb aber plötzlich stehen, drehte sich um und ging weg.

iii. Heranrücken and **näherrücken** are 'to move [up] close[r] to' and can be trans. and intr. *Sie rückte den Stuhl an das Feuer heran* and *Er rückte dicht an sie heran.*

Wenn du ein wenig heranrückst/näherrückst, können wir uns besser unterhalten.

iv. Herantreten implies close proximity, coming at least to within a few steps of s.o./sth., whereas *sich nähern* leaves the distance unspecified. *Herantreten* suggests that the purpose of moving closer is a further action, while with *sich nähern* another action may, but need not, follow.

Als sie an die Autotür herantrat, öffnete er das Fenster.

Er trat an ein parkendes Taxi heran, um den Fahrer nach dem Weg zu fragen.

v. Herankommen is 'to approach the speaker'.

Das Reh kam ganz nahe an mich heran.   *Das Kind traute sich nicht heranzukommen.*

3. Approach in time. **Sich nähern** is used with a dat. *Der Sommer/Unser Aufenthalt in den Bergen nähert sich dem Ende.* **Nahen**, which is now no longer usual for coming near in space, is still used for approaching in time. It is an emotionally coloured word and occurs often, though not exclusively, with ns. denoting danger, calamity, catastrophe, etc. *Sie sahen die Katastrophe/das Unheil nahen, konnten sie/es aber nicht abwenden.*

Die deutlich steigenden Temperaturen zeigen, daß das Ende des Winters naht.

Die Zeit naht, zu der/wo wir eine Entscheidung treffen müssen. Or *Wir nähern uns der Zeit ...*

More common words are **heranrücken** or **näherrücken**, to come closer, draw near, approach.

Der Tag der Urteilsverkündung rückte heran/näher.   *Der Urlaub rückte langsam heran.*

Der Termin, zu dem er die Zeichnungen fertig haben mußte, rückte heran.

Herankommen is also possible. *Weihnachten kam/rückte langsam heran.*

4. Approach s.o. **about** sth. or **with** a request or suggestion.

i. One of the simplest ways to express this concept is to use **ansprechen**, to speak to, address, or approach a person. It implies a request in speech, not in writing. *About* is *um* when the subj. wishes to get something and *wegen* when a matter or suggestion etc. is involved. *Er hat mich um ein Darlehen/um Geld angesprochen* but *wegen eines Vorschlags. Bezüglich*, 'with regard to', is possible in formal language instead of *wegen*.

> *Wann kann man ihn am besten wegen einer Gehaltserhöhung ansprechen?* Or . . . *ihn mit der Bitte um eine Gehaltserhöhung ansprechen?*   *Sie sprach mich um Rat/um Hilfe an.*

ii. Sich wenden an, 'to turn to s.o. for help, advice, etc.', expresses the same idea, but, unlike *ansprechen*, it includes requests in writing.

> *Er hat sich an seinen Bruder um Rat/um Hilfe gewandt/gewendet.*
> *An deiner Stelle würde ich mich an den Direktor wenden und ihm alles erklären.*
> *An wen muß ich mich [mit diesem Vorschlag/mit dieser Bitte] wenden?*

iii. Herantreten is used with requests and with words like *Idee* and *Vorschlag*. With requests it suggests considerable politeness. (Cf. *angehen*, discussed under ASK 3. v., which can suggest less politeness.)

> *Man sollte einen günstigen Augenblick abwarten, um an sie wegen der noch ausstehenden Entscheidung heranzutreten.* Or . . . *um sie wegen der . . . Entscheidung anzusprechen.*
> *Es scheint, daß die Gewerkschaften beabsichtigen, mit unerfüllbaren Forderungen an die Arbeitgeber heranzutreten.*
> *Er trat an einen befreundeten Geschäftsmann mit dem Vorschlag heran, ihre beiden Unternehmen zu fusionieren.*

iv. Angehen is the usual v. for approaching or making a request to an institution or a person in a business capacity. *Wir müssen die Bank um ein Darlehen angehen.*

5. Approach = 'to tackle a problem, difficulties, a task, etc. in a certain way'. **Anpacken**, which is probably the more common word, and **angehen** mean 'to set about a task', 'tackle a piece of work etc.' and are both used with *ein Thema*, 'a topic or subject', as obj. *Du hast das Thema richtig/falsch angepackt. Man kann das Thema/das Problem von einer anderen Seite anpacken/angehen.* **Herangehen** is used in similar contexts, but usually with an adv. or phr. showing how the task is approached. *Sie ging mit Begeisterung/mit Unlust an ihre neue Arbeit heran.* **Anfassen** means 'to tackle sth. in a certain way'. *Sie hat die Aufgabe geschickt/mit Eifer angefaßt.*

> *Ich weiß schon, wie ich die Aufgabe anpacken muß.*   *Er hat das Problem klug angefaßt.*
> *Er ging die Aufgabe/das Problem mit der gebührenden Sorgfalt/mit Umsicht an.*

6. Approach = 'to come close to in quantity or in nature'. **Sich nähern** is used in both cases.

> *Da unsere Jahresproduktion von Stahl in den letzten Jahren ständig gestiegen ist, nähert sie sich nunmehr 100 000 Tonnen.* Or . . . *reicht fast an die 100 000 Tonnenmarke heran.*
> *Unser Absatz nähert sich dem unseres größten Konkurrenten.*
> *Seine Auffassung nähert sich mittelalterlichen Vorstellungen.*
> *Er glaubte, sich seinem Ideal genähert zu haben.*
> *Seine Sammelleidenschaft nähert sich einem Wahn.*   *Ihre Begeisterung nähert sich der Hysterie.*

An alternative in the last two sents. is **nahekommen**. *Seine Sammelleidenschaft kommt einem Wahn nahe. Ihr Verlangen nach Sauberkeit kommt schon der Besessenheit nahe.*

7. Approach = 'to come close to in quality or in another aspect'. *Ein Schüler, der einem anderen an Fleiß nachsteht*, or *eine Ware, die einer anderen an Qualität nachsteht*, is inferior to him, her, or it in that respect. *Nicht nachstehen* therefore means 'to be the equal of'. *Er steht seiner Schwester an Fleiß nicht nach.* **Kaum/wenig nachstehen** thus resembles **approach**. *Leather now approaches plastic in price/cheapness* could become *Was den niedrigen Preis angeht/betrifft, steht Leder dem Kunststoff nicht/kaum nach.* (A very simplified alternative is *Leder ist fast so preiswert/billig wie Kunststoff.*) Similarly, *Marlowe steht Shakespeare an/in poetischer Ausdruckskraft kaum nach* or

Marlowe's poetische Ausdruckskraft steht der Shakespeares nur wenig/kaum nach, M. approaches S. in . . . Another v. is **heranreichen**, to come near to, measure up to, approach. *Marlowes poetische Ausdruckskraft reicht an die Shakespeares heran.* **Herankommen** is used in the same way in informal speech.

Kein Komponist nach ihm reicht an ihn heran.

Kein anderes Waschmittel reicht in der Qualität an dieses heran.

Die Aufführungen in diesem kleinen Theater reichen an die einer großen Bühne heran.

An den Rekord war er nahe herangekommen. Or . . . *war er bis auf eine Sekunde herangekommen.*

area, district, region *ns.*

1. When **area** means 'size or amount of surface', generally expressed as a square measure, **die Fläche** is the usual equivalent.

Man berechnet die Fläche eines Kreises mit der Formel πr².

Das Zimmer hat eine Fläche von dreißig Quadratmetern.

Das Feld hat eine Fläche von 4 Hektar.

Fünfzehn Millionen Australier wohnen auf einer Fläche von 7,7 Millionen Quadratkilometern.

An alternative for a large area, particularly that of countries, is the expression **umfaßt ein Gebiet von**.

Die Bundesrepublik umfaßt ein Gebiet von fast 96 000 Quadratmeilen.

2. District = 'a division of territory for an administrative or official purpose'. *A postal, police,* or *administrative district.* **Region** can be used in the same way.

i. The G. word is **der Bezirk.** Thus *der Postbezirk, der Polizeibezirk, der Verwaltungsbezirk.* It is also applied to a similar division made, for example, by firms for salesmen etc. where the E. word is **area**.

In den meisten Großstädten ist das Stadtgebiet in Bezirke eingeteilt.

Jeder Vertreter der Firma hat seinen eigenen Bezirk.

ii. Das **[Polizei]revier** is either 'a police district', *Das Revier dieser [Polizei]dienststelle umfaßt zwei Vororte,* 'a policeman's beat', *Der Polizist machte einen Kontrollgang durch sein Revier,* or 'a police station' (here also *die Polizeiwache*), *Der Polizist nahm den Täter mit aufs Revier. Das Revier* is used in other fields with a similar sense. *Das Forstrevier* is 'a forestry district'; hence *der Baumbestand des Reviers. Revier* is used for the area or territory of an animal, *Der Hirsch markiert und verteidigt sein Revier,* and for a person's area of activity, *Der Garten ist ausschließlich mein Revier.*

3. Area = 'a particular extent, part, expanse, or tract of the earth's surface'. A tract of land of vaguely defined limits can also be called a district.

i. The usual word is **das Gebiet**, which denotes an area of land which can be seen as forming a unit in some way, a region.

Südlich der Stadt ist ein fruchtbares Gebiet, in dem Gartenbau betrieben wird.

Das Gebiet, in dem Deutsch gesprochen wird, ist erheblich kleiner als vor 1945.

Ich halte die Rhein- und Moselgebiete für die schönsten in Deutschland.

Das Gebiet, das zum Nationalpark erklärt worden ist, soll mehreren bedrohten Tierarten eine Zufluchtsstätte bieten.   *Weite Gebiete Australiens sind noch unbewohnt.*

Durch Bewässerung will man neue Gebiete für die Landwirtschaft erschließen.

Das Absatzgebiet für unsere Produkte hat sich in letzter Zeit erheblich vergrößert.

There are numerous compounds: *Das Küstengebiet, Grenzgebiet, Westgebiet, Katastrophengebiet,* 'disaster area', *Notstandsgebiet,* 'disaster or distressed area', *Hochdruckgebiet,* 'area of high air-pressure', *Industriegebiet, Stadtgebiet, Naturschutzgebiet, Kampfgebiet, Operationsgebiet, Wohngebiet,* 'residential area' in contrast to the commercial and industrial areas, *Kartoffelanbaugebiet,* 'potato-growing area', *Bergbaugebiet,* etc. *Das Gebiet* is the usual word for an area, region, district, or territory belonging to or under the political control of a country. (In compounds *Bereich* also has this sense. Thus *Hoheitsbereich* and *Hoheitsgebiet.*)

Die Armee des Landes X hat das Gebiet des Nachbarstaates besetzt.

In der Schweiz und den angrenzenden Gebieten sind wirksame Maßnahmen zur Reinhaltung der Flüsse dringend notwendig.

ii. Die Region is a learned geographical syn. of *Gebiet* denoting, like the E. word, a large area of land which has no definite boundaries but which has certain features or qualities such as climate, vegetation, or economic structure which distinguish it from other areas. *Die alpine/arktische Region. Die Region des ewigen Schnees. Die dünn besiedelten Regionen des Landes.*

iii. Die Fläche can also mean 'an expanse or stretch of land or water' and includes small areas.

Weite Flächen des Landes sind mit Weizen bebaut.

Eine Fläche/Ein Gebiet von zwanzig Hektar wurde mit Bäumen bepflanzt.

Nomadische Indianer pflanzten ihr Korn überall an, wo sie eine freie Fläche im Urwald fanden.

Das Betreten der Rasenfläche ist verboten.

iv. Das Viertel, 'quarter', is applied to an area or a part of a town and occurs also in compounds such as *Geschäftsviertel, Hafenviertel, Regierungsviertel, Studentenviertel, Einkaufsviertel, Elendsviertel, Stadtviertel*, etc.

Wir wohnen in einem ruhigen Viertel.

Die historischen Bauten im ältesten Viertel der Stadt stehen unter Denkmalschutz.

4. Whereas *Gebiet* refers to an area which is bounded in some way, **die Gegend** suggests an area in a vague way without marking its limits. It is determined by its characteristics and is not very large. Usually one can see all of it or travel through it in a fairly short time. Applied to non-urban areas, it denotes an area of countryside and is often combined with an adj. showing what it is like. It also denotes the area around a person or thing, i.e. any area around me, us, them, here, etc. *Banden von jugendlichen Rowdys machen die Gegend unsicher.* It is often used for the area around a town etc. In *Wir sind ein bißchen durch die Gegend gefahren, Gegend* could be translated as *countryside* or *area round about. Eine Gegend* can also be a vaguely defined part of a town. *Sie wohnen in einer vornehmen Gegend [der Stadt].*

Der Harz ist eine schöne Gegend.   *Die Gegend um Hannover ist flach.*

In der Gegend um Berlin sind viele Seen.

In unserer Gegend, die noch sehr ländlich ist, gibt es riesige Waldgebiete.

A transl. of *the Sydney area*, which encompasses the city and its surroundings, is *Sydney und das umliegende Gebiet.* An alternative is *Sydney und [die] Umgebung.*

5. i. When **area** means 'a definitely bounded piece of ground set aside for a special use or purpose', the main equivalent is one sense of **das Gelände**. In *Die Polizei sperrte das Gelände ab, Gelände* implies land used for a special purpose. It is often found in compounds. Thus *Industriegelände*, 'area for industry', *Sportgelände, Fabrikgelände*, 'the area on which the factory stands', *das Flughafengelände, das Universitätsgelände*, usually translated as *campus, Bahnhofsgelände, Erprobungsgelände*, 'area for testing or carrying out trials', *Versuchsgelände*, 'area for carrying out experiments', *Truppenübungsgelände*, 'military training area'. The other meaning of *Gelände* is 'country' or 'area' as syns. of *terrain*, i.e. 'a tract of land considered with regard to its natural features'. *It's hilly country/a hilly terrain/a hilly area.* With an adj. *Gelände*, like *terrain*, states what the land, country, or area is like. Hence *ein hügliges/ebenes/ansteigendes/welliges Gelände.*

Auf dem neuen Sportgelände kann man fast jede Sportart treiben.

Das Militärgelände wird scharf bewacht, damit keine Unbefugten es betreten.

ii. Some things we call an area are in G. **ein Platz**. *A rest area* on the *Autobahn* is *ein Rastplatz; a parking area, ein Parkplatz; the playing area, der [Kinder]spielplatz;* and *the barbecue area, der Grillplatz.*

6. Area also means 'the extent, range, or scope' of power, influence, knowledge, interest, an activity, life, experience, etc. *A country's area of influence. The area of electronics. New areas of experience. In which area of G. literature does your special interest lie?*

i. Der Bereich is connected with *reichen*, 'to reach or extend', and denotes the area over which something extends or an area dominated or determined by the presence of some factor. The E. equivalent is frequently *area* but also *field* or *sphere*. *Der Machtbereich* and *der Einflußbereich*, usually translated as *sphere of influence*, are thus the areas over which a person's or country's influence or power extends. *Der Mond kreist im Bereich der Anziehungskraft der Erde* means that it is within the range of the earth's gravity. *Der Geltungsbereich eines Gesetzes* is 'the area over which the law is in force'. *Mein Tätigkeitsbereich, Arbeitsbereich*, or *Aufgabenbereich* is 'the area[s] over which my activity, work, or duties extend'. In some cases both *Gebiet* and *Bereich* are possible but express a different perspective. *Das Grundstück liegt im Stadtgebiet* means that it lies within the official area of the town. *Im Bereich der Stadt* suggests in the area influenced by the town, the metropolitan area in a vague sense. *Bereich* has this sense in *Die Stadt liegt im Bereich der Küste* and *Deutschland liegt im Bereich eines Tiefs* (or *eines Tiefdruckgebiets*). *Das liegt im Bereich des Möglichen* is translated as *in the realm of possibility*.

> *In meinem Zimmer habe ich die Bücher so angeordnet, daß ich im Bereich des Schreibtisches alle wichtigen Nachschlagewerke habe.*
>
> *Im Bereich der Fabrik ist der Geruch der Abgase unerträglich, auch die Felder zeigen Spuren der Umweltverschmutzung.*

ii. Areas of ground or space called **Bereiche** are usually seen in connection with some activity. The areas concerned can be smaller than ones called *Gebiete*. Thus *die Schlaf-* and *Eßbereiche eines Hauses/einer Wohnung* and *der Wohnbereich eines Hauses* and *Die Wohnung hat einen großen Küchenbereich. Innerhalb der Wohnung hat jeder seinen eigenen Bereich* means 'an area or place for his or her activities'. The areas into which an organization is divided are called *Bereiche. Das Institut hat vier Bereiche. Bereiche* suggests sections or areas in the compound *Erfahrungsbereiche*.

> *Die Erfahrungsbereiche, die im Roman behandelt werden, haben sich allmählich erweitert.*

iii. For **area** or *field* when they mean 'range or scope of an activity, work, subject of study', both **der Bereich** and **das Gebiet** are used and are frequently interchangeable, although in some cases one tends to be more usual. *Jmds. Interessengebiet* or *Interessenbereich* is 's.o.'s field of special interest'. Both *der ganze Bereich der Außenpolitik* and *das ganze Gebiet der Außenpolitik* are used. In *Diese technische Neuerung greift auf andere Gebiete über, Bereiche* could be used. *Auf dem Gebiet der Wirtschaft* can be *im Bereich der Wirtschaft* and *auf dem Gebiet der Finanzen* can be *im Finanzbereich. Er ist auf sportlichem Gebiet gut unterrichtet* is the usual expression, but *im sportlichem Bereich* is possible. *Unsere Firma ist auf diesem Gebiet führend* is usual, though *in diesem Bereich* is possible. *Eine Frage, die in meinen Bereich gehört*, comes within my area of responsibility. Students often say some field or topic is *ihr Gebiet, Fachgebiet*, or *Spezialgebiet. Bereich* is also possible. Both *Diese Frage gehört/fällt in den Bereich der Biochemie* and *fällt ins/gehört zum Gebiet der Sprachwissenschaft* are used. As a general rule, *Bereich* is likely to be correct.

> *Im Bereich der Autoindustrie sind einige neue Erfindungen auf den Markt gekommen.*
>
> *Mein Fachgebiet in der Anglistik ist der Roman des 19. Jahrhunderts.*

7. When **area** means 'part of the surface of the body', **die Stelle** is used. Cf. PLACE.

> *Wenn das Äthyl die Haut berühren sollte, muß die Stelle sofort gewaschen werden.*

A larger part of the body containing a major organ is called **die Gegend**. *Die Herzgegend. Die Nierengegend. Die Magengegend.*

arm, disarm *vs.*

1. The sense 'to provide an individual or group of people with a weapon or weapons' is expressed by **bewaffnen**, the base v. *waffnen* being obsolete. Sich **bewaffnen** means 'to arm oneself'. *Bewaffnen* is frequently used in the past part., both in the lit. sense, *Die bis an die Zähne bewaffneten Räuber nahmen fünf Geiseln mit*, and in fig. expressions, *Mit Fotoapparaten und Ferngläsern bewaffnet, machten sich die Touristen auf den Weg.* Hence *schwer bewaffnet*, heavily armed. To **disarm** a pers. is **entwaffnen**.

> *Die Aufständischen brachen in das Waffenarsenal ein und bewaffneten sich und die Gefangenen, die sie befreit hatten, mit den erbeuteten Gewehren.*
>
> *Die Mutter bewaffnete sich mit einem Stock und ging auf die Suche nach der Schlange, die sie gerade gesehen hatte.*   *Die Soldaten sind mit Maschinenpistolen bewaffnet.*

2. When the obj. is not a person but ships, tanks, or an aircraft, *bewaffnen* is possible, but not common, even though one speaks of *die Bewaffnung eines Schiffes.* The usual words are **ausrüsten**, 'to equip', and **bestücken**, 'to fit [out] with technical devices', as in *Alle vier Räder sind mit Scheibenbremsen bestückt.* Both can mean 'to provide with' when the arms or armaments involved are specified.

> *Die Schiffe/Panzer/Flugzeuge sind mit Raketen/Laserkanonen/Bomben bestückt/ausgerüstet.*
> *Der Panzer ist mit einer 130 mm Kanone bestückt/ausgerüstet.*
> *Das Schiff ist mit schweren Geschützen bestückt.*

3. If a country arms, the v. is **rüsten**. Hence **aufrüsten**, 'to increase armaments', and **abrüsten**, 'to disarm'. Also *die Rüstungsindustrie*, armaments industry. (*Rüsten* is used with a personal subj. only in the refl. when it means 'to prepare'. *Sie rüsteten sich zum Aufbruch.*)

> *Statt abzurüsten, rüsteten die Großmächte weiter.*
> *Viele Entwicklungsländer haben unsinnige Summen für Rüstung ausgegeben.*

4. Sich wappnen is used only fig. and means 'to be ready to display a quality' like patience, or 'to have arguments etc. ready', or 'to be prepared for' attacks, surprises, etc. **Arm** expresses some of these senses.

> *Wenn du mit ihm verhandelst, wappne dich mit Geduld! Konzessionen macht er nur ungern und meist erst nach langem Sträuben.*
> *Als sie in die Versammlung ging, glaubte sie gegen alle zu erwartenden Angriffe/Überraschungen gewappnet zu sein.*
> *Der Redner hatte sich mit glänzenden Argumenten für die geplante Reform gewappnet.*

arrange, order *vs.* For **order** as a syn. of *command* see ORDER v.

1. Arrange = 'to put in a particular position, sequence, or order'.
i. Ordnen is the usual v. meaning 'to put thgs., material, thoughts, events, etc. systematically in a certain order or sequence', for which E. uses both **arrange** and **order**. *Ordnen* can be followed by *nach* or *in* and also means 'to bring order to'.

> *Ich habe die Bücher alphabetisch nach den Namen der Verfasser geordnet.*
> *Die Briefe sind nach dem Eingangsdatum geordnet.*
> *Wir müssen die Betonplatten nach der Größe ordnen. Also . . . der Größe nach ordnen.*
> *Ich habe die Akten im Schrank/auf dem Schreibtisch geordnet.*
> *Bevor sie anfing, den Aufsatz zu schreiben, hat sie ihre Gedanken geordnet.*
> *Er versuchte, die zusammengewürfelten Photos nach Lebensabschnitten/Orten zu ordnen.*
> *Da Papiere überall herumlagen, sah er sich einem heillosen Chaos gegenüber, und es dauerte Tage, bis er es einigermaßen geordnet hatte.*

Ordnen also means 'to [re]arrange' things which have got out of order or have become untidy. *Sie versuchte, ihr wirres Haar zu ordnen. Er ordnete seine Kleidung.* It is used for putting one's affairs etc. in order, and the past part. often occurs in expressions like *in geordneten Verhältnissen leben* or *ein geordnetes Leben führen*.

> *Bevor er die lange Reise antrat, ordnete er seine persönlichen Angelegenheiten/seine privaten Verhältnisse.*

Sich ordnen is applied to people who arrange themselves in a certain way.

> *Man hat die Touristen gebeten, sich nach Sprachgruppen zu ordnen.*
> *Die Teilnehmer ordneten sich zum Festzug.*   *Die Demonstranten ordneten sich in Reihen.*

ii. Anordnen means 'to arrange thgs. in space', 'to put or place thgs. in a certain relation to each other or other thgs. so that some kind of practical or aesthetic effect is produced'. (*Dinge*) *so anordnen, daß* . . . often occurs. *Anordnen* is occasionally found in the sense of arranging systematically, *Die Kartei ist alphabetisch/nach Sachgebieten angeordnet,* but *ordnen* is the normal word.

> *Die Bücher auf dem Schreibtisch sind so angeordnet, daß ich sie immer gleich zur Hand habe.*
> *Die Bilder an der Wand waren geschmackvoll/künstlerisch/in auffallender Weise angeordnet.*
> *Er hat die Bücher so angeordnet, daß man sich leicht in der Bibliothek zurechtfinden kann.*
> *Der Architekt hat die Säulen in zwei Reihen angeordnet.*

iii. Einordnen presupposes that the order already exists and that things are placed where they belong or put in their places within this order. It is broader than **arrange** and can mean 'to classify' in the sense of assigning something a place in an existing classification or putting behaviour etc. in a category. Applied to road traffic, **sich einordnen** means 'to get into the correct lane'. Also *Jmd. ordnet sich in eine Gemeinschaft ein,* fits in.

> *Er mußte das neue Material erst einordnen* (assign it its place among that which he already has).
> *Wir müssen die neuen Bücher in die alphabetische Reihenfolge/in die Regale einordnen.* (The order exists already, and we put them in the correct places.)
> *Ich weiß nicht, wo/in welche Kategorie ich ihn einordnen soll.*
> *Ist dieses Buch unter die Nachschlagewerke einzuordnen?*
> *Wenn du abbiegen willst, mußt du dich rechtzeitig einordnen.*

iv. In one sense **zurechtmachen** means 'to prepare for a particular purpose', mostly rooms, food, or a bed, and sometimes corresponds to *arrange*.

> *Sie machten die Möbel im Zimmer für eine Fete zurecht.* Also . . . *machten das Zimmer . . . zurecht.*
> *Er machte die Kissen auf dem Bett zurecht.*

2. Arrange with s.o. **to do** sth. or **arrange** a meeting etc. **with** s.o., meaning 'to come to an agreement or understanding about'.

i. The everyday words are **ausmachen** and **abmachen**, which do not differ except that *abmachen* is preferred to stress the idea that an arrangement is settled or finalized. *Das ist also abgemacht.* They are used with an obj., an infin., or a *daß*-clause. The infin. after *what, how, when, where,* as in *We arranged what to do/where to meet*, etc., must be expressed as a clause. *Wir haben schon ausgemacht, was wir machen werden/wo wir uns treffen.* **Vereinbaren**, which is somewhat more formal, is used both for everyday arrangements and for weightier agreements. Cf. AGREE 1. v.

> *Habt ihr schon einen Preis/einen Lohn für die Arbeit/einen Termin/einen Treffpunkt/eine Zeit etc. ausgemacht/abgemacht/vereinbart?*
> *Wir haben schon ausgemacht, uns morgen zu treffen.* Or . . . *ausgemacht, daß wir uns morgen treffen.*
> *Wir haben mit den anderen ausgemacht, wann und wo wir uns treffen.*
> *Sie machten [unter sich] ab/aus, sich bei der Examensvorbereitung zu helfen/daß der eine zu der Vorlesung gehen und dem anderen seine Mitschrift geben würde.*
> *Wir haben mit unseren Nachbarn abgemacht, daß sie während unserer Abwesenheit die Kirschen ernten dürfen.*
> *Du hättest kein Treffen mit ihnen vereinbaren sollen, wenn du wußtest, daß du nicht genug Zeit hast, um hinzugehen* (arranged to see/meet or arranged a meeting with).

Wir vereinbarten [untereinander], daß wir uns um sechs Uhr früh vor dem Bahnhof treffen würden.
    Or . . . *vereinbarten, uns . . . zu treffen.*
Er erschien zum vereinbarten/ausgemachten Zeitpunkt.

ii. Verabreden is used with an obj., infin., or clause in contexts relating both to meetings and other matters. It implies a verbal agreement and is used both for everyday and more important arrangements. **Sich verabreden** means 'to arrange to meet'. The possible constructions are: *Wir haben uns für Mittwoch um vier zu einer Partie Tennis verabredet* and *Ich habe mich mit ihr um vier zum Kaffee verabredet. Ich bin schon verabredet* means that I have already arranged to meet someone else.

Wir haben schon eine Zusammenkunft für die nächste Woche verabredet.
Sie hatten sich in einem Café am Rheinufer verabredet.
Die Kartenspieler verabredeten bestimmte Handzeichen, um die Mitspieler zu täuschen.
Die Schüler hatten [untereinander] verabredet, bei Nennung eines bestimmten Namens in prustendes Gelächter auszubrechen. Also . . . *daß sie . . . ausbrechen würden.*
Erst nach wochenlangen Verhandlungen gelang es den Koalitionspartnern, eine gemeinsame Strategie zu verabreden.

3. Arrange for sth. **to be** done can often be translated by **lassen**, to have/get sth. done. *Ich rufe bei der Firma an und lasse die Waren sofort zustellen/abschicken. Ich lasse ihn von dem Flughafen abholen. Ich lasse den Fernseher reparieren.* Cf. MAKE.

4. One sense of **einrichten** is 'to make possible', so that it corresponds to **arrange** in a sent. like *Can you arrange to be here at six? Einrichten* here suggests making the necessary changes or adjustments or manipulating matters so that something can happen. It can take an obj., *Er wird seine Teilnahme an der Konferenz hoffentlich noch einrichten können,* but it occurs mostly with an infin. or a *daß*-clause which is frequently preceded by *es* and *so. Er wird es hoffentlich noch so einrichten können, an der Konferenz teilzunehmen/daß er an der Konferenz teilnimmt. Kannst du es so einrichten, um sechs Uhr hier zu sein/daß du um sechs Uhr hier bist?* If **arrange** is used with **for**, as in *Can you arrange for Michael to get a few hours off tomorrow?, for* drops out, and the word after it becomes the subj. of a *daß*-clause. An infin. is not possible in such a case. *Kannst du es so einrichten, daß Michael morgen ein paar Stunden freihat?*

Kannst du es so einrichten, daß du heute nach der Arbeit zu mir kommst?
Wenn ich es einrichten kann, komme ich heute noch vorbei.
Ich will versuchen, es so einzurichten, daß ich an der Sitzung teilnehme.
Kannst du es so einrichten, daß Uwe um zwei Uhr frei ist?

Einrichten also translates *to arrange thgs. so that. Die Kinder hatten es so eingerichtet, daß die Eltern für zwei Wochen verreisen konnten.* **Sich auf etw. einrichten** means 'to prepare for', both mentally and otherwise. In a sent. like *Teile mir die Zeit deiner Ankunft mit, damit ich mich darauf einrichten kann,* it could be a transl. of *so that I can arrange thgs. accordingly.*

5. Arrange = 'to plan beforehand', 'make preparations for'.

i. Arrangieren is often heard, particularly for arranging journeys, dinners, meetings, etc. *Das Reisebüro hat alles für meine Reise nach Neuseeland arrangiert. Für den Tag seiner Rückkehr hatte seine Familie ein Essen für einige seiner Freunde arrangiert. Sie haben ein Fest/ein Treffen aller Interessierten arrangiert.*

ii. Like *to plan,* **planen** may denote only the intention to do something, *Wir planen eine Reise nach Neuseeland;* or it may mean 'to work out in detail' what one wants to do and how to do it, *Die Tagung/Reise verlief genau wie geplant.* Although *planen* does not correspond exactly to **arrange**, it is appropriate in contexts in which *plan* and **arrange** are syns. *Man plant eine Konferenz sorgfältig, damit alles reibungslos abläuft.*

Da Montag ein gesetzlicher Feiertag ist, haben wir einen Ausflug ins Gebirge geplant.

Hast du fürs Wochenende schon etw. geplant?   Für den Herbst ist ein Sportfest geplant.

Wir sind gerade dabei, die Lehrveranstaltungen für das nächste Semester zu planen.

iii. Veranstalten means 'to prepare, organize, and run' a function such as *eine Tagung, eine Konferenz, ein Fest, eine Versammlung, eine Kundgebung, ein Ball, ein sportlicher Wettbewerb, ein Autorennen, eine Ausstellung, ein Konzert*, etc. Because it always includes the running of such things, it is broader than **arrange**. *Ein Reisebüro, das eine Reise veranstaltet,* makes the necessary arrangements for it to take place.

6. Vermitteln means 'to see to it that s.o. gets sth.' or 'to help s.o. to get sth.' and suggests that the subj. acts as an intermediary between the people involved. It is the equivalent of **arrange** in the context of arranging a job etc. for someone arranging for someone to get an interview with a third person, etc.

Sie hat ihrem Bruder eine Stelle vermittelt bei der Firma, wo sie arbeitet.

Er hat der Firma seines Vaters Aufträge vermittelt.

Der Makler/Ein Freund hat den Hausverkauf vermittelt.

Unser Abgeordneter hat uns eine Unterredung mit dem Premierminister vermittelt.

7. If none of these words suits the E. context, **vorbereiten**, 'to prepare', may be appropriate. The n. **Vorbereitungen** is used with **treffen**, to make preparations or arrangements. A related word is **die Vorkehrungen**. **Vorkehrungen treffen** means 'to take steps to prevent possible or anticipated adverse developments from happening' or 'to ward them off'. If this idea of precautionary measures is not present, *Vorbereitungen* is used.

Da sie alles sorgfältig vorbereitet hatten, ist die Tagung planmäßig abgelaufen.

Zwei Kollegen haben alle Vorbereitungen für die Konferenz getroffen.

Alle Vorkehrungen waren nutzlos. Alles, was nur schief gehen konnte, ging schief.

Er wollte den Erfolg durch bestimmte Vorkehrungen sichern.

Damit alles reibungslos abläuft, müssen wir einige Vorkehrungen treffen.

8. Arrange = 'to adapt a musical composition for voices or instruments other than those for which it was originally written'. The usual word is **bearbeiten**.

Sie hat den Walzer, der für ein kleines Orchester geschrieben wurde, fürs Klavier bearbeitet.

ask, request *vs.* Some related words.

1. Both *fragen* and *bitten* are equivalents of **ask**. *Fragen* means 'to enquire' or 'to put a question seeking information', whereas *bitten* means 'to request sth. desired'. *Man fragt, wie man zum Bahnhof kommt*, but *bittet um Auskunft/Hilfe/etw. zu essen.* The two words overlap only in a few cases.

i. Fragen differs from **ask** syntactically. **Ask** is used: *a.* Without mention of the person addressed, with an obj. or a clause: *He asked the way/my name* or *He asked if you were ready. b.* With a person as obj.: *I asked her, and she said, 'tomorrow'. c.* With two objs.: *They asked us the way. Fragen* takes only a person as obj. The thing or person asked about must follow *nach* whether a personal obj. is present or not. *Sie fragte nach dem Preis/nach meinem Namen* or *Er fragte mich nach der Uhrzeit. Nach* also translates *about* and *for* a person and the somewhat old-fashioned *after* a person. *Sie fragte nach meinem Bruder/meiner Arbeit. Hat jmd. heute nachmittag nach mir gefragt? Über* is also possible but suggests detailed questions and answers. The only non-personal objs. used with *fragen* are indefinite expressions like *etw., viel[es], einiges, verschiedenes. Ich möchte dich etw. fragen. Sie hat nichts gefragt. Der Lehrer fragte einiges, was die Schüler noch nicht wissen konnten. Sie fragte uns verschiedenes, was wir ohne Schwierigkeit beantworten konnten. Fragen* is used with *wegen*, 'with regard to or about', a formal syn. of which is *in Bezug auf. Ich muß den Chef wegen meines Urlaubs* *fragen* means that I shall ask when I can have it. *Sie fragte mich nach meinem Urlaub* means she asked what it was like. *Fragen um* means 'to ask for, request', but is used only with *Erlaubnis* and *Rat* as objs. *Bitten* is also common with these objs. *Fragen* corresponds to **ask** in direct and indirect speech, but in the case of requests, *bitten* is also possible in writing down direct speech. *'Wann fängt der Film an?' fragte sie. Er fragte, wie spät es sei. 'Kann ich mir das Buch ausleihen?' fragte/bat sie.* To **ask** [s.o.] a question is [jmdm.] **eine Frage stellen**. *Ich muß Ihnen leider ein paar persönliche Fragen stellen.*

> *Sie fragte mich, wo Riedel wohnt, aber ich wußte es nicht.*
> *Der Kommissar fragte ihn nach Dingen, von denen er nie etw. gehört hatte.*
> *Kleine Kinder fragen zuerst ihre Eltern um Rat.*   *Kinder fragen viel.*
> *Bei jeder Kleinigkeit muß das Kind seine Eltern erst um Erlaubnis fragen/bitten.*
> *Ich habe ihn nach seinen Plänen gefragt.*
> *Hast du ihn wegen des Zimmers gefragt?*   *Er hat [mich] nach meiner Meinung gefragt.*
> *Du brauchst nicht erst lange zu fragen, sondern kannst dir das Buch jederzeit ausleihen.*

ii. Bitten usually implies confidence in or dependence on the goodwill of the person to whom the request is made. It too takes only a personal obj. What is asked for or requested follows *um*. E. usage varies. *I ask s.o. for sth.*, but *I ask a favour of s.o.* or *ask s.o. a favour/ask* or *request permission*. The only G. constructions are: *Ich möchte dich um einen Gefallen bitten* and *Ich bitte um Erlaubnis. Bitten* also takes an infin. *Er bat uns, ihm beim Umzug zu helfen.* A clause is possible like the E. *He asked that we forgive him*, but is not very common, is formal in tone, and needs the subjunctive.

> *Er bat seinen reichen Onkel um finanzielle Unterstützung.*
> *Ich bitte alle Mitarbeiter, pünktlich zu erscheinen. Also Um pünktliches Erscheinen wird gebeten.*
> *Um einen kleinen Beitrag für die entstandenen Unkosten wird gebeten.*
> *Ich bat sie um Verzeihung. Or Ich bat sie, mir zu verzeihen. Or Ich bat sie, sie möge [mir] doch verzeihen.*
> *Die Minister baten den König, er möge den zum Tode verurteilten Rebellen begnadigen.*

2. Derivatives of *bitten* denoting a request.

i. Sich (dat.) **ausbitten** is an unusual word confined to a few set expressions such as *Ich habe mir eine Bedenkzeit ausgebeten*. More common is *Ich bat um eine Bedenkzeit. Sich ausbitten* is also used when someone who is annoyed at the lack of something like *Ruhe, Höflichkeit, Sauberkeit,* or *Ordnung* requests or practically demands this. *'Ich bitte mir Ruhe aus', rief der Offizier. Das möchte ich mir auch ausgebeten haben* means that I ask or demand it, in the sense that I regard it as essential.

> A. *Herr Schneider wird Ihren Forderungen nachkommen, Herr Direktor.*
> B. *Das möchte ich mir aber auch ausgebeten haben, sonst kann er sich eine neue Stelle suchen.*

ii. Erbitten implies a polite request, but is formal and found mostly in the past part. in set expressions.

> *Ich erbat mir die Hilfe/den Rat eines Freundes.*   *Er erbat meine Zustimmung für den Plan.*
> *Ihre Anwesenheit ist erbeten.*   *Sofortige Antwort/Benachrichtigung erbeten.*

3. Syns. of *bitten*.

i. Ersuchen implies a polite formal request, but is used only on higher stylistic levels. In official language it expresses a command in the form of a request or a request that one must comply with.

> *Hiermit ersuche ich Sie um Ihre Unterstützung unserer dem Gemeinwohl dienenden Aktivitäten.*
> *Ich ersuche Sie um baldige Nachricht.*   *Ich ersuche Sie, den Raum zu verlassen.*
> *Sie werden ersucht, sich morgen auf Zimmer 212 des neuen Rathauses zu melden.*
> *Sie werden ersucht, das Land binnen 48 Stunden zu verlassen.*

ii. Nachsuchen, also a fairly elevated term, is often used for requests in official language. It usually implies a formal application for something.

> *Wir müssen beim Ministerium um eine Ausnahmegenehmigung nachsuchen.*

Der Botschafter suchte um eine Unterredung mit dem Premierminister nach.

iii. Anfordern has spread from the language of the civil and military administration. It means that men, materials, etc. are requested from the authority in control which has to give its approval and then supply what has been asked for. *Der Polizist forderte einen Krankenwagen an. Ich werde den Fall bearbeiten und habe die Akten angefordert. Interessenten können einen Katalog anfordern.*

Zur Bekämpfung des Waldbrandes hat die Feuerwehr Verstärkung angefordert.
Die Leiter der Baustelle forderte Hilfskräfte von der Baufirma an.
Nach dieser Drohung forderte der Abgeordnete verstärkten Polizeischutz an.

iv. Beschwören and **anflehen** mean 'to beseech', 'to implore'. Both suggest an intense and urgent request, but *anflehen* implies also a humble and desperate appeal to the person's good nature.

Er beschwor sie, von ihrem Vorhaben abzulassen.   *Sie flehte mich um Hilfe an.*
Ich flehe dich an, bleib' bei mir!   *Das sagte er in beschwörendem Ton.*

v. Angehen is used for a request to an institution or person with one of two implications. It can suggest a request when a business relation exists between the people concerned. It is thus used for approaching an institution like a bank for a loan. *Ich ging die Bank um ein Darlehen an* is usual, as *bitten* suggests a request by a person of lower status to a superior. However, if *angehen* is used when *bitten* would be normal, e.g. among people between whom a personal relationship exists, such as members of a family, *angehen* implies an adverse judgement on the action, that the request is not proper, reasonable, or justified.

Sie ging den Lehrer um Hilfe bei der Lösung der Mathematikaufgaben an.
Er ging seinen Großvater um Geld für ein Auto an.
Sie gingen die Passanten um Spenden für die Opfer der Hungersnot an.

vi. Anhauen is colloquial and implies effrontery and over-familiarity on the part of the person asking for something.

Er hat einen Fremden angehauen, ihn im Auto mitzunehmen/ob er ihn mitnehmen würde.
Er hat mich um fünfzig Mark angehauen.

4. Derivatives of *fragen*.

i. Anfragen is common in business and official style in the meaning 'to enquire'. It can refer to a personal, written, or telephone enquiry. *Bei* shows to whom the enquiry is directed, *wegen* what it concerns. *Anfragen* implies that the enquiry is directed to the person in whose field of responsibility the matter lies. It can also mean 'to enquire in order to obtain sth.' *Broschüren sind beim Fremdenverkehrsverein anzufragen. Ich frage morgen bei der Universität wegen der Formulare an.*

Ich werde morgen bei der Baubehörde telefonisch anfragen, ob der Bau einer Garage grundsätzlich möglich ist.
Ich habe bei dem Hotel angefragt, ob in der Zeit vom 4. bis 14. Juli noch Zimmer frei sind.
Er fragte bei dem Zahnarzt an, ob er morgen einen Termin bekommen könnte.

ii. Abfragen means to ask questions to see whether someone has learnt something or possesses certain knowledge. It is usual to have both ns. in the acc. *Ich fragte den Schüler die Vokabeln ab.* A dat. of the person is possible.

Ich frage meine Tochter jeden Tag das Einmaleins ab.
Er muß viele Formeln lernen, und ich frage sie ihn ab.

iii. Befragen means 'to question individuals fully and precisely' or 'to question a number of people on particular matters'. It is used for police questioning of witnesses, for courts or committees questioning experts, for questioning people in *Umfragen*, 'surveys of public opinion', *Marktforschung*, and *(statistische) Erhebungen*, 'surveys'. In political language *das Volk befragen* means 'to hold a referendum or plebiscite'.

Bei der letzten Meinungsumfrage wurden 2 000 Personen zur Frage der Atomkraftwerke befragt.

Der Detektiv befragte alle ihm zur Verfügung stehenden Zeugen, kam aber dennoch zu keinem befriedigenden Ergebnis.

Nachdem die Polizei sie stundenlang befragt hatte, durften sie gehen.

Der Untersuchungsausschuß/Das Gericht hat mehrere Sachverständige/Experten befragt.

Alle Umstehenden wurden [von der Polizei] befragt, doch keiner konnte Auskunft geben.

iv. Ausfragen means 'to get or try to get information from s.o. by continuous questioning'. Unlike *befragen*, it is not restricted to police, courts, and inquiries, but is used in private life. One sense of **ausforschen** conveys the same idea, but suggests that the information is obtained subtly and indirectly, by stealth, so that the person does not notice it.

Unverblümt versuchten die Frauen, sie über ihr Privatleben auszufragen.

Es hat keinen Zweck, ihn über seine finanzielle Situation ausfragen zu wollen. Er wird dir gar nichts sagen.

Als ich merkte, daß er sich nicht mit direkten Fragen ausfragen ließ, forschte ich ihn mit verdeckten Fragen aus.

Wenn Sie versuchen wollen, mich in dieser Sache auszuforschen, so muß ich Sie enttäuschen. Ich weiß gar nichts darüber.

v. Nachfragen means in strict use 'to ask a second time'. Usually *wieder*, 'AGAIN', or a syn. is added. The person asked follows *bei*. It may suggest trying to obtain accurate information. However, in everyday use the implication of asking a second time is often ignored so that *Ich frage bei jmdm. nach* is a stylistically higher variant on *Ich frage jmdn. [nach etw.]*. Thus *Ich frage bei meinem Kollegen nach* = *Ich frage ihn*.

'Ich werde versuchen, Ihren Antrag morgen früh zu bearbeiten', sagte der Beamte. 'Fragen Sie deshalb morgen nachmittag noch einmal nach!'

Der Verkäufer wußte nicht, ob das bestellte Buch schon eingetroffen war, und fragte bei einer Kollegin nach.

Fragen Sie morgen wieder nach, ob ein Zimmer frei geworden ist.

Jedesmal, wenn er etw. nicht ganz verstanden hat, fragte er am Ende der Vorlesung bei dem Dozenten nach.

5. i. Verlangen, which often means 'to DEMAND', is the equivalent of **ask** in certain situations: *a.* Asking others to pay a price. *b.* Describing what someone asks for in a shop etc. *c.* Saying that someone has been asked for or is wanted on the phone or at the door. *d.* Asking for passports, driver's licences, or official papers to be produced. *e.* Asking or expecting something of a person.

Er verlangt für den Wagen einen unannehmbaren Preis.

Er hat für die Reparatur nichts verlangt.   *Die Kundin verlangte ein Paket Waschpulver.*

Sie hat zuerst 5 000 Mark verlangt, bekam aber keine Angebote.

Du wirst am Telefon verlangt.   *Telefonistin: 'Wen haben Sie verlangt?'*

Bei Ihrem nächsten Anruf verlangen Sie bitte Apparat 215/Herrn Braun!

Der Grenzbeamte verlangte unsere Pässe. (Bitten um is also possible.)

Bei der nächtlichen Fahrzeugkontrolle verlangte der Polizist neben meinem Personalausweis auch noch meinen Führerschein.

Was ich von ihm verlange, ist nur gerecht.   *Man kann wirklich nicht mehr von ihr verlangen.*

Es wäre zu viel verlangt, wenn wir erwarteten, daß er die Arbeit umsonst macht.

Er glaubte, für diesen schlecht bezahlten Job auch noch Höchstleistungen verlangen zu können.

ii. The less common **abverlangen** has the same meaning as *verlangen*, but involves a change of construction: *Ich verlange ihm etw. ab* instead of *verlange etw. von ihm*. *Abverlangen* also varies in meaning between 'demand' and 'ask'. It implies that the subj. gets what is demanded, whereas *verlangen* need only be the uttering of the request or demand. If someone says, *'Mit barscher Stimme verlangte der Grenzbeamte uns die Pässe ab'*, this suggests that he was given them and took them away at least for a short time.

Sie hat ihm für das alte Auto einen viel zu hohen Preis abverlangt.

Sie hat ihm die Schlüssel abverlangt.

Einem Missionar werden sehr große Opfer abverlangt/abgefordert.

iii. Abfordern can be used instead of *abverlangen*, but it is not often encountered. It is, however, the usual word when someone asks for the repayment of a debt. *Er ging zu dem Schuldner, um ihm das geliehene Geld abzufordern. Bitten* would normally be felt to be too weak in this context.

6. Ask = 'to invite'. To ask s.o. in is either *jmdn.* **bitten hereinzukommen** or *jmdn.* **hereinbitten.** Otherwise, in contexts like *to ask s.o. to dinner,* **einladen,** 'to invite', is necessary.

Ich habe sie für morgen abend eingeladen (invited/asked them round, asked them to visit us).

Sie hat uns zum Abendessen eingeladen.   Hast du sie zu unserer Fete eingeladen?

Bitten is sometimes found in this context, but implies a highly placed person issuing the invitation. *Der Bundespräsident hat zweihundert Jugendliche in die Villa Hammerschmidt (seine Residenz in Bonn) gebeten. Der Chef hat die Sachbearbeiterin zu sich gebeten* means that he asked her to come and see him, but this is an order couched in polite language. *To ask s.o. to dance* is usually *bitten.* A formal word is **auffordern.** When this refers to joining in an activity like dancing, it is a polite syn. of *bitten. Wir forderten sie zum Mitspielen auf.* (In other contexts *auffordern* suggests a firm request, akin to a demand, compliance with which is expected. *Der Polizist forderte die Jugendlichen zum Weitergehen auf. Er forderte uns auf, den Saal zu verlassen/sofort zu zahlen.*)

Darf ich Sie zum nächsten Tanz auffordern?   Ich bat sie um den ersten Tanz.

Ich habe sie zum Tanz aufgefordert, aber sie hat mir einen Korb gegeben.

attack v.

1. The general term **angreifen** can be both trans. and intr.: *Die Armee griff den Feind in der Flanke an* and *Der Feind griff mit Raketen an. Um ein Unentschieden zu erreichen, griff die unterlegene Mannschaft hektisch an.* It is used in military contexts and in sport as well as with a single person or a group and animals as subj. and can mean 'to attack with words'. **Attackieren** is a more learned word which is most frequently used for attacks with words, but is sometimes found in military contexts.

Das Bataillon griff die Festung im Sturm an.   Die Verbrecher griffen den Polizisten tätlich an.

Die Hauptnahrung der Hyäne ist Aas, doch greift sie, wenn sie Hunger hat, auch Viehherden an.

Der Minister wurde in allen Zeitungen scharf angegriffen/attackiert.

Um einen solchen Gegner zu besiegen, muß man ständig angreifen.

2. i. Anfallen means 'to attack suddenly and without warning', but does not imply as severe an attack as *herfallen* and *überfallen.* It is common with animals, being the usual word for a dog. *Ein bissiger Hund hat uns angefallen. Ein Wolf fiel die Herde an. Der Löwe fällt das Zebra an.* It is occasionally found with bodily conditions and feelings. *Schwäche/Wut/Heimweh/Jammer fiel mich an.* The usual expression would be *überkam mich* or *kam über mich.*

ii. Überfallen implies an unexpected attack carried out by robbers, thieves, pirates, etc. *Er ist auf dem Heimweg von zwei Jugendlichen überfallen worden.* In military contexts it suggests a barbaric action without the due formalities such as a declaration of war. *Deutschland überfiel Polen.* When these are observed, *angreifen* is used. A place can be the obj.: *Um zehn Uhr hat eine maskierte Gangsterbande eine Bank überfallen;* in this case *raid* may be the appropriate equivalent. *Überfallen* is sometimes used with moods, feelings, or states as subj. *Plötzlich überfiel mich der Schlaf. Heimweh überfiel uns.*

iii. Herfallen is the strongest term, implying brutality or barbarity. It is used e.g. for a number of animals, such as wolves, which spring on their victims or prey, whereas with *anfallen* only one need be involved and it may suggest only an attempted attack. *Die Wölfe fielen über die Schafe her. Die Wölfe versuchten, den Schlitten anzufallen. Herfallen* also suggests an attack by a number of brutal people. *Die rohe Horde fiel über die Stadt her und plünderte sie aus.* With things to eat as obj. it loses some of its connotation and, like **attack**, means 'to eat ravenously'. *Beim Geburtstagsfest fielen die Kinder über den Kuchen her. Die ausgehungerten Flüchtlinge fielen über die Vorräte her. Die Stare sind in Scharen über die Kirschen hergefallen.*

iv. Sich hermachen über is used colloquially like *herfallen* and *überfallen*, but only with people as subj., and usually does not suggest so severe an attack. *Die Einbrecher machten sich über den Nachtwächter her.* It is used for food, *Die Kinder machten sich über die Torte her*, and also means 'to get down to doing sth.', *Sie machten sich über die Arbeit/über das schmutzige Geschirr her.*

3. Befallen means 'to attack' in reference to diseases, but only when a number of people are affected or when the attack is fairly severe. *Das ganze Dorf wurde von einer geheimnisvollen Krankheit befallen. Befallen* is also used for pests which attack plants etc., *Die Weizenernte wurde von Schädlingen/Ungeziefer befallen*, and for emotions. *Befallen mit* can translate *stricken with*.

> *Er war von einer schlimmen Krankheit befallen.*
> *Er war von tiefer Mutlosigkeit/von Anwandlungen des Größenwahns befallen.*
> *Sie wurde plötzlich von einem Gefühl der Unruhe befallen.*

The n. **der Befall** is usually restricted to attacks on plants by pests, diseases, etc. *Der Befall durch Schädlinge/Blattläuse.* **Der Anfall** is used when human beings are affected by a disease, but is usually limited to fairly severe attacks which occur suddenly. *Der Grippeanfall* is used, but does not suggest a mild illness. *Sie hatte den Grippeanfall gut überstanden.* If people are only mildly affected by influenza, they say, *'Ich hatte die Grippe bekommen/gehabt.'*

attend *v.* As **attend** is a fairly formal term, its sense can often be expressed in simpler words. The simpler E. vs. are a guide to the appropriate G. equivalent.

1. Attend a meeting, wedding, funeral, conference, school, course, etc. = 'take part in' or 'go to'. **Teilnehmen an**, 'to take part in', is the usual word for conferences, meetings, etc. *Sie nimmt an einer Tagung/einer Konferenz/einer Sitzung/einem Kurs teil.* For weddings, funerals, school, etc. **gehen zu** would be used in everyday language. *Wir gehen zu einer Hochzeit/zu einer Beerdigung/in die Kirche. Heinz geht noch zur Schule.* **Besuchen** is used for attending school and other activities, but is a formal expression. In conversation *Ich besuche das Heine-Gymnasium* would be unusual, but could well occur in a *Lebenslauf*. The n. **der Besuch**, 'attendance', also belongs to formal language. *Alle Kinder, die das fünfte Lebensjahr erreicht haben, müssen die Schule besuchen.* Or *Der Besuch der Schule ist Pflicht für alle Kinder, die . . .* There are compounds like *Kirchenbesuch, Theaterbesuch, Vorlesungsbesuch, Universitätsbesuch*. The past part. *besucht* is commonly used with *gut* and *schlecht* meaning that something is well or poorly attended. *Das Theater/Das Kino/Die Versammlung war gut besucht.* With meetings etc. **beiwohnen** also occurs, but it is a not very common, formal expression. *Sie wohnten der Versammlung/dem Gottesdienst bei.*

2. Attend in *A doctor attends a patient* is **behandeln**, to treat. *Welcher Arzt behandelt Sie? Ein Arztbesuch* implies that the doctor comes to the patient's home. *Die Krankenkasse zahlt für Arztbesuche in Notfällen.*

3. In very formal language **attend [to]** means 'to pay attention'. *You're not attending—sit up and listen! Du paßt nicht auf. Setz' dich gerade hin und hör' gut zu! Paß auf, was ich dir sage!* expresses the meaning of *Attend/Pay attention to what I say!* but

belongs to a lower stylistic level. More like **attend** is *Achte auf das, was ich sage! Hören Sie sich meine Anweisungen genau an!* could translate *Attend to my instructions!* if we assume that *attend* = 'pay attention'. Cf. [TAKE] CARE and LISTEN.

4. Attend to a matter means 'to deal with it'. *I have two items of business to attend to* could be *Ich muß zwei Angelegenheiten erledigen* or *Ich muß mich mit zwei Angelegenheiten beschäftigen.* Cf. SETTLE 5. i and CONCERN 4. i. On a lower stylistic level: *Ich kümmere mich um diese Angelegenheit.* In *I shall attend to your instructions*, **attend** means 'to carry out', so that the sent. becomes *Ich werde Ihre Anweisungen ausführen.*

5. Attend to *customers in a shop* is *Kunden bedienen.*

6. In another very formal use, *She considered the consequences that might attend these experiments*, **attend** means 'to arise as a result of'. Transls. are *Sie bedachte die Folgen, die sich aus diesen Versuchen ergeben könnten/die diese Versuche zur Folge haben könnten/die diese Versuche nach sich ziehen könnten.*

attitude *n*. The main meanings are: (i) Originally a term in fine arts denoting the posture of a figure in a sculpture or painting, **attitude** was extended to the position, bearing, or posture of the body or way of holding the body in general with the added idea that this indicates a mental state, feeling, mood, or an action, e.g. *He stood there in a threatening attitude.* Thus *a defiant* or *disdainful attitude, a relaxed attitude, an attitude of deference/humility/pride/grief/despair.* Hence *to strike an attitude*, to take up dramatically or theatrically a posture indicative of a mental state, which is translated as *sich in Positur werfen*, to strike a pose. (ii) **Attitude** was then applied to people's behaviour or manner of acting, again with the idea that this is representative of feeling, conviction, or opinion. *My attitude to work* is my feeling or opinion about it as well as the way this manifests itself in what I do or do not do. Similarly, *We must maintain a firm attitude. Belligerent, aggressive,* or *casual attitudes* are mental states which can determine behaviour. (iii) In a further extension, the idea of the posture or behaviour is lost, and the mental state, feeling, or conviction becomes the only meaning. It is often difficult to know whether **attitude** includes behaviour or is restricted to mental processes. When the latter is meant, 'an **attitude** of mind' designates in strict use a habitual way of regarding a matter, but in looser use it is a weightier syn. of *opinion*. *A broad-minded, liberal,* or *scientific attitude* would usually suggest a habitual way of thinking, as would *someone's religious* or *political attitude. What is her attitude on this question?* may, however, ask for little more than her opinion.

1. i. Die Haltung denotes firstly the way someone holds his or her body or parts of it. It means 'posture, position and bearing', but also translates **attitude** in senses i and ii when, through the way the body is held and the facial expression, a mental state is or is intended to be expressed. In *Jmd. hat eine gute oder schlechte Haltung* or *eine stramme oder gerade Haltung* or *sitzt in gebeugter Haltung, Haltung* means 'posture or position'. But *eine drohende Haltung, eine respektlose Haltung,* or *eine servile Haltung* point to both the position of the body and the state of mind behind it and correspond to **attitude**. *Eine lässige Haltung*, 'a casual attitude', refers both to a person's bearing and to a frame of mind.

> *Dem Turner wurden wegen schlechter Haltung Punkte abgezogen.*
> *Das Schwimmen ist besonders gut geeignet, die Haltung zu verbessern.*
> *Er setzte sich an den Schreibtisch und nahm eine amtliche Haltung ein.*

ii. Die Haltung is also applied to behaviour which reflects a state or quality of mind. *Jmd. zeigt eine mutige/tapfere/entschlossene/loyale/feindselige/trotzige Haltung.*

> *Er hatte eine arrogante Haltung jungen Mitarbeitern gegenüber.*

A similar meaning to *eine* + adj. *Haltung einnehmen* can often be conveyed by **sich verhalten**, 'to behave', which often implies a reaction. *Er verhielt sich neutral* and *Er nahm eine neutrale Haltung ein* can be translated as *He took [up] a neutral attitude*. Thus *Sie nahm eine abwartende Haltung ein* and *Sie verhielt sich abwartend* both mean that she took [up] a wait-and-see attitude. *Wer sich ablehnend verhält* or *eine ablehnende Haltung einnimmt*, takes [up] a negative attitude or refuses to have anything to do with a matter. **Das Verhalten** means 'behaviour', but in some contexts it is the equivalent of **attitude**.

> *Sein neutrales Verhalten in einer so wichtigen Angelegenheit enttäuschte seine Freunde, die mit seiner Unterstützung gerechnet hatten.*

2. i. Both **die Haltung** and **die Einstellung** are applied to what or how people think and express sense iii of **attitude**. Although in numerous cases it does not matter which one is used, the difference lies in the nature of the attitude. *Eine Haltung* is seen as being connected with the character and determining a person's action and thinking. Someone has a particular *Haltung* because of the type of human being he or she is. *Einstellung* refers to a position or point of view arrived at by thinking and denotes a more comprehensive view than *die Meinung, die Ansicht*, or *der Standpunkt*. It can, however, change even from day to day, whereas someone's *Haltung*, if it changes at all, does so only slowly and over a period of time because it is part of the character. If talking of a person's attitude, a speaker would use *Einstellung* if he or she meant a point of view regarding a question which could well alter. *Ich habe sie nach ihrer Einstellung zum Tempolimit gefragt. Was ist seine Einstellung zu dieser Frage?* (More formally *in bezug auf diese Frage.*) *Ich habe in dieser Sache dieselbe Einstellung wie du.* *Haltung* and *Einstellung* are used to describe the nature of someone's views or thinking, *eine fortschrittliche/liberale/reaktionäre/ konservative/moderne/altmodische/kritische Haltung/Einstellung*, but here too *Haltung* would lie deeper and be part of the character, while *Einstellung* would refer to particular issues. In addition, *Er legte eine fortschrittliche Haltung an den Tag* suggests that this shows itself in his actions—he was open to new ideas and put innovations into practice—whereas *eine fortschrittliche Einstellung* would be apparent in what someone says or in his or her opinions. Both also refer to the field in which attitudes are held, *eine politische/religiöse/soziale Haltung/Einstellung* or *jmds. Haltung/Einstellung in politischen* etc. *Fragen*. Both are used with *haben* and *einnehmen*, to take [up].

> *Auf Grund seiner Haltung zum Militär verweigerte er den Wehrdienst.*
> *Der Mann änderte seine Einstellung zur Kindererziehung so oft, daß seine Frau nie wußte, was er billigen oder mißbilligen würde.*
> *Ich habe mir die verschiedenartigsten Einstellungen angehört und weiß nicht, was ich selber denke.*
> *Ihre Einstellung zur Arbeit/zu dieser Frage hat sich nicht geändert.*
> *Er nahm eine kühle/kritische/reservierte Haltung zu dem Reformplan ein.*

ii. In one of its senses **die Stellung** is similar to *Einstellung* and means 'position in or attitude to a matter'. *Stellung zu einer Frage nehmen* means 'to state one's attitude to it or to comment on it', mostly in speech, though sometimes in writing. *Wenn ich Stellung für oder gegen etw. nehme/beziehe*, I state my support for or opposition to it or speak in favour of or against it. **Die Stellungnahme** is 'a comment on' or 'the statement of one's attitude' to a matter. The v. is **sich stellen zu**. To ask [about] someone's attitude or point of view, I say, '*Wie stellst du dich zu dem Vorschlag/zu dem neuen Kollegen?*' Typical uses are *sich positiv/negativ zu einer Frage stellen*, which could translate *take [up] a . . . attitude to*.

> *Bei der politischen Diskussion mußte jeder Schüler die Stellung, die er bezogen hatte, auch begründen.*
> *In dem Flugblatt hat der Verfasser eine extreme Stellung bezogen.*

In dem Interview mußte der Kanzler zu verschiedenen Plänen der Regierung Stellung nehmen.

iii. Other words that express a meaning similar to **attitude** in sense iii are **der Standpunkt**, 'point of view', which is an everyday word, and **die Position**, which is a more learned one. Alternatives are *die Meinung* and *die Ansicht*, OPINION.

Der Bundestagsabgeordnete vertrat seine Position zur Änderung des Streikgesetzes mit Überzeugung.
Mein Standpunkt in dieser Frage hat sich in letzter Zeit kaum geändert.

attract *v.*

1. Attract, meaning 'to pull to or towards itself' in relation to natural phenomena, is **anziehen**. For the use of the refl. see 2. i.

Ein Magnet zieht Eisen an.
Salz zieht Feuchtigkeit an.

2. If something attracts people or animals, it causes them to come to it. People or their qualities which attract others cause them to like or admire them.

i. Anziehen is used when people or animals are attracted to a place without the place being stated, *Die Wettkämpfe zogen viele Zuschauer an,* or when someone or something arouses a sympathetic response, *Sie zog ihn sehr an.* Anziehen always needs an obj. Neither in this sense nor in sense 1 can *anziehen* be intr. as can **attract** in *Opposites attract.* This must be refl. in G., as it can be in E. *Ungleichnamige Pole ziehen sich an, gleichnamige stoßen sich ab. Es scheint, daß Menschen mit entgegengesetzten Charaktereigenschaften sich oft anziehen.*

Die Ausstellung zieht viele Besucher an. *Alles Neue zieht ihn unwiderstehlich an.*
Die Industriemesse zieht nicht nur Käufer an, sondern auch viele Schaulustige.
Er hat uns alle durch sein freundliches Wesen angezogen..

Anziehend means 'attractive'. *Sie hat viele anziehende Eigenschaften. Alle fanden sie sehr anziehend.*

ii. An alternative is **hinziehen**, a less common, stylistically higher word than anziehen. It is mostly found in the past part. applied to people. *Ich fühlte mich von jmdm. stark angezogen* or *zu jmdm. stark hingezogen* are both possible.

Schon in der Jugend fühlte er sich zu den schönen Künsten hingezogen.

iii. In one intr. use, **ziehen** means 'to attract or draw people, mostly patrons'.

Schon der Filmtitel zieht. *Solche Filme ziehen nicht mehr.*

iv. Anlocken was originally used for luring or attracting animals, but is now also used for people. It suggests a stimulus which is difficult to resist. *Anlocken* means 'to attract somewhere' without the place being stated. If the place is given, the base v. **locken** is used. *Die Musik lockte viele an,* but *Die Musik lockte viele in die Kneipe. Der Sonnenschein lockte uns ins Freie.*

Honig/Konfitüre lockt Wespen an. Also . . . zieht Wespen an.
Die Farben, der Duft und der Nektar der Blüten locken viele Insekten an, die in den Blüten Nahrung suchen und die unabsichtlich die Bestäubung vollziehen.
Mit ihrer blendenden Figur und den langen blonden Haaren lockte sie die Männer scharenweise an.
Mit diesen Preisen wirst du keine Käufer anlocken. Or . . . nicht viele Käufer in dein Geschäft locken.

3. Attract also means 'to induce s.o. to do or see sth., or to take on a task'. **Reizen** means 'to please' or 'appeal to' a person, but has the connotation of prompting to action. *Die Aufgabe reizt mich,* the task attracts me. Both *Dieser Film reizt mich [nicht]* and *Es reizt mich [nicht], den Film zu sehen* are used. Although *anziehen* usually does not suggest action, it overlaps to some extent with *reizen.* In *Einige Leute zieht das Kino nicht an, reizt* is possible.

Er war ein Gebirgsmensch. Strand, Wellen und Fischerboote konnten ihn nicht reizen.
Es würde mich reizen, es zu versuchen.
Das Theaterstück reizt mich, weil es viel positive Kritik bekommen hat.

4. Attract attention etc. The usual expression with *Aufmerksamkeit* and *Blicke* is **auf sich ziehen**, to draw to oneself. *Sie war eine so auffallende Erscheinung, daß sie die Aufmerksamkeit aller auf sich zog. Auf sich ziehen* is also used with *das Interesse*, mostly when people are the subj. With things as subj., *erregen*, 'to arouse, excite', is usual. *Diese Pläne haben sehr viel Interesse erregt.*

avoid *v.* **Avoid** has three meanings: 1. 'To keep away from a person or place'. 2. If I avoid something undesirable like an accident, I take action to prevent it happening. 3. If I avoid doing something, I make an effort not to do it. The obj. of **avoid** can thus be personal or non-personal, *I avoid a person, a collision, mistakes* or *I couldn't avoid it.* It also takes a gerund. *We could not avoid meeting them.*

1. The main G. equivalents are *meiden* and *vermeiden*. As only *vermeiden* can take an infin., it translates the E. gerundial construction. Both occur with an obj., but what the objs. designate is mostly of a different nature.

i. Meiden means 'to keep away from', or 'to attempt not to come into contact with', and is used with an obj. only. The obj. can be a person or a thing which stands for, or is associated with, people, such as someone's company, house, shop, glance, as well as places and food.

> *Nachdem er gestohlen hatte, mieden ihn alle seine früheren Freunde.*
> *Du mußt schlechte Gesellschaft/den Umgang mit solchen Menschen meiden.*
> *Spaziergänger meiden diesen Teil des Waldes, weil man dort immer Schwärmen von Mücken begegnet.*
> *Sie hat meinen Blick den ganzen Abend gemieden.*
> *Gefahrenzonen im Gebirge, wie z. B. stark gefährdete Lawinengebiete, sollte man, um sein Leben nicht zu riskieren, möglichst meiden.*
> *Seitdem er dort überfallen wurde, meidet er den Ort.*
> *Ich meide die Stadt in den Hauptverkehrszeiten.*
> *Wegen seines Magenleidens meidet er scharfe, fette Speisen.*
> *Wenn du weißt, daß du Gurken nicht vertragen kannst, mußt du sie in Zukunft meiden.*

ii. Vermeiden means 'not to let sth. happen' or 'to see to it that sth. does not happen'. While *meiden* means 'to keep away from' something that exists, *vermeiden* implies preventing a situation coming into existence or not doing something. It is used with *es* and *das* as obj. and with ns. which denote situations, difficulties, and states of mind, such as *ein Konflikt, eine Panik, Schwierigkeiten, Unannehmlichkeiten, ein Streit, Streitigkeiten, ein Zwischenfall, Gefahr, Fehler, Ärger, Aufsehen, Aufregung, Mißverständnisse*, etc. Only *vermeiden* takes an infin., usually with a preceding *es. Ich möchte es vermeiden, ihnen zu begegnen.* A *daß*-clause may follow. *Ich konnte es nicht vermeiden, daß wir uns trafen/daß man ihm diese Frage stellte.*

> *Weil er ein schlechtes Gewissen hatte, vermied er es, sie anzusehen.*
> *Glaubst du, ich hätte dich mit dieser Sache belästigt, wenn ich es hätte vermeiden können?*
> *Ich gehe nicht hin, wenn ich es vermeiden kann.   Das läßt sich nicht vermeiden.*
> *Sie hofft, einen Streit zu vermeiden.   Genau das/die Situation wollte ich vermeiden.*
> *Er ist übervorsichtig und stets darauf bedacht, Fehler zu vermeiden.*

iii. With some ns. either word is possible, sometimes with a slight difference in meaning. *Ich meide solche Situationen grundsätzlich* means that I do not go to places where such situations (might) exist; however, *Wenn es geht, vermeide ich solche Situationen* means that I do everything possible to prevent them coming about. *Wir haben das Thema gemieden* and *vermieden* amount to the same thing, as do *Ich meide* and *vermeide diesen Ausdruck. Vermeiden* is more common.

2. Ausweichen, the basic meaning of which is 'to get out of the way of', is similar to *meiden*, but as it implies that the danger is imminent, it is often closer to *elude* or *evade. Er wich dem Feind/der Gefahr/der Frage aus. Sie war bestrebt, allen*

Entscheidungen diplomatisch auszuweichen. However, in contexts like *Er wich dem Schlag/dem Stoß/dem Angriff aus,* **avoid** would be the appropriate v. *Ausweichen* is also the usual word for avoiding someone or something on a road. *Er wich dem anderen Auto/dem Radfahrer/dem Hund/dem Kind aus. Ausweichen* is used without a dat., but it is then translated as *get out of the way* or *swerve. Er ist im letzten Augenblick ausgewichen. Sie wich links/rechts aus.*

3. i. Umgehen (insep.), the primary meaning of which is 'to go round', is also used in the sense 'to get round or avoid' difficulties, impediments, and also rules, regulations, taxes, etc. which would normally have to be observed or paid. It also translates *to circumvent.*

> *Viele reiche Deutsche umgehen die höheren Steuern in der Bundesrepublik, indem sie Gesellschaften in Liechtenstein gründen.*   *Diese Vorschrift kann man nicht umgehen.*
>
> *Er hat den kritischen Punkt/die Frage geschickt umgangen.*
>
> *Wir wollen versuchen, diese Schwierigkeiten/diese problematische Situation zu umgehen.*
>
> *Es läßt sich nicht umgehen/vermeiden, daß ich Ihnen ein paar persönliche Fragen stelle.*

The v. in *She avoided the question* can be translated by *vermeiden, umgehen,* and *ausweichen. Sie vermied die Frage* means that she did not ask it. *Sie umging die Frage* means that someone asked it, but she avoided answering it, a meaning which can also be expressed by *Sie wich einer Antwort [auf die Frage] aus.*

ii. In one sense, **herumkommen um** means 'to get round or out of', or 'to avoid'. When an infin. follows, the construction is *Du kommst nicht drum herum, diese Prüfung abzulegen, drum* being a shortened form of *darum.*

> *Um eine Erhöhung der Steuern wird die Regierung nicht herumkommen.*
>
> *Um diese Aufgabe/Arbeit kommen wir nicht herum.*

b

bad, evil, wicked *adjs.* The main equivalents are *schlecht* and *schlimm*. *Böse* and *übel* are usually stronger. *Schwer* sometimes corresponds to **bad[ly]**. Order of meanings. 1. **Bad** = 'of unacceptably low quality'. 2. **Bad** = 'unpleasant, harmful, undesirable'. 3. **Bad** = 'morally unacceptable, evil, wicked'. 4. **Bad** as an intensifier. 5. Other uses. 6. **Badly**.

1. i. Bad and *poor* describe something of defective or inferior quality, what fails to come up to an acceptable standard, and are applied to aspects of the natural world, *bad soil, bad light, bad weather*, to natural products, *a bad crop, bad timber*, to things produced by human effort, *a bad film, a bad painting, a bad translation*, and to people performing work or tasks, *a bad teacher* or *carpenter*. The equivalent is **schlecht**, which expresses these senses both as an adj. and as an adv.

> *Der Boden ist hier so schlecht, daß der Ertrag der Felder auch niedrig bleibt.*
> *Das Essen/Der Wein/Der Kaffee/Der Roman/Der Vortrag war schlecht.*
> *Die Luft ist hier schlecht.*   *Das Wetter ist heute schlecht.*
> *Die Straßen sind in sehr schlechtem Zustand.*
> *Ich habe ein schlechtes Gedächtnis/ein schlechtes Gehör/schlechte Augen.*
> *Ihre schlechte Gesundheit wirkte sich nachteilig auf ihre Schaffenskraft aus.*
> *Er ist ein schlechter Lehrer/Arbeiter/Sänger.*   *Das ist ein schlechtes Ergebnis.*
> *Udo ist der schlechteste Schüler in der Klasse.* (This would refer to the quality of his work; *der schlimmste Schüler* would refer to his behaviour.)
> *Der Schüler schrieb eine schlechte Arbeit nach der anderen.* (Klassenarbeit, 'test', is meant.)
> *Wegen der Nachrichtensperre war die Bevölkerung über die Vorgänge im eigenen Land schlecht informiert.*   *Der Anzug sitzt/paßt schlecht.*
> *In einem so heißen und schlecht gelüfteten Zimmer kann man nicht richtig arbeiten.*

ii. Bad at *maths* etc. is **schlecht** or **schwach in**. *Sie ist schlecht in Mathe/schwach in Mathe.*

iii. Schlecht is used in the neg. as praise. *Das war keine schlechte Idee/kein schlechter Film.*

> *Er ist kein schlechter Schüler.*
> *Ich fand den Roman gar nicht schlecht.*

iv. Schlecht is used in the sense 'faulty, incorrect'.

> *Er spricht ein zu schlechtes Deutsch, um als Empfangschef arbeiten zu können.*
> *Das ist eine schlechte Übersetzung.*   *Sie haben den Text schlecht übersetzt.*
> *Ihr Französisch ist schlecht. Sie kann sich kaum verständigen.*

v. Schlecht means 'unsatisfactory with regard to quantity', i.e. in number, amount, profit, payment, etc.

> *In Zeiten hoher Arbeitslosigkeit ist ein schlechtes Gehalt/ein schlechter Lohn immer noch besser als gar kein Einkommen.*   *Die Theatervorstellung war schlecht besucht.*
> *Das Zweigwerk Essen wirft ständig die schlechteste Rendite des Konzerns ab.*
> *Die Firma wäre beinahe zugrundegegangen, weil sie eine Zeitlang nur schlechte Geschäfte gemacht hat.*
> *Die Kinder sehen schlecht ernährt aus.*   *Das war [eine] schlecht bezahlte Arbeit.*

vi. A common colloquial syn. of *schlecht* is **mies**, which can be translated by colloquial syns. of **bad** such as *lousy, rotten*, or *miserable*. *Mieses Wetter. Am Wochenende* *gibt's meist ein mieses Fernsehprogramm. Der Chef hat heute miese Laune. Das Essen wurde immer mieser. Eine mies bezahlte Arbeit.*

2. i. Both **schlecht** and **schlimm** correspond to **bad** meaning 'unfavourable, disadvantageous, harmful, unpleasant'. Although in some contexts both are possible, often with nuances in meaning, in others only *schlimm* is possible. E. Leisi (1961: 42) has pointed out that, whereas **bad** is used without restriction in its field of application, *schlecht* can be applied only to ns. which as a class can also be good. With things which by nature are exclusively bad, such as an illness, accident, or crime, only *schlimm* is possible. Some ns. of this kind are *der Unfall, die Krankheit, die Erkältung, die Entzündung, ein Anfall (von Epilepsie etc.), die Seuche, das Verbrechen, die Schuld, die Niederlage, die Folter, die Erniedrigung, die Qualen, der Fehler, der Verlust,* and *das Ungeziefer,* vermin in houses and pests on trees, crops, etc.

Sie hatte eine so schlimme Erkältung, daß sie eine Woche lang nicht aus dem Haus gehen konnte.
Die Eltern bangten nächtelang um das Kind, das einen schlimmen Keuchhusten hatte.
Sich so zu verrechnen war ein schlimmer Fehler, der einem Fachmann nie hätte unterlaufen dürfen.
Die Entzündung war so schlimm, daß sie unverzüglich behandelt werden mußte.
Im Mittelalter rafften oft schlimme Seuchen einen beträchtlichen Teil der Bevölkerung ganzer Landstriche hin.   Die Schmerzen waren schlimmer als vorher.
Die Mannschaft hatte mehrere schlimme Niederlagen hintereinander erlitten.
Nachdem seine junge Frau bei einem Autounfall ums Leben gekommen war, sah es längere Zeit so aus, als würde er einen so schlimmen Verlust nie verwinden.

ii. Closely related to *schlimm* in this sense is **schwer**, which besides meaning 'HEAVY' and 'DIFFICULT' expresses the sense 'of great strength' or 'to a high degree'. Applied to what is not beneficial in nature, *schwer* intensifies the unpleasant effect and corresponds to **bad** and SEVERE. *Schwer* is also used with words like those given for *schlimm,* such as *die Krankheit, der Anfall, der Fehler, das Verbrechen, das Vergehen, der Verlust, die Schuld, die Erniedrigung, die Verletzung, die Niederlage, die Qualen, die Grippe, die Erkältung. Schwer* is used with storms and natural disasters, *ein schweres Gewitter/Unwetter, ein schwerer Sturm, ein schweres Erdbeben,* though *schlimm* is heard in the spoken language. *Schwer* tends to be stronger and more objective than *schlimm,* which is emotionally coloured and somewhat colloquial. As *schlecht* and *schlimm* are not used as advs. in this meaning (although *schlimm* is sometimes used in colloquial speech), *schwer* is the usual equivalent of **badly** in this sense. Thus *schwer erkrankt* or *verletzt, schwer beschädigt.*

Der Schüler machte im Diktat mehrere schwere/schlimme Rechtschreibefehler. (Both mean that he badly misspelt some words; *schlimm* is colloquial and subjective, while *schwer* belongs to the standard language.)
Der Tod seiner Braut hat bei ihm eine schwere seelische Erschütterung hervorgerufen. Also . . . hat ihn schwer erschüttert.
Bei dem Aufprall wurde der Wagen schwer beschädigt. Es entstand schwerer Sachschaden.
Die Familie wurde von dem Unglück im Bergwerk schwer getroffen. Die vom Vater erlittenen Verletzungen waren so schlimm/schwer, daß er beinahe daran gestorben wäre.
Ein schweres Gewitter hat die Ernte vernichtet.   In den Bergen tobte ein schlimmes Unwetter.
Der Trainer war schwer enttäuscht, weil seine beste Schwimmerin wegen einer schlimmen Erkältung nicht antreten konnte.

iii. In cases in which ns. do not denote something bad by nature, both **schlecht** and **schlimm** occur. The general distinction is that whereas *schlecht* conveys an objective judgement and refers to the ascertainable concrete disadvantages of a situation, *schlimm* is a subjective judgement. It means 'bad in its effect on the person spoken about' and stresses the emotional involvement of the speaker in the situation, often expressing sympathy. Because of the emotional involvement, *schlimm* acts as an intensification of *schlecht. Eine schlimme Lage* is worse than *eine schlechte Lage. Eine schlimme Nachricht* would announce things having direr consequences than *eine schlechte Nachricht*. Thus, if *schlecht* = 'bad', *schlimm* = 'very bad'. *Schlechte Verhältnisse* refers to conditions of work or living judged objectively to be not good. *Schlimme Verhältnisse* could refer to the same trying conditions, but stresses how difficult they are to endure and/or expresses sympathy or perhaps indignation, or it could denote purely mentally bad conditions, intimidation or a depraved atmosphere. *Schlechte Zeiten* would refer to living standards, rates of pay, unemployment, etc., *schlimme Zeiten* to the general burdens, troubles, and difficulties seen subjectively. *Schlechte Erfahrungen mit einem Geschäft oder einer Person machen* implies that the goods are bad, the prices too high, the service poor, etc. or that the person is unreliable, untrustworthy, etc. *Eine schlimme Erfahrung* is a painful experience, even though it might ultimately lead to beneficial results. *Jmd. hat das Schlimmste überwunden* (also *das Schwerste*) expresses sympathy with the person's plight. *Die Radsportler haben nun das schlimmste Stück ihres Weges hinter sich* concentrates attention on the difficulties, the exertion and strain, etc. *Das schlechteste Stück einer Straße* refers primarily to the quality of the road—it could be badly constructed, have a broken surface, be full of potholes, and so on—and only by implication to the effort involved in negotiating it.

iv. In certain cases only **schlimm** is possible. In such expressions as *Du machst die Sache nur noch schlimmer*, *schlecht* would mean 'qualitatively bad'.

> *Etw. nimmt ein schlimmes/übles Ende*. But *Es wird wohl schlecht/schlimm/böse/übel ausgehen.*
> *Du mußt auf das Schlimmste vorbereitet/gefaßt sein.* Or *. . . mit dem Schlimmsten rechnen.*
> *Man wird den Patzer vergessen. Es gibt Schlimmeres auf der Welt.*
> *Es gibt Schlimmeres, als einmal eine Prüfung nicht zu bestehen.*
> *Wie kann man aber auch ohne Helm aufs Motorrad steigen? Das Schlimmste hätte passieren können.*
> *Das Schlimmste ist, daß er nun von allen Seiten verspottet wird.*

v. **Übel** also means 'very unfavourable or unpleasant', 'having disadvantageous consequences'. *Eine üble Situation. Die Sache nahm ein übles Ende* (or *ging übel aus*). **Böse** is a syn. in some contexts. *Eine böse Krankheit. Böse Jahre. Die Sache ging böse aus.* Like *schlimm*, *übel* and *böse* denote a higher degree of badness than *schlecht*. *Üble, schlimme*, and *böse Folgen* all emphasize the evil or harmful results. In this context *schlecht* is too weak. *Nicht übel* is used like *nicht schlecht. Das Kleid steht dir nicht übel.* (*Er hat die Bemerkung übel aufgenommen* means that he took it amiss.)

> *Die Wirtschaft des Landes befindet sich in einer üblen/schlimmen Lage.*
> *Deine Unvorsichtigkeit kann üble Folgen haben.*
> *Der Arzt sagte, es stehe übel um seine Gesundheit.*
> *Sie sind wirklich übel/schlimm dran* (are in a bad position).

3. Bad = 'morally depraved, evil, wicked, vicious'.

i. Schlecht is applied to people, their behaviour and actions. *Ein schlechter Mensch* is bad in character or in a moral sense, unreliable, a liar, untrustworthy. (Note that *ein schlechter Mann* is 'a bad husband'; *schlecht* is a judgement on his quality as an *Ehemann*.) In this sense **böse**, like **evil, wicked**, or *malicious*, expresses a higher degree of badness than *schlecht. Ein böser Mensch* might be dangerous, unpredictable, a thief, or violent and brutal. *Böse* is linked with *gut* in talking of good and bad/evil. *Er scheint nicht zu verstehen, was Gut und Böse ist.* The n. *evil* in an abstract sense is **das Böse** (without an article **Böses**), less commonly **das Übel**. Hence *Das Böse in der Welt ist nicht zu leugnen.* The line of the Lord's Prayer is either *Erlöse uns von dem Bösen!* or *Erlöse uns von dem Übel! Böses* can also mean 'bad or evil thgs.' *Er hat ihr viel Böses angetan. Ein Übel* denotes an evil, a condition causing harm. *Der Rauschgifthandel ist ein Übel, das man mit allen Mitteln bekämpfen muß.* The colloquial **mies**, applied to people, suggests false, selfish, untrustworthy. *Jmd. ist mies* or *ein mieser Typ.* **Übel** and **schlimm** are also applied to people and actions. *Der Junge hat schlechte Sachen angestellt* states that what was done was not morally good; *schlimme Sachen* is slightly stronger. *Schlimm* often carries a note of moral censure and criticizes actions which, even if not particularly evil, point to undesirable qualities. *Böse Sachen* implies actions causing evil and harm to others, as does *üble Sachen;* both point more to the underlying bad motive or evil intent. *Schlechte Gesellschaft* is in general not good; *böse* and *üble Gesellschaft* have a stronger overtone of depravity and express moral condemnation. With this overtone, *ein böser, übler,* and *schlimmer Ruf* are stronger than *ein schlechter Ruf. Wegen ihrer Unzuverlässigkeit hat sie einen schlechten Ruf bei ihren Kunden. Wegen ihrer Brutalität haben die Rocker einen üblen/schlimmen/bösen Ruf in der Stadt. Der Film war gar nicht so schlecht* is a judgement on its quality; *nicht so schlimm* suggests not so morally objectionable, e.g. not as pro-Nazi, as the speaker had been led to believe. *Ein übler Trick* expresses moral condemnation of the action and its motive; *ein böser* or *schlimmer Trick* is also an adverse moral judgement. *Ein übler Geselle/Bursche,* both = 'fellow', is someone with no moral principles. *Solche Leute tun die übelsten Dinge* expresses strong censure. *Jmdm. übel mitspielen,* 'to treat s.o. shabbily/badly', is a fixed phr., as is *jmdn. auf die übelste Weise/in der übelsten Weise hereinlegen,* 'to cheat or deceive s.o. despicably'. With *Absicht, böse* implies evil or malicious intent. *Schlecht* is weaker. With *meinen, böse* is not particularly strong either in pos. or neg. sents. In *Diese Bemerkung war nicht böse gemeint, nicht böse* means that no harm was meant.

> *Eine alte Frau zu bestehlen—diese schlimme Tat bestätigt, daß wir es hier mit einem von Grund auf schlechten Menschen zu tun haben.*
>
> *Er ist ein schlechter/böser Mensch, weil er selbst seine Mutter für Geld verkaufen würde.*
>
> *Diese charakterlosen Individuen sind für unseren Sohn die schlechteste Gesellschaft, die man sich denken kann. Also . . . der schlechteste Umgang.*
>
> *Da drei seiner fünf Freunde aus Hamburg wegen Körperverletzung vorbestraft sind, darf ich wohl behaupten, daß er dort in böser Gesellschaft lebte.*
>
> *In der Großstadt sind sie in ganz üble Gesellschaft geraten.*
>
> *Sie hat schon so viel Böses in ihrem Leben getan, daß niemand ihr mehr traut, nicht einmal ihre Mutter.*
>
> *Man tritt doch niemanden derart durch Zufall. Das war klar böse Absicht.*
>
> *Unter Ausnutzung meines Vertrauens ihm gegenüber hat er mich beim Verkauf dieses fahruntüchtigen Autos in der übelsten Weise hereingelegt.*

ii. With *Gewissen,* **schlecht** and **böse** are used. *Sein schlechtes Gewissen steht ihm im Gesicht geschrieben. Man sieht ihr das böse Gewissen an.*

4. i. Bad is an intensifier of words expressing undesirable effects. *A bad* (or *nasty*) *fright* is 'a very great fright'. For some examples see 2. ii. **Böse** occasionally has this function. As an adv. it is a syn. of *sehr.*

> *Ich bekam einen bösen Schrecken, als mich jmd. im Dunkeln an der Schulter faßte.*
>
> *Kein Geld und keine Freunde erreichbar, und der Gerichtsvollzieher in der Tür—er war in böser Bedrängnis.*   *Sie hatte ihre Familie böse blamiert.*

ii. In the language of the north **arg**, 'bad', is now confined to certain more or less fixed expressions, but it is not uncommon in some parts of the country. It does not introduce any new nuance and can usually be replaced by other words.

> *Das würde ich nicht einmal meinem ärgsten Feind antun.* (Fixed expression.)
>
> *Man muß auf das Ärgste/Schlimmste gefaßt sein.*   *Ich dachte an nichts Arges/Böses.*
>
> *Er hatte einen argen/bösen Schrecken bekommen.*
>
> *Man hatte ihm einen argen/bösen Streich gespielt.*
>
> *Die Krankheit hat ihn arg/böse/sehr mitgenommen.*
>
> *Das Buch ist schon hundertmal gelesen worden und hat schon arg/böse/sehr gelitten.*

5. Other uses of **bad.**

i. Taste and smell. *Etw. schmeckt schlecht* is a judgement on its quality—it is not up to the standard expected. Since *das Fleisch ist schlecht geworden* means that it has gone bad or off, *schlecht schmecken* could also mean 'to taste bad' in this sense. With *der Geschmack*, taste in the mouth, **schlecht** is weaker than **übel**. *Von der Arznei hatte ich einen schlechten/übeln Geschmack auf der Zunge. Etw., was schlecht riecht*, smells as if it has gone bad. *Etw., was übel riecht*, emits an offensive smell.

> *Mein Bruder kann einfach nicht kochen. Sogar die Spiegeleier, die er zu braten versucht, schmecken schlecht.*
>
> *Kaum machte er die Schatulle auf, als ihm ein äußerst schneidender, übler Geruch entgegenquoll, als wäre etw. Verfaultes darin.*

ii. Bad, applied to children meaning 'naughty', is either **schlimm** as in *Ihr seid aber heute schlimm!*, or **böse**, *Du bist ein böses Kind*. This is an exaggerated use of sense 3, but is no longer felt as such. Otherwise a word like *unartig*, 'naughty', can be used.

iii. Bad = 'painful, sore'. **Schlimm** and **böse** are applied to parts of the body causing pain. *Böse* can mean inflamed. *Ich habe einen bösen/schlimmen Finger/Zahn* is colloquially *einen wehen Finger* etc. *Sein schlimmes Bein ließ ihn ein Gewitter sicher vorausfühlen. Mir ist schlecht*, less frequently *Mir ist übel*, means that I feel unwell. *Mir wird übel* means that I am overcome by nausea.

iv. In *I feel bad about slighting such a good friend*, **bad** implies qualms or pangs of conscience, an idea which must be clearly translated. Possibilities are: *Ich habe Gewissensbisse, weil ich einen so guten Freund geringschätzig behandelt habe (or gekränkt habe), Ich habe ein schlechtes Gewissen, weil . . .*, or *Ich mache mir Vorwürfe, weil . . .*

6. Badly. **Schlecht** is used as an adv. and refers to quality. *Ich war schlecht vorbereitet.* **Badly** also means 'very much', 'to a great or intense degree'. **Schwer** and sometimes **böse** and **arg** can express this sense. *Sie haben mich schwer enttäuscht. Der Mantel hat schon böse/arg gelitten. Er hat mich arg/böse blamiert.* In some contexts **badly** must be translated by intensifiers such as **sehr**, **unbedingt**, and **stark**. *I miss you badly* is *Ich vermisse dich sehr*. *They needed help badly* is *Sie brauchten dringend Hilfe* or *brauchten unbedingt Hilfe*. With *to want*, **badly** is *sehr* or *unbedingt*. *Du wolltest unbedingt hingehen. Der Junge will unbedingt ein Fahrrad haben. Die Seile der Brücke hängen stark durch*, are sagging badly. In the spoken language, **ganz schön** functions as an intensifier both as an adj. and adv. It sometimes translates **bad[ly]**.

Du irrst dich sehr, wenn du das glaubst.	*Der Junge lispelte stark.*
Er hat einen ganz schönen Schrecken bekommen.	*Ich war ganz schön in Verlegenheit.*
Die Krankheit hat ihn ganz schön mitgenommen.	*Das Buch hat ganz schön gelitten.*

banish, ban *vs.*

1. i. Der Bann was a punishment for a breach of law in the form of exclusion from the community of the church so that expressions like *den Bann über jmdn. aussprechen* or *jmdn. mit dem Bann belegen* mean 'to excommunicate' (*exkommunizieren*). However, *der Bann* and **bannen** are now used in this sense only in historical contexts, sometimes also with the idea of excluding from secular society. The corresponding v. for civil jurisdiction was **ächten**, 'to proscribe, ban a pers.', 'declare s.o. to be an outlaw', and the n. **die Acht**. *Wer in Acht und Bann getan oder erklärt wurde*, was excluded from both the community of the church and civil society. The expression is occasionally found in the meaning 'to exclude s.o. from society or a group'. *Die politische Zeitströmung ist auch heute noch mächtig genug, jeden, der ihr widerspricht, in Acht und Bann zu tun—wer nicht 'zeitgemäß' denkt, ist 'reaktionär', und 'reaktionär' zu sein bedeutet seit 1789 einen sittlichen Makel.* In the literal sense, *ächten* is confined to historical descriptions, but it survives in the meaning 'to exclude s.o. from a group, ostracize', or 'to declare sth. to be harmful to the community, ban, outlaw'.

> *Der Papst hatte den Kaiser gebannt.*   *Ächtet die Atomwaffen!*

Die anderen Häftlinge haben den Kindesmörder geächtet.

ii. The second meaning of *Bann* is 'a spell'. *Er hielt alle in [seinem] Bann. Er war in ihren Bann geraten/stand ganz in ihrem Bann. Der Bann war endlich gebrochen.* **Bannen** thus meant 'to compel to remain in a place' or 'to make powerless to move by magic power or witchcraft' and is still found in fig. uses. *Das Stück bannte die Zuschauer auf ihre Plätze. Seine Augen hingen wie gebannt an ihr. Er starrte sie [wie] gebannt an. Eine Szene* etc. *auf die Leinwand* or *Seine Gedanken auf das Papier/in Sätze bannen* is 'to fix, hold, or capture' as a painting on canvas or in words. *Gebannt* is often translated as *spellbound*. A further meaning of *bannen,* 'to make powerless and/or drive away or remove', originally by magic power, something like *böse Geister* or *der Teufel,* has been extended to the use with *die Angst, die Gefahr, die Not,* or *die Sorge* as obj. It suggests causing something harmful to have no further influence or effect, sometimes only for a limited time. *Banish* is sometimes the appropriate transl.

> *Da in den letzten 24 Stunden eine Änderung der Wetterverhältnisse eingetreten ist, scheint die Smoggefahr vorerst gebannt zu sein.*
>
> *Mit der Ankunft von zwölf mit Lebensmitteln voll beladenen Lastwagen war die Not im Hungergebiet fürs erste gebannt.*
>
> *Wir haben Kredit für die nächsten vier Monate bekommen. Damit ist unsere Hauptsorge einstweilen gebannt.*   *Die Narkose hat die Angst vor Operationen weitgehend gebannt.*

2. Banish meaning either 'to exile s.o. permanently or for a specified time' or 'to send away from a place' is **verbannen**. It is also applied to something which is removed from a prominent position to a less important one, and to things occupying the thought which one puts out of one's mind, such as *Gedanken, Zweifel,* and *Sorgen.*

> *Der Diktator verbannte seine politischen Gegner aus der Hauptstadt/hat sie in kleine Dörfer verbannt.*
>
> *Zwei Tage nach Einnahme der Stadt hat der kommandierende General alle Journalisten daraus verbannt.*   *Er wurde für fünf Jahre auf eine Insel verbannt.*
>
> *Das Bild des Neffen, der bei seiner Tante in Ungnade gefallen war, wurde aus ihrem Wohnzimmer in die Rumpelkammer verbannt.*   *Ovid wurde aus Rom verbannt und starb im Exil.*
>
> *Den Gedanken an Nachgeben habe ich aus meinen Überlegungen verbannt.*
>
> *Sie verbannte alle Zweifel an der Richtigkeit ihres Vorgehens und machte sich an die Arbeit.*

3. Ban sth. or **ban** s.o. **from** doing sth. means 'to state officially that it must not be done or that s.o. is not allowed to do sth.' The equivalent is usually **verbieten**. *Das Abkommen verbietet die Herstellung von chemischen Waffen. Der Film wurde vom Zensor verboten. Ihm wurde verboten, an der Versammlung teilzunehmen,* he was banned from attending. *Das Mitnehmen von Hunden in den Park ist verboten,* dogs are banned from the park. That something is banned can sometimes be expressed by compounds of **das Verbot**, prohibition, ban. *Für diese Vogelarten gilt ein Ausfuhrverbot,* their export is banned. *Das Gericht verhängte ein Fahrverbot über ihn für die Dauer von einem Jahr. Die neue Regierung erließ ein Streikverbot. Der Arzt wurde mit Berufsverbot belegt.*

> *Es ist verboten, Rauschgift zu besitzen oder mit ihm zu handeln.* Or *Der Besitz von Rauschgift ist verboten.*

be *v.* there is, are

A. Be. In some cases a v. other than *sein* is necessary in G., in others it may be preferable for reasons of style to use a different word, and in others again a word other than *sein* is commonly used. The following are some suggestions.

1. Betragen. The literal meaning is 'to amount to', but it occurs more frequently than the E. term because E. often uses *to be. Betragen* is applied to bills, loans, salaries, fees, debts, etc. to state how much they are or amount to, and is also common when stating a distance, size, or measurement of any kind. When a sum of money comprises two or more items, or when at least two numerical items of any kind yield a total, **sich belaufen auf** is also used. Cf. ADD 5.

Sein Gehalt beträgt DM 3 200 im Monat ohne Abzüge/brutto.
Der von dem Sturm angerichtete Schaden betrug mehrere Millionen Mark.
Die Miete beträgt 800 Mark im Monat.   Die Rechnung betrug/belief sich auf 140 Mark.
Seine Schulden betragen/belaufen sich auf etwa DM 12 000.
Die Entfernung von Hannover nach Köln beträgt 339 Kilometer.
Wegen des Nebels betrug die Sicht nur wenige Meter.
Der normale Zeitunterschied zwischen Großbritannien und Australien beträgt 10 Stunden.

2. Sich befinden often states that someone or something is in a place, state, or condition, where E. has **be**. *Sein* is also possible.

Die Universität befindet sich im Norden der Stadt.   Herr von Holtei befindet sich auf Reisen.
Das Anwaltsbüro befindet sich im dritten Stock.
Die beiden Länder befinden sich zur Zeit im Kriegszustand/in einer schweren Finanzkrise.

3. Bestehen in, which is used with a n. or in the form *darin, daß*, means 'to consist or lie in', but it is often best translated as a form of **be**. It is the preferable equivalent of **be** in constructions like *The advantage/difference is that . . .* An alternative is **liegen in**.

Der besondere Vorzug dieses Farbfilms besteht in seiner starken Lichtempfindlichkeit.
Ihre Arbeit bestand darin, daß sie die spanische Geschäftskorrespondenz erledigte.
Das Problem besteht darin, daß das Land zu viel einführt und nicht genug ausführt.
Der Unterschied zwischen den beiden Motoren besteht/liegt darin, daß dieser mehr leistet und weniger
    Treibstoff verbraucht.
Der Vorteil dieser Maschine liegt in ihrer Vielseitigkeit/ . . . liegt darin, daß sie vielseitig verwendet
    werden kann.

4. Liegen is used to state geographical location and the position of things which can be regarded as lying somewhere. *Der Ort, wo wir unseren Urlaub verbrachten, liegt 2 000 Meter hoch.*

Paris liegt an der Seine.   Unser Grundstück liegt am Stadtrand.
Das Buch liegt auf dem Tisch. But *. . . steht im Regal*, when it is in a standing position.

Some expressions containing *liegen* are: *Es liegt in deinem/seinem*, etc. *Ermessen, Das lag in unserem Interesse*, and *Das lag nicht in meiner Absicht*.

5. Stehen is used when stating where something is written, printed, or can be read.

Es stand gestern in der Zeitung, daß die Premierministerin ihr Kabinett umbilden will.
Was steht in dem Brief?   Was steht auf dem Schild?
Sein Name steht noch auf der Liste.   Davon steht nichts in dem Vertrag.

6. Haben is used in certain cases where E. has **be**. *Man hat ein Gewicht*, also *eine Größe*, size of shoe, collar, etc. It is needed when *Farbe* is the obj. *Die Perlen haben eine gelbliche Farbe. Welche Farbe hat das Kostüm?* Also *Man hat Recht oder Unrecht* and *Jmd. hat morgen Geburtstag.*

Welche Größe haben Sie?   Jeder dritte Deutsche hat Übergewicht.
Der Koffer hat ein ganz schönes Gewicht (is very heavy).
Rate mal, welche Farbe mein neuer Pullover hat!
Welche Farbe hat das Auto? Answer: *Es ist blau.*

7. Handeln, used with **von** or **über**, means 'to be about' or 'to deal with', but the subj. can only be a film, book, etc., not a person. *To deal with*, when either a person or a book etc. is subj., is *behandeln*.

Der Vortrag handelte von einigen zeitgenössischen Schriftstellern.
Das Buch handelt vom Ausbruch des ersten Weltkrieges. Or *. . . handelt über die/von der Entdeckung*
    Australiens. Also *Das Buch/Der Autor behandelt die Entdeckung . . .*

Es handelt sich um has the general meaning 'it is a question of'. *Es handelt sich um unsere Zukunft* can be translated as *It is a question of our future* or *Our future is involved/concerned/at stake*. Similarly, *Es handelt sich um einen großen Betrag*. If I had asked to see someone, that person might ask, '*Worum handelt es sich?*', what is it that you would like to see me about? If *bei* is added, *sich handeln um* can become an equivalent of **be**. *Bei dieser Substanz handelt es sich um ein gefährliches Gift* is usually translated as *This substance is a dangerous poison*. A lit. transl. is *In the case of this substance it is a question of a dangerous poison*.

> *Bei dem Fremden, der seit zwei Tagen bei unseren Nachbarn wohnt, handelt es sich um den jüngsten Bruder von Frau Köhler.*
> *Bei dem Bild handelt es sich um eine Fälschung.*
> *Bei Amnesie handelt es sich um das Aussetzen des Erinnerungsvermögens infolge einer Bewußtseinsstörung.*

8. One sense of **herrschen** is 'to prevail' or 'be prevalent', but this meaning has been weakened to such an extent that it can now be an equivalent of **be**.

> *Zwischen uns herrschte ein offenes, herzliches Verhältnis.*
> *Auf allen Straßen herrschte extreme Eisglätte.*
> *Es herrschte drückende Hitze in der ganzen Stadt.*
> *Im Spind eines Soldaten soll Ordnung herrschen.*

9. Stattfinden is often preferred to *sein* in statements about when events take place.

> *Die Hochzeit findet Ende Juli statt.*
> *Das Konzert findet heute abend statt.*

10. Stecken is used like *sich befinden* and *sein*, particularly in the spoken language, and means 'to be in a place, position, or condition'. People can be the subj. *Wo steckst du denn die ganze Zeit? In diesem Buch steckt viel Arbeit* means that it contains or involves a lot of work, there is a lot of work in it.

> *Der Schlüssel steckt im Schloß.*   *Der Brief steckt im Kasten.*
> *Er steckt immer hinter seinen Büchern.*   *Der Junge steckt voller Dummheiten/voller Pläne.*
> *Ich weiß nicht, wer/was hinter diesem Projekt steckt.*
> *Herr Mertens steckt bis über die Ohren in Schulden.*
> *Wo hast du denn so lange gesteckt?*   *Ich weiß nicht, wo sie steckt.*
> *Er steckt immer in der Wohnung und geht nie aus.*   *In diesem Sprichwort steckt viel Wahrheit.*
> *In ihm stecken viele gute Eigenschaften/Fähigkeiten.*

11. To state or ask what someone wants to be, **werden** is used. *Was willst du werden? Mein jüngerer Bruder will Matrose werden. Meine Freundin hat beschlossen, Bibliothekarin zu werden.*

12. Vorliegen is often used in bureaucratic and formal language as an equivalent of **be**. *Es liegt offenbar ein Mißverständnis vor* means that there is obviously a misunderstanding.

> *Hier liegt ein Fall von Notwehr vor.*
> *Für sein Verhalten liegen besondere Gründe vor.* (*Es gibt* would be simpler G.)

B. There is, there are.

1. i. Es is the equivalent of *there* used as a formal subj. in e.g. *There is a man at the door* or *There are two versions of the story*. *Es* resembles *there* in being followed by a sing. or pl. v. depending on whether the real subj. is sing. or pl., but differs from it in that it can be used with any v., *there* being restricted to a small number of vs. Apart from **there is/are**, only *there exists, there remains, there followed, there has developed* are reasonably common. We thus get G. sents. with *es* in which *there* is impossible in E. *Es werden schon Vorbereitungen getroffen, das Schiff auf schnellstem Wege zu entladen. Es meldeten sich mehr als 200 Leute, die sich die Vorträge anhören* *wollten*. Although **es ist** and **es sind** are the equivalents of **there is/are**, there is another difference between E. and G. usage. *Es* is only used if it is the first word in the sent. If it is not the first word, it is omitted. *Es sind/waren mindestens fünfzig Leute im Saal* is usual, but in a question *es* drops out: *Wieviele Leute sind/waren im Saal?* This also holds if other words are put at the beginning: *Im Saal waren mindestens fünfzig Leute. There* needs to be added in translating from G. or omitted when translating from E. *Ist hier jmd., der Polnisch kann?* is *Is there anyone/anybody here . . . ?*

ii. The last sent. could also be *Gibt es hier jmd[n.], der Polnisch kann?* **Es gibt** takes an acc., *Es gab starken Widerstand*, has only one form for sing. and pl., and *es* is never omitted. A common explanation of the difference between *es ist* and *es gibt* is that *es gibt* denotes a fact of nature, something produced by nature, or a broad or permanent fact of history or life, and resembles *there exists*, whereas *es ist/sind* is applied to things which exist more or less by chance. This helps to a certain extent. In the following *es gibt* is the usual expression. *Es gibt neun Planeten in unserem Sonnensystem. Es gibt 92 Elemente, die in der Natur vorkommen. Känguruhs gibt es nur in Australien. Es gibt Menschen vielerlei Hautfarbe. Es gibt nur wenige Hunderassen, die sich als Blindenhunde eignen. Es scheint kein Leben auf dem Mars zu geben. Tyrannische Menschen hat es immer gegeben, und es wird sie wohl immer geben.* On the other hand, in stating that a certain number of people etc. are, as if by chance, in a place at a certain time, it is usual to use *es ist/sind. Es sind 16 Mädchen und 15 Jungen in der Klasse. Es sind zwei Japaner in unserer Gruppe. Es war niemand im Zimmer.* However, in many other cases both are heard, and in the spoken language, *es gibt* is very common. *Es gibt rote und schwarze Johannesbeeren* is a fact of nature. *Es sind mehrere Johannesbeerstauden im Garten* and *Es sind ein paar Äpfel im Kühlschrank* are chance occurrences, but in both sents., *es gibt* would be just as common as *es sind.* Likewise, *Heutzutage gibt es Löwen nur noch in einigen Teilen Afrikas* and *Es sind mehrere Löwen im Zoo* follow the rule, but just as frequently heard is *Es gibt mehrere Löwen im Zoo.* Thus *Im Zoo gibt es/sind viele Flamingos. Es gab einen guten Grund (für seine Weigerung)* is the usual expression, but with *Argumente* both occur. *Es gibt/sind andere Argumente, die für die Theorie sprechen. In dieser Stadt gibt es/sind zwei gute Kinos.*

> *Gibt es denn so was? Ja, das gibt es.*   *Es gibt eine andere Erklärung.*
> *Das gibt es ja gar nicht.*   *Ich glaube nicht, daß es Gespenster gibt.*
> *Autos gab es damals noch nicht.*   *Er ist der beste Spieler, den es gibt.*
> *Im Botanischen Garten gibt es/sind mehrere Gewächshäuser. In einem gibt es/sind hohe Farne.*

iii. Sein is used with an act. infin. where E. usually has a pass. infin. *Wie zu beweisen war*, as was to be proved. With **there is** both act. and pass. infins. are used. *There is a lot to say/to be said. There was a lot to discuss/to be discussed.* The latter can become *Es war viel zu besprechen*, but **es gab** is probably more common. It also takes an act. infin. only. *Es gab viel zu besprechen.*

> *Es gibt viel zu tun. Packen wir es an!*   *Es gab eine ganze Menge zu erledigen.*
> *Hier gibt es nichts mehr zu tun.*   *Hier ist nichts mehr zu machen.*
> *Was ist da zu machen?*   *Was gibt es hier zu überlegen?*
> *Was gibt es da zu lachen?*   *Was ist daran zu lachen/zum Lachen?*
> *Es war nichts zu sehen* (nothing to be seen).   *Es gab nichts zu sehen* (nothing to see).

iv. The equivalent of **there is** in *There was no going back* is **es gibt**. *Es gab kein Entweichen [mehr].*

> *Es gibt kein Halten mehr.*   *Da gibt es keine Widerrede.*
> *Da gab es kein Vor und kein Zurück.*

v. Only **es gibt** has the sense 'to happen, arise, take place', applied to weather and events.

> *Morgen gibt es schönes Wetter.*   *Dann gab es ein Gewitter.*
> *Wenn solche Grenzzwischenfälle sich wiederholen, wird es Krieg geben.*

Eine Zeitlang gab es viele Streiks in der Autoindustrie.
Es sah so aus, als ob es bald eine Schlägerei geben würde.
Wenn du so weitermachst, gibt es Streit/Krach/Scherereien.

vi. For what is on television, in a theatre or cinema, and what there is for a meal, **es gibt** is used.

Was gibt es zum Mittagessen?   *Was gibt es heute abend im Fernsehen?*
Ab nächster Woche gibt es einen neuen Film im Kino.
Was hat es heute in der Mensa gegeben? Es gab Rinderbraten.

vii. The widespread use of *es* makes it sometimes possible to translate the E. construction *There were a lot of students lying round on the lawn* not by *es waren* but by *es* and *liegen*. *Es lagen viele Studenten auf dem Rasen herum.* If *viele Studenten* is put at the beginning, the *es* drops out. Similarly *Es krabbelten über den Weg zwei Käfer, die glänzende Rücken hatten*, there were two beetles . . . crawling . . .

2. There is **da** when stressed in E., i.e. when someone is virtually pointing to something and says, 'There is the book you were looking for'. *Da ist/liegt das Buch, das du gesucht hast. Who is there?* is *Wer ist da?* The double *there, Is there anyone there?* or *There was s.o. there/no one there*, is translated by one *da* in a question, *Ist da jmd.?*, but in a statement as *Es war jmd./niemand da.*

3. In a sent. like *There was a joke I heard yesterday which will amuse you*, it is best to omit *there was. Ein Witz, den ich gestern hörte, wird dich amüsieren.* Or *Ich habe gestern einen Witz gehört, der . . .*

bear, stand, endure *vs.* A few uses.

1. The original meaning of **bear** was 'to support the weight of sth. while moving it from place to place', but in this sense it is now restricted in use, the idea being mainly expressed by *carry*. Still current are *The cheering fans bore the players from the field* and *He was borne unconscious from the ring*. These can only be translated by **tragen**.

Jubelnde Fans trugen die siegreiche Mannschaft im Triumph vom Spielplatz.
Man trug den Bewußtlosen aus dem Ring.

2. Bear also means 'to sustain a weight or pressure'.
i. Tragen occurs in a few related senses. *Man trägt eine Last* can imply carrying an actual load, but it can also mean 'to bear a burden'. *Das Flugzeug trägt eine schwere Last. Er hat die größte Last der Arbeit getragen. Tragen* is used for bearing a weight. *Die Brücke trägt zehn Tonnen/auch schwere Lastwagen. Die Balken tragen einige Tonnen. Der Ast wird dich tragen. Das Eis trägt noch nicht*, it won't bear/support a pers.'s weight.
ii. Standhalten means 'to withstand or stand [up to] pressure, weight, an attack etc.' and is sometimes translated as or translates **bear**. *Die Eisdecke hielt dem Gewicht des Kindes [nicht] stand. Man baut Häuser, die einem Erdbeben standhalten sollen. Die Tür hielt seinen wütenden Hieben stand. Eine Woche lang hielten die Verteidiger der Beschießung/dem Ansturm stand. Unsere Mannschaft hielt dem Angriff des Gegners stand. Standhalten* also means 'to bear or stand up to' an examination, investigation, etc. *Die Angaben des Zeugen hielten einer genauen Überprüfung nicht stand.*

Die Ergebnisse seiner Versuche hielten wiederholten Prüfungen stand (Versuche = 'experiments').

3. Tragen also means 'to take on oneself' or 'bear', but only with a few ns. such as *[Un]kosten, die Verantwortung, die Schuld, die Konsequenzen*, etc. For alternatives cf. ACCEPT 4.

Der Chef der Firma trägt die Verantwortung für seine Angestellten.
Es wird noch festgestellt, wer die Schuld an dem Verkehrsunfall trägt.
Wenn du verlierst, mußt du die Kosten des Gerichtsverfahrens tragen.
Wenn du so handelst, mußt du die Folgen/Konsequenzen deines Verhaltens tragen.

4. Bear may mean 'to endure or suffer sth. painful or trying'. *The heat was hard to bear.*

i. Tragen is still used in the sense of *ertragen* (cf. 4. ii), but its objs. can only be things which seem imposed by fate, and, though difficult to bear, are endured without complaint. *Sein Schicksal tragen* is a more or less fixed expression. *Das Volk wurde schwer unterdrückt, doch es trug sein Schicksal ohne Klagen. Er hat ein schweres Los zu tragen* and *Sie trugen ihr Unglück tapfer/mit Fassung und Würde. Jmd. trägt schwer an etw.* or *hat schwer an etw. zu tragen* means that what is endured is felt to be a great burden and the person suffers from it. *An dieser Verantwortung hatte sie schwer zu tragen.*

ii. The main equivalent is **ertragen**, which means 'to put up with sth. unpleasant or burdensome either permanently or for a time without protest or being over-whelmed'. It thus corresponds to **bear**, **stand**, and **endure** in this sense. It stresses in the positive the patience with which something trying is borne. The obj. can also be a person or some feature of a person. *Ich kann ihn/sie/diese Stimme nicht mehr/länger ertragen. Ertragen* occurs without *können* where *can* would be usual in E. Cf. sent. 3 below. When an infin. or clause follows, *ertragen* usually has *es* as obj. *Er erträgt es nicht, kritisiert zu werden/wenn man ihn kritisiert.*

> *Ich weiß nicht, wie ich diese Ungewißheit ertragen kann.*
> *Sie sagte, sie würde die Schmerzen nicht mehr lange ohne Betäubungsmittel ertragen können.*
> *Die Mutter erträgt es nicht, wenn die Kinder nicht pfleglich/schonend mit ihren Sachen umgehen.*
> *Ich kann den Gedanken nicht ertragen, daß etw. schief gehen könnte.*
> *Wie lange kannst du dieses Leben noch ertragen?*
> *Die Hitze in den letzten Tagen war kaum noch zu ertragen.*

iii. Vertragen suggests that by nature or constitution someone is unable to bear something. The obj. is not necessarily unpleasant in itself, but something which does not please or agree with a particular person. In pos. sents., in which it is often, but not always, used with *gut*, it is translated as *can take* or, with the subj. and obj. reversed, as *agree with. Sie verträgt viel Spaß* and *Ich kann das heiße Klima gut vertragen.* Cf. AGREE 6. In neg. sents. it corresponds to *cannot stand/bear/endure*, but because it makes a general statement it is weaker than *ertragen. Vertragen* is used in the same constructions as *ertragen*.

> *Meine Augen vertragen kein starkes Sonnenlicht.   Die Haut des Kindes verträgt keine Sonne.*
> *Er vertrug keine Kritik/vertrug es nicht, wenn man ihn kritisierte.*
> *Der Hund vertrug es nicht, daß ein Fremder ihn anfaßte.*
> *Der Inder verträgt das naßkalte Herbstwetter im nördlichen Europa nur schlecht.*

iv. Ausstehen means 'to stand or bear' with people or particular features or things as obj. *Ich kann ihn/seine Stimme/dieses Gerede nicht ausstehen. Ertragen* tends to be used in a definite situation, especially with *nicht länger/mehr. Ich kann ihn nicht länger ertragen. Ausstehen* refers to a general fact rather than one situation. It can express an aversion to things which for others may not be unpleasant. *Ich kann diese Farbe nicht ausstehen. Wenn du dieses Bild nicht ausstehen kannst, werde ich es nicht aufhängen.* With unpleasant things such as pain, anxiety, and fear as obj., it means 'to endure'. *Sie hat durch ihn viel ausstehen müssen. Ausstehen* is also often used when the painful or trying time is past and looked back on. *Beruhige dich! Nun ist es ja ausgestanden.* **Durchstehen** stresses even more strongly success in getting or coming through difficulties, troubles, and setbacks. *Er hat die Belastung/die Krisis durchgestanden.*

> *Er konnte es nicht ausstehen, wenn man in diesem Ton zu ihm sprach.*
> *Den neuen Freund ihrer Freundin konnte sie nicht ausstehen.*
> *Jmd. mußte großen Hunger/großen Durst/die strenge Kälte/die Hitze/solche Schmerzen/die große Anstrengung/die Verunglimpfungen ausstehen.*

Was hat sie alles auszustehen gehabt! Erst die Schwierigkeiten im Beruf, dann der Unfall des Kindes und nun auch das Gerede der Nachbarn und Kollegen.

Wieviel Angst haben wir ausgestanden, bis wir das Kind wieder bei uns hatten?

v. Aushalten has the same sense as *ertragen,* but is more common in everyday situations. It is not used with people as obj., but with mental and physical conditions, including being in a place. Like *aus* in *ausstehen,* the prefix suggests the whole process until completion, while *ertragen* implies bearing something at a particular time. The distinction is, however, lost in the neg. *Etw. ist nicht zum Aushalten* means that it is unbearable. *Es irgendwo aushalten* means 'to bear, stand, or stick it out in a place' or 'to bear being somewhere'. *In diesem Nest habe ich es drei Jahre ausgehalten. Ich kann es hier nicht länger aushalten.* Without *es* it means 'to persevere'. *Trotz schwerer Arbeit hat das Mädchen in der Stellung ausgehalten.* An idiom: *Eine Sache hält den Vergleich mit einer anderen [nicht] aus,* it [does not] bear[s] comparison with it.

Ich kann diesen Lärm/dieses Geschrei/diese Kälte nicht mehr lange aushalten.

Leicht verderbliche Waren halten den Transport nicht aus.

Wenn Sie sich nicht sicher sind, ob Sie die Anstrengungen auch wirklich aushalten können, dann sollten Sie lieber zu Hause bleiben.

Es ist schrecklich heiß heute, doch hier im Garten im Schatten der Bäume kann man es aushalten/läßt es sich aushalten.   *Diese Ungewißheit war schwer auszuhalten.*

In diesem Zimmer kann ich es nicht aushalten. Die Luft ist viel zu stickig.

beat [up] *v.* A few senses of **hit, knock,** and **thrash** *vs.* Senses treated: (i) **Hit** = 'to strike with the hand or a stick etc.' (ii) **Beat** = 'to strike repeatedly'. While *to give s.o. a beating* may mean 'to administer punishment by hitting repeatedly', **beat** leaves the intention open. It may imply punishment or some other motive. (iii) **Thrash** is 'to beat by way of punishment', often with a stick. (iv) **Beat up** = 'to strike so often and severely as to cause bodily harm and/or knock unconscious'. (v) **Beat** = 'to defeat or conquer'. **Thrash** when a syn. of this sense of **beat** means 'to defeat completely'.

1. i. Equivalents of E. senses i–iv.

While **schlagen** like HIT need only involve one blow either with the hand or a stick etc., **prügeln,** like **beat,** implies more than one. As *der Prügel* is a stick or cudgel, *prügeln* suggests beating with a stick, but the blows can also be given with the fists. *Prügeln* frequently has the connotation of inflicting punishment. Although the pl. *die Prügel* can be a syn. of *Schläge,* blows, *Prügel bekommen/kriegen* means 'to get a thrashing', and *eine gehörige Tracht Prügel bekommen/kriegen* is 'to get a good hiding/thrashing'. Also *die Prügelstrafe* = 'corporal punishment'. However, *wer Prügel austeilt,* deals out blows or lays about a victim and is not punishing him. Thus *wer jmd[n.] prügelt* can act from revenge, brutality, or sadism as well as from a desire to punish. The context must make the intention clear. *Prügeln* implies a certain limit in inflicting punishment or dealing out blows, whereas **verprügeln** implies corporal punishment or blows limited only by the physical endurance of the recipient. They differ also syntactically because *verprügeln,* like **beat up,** is not used with phrs. Only *prügeln* is used with adjs. and phrs. such as *windelweich,* 'black and blue', or *zu Tode* and with preps. giving a direction, *Man prügelte ihn aus dem Lokal.* While *schlagen* is common both in speech and writing, **hauen** is colloquial. *Der Vater haute den Jungen.* Without an adj. or phr. it mainly refers to children. *Der große Junge hat den kleinen gehauen. Schlagen* and *hauen* are also used with adjs. or phrs. indicating the state the blow[s] reduce[s] the person to. The E. v. is either **knock** or **beat**. *Der Polizist schlug den Einbrecher zu Boden/schlug ihn bewußtlos, Sie*

haben ihn windelweich geschlagen/gehauen or *haben ihn zum Krüppel geschlagen/gehauen.*
Verhauen implies a more severe beating than *hauen* but less than *verprügeln,*
either as a punishment, i.e. 'to spank', or otherwise. In *Der Vater hat dem Jungen den*
Hintern verhauen, the intention is clear. In one sense **zusammenschlagen** is a syn.
of *verprügeln.* It implies that the victim collapses, *zusammenbricht.*

> *Er hat ihr/sie mit der Faust ins Gesicht geschlagen.*   *Sollte man Kinder schlagen?*
> *Er schlug mir/mich [mit der Hand/einem Stock] auf die Finger/auf den Kopf/über den Rücken.*
> *Der Junge hat seinen kleinen Bruder gehauen.*
> *Bis in unser Jahrhundert hinein war es durchaus üblich, einen Knecht zu prügeln, wenn er etw. falsch*
>   *gemacht hatte.*   *Er prügelte die Kinder bei dem geringsten Anlaß.*
> *Die Nachbarn glaubten, daß er seine Frau gelegentlich prügelte.*
> *Die beiden Schüler beschlossen, den Streber, der sie verpetzt hatte, zu verprügeln.*
> *Nachdem sein Pferd nicht den gewünschten Sieg erlaufen hatte, prügelte er es in einem Anfall von*
>   *blinder Wut halb zu Tode.*   *Der Junge von nebenan hat Kai verhauen.*
> *Er wurde von zwei Rowdys zusammengeschlagen und beraubt.*

Dreschen, 'to thrash or thresh corn', is used colloquially like **thrash** in the sense
'to give s.o. a thrashing/hiding'. **Haue** or **Dresche kriegen** is used in children's language in the same sense. **Verdreschen** is stronger. *Wegen dieses harmlosen Vergehens*
verdrosch er den Jungen.

ii. Beat sth. so as to clean it or free it from something is **klopfen.** *Sie klopfte den*
Teppich/den Schnee von ihrem Mantel. The common factor in its uses is that a sound
is produced. Hence *an die Tür klopfen.*

iii. In *Er klopfte mir/mich auf die Schulter,* **klopfen** means 'to hit lightly, to pat'. In this
context **schlagen** suggests a harder hit and is translated as *slap. Er schlug mir*
wohlwollend auf die Schulter.

iv. In *Jmds. Herz schlägt (regelmäßig/ruhig,* etc.), **schlagen** is the equivalent of **beat**
and suggests normal action. *Jmds. Herz klopft* denotes a heightened action, 'to
pound or throb', but it can be *vor Freude* or *Schrecken.*

2. Equivalents of E. sense v. **Schlagen** can mean 'to defeat' in battle, sport, or some
kind of competition. **Besiegen** is a syn. Like **beat**, both require an obj. **Siegen** is
intr. and means 'to be victorious', 'to win', a syn. of *gewinnen.* As it takes *über,* both
Das Heer besiegte den Feind or *siegte über den Feind* are used without distinction in
meaning. **Thrash** in this sense is *jmdn. vernichtend schlagen/besiegen.*

> *Die preußische Armee schlug die österreichische Armee in mehreren Schlachten.*
> *Mannschaft X hat Mannschaft Y 3 : 0/mit 3 : 0 Toren geschlagen/besiegt.*
> *Der 18-jährige Spieler hat den Weltmeister geschlagen/besiegt.*
> *Er hat die anderen Kandidaten bei der Wahl besiegt.*
> *In dem Wettbewerb schlug sie alle Mitbewerber.*   *Wer hat im Fußballspiel gesiegt/gewonnen?*

before *conj.* and *adv.*

1. Both **bevor** and **ehe** introduce clauses of time. *Bevor* is the everyday word, while
ehe is somewhat more literary, but it is still commonly used in speech as well as
in writing. **Before** also means 'sooner or rather than'. *She would starve before she*
would steal. In this sense only *ehe* is used, and *lieber* is usually added to the main
clause.

> *Ich muß es selbst sehen, bevor/ehe ich es glauben kann.*
> *Ihr dürft nicht spielen gehen, bevor/ehe eure Hausaufgaben fertig sind.*
> *Ich lasse dich nicht weg, bevor/ehe du uns alles erklärt hast.*
> *Ehe sie stehlen würde, würde sie lieber verhungern.*
> *Ehe ich ihn um das Geld bitte, verzichte ich lieber auf das Vergnügen.*

2. The adv. **before** can be either **vorher** or **zuvor**, the former being the everyday
term and the latter a more refined word. *Zuvor* is, however, often heard in the

expression *nie zuvor*, although *nie vorher* is also used. Both mean 'before this/that', i.e. 'prior to some time or occurrence'.

Ich gehe um elf zu einer Sitzung, muß aber vorher ein paar Briefe schreiben.
Warum hast du uns vorher nichts davon gesagt?
Ich hatte sie erst am Tag vorher/am Tage zuvor kennengelernt.
Wir erhielten großen Beifall wie nie zuvor.   Ich hatte sie nie zuvor gesehen.

3. Noch nie means either 'never before this occasion' or 'never yet'. Which is meant must emerge from the context. If I am in London for the first time I can say, *'Ich bin noch nie in London gewesen'*, while in *'Ich habe mir vor drei Jahren einen Pelzmantel gekauft, aber ihn noch nie getragen'*, the meaning of *noch nie* is 'never yet'.

4. When **before** means 'already', as in *Have you read/seen*, etc. *sth. before?*, it is **schon einmal**.

Hast du den Film schon einmal gesehen?   Den Witz habe ich schon einmal gehört.

behave *v.* **behaviour, conduct** *ns*. **Behave** is broader in its range of application than any of the G. vs., each of which covers certain aspects of the E. word.

1. i. Sich benehmen and the n. **das Benehmen** refer mainly to conduct in relation to others in a social group. It is the usual word when good manners and the normal rules of decent behaviour in a group are meant and corresponds to *behave* [*oneself*] when this means 'to conduct oneself in a correct or proper manner', 'to conform to the accepted patterns of society', and in the case of children 'to be obedient and do what is considered right'. Unlike **behave [oneself]**, which implies good behaviour, *sich benehmen* is neutral, and *gut* and *schlecht* usually need to be added to show what kind of behaviour is meant. *Das Kind hat sich gut benommen.* However, *Benimm dich!* said as a warning usually to children, *Er weiß sich zu benehmen*, and *Er hat kein Benehmen* imply good behaviour, while *Was für ein Benehmen!* would, like *What behaviour!*, imply bad or unusual conduct. *Sich benehmen* is used normally only of people, but may be extended to house-trained animals. *Dieser dressierte Hund benimmt sich immer gut.*

Sie benahm sich wie eine Dame, und er wie ein Kavalier.
Sie haben sich anständig/korrekt/höflich/flegelhaft/dumm/unpassend benommen.
Ein junger Mann half ihr in den Mantel, und sie sah gleich, daß in der Gruppe wenigstens einer war, der sich zu benehmen wußte.
Der Hund hat sich heute schlecht benommen—er ist auf den Tisch gesprungen.

ii. Sich benehmen sometimes occurs in the sense of behaving in a specified way, a meaning which is usually expressed by *sich verhalten*. Cf. 2. i.

Er hat sich mir gegenüber zurückhaltend/freundlich benommen.
Ich ärgerte mich darüber, daß ich mich wie ein Idiot benommen hatte.

iii. Sich betragen and **das Betragen** also suggest conformity to codes of behaviour. They are like **conduct [oneself]** and **conduct**. Although *sich betragen* and the n. are less common than *sich benehmen* and *das Benehmen*, some people still say, *'Ich hoffe, daß sich der Junge bei Meyers gut beträgt.'*

Schwere Vorwürfe waren für die Beiden zu erwarten, nachdem die Eltern sie zum ersten Mal mitgenommen hatten und sie sich prompt schlecht betragen hatten.
Er hat sich nicht wie ein Offizier betragen.

iv. Sich führen is used for prisoners. The n. is **die Führung**.

Der Strafgefangene hatte sich gut/schlecht geführt.
Er ist wegen guter Führung vorzeitig aus der Haft entlassen worden.

2. i. Sich verhalten is the main equivalent of **behave** meaning 'to act or react in a particular way'. It always needs an adv. or phr. to show how the person acts or reacts. It is neutral in that it implies neither good nor bad. Although combined with *richtig*, *korrekt*, and *falsch*, it is not used with *gut* and *schlecht*. It is the usual scientific term in psychological descriptions of human behaviour, in talking of animal behaviour, and in referring to the behaviour of substances in chemistry. The n. is **das Verhalten**.

> *Sie verhielt sich ruhig/vorsichtig/tapfer/mutig.*
> *Ich weiß nicht, wie ich mich in dieser Angelegenheit verhalten soll.*
> *Kaum trinkt er ein paar Glas Bier, und schon verhält er sich wie ein Kind.*
> *Alle müssen sich im Straßenverkehr richtig verhalten, sonst sind Unfälle nicht zu vermeiden.*
> *Die Legierung verhielt sich bei hohen Temperaturen anders als erwartet.*
> *Das zentrale Anliegen der von ihm betriebenen Forschung sah Konrad Lorenz darin, das Verhalten von Tieren und Menschen aus den angeborenen Mechanismen und Erbkombinationen sowie aus der Wechselwirkung zwischen diesen und der Umwelt ableiten zu können.*

ii. When **behave** means 'to act towards s.o.', **sich verhalten** or **handeln** are used. The former takes *gegenüber* + dat., the latter *an* + dat. *Er verhielt sich kameradschaftlich/wie ein Freund mir gegenüber. Er handelte an mir wie ein Freund.*

iii. **Sich gebärden** implies an unfavourable judgement on the way someone acts and is applied to behaviour which is in some way out of the ordinary, strange, uncontrolled, or exaggerated.

> *Er hat sich wie wahnsinnig/wie ein Verrückter gebärdet.*
> *Sie haben sich sehr unvernünftig gebärdet.*

iv. **Sich aufführen** refers to the impression one person makes on another or to someone's reaction to another's behaviour and suggests unusual conduct. Unlike *sich gebärden*, it can express a favourable as well as an unfavourable judgement. *Sie haben sich untadelig/tadellos aufgeführt.*

> *Er führte sich auf wie ein Rasender/wie ein Mann von Manieren.*
> *Mehrere Schüler haben sich auf dem Tanzabend rüpelhaft/unverschämt aufgeführt.*

v. **Sich geben** implies giving prominence to a certain characteristic so as to create deliberately a particular impression on others. It may, but need not, involve pretence or dissimulation.

> *Sie gab sich sehr liebenswürdig.*   *Er gibt sich gern als Sachverständiger.*
> *Ich habe es nie erlebt, daß sie sich anders als natürlich gegeben hat.*

3. The idea that a car behaves well or badly can be expressed by the ns. **die Fahreigenschaften** and **das Fahrverhalten** and an adj. *Das Auto zeigte gute Fahreigenschaften/gutes Fahrverhalten.* A common everyday expression is *Das Auto fährt sich gut.*

belief, faith *ns.* E. senses: (i) In one sense **belief** denotes either the mental acceptance of a statement or proposition as true or the conviction of the reality of some being or phenomenon. The belief may result from objective evidence or from an examination of the grounds for accepting it or arise from another's testimony or authority. *His belief in ghosts/the goodness of human nature/the value of parliamentary democracy was unshakeable.* (ii) The other sense is 'sth. believed'. It may refer to a statement or opinion held to be true or a basis for action in various spheres of life, but it has been weakened to such an extent that it can be a syn. of *opinion* or *view*. *It is my belief that more women should stand for parliament.*

1. i. **Der Glaube** or **der Glauben** can mean 'credence', 'the acceptance of sth. as true' without any further implication. It has this sense mainly in the expressions *jmdm. Glauben schenken*, 'to believe', and *Glauben finden*, 'to be believed'. *Niemand wollte ihm Glauben schenken, weil das, was er erzählte, sich so phantastisch anhörte. Der Bericht fand keinen Glauben. Warum verdient sie mehr Glauben als ich? Im Glauben* can mean 'in the belief'. *Er kam hierher im Glauben, daß er uns helfen könnte.* [Un]worthy of belief is [un]glaubwürdig or [un]glaubhaft.

ii. Der Glaube is applied to religious belief, conviction, or faith defined as 'the state of wholeheartedly and steadfastly believing in the existence, power, and benevolence of a supreme being, of having confidence in his care, and of being loyal to his will as revealed'. *Der Glaube* is used in the Bible where **faith** occurs in E. *Durch den Glauben wurde Abraham gehorsam, als er berufen wurde, in ein Land zu ziehen, das er erben sollte, und nicht wußte, wo er hinkäme* (Hebrews 11: 8).

> *Sie wollte ihn in seinem Glauben stärken.*   *Er hat seinen Glauben an Gott nie verloren.*

The *OED* points out that **belief** was the earlier word for what is now called **faith**. **Faith** originally meant 'loyalty to a pers. or to one's promise or duty', as in *to keep* or *break faith*. When in the fourteenth century **faith** began to be used as a transl. of Latin *fides*, it gradually displaced **belief**, leaving it in great measure to the merely intellectual process of accepting something as true. Thus *belief in God* no longer means as much as *faith in God*. *Belief in the divine right of kings* is now understood as acceptance of its validity. As *Glaube* means both 'belief' and 'faith', it retains senses **belief** earlier had.

iii. Der Glaube also means 'religion, faith'. Thus *der christliche* or *mohammedanische Glaube. Die Freiheit des Glaubens* is 'religious freedom' or 'freedom of worship'. *Sie sind tolerant in Glaubensfragen*, religious matters. *Sie kämpften für ihren Glauben. Sie wurden zum christlichen Glauben bekehrt.*

iv. In the non-religious sphere, **der Glaube** suggests inner certainty or conviction which is more emotional than rational, does not arise from objective facts, and seeks no proof. It is applied to belief in ideas and phenomena considered correct or real, and to trust in an authority. Adjs. often used with *Glaube* are *tief, fest, blind, fanatisch, falsch*, and *irrig*. Some compounds are *Fortschrittsglaube, Autoritätsglaube, Schicksalsglaube. Glaube* also includes the idea of faith or confidence in s.o./sth., particularly in the expressions *Glauben an jmdn./etw. haben* and *den Glauben an jmdn./etw. verlieren. Sie scheint den Glauben an ihn/ihre eigenen Fähigkeiten verloren zu haben.*

> *In vielen Menschen lebt der Glaube an das Gute im Menschen.*
> *Nichts konnte seinen Glauben an den Sieg der Vernunft erschüttern.*
> *Meinen Glauben an Gespenster hat mir mein Vater mit dem Stock ausgetrieben.* (Fontane)
> *Er gab sich dem törichten Glauben hin, ihm könne nichts schiefgehen.*
> *Der Glaube an den Nutzen militärischen Drucks scheint in Deutschland unausrottbar zu sein.*

Glaube sometimes suggests a wrong or naïve belief. *Jmdm. den/seinen Glauben lassen* usually means 'to let s.o. cling to wrong ideas' or 'to give up trying to enlighten s.o.' The context often implies a mistaken belief. *Er wiegt sich in dem Glauben, daß er nie einen Fehler machen könne.*

v. Im guten Glauben or **in gutem Glauben** mean 'in good faith'.

> *Ich habe in gutem Glauben unterschrieben, ohne die Einzelheiten nachprüfen zu können.*

2. For the sense 'sth. believed' there are various equivalents. **Der Glaubenssatz** is used for religious beliefs but is usually translated as *dogma* or *tenet*. What someone's beliefs are is often best translated by the v. **glauben**. *Woran glaubt der Durchschnittsbürger heutzutage?* Otherwise **die Meinung** or **die Ansicht**, 'OPINION', **die Annahme**, 'assumption', or **die Überzeugung**, 'conviction', cover the shades of meaning **belief** can have. Cf. POPULAR 2.

> *Über deine Annahme, daß ich dir in dieser Lage nicht helfen würde, bin ich tief gekränkt.*
> *Meine Ansicht ist, daß sie der Aufgabe durchaus gewachsen ist.*
> *Als Falkenhayn 1915 Generalstabschef wurde, hielt er die Lage für sehr ernst, doch hat er in seinem Herzen die Überzeugung nicht aufgegeben, daß ein deutscher Sieg im Westen allein entscheidend sein könnte und noch möglich war.*

belong *v.*

1. Gehören + dat. denotes possession and means 'to be the property of'.
Der Hund/Das Fahrrad/Das Buch gehört meinem Bruder.
Wem gehört das Auto, das vor dem Haus steht?

2. i. With preps. + acc. **gehören** means that something belongs or has its proper place somewhere.
Dieses Wörterbuch gehört unter die Nachschlagewerke.
Das Fahrrad gehört in die Garage, nicht in das Haus.   *Das Buch gehört ins oberste Regal.*
Gehört dieser Betrag von 1 200 Mark unter Personalkosten oder unter Reisekosten?

ii. Hingehören is a syn. of *gehören* when it means 'to belong in a certain place'. *Hingehören* must be used when the place is not stated. *Where does it belong?* is *Wo gehört das denn hin?* or *Wohin gehört das?* or *Put the book back where it belongs!* is *Stell' das Buch dorthin zurück, wo es hingehört.*
Beim Tischdecken hatte Hans die Gabeln an die rechte Seite der Teller gelegt, obwohl er hätte wissen müssen, daß sie dort nicht hingehören.

iii. Belong here is **hierhergehören.** *Gehört dieser Stuhl hierher?*

iv. Like **belong**, **gehören** states where in the opinion of the speaker someone should be.
Er gehört hinter Schloß und Riegel.   *Sie gehört vor ein Gericht/ins Gefängnis.*

v. Gehören zu can mean that a quality is necessary to achieve a certain result.
Es gehört viel Fleiß dazu, ein solches Buch zu schreiben.
Es gehörte schon große Frechheit dazu, sich so zu benehmen.

3. i. With **zu**, **gehören** also means that the subj. belongs to or is part of a larger whole. The subj. can be people who belong to a group or to a type displaying certain characteristics, or a country or territory which belongs to a larger unit, or a thing which is part of something else. *Gehören zu* is sometimes best translated as *is one of/are some of. Sie gehört zu den besten Schülern in der Klasse. Diese Frage gehört nicht zum Thema* or *Diese Bemerkung gehört nicht zur Sache,* the question or remark is not relevant to the issue.
Der Verlobte unserer Tochter gehört schon zur Familie.
Sie gehören zu unseren Freunden/zu unserem Bekanntenkreis.
Mein Herr, gehört dieser kleine Junge zu Ihnen?
Dieser Motor gehört zu den neuen Erfindungen.
Dieser Deckel gehört zum Topf auf der vorderen Kochplatte.
Dieser Schlauch gehört zum Staubsauger.   *Südtirol gehört nicht mehr zu Österreich.*
Ich habe alle Knöpfe angenäht, die zum Kleid gehören.
Seit dem 1. Januar 1986 gehören Spanien und Portugal zur Europäischen Union.
Er gehört zu den Leuten, die immer das letzte Wort behalten wollte.

ii. Angehören means 'to be a member of an organization, club, society, association, etc., membership of which requires an application'. A personal subj. is necessary. *Jmd. gehört einer Partei/einer Kirche/einem Verein/einem Club* etc. *an.* Where official membership is involved, *angehören* is the appropriate v., but **gehören zu** also occurs, particularly when an application to join is not involved. *Jmd. gehört zu einer Delegation/einer Kommission* or *gehört einer Delegation/einer Kommission an.* It is, however, best to make the distinction just given. *Ich gehöre zum Chor* need only mean that I am a singer, whereas *Ich gehöre dem Chor an* states that I am an official member.
Warum gehörst du keinem Sportverein an, wo du doch so gut im Rudern bist?
Im Betrieb ist am Schwarzen Brett der folgende Aushang angeschlagen: Alle Beschäftigten, die der Gewerkschaft angehören, treffen sich am Montag, dem 18. April, um 17 Uhr im Raum 501 zu einer Vollversammlung.   *Welchen studentischen Clubs gehörst du an?*
Wie viele Unterhausabgeordnete gehören der Labourpartei an?

iii. Angehören means 'to belong to a class, category, genus, etc.' *Gehören Mäuse und Eichhörnchen derselben Familie an? Diese Kirche gehört der Spötgothik an. Das Gedicht gehört seiner frühen Schaffensperiode an.* This meaning is also expressed by **gehören zu**, particularly in speech. *Auch der Wal gehört zu den Säugetieren. Die zu den Amphicoelen gehörenden Arten zeigen noch primitivere Merkmale als die übrigen Froschlurche. Das Stück gehört zu ihrer frühen Schaffensperiode.*

iv. Angehören is used when something belongs to a period of time. In colloquial speech **gehören zu** is also used. *Das gehört zu meinem früheren Leben.*

> *Diese Mode gehörte dem 18. Jahrhundert an.*
> *Diese Mißstände gehörten schon der Vergangenheit an.*

v. Angehören expresses the meaning that people belong to one another. *Sie gehörten einander ihr ganzes Leben an.*

bend, bow *vs.* **Bend** is one of the most complicated words to translate into G. To understand the use of the G. words, it is necessary to make the distinctions listed here with their usual equivalents. Order of treatment: 1. **Bend** sth. in a useful way which is desired or intended—*biegen.* 2. When a tree, pole, or mast bends or sways, as it were, by itself (intr. use)—*sich biegen.* 3. **Bend** the body or parts of it—usually *beugen,* but sometimes *biegen.* 4. When a person bends over s.o./sth.—*sich beugen.* 5. When a person or some force bends something in a way not intended or desired, or when someone bends something in order to make it useless—*verbiegen.* 6. When something bends in a way not desired, as it were, by itself—*sich verbiegen.* 7. When a person bends over or stoops [down]—*sich [herunter]bücken.* 8–10. Related words.

1. Biegen.

i. 'To bend sth. deliberately so as to bring about a result that serves a useful purpose'. *Die Arbeiter bogen die Eisenstange. Etw. gerade biegen,* to make sth. bent or crooked straight.

> *Der Meister bog die Rohre in die gewünschte Form.*   *Man kann den Draht leicht biegen.*
> *Sie bog die Zweige zur Seite, um das Nest besser sehen zu können.*

ii. The intr. use, **bend** meaning 'can be bent', as in *The wire bends easily,* must be translated by **sich biegen lassen.** *Diese Äste lassen sich leicht biegen. Der Draht läßt sich leicht biegen.*

2. Sich biegen, applied to things, means 'to move either in one direction or backwards and forwards', i.e. 'to bend or sway'. *Die Bäume biegen sich im Wind.* For people there is the idiom *Er bog sich vor Lachen.*

> *Der Mast des Segelschiffes bog sich leise knarrend im Wind.*
> *Die Zweige biegen sich unter der Last des Schnees.* (But will later go back to their original position. *Sie sind gebogen* would be permanent.)

3. i. Beugen is now the usual word for bending parts of the body.

> *Sie beugte den Arm/das Knie.*   *Er hielt den Kopf gebeugt.*
> *Sie beugte den Oberkörper nach vorne/nach hinten.*

ii. In earlier G., **biegen** was used with parts of the body. Schiller wrote: *Nicht unter Fürsten bogen wir das Knie,* whereas nowadays *beugten* would be used. *Biegen* does, however, still occur with the body or parts of it as obj., but has acquired special meanings. It is used: *a.* When one person bends another's arm.

> *Zwei Burschen hatten Simrock bei einem nächtlichen Spaziergang überfallen. Als aber ein Streifenwagen in die Straße einbog, lief einer davon. Simrock faßte den anderen und bog ihm den Arm so, daß es weh tun würde, wenn er sich bewegte.*

b. When someone bends the body or part of it in a way which is not usual for most people. It is a movement acquired by training, e.g. in gymnastics or dancing, and one which arouses admiration.

Wenn man sieht, wie diese Tänzerin ihren Körper beim Tanz biegt, staunt man darüber, wie biegsam
der menschliche Körper sein kann.   Die Ballettänzerin bog sich graziös nach vorn.

iii. Other uses of *beugen*. *Das Recht beugen* means 'to stretch the law, warp justice'.
In earlier G., *biegen* had this sense. *Jmds. Stolz beugen* occasionally occurs, although
jmds. Stolz brechen is more common.

4. Sich beugen, often + *über*.

i. Of people. 'To bend over s.o./sth.'
Die Offiziere beugten sich über die Karten, die auf dem Tisch ausgebreitet waren.
Die Mutter beugte sich über das schlafende Kind.   Er beugte sich aus dem Fenster.
Sie beugte sich nach vorn, um besser hören zu können, was die kranke Frau sagte.

ii. Sich beugen + dat., occasionally + *vor*, means 'to bow or submit to' fate, some-
one's will, authority, etc.
Schließlich beugten sie sich der Übermacht/der Gewalt.
Er mußte sich [vor] dem Schicksal beugen.
'Ich beuge mich dem System nicht', rief der junge Mann.
Er beugte sich dem Willen seiner Vorgesetzten.

5. Verbiegen.

i. 'To bend unintentionally, in a way not desired'.
Er verbog den Schlüssel, als er ihn gewaltsam im Schloß zu drehen versuchte.
Ich bin gegen einen Baum gefahren und habe die Stoßstange verbogen.
Der Nagel ist verbogen, aber ich kann ihn vielleicht gerade biegen.

ii. 'To bend deliberately so as to make useless'.
Er hatte den Schlüssel [absichtlich] verbogen, damit wir ihn nicht benutzen könnten.

6. Sich verbiegen is used when something bends in a way not desired, as it were,
by itself.
Der Nagel hat sich verbogen, als ich ihn einschlug.
Die alten Bronzeschwerter verbogen sich im Kampf sehr leicht.

7. Sich bücken or **sich herunterbücken** mean 'to bend down or over' either to
pick up something from the ground or floor or to get through a low opening.
Ich bückte mich [herunter], um die Münze aufzuheben. Also Ich bückte mich nach der Münze.
Als der Handschuh zur Erde fiel, bückte sie sich eilig danach.
Um nicht entdeckt zu werden, bückte sich der Späher blitzschnell herunter.
Du mußt dich bücken, wenn du durch den Eingang gehst, sonst stößt du dich am Kopf.

8. Both **gebückt** and **gebeugt** mean 'bent, stooped'. *Gebückt* denotes simply a bent
position of the body.
Sie stand gebückt vor dem niedrigen Fenster.   Geht er denn immer so gebückt?
Gebeugt can, but need not, add to the idea of being bent the suggestion of being
mentally oppressed by misfortune, sorrow, age, etc. Hence *vom Kummer gebeugt*.
Er saß gebeugt/mit gebeugtem Rücken an seinem Schreibtisch.
Sie saß am Tisch und las, tief über das Buch gebeugt.
Von Alter und Kummer gebeugt, humpelte er die Straße hinauf.

9. Knicken is 'to bend sth. so that it forms a sharp angle, but without severance
into two parts'. Applied to things made of paper, it means 'to bend or crease in
an undesired way'. Hence the request or warning on envelopes: *Bitte nicht
knicken!—Im Umschlag sind Fotos. Knicken* is both trans. and intr.
Ich habe aus Versehen die Seiten des Buches geknickt.
Er hat das Foto geknickt, als er es sich ansah.
Der Sturm hat viele Bäume geknickt.   Im Sturm knickten die Bäume wie Strohhalme.

10. The usual word for to **bow** as a salutation is **sich verbeugen**. **Sich verneigen**
is an elevated syn. *Die Etikette verlangt, daß man sich vor dem Staatsoberhaupt
verbeugt.*

blame, censure, criticize, find fault, reprove, rebuke, reproach, reprimand, scold *vs.* The current leading sense of **blame** is 'attribute responsibility to'. However, the original meaning was 'find fault', i.e. the opposite of *praise*. Though this sense survives in the n. when it is linked with *praise* in *praise and blame*, a sent. like Matthew Arnold's *Heine cared whether people praised his verses or blamed them* would nowadays be formulated differently, **blame** having given way to **criticize** or **censure** when the opposite of *praise* is meant. **Blame** meaning 'criticize, censure' still survives, however, in some expressions. *You cannot blame starving children who steal food, I don't blame you for giving up such a job, I don't blame her for leaving him,* and *I have nothing to blame myself for* still show the original meaning. In this original sense **blame** is usually neg. In a pos. sent. like *You can blame him for what has happened,* it would be construed as 'criticize' only if countering the opposite statement *You can't blame him.* Otherwise it would be understood in the sense of imputing wrongdoing or responsibility. When **blame** means 'to lay the blame or fix responsibility on s.o. or sth. for sth. bad', it occurs frequently as an infin. with *to be*: *S.o./Sth. is to blame for sth. done wrongly, badly, or not at all* or *for an accident, poor result,* etc. It is also used with a personal subj. either with *for* or *on. She blamed the teacher for her failure* or *She blamed her failure on her teacher. He blamed the bad weather for the poor harvest* or *He blamed the poor harvest on the bad weather.*

1. i. Be to blame [for] is **schuld sein [an]**, which can be applied to people and things. A n. in the dat. follows *an*, which also appears as *daran* + *daß*-clause. It can also be used alone without *an*.

> *Die unzulängliche Planung ist schuld an dem schlechten Ergebnis.*
> *Du bist schuld, wenn dem Kind etw. zustößt.*
> *Der anhaltende Regen ist an der schlechten Ernte schuld.*
> *Er behauptete, der andere Fahrer/die vereiste Straße sei an dem Unfall schuld gewesen.*
> *Die Unnachgiebigkeit beider Verhandlungspartner war schuld daran, daß man wieder auseinanderging, ohne einen Kompromiß ausgehandelt zu haben.*
> *Seine Unachtsamkeit ist schuld daran, daß wir statt 20 Exemplare 200 bekommen haben.*

A variant is **schuld haben an**. *Der Autofahrer, nicht der Fußgänger, hatte schuld an dem Unfall.*

> *Ich soll an allem schuld haben/sein.*

ii. In all the above cases **verantwortlich sein für**, 'to be responsible for', can also be used. It is stylistically higher and stronger than *schuld haben an*. Like *responsible* it expresses the meaning 'blame' only if something undesirable follows. (In other contexts *verantwortlich* means 'RESPONSIBLE' = 'legally or morally obliged to take care of s.o./sth. or to carry sth. out'. *Der verantwortliche Minister. Sie ist für die Durchführung des Planes verantwortlich. Ihr seid dafür verantwortlich, daß die Unordnung beseitigt wird.*)

> *Er allein war für diesen Fehler verantwortlich.*
> *Die starken Regenfälle waren für die Überschwemmung verantwortlich.*
> *Mangelhafte Planung war für den schleppenden Ablauf der Konferenz verantwortlich.*

2. Blame s.o./sth. **[for** sth.**]** or **blame** sth. **on** s.o./sth.

i. The commonest expression is **jmdm./etw. die Schuld an etw. geben**. *An* also appears as *daran* + *daß*-clause. The neg. is **keine Schuld geben**.

> *Er gab mir die Schuld an der Verspätung.*   *Ich gebe dir keine Schuld.*
> *Er gab mir die Schuld daran, daß wir uns verspätet hatten.*
> *Sie gab immer anderen die Schuld an ihren Mißerfolgen.*
> *Er hat einem Kollegen die Schuld daran gegeben, daß die Bestellung nicht ausgeführt wurde.*
> *Man gab dem schlechten Wetter die Schuld an dem mißlungenen Ausflug.*

A less frequent variant is **schuld geben an**, which is only used with people in the dat., i.e. the obj. in E.

Sie gab ihrer Freundin schuld an dem Streit.

Der Firmeninhaber gab seinen Beratern schuld an dem Scheitern des Unternehmens.

ii. Verantwortlich machen für occurs particularly with things as obj., but sometimes with people. It sounds stronger, more formal, and more official than *die Schuld geben.*

Die schweren Regenfälle der letzten Tage werden für die schlechte Heuernte verantwortlich gemacht (are to blame for). Also . . . *sind für die schlechte Ernte verantwortlich zu machen.*

Er machte den Hausbesitzer für seinen Sturz verantwortlich, weil er den Weg vor seinem Haus nicht geräumt und gestreut hatte.

Sie machte das drückende Wetter verantwortlich für ihren schlechten Gesundheitszustand.

Ich mache ihn dafür verantwortlich, daß so viel Geld verschwendet worden ist.

3. Blame = 'to criticize'.

i. Jmdm. einen Vorwurf machen aus or **jmdm. etw. zum Vorwurf machen** are interchangeable and only involve a variation in construction. The sense is 'to reproach s.o. with sth. or for doing sth.' or 'to criticize for', thus in the neg. 'cannot or do not blame for'. Both also take a clause or infin., in which case the first needs *daraus* and the second usually has *es*.

Notwehr kann man niemandem zum Vorwurf machen.

Sie machte es ihm zum Vorwurf, daß er ihr nicht richtig zugehört und darum alles falsch gemacht hatte.   Aus Notwehr kann man niemandem einen Vorwurf machen.

Niemand wird Ihnen einen Vorwurf daraus machen, daß/wenn Sie sich nach der Krankheit erst einmal ein paar Tage zu Hause erholen.

Martin Luther King vertrat die Auffassung, daß man es den Schwarzen nicht zum Vorwurf machen könne, ungerechte Gesetze nicht zu beachten. Or . . . daß man den Schwarzen keinen Vorwurf daraus machen könne, ungerechte Gesetze nicht zu beachten.

ii. The fourth sent. in 3. i could be formulated as *Niemand wird es Ihnen verdenken, wenn Sie sich ein paar Tage zu Hause erholen.* **Verdenken** means 'to think ill of s.o. for doing sth.' and is often translated as *blame.* It is usually neg. in a statement. *Ich verdenke es Ihnen nicht. Niemand/Keiner wird es dir verdenken.* Questions are positive. *Wer wird/kann es ihr verdenken, wenn sie etwas mehr verdienen möchte?* It is usually found with a clause, but an obj. is possible. *Bei einer so wichtigen Entscheidung kann man ihr das Zögern nicht verdenken.* Though in many cases similar to the expressions with *Vorwurf*, it is not used for criticism by someone in authority. *Der Chef hat es ihm zum Vorwurf gemacht, daß er oft zu spät zur Arbeit kam.* But *Da er oft nach Feierabend im Büro weiter arbeitete, hat man ihm seine Unpünktlichkeit nicht verdacht.*

Ihre gereizten Worte kann man ihr angesichts so viel Dummheit und Egoismus nicht verdenken.

Man kann es ihr nicht verdenken, daß sie diesen jähzornigen Mann verlassen hat.

iii. Verargen is a syn. of *verdenken*, but it has gone out of use. **Übelnehmen**, 'to take amiss or resent', though broader in sense than **blame**, is used like *verdenken*, but is stronger than it and not limited to the neg. **Verübeln** is a less common syn. In sents. 1 and 2 below the vs. mean 'blame'; in 3 and 4 'resent'.

Ihre Entscheidung auszuwandern kann ihnen niemand verdenken/verübeln/übelnehmen/zum Vorwurf machen.

Ich kann [es] dir nicht übelnehmen, wenn dir deine Arbeit im Moment wichtiger erscheint als ein Theaterbesuch.   Sie hat ihm seine groben Worte sehr übelgenommen.

Ich würde es dir sehr übelnehmen/verübeln, wenn du mich in einer so schwierigen Lage im Stich ließest.

4. Reprove, rebuke, reproach, reprimand, and **scold** mean 'to criticize adversely', but with the aim of warning against mistakes and faults and urging that they be corrected.

i. Tadeln has become unusual in the spoken language, but survives in official and formal diction, particularly in schools. It combines the idea of clear, but relatively mild, censure with a call to improve and is thus like **reprove** or **rebuke**. Outside the school situation, it presupposes a relationship like that between teacher and pupil, someone with authority correcting a person under his or her charge. It takes either *wegen* or *für*. **Der Tadel**, 'censure, reproof', is as formal as *tadeln*, but *tadellos* and *untadelig*, 'faultless, perfect', are still common.

> Der eigentlich harmlose Streich der beiden Jungen wurde dem Direktor der Schule gemeldet, und sie wurden von ihm dafür streng getadelt.
>
> Der Meister tadelte zwei Lehrlinge wegen ihres Leichtsinns.
>
> Lehrer: 'Ich muß dich wirklich tadeln, Kai. Diese Nachlässigkeit ist sonst nicht deine Art.'
>
> Der Schüler hat vom Lehrer einen Tadel wegen ungebührlichen Verhaltens bekommen.

ii. Rügen has also gone out of general use and is now found only in formal or official language. It suggests a relatively mild reprimand.

> Der Lehrer rügte die Schüler wegen der Unordnung, in der sie den Klassenraum zurückgelassen hatten.
>
> Sie wurde wegen wiederholter Unpünktlichkeit streng gerügt.

iii. Although **Verweis** in the phrase *einen Verweis erteilen* means 'reprimand', it is now not commonly used, and **verweisen** in the same sense has dropped out of use. The normal equivalent of **reprimand** is now **zurechtweisen**. It implies a person in authority censuring another and urging a change in his/her behaviour.

> Die Kinder wurden ziemlich frech, und der Polizist wies sie schließlich zurecht.
>
> Der Staatsanwalt bombardierte den Angeklagten förmlich mit Fragen, bis der Richter ihn zurechtwies und ermahnte, den Angeklagten nicht absichtlich zu verwirren.

iv. Maßregeln extends from reprimanding, which involves no more than words, to disciplining, which entails the imposition of a penalty.

> Der Minister maßregelte verschiedene Beamte seines Ministeriums.
>
> Man maßregelte den Angestellten wegen verschiedener Versäumnisse.

5. Criticize and **censure** mean 'pronounce an adverse judgement on' or 'express dissatisfaction with' and may, but need not, have the secondary associations of **reprove, rebuke, reproach**, etc.

i. Vorwerfen means 'to reproach', but is more commonly used than the E. word and is often best translated as **criticize** or accuse, as is **jmdm. Vorwürfe machen**. Both combine the idea of criticism and disapproval directed to the person concerned with the wish for different behaviour. *Ich habe mir nichts vorzuwerfen*, I have nothing to blame or criticize myself for. **Vorhalten** expresses the same meaning, but it suggests greater forcefulness in making the fault clear, often that someone criticizes for a fairly long time or on several occasions. Likewise **jmdm. Vorhaltungen machen**. For *vorwerfen* cf. ACCUSE 1 and 2.

> Er machte sich bittere Vorwürfe, weil er dem Freund nicht geholfen hatte, als die Gelegenheit sich dazu bot.   Sie warf ihrem Bruder Rücksichtslosigkeit vor.
>
> Ihr wurde vorgeworfen, im entscheidenden Moment geschwiegen zu haben.
>
> Er warf den Kindern dauernd vor, zu viel Krach zu machen/daß sie zu laut seien.
>
> Du hast mir oft genug meine Fehler vorgeworfen/vorgehalten.
>
> Sie hatte recht, als sie mir meine Unentschlossenheit/meine Unpünktlichkeit vorhielt.
>
> Man machte ihm Vorwürfe wegen seiner mangelnden Kompromißbereitschaft.
>
> Sie hat ihm wegen seines schlechten Lebenswandels Vorhaltungen gemacht. Or . . . Vorhaltungen gemacht, daß er einen schlechten Lebenswandel habe.

ii. A common equivalent of **criticize** is **kritisieren**. As obj. it takes the thing criticized, *Man kritisierte seine Handlungsweise*, or a person, *Man kritisierte uns*. A phr. with *wegen* may be added. *Man kritisierte ihn wegen seiner Unzuverlässigkeit*. It also takes *an* followed by a n. denoting the person or thing criticized, and an indefinite expression like *etw.* or *vieles* or a *daß*-clause. *Man kritisierte vieles an mir*. This construction must be used to translate *to criticize s.o. for doing sth. Man kritisierte an ihm, daß er immer zu viel Geld ausgab*, criticized him for spending.

Er hat immer an jedem/allem etw. zu kritisieren.

Sie kritisierte an ihrem Vorgesetzten, daß er wichtige Entscheidungen immer hinausschob.

Man kritisierte an dem neuen Plan, daß er zu wenig durchdacht war.

iii. Kritik üben is a common alternative to *kritisieren*. It is used alone or with *an* + dat. *Der Meister begutachtet die Arbeit der Lehrlinge und übt—wenn es nötig ist—auch Kritik. Sie übte Kritik an mir/an meiner Arbeit.*

Der Oppositionsführer übte scharfe Kritik an der Wirtschaftspolitik der Regierung.

Die Lehrerin übte Kritik an mehreren Schülern ihrer Klasse, mit deren Leistungen und Verhalten sie unzufrieden war.

iv. Kritisieren also means 'to write a criticism or review of' a book, play, film, etc. *In der Zeitung wurde die Aufführung/der Film gut/abfällig kritisiert.*

v. Aussetzen an is used with *haben* or *sein* or the equivalent of *sein, es gibt*. It means 'to criticize s.o./sth. for or about sth.', but other words are often a better transl. *Have you any objection? Haben Sie etw. daran auszusetzen? Daran ist nur eines auszusetzen,* there is only one objection/one thing wrong.

An diesem Plan habe ich folgendes auszusetzen.   An seinem Verhalten ist nichts auszusetzen.

An der Konstruktion dieser Maschine gibt es viel/nichts auszusetzen (there is a lot/nothing to criticize about it).   *Was hast du nun schon wieder an mir auszusetzen?*

vi. Bemängeln is 'to criticize' in the sense of pointing out *Mängel,* faults, deficiencies, or shortcomings. The obj. can only be the thing criticized. It is used with *an* like *kritisieren.*

Die deutschen Urlauber bemängelten den schlechten Service in dem Hotel.

Sie bemängelte seine Manieren/die Höhe der Ausgaben.

Der Gesetzentwurf wurde von allen Seiten bemängelt.

Er bemängelte an dem Theaterstück, daß es zu lang war.

An der Wohnung kann bemängelt werden, daß es keine Waschmaschine gibt.

6. Scold, which is restricted to children and adolescents, is now **schimpfen mit** or **ausschimpfen** + acc. **Schelten** is no longer generally used, but it may occasionally be found in elevated style or in one which is consciously old-fashioned. *Frau von Schrickwitz war ungehalten und schalt mit der Köchin wegen des nicht eingehaltenen Speiseplans.* (**Schimpfen,** used alone or with *auf* and *über,* also expresses the idea of grumbling about s.o./sth., but it is often stronger than the E. v. *Die deutschen Bauern schimpfen auf die Regierung. Er hat sehr über seinen Chef geschimpft.*)

Nach diesen frechen Bemerkungen hat der Vater den Sohn tüchtig ausgeschimpft. Or . . . hat tüchtig mit ihm geschimpft.

Da die Mutter mit dem Jungen heftig geschimpft hatte, verkroch er sich in die letzte Ecke des Gartens.

7. Of the pejorative terms which resemble **find fault with, meckern** is probably the most common in colloquial speech. It suggests petty fault-finding and grumbling, grousing, or bellyaching and implies disapproval of this way of behaving. It is used alone or with *über* and only for spoken criticism. *Die Studenten meckerten ständig über das angeblich eintönige Essen in der Mensa.* **Mäkeln,** which is stylistically higher, is also applied to petty fault-finding. It takes *an,* sometimes *über. Er mäkelte ständig am Essen/an seiner jüngeren Schwester/über die Lehrer.* With an obj., **bemäkeln** is used. *Sie haben jede Einzelheit bemäkelt.* **Kritteln** implies petty criticism which is usually felt to be unjustified. It takes *an. Du kannst nichts anderes als immer nur [an uns] kritteln.* **Bekritteln** takes an obj. *Sie bekrittelt ständig ihre Mitarbeiter.* **Nörgeln** means 'to criticize continuously, grumble about'. *Man hat immer an ihm genörgelt.* There are also compounds with *herum* which suggest repeated fault-finding, **herumkritisieren, herummeckern, herummäkeln, herumkritteln,** and **herumnörgeln.** All take *an.*

Was gibt es denn da schon wieder zu meckern, Kinder?

Er hat sich nicht verändert. Heute würde er genauso meckern wie damals.

Nichts war ihm recht. Er mäkelte/nörgelte an allem/hatte an allem zu mäkeln/nörgeln.
Es ist kleinlich, andere Leute wegen ihrer Unzulänglichkeit zu bekritteln.
Er kann nie einen Roman lesen, ohne ihn zu bekritteln.
Immer mußt du an mir herummäkeln.   *Bitte krittle nicht immer an den Nachbarn herum!*

blind *adj.* **blindly** *adv.* **blind, dazzle** *vs.*

A. Adj. and adv.

1. Blind covers the lit. and fig. meanings of the E. adj. **blind**.

i. 'Lacking the sense of sight'.
> *Er war durch einen Unglücksfall blind geworden.*   *Er war blind geboren.*
> *Ich führte den Blinden über die Straße.*   *Sie ist auf einem Auge blind.*

ii. 'Temporarily unable to see'.
> *Starkes Sonnenlicht macht anfangs blind.*   *Ihre Augen waren von Tränen blind.*

iii. Blind meaning 'unable to judge', 'lacking in perception', as in *blind to s.o.'s faults* or *blind to the dangers*, is **blind gegenüber** or **für**.
> *Er war blind für die Schönheiten der ihn umgebenden Natur/für ihre Reize.*
> *Er liebte sie so sehr, daß er gegenüber ihren Fehlern blind war.*
> *Wegen seines übermäßigen Selbstvertrauens war er gegenüber allen Gefahren blind.*
> *Ihre Tagträumereien machte sie blind für die/gegenüber der Wirklichkeit.*

iv. Applied to emotions and those experiencing them, both E. **blind** and G. **blind** mean 'immoderate, heedless, reckless'. *Blind prejudice, blind hatred, blind fury* are *blindes Vorurteil* or *blinde Voreingenommenheit, blinder Haß*, and *blinde Wut. Blind with rage* is *blind vor Wut.*
> *In blinder Angst liefen sie davon.*

v. Both are applied to people and behaviour which lack discrimination and judgement.
> *Nichts konnte seinen blinden Glauben an die Partei erschüttern.*
> *Seine ihm blind ergebenen Anhänger stimmten jedem auch noch so sinnlosen Plan zu.*
> *Von preußischen Soldaten erwartete man blinden Gehorsam.*

2. While G. *blind* is both an adj. and adv., **blindlings** is an adv. only and the usual equivalent of **blindly**. *Blindlings* is used when confusion with the lit. sense of G. *blind* is possible. *Er stürzte blindlings vorwärts* and *Sie rannte blindlings in ihr Unglück* suggest without judgement, under the overpowering influence of a feeling, whereas *blind* could mean 'lacking sight'. When such confusion is not possible, either can be used, though with fig. expressions it is usual to use *blindlings. Sie gehorchten blindlings.* (Here *blind* is possible as well as in *Sie waren blind gehorsam.*)
> *Sie begaben sich blindlings in Gefahr.*   *Er stürzte sich blindlings ins Verderben.*
> *Sie ließen sich blindlings führen.*   *Er führte den Befehl blindlings aus.*
> *Sie vertraute/folgte/glaubte ihm blind/blindlings.*

B. Vs.

1. While the E. v. **blind** can mean 'to deprive permanently of the power of vision', it also means 'to render temporarily unable to see' and is a syn. of **dazzle**. *Coming out of the dark, we were dazzled/blinded by the bright sunlight.* Someone can also be blinded by pain or tears. Applied fig. to brilliant or showy qualities and people displaying them, **dazzle** means 'to overpower the judgement' or 'cause s.o. to be unable to think clearly'. To **blind** s.o. **to** sth. is also 'to deprive of judgement'. *His feelings for her blinded him to her faults.* To what the person is blinded need not be expressed. *His greed blinded him [to the risks involved in the enterprise].*

i. Blenden is the equivalent of **dazzle** in both the lit. and fig. senses, including deceiving and deluding by outward show or display. It also translates the fig. sense of **blind** except when it is used with a following *to*. For this cf. 1. ii.

Das Scheinwerferlicht blendete sie im Dunkeln auf der nassen Fahrbahn.
Der Blitz des Elektronenblitzgerätes blendete ihn. Er konnte minutenlang nicht richtig sehen.
Wenn man aus dem Dunkeln ins Helle kommt, ist man anfangs geblendet.
Von der Aussicht auf Macht und Reichtum geblendet, vergaß er alle seine Ideale und stellte sich in den Dienst der Machthaber. *Er war von ihrer Schönheit ganz geblendet.*
Von den Gewinnaussichten geblendet, stürzte er sich in ein Geschäft, das nie gut gehen konnte.
Sie blendet alle. *Ich lasse mich nicht vom Reichtum/vom Glanz/vom äußeren Schein blenden.*
Der Führer der rechtsradikalen Partei blendete weite Kreise mit seinen Versprechungen.

Blendend, 'dazzling', is applied to white. *Die Wäsche war/Ihre Zähne waren blendend weiß.* With other colours **leuchtend** translates **dazzling**. *Leuchtend rot. Blendend* is used colloquially in the sense 'brilliant, very impressive'. *Er hielt eine blendende Rede/erlebte einen blendenden Aufstieg.*

ii. Blind machen also expresses the fig. sense of **blind** but, unlike *blenden*, it can be used with *für* and *gegenüber*, which are the equivalents of *to*, as well as alone.
Ihre Liebe machte sie blind für seine Schwächen/gegenüber seinen Schwächen.
Die politische Erziehung machte die Menschen blind für alle Ansichten, die von den offiziell genehmigten abwichen. *Vorurteile machten sie den Tatsachen gegenüber blind.*
Haß/Wut/Leidenschaft machte ihn blind für die/gegenüber der Wahrheit.
Seine Habgier machte ihn blind gegenüber den Risiken, die das Projekt in sich barg.

iii. Verblenden means 'to deprive of the ability to think clearly or to judge properly'. It is a stronger, but less common, variant of *blenden* in the same sense. It is usually applied to feelings and desires which arise within a person. *Seine Geldgier hatte ihn verblendet.* The past part. often means 'deceived' or 'misled'.
Ihr Haß auf Männer hatte sie so verblendet, daß sie allem, was von einem Mann gesagt oder getan wurde, mit Mißtrauen begegnete.
Vom eigenen Glück und Erfolg verblendet, vergaß er seine früheren Freunde.

2. i. Erblinden, 'to go blind', sounds more elevated than **blind werden**.
Da sie im Alter von 80 Jahren erblindet war/blind geworden war, hat sie die Blindenschrift nicht mehr erlernt. *Er war auf einem Auge erblindet.*
Als das Medikament zur Erblindung mehrerer Versuchstiere geführt hatte, wurde seine weitere Entwicklung aufgegeben.

ii. To render the E. trans. v. **blind** when this denotes an accidental result, as in *An explosion blinded him*, **erblinden** or **blind werden** can be used with a change of construction or with *lassen*.
Sie ist infolge eines Unfalls erblindet/durch eine Explosion erblindet/blind geworden.
Der Mangel an Vitaminen ließ ihn vollständig erblinden.

Jmdm. das Augenlicht nehmen and **das Augenlicht verlieren** are elevated expressions which convey the meaning 'to deprive s.o. accidentally of his/her sight'.
Eine Explosion nahm ihm das Augenlicht. *Durch eine Explosion verlor er das Augenlicht.*

iii. Blenden, defined as *jmdm. die Augen ausstechen*, means 'to blind deliberately', 'put out s.o.'s eyes'.

block v. One sense of close v.

1. Block = 'to make unpassable by an obstruction'.

i. To state that *eine Straße, eine Brücke, ein Tunnel*, etc. is closed to traffic and pedestrians or is blocked off by official action, this being shown by barriers, a rope, chain, etc., G. uses **sperren**, which implies the carrying out of an intention on the part of the police or an administrative body. It does not necessarily imply that there is an actual obstruction present.
Die Straße ist wegen Bauarbeiten für Fahrzeuge gesperrt, aber Fußgänger dürfen die Bürgersteige noch benutzen. *Der Tunnel ist wegen Einsturzgefahr gesperrt.*
Während der Ausbesserungsarbeiten bleibt die Brücke gesperrt.

ii. Sperren is also used in *eine Grenze sperren*, 'to close', *die Einfuhr/die Ausfuhr/den Handel sperren*, 'to block or prohibit', *ein Bankkonto sperren*, 'to block or freeze', and [*weiteren*] *Kredit sperren*, 'to block'. It also translates *to cut off* with *das Telefon*, *der Strom*, or *das Gas* as objs., usually in cases in which accounts have not been paid.

> *Die Polizei sperrte die Grenze und durchsuchte alle Wagen in der Hoffnung, drei Bankräuber abfangen zu können.*
> *Die Firma befindet sich in einer üblen Lage, weil man ihr den Kredit gesperrt hat.*
> *Da er die Telefonrechnung längere Zeit nicht bezahlt hatte, wurde ihm das Telefon gesperrt.*

iii. Absperren is also 'to block, shut, or cordon off' an area, but implies greater thoroughness or completeness than *sperren*. It is often used with *hermetisch* or *vollständig* to emphasize the idea. A syn. is **abriegeln**. *Die Polizei hat die Unfallstelle hermetisch abgesperrt/abgeriegelt.*

> *Das Gefahrengebiet wurde vollständig abgesperrt, und niemand durfte es betreten.*

iv. Versperren is used: *a.* When someone blocks another's passage either with his/her body or by putting an obstruction in the way. *b.* When a car, truck, or something under human control causes a street, passage, entry, etc. to be blocked, either as a result of an accident or through carelessness. *c.* When something natural does this without human intervention. *d.* When something blocks a view. *Versperren* takes an acc. and a dat. *Er versperrt mir den Weg.* **Verstellen** in one sense is a syn. *Die Menge verstellt den Eingang/verstellt uns den Weg.*

> *Jmd. hatte die Einfahrt mit Kisten versperrt.*　*Große Kisten versperrten die Einfahrt.*
> *Streikposten versperrten die Fabriktore.*　*Ein parkendes Auto versperrte die Einfahrt.*
> *Er stellte sich vor mich im engen Gang und versperrte mir den Weg/den Durchgang.*
> *Ein Lastwagen hatte eine Panne mitten auf der Straße gehabt und versperrte sie völlig.*
> *Vom schweren Schnee gefällte Bäume versperrten Fußgängern den Weg.*
> *Das neue Haus auf dem nächsten Nachbargrundstück versperrt uns die Aussicht auf den See.*
> *Der Durchgang war mit Fahrrädern verstellt.*　*Ein Wagen verstellt die Ausfahrt/die Straße.*

v. *Ein Lastwagen, der eine Straße versperrt*, blocks the street by causing an obstruction which other vehicles cannot pass. It does not necessarily mean that other traffic blocks up on either side of it. If, however, other vehicles are forced to stop and fill or block up the street, the street is said to be *verstopft*. The concept expressed by **verstopfen** is that the free passage of water through a pipe is obstructed. The material causing the obstruction can be the subj., *Teeblätter verstopfen den Ausguß*, but it is most frequently found as a past part. after *sein*, *Der Abfluß im Bad ist verstopft*. It is also applied to parts of the body. *Meine Nase ist/Meine Nasenlöcher sind verstopft.*

> *Alle Kreuzungen waren von Fahrzeugen verstopft.*
> *Die Düse ist verstopft und muß gereinigt werden.*

vi. Zustopfen presupposes an intention whereas *verstopfen* suggests that the blockage comes about by accident. *Zustopfen* is used with objs. like *eine Ritze, eine Fuge, ein Loch, eine Spalte*. If used with *ein Rohr*, it would mean that someone deliberately blocks it by stuffing something into it, while *verstopfen* implies no intention. *Ohren* can be the obj. of *zustopfen*. *Bei dem Lärm muß ich mir die Ohren zustopfen.*

vii. Besides 'to blockade', **blockieren** means 'to prevent access to or passage through sth.' with and without intention, thus combining the meanings of *versperren* and *verstopfen*.

> *Die Zufahrtsstraßen wurden durch eine große Menge Schnee blockiert.*
> *Ein entgleister Güterzug blockierte die Strecke.*
> *Eine Menschenmenge blockierte den Eingang.*　*Streikposten blockierten die Fabriktore.*
> *Die Straße durch das Tal wurde durch eine Lawine blockiert.*

2. Block = 'to prevent sth. being accomplished' or 'to stop s.o. achieving sth.' *They did everything possible to block her election. The upper house blocked the legislation. His* *brother blocked him at every turn.* While **block** suggests that what is blocked fails to take place, **blockieren** only sometimes has this sense and may only mean that something is held up, delayed, or impeded. It means, therefore, both 'to block' and 'to obstruct'. In *Der Senat blockierte den Gesetzentwurf* and *Durch diese nutzlosen Diskussionen haben sie die Verhandlungen blockiert,* it is understood as 'obstruct'. Because of this ambiguity, if **block** implies that something was successfully prevented, it is best to use words like **vereiteln** or **durchkreuzen,** 'to thwart or foil' (cf. FRUSTRATE 1), or **etw./jmdn. zu Fall bringen,** 'to deliberately cause s.o./sth. to fail', or the sent. can be rephrased with **verhindern,** 'to PREVENT'. *Sie durchkreuzten seine Ernennung zum Vorsitzenden. Er vereitelte den Reformplan. Der Senat brachte den Gesetzentwurf zu Fall. Brauns Gegner verhinderten, daß er zum Vorsitzenden ernannt wurde.* A new word which means that something is successfully prevented is **abblocken.** It comes from the language of sport, *Der Spieler blockte den Angriff ab,* but is used in other fields and suggests great effort to stop something succeeding. *Sie blockten den Plan/das Vorhaben/diesen Versuch ab.*

> *Er hat die Pläne seines Konkurrenten durchkreuzt/vereitelt.*   *Jmd. blockte seine Beförderung ab.*
> *Sie haben alles Mögliche getan, um ihre Wahl zu verhindern.* Or . . . *um zu verhindern, daß sie gewählt wurde.*
> *Sie blockten alle Argumente der Gegenseite ab.*

Block s.o. needs to be expressed differently. *His brother blocked him* . . . could be translated as *Sein Bruder versuchte, alle seine Pläne zu durchkreuzen/jedes seiner Vorhaben zu vereiteln.* Other expressions with a similar meaning are *jmdm. Schwierigkeiten machen* or *jmdm. Steine in den Weg legen,* to put obstacles in s.o.'s way.

boast, show off *vs.* **Sich rühmen** means 'to boast', but lies on the borderline between boasting which expresses one's justified pride and boasting which is excessive and reflects badly on the person. It is used neutrally in sents. like *Ich kann mich rühmen, das alles allein gemacht zu haben,* and *Die Fluggesellschaft kann sich rühmen, daß keine ihrer Maschinen in den letzten zwanzig Jahren abgestürzt sei.* Elsewhere, it can express disapproval. *Er rühmte sich, ein verkanntes Genie zu sein.* It is occasionally found with the gen. *Sie rühmten sich ihres Erfolges.* **Prahlen** is always pejorative. A colloquial equivalent is **sich brüsten.** Strongly pejorative is **protzen,** which means 'to show off' with something and occasionally 'to boast or brag' about it. [**Mit etw.**] **angeben** is also 'to show off', but it is not as strong as *protzen* and is used particularly for children. It can also mean 'to boast'. **Aufschneiden** is 'to boast or brag by exaggerating when telling something, by embellishing what one says with invented incidents which are presented as true, and by giving undue prominence to oneself'. A speaker uses the word to describe someone else's behaviour and to criticize the way the person referred to gives prominence to himself and falsifies events by exaggeration.

> *Er prahlt mit seinem Geld/mit seinen Sprachkenntnissen.*
> *Wie der wieder mit seiner Freundin geprahlt hat!*
> *Ich an deiner Stelle würde mich mit so etw. nicht brüsten.*
> *Er brüstet sich damit, daß er zu den Spitzenverdienern gehört.*
> *Er protzt mit seinem Vermögen/mit seinen geschäftlichen Erfolgen.*
> *Er fährt den dicken Wagen doch nur, um damit zu protzen.*
> *Das Kind gibt mit dem neuen Fahrrad an.*
> *Wir wollten ein bißchen angeben, um die Mädchen zu beeindrucken.*
> *Nun begann B. Geschichten über Gefechte mit den Engländern zum besten zu geben. Er schnitt fürchterlich auf und erfand die tollsten Dinge. Die viermotorigen Bomber hätten er und seine Kameraden abgeknallt wie die Spatzen.*

body *n.*

1. *Der Körper* and *der Leib* both denote the body of a human being or an animal, but although *Leib* is still often heard, its use in the literal sense, in which it has a poetical ring, is now confined to literary or elevated language. It survives, however, at all levels of the language in a number of commonly used expressions. **Der Körper** is now the usual equivalent of **body** in the basic meaning.

> *Die Athleten erhalten ihre Körper leistungsfähig.*
> *Als er ankam, schwitzte er am ganzen Körper.*
> *Sie hatte einen gesunden/kräftigen/gut trainierten Körper.*
> *Er rettete nur das, was er auf dem Körper trug.*
> *Nach dem Ritt dampften die Körper der Pferde.*
> *Es gibt verschiedene Abwehrreaktionen des Körpers auf eine Infektion.*

2. Examples of fixed expressions still in use.

i. **Der Leib** is usually linked with *Seele, Leib und Seele,* 'body and soul' or 'body and mind'. *Sie waren gesund an Leib und Seele.* (Besides meaning 'soul', *Seele* denotes that part of a human being which feels and thinks, the consciousness or psyche.) *Er hing mit Leib und Seele an seinem Beruf,* with heart and soul. *Sie war mit Leib und Seele Lehrerin.* A few vs. are used with the expression *die Seele aus dem Leib* to indicate an intensification of the action. *Das Kind schrie/weinte sich die Seele aus dem Leib. Er fragte mir die Seele aus dem Leib. Man prügelte ihm die Seele aus dem Leib.*

ii. *Man spürt* or *erfährt etw. am eigenen Leibe. Nun sollten sie die wirtschaftliche Not des Landes am eigenen Leibe spüren. Ein Kleidungsstück wird jmdm. auf den Leib geschneidert* or *eine Rolle wird einem Schauspieler auf den Leib geschrieben.* **Bleib' mir vom Leibe!,** keep away!, and **Bleib' mir damit vom Leibe!,** don't tell me about it/involve me in it! *Peter ist mir unheimlich—ich werde ihn mir vom Leibe halten. Jmdm. auf den Leib rücken* is 'to come closer to s.o. in a way which that person feels to be unpleasant'. *Bleibe doch auf deinem Platz und rück' mir nicht so dicht auf den Leib! Zu Leibe rücken/gehen* is 'to attack s.o./sth.' or 'to tackle' a difficult or unpleasant task. *Als der angeschossene Bär ihm zu Leibe gehen wollte, packte den Jäger die Angst. Wir müssen diesem Mißstand zu Leibe gehen.*

3. Body also denotes the main part of a person's body excluding the neck, head, and limbs. *He received a blow to the body.* The specific term is **der Rumpf,** but *Körper* is also possible. *Der Kopf sitzt auf dem Rumpf. Der Boxer hatte seinen Gegner mehrfach am Körper/Rumpf getroffen.*

4. *A dead* **body** must be **die Leiche.** *Die Leiche eines älteren Mannes wurde gestern an einen Strand südlich von Sydney angeschwemmt.*

5. Body also means 'an organized group of people who are in charge of sth. or who work together'. **Die Körperschaft** denotes either a group of people who join and work together for some purpose, *eine karitative/gewerkschaftliche Körperschaft,* or an organization or body which possesses political rights granted by law, *eine gesetzgebende Körperschaft. Eine Gemeinde ist eine Körperschaft des öffentlichen Rechts.*

6. A **body** of people means 'a group of people'. The general equivalent is **die Gruppe.** *Große Gruppen von Arbeitslosen zogen durch die Straßen und forderten Arbeit,* large bodies of unemployed people. *Die Studenten gingen als geschlossene Gruppe zum Rektor* is a transl. of *They went in a body.*

bother, pester *vs.* Some senses of **trouble, worry,** and **concern** *vs.*

1. Bother = 'to annoy or upset by petty provocations'. *Don't bother me with foolish questions!* **Pester** = 'to trouble or harass with petty and repeated irritations', especially questions or requests. *He pestered me all day with requests for help.* **Worry** = either 'to plague' with repeated demands, requests, etc., *The teacher began to worry [the life out of] me with requests and demands to finish the work,* or 'to distress or inconvenience by inconsiderate behaviour'. If I worry someone with a problem, I tell him or her about it and may cause trouble or irritation by doing so. *Why worry her with it now when it's all over?*

i. Plagen means 'to annoy or irk' with persistent questions and requests, 'to give s.o. no peace'. Although **quälen** can mean 'to cause great physical or mental pain' and be stronger than **bother**, it is also common in less serious situations in which someone pesters or plagues another continuously with questions, requests, etc. It can be followed by *mit*, a clause with *sollen*, or an infin.

Die Kinder plagten die Eltern den ganzen Tag mit Fragen und Wünschen.
Der Lehrer fing an, mich endlos zu plagen mit Bitten und Forderungen, die Arbeit zu erledigen.
Warum plagst du sie mit der Sache, wo alles doch schon vorbei ist?
Die Jungen plagten/quälten die Mutter so lange, bis sie ihnen erlaubte, in den Zoo zu gehen.
Die beiden quälten mich, ich sollte sie mitnehmen.
Quäl' uns doch nicht so mit diesen dummen Fragen!

ii. Both **plagen** and **quälen** are used when the cause is within the mind. *Quälen* is stronger than *plagen*. As **bother** is weak, stronger words like *trouble* or *torment* may be a more appropriate transl.

Skrupel und Zweifel plagten ihn.   *Ein Gefühl der Unsicherheit quälte sie.*
Die Ungewißheit darüber, wie alles ausgehen würde, plagte ihn.
Das böse Gewissen plagte/quälte sie.

iii. Jmdm. mit etw. auf die Pelle/den Pelz rücken and **jmdm. mit etw. in den Ohren liegen** mean 'to pester' someone with requests, wishes, etc. and are colloquial syns. of the vs. in 1. i.

Nächstes Wochenende muß ich unbedingt mal meine Schwester in ihrem neuen Haus besuchen. Schon seit Wochen liegt sie mir damit in den Ohren.
Immer wieder rückt er mir mit der alten Bitte/mit unerfüllbaren Wünschen auf die Pelle.

2. Pester s.o. **to do** sth. **Drängeln** means 'to try impatiently to get s.o. to do sth.' or 'to beg s.o. repeatedly to do sth.' It is used with an infin. or alone and mostly with children as subj. Cf. vs. under 1.

Die Kinder drängelten die Mutter, ihnen Eis/Bonbons zu kaufen.
Hört doch endlich auf zu drängeln! Ich nehme euch heute nachmittag mit zum Strand.
Seit Tagen drängelt er mich, den Bericht abzuschließen.

3. Bother = 'to cause to suffer mild discomfort'. *Do the mosquitoes bother you?* **Plagen** is used in pos. sents. *Die Mücken im Wald haben uns sehr geplagt. Mich plagte die Hitze.* In neg. sents. **jmdm. nichts ausmachen**, 'not to MATTER TO', expresses the sense. *Die Hitze machte mir nichts aus.* **Bother** and **trouble** are applied to something which causes bodily pain or inconvenience. *Plagen* is used for pain, hunger, thirst, and diseases, *Seit ein paar Tagen plagen mich Zahnschmerzen* or *Mich plagt Hunger/Durst/ein Husten,* but not to parts of the body causing it. *His stomach was bothering/troubling him* would be *Er hatte [leichte] Magenschmerzen. Quälen* is stronger than *plagen. Fortlaufend quälten sie starke Schmerzen.*

4. Bother = 'to force unwelcome attention or company on', 'to intrude upon'. *I don't want to bother her.* Disturb is closely related.

i. *Don't bother me!* can be **Laß mich in Ruhe!**, leave me alone/in peace! A phr. with *mit* can be added. *Laß mich mit dieser dämlichen Sache in Ruhe!* A common syn. is **stören**, to keep s.o. from or interrupt s.o. in work or an activity, to disturb, trouble, bother, or worry.

Stört Sie die Schreibmaschine?   *Stört es Sie, wenn ich mit der Maschine schreibe?*
Darf ich Sie einen Augenblick stören?   *Soll ich den Chef mit dieser Sache stören?*

ii. Belästigen belongs to a higher stylistic level, but has a similar meaning. Although the basic sense is 'to cause inconvenience', often by questions, wishes, demands, etc. or by saying unwelcome things, it can be stronger and mean 'to molest'. In some contexts it is a syn. of the vs. in 1 and 3.

> *Es tut mir leid, Sie mit dieser Angelegenheit belästigen zu müssen.*
> *Ich wurde durch das dauernde Geräusch sehr belästigt.   Die Mücken haben uns sehr belästigt.*

iii. Behelligen is on the same stylistic level as *belästigen*, but is less common. It implies disturbing someone, often repeatedly.

> *Darf ich Sie mit einer anderen Angelegenheit behelligen?*
> *Er hat seinen Vorgesetzten mit Fragen/Bitten/Forderungen/Briefen behelligt.*
> *Sie wird wohl Verständnis haben, wenn ich sie mit dieser Sache behellige.*

5. Bother = 'to cause to be mildly anxious'. *Don't let it bother you! What bothers me is that it is not quite legal.* To **bother oneself** and to **bother one's head** mean 'to become mildly anxious'. *It's not important—don't bother yourself/your head about it!* **Bother** is weaker than **trouble** and **worry**. To **trouble** = 'to put into a state of mental distress or disquiet'. *I believe sth. is troubling him.* **Trouble** is also used in the refl. in the sense 'to become mentally agitated about', this form thus being the equivalent of the pass. **be troubled.** *He allowed the reformers to have their way and never troubled himself about the consequences* or *. . . was not troubled about the consequences.* To **worry** means 'to cause distress of mind to'. *It worried him to think that Sylvie was alone.* **Worry** is used intr. meaning 'to give way to mental disquiet', the sense of the pass. *She told me not to worry/be worried. I worry/am worried about him.* To **concern** means 'to worry'. *Don't let my illness concern you! His parents were concerned about his safety.*

i. For the act. forms *Sth. is bothering/troubling/worrying her*, **beunruhigen** is used as well as **jmd./etw. macht jmdm. Sorgen**. The past part. **worried** is **besorgt** as well as **beunruhigt**.

> *Irgendetwas beunruhigt sie, aber ich weiß nicht, was es ist.*
> *Was beunruhigt dich?*
> *Er gewährte den Reformern alles, worum sie ihn baten, und ließ sich von den Folgen nicht beunruhigen.*
> *Es beunruhigt mich, daß die Sache nicht ganz astrein (= moralisch einwandfrei) ist.*
> *Sie sah sehr besorgt aus.   Die besorgten Eltern.*
> *Es macht mir Sorgen/beunruhigt mich/macht mich besorgt, daß sie stets dieses Thema fallen läßt, sobald es angeschnitten wird.   Was macht dir Sorgen?*
> *Ich bin über dein schlechtes Aussehen besorgt. Also . . . wegen deines . . .*

ii. Equivalents of the intr. and refl. forms and the pass. **Sich Gedanken machen über/wegen** means 'to feel anxiety or concern about'. **Ich mache mir Sorgen** and **ich sorge mich um jmdn./etw.** are stronger and are usually translated as **worry**. **Ich beunruhige mich über/wegen**, I feel uneasy about. *Wegen* is more formal than *über*.

> *Die Sache ist nicht weiter wichtig. Mach' dir keine Gedanken darüber!* (Don't worry/bother [your head] about it/let it bother/trouble you!) *Also Mach' dir deswegen keine Gedanken!*
> *Wo bleibt sie nur? Ich mache mir ihretwegen Gedanken.*
> *Es hat keinen Sinn, dir Gedanken/Sorgen zu machen. Ihr wird bestimmt nichts passiert sein.*
> *Du brauchst dich seinetwegen nicht zu beunruhigen. Or . . . dich darüber nicht zu beunruhigen.*
> *Sie sorgte sich um die Gesundheit ihres Mannes/um die finanzielle Lage der Familie.*

(*Sich über etw. Gedanken machen* also means 'to think about'. *Dies ist eine wichtige Frage, über die Sie sich zu Hause ruhig einmal Gedanken machen können.*)

6. i. Bother about/with means 'become concerned or interested', 'devote time, energy, or attention to'. *I haven't time to bother about such trifles. She needed help, but they didn't bother about her/that.* It can be refl. *My wife doesn't bother herself with money* *matters*. To **concern oneself with** is stylistically higher, if interchangeable with **bother**, but it is usual in pos. sents. while **bother** is mostly neg. **Sich kümmern um** covers all these senses and translates both *to bother* and *concern oneself*.

Sie brauchte Hilfe, aber niemand kümmerte sich um sie.
Niemand kümmerte sich um die neue Anweisung (bothered about/paid attention to).
Ich habe keine Zeit, mich um solche Bagatellen zu kümmern.
Kümmere dich nicht um Dinge, die dich nichts angehen!   *Sie kümmert sich nicht um Politik.*
In den vier deutschen Besatzungszonen setzten die Militärbefehlshaber weitgehend die politischen und ökonomischen Konzeptionen ihrer Regierungen durch, ohne sich um die Frage einer gemeinschaftlichen Regelung für ganz Deutschland zu kümmern.

ii. Sich kümmern um also means 'to take care of' a person or thing, *Während die Eltern verreist waren, kümmerte sich die Oma um die Kinder*, and 'to do sth. about getting or doing sth.', *Ich muß mich um ein Geschenk kümmern*. Cf. SEE TO S.O./STH. In both senses it translates *not to bother* in some contexts. *Sie kümmerte sich nicht um meine Pflanzen, während ich weg war*, and *Er kümmerte sich nicht um die Karten.*

iii. Kümmern is used in neg. sents., or in questions which imply a neg. answer. *Das braucht dich nicht zu kümmern*, it needn't bother/concern you.

Was kümmert mich der Klatsch?   *Das soll mich wenig kümmern.*

7. i. Bother = 'to take pains', 'to take the trouble to do sth.' It is used with an infin. or gerund. *Don't bother to get/bother getting breakfast for me!* To **trouble**, which can also have this meaning, is followed by an infin. *Don't trouble to meet me at the station!* **Sich Mühe geben**, 'to make an/the effort, take pains', and **sich bemühen**, 'to endeavour, try, trouble oneself', can be used, but it often sounds better if **bother** is not translated. *I said I was interested, but he didn't even bother to write down my name* could be *Ich sagte, ich würde mich dafür interessieren, aber er hat nicht einmal meinen Namen aufgeschrieben*. In full: . . . *er hat sich nicht einmal die Mühe gegeben, meinen Namen aufzuschreiben. Ich bügle meine Hemden nie*, never bother to iron them. *Why bother learning all these facts?* can be *Warum soll ich mir die Mühe geben, mir alle diese Tatsachen einzuprägen?* or *Warum soll ich mir . . . einprägen? Bitte bemühen Sie sich nicht!* is a polite formula meaning 'Please don't trouble/bother to do sth.' *Du kannst dir die Mühe sparen*, 'you can save yourself the effort/trouble', can translate *You needn't bother*, but is not very polite. Cf. SAVE 6. *I can't be bothered doing sth.* is *Ich habe keine Lust, das zu machen.*

Bitte bemühen Sie sich nicht, mich nach unten zu begleiten/mich vom Bahnhof abzuholen!

The idiom **nicht erst lange** can sometimes express the meaning 'not to bother'. *Du brauchst es gar nicht erst lange zu versuchen—es klappt nicht*, you needn't bother trying—it won't work. *Such' es gar nicht erst lange—es ist nicht da.*

ii. Trouble is used in polite or irritated requests. Both can be expressed by **bitten**. *Dürfte/Darf ich Sie bitten, den Senf herüberzureichen?*, 'may I trouble you to pass', is very polite. *Ich möchte dich doch [wirklich] bitten, dir die Schuhe abzutreten, wenn du das nächste Mal ins Haus kommst*, 'I'll trouble you to wipe your shoes . . .', is less so.

bottom *n.* and *adj.*

1. Bottom = 'the lowest surface or part of sth.' *The bottom of a box, bag, case, drawer, barrel, cup*, etc. The usual word for most objects is **der Boden**. However, with things like a saucepan or pot, the inside bottom is called *der Boden*, the outside bottom **die Unterseite**. *Die Unterseite eines Blattes, eines Tellers*, or *die Unterseite des Stoffes* is 'the underside or back'.

Der Boden eines Eimers/einer Kiste/einer Schachtel/einer Schublade/eines Schrankes etc.
Die Teeblätter sinken nach ein paar Minuten auf den Boden der Kanne.

Der Koffer des Schmugglers hatte einen doppelten Boden.
Der Boden des Topfes hat ein Loch. *Die Unterseite des Topfes war ganz schwarz.*

2. Both **der Boden** and **der Grund** are equivalents of **bottom** meaning 'the ground or bed under the water of a lake, sea, river, etc.' They are in practice often interchangeable, though *Boden*, like *bed*, suggests more strongly what the bottom is like, *Grund* that it is the layer of matter where the water ends. *Der Meeresboden* would be used in a geographical or geological description, *die Struktur des Meeresbodens; der Meeresgrund* is somewhat poetical in tone and can imply great depth, but *Grund* by itself is common. In certain expressions only one is used. *Ein Boot/Schiff gerät/läuft auf Grund*, runs aground or touches bottom. *Der Schwimmer hatte/fand keinen Grund*, was out of his depth, could not touch the bottom. Thus *Der Schwimmer hatte [endlich] wieder [festen] Grund unter den Füßen. Man pumpt einen Brunnen bis auf den Boden aus*, but *Grund* is also used and suggests greater depth. *Bottomless* is *bodenlos* or *ohne Boden*, as *grundlos* and *ohne Grund* mean 'without reason, unfounded, groundless'. Although *Grund* is no longer used for the bottom of a drinking vessel, it still occurs in the phr. *ein Glas bis auf den Grund leeren*, to drain (to the dregs).

Tang gedeiht nur dort, wo der Untergrund felsig ist und wo er sich festsetzen kann. An solchen Stellen bedecken ausgedehnte Bestände brauner Algen den felsigen Meeresboden.
Das Wasser im See war so klar, daß man bis auf den Grund sehen konnte.
Auf dem Grund des Teiches war eine dicke Schlammschicht.

3. i. Applied to things having elevation, **bottom** or *foot* means 'the lower or lowest part' as opposed to the upper or topmost part and is usually **der Fuß**. *Der Fuß des Berges/des Hügels/der Felsenwand/der Mauer/des Turmes/der Leiter/der Treppe.* It is also used for a page. *Die Anmerkungen befinden sich am Fuß der Seite.*

ii. Bottom is used with things like a garden, field, or street meaning 'the end', but it usually suggests that the ground slopes downward. This is **das Ende**.

Das Geschäft befindet sich am Ende der Hauptstraße.
Am Ende des Gartens steht ein Kirschbaum.

iii. *My name is at the bottom of the list* is *Mein Name ist am Ende der Liste* or *der letzte in der Liste*. This says no more than that it is the last one to be added. **At the bottom** also means 'at the lower end with regard to dignity or precedence'. *I am at the bottom of the class in mathematics.* This can only be **der/die letzte**. *In Mathe bin ich der letzte in der Klasse.*

iv. [Right] at the bottom, referring to position in space or in a hierarchical structure only, can often be translated by **[ganz] unten**. *Der Brief, den ich suchte, war ganz unten im Stapel.*

Das blaue Hemd ist ganz unten im Koffer/im Schrank.
Sie wollten die Treppe nicht hinaufsteigen und blieben unten.
Das Wort finden Sie auf Seite 10, vier Zeilen von unten. (*Seite 10 unten* means 'the bottom half of page 10'.) *Mein Name steht ganz unten auf der Liste.*
Ich habe ganz unten angefangen, habe mich aber allmählich heraufgearbeitet.

4. Bottom means 'the fundamental character or nature', but this survives mainly in the expressions *to get to the bottom of* and *at bottom*. These are **einer Sache auf den Grund gehen** and **im Grunde**. **Ergründen** is a stylistically higher syn. of the former.

Sie will das Geheimnis um jeden Preis ergründen/ . . . dem Geheimnis auf den Grund gehen.
Die Demonstranten, die im Straßenkampf mit der Polizei verletzt wurden, waren im Grunde gutmütige Burschen.

5. *They are* **at the bottom of** *every such scheme* can be *Sie* **stecken hinter** *jeder Machenschaft dieser Art.*

6. The human **bottom** is das Gesäß or colloquially **das Hinterteil** or **der Hintern**.
Er hat dem Jungen ein paar [Schläge] aufs Hinterteil/auf den Hintern gegeben.
Der Vater hat dem Jungen den Hintern verhauen/vollgehauen.
Da das Eis sehr glatt war, sind sie aufs Hinterteil gefallen. (Children's language: . . . *auf den* **Po**.
Cf. *Diese Illustrierte ist ein Po- und Busenblatt der schlimmsten Sorte.*)

7. The adj. **bottom** is **untere** if two things are involved, **unterste** if more than two.
Das Buch steht im unteren Regal or *im untersten Regal*, depending on the number. *Die untere Hälfte der Seite. Der untere Teil des Schrankes. Die untere/unterste rechte Schublade. Die unterste Sprosse der Leiter.*

box, case, crate, carton, bag, wallet, purse *ns.*

A. Boxes, **cases**, and **crates** differ in size, but as there is some overlapping, the line of demarcation is not clear. *A box* and *a case of apples* are different names for the same thing. **Crates** are large containers, but some crates could be called packing-cases. A **carton** is determined by the material it is made of, but must be of a certain minimum size—shoes are supplied in a box. *Die Schachtel, der Kasten,* and *die Kiste* also differ in size, but in different ways from the E. words.
Die Schachtel is a small, relatively flat, thin-walled rectangular or round container with a lid made usually of *Pappe*, 'cardboard', but sometimes of thin wood or *Kunststoff*, 'plastic', and is used mainly for packaging goods. It also denotes the quantity of goods such a box contains. **Boxes** are called *Schachteln* up to the size of a *Schuhschachtel*, but this can also be called a *Schuhkarton*. Only a *Hutschachtel* may be bigger.
Ich kaufe eine Schachtel Streichhölzer/Bonbons/Pralinen/Zigaretten etc.
Er bewahrt einige alte Photos in einer Schachtel auf.
Sie nahm den Deckel der Schachtel ab/öffnete die Schachtel und nahm eine Praline heraus.
Der Karton must be made of cardboard and begins in size with a shoe-box.
Die Geschenke, die wir verschicken wollten, packten wir in einen Karton.
Ich habe die Kartons, in denen das Stereogerät verpackt war, aufgehoben.
Der Kasten is a small or middle-sized, firm, rectangular container made of wood, metal, or plastic, frequently with a lid and principally used for storing things, though something stored in a *Kasten* can be transported in it. It is used for boxes for tools, instruments, etc. *Der Werkzeugkasten, Arzneikasten, Instrumentenkasten, Besteckkasten, Brotkasten, Schuhputzkasten, Verbandkasten, Zettelkasten,* 'card index box'. *Kasten* is also applied to firm containers, called **cases** in E., in which musical instruments are carried or kept. *Er holte die Geige aus dem Kasten. Der Briefkasten* is either a box for posting mail or the one into which the postman puts the mail he is delivering. Containers (not made of cardboard) used for the transport or sale of usually a dozen bottles of drink are called *ein Kasten*, but *eine Kiste* is also common and is the only possibility for wine.
Wir kauften einen Kasten/eine Kiste Limonade/Brause/Apfelsaft/Mineralwasser/Bier etc.
Kasten, in full **der Schaukasten**, is used for the **cases** in which exhibits in museums and elsewhere are displayed and for display cases attached to a wall. **Die Vitrine** is a syn.
In diesem [Schau]kasten/dieser Vitrine sind römische Münzen.
Eine Kiste is made of wood, except that those made for drinks can be of *Kunststoff*, and is usually used for transport. It extends from middle-size upwards and thus covers **crate** as well as **box** and **case**. It is the only word used for a **box** or **case** of fruit. *Wir kauften eine Kiste Äpfel.*
Wir packten die Waren in zwei große Kisten und ließen sie durch die Bahn befördern.
Wir müssen die zerbrechlichen Sachen in dieser Kiste verpacken.

Das Kästchen is usually a well-made, small, or not very big container used for articles which are small and delicate or valuable. *Das Nähkästchen. Das Schmuckkästchen.* **Die Büchse** is a small container for money, either *eine Sammelbüchse* or *eine Sparbüchse.* A child's money-box is often *ein Sparschwein.* **Die Dose** is also a small container with a lid for storing things in, and would sometimes be called a box. *Eine kleine runde Dose aus Holz.* (*Dose,* in full *Konservendose,* and *Büchse* mean 'can or tin' of preserved fruit etc., *Dose* being more usual.)
Der Koffer is 'a suitcase'. **Das Etui** is a fairly flat container or case for things up to about 25 cm. in length. The most common compounds are *das Brillenetui, Maniküreetui, Füllhalteretui, Nähzeugetui, Zigarettenetui.* The less common **das Futteral** is applied to containers of flexible material made to fit closely over certain things. A related word is *die Hülle,* cover.
Er zog den Notenständer/die Fahne aus dem Futteral.

B. Bag. A paper **bag** into which small quantities of goods are put in shops is called **die Tüte**. This term is also used for containers of similar shape made of plastic, in full **die Plastiktüte**, and includes containers which have some kind of handle and into which clothes etc. bought in shops are put. What is called **der Beutel** is made of flexible material, is open at the top, and closed by a cord which may be used for carrying it. There are two main shapes. Either two pieces of material of identical size and shape, often with a rounded bottom, are sewn up around the edges, or a round piece of material forms a flat bottom to which the sides, consisting of a single piece of material, are attached. It also translates *pouch,* including that of marsupials, which are called *Beuteltiere.* Some compounds are *der Sportbeutel, Frischhaltebeutel, Wäschebeutel, Klingelbeutel.* Perhaps the most frequent equivalent of **bag** is **die Tasche**. *Taschen* are made of flexible or firm material, are usually rectangular, have one or two handles, and are used for carrying things. *Tasche* corresponds sometimes to **bag**, sometimes to **case**. A handbag is *die Handtasche,* a shopping-bag is *die Einkaufstasche,* a briefcase is *die Aktentasche. Eine [Umhänge]tasche* is the bag in which a postman carries mail. Also *Instrumententasche, Werkzeugtasche, Schultertasche, Reisetasche,* etc. *Eine Schultasche* is 'a bag or case' carried in the hand. **Der [Schul]ranzen** is 'a school-bag' worn on the back by younger schoolchildren. **Die Mappe** is basically 'a folder', i.e. two pieces of cardboard of equal size joined on one side and tied on the others in which drawings and paintings or papers are kept. The sense has been extended to include a briefcase, but with the implication that it is fairly flat. *Aktentasche* is, however, more common than *Aktenmappe. Die Schulmappe* is sometimes used for *Schultasche.* A pack carried on the back is either **der Rucksack**, in particular for hikers, or **der Tornister** for soldiers, occasionally for schoolchildren. **Der Sack** is a large bag for potatoes, coal, fertilizer, cement, etc. *Der Postsack* is 'a mail-bag'.

C. Wallet, purse. **Die Brieftasche**, in which one keeps papers and *Geldscheine,* 'banknotes', is now the usual equivalent of a **wallet**, and **das Portemonnaie** of a **purse** in which one carries coins and notes. **Die Geldbörse** is a refined syn. of the latter. **Der Geldbeutel** has gone out of use in the lit. sense, but survives in expressions in which it is often shortened to *Beutel. Er hat einen dicken/vollen Geldbeutel,* has a lot of money. *Tief in den [Geld]beutel greifen müssen,* to have to pay a lot of money. *Mein Beutel ist leer,* I have no money. *Den Beutel festhalten* or *den Daumen auf den [Geld]beutel halten,* not to spend any money.

boy *n*. Although everyone knows what **der Knabe** means, it is now hardly used. It survives only in *der Knabenchor* and *die Knabenstimme.* The usual word in the

North is **der Junge** and in the South **der Bub**. *Der Junge* is also used for a young man. *Die Sportler sind prächtige Jungen* (sometimes *Jungs*).

brain *n*. Both **das Gehirn** and **das Hirn** denote the brain as an organ and the mind or intelligence. *Das Gehirn* is used in scientific or medical contexts to denote the brain of either a human being or an animal. *Das Hirn* is used in cooking when the brains of animals are prepared for eating, *gebratenes Schafhirn*, and in three pejorative compounds in which it implies intelligence or lack of it, *hirnverbrannt*, 'demented, crazy', *hirnlos*, 'brainless, stupid', and *das Hirngespinst*, 'figment of the mind, fantasy'. *Er strengte sein Hirn/Gehirn an* are possible, but as an equivalent of **brain[s]** in the sense 'intelligence or mind', **der Kopf** would now be the most common word. *Jmd. ist ein kluger/gescheiter/heller/fähiger Kopf* or *hat einen klugen/hellen/ guten Kopf* means that he/she has brains or a good brain. **Der Verstand, der Sinn**, and **der Geist** occur in certain expressions. Cf. MIND. *Jmd. hat Verstand [im Kopf]* and colloquially *hat Köpfchen* or *Grütze/Grips im Kopf* are also used, implying intelligence. *Jmd. ist der fähigste Kopf der Gruppe* could translate *its brains*. *Er ist der Kopf des Unternehmens* also occurs. *Sich den Kopf zerbrechen* is 'to rack one's brains'. *To have sth. on the brain* can be *Eine Melodie/Eine Erinnerung/Ein Gedanke geht mir nicht aus dem Kopf/Sinn* or *Er hat nichts als Fußball im Kopf/Sinn*. For *Use your brains!* there is also *Streng' deinen Geist mal ein bißchen an!* *Brain work* is usually *Geistesarbeit* or *geistige Arbeit* although *Kopfarbeit* is also used.

> *Die Verletzungen des Gehirns bewirkten partiellen Gedächtnisausfall.*
> *Dieses Kapitel beschreibt den Bau des menschlichen Gehirns.*   *Sein Hirn arbeitet nur langsam.*
> *Sie verwarf alle diese Pläne als Hirngespinste, die man nie durchführen könne.*
> *Die Schulaufgaben erschienen ihr völlig hirnverbrannt.*
> *Was geht in seinem Kopf/Hirn vor?*

break *v*. Order of treatment: 1. **Break** relating to a branch, plate, string, etc. and a coalition, friendship, etc. 2. **Break** with a law, an agreement, etc. as obj. 3. Other senses of **break** expressed by *brechen*. 4. Senses of **break** expressed by derivatives of *brechen*. 5. **Be broken, break down**, and **break** applied to mechanical devices, cars and negotiations. 6. **Be /go broke**.

1. When it is trans., **break** means 'to smash into pieces or parts', 'to pull apart' either deliberately or by accident. *He broke the glass.* If intr., it means 'to come apart' or 'split into pieces'. *The glass broke.*

i. Both **brechen** and **zerbrechen** express these senses of **break** in relation to hard objects (cf. 1. iv), but *zerbrechen* has the connotation that what is broken becomes completely useless and worthless. *Zerbrechen* is therefore used for things which, if broken, can no longer be used, such as *Glas, Porzellan*, and *Geschirr*, and relatively small objects of wood or plastic like *ein Stuhl, Spielzeug, Modellhaus*, etc. Note that the intr. senses of *brechen* and its derivatives take *sein* in the perf. *Der Ast ist gebrochen. Die Tasse/Fensterscheibe ist zerbrochen.*

> *Man kann diese dürren Zweige leicht brechen.*   *Er hat den Stock in Stücke gebrochen.*
> *Das dünne Brett wird brechen, wenn ihr beide euch darauf setzt.*
> *Der Mast des Schiffes ist im Sturm gebrochen.*   *Der Junge hat das Spielzeug zerbrochen.*
> *Ich habe beim Abwaschen leider eine Tasse zerbrochen.*
> *Der Teller fiel auf den Boden und zerbrach.*   *Der Stuhl lag zerbrochen in einer Ecke.*
> *Ich habe das Bild fallenlassen/fallengelassen. Das Glas ist dabei zerbrochen.*

ii. With *zerbrechen*, the breakage is usually taken to be accidental, but it can be deliberate if this is clear from the context. In the latter case, **zerschlagen**, 'to smash', is often preferred, because with a personal subj. it always implies intentional breaking. In other circumstances, no intention is suggested. *Ein Stein hat die Windschutzscheibe zerschlagen.* Note that when a phr. is added, the base v. *schlagen* is used. *Er schlug den Stuhl kurz und klein,* smashed or broke it to bits. *Er wollte alles in Stücke schlagen.*

> *Mutwillig zerbrach/zerschlug er alles, was im Zimmer stand.*
> *Die Einbrecher zerschlugen das Küchenfenster, um in das Haus einsteigen zu können.*

iii. Zerbrechen is also applied to the breaking up of associations between people, *die Freundschaft, die Ehe, ein Bündnis, eine Koalition, die Einheit der Partei, Kinder aus zerbrochenen Familien,* 'from broken homes', and to people or their beliefs which are broken or destroyed. It is common in intr. use, often with *an*, but sometimes occurs as a trans. v. *Die Freundschaft ist an einer politischen Meinungsverschiedenheit zerbrochen* and *Eine Meinungsverschiedenheit zerbrach die Freundschaft.*

> *Die Koalition zwischen Sozialdemokraten und Grünen zerbrach nach vierzehn-monatiger Dauer.*
> *Die Einheit der Opposition zerbrach.*
> *Sie wäre an dem Kummer/an den Sorgen beinahe zerbrochen.*
> *Sein Glaube an ein neues, soziales Deutschland zerbrach nur allzu bald.*

iv. Break is used both for hard and flexible objects. *The branch broke* and *The string broke. Brechen* and *zerbrechen* are applied only to the former. For the latter, **reißen** and **zerreißen**, which for certain materials correspond to TEAR, are used. The distinction in normal use is that *zerreißen* is trans. and *reißen* intr., so that both can be used with the same material without requiring a different E. v. *Beim Zubinden des Pakets habe ich den Bindfaden zerrissen.* But *Als ich das Paket zubinden wollte, ist der Bindfaden gerissen.* (Or . . . *riß der Bindfaden.*) They are used with *der Faden, das Seil, das Tau, die Leine, der Schnürsenkel, das Netz, die Saite, der Draht, das Band, die Kette,* and *der Film* (usually intr., thus *reißen*). *Das Glied* (link) *einer Kette bricht* because it is hard, but *eine Kette,* being flexible, *reißt.* Both words denote an unintentional break. If it is deliberate, **durchreißen** is used. *Kannst du den Faden durchreißen?*

> *Der Hund zerrte heftig an der Leine und hat sie zerrissen. Die Leine ist gerissen, als der Hund daran*
> zerrte. *Als der Geiger zu spielen anfing, riß eine Saite.*
> *Der Faden ist schon wieder gerissen. Er hält dem Druck der Nähmaschine nicht stand.*
> *Der Bindfaden ist sehr dünn. Er reißt sehr leicht.*

Zerreißen can also be used intr., but involves a difference in degree from *reißen*, implying either a more forceful separation of the parts, *Das Seil zerriß plötzlich in zwei Stücke,* or breaks in several places, *Das Netz zerriß.*

2. Break = 'violate by failure to follow or act in accordance with'. *I break the law/an agreement/a promise.*

i. Although *der Gesetzesbrecher, Rechtsbrecher,* and *der Rechtsbruch* exist, *brechen* is now found only in elevated language with the equivalents of *law* etc. as obj. The usual vs. with an obj. like *Gesetz, Vorschrift, Verordnung, Regel,* or *Bestimmung* are now **verstoßen gegen** and **übertreten.**

> *Ein Schüler, der gegen die Schulordnung verstößt, muß mit Bestrafung rechnen.*
> *Er ist vierzig Jahre lang unfallfrei gefahren und hat die Verkehrsvorschriften nie übertreten/hat nie*
> *gegen die Verkehrsbestimmungen verstoßen.* *Wir übertraten aus Versehen ein Landesgesetz.*

ii. Brechen is still used with ns. which presuppose an agreement between two or more people, such as *ein Versprechen, sein Wort, ein Eid, ein Tabu, ein Vertrag, eine Vereinbarung, ein Abkommen, der Waffenstillstand,* or *ein Gelübde.* With *der Termin,* 'appointment', the usual v. is **nicht einhalten**, not to keep. Cf. APPOINTMENT and KEEP 1. iii.

> *Die Rebellen drohten, den Waffenstillstand zu brechen, falls die Regierung ihre Truppen weiter ver-*
> *stärkte.*
> *Das Unternehmen war in finanzielle Schwierigkeiten geraten und mußte den Vertrag mit einem*
> *Rohstofflieferanten brechen.*

Es würde uns nie einfallen, diese Vereinbarungen zu brechen. Sie bieten uns so viele Vorteile.

3. Cases in which **brechen** corresponds to **break**.

i. Of arms, legs, etc. *Er hat sich den Arm gebrochen.*

ii. Of the heart. *Der Anblick des Elends unter den halb verhungerten Menschen hat ihr fast das Herz gebrochen.*

iii. Brechen means 'to make ineffective or overcome' with objs. like *Widerstand, Stolz, Willen, Macht, Tyrannei, eine Blockade, ein Streik,* etc. Related uses: *Jmd. hat den Weltrekord gebrochen. Er hat sein Schweigen gebrochen,* broke his silence, began to reveal what he knew.

Die Eltern haben endlich den Trotz des Jungen gebrochen.

Ist es der indonesischen Armee gelungen, den Widerstand in Osttimor zu brechen?

Der Bann ist gebrochen (the spell is broken).

be broken in will or strength. *Nach der Niederlage bei Waterloo war Napoleon ein gebrochener Mann. Jmds. Lebensmut schien gebrochen zu sein.*

iv. Of water, waves, etc. *Eine Mole* (breakwater) *bricht die Wellen. Eine Reihe von Bäumen bricht die Kraft des Windes.* With waves as subj., **sich brechen** is used. *Die Wellen brechen sich an den Felsen.*

v. Break with s.o./sth. is **brechen mit**. *Wir müssen mit solchen sinnlosen Traditionen brechen.*

Mit meiner Familie/Mit der Vergangenheit will ich nicht vollständig brechen.

vi. *Seine Stimme bricht,* is breaking.

4. Derivatives of **brechen** which correspond to meanings carried by **break** or **break** + a prep.

i. Anbrechen means 'to begin'. Thus *Der Tag bricht an,* day or dawn breaks. *Anbrechen* occurs also with ages or epochs as subj. *Mit dem Sieg der Revolution im März 1848 glaubten viele Mitteleuropäer, daß ein neues Zeitalter für die Menschheit angebrochen sei.* (*Anbrechen* also means 'to start to use' a supply of some kind. *Ich habe die Tafel Schokolade angebrochen.*)

ii. When trans. **aufbrechen** means 'to break open by force'. *Sie haben die Tür/den Schrank/das Auto/den Kiosk aufgebrochen. Man bricht eine Straße/eine Betondecke auf,* breaks it up. In intr. use *aufbrechen* means 'to break or burst' applied to abscesses or boils, *Das Geschwür brach auf,* to wounds, *Die alte Wunde ist wieder aufgebrochen,* and to flowers and buds, *Die Knospe bricht auf.*

iii. Break + obj. or **break through** = 'make a way through'. *The excited crowd broke the barrier/broke through the police cordon.* With a following n., the usual word is inseparable **durchbrechen**. When no n. follows, i.e. when what is broken through is understood, separable **durchbrechen** is used. Thus *Der Mittelstürmer hat die Verteidigungslinie durchbrochen* and *Der Mittelstürmer ist durchgebrochen.* The obj. of inseparable *durchbrechen* can also be *der Teufelskreis,* 'vicious circle', and *der Kreislauf,* 'cycle' = 'a series of events or processes that is repeated again and again, always in the same order'. *Ist es nicht möglich, den Kreislauf von Boom und Rezession zu durchbrechen?*

Die aufgeregte Menge durchbrach den Polizeikordon/die Barriere.

Die Zuschauer haben die Absperrung durchbrochen und sind auf das Spielfeld gelaufen.

Der Düsenjäger hat die Schallmauer durchbrochen.

Unsere Truppen/Die Panzer sind an der vordersten Linie nach schweren Kämpfen durchgebrochen.

Bundesjustizminister Kinkel erklärte, wenn die (terroristische) Rote-Armee-Fraktion bereit sei, auf Gewalt zu verzichten, sei das eine Chance, den Kreislauf zu durchbrechen.

(Note: *Nach vier Regentagen brach die Sonne endlich durch die Wolken.*)

iv. Break = 'disrupt the continuity of an action or of sth. uniform'. *Sth. broke the silence/the monotony.* **Unterbrechen** expresses this idea. *To break a journey is eine*

Reise/Fahrt unterbrechen. To break the silence among people, *das Schweigen unter-brechen. To break natural silence* or *stillness* is *die Stille unterbrechen. Etw. unterbrach den Fluß der Unterhaltung.* It occurs with words denoting uniformity in time, *Der Besuch unterbrach für ein paar Tage die Einförmigkeit seines einsamen Lebens,* and in space, *Kein Baum unterbrach die Eintönigkeit der Steppe. Unterbrechen* is used with *Bahn-/Telefonverbindungen* where E. has *cut* or *cut off.* Hence *Die Telefonverbindungen nach Berlin wurden unterbrochen,* 'cut', and *Mein Telefongespräch nach Frankfurt wurde unterbrochen,* 'cut off, interrupted'. *Spiele oder Verhandlungen, die unterbrochen wer-den,* stop only for a time; *wenn sie abgebrochen werden,* they are broken off com-pletely. With *Beziehungen,* 'relations', either personal, commercial, or diplomatic, **abbrechen** is used. *Das Land X hat die diplomatischen Beziehungen zu dem Land Y abgebrochen.*

> *Der Kaufmann hat die Beziehungen zu der Lieferfirma abgebrochen.*

v. Break one thg. **off** another is now **abbrechen**, though *brechen* is possible in more poetical language. *Abbrechen* is also intr. *Der Henkel ist abgebrochen.*

> *Wir haben die Zweige vom Baum abgebrochen. Also Ich habe den Bleistift/die Bleistiftspitze abge-brochen. (Ich habe den Bleistift gebrochen* means that I broke it in two.)

vi. Losbrechen, 'to begin suddenly and with force', is applied both to natural and fig. storms. Sometimes it must be translated as *break out.*

> *Ein Sturm/Ein Gewitter/Ein Regenguß brach los.*   *Ein Tumult/Lauter Jubel brach los.*
> *Ein Sturm der Entrüstung/des Beifalls brach los.*   *Über diese Frage ist ein Streit losgebrochen.*

vii. Break out of. Hervorbrechen is 'to break or burst out of' an ambush, hiding place, etc.

> *Die Soldaten brachen aus dem Hinterhalt/aus dem Gehölz/aus ihren Verstecken hervor.*

Where imprisonment is implied, **ausbrechen aus** is the appropriate v.

> *Zwei Häftlinge sind aus dem Gefängnis ausgebrochen.*
> *Ein Löwe brach aus dem Käfig aus.*

5. i. Of mechanical devices, **be broken**, **break [down]**, **break**. The frequently heard word **kaputt** is applied to a large range of things which do not work properly. *Meine Uhr/Der Lichtschalter ist kaputt.* **Defekt** is a formal syn. *Die Tür öffnet sich nicht—der Mechanismus ist wohl defekt.* The intr. v. corresponding to **break down** is **kaputtgehen**. *Die Waschmaschine ist kaputtgegangen.* The trans. v. **kaputtmachen** means 'to break a mechanical device'. *Das Kind hat das Spielzeug kaputtgemacht.*

> *Der Fernseher ist kaputt. Wir müssen ihn reparieren lassen.*
> *Nimm die Uhr nicht auseinander! Du verstehst nichts davon und machst sie nur kaputt.*

ii. Break down in relation to a car is **eine Panne haben**. There are two construc-tions. *Das Auto hatte eine Panne* or *Wir hatten mit dem Wagen eine Panne.*

iii. Break down in relation to negotiations is **zusammenbrechen**, to collapse. *Die Verhandlungen sind schon am dritten Tag zusammengebrochen—niemand war bereit, Konzessionen zu machen.*

6. *I'm* **broke** = 'have no money' is usually **Ich bin pleite**. Syns. are **blank** and **abge-brannt**. *Leider kann ich dir nicht aushelfen, ich bin im Augenblick selbst blank/pleite/abge-brannt. Pleite* is a colloquial word for **bankrott**, bankrupt. **Bankrott gehen** or **pleite gehen** and **Bankrott** or **pleite machen** mean 'to go bankrupt or broke'. Another exp. is *Die Firma* **ging in Konkurs**. The act. form, *These losses broke the firm,* is **ruinieren**, colloquially **kaputtmachen**.

> *Völlig blank/pleite reiste er nach Hause.*   *Ich bin schon wieder pleite.*
> *Wegen der Rezession sind viele kleine Firmen Bankrott/pleite gegangen/haben viele kleine Firmen Bankrott/pleite gemacht/sind viele kleine Firmen in Konkurs gegangen.*
> *Die hohen Verluste hatten die Firma ruiniert/kaputtgemacht.*
> *Jeder Supermarkt ruiniert viele kleine Geschäfte/macht viele kleine Geschäfte kaputt.*

broad *adj.* Some senses of **wide** *adj.* **Broad** and **wide** do not differ in their basic meaning 'to have an ample extent from side to side, a relatively large distance between sides or limits'. In some cases they are interchangeable. A road or river can be wide or broad, although there is a subtle distinction in that **broad** suggests imposing size. **Wide** is preferred when an actual measurement is given or implied. With parts of the body, only **broad** is possible, *a broad back, broad shoulders,* but with clothes only **wide** is found, *wide sleeves.* Both have further senses which coincide only in a few cases, such as *broad* or *wide interests. Weit* and *breit* differ in other ways than the E. terms, and it is not possible to express with one G. word the fine distinctions between **broad** and **wide**. (*Weit* also means 'far', *Wie weit ist sie gesprungen?,* and sometimes 'long', *ein weiter Weg.*) The following gives the uses of *breit* and *weit* meaning 'broad, wide'.

1. In giving a value for the width or breadth, only **breit** is possible. *Der Fluß ist 600 Meter breit. Wie breit ist das Zimmer/die Straße? Der Weg ist schmal, nur einen Fuß breit.* (With expressed or implied measurements, *weit* states a distance. *Wir sind nicht sehr weit vom Gipfel. Wie weit ist es bis Adorf?*)

2. Breit is used without a measurement in the sense 'to be a considerable or relatively large distance across', the opposite of *schmal,* narrow. *Eine breite Straße, eine breite Brücke, eine breite Treppe, ein breiter Fluß, ein breiter Gang, ein breiter Gürtel, ein breites Bett, ein breites Band.*
> *Lassen Sie einen breiten Rand!* (margin).

3. Breit only is used with parts of the body. *Ein breiter Rücken. Breite Hüften. Eine breite Nase/Stirn.*

4. Only **weit** is used for clothes and means 'loose' or 'wide'. *Weite Ärmel. Ein weiter Rock. Ich habe in letzter Zeit stark abgenommen, und alle meine Sachen sind mir zu weit.*

5. Both **broad** and **wide** are used without precise measurements in mind to state that something is of great extent. *The broad western plains. Broad lands. The broad lake/sea. The broad/wide Atlantic. The wide world.*
i. *Weit* only has this sense as it means 'extending a long way in all directions', while *breit* denotes only the distance across. *Zum Schloß gehörte ein weiter Park, in dem Rehe grasten.* To express *distant* or *far off, entfernt* is added to *weit. Ein weites Tal* is 'a broad valley', *ein weit entferntes Tal* is 'a distant valley'.
> *Weite Wälder bedeckten das Gebirge.*   *Ein weites Gelände zog sich hin, so weit das Auge reichte.*
> *Als die Bergsteiger die Baumgrenze passiert hatten, breitete sich vor ihnen eine weite Ebene/das weite Meer aus.*   *Er wollte unbedingt in die weite Welt hinaus.*

ii. *Broad sections of the population* is *breite* or *weite Kreise der Bevölkerung,* but the sing. *a broad section* has to be *ein großer Teil der Bevölkerung.* Other expressions are *die breite Masse des Volkes* and *Das spricht eine breite Öffentlichkeit an,* i.e. a large section of the general public.

6. Suggestions for other senses of **broad**.
i. Broad *day[light].* *Heller Tag* is the normal expression, *hellichter Tag* a more emphatic variant.
> *Das Verbrechen geschah am hellen Tag/am hellichten Tag.*
> *Als ich aufwachte, war es hellichter Tag.*

ii. In *a broad hint,* **broad** means 'plain or clear'. Therefore *ein* **klarer/deutlicher** *Hinweis/Wink.*

iii. Broad = 'coarse, indelicate, risqué' is **derb**. *Derber Humor, ein derber Witz.*

iv. *Eine breite Aussprache* is a slow way of speaking in which the vowels are unduly extended. Only if it is clear that a dialect is referred to does it correspond to *broad* *accent* or *broad Cockney*, etc. *Sie hatte eine breite mecklenburgische Aussprache.* Otherwise use **stark**: *ein starker Akzent.*

v. Broad = 'having to do with the main, essential, or general aspects of a problem', 'not minute or detailed'. *In broad outline* is *in groben Zügen* or *in großen Zügen*, which do not differ in meaning. These phrs. can be adapted to translate *broad outline[s]* in other cases. *A knowledge of the broad outline[s] of scientific development* could therefore be *Die Kenntnis der Entwicklung der Naturwissenschaften in großen Zügen. Man beschreibt etw. in großen Zügen*, gives a broad outline of it. If this is not possible, **die Hauptzüge**, 'the main features', may be used. *Eine allgemeine Übereinkunft* is used in the sense of 'a broad agreement', as well as *eine Übereinkunft in großen Zügen*.

> *Die Außenminister hatten eine allgemeine Übereinkunft erzielt und überließen es den Diplomaten, die Einzelheiten auszuhandeln.*

vi. Broad = 'having a wide range, extensive, inclusive, general'. The transl. varies according to the context. *A broad generalization* is *eine* **grobe** *Verallgemeinerung; the widest/broadest sense of the word* is *der* **weiteste** *Sinn des Wortes.* **Allgemein,** 'general' in the sense 'not going into details', or **umfassend,** 'comprehensive, including much', may convey the sense. *Eine allgemeine/umfassende Definition/Frage. Wide* or *broad interests* can be *vielseitige, umfassende*, or *weitgespannt* (extensive) *Interessen.*

vii. People are broad-minded or have a broad mind, views, or sympathies. As well as meaning 'generous with money', **großzügig** is the opposite of *kleinlich*, petty. It implies that someone rises above things which he/she thinks of lesser importance and is tolerant towards the opinions and actions of others, though these are different from his/her own. It is applied to people and their views. *Ein großzügiger Mensch. Eine großzügige Natur.* (The context needs to make the sense clear.) *Von ihnen war keine großzügige Haltung zu erwarten.* **Weitherzig** is less common, but expresses the same idea of tolerance towards the opinions and actions of others that are different from one's own. **Tolerant** is used particularly for political and religious beliefs.

> *Er ist ein weltoffener, erfahrener Mann, dabei weitherzig und zu Kompromissen geneigt.*
> *Du kannst dich ruhig an ihn wenden. Er ist ein gütiger und toleranter Herr.*
> *Bildung sollte die Menschen toleranter machen.*
> *Mit dem sanften Bischof Jeremias verstand sie sich gut. Seine tolerante Haltung gefiel ihr.*

burn v. Order: A–C: The three important vs. and their main uses. D: Other derivatives. E: Sunburnt.

A. Brennen.

1. 'To be (easily, etc.) combustible'. *Trockenes Holz brennt leicht.*

2. 'To burn or be on fire either by accident or by design'. *Es brennt* means that something is on fire.

Das Haus brennt.	*Die Scheune brannte wie Zunder/lichterloh.*
Irgendwo in der Stadt brennt es.	*Das Schiff trieb brennend auf dem Meer.*
Das Feuer brennt heute schlecht/brennt noch nicht.	*Im Kamin brennt ein Feuer.*

Occasionally used in reference to strong emotions. *Haß/Wut brannte in ihm. Er brannte vor Neid und Wut.*

3. Of the sun. 'To be extremely hot'.

> *Die Sonne brannte sehr stark auf die Erde.*   *Leg' dich doch nicht in die brennende Sonne!*
> *Die Sonne brannte auf die Wüste herunter.* Or in elevated style: *Die Sonne brannte . . . hernieder.*

4. Of candles and lights. 'To be burning or on'.

> *Die Kerze brennt nur noch ganz schwach.*   *Nur die Stehlampe brennt.*

5. Sengen und brennen means 'to burn and lay waste' a country etc.

> *Die Horden der Wikinger zogen sengend und brennend durch die Gegend.*

6. 'To burn in [to]'. *Das Muster ist in das Porzellan gebrannt.* Also *eingebrannt.*
Er hat sich mit der Zigarette ein Loch in den Anzug gebrannt.

7. 'To treat with heat, by fire'. *Man brennt Ziegel/Porzellan.*

8. i. Of parts of the body, wounds. 'To be extremely painful'.
Nach dem langen Marsch brannten mir die Fußsohlen.   *Die Wunde brennt.*
Die Augen brennen mir vor Müdigkeit/vom vielen Lesen.

ii. Of things which produce a sharp sensation in the mouth.
Pfeffer brennt auf der Zunge.   *Der Schnaps brannte mir in der Kehle.*

9. Brennen auf/nach, to desire strongly. *Er brannte auf ein Wiedersehen/auf Rache.*

10. Fig. use. *Die brennendsten Fragen bleiben noch offen.*

B. Verbrennen.

1. The general sense is 'to expose to the action of fire'. Therefore
i. Trans. use. 'To destroy by burning', i.e. deliberately. *Sie hat die alten Briefe im Ofen verbrannt. Verbrennen* is also used for burning human beings. *Ketzer wurden im Mittelalter auf dem Scheiterhaufen verbrannt.*
Alte Zeitungen soll man nicht verbrennen, sondern der Altpapiersammlung geben.
Zu dieser Jahreszeit verbrennen viele Leute Laub.   *Wir haben die Abfälle schon verbrannt.*
Ich habe alle Brücken hinter mir verbrannt und kann nicht zurück.

ii. 'To use up or consume by burning'. The obj. is often the amount of fuel used.
Wir haben in diesem Jahr unseren ganzen Kohlevorrat/vier Tonne Holz verbrannt.
Diese Bretter sind viel zu gut zum Verbrennen.

iii. Intr. use. *Etw. verbrennt*, is destroyed by fire, *jmd. verbrennt*, is burnt to death.
Die wichtigsten Dokumente verbrannten/sind verbrannt.
Bei dem großen Brand ist das Haus zu Schutt und Asche verbrannt.
Einige wertvolle Gemälde verbrannten beim Schloßbrand.
Bei dem Flugzeugunglück verbrannten mehrere Menschen.

2. The other meaning is 'to expose to the action of heat'.
i. 'To hurt by contact with a very hot object'. Hence *I burnt myself* is *Ich habe mich verbrannt.* A phr. with *an* or *mit* can be added. *Das Kind hat sich die Finger am Bügeleisen verbrannt.* Or . . . *hat sich mit dem Bügeleisen verbrannt.*
An der heißen Suppe kannst du dir die Zunge/den Mund verbrennen.
Hence **die Verbrennung.** *Er erlitt Verbrennungen ersten und zweiten Grades.*
ii. Of food. 'To burn so that it is unusable'. *Der Kuchen/Das Essen ist [mir] verbrannt.* Cf. *anbrennen.*
iii. Of vegetation, land. 'To be completely dried up by the sun'.
Die Vegetation/Das Land ist von der glühenden Hitze völlig verbrannt.
Die Wiesen waren von der langanhaltenden Hitze total verbrannt.

C. Anbrennen can mean 'to burn' in the sense 'to begin to burn', *Das Holz will nicht anbrennen,* but it is also applied to food when it is spoilt by being subject to heat which is excessive or continues for too long and which causes what is being cooked to stick to the pan or saucepan. Food which is *angebrannt* may still be used; if it is *verbrannt* it is completely ruined. The trans. use *He burnt the cakes* can only be **anbrennen lassen.**
Nach der Sage ließ König Alfred die Kuchen anbrennen.   *Der Braten ist angebrannt.*
Sie hat den Reis anbrennen lassen.   *Milchsuppe brennt leicht an.*

D. Other derivatives of *brennen.*

1. Applied to buildings, ships, cars, railway carriages, etc., **ausbrennen** means that the interior has been completely destroyed by fire.
Der beim Zusammenstoß zertrümmerte Wagen brannte aus.
Da es nicht gelang, den Brand unter Kontrolle zu bringen, brannte das Gebäude aus.

Applied to people *ausbrennen* means 'to lose one's dwelling and possessions as a result of a fire'. *Die Familie war im Krieg ausgebrannt.* With a thing that burns as subj., it means 'to burn itself out'. *Das Feuer im Herd war ausgebrannt.* In reference to people, the past part. *ausgebrannt* can mean 'physically or mentally and emotionally exhausted', 'burnt out'. *Der Läufer Uhlisch scheint völlig ausgebrannt zu sein.*

> *Sie hatte nur eine Woche unter den verhungernden Flüchtlingen gearbeitet, fühlte sich aber leer und ausgebrannt.*

2. Both **abbrennen** and **niederbrennen** mean 'to burn down', the only difference being that the compound with *nieder* is more elevated in tone. Both are trans. and intr.

> *Nachdem die Bewohner die Flucht ergriffen hatten, brannten die Soldaten das Dorf nieder.*
> *Die Scheune brannte bis auf die Grundmauern nieder.*
> *Nur ein Haus wurde abgebrannt* (deliberately).
> *Der Schuppen fing Feuer und brannte ab* (by accident).

Both also occur in a different sense of **burn down**. *Das Feuer ist fast ganz abgebrannt. Die Kerzen sind halb/fast abgebrannt/niedergebrannt.* Also used is *heruntergebrannt.*

E. Sunburnt.

i. Der Sonnenbrand involves pain and discomfort. *Weil ich zu lange in der Sonne gelegen habe, habe ich mir einen Sonnenbrand geholt.* Also *Jmd. hat/bekam/kriegte einen Sonnenbrand.* **Verbrennen** also implies discomfort.

> *Sie hat ein ganz verbranntes Gesicht.*   *Die Sonne hat ihm die Schultern verbrannt.*

ii. [Sun]tan. *Die Sonne hat mich/mein Gesicht/meine Haut* **gebräunt.**

> *Da sie Urlaub in Nordafrika machte, wollte sie sich ein bißchen bräunen.*
> *Die [sonnen]gebräunten Urlauber stiegen aus dem Flugzeug aus.*

Braungebrannt indicates a deeper brown and is probably more common.

> *Sie kehrten braungebrannt aus dem Urlaub in Spanien zurück.*

burst *v.* A few senses.

1. The basic meaning of **burst** is 'to break suddenly, fly apart, break into pieces', especially because of pressure from within.

i. The equivalent is **platzen**, to burst suddenly and often noisily through pressure usually from the inside. It is applied to *eine Tüte*, 'a paper bag', for which E. uses *break* and **burst**, to tyres, balloons, bubbles, etc., *Der Reifen/Der Luftballon/Die Seifenblase platzte*, and to boilers and pipes, *Der überhitzte Kessel ist geplatzt.* (For seams of clothes, for which E. uses *split*, the v. is *aufplatzen. Die Naht platzt auf.*) *Platzen* is also used for the imagined consequences of eating to excess, *Wenn du noch einen Bissen ißt, wirst du platzen*, and for *Bomben, Geschosse, Granaten*, etc., though **explodieren** is now usual. *Die Bombe explodierte im Garten.* With *vor* + a few ns., *platzen* means 'to be unable to contain oneself', 'to be bursting with' rage etc. *Er platzte vor Neid/Wut/Ärger/Neugier. Wir platzten beinahe vor Lachen.* With things planned or begun, *platzen* means 'to fail' or 'come to nothing', or with dishonest ones 'to be found out'. *Das Schwindelunternehmen ist geplatzt.*

> *Ich habe so viel in die Tüte gesteckt, daß sie geplatzt ist.*
> *Da das Wasser gefroren ist, ist das Rohr geplatzt.*
> *Etwa zehn Meter von uns platzte eine Granate.*
> *Ein Reifen platzte einmal, als ich bei hoher Geschwindigkeit fuhr.*
> *Die Mine explodiert in dem Moment, wo ein Mensch oder Tier darauf tritt.*
> *Sein Vorhaben ist geplatzt, weil ihm das Geld ausging.*

ii. Zerplatzen, which implies that nothing remains when the object bursts, is sometimes used as a stronger variant on *platzen* when this condition is fulfilled. *Die Seifenblase/Die Bombe zerplatzte. Raketen stiegen in den Himmel und zerplatzten.*

Bersten now belongs to literary language and is applied to bombs etc. as well as to large natural objects which consist of hard material. *Die Eisdecke am Fluß ist geborsten. Mit einem dumpfen Geräusch barst das Hauptleitungsrohr.* One still encounters, however, *Der Saal war zum Bersten voll* as well as *zum Platzen voll.* The not very common **zerbersten** means 'to break into pieces with great force'. *Bei dem Erdbeben zerbarsten viele Häuser. Die riesigen Tanks hielten dem Druck nicht stand und zerbarsten.*

2. Burst into or **out**, used in expressions like *S.o. burst into tears* or *burst out laughing*, is **ausbrechen**, to begin suddenly to show signs of some emotion. It also translates *to break [out] into a laugh.*

   Sie brachen in [lautes/fröhliches] Lachen/Gelächter aus.
   Die Klasse brach in ein wildes Geschrei/in Kichern aus.
   Das Kind brach in heftiges Weinen aus.   *Als er seinen Feind sah, brach er in Wut aus.*
   Das kleine Mädchen brach in Tränen aus, als sie merkte, daß ihre Mutter nirgendwo zu sehen war.

Herausplatzen, used without a phr., means 'to burst out laughing' if laughter is clear from the context.

   Hatte ich bisher mit Mühe das Lachen unterdrückt, länger war es unmöglich, ich platzte heraus.
   Ich mußte mich sehr zusammennehmen, um nicht laut herauszuplatzen.

Herausplatzen also corresponds to **burst out** when this means 'to say or tell s.o. sth. unexpectedly and impetuously'. It is used alone or with *mit.*

   'Ich habe eine wichtige Nachricht für Sie', platzte er heraus.
   Wenn der Junge anfängt zu reden, platzt er mit allen Fragen heraus, die ihm gerade einfallen, wie peinlich sie auch sein mögen.

3. Burst into = 'to come suddenly and impetuously' into a room etc. is **hereinplatzen**, if seen from the perspective of someone in the room, or **hineinplatzen**, if seen by someone outside it.

   Als wir beim Essen waren, platzten Onkel und Tante herein.
   Du kannst doch nicht so in mein Zimmer hereinplatzen, ohne auch nur zu klopfen.
   Ich hatte dem Kollegen etw. Wichtiges mitzuteilen, platzte aber in eine wichtige Arbeitsbesprechung hinein, von der ich nichts wußte.

4. Some trans. uses.
i. As well as 'to blow up', as in *Die Soldaten sprengten die Brücke,* **sprengen** means 'to burst or break' bonds or barriers both lit. and fig.

   Der Gefangene hatte seine Fesseln/seine Ketten gesprengt.
   Diese Ideen sprengten die Schranken/Grenzen des herkömmlichen Denkens.

ii. *The river* **burst** *its banks* is *Der Fluß* **trat über** *die Ufer* if the water rose so high that it flowed over the banks and covered the land round about. If a wall constructed to keep back the water is meant and this is breached, the v. is *Der Fluß/Das Wasser* **durchbrach** *den Damm,* broke through/burst the dam/wall. The intr. v. *The dam broke/burst* can only be *Der Damm* **brach.** *Durchbrechen* is used for bursting or breaking through other barriers. Cf. BREAK 4. iii.

5. For **burst** in relation to a boil, abscess, etc. cf. **aufbrechen** under BREAK 4. ii.

bury *v.* funeral *n.*

1. Bury = 'to dispose of a corpse by placing it in the earth, a grave, or tomb or by consigning it to the water'.
i. Beerdigen, which means 'to inter with the due funeral rites', refers usually to the ceremony. It is the normal word, whereas **beisetzen** and **bestatten** are more elevated terms which are appropriate when more than the usual ceremony is involved. *Die Gefallenen wurden mit militärischen Ehren beigesetzt/bestattet. Der verstorbene Graf wurde in der Familiengruft bestattet/beigesetzt.* They are, however, sometimes

used as refined variants on *beerdigen*. *Beisetzen* is used for burial at sea. *Sie wurde auf hoher See beigesetzt*. *Bestatten* is a general term for disposal of the dead and is used for forms other than burial as well as in descriptions of funeral rites of other peoples. All three words are used only for human beings.

Der Verstorbene wird morgen nachmittag auf dem Stadtfriedhof beerdigt.
Alle Familienmitglieder werden in dem Mausoleum beigesetzt/bestattet.
Dieser Stamm bestattet seine Toten sitzend auf dem steilen Abhang eines Berges.

ii. Begraben can be a syn. of *beerdigen*. *Sie wurde mit großem Pomp/unter großer Anteilnahme der Bevölkerung begraben*. It need not, however, refer to a ceremony and is used when saying where a person is buried or that someone was buried rather than cremated. It can mean 'to put in the earth without ceremony' and is used for animals as well as for people.

Die Flüchtlinge begruben den Toten bei Nacht und Nebel in ungeweihter Erde.
Wir haben den Hund am Ende des Gartens begraben.   *Es liegen drei Kaiser begraben in Prag.*

iii. Related ns. **Das Begräbnis** and **die Beerdigung** are the usual equivalents of **funeral** or *burial*, while **die Beisetzung** and **die Bestattung** are more refined expressions.

Die Beerdigung findet morgen nachmittag statt.   *Viele nahmen an dem Begräbnis teil.*

iv. *Scharren* means 'to scrape or scratch with the feet' and is mostly used for birds and animals. *Ein Tier scharrt seine Beute ein*, it scratches a hole in the ground and buries the prey. Applied to a human corpse or an animal carcass, the syns. **einscharren** and **verscharren** mean 'to put in a shallow hole and cover with earth without much care or affection'.

Der Verbrecher hat sein Opfer eingescharrt.
Noch in den letzten Wochen und Tagen des Krieges sind viele der eingekerkerten Widerstandskämpfer nachts von SS-Kommandos hinausgetrieben und durch Genickschuß getötet oder erhängt, in Massengräbern verscharrt worden.

2. Begraben is used when people, villages, etc. are buried under the rubble of a collapsed building, avalanche, landslide, etc. *Unter sich* is often added when an avalanche, landslide, etc. is the subj.

Schlammassen rutschten den Berg hinunter und begruben das ganze Dorf unter sich.
Ein Erdbeben zerstörte fast die ganze Stadt. Ein Junge, der unter den Trümmern [lebendig] begraben wurde, konnte erst drei Tage später gerettet werden.

A fig. meaning is 'to put out of sight or mind'. *Man begräbt Pläne, Hoffnungen, Träume*, 'gives them up', or *begräbt einen Streit*, 'consigns it to oblivion'.

Die Hoffnung auf eine baldige Versetzung mußte er begraben.
Das sind längst begrabene Wünsche/Träume. Ich sah ein, daß sie sich unmöglich verwirklichen ließen.
Wir sollten diesen alten Streit endlich begraben.

3. Vergraben means 'to place in the earth and cover with soil'. The aim may be to hide something which can be retrieved later, but it can also suggest disposing of things in this way or preventing them falling into others' hands. It usually implies an intention.

Der Hund hat den Knochen im Garten vergraben.   *Der Mörder vergrub die Mordwaffe im Wald.*
Die Piraten gingen auf einer unbewohnten Insel an Land und vergruben den Schatz, den sie erbeutet hatten.
Hier gibt es keine Mülleimer, deshalb muß man alle Abfälle vergraben.

To state that a letter etc. was unintentionally buried under [a pile of] other things, *vergraben* is usual, but *begraben* also occurs. *Dieser Aufsatz lag irgendwo zwischen meinen Papieren vergraben—war er für dich? Vergraben* is used for burying one's face in one's hands. *Sie vergrub das Gesicht in beide Hände.* **Sich vergraben** means 'to occupy oneself intensively with sth.', *Er vergrub sich in seine Arbeit*, and can suggest withdrawing from the world, *Nach dem Skandal hat er sich auf dem Land vergraben.*

With an animal as subj., it means 'to cover itself with earth'. *Maulwürfe vergraben sich in der Erde.*

business *n.* The basic sense of **business** is 'that with which one is busy'. The range of meanings that have developed from this sense have G. equivalents which are seldom the same word.

1. Business = 'an activity engaged in as normal or logical and usually extending over a considerable period of time', 'a person's duty or function'. *Study is the main business of a student. Historians are scholars whose business it is to explain the past to us.* The main equivalent is **die Aufgabe**. **Die Pflicht**, 'duty', would stress moral obligation.

    Das Lernen ist die Hauptaufgabe eines Studenten/eines Schülers.
    Historiker sind Gelehrte, deren Aufgabe es ist, uns die Vergangenheit zu erklären.
    Es ist die Aufgabe/die Pflicht eines Lehrers, die Schüler zu unterrichten.

2. Business = 'that on which one is engaged at a particular time', 'an activity engaged in towards an immediate end and usually extending over a limited period'. *What business brings you/him to this part of town? What is your business here at the moment? Make it your business to find out!* A possible n. for **business** is **die Angelegenheit**, matter. *Welche Angelegenheit bringt Sie hierher?* The simplest way to deal with it is to omit *business* and translate the rest as *Was bringt Sie hierher/in diesen Teil der Stadt?* A simplified alternative is *Was machen Sie hier? She got on with the business of cleaning up* can be *Sie fuhr mit der Aufräumearbeit fort. Make it your business to find out!* can be **Mach es dir zur Aufgabe,** *das zu erfahren!* **Ich lasse es mir angelegen sein** or *Ich lasse mir die Sache angelegen sein,* 'I will make it my concern or business', is stylistically higher. It suggests a moral obligation. An infin. may follow. *Ich werde es mir angelegen sein lassen, möglichst viel über den Fall zu erfahren.*

3. The general sense of **business** discussed in this section is 'a pursuit or occupation, usually of a commercial nature, demanding time and attention and customarily engaged in as a means of livelihood'. *Geschäft* (cf. 3. iv) is the main equivalent, but particular contexts require other words.

i. The business someone is in is the area in which that person works to earn a living. **Business** is thus a syn. of *occupation* or *trade. They must apply themselves to their business. What business is he in? What is his business? They are in the hotel business.* The most comprehensive term is **der Beruf**, 'occupation', which covers all work including professions and trades. It is broader than **business**. *Das Sammeln von alten Waffen ist mein Beruf, nicht mein Hobby. Jmd. übt einen Beruf aus,* carries on a profession or trade. (Professions are called *freie Berufe* if it is necessary to distinguish them from other *Berufe.*) A *trade* which has to be learnt, i.e. a skilled one, is **das Handwerk. Das Gewerbe** is a legal and bureaucratic term which covers trades and small and medium-sized businesses, e.g. *das Hotel- und Gaststättengewerbe,* but excludes agriculture, forestry, fishing, and mining. *Gewerbetreibende* are people running such businesses. *To run or carry on a business* is *ein Handwerk/Gewerbe betreiben* or *ausüben.* Both *Handwerk* and *Gewerbe* are used in fixed expressions in a general way without any restriction as to the kind of work. *Jmd. versteht sein Handwerk* can be said of anyone who knows his/her job or business. *Dieser Fernsehmechaniker versteht sein Handwerk.* (*Sein Geschäft verstehen* is also used.) *Er suchte Leute, die ein Gewerbe daraus machten, Bürger der Ostblockstaaten heimlich in den Westen zu überführen.*

    Was ist er von Beruf? Was ist sein Gewerbe? Answer to both: *Er ist Bäcker/Klempner.*
    Er konzentriert sich auf seinen Beruf und hat nur ein paar andere Interessen.

Niemand sollte einen Beruf ausüben, für den er nicht qualifiziert ist.
Wir brauchen einen Rechtsanwalt, der sein Handwerk versteht.
Der Waffenhandel ist ein schmutziges Gewerbe.   *Das Hotelgewerbe muß sehr einträglich sein.*

ii. Die Branche can denote a particular branch or field of economic activity. *Die ganze Branche verzeichnet einen Rückgang im Umsatz.* For individuals it means 'line of business'. *Was ist seine Branche? In welcher Branche ist er [tätig]? Er ist in der Wollbranche [tätig].* (*Tätig sein*, to WORK, be employed.)

iii. Business when opposed to pleasure or recreation is usually **die Arbeit**. *Arbeit und Vergnügen sollten sich abwechseln.*

iv. Business = 'a commercial or industrial enterprise regarded as a going concern'. The usual equivalent is **das Geschäft**. There are numerous compounds such as *Exportgeschäft, Geschäftsviertel, Geschäftsmann, Geschäftsbrief, Geschäftszeiten, Geschäftsleben, Geschäftsführer, Geschäftsinhaber.* While *ein Geschäft* is mostly of small or medium size, **das Unternehmen** is used for large industrial and commercial enterprises or businesses.

Sie hat ein eigenes Geschäft angefangen/aufgemacht, das gut zu gehen scheint.
Die Familie hat sehr viel in das Geschäft hineingesteckt/investiert.
Er hat das Geschäft seines Vaters übernommen und es ausgebaut. Seitdem blüht es auf.
Alle Mitglieder der Familie hatten einen ausgeprägten Geschäftssinn.
Der Rauschgifthandel ist ein krummes Geschäft.

v. When **business** is a collective term for all the people running such enterprises, as in *Business is for/against agricultural subsidies*, either **Die Geschäftswelt** *ist für/gegen Agrarsubventionen*, which would include all businesses, or **die Geschäftsleute und die Unternehmer** can be used.

vi. Das Geschäft is also applied to the place where a business is conducted and has become a common syn. of *der Laden*, shop. *Business premises* are *die Geschäftsräume.* In the sense of 'shop, business', **die Handlung** also occurs in certain combinations or alone if it is clear that one of these types of business is meant. *Die Buchhandlung, Blumenhandlung, Gemüsehandlung, Lederhandlung, Weinhandlung.*

Die Geschäfte öffnen um 9 Uhr und schließen um 17.30 (shops and/or businesses).
Ich war den ganzen Tag im Geschäft.   *Ich gehe morgen nicht ins Geschäft.*
Unser Geschäft befindet sich im Erdgeschoß.

4. i. In *We do business with several French firms*, **business** is a collective n. meaning 'one or more commercial transactions'. A single transaction can be called a piece of business or a business deal. In *Business is brisk/improving*, **business** is a collective term for the state of business or business activity. **Das Geschäft** can mean 'a single transaction, a piece of business, or a [business] deal'. *Die ganze Zeit haben wir kein einziges Geschäft abgeschlossen/gemacht. Er witterte ein Geschäft. Er hat mit dem Grundstück ein glänzendes Geschäft gemacht*, a very profitable deal/piece of business. The pl. is used when **business** refers to several or continuous transactions. *Wir machen Geschäfte mit China.* The pl. is also common in the second collective sense, 'business activity, sales, turnover'. *Die Geschäfte gehen gut/schlecht/flott.* The sing. also occurs, but is ambiguous as it could mean a particular person's business. *Das Geschäft ist flau.*

Der Betrieb macht Geschäfte mit mehreren deutschen und französischen Firmen.
Glücklicherweise hat der Firmenleiter das betrügerische Geschäft durchschaut.
Was machen die Geschäfte? Was macht das Geschäft? (Both = 'How's business?')
Das Geschäft stockt/belebt sich.

ii. When the state, not of a particular business, but of the level of economic or business activity of a country or of a sector of the economy is meant, G. uses **die Konjunktur**, the basic sense of which is 'business, trade, or economic cycle'. It is also used for the level of business activity at a particular time with the implication that this can develop one way or the other.

Die Konjunktur ist gut/normal/stabil/rückläufig (declining, deteriorating).
Die Regierung versucht, die Konjunktur zu beleben/anzukurbeln.

In a particular area: *Die Konjunktur in der Schiffbauindustrie ist rückläufig.* It also means 'good economic activity', a shortened form of **die Hochkonjunktur**, boom.

Zwei Jahre nach der Rezession setzte eine neue Konjunktur ein.
Im Augenblick herrscht Konjunktur/Hochkonjunktur.

iii. In *The firm is looking for business*, **business** means 'orders for work to be carried out'. This is **der Auftrag**, 'order for goods or services', but as an equivalent of **business** it is usually in the pl.

Die Firma sucht [neue] Aufträge.   Die Auftragslage ist befriedigend.

5. Two phrases.
i. On business. The usual word is now **geschäftlich**. The expressions *in Geschäften* and *Geschäfte halber* may still be found in literary prose, but not in commercial language. *Sind Sie geschäftlich in London oder zum Vergnügen? Geschäftlich* translates the adj. *business* and sometimes *businesslike*, but it is not used with people. *Unsere geschäftlichen Interessen. Er sprach in geschäftlichem Ton. Ein geschäftstüchtiger Mann* is one who is businesslike or efficient or smart in business dealings.
ii. In business. *A person is in business* can be *Er ist Geschäftsmann* or *Sie ist Geschäftsfrau* or *Er/Sie betreibt ein Geschäft.* A general expression meaning that someone works in business or industry rather than as a civil servant, lawyer, etc. is *Er/Sie ist in der freien Wirtschaft tätig.* If a particular business is meant, see *Branche* under 3. ii. *In my business* is *in meiner Branche. The firm is still in business* is *Die Firma besteht noch. The firm is back in business* becomes, when a manufacturing plant is referred to, *Die Firma hat den Betrieb wieder aufgenommen (der Betrieb,* operation).

6. Business also refers to matters or affairs which someone has to discuss or deal with. These can be private and not of a commercial nature. *We have some important business to talk about. Wer die Geschäfte führt,* 'deals with or attends to the business of any organization', e.g. a university department or a club. *Der Geschäftsführer* is 'the secretary or manager who looks after the day-to-day affairs of the organization'. In the personal sphere the normal words are **die Angelegenheit** and the less formal **die Sache**, both of which mean 'matter'. *Geschäfte* is possible, but suggests commercial matters of some kind. Cf. 2.

Ein paar dringende/wichtige Angelegenheiten/Sachen, die meine Familie betreffen, muß ich nächste
*   Woche in Launceston erledigen* (deal with/attend to some urgent business/matters).
Während meiner Abwesenheit hat er alle Geschäfte für mich besorgt/erledigt.

7. Business can mean 'a matter with which one has the right to meddle, sth. felt to be s.o.'s particular concern, responsibility, or right' and is frequently, but not always, neg. There is no one G. equivalent so that the idea of each E. expression has to be rendered. *Mind your own business!* is *Kümmere dich um deine Angelegenheiten! That's my business* is *Das ist meine Sache. That is no business of yours/none of your business: Das geht dich nichts an,* doesn't CONCERN you. *S.o. has no business [being] here/in a place* or *going there/to a place: Er hat hier/dort nichts zu suchen,* which implies that the person should not be or has no right to be in the place. *Etw./nichts zu suchen haben* is also used in questions. *Was hat er denn hier zu suchen? You had no business hitting him* means that you should not have hit him and could be *Du hättest ihn nicht schlagen dürfen* or *hattest keinen Anlaß/Grund, ihn zu schlagen,* had no cause/reason.

8. Business is used vaguely meaning 'affair' or 'matter' and usually expressing some degree of contempt or impatience. *It's an odd/bad business. I'm fed up with the* *whole business. I'm sick and tired of the whole stupid business.* **Die Sache**, 'matter or affair', is neutral in tone, but with certain adjs. it can be like **business**. **Die Affäre** is an unpleasant and dishonest matter, often related to politics. **Die Geschichte** is also used colloquially in the sense of 'an unpleasant or disagreeable matter'. *This boat business must be part of a larger (crooked) scheme* could be *Die Sache/Geschichte mit dem Boot muß Teil eines größeren Schwindelunternehmens sein.*

> *Das ist eine böse/gefährliche/riskante/üble/unangenehme/dumme/blöde/faule/krumme Sache.*
> *Ich will nichts mehr mit dieser Sache/Geschichte zu tun haben.*
> *Eure Streitereien kann ich nicht mehr mit anhören. Die ganze Sache hängt mir zum Hals heraus.*
> *Man wollte ihn in eine dunkle Affäre hineinziehen.*   *Ich bin in diese dumme Affäre verwickelt.*
> *Das ist eine schlimme/böse/üble Geschichte.*
> *Ich habe die ganze Geschichte satt.*   *Die ganze Sache/Geschichte stinkt mir.*

busy *adj.* **Busy** is applied to: 1. Living beings, mostly people. *A busy woman.* 2. Periods of time. *A busy day.* 3. Places. *A busy intersection.* No one G. term covers all three areas.

1. i. Applied to people and sometimes animals, **busy** means 'engaged in sth. requiring time and attention', 'occupied', 'not idle or at leisure'. The equivalent is **beschäftigt**, but when used attributively, as in *The editor is a busy man*, it can only be **vielbeschäftigt** or **sehr beschäftigt**. *Der Redakteur ist ein vielbeschäftigter Mann* or *ein sehr beschäftigter Mann.* A stylistically slightly higher alternative to the predicative use *Jmd. ist beschäftigt* is **Jmd. hat zu tun.** *I'm busy at the moment—could you come back in an hour's time?* could be either *Ich bin im Augenblick/im Moment/momentan beschäftigt* or *Ich habe im Augenblick zu tun—könnten Sie in einer Stunde wiederkommen? Less busy is Könnten Sie wieder kommen, wenn ich weniger beschäftigt bin/weniger zu tun habe?* or *. . . wenn ich nicht so viel zu tun habe.*

> *Der Direktor ließ durch die Sekretärin ausrichten, daß er im Moment beschäftigt sei/zu tun habe.*
> *Unterbrich mich bitte nicht! Du siehst doch, daß ich beschäftigt bin/zu tun habe.*

ii. Busy with sth., as in *She was busy with the report*, and **busy** doing sth., as in *She was busy reading/writing the report*, mean that the activity takes all the person's attention. **Gerade dabei sein, etw. zu tun** means 'to be engaged in or in the middle of doing sth.' and can be used as an equivalent of the E. continuous tenses. *Ich war gerade dabei, den Koffer zu packen/den Bericht zu schreiben*, I was just packing etc. It is not exactly the same as **busy** but fairly close to it. In *Sie war mit dem Bericht beschäftigt*, **beschäftigt** means either 'occupied with' or 'busy with'. *Beschäftigt* is used with *mit* + a n. denoting an action and with *damit* + infin.: *Sie war mit den Vorbereitungen für die Reise beschäftigt* or *Sie war damit beschäftigt, alles für die Reise vorzubereiten.* The nuance distinguishing **busy** and *occupied* can be conveyed by *voll und ganz* or *vollauf* which mean 'completely'. *Eine Woche lang war ich voll und ganz mit der Organisation . . . beschäftigt* or *. . . mit der Organisation der Reise vollauf beschäftigt. She was busily typing letters* can be *Sie war vollauf damit beschäftigt, Briefe zu tippen.* **Emsig** means 'active' or 'busy', but is no longer much used in the spoken language except perhaps in *eine emsige Biene*. It is still found in the written language. *Die Kinder waren emsig damit beschäftigt, Muscheln für ihre Sandburg zu sammeln.*

iii. As a lit. transl. of **busy** in *to keep s.o. busy* is not used, other expressions must be employed. Common equivalents of *The garden keeps me busy* are *Der Garten* **macht mir viel Arbeit** and **gibt** *mir* **viel zu tun** or colloquially **hält** *mich* **in Trab. Zeit in Anspruch nehmen**, 'to take or require time', can also express the idea, especially with the addition of *stark. Die Übersetzung hat zwei volle/ganze Wochen in Anspruch genommen*, lit. 'required two whole weeks', could translate *kept me busy for . . . Die vielen Sitzungen haben meine Zeit stark in Anspruch genommen* is also close to *kept me* *very busy.* Another transl. is *Mit der Übersetzung hatte ich zwei Wochen lang vollauf zu tun. Let's/We must get busy!* could be *Machen wir uns an die Arbeit!*, simply *An die Arbeit!*, or *Wir müssen doch [endlich] anfangen zu arbeiten.*

2. Busy is used with expressions of time, as in *I've had a busy day,* an idea conveyed by **arbeitsreich**. *Ich hatte heute einen arbeitsreichen Tag.* **Anstrengend**, 'strenuous', is an alternative, or the sent. can be paraphrased as *Ich habe heute mehr erledigen müssen als sonst.*

Nach zwei nicht so arbeitsreichen Wochen bereite ich mich nun im Ernst für die Prüfungen vor.

Die beiden letzten Wochen sind besonders anstrengend gewesen.

3. Places. a **busy** shop, street, port, station, crossing, etc.

i. One sense of **der Betrieb** is 'movement, bustle, commotion'. It suggests a lot of people and activity in shops, streets, towns, offices, exhibitions, etc. *In allen Geschäften herrschte reger Betrieb* or *war viel Betrieb,* all the shops were busy. **Der Hochbetrieb** has the same sense. *Vor den Feiertagen herrscht auf den Bahnhöfen Hochbetrieb.*

In der Vorweihnachtszeit herrscht reger Betrieb/Hochbetrieb in den Geschäften/auf den Straßen.

Sydney ist ein Hafen mit regem Betrieb (a busy harbour; *rege*, 'active, lively', is used with ns. denoting activity, not places like *Hafen*).

In diesem Geschäft/Restaurant ist immer viel Betrieb.

ii. *Eine* **belebte** *Straße* refers also to the people in it.

Wir traten aus der U-Bahn-Station auf eine belebte Geschäftsstraße.

iii. When traffic is meant, **verkehrsreich** and **stark befahren** are the specific terms. Alternatives which cover both people and traffic are **viel/oft/häufig benutzt**. **Hektisch** implies an adverse judgement. The expressions with *Betrieb* can also refer to traffic. *Auf den Straßen der Großstadt herrscht immer starker Betrieb.*

Die Autobahn zwischen Frankfurt und Heidelberg ist eine stark befahrene Strecke.

Das Universitätsgelände liegt zwischen zwei verkehrsreichen Straßen.

Die Bahnlinie ist so stark befahren/so oft benutzt, daß man hier eigentlich eine Überführung bauen müßte und den Bahnübergang beseitigen.

Dies ist eine der belebtesten/hektischsten/am meisten benutzten U-Bahn-Stationen in London.

C

calculate, reckon, work sth. out (numerically) *vs.* Order of treatment:
1. Vs. meaning 'to find out by working with numbers'. 2. Other senses of *rechnen*.
3. Senses of its derivatives. *Rechnen* and its derivatives carry some meanings
expressed by **reckon** and **calculate**. 4. **Reckon** = 'think'.

1. The now somewhat old-fashioned v. **reckon [up]** means 'to ascertain a number, quantity, cost, etc. by counting or by calculation'. **Calculate** means 'to ascertain or determine by mathematical processes' often of some intricacy. *They
reckoned/calculated that production would increase by 5 per cent in the next year. Hire
charges are reckoned/calculated from the date of delivery.* Both are trans., *She calculated
the area*, and intr., *Computers calculate more quickly than human beings. Children reckon
on their fingers.* **Work out** is an everyday syn. of both, but is trans. only. *I've worked
out your share of the expenses to be £10. Rechnen, ausrechnen, berechnen, errechnen*, and
zusammenrechnen express senses related to those of the E. words. While *rechnen* is
mostly intr., the others require an obj.

i. Rechnen, 'to perform mathematical computations', translates **reckon** and **calculate** used intr. *Sie haben stundenlang gerechnet.* Particularly with younger schoolchildren as subj., it is translated as *to do arithmetic. Das Kopfrechnen* is 'mental
arithmetic', and *im Kopf rechnen* 'to calculate in one's head'. In *Der Lehrer unterrichtet
Rechnen*, it would mean 'arithmetic'. Although mostly intr., *rechnen* is sometimes
found with *die Aufgabe*, '(mathematical) exercise', as obj. instead of the usual *ausrechnen*. Cf. 1. iii.

> *Ein Computer rechnet viel schneller als der intelligenteste Mensch.*
> *Mit einem Taschenrechner rechnen kann jeder! Du mußt dir angewöhnen, öfter im Kopf oder auf dem
> Papier zu rechnen. Sonst wirst du das Rechnen verlernen.*
> *Lutz und Sabine rechnen schnell im Kopf und sind immer die ersten, die das Ergebnis haben.*
> *Diese Aufgabe hast du richtig gerechnet.*   *Alle haben die Rechenaufgabe ausgerechnet.*

ii. Zusammenrechnen is limited to one mathematical process, adding up. It corresponds to **reckon up** with expressions such as the costs, how much one owes,
the total, etc. Cf. ADD 1.

> *Wenn man alle Ausgaben zusammenrechnet, so war die Reise doch sehr teuer.*
> *Ich habe alle Kosten zusammengerechnet, und es ergibt sich eine Gesamtsumme von 670 Mark.*

iii. *Ausrechnen, berechnen*, and *errechnen* all mean 'to determine or work out by calculation' and include all arithmetical processes. **Ausrechnen** is a frequently
encountered everyday word like **work out**. **Berechnen** is stylistically higher. It can
be used with the same objs. as *ausrechnen*, but is more appropriate for contexts
presupposing more difficult calculation. **Errechnen** is the most formal word,
implying long and/or careful calculation, that the result is accurate, and that this
is the definitive solution. It is usual in scientific contexts. It can be replaced by
berechnen, but the special implications are lost. It is also used in commercial language. The refl., meaning 'to be calculated from', is occasionally found. *Der
Lebensstandard errechnet sich aus mehreren Faktoren.*

> *Die Schüler rechneten die Zahl bis auf 5 Stellen hinter dem Komma aus (das Komma = 'decimal
> point').*

Wir rechnen die Fläche des Zimmers/die Höhe des Turmes/die Entfernung/den Preis/den Umfang des Kreises aus.

Ich habe noch nicht ausgerechnet, wieviel ich dir schuldig bin.

Die Schülerin wies jede Hilfe ab und war nachher umso stolzer und zufriedener, als sie die schwierige Aufgabe allein ausgerechnet hatte.

Da er in Mathematik sehr begabt war, hatte er die Lösung immer schneller ausgerechnet als die anderen.

Wir haben alle Kosten genauestens berechnet und sind sicher, daß der Kostenvoranschlag richtig ist.

Mit dem Sextanten berechnete der Kapitän die Position des Schiffes und trug sie in die Karte ein.

Die Kosten eines Mietwagens werden vom Tag der Übernahme an berechnet.

Als Summe ihrer Schulden habe ich 2 500 Mark errechnet/ausgerechnet.

Die Wissenschaftler errechneten den Aufprall der Raumkapsel auf die Minute genau.

Die Raumsonde ist von der errechneten Bahn kaum abgewichen.

2. Other meanings of *rechnen*.

i. Rechnen can mean 'to be economical', 'to budget carefully'. *Sie verdient so gut, daß sie nicht zu rechnen braucht. Mit jedem Pfennig rechnen*, to count every penny.

In den ersten Nachkriegsjahren mußten fast alle deutschen Familien mit jedem Pfennig rechnen.

ii. With an obj. which is a quantity, price, or amount of time, **rechnen** does not suggest an accurate calculation and therefore means 'ESTIMATE' or 'calculate roughly'. Cf. 3. iii. It can sometimes be translated as **reckon with**. *Grob, gut, hoch,* and *niedrig gerechnet*, mean '[at] a rough, generous, high, and low estimate' respectively. They are used as phrs. or after *sein*. *Grob gerechnet, brauchen wir zwei Monate für diese Arbeit. Das ist hoch gerechnet*, a generous estimate.

Man rechnet bei diesem Gericht 200 gr. Fleisch pro Person.

Wir rechnen etwa 200 Mark für die Transportkosten.

Alles in allem gerechnet, wird der Ausflug an die 200 Mark kosten.

Für den Rückweg müssen wir zwei Stunden rechnen.

Grob gerechnet, fahren wir noch zwei Stunden.

Gut gerechnet, brauchen wir für die Entfernung vier Tage und 600 Liter Benzin.

300 Mark für eine solche Reparatur—das ist niedrig gerechnet.

iii. Rechnen zu/unter + acc. = 'to reckon as belonging to or being one of a group or class', 'to include or count among'. *Man rechnet Schneider zu den Experten/unter die Experten auf diesem Gebiet.*

Ich rechne die beiden noch zu meinen Freunden/unter meine Freunde.

Man rechnet dieses Hotel zu den besten in der Stadt.

Man rechnet ihn zu den fähigsten Arbeitern.

Zurechnen has the same meaning but takes an obj. and a dat. It is a more learned word and can mean 'to classify as belonging to a group' or 'to attribute to a period'.

Diese Kirche ist der Spätgotik zuzurechnen.   *Er ist dem rechten Flügel der Partei zuzurechnen.*

iv. Rechnen mit/auf + a person or thing means 'to reckon on or rely on'.

Er ist ein Mensch, auf den/mit dem man immer rechnen kann.

Ich rechnete mit der Unterstützung der meisten Kollegen.

Sie rechnete auf seine Hilfe und täuschte sich nicht in den Erwartungen, die sie in ihn gesetzt hatte.

Ich rechne mit deinem Verständnis in dieser Angelegenheit.

Rechnen mit also means 'to reckon on sth.', i.e. 'to feel certain that it will happen', or 'to reckon with sth.', i.e. 'to expect, be prepared for it'. With a clause or infin. it appears in the form *Wir rechnen damit, daß 200 Leute erscheinen*, reckon on 200 people turning up.

Alle rechnen mit einer weiteren Abwertung der französischen Währung.

Obwohl der Arzt sagte, daß wir mit dem Schlimmsten rechnen müßten, ist eine Besserung doch eingetreten.   *Sie rechnet mit guten Noten in Deutsch und Englisch.*

Die Angestellten rechneten fest damit, eine Gehaltserhöhung zu bekommen. Also . . . daß sie . . . bekommen würden.   *Mit so vielen Schwierigkeiten hatte er nicht gerechnet.*

3. Derivatives of *rechnen*.

i. Ausrechnen is used with the refl. dat. meaning 'to find out by thinking', 'to calculate, work out'. *Sie hatte sich ausgerechnet, daß sie mit dem ersparten Geld eine Mittelmeerreise machen könnte.* The result need not be purely numerical. *Er hatte sich gute Erfolgschancen ausgerechnet.* It also expresses the meaning that someone ought to be able to work out the consequences, outcome, etc. for him/herself. *Du kannst dir ja selbst ausrechnen, daß das nicht gut gehen wird/wie das enden wird.*

> *Nach dem Vorstellungsgespräch rechnete er sich gute Chancen aus, die Stelle zu bekommen.*
> *Du könntest dir doch ausrechnen, daß alles nicht so wie geplant verlaufen würde.*
> *Er konnte es sich an den fünf Fingern ausrechnen, wohin solche unausgegorenen Pläne führen würden.*

ii. Berechnen + dat. means 'to charge for', i.e. 'to make s.o. pay for'.

> *Er hat mir für die Arbeit keinen hohen Preis berechnet.*
> *Wir müssen Ihnen das Porto und die Verpackung berechnen.*
> *Für das leicht beschädigte Exemplar berechnen wir Ihnen weniger.*

iii. Berechnen auf means 'to calculate sth. at/to be a number or amount'. Unlike *rechnen* under 2. ii, it suggests accuracy.

> *Der Architekt berechnet die Kosten des Umbaus auf DM 15 000.*
> *Man hat die Bauzeit auf vier Monate berechnet.*
> *Die gesammelten Werke des Autors sind auf fünf Bände berechnet.*

iv. More in the written language **berechnen** means 'to calculate' in the sense of arranging, designing, or planning for a purpose. It may relate to something concrete, *Der Aufzug ist für zehn Personen berechnet,* but frequently refers to producing an effect. It takes an obj., *Der Redner hatte die Wirkung seiner Worte genau berechnet,* and the past part. is found with *sein* and *auf* followed by *Effekt, Wirkung,* and *Schau, Der ganze Auftritt war nur auf Schau berechnet.* It is also used with *darauf* + infin. *Das Gericht war der Meinung, daß die Bemerkungen des Politikers darauf berechnet waren, die Geschworenen zu beeinflussen,* were calculated to influence. (In less formal language: . . . *waren darauf angelegt, die Geschworenen zu beeinflussen.* Cf. AIM 2. iv.)

> *Seine Rede/Sein Auftreten war ganz auf Effekt berechnet.* Also . . . *auf maximalen Effekt berechnet.*
> *Diesen klug berechneten Plan begann er nun Schritt für Schritt auszuführen.*
> *Alle diese Schritte waren bis ins Einzelne berechnet.*

Berechnend is pejorative, suggesting a person who is self-seeking or out for personal advantage. *Er ist schlau und berechnend/ein kalt berechnender Mensch.*

v. Reckon in = 'to include, take into account when reckoning'. *Did you reckon in the cost of the taxi to the airport?* **Rechnen** can be used when a phr. with *in* does not follow.

> *Wir waren zwanzig Personen, die Kinder nicht gerechnet.*
> *Die Reise kostete 500 Mark, die Verpflegung nicht gerechnet.*

Einrechnen, to which *mit* is often added, is a syn. and takes a phr. with *in*. *Sind die Trinkgelder in dem Preis mit eingerechnet?* **Mitrechnen** is a further syn. and takes an obj. but not *in*. *Wir haben sämtliche Spesen mitgerechnet. Hast du die Taxifahrt eingerechnet/mitgerechnet?* (Mitrechnen also means 'to calculate at the same time as s.o. else'. *Ich rechne es aus. Rechne du mit, dann vergleichen wir die Ergebnisse!*)

> *Porto und Verpackung sind bei dem Betrag nicht eingerechnet.*
> *Allein der Flug kostete DM 2 400, Unterkunft und Verpflegung gar nicht mitgerechnet.*

vi. Reckon up with s.o. means 'to settle accounts' with that person both lit. and fig. The *OED* quotes Scott for the fig. use (without *up*): *The blame rests not with thee but with those with whom I hope to reckon roundly.* This expression is still sometimes used: *When the war is over, we'll reckon up with the enemy's sympathizers in our ranks* or *There will be a day of reckoning. To settle accounts* or *scores with* is now usually preferred. **Abrechnen** means 'to settle accounts' in the lit. and fig. senses. Lit. sense:

Am Ende der Woche rechnen wir miteinander ab. In a moral sense: *Sobald die Wahlen vorüber sind, rechnen wir mit den Verrätern in den eigenen Reihen ab. Die Stunde der Abrechnung wird kommen.*

4. The informal use of **reckon** as a syn. of *think* can be expressed by **glauben, denken,** or **meinen.** *Ich glaube/denke, daß ich bis zwei Uhr fertig sein werde. Ich meine, daß sie recht hat.* Cf. THINK 2. An alternative is **annehmen,** to assume. *Ich nehme an, daß wir spätestens um sechs dasein werden.*

call [out, for, on, in], name *vs.* Order of treatment: 1. Discusses *rufen,* which translates **call** = 'say sth. in a loud voice'. 2. Its derivatives. 3. **Call** = 'visit'. 4–8. **Call** = 'give a name to', 'refer to as', and **name.** The senses discussed in 4–8 are expressed by *nennen* and its derivatives.

1. Rufen corresponds to **call** or **call out** when they mean 'to speak loudly or shout so as to be heard at a distance and attract s.o.'s attention'.
i. Rufen is used alone and often with an adv.
> *Ruft da jemand? Ich dachte, ich hörte jmd[n.] rufen.*
> *Ich rief und rief/habe wiederholt gerufen, aber erst nach zwei Stunden kam jmd. zu Hilfe.*
> *Sie ist noch nicht so weit weg, daß sie dich nicht hören wird, wenn du rufst.*
> *Er rief laut/leise/wütend/kräftig/aus Leibeskräften/aufgeregt etc.*

ii. The obj. of **rufen** can be either the person whose attention is to be attracted or what is called, often only a word or name. The latter is direct speech, but it is not always printed as such. *'Hilfe!' rief sie,* but *Sie riefen Feuer. Er rief Hilfe.*
> *Die Mutter rief den Jungen. 'Werner' rief sie.*   *Obwohl sie ihn rief, hat er nicht geantwortet.*
> *Sie riefen mich/meinen Namen vom anderen Ufer des Flusses aus.*
> *Eine Stimme rief etw. Unverständliches aus der Nachbarwohnung.*

iii. A phr. denoting where the person called is to go or what he/she is to do can be added. *Die Mutter rief die Kinder zum Essen/ins Haus.* As in E., the idea of raising one's voice disappears in cases like *einen Arzt/die Feuerwehr/die Polizei rufen* or in *Sie haben mich rufen lassen,* and the place may be only implied. When **call** or **call for** means 'to ask s.o. to come to a place or bring sth.', *rufen* is usually followed by *nach, Der Patient rief nach der Schwester,* but with *Hilfe, um* is normal, *Sie rief um Hilfe.* Also *Sie rief einen Passanten zu Hilfe,* called him to her aid.
> *Das Publikum rief die Schauspieler wiederholt auf die Bühne.*
> *Der Arzt wurde zu dem Patienten gerufen.*   *Wir müssen den Arzt rufen.*
> *Der Gast rief nach dem Ober/nach einem Bier.*   *Der Ertrinkende rief um Hilfe.*

iv. Some other uses of *rufen. Der Vorsitzende rief ein paar Studenten, die den Redner mit Zwischenrufen dauernd unterbrachen, zur Ordnung,* called them to order. *Eine Organisation ins Leben rufen,* to bring or call it into existence. *Rufen* is used with and without an obj. in expressions like *Die Pflicht ruft, Die Arbeit ruft mich.* In radio jargon it is used when asking someone to answer a call. *Alpha 1 ruft Delta 2. Bitte melden!*

2. Derivatives of *rufen.*
i. Zurufen needs a dat. and means 'to call to s.o.', but it implies that a message is communicated. It takes an infin., a clause with *sollen,* or an obj. which is the contents of the message. *Sie riefen uns einen Gruß/einen Befehl/Abschiedsworte zu.*
> *Als ich das Büro verließ, rief sie mir zu, ich sollte morgen pünktlich sein.*
> *Ich rief ihr zu, sich vorzusehen/sich zu beeilen/sie sollte endlich mal die Klappe halten.*
> *Als der Zug anfuhr, rief er ihr noch 'Lebe wohl!' zu.*

ii. Anrufen can mean 'to call to s.o.' but takes an acc. and implies a message, non-compliance with which will result in dire consequences. It is applied to sentries, guards, and the police, or to someone who at least has a gun. It needs a person as obj. and either an infin. or a clause with *sollen*, or direct speech. Hence one use of *der Anruf: Wenn man auf Anruf nicht stehenbleibt, dann wird geschossen.*

> *Der Posten wurde angewiesen, alle Eindringlinge mit den Worten anzurufen: 'Halt! Stehenbleiben! Oder ich schieße!'*
>
> *Ich rief ihn an, stehenzubleiben/er sollte stehenbleiben* (said by guard etc.).

iii. Anrufen now mostly means 'to ring up, telephone, or call s.o. [up]'. *Rufen* is used in this sense only when giving a number at which one can be reached. *Rufen Sie mich unter der Nummer 61 22 46! Der Anruf* is thus 'a telephone call'. *Ich erwarte einen Anruf aus Paderborn.* The question *Who is calling?* is *Wer ist da, bitte?* **Call back** on the telephone is **zurückrufen**. *Ich gehe zu einer Sitzung, die in zwei Minuten anfängt. Kann ich heute nachmittag zurückrufen?* The n. is *der Rückruf. Herr Schneider hat angerufen, während Sie weg waren, und bittet um Rückruf.*

iv. Other meanings of **zurückrufen** are 'to call s.o. back somewhere', *Man rief sie ins Zimmer zurück*, and 'to shout an answer back', *'Ich komme gleich', rief er zurück. Etw. ins Gedächtnis zurückrufen* is 'to recall or call to mind'.

v. Call [out] names, numbers, etc. **Aufrufen** means 'to call one name from a number of names for a special purpose'. It usually implies some kind of authority. *Der Lehrer ruft die Namen der Schüler nach dem Alphabet auf. Wer da ist, sagt 'Hier'.* That would be the equivalent of *calling the roll. Ein Lehrer ruft einen Schüler auf, mit der Übersetzung fortzufahren*, calls his name. *Zeugen werden [zur Aussage] aufgerufen*, the witnesses[' names] are called. *Bei einigen Ärzten werden die Patienten aufgerufen, wenn sie an der Reihe sind.* Thus *Bitte warten Sie, bis Sie aufgerufen werden!*

vi. Ausrufen means 'to announce', 'to make known by calling', though now usually by loudspeaker. *Der Busfahrer ruft die Stationen aus. Die Zeitungsverkäufer riefen die Abendzeitung/die Schlagzeilen aus.* It is used when one person is trying to find another in a railway station, airport, etc. *Der/Die Suchende läßt jmd[n.] [über/durch die Lautsprecher] ausrufen.*

> *Sie ließ ihren Mann über den Informationsschalter im ganzen Flughafen ausrufen.*

(*Ausrufen* also means 'to exclaim'. *'Wie schön! ' rief sie begeistert aus.*)

vii. Aufrufen zu is the usual expression for **call on** (or *appeal* to) someone to do something. *Man rief die Bevölkerung zu Spenden für die Opfer der Hungersnot auf. Die IG-Metall rief alle Metallarbeiter zu einem Streik auf*, called on them to strike. Cf. next section. (*Appellieren* is also used. *Man appellierte an die Öffentlichkeit, großzügig zu spenden. Anrufen um* is occasionally found in the sense 'to call on or appeal to s.o. to grant help, protection, etc.' *Die verfolgten österreichischen Protestanten riefen den König von Preußen um Schutz an.*)

> *Die Mitglieder des Studentenparlaments riefen alle Studenten zur Teilnahme an einer Protestkundgebung auf. Or Sie riefen alle Studenten dazu auf, an der Protestkundgebung teilzunehmen.*

viii. Die Gewerkschaft rief einen Streik aus, called a strike. Here **ausrufen** means 'to proclaim'. *Am 9. November 1918 rief Philip Scheidemann die deutsche Republik aus, um der beginnenden Revolution entgegenzuwirken. Im Überschwemmungsgebiet hat man den Notstand ausgerufen.*

ix. The formal word for **call** or *convene* a meeting is **einberufen**. *Man beruft eine Versammlung/das Parlament ein.* A less formal syn. is **ansetzen**. *Der Direktor hat eine Kollegiumssitzung für nächsten Donnerstag angesetzt. Einberufen* also means 'to call up for military service' as does **einziehen**. *In vielen Ländern werden alle tauglichen zwanzigjährigen Männer zum Wehrdienst einberufen/eingezogen.*

> *Der Parteivorstand beschloß, einen Sonderparteitag einzuberufen.*
>
> *In diesem Jahr wird der Jahrgang 1973 eingezogen/einberufen.*

x. Someone can feel called by God, destiny, etc. to do something. This is expressed by one sense of **berufen**. Only in a few expressions are the act. forms translated by **call**. *Jesus berief seine Jünger. Viele sind berufen, aber nur wenige auserwählt.* The past part. means 'especially suited or endowed for a task'. *Sie ist zu größeren Aufgaben berufen. Er ist berufen, in der Mathematik Großes zu leisten. Er wurde Priester, ohne berufen zu sein. Ein berufener Fachmann* is 'a specially qualified or competent expert'. *Die Berufung* is 'vocation'. *Um Mönch zu werden, braucht man eine wirkliche Berufung.* Cf. APPOINT 4. i.

3. In *I'll call [in] tomorrow* or *He called on us*, or *We called at their place*, **call** means 'to visit'. **Call in** or *drop in*, i.e. 'to make a short informal visit', is **vorbeikommen**. *Wenn du morgen nachmittag zu Hause bist, komme ich vorbei.* Vorbeikommen is used only when speaking to the person to be visited. If I tell someone I am going to call on a third person, I say, *'Ich* **gehe** *heute machmittag bei Martin* **vorbei** *und kann ihm das Buch geben.'* **Vorbeischauen** can be used in both situations. *Ich schaue gegen Abend [bei Anna] vorbei.* Alternatives are **besuchen**, 'to visit', and **aufsuchen**, 'to pay a short visit to, to look up'. *Ich möchte einen früheren Studienkollegen in Oldenburg aufsuchen.* When the call is for business purposes, **dasein**, 'to be present', is used as well as *vorbeikommen. Der Mann, der die Heizung nachsieht, war heute früh da/kam heute früh vorbei. Ein Mann war da, um ein Paket abzugeben.* A ship also calls at a port. This is *einen Hafen* **anlaufen**. *Nur ein Schiff im Monat läuft den Hafen an.*

4. Both **call** and **name** mean 'to give a name to s.o./sth.' with the implication that the person or thing has just come into existence or been discovered. Only **name** is possible when the name is not stated. *The local council names new streets.* **Call** needs the name or a question introduced by *what. They called the new state Bangladesh. What did Röntgen call the rays he discovered?* When the designation follows, **call** is the everyday word, **name** more formal. *They called/named the new baby John. What are you going to call/name the rose you have bred?* Both can take *after.* **Call** also means 'to address or refer to as sth.' It may state the real name, *My students call me by my first name,* or another one in contrast to the real name, *Her name is Elizabeth, but everyone calls her Liz.* The pass. *S.o./Sth is called sth.* states the name by which a person or thing is known. *She had a boyfriend called David. This device is called an autocue.*

i. Nennen covers these uses of **name** and **call** when a person is the obj., when talking of pets' names, and when stating what people usually call a person, animal, or place. The equivalent of the pass. is **heißen**, which is used to give or ask the name of a person or thing. The pass. of *nennen*, applied to people, states what someone is called in contrast to the real name. *Wie* is used in combination with *nennen* and *heißen* where E. uses *what.* The question *What do you call it/that thg.?* or *What is it/that thg. called?* when asking for a word or name in one's own or another language is *Wie heißt es [auf Deutsch]?*

    Wie wollt ihr das neue Kind nennen? Wir wollen sie/es Annette [nach der Großmutter] nennen.
    Wir wollen die beiden Größen, die wir suchen, x und y nennen.
    Ich wußte, daß die Frau, die ich Mutter nannte, nicht meine Mutter war.

Wir nennen den Hund Bello.	*Der Hund heißt Bello.*
Sie hatte einen Freund, der David hieß.	*Diese Vorrichtung heißt ein Teleprompter.*
Wie heißt er?	*Wie heißt er mit Vornamen/Nachnamen?*
Nennen Sie mich bitte beim Vornamen!	*Wie heißt diese Straße?*

    Eigentlich heißt sie Brigitta, aber alle nennen sie Gitte. Or *Sie wird von allen Gitte genannt.*

ii. Benennen means 'to name a thg.', i.e. 'to give it a name for the first time'. It needs an obj. such as a new street, an invention, or a newly discovered plant, place, animal, etc. A phr. with *nach* may follow.

    Die Gemeindeverwaltung sucht 25 noch nicht benutzte Namen, um die Straßen der neuen Siedlung zu benennen.   *Welches antike Volk hat die Planeten benannt?*

Man benennt eine neue Pflanzenart oft nach dem Züchter.

Die Pflanzengattung Banksia und zahlreiche Pflanzenarten sind nach dem englischen Naturforscher Joseph Banks benannt, der Cook 1768-71 auf seiner ersten Reise begleitete.

iii. A more learned syn. of *nennen* in the sense 'to refer to sth. by a particular name' is **bezeichnen als,** which can be translated as *to denote* or *designate as.*

Die Elemente der 7. Hauptgruppe des Periodensystems, Fluor, Chlor, Brom und Jod, bezeichnet man als Halogene. Also Die Elemente . . . nennt man Halogene. Or Die Elemente . . . heißen Halogene.

Das Nomen, das angibt, wer oder was die Handlung des Verbs ausführt, bezeichnet man als das Subjekt.

iv. Umbenennen means 'to change the name of or to rename'. It may take *nach.*

Die Nationalsozialisten haben viele Straßen umbenannt.

Van Diemens Land wurde 1855 in Tasmanien nach dessen Entdecker A. J. Tasman umbenannt.

v. The refl. **sich nennen,** 'to call oneself sth.', need not, but often does, imply that the designation does not correspond to reality.

Erst nachdem er die Prüfung bestanden hat, darf er sich Doktor nennen.

So was nennt sich Fachmann!   Und das nennt sich nun Luxushotel!

Er ging bis zur nächsten Ecke und kam zurück—das nennt sich spazierengehen.

5. i. Nennen corresponds to **call** when it means 'to designate s.o./sth. with a word which characterizes it'. *I call that dishonest. That's what I call a good meal. I would call that a bargain.* A n., adj., infin., or past part. can follow *nennen.*

Das nenne ich Mut/mutig! (That's what I call courage/courageous.)

Das nenne ich aber ein gutes Essen!   Das nenne ich klug handeln/klug gehandelt.

Großzügig kann ich ihn gerade nicht nennen!   Das nennst du arbeiten? Ich nenne es faulenzen.

Bezeichnen als is a more learned syn. of *nennen.* It is often translated as DESCRIBE.

Ich würde sein Verhalten als unsportlich bezeichnen.

Sie bezeichnete es als Schwäche, daß die eigentliche Handlung des Romans zu spät einsetzt.

ii. Both **call** and **nennen** mean 'to use a particular word to describe people or thgs. when this makes it clear what one thinks of them'. *Nixon called his opponents traitors. Nixon nannte seine Gegner Verräter.*

Er hat mich gestern vor allen Leuten einen Dummkopf/einen Lügner genannt.

Call s.o. **names** is **beschimpfen,** to abuse. *Er beschimpft mich mit gemeinen Worten.*

Vernünftig handeln nenne ich es nicht, wenn du jmd[n.], der deine Meinung nicht teilt, beschimpfst.

6. Nennen also means 'to give or state' one's own or someone else's name or address, the name of something, a price, or a piece of information in order either to inform someone or to show that one knows it. *Nennen Sie die fünf höchsten Berge der Welt!* It thus translates *to give, give the name of,* or **name.**

Er trat an sie heran und nannte seinen Namen.

Nennen Sie bitte Namen, Adresse und Geburtstag!

Hat er seine Gründe für seine Ablehnung der Stelle genannt?

Kannst du mir dort ein gutes, aber nicht zu teures Hotel nennen?

Können Sie andere Beispiele nennen?   Haben sie den Preis genannt?

Nennen Sie die wichtigsten Unterschiede zwischen den Verfahren!

7. i. Name meaning 'to mention s.o./s.o.'s name in connection with a particular matter' is expressed by **nennen.** *Mehrere Studenten wurden im Parlament als Terroristen genannt.*

Herr Frank sprach von einigen Schülern, mit deren Leistungen er nicht zufrieden war. Er hat einige von euch genannt, aber ihr beide wart nicht unter den Genannten.

ii. Benennen meaning 'to name' is used with ns. like *die Kandidaten* or *die Zeugen.* It is a formal or bureaucratic word and implies that the information given is correct and definite. *Die Partei hat ihren Kandidaten benannt* implies that the one named will definitely be nominated. *Jmd. konnte zwei Zeugen benennen* is a formal expression which has become usual in this context, though *nennen* is not wrong.

iii. *Als möglicher Nachfolger des Außenministers ist der Innenminister genannt worden* means that his name has been mentioned in that connection. Cf. 7. i. If **name** means 'to appoint', the equivalent is **ernennen**. *Der Premierminister hat den neuen Außenminister ernannt.* Cf. APPOINT 3.

8. Benennen also means 'to name or give the name of' when these mean 'to identify'. It implies that someone is shown or given (part of) a tree, plant, etc. and has to say what it is. The examples given for *nennen* in 6 do not suggest identification but that someone can give certain information like *die Hauptstädte der kanadischen Provinzen* when required.

> *Der deutsche Forststudent muß alle Bäume des mitteleuropäischen Raumes benennen können.*
> *In der Botanikprüfung mußten wir eine Anzahl von Pflanzen benennen.*
> *Wenn ich Ihnen ein paar Apfelarten zeige, können Sie sie benennen?*

cancel, call off, lift (a ban, prohibition, etc.) *vs.*

1. Cancel an order, law, contract, etc. The original sense of **cancel** was 'to deface or obliterate writing by drawing lines across it to show that it was null and void'. The word now means 'to make null and void' and is applied to anything that has legal force.

i. Aufheben is applied to the ending of any kind of legal regulation or obligation. For this action there are a number of E. words like *annul, rescind, repeal, revoke,* and *abolish,* although **cancel** and **lift** are common general terms. The obj. of *aufheben* can be *Verträge,* 'contracts', or *eine Klausel,* 'clause' (of a contract, etc.), or *ein Absatz,* 'paragraph of a contract or law', *ein Gesetz, die Todesstrafe, die Zensur, Bestimmungen,* 'regulations', *Verfügungen,* '(administrative) orders or decrees', *Verbote, Beschränkungen, der Visumzwang, ein Befehl,* 'military command', and *ein Haftbefehl,* 'warrant for s.o.'s arrest'. Also *Urlaub für Soldaten wird aufgehoben.*

> *Nach dem Staatsstreich haben die neuen Machthaber die Verfassung aufgehoben.*
> *Die Vertragspartner kamen überein, daß der Vertrag grundsätzlich gelten solle, der Absatz/die Klausel bezüglich des eingeschränkten Rücktrittsrechts jedoch aufgehoben werden solle.*
> *Bereits am gleichen Nachmittag wurden die im Rahmen des Smog-Alarms 1 verfügten Beschränkungen des Kfz-Verkehrs wieder aufgehoben.*
> *Zum Glück wurde der Befehl von der obersten Heeresleitung wieder aufgehoben.*
> *Unverzüglich hob der Untersuchungsrichter den Haftbefehl wieder auf.*

Where we write *cancelled* across something, a G. writes *ungültig,* invalid. **Etw. für ungültig erklären,** 'to declare invalid', can express the same meaning as *aufheben.* *Beide Partner erklären hiermit den bisherigen Vertrag für ungültig.*

ii. Streichen means 'to delete'. In relation to a contract it implies one that has been drawn up for signing, but is not yet in force. The contracting parties could agree that one or more clauses should be cancelled or deleted.

> *Dieser Passus muß gestrichen werden, bevor ich bereit bin, den Vertrag zu unterschreiben.*
> *Die Stelle über den Haftungsausschluß ist ersatzlos aus dem Vertrag zu streichen.*

iii. Aufheben can be used for cancelling debts. *Schweden hat die Schulden der Entwicklungsländer aufgehoben.* The technical term is **annullieren.** *Die Hälfte der Schulden wurden annulliert.*

iv. Rückgängig machen is used in some of the same legal contexts as *aufheben. Der Befehl/Der Haftbefehl/Der Vertrag/Die Einreisegenehmigung wurde rückgängig gemacht.*

> *Nachdem man im Generalstab die Aussichtslosigkeit des Unternehmens eingesehen hatte, wurde der Befehl zum Angriff rückgängig gemacht.*

v. Jmdm. die Erlaubnis entziehen means 'to withdraw permission granted to do sth.' *Einem Kraftfahrer wird der Führerschein entzogen, z. B. wegen Trunkenheit am Steuer, oder wenn man ihm Alkohol im Blut nachweist.* Also *man nimmt die Erlaubnis zurück.*

Zurücknehmen, applied to *Verbote, Bestellungen, Aufträge,* 'orders for goods', means 'to withdraw'. *Die Firma war in Zahlungsschwierigkeiten geraten und mußte den Auftrag zurücknehmen.*

vi. Cancel *a cheque* is *einen Scheck* **sperren**. *Falls ein Scheck oder Ihr Scheckheft gestohlen wird, unterrichten Sie die Bank sofort, damit sie die abhandengekommenen Schecks sperren kann.*

vii. Cancel a postage stamp or to make a mark on a ticket to show that it has been used is **entwerten**.

> *Beim Einsteigen in den Bus oder die Straßenbahn muß man Fahrscheine selbst [im Entwerter] entwerten.*

2. Cancel an order for goods or services.

i. Rückgängig machen, 'to declare to be no longer in force', is the usual term for cancelling orders and purchases.

> *Sie machten den Kauf/die Bestellung/den Auftrag/die Vereinbarung/das Abonnement rückgängig.*

ii. When the obj. is the thing cancelled, i.e. something previously ordered, **abbestellen** is used. It is also used with a person whose services have been ordered or requested as obj. *Wir müssen den Klempner/den Elektriker abbestellen. Abbestellen* is also used without an obj., with what is cancelled being implied.

> *Ich habe die Zeitung für drei Wochen abbestellt.   Ich bestelle das Hotelzimmer ab.*
> *Wir bestellen den Flug nach Teneriffa eben wieder ab* (cancel the reservation for the flight).
> *Wenn du lieber zu Fuß gehen willst, dann bestellen wir das Taxi wieder ab.*
> *Wenn Sie zu diesem Zeitpunkt noch abbestellen wollen, kann ich Ihnen aber nicht den vollen Preis zurückerstatten.*

iii. Stornieren is a commercial term which means either 'to reverse an erroneous entry in a financial statement', *Die Bank wird die falsche Gutschrift stornieren*, or 'to cancel an order', *Bis auf weiteres sollten alle Bestellungen storniert werden, da die Firma in Zahlungsverzug geraten ist. Die Fahrkarten stornieren* means 'to cancel tickets'. A synonymous expression often used in speech is *die Fahrkarten zurückgeben*.

> *Stornieren Sie Ihre Buchung umgehend, falls Sie Ihre Reisepläne ändern!*

3. Cancel, call off = 'to say that sth. already arranged or decided on will not be done or take place', i.e. *to cancel a meeting, appointment, lecture,* etc.

i. Absagen means 'to cancel sth. already planned, arranged, or agreed to'. *Der Veranstalter hat die geplante Tibetreise abgesagt.* It can be used alone so that what is cancelled is implied. *Es wird schwer sein, Ersatz zu finden, nachdem der Tenor so kurzfristig abgesagt hat. Ich mußte absagen, obwohl ich gern hingegangen wäre.* A dat. of the person one has arranged to meet or who gave the invitation etc. may be included. *Es fällt mir nicht leicht, ihr abzusagen, aber die Prüfung läßt mir keine Zeit.*

> *Man sagt eine Konferenz/eine Versammlung/eine Verabredung/einen geplanten Besuch ab.*
> Or *Man sagt seine Teilnahme an der Konferenz ab.*
> *Das Fußballspiel mußte wegen des anhaltenden, schweren Regens abgesagt werden.*
> *Der Dirigent mußte sämtliche Konzerte der Spielzeit absagen.*
> *Ich habe den Termin beim Arzt abgesagt.* But *Ich habe dem Arzt abgesagt.*

ii. Abschreiben and **abtelefonieren** are used when someone calls an engagement off or declines an invitation in writing or by phone.

> *Wir müssen ihm noch vor den Festtagen abschreiben, damit er uns nicht mehr mit einplant.*
> *Die Probe ist aber nun wirklich wichtig, da kannst du doch deinem Friseur abtelefonieren.*

iii. Ausfallen in *Das Seminar fällt heute aus* means that it is not taking place, i.e. it is cancelled. The equivalent of the act. form *S.o. cancels sth.* is **ausfallen lassen**. *Ich muß das Seminar morgen ausfallen lassen. Ausfallen* means that the cancellation happens once only and is an exception to the rule. *Absagen* can be used in this situation only if it is clear that it refers to one occasion only, because it could also mean 'to call off or cancel completely'. *Weil sich nicht genug Teilnehmer angemeldet haben, hat die Volkshochschule den Chinesisch-Kurs abgesagt. Die heutige Vorstellung ist abgesagt worden.* Or *Die Vorstellung fällt heute abend aus.*

iv. In reference to *Züge* or *Flüge* **streichen** means 'to cancel'. *Die Bundesbahn hat den Sonderzug nach Rom gestrichen.* **Annullieren** is also used for *Flüge*.

4. Cancel [out] = 'to balance a quantity of opposite sign so that the result is zero'. The mathematical term is **aufheben**, which is also used fig. for two things which equalize each other.

Eine negative Zahl hebt die gleiche positive auf.
Eine positive und dieselbe negative Zahl heben sich auf. Or *−x and +x heben einander auf.*
Dieser Verlust hebt den früheren Gewinn wieder auf.   *Die Vor- und Nachteile heben sich auf.*
Seine durchaus positiven Charaktereigenschaften werden alle durch seine unglaubliche Unbeherrschtheit wieder aufgehoben.

care, worry, caution *ns*. Some uses of **care for** and **look after** *vs*.

1. Care and the syns. **worry**, *concern*, and *anxiety* denote a burdened state of mind arising from fear or uncertainty about someone or something.

i. Die Sorge is defined as 'an oppressive uneasiness which is caused by a future adversity which s.o. fears might afflict him, her, s.o., or sth., or by present adversity when one is uncertain how long it will last'. It is often seen as a rational reaction. Like **cares** and **worries**, it is frequently used in the pl. and denotes both the feeling and what causes it. It often refers to difficult external circumstances and to the future. *Ich mache mir Sorgen um jmdn./etw.* or *über etw.* or *wegen einer Sache,* I worry about s.o./sth.

Sie wußte vor Sorgen weder aus noch ein.   *Meine Sorgen um sie waren grundlos.*
Jmd. hat große/schwere/berufliche/familiäre/finanzielle Sorgen.
Hier kann man für kurze Zeit seine Sorgen vergessen.   *Er hat keine Sorgen.*
Auf ihm lastet die Sorge vor der drohenden Kündigung.
Vor allem in Polen und Großbritannien sprach sich ein großer Teil der Bevölkerung gegen die deutsche Einigung aus. Viele Menschen äußerten die Sorge, der Faschismus könne wieder aufkommen oder das wieder vereinigte Deutschland könnte territoriale Ansprüche stellen oder wirtschaftlich zu stark werden.

ii. In strict use **der Kummer** is 'a sad, depressed state of mind caused by adversity, hard blows of fate, or misfortune one is suffering'. Equivalents are *sorrow, distress, trouble,* **worry**, *concern,* **care**, or *grief.*

Sie hat großen Kummer.   *Ihr Mann macht ihr viel Kummer.*
Ein heimlicher Kummer zehrte an ihr.   *Der Kummer hat sie vorzeitig alt gemacht.*
Aus Kummer über den Verlust seines Arbeitsplatzes ist er krank geworden.
Er versuchte, seinen Kummer im Alkohol zu ertränken.

Colloquially, however, it means 'mild sorrow about sth. which has gone wrong or about difficulties one is unable to surmount'. In *Zu ihrem Kummer ist der Sohn in schlechte Gesellschaft geraten,* it suggests distress or sorrow, but in *Zu meinem Kummer habe ich keine Karte für das Konzert bekommen,* little more than regret. Similarly *Ihr größter Kummer sind ihre Sommersprossen. Darüber werde ich mir wenig Kummer machen* and *Das ist mein geringster Kummer* refer to relatively unimportant sources of concern.

iii. Die Kümmernis is 'a small or trifling care, worry, or trouble'.

Die Kinder erzählten der Lehrerin ihre Kümmernisse.

2. Care = 'serious attention or thought paid to what one is doing', 'taking pains'. *Whatever she does is done with great care.* The equivalent is **die Sorgfalt**. To take care with sth. in this sense is lit. *Sorgfalt auf etw. verwenden. Sie hat große Sorgfalt auf die Zeichnungen verwendet.* However, it is often simpler to express the idea with *sorgfältig*, 'CAREFULLY', or a phr. *Sie haben die Abbildungen sehr sorgfältig/mit großer Sorgfalt gemacht.*

Bei dieser Arbeit ist besondere Sorgfalt nötig.   *Sie kleidet sich immer mit Sorgfalt.*
Er schreibt seine Berichte mit großer Sorgfalt.   *Die Arbeit läßt große Sorgfalt erkennen.*
Man sieht der einfachen Statue die Sorgfalt an, mit der sie geschnitzt worden ist.

3. Care often means 'caution' and *careful* 'cautious'. *Always drive with care! We must proceed carefully.* **Care** is **die Vorsicht**, and **vorsichtig** is 'careful[ly]' or 'with care'. *Man muß immer vorsichtig fahren. Diese Sache muß mit Vorsicht angegangen werden. Handle with care!* on packages is *Vorsicht Glas!* or *Vorsicht zerbrechlich!* For *to treat with care* and *to take care with* in this sense see CAREFUL 4.

Wir müssen vorsichtig vorgehen/mit großer Vorsicht vorgehen.
Sie gingen mit der gebührenden Vorsicht an die Aufgabe heran.
Solche Verhandlungen erfordern sehr viel Vorsicht, weil man leicht alles verderben kann.

4. Care = 'protection, responsibility, or supervision with a view to preserving, or guiding'.

i. Pflegen means 'to take care of', 'to care for'. It implies looking after or keeping in a good, tidy condition when used with things as obj., such as *ein Garten, eine Wohnung, eine Pflanze, das Äußere*, 'appearance', the body and parts of it. *Das Auto/Der Garten/Die Wohnung/Das Haus war sehr gut gepflegt worden/sah gepflegt aus. Die Körperpflege* is 'care of the body' or 'personal hygiene'. With a baby or child that cannot look after itself as obj., *pflegen* means 'to care for'. Hence *die Säuglingspflege*. Normally, with people and animals as obj., it implies that they are sick or in need of special care. It is the usual v. meaning 'to care for' when talking of hospitals and nurses. However, with *Pflegemutter* etc. as subj., it implies looking after normally. *Die Pflegemutter pflegte über Jahre hin die beiden Kinder wie ihre eigenen.* **Die Pflege** is the n. *In Pflege geben*, 'to give to someone to look after', and *in Pflege nehmen*, 'to take to look after', imply only normal care. *Wir haben die Katze bei den Nachbarn in Pflege gegeben.*

Sie hatte eine gepflegte Frisur/ein gepflegtes Äußeres.   *Du mußt dein Äußeres mehr pflegen.*
Die Pflege des Gartens nimmt viel Zeit in Anspruch.
In diesem Krankenhaus bekommen alle Kinder die beste Pflege.
Die Kranke wurde in häusliche Pflege entlassen.   *Die Pflanze erfordert viel Pflege.*

ii. Sorgen für with a person as obj. implies the effort or endeavour to maintain that person's well-being, and is the usual equivalent of **care for** or **look after** (sometimes temporarily) under normal circumstances. *Er/Sie sorgte vorbildlich für die Familie.* It need only mean 'to provide for financially', but may include everything the words **care for** imply, particularly when talking of parents and children. To make the sense of financial provision clear *für jmds. Lebensunterhalt sorgen* is often preferred. When the n. after *für* is not a person, as in *Sie sorgte für einen reibungslosen Ablauf der Konferenz*, *sorgen* means 'to see to it' (that the conference went off smoothly.) Cf. SEE TO S.O./STH. The n. **die Sorge** has the two senses 'caring for or looking after people' and 'seeing to it that sth. happens or is done'. In the meaning 'caring for', *die Sorgepflicht der Eltern für ihre Kinder* is 'the obligation to care for them', *das Sorgerecht* 'the right to care for', i.e. 'custody'. *Das Gericht hat der Mutter/dem Vater das Sorgerecht zugesprochen. Sorge* in this sense is followed by *für*. *Die elterliche Sorge für die Kinder.* **Sorge für etw. tragen** is a formal variant on *sorgen für*. *Ist niemand da, der für das Kind Sorge trägt?* In the sense 'seeing to it that sth. is done', *Sorge* is found mainly in fixed expressions. *Das ist meine Sorge,* I will [have to] see to/take care of that. *Das laß nur meine Sorge sein!,* let me see/attend to/take care of that!

Nach dem Tod der Eltern hat der Fünfzehnjährige für drei Geschwister gesorgt.

Während der Abwesenheit der Eltern sorgte die Großmutter für den Haushalt und die Kinder.
Die Sorge für eine große Familie verlangt ihre ganzen Kräfte.
Nach der Scheidung sorgt der Vater weiterhin für die Kinder und sieht sie dreimal in der Woche.

Die Fürsorge has the same meaning as *Sorge für* applied to people. *Fürsorge* is used when *Sorge* cannot be followed by *für*. *Sorge* without *für* would be taken to mean 'worry', and *Fürsorge* avoids ambiguity. Thus *Das verwaiste Kind wurde der Fürsorge einer Tante übergeben. Bei diesen Kindern vermißt man die elterliche Fürsorge.* In contexts like *öffentliche/staatliche/kirchliche Fürsorge*, it means 'welfare' or 'welfare work or service'. *Fürsorgeempfänger* are 'those receiving welfare payments'. (Welfare provided for the needy in Germany is now called *Sozialhilfe* and is administered by the municipalities, *die Gemeinden*.)

iii. Die Aufsicht means 'supervision'. It translates **care** in *under the care of* if supervision is implied.

Man stellt alle jungen Mitarbeiter eine Zeitlang unter die Aufsicht eines erfahrenen Kollegen.
Der Leseraum der Bibliothek steht unter der Aufsicht von Herrn Schmidt.

iv. Die Obhut is a formal and legal term meaning 'protective supervision' and is translated as **care**, *charge*, or *care and protection*. It can be applied to people and things. Expressions in common use are *jmd. nimmt jmdn./etw. in/unter seine Obhut* or *hat jmdn./etw. in/unter seiner Obhut*, *jmd./etw. steht unter jmds. Obhut.*

Sie hatte die Kinder ihrer verstorbenen Schwester unter ihrer Obhut.
Während der Klassenfahrt hatte ich zwanzig Schüler unter meiner Obhut. Or Ich betreute zwanzig Schüler.
Er nahm seine Nichte unter seine Obhut.

v. Betreuen can mean 'to have s.o./sth. under one's care' or 'to look after'. It is used in a wide range of situations including taking special care as with the sick. It stresses the personal care for each individual.

Die Nonnen betreuen die Patienten wirklich aufopferungsvoll.
Die Fluggäste werden von den Stewardessen betreut.
Säuglinge werden in der Kinderkrippe betreut.
In den nächsten zwei Wochen betreue ich eine Gruppe von deutschsprechenden Touristen.
In der Abwesenheit seines Bruders betreut er dessen Geschäft/dessen Laden.

[take] care, mind, beware, be careful [+ infin.], pay attention *vs.* Order of treatment: 1. **Take care**, used as a warning to avoid harm or damage, is discussed. 2. A stronger meaning in which **take care** = 'to beware of'. As the three equivalents in sense 1 also mean 'to pay attention', this is dealt with in 3. 4 and 5. Meanings of **mind**. 6. Meanings of **take care** treated elsewhere.

1. Take care can be a syn. of **be careful**. *Take care/Be careful when you cross the road!* **Mind [out]** is similar, but suggests imminent danger. *Mind out!—there's a car coming.* The E. expressions occur in a variety of constructions:

a. Each can be used alone. *Take care! Mind [out]! Be careful! You'll hurt yourself, if you don't mind out/take care/if you're not careful.*

b. All three take a clause introduced by an interrogative. *Take care/Be careful/Mind what you say/how you behave/where you go/how you carry it! Mind what you're doing/what you're about!*

c. **Take care** and **be careful** are used with an infin. or a clause, **mind** only with a clause. All three occur when the clause or infin. is neg. *Take care/Be careful not to break the eggs! Mind you don't break the eggs! Take care/Be careful not to get run over! Mind you don't get run over!*

d. With a pos. clause or infin. **be careful** may be used, *Be careful to avoid spilling any!*, **mind** sometimes is, *Mind you post the letters!*, and **take care** can be, *Take care to see that all the windows are locked!*, or *Take care to wipe your shoes well before you come* *inside!* More common with a pos. clause or infin. are *Make sure you arrive on time!* and *See [to it] that you hand in your essay on time!* Cf. SEE TO S.O./STH.

Aufpassen is common in everyday speech and covers almost all senses. It is appropriate in all but the most formal contexts. *Achten* implies a higher degree of attention, but in cases in which *aufpassen* is also possible it is somewhat more formal. *Achtgeben* implies a still higher degree of caution than *achten*.

i. Aufpassen means 'to take care to avoid either suffering harm or causing it' so that the imp. *Paß auf!* can be translated either as *Take care!, Be careful!,* or *Mind out! Paß auf!—da kommt ein Lastwagen!* It takes a *daß*-clause but not an infin. and can translate all three E. words in *c* above if the construction is changed. It is mostly used when the following clause is neg. and when the action of the clause is related to the subj. of *aufpassen*. *Paß auf, daß du bei dem Glatteis nicht ausrutschst! Ich passe gut auf, daß sie mich nicht übervorteilen! Paß auf, daß du das Baby nicht weckst!* A pos. clause is possible but not common. *Der Lehrer paßt auf, daß die Kinder ihre Arbeit ordentlich machen.* It is used in the spoken language in constructions like the E. ones under *b* above. *Paß auf, was du da machst! Paß auf, was du sagst! Paß auf, wohin du trittst, weil der Boden an vielen Stellen sumpfig ist, und du könntest leicht einsacken.*

ii. Achten auf also means 'to take care', 'be careful'. It is used with a *daß*-clause which can be either pos. or neg. *Achte darauf/Paß auf, daß du nicht zu spät zum Termin kommst! Achte darauf, daß du rechtzeitig zum Termin kommst!* The clause can describe something not connected with the subj. of *achten*. *Wir müssen darauf achten, daß die Temperatur nicht zu hoch wird. Sie achtete darauf, daß die Handwerker die Arbeiten gewissenhaft ausführten.* Unlike *aufpassen*, *achten* takes an infin. *Achte darauf, die Anweisungen genauestens auszuführen! Sie achtet darauf, immer gepflegt auszusehen, wenn sie zur Arbeit geht.* It is the normal v. for E. construction *b* above. *Achte darauf, wie du mit ihm redest! Achte auf das, was du ihm sagst! Achte darauf, wie du das Paket trägst!*

iii. Achtgeben also means both 'to be careful or cautious' or 'to take care'. It is used alone or with *auf*. The imp. *Gib acht!* often means 'take care!' or 'look out!' *Gib acht!—da kommt ein Auto. Gib acht/Paß auf!—die Tür ist sehr niedrig, und du mußt den Kopf einziehen, wenn du dich nicht stoßen willst. Achtgeben* is also used with a *daß*-clause. *Im Wald geben die Kinder darauf acht, daß sie nicht vom Weg abkommen. Gib acht, was du machst!* is possible, but *aufpassen* and *achten auf* are more common in this construction.

> *Kannst du nicht besser achtgeben? Du hättest mich beinahe mit deinem Fahrrad angefahren.*
> *Der Boden ist voller Scherben—gib acht/paß auf, daß du dich nicht schneidest!*
> *Gib acht auf das neue Kleid, damit es nicht schmutzig wird!*

2. Take care has a stronger meaning 'to protect oneself in a dangerous situation or when s.o. is trying to cause one harm' and is close to **beware of** or *be on one's guard. Take [great] care! He has a reputation for sharp practice.*

i. Sich in acht nehmen is used only to warn against an imminent or potential danger. The danger can arise either from human qualities like dishonesty or treachery or perils in nature. It can be used alone, but also takes *vor*. It corresponds to **take care** when this means 'to be on one's guard [against]' or 'to beware of'. **Sich vorsehen** is a syn.

> *Nimm dich in acht vor den beiden! Sie sind die hinterhältigsten Menschen, die ich kenne.*
> *Nimm dich in acht! Ich traue ihm nicht. Or Bei ihm muß man sich vorsehen.*
> *Die Mutter sagte, Rotkäppchen solle sich vor dem bösen Wolf in acht nehmen.*
> *Wenn man im Busch wandert, muß man sich vor Schlangen in acht nehmen.*
> *Der Vater sagte zu den Kindern: 'Seht euch vor vor Fremden! Geht nie mit ihnen mit!'*
> *Sieh' dich vor! Du könntest in deiner Wut etw. sagen, was du später bereuen wirst.*

ii. Sich vor jmdm./etw. hüten also means 'to be on one's guard against' or 'to beware of' a person or 'to avoid sth. under all circumstances'. With an infin., it means 'to take care *not* to do sth.' *Ich werde mich [schon] hüten, mich da sehen zu lassen,* I'll take [good] care *not* to be seen there. *Ich werde mich hüten,* as an answer to a suggestion, means that I will do no such thing or will not do something under any circumstances.

Ein Politiker muß sich vor skrupellosen Gegnern in den eigenen Reihen hüten.

Sie müssen sich vor Aufregungen und Anstrengungen hüten, bis Sie wieder völlig gesund sind.

Hüte dich davor, Kaufverträge an der Tür zu unterschreiben!

A. *Wirst du ihm 10 000 Mark leihen?* B. *Ich werde mich hüten, ihm auch nur eine Mark zu leihen. Ich bin doch nicht verrückt. Das Geld würde ich nie wiedersehen.*

iii. Vorsicht is used in notices and in speech to draw attention to a source of danger. *Vorsicht, Bissiger Hund! Vorsicht, Stufe!* **Achtung** suggests greater danger. *Achtung! Hochspannung! Lebensgefahr!*

3. i. The basic sense of **aufpassen** is 'to pay attention'. *Du mußt in der Schule besser aufpassen.*

Du mußt jetzt gut aufpassen, damit du beim nächsten Mal den Kuchen ohne meine Hilfe backen kannst.

Paß gut auf! Ich muß dir etw. Wichtiges erklären.

ii. Achten auf means 'to pay attention to'. *Der Junge achtete nicht auf die Worte des Lehrers.* Unlike *aufpassen*, *achten* needs *auf* + a n. or pronoun. *Achte auf die Erklärung!*

Du mußt auf alles achten, was ich dir sage.

Beim Überqueren eines Gletschers muß man sehr auf den Weg achten, damit man nicht in eine Spalte fällt.   *Achte auf das, was du tust!*

iii. In an appropriate context **achtgeben** also means 'to pay attention'. *Gib acht auf das, was ich dir sage! Geben Sie mal ganz genau acht!*

4. Mind and **take care of** are used for looking after people, animals, and things temporarily. **Aufpassen auf** means 'to watch so as to see that a pers. or thg. suffers no harm or damage or causes none'. It implies only for a limited time and frequently, but not always, suggests that the subj. concentrates on the task and does not just do it in addition to something else. It thus varies between *keep an eye on* and **mind**. *Er verdient sich ein wenig Taschengeld, indem er gelegentlich auf die Kinder der Nachbarn aufpaßt. Du mußt auf die Milch aufpassen, damit sie nicht überkocht.* **Achten auf** is also used for minding children, pets, houses, etc., but is less common than *aufpassen*. It implies keeping an eye on them so as to be able to intervene in case of need. *Während wir weg waren, hat der Junge von nebenan auf das Haus/den Hund geachtet.* **Achtgeben** is also sometimes found in the sense 'to mind, look after, see that s.o./sth. is in order'. *Gib bitte acht auf das Baby! Geh du nur telefonieren! Ich gebe auf das Gepäck acht. Ich gebe auf das Feuer im Herd acht* could mean that I see to it that it does not go out or set the house on fire.

Während wir im Urlaub waren, paßten die Nachbarn auf unser Haus auf.

Achte mal ein bißchen auf die Kinder, während ich einkaufe!

Gib auf den Hund/den Kuchen im Backofen acht!

Sorge dich nicht wegen der Kinder! Ich werde auf sie achtgeben, während du weg bist.

5. Mind is used with an obj. *Mind the step! Mind the broken rung on the ladder! Mind the eggs/the garden/the plants!* The sense is either 'not to hurt oneself' or 'not to inflict harm or damage on s.o. or sth.' *Mind the dog!* can be paraphrased as *Take care it doesn't bite you!* or *Don't tread on it!* To be **careful** of something also means 'not to cause harm to sth.' *Be careful of the plants!* One equivalent is **achtgeben**, but it is limited to things which can cause harm. *Gib acht auf die Stufe!,* mind the step! *Gib acht auf die zerbrochene Sprosse! Ich passe auf den Garten auf* means that I will mind or look after it. For *Mind/Be careful of the garden!* implying *Don't do any damage to it!*, a more specific expression is needed. *Paß auf, daß du die Rosen nicht kaputt machst/die Sträucher nicht abknickst/daß du nicht auf die Pflanzen trittst!* Thus *Mind the eggs!* would become *Paß auf, daß du die Eier nicht zerbrichst! Mind the dog!* meaning 'don't let it harm you' becomes *Paß auf, daß der Hund dich nicht beißt! Ich gebe auf den Hund acht* implies looking after it.

6. Other meanings of **take care** are dealt with elsewhere. To **take care of** a person or animal meaning 'to look after' by providing food etc. is *sorgen für.* Cf. CARE **4. Take care of** a thing for someone for a time, i.e. 'to see it is not lost, stolen, etc.', is *aufheben* or *aufbewahren.* Cf. KEEP 7. For **take care** of a matter meaning 'to deal with it', see *erledigen* under SETTLE 5.

careful[ly], cautious[ly] *adjs.* and *advs.*

1. Careful means 'applying care or attention to' or 'taking pains with' what one does. It is applied to people, *a careful worker* or *He always plans everything carefully,* or to work which shows the result of such attention, *a careful translation, a careful examination of the facts.* **Sorgfältig** expresses this concept in reference both to people and their work.

 Die beiden sind sorgfältige Arbeiter. *Das ist eine sorgfältige Arbeit.*
 Er hat sich gründlich und sorgfältig auf die Prüfung vorbereitet.
 Sie war bemüht, den Brief sorgfältig ins Deutsche zu übersetzen.
 Hier ist eine sorgfältige Prüfung/Auswahl nötig.

2. Sorgsam is a syn. of *sorgfältig,* but is now old-fashioned and restricted in use. It still occurs in contexts which refer to looking after others carefully or keeping things in good condition, *Sie war eine sorgsame Mutter,* but instead of *Sie wählen ihre Worte sorgsam,* most people would now use *sorgfältig.*

 Sie deckte das Kind sorgsam zu/hat das Kind sorgsam gepflegt.
 Sie legte ihre Strickarbeit sorgsam zusammen, um keine Maschen zu verlieren.

3. When **careful** implies close attention to detail, it can be translated by **genau,** which in one sense means 'careful, meticulous, thorough'. *Sorgfältig,* however, suggests greater care. *Jmd. arbeitet genau/richtet sich genau nach der Vorschrift/hat alles genau durchdacht/achtet genau auf Klarheit des Ausdrucks. Bei genauem Hinsehen,* on looking carefully/closely, on close/careful inspection.

 Wir müssen die beiden Begriffe genau unterscheiden.
 Wir haben die Kosten genauestens berechnet.
 Man muß die Gebrauchsanweisungen genau befolgen.

4. In certain contexts **careful** is a syn. of **cautious**. Both mean 'avoiding harm, damage, or risks'. *Be careful! A careful driver. We must proceed carefully.* This sense is expressed by **vorsichtig.** *Ein vorsichtiger Fahrer. Be careful!* can be *Seien Sie vorsichtig!,* but an infin. construction is not added as in *Be careful not to break the eggs!* For the equivalent cf. [TAKE] CARE 1. To be careful with sth. in this sense, *to treat* or *handle sth. carefully/with care,* and *to take care with sth.* can often be translated by *vorsichtig mit etw. umgehen. Man muß mit der Kiste vorsichtig umgehen—sie enthält nämlich Porzellan.*

 Sie näherte sich vorsichtig dem verwundeten Tier.
 Vorsichtig öffnete er die Tür, damit sie nicht knarrte.
 Da sie noch nie auf Schlittschuhen gestanden hatte, machte sie nur vorsichtig an der Hand des
  Bruders die ersten Fahrversuche. *Sei doch vorsichtig mit dem Gewehr!*
 Das war eine vorsichtige Frage/Antwort.
 Man muß sehr vorsichtig fahren, weil die Straße glatt ist.
 Der Chemielehrer schärfte den Schülern ein, daß man vorsichtig mit organischen Lösungsmitteln
  umgehen muß und sie nie in die Nähe von offenen Flammen bringen soll.
 Er war viel zu vorsichtig, um ein solches Risiko einzugehen.

5. With regard to the treatment of people, **behutsam** implies an endeavour to avoid doing anything wrong or giving any offence. In relation to things, it means 'endeavouring not to damage them'. It is also often translated as *gentle*.

Sie legte das Baby behutsam in die Wiege zurück.

Behutsam und ganz langsam öffnete das kleine Mädchen das Paket.

Er fragte behutsam, was sie nun vorhabe.   Ich hätte sie behutsamer behandeln sollen.

6. Applied to the way people behave to one another, **schonend** means 'showing consideration', 'sparing others' feelings', and with regard to the treatment of things 'avoiding damage'. *Schonend mit etw. umgehen* means 'to look after it carefully' or 'to take good care of it'. *Behutsam* in the same construction suggests that the thing is fragile and could easily be damaged. *Schonend* is also translated as *gentle* or *gently*.

Die Benutzer der Bibliothek werden gebeten, die Bücher schonend zu behandeln (carefully).

Du mußt mit deinen Sachen schonender umgehen.

Man hatte ihn in schonender Weise auf die schlechte Nachricht vorbereitet (gently).

Das mußt du ihm schonend beibringen (break it gently).

casual[ly] *adj.* and *adv.*

1. The original meaning of **casual** is 'produced as a result of chance', but this sense survives only in a few expressions, the most common of which is *a casual encounter*, i.e. 'a chance or accidental meeting'. This is *eine* **zufällige** *Begegnung* or **eine Zufallsbegegnung**. Cf. ACCIDENT 3.

Ich traf auf der Straße eine Kommilitonin aus alten Studientagen. Es war eine rein zufällige Begegnung.

2. From sense 1 there has developed the sense 'happening as if by chance' applied to actions, mainly things said, which occur apparently without plan, premeditation, or prior consideration, as in *I made some casual remarks about the weather*.

i. One equivalent is **beiläufig**, which in general suggests that one attaches no great importance to something. In *Sie hat es nur beiläufig erwähnt* it means '(mentioned) incidentally' or 'in passing'. It also means 'coming about by chance' and can imply lack of concern. *Eine beiläufige Bemerkung* can therefore be 'an incidental or a casual remark'. *Ein beiläufiger Blick* is 'a casual glance', i.e. 'one arising when s.o. looks only by chance at s.o./sth.'

Ich machte einige beiläufige Bemerkungen über das Wetter.

Er hatte es nur ganz beiläufig gesagt, und wunderte sich, als sie ganz blaß wurde.

Manchmal gelingt es mir, meiner Stimme am Telefon jenen beiläufigen Klang zu geben, der den Kredit stärkt. (Böll)

Beiläufig möchte ich Ihnen mitteilen, daß ich Ihnen nicht rate, das Testament anzufechten.

ii. Leichthin, which is applied mostly to the way things are said, means 'without much consideration or seriousness', hence 'lightly or casually'.

Sie hatte es nur leichthin gesagt, ohne langes Nachdenken.

Das läßt sich leichthin behaupten. Bringen Sie aber die Beweise!

Er sagte, so leichthin ihm das vom Mund gehen wollte, daß er die ganze Arbeit sinnlos finde.

3. Applied to work, jobs, and workers, **casual** means 'without regularity or permanence'. **Die Gelegenheitsarbeit** suggests non-permanent work of a varied nature and of varying duration for which no special training is required. It translates both *casual work* and *odd jobs*.

Er war Gelegenheitsarbeiter. Im Sommer fand er Beschäftigung auf dem Bau oder beim Straßenbau, im Winter erledigte er Reparaturarbeiten oder übernahm Tapezier- und Malerarbeiten.

Vom Gelegenheitsarbeiter hatte er sich systematisch emporgearbeitet und besaß nun eine gutgehende Werkstatt mit mehreren Angestellten.

Gelegenheitsarbeit is also used for casual work undertaken by students etc. *Viele Studenten suchen nach einer Gelegenheitsarbeit.* However, **der Job** has become common in this sense. It implies temporary work of any kind from which some money can be earned. The v. **jobben**, 'to do casual work to earn money', has developed from it. (*Der Job* is sometimes used in the senses 'a position', *ein hochbezahlter Job*, and 'kind of work', *Mein Job ist sehr anstrengend.*)

> *Jeder dritte Schüler sucht sich in den großen Ferien einen Job.*
> *Mehrere Studenten im Wohnheim sehen sich nach einem Job/nach Gelegenheitsarbeit um.*
> *Da das Geld oft nicht ausreicht, müssen viele Studenten in den Ferien jobben.*
> *Er hat für drei Monate als Taxifahrer gejobbt.*

4. In another sense **casual** means 'feeling or showing little concern or interest', 'not giving close attention', 'indifferent to what is going on and to formal standards of behaviour, or pretending to be this'. It is applied to the way people work, behave, and act towards others, and may suggest informality. Although **too casual** and **over-casual** always express criticism, some people see casual behaviour as a virtue, while others disapprove of it. For some people, **casual** means 'not to be depended on, haphazard, happy-go-lucky'. *He does his work in a very casual manner.*

i. Lässig is applied to the way people bear themselves and act. It implies relaxed, free and easy bearing, or behaviour which lacks discipline and springs from great self-assurance. Whether *lässig* expresses approval or criticism depends on the speaker's attitude and on the situation; only *zu lässig* always expresses disapproval. *Lässig* is also applied to the mental attitude behind such behaviour and to the results it leads to. Thus *eine lässige Haltung* can refer to casual bearing or posture as well as to a casual mental attitude. *Er hat eine sehr lässige Haltung/Einstellung seiner Arbeit gegenüber. Er hat die Arbeit lässig gemacht/getan.* (**Nachlässig** denotes careless or slovenly work etc.) If *lässig* is pejorative, this may be expressed by the v. in E. *Er saß lässig in dem Sessel* can be translated as *lounged*, and *er lehnte lässig an der Mauer* as lolled.

> *Du gehst diese Aufgabe zu lässig an. Du könntest dir mehr Mühe geben.*
> *Er kam zehn Minuten zu spät zu der Sitzung, setzte sich lässig auf seinen Platz und grüßte nach allen Seiten hin.*   *Er hat eine lässige Art zu sprechen.*
> *Er ist ein lässiger, aber trotzdem guter Schüler.*   *Er stellte lässig ein paar Fragen.*

ii. Leger also denotes free and easy or relaxed behaviour or bearing, and can be applied to the way people work. It is like the E. word *nonchalant*. It is usually neutral, implying no criticism and suggesting casualness combined with joviality, but may sometimes express disapproval.

> *Du solltest die Sache nicht so leger behandeln.*   *Er hat die Abrechnung leger gehandhabt.*
> *Die Opposition warf der Regierung vor, die Waffenverkäufe an den Irak lässig/leger gehandhabt zu haben.*
> *Er saß ganz leger in dem Sessel und pfiff eine Melodie nach der anderen vor sich hin.*
> *Sie überspielte die Andeutungen und Sticheleien ganz leger und schnitt ein anderes Thema an.*

iii. Zwanglos means 'not showing the constraint of rules or conventional formality'. It can mean 'informal', but also 'casual' or 'free and easy' applied to behaviour or conversation. It is quite neutral.

> *Das soll keine formelle Einladung sein. Wir wollen nur zwanglos beisammensitzen und uns unterhalten.*
> *Es soll ein ganz zwangloses Treffen sein ohne großartige Formalitäten.*
> *Unter den Lehrkräften herrscht eine zwanglose Atmosphäre. Jeder redet jeden mit Vornamen an.*
> *Geben Sie sich ganz zwanglos!*   *Es war eine ganz zwanglose Unterhaltung.*

iv. Ungezwungen expresses no judgement. It means 'without stiffness, formality, tension, or inhibitions', 'free'. It is applied to people, their behaviour, conversation, etc. and may occasionally translate *casual*.

Die Umgebung war ihr neu und eigentlich auch ganz fremd, aber sie bewegte sich so ungezwungen, als sei sie dort aufgewachsen.   *Reden Sie frei und ungezwungen!*
Wenn Sie daran gewöhnt sind, sich ungezwungen zu benehmen, müssen Sie Ihr Verhalten ändern, um sich der formalen Atmosphäre anzupassen.
Sie würden eine bessere Reaktion erzielen, wenn Sie mit den Leuten zwangloser/ungezwungener umgingen.
Es war eine ganz ungezwungene Unterhaltung/Begegnung.
Sie können es mir ungezwungen sagen.

v. Nonchalant is sometimes used in educated speech with the same meaning as in E. *Er winkte uns mit einer nonchalanten Gebärde. Er grüßte nonchalant. Sie warf ihren Hut nonchalant auf den Tisch.*

vi. Hemdsärmelig means lit. 'in shirt-sleeves', but it has developed the sense of 'casual' and, depending on the point of view, 'over-casual'.

Hemdsärmelig stand der Firmenchef mitten unter seinen Arbeitern und packte kräftig mit an, wo Not am Mann war.
Seine hemdsärmelige Art und Redeweise spricht die einfachen Leute an.

vii. Salopp means 'not adhering to the existing conventions or prescriptions in manner, behaviour, speech, or clothing', 'very informal', 'free and easy'. Whether it expresses disapproval or not depends on the speaker's point of view and the situation. *Diese saloppe Haltung gefällt mir nicht.* Only *zu salopp* is clearly pejorative. It is translated as *casual*, but also as *sloppy* and *slovenly* or, for speech, *slangy*.

Er würde einen besseren Eindruck machen, wenn er sich nicht so salopp geben würde.
Ihre saloppen Bemerkungen sollten Sie lieber für den Stammtisch behalten.
Salopp gesagt: Der Vertrag ging in die Hose.   *Diese Ausdrucksweise finde ich sehr salopp.*

5. Lässig, leger, and **salopp** are used for clothes. Although *lässige Eleganz* occurs, all three suggest not elegant but informal. *Sie waren lässig gekleidet in Jeans und Pullovern. Eine legere Jacke. Ein legeres Kleid. Das Halstuch gibt dem Kleid eine saloppe Note.* The general term for *casual clothes* is *Freizeitkleidung.*

Der junge Mann wurde sich plötzlich seines saloppen Aufzugs bewußt.

catch, capture *vs.* Order of treatment: 1. **Catch** = 'to capture' and a fig. sense. 2. 'To take by surprise'. 3. 'To reach' a train etc. and 'to intercept' a person/thing. 4. 'To hit a part of the body'. 5. 'To take hold of forcibly'. 6. **Catch** *fire.* 7. Sth. is **caught** or entangled **in** sth. or **catches on** or **in** sth. 8. 'To seize sth. passing through the air'. 9. 'To be infected by a disease'. 10. 'To apprehend by the senses'. 11. **Catch** or **capture** an expression, mood, etc. 12. **Catch** s.o.'s attention.

1. i. Catch = 'to capture or lay hold of by superior force or speed or by a trap, snare, net, etc. that which tries or would try to escape'. It may also involve pursuit. Subj. and obj. can be people and animals. **Capture** is a syn. which implies greater opposition and difficulty. **Fangen** is the equivalent of both vs.

Man hatte das Känguruh in einer Falle gefangen.   *Die Spinne fängt Insekten in ihrem Netz.*
Wir haben den Vogel, den die beiden Jungen gefangen hatten, wieder freigelassen.
Die Katze hat schon wieder eine Maus gefangen.   *Ein Polizist hat den Dieb gefangen.*
Die Raubtiere fraßen die Beute, die sie gefangen hatten.
Die Grenzpolizei hatte die Schmuggler an der Grenze gefangen.

In relation to criminals **erwischen** and **schnappen** are common in speech. Cf. *fassen* under SEIZE 1.

Die Polizei hat die drei Bankräuber noch nicht erwischt.
Bei der Razzia hat die Polizei den Falschen erwischt.   *Die Polizei schnappte die Schmuggler.*

In reference to soldiers **gefangennehmen** is the usual v., but *gefangen* is the past part. used as an adj.

Im Laufe des erfolglosen Feldzuges wurden Tausende von Soldaten gefangengenommen.
Der Spähtrupp wurde hinter den gegnerischen Linien gefangengenommen.
Man hat die gefangenen Truppen/Soldaten wieder freigelassen

Einfangen has the same meaning as *fangen*, but implies that the person or animal caught has escaped and is fleeing. It is usually used with *wieder*.

Nach großer Aufregung haben die Kinder den entflogenen Vogel [wieder] eingefangen.
Die Häftlinge, die aus dem Gefängnis ausgebrochen waren, wurden schnell wieder eingefangen.

ii. Like **catch**, **fangen** also means 'to trap or ensnare people into admitting sth. they wanted to hide' or 'to win them for one's side etc.'

Der Kommissar versuchte durch geschickte Fragen den Verdächtigen zu fangen.
Es gelang dem Staatsanwalt, den Angeklagten zu fangen.
Durch Versprechungen, die wahrscheinlich nie erfüllt werden, versucht die Regierung, Stimmen zu fangen.
Ich lasse mich mit/durch Schmeicheleien nicht fangen.

2. Catch = 'to take by surprise'.

i. Catch is applied to rain, storms, etc. which overtake one before one reaches one's destination. *We were caught in the rain. The storm caught us just as we reached the top of the hill.* **Überraschen** suggests that the rain etc. arrived suddenly and that the people were unprepared.

Bei der Rückfahrt überraschte uns ein Schneesturm, und wir mußten sehr langsam fahren.
Auf dem Spaziergang wurden wir vom Regen überrascht und mußten Schutz suchen.

ii. Catch = 'to come upon s.o. suddenly or unexpectedly', 'to surprise s.o. in or at some action or doing sth.' *They were caught in the act/stealing apples. The police caught them at their little game.* **Ertappen** is the normal word in the standard language and **erwischen** in the spoken language. *Der Handtaschendieb wurde auf frischer Tat ertappt/erwischt*, caught in the act, caught red-handed. The usual prep. after both vs. is *bei*, either with a n., *Sie wurde bei einem Diebstahl ertappt*, or in the form *dabei* + a clause with *als, daß*, or *wie. Er wurde dabei ertappt/erwischt, wie er ein Auto aufbrach.*

Er ertappte die Nachbarskinder dabei, als sie gerade im Kirschbaum saßen und sich die Kirschen schmecken ließen.
Ich ertappe mich manchmal bei dem Gedanken, daß das Ganze keinen Sinn mehr hat.
Sie ertappte sich dabei, wie sie immer wieder dasselbe Wort gebrauchte.
Man hat sie bei einer krummen Sache erwischt.   *Er wurde bei einem Einbruch erwischt.*

3. Catch = 'to reach a train etc.' and 'to intercept s.o./sth.'

i. Catch means 'to reach or get to a pers. or thg. before he/she/it moves away' where the idea of being in time is paramount, *to catch a train, bus, the post*, etc. The equivalent in the standard language is **erreichen** and in the spoken language **erwischen**, but they are only used when being in time is implied. *Ich habe den Bus gerade noch erreicht/erwischt.* Both can be used for catching someone before he or she leaves a place.

Im Galopp ging es zum Bahnhof. Nur mit Mühe und Not erreichte/erwischte er noch den Zug.
Wir können die letzte Straßenbahn hoffentlich noch erwischen/erreichen.
Herr Behrens ist gerade hinausgegangen, aber vielleicht erreichen Sie ihn noch, bevor er das Gebäude verläßt.
Du hast Glück gehabt, daß du mich noch erwischt hast. Ich wollte gerade einkaufen gehen.

In sents. like *What train are you catching?, You catch the bus outside the Post Office*, or *I catch the ferry to work every day* where there is no implication of being in time, vs. like **fahren** or **abfahren** must be used. Cf. GO 2 and LEAVE 1.

Mit welchem Zug fährst Du nach Paderborn?   *Ich fahre jeden Tag mit der Fähre zur Arbeit.*
Der Bus zur Universität hält vor dem Postamt/fährt vom Postamt ab.

ii. One sense of **abfangen** is 'to intercept'. *Die Maschine wurde von sowjetischen Jägern abgefangen* (i.e. *Abfangjäger*, interception-fighter). It also means 'to wait at a place

in order to meet s.o. going past', an idea which would usually be expressed in E.
by **catch**.

> *Es gelang ihm endlich, den Sänger am Theatereingang abzufangen und ein Autogramm zu erhalten.*
> *Der Briefträger wird erst in einer Stunde hier sein, aber wenn du an der übernächsten Ecke wartest,*
> *kannst du ihn vielleicht abfangen.*
> *Die Polizei fing den Spion auf seinem Fluchtweg ab.*

4. Catch used with blows, falling objects, missiles, etc. means 'to hit some part of
the body'. *The ball caught him on the side of the head.* The normal equivalent is **treffen**, 'to hit (the mark)', (the opposite of *miss*) and **erwischen** in the spoken language. The subj. must be the moving or falling object. Cf. HIT 1.

> *Der Stein traf ihn an der Seite des Kopfes/am Bein.*
> *Ein fallendes Stück Holz traf/erwischte ihn an der Stirn, und er wurde bewußtlos.*

5. Catch can mean 'to take hold of suddenly or forcibly', 'to seize'. *He
caught/grabbed/seized the child just as it was about to step in front of the car.* To take hold
of is **fassen**, to seize **packen**. Cf. SEIZE 1. **Erwischen** can mean 'to manage to get hold
of just in time'.

> *Er erwischte den Jungen am Kragen und zog ihn zurück vom Felsenrand.*
> *Er faßte mich bei der Hand/beim Arm.*   *Der Polizist packte den Burschen beim Kragen.*

6. Catch *fire* is **Feuer fangen**. *Durch einen Funken fing das trockene Gras Feuer.*
However, *The flames were catching the bed* becomes *Die Flammen* **erreichten** *gerade das
Bett* or *griffen auf das Bett über.* **Übergreifen**, to SPREAD TO. *Das Feuer griff auf das
Nachbarhaus über.*

7. Catch is applied to inanimate things which hold a person or animal against its
will or prevent a thing from moving. *The branches caught the deer's antlers. The ram
was caught in the thicket by its horns.* Used intr. in a related sense, **catch** means 'to
be held or entangled'. *The kite caught in the branches. Her sleeve caught in the thorn-
bushes.*

i. The main v. is **sich verfangen**, 'to become caught or entangled', which is usual
in speech and is found on other levels of style. The animal etc. must be the subj.,
and the part of the body caught is expressed with *mit*. *Ein Tier hatte sich mit den
Hörnern im Dickicht verfangen.* Sich verfangen implies that escape is difficult. *Ein Vogel,
der sich im Netz verfangen hatte*, could normally only be freed by outside help. *Eine
Drachenschnur* (string, cord of a kite), *die sich in den Ästen eines Baumes verfangen hat,*
would be difficult or impossible to retrieve. *Sich verfangen* is used fig., as in *Er hat
sich in Widersprüchen verfangen.* In literary G. **sich fangen** is used in two contexts.
Ein Insekt fängt sich in einem Spinnennetz when by its own movements it seems to
cause itself to be caught. *Die Fliege hatte sich im Spinnennetz gefangen.* For people *sich
fangen* is used fig. in relation to a trap, but also has the idea of causing oneself to
be caught. *Mit diesen Fragen legen sie eine Falle, in der ich mich fangen soll.*

> *Ihr Halstuch verfing sich im Gestrüpp, und sie mußte es zurücklassen.*
> *Die Angel hatte sich im Schilf verfangen.*
> *Beim Abrutschen hatte er sich mit dem Fuß in einem Netz verfangen. Das hielt ihn auf und hat ihm*
> *wahrscheinlich das Leben gerettet.*
> *Der Springer muß immer ein Messer mit sich führen, da es immer wieder bei der Landung vorkommt,*
> *daß er sich im Fallschirm verfängt und sich freischneiden muß.*
> *Ihr Haar fing sich im Geäst, aber mit Hilfe ihrer Begleiter konnte sie sich wieder losmachen.*

ii. A nail, hook, etc. is also said to catch something which comes against it in passing. *A nail caught her dress, Her dress caught on a nail*, and *She caught her dress on a nail.*
The usual v. is **hängenbleiben**, 'to be/get caught', also 'to stick or get stuck'. The
construction is usually *Sie blieb mit dem Kleid im Stacheldraht hängen*, but the article
of clothing can be the subj., *Das Kleid blieb im Stacheldraht hängen. Ein Kleid, das an*

einem Nagel/am Stacheldraht hängenbleibt, would only suffer slight damage. *Eines, das sich verfangen hatte,* would be more or less ruined. **Steckenbleiben,** 'to become stuck', as in *Wir sind im Schlamm steckengeblieben,* translates **catch** referring to a bone caught or stuck in one's throat. *Ihm blieb eine Gräte in der Kehle stecken.*

> Sie blieb mit ihrem Jackenärmel an der Türklinke hängen.

iii. In *I caught my foot against a root and stumbled,* or *My foot caught . . . , and I stumbled,* **caught** means 'hit or banged', which is **stoßen.** *Ich bin mit dem Fuß an eine Wurzel gestoßen und bin [darüber] gestolpert.* Cf. HIT 7. *Ich bin mit dem Fuß/Mein Fuß ist an einer Wurzel hängengeblieben* is also used.

iv. If **catch** means 'to jam', **klemmen** is used. *Ich habe mir den Finger in der Tür geklemmt.*

v. If someone is caught [up] or entangled in something which is not concrete, for example prejudices or illusions, this is expressed by one sense of **befangen.** *Er war in Illusionen/Vorurteilen/in einer Täuschung befangen.*

> Sie ist in den eigenen Anschauungen so befangen, daß sie nichts anderes mehr gelten läßt.

8. Catch = 'to intercept or seize sth. passing through the air or falling'. The usual word is **auffangen.** However, when it is clear that the obj. is meant to be caught, *auf* is omitted, and the base v. *fangen* is used. A child who wants to throw a ball to someone will simply say, '*Fang mal!'* Similarly, *Ich konnte den heruntergeworfenen Schlüssel nicht fangen.* However, *auffangen* would not be incorrect in both cases. It is used when the idea of catching something is not clear from the context, when **catch** means 'to collect water or other liquids in a vessel', *Wir fangen Regenwasser in einem großen Faß auf,* or when someone catches or overhears some words of a conversation etc., *Die Mutter hatte nur das Wort 'Verdacht' aufgefangen. Einen Funkspruch auffangen,* to intercept a radio message.

> Der Vogel fing das ihm zugeworfene Stück Brot geschickt im Fluge auf.
>
> Seine Arme waren viel zu kurz, und es machte ihm Mühe, den großen, schweren Ball zu fangen/aufzufangen.   Spring' mal runter! Ich fang dich auf.
>
> Aus den aufgefangenen Wortfetzen konnte sich der Direktor nur ein ungefähres Bild von dem machen, was die Schüler wirklich über ihn dachten.

9. Catch can mean 'to get or take passively'. It is used most frequently with diseases, but is also found in other contexts.

i. Bekommen is often used for illnesses. *Man bekommt eine Erkältung/die Masern,* etc. The alternative **sich holen** is broader than **catch** in the range of bad things it is applied to, but includes catching by infection. *Ich habe mir einen Schnupfen/eine Erkältung/die Grippe geholt.* **Anstecken** is 'to infect'. The pass. **angesteckt werden** or the refl. **sich anstecken** imply catching by contagion or infection. Thus *Ich wurde von ihm angesteckt* or *Ich habe mich bei ihm angesteckt. Ansteckende Krankheiten* are contagious, infectious, or catching. *Grippe steckt an.* It is also applied to feelings, good humour, and ideas which spread to others. *Seine gute Laune/Die Begeisterung steckt alle an/wirkte ansteckend. Gähnen steckt an.*

The expression *Dabei kannst du dir den Tod holen* can be adapted to translate *catch your death of cold. Wenn du bei diesem Wetter ohne Mantel ausgehst, wirst du dir den Tod holen.* Being broader than the E. expression, it occurs in other contexts. *Bei deinem unvorsichtigen Motorradfahren wirst du dir den Tod holen.*

ii. The ship caught the full force of the storm is *Das Schiff bekam die volle Wucht des Sturmes zu spüren.*

10. Catch = 'to apprehend by the senses or intellect', 'to succeed in hearing, seeing, understanding, etc.' **Verstehen** can mean 'to succeed in hearing and understanding'. A colloquial syn. is **mitbekommen.** *To catch sight of* is **erblicken,** and *to catch a glimpse of* **flüchtig zu sehen bekommen.**

Ich habe bei dem Lärm kein Wort verstanden (understood/heard/caught).
Ich habe das Ende des Satzes nicht mitbekommen/verstanden.
Worum es eigentlich ging, habe ich nicht mitbekommen.
Den Sinn Ihrer Worte habe ich nicht mitbekommen/verstanden.
Ich habe ihn nur ganz flüchtig in der Menschenmenge zu sehen bekommen.
Als ich die Straße entlang ging, erblickte ich meine Freundin auf der anderen Straßenseite.

11. The idea that an artist catches or captures the expression on someone's face is translated by **treffen**. To state that a writer catches or captures an atmosphere etc., G. uses **einfangen**.

Der Künstler hat den hochmütigen Gesichtsausdruck genau getroffen.
Der Film/Der Roman konnte die Stimmung am Ende des Krieges genau einfangen.
Der Maler versuchte, die Herbststimmung/das Leben auf dem Lande in seinen Bildern einzufangen.

12. Catch s.o.'s attention = 'to attract'. *Jmds. Aufmerksamkeit/Blicke auf sich ziehen* or *lenken.* Cf. ATTRACT 4.

cause *n.* Some senses of **reason** and **occasion** *ns.*

1. One meaning of **cause** is 'that which produces an effect or gives rise to any action'.

i. The equivalent is **die Ursache**. *Cause and effect is Ursache und Wirkung.* Sometimes *Ursache* can only be translated as *reason. Der Wagen ist aus unbekannter Ursache von der Straße abgekommen.*

Das Fahren mit überhöhter Geschwindigkeit ist die Ursache vieler Unfälle.
Die Polizei versuchte, die Ursache des Brandes festzustellen.
Die Ursachen der Mißstände wurden aufgedeckt und behoben.

ii. People who bring something about and are said to be the cause of it. *They were the cause of our misfortune/failure.* This idea is mostly expressed by **verschulden**, to be to blame for. *Sie haben den Mißerfolg/unser Unglück/den Unfall verschuldet.* Alternatives are **schuld sein an** and **verantwortlich sein für**. Cf. BLAME 1. *Die beiden sind an dem Scheitern des Unternehmens schuld/für das Scheitern . . . verantwortlich.*

2. Cause also denotes a fact or condition moving someone to action, the reason for action. It occurs mostly in fixed expressions and is usually interchangeable with **reason,** which denotes a rational ground or motive leading to action. *There is no cause/reason for anxiety. I have cause/reason to believe that he is dishonest. You have no cause/reason for alarm. They distrusted him without cause/with good cause. He complains, and with reason, that he has been unfairly punished.*

i. Die Ursache does express this sense, mainly in the phr. *alle Ursache* or *keine Ursache haben* + infin., but it is less common than **der Grund**, reason. *Er hatte alle Ursache, mit seinem Arbeitsplatz zufrieden zu sein. Du hast alle Ursache/jeden Grund, dich über diese Lösung zu freuen. Ich habe keine Ursache, unzufrieden zu sein. Du hast keinen Grund, dich zu beklagen/zur Klage.*

Ich habe Grund anzunehmen/zur Annahme, daß er unehrlich ist.
Sie mißtraut ihm ohne jeden Grund/mit gutem Grund.
Es gibt keinen Grund zur Beunruhigung.
Ohne guten Grund sollte man nicht wegbleiben.   *Sie haben alle Ursache, sich zu beklagen.*

ii. One sense of **der Anlaß** is 'sth. that brings about an action or mental reaction'. It thus refers to what prompts human behaviour and is translated as **cause, reason,** *motive,* or **occasion**. When **cause** refers to a motive, *Anlaß* is the appropriate word, although the idea can also be expressed by *Grund. Anlaß geben zu,* to give rise to or cause for.

Er ist ohne den geringsten Anlaß weggelaufen.   *Sie haben uns ohne jeden Anlaß beleidigt.*

Wenn wir einen Anlaß sehen, neue Arbeitsmethoden einzuführen, werden wir die entsprechenden Änderungen durchführen.   *Krawalle brachen aus, deren Anlässe völlig nichtig waren.*
Die Erkrankung gibt keinen Anlaß zur Besorgnis/zur Beunruhigung.

iii. Die Veranlassung is more formal and also stresses the idea of a motive leading to action.

Sie hat nie die geringste Veranlassung zu einem Streit gegeben.
Er hatte keine Veranlassung, unzufrieden zu sein.   *Dazu besteht/gibt es keine Veranlassung.*

3. i. In one sense **occasion** is a syn. of **cause** and denotes something which produces an effect. *This wording has been the occasion for a considerable amount of misunderstanding.* This could be translated by *sein* with *Ursache* or by *Anlaß geben: Dieser Wortlaut war die Ursache vieler Mißverständnisse* or *Dieser Wortlaut hatte Anlaß zu vielen Streitereien gegeben.*

ii. Occasion is also applied to circumstances requiring or calling for action. *There is no occasion/cause/reason for alarm* is *Es gibt keinen Grund zur Panik* or the alternatives in 2.

iii. Der Anlaß means 'occasion' when it refers to the time at which something happens. *On the occasion of her seventieth birthday* is *aus Anlaß ihres siebzigsten Geburtstages. Aus Anlaß des hundertjährigen Bestehens der Firma bekamen alle Beschäftigten eine zusätzliche Woche Urlaub. That's an occasion for celebration* is *Das is ein Anlaß zum Feiern. Grund zum Feiern* means 'a reason for celebration'.

4. Cause meaning 'a principle worth defending' or 'a movement which calls forth the efforts of its supporters' is expressed by one meaning of **die Sache**. When it is not followed by a gen. or a clause, it is usual to add an adj. like *gut* or *gerecht*. Thus *Er widmete seine ganze Kraft der Sache des Friedens/des Sozialismus*, or *Die Sache, für die sie kämpften, war hoffnungslos*, but *Sie waren bereit, für die gute Sache zu sterben. To make common cause* is *mit jmdm. gemeinsame Sache machen.*

Sie haben es um der guten Sache willen getan.   *Die Sache der Gerechtigkeit wird siegen.*
Sie kämpften/arbeiteten für eine gute/gerechte/verlorene Sache.
Wenn wir so handelten, wären wir Verräter an der Sache, der wir zu dienen gelobt haben.

cause, bring about *vs.* **Cause** means 'to make sth. happen' or 'to result in s.o. doing sth.' **Bring about** means 'to cause to happen'. Several G. vs. express variations on the sense of these syns. **Cause** + a non-personal obj. is mainly *verursachen*, and **cause** + a pers. + infin. *veranlassen*.

i. Verursachen and **bewirken** express the same meaning as the E. expressions, but differ slightly from each other in the way the process of cause and effect is seen. Being formed from *die Ursache*, *verursachen* stresses the cause or actuating factor, while *bewirken*, being related to *die Wirkung*, draws attention to the effect, as does **bring about**. Both imply a direct connection between cause and effect and are in some cases interchangeable, although each is particularly appropriate in the situations just described. *Der Bau der neuen Bibliothek verursacht viel Lärm. Die Tablette bewirkte eine Linderung der Schmerzen.* There are some syntactic differences. *Verursachen* can take a dat. as well as an acc. and thus corresponds to *cause s.o. pain* etc. This use is, however, common only in formal language and mostly with unpleasant effects. *Mit seinen schlecht durchdachten Plänen hat er uns große Unannehmlichkeiten verursacht. Diese Angelegenheit hat ihm viel Ärger/unnötige Kosten/viel Mühe verursacht.* (The usual vs. meaning 'to give or to cause' someone pleasure or pain are *machen* and *bereiten*. Cf. GIVE 9.) **Cause** with a thing as obj. and an infin., as in *This caused the government to fall*, needs a different construction, as neither *verursachen* nor *bewirken* is used with an infin. Both can be used if the idea of the infin. can be expressed as a n. *Das hat den Sturz der Regierung verursacht* or *bewirkt. What caused the forests to die?* could be *Was hat das Waldsterben verursacht?* (Or *das Absterben der Wälder.*) Besides taking an obj., *bewirken* takes a *daß*-clause. Thus *Die Tablette bewirkte, daß die Schmerzen bald vergingen*, caused the pain to disappear. **Zur Folge haben**, 'to have as a consequence or result in', is a common expression which takes an obj. or *daß*-clause. *Die außergewöhnlich starken Regenfälle hatten eine Steigerung des Ertrags zur Folge/hatten zur Folge, daß die Ernte besonders gut ausfiel.*

> *Eine Zigarette, die jmd. ohne die nötige Vorsicht weggeworfen hatte, verursachte den Waldbrand.*
> *Diese Meinungsverschiedenheit hat eine Entfremdung zwischen den beiden verursacht/bewirkt.*
> *Das Lesen bei schlechtem Licht verursacht Augenschäden.*
> *Wenn du so streng bist, wirst du das Gegenteil von dem bewirken, was du erreichen willst.*
> *Vitamin C bewirkt eine größere Widerstandsfähigkeit des Körpers gegen Erkältungen.*
> *Durch seinen Zuspruch hat er bewirkt, daß die beiden sich wieder aussöhnten.*
> *Die neuen Richtlinien hatten eine Verbesserung der Arbeitsverhältnisse zur Folge.*
> *Unvorhergesehene Umstände haben meine Verspätung verursacht.* Or . . . *hatten zur Folge, daß ich mich verspätete.*

ii. Hervorrufen means 'to cause or produce' some kind of mental reaction or a disease. *Bei* states the person experiencing the reaction. *Diese Bemerkungen riefen bei allen Heiterkeit/ein Lächeln/stürmischen Protest/berechtigte Empörung/nur Widerspruch hervor.*

> *Der Brand hat eine Panik/allgemeine Verwirrung hervorgerufen.*
> *Das Fieber wurde durch eine Entzündung hervorgerufen.*

iii. Bedingen is related to *die Bedingung*, condition. The meaning is that if certain conditions are fulfilled, a particular result follows. In strict use, it therefore means 'to cause in an indirect way'. It mostly occurs in the past part. with *sein*. *Die niedrigen Preise sind durch das Überangebot bedingt* suggests that because the market is oversupplied, the prices are low. It can be translated as *caused by*, but also as *conditional* or *dependent on*. Behaviour is said to be *psychisch bedingt*, which suggests that because certain mental conditions obtain, a certain type of behaviour ensues. The relation between cause and effect is less direct than with *verursachen* and *bewirken*.

> *Das rasche Voranschreiten der Arbeit ist durch den großen Fleiß der Mitarbeiter bedingt.*
> *Es gibt Krankheiten, die durch Vitaminmangel bedingt sind.*
> *Der Produktionsrückstand ist durch den Streik bedingt.*

iv. Herbeiführen also means 'to bring about'. It suggests a less direct connection between cause and effect than *verursachen* and *bewirken*, but a more direct one than **führen zu**, to lead to. It often suggests that what is brought about is in its way decisive. *Sein Eingreifen in die Verhandlungen führte eine Wende herbei.* With people as subj., it presupposes an intention, so that *Er hat den Untergang der Firma herbeigeführt* would imply that he did it on purpose. This does not hold, of course, when no intention can be present, as in *Die Wirtschaftskrise führte den Ruin der Firma herbei. Bewirken* does not presuppose an intention, so that *Die Wirtschaftskrise bewirkte* . . . expresses the same meaning as the previous sentence. *Die Wirtschaftskrise führte zum Ruin der Firma* is also possible.

> *Sie versuchte, eine Einigung/eine Versöhnung zwischen den Brüdern herbeizuführen.*
> *Hitler wollte Deutschland die Vormachtstellung in Europa verschaffen. Dazu plante er einen Hegemonialkrieg und führte ihn herbei.*   *Die Hungersnot führte zu Unruhen.*
> *Die falsche Einschätzung der Lage führte zu dieser Fehlentscheidung.*

v. In one use **veranlassen** has a person as obj. + an infin. or + *zu* + an action. *Was hat ihn veranlaßt, sein Amt niederzulegen?* Or *Was hat ihn zum Rücktritt veranlaßt?* It is the main equivalent of *to cause s.o. to do sth. Veranlassen* is mostly restricted to situations in which the resulting action is a considered decision, an act of free will, not involuntary. With an involuntary action as in *A sudden noise caused me to jump* *back*, the v. is **lassen**. *Ein plötzliches Geräusch ließ mich zurückspringen.* Although *veranlassen* is not impossible in this context, it makes the sent. sound very formal. There is, however, an area of overlap. *Das Verhalten der Schüler veranlaßte den Lehrer einzugreifen* or *ließ den Lehrer eingreifen.* Cf. MAKE 1.

> *Sein auffälliges Benehmen veranlaßte die Gäste, frühzeitig aufzubrechen.*
> *Das hat mich zum Nachdenken veranlaßt/hat mich veranlaßt, noch einmal über die Sache nachzudenken.*

Cause + a non-personal obj. + infin. is expressed by *lassen*.

> *Die starken Regenfälle ließen den Fluß über die Ufer treten.*
> *Die anhaltende Trockenheit hat den Pegel aller Flüsse dramatisch fallen lassen.*

vi. In one sense **anrichten** means 'to cause or give rise to sth. evil or baneful' such as *Schaden, Unheil, große Verwirrung, ein Blutbad*, or *Verwüstungen*. **Verursachen** is also used in relation to damage etc. The subj. can be human beings or forces of nature. *Anrichten* can be used ironically with people as subj., but does not necessarily imply that the bad effect was intended. *Da habt ihr was Schönes/Nettes angerichtet*, you've done something stupid, caused a lot of trouble. *Anrichten* is used with a phr. stating a place, but it does not take a dat. With a dat., e.g. to cause s.o. harm, **zufügen**, 'to inflict on', is necessary. *Dieser Mann hat mir/der Firma viel Schaden zugefügt.*

> *Der Orkan hat im ganzen Küstengebiet Verwüstungen angerichtet.*
> *Besonders in Hamburg haben randalierende Fans großen Schaden angerichtet.*
> *Der Angreifer fügte seinem Opfer schwere körperliche Verletzungen zu.*

vii. In one sense **stiften** means 'to bring about, cause, or produce'. The obj. can be something beneficial like *Frieden* or *Eintracht* or something undesirable like *Verwirrung, Zwietracht*, or *Unfrieden*. Thus *Sie stiftete Frieden zwischen den Parteien* and *Sie versuchte, Unfrieden zwischen den Kollegen zu stiften.* The result can be intended or, as in the first example below, unintended. **Anstiften** means 'to bring about deliberately' something objectionable and harmful like *Unruhe, Streit, Verwirrung, Unfrieden.* (With *zu* + n. or infin. *anstiften* means 'to incite', 'egg on'. *Der große Junge stiftete den kleinen zum Diebstahl an. Der Soldat stiftete seinen Kameraden dazu an, seinen Panzer kaputtzufahren.*)

> *Die unbedachte Äußerung des Präsidenten stiftete Verwirrung und Zwietracht unter den Delegierten.*
> *Die beiden Kinder stritten sich solange, bis die Mutter eingriff, um Ruhe/Frieden zu stiften.*
> *Diese Streitereien unter den Kollegen—das hat dieser Mann angestiftet.*

change, alter, exchange, transform, convert *vs.* Order of treatment: 1. The meaning 'to make or become different' and *ändern* and its derivatives. 2. The meaning 'to substitute one thg. for another', senses carried by *wechseln* and its derivatives. 3. The sense 'to transform' and *wandeln* and its derivatives. 4. *Tauschen* and its derivatives and the sense 'to exchange'. 5. Other equivalents of **change**. 6. Vs. meaning 'to change [over] from one thg. to another'.

1. Change or **alter** = 'make a thg. different without putting another in its place'. **Alter** and **change** do not suggest a degree of difference. Both occur with *slightly, drastically*, and *radically*. While **change** has other senses, **alter** is limited to this meaning. Only **alter** means 'to make clothes different'. **Alter** and **change** are both trans., meaning 'to make different', *The defeat of the government altered/changed the situation*, and intr., meaning 'to become different', *The situation has altered/changed.* The latter is the refl. in G.

i. Ändern, the general term, means 'to make different by adding or taking away or by modifying parts of a whole' and thus corresponds to both E. vs. The degree of change varies from slight to considerable to more or less complete. It means 'to alter' clothes and 'to change' things which are fixed in writing or have a definite shape in one's mind. It thus occurs with words like *Einzelheiten, Testament, Preis, Programm, Vertrag, Gesetz, Name, Bestimmungen, Text, Verfassung, Plan, Richtung, eine Politik*, 'policy', and with relatively clearly defined things like *Meinung, Ansicht, Entschluß, Taktik, Ton, Kurs, Strategie, Bedeutung, Sinn*, 'sense' = 'meaning', *Benehmen*. It is also the usual word when the subj. or obj. is indefinite, *das, es, einiges, etw., nichts*. The refl. is necessary when in E. the thing changed is the subj. *My opinion has changed/altered: Meine Ansicht über diese Frage hat sich geändert*. With a person as subj., the refl. implies a change in behaviour for the better. *Er hat sich geändert* may suggest a considerable change, but may mean no more than that he is more punctual or tidier, does not drink so much, or similar improvements. Cf. AFFECT 1. iv.

Das Kleid ist zu lang. Ich muß es ändern.	*Ich habe den Text an einigen Stellen geändert.*
Das Flugzeug änderte seinen Kurs um 30 Grad.	*An der Sache läßt sich nichts ändern.*

Aller Anlaß war gegeben, die bisherige Politik zu ändern und sie der neuen Lage anzupassen.

Ich kann es leider nicht ändern.	*Es ist leider nicht zu ändern.*

Refl.: *In den letzten Monaten hat sich die Lage geändert.*

Einiges hat sich von Grund aus (or auf) geändert.

Daran hat sich bis heute gar nichts geändert.

ii. Verändern is 'to change in nature or appearance', i.e. to give something a different form or shape, composition, or order, the degree of change often being stated. With *verändern*, the obj. changed tends to be large and often amorphous like *Welt, Verhältnisse*, conditions, *sein Leben, die Situation*, not clearly outlined as with *ändern*. It often implies a more substantial or fundamental change than does *ändern*. With some ns. such as *Verhältnisse, Verhalten, Leben*, or *die Lage*, both *ändern* and *verändern* occur, but *ändern* suggests a less drastic or radical change. *Verändern* often has *viel* as obj. *Diese Reform hat viel verändert*. (This does not mean that a change denoted by *ändern* is always slight; one can speak of *grundlegende Änderungen* or say *Gegebenheiten können sich entscheidend/von Grund auf ändern*.) Applied to people, *verändern* can refer to appearance or character. If I say to someone I have not seen for a long time, *'Du hast dich aber gar nicht verändert'*, his or her appearance would usually be understood. If in talking of someone's behaviour someone says, *'Er hat sich ganz verändert'*, it would usually be assumed that the character is meant.

Die Wolken veränderten schnell ihre Form.	*Die Rohstoffe werden im Arbeitsprozeß verändert.*

Das Fernsehen hat die Lebensgewohnheiten vieler Menschen verändert.

Was soll in dieser Situation geschehen? Die Antwort lautet kurz und bündig: Nichts, was die Verhältnisse grundsätzlich verändern könnte.

Die bisherigen Philosophen haben die Welt nur verschieden interpretiert. Jetzt kommt es darauf an, sie zu verändern. (Marx/Engels)

In Hugo war eine gewaltige Veränderung vorgegangen. Er war nicht mehr derselbe Mensch.

Sie spürte, diese Nachricht würde ihr ganzes Leben verändern.

Die Stadt hat sich in den letzten zwanzig Jahren kaum verändert.

Einer bestimmten Politik kann der Boden entzogen werden, wenn sich entweder die Lage oder die öffentliche Meinung verändert.	*Er hat sich zu seinem Vorteil verändert.*

Cf. 2. ii for the meaning *sich [beruflich] verändern*.

iii. Abändern implies making slight additions, deletions, or alterations, but it is hardly used in the spoken language. It occurs in the phr. *In Abänderung (unseres Programms). In Abänderung unseres gedruckten Programms bringen wir jetzt eine Ansprache des Bundespräsidenten.*

Wegen des Todes des Präsidenten ändern der Rundfunk und das Fernsehen heute ihre Programme ab.

In den ersten Takten hat er die Klavierbegleitung abgeändert.

iv. Umändern, to give sth. a new form, to remodel, to change so that sth. completely different is formed from old materials. As well as to clothes, it can be applied to products of the mind which are recast or refashioned without the substance being affected. It can be followed by *in, into*.

Meinen alten Wintermantel habe ich mir total umgeändert.
Der Schriftsteller änderte die ursprüngliche Fassung des Romans um.
Er hat das Haus in eine kleine Fabrik umgeändert.

2. Change = 'to put or take one thing for another of the same kind', 'to substitute for'. This meaning is expressed by *wechseln*, the difference between it and *ändern* being the same as that between *to change one's dress* and *to alter a dress*. *Wechseln* has, however, several meanings, and there is some overlapping between it and *ändern* and *tauschen*. i–vii give the uses of *wechseln*, and viii those of a derivative.

i. Wechseln = 'to replace one thg. which may have become unusable by another of the same kind'. *Man wechselt die Bettwäsche/ein Hemd/Kleider/die Schuhe/Handtücher/ einen Reifen/ein Rad/das Öl (in einem Auto)* etc.

ii. Wechseln = 'to give one thg. up and take or go to another of the same kind'. *Man wechselt den Arbeitsplatz/die Schule/die Wohnung/den Platz/das Thema/die Branche/den Beruf/den Betrieb* etc.

  Das Geschäft hat den Besitzer gewechselt (changed owners or hands).

  Der Koffer ist schwer, ich muß mal die Hand wechseln. Or . . . *ich muß ihn mal [von dieser] in die andere Hand wechseln.*

N.B. *Man wechselt die Wohnung,* but *Man ändert die Adresse.* **Change** *jobs* is lit. *die Stelle wechseln.* With a person as subj. **sich verändern** can mean 'to change one's job'. *Beruflich* may be added. *Sie hat sich [beruflich] verändert und verdient jetzt 300 Mark im Monat mehr.*

iii. Wechseln is intr. in a sense which implies that one thing takes the place of another and which is therefore related to the meanings defined in i and ii. In *Das Kino wechselt das Programm alle vierzehn Tage,* it is trans., but *Programm* can become the subj. so that it is intr., *Das Programm wechselt alle vierzehn Tage.* Also intr. are *Die Regierung hat gewechselt* and *Die Bewölkung/Mode wechselt ständig.*

iv. Wechseln is also intr. in the meaning 'to become different' and is thus synonymous with *sich [ver]ändern,* but it often has the connotation that the change happens more than once. It is used often, but not exclusively, in connection with the weather. Hence the synonymous adjs. *wechselhaftes* and *veränderliches Wetter.*

  Seine Stimmung konnte sehr schnell wechseln.

  Während unseres kurzen Urlaubs an der Nordsee wechselte das Wetter mehrmals.

v. Wechseln means 'to alternate', mostly in reference to major phenomena of nature and life. *So wie die Ernte wechselt und mal gut und mal schlecht ist, wechseln auch die guten und schlechten Zeiten.* (*Sich abwechseln* is the usual equivalent of *alternate*. *Regen und Sonnenschein wechseln sich ab. Wir wechseln uns bei der Arbeit ab.*)

  An dieser Küste kann man gut beobachten, wie Ebbe und Flut wechseln, weil der Wasserspiegel bei Ebbe vier Meter niedriger ist als bei Flut.   *In rascher Folge wechselten Rede und Gegenrede.*

vi. Wechseln means 'to change to another place' in the sense of moving to it. Cf. 6. iii.

  Der Justizminister soll ins Auswärtige Amt wechseln.

  Wir müssen in die linke [Fahr]spur wechseln (die Fahrspur = 'traffic lane').

vii. Wechseln means 'to give s.o. one thg. and receive in return another/others of the same value', i.e. 'to exchange', which is usually *tauschen.* Cf. 4. i. *Wechseln* is used mainly for money and with *Briefe, Worte,* and *Blicke.* It is the normal v. in *Das Brautpaar wechselte die Ringe.* With money *wechseln* means 'to change either into smaller notes or coins or into another currency'. (**Einwechseln** and **umwechseln** are alternatives for money in both senses, but less common. *Können Sie mir einen Fünfzigmarkschein einwechseln? Ich habe 300 DM in französische Francs eingewechselt. Ich* *muß noch [um]wechseln (d. h. von DM in Francs). Umtauschen* is a syn. in the latter sense. Cf. 4. iv.)

> *Wir haben im Gang ein paar Worte [miteinander] gewechselt.*
> *Die beiden Schriftsteller haben jahrelang Briefe gewechselt.*
> *Ich kann [dir] zehn Mark [in zwei Mark-Stücke] wechseln.*
> *Im Flughafen habe ich DM in/gegen Pfund gewechselt/umgetauscht.*

viii. Auswechseln means 'to change' as a syn. of *replace*. With things as obj., it often, though not always, implies that the thing replaced is worn out or unusable. *Man wechselt eine Glühbirne/die Zündkerzen/die Batterie aus.* However, *Ich muß diese Glühbirne gegen eine stärkere auswechseln* does not imply being worn out. *Auswechseln* is also used in sport. *Der Torwart mußte wegen einer Verletzung ausgewechselt werden. Der Trainer entschloß sich, bei der Halbzeit zwei Spieler auszuwechseln.*

3. Change = 'to turn, convert, transform into sth. else'. The words in this group are derivatives of *wandeln*. While the base v. ranges in meaning from making or becoming considerably different to making or turning into something else, *umwandeln* and *verwandeln* denote only the latter.

i. Wandeln is elevated and uncommon, though the refl. is occasionally met with. It usually implies a gradual development rather than a sudden change. The refl. of *wandeln* and of the derivatives is necessary if the thing changed is the subj. *Die Mode wandelt sich ständig.* [Sich] *wandeln* can be followed by *in. Seine Angst hatte sich in Zuversicht gewandelt.* More commonly: *verwandelt.*

> *Die Erlebnisse im Krieg haben ihn gewandelt.* (More commonly: . . . *haben ihn verändert.*)
> *Der Begriffsinhalt des Wortes* Demokrat *hat sich in den letzten 150 Jahren sehr gewandelt.*
> *Der Geschmack wandelt sich/Jmds. Anschauungen wandeln sich im Laufe der Jahre.*
> *Der Charakter eines Menschen kann sich im Laufe der Zeit wandeln.*

ii. Verwandeln usually implies a complete, mostly quick, and striking change which produces or seems to produce something so new or different that the former state is practically unrecognizable. It is used for magic transformations and also for natural ones and is followed by *in*. It occurs in scientific contexts, but here *umwandeln* is more common. *Man verwandelt Energie in Bewegung/Wasser in Dampf.*

> *Im Märchen verwandelte die Hexe den Prinzen in einen Frosch.*
> *In der Geschichte* Das häßliche Entlein *verwandelt sich die kleine unansehnliche Ente in einen schö-
> nen Schwan.   Der Frühling wird bald die Landschaft verwandeln.*
> *Der Regen hat die ausgetrockneten Wiesen in grünes Weideland verwandelt.*
> *Das Haus wurde durch die Explosion in einen Schutthaufen verwandelt.*
> *Wenn es regnet, verwandelt sich der Spielplatz in eine Schlammwüste.*

iii. Umwandeln is used for conscious and deliberate actions which produce something new and different, and for natural transformations which do not proceed quickly. It can also be applied to a person whose behaviour undergoes a considerable change. *Peter war heute wie umgewandelt, richtig gut gelaunt.*

> *Sie haben die Scheune in einen Saal umgewandelt.*
> *Die stahlharte Energie Stüves tat dem König Ernst August und dem Staat Hannover gut. Er wandelte
> den Despoten in einen zwar manchmal mürrischen, aber doch loyalen konstitutionellen Monarchen
> um.   Die Raupe wandelt sich in einen Schmetterling um.*
> *1848 machten sich Bürger und Bauern mutig daran, den alten absolutistischen Militärstaat Preußen
> in einen modernen Verfassungsstaat umzuwandeln.*
> *Der Fabrikbesitzer wandelte seine Firma in eine Aktiengesellschaft um.*

4. The main v. expressing the meaning 'to give and receive reciprocally' is **exchange**, but **change** is used in *He changed places with her.*

i. The G. word is **tauschen**. *Die Sammler tauschen Münzen. Er tauschte das Fernrohr gegen einen Fotoapparat. Ich wechsle den Platz* and *Wir wechseln die Plätze* mean that we go to another place or other places without any idea of exchange. For *die Plätze* *tauschen* to be used, at least two people must be involved, and one takes the other's place. The addition of *mit* to *wechseln* results in the same meaning, just as the addition of *with* to **change** makes it a syn. of **exchange**. *Ich habe mit ihr den Platz getauscht* or *gewechselt*. *A wechselt den Platz* and *A und B wechseln die Plätze* imply simply a change of place. *A und B tauschen die Plätze* and *A tauscht den Platz mit B* and *A und B wechseln die Plätze miteinander* imply an exchange. *Tauschen* is the more commonly used v. in this sense. Cf. 2. vii.

> *Die Bewohner dieser Inseln kannten Geld nicht, aber tauschten regelmäßig Waren.* (Cf. *der Tauschhandel*, barter trade.)   *Die Schüler tauschen Briefmarken/Abzeichen.*
> *Er möchte seine Wohnung gegen eine kleinere tauschen.*
> *Die Freunde tauschten ihre Theaterkarten.*   *Mit dieser Frau möchte ich nicht tauschen.*
> *Der Bankräuber hat mit einem Komplizen die Kleider getauscht.*

ii. Eintauschen gegen means 'to exchange one thg. for another of the same value'.

> *Weil Lebensmittel damals knapp waren, tauschten sie fast alles, was sie hatten, gegen Brot ein.*

iii. Austauschen is used instead of *tauschen* when what is exchanged is more important in nature, i.e. people, *Botschafter, Kriegsgefangene,* or ideas, opinions, experiences, etc.

> *Die Universitäten haben einen Studentenaustausch organisiert.*
> *Die beiden Männer haben Erinnerungen/Gedanken ausgetauscht.*
> *Eine Diskussion ist nur dann sinnvoll, wenn alle Teilnehmer ihre Meinungen friedlich austauschen.*
> *Von dem Erfahrungsaustausch haben wir alle profitiert.*

iv. Umtauschen. The first meaning is 'to exchange goods bought in a shop'.

> *Das Geschäft hat die Waren ohne weiteres umgetauscht.*
> *Ich habe dieses rote Hemd als Geschenk bekommen. Kann ich es gegen ein grünes umtauschen?*
> *Der Umtausch ist bei Batterien ausgeschlossen.*

Umtauschen also means 'to change money into another currency'. Cf. 2. vii.

> *Vor der Reise habe ich australische Dollars in kanadische Dollars umgetauscht.*

v. Vertauschen means 'to take sth. that does not belong to one instead of the thg. that does, either by mistake or sometimes deliberately'.

> *Unsere Hüte wurden vertauscht* (someone took mine and left his).
> *Ich scheine meinen Schirm mit dem eines anderen vertauscht zu haben.*

Another sense is 'to give up what one has previously done and begin a new kind of work'.

> *Sie hat das Schulzimmer mit dem Fernsehstudio vertauscht.*

5. Other equivalents of **change**.

i. *Der Termin,* 'APPOINTMENT or time at which something is to take place', is used with **ändern** when no phr. with *from* and/or *to* follows. *Wir müssen den Termin für die Sitzung ändern. Eine Terminänderung ist nicht möglich.* **Verlegen,** 'to MOVE or shift', can be used instead. *Sie mußte den Termin beim Zahnarzt verlegen. Verlegen* must be used when a phr. with *from* and *to* or either of them follows. *Die Sitzung wurde von Montag auf Donnerstag verlegt.* (*Verschieben,* 'to POSTPONE', is also possible.) *Zum Glück konnte die Seminarsitzung auf einen anderen Tag verlegt werden.* When 'moved forward' is meant, **vorverlegen** is used. *Die Sitzung ist von Freitag auf Mittwoch vorverlegt worden.*

ii. Change channels on a television set is **umschalten**. *Mit Hilfe der Fernbedienung kann man, ohne aufzustehen, von einem Programm auf ein anderes umschalten. Ich habe gerade vom ersten Programm auf das zweite umgeschaltet.*

iii. Change clothes = 'to take off one thg. and put on another'. **Wechseln** is used with *Kleider* or *Kleidung,* 'clothes', *ein Kleid,* 'dress', or an article of clothing. When a more or less complete change is meant, as in *I must change/get changed before I go out,* **sich umziehen** is the usual v. **Sich umkleiden** is a formal syn. like *dress*. There is no equivalent of *He changed into shorts* etc. The idea can be expressed as *was man anhat, ausziehen und eine kurze Hose anziehen. Ich ziehe das Kleid aus und die Jeanshose an.*

Die Schauspielerin hatte zwischen zwei Auftritten gerade zehn Minuten Zeit, um ihr Kostüm zu wechseln.

Weil er vom strömenden Regen durchnäßt war, mußte er seine Kleidung wechseln.

Sie kleideten sich für das Diner im Palast um.

Ich muß mich umziehen, bevor wir ins Theater gehen.

Der Junge hatte keine Lust, sich für den Besuch umzuziehen.

iv. Change one's *mind.* The usual expression is **sich etw. anders überlegen.** Cf. MIND 2. *Ich habe es mir anders überlegt und mache jetzt mit.*

v. Change trains, buses, etc. is **umsteigen** which can be used alone, with *in* + a place, and with *in* + another train. *In Hannover steigen Sie in den Intercity-Zug nach Frankfurt um.*

Mußt du umsteigen, oder gibt es eine direkte Verbindung?

6. Change [over] from one thg. **to** another.

i. Übergehen zu, to change over to or go on/over to. *Zu* can appear as *dazu* + infin.

Der Betrieb ist dazu übergegangen, Arbeitskräfte durch Roboter zu ersetzen.

> *In den letzten Jahrzehnten ist man immer mehr zur Automatisierung der Arbeitsprozesse übergegangen.*
> *Australien ging 1966 zur Dezimalwährung über.*
> *Nach einer kurzen Einleitung ging der Redner zum eigentlichen Thema über.*

ii. Umstellen means 'to rearrange or change around'. *Wir haben die Möbel in der ganzen Wohnung umgestellt. Die Fußballmannschaft wurde vom Trainer umgestellt.* With *auf,* **umstellen** means 'to change sth. over to sth. different'. It suggests adopting something new in response to definite requirements or circumstances. *Wir haben die Heizung von Öl auf Gas umgestellt.* The E. intr. form *They changed over to sth. new/different* is translated by **sich umstellen auf** or occasionally by *umstellen* used intr. The meaning can be expressed by *übergehen,* but whereas *übergehen* refers to a process which can take some time, *[sich] umstellen* usually denotes one which proceeds fairly quickly, possibly from one day to the next. *Wir haben unser Rechnungswesen auf elektronische Datenverarbeitung umgestellt.*

> *Die Fabrik hat die Produktion von Traktoren auf Autos umgestellt.* (It is usual to include *die Produktion.*)   *Die meisten Züge sind auf Elektrizität umgestellt worden.*
> *Fast alle Lebensmittelgeschäfte haben sich auf Selbstbedienung umgestellt.*

With people as subj. *sich umstellen* means 'to adapt [to]' or 'change'.

> *Sie konnten sich nur schwer von dem Gebirgsklima auf das schwüle, tropische Klima umstellen.*
> *Ich bin doch nicht so alt, daß ich mich nicht umstellen kann.*

iii. Überwechseln, which is similar to the sense of *wechseln* discussed under 2. vi, differs from it syntactically. *Wechseln* is the normal v. in *Der Student wechselte das [Studien]fach.* However, when the subject being dropped and the one being taken up are mentioned, the usual expression is *Er ist von Biologie zur Chemie übergewechselt.* This also applies in other circumstances when *von* and *zu* are used. *Ein Politiker wechselt die Partei,* but *Er wechselt von der konservativen zur liberalen Partei über.* When nothing is added, the usual expression is *Ich wechselte das Thema,* but *Mitten in der Rede wechselte sie von dem angekündigten Thema zu einem ganz anderen über.* Similarly, *Man wechselt die [Fahr]spur,* '(traffic) lane', but *wechselt von der linken Spur in die rechte über.*

cheek *n.* The more frequently heard word is **die Backe.** It implies that the cheeks are so formed and of such an appearance that they express health and strength. **Die Wange** is a less common, somewhat more elevated expression which suggests that the cheeks appear delicate and tender. As *Backe* is used only with adjs. suggesting health and strength, *Wange* needs to be used with words like *bleich* or *blaß* or others suggesting the absence of strength and health. When nothing is implied, either is possible, but *Backe* would be the everyday word, *Wange* stylistically higher. *Jmdm. die Wange[n] streicheln* is a fixed expression.

Das Kind hatte runde/blühende/frische/pralle Backen.

Er hatte eine geschwollene Backe. (Fixed expression.)

Er hatte eingefallene Wangen und Ringe unter den Augen.

Die roten Backen des Kindes zeigten, daß es kerngesund war.

Der Großvater zwinkerte und kniff dem Jungen in die Backe/Wange.

Als sie ihn erblickte, erröteten ihre Wangen leicht.   *Nach dem Schlag rieb er sich die Backe.*

choice, selection *ns.* Like the E. words, *die Wahl* and *die Auswahl* overlap in some senses, but not in others. *Die Wahl* also means 'election'.

1. Choice and **selection** denote the act or an instance of choosing between persons or things proposed or on offer. *Wahl* and *Auswahl* express this sense.

i. Die Wahl is used in general statements about choosing.

Er schilderte die verschiedenen Möglichkeiten und überließ mir dann die Wahl. Also *Ich überlasse dir die Wahl des Films.*   *Wer die Wahl hat, hat die Qual.*

Sie steht vor einer schwierigen Wahl.   *Er war nicht zimperlich in der Wahl seiner Mittel.*

ii. When the choice is between two persons or things only, or when only one is to be chosen out of a larger number, **die Wahl** is usual. When several things can be chosen, **die Auswahl** is normal and resembles *selection* (cf. 4). This applies to the expressions *Jmd. trifft eine gute/schlechte Wahl* or *trifft eine Auswahl.* If, from the original entries for a competition, the selection of a number of possible winners is made, this would be called *eine Auswahl* or *die erste Auswahl*. The choice of a winner would be called *die Wahl. Nachdem wir die erste Auswahl ohne große Schwierigkeit getroffen hatten, fiel uns die Wahl des Gewinners sehr schwer.* Both words occur in similar contexts, the only difference being the number to be chosen. *Die Wahl/Auswahl unter verschiedenen Möglichkeiten.*

Die Auswahl der passenden Möbelstücke für unsere Wohnung war nicht leicht.

Im großen und ganzen war die Auswahl, die er unter seinen Leuten getroffen hatte, eine vortreffliche gewesen.

Die Wahl eines Erziehers für den Kronprinzen wurde von der Königin sorgfältig überwacht.

iii. In some cases the question of the number may be open, or the distinction described in ii is not carefully made, so that both words are found. *Sie haben die Wahl/die Auswahl zwischen zehn Modellen.* Fixed expressions are *in die engere Wahl ziehen*, 'to put on the short list', and *in die engere Wahl kommen*, 'to get on the short list'. **Zur Auswahl**, 'to choose from', is also often found no matter how many things are to be chosen. *Fernsehapparate verschiedener Größen standen zur Auswahl. Der Verkäufer legte uns preiswerte Artikel zur Auswahl vor.* **Zur Wahl** *stehen* can be used, but it usually implies the choice of only one. *Mehrere Methoden/Verfahren/Interpretationen stehen zur Wahl.* With a person as subj. *zur Wahl stehen* means 'to be standing or running for election'. In certain contexts involving the choice of one person *Auswahl* is preferred to make clear that *selection* is meant and to avoid a clash with the sense of 'election'. *Die Auswahl eines Bewerbers zur Besetzung einer Stelle ist sehr schwer, wenn viele qualifizierte Leute sich darum beworben haben.*

Die Auswahl des Kandidaten, den die Partei in den nächsten Wahlen aufstellt, steht einem Ausschuß der Parteimitglieder in dem Wahlkreis zu.

2. Some expressions.

i. To do sth. **by choice** is usually **aus freier Entscheidung**, sometimes **aus freier Wahl**. *Viele berufstätige Frauen arbeiten nicht aus Notwendigkeit, sondern aus freier Entscheidung/Wahl.*

ii. *To take one's* **choice** = 'choose what one wants to take or have' must be translated by expressing its meaning. *Nimm, was du willst! Tue, wie du willst!*

iii. Choice in *What is your choice?* is translated by *Welches (Buch* etc.) *hast du gewählt?*

3. Choice = 'the power, right, or possibility of choosing', as in *You have a free choice* or *We had no choice.* Only **die Wahl** has this sense. *Sie haben die freie Wahl.* The neg. is *keine andere Wahl haben,* 'to have or be left with no choice', or, if expressed impersonally, *Es gab keine andere Wahl.* But in *no choice but to do sth.* is *als* + infin. *Sie hatten keine andere Wahl als zu gehorchen. Es gab keine andere Wahl als zu gehorchen.* An alternative is *Es* **blieb ihnen nichts anderes übrig als** *zu gehorchen.*

> *Ich würde keinen Augenblick zögern, wenn ich die Wahl hätte.*
> *Für unseren Urlaub hatten wir die Wahl zwischen dem Gebirge und dem Meer.*
> *Den Hochschulabsolventen blieb schließlich keine andere Wahl, als sich mit eintöniger Arbeit zu begnügen oder arbeitslos zu werden.*
> *Ihm blieb keine andere Wahl als den Krieg zu erklären.* Or *Ihm blieb nichts anderes übrig als . . .*
> *Ich habe keine andere Wahl als seine Bedingungen anzunehmen.* Also *Es bleibt mir keine andere Wahl als . . .* and *Mir bleibt nichts anderes übrig als seine Bedingungen anzunehmen.*

The expressions in the last sent. can translate **choice** when it means 'alternative'.

In dealing with William the Conqueror there were only two choices, unconditional submission or resistance to the last.

> *Die mittelalterlichen Missionare ließen den Heiden nur die Wahl zwischen der Bekehrung und dem Tod.*
> *Gegenüber Wilhelm dem Eroberer hatte man nur die Wahl zwischen bedingungsloser Unterwerfung oder Widerstand bis zum Letzten.*

4. Selection means: (i) 'A number, abundance, or variety of thgs. to choose from', (ii) 'A collection or group of thgs., pers., or examples selected'. In sense i it is interchangeable with **choice**. *The shop had a large selection/wide choice of jumpers.* **Die Auswahl** covers both senses. *Of* is *an* or *von.*

> *Das neue Kaufhaus hatte eine große Auswahl an Sportgeräten.*
> *Dieser Laden führt/hat eine reichhaltige Auswahl an Gardinen.*
> *Wenn man Kleider kaufen will, muß man in die Stadt fahren. Hier im Dorf hat man wenig Auswahl.*
> *Er hat eine Auswahl von Goethes Gedichten herausgegeben und erläutert.*
> *Die deutsche Auswahl an Fußballspielern versagte im Weltmeisterschaftsspiel völlig.*

5. Die Auslese implies choosing s.o./sth. specially on account of his/her/its excellence. It denotes either the process of choosing such excellent examples, i.e. the selection; or the result, i.e. the outstanding products or people, thus the pick or cream. It can refer to natural products, to pupils, students, etc. and is used in sport. *Die natürliche Auslese* is 'natural selection'.

> *Die Steigerung des Milchertrages wurde durch bewußte Auslese erreicht.*
> *Der Weinbauer bemühte sich um die Auslese der besten Trauben, um einen Spitzenwein zu erzeugen.*
> *Die Universität unterwarf die Studienbewerber einer strengen Auslese.*
> *Der Herausgeber hat eine mustergültige Auslese der deutschen Dichtung zusammengestellt.*
> *Zur Weltmeisterschaft trat die Auslese der Sportler an.*

6. Die Wahl denotes the grade or quality of goods. *Waren erster/zweiter/dritter Wahl. Die Waren sind zweiter Wahl. Sie haben kleine Mängel.*

choose, select *vs.* One sense of **pick [out]** *v.*

1. The basic sense of **choose** and **select** is 'to take by preference out of all that are available'.

i. This meaning is expressed by **wählen** and **auswählen**, which differ only slightly in the way they are used and in what they imply. Only *wählen* is intr. as *auswählen* needs an obj. Thus *Haben Sie schon gewählt?* or *Du mußt zwischen mir und ihm wählen. Ich wähle Geschenke/Beispiele aus.* An alternative to intr. *wählen* is **eine** or **seine/ihre,** etc. **Wahl treffen.** *Haben Sie schon eine Wahl (z. B. zwischen den beiden Angeboten)* *getroffen?* When the choice is between two things, people, or possibilities, *wählen* is usual, and is both trans. and intr. *Welche Fächer hast du gewählt? Wähle sorgfältig!* It is also common when one person or thing is chosen from more than two. It is followed by *zwischen* when the choice is between two possibilities, and by *unter* when there are several to choose from. *Sie wählte genau und gründlich zwischen den beiden Möglichkeiten. Du kannst unter allen diesen Kleidern/Möglichkeiten wählen.* *Auswählen* implies that the choice is to be made from at least three possibilities and that the number to be chosen is greater than one. *Wir haben die Besten ausgewählt* and *Der Hauptmann wählte drei Männer aus, die ihn zum Gipfel des Berges begleiten sollten.* In a context describing how an initial choice of several is narrowed down to one, both words could occur. *Die Preisrichter haben zuerst aus 25 Zeichnungen fünf ausgewählt und aus diesen dann eine zur Prämierung gewählt. Auswählen* also occurs when the result is one person or thing, but it implies that a careful choice is made from several possibilities whereas *wählen* carries no special implication. (It may also avoid a clash of meaning with 'to elect'. Cf. 1. ii.) *Horst wurde als fähigster Schüler ausgewählt und vertrat die Klasse.*

> *Er wählte den richtigen/falschen Moment, um sie anzusprechen.*
> *Sie wählte ein Kostüm in der mittleren Preislage.*   *Von den zwei Üblen wählte er das Kleinere.*
> *Er wählte den Schriftstellerberuf/die Schriftstellerei als Beruf.*
> *Sie können zwischen der einfachen Ausführung und dem Luxusmodell wählen.*
> *Wir müssen von den sieben Vorschlägen drei auswählen.*
> *Wähle unter den Studenten, die du kennenlernst, die zuverlässigsten als Freunde aus!*
> *Man hat ihr vier Stellen angeboten. Sie kann also unter vier Firmen wählen.*

ii. Wählen also means 'to elect' and must be used when **choose** implies this. *Morgen wählt die Bevölkerung von Großbritannien eine neue Regierung,* will choose a new government. *Er wurde zum Vorsitzenden gewählt.* When *wählen* could mistakenly be taken to mean 'elect', *auswählen* is preferred. *Die Partei muß geeignete Kandidaten für die nächste Landtagswahl auswählen,* select suitable candidates.

iii. Wählen alone is applied to words and language. *Er wollte nicht verletzen und wählte seine Worte mit großer Sorgfalt.* **Gewählt** in this context means 'choice, refined, or elegant'. *Der Detektiv in dieser Fernsehserie spricht ein gewähltes Deutsch.* **Ausgewählt** means 'selected'. *Ausgewählte Gedichte der Romantik. Ausgewählte Werke Kellers.*

iv. Special uses. *There are so many models etc. to choose from* can be translated as *Es stehen so viele Modelle etc. zur Wahl/zur Auswahl.* Cf. CHOICE 1. iii. *There is not much/little/nothing to choose between them* must be rendered as the underlying idea: *Sie unterscheiden sich kaum* or *Sie sind gleich gut/gleich schlecht. He cannot choose but to obey* is *Er hat keine andere Wahl als zu gehorchen.* Cf. CHOICE 3.

v. Common in the spoken language is **aussuchen**, which is often used with the refl. dat. when the choice is in some way related to the person choosing. It is applied to choosing or picking one or more people or things either from two or from a larger number.

> *Ich habe [mir] Möbel für das Wohnzimmer ausgesucht.*
> *Klage nicht! Das hast du dir selbst ausgesucht.*
> *Habt ihr euch schon ausgesucht, was ihr essen möchtet?*
> *Wir hatten uns zum Zeltplatz eine sehr unpassende Stelle ausgesucht.*
> *Warum suchen Sie mich immer aus, wenn unangenehme Arbeit getan werden muß?*

vi. Küren is an otherwise archaic v. meaning 'to choose' which is still sometimes used in the language of sport, *Er wurde zum Sportler des Jahres gekürt,* of Fasching, *Heute kürt man die Faschingsprinzessin,* or elsewhere ironically. *Die Kür* is used in sport for a sequence of exercises which the competitor chooses him- or herself. *Die Kür beim Eiskunstlauf/beim Turnen.*

2. Choose, pick out = 'to identify among several'.

i. Heraussuchen means 'to examine a number of similar thgs. or people and separate some from them for a particular purpose'. It is applied like **pick out** to separating the bad from the others or like **choose, select**, and **pick [out]** to taking those of a particular kind. In the latter case, it emphasizes the difficulty of choosing and may imply taking what is picked out into one's hand. (*Heraussuchen* also means 'to find among a number of people or thgs. the one that is being sought', i.e. 'to look sth. out'. *Trotz der Unordnung hat er das gewünschte Buch schnell herausgesucht. Würdest du mir bitte ein sauberes Hemd heraussuchen?*)

Der Beamte bemühte sich, die wichtigsten Akten herauszusuchen.
Der Zeuge versuchte, den wirklich Schuldigen unter den vorgeführten Männern herauszusuchen.
Ich habe die schlechten Äpfel aus den Kisten herausgesucht.
Die gefräßigen Jungen haben [sich] die größten Äpfel herausgesucht.

ii. Auslesen means either 'to sort out or remove what is bad or of inferior quality', *Wir lesen die faulen Äpfel/die schlechten Kirschen/die schimmeligen Pilze aus*, so that it is a syn. of *heraussuchen*, or 'to select' in the sense 'to choose the best', *Der Weinbauer bemühte sich, die besten Trauben auszulesen, um einen hervorragenden Wein zu machen.* In the latter sense it is a syn. of *auswählen*, but stresses quality.

3. Choose is used with an infin., as in *He chose to stay where he was* or *I would not choose to live in such a remote place.* The original sense is 'to decide in favour of one course of action in preference to another'. *Rather* is usually added. *The minister chose to resign rather than to betray his principles.*

i. When there is a clear or implied choice between alternatives, a word expressing preference like **vorziehen** or **lieber** can be used. *Der Minister zog es vor, von seinem Amt zurückzutreten, als seinen Grundsätzen untreu zu werden. Sie zog es vor, zu Hause zu bleiben.* (The alternative would be clear in the full context.) *Er wollte lieber dort bleiben, wo er aufgewachsen war.*

ii. The second example *I would not choose* . . . implies that if I had the choice I would not do something. This must be expressed by **wenn ich die Wahl hätte**. *Wenn ich die Wahl hätte, würde ich nie in einem so abgelegenen Ort leben.*

iii. The notion of a choice between alternatives can fade into the background, and **choose** becomes little more than an emphatic syn. of *think fit* or *wish*. *Pendennis chose to assume a very gloomy countenance. I did not choose to be a candidate.* **Ich hielt es für angebracht** can convey the sense 'to think fit'. *Angebracht* = 'appropriate, suitable, fitting'. *Er hielt es für angebracht, eine traurige Miene aufzusetzen.* **Wollen** or **Lust haben**, 'to feel inclined', can convey the idea 'to wish'. *Ich wollte nicht kandidieren/hatte keine Lust zu kandidieren. Do as you choose!* could be *Tu[e], was/wie du willst!* or *Tun Sie, was Sie für richtig/angebracht halten!*

claim, assert, maintain vs.

Only one sense of **claim** is dealt with here, its use usually with an infin. or clause, but sometimes with an obj., as a syn. of **assert** or **maintain**. For other senses cf. DEMAND v. **Claim** can mean 'to assert and demand recognition of' a right, possession, attribute, skill, etc. *He does not in fact have the knowledge he claims.* The idea of a right etc. disappears, and it comes to mean 'to assert sth. especially with conviction and in the face of possible contradiction or doubt'. *She claimed she had seen a ghost.* **Assert** means 'to declare sth. to be a fact although the evidence for this is not conclusive'. *He asserted that his account of events was correct, but I have my doubts.* **Maintain** means 'to assert as true, usually more than once or for a longer period of time'. *He maintained his innocence throughout the trial* or *maintained that he was innocent.*

i. Für sich in Anspruch nehmen means either 'to claim a right, privilege, or sth. concrete for oneself as one's entitlement' or 'to claim that one possesses certain qualities or skills, is sth., or has done sth.' It is used with an obj. or an infin. (One sense of *beanspruchen* is a syn. of the first meaning. *Er beanspruchte die Belohnung.* Cf. DEMAND v.)

> Als ältestes Mitglied des Lehrerkollegiums nahm sie den Vorsitz bei der Sitzung für sich in Anspruch.
> Beide Seiten nahmen den Sieg für sich in Anspruch.
> Der Angeklagte nahm mildernde Umstände für sich in Anspruch.
> Sie zeigt Geduld, wie sie nur wenige für sich in Anspruch nehmen können.
> Eigentlich besitzt er nicht die Kenntnisse, die er für sich in Anspruch nimmt.
> Er nahm für sich in Anspruch, der beste Tennisspieler in der Schule zu sein. Also Er behauptete . . .

ii. Behaupten, 'to declare something to be true without proof being available', is a more general term used for assertions both about oneself and about anyone or anything else. It is used with an infin., a *daß*-clause with the subjunctive, and *es, das, etw., was, nichts,* and *das Gegenteil* as obj.

> Sie behauptete, die Wahrheit gesagt zu haben/alles allein gemacht zu haben. Or . . . daß sie die Wahrheit gesagt hätte. Er hat etw. behauptet, was sich nicht beweisen läßt.
> Sie behauptet, daß alles, was in ihrem Bericht steht, wahr sei, aber ich habe da meine Zweifel.
> Obwohl er mit großer Entschiedenheit das Gegenteil behauptet, glaube ich, daß er hinter diesen Machenschaften steckt. Er hat wiederholt behauptet, daß er unschuldig sei.

iii. To convey the sense of **maintain** with an obj., the sent. can be rephrased with *behaupten*, or **festhalten an** + dat., 'to stick to (a claim, an assertion)', can be used. **Bleiben bei** expresses a similar meaning. Both are also used with a clause or infin.

> Er hielt während der Gerichtsverhandlung an seiner Unschuld fest.
> Sie hielt daran fest, daß sie mit dem Verbrechen nichts zu tun gehabt hatte.
> Der Angeklagte blieb dabei, zur Zeit des Einbruchs zu Hause gewesen zu sein.
> Der Schüler blieb dabei, daß der Lehrer seine Worte nicht als Beleidigung hätte auffassen sollen.

iv. Mostly with people as subj. and usually a perf. infin., **wollen** expresses the meaning 'to claim or assert', but implies doubt about the correctness of the claim. *Ein Zeuge will Müller gegen elf Uhr in der Nähe des Tatortes gesehen haben.* A pres. infin. is only used in a context in which *wollen* would normally not be understood as 'to want'. *Du willst krank sein?* thus suggests a claim to be ill. In *Das Buch will mehr als eine bloße Kompilation sein, will* is understood as 'claims' because of the impersonal subj. even though a person obviously makes the claim.

clean v.

i. Putzen and **saubermachen** are both applied to cleaning the interior of a house or other dwelling and can be trans. and intr. *Ich putze die Küche. Ich mache die Wohnung sauber. Ich muß noch saubermachen/putzen.* Putzen implies thorough cleaning with a brush, mop, cloth, etc. *Die Treppe putzen* suggests washing it thoroughly. Under some circumstances, *saubermachen* means 'to remove the worst of the dirt without washing completely clean'. *Die Treppe saubermachen* could imply removing dirt which has got on it without necessarily washing it. Shoes which have become covered with mud *werden saubergemacht,* i.e. the mud is removed. If they are then cleaned with shoe polish, the v. is *putzen.* If your clothes have become dusty or spattered with dirt and you brush, wipe, or clean this off yourself, this is denoted as *saubermachen.* Hence *Die Windschutzscheibe ist schmutzig. Ich werde sie saubermachen.* **Abputzen** is a syn. *Sie putzte den Staub von dem Mantel ab. Ich putze mir die Schuhe ab.* Putzen is used for the *Zähne, Schuhe, Fenster, eine Brille, Silber,* etc. Animals, e.g. *Katzen, putzen sich.*

ii. Clean *with a vacuum cleaner* is **staubsaugen**, which is intr. and weak. *Ich habe heute staubgesaugt.* The trans. form is **saugen** used as a weak v. *Ich habe das Zimmer* *gesaugt.* **Durchsaugen** is 'to clean quickly with a vacuum cleaner' and is also intr. *Soll ich hier [schnell] durchsaugen?*

iii. Reinigen applied to clothes now means 'to dry-clean'. *Reinigen* is the formal v. meaning 'to clean', used in legal and official language. *Die Straßenreinigung* is the official word for *street-cleaning*. *Die Treppe reinigen* would be used in a rent contract listing the tenant's obligations. It is also used in scientific and medical contexts. Hence *chemische Reinigung* for dry-cleaning. *Um den sauren Regen zu verhindern, müssen die Abgase aus Kohlekraftwerken gereinigt werden. Die Wunde muß gereinigt werden, bevor man sie verbindet.*

iv. In the lit. sense of 'to clean', i.e. 'to free from dirt', **säubern** is now a formal word. It is used in medical contexts, *eine Wunde säubern*, but is mostly fig. *Der Hafen wird von Minen gesäubert*, 'cleared', and *Das Regime hat die Verwaltung von politischen Gegnern gesäubert*, 'purged'.

v. Aufräumen, which implies considerable disorder, corresponds to **clean**, *clear up*, or *tidy up*. *Ich muß dringend mein Arbeitszimmer aufräumen—alles liegt durcheinander wie Kraut und Rüben.*

Ihr müßt die Werkstatt aufräumen, bevor ihr Feierabend macht.
Die Aufräumungsarbeiten nach dem Orkan dauerten mehrere Wochen.

clear *adj.*

1. Klar means 'easy to see through', 'transparent', applied to liquids and solids. *Das Wasser im Bach ist so klar, daß man alle Steine auf dem Grund sehen kann.* In the sense 'free from what is unwanted', *klar* is applied to the air, *klare Luft*, to visibility, *klare Sicht*, and to the sky and weather, *klares Wetter, ein klarer Himmel*. With sounds, particularly the voice, it means 'free of roughness, harshness, or hoarseness'. *Der klare Ton einer Glocke. Da hörten sie plötzlich eine klare Knabenstimme.* It is applied to thinking, either to *der Kopf* and *der Verstand*, or as an adv. with *denken*.

Wenn man die Flüssigkeit eine Zeitlang stehen läßt, wird sie wieder klar.
Die Nacht/Der Tag war klar und kalt.   *Ich kann heute nicht klar denken.*
Er ist ein Mensch, der in jeder Situation einen klaren Kopf behält/bewahrt.
Nachdem er zwei Flaschen Bier getrunken hatte, war er nicht mehr klar im Kopf.

2. Although *deutlich* originally meant 'clear to the senses, distinct, easily perceivable by the eyes, ears, or touch', and *klar* meant 'clear to the understanding', the distinction has been obliterated to a considerable extent, so that in many cases they are now interchangeable. In some cases *klar* is the everyday word, while *deutlich* is somewhat weightier. In others, however, it is necessary to bear the original meanings in mind.

i. *Spüren* and *fühlen* occur only with **deutlich**. *Als sie mit geschlossenen Augen da saß und beinahe eingeschlafen wäre, spürte sie deutlich, wie etw. ihr Gesicht berührte.*

ii. With *hören*, **deutlich** is usual, though **klar** is possible. *Ich habe das Geräusch deutlich gehört. Ihre Stimme war im Nebenzimmer deutlich zu hören.*

iii. In *Man drückt sich/seine Gedanken klar aus*, **klar** means 'clear to the mind'. However, *eine Aussprache* can be *klar* or **deutlich**, and both refer to its acoustic properties. With *sagen, sprechen*, and *reden*, *klar* could refer to the clarity of expression, *deutlich* to the pronunciation of the words, but the distinction is not always observed, and they are often joined together in the sense 'absolutely clearly both to the ears and the mind'. *Er hat klar und deutlich gesprochen. Sie hat es klar und deutlich gesagt. Er hat seine Gedanken klar/deutlich/klar und deutlich ausgesprochen. Wir erwarten von ihnen eine klare/deutliche Antwort. Klar* is, however, always correct. **Klipp und klar**, 'quite plainly or perfectly clearly', is common in speech. *Sie hat ihre Meinung klipp und klar gesagt.*

iv. With things that are seen, both **klar** and **deutlich** are found. *Ich habe alles deutlich gesehen. Wir haben es alle klar gesehen. Die Berge traten deutlich aus dem Nebel hervor.*

> *Das Schiff ist deutlich am Horizont zu sehen.*   *Das Schloß hebt sich klar vom Hintergrund ab.*
> *Der Umriß des Schiffes hob sich deutlich gegen den Himmel ab.*

v. With *verstehen*, **deutlich** is usual, but **klar** is also possible. *Man gibt jmdm. klar/deutlich zu verstehen, daß er pünktlich erscheinen muß.* Also *Man muß die beiden Begriffe klar/deutlich unterscheiden.*

vi. With all senses of *erkennen*, 'to recognize', 'to make something out optically', and 'to realize mentally', both **klar** and **deutlich** occur. *Obwohl es dunkel war, konnte ich das Haus unter den Bäumen klar/deutlich erkennen. Obwohl sie ihn im Kino deutlich erkannt hatte, behauptete er, nicht da gewesen zu sein. Erst später habe ich klar [und deutlich] erkannt, daß ich unrecht hatte.* Also *Ich erinnere mich noch klar/deutlich an den Vorfall.*

vii. With *erklären*, only **deutlich** is used, probably because of the clash of sounds, were *klar* used. *Er hat den Unterschied deutlich erklärt.*

viii. With *der Wink*, 'hint', *der Hinweis*, 'indication', *das Zeichen*, 'sign', *der Beweis*, 'proof', *die Aufforderung*, 'request or demand', *die Anspielung*, 'allusion', *ein Sieg*, 'victory', *die Mehrheit*, 'majority', and *die Warnung*, **klar** and **deutlich** can be used. With *die Schrift*, 'handwriting', both mean 'clearly legible'. With *der Fall*, *klar* is used. *Das ist ein klarer Fall von Bevorzugung.*

ix. **Klar** is the normal transl. of *it is* **clear** + clause. *Es ist klar, daß er gelogen hat.* A dat. can be added. *Es ist mir klar [geworden], daß ich vieles falsch gemacht habe.* Also *Ist das klar? Das ist nun hoffentlich klar.* The synonymous variants *Wir sind uns noch nicht klar, was wir machen wollen*, and *Wir sind uns noch nicht im klaren, was wir machen sollen* mean 'clear in our mind'.

x. *It is* **clear from** *sth. that* . . . Here both **klar** and **deutlich** are used, but with *werden*, not with *sein*.

> *Aus diesen Bemerkungen wurde klar/deutlich, daß ihre Vorstellungen über unsere weitere Zusammenarbeit sich erheblich von den unseren unterschieden.*

xi. *To make sth.* **clear** *to s.o.* is **jmdm. etw. klar machen.** *Ich weiß nicht, ob ich es ihnen klar gemacht habe.* **Deutlich werden** has the special sense 'to speak plainly or bluntly with s.o.' *Habt ihr mich verstanden? Oder muß ich deutlich werden?* Also . . . *noch deutlicher werden?*

3. Clear = 'easy or safe to pass along, free from obstacles, dangers, etc.' *The road is clear.*

i. Frei mostly carries this sense as *free* often does. *Bahn frei!* means lit. 'make the way clear!' or 'clear the way!' *Einfahrt freihalten* is the notice on entrances which are to be kept clear. *Frei*, like *free* and **clear**, is applied to people with regard to financial liabilities and suspicion.

> *Zwei Lastwagen, die zusammengestoßen waren, hatten die Straße versperrt, aber sie ist jetzt wieder frei. Ist der Fluß schon eisfrei?* Also *Die Straße ist schneefrei.*
> *Der Weg ist nunmehr frei für eine Einigung.*
> *Er arbeitet schwer, kann aber nicht schuldenfrei werden.*
> *Sie blieb frei von Verdacht, weil alle wissen, daß sie grundehrlich ist.*

ii. *The coast is* **clear** is *Die Luft ist rein*. **Rein** is also used with *das Gewissen*, conscience. *Ich habe ein reines Gewissen. Mein Gewissen ist rein.*

iii. The naval term **klar**, which like **clear** means 'ready for action etc.', is also used for aircraft.

> *Das Flugzeug ist klar zum Start.*   *Das Schiff ist klar zum Auslaufen/zur Abfahrt/zum Gefecht.*

4. Clear = 'whole, complete'. *Three clear days* is *drei* **volle/ganze** *Tage*. *We made a clear profit of £100* could be *Wir erzielten einen Reingewinn or Nettogewinn von* . . . **Netto**

means 'clear of deductions, expenses, tax, etc.' *Ich verdiene DM 3 400 im Monat brutto, aber nur DM 2 200 netto. Wenn man 1 000 Mark in der Woche bekommt, wie viel hat man dann netto?*

5. Clear of = 'without touching','at a [safe] distance from'. There is no G. term, and the idea needs to be expressed by other words. *To keep clear of a pers.* could be **meiden**, to AVOID. *Du solltest diesen Kerl in Zukunft meiden. Also Eine Gefahr[enzone] meiden. Stand/Keep clear of the doors/machinery!* could be *Geh' nicht in die Nähe der Tore!* or *Bleib weg von der Maschine! We are now clear of the undergrowth* could be *Wir sind nun aus dem Gestrüpp heraus.* **Der Abstand**, 'DISTANCE', can sometimes express the idea. *Wir müssen Abstand zum nächsten Schiff halten. Der Abstand zwischen der Tür und dem Boden muß ungefähr einen Zentimeter betragen,* the door must be about one centimetre clear of the floor.

clever, shrewd, cunning, sly, crafty, skilful *adjs.* Applied to people, **clever** means 'able to use hand and/or mind readily and effectively'. When it refers to skill in using the hands or in other bodily movements, this must be stated. *The boy was clever with his hands.* Otherwise, it is taken to mean 'displaying mental quickness, intelligence, or resourcefulness'. **Clever** can be applied to people, their behaviour, and to things people produce which show ingenuity and sometimes wit. *Emma is spoiled by being the cleverest of her family. A clever artisan. A clever poem. The audience applauded the clever speech.* **Clever** is in itself neutral, but can be used with words indicating something bad. *He was a clever crook. They were the victims of a clever deception.* In *He was too clever for us,* **clever** also means 'smart' in a bad sense if it implies outwitting another person. **Shrewd** implies cleverness and an ability to see beneath the surface and judge a situation quickly and to use this understanding to one's own advantage. It need not be pejorative, although it often suggests wiliness and self-seeking. *A shrewd observer. A shrewd remark. He is sensible and shrewd with a considerable fund of humour. A shrewd operator. A shrewd exploiter of loopholes in the law.* In the prevailing current sense, **cunning** mostly has a neg. connotation, suggesting trickery or covert means in attaining one's ends or circumventing what is disadvantageous. The degree of censure it expresses varies considerably from strong to very slight. *The cunning thieves drove their victims into a well-laid trap. Infants are far more cunning than grown-up people are apt to suppose; if they find that crying produces agreeable results, they will cry.* **Sly** stresses secretiveness and dishonesty in one's dealing with others, but does not always express strong condemnation. **Crafty** now has a bad sense. Applied to people and their faculties, it means 'skilful in devising and carrying out underhand or evil schemes'. *He thought a crafty cheat would make a good politician. We were taken in by this crafty trick. One of his crafty schemes had been discovered.* **Skilful** means 'having the ability to do sth. expertly and well'. *It was a very skilfully organized election campaign.*

1 treats words expressing praise, 2 those expressing censure, and 3 the equivalents of **skilful**.

1. Words with a positive sense or only mildly pejorative.

i. Applied to people, **klug** means 'possessing understanding and the ability to think clearly and acutely', thus 'clever' or 'intelligent'. With words denoting actions, it means that the actions display these qualities and are thus sensible, wise, shrewd, or prudent. *Klug* cannot be used with something bad, so that it does not translate *a clever crook* or *deception.*

Er ist eine kluger Kopf/ein kluger Geschäftsmann.
Sie ist eine sehr kluge Frau/ein kluges Kind.

Dieter und Inge sind die klügsten Schüler der Klasse.   Das war eine kluge Antwort.
Er ist klug genug gewesen, sich rechtzeitig aus dem Staub zu machen.
Ich halte es für das Klügste, erst einmal abzuwarten.

ii. Gescheit also means 'possessing intelligence and sound judgement', but often suggests that this expresses itself in practical matters and action. It is applied to people, *ein gescheites Mädchen, ein gescheiter Bursche,* and to what people say, think, and do when this displays intelligence and judgement, is sensible, *Das war eine gescheite Antwort/Äußerung. Ein gescheiter Einfall.* It is also used only with things which are good by nature.

Sei doch gescheit und tue, was man dir geraten hat!
Es wird nichts Gescheites dabei herauskommen.
Es wäre gescheiter/das Gescheiteste, wenn wir gleich losfahren würden.

iii. Intelligent is used as in E. **Begabt,** 'gifted', is often used in the sense 'particularly intelligent', mainly of children. *Mehrere Schüler in der Klasse sind sehr begabt.* **Aufgeweckt** means 'showing surprising mental agility and soundness of judgement for his/her age' and is used to describe children. *Der Lehrer hatte seine Freude an den aufgeweckten Schülern.*

iv. Schlau means 'possessing the ability to gain one's ends by calculated means which are hidden from others or which they do not suspect'. *Er hat alles schlau eingefädelt, damit das Ergebnis herauskam, das er haben wollte. Ein schlauer Bursche* combines intelligence with the ability to think ahead and use a favourable situation to his own advantage. It is a quality traditionally associated with a fox, *ein schlauer Fuchs.* The word is usually not pejorative. Although it may suggest some measure of reprehensible cunning, it usually expresses admiration rather than condemnation.

Er ist zu schlau, um auf eine solche List hereinzufallen.
Sehr schlau hatten sie die Sache gerade nicht angepackt.
Der ist schlau, der weiß, wie man so was anstellen muß.
Das hast du aber ganz schlau gemacht! (Can be ironical and mean 'not very sensibly'.)

Schlau is used colloquially about people as a syn. of *klug* or *gescheit. Ein schlaues Kind* or *ein schlauer Schüler* is one who knows a lot and gets good results. It is usually confined to children. For adults, *intelligent, klug,* or *gescheit* are more usual.

v. Clever is close to *schlau,* but is less broad than the E. word. It is applied to people who know how to use their abilities and to adjust to situations in a way which serves their ends or interests. Although it expresses admiration for the skill involved, it also carries reservations about the lack of scruples in overcoming difficulties. These reservations are suggested in *Er ist ein cleverer Geschäftsmann,* but in sport, *eine clevere Taktik* means 'skilful and successful' without any overtones. The *Bundespost* has been promoting its savings bank accounts for some time as *das clevere Konto.*

vi. Listig is also applied to people and what they do. The meaning is 'achieving one's purposes by using tricks and dodges, hiding one's real intentions, and exploiting for one's own advantage circumstances which are not known to others'. The censure expressed varies considerably depending on the situation and the point of view of the speaker. It may suggest no more than that one uses unusual means to achieve an end which may be good as well as bad, or it may imply deceit. Although it is mostly somewhat pejorative, it is not as strong as *gerissen* or *durchtrieben.* Cf. 2. i and ii.

In dieser Situation konnte ihnen nur ein listiger Plan helfen.
Der listig ausgeklügelte Plan mißlang gründlich.
Sie mußten sehr listig vorgehen, um das Ziel zu erreichen.

vii. Gewieft and **gewiegt** are colloquial words which express similar meanings, except that *gewieft* tends more towards *gerissen* (cf. 2. i) and thus corresponds to *cunning,* while *gewiegt* means 'shrewd or astute'. Both are used in reference to people and actions. *Gewieft* suggests wide awake in any situation and able to react quickly to secure one's advantage or not to be duped. *Ein gewiegter Geschäftsmann* has become skilled through experience and knows all the tricks.

> *Um sich als Geschäftsmann bei der großen Konkurrenz behaupten zu können, muß man sehr gewieft vorgehen.*
>
> *Mit diesem gewieften Zug überraschte der Schachspieler seinen Gegner.* (Also *gewiegt.*)
>
> *Der Trainer war ein gewiegter Taktiker, der immer im rechten Augenblick reagierte.*
>
> *Der Anwalt war in solchen Sachen sehr gewiegt.*

viii. Pfiffig is mostly applied to young people, particularly boys, though it occasionally describes older people, *ein pfiffiger Alter.* It suggests someone who knows how an aim can be carried out or who finds clever and ingenious ways out of difficult situations. It is like *smart* and *bright* in not usually expressing censure. If any is meant, it implies that the person is a lovable rascal. *Pfiffig* can refer to facial expression, ideas, etc. as well as directly to people.

> *Er war ein pfiffiger Kerl und verblüffte seine Eltern immer wieder.*
>
> *Zuerst kamen einige pfiffige Jungen auf die Idee, wie man Karten kriegen konnte.*
>
> *Sie hatten eine pfiffige Idee, wie sie das Produkt besser absetzen konnten.*

ix. Gewitzt is like *pfiffig* and suggests practical understanding and abilities, and finding clever and practical solutions for problems as a result of having been made wise by experience.

> *Er war ein gewitzter Bursche und bei allen beliebt.*
>
> *Der Junge war klüger und gewitzter als die anderen.*

x. Geistreich means 'witty' or 'sparkling' and is applied to people, conversation, writing, or style. It can be used to express **clever** in contexts like *a clever answer/remark,* etc. Thus *eine geistreiche Antwort/Bemerkung* and *eine geistreiche Rede/Komödie.* It implies not only that the thoughts are presented with wit but also that the speaker or author has something of importance to say. By contrast, *eine kluge Antwort* suggests intelligence or wisdom, and *eine gescheite Antwort* is 'a sensible answer'.

2. Words with a pejorative sense.

i. Someone who is **gerissen** knows all the tricks and dodges, so that he or she cannot be tricked, but tries to outwit or deceive others to gain an advantage. Although it always has a neg. connotation, it does not always express strong condemnation, particularly if what is achieved benefits the speaker or the community. *Die Chancen des Angeklagten standen nicht schlecht, denn sein Anwalt war sehr gerissen. Der Detektiv/Kriminalkommissar gilt als gerissener Bursche. Ein gerissener Geschäftsmann* is, however, usually unscrupulous. *Gerissen* thus varies between the meanings 'cunning' and 'crafty'. It is also applied to actions and is the equivalent of **clever** used in a neg. sense. Hence *ein gerissener Gauner* and *Er ist mir zu gerissen* and *Sie war das Opfer eines gerissenen Betrugs.*

ii. Durchtrieben, which is only applied to people, means 'experienced in devising and carrying out schemes which serve one's own advantage'. It expresses a complete rejection of the person's behaviour. Such a person is completely unreliable as he/she might deceive those dealing with him or her at any time. It is frequently used for people in business, but can also be applied to young people in whom one is surprised to find such characteristics. *Ein durchtriebener Bengel.*

> *Der ist ein ganz durchtriebener Geschäftsmann. Er verkauft zwar mit 30% Rabatt, aber vorher hat er die Preise um 50% heraufgesetzt.*

iii. Raffiniert either means 'extraordinarily effective because of the skilful choice of means employed', *Das hat er raffiniert dargestellt/konstruiert* and *eine raffinierte Regie/Taktik,* or it is a syn. of *gerissen* and *durchtrieben, ein raffinierter Betrug/ Diebstahl/Gauner/Trick/Bursche. Sie sind äußerst raffiniert vorgegangen. Die Sache haben sie raffiniert eingefädelt.* Out of context it is not clear whether *Er nutzte die Gesetzeslücke auf raffinierte Weise aus* expresses admiration or condemnation. The context would normally indicate one or the other. By contrast *auf gerissene Weise* mostly expresses condemnation, though some people might admire the cunning involved.

iv. Verschlagen also has a bad sense and stresses the lack of straightforwardness. It is applied to people who hide their intentions, never say what they really think, and try to outwit others by pretending to be the opposite of what they are or by wearing the mask of goodness to conceal selfish aims or malice. It is applied directly to people and to their facial expressions. *Er lächelte verschlagen/sah mich mit verschlagenen Augen an.*

> *Eine halbe Stunde lang ließ ich die Worte des Lehrers über mich ergehen. Dann sagte ich kleinlaut und verschlagen: 'Wahrscheinlich haben Sie recht, Herr Oberstudienrat.'* (He would be posing as *ein braver Schüler* and mean the opposite.)

v. Mit allen Wassern gewaschen and **mit allen Hunden gehetzt** mean 'as cunning as a fox' or 'knowing all the tricks of the trade'.

> *Den Quertreibereien des neuen Kollegen bin ich nicht gewachsen. Der ist überschlau und mit allen Wassern gewaschen.*
>
> *Wir haben hier in der Stadt keinen hervorragenden Anwalt, der mit allen Hunden gehetzt und in den bedenklichsten Sachen versiert wäre.* (Thomas Mann)

vi. Abgefeimt is the strongest word, suggesting that there are no redeeming features. With neutral words like *der Bursche,* it means 'cunning' or 'crafty'. *Er ist ein abgefeimter Bursche.* With words denoting evil or the perpetrators of it, it means that there is nothing to relieve the villiany etc., thus 'out and out', 'unmitigated'. *Ein abgefeimter Schurke/Spitzbube/Lump. Ein abgefeimter Lügner.*

vii. Hinterlistig is stronger than *listig* and always expresses censure; it suggests acting to a person's disadvantage behind his or her back and is translated as *treacherous, deceitful,* or *crafty.*

> *Er mißbrauchte ihr Vertrauen in hinterlistiger Weise.*
>
> *Er ist ein gemeiner, egoistischer und hinterlistiger Mensch.*

3. Skilful.

i. Like **skilful**, **geschickt** refers to manual or physical dexterity and to the way work or actions are carried out and people or situations are dealt with. It translates *clever with one's hands.*

> *Er ist ein geschickter Arbeiter/Handwerker/Spieler/Tänzer usw.*
>
> *Sie hat geschickte Hände/hat die Blumen in der Vase geschickt arrangiert.*
>
> *Sie hat sich geschickt verteidigt/die Verhandlungen geschickt geführt.*
>
> *Sie ist sehr geschickt im Umgang mit Kindern.*
>
> *Die Wahlkampagne war geschickt organisiert/wurde geschickt durchgeführt.*

ii. Someone who is **gewandt** displays self-assurance and ease in behaviour and movement, and skill in speech and dealing with people. Applied to activities, it means that the person has mastered the techniques involved and, in the way they are carried out, or in the movement of the body, expresses neatness and elegance, thus making a pleasing impression. For physical activities, it corresponds to *skilled, agile,* or *nimble.* It is used for people, *ein gewandter Tänzer/Redner,* and actions, *ein gewandtes Auftreten, eine gewandte Redeweise.*

> *Das Pferd sprang gewandt über den Zaun.*
>
> *Das war eine gewandte Abwehr.* (A clever/skilful defence carried out with a certain elegance either in sport or in a discussion e.g. *eine gewandte Abwehr aller Gegenargumente.*)

Er findet sich überall zurecht, denn er ist gewandt und weiß mit Menschen umzugehen.

iii. Patent means 'skilful and ingenious in practical matters' and suggests that this skill is combined with a pleasant nature. As well as to people, *ein patentes Mädchen, ein patenter Kerl/Junge,* it is applied to ideas, methods, solutions, etc. which show ingenuity, *Das ist eine patente Methode/Idee/Lösung.*

climb, go up *vs.*

1. The usual equivalent of **go up** in relation to stairs is *die Treppe* **hinaufgehen**. It implies no special effort. *Ich habe sie vor fünf Minuten die Treppe hinaufgehen hören.* A syn. in everyday speech is **hochgehen**. *Er ist gerade die Treppe hochgegangen.* Without an obj. both vs. mean 'to go up to a previously mentioned higher place' or 'to go upstairs'. A syn. in the latter sense is **nach oben gehen**. *Sie sind vor fünf Minuten nach oben gegangen/hochgegangen. Die Treppe* **hinaufsteigen** implies a degree of difficulty greater than *hinaufgehen,* in the same way that **climb** can in comparison with **go up**. *Ich bin die steile Treppe bis unter das Dach hinaufgestiegen. Die Treppe ist zwar sehr schmal, aber wir sind trotzdem auf den Turm hinaufgestiegen.*

2. With hills and mountains, **go up** on foot or **climb** is **gehen auf** when no great difficulty is involved. *Wenn man auf den Hügel/die Anhöhe geht, hat man eine schöne Aussicht über die Flußmündung. Morgen gehen wir auf den Berg.* **Steigen** implies more difficulty, but this need not be very great. *Steigen* is the usual word for climbing a ladder or something having rungs, and for going up or down. *Ich brauche eine Leiter, um auf das Dach zu steigen. Um alle Äpfel zu erreichen, muß man auf die Leiter steigen. Er stieg in den Brunnen, um die Pumpe zu reparieren.* **Hinaufsteigen** is used when what is climbed is not expressed, but is clear from the context. *Wir haben vier Stunden gebraucht, um hinaufzusteigen,* get up, get to the top. It is also used if ladder is only implied. *Wenn wir die Leiter an die Wand anlegen, kannst du hinaufsteigen und die Dachrinne dicht machen. Er stieg auf das Dach hinauf* is heard, but is avoided in educated speech as *hinauf* only repeats the idea of the prepositional phr. Thus in *Wir sind auf den Berg hinaufgestiegen,* *hinauf* is optional, as is *up* with **climb**. *Hinaufsteigen* can also take an obj., in which case *hinauf* is not omitted. *Heute steigen wir den Berg hinauf.* **Besteigen** implies climbing which involves a degree of difficulty and some preparation. It is the usual word when referring to *Bergsteiger,* mountain climbers. The general sense of **bezwingen** is 'to defeat or overcome'. When used with mountains, it implies great difficulty and effort and an achievement in mountain climbing. It is appropriate for the climbing of a difficult peak, but occurs also in other contexts. *Die Gruppe von Bergsteigern hatte alle 3 000er in den Alpen bezwungen.*

Um die Schornsteine zu fegen, steigt der Schornsteinfeger auf das Dach [hinauf].

Reinhard Messner ist zur Zeit unterwegs, einen weiteren Achttausender zu besteigen. Er hat schon viele hohe Berge bezwungen.

Nach vielen mißglückten Versuchen gelang es Hilary und Tensing, Mount Everest zu bezwingen/besteigen.

3. Klettern implies using the hands as well as the feet in order to climb. It usually has a prep. such as *auf, in,* or *aus,* but can be used alone. It is the usual word for animals and for people when referring to trees. *Sie kletterte auf den Ast. Die Jungen sind in den Baum geklettert. Die Passagiere kletterten aus dem notgelandeten Flugzeug.* With *über einen Zaun,* **steigen** is used if the fence is low and easily surmountable. If, for example, I use my hands to pull myself up, *klettern* is the appropriate v. *Er ist über die Mauer/den Zaun geklettert.* In many cases either *klettern* or *steigen* is possible. *Er ist durchs Fenster gestiegen/geklettert. Klettern* also means 'to go mountain climbing'. *Er ist in seiner Jugend viel geklettert.*

Die Kinder sind auf den großen Felsbrocken geklettert.   Der Junge klettert wie ein Affe.
Auf dem Spielplatz klettern die Kinder gern in den Gerüsten herum.
Die Eichhörnchen klettern von Baum zu Baum und springen von Ast zu Ast.

4. Klettern and **sich ranken** mean 'to climb' in relation to plants. *Mehrere Pflanzen ranken sich an den Seitenwänden des Balkons. Die Liane klettert an dem Baum nach oben. Die Reben klettern/ranken sich am Spalier nach oben.*

5. Both **steigen** and colloquially **klettern** are used:
i. With aircraft. *Das Flugzeug stieg auf 12 000 Meter Höhe/ist über die Wolken geklettert.*
ii. With instruments. *Das Thermometer stieg/kletterte auf 43°. Der Tachometer kletterte auf 140.*
iii. With prices. *Die Preise steigen seit einiger Zeit nicht mehr. Die Preise kletterten um 20%.*

6. Climb, applied to roads etc., is **ansteigen**, which expresses the concept that ground rises. *Die Straße steigt bis auf 3 000 Meter an.* We are still climbing/going up used for a car on the road is *Wir* **fahren** *noch* **bergauf** or **steigen** *noch.*

coat, jacket *ns.* An **overcoat** is der Mantel, a **raincoat** der Regenmantel. For the garment which covers only the upper part of the body and reaches to just below the hips, there are several terms. **Der Rock** was formerly used for a coat of this kind for men, but it has gone out of use. It survives in this sense only in **der Morgenrock**, 'dressing gown', for which there is now the alternative, **der Bademantel**. *Der Rock* now means 'a skirt'. The general word for **coat** is now **die Jacke** which is used both for men's and women's clothing. It is the usual word for the coat of a costume and for a suit coat (in full *die Anzugsjacke*), but it does not have to be part of a suit. **Das Jackett** was originally the coat of a man's suit, but it may also be used for something like a sports coat which is not part of a suit. In the latter sense **der/das Sakko** is also common. **Der Kittel** is always associated with work. It is a coat resembling an overcoat in shape but of light material and worn for protection or for reasons of hygiene. *Der weiße Kittel des Arztes. Der Laborkittel. Der Malerkittel. Der Arbeitskittel.*

Sie trug eine schwarze Hose zu einer weißen Jacke.   Seine Jacke paßt gut zu der Hose.
Ein Kostüm besteht aus Jacke und Rock.   Alle Arbeiter trugen graue Kittel.
Er trägt einen modischen, schwarzen Sakko zu einer grauen Hose. Or *ein modisches, schwarzes Sakko.*
Er hat zugenommen und kann nun sein Jackett nicht mehr zuknöpfen.
Sie trug ihren Morgenrock/Bademantel den ganzen Vormittag und zog sich erst am Nachmittag um.
Alle Schülerinnen haben lange Röcke zu der Abschiedsfeier getragen.

comfortable, cosy *adjs.*
1. i. In its basic sense **bequem** describes something which offers bodily ease and comfort. It is applied to furniture, *ein bequemer Stuhl, bequeme Sitze, ein bequemes Bett,* to living areas, *eine bequeme Wohnung,* and to clothes, *eine bequeme Hausjacke, bequeme Schuhe.* To make someone **comfortable** must be expressed with *es* as obj. and the dat. of the person. *Ich machte es dem Kranken so bequem wie möglich. Es* is also necessary in the refl. *Machen Sie es sich bequem!* is lit. *Make yourself comfortable!,* but it also implies easy and informal behaviour and is then translated as *Make yourself at home! Bequem* after *sein* means 'comfortable' only with things as subj. *Der Sessel ist bequem.* This use is not possible with people because of the clash with the meaning 'indolent'. Cf. 1. iii. To state that a person is comfortable, it is necessary to use *sitzen* or *liegen. Ich sitze hier sehr bequem.*

In diesem Bett liege ich sehr bequem.   In diesem Sessel wirst du bequemer sitzen.

ii. Applied to things, **bequem** also means 'well adapted to the body for easy use', 'easy', 'convenient'. *Dieser Koffer ist sehr bequem zu tragen.* It then acquires the sense 'causing no effort', 'able to be used, reached, or carried out without exertion or trouble', as both an adj. and adv. *Ein bequemes Leben*, an easy life. *Ein bequemer Weg. Das Dorf ist bequem in einer halben Stunde zu Fuß zu erreichen.*

Der Apparat ist sehr bequem zu handhaben.   *Das Hotel liegt sehr bequem zum Strand.*
Wir können in zwei Stunden bequem dort sein. *Ich konnte alles bequem beobachten.*
Den Schirm kann man bequem in der Handtasche tragen.
Von Fulda aus sind Städte wie Weimar, Erfurt, Eisenach, Marburg und Würzburg in Tagesausflügen
 bequem mit der Bahn oder mit dem Auto zu erreichen.

iii. Applied to people, **bequem** means 'disinclined to exert oneself' and is pejorative, implying indolence.

Er war viel zu bequem, um mitzugehen.

2. Behaglich presupposes bodily comfort, but it refers to the total atmosphere that arises when, in addition, a relaxed feeling, ease of behaviour, contentment, friendly companionship, and warmth are present. A room, no matter how *bequem* its furniture, could not be *behaglich* if it were unpleasantly cold or if the people in it despised one another. *Behaglich* resembles **cosy**, which may refer to comfort and warmth, but can also imply a pleasant and friendly atmosphere involving a close relationship between people. *Behaglich* is applied to places which radiate such an atmosphere and to the people who react to it.

Es ist behaglich bei euch.   *Er streckte die Beine behaglich aus.*
Ich fühle mich hier sehr behaglich.   *Mein Zimmer ist klein, aber behaglich.*

3. Gemütlich too describes an atmosphere which presupposes physical comfort, but also makes an agreeable impression on the mind and feelings because of the friendly intimacy, the easy and relaxed behaviour, and lack of formality. It denotes a physical and emotional reaction rather than an intellectual or aesthetic one. It is applied to houses, flats, rooms, etc. which seem to have such an atmosphere. *Eine gemütliche Wohnung. Eine gemütliches Lokal. Eine gemütliche Sitzecke. Hier finde ich es sehr gemütlich.* It is used for periods of time or occasions people spend together. *Wir verlebten bei Ihnen einen gemütlichen Abend. Nach der Theatervorstellung saßen wir noch ein Stündchen gemütlich beisammen. Wir haben den ganzen Abend gemütlich geplaudert. Es war sehr gemütlich bei Ihnen.* The usual transls. are *snug*, **cosy**, *agreeable*, or *pleasant. Ein gemütlicher Mensch* is one who is friendly and easy to get on with. *Unsere Nachbarn sind gemütliche Leute.*

4. Komfortabel is a term much used in the commercial area. Both it and **der Komfort** are slightly different from the E. terms. *Der Komfort* includes comfort, but suggests all the latest conveniences and at least a degree of luxury. *Die Ferienhäuser bieten allen Komfort. Das Hotel ist mit allem Komfort ausgestattet. Ein Auto mit höchstem technischem Komfort. Ich verzichte auf Komfort.* Thus *komfortabel* means 'equipped with all the latest conveniences'. *Eine kleine Wohnung* can be *bequem*, but *eine komfortable Wohnung* would be spacious, well appointed, and at least approaching luxurious. *Luxuriös* suggests an even higher degree of luxury.

Das neue Hotel ist komfortabler als die anderen.
Sie haben ihre Wohnung komfortabel eingerichtet.

5. Gemütlich is also used for activities carried out at a leisurely, comfortable pace. *Er macht alles ganz gemütlich—Hetze kennt er nicht.* **Gemächlich** means 'slowly and without haste', thus 'at a leisurely or comfortable pace'. *Wir schlenderten gemächlich nach Hause/am Fluß entlang.*

Wir sind gemütlich spazierengegangen. *Wir hatten noch Zeit, gemütlich Kaffee zu trinken.*
Sie gingen gemächlich zum Bahnhof.   *Sie schlugen ein gemächliches Tempo ein.*

6. i. Comfortable/*Uncomfortable in one's conscience.* **Mir ist bei etw. [nicht] wohl zumute.**

Bei diesem ganzen Unternehmen war mir nicht wohl zumute.

Bei dem bloßen Gedanken an einen solchen Plan war mir nicht wohl zumute.

ii. Comfortable *financially.* **Die Familie ist [finanziell] gut gestellt,** *ist* **wohl/gut situiert,** and **lebt in guten/gesicherten Verhältnissen** all express this idea.

iii. Leicht expresses the idea of winning or passing e.g. an examination easily or comfortably.

Unsere Mannschaft hat das Spiel leicht gewonnen.

Es war ein leichter Sieg.   Sie hat die Prüfung leicht bestanden.

common, joint *adjs.* Some uses of **general** and **ordinary** *adjs.*

1. Common = 'possessed or shared alike by both or all of the pers./thgs. in question', 'experienced or participated in by a number of individuals'. It is used attributively and with *to* after *to be. They have some common interests. We will help our allies against our common enemy. The two triangles have DE as their common base. Sharp teeth are common to all cats. Sharp teeth are a characteristic common to all cats.* After *have* + *obj.,* **in common** is used in two constructions: *Goats have many features in common with sheep* and *Goats and sheep have many features in common.* An extended meaning 'belonging to more than one as a result of co-operation or agreement' is now restricted to a few expressions. *By common consent the partnership was dissolved. This house was the common property of the tribe.* More usual is *joint* or *concerted* action etc.

i. The equivalent in the sense 'common [to]' is **gemeinsam.** It is used alone, *Die beiden Sprachen weisen gemeinsame Merkmale auf,* with a dat., *Scharfe Zähne sind allen Katzen gemeinsam,* and with *haben.* In earlier G., **gemein** had this sense, but it is now archaic except as a syn. of *gemeinsam haben. Bruder und Schwester haben diese Eigenschaft gemein/gemeinsam.*

Die beiden Dreiecke haben die gemeinsame Basis DE.

Die Straßen laufen von einem gemeinsamen Mittelpunkt auseinander.

Ziegen und Schafe haben viele gemeinsame Merkmale/ . . . haben viele Merkmale gemeinsam.

Ziegen haben viele Merkmale mit Schafen gemeinsam.

Die neue Fassung des Romans hat nur sehr wenig mit der alten gemein/gemeinsam.

ii. *Eine Gemeinschaft* is 'a number of people who form a group for some purpose'. The adj. **gemeinschaftlich** and the n. in compounds are used to express the same idea as *gemeinsam,* but are more formal and legal and imply *eine Gemeinschaft* of some kind. *Gemeinsamer Besitz* is the everyday expression for *the common* or *joint property* of two or more people. The owners/occupiers of a block of flats form *eine Gemeinschaft. Der Treppenraum ist also gemeinschaftlicher Besitz. Der Gemeinschaftsraum,* 'common room', is open to all members of a *Gemeinschaft* such as *ein Wohnheim* or *ein Betrieb. Ein Gemeinschaftskonto* is 'a joint (bank) account'.

iii. Gemeinsam, gemeinschaftlich, and **Gemeinschafts-** all mean 'undertaken with another or others'. *Gemeinsam* is the normal word and also translates **joint,** *mutual, concerted,* and *united. Die Fotos sind eine schöne Erinnerung an unsere gemeinsame Reise. Diese Schritte wollen die beiden Gruppen gemeinsam unternehmen. To make common cause with* is *gemeinsame Sache mit jmdm. machen. Gemeinschaftlich* can be a legal term. *Die drei wurden wegen gemeinschaftlichen schweren Diebstahls angeklagt. Das Buch ist eine Gemeinschaftsarbeit mehrerer namhafter Sprachwissenschaftler. Das Flugzeug wurde in britisch-französischer Gemeinschaftsproduktion hergestellt.*

Ein gemeinsames Vorgehen hätte bessere Aussichten auf Erfolg.

Unsere gemeinsamen Anstrengungen haben das gewünschte Ergebnis gehabt.

Das Gericht befand die beiden ehemaligen DDR-Grenzsoldaten des vorsätzlichen gemeinschaftlichen Totschlags für schuldig. Sie hatten im Dezember 1984 einen Flüchtling an der Mauer erschossen.

iv. The meaning of **common** in *by common consent* has to be expressed. One possibility is *Mit [der] Zustimmung aller wurde die Partnerschaft aufgelöst*.

2. i. The meaning of **general**, i.e. 'common to all', 'shared by all, not just by a few people', is expressed by **allgemein**. *Das allgemeine Wahlrecht* is 'universal suffrage', *die allgemeine Schulpflicht* means 'the obligation of all to attend school', and *eine Angelegenheit von allgemeinem Interesse* is 'a matter of interest to all'. **Gemein** used to have this meaning and also the sense 'pertaining to all the citizens of a country', but it has been displaced except in a few expressions. **Common** has also been replaced by *public* and **general**, except in a few expressions like *the common good*. **Gemein** survives in a few compounds: *Gemeinnützig*, existing in the public interest or for the general good of the community; *gemeingefährlich*, liable to cause damage to everyone. *Das Gemeinwohl* means 'the general good' or 'the good of the whole community', but *das Allgemeinwohl* is now just as usual. Both *gemeinverständlich* and *allgemeinverständlich* mean 'generally comprehensible'.

ii. Like **general**, **allgemein** also means 'widespread', 'shared by most or all'. *Das ist die allgemeine Ansicht. Die allgemeine Empörung zwang die Regierung einzugreifen. Der Inhalt des Briefs wurde allgemein bekannt*, it became common knowledge or generally known.

iii. The advs. **commonly** and **generally**, meaning 'accepted by most people or by most people in a particular group', are usually **allgemein**, sometimes **gemeinhin**, which is stylistically higher. *Es wird allgemein angenommen, daß der Premierminister bei der nächsten Wahl nicht kandidieren wird. Das geht schneller, als gemeinhin angenommen wird.*

3. Like **general**, **allgemein** also means 'concerned with the main elements rather than with details'. *Eine allgemeine Definition. Seine Ausführungen blieben zu allgemein.* Cf. BROAD 6. v.

Das Buch bringt einen allgemeinen Überblick.   *Die Darstellung war zu allgemein gehalten.*

4. Common = 'occurring frequently or in large numbers, prevalent'. *These trees are common in most areas. A common view/mistake/experience.*
i. The usual equivalent is **häufig**, 'frequent', but it is often necessary to add a v. such as *Etw. ist häufig anzutreffen*, 'frequently met with', or *häufig vorkommen[d]*, 'occur[ring] frequently'.

Das ist ein häufiger Fehler/ein häufig vorkommendes Erlebnis.
Dieser Fehler ist unter Männern häufig anzutreffen.
Echter Kunstsinn ist nicht häufig/oft anzutreffen.
Dieser Baum ist in feuchten Gegenden häufig anzutreffen. Diesen Baum findet man häufig . . .

ii. Weit verbreitet, 'widespread', is similar to *häufig*. *Das ist eine weit verbreitete Ansicht.*
iii. With reference to words and expressions **gebräuchlich** is used. *Ein gebräuchlicher Ausdruck. Allgemein* is often added: *Ist dieses Wort allgemein gebräuchlich?*, in common use. Also used is *Wird dieser Ausdruck häufig verwendet? Gebräuchlich* occurs in other contexts. *Die gebräuchliche Methode. Das allgemein gebräuchliche Verfahren.* [Allgemein] **üblich**, 'usual', is close in meaning. *Die allgemein übliche Methode.*

5. In *common gratitude, common decency*, etc. **common** suggests behaviour which people in general expect other people to share. The idea can be expressed by **einfach** or **normal**. *Es war einfach ein Gebot der Dankbarkeit, daß wir ihnen geholfen haben. Daß wir mitgehen, erfordert einfach der Anstand. Nicht daran teilzunehmen wäre ein Verstoß gegen die normale Höflichkeit. Die Sitte* can denote rules of behaviour or standards accepted in a society in the ethical or moral spheres and in the pl. with *gut*

COMMUNITY   168

can translate *common decency*. *Nackt auf der Bühne?—vor 20 Jahren hätte man das fraglos als Verstoß gegen die guten Sitten empfunden.*

6. Common = 'having ordinary qualities', 'characteristic of ordinary people, life, language, etc.', 'not distinguished by special or superior characteristics or by rank or position'. It is a syn. of **ordinary** and *average*, which are more usual nowadays.
i. The main equivalents are *gewöhnlich* and *durchschnittlich*. **Gewöhnlich**, used without modification, means 'ordinary' without any depreciatory sense. *Ein gewöhnlicher Sterblicher*, an ordinary mortal. *Im gewöhnlichen Leben*. **Durchschnittlich** means 'average'. *Ein Schüler von durchschnittlicher Intelligenz. The common people* used to be *das gemeine Volk*, but it has gone out of use. *Die einfachen Leute* is now the normal term and suggests people with an average standard of living and education. **Einfach** means 'simple, ordinary, plain'. *Ein einfacher Arbeiter. Das 20. Jahrhundert soll das Zeitalter des einfachen Mannes sein. Die Durchschnittsbürger* is often used instead. The compound *ein Durchschnittsmensch* means the same as *ein durchschnittlicher Mensch*, i.e. 'average, ordinary'. **Alltäglich** (or **Alltags-**), 'what can be met with any day, ordinary, usual', have no depreciatory overtones. *Ein alltäglicher Mensch* is 'an ordinary, everyday human being', *die Alltagssprache* is 'ordinary lang.', and *ein alltägliches Ereignis* is 'common' in the sense that it could happen every day. (If **common** means 'frequent', the transl. is *ein häufig vorkommendes Ereignis*. Cf. 4.)

> *Er sah sich gezwungen, die Stelle eines gewöhnlichen Hilfsarbeiters anzunehmen.*
> *Der Lohn eines gewöhnlichen Landarbeiters war damals sehr niedrig.*
> *Er sammelte die Lieder und Geschichten, die unter den einfachen Leuten im Umlauf waren.*
> *Wenn die Alltagssprache der Durchschnittsmenschen unserem Zweck dient, werden wir sie benutzen.*

ii. Gemein in this sense occurs now in zoological and botanical names only. *Die gemeine Hausfliege. Der gemeine Löwenzahn.*

7. i. **Gewöhnlich** also corresponds to **common** in the sense of 'vulgar and unrefined'. What sense is intended depends on the context, but it is generally true to say that with *sehr, ganz, zu*, and *ausgesprochen, gewöhnlich* means 'vulgar'. *Er war ihr zu gewöhnlich. Sein Benehmen war sehr gewöhnlich. Er benahm sich ausgesprochen gewöhnlich.* Applied to people and their behaviour, **ordinär** always means 'vulgar'.

> *Seine Ausdrucksweise ist mir viel zu ordinär.*   *Er ist ein ganz ordinärer Kerl.*
> *Er benahm sich ordinär.*   *Solches Benehmen ist ordinär.*

ii. Applied to people's language and appearance, **gemein** also means 'coarse and vulgar'.

> *Ein gemeiner Ausdruck.*   *Er hat mich mit gemeinen Worten beschimpft.*
> *Er hatte einen gemeinen Gesichtsausdruck.*   *Gemeine Witze.*

iii. Gemein is now most frequently found in the sense 'vile, mean, nasty, or malicious' applied to people and their behaviour. *Sie haben uns gemein behandelt. Er hat an mir gemein gehandelt. Das war gemein von dir. Das war eine gemeine Handlungsweise.* It is used in an exaggerated way, particularly by children, to denote something unpleasant or annoying. *Ich finde es ganz schön gemein, daß der Bus uns vor der Nase weggefahren ist.*

community *n*.

1. The **community** denotes the people of an area or a country as a whole, the public, the body to which all belong. The group it designates ranges in size from small, *the village community, The members belong to all sections of the [town/local] community*, to society in general. To distinguish the latter *the community at large* is often used.
i. Die Gemeinschaft is applied to groups or associations of people who feel themselves united in some way. It varies in size from two or a few, *die Gemeinschaft der*

Familie, to groups who are united by common interests or views or who pursue a common aim, to bodies of people who are organized into a political unit, and to associations between nations for a common goal. Some common compounds are *die Dorfgemeinschaft,* 'the people living in a village, village community', *die Wohngemeinschaft,* 'a group of people, e.g. students, living together in a house or flat', *die Interessengemeinschaft,* either 'an association of people to preserve or promote common interests' or 'a number of independent business enterprises which join together in the pursuit of common aims', *die Sprachgemeinschaft,* 'linguistic community', *die Glaubensgemeinschaft,* 'body of people sharing the same religious views', *die Hausgemeinschaft,* 'the people living in a house'. *Eine Arbeitsgemeinschaft* is a usually small group who work together. *Die Klasse teilte sich in Arbeitsgemeinschaften auf, die je eine bestimmte Aufgabe bearbeiteten.*

ii. When **community** refers to the people in a place or country in a vague way, **die Gemeinschaft** is used. Actions can be *zum Wohl* or *im Interesse der Gemeinschaft* or *zum Nachteil der Gemeinschaft. Einem Verbrecher Gnade vor Recht ergehen zu lassen heißt oft, der Gemeinschaft ein Unrecht tun. Die Soldaten, die mehrere Jahre im Dschungel gedient hatten, mußten sich wieder in die Gemeinschaft eingliedern.* If, however, a branch of government which provides money or assistance is meant, **die Gemeinde,** 'the local authority', or, on a national level, **der Staat** is used. *Sie wollten nicht der Gemeinde/dem Staat zur Last fallen,* be a burden to/on the community. Cf. 2. **Das Gemeinwesen** is a formal term occasionally met with which denotes the people in an area as an organized body or unit. Both *eine Gemeinde* and *ein Staat* in the sense of 'country' can be called *ein Gemeinwesen. In unruhigen Zeiten ist es notwendig, dem Gemeinwesen Sicherheit zu verschaffen.*

iii. When **community** refers to society in general or when it is used with this sense in such expressions as *the community at large* or *in general* or *the wider community,* it can be translated by **die breite Öffentlichkeit,** the general public. *Das Schicksal dieser vernachlässigten Kinder scheint die breite Öffentlichkeit nicht zu interessieren.* Alternatives are **die Allgemeinheit** and **die Gesamtheit.** *Etw. dient der Allgemeinheit/ist der Allgemeinheit förderlich. Jmd. erwirbt sich große Verdienste um die Allgemeinheit. Sie haben vieles zum Wohl der Gesamtheit getan.* In some contexts **die Bevölkerung,** 'population', is the appropriate transl. *Alle Schichten der Bevölkerung sind in unserem Verein vertreten.*

iv. Community *work* or *service* means 'activities designed to help others, particularly the disadvantaged'. **Die Sozialarbeit** denotes work intended to assist those in need because of their social position, health, age, etc. Hence *der Sozialarbeiter, der Sozialberuf,* and *Jmd. ist im Sozialbereich tätig.*

2. Other senses of *Gemeinschaft.*

i. Die Gemeinschaft can, but need not, suggest that a spirit or sense of belonging together unites the group. *In unserer Klasse herrscht [k]eine echte Gemeinschaft.* Although the meaning is clear here, this sense is often best expressed by the compounds **der Gemeinschaftsgeist** or **das Gemeinschaftsgefühl,** spirit or sense of community or belonging together. One of these compounds is an unambiguous transl. of **community** when it means 'friendship created and maintained between people who are in some way different'. *Sie war bemüht, dieses Gemeinschaftsgefühl/ diesen Gemeinschaftsgeist zu stärken,* anxious to strengthen this sense of community.

ii. In the wider political sphere, **community** denotes a group of countries who work together or have common interests. This is also expressed by **die Gemeinschaft.** Thus *die europäische Gemeinschaft* and *die atlantische Gemeinschaft.* The Russian words which we translate as *Commonwealth of Independent States* are rendered in G. as *die Gemeinschaft unabhängiger Staaten.*

iii. Die Gemeinschaft can mean 'an association or a society', the normal word for which is *die Vereinigung. Sie traten in eine Gemeinschaft/Vereinigung zum Schutz der Umwelt ein.*

iv. Die Gemeinschaft can refer to working, living, or being together. *Als Mitglied der Polarexpedition mußte er in enger Gemeinschaft mit zehn anderen leben. Gemeinschaft mit Gott* is translated as *communion* or *fellowship*.

3. i. In two compounds *Gemeinde-* is translated as *community. Das Gemeindezentrum* is 'the community centre', and *das Gemeindehaus* is 'the community hall', but can be 'the parish hall'. Cf. ii below. In other compounds *Gemeinde-* means 'municipal' or 'local government'. *Der Gemeindebeamte.* **Die Gemeinde** or **die Kommune** is the lowest unit in civil administration, the local authority, called a municipality or shire in Australia and a borough or parish in the UK. *Eine kleine/große/ländliche/ reiche Gemeinde. Die Gemeinde hat 20 000 Einwohner. Die benachbarte Gemeinde baut ein neues Schwimmbad. Die Müllabfuhr und die Straßenbeleuchtung sind Aufgaben der Kommune/Gemeinde.* Both can also denote the population of such a unit. *Morgen wählen alle Gemeinden/Kommunen in Niedersachsen neue Gemeinderäte.*

ii. In connection with a church, **die Gemeinde** is 'a parish', the area for which a particular church is responsible, *Die Gemeinde hat einen neuen Pfarrer bekommen,* and the people belonging to that church in that area, *Die Gemeinde sammelt für eine neue Orgel.* In addition it means 'the people attending a particular church service', i.e. 'the congregation'. Clergymen often address the congregation as *liebe Gemeinde. Die Gemeinde stimmte ein bekanntes Kirchenlied an/folgte der Predigt aufmerksam.*

4. In an expression like *the German community in Sydney,* **community** denotes a group of people who have a characteristic such as nationality in common, but who live in a larger society which does not share this. This is one sense of **die Kolonie**. *Die deutsche Kolonie in Sydney.* If the people are united by religion, *die Gemeinde* is possible. *Die jüdische Gemeinde in New York.* An alternative without implications is **die Bevölkerungsgruppe**. *Die jüdische Bevölkerungsgruppe in London. Die islamische Bevölkerungsgruppe in Bradford. Community relations* when it refers to relations between ethnic groups is *das Verhältnis* or *die Beziehungen zwischen den verschiedenen Bevölkerungsgruppen.*

5. We speak of people having common interests etc. The n. for this is **community** *of interests.* As *common interests* is *gemeinsame Interessen,* the n. is **die Gemeinsamkeit** *der Interessen.*

complain *v.* While the general sense of **complain**, i.e. 'to express discontent, dissatisfaction, resentment, or regret as though expecting sympathy', is covered by *klagen,* G. makes with *sich beklagen* aand *sich beschweren* distinctions not present in E.

i. Klagen now usually means 'to complain' in the sense 'to express discontent, mostly with the aim of arousing sympathy'. It is a general term and does not necessarily lay the blame on anyone. Applied to bodily ailments, it means little more than 'to have' them. It is used alone, with *über,* or with *darüber* + clause.

> *Warum mußt du ständig klagen?*   *Sie klagten dauernd über das schlechte Wetter.*
> *Die Hausbewohner klagten über ständigen Lärm.*
> *Der Patient klagte über Schmerzen im Rücken.*
> *Er klagte darüber, daß er fast täglich bis spät in die Nacht arbeiten mußte.*

Used with a dat., *klagen* means 'to pour out one's woes/troubles/sorrows to s.o.' *Sie klagte mir ihr Leid/ihre Not/ihren Schmerz/ihren Kummer* etc. It occasionally means 'to

express one's pain or grief, either by groaning or by tears and wailing. *Sie weinten und klagten um den Verstorbenen.*
> *Er klagte und jammerte den ganzen Tag vor Schmerzen.*

ii. Sich beklagen adds to the idea of expressing discontent about a wrong suffered, bad treatment, etc. a strong reproach against the person responsible. It is, however, not directed at the one who gives rise to the dissatisfaction, but to a third person.
> *Wenn er mit anderen Kollegen zusammen ist, beklagt er sich oft über seinen Vorgesetzten.*
> *Sie beklagte sich bei allen ihren Bekannten über die schlechte Behandlung, die ihr am Arbeitsplatz widerfahren war.*
> *Die Gäste des Ferienhotels beklagten sich ständig über den mangelnden Service.*
> *Seine Schwierigkeiten waren alle unerheblich, und er hatte keinen Grund, sich zu beklagen.*

iii. While the person, *bei der ich mich beklage,* may have nothing to do with the matter, **sich beschweren** means 'to direct the complaint (*die Beschwerde*) either to the pers. who is to blame for what has given rise to the dissatisfaction or to s.o. else within whose area of responsibility the grievance has arisen'. It thus implies making or lodging a formal complaint.
> *Die Kunden beschwerten sich beim Kellner über das schlechte Essen.*
> *Die Dame drohte, sich bei der Direktion des Kaufhauses über die schlechte Bedienung zu beschweren.*
> *Ich werde mich bei Ihrem Vorgesetzten über Sie beschweren.*

iv. Lamentieren implies that someone complains repeatedly about unimportant things in a way which is more likely to try others' patience than to arouse their sympathy. It is colloquial like *to grouse* or *to gripe. Du mußt nicht bei jeder Kleinigkeit lamentieren.* **Jammern [über]** suggests a continued expression of dissatisfaction about troubles, difficulties, being hard done by, etc. like *to moan [about]. Hör' doch endlich auf zu jammern! Jammere doch nicht den ganzen Tag über diese Kleinigkeit!*
> *Hör' doch auf zu lamentieren! Wir haben deine Klagen satt.*
> *Sobald er aufhörte zu jammern und die Sache in die Hand nahm, glückte sie ihm.*
> *Hör' endlich auf herumzulamentieren/herumzujammern, denn du gehst uns allen gehörig auf die Nerven!*

v. Murren has the general sense of expressing dissatisfaction. The notion is to make vague or inarticulate noises signifying displeasure. *Das Kind murrt dauernd über das Essen.* Similar E. words are *grumble, mutter,* or *murmur.* Applied to groups of people, it means 'to express their discontent in protests'.
> *Er murrte über diese Ungerechtigkeit, unternahm aber nichts.*
> *Sie ertrug das schwere Schicksal ohne Murren.*
> *Er tat seine Pflicht, ohne zu murren.*
> *Als das Volk anfing zu murren, gab der Fürst nach.*
> *Das Murren der Arbeiter wurde zur Meuterei.*

complete, perfect, entire, total *adjs.*

1. The basic sense of **complete** is 'having all or not lacking any of the necessary parts' or 'embracing all the requisite items, details, components, topics'. *A complete set of teeth. A complete edition. The complete works. The list is not yet complete.* This is the meaning of **vollständig** which is used as an attributive and predicative adj. and as an adv. It refers to concrete things and to something in writing, like a list or an account of events. *Ein vollständiges Gebiß. Die Sammlung ist noch nicht vollständig. Eine vollständige Darstellung der Ereignisse lag nicht vor.* It occurs with ns. denoting a process when the idea of using up every part is present. *Wieviel Luft wird zur vollständigen Verbrennung von einem Kilogramm Kohle benötigt?* As an adv., *vollständig* can be used like *völlig.* Cf. 6. *Die Stadt wurde vollständig zerstört. Ihre Gesundheit ist vollständig wiederhergestellt.*

Die Liste der Schüler, die an der Klassenfahrt teilnehmen, ist noch nicht vollständig.
Das ist kein vollständiger Satz/ein vollständiges Verzeichnis der Bilder.
Ich habe eine vollständige Ausgabe der Gedichte Mörikes.
In einer Höhle in Neuseeland hat man ein fast vollständiges Skelett einer ausgestorbenen Vogelart gefunden.
Wir haben nun die Einzelteile vollständig beisammen.
Ohne Haferflocken würde ich das Frühstück nicht als vollständig betrachten.
Er vermittelte uns ein beinahe vollständiges Bild von der Kultur der Balinesen.

2. Vollzählig means that all members of a group or all parts of something are present. In *Die Gruppe ist nun vollzählig*, it can be translated as *complete*, but it has other equivalents. *Sind wir nun vollzählig?* is like *Are we all here?*

3. In *The report is now complete*, **complete** means 'finished' and is translated by **fertig**, 'finished', or **abgeschlossen**, 'completed'. *Der Bericht ist nun fertig. Die Arbeit ist jetzt abgeschlossen.*

4. In reference to time, **complete** is often interchangeable with *whole* and **entire**. *I need a complete lecture to explain the basic concepts. That simple job took a complete/whole hour. That was the only time in his entire life that he was off the farm for more than a few days.* These three words are translated by **ganz**.
Ich brauche eine ganze Vorlesung, um die Grundbegriffe zu erklären.
Ich brauchte eine ganze Stunde, um diesen kurzen Brief zu schreiben.
Das war das einzige Mal in seinem ganzen Leben, daß er für mehr als ein paar Tage vom Hof weg war.

5. When **entire** refers to the whole of something other than time and can also be replaced by *whole*, the equivalent is also **ganz**. *Die ganze Klasse*, the whole/entire class, *das ganze Gebiet*, the whole/entire area. In contexts such as *his entire ignorance of the subject* or *entirely different*, it is a syn. of **complete** and can be translated by the words discussed in 6, mainly *völlig*. *Seine völlige Unwissenheit über das Thema. Das ist völlig/ganz anders.*

6. i. While *vollständig* mostly refers to something concrete which consists, or is thought of as consisting, of parts, **völlig** is applied to more abstract qualities or states. It is the usual equivalent of **complete** when it describes an action carried through to its full extent. *A complete change. A complete break with the past.* It is used both as an adv. and as an attributive adj., but cannot be used predicatively.
Es herrschte völlige Ruhe/völlige Windstille/völlige Dunkelheit.
Wir rechnen mit der völligen Wiederherstellung ihrer Gesundheit/mit ihrer völligen Genesung.
Ein völliger Bruch mit der Vergangenheit ist kaum möglich.
Ich wunderte mich über seine völlige Gleichgültigkeit meinem Vorschlag gegenüber.
Sein Vorgehen war völlig gerechtfertigt/völlig verständlich.
Es ist völlig unmöglich, ihm zu helfen.   *Wir tappten völlig im Dunkeln.*
Du hast die Uhr völlig kaputt gemacht.   *Das habe ich völlig vergessen.*
Es ist völlig überflüssig, dem, was schon gesagt wurde, noch mehr hinzuzufügen.
Wir haben eine völlige Einigung erzielt.   *Die Symptome sind völlig verschwunden.*
Von Ihrem früheren Standpunkt sind Sie völlig abgerückt.

ii. Vollkommen is used like *völlig* as an adj. and adv., but some people avoid it in contexts expressing undesirable qualities. When both are possible, *vollkommen* sounds weightier. *Sie erzielten eine völlige/vollkommene Einigung. Er bat um völlige/vollkommene/absolute Ruhe.* Cf. 7.
Das habe ich völlig/vollkommen verstanden.   *Ich bin völlig/vollkommen/ganz deiner Meinung.*

7. Perfect means 'complete with everything needed' or 'not lacking in any particular'. Applied to qualities, it is often a syn. of **complete** or *absolute*. *Perfect/Complete/Absolute sincerity/honesty.* It also means 'without fault', 'free from

imperfection', or 'corresponding exactly to an ideal, definition, or pattern'. *A perfect copy/representation/example/circle/body. Perfect beauty.* For a work of art it means 'faultless', *a perfect poem*, and for people 'morally faultless', *Few people are perfect.*
i. The general word expressing these concepts is **vollkommen. Vollendet** usually refers to the faultless way a quality is displayed. **Absolut** is used with qualities and states.

Alle waren von seiner absoluten/vollkommenen Ehrlichkeit/Aufrichtigkeit überzeugt.
Im Haus herrschte vollkommene/vollendete Eintracht/Harmonie/absolute Ruhe.
In ihr sah er die vollkommene Frau.   Viele Leute halten dieses Gedicht für vollkommen.
Kein Mensch ist vollkommen.   Sie ist zu einer vollendeten Schönheit herangewachsen.
Er war von der vollkommenen Schönheit der Blüten überrascht.
Das kann ich mit absoluter/völliger Sicherheit sagen. (Some people would also use *vollkommen.*)

ii. Perfect and **complete** are applied to people who embody a quality to the greatest possible extent. **Complete** is now used only for bad qualities, *a complete villain/fool*, although *a complete gentleman* was formerly normal. **Perfect** is used for good and bad qualities: *A perfect gentleman* and *a perfect fool. Stranger* is a borderline case as both these words and *total* are possible. *Absolute* is a syn. *He's an absolute dimwit.* **Vollkommen** is used here, although some speakers restrict it to pos. qualities, as well as **völlig** and **absolut. Vollendet** is limited to favourable judgements. Another expression is **durch und durch.** *Er ist ein Schurke durch und durch. Er ist durch und durch ein Egoist.* One sense of **ausgemacht** expresses a related meaning and is confined to neg. characteristics. *Er is ein ausgemachter Dummkopf/ein ausgemachter Schurke.*

Er ist ein vollkommener Kavalier, und sie eine vollendete Dame.
Sie ist mir völlig/total fremd (a complete stranger).
Er ist ein völliger/totaler Idiot. (For *total* see 8.)
Er ist eine absolute/völlige Niete. (Many people also use *Eine vollkommene Niete.*)

iii. Perfect, complete, and *absolute* also mean 'unmitigated'. *Perfect/Complete/Absolute nonsense.* The adjs. listed in ii also express this sense. *Das ist völliger/absoluter/vollendeter/vollkommener Unsinn/Blödsinn. Das ist ein ausgemachter Schwindel.*

iv. Perfect, relating to the carrying out of skills, can be **vollendet.** *Ein vollendeter Redner/Schauspieler. Eine vollendete Hausfrau.* **Vollkommen** is also used. *Sie hat das Musikstück vollkommen gespielt.* **Perfekt** is common. It means 'excellent', 'without fault'.

Englisch spricht sie perfekt.   *Sie ist perfekt in der Buchhaltung.*
Er hat in perfektem Deutsch geantwortet.   *Die Schüler beherrschten den Lehrstoff perfekt.*
Wegen der perfekten Planung verlief alles reibungslos.

8. Total(ly).

i. Total is frequently encountered, particularly in the spoken language. Originally, it was applied only to neg. qualities and events. *Ein totaler Mißerfolg. Ein totales Fiasko. Eine totale Niederlage. Das ist ja totaler Wahnsinn. Ich war total erschöpft. Sie sind ja total verrückt. Sie machen alles total falsch/verkehrt. Die Reise war total chaotisch.* This does not apply to scientific or learned contexts. *Eine totale Mondfinsternis. Eine totale Neuordnung.* Particularly in the current *Jugendsprache, total* is used with pos. qualities. *Alle waren total begeistert/total freundlich.*

ii. From its derivation **restlos** means that nothing is left over; it has become a common syn. of *völlig.*

Die billigen Pullover waren restlos ausverkauft.   *Wir arbeiteten bis zur restlosen Erschöpfung.*
Die Sitzungen, in denen man dauernd über Lappalien redet, habe ich restlos satt.

iii. Gänzlich, which is not very common, is a stronger form of *ganz* and sometimes corresponds to *utter.* It is used only as an adv. and attributive adj. *Diesen Plan habe ich gänzlich aufgegeben. Der gänzliche Mangel an Hilfsbereitschaft. Gänzliche Hilflosigkeit.*

Wir haben es mit gänzlich verschiedenen Menschen zu tun.

iv. The adv. **vollends** is also not often met with. It means that a process which has already begun is completed in the intervening period. *Es war inzwischen vollends dunkel geworden.*

Dieser weitere Verlust hat die Firma vollends ruiniert.

v. In reference to money, the E. adj. **total** is **gesamt**, which is used attributively only and forms numerous compounds. *Er hinterließ sein gesamtes Vermögen dem Waisenhaus. Mein gesamtes Einkommen. Haben Sie den Gesamtbetrag schon ausgerechnet? Wieviel beträgt die Gesamtschuld des Landes?* Cf. ALL 2. iii.

concern *v.*

1. i. The first sense is 'to relate or refer to', 'to have a bearing on', 'to be of relevance to', and is expressed by **angehen** and **betreffen**. With a person as obj. they are interchangeable. *Das geht auch Sie an* and *Das betrifft Sie auch. Dieses Gesetz betrifft alle Bürger/geht alle Bürger an.* The difference in meaning is slight; *angehen* is the everyday word and suggests something like having a bearing on or being of importance to, while *betreffen* is more formal and often implies that something has practical consequences for someone. As *angehen* needs a person as obj., only *betreffen* is possible when a thing is obj. *Das neue Gesetz betrifft chemische Zusätze in Lebensmitteln.* The abbreviation *betr.* = *betrifft* is used in business letters like *re* or *ref(erence).* Only the pres., past., and future act. of both vs. are found in the sense defined here. In the perf. and pass. *betreffen* means 'to AFFECT'.

> *Die fünf ersten Punkte der Tagesordnung betreffen die Unterbringung der Teilnehmer an der Konferenz.*
> *Die Neuregelung betrifft alle Studenten.   Dieser Fall geht uns alle an.*
> *Die Luftverschmutzung betrifft uns alle, und niemand kann sagen, sie ginge ihn nicht an.*

ii. Angehen has a somewhat stronger sense which resembles **concern** meaning 'to be s.o.'s business'. It is mostly neg., this being expressed by *nichts. Misch' dich nicht in Sachen ein, die dich nichts angehen!* It is pos. in questions, *Was geht mich das an?,* and when disputing a neg. assertion. In this case the sent. usually contains *etw.* In reply to *Das geht mich nichts an,* someone might say, '*Das geht dich doch etw. an, auch wenn du dich dagegen mit aller Macht zu wehren versuchst.*'

> *Der Diplomat wurde in Streitigkeiten verwickelt, die weder ihn noch sein Land etw. angingen.*

2. Concerned. Betreffend means 'concerned' or 'in question', i.e. 'referred to, involved in what we have been talking about'. *Die betreffenden Studenten werden gebeten, sich im Sekretariat zu melden.* (*Die betroffenen Studenten* = 'the students affected'.) *Zu der betreffenden Zeit. Am betreffenden Ort.* The people concerned also means 'those involved or taking part in sth.', which is **die Beteiligten**. In reference to a play or team a teacher might ask those concerned to meet. *Der Lehrer bat alle Beteiligten, sich nach der Schule in der Aula zu versammeln.* Thus *Der Direktor dankte allen Beteiligten,* everyone concerned. Cf. INVOLVE 1.

3. As far as s.o./sth. **is concerned.**
i. The everyday expressions are **was** *mich/diese Angelegenheit* **angeht**, and **was . . . betrifft.** *Angehen* is here not restricted to a personal obj. **Was . . . anbelangt** is a formal variant, and **was . . . anbetrifft** is found only in business and official style. The v. *anbetreffen* has gone out of use except in this expression.

> *Was mich angeht/betrifft, so ist die Sache schon erledigt.*
> *Was den Vertrag angeht/betrifft/anbetrifft/anbelangt, so finden Sie darin die Rechte and Pflichten beider Vertragsparteien eindeutig festgelegt.*
> *Was die Tatsache Ihres Nichterscheinens angeht/betrifft/anbetrifft/anbelangt, so werde ich noch einmal darüber hinwegsehen.*

ii. Von mir/ihm/ihr aus and **meinetwegen/seinetwegen/ihretwegen**, etc. translate *as far as I'm* etc. *concerned* when this means that I etc. have no objection.

Von mir/ihm aus können wir das machen.   *Meinetwegen könnt ihr gehen.*

4. Concern oneself with = 'occupy oneself with', 'be concerned with'.
i. Sich befassen mit implies a basic level of concern and interest, while **sich beschäftigen mit** suggests greater involvement, sometimes working on something. Though the distinction is not always observed, *sich befassen mit* is more likely to be found when the degree of involvement is not stated and in neg. sents. *Sich beschäftigen mit* needs a person as subj., or something that stands for people. *Seine Gedanken beschäftigten sich oft mit dem Problem* or *Der Bundestag beschäftigt sich mit dem Haushaltsplan. Sich befassen mit* can have as subj. a book, chapter, etc. and means 'to be about'. *Das nächste Kapitel befaßt sich mit den frühen Dramen. The novel concerns two soldiers* can be *Der Roman befaßt sich mit zwei Soldaten*, but *Der Roman handelt von zwei Soldaten* is a common alternative. Cf. BE A. 7.

> *Mit diesem Fall will ich mich nicht weiter befassen/beschäftigen.*
> *Er gehörte zu den Menschen, die sich nicht gern mit Bagatellen befassen.*
> *Die Mutter hatte keine Zeit, sich mit dem Kind zu beschäftigen.*
> *Die Polizei mußte sich mit dem Fall befassen/beschäftigen.*

ii. *Three important questions will concern us today* or *We are today concerned with three important questions* can be *Wir befassen uns heute mit drei wichtigen Fragen.* **Es geht um etw.** means that something is the issue, concerned, or at stake, or that something is referred to. *Bei der heutigen Sitzung geht es um drei wichtige Fragen* is a common variant on the first transl. *Jeder weiß, worum es hier geht*, what is concerned, what it's about. *Bei dem Gespräch ging es um die neue Wohnung. Um wen geht es hier?* **Es handelt sich um** means that (in what we are dealing with or talking about) something is concerned or involved, or it is a question of something. *Worum handelt es sich?* implies *What is it (that you want to talk to me) about?* or *What does it concern? Es handelt sich um eine wichtige Angelegenheit*, an important matter is concerned/involved. *Bei diesem Geschäft handelt es sich um eine beträchtliche Summe Geld, . . .* is concerned/involved. *Es geht um/handelt sich um eine wichtige Angelegenheit. Die Schüler, um die es sich handelt*, the pupils concerned.

iii. Wir haben es mit etw./jmdm. zu tun means that we are dealing, concerned, or confronted with a person or thing of a particular kind. The sents. below could be translated as *We are here concerned with . . .*

> *Wir haben es mit einer gefährlichen Verbrecherbande zu tun.*
> *Hier haben wir es mit einem ungewöhnlichen Fall zu tun.*

5. In *The shaky financial position of the firm concerns me greatly* and *His father is very concerned about his poor behaviour*, **concern** means 'to worry'. *Die wackelige finanzielle Lage der Firma* **beunruhigt** *mich sehr. Sein Vater ist über sein schlechtes Benehmen sehr beunruhigt.* Cf. BOTHER 5 for alternatives.

6. The pass. of **concern** is used with an infin., meaning 'to feel interested in', 'to be anxious to secure'. *She is more concerned to raise productivity than to increase profit. He was not concerned to extend his territory.* **Es geht um** or **es geht darum** + infin., mostly with, but sometimes without, a dat., means that something is important to someone, that he or she is concerned or anxious to do something. *Es geht mir sehr darum, ihr diese Enttäuschung zu ersparen. Es geht darum, die letzten Zweifler zu überzeugen.*

> *Es geht ihr mehr darum, die Produktivität zu steigern, als den Gewinn zu erhöhen.*
> *Es ging ihm nicht darum, seinen Beseitz zu erweitern. Also Es lag ihm nicht daran . . .*
> *Es geht mir darum, sie von der Richtigkeit unseres Vorgehens zu überzeugen.*

7. To be **concerned for** means 'to care about', 'to consider important', 'to want to take care of the welfare of'. *An employer should be concerned for the safety of his workers. Politicians continually tell us how concerned they are for the well-being of the housewife.* The idea can be conveyed by **es liegt mir [viel] an etw., es liegt mir [viel] daran** + infin. or *daß*-clause, or **an etw. ist mir [viel] gelegen**, all of which mean that something is important to me. Cf. EAGER 2. ii. *Es geht mir um* is also possible.

> *Es liegt mir viel daran, daß die beiden an dem Projekt mitarbeiten. Also Mir ist an ihrer Mitarbeit viel gelegen.   Ihm lag daran, jedes Risiko auszuschließen.*
> *An der Sicherheit seiner Arbeiter sollte einem guten Arbeitgeber viel gelegen sein.*
> *Die Politiker versichern uns dauernd, es liege ihnen sehr viel am Wohlergehen aller Hausfrauen.*

confess, admit, concede *vs.*

1. Admit = 'to acknowledge voluntarily or accept as true', 'declare to be correct'. *I admitted my mistake/that I had made a mistake. He admitted his guilt.*

i. Zugeben is the everyday equivalent of **admit** in this sense. It can be used for admitting [to] a crime or [to] less serious wrongdoing, for admitting that one has made a mistake, not done something expected, or for conceding the correctness of another's point of view etc. It needs an obj. which can be a n., *Sie gab ihren Fehler zu*, or *das* or *es*, *Gib's doch endlich zu!* It is also used with an infin. or clause.

> *Der Angeklagte hat die Tat/das Verbrechen/seine Schuld zugegeben.*
> *Sie gab zu, eine wichtige Tatsache verschwiegen zu haben.*
> *Er mußte zugeben, daß er sich in Bezug auf die Länge der Donau geirrt hatte. Sie ist nämlich länger als der Rhein.   Ich gebe gern zu, daß er die Arbeit sehr gut gemacht hat.*

ii. The past part. **zugegeben** is used like *granted, I admit. Zugegeben, ich habe mich geirrt, aber das rechtfertigt sein Verhalten mir gegenüber nicht. Es war, zugegeben, viel Glück dabei.*

iii. *Admittedly,* when it does not imply that someone admits something, is **zwar.** *Das ist zwar verboten, aber keiner hält sich daran. Das ist ein zwar guter, aber kein neuer Gedanke.*

iv. Gestehen is the usual word for confessing a crime to the police or other relevant authority. It can be used alone, *Der Mann, den die Polizei festgenommen hat, hat gestanden*, with an obj., *Er gestand den Diebstahl/seine Schuld*, a clause, *Er gestand, daß er bei dem Banküberfall Beihilfe geleistet hatte*, and an infin., *Sie gestand, gelogen zu haben/das Verbrechen begangen zu haben.* It is also used for admitting wrongdoing of a less serious nature, and for admitting to feelings and views which might differ from those generally held. It is used as a formula to introduce a view which might not be well received. *Ich gestehe, daß ich Bedenken habe/daß ich das Essen nicht sonderlich mag. Jmdm. seine Liebe gestehen* is a fixed expression.

> *Das Kind gestand der Mutter, daß ihm ein Teller kaputt gegangen war.*
> *Der Soldat mußte dem Feldwebel gestehen, daß er während der Ausübung seiner nächtlichen Pflichten eingeschlafen war.*

v. Beichten is the main religious term which can be used alone, *Wann haben Sie zuletzt gebeichtet?*, or with either dat. or acc. or both, *Er hat dem Priester seine Sünden gebeichtet.* **Bekennen** is also used with *Sünden* as obj. It is normal in a sent. which contains *Beichte. Während der Beichte bekennt man seine Sünden und wird durch die Erteilung der Absolution von ihnen freigesprochen.* While *beichten* suggests confession in a confessional, *bekennen* is used in other situations, especially with a first person subj. *Ich bekenne meine Schuld/die Tat.* One introduction to the *Sündenbekenntnis der evangelischen Kirche* reads: *Da wir hier versammelt sind, um miteinander Gottes Wort zu hören . . . so lasset uns . . . vor Gott bekennen, daß wir gesündigt haben mit Gedanken, Worten und Werken.*

vi. Beichten occurs in non-religious contexts, either for confessing important things, *Die Tochter beichtete der Mutter ihre erste große Enttäuschung*, or in a more ironical or jocular way when one's conscience is somewhat troubled, *Ich muß dir beichten, daß ich eine Menge Geld ausgegeben habe*, or *Nun beichte mal!—wo bist du denn gestern abend gewesen?* **Bekennen** is used for admitting things about which one feels guilt although one is not obliged to divulge them, but it has a religious ring. It is restricted to private life, for admitting things to friends, relatives, etc. and is not used for confessing crimes to the police. It is much less common than *zugeben* and *gestehen* and now sounds very formal. Sometimes it denotes an unreserved expression of likes or dislikes, but here too *gestehen* is more usual. *'Nein, ich fühle mich hier nicht mehr wohl', bekannte Bernadette frank und frei.*

> *Er bekannte, daß er im Unrecht gewesen war.*
> *Sein Unrecht zu bekennen soll sich niemand schämen.*
> *Ich bekenne aufrichtig, einen Fehler gemacht zu haben.*

Other uses. *Seinen Glauben bekennen*, to profess one's faith. Hence *das Glaubensbekenntnis*. *Sich zu etw. bekennen*, to state openly one's allegiance to a movement, person, or view. *Sie bekannten sich zum Christentum/zum Kommunismus/zu Mohammed. In seinen Reden bekennt sich unser Abgeordneter immer zu liberalen Grundsätzen. Zu der Meinung, die er in den letzten Monaten oft vertreten hat, will er sich jetzt nicht mehr bekennen.* In court language **sich** *schuldig* **bekennen** is 'to admit one's guilt' or 'to plead guilty'. *Vor dem Gericht bekannte sich der Angeklagte schuldig und bereute die Tat.* An alternative expression is *Der Angeklagte bekannte sich als Täter. Sich bekennen zu* also means 'to admit to, own up to, or confess to'. *Einer 1992 durchgeführten Umfrage zufolge bekennt sich fast ein Drittel der Jugendlichen in Deutschland zu ausländerfeindlichen Einstellungen.* In reference usually to bombings, assassination attempts, etc. it also translates *to claim responsibility for. Nach dem Mordanschlag auf den Botschafter bekannte sich eine Terroristengruppe zu der Tat.*

vii. Eingestehen is the only word used with a refl. dat. and thus translates *to admit to oneself. Endlich mußte er sich eingestehen, daß er sich zu viel zugemutet hatte.* Without the refl. it means 'to admit sth. one feels uneasy or guilty about, often to s.o. close'. *Er gestand mir sein Versagen ein.* It is like *bekennen*, but does not have the religious overtone. Mostly it suggests some hesitation or reluctance to own up, and/or yielding to pressure. Cf. 2.

> *Er gestand (z. B. seiner Frau) seine Schuld ein/daß er den ganzen Wochenlohn ausgegeben hatte.*
> *Erst Jahre später, als die Kinder schon längst nicht mehr zu Hause wohnten, mußte der Vater eingestehen, daß er den ältesten Sohn vor dessen Geschwistern vorgezogen hatte.*
> *Ich habe mich damals noch der Einsicht widersetzt und konnte dir nicht bekennen, was ich mir selbst nicht eingestehen wollte.*

2. Concede means either 'to grant or admit the correctness of a view, an opponent's claim, etc.', *He conceded that they had tried very hard*, or 'to grant or permit rights, conditions, etc.', *He conceded us the right to cross his land.* **Einräumen** and **zugestehen** cover both senses and are, like **concede**, learned words.

> *Er räumte ein, daß sie sich große Mühe gegeben hatten.*
> *Ich räume ein, ich könnte mich geirrt haben.*
> *Er wollte nicht zugestehen, daß seine erste Behauptung nicht stimmte.*
> *Wir haben diesen Mitarbeitern besondere Rechte eingeräumt.*
> *Diese übertriebenen Forderungen können wir unter keinen Umständen zugestehen.*
> *Er gestand uns das Recht zu, durch sein Land zu fahren.* Also *Er räumte uns das Recht ein . . .*

Eingestehen is the usual v. for conceding or admitting defeat. *Der Kanzler gestand die Wahlniederlage ein.*

3. Admit, when it means 'to let s.o. in through a door/into a room, etc.', is **hereinlassen** when seen from the inside and **hineinlassen** when seen from outside. *An der Tür ist ein Polizist. Sollen wir ihn hereinlassen? Sie stand vor der Tür und wartete darauf, hineingelassen zu werden.* When **admit** means 'to give official permission to attend or enter', as in *Children under 14 are not admitted*, the equivalent is **zulassen**. *Kinder unter vierzehn Jahren werden nicht zugelassen. Nur Mitglieder des Vereins werden zu diesen Sitzungen zugelassen. Zulassen* also means 'to admit' to a university etc. *Sie wurde zum Studium an der Universität Göttingen zugelassen.* A syn. is **aufnehmen** with and without *in. Wie viele Studenten nimmt die Universität jedes Jahr auf?* Cf. ACCEPT 5.

consider *v.* One sense of **think** and **reflect on** *vs.*

1. Consider = 'to occupy one's mind with, think about, reflect on, ponder'. *I've considered the matter carefully. Nachdenken* and *überlegen* are the main equivalents.

i. Nachdenken, which implies expending mental activity on or attempting to gain clarity in thought about a situation, question, problem, person, etc. is usually translated as **think** or **consider**. It is used alone, with *über*, or *darüber* + clause.

> *Ich hatte keine Zeit nachzudenken.   Denke mal gut nach!*
> *Der Schüler dachte lange über die mathematische Aufgabe nach, ohne eine Lösung zu finden.*
> *Ich habe angestrengt darüber nachgedacht, wie man diese mathematische Aufgabe lösen kann.*
> *Ich habe über das Aufsatzthema gründlich nachgedacht und weiß nun, was ich schreiben will.*
> *Er dachte lange über das seltsame Verhalten seines Freundes nach.*

While **überlegen** is close in meaning to *nachdenken*, it implies thought or reflection with regard to future action, i.e. making a choice or judgement or reaching a decision about what one will say or do. *Ich überlege [mir], was ich machen soll. Nachdenken* means 'to occupy oneself in thought with sth.' without necessarily making a decision etc. Although the distinction is sometimes very fine, and both are often possible, *nachdenken* is the appropriate word when, with reference to past events or a question, **consider/think about** means 'to turn sth. over in one's mind'. *Sie dachte über alles nach, was in den letzten Wochen passiert war.* In a similar context, *überlegen* would imply coming to a judgement or decision. *Er überlegte, ob er in letzter Zeit richtig gehandelt hatte. Er hatte sich alles, was passiert war, genau überlegt und beschloß, nicht weiterzumachen. Überlegen* is used with the refl. dat. without a change in meaning, but the dat. is necessary only when a n. follows. *Ich überlege mir den Plan.* When *überlegen* is used alone or with a clause, the dat. is often omitted. *A. Was machst du? B. Ich überlege.*

> *Sie überlegte kurz und gab dann eine für alle Beteiligten befriedigende Antwort.*
> *Da er sich morgen an seinem neuen Arbeitsplatz vorstellt, überlegt er sich, was er sagen will.*
> *Sie überlegte hin und her und konnte doch zu keinem Entschluß kommen.*
> *Es ist zu überlegen, ob die Firma im Falle einer Rezession die vereinbarten Rückzahlungen einhalten kann.   Überlege es dir gut, bevor du dich entscheidest!*
> *Ich muß mir die Sache noch einmal gründlich überlegen.*
> *Moment mal, ich überlege. Also Ich bin am Überlegen.*

Überlegen can also mean 'to think about in order to find', 'to think out'. *Er überlegte sich eine bessere Lösung. Überleg' dir ein paar gute Witze für deine Rede morgen abend!* Cf. *ausdenken* under THINK 4. v. As the examples show, *überlegen* and *nachdenken* translate **consider** when it is intr., as in *I stood still for a moment to consider. Ich blieb einen Augenblick stehen, um zu überlegen/nachdenken.* If **think about** means 'to reflect on', it must also be translated as *nachdenken* or *überlegen. Denken über* or *von* is 'to think about' only when this means 'to have an opinion about'. Cf. THINK 2. *Was denken Sie über den Fall?* asks for an opinion, while *Ich werde über den Fall nachdenken* states that I will think about it. Thus *Über diesen Vorschlag denkt sie anders als ich* and *Sie dachte lange über den Vorschlag nach.*

ii. In the sense 'to reflect on' **bedenken** is now confined to objs. referring to consequences, *Du mußt die Folgen gut/reiflich/gründlich bedenken,* and to fixed expressions such as *Wenn ich es recht bedenke, so ist er doch schuldig,* and *Wenn man bedenkt, wie er sich benommen hat . . .* and *Bedenke, was geschehen ist! Bedenk' es wohl!* sounds antiquated. *Überleg' es dir gut!* is now used. Even in reference to consequences, **bedenken** belongs more to the written language. **Denken an** is used in speech. *Denk' an die Folgen, wenn du zurücktrittst!*

   Bedenke, daß es noch ein paar Grad unter Null ist! Wir können nicht allzu lange draußen bleiben.
   Also Denk' daran, daß es draußen sehr kalt ist!

iii. Both **durchdenken** and **überdenken** suggest thinking over or considering thoroughly.

   Er hat den Plan gründlich durchdacht und weiß nun, was er machen will.
   Sie muß jetzt die ganze Angelegenheit in Ruhe überdenken und allein einen Entschluß fassen.
   Ich muß das Ganze/alle Einzelheiten noch einmal durchdenken.

iv. Sich (dat.) **durch den Kopf gehen lassen** is a colloquial syn. of *nachdenken* and *überlegen.*

   Ich werde mir Ihren Vorschlag durch den Kopf gehen lassen und Ihnen bald Bescheid geben.

v. Erwägen also means 'to consider' or 'deliberate on', but belongs to a higher stylistic level than *überlegen* and *nachdenken.* Being formal, it is used of governments, deliberative bodies, companies, etc. and usually implies examining a plan, proposal, project, question, suggested steps or action, etc. with a view to implementation or acceptance or rejection. An individual can be the subj. only in formal style. In reference to oneself, it is used only when a weighty decision is involved.

   Das Kabinett erwog weitere Maßnahmen zur Ankurbelung der Wirtschaft.
   Die Deutschlehrer erwägen die Einführung eines neuen Lehrbuchs.
   Der Ausschuß hat den Plan reiflich/gründlich erwogen und empfahl, daß der größte Teil davon verwirklicht werden sollte.   *Ich werde Ihr Angebot sorgfältig erwägen.*

2. Consider doing sth. **Überlegen** and **nachdenken** can be used in this sense only with an *ob*-clause. *Ich überlege, ob ich hingehen soll,* I am considering going. *Wir überlegten, ob wir aus Sydney wegziehen sollten,* considered moving from Sydney. **Erwägen** is used with a infin., but remains formal in tone. *Sie erwägt, ihren Beruf zu wechseln.* For everyday situations **denken daran** + infin. in a pos. sent. means 'to think about a possible course of action', 'to think of doing sth.' However, when neg., as in *Ich denke nicht daran hinzugehen,* the sense is 'I have no intention of going' or 'I wouldn't consider going'. Another possibility is *Es/Das kommt gar nicht in Frage.* Cf. 3.

   Sie dachte darüber nach, ob sie ihm ihre Hilfe anbieten sollte, entschied sich aber dagegen.
   Die Firma erwägt, die Produktion von Europa nach Taiwan zu verlegen.
   Ich denke daran, nach Kanada auszuwandern.
   Sie denkt nicht daran, mit ihm auszugehen.
   Ich denke nicht daran, mich auf einen so blöden Plan einzulassen.

3. In Betracht ziehen means 'to consider s.o./sth. as a possibility'. *Würden Sie Frau Friedrich bei der Besetzung dieser Stelle in Betracht ziehen?* The pass. is **Etw./Jmd. kommt in Betracht/in Frage,** 's.o./sth. can be considered', is a possibility. *Er kommt als Abteilungsleiter durchaus in Frage/Betracht.* Would you consider selling the house? can be translated lit. as *Würden Sie den Verkauf des Hauses in Betracht ziehen?* A possibly more common alternative is *Kommt der Verkauf des Hauses in Frage?*

4. Consider meaning 'to weigh up factors against each other' is **abwägen.** *Du mußt das Für und das Wider der Sache abwägen.* Also *. . . das Pro und Kontra abwägen.*

Um zu entscheiden, ob der Ausbau des Flughafens wünschenswert ist, muß man die wirtschaftlichen Vorteile gegen die ökologischen Nachteile abwägen.

5. When **consider** means 'to fix one's attention on sth.' or 'to analyse' in a context like *Let us consider another example!*, G. uses **betrachten**. *Betrachten wir ein anderes Beispiel!* It also expresses the idea of considering or looking at questions or problems in a particular way or from a particular point of view. *Wir wollen den Vorgang unter verschiedenen Gesichtspunkten/von zwei Seiten betrachten.* However, if someone gives an example to illustrate a point just made rather than analysing one case in some detail, the v. is **denken an**, to think of or consider. *Die Vorsilbe un- kann das Grundwort nicht nur verneinen, sondern es auch verstärken. Denken wir an Bildungen wie Ungewitter, Unmenge, Unzahl, Unding!*

Wir wollen nun einen weiteren Fall betrachten.
Später werden wir diesen Vorgang gesondert/isoliert betrachten.
Man kann die wirtschaftliche Entwicklung von einem anderen Standpunkt aus betrachten.
Er hat sich bemüht, die politische Lage objektiv zu betrachten.

6. In *We have considered all applications carefully*, **consider** means 'to give due attention to [and think about] in order to come to a conclusion'. **Sich befassen mit** means 'to CONCERN or occupy oneself with', either together with others or in one's own mind. *Wir haben uns mit allen Bewerbungen eingehend befaßt. Wir müssen uns noch mit Punkt zehn der Tagesordnung befassen. Die Geschworenen müssen sich mit den Aussagen aller Zeugen befassen.* **Berücksichtigen** also means 'to give attention to, deal with, take into consideration'. The subj. can be either one person or several forming a group. *Wir haben alle Bewerber/alle Anträge berücksichtigt. Dieser Punkt braucht nicht berücksichtigt zu werden.* While *sich befassen* suggests that the matter dealt with is the main topic, or an important one, considered on a particular occasion, *berücksichtigen* implies that the matter is not ignored in carrying out a broader task.

7. Consider has developed the nuance 'to make allowance[s] for'. *You must consider his youth/the conditions under which they live/that the text is extremely difficult.* **Berücksichtigen** expresses this nuance. **Bedenken** is an alternative in formal style. **Daran denken** is common in speech and is like REMEMBER or *not to forget*. **In Betracht ziehen** also means 'to take special factors into consideration and make allowances'.

Bei der Bewertung seiner Leistung muß man sein Alter berücksichtigen/bedenken.
Sie müssen berücksichtigen/bedenken, daß der Text äußerst schwierig ist.
Auch wenn er die Tat begangen hat, muß man doch bedenken/daran denken, daß er noch sehr jung ist.
Bevor du diese Schüler verurteilst, mußt du die Verhältnisse berücksichtigen, in denen sie leben.
Bei der Beurteilung dieser Schülerin muß man ihre besonderen Umstände in Betracht ziehen.

8. Consider s.o./sth. **to be** or **as**, as in *I consider him [to be/as] a good friend* or *She considers money [to be/as] of little importance*, is either **halten für** or **betrachten als**. While in many cases either is possible, *betrachten als* is more formal than the everyday word *halten für*. Whereas *halten für* expresses an opinion or conjecture, *betrachten* is more definite, and when that which one considers to be true corresponds without doubt to the facts, it alone is used, particularly in the imp. *Betrachten Sie sich als verhaftet/entlassen/eingestellt! Betrachte dich als enterbt!* Both these vs. can be used in the pass., but the pass. sense is often expressed by **gelten als** or **für**, to be considered or regarded as. *Er gilt als Dummkopf/Witzbold. Er gilt für einen Sonderling. Er gilt als/für unwissend und arrogant.*

Ich halte ihn für einen Schwindler/Angeber.   *Wofür hält sie sich eigentlich?*
Ich halte es für/betrachte es als meine Pflicht, diesem Menschen zu helfen.

Ich halte es für wahrscheinlich, daß sie die Stelle bekommt.
Geld hält sie für nicht besonders wichtig.   *Sie galt als reich, war es aber nicht.*
Er galt als [ein] großer Künstler/für einen ehrlichen Mann.

9. If **consider** means 'to show consideration for people', the equivalent is **Rücksicht nehmen auf**.

Du mußt immer Rücksicht auf die anderen Mitglieder der Familie nehmen.
Wir müssen Rücksicht auf die Gefühle unserer Mitmenschen nehmen.

consolidate, merge *vs.*

1. Consolidate = 'to make firm or strong' or 'strengthen', chiefly power, someone's position, established systems, regimes, etc. *Festigen* and *befestigen* are the possible equivalents. Current usage seems to have assigned them to different contexts, *festigen* being used with abstracts and *befestigen* with concrete objects. A difficulty arises, however, because G. dictionaries give examples of *befestigen* used with abstracts like *Vertrauen, Ansehen,* and *Autorität,* or in *Diese Tat befestigte seinen Ruhm.* This may be a survival of older usage which is still found on higher stylistic levels, but it does not occur in normal usage. **Befestigen** is restricted to contexts in which something is made firm in a concrete sense, i.e. is fastened. *Das Seil des Bootes wurde am Steg befestigt. Wir haben ein Schild an der Tür befestigt. Den Wandschrank kann man mit Schrauben an die Wand befestigen. Man befestigt das Ufer,* secures it from being washed away. *Nach dem furchtbaren Unwetter mußten einige beschädigte Deiche befestigt werden. Eine Stadt* or *eine (militärische) Stellung befestigen* is 'to fortify it'. With abstract ns. **festigen** is usual and is therefore the equivalent of **consolidate**. *Jmd. festigt seine Macht/seine Autorität/seine Stellung/ein Bündnis/ein Regime* etc. The refl. in *Seine Macht festigte sich,* can be translated by the E. pass., *His power was consolidated* or in other contexts by *to become stronger.*

> *Im Jahr 284 n. Chr. machte ein Heer in Kleinasien seinen Feldherrn Diokletian zum neuen Kaiser des römischen Reiches. Dieser ging mit ernster Energie daran, das Reich wieder zu festigen.*
> *Das Unternehmen hat durch eine Steigerung des Absatzes seine führende Stellung gefestigt.*
> *Der neue Parteiführer hat seine Stellung in der Partei durch eine ausgezeichnete Rede im Parlament gefestigt.*   *Die gegenseitige Hilfe festigte ihre Freundschaft.*
> *Der Diktator festigte seine Herrschaft dadurch, daß er alle Gegner ins Gefängnis warf.*
> *Erst allmählich festigte sich das Vertrauen zwischen der Klasse und dem neuen Lehrer.*
> *Ihre Freundschaft festigte sich durch die vielen gemeinsamen Interessen und Unternehmungen.*

2. In its other sense **consolidate** is trans. and intr. When trans. it means 'to combine estates, companies, commercial operations, etc. into one connected whole'. *The company bought the small farms and consolidated them for greater efficiency.* The usual transl. is **vereinigen**, to UNITE. *Die Lebensmittelverarbeitungsfirma kaufte die kleinen Bauernhöfe und vereinigte sie zu einem Gut zum Zweck der rationelleren Bewirtschaftung. Er vereinigte die Geschäfte zu einer Kette.* When intr. it means 'to merge'. *The three banks consolidated/merged and formed a single large bank.* This sense is expressed by **sich vereinigen** or **sich zusammenschließen**, 'to UNITE', or by **fusionieren**, 'to merge or amalgamate'. *Die drei kleinen Banken vereinigten sich zu einer großen Bank/schlossen sich zu . . . zusammen. Die drei kleinen Banken haben fusioniert.*

constant *adj.* Some senses of **steady, continual, permanent** *adjs.*

1. The original sense of **constant**, which still occasionally occurs, is 'standing firm in mind and purpose, not vacillating, resolute, steadfast in attachment to a pers. or cause'. *A constant friend. A man constant in his endeavour to live according to his ideals.*

i. Standhaft, 'steadfast', now expresses the meaning just defined. *Er blieb trotz aller*

Anfeindungen standhaft. Diesen Mann, der sich standhaft bemühte, seinen Idealen nachzuleben, haben wir alle bewundert.

Diese Enttäuschungen hätten sich auf die Entschlußkraft eines weniger standhaften Gemüts als das von Herrn Quitek nachteilig ausgewirkt.

Treu is the adj. normally combined with *Freund* and *Anhänger. Ein treuer Freund/Anhänger.*

ii. Beständig has the sense of **constant** given in 1, but it is now rare in this sense. *Ein beständiger Mensch* is still understood, but, like **constant** in this sense, no longer belongs to the normal language *Beständig* now occurs in other meanings. In *beständiges Wetter* it means 'settled', i.e. 'good and likely to remain so'. Hence *unbeständiges Wetter. Das Glück ist nicht beständig,* it does not last. A new sense is 'resistant'. *Diese Pflanze ist gegen Frost beständig.* Hence *feuerbeständig. Das Laboratorium hat feuerbeständige Wände.*

2. Constant also means 'remaining the same, invariable'. *A constant flow of water. Her constant friendliness.* **Steady** also means 'unchanging' and is a syn. of **constant**. *There's a steady demand for these goods.* In technical and scientific language **konstant** is usual. *Wir halten die Luftfeuchtigkeit im Treibhaus konstant.* The v. **gleichbleiben**, 'to remain unchanged', can express the sense. *Die Zahl der Germanistikstudenten ist gleichgeblieben.* **Gleichbleibend** is used as an. adj. and means 'constant' or 'steady'. (With a personal subj. *sich gleichbleiben* is used, *In Glück und Unglück blieb sie sich gleich,* but this does not translate *constant.*)

Die innere Körpertemperatur des Menschen bleibt konstant, auch wenn die Temperatur der Umgebung sich verändert.   Man muß darauf achten, daß der Druck konstant bleibt.

Ihre gleichbleibende Freundlichkeit nimmt alle für sie ein.

Der Preis ist zwölf Monate lang gleichgeblieben. Jetzt fängt er an zu steigen.

Bei gleichbleibender Nachfrage können wir mit guten Absatzmöglichkeiten rechnen.

3. Applied to actions, conditions, or processes, **constant** means 'continuing without interruption', 'continual'. *The books are in constant use. The constant ringing of the bell. The expenses are subject to constant scrutiny.* For people, it implies being continually engaged in the action denoted by the n. *He was her constant companion/a constant reader of Shakespeare's works.*

i. This sense is mainly carried by **ständig**. Sometimes a change of construction is necessary.

Die Qualität unserer Produkte unterliegt der ständigen Kontrolle.

Die Bücher werden ständig benutzt.

Er war ihr ständiger Begleiter/Ratgeber.

Er hat ständig in Shakespeares Werken gelesen.

Die Kinder, die alle paar Minuten herein- und hinausliefen, waren ein ständiges Ärgernis.

Er ist ständig unterwegs/steht unter ständigem Druck.

ii. Stet is an elevated word which has the same sense as *ständig. Die stete Bewegung des Wassers. Seine Schwester ist seine stete Begleiterin. Steter Tropfen höhlt den Stein.*

iii. Dauernd, 'continuous, constant', often expresses displeasure at the way something continues or at the frequency with which it is repeated. **Andauernd** is stronger. *Es regnet andauernd.* Cf. KEEP 12. They are the appropriate terms when **constant[ly]** expresses annoyance.

Die Fernsprechauskunft ist dauernd besetzt.   Er kommt dauernd zu spät.

Diese dauernden Störungen!   Er fragt andauernd dasselbe.

4. Steady means 'continuing or developing uniformly and without interruption'. *Slow but steady progress/growth. A steady rise in prices.*

i. Stetig means 'continuing uniformly', i.e. 'steady'. *Ein stetiger Wind wehte. Die Zahl der Besucher nimmt stetig zu.*

Seit mehreren Stunden fällt ein stetiger Regen.
Die durchschnittliche Lebensdauer des Menschen steigt stetig.
Durch stetige Arbeit/Bemühungen hat er dieses Ergebnis erzielt.
ii. Kontinuierlich means 'proceeding without interruptions', 'steady'. *Eine kontinuierliche Entwicklung. Jmd. arbeitet kontinuierlich. Etw. verläuft kontinuierlich. Die Preise stiegen kontinuierlich an.*

5. Permanent means 'continuing or enduring for ever or for a very long time without marked change, lasting'. *A permanent residence/job/income. This experience was of permanent/lasting value for me. Excessive doses of this drug can cause permanent damage.*
i. Ständig and **fest** are applied to where one lives and works. *Sein ständiger/fester Wohnsitz. Ihr ständiger Arbeitsplatz* is found, but *fest* is the usual adj. in relation to employment. *A permanent position is eine feste Anstellung.* Hence *Jmd. ist irgendwo fest angestellt. Er ist ohne feste Beschäftigung/hat keinen festen Beruf.* Used attributively, *ständig* means 'continuously employed in a certain function'. *Er ist ständiger Korrespondent unserer Zeitung. Der Minister hat einen Stab ständiger Mitarbeiter.* (*Fest angestellt* expresses the same meaning.) *Ständig* is applied to a committee and translates *standing* = 'permanently in existence, rather than being formed only when it becomes necessary'. *Ein ständiger Ausschuß. Eine ständige Garnison.* (But *a standing army is ein stehendes Heer.*) Both are used with *das Einkommen* etc., but here the equivalent is *regular. Sie hat ein ständiges/festes Einkommen. Er bezieht ein festes Gehalt.*
Es gab eine ständige Bevölkerung von etwa 200 Familien im entlegenen Bergarbeiterdorf.
New York ist der ständige Sitz der Vereinten Nationen.
Fest is used in *Der Autor hat sich einen festen Platz in der Literaturgeschichte erobert* and *Eine Fremdsprache ist [ein] fester Bestandteil unserer Ausbildung.*
ii. Dauerhaft means 'lasting for a long time'. It is applied to relations and agreements between people, institutions, and mental states. It is normally only applied to what has a value in itself.
Sie lebten eine Zeitlang in Ruhe und Zufriedenheit, doch dieses Glück und dieser Friede waren nicht dauerhaft.   Die beiden Männer verbanden eine dauerhafte Freundschaft.
Karl der Große schuf ein dauerhaft geeintes Reich.   So entstand ein dauerhaftes Bündnis.
Um Kindern in Senegal dauerhaft bessere Lebenschancen zu geben, führt UNICEF dort zur Zeit eine Impfkampagne gegen Infektionskrankheiten durch.
(*Dauerhaft* also means 'durable, hard-wearing'. *Dauerhafter Stoff. Ein dauerhaftes Kleidungsstück.*)
iii. Bleibend means 'maintaining its effect, significance, or value despite the passage of time'. It translates *lasting* and **permanent**. *Etw. war ein bleibender Erfolg/ein bleibender Gewinn.*
Diese Erlebnisse in Indien waren von bleibendem Wert/von bleibendem Nutzen für ihr weiteres Leben.

continue, go on, keep on vs. To understand the G. usage, it is necessary to distinguish the following E. constructions: (i) **Continue** + obj. *They continued the conversation/the negotiations/the struggle.* See 1. (ii) **Continue/go on/keep on** + infin. or gerund. *They continued to fight/fighting/went on/kept on working.* See 2. ii and 3. (iii) **Continue/go on/keep on** + **with**. *She continued/went on/kept on with her work/studies.* See 2. iii. (iv) Intr. use. *a. She continued/went on after a pause. 'It was now dark,' she continued/went on.* See 2. i. *b. The rain continued for another three days. The discussion is still going on. The fighting continued/went on/kept on all night.* See 4 and 1. ii.
1. The main equivalents *fortsetzen* and *fortfahren* do not differ in meaning, but require different constructions.

i. Fortsetzen needs an obj. and translates E. construction i. *Wir setzen die Diskussion morgen fort.* Ns. such as *ein Krieg, eine Tradition* or *eine Überlieferung, ein Gedankengang, die Arbeit, ein Spiel, die Verhandlungen, meine/seine/ihre Bemühungen, die Debatte* can be the obj. of *fortsetzen.*

Sie setzten ihr Gespräch bis in die späten Nachtstunden fort.

Die Arbeiter setzten ihren Kampf für die Mitbestimmung fort.

ii. Ns. which are possible objs. of *fortsetzen* can be made the subj. of **sich fortsetzen,** which means that something continues (in time) and is one equivalent of E. construction iv. *b.*

Das Gespräch hat sich bis in die Nacht fortgesetzt.

Die schweren Kämpfe um die Hauptstadt von San Salvador setzen sich unvermindert fort.

2. When it means 'to continue', **fortfahren** needs a personal subj. It is used:

i. Alone, i.e. without an obj., infin., or prep. *Fahre nur so fort, wie du begonnen hast!*

Wir wollen heute fortfahren, wo wir gestern stehengeblieben sind.

This translates E. construction iv. *a, She continued/went on,* i.e. 'resumed'. *Nach einer kurzen Pause fuhr sie fort.*

'Und dann', fuhr er fort, 'hat es angefangen, in Strömen zu regnen.'

ii. With an infin., E. construction ii. *Trotz aller Ermahnungen fuhr der Junge fort, den neuen Schüler zu hänseln.*

iii. With *mit* and less commonly *in.* This translates E. construction iii. *Sie fuhren eifrig mit der Arbeit fort.*

Der Vortragende fuhr trotz des störenden Lärms in seiner Rede fort.

Variations are possible. The sense of *Sie fuhr fort zu studieren* or *Sie fuhr mit dem Studium fort* can be expressed as *Sie setzte das Studium fort.* Another variation is *Sie studierte weiter.*

3. Weiter, added to a v., means that the action denoted by the v. is continued. *Sie spielten trotz des Regens weiter.* **Weitermachen** means 'to continue what one is doing' and is used when the activity is not specified. *Wir müssen weitermachen.* Both *weiter* and *weitermachen* are more common in conversation than the fairly formal vs. *fortsetzen* and *fortfahren.* In formal language **weiterhin** is used instead of *weiter.* *Der Präsident sagte, die Vereinigten Staaten würden die Staaten Mittelamerikas weiterhin unterstützen.*

Fahre fort wie bisher! Or *Mache [nur] so weiter wie bisher!*

So könnt ihr hier nicht weitermachen.   *Wir machen morgen weiter.*

Der Redner fuhr trotz der Störung in seinem Vortrag fort. Or *Der Redner sprach trotz der Störung weiter.* (The first suggests that he continued after a pause, the second that he kept on regardless, but the difference is slight.)

Er wird weiterhin seinen Dienst als Verkehrspolizist versehen.

4. To express E. sense iv. b, the idea that an activity or state is not yet over, G. uses *anhalten, andauern,* or *weitergehen* as well as *sich fortsetzen,* mentioned in 1. ii. **Anhalten** and **andauern** do not differ in sense, but only in the contexts in which they occur, and are often interchangeable. For weather and other natural phenomena, *anhalten* is usual, but *andauern* quite possible. Both are used for moods or states of mind which continue, last, or keep on. However, for activities which depend on the human will, *andauern* tends to be preferred. **Weitergehen** is the everyday, conversational word. *Anhaltend* is used like *continuous* and is neutral. *Andauernd* is a syn. which often expresses a certain irritation. Cf. KEEP 12 and CONSTANT 3. iii.

Der Regen/Die Kälte hielt den ganzen Tag/ununterbrochen an/ . . . hielt lange an.

Seine schlechte Stimmung hielt an, und auch die Bemühungen seiner Freunde vermochten ihn nicht auf fröhliche Gedanken zu bringen.

Die seit 1979 anhaltende Trockenheit in Ostafrika hat den Pegel des Nils dramatisch fallen lassen.
A. Ist die Sitzung schon zu Ende? B. Nein, sie dauert noch an.
Die Kämpfe um den Stützpunkt der Rebellen dauern noch an/ . . . gehen weiter.
Die Verhandlungen dauern noch an.   *Der Streik in der Autoindustrie dauert an.*
Der Streit ging weiter.   *Wie geht die Geschichte weiter?*
Wie lange kann das noch so weitergehen?   *So kann das nicht weitergehen.*

5. In a further sense, *She hopes to continue at school for another two years* and *He continued as mayor*, **continue** means 'to remain' and is translated by **bleiben**.
Sie will noch zwei weitere Jahre an der Schule bleiben. Er blieb Bürgermeister.

6. A road **continues/goes on** to . . . is *Die Straße* **geht** *zum Fuß des Berges* **weiter**.

contribute v.

i. Beisteuern is the equivalent of **contribute** when [a sum of] money is the stated or implied obj. *Jeder Teilnehmer muß zwanzig Mark beisteuern. Sie hat bei der Spendensammlung etw./nicht viel/reichlich/ihr Scherflein beigesteuert.* If **contribute** means 'to donate', it may be translated by the equivalent of *donate*, **spenden**. *Viele haben Lebensmittel/Geld für die Flüchtlinge gespendet.*
ii. If something contributes to a result, event, or situation, it is one of the causes of it. *The recession contributed to the failure of the firm.* **Beitragen** means that one thing plays a part in bringing something about. *Sein unermüdlicher Fleiß trug erheblich zum Erfolg des Unternehmens bei.* It can take an infin. construction. *Alles trug dazu bei, ihn unzufrieden zu machen.* A person can be the subj. if what he or she does helps bring about a result. *Dieser Zeuge hat mit seinen Angaben erheblich zur Klärung des Falles beigetragen.*
> *Die Offenheit dieses Politikers hat sehr zu seiner Popularität beigetragen.*
> *Dadurch, daß man Tausende von Bäumen pflanzte, hat man zur Verschönerung der Stadt beigetragen.*
> *Die Rezession trug zum Bankrott der Firma bei, war aber nicht die einzige Ursache.*

iii. Contribute also means 'to do or say sth. that helps to make sth. successful'. *Students contributed many useful ideas for the Open Day.* If people contribute to a magazine, book, etc., they write articles, poems, etc. for it. Here both **beisteuern** and **beitragen** are possible, although some speakers may only use one or the other. *Sie hat viel Interessantes zur Unterhaltung beigesteuert/beigetragen. Der Professor hat einen Artikel zum Sammelband beigesteuert/beigetragen.*
> *Die Studenten haben viele wertvolle Gedanken zur Gestaltung des Tages der offenen Tür beigesteuert/beigetragen.*

control, regulate, check vs.

1. The original sense of **control** is 'to check or verify', hence 'to regulate' payments, receipts, expenditure, etc. It is still common in this sense. The equivalent is **überwachen**. The lit. meaning is 'to watch over', but it implies control, ensuring that everything is done properly. *Zwei Ingenieure überwachen die Ausführung der Arbeit.* However, although not displaced, *überwachen* has largely given way to **kontrollieren**. **Beaufsichtigen**, 'to inspect or supervise', expresses a similar meaning. If **control** has a broader meaning like 'to be in charge of', **verwalten**, 'to administer', or **für etw. zuständig sein**, 'to be RESPONSIBLE for', can be used. *Er verwaltet die Finanzen* or *Er ist für die Finanzen zuständig.*
> *Er beaufsichtigt die Einnahmen und Ausgaben der Firma.*
> *Sie müssen alle Ausgaben überwachen/kontrollieren. Geld darf nur zu den Zwecken ausgegeben werden, für die es bewilligt worden ist.*   *Die Polizei überwacht den Verkehr.*

2. From the original sense **control** has developed the sense of exercising restraint on the free action of another and has come to mean 'to exercise power or authority over' in numerous contexts.

i. For **control**/*have control of a horse*, the usual expression is **Gewalt** *über ein Pferd* **haben**, and the opposite, *Er verlor die Gewalt über das Pferd. Gewalt* is also used with a motor vehicle, *Es schien, als hätte der Fahrer hinter mir die Gewalt über sein Fahrzeug verloren*, but **die Kontrolle** *über ein Fahrzeug usw.* **haben/verlieren** is more common, *Der Fahrer hatte die Kontrolle über den Wagen verloren*.

ii. Control a crowd, meaning 'to prevent it from becoming unruly', is **unter Kontrolle halten**. *Die Polizei hält die Menge unter Kontrolle*. If the crowd has got out of control, the expression is **unter Kontrolle bringen**. *Ein starkes Polizeiaufgebot hielt die Tausende von Fußballfans unter Kontrolle. Schließlich gelang es der Polizei, die Randalierer unter Kontrolle zu bringen*. **Control** pests or other harmful thgs., meaning 'to prevent them from becoming too numerous or spreading', can also be expressed by *unter Kontrolle halten* or *bringen. Man hält Schädlinge unter Kontrolle.* Hence *einen Brand unter Kontrolle bringen*, to control it or to bring it under control. *Schädlinge/Ungeziefer* **bekämpfen**, which suggests combating or taking action against them, is another possibility.

iii. Kontrollieren has two senses, the main one being 'to check' in various situations. *Reisende/Die Ausweise werden an der Grenze kontrolliert. Zollbeamte haben unser Gepäck kontrolliert. Die Qualität der Produkte wird ständig kontrolliert.* **Kontrollieren** also means 'to control or dominate', especially economically. *Durch Aktienkäufe gelang es dem Unternehmer, einen der größten Konzerne des Landes zu kontrollieren. Vier Banken kontrollieren einen großen Teil der Industrie*.

iv. Control territory etc. is expressed by **kontrollieren** or frequently **beherrschen**, to rule or control. *Das von den Rebellen kontrollierte/beherrschte Gebiet erweitert sich ständig. Die Situation beherrschen* is 'to control the situation'.

Die Türkei beherrschte damals weite Teile des Mittleren Ostens.

Eine Militärjunta beherrschte bis vor kurzem das Land.

v. Control or **regulate** s.o. else's life and **control** what people do can often be expressed by **vorschreiben**, to prescribe. *Der Trainer wollte vorschreiben, wie die Spieler außerhalb der Spiel- und Trainingszeiten leben sollten. Die Schule schreibt vor, wie sich die Schüler in der Öffentlichkeit verhalten sollen. Sein Leben selber bestimmen* is a fixed expression. Cf. ORDER v. 4. i; DETERMINE 2. i. *Junge Menschen in allen Ländern der Welt wollen ihr Leben selber bestimmen, statt anderen zu gehorchen*.

vi. Lenken means 'to control' in a few contexts. In *Der Kanzler lenkt die Geschicke seines Landes* and *Das Schicksal läßt sich nicht lenken* it is formal, but expresses no judgement. However, in *eine zentral gelenkte Wirtschaft* and *eine gelenkte Presse* it normally expresses disapproval of the control exercised.

3. Control and often **regulate** mean 'to make sth. work in the way it is intended to work'. The things controlled or regulated range from traffic, *Lights control/regulate the traffic*, to machines and other devices, *This knob regulates/controls the volume, The thermostat controls/regulates the temperature automatically*, and to complete systems, *A computer controls the whole production process*. A person can also be the subj.

i. Regeln is the everyday word for controlling or regulating traffic, volume, temperature, etc. A control knob is called *der Regler*, e.g. *der Lautstärkeregler*.

An den Kreuzungen in der Mitte der Stadt wird der Verkehr von Ampeln/Polizisten geregelt.

Diese Automatik regelt die Temperatur/die Geschwindigkeit.

Das Pendel regelt den Gang des Uhrwerks.

ii. Regulieren has the same meaning as *regeln*, but seems to be preferred in technical contexts.

Diese Vorrichtung reguliert die Zufuhr von Luft.
Ein Thermostat reguliert automatisch die Temperatur.
Mit diesem Knopf kann man die Temperatur/die Lichtstärke im Saal regulieren.
Das Nervensystem reguliert die Produktion der meisten Hormone.

iii. Steuern, the basic sense of which is 'to STEER', has acquired the sense of influencing something so that it proceeds in the way intended. Whereas *regeln* and *regulieren* tend to be limited to a single operation, *steuern* is broader and often embraces a whole system. It is used for bodily processes and for all or part of the production in an industrial plant. *Eine automatisch gesteuerte Produktionsanlage. Elektronisch gesteuerte Apparate.*

Der Kreislauf des Menschen wird vom Nervensystem gesteuert.
Die neu errichtete Anlage zur Herstellung von Isolatoren wird automatisch gesteuert.
Ein Computer steuert die Geschwindigkeit des Fließbandes/die Produktionsprozesse.

4. With a law, rule, contract, etc. as subj. **regeln** means 'to lay down how sth. is to happen or regulate a procedure'. What is to happen under certain circumstances or how something is to be done can be *gesetzlich geregelt*, laid down or regulated by law. *Die Prüfung der Examenskandidaten erfolgt nach einem streng geregelten Verfahren*, the examination procedure is governed by strict rules or regulations.

5. When **control oneself** means 'to keep one's emotions in check' or 'to prevent one's feelings from getting out of control', it can be expressed by **sich im Zaum halten, an sich halten, seine Gefühle beherrschen**, or **sich beherrschen**. Also occasionally **sich bezähmen** and **sich bändigen**.

Sie war so wütend, daß sie nur noch mit Mühe an sich hielt.
Du mußt deine Zunge im Zaume halten.
Er war so aufgebracht, daß er sich/seine Gefühle nicht mehr im Zaume halten konnte.
Man sah ihm an, daß er sich nur mühsam beherrschen konnte.   *Er erschien stets beherrscht.*
Er beherrschte seinen Zorn/seine Worte/seine Leidenschaft.
Es steht einem Mann in leitender Stelle übel an, so unbeherrscht zu sein.
Er bändigte sich/seinen Zorn und sprach mit beherrschter Stimme weiter.

If someone has lost control of his emotions so that *Control yourself!* implies getting back to normal, **mäßigen**, 'to moderate', or **sich mäßigen** is used. Both imply that normal control has been lost.

Wenn er einmal aufgeregt ist, fällt es ihm schwer, sich zu mäßigen.
Mäßige dich, sonst wirst du etw. sagen, was du später bereuen wirst!
Mäßige deinen Zorn!

conventional, unconventional *adjs.*

1. Whether **conventional** is used in a pos. or neg. sense depends on the attitude of the speaker. With things, such as *conventional methods*, it is mostly neutral. In relation to people and behaviour, the primary meaning is 'conforming to or based on (social) convention, custom, traditional usage or attitudes'. It can, however, mean 'conforming to accepted artificial standards of conduct or taste', 'stiffly formal', and in reference to both behaviour and thought, 'not natural, original, or spontaneous'.

i. Herkömmlich is derived from *das Herkommen*, social custom or usage, and is quite neutral in tone meaning 'customary, usual, and conventional'. It is applied to behaviour, *herkömmliche Bräuche/Formen*, and is common in reference to methods of working, teaching, or performing a task. It can be used for weapons, *herkömmliche Waffen*, but *konventionell* is frequently employed in the discussion of warfare.

Ich unterrichte immer in der herkömmlichen Weise und habe immer gute Ergebnisse dabei erzielt.
Dieses neue Verfahren bietet beträchtliche Vorteile gegenüber den herkömmlichen Methoden.

Ist es sinnvoll, die herkömmlichen Energiequellen durch Atomenergie zu ersetzen?
Die Bienenstöcke hatten die herkömmliche Form.   Die ganze Familie hängt am Herkömmlichen.

ii. Konventionell is a learned word that has become well known in most circles. It originally referred to the conventions of social behaviour, but has spread to the same areas as *herkömmlich*, and is now usual in talking of weapons and warfare, *konventionelle Waffen, konventionelle Streitkräfte*, or *ein konventioneller Krieg*.

Die Neuinszenierung des Stückes ist ganz konventioneller Natur.

Die neue Methode unterscheidet sich in wesentlichen Punkten vom konventionellen/herkömmlichen Herstellungsverfahren.

iii. Konventionell alone has developed a pejorative sense, 'stiff or stiffly formal and lacking naturalness and spontaneity'. An alternative is *förmlich*, FORMAL. The other pejorative E. sense 'lacking spontaneity and originality in thought' can be expressed to a certain extent by *konventionell. Jmd. denkt in konventionellen Begriffen* or *in Begriffen, die in konservativen Kreisen konventionell/üblich* (customary) *sind*.

Solche konventionellen Redensarten hört man oft in diesen Kreisen.

In dieser Gesellschaft geht es sehr konventionell zu.   Alles Konventionelle war mir verhaßt.

Alle haben sich sehr konventionell verhalten/haben fast nur konventionelle Höflichkeiten ausge-tauscht.

2. Unkonventionell serves as a neg. for both *herkömmlich* and *konventionell. Unkonventionelle Mittel. Unkonventionelle Methoden. Das scheint mir ziemlich unkonven-tionell zu sein.* It is also applied to behaviour and means 'not sticking rigidly to what is usual'.

Effi sagte: 'Verzeih', . . . ich kann auch rasch sein, und in fünf Minuten ist Aschenpuddel in eine Prinzessin verwandelt.' Frau von Briest aber, die unter Umständen auch unkonventionell sein konnte, hielt die schon forteilende Effi zurück und sagte: 'Es ist am Ende das Beste, du bleibst, wie du bist.' (Fontane)

Ausgefallen, 'out of the ordinary, unusual, striking', may convey the meaning 'unconventional'. *Eine ausgefallene Idee/Meinung. Er hat einen ausgefallenen Geschmack. Eine ausgefallene Ware.*

cook, boil, seethe *vs.*

1. The everyday equivalent of intr. **boil** is **kochen.** *Kocht das Wasser schon?* **Sieden** is now only used in scientific contexts and as a weak v. *Bei normalem Druck siedet das Wasser bei 100°. Die Lösung siedete.* Hence *der Siedepunkt.* Boiling water is *kochendes Wasser* or *siedendes Wasser.* In relation to natural phenomena, both are found. *Kochender Schlamm, siedender Schlamm.* Neither is used trans. with water or a liquid as obj., as in *I'll boil some water.* **Boil** + obj. is expressed by **zum Kochen bringen** or **zum Sieden bringen.** *Man bringt einen Liter Wasser zum Kochen.* **Aufkochen** is 'to bring to the boil for a moment'. *Man kocht die Suppe auf.* In the sense 'to sterilize by boiling', **abkochen** is used. *Der Arzt muß die Instrumente abkochen. Wegen der Ansteckungsgefahr darf nur abgekochtes Wasser getrunken werden.*

2. i. Kochen is used trans. with an item of food as obj. It means both 'to boil' and 'to cook'. *Ich koche das Gemüse/die Eier/Reis/die Kartoffeln/das Fleisch/ein Huhn/das Obst,* etc. *Mein Mann hat das Essen heute abend gekocht.* Boiled eggs are *gekochte Eier.* (*Gesotten* is sometimes found in the names of recipes, but other forms of *sieden* are not used for cooking. *Gesottener Fisch. Gesottenes Fleisch.*)

ii. Kochen is also intr., meaning 'to cook' when this implies preparing a meal or doing the cooking. *Inge ist bei Hans zum Abendessen eingeladen—er kocht selbst. Wo haben Sie kochen gelernt? Sie muß täglich für zehn Personen kochen. Er kocht oft/gern.*

3. Fig uses.

i. Kochen and occasionally **sieden** are used fig. in reference to anger. *Er kochte innerlich vor Wut. Vorsicht!—der Chef kocht [vor Wut]! Wut/Ärger kochte in ihr. Er siedete vor Wut. Mir kocht das Blut, wenn ich diese Ungerechtigkeit sehe.*

ii. Seethe, which also meant 'to boil', is now used mostly in the fig. sense 'to be in a state of inward agitation, turmoil, or ferment'. *Er kochte/siedete vor Wut* given in 3. i translates *seethe with rage* or *anger*. Another use of **seethe** is *The city was seething with discontent*. **Brodeln** means 'to produce bubbles and steam', 'to simmer'. It is applied to food, *Die Suppe brodelt im Topf*, to natural phenomena, *brodelnde Lava*, and fig. to discontent among numbers of people, *Es brodelte in der Stadt/unter der Bevölkerung/unter den ausgebeuteten Arbeitern*. An alternative is **gären**, 'to ferment', which is applied fig. to people who are seething with discontent. *Unter weiten Kreisen der Bevölkerung gärte es.*

copy *v.* and *n.* **imitate, mimic, ape** *vs.* 1. **Copy** = 'to make a duplicate of sth.' and **copy** = 'to cheat by writing down what a neighbour has written' (see 1. v), and the corresponding ns.

i. The original sense of **kopieren**, which still survives, is 'to copy' a work of art, painting, sculpture, design, piece of furniture, etc. It has no secondary associations. The n. is **die Kopie**.

> *Als Kunststudent habe ich manchmal in der Galerie kopiert.*
> *Sie hat das Gemälde/die Statue kopiert.*   *Dürer kopierte italienische Muster.*
> *Die Pariser Moden werden in der ganzen Welt mit großer Genauigkeit kopiert.*
> *Die Kopie ist von dem Original kaum zu unterscheiden.*
> *Das ist eine von einem Studenten angefertigte Kopie eines Bildes von Picasso.*

ii. Kopieren is now used for photocopying. *Könnten Sie heute nachmittag einen Text von 150 Seiten für mich kopieren?* A **copy** is **die Kopie**. *Würden Sie bitte fünf Kopien des Briefs machen?*

iii. Nachbilden implies making an exact copy or replica. *Für den Film hat man die Stadt historisch getreu nachgebildet.* Hence **die Nachbildung**. *Die Statue ist eine Nachbildung—das Original steht im Museum.*

iv. If a document is copied in writing or by typing, the v. is **abschreiben**. The n. is **die Abschrift**.

> *Bis zur Erfindung der Buchdruckerkunst haben Mönche die alten Handschriften abgeschrieben.*
> *Ich habe den Aufsatz schon aufgesetzt und werde ihn morgen abschreiben.*
> *Der Rechtsanwalt ließ eine Abschrift des Testaments machen.*

Copy [out], not the full text, but a part, perhaps the most important facts, is **herausschreiben**.

> *Ich habe mir die wichtigsten Tatsachen aus dem Artikel herausgeschrieben.*
> *Ich habe nur ein paar Stellen aus der Rede herausgeschrieben.*

v. Abschreiben is also used for copying deceitfully in examinations etc.

> *In der Prüfung hatte der Schüler von seinem Nachbarn abgeschrieben.*

vi. Copy an audio or video tape is **überspielen**. *Ich habe die Sendung auf ein Videoband aufgenommen und werde sie für dich überspielen. Ich überspiele das Hörspiel auf eine [Musik]kassette, damit du es dir beliebig oft anhören kannst.* If a change of medium is involved, **übertragen**, 'to transfer', is used. *Mit dieser Maschine kann man Filme auf Videoband übertragen.*

2. Other ns. corresponding to **copy** = 'a duplicate'.

i. A **copy** of a book or printed material or a document is **das Exemplar**.

> *Nur 500 Exemplare des Buches wurden gedruckt.*
> *In der Buchhandlung sind noch ein paar Exemplare des Romans.*

ii. Ein Durchschlag is 'a carbon copy'. *Du mußt fest drücken, sonst kann man den Durchschlag nicht lesen.*

iii. One sense of **abziehen** is 'to print, run off, or duplicate' on a duplicating machine. *Die Studenten haben 1 000 Exemplare des Flugblattes abgezogen und verteilt.* The n. is **der Abzug.**

    Ich brauche zwanzig Abzüge dieses Gedichts.

iv. Imitieren is used for imitation products. *Imitiertes Holz. Imitierter Marmor.* **Die Imitation** is 'the copy or replica of a valuable original or an objet d'art'. It implies no value judgement, but is found with a range of adjs. which express one. *Eine minderwertige/billige/schlechte* or *gute/verblüffende Imitation.*

    Was sie bisher für echten Schmuck gehalten hatte, erwies sich als geschickte Imitation.

    Diese Brillanten sind Imitation, aber lassen sich vom Original kaum unterscheiden.

v. Der Abklatsch implies a copy in a neg. sense, either a poor reproduction, or a slavish imitation of someone's style, or something composed in a certain style but without any artistic originality.

    Dieses Gedicht ist ein bloßer Abklatsch der romantischen Naturlyrik.

3. Copy also means 'to do what another pers. does'. *They copied in dress and speech the oldest members of their gang.* **Imitate** can also mean 'to behave either consciously or unconsciously as s.o. else does'. *He suddenly realized how much he tended to imitate his father's way of talking.* It also means 'to reproduce consciously certain features of a model with and without the intention of being funny'. *He imitated bird calls/the teacher's way of walking and talking.* **Mimic** implies imitating someone in a way that is meant to be amusing. *She savagely mimicked the nasal whine of their teacher.* **Ape** a certain feature of a person is 'to mimic it in a way that makes it look ridiculous'. *She aped the receptionist's dumb-blond voice.* Both **ape** and **mimic** can express contempt for the way some people copy others. *The social climbers mimicked the officers. Adults who ape the latest crazes of the young.*

i. *a.* **Nachahmen** can mean 'to imitate' a person, 'to act or behave as a model does', without any implications. *Kinder ahmen Erwachsene nach. Er kann Vogelrufe vortrefflich nachahmen. Sie ahmte die Sprache und Bewegungen der Filmschauspielerin nach. Ich habe seinen Stil nachgeahmt.*

    Sie ahmte unwillkürlich den Tonfall/die Redeweise des Chefs nach.

    In ihrer Kleidung und Redeweise ahmten sie die ältesten Mitglieder der Gang nach.

b. **Nachahmen** also means 'to imitate or mimic' people or their peculiarities, with the aim either of amusing others or of making fun of the person imitated. *Thomas amüsierte sich aufs köstlichste, wenn Christian, welcher Gymnasiast war, die Lehrer mit ungeheurem Geschick nachahmte* (T. Mann).

c. **Nachahmen** also implies taking someone or a particular characteristic someone displays as a model and endeavouring to act likewise. It thus also corresponds to *emulate*, meaning 'to copy a pers. because one admires him or her so much'. *Er ahmte den stillen und zähen Fleiß des Vaters nach* (T. Mann). Cf. 3. v.

    Er würde am liebsten Robinson Crusoe nachahmen und sich auf eine Insel zurückziehen.

    Man sollte seine guten Eigenschaften, nicht die schlechten, nachahmen.

ii. Nachmachen has several meanings. It is a syn. of *nachahmen* in senses 3. i. *a* and *b*, but is somewhat vaguer. It is the most general term and means 'to do as s.o. else does', not necessarily consciously. *Er machte dem älteren Bruder alles nach.* As an equivalent of **mimic**, it is used when an exact imitation is not aimed at, but when the peculiarities are indicated or imitated approximately, often with a certain ill-will.

    Schämt ihr euch nicht, die arme, hinkende Frau nachzumachen?

    Die anderen amüsierten sich, wenn er die Bewegungen und Sprechweise des alten Lehrers nachmachte.

    Sie kann die Stimme des Polizisten/das Miauen der Katze vortrefflich nachmachen.

Nachmachen also means 'to forge'. *Die nachgemachten Geldscheine sehen wie echte aus. Sie versuchten, die Unterschrift des Vaters nachzumachen.*

iii. Kopieren also means 'to copy' a person's behaviour, movements, etc. The purpose may be either to copy a model worthy of imitation or to amuse others. It thus corresponds to senses of both **imitate** and **mimic**.

Die Schauspielerin kopierte die Gestik und Redeweise ihres Vorbilds.
Der Schüler kopierte den Lehrer.
Er kopierte den alten Sonderling so treffend, daß die ganze Gesellschaft in lautes Gelächter ausbrach.
Sie verstand es sehr gut, die Bewegungen und Gesten des Chefs zu kopieren.

iv. Imitieren means 'to imitate s.o. or his/her mannerisms'. The aim is usually to cause amusement. It also translates *to impersonate*.

Der Schauspieler hat den Gang, die Sprechweise und die Gestik des Kanzlers genau imitiert.
Er hat am Telefon deine Stimme so verblüffend genau imitiert, daß ich glaubte, du wärst es.

v. Nacheifern + dat. is a syn. of *nachahmen* meaning 'to copy or emulate' and suggests zeal in doing so.

Jeder braucht ein Vorbild, dem er nacheifern kann.
Ihr solltet seinem Mut nacheifern.
Im Grunde ist es zeitlebens mein Bemühen gewesen, diesem großen Lehrer nachzueifern.

vi. Nachäffen is 'to mimic' a person as a whole or certain peculiarities or habits with the aim of making fun of him or her. It implies exaggeration which distorts the peculiarities. It also means 'to follow a model slavishly', 'to ape' a person, and expresses an adverse judgement by one person on the way someone else copies a third person.

Ein Mädchen äffte in alberner Weise das Rechtsum, Linksum der Soldaten nach.
Die Schüler äfften die Stimme und die Gebärden des Lehrers nach.
Vielleicht bewundert er den Chef, aber muß er ihn in so übertriebener Weise nachäffen?

corner *n.*

i. Die Ecke is the normal equivalent of **corner** either of a street, a building or room, or any other object. *Ich warte an der Ecke auf dich. Ich habe mich an einer Ecke des Schranks gestoßen.* With regard to buildings, *der Winkel* is a more poetical word than *Ecke*, but is rare. *In einem Winkel des Zimmers stand ein Gestell mit Fahnen.* With a v. meaning 'to look for or search', *in allen Winkeln* means 'everywhere, high and low, in all places'. *Ecke* is often added. *Sie suchten in allen Ecken und Winkeln*, in every nook and cranny. *Er verkroch sich im hintersten Winkel des Hauses* suggests the most out of the way place he could find. *(Winkel* can mean 'a recess or niche'. *Der Hof hatte viele Ecken und Winkel.* The usual meaning of *der Winkel* is 'angle'. *Die Straßen kreuzen sich in einem Winkel von 45°.)*

Es liegt im Schrank, hinten rechts in der Ecke.
Sie setzten sich in eine gemütliche Ecke des Saales.
In der linken oberen Ecke des Zimmers hängt ein Spinnennetz.
Wir haben auch in den dunkelsten Winkeln gesucht, aber nichts gefunden.

ii. Der Winkel is used with certain adjs. and describes an area of the countryside, a town, or the earth which is picturesque or remote or has a particular characteristic. *Ein Winkel der Erde* is a fixed expression.

Wir wohnen in einem idyllischen/verträumten/stillen Winkel [des Landes].
Die Teilnehmer waren aus den entferntesten Winkeln des Landes gekommen.
Er kennt die entlegensten Winkel der Stadt/des Landes.
In keinem anderen Winkel der Erde hat die Geschichte solche unmittelbare Bedeutung für die aktuelle Politik erlangt wie in Jerusalem.
Kataganga war für mich der letzte Winkel der Erde.

iii. Der Winkel is applied to the eyes and mouth and fig. to mind and heart. *Sie warf mir einen Blick aus den Augenwinkeln. Im tiefsten Winkel meines Herzen war ich zur Aussöhnung geneigt.*

Durch angestrengtes Nachdenken habe ich diese Erinnerungen aus den dunkeln Winkeln meines Gedächtnisses heraufbeschworen.   Ein Lächeln spielte um ihre Mundwinkel.

corpse, carcass *ns.*

i. Die Leiche is the usual equivalent of *a dead human body* or **corpse**. *Die Leiche des Ermordeten wurde auf die Todesursache untersucht.* It is an unemotional word. It does not have the harsh ring that **corpse** has and is used when E. often has *body*.

Die Leiche des Verstorbenen wurde in seine Heimatstadt überführt und dort begraben.
Fünf Leichen wurden aus dem abgestürzten Flugzeug geborgen.

ii. Der Leichnam is a more elevated word which sounds more respectful than *die Leiche*. It is the usual word when talking of lying in state.

Der Leichnam des Staatsmannes wurde vor der Beisetzung in der Kathedrale aufbewahrt.

iii. Der Kadaver is basically 'the carcass of an animal'. *Wir haben die Kadaver der verreckten Kühe begraben. Fliegen umschwärmten den Kadaver des Hundes.* If applied to a human being, it shows either complete lack of respect or the speaker's insensitivity or callousness.

iv. Das Aas is also 'an animal carcass', often in its natural surroundings and sometimes in the process of decomposition. *Wo ein Aas ist, da sammeln sich die Geier. Der Aasfresser* is 'a (natural) scavenger'.

costly, expensive, precious, dear, valuable *adjs.*

1. In the sense 'high in price', *teuer* is the usual word.

i. Teuer refers: *a.* To things which cost a lot of money. *Er hat den teuren Anzug gekauft. Wie teuer ist dieser Mantel? Das ist mir zu teuer. Alles ist in letzter Zeit sehr teuer geworden. b.* To the way people live. *Nach diesen Verlusten war die teure Lebensweise nicht mehr möglich. c.* To places and people that charge high prices. *Ein teures Restaurant. Ein teurer Schneider. d.* To activities which cost a lot. *Eine teure Reise. Das war ein teurer Urlaub. e.* To times when prices are high. *Teure Zeiten.*

ii. Kostspielig is a syn. applied to activities, things, and places. *Niemand verstand, wie er sich ein so kostspieliges Leben leistete. Kostspielige Reparaturen. Äußerst kostspielige Waren. Es war ein hübsches, kleines, aber kostspieliges Restaurant. Die Entwicklung des Verfahrens war für die kleine Firma zu kostspielig.*

iii. Aufwendig is derived from *der Aufwand*, 'expenditure, cost', and expresses the same meaning as *teuer* and *kostspielig*. It refers to the carrying out of projects as well as to functions and activities and may suggest that the latter are engaged in for reasons of ostentation.

Einen zweiten so aufwendigen Film dürfen wir erst dann drehen, wenn die Ausgaben für den ersten gedeckt worden sind.   Der Plan wurde als zu aufwendig/kostspielig abgelehnt.
Die Familie führte ein aufwendiges Leben/veranstaltete aufwendige Gesellschaften.

iv. Unerschwinglich means 'too dear or expensive', 'unable to be afforded'. It is often followed by *hoch* or *teuer*, *Das ist für mich ein unerschwinglich hoher Preis/ein unerschwinglich teures Grundstück*, but the idea can be formulated without them, *Das ist ein unerschwinglicher Preis. Dieses Auto/Eine solche Reise/Ein solcher Urlaub ist für uns einfach unerschwinglich.*

2. Wertvoll means 'valuable'. It can refer to monetary or artistic value, to worth or quality as an abstract idea, or to value in other respects. *Er hat seiner Frau einen wertvollen Ring gekauft. Sie hat eine wertvolle Briefmarkensammlung. Das wertvollste Stück der Sammlung ist diese alte Uhr. Sie hat mir viele wertvolle Ratschläge gegeben. Er wäre ein wertvoller Mitarbeiter in jeder Organisation. Sie haben wertvolle Arbeit geleistet. Wir dürfen wertvolle Zeit nicht vergeuden.*

3. Kostbar, 'precious, valuable', refers:

i. To things which are costly or expensive. *Ein kostbarer Ring/Teppich. Kostbare Möbelstücke. Kostbarer Schmuck.*

ii. To a few intangibles like time, health, or an opportunity. *Kostbare Zeit verstrich ungenutzt. Kurz vor dem Ziel stolperte er und verlor kostbare Sekunden. Die Gesundheit ist zu kostbar, um aufs Spiel gesetzt zu werden. Eine so kostbare Gelegenheit muß man nutzen.* Note that **köstlich**, which expresses an emotional judgement, now means either 'delicious', *köstliche Erdbeeren, köstliche Speisen*, or 'very amusing or funny', *Du mußt diese köstliche Geschichte unbedingt erzählen. Das war ein köstlicher Einfall.* **Preziös** is a learned word which means 'artificial or affected'. *Ein preziöser Stil. Eine preziöse Ausdrucksweise.*

4. Teuer is a formal equivalent of **dear** = 'regarded with affection', *Er war mir ein teurer Freund*, the usual word being **lieb**. *Er ist mein liebster Freund. Das ist ein Andenken an meine lieben Eltern.*

5. Teuer also has the fig. sense of **dear** = 'at great price/cost'. *Das war ein teuer erkaufter Sieg. Dieser Leichtsinn wird ihn teuer zu stehen kommen*, he will pay dearly for it.

cost[s], price, expense[s], expenditure *ns.*

1. The **price** is 'the amount of money a seller asks and a purchaser has to pay'. The **cost** of sth. is 'the amount the purchaser needs in order to buy, do, or make sth.' *The total cost of the holiday came to £300.* My **costs** are 'the total amount I must spend on running my house, business, etc.' *I had to cut my costs by half.* **Expense** is 'the spending of money'. *They spared no expense.* **Expenditure** is a collective n. denoting money spent. *We must reduce our expenditure.* **Expenses** are 'costs incurred in doing sth.' *We reduced our household expenses.* It can refer to amounts of money spent in the course of one's work which will be refunded.

i. Der Preis is 'what is asked for sth.' While *die Kosten* means 'costs', it exists only in the pl. When **cost** and **price** are interchangeable, both are translated by *der Preis*. *The price/cost of a telephone call is Der Preis eines Telefongesprächs ist in den letzten fünf Jahren nur geringfügig gestiegen. The price/cost of a ticket/journey is Der Preis einer Fahrkarte/einer Reise. The cost/price of electricity is der Strompreis. Die Bergsteiger fanden, daß die Preise für Proviant in den Bergdörfern höher waren als in den größeren Städten,* price/cost of/prices for.

ii. Die Kosten means 'what s.o. spends or has to spend to get or maintain sth.', i.e. 'costs or expenses'. Like **costs**, it is often thought of as involving more than one expense. However, in compounds it can refer to one cost and translate the E. sing. *cost* and pl. *costs. The cost of transport* or *transport costs* would usually be *Die Transportkosten sind nicht sehr hoch. The price of this article is well below the cost of manufacture is Der Preis für diesen Artikel liegt weit unter den Produktionskosten. The cost of keeping up a house: Die Kosten für die Unterhaltung eines Hauses sind tragbar, wenn man alle anfallenden Arbeiten (am Haus) selbst macht. Die Baukosten* can be either 'the cost of building' or 'building costs'. *Die Kosten* is used with a gen., and there are numerous compounds: *Die Kosten der Reparatur, die Reparaturkosten, die Behandlungskosten, die Instandhaltungskosten, die Reinigungskosten, die Frachtkosten, die Versandkosten.* It is also used for costs imposed by a court. *Die Kosten des Verfahrens wurden dem Kläger auferlegt.*

Wir haben nur wenig Kosten gehabt, weil wir alles selbst gemacht haben.

Die Kosten sind gerade gedeckt worden.

Sie scheuten keine Kosten, um ihren Kindern eine gute Schulbildung zu geben.

Die bei der Erledigung der Aufgabe anfallenden Kosten übernimmt die Firma.

iii. While *die Kosten* is neutral, **die Unkosten** has a neg. connotation. *Un-* strengthens the neg. meaning (as in *Unzahl*, 'huge number', and *Unmenge*, 'enormous amount') and suggests costs which arise in addition to the normal expenses, which do not bring any return and are felt to be a loss. In commercial language *Kosten* refers to everything which is directly related to production, the cost of material, plant, labour, power. The cost of items that have nothing to do with the manufacture of goods, e.g. what is needed in the office, is called *Geschäftsunkosten*. The cost of new machinery is part of the *Kosten* while the purchase of a typewriter or photocopier is referred to as *Unkosten*. In the private sphere *Unkosten* is often reserved for expenses which go beyond the normal cost of living. If someone has a large dentist's bill to pay or an expensive car repair, these are called *Unkosten*. Thus *Wir haben in diesem Monat hohe Unkosten gehabt* suggests costs in addition to normal expenditure. If A is carrying out some work for B, B could ask, *'Sind Ihnen irgendwelche Unkosten entstanden?'*, i.e. expenses apart from those anticipated or allowed for. B might also say, *'Die Ihnen dabei entstandenen Unkosten werde ich selbstverständlich bezahlen.'* *Braun hat sich in Unkosten gestürzt* means that he incurred needless expense. The line of demarcation between *Kosten* and *Unkosten* is not completely clear because it is often a matter of opinion whether particular items belong to one category or the other.

Hatten Sie Unkosten während der Dienstreise?
Durch den Unfall sind uns nur geringe Unkosten entstanden.
Es kommen noch die Unkosten/Kosten für den Einbau dieser Vorrichtung hinzu.
Die Kosten/Unkosten für die Saalmiete übernimmt der Betrieb.
Wir haben die Kosten/Unkosten der Veranstaltung auf alle Beteiligten umgelegt.

Der Unkostenbeitrag is 'an amount all those taking part in some function are asked to contribute'.

Für diese Veranstaltung wird ein Unkostenbeitrag von fünf Mark erhoben.

iv. Die Spesen is a commercial term denoting the expenses incurred in carrying out business, e.g. meals with possible clients, tips, taxis, etc. They are mostly refunded by the employer. *Außer Spesen nichts gewesen* means that a visit etc. achieved no result apart from expenses, i.e. was a waste of time and effort.

Die während der Dienstreise entstandenen Spesen wurden ihm vom Betrieb erstattet.
Ich lade Sie zum Essen ein. Keine Sorge! Es geht alles auf Spesen.
Sie haben auf dieser Fahrt reichlich hohe Spesen gehabt.

v. A neutral and common word is **die Ausgabe**, expense, expenditure, or money spent. It is often found in the pl., *Ich habe in den letzten Monaten hohe Ausgaben gehabt*, but can be sing., *Du kannst dir diese Ausgabe [er]sparen.*

Die Ausgaben der bundesdeutschen Bevölkerung für Luxusartikel sind im letzten Jahr enorm gestiegen.
Hatten Sie irgendwelche unvorhergesehenen Ausgaben, die ich Ihnen nun [zurück]erstatten muß?
Die Ausgaben im Verteidigungshaushalt stehen in keinem Verhältnis zu den geplanten Ausgaben im Sozialbereich.   *Meine Ausgaben übersteigen mein Einkommen/meine Einkünfte.*

vi. Die Auslagen can be a syn. of *Unkosten*, but usually refers to money which has been paid out on another's behalf and which will be repaid. *Ich werde Ihnen Ihre Auslagen sofort erstatten.*

2. Expenditure is 'the using of money, energy, or time for a particular purpose'. From *aufwenden*, 'to expend' (cf. SPEND), two ns. *der Aufwand* and *die Aufwendung* are derived. **Der Aufwand** is used for intangibles like *Zeit, Kraft,* and *Energie* and sometimes money. *Der Aufwand an Zeit und Energie hat sich also doch gelohnt. Der Aufwand an Geld, Zeit und Kraft steht in keinem Verhältnis zum Ergebnis.* **Die Aufwendung** is a

formal word meaning 'the expenditure of money', 'the amount spent'. *Die Aufwendungen für Straßen sind weiter gestiegen.*
Die Aufwendungen für die neue Schule betragen 800 000 Mark.
Eine einmalige Aufwendung von 10 000 Mark könnte diese alte Kirche vor dem Verfall retten.
(*Aufwand treiben* means 'to be extravagant'. *Bei der Einrichtung des neuen Hauses haben sie großen Aufwand getrieben.* The n. has the same meaning in *Alle waren ohne Aufwand gekleidet. Aufwendung* sometimes means 'expending, summoning up'. *Unter Aufwendung seiner ganzen Beredsamkeit überzeugte der Anwalt die Geschworenen von der Unschuld seines Mandanten.*)

3. In fig. senses, **cost** and **price** mean 'that which must be sacrificed or done to obtain, achieve, or keep sth.' *The price of freedom is eternal vigilance. Loss of independence would be too high a price to pay for peace. No matter at what cost to herself, she is determined to succeed.*

i. Der Preis is used fig. and translates **cost** and **price** depending on the context. *Die Freiheit hat ihren Preis. Er mußte ihm die Wahrheit sagen, auch um den Preis seiner Freundschaft. Er vollendete das Werk um den Preis seiner Gesundheit. Der Verlust der Unabhängigkeit wäre ein zu hoher Preis für den Frieden. Um jeden Preis* is 'at any price, at any/all cost'. *Sie will um jeden Preis erfolgreich sein.*

> *Ein Vergleich mit den anderen westlichen Ländern zeigt, daß die Bundesrepublik die mit den siebziger Jahren allgemein einsetzende Phase schwieriger wirtschaftlicher Entwicklungen relativ gut überstanden hat—wenn auch um den Preis höherer staatlicher Verschuldung.*

> *Das föderative Element des Grundgesetzes—ein Grundpfeiler der deutschen Demokratie seit 1949—wird mit der politischen Vereinigung Europas empfindlich geschwächt. Das ist ein hoher Preis.*

ii. Auf Kosten means 'at the cost of', 'to the disadvantage or at the expense of'. *Er wurde reich, aber auf Kosten seiner Gesundheit. Sie hat den Bericht in ein paar Stunden geschrieben, aber diese Schnelligkeit ging auf Kosten der Genauigkeit.* It can be applied to what people do. *Er machte seine Witze immer auf Kosten anderer.* To my cost must be translated as the idea it expresses: *Wespenstiche sind schmerzhaft, wie ich* **aus eigener [bitterer] Erfahrung** *weiß.*

course *n.* **proceed** *v.* Two related meanings of **course** are treated here: (i)'The progression through a series of acts or events, through a development, or through time'. *What effect did this have on the course of the war? In the course of the conversation she said . . . I hope they'll change their minds in the course of the next two or three weeks.* (ii) 'The habitual or ordinary manner of procedure'. *The law must take its course.* The two common equivalents *der Ablauf* and *der Verlauf* are close in sense and can perhaps best be understood through the vs.

1. Proceed and *go [off]* are syns. in a sent. like *The meeting went [off] well/proceeded as planned.* One equivalent is one sense of **verlaufen**. *Wie ist die Versammlung/die Feier verlaufen? Die Fahrt verlief planmäßig/ohne Zwischenfälle/reibungslos* etc. **Ablaufen** has several meanings, one being 'to flow or drain off', *Das Wasser läuft aus dem Schwimmbecken ab,* another relating to things which run off or unwind from a spool, *Der Faden/Die Schnur läuft von der Spule ab,* or *Das Kabel läuft von der Trommel ab,* and another being 'to come to an end or expire', *Seine Amtsperiode läuft am Ende des Jahres ab. Ablaufen* is also applied to something which proceeds in time and is a syn. of *verlaufen,* but, unlike it, implies a conclusion and may suggest the unwinding of a plan. *Alles lief nach Plan ab.* With regard to something still going on, *verlaufen* is the usual v. *Wie verlaufen die Verhandlungen? Wie verläuft die Sitzung? Sie ist bisher sehr stürmisch verlaufen.* For something that has concluded either is possible. *Die Verhandlungen sind reibungslos verlaufen* or *abgelaufen. Das Programm ist wie geplant verlaufen/abgelaufen.* Both occur in relation to something which will take place or end in the future. *Ich hoffe, daß alles gut abläuft/verläuft.* Although *verlaufen* is the normal word, *ablaufen* is often used in similar contexts without any distinction being made.

2. Course.

i. **Der Verlauf** and **der Ablauf** are the corresponding ns. and are in many cases used without distinction. *Der Verlauf* has no implications while *der Ablauf*, like *ablaufen*, suggests the running off of events which are in some way planned. Hence *der Ablauf* is usual where planning is stressed, *Nur gründliche Planung sichert den reibungslosen Ablauf einer Unterrichtsstunde,* and *Verlauf* is preferred where planning is impossible, *Der Tod des Kaisers änderte wesentlich den Verlauf des Krieges. Verlauf* is more common.

> *Immer wieder spielte er in Gedanken den Ablauf des Einbruchs durch, bis er sicher war, daß nichts schief gehen konnte. Dann verlief aber doch alles anders, als er gedacht hatte.*
> *Sie berichtete über den Verlauf der Reise/Kampfhandlungen.*
> *Der Arzt ist mit dem bisherigen Verlauf der Kur zufrieden.*

ii. With *nehmen* + adj., only **der Verlauf** is used. *Der Heilungsprozeß nahm seinen normalen Verlauf. Die Verhandlungen nahmen einen befriedigenden/stürmischen/verhängnisvollen Verlauf.*

iii. If there is no adj. **der Lauf** is used. *Lauf* expresses sense ii of **course,** 'the ordinary manner of procedure'. *Die Gerechtigkeit nimmt ihren Lauf. Damit nahm das Verhängnis seinen Lauf.* **Der Gang** is a syn. of *Lauf* and is used with *gehen* instead of *nehmen*. Both *Die Sache geht ihren Gang* and *Die Sache nimmt ihren Lauf* are used. *Der Gang/Lauf der Geschichte,* course of history. *Der Lauf der Geschichte beweist die Unrichtigkeit dieser Beschuldigungen. Der Lauf* occurs mostly in fixed expressions. *Das ist der natürliche Lauf der Welt. Der Lauf der Dinge hat es mit sich gebracht.*

iv. **Der Gang** means 'course' in a few fixed expressions and has the same meaning as *Verlauf. Der Gang der Entwicklung. Der Gang der Handlung,* course of events in the plot of a literary work. *Der Gang der Geschäfte. Der eintönige Gang ihres Lebens. Der Gang der Ereignisse/der Dinge,* course of events. *Der Gang der Untersuchung. Der Gang der Verhandlungen war mühsam—über jeden Punkt gab es Gerangel* is possible, but *Verlauf* is usual with *Verhandlungen.*

> *Zu dem Zeitpunkt hätte ein beherztes Eingreifen den Verlauf/den Gang der Ereignisse entschieden zum Guten wenden können.*
> *Alles geht seinen ruhigen, alten Gang.*
> *Ich habe wohl keine Einzelheit vergessen. Ja, das war der Gang der Dinge.*

v. In the course of is usually **im Laufe,** but **im Verlauf** is used in formal and bureaucratic language. *Im Laufe der Debatte kam es zu einer Annäherung der Standpunkte. Im Verlauf des Grundstudiums sollen Studierende ein allgemeines Bild ihres Faches gewinnen.* (*Nach Verlauf einiger Tage,* after [the passage of] a few days. *Nach Ablauf der Frist,* on the expiry of the time allowed.)

> *Komm doch bitte im Lauf[e] des Abends vorbei!*
> *Im Verlauf/Lauf einer Woche gelang es ihm zweimal, seinen eigenen Weltrekord zu brechen.*

vi. **Der Hergang** means 'course of events', but is used only when these are reported or recorded in some detail in speech or writing. *So, erzählen Sie dann mal genau den Hergang!*

> *Der Zeuge stand zu weit ab, um den Hergang des Unfalls beschreiben zu können.*

cover v. Main equivalents.

1. i. In the sense 'to put or lay one thg. over another', **bedecken** is the general equivalent and is common in act. and pass. It need not imply covering completely.

> *Der Schreibtisch war vollständig mit Akten bedeckt.*   *Dichter Wald bedeckte die ganze Insel.*
> *Die Kartoffeln sind gerade mit Wasser bedeckt.*   *Schnee bedeckte das Tal.*

Der Himmel bedeckt sich [mit Wolken]. (It is clouding over.) *Ein bedeckter Himmel* (overcast).
Like **cover**, *bedecken* denotes a large number or amount of something on a surface.

Sein Körper war mit Narben bedeckt.   *Er war am ganzen Körper mit Narben bedeckt.*
Die Fußballspieler waren über und über mit Schlamm bedeckt.
Der Strauch war mit Blüten bedeckt.   *Schweiß/Tiefe Röte bedeckte sein Gesicht.*

ii. Zudecken is more specific, meaning 'to cover, usually a pers., with a blanket, rug, bedclothes, etc.' It stresses care and protection and implies covering up to the neck. *Bedecken* need only involve covering part of the body. *Sie legte sich hin und deckte sich mit einer Wolldecke zu.* But . . . *bedeckte sich die Beine.*

Bei einer Schlittenfahrt müssen die Fahrgäste gut zugedeckt sein, damit sie nicht frieren.
Die Mutter deckte das kleine Kind, das sich im Schlaf bloßgestrampelt hatte, sorgsam zu.
Da ihm sonst nichts zur Verfügung stand, deckte er sich mit Zeitungen zu.

Zudecken can suggest that something is covered completely, though this may only be an impression.

Während der Nacht hatte Schnee das Land zugedeckt.   *Die Brecher deckten das ganze Boot zu.*

iii. Überziehen means 'to cover sth. on all sides or on all sides except one'. Whereas *bedecken* means 'to place one solid thg. over another', *überziehen* implies that the covering material is liquid when applied.

Nachdem der Kuchen abgekühlt ist, wird er mit einer Schokoladenglasur überzogen.
Das Holz der Möbelstücke wird mit einer Grundierschicht und dann mit Klarlack überzogen, damit die Holzmaserung deutlich sichtbar bleibt.   *Die Drähte sind mit Isoliermaterial überzogen.*

iv. Abdecken means 'to cover as protection' in a few contexts, but never with a person as obj.

Wenn man den Brunnen nicht abdeckt, wird jmd. bestimmt hineinfallen.
Mehrere mit Planen abgedeckte Fahrzeuge standen im Hof.
Zum Schutz gegen Frost werden die Pflanzen mit Stroh abgedeckt.
Das Schwimmbecken wird im Winter mit einer Plane abgedeckt, damit es nicht völlig verschmutzt.
Ich decke das Loch im Dach ab, bis der Regen aufhört, und wir es ausbessern lassen können.

Note that *abdecken* also has the opposite meaning 'to uncover or take the covering off'. *Als das Schiff in den Hafen einfuhr, deckten die Matrosen die Laderäume ab. Den Tisch abdecken* is 'to clear the table'. *Der Orkan hat mehrere Häuser abgedeckt*, it blew their roofs off.

2. Verdecken means 'to hide or screen from view', thus 'to cover [up]'.

Das neue Haus verdeckt uns die Aussicht auf den See.
Das Bild verdeckt einen Fleck an der Wand.
Er verdeckte die Spielkarten mit der Hand.
Dunkle Brillengläser verdeckten ihre Augen.

3. *Decken* now expresses only fig. senses of **cover**. It has a meaning similar to 1 only in *ein Haus decken*, to put the roof on it. *Das Haus ist mit Stroh/Ziegelsteinen gedeckt*, has a roof of.

i. Decken is the equivalent of **cover** meaning 'to shield or protect', 'to protect from or deter an attack'. It is used in military contexts, in sport, and in chess. *Die Artillerie deckte den Rückzug der Kompanie.* In sport it means 'to mark' as well as 'cover'.

Dichter Wald deckte unseren Rückzug.   *Der Turm wird vom Läufer gedeckt.* (Chess.)
Ein Fußballer deckt den gegnerischen Spieler, indem er ihn beobachtet und auf ihn reagiert.

Die Deckung is 'cover'. *Das Gelände bot keine Deckung. Die Soldaten gingen in Deckung.*
ii. Decken is used for shielding someone who has done something wrong. *Die Geheimorganisation deckte lange Zeit das kriminelle Verhalten eines ihrer Mitglieder, bis es schließlich unmöglich wurde, ihn weiterhin zu schützen.*
iii. Decken is common in the language of commerce and economics, meaning 'to cover or meet' needs, requirements, expenses, costs, losses, etc.

Der Scheck ist gedeckt.   Der Schaden ist durch die Versicherung voll gedeckt.
Wir müssen Waren einführen, weil die heimische Industrie den Bedarf der Bevölkerung nicht decken kann.
Die Versorgung ist für eine Woche gedeckt.   Das Darlehen ist durch eine Hypothek gedeckt.
Der Preis deckt die Kosten kaum.   Dieser Gewinn deckt den bisherigen Verlust.

When an insurance policy is the subj., *decken* can be used. *Meine Reiseversicherung deckt mich gegen Krankheit sowie gegen Unfälle und Verluste.* When a person is the subj., as in *I am covered against . . .*, it is necessary to say *Ich bin gegen Unfälle versichert.*

iv. Sich decken, originally applied to congruent triangles, *Die beiden Dreiecke decken sich*, is used in other spheres to state that two things are identical or tally.

In dieser Frage decken sich unsere Ansichten.   Die beiden Begriffe decken sich nicht.
Was Onkel Moritz ihr sagte, deckte sich zum Teil mit dem, was der Großvater ihr erzählt hatte.
Seine Interessen decken sich mit denen seiner Frau.

4. Some fig. uses of **cover**.

i. Cover a distance. *Wir haben heute [eine Strecke von] 600 km* **zurückgelegt**. Colloquially **geschafft**. *Wir brauchen drei Tage, um diese Entfernung zurückzulegen.*

ii. Cover an area of ground. **Einnehmen**, 'to occupy', **umfassen**, 'to comprise', can express this sense. *Das Fabrikgelände nimmt 2 000 Quadratmeter ein. Der Hof umfaßt eine Fläche von 100 Hektar.*

iii. Umfassen is applied to a book, field of study, regulation, etc. which covers a certain area or certain points.

Sein Aufgabenbereich umfaßt die deutsche Literatur von der Frühaufklärung bis zum Ende der Klassik.
Diese Definition umfaßt alle zu berücksichtigenden Merkmale.
Das Buch umfaßt die deutsche Geschichte von den Befreiungskriegen bis zur Reichsgründung.
Diese Erklärung umfaßt alles, was zu berücksichtigen ist.
In seiner jetzigen Form umfaßt der Beschluß unterschiedliche Standpunkte.
Die im Gesetz eingeführten Einschränkungen umfassen alle Arten von Transport.
Diese Bestimmungen umfassen jeden denkbaren Fall.
Das englische Wort 'set' umfaßt eine Vielfalt von Bedeutungen.
Diese Zahlen umfassen alle verfügbaren statistischen Angaben aus den Jahren 1980–90.

Behandeln, 'to deal with', is used with *Bericht*, *Buch*, etc. as subj. as well as *umfassen*. If a person is the subj. of **cover**, *behandeln* is necessary. *Die Verfasser des Berichts behandeln alle Bereiche des Wirtschaftslebens*, but *Der Bericht des Finanzministers umfaßt/behandelt alle Bereiche des Wirtschaftslebens.*

In den Fällen, die in den gesetzlichen Bestimmungen nicht behandelt sind, darf der Beamte, der den Antrag bearbeitet, nach eigenem Gutdünken entscheiden.
In unserer Diskussion haben wir viele Punkte behandelt. (Could be: *covered a lot of ground.*)

iv. Jmdn./Sich bedecken *mit* means 'to cover s.o./oneself with' glory, honour, shame, etc.

Er hatte sich/seine Familie mit Ruhm/Schmach und Schande bedeckt.

v. Cover, meaning 'to point a gun at s.o. who might attack', can be expressed by **richten**, to point, AIM. *Er hatte/hielt die Waffe/das Gewehr/die Pistole auf mich gerichtet,* had me covered.

vi. For **cover** when it means 'to report on', see *berichten* under ANNOUNCE 3.

vii. Cover [up] = 'hide or veil'. *Verdecken* is possible with *Absichten. Er hat seine wahren Absichten verdeckt.* With words like *Betrug, Mißstände, ein Skandal*, or *Absichten*, **verschleiern**, 'to veil', and **verbergen**, 'to HIDE', are more usual as transls. of **cover up**.

Er lachte, um seine Angst und Verwirrung zu verschleiern.
Die Mißstände in dem Lande wurden durch eine alles umfassende Propaganda verborgen.
Das Zahlen von Bestechungsgeldern ist durch die Ausstellung von Belegen verschleiert worden, denen zufolge das Geld Wohltätigkeitsvereinen zugewendet wurde.

cross, go over, intersect vs.

1. This section discusses vs. expressing two meanings of **cross**, 'to pass over a line, boundary, river, etc.' and 'to pass from one side of any space to the other'.

i. Überqueren means 'to go over' either something seen as a line, e.g. *die Grenze, die Eisenbahnschienen,* or a space seen as a surface only, i.e. in two dimensions, such as *eine Straße, ein See, ein Fluß, ein Kanal.*

Als die Ampel grün wurde, überquerte das Kind schnell die Straße.
An dieser Stelle haben die Römer den Rhein überquert.
Man muß den Fluß mit der Autofähre überqueren, es gibt keine Brücke.

ii. Durchqueren means 'to pass from one side to the other' of a space seen in three dimensions, hence 'to go through, traverse'. It is used with ns. like *ein Wald, ein Erdteil, ein Saal, ein Zimmer, eine Stadt, eine Wüste,* and does not necessarily imply that the person stops on reaching the other side.

Sie durchquerten das Dorf in ein paar Minuten.
Sie durchquerte die Galerie, um sich ein Bild an der gegenüberliegenden Wand näher anzusehen.
Wie lange braucht man, um die Sahara auf dem Landweg zu durchqueren?

Whether *überqueren* or *durchqueren* is used may depend on the perspective. *Livingstone war der erste Europäer, der Afrika durchquerte* implies on foot or on land, i.e. a journey through three-dimensional space, but in *Moderne Flugzeuge überqueren Afrika in ein paar Stunden, überqueren* is used because from the air it is only a surface. *Ich durchquere einen Fluß* if I swim across it, i.e. I am in it, but *überquere den Fluß,* if I cross it on a bridge or a boat. (With ships, *den Ozean durchqueren* is occasionally found instead of the more usual *überqueren.*)

iii. In conversation, it is more usual to use a v. of motion with *über*.

Man soll nur beim Zebrastreifen über die Straße gehen.
Der Zug fuhr über die Brücke.   Man fliegt in zwölf Stunden über den Pazifik.

iv. *Über die Straße hinübergehen* is also found, but with a phr. with *über* or another prep. *hinüber* is not necessary as it adds nothing new, and is mostly omitted. If a n. like *Straße* is not present, i.e. when **cross** is intr., as in *You can cross now,* **hinübergehen** is necessary; it is modified in speech to *rübergehen*.

Wir wollen hier auf die andere Seite hinübergehen. Or Gehen wir hier hinüber/rüber!
Die Ampel ist grün, du kannst jetzt rübergehen.

v. If an army crosses a border with hostile intent, **überschreiten** is used.

Wenn die Armee des Landes X die Grenze des Landes Y überschritten hat, so heißt das, daß die beiden Länder sich im Kriegszustand befinden.
Dadurch, daß Cäsar den Rubikon überschritt, hat er dem Senat den Krieg erklärt.

Überschreiten is also used, without implying warlike intentions, in official language instead of *überqueren*.

Überschreiten der Gleise ist [Unbefugten] verboten. (Sign in many railway stations. *Überqueren* would be the normal word.)
Pfähle markieren die Grenze. Wer auch aus Versehen die Grenze überschreitet, muß mit sofortiger Verhaftung rechnen.

vi. When a bridge is the subj. of **cross**, the G. v. is **führen**. *Nur eine Brücke führt über den Fluß.*

2. Cross is trans. meaning 'to put one thg. across another', *He crossed his legs, The road crosses the railway line,* and intr. meaning 'to lie across one another or intersect', *Two roads cross.*

i. Arms and legs. **Verschränken** is the usual v. in relation to arms, and **übereinanderschlagen** to legs. **Kreuzen** is possible in both cases, but less common. **Überschlagen** is also used for the legs.

Er hatte die Arme verschränkt/gekreuzt.
Sie hatte ihren Kopf auf die verschränkten Arme gelegt.

Er lag auf dem Sofa und hatte die Arme/Hände unter dem Kopf verschränkt.
Er hatte die Beine übereinandergeschlagen/übergeschlagen/gekreuzt.

ii. Lines, roads, letters, paths, etc. If **cross** is trans., the equivalent is **kreuzen.**

Zweihundert Meter von hier kreuzt Straße a Straße b.
Dort wird man oft aufgehalten, weil die Straße eine Bahnlinie kreuzt.
Auf der Flasche war ein Etikett mit Totenkopf und zwei gekreuzten Knochen.

If **cross** is intr., it is translated by **sich kreuzen.** *Sich kreuzen* therefore means 'to intersect'.

Die beiden Linien kreuzen sich im Punkt A.   Dort kreuzen sich zwei Hauptstraßen.
Ihre Wege kreuzten sich immer wieder (their ways/paths crossed).
Unsere Briefe haben sich gekreuzt.

3. Cross = 'to cause plants and animals to interbreed'. This sense is also carried by **kreuzen.** *Der Züchter kreuzte zwei Schafrassen miteinander.*

Zur Verbesserung der Eigenschaften des Roggens wurden zwei Sorten gekreuzt.

4. Cross out or **off.** The usual word is **durchstreichen,** to draw one or more lines through something. In forms, however, **streichen** is used. *Nicht Zutreffendes bitte streichen!*

Sie hatte mehrere Wörter falsch geschrieben, durchgestrichen und dann richtig geschrieben.
Der Vater hat die fehlerhaften Rechenaufgaben des Jungen durchgestrichen.

Ausstreichen expresses the same meaning, but suggests removing something from a text, list, etc. *Ich strich meinen Namen aus* and *Ich strich meinen Namen in der Liste aus.* When, however, the sent. contains a phr. with *aus,* **streichen** is used. *Ich strich meinen Namen aus der Liste.*

Ich habe zwei Sätze ausgestrichen.
Wo ist die Teilnehmerliste? Ich streiche meinen Namen aus, weil ich nicht mitfahren kann.

curse, swear, vow *vs.* damned *part.*

1. Curse and **swear** mean 'to give vent to one's anger about s.o./sth. in profane and/or obscene words'. They are intr. *He began to curse/swear.* **Curse** can be trans. *He began to curse the driver/car.* **Swear** is used with *at. He swore at the driver.*

The usual equivalent **fluchen** can be used alone like the E. vs. With *über* and *auf* it translates **curse** + obj. or **swear at. Wettern** too has the sense 'to utter [a string of] abusive or swear words', but is less frequently used than *fluchen.* It is used alone or with *auf* and *über.* Like **curse** and **swear,** *fluchen* and *wettern* are often combined. *Da wird der Chef fluchen und wettern. Wettern gegen* also means 'to rail against'. *Die Mutter wettert gegen jeden Freund, den die Tochter ins Haus bringt.* **Schimpfen** means 'to give vent to one's annoyance and dissatisfaction in strong words'. Used alone, it can mean 'to be abusive, to curse', but it is not as strong as *fluchen.* While *schimpfen* presupposes a listener, *fluchen* can be to oneself. *Schimpfen auf* and *über* is usually translated as *to grumble* or *moan about.*

Ohne über den Vorfall nachzudenken, begann er wie wild zu fluchen.
Der Feldwebel wetterte lauthals über den Kasernenhof.   Du sollst nicht fluchen.
'Verdammt noch mal!' fluchte/wetterte er.   Die Männer im Boot fluchten vor Zorn.
Er machte seinem Ärger durch lautes Fluchen Luft.   Fluche bitte nicht!
Der Vorarbeiter fluchte/wetterte auf/über die Arbeiter/über das Auto.
Nach der letzten Gebührenerhöhung fluchen/schimpfen alle über die Post.

2. Curse = 'to utter against pers. and thgs. words which consign them to evil'. *In this scene King Lear curses Goneril.* This is the basic sense of **verfluchen,** to call down misfortune or the wrath of God on a person. *Die Mutter verfluchte ihren Sohn, nachdem er sie verraten hatte. In seinem Zorn verfluchte er alle, die ihm etw. angetan hatten.* **Verwünschen** means 'to wish evil upon' or 'to wish away from oneself or out of the world' and is a weaker syn. of *verfluchen*. *Sie verwünschte den Tag, an dem sie diesem Mann zum ersten Mal begegnet war.* Both words are now mostly found in a weaker sense 'to be very angry about and wish sth. had or had not happened'. *Ich verwünschte/verfluchte diese unüberlegte Handlung.* **Sich verfluchen** means 'to curse oneself', usually for having done something stupid or not having done the right thing. *Ich könnte mich verfluchen, daß ich nicht auf diese Idee gekommen bin. Er verfluchte sich für seine Rücksichtslosigkeit ihr gegenüber.* The past part. **cursed** can mean 'afflicted with such evils as indicate divine wrath or a malignant fate'. *The family seemed cursed* is now usually *Auf der Familie schien ein Fluch zu liegen.* The idiom *I am cursed with a bad memory* can be *Ich werde von einem schlechten Gedächtnis geplagt*, I am plagued by.

> *Später verfluchte er seine Abwesenheit bei dieser wichtigen Besprechung.*
> *Ich habe meinen Leichtsinn verflucht/verwünscht.*
> *Ihre Überheblichkeit gegenüber dem jungen Mann hatte sie oft verflucht.*
> *Nachdem er den Schmuck seiner Mutter verkauft hatte, verwünschte ihn die Familie.*

3. Verwünscht is used as an adj. like **damned** or **cursed** to express anger or annoyance. *Ich habe die ganze verwünschte Geschichte satt. Der verwünschte Plattenspieler funktioniert schon wieder nicht.* More usual are **verdammt**, **verflucht**, and **verflixt**, which can also all be used alone like *Damn!* (*Ein verwünschenes Schloß*, one 'having a curse on it, bewitched', belongs to literary language.)

> *Die verflixte Geschichte wird mich noch meine Stelle kosten.*
> *Verdammt/Verflucht noch mal! Jetzt ist mir ein Reifen geplatzt.*
> *Verflixt und zugenäht! Jetzt habe ich meine Eintrittskarte vergessen.*
> *Verflucht! Ich habe meinen Regenschirm im Bus liegengelassen.*

4. Swear = 'to take an oath to do sth.' *He swore to tell/that he would tell the truth.* It is also used when soldiers, ministers, and officials swear to serve their country or sovereign faithfully or to uphold the constitution etc. In looser use it indicates a feeling of near certainty. *I could have sworn that there was s.o. in the next room.*

i. Schwören covers all these uses. With *der Eid*, 'oath' (to tell the truth or serve loyally) as obj. either *schwören* or *leisten* is used. *Ich schwöre/leiste den Amtseid. Schwören* is also used like **swear** when someone vows to do something without an oath. *Nach der Auseinandersetzung schwor er, sich nie wieder so schlecht zu benehmen.* A syn. in the last sense is **sich geloben**, to vow to do something. *Er gelobte sich, nie wieder in eine Spielbank zu gehen/ein anderer Mensch zu werden.* **Geloben** takes an obj. *Er gelobte Besserung/Stillschwiegen.*

> *Die Zeugin schwor, die Wahrheit zu sagen/daß sie die Wahrheit sagen würde.*
> *Ich hätte schwören können, daß sich jmd. im Nebenzimmer befand.*
> *Ich könnte schwören, ihn dort gesehen zu haben.   Die beiden schworen sich ewige Treue.*
> *Die Wehrpflichtigen mußten ihren Fahneneid in aller Öffentlichkeit schwören.*
> *Gestern schworen die Beamtenanwärter ihren Diensteid.*
> *Ich schwöre bei allem, was mir heilig ist, daß ich schweigen werde.*

Swear by when it means 'to have great confidence in' is **schwören auf**.

> *Er schwört auf seine Methode. Es ist nie etw. schief gegangen.*
> *Ich schwöre auf ihn. Er ist der zuverlässigste meiner Mitarbeiter.*
> *Ich hätte darauf schwören können, daß unsere Mannschaft gewinnen würde.* (*Darauf* is optional.)

ii. Swear s.o. **to** secrecy, etc. As *schwören* does not take a person as obj., **jmdn. schwören lassen** must be used. *Er ließ den Freund schwören, daß er über diese Sache schweigen würde.*

iii. Swear an official, minister, etc. **in** or **swear** a witness is **vereidigen**. *Der Bundespräsident hat die neuen Minister/das neue Kabinett vereidigt. Soldaten werden am Anfang ihrer Dienstzeit vereidigt. Der Zeuge wurde zunächst vereidigt.*

iv. Beeiden and **beeidigen** are legal terms meaning 'to swear an oath as to the correctness', usually of evidence. In G. courts, a witness usually gives evidence and then swears it is correct.

> *Die Zeugin beeidete die Richtigkeit der Behauptung.*   *Er beeidete seine Aussage* (evidence).
> *Der Bestohlene beeidete, daß er in dem jungen Mann, der vor ihm stand, den Dieb erkannte.*

v. Beschwören, which also means 'to entreat or implore', is limited in use when it means 'to swear'. It occurs with *Aussage*, evidence. *Er beschwor seine Aussage vor Gericht.* With a *daß*-clause, it differs from *schwören* only in being more formal. *Ich kann beschwören/schwören, daß er dabei war. Beschwören* is also used with *es* and *das* as obj. and here too is more formal then *schwören. Ich kann es beschwören. Das kann ich beschwören.*

vi. Abschwören + dat. in one sense is 'to swear off'. *Nach dem Autounfall schwor er dem Alkohol ab.*

cut *v.* Some equivalents.

1. i. When **schneiden** is used with an obj without a prep., the normal implication is that the cutting produces several pieces. When one new piece results or something is cut in two, the derivatives discussed in iii and iv are used. This implication does not apply to ii nor when *aus* follows. *Ich schnitt ein Bild aus der Zeitung/eine faule Stelle aus dem Apfel. Schneiden* can be intr., *Die Schere schneidet gut*, but is mostly trans. It is used with everyday things which do not require much force like *Brot, Käse, Wurst, Bohnen, Kohl, Obst, Gemüse*, etc. as well as when more force is required, *Rohre schneiden* or *Bleche/Metallplatten schneiden* or *Die Waldarbeiter schnitten die Äste auf zwei Meter Länge*. The result is specified by *in. Ich habe das Papier in Streifen/das Fleisch in Stücke geschnitten.*

> *Ich kenne keinen, dem die Augen nicht tränen, wenn er Zwiebeln schneidet.*
> *Der Fleischer wetzte sein Messer, bevor er das Fleisch zu schneiden begann.*
> *In Ägypten auf dem Bazar sieht man noch Schneider ihr Tuch schneiden.*

ii. Parts of the body can be the obj. of **schneiden**, either when the cutting is deliberate, *Ich schneide mir die Fingernägel*, or accidental. In reference to a wound produced by cutting, the constructions are *Ich habe mich geschnitten*, or, when the part of the body is mentioned, *Ich habe mir* (or *mich*) *in den Finger geschnitten.*

> *Es wird Sommer, und ich lasse mir das Haar wieder ganz kurz schneiden.*

iii. Abschneiden means 'to cut off'. *Ich habe ein Stück vom Brett abgeschnitten.* It is sometimes used where E. only has *cut. Ich schneide das Brot* usually means 'I cut all or part of a loaf into slices'. When only one slice is cut, the v. is *abschneiden. Schneide mir bitte noch eine Scheibe ab!*

> *Die Mutter schnitt dem Kind eine Scheibe Brot ab.*

iv. Durchschneiden is used when something like *Faden, Bindfaden, Draht*, or *Seil* is cut so that two pieces are formed. In this use it is always separable. **Entzweischneiden** means 'to cut in two'. *Ich schneide das Blatt Papier entzwei.*

> *Haben Sie eine Schere, mit der ich den Faden durchschneiden kann? Ich kann ihn nicht durchreißen.*
> *Um diesen Draht durchzuschneiden, braucht man eine besondere Schere.*
> *Vor dem Einbruch hatte die Bande die Telefonleitung durchgeschnitten.*
> *Da sie es sehr eilig hatte, machte sie den Bindfaden nicht auf, sondern schnitt ihn durch.*
> *Sie hat beim Ausschneiden die Tischdecke entzweigeschnitten.*

Inseparable *durchschneiden* is used with geographical features which cut or intersect a landscape. *Mehrere Kanäle durchschneiden die Ebene.* It is the normal v. with *Band*, 'ribbon', as obj. when a symbolic action is involved. *Der Ministerpräsident durchschnitt das Band und gab damit die neue Autobahnstrecke frei. Er schnitt das Band durch* would have no symbolic significance.

v. Anschneiden is 'to cut the first piece' or 'put the first cut in'. *Wir schneiden jetzt den Kuchen an. Ich habe die Wurst schon angeschnitten.* (It also means 'to broach or start talking about' a subject. *Warum hast du dieses Thema beim Mittagessen angeschnitten?*)

vi. Zerschneiden means 'to cut into more than two pieces'. *Ich habe mich an einer Scherbe geschnitten* mostly implies one cut. *Wer sich an den Scherben die Fußsohlen zerschnitten hat,* has several cuts. *Wer eine Schnur durchschneidet,* has two pieces. *Wer eine Schnur zerschneidet,* has several pieces. With a thing as obj. *zerschneiden* also suggests that the thing is spoilt by being cut. *Warum hast du das schöne Bild zerschnitten?* (*Zerschneiden* also has the fig. sense 'to ruin completely'. *Das Band der Freundschaft war mit dieser scharfen Kritik für immer zerschnitten.*)

2. Hauen is 'to cut or hew' stone or hard material. *Man hat Stufen in den Fels gehauen. Sie haben ein Loch in das Eis gehauen. In Stücke hauen* implies wanton destruction, smashing something to pieces. *Sie drohten, alles im Zimmer in Stücke zu hauen.*

3. Hacken implies using a sharp instrument, mostly a knife or an axe, and by repeated blows making something considerably smaller than it was. It means 'to chop [up]' or 'cut up' wood or vegetables, etc. **Klein schneiden** and **zerkleinern** are also used for vegetables, and **spalten,** 'to split', for wood.

> *Seit sie sich einen offenen Kamin zugelegt haben, müssen sie dauernd in den Wald, um Brennholz zu hacken.*   *Ich habe die alten Kisten in Stücke/zu Feuerholz gehackt.*
>
> *Sie nahm die neue Maschine und mit ein paar Stößen war die erste Zwiebel fein gehackt.*
>
> *Zuerst schneidet man das Gemüse/das Obst/den Käse klein. Or Man zerkleinert das Gemüse/das Fleisch.*
>
> *Dieses trockene Holz kann man leicht spalten. Or Dieses Holz läßt sich leicht spalten.*

4. Although *schneiden* is not used in relation to chopping wood or cutting down trees, it is used for cutting timber into boards and suggests a fine edge. *Hier werden die Stämme zu Brettern geschnitten.* **Cut up** or *saw up* without any implication is **zersägen.** *Jetzt werden die Baumstämme zersägt.* **Cut down** a tree is *einen Baum* **fällen** or **umhacken.** *Zwei alte Bäume im Park mußten gefällt wurden. Den Apfelbaum mußte ich umhacken—er war fast abgestorben.*

5. *Schneiden* can be used with *Gras, Getreide,* or *Korn* as obj., but the usual word is **mähen,** to mow.

> *Vater. Es sieht aus, als hättest du den Rasen nicht gemäht. Sohn. Ich habe ihn doch gemäht.*

d

damage *v.* and *n.* **hurt, harm, injure** *vs.*

1. Damage means 'to harm or spoil sth. so that it does not work properly or is not in as good a condition as it originally was'. *The car was damaged in the accident.*
i. The main equivalent **beschädigen** is applied only to things in normal use. Only in bureaucratic language does *die Kriegsbeschädigten* refer to people who suffered injuries or whose health was impaired by the war; the disabled whose working capacity was diminished by more than half used to be called *schwerbeschädigt*, but this has been replaced by *schwerbehindert*.

> *Mehrere Häuser wurden vom Sturm schwer beschädigt.*
> *Die Uhr funktioniert nicht—sie ist beschädigt.*
> *Obwohl der Tanker von einer Mine beschädigt worden war, setzte er seine Fahrt fort.*
> *Der Unfall war nicht schlimm. Nur die Stoßstangen der Autos sind beschädigt worden.*
> *Dieses Exemplar [des Buches] ist leicht beschädigt und kostet deshalb weniger.*

ii. A colloquial syn. meaning 'to damage fairly badly' is **ramponieren**. *Am Morgen nach dem Zeltfest stellten die Verantwortlichen fest, daß mehrere Tische und Stühle stark ramponiert waren.*

2. Harm, hurt, and sometimes **damage** mean 'to have a detrimental effect on'. *This mistake hurt/harmed the firm. Strikes were damaging the economy.*
i. Schaden + dat. means 'to cause or do harm to' or 'to be harmful or disadvantageous to'. *Diese Fehlentscheidung in der Investitionsplanung hat der Firma sehr geschadet.* The neg. is usually *nichts*, sometimes *nicht. A bit of exercise won't hurt you/do you any harm* usually becomes *Ein bißchen Bewegung wird dir nichts schaden. Schaden* can be followed by an infin. or a clause with *daß* or *wenn. It won't hurt to postpone/if we postpone the meeting for a week: Es schadet nichts, die Versammlung um eine Woche zu verschieben,* or *Es schadet nichts, wenn wir die Versammlung um eine Woche verschieben. Es schadet nichts, das noch einmal zu sagen. Es schadet ihm gar nichts, daß er durch die Prüfung gefallen ist.*

> *Das schadete seinem Ansehen/seinem Ruf.*   *Die schlechte Luft schadet der Gesundheit.*
> *Den Kirschbäumen, die zur Zeit in Blüte stehen, hat der Frost sehr geschadet.*
> *Die wiederholten Streiks schadeten der Wirtschaft/der Industrie.*
> *Es kann dir nichts schaden, wenn du noch etw. dazu lernst.*
> *Es kann nichts schaden, wenn er wieder mehr Sport treibt. Er ist so träge geworden.*

ii. Whereas *schaden* means 'to harm or damage' in a vague and general way, **schädigen** refers to something specific in a definite area. *Rauchen schadet der Gesundheit* is general, but with a specific organ the v. is *schädigen. Alkohol schädigt die Leber. Zu laute Musik schädigt auf die Dauer die Ohren.* Living things can be the obj. *Industrieabgase haben einen großen Teil der Bäume geschädigt.* Other objs. are *der Ruf, das Ansehen,* and financial or economic factors. With the latter too it denotes something specific. *Durch seine Unterschlagungen hat der Kassierer die Firma sehr geschädigt* or *um mehrere Tausend Mark geschädigt. Schaden* used with *das Geschäft,* or *jmdm. geschäftlich schaden,* suggests harm in a less precise and clear way. The past part. of *schädigen* is used as an adj. *Alle geschädigten Bäume werden gefällt. Fast die Hälfte aller Bäume im Harz sind geschädigt.* As *schaden* takes the dat. its past part. is not used as an adj.

3. Damage n. **Der Schaden** denotes concrete material damage. *Der durch den Unfall an meinem Auto entstandene Schaden muß so bald wie möglich repariert werden.* It also occurs in the pl. *Das Ausmaß der Schäden im Überschwemmungsgebiet kann noch nicht festgestellt werden.* In addition it means 'an injury', *Er hat sich durch den Unfall einen Schaden an der Wirbelsäule zugezogen,* and 'harm' in an abstract sense, *Davon haben wir mehr Schaden als Nutzen. Sie wollte die Firma vor Schaden bewahren.*
> *Trotz aller Schädlingsbekämpfungsmittel fügt der Kartoffelkäfer der Landwirtschaft immer noch großen Schaden zu.*

4. The formal v. **beeinträchtigen** means 'to have a detrimental or prejudicial effect on', 'to harm'. It is not used for concrete objects, but for abstracts like rights, interests, reputation, people's moods and abilities, and sales. *Alkohol beeinträchtigt die Reaktionsfähigkeit des Autofahrers.* A person can be the obj. and is linked to these factors by *in. Diese neuen Bestimmungen beeinträchtigten ihn in seiner Freiheit/in seinem Handeln/in seinen Rechten.*
> *Das Regenwetter konnte die gute Laune nicht beeinträchtigen.*
> *Der Warenabsatz der heimischen Industrie wird durch billige Importe beeinträchtigt.*

5. Hurt meaning 'to cause pain' is **wehtun** or **schmerzen**. *Tut die Hand noch weh? Der Fuß, den ich mir letzte Woche verrenkt habe, schmerzt immer noch/tut immer noch weh. Nach der langen Wanderung tun mir die Füße weh.* Man tut sich/einem anderen weh, causes oneself/someone else bodily pain. *Haben Sie sich beim Sturz wehgetan? Du tust mir ja weh.*

6. Hurt oneself or part of the body and **be/get hurt** imply more than pain. They are syns. of **injure**, meaning 'to cause damage to the body'. The equivalent is **verletzen**. *Der Fahrer und Beifahrer wurden im Unfall verletzt. Er hat sich beim Fußball verletzt. Ich habe mir das Bein verletzt.*

7. Hurt and **injure** also mean 'to inflict mental pain on, cause distress to s.o.'s feelings, offend'. **Jmdm. wehtun** also carries this sense. *Es tut weh, wenn man sich von seinen Freunden verlassen fühlt.* A common alternative is **kränken**, to hurt or wound s.o./s.o.'s. feelings. *Ich wollte dich nicht kränken.* **Verwunden**, which also means 'to wound' in the lit. sense, and **verletzen** are syns. of *kränken*, but they belong to a stylistically higher plane. *Diese ungerechte Kritik hat mich sehr verwundet/verletzt.*
> *Er war gekränkt, weil man ihn nicht nach seiner Meinung fragte.*
> *Diese harmlose Bemerkung hat sie offenbar verletzt.*
> *Dieses so deutlich geäußerte Mißtrauen verwundete ihn.*

dare, venture, risk *vs.*

1. Dare = 'to be bold, brave, or courageous enough to do sth. despite the risk involved'. It is used either with an infin., *No one dared to contradict him, I dare not ask them,* or alone with the infin. implied, *I wouldn't dare, Try it if you dare!*
i. The main equivalent is **wagen** which means 'to have the courage to undertake sth., despite the risks or possiblity of failure'. *Wagen* sometimes has an obj. Cf. 3. If it has no obj., it needs *es*, but this is optional when an infin. follows. *Vor ihm hatte [es] niemand gewagt, die fast steile Gesteinswand zu besteigen. Er hatte die Reformer so weit unterstützt, wie er es wagte. Versuch' es, wenn du es wagst!*
> *Niemand wagte, dem Chef zu widersprechen, obwohl das, was er sagte, ganz offensichtlich ein Fehler war.*
> *Die Strafen waren so hart, daß kein Soldat [es] wagte zu desertieren.*
> *Hat sie es gewagt, sich an dich zu wenden, nach dem, was passiert ist?*
> *Sollte er es dennoch wagen, werden wir ihm einen gehörigen Denkzettel verpassen* (teach a good lesson).

ii. Sich trauen means 'to possess the courage to do sth.' It is a common expression among children and suggests timidity and faint-heartedness, or implies *eine Mutprobe*, a test of courage. *Wagen* is stronger and is used when there are clear objective disadvantages or risks, *Bei der augenblicklichen Situation wage ich es nicht, in dieser Firma zu investieren*, whereas *sich trauen* stresses (overcoming) a lack of self-confidence. *Sich trauen* is also used by and for adults. *Ich traue mich nicht, es ihm zu sagen*, although *ich wage es nicht* would imply an objective assessment of the risks and is stylistically slightly higher. *Sich trauen* takes an infin. or stands alone and is often neg. or found in questions. *Traust du dich, vom Zehnmeterbrett zu springen? Ich traue mich nicht.* In colloquial speech it is used with an impersonal obj., like *das, alles, viel, wenig*, etc. *Das traust du dich ja doch nicht!*, you won't dare to do it. The standard language uses an infin. *Du traust dich ja nicht, das zu machen.*

> *Das Kind traute sich nicht, auf den Baum zu klettern/ins Wasser zu springen.*
> *Wer sich traut, zum anderen Ufer und zurück zu schwimmen, bekommt von mir ein Eis.*
> *Komm' doch 'rüber, wenn du dich traust!*
> *Sie gingen so nahe an die Stelle heran, wie sie sich trauten/es wagten.*

iii. Sich getrauen has the same sense as *sich trauen*, but has become uncommon. *Wer sich das getraut, ist in meinen Augen fast schon ein Held.*

2. Both **sich wagen** and **sich trauen** are used with a phrase stating a place and differ in the way described in 1. ii. In E., this idea is expressed by either **venture** + a place or **dare** to go.

> *Er traute sich nicht auf das Eis, und die anderen Kinder waren sich darüber einig, daß er ein Angsthase war.* *Sie traute sich nicht allein in das dunkle Zimmer.*
> *Er wagte nicht, das Eis zu betreten/wagte sich nicht auf das Eis, denn noch gestern hatte es gefährlich geknistert, als er nur einen Schritt darauf getan hatte.*
> *Sie wagte sich auf die wacklige Brücke.* *Er hatte sich in die Höhle des Löwen gewagt.*

Sich wagen an is used with a task. *Die junge Schauspielerin wagte sich an die Titelrolle.*

3. i. Dare is occasionally found with an obj., but the usual v. is now **risk**. *Columbus dared the perils of the sea. He will dare any danger. The missionary was prepared to dare all thgs. and bear all thgs. for his Lord's sake.* **Wagen** is used in a few cases with an obj. in the sense 'to do sth. despite the danger of loss or unpleasant consequences in the hope of achieving a pos. result' and can be translated as **risk**. *Der Missionar war bereit, im Dienste Gottes alles zu wagen und alles zu ertragen. Er hat viel gewagt. Für sein Kind hat er sein Leben gewagt. Sollen wir einen Versuch wagen?*, risk a trial or dare to attempt sth. **Sich aussetzen** expresses the meaning 'to expose oneself to danger etc.' *Columbus setzte sich den Gefahren des Meeres aus. Er hat sich jeder Gefahr ausgesetzt.* **Risk** is usually **riskieren**. In some contexts it stresses, like *wagen*, the courage required to do something and is like *to take the risk of doing sth. Er riskierte/wagte einen Einspruch*, took the risk of objecting, ventured an objection. *Sie riskierte es/wagte es, diese heikle Angelegenheit zur Sprache zu bringen.* Mostly it draws attention to the unpleasant consequences or loss that may result from doing something. *Er hätte alles riskiert, nicht nur seine Stellung. Sollen wir es riskieren? Sie riskieren einen Prozeß. Wer sich betrunken an das Steuer eines Autos setzt, riskiert seinen Tod/sein Leben.*

ii. Risk also means 'to put s.o./sth. in a dangerous position in which death or destruction might result'. *He was not willing to risk a single soldier in such a foolhardy enterprise.* *Riskieren* can be used here, but an expression which emphasizes the unnecessary risk is **aufs Spiel setzen**. *Er war nicht bereit, das Leben einen einzigen Soldaten aufs Spiel zu setzen in einem so leichtsinnigen Unternehmen.*

4. Dare = 'to challenge or defy s.o. to do sth. which requires courage'. *I dare you to jump over the stream. The other boys dared him to dive from the bridge.* In direct speech, children use **wetten** + a clause with **sich trauen**. *Ich wette, du traust dich nicht, über* *den Bach zu springen.* This can be adapted to other circumstances. *Die anderen Jungen wetteten, er würde sich nicht trauen, von der Brücke zu springen.* Vs. related in meaning are **anstacheln**, 'to incite, goad', **anspornen**, 'to urge, incite, or encourage s.o. to do sth.', or **herausfordern**, 'to challenge'.

Ich wette, du traust dich nicht, vom Zehnmeterbrett zu springen.
Kinder stacheln sich oft gegenseitig an, dumme Dinge zu tun.
Er stachelte mich dazu an, den Aushang vom schwarzen Brett zu reißen.
Sie wußte, daß sie ihn herausforderte, ihr zu widersprechen.
Die anderen Jungen spornten ihn an, von der Brücke zu springen.

5. Dare means 'to have the impudence to do sth.' This is a variation on sense 1 seen from the point of view of the person who suffers the (supposedly) bad effects of the action and who expresses his/her indignatiion. *He dared to question my authority. How dare you take my car? Don't you dare steal those apples!*
i. Wagen is possible in all cases. In the imp., stressed *ja* or *bloß*, which express a threat or warning, are usually added. *Wagt es ja/bloß nicht, diese Äpfel zu nehmen! Ja* und *bloß* are used with other vs. *Komm' ja/bloß nicht auf die Idee, diese Äpfel zu stehlen!* could translate *Don't you dare steal them!*

Er hat es gewagt, die Aufrichtigkeit meiner Absichten in Zweifel zu ziehen.
Der Wachtposten hat es doch tatsächlich gewagt, meinen Paß zu verlangen.
Wie kannst du es wagen, [einfach] mein Auto zu benutzen?
Wie kannst du es wagen, so zu mir zu sprechen?

ii. Sich unterstehen means 'to have the audacity or effrontery to do sth.' and translates *dare* in this sense. *Wie kannst du dich unterstehen, gegen diese Verordnung zu verstoßen? Wie kannst du dich unterstehen, ohne meine Erlaubnis das Auto zu benutzen? Er hat sich unterstanden, ihm zu widersprechen.* The imp. *Unterstehen Sie sich!* is used in the pos. in the sense 'don't you dare [do that]!'
iii. Sich hüten + infin. means 'to avoid doing sth.' and can translate *not to dare. Sie hatte sich gehütet, diesen Vedacht zu äußern. Hüte dich* introduces a warning *not to do* something and can translate *Don't you dare! Hüte dich, ihm das zu erzählen!*

6. I dare say is **ich nehme an** or **ich vermute**, I assume or presume. This meaning can also be expressed by the particle **wohl**. *I dare say you've spent a lot of money: Ich nehme an/vermute, du hast sehr viel Geld ausgegeben* or *Du hast wohl sehr viel Geld ausgegeben.*

Ich nehme an/vermute, diese Regelung wurde getroffen, ohne die Praxis an den Gerichtshöfen zu berücksichtigen.   *Ich nehme an/vermute, du hältst mich für sehr nachlässig.*

data *n.* The only rarely encountered sing. of this word *datum* is defined in its basic sense as 'a thg. given, known, or assumed as a fact and made the basis of reasoning or calculation, of a theory, or of an explanation'. The pl. is applied to material serving as a basis for discussion etc., as in *No general appraisal will be possible until more data are available,* and to detailed information of any kind.
i. The word of G. origin is **die Angabe**, which has several senses. The basic meaning is 'a piece of information given'. It can be what a witness says, i.e. his/her evidence, *nach Angaben mehrerer Zeugen,* as well as instructions or directions, *Wir haben den Schrank nach den Angaben des Kunden angefertigt,* and the giving of any information, *mit/ohne Angabe des Namens/der Adresse.* As a mathematical term it means 'the data or given information of a problem' and translates *data* in other fields.

Das Buch bringt Angaben über Agrarsubventionen in verschiedenen Ländern.
Wir haben keine näheren Angaben, die uns weiter helfen würden.
Eine Beurteilung der Lage wird erst dann möglich sein, wenn weitere Angaben vorliegen.

In Hamlet wie in jedem Literaturwerk gibt es gewisse, naheliegende Angaben. Bei der Interpretation muß man alle diese Angaben berücksichtigen und darf keine verzerren.

ii. Die Daten was originally a learned word and referred to information or findings, often in the form of figures, which are obtained by observation, measurements, statistical investigations, etc. It has, however, been extended to all kinds of information and is the usual word in connection with computers. *Die Datenverarbeitung* is 'data processing'.

Fast alle Wissenschaften benötigen Daten als Ausgangsmaterial, aus dem man Regeln, Hypothesen and Gesetze ableiten kann. In vielen Disziplinen sind die anfallenden Daten so zahlreich, daß zu ihrer Verarbeitung datenverarbeitende Maschinen verwendet werden müssen.
Die Broschüre enthält die exakten technischen Daten des neuen Autotyps.

deceive, cheat, delude, be mistaken *vs.*

1. Deceive and **delude** = 'to make s.o. believe sth. that is not true'.

i. Trügen, which is now old-fashioned and very restricted in use, surviving only in a few fixed expressions, has things, senses, or feelings as subj. and means 'to give rise to a false impression' or 'to create an illusion'. It is mostly intr., but sometimes takes an obj. In both intr. and trans. uses, *täuschen* is the more usual word in current usage.

Der Schein trügt, die Straße ist nämlich gar nicht naß.
Die Sinne trügen oft.   Die Ahnung trog nicht.
Wenn mich mein Gedächtnis/meine Erinnerung nicht trügt, so war das vor drei Jahren.
Wenn mich nicht alles trügt, geht dahinten ein ehemaliger Schulkamerad von mir.

ii. Täuschen means 'to make s.o. believe sth. which is wrong or does not correspond to the facts' or 'to mislead'. It can refer either to a false impression which comes about without any intention or to one which is purposely created. *Ihre Augen haben Sie getäuscht.* In sport *Er täuschte geschickt* means that he pretended to be going to do something in order to outwit his opponent. It translates **deceive** and **delude** meaning 'to cause s.o. to believe what is false' or 'to mislead as to a matter of fact' in sents. such as *Wolsey was too wise to be deceived by outward show* or *He deceived us as to his real intentions* or *He deluded them with promises he did not mean to keep*. It does not in itself imply cheating someone of something. *Täuschen* usually has an obj., but can be intr. *Wenn mich mein Gedächtnis nicht täuscht, hat sie recht.* *Der äußere Schein täuscht.* Phrs. like *(deceived/deluded) into believing* or *doing sth.* must be expressed as a clause. *Er hatte sie dermaßen getäuscht, daß sie glaubten, er würde ihre Interessen wahrnehmen. Er hatte sie dermaßen getäuscht, daß sie ihm eine größere Geldsumme anvertrauten.* Cf. 2 for the refl.

Er hatte seinen Freund über seine wahren Absichten getäuscht.
Wir haben alle geschossen, um die Männer im Boot zu täuschen.
Der Erfolg täuscht.   Laß dich nicht von ihm täuschen!
Sie täuschte uns mit ihrer angeblichen Notlage, damit wir sie weiterhin unterstützten.
Das Haus ist gar nicht so hoch. Das täuscht nur.   Wenn mich nicht alles täuscht, stimmt das.
Wolsey war zu klug, um sich vom äußeren Schein täuschen zu lassen.
Er täuschte sie mit Versprechen, die er nicht zu halten beabsichtigte.

Like **deceive**, *täuschen* is used in connection with *Hoffnungen* and *Erwartungen*, although the usual v. in this context is **enttäuschen**, to disappoint. *Ich sehe mich in meinen Erwartungen getäuscht/enttäuscht.*

2. The usual equivalent of **be mistaken** in the sense 'to be wrong about a matter of fact' is **sich irren**. It is mostly refl., but can be non-refl. without any change of meaning. *In diesem Punkt irren Sie [sich].* It refers to something which can be readily confirmed. *Ich habe mich im Preis geirrt. Sie habe sich im Datum geirrt.* **Sich**

täuschen means 'to have the wrong impression about s.o. or sth.', 'to be deceived or mistaken in one's estimation of a pers. or situation', or 'to delude or deceive oneself about sth.' It usually refers to something which cannot be verified easily by checking or looking. It is used alone or with *in* + a person and *über* + a thing. If someone mistakes one person for another, *sich täuschen* is usual, but *sich irren* is possible. *Das war gar nicht der Michael—ich habe mich getäuscht/geirrt und ihn mit einem anderen verwechselt.*

> *Du täuschst dich, wenn du ihn für glaubwürdig hältst.*
> *Wenn du glaubst, der Ast hält deinem Gewicht stand, so täuschst du dich.*
> *Du täuschst dich in ihr. Sie ist ganz anders als du denkst.*
> *In diesem Menschen habe ich mich sehr getäuscht.   Er täuscht sich über seine wirkliche Lage.*
> *Du täuschst dich über den Schwierigkeitsgrad der Sache.*

3. Cheat.

i. Betrügen means 'to deceive deliberately' or 'to cheat or trick', chiefly with regard to money or a concrete advantage. It can be intr., *Er betrügt oft*, but is mostly trans., *Sie hat mich beim Verkauf dieses Autos betrogen.* With *um* it means 'to cheat or swindle out of'. *Er hat mich um eine beträchtliche Summe/um 500 Mark betrogen.* With reference to married couples, it means 'to be unfaithful'. *Er hat sie mit einer Jugendfreundin betrogen.*

ii. Mogeln and **schummeln** are interchangeable and refer to cheating at cards and other games. They are used colloquially for cheating in examinations. *Täuschen* is the normal v. in formal language. A teacher might say to a pupil caught cheating, *'Du hast versucht, mich zu täuschen'*, and the pupil could reply, *'Ich habe versucht zu mogeln/schummeln, aber es hat nicht geklappt.'* Both are intr. If an obj. follows, **bemogeln** and **beschummeln** are used.

> *Er versucht jedesmal beim Kartenspiel zu mogeln/schummeln, indem er die Karten vertauscht.*
> *Er hat mich wieder bei der Abrechnung bemogelt/hat mich beim Kartenspiel beschummelt.*

4. If **deceive** means 'to lie to s.o. deliberately', it is **belügen**. Cf. LIE.

5. Further syns.

i. From the original idea of going round the back of an enemy and taking him by surprise, **hintergehen** has come to mean 'to deceive by lack of sincerity', e.g. by hiding important facts, and then, behind someone's back, doing something which is not expected and causes loss or harm.

> *Du hast mich hintergangen. Du hast mir nicht die Wahrheit gesagt.*
> *Er ist viel zu anständig, um jmd[n.] zu hintergehen.*
> *Die hintergangenen Käufer protestierten alle.*

ii. Übervorteilen means 'to get some benefit, mostly money, for oneself by sharp practice or trickery', usually by taking advantage of the other's ignorance or inexperience.

> *Bei dem Hauskauf ist er sehr übervorteilt worden.   Paß auf, daß er dich nicht übervorteilt!*

iii. Prellen means 'to cheat s.o. of what is his or her due'. It is used with *um* and ns. like *die Belohnung, das Erbe, das Honorar. Die Zeche prellen* means 'not to pay for the food and drinks one has received'; hence *die Zechprellerei*, bill-dodging.

> *Der Händler hat die alte Dame um 200 Mark geprellt, weil er ihr den Preis nicht zahlte, den das Bild, das sie verkaufte, wert war.*
> *Er kann sich nicht mehr im Gasthof sehen lassen, weil er die Zeche geprellt hat.*

iv. Hereinlegen, in speech often shortened to *reinlegen*, is a common colloquial word meaning 'to cheat or take in'. *Bei diesem Geschäft sind wir ganz schön hereingelegt worden.* **Hereinfallen** corresponds to the pass., *to be taken in by. Auf diesen Hochstapler fallen sicher viele herein.*

Beim Abschluß des Geschäfts hat er den Vertragspartner mit Hilfe eines geschickt formulierten Paragraphen hereingelegt.   Laß dich nicht hereinlegen! Er ist ein gerissener Geschäftsmann.

v. Jmdn. übers Ohr hauen and **aufs Kreuz legen** are colloquial expressions with the meaning of *betrügen*, while **jmdm. ein X für ein U vormachen** is a colloquial syn. of *täuschen*.

'*Wie gefällt dir diese antike Vase? Ich habe sie letztens für 300 Mark gekauft.' 'Für 300 Mark? Da hast du dich aber gehörig übers Ohr hauen lassen. Das ist eine billige Nachahmung, die keine zehn Mark wert ist.'*

Das soll ein Perserteppich sein? Sie können mir doch kein X für ein U vormachen.

Von diesem Hausierer bin ich ganz schön aufs Kreuz gelegt worden.

vi. [Jmdm.] auf den Leim gehen means 'to be tricked or duped'.

Stell dir vor, dieser Gauner hat sich als Vertreter eines Wohlfahrtswerks ausgegeben und in unserem Haus um Spenden gebeten. Sogar Quittungen hat er ausgestellt. Kein Wunder, daß ihm mehrere Hausfrauen auf den Leim gegangen sind.

In one meaning, **aufsitzen** + dat. is a syn. of *auf den Leim gehen*, but it is only used in the perf. *Sie sind einem Betrüger aufgesessen. Viele Käufer sind diesen Verkaufsmethoden aufgesessen.*

decide *v.* make up one's mind *v. phr.*

1. Decide means 'resolve', 'to make up one's mind'. *My brother has decided to become a sailor/that he will become a sailor.*

i. One equivalent of **decide** in this sense is **sich entschließen**. It means that one considers the issue, reaches a conclusion, and has the necessary will-power, determination, or resolve to carry this out, although these implications may not always be apparent in everyday instances. The idea is thus that one either summons up the necessary resolution to do something or does not do it at all. The subj. can only be a person seen as an individual, not a group of people like a committee, a parliament, etc. *Sich entschließen* cannot refer to a decision about what someone else should do. It is used when someone is unable to make up his or her mind to do something. *Sie kann sich nicht [dazu] entschließen. Ich habe mich noch nicht [dazu] entschlossen* means that I haven't decided/made up my mind to do something, but in some cases, like the last two examples below, it is translated as *see my way clear (to doing sth.)* It is used with an infin. or with *zu* + a n. denoting an action *Er hat sich entschlossen, ein Haus zu kaufen* or *Er hat sich zum Kauf eines Hauses entschlossen.* With an infin. and a personal subj., it is interchangeable with *beschließen*. Unlike *beschließen, sich entschließen* can be used alone, as in *Hast du dich entschlossen?* The question is *Wozu hast du dich entschlossen?*, what have you decided [to do]?

Sie entschloß sich, sofort abzufahren/das Studium aufzugeben/nun doch mitzukommen/ein neues Leben zu beginnen.   Ich habe mich entschlossen, die volle Wahrheit zu sagen.

Ich habe mich zu einer Reise nach Europa entschlossen.

Ich kann mich noch nicht dazu entschließen, meine Stelle zu wechseln.

Ich würde mich sehr freuen, wenn Sie sich dazu entschließen könnten, ihr zu helfen.

Note the idiom: *Kurz entschlossen gingen wir ins Theater*, we made up our minds quickly, on the spur of the moment; a suggestion was accepted without hesitation.

Kurz entschlossen trat er in das Geschäft und kaufte den Verlobungsring.

ii. Beschließen usually implies that a firm or binding decision has been or is to be made after consultation or careful consideration. Although used for personal decisions, it is the usual word when a group of people or a deliberative body, a council, parliament, committee, trade union, etc., decides or resolves something, mostly by a vote. It is followed by *über* when the matter still has to be decided or voted on, or by an obj. or clause when it has been agreed on.

Der Bundestag muß heute über die neue Steuergesetzgebung beschließen.
Das Parlament hat die Abschaffung der Todesstrafe beschlossen.

In the private sphere, *beschließen* is usually followed by an infin. when the decision concerns the subj., *Sie beschloß, sofort abzureisen,* although a *daß*-clause is possible, *Sie beschloß, daß sie in einer Woche abreisen würde.* However, when the decision concerns someone else, a *daß*-clause is necessary. *Der Vater beschloß, daß seine Töchter studieren sollten.* The question is *Was hast du beschlossen?* If *beschließen* is used, it is usually expected that the action decided on will be carried out. If X had decided to give up smoking, someone who doubted his ability to carry it out might say, 'X *hat sich entschlossen, das Rauchen aufzugeben, aber er wird es diesmal auch nicht halten.*' Another person, who thought the decision was serious and that X would persevere, might say, '*Er hat doch beschlossen, das Rauchen aufzugeben.*'

Er beschloß, ihr die ganze Wahrheit zu sagen.   Er beschloß, ein neues Leben anzufangen.
Er beschloß, das Auto zu verkaufen/Chemie zu studieren/Matrose zu werden.

2. Decide also means 'to settle a question in dispute', 'give a judgement'. *The jury must decide whether the accused is innocent or guilty. Galileo decided the question by an experiment.* It often implies making a personal choice. *You must decide what to do. I can't decide which subjects to take/which offer I should accept.*

i. Entscheiden is the usual v. in the sense 'to settle a question'. It means 'to come to a decision about sth.', either in the sense of resolving an issue in doubt or of opting for one of several courses of action. It can be used alone. *Entscheiden Sie! Das Los wird entscheiden.* It takes an obj., *Das Gericht wird die Frage entscheiden,* an infin. or a clause, *Die Mitglieder entschieden, nichts zu unternehmen/daß sie nichts unternehmen würden,* and is used with *über, Wir müssen über diesen Fall entscheiden.*

Ich wage nicht zu entscheiden, wer hier recht hat.
Das Zielfoto entschied über den Sieger des 100-Meter-Laufes.
Die Geschworenen müssen entscheiden, ob der Angeklagte schuldig ist oder nicht. Sie entschieden, ihn
*   freizusprechen.   Der Streit wurde vor Gericht entschieden.*
Der Kanzler wird heute endgültig darüber entscheiden, ob er bei den nächsten Wahlen kandidieren
*   will.*
Versuche werden entscheiden, welches Verfahren das geeignetere ist.
Der Chef muß entscheiden, wer versetzt wird/was geschehen soll.

Deliberative bodies *entscheiden über eine Frage/über die zu ergreifenden Maßnahmen* in the sense of determining or choosing what action is to be taken. *Beschließen* would imply a binding vote, but in practice there is little difference between the two words in this context. *Das Kabinett muß über den Einsatz von Truppen entscheiden/beschließen.* When a decision has been reached *beschließen* is the usual v. *Das Kabinett beschloß, Truppen zur Bekämpfung der Drogenmafia einzusetzen.*

ii. The refl. **sich entscheiden** is used when the decision concerns oneself. *Entscheiden* + infin. tends to suggest some kind of authoritative and important decision, whereas *sich entscheiden* + infin., being personal, can also be used for trivial matters. The question is *Wie hast du [dich] entschieden?* Note that the E. construction **decide** + interrogative + infin., *to decide what to do* or *how to do sth.,* must be turned into a clause. *Du mußt dich entscheiden, was du tun willst/wie du das machen willst.*

Du kannst dich frei entscheiden.   Du hast die Freiheit, dich so oder so zu entscheiden.
Jetzt mußte sie sich entscheiden, ob sie studieren wollte.
Jetzt mußt du dich entscheiden, welche Fächer du studieren willst.
Wir haben uns entschieden, ins Kino zu gehen (implies that there were other possibilities).

In practice, there is often little difference between *sich entscheiden* and *sich entschließen,* because in many decisions there is a choice between various alternatives. Thus *I can't make up my mind* can be either *Ich kann mich nicht [dazu] entschließen,* 'find the will-power to do something', or *Ich kann mich nicht entscheiden,* 'decide between two or more possibilities'.

iii. Entscheiden is used with games, battles, wars, etc. as obj. *Diese Schlacht entschied den Ausgang des Krieges. Dieser Zug (move) entschied die Schachpartie.* The refl. is used with the thing decided as subj. *Die Schlacht entschied sich am zweiten Tag.* With *es* as subj. the refl. means that something will be decided. *Morgen wird [es] sich entscheiden, wer recht behält.*

3. Decide on means 'to choose'. *In the end, she decided on the green hat.* **Sich entscheiden für** expresses this meaning. The question is *Wofür hast du dich entschieden?* or *Für welches Modell habt ihr euch entschieden?*

> *Ich habe mich für diesen Anzug entschieden.*
> *Er hatte die Wahl, entweder in Sydney zu bleiben oder eine Versetzung nach Melbourne anzunehmen. Er entschied sich für Sydney.* Alternatives: *Er hat sich dafür entschieden, in Sydney zu bleiben.* Or *Er entschied sich, in Sydney zu bleiben.*

4. Decide can mean 'to cause s.o. to do sth.' *What decided you to give up your job?* An alternative, which is more common, at least in Australia, is *What made you decide to change your job?* **Decide** in this sense or *make s.o. decide to do sth.* are mostly translated by **veranlassen**, to CAUSE. Stylistically higher are **bestimmen**, 'to induce, move s.o. to do sth.' (cf. DETERMINE 3), and **bewegen**, 'to MOVE'.

> *Was hat sie veranlaßt, aufs Land zu ziehen/das Studium aufzugeben/an der gefährlichen Expedition teilzunehmen?   Was hat ihn zur Teilnahme an der Tagung bestimmt?*
> *Was hat sie bestimmt/veranlaßt, die Stelle zu wechseln?*
> *Nichts wird mich dazu bestimmen, den Plan aufzugeben.*

demand, claim, require *vs.* Some uses.

1. Claim means 'to ask for sth. to which one has a right'. *Every citizen should claim his rights.* **Demand** can also mean 'to ask for sth. one is entitled to', but suggests greater insistency, and when it and **claim** are both possible, **demand** is stronger. *He demanded his rights. The doctor demanded the payment of his bill. The court demands fair treatment of the accused by the prosecutor.* **Demand** also means 'to ask for sth. peremptorily and imperiously' without any suggestion of entitlement. *He came to my house and demanded money/help. She demanded to speak with Sherland/to be told everything/that we tell her what had happened.*

i. Both **fordern** and **verlangen** are translated as *demand*, and there is now little difference between them. One explanation of the distinction is that *fordern*, like **claim**, is used when *der/die Fordernde* believes that he or she has a right to what is demanded. This explains the frequent use of *fordern* in cases in which a right is involved. *Er fordert sein Recht. Sie forderten Genugtuung. Sie forderte von ihm das Geld, das sie ihm geliehen hatte. Der Anwalt forderte Freispruch. Die Arbeiter fordern eine Lohnerhöhung.* Verlangen is used in similar contexts, *Jmd. verlangt sein Recht, Rechenschaft, Schadensersatz,* or *eine Erklärung,* etc., the difference, if any, being that *verlangen* is more emphatic or ultimative. In most cases either is possible. *Das Einzige, was er fordert/verlangt, ist Gerechtigkeit.* When the demand is completely without entitlement, *verlangen* is used. *Er verlangte Geld.* When someone insists that something be done, only **demand** is used. A *daß*-clause can follow *verlangen* and *fordern,* the former being more common. A pass. infin. also follows *verlangen.* *Ich verlange, daß du schweigst. Er verlangte, daß man ihn hineinließ/hineingelassen zu werden. Er forderte Einlaß. Sie verlangte/forderte, daß man ihr alles erzählte, was passiert war. Ich verlange/fordere, daß dieser Schaden so bald wie möglich behoben wird/daß die Rechnung sofort beglichen wird.* Thus while *fordern* is similar to **claim**, *verlangen* does not differ from it in all respects in the same way as **demand** does from **claim**.

ii. Demand that s.o. **do** sth. can also be expressed by **auffordern** + infin., which implies a forceful request or demand. As *fordern* does not take an infin., *aufforden* is used with one in the meaning 'to demand or call on s.o. to do sth.' *Er forderte mich auf, den ausstehenden Betrag zu zahlen. Auffordern* is not always as strong as **demand**; in relation to joining in an activity it means 'to ask'. Cf. ASK 6.

Der Polizist forderte die Ruhestörer auf, den Saal zu verlassen/sofort zu verschwinden.

iii. Beanspruchen in one sense means 'to claim or lay claim to sth.', usually what one has a right to. It is less strong than *fordern.*

Er beanspruchte den Urlaub, der jedem Arbeitnehmer zusteht.

Sie beanspruchte Schadensersatz/ihr Erbteil/einen Anteil am Gewinn/ihr Recht.

iv. *The teacher* **demands** *a lot of his pupils* can be *Der Lehrer stellt hohe Anforderungen an seine Schüler.* Cf. DEMAND n. 2. For *This work demands all/a lot of my time/energy* see DEMAND n. 3.

2. With an activity or task as subj., **demand** means 'to call for' or 'need' and is interchangeable with **require.** *Governing a country demands/requires skill, patience, and energy. This work demands/requires great concentration.* **Claim** also has this sense in a few contexts. *There are several matters which claim/require/demand my attention.* **Fordern** is used in a few cases with an abstract n. as subj. *Das Gesetz fordert von uns Gehorsam. Das Leben fordert sein Recht.* These are more or less fixed expressions. In the first sent. *fordern* could be replaced by **erfordern,** which usually translates *require* and *demand* when they are synonymous, but it would be weaker, as *fordern* expresses a strong demand. The meaning of *Das Gesetz erfordert von uns Gehorsam* could be expressed as *The law requires obedience (if it is to fulfil its function).* **Verlangen** with a thing as subj. is a syn. of *erfordern* and differs only in being slightly stronger. *Diese Arbeit erfordert/verlangt ein hohes Maß an Konzentration.*

Die verzweifelte Lage fordert eine Entscheidung. Also with a slight difference: *erfordert/verlangt. Das Erlernen dieser Sprache erfordert ein intensives Studium.*

3. Claim in *An accident claims lives* is translated by **fordern.** *Das Unglück hat zwei Menschenleben gefordert.*

demand n.

1. A **demand** is 'a firm request' and is made by a person for something specific. *The workers' demand for higher wages. The demand for justice/more information/s.o.'s resignation/money.*

i. Die Forderung is 'demand' in the sense just defined. *Die Unternehmer lehnten die Forderung der Arbeiter nach einer Lohnerhöhung ab. Forderung* also denotes a claim for the honouring of financial obligations. *Unsere Forderungen an diese Firma betragen 20 000 Mark,* our claims, the amount it owes us.

Diese moralische Forderung kann man nicht umgehen.

Es ist den Beamten nicht gelungen, ihre Forderung nach einer verkürzten Arbeitswoche durchzusetzen.

Er erhob Forderungen, die niemand erfüllen konnte.

ii. Demand, followed by an infin., is **die Aufforderung.** *Der Aufforderung des Gläubigers, diese Schulden zu tilgen, ist er nur mit Mühe nachgekommen.* In *Auf wiederholte Aufforderung hin öffnete der Pförtner die Tür,* the infin. is implied. Cf. DEMAND v. 1. ii.

Die Jugendlichen widersetzten sich der Aufforderung der Polizisten, den Platz zu räumen.

2. Tasks, situations, and people make demands on a person in the sense of requiring a certain level of achievement. **Demand** meaning 'level or standard of achievement' is **die Anforderung.** It is used with *stellen,* 'to make', and the subj. can be work, a position, task, or a person.

Diese Aufgabe stellt hohe Anforderungen an einen jungen Juristen.

Der junge Fußballer wurde den Anforderungen des Vereins [nicht] gerecht.

Die beiden Angestellten waren den Anforderungen des Geschäfts gewachsen. Or . . . *haben den Anforderungen genügt.*

Der Direktor stellt hohe/große Anforderungen an die Angestellten.

A difficulty arises because *Forderungen* is used in the same sense as *Anforderungen.* Someone could say, *'Der Lehrer stellte hohe Forderungen an die Schüler.'* This would normally be taken to mean *Anforderungen*, which could also be used and would be unambiguous. *Forderungen* is, however, ambiguous in this sent. as it could imply demands for help or attention, or money for damage to books etc. Likewise *Eine Aufgabe stellt hohe Forderungen* or *Anforderungen.* The non-native speaker is best advised to use *Anforderungen* always in this sense, but will encounter *Forderungen.*

3. In *The work makes [heavy] demands on s.o.'s time/energy* and in *This work demands all/a great deal of my time/energy*, the n. and v. **demands** means that the work requires a large amount of time or energy. Both n. and v. are expressed by **in Anspruch nehmen** or **beanspruchen.** *Sie ist von ihren Aufgaben sehr beansprucht* and *Die Arbeit nimmt sie sehr in Anspruch.*

Der Beruf nimmt meine ganze Zeit/sehr viel Zeit/alle meine Kräfte in Anspruch.

Die Arbeit/Der Beruf beansprucht ihn voll and ganz/nimmt ihn voll und ganz in Anspruch.

4. Demand in the economic sense means 'the desire to buy'. *The demand for personal computers is still rising.* For this meaning G. has *der Bedarf* and *die Nachfrage.* **Der Bedarf** refers either to what is required by the population for normal life or to what industry etc. needs for production. *In den letzten Jahren hat sich der Bedarf an Elektrizität verdoppelt.* **Die Nachfrage** is 'the desire to buy'. It is used in statements about the level of demand. *Die Nachfrage nach Personalcomputern steigt immer noch. Das Angebot* is 'supply'. *Das Verhältnis von Angebot und Nachfrage.* **In demand** is **gefragt.** *Diese Waren sind sehr gefragt.*

Der Bedarf des In- und Auslandes an Eisenerz ist in den letzten Jahren kaum gestiegen.

Der Bedarf an Lebensmitteln ist gedeckt.

Es besteht/herrscht große Nachfrage nach diesen Waren.

Die Nachfrage übersteigt das Angebot.

Es besteht eine rege/schwache Nachfrage nach dem Brot.

deny *v.*

1. Deny means 'to declare what is alleged or stated to be untrue'. *I denied the accusation/being involved.*

i. Leugnen is commonly used when someone who has been accused of doing something declares the accusation to be false. While **deny** always needs an obj., *leugnen* can be used without an obj. *Leugne nicht! Es hat keinen Sinn zu leugnen. Er hat auf das bestimmteste geleugnet.* In E. it would be added. In addition, *leugnen* is used with a n. obj., a clause—usually *daß*—or an infin.

Er hat seine Schuld/seine Identität/die Beschuldigung/die Anklage/die Mitwisserschaft an der Tat/den ihm zur Last gelegten Diebstahl geleugnet.

Er leugnet jetzt alles, was er früher zugegeben hatte.

Der Mann, dessen Gewehr man in der Nähe der Mordstelle gefunden hatte, leugnete, die Frau erschossen zu haben.   Sie leugnete, daß sie das Geld gestohlen hatte.

In connection with statements or assertions, *leugnen* is now mostly neg. and is a way of confirming that a statement is true. *Niemand kann leugnen, daß dieser Forscher hervorragende Arbeit geleistet hat.*

Es ließ sich nicht leugnen/Es war nicht zu leugnen, daß das Geld fehlte. (Could translate: There was no denying.)   *Niemand kann Schmidts Tüchtigkeit leugnen.*

ii. Abstreiten, which needs an obj., an infin., or a clause, suggests a forceful denial and is perhaps more common than *leugnen*, particularly in the spoken language, when an accusation is rejected.

Sie stritt energisch ab, jemals so etw. gesagt zu haben.

Maria Stuart stritt energisch jede Beteiligung an einer Verschwörung gegen das Leben der Königin Elisabeth ab.

Es half dem Mann nun nicht mehr, die Tat abzustreiten. Die Last der Beweise war erdrückend.

iii. Ableugnen implies a stronger denial than *leugnen*, but it is not particularly common.

Nachdrücklich leugnete er seine Schuld an dem Unfall ab.

Sie hat das Verbrechen verbissen abgeleugnet.

iv. For the use of **zurückweisen** with *eine Beschuldigung*, i.e. to reject/deny an accusation, cf. REFUSE 5.

v. Bestreiten means 'to dispute the correctness of'. It suggests using arguments to question the accuracy of what is stated. The obj. is what someone says or claims as well as accusations or allegations. *Jmd. bestreitet eine Behauptung/ein Argument/eine Theorie/eine Feststellung.* It also translates *deny* in the occasional use in the pos. with statements, when it is interchangeable with *dispute*, as in *I deny/dispute that this is the correct interpretation of the law. Ich bestreite, daß das die richtige Auslegung des Gesetzes sei.*

Die Eisenbahnverwaltung bestritt hartnäckig jede Schuld an der Entgleisung und behauptete, die Schienen seien absichtlich gelockert worden.

Er bestritt, daß Goethes Werke Bedeutung für die heutige Welt hätten.

vi. Verneinen basically means 'to answer no to a question'. It can have *Frage* as obj., but is often found without an obj. With an infin. or a *daß*-clause, it means that someone answered no to a question, the contents of which is given by the infin. or clause. Unlike *leugnen*, it does not presuppose an accusation, only a question.

Sie verneinte, als ich sie fragte, ob sie jemals in London gewesen sei.

Einer der Umstehenden, den ein Polizist danach fragte, verneinte, den Unfall gesehen zu haben.

Er verneinte, daß seine Barocktruhe großen Wert hat.

vii. Dementieren is 'to issue an official denial' about a rumour or reported claim that a particular action has occurred or will occur. The n. is **das Dementi**.

Der Regierungssprecher hat die Meldung scharf dementiert, daß das Kabinett eine Steuererhöhung beschlossen hatte.

viii. Absprechen + dat. and acc. means 'to state or claim that s.o. does not possess a quality or ability' and is sometimes translated as *deny*. *Er spricht mir jedes Talent ab*, denies that I have any talent.

Organisatorische Fähigkeiten kann man ihm nicht absprechen (cannot deny he has them).

Sie spricht ihm jedes Verständnis dieser Frage ab.

2. i. Deny and **leugnen** also mean 'to refuse to admit the validity of a doctrine or belief' or 'to reject sth. as non-existent or unreal'. *She denies the existence of ghosts.*

Er leugnet das Dasein Gottes/die Unsterblichkeit der Seele/die Existenz von Gespenstern.

Das Übel in der Welt ist nicht zu leugnen.

Er leugnet die Existenz eines angeborenen aggressiven Triebs im Menschen.

ii. Verneinen also means 'to reject or not to accept the value of a doctrine or of some commonly accepted way of behaving' and corresponds to **deny** in some contexts. A syn. is *ablehnen*. Cf. REFUSE 5.

Er verneint den Wert der Nächstenliebe.

Sie verneinen überhaupt den Sinn des Lebens (deny that life has any meaning).

3. Deny means 'to refuse to acknowledge' or 'to disown' someone or someone's claims, one's convictions, personal characteristics, etc. *Peter denied Jesus.*

Verleugnen means 'to claim that that which another believes to be the case, or which seems obvious, is not so'. *Jmd. verleugnet einen Freund*, claims he/she does not know him, he is not a friend. **Sich verleugnen** can imply denying or acting contrary to one's beliefs or convictions. *Ich müßte mich verleugnen, wenn ich so handelte. Schmidt läßt sich verleugnen*, he gets someone to say he is not at home when he is. *Ich bin sicher, daß er zu Hause war, aber er ließ sich verleugnen.*

> *Jesus sagte zu Petrus: 'Ehe der Hahn zweimal kräht, wirst du mich dreimal verleugnen.'*
> *Da er sich seiner tieferen Gefühle zu schämen scheint, hat er sie verleugnet.*
> *Wenn ich einem solchen illiberalen Gesetz zustimmte, dachte der Abgeordnete, hieße es, meine Überzeugungen verleugnen/mich verleugnen.*

4. Deny means 'to withhold from' or 'to refuse to grant'. *We cannot deny him his just reward. It is unfair to deny recognition to the Palestinians. She denied herself every luxury.*

i. In the first two sents. *refuse* is the everyday word, **deny** being stylistically higher. **Versagen** is a stylistically similar equivalent. **Verweigern** is also close in meaning. Cf. REFUSE 1.

> *Ich konnte ihm meine Bewunderung nicht versagen.*
> *Zwar versicherten sie alle ihren guten Willen, aber sobald es darum ging, die Worte in Taten umzusetzen, versagten ihm alle ihre Unterstützung.*
> *Die Belohnung kann man ihnen nicht verweigern.*
> *Den Palästinensern sollte man nicht länger die Anerkennung als Nation verweigern.*

ii. With a dat. refl. pronoun and an acc. **versagen** expresses the idea of denying oneself something. *Ich mußte mir diesen Wunsch versagen.* A colloquial syn. is **sich verkneifen**. *Sie hatten gespart und sich alles verkniffen.* Both imply making a sacrifice. At the neutral level of language **verzichten auf**, 'to forgo, do without', would be usual, but it does not necessarily imply a sacrifice.

> *Da sie versuchte, so sparsam wie möglich zu leben, versagte sie sich jeden Luxus.*
> *Warum sollte ich mir dieses Vergnügen verkneifen? Or Ich muß auf dieses Vergnügen verzichten.*
> *Das muß ich mir vorläufig noch verkneifen, es ist mir nämlich zu teuer.*

Deny oneself without an obj. is **sich verleugnen**. *Will mir jmd. nachfolgen, der verleugne sich selbst und nehme sein Kreuz auf sich!* **Die Selbstverleugnung** is thus 'self-denial'.

depend on, rely on, count on *vs.* dependent *adj.*

1. Depend on means 'need s.o. else or another pers.'s action or characteristic in order to survive physically or financially'. *Children depend on their parents for food and clothing. We depend on his help/their goodwill.* This sense is partly carried by **abhängen von**, which implies that one person/thing needs another for survival. In *Kinder hängen von ihren Eltern ab* it is translated as *are dependent on*, but in *Die Insel regiert sich zwar selbst, hängt aber wirtschaftlich von Frankreich ab*, the second v. could be either *is dependent* or *depends*. This sense of *abhängen von* suggests that the person is not completely free in his actions, but is subject in an important respect to the will of another. In this sense it is not used with a prep. other than *von*. A related expression is **angewiesen sein auf**, which means that one person needs or cannot get by or would be in difficulties without another. *Wir sind auf diesen Lieferanten angewiesen.* It is also used with characteristics and actions. *Wir sind leider auf die Gunst dieses Mannes/auf Aufträge aus dem Ausland angewiesen. Angewiesen* may suggest that someone has to rely on or is thrown back on s.o./sth. because nothing else is available. *Wer die Zahl der Deportierten nennen will, ist auf Schätzungen angewiesen.* Besides *auf, angewiesen* takes *für* which means that one person or thing needs another in a specific way. *Für Kleidung und Ernährung sind Kinder auf ihre Eltern angewiesen.* With abstracts the E. construction *We depend on him for support* must be rephrased as a possessive: *Wir sind auf seine Unterstützung angewiesen. Er ist auf sich selbst angewiesen,* he gets no outside help, is thrown back on his own resources.

Viele Studenten hängen noch finanziell von ihren Eltern ab.

Sie ist auf jmds. Hilfe/auf jmds. Wohlwollen/auf den Rat eines Freundes/auf eine kleine Rente angewiesen.

Wir sind auf Kohle angewiesen—wir haben keine andere Energiequelle.

Angewiesen is similar to **abhängig**, dependent. When the dependence is on a thing, they do not differ, *Das Dorf war von dieser einen Quelle abhängig/auf diese eine Quelle angewiesen,* but when the dependence is on a person, *abhängig* is much stronger. *Er war von diesem Mann abhängig* suggests total dependence, whereas *Er war auf diesen Mann angewiesen* means merely that the first person needed or had to rely on the other to do something or provide help, information, something concrete, etc.

2. With a thing as subj. **depend** means that something will happen only if the circumstances are right for it or if a particular condition is fulfilled. *The success of a meeting depends on how well it has been prepared.* **Abhängen** is also used here, an alternative being **ankommen auf**. When the subj. is *es* they are interchangeable, but only *abhängen* takes a subj. other than *es* or *das*. Thus *Es hängt von den Umständen/dem Wetter ab* or *Es kommt auf die Umstände/das Wetter an,* but *Der Erfolg hängt meist vom Fleiß ab. Meine Zukunft hing von dieser Entscheidung ab.* A clause can follow both. *Es kommt darauf an/hängt davon ab, ob ich genug Geld habe. Es hängt davon ab/kommt darauf an, wie man die Aufgabe anpackt.* The elliptical phr. *That depends* (i.e. on circumstances) is usually *Das kommt darauf an,* but *Es hängt davon ab* is not uncommon. Cf. 4.

Ob eine Sitzung erfolgreich ist, hängt davon ab, wie gründlich sie vorbereitet worden ist.

'Was wirst du machen?' 'Ich weiß es noch nicht. Es kommt darauf an.'

Von dieser Entscheidung hängt sehr viel für mich ab.

'Wie soll ich über diese Ereignisse berichten?' 'Es kommt darauf an/hängt davon ab, für welche Zeitung Sie arbeiten.'   *Der Ausgang einer Wahl hängt von vielen Faktoren ab.*

3. Depend on also means 'to rely on', 'trust', or 'be certain about'. *You can always depend on John. You can depend on her to help. You can depend upon it that she will help.*
i. The usual v. is **sich verlassen auf**, to rely on. *Du kannst dich immer auf Hans verlassen.* When an infin. or clause follows *depend,* it is translated by the construction *Du kannst dich darauf verlassen, daß sie uns hilft.* An alternative is **zählen auf**, to count on. *Kann ich auf dich zählen? Sie zählt auf meine Hilfe* would be translated as **count** or **rely on** because **depend** would suggest dependence rather than reliance.

Er hat zwar versprochen, dabei zu sein, aber ich weiß nicht, ob ich mich auf ihn verlassen kann.

ii. *It will rain tomorrow, [you can] **depend on** it!* The closest equivalents are *Es wird morgen regnen—darauf kannst du dich verlassen* or *verlaß dich drauf!* There are several alternatives. One on a fairly high stylistic level is *Dessen kannst du sicher sein!* At a neutral level *ganz gewiß* or *bestimmt* can be added to the sent. *Es wird morgen ganz gewiß/bestimmt regnen.* Colloquially, *Du kannst Gift darauf nehmen!* expresses assurance. *Neuseeland wird gewinnen—du kannst Gift darauf nehmen.*

Es wird schon klargehen—darauf kannst du dich verlassen.

Es wird klappen—verlaß dich drauf!

4. Je nach means 'depending on'. Before a clause it appears in the form **je nachdem**. When the possibilities are specified, *ob* usually introduces the subordinate clause, but may be omitted. *Je nachdem [ob] die Reise billig ist oder teuer, fahre ich, oder fahre ich nicht.* When the possibilities are not specified, the clause is introduced by *wie*, which may also be omitted. *Sie können zu jeder Zeit vorbeikommen, je nachdem wie*

es Ihnen paßt. Je nachdem, used alone, means 'that depends' and is thus the same as *Das/Es kommt darauf an. A. Gehst du mit? B. Je nachdem.*
Man verkauft frisches Obst je nach der Jahreszeit.
A. Wann kommst du? B. Je nachdem, wann ich fertig bin.
Je nachdem wie der Zustand des Autos ist, kaufe ich es oder nicht.
Es ist bekannt, daß die Patienten in Krankenhäusern verschieden verpflegt werden, je nachdem ob sie in der ersten oder der dritten Klasse untergebracht sind.

describe *v.*

1. Schildern is 'to give a vivid and lively picture of sth.', 'to present sth. in some detail', while **beschreiben** means 'to give a clear idea or impression of s.o. or sth.', mostly by giving the essential features or peculiarities. As the difference thus often lies in the fullness of the description, an area in which the two words overlap is to be expected. For a description of a person or a stolen object to the police only *beschreiben* is used. *Sie beschrieb der Polizei genau den Täter/den gestohlenen Gegenstand. Beschreiben Sie mir seine Größe, sein Aussehen, seinen Gang!* It is used for an objective or scientific description. *Man beschreibt jmdm. den Weg. Man beschreibt ein Experiment/eine Landschaft/eine Maschine. Der Botaniker muß eine Pflanze, die er entdeckt hat, genau beschreiben.* It is usual when only a few words are required, *etw. kurz beschreiben*, or when something cannot be described, *Wer wollte beschreiben, wie wunderbar das Konzert war? Sein Entsetzen war kaum zu beschreiben. Diese Empfindung läßt sich mit Worten nicht beschreiben.* With regard to describing symptoms to a doctor, *beschreiben* is the normal v., but *schildern* is possible and would imply that the complaint is of a varied and complicated nature. *Er beschrieb/schilderte dem Arzt seine Beschwerden.* With *Experimente* which are long and involved, *schildern* is also possible. Although *schildern* suggests a more detailed account while *beschreiben* implies the essentials, the distinction is not always made. *Er schilderte uns seine Reise so lebhaft, daß wir nachher glaubten, dabei gewesen zu sein* follows the definition. However, *Sie beschrieb uns peinlich genau ihre Reise mit der transsibirischen Eisenbahn, wobei sie kaum einen Halt zu erwähnen vergaß,* also occurs. *Er schilderte uns seine Erlebnisse in Afrika. Er beschrieb seine Erlebnisse in der Osttürkei in den düstersten Farben.* Schildern sometimes has people as obj. and suggests habits and character rather than appearance. *Wenn ich ihn schildern wollte, würde ich vor allem seine Marotten hervorheben.*
Schildern Sie den Hergang der Tat vom Zeitpunkt an, als der Wagen auftauchte!
Alles ging so schnell. Wie soll ich da den Hergang beschreiben können?
Bevor ein Lehrling an eine neue Maschine gelassen wird, schildern Sie ihm bitte immer den Arbeitsgang vom Rohteil bis zur Fertigstellung.
Der Arbeitsgang ist schnell beschrieben. Man dreht an diesem Regler, und das Teil ist gestanzt.
In diesem Buch wird geschildert, wie der Norden Australiens erschlossen wurde.

2. Describe also means 'to characterize by a word'. *I wouldn't hesitate to describe her as clever/a genius. The opposition described this answer as insensitive.* The usual v. is **bezeichnen als.** *Die Opposition bezeichnete diese Antwort als kaltschnäuzig.* (For *bezeichnen* cf. CALL 4.) **Qualifizieren als** is a learned syn. *Ich würde die Konferenz als Erfolg qualifizieren.* **Beschreiben** is also followed by *als* but implies a description with several details, *bezeichnen* only one point. *Die Nachbarn beschrieben Katharina als eine tief religiöse und wohltätige Frau, die immer bereit war, anderen zu helfen.*
Ich würde ihn als guten Freund/Genie/einen Lügner/geistreich/dumm bezeichnen.
Diese Länder kann man als unterentwickelt qualifizieren.

destroy, annihilate *vs.*

1. Zerstören means 'to damage to such an extent that the thg. becomes unusable or that only ruins, remnants, or rubble remain'. *Der Wirbelsturm/Das Erdbeben hat die Stadt/das Haus/die Brücke völlig zerstört. Der Brand hat die Fabrik zerstört. Die Flugzeuge wurden durch Bombenangriffe am Boden zerstört.* **Vernichten** means 'to destroy sth. so completely that nothing of its previous form remains'. In its strict sense, it is applied mostly to things which burn so that only ashes remain. *Er hat die Briefe/die Akten/die Unterlagen vernichtet, damit man ihm nichts nachweisen könnte. Das Feuer hat alle Vorräte vernichtet.* In reference to buildings destroyed by fire, *zerstören* is the usual v., but *vernichten* also occurs and suggests more complete destruction. *Gestern hat ein Großbrand das Zentrum der alten Stadt zerstört/vernichtet.* *Vernichten* is also used for a harvest which is ruined or destroyed by untoward weather. *Der Sturm, der letzte Nacht über Norddeutschland wütete, hat die Ernte vernichtet.* When an army or fleet is annihilated or wiped out, the v. used is *vernichten*; hence *eine vernichtende Niederlage. Vernichten* is used with *Ungeziefer*, 'vermin', *Schädlinge*, 'pests', and *Unkraut*, 'weeds', as obj., and in this context is synonymous with **ausrotten, austilgen**, and **vertilgen**, 'to exterminate, wipe out'. *Man tilgte das Unkraut aus. Die Vögel haben das Ungeziefer vertilgt. Chemische Mittel, die man zur Ausrottung/Vernichtung von Schädlingen und Unkraut benutzt hat, haben oft unerwartete Nebenwirkungen gehabt.*
> *Die Saboteure haben die Telefonleitungen planmäßig zerstört.*
> *Ein Fanatiker hat das Gemälde mutwillig zerstört.*
> *Diese Fabriken haben die Landschaft/die Natur in der Umgebung gänzlich zerstört.*
> *Geschlagen aber nicht vernichtet, zog sich die preußische Armee nach Brüssel zurück.*
> *In den letzten Jahrzehnten sind viele Beuteltierarten in Australien ausgerottet worden.*
> *Die Rodung des Regenwaldes hat mehrere Indianerstämme ausgerottet.*

2. Destroy is applied fig. to hopes, dreams, plans, someone's reputation, love, friendship, etc. and to people themselves. **Zerstören** is the usual v. in such contexts, but **vernichten** sometimes occurs. *Diese schweren Rückschläge haben ihre Existenz/sein Leben/ihre Ehe/unser Glück/mein Vertrauen auf seine Fähigkeiten/meine Freude an der Sache zerstört. Das hat alle meine Hoffnungen vernichtet/zerstört. Diese unsauberen Praktiken haben seinen Ruf zerstört/vernichtet.*
> *Durch ihre Unehrlichkeit hat sie unsere Freundschaft/unser gutes Verhältnis zueinander zerstört.*
> *Das ausschweifende Leben hat seine Gesundheit zerstört.*

determine *v.* Some uses of **fix** *v.*

1. Determine = 'to settle or decide a dispute, question, or a matter in doubt, authoritatively or as a judge'. What determines something is mostly a person, *It is left to the judge to determine what sentence a convicted criminal will receive*, but occasionally a thing, *The financial position of the company will determine whether we develop a new model.*
i. The usual equivalent is **entscheiden** with and without *über*. For its use see DECIDE 2. *Die finanzielle Lage der Firma wird [darüber] entscheiden, ob wir ein neues Modell entwickeln.* In the following examples *entscheiden* could be translated either as *decide* or **determine**.
> *Das Gesetz legt gewöhnlich eine Höchststrafe fest. Es bleibt dem Richter überlassen, in jedem Fall über das Strafmaß zu entscheiden.*
> *Wir müssen entscheiden, welche Schritte wir unternehmen können.*
> *Wir haben darüber zu entscheiden, wieviele Gäste wir einladen können.*
> *Hat man entschieden, was für eine Schule gebaut werden soll?*
> *Wir müssen entscheiden, wann die nächste Sitzung stattfinden soll.*

ii. Closely related is another sense of **determine**, 'to decide upon one of several people or alternatives'. *Rigorous tests will determine which men can become astronauts.* **Entscheiden** could be used here. *Strenge Tests werden darüber entscheiden, welche Männer Astronauten werden können.* **Bestimmen** in such a context means 'to determine' as a syn. of *find out* or *discover.* Cf. 4.

2. If people determine the price at which something is to be sold, someone's salary, the time and place of a meeting, who is to be promoted, etc., they lay it down by virtue of their authority. *We have the right to determine how the money will be spent. The date of the match is still to be determined.* **Fix** is also used for laying down a time for a meeting etc. or a price. *All that remained to do was to fix the date of the wedding.* This sense differs from 1 by suggesting someone with the authority to impose his or her decision.

i. Bestimmen with a person as subj. suggests in such contexts that someone has the power or authority to determine what is to happen. *Man bestimmt den Preis/jmds. Gehalt/einen Termin/den Ort, wo eine Sitzung stattfindet,* all imply the exercise of authority. *Wenn hier einer bestimmt, wann wir losgehen, dann bin ich das. Der Chef bestimmt, wer versetzt wird. Bestimme selbst den Tag deines Besuchs!* *Bestimmen über* means 'to have the power of decision with regard to people or thgs.' *Er hat über mich/über mein Geld nicht zu bestimmen.* *Bestimmen* thus translates **determine** or **fix** with this implication.

> *Wir haben das Recht zu bestimmen, wie das Geld ausgegeben werden soll.*
> *Die Fakultät hat bestimmt, daß Doktoranden ihre Dissertationen innerhalb von fünf Jahren abschließen müssen,*

ii. Festlegen and **festsetzen**, which do not differ in meaning, suggest deciding and laying something down which others are obliged to comply with. Whatever is *festgelegt* is in effect just as binding as what is *bestimmt,* but while *bestimmen* implies the imposing of authority, *festlegen* and *festsetzen* need only suggest an agreement which, once acceded to, becomes binding. They are, therefore, less strong than *bestimmen. Man setzt eine Zeit/den Termin für eine Sitzung/den Ort eines Treffens/den Preis/die Höhe des Steuersatzes/Bedingungen* etc. *fest. Man legt die Reihenfolge der startenden Springer/das Programm/einen Termin/die Ausbildungsdauer* etc. *fest.* With *auf, festsetzen* is usual, *Man hat die Ausbildungsdauer auf drei Jahre/den Preis auf 5 000 Mark festgesetzt,* but *festlegen* is possible. In reply to *'Die Filme sind bereit—wir müssen nur noch die Reihenfolge festlegen, in der sie gezeigt werden',* someone might say, *'Bestimme du die Reihenfolge! Ich halte mich ganz zurück.'* The past part. *bestimmt* is not used after *sein* in this sense so that *Die Reihenfolge ist noch nicht genau festgelegt* is the only possibility.

> *Man hat den Beginn der Veranstaltung auf 15 Uhr festgesetzt.*
> *Wir müssen noch ein Datum für das nächste Treffen festsetzen/den Tag der Hochzeit festlegen.*
> *Da in diesem Betrieb mit flexibler Arbeitszeit gearbeitet wird, kann sich jeder seinen Arbeitsbeginn selber festlegen.* *Die Partei legte ihren Kurs fest.*

3. Bestimmen is the equivalent of **determine** meaning 'to fix or decide causally', 'to be the cause of' or 'to bring about as a result'. *Seine religiösen Überzeugungen bestimmen sein Verhalten.* A related meaning is 'to influence decisively'. *In der verwüsteten und ausgeplünderten Stadt bestimmte der Kampf ums Überleben die Existenz des einzelnen und der Gemeinschaft.*

> *Die Nachfrage bestimmt den Preis.* *Die Größe unserer Füße bestimmt unsere Schuhgröße.*
> *Unsere Erfahrungen bestimmen unsere Handlungen.*
> *Bestimmen Erbanlagen und Umgebung den Charakter eines Menschen?*

4. Determine and **bestimmen** also express the meaning 'to ascertain definitely by observation, examination, calculation, etc. a point previously unknown or uncertain'. *Der Wert von x in der Gleichung ist zu bestimmen. Bestimmen* often implies a scientific investigation or procedure to find something out. *Wie bestimmen Astronomen die Entfernung der Sterne von der Erde?* An alternative is one sense of **feststellen**. Cf. DISCOVER 2. iii. *Man stellt die Windrichtung/die Ursache einer Krankheit fest.*

Oft ist es schwer, die genaue Bedeutung eines Wortes in einem mittelalterlichen Text zu bestimmen.
Die Höhe eines Bergs kann man mit Hilfe der Trigonometrie bestimmen.
Eine gerichtsmedizinische Untersuchung stellte [die] Zeit und [die] Ursache des Todes fest.

5. Determine also means 'to resolve definitely to do sth.' and is translated by equivalents of DECIDE, usually **sich entschließen** or **beschließen**. **Be determined** to do sth. is *entschlossen sein*.

Wann hat sich Thoreau dazu entschlossen, Schriftsteller zu werden? Also beschlossen.
Sie war entschlossen, einen reichen Mann zu heiraten.
Er war entschlossen, nichts mehr mit seinen früheren Bekannten zu tun zu haben.

die v. Some equivalents.

1. i. The main v. meaning 'to die' in reference to human beings, animals, and plants is **sterben**. *Er starb durch einen Autounfall. Der alte Hund ist gestorben. Der Wald/Der Baum stirbt.* **Versterben** expresses the same meaning, but is restricted to people. It is a refined or genteel word which sounds impersonal, detached, respectful, and official. It is usual in *Todesanzeigen* in newspapers and in similar announcements, but only in the past tenses. The past part. is the equivalent of *late* or *deceased*. Thus *der/die Verstorbene*.

Nach kurzer Krankheit verstarb gestern im Alter von 65 Jahren unser verehrtes Vorstandsmitglied H. K. Müller.
Mein verstorbener Großvater pflegte in solchen Situationen 'Trau, schau, wem!' zu sagen.

ii. Sterben an is 'to die of' when this means 'to lose one's life through an illness'. *Immer mehr Menschen sterben an Lungenkrebs.*

iii. Sterben vor is 'to die of' when this means 'to experience a high degree of'. *Ich sterbe vor Langeweile/Angst/Neugier.* A syn. is *vor Hunger/Sehnsucht/Scham* **vergehen**. *Ich vergehe vor Durst.* With a few vs. **zu Tode** means 'extremely'. *Ich habe mich zu Tode geschämt/gelangweilt.*

Hoffentlich kommt bald was auf den Tisch—ich sterbe vor Hunger.
Ich bin/wäre vor Heimweh/Schmerz/Langeweile fast vergangen.

I'm dying for a drink is *Ich brauche dringend etw. zu trinken. I'm dying to know/find out* can be *Ich bin sehr gespannt, wie die Wahl ausgeht.* Cf. EAGER 2.

iv. Absterben means 'to die gradually or slowly'. It is now not used for human beings or animals, but it is found with parts of the body such as a limb. It is common in connection with plants and trees, whether the whole organism or parts of it are referred to. It is the usual word in the past part. for trees. *Abgestorbene Bäume.* It is also used for parts of the body which become numb or lose sensation through extreme cold (usually after *wie*) and sometimes for customs which die out. (In the latter context *aussterben* is the normal v. Cf. 2.)

Schon einige Monate nachdem das Gift in die Erde gelangt war, konnte man entlang seiner Ausdehnung sehen, wie der Wald abstarb. Or . . . wie Baum für Baum abstarb.
Wir müssen einige abgestorbene Äste abschlagen, weil sie herabzufallen drohen.
Sein rechter Arm war abgestorben und mußte amputiert werden.
Er hatte seine Füße stark unterkühlt—sie waren wie abgestorben.
Tal für Tal sterben Brauchtum und Sitten im Schwarzwald ab.

v. In one sense **eingehen** means 'to die'. Plants and animals can be the subj., but not human beings. It says nothing about the manner. *Der Baum/Die Pflanze/Das Kalb ist eingegangen.*

vi. There are numerous colloquial or slang expressions meaning 'to die', e.g. **abkratzen, ins Gras beißen, draufgehen, hopsgehen,** and one sense of **daran glauben müssen.**

'Was schadet es schon, wenn von den Bullen einer abkratzt?' dachte der Terrorist.

Es war klar, daß der Einsatz kein Zuckerlecken werden würde und daß einige von uns draufgehen/hopsgehen würden.

Trotz der Bunker haben wieder mehrere Soldaten im Sperrfeuer dran glauben müssen.

vii. Verenden is a stylistically neutral word applied to the death of bigger animals. *In dem strengen Winter ist viel Wild verendet.* **Verrecken** and **krepieren** are slang words meaning 'to die miserably or under wretched circumstances', primarily of animals, but also of human beings. When used in reference to human beings they express, in some cases, pity that people should die under such circumstances, but in others they show a lack of feeling.

Viele Tiere sind an der Seuche verendet.

Während der Dürre sind mir fast alle Schafe verreckt/krepiert/verendet.

Man kann die Männer doch nicht hier vor der Tür des Feldlazaretts verrecken lassen!

Die Kameraden sind in einem sinnlosen Kampf einfach krepiert.

'Wenn du nicht genau machst, was ich dir sage, lasse ich dich hier mitten in der Wüste ohne einen Tropfen Wasser verrecken.'

Von mir aus sollen sie doch verrecken. (Could refer to animals or people.)

2. Aussterben is 'to die out' or 'to become extinct'. *Viele Tier- und Pflanzenarten sind in den letzten Jahrzehnten ausgestorben, und andere sind noch vom Austerben bedroht. Diese Sitte stirbt aus.*

3. Die away. For sounds which die away, there are two vs., **abklingen** and *verklingen*. **Abklingen** denotes the interval between very loud and barely perceptible, and **verklingen** is applied to the transition from soft to nothing. **Sich verlieren** is also used for sounds.

Der tosende Beifall klang erst nach vier Vorhängen allmählich ab.

Seine Schritte verklangen langsam in den weiten Fluren.

Als der Zug sich immer mehr entfernte, verlor sich das Geräusch der Räder.

different, various, variable *adjs.*

1. In one sense **different** states that two or more things are unlike or not the same. *These two insects are different.*

i. This concept is expressed both by **verschieden** and **anders**, which differ only syntactically. With a pl. subj. or words implying at least two persons or things, *verschieden* is used; with a sing. subj., *anders*. This means that the idea of many sents. containing *verschieden* can be expressed by *anders* if the sent. is altered. Thus *A und B sind verschieden*, but *A ist anders als B. Wir sind verschiedener Meinung über diese Sache*, but *Ich bin über diese Sache anderer Meinung als du. Wir haben verschiedene Ansichten über diese Frage*, but *Ich habe eine andere Ansicht über diese Frage als du* or *Meine Ansicht über diese Frage ist anders als deine.* The same distinction holds for their use as advs. *Die beiden reagierten verschieden auf den Vorfall*, but *A reagierte anders als B.* While *verschieden* states that two or more things are not alike, *anders* is used when a comparison or contrast with s.o./sth. else is made. *Darüber denke ich anders [als er].* Two or more things are said to be *verschieden lang/groß*, etc., different in length or size.

Diese beiden Insekten sind nur der Größe nach verschieden.

Insekt A ist nach Farbe und Form anders als Insekt B.

Das Klima in den beiden Orten ist verschieden. Hier ist das Klima anders als dort.

ii. Verschieden is found with a sing. subj., but at least two points of comparison are implied. In *Die Spielweise der beiden Mannschaften ist verschieden*, two different ways of playing are implied. *Das ist von Fall zu Fall verschieden* and *Das ist individuell* *verschieden* also imply at least two people or things which are different. *Darüber kann man verschieden denken* means that different people have different ways of interpreting or considering it.

iii. In the examples given in 1. i **anders** is followed by **als**. *Als* need not always be expressed. *Ich hatte eine bestimmte Vorstellung von den Verhältnissen dort, fand aber, als ich ankam, daß sie ganz anders waren. Anders als* is the usual way of stating that one person or thing is different from another or others. The subj. can also be pl., but this implies that, although a number of things or people are referred to, they form one group which differs from another group. *Diese Bienen sind anders als die ersten, die wir gesehen haben.* As an adv.: *Wir haben die Arbeit anders angepackt als ihr.* **Verschieden von** is a syn. of *anders als* and need not have a pl. subj., but it is restricted to formal language. *Insekt A ist verschieden von Insekt B.*

    Ich bin ganz anders als du denkst.   *Der Fall liegt anders, als man ihn mir dargestellt hat.*

iv. Anders is used when s.o./sth. has changed in comparison with a previous time whether the subj. is sing. or pl. *Er ist inzwischen ganz anders geworden. Die Insekten sind jetzt anders als vor zwei Tagen.*

2. In its second meaning, **different** does not state that two things are not alike, but that one thing is a separate entity from another. It is closely related either to **various** or to *another*. In some cases, **different** and **various** are interchangeable. *He studied the behaviour of children in different/various age groups. They are sold in different/various colours.* In other cases, they are not interchangeable because they have different meanings. *We (= she and I) shop in different supermarkets* is not the same as *We shop in various supermarkets.*

i. When **different** and **various** are interchangeable, both are expressed by **verschiedene**. *Er untersucht das Verhalten von Kindern in verschiedenen Altersgruppen. Dieses Modell wird in verschiedenen Farben angeboten.*

ii. Where **different** and **various** are not interchangeable, the sense needs to be expressed by **anders**, usually with a sing. subj., as it is unambiguous. In *Wir kaufen in verschiedenen Supermärkten ein, verschiedenen* would normally be understood as 'various', so that to avoid ambiguity it is necessary to formulate the thought as *Ich kaufe in einem anderen Supermarkt ein [als sie].*

iii. When **different** and *another* are interchangeable, both are **anders**. *She put on a different/another dress* both become *Sie zog ein anderes Kleid an. Da ihm das erste Buch nicht gefiel, nahm er ein anderes,* he took a different/another one. In E., only **different**, not *another*, can be qualified by an adv. *That is another matter [entirely]* but *a completely different matter. Anders* can be qualified, so that both E. versions become *Das ist eine ganz andere Angelegenheit.*

3. Unterschiedlich basically means 'varying' or 'variable'. *Die Leistungen dieses Schülers sind unterschiedlich,* his marks vary between subjects. *Die Qualität der Produkte ist recht unterschiedlich. Unterschiedlich* is also a syn. of *verschieden* = 'different[ly]'. *Gebiete von verschiedener/unterschiedlicher Größe. Wir sind unterschiedlicher/verschiedener Meinung darüber.* Although *unterschiedlich* has enjoyed a vogue in recent years, it is only really necessary to use it to avoid a clash of meaning with *verschiedene* = 'various'. In *Verschiedene Ansichten wurden vertreten* it could, in theory, mean 'various' or 'different', but would normally be taken to mean 'various'. *Unterschiedliche Ansichten* makes it clear that the views differed and could be translated as *differing* as well as *different.*

    Ein Lehrer sollte Schüler nicht unterschiedlich behandeln.

    Die Studenten haben verschiedene Lösungen vorgeschlagen (various). *Sie haben unterschiedliche Lösungen vorgeschlagen* (different).

difficult *adj.* Some uses of **hard** *adj. Schwer* and *schwierig* overlap in the meaning 'causing trouble and exertion', 'requiring effort', or 'not of a simple nature', but differ sometimes in the contexts in which they are used, sometimes in implication, and sometimes syntactically.

i. Schwer alone is used in reference to physical work. *Auf dem Bauernhof mußte ich schwer arbeiten. Er ist schwere, körperliche Arbeit gewohnt. Trotz der Mechanisierung ist der Beruf eines Bergmanns noch sehr schwer. Bis vor kurzem dachte man, diese Arbeit wäre für Frauen zu schwer.*

ii. Schwierig alone is applied to people who are difficult, hard to please or satisfy, or not easy to get on with. *Er ist ein schwieriger Mensch/Charakter. Ich habe einige schwierige Kinder in meiner Klasse. Sie sieht sich nach einem weniger schwierigen Verehrer um. Sie wurde mit zunehmendem Alter immer schwieriger. War er denn immer so schwierig?* When an infin. follows, the syntactic rules explained in vi apply. *She is difficult to please* is *Es ist schwer/schwierig, ihr zu gefallen. He is a difficult man to get on with: Es ist schwer/schwierig, gut mit ihm auszukommen.* [*Not*] *to be difficult about food* is [*keine*] *Schwierigkeiten wegen des Essens machen.*

iii. Both **schwer** and **schwierig** mean 'hard to understand or follow'. *Das verstehe ich nicht—es ist für mich zu schwer/schwierig. Ein schwerer/schwieriger Text. Dieser Roman ist eine schwierige Lektüre,* is difficult reading.

iv. Both **schwer** and **schwierig** express the sense 'not simple and requiring effort', but are not always interchangeable. *Schwierig* often expresses the nuance that something is complex or involved, or contains obstructions and complicating factors. Non-physical work can be *schwer* and *schwierig*, as can *eine Aufgabe, eine Prüfung, eine Übersetzung,* and *eine Entscheidung. Ein schweres Amt* and *ein schwerer Kampf* are the normal expressions, as are *ein schwieriges Unternehmen, ein schwieriger Fall, schwierige Verhandlungen, ein schwieriges Problem, ein schwieriges Thema,* and *eine schwierige Angelegenheit. Eine schwere Frage* is 'a question that is hard to answer', *eine schwierige Frage* is 'a difficult issue'.

v. With regard to situations and conditions, **schwierig** means 'hard to deal with' and/or 'having unpleasant consequences'. *Sie befindet sich in einer sehr schwierigen Lage/Situation. Die Verhältnisse hier sind sehr schwierig geworden.* **Schwer** often means 'hard' in the sense 'difficult to bear and/or economically bad'. *Sie hat ein schweres Leben hinter sich* and *Sie hat es im Leben schwer gehabt,* has had a hard life. *Schwere Zeiten. Sie haben viel Schweres durchgemacht. Eine Operation ist schwer für den Patienten, schwierig für den Chirurgen. Das Schwerste haben wir schon überwunden/überstanden/hinter uns.* (Usual transl. *the worst.*) *Einen schweren Stand haben* means 'to have a hard time of it'.

vi. With an infin. **schwer** is the usual word, whether a n. or *es* is the subj. *Es ist schwer zu sagen, wer gewinnen wird. Die Frage ist schwer zu beantworten. Die Maschine ist schwer zu bedienen. Ich stelle es mir sehr schwer vor, den Premierminister persönlich zu sprechen. Es war nicht schwer für uns, unsere Pläne durchzusetzen. Die beiden Begriffe sind schwer zu unterscheiden. Es ist schwer, die beiden Begriffe zu unterscheiden.* **Schwierig** is also occasionally found after *es*. It is somewhat stronger than *schwer* and may suggest an involved and complicated process. *Es war [äußerst] schwierig, das Geschäft vor dem Konkurs zu retten. Es ist schwierig/schwer, eine befriedigende Antwort auf eine so komplizierte Frage zu genen.* With *zu* and the present part., *schwer* is normal, but *schwierig* is also possible. *Ein schwierig zu lösendes Problem* is less common than *ein [nur] schwer zu lösendes Problem.* (*Nur schwer* means 'only with difficulty'. *Ich konnte mich nur schwer von dieser Stadt trennen.*)

vii. Etw. fällt jmdm. schwer, 'someone finds something difficult', is an idiom. *Die*

Trennung von ihrer Familie fiel ihr schwer. Es fällt mir schwer, solches Verhalten zu erklären. Du mußt hingehen, auch wenn es dir schwerfällt.

disappear, vanish vs.

1. The everyday equivalent of both words is *verschwinden*. If the nuance conveyed by **vanish**, i.e. 'to disappear in a rapid and mysterious way', is important, it can be conveyed by adding *plötzlich, auf geheimnisvolle Weise*, or similar words. **Verschwinden** means 'to cease to be visible', 'to pass from s.o.'s sight', and is used both for people and things. *Sie verschwand um die Ecke. Er verschwand im Gewühl/in der Menschmenge. Sie verschwanden zwischen den Bäumen. Sie sah dem Flugzeug nach, bis es in der Ferne verschwunden war. Der Mond verschwand hinter einer Wolke. Als der Anführer der Herde etwa zwei Drittel des Flusses durchschwommen hatte, sah ich ihn plötzlich sinken und [vor meinen Augen] verschwinden. Der Zauberer ließ allerlei Gegenstände verschwinden.* It is used of people who disappear or drop out of the public eye, particularly in the expression *von der Bildfläche verschwinden. Nach der Wahlniederlage verschwand dieser Politiker von der Bildfläche/aus dem öffentlichen Leben. Jmd. verschwindet aus dem Leben eines anderen.* It is also used for customs, fashions, beliefs, empires, species, etc. which pass away.

> *Dieser alte Aberglauben ist gänzlich verschwunden.*   *Die Mode ist schnell verschwunden.*
> *Das Verschwinden dieses einst mächtigen Reiches um etwa 1400 n. Chr. ist ein Rätsel.*
> *Wir müssen das Verschwinden weiterer alter Bauten dieser Art verhindern.*
> *Die letzten Spuren zivilisierten Verhaltens waren verschwunden.*
> *Pflanzen- und Tierarten sind verschwunden, um für besser angepaßte Arten Platz zu machen.*

Verschwinden is common, particularly in colloquial speech, in the meaning 'to cease to be present', 'get out of s.o.'s sight'. *Verschwinde!* is often used like *Go away!* or *Clear out! Gleich nach dem Essen sind sie von der Party verschwunden. Er hatte sie zum Ball eingeladen, doch nach drei oder vier Tänzen verschwand er mit einigen Freunden in die Bar.*

2. Entschwinden, to which *den Augen* is often added, suggests a slow disappearing from sight, but it has a poetical and archaic ring. Apart from quotations, like *O alte Burschenherrlichkeit, wohin bist du entschwunden?*, it is only rarely found in this sense in the current language. *Das Schiff segelte davon und entschwand schließlich meinen Augen.* It is occasionally used for things which disappear from one's memory, *Dieser Name war mir aus dem Gedächtnis entschwunden*, and for the disappearance of mental states, *Plötzlich entschwand alle Furcht.*

> *Die Liebe entschwand, und zurück blieb nur noch Gleichgültigkeit.*
> *Er trauerte den entschwundenen Illusionen nach.*   *Das Glück entschwand schnell.*

3. The usual v. for the waning, fading, or disappearing of mental states and sensations is **vergehen** although **verschwinden** is possible. *Meine Angst ist plötzlich vergangen/verschwunden.*

> *Die Hoffnung auf ein Wiedersehen verging, und mit ihr auch die Sehnsucht.*
> *Die Freude daran ist mir vergangen.*   *Die Schmerzen sind schon vergangen.*

Alternatives. **Schwinden**, which is now confined to the written language, means, when applied to stores and reserves, 'to dwindle or decrease'. *Meine Barschaft/Die Vorräte/Die Reserven schwinden von Tag zu Tag mehr.* It is also used for the waning or disappearing of mental states and influence. *Ihm schwand immer mehr die Hoffnung/der Mut. Sein Einfluß/Das Mißtrauen schwand nach and nach. Ihr schwanden die Sinne*, 'she fainted', occurs occasionally. *Plötzlich war das Lächeln von ihrem Gesicht geschwunden* is elevated literary style. *Verschwinden* is the everyday word. *Im Schwinden begriffen*, 'to be on the wane/waning', is more common. *Der Erfolg und die Popularität des Sängers waren im Schwinden begriffen.* **Dahinschwinden** is also an elevated v., but perhaps a more common one than *schwinden* and *entschwinden;* it is mainly applied to the waning and disappearance of mental states, *Sein Interesse/Sein Groll schwand dahin,* sometimes to the dwindling of supplies, *Die Vorräte schwanden dahin.*

Die Erinnerung an diese Ereignisse schwand allmählich aus ihrem Gedächtnis.
Sein Ruhm ist im Schwinden begriffen. *Ihre guten Vorsätze sind schnell dahingeschwunden.*
Ihre Sicherheit verschwand plötzlich/schwand plötzlich dahin.
Seine Hoffnung ist fast schon völlig dahingeschwunden.

discover *v.* One sense of **find** *v.* **find out** *v.* One sense of **learn** *v.*

1. i. Discover meaning 'to find, come upon, or obtain sight or knowledge of sth. previously unknown' when talking of explorers, scientists, researchers, etc. is **entdecken.** *Im Jahre 1895 entdeckte Wilhelm Röntgen die sogenannten X- oder Röntgenstrahlen. 1642 entdeckte Abel Tasman Tasmanien.*

Mit Hilfe des von Lippeschey erfundenen Fernrohrs hat Galilei die Jupitermonde entdeckt.
Ein großes Uranvorkommen wurde vor kurzem in Südaustralien entdeckt.

ii. The sense of both **discover** and **entdecken** has been extended to finding something hidden or sought, and to coming across s.o./sth. unexpectedly, for which **find** and **finden** can also be used. *Schließlich entdeckte sie ihn und seinen Wagen in einer Seitenstraße. Die Kinder entdeckten ein Vogelnest in einer Hecke. Sie entdeckte in sich eine Fähigkeit, die sie nie geahnt hatte. Ich entdeckte ihn zufällig unter den Gästen. Ich entdeckte, daß man mich belogen hatte.*

iii. Auffinden means 'to discover or find people or thgs. lost or missing'. In contrast to the first sense of *entdecken,* it implies that they are known to exist, but that their whereabouts are unknown. *Man hat die vermißten Kinder in einer kleinen Höhle aufgefunden. Der Verunglückte wurde bewußtlos aufgefunden. Der Schlüssel ist nirgendwo aufzufinden.* Usually *man entdeckt* or *findet eine Spur,* trace. *Man hat noch keine Spur von den vermißten Wanderern entdeckt/gefunden.* Cf. FIND.

2. Find out and **discover** = 'to ascertain a piece of information'.

i. Ausfindig machen implies a deliberate effort and a keen and skilful search to discover something which is hidden or unknown or about which one would like certainty. The objs. are a wide range of things. *Man macht jmds. Adresse/ein Quartier/ein Versteck/den Eigentümer von etw./ein anderes Mittel/Mittel und Wege etc. ausfindig. Ich habe eine Dame ausfindig gemacht, die den polnischen Text übersetzen kann.* It is also used with a clause. *Wir versuchen, ausfindig zu machen, wo das Geld geblieben ist/wer ihm dabei geholfen hat/wo sie sich aufhalten.*

ii. Ermitteln, which also means 'to INVESTIGATE', is a syn. of *ausfindig machen,* but it is more formal. People in some official position are generally its subj., often the police or in Germany *der Staatsanwalt,* who by a skilful search and investigation bring facts to light. Because it refers to an important activity, it is often best translated as *establish* or *ascertain facts, s.o.'s whereabouts, identity,* etc. although it expresses the same sense as **find out** or **discover.**

Alle Versuche der Polizei, den Täter/sein Versteck/die Wahrheit zu ermitteln, schlugen fehl.
Es dauerte sehr lange, bis die Polizei ihn und seinen Wohnsitz ermittelt hatte.
Es ließ sich nicht mehr ermitteln, wohin die Familie gezogen war.
Als die Bachgesellschaft Ende des vorigen Jahrhunderts ein Bachhaus gründen wollte, ließ sich nicht mehr ermitteln, in welchem Haus Bach geboren worden war.

iii. In one of its senses, **feststellen** also means 'to establish, ascertain, or find out' a fact, someone's whereabouts, etc. It is also a fairly formal word.

Die Jungen haben zuerst festgestellt, in welchem Zimmer der Dieb wohnte.
Wie können wir feststellen, ob sie die Wahrheit sagt?

Er glaubte, mit Genauigkeit feststellen zu können, was die Konkurrenz plante.
Ich hoffe, seinen Aufenthaltsort/seine Adresse/seinen Verbleib bald festzustellen.

iv. The equivalents in everyday language are **herausfinden**, 'to find out', and **herausbekommen** and **herauskriegen**, 'to find out, solve, work out, find the answer to'. The last two are more colloquial than the first. The result can be achieved by search, enquiry, or logical deduction from known facts, or by chance.

Ich habe noch nicht herausbekommen, wie man den Apparat bedient.
Hast du herausgekriegt, wieviel Herr Müller verdient?
Der Forscher wollte das Geheimnis der Inschrift um jeden Preis herausbekommen.
Die Post findet immer die richtige Anschrift heraus.
Es dauerte nicht lange, bis die Techniker den Grund der Störung herausgefunden hatten.
Nach langem Suchen habe ich herausgefunden, wo er sich herumgetrieben hat.

v. Hinter etw. kommen means 'to find out or discover (the truth about) sth.' which is not necessarily bad, but which the other person would like to keep secret. When a clause follows, it becomes **dahinterkommen**. *Ich bin hinter seine Pläne gekommen* or *Ich bin dahintergekommen, was er vorhatte.*

Sie ist hinter sein Geheimnis gekommen.   *Ich bin dahintergekommen, daß sie gelogen hat.*

3. Learn [of/about] is a syn. of **find out** in sents. like *How did you learn [of] his whereabouts? The Prime Minister only learnt of the incident last week. We learnt that she was ill.* **Erfahren** means 'to come by or receive information or news' when one either finds something out through questions or learns it by chance in conversation or reading. *Durch Zufall*, 'by chance', may be added. *Erfahren* takes *das, etw., alles, nichts, Einzelheiten, eine Nachricht*, or a clause as obj.

Er hat erst später von dem Vorfall erfahren.   *Von wem haben sie das erfahren?*
Ich habe es von einem Freund/aus der Zeitung erfahren.
Wenn wir uns sehen, erzähle ich dir, was ich über den Fall erfahren habe.
Wo kann ich erfahren, wann der nächste Bus fährt?
Wir haben noch keine Einzelheiten erfahren.   *Ich habe durch Zufall erfahren, daß sie krank ist.*

distance *n.* distant *adj.*

1. i. When **distance** denotes a place or area which is near the limit of vision, as in *In the distance you can see a village*, the equivalent is **die Ferne**.

In der Ferne sehen Sie ein Dorf und eine Kirche.   *Schwarze Wolken zogen in der Ferne auf.*

In literary language and some fixed expressions, *die Ferne* also means 'a place or country far away'. *Ich überbringe Ihnen Grüße aus der Ferne. Mit zwanzig Jahren zog er in die Ferne.* (One transl.: '. . . into the wide world'.) *Die Ferne* can refer to a period of time which lies at a great distance in the past or in the future. *Dieses Ereignis rückt immer mehr in die Ferne*, the time separating us from it is becoming greater and greater, it is becoming more and more remote. *Die Verwirklung dieser Pläne liegt noch in weiter Ferne*, lies in the distant future. *Diese Aussicht ist in die Ferne gerückt*, has become remote.

ii. *I looked at the picture* **from a distance** is *Ich betrachtete das Bild* **von weitem. Aus der Ferne** or **von fern** are also used with *sehen* etc., but imply a greater distance.

2. Distance meaning 'the length of space lying between any two objects' is expressed by *der Abstand* and *die Entfernung*.

i. Whereas *die Ferne* is an unspecified distance away, **die Entfernung** designates a precise distance and is the usual word if one is giving the distance between two towns etc. or from one place to another. With preps., *Entfernung*, when compared with *Ferne*, also implies a relatively specific distance. *Bei/Aus dieser Entfernung kann man nichts Genaues erkennen. Aus der Ferne* is much less exact.

Die Entfernung zwischen Kassel und Hannover beträgt 155 Kilometer.

Wie berechnen die Astronomen die Entfernung eines Sterns von der Erde?
Die Entfernung zur nächsten Ortschaft beträgt acht Kilometer.
Hast du die Entfernung zwischen deinem Haus und der Schule gemessen oder nur geschätzt?
Wir beobachteten alles aus einiger Entfernung. *Er folgte ihr in kurzer Entfernung.*
Hunde sehen gut auch auf eine große Entfernung.
Ich kann nur auf kurze Entfernungen gut sehen—ich habe eine Brille für die Ferne.

ii. Der Abstand is used when two or more persons or things form an order of some kind or belong together. It is thus the usual word when the distance apart of, or the gap or space between, a number of things is referred to. *Der Abstand der Häuser voneinander beträgt nur wenige Meter. Die Bäume wurden in Abständen von je zehn Metern gepflanzt. Die Soldaten gingen in Abständen von fünf Metern vor. Abstand* and *Entfernung* could occur in the same sent. *Mit zunehmender Entfernung von der Sonne wird der Abstand zwischen den Planeten größer. Abstand* is used for the distance between cars on the road. *Abstand halten* means 'to keep the proper distance from the car ahead'. When two persons or objects are involved, both *Abstand* and *Entfernung* occur: *Die Entfernung zwischen der Erde und der Sonne* or *der Abstand der Erde von der Sonne. Er folgte ihr in einer Entfernung/einem Abstand von fünfzig Metern. Abstand* tends to be used for very short distances, *der Abstand zwischen den Atomen,* and is usual with parts of the body, *der Abstand zwischen den Augen,* and in technical contexts. There are the compounds: *Der Radabstand, der Gleisabstand, der Balkenabstand, der Zeilenabstand.* **Die Distanz** also exists. *Die Distanz zwischen den beiden Punkten beträgt 200 Meter.* It is a fairly learned word except in the language of sport. *Ein Lauf über eine Distanz von 1 000 Metern. Die Reiter hatten die Hälfte der Distanz zurückgelegt.*

iii. Der Abstand also means 'an interval in time'. *Die Läufer starten in Abständen von 15 Sekunden.*

3. i. Der Abstand translates *distance* when this refers to reserve in relations between people. **Die Distanz** also has this sense, but is often restricted to an intentional lack of friendliness.

Man sollte den angemessenen Abstand wahren/halten.

Indem er ziemlich förmlich spricht, wahrt er eine gewisse Distanz zwischen sich und seinem Gesprächspartner.

ii. Der Abstand also means 'detachment', either in judging what one has experienced or in depicting events. **Die Distanz** is a more learned syn. *Der Historiker muß die Ereignisse mit Distanz sehen und darstellen.*

Es fehlt ihr noch der innere Abstand zu den Erlebnissen der letzten Zeit.

Er hatte noch nicht den nötigen Abstand, um sachlich über das Geschehen reden zu können.

4. To translate *the distance to be covered,* die Entfernung can be used, but **die Strecke** is also common. In such contexts it means 'a stretch of road, railway line, etc.' It conjures up a picture of the actual road etc., not the number of kilometres.

Wir können die Strecke von Hannover nach Bremen in anderthalb Stunden zurücklegen.

Die Entfernung von Sydney bis Melbourne beträgt 950 Kilometer, aber die Strecke ist leicht zu befahren.

Wir sind eine Strecke von zehn Kilometern marschiert.

Der Zug war schon eine gute Strecke entfernt (a good distance).

Das ist eine ziemliche/ordentliche/ungeheure Strecke [bis dahin].

Wir sind eine gute/kleine/große Strecke gefahren. *Ich bin eine Strecke mit ihr gegangen.*

Ihr seid, wie ich höre, im Urlaub unwahrscheinliche Strecken/Entfernungen gefahren.

5. E. expressions like *The shops are only a short distance from here* or *. . . are no distance away* are mostly translated as the idea. *Von hier bis zur Uni. ist keine Entfernung* is close to the second E. expression. Alternatives when this construction is not possible are *Die Geschäfte/Läden sind nicht sehr weit [von hier]* or *. . . sind gar nicht weit* [weg/entfernt]. Similarly *He lives within easy distance of his work: Er wohnt gar nicht weit vom Arbeitsplatz. The school is within walking distance: Die Schule ist gut zu Fuß zu erreichen.* An alternative for [only] *a short distance away* is [ganz] *in der Nähe: Der nächste Briefkasten ist ganz in der Nähe.*

6. Distant.

i. With precise distances, **entfernt** is used. It corresponds to **distant**, *Er arbeitet in einem entfernten Teil des Landes,* but is also used to state a distance where E. has *away* or, in a question, *far. Das nächste Dorf ist fünf Kilometer entfernt. Das Dorf ist acht Kilometer von Göttingen entfernt. Wie weit ist das nächste Dorf entfernt? Wie weit ist Adorf von Behausen entfernt?* But *Wie weit ist es bis zum nächsten Dorf?* and *Wie weit ist es von Adorf bis Behausen?* When the sent. contains *von hier*, entfernt is optional. *Das Dorf ist fünf Kilometer von hier [entfernt].* **Weg** is used with *weit* like *away. Die Schule ist nicht sehr weit weg. Weg* is heard in speech with distances, but *entfernt* is usual in writing. *Das Dorf ist neun Kilometer weg/entfernt.* **Fern** is used in imprecise statements, but has a poetic ring. It is, however, common in the phrs. *von fern* and *von nah und fern,* and to refer to the distant past or future. It forms numerous compounds: *der Fernfahrer, das Ferngespräch, das Fernsehen, das Fernrohr, die Fernbedienung, die Fernlenkung,* etc.

> *Er stand ein Stück entfernt/weg vom Menschengetümmel.*
> *Er ist ein so begeisterter Bergsteiger, daß er zum entferntesten Punkt der Erde fahren würde, wenn sich dort ein hoher Berg befände.*
> *Er träumt von fernen Ländern/einer fernen Insel in der Südsee.*
> *Von fern konnte ich ihre Stimmen hören.*   *Die Besucher kamen von nah und fern.*
> *Die alten Männer tauschten Erinnerungen aus fernen Zeiten aus.*
> *Das ist ein Plan für die ferne Zukunft.*

ii. Entfernt is applied to a distant or slight resemblance and a distant relative. *Eine entfernte Ähnlichkeit.*

> *Sie ist eine entfernte Verwandte von mir.*   *Sie ist entfernt mit mir verwandt.*

dive *v.* **Dive** from a height above the surface of the water is **springen**. It is thus used for diving from a diving-board or the bank of a river, and for diving as a sport. *Springen* also means 'to jump', but the context usually makes it clear which is meant. To distinguish *He jumped into the river* from *He dived into the river* it is possible to use *Er sprang mit den Füßen zuerst in den Fluß,* but it would be unusual. **Tauchen** implies that someone is in the water, goes under the surface, and there moves along. This can be carried out either by holding one's breath or by using a diving suit or other diving equipment. It concentrates attention on the length of time someone stays under the water and on the distance moved or dived. The momentary act of going under the water is called **untertauchen**. *Ein Unterseeboot taucht unter,* 'submerges or dives', but when a distance or time is given the v. is *tauchen. Dieses Unterseeboot kann bis 500 Meter Tiefe tauchen* or *hat mehrere Tage getaucht. Untertauchen* also takes an obj. and means 'to duck (s.o.)'. *Beim Schwimmen hat er die Freundin zum Spaß untergetaucht, was sie ihm aber ziemlich übelgenommen hat.*

> *Sie ist vom Zehnmeterbrett gesprungen.*   *Er ist von der Steilküste ins Meer gesprungen.*
> *Sie kann drei Minuten tauchen, ohne ein Tauchgerät zu benutzen.*
> *Er ist gerade untergetaucht.*   *Er ist fünf Meter tief getaucht.*

divide, distribute, share *vs.* Some uses.

1. The general term is *teilen,* which means both 'to divide' and 'to share'.
i. When **teilen** means 'to divide', the division can be natural or man-made; *teilen* implies nothing more than that a unity does not exist or no longer exists.

Sie teilte den Kuchen in zwölf Stücke.   *Man hat den großen Raum in zwei kleinere geteilt.*
Der Fluß teilt das Tal in zwei Hälften.   *Durch diese Umstände wurde die Familie geteilt.*

Divide used intr., as in *The marchers divided into two groups*, must be **sich teilen**.
An der Ecke teilten sich die Marschierenden in zwei Gruppen.
Der Weg teilte sich, und sie waren im Unklaren über den richtigen.

ii. When it means 'to share', **teilen** is both trans., *Sie hat ihr Essen mit mir geteilt* or *Es ärgerte ihn, den Tisch mit mir zu teilen*, and intr., *Wir haben immer redlich [miteinander] geteilt*.

iii. Aufteilen means 'to divide up a whole into smaller parts and give his/her portion to each pers. entitled to a share'. It is often followed by *unter*. *Sie hat den Kuchen [unter die Kinder] aufgeteilt* implies both cutting it into pieces and handing them out. *Teilen* is used when the number of pieces is stated. Cf. first sent. in 1. i.
Die Piraten teilten die Beute unter sich auf.
Das Land der Großgrundbesitzer wurde unter die Bauern aufgeteilt.

iv. Einteilen suggests a careful division according to some principle and can imply a classification. With time, money, or work as obj. and often the refl. dat., it suggests a careful plan so that everything is done on time or that the money etc. does not run out before more is due. *Teile dein Geld ein!* suggests not spending it all now so that none is left for later. *Teile dir die Zeit ein!*, plan how to use it so that everything fits in.
Die Stadt ist in vierzehn Bezirke eingeteilt.   *Man teilt die Pflanzen in Arten und Gattungen ein.*
Wenn ihr euch die Vorräte richtig einteilt, werden sie auch für den Rückweg reichen.

v. In reference to dividing up groups of people, **teilen**, **aufteilen**, and **einteilen** are used. *Man teilte die Klasse* states the fact that it has been divided. *Man teilte die Klasse in drei Gruppen auf* stresses the result. It implies that the division into groups serves some purpose and may suggest that the groups become independent. *Man teilte die Klasse in drei Gruppen ein* implies a division according to some principle, e.g. performance. Often the only difference is in perspective, so that all three occur in similar contexts.
Als man die Klasse teilte, wurde manche Freundschaft zerrissen.
Für das Spiel teilte der Sportlehrer die Schüler in vier gleichgroße Gruppen auf.
In der Orientierungsstufe werden die Schüler nach ihren einzelnen Leistungen in A-, B- und C-Kurse eingeteilt.
Da die Interessen der Reisenden sich als äußerst unterschiedlich erwiesen, wurden sie in drei Gruppen eingeteilt/aufgeteilt.

vi. Teilhaben an means 'to share in', 'to have a share in'. *Alle Bürger sollen am Wohlstand des Landes teilhaben. Der Restaurator ließ einige Studenten an seiner Arbeit teilhaben.*
Die Rentnerreform von 1957 wurde damit begründet, daß nicht alle Bevölkerungsgruppen am ökonomischen Aufstieg der Bundesrepublik teilgenommen hätten. Bundeskanzler Adenauer führte aus, es sei die Aufgabe der Bundesregierung, die wirtschaftliche Lage der Rentner, Invaliden, Waisenkinder und Hinterbliebeneen zu verbessern.
Der universale Konsum der industriellen Massenproduktion sorgt dafür, daß fast jedermann das Gefühl entwickeln kann, nicht mehr ganz unten zu sein, sondern an der Fülle und dem Luxus des Daseins teilhaben zu können

2. Divide denoting an arithmetical process is either **teilen** or **dividieren**. *By* is expressed by *durch*. *20 geteilt/dividiert durch 5 ist/ergibt 4.*

3. Austeilen and **verteilen** both mean 'to distribute'. *Flugblätter/Werbezettel verteilen* suggests standing somewhere and handing leaflets to anyone who comes along and is interested in taking one. *Austeilen* also means 'to hand out', but suggests that the number of recipients is limited, that everyone has the right to receive what is being handed out, and that each gets what is meant for him or her. *Man* *teilt die Post/das Essen/die Ration aus. Die Lehrerin teilt die Hefte/die Klassenarbeiten aus.* When things are distributed without each person being handed his or her own, *verteilen* is used. *Man verteilt Vorräte/Lebensmittel [an die Opfer der Katastrophe]/Eintrittskarten gratis an Studenten/die Tagesordnung einer Sitzung. Austeilen* is used if the people concerned are handed theirs individually. *Verteilen* is the usual v. in *Die Rollen in einem Theaterstück werden verteilt.* The refl. in *Menschen verteilen sich auf einer/über eine Fläche* means 'to distribute themselves or spread out over an area'. *Die Menschen verteilten sich über den ganzen Platz.*

> *Mehrere Studenten verteilen Flugblätter am Eingang zur Mensa.*
> *Um sein Taschengeld aufzubessern, verteilt er Werbezettel vom Einkaufszentrum.*
> *Beim Anpfiff verteilen sich die Spieler auf dem Fußballfeld.*
> *Die Gäste verteilten sich über alle Räume.*

4. Divide one thg. from another can only be **trennen**, to separate.
> *Der Bach trennt mein Land vom Nachbarhof.*
> *Die Wand, die die beiden Büros trennt, ist sehr dünn.*

5. The idea that something written falls, or is divided, into parts or sections is expressed by **zerfallen** or **sich gliedern in**. *Die Abhandlung zerfällt/gliedert sich in fünf Teile.*
> *Das Referat zerfällt/gliedert sich in sechs Abschnitte.*

do v. Both *tun* and *machen* are equivalents to **do** meaning 'carry out', 'perform and finish', 'be engaged in sth.', or 'take action'. Although *machen* is preferred in the spoken language, both can be used in many contexts. In a few cases only *tun* is possible. In some others it is preferred in the standard language.

1. With an interrogative or an indefinite expression as obj.

i. To ask what someone is doing at the moment, it is usual to use **machen**. *Was machst du gerade? Was tust du gerade?* is also possible, and, in a question which expresses no more than a desire for information, **tun** differs from *machen* only in being stylistically somewhat higher. *Was machen wir heute abend? Was macht sie in ihrer Freizeit? Was soll ich als Nächstes machen? Was macht ihr, falls es regnet? Was wollen Sie in der heutigen Grammatikstunde machen? Was macht er im Büro?* suggests either *What is his work?* or *What is he doing in the office?* When the question not only seeks information, but also implies a reproach, *tun* is usual. While *Was machst du da?* is quite neutral, *Was tust du da?* suggests a reproach, that the person addressed is doing something harmful or stupid. *Was tust du hier?* or *Was tut er hier?* suggests that the person should not be here or has no right to be here. *Wer hat das getan?* and *Was hat er denn getan?* imply wrong or foolish behaviour. *Du blutest ja. Was hast du gemacht?* is neutral. *Was hast du getan?* would be reproachful and be said, for example, to a boy who is always fighting or hurting himself. Unless the question is to be taken to be a reproach, it is best to use *machen*.

ii. Machen and **tun** are used when indefinite expressions such as *alles, viel, nichts, manches,* or *etwas* are obj. *Das machen wir am besten gleich. Die Kinder dürfen nicht alles machen, was ihnen einfällt. Tun* belongs to a higher plane stylistically and may suggest a more important action or activity. As the borderline is not clearly marked, both often occur in similar contexts, *machen* being the everyday word and *tun* sounding somewhat weightier or more refined. *Ich weiß nicht, was ich in diesem Fall machen/tun soll. Ich will sehen, was sich machen/tun läßt. Ich werde alles tun/machen, was du sagst. Er tat/machte, was ihm befohlen wurde. Sie macht, was sie will. Tu', was du willst! Das macht man doch nicht* and *So etw. tut man nicht* both mean that such behaviour is unacceptable. *Daran ist nichts mehr zu machen* and *Da ist nichts zu machen,* 'it can't

be altered', are fixed expressions. *Dagegen ist nichts zu machen* and *Dagegen kann man nichts tun*, 'nothing can be done about it', are also common. *Ich kann nichts für Sie tun* exists beside *Es läßt sich nichts machen*. So, *diese Arbeit ist/wäre getan* and *Die Arbeit war schnell getan* are often heard, but also *Wir haben die Arbeit schnell gemacht*. In reference to important or serious action, *Wir haben alles getan, was man tun konnte*, would be normal. With *etw.* + adj., both are found: *Er hat etw. Dummes/Verrücktes gemacht* and *Sie haben etw. Unverständliches getan*. Machen often relates to work. *Haben wir alles gemacht? Ich habe gestern nichts gemacht. Sie will immer alles alleine machen.* The following are more or less fixed expressions. *Ich will heute noch etw. tun. So, tu' doch was/etw.! Kann ich etw. für Sie tun? Sie haben alles getan, um die Niederlage zu verhindern. Ich habe alles getan, was in meiner Macht stand. Wir wollten einmal nichts tun.*
iii. There are cases in which only **tun** is used or in which it is usual. Apart from the sents. containing *ist zu machen* given in ii (*Daran ist nichts mehr zu machen* and *Da/Dagegen ist nichts zu machen*), tun is used with *zu*, mostly after *haben* and *es gibt*. *Wir haben heute viel zu tun. Wir hatten gestern wenig/nichts zu tun. Es gibt viel zu tun, packen wir es an! Dort gibt es noch manches zu tun.* Tun is used in the expressions *etw./nichts zu tun haben mit. Seine Gereiztheit hat wohl etw. mit seiner Arbeit zu tun. Seine Bemerkung hat mit dem Thema etw./nichts zu tun. Er hatte mit dem Einbruch nichts zu tun.* Tun is the usual v. in the following constructions. *Wenn du nichts Besseres zu tun hast, so komm' doch mit ins Kino! Ich habe Wichtigeres zu tun, als den ganzen Tag hier herumzusitzen. Er tut nichts als faulenzen/schimpfen.*
iv. **Tun** is used with an indefinite superlative. *I did my best* becomes *Ich habe mein Bestes getan. Obwohl er sein Bestes getan hatte, ist er doch durch die Prüfung gefallen.* There is the idiom *Wir haben unser Möglichstes getan, um ihnen zu helfen.* The E. idiom *His threats don't trouble me—let him do his worst!* could be translated as *Seine Drohungen kümmern mich nicht, soll er sie doch wahrmachen* or *soll er es doch versuchen!*
v. In certain expressions **tun** is normal. *Was kann ich für Sie tun? Was kann man tun, um ihnen zu helfen? Ich werde das nie wieder tun. Man tut, was man kann. Ich tue, was ich kann. Ich habe bei dem Umzug getan, was ich konnte. Tu', was du nicht lassen kannst! Leichter gesagt als getan.*

2. Machen, used with *mit*, means 'to do with or to'. Thus in *Was hast du mit meinem Fahrrad gemacht?*, *mit* could correspond to *with* and mean 'what have you done with it?—I lent it to you, and where is it?', or to *to* and mean 'what have you done to it?—it's broken'. *Was hast du mit deinem Bein gemacht?*

3. Do in the sense 'to carry sth. out', 'to achieve sth.', the manner often being stressed, is usually **machen**. *Keine Sorge, das werden wir schon machen. Wie willst du das machen? Wie macht man das? So wird's gemacht. Das habe ich alleine gemacht. Laß mich das machen! Laß mich nur machen! Das hast du richtig/falsch/gut/schlecht gemacht.* To a child: *Das hast du fein gemacht. Das machte sich von selbst*, came about by itself. *Das muß sich irgendwie machen lassen*, there must be some way of doing it. *Der Klempner sagte, er könnte die Reparatur unter 500 Mark nicht machen.* Although *Einer muß es machen* is common, at least in speech, tun can be also used.

4. Do refers to, or replaces, a v. which has just been used. *She plays better now than she did a year ago. He works in a factory as his father had also done. We went to Tasmania last summer as did two other families in our street. 'Who broke the window?'—'I did.'* **Tun** has this function, but it needs *das* or *es* or *was* = 'which'. *Du solltest deine Frau öfters ausführen, wie es andere auch tun. Wir müssen unsere Unkosten verringern, wie das andere Firmen auch tun. Ich habe ihm geraten, sofort zu verschwinden, was er auch tat.* Or *Das hat er auch getan*. Es can correspond to *so* in E. *Wenn du Lust hat mitzuspielen, dann tu' es doch!* **Tun** belongs to the standard language. In colloquial speech machen is also used. *Wenn die Kinder unbedingt auf die Bäume klettern wollen, dann sollen sie es auch tun/machen.* Although the E. sents. can be translated word for word, the equivalent of **do** is often omitted. *Er arbeitet in einer Fabrik, wie sein Vater es auch getan hatte* is quite correct, but *wie sein Vater auch* is mostly used. *Wie* means 'like'. Thus *Wir sind nach Tasmanien gefahren, wie zwei andere Familien in unserer Straße auch. Sie spielt besser als vor einem Jahr. 'Wer hat das Fenster zerbrochen?'—'Ich.'*

'Irgend jmd. muß mit ihm sprechen. Wollen Sie es tun?' 'Ich habe es schon getan' (also *gemacht*).
Heinz hatte besonnen gehandelt. Sein Bruder tat es aber nicht.
Er handelte nicht besonnen, wie sein Bruder es getan hatte.
Es sollte am nächsten Tag regnen, und das tat es auch.

5. Other vs. sometimes translated as **do**.
i. Anfangen can mean 'to do' in the sense 'to achieve or succeed in bringing about'. *Wie haben Sie es bloß angefangen? Er hat das schlau/geschickt/richtig/verkehrt angefangen.* Sometimes it is an exact syn. of *machen. Was können wir nachher anfangen?* It is mostly found with *nichts, wenig, etw., [nicht] viel* as obj., and with *können, wissen,* or *sein + zu* meaning 'to be able to make some use of or achieve sth. with'. The context is often not knowing what to do with something. *Mit dem komplizierten Gerät konnten sie nichts anfangen.*

Sie wußten nicht viel mit ihrer Freizeit anzufangen.   *Mit ihm ist [heute] nichts anzufangen.*
Sie wissen nicht, was sie mit dem Zeug anfangen sollen.

ii. In one sense **anstellen** means 'to do, or to get up to, sth. not allowed'. It implies something stupid that the person, usually a child, does while not being observed. *Wenn man die Kinder allein läßt, stellen sie immer etw. an. Was hast du da nun wieder angestellt?*

iii. Treiben is used in the sense of 'do' in familiar speech, i.e. among people between whom a close relationship exists. It often, though not always, suggests an activity which goes on for some time. *Machen* would be used in other circumstances. For sport cf. 8. iii.

Was habt ihr in den Ferien/bei dem schlechten Wetter getrieben?
Was treibst du hier?
Was treibst du den ganzen Tag/in deiner Freizeit?

6. Do good/evil. **Do** s.o. **good. Do** right/wrong. **Do** well/badly [at an activity].
i. With *Gutes* and *Böses*, **tun** is usual. *Sie hat [in ihrem Leben] viel Gutes getan. Wir sollten uns bemühen, jeden Tag Gutes zu tun. Ohne es zu wollen, hat er Böses getan.*
ii. Do s.o. **good** in the sense of benefiting the health is **gut tun.** *Der Urlaub hat ihr [sehr] gut getan.*
iii. Do some good or **not do any good**, meaning 'to benefit generally', is **nutzen** (or **nützen**) or **helfen.** *Sein Eingreifen hat etw. genutzt. Die Änderungen haben gar nichts genutzt. Die Medizin hat ihr nichts genutzt. Hat das etw. geholfen? Das hat gar nichts geholfen.*
iv. With *recht, unrecht,* and *gut,* to which *daran* is often added, **tun** means 'to do right, well, or wrong' in the sense of behaving or acting correctly or wrongly. *Du hast ganz recht getan, sein Angebot abzulehnen. Du hast unrecht getan, nicht sofort auf den Brief geantwortet zu haben. Er täte gut daran, zu einem Rechtsanwalt zu gehen,* means 'he would do well', but is very formal. *Du wärst gut beraten,* 'well-advised', is more common. *Du wärst gut beraten, dich über das Thema genauestens zu informieren.*
v. Do well/badly meaning 'to get on' is in some contexts **gut/schlecht gehen.** *Ich höre, daß es dieser Firma in letzter Zeit gut/nicht gut/schlecht/geht.*
vi. Do or get on [well/badly] in an examination or competition is **abschneiden.** *Wie hat sie in der Prüfung abgeschnitten? Sie hat gut/schlecht /besser als erwartet abgeschnitten.*
vii. Do = 'make progress' or 'thrive'. *S.o. is doing well* can be *Er* **macht sich** *gut* in

speech. *Er macht sich gut im Geschäft. Sie geht zum Gymnasium und macht sich gut. How is your son doing at school?* is *Wie macht er sich in der Schule?* In the standard language **vorankommen**, 'to get on', is probably more usual. *Er kommt in seinem Beruf gut voran. Sie kommt mit der Arbeit zügig/schnell/gut voran. Everything in the garden is doing splendidly: Alles im Garten* **gedeiht**, is thriving. *Ein Geschäft gedeiht/floriert/blüht.*

viii. For **be doing** *well* relating to health cf. WELL 6.

7. Do = 'to cause harm, pain, injury, etc. to a pers.' *What have they done to you?* Both **tun** and **antun** are used with a dat. in this sense. *Was hat man dir getan?* implies that the person has suffered physical harm and seeks to find out what. Although *antun* does not exclude physical injury, it goes beyond it and includes the moral sphere. It stresses more strongly than *tun* the personal relationship between the perpetrator and the victim and implies that the action of the former causes the latter severe mental pain. *Das wirst du mir doch nicht antun.* The hurt could result from a severe insult or defamatory remarks. *Was hat man dir angetan?, Wer hat dir das angetan?*, and *Wer weiß, was sie mir alles noch antun werden?* suggest something causing anguish. *Das kannst du deiner Mutter doch nicht antun* implies doing something which would badly hurt her feelings. A speaker trying to reassure someone that no harm will come to him or her would use *tun. Hör' auf zu weinen! Hier tut dir niemand was.* Or *Niemand will dir etw. tun.* With *nichts, tun* is usual. *Ich tu' dir nichts. Man hat ihnen nichts getan.* With [etw.] *Schlimmes/Böses*, both are possible. In pos. sents., *antun* is usual, *Er hat ihr Schlimmes/Böse/Übles angetan*, but in neg. ones, often as reassurance, *tun. Ich will dir doch nichts Böses tun.* In some contexts *antun* is translated as *inflict. Eine solche Schmach können Sie Ihrer Frau und Ihrem alten Vater doch nicht antun.*

> *Sie drohte, ihm bei der ersten Gelegenheit das zu tun, was er ihren Freunden getan hatte.*
>
> *Alles Böse, was sie ihm antat, vergalt er mit Güte.*

There are a few idioms. *Er sieht aus, als könnte er keiner Fliege etw. zuleide tun*, hurt or harm. *Sich ein Leid antun* implies suicide, but is a fairly literary expression. *In seiner Darstellung der Ereignisse tat er den Tatsachen Gewalt an*, did violence to.

8. Some other senses.

i. The question corresponding to *What does he do for a living?* is *Was ist er von Beruf? She graduated in July, but still hasn't got anything to do: Sie war im Juli mit dem Studium fertig, hat aber noch keine Stelle/Anstellung.*

ii. Do = 'to cause, bring about'. *The storm did a lot of damage: Der Sturm hat sehr viel Schaden* **angerichtet**. Cf. CAUSE v. *A fuse must have gone—I wonder what did/caused it: Eine Sicherung muß durchgebrannt sein—was wird das wohl* **verursacht** *haben?* Cf. CAUSE v. *See/Try what patience/kindness will do!: Probier mal, was du mit Geduld/Güte* **ausrichten** *kannst!* Cf. ACHIEVE 1. *Patience and perseverance will do/work wonders: Geduld und Ausdauer werden Wunder* **vollbringen/wirken**.

iii. Do forms fixed expressions with various ns. **Tun** and **machen** are also combined with certain ns. Some ns. the E. equivalents of which require **do** are: *Sie macht Hausaufgaben. Hast du den Aufsatz gemacht? Mein Bruder muß seinen Wehrdienst machen. Ich mußte die Arbeit alleine machen. Er macht Botengänge für einen Arzt. Meine Mutter macht Einkäufe/Besorgungen. Die Firma macht [gute] Geschäfte. Man macht den Abwasch* is used, but *abspülen* is more common. *Man macht die Wäsche/eine Übersetzung/ Leibesübungen/ein Bett. Ich mache mir die Haare. Einen Versuch* or *ein Experiment machen*, to make or do an experiment. *Einen Versuch machen* can also mean 'to make an attempt'. *Jmd. macht/tut seinen Dienst*, 'does his duty or work', but *Man erweist jmdm. einen guten/schlechten Dienst*, 'does s.o. a good/bad turn/disservice'. *Man tut seine Pflicht. Man tut jmdm. einen Gefallen. Man tut Unrecht. Sport* and *Gymnastik treibt man.*

iv. With subjects of study, **machen** is used colloquially. *Ich mache Geschichte, Mathematik, Französisch* or *Alle machen vier Fächer.* The usual word is **nehmen.** Cf. TAKE 1. ix.

v. Do = 'to clean'. *Ich mache mein Zimmer selbst. Wir lassen die Küche machen* could imply cleaning or painting, renovating, etc.

vi. It is often necessary or advisable to use the precise v. to denote the activity implied by **do.** *She does a lot of knitting: Sie strickt viel. He does the cooking: Er kocht selbst.* **Do** the + gerund can always be translated in this way. *I'll do the typing: Ich tippe. He did a picture/drawing of her: Er hat ein Bild von ihr gemalt/gezeichnet* (*gemacht* is possible, but is best avoided). *The students are doing a play: Sie führen ein Stück auf. Who is doing/playing Hamlet?: Wer spielt Hamlet? He did all the talking: Er hat das ganze Gespräch bestritten. Do/solve a problem: Eine Aufgabe lösen* or *machen.*

vii. *We did the journey in five hours* can be *Wir haben die Fahrt in fünf Stunden gemacht.* **Schaffen,** 'to manage to do', is common both for work done and for distances. *Ich habe heute mein Pensum geschafft. Ohne fremde Hilfe schafft sie das nicht. So, das hätten/haben wir geschafft!* With distances *zurücklegen,* 'to COVER', is the standard word, but *schaffen* is often encountered, particularly in conversation. *Wir haben die Strecke von 680 km. in sechs Stunden geschafft. In zwei Tagen haben wir 1 400 km zurückgelegt/geschafft.* A simple statement of speed uses **fahren,** *Das Auto fuhr mit 90 Stundenkilometern,* 'it was doing', but in reference to possible speed *schaffen, Dieses Auto schafft nicht mehr als 120 Stundenkilometer.* Or . . . *schafft 180 spielend leicht.*

viii. Not to do + infin. = 'to be advisable'. *It doesn't do to complain: Es ist* **nicht ratsam** *zu klagen. Es ist nicht ratsam, Kindern alles durchgehen zu lassen.* An alternative is *Es* **geht nicht an,** *daß man ihnen alles durchgehen läßt. Man wird sich wahrscheinlich um die Karten reißen—darum wäre es nicht ratsam, zu spät zu kommen,* it wouldn't do to be late.

ix. Sth. **will do** = 'it will be sufficient or good enough'. **Es tun** in *Das tut's auch* and *Das tut's nicht* mean that something will [not] suffice or do. *Worte allein tun es nicht. Mit ein paar netten Worten ist es nicht getan* has the same sense, i.e. 'a few nice words won't be enough/all that is required'. For an amount of material: *Wenn du mir nicht ein Dutzend Eier geben kannst, werden es sechs auch tun.* **Genug** may express the meaning. *Ist es früh genug, wenn ich Ihnen meine Antwort am Freitag gebe?,* will it do if I let you have . . . *Auch wenn die Pflaumen nicht reif genug zum Essen sind, sind sie gut genug, um Marmelade daraus zu machen,* they will do to make/for jam. *Dieses Hotel ist uns gut genug,* will do us. *If you write five pages, that will do: Wenn Sie fünf Seiten schreiben, wird das genug sein/reichen.*

> *Ich kann diese alte Hose nicht im Büro tragen, aber sie ist zur Gartenarbeit gut genug.*
> *Dieser Baumstamm ist als Sitzgelegenheit gut genug.*
> *Diese Schuhe sind nicht gut genug zum Klettern.*
> *Wirf die Abfälle nicht weg, sie sind für den Hund gut genug!*

In relation to a quantity, **reichen** means 'to do or last for a certain time'. *Ein halbes Pfund wird wohl reichen.* Cf. LAST 5. **Langen** is a colloquial syn. *Ich glaube, das Brot* (or *diese Menge Brot*) *langt bis Montag,* will do us. The. person is usually omitted after *reichen* and *langen.* **Genügen** in *Das genügt fürs erste/für diesen Zweck* is more formal and refers to work done. To make sth. **do** can be expressed by *reichen* and **auskommen.** *Can you make £5 do?: Werden dir fünf Pfund reichen? Kommst du mit fünf Pfund aus?* (However, *The soldiers made the helmet do as a frying pan* becomes *Sie benutzten den Helm als Bratpfanne.*)

x. If *That* **will do!** is a command to stop something, it can be *Jetzt Schluß [damit]!,* but *Jetzt reicht's mir aber!* and *Jetzt langt's mir aber!* are also common.

xi. Done meaning 'finished' is **fertig**. *When will the shoes be done? Wann werden die Schuhe fertig sein?*

xii. Do can express a protest. *What is he doing here?* The implication is that he has no business being here. This sense is carried by **zu suchen haben** which can have people and things as subj. *Was hat er hier zu suchen? Was haben deine schmutzigen Schuhe im Schrank zu suchen?* Cf. BUSINESS 7.

doubt *v.* *Zweifeln, bezweifeln,* and *anzweifeln* all express the concept of doubting. The first two differ in the main syntactically, whereas the third is restricted to a specific context.

i. Zweifeln alone can translate the intr. use **doubt** or *be in doubt*, as in *Why do you doubt? Warum zweifelst du noch? Gib dir doch einen Ruck und nimm das Angebot an!*

ii. With **an** + n. or **daran** + clause, **zweifeln** expresses the same meaning as **bezweifeln**, which needs a n. or clause as obj. They are generally interchangeable, but *bezweifeln* is probably more common. It tends to be used to express doubt about a preceding statement, criticism, etc. *Das möchte ich stark bezweifeln* presupposes a statement, while *zweifeln an* can be used without being a response to what someone has just said. *Ich zweifle nicht an seiner Zuverlässigkeit.* However, the dividing line is by no means clear, and both are often possible. *Ich zweifle an der Glaubwürdigkeit dieses Zeugen. Ich bezweifle die Glaubwürdigkeit dieses Zeugen. Ich zweifle an dem Nutzen dieser Neuerung. Ich bezweifle den Nutzen dieser Neuerung. Ich zweifle nicht an seiner Ehrlichkeit. Ich bezweifle seine Ehrlichkeit nicht. An seinen Fähigkeiten ist nicht zu zweifeln. Seine Fähigkeiten sind nicht zu bezweifeln.* Bezweifeln is used mostly with a *daß*-clause, *zweifeln* with *ob* but also with *daß*. *Ich bezweifle, daß sie genau im Kursbuch nachgesehen hat. Ich zweifle [daran], ob das alles noch Sinn hat. Sie zweifelte nie [daran], daß er sein Wort halten würde. Ich zweifle nicht daran, daß er uns helfen wird.* An idiom in which only *zweifeln* is possible is *Was man mir da erzählt hat, läßt mich an meinem Verstand zweifeln.*

iii. Anzweifeln is translated as *to cast doubts on* or *to have one's doubts about*. *Bezweifeln* expresses the same meaning. Often either is possible. *Sie konnten seinen Bericht nur bezweifeln/anzweifeln, so ungeheuerlich klang er.* The difference, if there is one, is that *anzweifeln* is preferred to express doubt about a specific matter. *Ich bezweifle seine Glaubwürdigkeit* refers to the person's credibility as a whole, but in *Er zweifelte die Richtigkeit dieser Angabe an, anzweifeln* refers to one point. *Anzweifeln* takes a n. or pronoun obj. only.

> *Die von den Wissenschaftlern aufgestellte Theorie wurde von vielen Seiten [stark] angezweifelt.*
> *Die Wahrheit/Glaubwürdigkeit der Aussage wurde angezweifelt.*

iv. An expression which is a syn. of **doubt** is **in Frage stellen**, to call in question, cast doubts on. *Sie stellen den Wert dieser Änderungen in Frage.*

v. In some contexts in which **doubt** is used, **nicht glauben** would be the normal G. v. *Glaubst du nicht, daß er gewinnen wird?*, do you doubt. *Ich glaube nicht/bezweifle, daß sie noch erscheinen werden. Wenn du ihm nicht glaubst, solltest du nichts mehr mit ihm zu tun haben,* if you doubt him.

dress, clothe *vs.*

i. Kleiden means 'to provide or supply with clothes regularly over a period of time' and is the equivalent of **clothe** in *It costs a lot to feed and clothe a family of six. Es kostet sehr viel Geld, eine sechsköpfige Familie zu kleiden und zu ernähren.* Kleiden also means 'to dress' when this refers to what someone habitually wears, as in *He dresses well* or *She is always dressed in the latest fashion*. It is often refl., but can take an obj. *Sie kleidet sich immer mit Sorgfalt.* The past part. is often found. *Jedesmal, wenn ich ihn sehe, ist er sorgfältig gekleidet.*

Wieviel müssen sie ausgeben, um ihre Kinder zu kleiden?

Sie weiß sich geschmackvoll zu kleiden.

Sie kleiden ihre Töchter nach der neuesten Mode. Or *Ihre Töchter sind nach der neuesten Mode gekleidet.*

(*Kleiden* can also mean 'to suit', for which *stehen* is usual, *Das neue Köstum kleidet sie gut,* and 'to clothe or couch' thoughts in words, *Bei der feierlichen Entlassung der Abiturienten kleidete der Direktor seine Gedanken in gewählte Worte.*)

ii. With a person as obj. **anziehen** means 'to dress' someone, while **sich anziehen** is the everyday v. meaning 'to get dressed or to dress oneself'. With an article of clothing as obj., *anziehen* means 'to put on'. *Ich zog das Hemd an. Ich ziehe dem Kind das Hemd an.* (Note that one says *den Hut aufsetzen* and *die Krawatte/den Schlips anbinden.*)

Nachdem die Mutter das Kleinkind gebadet hatte, zog sie es an.

Klärchen zieht ihre Puppen ständig an und aus.

Hast du dich immer noch nicht angezogen? Bist du noch nicht fertig angezogen?

'Steh endlich auf und zieh dich an!' schimpfte die Mutter.

Ich weiß nicht, was ich anziehen soll.   Für den Theaterbesuch zog sie ihr neues Kleid an.

iii. Sich anziehen and **angezogen sein** with an adv. of manner also denote the way someone is dressed, but, unlike *kleiden*, refer to a particular situation or occasion. *Sie waren sommerlich/elegant angezogen. Die Besucher hatten sich sonntäglich angezogen.* With the addition of *immer* it expresses the same meaning as *kleiden*. *Sie ziehen sich immer geschmackvoll an. In seiner Stellung muß er immer gut angezogen/gekleidet sein/ . . . muß er sich immer gut anziehen/kleiden.* Sich anziehen is the usual v. for dressing warmly or lightly. *Ihr müßt euch warm anziehen, wenn ihr bei dieser Kälte spazierengeht. Im Winter muß man sich wärmer anziehen als im Sommer. Bei der Hitze waren alle leicht/sportlich angezogen.* Kleiden is sometimes used for the way someone dresses on one occasion. It is more formal than *anziehen* and may be used ironically. *Heute seid ihr aber königlich gekleidet! Heute habt ihr euch aber königlich gekleidet!*

iv. Kleiden is the only possibility for the meaning 'dressed in a particular colour'. *Sie war ganz in Weiß gekleidet und sah fabelhaft aus.*

v. Bekleiden means 'to provide with clothes on one occasion'. It is found in the act. and refl. but most frequently in the phr. **mit etw. bekleidet sein**, 'to be dressed in', a refined syn. of *anhaben*, 'to have on', or *tragen*, 'to wear'. Thus *unbekleidet*, undressed, without clothes. *Die Kinder liefen unbekleidet am Strand herum.*

Die notdürftig bekleideten Hotelgäste, die sich vor dem Brand über das Dach gerettet hatten, wickelten sich in Wolldecken ein.

Weil die Mädchen nur mit Shorts und leichten Blusen bekleidet waren, wollte man ihnen den Zutritt zur Kirche verwehren.

Der entflohene Häftling war mit Jeans und einer braunen Jacke bekleidet.

vi. Ankleiden is a formal syn. of *anziehen*, used particularly of important personages. *Während der Audienz mit Galilei wird der Papst angekleidet. Mit der Hilfe ihrer Zofe kleidete sich die Herzogin an.* It is used in formal bureaucratic language instead of *anziehen. Die Krankenschwester war der Patientin beim Ankleiden behilflich.* It is sometimes used for ordinary people on special occasions but may be ironic. *Die gesamte Verwandschaft kam festlich angekleidet zur goldenen Hochzeit meiner Eltern. Gekleidet* and *angezogen* could also be used here.

drink n. and v.

1. Drink n.

i. When a **drink** means 'what s.o. drinks on a specific occasion', the usual expression is **etw. zu trinken**. (*Zu* is omitted with vs. which do not require it. *Möchtest du* *etw. trinken? Ich habe Durst—ich muß etw. trinken.*) The normal equivalent of both *We all need a drink* and *We all need sth. to drink* is *Wir brauchen alle etw. zu trinken. Hast du den Gästen schon etw. zu trinken gegeben/angeboten?* (*Etw. zum Trinken geben* is also common in colloquial speech.) *Es ist aber heiß heute—hast du mal etw. zu trinken für mich?* An adj. can be added. *Wir haben etw. Heißes/Kaltes/Erfrischendes zu trinken bekommen. Nach der Arbeit in der sengenden Sonne gab er uns etw. Eisgekühltes zu trinken. Ich möchte etwas Saft trinken* means 'some juice to drink' or 'a drink of juice'. With a n. *etw.* can be omitted. *Give me a drink of water!* is either *Gib mir bitte etw. Wasser zu trinken!* or *Gib mit bitte Wasser zu trinken!*

ii. Das Getränk is used in general statements about drinks of all kinds. *Hanna sorgt für die Getränke* or *kümmert sich um die Getränke,* 'is looking after the drinks', e.g. for a party. *Was für alkoholfreie Getränke hat das Hotel auf der Speisekarte? Die Getränke sind noch im Flur, aber ich werde sie gleich in den Keller bringen* could refer to drinks of any kind that had just been delivered. *Die Zuschauer dürfen keine alkoholischen Getränke ins Fußballstadion mitnehmen. Getränk* is also used in reference to trying or tasting a particular drink. *Dieses Getränk hatte sie noch nie getrunken/probiert, und sie fand, daß es gut/schleußlich schmeckte.* It is possible for a drink on a specific occasion, but *etw. zu trinken* is more usual and would be normal in a request for a drink. *Sie bestellen die Getränke/etw. zu trinken. Ich hätte nichts gegen ein heißes/kühles Getränk/gegen etw. Heißes/Kühles zu trinken.*

iii. The other ns. derived from *trinken,* **der Trank** and **der Trunk,** have become uncommon except in a few fixed expressions. *Trank* survives more or less only in *der Zaubertrank,* magic potion. *Trunk* is a formal word in the lit. sense. *Darf ich Sie nach der Besichtigung der Anlagen zu einem kleinen Trunk einladen?*

iv. Der Trunk also refers to drinking alcohol, with the implication of drunkenness. *Er hat seinen Kummer im Trunk begraben* is possible, but *im Alkohol* is more usual. *Jmd. ist dem Trunk ergeben* (colloquially *dem Suff*) also occurs.

v. Der Alkohol is used in talking about **drink** meaning 'the consumption of alcoholic liquor'. *Der Alkohol hat ihn zugrundegerichtet.*

2. Drink v.

i. When people are the subj., the normal equivalent of **drink** is **trinken.** *Sie trank einen Schluck/eine Tasse Kaffee. Er trank das Bier aus der Flasche. Ich habe zu schnell getrunken.*

ii. Trinken also means 'to drink [large amounts of] alcoholic beverages' either habitually or on one occasion. Habitually: *Ihr Mann trinkt. Sie trinkt nie. Damals hatte er angefangen zu trinken. Sie sind Trinker,* alcoholics. **Das Trinken** can refer to habitual drinking. *Sie können das Trinken nicht mehr lassen.* On one occasion: *Er hatte getrunken und konnte nicht mit dem Auto nach Hause fahren. Er hatte zuviel getrunken.*

iii. Saufen means 'to drink' when talking of animals. *Der Elefant soff aus dem Wasserloch. Wir müssen dem Vieh zu saufen geben.* (Or *Wir müssen das Vieh tränken.*) Applied to people, *saufen* means, firstly, 'to drink anything in great quantity, in large greedy gulps, and in a noisy and ill-mannered way'. *Er säuft den Rotwein geradezu, trinken kann man es nicht mehr nennen.* Secondly, when drinking alcohol is implied, it means 'to drink habitually, immoderately, and in an uncontrolled way' and is stronger than *trinken* used in the same context. *Damals hatte er aus Verzweiflung angefangen zu saufen/trinken.*

eager, anxious, keen, ardent, fervent, zealous *adjs.*

1. Eager = 'showing a strong desire to do, attain, or hear sth.' It is used alone, *eager faces, They are very eager,* or with *for, eager for success,* or an infin. (Cf. 2.) **Keen** means 'showing interest or enthusiasm' and is a syn. of **eager**. It is used attributively, *a keen student/chess player/gardener,* and predicatively, *They are very keen.* **Fervent** and **ardent** mean 'enthusiastic, displaying strong feelings'. *An ardent supporter of the Labour Party. A fervent admirer of the Chancellor.* **Zealous** is applied to people who spend a lot of time or energy in supporting something, especially a political or religious ideal, that they believe in very strongly. *He was a zealous anti-smoker.*

i. *Der Eifer* implies enthusiasm and a serious endeavour to do or achieve something. Depending on the context, it can be translated as *eagerness, fervour,* or *zeal.* **Eifrig** means 'displaying such enthusiasm', and, in appropriate contexts, can be translated as **eager, keen,** *enthusiastic,* **fervent, ardent,** and **zealous.** It is used attributively, *ein eifriger Schüler/Student, ein eifriger Schachspieler/Sportler/Bergsteiger,* and predicatively, *Sie ist sehr eifrig und gibt nicht schnell auf.* (E. mostly = 'keen'.) In *ein eifriger Anhänger einer Partei, ein eifriger Verehrer des Kanzlers,* and *ein eifriger Kirchgänger,* the E. adj. could be *ardent, fervent,* or *zealous* as well as *keen. Eifrig* is used with *bei. Sie waren eifrig bei der Arbeit. Eifrig* refers to the enthusiasm with which the work is being tackled, but it comes close to *busy. Die Kinder haben eifrig gelernt.* An infin. is possible after *dabei* and translates *eagerly, keenly,* or *busily doing sth. Die Kinder waren eifrig dabei, das Laub zusammenzuharken.*

> *Sie machten sich eifrig an die Arbeit. Sie haben eifrig musiziert.*
> *Er war eifrig damit beschäftigt, dem Referat den letzten Schliff zu geben.*

ii. Begeistert and the emotionally charged **glühend** are stronger than *eifrig* and may be preferred as a transl. of **fervent, ardent,** and **zealous.** *Er war ein begeisterter Anhänger der Labourpartei. Ein glühender Verteidiger der Freiheit. Ein glühender Bewunderer des Kanzlers. Er schrieb einen glühenden Liebesbrief.*

> *Als glühender Verfechter des freien Wettbewerbs befürworten Sie wohl die völlige Deregulierung der Luftfahrt.* (from a *Spiegel-Gespräch*) *Er war ein glühender Patriot.*

2. Keen and **eager** are used with an infin. and mean 'desirous'. *He is keen to see his birthplace again. They are eager to please/learn/help. Keen/Eager to assist.* **Keen** on doing sth. can have the same meaning. *She is keen to go/on going to India. Mrs Hills is keen on Jack marrying Mary/that J. should marry M.* **Anxious** = 'earnestly desirous to carry out an aim or find sth. out'. *He was anxious to meet you/for his brother to meet you/that help should be sent/for help to be sent/to find out how thgs. turned out.* For **anxious** = 'fearful', see TIMID.

i. Bemüht + infin. means 'to be endeavouring or keen to do sth.' *Eifrig* may be added as an adv. *Sie waren [eifrig] bemüht, einen guten Eindruck zu hinterlassen. Bemüht* is also used with *um: Er war um Erfolg eifrig bemüht,* eager for success. **Bestrebt** + infin. is a more refined and formal syn. *Er ist bestrebt, mit Ihnen ins Geschäft zu kommen,* keen on doing, anxious to do business with you. **Auf etw.** (acc.) **bedacht sein,** 'to be anxious to secure or intent on gaining something', is also formal, and is somewhat stronger than *bemüht*. It is used with a n., infin., or clause. *Er ist immer auf seinen Vorteil bedacht. Er ist darauf bedacht, ihre Gunst zu gewinnen. Sie war stets darauf bedacht, daß alles ordentlich gemacht wurde.*

> *Er war bemüht, ihr alles recht zu machen.*
>
> *Die Firma war bemüht, den Wünschen der Kunden so schnell wie möglich nachzukommen.*
>
> *Da er bestrebt ist, seine Chancen auf dem Arbeitsmarkt zu verbessern, besucht er Fortbildungskurse.*
>
> *Die Reaktion der Staatsgewalt auf die zahlreichen Protestdemonstrationen der Studenten war harsch und ganz auf die Wiederherstellung von Ruhe und Ordnung bedacht.*

ii. A common expression related to those in 2. i is **möchte gern. Eager/Anxious/Keen** to please/help/succeed could be *Sie möchte gern gefallen/helfen/Erfolg haben. Ich möchte ihn gern kennenlernen.* Related expressions which take an infin. are **es liegt jmdm. daran**, 'it is important/matters a great deal to s.o.', or the stronger **es kommt jmdm. darauf an.** *Anxious to* would be the main E. equivalent in the following sents. *Es lag ihm sehr daran, sie von seiner Glaubwürdigkeit zu überzeugen. Allen kam es darauf an, die Diskussion nicht weiter in die Länge zu ziehen. Es liegt mir sehr daran, Näheres über die geplanten Maßnahmen zu erfahren.* To translate *anxious for sth. to happen* or *that sth. should happen*, all three expressions can be used with a *daß*-clause, the subj. of which is the n. after *for. I am anxious for my brother to meet you* becomes *Ich möchte gern/Es liegt mir daran/Es kommt mir darauf an, daß mein Bruder Sie kennenlernt. Es lag den Eltern daran/kam den Eltern darauf an, daß die Kinder eine gute Schulbildung erhielten.*

> *Sie möchte gern nach Indien fahren.*   *Seine Heimat möchte er gern wieder sehen.*
>
> *Es kommt mir darauf an, daß dieser Fall vertraulich behandelt wird.*

iii. Anxious, combined with expressions like *to find out how sth. turned out/how s.o. got on*, and **eager** followed by *to hear* or *find sth. out*, are **gespannt** or **neugierig**. *Gespannt* implies expectancy and tension caused by uncertainty about an outcome; *neugierig* suggests curiosity for its own sake. They include the meaning of the E. infin. *to find out, to see, to discover*, etc. Both are used with *auf* + a n. or a clause. *Ich bin gespannt auf deine neue Freundin. Alle waren gespannt/neugierig auf den Urlaubsort. Ich bin gespannt, was für eine Note ich in der Prüfung bekommen werde. Ich bin neugierig, wie das alles enden wird. Ich bin gespannt/neugierig auf das, was er uns zu berichten hat. Alle verfolgten ihre Ausführungen mit gespannter Aufmerksamkeit.*

3. Be keen on s.o./sth./doing sth. means 'to LIKE'. *He's very keen on dancing. Jack is keen on Mary.* The main equivalents of *like* with a personal subj. are **mögen**, and a v. + **gern.** Cf. LIKE. *I'm not keen on westerns* becomes therefore *Wildwestfilme mag ich nicht. Meinen neuen Kollegen mag ich nicht sonderlich.* With food: *Sauerkraut mag ich sehr/gar nicht. She is keen on dancing/swimming* is *Sie tanzt/schwimmt gern.* When more than a normal liking for a person is involved, **sich sehr interessieren für** can be used. *Hans interessiert sich sehr für Inge. Peter scheint sich in letzter Zeit sehr für Anna zu interessieren. Mrs Hills is keen on Jack marrying Mary/that J. should marry M.* could be *Sie ist an einer Heirat zwischen Jack und Mary sehr interessiert* or *sehr daran interessiert, daß Jack Mary heiratet.* The expressions in 2. ii are also possible. *He's keen to go/on going for us to go: Er möchte gern nach Indien fahren/daß wir nach Indien fahren.* **An etw. interessiert sein** can also be used. *Er ist sehr daran interessiert, seinen Geburtsort wiederzusehen. Sie sind sehr daran interessiert, die Arbeit so bald wie möglich abzuschließen.* The infin. may only be implied. *Zeig' dich nicht allzu sehr interessiert, denn sonst werden sie von dem Preis, den sie verlangen, nicht heruntergehen!, don't be too keen.* Other alternatives: *Er interessiert sich sehr für seine Arbeit* or *zeigt großes Interesse daran, is keen on. Keen on a plan: Der Plan interessiert mich sehr,* or in the neg., *Ich kann mich für diesen Plan nicht begeistern.*

4. Fervent and **ardent**, applied to emotions, mean 'very strong'. *An ardent/fervent desire for reconciliation. Ardent/Fervent love/hatred.* **Fervent** is applied to pleas, wishes, hopes, etc. that are heartfelt. *A fervent plea for peace. We were struck by her fervent request to put an end to this injustice.*
i. Glühend is applied to all emotions whether good or bad. *Seine glühende Verehrung ihrer Kunst.* **Innig**, 'heartfelt, deep', is used only with good feelings, but is not very common. *Er liebte sie heiß und innig. Innige Zuneigung. Glühende or innige Liebe* and *ein glühendes or inniges Verlangen nach Versöhnung* occur, but only *glühender Haß*.
ii. With pleas, requests, wishes, etc., **dringend** or **dringlich**, 'urgent', or the elevated **inbrünstig** are the usual equivalents. *Sie richteten einen dringenden Appell um Frieden an beide Regierungen. Wir waren betroffen von der mit solcher Dringlichkeit vorgebrachten Forderung, dieser Ungerechtigkeit ein Ende zu machen. Sie hoffte inbrünstig, daß ihre Erwartungen diesmal nicht enttäuscht würden.*

edge *n.* **Die Kante** denotes the line dividing two surfaces at right angles to each other. *Die Bordsteinkante. Ich habe mich an der Kante des Schrankes gestoßen. Kindermöbel sollten keine scharfen Kanten haben, sondern nur abgerundete.* **Der Rand** means 'the area at the edge' and is used when **edge** is not a line but a space similar to a margin or strip. *Der Rand des Waldes/des Spielfeldes/der Wiese/der Stadt/der Felsenwand/der Seite/der Wüste.* In some cases both are found, but *der Tischrand* suggests the area along the edge, while *die Tischkante* is the line where the horizontal surface meets the vertical. *Rand* is also used fig. like **edge**. *Am Rande des Bankrotts/des Ruins.* In *am Rande des wirtschaftlichen Zusammenbruchs*, *Rand* also translates *verge*. (*Der Rand* is also 'the brim or rim' of a drinking vessel or container, *Er füllte das Glas bis zum Rand, Wasser schwappte über den Rand des Eimers,* 'the rim' of spectacles, *eine Brille mit dunkeln Rändern,* 'rings around the eyes', *dunkle Ränder um die Augen,* and 'the margin' of a sheet of paper, *Der Rand muß drei Zentimeter breit sein.*)

educate *v.* **education** *n.* **bring up, rear, train** *vs.* **Educate** can mean 'to bring up children so as to form habits, manners, desirable qualities of mind or character, general competence and knowledge, and intellectual and physical aptitudes'. It also means 'to provide with schooling or a course of instruction'. Often the two meanings run together in a sense defined as 'to provide or assist in providing with knowledge, wisdom, moral balance, and a good physical condition by means of formal education'.

1. Rear. **Aufziehen** and **großziehen**, which are interchangeable for human beings, mean 'to bring up or rear' in the sense 'to provide with food, clothing, shelter, and care'. *Nachdem die Eltern verunglückt waren, haben die Großeltern die Kinder aufgezogen. Sie haben sechs Kinder aufgezogen/großgezogen. Sie zogen den fremden Jungen als eigenes Kind auf.* **Aufziehen** is also used for animals. *Die Kinder haben das verletzte Hundebaby aufgezogen.*

2. Educate and **bring up**.
i. Erziehen means 'to develop the mind, character, and abilities of a child or young pers. and to bring his or her behaviour into conformity with the standards of the society'. It is the comprehensive term, including everything that contributes to making a child a responsible and informed adult. It refers primarily to behaviour, *ein gut erzogenes Kind* being well behaved or well brought up, then to values, desirable characteristics, and attitudes. Skills and knowledge are not excluded, but the emphasis on one or the other varies from situation to situation. If parents are the subj. the v. used in E. is **bring up**; if a school or teachers are the

subj., the E. v. is **educate** in either or both of the senses defined above. *Erziehen*, not *bilden*, is used to state where and how someone has been educated. *Er wurde in einer Jesuitenschule erzogen*. *Erziehen zu* means that a particular quality is inculcated. *Unsere Kinder sind zur Selbständigkeit erzogen worden. Ein schwer erziehbares Kind* is one who is difficult, a problem child, or hard to bring up. *Heimerziehung* refers to the bringing up of children in an institution like an orphanage.

> *Sie sind von den Eltern/vom Vormund gut/schlecht/mit Strenge erzogen worden.*
> *Das Kind wurde von den Großeltern/von Nonnen/in einem Internat erzogen.*
> *Die Eltern haben die Kinder zur Sparsamkeit/im christlichen Geist erzogen.*
> *Die Schule/Der Lehrer erzog sie zur Toleranz/Gewissenhaftigkeit etc.*

ii. Bilden refers to gaining knowledge and understanding both in particular fields and in what is regarded as general education, but apart from the past part., as in *gebildete junge Leute*, the v. is not much encountered. *Man bildet seinen Geist/seinen Verstand. Man muß die Jugend politisch bilden*. As an intr. and refl. v. it denotes a process not confined to educational establishments. *Lesen/Reisen bildet. Man bildet sich durch Lesen/Reisen. Der kluge Mann bildet sich ständig.*

3. Education. **Die Erziehung** refers to gaining both good behaviour and attitudes, and to knowledge. *Die Erziehung der Jugend durch Elternhaus und Schule. Die elterliche Erziehung dieses Kindes ließ nichts zu wünschen übrig*. In particular situations one or the other may be stressed, but both are often implied. *Sie gaben ihren Kindern eine gute Erziehung. Sie hatte eine gute/sorgfältige Erziehung erhalten. Körperlich* and *moralisch* or *sittlich* are combined only with *Erziehung*, as are mostly *musisch*, artistic, and *ästhetisch*. **Die Bildung** is the usual equivalent of **education** when it means 'instruction in schools etc.' and refers to specific or general knowledge. *Sie haben eine gute musikalische/künstlerische/literarische/ naturwissenschaftliche Bildung erhalten. Sie hatte eine gründliche/ausgezeichnete Bildung genossen. Die Schule vermittelt eine vielseitige Bildung. Bildung* stresses knowledge and skills, but it also suggests that these are combined with desirable attitudes and good behaviour. *Jmd. besitzt eine umfassende Bildung* or *ist ein Mann von Bildung. Das gehört zur allgemeinen Bildung* suggests something every educated person should know. *Ein Mensch ohne Bildung* can be ignorant or badly behaved, or both. Compounds of either word refering to educational systems are synonymous. **Das Bildungswesen** is 'the education system'; it includes all institutions involved in providing knowledge and instruction, mainly schools and tertiary institutions. **Das Erziehungswesen** is for all practical purposes a syn. of *Bildungswesen. Die gesellschaftlichen Veränderungen hatte auch eine Umwälzung des Erziehungswesens zur Folge*. In some compounds *Bildung* denotes the organized instruction of the young. *Bildungspolitik* is 'educational policy', and there has been much discussion of *Bildungsreform* in West Germany in recent decades. In other compounds *Bildung* refers to knowledge. *Der Bildungsdrang*, desire for education. *Das Bildungsniveau* and *der Bildungsgrad*, level of education. *Der Vortrag war dem Bildungsniveau der Zuhörer angepaßt*. In some compounds *Erziehung* implies inculcating appropriate behaviour. *Bei diesem Jungen sind besondere Erziehungsmaßnahmen erforderlich*. When confined to schools, **education** can be translated by **die Schulbildung**, which can be either general or in specific subjects. *Sie ermöglichten ihren Kindern eine gute Schulbildung. Die Schulbildung, die die Kinder im literarischen Bereich/in den Naturwissenschaften bekommen haben, ist bemerkenswert*. Primary education is *Grundschulbildung*, and *secondary education Realschul- und Gymnasialbildung*. Tertiary education can be *das Hochschulstudium, Das Hochschulstudium sollte für alle kostenlos sein*, or *die Hochschulbildung*. The ministry or department in charge of education in G. states (*Länder*) is **das Kultusministerium**. The corresponding institution in E.-speaking countries is called by G. speakers **das Erziehungsministerium** or **das Ministerium für das Bildungswesen**.

4. Train.

i. When **education** implies or involves specific training, the equivalent is **die Ausbildung**, training. *Die technische Ausbildung*, technical education. *Die kaufmännische Ausbildung findet in speziellen Schulen statt*, commercial education. **Ausbilden**, 'to train', can be applied to abilities, *Man bildet seine Anlagen/seinen Verstand aus*, but mostly has a person as obj., *Jmd. bildet Lehrlinge/Lehrer/Rekruten/Facharbeiter aus. Sie ließen sich als Sänger/Dolmetscher/Stenotypisten ausbilden. Ich wurde als Bankkaufmann ausgebildet.* **Schulen** is 'to train intensively for a specific task or occupation'. *Für die neue Aufgabe hat die Firma mehrere Mitarbeiter in Sonderkursen geschult.* It is also used with mental faculties. *Man schult das Gedächtnis durch Auswendiglernen. Der Geschmack wird systematisch geschult.*

ii. Abrichten and **dressieren** mean 'to train animals'. *Ich habe den Hund zum Apportieren abgerichtet. Der Dompteur hat den Löwen für eine Zirkusnummer dressiert.* They are used for people when a mindless discipline is involved. *Diese Soldaten waren nur auf blinden Gehorsam abgerichtet/dressiert.*

iii. Trainieren and **das Training** are only used for sport and similar activities. *Trainieren* is both intr., *Sie trainieren hart*, and trans., *Dieser Trainer/Teamchef hat schon mehrere erfolgreiche Mannschaften trainiert. Hartes Training ist nötig, wenn man gewinnen will.*

embarrass v. **embarrassing** *part.* or *adj.* The sense of the v. is 'to cause s.o. to experience a state of self-conscious distress'. *It embarrasses many people to walk into a room full of strangers.*

i. Peinlich is an adj. meaning 'embarrassing'. It is applied attributively and predicatively to things which produce embarrassment. *Eine peinliche Angelegenheit/Äußerung/Situation. Ein peinlicher Zwischenfall. Das Schweigen war sehr peinlich.* **Etw. ist jmdm. peinlich** means that someone finds something embarrassing or is embarrassed by/about something. The subj. must be a thing or *es. Diese Bemerkung war mir sehr peinlich. Es ist mir sehr peinlich, daß ich Sie stören muß. Es war mir peinlich, ihn darum bitten zu müssen.*

ii. While *peinlich* is applied to things, the adj. **verlegen** is used for people. *In einer peinlichen Situation ist/wird jmd. verlegen. Er wurde ganz verlegen, als er um Hilfe bitten mußte.* It suggests a feeling of distress or awkwardness often resulting from not knowing what to do. *Verlegen* is applied as an adv. to actions which reveal someone's *Verlegenheit. Sie lachte verlegen/stand verlegen da. Verlegen drehte er seinen Hut in der Hand.* It can be applied as an adj. to such actions. *Ein verlegenes Lächeln, ein verlegener Blick.* Um etw. **verlegen sein** means 'to be at a loss for sth.' *Jmd. ist um eine Antwort/Ausrede [nicht] verlegen. In finanzieller Verlegenheit*, financially embarrassed. The act. form expressing *Sth.* **embarrasses** *s.o.* is **jmdn. verlegen machen** or **jmdn. in Verlegenheit bringen**. *Diese Frage machte mich verlegen/brachte mich in Verlegenheit.*

Viele Menschen werden verlegen, wenn sie in ein Zimmer voll Fremde treten müssen.

iii. While *verlegen* suggests that someone is embarrassed because he or she feels helpless or does not know what to do, the adj. **betreten** suggests embarrassment arising from a feeling of guilt or shame. *Es herrschte betretenes Schweigen, als die betreffende Person eintrat. Als sie das sagte, blickte er betreten vor sich hin.*

Bei diesem Anblick schwieg sie betreten/wandte sie sich betreten ab.

iv. Sich genieren means 'to be or feel embarrassed' or 'to feel awkward or self-conscious'. *Ich genierte mich, ihm die Wahrheit zu sagen. Er genierte sich vor den anderen.*

It is often used in the neg. imp. to encourage someone not to feel embarrassed about doing something. *Genieren Sie sich nicht, Ihre Meinung offen zu sagen!*

emotion, feeling *n.*

1. Emotion is 'a strong feeling' such as fear, love, hatred, joy, pity, grief, disgust, anger, or jealousy. *She began to feel a new emotion—pride.* **Das Gefühl** translates both **the feeling** and **the emotion**, i.e. a specific one. *Die Liebe, der Haß und die Furcht sind Gefühle. Sie empfand ein Gefühl der Liebe/der Erleichterung/der Freude/der Schuld. Er fühlte plötzlich Wut in sich aufsteigen, aber wie immer wurde er solcher Gefühle Herr*, controlled such emotions. Closely related is **die Gefühlsregung** or, if the emotion is specified or the sense clear, **die Regung** alone. *Regung* denotes the stirring or arousal (of a feeling or emotion). *Er zeigte keine Gefühlsregung. Sie empfand eine Regung des Mitleids/der Eifersucht. Eine menschliche Regung* is '(human) sympathy or pity'. **Die Empfindung** also refers to a feeling of a specific kind. *Die Empfindung von Dankbarkeit/von Scham/von Freude/von Zorn/von Ekel.* **Die Emotion** is only used in learned language. *Sie ließ ihren Emotionen freien Lauf. Er antwortete ohne jede Emotion.* (For *Feelings were running high* cf. EMOTIONAL 5.)

> *Sie wurde von dem Kummer über den Tod des Freunds überwältigt. Sie hatte nie zuvor so starke Gefühle/eine so starke Gefühlsregung erlebt.*
>
> *Er empfand eine Regung des Erbarmens.   Ihre erste Regung war Freude/Abneigung.*
>
> *Beim Anblick des Schmutzes und des Elends empfand ich zuerst Abscheu, aber dann schämte ich mich dieser Empfindung.   Es überkam mich eine Empfindung von Reue.*

2. Without *an, the, this*, etc., but sometimes with a possessive, **emotion** denotes the turmoil, agitation, or disturbance of the mind brought about by experiencing strong feeling such as love, grief, anger, desire, etc. *Her voice was choked by emotion. He did not want his face to show his emotion. How can I describe my emotion at this catastrophe?* **Emotion** is here a general term which does not specify which emotion is felt.

i. Although **die Rührung** is often translated as *emotion*, it implies pity, compassion, or sadness, feelings which bring someone at least close to tears. *Ihre Stimme wurde von Rührung erstickt.* In *Sie wurde von Rührung ergriffen*, 'was seized by emotion', *Er konnt vor Rührung nicht sprechen*, 'was too moved to speak', and *Sie vergoß Tränen der Rührung, Rührung* could suggest compassion.

ii. Die Ergriffenheit denotes strong emotion, but it also suggests feelings akin to sadness. *In tiefer Ergriffenheit standen die Menschen vor den Opfern des Unglücks*, deeply moved, overcome by emotion. *Auf den Gesichtern der Anwesenden spiegelte sich ihre innere Ergriffenheit wider*, their deep emotion was reflected in their faces. *Sie schwieg vor Ergriffenheit*, was too moved to speak, could not speak for emotion.

iii. Die Gefühle means either 'feelings' or 'emotion'. *Er ließ seinen Gefühlen freien Lauf/machte seinen Gefühlen Luft.* **Die Empfindungen** means 'feelings' and can be used for an unspecified emotion or one which is clear from the context. *Ich kann meine Empfindungen nicht in Worte fassen.* **Erregen** means 'to arouse' strong feelings of any kind. Cf. EXCITE 1. ii. **Die Erregung** denotes the state of experiencing any strong emotion (as well as excitement). *In heftiger Erregung sagte er . . . Eine freudige Erregung*, an intense feeling of joy. **Die Gemütsbewegung** denotes an unspecified emotion. *Die tiefe Gemütsbewegung war ihr äußerlich nicht anzumerken.* (The meaning is the same when the two parts of this compound are separated. *Sein Gesicht zeigte deutlich die Bewegungen seines Gemüts.*) **Der Affekt** is a learned word denoting strong or violent emotion, often one which results in a violent action or crime, *ein im Affekt begangenes Verbrechen*, but can be more general, *Ein Entschluß, den man im Affekt gefaßt hat, wird kaum vernünftig sein.*

Wie kann ich meine Gefühle angesichts dieser Katastrophe beschreiben?
Sie versuchte, ihre Gefühle/ihre Empfindungen/ihre Erregung zu verbergen.
Voller zwiespältiger Empfindungen stand sie ihm gegenüber.
Sie verriet durch eine unwillkürliche Handbewegung die immer stärker werdende Erregung, die sie
   ergriffen hatte.   *Der Film weckte bittere Gefühle in ihnen.*
Er bemühte sich, seiner Erregung Herr zu werden.   *Seine Erregung flaute ab/verging.*
'Die weiß eben, was Krieg ist—besser als wir', kommentierte der italienische Grenzer die Tränen und
   das Schluchzen der alten Frau, die gerade von Slowenien nach Italien gefahren wurde. Vielleicht
   wurde die Gemütsbewegung ausgelöst, als sie an den ausgebrannten Panzern unmittelbar bei der
   Grenzstation vorbeikam.

3. Other expressions. *He showed no emotion* can be *Er blieb unbewegt/unberührt,* unmoved, or *Ihm war nichts anzumerken. Sie sprach mit bewegter Stimme,* in a voice touched with emotion. *Die Rede/Der Film war reine/pure Gefühlsduselei,* mawkish sentimentality, a cheap display of emotion, slush, gush.

4. Another way of translating **emotion** is is to use the specific emotion that is being felt. *He thought of his dead wife with deep emotion* could be *Er dachte an seine tote Frau mit tiefer Trauer. Rührung* is also possible. *Jmd. ist von Angst/von Freude überwältigt* or *von Freude/von Zorn/von Bitterkeit/von Haß/von Grauen/von Verzweiflung erfüllt. His face showed no emotion* can be *Sein Gesicht zeigte/verriet keinen Ärger/keine Enttäuschung,* etc. *He/His face showed no emotion* can also be *Ihm/Seinem Gesicht war kein Ärger/keine Enttäuschung/keine Reue anzumerken.*

5. When **emotion** means 'feeling or the affective aspect of consciousness when contrasted with reason', as in *The speech appealed to our emotions, not to our reason,* **das Gefühl** or **die Gefühle** is used. Cf. **das Gemüt,** the emotional nature or make-up, under MIND 3. iii.
   Diese Rede sprach unsere Gefühle eher an als unsere Vernunft. Or . . . sprach unser Gemüt an.
   Wir sind Geschöpfe des Verstandes, nicht des Gefühls.
   Die Vernunft eher als das Gefühl bildete die Grundlage ihrer Ehe.

emotional *adj.*

1. One meaning of **emotional** is 'concerned with the emotions and the way the pers. feels rather than with the physical health or condition'. *There are emotional problems too. Emotional states affect our hormone levels.* The general term is **seelisch,** psychological, mental, and emotional. **Psychisch** is a learned syn. *Seelische Probleme/Belastung. Seelische/Psychische Störungen. Die psychische Entwicklung eines Kindes.* Compounds of *Gemüt,* cf. MIND 3. iii, express a similar meaning. **Die Gemütslage, die Gemütsverfassung,** and **der Gemütszustand** refer to someone's emotional state. Other compounds are **das Gefühlsleben,** 'emotional life', and **die Gefühlswärme,** 'emotional warmth'.
   Sie befindet sich in einer depressiven Gemütslage.   *Sein Gemütszustand machte allen Sorgen.*
   Sie befand sich in einer heiteren Gemütsverfassung.

2. Applied to people or attitudes **emotional** means 'influenced by feelings rather than by rational thinking' and in relation to language, words, speech, etc. 'expressing more than the usual emotion'. *An emotional expression of thanks.*
i. Gefühlsbetont is applied both to people and things. **Gefühlsgeladen,** lit. 'laden or charged with emotion', is considerably stronger and is used mostly for things, but sometimes for people.
   Sie ist ein sehr gefühlsbetonter/gefühlsgeladener Mensch.
   Die Formulierungen dieses Briefs sind sehr gefühlsbetont und entsprechen nicht den landläufigen
      Vorstellungen eines Geschäftsbriefs.   *Es war eine sehr gefühlsbetonte Rede.*
   Bei diesem Treffen herrschte eine bewußt gefühlsbetonte/gefühlsgeladene Atmosphäre.

Es war ein sehr gefühlsbetonter/gefühlsgeladener Film, und so mancher Zuschauer wurde zu Tränen gerührt. (Note *rührselig*, over-sentimental, tear-jerking.)

ii. Pathetisch has little in common with *pathetic*, which is applied to what arouses sorrow or pity and in colloquial use means 'contemptible'. The G. word means 'impassioned', *eine pathetische Rede*, or 'emotional', *ein pathetischer Stil*, and is often pejorative suggesting over-emotional or unduly solemn.

Was sollen all diese pathetischen Worte? Sag es doch einfacher und weniger weihevoll!
Das klingt sehr pathetisch. Drück dich sachlich aus!   Das ist mir zu pathetisch, zu feierlich.
Er begleitete seine Rede mit pathetischen Gesten, die manche als lächerlich empfanden.

3. For people **emotional** also means 'prone to the arousal of emotions'. [**Leicht**] **erregbar** and [**leicht**] **erregt** mean 'getting worked up easily' and 'easily excited or stirred up' and can translate **emotional** if it expresses this nuance. *He became emotional* can be *Er wurde sehr erregt und fing an zu schreien/zu weinen.*

4. Another sense of **emotional** is 'motivated by emotion as opposed to the intellect' with reference to judgements, reactions, acceptance, rejection, etc. **Gefühlsmäßig** means 'relating to or based on feeling or emotion'. It is quite neutral. As an adv., it is used to state that an opinion or judgement is based on feeling rather than reason, as in *Emotionally, I'm against it.* **Vom Gefühl her** is also used.

Meine erste, rein gefühlsmäßige Reaktion war, daß ihm nicht zu trauen ist.
Vom Gefühl her lehne ich diesen Roman ab, obwohl in erzähltechnischer Hinsicht nichts an ihm auszusetzen ist.   Diese Bilder lassen mich gefühlsmäßig vollkommen kalt.
Rein gefühlsmäßig glaube ich, daß man zu diesem Menschen nie Vertrauen haben kann.

5. A situation or issue described as **emotional** is one that causes people to have strong feelings. *Disarmament was a very emotional issue.* This is best expressed by *Über die Abrüstung haben sich die Gemüter sehr erhitzt* or *Die Gemüter waren über diese Frage sehr erregt.* Both are often translated as *Feelings were running high.*

end, finish, complete *vs.* Some equivalents of **conclude** *v.*

1. Intr. use.
i. End, finish, conclude = 'to come to an end in time'. *When does the film end? The holidays end/finish next week. The Civil War ended/finished in 1865. The meeting ended/finished/concluded at eleven.* **Enden** is only intr. Although *Wann endet der Film?* is possible, **zu Ende sein** and **zu Ende gehen** are much more usual, at least in conversation and for everyday situations. *Wann ist der Film zu Ende? Die Ferien gehen nächste Woche zu Ende.* **Enden** in this sense is mostly found, not with everyday occurrences, but with more important events. *Der amerikanische Bürgerkrieg endete 1865.* **Endigen** has gone out of use.

Die Regierungszeit der Königin Viktoria endete 1901.
Als der Redner endete, brach der Beifall los.
Die Schwierigkeiten scheinen nie enden zu wollen.   Die Vorstellung war erst um elf Uhr zu Ende.
Das Finanzjahr geht in Australien am 30. Juni zu Ende.   Der Prozeß wird bald zu Ende sein.

Enden is, however, usual when the manner of ending or finishing is described. It is used with an adv., and with *wie, so, mit* + a n., or *damit, daß*. In this use, it is a syn. of one sense of **ausgehen**, to end with a certain result, turn out in a certain way, or have a particular outcome.

Wer hätte gedacht, daß die Sache so enden würde?   Der Streit endete mit einer Versöhnung.
Das Gespräch endete damit, daß der Bruder verärgert nach Hause fuhr.
Der Roman endet tragisch/geht glücklich aus.   Wie sind die Wahlen ausgegangen?
Das Spiel endete unentschieden/ging unentschieden aus.
Das Spiel endete mit einem Sieg unserer Gegner.   Wie wird das alles wohl enden/ausgehen?
Die Angelegenheit kann für ihn günstig/schlecht ausgehen.

Schließen, which corresponds to **conclude** in various senses, is a syn. of *enden*. *Schließen* means 'to end in time', *Die Versammlung schloß um elf Uhr*, and 'to end with a certain result', *Der Prozeß schloß mit einem Freispruch*. A person can also be the subj. *Er schließt immer mit einem Zitat.*

> *Die erste Fassung des Stückes schließt mit dieser Szene.*   *'Es gibt also viel zu tun', schloß er.*

Abschließen is used intr. with *mit* meaning 'to end or conclude'. It is usual with periods of time in relation to finances, *Das Geschäftsjahr schloß mit einem Gewinn ab*, but elsewhere it does not differ from *schließen*. *Das Fest schloß mit einem Feuerwerk* [*ab*]. *Das Buch schließt mit dem Ersten Weltkrieg* [*ab*].

ii. Enden also means 'to end in space'. *Bitte alle aussteigen! Der Zug endet hier. Der Weg endete an einer Bretterhütte. Die Gebirgslandschaft endet hier, und eine weite Ebene beginnt.* An alternative is *Der Weg ist hier zu Ende*.

iii. Enden and **ausgehen** are used with **auf** to state how a word ends. *Für mein Gedicht brauche ich ein Wort, das auf -tet endet/ausgeht.*

2. Trans. use **Finish, complete, conclude** a piece of work, an activity, etc.

i. Beenden is 'to bring an activity or state to an end'. **Abschließen** is 'to bring to an end' something which has already gone on for some time. Both translate **finish** or **complete** + obj. and can take a phr. with *mit*. **Beendigen** is still occasionally found, but does not differ from *beenden*. To conclude or end a speech etc. with a quotation etc. can be translated by *beenden*, but **schließen** is frequently used. *Er schloß die Rede mit einer Strophe aus einem Gedicht von Byron.*

> *Sie hat das Studium Ende letzten Jahres abgeschlossen/beendet.*
> *Man forderte die beiden Regierungen auf, den Krieg zu beenden.*
> *Die Versammlung wurde mit einem Musikstück beendet.*
> *Wir schlossen die Rundreise mit einem Besuch der Burg ab.*
> *Wir hoffen, die Untersuchung/die Verhandlungen bald abschließen/beenden zu können.*
> *Ovid wurde aus Rom verbannt und beendete sein Leben im Exil.*

ii. Vollenden means 'to complete what has already been begun'. It often refers to work of an artistic nature and suggests that, through completion, such works reach perfection or high quality. *Der Dichter hat dieses Werk in hohem Alter vollendet.* It is sometimes found with abstract ns. as obj. *Die Reichsproklamation am 18. Januar 1871 vollendete die deutsche Einheit.* The expression *Jmd. hat sein/ihr sechzigstes etc. Lebensjahr vollendet* is used in formal language. *Jmdn. vor vollendete Tatsachen stellen*, to present someone with a *fait accompli*.

> *Der Maler nahm die Arbeit am Bild wieder auf und vollendete es in kurzer Zeit.*
> *Dieser Roman ist das letzte Werk, das er vollendet hat.*

iii. Vervollständigen is 'to complete' in the sense of filling gaps by adding the missing part or parts. *Ich brauche noch zwei Münzen, um meine Sammlung von australischen 'shillings' zu vervollständigen.*

> *Den Bericht muß ich noch vervollständigen. Es fehlen noch einige Absätze/einige Einzelheiten.*

iv. Fertigstellen refers mostly to manual and mechanical work.

> *Die neue Brücke/Die neue Autobahnstrecke wird demnächst fertiggestellt.*
> *In den letzten drei Monaten hat die Firma 10 Häuser fertiggestellt.*

v. Fertigmachen is used in speech like **finish off**. *Ich mache eine Arbeit/eine Aufgabe fertig.* (Note: In colloquial speech it means 'to wear out, exhaust'. *Die schwere Arbeit bei der sengenden Hitze hat mich fertig gemacht.* The refl. means 'to get ready'. Cf. PRE-PARE 3. *Macht euch fertig, das Taxi kommt!*)

3. Both **schließen** and **abschließen** express senses carried by **conclude**. Both are used with *das Abkommen*, 'agreement', and *das Bündnis*, 'alliance', as obj. *Vertrag* is found with both: *Die Firma hat einen langfristigen Vertrag mit einem Lieferanten geschlossen* and *Man schließt einen Arbeits-, Miet- und Handelsvertrag ab*. *Schließen* is the usual v. with *der Waffenstillstand, der Pakt*, and *die Vereinbarung. Eine Versicherung abschließen* means 'to take out insurance', and *ein Geschäft abschließen* 'to conclude a business deal'.

4. Schließen corresponds to **conclude** = 'to make a logical deduction'. *Aus der Aussage dieses Zeugen kann man schließen, daß der Verdächtigte unschuldig ist. Aus etw. auf etw. schließen* means 'to conclude from one thg. that sth. else is the case'. *Man kann nicht von einem afrikanischen Staat auf alle anderen schließen*, conclude from one what all the others are like. *Wir haben aus deiner Miene auf deine Zustimmung geschlossen*, concluded from the way you looked that you were in agreement.

5. End sth. when it means 'to put an end to it' is **etw. ein Ende machen** or **setzen**. A distinction made by some, but not all, speakers between the two vs. is that *machen* refers to an end one welcomes, whereas *setzten* suggests an end one regrets. The two examples follow this usage.

> *Wir müssen diesem Mißbrauch/dieser Ungerechtigkeit/diesem Unsinn ein Ende machen.*
> *Der Ausgang des 20. Juli 1944 setzte dem innerdeutschen Widerstand ein blutiges Ende und gab den Weg frei für eine letzte Steigerung der NS-Herrschaft.*

Ein Ende bereiten and **beenden** express neither satisfaction nor regret about an outcome. *Diese Niederlage hätte der politischen Karriere eines weniger ehrgeizigen Mannes ein [schnelles] Ende bereitet* or *. . . hätte die Karriere . . . [schnell] beendet. Wir müssen dieser Sache irgendwie ein Ende bereiten* or *. . . diese Sache irgendwie beenden.*

6. Finish sth. and **finish doing** sth., be ready.

i. With some vs. **zu Ende** states that the activity is finished. *Ich muß den Brief noch zu Ende schreiben/das Buch zu Ende lesen.* It is not used with *haben*.

> *Sie wollten den Fernsehfilm unbedingt zu Ende sehen/die Radiosendung zu Ende hören.*
> *Sie sangen das Lied zu Ende/spielten das Spiel zu Ende.*

ii. Fertig is used in the same way but, unlike *zu Ende*, can be combined with *haben. Ich habe den Brief fertig*, and *ich habe den Aufsatz fertig*, finished writing it. *Ich habe die Hausaufgaben fertig.*

> *Wir müssen die Koffer noch fertig packen.*   *Ich habe mich noch nicht fertig angezogen.*
> *Gestern haben wir den Schuppen fertig gebaut.*   *Ich habe die Zeitung fertig gelesen.*

iii. Fertig, mostly + *sein*, means that people and things are ready to go or to be used. *Ich bin fertig—wir können gehen. Das Essen ist fertig.*

> *Auf die Plätze! (or Achtung!) Fertig! Los!*
> *Der Zug ist fertig zur Abfahrt.*

Fertig also means 'finished, completed'. The result of the completed action must be visible and tangible. *Die neue Brücke ist fertig. Fertig* cannot be used when **finished** can be replaced by *over*, which is *zu Ende. Das Spiel ist zu Ende.* Cf. 1.

iv. Fertig is also used attributively, *Ich muß das fertige Manuskript Ende Februar abliefern*, and can mean 'ready-made', *ein fertiger Kuchenboden.*

> *Das Haus/Die Arbeit ist fertig.*   *Der Aufsatz ist noch nicht fertig.*
> *Sind die Briefe, die Sie für mich tippen, schon fertig?* (finished or ready).

v. With people as subj., **fertig sein mit** means 'to have finished doing or using sth.' *Ich bin mit dem Buch fertig* usually means that I've finished reading or using it, but could mean writing it. *Bist du mit dem Wörterbuch fertig? Wenn du mit den Hausaufgaben fertig bist, darfst du gehen.* (When *mit* is not included, the context must make it clear whether *Ich bin fertig* means 'I've finished' or 'I'm ready'.) *Fertig sein mit* is often used with a verbal n. or a n. denoting an action. *Bist du mit dem Packen fertig? Seid ihr mit dem Abwasch fertig?* **Fertig werden mit etw.** is 'to finish sth.' or 'to get sth. finished'. *Er ist gerade mit der Lehre fertig geworden. Wann wirst du endlich mit dem Aufsatz/mit dem Studium fertig? Ich bin gestern abend mit der Übersetzung fertig geworden.* (In fig. use it means 'to cope or manage with sth.' *Sie ist mit dem*

Problem/mit den Kindern leicht fertig geworden.) *Fertig sein mit jmdm.* means 'to be finished with' or 'not to want to have anything more to do with s.o.' *Mit diesem Individuum bin ich restlos fertig. Fix*, which is often added to *fertig* in speech, strengthens any of the latter's senses without changing it. *Alles ist fix und fertig. Innerlich war sie fix und fertig mit dem Mann.* (*Fertig* also means 'completely exhausted'. *Nach dem Gewaltmarsch waren wir fertig. Nach der ungewohnten Anstrengung war ich fix und fertig.*)

7. Finish = 'to use up'. **Alle** is used to state that food or drink is all gone or finished. *Der Kuchen/Der Saft ist alle. Die Torte muß alle werden.* **Aufessen** means 'to finish [off] or eat what remains'. *Ich habe die Torte aufgegessen.* **Aufbrauchen** means 'to use up'. Cf. USE 4. *Wir haben unsere Vorräte aufgebraucht.*

8. Finish *first* etc. *in a race* is **durchs Ziel gehen**. *Der kanadische Läufer ging als erster durchs Ziel.*

enjoy *v.*

1. Enjoy means 'to find pleasure and satisfaction in doing or experiencing sth.' The degree of pleasure varies from only moderate to great, the latter being expressed by advs. like *really* or *very much*.

i. Genießen implies doing something with great pleasure, experiencing things seen or heard, or participating in activities with relish. It is often found with aspects of nature, but most activities can be the obj. if the condition of a high degree of enjoyment is fulfilled. *Man genießt den herrlichen Ausblick/den Duft der Blumen/die frische Luft und den Sonnenschein/die Schönheit der Natur/den Sonnenuntergang/die Einsamkeit des Gebirges/den Frühling/die Ruhe nach der Arbeit/das Leben in vollen Zügen.* It is also used with *es* and an infin. or clause. *Ich genieße es, im Gebirge zu wandern. Wir genossen es, daß es endlich mal kühl wurde.* Although the obj. is mostly of a desirable nature, a statement is possible like *Er genoß seine Rache.* In cases in which *gefallen* (cf. LIKE) is the basic state, *genießen* denotes something more and is often found with *sehr* or *wirklich. Der Film/Die Musik/Der Vortrag/Die Erzählung/Die Aufführung* (*des Theaterstücks*) *hat mir gut gefallen* or *Ich habe den Film/die Aufführung/die Musik wirklich/sehr genossen.* In the imp., *genießen* means 'to enjoy to the full', *Genießen Sie den Urlaub/die Ferien/die Schiffsreise/den Aufenthalt auf dem Lande/das schöne Wetter!*, but here it is the only possibility, as *gefallen*, like *like*, cannot be used in the imp. *Genießen* can also be used to express the wish that someone will enjoy something. *Ich hoffe, daß du nicht die ganze Zeit zu arbeiten brauchst und den Aufenthalt in Göttingen mehr genießen kannst.* Such wishes are, however, often formulated differently. *Wir wünschen Ihnen einen angenehmen Aufenthalt in Australien,* hope you enjoy your stay there. The idiom *Etw. war mir ein Genuß* means 'I enjoyed it very much'.

Wir genossen es geradezu, daß ihm endlich mal einer so richtig die Meinung sagte.

ii. In many cases, **enjoy** does not suggest such a high degree of pleasure as implied by *genießen* and needs to be translated by an equivalent of LIKE. In generalizations about what people enjoy, **genießen** is occasionally used with *immer. Hochgebirgswanderungen/Solche Gespräche habe ich immer genossen.* The main equivalents of *like* are **gern, mögen,** and **gefallen.** *Ich schwimme gern,* I enjoy/like swimming. *Ich mag Krimis nicht,* don't enjoy/like them. *Das Konzert hat mir gut gefallen,* I liked/enjoyed it. In relation to food the v. is **schmecken**. A waiter asks, *'Hat es Ihnen geschmeckt?'*, did you enjoy the meal. Note *Ich habe das Essen sehr genossen,* I enjoyed it very much. An alternative for enjoying one occasion is *Der Ausflug hat mir viel* **Vergnügen gemacht.**

iii. Enjoy oneself or *have a good time* is **sich amüsieren**. *Wir haben uns alle gut amüsiert. Enjoy yourselves!* can be *Amüsiert euch gut [beim Ball]!*, but *Viel Spaß!* and *Viel Vergnügen!* are very common. **Viel Spaß haben** or, with an activity as subj., **viel Spaß machen** often express the sense of enjoying oneself or something. *Die Kinder hatten viel Spaß beim Zoobesuch und sprachen tagelang davon* or *Der Zoobesuch machte ihnen viel Spaß.*

Um alles zu vergessen, fuhren wir in die Stadt. Wir wollten uns ein paar Stunden amüsieren.

2. Enjoy also means 'to have the benefit of sth.' *They enjoyed a good education. She enjoys good health/the respect of her subordinates/the confidence of her employer.* **Genießen** is used in this sense. *Alle haben eine gute Ausbildung genossen.* **Sich erfreuen** + gen. is a more elevated syn. which occurs mostly in fixed expressions, such as *Der Roman erfreute sich großer Beliebtheit* or *Sie erfreute sich bester Gesundheit.*

Alle Kinder hatten eine gute Schulbildung genossen.

Er genießt die Achtung seiner Untergebenen/das Vertrauen aller Kollegen/einen guten Ruf.

(Note: With food and beverages as obj. **genießen** means 'to eat, drink, or consume', but is unusual except in bureaucratic or formal style. *Der Patient hat noch nichts/nur eine Kleinigkeit genossen. Ich habe heute noch nichts genossen* is very formal style. **Genießbar** and **ungenießbar** mean 'edible' and 'inedible'. The idea can also be expressed by *genießen*. *Die Früchte dieses Baumes sind genießbar, schmecken aber nicht besonders gut. Diese Früchte kann man ohne Schaden genießen. Diese Pilze sind ungenießbar/sind nicht zu genießen. Der Fisch ist ungenießbar/ist nicht mehr zu genießen,* it's gone bad. **Der Genuß** can mean 'the consumption' of something. *Der übermäßige Alkoholgenuß hat zu dem Unfall geführt.*)

enter *v.* Some uses of **come, go, get in[to]** *vs.*

1. Enter a room or building. In its basic sense **enter** expresses the same meaning as **come** or **go in[to]**, but belongs to a higher stylistic level and tends to be used in formal language for an important person. *The Prime Minister entered the room.* It often stresses the manner. *The procession slowly entered the church.*
i. The ordinary words are **gehen** and **kommen** + **in**. *Sie ging ins Zimmer und setzte sich an den Schreibtisch. Er kam ins Schlafzimmer und legte sich hin.* **Hinein** may be added to *gehen*, and *herein* to *kommen*, but they are not necessary with a phr. with *in* as they only emphasize the meaning without adding anything to it. They must, however, be used when a phr. with *in* is not present. Thus *Er ging durch eine Seitentür in den Sitzungssaal*, but *Er ging durch eine Seitentür hinein*, went in, entered. *Als ich sah, wie sie mit Paketen hoch beladen ins Zimmer kam, stand ich auf, um ihr zu helfen. Er kam herein, ohne zu klopfen.*
ii. The appropriate v. of motion, mostly **fahren**, is used when vehicles, ships, etc. enter something. *Der Zug fuhr in den Tunnel. Wir sahen zu, wie das Schiff in die Schleuse fuhr. Der Hafen ist breit und tief, und Schiffe fahren ohne die Hilfe eines Bugsierers hinein.* **Einfahren** and **einlaufen** are used when **enter** means 'to arrive', particularly when a time is given. *Der Schnellzug aus Hamburg fährt gleich ein/ist gerade eingelaufen. Das Schiff fuhr/lief um Mitternacht in den Hafen ein.*
iii. For people, **treten in**, 'go into, enter', is often used and like **enter**, but unlike **go/come in[to]**, is not affected by the position of the speaker. *Er trat in die Bank und ging zur Kasse. Als sie in die Kirche traten, bekreuzigten sie sich mit Weihwasser.* **Eintreten** has the same sense and must be used when a phr. with *in* is not present. When a phr. with *in* is present, *ein* is optional. *Sie klopfte an und trat ein*, but *trat ins Zimmer [ein]. Wir wagten nicht einzutreten. Bitte eintreten, ohne zu klopfen!* If the place entered would otherwise be the last word in the sent., *ein* tends to be used,

possibly because it rounds off the sound of the statement. *Sie trat in das Zimmer ein.* Thus *Als ich in den Dom trat, überkam mich ein Gefühl andächtiger Stille,* but *In andächtiger Stimmung traten wir in den Dom ein.* The usual word for *Come in!* called through a closed door, is *Herein! Treten Sie ein!* is also used, particularly when the speaker sees someone hesitate at the door. It is more formal than *Herein! Nur herein!* is translated as *Come right in!* or *Come on in!*

iv. Betreten is a syn. of *eintreten* and *treten in,* but it is more formal. It means 'to come right into the room etc.', while *treten in* and *eintreten* need only mean 'to get just past the entrance'. *Betreten* needs an obj. *Fast jeden Tag betritt sie das Büro um 5 vor 9. Als er das Zimmer betrat, verstummten alle sofort. Betreten* is always used when official permission to enter is involved. *Betreten der Baustelle verboten!*

> *Er verbot uns, das Laboratorium zu betreten.*
>
> *Unter normalen Umständen darf die Polizei ein Haus ohne Durchsuchungsbefehl nicht betreten.*

(*Betreten* also means 'to set foot on'. *Morgen werden Sie zum ersten Mal australischen Boden betreten. Nach der wochenlangen Fahrt auf dem ständig schlingernden Schiff war ich froh, endlich wieder festen Boden zu betreten.* With *die Schwelle,* 'threshold', E. uses cross. *Du betrittst mir nie wieder die Schwelle!*)

v. Einsteigen is the usual v. in relation to burglars who enter a house. *Die Einbrecher sind durch das Küchenfenster in die Wohnung eingestiegen.* **Eindringen** is an alternative and in this situation suggests force or violence. *Die Räuber sind in den frühen Morgenstunden in das Geschäft eingedrungen, ohne bemerkt zu werden. Eindringen* also means 'to enter where one should not be'. *Der Mann war unbemerkt in den Palast geschlichen und drang in das Schlafgemach der Königin ein.*

> *'Wer erlaubt Ihnen eigentlich, so einfach hier einzudringen?' fuhr er mich an. 'Haben Sie noch nie gehört, daß man sich anmeldet, wenn man einen Oberregierungsrat sprechen will?'*

2. Enter a country, territory, place.

i. Of armies etc. **Einfallen** and **eindringen** always imply an aggressive intention and are like *invade.* **Einziehen, einrücken,** and **einmarschieren** can be used for entering with warlike intent, but in other contexts suggest only peaceful aims. *Feindliche Truppen sind in das Land eingefallen/eingedrungen/einmarschiert. Das siegreiche Heer zog/rückte im Triumph in die Hauptstadt ein. Die Sportler zogen/marschierten ins Stadion ein.*

ii. Einziehen is also used for parties entering parliament and for entering/getting into a round of a competition. The normal v. for the latter is *kommen.* Cf GET 7. i. *Die Grünen ziehen zum ersten Mal in den Landtag ein.*

> *Zwei rechtsradikale Parteien, die Republikaner und die Deutsche Volksunion, haben ihren Stimmenanteil bei den Landtagswahlen in Baden-Würtemberg und Schleswig-Holstein erhöht und ziehen ins Parlament ein. Die Mannschaft ist in die Endrunde gekommen/eingezogen.*

iii. Hereinkommen and **hineinkommen** mean 'to get into an area', often a country, sometimes a building. The first is used by people who are in the area, the second by those outside it. They are used as a general comment and do not refer to a specific point of entry nor to permission. *Es war für Ausländer schwer oder sogar unmöglich, in bestimmte Gebiete der Sowjetunion hineinzukommen. Eine Zeitlang konnten Westdeutsche nur schwer in die DDR hineinkommen/hereinkommen.*

iv. The official term meaning 'to enter a country' in relation to people is **einreisen,** the n. **die Einreise.** It implies conformity with the existing regulations whether these require permission or not. *Die Familie ist am 21. Juli 1991 in die BRD eingereist.* For goods entering a country, the usual vs. are **einführen** and **importieren,** both of which mean 'to import'. *Immer mehr Waren werden eingeführt/importiert.* For goods or people entering illegally, **[ein]schleusen** is used. *Rauschgift wird über Holland in die Bundesrepublik [ein]geschleust* and *Mehrere Agenten wurden in das Land [ein]geschleust.*

3. Einsteigen is 'to GET into' or 'enter' a vehicle. *Ein* is optional if a phr. with *in* follows. *Der Bus hielt, und wir stiegen ein,* but *Ich bin in den falschen Zug gestiegen. Ein* could be added here.

4. Enter = 'penetrate'. With a thing as subj., **dringen in** means 'to penetrate, get, or make its way into'. It implies overcoming what might prevent entry, but not great force. *Bei einem Sandsturm in der Wüste dringt der Sand in alle Fugen und Ritzen des Gepäcks und der Kleider. Der Rauch dringt mir in die Nase. Der Regen dringt in meine Schuhe.* **Eindringen** denotes the same action, but implies some kind of force or violence and sometimes corresponds to **enter**. The subj. can be bullets or splinters entering the body. *Die Kugel ist in die rechte Schulter eingedrungen. Der rostige Nagel/Der Splitter ist tief in den Fuß eingedrungen. Im Fall eines Schlangenbisses muß man verhindern, daß das Gift in den Blutkreislauf eindringt.* It is also used fig. *Diese Ideen sind in das allgemeine Bewußtsein eingedrungen.*

5. Enter a firm, the army, etc., government service, a profession. (Cf. JOIN 4.) **Enter** a firm as employee or in another capacity. *Mit 25 ist er in die väterliche Firma eingetreten. Sie ist als Teilhaberin in das Geschäft eingetreten. Sie traten in die Armee/Marine/Luftwaffe ein.* **Enter** a specified branch of government service is expressed as *Jmd. tritt in den Schuldienst/in den Justizdienst/in den diplomatischen Dienst ein.* For other professions, different expressions are necessary. *To enter the medical profession: Arzt werden. To enter the church: Pfarrer/Priester werden. Er trat in ein Kloster ein* or *wurde Mönch. To enter parliament: Er wurde Abgeordneter/wurde ins Parlament gewählt. To enter politics* in the sense of being actively engaged in it is colloquially *Sie sind in die Politik eingestiegen.* If becoming a politician is meant, *jmd. wird Politiker* or *geht in die Politik* is used. *To enter s.o.'s service* could be *bei jmdm. zu arbeiten anfangen,* but *eine Stelle bei jmdm.* **antreten** would be used in more formal language and is like *to take up a position. She entered a university* is normally *Sie fing an zu studieren,* but in formal language *Sie trat das Studium an der Universität X an* is found.

6. Other uses of **eintreten. Enter** a stage/period of time/history. *Die Verhandlungen treten in die kritische/entscheidende Phase [ein]. Mit dem Untergang des römischen Reiches trat Europa in ein Zeitalter der Barbarei ein. Als Kinder einer wohlhabenden Familie sind sie mit vielen Vorteilen in das Leben eingetreten.* **Enter** a war. *Amerika ist erst 1941 in den Krieg eingetreten.*

7. Eintragen is 'to enter sth. in writing' into a book, list, account, etc. *Ich habe alle Namen/mich in die Liste eingetragen. Die Eintragung im Tagebuch* is 'an entry in a diary'. *Ich trage immer alle Ausgaben in dieses Heft ein.*

8. Enter = 'to enrol or register for'. *I enter a competition/for an examination.* **Anmelden** can mean 'to enrol or register'. *Charlotte ist gerade zwei geworden, aber wir haben sie schon für den Kindergarten angemeldet.* It also means 'to enter s.o./sth. for a contest or competition'. *Ich habe meinen Pudel für den Hundeschönheitswettbewerb angemeldet.* For the E. intr. use *Five [runners] have entered* or *I entered for the high-jump/enrolled for a course,* **sich anmelden** is used. *Ich habe mich für den Hochsprung/den Russischkurs angemeldet. Zwanzig Läufer haben sich angemeldet.* A phr. with *mit* can be added. *Sie hat sich mit einem Landschaftsbild für den Malwettbewerb angemeldet. Dreißig Fahrer haben sich mit ihren Autos für das Rennen angemeldet.* (*Ein Auto anmelden* means 'to register a car'.) *To enter for an examination* is either **sich zu einer Prüfung melden** or **sich für eine Prüfung anmelden**. *Ich habe mich gerade zum Staatsexamen gemeldet* or *mich für das Staatsexamen angemeldet.* Without a prepositional phr. *sich anmelden* is necessary. *Wenn Sie das Staatsexamen nächstes Jahr machen wollen, müssen*

Sie sich vor Ende dieses Jahres anmelden. (Note that *sich zu einer Arbeit/Aufgabe melden* means 'to volunteer for it'.)

9. Some other uses of **enter**. **Enter** *into* negotiations: *Wir sind vor kurzem in Verhandlungen mit der Firma N. getreten.* **Enter/go into** *details/particulars/a* question: *Auf Einzelheiten/eine Frage* **eingehen.** *Auf Einzelheiten kann ich im Augenblick nicht eingehen—ich erkläre nur das Wesentliche.* **Enter**/get into/start *a conversation* is usually *ein Gespräch mit jmdm.* **anknüpfen.** *Ich lernte ihn kennen, als wir zusammen in einem Zugabteil saßen und er ein Gespräch mit mir anknüpfte.* **Sich einlassen auf** usually has a neg. connotation suggesting that the activity is bad, disadvantageous, or dangerous. It often occurs in the neg. *Mit dem lasse ich mich auf kein Gespräch ein—unter zwei Stunden kommt man nicht weg.* One transl. of *The question of cost never* **entered into** our considerations is *Die Preisfrage ist in unseren Überlegungen nie aufgetreten.* **Auftreten**, to OCCUR, come up. *The thought* **entered** my mind can be *Mir kam der Gedanke, daß ich eine andere Arbeitsweise versuchen sollte* or *Der Gedanke kam mir in den Sinn* . . .

escape *v.*

A. This section deals with two meanings of **escape**. 1. 'To gain one's liberty by flight', 'to get free from detention or control or from an oppressive or irksome condition'. The situations to which it is applied vary considerably. (*a*) *A prisoner has escaped.* (*b*) *He escaped from the burning building.* (*c*) *The animal escaped from the trap.* 2. 'To get clear of or away from pursuers', 'to elude s.o.'s grasp', and 'to succeed in avoiding anything painful or unwelcome which threatens or could happen'. In this case the person is not in the power of the pursuer or the unwelcome conditions. (*a*) *He escaped by fleeing when he saw the policeman.* (*b*) *S.o. escapes punishment/ arrest/death.* (*c*) *The infection was so general that few escaped.* No G. word is as comprehensive as **escape**. For other senses of **escape** see section B.

1. Vs. appropriate to three situations listed above are treated here. 1*a*. *Two prisoners have escaped. They escaped from prison/their guard. A tiger escaped from its cage.* 2*a*. *The policeman was about to grab the boy, but he ducked and escaped/got away.* 2*b*. *Murderers sometimes escape punishment. People escape death/danger/a particular fate/arrest/a disaster.*

i. The v. with the broadest meaning, **entkommen**, 'to escape from actual or threatened captivity or danger', mainly occurs in meanings 1*a* and 2*a*, but can also express meaning 2*b*. Even in *Die Verbrecher konnten [unbemerkt] entkommen*, it suggests a situation which normally results in capture. **Entwischen** is a common colloquial syn. It implies getting away quickly and unobtrusively, often by a trick, mostly from one person or more. Both can be used with a phr. denoting direction. *Der Einbrecher konnte durch das Fenster entkommen/entwischen.*

Er entkam/entwischte seinen Bewachern/seinen Verfolgern.

Zwei Geiseln sind den Geiselnehmern entwischt/entkommen.

Der Polizist war gerade im Begriff, den Jungen zu fassen/packen, aber er duckte sich und entkam/entwischte.   In letzter Minute entwischte der Junge den Polizisten.

Es gelang den Bewohnern des brennenden Hauses, den Flammen zu entkommen.

Sie sind aus dem Gefängnis/über die Mauer/ins Ausland entkommen/entwischt.

ii. Alternatives for situations 1*a* and 2*a*. **Ausbrechen**, 'to break out', implies captivity and some measure of violence. *Der Schwerverbrecher brach aus dem Gefängnis/aus der psychiatrischen Anstalt aus. Die Löwen sind aus ihrem Käfig ausgebrochen.* **Entspringen** implies escaping from legal custody, but it is not particularly common. Only the perf. and the past part. occur. *Zwei Häftlinge waren auf dem Transport entsprungen. Nach zwei Tagen konnten die entsprungenen Häftlinge wieder* *gefaßt werden.* **Entweichen** is often encountered in official language and in newspapers, but rarely in conversation. *Ein Jugendlicher ist aus dem Erziehungsheim entwichen. Mehrere Giftschlangen sind aus dem Toxikologischen Institut entwichen. In der allgemeinen Verwirrung konnte der Dieb entweichen.* **Entfliehen** is a more elevated word than *entkommen.* It means 'to flee from s.o.'s power, area of influence, a threat, or danger in order to get to safety or freedom'. It is used for escaping from captivity, *Er ist seinen Bewachern/aus dem Gefängnis/der Gefangenschaft entflohen* or *Der Gefangene konnte entfliehen,* and from large areas, *Die norwegische Regierung entfloh im zweiten Weltkrieg nach Großbritannien. Entfliehen* is also used for getting away from unwelcome conditions. *Sie entflohen dem Lärm/der Unruhe/dem Menschengetümmel.* **Entschlüpfen** means 'to elude or slip away from one or more people who have captured or would like to capture s.o.' It is used alone or with a dat. *In dem dichten Gewühl riß er sich los und entschlüpfte. Obwohl das Haus umstellt war, konnte er entschlüpfen. Er entschlüpfte seinen Bewachern/seiner Bewachung.* **Jmdm. durch die Lappen gehen** is a colloquial expression for evading capture. *Der Inspektor fluchte, weil ihm der Gauner wieder durch die Lappen gegangen war.* **Entlaufen** is now unusual in reference to people except as a past part., as in *der entlaufene Gefängnisinsasse/Sklave.* (*Das entlaufene Kind* means 'the child who has run away'. The v. *to run away* is *weglaufen. Das Kind ist von zu Hause weggelaufen.*) *Entlaufen* is used as a v. when an animal, mostly a pet, is the subj. *Unseren Nachbarn ist der Hund entlaufen.* For birds, the v. is **entfliegen.** *Ihnen ist der Wellensittich entflogen.*

iii. Other equivalents for situation 2*b*. **Escape** punishment, death, etc. The main equivalent **entgehen** means 'to be able to avoid or not to become involved in a dangerous or unpleasant situation'. It is used with *Tod, Gefahr, Strafe,* a certain kind of fate, or any potentially unpleasant circumstances. *Nur wenige Verschwörer entgingen dem Blutbad, das die Nazis aus Rache anrichteten.* **Entkommen** is also used with *Strafe, Tod,* etc. *Er wird seiner Strafe nicht entkommen/entgehen.* **Entrinnen** also means 'to escape' danger, disaster, etc., but it is an elevated and not very common word. These words usually imply that, by favourable circumstances, an untoward fate did not befall a person. Although *entkommen* presupposes more activity than the other vs., none suggests active evasion. If **escape** implies activity to avoid something, the equivalent is **sich entziehen.** *Manchmal entgehen Mörder der Strafe/Bestrafung,* they are not punished. *Sie entziehen sich der Strafe* means that they evade it.

Sie sind dem Verderben/der Gefahr mit knapper Not entgangen/entkommen.

Sie beschlossen, den Flug um eine Woche zu verschieben, und entgingen dadurch dem Flugzeugabsturz.

Mit knapper Not entging er der Festnahme/der Verhaftung.

Einem ähnlichen Schicksal ist die Stadt glücklicherweise entgangen.

Der Kranke ist dem Tod entronnen/entgangen.

Er hat sich der Verhaftung durch die Flucht entzogen.

iv. E. situation 1*b*. *They* **escaped** *from the burning building/the sinking ship.* **Sich retten**, to escape from an impending disaster, shipwreck, fire, or a [raging] mob. It needs a phr., e.g. with *vor* = 'from', or *durch (die Flucht),* or with *in, über, auf,* etc., unless the context makes it clear that one is implied. In *Der Minister konnte sich vor den unangenehmen Fragen der Journalisten nicht retten,* it is used with a certain irony.

Nach dem Kentern des Bootes retteten wir uns ans Ufer/auf eine nahegelegene Insel.

Der Pilot konnte sich mit dem Fallschirm/mit dem Schleudersitz retten.

Da das Feuer andere Fluchtwege abgeschnitten hatte, retteten sich die Hotelgäste auf das Dach.

Er wurde von zwei Schlägertypen angegriffen, es gelang ihm jedoch, sich zu retten/ihnen zu entkommen/entwischen. Or Er konnte sich aber durch die Flucht vor ihnen retten.

v. E. situation 1*c*. *The animal* **escaped** *from the trap. They escaped from the rubble of the collapsed house.* **Sich befreien**, 'to free oneself', either from something concrete like a trap or something less tangible like *Angst, Sorgen, Illusionen,* or *Schulden.* The prep. is either *aus* when the body is held in or under something and in the phrs. *aus einer unangenehmen Situation* and *aus Not und Elend,* or *von* when one is oppressed by cares etc., *Man befreit sich von Sorgen.*

Das Känguruh konnte sich aus der Falle befreien.
Sie konnten sich aus den Trümmern des eingestürzten Hauses befreien.
Der Ringer befreite sich aus der Umklammerung seines Gegners.
Das Volk befreite sich durch eine Revolution von der Unterdrückung.

vi. E. situation 2c. A transl. of *The infection was so general that few* **escaped** is *Die Seuche war so weit verbreitet, daß nur wenige dem Tod entkamen/entgingen,* or *daß nur wenige mit dem Leben davonkamen.*

B. Other meanings of **escape**.

1. 'To get off safely when imperilled', 'to remain unhurt', or 'to be less seriously injured than might have been expected'. *The car was a wreck, but the passengers escaped with a few bruises.* This sense is expressed by **davonkommen**, which is often combined with a phr. with *mit*. *Er ist mit einer leichten Verletzung davongekommen. Das Boot war an den Felsen auseinandergebrochen, aber die Besatzung kam mit dem Leben davon/konnte sich retten.* Without a *mit* phr., as in *Er ist gerade noch einmal davongekommen,* it implies with less harm than might have been expected.

Das Auto war ein Wrack, aber alle Insassen kamen mit ein paar blauen Flecken davon.
Sie sind mit einer leichten Strafe davongekommen.

2. With gases and liquids as subj. **escape** means 'to issue from a pipe or container'. **Ausströmen** is the everyday word in reference to gas and liquid and implies a large amount. **Entweichen**, which is only used for gas, belongs to the written language. *Infolge eines Brandes in einer Chemiefabrik ist Chlorgas entwichen.*

Das Gas, das aus der Hauptleitung ausgeströmt war, konnte man im ganzen Haus riechen.
Das Wasser ist an mehreren Stellen ausgeströmt.

3. Escape in *A remark/sound escaped s.o./s.o.'s lips* is **entfahren**.

Ein leises Stöhnen entfuhr den Lippen des Jungen.
Ein Seufzer/Ein Fluch entfuhr ihm.

4. Escape = 'to elude observation or notice' as in *The significance of this fact had escaped us* or *I hope no further mistakes have escaped us/our attention* is **entgehen**.

Die Bedeutung dieser Tatsache war uns entgangen.
Wir wollen hoffen, daß uns/unserer Aufmerksamkeit keine weiteren Fehler entgangen sind.

5. Escape = 'to elude s.o.'s memory'. *Her name escapes me at the moment. Der Name ist mir völlig/ganz* **entfallen**. *Die Angelegenheit ist mir vollkommen/ganz entfallen.*

estimate, assess *vs.*

1. Estimate means 'to calculate approximately' any numerical value. **Assess** means 'to calculate the amount of money that sth. is worth or that should be paid for it' and implies greater accuracy than **estimate**. **Schätzen** is the main v. meaning 'to estimate', but in certain contexts it also translates **assess**. See 2 for **estimate** *costs* referring to a tradesman etc.

i. When a non-expert result is being given, **schätzen** means 'to attempt to ascertain the value, weight, size, height, distance, age, amount, cost of sth., etc., either approximately without thorough knowledge or on the basis of reasonable probability'. It is used with an obj. with and without *auf* = 'at, to be', or with a clause.

Sie haben die Größe/die Geschwindigkeit/das Gewicht/die Breite der Straße richtig geschätzt.
Ich schätze die Entfernung auf zwanzig Kilometer. Ich schätze, daß ihr um zwei Uhr losfahren müßt, wenn ihr vor dem Dunkelwerden in Hamburg ankommen wollt. When

schätzen is interpolated into a sent. the construction can be either *Wann, schätzt du, wirst du fertig sein?* or *Was schätzen Sie, wie lange die Untersuchung dauern wird?*

Ich schätze ihn auf Mitte dreißig.   Sie schätzten den Schaden auf 2 000 Mark.

Auf wie hoch schätzt du den Turm?   Ich kann nicht schätzen, wieviel der Koffer wiegt.

ii. Überschlagen means 'to work out a numerical value quickly and roughly in one's head'. The result is a rough approximation. *Überschlagen* is used with an obj. or clause, but not with a prep.

Sie überschlug, was die Reise kosten würde/wieviel sie ausgegeben hatte/wie lange wir für die Fahrt brauchen würden.   Ich habe die Kosten überschlagen.

Der Lehrer riet den Schülern, bei komplizierten Rechenaufgaben immer das Ergebnis zuerst zu überschlagen.

iii. Abschätzen means 'to look at sth. carefully in order to form an accurate estimate'. It is, however, rarely used alone, but occurs mostly with a modal v. and in the constructions *läßt sich abschätzen* and *ist abzuschätzen*, and is often neg. Thus *Ich kann die Größe des Feldes nicht leicht abschätzen* or *Können Sie die Kosten abschätzen?* or *Es läßt sich nur schwer abschätzen, wie lange wir für diese Arbeit brauchen*, but in a sent. without a modal v. or *lassen*, **schätzen** is used, *Ich habe die Größe/die Kosten falsch/richtig geschätzt*. If the obj. is something concrete, *abschätzen* is interchangeable with *schätzen*, but only *abschätzen* is used with abstracts, including effects. *Die Dynamik der Entwicklung ist schwer abzuschätzen.*

Ich kann die Höhe des Baumes/das Ausmaß der Unzufriedenheit nicht abschätzen.

Die Wirkung solcher Maßnahmen läßt sich nur schwer abschätzen.

Abschätzen is used with people as obj. in the sense 'to classify socially, estimate s.o.'s social position'. *Der Ober schätzte den Gast ab. Sie sahen sich an und schätzten sich ab. Schätzen* with a person as obj. means 'to esteem' and would not convey this sense.

iv. Grob gerechnet means 'at a rough estimate' or 'estimated roughly'. Cf. CALCU-LATE 2. ii. Also used are *grob/niedrig* etc. *geschätzt. Gerechnet* used with *grob* or other advs. like *hoch* and *niedrig* forms fixed expressions. If the idea is to be expressed as a v., *schätzen* must be used. *Grob gerechnet brauchen wir zwei Tonnen Sand*, but *Ich habe die Menge Sand, die wir brauchen, nur grob geschätzt.*

2. Although **der Kostenvoranschlag** is 'an estimate of cost' prepared by a trades-man, architect, etc., the v. *anschlagen* is now not used in this sense. It has been replaced by **veranschlagen**, to calculate in advance the amount of money, time, material, etc. something will take. It implies an expert opinion which is in writ-ing and binding, while *schätzen* may be merely an informed guess. An amount or number can be the obj. of *veranschlagen*, in which case what is being built etc. fol-lows *für. Für den Bau der Brücke hat man zwei Millionen Mark veranschlagt.* What is being constructed etc. can also be the obj. and the price etc. follows *mit. Man hat den Bau der neuen Universitätsbibliothek mit 20 000 000 Mark veranschlagt.*

Er veranschlagte ein Drittel der zur Verfügung stehenden Zeit für die Vorbereitungsarbeiten.

3. The specific v. for assessing the (monetary) value of something is **taxieren**. *Das Grundstück wurde auf 200 000 Dollar taxiert* (or *geschätzt*). With an expert as subj. and, as obj., something whose monetary value is to be determined, **schätzen** means 'to assess'. *Jmd. schätzt einen Gebrauchtwagen/ein Haus.* A non-expert who says, '*Ich schätze dieses Bild hoch ein*', believes that either its artistic or monetary value is high (cf. 4) without, however, putting a precise figure on the latter; the v. used when an expert assesses value precisely is *schätzen. Ich lasse das Bild/den Schmuck schätzen.*

4. Estimate can also refer to a result of a non-numerical nature. *How do you esti-mate our chances?* **Assess** a situation means 'to consider all the facts and to decide what is likely to happen' and **Assess** s.o. or sth. 'to judge his/her/its quality or worth in an abstract sense'. **Einschätzen** corresponds to **estimate** and **assess** when they mean 'to judge' or 'to form an opinion of'. Its use is limited to objs. like *die Lage* or *die Situation, der Wert*, 'value in an abstract sense', *die Bedeutung*, 'significance', *jmds. Charakter, jmds. Fähigkeiten*, and people. It needs an adv. like *hoch, niedrig, falsch*, or *richtig*, or *so* or *wie*, or a phr. with *als*. *Wie schätzt du die Lage ein? Alle schätzen dieses Vorgehen als Mißgriff ein.* A syn. is **beurteilen**, to JUDGE. *Wie beurteilst du unsere Chancen? Wie schätzt du unsere Chancen ein?*

> *Wir hatten die Verhältnisse/die Situation/die Gefahr falsch/richtig eingeschätzt.*
> *Der künstlerische Wert dieser Bauten wurde früher sehr hoch/sehr niedrig eingeschätzt.*
> *Seine Mitarbeit/Die Bedeutung dieses Abkommens kann man nicht hoch genug einschätzen.*

even *adv.*

1. Sogar is one equivalent of **even** when it introduces something surprising or unexpected, or an extreme case. *Even a young child can use the machine. Sogar* occurs only in pos. sents. **Auch** and **selbst**, which are often syns., mean 'even' only when they precede the subj. Elsewhere in the sent. or clause, they are taken to have their other senses, 'also' and 'himself etc.' *Auch/Selbst/Sogar der kleine Junge hat eingekauft* are all possible, but only *Der kleine Junge hat sogar eingekauft. Der kleine Junge hat auch eingekauft* and *hat selbst eingekauft* are correct sents., but here *auch* and *selbst* do not mean 'even' as they do not precede the subj. Likewise *Auch/Selbst/Sogar wir wurden mit dem Dienstwagen des Chefs abgeholt* and *Wir wurden sogar mit dem Dienstwagen des Chefs abgeholt.* A sent. containing both *sogar* and *selbst* in different senses is possible. *Sie ging sogar selbst hin. Auch* is the weakest word, *sogar* the strongest, but there is little difference between *selbst* and *sogar. Sogar* is sometimes shortened to *gar*.

> *Viele behaupten, daß auch/selbst/sogar die umfassendsten Sicherheitsvorkehrungen eine absolute Sicherheit von Atomkraftwerken nicht garantieren können.*
> *Auch/Selbst/Sogar der größte Dilettant könnte es in dieser Regierung zu etw. bringen.*
> *Ich traue dem Mann nicht. Ich betrachte ihn sogar als Betrüger.*

2. Not even. The usual equivalent is **nicht einmal**, as neither *sogar* nor *selbst* is used in the neg. *Nicht einmal diesen kleinen Betrag wirst du sparen können.* **Auch nicht** is also used, but it is stylistically higher and stronger. It is often preferred to *nicht einmal* to avoid the repetition of *ein. Auch nicht eine Mark wirst du sparen können. Nicht einmal* is also possible.

> *Nicht einmal/Auch nicht der stärkste Mann könnte dieses Gewicht heben.*
> *Er hat uns auch nicht einen Pfennig gegeben.*
> *Es ist auch nicht einer mit dem Leben davongekommen.*

3. In a neg. sent. **auch nur** means '(not) even as much as what is stated'. It must be used to translate **even** when it is preceded by a neg. or *without. No one believed this report even for a moment* becomes *Niemand glaubte auch nur einen Augenblick an die Richtigkeit dieser Meldung. He left the house without even locking the door* is *Er verließ das Haus, ohne auch nur die Tür abzuschließen. Der nächste Tag verging, ohne daß die Schwester sich auch nur gesehen hätten* (Fontane). *Auch nur* is also found in pos. contexts and means 'even as little as'. *Sogar* cannot be substituted for it, since it does not express this meaning. *Wer auch nur einen Augenblick über das Unglück nachdenkt, muß erkennen, daß es weitreichende Konsequenzen für sein Handeln hat. Wer ihn auch nur oberflächlich kennt, muß wissen, daß die Gerüchte, die über ihn im Umlauf sind, völlig aus der Luft gegriffen sind.*

> *Sie ließ sich verhaften, ohne auch nur nach dem Grund zu fragen.*
> *Er stahl der alten Frau die Handtasche, ohne auch nur einen Hauch von Mitleid zu spüren.*
> *Niemand zweifelte auch nur einen Moment lang an seiner Aufrichtigkeit.*
> *Auch nur der geringste Fehler beim Fliegen dieses Flugzeugs kann zum Absturz führen.*

4. Even though can either be a strengthened form of *though* or *although*, *Even though I was sitting in the front row, I couldn't understand everything*, or a syn. of **even if**, *He will never be dishonest, even if/though he should be reduced to poverty*.

i. As *obwohl* and *obgleich* are not combined with *selbst*, *sogar*, and *auch*, there is no strengthened form, and **even though** in the first sense must be translated as **obwohl/obgleich**, i.e. *even* is not translated. *Obwohl ich im Augenblick kein Geld habe, plane ich schon eine Reise fürs nächste Jahr.*

> *Obwohl/Obgleich ich in der ersten Reihe gesessen habe, habe ich nicht alles verstanden.*

ii. When **even if** and **even though** are syns., they are expressed by **wenn** preceded by **auch**, **selbst**, or **sogar**. *Auch/Selbst/Sogar wenn sie unschuldig sein sollte, wird ihr Ruf als Folge der Presseberichte für immer geschädigt sein. Selbst wenn ich wollte, könnte ich das nicht tun. Auch wenn wir ein Taxi nehmen, können wir den Zug nicht erreichen.*

> *Auch wenn man in der ersten Reihe sitzt, versteht man nicht immer alles, was gesagt wird.*

Auch can also be placed in the clause, but this construction is less common and belongs to a higher stylistic plane. *Er hat Zeit, wenn er auch das Gegenteil behauptet.* It occurs most frequently in the combination **wenn auch . . . so doch**, the latter part introducing a pos. feature. *Wenn auch nur wenige dabei waren, so war es doch ein unterhaltsamer Abend.* In this case, *wenn* can be omitted in formal style, and the v. comes to the beginning. *Hat sie auch keine gute Note bekommen, so hat sie doch fleißig gearbeitet.*

5. Even + a comparative is usually **noch**. *Noch besser. Sie scheinen noch weniger darüber zu wissen als wir.* **Sogar** is slightly stronger, but is found only with adjs. used predicatively or with advs. *Das ist sogar besser. Diesmal spielten sie sogar schlechter.* With an attributive adj., *noch* is necessary: *Eine noch einfachere Lösung.*

event, occurrence, incident *ns.*

1. Occurrence is the general term for anything that happens. **Event** is a syn., though not always interchangeable, as e.g. in the fixed expressions *the course* or *sequence of events*. In *Unexpected events made him leader*, *occurrences* is possible, but would be unusual. **Event** is often restricted to occurrences of some importance. *The events of the year. The event of their childhood was a trip to Europe. It was a real event/quite an event.* An **incident** is often 'an occurrence of secondary importance', *the incidents of everyday life*, but it also denotes a single happening that stands out or is significant, *The book narrates a series of thrilling incidents. He looked on the incident as an adventure. A dangerous incident. A border incident* is 'a critical event that provokes a break in or strains relations or may lead to war'.

i. Der Vorgang is something that happens. *Ein Vorgang* can be important or insignificant. *Die Vorgänge des täglichen Lebens. Ich habe nichts von dem Vorgang gehört. Der Vorgang wurde mir nicht gemeldet. Es war ein ganz gewöhnlicher Vorgang. Ein starker Regenguß ist in diesem Teil Afrikas ein alltäglicher Vorgang;* also . . . *ein alltägliches Ereignis.*

ii. Das Ereignis resembles **event** in that it can refer to an ordinary occurrence and so be a syn. of *Vorgang*, but also often occurs when talking of something which, by its unusual nature, breaks the everyday run of things. *Ich bin auf alle Ereignisse vorbereitet. Darauf folgte ein sensationelles Ereignis.* In the latter use it translates **event** and **incident** when they denote significant occurrences. It is used with a range of adjs. such as *ein glückliches/trauriges/tragisches Ereignis* or *ein sonderbares/merkwürdiges/außerordentliches Ereignis* or *ein bedeutendes/einschneidendes Ereignis. Etw. war ein Ereignis für jmdn.* implies importance. *Der Besuch des Bundespräsidenten war ein Ereignis für die kleine Stadt. Groß* can be added if the implication is not clear. *Das* *große Ereignis ihrer Kindheit war eine Reise nach Europa. Der Gang der Ereignisse* is 'course of events'. *Der Gang der Ereignisse hat uns recht gegeben.* The birth of a child is called *ein freudiges Ereignis.*

iii. Die Begebenheit is an occurrence somewhat out of the ordinary, but it is not a common word and is slightly old-fashioned. **Das Geschehnis** is also an important occurrence, but it is an elevated word now little used.

> *Sie hörte sofort nach ihrer Ankunft von den seltsamen Begebenheiten in der Stadt.*
> *Die Novelle beruht auf einer lustigen Begebenheit, die er als Kind erlebte.*
> *Kurz danach ereignete sich ein ebenso unheimliches Geschehnis.*

iv. Das Vorkommnis is also something that happens, but it implies that this concerns others and should be reported. It is the usual word in police, military, and official language. *Keine besonderen Vorkommnisse,* used as a report by a policeman etc., corresponds to *Nothing to report.*

> *Folgende Vorkommnisse trugen sich kurz vor Mitternacht in der Bahnhofstraße zu.*

v. Der Vorfall suggests an unexpected occurrence which disturbs the previous or normal course of events and is mostly unpleasant for the people involved. While *Vorgänge* may be predicted, *Vorfälle,* which happen without warning, cannot be. The usual transl. is **incident**.

> *Dieser Vorfall veranlaßte ihn, nach Australien auszuwandern.*
> *Alle redeten von einem Vorfall, der sich kurz vorher ereignet hatte.*
> *'Sie müssen diesen Vorfall auch unbedingt melden', beschwor der Mann den anderen Tatzeugen.*

vi. Der Zwischenfall is also something which happens unexpectedly and disturbs the normal smooth flow of things. In many cases it is embarrassing for the people concerned, but there are also *heitere Zwischenfälle.* It is also mostly translated as **incident**. *Ein Grenzzwischenfall* is 'a border incident'.

> *Es gab einen kleinen/lästigen/bedauerlichen Zwischenfall.*
> *Der Abend verlief ohne besondere Zwischenfälle.*
> *Am Anfang der Verhandlung kam es zu einem peinlichen Zwischenfall.*

2. In the event of *war* etc. can be **im Falle** *eines Krieges,* or the idea can be expressed in a **falls**-clause. *Falls ein Krieg ausbricht/ausbrechen sollte. In the normal course of events: Wenn/Falls alles normal verläuft, wird er Chef der Firma werden.*

evidence *n.*

1. Legal uses. **Evidence** = 'information from personal testimony, documents, or the production of material objects to establish a fact'.

i. *Personal testimony* is **die Aussage** or **die Zeugenaussage**. *Die Aussage des ersten Zeugen stimmt mit der des zweiten überein. Der Zeuge wurde zur Aussage aufgerufen,* called in court to give evidence. *Jmd. wurde zur Zeugenaussage vorgeladen,* was summoned to give evidence. *Eine Aussage machen* is 'to give evidence' or 'make a statement' to the police. To translate *The witness said/stated in evidence,* the v. **aussagen** is used. *Der Zeuge sagte aus, daß er den Angeklagten in der Nähe des Tatorts gesehen habe. To give evidence for/against s.o./about sth. is für/gegen jmdn./über ein Verbrechen aussagen.* In more formal language: *Er sagte zugunsten/zuungunsten des Angeklagten aus.*

> *Die Aussagen der beiden Zeugen widersprachen sich.*
> *Die Aussagen der Zeugen haben den Angeklagten entlastet/stark belastet.*

ii. Das Zeugnis means 'testimony in court', but it is now an elevated word which may be dropping out of use in this sense. *Man legt Zeugnis für/gegen jmdn. ab.*

iii. Der Beweis, 'proof', translates **evidence** when this refers to things other than personal testimony. It is used in the sing. in statements about evidence or proof of something, or for a single piece of evidence. *Das ist der Beweis seiner Schuld/für seine Schuld. Wir haben keinen Beweis dafür, daß er das Auto gestohlen hat. Ein Fingerabdruck war* *der einzige Beweis.* The pl. expresses the collective sense of **evidence**, a number of things of all kinds proving a fact. *Die Beweise seiner Unschuld häufen sich.* **Das Beweisstück** is a single concrete obj., e.g. *eine Waffe,* or a document which proves something. **Das Beweismaterial** is a collective term for all such evidence. *Das Beweismaterial reicht für eine Anklage aus. Auf Grund des vorliegenden Beweismaterials,* on the evidence available. *Lack of evidence* is in legal language in strictly correct use *mangels Beweises,* but now *mangels Beweis* is often used. In the pl. both the gen. *mangels [eindeutiger] Beweise* and dat. *mangels Beweisen* occur. In ordinary language the expression is *Aus/Wegen Mangel an Beweisen wurde der Angeklagte freigesprochen.*

> *Der Staatsanwalt konnte zwingende Beweise für die Schuld des Angeklagten anführen/erbringen.*
> *Der Verteidiger versuchte, die seinen Mandanten belastenden Beweise zu entkräften.*
> *Die Polizei fand mehrere Beweisstücke, die den Mordverdacht bestätigten.*
> *Das Beweismaterial, das die Staatsanwaltschaft vorlegte/für die Schuld des Angeklagten gesammelt hatte, war nicht so überzeugend wie das, das die Verteidigung vorbrachte.*

2. Evidence = 'ground for belief', 'testimony or facts tending to prove or disprove any conclusion'. *What evidence is there for this view/theory/claim/assertion?*

i. Der Beweis is the usual word. *Sie lieferte den Beweis für ihre Behauptung. Das ist ein überzeugender Beweis gegen die gängige Erklärung.* With a clause: *Das ist der beste Beweis dafür, daß ich recht habe. Bringen Sie den Beweis!* suggests something concrete as evidence, *Erbringen Sie den Beweis!* a logical deduction. *Beweis* also refers to something which proves, or is a sign of, ability or a characteristic. *Zum Beweis seiner Dankbarkeit überreichte er uns ein wertvolles Geschenk. Man stellt seinen guten Willen/seine Intelligenz/sein Können unter Beweis,* gives evidence of. **Beweismaterial** is also used in non-legal fields. *Das Beweismaterial, das er für die Theorie vorlegte, war nicht besonders überzeugend.*

> *Das ist ein eindeutiger/sicherer/schlagender Beweis für die Richtigkeit/Unhaltbarkeit der Theorie/meiner Ansicht/dieser Annahme.* Or *Das ist ein Beweis gegen die Richtigkeit dieser Auffassung.*
> *Ich sehe in dieser Äußerung einen Beweis ihrer Charakterfestigkeit.*
> *Diese Arbeit ist ein guter Beweis seines Könnens/seiner Fähigkeiten.*

ii. Das Zeugnis is also an elevated syn. of *Beweis* meaning 'evidence for a quality etc.' *Diese Entscheidung ist Zeugnis seiner liberalen Gesinnung. Sein Schweigen war Zeugnis eines schlechten Gewissens.* **Bezeugen** with a person as subj. means 'to bear witness to' or 'to testify', *Ich kann seine Unschuld bezeugen,* and with a thing as subj. 'to provide evidence of sth.', *Diese Handlungen bezeugen seine Freundschaft.*

> *Er bezeugte vor Gericht, daß er den Angeklagten zur fraglichen Zeit gesehen habe.*
> *Sie können nicht gut bestreiten, was Ihnen die Augen bezeugen* (the evidence of your eyes).

3. Evidence = 'sth. visible from which inferences may be drawn', 'an indication, mark, sign, trace'. *The country gave evidence of careful cultivation. The ship bore abundant evidence of having been through a severe storm.* **Die Spur**, 'trace', is used when the evidence on which the conclusion is based can be clearly seen. If it is less clear, **das Zeichen**, 'sign', would be more appropriate. *Das Schiff trug deutliche Spuren davon, daß es kurz vorher gegen einen schweren Sturm angekämpft hatte. Am Auto entdeckten sie Spuren, daß es beschädigt worden war. Keine Zeichen des Verfalls waren am Haus zu sehen.* When the equivalents of *trace* and *sign* do not express the sense, **ist deutlich zu sehen** may do so. *Es war deutlich zu sehen, daß das Land sorgfältig bebaut wurde.*

4. [Not] to be in evidence, to be much in evidence. The meaning needs to be expressed. *Jmd. war überall zu sehen* or *hatte immer was zu sagen* could translate *was much in evidence* depending on the circumstances. *Smith war nirgendwo zu sehen* or *Von Smith war keine Spur zu sehen,* he was not much in evidence. *This politician has been very much in evidence of late: Dieser Politiker macht in letzter Zeit viel von sich reden.*

He likes to be much in evidence: Er setzt sich gern ins Licht. Ideas which have been much in evidence: Gedanken, von denen man viel geredet hat.

5. Der Beleg is 'proof in writing', either of expenditure or payments, *Die Quittung dient als Beleg, daß die Rechnung bezahlt worden ist,* or of something historical, *Er hat historische/urkundliche Belege für seine Auffassung,* or of the use of words and constructions, *Ich habe mehrere Belege für diesen Satztyp bei Schiller. Haben Sie einen Beleg für den Gebrauch dieses Wortes?*

exceed, surpass *vs.*

1. The first meaning of **exceed** is 'to go beyond what is allowed, necessary, or advisable'. *They exceeded the speed limit/their authority.* The equivalent is **überschreiten.** If in *die Grenze überschreiten, Grenze* has its lit. sense 'border', the v. means 'to CROSS', but when *Grenze* is used fig. meaning 'limit', *überschreiten* is translated as **exceed.** Hence its use with other words which suggest a limit of some kind.

Ich habe die zulässige Höchstgeschwindigkeit nicht überschritten.
Er hat seine Befugnisse überschritten. *Diese Ausgaben überschreiten den Etat.*

2. Exceed also means 'to be greater than, to go beyond'. *Their success exceeeded all expectations. The demand exceeded the supply.* **Surpass** means either (i) 'to be better than', *He surpasses me in strength,* or (ii) 'to go beyond', *The beauty of the scenery surpassed my expectations.* In the second sense it is a syn. of **exceed** though they are not always interchangeable. **Übertreffen** means 'to surpass' in both senses. In sense i, either the field in which one person surpasses the other is expressed by *an, Sie übertrifft mich an Intelligenz* or *Er übertrifft mich an Kraft,* or it has an obj. only, *Ihre Leistung hat meine übertroffen.* Its second sense is 'to go beyond' what was anticipated or previously achieved or experienced. It is found in contexts which suggest exceeding hopes or expectations either for good or bad; hence both *Der Erfolg übertraf alle unsere Erwartungen* and *Der Ruin übertraf meine schlimmsten Befürchtungen* occur. While *übertreffen* suggests going beyond something either in good or bad quality, **übersteigen** implies going beyond something which is expressible at least vaguely as a number. Thus *Etw. übersteigt meine finanziellen Möglichkeiten/meine Kräfte/meine Auffassungskraft,* power of comprehension. It is used in the idiom *Etw. übersteigt jedes Maß,* goes beyond all measure. *Diese Gemeinheit übersteigt jedes Maß.* Both *übertreffen* and *übersteigen* are possible when the increase or excess can be seen either in terms of quantity or quality. *Der diesjährige Gewinn hat den des Vorjahres um 10% übertroffen/überstiegen.* While *Der Preis übersteigt den Voranschlag* (= 'quote') is normal style, **überschreiten** is used in more formal language, the amount being seen as a limit. *Wir dürfen/Der Preis darf den Voranschlag nicht überschreiten.* However, only *überschreiten* is used in the pass. on all levels of style. *Der Voranschlag darf nicht überschritten werden.*

Die Nachfrage übersteigt das Angebot.
Die Reparaturkosten werden voraussichtlich 200 Mark nicht übersteigen.
Der Erfolg/Diese Wohnung übertrifft alle meine Hoffnungen.
Das übertrifft alles bisher Dagewesene. *Das übersteigt alles, was wir bisher erlebt haben.*

excite, incite *vs.* Some uses of **agitate, stimulate** *vs.*

1. Excite means 'to stir up the feelings' or 'to cause to feel strongly'. The feeling stirred up can be pleasurable or painful. It now often refers to strong feelings arising from the keen anticipation of something that will give pleasure, *We were all excited at the prospect of a few days off,* but in *Don't excite yourself/get excited!,* it means 'to agitate' and suggests a feeling of disquiet, anxiety, worry, or annoyance.

i. Aufregen means 'to stir up emotions' and implies that they are clearly visible in the way the person behaves. The emotions implied are more of a painful nature, like *Beunruhigung, Angst, Nervosität,* or *Ärger,* so that *aufregen* often corresponds to **agitate**, *upset, work up,* or *worry.* If not modified, it has this neg. sense. It is, however, used with *Freude,* as in *Ich war vor Freude so aufgeregt, daß ich den Stuhl umstieß.* Particularly in reference to children it means 'excited in anticipation of sth. pleasant'. *Die Kinder waren über die/wegen der Reise so aufgeregt, daß sie nicht schlafen konnten.* **Sich aufregen** means 'to become agitated, upset, or worried' or 'to get worked up' and is often close to *sich ärgern,* to be annoyed. It also implies that the feelings are perceptible in the way the person behaves. *Sich über jmdn./jmds. Verhalten aufregen* implies making derogatory remarks.

> *Sein andauerndes Meckern regt mich langsam, aber sicher auf.*
> *Der Lärm/Seine Unverschämtheit/Die schlechte Nachricht hat uns alle aufgeregt.*
> *Sie gestikulierte sehr aufgeregt; dann schimpfte sie auf ihn los.*
> *Es lohnt sich nicht, sich darüber/deswegen aufzuregen.*

ii. Erregen also means 'to stir up strong feelings', but suggests that the emotion is controlled and not clearly visible to others, although this produces a tension in the person's mind which may show itself in subtle ways. It is often used when the cause is justified or understandable. *Die Unverschämtheit des Burschen erregte ihn* implies that his agitation was not outwardly visible, *regte ihn auf* that it was. *Erregen* refers to pleasurable emotions as well as to painful or neg. ones. *Die Aussicht, Geschenke zu bekommen, hatte die Kinder erregt. Freudig erregt* is often found, but **sich erregen**, like *sich aufregen,* now also refers to worry or annoyance. In general, *erregen* is stylistically higher and less used than *aufregen. Sei doch nicht gleich so erregt!* is a refined way of saying *Sei doch nicht so aufgeregt!* The past part. is not uncommon. *Man beruhigte die erregten Gemüter/die erregte Menge* are often found, though *aufgeregt* is also used. *Eine erregte Atmosphäre/Auseinandersetzung/Stimmung* is potentially explosive. *Jmd. spricht mit erregter Stimme* or *spricht sehr aufgeregt.* Here the difference disappears, but if the cause is something like an ideal, only *erregt* would be used. *Erregen* alone is used for exciting sexually. It also means 'to call forth or arouse' feelings or emotional responses, but often requires an E. v. other than **excite**. Some ns. *erregen* takes as obj. are *das Aufsehen,* 'a stir or sensation', *der Anstoß,* 'offence', *das Mißfallen, das Mitleid, das Interesse, die Bewunderung. Diese Berichte haben großes Interesse erregt. Diese großartige Leistung hat meine Bewunderung erregt.*

2. Anregen means 'to stimulate', i.e. 'to encourage to begin and to develop', 'to rouse and quicken thought or feeling'. It is applied to the mind and body. *Etw. regt den Appetit/die Phantasie an. Eine Diskussion/ein Roman ist [geistig] anregend.* Used alone as in *Starker Kaffee regt an,* it means 'to act as a stimulant'. *Jmd. regt ein Thema an,* suggests it gives the impetus to a discussion or treatment of it. *Sie regte an, daß die Arbeit gleichmäßiger verteilt würde.* With a person and *zu* + n. or infin., it means 'to stimulate to do sth.' *Dieser Film wird viele Menschen zum Nachdenken anregen. Die Frauenzeitschrift will jede Leserin dazu anregen, ihr Heim schöner zu gestalten.*

3. *Anregen* is only used for good activities. For something bad like mutiny or rebellion, when **incite** meaning 'to encourage people to do sth. by making them angry or excited' is the usual v., the equivalents are **aufhetzen**, **aufwiegeln**, and **aufreizen**. *Sie hetzten die Matrosen zur Meuterei auf. Sie wiegelten/reizten das Volk gegen die Regierung auf. Jmds. Sinne/Leidenschaften aufreizen* is 'to excite or strongly arouse'.

excuse, pardon, apologize *vs.* **excuse, apology, pretext** *ns.*

1. Vs.

i. The usual equivalent of **excuse** or **pardon** s.o./sth. is **entschuldigen**. *Ich bitte, den Fehler/den Vorfall zu entschuldigen. Solches Benehmen kann ich nicht entschuldigen. Entschuldigen Sie bitte die Störung!* **Sich entschuldigen** means 'to excuse oneself' [for sth.], 'to apologize', or 'to make an apology'. Certain preps. extend the meanings of the refl. and non-refl. forms. *Bei* states the person to whom the excuse or apology is addressed. *Sie entschuldigte den Kollegen beim Chef. Du mußt dich bei der Kollegin entschuldigen. Für, wegen,* or *dafür, daß* state the behaviour that calls for pardon. *Ich entschuldigte mich für meine Taktlosigkeit. Sie entschuldigte sich dafür, daß sie zu spät gekommen war. Mit* or *damit, daß* give the reason why someone should be excused. *Der Schüler platzte mitten in die erste Stunde hinein und entschuldigte sich damit, daß die Straßenbahn wegen eines Stromausfalls stehengeblieben war.* **Excuse** s.o. **for** doing sth. is translated by a *daß*-clause whose subj. is the obj. of **excuse**. With a non-personal subj., *That doesn't excuse him for not having got in touch,* it becomes *Er hat zwar viel zu tun, aber das entschuldigt nicht, daß er seit Wochen nichts von sich hören läßt.* With a personal subj., the construction is *Ich kann sie nicht dafür entschuldigen, daß sie die Arbeit so nachlässig gemacht hat,* can't excuse her for having done the work so carelessly.

Sie entschuldigte den Fehler mit mangelnder Erfahrung.
Ich möchte mich [bei Ihnen] für das entschuldigen, was ich vorhin sagte.
Du mußt dich unbedingt bei ihm wegen deines schlechten Benehmens entschuldigen.
Er entschuldigte sich/sein Fehlen bei der Sitzung mit dringenden Geschäften.
Er entschuldigte sich/sein Fehlen damit, daß er gestern abend eine dringende Angelegenheit unbedingt erledigen mußte.

Entschuldigen is used for excusing one's temporary absence, and someone's absence from school. *Entschuldigen Sie mich bitte für ein paar Minuten!, Ich möchte meine Tochter [dafür] entschuldigen, daß sie gestern nicht zur Schule gegangen ist.* In *Make my excuses/apologies at the meeting tomorrow!,* **excuses** and **apologies** mean 'an expression of regret for one's absence'. This is expressed by *entschuldigen. Entschuldigen Sie mich bitte beim Direktor in der Sitzung morgen früh!* **Entschuldigen** is also used for excusing someone [from doing something] temporarily. *Wegen der Beinverletzung wird er vorübergehend vom Turnen entschuldigt.* If permanently is implied, **befreien**, to 'free or exempt', is usual. *Sie wurde vom Sport befreit.*

ii. Excuse me!, said when having to push past or go between people etc., is in formal language **Gestatten Sie!**, lit. *Permit me!,* or more usually **Entschuldigen Sie bitte!** or **Entschuldigung!** The latter are also used when one person asks another for information. *Entschuldigen Sie bitte, können Sie mir sagen, wie ich zum Bahnhof komme? Entschuldigung, können Sie mir sagen, wie spät es ist?* They are also used when something has happened which the speaker regrets, such as treading on someone's foot, when in E. we use [*I'm*] sorry. **Verzeihung!** is an alternative. Both ns. are the shortened forms of *Ich bitte um Entschuldigung/um Verzeihung.*

iii. Abbitten implies that someone feels that he or she has done another person an injustice and wishes to make amends or to ask to be forgiven. It is used in formal situations or in elevated language. The n. *die Abbitte,* 'apology', is only used in the expressions *Abbitte leisten* or *tun,* to make an apology.

Ich möchte ihm die Beleidigung abbitten.   *Er hatte ihr vieles abzubitten.*

2. Ns. An **excuse** is 'a reason to explain or defend one's conduct', but it can be true or invented. An **apology** is 'an expression of regret for having hurt or upset s.o. or for having caused s.o. trouble'.

i. Die Entschuldigung is 'a reason which justifies or explains an action which seems to deserve blame', i.e.. an excuse. Unless otherwise stated, the implication is that it is true and reasonable. *Ich nehme Ihre Entschuldigung an. Als Entschuldigung für mein Zuspätkommen muß ich sagen, daß es mir heute früh nicht gut ging. Sie bringt immer eine stichhaltige/triftige/fadenscheinige/unglaubhafte Entschuldigung vor. Entschuldigung* also means 'apology'. In many cases **apology** is translated by *sich entschuldigen. Er entschuldigte sich bei ihr,* made an apology to her. *You owe him an apology* is *Du mußt dich bei ihm entschuldigen. Entschuldigung* translates *apology* in *Wir bitten vielmals/tausendmal um Entschuldigung,* 'please accept our apologies', and *Ich stammelte/murmelte eine Entschuldigung.*

ii. Die Ausrede implies giving a false, or at least not completely correct, reason as an attempt to justify what one has done or is doing. *Faul,* which here means 'lame', or *billig,* 'cheap', are often added. *Das ist nur eine faule Ausrede.*

Mit einer billigen Ausrede versuchte er sich zu entschuldigen; da kannte er aber den Lehrer schlecht.
Für alles, was er anstellt, hatte er eine Ausrede.   An Ausreden fehlt es ihm nie.
Er konnte doch nicht zugeben, daß er wieder verschlafen hatte; deshalb behalf er sich mit einer Ausrede.

iii. Die Ausflucht is now mainly found in the pl. *Ausflüchte.* It does not belong to everyday language, like *Ausrede,* but to educated speech. It suggests the attempt to justify a refusal to do something or to get out of a situation which could become embarrassing, either by inventing reasons or by evading the issue or talking of something else. *Bitte keine Ausflüchte!* or *Mach' keine Ausflüchte!* can be translated as *Don't prevaricate! Anstatt aufrecht die Wahrheit zu sagen, bedient ihr euch einer schäbigen Ausflucht.*

Wärt ihr ehrlich gewesen, hätte ich euch verziehen; solche Ausflüchte erregen nur meinen Zorn.
Gib zu, daß du dort gewesen bist! Wir glauben dir deine Ausflüchte schon lange nicht mehr.

iv. Der Vorwand is 'a pretext' and translates **excuse** when this means 'pretext'. It implies inventing a reason for not doing what someone else wants or for doing something unreasonable oneself.

Sie benutzte die Ankunft ihrer Mutter als Vorwand, nicht an der Sitzung teilzunehmen.
Er wies mich ab unter dem Vorwand, verreisen zu müssen.
Er suchte einen Vorwand, den kritischen Mitarbeiter zu versetzen.

experience *n.* and *v.*

A. Experience n. The E. n. has three main meanings: (i) 'Sth. that has been experienced'—it may be an event that has happened to the speaker or something observed. *I had a strange experience yesterday.* (ii) 'Knowledge or practical wisdom gained from what one has observed, encountered, or undergone'. *We all learn best from our own experience. I speak from personal experience.* (iii) 'The state of having been occupied in work, study, or practice of some skill, or in dealings with others and the qualifications, knowledge, or ability acquired from this'. *A secretary with four years' experience. Das Erlebnis* corresponds to sense i, *die Erfahrung* to ii and iii.

1. Experience = 'sth. that happens to s.o.'
i. Das Erlebnis is an event which someone has experienced and which makes a fairly strong or lasting impression. It is used with *haben* and can be good or bad. *Ich habe ein interessantes/schreckliches Erlebnis gehabt.* It refers to an occurrence which is at least to a certain extent different from the ordinary run of things, and can be something seen or heard as well as an event involving the speaker. In sents. like *Das Konzert/Die Aufführung war für mich ein [einmaliges] Erlebnis* or *Das Gebirge wurde ihm/für ihn zum [einmaligen] Erlebnis,* it means 'an outstanding or memorable experience'.

Die Reise war ein schönes/großes/eindrucksvolles/nachhaltiges/außergewöhnliches/aufwühlendes/ erschütterndes Erlebnis.

Der Autor schrieb seine frühesten Erlebnisse nieder.

Ich habe gestern ein unangenehmes Erlebnis gehabt, ich bin mit einem anderen Auto zusammengestoßen.

Ich habe ihn nach seinen Erlebnissen in Indien gefragt.

ii. Less common and more elevated is the verbal n. **das Erleben,** which means either 'the process of experiencing or going through sth.' or 'experience' as a collective term, i.e. 'all thgs. experienced'.

Das Erleben der Scheidung ihrer Eltern wirkte sich äußerst nachteilig auf die beiden Brüder aus.

Ich zweifle nicht daran, daß den Vorgängen in Hallers Erzählungen auch ein Stück wirklichen, äußeren Erlebens zugrundeliegt. (Hesse)

Der Dichter schöpfte aus seinem unmittelbaren Erleben. Or . . . aus seinen persönlichen Erlebnissen.

2. Experience in life and with work. **Die Erfahrung** denotes knowledge, insights or wisdom, or practical ability which a person or group acquires either generally in life (cf. i below for examples) or in work or an activity (cf. ii below). It does not refer to an event one goes through, but rather to the knowledge gained from doing, observing, or undergoing something, often more than once. The idea of gaining knowledge or becoming wiser is always present even if the context seems to refer to an event. It is used with *machen. Die Erfahrung machen, daß* means 'to discover from experience that'. *Sie machte sehr früh die Erfahrung, daß man nicht jedem Menschen trauen kann. Das weiß ich aus Erfahrung,* know from experience.

i. *Indem man über Erlebnisse nachdenkt, kann man Erfahrung gewinnen.*

Ich habe die Erfahrung gemacht, daß der Lebensrhythmus in Griechenland anders ist als in Deutschland.

Durch Erfahrung wird man klug. (We learn from experience.)

Ich weiß aus eigener/persönlicher Erfahrung, daß man ihm voll und ganz vertrauen kann.

Die Erfahrung hat gezeigt, daß die Hoffnungen dieser Geschäftsleute übertrieben waren.

Er ist ein Mann mit keiner Lebenserfahrung/mit einer reichen Lebenserfahrung.

ii. *Jmd. hat große/reiche/langjährige Erfahrungen auf einem Gebiet.*

Seine Erfahrung half ihm, sich so geschickt zu verbergen, daß niemand sein Versteck entdeckte.

Alle Bewerber besitzen genügend berufliche/praktische Erfahrung.

Wir müssen uns seine Erfahrung zunutze machen.

Erfahrung may imply bad experience. *Ich habe da so meine Erfahrungen gemacht,* have become wise, cautious, by suffering or loss. Note: *Mit jmdm./etw. gute Erfahrungen machen,* to find s.o./sth. satisfactory, *Ich habe mit diesem Material nur gute Erfahrungen gemacht,* and *mit jmdm./etw. schlechte Erfahrungen machen,* to find s.o./sth. unsatisfactory, to be disappointed with, *Er hat mit diesem Restaurant schlechte Erfahrungen gemacht.*

B. Experience v.

1. The normal equivalent of **experience** is *erleben.* It can refer either to something one goes through and is involved in, or to seeing, witnessing, or observing something. *Erleben, daß* suggests seeing or observing something happening. *Ich habe es erlebt, daß er zwanzig Stunden hintereinander gearbeitet hat* can be translated as *I have known him to . . .* (*Erleben* also means 'to live to see'. *Werden wir alle das Jahr 2 000 noch erleben?*)

Eine solche Gemeinheit/Frechheit habe ich noch nie erlebt.

Erleben Sie die Faszination einer Reise in ein fast unbekanntes Land!

Das Schrecklichste, was mein Vater erlebte, war die Kriegsgefangenschaft bei den Japanern.

Diese Aufführung muß man unbedingt erlebt haben. Sie ist ausgezeichnet.

Rote Känguruhs können ihren menschlichen Gegnern mit ihren scharfen Fußkrallen tödliche Verletzungen beibringen. Andererseits erlebt man vielfach in Freiluftzoos, daß sich auch Drei-Meter-Känguruhs von Kindern füttern und streicheln lassen, ohne ihnen etw. zu tun.

2. As a syn. of *erleben,* **erfahren** belongs to a higher stylistic level. It means 'to be subjected to' something. Although *Freude* can only be the obj. of *erleben, erfahren* is found with good and bad experiences. *Ich habe dort Gutes/Schlechtes erfahren.* Both *erleben* and *erfahren* are found with *am eigenen Leibe*, lit. 'to experience on one's own body, to be subjected to something oneself'. A synonymous expression is *an sich erfahren*. *Erfahren* also means 'to find out' or 'learn' (cf. DISCOVER 3) and cannot be used in the sense of 'to experience' in contexts in which it could be taken to mean 'learn or find out'. *Er sagte nichts über das, was er dort erfahren hatte* and *Sie haben etw. Schlechtes/Neues erfahren* would be understood as 'learned or found out'. To avoid ambiguity in such contexts *erleben* or *widerfahren* is used. Sents. like *Sie haben in ihrem Leben viel Leid/Kummer/Unrecht/nur Undank erfahren* and *Sie hatte viel Schlimmes/Böses/Schmerzliches erfahren* can also be formulated with **widerfahren**, 'to happen to or befall', with subj. and obj. reversed. *Viel Leid/Ein großes Unrecht/Viel Böses ist ihnen widerfahren.* Cf. MEET 9.

> *Sie hatte ihren Fuß gebrochen und erfuhr nun am eigenen Leibe, was es heißt, gehbehindert zu sein.*
> *Sie erzählte uns, was ihr auf der Reise widerfahren war.*

3. i. Both **erfahren** and **erleben** are used like **experience** in the sense 'to undergo'. Certain ns. are found with each, in a few instances with both.

> *Das Unternehmen/Der Sportler hat in letzter Zeit einen großen Aufschwung erlebt/erfahren.*
> *Er hat sich redlich bemüht, erfuhr aber immer wieder Rückschläge.*
> *Der Betrieb hat mehrere Rückschläge erfahren/erlebt.*
> *Teile von Australien erleben zur Zeit eine schwere Dürre.*
> *Der Sänger erlebte ein Comeback.*
> *Nach der Rezession erlebt die Wirtschaft wieder eine Hochkonjunktur.*
> *Der Dichter erlebte seine Blütezeit. Das Buch erlebte eine fünfte Auflage.*

ii. Both vs., but particularly *erfahren*, are used to replace the pass., but often result in a stilted kind of language. *Das Meßgerät muß eine sorgfältige Behandlung erfahren* may be found in a set of instructions for use (*Gebrauchsanweisung*), but in everyday language the sent. would be formulated as . . . *muß sorgfältig behandelt werden.* Similarly *Jmd. hat eine Demütigung erfahren* is more simply *wurde gedemütigt,* and *Jmd. hat eine Überraschung/eine Enttäuschung erlebt* is *wurde überrascht/enttäuscht. Der Umsatz hat eine Steigerung erfahren* is in everyday language *wurde gesteigert* or *ist gestiegen.*

4. Experienced. *Erfahren in* means 'experienced, well-versed, proficient, well up in'.

> *Die Firma suchte eine in Buchhaltung erfahrene Sekretärin.*   *Im Kochen war ich nicht erfahren.*
> *Er ist auf diesem Gebiet/in allen Fragen des Bergbaus erfahren.*   *Ein erfahrener Lehrer/Pilot.*

express *v.*

1. Express means 'to represent in language', 'to put into words' a meaning, thought, intention, feeling, etc. The refl. means 'to put one's thoughts into words', 'to formulate what one thinks'.

i. Ausdrücken refers primarily to the way something is formulated or put into words. The obj. is something which can be put into words, *ein Gedanke, eine Überlegung, eine Absicht, eine Vorstellung, ein Wunsch*, etc. Besides an obj. it needs an adv. or phr., *wie* in a clause or question, or *so. Ich will es anders/besser ausdrücken. Wie soll ich das ausdrücken? Wie dein Vater es ausdrückt. Wenn ich es/mich so ausdrücken darf.* The refl. also refers to the manner in which someone expresses something, *Er drückte sich/seine Gedanken in Worten aus, die jedem verständlich waren,* and is used for expressing oneself in a foreign language. The mode of expression can be a figure or sign. *Das Ergebnis wird in Prozenten ausgedrückt.* When the obj. is *Bedeutung*, 'meaning', the subj. can be *ein Wort, eine Zahl,* or *ein Zeichen. Die Bedeutung, die das Wort 'Kunst' ausdrückt, hat sich seit dem Mittelalter erheblich geändert.*

Den Unterschied hast du gut/klar/verständlich/präzise/in einfachen Worten ausgedrückt.
So kann man das nicht ausdrücken. Formulieren Sie den Gedanken anders!
Ihre Verachtung hat sie zwar sehr vornehm, aber doch unverkennbar ausgedrückt.
Jmd. hat sich gut/passend/unbeholfen/taktvoll/verschwommen/geschwollen/poetisch/derb/grob/ unklar/vorsichtig/schlecht ausgedrückt.
Ich hatte noch gelegentlich Mühe, mich in der fremden Sprache auszudrücken.
In keinem seiner Berichte verstand er es, sich kurz und bündig auszudrücken; stets schweifte er uferlos ab.   Wie soll ich bloß ausdrücken, wie uns damals zu Mute war?

ii. Ausdrücken also means 'to show or reflect' an emotion or state with a thing as subj., usually spoken or written words, behaviour, facial features, or a work of art. *Das Gedicht drückt seine Schwermut/seine Freiheitsliebe aus.* Occasionally people can be the subj., with the action expressed as a phr. *Mit lang anhaltendem Beifall drückten die Zuschauer dem Solisten ihre Bewunderung aus.* When the feeling etc. is made the subj., the v. becomes refl., as it can in E. *Seine Überraschung drückte sich in seinen Worten aus.*

Jmds. Gesicht/Blick drückt Zufriedenheit/Kummer/Bestürzung/Verachtung/Schadenfreude aus.
Ihre Haltung drückte ihr ruhiges Wesen/ihre Enttäuschung/ihre Müdigkeit aus.
Jeder Gesichtszug drückte unmittelbares Ergriffensein aus.
Die Antwort drückte Erstaunen aus.

iii. Zum Ausdruck bringen has the same meaning as the second sense of *ausdrücken* and can be used when emphasis is required. *Diese Worte sollen meine Zuneigung und Dankbarkeit zum Ausdruck bringen.* With a person as subj. it can sound like an inflated way of saying what can be expressed more simply. Thus *Er brachte seinen Dank zum Ausdruck* instead of *Er sprach seinen Dank aus* or *bedankte sich.*

In zahlreichen Protestdemonstrationen brachte das Volk seine Verachtung der Machthaber zum Ausdruck.

2. i. Another sense of **express** is 'to state or make known one's opinion, feelings, etc.', a meaning carried by **aussprechen**. Whereas *ausdrücken* denotes the manner in which something is couched in words, *aussprechen* refers to the action by which something is made known in speech or writing to others. It is the opposite of *to keep to oneself.* In *Sie sprach es offen aus* or *Er sprach klipp und klar aus, daß er dagegen ist*, it is translated as *say* or *state*, but in *Jmd. spricht eine Meinung/einen Gedanken/einen Wunsch/eine Bitte/eine Befürchtung/eine Vermutung/seinen Verdacht aus*, as **express**. *Ich weiß nicht, wie ich meinen Dank angemessen ausdrücken kann*, refers to formulating it adequately, but *Ich möchte ihnen meinen Dank aussprechen* suggests seeking an occasion for expressing my gratitude. Emotions are often the obj. of *aussprechen. Er sprach sein Bedauern/seine Verwunderung/seine Bewunderung aus. Sie sprach ihre Zustimmung aus* and *sprach dem neuen Mitarbeiter ihre volle Anerkennung seiner Leistung aus. Das Parlament sprach der Regierung das Vertrauen aus* means that it passed a vote of confidence. *Ausdrücken* is sometimes used with emotions and opinions as obj. meaning 'to state', but in such contexts it is an elevated word, *aussprechen* being the normal one. *Er drückte dem Freund zum Tod seines Vaters sein Beileid aus* would in everyday language be *sprach ihm sein Beileid aus.*

'Sprechen Sie bitte klar und detailliert aus, was Sie gesehen haben, Herr Zeuge!' sagte der Richter.
Sie sprach offen aus, was alle dachten.
Er scheute sich nicht, seine innersten Überzeugungen auszusprechen.
Keiner der Sechs wagte die Vermutung auszusprechen, es könnte vielleicht kein Entkommen geben; doch ihre verängstigten Blicke drückten ihre Befürchtungen und das Bewußtsein um ihre Lage aus.

ii. With a personal subj. + *über* + adv., **sich aussprechen** states someone's feeling, opinion, or judgement about s.o./sth. *In dem Brief hat sie sich mißbilligend über sein Verhalten ausgesprochen*, expressed her disapproval of. *Er hat sich lobend/zufrieden/ anerkennend über Ihre Leistung ausgesprochen. Sich für/gegen jmdn./etw. aussprechen* is 'to express views in favour of or against'. *Sie haben sich gegen die Atomkraft/für die Reformen/für den Bewerber ausgesprochen.*

iii. Like *aussprechen*, **äußern** is an equivalent of **express** when this means 'to say or state', but it is somewhat more formal. In *Jmd. äußert seine Meinung/seine Gedanken/seine Ansicht freimütig, etc.* it could be translated as **expresses** or *states. Man äußert einen Wunsch/eine Bitte/einen Verdacht/Zweifel/Bedenken* etc. Unlike *sich aussprechen, sich äußern* is followed by *zu.* **Sich zu etw. äußern** means 'to state one's opinion about sth.' and can be used to ask someone to express a view, or to state that one would like to express an opinion. *Wer möchte sich zu dieser Frage äußern? Ich möchte mich zu mehreren Fragen/Punkten äußern.* Unlike *sich aussprechen, sich äußern* is not followed by *für* and *gegen*, but both are used with *über. Man äußert sich abfällig/wegwerfend/lobend/vorsichtig über etw./jmdn.*

3. Two other uses of **express**.

i. With an emotion as subj., **sich aussprechen** and **sich ausdrücken** mean 'to show itself', 'to be expressed'. *In ihren Gesichtern sprach/drückte sich Angst/Mitleid aus.*

ii. States and emotions express themselves in certain behaviour or reactions. Here **sich äußern** is used. *Die Krankheit äußert sich durch Fieber. Ihre Erregung äußerte sich im Zittern ihrer Hände.*

extent, degree *ns.* Some uses of **measure, moderation,** and **scale** *ns.*

1. Degree originally denoted one of a flight of steps or a rung of a ladder and was then applied to a step or stage in a process, especially one in an ascending or descending scale. This sense survives only in the phr. **by degrees**, which can be **stufenweise**, *die Stufe* being the equivalent of *step* or *rung*, or **schrittweise**, *der Schritt* being 'a step taken by the feet'.

> *Die Handelsbeziehungen zwischen den beiden Ländern wurden stufenweise ausgebaut.*
> *Durch die Verhandlungen haben sich die Standpunkte schrittweise angenähert.*

2. Degree was then applied to a step or stage in intensity or amount and now denotes the relative intensity, extent, or amount of a quality, attribute, or action. Burns, e.g., are classified as first, second, etc. degree according to their severity. In *a high degree of tolerance*, **degree** means 'a large amount of it'; the idea of a scale is perhaps not prominent, but can easily be imagined.

i. Der Grad is derived from Latin *gradus*, 'step', as is ultimately **degree**, but like the E. word, it has lost the basic sense. It now covers most meanings of **degree**. **Degrees** of the thermometer. *Es ist heute fünf Grad unter Null/40 Grad im Schatten.* Angles are measured in *Grade*, and degrees of latitude and longitude are *Breiten- und Längengrade. Der Ort liegt 41 Grad südlicher Breite und 147 Grad östlicher Länge. Grad* is used for academic degrees. *Sie ist das erste Mitglied der Familie, das einen akademischen Grad erworben hat.* (In G. this could also be expressed as *Sie ist die erste, die studiert hat.*)

ii. Der Grad is also applied to degrees of intensity and severity, the extent to which a feature or state is present. *Grad der Konzentration/der Entwicklung/der Feuchtigkeit/der Helligkeit*, etc. *Verbrennungen ersten/zweiten Grades.* There are compounds like *Schwierigkeitsgrad, Wirkungsgrad, Reinheitsgrad*, etc. In certain contexts it becomes a syn. of *amount. Alle Schüler zeigen einen hohen Grad von Intelligenz. In hohem Grade* means 'to a high degree' or 'very much'. *Bis zu einem gewissen Grad* means 'to a limited degree' or 'to a certain extent'.

> *Die Annahme hat einen hohen Grad von Wahrscheinlichkeit.*
> *Nach den neuesten Ermittlungen übersteigt der Grad der Grundwasserverschmutzung alle Befürchtungen.*

Es gibt einen Grad von Müdigkeit—welcher Soldat kennt ihn nicht?—der geradezu tödlich ist für Leib und Seele. Man würde einen Mord begehen für eine einzige Nacht voll Schlaf, alles ist einem gleichgültig außer Schlaf. (Böll)
Die Jungen zeigen verschiedene Grade der Geschicklichkeit in der Behandlung der Werkzeuge.
Ich wunderte mich über den hohen Grad von Toleranz, den diese angeblich primitiven Menschen zeigten.
Bis zu einem gewissen Grade stimme ich mit dir überein.
Diese Lieder sind mir in hohem Grade verhaßt.

3. *Das Maß* is connected with *messen,* 'to measure', and has some senses for which we use **measure**, as well as others, the equivalents of which are *measurement,* **moderation**, and **extent**.

i. *Die Elle ist ein altes* **Maß**, '(unit of) measure'; thus *metrische Maße und Gewichte,* 'weights and measures', and *die Maße eines Schranks/für die Gardinen. Der Schneider nimmt Maß,* takes someone's measurements. *Das Maß ist voll* is derived from the idea of a *Maß,* an old measuring jar, becoming full, and means that one person's patience with another is at an end, that what someone is doing is the last straw.
'Benimm dich jetzt anständig! Dein Maß ist gleich voll', schimpfte die Mutter mit dem Jungen.

ii. *Das Maß* means 'an amount' as **measure** does in *We all seek a measure of security for ourselves* and *In such ideas there is a measure of truth and a measure of nonsense. Maß* needs an adj., so that where E. has none, *gewiß* needs to be added. *Wir suchen alle ein gewisses Maß an Sicherheit. Man reduziert den Lärm auf ein erträgliches Maß,* reduces the noise to a bearable/acceptable level. *Die Zahl der Verkehrsunfälle geht über das übliche Maß hinaus,* goes beyond the level that is usual.
Solche Vorstellungen enthalten ein gewisses Maß an Wahrheit und ein gewisses Maß an Unsinn.
Diese Klavierübung erfordert ein hohes Maß an Konzentration und Fingerfertigkeit.
Um Erfolg mit diesen Kindern zu haben, braucht man ein hohes Maß an Geduld.
Sie brachten uns ein hohes Maß an Vertrauen entgegen.

iii. A now more or less literary sense of **measure** is 'extent or degree that is not excessive', 'a sense of proportion or restraint'. *This lack of measure was characteristic of her.* This sense is now mostly found in expressions like *irritated beyond measure* and *to know no measure,* in which it suggests going beyond what is normal or moderate. *Das Maß* also means 'moderation'. *Jmd. kennt kein Maß in seinen Forderungen,* knows no moderation, is quite immoderate. *Das rechte Maß halten* is 'to keep within the bounds of moderation'. *Etw. überschreitet jedes Maß,* is completely immoderate. The old pl. has survived in the phr. *in/mit Maßen,* in moderation. *Man muß mit Maßen essen und trinken.*

iv. In some/great measure mean 'to some or a great extent'. With an attributive adj., **das Maß** is mostly translated as **extent** or **degree**, which are more common than the formal **measure**. *In beschränktem Maß,* to a limited extent/degree. *In zunehmenden Maße. Seinen Bemühungen ist der Erfolg in hohem Maße zuzuschreiben.* (*In hohem Grade* could also be used.) *In dem Maß[e], wie* is 'to the extent that' or 'in proportion as'. *In dem Maße, wie die allgemeine politische Lage im Land sich verschlechterte, wuchs auch die Unruhe in den kleineren Nachbarstaaten.*
Der Grad der Verletzungen gibt Grund zur Sorge. In welchem Maße auch die inneren Organe betroffen sind, ist im Augenblick nicht feststellbar.   *Wir waren auch in kleinerem Maße betroffen.*
Wir waren nicht im selben Maße betroffen wie die anderen.
In dem Maße, wie mehr Rohmaterial verfügbar wurde, steigerte man die Produktion.

4. Extent can mean 'the amount of space over which sth. extends'.
i. When **extent** means 'size or area' in a precise way, **die Ausdehnung** is used. Thus *Von hier aus sieht man die volle Ausdehnung des Parks,* 'the full extent of it', and *Ich wurde von der kollosalen Ausdehnung des Industriegeländes sehr beeindruckt.*
ii. Das Ausmaß in its basic sense refers to great size, but in a vague way. *Der Rumpf*

des neuen Flugzeugs hat riesige Ausmaße. It is frequently found in the gen. or after *von*, like *dimensions* and *proportions* in *of vast dimensions* or *of huge proportions*, or like **extent** in *of great extent, Eine Bergmassiv von gewaltigen Ausmaßen. Ein Krater riesigen Ausmaßes.* Fig. use. Etw. *nimmt erschreckende/gefährliche* etc. *Ausmaße an,* takes on/assumes terrifying etc. proportions.

Ein Weizenfeld riesigen Ausmaßes erstreckte sich vor den Augen der Reisenden.
Die Aufsässigkeit der Klasse nahm bedrohliche/bedenkliche Ausmaße an.

5. Extent is applied to the fig. area covered by some effect. *The full extent of the problem/damage is not yet known.* **Scale** means 'relative size, extent'. *The scale/extent of the operation was impressive.*

i. This concept is expressed by **das Ausmaß.** It is used without an adj. *Das Ausmaß des Erfolges hat alle überrascht. Das Ausmaß des Schadens ist noch nicht bekannt. Das Ausmaß der Katastrophe ist noch nicht überschaubar.* It also occurs with a few adjs. in the gen. and could be translated by **scale** as well as by **extent**. *Ein Unglück nie dagewesenen Ausmaßes/unvorstellbaren Ausmaßes. In großem Ausmaß* is 'on a large scale', *in geringem Ausmaß* the opposite. Cf. 5. ii. *Diese Waren können in großem/ geringem Ausmaß exportiert werden. Voll* or *ganz,* used with *Ausmaß* and *Umfang,* translate *the full extent. Das volle Ausmaß des Unglücks. Die Versicherungsgesellschaft haftet für den Schaden in vollem Umfang.*

ii. The basic sense of **der Umfang** is 'the distance round sth.' *Der Umfang eines Baumes.* It thus means 'circumference of a circle' or 'perimeter' of another figure. *Der Umfang eines Kreises/eines Vierecks.* In fig. use it is very like *Ausmaß.* While *Ausmaß* suggests the area occupied, *Umfang* implies the length round, the area, but in fig. use such differences are of no importance. *Der Umfang einer Katastrophe/einer Krise. In großem Umfang* is the usual equivalent of *on a large scale.* Also *Reformen größeren Umfangs. Der Umfang eines Buches* refers to its size, the number of pages it has.

Das Ausmaß/Der Umfang der Verluste läßt sich noch nicht überblicken.
Der Umfang der vorzunehmenden Untersuchungen überschreitet die Leistungskapazität dieses Labors bei weitem.   Die Ausgrabungen wurden in großem Umfang betrieben.
Er scheint die Bedeutung der Sache in ihrem vollem Ausmaß/Umfang nicht erkannt zu haben.

6. Other equivalents of **extent**. It is often better not to use either *Ausmaß* or *Umfang* discussed in 5 but to rephrase the E. sent. containing **extent**, as the meaning can easily be expressed more simply. *No one knew the **extent** of his debts* could be *Niemand wußte, wie tief verschuldet er war. He owed people money to the **extent** of £5,000: Seine Schulden beliefen sich auf . . . I am amazed at the **extent** of his knowledge: Ich staune über sein [ausgesprochen] großes Wissen. To what **extent** is he to be trusted?: Wie weit kann man ihm vertrauen? Inwiefern* and *inwieweit* mean 'in what respect' or 'to what extent' *Ich kann nicht sagen, inwiefern der eine Vorschlag besser ist als der andere. Inwiefern hat sich die Lage geändert? Inwieweit hat er die Wahrheit gesagt? Ich weiß nicht, inwieweit sie recht hat.*

extinguish, put out, go out *vs.*

1. The everyday v. meaning 'to put out' is **ausmachen.** *Man macht ein Feuer/das Gas/eine Kerze/eine Zigarette aus.* **Löschen,** which is more formal, like **extinguish,** is used with fires and candles. *Die Feuerwehr hat den Brand gelöscht. Man löscht ein Feuer/eine Kerze.* **Löschen** must be used when no intention is present. *Der Regen hat den Waldbrand gelöscht.* **Auslöschen** means 'to extinguish completely'. *Er hat die Öllampe ausgelöscht/gelöscht. Auslöschen* is used fig. with memories or places. *Die Jahre konnten die Erinnerung an diesen Sommer nicht auslöschen. Die Lavamassen haben ein ganzes Dorf ausgelöscht.*

2. Go out, applied to fires and a light produced by burning, is **ausgehen** or **erlöschen**, the first being the everyday word while the second is more formal. *Die Kerze/Die Lampe/Das Feuer war ausgegangen. Die Pfeife war ihm ausgegangen. Das Lichtsignal flammte auf und erlosch wieder. Das Feuer/Der Brand/Die Kerze ist erloschen.* Erlöschen is used fig. for interest, hopes, or emotions which die away or wane, and for rights which run out or expire. *Sein Interesse an dem Projekt ist erloschen. Die Liebe erlosch mit der Zeit. Ihr Anspruch auf Garantieleistungen erlischt ein Jahr nach Kauf des Geräts. Damals erlosch das Urheberrecht fünfzig Jahre nach dem Tod des Verfassers.* **Verlöschen** has the lit. and fig. senses of *erlöschen*, but seems to be confined to certain parts only of the country. *Die Flamme verlosch. Ihre Liebe war verloschen.*

fact *n.*

1. A **fact** is 'a piece of information that is true'.

i. The general term is **die Tatsache**. **Das Faktum** or **der/das Fakt** are exact, but more learned, syns. *Wir müssen den Tatsachen ins Auge sehen*, face up to the facts. *Die Tatsache bleibt bestehen*, the fact remains. *Das ist ein interessantes Faktum. Diese Erscheinung* (phenomenon) *ist ein unbestrittener historischer/naturwissenschaftlicher Fakt.*

> *Das ist eine unleugbare/unabänderliche Tatsache.*   *Du mußt dich mit dieser Tatsache abfinden.*
> *Ihre Darstellung der Ereignisse entspricht nicht den Tatsachen/ist eine Verzerrung der Tatsachen.*
> *Sie untermauerte ihre Auffassung mit Fakten und Zahlen.*
> *Die Fakten sprechen gegen diese Ansicht.*
> *Dieser idealistische Plan setzt sich einfach über die Fakten der Geschichte hinweg.*

I know it for a fact could be translated as *Ich weiß es ganz genau*, I know it for certain.

ii. Sth. is a **fact**. *Es ist [eine] Tatsache, daß* is the lit. equivalent. A simple way to state that something is a fact is to use the v. **feststehen**, to be certain or a fact. Thus *Das steht fest* can translate *That is a fact*. It is often followed by a *daß*-clause. *Es steht fest, daß die Atmosphäre sich langsam erwärmt*. If *es* is not the first word, it is omitted: *Fest steht, daß* . . . As it is also used in combination with *die Tatsache*, a sent. like *Diese Tatsache steht fest* is translated as *This fact is certain*. *Eine feststehende Tatsache* is 'an established or incontrovertible fact'. (*Feststehende Anschauungen* are, however, 'settled or fixed views', and *Ein Entschluß steht unwiderruflich fest* means that the decision is firm and will not be changed.) Another way of expressing *That's a fact* is **Daran ist nicht zu zweifeln** or in speech *Daran gibt's nichts zu zweifeln*. The question *Is that a fact?*, expressing surprise or interest, can be translated by **tatsächlich**.

> *A. Peter hat sich voriges Jahr endlich verheiratet. B. Tatsächlich?*
> *Es ist eine Tatsache,/Es steht fest, daß in Teilen Australiens Dürren sich alle 10 bis 15 Jahre ereignen.*
> *Fest steht, daß diese Seesterne einem Korallenriff beträchtlichen Schaden zufügen.*

iii. Tatsache ist, daß is used like *The fact is* or *The fact of the matter is* when they emphasize the truth or reality of a situation in contrast to an incorrect view or statement. *Es wurde behauptet, ich sei ein Duzfreund des Kanzlers—Tatsache ist, daß ich dem Kanzler nur dreimal im Leben begegnet bin. Der Minister sagte, die Zuwendungen für Universitäten seien nicht gekürzt worden—Tatsache ist, daß alle Universitäten in diesem Jahr weniger bekommen als im vorigen.*

2. The fact + *that*-clause.

i. Die Tatsache, daß is used, but just as common is **der Umstand, daß**. *Der Umstand* means 'circumstance', but it is often used like **fact**. *Der Bericht verhehlt einen Umstand, der für den General unangenehm, wenn nicht sogar peinlich ist.*

> *Die Tatsache, daß er in Afrika gelebt hat, gibt seiner Meinung über dortige Zustände Gewicht.*
> *Unser Verständnis der Lebensweise dieser Tiere verdanken wir dem Umstand, daß eine kleine Gruppe*
> *von Forschern längere Zeit auf jede Bequemlichkeit verzichtete und sie beobachteten.*
> *Das Spiel wurde trotz der Tatsache, daß es stark regnete, fortgesetzt.*

ii. Certain G. constructions replace *the fact that*. One is the **da** + prep. + **daß** construction.

Der Grund des Mißlingens liegt darin, daß die Anweisungen nicht genau beachtet wurden (lies in the fact that).

Wer trägt die Schuld daran, daß diese Arbeit liegengeblieben ist? (is to blame for the fact that . . . or . . . for the work not having been done).

iii. Owing/Due to the fact that is *weil. Es war eiskalt im Zimmer, weil er die Tür offen gelassen hatte.*

iv. W. Friedrich has pointed out in *Technik des Übersetzens* (1981: 124 ff.) that certain E. expressions are linked to a *that*-clause by **the fact**. Some of these are *to overlook (the fact that)*, *[not] to ignore*, *to disguise*, *to conceal*, *to hide*, and *to take into account/consideration*, *to make no mention of*, and *to take account of*. The G. equivalents *übersehen*, *beachten* (*nicht beachten*, 'to ignore', and *beachten*, 'not to ignore'), *verschleiern*, *verbergen*, *verheimlichen*, *verschweigen*, and *berücksichtigen* take a *daß*-clause without any link. Understanding this can rid transl. from E. into G. of many a superfluous *Tatsache*.

Sie müssen beachten, daß alle Kollegen schon überlastet sind und keine zusätzliche Arbeit bewältigen können.

Wir müssen berücksichtigen, daß Rohstoffpreise auf kurzer Sicht noch weiter fallen werden.

Übersehen Sie nicht, daß für die erfolgreiche Abwehr feindlicher Angriffe in erster Linie die moralische Haltung der Truppe ausschlaggebend ist!

Sie müssen Rücksicht darauf nehmen, daß die beiden noch sehr jung und unerfahren sind.

Es hat keinen Sinn zu verheimlichen/verschweigen, daß er unehrlich ist.

Es läßt sich nicht weiter verbergen, daß einige unserer Erwartungen sich nicht erfüllt haben.

v. When **the fact that** begins a sent., it need not be translated, and the sent. begins with *daß*. Both the following sents. would probably begin with *the fact* in E.

Daß sie es nicht tun dürfen, wird sie keineswegs daran hindern, es zu tun.

Daß Eis leichter als Wasser ist, stellt die einfache Erklärung dieses Phänomens dar.

3. Die Gegebenheit denotes an existing circumstance or factor which has to be taken into consideration, and can often be translated as **fact**. *Seine Opposition ist eine Gegebenheit, die sich durch Wunschdenken nicht aus der Welt schaffen läßt. Mit diesen Gegebenheiten müssen wir uns abfinden.*

4. *Der Tatbestand, die Sachlage,* and *der Sachverhalt* express meanings similar to that of **the facts of the case/matter**. *Der Tatbestand* is a legal or police term denoting all the facts relevant to a case or the circumstances pertaining to an issue. *Man stellt den Tatbestand fest*, establishes the facts, *nimmt den Tatbestand auf*, records the facts. *Jmd. versucht, den Tatbestand zu verschleiern. Was sie getan haben, erfüllt den Tatbestand des Betrugs* is a legal expression usually translated as *constitutes [a] fraud*. **Die Sachlage** is 'the situation or position with regard to a certain matter'. It is used in legal language, but not exclusively. It is translated as *the state of affairs* and as *the facts of the matter/case. Wie ist die Sachlage?* is a stylistically higher way of saying *Wie liegen die Dinge?* **Der Sachverhalt** is closer to conversational language, though not really a very common word in speech. It refers to the circumstances bearing on a matter, the events or things relating to a matter. *Sie erklärte mir den [wirklichen] Sachverhalt*, she explained the [real] facts or circumstances of the case or regarding a matter.

Das Gericht prüft den Tatbestand.   *Über den Tatbestand besteht gar kein Zweifel.*

Die Sachlage hat sich geändert. Eine Firma ist aus dem Vertrag ausgetreten.

Nach Beurteilung der Sachlage kam der Sachverständige zu folgendem Schluß.

Die Tochter erzählte zu Hause, daß sie am Unfall keine Schuld trage, der wahre Sachverhalt sah aber anders aus.

Ich glaube, du siehst den Sachverhalt falsch. Wenn die Bestechung ans Licht kommt, ist die Firma ruiniert.

5. In E. we talk of someone's facts, meaning 'what s.o. asserts to be true or the facts'. This can be **die Angabe**, i.e. what someone states or declares to be true, especially in legal language. *Seine Angaben halten einer näheren Prüfung nicht stand.* Another equivalent would be **die Behauptung**, 'assertion', cf. CLAIM. *Ihre Behauptungen erwiesen sich als unhaltbar.* In *to marshal one's facts*, **facts** suggests evidence or arguments and is *seine Beweise/Beweisgründe/Argumente ordnen und darlegen.*

fail *v.*

1. The original meaning of **fail** is 'to be absent or lacking', but this sense, which the cognate *fehlen* still has, now survives only in a few phrs., mainly *failing this/that* or *failing* + n. The simplest transl. of *failing this/that* is a clause with **wenn** + **nicht** or other neg. *Wenn das nicht klappt/nicht möglich ist*, i.e. if something you were hoping/advised to do turns out not to be possible. *Ask Michael, or failing him, Mary!* is, depending on the sense, *Frag Michael danach, oder wenn er nicht da ist/wenn er dir nicht helfen kann/wenn er es nicht weiß, Maria!* Phrs. like *failing receipt/submission of conclusive evidence, failing proof of this claim* can be expressed by a clause: *Wenn/Da man keine schlüssigen Beweise (für diesen Anspruch) vorgelegt hat*, or *Da/Falls zwingende Beweise fehlen*, or by the prep. **mangels**, 'for lack of', *Mangels schlüssiger Beweise.* Note that **fehlen** translates **fail** only with *Worte*. *Mir fehlen die Worte, um meine Freude/meine Verachtung auszudrücken*, I cannot find adequate words, words fail me.

2. Fail also means 'to become exhausted', 'come to an end', 'run short or out' applied to (the supply of) water and other things. For wells, springs, etc., G. uses **versiegen**, to dry up. *Nach einer längeren Trockenheit versiegten alle Brunnen. Die Quellen, die das Dorf mit Wasser versorgten, sind allmählich versiegt.* For other supplies, the pass. of **erschöpfen**, 'to exhaust', can be used.

   Die Vorräte der Verteidiger wurden erschöpft.   *Sein Kredit war erschöpft.*

3. Fail = 'to lose power or strength', 'become enfeebled', 'decline in vigour or vitality', or 'not to do what is expected'. *S.o.'s strength/health/memory failed. The wind/engine failed.*

i. Versagen, here = 'not to function', covers several contexts. *Plötzlich versagte ihre Stimme [vor Aufregung]. Seine Kräfte versagten* or *verließen ihn. Da versagt mir das Gedächtnis* or *Da läßt mich mein Gedächtnis im Stich.* For legs/feet: *Meine Beine/Füße versagten mir den Dienst. Die Bremse versagte. Das Herzversagen*, heart failure.

ii. Versagen is also used with *der Motor* or *das Triebwerk*, 'plane engine', but **ausfallen** would be more usual. This means that something which normally operates ceases to work. *Dann fiel der Motor/die Bremse/eines der Triebwerke/die Ampel/die Elektrizität* or *der Strom aus.* **Aussetzen**, used of a motor etc., means that it STOPS suddenly, sometimes only temporarily. *Dann setzte der Motor völlig unerwartet aus.*

iii. Ausbleiben is used for what is expected or predicted, but fails to materialize or eventuate. *Der Sommermonsun/Der Regen ist in diesem Jahr ausgeblieben. Die für diese Woche vorausgesagten Nachtfröste blieben aus. Die Aufträge sind leider ausgeblieben.* It is often used in the neg. and with *können. Der Erfolg/Die Strafe wird nicht ausbleiben. Die Katastrophe kann/wird nicht ausbleiben.* Ausbleiben is also applied to a crop failure. *Die Apfelernte blieb aus*, there was none. (If *The crop failed* means that it turned out to be bad, this is *Die Ernte fiel schlecht aus.*) *The wind failed* is *Der Wind* **hörte** plötzlich **auf**.

iv. Nachlassen, 'to decline in strength or intensity', and **abnehmen**, 'to decrease', can express the meaning of **fail** defined in 3. *Ihre Gesundheit ließ nach/nahm ab. Die Geisteskräfte der alten Dame lassen nach.* Other expressions can convey the meaning. *Seine Augen wurden schwächer*, were failing/beginning to fail. *The light was failing: Es*

dämmerte/wurde dunkel or *Das Licht nahm ab. His courage failed: Sein Mut ließ nach,*
schwand dahin, 'waned' (cf. DISAPPEAR), or *Er ließ seinen/den Mut sinken.*

4. With a person as subj. and obj., **fail** means 'not to render the due or expected
service or aid'. This is **im Stich lassen**, to let down, leave in the lurch, desert. *Er*
hat uns nie im Stich gelassen, has never failed us.

> *Als die Schlacht bevorstand, befürchtete er, alle Verbündeten würden ihn im Stich lassen.*

5. Fail + an infin. means 'to leave undone', 'not to perform or carry out some
action'. *He failed to inform us.*

i. When no conscious effort or obligation is involved, **fail** is simply an alternative
to a neg. and is best translated as such. *Er hat sein Wort nicht gehalten*, failed to keep
his word. *Sie ist unserem Rat nicht gefolgt*, failed to take our advice. *Ich sehe nicht ein,*
warum ich das machen soll, fail to see. *Sie reagierten nicht auf die Drohungen*, failed to
react. *Die Bombe explodierte nicht*, failed to explode.

ii. When the action which someone fails to carry out appears necessary or is the
person's duty, *unterlassen* and *versäumen* are used. **Unterlassen** can mean 'not to
do sth.' without any implication of neglecting one's responsibility. *Zuerst wollte ich*
anrufen, dann habe ich es aber doch unterlassen. With an infin., *unterlassen* is a syn. of
versäumen, to fail or neglect. *Er unterließ es/versäumte, uns zu benachrichtigen.*

> *Sie unterließ es, mir mitzuteilen, daß sie verreisen wollte.* (*Es* usually precedes the infin.)
> *Er unterließ es nicht, seine Schulden zu bezahlen, bevor er das Land verließ.*
> *Die Polizei unterließ es, den Fall weiter zu untersuchen.*
> *Der Pförtner hatte es versäumt, die Feuerwehr anzurufen.*
> *Sie versäumte nicht, uns über den Vorfall zu berichten.*

iii. Fail in *I will not fail to do my share* can be expressed by **auf jeden Fall** or **be-**
stimmt, both = 'definitely'. *Ich werde auf jeden Fall/bestimmt meinen Beitrag leisten.* An
alternative is *Ich werde nicht versäumen, meinen Beitrag zu leisten. Bestimmt* in a sent.
like *Die Regierung wird bestimmt fallen* could be a transl. of *cannot fail (to fall).*
Unfehlbar, in one sense = 'without fail', 'certainly', is close in meaning to **be-**
stimmt. *Er wird unfehlbar etw. Dummes machen*, he won't fail to do sth. stupid—you
can be sure of that. **Cannot fail** or **can hardly fail** to do sth. can be **nicht**
umhinkönnen, but this is not very common in conversation. *Sie können nicht*
umhin, ihn zu erkennen, er überragt alle anderen um Kopfeslänge. Er kann nicht umhin, von
dem, was wir getan haben, beeindruckt zu werden. An alternative would be *Er* **kann**
nicht anders als *beeindruckt werden. Sie kann nicht anders als dem Plan zustimmen.*

6. Fail = 'to be unsuccessful'.

i. That someone fails to do something attempted is expressed by **es gelingt jmdm.**
nicht + infin., 'not to SUCCEED', which implies an effort and is applied only to people or an institution (which implies people). *Es gelang ihr nicht, ihn zu überzeugen. Es*
gelang der Erziehungsanstalt nicht, den Jugendlichen zu bessern. When a thing is subj.,
as in *The jack failed to lift the truck*, the transl. is *Der Wagenheber* **konnte** *den Lastwagen*
nicht *heben* or **schaffte es nicht**, *den Lastwagen zu heben.*

> *Es gelang den Truppen nicht, die gegnerische Stellung einzunehmen.*
> *Es ist ihm nicht gelungen, die nötige Summe zusammenzubringen.*

ii. When the subj. is an attempt, someone's efforts, a plan, etc. there are several
vs. with a similar sense. In rising order of stylistic level, they are **fehlschlagen,**
mißlingen, mißglücken, and **scheitern**. All are found with words like *der Versuch,*
der Plan, jmds. Bemühungen, etc. as subj., although for *eine Ehe*, only *scheitern* is used.
Mein erster Versuch schlug fehl/mißlang. Das Projekt/Das Unternehmen mißglückte. Die
Friedensbemühungen scheiterten. Mißlingen and *mißglücken* take a dat. of the person,
but not an infin. *Du wolltest uns hereinlegen, aber das ist dir gründlich mißlungen. Alles,*
was ich anfange, mißglückt mir. Since *der Versuch* etc. must be the subj. in G., the E.

construction with a personal subj., such as *The enemy had failed in his attempt to take the fort,* has to be rephrased with *attempt* as subj. *Der Versuch des Feindes, die Festung zu erobern, war fehlgeschlagen.* An alternative which makes it possible to retain the E. construction is **keinen Erfolg haben.** *Sie hatte mit ihren Bemühungen, die Schule zu reformieren, keinen Erfolg. Nicht gelingen* could be used as well as *scheitern mit,* cf. 6. iii. Colloquial expressions are **danebengehen** and **schiefgehen,** 'to go wrong or fail', and *Sein erster Versuch war* **ein Reinfall,** 'failure, flop', or 'it failed badly'.

> *Da alle Vermittlungsversuche fehlgeschlagen sind, ist alle Hoffnung auf eine Versöhnung dahin.*
> *Auch der zweite Angriff schlug fehl/mißlang.*   *Der Raketenstart ist mißglückt.*
> *Alle meine Bemühungen um einen größeren Kredit sind gescheitert/fehlgeschlagen.*
> *Trotz anfänglicher Erfolge war es nach einigen Monaten klar, daß die Revolution gescheitert war.*
> *Diesmal wird das Experiment bestimmt nicht danebengehen.*
> *Die Sache hätte leicht schiefgehen können.*   *Es wird nichts schiefgehen.*

iii. Fail is used with a person, institution, or skill, etc. as subj., either without a phr. or with one like *at/in a job. They tried hard, but failed. If s.o. has failed in one job, this does not mean that he will fail in another. The reform school does not fail in all cases.* Apart from *keinen Erfolg haben, scheitern,* and *versagen* are used. **Scheitern** is quite objective and says nothing about the cause, while **versagen** attributes some measure of blame and may suggest weakness or inadequacy on the part of the person or institution. *Scheitern* is used without a prep., *Vielleicht hat sie diesmal mehr Erfolg—sie darf kein zweites Mal scheitern,* but also takes *mit, Sie ist mit diesem Plan gescheitert,* and *an, Er scheiterte an mangelnder Erfahrung.* It is the only word used when discussing the failure of a character in a tragedy. *Woran scheitert der Held dieser Tragödie? Bei diesen Kindern hat das Elternhaus/die Schule versagt.* (Note that *Er hat versagt* does not express such strong condemnation as *Er ist ein Versager.*)

> *Hier versagt die ärztliche Kunst.*   *In dem entscheidenden Augenblick versagte er.*
> *Wenn jmd. in einem Beruf gescheitert ist, heißt das nicht, daß er in einem anderen keinen Erfolg*
>   *haben wird.*   *Beide haben in/bei der Prüfung völlig versagt.*
> *Es stimmt nicht, daß die Erziehungsanstalt bei allen Jugendlichen keinen Erfolg hat/versagt.*

7. Fail [in] *an examination* is either **durch eine Prüfung fallen** or **durchfallen.** Both are used when the name of the examination is not stated so that *I failed* is either *Ich bin durch die Prüfung gefallen* or *Ich bin durchgefallen.* With the first expression the nature of the examination can only be combined with *Prüfung. Ich bin zum zweiten Mal durch die Fahrprüfung gefallen.* With *durchfallen* the name of the subject or examination follows *in. Ich bin in der theoretischen Fahrprüfung/im Abitur durchgefallen. Ich bin leider in Mathematik durchgefallen.* When trans., as in *S.o. fails a student,* **fail** is **durchfallen lassen.** *Die Prüfer ließen ein Fünftel der Prüflinge durchfallen.*

8. Durchfallen is used for a play which fails. *Das neue Theaterstück ist durchgefallen.* An alternative is *Das Stück war/wurde* **ein Durchfall.** These words can translate *His second novel failed.* If **fail** means that no one read or bought it, an alternative is *Sein zweiter Roman kam nicht beim Publikum an.*

9. *A firm/bank* **fails** is *Eine Firma/Bank* **geht in Konkurs,** goes bankrupt. For alternatives cf. BREAK 6.

fairly, pretty, rather, somewhat *advs.*

1. All mean 'moderately' or 'to a certain extent'. **Fairly** and **rather** are syns., although not always interchangeable. **Pretty,** used colloquially, is normally a step higher towards *very,* so that the rising order would be *fairly/rather good, pretty good, very good.*

i. Fairly and **rather** are ziemlich, recht lies between *ziemlich* and *sehr* and is like

pretty, and *sehr* is 'very'. In the spoken language **ganz schön** is common and close to *sehr*. The progression is *ziemlich kalt, recht kalt, ganz schön kalt,* and *sehr kalt. Ich kenne ihn ziemlich gut. Es is heute recht kalt/windig. Wir haben ganz schön geschuftet. Ziemlich* + an adj. translates *rather* either before or after the definite article. *A rather surprising result* and *rather a surprising result* become *eine ziemlich überraschendes Ergebnis.*

  Es ist ziemlich heiß heute.   Es waren ziemlich viele Leute da.
  Es ist ziemlich spät.   Die Kinder sind ganz schön dreckig.
  Wir waren ziemlich abgespannt/ziemlich aufgeregt/ganz schön müde.

ii. Etwas, used with an adv. or an adj. without an ending (not e.g. *etwas Gutes*), means 'somewhat'. *Etwas ungeschickt. Etwas enttäuscht.* Unlike *ziemlich, recht,* and *ganz schön*, it can be used with a comparative and before *zu*, as **rather** and **some-what** are in E. An alternative is **ein bißchen**, a bit.

  Dieses Auto ist etwas zu groß.   Ich bleibe morgen etwas länger.
  Die Rechnung/Der Preis ist etwas höher als ich erwartet hatte.
  Heute geht es meinem Bruder etwas besser.
  Dieses Buch ist etwas/ein bißchen zu schwer für Schüler der achten Klasse.

iii. Fairly and **rather** differ in a nuance. *This is a fairly easy book and is therefore suitable,* but *This is a rather easy book and therefore unsuitable;* the second sent. suggests it is too easy. The first would be *Dies ist ein ziemlich leichtes Buch und deshalb geeignet.* The idea of the second would have to be clearly stated. *Dies ist ein etwas zu leichtes Buch/Dieses Buch ist etwas zu leicht und deshalb ungeeignet.*

2. Rather + n. can, in a few cases, be translated by **ziemlich** used as an adv. *Rather a pity: Ziemlich schade. $100 is rather a lot to pay for a dress* can be *Hundert Dollar ist ziemlich viel für ein Kleid. Ziemlich* is used as an adj. meaning 'a fair or considerable degree of'. *Das kann ich mit ziemlicher Sicherheit behaupten*, with a fair degree of certainty. In some cases this translates **rather**. *Das war eine ziemliche Enttäuschung,* rather a disappointment. *Das war eine ziemliche Anstrengung,* rather/quite an effort.

3. Pretty much, **pretty nearly**, and **pretty well** all mean 'almost' and are trans-lated by **fast** or **beinahe**. *Sie sind fast gleich,* pretty much the same. *Wir haben fast alles erledigt,* pretty nearly/pretty well everything. Cf. NEARLY. A colloquial alterna-tive which is possible in some cases is **so ziemlich**. It also translates *just about. A fragt: 'Seid ihr fertig?' B und C antworten: 'So ziemlich.'*

  Wir haben so ziemlich alles erledigt, was wir uns vorgenommen haben.
  Das Ergebnis der Abstimmung ist so ziemlich das, was wir erwartet haben.

4. Rather and *sooner* = 'more willingly', 'by preference or choice'. *I'd rather/sooner stay here.* The usual transl. is **lieber** with *haben* or another v. when the person car-rying out the action is the subj. *Ich hätte lieber Fisch. Ich würde lieber hier bleiben* or *Ich bleibe lieber hier.* When someone else performs the action as in *I would rather/sooner you came tomorrow*, **Mir wäre es lieber, wenn** . . . is used. *Es wäre mir lieber, wenn du morgen vorbeikämest.*

  Er würde lieber gleich hingehen.   Sie wäre lieber dort geblieben, aber es ging nicht.
  Ich ginge lieber zu Fuß/würde lieber zu Fuß gehen.
  Ich hätte lieber den braunen Anzug.
  Ich hätte lieber ein Haus als ein Auto.
  Sie würden lieber auf dem Lande leben als in der Großstadt.
  Möchtest du nicht lieber geliebt als gefürchtet sein?
  Ihm wäre es lieber, wenn wir alles in einem Brief erklären würden.

An alternative is one sense of **eher**, but *lieber* is commoner. *Er legte sein Amt eher/lieber nieder, als sich auf das unlautere Unternehmen einzulassen. Ich würde eher* *sterben als mit solchen Leuten gemeinsame Sache machen. Ich stehe eher zeitiger auf, als mich zu hetzen.*

5. Rather also means 'more truly, accurately, or precisely', and, when put in opposition to a previous statement, it corrects it or makes it more precise. *Suddenly there stood before him, or rather above him, a gigantic figure.* **Eher** is usual when a phr. with *als* follows. *Es war mir eher unangenehm als angenehm. Er ist eher egoistisch als despotisch. Er ist nicht despotisch, sondern eher egoistisch.* In the last sent. **vielmehr** could also be used. *Er ist nicht despotisch, sondern vielmehr egoistisch.* It is usual when a phr. with *als* does not follow, but *eher* is also possible.

> *Das ist eher eine Wildnis als ein Garten.   Das ist kein Spaß, sondern vielmehr bitterer Ernst.*
> *Sie sind gestern abend spät angekommen oder vielmehr in den frühen Morgenstunden.*
> *Plötzlich stand vor ihm, oder eher/vielmehr über ihm eine riesige Gestalt.*
> *Ich kann deine Meinung nicht teilen, vielmehr glaube ich, daß das Gegenteil zutrifft.*

(With the suppression of *als*, **eher** means 'more likely'. *Das ist schon eher möglich*, more likely to be possible or the case than what has just been said. *Das ist eher der Fall. Das eher.* It also means 'more likely' when an *als*-clause follows. *Als* then means 'as'. *Er wird um so eher damit einverstanden sein, als es ihm so bequemer ist*, all the more likely to agree as . . .)

6. Rather than, as in *I have used the familiar E. names rather than the scientific Latin terms*, can be translated by **statt** or **anstatt**. *Ich habe die geläufigen englischen Namen benutzt statt/anstatt der wissenschaftlichen lateinischen Bezeichnungen.*

fall [over/down/into], crash, tip over, knock over *vs.* Some uses.

1. Fall.

i. **Fallen** and **hinfallen** both mean 'to get into a downward movement', are used for people and things, but differ syntactically. *Fallen* is used when an expression of direction is present, but without this *hinfallen* must normally be used. With an adv. or phr. of manner *hin* can be omitted, as *over* is in E. At the end of a sent. *hin* may be left out. *Hilfe! Ich falle. Halt mich fest!—ich habe Angst, daß ich [hin]falle.*

> *Sie fiel auf den Boden/auf die Erde/nach vorn/nach hinten/auf den Rücken/auf das Gesicht.*
> *Er ist auf dem Eis ausgerutscht und hingefallen.*   *Das Kind stolperte und fiel hin.*
> *Der Spaziergänger rutschte aus und fiel gegen die Bank.*   *Er fiel der Länge nach hin.*
> *Das Kind fiel unglücklich und brach sich den Arm.*   *Das Pferd fiel hin.*
> *Jmd. fällt sanft/weich/hart/mit großer Heftigkeit.*
> *Sie ist beim Laufen hingefallen.*
> *Die Pflaumen sind reif und fallen vom Baum.*
> *Er stellte das Fahrrad so ungeschickt neben die anderen, daß sie alle hinfielen.*
> *Dir ist etw. hingefallen.* (Sth. has fallen out of your pocket, bag, etc.)

ii. In one of its senses, **stürzen** means 'to fall with some force'. It is used only for human beings and for objects which are at least as big as a human being. Therefore *Ein Bleistift fiel vom Tisch* and *Ein Reiter stürzte vom Pferd. Stürzen* also implies that the fall had some adverse effect. *Er fiel hin* means that an action took place which may or may not result in an injury. *Er stürzte* suggests that at least pain was caused, if not an injury. *Stürzen* thus implies more consequences than *fallen*, although just what may remain unspecified. *Er ist von der Leiter gefallen* suggests no consequences to speak of. *Er stürzte von der Leiter* or *sie ist gestürzt* suggests at least a shaking or injury. Only in poetical or literary language is *stürzen* used in reference to liquids. *Tränen stürzten ihr aus den Augen. Wie aus Kannen stürzte der Regen auf uns herab.*

> *Er war im Winter auf dem Eis gestürzt und hatte sich ein Bein gebrochen.*
> *Einer der Radfahrer stürzte, aber der Nachfolgende konnte noch rechtzeitig ausweichen.*

2. Crash. With aircraft, **abstürzen** means 'to crash' when no phr. follows. *Das Flugzeug stürzte ab*. With a phr. in the acc., *stürzen* is used. *Das Flugzeug stürzte ins Meer/in den Wald*. *Ab* is, however, included with a phr. in the dat. *Das Flugzeug stürzte im Meer/im Wald ab*.

3. Fall over, tip over (intr.).

i. Umfallen, to fall over or down, is used for things and living beings. With the latter, it suggests in strict use falling over from inner weakness, but it is often used when something surprises someone greatly. In such cases *fast* and *beinahe* are often added.

> *Er ist aufgestanden und einfach umgefallen. Wir waren alle ziemlich erschrocken.*
> *Das Pferd hatte sich total verausgabt und fiel nach dem Rennen tot um.*
> *Ich wäre beinahe vor Schreck umgefallen, als ich den Preis hörte.*
> *Der Zaun ist während des Sturms umgefallen.*   *Ich bin fast umgefallen vor Lachen.*
> *Es ist eine große Überraschung. Du fällst um, wenn du es hörst.*

ii. Umkippen, 'to fall over or tip over', is common in speech. *Die Vase ist umgekippt. Der Stuhl kippte um*, fell, toppled over. For people it suggests fainting. *Bei der Hitze kippten viele Menschen um*. When a person is the subj., a *mit*-phr. can be added. *Er kippte mit dem Stuhl um*. In *Das Boot ist umgekippt*, capsized, *umkippen* replaces the v. of the standard language *ist gekentert*.

4. Knock over. Umkippen is also trans. *Sie hat die Vase umgekippt.* **Umwerfen** and **umstoßen** are syns., but suggest somewhat more force. *Ich stieß gegen den Stuhl und warf ihn um. Er hat das Glas umgestoßen.* (Fig. uses: *Diese Nachricht warf uns alle um*, stunned, shocked. *Diese Änderungen haben alle unsere Pläne umgestoßen*, upset, wrecked.)

> *Der Anprall hätte mich beinahe umgeworfen.*
> *Er wußte nicht, daß das Kind hinter ihm stand und hat es umgestoßen.*

5. i. For **fall into**, meaning 'to pass or lapse into a state', both **fallen** and **verfallen** are used. With *in, fallen* denotes a change of state and is the more frequently used v. *Er fiel in tiefen Schlaf.* Although in some contexts both occur, *verfallen* is now mostly confined to undesired and undesirable states, frequently mental ones. *Jmd. verfiel in Stumpfsinn. A fällt bei B in Ungnade*, 'falls into disgrace', is a fixed expression.

> *Man fällt in einen sanfteren Ton/in seinen Dialekt/in seine Muttersprache/in Trance/in Krämpfe.*
> *Während der Diskussion fiel der Politiker von einem Extrem ins andere.*
> *Man verfällt in Schwermut/in Lethargie/in tiefe Grübelei/in tiefes Nachdenken.*
> *Er verfiel in eine Stimmung der absoluten Gleichgültigkeit.*
> *Die Bevölkerung fiel/verfiel in Angst und Schrecken.*   *Das Land verfiel in Anarchie.*

Verfallen + dat. means that something has a hold on someone, that he/she is a victim of it or has fallen victim to it. *Er/Sie ist dem Trunk/dem Spiel/der Verzweiflung verfallen. Jmd. ist einem Irrtum verfallen.*

ii. Some other senses of *verfallen*. 'To fall into disrepair'. *Ein Gebäude/Bauwerk verfällt.* 'To decline, lose strength' of people. *Jmd. verfällt zusehends. Das Römische Reich verfiel*, declined, lost power.

falsify, forge, adulterate *vs.* While **forge** means 'to make a fraudulent imitation of sth.', **falsify** implies making some modifications or partial changes which are not true.

1. i. Fälschen means both 'to forge' and 'to falsify'. It is used when something like *Banknoten, Urkunden*, 'certificates', *Bilder*, etc. are copied and passed off as genuine, but also when items or parts of something like a *Bilanz, Rechnung*, or *Testament* are fraudulently altered. It implies intentionally changing what one knows to be true or genuine, usually to one's own advantage.

Es scheint nicht schwer zu sein, einen Paß zu fälschen. (Could either be partial, just changing the photograph etc., or forging the whole thing.)

Er setzte sich hin und fälschte die Unterschrift seiner Frau auf dem Reisescheck.

Das Gemälde ist nicht das Original, es ist gefälscht. Also . . . eine Fälschung.

Bei genauer Nachrechnung der in den Büchern aufgelisteten Beträge ergab sich, daß die Bilanz vom Buchhalter gefälscht worden war.   Die Verbrecher hatten Banknoten gefälscht.

ii. The basic meaning of **verfälschen** is 'to make a partial change or falsification', so that it is a syn. of one sense of *fälschen. Verfälschen* has two other meanings, the first being 'to present facts, events, etc. wrongly'. When the obj. is a word like *die Geschichte,* 'history', *die Wahrheit, der Hergang, die [Darstellung der] Tatsachen, das Charakterbild,* both words are possible. *Mit dem gefälschten Tagebuch Hitlers wurde der Versuch gemacht, das Charakterbild des Naziführers zu fälschen,* means that the attempt was made to pass off as real a depiction of his character which bore no resemblance to what his character actually was. *Jmd. fälscht die Geschichte/die Ereignisse* means that the person consciously presents as true what he or she knows to be false. The whole, or a significant part, is invented. *Jmd. verfälscht die Geschichte/die Tatsachen/das Charakterbild* means that the result is not completely accurate. A further difference is that with *verfälschen,* the partial inexactness can be unintentional as well as deliberate.

Er fälschte/verfälschte seinen Paß dadurch, daß er das Geburtsjahr änderte.

Der Überfallene verfälschte den Tathergang ein wenig, wahrscheinlich um Mitleid zu erregen.

Die Nachricht ging von Mund zu Mund, jeder fügte etw. hinzu oder ließ etw. weg, und so wurde der eigentliche Sachverhalt so sehr verfälscht, daß am Ende niemand wußte, wie es wirklich war.

iii. Nachmachen, which can mean 'to COPY', is also used for forging a signature or banknotes.

Wer Banknoten nachmacht, wird bestraft.   Jmd. hat meine Unterschrift nachgemacht.

2. With food as obj. **verfälschen** means 'to adulterate'. *Sie haben den Wein durch Zusatz von Zucker verfälscht. Auf Lebensmittelverfälschung steht eine Gefängnisstrafe.*

farm, farmer *ns.*

1. A **farm** is **ein Bauernhof,** but if it is clear what is meant, **der Hof** alone is sufficient. *Ich bin auf einem Bauernhof großgeworden. Mein Vater war Bauer, aber nach seinem Tod verkaufte meine Mutter den Hof. Die Höfe in dieser Gegend sind alle mittelgroß.* **Das Gut** or **das Landgut** is 'an estate or property' and suggests a larger area than *ein Bauernhof,* but the dividing line is by no means clear, and *ein großer Bauernhof* could well be larger than some *Güter.* The former aristocratic estates east of the Elbe were called *Güter,* originally *Rittergüter,* and their owners *Gutsbesitzer.* **Die Farm** is used for farms in Anglo-Saxon countries other than the UK. The word usually suggests an area larger than the average G. *Bauernhof,* but there are *kleine Farmen.* In technical literature about farming, **ein landwirtschaftlicher Betrieb** is often found. It means lit. 'an agricultural enterprise' and is applied to farms of all types. **Der bäuerliche Betrieb** is also used.

2. The usual word for **farmer** is **der Bauer.** In historical contexts it is translated as *peasant.* The slightly pejorative tone which the word has had, with regard both to social status and to manners and behaviour, has disappeared, and the G. farmers' association calls itself *der deutsche Bauernverband.* A word with no overtones is **der Landwirt.** *Mein Bruder ist Bauer/Landwirt.* If he has studied agriculture, only *gelernter Landwirt* is used. **Der Farmer** is used only for someone who owns or runs *eine Farm.*

farming, agriculture *ns.* The general word, which includes all types of primary production, is **die Landwirtschaft.** It refers to the carrying on of farming as a

means of livelihood, to the section of the economy which derives its income from farming, and to agriculture as a subject of study. The two main branches of agriculture are **der Ackerbau**, 'the cultivation of the soil and the planting of crops', and **die Viehzucht**, 'the keeping of animals, mainly sheep and cattle'. In compounds, **Agrar-** is often used, although *landwirtschaftlich* expresses the same sense. *Das Agrarprodukt, das Agrargebiet, das Agrarland. Landwirtschaftliche Produkte. Agrarprodukte.*
> *In Industriestaaten ist nur ein kleiner Teil der Bevölkerung in der Landwirtschaft tätig.*
> *In den meisten kommunistischen Ländern wurde die Landwirtschaft kollektiviert.*
> *Der Landwirtschaft in Australien geht es zur Zeit ziemlich schlecht.*
> *In dieser Gegend überwiegt der Ackerbau/betreibt man Ackerbau und Viehzucht.*

fatal *adj.* **Tödlich** means 'resulting in or causing death'. *Ein tödlicher Unfall/Schlag. Er erlitt tödliche Verletzungen. Der Biß dieser Schlange ist/wirkt selten tödlich. Die Kugel hatte ihn tödlich getroffen.* **Verhängnisvoll** means 'of such a nature that it leads to doom or disaster' and corresponds to **fatal** = 'disastrous'. *Ein verhängnisvoller Fehler/Irrtum. Verhängnisvolle Folgen. Sie gewann einen verhängnisvollen Einfluß auf ihn. Die Wahl dieses Vorsitzenden erwies sich als verhängnisvoll für die Partei. Ein verhängnisvoller Tag* is 'a fatal day, one destined by fate to see some disaster'. G. **fatal** means 'extremely unpleasant', and often implies highly embarrassing. *Ein fatale Angelegenheit* is 'a bad, disagreeable, or odious business'. *Wir sind in einer höchst fatalen Lage. Er sah sich zu einem für ihn fatalen Eingeständnis gezwungen.*

fate, destiny, lot (in life) *ns.* **Fate** and **destiny** are syns. in denoting a power or agency by which events are unalterably predetermined. *He had hoped to become president, but fate decided/decreed otherwise. Such are the tricks played on human beings by destiny.* Both also denote that which is fated or destined to happen, the future or events of life as determined by fate or destiny. While **fate** suggests something bad which is to be feared, often death, destruction, or ruin, **destiny** mostly says nothing about the nature of what happens except that it is irrevocably predetermined by fate, providence, nature, God, etc. *She deserves a better fate. They left/abandoned the men to their fate. He went to/met his fate with dignity. This decided/sealed our fate. It was his destiny to spend his life in a country far from his family and the friends of his youth. His belief in the splendid destiny of the human race was unshakeable.* **Fate** can also mean 'what has or will become of a pers.' *The fate of the overdue hikers is still uncertain.* S.o.'s **lot** means 'his/her destiny or condition in life', whether good or bad. *His lot has been a hard one. Poverty has been their lot. Such good fortune is the lot of few men.*

1. Das Schicksal is 'fate or destiny', i.e. 'the power that determines events'.
> *Ein gütiges Schicksal bewahrte sie vor dem Schlimmsten.*
> *Das Schicksal hat es gut mit uns gemeint.*
> *Das grausame/unerbittliche Schicksal hat sie schwer geprüft.*
> *Er hatte gehofft, Präsident zu werden, aber das Schicksal hatte es anders gewollt.*

Das Schicksal also means 'what happens or is destined to happen to s.o./sth.' and can be good or bad. *Jmd. rennt in sein Schicksal* implies ruin or downfall, and *Jmd. überläßt andere ihrem Schicksal* suggests an untoward fate.
> *Sie hatten beide das gleiche freundliche/schwere/tragische Schicksal.*
> *Sein Schicksal war besiegelt/hatte sich entschieden.*　　*Etw. entscheidet über jmds. Schicksal.*
> *Man muß sich mit seinem Schicksal abfinden.*　　*Sie verdient ein besseres Schicksal.*
> *Was wird das Schicksal dieser alten Häuser sein?*
> *Ihn ereilte das gleiche Schicksal wie seinen Vorgänger.*

Das Schicksal also means 'what has become of s.o.' *Man stellt Nachforschungen über das Schicksal des entlaufenen Kindes an.*

2. A syn. of *Schicksal* in the sense 'what happens or is destined to happen to s.o./sth.' is **das Geschick**, but it is an elevated word, now slightly antiquated. *Niemand kann seinem Geschick entgehen.*
Die Stadt traf ein gütiges/schweres/widriges/trauriges Geschick.
Geschick is still used in the pl. meaning 'the political and economic fortunes of a country, town, or enterprise', but here too it belongs to a high stylistic level.
Die Geschicke des Landes/der Stadt lagen in den Händen eines einzigen Mannes.
Als viele glaubten, der Konkurs sei unabwendbar, hat er die Geschicke des Unternehmens erfolgreich gelenkt.

3. Das Los means 'lot in life'. Like *Geschick* it is an elevated and rather poetic word. *Ich bin mit meinem Los zufrieden. Sie hatten ein schweres/hartes/bitteres/beneidenswertes Los.* (*Das Los* is also 'a lot', as in *to draw or cast lots, Die Reihenfolge wurde durch das Los entschieden*, and 'a lottery ticket', *Ich habe zwei Lose gekauft. Das große Los* is 'the first prize'.)

4. Destiny meaning 'sth. good or bad pre-ordained for a pers.' is **die Bestimmung**.
War es Zufall oder Bestimmung, daß ich gerade diese Frau traf?
Im Rausch des Sieges verschwanden die Zweifel, die in Hitler aufgestiegen waren; der Glaube an seine Bestimmung übertönte alle Bedenken.
Ich bin mit Glücklichsein nicht zufrieden, ich bin nicht dafür geschaffen, es ist nicht meine Bestimmung. Meine Bestimmung ist das Gegenteil. (Hesse, *Der Steppenwolf*)
Es war seine Bestimmung/sein Schicksal, sein Leben in einem fremden Land zu verbringen.

5. Das Verhängnis implies an untoward fate, often ruin or downfall, imposed (i.e. *verhängt*) by a higher power. *Etw. wurde jmdm. zum Verhängnis*, sth. proved fatal, was s.o.'s undoing, downfall.
Die Spielleidenschaft/Die Raserei/Diese Frau wurde ihm zum Verhängnis.
Das Verhängnis nahm seinen Lauf/ließ sich nicht aufhalten/brach über das Land herein.

fear *v.* and *n.* be afraid, dread *vs.*

1. Fear v.
i. Sich fürchten and **Angst haben** denote real fear and correspond to the basic sense of **be afraid** or *frightened*, 'to regard with fear', because the person or thing is a source of danger or will cause something painful or evil. The only difference between them is that *Angst haben* is the everyday word, while *sich fürchten* is formal. *I'm afraid/frightened* is either *Ich habe Angst* or *Ich fürchte mich*, and *Don't be afraid!* can be *Hab' keine Angst!, Nur keine Angst!*, or *Fürchte dich nicht!*, but the latter has a biblical ring. Both can take *vor* + a n., or an infin. When **dread** denotes a heightened degree of fear, it can be expressed by strengthened forms of these expressions. *Ich hatte große Angst vor diesem Lehrer* or *Ich fürchtete mich sehr vor diesen Stunden.*
Der kleine Junge fürchtet sich im Dunkeln/fürchtete sich vor dem großen Hund.
Er hat Angst vor dem Bullen/vor Haien.   *Als Kind fürchtete ich mich vor Gespenstern.*
Vor Gespenstern habe ich keine Angst.   *Sie fürchtet sich, allein durch den Wald zu gehen.*
Wegen der Haie habe ich Angst, im Meer zu schwimmen.

ii. Fürchten is used with an obj. Like **fear**, it means 'to regard with reverence', 'feel respect or awe for'. *Gläubige Menschen fürchten Gott. Als Kinder haben wir unsere Großeltern gefürchtet.* Its main sense is 'to feel fear' because you believe you will suffer something bad or unpleasant from the person or situation which is the obj. *Er fürchtet diesen/keinen Gegner.* With *um* and *für*, it means 'to fear for', 'to be very worried about'. *Er fürchtet um seine Stellung.* It can also take an infin. *Seine Kehle war verstopft, und er fürchtete zu ersticken.* *Fürchten* also translates **dread** meaning 'to anticipate with terror or foreboding'. *Alle fürchteten die Ankunft des neuen Chefs. Der gefürchtete Augenblick war da*, the dreaded moment had arrived.

Alle Schauspieler fürchten diesen Kritiker. Er ist allgemein gefürchtet.
Sie fürchtet die Wahrheit.   *Alle fürchten ihn wegen seiner Grausamkeit.*
Er fürchtet für ihre Gesundheit.   *Sie fürchtet um das Leben ihres Sohnes.*

iii. Befürchten means 'to have an uneasy sense of the likelihood of some unwelcome or unpleasant occurrence in the future'. *Was befürchtest du?* refers to something bad you feel is going to happen, *was fürchtest du?* to something you fear or dread. *Ich befürchte eine Begegnung mit jmdm.*, I think an encounter is likely and will be unpleasant. *Ich fürchte eine Begegnung mit jmdm.*, I dread it. *Wir brauchen keinen Angriff zu befürchten* is a prediction that an attack will not take place, whereas *Wir brauchen keinen Angriff zu fürchten* means that we are strong enough to ward off any attack and need not be afraid. *Weitere Schwierigkeiten sind nicht zu befürchten*, they will not happen. In speech, particularly when *ich* is subj. and when a clause follows, the *be-* is often omitted and *fürchten* is used, provided there is no ambiguity. *Ich [be]fürchte, das wird nicht gutgehen. Ich fürchte, du hast recht.* However, in other constructions, *befürchten* is usual. *Sie haben von der Polizei nichts zu befürchten. Das ist nicht zu befürchten.* With *nichts*, only *befürchten* is found, because *fürchten* would mean 'to be afraid of nothing'. *Die Genehmigung des Kredits ist nur noch eine Formsache; in dieser Hinsicht haben/brauchen Sie nichts zu befürchten.* In colloquial speech **Angst haben** + clause expresses this sense of anticipating something unpleasant. *Ich habe Angst, du fällst aus dem Fenster.*

> *Das, was ich seit langem befürchtete, ist nun eingetreten.*
> *Wie alle befürchtet hatten, regnete es am folgenden Tag.*
> *Er [be]fürchtet, daß er auch diese Arbeitsstelle nicht bekommen wird.*
> *Ich glaube nicht, daß wir in dieser Hinsicht etw. zu befürchten haben.*
> *Er [be]fürchtete, keinen Vorschuß zu bekommen/daß er keinen Vorschuß bekommen würde.*
> *Sie befürchteten das Schlimmste.*   *Ich habe Angst, unser Ausflug fällt morgen ins Wasser.*

2. Fear n. **Die Angst** corresponds to **fear** meaning 'an unpleasant and often strong emotion caused by the awareness of danger'. **Die Furcht** suggests somewhat weaker fear, but is stylistically higher. **Die Befürchtung** is 'fear' meaning 'a feeling that sth. unpleasant will happen'. It is often found in the pl. and suggests worried thoughts about what could happen. The pl. often translates **fears**. *Diese Nachricht hat alle meine Befürchtungen zerstreut.*

> *Er zitterte vor Furcht/überwand seine Furcht/wurde von starker Furcht erfaßt.*
> *Befürchtungen wurden laut, daß es zum Streik kommen könnte.*
> *Was für Befürchtungen haben Sie?*   *Ihre Befürchtungen erwiesen sich als grundlos.*

3. I dread to think what might happen suggests worry because what could happen is likely to be unpleasant. Such sents. could become *Es beunruhigt mich sehr, wenn ich an die möglichen Folgen denke/wenn ich daran denke, wie die Sache ausgehen könnte/wenn ich mir vorstelle, was geschehen könnte/was sie uns antun könnten.* **Beunruhigen**, to worry. In a less serious situation: *Ich mag gar nicht an die möglichen Folgen denken. Ich mag gar nicht daran denken, wie die Sache enden könnte.*

4. I'm afraid is used as a polite phr. to introduce a statement containing information which might be unwelcome to another. *I'm afraid Mr Jones has already left.* This can be **es tut mir leid** or **ich bedaure [sehr]** often with *aber*. *Es tut mir leid, [aber] Herr J. ist schon weg. Ich bedaure [sehr], aber Herr J. ist schon weg. Es tut uns leid,/Wir bedauern [es] sehr, aber wir können die Einladung nicht annehmen.*

5. i. Fear/be afraid can also mean 'to hesitate to do sth. for fear of doing wrong or causing unhappiness or inconvenience'. *I feared/was afraid to disturb you at work/to tell them the truth.* This is **sich scheuen** + infin. *Ich scheute mich, ihnen die Wahrheit zu sagen/Sie bei der Arbeit zu stören.*
ii. With *work* as obj., **scheuen**, 'to shy away from', is usual, *Sie scheuen die Arbeit*, but *fürchten* is possible, *Er fürchtet keine Arbeit.*

feed *v.*

1. Feed means 'to supply a pers. or a group of people with food', *The farmers grow only enough corn to feed their families*, and 'to prepare the food for s.o.' In the latter sense the manner is often stated. *Are you feeding yourself properly? They look well fed.*
i. The equivalent of **feed** meaning 'to provide with food on a regular basis', 'to maintain or support', as in *He has to feed and clothe a large family*, is **ernähren**. *Er hat eine große Familie zu kleiden und zu ernähren.* A place can be the subj. *Die Insel konnte nur zwei Familien ernähren. Ein Beruf ernährt seinen Mann [nicht]* means that the occupation provides someone with [in]sufficient income to live on.
  Diese Bauern bauen nur die Menge Getreide an, die sie brauchen, um ihre Familien zu ernähren.
ii. Sich ernähren can mean 'to feed or support oneself'. *Als Lehrling verdiene ich genug, um mich zu ernähren. Sich von etw. ernähren* means 'to live or feed on a particular kind of food' at least for a certain length of time, if not always. *Auf der unbewohnten Insel ernährten sich die schiffbrüchigen Matrosen von Austern, Nüssen und Obst. Kühe ernähren sich von Gras und anderen Pflanzen.*
  Der Student wollte kein Geld von seinen Eltern annehmen und ernährte sich von Gelegenheitsarbeit.
  Nicht alle Fledermäuse ernähren sich von Insekten.
iii. Ernähren also means 'to feed s.o. in a certain way', i.e. well, badly, adequately, and is the usual word when talking of nutrition, which is *die Ernährung. Die Kinder wurden auf Grund der neuesten Erkenntnisse ernährt.* With *gut* or *richtig*, it translates *nourish. Es ist wichtig, daß Kleinkinder richtig ernährt werden.* **Sich ernähren** also expresses this sense. *Man muß sich richtig ernähren.*
iv. Nähren is now restricted to a few contexts. One is 'to breast-feed' or, for animals, 'to suckle'. It refers to the fact that a child is nourished in this way for a certain period, not on a particular occasion. **Stillen** is the normal v. meaning 'to [breast-]feed' and denotes both a single occasion or the continuing or whole process. For animals, **säugen**, 'to suckle', is used in the same way. *Die Kuh säugt das Kalb. Eine Schlange an seiner Brust nähren* is a fixed expression.
  Sie hat alle ihre Kinder selbst genährt.   Sie konnte das Kind nur acht Wochen nähren/stillen.
  Das Kind wird in regelmäßigen Abständen gestillt.
  Die ersten Wochen nach der Geburt nährt das Muttertier die Jungen.
Nähren also means 'to feed in a certain way', but occurs in this sense only in the past part. *Genährt* is an exact syn. of *ernährt*, except that *ernährt* alone forms compounds, *überernährt, unterernährt.*
  Die Kinder scheinen wohl genährt zu sein.   Die Tiere sehen gut/wohl genährt aus.
  In diesem Heim wurden die Kinder offenbar nicht zureichend genährt/ernährt.
With food as subj., *nähren* means 'to be nutritious'. *Die Speise/Kost nährt.*
v. With human beings, **füttern** is used only when the food is put into their mouths. *Das Baby wird von seiner Schwester gefüttert.*

2. Feed animals. **Füttern** is the usual word for feeding animals. The obj. is usually a farm animal, and a phr. with *mit* can be added. *Wir füttern die Kühe [mit Rüben].* The food can be the obj. *Wir füttern Rüben an die Kühe.* **Verfüttern** could be used in the last sent. *Wir verfüttern Hafer [an die Pferde]. Verfüttern* also means 'to use up by giving as fodder'. *Wir haben zwei Zentner Heu [an die Kühe] verfüttert.*
  Wir füttern die Schweine mit Kartoffeln.   Er füttert gerade die Hühner.
  Bitte füttern Sie die Tiere nicht mit Abfällen!   Der Bauer hatte das gesamte Heu verfüttert.
An alternative is **zu fressen geben** or **sein Fressen geben** and, for the pass., **zu fressen bekommen** or **sein Fressen bekommen**. *Ich muß der Katze zu fressen geben/ihr Fressen geben. Der Hund bekommt um sechs Uhr zu fressen/sein Fressen.*

3. Feed = 'to provide with a meal or meals'. The expressions discussed here are not always translated as **feed**.

i. The general expression is **zu essen geben** or **das/sein/ihr Essen geben**. The kind of food can be added to the first. *Ich gebe dem Baby Apfelmus zu essen.* The equivalent of the pass. *to be fed* or of *to get a meal/one's meals* is **zu essen/das Essen bekommen**. These expressions are used when the time or number of meals is referred to, but not when the manner, well/badly, etc., is stated.

> *Man muß Kindern dreimal täglich zu essen geben. Or Kinder müssen dreimal täglich zu essen bekommen.*
>
> *Die Kinder sind hungrig. Ich muß ihnen zu essen/ihr Essen geben. Or Sie müssen ihr Essen/zu essen bekommen.*
>
> *Studenten bekommen das Essen in der Mensa zu verbilligten Preisen.*
>
> *Während der Manöver bekamen die Soldaten ihr Essen regelmäßig im Freien.*

ii. Verpflegen means 'to provide or supply with meals', usually for some time, and suggests ordinary, everyday food. It is usual for *die Streitkräfte, Jugendherbergen,* and *Kantinen* as well as for *Pensionen* and small hotels. *Jmd. verpflegt sich selbst,* gets his/her own meals. *Full board* or *all meals [provided]* is *volle Verpflegung,* but for guesthouses and hotels often *volle Pension.*

> *Alle Arbeiter haben eine eigene kleine Wohnung, werden aber zentral verpflegt.*
>
> *Bei der Wanderung durch das unbewohnte Gebirge mußten die Pfadfinder sich selbst verpflegen.*
>
> *Auch im Manöver werden die Soldaten regelmäßig warm verpflegt. Also . . . gut verpflegt.*

iii. Beköstigen is also 'to supply with meals', but is a formal word and, unlike *verpflegen,* suggests a certain quality. It is still used, although it now sounds somewhat old-fashioned. **Verköstigen** has the same sense, but is confined to south Germany, Switzerland, and Austria.

> *In dem Krankenhaus, wo ich arbeite, werde ich beköstigt.* (Suggests a certain level, otherwise *verpflegt.*)
>
> *Als Gourmet interessierte er sich besonders dafür, wie die Reisegruppe in den verschiedenen Hotels beköstigt wurde.*   *Heute sind wieder 150 Feriengäste zu beköstigen.*
>
> *Es grenzte an ein Wunder, daß es der Küche gelungen war, weitere 200 Gäste zu verköstigen.*

iv. Bewirten means 'to provide guests with food and drink'. In the private sphere it suggests everything that goes with receiving guests, and for hotels, general service as well as meals, and is often like *look after.*

> *Sie hatten sich viel Mühe gegeben, den Besuch/die Gäste gut/reichlich zu bewirten.*
>
> *Sie wurden mit Kaffee und Kuchen bewirtet.*
>
> *Beim Abschied haben wir uns für die freundliche Bewirtung bedankt.*

v. Although the term *der Speisesaal* is still used, the v. **speisen**, meaning 'to eat or dine', is an elevated term, used only for highly placed people or ironically instead of *essen.*

> *Die Abgeordneten speisten gemeinsam im Speisesaal des Landtags.*
>
> *Dienstbeflissen versuchte der Butler in Erfahrung zu bringen, ob die Herrschaften im großen oder kleinen Salon zu speisen wünschten.*
>
> *Am zehnten Hochzeitstag speisten sie im Ratskeller.*

Speisen is sometimes used with people as obj., and is stylistically higher than the usual *verpflegen.* Because of its use in the Bible, it is found in religious language, *die Armen/Hungrigen speisen,* and in similar contexts, *Wohltätige Organisationen haben die Flüchtlinge gespeist,* and occasionally elsewhere, *Die Hotels speisten die Feriengäste.*

4. Feed a feeling. **Nähren** is used like **feed** with feelings and states of mind as obj. in the sense 'to arouse and cause to develop'. *Etw. nährt einen Wunsch/eine Vorstellung/Hoffnungen/jmds. Haß/einen Verdacht.*

5. Technical uses.

i. Speisen is common in technical language in the sense of providing a plant, machine, etc. with what is necessary to make it operate. *Das Kraftwerk wird mit*

Wasser aus zwei Seen gespeist. Die Taschenlampe wird von/aus drei Batterien gespeist. Another meaning is 'to feed into'. *Das neue Kraftwerk hat den ersten Strom in das Stromnetz gespeist.*

ii. The usual word for feeding data or information into a computer is **eingeben.** *Man gibt Daten/Informationen in einen Computer ein.* Colloquially, **füttern** is used.

> *Man füttert einen Computer falsch/mit einem Programm/mit Informationen.*
> *Er fütterte die Flugdaten in den Computer. Or Er gab die Flugdaten in den Computer ein.*

feel *v.* The three common vs. *fühlen, spüren,* and *empfinden* have some uses of their own, but overlap in many others. *Fühlen* is the general term. *Spüren* originally meant 'to become aware of sth.', whether one was paying attention or not, and still retains this idea to some extent. *Empfinden* often suggests that someone is sensitive enough to feel something.

1. Feel = 'to perceive through a sensation on the skin'. **Fühlen** and **spüren** carry this sense. *Fühlen* is probably more frequently used, but *spüren* is by no means uncommon.

> *Haben Sie den Luftzug/die Berührung/den Nadelstich nicht gespürt/gefühlt?*
> *Ich spürte/fühlte, daß mir Wasser auf den Kopf tropfte.*
> *Sie spürte/fühlte, daß sie angefaßt wurde/daß jmd. sie berührte/daß sie etw. berührte.*
> *Ich fühlte einen herben Geschmack auf der Zunge. Also . . . spürte.*
> *Sie spürte/fühlte, daß ein Insekt sie gestochen hatte.*
> *Ich fühlte/spürte etw. Kaltes/Feuchtes am Arm.*

Both *fühlen* and *spüren* occur with an infin. *Die Mutter fühlte ihr Herz/das Herz des Kindes lebhaft schlagen. Er spürte sein Herz schneller schlagen.*

With *ob,* only *fühlen* is used in the sense 'to feel for sth.'. *Ich fühlte, ob die Brieftasche noch in der Tasche war.* This implies using one's hand to find out. Cf. 9. *Ich spürte, daß die Brieftasche noch in der Tasche war,* means that without using a hand, I could tell from the way it felt that it was there.

Fig. uses. *Am eigenen Leibe spüren,* to experience, is a fixed expression. *Ich habe ihren Egoismus am eigenen Leibe gespürt. Etw. zu spüren bekommen* means 'to feel' in the sense 'to be subjected to'. Although *spüren* is the normal expression, *fühlen* is also found. *Ich habe seine Wut zu spüren bekommen. Sie hat seine grobe Art zu fühlen bekommen. Sie bekamen den Stock/seine Fäuste zu spüren/fühlen.*

2. Feel sensations within the body. **Fühlen** and **spüren** are used with pain, hunger, and effects. **Empfinden** occurs as well, but may suggest a sensation of a definite duration. With *Müdigkeit, Hitze,* and *Kälte,* all three are used, but *spüren* and *empfinden* seem to occur more frequently. *Jmd. spürt/empfindet die Kälte/Hitze nicht,* doesn't feel it, is not affected by it.

> *Ich hatte mich an einem Nagel geritzt und spürte/fühlte einen heftigen Schmerz.*
> *Sie spürte, wie sich ihr Magen zusammenzog.   Im Heu spürten wir die Kälte nicht.*
> *Spürst/Fühlst du schon die Wirkung der Tablette?*
> *Sie spürte, wie die Kälte langsam in ihr hochkroch.*
> *In diesem Augenblick empfand er wieder starke, stechende Schmerzen.*
> *Ich freute mich, als ich die Wärme der Sonnenstrahlen empfand/die warmen Sonnenstrahlen empfand.*

3. Feel = 'to experience an emotion or feeling'.

i. With *die Achtung, die Verachtung, das Mitleid, die Freude, die Angst, der Haß, die Liebe, die Dankbarkeit, die Reue, der Stolz, die Abneigung, die Zuneigung, die Schadenfreude, die Genugtuung, die Bitterkeit,* and *der Zorn,* **empfinden** is the usual word in educated speech, although **fühlen** is also found. With *das Bedürfnis* and *die Verpflichtung,* *fühlen* is usual, but *empfinden* also occurs. Both occur in *Man fühlt/empfindet einen Verlust tief/schmerzlich.*

Nach seinen schlechten Erfahrungen empfand er nichts als Verachtung für das System.
  Sie empfanden nicht gerade Freundschaft füreinander/Achtung voreinander, doch wenn es darauf
    ankam, hielten sie zusammen.   *Er empfand Zuneigung/Liebe für sie.* (Fühlen is possible.)
  Wir haben nur noch Haß füreinander empfunden. (Fühlen is possible.)
  Sie fühlte/empfand das Bedürfnis, sich mit jmd[m.] auszusprechen.
  Er fühlte/empfand die Verpflichtung, den anderen nach Kräften zu helfen.
  Als die Spannung der letzten Tage von ihr wich, fühlte sie nur eine große Leere in sich.

ii. When an infin., often expressed by a part. in E., follows, **fühlen** is used. *Er fühlte seinen Mut sinken/seine Sicherheit dahinschwinden. Bei diesen Worten fühlte sie eine Wut in sich hochsteigen, die sie nur schwer bezähmen konnte.* With a *daß*-clause, *fühlen* is common, but **empfinden** is also used. *Er fühlt/empfindet, daß er ihr Unrecht getan hat. Sie fühlt, daß er in Gefahr ist. Er fühlte, daß das nicht die Wahrheit war.*

iii. Both occur with indefinite expressions *etw.*, *nichts*, etc., but **fühlen** is probably more usual. *Was man in solchen Augenblicken fühlt, ist nicht mit Worten zu beschreiben. Ich habe etw. dunkel gefühlt/empfunden. Er empfand gar nichts dabei* means that in doing something dishonest, cruel, etc., someone felt no qualms. There are fixed expressions. *Die Menschen empfinden sehr verschieden. Ich bin kein Stück Holz, das nichts fühlt und empfindet. Sie kann nichts für ihn empfinden* implies affection or love; thus *Sie empfanden viel füreinander, wollten es sich jedoch nicht eingestehen.*

iv. Fühlen is usual with *mit*, but **empfinden** is possible. *Alle fühlen mit dir.*

4. Verspüren means 'to feel through the senses', 'to feel a bodily sensation', and 'to feel an emotion'. It does not add any new meaning to those of the three vs. already discussed. *Jmd. verspürt Schmerz/[keine] Müdigkeit/die Wirkung von etw./das Verlangen nach Abwechselung.* Whether it is used is a matter of style. It is slightly old-fashioned and now belongs to refined speech only, but may be used ironically. *Ich verspüre Hunger* is a genteel variant on *Ich habe Hunger.* Likewise *Ich verspüre [keine] Lust dazu* is much more refined than the normal *Ich habe [keine] Lust.*

5. i. When **feel** means 'to become aware of' what others are feeling, all three vs. can be used, but **spüren** occurs very frequently. **Empfinden** may suggest greater sensibility. *Ich spürte/fühlte seine Kälte mir gegenüber. Sie fühlte/empfand seinen Kummer/seinen Zorn. Man spürt die Achtung/die Verachtung der anderen/jmds. Enttäuschung. Sie empfand die Verzweiflung der Umstehenden. Von Kameradschaft/gutem Willen war dort nichts zu spüren.*

ii. When **feel** means 'to realize or become aware of sth.', the equivalents are **spüren** and **fühlen**. *Hast du nicht gespürt, daß sie dir damit helfen wollte? Er spürte/fühlte, daß er angestarrt wurde. Sie spürte, daß es zwischen den beiden nicht zum Besten stand, doch hätte sie nicht sagen können, woher dieses Gefühl kam.*

iii. To *make/let s.o.* **feel** *one's emotions* is **spüren lassen** or **fühlen lassen**. *Er ließ sie seine Ablehnung deutlich spüren/fühlen. Sie ließ ihn ihre Geringschätzung/ihre Abneigung/ihre Überlegenheit spüren/fühlen. Sie ließ ihn spüren, daß sie ihn nicht mochte.*

6. When a person feels him/herself to be in a certain bodily or mental condition, **sich fühlen** is used. It takes an adj., part., and occasionally *als. Ich fühle mich krank. Sie fühlten sich als Verteidiger der Freiheit.* (It is not used for *I feel hot/cold*, which is *Mir ist heiß/kalt. My feet feel sore* would usually be *Die Füße tun mir weh.* For *Her hands felt cold* when this implies to someone else's touch, cf. *sich anfühlen* under 8.)

  Sie fühlte sich gesund/gut/wohl/unwohl/elend/schwach/stark/müde und zerschlagen/wie gerädert.
  Wie fühlt man sich denn als frisch gebackener Vater?
  Er fühlte sich glücklich/bedroht/beleidigt/verfolgt/verkannt/erleichtert/der Aufgabe (nicht) gewach-
    sen/zu jmdm. hingezogen.   *Ich fühle mich verpflichtet, ihnen zu helfen.*

7. Only **empfinden** is used with *als* in the meaning 'to feel or consider sth. to be'. *Sie hat diese Worte als Beleidigung/Lob empfunden. Diese Bemerkung wurde allgemein als* *taktlos empfunden. Ich empfinde diese Forderung als Zumutung. Den Lärm empfinden sie als sehr störend.* In cases in which an intellectual conviction rather than a feeling is involved, as in *measures felt to be inexpedient*, it is best to use an equivalent of CONSIDER. *Maßnahmen, die viele für unklug hielten.*

8. Feel meaning 'to produce a certain kind of sensation when touched or felt', as in *The stone/Your hand feels cold/wet*, etc., is expressed by **sich anfühlen.** *Der Stein fühlt sich kalt/naß an.*

> *Die Luft/Der Wind fühlt sich kalt [an der Haut] an.* *Die Haut des Babys fühlt sich an wie Samt.*
> *Ihre Hand fühlte sich eiskalt an.* *Der Stoff fühlt sich weich an.*
> *Dieser Stoff fühlt sich zu rauh an, als daß ich ihn jemals auf meiner Haut tragen könnte.*

9. Feel for sth. and **feel one's way**. Tasten means 'to try to find sth. by using the sense of touch in one's hands'. When a person remains more or less in the same spot, *tasten nach* is used. *Im Dunkeln tastete sie nach dem Lichtschalter.* **Fühlen** is an alternative. *Im Dunkeln fühlte sie nach dem Lichtschalter.* When the subj. changes position, only **sich tasten** with a phr. of direction is possible. *Im Dunkeln tastete sie sich vorsichtig zur Tür, felt her way. Er tastete sich vorsichtig die Wand entlang. Er hatte sich mühsam durch das dunkle Gebäude getastet.*

10. Feel = 'to examine by touching', 'to search by touching'.
i. Befühlen is 'to feel' when it means 'to examine by touching or feeling'. *Man befühlt einen Stoff* etc. to find out something about it, what it is like. It suggests touching an object with one's fingertips or moving it around between them or running one's hand over it. *Sie befühlte das Papier, um festzustellen, ob es fest genug war.*

> *Er befühlte sein schmerzendes Knie.*   *Der Arzt befühlte meinen Arm.*
> *Er befühlte die Bootswand, konnte aber keinerlei Risse feststellen.*

ii. Anfühlen is a syn. of *befühlen*, but it suggests lighter touching or simple contact with the hand to find out what something is like or what state it is in. *Sie fühlte den Stoff/die erfrorenen Füße des Kindes an. Fühl einmal meinen Kopf an, wie heiß er ist!*

iii. Betasten means 'to touch a thg. in a number of places, generally with the fingertips, in order to find out sth. about it'. *Das Betasten der Waren ist verboten.*

> *Der Arzt betastete behutsam den Knöchel, um festzustellen, wo er gebrochen war.*

iv. Abtasten means 'to touch or feel systematically at various places in order to discover sth.' It occurs most frequently in *jmdn. [nach versteckten Waffen] abtasten*, usually translated as to *search*.

> *Der Arzt tastete den Kranken ab.*
> *Die Wand wurde nach Unebenheiten abgetastet.*
> *Er tastete alle Taschen nach dem Schlüssel ab.*

fellow *n.* and *adj.* **chap, guy** *ns.*

1. These three ns. are variants on *man* or *boy*. The G. equivalents are not as frequently used as the E. words so that **der Mann** is often the appropriate equivalent. *Der Mann, mit dem sie tanzte, war ein Freund von mir*, the chap she was dancing with. *Ein junger Mann hat nach Ihnen gefragt*, a young fellow. *Der Mann, der den Schulbus fährt*, the guy who drives the school bus. *Kerl* would be pejorative in these sents. *He's a nice guy* can be *Er ist ein netter Kerl* or *ein netter Typ* in the *Jugendsprache*. The normal expression in the standard language is *ein netter Mensch*.

i. Der Kerl denotes a male person, but always contains a value judgement which, depending on the context, can be favourable or unfavourable. It refers first to the impression someone's physical build and appearance make, then to conclusions drawn from this about the character and the behaviour to be expected. *Ein großer/junger/starker/anständiger/tapferer Kerl* or *ein schlechter/gemeiner/widerlicher/liederlicher/dummer Kerl*. Without an adj. it is usually pejorative, but in a few cases the tone of voice makes it clear that praise is meant. *Das war ein Kerl!*, he was a [real] man. *Ein Kerl ist mir auf der Straße nachgelaufen* suggests an unfavourable judgement, and *Es standen drei Kerle an der Theke* could. With a pejorative adj., it can be a term of reproach or abuse. *Du blöder/schwachsinniger Kerl! Der verdammte/brutale Kerl!* *Der Kerl* is occasionally applied to a woman, but suggests one who is reliable, unsophisticated, and *kameradschaftlich*. *So ein feiner Kerl wie die ist, die läßt uns nicht hängen. Sie macht uns nie Schwierigkeiten, ist halt ein netter Kerl.*

Basketballspieler sind in der Regel ellenlange Kerle.

So ein starker Kerl, wie du einer bist, hebst du doch den Sack allein.

Er ist immer ein ehrlicher Kerl gewesen. Ich glaube nicht, daß er uns belogen hat.

Du elender Kerl würdest wohl eher deine Mutter krepieren lassen als das Spielen aufgeben.

Man muß schon ein verrückter Kerl sein, um freiwillig mit dem Rad durch Afrika zu fahren.

Der Kerl zog sein Messer und wollte Geld erpressen.

ii. Particularly in the *Jugendsprache*, **der Typ** is used for a young male. It is found with adjs. which are good and bad, but it is neutral when not modified. *Ein prima/netter/dufter/mieser Typ. Sie trifft sich mit einem Typ, den sie vorige Woche kennengelernt hat.*

iii. In *Could you fellows show a bit of consideration?* **fellows** is best omitted in transl. *Könnt ihr nicht ein bißchen Rücksicht zeigen?* *Ihr Typen* is possible, but depreciatory. Likewise *You chaps are doing an excellent job* becomes *Das macht ihr ausgezeichnet* or *Ihr macht die Arbeit ausgezeichnet*. The fellows *at school* or *at work* can be **meine Klassenkameraden** or **meine Arbeitskollegen** or **-kameraden**. **Der Kumpel** is used colloquially for the latter but implies a close personal relationship as well as working together. *Die Sache will ich mit ein paar Kumpels besprechen.*

iv. Der Bursche is basically a *halbwüchsiger* (adolescent) male or young man. Although the word is itself neutral, the context may imply a daring and sometimes rough or uncouth nature. Such young men usually cease to be *Burschen* when they settle down. Theodor Storm refers to an exception: *Obwohl ein Mann an die Dreißig, galt er immer noch für einen ziemlich wilden Burschen. Bursche* is used with adjs. which denote good and bad qualities. *Ein flinker/strammer Bursche. Ein roher/ungesitteter Bursche.* It is often applied to boys, particularly older and bigger ones. It can be used for animals. In another use *Bursche* is applied to males of any age when the speaker considers them capable of something bad. This sense is now restricted to the use with a few pejorative adjs., mainly *ein übler* or *ein gerissener Bursche*. **Der Geselle** is a syn. in this sense, *ein wüster Geselle*, but it is now somewhat old-fashioned. *Geselle* is occasionally found with good qualities. *Ein lustiger Geselle.*

Alle sprechen gut über ihn, er scheint ein netter Bursche zu sein.

Klaus ist der hochgeschossene Bursche, der alle in der Klasse überragt, und der schon größer ist als die meisten Lehrer.

Die drei Burschen luden ihre Räder und fuhren, obwohl sie erst zehn waren, allein in den Harz.

Jahrelang legte dieser durchtriebene Bursche ältere Menschen herein und ergaunerte sich ein kleines Vermögen.

Er könnte sich alles leisten und läuft dennoch wie ein Bursche von achtzehn Jahren herum.

Die Flanken des Hengstes glänzten in der Sonne, und Franz war stolz, diesen prächtigen Burschen in seinem Stall zu haben.

2. Fellow used adjectivally also describes a person or people who have something in common with someone. In some cases compounds with *mit* express this meaning. *Unsere Mitmenschen*, fellow men/human beings. *Der Mitschüler*, fellow pupil. *Der*

Mitreisende, fellow passenger. Other words are: *der Kommilitone*, 'fellow student', *der Arbeitskollege*, 'fellow worker', *der Landsmann*, 'fellow countryman'.

few, a few *adjs*. **A few** differs from **few** in suggesting something pos., whereas **few** is neg., meaning 'hardly any'. *There were a few students there. Few people live to be 100. A man of few words*. In some contexts both are possible: *There are few/a few mistakes in the essay*, **few** meaning 'as good as none' and **a few** 'some though not many'. There are three equivalents, *einige*, *ein paar*, and the pl. of *wenig* which, when a n. follows, appears either in the inflected form *wenige* or in the uninflected form *wenig*.

i. Einige und **ein paar** are used when what is described is seen positively. If it has been predicted that no students will attend a lecture and a few or some do go, someone can say, *'Es waren doch einige Studenten da.' Einige* is not used with *nur*. **Only a few** is *nur ein paar* or *nur wenig[e]*. *Ein paar* means the same as *einige*, the only difference being that *ein paar* may suggest a slightly smaller number. *Sie gingen mit ein paar Freunden aus. Ein paar der Anwesenden protestierten*. Both are used with a number. *Einige/Ein paar hundert Bücher*. With *die, alle, diese, meine*, etc., *einige* is not possible, but *paar* without *ein* can be combined with them. *Warte doch die paar Minuten! Alle paar Wochen/Kilometer. Diese/Meine paar Sachen*.

ii. In *Er hatte wenige Zuhörer*, **wenige** means 'a very small number'. *Einige* would mostly be a few more, but could be the same number, the word chosen depending on whether the speaker sees the number in a pos. or neg. light. *Einige* is like **a few**, *wenige* like **[very] few**. *Wenige* is frequently preceded by *nur*. *Der Film hat nur wenigen Leuten gefallen*. There is no difference in meaning between the inflected pl. *wenige* and the uninflected form **wenig**. *Wenige* sees what is referred to individually, *wenig* sees it as a group or class. *Er hat mir wenig Sorgen gemacht* means that of the class of things called *Sorgen* I had very little or few. In *In dieser Höhe wachsen nur noch wenig/wenige Pflanzen*, the choice of word indicates a difference in perspective. *Wenig* suggests something like 'little plant life'. With *wenige* the small number of plants is seen individually. *Wenig* may imply a smaller number than *wenige*. *Ich hatte wenig Bedenken* and *Wir hatten wenig Kosten* suggest 'hardly any'. Both *wenig* and *wenige* are usually possible. *Auf dieser Insel gab es wenig Menschen/nur wenige Menschen. Er hat es mit wenig/wenigen Worten erklärt. Sie haben wenig/wenige Chancen. In dem Aufsatz sind wenig/nur wenige Fehler. Es waren so wenig/wenige Leute/Zuhörer da, daß der Vortrag nicht stattfand*. The uninflected form is mostly found in the nom. and acc., occasionally in the dat. Only *wenige* can be used when no n. follows. *Es waren so wenige gekommen, daß der Raum viel zu groß war*. The inflected form is used after *die. Die wenigen Studenten, die da waren*.

iii. Einige wenige means 'only a very few'. *Nur noch einige wenige Äpfel hängen am Baum. Nur einige wenige verstehen etw. davon*.

iv. Quite a few and **a good few** are *ziemlich viele. Es waren ziemlich viele Leute da*.

field, meadow, paddock *ns*. (*Paddock* is meant here in the Australian sense of a fenced area used for either cultivation or pasture, and is thus a syn. of the other words.) G. makes a distinction between **die Wiese**, 'a field used for pasture', i.e. a meadow, and **der Acker**, 'a field which is cultivated and planted with crops'. The only word in everyday use which combines both ideas is the pl. of *das Feld*, field, **die Felder**. *Soweit das Auge reichte, erstreckten sich Felder, die durch Hecken voneinander getrennt waren*. The sing. **das Feld** means 'a cultivated field' and is a syn. of *Acker*. *Der Bauer bestellt/bebaut/bearbeitet/düngt/pflügt das Feld/den Acker. Er arbeitet auf dem*

Feld/Acker. Ein ertragreicher Acker. Ein fruchtbares/steiniges Feld. Die Weizenfelder.
Compounds are *der Kartoffelacker* or *-feld, der Rübenacker, das Getreidefeld, das Maisfeld,*
etc. **Die Aue** is applied to a flat area of pasture along a watercourse on which there
are also usually a few bushes and trees growing. **Die Flur** is a technical term for
all land used for agricultural purposes. *Er kennt alle Tiere und Vögel in Wald und Flur.*
Der Hagel hat auf allen Fluren großen Schaden angerichtet.

fight, struggle *vs.*

1. Fight = 'to use the force of the body or weapons against'. The main equivalent
of **fight** is **kämpfen**. It is used alone or with the preps. *für, gegen, mit,* and *um* and
occasionally with *der Kampf* as obj. Two or more people who fight either with their
fists or with weapons can be the subj., as can animals. It is used for fighting in
wars, but does not take *Krieg* as obj. Like *with, mit* can mean 'against'. *Die beiden*
Gegner kämpften verbissen miteinander/gegeneinander.
   Mein Großvater hat im ersten Weltkrieg gekämpft.
   Um jeden Fußbreit Erde wurde hart gekämpft.   Sie haben einen harten/guten Kampf gekämpft.
   Bei der Seeschlacht von Salamis kämpften die Griechen erfolgreich gegen die Perser.
Fight *a battle* is *eine Schlacht schlagen.* **Fight** or *wage a war* is *Krieg [gegen jmdn.]*
führen.

2. Fight or **struggle for/against** s.o./sth. **Kämpfen** also means 'to use all available
resources and all one's strength either to combat sth. or to bring about a result'.
Gegen die Ungerechtigkeit/Gegen Schwierigkeiten/Vorurteile kämpfen is 'to fight or struggle against' it/them. *Um* and *für* mean 'in order to obtain sth.' *Sie kämpften um*
bessere Arbeitsbedingungen/um ihr Recht. Man kämpft für die Freiheit/um höhere Löhne/für
eine gute Sache, for a cause. It is used in sport. *Die Mannschaft kämpfte verbissen gegen*
die drohende Niederlage/um den Sieg. In der letzten Runde kämpfte er wie ein Löwe. What
people fight or struggle against can be natural forces and disease, *Der Schwimmer*
kämpfte gegen die Strömung or *Die Ärzte kämpften gegen die Malaria,* something that
threatens to overwhelm someone, *Sie kämpften mit dem/gegen den Schlaf/gegen die*
Tränen, and something within oneself, *Er kämpfte lange mit sich, ob er die Wahrheit*
sagen sollte or *Sie kämpfte mit dem Entschluß, ihren Mann zu verlassen.*

3. Vs. meaning 'to fight or struggle against'. **Bekämpfen** means 'to combat or
fight against' some undesirable development, state, plan, etc. *Jmd. bekämpfte die*
Korruption/eine Seuche/eine Politik. It implies attacking it as a whole and is stronger
than *ankämpfen,* which suggests attacking part of a whole. **Ankämpfen** is always
used with *gegen* and is the appropriate v. when intellectual opposition to one feature of something is implied. *Man kämpft gegen eine bestimmte Haltung an. Man muß*
gegen eine solche irrige Meinung ankämpfen. It is translated as **fight, struggle**
against, or *oppose,* but is restricted to intellectual opposition. **Kämpfen gegen**
suggests greater resistance by what is being opposed and greater difficulties in
general. All three vs. are often found in similar contexts. *Ankämpfen* suggests
opposition confined to words, *bekämpfen* taking energetic action, and *kämpfen*
gegen words and action. *Die deutschen Liberalen kämpften gegen den militäristischen*
Geist an suggests by means of arguments. *Sie kämpften gegen diesen Geist* does not
exclude arguments, but suggests prolonged action such as, in this case, political
rallies or demonstrations, while *sie bekämpften den militäristischen Geist* implies
measures to curb or suppress the spirit of militarism. On the personal level
ankämpfen seems to be preferred for fighting both against natural difficulties,
such as storms, and against feelings which threaten to overwhelm one. *Jmd.*
kämpft gegen die Wellen/gegen Müdigkeit/gegen eine Neigung/gegen eine Sucht/gegen

Versuchungen an. Ankämpfen in itself does not say anything about success. With emotions, **niederkämpfen** implies success. *Sie kämpfte die Müdigkeit/den Ärger nieder*. After *versuchen*, both *ankämpfen* and *niederkämpfen* are possible in relation to emotions, but *Er versuchte, seinen Zorn niederzukämpfen* suggests that the probability of success was greater than *Er versuchte, gegen seinen Zorn anzukämpfen*.

> *Gegen den bayerischen Partikularismus noch weiter anzukämpfen, hatte der Kanzler keine Lust mehr.*
> *Bald nachdem die Sahara-Expedition aufgebrochen war, mußte sie gegen einen Sandsturm ankämpfen.*
> *Der Inder kämpfte gegen den Starrsinn seiner Mitschüler an, die ihn nicht akzeptieren wollten.*
> *Gegen die Enttäuschung, die plötzlich über sie gekommen war, kämpfte sie mit ganzer Kraft an.*

4. Other vs. meaning 'to fight with one's fists'.

i. Sich balgen is applied primarily to dogs. *Die beiden jungen Hunde haben sich [um die Beute] gebalgt*. Transferred to boys, it implies a friendly, playful scuffle on the ground. *Die Kinder balgten sich auf der Wiese.*

ii. Sich raufen suggests a more serious fight than *sich balgen*. Clothes may be torn and some harm done, but it does not cause serious injuries. The subj. can only be boys or youths. Like all the words in this group, it is used with a pl. subj.: *Die Beiden (or X und Y) rauften sich;* with a sing. subj. it needs a phr. with *mit: X raufte sich mit Y.*

> *'Wenn die Burschen sich zu raufen anfangen, schmeiß ich sie raus', sagte der Wirt.*
> *Auf dem Schulhof hatte er sich mit einem Mitschüler gerauft.*

iii. Sich hauen is a colloquial word, and **sich kloppen** is slang. Both are used only of children and *Jugendliche* and belong to their language. When used by adults, they either suggest that the fight was a harmless scrap or express disparagement.

> *Die Jungen hatten sich zuerst beschimpft und dann gehauen.*
> *Zwei kleine Jungen kloppten sich auf dem Spielplatz.*   *Sie kloppen sich beinahe den ganzen Tag.*

iv. Sich schlagen means that two people fight each other with their fists or with weapons. In *Die beiden Offiziere schlugen sich*, it implies a duel. For other uses, cf. 5. ii and iii.

> *Peter hatte sich mit dem Nachbarsjungen geschlagen und kam zerkratzt im Gesicht und mit blutender Nase und einem blauen Auge nach Hause.*
> *Der Lehrer griff ein, als er zwei Jungen sah, die sich stark schlugen.*

v. Sich prügeln suggests a violent and rough attack with repeated blows from the fists or *Schlagwaffen*. *Verprügeln* means 'to beat s.o. up'. Cf. BEAT 1. **Sich verprügeln** implies a fight between two people, but suggests worse consequences than *sich prügeln*. *Die beiden haben sich verprügelt.*

> *Am Ende der ersten Halbzeit prügelten sich fanatische Anhänger beider Mannschaften.*
> *Mit zerfetzter Hose und Prellungen an Armen und Beinen kam er schlechten Gewissens nach Hause.*
> *'Warum müßt ihr euch dann immer verprügeln, wenn ihr euch mal in den Haaren liegt?' fragte die besorgte Mutter.*

vi. Handgemein werden means 'to come to blows' after a quarrel has become increasingly bitter. *Alle befürchteten, die beiden würden bald handgemein werden, wenn der Streit noch weiter andauerte, und versuchten, sie zu beruhigen.* Cf. *handgreiflich* and *tätlich* under VIOLENT 3. ii.

5. Other expressions.

i. Aufeinander losgehen means 'to approach one another with hostile intent' and implies coming to blows. *Die Rivalen zogen Messer und gingen aufeinander los.* It is also used for animals. *Die beiden Hähne gingen aufeinander los.*

ii. Sich schlagen also means 'to acquit oneself in a certain way', originally in battle, *August-Wilhelm schlug sich tapfer bei der Schlacht*, and now in sport and other areas, *Der junge Tennisspieler hat sich tapfer geschlagen,* put up a good fight, acquitted himself well. *Du hast dich in der Diskussion wacker geschlagen. Unsere Mannschaft hat sich ganz ordentlich geschlagen.*

iii. Fight for tickets etc. = 'to make a determined effort to get'. **Sich um etw. schlagen** suggests fighting to gain possession of something. *Man schlug sich fast um die Eintrittskarten.* Possibly more common is **sich um etw. reißen,** to try desperately to obtain sth. *Man riß sich [förmlich] um die Karten.*

> *Österreich und Preußen hatten sich ineinander verbissen und schlugen sich um ein paar Dörfer.*
> *Die Kinder schlugen sich um das Spielzeug.*   *Die jungen Männer rissen sich um sie.*
> *Im Sommerschlußverkauf rissen sich die Leute um die verbilligten Waren.*

iv. Fight when it means 'to quarrel' is [**sich**] **streiten.** Colloquial syns. are **sich in die Haare geraten,** 'to get into a quarrel', and **sich in den Haaren liegen,** 'to quarrel or be at loggerheads'.

> *'Hoffentlich gibt es heute abend nicht wieder Streit!'—'Da bin ich nicht so sicher. Wenn Horst mitkommt, geraten sich die Männer bestimmt wieder in die Haare'.*
> *Die beiden streiten sich um jede Kleinigkeit/um nichts und wieder nichts.*
> *'Jetzt hört endlich auf mit der Streiterei!—ich verstehe einfach nicht, wieso ihr euch wegen einer solchen Lappalie wieder in den Haaren liegen müßt!'*

fill, fulfil *vs.*

1. Fill = 'make a space full with sth. liquid or solid, or with people'.

i. Füllen means 'to put or pour sth. into a receptacle until it is full'. The obj. is normally the receptacle. *Ich füllte das Glas mit Limonade.* This suggests that the glass is more or less full. When the material is the obj., the construction is *Ich habe Milch in die Kanne gefüllt,* which does not necessarily imply that the receptacle is full. *Füllen in* can be translated as *pour. Sie hat Suppe in die Teller gefüllt. Ich fülle Kartoffeln in die Säcke.*

> *Füll' mal bitte den Eimer mit Wasser!*   *Die Kinder füllten ihre Taschen mit Kirschen.*
> *Wir haben das Loch mit Sand/den Sack mit Kartoffeln gefüllt.*
> *Wir füllen unsere Köpfe mit belanglosen Tatsachen.*   *Der Sänger füllte das Stadion.*

ii. Fill, used intr. with the thing filled as subj., as in *The hole soon filled with water,* is **sich füllen.** *Das Loch füllte sich mit Wasser, sobald es anfing zu regnen. Die Segel füllten sich mit Wind. Ihre Augen füllten sich mit Tränen. Eine halbe Stunde vor Anfang der Vorstellung begann sich das Theater zu füllen.*

iii. Abfüllen is now used mostly for the commercial process of filling large numbers of containers, usually automatically. The obj. or subj. in the pass. is usually the container, *Die Flaschen werden jetzt automatisch mit Apfelsaft abgefüllt,* but it can be the material, *Zucker wird in Tüten abgefüllt. Abfüllen* need not, however, refer to a commercial process. *Er füllte das selbstgebraute Bier in Flaschen ab.*

iv. Füllen also means 'to occupy the whole capacity or space of sth.' In this sense the thing filling the space is the subj. in the act. *Meine Sachen füllen zwei Koffer.* It is often found in the pass. *Der Schrank ist mit alten Kleidungsstücken gefüllt. Füllen* is used fig. with *die Lücke,* gap. *Dieses Werk füllt eine spürbare Lücke auf dem Büchermarkt.* To fill a gap in one's knowledge is *eine Wissenslücke füllen* or *schließen.*

> *Zehn Liter Wasser füllen den Eimer.*   *Tränen füllten ihre Augen.*
> *Die Hochzeitsgäste füllten die kleine Kirche.*   *Der Bericht füllte drei dicke Bände.*
> *Der Saal war bis auf den letzten Platz gefüllt.*   *Das Bett füllt fast das ganze Zimmer.*

v. With space as obj. **ausfüllen** differs from *füllen* in implying that the space is completely filled.

> *Beim Einpacken von Gläsern füllt man die Zwischenräume mit Holzwolle aus.*
> *Der dicke Gastwirt stand breit und behaglich in seiner Haustür, die er ganz ausfüllte.*

vi. Auffüllen means 'to fill again what is [almost] empty'. *Ich muß den Kanister auffüllen.*

vii. Erfüllen means 'to fill space' with less tangible things than those used with *füllen*, such as *der Rauch, der Qualm, das Gas, der Duft,* and *der Lärm.*

> *Der Rauch/Das Gas/Der Duft erfüllte die ganze Wohnung.*
> *Lautes Geschrei/Der Gesang der Vögel erfüllte die Luft.*
> *Die Kinder erfüllten das Haus und den Garten mit Leben.*

The use with intangibles as obj. can be described as fig. *Der Lehrer versuchte, den toten Stoff mit Leben zu erfüllen. Sie hatte ein mit Sorgen erfülltes Leben geführt.*

viii. Überfüllt means 'crowded'. *Alle Züge waren überfüllt. Die beiden quetschten sich in die schon überfüllte Straßenbahn.*

ix. Filled with can often be translated as **voll**. *Der Wartesaal war voll Passagiere.*

x. For **fill** (a car) with petrol, *füllen* is possible. *Ich habe den Tank mit Benzin gefüllt.* **Tanken** is the usual v. *Wir müssen bald [Benzin] tanken.* **Auftanken** means 'to fill up with' or 'take on' fuel and is usual for aircraft. It is trans., *Man tankt das Flugzeug/den Rennwagen auf,* and intr., *Das Flugzeug tankt auf.*

> *Auf dem Flug zwischen Sydney und London muß die Maschine mindestens einmal auftanken.*

2. Fill time. The main meaning of **ausfüllen** is 'to fill or occupy a period of time'.

> *Die Vorbereitungen füllten jede Minute des Tages aus.*
> *Das Material, das ich bis jetzt vorbereitet habe, füllt keine ganze Stunde aus.*
> *Ihre Hobbies füllen ihre ganze Freizeit aus.*   *Dieses Gespräch füllte die Wartezeit aus.*

3. Fill the mind.

i. Erfüllen also means 'to fill s.o./s.o.'s mind with an emotion of some kind', such as *Freude, Bitterkeit, Mißtrauen, Haß, Angst, Kummer,* or *Verzweiflung.*

> *Diese Nachricht erfüllte uns alle mit Trauer.*   *Mein Herz war von Dankbarkeit erfüllt.*
> *Der Ausgang des Prozesses erfüllte uns alle mit Genugtuung.*
> *Seine Versuche erfüllten alle mit Bewunderung.*   *Sein Verhalten erfüllte mich mit Sorge.*

Füllen was formerly used in this way, especially with *Herz* as obj., *Trauer füllte ihr Herz,* and may still occasionally be found in elevated prose. *Erfüllen* is, however, now the normal word.

ii. Erfüllen also states that something completely occupies someone's thoughts. *Sie kehrten, erfüllt von neuen Eindrücken, von der Reise zurück und erzählten die halbe Nacht davon.* With ideas as subj. **ausfüllen** means 'to dominate or occupy' someone's thoughts. *Der Gedanke an eine baldige Rückkehr füllte sie ganz aus.*

4. Fulfil.

i. Erfüllen means 'to fulfil' in the senses 'to carry out or satisfy s.o.'s wishes etc.' or 'to meet an expectation, obligation, hope, condition, etc.'

> *Man erfüllt eine Bitte/jmds. Ansprüche/einen Vertrag/ein Versprechen/seine Pflicht/eine Aufgabe.*
> *Die Eltern erfüllten dem Kind jeden Wunsch.*
> *Eltern dürfen ihren Kindern nicht jede Bitte erfüllen.*
> *Der neue Mitarbeiter hat die in ihn gesetzten Erwartungen erfüllt.*
> *Um zum Studium an der Technischen Universität zugelassen zu werden, muß man bestimmte*
>   *Bedingungen erfüllen.*   *Wir haben alle Verpflichtungen erfüllt.*

ii. In relation to wishes, expectations, etc., **be fulfilled** means 'come to pass'. *They expect improvements—are their expectations being fulfilled?* The refl. **sich erfüllen** is used when *Wunsch* etc. is the subj., and corresponds to the E. pass. *Unsere Erwartungen haben sich erfüllt. Diese Prophezeiung/Diese Befürchtung hat sich erfüllt.* The pass. of **erfüllen** is also possible. An alternative is **in Erfüllung gehen**. *Der Wunsch wurde erfüllt/hat sich erfüllt/ging in Erfüllung.*

iii. Fulfil also means 'to make s.o. feel happy and satisfied with what he or she is doing or has achieved'. **Etw. füllt jmdn. aus** combines the idea of occupying time with that of satisfying and bringing fulfilment. *Die Arbeit/Der Beruf füllt sie ganz aus. Meine Tätigkeit füllt mich nicht aus. Sie hat ein ausgefülltes Leben.* In *Die Arbeit/Die neue Aufgabe erfüllt ihn ganz, erfüllen* means 'to occupy completely'. The idea of satisfaction is expressed by **Erfüllung finden**. *Jmd. findet Erfüllung im Beruf/in der Arbeit.* **Sich verwirklichen** means 'to realize one's potential' or 'to fulfil oneself' and implies gaining satisfaction. *Sie konnte sich im Beruf/in der neuen Arbeit verwirklichen. Die Möglichkeit, sich zu verwirklichen, bleibt heutzutage vielen jungen Menschen versagt.*

5. Fill a position well. **Fill** a position. With a person as subj. and employment as obj., **ausfüllen** means that the person discharges his/her duties or fills a position in a certain way, as in *He fills the post satisfactorily. Er füllte die Stelle gut/schlecht/gewissenhaft/unzureichend aus.* **Ausfüllen** does not mean 'to fill' a position when this means 'to appoint s.o. to it', which is *eine Stelle* **besetzen**. *Wir müssen die vakante Stelle so bald wie möglich wieder besetzen.* **Besetzen** is used with *mit: Wir wollen die Stelle mit einer Fachkraft besetzen. We are looking for an experienced person to fill the position* is usually *Wir suchen eine erfahrene Kraft für die Stelle/für diese Aufgabe.*

6. Fill in or **fill out** a form. **Ausfüllen** expresses this sense. *Ich habe das Formular/den Fragebogen ausgefüllt.* It implies the whole form or section. If only one item is meant, as in *You have forgotten to fill in your place of birth*, **angeben**, 'to give or state', is used. *Sie haben vergessen, Ihren Geburtsort anzugeben.*

find *v.* A few uses.

1. There is a fundamental difference between **find** and *finden*. **Find** means either 'to come upon by chance' or 'to discover by search or effort'. **Finden** corresponds exactly to the first sense. It also includes expending effort on looking for something, but it does not suggest that the result is self-evident. The pres. and future of **find** often need to be translated by **suchen**. *I'll find a chair for you* can only be *Ich suche einen Stuhl für Sie*, because it cannot be predicted that *finden* will have a result or that what is sought will be found. Someone who has succeeded in finding a chair, could, however, well say, '*Ich habe einen Stuhl für Sie gefunden.*' If A, an impatient superior, has been told by B that B does not know where a certain map is, A might say, 'Then find it!' or 'Then go and find it!' Both expressions become *Dann suchen Sie sie!* **Try to find** and **try and find** also become *suchen. Ich suche den Brief. Die Partei sucht einen neuen Führer.*

Ich habe eine Zweimarkstück auf der Straße gefunden.
Er fand den vermißten Schlüssel in seinem Mantel.
Das Dorf habe ich endlich auf der Karte gefunden.   *Nach einigem Suchen fand sie die Karte.*

2. Vorfinden means that on arrival in a place, someone finds a person or thing there or finds in a particular place s.o./sth. in a specified condition. For this E. uses **find**, as in *Leave things as you find them!*

Bei unserer Rückkehr haben wir die Wohnung in musterhafter Ordnung vorgefunden.
Die Verhältnisse, die er in dem halbzerstörten Krankenhaus vorfand, waren katastrophal.
Das Labor ist gut ausgerüstet. Sie werden dort alle für Ihre Arbeit erforderlichen Gerätschaften vorfinden.   *Wenn du ankommst, wirst du mich da vorfinden.*

3. Sich befinden means 'to be in a place or condition'. *Wir befinden uns hier auf dem höchsten Berg Deutschlands. Die Schule befindet sich im Süden der Stadt.* It often refers to health. *Sie befindet sich in bester Gesundheit.* The E. equivalent is mostly *to be.* It needs to be distinguished from *sich finden.*

Wo befindet sich das Rathaus?   *Die Wirtschaft befindet sich in einer katastrophalen Lage.*
Wie befindet sich der Patient heute?   *Die beiden Länder befinden sich im Kriegszustand.*

4. Sich finden has several senses.

i. Of something lost or mislaid 'to be found again'. *Das Buch wird sich schon finden,* it will turn up, be found. *Der verlorene Handschuh hat sich wieder gefunden.*

ii. 'To be met with or be able to be found somewhere'.

Diese Steine finden sich häufig da.   *Es fand sich niemand, der die Arbeit machen wollte.*

Dieses Wort findet sich oft bei Lessing.   *Es werden sich Stellen für alle Studenten finden.*

In dieser Sammlung finden sich die besten Gedichte der Nachkriegszeit.

iii. Idiomatic uses are *Es wird sich finden, ob du recht hast*, 'it will become apparent, we'll see whether . . .' and *Es wird sich alles schon finden*, 'things will turn out all right'.

5. Find expresses an opinion or judgement. *I don't find that funny. The jury found him guilty.*

i. Finden gives an impression and is always fairly subjective. An adj. or a clause follows.

Wie hast du den Film gefunden? Ich fand ihn gut/langweilig/mittelmäßig usw.

Findest du es hier auch sehr heiß?   *Ich finde den neuen Kollegen sehr freundlich.*

Der Kritiker fand es nicht der Mühe wert, mehr als das erste Kapitel zu lesen.

Ich finde, wir müssen uns beeilen.   *Solche Bemerkungen finde ich gar nicht lustig.*

ii. Befinden suggests an expert judgement. It is used with *für*, so that *He was found guilty* becomes *Er wurde für schuldig befunden.* *Über etw. befinden* is a legal term meaning 'to pass or reach a judgement on s.o./sth.', but has spread to other spheres and is a syn. of *entscheiden*, to DECIDE.

Die Prüfungskommission hat die Examensarbeit für gut befunden.

Die neue Maschine wurde von den Sachverständigen für brauchbar befunden.

Die Ärzte haben mich für tauglich befunden, bei der Bundeswehr zu dienen.

Das Gericht hat darüber zu befinden, ob der Beamte der Korruption schuldig ist.

iii. When a feeling, not an opinion, is involved, it is necessary to use **empfinden als**, 'to feel to be' (cf. FEEL). *Ich empfand den Frühlingssonnenschein als sehr angenehm. Sie empfand das warme Klima als ihrer Gesundheit zuträglich.* Other expressions may convey the meaning of **find**. *I find it embarrassing* could be *Es ist mir peinlich, ihn auf solche Fehler aufmerksam machen zu müssen.* Cf. EMBARRASS.

fire *n*. **Das Feuer** denotes in one sense the element fire. *Das Gebäude wurde durch Feuer zerstört*, by fire = 'combustion', not perhaps by an explosion. It is also used for a controlled fire. *Im Kamin brannte ein Feuer.* In everyday language it is the normal word for a destructive fire. *Die Explosion löste das Feuer aus, das Sie da sehen. Wie ist das Feuer entstanden?* In the latter use it is a syn. of **der Brand**, which is a more official word for a destructive fire. *Die Explosion löste einen Brand aus.* In *Die Scheune ist durch einen Brand zerstört worden*, a fire, not fire = 'combustion', is meant. *Brand* is used on all stylistic levels to avoid ambiguity and in compounds such as *der Waldbrand, der Hausbrand, die Brandversicherung, der Grubenbrand, die Brandstiftung.* A fire of great proportions can be called **eine Feuersbrunst**, 'a conflagration', but the word is as little used as the E. equivalent. *Alle Häuser auf dieser Seite der Straße fielen der Feuersbrunst zum Opfer.*

Die Pfadfinder saßen bis in die frühen Morgenstunden um das Lagerfeuer, grillten Würstchen und Kartoffeln, sangen und erzählten sich Gruselgeschichten.

Das Feuer/Der Brand im Dorf hat viele Familien obdachlos gemacht.

Es ist der Feuerwehr gelungen, einen gestern ausgebrochenen Waldbrand zu löschen.

Der Chronist berichtet von einer Feuersbrunst, die die ganze Stadt in Schutt und Asche legte.

first *adv.* and *adj.* **at first** phr. used as *adv.*

1. Meanings of **zuerst**.

i. 'In the initial or early stages', 'at the beginning'. In this sense, E. mostly has **at first**, but **first** is used under certain circumstances. *I didn't understand at first. I am even more impressed by it now than I was at first or than I first was. The assurance which he had displayed at first . . . or . . . which he had first displayed . . .* An alternative to *zuerst* is **anfangs**, in/at the beginning.

> *Die Zuversicht, die er zuerst an den Tag gelegt hatte, machte bald deutlicher Verlegenheit Platz.*
> *Zuerst habe ich nicht recht/richtig verstanden.*
> *Ich bin jetzt noch mehr beeindruckt davon, als ich es anfangs/zuerst war.*

ii. 'For the first time'. Here E. uses both **first** and **for the first time**. *When did you first hear of this? I first met her when I was working in Brighton. I saw him for the first time/I first saw him only last week.* **Zuerst** is used if there is no confusion of sense. An alternative is **zum ersten Mal**, which is unambiguous. Both *zuerst* and *zum ersten Mal* mean 'for the first time ever' or 'for the first time on a particular occasion'.

> *Ich habe zuerst 1985 mit ihr in Brighton zusammengearbeitet.*
> *Wann haben Sie den Mann zuerst/zum ersten Mal bemerkt?*

iii. 'Before all other thgs. or people in a series or situation'. **First** can mean 'before anyone else', *I arrived first,* 'before anything else is done or takes place', *We will consider this case first,* or 'before any other in time, space, order, rank, etc.' *Women and children first.* **Zuerst** implies by the nature of its meaning that something else follows, but this is left vague. *Wer von euch war zuerst da? Wir betrachten diesen Fall zuerst. Frauen und Kinder zuerst!* A syn. is **zunächst**, which suggests more strongly that what is first is of greater importance. *Zunächst* often occurs in the form *zunächst einmal*, but *einmal* does not change the meaning. *Zunächst [einmal] müssen wir entscheiden, ob der Versuch überhaupt gemacht werden soll.* **Zuallererst** corresponds to the strengthened form *first of all. Zuallererst muß ich diesen Brief zu Ende schreiben.* A further alternative is **als erster/erste/erstes**. *Sie hat als erste gesprochen. Welcher Teil der Universität wird als erstes gebaut?* **Erst einmal** is also a syn. and is discussed below (2. ii). **Erstens** is used in an enumeration when several points are mentioned in succession. *Erstens erkläre ich den Zweck der Untersuchung, zweitens beschreibe ich unsere Arbeitsweise, dann teile ich die Ergebnisse mit.*

> *Wer zuerst kommt, wird zuerst bedient. Or Wer zuerst kommt, [der] mahlt zuerst.*
> *Er ist mit dem Kopf zuerst ins Wasser gesprungen.*
> *Wir müssen uns zunächst einmal/zuerst mit Punkt vier befassen.*
> *Er ist zuerst angekommen.*   *Er ist als erster angekommen.*

2. First also means 'before some other stated action'. *I must first finish this letter, then I can help you. First do your homework, then you can play!*

i. In this case, **erst** is an alternative to **zuerst**. *Erst* is used in this sense only when what follows is specified, and it stresses what follows. The second part of the sent., which may, but need not, be conditional on the first, is introduced by words like *dann, danach,* or a clause with *bevor* or *ehe.* It can be replaced by *zuerst,* but some expressions such as *Erst überlegen, dann reden!* and *Erst so, dann so,* 'first someone acts one way and then quite differently', are fixed phrs., and only *erst* is used.

> *Sie handeln nach dem Motto: Schieß' erst, frag' später!*
> *Wir waren erst im Kino, danach zu Hause.*
> *Ich werde erst/zuerst dich bezahlen und dann die anderen.*
> *Ich muß diesen Brief erst zu Ende schreiben, dann kann ich euch helfen.*
> *Ich muß dieses Kapitel erst zu Ende lesen, bevor ich euch helfen kann.*
> *Mach' erst deine Hausaufgaben, dann kannst du spielen!*

ii. When *einmal* is added to *erst*, often in the shortened form *mal*, the sequence is not so strongly stressed, so that **erst [ein]mal** is a syn. of *zuerst*. It is used like *erst* with the subsequent action specified, but also occurs without this. *Wir wollen erst mal essen.*

> *Ich will mir die Sache erst einmal überlegen.*
> *Iß erst einmal deine Suppe auf, und dann bekommst du die Erdbeeren!*

iii. Note that *erst* also means 'ONLY', 'not until'. With a following time phr. there is a difference in meaning between *zuerst* and *erst*. *Dieser Begriff tritt zuerst im 18. Jahrhundert auf*, first or for the first time. *Frauenrollen im Theater wurden erst im 18. Jahrhundert von Frauen gespielt*, not until.

3. In E. an infin. is usual after **the first**, *They were the first to discover gold*, although a relative clause is possible, *He was the first (doctor) who noticed the harmful side-effects.* A clause is needed after **der/die/das erste**, but the idea is often best expressed differently. *We were the first to arrive* can be *Wir waren die ersten, die angekommen sind*, but *Wir sind als erste/zuerst angekommen* are common alternatives. Thus *Sie waren die ersten, die Gold entdeckten* or *Sie haben als erste Gold entdeckt.*

> *X war der erste (Arzt), der auf die schädlichen Nebenwirkungen dieser Arznei hingewiesen hat.*

4. First in a race, contest, etc. is *Er war/wurde der erste, Sie war/wurde die erste*, or for a race only *ging als Erste[r] durchs Ziel.* Note that *the first two/three* is *die beiden/zwei ersten* or *die drei ersten*.

flat, shallow *adjs.*

1. *Flach* and the less common *platt* both express the basic sense 'horizontally level' and differ mostly in the contexts in which they are used.

i. In reference to natural landscape, only **flach** is used and means 'flat' or 'low'. *Ein flaches Gelände. Eine flache Küste. Auf dem flachen Lande* means 'in the country'. *Platt* used to be used in this expression, but is now rare.

> *Das Land ist total flach. Keine Erhebung versperrt einem die Sicht, und man scherzt, daß man morgens schon sehen kann, wer abends zu Besuch kommt.*
> *Er liebt das flache Land seiner Heimat.   Die Straße führt durch flaches Gelände.*

Flach is also applied to things made flat, low, or not deep or high. *Ein flaches Dach. Schuhe mit flachen Absätzen. Ein flacher Teller.*

ii. For parts of the body, **flach** is normal, but **platt** is used colloquially. *Er fiel durch die flache/platte Nase auf. Die flache Hand*, the flat of the hand. *Sie hielt den Vogel in der flachen Hand. Er schlug mit der flachen Hand auf den Tisch.* To lie flat is *flach liegen. Man liegt flach auf dem Boden. Bei dieser Übung müßt ihr euch flach auf den Boden legen.*

iii. *Platt* now mostly suggests that something is pressed or squashed flat, whether intentionally or not, i.e. it is combined with vs. like *drücken* 'to press', *walzen*, 'to roll', or *treten*, 'to tread'. *Flach* is not impossible.

> *Das Kind drückte die Nase an der Fensterscheibe platt.*
> *Jmd. hat sich auf meinen Hut gesetzt und ihn ganz platt gedrückt.*
> *Nach dem Manöver waren die Felder platt gewalzt.*
> *Die spielenden Kinder hatten einen Teil des Getreides platt getreten.*

2. Both also mean 'shallow'. *Flach* is used occasionally in the lit. sense, *Der Rhein ist im Augenblick flach* (or *niedrig*, LOW), and both **flach** and **platt** are applied to remarks, products of the mind, etc. *Ein flacher Film. Ein flaches Urteil. Ein plattes Gespräch.* **Seicht** is 'shallow' in the lit. sense, *ein seichtes Gewässer*, and in fig. use it is the strongest word, expressing the most scorn, *seichtes Geplauder/Gerede.*

> *Die Diskussion war eher flach und ging nicht in die Tiefe.*
> *Der Vortrag war flach und oberflächlich.   Die Witze waren platt und geschmacklos.*

Die Unterhaltung artete im Laufe des Abends in plattes Geschwätz aus.
Seine Theaterstücke sind immer ziemlich seicht.   *Rede doch nicht so seicht daher!*

3. Platt also means 'astounded, flabbergasted'.
Sie war platt über die Dreistigkeit des jungen Mannes.   *Da war ich erst einmal platt!*

follow, ensue, pursue, persecute, prosecute *vs.*

Order of treatment: 1–10 deal with senses of **follow**, all of which except 7 are expressed by *folgen*, and give syns. in several senses; 11 treats **ensue**; and 12 *verfolgen* in the senses 'pursue', 'persecute', and 'prosecute'.

1. Follow means 'to go or come after s.o. in space'. *Please follow me!*
i. The equivalent is **folgen**.
Folgen Sie mir bitte!   *Ich folgte ihr zur Tür, ging aber nicht hinaus.*
Später entdeckte er, daß einer der Polizisten ihm unauffällig gefolgt war.
Von seinem Kollegium gefolgt, betrat der Direktor die Aula.
Ein dichter Schwarm von Photographen und Anhängern folgten dem Sänger.
Es führt Nr. 10, dicht gefolgt von Nr. 5.

ii. Nachkommen can mean 'to follow' in the sense 'to come after in space'. *Sie kommt später nach, wenn sie mit der Arbeit fertig ist. Geh' du voran!—ich komme in zehn Minuten nach.*

iii. Nachfolgen means 'to come after or behind'. *Als das Auto mit dem Lastwagen zusammengestoßen ist, mußten die nachfolgenden Wagen scharf bremsen.* If *folgend* were used here, it would suggest that a list follows. *Ich folge nach* translates **follow** or *come after/behind* when nothing else follows. *Seine Freunde folgten nach.* With *folgen* in this sense, a dat. is usual. *Seine Freunde folgten ihm. Nachfolgen* is also found with the dat. of the person in the sense 'to come after', but then is more emphatic than *folgen. Seine Frau wollte ihm erst dann nachfolgen, wenn er eine Wohnung gefunden hatte.*

2. Both **follow** and **folgen** express the sense 'to keep on or near'. *We followed the track for ten kilometres/the footsteps in the snow. The road follows the coast.*
Wir sind dem Ufer des Baches gefolgt.   *Sie folgten den Fußstapfen im Schnee.*
Wir sind davon überzeugt, daß wir der richtigen Fährte folgen.
Folgen Sie dieser Straße, bis Sie zum nächsten Dorf kommen!
Folgen Sie den roten Wegmarkierungen, und Sie werden Ihr Ziel nicht verfehlen!
Die Straße folgt der Küste für die nächsten fünfzig Kilometer.

3. Follow also means 'to come after in time', 'to succeed s.o.', 'to be next in a series'. *A mild spring followed the severe winter. One success followed another. He followed his father as chairman of the firm. Wilhelm II followed Friedrich III.*
i. Folgen is used with *auf* as well as with the dat. Thus both *Auf König David folgte sein Sohn Salomon*, and *Wilhelm II folgte seinem Vater Friedrich III (dem dritten)* are found.
Auf den strengen Winter folgte ein milder Frühling.   *Ein Erfolg folgte dem anderen.*
Ein Unglück folgte auf das andere/dem anderen.   *Er folgte seinem Vater im Amt.*
Although *der Nachfolger* means 'successor', *folgen* means 'to follow or succeed s.o. in a position'. *Herr X folgte Herrn Y als Bürgermeister/im Amt des Bürgermeisters* or *wurde sein Nachfolger.*
ii. Sich anschließen + dat. or + *an* + acc., 'to follow immediately (in time)', is used of planned activities. Thus either *Dem Vortrag schloß sich die Diskussion an* or *An den Vortrag schloß sich die Diskussion an.*
An den Trachtenumzug schloß sich ein Konzert auf dem Marktplatz an.

4. Follow means 'to act in accordance with'. *We followed the instructions. They followed her advice. He followed his conscience/his own wishes.*

i. Folgen expresses this sense, but there are several alternatives.

Wir sind den Gebrauchsanweisungen/der Regel/den Anordnungen/dem Befehl/den Vorschriften/den Richtlinien/seinem Wink/ihrem Rat gefolgt.
Als sie diese Entscheidung traf, folgte sie ihrem Gewissen.
Man folgt einem Gefühl/einem Impuls/einem Antrieb/einer Neigung etc.
Viele glauben, der Mode folgen zu müssen. *Wir folgen ihrem Beispiel/dem Brauch.*
Der Koalitionspartner wollte dem Kurs der Regierung nicht weiter folgen.

ii. Befolgen + acc., 'to follow, act upon, comply with', is used with ns. like *ein Befehl, Vorschriften, jmds. Rat, ein Vorschlag, ein Gesetz,* and *Anweisungen,* as is *folgen,* the difference being that the *be-* prefix intensifies the meaning so that it implies an exact carrying out of the instruction etc. This is often made even clearer by an adv. like *genau, streng,* or *gewissenhaft.*

'Wenn ich Ihnen einen Befehl erteile, so haben Sie diesen ohne weitere Fragen augenblicklich zu befolgen.' *Gewissenhaft befolgte sie die Dienstvorschriften.*

iii. Sich richten nach, to follow, act in accordance with.

Der Beamte hat sich nach der Vorschrift zu richten.
Wir müssen uns nach den Wünschen unserer Kunden richten.
Mit meinen Urlaubsplänen richte ich mich ganz nach dir (fit in with).

iv. Sich leiten lassen von, to follow, be guided by a principle, feeling, someone's advice, etc.

Als wir diese Entscheidung trafen, haben wir uns nur von wirtschaftlichen Gesichtspunkten/von politischen Motiven/von unseren Gefühlen leiten lassen.
Bei der Wahl ihres Wohnortes ließ sie sich von den Wünschen ihrer Eltern leiten.

5. i. Follow and **folgen** mean 'to treat as a leader', 'espouse the opinions of'. *The masses followed the demagogue blindly. Die Massen folgten dem radikalen Demagogen blindlings.*

Die Mitglieder der Bande folgten ihrem Führer.

ii. *Christus nachfolgen* is 'to follow Christ'. In other contexts, **nachfolgen** means 'to become an adherent of'. *Matisse entwarf eine neue Theorie der Malerei, und viele Künstler folgten ihm nach.*

6. Follow and **folgen** mean 'to watch the progress or course of a moving object'. *My eyes followed the train until it disappeared in the distance. Ich folgte dem Zug mit den Augen, bis er in der Ferne verschwand.*

7. Follow means 'to watch', 'occupy oneself mentally with', or 'take an interest in'. *Did you follow the tennis at Wimbledon? They follow the events/developments in Africa.* **Verfolgen,** 'to observe carefully, attentively', expresses this sense. (Cf. 12 for other senses of *verfolgen*.)

Ich habe den Prozeß in der Zeitung verfolgt.
Die Journalisten verfolgten den Verlauf der Konferenz.
Millionen verfolgten gespannt das Fußballspiel im Fernsehen.
Hast du die politischen Ereignisse in den letzten Tagen verfolgt?

8. Follow means 'to understand or keep up with an argument, train of thought, or a pers. speaking'. *The reasoning is too difficult for them to follow. He spoke so fast that I couldn't follow him.* **Folgen** means 'to listen to with understanding' or 'to understand'.

Können Sie mir folgen, oder soll ich es Ihnen noch einmal ausführlicher erklären?
Sie folgten der Rede/dem Redner/dem Vortrag/den Ausführungen des Redners aufmerksam.
Die Schüler folgten dem Unterricht mit Interesse.
Ich konnte seinem Gedankengang nicht folgen.
Wir folgten dem Schauspiel mit wachsender Begeisterung.

9. Follow and **folgen** are intr. in the sense 'to come after or next or be sent subsequently'. *The news follows in a minute. We have sent off some of the books; the rest will follow in a few days.*

Erst kam ein Tango, nun folgt ein Walzer.
Weitere Einzelheiten folgen in einem Brief. Or *Brief folgt.*
Es folgt die dritte Symphonie von Beethoven gespielt von den Wiener Philharmonikern.
Rest folgt. Also *Den Rest der Waren lassen wir nächste Woche folgen.* (Commercial language.)

10. Follow is also intr. in the meaning 'to result logically'. *From the evidence it follows that he is innocent.*

i. Folgen has this meaning. The *es* of *es folgt* is omitted if it is not the first word in the sent.

Es folgt aus der Aussage der Zeugen, daß der Angeklagte unschuldig ist.
Aus dem bisher Gesagten folgt, daß Sie der Theorie zustimmen.
Aus unserem Charakter folgt unser Verhalten.

ii. Sich ergeben aus means 'to be a consequence of, to follow either logically or as a result'. *Dieser Lehrsatz ergibt sich aus dem vorigen. Es* in *es ergibt sich* is also omitted if it is not the first word in the sent. *Ergeben* means 'to yield' a result or conclusion, and the following transformation is often possible: *Die Dokumente ergaben seine Unschuld* and *Aus den Dokumenten ergab sich seine Unschuld* or *Es ergab sich aus den Dokumenten, daß er unschuldig war.*

Daraus/Aus dem soeben Gesagten ergibt sich, daß die gängige Erklärung unzureichend ist.
Aus der Untersuchung ergab sich, daß der junge Mann an der Schlägerei völlig unbeteiligt war.

11. Ensue.

i. Erfolgen means in its original sense 'to ensue or follow', i.e. 'to happen as a result of sth. else'. However, it has become common, particularly in officialese or journalese, in a looser sense 'to happen or take place' without the idea of a consequence.

Als das Feuer auf das Benzinlager übergriff, erfolgte eine gewaltige Explosion.
Auf diesen Skandal hin erfolgte der Rücktritt des Ministers.
Loose use: *Die Auszahlung der Gehälter erfolgt am 15. des Monats.*

ii. Sich ergeben [aus] can mean 'to ensue or result [from]'. *Aus dieser Nachläßigkeit können sich böse Folgen ergeben. Neue Schwierigkeiten haben sich ergeben.*

12. Pursue, persecute, and prosecute.

i. Verfolgen means 'to pursue, chase, follow with the intention of capturing'. *Die Polizei verfolgte den fliehenden Verbrecher.*

Die Hunde verfolgten das Reh, aber es entkam im dichten Wald.
Fig. meanings have developed from this. *Er scheint vom Unglück verfolgt zu sein,* dogged by. *Eine trübe Ahnung verfolgte sie seit einiger Zeit,* haunted. *Der Gedanke verfolgt mich. Er verfolgte sie mit Vorwürfen/Bitten/seiner Eifersucht,* etc. tormented, plagued.

ii. Verfolgen expresses the sense of **pursue** 'to continue an action already begun'. *Wir haben das Thema nicht weiter verfolgt,* did not pursue the subject any further. *Ich werde die Sache weiter verfolgen.*

iii. Verfolgen corresponds to **pursue** meaning 'to try to carry out, put into effect'. *Man verfolgt ein Ziel/einen Zweck/einen Plan/eine Absicht/ein Prinzip/eine Idee/einen Gedanken/eine Politik.*

Die Regierung verfolgte eine selbständige Außenpolitik.
Was für einen Zweck verfolgt er mit seinem Verhalten?

iv. It also means 'to persecute'. *Das Regime verfolgte erbarmungslos alle oppositionellen Kräfte.*

In der Nazizeit wurden Millionen Menschen aus rassischen und politischen Gründen verfolgt.

v. Prosecute means 'to take legal action against', but it is used only with people as obj. in the act. *They will prosecute any offender.* **Verfolgen** + **strafrechtlich** or **gerichtlich** expresses this meaning and is applied both to people or offenders and offences. *Übertreter dieses Verbots werden gerichtlich verfolgt.* In relation to an offence, as in *Zuwiderhandlungen* (or *Verstöße*) *werden strafrechtlich verfolgt*, the E. equivalent could be *Contraventions/Infringements/Breaches are subject to prosecution.* **Gerichtlich belangen** is a syn. applied only to people. *Wer gegen dieses Verbot verstößt, wird gerichtlich belangt. X prosecuted at a trial is X vertrat/führte die Anklage.* In Germany the prosecutor is *der Staatsanwalt.*

food, nourishment, nutrition, foodstuff *ns.* Food denotes that which is either eaten by human beings or animals or taken in by plants to sustain life and permit growth, as in *How long can you survive without food?*, or a particular kind of such nutriment, *baby food, packaged food, the food in the canteen*, or *dog food.* **Nourishment** can mean 'food required to grow and remain healthy', but also refers to the way people are nourished or the kind or amount of food they eat. *Illnesses can be caused by poor nourishment.* **Nutrition** also refers to the way people are nourished or what they eat. *The standard of nutrition must be improved.* A **foodstuff** is 'a material used as food'.

1. Die Nahrung is 'the food which a living being needs to maintain life and growth'. It is the general term, but is more used in specialized than in everyday language. It is also translated as **nourishment**. It denotes the food of plants and what animals live on under natural circumstances. Hence *Die Nahrung der Blindschleiche besteht hauptsächlich aus Regenwürmern und Nachtschnecken*, or *Die Vögel/ Tiere gehen auf Nahrungssuche.* For animals and human beings it often also refers to the kind of food in a general way. *Tierische/Pflanzliche/Vitaminreiche Nahrung. Der Patient durfte zwei Tage lang nur flüssige Nahrung zu sich nehmen.* In more specialized language a doctor might say of a patient, '*Er verweigert die Nahrungsaufnahme.*' Fig. *Nahrung* is applied to the mind, to rumours, and to emotions. *Bücher sind Nahrung für den Geist. Das Gerücht/Der Verdacht fand neue Nahrung. Dieser Vorfall gab seiner Unzufriedenheit neue Nahrung.*

2. i. Das Futter is 'fodder' or 'food for animals', but is mostly restricted to pets or farm animals.

Wir brauchen mehr Futter für das Vieh.   *Dieses Fleisch wird zu Hundefutter verarbeitet.*

ii. Der Fraß is 'the food of carnivorous animals or birds'. *Man warf den Löwen Fleisch als/zum Fraß vor.*

Früh wird euer Fleisch den Geiern ein Fraß sein, Soldaten. (Dürrenmatt)

3. Die Ernährung denotes either the action of feeding, *die künstliche Ernährung eines Kranken*, providing others with food or keeping them, *Der Vierzehnjährige war für die Ernährung seiner Geschwister verantwortlich*, or nutrition, which can denote the process of taking nourishment or nutrients into the body, but usually refers to the value or quality of what is eaten. Thus the use with adjs. denoting quality: *Eine gesunde/gute/schlechte/hochwertige/unzureichende Ernährung. Die Ernährungslage* denotes the general state of nutrition in an area. *Die Ernährungswissenschaft*, dietetics.

4. Das Nahrungsmittel, which is applied to natural or processed human food only, denotes an item of nutrition. It is often translated as **foodstuff**, and, like it, is more a technical term and usually has an adj. It is used when stating that something has special nutritive value, in contrast to *Lebensmittel* which implies necessities of life without saying anything about their food value.

Obst ist ein vitaminreiches Nahrungsmittel. Also . . . eine vitaminreiche Nahrung.

Daß Milch ein hochwertiges Nahrungsmittel ist, wird wohl nicht ernstlich bestritten werden.

5. i. Die Lebensmittel are products which, either in a natural or processed state, are suitable for human consumption and are necessary for normal life and nourishment.

It now refers to groceries, fruit, vegetables, and meat, and is the appropriate word when **food** means that. This is its sense in *Lebensmittelherstellung, -industrie, -konservierung,* or *-rationierung. Das Lebensmittelgeschäft* is 'a grocery shop', though *der Supermarkt* is now more usual. In technical language **die Genußmittel** denotes items such as tea, coffee, spices, and alcoholic drinks, which are not necessities like *Lebensmittel,* but are consumed for enjoyment.

> *Die Lebensmittelpreise sind in letzter Zeit kaum gestiegen.*
> *Die Italiener essen mehr Lebensmittel, die aus Getreide hergestellt werden, als andere Europäer.*

ii. We haven't got much food left in the house is best translated as *Im Haus ist nur wenig zu essen. I'll have to buy some food* is usually *Ich muß einkaufen,* although *Lebensmittel einkaufen* is heard.

6. Food means 'meal or meals'.
i. Das Essen is the normal equivalent. With adjs. it can denote the type or quality of the food. *Das Essen ist gut/schlecht/unzureichend.*

> *Laß doch dein Essen nicht kalt werden!*   *Das Essen zu Hause ist besser.*
> *In diesem Wohnheim kocht jeder das eigene Essen selbst.*
> *Das Essen im Hotel war nicht besonders/nicht ausgezeichnet.*
> *Das Essen hier schmeckt mir immer.*

ii. Die Kost suggests a special type of food, sometimes a particular diet; it is mostly confined to food for people, but is occasionally used for animals' food. It is a more formal or technical word than *das Essen. Babykost* is the general name for *baby food,* but in a particular case, i.e. where E. has *the baby's food* or [the] *food for the baby,* the expression is *das Essen für das Baby.*

> *Vorläufig verträgt der Patient nur leichte Kost.*
> *Wenn es die Umstände erfordern, gehen viele Tiere, die auf eine bestimmte Nahrung eingestellt sind, zu einer anderen Kost über.*
> *Auf dieser Station im Krankenhaus bekommt man nahrhafte Kost.*

Die Kost also means 'board', i.e. 'meals supplied with accommodation or as part payment for service'. *Neben seinem Lohn bekommt der Hotelpförtner freie Kost,* he gets free meals/board. *Board and lodging* is *Kost und Logis* or *Verpflegung und Unterkunft.*

iii. Die Verpflegung is 'the food regularly provided for a period of time', e.g. in the armed forces, schools, canteens, boarding-houses, simple hotels, etc. It suggests everyday food of average quality and is more an official term which can be replaced by *das Essen.* Cf. FEED 3. ii. For more expensive hotels, **die Beköstigung** is often found.

> *Die Verpflegung in der Jugendherberge ließ zu wünschen übrig.*
> *Die Soldaten klagten über die Verpflegung beim Manöver/in der Kaserne.*
> *Entgegen den Versprechungen des Prospekts war die Verpflegung während der Reise sehr schlecht.*
> *In diesem Hotel ist die Beköstigung vorzüglich.*

iv. When **food** means 'the provisions needed for a journey', the specific term is **der Proviant.**

> *Bei der Hochgebirgswanderung haben wir Proviant/Verpflegung für drei Tage mitgenommen.*

v. Der Fraß is also a colloquial or slang term for very bad food. *Er ließ den Fraß stehen.*

> *Ich hatte einen Mordshunger, konnte den Fraß aber kaum herunterwürgen.*

fool *n.* **foolish, stupid** *adjs.* **make a fool of** *v.*

i. Der Tor denotes someone who is naïve or foolish through lack of experience, but who does not necessarily lack intelligence. It is now a purely literary term. **Töricht,** however, survives, but it belongs to a higher stylistic level than the other adjs. discussed here. It is not as strong nor as derogatory as *dumm* or *blöd.* **Der Narr** still occurs in everyday language, whereas **närrisch** is little used except in the language of *Karneval*, e.g. *die närrische Zeit*. *Der Narr* was a court fool or jester and is also much used in *Karneval*. For *You fool!*, there are relatively mild expressions like **Du Dussel!** or **Du Esel!** Stronger are **Du Dummkopf!** and **Du Narr! Du Idiot!** is stronger again.

> *Das weiß jeder Dummkopf/jeder Narr* (any fool . . .).   '*Spiel doch nicht den Narren!*'
> *Er ist mehr ein Dummkopf als ein Schurke.*
> *Nur ein Narr könnte sich so verhalten, wie er es getan hat.*
> *Jeder Idiot weiß doch, wie gefährlich diese Strecke ist.*   '*Sei doch kein Narr!*'
> *Diese Idioten, wie können sie bloß so fahrlässig handeln?*

ii. Fool is often best translated by the adj. **dumm**, stupid, silly, foolish. *Wie dumm waren wir doch, die Falle nicht zu sehen!*, what fools we were . . . A common alternative in everyday speech is **blöd**, which is applied to people and things. *Ein blöder Kerl. Ein blödes Buch.* There are also the strengthened colloquial forms **saudumm** and **saublöd**. *Ein saudummer Kerl. Ein saublöder Einfall.* **Blödsinnig** is a somewhat strengthened variant on *blöd*, as is another syn., **schwachsinnig**. *Das ist ein blödsinniger Gedanke. Der Plan ist schwachsinnig.* **Idiotisch** is stronger. *Das ist doch idiotisch, was du jetzt vorhast.* **Dumm** and **blöd** also mean 'stupid' in the sense of 'unpleasant'. *Diese dumme/blöde Sache hat mir sehr viel Lauferei verursacht.*

> *Sie war so dumm, ihm zu glauben* (she was fool/foolish enough to . . .).
> *Er ist nicht so dumm, wie er aussieht.*
> *Es war dumm von ihm, alle Freunde zu verlassen* (he was a fool/foolish to . . .).
> '*Du bist mir viel zu blöd, Müller, mit dir unterhalte ich mich gar nicht mehr.*'
> '*Stell' dich nicht so dumm/idiotisch an!*'   *Er hat eine idiotische Frage gestellt.*

iii. Blamieren ranges from embarrassing someone or making someone look ridiculous or a fool to disgracing someone. *Er hat mich vor allen Anwesenden blamiert.* **Sich blamieren** means 'to make a fool of oneself'. *Ich will mich nicht vor diesem Publikum blamieren.* To make someone look a fool/foolish deliberately is **jmdn. zum Narren halten**. *Was er dir da erzählt hat, stimmt gar nicht—er will dich bloß zum Narren halten. Laß dich nicht zum Narren halten!*

footpath, pavement, sidewalk *ns.* The meaning of all three words is 'a paved and usually elevated section along each side of a street for people on foot'. The usual equivalent nowadays is **der Bürgersteig**. The other words are regional variants. **Der Gehsteig** is used in south-west Germany, **der Gehweg** in the south-east, and **das Trottoir** in Switzerland and the south-west. For **footpath** = 'a track across fields or open country' cf. STREET.

formal *adj.* G. has three words *formal*, *förmlich*, and *formell*, each of which expresses some senses of **formal**.

1. G. **formal** alone means 'pertaining to the shape, arrangement, or composition mostly of a novel, drama, or work of art' as distinguished from its contents. *Die formale Struktur des Romans.*

> *Die formale Gliederung des Dramas.*   *Der Aufsatz ist in formaler Hinsicht gut.*

2. E. **formal** means 'in accordance with the recognized or prescribed forms, social customs, conventions, or rules of behaviour'. *A formal welcome. Formal politeness. The letter was stiff and formal.* **Formell** and **förmlich** mean 'in strict conformity with social conventions or the rules of good behaviour'. *Ein formeller Antrittsbesuch. Der Brief war steif und formell. Es folgte eine formelle Begrüßung. Wir wurden förmlich empfangen. Die Urkunde wurde mir förmlich überreicht.*

> *Alle Gäste trugen den formellen Abendanzug.* (Formal dress/clothes can also be *Gesellschaftskleidung*.)

'Wie geht es eigentlich Ihrer Mutter?' fragte Böhm mit formeller Höflichkeit.
Sie empfingen uns ganz formell.   Ich erhielt eine förmliche Einladung.

3. Applied to people, E. **formal** means 'rigorously observant of the conventions of good behaviour' and often implies a reproach for being unduly stiff, serious, and correct instead of relaxed and friendly. **Förmlich** can mean 'punctiliously observing the rules of correct behaviour' and implies a lack of warmth, a certain reserve and solemnity. **Formell** has the same pejorative sense and suggests that the person avoids close personal contact and limits himself or herself to a non-committal kind of correct behaviour.

'Sei doch nicht so förmlich!'   Sein förmliches Wesen stieß mich ab.
Engländer gehen weniger förmlich miteinander um als wir.
Sie schrieb mir einige nichtssagende, formelle Zeilen.

4. E. **formal** = 'done or made with the forms recognized as ensuring validity', often as opposed to a tacit understanding. *It will have to go to Parliament for formal approval. No formal declaration of war had been made.* Both **förmlich** and **formell** mean 'in accordance with the law or regulations' or 'official'.

Die Ernennung/Die Kündigung war noch nicht förmlich erfolgt.
Ich habe förmlich um Sonderurlaub ersucht.
Die förmliche Übergabe des Amtes findet morgen statt.
Die Nationalsozialisten haben den Reichstag zwar nicht formell beseitigt, aber er wurde zur völligen
*   Bedeutungslosigkeit verurteilt.   Eine formelle Kriegserklärung war noch nicht erfolgt.*
Die formelle Bestätigung durch das Parlament ist erforderlich.
Die Vollversammlung beschloß formell, den jährlichen Mitgliedsbeitrag zu erhöhen.

5. E. **formal** = 'done for the sake of form or convention only',' having the form or appearance without the spirit or substance'. **Formell** can mean 'in accordance with convention or regulation but without real value', 'simply to keep up appearances'. G. **formal** means 'for the sake of form, without the spirit, not real'. *Jmd. ist formell/formal im Recht* means that he has obeyed the letter, but not the spirit, of the law. *Eine formale Demokratie* has the forms of democratic government but not its reality.

Meine Beziehungen zu ihm wurden immer formeller.

found, establish, set up *vs.* Some equivalents of base, substantiate *vs.*

1. Gründen means 'to take the steps to bring sth. into existence', 'to set up or establish' a settlement, firm, family, etc. *Man gründet eine Siedlung/eine Kolonie/ein Dorf/ein Geschäft/eine Firma/ein Unternehmen/eine Zeitung/eine Zeitschrift/einen Verein/eine Familie/einen Hausstand.*

Der Urgroßvater des jetzigen Inhabers hat die Firma gegründet.
Das Dorf Gutingi, aus dem sich später Göttingen entwickelt hat, wurde um 950 gegründet.
Er siedelte nach Neuseeland über und gründete dort eine Familie.

2. Begründen means 'to create the basis for', 'lay the foundation of'. It is used with intangibles like *jmds. Ruf, Ruhm,* or *Glück* and with things which do not have a clear beginning like *das Vermögen. Der Großvater begründete das Vermögen der Familie.* Applied to a movement, meaning 'a group of people sharing similar views and pursuing particular aims', *begründen* means 'to provide a foundation of ideas on which it can grow and develop'. *Er begründete eine Schule/eine neue Richtung in der Architektur. Der Begründer einer Weltanschauung* provides its theoretical basis.

Vor allem der Roman Werther *begründete Goethes Ruhm/Popularität weit über die Grenzen*
*   Deutschlands hinaus.*
Wer hat den Dadaismus/das ökologische Denken begründet?

3. Stiften, 'to endow', translates **found** meaning 'to provide the money to establish or get sth. going'.

Der reiche Bankier hat mehrere Stipendien/ein Krankenhaus/eine Schule/eine Kirche gestiftet.

4. Other meanings of *gründen* and *begründen*.

i. Gründen auf + acc. means 'to base sth. on'. *Er gründete seinen Verdacht auf die Aussage eines Zeugen. Sie gründete ihre Theorie auf ihre Beobachtungen.* The refl. **sich gründen auf** corresponds to the E. pass., *to be based* or *founded on. Die Theorie gründet sich auf die Ergebnisse ihrer Versuche. Worauf gründet sich Ihr Verdacht? Ihre Forderungen gründen sich auf das Testament ihres Großvaters. Die Romanhandlung gründet sich auf eine wirkliche Begebenheit/auf historische Tatsachen.* An alternative for the last sent. is . . . *ist auf historische Tatsachen gegründet.* (*Begründet* is occasionally found instead of *gegründet*, but is not the usual word in this context.)

ii. Begründen means 'to give reasons for', 'to substantiate'. *Man begründet eine Behauptung/eine Beschuldigung/einen Einwand* etc. *Können Sie Ihren Entschluß begründen?* The past part., as in *begründete Hoffnung/Abneigung* or *begründeter Optimismus*, means 'well-based' or 'well-grounded'. *Etw. liegt/ist in etw. begründet* means it has its reasons in something, is derived from it. *Das liegt in der Natur der Sache begründet. Gut begründete Argumente* are well based, founded, or substantiated. A more learned expression is *gut/wohl fundierte Argumente.* **Fundieren** in one sense means 'to support or back up by reasons, evidence, etc.' *Er hat seine Erklärung der historischen Vorgänge durch reiches Quellenmaterial gut fundiert.*

freeze *v.* There are four main senses: (i) Of water and liquids, 'to become ice or solid'. See 1. (ii) Of the weather, 'to be very cold'. *It's freezing today.* See 2. (iii) Of people, 'to be or feel very cold'. *I'm freezing.* See 2. A phr. can be added such as *They almost froze to death.* See 7. (iv) 'To preserve by keeping at a low temperature'. See 4.

1. Gefrieren corresponds to E. sense i. **Der Gefrierpunkt** is the freezing point of water and of other liquids. The v. is occasionally used fig. *Das Lächeln gefror ihr auf den Lippen.*

Wasser gefriert, wenn die Temperatur unter Null Grad sinkt.

In einem strengen Winter gefriert der Erdboden hart.

Das Wasser im See ist nur in der Nähe des Ufers gefroren.

2. Frieren is occasionally found in the sense of *gefrieren*. They are, of course, indistinguishable in the past part. *Frieren* occurs mostly in E. senses ii and iii. Referring to the weather, *es friert* means that the temperature has fallen below zero. *Es wird heute nacht frieren*, there will be a frost tonight. *Es friert anhaltend. Es hat in der Nacht stark gefroren. Ich friere* means 'I'm freezing'. A phr. showing which part of the body is affected can be added. *Ich friere an den Händen/an den Füßen/am ganzen Körper.* An impersonal construction + acc. also occurs, but is less common. *Es friert mich entsetzlich.*

3. i. Einfrieren means that something becomes unusable by freezing and is the appropriate word for water in pipes. *Die Wasserleitung/Das Wasser in den Rohren ist eingefroren. Wir müssen die eingefrorenen Wasserrohre auftauen. Einfrieren* also means 'to imprison in ice'. *Das Schiff war im Packeis eingefroren.*

ii. Einfrieren is used fig. for freezing positions, projects, etc. meaning 'not to fill or continue with them'. *Die Stelle wird zwar nicht gestrichen, aber bis auf weiteres eingefroren.* Also *Ein Guthaben bei einer Bank wird eingefroren. Man hat das Projekt/die Löhne eingefroren.*

4. Einfrieren is also the usual v. for E. sense iv, 'to preserve by freezing'. *Ich habe das Fleisch/das Gemüse/das Brot eingefroren.* A syn is **tiefkühlen**. *Ich habe einige Gerichte* *tiefgekühlt.* For the past part. or adj. **frozen, tiefgefroren** is usual. *Ich kaufe lieber tiefgefrorene Erbsen.* The infin. is *tiefgefrieren.*

5. Überfrieren is 'to cover with a thin layer of ice'. It can be applied to a body of water, but is mostly used for solid surfaces covered with moisture. *Eine Straße überfriert.*

> *In geschützter Lage, z. B. im Wald, überfrieren Landstraßen weniger schnell.*

6. Zufrieren, 'to freeze over solidly', is applied to any body of water.

> *Eine Pfütze/Ein Teich/Ein See/Ein Fluß friert zu.*
> *Wir können auf dem Teich Schlittschuhlaufen. Er ist nämlich in der Nacht zugefroren.*

7. Erfrieren means that human beings and animals freeze to death or that plants are killed by frost. *Einer der Bergsteiger war erfroren. Mehrere Pfirsichbäume waren erfroren.* Applied to toes, fingers, etc., it means 'to be frostbitten'. *Zwei Zehen sind ihm erfroren.* Colloquially, it means 'to be extremely cold', 'frozen to the marrow'. *Ich bin halb erfroren. Völlig erfroren kamen sie nach Hause.*

8. Durchfrieren is 'to freeze right through', but for people it often means 'to be extremely cold'.

> *Wenn man bei der Kälte draußen stehen muß, friert man ganz schön durch.*
> *Er kam völlig durchgefroren zu Hause an.*

fright *n.* get a fright, frighten *v.*

1. Der Schreck and **der Schrecken** both mean 'fright, the reaction caused by the sudden realization of impending danger'. Although the dividing line is not clear, *der Schreck* is best kept for relatively harmless everyday situations, and *der Schrecken* for stronger and longer-lasting reactions when people feel gravely threatened or fear for their lives. With *heftig* both are found. *Ein heftiger Schreck/Schrecken ergriff ihn. Der Schreck* is also used for the reaction when someone unexpectedly receives good news or a pleasant surprise, where E. uses *a (pleasant) shock* or *surprise.* Common expressions are *einen Schreck bekommen/kriegen,* to get a fright; *jmdm. einen Schreck bereiten* or, in everyday language, *einjagen,* to give s.o. a fright. *Man erholt sich von einem Schreck* or *überwindet einen Schreck,* recovers from, gets over a fright.

> *Unerwartet sprang eine Maus vorüber, und ich bekam einen Schreck.*
> *Ich komme spät zurück. Krieg' keinen Schreck, wenn du die Tür um zwei gehen hörst!*
> *Als ich die Rechnung sah, wäre ich vor Schreck beinahe umgefallen.*
> *Bei dem Zusammenstoß ist er mit dem bloßen Schreck/Schrecken davongekommen.*
> *Als die Zuschauer den Rauch erblickten, ergriff sie ein panischer Schrecken.*
> *Die Nachricht, daß feindliche Truppen die Grenze überschritten hatten, verbreitete Schrecken unter der Bevölkerung/versetzte alle in Schrecken.*
> *Beinahe wäre ich von der Straße abgekommen, da mußte ich mich erst mal eine halbe Stunde erholen, so lag mir der Schrecken in den Gliedern.*

2. The v. is **erschrecken.** When trans., it is weak, *Sein Messer hat mich sehr erschreckt,* 'gave me a fright', but when intr., it is strong, *Ich erschrak beim Anblick des Messers,* 'I was frightened or alarmed'. *Vor jmdm. erschrecken* suggests shock either at a person's unexpected or altered appearance or because of an unexpected action which could represent a danger. *Erschreckend* means 'terrifying, alarming'. *Zu Tode erschrocken,* frightened to death.

> *Du hast mich aber erschreckt, ich hätte nicht gedacht, daß zu dieser Zeit noch jmd. hier sitzt.*
> *Bei der Eröffnung, daß sie noch weitere zwei Wochen bleiben wollten, erschrak ich sehr/zutiefst.*
> *Das Waldsterben hat in den Mittelgebirgsregionen erschreckende Ausmaße angenommen.*

3. From *die Angst* three vs. are formed, *ängstigen, beängstigen,* and *verängstigen,* but with the exception of the pres. part. *beängstigend,* none is common in everyday language.

i. Ängstigen, 'to cause anxiety or disquiet', and **sich ängstigen**, 'to feel anxiety', both belong to the more formal written language. *Sich ängstigen* is weaker than *sich fürchten*, to FEAR.

Bloß die Vorstellung, allein reisen zu müssen, ängstigt sie schon.

Sie werden die Kleinen mit diesem Aufzug nur unnötig ängstigen.

Das Mädchen ängstigte sich um ihren kleinen Bruder.

ii. Beängstigen, which is also not common, means 'to cause s.o. to fear' and suggests arousing anguish or mental suffering. *Beängstigend* is, however, often encountered in the sense 'alarming or disquieting'.

Diese Drohungen beängstigten alle Zuhörer.

Die Gefahr eines nuklearen Krieges beängstigte viele Menschen in vielen Ländern.

Die Stimmenzunahme der radikalen Parteien muß als beängstigendes Zeichen gewertet werden.

iii. Verängstigen suggests that the state of anxiety either continues for some time or becomes permanent. *Man darf Kinder nicht verängstigen.* It is mostly found as a past part. used as an adj.

Verängstigen Sie die Welpen nie, sonst bleiben die Hunde immer menschenscheu!

Mit verängstigter Miene schilderte sie den Vorgang.

Als er mit der Flinte erschien, liefen die verängstigten Wildschweine keifend auseinander.

frustrate *v.*

1. In one sense, **frustrate** means 'to thwart, balk, foil, or bring to nothing' a plan, purpose, intention, someone's hopes, expectations, ambitions, etc. A person can be linked to the plan etc. by *in*. *He was frustrated in his ambitions.* The G. vs. are **vereiteln** and **durchkreuzen**, which hardly differ except that *durchkreuzen* suggests that the person has already begun to put the plan etc. into effect, while *vereiteln* can be applied to what exists only as an idea. *Man vereitelt ein/jmds. Vorhaben/einen Plan/einen Versuch/seine Hoffnung auf eine Versetzung. Man durchkreuzt Absichten/Pläne.* A person cannot be the obj. of either G. v. in the act. nor the subj. in the pass. As **frustrate** often occurs with a person as subj. in the pass., this E. construction needs to be rephrased. *She was frustrated in her efforts to bring about a reconciliation* becomes *Man/Jmd. vereitelte alle ihre Bemühungen, eine Versöhnung herbeizuführen.* An alternative is *Alle ihre Bemühungen waren vergebens*, in VAIN.

Die Gewerkschaften versuchten, die Politik der Regierung zu durchkreuzen.

Ungünstige Umstände haben seine Ambitionen vereitelt.

2. Applied to people when the area is not specified by *in*, **frustrate** means 'to induce a feeling of disappointment, dissatisfaction, or discouragement about the fact that one is, or one's expectations are, not being fulfilled'. *A group of discontented and frustrated young men who after returning from the war, found inadequate scope for their energies.* **Frustrieren** has become usual in this sense. **Der Frust**, 'the feeling or state of being frustrated', is a common colloquial word. *Wer für die Tätigkeit, die er ausübt, überqualifiziert ist, fühlt sich unterfordert—statt Berufsfreude kommt es zum Frust.*

Dieses Erlebnis war für sie frustrierend, weil es zeigte, daß ihrer Handlungsfreiheit enge Grenzen gesetzt waren.   Seine eintönige Arbeit frustrierte ihn.

Nachdem diese Gruppe von jungen Männern aus dem Krieg zurückgekehrt war, fühlten sie sich unzufrieden und frustriert, weil sie ihre Energien nicht hinreichend entfalten konnten.

3. If **frustrated** means 'fed up with', as in *He was frustrated by army routine*, there are other expressions. *Ihm reichte der Kommis bis hier* (with a gesture, *bis zum Hals*). *Etw. hängt mir zum Hals heraus.*

funny, amusing *adjs.* Like **funny**, komisch means both 'amusing' and 'strange'. The dominant sense is, however, 'strange', and if it is not clear from the context which is meant, komisch will be taken to mean 'strange'. *Der ist ein komischer Mensch—mit dem komme ich nicht klar. Der Film war aber komisch!*, means 'peculiar or strange'. In *Der Film war aber lustig!*, **lustig** means 'producing amusement', 'funny', and is unambiguous. *Er hat ein paar lustige Geschichten erzählt. Ein lustiges Erlebnis. Eine komische Geschichte/Situation* or *Das klingt komisch* will be understood as 'amusing' only when this is clear from the context. A syn. of komisch in both senses informal language is **ulkig**. *Jmd. ist ein ulkiger Nudel/Charakter*, strange. *Das hat sie sehr ulkig erzählt*, amusingly. *Eine ulkige Geschichte*. **Spaßig** has the one meaning 'amusing' and is applied to people and what they say. *Ein spaßiger alter Herr. Das hat sie spaßig erzählt. Er hat einen Vorrat an spaßigen Anekdoten. Spaßige Bemerkungen*. Applied to films etc. spaßig and lustig suggest a knockabout type of humour. **Spaßhaft** means '(meant) as a joke'. *Diese Bemerkungen waren spaßhaft gemeint, um die Diskussion aufzulockern*. **Belustigend** and **erheiternd** mean 'amusing', but belong to formal or written language. *Die Rede erhielt ein paar belustigende Bemerkungen*. **Witzig** means 'witty, amusing', but does not imply that what it describes has any great intellectual depth. *Eine witzige Antwort. Ein witziger Einfall. Witzige Bemerkungen*. **Geistreich**, applied for example to *eine Rede*, suggests that the author has not only a sparkling wit but also something of substance to say. *Einige geistreiche Bemerkungen. Eine geistreiche Person* has intellect and wit.

gather, collect, assemble, accumulate vs.

1. **Sammeln** expresses the basic meaning of **gather** and **collect**, 'to bring together into one place or group', and is used in several contexts.

i. 'To gather or collect thgs. which will be consumed or used'. *Man sammelt Pilze/Beeren* or *Brennholz/Reisig. Bienen sammeln Honig. Die Eichhörnchen sammeln Vorräte für den Winter. Lumpen und Altpapier werden regelmäßig gesammelt und wiederverwertet.*

ii. 'To collect as a hobby or pastime' or 'to make a collection' of stamps, rare books, paintings, etc. *Die Kinder sammeln Briefmarken/Münzen/Abzeichen/Steine/ Schmetterlinge. Der Bankier hat Gemälde/alte Bücher gesammelt.*

iii. 'To collect [donations]'. *Die Schüler sammelten [Spenden] für die Heilsarmee/für das Rote Kreuz.*

iv. 'To bring together' facts, information, material, and signatures and 'to gain' experience. *Der Journalist sammelte Fakten/Informationen/Material über die Lage der Reisbauern. Man sammelt Unterschriften zur Ächtung von Atomwaffen. Während er dort arbeitete, hat er reiche Erfahrungen in Verhandlungen mit Gewerkschaften gesammelt.*

v. With a personal obj., it is now used only in more formal language, e.g. in military contexts. *'Versuchen Sie, die fliehenden Truppen wieder zu sammeln!' befahl der General seinen Offizieren.* Cf. 4 for *versammeln*, now the usual word for people.

vi. Collect oneself and **collect one's thoughts** both imply making an effort to calm oneself. The second also suggests preparing oneself for or concentrating on something. *They were excited and needed time to collect themselves. I had only five minutes to collect my thoughts before the interview.* **Sich sammeln** and **sich fassen** mean 'to regain one's composure or inner balance'. *Sie waren aufgeregt und brauchten Zeit, um sich zu sammeln. Sie hatte sich nach dem Schreck schnell gefaßt.* **Sich sammeln** and **seine Gedanken sammeln** suggest regaining mental balance to deal with a person or thing. *Ich hatte nur fünf Minuten, um meine Gedanken zu sammeln, bevor das Vorstellunggespräch begann. Ich gab mir Mühe, mich zu dieser Aufgabe zu sammeln.*

2. The main difference between **collect** and *sammeln* is that *sammeln* can only be used when several things are brought together on different occasions and over a period of time, which is usually fairly long, but is occasionally short. *You can collect your passport at the beginning of next week* involves only one object and one occasion, and **collect** means 'to go/come and get'. Here **abholen** is used.

> *Ich hole meinen Paß Anfang nächster Woche ab.*
> *Ich muß meine Tochter vom Kindergarten abholen.*
> *Ich muß meinen Koffer vom Schließfach im Bahnhof abholen.*

3. Vs. related in meaning to *sammeln*.

i. **Zusammenpacken** means 'to gather up or together or pack up', with the connotation of leaving or finishing work. *Er packte seine Sachen/die Papiere/das Werkzeug zusammen und ging weg. Die Maurer packten zusammen und machten Feierabend.*

ii. **Zusammentragen** is 'to bring together or collect' either objects or facts, etc. *Im Museum trägt man Funde aus der Umgebung zusammen. Sie trägt Stoff/Fakten für einen Vortrag zusammen.*

iii. Zusammenkommen is applied to the result of a *Spendensammlung*, collection of donations. *Bei der Sammlung ist ziemlich viel Geld zusammengekommen*, a lot of money was collected.

4. i. Versammeln has people as obj., and when trans. means 'to call or bring together, gather, assemble'.
Der Direktor versammelte die Schüler der elften Klasse in der Aula.
Der Kranke versammelte seine Familie um sich.
Der Redner versammelte einen Kreis von Zuhörern um sich.

ii. The E. intr. use *Participants began to assemble/gather/collect* is expressed by **sich versammeln**, which is also used only of people. It implies coming together intentionally at a previously designated place for a particular purpose and is used when a formal meeting is involved. **Sich sammeln** is also used when a number of people come together intentionally for a particular, previously known purpose. Nowadays it is used in military and similar contexts, *Sammeln!* and *Sammelt euch!*, 'gather together, gather round me', being the normal commands. It is also used when people gather at a place for a time prior to going somewhere else. *Die Gäste sammelten sich in der Halle* suggests that they gathered there and waited before going to another place. *Sich versammeln* implies that they stay where they gather. Only *sich sammeln* is used for animals, *Auf allen Strommasten der Umgegend hatten sich Vögel in Scharen gesammelt, um gemeinsam gegen Süden zu ziehen*, and in optics, *Im Brennpunkt der Linse sammeln sich die Strahlen*. **Sich ansammeln** means that a crowd gathers, but without prior intention; something attracts their attention, and they come together to watch, as in *A crowd soon gathered/collected near the burning building*. *Viele Neugierige hatten sich an der Unfallstelle angesammelt. Viele Schaulustige sammelten sich an, um bei der Bekämpfung des Brandes zuzusehen.*
Viele Interessierte hatten sich versammelt, um den Vortrag zu hören.
Die Studenten versammelten sich vor dem Verwaltungsgebäude zu einer Kundgebung.
Die Besatzung des sinkenden Bootes hatte sich auf der Back versammelt/gesammelt.
Noch bevor die Kavallerie sich sammeln konnte, brach der feindliche Angriff los.
Die Teilnehmer an der Exkursion sammeln sich um acht Uhr vor der Schule und fahren mit Bussen nach Frankfurt.
Wir sammeln uns um neun Uhr vor dem Haupteingang des Museums und gehen dann hinein.

5. Vs. related in meaning to [*sich*] *versammeln*.
i. Zusammentreten means 'to convene' of parliaments or similar bodies. *Der neue Bundestag tritt Anfang Oktober zusammen. Der Ausschuß tritt morgen zu Beratungen zusammen.*
ii. Zusammenkommen means, like *sich versammeln*, 'to come together at a certain time for a purpose'. *Eine große Menschenmenge war auf dem Rathausplatz zusammengekommen, um den Kanzler zu hören.*

6. Aufsammeln means 'to collect' or 'gather up' at least a few things which are lying around. *Man sammelt Papier/Scherben/Büroklammern/Fallobst/Münzen/das Spielzeug, das zerstreut im Zimmer herumliegt, auf.*

7. Einsammeln has two main meanings.
i. One is 'to gather up or collect together again' what has already been together, but has become separated. *Kartoffeln, die aus einem Sack gefallen sind, sammelt man ein. Ich sammelte die heruntergefallenen Sachen wieder ein.*
ii. The other is 'to collect' in the sense of getting a group of people to hand over or hand in something of the same kind for a particular purpose. Thus *Der Lehrer sammelt die Hefte/die Klassenarbeiten ein. Er sammelt das Geld für den Ausflug ein. Der Reiseleiter sammelt die Pässe der Passagiere im Bus ein und bringt sie der Grenzkontrolle.*

8. Accumulate is trans., *I've accumulated a lot of stuff in just one year*, and intr., *A lot of old newspapers have accumulated in the study*.

i. Ansammeln is trans., meaning 'to accumulate, amass'. *Er hatte im Laufe seines Lebens viele Kunstwerke angesammelt.* In contrast to *sammeln* in sense 1. ii, it suggests a large number and a complete lack of discrimination.

ii. A syn. of *ansammeln* is **anhäufen**, to accumulate, pile up, amass. It is slightly pejorative. *Jmd. häuft Geld/Vorräte/Reichtümer an. Der Geizige häufte Geld an, der Hamsterer Lebensmittel.*

iii. With things as subj. **sich ansammeln** corresponds to the intr. vs. in *Water/Dust/Rubbish accumulates/collects/gathers. Viel Staub hat sich angesammelt.* When **accumulate** is trans. but does not suggest a real intention as in the first sent. in 8, it is best to use the refl. *Es hat sich bei mir viel Zeug in bloß einem Jahr angesammelt.* With *Staub* as subj., **sich absetzen**, 'to settle, to be deposited', is a syn. *Eine Menge Staub hat sich hier abgesetzt.*

> *Bei uns haben sich viele Zeitungen angesammelt, die wir der Altpapiersammlung geben wollen.*
> *Es regnet so oft, daß sich Wasser in jedem Loch ansammelt.*
> *Im Behälter sammelt sich Regenwasser an.*
> *Erst seit einer Woche streikte die Müllabfuhr, und niemand hatte damit gerechnet, daß sich in so kurzer Zeit ein so großer Berg Müll auf den Straßen ansammeln würde.*

iv. Sich häufen means 'to accumulate, pile up' in the sense 'to become more frequent or numerous'. It refers to events, to examples of a certain type of behaviour etc., or something intangible like evidence. *Die Fälle von Gewaltverbrechen häufen sich in letzter Zeit. Die Beweise für seine Unschuld/Die Beispiele der Schlamperei häufen sich.* **Sich anhäufen** refers to concrete objects which accumulate or pile up. *Rechnungen/Akten häufen sich auf meinem Schreibtisch an.*

v. For emotions, **sich aufstauen**, 'to build up, accumulate', is the usual v. *Wut hatte/Aggressionen hatten sich in ihnen aufgestaut.* **Sich ansammeln** sometimes has this sense. *Empörung hatte sich in ihm angesammelt.*

9. Gather = 'to conclude or deduce', as in *I gather from what you said that you agree with us.* **Entnehmen** or **schließen** are general terms for drawing a conclusion. The formal **ersehen** means 'to deduce sth. from what is seen or read'. *Ich ersehe aus dem Bericht, welche Schwierigkeiten Sie überwinden mußten.*

> *Seinen Bemerkungen haben wir entnommen, daß wir mit weiteren Aufträgen rechnen können.*
> *Aus dem, was sie sagten, schließe ich, daß sie mit dem Plan einverstanden sind.*
> *Aus dem Brief ersehe ich, daß sie demnächst hierher kommen will.*

German and other languages

1. In German is usually **auf deutsch**. *Wie heißt das auf deutsch? Er hält den Vortrag auf deutsch. Ich habe den Aufsatz auf deutsch geschrieben.* A variant is **deutsch** alone. *Der Roman wurde deutsch/auf deutsch geschrieben. Das kann man deutsch sagen. Sie haben sich deutsch unterhalten.* (This means that on a particular occasion G. was the medium of communication. This also applies to *Die Unterhändler haben deutsch gesprochen.* Cf. *Deutsch* in 2.) Another alternative is **in deutscher Sprache**. *Er hielt die Rede auf deutsch/in deutscher Sprache.* Another possibility is **in deutsch**. This is not a new expression, but has probably increased in use under E. influence and is best avoided by E. speakers. *Auf deutsch* is always correct. *Die Erklärung erschien in deutsch/auf deutsch/in deutscher Sprache.* The idiom *Auf [gut] deutsch gesagt, er will nichts davon wissen* means 'to put it plainly'. (For Latin there is an additional n. *Als mittelalterlicher Historiker muß man Quellen lesen, die in Latein/in lateinischer Sprache/auf lateinisch abgefaßt sind.*)

2. Deutsch, a neuter n. written with a capital letter, is 'the German language'. It is used with *können, sprechen, schreiben*, and *verstehen*, often with an adv. *Er kann [gut] Deutsch. Sie spricht [gut/fließend] Deutsch.* Both ns. in *Deutsch unterscheidet sich stark von Französisch* suggest the language as a whole. An alternative is **Das Deutsche** *unterscheidet sich stark vom Französischen.* The latter forms always refer to the language. Although *Deutsch, das Deutsche* are often both possible, the latter is always used in connection with translating. *Dieser Roman wurde von Ulrike Meyer aus dem Spanischen ins Deutsche übersetzt/übertragen.*

3. Deutsch is also used for the German of a person or of a group or period, like the E. expressions *Goethe's German, sixteenth-century German, his/her/their German.*
Goethes Deutsch unterscheidet sich vom heutigen Deutsch.
Das Deutsch dieser Studenten läßt zu wünschen übrig.
Jmd. spricht fehlerfreies/akzentfreies Deutsch.
Sie spricht ein gutes/gepflegtes/gewähltes Deutsch.
Sein Deutsch ist einwandfrei/sehr idiomatisch.

4. Deutsch with a capital letter also denotes German as a school or university subject. For the latter **die Germanistik** is an alternative. *Die Zahl der Germanistikstudenten ist gestiegen/zurückgegangen.*
Herr Maclean unterrichtet Deutsch an einer höheren Schule in Aberdeen.
In unserer Schule haben 200 Schüler Deutsch als Fach/lernen . . . Deutsch.

5. Zu deutsch is used when giving the meaning of a non-German word or phr. *'Discipulus', zu deutsch Schüler.* There is no comparable expression for other languages.

get, receive, obtain, fetch, procure *vs.* Order of treatment: 1–3 treat *bekommen*, its derivatives, and *kriegen*, 4 *hernehmen*, 5 *holen*, 6 **get** = 'to procure', 7 **get** = 'to reach a place', and 8 **get** = 'to become'. For **get** s.o. to do sth. and **get** sth. done cf. MAKE.

1. Bekommen, being derived from *kommen*, suggests receiving what comes to one in the natural course of events. It is thus the equivalent of **get, obtain**, and **receive** when they mean 'to come by sth. passively'. It is used for getting what one deserves, expects, or has striven for, and although it does not exclude some activity, it is not used in the imp. or when a special effort to obtain something for oneself or others is implied. *Ich kann das Buch für dich dort bekommen* suggests that it is there to be had. *Bekommen* is used in the following senses and contexts.
i. 'To receive'. *Was hast du zum Geburtstag bekommen? Jmd. bekommt ein Geschenk/einen Preis/eine Belohnung/Nachricht von jmdm./mehrere Briefe/eine Antwort/einen Kuß/die Erlaubnis, etw. zu tun/einen Besuch etc. Die Firma hat neue Aufträge bekommen.*
ii. 'To find or get, possibly as a result of one's endeavours'. *Jmd. hat Arbeit/eine Stelle bekommen.*
So wirst du keine Frau/keinen Mann bekommen.   Ich habe keinen Platz mehr bekommen.
iii. 'To get, obtain, or receive'. Some activity or purchase may be involved, but the idea is usually that something is there to be had or comes normally into a person's experience. *Wo haben Sie das Buch bekommen? Kann ich hier ein Zimmer bekommen? Ich habe das Auto billig bekommen. Ich bekomme 2 500 Mark im Monat netto. Du hast dein Motorrad verkauft—was hast du denn dafür bekommen?* Less tangible things can be the obj. *Man bekommt Erfahrung/Übung/die Oberhand/eine Vorstellung von etw./Macht oder Gewalt über andere. Jmd. bekommt seinen Willen. Ich habe einen ganz anderen Eindruck bekommen.* The obj. can be something unpleasant, including punishment. *Ich bekam einen elektrischen Schlag. Er hat einen Fußtritt/einen Stoß/einen Schlag auf den Kopf/eine Ohrfeige bekommen. Der Dieb bekam ein Jahr Gefängnis.*

Note: The perf. of **get** often replaces *have* in spoken E. People say *Have we got enough money?* instead of *Do we have* or *Have we enough money?* In G. only **haben** is possible here. *Haben wir genug Geld? Haben wir genug Geld bekommen?* means 'did we receive enough money?'

iv. The E. pass. with **get**, *They got arrested*, is usually translated by *werden*. *Sie wurden verhaftet. Bekommen* is used with a past part., but retains the idea of receiving something. *Ich habe die Schallplatte geschenkt bekommen*, I received/got it as a present. *Ich bekam es geliehen*, received it as a loan, or it was lent to me.

v. With preps. *Man bekommt etw. in seine Macht/in die Hände.*

Die Mutter bekam den Jungen nicht aus dem Bett.

Wir bekommen das Klavier nicht durch die Tür.

vi. With an infin. *Wir haben etw. zu essen und zu trinken bekommen. Bekommst du ihn jemals zu sehen? Ich habe etw. zu hören bekommen, was dich bestimmt interessieren wird.*

vii. With the weather. *Wir bekommen gutes/schlechtes Wetter/ein Gewitter.*

viii. Changes such as illness, different emotional states, changes in the body and in living things (E. sometimes uses *catch*). *Sie hat eine Erkältung/Kopfschmerzen bekommen. Das Baby bekommt Zähne. Ein Läufer bekam einen Krampf im Bein. Ich bekam Angst/Heimweh/einen Schreck/Hunger/Durst/Lust, wieder zu reisen.*

ix. With an adj. or phr., *bekommen* means 'to get' in the sense of being successful in achieving something. *Der Anwalt hat den Gefangenen frei bekommen. Ich muß den Aufsatz bis morgen fertig bekommen.*

Er hat das marode Unternehmen wieder auf die Beine bekommen.

2. Derivatives. **Abbekommen**, to get off. *Ich kann den Verschluß von der Flasche/den Schmutz von den Händen nicht abbekommen.* **Aufbekommen**, to get open. *Es dauerte einige Zeit, bis ich die Tür aufbekam.* **Herausbekommen**, to get sth. out. *Ich bekomme den Korken nicht heraus. Ich habe den Fleck aus dem Kleid herausbekommen. Aus ihm ist nichts herauszubekommen*, you can't get any information/secrets out of him. **Hereinbekommen**, to get sth. in. *Wir haben gestern neue Waren hereinbekommen.* **Wiederbekommen** or **zurückbekommen**, to get back. *Sie hat das Geld, das sie der Freundin geliehen hatte, nocht nicht wiederbekommen/zurückbekommen.*

3. Kriegen is the common colloquial equivalent of *bekommen* which has all its senses connected with getting, obtaining, or receiving. It is not at all formal and is best avoided in writing. Unlike *bekommen*, *kriegen* can mean 'to catch or arrest'. *Mich kriegst du nicht. Die Polizei wird den Dieb/den Verbrecher/den Flüchtigen bald kriegen.* The numbers i to ix follow the meanings of *bekommen* in 1. *Kriegen* is also used with the prefixes given in 2.

i. 'To receive'. *Sie hat 50 Mark Finderlohn gekriegt. Man kriegt Post/ein Geschenk/etw. zum Geburtstag/ein paar Tage Urlaub.*

ii. 'To find'. *Er hat die Arbeitskräfte, die er suchte, gekriegt. Ich habe Arbeit/noch einen Platz gekriegt.*

iii. 'To get, obtain, receive' including by purchase. *Sie kriegt fünfzehn Mark für die Stunde. Was hast du für dein Fahrrad gekriegt? Du kriegst noch zehn Mark von mir. Ich kriege mein Gehalt morgen. Sie hat eine schlechte Meinung von uns gekriegt.* Unpleasant things: *Er hat Prügel/eine Geldstrafe/einen Schlag/ein Jahr Gefängnis gekriegt.*

iv. With past parts. *Er kriegt nichts von mir geliehen. Ich kriege jeden Abend ein gutes Essen vorgesetzt.*

v. With preps. *Er hat diesen Brief versehentlich in die Finger gekriegt. Der Mittelstürmer kriegte den Ball nicht ins Tor.*

vi. With an infin. *Wann kriegen wir endlich was zu essen?*

vii. Weather. *Wir kriegen bald Regen/Schnee.*

viii. Changes. *Er kriegt graue Haare/Angst/Heimweh/Schnupfen. Der Baum kriegt Knospen. Die Hündin hat Junge gekriegt.*

ix. With adjs. etc. *Ich kriege die Arbeit heute nicht mehr fertig.*

4. Hernehmen is used only with *wo* and usually asks where someone is to/shall find/get sth./s.o. from. *Wo nehme ich denn das Geld her?* or *Wo soll ich denn das Geld hernehmen?*

Wir wissen nicht, wo wir die Fachkräfte hernehmen sollen.

5. i. Holen is 'to get' when it means 'to fetch' or 'to go and get' either people or things, and can include buying. *Ich hole jeden Morgen Brötchen vom Bäcker.* In this sense the refl. means 'for oneself'.

Der Junge holte seinen Bruder vom Spielplatz.   *Wir müssen den Arzt/die Polizei holen.*
Ich hole [mir] das Essen/etw. zu essen aus der Küche.
Hol mir bitte mal ein Glas Wasser!   *Das Kind holte dem Vater die Zeitung.*
Er holte die Schuhe aus dem Schrank/einen Apfel aus der Tasche (E. took).
Sie holt das Auto aus der Garage/das Fahrrad aus dem Keller.

ii. Sich holen is colloquial and has three senses.

a. 'To get' advice, help, permission, etc.
  Das Kind holte sich beim Lehrer Hilfe bei der Lösung der Rechenaufgabe.
  Du solltest dir eine Sondergenehmigung/Rat beim Fachmann holen.

b. 'To win or gain' a prize, victory, etc. at sport or in a competition. *Die Sportlerin holte sich den Sieg.*
  Sie hat sich den ersten Preis/eine Goldmedaille geholt.
  Du wirst dir nur eine Niederlage holen.

c. 'To get or catch' an infection or disease. *Ich habe mir einen Schnupfen/die Grippe geholt.*

iii. Einholen is a formal syn. of *sich holen* in sense *a*, 'to get' help, advice, permission, etc. *Jmd. holt die Erlaubnis/jmds. Rat/jmds. Zustimmung/ein Rechtsgutachten ein. Ich hole Auskunft bei jmdm. über eine Person oder eine Sache ein.*

6. Get or **obtain** = 'to procure or secure for oneself or others by effort'.

i. The everyday word is **besorgen**, which is used with a dat. and acc., or an acc. alone. It means that someone sees to it that he/she/someone else gets something which is needed. Very often it means 'to buy', but it can mean 'to obtain for a time' by other means, such as borrowing. The obj. is mostly something concrete. The dividing line between *bekommen* and *besorgen* is not always clear. *Ich habe die Zeitschrift hier bekommen* or *Man kann die Zeitschrift hier bekommen* suggests that it is on sale here. In the future *Ich werde mir morgen ein Exemplar besorgen*, *besorgen* is used because it implies that I shall go somewhere and procure a copy, whereas *Ich werde es dort bestimmt bekommen* is appropriate when someone is certain that a copy is available somewhere. However, with a dat. only *besorgen* is possible. *Ich werde dir/ihr ein Exemplar besorgen.*

Ich habe ihm ein Zimmer/eine Wohnung in einem ruhigen Stadtteil besorgt.
Können Sie uns die Eintrittskarten besorgen, wenn Sie in der Stadt sind?
Ich besorge Ihnen ein Taxi/die Getränke für die Fete/etw. zum Essen.

ii. Beschaffen also means 'to ensure that the subj. or another pers. gets what is needed'. It refers mostly to concrete things and suggests, with individuals as subj., overcoming more difficulties than *besorgen*. *Ich habe mir das Geld/die Genehmigung beschafft.* It is also used in formal contexts with a government, official, firm, etc. as subj. and is then translated as **procure** or *provide. Das Beschaffungsamt* is the division, e.g. of the *Bundeswehr*, which purchases supplies.

Es war schwierig, für alle Messegäste ein Quartier zu beschaffen.
Die Regierung sollte allen arbeitslosen Jugendlichen Arbeit/Arbeitsplätze beschaffen.

Kannst du mir bis morgen diese Summe beschaffen?
Diese Waren sind noch schwer zu beschaffen.

iii. Verschaffen suggests special tactics or manœuvres, use of personal influence, and often even dishonest methods to get something which is difficult to obtain. *Wer sich Zugang zu einer Sitzung verschafft*, would not normally be admitted and has to employ questionable means or tactics to gain admission. With abstracts, *Er hat sich Respekt verschafft*, or a non-personal subj., *Ihr Ausweis verschaffte ihr Zutritt zum Militärgelände*, it means 'to secure or gain' and implies only the overcoming of difficulties. *Es dauerte einige Zeit, bis er sich Gehör verschaffen konnte.*

Er versuchte dem Komplizen ein Alibi zu verschaffen.
Der Bürgermeister verschaffte seinem Neffen eine gute Stellung in der Stadtverwaltung.
Er hatte sich das Geld auf unrechtmäßige Weise verschafft.
Ich möchte mir Gewißheit über diese Sache verschaffen.

iv. Auftreiben means 'to get, find, or get hold of sth. which s.o. needs or would like to have and which is either hard to come by in general or difficult for s.o. to lay his/her hands on at the time'.

Es war für mich nicht leicht, diesen Betrag/das Geld für die Reise aufzutreiben.
In dem Dorf war um drei Uhr morgens kein Taxi aufzutreiben.
Wo können wir eine Kleinigkeit zu essen auftreiben?

7. Get = 'to move, go, or reach somewhere'. *How do you get to the station? They had to get across a river. When did they get to their destination?*

i. The general equivalent is **kommen**. *Können Sie mir bitte sagen, wie ich zum Bahnhof komme?* G. does not make the distinction between *come* and **get** made in E. *Sie kamen dicht an das Tier heran. Ans Ziel kommen* is 'to get to one's destination'.

Wie weit sind Sie am ersten Tag gekommen?
Das Haus war abgeschlossen, und wir kamen nicht hinein.
Wie kommen wir über den Fluß? Note: Der Fluß ist breit. Wie kommen wir hinüber?

ii. Geraten + a prep. means 'to get into a place or state by accident, without intention'.

Auf der Wanderung haben wir den Weg verfehlt und sind in ein ganz abgelegenes Dorf geraten.
Auf der Rückfahrt sind wir in einen Schneesturm geraten.
Die Straße war naß, und das Auto geriet in der Kurve ins Schleudern.
Sie sind in Schwierigkeiten/in schlechte Gesellschaft/in eine mißliche Lage geraten.
Als er diese Verleumdung hörte, geriet er in Wut.

iii. In *When does the train get to Bern?*, **get to** means 'to arrive' and is **ankommen**. *Wann kommt der Zug in Bern an? Wir sind um Mitternacht in Rom angekommen.*

iv. In *Where did we get to yesterday?*, **get to** means 'to stop reading or discussing a text, etc.' **Stehenbleiben** expresses this sense. *Wo sind wir stehengeblieben?*, where did we stop/get to? **Wie weit sind wir gekommen?** is also used. Possible answers are *Wir sind auf Seite 9 stehengeblieben* and *Wir sind bis zum Ende des zweiten Akts gekommen.*

v. A person wondering why someone has not arrived or turned up by a certain time asks, 'Where [on earth]/Wherever has he got to?' or 'What's keeping him?' or 'What's become of him?' **Bleiben** translates **get to** meaning 'to become of'. *Kurt hätte vor einer Stunde hier sein müssen—wo bleibt er nur?* or *Wo bleibt er bloß?* It is not confined to people. *Ich frage mich, wo das Geld geblieben ist.*

vi. In one sense **hinkommen** means 'to get to a place'. *Wie willst du hinkommen? Als ich hinkam, war er weg.* In combination with *wo*, it asks where something that cannot be found has got to or gone. *Wo ist mein Hut hingekommen? Wo kann bloß meine Uhr hingekommen sein? Ich weiß nicht, wo das Buch hingekommen ist.*

vii. Einsteigen and **aussteigen** mean 'to get into or out of' a bus, train, car, etc., but the prefixes are optional when the sent. contains a phr. with *in* or *aus*. *Bitte* *alle einsteigen!*, but *Ich bin in den falschen Zug [ein]gestiegen. Der Zug hielt, und alle stiegen aus*, but *Alle stiegen aus dem Zug [aus]*.

8. Get + adj. or past part. = 'to become'. *It got very cold. S.o. got rich.* When *become* is also possible, **werden** is used. *Es ist wieder kalt geworden. Mir wurde sehr kalt. Es wird hier schnell dunkel. Durch Überanstrengung wurde er krank. Er wurde sehr aufgeregt.* In some cases there is a specific v. such as **sich betrinken**, 'to get drunk', and **sich erholen**, 'to get well or recover'. For *to get used to sth.* cf. ACCUSTOM.

give, give away *vs.* Some equivalents.

1. Give = 'to hand or pass to s.o.' *The postman gave me the letters.*
i. Geben has this sense. It can imply handing someone something to keep to which he or she has a right or passing someone something to make [temporary] use of. *Der Briefträger gab mir die Briefe. Würden Sie mir bitte meinen Mantel geben?* What is given can be the due payment. *Ich habe dem Taxifahrer das Geld noch nicht gegeben.* It is not used for giving someone something as a present, for which *schenken* is necessary. Cf. 3. *Sie gab mir das Buch* would normally be understood as 'handed it over so that I can use it'. *Sie gab mir die Speisekarte/den Schlüssel/den Paß/das Wechselgeld. Man gibt jmdm. das Essen/etw. zu essen und zu trinken. Wir müssen dem Vieh Futter geben.*
ii. Syns. of *geben*. **Reichen** means 'to pass s.o. sth.' Being more formal, it sounds more polite in requests or commands than *geben*. *Würden Sie mir bitte die Speisekarte/die Butter reichen? Reich' mir [bitte] mal das Salz! Sie setzte sich und reichte dem Schaffner den Fahrschein.* Without a dat. **hergeben** means 'to give to the speaker'. *Gib her!*, give it to me, hand it over. *Gib sofort die Schere/das Messer her!* With a dat. it is a colloquial syn. of *reichen*. *Gib mir bitte mal den Bleistift her! Gib mir mal den Hörer her!* **Langen** is colloquial and suggests stretching out one's arm to give someone something. *Du stehst gerade auf der Trittleiter; lang' mir doch bitte das dritte Buch aus dem obersten Regal!* **Aushändigen** means 'to hand over to the pers. entitled to receive it sth. of importance or value to the recipient'. *Er händigte mir meinen Wochenlohn/meinen Paß/den Einschreibebrief/meine Papiere aus. Der Hausbesitzer händigte dem neuen Mieter den Wohnungsschlüssel aus.* **Übergeben** means 'to hand over to the proper recipient and thereby ensure that it is in his or her possession'. *Du mußt ihm den Brief persönlich übergeben. Der Bote übergab dem Offizier das Päckchen sofort nach dessen Ankunft. Sie hat mir die Schlüssel/die Post übergeben. Er übergab dem Gericht die Beweisstücke/die Akten.* **Überreichen** suggests handing over something in a ceremony in the presence of an audience. *Der König überreichte dem Preisträger die Urkunde. Die Preise wurde während der Feierstunde an die Sieger überreicht.*
2. The specific v. meaning 'to donate' is **spenden**. It is mostly used for giving to charities. *Sie spendete Geld/Kleidungsstücke für das Rote Kreuz.* In the first sent. below it can be translated as **give** or *donate* (generously). **Geben** is also used for giving to those in need and is less formal than *spenden*. *Spenden* is mostly used of a third person. People who have already donated say, *'Ich habe schon gegeben.' Geben* is the usual v. for giving to beggars, *Ich habe dem Bettler zwei Mark gegeben*, and takes *Almosen* (alms) as obj.

> *Der Bundespräsident rief die Bevölkerung auf, für die Hungernden in aller Welt großzügig zu spenden.*
> *Jeden Monat spendet sie Wohltätigkeitsorganisationen DM100.* Also *Sie gibt jeden Monat etw.*
> *Geben ist seliger als nehmen.*   *Viele Studenten spenden Blut.*
> *Ich gebe nichts/ein paar Mark für die Heilsarmee.*

3. i. Schenken is the usual v. for giving something as a present and naturally implies that the recipient should keep what is given. *Schenken* suggests the desire either to give pleasure to or to thank someone. It takes the thing given as obj. *Zum Geburtstag hat mir meine Schwester einen Pullover geschenkt.* When *das Geschenk* is the obj., the v. is **geben**. *Sie haben uns ein wertvolles Geschenk gegeben. Geben* is also used with the phr. *als Geschenk. Er hat mir die Uhr als Geschenk gegeben. Geben* is used with *das Trinkgeld. Wir haben dem Kellner ein Trinkgeld gegeben. Geben* is also found in everyday situations or when the meaning is clear. *Die Mutter gab den Kindern Bonbons/Geld, um Eis zu kaufen. Sie gab den Kindern je eine Tafel Schokolade. Er gab der Gastgeberin einen Blumenstrauß.* (*Geben* could in the last three sents. also be understood as having meaning 1.) *Schenken* is needed to avoid ambiguity. When *I'll give it to you* means 'give to keep', it becomes *Ich schenke es Ihnen/Dir* and cannot be misinterpreted.

> *Dem jungen Mann, der das Mädchen vorm Ertrinken gerettet hatte, schenkt der Vater seine Armbanduhr.*
> *Er hat seiner Frau zum Geburtstag/zu Weihnachten Schmuck geschenkt.*
> *Die Großeltern schenkten dem Jungen ein Fahrrad. Er bekam das Fahrrad geschenkt.*

ii. Verschenken has two meanings, 'to give as a present' and 'to give away'. In the first it is a syn. of *schenken*. While *schenken* is required with a dat., either *schenken* or *verschenken* can be used when there is only an acc.

> A. *Was willst du deinen Nichten und Neffen zu Weihnachten schenken?*
> B. *Ich habe so oft Bücher geschenkt/verschenkt, daß ich mir was Neues einfallen lassen muß.* But *Ich habe ihnen so oft Bücher geschenkt.*

A not very common alternative to *schenken* + dat. is *verschenken an. An jede Dame verschenkte er Rosen* is possible instead of the normal *Jeder Dame schenkte er Rosen.*

4. i. In the sense 'to give away', **verschenken** retains the idea of making a present and means 'to give away out of kindness or generosity'. If A notices that some of B's books are not where they used to be and asks where they are, B could answer, '*Ich habe sie verschenkt*', given them away or given them to someone unspecified. With a dat.: *Ich habe sie Freunden geschenkt.* Thus *Das ist verschenkt* or *Das schenke ich Ihnen—ich nehme nichts dafür.*

ii. Verschenken is also used to indicate that a good chance or opportunity has been allowed to pass by without being taken advantage of. *Ein Spieler/Eine Mannschaft hat den Sieg verschenkt. Er hatte die Möglichkeit, eine sichere Ausbildungsplatz zu bekommen, verschenkt* (also *vergeben*).

iii. Weggeben means 'to give away what one no longer wants to keep'. *Diese Kleider/Den Kinderwagen/Das Schaukelpferd können wir weggeben.* **Hergeben** also means 'to give away', but, unlike *weggeben*, suggests that the thing given is of value or use and parting with it involves a sacrifice. *Er würde sein letztes Hemd für Notleidende hergeben.* Particularly in the neg. *Das Buch gebe ich ungern her*, it can be translated as *part with*. In the refl. or with *Namen* as obj., *hergeben* means 'to lend oneself to or put one's name in the service of sth. bad' and is mostly neg. *Zu Spitzeldiensten gebe ich mich nicht her.*

> *Die Bücher, die wir nicht mehr brauchen, habe ich weggegeben.*
> *Sie möchten alles behalten und nichts hergeben.*
> *Sie gab ihre Ersparnisse her, um der armen Familie zu helfen.*
> *Für dieses fragwürdige Unternehmen gab er seinen Namen nicht her.*

5. Geben can mean 'to pay'. *Was hat er dir dafür gegeben? Ich habe zwölf Mark für die Blumen gegeben.* It also means 'to give up or sacrifice'. *Ich gäbe viel darum, wenn ich dabei sein könnte.*

6. Schenken is used with the abstracts *Aufmerksamkeit, Beachtung, Glauben, Liebe, Vertrauen,* and *Gehör* as obj. *Sie schenkten uns ihre volle Aufmerksamkeit. Man hat diesen*

Einwänden keine Beachtung geschenkt. Man schenkte dieser Meldung keinen Glauben/keine Beachtung. Ich schenkte ihr [mein] volles Vertrauen.

7. i. Give one's life to sth. = 'to devote'. The normal equivalent is **widmen**, to devote. *Sie beschloß, ihr Leben ganz der Sache des Friedens/der Kunst zu widmen*, to give her life to the cause of peace/art. **Sich widmen** means 'to devote oneself to'. *Sie widmete sich der Musik/der Familie. Ich brach das Studium ab, um mich anderen Plänen zu widmen.*

ii. Sich hingeben is a syn. when used with an activity. *Sie gab sich der Arbeit/der Aufgabe hin.* It also means 'to give oneself up to desirable and undesirable states of mind'. *Er gab sich dem Genuß/dem Wahn/Illusionen hin.* With an obj. like *Leben, hingeben* means 'to give oneself up to desirable and undesirable states of mind'. *Er gab sich dem Genuß/dem Wahn/Illusionen hin.* With an obj. like *Leben, hingeben* means 'to SACRIFICE'.

8. Give one's name/address, etc. With a dat. **geben** is used. *Geben Sie mir bitte Ihre Telefonnummer!* Without a dat. **angeben**, which can also be translated as *state*, is necessary. This is the normal v. in forms or in official language and usually implies in writing. *Man muß nicht nur die Semesteradresse angeben, sondern auch die Heimatanschrift.* **Nennen** often means 'to say, give, or state' a name, number, price, reason, example, etc. *Nennen Sie Namen, Adresse, Geburtsort! Können Sie andere Beispiele nennen?*

Lassen Sie sich von Helmut unsere Adresse und Telefonnummer geben!
Alle Teilnehmer werden gebeten, ihre Adressen und Telefonnummern im Sekretariat anzugeben.
Sie müssen Ihr Alter/Ihren Geburtsort angeben.   *Einen anderen Grund hat er nicht genannt.*

9. Give s.o. pleasure/trouble, etc. The everyday word is **machen**; **bereiten** is more formal. *Etw. macht jmdm. Freude/Kummer/großen Ärger/Vergnügen/Sorgen.* Cf. CAUSE v. i.
Die Durchführung dieser schwierigen Aufgabe hat mir beträchtliche Schwierigkeiten bereitet/gemacht.
Ihr Erfolg hat den Eltern große Freude bereitet.

glad, pleased, happy, cheerful, joyful *adjs.*

1. i. The usual way of saying *I am* **pleased/glad/happy** *about s.o./sth.* or *to see s.o./do sth.*, etc. is to use **sich freuen**. *Ich freue mich über ihren Erfolg. Ich freue mich, Sie wiederzusehen.* Freuen is now used only in the refl. or impersonally with *es* or *das* as subj. The impersonal *es/das freut mich* means the same as *ich freue mich*, but is more detached and less emotional. *Ich freue mich/Es freut mich, das zu hören.* Sich freuen an means 'to get pleasure from'. *Er freut sich an den Blumen.* Sich freuen auf is 'to look forward to'. *Wir freuen uns auf die Ferien.*
Der Lehrer freut sich über die Fortschritte der Schüler.
Es wird uns freuen, Ihre Aufträge zu erhalten.

ii. Please s.o. with a subj. other than *es* and *das* is expressed by **erfreuen**, and it alone forms a pass. *Das Geschenk hat uns sehr erfreut. Die Eltern waren sehr erfreut über die guten Zensuren des Kindes.* The sense is, however, frequently expressed by **sich freuen**. *Wir haben uns über das Geschenk sehr gefreut. Die Eltern haben sich über die guten Zensuren des Kindes sehr gefreut.*

iii. Froh sein [über etw.] expresses pleasure which is often, but not always, mixed with relief that things have turned out well. In the future, it is a prediction that someone will be relieved when something is over or has gone off well.
Ich bin ja so froh, daß alles geklappt hat/daß nichts schief gegangen ist.
Ich werde froh sein, wenn endlich alles vorbei ist.
Ich bin froh, daß ich gekommen bin. Es war ein interessanter Abend.

2. In *die Frohe Botschaft*, the glad tidings, gospel, **froh** means 'bringing joy', but is, like its E. equivalent, a survival of an older usage. This is true too of set expressions like *frohe* (or *fröhliche*) *Weihnachten/Ostern, Frohes Neues Jahr*. Referring to people (except in the construction given in 1. iii) *froh* means 'happy and contented' and is a less strong syn. of *glücklich*, though not very common. *Er|Sie ist ein froher Mensch*. It is also applied to what shows happiness. *Ein frohes Gemüt. Ein frohes Gesicht. Fröhlich* (cf. 3. iii) is probably more usual. *Froh* occurs in compounds. *Die Frohnatur*, cheerful, happy nature; *der Frohsinn*, cheerfulness; *frohgestimmt*, in a cheerful mood.

> *Ich habe das Gefühl, nie wieder froh werden zu können nach all den schrecklichen Ereignissen.*

3. i. *Das Glück* means either 'happiness' or 'good fortune, luck'. **Glücklich** means 'happy' or 'lucky, fortunate'. *Eine glückliche Familie. Der glückliche Gewinner.* Although *Ich bin über diese Entscheidung sehr glücklich* is possible, *Ich freue mich darüber* would be more usual, *glücklich* being reserved for states of happiness which last for some time. It is applied directly to people, *Die beiden waren sehr glücklich*, to things connected with people, *eine glückliche Stimmung, eine glückliche Natur, eine glückliche Ehe*, to periods of time in which people experience happiness, *ein glückliches Leben, eine glückliche Kindheit, glückliche Tage/Zeiten*, and to something which creates happiness, *ein glückliches Ereignis*.

ii. In one sense **heiter** means 'cheerful' and suggests inner balance and a pos. attitude to life and events. It is applied to people and to things connected with people which express the state it designates. *Ein heiteres Gesicht. Der heitere Ton seiner Worte. Heitere Gespräche*. It is a somewhat elevated term which was formerly more used than now. (Besides 'cheerfulness', *die Heiterkeit* means 'hilarity, laughter'.)

> *Sie ist immer froh und heiter/hat ein heiteres Wesen/Gemüt.*

iii. **Fröhlich** suggests a cheerful, calm, and untroubled nature, good spirits, and a pos. attitude to things and other people. It is applied directly to people, *ein fröhlicher Mensch, eine fröhliche Gesellschaft*, to what shows this frame of mind, *eine fröhliche Stimmung, ein fröhliches Gesicht, eine fröhliche Atmosphäre, fröhliches Gelächter*, and to time, *fröhliche Ferientage*.

iv. Applied to people, **lustig** suggests high spirits, much laughter, jokes, fairly noisy and unrestrained merriment which borders on *ausgelassen*, boisterous, exuberant. *Ein lustiger Mensch* laughs a lot, likewise *eine lustige Gesellschaft. Bei euch geht es immer lustig zu.*

v. **Freudig** means 'full of joy'. It is applied to people only indirectly, i.e. to what they do and feel, how they look, and as an adv. *Mit freudigem Gesicht. Freudig erregt/überrascht. In dem freudigen Bewußtsein erfüllter Pflicht. Man hörte freudige Zurufe. Der Hund begrüßte den Jungen mit freudigem Gebell*. It also means 'bringing or giving joy'. *Ein freudiges Erlebnis. Eine freudige Begegnung. Ein freudiges Ereignis.*

go *v*. Some uses.

1. Gehen means 'to go on foot' and may need to be translated as *walk*. Cf. RUN 1. ii.

> *Sie ging die Straße hinauf/hinunter*. Colloquially *rauf/runter*.
> *Wir sind den gleichen Weg gegangen.*
> *Sie ging an meiner Seite/auf Zehenspitzen/über die Straße etc.*
> *Wenn ich nicht mitfahren kann, dann geh' ich.*   *Wir sind drei Kilometer gegangen.*

2. Fahren means 'to move by means of a propelling force'.

i. A vehicle or means of conveyance can be the subj. *Der Zug/Das Auto/Der Lastwagen/Die Straßenbahn/Das Schiff/Das Boot/Der Aufzug fährt irgendwohin.* The propelling force can be a horse. *Die Kutsche/Der Schlitten fuhr langsam den Hügel hinauf.*

> *Heute fahren viele Autos auf der Autobahn nach Süden.*
> *Nur wenig Passagierschiffe fahren heutzutage von Australien nach Europa.*
> *Der Aufzug fährt schnell ins dreißigste Stockwerk.*

ii. Fahren is used with people as subj., the means of conveyance being expressed by a *mit*-phr. *Wir fahren mit dem Zug nach Frankfurt*. *Mit dem Auto fahren* is often translated as *to drive*. *Fahren* is used in connection with *ein Fahrrad*. *Ich bin gestern mit dem [Fahr]rad um den Bodensee gefahren*.

> *Ich fahre immer mit der Straßenbahn/dem Bus zur Arbeit.*
> *Wir fahren morgen nach Italien/nach Wien/in/auf Urlaub.*
> *Wir fuhren den ganzen Morgen mit dem Boot stromaufwärts.*
> *In zehn Minuten fahren wir zur Universität/über die Grenze.*
> *Wie lange fährt man nach Bremen?* (How long does it take to go/get/drive there?)

iii. Specific vs. are often preferred. **Fliegen** is used for travelling by plane. *Er fliegt nach Boston*. Other specific terms: a person on a horse, **reiten**; in a rowing boat, **rudern**; a sailing boat, **segeln**; a canoe, **paddeln**.

3. i. For **go** somewhere, both *fahren* and *gehen* occur. When someone walks, only **gehen** is possible. *Wir gehen baden/einkaufen/spielen. Ich gehe ins Kino/zu meinem Freund/ins Büro/in die/zur Kirche.* In some of these cases, the person might go by car or another vehicle, and **fahren** would be the usual v. *Ich fahre einkaufen/zu Wolfgang/ins Büro.* However, *gehen* occurs when *fahren* might be expected. When the purpose of going somewhere is the main issue, *gehen* can be used irrespective of how the person gets there, but when the means of transport is uppermost in the speaker's mind, *fahren* is usual. *Heute nachmittag gehen wir einkaufen/in die Stadt. Ich fahre meistens zur Uni. Ich gehe jetzt zur Uni.*

ii. Gehen is also used if someone is going to settle somewhere or stay there for a long time. *Ich fahre morgen nach Newcastle* suggests a temporary visit, while *Ich habe beschlossen, nach Newcastle zu gehen,* is understood as a permanent move. For regular attendance, *gehen* is normal. *Sabine geht schon zur Schule. Sie fährt zur Schule* states the means of getting there. *Sie gehen jeden Sonntag in die Kirche.*

iii. With modal vs. *gehen* and *fahren* are often omitted. *Hier können Sie nicht weiter.*

> *Ich muß morgen in die Stadt/nach Canberra.*

iv. Hingehen, hinfahren. With a phr. showing where someone is going, *gehen/fahren* are used without *hin*. *Ich gehe zur Vorlesung.* However, when there is no such phr., where E. uses **go** alone, it is necessary to add *hin*. *Are you going?* (i.e. *to sth./somewhere*) is *Gehst du hin? (Gehst du?* would be understood as **go** = 'leave'.) Similarly, *Wir fahren morgen hin.* In a question, *hin* can be attached to *wo* or to the v.: *Wohin gehst du denn?* or *Wo gehst du denn hin?*, where are you going [to]?

4. Go [away] or *leave*.

i. Of people. If the meaning is clear, **gehen** alone is enough, but **weg** can be added. *Wir müssen jetzt gehen. Ich gehe in einer halben Stunde. Meine Frau bleibt, aber ich gehe. Sie geht immer um fünf Uhr weg.* In the past and perf. it is usual to add *weg*. *Er ging mit seiner Frau vor zehn Minuten weg. Er ist gerade weggegangen.* To state that someone has gone, *weg* is used with *sein*. *Es tut mir leid, aber Herr Bastert ist schon weg.*

ii. Of trains, buses, etc. **Gehen** and **fahren** can be used to state when trains, buses, etc. go or leave, except in the perf. **Abfahren** is the more precise term which can always be used, but is needed in the perf. Cf. LEAVE. *Wann geht der nächste Zug? Wann fährt der nächste Bus? Der Bus geht in fünf Minuten,* but *Der Bus ist gerade abgefahren,* has just gone/left. *Wann geht/fährt die letzte Straßenbahn?*

grant, allow, permit, approve [of] *vs.*

1. Both **grant** and **allow** still mean 'to admit, acknowledge, or concede'. *I grant that I was wrong. I grant that there is some merit in their claim. You must allow that he has some expertise in that field.* Equivalents of *admit* (cf. CONFESS) translate the vs. in these sents., the main one being **zugeben**. *Ich gebe zu, daß ich mich geirrt habe. Ich gebe zu, daß ihr Anspruch etw. für sich hat. Ich gebe zu, daß er Fachkenntnisse und Erfahrung auf diesem Gebiet besitzt.*

2. Allow and permit.

i. The usual equivalent of these vs. in the sense 'not to forbid' or 'to agree that s.o. might do sth.' is **erlauben**. **Gestatten** is more formal. They also translate *to grant permission to do sth.* The subj. is mostly a person, *Der Arzt erlaubte dem Patienten aufzustehen*, but can be a thing as in *Meine Zeit erlaubt es mir nicht hinzugehen*. They take an infin. or *daß*-clause, often preceded by *es*. *Die Eltern erlaubten es den Kindern nicht, allein zum Strand zu gehen. Erlauben/Gestatten Sie, daß ich rauche?* An obj. is also possible. *Das gestattet andere Schlüsse als den, den Sie gezogen haben.* To state that something is not allowed, *verboten* is common, but *nicht erlaubt/gestattet* also occur. *No smoking allowed* is *Rauchen verboten/nicht gestattet.* **Be allowed** to do sth. is mostly expressed by **dürfen**. *Darf man hier halten?*

> *Erlauben Sie mir, Ihnen eine Tasse Tee zu geben?*   *Das ist eine erlaubte Handlungsweise.*
> *Meine Stellung im Betrieb erlaubt es mir, die Mittagspause ein wenig auszudehnen.*
> *Wenn es das Wetter erlaubt, fahren wir morgen in die Berge.*
> *Es ist verboten/nicht erlaubt, die Tiere zu füttern. Or Man darf die Tiere nicht füttern.*

ii. *Erlauben* and *gestatten* refer to permission given to people. When **allow/permit** mean that one thing lets something happen, the idea is best rephrased. *The pipe is there to allow the heated air to escape* could be *Das Rohr ist da, damit die erwärmte Luft entweichen kann. Sie hielten an der Straßenseite an, damit das andere Auto vorbeifahren könnte*, to allow it to pass.

iii. Sich erlauben means 'to permit or allow oneself' luxuries etc. or behaviour that may be out of the ordinary or seem strange. *Den Scherz, den er sich erlaubte, empfand sie als ungehörig. Was erlauben Sie sich [denn]?* is a protest against behaviour or remarks felt to be offensive or inappropriate. *Sich erlauben* also translates *to take the liberty (to do sth.)* and can be used as a polite formula. *Ich erlaube mir, Sie darauf aufmerksam zu machen, daß die Zeit drängt.* It can mean 'to afford to buy'. *Wir können uns nun ein größeres Auto erlauben.* **Sich gestatten** has the same senses, but is less common. *Ich gestatte mir dieses Vergnügen. Ich gestatte mir ein paar Bemerkungen.*

> *Er hatte sich allerlei Frechheiten/Übergriffe erlaubt.*
> *Sie kann sich diesen Luxus erlauben/gestatten.*   *Ich erlaube mir, Sie morgen zu besuchen.*
> *Du kannst es dir nicht erlauben, zu spät zur Arbeit zu kommen.*

iv. Ermöglichen, 'to make possible', is close in sense to *erlauben* when the subj. refers to external factors.

> *Ich gehe hin, sobald es mir meine Verpflichtungen ermöglichen.*
> *Dieses Geld ermöglichte es ihr, weiter zu studieren.*

v. Zulassen means 'to allow sth. to happen' rather than 'to give permission'. The idea is to tolerate without protest something that someone else would like to do or proposes to do, or not to do anything to prevent something which one views with disfavour. *Warum lassen Sie das zu?* suggests that the person addressed disapproves, or could be expected to do so, but does not intervene to stop it. It is used only with an obj. or *daß*-clause. It is often neg. as in the examples below, but can be pos., particularly in questions. *Wie konnte man zulassen, daß dieser Amtsmißbrauch monatelang getrieben wurde?*

> *Dieses Unrecht darf man unter keinen Umständen zulassen.*
> *Man hätte es nicht zulassen sollen, daß solche Zustände sich entwickelten.*
> *Sie ließ es nicht zu, daß er das Essen bezahlte.*
> *Diese Worte lassen keinen anderen Schluß zu.*
> *Diese Bestimmung gilt für alle. Ausnahmen werden nicht zugelassen.*

Ihr Stolz ließ es nicht zu, daß sie ihn um Hilfe bat.
Die nasse Fahrbahn läßt kein höheres Tempo zu.

Zulassen also means 'to give official permission for s.o. to do sth.' *Jmd. wird als Arzt zugelassen*, permitted to practise. *Ein Student wird zur Prüfung zugelassen*, permitted to sit for it. *Neue Medikamente werden erst nach der Erprobung zugelassen. Dieser Film ist für Jugendliche [nicht] zugelassen.*

3. Grant or approve.

i. Bewilligen is 'to give approval to' a request, mostly in the form of an application. It is thus the general term for granting someone something or approving something. It is used with acc. and dat. Cf. *einwilligen* under AGREE 2. ii.

Die Verlängerung der Aufenthaltsgenehmigung wurde von der Behörde anstandslos bewilligt.
Das Ministerium/Der Landtag hat eine Million Mark zum Bau einer neuen Brücke bewilligt.
Die Firmenleitung bewilligte den Antrag des Abteilungschefs, zwei neue Mitarbeiter anstellen zu dürfen.
Das Gremium hat zehn Studenten Stipendien bewilligt.
Die bewilligte Gehaltserhöhung für alle Lehrer tritt am 1. Januar in Kraft.

ii. Gewähren also means 'to grant' a request, wish, application, etc., but it stresses the superior position of the person giving approval and suggests that he/she acts voluntarily and often out of generosity. High-standing personages can be the subj., *Der Papst/Der König gewährte jmdm. eine Audienz/eine Unterredung,* and the state or someone in authority representing it, *Der Nachbarstaat gewährte den Flüchtlingen Asyl/Zuflucht/Schutz* or *Der Minister gewährte den von der Dürre betroffenen Landwirten großzügige, finanzielle Unterstützung.* It is also used for the granting of loans and credit by banks etc. *Nachdem der Kreditdirektor die laufenden Eingänge des Kunden geprüft hatte, gewährte er ihm weiteren Kredit.*

iii. Genehmigen means 'to approve' or 'to give official approval for'. The obj. is either the thing applied for, *Die Baubehörde hat den Umbau des Hauses genehmigt,* or the application, *Die Behörde hat den Antrag auf Umbau des Hauses genehmigt.*

Man hat der Familie den Aufenthalt in der Bundesrepublik genehmigt.
Das Protokoll der letzten Sitzung muß zuerst genehmigt werden.

iv. Stattgeben is a bureaucratic term meaning 'to approve or grant' an application or request. The thing approved is in the dat. *Das Ministerium gab seinem Antrag statt. Dem Gnadengesuch wurde stattgegeben.*

Das Gericht gab der Klage statt (found in favour of the plaintiff, granted the plaintiff's petition).

v. In everyday situations, **erfüllen**, 'to fulfil', is used for granting wishes or requests. *Er erfüllte ihr jeden Wunsch. Der Lehrer war nicht bereit, die Bitte des Schülers um Befreiung von Sport zu erfüllen.* Cf. FILL 4.

vi. Billigen is used for approval given by parliaments etc. *Das Parlament hat die Steuererhöhung gebilligt.* The usual v. for passing or approving a parliamentary bill is **verabschieden**. *Der Bundestag hat die Gesetzesvorlage verabschiedet. Der Senat verabschiedete die Gesetzesänderung mit knapper Mehrheit.*

4. Approve of means 'to have or express a favourable opinion of'.

i. The normal word is **gutheißen**, which states a personal reaction.

Er konnte diese zweifelhafte Sache/die skrupellosen Methoden niemals gutheißen.
Man heißt eine Entscheidung/einen Plan/eine Neuerung/eine Reform usw. gut.

ii. Billigen also has people's actions and plans and the principles underlying them as obj., but it is stylistically higher than *gutheißen* and presumes a certain competence, or a feeling of competence, based on a consciousness of responsibility for others.

Man billigt jmds. Entschluß/jmds. Vorhaben/jmds. Haltung/einen Plan etc.
Die Politik der Regierung billige ich [ganz und gar nicht].

Ich kann es nicht billigen, daß du dich an einer solchen Demonstration beteiligst.

iii. Bejahen means 'to find sth. in conformity with one's basic views'. It is only used in the pos., and often in more philosophical contexts. *Sie bejaht diese Gesellschaftsform/diese Weltanschauung.*

5. Allow = 'to allot, allocate'.

i. *They* **allowed** *each child $1 a week [for] pocket money.* The simplest way to translate this is to use **geben**. *Sie gaben jedem Kind einen Dollar Taschengeld pro Woche.* A more formal term with the same sense is **zuwenden**. *Während des Studiums haben die Eltern allen drei Kindern 800 Mark im Monat zugewendet.*

ii. Allow so much time, material, etc. **for** s.o./sth. **Rechnen** in the sense 'to estimate' expresses this meaning. Cf. CALCULATE 2. ii. *Für den Rückweg müssen wir vier Stunden rechnen.*

> *Für die Fahrt durch die Stadt rechne ich immer eine Dreiviertelstunde.*
> *Wir rechnen pro Person eine halbe Flasche Wein oder Saft.*

6. i. Allow for means 'to include a factor, cost, etc. in one's calculations', a sense carried by **einkalkulieren**. *Haben Sie die Transportkosten/die Verpackungskosten schon einkalkuliert?*

ii. Allow for also means 'to bear in mind and to make allowances for as a modifying or extenuating circumstance'. *You must allow for* (or *make allowances for*) *the changed circumstances.* The main equivalents are **berücksichtigen** and **in Betracht ziehen**, to CONSIDER. **Rechnung tragen** + dat. is a syn., and **einkalkulieren** is also used. *Man muß seine Jugend/die veränderten Verhältnisse berücksichtigen/in Betracht ziehen. Der veränderten Lage muß man Rechnung tragen. Sie müssen das Risiko/die anderen Umstände einkalkulieren.*

greet, salute, welcome *vs.*

i. Grüßen means 'to show a friendly sign of recognition when encountering or seeing another pers. unexpectedly'. The sign may be a gesture with the hand, nodding the head, smiling, etc. and may or may not be accompanied by words. In the armed forces, *grüßen* means 'to salute'. In contexts in which misunderstanding might arise, *militärisch* can be added or **salutieren** used. *Als er dem Major außerhalb der Kaserne begegnete, grüßte er ihn militärisch/salutierte er ihn. Grüßen* also means 'to pass on or convey s.o.'s greetings or regards to a third pers.' *Grüßen Sie Ihre Eltern von mir!* An alternative is *Bestellen Sie ihnen einen Gruß von mir!* The person passing on such greetings says, *'Jutta läßt euch grüßen'* or *'Ich soll euch von Jutta grüßen.'*

> *Er grüßte mich mit einem Nicken/einem Lächeln, als wir uns gestern auf der Straße begegneten.*
> *Als sie sich in der Bibliothek sahen, grüßte der Student den Professor.*
> *Wir kennen uns zwar nicht näher, aber wir grüßen uns immer.*

ii. Begrüßen means 'to greet or welcome' guests at one's house or official visitors to a country, city, firm, etc. or participants in some function etc. Hence sents. like *Der Bürgermeister begrüßte die Teilnehmer, Die offizielle Begrüßung fand im Rathaus statt,* and compounds like *die Begrüßungsansprache* or *-rede.* An alternative to *Ich begrüße Sie* is *Ich* **heiße** *Sie* **willkommen**. *Begrüßen* is also used when a crowd greets players, stars, etc. Animals can be the subj., and natural phenomena such as seasons the obj.

> *Die Gastgeber standen in der Tür und begrüßten die ankommenden Gäste.*
> *Er begrüßte die Teilnehmer mit einem Handschlag.*
> *Die Spieler wurden mit lautem Beifall begrüßt.*
> *In einer kurzen Ansprache begrüßte der Präsident des Vereins alle Teilnehmer an der Tagung.*
> *Als sie in den Flur trat, wurde sie von dem Hund ihrer Freundin begrüßt.*
> *Die Kinder begrüßten den ersten Schnee mit lautem Freudengeschrei.*

iii. Begrüßen also means 'to welcome' news, suggestions, decisions, actions, etc. *Alle haben diesen Vorschlag begrüßt.* Unlike **greet**, it denotes a favourable response only. If an unfavourable response is meant, as in *The news was greeted with dismay*, it could be translated as *Die Nachricht wurde mit Bestürzung aufgenommen* or *Man reagierte mit Bestürzung auf die Nachricht*. (For *aufnehmen*, 'to take news well/badly', cf. TAKE 5. ii. *c* and for *reagieren* ANSWER 7. iii.)

> *Alle begrüßten seinen Entschluß, weiter zu studieren.*
> *Wir begrüßen es sehr, daß eine Fremdsprache jetzt zu den Pflichtfächern gehört.*
> *Wir würden es begrüßen, wenn zukünftig alle solche Aufträge in 48 Stunden ausgeführt werden könnten.*

ground, land, soil, earth *ns.*

1. The planet **Earth** is **die Erde**.
> *Die Erde ist der der Sonne drittnächste Planet und liegt zwischen Venus und Mars.*

2. Land = 'the solid part of the earth's surface as contrasted with sea, water, and air'. **Ground** and **earth** also express this idea. *I was glad to feel the earth/firm ground/land under my feet after the rough voyage.* The usual word is **das Land**; **der Boden** and **die Erde** also occur in certain cases. *Ground forces are Bodenstreitkräfte.*
> *Lurche leben sowohl im Wasser als auch auf dem Land.*
> *Ganz in der Ferne wurde das Land sichtbar.*
> *Einige Wrackteile wurden an Land geschwemmt.*   *Die Passagiere gingen an Land.*
> *Nach der stürmischen Fahrt mit dem kleinen Schiff waren alle froh, wieder [festen] Boden/festes Land unter den Füßen zu haben.*   *Die Erde bebte.*
> *Der Boden schwankte unter unseren Füßen.*
> *Vor Scham wäre ich am liebsten in die Erde versunken. Also . . . in den Boden versunken.*

3. Ground = 'surface of the earth'. *The window is sixty feet above the ground. The apple fell to the ground.* Both **der Boden** and **die Erde** have this sense. *Das Fenster ist ungefähr zwanzig Meter über dem Boden. Etw./Jmd. fällt auf die Erde/zur Erde/auf den Boden/zu Boden. Man hebt etw. vom Boden/von der Erde auf. Er liegt auf dem Boden/auf der kalten, nassen Erde. Wasser quillt aus dem Boden. Mehrere Flugzeuge wurden gleich nach Ausbruch des Krieges am Boden zerstört.* **Der Erdboden** means 'the ground under our feet', but it occurs mostly in fixed expressions. *Die Stadt wurde dem Erdboden gleichgemacht,* razed to the ground. *Er war nirgends zu finden. Es war, als hätte ihn der Erdboden verschluckt/als wäre er vom Erdboden verschwunden.*
> *Wir mußten stundenlang auf dem Boden/auf der Erde/auf dem Erdboden herumkriechen.*

Fig. uses. *An Boden gewinnen* is 'to gain ground' and can be fig. *In letzter Zeit hat das Radfahren wieder sehr an Boden gewonnen, und zwar unter Menschen jedes/jeden Alters. Ich kann es nicht aus dem Boden/der Erde stampfen,* I can't produce it by magic.

4. For the meaning 'the material composing the uppermost layer of the earth's crust in which plants and trees grow', E. uses **ground**, **earth**, **soil**, and **land**. They refer to the soil or its nature. *Cover the roots of the plants with earth/soil. It's good/fertile soil/ground/land.* **Der Boden** and **die Erde** are the usual words. Thus *guter/ertragreicher/lehmiger/felsiger/vulkanischer Boden* or *fruchtbare/feuchte/sandige Erde. Erde* is used for the soil in flowerpots, window-boxes, etc. *To till, cultivate,* or *work the soil* is *den Boden bestellen/bebauen/bearbeiten;* hence *Bodenentwässerung* and *-bewässerung* and *Bodenerosion.* **Das Land** also refers to the nature of the ground or soil. *Gutes/Fruchtbares/Steiniges Land.* Another syn. is **das Erdreich**. *In dieser Gegend ist das Erdreich hart/steinig/fruchtbar.*
> *Im vorigen Winter war der Boden hart gefroren.*
> *Man bedeckt die Wurzeln der Pflanzen mit Erde.*

Diese Böden sind für den Weizenanbau nicht geeignet.
Man muß das Erdreich zuerst auflockern.

5. E. **land** and **das Land** refer to the kind of surface an area has, i.e. the terrain. *Rough/Even/Undulating land* or *country. Steiniges/Flaches/Kahles/Hügeliges Land. Bewaldetes/Gerodetes Land.* For a syn. cf. *Gelände*, 'terrain, landscape', under AREA 5.

6. i. E. **land** and **das Land** denote ground used for agriculture. *Er bebaut/bestellt sein Land. Er pflügt sein Land. To work on the land is in der Landwirtschaft tätig sein as auf dem Lande* means 'in the country'.

ii. For **land** = 'the property that s.o. owns' **das Land** and **der Boden** are used. *Wie weit erstreckt sich Ihr Land? Die Familie hat zwanzig Hektar Land/fünfzig Morgen fruchtbaren Boden.*

Nach dem zweiten Weltkrieg wurde das Land der Großgrundbesitzer östlich der Elbe unter den Bauern aufgeteilt.

Der Grund und Boden and **der Grundbesitz** also denote the land someone owns. *Sie haben einen Teil ihres Grund und Bodens verkauft. Im Laufe seines Lebens hat er seinen Grundbesitz allmählich vergrößert.* The land for a house is **das Grundstück**, block of land.

7. Grounds = 'land and garden around a building'. One sense of **die Anlage** denotes laid-out parks and gardens. *Die Schloßanlagen*, the castle grounds. *Ein von Anlagen umgebenes Haus*, one standing in its own grounds. *Die Anlagen der Universität* refers to parkland and gardens. Cf. *Gelände* in 8.

8. Ground = 'area used for a special purpose'. The usual word is **der Platz**. Hence the compounds *der Fußballplatz, der Paradeplatz, der Campingplatz.* For a more extensive area, **das Gelände** is used. *Das Sportgelände.* Also *Sportanlagen.* If by *the grounds of the university* the area on which it stands is meant, this is *das Gelände*. Cf. AREA 5. *Das Universitätsgelände liegt zwischen zwei stark befahrenen Straßen.*

9. Ein Nährboden is 'a breeding-ground' in the lit. and fig. senses and translates **ground** used fig. *Die Arbeitslosigkeit ist der Nährboden für Gewalttätigkeit und Haß*, a breeding-ground or fertile ground for . . .

grow v. Order of treatment: 1–4 discuss intr. uses. S.o./sth. **grows [up]**. S.o./sth. **grows** tall/fat. 5 deals with the trans. uses. S.o. **grows** sth.

1. i. Wachsen is intr. only and means 'to become larger, taller, or longer', 'to develop'. For plants it is used in talking of the habitat, in saying how things grow, but only in a restricted way to state the result of growth, as in *The trees grow very tall.* For this sense cf. *werden* in 3.

Diese Bäume wachsen nur in den Tropen.	*Unkraut wächst überall.*
Im Wald wachsen Pilze nicht.	*Das Gras wächst sehr schnell.*
Auf diesem Boden/In diesem Tal wächst das Getreide gut.	*Der Baum wächst gerade.*
Diese Sträucher wachsen in die Höhe/in die Breite.	*Der Baum ist krumm/schön gewachsen.*

For human beings and animals *wachsen* refers to development, and only rarely to the result of growth. In the use with the adjs. *schlank und muskulös* below, *wachsen* belongs to literary language. In everyday language *werden* would be used.

Jugendliche wachsen noch.	*Der junge Hund wuchs zusehends.*
Der Junge war in letzter Zeit stark/sehr gewachsen.	*Du bist aber schnell gewachsen!*
Er ist schlank und muskulös gewachsen.	*Haare/Nägel wachsen ständig.*

ii. Aufwachsen, which is applied to people only, refers to the whole process of developing from a baby to an adult, i.e. to growing up. It is usually accompanied by a phr. stating where or under what conditions this happened, although it is occasionally found alone. *Eine neue Generation wächst auf.* An alternative is **groß werden**. *Ich bin in Neuseeland aufgewachsen/groß geworden.*

Ich bin auf dem Lande/in einer Kleinstadt aufgewachsen/groß geworden.

Sie sind in Not und Elend aufgewachsen.

iii. Heranwachsen means 'to be gradually reaching maturity' and refers to the last stage in growing up before becoming adult. *Die heranwachsende Generation* is 'the oncoming generation', 'the generation growing to maturity', roughly the age group 14 to 18 or 19. *Die Kinder sind [sehr schnell] herangewachsen* means that [in a short time] they have ceased to be children and have become (independent) young people. In addition *heranwachsen* is used with *zu*, meaning 'to grow into'. *Das Mädchen ist zu einer schönen Dame/einer ernsten jungen Frau herangewachsen.*

iv. Erwachsen used as a past part. means 'grown up or adult' in reference to people. It usually implies mental as well as physical maturity. *Ein erwachsener Mensch benimmt sich nicht so.* Physical maturity alone is expressed by **auswachsen**, applied to people, plants, and animals. *Ein ausgewachsener Löwe* is 'a fully grown lion'. A young man who has reached his full stature is sometimes described as *ausgewachsen*.

Ihre Kinder sind schon erwachsen.   *Sie haben erwachsene Kinder.*

Er sieht schon sehr erwachsen aus.   *Du bist nun erwachsen.*

Der Baum/Der Hund ist noch nicht ausgewachsen.

2. Grow also means 'to increase in quantity or number'.

i. Wachsen has this meaning in some cases. Concrete growth can be meant. *Die Bevölkerung/Der Handel/Jmds. Vermögen/Seine Familie/Die Stadt wächst [ständig].* The subj. can be less tangible things. *Der Widerstand/Ihr Interesse/Die Spannung/Der Lärm/Sein Zorn wuchs.* The pres. part. is also often found. *Wachsende Unruhe. Wachsende Arbeitslosigkeit.*

ii. Anwachsen means 'to increase steadily, slowly, and regularly' and is applied to numbers, amounts, and intensity. Unlike *wachsen*, it is used with *auf* or [*bis*] *zu* meaning 'to increase [up] to a certain point'. Without these preps., it is interchangeable with *wachsen*. *Die Einwohnerzahl wuchs noch [an].*

Der Lärm war bis zur Unerträglichkeit angewachsen.

Die Schulden sind auf eine beträchtliche Summe angewachsen.

Die Literatur über den Ersten Weltkrieg ist zu einer unübersehbaren Flut angewachsen.

Gegen 15 Uhr wuchs die Besucherzahl so an, daß die Ausstellung wegen Überfüllung vorübergehend geschlossen werden mußte.

3. i. When the result of growth is stated, as in *These crocodiles grow to three metres in length/to a length of three metres*, **werden** is the usual v. and is applied to people, animals, and plants.

Du bist aber groß geworden, seitdem ich dich zuletzt sah (have grown tall).

Diese Frösche werden zehn Zentimeter lang.   *Diese Bäume werden zwanzig Meter hoch.*

ii. Grow + an adj. meaning 'to become', as in *It was growing dark* or *She grew pale*, is expressed by **werden**. *Es wurde dunkel. Sie wurde blaß.*

Er ist in letzter Zeit dick geworden.   *Die Schutthalden werden immer größer.*

4. i. Grow up means 'to develop' or 'to arise' in *A warm friendship grew up between the two*. The general equivalent is **entstehen**, to arise or originate. *Zwischen den beiden entstand eine warme Freundschaft.*

ii. Aus etw. wurde etw. can translate **grow into**. *Aus der Hungerrevolte wurde eine Revolution.*

Aus der Freundschaft wurde Liebe.   *Aus Jungen werden Männer.*

iii. Erwachsen means 'to arise gradually'. *Der Roman ist aus einer Erzählung erwachsen.*

Diese Schwierigkeiten sind aus seiner steten Gereiztheit entstanden/erwachsen.
Daraus können uns gewisse Vorteile entstehen/erwachsen.

iv. Sich zu etw. auswachsen means 'to develop into sth.' both lit. and fig. *Der schmächtige Junge hat sich zu einem kräftigen jungen Mann ausgewachsen. Der Setzling wächst sich zu einem Baum aus. Die Unruhen haben sich zu einer Rebellion ausgewachsen.*

5. Trans. uses.

i. The construction *Sie ließ ihre Haare wachsen* or *ließ sich die Haare wachsen* can be used to translate *He grew a beard: Er ließ sich einen Bart wachsen.*

ii. Grow wheat, vegetables, etc. **Anbauen** means 'to plant' a crop or 'grow' corn, potatoes, etc. on a large or commercial scale. *In diesem Gebiet wird nur Weizen angebaut.* **Grow** on a small scale, for instance in one's garden, is **ziehen**. *Ich ziehe Tomaten/Bohnen und Erbsen/Gemüse/Blumen/Rosen im Garten. Er hat die Pflanzen aus Samen/aus Stecklingen gezogen.* Anbauen means 'to plant' and does not necessarily mean that a crop will result.

iii. The vs. in 5. ii do not convey the sense 'to grow a certain quantity'. **Erzeugen**, 'to PRODUCE', can express this meaning. *Ägypten erzeugt sehr viel besonders hochwertige Baumwolle. Indien erzeugt genug Nahrungsmittel, um den eigenen Bedarf zu decken.* Erzeugen is used in relation to *die Wolle*, for which E. uses **grow** and *produce. In Australien wird mehr Wolle erzeugt als in jedem anderen Land.* An alternative with *Getreide, Obst, Kartoffeln*, etc. as obj. is **ernten**, to harvest. *Wir haben in diesem Jahr 100 Tonnen Getreide/Kartoffeln/Äpfel geerntet.*

guard, sentry, warder, keeper *ns.*

1. Guard meaning 'a body of men stationed to protect or watch military establishments, buildings, etc.' is **die Wache**. *Die Wache zieht auf,* marches up, comes on duty. *Die Wache wird alle zwei Stunden abgelöst,* relieved, changed. **Die Leibwache** is 'the bodyguard', i.e. 'several guards or a body of men protecting a pers.' *Die Leibwache des Papstes. Die Leibgarde* also has this sense, but is little used.

Die Wache, die aus drei Mann besteht, kontrolliert die Ausweise.

2. A single military guard or sentry is called **der Wachposten** or **Wachtposten**, but this is usually shortened to **der Posten**. *Man stellt einen Posten/Posten auf. Ein Soldat steht [auf] Posten.* In *Wachen aufstellen,* to post sentries or guards, **Wachen** denotes individuals and is a syn. of *Posten.*

Vor dem Denkmal stehen zwei Posten unter Gewehr, die ihre Strecken alle paar Minuten abschreiten.
Die Botschaft wird von Posten bewacht.
Bei Regen tritt der Posten ins Schilderhäuschen/Wachhäuschen.

3. Die Wache also means 'guard duty' and is a syn. of **der Wachdienst**. *Ein Soldat hat/hält Wache/Wachdienst.* Colloquially: *Er schiebt Wache. Der junge Soldat konnte am Wochenende nicht nach Hause fahren, weil er Wache halten/schieben mußte. Die Wache* also means 'a watch', 'the period s.o. keeps watch'. *Wir sind zum Wachdienst eingeteilt und übernehmen die Wachen, die um sechs Uhr und um Mitternacht anfangen. Die Wache* also means 'guard-room', *Du mußt dich auf der Wache am Eingang der Kaserne melden,* and 'police station', *Der betrunkene Autofahrer wurde zur Ausnüchterung auf die Polizeiwache gebracht.*

4. Der Wächter is someone whose work it is to watch or guard a building or area. Common compounds are *der Nachtwächter,* 'night watchman', *der Parkwächter,* 'car-park attendant', *der Grenzwächter,* 'border guard', *der Leibwächter,* 'bodyguard' (one person). Cf. *die Leibwache* under 1.

Der Wächter machte seinen Rundgang/seine Runde durch das Fabrikgelände.

5. Der Wärter is derived from *warten* meaning 'to care for, look after', and denotes a person whose task it is to look after people, animals, or things. For prisons E. uses **warder** (the G. equivalent is in full *der Gefängniswärter*), and for zoos **keeper** (in full *der Tierwärter*). *Der Museumswärter* is 'an attendant'. *A prison warder* is also called **der [Gefängnis]schließer**.

6. i. Die Garde is the designation for the regiment[s] whose duty is the protection of the sovereign or ruler. *Die königliche Garde war vor dem Schloß aufgezogen. Der Gardist* or *Gardesoldat* is a member of such a regiment. Nowadays *Garde* is mostly used in *die Ehrengarde*, 'guard of honour', and the *Prinzengarde* of *Karneval* or *Fastnachtsgarde*.

ii. Die Garde is used like *the old guard*. *Der ist noch von der alten Garde* suggests unwillingness to change, but also reliability. *Die neue* or *junge Garde* is applied to a group of younger people with common, usually innovatory, aims. *Er gehört zu der jungen Garde der achtziger Jahre.*

guess *v.* The general sense is 'to attempt to find the correct answer when one does not have the specific knowledge merely by thinking about it'. Such a guess can be completely at random, on grounds of probability, or on the basis of uncertain or inconclusive indications. When the answer is given more or less at random or as merely the most probable solution, G. distinguishes between simply making a guess at the answer and guessing correctly. *Guess what I found!* or *I'm just guessing* suggest guessing randomly, whereas in *It's not difficult to guess* or *You've guessed it* or *She guessed my age the first time*, **guess** means 'to hit upon the correct answer'. *Right* or *correctly* make the second sense clear.

i. Raten means 'to have or hazard a guess'. It is used alone. *Ich weiß es nicht, ich habe nur geraten.* It also takes a clause. *Rate mal, wem ich heute begegnet bin!* Raten is used in the imp., *Rate mal, wen ich gesehen habe!*, but not with *können* in questions. E. questions such as *Can you guess how much it cost?* can be expressed as an imp. *Rate mal, wieviel es gekostet hat!* Alternative constructions are *Du rätst nie, wieviel . . .* and *Wetten du rätst nicht, wieviel . . .* **Erraten** means 'to guess right or correctly'. It needs an obj. which can be a n. or a clause and is often *es*. *Sie hat seine Absicht erraten. Sie erriet, was er vorhatte. Sie wußte nicht, worum es ging, hat es aber sofort erraten.* Neg. sents. mostly have *erraten* since *Ich habe es nicht erraten* and *Ich kann es nicht erraten* imply not guessing correctly. The obj. of *erraten* is a n. like *Wunsch, Gedanken, Grund, ein Geheimnis, Pläne, Absichten, einen Namen*, etc. *Erraten* is used with *aus* = 'from'. *Aus den Andeutungen habe ich erraten, welches Ziel sie verfolgten.* In the standard language *raten* is only rarely found with an obj., but it does occur in colloquial speech with one. Hence *Sie hat mein Alter [richtig] geraten*, or *. . . mein Alter erraten.* In the spoken language *raten* can mean 'to guess correctly', when this is clear from the context. Thus *Das rätst du nie* and *Das errätst du nie* are both heard. With *richtig*, *raten* has the meaning of *erraten*, so that both *Du hast richtig geraten* and *Du hast es erraten* are used. With *Rätsel*, 'riddle, puzzle', *lösen*, 'to solve', is the usual v., but *raten* is a syn. *Du hast das Rätsel gelöst/geraten* or *Kinder lösen/raten gern Rätsel.*

> Sie rieten lange, wer es gewesen sein könnte.   Sie hat das Geheimnis erraten.
> Ich kann leicht erraten, was er denkt.   Soll ich mal raten, was du denkst?
> Aus seinem Verhalten konnte ich schon den Grund seines Besuchs erraten.
> Seine Absicht war nicht schwer zu erraten/war leicht zu erraten.   Wie hast du das erraten?
> Aus seiner Verhaltensweise habe ich erraten, daß etw. schief gegangen sein muß.

ii. In reference to the future or to unexplained events in the past, such as *We can only guess what consequences this action will have* and *In the absence of evidence we can only guess how it happened*, **guess** means 'to give an opinion' or 'to suggest a hypothesis'. If the opinion or hypothesis is based on indications or probability, the usual equivalent is **vermuten**, to surmise, conjecture, draw a conclusion on the basis of reasonable probability. *Raten* would indicate a stab in the dark with no, or the barest, evidence.

> *Hier vermute ich bloß, statt zu wissen* (I'm guessing). *Also Ich rate nur.*
> *Man kann nur vermuten, was für Folgen dieser Schritt haben wird.*
> *Da wir keine Zeugnisse haben, können wir nur vermuten, wie es sich abgespielt hat.*
> *Daß die Tür verschlossen sein würde, hätte ich vermuten können* (I could have guessed).

iii. When the obj. is a precise value, size, number, price, distance, etc., **guess** means 'to form an approximate judgement without measurement or calculation', i.e. 'to ESTIMATE roughly'. If someone says *Rate mal, wieviel die Kiste wiegt!*, he/she is setting the other a puzzle. When a rough estimate is expected, **schätzen** is used. *Schätzen* is always found with a obj. like *die Entfernung, das Gewicht, der Preis*, etc., as *raten* is not normally followed by a n. (*Raten* is possible if the meaning of the n. is expressed as a clause, e.g. *wie weit es ist*, but the intention behind the utterance is different.)

> *Kannst du das Gewicht des Koffers mal schätzen? Also Schätze mal das Gewicht des Koffers!*
> *Die Zahl der Anwesenden habe ich nur geschätzt* (I only guessed). *Ich habe sie nicht gezählt.*
> *Das Zimmer habe ich nicht ausgemessen. Ich habe die Größe/die Länge, Breite und Höhe geschätzt.*
> *Ich schätze ihn auf ungefähr vierzig.* (I guess him/his age to be about 40.)
> *Ich schätze die Entfernung auf fünfundzwanzig Kilometer.*

iv. Guess at the distance etc. should be treated like **guess** and translated by **raten, vermuten**, or **schätzen** as appropriate. In *There is no point in guessing at the answer, at the answer* is best omitted: *Es hat keinen Sinn, bloß zu raten, rechne es aus! We can only guess at the number of deaths this has caused* can be *Wir können die Zahl der Todesfälle nur schätzen* or *Wir können nur vermuten, zu wie vielen Todesfällen dies geführt hat. I'm only guessing at the price/distance* becomes *Ich schätze die Entfernung/den Preis nur.*

gun *n.* The general term for a portable firearm is **das Gewehr**, which is a gun with a long barrel, i.e. a rifle. It is the normal word for a gun carried by a soldier, hence its use in *Präsentiert das Gewehr!* or *Die Soldaten standen Gewehr bei Fuß.* A rifle used for hunting is **die Büchse**, and a shot-gun is **die Flinte**. *Er schoß alles, was ihm vor die Flinte/Büchse kam.* Soldiers may refer to their *Gewehre* as *Flinten. Die Soldaten nahmen ihre Flinten auf den Rücken und marschierten los.* **Das Maschinengewehr** is 'a machine gun', and **die Maschinenpistole** 'a sub-machine gun'. Small guns are called **die Pistole** or **der Revolver. Die Feuerwaffe** denotes a firearm using gunpowder. *Es gibt Feuerwaffen in Europa seit dem vierzehnten Jahrhundert.* **Die Schußwaffe** refers to revolvers or guns used by police, criminals, etc. *Unter welchen Umständen dürfen Polizisten von Schußwaffen Gebrauch machen?* If it is clear that a gun (rather than another weapon) is meant, *Schuß* is omitted. *Die Polizisten führen im Dienst Waffen mit sich. Werfen Sie die Waffe weg!* Large guns, used by the artillery or on tanks or ships, are called **das Geschütz** or **die Kanone**. *Sie richteten die Kanone des Panzers und feuerten. Die Geschütze feuerten etwa zehn Minuten lang. To force s.o. to do sth.* **at gun-point** is *jmdn.* **mit vorgehaltener Pistole/vorgehaltenem Gewehr** zwingen, *etw. zu tun.*

habit, custom *ns.*

1. Habit refers to someone's customary manner of acting. In reference to individuals **custom** also denotes a settled practice or long established way of behaving. *It was Tony's custom to get up early and go for a walk before breakfast.* **Custom** is neutral or pos., whereas **habit** often implies that the practice is hard to give up, and it alone is used with *bad.*

i. Die Gewohnheit denotes something a person habitually does and implies neither good nor bad. Such judgements are conveyed by an adj. Thus *eine gute Gewohnheit* and *eine schlechte/üble Gewohnheit.* Common expressions are *Es ist mir zur Gewohnheit geworden* + infin., *Jmd. tut etw. aus [alter] Gewohnheit,* and *entgegen aller Gewohnheit.* It is s.o.'s **custom** *to do sth* and s.o. is **in the habit** *of doing sth.* can be translated by *Es war seine Gewohnheit, etw. zu machen* or by *er war gewohnt, etw. zu machen.* Cf. ACCUSTOM for *gewohnt* and for *to get into the habit of doing sth.*

> *Es war seine Gewohnheit, bei jedem Arbeitsessen die Kunden mit Schwänken* (stories about funny happenings) *aus seinem Leben zu unterhalten.*
>
> *Nach alter Gewohnheit trinken sie ein Gläschen Portwein nach dem Abendessen.*
>
> *Jetzt bin ich seit mehr als fünf Jahren mit ihm verheiratet, aber an seine Gewohnheiten werde ich mich wohl nie gewöhnen.*
>
> *Entgegen aller Gewohnheit wollte sie ihren Geburtstag dieses Mal nicht zu Hause feiern.*

Break **a habit** or get s.o. out of **a habit** is **abgewöhnen** with a dat. or refl. dat. *Er hat sich das Trinken abgewöhnt. Seine Frau hat ihm die Unpünktlichkeit/das Rauchen abgewöhnt.*

ii. Die Angewohnheit is 'a mannerism or way of behaving which s.o. has taken on, often without being aware of it, and which has become so ingrained that it is difficult to stop'. Even in a sent. which seems pos., such as *Er hatte die Angewohnheit, nicht viel zu reden, Angewohnheit* implies that the habit is at least strange, if not bad or unpleasant, and that it should be broken. It is often strengthened by adjs. denoting badness. *Man nimmt eine schlechte/üble Angewohnheit an* or *legt eine schlechte Angewohnheit ab.*

> *Die schreckliche Angewohnheit, mit sich selbst Gespräche zu führen, hatte stark zugenommen.*
>
> *Er hat die Angewohnheit/üble Gewohnheit, an den Fingernägeln zu kauen, immer noch nicht abgelegt.*
>
> *Sie hatte die dumme Angewohnheit, dauernd zu meckern.*

iii. Die Unart denotes a bad habit which strikes others as unpleasant. *Du mußt dir diese Unart abgewöhnen (z. B. auf/an den Fingernägeln zu kauen). Warum hast du diese Unart angenommen? (Unart* also means 'bad behaviour or sth. naughty done by a child'. *Er wurde für diese Unart bestraft.)*

iv. Die Gepflogenheit is a stylistically more elevated word for an individual's habitual behaviour. It is always seen pos. and may be something deliberately cultivated which serves to regulate the day. It suggests a refined style of living, mostly among the richer classes.

> *Es entsprach alter Gepflogenheit im gräflichen Hause, den gesamten Adel der Nachbarschaft zur Jagd zu bitten.*
>
> *Es hätte allen Gepflogenheiten meines Elternhauses widersprochen, uns Kinder zu Mitwissern solcher Skandalaffären zu machen.*

2. Customs of groups of people.

i. Die Sitte denotes a way of behaving which has become usual or habitual among a smaller or larger group of people and is felt to be binding. Especially in the expression *Es ist [bei uns/hier] Sitte* + infin., it means that a way of acting is the custom or usually done here. *In Deutschland ist es Sitte, sich zur Begrüßung die Hand zu reichen. Die Sitten eines Landes* are 'its customs' or 'the usual ways of behaving there'. (*Die Sitte* also refers to behaviour and ethical standards. *Hier herrschen Anstand und Sitte. Sie legen Wert auf gute Sitten/bewahren Anstand und Sitte. Verfall der Sitten,* decline of moral/ethical standards. Less commonly it means 'manners'. *Sie achteten bei den Kindern auf gute Sitten. Ein junger Mensch von guten/schlechten Sitten.*)

  In diesem Land ist die Verbeugung Sitte und hat nichts mit Unterwürfigkeit zu tun.

  Es empfiehlt sich, die herrschenden Sitten einzuhalten, wenn man weiterkommen will.

  Es war in diesem Betrieb Sitte, daß der Einstand mit einem Kasten Bier zu bezahlen war.

ii. An adj. with a related, but wider, sense is **üblich**, usual, normally done. *Die übliche Methode. Wir gehen in der üblichen Weise vor. Es ist üblich anzuklopfen, bevor man in ein Zimmer tritt.*

iii. Der Brauch also denotes something which has become a practice among a group of people, often a social class or those in a certain occupation. In reference to the way an individual acts it is similar to *Sitte*, but suggests something time-honoured as well as usual in a group. *Wir akzeptierten den Brauch und zogen die Schuhe aus, bevor wir den Tempel betraten. Das ist bei uns so Brauch.* The dividing line between *Sitte* and *Brauch* is not clear, and in some situations both are found. *In dieser Familie war es Sitte/Brauch, vor dem Essen zu beten.* In reference to a larger group of people *Brauch* also denotes a tradition which is hallowed by being handed down from earlier generations and is often ceremonious. *Es war im Dorf von alters her Brauch, das Ende der Ernte zu feiern. Militärische Bräuche* are e.g. standing at attention when talking to a superior, firing a certain number of gun salutes on special occasions.

  Leider ist der schöne Brauch, Frauen in ihren Mantel zu helfen, bei uns in Verruf geraten.

  In allen Gewässern ist es Brauch, daß der Kapitän als Letzter das sinkende Schiff verläßt.

  Entgegen allen militärischen Bräuchen legte der verwundete Soldat seine Hand auf die Hand des Artzes.

iv. Der Gebrauch, in the sense of 'custom', is only used in the pl. and mostly combined with *Sitten, die Sitten und Gebräuche*, customs and traditions, practices and ceremonies. Without *Sitten, Gebräuche.* is a syn. of *Bräuche*, customs, traditions. *In entlegenen Gebieten haben sich die alten Gebräuche erhalten.*

  Es ist erstaunlich, wie in dieser Inselgruppe die Sitten und Gebräuche sich von einer Insel zur nächsten unterscheiden.

  Bei einigen Bevölkerungsgruppen haben sich die Sitten und Gebräuche der vorindustriellen Welt noch bis in die heutige Zeit erhalten können.

half *n., adj.,* and *adv.*

1. Both *die Hälfte* und *halb* mean 'half'. The first is a n., and the second an adj. or adv.

i. Die Hälfte must be used when **half** is used alone without a following n. *We each paid half: Wir haben je die Hälfte bezahlt. So viel Arbeit kann dir niemand zumuten—ich übernehme die Hälfte. Die Hälfte* is needed when E. has *half of it/them, of it/them* being *davon* or, if *them* refers to people, *von ihnen. Er hat mir die Hälfte davon versprochen. Die Hälfte davon ist verdorben.* I understood only half of what he said becomes *Ich verstand nur die Hälfte von dem, was er sagte. Die Hälfte* is also necessary when a pl. n. follows **half**. *Of* is optional after **half**, *half [of]* the children, but *Hälfte* needs the gen. or *von*.

Die Hälfte der Kinder fehlten. Die Hälfte der bestellten Bücher wurde gestern abgeschickt. Only *Hälfte* can be qualified by an adj. *In the second half of August* is *in der zweiten Hälfte von August. Sth. rose or fell by half* is *Es stieg oder fiel um die Hälfte. Wir verringerten unsere Ausgaben um die Hälfte.*

ii. In expressions stating a quantity, distance, or a length of time in which **half** is followed by *a* or *an*, such as *half a litre/mile* or *half an hour*, **halb** is used as an adj. *Ein halber Liter. Eine halbe Meile. Ein halbes Pfund. Eine halbe Minute. In einer halben Stunde. Eine halbe Tasse Tee. Eine halbe Million Soldaten.*

iii. When a sing. n. with the definite article follows **half**, as in *half the class* (of is again optional), either **die Hälfte** or **halb** is possible. *Die halbe Klasse* or *die Hälfte der Klasse. Wir haben die halbe Strecke/die Hälfte der Strecke geschafft. Die halbe Wand/Die Hälfte der Wand ist von einem Schrank verdeckt. Ich habe den halben Tag/die Hälfte des Tages vertrödelt. Sie hat die halbe Nacht/die Hälfte der Nacht gearbeitet. Die Hälfte* suggests greater precision, but in spoken G. the tendency is to use *halb*. Sometimes *halb* sounds very colloquial. While *Ich habe die Hälfte der Milch verschüttet* is normal in the standard language, *die halbe Milch* is used in colloquial speech. Likewise *Wir brauchen nur die Hälfte der Menge* can be *nur die halbe Menge*. When an adj. precedes the n. following **half**, *half the normal price*, only *Hälfte* is possible. *Wir zahlten nur die Hälfte des normalen Preises.*

> *Die Hälfte der Zeit/Die halbe Zeit ist er nicht hier.*
> *Er überließ mir den halben Gewinn/die Hälfte des Gewinnes.*
> *Kinder bezahlen den halben Fahrpreis/die Hälfte des Fahrpreises.*

iv. Die Hälfte forms a pl. *Der Durchmesser teilt einen Kreis in zwei Hälften.* In reference to beer and other alcoholic drinks **der/die/das Halbe** denotes a half measure or half a litre and can form a pl. *Ich trinke einen Halben/ein Halbes. Sie bestellten zwei Halbe.*

v. Die Hälfte is used inexactly. *Die größere/kleinere Hälfte. Ich habe gut die Hälfte gemacht*, a good half. **Halb** has the imprecise meaning 'a fairly large proportion of'. *Die halbe Klasse fehlt* need not be based on an accurate count.

2. Halb is also an adv. and modifies an adj. *Half-finished* is *halb fertig. Das Glas ist halb voll. Die Birnen sind erst halb reif.* **Zur Hälfte** is a syn. *Die Arbeit ist zur Hälfte fertig.* Both are used with a v. *Das habe ich nur halb verstanden. Er hat den Apfel halb/zur Hälfte gegessen. Sie hatte sich nur halb angezogen. Man füllt die Schale zur Hälfte mit Wasser. Ich habe das Glas halb/zur Hälfte gefüllt.*

3. In sport the first/second **half** is **die Halbzeit**. *Die Tore fielen in der ersten/zweiten Halbzeit. Halbzeit* also means 'half-time'. *In der Halbzeit gab der Trainer den Spielern neue Anweisungen.* **Die Hälfte** refers to a half of the field. *Die überlegene Mannschaft spielte meist in der Hälfte des Gegners.*

hang [up] *v.*

1. Hang can be intr., *Your suit is hanging in the cupboard*, or trans., *Hang your suit in the cupboard!*

i. Hängen, 'to hang', can be strong or weak. The strong forms *hing, gehangen* are intr. and have as subj. something that is hanging, fastened, or suspended, *Die Wäsche hing auf der Leine zum Trocknen*, while the weak forms are trans. and have as subj. someone who hangs something somewhere, *Sie hat die Wäsche auf die Leine gehängt.*

> *Ein Bild hängt über dem Kamin.*   *Das Bild hängt schief.*
> *Die Kinder hingen über dem Brückengeländer/aus den Fenstern.*
> *Dunkle Wolken hingen über dem Gipfel.*   *Haare hingen ihm ins Gesicht.*
> *Gestern haben wir das Bild an die Wand gehängt.*   *Häng' doch dein Kostüm in den Schrank!*
> *Er hat seinen Hut an einen Kleiderhaken und seinen Mantel auf einen Bügel gehängt.*

ii. Aufhängen, 'to hang up or out', does not differ in meaning from *hängen*, but is used, like **hang up**, with an obj. only, without the place being stated. *Sie hängte den Mantel auf* as against *Sie hängte den Mantel in den Schrank.* A prep. + dat. states on what the garment is hung. *Ich hängte den Mantel auf einem Bügel auf.*
Er hängte die Wäsche auf.

2. Henken now means 'to execute by hanging'. *Der Mörder wurde verurteilt und gehenkt. Hängen* used to have this sense, but now survives only in the proverb *Die kleinen Diebe hängt man, aber die großen läßt man laufen.* (In this case, the pronunciation is the same as *henkt*.) **Erhängen** is a syn. of *henken. Die Piraten wurden zum Tod durch Erhängen verurteilt.* **Hang oneself** is *sich erhängen. In den letzten Jahren haben sich mehrere etwa zwanzigjährige australische Ureinwohner in Gefängniszellen erhängt.* In everyday language *aufhängen* means 'to execute by hanging', *Die ganze Bande sollte aufgehängt werden,* and **sich aufhängen** is used instead of *sich erhängen. Hauptmanns Stück* Fuhrmann Henschel *endet damit, daß Henschel sich aufhängt.*

3. One meaning of **hang about/around**, applied to people, is 'to be standing or loitering about doing nothing definite'. This sense is expressed by **herumstehen** or **herumsitzen**, to stand or sit around doing nothing. *Halbstarke standen im Hauseingang herum. Müßig* or *untätig*, 'idly', are often added. *Ich will nicht hier den ganzen Tag untätig herumsitzen.* **Hang around (with)** also means 'to spend a lot of time in s.o.'s company or in a place'. **Sich herumtreiben [mit jmdm.]** means 'to wander, roam, or knock about or around without any aim [with s.o.]'. It expresses disapproval. At its strongest it implies leading a dissolute life. *Mit welchem Gesindel treibst du dich herum? Er hat die Lehrstelle geschmissen und treibt sich jetzt nur noch herum. Er treibt sich in Spelunken/in Bars herum. Wo treibst du dich eigentlich die ganze Zeit herum?* While *sich herumtreiben* implies an action which continues for a fairly long period of time, **sich herumlungern**, 'to loaf around', may be on one occasion. *Viele Jugendliche lungerten vor dem Kino/in der Kneipe herum.* If **hang around** is neutral, as in *I used to hang around a lot with journalists*, **verkehren mit**, 'to mix or associate with', can be used. *Damals verkehrte ich viel/oft mit Journalisten.*

hearty, cordial *adjs.* As **cordial** is derived ultimately from the Latin word meaning 'heart', both these adjs. denote feelings which were supposed to come from the heart. While **hearty** implies a certain physical vigour, as in *a hearty laugh*, **cordial** suggests a quieter manifestation of goodwill, *cordial reception.* Two adjs. are formed from *das Herz, herzlich* and *herzhaft.*

i. Herzlich implies firstly full of kindly sentiment or goodwill and means 'cordial or warm' applied to a reception, welcome, etc. *Alle waren sehr herzlich zu mir. Man begrüßt/beglückwünscht/verabschiedet jmdn. herzlich* or *dankt/gratuliert jmdm. herzlich* or *schüttelt jmdm. herzlich die Hand.* It also implies genuineness or sincerity. *Herzliche Worte. Ein herzliches Lächeln. Herzliche Zuneigung.* It occurs frequently in fixed expressions of thanks and greeting. *Herzlichen Dank! Herzliche Grüße! Ich heiße Sie auf unserer heutigen Veranstaltung herzlich willkommen.* (In colloquial usage *herzlich* also means 'very'. *Herzlich wenig*, very/precious little. *Die Erzählweise dieses Autors finden viele Schüler herzlich langweilig.*)

ii. Hearty means 'giving unrestrained expression to the feelings', 'vigorous', as in *a hearty laugh* or *a hearty slap on the back*. The equivalent is **herzhaft**. *Ein herzhaftes Lachen/Gelächter. Er schlug mir herzhaft auf die Schulter. Ein herzhafter Händedruck. Sie gab ihm ein herzhaften Kuß.*

iii. *Hale and* **hearty** is **gesund**, healthy. Of old people, **rüstig**, 'strong and vigorous', is used.

iv. *Er aß herzhaft* or *griff/langte herzhaft zu* means 'he ate with gusto, enjoyment'. As an adv. **herzhaft** does not necessarily suggest a large amount, as does **kräftig**. *They ate heartily* is *Sie haben kräftig gegessen/zugegriffen/zugelangt* or *dem Essen kräftig zuge-sprochen.* As an adj. *herzhaft* implies a large amount. It also suggests simple food which is nourishing and invigorating. *Eine herzhafte Mahlzeit. Ein herzhaftes Frühstück/Essen. Er nahm einen herzhaften Schluck. Ein kräftiger Schluck* is also used. *A hearty meal* can also be *eine üppige Mahlzeit* and *eine handfeste Mahlzeit.* (*Üppig* also translates *sumptuous.*)

v. Applied to food, **herzhaft** refers primarily to the taste and means 'savoury, tasty'. *Die Suppe schmeckt herzhaft. Sie ißt gern etw. Herzhaftes.*

heat *v.*

1. Heizen means 'to heat' a space such as a room, house, etc., not food. It can be trans. and intr. *Man heizt ein Zimmer/eine Wohnung/ein Haus. In Deutschland muß man ab Oktober heizen. Wir heizen mit Gas/Kohle/elektrisch. Der Ofen heizt gut.* **Beheizen,** which needs an obj., is used in technical language in the same way as *heizen* + obj. *Treibhäuser werden beheizt. Im Sommer werden die Freibäder beheizt. Die Büros werden mit Gas geheizt* is everyday language while *Die Büros werden mit Gas beheizt* is technical style. *Beheizen* draws attention to the method of heating. Hence *gasbeheizte Wohnungen.* **Einheizen,** applied to rooms, flats, etc., means 'to see to it that they are well heated or thoroughly warm'. While *heizen* suggests heating regularly for a time, *einheizen* implies for some special reason at a particular time. *Sie haben das Zimmer tüchtig eingeheizt. Bei großer Kälte heizen wir eben tüchtig ein.*

2. Erhitzen, which belongs to scientific and technical language, means 'to heat to a certain temperature'. The resulting temperature may or may not be stated. *Man erhitzt die Flüssigkeit auf 60°/bis zum Sieden/Siedepunkt.* In everyday situations **heiß machen** is used. *Ich mache etwas Wasser heiß. Soll ich Milch heiß machen?*

3. Sich erhitzen means 'to become hot' in reference both to things, *Die Kugellager hatten sich erhitzt,* and to people, *Man erhitzt sich schnell beim Tanzen/Laufen.* In rela-tion to people *sich erhitzen* means 'to become heated' about an issue. *Wir erhitzten uns über politische Fragen.* In a similar context, **erhitzen** means 'to cause to become heated'. *Diese Frage/Der Streit erhitzte die Gemüter/die Köpfe/die Geister.*

hide, conceal *vs.*

1. i. Hide means 'to put or keep people, animals, or thgs. out of sight' or 'conceal them intentionally from the notice of others'. **Verstecken** is the usual equivalent in everyday language. **Verbergen** may still be used for hiding people, but applied to things it is old-fashioned or formal. From its derivation, *verbergen* means 'to protect from being found', *verstecken* 'to put somewhere so that it is not seen'. Both are used with *in* + dat. and *vor* + dat. = 'from'.

Ich habe das Geld im Schreibtisch versteckt.   *Wo hast du den Schlüssel versteckt?*

Wir müssen die Weihnachtsgeschenke vor den Kindern verstecken.

Der Falschspieler hatte Karten in seinen Ärmeln versteckt.

Er versteckte den Blumenstrauß hinter dem Rücken, um sie zu überraschen.

Sobald sie ihren Mann kommen hörte, versteckte sie den Liebhaber im Schrank.

Vergeblich versuchten sie, den Flüchtling vor der Polizei zu verbergen.

ii. Although the refl. *They hid themselves* exists in E., **hide** used intr. conveys the same idea. *We hid in the shed.* Both the refl. and non-refl. form must be translated by **sich verstecken** or **sich verbergen.**

Wir versteckten uns in dem Keller/hinter einem Felsen/im Schuppen.
Der Flüchtling verbarg sich vor der Polizei in einem Schuppen.

2. In certain contexts only *verbergen* can be used.

i. Verbergen alone is used for things hidden by nature or the passage of time. *Die Galleone lag seit Jahrhunderten im Meer verborgen. Man legte die im Wüstensand verborgene Stadt frei.*

ii. Only **verbergen** means 'to hide facts, information, etc. from others' and takes a dat. Similar are **verheimlichen**, 'to keep secret', and **verschweigen**, 'not to tell or reveal'. A formal syn. is **verhehlen**. *Er hat mir die Wahrheit/seine wahre Meinung verhehlt.*

> *Ich habe nichts zu verbergen. Ich habe euch nichts verschwiegen/verheimlicht/verborgen.*
> *Der Jürgen ist so bedrückt; ich fürchte, er verbirgt uns etw.*
> *Sie konnte uns ihre wirkliche Meinung nicht verbergen.*
> *Ich will dir nicht verbergen, daß ich dein Vorgehen mißbillige.*
> *Er hat ihr die Wahrheit verschwiegen/ . . . ihr verschwiegen, daß er schon verheiratet war.*
> *Sie konnte ihrer Mutter nicht verheimlichen, daß sie sich stark zu Dieter hingezogen fühlte.*

iii. Verbergen also means 'to hide' an undesirable characteristic or an inadequacy.

> *Er versuchte, seine Unsicherheit durch forsches Auftreten zu verbergen.*
> *Die Linke hatte schnell Gagerns Mangel an Originalität herausgefunden, die er durch überlegene Feierlichkeit verbarg.*

iv. Verbergen only is used for hiding feelings or emotions.

> *Wenn einer so flapsig daherredet, kann ich meinen Unmut nicht verbergen.*
> *Er konnte seine Freude über den glücklichen Ausgang des Spiels nicht verbergen.*
> *Er gab sich alle Mühe, seinen Ärger/seine Abneigung/das Lachen/seine Enttäuschung/seine Gefühle/seine Verlegenheit zu verbergen.*

(The past part. *versteckt* occurs with some words such as *Vorwurf, Absicht, Drohungen, Schadenfreude,* or *Lächeln* meaning 'veiled' or 'disguised'. The purpose of *eine versteckte Drohung* is clear to the hearer. If a feeling is successfully *verborgen*, no one knows of its existence. *Verborgen*, however, can be modified. *Nur schlecht verborgene Enttäuschung.*)

3. When **hide** means 'to keep from view' or 'prevent from being seen' without implying an intention, the equivalent is **verdecken**. It also translates COVER [UP].

> *Die Sonne war von/hinter dichten schwarzen Wolken verdeckt.*
> *Die Bäume verdecken [uns] die Aussicht auf den See.   Ein Schleier verdeckte ihr Gesicht.*

hit, strike, bang, bump *vs.* A few senses.

1. i. While *schlagen* means 'to strike a pers. or animal deliberately', **treffen** means that a blow or a missile thrown or shot or a falling object comes into contact with s.o./sth. This contact can be intended or accidental, so that *treffen* means 'to hit' a target, *Du hast genau die Mitte der Zielscheibe getroffen,* or 'to hit or strike' what is aimed at, *Er schlug zu und traf mich [mit der Faust] ins Gesicht,* or 'to hit or strike' both when no intention can be present, *Sie wurde von einem herabfallenden Dachziegel getroffen,* and when something thrown etc. hits s.o./sth. without being meant to, *Ein Stein, den der Junge ins Wasser werfen wollte, traf seinen Freund am Kopf. Schlagen* and *treffen* could occur in the one sent. *Er wollte den Jungen schlagen, hat ihn aber nicht getroffen.* (The most likely transl.: . . . *but missed* [him].) When a person is subj., a phr. with *mit* can be added. *Er traf ihn mit dem Stock/mit der ersten Kugel.* The blow or missile can be the subj. *Der Schlag/Der Pfeil/Die Kugel hat ihn getroffen.* Unlike **hit**, *treffen* is used without an obj. when it is clear what the obj. is. *Der Schuß/Der Schütze hat [nicht] getroffen.*

ii. Treffen is used for lightning. *Der Blitz hat die Scheune getroffen.* **Einschlagen** is used for lightning and for bombs and shells which hit, strike, or land on something. *Der Blitz schlug in die Scheune ein. Die Bombe schlug in das Nebenhaus ein. Treffen* differs only in taking an acc. *Die Bombe traf das Nebenhaus.* With *einschlagen* what is hit need only be implied. *Schrapnells schlugen um ihn herum ein.*

2. i. Schlagen means 'to strike intentionally with force with the hand, a stick, or other object so as to hurt'. It can imply one or more blows, but covers a range of intensity, so that it also translates *smack* or *slap.* To convey the special meaning of *slap* it is necessary to say *mit der offenen Hand schlagen. Schlagen* can mean 'to punch', which can be made clear by adding *mit der Faust.* These additions are, however, unusual, so that *Er schlug ihn aufs Kinn* can translate **hit** or *punched.* A phr. stating where the blow falls can be added. *Sie schlug ihm mit der Hand/mit dem Stock ins Gesicht/auf die Finger/auf den Kopf. Schlagen* also translates *slap* when it is friendly, not a punishment. *Er schlug mich freundlich auf die Schulter.* Cf. beat 1. iii.

ii. Schlagen nach leaves it open as to whether the blow actually connects and is like **hit at.** *Das Kind schlug nach dem Hund.*

iii. Schlagen auf is used for banging on a table etc. intentionally. *Bei diesen Worten schlug der alte Herr kräftig auf den Tisch.*

iv. Schlagen is the usual v. for hitting a ball. *Tennis ist ein Ballspiel, bei dem zwei Spieler mit ihrem Tennisschläger einen Ball über ein Netz hin- und zurückschlagen.*

3. In one sense **zuschlagen** is intr. and means 'to begin to strike' or 'to deal one or more blows'. It translates **strike** used intr., *He was ready/waiting to strike,* or **hit out** and **strike out** in *He lost his temper and hit/struck out wildly. Er verlor die Beherrschung und schlug wild zu.* A phr. with *mit* is occasionally added, but the obj. is still implied. *Er schlug mit dem Stock zu.* A partial syn. is **Jmd. schlug um sich**, hit/struck out wildly in all directions.

> *Der Lehrer hatte beobachtet, welcher der beiden Jungen zuerst zugeschlagen hatte.*
> *Er holte aus und schlug zu.   Der Täter schlug rücksichtslos zu.*

In another sense *zuschlagen* is applied to armies etc. *Die Polizei schlug zu,* suddenly intervened or took strong action. *Niemand verstand, warum die Armee bei einer so günstigen Gelegenheit nicht zuschlug.*

4. *Auf jmdn./ein Tier* **einschlagen** means 'to hit repeatedly and violently'. *Der Räuber schlug auf sein Opfer ein.*

5. Hit/strike sth. in falling. When what the person or thing falling hits is stated, **schlagen** is used. *Er ist mit dem Kopf gegen die Wand/auf den Stein geschlagen.* When hitting the ground or floor is meant, **aufschlagen** is usual. One sense of *der Aufschlag* is 'the impact' of something falling, of a crash-landing aircraft, etc. The v. contains the idea of hitting the ground, but a phr. with *auf* may be added.

> *Er schlug hart [auf die Erde/auf die Wasseroberfläche] auf.*
> *Er wurde umgeworfen und fühlte, wie sein Hinterkopf hart aufschlug.*
> *Krachend schlug das abstürzende Flugzeug auf den Boden auf.*

6. For cars and other vehicles which hit or run into s.o./sth., **fahren** can be used. *Ich bin/Das Auto ist gegen einen Baum/einen Laternenpfahl gefahren.* **Prallen** suggests a stronger impact. *Das Auto prallte an/gegen den Baum.* **Anfahren** means 'to run into and injure'. *Das Kind wurde von einem Motorrad angefahren.* **Erfassen** means that one vehicle runs into another or a person and knocks it/him/her to the side or drags it/him/her along with it. *Der Bus wurde von einer Lokomotive erfaßt und zertrümmert. Ein Fußgänger wurde beim Überqueren der Straße von einem Auto erfaßt.* **Auflaufen** is used for a ship which hits/strikes a rock. *Das Schiff ist auf einen Felsen aufgelaufen.*

7. The meaning of **hit, bang**, and **bump** in *I hit/banged/bumped my head/elbow*, etc. *on/against sth.* is expressed by **stoßen**. With *an, auf*, and *gegen*, it means 'to bump into or bang against' and suggests no or very little pain. *Ich bin an den Stuhl/gegen den Tisch gestoßen*. A phr. with *mit* can be added. *Ich bin mit dem Staubsauger an den Glastisch gestoßen*. **Sich stoßen** also means 'to come unexpectedly and with at least some force into contact with sth.', but implies pain and sometimes injury. There are several constructions. The simplest is *Ich habe mich gestoßen*. Thus *Paß auf, daß du dich nicht stößt!* could imply banging the head or another part of the body. What is banged against is given by *an*. *Ich habe mich am Schrank gestoßen. Man stößt sich leicht an dem niedrigen Türrahmen*. When a part of the body is stated, either *Ich habe mir den Kopf gestoßen* or *Ich habe mich am Bein gestoßen* can be used. However, only *sich den Kopf* etc. *stoßen* is possible with *an* and the thing banged against, as with the other construction *an* would occur twice. *Paß auf, daß du dir nicht den Kopf am niedrigen Eingang stößt! Blutig* can be added. *Der Junge hat sich das Knie blutig gestoßen*, banged it against sth. and made it bleed.

> *Ich habe mich hinten am Kopf/an der Stirn gestoßen.*
> *Ich habe mir die Stirn [am Fenster] gestoßen.*

In *Er ist mit dem Kopf [an die Wand] angeschlagen*, **anschlagen** suggests a stronger impact than *sich stoßen*, but it is not used in this sense in north Germany. In the north **anstoßen** is only found in the sign *Nicht anstoßen!*, which is a warning not to bump or bang one's head. **Prallen** implies a violent impact and is the strongest word. *Er ist gestürzt und mit dem Kopf gegen die Wand geprallt.*

8. For to be **hit** by famine, flood, a calamity, etc. cf. **treffen** and **betreffen** under AFFECT 2.

holiday[s], leave, vacation *ns.*

1. A single day on which the whole community is freed from work is **der Feiertag**. *A public holiday* is *der gesetzliche Feiertag*.

> *Das Museum ist an Sonn- und Feiertagen geschlossen.*

2. For **holidays** or *annual leave*, there are two words, *die Ferien*, which is always pl., and *der Urlaub*. **Die Ferien** is the time during which certain public institutions do not operate, mainly *Gerichte, Universitäten, Schulen*, and *Parlamente. Die Gerichtsferien dauern drei Wochen. Deutsche Universitäten haben Ferien von Mitte Juli bis Mitte Oktober. Die Schüler freuen sich auf die Sommerferien. Das Parlament geht nächste Woche in die Ferien. Betriebsferien* is used for the period when a whole factory or business closes down for a certain time and all employees take their holidays. **Der Urlaub** is applied to the leave individuals in paid employment get and implies that they are freed from work and continue to be paid. *Ich bekomme Urlaub im Mai. Ich habe ab nächster Woche Urlaub. Schüler* and *Studenten* have *Ferien* when the school or university is closed. If they go away during this time, they say, 'Wir machen Urlaub (in Spanien)'. *Urlaub* is always used when talking of leave in a general way. *Jedem Arbeitnehmer stehen vier Wochen [Jahres]urlaub zu*. However, in talking of someone's holiday, both *Ferien* and *Urlaub* are possible. *Wir haben unseren Urlaub/unsere Ferien am Meer verbracht.*

> *Du müßtest mal wieder Urlaub machen und richtig ausspannen.*
> *Unsere Ferien waren/Unser Urlaub war in diesem Jahr total verregnet.*

There are fixed expressions. *Man nimmt Urlaub*. Colloquially: *Man macht Ferien/Urlaub. Ich gehe Ende Juni in den Urlaub. Wir fahren nächste Woche in die Ferien/in den Urlaub. Wohin fährst du in Ferien/in Urlaub?* **Leave** for a special purpose is always **der Urlaub**. *Der Sonderurlaub, der Studienurlaub, der Schwangerschaftsurlaub.*

3. Frei haben is 'to have a day, etc. off or free'. *Morgen habe ich frei.* In the armed forces **der Ausgang** is used for a short period, hours, an evening, a day or so, **der Urlaub** for a longer period. *Drei Soldaten aus unserer Abteilung* (unit) *haben heute Ausgang; die anderen haben Wachdienst* (or *schieben Wache*).

however, but, yet *conjs.* One sense of **still** *adv.* **all the same, just the same, in spite of this/everything** phrs. used as *advs.*

1. Position of *aber.*

i. The usual equivalent of **but** and **however** is aber. It can be the first word in its clause or phr., *Er hat es mir auch erzählt, aber ich glaube es nicht,* or like **however** can be placed elsewhere. The second part of *Die Schwerkraft ist eine bekannte Kraft, aber wir wissen nicht sehr viel darüber* could equally well be . . . , *wir wissen aber nicht sehr viel darüber,* or . . . , *sehr viel darüber wissen wir aber nicht,* or . . . , *darüber wissen wir aber nicht sehr viel.* (Note that in two similar syntactic patterns, *aber* has different meanings. The first, *Der Film war aber lustig!,* is an exclamation like *What a funny film that was!* or *That film was really terribly funny.* The second is when *aber* strengthens a command. It is mostly not translated. *Jetzt komm aber endlich! Nun aber schnell! Jetzt ist es aber genug!*)

ii. When the sent. begins with *ja,* **aber** can either follow immediately or be placed in the middle of the sent. A. *Hast du Michael angerufen?* B. *Ja, aber er war nicht zu Hause.* Or *Ja, er war aber nicht zu Hause.*

2. For **but** beginning a sent., and possibly implying a reproach, as in *But you promised!,* there are four variations. *Du hast es* **doch** *versprochen* is weakest and little more than a reminder. *Du hast es* **aber** *versprochen* is stronger and makes a protest. **Aber** combined with **doch** is stronger again. They can either be together in the middle of the sent., *Du hast es aber doch versprochen,* or separated *Aber du hast es doch versprochen! Aber* at the beginning without *doch* is possible, but not very common. *Doch* in this use strengthens *aber.*

3. But after a neg.

i. When **but** follows a neg. both *sondern* and *aber* are found. Which is required depends largely on the intention behind what is to be communicated. The function of **sondern** is to introduce the correct information after a neg. in the first part of the sent. states what is not true. *Werner ist nicht fleißig, sondern stinkfaul,* would be said when someone mistakenly believes him to be hard-working. *Sondern* thus corrects what is mistakenly considered correct. *Max ist nicht mein Bruder, sondern mein Vetter. Sie sind nicht ins Kino gegangen, sondern zum Fußballspiel.* **Aber** also follows a neg. which states that something is not true, but stresses a common or pos. factor, so that the two parts of the sent. are not mutually exclusive. *Jörg ist nicht in seinem Zimmer, aber er ist zu Hause.* The pos. factor is *Er ist hier* or *in der Nähe. Aber* would be used in *Jörg ist nicht in seinem Zimmer, aber im Keller* when the second part represents a pos. feature, not a correction, i.e. the assurance that he is at home. In *Die zweite Auflage haben wir nicht, aber wir haben die erste, aber* brings out the pos. feature that we do have a copy instead of not having one at all. If I mistakenly think I am using the second edition, someone might say, *'Das ist nicht die zweite Auflage, sondern die erste.'* (The transl. of the sent. with *aber* is likely to be: *We don't have the second edition, but/however we have/do have the first.* The sent. with *sondern* could be translated as *That's not the second edition, but the first* or as *That's not the second edition, it's the first.*)

ii. Certain words make it necessary to use either *sondern* or *aber.*

a. When either part of the sent. contains *nur*, only **sondern** is used. Hence *nicht nur . . . sondern auch.*

Du hast nicht nur gesprochen, sondern auch gelacht.

Er hat nicht gesprochen, sondern nur gelacht.   *Sie kann nicht gehen, sondern nur humpeln.*

b. Only **sondern** is used if the two parts of the sent. being contrasted contain antonyms.

Sie ist nicht krank, sondern gesund.   *Das Wasser ist nicht heiß, sondern kalt.*

c. **Sondern** is used if the second part of the sent. represents a semantic variant on the first, one which intensifies the meaning. *Es regnet nicht, sondern es gießt,* it's not raining, it's pouring.

d. Only **sondern** is possible in sents. of the type *Nicht Klaus hat angerufen, sondern Inge* or *Auf dem Tisch lagen nicht Bücher, sondern Schallplatten.*

e. **Sondern** is used when the second part of the sent. contains *eher, vielmehr, höchstens,* or *allenfalls,* all of which correct or modify a previous statement.

Er ist nicht dumm, sondern eher/höchstens/vielmehr/allenfalls faul.

f. **Aber** is used when the second part of the sent. contains the particles *wohl, schon,* or *auch.* In *Das Paket habe ich nicht bekommen, aber den Brief wohl/schon, wohl* or *schon* strengthen the meaning of *aber* without adding anything new to it. They can be translated as . . . but I <u>have</u> received the letter, with *have* stressed. *Es ist nicht ganz richtig, aber auch nicht falsch.*

g. Only **aber** is possible when the first part of the sent. contains *zwar,* admittedly, it is true.

Das ist zwar verboten, aber keiner hält sich an das Verbot.

Sie schlug eine zwar ungewöhnliche, aber höchst interessante Lösung vor.

h. When the second part of the sent. contains *wenigstens* or *immerhin,* both = 'at least', or *doch,* only **aber** is used. In all cases *zwar* may be added to the first part of the sent.

Sie ist [zwar] nicht klug, aber wenigstens/immerhin/doch fleißig.

i. Only **aber** is used if the n. in the second part denotes a category which includes the n. in the first part. *Das ist kein Papagei, aber es ist ein Vogel. Das ist keine Rose, aber es ist eine Blume.* This explains the use of *aber* in *Das ist kein großer Mißerfolg, aber es ist ein enttäuschendes Ergebnis.*

j. The E. constructions without a conjunction, *John didn't ring up, Mary did* or *Anne didn't go to London, it was Ruth* or *It wasn't John who rang up, it was Mary* or *What we need is not sugar, it's flour,* are best translated by **sondern**. *John hat nicht angerufen, sondern Mary. Nicht John hat angerufen, sondern Mary. Was wir brauchen ist nicht Zucker, sondern Mehl. Zucker brauchen wir nicht, sondern Mehl.*

iii. When a pos. factor follows a neg., **wohl aber** is used in educated speech in an elliptical construction. *Ich habe ihn nicht gesehen, wohl aber gehört, daß er wieder hier ist. Er ist kein guter Läufer, wohl aber ein guter Schwimmer. Die zweite Auflage haben wir nicht, wohl aber die erste.* In everyday speech *aber* and *wohl* are separated as explained in ii. *f.*

4. Jedoch is a syn. of *aber* or *doch* when they link two clauses, but it belongs rather to the written language and is more like **however**. Unlike *doch* used as a conj. (cf. 6) it need not be at the begining of its clause.

Meiner Frau hat es in Spanien gar nicht gefallen, mir jedoch hat der Urlaub dort gut gefallen.

Er sagt, daß er im Augenblick keine Zeit hat, jedoch bereit ist, uns später zu helfen.

5. In one sense **allerdings** is translated as **but** or **however**, but it introduces a qualification or reservation about something just stated rather than a complete contrast.

Ich komme gern mit. Allerdings kann ich nur eine halbe Stunde bleiben.

Er ist sehr stark und hilfsbereit, allerdings wenig geschickt.

6. The conjs. **yet** and **and yet** mean 'but in spite of that' or 'nevertheless' and introduce a statement which is surprising in view of what has just been said. *Everything around him was blown to pieces, yet he escaped without a scratch. She's vain and foolish, and yet people like her.* **Doch, trotzdem,** and **dennoch** are used as conjs. They stand at the beginning of a sent. or clause and are stronger than *aber. Sie ist dumm und eitel, dennoch/trotzdem haben sie alle gern.* Or . . . *doch alle haben sie gern.* Cf. 7. And in *and yet* is not translated. When *doch* begins a clause, v. and subj. are usually not reversed; inversion is only found in literary style. *Er hat sich sehr bemüht, doch es gelang ihm nicht.* These conjs. are often the best equivalent of **still** at the beginning of a sent. or clause. *That's true—still, there's more to be considered than that: Das stimmt [schon]—doch man muß auch mehr berücksichtigen als das.* Cf. 7. ii.

> *Ich wollte nie wieder hinfahren, trotzdem habe ich mich dazu überreden lassen.*
> *Alles um ihn herum wurde zertrümmert, dennoch kam der Minister unversehrt davon.*

7. Still, all/just the same, in spite of this/that/everything. All are used after **but.** *I didn't win, but it was still an enjoyable experience. She knew he wasn't listening properly, but she went on all the same. You're a nuisance sometimes, but we love you just/all the same.* They are also used after a concessive clause or phr. *Although I didn't win, it was still an enjoyable experience/it was an enjoyable experience all the same/in spite of that. Whatever they have done or not done, they are still your parents. Whoever he is, he still needs a pass. With all her faults, we love her still. They still kept on despite the setbacks.*

i. Aber is combined with **doch, trotzdem,** and **dennoch.** These function like **in spite of that, all/just the same,** and **still.** *Doch* is the weakest, and *dennoch* the strongest as it indicates a considerable contrast between what one is led to expect by the first clause and the actual result stated in the second. *Doch* and *trotzdem* belong to the everyday language, *dennoch* is stylistically somewhat higher. *Aber* + one of these words translates **and yet** when it joins two adjs. (not two clauses). *He was an embittered man and yet very funny* (or *but still very funny*): *Er war ein verbitterter Mensch, aber trotzdem sehr witzig.* The sents. given in 6 with *doch* etc. used as conjs. can also be formulated with *aber* + *doch* etc.

> *Er hat nicht viel gearbeitet, aber die Prüfung doch bestanden.* Also . . . *die Prüfung hat er aber doch*
>   *bestanden.   Es regnete oft, aber der Urlaub war trotzdem schön.*
> *Keiner hatte ihm eine Chance gegeben, aber er hat es trotzdem/dennoch geschafft.*
> *Es war ihr klar, daß er nicht richtig zuhörte, aber sie erzählte trotzdem weiter.*
> *Du bist zwar ein richtiger Plagegeist, aber wir haben dich trotzdem lieb.*
> *Alles um ihn herum wurde zertrümmert, aber der Minister kam dennoch unversehrt davon.*

ii. Doch, trotzdem, and **dennoch** are used in combination with a concessive clause or phr. introduced by *trotz* or *obwohl. Obwohl keiner ihm eine Chance gab, hat er es doch/trotzdem/dennoch geschafft. Trotz aller Rückschläge arbeiteten sie dennoch weiter.* Sometimes what is conceded or admitted to be true is in a previous sent. The next sent. begins with **still** or one of the other expressions. *He's treated you badly. Still/In spite of that/All the same he's your brother, and you ought to help him now: Er hat dich [zwar] schlecht behandelt, doch er ist dein Bruder, und du solltest ihm jetzt helfen. Ich will es trotzdem/dennoch/doch versuchen* translates *I'll still try, I'll try all/just the same/in spite of that* when these refer to something said previously.

> *Obwohl ich nicht gewonnen habe, war es doch/trotzdem sehr angenehm, am Wettkampf*
>   *teilzunehmen.*
> *Was sie auch immer getan oder unterlassen haben, sie sind trotzdem/dennoch deine Eltern.*
> *Wer er auch sein mag, er braucht trotzdem einen Passierschein.*
> *Trotz aller Fehler lieben wir sie doch.   Trotz der Dunkelheit habe ich ihn doch erkannt.*
> *Ihre Argumente sind stichhaltig, das bestreite ich nicht. Trotzdem gibt es andere Gesichtspunkte, die*
>   *Sie nicht berücksichtigt haben.*

hurry *v.* and *n.* **hasten** *v.*

1. Hurry. intr.

i. The main equivalent is **sich beeilen** which means both 'to move at a faster pace than normal' and 'to do sth. more quickly than usual'. *Wir müssen uns beeilen, sonst wird der Bus weg sein.* It is the normal word in the imp., *Beeil' dich doch ein bißchen!*, it is used with *mit*, *Er beeilte sich mit der Arbeit/den Besorgungen*, and can take an infin., *Alle Länder beeilten sich, den Vertrag zu unterzeichnen*, hurried or hastened to sign.

    Wenn wir den Zug noch erreichen wollen, müssen wir uns sehr beeilen.
    Unser Werk ist angewiesen worden, sich mit diesem Auftrag zu beeilen.
    Sie beeilte sich, den Fehler wiedergutzumachen.   *Er beeilte sich, die Sache zu erledigen.*

ii. **Eilen** denotes hurried movement towards a place. It is now used only with a phr. stating where someone is hurrying to, and usually implies on foot. *Als das Telefon klingelte, eilte ich nach unten.*

    Als er die Nachricht bekam, eilte er nach Hause/eilte er sofort zu dem Freund.
    Der Dame waren einige Pakete heruntergefallen, aber ein Junge eilte ihr zu Hilfe.

iii. **Schnell machen**, **sich sputen**, **sich ranhalten**, and **hinmachen** are common in speech and mean 'to hurry up' or 'to get a move on'. *Mach schon!* is a command like *Hurry up!* or *Get on with it!*

    Spute dich!   *Ich werde mich sputen, damit ich bis sechs wieder hier bin.*
    Du mußt dich mit der Arbeit aber gewaltig sputen, wenn du bis zum Abend noch fertig werden willst.
    Hole deine Sachen, aber mach' schnell!
    Nun müssen wir aber schnell machen, sonst kommen wir zu spät.
    Ihr Zug geht in einer Viertelstunde, aber wenn Sie sich ranhalten, schaffen Sie es vielleicht noch.
    Nun mach' ein bißchen hin, denn wir müssen weg! (Only in the north.)
    Macht mal hin, damit ihr fertig werdet!

2. Hurry trans. None of the vs. in 1 is trans. The idea of hurrying s.o./sth. [up] is expressed in various ways.

i. *It always takes Jim an age to get ready. Can you hurry him up a bit?* could be *Kannst du dafür sorgen, daß er sich beeilt?* To hurry people with work is *zur Eile antreiben*. *Wenn Sie die Restaurateure zur Eile antreiben, werden Sie alles verderben.* For *The troops were hurried to the border*, the simplest transl. is *Truppen wurden eiligst/schleunig zur Grenze gebracht* or *an die Grenze verlegt*. *Sie wurden an die Front geworfen* is also used.

ii. **Beschleunigen**, 'to accelerate', can mean 'to make sth. happen more quickly or sooner than usual' and can translate **hurry**, **hasten**, *expedite*, or *speed up*.

    Man hat die Reiseformalitäten beschleunigt.   *Sie beschleunigten ihre Abreise.*
    Der Verlag beschloß, den Druck des Buches zu beschleunigen.

iii. Hurry food/a meal. One transl. is *Du brauchst das Essen nicht hinunterzuschlingen*, gulp it down.

4. Two vs. related to *eilen*.

i. Sich übereilen means 'to hurry too much', 'to rush', or 'to act precipitately, without due consideration'. *Übereil' dich nicht beim Kauf des Wagens!* **Übereilen** is trans. *Sie übereilten die Sache.* **Übereilt** means 'over-hasty, rushed'. *Eine übereilte Handlung. Tu' nichts übereilt!*

    Man sieht der Arbeit an, daß er sich damit übereilt hat.   *Eine übereilte Schlußfolgerung.*

ii. *Eine Entscheidung* **überstürzen** is 'to make a decision in far too great a hurry', 'to rush it'. It is stronger than *übereilen*. **Sich bei etw. überstürzen** is 'to do sth. in far too great a hurry or rush'.

    Soweit ich weiß, hat er sich nie bei solcher Arbeit überstürzt.
    Sie handelten überstürzt, als sie das Angebot ablehnten. Es hätte ihnen viele Vorteile geboten.

5. Hurry. n.

i. Die Eile means 'hurry or rush'. *Warum die Eile? Ich mußte die Arbeit in großer Eile erledigen. Die Sache hat keine Eile* and *Damit hat es keine Eile* are fixed, synonymous expressions without a pos. form. **Eilig** means 'hurried'. *Wir hörten eilige Schritte. Ich habe es eilig, Ich habe Eile,* and *Ich bin in Eile* all mean that I'm in a hurry. *Es eilig haben mit* etc. means 'to be in a hurry for sth.' *Ich habe es nicht eilig mit der Übersetzung.* An infin. can also follow. *Er hatte es nicht eilig, uns zu benachrichtigen.*

    In der Eile habe ich den Brief liegengelassen.   *Ich lief eilig davon.*

    Man sieht der Arbeit die Eile an, in der sie gemacht worden ist.

ii. Eilen with a thing as subj. means that the thing is pressing or urgent, and can convey the sense of the E. n. *Die Sache eilt [sehr].* The impersonal expression *es eilt mit* has the same meaning. *Mit dieser Angelegenheit eilt es sehr.* The neg. means that there is no hurry with something. *Mit der Übersetzung eilt es nicht—laß dir Zeit! Eilt* on letters means 'urgent'. (The adj. *eilig* also means 'pressing, urgent'. *Eine eilige Angelegenheit.*)

i

idea, concept, conception *ns.* **Idea** and *die Idee* do not coincide in all uses, so that other words may be better transls. of *idea*.

1. One sense of **idea** is 'a conception or notion of sth. to be done or carried out', 'an intention or plan for action'.

i. In one of its main senses, **die Idee** denotes a thought according to which one can act. It refers to just the germ of a plan which occurs to someone suddenly, not something thought out or worked out in detail, and can be a clever thought about the way something can be done. A following *wie*-clause is common. *Auf meine Idee, wie wir das Produkt verbessern könnten, ging sie sofort ein.* What is to be done is also often given in a new sent. *Ich habe eine Idee! Laßt uns das Haus neu dekorieren!* An infin. suggests a spontaneous action. *Es war eine gute Idee von dir, hierher zu kommen.* When a considered decision is involved or when concrete details of an action are implied, *der Gedanke* or *der Plan* are more appropriate transls. of **idea**. Particularly in speech, *Idee* often has the connotation of a good idea, but it is also often used ironically and means a not particularly deep or intelligent thought. *Idee* can also suggest a fanciful notion or one remote from reality. It may thus have a pos. or neg. connotation even if an adj. does not make this clear. *Er ist nie dazu gekommen, seine Ideen auszuführen* would mostly be neutral. *Jmd. steckt voll Ideen* is praise, as *Sie kam plötzlich auf eine neue Idee* can be. *Du hast vielleicht Ideen!* suggests unusual, if not outrageous, ideas. Thus *Wie kommst du denn auf so eine Idee?* and *Er wurde von der Idee ergriffen, er könnte die Gesellschaft neu ordnen. Etw. bleibt bloße Idee* or *nur Idee* or *ist bloß/nur als Idee vorhanden*, 'something exists only as an idea', may, but need not, suggest unrealizability.

> *Das ist eine gute/glänzende/kindische/gefährliche Idee.*   *Alle waren von dieser Idee begeistert.*
> *Die Schriftstellerin hatte die Idee zu einem neuen Roman.*
> *Die anderen haben ihre Idee verworfen.*
> *Das ist keine schlechte Idee, aber ob sie sich ausführen läßt?*

ii. Ein Gedanke means 'a thought', but as it often suggests one which gives rise to action, it can translate **idea**. It implies more consideration than *Idee*. *Das ist ein guter Gedanke*, plan or idea. *Das bringt mich auf einen Gedanken*, gives me an idea. *Auf diesen Gedanken wäre ich ohne ihre Ratschläge niemals gekommen. Gedanke* can be applied to foolish thoughts and ideas, *ein dummer Gedanke*, and can be used ironically, *Das ist ein grandioser Gedanke—wir gehen heute mal ins Kino.*

> *Ich trage mich seit einiger Zeit mit dem Gedanken, die Stelle zu wechseln.*

Gedanke translates *the very idea/mere thought of* [*doing*] *sth. Der bloße Gedanke, eine Regierung durch einen Staatsstreich zu stürzen, erfüllt ihn mit Entsetzen.*

iii. Der Einfall is 'an idea which occurs to s.o. suddenly'. It can be a witty or amusing remark, or the thought of doing something which can be sensible or foolish.

> *Er hat immer seltsame Einfälle.*   *Sie hat oft geistreiche Einfälle.*
> *Als sie nach Hause ging, kam ihr der Einfall, übers Wochenende zu verreisen.*
> *Der Autor hatte einen glänzenden Einfall, wie er den Roman abschließen konnte.*

iv. Other equivalents. *Das denkst du dir nur*, it exists only in your mind, it's just an idea you have. *What an idea!* or *What a ridiculous idea!* can be *Das ist doch Unsinn!* or

Das ist doch lächerlich! but also *Was für eine blöde Idee/ein blöder Gedanke! Eine Schnapsidee* or *Kateridee* is 'a hare-brained or crackpot idea'. *Damals schien es mir richtig zu sein* is an adequate transl. of *It seemed a good idea at the time*.

2. Die Idee can also be 'an idea determining s.o.'s thinking and action', or 'the plan or design according to which sth., particularly a work of art, is constructed or created' and, mostly in the pl., 'formulated thoughts or opinions, the products of s.o.'s reflection, the basic conceptions of a political or other system of thought'. Thus *Sie kämpften für diese Idee. Mehrere Abgeordnete traten für diese Idee ein. Die Idee der Freiheit bei Schiller. Die Idee eines Dramas/eines Romans. Marxistische/Fortschrittliche/ Liberale Ideen. Die Ideen der Demokratie.* **Der Leitgedanke**, 'main idea or central/dominant theme', is occasionally used in connection with works of art, conferences, etc. *Der Leitgedanke spiegelt sich in allen Kapiteln des Romans wieder.* **Das Gedankengut** is a collective term for the ideas of a particular system, of a philosophy, or of an age. *Das christliche Gedankengut* is 'the body or system of Christian ideas or thought'. *Das westliche Gedankengut hat alle Völker der Erde beeinflußt.* Also *Westliche Ideen*.

3. S.o.'s **ideas** can mean 'that pers.'s OPINIONS'. *Dränge anderen deine Ansichten nicht auf!*, don't force your ideas on others!

4. S.o.'s **idea** of sth. is 'a mental image, conception, or impression of what sth. is or should be like'.

i. The equivalent is **die Vorstellung**, what someone pictures something as or conceives it to be. *Dieses [Theater]stück entspricht nicht meiner Vorstellung einer Komödie*, is not my idea of a comedy.

> *Das Buch gibt/vermittelt eine gute Vorstellung vom Leben im alten Rom* (gives a good idea of).
> *Über den Ort hatte ich so viel gehört, daß ich mir eine Vorstellung von dessen Herrlichkeit gebildet hatte.*
> *Kann ein Blinder eine Vorstellung von Farben haben?*
> *Ihre Vorstellung von der Bedeutung des eigenen Landes war nicht übertrieben.*
> *Ich habe mir eine klare Vorstellung von den Ereignissen verschafft.* Also . . . *ein klares Bild*.
> *Du kannst dir keine Vorstellung [davon] machen, welche Mühe das gekostet hat.*

ii. Der Begriff is a syn. of *Vorstellung* but is mostly confined to the ethical and aesthetic spheres. *Sich einen Begriff von etw. machen* is 'to form an idea or mental picture of it', often of its essential features in order to understand it. *Du kannst dir keinen Begriff davon machen* means that you cannot form a mental picture of it, i.e. you cannot imagine it. *Vorstellung* can be used in both these expressions and now seems to be more common.

> *Sie war nicht hübsch nach landläufigem Begriff.*   *Ihre Schönheit übersteigt alle Begriffe.*
> *Es wird mir nie gelingen, mir einen Begriff von deiner Denkwelt zu machen.*

iii. Das Bild can also mean 'an image in the mind, a conception, idea, or impression'. Although *das Weltbild* or *Menschenbild* mean 'view or conception of the world or man', *Bild* suggests a direct connection with reality, while *Vorstellung* is more abstract. *Ich mache mir ein [klares] Bild von den Zuständen irgendwo* could imply going and looking at the conditions in the place, but it may also refer to a view or impression formed in other ways. *Bild* does not, however, imply that the idea something gives is correct. Thus *Der Bericht vermittelt/gibt ein realistisches Bild der Lage* is just as usual as *Er gibt ein schiefes Bild davon*. Only the sing. is common.

> *Du hast ein falsches Bild von der Bedeutung dieser Politiker.*
> *Ein Schauspieler muß sich ein klares Bild machen von der Gestalt, die er darstellt.*

5. Der Begriff is 'a concept', meaning 'a general idea or notion of the essential features of a phenomenon or class of phenomena'. *Wir bilden den Begriff Pferd, indem wir viele Pferde sehen. Der Begriff der Demokratie. Begriff* also denotes a word, term, or concept which expresses such a general idea, often one used in a particular field. *Ein grammatikalischer/ästhetischer Begriff. Etw. ist mir ein Begriff* means that it is known to me, I am familiar with the idea/name, it means or conveys something to me.

> *Können Sie den Begriff der Pflicht definieren?*
> *Die Entropie ist ein physikalischer Begriff.*
> *Sie haben die beiden Begriffe miteinander verwechselt.*
> *Ein festumrissener/verschwommener Begriff.*

6. When **idea** refers to knowledge, *I had no idea that this land could be flooded*, to the suspicion that something is true, *I had an idea that this was wrong*, or to a presentiment about what will happen in the future, *I had an idea/no idea that I would meet her there*, it is expressed by **die Ahnung** or the v. **ahnen**. *Ich habe nicht die geringste Ahnung* or *keine blaße Ahnung*, I haven't the faintest/slightest/remotest/foggiest idea.

> *Habt ihr eine Ahnung, wann er kommt?*   *Ich habe geahnt, daß diese Behauptung nicht stimmte.*
> *Nicht einmal seine engsten Freunde ahnten, daß etw. nicht in Ordnung war.*
> *Sie ahnte nicht, daß dieser Wunsch sich bald erfüllen würde.*
> *Ich hatte keine Ahnung, daß dieses Land überschwemmt werden könnte.*
> *Ich hatte eine Ahnung/ahnte, daß sie dabei sein würde/daß alles schief gehen würde.*

ignorance *n.* **Die Unkenntnis** can only mean 'ignorance of a specific matter or in a specific field'. The matter or field must be stated. *Unkenntnis der Gesetze schützt nicht vor Strafe. Sie ließen uns in Unkenntnis über den wahren Sachverhalt. Ihre Unkenntnis der Lebensweise der Gebirgsstämme führte zu diesen Fehlentscheidungen.* Unkenntnis belongs to formal language. **Die Unwissenheit** is both 'a lack of the knowledge normally expected among educated and civilized people', *In vielen Ländern herrscht noch große Unwissenheit*, and 'ignorance of a matter or in a field'. The matter or field may, but need not, be stated. *Unter diesen Leuten herrschte völlige Unwissenheit hinsichtlich ihrer Rechte. Sie hat es aus Unwissenheit falsch gemacht.*

imagination *n.*

1. i. **Die Phantasie** is the usual equivalent of **imagination** meaning 'the power or ability to form pictures or ideas in the mind'. It also translates the less common syns. of **imagination**, i.e. *fancy* as in *let one's fancy roam*, and *phantasy/fantasy* meaning 'the power of imagination'. *Jmd. hat viel/wenig/keine/eine rege Phantasie. Der Dichter bevölkerte seine Werke mit den Gestalten seiner Phantasie. Er ließ seiner Phantasie freien Lauf. Das Spiel/Die Welt der Phantasie. Der Plan besteht nur in deiner Phantasie.*
ii. **Die Einbildungskraft** was coined as a G. equivalent of *die Phantasie* but remains a learned word. **Die Vorstellungskraft** and **das Vorstellungsvermögen** are 'the power of picturing thgs. in the mind' and can be translated as **imagination** or *power of conception. Das geht über meine Vorstellungskraft hinaus.* Both are confined to learned discourse.

2. **Die Phantasie** also denotes the result of using the faculty of imagination, i.e. *a fancy or fantasy*, and, like the E. words, can be neutral or pejorative. *The fancies of a poet. Sth. is a mere fantasy.* In this use, *die Phantasie* is often pl., and as a medical term can mean 'hallucinations'. *Die schönen Phantasien eines Dichters. Die seltsamen Phantasien des Kindes. Was sie da behauptet, ist reine/bloße Phantasie.*

3. **Die Einbildung** is occasionally a syn. of *Phantasie* 1. i meaning 'faculty of imagination'. *Das Schloß existiert nur in seiner Einbildung.* Its chief meaning is 'an unfounded or untrue idea or belief'. It corresponds to **imagination** when it means 'sth. falsely imagined'. *You didn't see a ghost—it was just imagination. Du hast doch kein Gespenst gesehen—das war bloß Einbildung. Diese Krankheit ist reine Einbildung. In seiner Einbildung gibt es unüberwindliche Schwierigkeiten* thus usually implies that what he imagines is mistaken, a false belief, or fantasy. (*Einbildung* also means 'conceit, excessive pride'. *Ihre Einbildung macht sie sehr unbeliebt.* Cf. IMAGINE 1. ii.)

imagine *v.*

1. In the basic sense 'to form a mental image of sth. not present to the senses', G., by using two words, makes a distinction which is not made clear in E., i.e. whether what is imagined is believed to correspond to reality or not.

i. **Sich einbilden** is used when the mental image or idea is unfounded, mistaken, or contrary to reality, but is believed to be correct. It suggests an illusion. It is used with an obj., an infin., or a clause and is common in the neg. imp. implying that the person addressed should not be under an illusion. *Bilde dir ja nicht ein, daß alle dich bewundern!*, don't imagine everyone admires you. The question *Do you imagine that I am satisfied?*, which implies that the belief of the person addressed is mistaken, is *Bildest du dir etwa ein, daß ich zufrieden bin? Etwa*, lit. = 'PERHAPS', strengthens the implication that the belief is mistaken and gives the clause a meaning like *you don't really believe.*

> *Er bildet sich Gefahren ein, die es gar nicht gibt.*   *Er hatte sich eingebildet, verfolgt zu sein.*
> *Ich bildete mir ein, Schüsse gehört zu haben.*   *Ich bildete mir ein, es hätte geklopft.*
> *Du solltest dir nicht einbilden, daß du die Zustände in der Firma ändern kannst.*
> *Der Weltmeister im Schachspiel bildete sich ein, daß seine Gegner ihn vergiften wollten.*

ii. With words like *viel* or *allerhand* and sometimes *etw.*, **sich einbilden** means 'to be unduly proud or conceited'. *Auf* = 'about'. *Er bildet sich viel auf seine Kenntnisse ein.* In *ein eingebildeter Mensch*, *eingebildet* means 'conceited', but in *eingebildete Krankheiten* and *ein eingebildeter Kranker* it has sense i and means 'imaginary'.

> *Sie bildet sich viel ein* (is conceited). Neg. *Bilde dir bloß nicht so viel ein!*
> *Auf diese Leistung darfst du dir wirklich etw. einbilden* (you can be proud of).

The neg. is formed with *nichts. Darauf brauchst du dir nichts einzubilden*, you needn't be proud.

iii. **Sich vorstellen** means 'to form a mental image or idea of sth. real or possible'. It is used whenever someone consciously tries to picture something in his/her mind and also when someone forms an idea of something in the future, although this may turn out not to be accurate. It is used with an obj. or a clause and with *als*. If what is imagined is only a very remote possibility or highly unlikely, the subjunctive is used. *Stell' dir vor, du wärst Millionär!* Unlike *sich einbilden*, *sich vorstellen* does not suggest that the state imagined is considered real. The E. gerundial construction *I can't imagine myself doing sth.* must be turned into a clause. *Ich kann mir nicht vorstellen, daß ich jemals im Dschungel arbeiten würde.*

> *Ich kann mir den Ort gut/genau vorstellen.*
> *Es ist schwer, sich diese Vorgänge vorzustellen.*
> *Er konnte sich gut vorstellen, wie sich das abgespielt hat.*
> *Unter diesem Begriff kann ich mir gar nichts vorstellen.*
> *Stell' dir vor, wir würden das große Los gewinnen!*
> *Ich stelle mir vor, daß das gar nicht so einfach ist.*   *Ich kann sie mir gut als Lehrerin vorstellen.*
> *Kannst du dir meine Überraschung vorstellen?*
> *Der Verkehr war nicht so schlimm, wie ich ihn mir vorgestellt hatte.*
> *Er ist der größte Hund, den man sich vorstellen kann.*

iv. The imp. of **sich vorstellen** is used like *Just imagine!* to express surprise. *Stell' dir vor!—wir haben gewonnen. Stell' dir vor, er will morgen abreisen!*

v. **Sich denken** also means 'to picture in the mind' and is a close syn. of *sich* *vorstellen.* They are in many cases interchangeable. *Sich denken* is particularly common in speech. *Das kann ich mir gut denken,* I can well imagine that. *Sich denken* is translated by *think* or by **imagine** depending on the context. *Das habe ich mir gleich gedacht,* I thought so/as much, thought that was the case. *Ich kann mir ihre Überraschung denken,* I can imagine her surprise. In all of the following sents. *sich vorstellen* could also be used.

> *Ich denke ihn mir als großen, stattlichen Mann.*   *Wie denkst du dir deine weitere Laufbahn?*
> *Wie das schmerzt, das kannst du dir nicht denken.*
> *Du kannst dir denken, wie entsetzt ich war.*
> *Ich denke mir das Leben auf dem Lande sehr erholsam.*
> *Ich habe es mir so gedacht—wir nehmen uns ein paar Tage frei und fahren ins Gebirge.*
> *Daß etw. schief gehen würde—das kann man sich doch denken.*

vi. When **imagine** means 'to create as a mental conception sth. which does not exist in reality', either **sich denken** or **sich vorstellen** can be used, but the only equivalent of the past part. **imagined** is *gedacht. Ein gedachter Punkt. Eine gedachte Linie.*

> *Die Landschaft ist flach und uninteressant, aber denk' dir einen See in der Mitte und dahinter einen Hügel! Or Stell' dir einen See in der Mitte vor! Or Stell' dir vor, es gäbe einen See . . .*
> *Das ist nur ein gedachter Fall (imagined, imaginary).*

vii. Sich ausmalen also means 'to picture in the mind', but it adds the idea that what is pictured is seen vividly and in all details. It is often applied to what someone wishes for or fears.

> *Er hatte sich [in der Phantasie] ein abenteuerliches Seemannsleben ausgemalt, fand aber, daß das Leben auf einem modernen Handelsschiff sehr eintönig war.*
> *Sie malte sich ihre berufliche Zukunft in den lebhaftesten Farben aus.*

viii. Sich vergegenwärtigen implies a conscious effort to picture something clearly to oneself. It is not used for purely imaginary situations and suggests drawing on memory or experience. It is translated as **imagine** or *visualize. Vergegenwärtige dir doch einmal die Folgen, wenn du jetzt zurücktrittst!*

> *Sie versuchte, sich die damalige Situation zu vergegenwärtigen.*
> *Vergegenwärtigen Sie sich die Lage, in der wir uns befanden!*

2. In *We can only imagine the cause of this prehistoric disaster,* **imagine** means 'to conjecture, surmise, or guess' and would be translated as **vermuten.** Cf. GUESS ii.

> *Wir können nur vermuten, was diese vorgeschichtliche Katastrophe herbeigeführt hat.*

3. In *Tilo found that Romola was a more unforgiving woman than he had imagined,* **imagine** means 'to think or suppose' and is translated as **[sich] denken, glauben,** or **annehmen,** to assume.

> *Tilo fand, daß Romola eine unversöhnlichere Frau war, als er [sich] gedacht hatte/als er geglaubt/angenommen hatte/als er sie sich vorgestellt hatte.*

immediately, straight away, directly *advs.* **at once** phr. used as *adv.*

i. Sofort means 'in the shortest possible time after sth. else'. It is emphatic and occurs more often in the imp. than the syns. discussed below. *Du sollst zum Chef gehen und zwar sofort. Rufen Sie ihn sofort an! Ich habe dich sofort erkannt, als du aus dem Zug gestiegen bist. Die Waren sind sofort lieferbar.* In *Diese Regelung gilt ab sofort, sofort* is the only possibility as the other words are not used with *ab.* With a v. in the pres., *sofort* indicates that someone will do something as soon as possible. *Nehmen Sie bitte Platz! Ich bin sofort wieder da.*

> *Der Verletzte wurde sofort operiert.*   *Wir geben Ihnen sofort Bescheid.*
> *Ich werde sofort nach dem Essen hingehen.*   *Meine Kollegin wird sofort zurück sein.*

ii. Sogleich is used only in the written language. *Er verabschiedete sich und fuhr*

sogleich nach Hause. **Gleich** is much used in everyday language and means 'in a relatively short time'. Like **directly**, it varies between *at once, without delay,* and *in a minute, in a short time.* It thus often denotes a longer time than *sofort* and is less categorical. *Gleich nach dem Essen gingen sie weg. Sie verstand nicht gleich, wen ich meinte. Ich komme gleich runter. Ich bin gleich wieder da.*
iii. Unmittelbar means 'directly or immediately after or before sth.' It is only used in statements, not in commands. *Unmittelbar nach dieser Auseinandersetzung kündigte er,* immediately after. *Er hatte das Gebäude unmittelbar vor der Explosion verlassen. Die Wahlen stehen unmittelbar bevor,* the elections are close or about to take place.
iv. Umgehend is common in business letters. *Wir bitten Sie, diese Angelegenheit umgehend zu erledigen. Teilen Sie uns Ihre Entscheidung umgehend mit!* **Prompt** is also common in business style. *Sie haben prompt geantwortet. Der Auftrag wurde prompt ausgeführt.* **Unverzüglich** means 'without delay' and is fairly formal. *Der Vorfall muß unverzüglich gemeldet werden.* **Auf der Stelle**, means 'on the spot, immediately'. *Als er das hörte, drehte er sich auf der Stelle um und ging weg.*

improve v. **Improve** is both trans. meaning 'to make better' or 'to increase the quality of', *These reforms improved the education system,* and intr. meaning 'to become better', *Your French is improving* or *My health has improved. Bessern* and *verbessern* correspond to the trans. sense, while the refl. forms *sich bessern* and *sich verbessern* express the intr. senses. The trans. meaning is also expressed by *to* **improve on/upon**. *She improved on her record. Our methods are being improved on daily.*
1. Trans. uses. As a trans. v., *bessern* has become uncommon and been largely replaced by *verbessern.*
i. Bessern still means 'to improve morally, to reform'.
   Verwandte versuchten, den Jugendlichen, der mit dem Gesetz in Konflikt geraten war, zu bessern.
(With *an,* as in *Der Dichter feilte und besserte an jedem Satz,* it is archaic.)
ii. Bessern = 'to improve in health'. *Verbessern* occurs, but *bessern* is still used. Hence *Gute Besserung.*
   Der Aufenthalt in den Bergen hat den Zustand des Kranken gebessert.
   Der Arzt hat noch Hoffnung auf Besserung.
iii. Verbessern is the usual word when the obj. is non-personal. As it does not necessarily imply that the thing was bad before, it means 'to improve on' as well as 'to improve'. It is applied to methods, processes, machines, (the quality of) products, personal relations, books, educational and other systems, one's marks or performance, and is also used in sport.
   Die Firma ist ständig bemüht, die Qualität ihrer Produkte zu verbessern.
   Die Fernsehanstalten wollen ihre Programme verbessern.
   Die Läuferin konnte den Weltrekord um 20 Sekunden verbessern.
   Die zweite Auflage des Wörterbuchs stellt eine große Verbesserung gegenüber der ersten dar. Also . . .
   eine große Verbesserung im Vergleich zu . . . (Both = 'is a great improvement on'.)
2. Intr. use.
i. With people as subj. **sich bessern** translates the intr. use of *reform* and **improve**, but, unlike *bessern* in 1. i, it is not restricted to serious situations. It can simply imply throwing off bad habits.
   Da er sich gebessert hatte, beschlossen sie, ihm zu verzeihen.
   Ich will mich bessern (d. h. ordentlich sein, nicht mehr zu spät kommen, nicht zu laut sein, nicht faul, sondern fleißig sein etc.)
ii. When a word which can be the obj. of *improve* becomes its subj., i.e. when **improve** is intr., e.g. *He improved his performance* and *His performance improved,* the refl. **sich verbessern** is used. *Alle Regierungen bemühen sich, die Lebensbedingungen der*

Bevölkerung/die Arbeitsbedingungen zu verbessern. But *Die Lebensbedingungen der Menschen haben sich in den letzten Jahrzehnten erheblich verbessert.*

Der Schüler hat seine Leistungen verbessert. But *Seine Leistungen haben sich verbessert.* Also *Der Schüler hat sich seit dem letzten Zeugnis deutlich verbessert.*

Die Qualität der Waren hat sich in den letzten Jahren erheblich verbessert.

iii. Sich bessern is still used without restriction in context to denote an unspecified degree of improvement, but *sich verbessern* is also common.

Das Wetter hat sich in den letzten 24 Stunden gebessert. Or . . . *sich verbessert/ist besser geworden.*

Die Lage/Die Situation hat sich gebessert/verbessert.

Ihr Verhältnis zueinander hat sich gebessert/verbessert.

Der Zustand des Kranken hat sich erheblich gebessert/verbessert.

iv. With people as subj., **sich verbessern** means 'to get a better job or higher salary/wage'.

Ich habe den Arbeitsplatz gewechselt, um mich zu verbessern.

Wenn sie die Stelle, um die sie sich beworben hat, bekommt, wird sie sich verbessern.

3. Verbessern also means 'to correct', but implies a less serious mistake than *berichtigen.* Hence *Der Redner versprach sich zwei- oder dreimal, verbesserte sich aber jedesmal sofort.*

Immer wieder mußten wir seine Aussprache verbessern.   *Hast du alle Fehler verbessert?*

Wenn ein Lehrer im Fremdsprachenunterricht die Schüler ständig verbessert, verlieren sie die Lust am Sprechen.

4. The less common **aufbessern** means 'to improve slightly in quantity or quality' and is applied: (i) To *Gehälter, Renten,* etc. (ii) To food, *Essen, Verpflegung.* (iii) Occasionally to one's knowledge, *Kenntnisse.*

Die Regierung hat versprochen, die Renten aufzubessern.

Der Schüler hat sein Taschengeld durch einen kleinen Nebenverdienst aufgebessert.

Die Studenten hoffen, daß man das Essen in der Mensa aufbessern wird.

Sie besuchte einen Englischkurs, um ihre Sprachkenntnisse aufzubessern. Also *verbessern.*

5. G. often prefers to use the v. normal in the specific context where E. uses **improve**. When **improve** is trans. and means 'to raise or increase sth.', *erhöhen* and *steigern* can be used, and when it is intr. meaning 'to rise or increase', *sich erhöhen* and *steigen* express the sense. Cf. INCREASE.

Man hat die Produktion allmählich gesteigert. Die Produktion ist gestiegen/hat sich erhöht.

Die Preise für Wolle sind in letzter Zeit gestiegen.

Die Bodenverbesserungsmaßnahmen haben die Ertragfähigkeit des Bodens erhöht/gesteigert.

Der Absatz hat sich im Vergleich mit dem Vorjahr um 10 Prozent gesteigert/erhöht.

Du kannst den letzten Versuch noch steigern (improve on your last effort).

With *knowledge* as obj. *erweitern* and *vertiefen* are the appropriate vs. *Sie müssen Ihre Kenntnisse auf diesem Gebiet erweitern/vertiefen.*

include *v.*

1. Include = 'to contain or comprise'. *One thg. includes another. One thg. is included in another.* **Include** differs from *contain* by suggesting that what is included is only one constituent or a secondary feature of something.

i. This distinction is not normally expressed in G. as **enthalten** can be used in all cases. Thus *Das Buch enthält dreißig Abbildungen* could be translated as *contains* or **includes**. *Contains* implies that this is the total number of illustrations to be found in it while **includes** suggests they are there along with other things. As the pass. **in etw. enthalten sein** suggests that the subj. is one of the parts that make up a whole, it is often preferred as a transl. of **include**, but it frequently does not matter which form of *enthalten* is used. *Im Buch sind dreißig Abbildungen enthalten.*

Der Artikel enthält wichtige wissenschaftliche Forschungsergebnisse.

Die Prüfung enthielt eine Frage über Grillparzer.   Der Brief enthielt eine wichtige Nachricht.
In der neuen Verkehrsordnung sind viele Verbesserungen enthalten.

ii. Whereas *einbeziehen* (cf. 4. ii) implies actively drawing s.o./sth. into something, **einschließen** denotes a state, one thing embracing something else or being included in a more comprehensive group.

Diese Definition schließt alle wichtigen Faktoren ein.   Mich eingeschlossen sind wir dreizehn.
Der Lehrplan schließt auch die Entwicklung der Bundesrepublik ein.
Ich schließe mich in die Kritik ein. (Usually *Ich beziehe mich . . . ein.*)

iii. Einbegreifen also states that one item is included in a number or total. It is most commonly used as a past part., which appears in two forms *einbegriffen* and *inbegriffen.*

Kinder unter zehn Jahren sind in dieser Zahl nicht einbegriffen/inbegriffen.

iv. Include meaning 'to be one of or among', as in *The subjects offered include Italian* or *The projects completed this year include the following,* is translated by **gehören zu,** to belong to. Cf. BELONG 3.

Zu Ihren Aufgaben gehört, die Kinder ins Bett zu bringen (Your duties include).
Zu den in diesem Jahr abgeschlossenen Projekten gehören die folgenden: . . .
Zu den in der Schule angebotenen Fächern gehören Russisch, Deutsch, Chinesisch und Japanisch.

2. A price **includes** sth. Sth. **is included in** a price.

i. Einschließen can refer to prices both in the act. and pass. *Der Preis schließt das Frühstück auch ein* or *Im Preis ist das Frühstück [mit] eingeschlossen.* Like *included, eingeschlossen* follows the n. *Die Zustellung eingeschlossen, kostet der Kühlschrank 820 Mark.*

Die Transportkosten sind im Preis [mit] eingeschlossen. (More commonly *mit inbegriffen.*)
Das Wörterbuch kostet DM 75, Verpackung und Porto eingeschlossen.

ii. The past part. **enthalten** + *sein* means that certain items are included in a price. *In diesem Betrag sind alle Gebühren [mit] enthalten. Die Verpackung ist im Preis [mit] enthalten.*

In dem Preis sind Unterkunft und Verpflegung [mit] enthalten.

iii. The two past parts. of *einbegreifen,* **inbegriffen** and **einbegriffen,** are also used in connection with prices. *In diesem Preis ist alles inbegriffen.*

Die Mehrwertsteuer ist im Preis [mit] einbegriffen/inbegriffen.
Die Miete beträgt DM 500, die Nebenkosten inbegriffen.

iv. Dabei sein means 'included' in reference to costs, and is common in speech. *Strom/Heizung ist dabei,* i.e. is included in the rent or price of the room.

3. Including is *einschließlich,* sometimes **darunter.** *Einschließlich* takes the gen., but this is not shown if the n. does not have an article. *Einschließlich aller Reparaturen kostet das Auto DM 5 250. Die Kosten einschließlich Porto betragen 220 Mark.* **Eingeschlossen** can translate **including.** Cf. 1. ii and 2. i.

In vielen Ländern, darunter der Schweiz, ist diese Entwicklung zu beobachten.
Jedes Jahr besuchen Tausende von Touristen, darunter viele Japaner, Schloß Schönbrunn.

4. Include one thg. **in** another.

i. Aufnehmen in + acc. is 'to make one thing part of a larger whole'. This whole is something which already exists or is planned, such as *eine Mannschaft, ein Programm,* or *eine Liste.* (With people as obj. *aufnehmen* also means 'to accept or admit'. Cf. ACCEPT 5.)

Wir wollen diesen Punkt in die Tagesordnung aufnehmen.
Der Intendant beschloß, das Stück des jungen Autors in den Spielplan aufzunehmen.
Wie viele Gedichte von Mörike haben Sie in die Anthologie aufgenommen?
Man hat zwei Nachwuchsspieler in die Mannschaft aufgenommen.

ii. Einbeziehen suggests greater action than *aufnehmen.* With people as subj. and obj., the idea is often that one person draws another into an activity. With things as obj. *einbeziehen* may suggest that the new fact or factor included can influence the outcome rather than just being part of something in a passive way.

> *Sie bemüht sich immer, Gäste in die Unterhaltung [mit] einzubeziehen.*
> *Wir müssen diese Tatsache/diesen Umstand in unsere Überlegungen einbeziehen.*
> *Der Chef bezog alle Mitarbeiter in das allgemeine Lob ein.*
> *Wenn ich von der heutigen Jugend rede, so beziehe ich meine Kinder [mit] ein.*
> *Sie wurde in seinen Freundeskreis einbezogen.*

5. Other senses.

i. Include in a class or category = 'to classify or regard as belonging to it' can be expressed by **einordnen**, 'to put something in its place', or **einreihen**, 'to put in its place, to class as'.

> *Dieses Tier ist unter die Säugetiere/in die Klasse der Säugetiere einzuordnen/einzureihen.*
> *Ich habe das Buch unter die Romane/Sachbücher eingereiht/eingeordnet.*

ii. When an invitation, regulation, order, etc. is subj., **include** means 'to APPLY to' and is **gelten**.

> *Die Einladung gilt natürlich auch für dich* (also includes you).
> *Seid doch ruhig! Das gilt für alle!* (includes everyone)

increase, rise, raise *vs.*

1. Intr. use. *Production has* **increased/risen**.

i. The general word is **zunehmen**, to become greater in number, size, amount, extent, intensity. Some ns. which can be the subj. are *der Wind, die Kälte, die Hitze, die Temperatur, die Produktion, der Verkehr,* and mental states, *jmds. Eifer/Angst/Nervosität. Zunehmen* is used with *an: Der Sturm nahm an Stärke zu* and *Die Schüler nehmen an Erfahrung, Weisheit und Größe zu. In zunehmendem Maße,* to an increasing extent. With people as subj., *zunehmen* means 'to put on weight', with days 'to become longer'.

> *Die Zahl der Studierenden nimmt immer noch zu.*   *Die Spannungen nehmen zu.*
> *Die Menge der abgebauten Kohle hat auch in diesem Jahr zugenommen.*
> *Die Krankheit hatte ihn sehr geschwächt, aber seine Kräfte nehmen jetzt wieder zu.*
> *Sie hatte stark zugenommen und wollte wieder abnehmen.*   *Die Aufregung nahm ständig zu.*

ii. Anwachsen means 'to grow in number or intensity by increasing slowly and steadily'. It is usually interchangeable with *zunehmen* or *steigen* and is used with *auf* like *steigen*. Cf. GROW 2. ii.

> *Er war stolz auf seine Schallplattensammlung, die schon auf über 500 Stück angewachsen war.*
> *Die Aufträge des kleinen Tischlerbetriebs sind in letzter Zeit so angewachsen, daß der Meister noch*
>   *zwei Leute einstellen muß.*

iii. Steigen and **ansteigen** are very close in meaning and correspond to **increase** used intr. and to **rise**. When the rise is quantifiable, either is possible. *Steigen* tends to be used in talking of a rise in an unspecified way. *Die Temperatur/Die Einwohnerzahl/Die Produktion/Sein Einkommen ist gestiegen. Ansteigen* seems to be preferred when the speaker has a clear idea of the difference or when the rise or increase continues, i.e. when after one rise a further one takes place. *Die Zahl der Arbeitslosen stieg weiter an.* However, the distinction is not clear, and sents. often end with *an* whatever the context.

> *Der Wasserspiegel ist seit gestern um einen Meter gestiegen/angestiegen.*
> *Die Preise steigen immer noch [an].*   *Die Preise stiegen um das Doppelte.*
> *Die Regierung konnte nicht verhindern, daß die Preise noch weiter anstiegen.*
> *Die Zahl der Abonnenten ist auf das Dreifache [an]gestiegen/ . . . ist auf 2 000 gestiegen.*
> *Commerzbankaktien steigen weiter—ich werde sie also nicht verkaufen.*

iv. Sich steigern and **sich erhöhen** express the same meaning as *steigen* and *zunehmen. Die Zahl der Erkrankten hatte sich von 20 auf über 100 erhöht* or *war von 20 auf* *über 100 gestiegen. Seine Angst vor der geheimnisvollen Gestalt steigerte sich immer mehr* or *nahm immer mehr zu. Mit dem Lob steigerte sich auch ihr Selbstvertrauen* or *stieg auch ihr Selbstvertrauen.* In the last sent. *sich steigern* sounds weightier than *steigen.* (*Sich steigern in,* used of people, means 'to work oneself up into a mental state'. *Sie steigerten sich in Begeisterung/Wut. Sie steigerte sich in den Wahn, weit intelligenter zu sein als alle Mitschüler.*)

> *Hoffentlich wird sich der Lebensstandard in der dritten Welt erhöhen. Or . . . wird . . . steigen.*
> *Das Ansehen des Bürgermeisters hatte sich beträchtlich erhöht.*

v. Steigen is used for emotions like *die Begeisterung, die Ungeduld, die Wut,* etc., as well as *das Ansehen* and *die Chancen. Die Spannung* and *die Aufregung* are used with *steigen* as well as with *zunehmen. In steigendem Maße* also means 'to an increasing extent' or 'increasingly'. *Jmd. ist in meiner Achtung gestiegen,* has risen in my estimation.

> *Er konnte seine steigende Wut/Ungeduld kaum beherrschen.*
> *Als die Spannung während des Raketenstarts bis zum höchsten Punkt gestiegen war, wurde er verschoben.*

vi. Steigen also means 'to rise in rank or position'. *Er wollte in dem Unternehmen von Stufe zu Stufe steigen.*

vii. Sich mehren means 'to become more numerous'. *Die Unruhen/Die Schwierigkeiten mehrten sich.*

> *Die Zeichen mehren sich, daß eine Umbildung des Kabinetts bevorsteht.*

viii. Sich vermehren is occasionally used for the numerical increase of things, *Die Zahl der Verkehrsunfälle hat sich vermehrt,* but mostly means 'to multiply, to increase by reproduction'. *Die aus England eingeführten Kaninchen vermehrten sich unter den günstigeren klimatischen Bedingungen in Australien so stark, daß sie zu einer wahren Landplage wurden.*

2. In reference to land **ansteigen** means 'to rise, to slope upwards'. *Das Land steigt steil/sanft an.*

3. Trans. use. *We must increase/raise* **production.**

i. The basic sense of **erhöhen** is 'to make higher'. *Man erhöhte den Deich, damit bei der nächsten Sturmflut das Dorf nicht überschwemmt werden könnte.* It also means 'to increase sth.' or 'to raise'. *Man erhöht Preise/Löhne/Steuern/die Miete/die Produktivität/ den Umsatz.* It is used with some intangibles such as *der Verdacht* and *die Aufmerksamkeit.*

> *Die Regierung beschloß, die Mehrwertsteuer von 12% auf 14% zu erhöhen.*
> *Man hat die Erträge der Landwirtschaft/die Produktion noch weiter erhöht.*
> *Die Polizei war am ganzen Abend in erhöhter Alarmbereitschaft.*

ii. Steigern is also trans., and in its basic sense is interchangeable with *erhöhen.* It is often used with *die Leistung* particularly in the language of sport.

> *Es gelang der Firma, die Produktion und den Absatz zu steigern.*
> *Der Student steigerte sein Arbeitspensum in den letzten Semestern vor dem Examen.*
> *Durch eine andere Technik steigerte er seine Hochsprungleistung so sehr, daß er Jugendmeister wurde.*
> *Nach dem stockenden Anfang fingen alle an, dem Redner mit gesteigertem Interesse zu folgen.*

iii. Heraufsetzen is 'to increase' or 'to put up' prices, taxes, etc.

> *Man setzt die Preise/die Mieten/die Steuern herauf.*

iv. Mehren, 'to increase', is now little used. It is occasionally found with *das Ansehen* as obj. but occurs mostly in the refl. Cf. 1. vii. *Dieser unerwartete Erfolg hat sein Ansehen beträchtlich gemehrt/vermehrt.*

v. Vermehren means 'to increase in amount, number, weight, extent, and intensity', but, except in relation to possessions and wealth, is less used than *erhöhen* and *steigern. Jmd. vermehrt seinen Besitz/seinen Reichtum/seinen Bestand an Büchern/seine*

Anstrengungen. Jmd. versucht, seinen Einfluß zu vermehren. Diese weisen Entscheidungen mehrten/vermehrten das Ansehen des Ministers.

inhabitant, population *ns.*

1. Der Einwohner is 'the inhabitant' of a city or smaller unit. *Die Einwohner von Göttingen.* The pl. is used to state the permanent population or number of inhabitants of cities, towns, or villages. For larger areas and for countries, states, and counties, **die Bevölkerung** is usual. Thus *München hat ungefähr eine Million Einwohner,* but *Bayern hat eine Bevölkerung von elf Millionen.* **Die Einwohnerzahl** is thus 'population' or 'number of inhabitants'. *Die Einwohnerzahl von München ist gestiegen.* For a larger area or a country, **die Bevölkerungszahl** is the strictly accurate term, *Wegen der geringen Bevölkerungszahl hat sich die Industrie nicht entwickelt,* but **die Bevölkerung** alone is frequently used, *Die ehemalige DDR hatte eine Bevölkerung von ungefähr 17 000 000.*

> *Die Bevölkerungszahl steigt ständig.*   *Die Bevölkerung Bayerns nimmt ständig zu/ab.*

2. Der Bewohner is 'a pers. living in or occupying a place'. It covers a wide range of places, and for some it is translated as *inhabitant. Die Bewohner des Zeltes/des Hauses/der Insel/des Dorfes/der Stadt/des Landes/der Erde.* It normally needs a gen., although this may be implied. *Viele Bewohner [des Dorfes] hatten ihre Häuser festlich geschmückt.* Also *die Dorfbewohner.*

3. Die Bevölkerung can mean 'the body of inhabitants', regarded as a group, not a number, 'all the people living in a place', and in this sense is applied to all areas. *Junge Leute aus allen Kreisen der Bevölkerung meldeten sich zur Bekämpfung der Waldbrände. Die ganze Bevölkerung des Dorfes/der Stadt/des Landes war empört.*

inherit, bequeath *vs.* and related words.

1. The usual equivalent of **inherit** is **erben**, which can be applied both to property and money and to abilities and features passed on from parents to their children. Thus *Sie haben das Vermögen/das Haus des Vaters geerbt* and *Alle Kinder haben die musikalische Begabung der Mutter geerbt.* **Ererben** is no longer used as a v. except in quotations, but survives as a past part. meaning 'inherited or acquired by inheritance'. It too can be applied to property, *das ererbte Vermögen,* and to abilities etc., *die von den Eltern ererbten Fähigkeiten.* Expressed using a v., the last sent. would now be *die Fähigkeiten, die er/sie . . . geerbt hatte. Geerbt* is also possible as a part. *Das geerbte Haus. Ererbt* is more emotional and stylistically more elevated.

2. Beerben, which can only have a pers. as obj., means 'to become s.o.'s heir' and refers only to property. *Sie hat völlig unerwartet eine reiche Tante beerbt. Alle Enkelkinder wollten die wohlhabende Großmutter beerben.*

3. Vermachen is a legal term meaning 'to bequeath'. *Er vermachte das alte Gemälde der Kunstgalerie.* **Vererben** means 'to leave property' or 'to pass on characteristics' to someone. It needs a dat. *Er hat dem ältesten Sohn den Hof vererbt. Er hat allen Kindern seine kräftige Konstitution vererbt.* **[Jmdm.] etw. hinterlassen**, 'to leave sth. [to s.o.]', is a syn. of *vermachen* and *vererben.* It is used with and without a dat. *Er hinterließ ein Vermögen/nur Schulden. Sie hinterließ dem Waisenhaus eine große Summe.*

4. Sich vererben is used when the characteristic passed on is the subj. *Ihre musikalische Begabung hat sich auf alle Kinder vererbt. Eine Anlage/Begabung vererbt sich in einer Familie. Diese Krankheit vererbt sich nicht [von den Eltern auf die Kinder].*

inheritance, bequest, legacy *ns.* One sense of **estate** *n.*

i. When **inheritance** refers to material possessions, the everyday equivalent is **die Erbschaft.** *Sie hat die Erbschaft angenommen/ausgeschlagen. Er wollte sich eine Erbschaft erschleichen. Ich habe eine Erbschaft gemacht,* I have inherited some money, property, etc. **Das Erbe** is a more elevated word. It can refer to a concrete possession as well as to a cultural, historical, intellectual, or spiritual heritage or legacy. *Er hat das väterliche Erbe angetreten. Sie wollte auf das mütterliche Erbe nicht verzichten. Das geistige Erbe der Antike. Zerstörte Städte waren das traurige Erbe des Faschismus.* **Das Erbteil** is 's.o.'s share of an inheritance'. *Der reiche Bruder hat auf sein Erbteil zugunsten seines jüngeren Bruders verzichtet.* It is also used for characteristics etc. passed down by parents. *Die künstlerische Begabung ist ein Erbteil der Mutter.*

ii. Das Vermächtnis is a legal term meaning 'bequest or legacy' and is occasionally used fig. *Sie forderte die Herausgabe ihres Vermächtnisses. Er hinterließ ihr ein Haus als Vermächtnis. Das Vermächtnis der deutschen Klassik.*

iii. Die Hinterlassenschaft is 'what a pers. leaves behind, the deceased's estate'. *Sein Bruder ist zum Verwalter der Hinterlassenschaft bestellt worden.* **Der Nachlaß,** 'what s.o. leaves either in the way of property or obligations', is a syn. of *Hinterlassenschaft. Der literarische Nachlaß eines Autors or seine nachgelassenen or hinterlassenen Schriften,* what he leaves in the way of unpublished manuscripts.

interest *v.* and *n.*

1. V.

i. Interessieren, 'to interest', is used with a thing as subj. *Das Thema interessiert mich sehr* or *Das Buch/Der Film hat uns sehr interessiert.* With people as subj. and obj. and *für* or *an,* it means 'to interest s.o. in sth.' or 'gain s.o.'s interest for sth.' *Er wollte seinen Bruder für das/an dem Projekt interessieren. Wir müssen weite Kreise an der Arbeit der Universität interessieren.*

> *Der Fall begann den Rechtsanwalt zu interessieren.*   *Der Vortrag hat mich sehr interessiert.*
> *Es würde mich interessieren zu erfahren, wie sie mit der Untersuchung vorankommen.*
> *Der Abteilungsleiter bemühte sich, alle Mitarbeiter für den Lehrgang zu interessieren.*

ii. To state that a person is interested in something **sich interessieren** can be used with **für,** *Ich interessiere mich für Politik/Musik/Sport,* or the past part. **interessiert** with **an,** *Ich bin an dem Plan [sehr] interessiert.* The only difference is that the refl. is stronger, suggesting deeper interest.

> *Ich würde mich für Ihre Antwort sehr interessieren.*   *Interessierst du dich für Fußball?*
> *Ich interessiere mich für den Vortrag/bin an dem Vortrag interessiert. Hast du Lust mitzukommen?*

iii. Both **sich interessieren** and **interessiert sein an** mean 'to be interested' in buying or renting something and in seeing that something is done.

> *Viele Käufer interessieren sich für diese Waren.*
> *Ich interessiere mich für diesen Fernsehapparat.*
> *Wir sind am Kauf des Hauses/an der zu vermietenden Wohnung interessiert.*
> *Ich bin daran interessiert, daß diese Angelegenheit so schnell wie möglich erledigt wird.*
> *Wir sind alle an der schnellen Erledigung dieser Sache interessiert.*

2. N.

i. Das Interesse is 'mental interest' in something *Jmd. zeigt großes/kein/wenig/reges Interesse an etw./jmdm.* or *für etw./jmdn. Sie brachte etwas Interesse für den neuen Plan auf. Er versuchte, unser Interesse auf einen anderen Punkt zu lenken/unser Interesse zu wecken.*

ii. Das Interesse is also applied to what people are interested in. *Sie hat vielseitige Interessen. Von der Arbeit abgesehen, scheint er keine Interessen zu haben. Die beiden haben viele gemeinsame Interessen.*

iii. Das Interesse also denotes the desire to buy. *Für diese Waren besteht großes/nur geringes Interesse.*

iv. Das Interesse also means 'what is to the advantage of a pers. or thg.' *Sie verfolgen private Interessen. Es liegt in meinem Interesse/in unserem beiderseitigen Interesse, das zu tun. Tun Sie das in Ihrem eigenen Interesse? Im Interesse der Deutlichkeit möchte ich einige Begriffe genau bestimmen.* A formal syn., used in the pl. only, is **die Belange**. *Die Belange des Staates/der Wirtschaft/der Rentner.*

> *Ein Rechtsanwalt vertritt die Belange/die Interessen seiner Mandanten.*

3. Interest = 'money paid on a loan or on money invested' is **die Zinsen**. *Diese Geldanleihe trägt 8% Zinsen.* **Der Zinssatz** is 'rate of interest'. *Die Zinssätze für Bundesanleihen sind in letzter Zeit gestiegen.*

4. Someone who has an interest in a company has a share in its ownership. *Ich beteiligte mich an einem Geschäft [finanziell]* means that I took a share or interest in it. Thus *to have a [financial] interest* in a property, firm, etc. can be expressed by **[finanziell] an etw. beteiligt sein**. *Mein Vater ist an diesem Geschäft beteiligt. X ist an Firmen in der ganzen Welt finanziell beteiligt*, has interests throughout the world. The ns. are **die Beteiligung** and **der Anteil**. *Ein Industrieller mit Beteiligungen an mehreren* or *verschiedenen* or *ein paar/einigen deutschen Firmen*, an industrialist with business interests in Germany. *Y erwarb eine Beteiligung/einen Anteil an einem Unternehmen*, acquired a share or interest. *A firm's cable-making interests* can become *Die Anteile der Firma Z an Kabelwerken werden nicht verkauft. Ihre Anteile an einer kanadischen Firma, die Papier herstellt.*

interpret, construe vs.

1. Auffassen, which is often used with *als,* means 'to understand, take, or interpret as possessing a certain meaning', 'to construe or put a particular construction on' words, actions, etc. It differs from the other words in denoting a more or less immediate reaction, i.e. someone takes remarks as having a certain meaning on hearing or reading them. *Wie hast du diese Worte aufgefaßt?*

> *Er hat meine harmlose Bemerkung falsch/als Beleidigung/als Vorwurf aufgefaßt.*
> *Soll ich diese Worte als Kritik auffassen, oder waren sie als Lob gemeint?*

2. i. When **interpret** means 'to explain the meaning of words or a passage or of sth. possibly abstruse or mysterious', *auslegen* and *deuten* are the equivalents. **Auslegen** means 'to make words or happenings comprehensible', **deuten** 'to see in words, events, a thg., etc. a certain meaning', but they do not differ greatly. *Auslegen* is mostly used for everyday matters, *deuten* for more important ones. With *das Gesetz* and *die Vorschrift*, only *auslegen* is used, while both are possible with *eine Textstelle* or *ein Text*. For *ein Bibelvers* or *ein Gleichnis*, 'parable', *deuten* is usual though *auslegen* is found. For *ein Traum* or *Zeichen*, 'signs', *deuten* is normal, although *auslegen* is not impossible. For *jmds. Benehmen/Verhalten* and *Handlungen*, *auslegen* (often + *als*) is usual, but *deuten* also occurs.

> *Da sprach Pharao zu Joseph: 'Ich habe einen Traum gehabt, und es ist niemand, der ihn deuten kann.'*
> Also *Josef legte zwei Gefangenen ihre Träume aus.*
> *Der Pfarrer deutete die Bibelstelle auf eine Weise, die nachzuvollziehen vielen seiner Hörer schwerfiel.*
> Also *Er legte sie aus.*   *Sein Nachgeben wurde als Feigheit ausgelegt.*
> *Nun wurde ihm seine Höflichkeit als Unterwürfigkeit ausgelegt/gedeutet.*

ii. For *ein Gedicht, ein Drama, eine Erzählung*, or *ein Roman*, both *deuten* and *auslegen* occur, but **interpretieren** has become the accepted word. It is a learned word and at the appropriate stylistic level can also be applied to *Äußerungen* or *Verhalten*.

> *Dieses Buch, ein Klassiker der Interpretationskunst, exemplifiziert eine früher gängige Methode, Literatur zu interpretieren.*

3. Interpretieren is also applied, as in E., to the way a piece of music is played. *Sie hat die Sonate einfühlsam interpretiert. Das Orchester hat die Sinfonie meisterhaft interpretiert.* For an actor who interprets a role in a certain way, **darstellen**, 'to perform', is the normal v., although *interpretieren* occasionally occurs. *Die Art und Weise, wie der junge Schauspieler Wallenstein dargestellt hat, hat alle stark beeindruckt.*

4. Dolmetschen is 'to interpret', i.e. 'to translate orally from one lang. to another'. *Sie hat auf der Tagung gedolmetscht. Ich habe gerade die Dolmetscherprüfung abgelegt.*

introduce *v.*

1. i. The meaning 'to make one pers. acquainted with another' is expressed by either **vorstellen** or **bekanntmachen**. There is hardly any difference except that *bekanntmachen* is slightly less formal, so that *vorstellen* should be used when formality is implied. The constructions are *Sie machte mich mit ihrer Freundin bekannt* or *stellte mich ihrer Freundin/Bekannten vor. Man macht zwei Menschen miteinander bekannt* or *stellt A und B einander vor. Darf ich mich/meine Frau vorstellen? Wir haben uns schon bekanntgemacht.* Vorstellen is also used for introducing speakers at meetings etc. *Der Vorsitzende hat den Redner vorgestellt.*
  Sie hat ihren Eltern den neuen Freund schon vorgestellt.
  Zwei seiner Freunde, die einander nicht kannten, machte er miteinander bekannt.
ii. Vorstellen is used for introducing new products to the public.
  Die Autofirma stellt auf der Messe ihr neuestes Modell vor.
2. In three contexts **introduce** is translated by **einführen**. The prep. is usually *in*.
i. 'To introduce people into a group, club, society, etc.'
  Den neuen Kollegen führte er in die Gruppe seiner Bekannten ein, die regelmäßig Golf miteinander spielen.
  Er hat seine Freundin in seinen Freundeskreis eingeführt.
ii. 'To bring a custom, practice, new method into use, fashion, etc.'
  Prinz Albert soll die deutsche Sitte des Christbaums in England eingeführt haben.
  Er hat neue Ideen/neue Methoden in das Geschäft eingeführt.
  Die neue Mode wurde letztes Jahr eingeführt.
iii. 'To bring plants and animals native to one country into another'.
  Die Kartoffel wurde aus Amerika in Europa eingeführt.

3. Introduce people to a thg. = 'make them acquainted with it' is **bekanntmachen**.
  Ich muß nun den Leser mit einer Szene bekanntmachen, die damals in England häufig zu sehen war, die aber jetzt unbekannt ist.   Er machte uns mit dem neuen Computersystem bekannt.

4. Introduce s.o. to a field of study, area of thought, etc. means 'to give a basic knowledge or understanding of it or a grounding in it'.
i. One v. is **einführen**, which sounds scholarly or academic. **Bekanntmachen** and **vorstellen** also express this sense. More usual than these vs. is **eine Einführung geben** in. *Eine Einführung in ein Fachgebiet* is 'a chapter, book, lecture [series], etc. which gives basic information'. *Die Einleitung* to a book, talk, etc. denotes the remarks which begin it. Cf. 5 below.
  In dieser Vorlesung stelle ich Ihnen die Werke Byrons vor/ . . . mache ich Sie mit den Werken Byrons bekannt. Or more commonly Ich möchte Ihnen eine Einführung in die Werke Byrons geben.
  Dieser Professor hat uns in das klassische Drama/in das Studium des Romans eingeführt.
  Der Lehrer hat die Schüler in die moderne deutsche Geschichte/in die Integral- und Differentialrechnung eingeführt.
ii. In one sense **einweisen** means 'to introduce s.o. to a particular kind of work'. *Eine erfahrene Mitarbeiterin hat die neue Kollegin in die Arbeit eingewiesen. Eingeführt* could also be used.

5. Introduce also means 'to begin or open sth. with preliminary or preparatory remarks'. This is one of the senses of **einleiten**, to begin or open sth. *Die Feier wurde mit Musik eingeleitet. Er wies einleitend darauf hin, daß* . . . , pointed out by way of introduction.

> *Sie leitete ihre Vorlesung mit ein paar geistreichen Anekdoten/mit einer Erklärung der wichtigsten Begriffe ein. Er leitete seine Rede mit einigen Begrüßungsworten ein.*

Einleitend + n. means 'introductory'. *Einleitende Bemerkungen. Die einleitenden Takte der Sinfonie.*

6. Einbringen is used for introducing a bill into parliament as well as for bringing a new topic into a conversation or discussion.

> *Der Gesetzentwurf wurde gestern in den Bundestag eingebracht.*
> *Sie haben ein neues Thema in das Gespräch eingebracht.*

investigate, examine, explore, research *vs.* Some uses of check *v.*

Investigate is 'to observe or study closely or to inquire into systematically in order to discover some relevant fact'. *The police are investigating the incident.* **Examine** is 'to look at carefully to learn about or from'. In some cases, it is much the same as **investigate**, *Scientists investigated/examined the theory,* but differs mainly in the contexts in which it is used. *The doctor examined the patient. I will examine the plan. Our luggage was examined by customs officials.* **Examine** is used for schools, universities, etc., and people examine themselves, their consciences, their past mistakes, their lives, etc. **Check** means 'to examine sth., sometimes by comparison with an original or standard, to see whether it is correct or in order'. For an important equivalent *kontrollieren,* cf. CONTROL, but other words discussed here often translate **check**. The main equivalents *untersuchen* and *prüfen,* discussed in 1 and 2 respectively, carry meanings of **investigate** and **examine**.

1. Untersuchen is a general word used in a large number of contexts.
i. It is the only equivalent of **examine** in reference to a doctor or dentist. *Der Arzt hat den Patienten genau untersucht.*

> *Ich muß meine Augen untersuchen lassen.*
> *Der Zahnarzt hat meine Zähne auf Karies [hin] untersucht.*

ii. Untersuchen is the appropriate v. in reference to an investigation into accidents or their causes, crimes, disputes, etc. or for the examination of the state of an industry etc. It is the usual v. in relation to the police. *Die Polizei/Ein Detektiv untersucht den Fall.*

> *Eine Gruppe von Sachverständigen untersucht den Unfall, der zum Untergang des Schiffes geführt hat.*
> *Ein Richter hat den Fall vollständig untersucht und fand die Beschuldigungen bestätigt, daß Beamte Bestechungsgelder angenommen hatten.*
> *Die Ingenieure untersuchten das Gelände nach dem günstigsten Standort für das Kraftwerk.*

iii. Untersuchen is commonly used for a scientific, scholarly, or other expert examination or investigation of a subject etc. *Wer eine Dissertation schreibt, untersucht eine bestimmte Frage.*

> *Der Verfasser hat die gesellschaftlichen Verhältnisse genau untersucht.*
> *Sie hat den Text sprachlich untersucht.   Er untersucht eine in der Antarktis lebende Pinguinart.*

iv. Untersuchen means 'to examine chemically' mainly by analysis or by other scientific or medical means. *Die vergifteten Lebensmittel wurden untersucht. Man untersucht die Blutprobe/die Beschaffenheit des Bodens.* **Etw. auf etw. untersuchen** means 'to examine for sth.' *Hin* is often added after the word governed by *auf,* but is optional. **Prüfen** and **kontrollieren** are also used, but are closer in meaning to **check** than to **examine**. **Analysieren** may also be appropriate.

Der Chemiker untersuchte/prüfte/kontrollierte den Wein auf seine Reinheit hin.
Die Studenten müssen ihre Bodenproben genau untersuchen.
Das Wasser wird regelmäßig auf Verunreinigungen hin untersucht/geprüft/kontrolliert/analysiert.

v. Untersuchen sometimes means 'to examine' as a syn. of *search*. Here *kontrollieren* would, however, be the normal word. **Durchsuchen** is the usual v. for searching a person, building, etc.

Soldaten untersuchten/durchsuchten die Fahrzeuge nach Waffen.
Mein Gepäck wurde von zwei Zollbeamten auf Rauschgift untersucht/kontrolliert.
Die Polizei hat das Haus durchsucht.   *Ich durchsuchte das ganze Zimmer nach der Brieftasche.*

vi. Ermitteln is used in official language for investigating a crime. It is used alone, *Die Staatsanwaltschaft begann zu ermitteln,* 'began to investigate/conduct an investigation', but does not take an obj. *Die Polizei untersucht den Fall* is normal style, but official style is *Die Polizei ermittelt in dem Fall. Ermitteln* also means 'to discover by investigation'. Cf. DISCOVER 2. ii.

vii. Forschen nach jmdm./etw. basically means 'to make an effort to find or trace' something unknown or s.o./sth. whose whereabouts are unknown. *Er forschte nach der Ursache des Unfalls,* investigated its cause. *Sie forschte lange nach ihrem vermißten Bruder/nach dem Verbleib ihres Bruders* could be a transl. of *She investigated where he had got to.* **Nachforschen** suggests investigating or inquiring into a matter with great intensity. With a dat. it represents only a syntactic variant on *forschen nach. Er forschte dem Verbleib der Unterlagen nach* or *Er forschte nach dem Verbleib der Unterlagen.* Thus *Die Polizei forschte der Ursache des Unfalls nach. Nachforschen* does not need a dat. *Sie haben lange vergeblich nachgeforscht* would be translated as *carried on their investigation* or *searched.* It also takes a clause. *Die Polizei forscht nach, wie das Rauschgift in die Bundesrepublik eingeschleust wird. Untersuchen* could replace *nachforschen* in this sent. and can also be used with *Ursache* as obj.

Die Frau forschte überall nach, doch sie konnte ihren vermißten Mann nicht finden.
Sie forschten nach, wie sich der Vorfall zugetragen hatte.
Wir werden nachforschen, wo das Geld geblieben ist.

2. *Prüfen* and some derivatives.

i. Prüfen is the v. for school and similar examinations and tests. *Der Lehrer prüft die Schüler in Geschichte. Die Schüler werden heute in Deutsch und morgen in Biologie geprüft. Im Examen werden alle behandelten Gebiete geprüft. Ich habe die Fahrprüfung bestanden.*

ii. Prüfen also means 'to check or examine for conformity to regulations, quality, suitability, or to see whether sth. is in order'. The obj. can be a thing or person. *Die Bauern luden Gemüse, Eier und Butter ab; die Hausfrauen prüften das Angebot mißtrauisch. Sich/Sein Gewissen prüfen,* to examine oneself/one's conscience. *Prüfen* is used with *auf* = 'for'. *Die Bewerber wurden auf ihre körperliche Eignung geprüft. Ich will diese Behauptung auf ihre Wahrheit prüfen.* It also takes a clause. *Er prüfte, ob das Gerät einwandfrei funktionierte/ob der Bewerber für die Aufgabe geeignet war. Prüfen* suggests a less thorough examination than *untersuchen.*

Andere Studenten haben die Richtigkeit unserer Ergebnisse geprüft.
Der Bankbeamte prüfte die Echtheit der Banknoten.   *Die Käufer prüfen die Sonderangebote.*
Die Waren werden auf ihren einwandfreien Zustand geprüft.
Alle zwei Jahre müssen alle in der Bundesrepublik zugelassenen Wagen vom TÜV (Technischen
*   Überwachungsverein) geprüft werden.*   *Er prüfte fachmännisch das Vieh.*
Wir müssen uns/unsere Einstellungen prüfen, um festzustellen, ob wir Vorurteile hegen.

iii. Überprüfen basically means 'to examine again' but also 'to examine carefully to see whether sth. is in order, works, etc.' With *ein Alibi, jmds. Aussagen, jmds. Personalien* as obj., it is translated as **check.**

Alle Rechnungen müssen nochmals überprüft werden, denn es gibt einen großen Fehlbetrag in der Kasse.

Ich werde die Maschine überprüfen.
Der Verfasser benutzte die Angaben im Text, ohne sie vorher überprüft zu haben.

iv. Nachprüfen is a syn. of *überprüfen*, but is restricted to matters of fact. *Wir prüfen die Richtigkeit der Angaben nach. Es läßt sich nicht mehr nachprüfen, ob diese Darstellung der Ereignisse stimmt.*

v. Nachsehen, 'to look and see', can express the meaning of **check**. It is used with an *ob*-clause and a n. Cf. LOOK 5. *Ich sehe mal nach, ob alle Schüler im Bus sind.* Someone can say either, '*Sehen Sie bitte die Reifen/das Öl nach!*' or '*Sehen Sie bitte nach den Reifen/dem Öl!*' *Kontrollieren* is also used.

3. Research suggests an exhaustive investigation, particularly of an academic nature, and is intr. and trans. *A lot of people are researching in this field.* In the trans. use *He researched the subject for some time*, it is interchangeable with **investigate**. **Research** is often used of journalists who investigate something.

i. Forschen means 'to do academic or scientific research' and is intr. It is used with *über* or *auf einem Gebiet*, or *nach* = 'in order to find'. *Sie bekam ein Stipendium und konnte zwei Jahre lang forschen. Viele forschen über dieses Thema/auf diesem Gebiet. Er forschte nach der Ursache der Krankheit.*

ii. Research + obj. is translated by **erforschen**. A syn. of *untersuchen* 1. iii, *erforschen* suggests a rigorous scientific or scholarly investigation. *Er hat als erster die Bedingungen des bemannten Raumflugs erforscht. Diese Forschungsgruppe hat das Verhalten von verschiedenen Tieren erforscht.*

iii. While *forschen* and *erforschen* are usually restricted to academic research, **recherchieren** is used for journalists who carry out investigations. It is both intr. and trans. *Wir haben lange, aber ergebnislos recherchiert. Diese Reporterin kann gut recherchieren. In dem Fall wird noch recherchiert. Zwei Journalisten haben die Hintergründe des Korruptionsfalles recherchiert.*

4. Explore. Land, an area, etc. is explored either for the first time, known land is explored for oil/minerals, etc. or for a special purpose. *The area has not been explored geologically.*

i. Erforschen means 'to explore' land, a cave, river, etc. for the first time. *Die Antarktis/Unser Planetensystem wird erforscht.*
Im Jahre 1770 entdeckte und erforschte James Cook die Ostküste Australiens.
Sie kehrten am nächsten Tag zurück, um die eben erst entdeckte Höhle zu erforschen.

ii. Durchforschen means 'to search or explore an area for sth. or for a special purpose'. *Man hat viel Geld ausgegeben, um entlegene Gebiete Australiens nach Erzen zu durchforschen. Sie durchforschten die Gegend nach einer Quelle. Man hat das Gebiet geologisch durchforscht.*

iii. For tourists etc. who explore the ruins, an old town, etc. **besichtigen** is used. Cf. LOOK 3. ii.
Wir verbrachten ein paar Stunden damit, die Ruinen/den alten Teil der Stadt zu besichtigen.

iv. Explore also means 'to examine thoroughly'. *The novel explores the effect of the past on a group of people.* The equivalent of this sense is **untersuchen**.
Der Roman untersucht die Auswirkung der Vergangenheit auf eine Gruppe von Menschen.

involve, entangle *vs.*

1. The first sense of **involve** is 'to engage s.o. in some kind of activity, a particular circumstance, etc.' The activity can be completely neutral like *200 people were involved in the project*, but circumstances are often implied from which it is difficult to extricate oneself, so that **involve** means 'to entangle or embroil in sth. unpleasant' such as a quarrel, scandal, trouble, difficulties, and so on. A word which, like **involve**, can be used with both good and bad activities is **beteiligen**. Words only used for something unpleasant are **verwickeln, verstricken,** and **hineinziehen.** However, *beteiligen,* which is neutral, can be used to express something which is bad by nature in an impartial way. A police report could include the words *die an dem Unfall beteiligten Personen/Fahrzeuge,* but one of those involved in it could well say, *er sei in den Unfall verwickelt. Verstricken* is stronger than *verwickeln,* suggesting that someone has become caught in a kind of net from which he or she cannot escape, and is like **entangle** or *embroil. Hineinziehen* implies drawing someone into something unpleasant against his/her will. It is stronger than *verwickeln,* but it too suggests that the person is unable to get out of the situation. *Man verwickelt jmdn. in ein Gespräch* suggests that the conversation is not welcome, at least at that time.

> *Diese Firma war auch am nationalen Verteidigungsprogramm beteiligt.*
> *Die Zahl der an der Arbeitsniederlegung beteiligten Arbeiter stieg bald bis über 1 000.*
> *Er wurde in einen Rechtsstreit verwickelt/hineingezogen.*
> *Der Streit/Die Auseinandersetzung zog bald auch andere hinein.*
> *Er hat einen Freund in dieses zweifelhafte Abenteuer verstrickt/hineingezogen.*
> *Die Detektive entdeckten, daß ein Vetter des Kindes an der Entführung beteiligt war.* Or . . . *in die Entführung verwickelt war.*   *Sie wurde auch in den Skandal verstrickt.*

He carried out an inquiry involving 200 families becomes *Er führte eine Umfrage durch, die 200 Familien zum Gegenstand hatte,* or *Um die Umfrage durchzuführen, befragte er 200 Familien. 200 Familien waren an der Umfrage beteiligt* means that they carried it out. *Don't involve yourself in unnecessary expense!* can be translated as *Stürz' dich doch nicht in unnötige Unkosten!*

2. Involve can mean 'to have within or as part of itself', 'to contain or include'. For equivalents when the sense is 'include or contain', cf. INCLUDE. Some examples: *The equation involves rational numbers* is *Die Gleichung* **enthält** *rationelle Zahlen. Part of the course involves the study of the latest economic developments* could be *Der Kursus* **schließt** *die Beschäftigung mit den neuesten ökonomischen Entwicklungen* **ein.** *Nur wenige Leute verstehen, was* **dazu gehört,** *einen Fernsehfilm zu drehen,* what is involved in making a TV film. The sense might be 'to consist of', **bestehen aus.** *The holiday programme involves cultural and recreational activities* could be *Das Ferienprogramm besteht aus einer Mischung von Kultur und Erholung* or *Es umfaßt Kultur und Erholung. Woraus besteht Ihre Arbeit?,* what does it involve. **Umfassen** means 'to comprise'. *You're doing European Studies. What does that involve?: Was umfaßt das?*

3. Involve also means 'to include as a necessary feature, circumstance, or consequence', 'to entail'. *The job involves a lot of work/constant travelling.* This sense is expressed by **zur Folge haben,** which refers to consequences, and **mit sich bringen,** which refers to accompanying circumstances, or **erfordern,** to require. *The difficulties involved in this work* becomes *die Schwierigkeiten, die diese Arbeit mit sich bringt,* or *die mit dieser Arbeit verbundenen Schwierigkeiten.* (Verbunden mit, connected with.)

> *Der Bau von Straßen bringt die Errichtung einer großen Anzahl von Brücken mit sich.* Also *erfordert.*
> *Die Arbeit bringt keinerlei Risiken mit sich.*
> *Der Übergang zu metrischen Maßen und Gewichten hatte grundlegende Änderungen in der industriellen Produktion zur Folge.*   *Dieses Amt bringt nicht viel Arbeit mit sich.*
> *Diese Arbeit bringt es mit sich/hat zur Folge, daß ich ständig unterwegs bin.*
> *Das Erlernen dieser Sprache erfordert ein intensives Studium* (requires, involves).
> *Die Behandlung dieser Krankheit erfordert einen Aufenthalt im Gebirge.*

4. Involve also means 'to affect, have an effect on', 'to concern or relate to'.
i. Where **involve** means 'to concern' as in *That does not involve me,* see *angehen, betreffen* under CONCERN 1, and *betreffen* under AFFECT 2. **ii.** *Die Einstellung der Produktion betraf mehr als 10 000 Arbeitnehmer* means 'affected', but could translate as *involved* in this sense.

Arbeiter erfahren oft nichts von wichtigen Entscheidungen, die sie betreffen/angehen.

ii. Es geht um and **es handelt sich um,** 'it is a matter of', can translate *Sth. is involved. Bei dieser Transaktion geht es um eine große Summe Geld. Es handelt sich [bei diesem Geschäft] um einen beträchtlichen Betrag. Um wieviel Geld geht es denn?* An alternative is *Wieviel Geld ist dabei im Spiel? The amount of money involved* can be *Der Geldbetrag, um den es geht/sich handelt, ist nicht sehr groß. Es geht um einen Grundsatz/ein Prinzip,* a matter of principle is involved.

iii. The people/Those **involved**. If 'involved in an activity' is implied, the transl. is *diejenigen, die an der Debatte teilnehmen* or *an der Debatte beteiligt sind.* If **involved** = 'concerned', it is *die Leute, um die es geht/sich handelt,* or *die Betreffenden,* those in question. If **involved** = 'affected', it becomes *die Betroffenen.* Cf. AFFECT 2.

5. i. People who are involved in their work or an activity are engrossed in or absorbed by it. *Jmd., der in seiner Arbeit* **aufgeht,** is taken up by it or devoted to it, i.e. absorbed or engrossed in it, not on one occasion only but over a longer period. **Sich vertiefen in** means 'to become deliberately engrossed or absorbed in' an activity on one occasion. *Ich vertiefte mich in die Arbeit/in die Lektüre. Sie ist ganz in ihre Arbeit vertieft. Wir hatten uns in ein Gespräch über Literatur vertieft. Die Kinder waren in das Spiel so sehr vertieft, daß sie unser Rufen überhörten.*

ii. Novels, films, etc. can be the subj. of **involve**. *The conflicts in these novels do not involve the reader. We do not see enough of the character to become involved in what she does.* In talking of novels etc., **ansprechen** means 'to appeal to'. *Die Konflikte im Roman sprechen den Leser nicht an.* **Fesseln,** 'to grip', is stronger. **Sich identifizieren mit** could also express the idea of becoming involved with a character. *Viele Jugendliche identifizierten sich mit dem Held in diesem Roman und ahmten ihn nach.*

> *Man erfährt nicht genug von diesem Charakter, um sich persönlich von dem, was sie sagt, fühlt und tut, angesprochen zu fühlen.*
>
> *Ich habe einen Film gesehen, der mich eigentlich nicht ansprach/der mich wirklich gefesselt hat.*

6. Involve is applied to relationships between people and ranges from relatively superficial contact to strong emotional attachment. **Sich einlassen** is pejorative, suggesting that the people with whom someone becomes involved are undesirable. *Er hat sich mit Betrügern/leichtsinnigen Menschen/zwielichtigen Gestalten eingelassen. Laß dich doch nicht mit ihm/ihr ein!* **Mit jmdm. etw./viel/nichts zu tun haben** is neutral. *Ich habe mit diesen Leuten etw. zu tun gehabt. Sie dachte nicht daran, etw. mit ihm zu tun zu haben.* **Mit jmdm. nichts zu schaffen haben,** which is colloquial, expresses aversion. *Mit diesen Leuten will ich nichts mehr zu schaffen haben.* Several expressions can translate **involve** implying an emotional or romantic attachment. *X und Y sind sich* (or *einander*) *näher gekommen,* which means that they have got on close terms with each other, may express the sense. Stronger is *A hat sich in B verliebt* or *Sie haben sich ineinander verliebt. Sie ließ sich mit ihm ein* usually suggests a sexual relationship, but throws an unfavourable light on it. Words meaning 'a relationship' (cf. RELATION) may express the sense. *Er knüpfte eine Beziehung zu/mit einer anderen Frau an. Er fing ein [Liebes]verhältnis/eine Affäre mit ihr an.*

7. Involve is also applied to people's activities. The expressions given in 6 are used in relation to activities with the same connotations. *Sie ließen sich auf ein gefährliches Unternehmen ein. Ich will mit dieser Sache nichts mehr zu tun/zu schaffen haben.* **Sich engagieren** can mean 'to become involved' with a cause or activity or in order to help [a group of] people. **Sich politisch betätigen** means 'to be in or take part in politics'. It suggests involvement in politics in addition to one's normal occupation. If someone is paid for his/her political activity, the expression is *Er/Sie ist in die Politik gegangen.* **[Aktiv] an etw. beteiligt sein,** to be [actively] engaged or involved in, could translate *Should religious leaders be involved in politics? Sollten religiöse Führer aktiv an der Politik beteiligt sein?* If a lesser degree of involvement is meant, *Sollten religiöse Führer in der Politik mitmischen* or *dreinreden?* could be used. They suggest an attempt to influence on certain occasions.

Sie engagierte sich stark/sehr für ausländische Arbeitnehmer und half ihnen besonders bei Sprachschwierigkeiten mit Behörden.

Er engagiert sich sehr/stark in der Kommunalpolitik.   *Er betätigt sich in der Landespolitik.*

Sie engagieren sich in mehreren Bürgerinitiativen/sind aktiv daran beteiligt.

Sie sind an der Organisation von Sportwettkämpfen für Kinder beteiligt.

j

join, adjoin vs.

1. Join = 'to connect two thgs. so that they become physically united'. **Verbinden** is a general term which like **join** covers different ways of holding things together. *Man verbindet zwei Bretter mit Leim/mit Schrauben. Ich habe die Bindfadenenden verbunden. Die Drähte werden durch Lötung miteinander verbunden.* The thing effecting the join can be the subj. *Schrauben verbinden die Teile der Maschine.* However, as in E. there are specific terms which are probably more common. *Man* **verknotet** *die Bindfadenenden* or **knotet** *sie* **zusammen**, ties them together. *Man* **lötet** *die Rohre* **zusammen** or **schraubt** *Platten* **zusammen** or **leimt** *Bretter* **zusammen. Fügen** is used in carpentry for joining pieces of board. It may suggest that they slot into each other, but need not. The constructions are either *Man fügt einen Stein an einen anderen* or *fügt zwei Steine zusammen. Der Fliesenleger fügt die Kacheln mit Mörtel aneinander. Man fügt die Bauteile zusammen.*

2. Verbinden is also used for making a link between two things. *Kanäle verbinden alle großen deutschen Flüsse. Eine Brücke verbindet die Insel mit dem Festland. Ein Tunnel verbindet die beiden Ufer des Flusses. Verbinden Sie die beiden Punkte mit einem Strich!*

3. Join hands is *sich* **die Hände reichen.** *Alle reichten sich die Hände und sangen* Auld Lang Syne. (Note: *Sie gaben sich die Hände*, they shook hands.)

4. Join means 'to come into contact, company, or union with a pers.' *Won't you join us?*

i. If one person is seated and another comes and sits with him/her, the v. is **sich zu jmdm. setzen.** *Eine zweite Person setzte sich zu der ersten.* In this situation *May I join you?* is *Darf ich mich zu Ihnen setzen?*, and *Join us!* is *Setzen Sie sich zu uns!*

ii. When **join** implies that someone accompanies another person somewhere or in doing something, the v. is **sich anschließen.** If one person sees another walking and wishes to join him/her, the question is *'Darf ich mich Ihnen anschließen?'* Thus *Man schließt sich einer Gruppe/einer Reisegesellschaft an. Man schließt sich einer Schlange an.* The pass. is not possible. *They were joined by two others* should be expressed in the act. *Zwei andere schlossen sich ihnen an. Sich anschließen* also expresses the idea of joining [with] others to do something. It takes a dat. and can be followed by an *um . . . zu* construction. *Die meisten Arbeiter schlossen sich dem Streik an.* A simple way to translate *My wife joins me in congratulating you* is to omit *me* and use a n. *Meine Frau schließt sich diesem Glückwunsch an.*

> *Die Abgeordneten der Linken schlossen sich den Sozialisten an, um den Gesetzentwurf zu Fall zu bringen.*   *Andere Länder schlossen sich dem Boykott an.*

iii. The idea that people or organizations join together (to do/form something) is expressed by **sich zusammenschließen,** to unite. *Die Spieler schlossen sich zu einer Mannschaft zusammen. Die Jugendlichen im Dorf schlossen sich in Clubs/Vereinen zusammen. Alle Abgeordneten der Linken schlossen sich zusammen, um die Regierung zu stürzen. Sich zusammenschließen* also translates *to join forces. Die Armee und die Polizei schlossen sich zusammen, und es gelang ihnen, einen im Gebirge schwer verletzten Jungen lebend zu* *bergen.* **Zusammenlegen** is trans. and means 'to join together or combine'. *Man hat die beiden Schulklassen/die Felder zusammengelegt.*

iv. Join in, if singing is meant, is **mitsingen**. *Alle, die den Text kannten, sangen mit.* Certain other vs. are combined with *mit* such as **mittanzen** or **mitspielen**. *Sie forderten die anderen auf mitzutanzen. Laßt die beiden Jungen doch mitspielen!* A general term is **mitmachen**. *Mitmachen* either takes an obj., *Alle Kollegen machen die Wanderung mit*, are taking part/joining in, or *bei*, *Wir machen bei dem Spiel/Wettbewerb mit*, or has neither, *Da mache ich mit.* *Three others joined in the fight* could be *Drei andere ließen sich in die Schlägerei ein.* For *einlassen*, cf. INVOLVE 6 and 7.

v. The usual word for joining a club or association is **eintreten**. *Ich bin in den Sportverein/in die Partei eingetreten.* **Beitreten** is more formal and takes a dat. *Die Türkei will der E.U. beitreten. Eintreten* is also possible. For **join** the army, a firm, and other professions cf. ENTER 5.

5. We still say, 'His land joins mine', but in most cases, **adjoin** is now the normal v. *The oval adjoins the school.* The usual word is **angrenzen an**. *Das Schulgelände grenzt an den Wald an. Sein Land grenzt an meines an. Im angrenzenden Feld/Zimmer.* The intr. form *The two fields adjoin* is *Die beiden/zwei Felder, (um die es hier geht), grenzen aneinander an.* The adjoining *house/room* is often expressed as *das Haus/Zimmer daneben* or *nebenan* or *das Nachbarhaus* or *das Nachbarzimmer.*

judge, evaluate *vs.*

1. The usual equivalent of **judge** or *pass judgment* when they refer to judges or courts is now **urteilen** or **ein Urteil fällen**. While **judge** is both trans. and intr., *urteilen* is intr. However, as both *urteilen* and *ein Urteil fällen* take *über*, this construction can translate the E. trans. use. *Das Gericht muß über einen schwierigen Fall urteilen* or *muß über einen schwierigen Fall ein Urteil fällen.*

Der Richter wartete das Gutachten des Psychiaters ab, bevor er über den Angeklagten urteilte.

In angelsächsischen Ländern entscheiden die Geschworenen, ob ein Angeklagter schuldig ist. In Deutschland urteilt ein Richter oder ein aus mehreren Richtern bestehendes Gericht über die Schuld oder Unschuld von Angeklagten.

Das Gericht hatte darüber zu urteilen, ob er des Mordes schuldig war oder nicht.

Alle glauben, daß das Gericht in diesem Fall ein gerechtes Urteil gefällt hat/gerecht geurteilt hat.

Although *a judge* is *der Richter*, **richten** meaning 'to judge' now sounds antiquated. It is still found in religious language. *Richtet nicht, auf daß ihr nicht gerichtet werdet!*, judge not that ye be not judged. *Richten* meant not only 'to pass judgment' but 'to carry the judgment out', so that it had the sense of *hinrichten*, to execute. This survives in literary usage and fixed expressions. *Die Wahrheit wird sie richten* (Frisch) could be interpreted as **judge** but also as *carry out the judgment. Jmd. hat sich selbst gerichtet* means the person executed judgment on himself.

2. Judge means 'to form an opinion about' and suggests careful consideration and an opinion which is sound and correct.

i. Beurteilen, which is not used for courts, is the usual word in this sense, although **urteilen [über]** is also used. Both take *nach* = 'by'. In some cases syntax determines the use of one or the other, and in others, both are possible. As *beurteilen* needs an obj., *urteilen* is used when there is no obj. *Sie urteilt sachlich und vorurteilsfrei. Man sollte nicht nach dem Aussehen urteilen*, but *Menschen sollte man nicht nach ihrem Aussehen beurteilen. Urteilen nach* is therefore used to translate phrs. like **to judge/judging by**. *Nach dem, was man dir erzählt hat, zu urteilen, wird er Erfolg haben.* (Or *Nach dem zu urteilen, was man dir erzählt hat, . . .*) *Nach dem ersten Eindruck zu urteilen, ist alles in bester Ordnung.* To translate *I cannot judge whether he is right or* *wrong,* either *urteilen, beurteilen,* or **entscheiden,** 'to DECIDE', can be used. *Ich kann nicht beurteilen/darüber urteilen/entscheiden, ob er recht oder unrecht hat.* Someone refraining from passing judgement on something can use either *Darüber möchte ich nicht urteilen* or *Das möchte ich nicht beurteilen.* Although both *beurteilen* and *urteilen über* are possible here, *beurteilen* is the normal word. *Urteilen über* is used only in giving a well-considered and even authoritative judgement on people and weighty matters. If someone were asked, *'Wie beurteilen Sie das Buch?',* an opinion would be expected. *Jmd., der über ein Buch urteilt* gives a balanced and reasoned assessment. Someone called on to *urteilen über* a person or his/her character would present the facts and substantiate the conclusions in some detail, whereas in response to *Wie beurteilen Sie ihn/seinen Charakter?* an opinion in a few words would be expected. Only *beurteilen* is used with *als. Alle Kollegen beurteilten den Plan als sehr aussichtsreich.* The judgement can be on a past event or on what might happen in the future. *Wie beurteilen Sie unsere Chancen?* Cf. 4.

> *Er urteilte sehr günstig über ihren Charakter.*   *Wie beurteilst du die Lage?*

ii. A syn. of *beurteilen* is **ermessen,** which occurs mostly with *können* or an equivalent such as *sein* + *zu* + infin. or *sich lassen.* Being derived from *messen,* it suggests an evaluation in a vague way. *Es ist schwer zu ermessen, ob das Projekt sich rentieren wird. Das Ermessen* means 'judgement or discretion'. *Das stelle ich in Ihr Ermessen. Das liegt in seinem/ihrem Ermessen* or *im Ermessen des Gerichts.*

> *Wer nie selbst unter einer Diktatur gelebt hat, kann den psychologischen Terror, dem die Menschen ausgesetzt sind, nicht/kaum ermessen.*
>
> *Daraus läßt sich ermessen, wieviel Einfluß er inzwischen verloren hat.*

3. Judge in a competition etc.

i. In sports in which the award of points decides the winner, *a judge* is called *der Punktrichter* and, in competitions in which the best entries receive awards, *der Preisrichter.* The vs. applied to both activities are **werten** and **bewerten.** As *bewerten* needs an obj., *werten* translates **judge** used intr. Thus *Die Punktrichter haben unterschiedlich gewertet,* but *Sie haben die Sprünge* (dives) *unterschiedlich bewertet.* Or *Die Preisrichter haben nicht gerecht gewertet,* and *Sie haben die Hunde nach verschiedenen Maßstäben bewertet.*

> *Die Preisjury bewertete den Film sehr positiv, und er bekam einen Preis.*
>
> *Zwei Viehzüchter bewerten die Kühe, um zu entscheiden, welche prämiert werden sollen.*

(Note that in sport etc. *werten* also means 'to be counted in a result'. *Die Punktrichter bewerten alle sechs Tänze/Sprünge, aber der schlechteste wird nicht gewertet. Dieser Durchgang wird nicht gewertet.*)

ii. Bewerten is used for evaluating or giving a mark to essays, tests, etc. *Zwei Lehrer bewerten die Abituraufsätze. Bewerten* is the usual word for evaluating a literary work or work of art, although **werten** is used intr. *Kritiker A bewertete den Roman anders als Kritiker B. Die jüngere Generation wertet im Bereich der Kunst anders als die ältere. Evaluation* is *die [literarische] Wertung. Werten* is occasionally found with an obj., mainly for evaluating a number of works. *Man wertet verschiedene Werke gegeneinander. Die Kritik hat das Stück positiv gewertet* is possible, but unusual.

4. Judge sth. [to be] + n. or adj.

i. Both **bewerten** and **werten** mean 'to decide what value or significance an event has', but *werten* is less common than *bewerten. Die meisten Zeitungen bewerteten/werteten die Konferenz als Erfolg/Mißerfolg. Die Presse bewertete die Handlung als Heldentat.* Both take *wie* in a question. *Wie hat die Presse das Gipfeltreffen gewertet/bewertet?* **Beurteilen** can also be used in these sents. Unlike [be]*werten* it can give a judgement on something in the future. *Sie beurteilte das Gipfeltreffen als Erfolg. Er beurteilte die Erfolgsaussichten als gut.* Cf. 2. i.

ii. Judge in this construction also means 'to CONSIDER' and can be expressed by **betrachten als** or **halten für.** *He judged it wiser to put an end to the quarrel: Er hielt es für ratsamer, diesem Streit ein Ende zu machen. The president shall recommend such measures as he shall judge necessary* could be *Der Präsident wird diejenigen Maßnahmen empfehlen, die er als notwendig betrachtet,* but a more elevated word like **judge** is **erachten.** *Er wird die Maßnahmen empfehlen, die er für notwendig erachtet.* Cf. *einschätzen* under ESTIMATE 4.

5. In *to judge a distance* or *speed*, **judge** means 'to estimate'. The equivalent is **einschätzen.** While *schätzen*, 'to ESTIMATE', suggests no more than giving a numerical value, *einschätzen*, like **judge**, implies making an assessment of something and then deciding whether a further action is possible. *Die alte Dame wollte über die Straße gehen, hat die Entfernung aber falsch eingeschätzt, so daß der Fahrer des auf sie zukommenden Autos scharf bremsen mußte.* If I wanted to jump across a stream, I might ask someone with me, '*Kannst du einschätzen, ob ich rüberkomme?*' An answer might be, '*Das kann ich nicht einschätzen.*' A driver might say, '*Ich versuchte, die Geschwindigkeit des anderen Autos einzuschätzen, um zu entscheiden, ob ich überholen sollte.*' Cf. ESTIMATE 4.

just *adv.*

1. The basic sense is 'exactly or precisely'. This is the meaning expressed by *gerade* and *eben. Genau* used as an adv., is a further, though stronger syn. When the first two are interchangeable, *gerade* is the everyday word, *eben* is more refined.
i. Just refers to place. **Gerade** is always possible, **eben** and **genau** often are.
    Sie wohnt gerade um die Ecke.   *Er saß gerade vor mir.*
    Die Bombe explodierte an gerade/eben/genau der Stelle, wo wir zehn Minuten früher gestanden hatten.
    An gerade/eben/genau dem Ort, wo das Haus gestanden hatte, wachsen jetzt Bäume.
ii. Just also refers to amount, number, quantity. **Gerade** and **genau** express this sense.
    Ich habe gerade 500 Mark gespart.   *Das Paket wiegt gerade/genau ein Kilo.*
    Ich habe einen Scheck über genau/gerade den Betrag bekommen, den ich ihm schuldete.
    Heute ist es gerade ein Jahr her, daß wir umgezogen sind.   *Das Auto ist genau vier Meter lang.*
iii. With *so (gut etc.) wie*, as . . . as, all three are used. *Sie ist* **ebenso** *begabt wie ihr Bruder. Er hat* **gerade** *so viel gegessen wie du. Du bist* **genau** *so groß wie er.*
iv. Just means that what follows is exactly what is stated, i.e. what was said, is needed, not known, why something happened, etc. *That's just what I was going to say. That's just what we don't know.* **Gerade** can always be used, **eben** frequently, and **genau** sometimes. *Eben/Gerade/Genau das wollte ich sagen. Von eben dem reden wir,* he's just the one we're talking about. *Eben/Gerade deshalb/darum ist sie zu Hause geblieben,* just for that reason or that's just why she stayed at home. *Gerade* and *genau* are used with *Gegenteil. Gerade das Gegenteil ist der Fall. Sie hat genau das Gegenteil gesagt.* Some E. sents. need expansion. *This is just the place: Gerade die Stelle haben wir gesucht* or *Gerade eine solche Stelle . . . Sam's just the man: Sam wäre gerade/genau richtig (für diese Aufgabe)* or *Gerade einen Mann wie Sam suchen/brauchen wir.*
    Das ist es ja gerade. (That's just it.)   *Gerade das weiß ich nicht.*
    Eben/Gerade jetzt brauchen wir das Geld.
v. In reference to time, **just** can mean: *a.* 'Exactly at the moment spoken of'. *It's just six. I'm just writing a letter. b.* 'A very little time before'. *She has just left. c.* 'A very little time after'. *We're just going.* **Gerade** and **eben** have all these senses. Examples follow under the same letters.
a. Es ist gerade fünf Uhr.   *Der Zug fährt eben/gerade ab.*

Sie telefoniert gerade/schreibt gerade einen Brief.   Wir waren gerade beim Essen.
Ein Mann, der eben/gerade vorbeiging, hat alles gesehen.   Eben tritt er ein.
Eben da ich das sage, fällt mir etw. anderes ein.
Wir kamen gerade zur rechten Zeit an.

b. Als ich ankam, war sie gerade/eben weggegangen.   Sie hat gerade angerufen.
  Sie hat gerade/[so]eben an dich geschrieben.   Er ist gerade hereingekommen.

c. Wir wollen gerade aufbrechen/weggehen/aussteigen.   Ich gehe gerade mal hin.

Soeben means 'at this moment' and 'a moment ago'. *Soeben schlägt es zwölf. Ihre Frau hat soeben angerufen.*

vi. Just now means either 'at this exact moment', *I'm very busy just now*, or 'only a very short time ago', when it has the same meaning as *just this minute/moment. You were speaking to her just now/just this minute.* **Only just** also has the second sense. *They have only just arrived.* The first sense of **just now** is im Augenblick. *Im Augenblick bin ich beschäftigt.* An alternative is **gerade jetzt**, just/right now. *Gerade jetzt kann ich Ihnen nicht helfen.* For the second sense **gerade** or **eben** can be used as explained in section v. b. *Tom ist gerade reingekommen—er wird wohl auf seinem Zimmer sein*, Tom came in just now/has just this minute come in. *Ich war gerade auf der Bank—jetzt muß ich wieder hin.*

Stronger expressions. Eben erst or **gerade erst** mean that something has only just happened, or occurred just this minute, or that someone has [only] just now heard, seen, or done something. In a few expressions **eben/gerade noch** also mean that something happened only just now or just this minute.

Ich habe es ihm gerade erst erklärt.   Das habe ich eben erst gehört.
Ich habe gerade noch/eben noch mit ihnen gesprochen.   Sie sind eben erst angekommen.
Ich bin gerade noch fertig geworden und gehe jetzt nach Hause.

vii. Vorhin also means 'just now, a short time ago'. The time extends from a few minutes to a few hours ago. *Sie haben vorhin gesagt, daß Sie in China gewesen seien. Vorhin hatte ich Angst, aber jetzt nicht mehr.* **Vor einer Weile** has the same sense. *Sie sagte, ein Mann hätte vor einer Weile nach mir gefragt.*

2. Just, only just = 'with nothing to spare'. *I had just enough time to duck. We only just caught the train. She [only] just passed the exam.* **Gerade** and *eben* can be used alone, but *noch* is usually added so that **gerade noch** and **eben noch** are the normal equivalents. *Ich kam gerade noch rechtzeitig an.*

Ich habe gerade genug zum Leben.   Das Geld reichte gerade [noch] aus.
Wir haben den Zug gerade noch erwischt.   Wir haben es gerade noch geschafft.
Er konnte den Wagen eben noch zum Halten bringen. Sonst hätte er einen Fußgänger angefahren.
Sie konnte sich eben [noch] in Sicherheit bringen, bevor das ganze Gebäude in Flammen aufging.

3. Just is used in commands and requests.

i. One of the functions of **just** is to soften a command. *Give me the book!* and *Hold the hammer!* sound very peremptory, and we tone them down by saying in a polite tone 'Just hold the hammer, would you?' A G. imp. is made milder by using **einmal**, which is usually shortened to **mal**. *Halt' mal den Hammer! Mach' mal den Fernseher an! Zeigen Sie mal her!* It is also added to an infin. used as a command, *Alle [ein]mal herhören!*, and to requests, *Können Sie mir mal einen Gefallen tun?* or *Würden Sie mir [bitte] mal Ihr Wörterbuch leihen?*, and occasionally to a n., *Augenblick mal! Mal* added to a statement, usually an expression of intention, makes this sound simple, modest, and casual as **just** also does. *Ich werde sie mal fragen, ob ich helfen kann. Mal* is also combined with *gerade* and *eben*. There is no difference in meaning between **gerade mal** and **eben mal**. (These are also occasionally found the other way round, *mal gerade* and *mal eben*, but still have the same sense.) Both suggest that what the person speaking wants the other to do requires no effort and will not take long. It is often like *just for a moment*. *Halt' eben mal/gerade mal den Hammer!* These expressions imply that the action is to be carried out at once. *Rufen Sie ihn mal an!* can, but need not, refer to the present, whereas *Rufen Sie ihn eben mal an!* implies ringing up now. Both *eben mal* and *gerade mal* are used in statements and mean 'just [for a moment]'. *Ich bin gleich wieder da—ich muß diese Briefe eben mal einwerfen,* I just have to post them, and it won't take long.

ii. Just also gives emphasis to an imp. *Just be quiet!* **Doch** makes an imp. more emphatic. *Beeil' dich doch!* is like *Do/Just hurry up! Doch* expresses mild impatience. Whereas *mal* does not refer to a previous action or remark, *doch* links up with a remark, the behaviour, or an attitude of the person addressed. The speaker expresses a wish for a change or criticizes the other person. *Freu' dich doch!* is said to someone who takes life unduly seriously or who is always getting annoyed or dejected. To a patient who complains to a doctor and seems to lack confidence in the way he is being treated, the doctor could say, '*Haben Sie doch ein bißchen Vertrauen zu mir!*' To an impatient person someone might say, '*Sei doch nicht so ungeduldig!*', and someone whose car is always breaking down and not being properly repaired might receive the advice, '*Bring doch das Auto in die Werkstatt!*' Commands with *doch* can express considerable annoyance, particularly when it is combined with *endlich*. *Halt doch endlich den Mund! Sei doch endlich ruhig!* or *Paß doch endlich auf!* **Doch mal**, on the other hand, is always polite and suggests that what is asked is simple and easy. *Doch* carries a note of surprise that this has not been done before. *Machen Sie den Fernseher doch mal aus!* (*d. h. wenn er Sie stört*). *Rufen Sie die Auskunft doch mal an, wenn Sie die Nummer im Telefonbuch nicht finden!*

iii. Just also occurs in warnings or threats. These tell someone [not] to do something in the future. **Ja** and **bloß** are used in pos. and neg. sents., and **nur** in neg. ones only. They are always stressed. *Sei ja vorsichtig!*, just be careful! *Mach' das ja/bloß/nur nicht noch einmal!* could be *Just don't do that again!* or *Don't you dare do that again! Komm bloß nicht wieder zu spät! Laß dich nur nicht reinlegen! Benehmt euch ja anständig!*

4. i. Just gives emphasis to a statement and may indicate that there is no alternative to doing what is said. *It just won't work. We'll just have to wait.* Unstressed **eben** and **halt** express the idea that a situation cannot be changed and that this fact must be recognized and accepted. *Eben* is more usual in northern Germany, *halt* in the south. *Es geht eben/halt nicht* means that something is just impossible and that we [just] have to reconcile ourselves to this fact. *Da kann man eben nichts machen* is like *There's just nothing you can do about it. Es ist eben nicht mehr zu ändern. Du hättest dich eben in acht nehmen sollen. Junge Menschen haben eben ihren Willen. Allen Menschen kann man eben nicht vertrauen.* With an imp. *eben* means that there is nothing else for it but to do what is stated. *Wenn du den Film nicht sehen willst, dann bleib eben zu Hause! Wenn der Lorenz nicht mitkommen will, dann geh' eben alleine zum Fußballplatz!* It is used with *müssen* in a similar situation. *Wir müssen eben warten. Wenn es wieder nicht klappt, dann mußt du es eben aufgeben.*

ii. Nun einmal, often shortened to *nun mal*, also suggests that a situation cannot be changed, but it points to something which is more impersonal and universal than *eben*. It refers not to a particular case but to a general fact which is true for all times and places. *Die Menschen sind nun einmal keine Engel. Ich bin nun einmal so* means that that's just what I'm like, and nothing can change it.

    Das Wetter in Deutschland ist nun einmal nicht besonders gut.

5. Eben, used as an exclamation, is like *That's just what I think/was saying* or *Quite/Just so!*

    A. *Wir wollen uns ja nicht streiten.* B. *Eben!*

6. Just also means 'only'. *He's just a normal human being. You just need to add boiling water! They were just thirty metres away. That's just one aspect of my work.* The equivalent is **nur**. *Er ist nur ein normaler Mensch—mehr können Sie von ihm nicht erwarten. Das ist nur ein Gerücht,* just a rumour. *Das sind nur einige der Fragen, die gestellt worden sind,* just a few. *Das ist nur eine Seite meiner Arbeit.*

Brandt war nur achtzehn Jahre alt, als Hitler an die Macht kam.

Sie waren nur dreißig Meter entfernt.   Man braucht nur kochendes Wasser hinzuzugießen.

7. In *That's just splendid*, **just** means 'simply, absolutely'. **Einfach** can be used.

Das ist einfach unmöglich.   Hier halte ich es einfach nicht länger aus.

Geradezu is used to intensify an adj. or adv. *Das ist geradezu fabelhaft/gemein.*

8. Just on, **just under**. With a number or something implying a number, **knapp** means 'just less than'.

Vor knapp einer Stunde fiel der Strom aus.

Für zwei Stunden beträgt die Parkgebühr knapp sieben Mark.

Das Flugzeug fliegt knapp unter der Schallgrenze.

9. For **just about** = 'almost' cf. NEARLY and *so ziemlich* under FAIRLY 3.

keep, maintain, preserve *vs.* Although *halten* also means 'to hold' and 'to stop', it and its derivatives express many of the meanings of **keep**. This article first deals with those senses of *halten* for which E. uses **keep**, but treats at the same time derivatives and other words with a related meaning. Order of treatment: 1. **Keep** = 'observe, abide by'. *She kept her promise.* 2. **Keep** animals, oneself/one's family, **maintain** roads, **keep** accounts, a diary, etc., **keep/maintain** a house in proper order. 3. **Keep** = 'cause to remain in a condition'. *Keep your room tidy!* 4. **Keep** = 'restrain from going away'. *I don't want to keep you.* 5. **Keep** = 'remain in good condition'. *Milk keeps for several days.* 6. **Keep** = 'remain in a specified position'. *Keep to the left!* 7. **Keep** = 'retain in one's possession' and 'withhold from present use'. *Keep the change! I'll keep a piece of cake for you.* 8. **Keep, maintain, preserve** = 'save or guard from harm'. *He kept them from harm. She maintained/kept her composure. Only a few of the early poems are preserved.* 9. **Keep** = 'have sth. where it is normally stored'. *Where do you keep the cutlery?* 10. **Keep** information **from** s.o. 11. **Keep** s.o. **from** doing sth. 12. **Keep on** doing sth.

1. Keep [to] trans. = 'to observe, to abide dutifully by sth. one has committed oneself to or is obliged to carry out' such as a promise, law, appointment, treaty, contract, etc.

i. Halten is used with *ein Versprechen* or *[sein/ihr] Wort, ein Schwur, ein Eid, die Gebote, Diät, eine Wette, ein Vertrag* as obj. *Jmdm. die Treue halten*, to keep faith with. *Frieden halten* is 'to keep the peace'. With *Disziplin, Ordnung,* and *Ruhe* as obj., *halten* implies observing them, i.e. remaining disciplined etc. *Die Schüler hielten Disziplin. Der Lehrer sorgt für Disziplin* means that it is the teacher's responsibility to ensure that the pupils remain disciplined and translates *The teacher keeps/maintains discipline* when this expresses the meaning just given. In reference to someone's ability to keep order etc. *Der Lehrer konnte [keine] Ordnung halten* is used. With regard to things: *Du mußt in seinen Sachen Ordnung halten.*

> *Ich hoffe, daß sie Wort hält und uns besucht.*   *Was man verspricht, sollte man auch halten.*
> *Er hat sein Wort gehalten, mir beim Tapezieren zu helfen.*
> *Die Bibliothekarin sagte zu den jungen Leuten, die sich im Lesesaal unterhielten: 'Ich muß Sie bitten, Ruhe zu halten, damit Sie die übrigen Leser nicht stören.'*
> *Der Film hält nicht, was die Reklame verspricht.*   *Die Fans haben diesmal Ordnung gehalten.*
> *Menschen, die uns betrügen, brauchen wir nicht die Treue zu halten.*

ii. Sich halten an is a syn. of *halten* i and is used with *eine Abmachung* or *Vereinbarung,* 'agreement', *ein Vertrag, eine Regel, eine Vorschrift, ein Gesetz, eine Verordnung.* A further meaning is 'to keep to, stick to, not deviate from' facts, something observed, an original (document), etc.

> *Der Autor des Drehbuchs hat sich eng/streng an den Roman gehalten, was bei Verfilmungen nicht immer geschieht.*   *Du solltest dich mehr an die Tatsachen halten.*

iii. Einhalten means 'to adhere, stick to, or keep' something regarded as an obligation. The obj. can be a word like *ein Termin, die Spielregeln, eine Abmachung, eine Vereinbarung, eine Verpflichtung, eine Bestimmung, ein Verbot, eine Vorschrift,* or something prescribed or agreed to, including a course, direction, speed, and position, customs regarded as laws, and arrangements to meet. *Die Frist einhalten* means 'to meet or keep to the time-limit or deadline'. *Eine Versprechung einhalten* is used in formal language instead of the everyday expression *ein Versprechen halten*.

> *Er konnte die Verabredung/den Termin wegen unvorhersehbarer Verkehrsverhältnisse nicht einhalten.*
> *Beim Bau des Tunnels zwischen Frankreich und Großbritannien hat man alle Termine einhalten können.*
> *Eine von den Betriebsangehörigen gebildete Kommission achtet stets darauf, daß die Arbeitsschutzbestimmungen eingehalten werden.*
> *Die Maschine hielt ihre Flugzeit genau ein.*
> *Jedes Flugzeug muß den ihm zugewiesenen Kurs einhalten.*

iv. Keep *early/late hours* must be translated as the idea. *Er kommt immer sehr früh/spät nach Hause. Meine Mutter geht immer früh ins Bett, aber meine Schwester bleibt sehr spät auf.*

2. The second sense of **keep** used trans. is 'to guard from external violence or injury', 'to preserve, maintain'. This sense is now often carried by **preserve** and **maintain**, and the equivalents are discussed in 8. Other E. uses have developed from this meaning.

i. Keep came to mean 'to own and to take care of' and was applied to animals kept to make money and as a hobby, thus to farm animals and to pets. **Halten** is used for animals kept for economic purposes, and **sich halten** for pets and animals kept for private use. (*Hüten* translates the archaic meaning of **keep** 'to tend'. *Mose hütete die Schafe seines Schwiegervaters.*)

> *Der Landwirt hat einen großen Schweinestall und hält ein paar hundert Schweine.*
> *Um frische Eier zum Frühstück essen zu können, halten wir uns ein paar Hühner im Garten.*
> *In diesem Mietshaus darf man sich keine Haustiere halten.* In the pass.: *... dürfen keine Tiere gehalten werden.*

Keep and *halten* are also occasionally found with servants, cars, newspapers, and periodicals as obj.

> *Als erfolgreicher Industrieller kann er es sich leisten, zwei Dienstmädchen, einen Butler, mehrere Autos und eine Mätresse zu halten.*
> *Ich halte mehrere Fachzeitschriften.* (More commonly: *Ich abonniere eine Zeitschrift.*)

ii. Keep also means 'to provide s.o./oneself with food, clothing, and other necessities of life'. **Maintain**, *support*, and *provide for* are syns. **Unterhalten** is now the usual word, *erhalten* in this sense having gone out of use. Close in meaning are *ernähren*, 'to FEED', *versorgen* and *sorgen für*, 'to PROVIDE FOR'. These vs. are often preferred because *unterhalten* also means 'to entertain'. **Aufkommen für**, 'to meet the cost of', is used when **keep** has a personal obj. + *in*, e.g. *to keep s.o. in clothes*.

> *Er muß von seinem Gehalt nicht nur seine fünfköpfige Familie, sondern auch noch zwei Geschwister unterhalten.*
> *Da er arbeitslos war, hatte er Schwierigkeiten, Frau und Kinder zu unterhalten.*
> *Ihr Vater bezahlt die Miete und gibt ihr genug Geld fürs Essen, aber sie kommt für ihre eigenen Kleider auf* (keeps herself in clothes).

iii. Unterhalten also means 'to maintain' in the sense of 'to bear the expense of'.

> *Die Heilsarmee unterhält mehrere Heime für Männer, die kein Zuhause haben.*
> *Das Kulturzentrum wird von der Stadt unterhalten.*
> *Die europäischen Länder unterhalten ein Kernforschungszentrum in der Schweiz.*

Die Gemeinde (local council) *unterhält die Straßen* means that it provides the money for the upkeep of the roads. **Instandhalten** denotes the actual work of keeping them in good order.

> *Die Straßenmeisterei hält die Straßen und Brücken instand.* Or *... hält sie in Ordnung.*

iv. Unterhalten also means 'to maintain or keep up' relations, correspondence, etc. *Firma A unterhält gute/enge Beziehungen zu/mit Firma B. Land X unterhält*

[Handels]beziehungen mit/zu Land Y. *Die beiden unterhielten jahrelang einen Briefwechsel/ eine rege Korrespondenz miteinander.* Unterhalten is a fairly formal word, but can be used in everyday life. *Ich unterhalte Kontakt/Fühlung/Verbindung zu/mit jmdm.* In *Ich erhalte die Verbindung zu jmdm. aufrecht,* the v. is also translated as **maintain**, but suggests effort to keep the relationship in a good state. Cf. 3. iv. In normal situations the usual expression is *mit jmdm. Verbindung/Kontakt haben* or *halten,* to keep/be/ remain in contact/touch with or maintain contact with s.o. *Wir haben nur briefliche Verbindung miteinander. Ich habe enge Verbindung mit ihr gehalten.*

Die beiden Institute arbeiten auf einigen wissenschaftlichen Gebieten eng zusammen. Seit Jahren unterhalten sie sehr gute Beziehungen.

v. Keep a record, journal, diary, accounts of money paid and received, etc. means 'to maintain them continuously in proper order'. In some cases, **führen** carries this sense. It is used with *Bücher* in the sense of *Geschäftsbücher* and with [*das*] *Protokoll,* either the minutes of a meeting etc. or a written record of events, testimony, etc. *Die Tochter führt die Bücher für ihren Vater. Über etw. Buch führen* means 'to keep a record of'. *Führen Sie genau Buch über alle Ausgaben! Man führt eine Liste, eine Kartei,* and *ein Tagebuch.* (*S.o. kept an account/record of events* is *Jmd. zeichnete alles auf, was geschah.* Cf. RECORD.)

In den Sitzungen des Lehrerkollegiums muß das jüngste Mitglied des Kollegiums das Protokoll führen.

vi. Applied to shops, businesses, or a house, **führen** means 'to keep or run'. *Er führt ein Geschäft,* carries on, conducts, runs, manages a business. *Das Ehepaar hat zehn Jahre lang ein Restaurant erfolgreich geführt. Sie führt ihrem verwitweten Sohn den Haushalt,* keeps house for.

vii. Führen also translates **keep** or *stock* meaning 'to have certain goods continually in stock'.

A. Haben Sie auch Regenschirme? B. Nein, die führen wir nicht.

Dieses Geschäft führt alles, was Kunstschüler brauchen.

viii. Keep = 'to maintain or preserve a house, garden, car, etc. in proper order'. **Halten** is used with an obj. + adj. or phr.: *Das Haus wird ordentlich/sauber/in bester Ordnung gehalten.* Cf. 3. **Pflegen** means 'to keep in good condition', 'to CARE FOR'. The past part. *gepflegt* means 'well-kept, well-cared for'.

Der Gärtner pflegt den Garten/den Rasen/die Anlagen.   *Die Wohnung sah gepflegt aus.*

3. Keep trans. = 'to cause s.o./sth. to continue in a specified condition, place, or action'. It is used with an obj. and an adj., *I keep sth. clean,* a pres. or past part., *I keep sth. going, He keeps the door shut,* a n., *They kept s.o. prisoner, He kept his misfortune a secret,* or a phr., *They kept s.o. in suspense/in prison, I keep sth. in good repair.*

i. Halten is possible in most cases with an adj., a past part., and a phr.

Adjs.: *Während des Versuchs muß man die Temperatur konstant halten.*

Die Kosten sind so niedrig wie möglich zu halten.	*Man muß diese Waren kühl halten.*
Wir müssen die Blumen bis heute abend frisch halten.	*Ich halte den Platz frei.*
Er hält sein Zimmer immer sauber und ordentlich.	*Ich werde dir das Essen warm halten.*
Dieser Mantel hält warm (obj. implied).	*Sport treiben hält jung.*

Past parts.: *Während sie meditiert, hält sie die Augen geschlossen.*

Freunde des Flüchtlings haben ihn versteckt/verborgen gehalten.   *Ich halte den Platz besetzt.*

Phrs.: *Wir müssen versuchen, ihn bei guter Laune zu halten.*

Du mußt dich etwas mehr im Zaume halten, auch wenn deine Kritik berechtigt ist.

Die Kinder halten ihre Zimmer in Ordnung.   *Man muß die Akten unter Verschluß halten.*

Durch tägliches Lesen der Zeitung hält man sich über das Tagesgeschehen auf dem Laufenden (keep abreast of/up with/up to date with).

Durch gesunde Ernährung und regelmäßige Bewegung wollte er sich bei Kräften halten.

Sie halten das Haus/den Wagen in gutem Zustand.

ii. Ns. and pres. parts. A n. may be able to be expressed as an adj. or part. *Er wurde* *gefangen gehalten*, kept prisoner/in prison. Cf. 4. *Er hat sein Unglück geheim gehalten*, kept it [a] secret. Unless there is a phr. with a similar sense such as *Die Maschine muß die ganze Nacht über in Gang gehalten werden*, 'be kept going/running', pres. parts. need to be expressed differently, as do some phrs. *Sorg' dafür, daß das Feuer nicht ausgeht!* could translate *keep it burning*. (Also here *Ich habe das Feuer im Kamin unterhalten*, maintained it, kept it going.) *Sie haben mich warten lassen*, kept me waiting. *Er sagt uns nie genau, was er vorhat/plant*, keeps us guessing/in the dark about his plans. Idioms with this construction can be translated as the underlying idea. *He kept his nose to the grindstone* could be *Er arbeitete fleißig*.

iii. Maintain + obj. + a phr., as in *We are maintaining production at the present level*, is translated by **halten**. *Wir halten die Produktion auf dem gegenwärtigen Stand. Wir müssen die Temperatur hoch halten* or *bei 800° halten*, maintain/keep it at a high level/at 800°.

iv. Aufrechterhalten means 'to ensure that sth. remains or continues in its existing (good) state'. In different contexts it corresponds to **maintain, keep**, or *uphold*. *Die Polizei erhält die Ordnung/die Ruhe/den Frieden im Lande aufrecht. Jmd. erhält sein Ansehen/seinen guten Ruf/seine Autorität aufrecht* and *erhält eine Fiktion/eine Täuschung/den Schein aufrecht. Jmd. erhält eine Behauptung aufrecht*, maintains a claim, an assertion. *Jmd. erhält eine Verbindung/den Kontakt/ein Verhältnis aufrecht.*

> *Seit Ausbruch des Golfkrieges bemüht sich der syrische Präsident, seinen Ruf als Freund des Westens aufrechtzuerhalten.*
> *Ich habe die Verbindung zu meinen Studienfreunden aufrechterhalten, obwohl wir uns nicht oft sehen.*

4. Keep trans. = 'to restrain from going away, or cause or induce to remain' and 'to hold as a captive or in custody' or 'to prevent from escaping, if necessary, by force'. *Extra work kept me at the office. Will they keep me in prison? Halten, festhalten, zurückhalten*, and *aufhalten* all express related ideas, but translate *hold* as well as **keep**.

i. Halten is used with *im Gefängnis* and also means 'to keep s.o. in a place'. If in the latter sense the subj. is or stands for a person and the sent. is pos., it implies that the person wishing to keep another has a strong desire, need, or interest in the other's remaining. It suggests that the other might want to go, without implying a specific goal, and that, if the efforts to keep the person are successful, he/she will remain more or less permanently. *Der Betrieb wollte die Facharbeiter halten*. It is, however, often neg. and also impersonal. *Es hielt ihn nicht länger in seinem Heimatdorf.*

> *Was hält dich hier noch [in der Stadt]?*   *Die Schulleitung will den erfahrenen Lehrer halten.*
> *Colet hätte Erasmus gern in Oxford gehalten.*   *Ich halte dich nicht, wenn du gehen willst.*

ii. Aufhalten is 'to keep' when this means 'to hold up or to detain for a short time'.

> *Wir wurden an der Grenze aufgehalten.*   *Ich brauche Sie nicht länger aufzuhalten.*

iii. Zurückhalten implies that the obj. intended to go somewhere specific but that s.o./sth. prevented him/her from going, at least for a time. It usually suggests a longer time than *aufhalten*, though it need not be very long. It is used when the subj. is something like *widrige Umstände* or *eine dringende Angelegenheit* and in this sense is interchangeable with **festhalten**.

> *Eine dringende Angelegenheit hielt mich in Frankfurt zurück.*   *Was hält dich hier noch zurück?*
> *Ich wurde durch eine Sitzung im Büro festgehalten.*
> *Obwohl er zu seiner Familie auf dem Lande zurückkehren wollte, verstand sie es, ihn unter allerlei Vorwänden in Wien zurückzuhalten/festzuhalten.*

iv. Besides having sense iii, **festhalten** can mean 'to detain by the (potential) use of force' or 'to arrest'. It has this sense in a sent. like *Er wurde an der Grenze festgehalten. Aufgehalten* would mean 'held up'.

5. Keep intr. = 'to remain in good condition' is used for food or things which deteriorate. For this G. uses **sich halten**. *Milch hält sich mehrere Tage im Kühlschrank.* (*Halten* is used for clothes and things subject to wear and tear for which E. uses LAST.)

> *Obwohl wir nur eine Woche weg waren, haben sich die Lebensmittel im Kühlschrank nicht gehalten.*
> *Die Pflaumen sind jetzt reif, aber weil sie sich nicht lange halten, verschenken wir den größten Teil davon.*
> *Wie lange hält sich Fisch/Fleisch?*

Keep, used intr., is applied to news etc. which can be reserved for a later occasion. *That will keep till later.* This is best expressed by a trans v. *Das heben wir für später auf.* Cf. 7. ix.

6. Keep intr. = 'to remain or continue in a specified position'. It is used with adjs., *Keep close to me!*, and with a prep. and/or a word indicating position, *Keep [to the] left!* or *We must keep in sight of the ocean.*

i. In relation to a position or direction **sich halten** means 'to take one up and remain in it'. **Bleiben** can be an alternative. *Sie hielt sich dicht hinter mir/an meiner Seite.* Or *Sie blieb dicht neben mir/an meiner Seite.*

> *Das Flugzeug hält sich auf einer Höhe von 10 000 Metern.*
> *Wenn Sie sich Richtung Süden halten, können Sie das Dorf gar nicht verfehlen.*
> *Solange der Lastwagen sich in der Mitte der Straße hält, können wir ihn nicht überholen.*
> *Um zur Stadtbibliothek zu kommen, brauchen Sie nur geradeaus zu gehen, sich am Marktplatz links zu halten und dann in die Otmarstraße einzubiegen.*

ii. Heraushalten is trans. meaning 'to keep s.o. out of sth.' **Sich heraushalten** has the intr. sense 'to keep out of sth.' *Ich will versuchen, dich aus der Sache herauszuhalten. Der Regierungschef hielt sich aus dem Streit zwischen Unternehmern und Gewerkschaften heraus. Das Land hielt sich aus dem Krieg heraus.*

iii. Related E. expressions. When **keep** means 'to remain in a condition', it is translated by **bleiben**. *S.o. keeps in good health* is *Jmd. bleibt bei guter Gesundheit. Ruhig bleiben* (or *Ruhe bewahren*), to keep calm. *Er blieb still/ruhig/fit*, kept still/quiet/fit. *I kept straight on* is *Ich ging geradeaus*, and *I kept on my way* is *Ich setzte meinen Weg fort.* Cf. also CLEAR 5. *Sich halten* is used for keeping one's feet when an effort is required to remain standing. *Auf den losen Steinen des steilen Gebirgspfades kann man sich nur mit Mühe auf den Füßen/Beinen halten. Ich konnte mich nicht mehr halten und rutschte den Berg hinunter.*

7. Keep trans. = 'actively to retain or hold in one's possession, power, or control'. *Keep the change! How long can you keep library books?*

i. The main equivalent is **behalten**, 'to keep or retain', which can be applied to people, *jmdn. in seiner Obhut behalten*, or things, *etw. in der Nähe behalten*.

> *Das Buch brauche ich nicht mehr. Sie können es behalten.*
> *Das Kleingeld können Sie behalten.*   *Ausgeliehene Bücher darf man einen Monat behalten.*
> *Man sollte Fundsachen nicht behalten, sondern beim Fundbüro abgeben.*
> *Behalten Sie unter allen Umständen einen klaren Kopf! Also Bewahren Sie . . . Cf. 8.*
> *Trotz des Bekanntwerdens seiner dunklen Vergangenheit durfte der Abgeordnete seinen Sitz im Parlament behalten.*   *Der Arzt behielt mich zehn Tage lang im Krankenhaus.*

ii. Behalten is also used for less tangible things. *Etw. behält seinen Wert. Jmd. behält sein Gleichgewicht. Die Blumen behalten ihren Duft. Die Fahrkarte behält ihre Gültigkeit. Er behielt die Herrschaft über sich.* **Keep** *one's temper* could be *sich beherrschen.* Cf. CONTROL 5.

iii. Behalten also means 'to keep, retain, or leave in a position'. *Trotz des Befehls behielt er die Hände in den Hosentaschen.* Hence **anbehalten** and **aufbehalten**, to keep on. *Sie behielt den Mantel an. Er behielt den Hut auf. Jmd. behielt die Zügel fest in der Hand* and *Die Regierung behielt die Außenpolitik fest in der Hand,* kept a firm grip on.

iv. Etw. für sich behalten means 'to keep sth. to oneself'. *Ich werde meine Meinung für mich behalten. Wenn ich dir etw. erzähle, kannst du es für dich behalten?* **Jmdn. bei sich behalten** is 'to keep s.o. in one's house etc.' *Sie behielten den Flüchtling mehrere Tage bei sich.*

v. Beibehalten means 'to stick to or not to give up' what already exists or what one is accustomed to doing. Thus *Man behält eine alte Lebensweise/eine Sitte/eine Gewohnheit/eine Methode/ein [veraltetes/überholtes] Verfahren/einen Namen bei.*

> *Trotz Bedenken behielten wir den ursprünglichen Wortlaut des Briefes/den einmal eingeschlagenen Kurs bei.*
> *Nach der Heirat behielt sie ihren Mädchennamen bei.*
> *Die neuen Besitzer haben den alten Firmennamen beibehalten.*
> *Die menschenunwürdigen Regelungen zur Behandlung von Asylanten werden trotz massiven Protests beibehalten.* *Der Stadtrat beschloß, die Parkuhren beizubehalten.*

vi. Keep = 'to withhold from present use', 'to lay up, store up, not to part with or throw away'. *I always keep old letters. I'll keep a piece of cake for you. We'll keep that for later.* It also means 'to look after for s.o. else'. *I'll keep the money for you.* **Aufheben** means 'to look after for future use'. It expresses all these senses, but it is the everyday word which says nothing about the value of the things kept. *Sie hebt immer alte Briefe auf. Ich hebe das Geld/das Paket für dich auf.* Only *aufheben* is used in connection with food. *Er hob ihr ein Stück seiner Geburtstagstorte auf. Ich hebe dir das Essen auf.*

> *Ich hebe diese Postkarten zum Andenken auf.*
> *Diesen Kram habe ich so lange für dich aufgehoben, und jetzt brauchst du ihn nicht mehr.*
> *Wir heben die Karten für euch auf. Ihr könnt sie abholen, wenn ihr nächste Woche in der Stadt seid.*

vii. Aufbewahren is used for keeping what is of greater value either in itself or to a person. There is some overlapping with *aufheben. Das Bild habe ich vierzig Jahre lang aufgehoben/aufbewahrt. Gepäck im Bahnhof aufbewahren,* to leave at the left-luggage. *Man bewahrt Gepäck in einem Schließfach auf.*

> *Das bewahre ich zur späteren Verwendung auf.*
> *Die Medikamente sind kühl aufzubewahren* (to be kept/stored in a cool place).
> *Sie hat dieses Foto ihres im Ersten Weltkrieg gefallenen Mannes ihr Leben lang aufbewahrt.*
> *Das Testament wird beim Rechtsanwalt aufbewahrt.*

viii. Verwahren means 'to keep very carefully'. It suggests that something is so securely kept that unwanted access is difficult, if not impossible. *Verwahren* is the formal word used for safe deposit.

> *Ihre kostbare Münzensammlung ist seit einiger Zeit in einem Banksafe verwahrt.*
> *Die Dokumente müssen sorgfältig verwahrt werden.*

ix. Keep or *save* a question, problem, news, remark, etc. up **for later** can be expressed by **aufheben**. *Diese Frage heben wir für später auf.* **Aufsparen**, to save for later use, expresses a similar meaning. *Diesen Witz/Diese Anekdote spare ich für den Schluß der Rede auf.* The E. intr. use *That (news) will keep till later* is translated by a trans. v. *Wir heben/sparen diese Nachricht bis/für später auf.*

8. Keep trans. = 'to save or guard from harm, deterioration, etc.' In this sense **keep** is now limited to certain expressions such as *She kept them from harm. He kept a clear head.* (In *The railing kept me from falling, kept* could be regarded as having the sense just defined or as being a syn. of *prevent*. In both cases it is translated by *bewahren.* Cf. 11.) **Preserve** means 'to save or protect from damage, loss, destruction, or decay'. *The paint preserves the metal from corrosion.* **Maintain** means 'to prevent from becoming weaker'. *I have maintained my friendship with them. He maintained/kept his composure. She maintained her independence.*

i. Bewahren has gone out of use in the sense of keeping a concrete object in good condition, but is used for intangibles. *Man bewahrt ein Geheimnis. Man bewahrt [die] Haltung/[die] Ruhe/die Fassung*, maintains one's calm, composure. *Er bewahrte einen klaren Kopf/ruhig Blut. Jmd. bewahrt sein Interesse an etw.* and *bewahrt Stillschweigen.* It is used with a dat. and refl. dat. *Bewahre mir die alte Freundschaft! Sie will sich die Freiheit bewahren.* (In the last two sents., also *erhalten*.)
  Diese Angelegenheit ist geheim. Also bewahre bitte Stillschweigen darüber!
  Das Reich zerfiel nach dem Tod Alexanders trotz der Bemühungen des Regenten, die Einheit zu bewahren.
  Mein oberster Grundsatz war, mir die Unabhängigkeit zu bewahren.
ii. The main use of *bewahren* is with *vor*. **Bewahren vor** means 'to keep, preserve, or SAVE from' harm, injury, loss, being hurt, killed, etc. *Man bewahrt Kinder vor Schaden/Unfällen. Man bewahrt Lebensmittel vor dem Verderben.* It can imply a special effort to ward off injury etc. or may mean that the result is brought about simply because something is there. *Das Treppengeländer bewahrte sie vorm Sturz.*
  Man bemüht sich, diese Tierart vor dem Aussterben zu bewahren. Or . . . diese Tierart davor zu bewahren, durch Jäger ausgerottet zu werden.
  Der geschickte Verteidiger konnte seinen Mandanten vor dem Gefängnis bewahren.
  Die Farbe bewahrt die Metallteile vor der Verrostung.
iii. Erhalten means either 'to cause sth. to remain in good condition' or 'to cause it not to decay or be lost' and is translated by **keep, preserve**, or **maintain**. It cannot be used with *vor* and suggests more activity than *bewahren*. It is applied to concrete objects and living beings. *Man hat das alte Bauwerk gut erhalten. Man muß die Vitamine in den Speisen erhalten. Ein Haus wird in gutem Zustand erhalten* implies, like **maintain**, special care and action over a long period, while *halten* (cf. 3. i) suggests normal care. *Man hat das Schloß vor der Verwahrlosung bewahrt* implies just enough care to keep it from becoming dilapidated or going to rack and ruin. *Trotz seiner Verwundungen konnte er am Leben erhalten werden* suggests great effort and special measures and is only used for people. Otherwise, to keep alive is *am Leben halten. Man wollte diese alten Bräuche am Leben halten. Erhalten* is used with abilities and less tangible things, often with a refl. or other dat. like *bewahren. Ich erhalte mir die Gesundheit. Sie erhielt sich die gute Laune. Erhalten Sie mir Ihr Wohlwollen!* The pass. can be *Etw. bleibt erhalten. Nur eine Handschrift dieses Epos ist erhalten geblieben.*
  Die Tänzerin erhält die Geschmeidigkeit ihres Körpers durch ständiges Üben.
  Die Regierung wollte diesen maroden Großbetrieb im Interesse der Vollbeschäftigung erhalten/vor dem Konkurs bewahren. Durch dieses Verfahren bleibt das Aroma erhalten.
  Dem Verletzten wurde das Augenlicht erhalten (saved/preserved).
  Nur wenige der frühen Gedichte sind erhalten.
iv. Sich erhalten means 'to be preserved or survive', 'to maintain itself'. *Die keltische Sprache hat sich erhalten* means that is has not died out, it is still spoken. *Dieser Brauch hat sich erhalten. Eine Art erhält sich durch Fortpflanzung. Beuteltiere haben sich fast nur in Australien erhalten.*
v. Other vs. **Wahren** is now restricted in everyday language to a few fixed expressions. *Den Schein wahren*, 'to keep up appearances', *die Formen wahren*, 'to keep to the rules of etiquette', and *das Gesicht wahren*, 'to save face'. It still occurs in elevated diction. *Wir sind entschlossen, die Sicherheit der Bundesrepublik Deutschland und den Zusammenhalt der deutschen Nation zu wahren, den Frieden zu erhalten und an einer europäischen Freidensordnung mitzuarbeiten* (Willy Brandt's inaugural speech to Parliament on 28 Oct. 1969). The G. Bible uses **behüten**, 'to PROTECT', where the AV has *keep* and *preserve. Der Herr segne dich und behüte dich* (Numbers 6: 24). *Der Herr behüte dich vor allem Übel, er behüte deine Seele* (Psalm 121).

9. Keep trans. = 'to have a thg. in the place where it is normally stored or housed'. *Where do you keep the cutlery? Halten* is not possible. Vs. meaning 'to PUT' are used as well as **haben, sein**, or **finden**.

> *Ich decke den Tisch. Wo sind die Teller?/Wo finde ich die Teller?* (Where do you keep them?)
> *Wo hast du die Briefmarken? Ich brauche eine achtziger, um diesen Brief abzuschicken.*
> *Ich stelle das Fahrrad immer in den Keller.*

10. Keep information **from** s.o. **Vorenthalten**, 'to withhold what is someone's by rights', can be applied to information. *Man hat uns die Nachricht vorenthalten.* More common would be **verschweigen** or **verbergen**, discussed under HIDE. Etw. **unterschlagen**, used without a dat., means 'deliberately not to mention or divulge'. *Er hat ein paar wichtige Tatsachen unterschlagen.*

11. Keep s.o. **from** doing sth. means 'to stop or prevent' and is trans. *Urgent business kept me from going. The cold spring kept the seed from germinating.* **Abhalten** has this sense, but **bewahren** and equivalents of PREVENT like *hindern* and *verhindern* are often necessary. *Abhalten* needs a pers. as obj. *Das Telefon klingelte dauernd und hielt mich vom Vokabellernen ab.* It implies that the person who is kept from doing something intended to do it. *Der Freund hielt ihn von dieser unüberlegten Handlung ab,* or . . . *hielt ihn davon ab, diese Dummheit zu machen.* Also . . . **hinderte** *ihn daran, eine Dummheit zu machen.* When the resulting action is not intended, **bewahren** is needed. *Er faßte mich am Arm und bewahrte mich vorm Stolpern,* or . . . *bewahrte mich davor, hinzufallen.* With a non-personal action, **verhindern** is the appropriate v. *Der ungewöhnlich kalte Frühling verhinderte, daß die Saat keimte.*

12. Keep [on] + a pres. part. means either 'to continue doing sth.' or 'to do sth. repeatedly' and is intr. *They kept on playing/fighting. Keep smiling! He keeps on slamming the door.* For the first sent. an equivalent of *continue* can be used. *Sie spielten weiter trotz des Regens. Er arbeitete weiter, obwohl er sehr müde war.* **Keep** moving or **keep** going = 'walking' is *weiter gehen. Obwohl sie erschöpft war, ging sie weiter.* Transls. of the fig. sense of **keep [on]** going are *Mach nur weiter!* and *Gib's doch nicht auf! Keep smiling!* could be *Den Mut nur nicht verlieren!* The sense of doing something repeatedly in the third sent. can be expressed by **jedesmal** or **immer wieder** or **wiederholt**, repeatedly. *Er schlägt jedesmal die Tür zu. Sie erzählt diese dummen Geschichten immer wieder. Der Bindfaden ist wiederholt gerissen.* **Dauernd** often expresses displeasure at the frequency with which something recurs. *Sie stören mich dauernd. Ruf mich nicht dauernd an!* **Andauernd**, 'constantly, continually', also often implies a certain irritation at the frequent repetition of an action. *Er stellt andauernd dumme Fragen* could translate *He keeps on asking . . . Sie belästigen uns andauernd mit diesen Angeboten.*

> *So lustig finde ich das gar nicht, dir andauernd sagen zu müssen, was du tun sollst.*

kill, murder, massacre, slaughter vs.

1. i. The main equivalent of **kill** is **töten**. It is both trans., meaning 'to cause s.o.'s death either intentionally or unintentionally', *Er tötete seinen Gegner,* and intr., *Du sollst nicht töten. Ein Soldat muß töten können. He shot to kill* is *Er schoß mit der Absicht zu töten.* Besides people and animals, the subj. can be behaviour which leads to a person's death or something which results in death like *eine Explosion, das Trinken,* or *ein Schlag des Propellers.*

> *Im Gericht ging man davon aus, daß sie ihren Mann mit Gift getötet hatte.*
> *Der Staatanwalt warf dem Angeklagten, der stark alkoholisiert eine Frau angefahren hatte, vor, sie fahrlässig getötet zu haben.*   *Er hat sich aus Lebensüberdruß getötet.*
> *Eine Explosion hat alle Insassen des Wagens getötet.*

Er hat seine arme, kranke Mutter durch Herzlosigkeit und Grausamkeit getötet.
Al Capone konnte man nicht nachweisen, selbst getötet zu haben.
Mit diesem Mittel töten Sie sicher sämtliche Ratten in Ihrem Keller.
Diese Insektizide töten Schädlinge rasch und sauber.
Ich konnte nie ein Kaninchen töten.

ii. Schlachten is 'to slaughter', i.e. 'to kill in order to use the meat for human consumption'. *Sie haben das Schwein geschlachtet.* If animals have to be killed because of a disease, drought, etc., the v. is **abschlachten**. *Die erkrankten Kühe mußten abgeschlachtet werden.*

2. Be killed in an accident, disaster, etc.

i. Getötet werden is mostly used when a number of people lose their lives. Expressions which are used for one or more people are **umkommen, ums Leben kommen**, and **den Tod finden**.

Bei dem Lawinenunglück sind alle fünf Mitglieder der Seilschaft getötet worden/ums Leben gekommen.
Obwohl das Boot gesunken ist, ist kein Mensch umgekommen.
Bei dem Erdbeben sind viele Menschen umgekommen/ums Leben gekommen.
Er ist nur deshalb ums Leben gekommen, weil er nicht angeschnallt war.
Bei dem Flugzeugabsturz haben achtzig Passagiere und die ganze Besatzung den Tod gefunden.

ii. Be killed in war or **killed in action** is expressed by **fallen**. *Mein Onkel ist im Ersten Weltkrieg gefallen. Tausende von Soldaten sind im erfolglosen Feldzug gefallen.*

3. Alternatives to *töten*.

i. Instead of *töten*, a specific term is often preferred. With a person as subj., **erschlagen** means 'to kill by one or more blows from the hands, a weapon, or another object'. *Er wurde von den überraschten Einbrechern erschlagen.* The subj. can also be falling objects or lightning. *Ödön von Horvath wurde in Paris von einem herabstürzenden Ast erschlagen.* **Erstechen** is 'to stab to death'. *Er wurde bei einer Schlägerei [mit einem Messer] erstochen.* **Niederstechen** is 'to stab' a defenceless person in an attack, hold-up, or fight so that the victim collapses, but is not necessarily fatally wounded. **Erdrosseln** and **erwürgen** mean 'to strangle'. *Der Mörder hat sein Opfer erdrosselt/erwürgt.*

ii. Umbringen means 'to put a violent end to s.o.'s life'. It is a strongly emotive word, stressing the violence and cruelty of the action. Animals as well as people can be the subj. and obj.

Die Bankräuber brachten ihre Geiseln um aus Furcht, identifiziert zu werden.
Der Tiger war zur Bestie geworden und hatte schon mehrere Bauern angefallen und umgebracht.
Wie kann ein Mensch bloß hilflose Robbenbabys umbringen?

iii. Totschlagen is 'to kill' small animals like *Fliegen, Insekten*, or *Ratten* with a blow. It is also applied to people. *Er hat den verhaßten Bruder im Streit mit einem Hammer totgeschlagen. Der Totschlag* is 'manslaughter'. **Totmachen** means 'to kill small animals quickly'. *Man macht Schädlinge tot.* The usual expression for destroying or putting an animal out of its misery is *Wir mußten den kranken Hund* **einschläfern** *lassen.*

Wie soll man denn so ein Ungeziefer totmachen?

iv. Abtöten is used in the standard language for killing bacteria and small organisms. In colloquial speech *töten* is usual. *Das Medikament tötet die Krankheitserreger/Bakterien ab.*

Die Giftkatastrophe im Rhein hat auf weiten Strecken sämtliche Mikroorganismen abgetötet.

4. Fig. uses of **kill**. **Abtöten** is also used for killing people's interest, enthusiasm, feelings, desires, etc. *Er wollte diese Begierden abtöten. Die Zeit* **totschlagen** is 'to kill time'.

Als Lehrer sollte man sich davor hüten, jemals die Motivation/die Begeisterung der Klasse abzutöten.
Kommt doch mit zum Sportplatz und spielt Tennis! Warum wollen wir hier herumsitzen und die Zeit
vor dem Fernseher totschlagen?

5. Murder. Morden is now used only intr. meaning 'to commit [a] murder or murders'. It is found with an obj. only in poetical or elevated language **Ermorden** is the usual v. with an obj.

Ich bin zwar ein Spion, habe aber nie gemordet.

Diese Horden zogen mordend und plündernd durchs Land.

Kaltblütig plante er, den Gegner zu ermorden. *Er ermordete seine Frau.*

6. Massacre.

i. Like all the words in this section, **niedermachen** presumes a number of victims and often a number of perpetrators. It means 'to kill defenceless people by shooting, stabbing, etc.'

Das Dorf wurde umzingelt, und die Bewohner bis auf den letzten Mann niedergemacht.

ii. Niedermetzeln implies a terrible bloodbath.

Aus Rache für den Überfall der Partisanen wurden alle Bewohner des Städtchens niedergemetzelt.

iii. Massakrieren is a more learned word for killing a number of people in an inhuman way.

Die Insulaner massakrierten die ganzen Bootsbesatzung mit Messern und Speeren.

iv. Hinmorden and **hinschlachten** mean 'to kill defenceless people in a brutal manner' but stress less the details of the action than the result. **Hinmetzeln** also refers more to the result, the killing of a large number of people.

Er richtete die Maschinenpistole in die Menge und mordete Passanten sinnlos hin.

Tausende sind in diesem Krieg sinnlos hingeschlachtet worden.

Nur weil die Soldaten einen wahnwitzigen Befehl nicht ausführen wollten, wurden sie von der Leibwache des Diktators hingemetzelt.

v. Abschlachten means 'to kill defenceless people one after the other in a brutal way'. It stresses less the bestiality of the perpetrators than the pitifulness of their victims.

Es war kein ehrlicher Kampf mehr. Die Gegner in ihrer verzweifelten Lage wurden regelrecht abgeschlachtet.

kind, species, sort, type *ns.* While **species** is used chiefly as a scientific term to designate a subdivision of a larger class or genus, **kind**, **sort**, and **type** are common words with a range of meanings which are not all carried by their direct equivalents. In particular, *die Sorte* is restricted in use.

1. i. Die Art originally denoted human beings, animals, and plants which belonged together because of common descent and characteristics. It is now the main equivalent of **species**. **Die Spezies** exists, but it is a learned word. Darwin's *The Origin of Species* is *Die Entstehung der Arten*. *Wer aus der Art schlägt,* is different from all his/her family or relatives.

Wie viele Arten von Eukalyptusbäumen gibt es?

Bedrohte und gefährdete Arten muß man vor dem Aussterben schützen.

ii. Die Art spread from living beings to inanimate things and became the normal word meaning 'kind or sort'. In *Bücher dieser/jeder Art*, *Art* can also be translated as **type**, *variety*, or *description*, which in such a context are all syns. of **kind** and **sort**. As the equivalent of *of all kinds*, *Art* is usually in the sing. irrespective of whether *alle* or *jeder* is used; thus *Pflanzen jeder/aller Art* because in *Pflanzen aller Arten* it would be taken to mean 'species'. *Of* following **kind/sort** is translated by the gen. or *von*, but *von* can often be omitted, and the nom. follows. *Ich lehne jede Art von Gewalt ab. Diese Art [von] Zeitung. Diese Art [von] Menschen schätze ich sehr. Eine Art grober*

Schotter. Eine Art von is used like **a kind/sort of** to denote something which resembles, but is not exactly the same as, the thing named. *Sie lag auf einer Art [von] Sofa.*
Diese Art von historischen Details las mein Vater mit großem Interesse.
Sie sind Verbrecher übelster Art/der übelsten Art.   *Diese Art Glück hatte sie noch nie erlebt.*
Das Bild ist einzig/vollkommen in seiner Art.   *Er grüßte Emmi mit einer Art von Scheu.*

2. Alternatives to *Art.* The meaning 'a particular kind of' is often expressed by words other than *Art.*

i. In *Welche Art Baum ist das?, Art* is like **species**. Usual in everyday language is **Was für** *ein Baum ist das?*

ii. *Sie ist nun einmal so* could translate *That's the sort of person she is.*

iii. **Allerlei** and colloquially **allerhand** mean 'all kinds of'. *Allerlei/Allerhand Gerümpel lag herum. Allerlei Ausgaben/Witze/Ausreden. Sie überwanden allerhand Schwierigkeiten.* Likewise **keinerlei:** *Sie machten keinerlei Konzessionen.*

iv. **Derartig** means 'such' or 'of this kind'. *Derartige Sträucher wachsen nur in den Tropen. Eine derartige Kälte erleben wir hier nur selten.* **Solche,** 'such', is close in sense. *Man muß sich hier an solche Hitze gewöhnen,* heat of this kind, this kind/sort of heat. **Dergleichen** means 'of this kind/sort'. *Dergleichen Vorfälle kommen oft vor. Etw. dergleichen muß passiert sein,* sth. of the/this kind.

v. So etwas can translate *sth. of this kind, this kind/sort of thg. So etwas ist mir noch nie passiert.* (Also: *Etwas Derartiges* and *etw. dergleichen.*) *So etwas kann ich nicht ausstehen.*

vi. The possessive adjs. are added to *gleichen* to form compounds like **meinesgleichen,** of my kind, **deinesgleichen, ihresgleichen,** etc.
Sie verkehrt am liebsten mit ihresgleichen (people of her kind/type/class).
Von ihm und seinesgleichen ist nichts anderes zu erwarten.
Meinesgleichen kann sich das nicht leisten.   *Hier sind wir unter unseresgleichen.*

vii. Alle combined with **möglich** means 'all kinds of', 'the most varied thgs. etc.'
Das Auto war mit allen möglichen Dingen beladen.   *Er hat alles mögliche versucht.*
Sie beschäftigt sich mit allen möglichen Problemen.

3. Der Schlag in one sense means 'kind or type'. It is applied to people and animals and occasionally to things. In reference to people, it is a shortened form of **der Menschenschlag** which refers to character and appearance. *(Möbel) alten Schlages* implies good quality as well as age.
Ein Mensch vom Schlag dieses Arztes macht sich nie Sorgen.
Im Hochland lebt ein ganz anderer Schlag von Menschen/ein ganz anderer Menschenschlag.

4. Die Sorte was taken into G. as a commercial term referring to the quality of goods, and this still determines its basic sense. *Die beste und schlechteste Sorte. Eine gute oder minderwertige Sorte.* It also means 'kind or variety' but refers mainly to what is bought and sold. *Man kann hier verschiedene Brotsorten kaufen. Die einzelnen Sorten sind am Geschmack zu unterscheiden. Diese Sorte (Kaffee* etc.) *kaufen wir wieder. Wir bleiben bei dieser Sorte.* It is used for fruit, vegetables, and plants, but only those which are traded commercially. *Eine frühe/späte Sorte Kartoffeln. Sie haben eine neue Sorte Äpfel gezüchtet.* It is also found in the sense of 'kind' in connection with things which are not commercial goods, but in such contexts it is often at least slightly pejorative. *Von dieser Sorte Musik hält sie nicht viel.* Applied to people, *Sorte* usually expresses contempt. *Mit dieser Sorte Menschen ist schwer auszukommen.*
Er ist ein Betrüger der schlimmsten/gefährlichsten Sorte.
Diese Sorte von Geschöpfen ist zum Sacktragen auf der Welt. (Schiller)

5. Type.

i. The first sense of **type** which concerns us here is 'a kind, class, or category of people or thgs. distinguished by certain common characteristics'. It hardly differs from **kind**. *This type of local government. The dominant weather type. Her beauty is of the*

Italian type. One G. equivalent is **der Typ**. **Der Typus** is used in learned language, but does not differ in sense. Some compounds are *der Charaktertyp, der Hauttyp, der Bautyp, der Schultyp*. Although not uncommon, *der Typ* does not seem to be as widely used as **type**, and the E. word is often best translated by **die Art**. *This type of work* is *diese Art [von] Arbeit. Problems of this type: Probleme dieser Art.*

> *Dieses Kapitel beschreibt die Typen des deutschen Nebensatzes.*
> *Sie gehört zu jenem Typ von Menschen, die immer sehr überlegt handeln.*
> *Einige Geschäftsleute wollen eine Universität neuen Typs gründen.*

ii. Another sense of **type** is 'a pers. or thg. that exhibits the characteristic qualities of a particular class', 'a representative specimen'. *He was an eccentric painter type*. **Der Typ** and **der Typus** express this sense, but are limited to people.

> *Er ist der Typ des Künstlers/des Intellektuellen.   Er ist der Typ des verschrobenen Malers.*
> *Er ist ein ruhiger/stiller/athletischer/ängstlicher/blonder Typ.*
> *Die beiden Schwestern sind verschiedene Typen. Sie ist ein anderer Typ als ihre Schwester.*

iii. Der Typ is used for types and models of cars or other industrial products. *Staubsauger verschiedenen Typs* or *verschiedener Typen.*

> *Fünf Düsenjäger desselben Typs flogen über der Stadt.*
> *Die Firma entwickelt einen neuen Autotyp.*

kind, kindly, friendly, good-natured *adjs.*

1. Kind, describing someone's character, means 'well-disposed, considerate, and sympathetic towards others'. *She was a very kind woman*. With *to*, it means 'exhibiting a friendly disposition to' people or animals. Actions which arise from or display this disposition are also called *kind*. **Kind** is often used in polite phrs.: *Would you be so kind as to . . . ?* **Kindly** means 'kind-hearted or good-natured' and is also applied to character and actions. The equivalent of both, *gütig*, is now not much used. Some common alternatives are, in ascending order of kindness, *nett, freundlich, liebenswürdig*, and *gut*, but a specific term like *hilfsbereit*, 'helpful', is often preferred.

i. Gütig corresponds in sense to both words, but although it is still generally understood, it is very little used and survives more or less only in religious language. *Er ist ein gütiger Mensch. Sie hat ein gütiges Herz. Die Familie war immer sehr gütig gegenüber Notleidenden. Sie lächelte gütig*. It is used ironically. *Sehr gütig von dir, mir zu helfen* implies that the bit of help given was the least to be expected.

ii. Nett is applied to people who act in a way which is to one's liking and gives pleasure.

> *Nett von dir, daß du daran/an mich gedacht hast.   Der Junge ist nett zu seinen kleinen Kusinen.*
> *Es war nett von ihm, uns seine Hilfe anzubieten.*

iii. Freundlich in one sense means 'displaying goodwill towards others, considerate, and obliging' and is used for actions which reveal such a disposition. Like *nett*, it takes *zu*.

> *Es war wirklich freundlich von Ihnen, uns zu helfen.*
> *Der Polizist war so freundlich, uns den Weg nach dem entfernten Vorort genau zu beschreiben.*
> *Sie lächelte freundlich/war sehr freundlich zu uns.   Sie sah uns mit freundlichen Augen an.*

iv. Liebenswürdig is somewhat stronger meaning 'very friendly' or 'kind, obliging, and polite'. It is applied to people, their characters, and actions, and takes *zu*.

> *Die Schüler waren sehr liebenswürdig zu den ausländischen Gästen.*
> *Das Kind war so liebenswürdig, mir die Tür aufzuhalten.   Er ist ein liebenswürdiger Mensch.*

Often either *nett, freundlich,* or *liebenswürdig* can be used, *Es war sehr nett/ freundlich/liebenswürdig von dem Taxifahrer, mein Gepäck bis in die Wohnung zu tragen*, but *liebenswürdig* expresses most recognition of the other person's kind action.

v. *He was very kind to his elderly relatives* can be translated as *Er war sehr nett/freundlich* *zu seinen älteren Verwandten.* This suggests courteous and considerate behaviour on one or certain occasions. If stronger permanent kindness is meant, **gut** is usual. *Er war sehr gut zu seinen alten Tanten/Eltern/seiner Großmutter* suggests considerate behaviour and could refer to financial support. For animals the expression is *Jmd. ist freundlich/gut zu Tieren.*

vi. In polite phrs. corresponding to *Would you be so kind as to help me?* or *Would you kindly tell me the time?*, **nett, freundlich, liebenswürdig**, and **gut** are used with little distinction.

> *Seien Sie so nett/freundlich/gut/liebenswürdig, diesen Brief für mich einzuwerfen!* Or *Würden Sie so gut etc. sein, mir zu helfen? Wären Sie so freundlich, mir zu sagen, wie spät es ist?*

2. Kind, referring to character, can be expressed by **gutmütig**, good-natured. **Gutherzig** is a less common syn. While both can express praise, they can also suggest that someone is too kind and is imposed upon.

> *Er ist ein äußerst gutmütiger Mensch.*　　*Meine Tante war ihr Leben lang gutherzig.*
> *Er ist zu gutherzig/gutmütig und kann niemandem eine Bitte abschlagen.*

3. i. Kindly in a peremptory and often irritated command is **gefälligst**. *Kindly take your feet off the table!* is *Nimm gefälligst die Füße vom Tisch! Kindly hurry up!* is *Beeilt euch gefälligst!*

> *Sagen Sie mir gefälligst, was Sie wollen!*
> *Laß sie gefälligst in Ruhe!*

ii. Not to take kindly to sth. can be translated by **nicht gern**. *Sie läßt sich nicht gern herumkommandieren. Er läßt sich nicht gern als Untergebener behandeln.*

4. In addition to 'kind', **freundlich** means 'friendly'. *Eine freundliche Stimmung. Die Leute im Dorf sind sehr freundlich. Sie haben uns freundlich gedankt/angehört/ behandelt/aufgenommen. Der Pfarrer hatte für jeden ein freundliches Wort.* It does not imply a close personal friendship. Such a relationship is expressed by **freund- schaftlich**. *Es bestehen freundschaftliche Beziehungen zwischen den beiden* means that the two are good friends. *Er schlug sofort einen freundschaftlichen Ton an. Ich klopfte ihm freundschaftlich auf die Schulter.* A und B sind **befreundet** or A ist mit B befreundet is a way of saying that A and B are friends. *Ein mit ihr befreundeter Lehrer*, a teacher who is a friend of hers.

know *v.* The following distinguishes *kennen* and *wissen* in the main by describing the constructions in which each occurs. Important syntactic differences are that *kennen* needs an obj. which is either a n. or a pronoun standing for one, whereas *wissen* is used with words like *es, das, etw., alles, nichts* as obj. or with a clause. Both vs. express virtually the same meaning i f the construction is changed. *Ich kenne ihre Adresse,* but *Ich weiß, wo sie wohnt. Ich kenne den Preis nicht,* but *Ich weiß nicht, wieviel es kostet. Wissen* is also used with certain ns. as obj. and in some cases involves a difference in meaning. The most important meanings of *kennen* are 1. i and ii, of *wissen* 2. i–iv, and of *können* all of 3.

1. Kennen.

i. With people as obj.

a. 'To be acquainted with a pers.' Intimacy is not implied.

> *Ich kenne ihn gut/kaum/schon lange/vom Ansehen.*　　*Wir kennen uns erst seit einigen Wochen.*

b. 'To know what a pers. is like', i.e. his/her nature or character. The obj. can be a person or traits of character. *Kennen* can also be followed by *als* = 'to know s.o. to be helpful etc.'

> *Das würde er niemals tun, ich kenne ihn.*　　*Ich kenne ihre Schwächen/Vorzüge.*
> *Von dieser Seite kenne ich sie doch gar nicht.*　　*Ich kenne ihn als hilfsbereiten Menschen.*
> *Ich kenne ihn als gewissenhaften Arbeiter.*

Da kennst du mich aber schlecht, wenn du glaubst, daß ich mich zu so was hergeben würde.

ii. With a thing as obj., **kennen** is the more common word and is the only one used in this context by some speakers. For *wissen* cf. 2. iv. The ns. used as obj. fall into four main categories.

a. Places. *Kennen* implies that the speaker has experience of the locality in question.

Ich kenne den Harz gut, da ich oft dort gewandert bin. *Kennst du die Gegend um Hamburg?*
Ich kenne einen schönen Ort, wo wir picknicken können.
Nur zwei Piraten kannten die Stelle, an der der Schatz vergraben war.

b. Works of art, music, literature. *Ich kenne das Buch [gut].*

Wir kennen Schillers Balladen/alle Symphonien Beethovens.
Meine Freundin kennt alle Romane Thomas Manns. *Kennst du das Bild schon?*

c. An occupation or trade, games. *Der Meister kennt sein Handwerk.* (Also *versteht.* Cf. 5.)

Das Schachspiel kennen die beiden gründlich. Es gibt wenig, wovon sie nicht gehört hätten.

d. Things observed, heard, understood, learned, etc. *Kennst du den Grund für sein Verhalten?*

Dieses Zitat kenne ich, ich habe es einmal gelesen und oft gehört. *Den Fall kenne ich gut.*
Diese Regel kennen die Schüler schon.
Er kannte nicht den Wert der Steine, die er gefunden hatte.
Ich habe sie zwar öfter gesehen, kenne aber ihren Namen nicht.

iii. Kennen is used in a few fixed expressions referring to people and their behaviour. It is usually neg.

Er kennt kein Maß beim Sport und weiß nicht, wann er aufhören soll.
Ihre Begeisterung kannte keine Grenzen.
Er kennt keine Furcht/keine Rücksicht/keine Schonung.

iv. Know also means 'experience'. *I had never known such happiness.* **Kennen** also expresses this meaning. *Als Junge hat er Armut und Entbehrung gekannt. Das kennen wir [schon]* means that someone has experienced or is familiar with something. It can refer ironically to dishonest or unreliable behaviour or someone's excuses. *A. Ich war gerade bei Jörg. Er will dir morgen deine Bücher zurückbringen. B. Das kennen wir schon.* Implied is that Jörg will not do what he says he will, as the speaker knows from experience. *Das kennen wir* (colloquially *Kennen wir*) may also refer to any kind of experience and to a n. like *ein Ort* or *ein Gedicht.* (Cf. the construction *erleben, daß* under EXPERIENCE B. 1.)

Die Gefahren einer Fahrt mit einem kleinen Boot auf offener See kennt er aus eigener Erfahrung.
Sie ist in einem Waisenhaus aufgewachsen und hat nie ein Zuhause gekannt.
Eine Katastrophe in noch nie gekanntem Ausmaß brach über das Land herein.

2. Wissen. i–iv are the main uses.

i. Wissen is used with impersonal, indefinite words and expressions as obj. *Das* and *es* refer to facts or information, not, like *kennen*, to a specific n. or to something experienced. Cf. 1. iv.

Er weiß viel/wenig/alles/eine ganze Menge/alles Mögliche/nichts.
Ich weiß es schon [lange]. *Ich weiß es nicht/nicht genau.*
Weißt du schon das Neueste/das Beste/das Schlimmste?
Niemand wußte etw. Bestimmtes/Genaues. *Das muß jeder wissen.*
Ich weiß genug von ihm, um ihn beurteilen zu können. Also Ich kenne ihn gut genug . . .
Ich weiß nichts Näheres davon/nichts von ihr/über sie.

ii. Wissen is used without an obj., clause, or prep. *Soweit ich weiß, ist alles in Ordnung. Ja, ich weiß [schon].*

iii. Only **wissen** is followed by a clause.

Ich weiß, auf wen ich mich verlassen kann. *Sie weiß, was sie will.*
Er wußte nicht, was er tun sollte. *Wer weiß, wie lange es noch dauert.*

Sie schauten sich lächelnd an, ohne recht zu wissen, warum.
Als sie aus der Ohnmacht erwachte, wußte sie nicht sogleich, was mit ihr geschehen war.

iv. Wissen is encountered in speech with certain ns. as obj., particularly those which denote a brief and precise piece of information, e.g. *jmds. Adresse, ein Beispiel, die Lösung, eine andere Möglichkeit, ihre Telefonnummer, der Titel des Buches, der Name des Verfassers, die Abfahrtzeiten der Züge, jmds. Alter.* In all these cases, *kennen* is also common and is considered by many speakers to be the correct v. With ns. like *Weg* or *Restaurant*, both are found; *kennen* implies personal experience, *wissen* acquired knowledge about it. *Ich weiß den Weg*, I know it from the map or from what others have told me, while *Ich kenne den Weg* suggests that I have been over it myself. Since *kennen* usually implies personal acquaintance, some people also use *wissen* in contexts like *Wissen Sie einen guten Rechtsanwalt/Arzt hier in der Nähe?* and *Weißt du jmd[n]., der uns helfen könnte?*, but *kennen* is certainly not wrong.

Niemand wußte eine bessere Möglichkeit/ein Beispiel.   *Ich kenne/weiß die Lösung schon.*
Schon am Ende des ersten Tages wußte/kannte der neue Lehrer die Namen aller Schüler.
Ich weiß/kenne ein gutes Restaurant hier in der Nähe.   *Seinen Beruf weiß/kenne ich nicht.*
Sie wußte bei jeder Schwierigkeit einen Ausweg.
Wenn er aus der Stadt zurückkehrt, weiß er immer eine Menge Neuigkeiten/Witze.

v. Wissen is followed by *von*, in literary G. also by *um*.

Er wußte von dieser Angelegenheit.
Zu viele wußten um unsere Absicht, als daß sie hätte verborgen bleiben können.

vi. Wissen can take an obj., which may be a person or thing, in the construction *wissen* + obj. + adj. or *wissen* + obj. + prep. + n. denoting a place or condition. *Jmd. wußte etw./einen anderen/sich irgendwo/in einem Zustand.* The sense of such constructions can also be expressed by a *daß*-clause.

Wir wußten uns frei von Schuld. Or *Wir wußten [genau], daß wir frei von Schuld waren.*
Haus, Garten und Kinder wußten wir gut versorgt.
Erst als er sich wieder in Sicherheit wußte, hörte er auf zu zittern.

vii. Wissen is used with an infin. In the spoken language, this construction occurs only in fixed expressions such as *Davon weiß sie ein Lied zu singen*, but in literary G. it can be used with any infin. Cf. 3. iii.

Wir wußten mit dem komplizierten Gerät nichts Rechtes anzufangen.
Sie wußten ihr Glück nicht zu schätzen.   *Sie weiß sich in jeder Lage zu helfen.*
Nach kurzer Zeit wußten sie sich schon nichts mehr zu sagen.
Literary: *Er wußte sich vor seinen Verfolgern zu verbergen.*

viii. Wissen also occurs in the idiomatic expression **Bescheid wissen über**, to be informed about something, to know one's way about a place. Cf. 8 for a syn.

In dieser Stadt weiß ich genau Bescheid.   *Ich weiß über Sie Bescheid.*
Er weiß in Geschichte/in einem Fach/auf einem bestimmten Gebiet Bescheid.
Du brauchst mir nicht alles zu sagen, ich weiß schon Bescheid.

3. i. Können must be used when **know** means 'to be able to say by heart or reproduce from memory'.

Ich kann das Gedicht auswendig. (*Hersagen* or *aufsagen* is implied.)
Kannst du die Vokabeln?
Die zweite Strophe kann ich nicht.   *Ich kann den Text des Liedes schon.*

ii. Können is also the usual word when knowing a language includes the ability to speak it. *Kannst du Deutsch? Er kann [gut] Russisch. Kannst du denn Japanisch? Ich kann kein Wort Italienisch. Kennen* occasionally occurs with a language as obj., but implies some knowledge about it rather than being able to speak it. *Sie kann gut Französisch und kennt auch zwei andere romanische Sprachen.*

iii. Know how to do sth. is best translated by **können**. *Kannst du mit einem Segelboot umgehen?* The meaning can also be rendered by *wissen, wie (man etw. tut). Weißt du,* *wie man mit einem Segelboot umgeht? Wissen* + infin. is best avoided unless a fixed phr. is involved. Cf. 2. vii and 5. ii. The infin. in sents. like *I don't know how to begin/what to do/where to go* must be turned into a clause with *sollen*.

> *Ich weiß nicht, wie ich es anfangen soll/was ich machen soll/an wen ich mich wenden soll/wohin ich gehen soll/was ich als Nächstes machen soll/welches Angebot ich annehmen soll.*

4. *Auswendig* can be used with the three vs. **kennen**, **können**, and **wissen**. *Etw. in- und auswendig kennen* means 'to be thoroughly familiar with it'. *Ich kenne die Stadt/das Gebäude in- und auswendig.*

> *Ich kann alle zwölf Strophen auswendig* (know by heart).
> *Ich habe so oft in diesem Restaurant gegessen, daß ich die Speisekarte auswendig kenne.*
> *Der Stationsvorsteher weiß die Abfahrtzeiten aller Züge auswendig.*
> *A. Kannst du mir mal Uwes Telefonnummer sagen? B. Die weiß ich nicht auswendig.*

5. Some senses of **verstehen** express meanings of **know**.

i. *Jmd. versteht sein Fach/sein Handwerk/seinen Beruf/seine Sache gründlich/meisterhaft/ausgezeichnet.*

> *Dieser Fernsehmechaniker versteht sein Handwerk.*
> *Sie versteht eine ganze Menge von Chemie und Physik.*   *Verstehst du etw. von Rosen?*
> *Ich verstehe nicht das Geringste von der Sache.*   *Ich verstehe nichts von Autos.*

ii. With an infin. *Er verstand [es], mit Menschen umzugehen.*

> *Dieser Politiker versteht es ausgezeichnet, andere zu überzeugen.*

6. Know can also mean 'to recognize' in sents. like *I don't think I would have known him again if I had seen him in the street* or *I know a good car when I see one.* The equivalent of this sense is **erkennen**.

> *Elmar, den ich seit achtzehn Monaten nicht gesehen habe, hat sich so stark verändert, daß ich ihn kaum wieder erkannt hätte, wenn ich ihm auf der Straße begegnet wäre.*
> *Ich habe sie sofort an ihrer Stimme erkannt* (knew or recognized).
> *Ich erkenne ein gutes Pferd, wenn ich eines sehe.*

7. Know one thg. **from** another = 'to distinguish' is **unterscheiden**.

> *Er kann Weizen von Roggen nicht unterscheiden* (doesn't know/can't tell wheat from rye).

8. Sich auskennen is very like *Bescheid wissen*. Cf. 2. viii. Applied to places, it means 'to know one's way about', 'to know a place well'. *Kennst du dich in Hamburg aus?* With ns. denoting a subject of study or areas of experience, it means 'to have a thorough knowledge of'. *Jmd. kennt sich mit Maschinen aus.*

> *Sie kennt sich in der Mathematik/Musik/auf diesem Gebiet/in dieser Materie gut aus.*
> *Ich bin auf einem Bauernhof großgeworden und kenne mich mit dem Vieh aus.*

knowledge *n.* The general distinction between *die Kenntnis* and *das Wissen* is that the former tends to refer to something specific, whereas the latter denotes general knowledge, but there is some overlapping.

i. In the sing., **die Kenntnis** designates knowledge of a specific matter or in a certain field. It is followed by the gen. or *von*. *Wir setzen bei einem Rechtsanwalt die Kenntnis der Gesetze/bei einem Schiffsoffizier die Kenntnis der Schiffahrtskunde voraus.* **Das Wissen** *um etw.* is used, but it is much less common. *Die Kenntnis der Beweggründe des Täters* could be *das Wissen um die Beweggründe des Täters.* Likewise *Ihm fehlte das Wissen um den Wert der Dinge* is more usually *Ihm fehlte die Kenntnis vom Wert der Dinge. Die Kenntnis* forms some expressions, all of which sound formal. In only a few is it translated by **knowledge**. *Jmdn. von etw. in Kenntnis setzen* means 'to inform s.o.' or 'to bring sth. to s.o.'s knowledge'. *Ich muß ihn über die veränderte Lage sofort in Kenntnis setzen. Das entzieht sich meiner Kenntnis* means that it is beyond my knowledge, but it is a high-flown expression. *Kenntnis erhalten von* means 'to receive news, be notified of'. *Wir haben erst gestern Kenntnis von ihrem Tod erhalten.* *Etw. zur Kenntnis nehmen* means 'to note or to take note of'. *Nehmen Sie bitte zur Kenntnis, daß die für morgen geplante Sitzung auf Freitag verschoben worden ist!*

ii. Die Kenntnisse is 'acquired or learned knowledge', but tends to be used for specific fields of study or branches of knowledge. **Knowledge** *of a lang.* is always *Kenntnisse* either with the gen., *seine Kenntnisse der polnischen Sprache*, or as a compound, *Ihre Deutschkenntnisse sind gut/ausgezeichnet. Kenntnisse* is used in other fields. *Jmd. hat umfangreiche Kenntnisse in der Chemie* or *umfassende Geschichtskenntnisse,* while *Sie ist mir an Kenntnissen überlegen* suggests a specific field or professional knowledge, *Sie ist mir an Wissen überlegen* implies general knowledge. **Das Wissen** is used in general statements about the nature and purpose of knowledge such as *Wissen ist Macht.* However, *Wissen* can be modified and is then interchangeable with *Kenntnisse. Sein politisches/geographisches Wissen* is usually *seine politischen/geographischen Kenntnisse.* Thus *ihr theoretisches Wissen* or *ihre theoretischen Kenntnisse.*

Jmd. eignet sich Kenntnisse an/erweitert/vertieft seine Kenntnisse/frischt seine Kenntnisse auf.
In nicht allzu ferner Zukunft werden Computer das gesamte Wissen der Menschheit speichern.
Sie hat ihr Wissen fast ausschließlich aus Büchern.

iii. Die Erkenntnis can denote a realization or recognition of some fact in some way concerning oneself, *Er ist endlich zur Erkenntnis seines Fehlers gekommen,* but it also means 'knowledge or insight gained by thinking about facts, experiences, or observations'. This is often of a scientific or philosophical nature and relates to the world, existence, human nature, the nature of art, etc. It may suggest newly acquired knowledge or knowledge to be acquired. *Der Stand der Erkenntnisse* refers to the state of knowledge in a particular field. *Der Baum der Erkenntnis* is 'the tree of knowledge' in chapters 2 and 3 of Genesis.

Letzten Sommer sind wir zu der Erkenntnis gekommen, daß es sinnlos ist, während der großen Ferien an die See zu fahren.
Die verschiedenen Raumsonden, die an dem Halleyschen Kometen vorbeigeflogen sind, brachten neue Erkenntnisse über die Beschaffenheit dieser Himmelskörper.
Der menschlichen Erkenntnis scheinen keine Grenzen gesetzt zu sein.

lack, be absent or missing *vs.* **Lack** varies in meaning between 'have too little of or be deficient in' and 'be without or not to have at all'. In *He is lacking in courage* and *They lacked the experience necessary for this work*, it would normally be understood as implying a deficiency, whereas in *German lacks a continuous tense* and *The soil lacked the necessary nutrients*, it suggests complete absence.

i. Mangeln means that there is not enough, but implies either a deficiency or complete absence. In most contexts it implies an insufficiency. *Geld mangelte überall.* However, in *Ihnen mangelte die Zivilcourage*, it can suggest the absence of the quality. The subj. of *mangeln* is whatever is lacking. It does not take a person as subj. The dat. is used to state that a person lacks something. *Ihr mangelte das Selbstvertrauen.*

ii. More frequently used than *mangeln* with a subj. is the impersonal expression **es mangelt [jmdm.] an etw.** which also carries both implications of *mangeln*. The E. subj. becomes a dat. so that *Es mangelt ihm an Mut/Selbstvertrauen/Entschlossenheit* translates *He lacks courage* etc.

> *Es mangelt uns an Geld/an nichts.*   *Es mangelt an Arbeitskräften.*
> *Dem Essen mangelt es an Vitaminen.*   *Es mangelt nicht an Aufträgen.*

iii. Mangelnd + a n. means 'lack of'. *Mangelnde Erfahrung/Aufmerksamkeit/ Selbstbeherrschung.*

> *Wegen mangelnder Nachfrage wurde die Produktion dieses Modells eingestellt.*

iv. With people as subj., **fehlen** means 'to be absent'. *Zwei Schüler fehlen heute. Bei dieser Sitzung darf niemand fehlen.* It can have the same sense with a thing as subj. and in some contexts is translated as **is missing**. *An der Jacke fehlt ein Knopf. In der Kasse fehlen 50 Mark.* In other contexts, however, the equivalent can be **lack**. *An diesem Aufsatz fehlt noch der letzte Schliff* could be translated as *The final polish is missing*, but an equally good transl. is *The essay lacks the final polish*. The thing that is without something can be the subj. of **lack**, but not of *fehlen*. E. sents. of the type *Sth. lacks sth.* must be reformulated as if they contained *to be missing in*. *Eine Verlaufsform des Verbs fehlt im Deutschen* translates *German lacks a continuous tense*. The construction *etw. fehlt* + dat. is also used when a person is the subj. of **lack**. *Ihm fehlt jeder Sinn für Humor. Fehlen* is the usual equivalent of **lack** when it denotes a complete absence. In spite of that *fehlen* may in certain contexts only denote a deficiency. *Uns fehlt das Geld für diese Reparaturen.*

> *In den ärmsten Entwicklungsländern fehlen Bodenschätze, die man exportieren kann.*
> *Diesen Kindern fehlte ein [richtiges] Zuhause.*   *Uns fehlen Beweise.*
> *Mir fehlen die Worte, um die Verwüstung zu beschreiben.*

v. Es fehlt [jmdm.] an etw. denotes a deficiency, rather than a complete absence. *Es fehlt an Ersatzteilen für diese Maschinen. Es fehlt an ausgebildeten Lehrern. Es fehlt mir an Übung.*

> *Es fehlt uns am nötigen Geld.*   *An allen Ecken und Enden fehlte es an Fachkräften.*
> *Es fehlt ihnen an Mut/an Tatkraft/an der nötigen Erfahrung.*

vi. Jmdm. geht etw. ab means 's.o. lacks or is without sth.' The subj. is usually a quality of character or of the mind. *Ihm geht der Humor/jedes Taktgefühl ab. Organisatorische Fähigkeiten gingen ihm ab.*

Was ihr an Begabung/Intelligenz abging, ersetzte sie durch Fleiß.
Mir gehen die Eigenschaften ab, die ein erfolgreicher Politiker unbedingt nötig hat.

vii. Colloquially, **es hapert an** expresses the sense 'to be lacking or in short supply'. *Es haperte [ihnen] am Material/an Geld.* **Es hapert + mit** or **in** means 'to be in a bad state'. *Mit der Versorgung haperte es. Bei diesem Schüler hapert es in der Mathematik.*

viii. Ermangeln + gen., to lack an abstract quality, is now used only in very formal prose. *Sein Vortrag ermangelte der Lebendigkeit* or *Ihre Worte ermangelten der Überzeugungskraft* can be expressed more simply as . . . *war[en] nicht lebendig/überzeugend.* **In Ermangelung** + gen. means 'for lack or want of'. *In Ermangelung schlüssiger Beweise. In Ermangelung eines Besseren behelfen wir uns mit dieser alten Schreibmaschine.*

ix. Entbehren, applied to people, means 'to do or go without what is necessary'. *In der Notzeit mußten wir vieles entbehren.* It is used in formal language with the gen. of something abstract and is then translated as **lack**. *Diese Behauptung entbehrt jeder Grundlage/der Glaubwürdigkeit.*

last *v.*

1. When **last** means 'have a certain duration or to take up a certain amount of time', the equivalent is **dauern**. *How long did the meeting last?* is *Wie lange dauerte die Sitzung ?*

Die Sitzungen dauern nur eine Stunde.   *Die Ferien dauern bis Anfang Februar.*
Der Krieg dauerte sechs Jahre.   *Es dauerte dreimal so lange, wie er erwartete.*

In some contexts, *dauern* must be translated as *to* BE or *to* TAKE.

Das wird lange dauern (i.e. to do sth.).   *Ein Weilchen wird es schon noch dauern.*
Wenn ich hier noch eine Stunde warten soll, dauert mir das zu lange.

2. Last means 'to continue or go on' in contexts like *While the civil war lasted, the farmers could not plant their crops* or *I hope this wet weather doesn't last.* **Andauern** or **anhalten** which most frequently correspond to *continue, go on,* or *keep on,* express this sense. Cf. CONTINUE 4. *Lange* must be added when the period of time is not expressed. *The heat won't last* becomes *Die Hitze wird nicht lange anhalten* or *hält/dauert nicht lange an.* Cf. *sich halten* in 3. i in relation to weather.

Solange der Bürgerkrieg andauerte, konnten die Bauern ihre Felder nicht bestellen.
Die starken Regenfälle hielten auch während des ganzen Monats an (lasted/continued/went on).
Hoffentlich hält das schlechte Wetter nicht lange an.

3. i. Last, applied to concrete objects which are subject to wear and tear, particularly clothes, means 'to remain in good condition or usable' and in reference to machines etc. 'to continue to work'. *This tyre/The suit has lasted well.* The usual G. word for concrete objects like clothes or machines is **halten**. *Die Schuhe haben gut gehalten. Das billige Radio hielt nicht lange. Sth. will last a lifetime* becomes *Etw. hält ein Leben lang.* For food and perishables, for which it is necessary to say KEEP in E., **sich halten** is used. *Wie lange hält sich Fleisch im Kühlschrank?* With flowers both are found. *Blumen halten* or *halten sich mehrere Tage in einer Vase.* The refl. is also used for weather. *Wenn sich das [schöne] Wetter hält, fahren wir morgen ins Gebirge* (= 'holds, lasts'). Or . . . *bis morgen anhält,* . . .

Diese Strümpfe/Reifen haben lange/gut gehalten.   *Die Frisur hat lange gehalten.*
Von einer so teuren Uhr erwartet man, daß sie lange hält.
Diese Mode hat sich lange gehalten.
Bundeswehrsoldaten bekamen gegen Ende 1992 neue Helme aus Aramit. Während die alten Stahlhelme dreißig Jahre hielten, halten die neuen nur vier Jahre.

ii. Halten is also used for friendship. *Ihre Freundschaft hält schon viele Jahre/hielt nicht lange.* With a n. like *Freundschaft* as subj., but not with ordinary things like food,

clothes, or flowers, **dauern** also occurs. It is more elevated in tone than *halten*.
Unsere Liebe wird ewig dauern.

iii. Last, applied to conditions or qualities of the mind, indicates that they remain fresh and undiminished. **Vorhalten** is the usual word in relation to mental states, such as someone's resolution, good mood, enthusiasm, etc., and for the effect of injections, therapy, etc.

> *Seine guten Vorsätze hielten/Seine Begeisterung/Die Freude hielt nicht sehr lange vor.*
> *Die gute Stimmung hielt den ganzen Abend vor. Also . . . hielt . . . an.*
> *Die Wirkung der Spritze hält nur zwei Stunden vor.*

iv. Last meaning 'to be permanent or of some duration' can be translated in some contexts by **von Dauer/Bestand sein** or **Dauer/Bestand haben**.

> *Sein Arbeitseifer war nicht von Dauer/war nur von kurzer Dauer. Also . . . hielt nicht lange vor.*
> *Die alte Jugendfreundschaft war von Dauer.*   *Sein Glück sollte nicht lange Bestand haben.*
> *Das Bündnis/Die Koalition hatte wider Erwarten Bestand/hatte keinen Bestand.*

v. Sich halten is used in other contexts, some of which require **last** in E. *Bei ihm hält sich keine Freundin lange*, doesn't last long. *Das Geschäft hat sich gegen alle Voraussagen in der Kleinstadt halten können*, kept going. *Das Stück hat sich wider Erwarten lange auf der Bühne gehalten. Der kleine Betrieb hielt sich trotz der starken Konkurrenz einiger Großbetriebe.* But *Eine Koalition* or *ein Bündnis hält*, holds or lasts.

4. Elevated and archaic is **währen**, which occurs in senses 1, 2, and 3. ii and iii. It is used in fixed expressions and sometimes ironically, otherwise only in formal and solemn prose.

> *Ehrlich währt am längsten.*   *Was lange währt, wird endlich gut.*
> *Seine nun über drei Jahrzehnte währende Tätigkeit wird in einer Woche vorüber sein.*
> *A. Roland hat sein Verhalten ganz schön verändert. B. Das währt nicht lange!*

5. i. With a subject such as a supply of money, food, petrol, etc. which can be used up or dwindle, **last** means 'to be enough for s.o. to use for the time indicated'. *That amount of food will last us for a month.* This sense is expressed by **reichen** or **ausreichen**, the latter being more emphatic. The meaning of both words is 'to suffice, be sufficient'. They are broader than **last**, which is used in this sense only with an expression of time stated or implied. The personal obj. in E., *It will last us for a week*, is often omitted in G.

> *Sie waren nicht sicher, ob der mitgeführte Wasservorrat bis zur nächsten Wasserquelle [aus]reichen würde.*
> *Das Brot muß bis Montag reichen.*
> *Diese Menge Lebensmittel wird für einen ganzen Monat reichen.*

ii. Make sth. **last. Auskommen mit**, to make do with, to get by with, can often express the meaning. While *reichen* and *ausreichen* do not take a person as subj., *auskommen* does. The meaning of *Wenn ich vorsichtig bin, reicht mein kleines Stipendium immer bis zum Anfang des nächsten Monats aus* can be formulated as *komme ich mit meinem kleinen Stipendium . . . aus*, which expresses the sense of *make it last.*

> *Die Expeditionsmitglieder gaben sich alle Mühe, mit den ihnen zur Verfügung stehenden Vorräten an Proviant und Benzin auszukommen.*
> *Dadurch daß der Kommandant sowohl die Bürger der Stadt als auch die Truppen auf Rationen setzte, schaffte er es, den ganzen Winter mit den knappen Vorräten auszukommen. Or . . . erreichte er, daß die knappen Vorräte ausreichten.*

iii. The construction *I have enough money to last me for two months* cannot be translated word for word. *Das Geld, das ich habe, wird für zwei Monate reichen* would be a common transl. *Mit dem Geld komme ich für zwei Monate aus* is equally idiomatic. Often the simplest solution is to omit **last**. *Ich habe genug Geld für zwei Monate.*

iv. Vorhalten is also a syn. of the everyday *reichen*. In pos. sents. there is a slight difference. *Die Vorräte werden bis zum Frühjahr reichen* means they will last as long as that, but there will not be any left. *Die Vorräte werden bis zum Frühjahr vorhalten* suggests that they will last that length of time and that some will still be left.

Das ersparte Geld wird nicht lange vorhalten/reichen, wenn du so viel ausgibst wie heute.

6. Last [out] can mean either 'to survive' or 'to continue in action as long as or longer than' or 'to endure'. *S.o. lasts the night/lasts the distance/lasts [out] another round. How much longer can we last out?*

i. If the meaning is 'to survive', **überstehen** or **überleben** are used. *Ohne ärztliche Hilfe wird der Verletzte die Nacht nicht überstehen/überleben.*

ii. Durchstehen means 'to get or come through sth. unpleasant imposed from the outside' such as *Schwierigkeiten, Krankheiten, Angst, eine Belastung, eine schwierige Situation,* and occasionally translates **last [out]**. *Wird der junge Boxer eine weitere Runde durchstehen?*

Mein Bruder hat die harte Ausbildung bei den Marinesoldaten durchgestanden (lasted out the training).

iii. Durchhalten, which is trans. and intr., means 'not to give up' and suggests keeping something up, often a task that one has taken on oneself, for a certain time. *Wie lange können wir noch durchhalten?,* last/hold out, stick it out.

Sie sind entschlossen durchzuhalten.   *Ich habe Angst , daß er nicht durchhält.*
Wir müssen bis zum Ende/Schluß durchhalten.   *Er hielt die ganze Strecke durch.*
Ich habe keine Kondition und halte beim Laufen nur eine kurze Strecke durch.

last, final[ly], eventual[ly] *adjs.* and *advs.* at last, in the end *phrs.* used as *advs.*

1. Last adv. **Zuletzt** is an adv. and expresses three uses of **last.**

i. 'Following all others in a series of thgs.' *I'll do that last [of all]. Diesen Brief werde ich zuletzt erledigen.* Because *zuletzt* has more than one sense, the syn. **als letztes** is often preferred. *Diesen Brief werde ich als letztes erledigen. Diese Angelegenheit wurde zuletzt/als letztes besprochen.* Note also *Das hebe ich bis zuletzt auf.*

ii. Zuletzt is also used in relation to people with the same meaning. *Ich bin zuletzt angekommen,* arrived last. Here too **als letzter/letzte** is often preferred. *Ich werde zuletzt/als letzter reden. Als letzter* can translate *the last to do sth. Der Kapitän verläßt als letzter das sinkende Schiff. S.o. was/came last in a race* or competition is *Jmd. war/wurde der letzte.* An alternative for races only is *Er ging als letzter durchs Ziel.*

Wir wurden zuletzt bedient.   *Wer zuletzt lacht, lacht am besten.*
Wer ist als letzter aus dem Haus gegangen?

iii. Zuletzt also means 'on the last occasion before the present', as in *When did you see him last? Wann hast du ihn zuletzt gesehen? Ich war zuletzt vor zwei Jahren in London. Als ich sie zuletzt sprach, ging es ihr gut.* Alternatives in this sense are **zum letzten Mal, das letzte Mal,** and **letztes Mal.** *Als ich zum letzten Mal/das letzte Mal/letztes Mal hier war, stand dieses Gebäude noch nicht. Zum letzten Mal* also means 'for the last time', e.g. in warnings, *Ich habe dir das zum letzten Mal gesagt.*

2. Finally, at last.

i. Zuletzt is one of three words meaning 'finally, in the end, at [long] last, at length', but is now more or less literary in this sense. The usual words are *endlich* and *schließlich. Zuletzt* suggests that something is the final point after other things have been tried.

Franz Daniel war der Spielwut verfallen. Ihr hatte er schon im ersten Jahr in Göttingen alles geopfert. Seine Mutter—der Vater war schon tot—hatte ihn zuletzt unter die Kuratel seines jüngeren Bruders stellen müssen. (Written 1880. *Zuletzt* still possible, but now mostly *schließlich.*)

ii. Endlich means 'after a time which is felt to be long', thus 'at [long] last, at length, or finally', and expresses the emotion of the speaker. Hence, in impatient or angry remarks, often questions, *endlich* only is found. *Bist du endlich fertig? Hast du es endlich begriffen? Endlich* occurs in sents. with a v. in the imp., but in this use it is only occasionally translated as **finally**. It suggests that the speaker has waited or put up with something a long time and that his or her patience is at an end. *Doch* is often added. *Hör' doch endlich auf! Macht doch endlich Schluß! Fahren wir doch endlich los! Komm' doch endlich!*

> *Endlich sah er ein, daß er sich geirrt hatte.*   *Sie ist endlich zu einem Entschluß gekommen.*

iii. Schließlich suggests that a number of things have happened before some occurrence and means 'at the end of a series of events, attempts, delays, etc.' and is unemotional. It is also the usual equivalent of **eventually**. Sometimes *schließlich* and *endlich* are joined to express both shades of meaning. *Schließlich und endlich erkannten wir, daß unsere Bemühungen keinen Sinn mehr hatten.*

> *Wir mußten schließlich erkennen, daß uns nichts anderes übrig blieb, als in den Plan einzuwilligen.*
> *Schließlich sind wir noch zu Hause angekommen.*
> *Er stimmte schließlich/endlich dem Vorschlag zu.*
> *Die Anerkennung dieser berechtigten Ansprüche war schließlich unvermeidlich.*

Schließlich translates **eventually** when it refers to the future. *Vorbereitungen sind schon im Gange, die schließlich einen bemannten Raumflug zum Mars ermöglichen werden.*

3. Und schließlich marks the final item in an enumeration. *Der Redner hatte A, B, C und D schon erwähnt. Dann sagte er: 'Und schließlich möchte ich Herrn Marks danken, der wesentlich zum Erfolg der Konferenz beigetragen hat.'* The less common **letztens** marks the last in a series and is contrasted with *erstens*. It can be joined to a number like *fünftens und letztens*, but often stands alone. *Erstens muß er Besorgungen machen, zweitens muß er die Koffer packen, und letztens muß er sie zum Bahnhof bringen.*

4. i. The adj. **schließlich** means 'final, eventual, or ultimate' = 'happening at the end of a process or series of events'. *Der schließliche Erfolg. Der schließliche Untergang des Reichs.* When **final** means 'last', the equivalent is **letzt**. *Das war unser dritter und letzter Versuch. Am letzten Tag des Wahlkampfes.* (Note: The adj. **endlich** means 'finite'. *Eine endliche Zahl. Eine endliche Größe.*)

ii. In several compounds **der Schluß** and **das Ende** express the meaning 'final': *Das Schlußkapitel, der Schlußakt, die Schlußminute, der Schlußpfiff, die Schlußphase, die Schlußabstimmung, das Endergebnis, das Endspiel, der Endspurt, das Endprodukt, der Endzustand.*

5. Final also means 'unable to be changed, conclusive', as in *The judges' decision is final* or *a final judgement*. **Finally** also means 'conclusively, once and for all'. **Endgültig** means that no further change is possible. *Wir warten die endgültige Entscheidung ab. Wir müssen diese Frage endgültig entscheiden,* decide/settle it finally/once and for all. *Die Frage wurde endlich entschieden* is a correct sent., but means that after the passage of a considerable period of time, a decision was reached. *Die endgültige Fassung des Romans* is translated as **final** or *definitive*.

> *Das endgültige Ergebnis der Wahl wird erst in zwei Tagen vorliegen.*
> *Erst die Entscheidung des Höchsten Gerichts stellt das endgültige Urteil dar.*

6. At/In the end. **Am Ende** without a gen. means 'in the end, finally, ultimately' and is like *schließlich* in 2. iii, but stresses the final result. *Am Ende mußte er zugeben, daß er sich zuviel zugemutet hatte.*

> *Er war äußerst träge und ließ die Arbeiten sich anhäufen, bis er sie am Ende nicht mehr bewältigen*
> *konnte und andere um Hilfe bitten mußte.*   *Am Ende hatte sie doch recht behalten.*

At the end when no gen. follows is usually **zum Schluß**, which also translates *in conclusion. Zum Schluß dankte sie den Zuhörern für ihre Aufmerksamkeit. Zum Schluß faßte* *der Redner seine Hauptthesen zusammen.* (*Am Ende* + a gen. means 'at the end of'. *Am Ende des Jahres. Am Ende/Schluß des Filmes war kein Auge trocken.* A speaker might say, '*Ich bin am Ende meiner Ausführungen*', but more usual is '*Ich bin zum Schluß/Ende meiner Ausführungen gekommen.*')

lead, guide, be guided *vs.* A few uses.

1. Führen expresses the basic sense of **lead**, 'to take s.o. somewhere, especially by going ahead', and also that of **guide**, 'to take s.o. somewhere'. In *Er führte uns durch den Wald* it could be translated as **led** or **guided**. *Der Fremdenführer* is 'a tourist guide'. *Sie führte den Blinden über die Straße* is everyday style; *sie leitete ihn über die Straße* is also possible, but as a syn. of the basic sense of *führen* **leiten** belongs to formal language. *Führen* is also 'to lead' animals. *Er führte das Pferd in den Stall.* In certain contexts *führen* is translated as *take*. The v. in *Er führte mich auf die Seite, um etw. mit mir zu besprechen*, could be translated as *took* or **led**. (*Nehmen* could also be used in this sent.)

> *Der Junge hat die Dame zum Postamt geführt.*   *Sie führte uns durch die Stadt/das Schloß.*
> *Der Direktor übernahm es selbst, die Gäste durch den Betrieb zu führen.*
> *Die Sekretärin führte den Besucher ins Büro des Direktors.*
> *Das entfernte Licht eines Hauses führte uns durch die Dunkelheit.*

You lead the way! is *Gehen Sie voran/vor, ich folge Ihnen!* **Vorangehen** and **vorgehen** both mean 'to go ahead'.

2. Both **führen** and **leiten** mean 'to be at the head of an organization or be in charge of sth.' *Führen* is used in relation to military forces. *General Riedel führte das Regiment. Ein Offizier führt seine Abteilung. Führen* is used for a political party or a movement. *X führt seit drei Jahren die liberale Partei.* Both vs. are used with *ein Geschäft* as obj. and are translated as *to conduct, manage,* or *run. Er führt ein Geschäft* may imply that he owns it, but it need not, *Während meiner Abwesenheit führt mein Sohn das Geschäft.* With objs. like *Geschäft, Unternehmen,* or *Schule, leiten* means that someone is entrusted with the management or direction of a business, school, institution, etc. *Ein Geschäft leiten* therefore means 'to manage a business'. Both **leitend** and **führend** can be translated as *leading. Ein leitender Angestellter* is 'an employee in a managerial position'. *Die leitenden Angestellten* are 'the senior staff' of a firm etc. *Jmd. steht an leitender Stelle* or *hat eine leitende Stelle inne* suggests a top or senior position in an organization. *Führend* suggests that in a scale comparing the people or organizations doing particular work the person or institution occupies a position at or near the top. *Eines der führenden Modehäuser Europas. Sie ist führend auf ihrem Gebiet. Dieses Institut steht an führender Stelle in der Gentechnologie.* In some contexts both *leiten* and *führen* occur without much difference in meaning. *Jmd. führt/leitet eine Expedition. Die Delegation wurde vom Außenminister geführt/geleitet.*

> *Er leitet eine Bankfiliale/eine Schule.*   *Senator Cheney führte die Opposition im Senat.*

In some contexts *leiten* is also translated by words other than **lead**, *eine Versammlung/eine Debatte/eine Dislussion leiten* being 'to preside at'. Cf. *eine Diskussion mit jmdm. führen*, to carry on. *Führen* or *führend sein* can translate *to be a leader in, to lead the way* or *to lead the world. Dieser Betrieb führt in der Stahlherstellung* or *ist in der Stahlherstellung führend.* Note that *die Führung übernehmen* means 'to take the lead (in a race)', while *die Leitung übernehmen* means 'to take over the management'.

3. Anführen is 'to be at the head of' in the literal sense. *Als die Truppen in die Stadt einmarschierten, führte sie der General an* means that he was at the head of the column. *Der Anführer* has a pejorative sense, referring to a leader of a band (of robbers), a gang, etc. It is a syn. of *der Rädelsführer*, ringleader. *Der Anführer einer*

Bande/einer Gang. Er hatte sich zum Anführer der Jungen in der Lindenstraße gemacht. Because of this use the v. has taken on a neg. colouring. *Der Junge führte eine Bande an.*

4. Lead = 'to be in the lead' is expressed by **führen**. *Nach der ersten Halbzeit führte der Sportverein Schwarz-Weiß mit 4 : 3 Toren. Es führt Nummer 9, dicht gefolgt von Nummer 4.*

5. Führen translates **lead** with a road, passage, steps, etc. as subj. *Viele Wege führen nach Rom.*

> *Die Spuren im Schnee führen zum Fluß.*   *Die Tür führt in den Garten.*
> *Die Treppe führt in den Keller.*   *Eine schmale Brücke führt über den Fluß.*

6. Führen zu means 'to lead to', i.e. 'to bring about, result in'. It can take *dazu* + a *daß*-clause.

> *Seine Bemühungen führten schließlich zum Erfolg.*
> *Diese Ereignisse führten zum Ausbruch des Krieges.*
> *Das Mißlingen der ersten Versuche führte dazu, daß er einen ganz neuen Plan ausdachte.*

With a personal obj. *führen zu* suggests that the result is of pos. value. If the result is undesirable, **verleiten** is used. *Der Erfolg verleitete ihn dazu, sich zu überschätzen. Die niedrigen Preise verleitete viele dazu, Waren zu kaufen, die sie gar nicht brauchten.*

7. Be guided by s.o., s.o.'s advice, a principle, etc. is **sich leiten lassen**. Cf. FOLLOW 4. iv. *Ich lasse mich von deinem Rat/vom gesunden Menschenverstand/von einem Prinzip leiten*, I shall be guided by.

8. Anleiten is 'to instruct s.o. how to do sth.' or 'to guide s.o. in doing sth.'

> *Der Lehrer leitet die Schüler bei der Arbeit an.*
> *Ein erfahrener Mitarbeiter hat den neuen Lehrling im Gebrauch der Maschinen angeleitet.*

learn *v.*

i. Lernen corresponds to **learn** when it refers to the acquisition of knowledge of a subj., *Wir lernen Deutsch/Chemie,* or of skill in an art, trade, game, etc., *Die Schüler lernen lesen/schwimmen/Klavier spielen/Auto fahren,* or of a way of behaving, *Du muß lernen, dich zu beherrschen/mit anderen Menschen umzugehen.* Lernen can also be intr. *Diese Kinder lernen schnell.* With *die Rolle* as obj., *lernen* implies learning by heart, but with other objs. *auswendig* is added. *Ich habe das Gedicht auswendig gelernt.*

> *Kleine Kinder müssen lernen, mit Messer und Gabel umzugehen.*

ii. Lernen is also used for learning a trade etc. In *Er lernt Tischler,* it implies being an apprentice. **Erlernen** is the v. used when stating that someone has completed an apprenticeship. *In Deutschland hat fast jeder Erwachsene einen Beruf erlernt. Die meisten brauchen drei Jahre, um dieses Handwerk zu erlernen.* Lernen can, however, also be used and is the only possibility in *ein gelernter Arbeiter,* a skilled worker.

iii. In other contexts **erlernen** means 'to pursue sth. so intensively that one masters it'. *Jiu-Jitsu läßt sich in kurzer Zeit erlernen. Wie lange braucht man, um diese Sprache zu erlernen?*

iv. Auslernen means 'to finish one's apprenticeship'. *Die meisten Lehrlinge lernen nach drei Jahren aus.* The idiom *Man lernt nie aus* means 'you never finish learning', or 'there's always something new to learn'.

v. Dazulernen means 'to learn sth. new or additional'. *Man kann immer [etw.] dazulernen.*

vi. Anlernen means 'to teach s.o. how to perform a certain task or do a particular job'. It suggests giving the person just the knowledge or skill required for the task, not a thorough training. *Ein angelernter Arbeiter* has been taught quickly to carry out one task and does not possess the skills of *ein gelernter Arbeiter. Anlernen*

should be contrasted to *ausbilden*, the v. applied to a thorough training. Cf. EDUCATE
4. Sich (dat.) **etw. anlernen** means either 'to acquire knowledge superficially', 'to learn up', *Ich habe mir die Prüfungskenntnisse angelernt*, or 'to acquire or pick up behaviour, how to do sth., etc. by observation or practice'. In the latter sense it is mainly found as a past part. and mostly implies that there is something not quite natural or genuine about the behaviour acquired. *Dieses Benehmen ist nicht natürlich, sondern angelernt. Mit dieser angelernten Weltgewandtheit hofft sie, alle zu beeindrucken.*

[at] least, at any rate phrs. used as *advs.*

1. When **at least** precedes a number, **mindestens** is the normal equivalent. *Für die Reise brauchen wir mindestens 200 Mark. Bis dahin fährt man mindestens zwei Stunden. Das Paket wiegt mindestens zwanzig Kilo.* It is also the usual word in statements which do not contain a number but for which a numerical value is conceivable. *Mein Aufsatz ist mindestens so gut wie deiner. Er ist mindestens teilweise verantwortlich.* In one instance, however, **wenigstens** is used. Someone who is asked to do a particular piece of work might answer, *'Für diese Arbeit brauche ich mindestens drei Wochen.'* If the other replied, *'Das geht leider nicht'*, the first might say, *'Dann gib mir wenigstens zwei Wochen!'* If the figure stated in *Wir brauchen mindestens 200 Mark* were not acceptable, the person involved could say, *'Dann gib uns wenigstens 150 Mark!'* *Wenigstens* indicates, on the one hand, a lower level someone is (reluctantly) prepared to accept, on the other a request not to go below this. It represents a lower figure after an initial assessment with *mindestens* proves impossible.

> *Weit und breit war kein Mensch zu sehen, und das nächste Dorf war mindestens 25 Kilometer ent-fernt.*
> *Er läßt das Telefon immer mindestens zwanzigmal klingeln, bevor er abnimmt.*
> *Dieser Staubsauger ist mindestens so gut wie der andere.*
> *Die Reparatur des Autos wird mindestens 500 Mark kosten.*
> *Ich habe mindestens zwanzig Minuten auf dich gewartet.*
> *Die Uneinigkeit in den Reihen des kleinen Koalitionspartners war mindestens teilweise die Ursache der Regierungskrise.   Es waren mindestens drei Täter.*
> *Ich hatte gehofft, daß du mindestens eine Woche bleiben würdest; wenn das nicht geht, dann bleibe doch wenigstens drei Tage!*

2. i. At least states a pos. feature among neg. ones. *He hasn't cleaned the house, but at least he's washed up.* The equivalent is **wenigstens**. *Er hat das Haus zwar nicht sauber gemacht, aber er hat wenigstens abgespült. Es ist zwar noch kalt und dunkel, aber jetzt ist wenigstens der Regenschauer vorbei. Das ist wenigstens etw.* means that at least some gain has been made, that in some fact lies some consolation or redeeming feature. *Jetzt weiß ich wenigstens, was ich machen soll,* at least I know that if not other things.
ii. Zumindest, 'at the very least', is a stronger syn. of *wenigstens*. *Ich wenigstens/zumindest habe mich gefreut. Zumindest/Wenigstens werde ich meine Meinung in dieser Angelegenheit noch sagen dürfen.*
iii. Wenigstens or **zumindest** translate **at any rate** when it means 'at least'. They were glad, or at any rate Dan was: *Sie waren froh, oder wenigstens/zumindest Dan war es.*
> *Er soll sehr tyrannisch sein—das zumindest/wenigstens behaupten seine Gegner.*
> *Nichts mehr konnte ihn erschüttern. Zumindest/Wenigstens glaubte er das.*

iv. *You could* **at least** *do sth.* = 'that is the least you could do/the least we could expect'. **Wenigstens** is the usual word. **Zumindest** is an alternative. *Du könntest dich wenigstens/zumindest für dein schlechtes Benehmen entschuldigen.* (The idea can also be expressed by the superlative. *Das (d.h. dich zu entschuldigen) wäre wohl das wenigste/mindeste, was du tun könntest/was man von dir erwarten könnte.*)

Wenn du schon keine Zeit zum Schreiben hast, könntest du wenigstens/zumindest ab und zu anrufen.
v. A partial syn. is one sense of **immerhin**. It refers only to something of pos. value which someone has done, not to what the person has not done or could have done. To a person who had not even washed up someone could say, *'Zumindest den Abwasch hättest du machen können'* or *'Du hättest wenigstens abwaschen können.'* Of a person who had at least washed up but not done much else, it could be said, *'Er hat immerhin/wenigstens abgewaschen.'* *Er hat es zwar nicht geschafft, aber er hat sich immerhin Mühe gegeben.* Cf. AFTER 2. vi.

Zumindest äußerlich war er ruhig und gelassen. Or Er war immerhin äußerlich ruhig.

Ihr Studium hat sie immerhin abgeschlossen, obwohl sie keine gute Note bekommen hat.

Er hat uns zwar nicht besucht, aber er hat immerhin zweimal angerufen.

leave *v.* Order of meanings: 1. **Leave** = 'to depart from a place or pers.' and 'to desert a pers.' 2. **Leave** = 'to allow to remain in a specified state'. 3. **Leave** = 'to go away allowing sth. to remain in a certain condition'. 4. **Leave** = 'to allow s.o./sth. to remain in a place deliberately or inadvertently'. 5. **Leave** = 'to move away allowing s.o./sth. to remain behind'. 6. **Leave** = 'not to do'. 7. **Leave** = 'to entrust sth. to s.o.' 8. **Leave** [s.o.] sth. **over**.

1. Leave = 'to go away or depart' referring to people and vehicles can be intr. *They left yesterday.* When the place left is stated, *He left the room,* it is trans. i–v deal with intr. uses, vi–viii with trans. ones.
i. When **leave** means 'to go away on foot', the appropriate vs. are **gehen** or **weggehen**. Cf. GO 4. *Ich muß jetzt leider gehen. Sie ist vor einer halben Stunde weggegangen.*
ii. **Fahren** and **abfahren** are used for a vehicle or for people travelling by one. *Ab* is optional in the pres. and past tenses if the sense is clear. *Wann fährt dein Zug?* or *Wann fährst du?* and *Er fährt/Ich fahre um 15 Uhr* are the normal questions and answers. Particularly when precise information is given or sought, *ab* can be added. *Mein Zug fährt um 17.10 von Gleis 6 ab.* Abfahren is used if the sense is unclear without it. *Die Großmutter, die einige Wochen bei uns zu Besuch gewesen ist, fährt morgen wieder ab.* If the person addressed knows she is leaving, *Sie fährt morgen um elf* is clear enough. Thus *Kurz nachdem er angekommen war, fuhr er plötzlich wieder ab.* In the perf. only abfahren is possible. *Der Zug/Der Bus ist schon abgefahren.* **Wegfahren** means 'to go away' other than on foot and can translate the meaning 'to leave'. *Sie ist vor einer halben Stunde weggefahren.*
iii. **Reisen** and **abreisen** are used in the same way as *fahren* and *abfahren*. *Reisen* implies a fairly long journey and sounds more important than *fahren. Ich reise morgen nach China [ab].* **Fliegen** and **abfliegen** are used for flying. *Er fliegt heute abend nach Tokio [ab].*
iv. **Losfahren**, applied to a vehicle, means 'to start (moving), to move off'. *Beim Losfahren fiel ein Teil der Ladung vom Lastwagen herunter.* For people, it means 'to leave, to set out or start [out]', mostly in one's private vehicle or by bicycle.The journey undertaken can be long or may be a short trip in the neighbourhood.

Wir wollen morgen vor Sonnenaufgang losfahren.

Da ich vor dem Kinobesuch noch einkaufen will, werde ich gleich losfahren.

v. **Aufbrechen** means 'to [get ready and] leave, to go, or to set off or out'. *Es wird Zeit, daß wir aufbrechen/abfahren/gehen.* It is fairly formal. **Sich auf den Weg machen** is a syn., as is the colloquial **sich aufmachen**. *Ich hatte mich gerade zum Friseur aufgemacht, da traf ich ihn.*

Die Soldaten brachen im ersten Morgengrauen zum Marsch in die Hauptstadt auf.

Bundesaußenminister Kinkel bricht morgen zu einer dreiwöchigen Reise nach Asien und Australien auf.

Wenn wir uns nicht sofort auf den Weg machen, kommen wir zu spät an.
Morgen muß ich mich früh in die Stadt aufmachen.

vi. Leave is trans. in *When did you leave Rome?* Such E. uses can be translated by G. intr. vs. *Wann sind Sie aus Rom abgefahren* or *weggefahren?* Another transl. is *Wann haben Sie Rom verlassen?* **Verlassen** always needs an obj. If the obj. is a place, it means 'to go away from it'. *Die Familie mußte ihre Heimat verlassen.* When the obj. is a person, it means either 'to separate from s.o.' or 'to leave, desert, or abandon s.o. for whom one is responsible'. *Ich muß Sie an der Kreuzung verlassen. Er hat seine Frau und Kinder verlassen.* Describing a place, the past part. means 'deserted'. *Die Straßen waren still und verlassen.* Hence *ein gottverlassenes Nest*, godforsaken.

> *Das Schiff verläßt den Hafen.*
> *Jeden Tag verläßt sie das Büro um 16.45 Uhr.*
> *Sie verließ die Karate-Gruppe, weil ihr diese Sportart zu anstrengend war.*
> *Der Wachtposten darf seinen Posten nicht verlassen.*
> *Der Kapitän verläßt als letzter das sinkende Schiff.*
> *Ich würde gern im Ausland arbeiten, aber ich kann meine alte Mutter nicht verlassen.*

vii. While *verlassen* belongs to the standard language in the sense 'to desert', two syns. *sitzenlassen* and *im Stich lassen* are fairly colloquial. Both express a certain indignation about the action described. **Sitzenlassen** means: *a.* 'To leave or abandon people for whom one is responsible'. *b.* 'To leave people unaided with unpleasant work with which one should help'. *c.* 'Not to turn up at an arranged meeting'. *d.* 'Not to marry s.o. to whom marriage has been promised'.

> *Eines Nachts verschwand er und ließ seine Frau mit drei Kindern und dem Schuldenberg sitzen.*
> *Nachdem sie die Wohnung ihrer Freundin in ein Chaos verwandelt hatte, ließ sie diese mit der ganzen Aufräumarbeit sitzen.*
> *Letzte Woche hat er eine Verabredung mit mir nicht eingehalten, und nun hat er mich wieder sitzen-lassen.* Alternative: *. . . mich wieder versetzt.*

Jmdn. im Stich lassen can also mean either 'to leave or desert s.o. for whom one is responsible', *Er ließ Frau und Kinder im Stich*, or 'not to do anything for s.o. who is in a difficult situation although this could be expected', *In guten Tagen war ich sein Freund, aber jetzt, wo es mir schlecht geht, läßt er mich im Stich.* Im Stich lassen is often translated as *to leave in the lurch.*

viii. Leave (= 'no longer attend') *school* is in formal language [**von der Schule**] **abgehen.** *Der Schüler ging schon nach der achten Klasse ab. Sie ging nach der zehnten Klasse von der Schule ab.* Die Schule verlassen is also used. *Wegen des Todes seines Vaters mußte er die Schule mit vierzehn Jahren verlassen.* **Leave** home can be expressed by **wegziehen** and **ausziehen.** *Sie ist von zu Hause weggezogen* suggests she has moved a fair way away. *Sie ist von zu Hause ausgezogen* means that she has moved to her own place in the same locality.

2. Leave = 'to allow to remain in a specified state'. *Leave everything as you find it!* **i.** This sense is carried by **lassen.** It does not suggest that someone goes away leaving a room etc. in a certain state but that the person stays there and changes nothing. *Wir haben die Sachen so gelassen, wie wir sie vorgefunden haben*, we have not changed the position of anything, we have left them as we found them. Thus *Obwohl einige Verbesserungen angebracht erschienen, ließ er das Manuskript so, wie es war.* It is mostly used with an adj., a past part., or a phr. *Soll ich die Tür offen lassen? Lassen Sie diesen Teil des Formulars frei!* A person can be the obj. *Diese Nachricht ließ die meisten kalt/unberührt. Man läßt jmdn. im Dunkeln/Ungewissen/Unklaren über etw. Man läßt jmdn. im Zweifel/bei seiner Meinung/in seinem Irrtum.* **Belassen** is an emphatic and formal alternative to *lassen* in a few contexts. It is often used for keeping or leaving someone in a position, although *lassen* is possible. *Der Chef beließ den Angestellten auf dem Posten, obwohl er nicht besonders zuverlässig war. Der Beamte wurde in seinem Amt* *belassen/gelassen. Belassen* is more formal and stronger and suggests a more considered action. *Wir haben die Dinge so belassen, wie wir sie vorgefunden haben. Wir belassen/lassen die Reden in der angegebenen Reihenfolge.* **Es bei etw. belassen/lassen** means 'to let an arrangement, sth. planned, etc. stand or remain as it is', 'to leave it as originally decided'. *Wir wollen es bei dieser Vereinbarung lassen/belassen. Wir lassen/belassen es bei der getroffenen Übereinkunft.*

> *Lassen Sie bitte alles so, wie es ist!*   *Sie haben alles beim alten gelassen.*
>
> *Es ist, glaube ich, besser, wenn ich das ungesagt lasse.*   *Sie ließen nichts unversucht.*
>
> *Belassen wir es dabei: Ich komme wie abgemacht am Donnerstag vorbei.*
>
> *Da kein anderer Termin allen paßte, beließen sie es schließlich bei Montag.*

ii. Leave alone has several equivalents. It can be translated lit. *Er schreibt einen Aufsatz zu Ende und will, daß wir ihn alleine lassen. Laß mich in Ruhe!* (cf. BOTHER) is a request not to be disturbed. *Laß mich zufrieden!* has the same meaning and often suggests a certain annoyance. *Laß mich mit dieser dämlichen Sache zufrieden! Jmdn. in Frieden lassen* is also used. *Leave the fire alone!* said to a child would be *Spiel' doch nicht mit dem Feuer! Laß die Katze zufrieden/in Ruhe!*, leave the cat alone! *Laß mich aus dem Spiel!*, leave me out (of what you're planning). *Laß mich nur machen!* is like *Don't interfere with me!* or *Let me go on/Leave me to go on* (doing this) my way! Also *Laß es ihn so machen, wie er es vorhatte/wie er es möchte!*, leave him to . . .

Jmd. gewähren lassen means 'to let, or leave, s.o. be'.

> A. *Ich glaube, er macht einen Fehler, wenn er kündigt.*
>
> B. *Laß ihn nur gewähren! Er muß schließlich seine eigenen Erfahrungen machen.*

iii. Stehenlassen means 'to leave mistakes', i.e. 'not to correct them'. *Diesen Satz kann man nicht so stehenlassen. Sie wollte nichts ändern und ließ mehrere Fehler stehen.* Another meaning is 'to leave food', i.e. 'not to eat it'. *Er ließ die Suppe stehen*, he didn't eat any. *Ich konnte nicht so viel essen und habe einen Teil stehenlassen. (Don't leave any of your dinner!* is usually *Iß alles auf!* or *Von deinem Essen soll/darf nichts übrigbleiben.)*

3. Leave = 'to go away allowing sth. to remain behind in a certain condition'. *They left the house in good order/in a mess.* Both **zurücklassen** and **hinterlassen** mean 'to depart allowing sth. to remain in a specified condition'. *Sie haben die Wohnung in bester Ordnung hinterlassen/zurückgelassen. Ihr habt alles in Unordnung zurückgelassen. Er hinterließ das Zimmer in ordentlichem Zustand.*

4. Leave = 'to allow to remain in a place either deliberately or inadvertently' or 'to deposit somewhere'. *We left our luggage at the station. I've left my umbrella on the bus.*

i. Lassen can mean 'to allow to remain' or 'not to remove from'. *Ich habe die Sachen im Koffer gelassen. Laß die Schüssel im Schrank!–Ich brauche sie im Augenblick nicht.*

ii. Lassen also means 'to put deliberately in a certain place and allow to remain there'. *Ich habe den Brief auf dem Tisch gelassen. Den Koffer lassen wir am Bahnhof. Wo kann ich meinen Mantel lassen?* (An alternative for the last two sents. is **abgeben**, to deposit for safekeeping. *Den Mantel kann man in der Garderobe gegen eine kleine Gebühr abgeben.)* People can be the obj. of *lassen. Während wir weg waren, haben wir die Kinder bei meinen Eltern gelassen. Etw. als Pfand lassen* means 'to leave as security'. *Ich lasse Ihnen den Fotoapparat als Pfand.*

iii. Lassen can also mean 'to forget or neglect to take with you', i.e. 'to leave inadvertently'. While *liegenlassen* usually means 'to forget', and *zurücklassen* (cf. 4. vi), means 'to leave intentionally', *lassen* can be either, and is mostly taken to mean 'to leave on purpose'. However, when it is clear from the context that something has not been purposely left, *lassen* can be used instead of *liegenlassen*.

> *Verdammt noch mal, ich habe meinen Schirm im Zug gelassen!*
>
> *Wo habe ich nur meine Brille gelassen?*   *Er hatte die Karten zu Hause gelassen.*

iv. Liegenlassen usually means 'to leave behind' or 'to forget'. *In der Eile hatte er den Fotoapparat im Zugabteil liegengelassen.* (Also *liegenlassen.*) It sometimes means 'to leave sth. lying where it is deliberately'. *Ich habe die Sachen auf dem Boden liegengelassen.* The idiom *Als sie diese Nachricht erhielt, ließ sie alles stehen und liegen und fuhr los* means that she left everything as it was.

v. Stehenlassen occasionally means 'to leave behind inadvertently' something which is in an upright or standing position. *Er ließ das Paket im Geschäft stehen.* It mostly means 'to leave intentionally'. *Nach dem reichlichen Alkoholkonsum ließen sie den Wagen stehen und fuhren mit einem Taxi nach Hause.*

vi. Zurücklassen means 'to leave sth. somewhere on purpose' and implies that the subj. moves away. *Wir lassen den Koffer am Bahnhof zurück.* It also means 'to leave one's possessions behind when one has no other choice'. *Wegen des Hochwassers mußten alle Dorfbewohner flüchten und ihr Hab und Gut zurücklassen.* It is used when people go on, leaving another/others behind. *Die vier Bergsteiger ließen ihren erkrankten Freund am Fuß des Bergs zurück. Man hat ihn tot zurückgelassen.*

vii. Dalassen is a colloquial v. meaning 'to leave s.o./sth. here or in a place deliberately [for a time]'. *Kann ich den Koffer/das Kind dalassen, während ich zur Post gehe? Wir waren dort und haben die Sachen dagelassen. Ich lasse das Gepäck bis zum Abend da.*

viii. Hinterlegen means 'to deposit for safe keeping', but does not always refer to something valuable.

Wir haben den Schlüssel beim Nachbarn hinterlegt.

5. Leave = 'to move away allowing sth./s.o. to remain behind'. *Mr Smith left a message for you. The storm left a trail of devastation.*

i. Hinterlassen and **zurücklassen** mean firstly 'to leave a family after one's death', *Er hinterließ eine Frau und drei Kinder. Sie ließ ihren Mann und zwei kleine Kinder zurück.* To leave a message/instructions for s.o. is usually *hinterlassen*, although *zurücklassen* is possible. *Der Chef hat einen Auftrag/Anweisungen für Sie hinterlassen. Da er nicht zur Verabredung kommen konnte, hinterließ er eine Nachricht für den Freund.* In colloquial speech **dalassen** is used. *Hat jmd. eine Nachricht für mich dagelassen?* Both *zurück-* and *hinterlassen* are used for leaving something tangible behind. *Die Wunde ließ eine Narbe zurück/hinterließ eine Narbe. Die Räder hinterließen tiefe Spuren im Boden/ . . . ließen tiefe Spuren . . . zurück. Der verschüttete Wein hat Schmutzflecken auf dem Teppich hinterlassen/zurückgelassen.* Both are also used with intangibles like a feeling or impression, but the constructions differ. *Etw. läßt jmdn. mit einem Gefühl zurück* and *hinterläßt [bei jmdm.] einen guten Eindruck/einen unangenehmen Nachgeschmack.* Thus *Der Krieg ließ die Besiegten mit einem tiefen Haß gegen die Sieger zurück* and *Der Krieg hinterließ bei den Besiegten einen tiefen Haß gegen die Sieger.*

    Der Sturm hat überall Verwüstung hinterlassen/zurückgelassen.

    Diese Nachricht ließ mich mit der Frage zurück, was als Nächstes geschehen würde (left me with the question, left me wondering). Or *. . . hinterließ bei mir die Frage, was . . .*

ii. Jmdn. hinter sich zurücklassen means 'to leave behind or outstrip'. *Im Marathonlauf hatte er die anderen Läufer bald weit hinter sich [zurück]gelassen. Zurück* is optional here because of the phr. *hinter sich*, but necessary without it.

iii. Hinterlassen can mean 'to leave' in the sense 'to bequeath sth. to s.o.' *Er hinterließ [ihr] ein großes Vermögen.* Cf. INHERIT.

6. Leave = 'not to do sth.' *I wanted to complain, but then decided to leave it. I didn't have enough time and had to leave that job.*

i. The three main vs. with the sense 'not to proceed with a possible or intended action' may need equivalents other than **leave**. The v. in the standard language is **unterlassen**, to refrain from doing something. It has a formal, even official ring. *Der schüchterne junge Mann hatte schon mehrmals vor dem Haus des mit ihm befreundeten*

Mädchens gestanden, um mit ihrem Vater zu sprechen, aber er unterließ es immer wieder, weil er voll Angst vor einer Begegnung mit dem verschlossenen und ihm unbekannten Mann war. In less formal language *Er unterließ es immer wieder* would be expressed as *Er ließ es immer wieder* or *Er ließ es immer wieder bleiben.* **Lassen** means 'not to carry out sth. one could well do'. It is often used in the imp. *Laß mal, das mache ich schon! Lassen wir das!* Although the syn. **bleibenlassen** may suggest more strongly that the action was planned, they are mostly interchangeable. *Zuerst wollte ich mich beschweren, aber dann habe ich es doch gelassen/habe ich es doch bleibenlassen. Das mit dem Kino heute abend wollen wir lieber [bleiben]lassen!* With a n. obj. *lassen* is much more colloquial than *unterlassen. Ich hatte mir vorgenommen, im Juni nach Italien zu fahren, aber wegen dringender Verpflichtungen mußte ich die Reise unterlassen. Lassen wir die Fahrt nach Hamburg!—das Wetter ist viel zu schlecht heute. Lassen* means 'not to go on talking about sth.', 'not to take sth. which one considered buying but decided against'. *Wir müssen dieses Thema jetzt lassen. Lassen wir das! Es kommt nicht in Frage—es ist mir viel zu teuer.* (Note that if an action has already begun, *unterlassen* and *lassen* mean 'to stop'. *Der Vorsitzende forderte die Anwesenden auf, Zwischenrufe zu unterlassen. Unterlassen Sie das!* is a strong formal command. *Laß das!* is everyday language.)

> *Wenn du mir nicht helfen willst, dann werde ich es eben lassen.*   *Laß mal, ich zahle schon.*
> *Ich wollte heute mit dem Wagen nach Frankfurt fahren, aber bei diesem Wetter lasse ich es lieber.*
> *Sie wollte im Herbst nach Rom fahren, aber dann mußte sie es doch bleibenlassen, weil ihre Mutter schwer erkrankte.*

ii. Liegenlassen also means 'to leave work undone'. It implies nothing about the cause, which may be adverse circumstances or just laziness. *Sie wurde plötzlich krank und mußte die Arbeit liegenlassen. Da der Schüler keine Lust hatte, seine Hausaufgaben zu machen, hat er sie liegenlassen.* The pass. is *Die Arbeit ist liegengeblieben*, which also says nothing about the reason. **Leave** work **for/until later**, i.e. intentionally, is expressed by **aufsparen**. *Die Hälfte der Arbeit spare ich für morgen auf.*

7. Leave means 'to entrust or hand over a matter to s.o.' *I'll leave this matter to you/in your hands* or *I'll leave you to deal with this matter. He left the decision to us*, and *He left it to us to decide.* Here G. uses **überlassen**. *Ich überlasse Ihnen die ganze Angelegenheit. Ich überlasse es Ihnen, die Sache zu erledigen. Ich überlasse Ihnen die Entscheidung. Ich überlasse es Ihnen zu entscheiden, was wir machen sollen. We'll leave you to paint the fence* can mean that we entrust this task to you and would be translated by *überlassen. Wir überlassen es euch, den Zaun zu streichen.* (The E. sent. can also be understood as meaning that we will not disturb you while you are painting the fence. This sense comes out more clearly in *We'll leave you to get on with your work.* One transl. of this is *Ich störe dich [bei der Arbeit] nicht weiter*; another is *Du kannst ungestört/in Ruhe weiter arbeiten/den Zaun weiter streichen.*)

8. Another meaning of **überlassen** is 'to leave or abandon s.o. to his/her fate, etc.' *Sie wurden ihrem Schicksal/dem Verderben/dem Elend überlassen.*

9. Leave [over] when act., as in *They haven't left anything [over] for us*, is expressed by **übriglassen** and when pass., as in *There's a bit/nothing left [over]*, by **übrigbleiben**. *Sie haben alles aufgegessen und uns nichts übriggelassen. Laß mir etw. davon übrig! Von dem Kuchen sind nur noch drei Stück übriggeblieben. Wenn ich sämtliche Rechnungen bezahlt habe, wird nicht sehr viel übrig bleiben*, there won't be much left, I won't have much left. (*Lassen* translates *to leave room/space for sth. Wir müssen Platz/Raum für die Bücher lassen. Also Lassen Sie bitte einen 4 cm breiten Rand für die Korrektur!*) **Übrig sein** means 'to be left [over]' and **übrig haben** 'to have left [over]'. *Von dem Stoff ist nichts mehr übrig. Ich habe nur fünf Mark übrig.* (In colloquial speech separable *überlassen* is used in the sense of *übriglassen*. *He, laß mir auch etw. über!* Inseparable *überlassen* can mean 'to let s.o. have sth.' *Mein Vater hat mir das Auto fürs Wochende überlassen*.) Idioms. *Etw./Jmd. läßt nichts/viel/sehr zu wünschen übrig*, he/she/it leaves nothing/much to be desired. *Ihnen blieb nichts anderes übrig, als das Haus zu verkaufen*, they were left with no other choice but to . . .

lend, borrow *vs.* These two vs. are clearly distinguished in E., **lend** meaning 'to grant s.o. the temporary possession of sth. on condition or in expectation of its return', while **borrow** is 'to take sth. to use temporarily'. The two main equivalents *leihen* and *borgen* have both senses. In *Ich habe der Nachbarin den Staubsauger geliehen*, the v. means 'lent'. In *Das Fahrrad habe ich [mir] nur geliehen* and *Das Fahrrad ist nur geliehen*, the same v. means 'borrowed'. In *Ich werde dir die Summe borgen, bis du sie zurückgeben kannst*, borgen means 'lend', while in *Er hatte überall Geld geborgt* and *Ich habe mir den Staubsauger von der Nachbarin geborgt*, geborgt means 'borrowed'. If not apparent from the context, the meaning is made clear by the addition of other words.

i. When it means 'to lend', **leihen** often has a dat. denoting a person to make the sense clear. The obj. can be any possession or money, and the loan can be private or commercial. *Sie hat mir 20 Mark bis Montag geliehen. Die Bank wird dir das Geld leihen. Kannst du mir bitte dein Wörterbuch leihen?* When it means 'to borrow', it usually has a refl. dat. and often *von*, occasionally *bei*. *Ich habe mir von ihr 20 Mark geliehen. Ich habe mir den Frack für die Hochzeit geliehen.* Used without a dat. or refl. dat., *leihen* is taken to mean 'to borrow'. In a sent. like *Ich habe Geld bei der Bank geliehen*, *mir* could be added, but whether it is or not, *geliehen* would be understood as 'borrowed'. The past part. also has this sense. *Der Wagen ist geliehen—er gehört mir nicht. Ich habe mir den Wagen geliehen* makes the sense unmistakable. If A sees B on a bike and asks, 'Hast du dir ein Fahrrad gekauft?', B could say, 'Nein, es ist nur geliehen', and this would mean 'borrowed'. If someone said to you, 'Dein Fahrrad ist nicht da' and you answered that you had lent it to Daniel, you could use the act. form 'Ich habe es Daniel geliehen' or say, 'Es ist ausgeliehen or verliehen', both of which mean 'lent'. Cf. ii and iv. **Borgen** also expresses both meanings, but it is less commonly used. It is restricted to money and relatively small possessions and to loans between individuals. *Ich habe dem Freund den Fotoapparat geborgt*, lent. With the addition of a refl. dat. and/or *von*, the meaning changes to 'to borrow'. *Ich habe mir von ihm etwas Geld geborgt*, borrowed. *Ich habe [mir] von der Nachbarin das Bügeleisen geborgt*, borrowed.

A. *Ich habe meine Schreibsachen vergessen. Könntest du mir einen Bleistift leihen?*
B. *Es tut mir leid, aber ich habe nur einen, und den habe ich mir selbst von meinem Nachbarn geliehen.*

ii. Ausleihen also has both senses. *Jmdm. etw. ausleihen* is 'to lend', often money, but also other possessions, mostly for use on one occasion. While *leihen* belongs to the neutral stylistic level, *ausleihen* is somewhat lower, and more common in speech. *Er hat mir die Leiter ausgeliehen*, he lent me the ladder. *Ich habe mir die Leiter ausgeliehen*, I borrowed the ladder. *Ausleihen* is the everyday word for borrowing a book from a library and a video-tape, etc., although *leihen* is possible, and *entleihen* is the formal term. Cf. vii. *Ausleihen* is mainly confined to the private sphere, but in the appropriate circumstances it can include taking or paying a fee. *Wir haben uns ein Ruderboot ausgeliehen.* As mentioned in i, the past part. *ausgeliehen*, used after *sein*, always means 'lent'. *Das Buch ist nicht da, es ist ausgeliehen.*

Ich würde dir gern helfen, aber ich habe kein Geld, das ich dir ausleihen kann.
Ich habe ihr mein Fahrrad ausgeliehen.   *Ihm werde ich nie etw. ausleihen.*

Ich habe mir das Buch ausgeliehen und muß es schnell lesen, weil die Leihfrist nur eine Woche beträgt.

iii. In non-commercial use, **verleihen** makes a statement about whether someone lends or does not lend his/her possessions, or whether something can be lent.

Bücher, die älter sind als 100 Jahre, werden nicht verliehen.

Ich verleihe meine Bücher nicht gern.

Einen Spaten kann man ohne Bedenken verleihen, vielleicht auch noch eine Bohrmaschine, aber mit deinem neuen Wagen wäre ich vorsichtiger gewesen.

The past part. means 'lent out', but belongs to more formal language. *Das Buch ist verliehen.* It is used with *an* on the same stylistic level. *Die Bank verleiht Geld an ihre Kunden* is sometimes found instead of the usual *Die Bank leiht ihren Kunden Geld. Er weiß nicht, an wen er das Buch verliehen hat.*

iv. In commercial use, **verleihen** implies a fee and means 'to hire out'. *Am anderen Ende des Sees werden Boote verliehen.* Hence compounds like *der Bootsverleih, der Filmverleih.* To hire, when the person who pays the fee and uses the thing hired is the subj., is mostly *mieten. Wir haben ein Boot/ein Auto gemietet.*

v. Verleihen means 'to lend' in a fig. sense, i.e. 'to give or contribute'. *The threatening gestures lent weight to his words. Durch drohende Gebärden versuchte er, seinen Worten Nachdruck zu verleihen. Der Hopfen verleiht dem Bier den bitteren Geschmack.*

vi. Pumpen and **sich pumpen** are colloquial terms used in the same way as *leihen* and *sich leihen.* They usually refer to loans of money and presuppose a close relationship between lender and borrower.

Hoffentlich pumpt er mir das Geld.

Ich muß mir erst Geld pumpen, bevor ich einkaufen kann.

vii. Entleihen is used in formal and elevated language and has the sense 'to borrow' only. *Studenten dürfen Bücher kostenlos entleihen.* The slip in a library book might read: *Dieses Buch ist aus der hessischen Landesbibliothek entliehen.*

viii. Entlehnen is 'to take over or borrow' in the intellectual sphere. The obj. is a style, ideas, words from other languages, etc. *Wir haben das Wort 'Charisma' aus der griechischen Sprache entlehnt.*

Die Griechen haben in der Baukunst vieles von den Ägyptern entlehnt. (Übernommen is less formal.)

lie *v.* and *n.* **tell a lie** *v.* **Lügen** is intr. only and translates *lie* and *tell a lie.* Hence *Er lügt* or *Sie lügt immer* or *Sie hat nie gelogen* and *'Ich war nicht dort', log sie. Das ist gelogen,* that's a lie. **Erlügen** survives only in the past part. *erlogen* which can be used instead of *gelogen* in the last sent., but is stylistically higher. Only *erlogen* occurs in the phr. *Das ist erstunken und erlogen,* a pack of lies, pure invention. Both **anlügen** and **belügen** need a personal obj. and differ only in that *anlügen* is somewhat more emphatic. *Du hast mich/deinen Lehrer belogen/angelogen. Er hat mich maßlos angelogen/belogen.* **Vorlügen** needs a dat. denoting a person and a *daß*-clause. *Er log uns vor, daß er am Freitag krank gewesen war und zum Arzt mußte.* The clause can be replaced by an indefinite expression like *das* or *etw. Das hat sie uns vorgelogen.* **Schwindeln** and its derivatives are used in colloquial speech when someone does not tell the truth, but they suggest a fairly harmless deviation from the facts, sometimes embellishing what one says with exaggerated or invented additions, or telling tall stories. *Ich glaube nicht, daß das passiert ist—du schwindelst ja. Jmdn.* **beschwindeln** is a syn of *belügen,* but also suggests nothing serious. *Das Kind hat die Mutter beschwindelt. (Beschwindeln* is also a syn. of *betrügen,* to CHEAT. *Er beschwindelte mich um 20 Mark.)* **Vorschwindeln** is used like *vorlügen. Er schwindelte mir vor, daß er alles alleine gemacht hatte. Das alles hat er uns vorgeschwindelt.* **Flunkern** is like *to [tell a] fib. Das Kind flunkert gern ein bißchen. Daß sie das alles kann, ist sicher geflunkert.*

light, ignite, illuminate *vs.*

1. i. Light = 'to make burn or set burning'. The usual equivalent of this trans. use is **anzünden**. *Ich zündete das Feuer/das Gas/eine Kerze an.*

ii. Anstecken is used colloquially for *anzünden. Sie steckte das Gas an.* In the standard language it is only used for setting fire to what should not be burnt. *Die Polizei stellte fest, daß der Bauer selbst seine Scheune angesteckt hatte, um die Versicherungssumme zu bekommen.* In this sense *anstecken* is a syn. of *in Brand setzen/stecken,* to set fire to.

iii. Zünden can be trans. The E. equivalent depends on the context. It means 'to ignite', *Er zündete das Gas durch Funken,* with bombs and explosives 'to detonate', *Sie zündeten die Bombe/den Sprengstoff,* and in connection with a rocket 'to fire', *Man hat die zweite Stufe der Rakete gezündet.* In fig. use, *Eine Rede zündete* means it roused the audience to enthusiasm.

iv. Entzünden is used as a syn. of *anzünden* only in elevated language. *Er entzündete das Feuer im Kamin.* It is occasionally found as a trans. v. in the fig. sense 'to kindle or arouse'. *Die schlechte Behandlung entzündete seinen Haß.*

2. Light is also intr. and means 'to start burning', as in *The matches are wet and won't light.*

i. Zünden used intr. conveys this meaning. *Die Streichhölzer sind naß und zünden nicht.*

ii. Sich entzünden means 'to catch alight or on fire', but is now only used for something that catches fire by itself. *Der Heuhaufen hatte sich von selbst entzündet.*

3. Light = 'to give light to a room etc.' or 'to provide with light'. *The streets are lit by electricity.* **Illuminate** means 'to throw light on' by floodlights or a spotlight and 'to decorate with lights' as for a celebration. These meanings are covered by *leuchten* and its derivatives.

i. Leuchten means 'to emit light' or 'to shine'. *Eine Kerze/Eine Lampe/Eine Flamme leuchtet. Der Mond leuchtet. Ihre Augen leuchteten vor Freude.* It also means 'to shine a light on sth.' *Sie leuchtet mir mit der Taschenlampe ins Gesicht. Ich leuchtete in jeden Winkel des Zimmers. Jmdm. leuchten* means 'to shine a light in order that s.o. can see the way'. *Er leuchtete mir, als ich die dunkle Treppe hinunterging.*

ii. Beleuchten means 'to provide with light'. It is used in stating how something is lit, either the means of lighting or whether something is well, badly, etc. lit. *Städte wurden früher mit Gaslampen beleuchtet. Die Straßenbeleuchtung. Der Hörsaal ist gut/schlecht beleuchtet.* A further meaning is 'to throw light on from the outside' and refers to floodlights, spotlights, lights of cars, and natural sources of light. *Der Dom und das Rathaus/Die Verkehrszeichen werden nachts beleuchtet. Der Scheinwerfer beleuchtete einen Schauspieler auf der Bühne. Die Sonne beleuchtete die Wolken/die Berge. Die Scheinwerfer des Autos beleuchteten plötzlich einen Radfahrer.* A syn. in the sense 'to floodlight' is **ausstrahlen**. *Die Stadt Hannover kann es sich nicht leisten, historische Gebäude in der Stadt auszustrahlen.*

iii. Erleuchten gives the impression of an observer seeing bright light in, or coming from, a room, house, town, etc. *Der Saal/Das Haus/Das Fenster war hell erleuchtet.* It is also used for the illumination of a town. *Zu Weihnachten war die Stadt festlich erleuchtet.*

iv. Ausleuchten means 'to fill completely with artificial light'. *Der neue Bahnhof/Der Hörsaal war taghell ausgeleuchtet.*

4. The equivalent of **illuminate** meaning 'throw light on a topic' is **beleuchten**. *Der Redner beleuchtete besonders die soziale Seite des Problems. Wir wollen diese Vorgänge näher beleuchten.*

like, love *vs.*

1. A common general equivalent is **mögen**, to like, be fond of, or care for. In pos. sents., *mögen* is often combined with *gern* or *sehr*. It is not as widely used as **like**, but is confined to special situations and meanings. i–iv give these uses; v deals with *möchte*.

i. In relation to people, **mögen** implies that one feels goodwill, friendship, and affection for another.

> Wir mögen die beiden sehr. Sie mochten ihn alle sehr.
> Ich mag sie nicht, und sie mag mich nicht. Ich habe ihn schon von jeher gemocht.

ii. With food, **mögen** expresses a permanent liking, not that someone likes the food on one occasion, but that he or she always likes it. *Mögen* is the everyday expression; *etw.* **gern essen/trinken** is more refined. Cf. 2. iv.

> Ich mag deutsche Wurstwaren nicht besonders. Deutsches Bier mag ich gern.
> Mein Vater mag Käse. Inge mag keinen Fisch.
> Sie essen gern Austern. Ich trinke gern Ananassaft.

iii. With plays, novels, films, etc. as obj., **mögen** mostly suggests a permanent liking. *Mögen Sie Barockmusik/Jazz? Ich mag Krimis/Wildwestfilme nicht.* In the spoken language it can refer to a single work and suggests an almost instinctive like or dislike that cannot be explained. *Diesen Film mag ich nicht. Den neuen Roman von Böll mag sie sehr gern. Der Roman gefällt ihr* is less emotional and weaker. Cf. 2. i.

iv. The pres. and past indicative of **mögen** are used with an infin., mostly in the neg., and mean '[not] to like' (disturbing/to disturb someone). *Ich mag ihn nicht stören. Seit dem Fernsehinterview mag sie kein Buch mehr von Graß lesen. Ich mochte es ihm nicht sagen. Er mochte sich nicht von ihr trennen.* These forms of *mögen* are stylistically higher and less common than *wollen* or *möchte*. *Mögen* is also used with *es* and a clause with *wenn* or *daß*. *Ich mag es nicht, wenn fremde Leute sich in meine Angelegenheiten einmischen. Ich habe es sehr gemocht, daß du die Wahrheit geradeheraus gesagt hast.* It is occasionally found with *gern* and an infin. with *zu*. *Ich mag es gern, durch die Stadt zu bummeln.* A clause may be needed for grammatical reasons, e.g. with a v. which cannot form the pass. *Er mag es nicht, daß man ihm widerspricht,* doesn't like being contradicted. *Ich mag es nicht, daß man mich warten läßt,* don't like being kept waiting.

v. Would like is **möchte** which, unlike other forms of *mögen*, is still commonly used. *Möchten Sie noch Tee? Ich möchte dir was sagen, wenn du ein paar Minuten Zeit hast.* It is often used because *Ich will* is felt to be too direct or even rude. It is found with and without *gern*. *Ich möchte gern helfen* is only slightly stronger than the form without *gern*. The E. acc. and infin. construction *I would like you to help me* must be expressed as a *daß*-clause: *Ich möchte, daß du mir hilfst. Ich möchte, daß Sie es ihnen erklären.*

2. Alternatives to *mögen*.

i. Gefallen expresses an opinion based on a judgement of taste. Syntactically it is like *to please*, but it occurs far more frequently than this equivalent and is used in contexts in which **like** is the normal E. v. The thing or person judged must be the subj., and the person making the judgement is in the dat. The subj. can be people, clothes, works of art such as films, plays, pictures, novels, stories, etc., aspects of nature, and places. It is not used in connection with food and drink. *Gefalle ich dir in diesem Kleid?* asks for a reaction to the appearance. The impersonal *Es gefällt uns hier gut* means that we like being here or that we like it here.

> Das Bild/Der Roman/Das Theaterstück/Die Fernsehsendung gefällt mir gut/gefällt ihr gar nicht/hat uns allen gefallen. Der neue Mitarbeiter gefällt mir.
> Es hat uns an der See/in Australien gut/ausgezeichnet gefallen.

ii. Gern haben is also used with things as obj. There is no difference in meaning between *Ich habe diese Möbel gern* and *Diese Möbel gefallen mir*. *Gern haben* is, however, preferred when someone has developed a fondness for something in the course of time. *Ich habe unsere alten Möbel recht gern*. It can be used with *es* and a clause. *Ich habe es gern, wenn die Kinder leise spielen*.

iii. A close syn. of *mögen*, used for people, is **jmdn. gut leiden können** or occasionally **jmdn. gern/gut leiden mögen**. Both are unemotional in tone. *Ich kann ihn gut leiden. Trotz seiner Schrullen mag sie ihn gern leiden*. **Sympathisch** is used to express a liking arising from a person's traits of character and is applied both to the person and individual characteristics. The constructions are *Ich finde sie sympathisch* and *Er ist mir sympathisch. Seine Stimme/Ihre Offenheit ist mir sympathisch*. **Etw./viel/nichts übrighaben für** is used colloquially to express a liking or a dislike for a person, or interest in a thing or activity. *Für den Jungen von nebenan hatte sie schon immer etw. übrig. Für Sport hatte er nichts übrig. Für diese Art Musik habe ich nicht viel übrig*.

iv. Like (or *enjoy*) on a single occasion in reference to food or drink is expressed by **etw. schmeckt jmdm.** *Hat Ihnen das Essen geschmeckt? Dieser Käse schmeckt mir. Wie schmeckt Ihnen der Wein?*

3. Like doing sth. is often expressed by **gern** and a v. *Ich bummle gern durch die Stadt. Ich tanze gern/schwimme gern/löse gern Kreuzworträtsel* etc. A common polite alternative to *ich möchte* (cf. 1. v) is **ich hätte gern**. *Ich hätte gern fünf Briefmarken zu eins achtzig* and *Ich hätte gern sechs Brötchen* are polite requests in shops etc. *Gern* means 'would like' or 'would have liked' when combined with a v. in the subjunctive. *Ich würde gern länger bleiben. Ich hätte gern gespielt, aber ich hatte zu viel zu tun*, I would have liked to play. *Ich wäre gern länger geblieben. Ich hätte gern Herrn X gesprochen* is a refined way of asking to speak to someone on the phone.

4. Love.

i. Lieben means 'to love' and takes as obj. *Menschen, ein Land, die Heimat, eine Stadt, eine Landschaft, ein Haustier* and what is of fundamental importance for mankind such as *die Natur, die Gerechtigkeit, die Wahrheit, die Freiheit, der Frieden, das Leben, die Kunst, die Musik*, etc.

Die Eltern lieben ihre Kinder.   *Man sollte seinen Nächsten lieben.*
Er liebt seine Frau.   *Die beiden lieben sich schon lange.*

Colloquially **love** means 'like or be fond of'. *She loves comfort/skiing. I'd love to help. Lieben* is sometimes used in this way with an obj. *Sie lieben den Luxus/teures Essen. Ich liebe den Duft dieser Blumen. Er hat schon immer schnelle Autos geliebt. Sie liebt das Alleinsein über alles*. Like **love**, *lieben* is apt to sound effusive and is avoided by many people. *Lieben* is also used with an infin. and *zu* and needs *es*, but here too, if used at all, it is best avoided for trivial activities. *Sie liebt es sehr, allein am Strand spazierenzugehen. Jmd. liebt es [nicht]* can also be followed by a *wenn*-clause which is sometimes necessary for grammatical reasons, e.g. with vs. that take the dat.

> *Er liebt es nicht, während der Vorlesung unterbrochen zu werden.* (More commonly *mag es nicht*.)
> *Der Chef liebt es nicht/mag es nicht, wenn man ihm widerspricht.* (Pass. infin. not possible.)

ii. To express affection for people to whom one is close, one's family, relatives, friends, or acquaintances, *lieben* is often felt to be rather theatrical, and **gern haben** and **liebhaben** are used. In ascending order of intensity, the vs. are *mögen, gern mögen* or *gern haben, liebhaben*, and *lieben*. *Liebhaben* suggests affection and/or close ties of friendship, but nothing erotic.

> *Er hat seine ältere Kusine sehr gern.*   *Ihr seid so gut zu mir. Ich habe euch alle lieb.*
> *Den dicken, kleinen Peter muß man einfach liebhaben.*

limit, restrict *vs.*

1. *Beschränken* and *einschränken* are both translated as **limit**, but differ slightly.

i. Beschränken [auf] means 'to see to it that sth. does not go beyond a certain limit', 'to set an upper limit which is not to be exceeded'. *Man beschränkte die Redezeit auf zehn Minuten. Ich muß meine Korrespondenz auf das Notwendigste beschränken*, see to it that it does not go beyond what is absolutely necessary. *Beschränken* forms the pass. with *werden* and, unlike *einschränken*, with *sein*. Hence *Die Redezeit wurde auf zehn Minuten beschränkt* as well as *ist auf zehn Minuten beschränkt*. The obj. can also be something intangible such as *[Handlungs]freiheit, Rechte*, or *Macht. Er wurde in seiner Handlungsfreiheit beschränkt.*

ii. Sich beschränken auf means with a person as subj. 'to limit or restrict oneself to doing sth.' *Ich beschränke mich darauf, die Vorgänge zu beschreiben.* With a non-personal subj., it means 'to be limited/restricted to'. *Diese neue Bestimmung beschränkt sich auf Studenten, die länger als vier Jahre studiert haben. Dieses Buch beschränkt sich auf die Geschichte Österreichs. Sein Einfluß beschränkte sich auf einen Teil der Industrie.*

iii. Einschränken is 'to limit' meaning 'to reduce, cut down or back, to make less than it was before'. *Die Zahl der Teilnehmer war beschränkt* means that at the outset a decision was made to set a maximum number, whereas *Die Zahl der Teilnehmer mußte eingeschränkt werden* suggests that the number had become excessive and had to be reduced. Similarly, *Ich muß meine Ausgaben beschränken* and *Die Ausgaben mußten eingeschränkt werden. Jmd. wurde in seiner Handlungsfreiheit/seinen Rechten/seiner Macht eingeschränkt* implies a reduction on what existed previously, as does *Sie müssen Ihr Rauchen stark einschränken.* The effect may be the same as with *beschränken*, but the perspective is different.

iv. Sich einschränken is applied to people and means 'to live [more] economically, to tighten one's belt'. *Die Familie mußte sich einschränken, weil das Einkommen des Vaters erheblich gesunken war.*

v. Alternatives. *Begrenzen* and *eingrenzen* mean 'to form the border of'. *Eine Hecke begrenzt das Grundstück* or *grenzt das Grundstück ein.* **Begrenzen** is also a syn. of *beschränken. Man hat die Redezeit begrenzt. In der Stadt ist die Geschwindigkeit auf fünfzig Stundenkilometer begrenzt. Die Maßnahmen hatten eine begrenzte Wirkung.* **Etw. auf etw. eingrenzen** expresses the same meaning as *begrenzen*, but is confined to the intellectual sphere, e.g. to limiting discussion etc. to, or concentrating it on, certain points. *Man grenzte die Diskussion auf die wichtigsten Fragen ein.*

2. [Un]limited.

i. Beschränkt can mean 'limited' in a general way without any implications. *Dieses Wort/Diese Vogelart ist auf den Norden des Landes beschränkt. Die Zahl der Studienplätze ist beschränkt.* Applied to people, *beschränkt* means 'of limited intelligence'. *Der Angeklagte ist offensichtlich beschränkt und nicht imstande, das Verwerfliche seiner Tat einzusehen.* In reference to views and outlook, it means 'narrow', *Sie haben beschränkte Ansichten/einen beschränkten Horizont*, and to economic circumstances, 'poor' or 'straightened', *Die Familie lebte in beschränkten Verhältnissen.*

ii. Unbeschränkt means 'not subject to any limitation', *unbeschränkte Kommando-gewalt*, and **uneingeschränkt** means 'not reduced or restricted in any way', *uneingeschränkte Macht.* In most cases they amount to the same thing. (*Eingeschränktes Lob* is, however, 'qualified praise', and *uneingeschränktes Lob* 'unqualified or unreserved praise'. Hence *Diesem Plan stimme ich uneingeschränkt zu.*)

line *n.* Three senses. **Die Linie** denotes a line carefully made on a surface. *Eine gerade/krumme/gestrichelte Linie. Man zieht eine Linie mit dem Lineal. Ein Schreibheft mit*

Linien. It is also used for a line in geometry, drawing, and in abstract senses. *Ziehen Sie eine gerade Linie! Parallele Linien. Denken Sie sich eine gerade Linie, die die beiden Punkte verbindet!* **Der Strich** is a line drawn by hand, sometimes with, but mostly without, a ruler. *Er zog einen Strich unter der Rechenaufgabe.* Also *unter die Rechenaufgabe.* **Die Zeile** is a written or printed line. *Die erste Zeile des Gedichts. In der vierten Zeile von unten. Sie haben beim Lesen eine Zeile ausgelassen. Wir gingen den Text Zeile für Zeile durch. Drop me a line!* can therefore only be *Schreib' mir ein paar Zeilen!*

listen [to] *v.* Some uses of **hear** *v.*

1. Listen [to] means 'to give one's attention to s.o. speaking, what is said, a sound of some kind, etc.' It is used without *to. They will be sure to listen, if they find you are a good speaker. Everyone listened carefully while she explained the procedure. To* is required when a n. or clause follows. *Listen to him/to what he has to say!* The main equivalents *zuhören* and *anhören* differ syntactically. Whereas **listen** presupposes the intention to hear, **hear** does not, except in special cases. *Hören* has the idea of intention more often than *hear* and may translate or be translated as **listen to**.
i. Zuhören can be used without a dat. *Sie hörte zu und sagte nichts.* What is heard is not stated but understood from the context, as is the case with *listen* in *They listened [attentively].* An adv. or phr. may state how the person listened. *Alle hörten aufmerksam zu, während sie die Arbeitsweise erklärte. Zuhören* implies that the sound is clearly audible and that, unless otherwise stated, the subj. follows with understanding. *Sie kann gut zuhören* implies being able to listen patiently to others or their problems etc.

> *Er beteiligte sich nicht an der Diskussion und hörte nur zu.*
> *Sie hörte ruhig/schweigend/staunend/höflich/geduldig/mit Vergnügen/mit Interesse/nur mit halbem*
> *Ohr zu.*   *Hör' gefälligst zu, wenn dein Vater mit dir spricht!*
> *Er kann nie richtig zuhören, wenn man ihm etw. erklärt.*
> *Sie werden bestimmt zuhören, wenn sie finden, daß du ein guter Redner bist.*

ii. Zuhören can take a dat., normally a n. or pronoun denoting a person, and means 'to listen to'. The dat. is often omitted if the meaning is clear without it. *Hört [gut] zu!* or *Hört mir [gut] zu!*

> *Als der Wortführer der Arbeiter ihr Anliegen vorbrachte, hörte ihm der Chef wohlwollend zu.*
> *Ein zahlreiches Publikum hörte den Rednern aufmerksam zu.*
> *Ihr müßt dem Lehrer gut zuhören, wenn er euch etw. erklärt.*

The dat. of a non-personal n. is used only if the reference to a person is clear. *Im Abteil waren zwei andere, die sich unterhielten und mir, nachdem sie erfahren hatten, woher ich kam, Fragen stellten. Ich habe auf ihre Fragen geantwortet, aber meistens habe ich nur ihrem Gespräch zugehört.* Implied . . . *ihnen zugehört. Zuhören* is not used with music except by implication or when the reference is really to people. *Sie spielte das [Musik]stück vor, und wir hörten alle zu.* In *Wir hörten dem Orchester beim Proben zu,* the players are meant. *Auf seinem täglichen Spaziergang kommt er an einem Haus vorbei, in dem eine Sängerin übt. Oft bleibt er stehen und hört einem Lied zu.* Here the singer is meant. The usual v. for listening to music is *sich anhören.* Cf. iii. *Er hört sich ein Lied an.* If the reader comes across examples in which *zuhören* is used with music, the use is metaphorical and is best not imitated by non-native speakers. *Zuhören* occurs with sounds of nature, but they are really personified. *Ich hörte dem Vogelgezwitscher/dem Meeresrauschen/dem Donner zu.*
iii. Anhören needs an obj. which can be personal or non-personal, and is thus like **listen to**. It implies attentiveness, is not restricted in its range of application, and is the normal equivalent of **listen to** with a non-personal obj. It is also often found with a refl. dat. **Sich anhören** means, in strict use, 'to listen to sth. with the aim

of forming an opinion or judgement', *Wir wollen uns mal anhören, was er zu sagen hat,* but it is often heard in the sense 'to listen to' in all kinds of contexts without any special implication.

Etwa hundert Leute haben ihn angehört.
Hast du dir den Sänger/das Lied/die Schallplatte angehört?
Ich habe [mir] den Bericht/die Rede/den Vortrag/die Oper angehört.
Heute abend höre ich [mir] im Radio ein Konzert und ein Hörspiel an.
Seine Reden werden immer von Hunderten von Zuhörern angehört.
Nachdem er sich die Kritik angehört hatte, sagte er, er würde sich später dazu äußern.

[*Sich*] *anhören* occurs with people's ideas, troubles, complaints, etc. as obj. and often suggests patience and goodwill on the part of the listener.

Der Chef hörte die Beschwerden der Arbeiter an und versprach Abhilfe.
Ich habe mir alle Vorschläge/alle Argumente angehört.
Ich hörte mir die Pläne meines Freundes geduldig an.
Ich mußte mir seine Klage zum dritten Mal anhören.

iv. With **mit**, **anhören** means 'to listen to involuntarily'. *Das Gespräch am Nachbartisch mußte ich mit anhören. Den Zank und Streit habe ich mit angehört.* With **können** and *nicht mehr*, *mit anhören* means 'not to be able to bear listening to sth. any longer'. *Die Streitereien kann ich nicht mehr mit anhören.*

v. Listen to and **hear** are interchangeable when it is a question of whether someone listened to a piece of music, talk, programme, etc. or not. *Did you hear/listen to the lecture by Doris Lessing [on the radio] last night?* When it is not a question of having heard something or not, only **listen** is possible. *I always listen to the science show.* **Hören** and [**sich**] **anhören** occur in both cases. *She was listening to a symphony when I arrived* can be *Sie hörte gerade eine Symphonie, als ich ankam,* or *Sie hörte sich gerade eine Symphonie an.* In general statements about what someone listens to, *hören* is used. *Ich höre gern/oft Jazz/klassische Musik/Wagner/Volkslieder/Bundestagsdebatten. Sie scheint den ganzen Tag nichts zu tun als Musik zu hören. Gestern abend habe ich eine Oper gehört* or [*mir*] *angehört. Hören* is the usual v. in *Man hört Radio/Rundfunk* and *Ich habe gerade die Nachrichten [im Radio] gehört.* In the future, however, [*sich*] *anhören* is normal. *Ich werde mir heute abend die Parlamentsdebatte/die Oper/die Schallplatte anhören.*

vi. Hinhören, which means 'to direct one's (auditory) attention in a particular direction but not towards the speaker', is used alone without an obj. or prep. It occurs most frequently in two situations: *a.* When someone makes an effort to hear something which may not be meant for him or her, or which is not very clear. (*Zuhören* implies that the sound is clearly audible.) *Hinhören* is often used with *genau*, closely. *Wenn man genau hinhört* is a fixed expression. *b.* When someone pays or does not pay attention to what is being said or announced. Common in speech is *Ich habe gar nicht hingehört, was er sagte.* (More formal is *Ich habe dem nicht zugehört, was er sagte.*) Cf. *herhören* under 3. iii.

In etwa zehn Meter Entfernung begann jmd. leise zu sprechen. Ich hörte hin, verstand aber doch nichts.
Wenn er etw. Wichtiges erklärt, lohnt es sich, genau hinzuhören. Also . . . zuzuhören.
Etw. wurde [durch die Lautsprecher] durchgesagt, aber ich hörte gar nicht hin.
Er hat nicht richtig/nur mit halbem Ohr/kaum hingehört.

2. Vs. expressing special senses of **listen**.

i. Listen to or **hear** what s.o. has to say for himself/herself, his/her explanation, etc. *You must listen to the other side before passing judgement . Won't you hear my side of the story? I've heard/listened to both sides.* With people and expressions like *the other side of the case* as obj., **anhören** means 'to give a hearing to' and is interchangeable with **hören**, as is **listen to** with **hear**. Both *hören* and *anhören* are also applied to witnesses or people appearing before an investigating commission/committee.

Man muß zu diesem Problem beide Parteien hören/anhören.
Sie dürfen ihn nicht verurteilen, ohne ihn angehört/gehört zu haben.
Das Gericht wird die neuen Zeugen morgen hören/anhören.   *Sie müssen mich anhören.*
Die Kommission hörte mehrere Sachverständige und Vertreter aller Interessenverbände an.

ii. Horchen means 'to strain one's ears or listen hard to catch an expected or possible sound'. It can be used alone and is the only v. meaning 'listen' followed by an *ob*-clause. With *ob*, it means 'to listen [and see] whether sth. is happening'. *Kannst du mal horchen, ob das Kind schon wach ist?* When *hinhören* and *horchen* are both possible, *horchen* suggests greater concentration. *Horchen* involves listening hard, but it does not necessarily suggest that something is heard, whereas *hören*, *zuhören*, and *hinhören* imply that there is something to hear. *Horchen* is now not used as an imp. in reference to people. With *auf*, it means 'to listen intently in order to hear or discover sth.' *Alle horchten auf seine Worte. Horchen* also means 'to eavesdrop'. *Er horchte an der Tür, um das Geheimnis zu entdecken.*

Er horchte, ob der vom Blitz getroffene Mann noch atmete.
Wir horchten, ob sich Schritte näherten.
Sie horchte gespannt auf die Ansage im Radio.
Ständig horcht er auf Fehler, wenn er Klaviersonaten hört .

iii. Lauschen is 'to listen with rapt attention and almost reverence', but it can also mean 'to eavesdrop', in which case it implies greater secrecy than *horchen*.

Die Zuhörer lauschten ergriffen der Stimme der Sängerin.   *Er lauschte ihren Worten.*
Wenn du das schon weißt, mußt du gelauscht haben.

iv. Listen for is **aufpassen** or **achten**. *Listen for the phone while I'm in the garden!* could be either *Paß auf das Telefon auf!* or *Achte auf das Telefon!* or *Achte darauf/Paß auf, ob das Telefon klingelt!* Cf. [TAKE] CARE.

3. The imp.: The imp. **Listen!** introduces a request for attention, as in *Listen! Isn't that someone knocking?* and *Listen! I've got an idea.* It also occurs in a protest or expostulation. *[Now] listen! That's going too far.*

i. The imp. of **zuhören** *Hör' [mal] zu!* calls on someone to pay attention usually to what is being or is about to be said. While *Hören Sie mir zu!* means 'Listen to me!', *Hören Sie mich an!* means 'Give me a hearing!' or 'Hear my side!' The imp. of **[sich] anhören** also translates *listen* with a thg. as obj. *Hör' [dir] bloß das Geschrei an! Hört [euch] die Anweisungen genau an!*

ii. The imp. of **hören** is used like **Listen!** in three situations: *a.* When one person wishes another to be alert to hear a sound. *Hör' mal! Da kommt jmd. Hör' mal! Es klopft. b.* When one person wishes to gain another's attention. *Hör' mal! Ich wollte dir noch was sagen. c.* When someone wants to protest either mildly or strongly. *Hör' mal, du mußt etwas sorgfältiger mit dem Buch umgehen. Na, hören Sie mal, wie können Sie so etw. behaupten? Das ist alles gelogen, die reinste Verleumdung.*

iii. Herhören always means 'to listen to the speaker'. It is common only in the imp. *Hört alle her!* or as an infin. used as a imp. *Alle[s] mal herhören!* In a statement *zuhören* is used. *Ich fing an zu reden, aber niemand hörte zu.*

4. Listen [to] means 'to give heed to, to allow oneself to be persuaded by s.o. or what is said'. *He won't listen to advice/reason/anyone who tries to help him. Don't listen to him!—he knows nothing about the matter.* **Hören auf**, 'to give heed to someone or what is said', expresses this sense. *Auf* cannot be omitted as *to* can be in E. In translating *I gave him some advice, but he didn't listen, auf* could appear either as *Er hörte nicht darauf* or *Er hört nicht auf das, was ich sagte*, or *Er hörte nicht auf meinen Rat.*

Sie hatte ihn gewarnt, aber er hörte nicht auf sie/auf ihre Warnungen.
Auf meine wohlgemeinten Ratschläge wollten sie nicht hören.

literal[ly] *adj., adv.*

1. In reference to a translation, transcript, or copy, **literal** means 'representing the actual words of the original' or 'reproduced word for word'. **Wörtlich** in its basic sense means 'corresponding exactly to the original' and is often translated by the more usual E. expression *word for word. Ein wörtliche Übersetzung. Das hat er wörtlich gesagt.* An alternative in some cases is **wortgetreu**, faithful to the original. *Eine wortgetreue Übersetzung. Sie hat alle Äußerungen wortgetreu protokolliert.*

> *Das Ergebnis wirkt natürlicher, wenn man nicht wörtlich aus dem Deutschen ins Englische übersetzt, sondern sinngemäß.   Würden Sie die Anweisungen bitte wörtlich wiederholen?*
>
> *Diese Formulierungen finden sich wörtlich in der vom Verfasser benutzten, aber nicht genannten Quelle.*

2. Literal denotes the primary, customary, or obvious sense of a word, or the sense expressed by the actual wording of a passage as distinct from any metaphorical or suggested meaning. *Should we take this remark literally?* **Wörtlich** also expresses this sense and is often found with *nehmen*. A syn. in reference to words is **eigentlich**. *Die eigentliche Bedeutung eines Wortes,* the literal, main, original meaning.

> *Du darfst nicht alles so wörtlich nehmen.   Das darfst du nicht wörtlich nehmen.*
> *Er hatte den ironisch gemeinten Auftrag wörtlich genommen.*
> *Um einen Text richtig zu interpretieren, muß man ihn nicht nur wörtlich nehmen, sondern zwischen den Zeilen lesen.   Sie waren reaktionär im wörtlichen Sinn.*

3. Wortwörtlich is an intensification of *wörtlich* in senses 1 and 2. It means 'exactly identical in the words used', *die wortwörtliche Übereinstimmung beider Aussagen,* or 'exactly what the primary meaning of the word says', *Sie war ihm in den Schoß gefallen—wortwörtlich sogar. Wortwörtlich übersetzen* is also used.

> *Sein Gedächtnis ist so phänomenal, daß er eine ganze Nachrichtensendung anschließend wortwörtlich wiedergeben kann.   So wortwörtlich war das doch nicht gemeint.*

4. Literally states that the following word or words is or are free from metaphor, exaggeration, or inaccuracy and is or are correct or true in its or their literal sense. *At the last moment, literally overnight, they changed their minds.* The equivalents are both adjs. and advs. The adj. **literal** is now rare in this sense.

i. Buchstäblich is the main equivalent. *Er schlotterte buchstäblich vor Angst.*

> *Die buchstäbliche Vernichtung eines ganzes Volkes ist kaum vorstellbar.*
> *Buchstäblich in letzter Sekunde konnte das Kind vor dem Ertrinken gerettet werden.*
> *Im letzten Augenblick, buchstäblich über Nacht, fielen sie um.*

ii. Förmlich means 'real' or 'true'. Both as an adj. and adv., it is close to **literal[ly]**.

> *Die Schülerin hatte eine solche Angst vor dem Lehrer, daß sie förmlich zu zittern anfing, wenn er sie nur ansah.   Hier herrscht ein förmliches Chaos.*

5. Literal is applied to people who understand words in a plain and simple way or who are apt to take literally what is spoken fig. or with humorous exaggeration. **Am Buchstaben kleben** is pejorative, suggesting that someone sticks unduly to the lit. sense. *Wer am Buchstaben klebt, wird den Humor dieser Verse nicht erkennen.* More general words are **nüchtern** and **prosaisch**, both of which mean 'unimaginative', 'down-to-earth' in certain contexts. *Er ist zu nüchtern veranlagt und wird den Humor nicht verstehen. Du siehst alles viel zu prosaisch—das war nicht so gemeint.*

live *v.* A few senses.

1. Wohnen means 'to have one's place of residence in a particular place'. It is used in giving an address and in stating what sort of dwelling someone lives in. *Ich wohne Burgstr. 17. Wir wohnen in einem Zweifamilienhaus am Stadtrand. Meine Schwester* *wohnt in einer kleinen Zweizimmerwohnung, die 1 200 Mark im Monat kostet.* It is also used when saying that someone lives in a larger area, such as a town, country, or a particular part. *Sie wohnt in Kassel/in einer vornehmen Gegend/auf dem Lande. Er wohnt nicht gern in der Großstadt.* Wohnen is also applied to temporary accommodation when *to stay* is usual in E. *In welchem Hotel wohnen Sie? Ich wohne für drei Tage bei Freunden.*

2. The basic sense of **leben** is 'to be alive'.

i. It is therefore used for asking or saying when someone lived or asking whether someone is alive.

> *Wann lebte Schiller? Er lebte von 1759 bis 1805.*   *Ich kann ohne dich nicht leben.*
> *Meine Urgroßeltern leben noch. Or ... sind noch am Leben.* Thus *Lebt sie noch? Ist sie noch am Leben?*
> *Alle Mitglieder der Expedition kehrten lebend zurück.*   *Wir leben im zwanzigsten Jahrhundert.*

ii. The obj. can be *das Leben* or a period of time. *Der Wunsch, sein eigenes Leben zu leben, beseelte ihn.*

> *Sie lebten dort ein glückliches/ruhiges/freies Leben.*   *Er hatte noch viele Jahre zu leben.*

iii. Leben refers to the way people live. *Sie lebten gut/ruhig/bequem/in Freiheit/im Wohlstand. Er lebte unter einem falschen Namen. Hier läßt es sich gut leben.* The way someone lives can also be expressed by *Leben führen. Jmd. führt ein einfaches/ friedliches Leben,* leads a simple/peaceful life.

iv. Leben means 'to live on or from' and refers to the way people earn their living and to the food they eat.

> *Die Gefangenen lebten von Brot und Wasser/von Reis.*   *Er lebt von einer kleinen Rente.*
> *Er lebt als freier Schriftsteller in Wien/von der Schriftstellerei.*
> *Von einem so kleinen Gehalt kann er nicht leben.*   *Sie haben kaum zu leben.*

v. Leben means 'to have one's dwelling somewhere', but it states not a precise location but a general area. There is therefore some overlapping with *wohnen. Sie leben/wohnen auf dem Lande/an der Küste. Ich lebe/wohne [nicht] gern in der Großstadt.*

vi. Only **leben** is used for animals. *Schafe leben in Herden.*

> *Schnabeltiere leben nur in Australien.*   *Diese Tiere leben im Wasser.*

vii. Leben + the dat. or *für* means 'to live for, to devote one's life to'.

> *Der Musiker lebt nur seiner Kunst.*   *Er lebt für seine Familie/für die Wissenschaft.*

viii. Leben is also used for something which lives on in the memory. *Homers Ruhm wird ewig leben.*

lively, vivid *adjs.*

1. In the sense 'full of life, spirit, movement, and vitality', **lebhaft** is the usual equivalent. It is applied to people, their appearance, and their activities.

> *Die Kinder sind heute sehr lebhaft.*   *Sie spielten/sprachen sehr lebhaft.*
> *Sie ist ein lebhafter Mensch.*   *Sie hat eine lebhafte Natur/lebhafte Augen.*

Other uses. *Die Diskussion war sehr lebhaft. Viele Menschen haben eine lebhafte Phantasie. Jmd. zeigt ein lebhaftes Interesse für ein Thema* etc. or *erzählt/berichtet lebhaft* or *schildert etw. lebhaft. Es besteht eine lebhafte Nachfrage nach Kuhlschränken. Das habe ich noch lebhaft in Erinnerung. Ein lebhaftes Gefühl,* strong and clear. *Ein lebhaftes Rot,* a bright or vivid red. *Der Verkehr war sehr lebhaft,* busy.

> *Sie erhoben lebhaften Widerspruch.*   *Das hat er lebhaft bedauert.*
> *Der Plan fand lebhafte Zustimmung/Ablehnung.*

2. The basic sense of **lebendig** is 'alive' in contrast to *tot. Die Säugetiere bringen lebendige Junge zur Welt. Der Verbrecher wird lebendig oder tot gesucht* or *soll lebendig oder tot eingeliefert werden.*

> *Nach den wochenlangen Anstrengungen waren sie mehr tot als lebendig.*

Lebendig is applied to intangibles. *Eine lebendige Tradition, ein lebendiger Glaube.* It is used in speech as a syn. of *lebhaft*. *Sie diskutierten lebendig. Der Erzähler fesselt uns durch seine lebendige Darstellung.* After *sein* it always needs *sehr* to avoid a clash with the meaning 'alive'. *Die Kinder sind heute sehr lebendig.*

3. Munter combines the ideas of lively and cheerful, but is now slightly old-fashioned. *Ein munteres Kind. Ein munteres Spiel. Ihre munteren Augen.* It is still used in reference to health, often combined with *gesund*. *Er ist wieder gesund und munter*, fit and well.

loan *n.* The general term for money lent is **das Darlehen**. It is used for a loan from one person to another and from a bank to an individual or to a firm. **Die Anleihe** is applied to loans raised by a governmental body of some kind. It could be a loan by a national or state government or a local authority and takes the form of *Wertpapiere*, 'bonds or securities', issued at a fixed rate of interest. In Germany, such loans are called *Bundesanleihen*, 'federal government bonds' (also *Bundesobligationen*), and there are numerous *DM-Auslandsanleihen*. A company can also raise *eine Anleihe* by issuing *Wertpapiere* which are similar to debentures. If a firm gets a loan from a bank, this is called *ein Darlehen*.

> *Die reiche Tante hat ihrem Neffen ein zinsloses Darlehen gegeben.*
> *Sie haben ihre Ersparnisse in Bundesanleihen angelegt.*
> *Er hat ein Darlehen von 3 000 Mark bei der Bank bekommen/aufgenommen.*

Could you give me a loan of sth.? is translated as *could you lend me sth.?*, and *Could I have a loan of sth.?* as *could I borrow sth.?* For both vs. cf. LEND.

lock, close, shut *vs.*

1. Lock.

i. The commonest equivalent is **abschließen**. **Zuschließen** has the same meaning, but it occurs less frequently. *Die Tür, das Fenster, das Zimmer, das Haus, das Auto, der Tresor, der Schrank, der Koffer, der Kasten*, etc. can be the obj. of *abschließen*.

> *Vergiß nicht, den Wagen abzuschließen, wenn du ihn abstellst/parkst!*
> *Ich hatte meinen Schlüssel vergessen. Deshalb fand ich, da niemand zu Hause war, die Tür abgeschlossen und kam nicht hinein.*   *Das Fahrrad stand abgeschlossen an der Hauswand.*
> *Sie hatte die Geldkassette abgeschlossen, den Schlüssel jedoch verlegt, so daß das Geld unerreichbar war.*
> *Man sollte nachts immer die Haustür abschließen.*
> *Ich habe die Haustür zugeschlossen, bevor ich weggegangen bin.*

ii. Schließen means 'to lock' only when it refers to locks and keys. In a sent. like *Er trat ins Zimmer und schloß die Tür hinter sich*, *schloß* would thus be understood in its normal current sense of 'shut'.

> *Er hängte das Vorhängeschloß in die Krampe ein und schloß es.*
> *Ich habe den Schlüssel vor ein paar Tagen leicht verbogen, und seitdem schließt er schlecht.*
> *Das Schloß schließt nicht richtig.*   *Du mußt zweimal schließen* (double-lock the door).

The only exception is the use with *in* in sents. like *Warum schließt er sich in sein Zimmer?* or *Man schloß den Gefangenen in eine Zelle* or *Sie schloß das Geld in den Schreibtisch*, but while *schließen* is possible in such sents., many speakers would probably use **einschließen**, which means 'to lock in'. *Er schloß sich/jmdn. in das Zimmer ein.*

> *Das Kind bekam in dem neuen Zimmer eine Schublade, in die es seine Kostbarkeiten einschließen konnte.*
> *Die Wärter haben die Häftlinge in ihre Zellen eingeschlossen.*

iii. Verschließen also means 'to lock' and stresses the idea of making something inaccessible. However, it is now less common than *abschließen*, and some people may find it slightly old-fashioned. It also means 'to lock [away] in' in a context such as *Er verschloß seine Wertsachen im Schreibtisch/in einem Tresor* (dat. because they are already in it) or *Empfindlich gegen Licht und Lärm, verschloß sich Proust in seiner Wohnung,* but in such contexts, **einschließen** is now more usual. While the past parts. **abgeschlossen** and **verschlossen** are frequently interchangeable, only *verschlossen* occurs in certain fixed expressions. *Die Verhandlungen fanden hinter verschlossenen Türen statt* or *Als Freunde von mir für das Rote Kreuz sammelten, kamen sie vor verschlossene Türen—niemand gab ihnen etw.*

> *Wir haben den Schrank/die Schublade/das Haus verschlossen.*
> *Die Tür war mit einem Vorhängeschloß verschlossen.*
> *Die Polizei mußte die abgeschlossene/verschlossene Tür aufbrechen.*

2. Fig. uses of *verschließen*.

i. **Verschließen** means 'to hide feelings, thoughts, etc.', an idea which is occasionally expressed in E. as *to lock a secret/one's love,* etc. *in one's breast.*

> *Sie verschloß ihre Liebe/Gedanken/Gefühle/Geheimnisse in ihrem Herzen/Inneren/in sich.*
> *Er verschloß seinen Kummer vor uns.*

ii. **Sich verschließen** implies hiding one's thoughts, feelings, etc. or being unwilling to communicate with others. *Er verschloß sich sogar seinen Freunden.*

> *Nachdem sie gemerkt hatte, daß er sie spöttisch behandelte, verschloß sie sich [vor] ihm ganz und gar.*

iii. **Sich verschließen** + dat. also means 'not to be accessible to' or 'to close one's mind to arguments, suggestions, etc.' *Solchen Gründen kann ich mich schwer verschließen.*

> *Sie verschloß sich unseren Argumenten/Vorschlägen/Wünschen.*
> *Er verschloß sich seiner eigenen besseren Einsicht.*

3. Shut or **close**.

i. Both **zumachen** and **schließen** mean 'to shut or close', the only difference being that *schließen* is slightly more formal in tone. *Zumachen* and *schließen* are used with objs. like *die Augen, der Mund, die Tür, das Fenster, der Koffer, der Schrank, die Schublade, der Deckel, der Vorhang, die Klappe,* etc. They are also intr.: *Wann machen die Geschäfte zu?* or *Wann schließen die Geschäfte?* In relation to shops, offices, exhibitions, etc. *schließen* is probably more usual. Only the past part. of *schließen* is used after *sein* or attributively: *Das Fenster war geschlossen* and *Sie lag mit geschlossenen Augen da. Das geschlossene Ventil.* Instead of *geschlossen* after *sein,* **zu** is common. *Die Tür ist schon zu.* It also occurs in commands, *Tür zu, es zieht!,* and in the spoken language with *haben, Er hat die Fenster immer zu. Die Läden haben sonntags zu.* (In the substandard language there also exists the form *eine zune Tür.*)

> *Das Museum ist dienstags geschlossen. Also . . . ist dienstags zu. Also Das Geschäft hat nachmittags zu.*
> *Er schließt seinen Laden über Mittag.*   *Die Gaststätte schließt um 23 Uhr.*

ii. Only **schließen** is combined with words stating how something closes. *Die Türen des Zuges schließen automatisch/selbsttätig/von selbst. Der Deckel/Die Tür/Das Fenster schließt nicht richtig.*

iii. With flowers and wounds, **sich schließen** is necessary. *Die Blüten schließen sich immer am Abend.*

> *Die Wunde hat sich noch nicht ganz geschlossen.*

4. Schließen also translates *to close* when this means 'to bring or come to an end'. *Da sich so viele angemeldet haben, müssen wir die Teilnehmerliste vorzeitig schließen. Die Sitzung schloß um fünf Uhr. Die Teilnehmerliste ist geschlossen. Hiermit möchte ich für heute schließen.*

> *Da es sehr spät geworden war, schloß der Vorsitzende die Sitzung.*
> *Der Vorsitzende erklärte die Versammlung [für] geschlossen.*

5. Schließen is used trans. and intr. when a business, school, etc. has to close or be closed temporarily or when a factory, business, mine, railway line, etc. ceases operating altogether, i.e. it closes [down] or is closed [down]. A syn. in the latter sense is **stillegen**. The past part is *stillgelegt*.

> *Die Gesundheitsbehörde hat die Schule wegen der Grippeepidemie bis auf weiteres geschlossen.*
> *In Australien schließen alle Schulen von Mitte Dezember bis Ende Januar oder Anfang Februar.*
> *Die Fabrik mußte schließen, weil die Zulieferungen ausgeblieben waren.*
> *Wegen der steigenden Erdöleinfuhren sollen mehrere Kohlegruben stillgelegt werden.*
> *Man hat die Fabrik stillgelegt, weil sich die Produktion nicht mehr rentierte.*
> *Obwohl die Bahndirektion die Strecke stillegen wollte, gab sie nach, als die Bürger dagegen protestierten.*

6. Close *a road* is *eine Straße* **sperren**. *Die Straße ist wegen Bauarbeiten gesperrt.* Cf. BLOCK.

[no] longer, not any more, how much longer *advs.*

1. i. Nicht mehr and **nicht länger** state that something will not last or did not last longer than a particular time. When the sent. contains *als* + a period of time, either is possible. *Sie wollten nicht länger als zwei Tage bleiben. Ich habe nicht vor, mehr als zwei Tage zu bleiben. Sie will nicht länger/nicht mehr als eine Stunde warten.* With *als* + a point of time *nicht länger* is used. *Ich kann nicht länger als 10 Uhr bleiben.*

ii. Both are also possible when a phr. with *als* is only implied. In such cases *als jetzt* can be understood. *Ich kann nicht länger warten. Ich warte nicht mehr. Ich ertrage es nicht länger. Ich ertrage es nicht mehr. Ich mache nicht länger/nicht mehr mit.*

iii. There are cases in which no *als*-phr. can be understood. These are sents. which state that something stopped in the past and is no longer operative in the present. In E. **no longer** and **not any more** are used, but in G. only **nicht mehr** is possible. Thus *He no longer works at Karstadt* or *He doesn't work at Karstadt any more* both become *Er arbeitet nicht mehr bei Karstadt. Sie ist nicht mehr berufstätig. Er wohnt nicht mehr hier. Es besteht keine Hoffnung mehr. Nicht mehr* is also used in a sent. in the past. which states that one thing had ceased before another happened. *Als ich sie kennenlernte, war sie nicht mehr Studentin.* (In older G. *nicht länger* also expressed this meaning. *Das ist nicht länger üblich* still occurs occasionally, but *Das ist nicht mehr üblich* is now usual.)

2. How much longer is *wie lange noch*.

> *Wie lange müssen wir noch warten?*   *Wie lange wird die Sitzung noch andauern?*
> *Wie lange bist du noch hier?*   *Wie lange kann diese Partei noch an der Macht bleiben?*

look, look at *vs.*

1. The general sense of **look** is 'to direct one's sight in a certain direction'. It is used with a phr. of direction, *I looked out of the window/through the keyhole*, or without a prep., *He looked closely but noticed nothing unusual* and *If you look [closely], you'll see what I mean.*

i. Sehen is the equivalent of **look** when a phr. or word states the direction.

> *Ich sah durchs Schlüsselloch.*   *Er sah geradeaus, weder nach links noch rechts.*
> *Sie sah in meine Richtung, und ich lächelte ihr zu.*   *Ich sah aus dem Fenster [hinaus].*

ii. An informal v. meaning 'to look', which is extremely common in spoken G., is **kucken** or **gucken**, depending on the region. It is used instead of *sehen* when 'to direct one's sight' is meant. *Laß mich doch mal gucken!*

> *Sie guckte aus dem Fenster/durchs Schlüsselloch/in den Kochtopf/in den Spiegel.*

iii. The imp. *Look!* is thus either *Sieh' [mal]!* or *Kuck' mal!* or *Guck' mal!* or *Sieh'/Kuck'* *doch!* A following n. can be nom. or acc. *Sieh'/Guck' mal, der Vogel da!* or *Sieh'/Guck' mal den Vogel da!*

> *Sieh' [mal]! Ein Segelflugzeug!*   *Guck' mal, was ich hier habe!*
> *Guck' mal/Sieh' mal, wer hier ist!*   *Sieh'/Kuck' mal, was sie gemacht haben!*

iv. When **look** is used without the direction being stated, the equivalent is **hinsehen**. It means 'to direct one's sight in a particular direction, i.e. the one implied in the context'. *'Guckt mal!' sagte er, und wir sahen alle hin. Wenn man genau/scharf hinsieht,* or *bei genauem Hinsehen,* if you look closely.

> *Sie antwortete, ohne hinzusehen.*   *Sie kann nicht hinsehen, wenn jmd. blutet.*
> *Wenn man näher hinsieht, erkennt man, daß die ganze Masse voll kleiner Löcher ist.*
> *Ich sah genau hin, mir ist aber nichts Ungewöhnliches aufgefallen.*

v. Look *where you're going/treading!* is *Paß auf, wo du hintrittst! Can't you look what you're doing?* becomes *Kannst du nicht aufpassen, was du machst?* For **aufpassen** cf. [TAKE] CARE.

2. Look is used with **at** + a pers. or thg. *She looked at me/at the car.* An adv. or phr. indicating a feeling may follow. *She looked at him enviously/sadly/in astonishment.*

i. Ansehen needs an obj. which can be a person or thing. An adv. is frequently added. *Ansehen* implies looking for more than the duration of a glance, unless otherwise stated. *Jmdn. ansehen* often, though not always, means 'to look a pers. in the face or eyes'. *Er sah sie beim Sprechen nicht an.* However, if *Gesicht* is used, it is necessary to use *sehen. Er sah ihr ins Gesicht.* For *sehen* cf. 1. i.

> *Sieh' mich an!*   *Sieh' mich nicht so an!*
> *Er sah seinen Vater an und wußte sofort, daß er wütend war.*
> *Sie kennen sich so gut, daß der eine weiß, was der andere denkt, wenn er ihn ansieht.*
> *Man sieht jmdn. fest/scharf/staunend/aufmerksam/genau/verwundert/finster/böse/lächelnd/mit Interesse/nur flüchtig an.*   *Sie war sich dessen bewußt, daß alle sie ansahen.*

ii. Sich (dat.) **etw. ansehen** is the usual expression when a thing is the obj., but it can also be applied to people. It often implies looking at s.o./sth. to see what he/she/it is like or to form an opinion, and thus is sometimes closer to **have a look at**. It can also be used with an adv.

> *Im Urlaub haben wir uns die Sehenswürdigkeiten Roms angesehen.*
> *Ich muß mir das Auto ansehen, bevor ich es kaufe.*   *Sie sah sich das Bild interessiert an.*
> *Im Schaufenster ist ein Buch, das mich interessiert. Kann ich es mir mal ansehen?*
> *Wir haben uns den Film/die Ausstellung/das Haus/die Stadt/das Bild usw. angesehen.*
> *Wir müssen uns die Bewerber ansehen, bevor wir entscheiden, wer sich für die Stelle am besten eignet.*
> *Der Arzt sah sich den Patienten an/sah sich sein geschwollenes Bein an.*
> *Sieh' dir nur mal die Kaffeemaschine an! Sie funktioniert nicht mehr.*
> *Sieh' dir bloß/mal an, was du angerichtet hast! Or . . . was du angestellt hast!*

The refl. dat. is sometimes omitted in speech. This often happens when the obj. is a thing made to be looked at. *Welchen Film/Welches Schloß wollen wir heute ansehen?* It is best for non-native speakers to use the dat.

iii. Ankucken and **sich ankucken** (**angucken** and **sich angucken**) are colloquial syns. of *ansehen* and *sich ansehen*.

> *Warum kuckst du mich beim Sprechen nicht an?*
> *Ich kucke mir das Buch/den neuen Kollegen an.*   *Er hat mich erstaunt/lächelnd angekuckt.*
> *Sieh'/Kuck' dir den Wagen mal an!*   *Kuck' dir das Boot an!*

iv. Sehen auf or **gucken auf** must be used if **look at** means 'to glance at' or to 'look for a fairly short time'. The action can be intentional, *Sie hielt an, um auf die Landkarte zu sehen,* or unintentional, *Als ich zufällig auf die Benzinuhr guckte, sah ich, daß der Tank fast leer war.*

> *Ich sah/kuckte auf die Uhr und erschrak, als ich erkannte, wie spät es schon war.*
> *Er hielt den Vortrag, ohne auch nur einmal auf das Manuskript zu sehen.*

v. Usually with *mit* and *nicht können,* **ansehen** means 'not to be able to bear looking at any longer'. *Ich kann diese Unordnung nicht mehr mit ansehen* or *Ich kann es nicht mehr mit ansehen, wie du so schlecht behandelt wirst.*

vi. *Etw. ist schön usw. anzusehen,* is beautiful to look at, is a beautiful sight. Thus *Sie ist in diesem Kleid hübsch anzusehen. Die von dem Erdbeben verwüstete Stadt war schrecklich anzusehen.*

vii. *Man sieht ihm das schlechte Gewissen an* means that anyone can tell by looking at him that he has a bad conscience. This construction is also used with things. *Man sieht es den Wörterbüchern an, daß sie viel benutzt werden. Man sieht ihm sein Alter an* translates *He looks his age.*

viii. Ansehen means 'to look at (mentally) or regard in a certain light, from a certain point of view, or as sth.'

> *Man kann die Sache auch von einem anderen Standpunkt ansehen.*
> *Auch viele Experten sahen das gefälschte Bild als ein Originalwerk des Künstlers an.*
> *Sie sieht ihn als Dummkopf an, weil er sich nur über Autos unterhalten kann.*

3. Syns. of [*sich*] *ansehen.*

i. Betrachten is a more formal syn. of *sich ansehen* in the sense 'to look at sth./s.o.' *Betrachten* means 'to look at carefully and thoughtfully', sometimes to the exclusion of the world round about. The obj. can be people and things. It is often used when talking of works of art.

> *Sie stand am Fenster und betrachtete die Fußgänger, die am Haus vorbeigingen.*
> *Er betrachtete mich von oben bis unten/lange/mißtrauisch/nachdenklich/schweigend/mitleidig/neugierig.*
> *Sie betrachtete gedankenvoll die alten Photographien.*
> *Beim Betrachten des Bildes vergaß er seine Begleiterin.*

ii. Besichtigen means 'to look or see round, through, or over' or 'to inspect' a town, factory, museum, school, or things like castles and cathedrals that tourists visit, or houses etc. that one might buy or rent. It also means 'to inspect' or 'review' troops.

> *Die Familie besichtigt gerade die Wohnung, die sie wahrscheinlich mieten will.*
> *Heute wollen wir das Schloß, den Dom und die Gemäldegalerie besichtigen/uns ansehen.*
> *Zwei Klassen haben heute mit ihren Lehrern eine große Autofabrik besichtigt.*
> *Morgen kommt General Röder, um die Truppen zu besichtigen.* Also . . . *inspizieren.*

4. To *watch* or **look at** television is **fernsehen.** *Wir sehen jeden Abend fern.* Very colloquially it is *Fernsehen kucken. Wir haben bis ein Uhr Fernsehen gekuckt. I watched a television programme* is *Ich habe mir eine Fernsehsendung angesehen.*

5. When an indirect question introduced by *who, what, how,* or *whether* follows, *see,* which is frequently combined with **look,** means 'to use one's sight to find out'. *See what they're doing! Look and see how much they've done! Look [outside] and see whether they've already gone/how they're getting on! Go and see* has the same meaning. *Go and see what they're doing!* The equivalent is **nachsehen,** to look in order to find out or ascertain. It translates *see* and the combinations *I'll [look and] see* or *I'll go [outside] and see. Ich sehe draußen nach, ob sie schon weg sind. Sieh' mal nach, was sie machen/wie weit sie gekommen sind!* Colloquially, *gucken* alone is used if the sense is clear, although **nachgucken** is by no means unusual. *Ich sehe mal nach, wer an der Tür ist* could be *Ich kucke mal, wer an der Tür ist.* The prefix *nach* is sometimes omitted in casual speech from both vs.

> *Sieh' bitte nach, ob alle Fenster geschlossen sind/was die Kinder machen!*
> *A. Soll ich auch Milch holen? B. Ich weiß es nicht, aber ich sehe/kucke mal im Kühlschrank nach.* (I'll just see/go and see/look and see (if we need any).)
> *Ich sehe draußen nach, wie weit sie gekommen sind.*
> *Wir hatten Geräusche im Garten gehört. Ich habe nachgesehen/nachgekuckt, konnte aber nichts sehen.*
> (looked/went to see/went and saw what it was).

6. Other senses of *nachsehen.*

i. Nachsehen also means 'to look sth. up' in a dictionary, timetable, etc. It is trans. and intr. It is synonymous with **nachschlagen** which is also used with and without an obj.

Haben Sie schon in der Enzyklopädie nachgesehen?   *Ich sehe/schlage im Lexikon nach.*

Das Wort kenne ich nicht. Ich muß es im Wörterbuch nachsehen/nachschlagen.

Onkel Ulrich sieht im Fahrplan nach, wann der Zug fährt.

ii. Nachsehen also means 'to look through or over in order to check for faults or mistakes'.

Die Mutter sieht die Hausaufgaben der Kinder nach und entdeckt meistens ein paar Fehler.

Ich muß den Computer von einem Fachmann nachsehen lassen.

Ich ließ das Öl wechseln und den ganzen Wagen nachsehen und abschmieren.

7. Zusehen + dat. is 'to look on (while sth. happens) or watch (s.o. doing sth.)'.

Wir sahen aus sicherer Entfernung zu, als das Bauwerk gesprengt wurde.

Viele Leute haben dabei zugesehen, wie mehrere ziemlich große Bäume umgepflanzt wurden.

Die Großeltern sahen den Kindern beim Spielen zu.

Ich sehe anderen Leuten gern bei der Arbeit zu.   *Sollen wir ruhig zusehen, wie er sich ruiniert?*

8. Look = 'to have the appearance of being or have a certain look or appearance'. *They looked tired.*

i. Aussehen covers most uses of **look** in this sense. It is applied to a person's facial expression or to the whole appearance and to things. *Warum sieht er so müde aus?* **Dreinsehen** is an elevated syn. *Sie sah traurig drein.* Colloquially **kucken/gucken** is used. It implies that someone's face conveys a certain impression and is thus restricted in use. *Jmd. guckte freundlich/böse/finster/ verständnislos.* In *Er hat ganz schön dumm gekuckt, dumm* means 'uncomprehending'.

Die beiden Studenten sehen klug aus.   *In ihrem neuen Kostüm sieht sie sehr gut aus.*

Er sieht gesund/müde/traurig aus.   *Eine blendend aussehende Dame trat ins Büro ein.*

Die Wohnung sah sehr gepflegt aus.   *Die Lage sieht nicht rosig aus.*

Er sieht aus, als ob er gestern nacht nicht geschlafen hätte.

ii. Look like is **aussehen wie** if similarity is meant. *Der Stoff sieht wie Seide aus. Sie sieht genau aus wie ihre Mutter. Jmdm. ähnlich sehen* also expresses similarity. *Sie sieht ihrer Mutter sehr ähnlich.* (*Das sieht ihm ähnlich* means that an action fits someone's character, can be expected of him.) If **look like** means that something is likely to happen or has probably happened, **aussehen nach** is used. *Der Himmel sieht nach Schnee aus. Es sieht nach Verrat aus.* No. 10 *looks like winning* needs to be expressed with the impersonal **es sieht so aus, als ob**, to look as if. *Es sieht so aus, als ob Nr. 10 gewinnen wird.*

iii. An infin. is not possible after *aussehen.* She **looks** to be in good health can be *Sie scheint bei bester Gesundheit zu sein,* or the infin. can be left out, *Sie sieht sehr gesund aus.* Likewise *Er sah stärker aus als er in Wirklichkeit war,* looked [to be] stronger. If the infin. cannot be omitted, use **scheinen**. *Scheinen* must also be used to translate a dat. It looks to me: *Es scheint mir, als ob wir uns in einer Krise befinden.*

9. Mit jmdm./etw. gut/schlecht usw. aussehen, used impersonally, expresses the idea that the position is or looks good/bad for s.o./sth. *Es sieht schlimm mit jmdm./der Firma aus.* The same thought can be formulated with a subj. if the sense is unambiguous. Thus *Die Sache sieht gut/schlecht aus* is found as well as *Es sieht mit der Sache gut aus.*

Es sieht mit unseren Vorräten noch gut aus.   *Mit ihm sieht es schlimm aus.*

Mit seinen Aussichten sah es mißlich/gut aus.

10. Ausschau halten nach means 'to look out for'. *Er stand am Bahnsteig und hielt nach seiner Freundin Ausschau.*

11. Look = 'to face', as in *The windows look north/into the garden/on to the river*. This is **hinausgehen auf**, but *hinaus* is often omitted. *Die Fenster gehen auf den Garten/nach Norden/auf den Fluß [hinaus].*

12. In the southern part of Germany **schauen** is used in the same way as *sehen* is in the north. *Schauen* is used by speakers in the north who consider it more refined than *sehen*. *Er traut sich nicht, dir ins Gesicht zu schauen. Sie schaute durchs Schlüsselloch. Ich schaute auf die Uhr/aus dem Fenster.*

loose *adj*. Main uses.

1. i. One meaning of **loose** is 'not rigidly fastened or securely attached', 'likely to come apart from an attachment'. Both **lose** and **locker** express the concept that something is not firmly attached. Thus *Ein Nagel/Ein Brett/Ein Knopf/Eine Schraube/Ein Ziegelstein ist locker oder lose*. *Locker* is the everyday word, but may suggest a less serious degree of looseness than *lose*. *Der Türgriff ist locker* implies that it is not firm, while *Der Türgriff ist lose* suggests that it will come off in one's hand. **ii.** *A loose tooth* can be *ein lockerer Zahn*, but more commonly it is *ein wackliger Zahn*. The main meaning of **wackelig** is 'wobbly, rickety'. It is applied to a chair, table, furniture, etc.

2. Lose means 'not tight or tightly fitting'. *Der Knoten ist zu lose. Lose aufgestecktes Haar. Ein loses Oberteil über einem engen Rock.*

3. Locker and **lose** express the meaning of **loose** 'having relative fredom of movement as a result of being partly attached or fixed only at one end'. *Loose ribbons hanging from her hat. Die Bänder hingen lose vom Hut herunter. Ihr lockeres/locker fallendes Haar. Loses/lockeres Gestein. Das Ende hing lose herunter.*

4. A rope which is not taut can only be **locker**. *Ein lockeres Seil*. **Locker** is also applied to relaxed limbs. *Er hielt seine Gliedmaßen locker.*

5. Locker is used for things which are not dense or compact in structure. *Lockere Erde. Lockerer Schnee.*

6. Lose is applied to things which are not joined together, *lose Blätter*, and to goods which are sold as single items, i.e. not in packages, *lose Ware*.

7. Both **locker** and **lose** have the meaning of **loose** 'characterized by limited cohesion between the elements' and 'permitting a wide area of freedom and action'. *A loose federation. Ein loser/lockerer Verband. Ein loser/lockerer Zusammenschluß*. Also *eine lose/lockere Vereinbarung*. Both are also used for a loose logical connection. *Eine lockere/lose Verbindung/Beziehung.*

> *Zwischen den beiden Teilen besteht nur ein loser/lockerer Zusammenhang.*
> *Die Gedanken sind nur lose/locker miteinander verknüpft.*
> *Die Abschnitte/Teile (z.B eines Buches) sind nur lose miteinander verbunden.*

8. For **loose** meaning 'inexact', as in *loose reasoning* or *thinking*, **ungenau** or **oberflächlich** can be used. *Eine ungenaue Beweisführung. Oberflächliches Denken.*

9. Both **locker** and **lose** are used in reference to morality. *Jmd. hat lockere Sitten/führt ein lockeres Leben/ist ein lockerer/loser Vogel. Lose Späße/Reden* are 'impudent or cheeky'.

10. Another sense of **loose** is 'free from a state of confinement or restraint'. *A lion loose in the streets. He let two rats loose in the classroom*. **Los** is used in this sense as a prefix of *lassen* and *reißen*. **Loslassen** and **losreißen** mean 'to let or break loose'. *Er ließ zwei Ratten im Klassenzimmer los. Er ließ den Hund [auf jmdn.] los. Der Hund riß sich von der Leine los. Los* is not used after *sein* in this sense. *Zwei Häftlinge sind aus der*

Haft ausgebrochen und sind noch auf freiem Fuß is like *on the loose, at large*. An alternative is *frei. Diese Verbrecher laufen noch frei herum.* (*Wieder frei* and *wieder auf freiem Fuß* mean 'free through having been released'. *Er war in Haft, ist aber wieder frei/wieder auf freiem Fuß.*) With an appropriate v. **frei** can express the meaning that animals are loose somewhere. An alternative is **unkontrolliert.** *Die Schweine sind aus dem Stall ausgebrochen und rennen frei/unkontrolliert im Garten herum. Den Löwen, der zwei Stunden lang frei durch die Straßen gelaufen ist, hat man wieder eingefangen.*

low *adj.*

1. In one sense **low** means 'extending upward for a relatively short distance from the bottom or ground'. *A low wall. A low table/ceiling. Low hills.* Another sense is 'close to the ground or another level'. *Low cloud. The plane flew low over the town. A low bridge.* While these uses mean 'rising relatively little above sth.' **low** also means 'situated relatively below the normal level, surface, or base of measurement'. *He pulled his cap down low over his face. He made a low bow. Low ground. She was writing, with her head bent low over the paper.* The sun and the moon are said to be low [in the sky], and a dress or blouse is described as low [cut] when it leaves a woman's shoulders and the upper part of her chest bare; in both cases **low** implies being below the normal level.

i. In reference to concrete objects **niedrig** means 'not rising far above a point of reference'. The reference point can be the ground or another surface. *Eine niedrige Mauer. Ein niedriger Tisch/Stuhl. Ein niedriger Durchgang. Die Decke ist ziemlich niedrig. Niedrige Hügel/Sträucher. Wir müssen das Bild niedriger hängen. Eine niedrige Brücke.* *Niedrig* can be paraphrased as *not high.* **Tief** means 'going below a point of reference which is considered normal for the thg. referred to'. *Der Eingang ist niedrig, man muß sich tief bücken,* i.e. bend one's head and shoulders below what is normally expected. *Er zog die Mütze tief ins Gesicht* again implies below the usual level, as does *ein tief ausgeschnittenes Kleid. Ein Tiefschlag* is below the belt. (In G. *unterhalb der Gürtellinie.*) *Jmd. machte ein tiefe Verbeugung. Während sie schrieb, beugte sie sich tief über das Blatt. Das Tiefland* is 'low-lying land'. In relation to aircraft *tief* and *niedrig* are used with *fliegen.* If the ground is taken as the point of reference, *niedrig* is usual. If a certain height is seen as normal, *tief* is used as it implies going below this height. *Das Flugzeug fliegt heute sehr niedrig/flog tief über die Stadt.* Hence *der Tiefflug.* Both *tief* and *niedrig* are used in relation to clouds. *Die Wolken hängen tief. Eine niedrige Wolke verdeckte uns die Aussicht auf den Berg.* Both are possible in *Das Haus liegt niedriger/tiefer als die Straße.* The basis of comparison for *niedrig* is the bottom of the rise, for *tief* the top. *Sie wohnen eine Etage tiefer* is a fixed expression, as is *Die Sonne/Der Mond stand tief am Himmel.*

ii. In reference to water level **low** means 'having less than or being below the normal level'. *The water in the reservoir is very low.* A river is low when it is carrying very little water. Only **niedrig** is used in relation to water, as *tief* also means 'deep'. *Der Fluß/Das Wasser ist/steht niedrig. Der Wasserstand/Der Pegelstand des Reservoirs ist sehr niedrig. Das Niedrigwasser* is 'low water or low tide'.

2. With reference to things measured by a scale **low** means 'small in number or amount, near the bottom of the scale'.

i. In this sense both **niedrig** and **tief** are used, but there seem to be standard combinations. *Tiefe/Niedrige Temperaturen. Die Temperatur heute ist niedriger als gestern. Die tiefsten Temperaturen der vergangenen Nacht* (occasionally *niedrigsten*). *Niedriger Luftdruck,* but *ein Tiefdruckgebiet. Das Barometer steht tief* (occasionally *niedrig*). *Der Niedriggang* is 'low gear'. Only *niedrig* is used with *der Verbrauch,* consumption. *Das*

Auto hat einen niedrigen Benzinverbrauch. Niedrig is used for numbers. *Die Zahl der Interessenten war sehr niedrig. Ich habe niedrige Noten bekommen.* (The perspective in these examples may be that explained in 1. i, so that *niedrig* means 'not far above nought', and *tief* 'below normal'.)

ii. With *die Qualität* and *die Intelligenz* only **gering** is used. *Waren von geringer Qualität. Solche Fehler deuten auf geringe Intelligenz hin. Gering* is a formal syn. of *niedrig* often found in more learned language. *Geringe Widerstandsfähigkeit gegen Ansteckungen. Geringe Dichte. Der Wagen hat einen geringen Benzinverbrauch* is less common than . . . *einen niedrigen Benzinverbrauch.*

iii. For prices **niedrig** is usual, *Der Preis ist so niedrig wie möglich zu halten,* but *Tiefstpreise* and *Die Preise sind zu tief/niedrig veranschlagt* also occur. *Sie haben uns eine niedrige Summe angeboten. Die Löhne/Mieten sind niedrig. Niedrige Zinssätze.*

iv. *Ein tiefer Ton* is 'a low (musical) note', and *eine tiefe Stimme* is 'of low pitch'. In *He spoke in a low voice*, **low** means 'soft' and is **leise**. *Er sprach mit leiser Stimme.*

3. In relation to supplies, rations, etc. **low** means 'nearly exhausted'. *Our supplies are low* can be *Unsere Vorräte sind* **fast verbraucht/fast aufgebraucht** (for these vs. see USE 4) or **fast erschöpft** or **knapp.** *Our rations are running low: Unsere Rationen* **gehen zu Ende** or *werden knapp. We are running/getting low on funds/petrol: Unser Geld/Benzin geht zu Ende* or *Uns geht das Geld/Benzin bald aus.*

4. The sense 'morally low' is expressed by **niedrig**. *Jmd. handelt aus niedrigen Beweggründen/Motiven. Er hat eine niedrige Gesinnung.* **Tief**, however, is used with *sinken. Wer hätte gedacht, daß er so tief sinken würde, um seine Kollegen zu bestehlen.* More common than *niedrig* is **gemein**, mean, base. *Sie ist auf einen gemeinen Trick eines Gauners hereingefallen.*

5. Low means 'depressed' in *S.o. is low* or *in low spirits* and can be translated as *Jmd. war* **niedergeschlagen** or **in gedrückter Stimmung.** Cf. PRESS 9 and 10.

6. Low describes the position of a person or thing in a hierarchy or order of precedence, a sense expressed by **nieder. Niedrig** is also used if no confusion with meaning 4 is possible. *Ein niederer/niedriger Offiziersrang. Eine niedrige/niedere Instanz. Die niederen Klassen* is a fixed expression, as is *Er stammt aus den niedersten Kreisen. Niedere Organismen.* (Socially) high and low is *Hoch und Niedrig. Er verschonte niemand mit seiner Kritik, weder Hoch noch Niedrig.*

7. *I have a* **low** *opinion of s.o./of s.o.'s talent* etc. can be *Ich schätze jmdn./jmds. Talent/Fähigkeiten niedrig ein.* For *einschätzen* cf. ESTIMATE 4. *Ich denke niedrig von jmdm.* is occasionally found.

8. *To turn the heating down* **low** is *die Heizung* **herunterdrehen.**

m

make, get, have *vs.* Some senses of **cause** and **let** *vs.* Most of this article deals with the equivalents of some closely related E. constructions containing these words. (i) **Make** + obj. + infin. without *to. The sudden noise made me jump. They made me repeat the story.* For the equivalents cf. 1. *Can you make the fire burn?* Cf. 5. *John made us laugh.* Cf. 8. iii. (ii) **Get** + obj. + infin. with *to. I got Tom to give me the number.* Cf. 3. *I can't get the wheel to move.* Cf. 5. (iii) **Get** + obj. + past part. *I must get my hair cut/my shoes mended.* Cf. 2. (iv) **Have** + obj. + past part. *I've had the car seen to. I'll have the text translated.* Cf. 2. (v) **Have** + obj. + infin. without *to. I'll have the plumber replace the pipe.* Cf. 3.

The E. *vs.* express more than one meaning. **Make** means 'to cause', which can in some cases replace it. *My irritation made me act in a way I regretted later. Despair made him run away.* Cf. 1. *The book makes the reader think.* Cf. 8. i. *That made me tremble/laugh.* Cf. 8. iii. *The film made us want to set off for Kashmir at once. His behaviour made me want to hit him.* Cf. 8. iv. In another sense **make** is close to *order* or *compel* and *force. I'll make him rewrite the report. I'll make the firm pay.* Cf. 1. iii. *You've got to make him heed our advice.* Cf. 6 and 7. **Get** also means 'to cause', is mostly interchangeable with **make**, and is applied to people and things. *You'll never get him to understand/make him understand.* Cf. 7. *I can't get the car to start. Can you get the fire to burn/make the fire burn?* Cf. 5. **Get** is also close to *persuade. We finally got her to tell us what she had seen. We might be able to get him to support us. We eventually got them to pay the bill.* Cf. 6. **Get** also means 'to ensure that s.o. else carries out a task'. *I'll get the car repaired/get him to repair the car.* It expresses a request or a mild order in direct speech. *I'll get my secretary to make you a copy.* Cf. 2 and 3. **Have** means 'to see to it that s.o. else does sth.' and in constructions iv and v expresses the same meaning as **get** in constructions ii and iii. *I must have/get these shoes repaired. I'll have the secretary type the letter* or *I'll get her to type the letter.* Cf. 2 and 3. *Lassen* translates *make, get,* and *have* in many of the senses illustrated. (*Lassen* also means 'to let'.)

1. Make s.o. **do** sth.

i. The general sense of **lassen** is 'to cause sth. to happen'. With a non-personal subj. and a person as obj., it refers both to sudden instinctive reactions, *Die laute Explosion ließ mich aufschrecken* (or in more informal language *ließ mich in die Höhe fahren*) or *Das plötzliche Geräusch ließ mich zurückspringen*, and to considered decisions, *Das Scheitern der ersten Versuche ließ sie über ihre Arbeitsweise nachdenken.* A partial syn. is **veranlassen** (cf. CAUSE v.) which is stylistically higher than *lassen* and is used mostly when a considered decision or reaction is involved. It usually takes an infin. in this sense. *Das Scheitern der ersten Versuche veranlaßte sie, ihre Arbeitsweise zu ändern.*

Das ließ mich aufmerken/aufhorchen.   *Der Wein ließ ihn seine Sorgen vergessen.*
Die drohende Gefahr eines Krawalls ließ die Polizei eingreifen.
Diese seltsamen Geräusche im Garten ließen ihn zur Waffe greifen.
Meine Ärger ließ mich in einer Art und Weise handeln, die ich später bereute.
Die Identifizierung mit einer Mannschaft läßt die Fans auf die Anhänger der anderen Mannschaft einschlagen.   *Die starke Strömung ließ uns umkehren.*

Sie fing an zu weinen; diese unerwartete Reaktion veranlaßte ihn, über sein Verhalten nachzudenken.
Was hat sie veranlaßt, das Angebot abzulehnen?
Seine Verzweiflung darüber, jemals einen Arbeitsplatz zu finden, ließ ihn von zu Hause weglaufen.
Or . . . *veranlaßte ihn, von zu Hause wegzulaufen.*

ii. Lassen is used when both subj. and obj. are phenomena of nature and corresponds to **make** or **cause**.

Die anhaltenden starken Regenfälle ließen viele Flüsse über die Ufer treten.
Die Hitze ließ die Blätter welk werden.   *Die Dürre ließ viele neu gepflanzte Bäume eingehen.*

iii. With a person as subj. and obj., **lassen** means 'to make' as a syn. of *order*, i.e. it presupposes a command in direct speech which is reported by *lassen. Der Feldwebel ließ die Soldaten strammstehen. Der Lehrer ließ den Jungen den Satz hundertmal schreiben. Lassen* also reproduces a request in direct speech and translates **have** and **get** with a personal obj. (Cf. 3.) Whether it is taken to mean 'make' or 'get' depends very much on the context. *Sie ließ ihn Platz nehmen und den ganzen Vorgang in aller Ruhe erzählen* suggests a polite request in direct speech and would be translated as **got**. *Der Dompteur ließ den Hund durch den Reifen springen* would usually be understood as **made**. In *Am Strand läßt er den Hund einen Stock aus den Wellen fischen*, it could mean 'to make, get, or let'. **Veranlassen** with a person or something standing for a person as subj. lies between a request and an order. It means 'to see to it that an action is carried out' and is used with a government or a person with power of some kind as subj. and a n. denoting action as obj. or a *daß*-clause. It implies that one person has another carry out his bidding. It is vaguer than *befehlen*, 'to command', or *anordnen*, 'to direct' (for both cf. ORDER *v*.), or the everyday word *lassen*, 'to make or have someone do something'. *X veranlaßte die Verhaftung von Y* expresses the same meaning as *X ließ Y verhaften*, but suggests a more roundabout procedure and is stylistically higher. With a clause: *Veranlassen Sie bitte, daß der Bote mir den Brief ins Haus bringt!*, have him bring/get him to bring it. In other contexts it could be translated as **make**. *Ich werde veranlassen, daß die Firma die Kosten übernimmt*, make/have the firm pay. *Ich werde das Nötige/alles Weitere veranlassen* is a fixed expression meaning that someone will see to it that further steps are taken, or will arrange for what is necessary so that a certain result is brought about.

Der Zirkusdirektor ließ die Kunstreiterin die Travers immer wieder reiten, bis auch das Pferd vor Erschöpfung nicht mehr konnte.
Der Hauptmann Krusche ließ den Soldaten Schneider zehn Strafrunden in voller Montur laufen.
Ich werde eine Überprüfung der ganzen Angelegenheit veranlassen.
Ich werde veranlassen, daß die Kasse Ihnen Ihre Auslagen sofort erstattet.
Rußland veranlaßte, daß die revolutionären Polen, die aus Frankreich in ihre Heimat zurückkehren wollten, an der preußischen Grenze festgehalten wurden.

2. With the pres. act. infin. **lassen** translates **get** and **have** in constructions iii and iv, *I get/have sth. done*. The E. past part. must be turned into an infin. *Ich lasse den Text übersetzen/den Brief tippen*, get/have it translated/typed. *Ich lasse eine Kopie machen. Du mußt das Auto nachsehen lassen. Ich lasse es ihr ausrichten/mitteilen*, have this passed on to her, i.e. have her informed. A refl. dat. is added to indicate possession or to show for whose advantage the action is being carried out. *Ich lasse mir das Haar schneiden. Sie lassen sich ein Haus bauen. Ich lasse mir einen Kostenvoranschlag machen/geben*. The lit. transl. of the last sent. is *I am having a quote made*. Probably more common in E. is *I'll get s.o. to give me a quote*. The agent is, however, often omitted in G. if it is not important. *Laß dir helfen!* translates both *Get s.o. to help you!* and *Let me/him/her*, etc. *help you!*

Du willst dir nicht wirklich den ganzen Vorfall nochmal erzählen lassen.
Sie ließ sich bei dem Gastgeber entschuldigen.   *Wo kann man Schuhe reparieren lassen?*

'Das Schreiben ist ein Handwerk, das man lernen kann, wie jedes andere auch', dachte Georg. 'Das erste Mal muß man sich helfen lassen.'

3. Constructions ii and v., **get** s.o./sth. to do sth. and **have** s.o. do sth., require special care. *I got her to tell me the story* is normal in E., whereas in G. the agent, as already mentioned in 2, can be omitted. *Ich ließ mir die Geschichte erzählen.* Her can be stated, but not as an acc., the usual way being to express it by *von*, so that the transl. reads *Ich ließ mir die Geschichte von ihr erzählen.* Thus *Ich ließ mir von Tom die Nummer geben*, got Tom to give it to me. In the third person sing. and pl., *sich* is necessary. *The boys got the driver to give them their luggage* is *Die Jungen ließen sich ihr Gepäck vom Fahrer geben. Ich ließ ihn mir den Vorfall erzählen* is correct G., but *ließ* in this construction would normally be understood as 'let' or 'made'. The construction in which it means 'got' or 'had' is *Ich ließ mir den Vorfall von ihm erzählen.*

Der Richter ließ sich den Vorgang genauestens vom Zeugen berichten.
Ich lasse den Brief von der Sekretärin tippen.   Ich lasse das Rohr vom Klempner ersetzen.
Lassen Sie sich von Ihrem Vorgesetzten die nötigen Anweisungen geben!
Sie ließ sich von ihm das Versprechen geben, daß er nicht zu viel trinken würde.
Sie ließen sich von dem Verkäufer sämtliche Ringe zeigen und konnten sich dann doch für keinen
*   entscheiden.   Laß dir von Kurt den Brief zeigen!*

Lassen in the imp. with a person as obj. means 'to let'. *Laß mich dich umarmen! Laß mich dir zur Beförderung gratulieren! Laß mich dir helfen! Laß ihn die Rechnung bezahlen!* The construction with *von* is also used when *lassen* means 'to let'. The context makes the meaning clear. *Sie ließ sich von ihm nicht vorschreiben, was sie anzuziehen hatte und was nicht.*

4. *Lassen* = 'let'. **Lassen** also means 'to let or allow'. *Laß sie doch schlafen! Wir lassen dich ungestört arbeiten. Laß doch den Jürgen durchs Fernrohr kucken! Er will mich nicht nach Hause gehen lassen. Sein schlechtes Gewissen ließ ihn nicht ruhig schlafen.* It is often used in the refl., and here too has the act. infin. where E. has a pass. one. *Laß dich nicht übervorteilen!*, don't let yourself be cheated. *Ich lasse mich nicht zu einem schnellen Kauf überreden.* (In *Ich lasse euch wissen, wann der Zug ankommt, lassen* means 'to cause to know', but in E. **let** is used.) *Das Kind ließ sich waschen* is ambiguous. It can mean either that the child had itself washed, i.e. had or got someone to wash it (with the person omitted) or that it let itself be washed. The context usually makes it clear which is meant. In cases in which **let** clearly implies giving permission, it may be best to use an equivalent of *allow* like **erlauben** (cf. GRANT) if ambiguity can arise. *Ich erlaubte ihm, den Bericht noch einmal zu schreiben* means 'I let him', whereas the v. in *Ich ließ den Bericht nochmal schreiben* is construed as **got** or **had**, and *ließ* in *Ich ließ ihn den Bericht nochmal schreiben* would most likely be understood as 'made'. *Ich lasse ihn mein Haus nicht mehr betreten, Laß sie doch auch mal dein Spielzeug benutzen!*, and *Sie läßt mich ihre Schreibmaschine benutzen* are unambiguous from the context.

5. Get a thg. **to do** sth., **make** a thg. **do** sth. **Bringen** with a thing as obj. and *zu* + a verbal n. means 'to bring to'. *Man bringt das Wasser zum Sieden.* It also translates **get** and **make** in the constructions given. *Wir können das Rad nicht zum Bewegen bringen*, get the wheel to move or make it move. *Wir haben das Holz endlich zum Brennen gebracht. Ich bringe das Radio nicht zum Laufen* or *bringe es nicht in Gang*, get it to go/work. *In Gang bringen* means 'to make go or get going'. *Kannst du die Uhr/das Auto/das Spielzeug wieder in Gang bringen?* (Note: *In Gang setzen*, to set going.)

6. Get meaning 'to persuade' can be expressed by **jmdn. zu etw. bringen,** which implies that a certain resistance has to be overcome in inducing someone to change an attitude or to do something. This expression also translates *S.o./Sth.*

made s.o. do sth. when the reaction is unexpected, not normal, or even extreme under the circumstances. It is either used with a verbal n., *jmdn. zum Reden bringen,* or in the construction *jmdn. dazu bringen, etw. zu tun/daß er etw. tut. Obwohl ich ihm mißtraute, brachte er mich dazu, ihm zu glauben. Soweit* and less commonly *dahin* are used with a *daß*-clause instead of *dazu* to stress that an unusual or extreme reaction is involved. *Ihr werdet mich nie soweit bringen, daß ich meine Beherrschung verliere.*

> *Wir haben sie dazu gebracht, dem Plan zuzustimmen.*
> *Ich habe ihn dazu gebracht, in Ruhe über die Sache nachzudenken.*
> *Die unheimlichen Geräusche im alten Haus brachten die Kinder zum Weinen.*
> *Weder Drohungen noch verlockende Versprechungen konnten ihn dazu bringen, seine Hausaufgaben sorgfältiger zu machen.   Wir brachten sie dazu, uns alles zu erzählen.*
> *Durch sein vertrauenerweckendes Verhalten brachte der Vertreter die alte Frau dazu, den Kaufvertrag zu unterschreiben.   Wie können wir ihn zum Schweigen bringen?*
> *Sie hatte ihren Ehemann durch ihre zur Schau gestellten Liebschaften soweit gebracht, daß er bereit war, sie bei der nächsten sich bietenden Gelegenheit zu verprügeln.*
> *Wie gelingt es ihm bloß, immer wieder Frauen dahin zu bringen, daß sie ihm anscheinend willenlos folgen?   Wir müssen ihn dazu bringen, auf unseren Rat zu hören.*

7. Machen sometimes translates **make** + infin. *Die Kälte machte mich zittern. Der eiskalte Wind machte mich frösteln. Glauben* is also used with *machen. Willst du mich denn glauben machen, daß alles in Ordnung sei?* In *He made himself look ridiculous, look* is omitted, and the transl. becomes *Er machte sich lächerlich. Es jmdm. verständlich machen* can translate *I made him understand* or *I got him to understand. Es ist mir endlich gelungen, es ihm verständlich zu machen. Vergebens versuchte er ihr verständlich zu machen, daß er nicht länger bleiben konnte.* (An alternative transl. of the neg. is *Ich habe mich sehr bemüht, aber er hat es trotzdem nicht kapiert.*)

8. Other transls. of **make**.

i. *Lassen* is not as strong as **zwingen**, and if **make** is much the same as *force* or *compel*, this should be used. *Ich werde sie schon zwingen, mir zu gehorchen,* I'll make them obey me. *Du mußt dich zwingen, den Atem anzuhalten,* make yourself. *Man kann ein Pferd zur Tränke führen, aber man kann es nicht zwingen zu saufen,* make it drink. *He made me pay the whole amount* can be *Er bestand darauf, daß ich den ganzen Betrag zahlte.* (*Er ließ mich die Rechnung zahlen,* he let me.) *Die Eltern bestanden darauf, daß das Kind Klavierspielen lernte.* One transl. of *If you wish your pupils to learn the language quickly, you should make them read a lot* is *Wenn Sie wollen, daß Ihre Schüler die Sprache schnell lernen, sollten Sie sie dazu anhalten, viel zu lesen.* **Anhalten,** to get s.o. into the way of doing sth. *Er trieb uns zur Eile an,* made us hurry. *Sorg dafür, daß die Kinder sich gut benehmen!,* make the children behave! Cf. SEE TO S.O./STH. *Das Buch regt den Leser zum Nachdenken an,* makes the reader think.

ii. Sometimes **make** need not be translated. *What made you say that?* would usually be *Warum hast du das gesagt? The good weather made her feel better* can be *Wegen des schönen Wetters fühlte sie sich besser,* although *Das gute Wetter bewirkte, daß sie sich besser fühlte* could be used. Cf. CAUSE *v.* Likewise *Wegen der Hitze wälzte ich mich die ganze Nacht im Bett herum,* the heat made me toss around. *Die Hitze ließ mich die ganze Nacht mich im Bett herumwälzen* is possible, but clumsy. *That made me realize my good fortune: Dadurch wurde ich mir bewußt, welches Glück ich doch hatte.*

iii. *A made B laugh* can be *A brachte B zum Lachen,* which suggests some effort. *The joke/This sight made me laugh* is often expressed as *Ich mußte über den Witz/über diesen Anblick lachen. Wir mußten über Johns Bemerkungen lachen. Ich mußte lächeln* is the only way of saying *Sth. made me smile,* as *lächeln* is too weak to use with *bringen.*

iv. *S.o./Sth* **makes** *s.o. want to do sth.* cannot be translated lit. The sense can be expressed. *Nachdem wir den Film gesehen hatten, wollten wir sofort nach Kaschmir fahren,* the film made us want to go. An alternative is *Der Film erweckte in uns den Wunsch, sofort nach Kaschmir zu fahren. Er hat sich so dumm gebärdet, daß ich ihn schlagen wollte,* his behaviour made me want to hit him.

9. Note that where we say a person or thing is made for s.o./sth., G. uses **geschaffen**, lit. 'created', usually preceded by *wie. Er war zum Lehrer wie geschaffen. Sie ist für diesen Beruf wie geschaffen. Dieser Beruf ist für sie wie geschaffen. Die beiden sind füreinander [wie] geschaffen.*

man *n.* **Man** denotes not only an adult male human being but also any human being irrespective of sex, *All men are born equal, No man could survive long on that island,* and the human race or all mankind, *Man is an animal/mortal.* The latter uses have been under attack for some time as sexist. This difficulty does not exist in G.

i. Der Mann refers to an adult male human being, while **der Mensch** and **die Menschen** mean 'human beings in general', and **ein Mensch** 'a member of the human race'. **Die Menschheit** is 'mankind' or 'man' referring to the whole of humanity. Thus *One man, one vote* is *Ein Mensch, eine Stimme. The most dangerous substance known to man: Die gefährlichste Substanz, die der Menschheit bekannt ist.* Only in fixed expressions does *Mann* include women. Cf. iv and v.

Er ist ein junger/alter/großer/kleiner/schöner/gebildeter Mann.
Ein Mann der Tat/von Geist/von Charakter.   *Der Mensch ist sterblich.*
Wodurch unterscheidet sich der Mensch von den Tieren?
Der Mensch verändert die Natur.
Alle Menschen sind gleich geboren/sind gleich vor dem Gesetz.   *Jeder Mensch hat seine Fehler.*
Sind die heutigen Menschen anders als die vor 2 000 Jahren?
Kein Mensch könnte lange auf dieser Insel überleben.

ii. Der Mann is often used as a shortened form of **der Ehemann**, husband. *Darf ich Sie mit meinem Mann bekannt machen?*

iii. Like the E. word, **der Mann** refers to the good qualities traditionally associated with men. *Sei ein Mann! Das hat er wie ein Mann ertragen.*

iv. In military and naval language the sing. and pl. of **der Mann** are identical. *Alle Mann antreten!,* all line up or fall in. *Alle Mann an Deck!* This pl. is found after numerals in other contexts when the number of men or people in a group is given. *Eine 150 Mann starke Belegschaft. Das Boot hat 30 Mann Besatzung.* Although it is still possible to say of a mixed group, '*Wir waren 20 Mann*', the usual expression now is '*Wir waren 20 Personen.*' Likewise instead of *Wir zahlen 12 Mark pro Mann,* people now use *pro Person.*

v. Some expressions in which **der Mann** can cover both males and females: *Mann über Bord. Das Schiff ging mit Mann und Maus unter. Ich habe meinen Wagen an den Mann gebracht,* sold it. *Er konnte es kaum erwarten, diese Geschichte/diesen Witz an den Mann zu bringen,* tell it to someone else. *Jmd. steht seinen Mann,* meaning 'he sticks up for himself', 'stands his ground', can be applied to women. *Sie steht ihren Mann. Sie waren bereit, bis zum letzten Mann zu kämpfen* may often be lit. correct.

vi. Der Mensch is also often used in describing a particular person's characteristics. In translating *He is a good man* or *She is a good woman, Mensch* can be used in both cases. *Er/Sie ist ein guter Mensch.*

Er/Sie ist ein aufgeschlossener/ehrlicher/stiller/verschlossener/sympathischer Mensch.
For *gentleman* see WOMAN 2. i and ii.

mark *v.*

1. The primary sense of **mark** is 'to put a mark or sign on sth. deliberately'. *I have marked the spot with a cross.*

i. The main v. expressing this sense is **kennzeichnen**, which means 'to make recognizable by a distinguishing mark or sign'. The mark may be a word, symbol, or name, but it can also be a line, cross, etc. **Markieren** is a syn. *Der Wanderweg war mit einem braunen Eichhörnchen gekennzeichnet/markiert.* With *als*, *kennzeichnen* means 'to mark as being of a certain kind'. *Die Fässer waren als gefährlich gekennzeichnet. Dieses Wort wird im Wörterbuch als veraltet gekennzeichnet,* marked [as] archaic.

> *Wir haben die Kisten mit Nummern gekennzeichnet.*
> *Ich habe die Stelle gekennzeichnet/markiert, an der Sie von der Hauptstraße abbiegen müssen.*
> *Das Kreuz kennzeichnet/markiert die Stelle, wo die Piraten den Schatz vergraben haben.*
> *Kennzeichnen Sie bitte die wichtigsten Punkte mit einem Kreuz!* Or *Ich markiere die Stellen, die mir besonders wichtig erscheinen.*
> *Ich habe die Stelle im Buch gekennzeichnet/markiert, wo wir stehengeblieben sind.* Also *Ich habe ein Zeichen gemacht, wo . . .   Die Einfahrt zum Hafen ist mit Bojen markiert.*
> *Auf der Landkarte sind die Brücken durch einen Strich markiert.*
> *Eine bestimmte Stelle ist als Abstellplatz für Motorräder gekennzeichnet/markiert.*
> *Die Bettwäsche ist mit dem Namen des Hotels gekennzeichnet/versehen.* (For *versehen* cf. 1. v.)

ii. In one sense **bezeichnen** is a syn. of *kennzeichnen* in sense 1. i, but it is less common. *Die Sitzplätze sind mit Nummern bezeichnet. Er bezeichnet die zu fällenden Bäume.* Both *bezeichnen* and *markieren* are found with *Grenze* as obj. *Ein Graben bezeichnet die Grenze. Eine Schneise markiert die Grenze.*

> *Der Bachlauf bezeichnet die Grenze zwischen den beiden Gemeinden.*
> *Das Kreuz bezeichnet den höchsten Punkt des Berges.*

iii. Something that marks a stage or point in the development of a person or thing is a sign that something different is about to happen. **Markieren** carries this sense, but **kennzeichnen** is also possible.

> *Dieser Krieg markiert den Beginn einer neuen Epoche.*
> *Dieses Buch markierte eine wichtige Etappe in der Entwicklung der Sprachwissenschaft.*

iv. Zeichnen can mean 'to mark with a name', but *kennzeichnen* is also used. *Sie hat die Wäsche mit Buchstaben/einem Monogramm gezeichnet;* the mit-phr. can be omitted. People's features and lives are the main obj. of *zeichnen* in the act. or the subj. in the pass. *Sorgen hatten ihr Gesicht gezeichnet. Ihr Gesicht war von Leid gezeichnet. Sein Gesicht war von Blatternnarben gezeichnet. Er war von der schweren Krankheit/von dem schrecklichen Erlebnis gezeichnet* means that each had left marks on mind and body.

v. The technical term for marking the price on something is **auszeichnen**. *Wir haben die neu hereingekommenen Waren noch nicht ausgezeichnet. Die Waren sind alle gut sichtbar ausgezeichnet.* (In another sense *auszeichnen* means 'to distinguish'.) Another v. which can express the idea of marking with a name, address, price, etc. is **versehen**, whose basic sense is 'to PROVIDE with sth.'

> *Pakete und Päckchen müssen gut sichtbar mit Namen und Adresse sowohl des Absenders als auch des Empfängers versehen werden.   Du mußt alle Kleidungsstücke mit deinem Namen versehen.*

2. In a less broad sense than 1, **mark** means 'to identify sth. by putting a sign against it, usually with pen or pencil'. **Kennzeichnen** can express this meaning, but certain vs. denote a specific mark. **Anstreichen** means 'to draw attention to sth. by putting a line against it'. *Jmd. hatte eine Stelle im Buch angestrichen. Ich habe die wichtigsten Stellen im Aufsatz angestrichen.* **Ankreuzen** means 'to mark with a cross'. *Ich habe die Annoncen angekreuzt, die für dich in Frage kommen. Zutreffendes bitte ankreuzen.* If **mark** means 'to underline', the v. is **unterstreichen**. *Die wichtigen Wörter, die ihr lernen müßt, habe ich unterstrichen.*

3. i. Anstreichen is used for marking [out] mistakes. If *Fehler* is the obj., the sense is clear. *Ich habe die grammatikalischen Fehler angestrichen.* Otherwise, *als falsch* must be added, as *wrong* is in E. *Warum haben Sie dieses Wort als falsch angekreuzt?*

ii. Mark meaning 'to correct' is generally **korrigieren**. *Ich habe das Wochenende damit verbracht, Aufsätze zu korrigieren.* If giving a numerical mark is stressed, **benoten** and **zensieren** are used. *Zwei Lehrer haben die Klassenarbeiten benotet/zensiert.* **Bewerten**, 'to evaluate', is also common. Cf. JUDGE.

4. A thing can leave a mark on something, i.e. mark it without intention, as in *The wet vase has marked the table with a ring.* This meaning could be expressed by **hinterlassen**, to LEAVE. *Die nasse Vase hat einen Ring auf dem Tisch hinterlassen.* While *The vase has marked the table* is enough in E., what the mark is needs to be specified in G. *Der verschüttete Kaffee hat einen Flecken auf dem Teppich hinterlassen*, has marked it, left a stain.

5. Mark also means 'to be a distinguishing feature of'. *What qualities mark a good teacher?* It is often used in the pass. *His style is marked by a predilection for metaphors.* The usual equivalent is **kennzeichnen** in its second meaning, 'to characterize'. As well as in the act. and pass., it occurs occasionally in the refl., **sich kennzeichnen**, to be marked by. *Sein Denken kennzeichnet sich durch logische Schärfe.* **Kennzeichnend für**, 'characteristic or typical of', is synonymous with **bezeichnend für**. *Dieses Verhalten ist für ihn bezeichnend. Diese Offenheit ist für sie kennzeichnend.*

> *Welches sind die Eigenschaften, die einen guten Lehrer kennzeichnen?*
> *Eine Vorliebe für Metaphern kennzeichnet ihren Stil.* Or *Ihr Stil ist gekennzeichnet durch eine Vorliebe für Metaphern.* *Die Automatisierung kennzeichnet die moderne Industrie.*
> *Dieses Verhalten kennzeichnet ihn als guterzogenen Jungen/hilfsbereiten Menschen.*

6. Mark *time* is **auf der Stelle treten**. The G. expression is also used fig. *In diesem Projekt treten wir nun schon seit drei Monaten auf der Stelle.*

7. Mark an anniversary, etc. *This year marks the 50th anniversary of the firm* can be *In diesem Jahr besteht die Firma 50 Jahre.* When a celebration is implied, **feiern**, 'to celebrate', or the more elevated syn. **begehen** are used. *In diesem Jahr feiern wir das 50-jährige Bestehen der Firma* or . . . *begehen wir das 50-jährige Jubiläum der Firma. 1988 fanden Feierlichkeiten statt, um die Besiedlung Australiens vor 200 Jahren durch die Briten zu begehen/feiern*, to mark the 200th anniversary. An alternative is *Aus Anlaß des 50-jährigen Bestehens der Firma* . . . Cf. CAUSE n.

8. [You] **mark** *my words!* is **Achte auf** *meine Worte!* or *Beachte, was ich gesagt habe!* It implies that the person will find that what I said will turn out to be true, and this may also need to be expressed. *Es wird sich herausstellen, daß ich recht habe.*

marriage *n.*

1. Die Heirat is 'the action of marrying s.o. or of getting married'. **Die Vermählung** is an elevated syn. not much used except in *Heiratsanzeigen*. **Die Eheschließung** is the bureaucratic term.

> *Ihre Heirat steht bevor.* *Vor der Heirat hat er ein unstetes Leben geführt.*
> *Ihre Eltern waren mit dieser Heirat nicht einverstanden.*
> *Nach der Heirat mit der Millionärstochter gab er seinen Beruf auf.*
> *Die Eheschließung erfolgte im Standesamt in Konz.*
> *Ihre Vermählung geben bekannt Camilla Richter und Rudolf Lamprecht.* (*Heiratsanzeige*)

2. Die Ehe is 'the state of being married over a period of time'. It is used in stating whether a marriage is happy, successful, or a failure, and in talking of the first, second, etc. marriage, about the children of a marriage, and about marriage as an institution; hence *die Einehe*, 'monogamy', and *die Vielehe*, 'polygamy'.

> *Ihre Ehe war glücklich und harmonisch.*
> *Sie sahen ein, daß ihre Ehe zerrüttet war, und ließen sich scheiden.*
> *Sie war in zweiter Ehe mit einem Rechtsanwalt verheiratet.*
> *Er hat einen Sohn aus erster Ehe.* *Aus der Ehe sind drei Kinder hervorgegangen.*

Die Ehe ist die gesetzliche und moralische Einrichtung für die Zeugung unter den Menschen.

3. Die Trauung is 'the marriage ceremony', while **die Hochzeit** is the festivity or celebration accompanying this, but often *Hochzeit* includes both.

In Deutschland darf die kirchliche Trauung erst nach der standesamtlichen Trauung stattfinden.
Wir müssen sämtliche Verwandte zur Hochzeit einladen.

marry *v.*

1. Like **marry** **heiraten** can be used intr. with one or two people as subj. *Sie hat mit 22 Jahren geheiratet. Sie haben jung geheiratet. Er hat nie geheiratet.* Heiraten is not used in the pass., and the act. intr. forms translate **is/are being/getting married** or **was/were/got married**. *Sie haben gleich nach dem Krieg geheiratet,* married or were/got married. *Sie wollen im Januar heiraten. Wir haben in Hannover geheiratet. Er heiratet zum zweiten Mal.* Heiraten is also used with an obj. *Er hat die Tochter eines Nachbarn geheiratet. Sie hat einen Pfarrer geheiratet.* The past part. of **verheiraten** is used to state whether a person is married in contrast to single. *Sind Sie ledig, verheiratet oder geschieden? Sie ist schon verheiratet.* It also states the nature of the marriage. *Sie sind glücklich verheiratet.* **Sich verheiraten** is occasionally found with a sing. subj. in the sense 'to get married' or 'to marry' (intr.). It stresses that a change in the person's status has taken place. *Hat er sich verheiratet, oder ist er immer noch ledig?* The person wedded is expressed by *mit*: *Er hat sich endlich mit ihr verheiratet.* With an obj., *verheiraten* means 'to marry one pers. [off] to another'. *Der alte Geizhals wollte seine Tochter mit einem viel älteren, steinreichen Bankier verheiraten.*

2. Sich vermählen is an elevated v. meaning 'to marry'. It belongs to the written language and was originally used only for highly placed people. It is, however, now often found in marriage notices in newspapers which might read *Wir haben uns vermählt* with the names following. The constructions are *A und B haben sich vermählt* or *A hat sich mit B vermählt.*

3. Trauen means 'to perform the marriage ceremony', and the subj. in the act. would be a clergyman or a registry office official. *Pfarrer Blank hat sie in der Marktkirche getraut.*

matter *v.* make a difference, not make any difference *v. phr.* The chief sense of **matter** is 'to be important'. In certain situations in which it is often neg., it means '[not] to inconvenience'. There are three main equivalents. *Etw. macht mir nichts aus* means 'sth. does not inconvenience me', while *es kommt mir auf etw. an* means 'sth. is of importance to me'. When someone has a choice between two or more things and does not mind which is chosen, *jmdm. gleich sein* or a syn. is used.

1. *Machen* and *ausmachen* imply inconvenience and differ only syntactically.

i. Machen is limited to the use with *es* and *das* as subj. and *nichts* as obj. without a dat. *Es macht nichts.* When the sent. contains not only *nichts* as obj. but also a dat., **ausmachen** is used. *Es macht uns nichts aus,* it doesn't matter to us. Ausmachen is used in a pos. sent. with *etw.* as obj. and a dat. *Es macht mir doch etw. aus,* it does matter to or inconvenience me. *Etw.* is also the obj. in a question. *Wir möchten hier bleiben. Macht das dir etw. aus?* Daß- or wenn-clauses can follow *ausmachen, Würde es Ihnen etw. ausmachen, wenn ich mitfahre?*, and are occasionally found after *es macht nichts, Es macht nichts, daß du zu spät gekommen bist.*

Das macht nichts.   *Das macht mir nichts aus.*

Macht es euch [et]was aus, wenn ich heute abend erst um neun Uhr ankomme?

Es macht gar nichts, wenn du dafür etwas länger brauchst.

Es macht mir nichts aus, daß ich den ganzen Tag stehe/wenn du länger bleibst.

ii. Related expressions. Less common than *es macht nichts* is **es schadet nichts**, sth. won't hurt [you], or no harm will come of it.

> A. *Beim Abwaschen habe ich diesen Teller zerbrochen.*
> B. *Das schadet nichts. Er hatte sowieso einen Sprung. Also Es macht nichts. Sei beruhigt!*
> *Es schadet nichts, daß sie im Schnee spazieren gegangen sind.*
> X. *Ich wußte nicht, daß wir nur drei Übungen aufhatten und habe sechs gemacht. Y. Das schadet nichts.*

Ich habe einen Tippfehler in dem Brief mit Kugelschreiber korrigiert—ist das schlimm?, does that matter? *Schlimm* = 'bad'. **Das ist nicht weiter schlimm** is used in speech when something of a neg. nature is felt not to be important. *Es ist nicht weiter schlimm, wenn du zu spät kommst.* Here *weiter* = 'besonders'.

2. Matter = 'to be important'.

i. Without a dat. **ausmachen** means 'to make a difference' or 'to matter'. It takes as obj. words like *nichts, etw., viel,* or *wenig.* Thus *Die paar Minuten machen nichts/nicht viel/wenig aus*, they make no/little difference. A clause with *ob* is occasionally found both in pos. sents., *Es macht doch etw. aus, ob man in der Stadt oder auf dem Lande aufgewachsen ist*, 'it does make a difference', and in neg. ones, *Es macht weiter nichts aus, ob die Wahlen jetzt oder erst in drei Monaten stattfinden*, 'it makes no great difference, doesn't matter greatly'. Also used is **Es ist doch ein/kein Unterschied, ob . . .** *Es ist doch ein Unterschied, ob ich den ganzen Tag stehe oder sitze.* This construction should be used only when there is an actual difference between the things talked about, not as a transl. of *It makes no difference whether you come today or tomorrow.* Cf. 3. **It makes a difference** should not be translated word for word. A common equivalent of *What difference does it make?* or *What does it matter?* is **Was macht das schon?** which is used e.g. to calm a person whose expectations have not been completely fulfilled. A parent might say it to a child who is upset because he or she has not done as well as anticipated in a *Klassenarbeit. Schon* implies a neg. answer—it doesn't matter. *Was macht das schon aus?* is also used. Someone who has tried to do something without success might say, **'Was soll's?'**, what does it matter?, so what? i.e. anyway it's not important or doesn't matter. *Does it matter?* = 'is it important?' is *Ist das denn wichtig?*

> *Das macht viel/wenig aus.*   *Als ob das was ausmachen könnte/würde?*
> *Es ist kein Unterschied, ob du es sagst oder ich.*

ii. Eine/Keine Rolle spielen means that something is/is not an important factor, it makes no difference.

> *Es spielt keine Rolle, wann du kommst. Hauptsache ist, daß du überhaupt da bist.*
> *Die Höhe der Ausgaben spielt keine Rolle.*
> *Geld spielt [bei ihm] keine Rolle.* (Money is no object [where he is concerned/with him].)
> *Für mich spielt es keine Rolle, ob er heute kommt oder nicht.*
> *Wenn du etwas zu spät kommst, so spielt das keine Rolle.*

iii. Ins Gewicht fallen means 'to be of importance or consequence'. It can express the sense 'to matter' and in particular 'not to matter'. *Bei einem guten Schüler fällt eine schlechte Note nicht ins Gewicht. Das englische Wort, mit dem ich dieses ungarische Wort übersetzt habe, entspricht ihm zwar nicht genau, aber der Unterschied ist so klein, daß er nicht ins Gewicht fällt.*

iv. Ankommen, which is used with **auf** + n., *Hier kommt es auf Genauigkeit an*, or with **darauf** + infin. or *daß*-clause, *Es kommt darauf an, Mißverständnisse zu vermeiden*, means that what is stated by the n., infin., or clause is important or what matters. A dat. indicating a person can be added to all three constructions. Thus *Es kommt ihm auf eine schnelle Erledigung der Sache an* and *Es kommt ihm darauf an, daß die Sache schnell erledigt wird.* It is often used when one thing is said to matter more than another [to s.o.] *Es kommt ihm mehr auf gute Behandlung als auf hohen Lohn an.*

Bei der Übersetzung kommt es mir auf eine genaue Wiedergabe des Sinns an.
Bei einem Traktor kommt es mehr auf Zugkraft als auf Schnelligkeit an.
Es kommt mir darauf an zu beweisen, daß die Theorie richtig ist.
Auf ein paar Mark kommt es mir nicht an. (It doesn't matter if sth. costs a few marks more.)
When something is important, but not very, i.e. it doesn't matter much, the expression is *Das ist nicht weiter wichtig*. Note that *es kommt mir auf etw. an* indicates the thing that matters or is most important. If one thing among others is important to someone, *jmdm. wichtig sein* is used. *Stilistische Schönheit ist mir bei der Übersetzung wichtig, aber ich möchte deswegen nicht auf Genauigkeit verzichten.*

3. i. The general sense of the expressions **es ist [jmdm.] egal/gleich/ gleichgültig/einerlei**, [*ob/was/wie* etc.] is that it is all the same, makes no difference, or doesn't matter [to s.o.] whether one or the other of a group of possibilities is chosen or whether someone does something or not. They translate **matter** when a *whether*-clause follows. *Es ist mir völlig egal/gleich, ob er geht oder bleibt.* Caution is required when using the dat., as the meaning can be like *I don't care* [*if s.o. does sth./what s.o. does*]. Egal is colloquial, *einerlei* fairly formal, and the others neutral.

> *Es ist [mir] egal, ob er das Buch morgen oder übermorgen zurückgibt.*
> *Es ist ganz gleich, was du tust: Er wird dir immer ablehnend gegenüberstehen.*

ii. Es/Das bleibt sich gleich, ob . . . means that it is all the same or makes no difference which of two alternatives occurs. *Es bleibt sich gleich, ob er dabei ist oder nicht.*
iii. Egal and **ganz gleich** can be used to translate the concessive clause *No matter what, how*, etc. in the spoken language. *Egal/Ganz gleich, was er sagte, niemand glaubte ihm. Was er auch sagte, niemand glaubte ihm* is stylistically higher.

4. *One pers.* **matters** *a lot to another* is expressed by **bedeuten**, to mean. *A bedeutet B viel.* Cf. MEAN 7.

mean *v.* While **mean** often has a personal subj., a person is the subj. of *bedeuten* only in meaning 7.

1. With a word, sent., passage of a text, statement, sign, symbol, etc. as subj., **mean** means 'to signify or convey a certain sense'. *A dictionary tells you what a word means. What does this symbol mean?* **Mean** also refers to the general significance of something. *You will learn what responsibility means.*
i. The basic meaning of **bedeuten** is 'to have a definite sense', and words, sents., symbols, etc. or something that has happened can be the subj. It is often used with *sollen*. *Sollen* does not change the meaning but may add an emotional nuance, like puzzlement or annoyance.

> *Hier wird erklärt, was dieses Wort/diese Stelle bedeutet.*   *Was bedeutet dieses Zeichen?*
> *Was bedeutet dieses Verkehrsschild?*
> *Was soll dieses Symbol bedeuten?*
> *Das Wort Gift bedeutete ursprünglich etwas anderes als heute.*

ii. A close syn. is **heißen**. While *bedeuten* is frequently used to give the meaning of a word, *heißen* often states the general significance of something. Both are, however, common in both uses. In reference to words in different languages, *heißen* usually implies an equivalent while *bedeuten* suggests a meaning. *Wie heißt* Butter *auf französisch? Das lateinische Wort* amo *bedeutet 'ich liebe'.*

> *Was heißt das, was soeben gesagt wurde?*   *Wenn ich nein sage, dann heißt das nein.*
> *Er muß lernen, was es heißt/bedeutet, Verantwortung zu tragen.*
> *Sie weiß nicht, was es heißt/bedeutet, kein Geld zu haben.*
> *Das Sinken der Verkaufszahlen bedeutet einen akuten Rückgang der Nachfrage.*

Es hieße occurs in formal style and means 'it/that would mean'. The everyday equivalent is *es würde bedeuten/heißen*. *Wenn wir diesem Rat folgten, hieße es, die ganze Sache verderben.*

2. Mean is used in connection with the purpose or motive of certain behaviour. Either the behaviour or the person can be the subj. *What does all this politeness mean? What does he mean by carrying on like that?* **Bedeuten** and **heißen** refer to behaviour when it, not a person, is the subj. *Was hat das alles zu bedeuten? Was soll das alles heißen? Was heißt das?* or *Was soll das heißen/bedeuten?* can be a neutral question but can also refer to behaviour and express indignation or a protest. *Was soll dieser Krach bedeuten/heißen? Was soll denn das nun wieder heißen?*, what's the meaning of this [behaviour]? **Was soll das?** is like *What do you/they*, etc. *mean by [doing] that?* It expresses surprise, protest, or annoyance. Similarly *Was soll diese übertriebene Höflichkeit?* If the idea is expressed in full, **erreichen**, 'to ACHIEVE', or **bezwecken**, 'to aim at, be supposed to achieve', can be used. *Erreichen* usually has a person as subj., but the subj. of *bezwecken* can be a person or an action. *Was wollen sie mit dieser übertriebener Höflichkeit erreichen?* or *Was bezweckt diese übertriebene Höflichkeit?*

> *Er wußte nicht, was das seltsame Verhalten seines Freundes zu bedeuten hatte.*
> *Was bezweckt dieses seltsame Verhalten?*   *Was bezweckt das alles?*

An alternative to *Das bedeutet nichts* and *Das hat nichts zu bedeuten* is *Etw.* **besagt** *nichts/wenig/nicht viel*, it doesn't mean or say anything, much, etc., has no/little significance. Cf. SAY 9. iii.

3. Applied to happenings and actions, **mean** implies that these are likely to result in something else. *The new frontier incident probably means war. The new orders for our goods will mean working overtime.* Both **bedeuten** and **heißen** express the sense that a happening means something. They are interchangeable when a clause follows; only *bedeuten* takes an obj.

> *Der graue Himmel bedeutet Schnee.*   *Das bedeutet nichts Gutes.*
> *Die vielen Aufträge, die die Firma bekommen hat, bedeuten/heißen, daß wir Überstunden machen müssen.*
> *Der neue Grenzzwischenfall könnte Krieg bedeuten.*   *Ein Hufeisen finden bedeutet Glück.*
> *Der Arzt sagt, die Wunde habe nicht viel zu bedeuten.*

4. With a person as subj., **mean** means 'to want to convey a certain sense when using a word or sent., or by saying sth.' *What does he mean? The remark was meant as a joke. By* often follows. *I don't understand what you mean by that [word/remark]. Mean* can indicate that a remark, allusion, or question refers to someone. *I wonder whether he meant any one of us by that remark. You asked for Mr Smith—do you mean Bill Smith or Peter Smith?* **Meinen** is the equivalent of **mean** in this sense. *What do you mean?* is *Was meinen Sie damit?* An alternative is *Was wollen Sie damit sagen?* (With *wie*, only *meinen* is used. *Wie meinst du das?*) The obj. can be a person or thing referred to, or a clause. *Meinen Sie meine Kollegin/unseren Brief von vorgestern? Er meinte nicht/wollte damit nicht sagen, daß wir nachlässig gearbeitet hätten. Meinen* also expresses how someone wants a remark to be taken. *Ich meine es ernst/als Witz.* To translate *I [really] mean it*, it is necessary to say *Ich meine es ernst/[wirklich] im Ernst.* The subj. in the pass. can be *das* or another word denoting what someone said, such as *Worte* or *diese Bemerkung. Diese Worte waren als Scherz gemeint, nicht als Vorwurf.*

> *Wen hat sie mit dieser Bemerkung/Kritik gemeint?*   *Welches Buch meinen Sie?*
> *Sie haben ihn mißverstanden. Er hat etw. ganz anderes gemeint.*
> *Wir sprechen nicht über dich, wir meinten Hans.*   *Meinen Sie mich?*
> *Du meinst doch nicht etwa, daß ich dich übervorteilen will? Or Du willst doch nicht etwa sagen, daß ich dich übervorteilen will.*   *Meinten Sie Peter Meier oder Hans Meier?*
> *Das/Diese Bemerkung war nicht ernst gemeint.*   *Ich meinte es nur als Scherz/Witz.*

5. In *They mean well [by you]* **mean** suggests that they have good intentions though not necessarily the will or capacity to carry them out. In *He means [you] no harm*, it also refers to someone's underlying intentions. **Meinen** also expresses this sense. *Es gut mit jmdm. meinen* is 'to mean well by a pers.' *Er meinte es nicht böse* or *Es war nicht böse gemeint*, no harm was meant.

> *Sie meint es gut mit dir und wollte dir nur helfen.*   *Der Vorschlag war gut gemeint.*

6. Mean also means 'to have in mind as a purpose or intention', 'to intend'. *I'm sorry I hurt your feelings. I didn't mean to. I didn't mean to disturb you. I didn't mean him to read that letter.* This and related meanings must be translated by equivalents of *intend*.

i. Es war [nicht] meine Absicht or **wollen** can express the sense of *I [do not] mean to do sth.*

> *Es tut mir leid, daß ich dich gekränkt habe. Das war nicht meine Absicht. Or Das wollte ich nicht.*
> *Ich wollte Sie nicht stören.*
> *Ich wollte dir das Geld gestern geben, aber ich habe es vergessen.* (I meant to).

ii. [Not] to **mean** s.o. to do sth. must be expressed as a *daß*-clause. *Es war nicht meine Absicht, daß er diesen Brief lesen sollte* or *Ich wollte nicht, daß sie diese Arbeit macht.*

iii. In *He means to succeed* and *They mean their children to succeed*, **mean** suggests determination. For this sense **unbedingt**, absolutely, can be added to **wollen**.

> *Er will unbedingt in der Geschäftswelt vorwärtskommen.*   *Sie will unbedingt Erfolg haben.*
> *Sie wollen unbedingt, daß ihre Kinder Erfolg haben.*

iv. Mean is applied to what one person intends for, or to give to, another. *I meant this book for my daughter. Is this valuable painting meant for me?* **Denken** or **bestimmen** are the usual equivalents. They are not confined to gifts. *Dieses Buch habe ich für meine Tochter gedacht/bestimmt. Das Buch ist für fortgeschrittene Studenten gedacht.* **Jmdm. etw. zudenken**, as in *Den Blumenstrauß hatte er seiner Frau zugedacht*, has the same meaning but is now very formal or old-fashioned. *Er hatte sich das größte Stück Kuchen zugedacht.*

> *Ist dieses wertvolle Bild für mich gedacht/bestimmt?*   *Das Geld ist für dich bestimmt.*
> *Dieses Lehrbuch ist für den Unterricht in der achten Klasse gedacht/bestimmt.*

v. Meant means 'destined for'. *He clearly seems meant to be a soldier. They are meant for each other.* **Bestimmen** carries this meaning. It suggests that something is preordained for the person.

> *Er scheint dazu bestimmt zu sein, Soldat zu werden.*
> *Die beiden scheinen füreinander bestimmt zu sein.*

7. With people or things as subj., **mean** signifies that something is of importance or value to a person. *She/Her friendship means a good deal to me.* **Bedeuten** alone has this sense and mostly has as obj. *vieles, wenig,* or *nichts. Was* is used in direct or indirect questions. *Was bedeutet er dir?*

> *Die gute Meinung der Nachbarn bedeutete ihm viel, und er vermied es peinlich, Aufsehen zu erregen.*
> *Sie war sich bewußt, was er für sie und ihre ganze Familie bedeutete.*
> *Dieser Mann/Diese Freundschaft bedeutete mir viel.*   *Schmeicheleien bedeuten mir nichts.*

The significance something has for someone is sometimes the obj. of *bedeuten*.

> *Die Rückkehr des Sohnes bedeutete für die Mutter einen großen Trost.*

In *The high cost of living does not mean anything/means nothing to some people*, **not to mean** has the sense 'not to MATTER'. Thus *Die hohen Lebenshaltungskosten machen einigen Leuten nichts aus.*

8. In *I am meant to go to the meeting at three*, **mean** expresses a strong expectation that this will happen. This could be **Es wird erwartet**, *daß ich bei der Sitzung erscheine, die um 15 Uhr anfängt.* Cf. WAIT 3. An alternative is **sollte**. *Ich sollte zu der Sitzung gehen, die um drei Uhr anfängt.* With *sollte* the question as to whether the person will actually go is more open than with *erwarten*.

Von Eltern wird erwartet, daß sie alle ihre Kinder in gleichem Maße lieben. Eltern sollten alle . . . lieben.

meet *v.*

1. Meet = 'to come together from different directions by chance or arrangement'.

i. The *OED* partly defines one meaning of **meet** as 'to come face to face with a pers. who is arriving at the same point from the opposite or a different direction'. If we add that this happens by accident, without prior arrangement, it is the chief meaning of **begegnen**, which implies that one person goes towards another who is coming from another, usually the opposite, direction and passes him or her. The people may greet each other or may stop to exchange a few words, but only one person need become aware of the other, and they may not be acquainted with each other. It cannot refer to an arranged meeting. Subj. and obj. are usually interchangeable. It is often found in the refl. with a pl. subj. It takes the dat. and *sein* in the perf.

Ich bin ihm kürzlich auf der Straße begegnet. Er ist mir begegnet. Wir sind uns begegnet.
Wir haben den ganzen Nachmittag im Wald verbracht und sind keiner Menschenseele begegnet.
Wir begegneten uns öfter auf dem Weg zur Arbeit.
Ich bin dem Ministerpräsidenten in der Stadt begegnet.

ii. **Treffen** can refer both to a chance meeting and to an arranged meeting. Applied to an accidental encounter, it implies unexpectedly coming across someone whom one knows and stopping at least for a short time to talk. It is immaterial whether the other person comes towards you or whether he or she is already at the place, so that when **meet** implies that the other person is at or in a place already, only *treffen* should be used.

Ich habe einen früheren Kollegen im Theater/auf der Straße getroffen.
Meine Mutter hat gestern in der Straßenbahn wieder einmal ihre alte Lehrerin getroffen.

For arranged meetings, only *treffen* is used. Although *Ich treffe dich*, 'I'll meet you', is possible, it is more usual to say *Wir treffen uns um Viertel vor acht vor dem Kino.* Whether the meeting is by design or accident is often uncertain, although the context may make it clear. *Die beiden trafen sich regelmäßig* normally suggests planned meetings. For an unexpected encounter *zufällig* can be added. *Ich traf ihn zufällig in der Stadt.* **Sich mit jmdm. treffen** is unambiguous as *A trifft sich mit B* presupposes an arrangement. *Er trifft sich heute abend mit seiner Freundin in der Stadt.*

iii. **Zusammentreffen** in one sense means 'to meet', usually by arrangement, but occasionally by accident. The people may be ordinary individuals but are mostly those in high positions. *Zusammentreffen* needs a pl. subj., except that when used with *mit*, the subj. can be sing. *A und B treffen zusammen. A trifft mit B zusammen.*

Der Bundesaußenminister und der US-Außenminister trafen in Bonn zusammen.
Der Bundesaußenminister traf gestern in Bonn mit dem US-Außenminister zusammen.
Gestern traf ich unverhofft mit einem alten Bekannten in der Stadt zusammen.

iv. **Sich treffen** is the equivalent of intr. **meet** used with an organized body, club, society, group of people, etc. as subj. *Die Diskussionsgruppe trifft sich jeden Donnerstag um 20 Uhr. Teilnehmer am Fontane-Seminar werden gebeten, sich am Mittwoch um 16 Uhr im Zimmer 881 zu treffen.* **Zusammenkommen** is also used for meetings of clubs etc. *Die Mitglieder des Sportvereins waren zusammengekommen, um über den Bau einer Turnhalle zu beraten.* For important deliberative bodies, such as parliaments, **zusammentreten**, 'to convene', is used. *Der Bundestag tritt nächste Woche wieder zusammen.*

Die Außenminister der Europäischen Gemeinschaft treffen sich morgen in Brüssel.

v. Eyes/Looks/Glances **meet** can be either **sich begegnen** or **sich treffen**. *Ihre Blicke begegneten sich. Ihre Augen trafen sich.*

2. Meet = 'to make s.o.'s acquaintance for the first time'.

i. The main equivalent is **kennenlernen**. (With advs. like *näher* or *richtig*, it means 'to get to know'.)

Ich freue mich, Sie kennenzulernen.   *Ich möchte ihn [näher] kennenlernen.*

Haben Sie den neuen Direktor schon kennengelernt?   *Er lernte seine Frau in einem Zug kennen.*

A. Kennen Sie sich schon? B. Ja, wir haben uns gestern kennengelernt.

ii. Begegnen is much used in statements about having or not having come into contact with someone and about meeting people of a certain type. Thus *Ich bin ihm nie begegnet. Ich bin ihr nur einmal begegnet. Ich bin ihm bei Sitzungen mehrfach begegnet, kenne ihn aber nicht gut. Einem besseren/fauleren Menschen bin ich nie begegnet.* A variant is *So ein Idiot ist mir noch nie im Leben vorgekommen. Treffen* is possible in all sents. but tends to be avoided as it suggests an arranged meeting. *Kennenlernen* could also be used, but it implies closer acquaintance while *begegnen* need only mean being in someone's company.

3. i. Treffen auf and more commonly **stoßen auf** mean 'to meet with or encounter', i.e. 'to come across unexpectedly, to hit upon by chance', or in some contexts 'to experience'.

Im Urwald traf die Expedition auf einen unbekannten Stamm.

Im Museum traf ich auf einen alten Bekannten.   *Wir stießen auf unerwartete Schwierigkeiten.*

Bei der Durchführung der Reformen ist man auf beträchtlichen Widerstand gestoßen.

Mit seinen Reformplänen traf er auf Ablehnung.

ii. Treffen auf is used in sport and translates **meet**. *Im Halbfinale trifft A auf B.*

Die australische Mannschaft trifft morgen auf die bisher unbesiegte schottische.

4. Come/go to meet meaning 'to go towards s.o. known or seen to be approaching' are **entgegenkommen** and **entgegengehen** or **entgegenfahren**. *Die Kinder wissen, wann ich nach Hause komme, und kommen mir oft ein Stück entgegen. Die Kinder gingen dem Vater bis zur Haltestelle entgegen. Ich fahre dir mit dem Rad ein Stück entgegen. Jmdm. auf halbem Weg entgegenkommen* is 'to meet s.o. half-way' in the fig. sense. *Der Möbelhändler erklärte sich bereit, mir hinsichtlich des Preises auf halbem Weg entgegenzukommen.*

5. Meet meaning 'go to a place where s.o. is going to arrive to welcome and then accompany or convey him/her somewhere' is **abholen**. *Ich hole dich vom Bahnhof ab. Alle Gäste werden mit dem Hotelbus vom Flughafen abgeholt.* If **meet** simply means 'to be somewhere when s.o. arrives', the vs. are **warten auf** or **da sein**. *Ich warte auf dich am Bahnsteig* or *Ich werde da sein, wenn du ankommst.*

6. Antreffen means 'to find or meet with sth.' *Echter Kunstsinn ist nicht oft anzutreffen. Dieses Wort ist in seinen Werken sehr oft anzutreffen.* With a personal obj. it is more like *to find*. It implies that one person has the intention or desire to meet another and goes to or rings up where the other usually is or could be expected to be, mostly a home, office, or place of work. When the meaning is 'to find s.o. in/at home', it is often not necessary to add *zu Hause*.

Wir sind zu ihrer Wohnung gegangen und haben sie glücklicherweise angetroffen.

Zu dieser Zeit werden Sie ihn im Büro antreffen.   *Wo kann ich sie am Nachmittag antreffen?*

Another sense is 'to find s.o. in a particular state'. *Wir trafen sie bei bester Gesundheit/unverändert an.*

7. Meet also means 'to satisfy demands or requirements' or 'to be able to discharge a pecuniary obligation'. *I have met all the demands/my obligations in full.* The main equivalents are **erfüllen** + acc., 'to fulfil', cf. FILL, **nachkommen** + dat., 'to carry out or discharge a promise or obligation or comply with a request', and **entsprechen** + dat., 'to comply with or answer s.o.'s needs'. Cf. *genügen* under SATISFY.

Ich habe alle Bedingungen erfüllt (met/fulfilled all conditions).

Haben Sie genug Geld, um Ihren Verpflichtungen nachzukommen?
Wir haben ihren Wünschen/Forderungen entsprochen/sind ihnen nachgekommen/haben sie erfüllt.
Entspricht das Ihren Vorstellungen/Ihren Bedürfnissen?
Wir kommen Ihnen/Ihren Wünschen gern entgegen suggests readiness to compromise or to make concessions in order to meet someone's wishes.

8. Meet also means 'to encounter or face the attacks of sth. impersonal in a certain way' or 'to cope or grapple with difficulties'. *He met these threats with defiance. They met the misfortune calmly/with composure.* **Begegnen** means 'to react to in a certain way and to take counter measures'.

Sie begegnete dem Unglück/dem Mißgeschick mit Gelassenheit.
Was können wir unternehmen, um der Konkurrenz zu begegnen?
Die Regierung begegnete dem Notstand mit energischen Maßnahmen.
Sie begegnete der Gefahr/allen Schwierigkeiten mit Umsicht.
Er begegnete ihrem Eigensinn mit Freundlichkeit/Gewalt mit Gewalt/der Drohung mit Trotz.

9. Meet with means 'to experience or undergo'. *They met with an enthusiastic reception/goodwill on every side/an accident.*
i. Begegnen also means 'to meet with or experience', *Sie sind großem Wohlwollen begegnet,* and with an adv. or phr. to receive and/or treat', *Sie begegneten uns höflich/kalt und verschlossen/mit Achtung/mit Hochmut.*
ii. In literary language **begegnen** is found in contexts stating that something remarkable, but mostly unpleasant, happens to someone. The person who meets with something is not the subj. but in the dat. *Das ist das Unerfreulichste, was einem begegnen kann. Ihm ist ein Unglück begegnet.* **Widerfahren** and **zuteilwerden** also translate **meet with**, but here too the E. subj. becomes a dat. Both mean that something happens to a person. *Ihm ist ein schweres Unglück widerfahren,* he met with a severe misfortune, a severe misfortune befell him. *Widerfahren* is mostly used with unpleasant things.

Den anderen ist das gleiche Schicksal widerfahren.
Uns ist nur gute Behandlung zuteil geworden.
He met with an accident is in everyday language *Ihm ist ein Unfall passiert* or *Er hatte einen Unfall.* On a higher stylistic level it is *Ihm ist ein Unfall zugestoßen.*
iii. *He **met** his death while mountain-climbing* is *Er fand den Tod beim Bergsteigen* or *kam beim Bergsteigen ums Leben.* Cf. KILL. *He met his death bravely* is *Er ging mutig in den Tod.*
10. Other uses. *Sich einer Herausforderung stellen,* to meet a challenge. *Jmd. begegnet einer Herausforderung mutig* etc. is also used. **Meet** with losses is *Verluste erleiden.* Cf. SUFFER B. 1. *There's more to it than **meets** the eye* is *Es steckt mehr dahinter, als man auf den ersten Blick erkennt.*

memory n. The E. word has two main meanings: (i) 'The mental capacity or faculty by which thgs. are remembered and impressions or experiences are revived or recalled'. *The memory can retain only a certain number of impressions.* It is usually considered as residing in a particular individual. *She has a good/bad memory.* An area can be added. *I have a good memory for faces.* (ii) 'A mental impression retained and revived, a recollection'. *My earliest memories of our neighbourhood are not pleasant. I only have a hazy memory of the incident.* i and ii correspond to the main meanings of *Gedächtnis* and *Erinnerung* respectively. The G. words share a sense, 'the store of recollections'.

1. Das Gedächtnis.
i. The first meaning is 'the ability of the mind to store and revive impressions, experiences, thgs. learnt, etc.' A more learned syn. is **das Erinnerungsvermögen.**

Jmd. hat/besitzt ein gutes/schlechtes/zuverlässiges Gedächtnis.

Er hat ein Gedächtnis wie ein Sieb.   *Der Verunglückte hat das Gedächtnis verloren.*
Ihr Gedächtnis läßt nach/versagt manchmal/läßt sie manchmal im Stich.
Der Unfall führte zum Verlust des Erinnerungsvermögens.

ii. The second sense is 'the store of remembered impressions, information, etc.'

Sein Gedächtnis reicht weit zurück.   *Seine Worte sind mir im Gedächtnis geblieben.*
Ich kann die Stelle aus dem Gedächtnis zitieren. Also *Man spielt ein Musikstück aus dem Gedächtnis/sagt ein Gedicht aus dem Gedächtnis auf.*
Ein solcher Vorfall prägt sich dem Gedächtnis ein.

2. Die Erinnerung.

i. The chief meaning is 'a mental impression retained and revived, a recollection'.

Meine Erinnerung an den Vorfall ist noch ganz klar/deutlich.
Ich habe nur eine schwache Erinnerung an den Vorfall.
Seine Erinnerungen reichen tief in die Vergangenheit zurück.
Der Anblick erweckt traurige Erinnerungen in mir.
Nach meiner Erinnerung war das ganz anders.
Sie zeichneten nach der Reise ihre Erinnerungen auf.

In some contexts *die Erinnerung* means 'the ability to recall'. It differs from *Gedächtnis* i in suggesting the memory of a particular occurrence. *Meine Erinnerung setzt hier aus* refers to my memory of something specific, while *Mein Gedächtnis setzt hier aus* means 'my ability to remember in general'.

Seine Erinnerungen an die Vorfälle lassen nach.   *Meine Erinnerung läßt mich im Stich.*

ii. Die Erinnerung also denotes the store of impressions etc. retained in the mind. The sing. *die Erinnerung* is a collective n. *Bei meinem guten Gedächtnis reicht die Erinnerung weit zurück.* With *etw. haben in* and *etw. bleibt jmdm. in* both *Erinnerung* and *Gedächtnis* occur.

Er schloß die Augen und döste eine Weile vor sich hin. Aus seiner Erinnerung stiegen angenehme Bilder auf. Er sah sich an seinem achtzehnten Geburtstag.
Diesen Vorfall habe ich noch gut in Erinnerung/im Gedächtnis.
Was damals geschah, ist mir ganz deutlich in Erinnerung geblieben, weil es so auffallend war. Also *im Gedächtnis geblieben.*

3. *The war is for most people* **only a memory** is *Den Krieg haben die meisten [Leute]* **nur noch schwach/blaß in Erinnerung.** Alternatives are *Die meisten haben nur noch eine schwache Erinnerung an den Krieg* and *Vom Krieg ist den meisten nur noch eine Spur im Gedächtnis/in Erinnerung geblieben.*

4. In the phrs. *in living memory* and *within the memory of,* **memory** means 'the length of time over which the recollection of a pers. or of a number of people extends'. *In living memory* can be translated by **seit Menschengedenken.** *Seit Menschengedenken hat sich noch keine so schwere Überschwemmung ereignet. Zum ersten Mal seit Menschengedenken* is 'for the first time in [living] memory'. *Es leben noch Leute, die* **sich an etw. erinnern [können],** could translate *Sth. is/happened within living memory. Es leben noch Leute, die sich an den ersten Weltkrieg erinnern.*

5. Memory also means 'the condition of being remembered or not forgotten'.

i. Like *in memory of* **zum Gedenken an** is used in solemn situations only and is mostly found on monuments. It refers either to the dead or to events which arouse feelings of sadness or awe. *Zum Gedenken an die Opfer der Nazi-Barbarei.* The same sentiment can be expressed as *Den Opfern der Nazi-Barbarei zum Gedächtnis.* **Zum Gedächtnis + an** or gen. is applied to memorable events, but not only to ones causing sadness. It is thus used like *to commemorate. Zum Gedächtnis an die Vereinigung der beiden deutschen Staaten wurde der 3. Oktober zum gesetzlichen Feiertag erklärt. Zum Gedächtnis ihres Mannes ließ die Witwe ein Waisenhaus bauen.*

Das Mahnmal wurde zum Gedenken an die Gefallenen errichtet.

Lassen Sie mich ein paar Worte zum Gedenken an unseren Kollegen sagen!
Das tut zu meinem Gedächtnis! (AV: This do in remembrance of me!)
Zum Gedächtnis an die letzte Schlacht im Befreiungskampf baute man ein kleines Museum.
Weihnachten wird zum Gedächtnis an die Geburt Jesu gefeiert.

ii. Common words expressing a related idea are **die Erinnerung** and **das Andenken**. Both are applied to what is solemn or serious, *zur Erinnerung/zum Andenken an meine Mutter*, but also often mean 'souvenir or memento'. *Das Andenken* is the usual word for *souvenir*, and *zum Andenken an* can mean 'as a souvenir or memento of'. In *Das Foto ist eine schöne Erinnerung an die gemeinsame Reise*, *Erinnerung* also means 'memento'. A syn. is *das Erinnerungsstück*. *Diese Halskette ist ein Erinnerungsstück an meine Großmutter.* *Als/Zur Erinnerung* also mean 'as a memento'. *Sie schenkte mir das Buch als Erinnerung.*

Ich habe diese Postkarte aufbewahrt zur Erinnerung an den schönen Urlaub. Also zum Andenken an.
Ich habe viele Fotos als/zur Erinnerung an unsere Schulzeit. Also als Andenken an unsere Schulzeit.
Dem aus dem Dienst scheidenden Lehrer wurde zur Erinnerung an seine Zeit an der Schule ein Bild überreicht.
Zum Andenken an Onkel Franz schenkte mir meine Tante seine Münzsammlung.
Seit kurzem gibt es im polnischen Lubowice einen Eichendorff-Verein, der das Andenken an den Dichter neu aufleben lassen möchte.

6. The **memory** of a computer is **der Speicher.**
Die Ergebnisse der Experimente wurden in den Speicher gegeben.
Der Computer hat sämtliche Adressen im Speicher, und wir können sie jederzeit abrufen.

million, billion *ns.* **Eine Million** is 'a million'. **Eine Milliarde** is 'a thousand million'. (**Billion** meaning 'a thousand million' used to be only American usage but has now spread to the rest of the English-speaking world especially in economics.) **Eine Billion** is 'a million million'. In E. we use the pl. of these numbers only when they are not preceded by a number. *Millions of dollars were wasted. It cost three million.* The pl. is necessary in G. in both cases. *Das Projekt hat Millionen/Milliarden verschlungen. Das Projekt hat drei Millionen [Mark] gekostet. Zwei Milliarden Mark.*

mind *n.* **Mind** has three main meanings: (i) 'Memory'. This is found only in expressions such as *come to mind, recall to mind, keep/bear in mind*, or *put a pers. in mind of s.o.* (ii) The sense 'what is in s.o.'s consciousness' also exists mostly in phrs. It refers either to thoughts or opinions, *We are encouraged to speak our minds*, or to intentions, *I've got a good mind to walk out.* (iii) In its main sense **mind** denotes the mental faculty or ability to think, the seat of a person's consciousness, thought, volition, and feelings, but this is often narrowed down to the cognitive or intellectual powers as distinguished from the will and emotions. G. makes a distinction between *der Geist* or *der Verstand*, which denote the ability to think, and *das Gemüt*, which refers to the emotions. Other words which express concepts carried by **mind** are *der Sinn*, which means 'sense' but also 'the faculty of thinking or s.o.'s thoughts', *die Gedanken*, 'thoughts', and *der Kopf*, 'head', which also means 'the faculty of thought'. The Arabic numbers below follow the E. senses.

1. Mind = 'memory'. *Aus den Augen, aus dem Sinn* is 'out of sight, out of mind'. *Wir müssen diese Tatsache im Auge behalten*, bear or keep in mind. *This put s.o. in mind of sth.* is *Dies erinnerte jmdn. an etw.*, reminded of. *To call to mind* is *sich erinnern an*, 'to REMEMBER', or *ins Gedächtnis zurückrufen*. The meaning of *to come to mind* is expressed in *Eine Erinnerung ging mir durch den Sinn* or *Ein Gedanke ging/fuhr mir durch den Kopf.* These G. expressions could also be a transl. of *went through my mind. Einfallen*, 'to OCCUR', could also translate *come to mind.*

2. Mind = 'what is in one's consciousness', i.e. 'opinion' or 'intention'. One sense of **mind** is 'what a pers. thinks about any subject or question, one's view, judgement, or opinion'. As a general rule, the equivalent is **die Meinung**, 'OPINION', but there are other expressions. **I'll speak my mind** could be *Ich halte mit meiner Meinung nicht hinterm Berg. I'll give him* **a piece of my mind** can be *Ich sage ihm klipp und klar meine Meinung.* **To my mind,** *that is a mistake: Meiner Meinung nach ist das ein Irrtum. We were all* **of one mind**: *Wir waren alle einer/derselben Meinung* or *Wir waren uns alle [in dieser Frage] einig.* Cf. AGREE 4. ii. The other sense is 'intention or desire'. *He doesn't* **know his own mind** can be *Er weiß nicht, was er will. I am* **in two minds** *about sth.: Ich bin unschlüssig, ob ich hingehen soll oder nicht. (Unschlüssig = 'undecided'.) I had* **a good mind** to: *Ich hatte nicht übel Lust, den Saal zu verlassen.* For *to* **make up one's mind** cf. DECIDE. **To set** one's **mind** or heart on [doing] sth. can be *sich etw. in den Kopf setzen* or *es sich in den Kopf setzen, etw. zu tun. Sie haben sich diese Reise eben in den Kopf gesetzt. Sie hat es sich in den Kopf gesetzt, die Welt allein zu umsegeln.* **I've changed my mind**, which can refer to an opinion or intention, is usually *Ich habe es mir anders überlegt*, but the more formal *Ich habe mich anders besonnen* is also heard.

3. Mind = 'power to think', 'the seat of consciousness'.

i. Der Geist, which can be 'spirit' in a religious context, denotes the mind as the seat of thought and consciousness both in a general way and in the restricted sense of 'intellect'. It is a fairly lofty term which is now restricted in use. As an equivalent of *mind* in everyday situations it sounds slightly antiquated. It occurs in *Geist und Körper*, 'mind and body', *die Geisteskrankheit*, 'mental illness', *die Geistesgegenwart*, 'presence of mind' (also *geistesabwesend*), and *Die Errungenschaften des menschlichen Geistes*, 'achievements of the human mind/spirit'. In *Streng' deinen Geist mal ein bißchen an, dann wirst du die Aufgabe schon lösen!*, *Geist* is used ironically. Only a superior would say this, e.g. teacher to pupil.

> *Der Geist ist das geheimnisvolle Etwas, das denkt und fühlt.* (Transl. of an example in the *OED*.)
> *Sie bemühte sich, ihren Geist zu bilden.*   *Sein Geist schien verwirrt/umnebelt zu sein.*
> *Sein beweglicher und lebendiger Geist war für literarische Arbeiten wie geschaffen.*

Geist is used with *haben* to state that someone has a particular kind of mind. The adjs. can denote good or bad qualities. *Er/Sie hat einen wachen/schnellen/langsamen/ prosaischen* or *einen umfassenden/überlegenen/kühnen Geist.* Such statements can also be formulated as *Jmd. ist ein wacher/prosaischer/kühner* or *ein schöpferischer/unruhiger Geist. Seine Antworten zeigen, daß er kein großer Geist ist. Geist* also denotes people with outstanding intellectual abilities, as **mind** can. *Er/Sie ist einer der großen Geister des Jahrhunderts.*

> *Unter der Führung der größten Geister der Zeit erreichte das Papsttum in diesen Jahrzehnten den Gipfel seiner Macht.   Viele bewunderten seinen feinen Geist.*

(*Geist* has several meanings. Some are: *Ein Mann von Geist* has something valuable to say and expresses it with sparkling wit and elegance. *Der Geist der Zeit*, the spirit of the age. *Im Geist der Humanität*, spirit. *Im Geist der Toleranz. Hier scheiden sich die Geister*, opinions are divided on this point. *Im Schloß geht ein Geist um*, a ghost/spirit. *Jmd./Etw. hat den Geist aufgegeben*, has given up the ghost.)

ii. Der Verstand denotes the ability to understand, think, judge, and reason. Like its closest E. equivalent the UNDERSTANDING, it means 'mind' in the sense of 'intellect', and when **mind** refers to reason, judgement, and intellectual ability, *Verstand* is now the usual equivalent.

> *Jmd. verfügt über/hat einen scharfen/klaren/nüchternen/praktischen Verstand.*
> *Man schärft den Verstand durch die Lösung solcher Aufgaben.*
> *Mit ihrem reifen Verstand hat sie die Zusammenhänge schnell erfaßt.*

iii. Das Gemüt is 'the emotional part of the mind', 'the seat of feelings and moods'.

Even in contexts in which it might seem to mean 'mind' in a general way, it stresses the emotional nature or feelings. Used with *haben* and an adj., it refers to the character or disposition as determined by the emotions, and adjs. commonly combined with it relate to the feelings or their absence. *Jmd. hat ein gutes/tiefes/warmes/ einfaches* or *ein freundliches/edles/offenes/ehrliches* or *ein ängstliches/ zaghaftes/aufrührerisches/verhärtetes Gemüt. Jmd. hat Gemüt*, possesses warmth of character or feeling. *Jmd. hat kein Gemüt* suggests he/she is deficient in feeling, soulless, has no warmth of feeling. *Du hast ein kindliches Gemüt* implies that the person is naïve. *Gemüt* can be pejorative. *Dieser Film ist etw. fürs Gemüt*, is [over-]sentimental.

Die Gedichte drücken den Zustand seines Gemüts aus.   *Sein sonniges Gemüt steckte alle an.*

Das Erlebnis bewegte das sanfte Gemüt des Kindes.   *Dieses Ereignis beunruhigte sein Gemüt.*

Die Gemütsverfassung means 'the (emotional) state of mind'. *In seiner augenblicklichen Gemütsverfassung wollte er nicht in die Kirche gehen.* A similar sense is expressed by *Ihm war nicht danach zumute, in die Kirche zu gehen*, he did not feel like going or was not in the mood to go.

iv. Die Gemüter means 'people's minds' or 'people' with no implications.

Der Skandal erregte die Gemüter.   *Die Gemüter erhitzten sich über diese Frage.*

Nach diesem Vorfall war es wichtig, die erregten Gemüter zu beruhigen.

4. Four other words express concepts carried by **mind**.

i. Der Sinn now occurs in fixed expressions in the meaning 'mind'. *Das kannst du dir aus dem Sinn schlagen*, get it out of your mind, forget it, i.e. because it's ridiculous, impossible, etc. *Die Melodie geht mir nicht aus dem Sinn* or *will mir nicht aus dem Sinn*, I can't get it out of my mind. *Er hatte nur das eine Ziel im Sinn*, kept his mind on the one goal. *So ein Gedanke war mir niemals in den Sinn gekommen*, had never entered my mind. *Jmd. ist von Sinnen*, out of his mind. *Bei Sinnen sein*, to be in one's right mind. See also 1.

ii. In everyday language **der Kopf** expresses the meaning 'mind' in the sense 'the faculty of thought, mental ability, or the contents of thought'. It is used with *haben, Jmd. hat einen hellen/wachen/guten Kopf,* and with *sein, Dieser Schüler scheint ein fähiger/kluger Kopf zu sein.* These expressions can translate *an able* etc. *mind. Gedanken/Sorgen gehen einem durch den Kopf. Jmd. hat nichts als Sport/Vergnügen im Kopf* or *hat nur Dummheiten im Kopf. Etw. geht/will mir nicht aus dem Kopf*, I can't get it out of my mind. Cf. BRAIN. *To turn over in one's* **mind**: *Sich etw. durch den Kopf gehen lassen.* Cf. CONSIDER 1. iv.

iii. Die Gedanken means 'thoughts, the contents of the mind', and in a few cases it is used like **mind**. *Jmds. Gedanken lesen* is 'to read s.o.'s mind or thoughts'.

Seine Gedanken waren/Sein Geist war von düsteren Vorahnungen erfüllt.

Seine Gedanken kehrten immer wieder zu seiner Familie zurück (thoughts or mind).

Du scheinst mit den Gedanken nicht bei der Sache zu sein. (Your mind is not on what you're doing.)

Meine Gedanken schweiften immer wieder ab. Or *Ich schweifte mit den Gedanken immer wieder ab.* (My mind wandered.)

iv. Die Seele means 'the psyche', 'what goes on in the consciousness', especially the person's deepest feelings and thoughts, a meaning the direct equivalent *soul* also has. *Her soul was in turmoil.* While thought is not excluded, *Seele* tends to stress feelings. It also often suggests an inner life not apparent outwardly. The lit. equivalent of the E. sent. *Ihre Seele war in Aufruhr* does occur, but the thought is more commonly expressed by *aufwühlen. Dieses Erlebnis hatte sie tief aufgewühlt. Sie war tief aufgewühlt.*

Der junge Romancier erweist sich als Kenner der menschlichen Seele.

Er hatte kein Verständnis für das, was sie tief in ihrer Seele bewegte.

Versetzen wir uns also einmal in die Seele und die Gedankenwelt eines Kindes/dieses Dichters!

5. Other expressions. For **close one's mind** *to sth.* see *sich verschließen* under LOCK. *To keep one's mind on sth.* can be *sich auf etw. konzentrieren. To have sth.* **on one's mind** meaning 'to be troubled by sth.' is *beunruhigen.* Cf. BOTHER. *Ich kannte meine Tante gut genug, um zu erkennen, daß irgendetwas sie beunruhigte. That* **takes my mind off** *my financial worries* is *Das lenkt mich von den Geldsorgen ab.*

miss *v.*

1. Miss means 'to fail to hit, meet, or light upon', a definition which fits both the trans. use, *I missed the target,* and the intr. use, *I fired, but I missed.*
i. When **miss** means 'to fail to hit' and is trans. with a target or something aimed at as obj., the equivalent is **verfehlen**, which needs an obj. The subj. can be either the person aiming or the missile. *Der Schütze hat das Ziel verfehlt* or *Der Schuß hat das Ziel verfehlt. Er war 15 Meter vom Tor, hat es aber verfehlt. Der Schuß verfehlte das Tor um ein paar Zentimeter.* A neg. syn. is **nicht treffen**, not to HIT. *Er schoß wieder, traf die Zielscheibe aber nicht.* The obj. of *verfehlen* can be something striven for, but it is not always translated as **miss**. *Der Läufer verfehlte den Rekord um den Bruchteil einer Sekunde. Diese Aktion hat ihren Zweck völlig verfehlt. Ihre Worte haben ihre Wirkung nicht verfehlt.*
ii. The trans. use of **miss** in which it means 'to fail to meet or find' with a person as obj. is also expressed by **verfehlen**. *Ich wollte meine Schwester vom Flughafen abholen, habe sie aber verfehlt.* It can be refl. with a pl. subj. *Wjr haben uns trotz der Verabredung verfehlt.*
iii. Verfehlen also means 'not to hit upon the right path', 'miss one's way'. *Ich habe den richtigen Eingang verfehlt und bin in das falsche Gebäude geraten. Sie müssen einen Kilometer von hier von der Straße abbiegen, aber Sie können den Weg/die Abzweigung gar nicht verfehlen.* In fig. use: *Er glaubte seinen Beruf verfehlt zu haben,* believed he had missed his vocation.
iv. Verfehlen also means 'to miss a step by mistake'. *Sie hat eine Treppenstufe verfehlt und ist gestürzt.*
v. When **miss** is intr., the obj. is understood. *He aimed carefully but missed.* **Danebenschießen** often corresponds to **miss** used intr. It needs a person as subj and implies either firing a gun or kicking a ball. *Er zielte scharf, schoß aber daneben. Der Mittelstürmer hat danebengeschoßen. Er warf daneben* means the object he threw failed to hit what he had aimed at. When the shot or blow is the subj., the v. is **danebengehen**. *Der Schuß/Der Wurf/Der Schlag ging daneben.* **Nicht treffen** is also intr. *Er schoß wieder, hat aber nicht getroffen.* Either the marksman or the shot can be the subj. *Der Schütze traf nicht. Der Schuß traf nicht.* Another intr. expression is **am Ziel vorbeischießen**, to miss one's aim, miss the target. *Zweimal schoß er am Ziel vorbei, erst mit dem dritten Schuß traf er die Zielscheibe.* (For the fig. use cf. 9.)
vi. Miss *one's footing* is **stolpern**, 'to stumble', or **ausgleiten**, 'to SLIP'. *Er stolperte und fiel hin.*

2. Miss means 'to fail to reach', 'to fail to perform or attend', or 'to fail to take advantage of'. *I missed the train/the lecture/the opportunity.*
i. Verpassen is the most frequently used word meaning 'not to catch' a train, bus, etc., 'not to take advantage of' an opportunity, and 'to fail to go to, hear, or see sth.' It suggests that, for lack of attention, someone arrives late or lets the appropriate time for doing something pass. *Wenn wir uns nicht beeilen, verpassen wir den Bus/den Zug. Er verpaßte die Stunde/die Vorlesung. Die Gelegenheit* or *die Chance* can be the obj. as well as something implying a time. *Ich will den Termin/die Verabredung/das Mittagessen nicht verpassen. Ein Schauspieler verpaßte sein Stichwort,* missed his cue.

Nachher wurde ihm klar, daß er eine Chance verpaßt hatte, die sich nicht so schnell wiederholen würde.

Eine so günstige Gelegenheit sollte man nicht verpassen.

Der Film ist so ausgezeichnet, daß man ihn nicht verpassen sollte.

ii. Versäumen means 'to fail or neglect to take advantage of by missing the right time'. It can suggest dilatoriness and undue delay but is also used when circumstances prevent someone from attending or doing something. In comparison with *verpassen* it stresses the value of what has been missed, i.e. not seen, heard, enjoyed, etc. It is used with words like *ein Termin, eine Verabredung, ein Treffen, eine Gelegenheit*, etc. With *viel, wenig*, and *nichts*, it states that someone did or did not miss much by doing or not doing something. *Als du nicht mit ins Theater gegangen bist, hast du nichts/nicht viel versäumt—die Aufführung/das Stück war schlecht. Du hast viel versäumt, weil du nicht am Ausflug teilgenommen hast. Ich möchte dieses Fest auf keinen Fall versäumen. Das Versäumte* is 'what has been missed'. *Ein Schüler, der längere Zeit krank gewesen ist, hat viel [Unterricht] versäumt und muß nun das Versäumte nachholen.* (Versäumen also means 'to neglect'. *Er hat seine Pflichten versäumt.*)

Sie versäumten keine Gelegenheit, sich mit uns zu unterhalten.

Um zwei Uhr ist ein wichtiger Termin, den ich nicht versäumen darf.

Schade, das du nicht zum Vortrag gekommen bist. Du hast wirklich etw. versäumt.

iii. Sich etw. entgehen lassen suggests letting an opportunity slip, depriving oneself of something valuable or interesting. The obj. can be an opportunity or something to be seen or heard. The blame lies with the person who has missed the opportunity, while with *versäumen* external factors can be the cause.

Dieser Film ist ein einmaliges Erlebnis, das Sie sich nicht entgehen lassen dürfen.

Eine so günstige Gelegenheit lasse ich mir nicht zum zweiten Mal entgehen.

iv. Miss also means 'to fail to attend school, church, etc. as an exception to the general rule'. *I missed school yesterday.* This sense is carried by **fehlen** with the E. obj. preceded by *in*. It states no more than that someone is not present. *Ich habe gestern in der Schule gefehlt. Sonntags fehlen sie nie in der Kirche.*

3. In *Sth. is missing [somewhere]* **missing** means either that it is not in its usual place, that it has been removed and not replaced, or that it has not been included when this could be expected. *Two pages are missing. A vital fact is missing in the report.* This sense is expressed by **fehlen**, to be absent or missing. *In diesem Buch fehlen 10 Seiten. An dem Hemd fehlt ein Knopf. A blanket has gone missing* could be either *Es fehlt eine Wolldecke* or *Eine Wolldecke ist verschwunden*.

Das Auto war ein Wrack. Es fehlten sämtliche Räder.

In dem Bericht fehlten einige wichtige Tatsachen.

Ihm fehlen zwei Vorderzähne. Man hat sie ihm in einer Schlägerei ausgeschlagen.

4. Miss used trans. means 'to perceive that a pers. or thg. is not in the expected or accustomed place', 'to notice its absence'. *When did you first miss your purse?* The equivalent is **vermissen**. *Wann haben Sie Ihr Portemonnaie zuerst vermißt? Seit einigen Tagen vermisse ich meinen Ausweis. Ich vermisse meinen Kugelschreiber—wo habe ich ihn bloß hingelegt? Wir haben dich in der Sitzung vermißt*, we missed you, or your absence was noticed. *Missing people* are *vermißte Personen* or *die Vermißten*.

5. Miss also means 'to feel that the absence of sth. is a drawback', a sense also carried by **vermissen**. *In der Wohnung vermisse ich eine Waschmaschine.*

6. When **miss** means 'to feel with regret the absence or loss of s.o./sth.', the equivalent is **vermissen**. *Das Kind vermißt seine Mutter. Mein älterer Bruder ist vor zwei Monaten zur Universität gegangen, und ich vermisse ihn sehr.* A syn. is **fehlen** + dat. with the subj. and obj. of *vermissen* reversed. *Die Mutter fehlt dem Kind* means that the child misses its mother. The obj. of *vermissen* or the subj. of *fehlen* can be a thing or an activity. *Ihm fehlt/Er vermißt sein tägliches Glas Bier mit seinen Freunden.*

7. Miss can mean 'to go without'. *They didn't want to miss their holiday.* **Missen** means 'to be or do without what one needs'. It is an elevated word only used with a modal v. Only in a few contexts does it translate **miss**. *Ich mag meinen abendlichen Spaziergang nicht missen. Sie wollten ihren Urlaub nicht missen.* (In other situations other E. vs. are needed. *Auf der Reise mußten wir alle Bequemlichkeit missen. Der Direktor möchte den neuen Mitarbeiter nicht missen.*) More common in speech is **verzichten auf**, to forgo either voluntarily or by necessity. *Er wollte nicht zum zweiten Mal auf den Jahresurlaub verzichten.*

8. Miss also means 'not to see sth. that is within view', 'to fail to hear part of what one is listening to', or 'to fail to understand'. **Entgehen** means 'to escape one's notice'. *Mir sind vielleicht ein paar Einzelheiten entgangen,* I may have missed a few details. *He didn't miss anything/much* is *Ihm ist nichts entgangen* or *Ihm ist so gut wie gar nichts entgangen.*

  Ihrem scharfen Auge ist nichts entgangen.   *Diese wichtige Kleinigkeit ist vielen entgangen.*

Miss meaning 'to fail to see' is **übersehen**. The failure to see can be intentional or unintentional.

  Ich habe überall im Haus gesucht, und der Brief lag die ganze Zeit auf dem Schreibtisch. Wie konnte ich ihn bloß übersehen?

  Sie haben beim Durchlesen des Aufsatzes ein paar Fehler übersehen.

Überhören means 'not to hear' both unintentionally and deliberately. *Ich habe leider überhört, was er eben sagte. Sie überhörte diese Frage/diese dumme Bemerkung absichtlich.* The alternatives **nicht hören** and **nicht verstehen** can only imply not hearing something unintentionally.

  Haben Sie die Durchsage verstanden? Ich habe sie überhört. Or *Ich habe sie nicht verstanden.*

9. Miss the point can be *Sie haben das Wesentliche* (the essential/important point) *nicht verstanden/begriffen.* (*Die Pointe* usually refers to a joke. *Ich habe die Pointe/den Witz nicht verstanden.*) An alternative is *Er hat das Thema verfehlt,* not written on/spoken about the actual question. *Am Ziel vorbeischießen* is used fig. *Sie schießen in Ihrem Referat am Ziel vorbei, da Sie das eigentliche Problem nicht behandeln, sondern sich mit Nebensächlichkeiten aufhalten.*

10. Miss and **miss out** mean 'to omit or leave out'. When the meaning is 'not to include', **auslassen** is the usual equivalent. *In Ihrer Übersetzung haben Sie einen ganzen Satz ausgelassen.* In *Two children were missed [out] in the distribution of presents,* *miss* is translated by **übergehen**, to pass over. As this can be on purpose or by accident, it is best to add *versehentlich/aus Versehen,* 'by mistake', or *absichtlich,* 'intentionally', to make the sense clear. *Bei der Verteilung der Geschenke wurden zwei Kinder aus Versehen übergangen.* **Miss out** meaning 'to skip' is **überspringen**. *Wir überspringen das nächste Kapitel.*

11. For *I narrowly* **missed** *being run over* see NARROW 4.

mistake, error, fault *ns.*

1. i. Der Fehler is 'a deviation from what is correct or the standard' and can translate all three E. words. It refers primarily to something concrete which is wrong or not as it should be. *Es gibt einen Fehler in der Berechnung. Ein Schreibfehler* is 'a spelling mistake'. Hence *ein Tippfehler. Einige Studenten machen noch grammatikalische Fehler. Es gibt Fehler in dieser Übersetzung. Ein Fehler* can be described as *schwer/schlimm/grob/leicht. Man macht,* or in formal language *begeht, einen Fehler.*

Other vs. commonly combined with *Fehler* are *Man stellt Fehler fest, deckt sie auf, korrigiert sie.*

ii. It is also applied to wrong decisions and actions. *Es war ein Fehler, nicht hinzugehen. Er sah seinen Fehler ein und entschuldigte sich. Wie kann ich diesen Fehler wiedergutmachen?*

iii. Der Fehler also means 'a fault or shortcoming in a pers.', *Jeder Mensch hat seine Fehler*, or 'a fault, flaw, or defect in (manufactured) goods', *Man hat den Fehler im Gerät behoben.* A syn. in these two senses is **der Mangel**, which mostly occurs in the pl. **die Mängel**. *Über diese kleinen charakterlichen Mängel, die sie wohl bald überwinden wird, wollen wir hinwegsehen. Der Apparat hat einige kleine Mängel, die sich aber leicht beheben lassen.*

> *Das Porzellan hatte kleine Fehler und wurde zu herabgesetzten Preisen verkauft.*
> *Dem Käufer sind die Mängel an dem Produkt nicht aufgefallen.*

2. There are some refl. vs. formed with **ver-** which mean 'to make a mistake in the action indicated' and sometimes correspond to a v. like *to miscalculate. Sich verzählen,* to miscount, *sich verrechnen,* to make a mistake in calculation, *sich verschätzen,* to make a wrong estimate, *sich verwählen,* to make a mistake in dialling, *sich verhören,* to hear wrongly. *Ich habe mich versprochen* means that I have either made a mistake in pronunciation or said something which does not make sense or is wrong. *Sich versehen* means 'to make a mistake in seeing'. *Sie hat sich in der Zeit versehen. Ich versah mich beim Lesen der Zahlen.*

> *Als ich den hohen Preis las, glaubte ich zunächst, mich versehen zu haben.*

3. When **mistake** suggests an error of judgement, a misconception, or a misunderstanding, i.e. a mistake which exists in the mind, the equivalent is **der Irrtum**, which means 'a mistaken or faulty belief, judgement, or idea'. It does not refer to something concrete like a mistake in calculation or spelling. *Ein Irrtum* manifests itself mainly in someone's judgements or views but can show itself in actions. *Man begeht einen Irrtum in der Einschätzung der Lage/in der Beurteilung eines Ereignisses. Man erkennt/verbessert/ beseitigt einen Irrtum* and *sieht einen Irrtum ein* or *gibt einen Irrtum zu.*

> *Es ist ein Irrtum, wenn du glaubst, sie werden dir helfen.*
> *Es war ein Irrtum zu glauben, er wollte sich ändern.*   *Alle diese Hoffnungen waren Irrtümer.*
> *Daß man Ihnen diese Arbeit gegeben hat, beruht auf einem Irrtum.*
> *Auf Grund eines Irrtums ist er nicht rechtzeitig benachrichtigt worden.*
> *Wenn du glaubst, das verhalte sich so, bist du sehr im Irrtum.*

4. Das Versehen is 'a mistake which results from lack of attention', but it extends from slight mistakes made inadvertently to ones with grave consequences. *Aus Versehen* means 'by mistake'. A syn. is the adv. **versehentlich**.

> *Wir bedauern sehr, Ihnen die falschen Waren zugeschickt zu haben und bitten Sie, das Versehen zu entschuldigen.*   *Das ist ein Versehen, das jedem passieren kann.*
> *Aus Versehen habe ich diesen Brief mitgenommen.*
> *Sie ist versehentlich ins falsche Zimmer gegangen.*

5. Der Mißgriff is applied to actions and decisions which turn out to be misguided or wrong. *Es war ein Mißgriff, diesen Mann zu wählen—er ist eine Niete. Der Kauf dieses Autos war ein Mißgriff. Fehler* can also be used in these sents.

mix, mix up vs.

1. i. The main equivalent of the primary sense of **mix** 'to bring different materials together and cause a uniform mass to be formed' is **mischen**. *Man mischt Zutaten, Farben, Chemikalien usw. Stoffe, die gemischt werden, lassen sich nicht mehr* *unterscheiden. Mischen* is used with *mit, in,* or *unter. Man muß das Backpulver gleichmäßig unter das Mehl mischen, damit der Kuchen nicht nur an einer Stelle geht.* It also means 'to produce sth. by mixing'. *Man mischt ein Getränk/einen Cocktail.* (**Mixen** is sometimes used for drinks. *Ich mixe dir einen Cocktail/einen Drink.*)

> *Die Zutaten zum Kuchen werden in einer Schüssel gemischt.*

Mischen is also applied to emotions. *Ihre Freude war mit Bedauern gemischt.* Hence *gemischte Gefühle.*

ii. Vermischen emphasizes the process more strongly, as well as the care and thoroughness with which this is carried out. To stress the idea, *gut* or *stark* is often added. *Vermischen* mostly occurs as a past part.

> *Das Mehl wird mit der Butter, etwas Salz und einem Ei vermischt und zu einem ausrollbaren Teig geknetet.*
>
> *Der Eischnee wird unter den übrigen Teig gemischt. Teig und Eischnee dürfen jedoch nicht so stark vermischt werden, daß der Eischnee nicht mehr sichtbar ist.*
>
> *Die Chemikalien werden im richtigen Verhältnis gemischt/vermischt.*

iii. Mengen is 'to mix two materials, one of which at least must be dry and consist of solid particles'. *Man mischt zwei Flüssigkeiten* but *mengt Sand mit/und Zement. Mischen,* however, can also be used in the latter case. *Mengen* is also used with *in* or *unter. Man mengt die Rosinen unter/in den Teig.* **Vermengen** stresses the process and suggests thoroughness. It, too, is often used with *gut.* Neither *mengen* nor *vermengen* is as common as *mischen* or *vermischen.*

> *Sie mengte die verschiedenen Zutaten in einem Topf.*
>
> *Er ist gerade dabei, das Futter für die Pferde zu mengen.*
>
> *Sie hatte Mehl, Zucker und Butter gut miteinander vermengt.*
>
> *Alle Zutaten müssen gut miteinander vermengt werden.*

iv. Special uses of *mischen* and *vermischen. Spielkarten mischen* is 'to shuffle cards' and *einen Salat mischen* 'to toss a salad'. *Eine gemischte Klasse* contains boys and girls, and *vermischte Nachrichten* are 'miscellaneous news'.

2. Refl. vs.

i. With a non-personal subj. *sich mischen* and *sich vermischen* correspond either to the E. intr. use, *Oil and water don't* **mix**, or to the E. pass., *Love* **was mixed** *with hatred in his mind.* Both express the idea that two or more things mix, combine, mingle, or blend, but one or the other seems to be preferred in particular contexts. In reference to groups **sich mischen** implies that they are no longer separate. *Die Gruppen haben sich gemischt.* Both *sich mischen* and **sich vermischen** are applied to emotions or qualities which combine in someone's mind, words, etc. *In seiner Antwort mischten sich Haß und Liebe. In seinen Erzählungen vermischen sich Phantasie und Wirklichkeit. In meine Freude mischte sich Angst.*

> *Im Grenzgebiet mischen sich die beiden Kulturen.*
>
> *In ihr mischen sich Entschlossenheit und Vorsicht.*
>
> *In die Bitterkeit seiner Antwort mischte sich Bewunderung.*
>
> *In den Maschinenlärm mischten sich menschliche Stimmen.*

Sich vermischen is the v. mostly used to state that two liquids mix or do not mix. *Öl und Wasser vermischen sich nicht. (Sich mischen* is also possible.) *Sich vermischen* is used for the mixing of races by intermarriage. *In kurzer Zeit hatten sich die Eroberer mit den Einheimischen vermischt.*

ii. Sich mischen unter with a person as subj. means 'to mix or mingle with a crowd, the people, spectators, etc.' *Einige Polizisten mischten sich unter die Menge/die Zuschauer.*

iii. With a person as subj., **sich mischen** means 'to interfere or meddle, to become involved in what is not one's business'. **Sich einmischen** has the same meaning and must be used when the sent. does not include a phr. with *in. Mischen Sie sich* *hier nicht ein!* With *in*, both are possible, i.e. *ein* is optional, but *einmischen* is probably more usual. *Ich will mich in diese Angelegenheit/Sache nicht [ein]mischen.*

Mischen Sie sich nicht in Sachen [ein], die Sie nichts angehen!

Da will ich mich lieber nicht einmischen.

3. When the obj. of **mix** is things which are not concrete, as in *to mix business and/with pleasure*, **verbinden**, 'to combine', is used. *Er wollte Arbeit mit Vergnügen verbinden.*

4. Mix with people meaning 'to associate with them' is **umgehen mit, Umgang haben mit**, or **verkehren mit**.

Sage mir, mit wem du umgehst, und ich sage dir, wer du bist. (Sprichwort)

Die beiden sind immer zusammen. Es scheint, daß niemand mit ihnen umgehen will.

Er hat Umgang mit einigen chinesischen Studenten und weiß über vieles, was in China passiert, gut Bescheid.   Sie verkehren mit Mitgliedern aller Klassen und Berufsgruppen.

5. Mix up = 'to confuse'. There are three meanings.

i. The usual v. when *confuse* or **mix up** mean 'to mistake one thg. for another' is **verwechseln**. *Sie haben die Begriffe verwechselt/haben Satyr und Satire verwechselt. Jmd.* **bringt** *Begriffe/Vorstellungen* **durcheinander** is also common.

ii. Vermischen, and less commonly **vermengen**, mean 'to mix up' in the sense 'to bring together arguments or fields of experience which do not belong together or are incompatible'. *Sie haben Tatsachen und/mit Vermutungen vermischt/vermengt. Sie vermischen wirtschaftliche und moralische Aspekte/Phantasie und Wirklichkeit.*

iii. Be mixed up applied to a person is **verwirrt sein**, confused. *Ich war wegen dieser vielen Fragen ganz verwirrt.* A product of the mind which is confused or mixed-up is **verworren** or **wirr**. *Verworrene/Wirre Gedanken/Vorstellungen.*

6. Be/get mixed up in sth. is **verwickeln**. Cf. INVOLVE. *Ich war in diese unangenehme Angelegenheit/in den Streit verwickelt.*

most *adj. and adv.* **mostly** *adv.*

1. As the superlative of *much* and *many*, **most** is used with and without the definite article. *Who made [the] most mistakes? Those who have [the] most money are not always the happiest.* **Meist** needs an article. *Wer hat die meisten Fehler gemacht? Diejenigen, die das meiste Geld haben, sind nicht immer die glücklichsten. Er hat von uns allen die meisten Bücher. Sie hat das meiste Talent.* When **most** is an adv., i.e. the superlative of the adv. *much*, the equivalent is **am meisten**. *Er arbeitet/verdient am meisten. Was hat Sie am meisten interessiert? Die am meisten befahrenen Straßen.*

2. i. Most forms the superlative of some adjs. and advs. *This is the most interesting book I've read for a long time* is *Dies ist das interessanteste Buch, das ich seit langem gelesen habe. The mistake occurring [the] most frequently* is *der am häufigsten vorkommende Fehler.*

ii. Most is also an intensifier meaning 'very' or 'exceedingly'. It is used without an article, *That was most interesting*, with the indefinite article, *It's a most useful book*, or with *some, a few*, etc., *She made some most interesting remarks.* The equivalent is **höchst** or **äußerst**. *Das war höchst/äußerst interessant. Das war ein höchst ungewöhnlicher Vorfall/ein äußerst interessanter Film. Sie machte einige höchst/äußerst interessante Bemerkungen.*

3. Most also means 'the majority of' or 'the greater part of' and is often used with *of*, as in *most of the money*.

i. Der größte Teil is the main equivalent of this meaning. *Den größten Teil des Geldes habe ich schon ausgegeben.* **Meist** also has this sense with pl. ns., and in the expression *die meiste Zeit*, which is the only case where *meist* is used with a sing. n. in this sense. Thus with pl. ns. *der größte Teil* and *die meisten* are interchangeable. *Der größte Teil der Schüler* and *die meisten Schüler*. Whereas in E. *of* is necessary with sing. ns. after **most**, *most of the class*, it is optional with pl. ones, *most [of the] pupils*. The usual G. construction with *meist* is without a gen. *Die meisten Tage. In den meisten Fällen. Die meisten Leute. Die meisten Kollegen fahren über Weihnachten nicht weg. Die meisten der Kollegen* is only possible when a relative clause follows or is implied. *Die meisten der Kollegen, die sich für das Thema interessieren, haben an der Diskussion teilgenommen.* It occurs without a clause if it is clear from the context which group is meant. *Die meisten der Kollegen waren da (der* stressed). When a possessive or *dieser* follows, a gen. is necessary. *Die meisten seiner Bücher. In den meisten dieser Fälle.*

ii. Most or **most of it/them** stand for a n. which has just been used. *There was a lot to do, but I've done most of it already.* Here both **das meiste [davon]** or **der größte Teil [davon]** are possible. *Das meiste* can stand for any preceding sing. n, and *der größte Teil* for any n. whether sing. or pl. *Die meisten* replaces a pl. n. *Ich habe es früher gewußt, aber das meiste schon vergessen. Ich habe das meiste/den größten Teil verstanden/gelesen. Einige Schüler haben sich gelangweilt, aber den meisten hat die Aufführung gut gefallen.*

> *Ich hatte sehr viel Arbeit, aber das meiste/den größten Teil [davon] habe ich schon erledigt.*

4. Mostly is **meistens** or **meist**, which do not differ in sense. *Abends bin ich meist/meistens zu Hause. Beim Schach gewinnt meist/meistens meine Tochter. Die Anwesenden waren meist jüngere Leute.*

5. At the most is **höchstens**. *Ich zahle höchstens 100 Mark. Es waren höchstens 50 Leute da.*

move *v.* 1. **Move** = 'to be put in motion' and *bewegen, sich bewegen*, and some syns. 2. The equivalents of **move** meaning, when trans., 'to change the place or position of', 'to take from one place to another' and, when intr., 'to change position'. 3. *Ziehen*, 'to move or go somewhere', and its derivatives related to moving house. 4. **Move** with a piece in chess etc. as obj. 5. Vs. meaning 'to move emotionally'. 6. **Move** = 'to induce s.o. to do sth.' 7. **Move** = 'to propose a motion at a meeting'.

1. [Sich] bewegen and syns.

i. In one sense **move** means 'to put and/or keep in motion', *The wind moved the leaves*, and 'to change the position of the body, or parts of it, or of thgs.', *He moved his arm*. **Bewegen** expresses these senses. It means 'to cause s.o./sth. to get out of a stationary position' and refers to an unspecified movement, one which of necessity changes the position of something, but the place to which it is moved is not stated. The only phr. indicating a change of position with which it is used is *von der Stelle*, from the spot. It is the usual word when stating whether someone can or cannot move something (without saying to where) and in reference to the body or parts of it. **Bewegt** is the opposite of *ruhend*, stationary. *Ein bewegter Körper* is 'a moving body or object'. In *Die stark bewegte See erschwerte die Rettung der Schiffbrüchigen, bewegt* means 'rough'.

> *Das Klavier war so schwer, daß er es nicht von der Stelle bewegen konnte.*
>
> *Der Hebel ist verrostet. Ich habe mich wie ein Ochs angestrengt, aber ich kann ihn nicht bewegen.*
>
> *Der Wind bewegte die Blätter/die Oberfläche des Wassers/die Gardinen.*
>
> *Der Schrank war aus massivem Eichenholz und fast nicht von der Stelle zu bewegen.*
>
> *Beim Bau der Tiefgarage unter der zukünftigen Universitätsbibliothek mußten Tausende von Kubikmeter Erde bewegt werden.*
>
> *Er war schwer gestürzt. Vorsichtig bewegte er Arme und Beine, um zu sehen, ob auch nichts gebrochen war.*

Die Kälte hatte ihre Hände ganz steif gemacht, und es bereitete ihr Mühe, die Finger zu bewegen.

ii. Move used intr., meaning either 'to be in motion' (often in contrast to being stationary or stuck) or 'to change position or exhibit physical activity' in reference to the body or parts of it, is expressed by **sich bewegen.** The movement is usually of an unspecified nature. Galileo's remark, 'It [the earth] does move', is in G. *'Und sie bewegt sich doch!'* Thus *Der festgefahrene Wagen bewegte sich nicht von der Stelle.* The movement need not involve going to a new place but, for example, only altering one's lying position. *Das Kind bewegte sich im Schlaf. Der Verletzte konnte sich vor Schmerzen kaum bewegen.* In *Ich sah, wie sich eine Gestalt im Dunkeln bewegte, sich bewegte* need only imply that the figure turns round, gets up, or makes a slight movement. Likewise *Das Wasser im Kessel begann sich zu bewegen. Die Gardinen bewegten sich im Wind hin und her. Die Büsche bewegten sich, und ein Hund sprang hervor.* A phr. stating a direction, or an adv. stating how s.o./sth. moved, is often added. *Der Festzug bewegte sich langsam durch die Stadt.* Sich bewegen can be used with a phr. expressing the velocity with which something moves, but in an everyday case, like a car, *fahren* would be usual. *Das Auto fuhr mit großer Geschwindigkeit durch die Stadt.* **Begin to move** is **sich in Bewegung setzen.** *Der Zug setzte sich in Bewegung.* (An alternative in this context is *Der Zug fuhr an.*)

> *Die Planeten bewegen sich um die Sonne.*   *Der Trauerzug bewegte sich zum Friedhof.*
> *Das Licht bewegt sich mit einer konstanten Geschwindigkeit, unabhängig davon, ob es von einem ruhenden oder von einem bewegten Körper emittiert wird.*
> *Ein Flugzeug bewegt sich gleichmäßig, unmerklich. Sieht man nicht zum Fenster hinaus, so merkt man nicht, daß man fliegt.*

Don't move! can imply either not moving part of the body or not moving from the spot. *Bewegen Sie sich nicht!* can have both senses, and *von der Stelle* can be added to make the second clear. A photographer might say, *'Bitte recht freundlich lächeln und nicht bewegen!'* (*Sich* is understood here.) *Stell dich dorthin und beweg dich nicht! Keine Bewegung!* is a strong command given, for example, when a policeman covers someone with a gun.

(*Bewegen* can mean 'to exercise'. *Pferde müssen täglich bewegt werden.* To get some exercise in reference to people is *sich bewegen* or *sich Bewegung machen* or *verschaffen. Sie fühlen sich unwohl, weil sie sich zu wenig bewegen. Wenn Sie sich regelmäßig Bewegung verschaffen, wird es Ihnen besser gehen.*)

iii. Move also means 'to frequent a particular sphere [in a certain manner]'. *They move in diplomatic circles.* **Sich bewegen** has this sense. *Sie bewegt sich [mit Sicherheit] in den vornehmsten Kreisen.* Thoughts, plans, and prices can also be the subj. *Seine Pläne bewegen sich in ganz anderer Richtung. Der Preis bewegt sich zwischen 50 und 70 Mark. Sich frei bewegen* can imply moving without inner or outer restrictions. *Die Diplomaten dürfen die Hauptstadt nicht verlassen, dürfen sich aber darin frei bewegen.*

iv. Sich fortbewegen means 'to move about, forwards, or in a direction'. *Der Kranke kann sich nur langsam fortbewegen. Er bewegt sich* need only imply moving his limbs. Particularly for animals *sich fortbewegen* describes the way they move as a natural characteristic. *Diese Eidechsen bewegen sich sehr schnell/mit großer Schnelligkeit fort.*

v. Rühren is 'to move a little' when limbs or wings are the obj. *Der Vogel begann die Flügel zu rühren.* **Sich rühren** suggests a slight, often hardly noticeable movement, in the neg. not even the slightest movement. *Er rührte sich nicht,* did not move or stir. A parent might say to a child, *'Ich gehe ins Geschäft. Bleib hier und rühr dich nicht von der Stelle!'* (*Bewegen* is possible but sounds stricter.) *Sich rühren* can imply showing a sign of energy, becoming active to help someone or do something expected or some work. *Komm', rühr' dich ein bißchen!,* bestir yourself, get a move on. *Er rührte sich nicht/rührte keinen Finger, um mir zu helfen.* (As a military command, *Rührt euch!* means 'stand at ease'.) **Regen** suggests the beginning of a movement, thus a very slight change in the position of something. *Der Verletzte regte kein Glied. Regen* and **sich regen** are syns. of *rühren* and *sich rühren* meaning 'to stir or move', but are stylistically higher. *Vor Kälte konnte sie die Finger kaum rühren/regen. Kein Muskel seines Gesichtes regte sich.* Sich regen is used with things which do not have the power to move themselves, *Die Blätter regten sich leise im Wind*, in contrast to *sich rühren*, which suggests moving by its/one's own strength.

> Als die Beute sich nicht mehr rührte/regte, ließ der Bär von ihr ab.
> Er war so verängstigt, daß er sich nicht mehr zu rühren/zu regen wagte.
> Ich habe ihm zweimal geschrieben, aber er hat sich nicht gerührt.
> Wir klingelten mehrere Male, aber im Haus rührte/regte sich niemand.
> Sie bat ihn um Hilfe, aber er rührte keinen Finger
> Wir stemmten uns mit allen Kräften gegen den Stein, aber er rührte/bewegte sich nicht.

2. Words denoting a change of position.

i. Move is intr. in the meaning 'to change one's position so as to get out of s.o.'s way'. *Could you please move?* When **move** suggests changing position to allow someone to pass, **Platz machen**, 'to make room', or **zur Seite treten**, 'to step aside', can be used. *Der hochbeladenen Dame, die vorbeigehen wollte, machte ich Platz. Ich trat zur Seite, damit die hochbeladene Dame durchkönnte.* A policeman asks, '**Gehen Sie bitte weiter!**', move on.

ii. Move is trans. in the meaning 'to take sth. out of the way'. *I'll move the books on the table.* **Wegnehmen**, 'to take away, remove', is used for anything that can be easily lifted. *Ich nehme die Bücher hier weg.*

> Nimm die Schuhe dort weg! Sie stehen sonst jedem im Wege.
> Erst im letzten Augenblick nahm er die Hand weg.

Schaffen means 'to take sth. at least moderately heavy either to or from a place' and sometimes corresponds to *move. Wir müssen diese Sachen in den Keller schaffen.* **Wegschaffen** means 'to move away' and may imply getting rid of something. *Wir müssen dieses alte Gerümpel wegschaffen.* When a phr. makes it clear that something is being moved out of, or away from, a place, *schaffen* is sufficient, but *weg* may be added. *Wir müssen dieses alte Gerümpel aus dem Haus [weg]schaffen.*

If **move** is trans. with a personal obj., as in *The policemen moved the group/the teenagers on*, it could be *Mehrere Polizisten versuchten, die Menge/die Jugendlichen zum Weitergehen zu bewegen*. Cf. 6.

iii. Rücken can be trans. and mean 'to move a short distance, often in stages'. It is the v. usually applied to moving furniture. It needs a phr. stating where something is moved to. *Rücken Sie Ihren Sessel näher ans Feuer!* If the place is not stated, **verrücken** is used. Someone who notices that a table has been moved might ask, 'Wer hat den Tisch verrückt?' or if asking who moved it to a certain place, '*Wer hat den Tisch ans Fenster gerückt?*' A distance does not fulfil the condition that the place to which the thing is moved be stated. *Wir haben den Schrank um 20 Zentimeter verrückt.* But *Wir haben den Tisch um 20 cm. zur Wand gerückt.*

> Sie rückte sämtliche Schränke von der Wand, aber die Münze war nicht zu finden.
> Schnell wurden Tische und Stühle zur Seite gerückt, um Platz zum Tanzen zu machen.
> Die schwere Kiste ließ sich um keinen Millimeter verrücken.
> Aus der oberen Wohnung war ein Lärm zu hören, als verrückten sie ihre Möbel.

Rücken is also intr. and can have a person as subj. *Er ist mit dem Stuhl näher an das Feuer gerückt. Mit dem Stuhl* can be omitted if it is clear what is meant. **Rücken** also means 'to move along in a row of seats' and has other uses which are expressed by **move** indicating a change of position.

> Er bat sie höflich, noch ein wenig zu rücken, damit auch er auf der Kirchenbank Platz nehmen könnte.

Würden Sie wohl mal einen Platz weiter rücken?
Durch großartige Erzählungen versuchte er, sich in den Mittelpunkt des Interesses zu rücken.
Die Mannschaft verbesserte sich und rückte auf den vierten Platz.

Heranrücken means 'to move closer to the speaker'. It can be trans., *Sie rückte den Stuhl näher heran, um besser verstehen zu können,* and intr., *Rücken Sie näher heran!*

iv. Schieben means 'to push or shove', and **verschieben** means 'to change the position of sth. by pushing or shoving'. Both can translate **move** when it is trans. provided that the thing whose position is changed is a large object. They stand in the same relation to each other as *rücken* and *verrücken* discussed in 2. iii. *Sie schob die Kiste in die Ecke.* But *Wir müssen den Schrank noch ein paar Zentimeter/ein Bißchen verschieben. The front seats (of the car) can be moved (backwards and forwards)* is *Man kann die Vordersitze verschieben* or *Die Vordersitze lassen sich verschieben. Die Grenze* can be the obj. of *verschieben. Man hat die Grenze um zwei kilometer nach Westen verschoben.*

Helfen Sie mir bitte, das Klavier ins Wohnzimmer zu schieben!
Er verschob die Bücher auf seinem Schreibtisch, um mehr Platz zu bekommen.

Sich verschieben means 'to move or shift' in the sense 'to become displaced'.

Sein Schlips/Ihr Kopftuch hatte sich verschoben.
Einige Platten des Bürgersteigs hatten sich verschoben.

v. Verstellen can mean 'to put in the wrong place'. *Ich habe das Buch im Regal verstellt und kann es nicht finden.* It also means 'to alter the way sth. is set'. *Jmd. hat meinen Rückspiegel verstellt.* A further meaning is 'to adjust to what one wants'. In *Die Rückenlehnen der Vordersitze lassen sich [in der Höhe] verstellen* it means 'to adjust for height' or 'to move up and down'. (Cf. 2. iv for backward and forward movement.) *Verstellen* also means 'to put furniture and other objects in a different position' and suggests a greater move than *verrücken. Wer hat die Möbel verstellt?*

vi. Verlegen means 'to move from one position to another', 'to set sth. up in a different place'. The obj. is something of some size, *ein Büro, die Geschäftsräume, der Sitz einer Firma, der Wohnsitz, ein Lager, eine Haltestelle, die Grenze,* as well as people, including *Truppen,* and activities. The move is usually over some distance. As explained under CHANGE 5. i, *verlegen* means 'to move a meeting etc. to another time' and can be used either alone or with one or both times mentioned. *Die Sitzung wurde von Montag auf Mittwoch verlegt. (Verlegen* also means 'to mislay'. *Ich habe meinen Schlüsselbund verlegt.)*

Da die Räume der germanistischen Abteilung zu klein geworden waren, wurde sie in ein Gebäude verlegt, wo ihr mehr Raum zur Verfügung stand.
Eine weitere Division wurde an die Front verlegt.
Die Firma hat ihren Sitz in eine kleinere Stadt/ins Ausland verlegt.
Das Fußballspiel mußte in ein anderes Stadion verlegt werden.
Man verlegt die Flüchtlinge aus dem grenznahen Gebiet in ein etwa 50 Kilometer entferntes Lager.

vii. With things as obj., **versetzen** means 'to move sth. which has a fixed position to a new position', but the things are relatively small, and the change of position relatively slight. *Man versetzt die Knöpfe an einem Kleid/die Lampen in der Decke/einen Lichtschalter* etc. *Man hat die Haltestelle versetzt* implies moving it a short distance. *Man hat die Haltestelle verlegt* suggests a new position at least some distance away. *Versetzen* is used for plants as an alternative to *verpflanzen,* to transplant. With people as obj., *versetzen* means 'to transfer'. *Im Laufe ihres Berufslebens werden Offiziere mehrmals zu anderen Einheiten versetzt. Einen Schüler versetzen* is 'to promote to the next class', but *Der Lehrer versetzte den Schüler nach vorn* means that he moved him to the front of the class[room].

Als die Straße verbreitert wurde, hat man die Straßenlaternen um anderthalb Meter versetzt.
Sie müssen das Komma um eine Stelle nach rechts versetzen (Komma here = 'decimal point').

Wir müssen das Bild um zehn cm. zum Fenster hin versetzen.
Ich muß die Büsche versetzen, bevor sie zu groß werden.

viii. Verlagern is applied to moving or shifting a weight. *Man verlagert eine Last von einer auf die andere Schulter. Man verlagert das Gewicht auf das andere Bein.* With *der Schwerpunkt* and *das Haupt-* or *Schwergewicht*, it means 'to shift the emphasis'. *Sie verlagerte den Schwerpunkt/das Schwergewicht der Arbeit auf eine andere Frage. Verlagern* also means 'to move sth. usually valuable to a different place in order to store it there'. *Während des Krieges verlagerte man die Kunstschätze des Museums aufs Land.* The intr. use of *shift* or **move** with weight or emphasis as subj. corresponds to **sich verlagern**. It is common in weather reports for the movement of areas of high or low pressure.

> *Bei dieser Turnübung verlagert sich das Körpergewicht abwechselnd auf das rechte und das linke Bein.*
> *Ein Hochdruckgebiet über den Alpen verlagert sich nach Osten.*
> *Im Laufe der Untersuchung verlagerte sich der Schwerpunkt auf eine Frage, die zuerst unbedeutend erschien.*

3. Move intr. = 'to go somewhere' and 'to change one's place of residence'.

i. Ziehen is applied to the movement of a mass of people or animals. It needs a phr. of direction or place, and is intr. in this sense, forming the perf. with *sein*. *Die Demonstranten sind durch die Straßen gezogen. Das Heer zog vor die Stadt. Die Vögel ziehen nach Süden.* Inanimate things, mainly natural phenomena, can also be the subj. *Eine Wolke zog über uns weg. Eine Regenfront zog durch die Wüste.* It is only rarely used for an individual. *Er zog durch die Welt*, moved around/about the world.

ii. Another meaning of **ziehen** is 'to leave one's previous place of residence and go somewhere else'. It can refer to an individual. *Er zog in die Fremde. Ziehen* is used for changing one's abode when the sent. contains a phr. of direction. *Sie ziehen nach Paderborn/aufs Land.* Without such a phr. **umziehen** is necessary. *Sie ziehen morgen um. Um* is found in sents. containing a phr., but it is optional. *Sie ziehen in eine kleinere Wohnung [um].* **Einziehen** and **ausziehen** are 'to move in and out'. *Unsere neuen Nachbarn ziehen morgen ein. Wir ziehen Ende Oktober aus.*

iii. For a move of some distance, for example from one country to another, **übersiedeln** is usual. *Die Familie ist von Irland nach Australien übergesiedelt.* **Move** (trans.) meaning 'to resettle', as in *A government moves people*, is **umsiedeln**. *Der Stamm wurde umgesiedelt, weil ihr Land zur Wüste geworden war.*

4. Move in reference to men or pieces in draughts, chess, etc. is either **ziehen** or **rücken**. Like **move**, both are trans. and intr. *Er zog den bedrohten Springer auf ein anderes Feld. Die Königin darf in jede Richtung ziehen/rücken. Du mußt ziehen/rücken*, it's your move. An alternative is *Du bist am Zug*.

5. Move means 'to affect with emotion', either with the emotion specified, as in *This sight moved them to tears* or *to pity/laughter/anger*, or with the emotion left vague, *She was deeply moved*.

i. *This* **moved** *s.o. to anger/laughter*, etc. can be translated as *aroused anger* etc., a meaning expressed by **erregen**. *Etw. erregte jmds. Zorn/Heiterkeit.* An alternative is **auslösen**. *Diese Bemerkungen lösten Gelächter aus.* **Rühren** is used with *zu Tränen*. *Dieser Anblick hat auch die härtesten Menschen zu Tränen gerührt.* Even without such a phr. *gerührt* suggests emotion which brings people close to tears. *Durch diese Geschichte war sie tief gerührt.*

ii. Bewegen is applied to a range of emotions, *Jmd. war von Angst/Kummer/Sorge/Freude/Hoffnung bewegt*, and can mean 'to stir up emotion' in a general way, *Die Frage nach der Schuld der Angeklagten bewegte die Gemüter. Seine warmherzigen Worte* *haben sie sehr bewegt.* It can mean 'to occupy people's minds', *Wir besprachen eine Frage, die uns damals sehr bewegte,* but it is mostly used when the emotion is sorrow, shock, or pity.

Voll Trauer und tief bewegt, verkündete der Präsident den Absturz der Raumfähre.

Die Trauerrede hatte die Anwesenden tief bewegt.

iii. Ergreifen is like *bewegen* but implies strong or deep emotion. *Das Elend dieser armen Menschen hat alle sehr ergriffen. Die Musik/Die Handlung des Romans hat mich tief ergriffen.*

6. In *Sth. moved s.o. to do sth.,* **move** means 'to operate as a motive'. **Bewegen** means 'to induce, cause, or move s.o. to do sth.' and is a strong v., *bewegen, bewog, bewogen.* It is followed either by an infin. or *zu* + a n. denoting an action. *Was hat dich bewogen, dich so zu verhalten?* or *Nichts konnte ihn zum Bleiben/zum Eintritt in den Verein bewegen.* Cf. *jmdn. zu etw. bringen* under MAKE 6.

Er fühlte sich nicht bewogen, in dieser Angelegenheit etw. zu unternehmen.

7. Move = 'to propose in a deliberative body, meeting, etc.' is **beantragen** or **den Antrag stellen**, to move a motion at a meeting. *Der Abgeordnete beantragte die Einsetzung eines Untersuchungsausschusses,* moved [for] the setting up of. **Move** + a clause, as in *He moved that sth. be done,* can also be translated by *beantragen* or *den Antrag stellen. Sie beantragte/stellte den Antrag, daß das übriggebliebene Geld zur Anschaffung neuer Bücher für die Bibliothek benutzt werden sollte.*

much, very much *advs.* **Much** and **very much** modify a participle, *a much discussed book, He wasn't much interested in the news,* or a v., *I love her very much* or *The film didn't interest me much.* There are two senses involved: one denotes frequency and means either 'on many occasions' or 'by many people'; the other refers to the intensity of the feeling or response.

i. Viel denotes frequency; **sehr** expresses intensity and means 'to a high degree'. *Ein viel besprochener Fall* is 'much discussed or talked about', i.e. 'on many occasions and/or by many people'. *Ich liebe sie sehr* means 'I love her very much', i.e. 'intensely, to a high degree'. *Viel* and the following part. are often written as one word. *Ein vielbesuchter Urlaubsort, ein vielgelesenes Buch.* The number of parts. used with *viel* is limited. *Much loved/beloved* used to be *vielgeliebt* but is now *sehr geliebt.* The comparative and superlative of both *sehr* and *viel* are *mehr* and *am meisten. Ich liebe sie jeden Tag mehr. Von allen Kollegen schätze ich ihn am meisten.*

Der Film hat mich sehr interessiert.   *Heute abend wird ein vieldiskutierter Film gezeigt.*

ii. The main difference between E. and G. is that **sehr** can modify a v. directly, *Das bedauere ich sehr,* whereas *very* cannot and must always stand together with **much**, *I regret it very much.* Thus *sehr* often translates **very much**. *Er bewundert sie sehr. Sie haßt ihn sehr. Ich vermisse sie sehr. Die Stadt hat sich nicht sehr verändert. Das wünsche ich mir sehr.* Note that both *etw. gefällt mir sehr* and *etw. gefällt mir gut* are commonly used without any difference in meaning.

iii. Very much also intensifies some phrs. with a prep. *They were very much against/in favour of this.* The equivalent is also **sehr**. *Sie waren sehr dagegen/sehr dafür.*

iv. The E. combination *to be* + past part. is intensified by *very* and an optional *much. I was very [much] concerned.* This is also translated by **sehr**. *Ich war sehr beunruhigt.*

Ich würde mich sehr wundern, wenn sie es nicht schafft (be very [much] surprised).

Wenn Sie das glauben, irren Sie sich sehr (are very much mistaken).

v. Sehr viel does occur in G., but it refers only to quantity. *Er ißt sehr viel/nicht sehr viel.* The pos. is translated as *He eats a lot,* and the neg. as *He doesn't eat a lot/very much.*

vi. Sehr viel is also used before a comparative. *Es geht ihr sehr viel besser.*

narrow[ly] *adj* and *adv.*

1. Narrow = 'not wide'. This sense is carried both by *schmal* and *eng*. **Schmal** is the opposite of *breit*. It refers to a surface or to something which looks like a surface, and is limited to the one dimension. *Ein schmales Band. Ein schmales Brett. Eine schmale Brücke. Eine schmale Treppe. Ein schmales Stück Land.* In one sense **eng** refers to space and states that this is very restricted or confined. It thus refers to three dimensions. *Ein enges Zimmer* or *eine enge Zelle.* With a dat., as in *Das Zimmer wurde mir zu eng,* it means that the person feels constricted or shut in in a confined space. However, when a horizontal surface is bordered or bounded by a vertical surface or structures, *eng* and *schmal* are interchangeable. Thus *a narrow street* with buildings on either side can be described as *schmal* or *eng*. Also *ein schmaler/enger Durchgang.* With *die Tür,* only *eng* is used, with *der Spalt* only *schmal.*

> *Sie durchschwammen den Fluß, wo er am schmalsten war.*
> *Wie eng ist die Pforte und wie schmal ist der Weg, der zum Leben führt, und wenige sind's, die ihn finden.* (Matthew 7: 14)

Only *schmal* is applied to parts of the body. *Schmale Schultern. Ein schmaler Kopf. Eine schmale Figur. Ein schmales Gesicht. Schmale Hüfte/Hände.*

2. Narrow in the sense 'without latitude' in reference to the limits set to people's activities, to the way something is interpreted, and to the way people think is expressed by **eng**. *Eng im Denken sein* means 'to be narrow in one's thinking or outlook'. *Einen engen Horizont/Gesichtskreis haben* is 'to have a narrow or limited horizon'. *Eng* is also applied to *Ansichten* and related words. *Im engeren Sinne des Wortes,* in its narrow sense. Alternatives are **begrenzt** and **beschränkt**, cf. LIMIT. *Diese Menschen haben einen begrenzten Horizont. Beschränkt* is not applied directly to people in the sense of 'narrow' as it means 'dim-witted', but can be applied to opinions. *Seine Ansichten sind beschränkt.* **Engstirnig** suggests prejudiced, one-sided, narrow-minded thinking. *Ein Mensch/Eine Haltung/Eine Einstellung ist sehr engstirnig.* **Borniert** means 'intellectually limited' as well as 'narrow in outlook'. *Ein bornierter Mensch. Eine bornierte Meinung. Bornierter Egoismus. Ich finde diese Einstellung borniert.*

> *Sie sind so eng in ihren Ansichten/Anschauungen, daß sie jeden, der anders denkt als sie, für einen Verräter halten.   Der Untersuchung sind sehr enge Grenzen gesetzt.*
> *Menschen, die ihre Gedanken immerzu auf eine Sache konzentrieren, müssen notwendigerweise ein wenig eng/beschränkt in ihrem Denken werden.*
> *Die Bedeutung dieser Ereignisse ist zweifellos durch das begrenzte/beschränkte/enge Blickfeld der Historiker dieser Zeit vermindert worden.*
> *Das oberste Gericht ist der Ansicht, daß der Wortlaut des Gesetzes nicht so eng auszulegen sei.*

(*Eng* applied to clothes means 'tight[-fitting]'. *Eine enge Hose.* For *eng* describing a connection, relation, etc., *ein enger Freund, enge Beziehungen,* cf. NEAR 4.)

3. Narrow means 'by a very small amount', 'only just sufficient'. *He won by a narrow margin. She was elected by a narrow majority. The bullet narrowly missed my head. The motion was narrowly defeated.* This sense is carried by **knapp**, as both an adj. and adv. *Es war ein knapper Sieg/eine knappe Niederlage. Wir haben das Spiel knapp gewonnen.* Sometimes E. requires *close. Der Wahlausgang war sehr knapp.*

Er gewann das Rennen/die Schachpartie nur knapp.
Die Kugel hat seinen Kopf [nur] knapp verfehlt.
Sie wurde von/mit einer knappen [Simmen]mehrheit gewählt.
Der Antrag wurde mit knapper Stimmenmehrheit abgelehnt (narrowly defeated).
Das Spiel wurde am Ende nur knapp von Australien verloren. Or Australien unterlag knapp.

4. Applied to an escape, **narrow** means 'barely effected' or 'only just successful'. *She had a narrow escape.*

i. The equivalent is also **knapp** which is often preceded by *nur*. The meaning is 'by a small margin', and *knapp* can translate E. idioms like *a close shave, a narrow squeak*, or *by the skin of one's teeth. Das war knapp* can, in the appropriate contexts, mean that it was a near miss/a narrow escape/a close shave. *Knapp* in this sense is an adv. only, so that *They had a narrow escape* needs to be rephrased as a v. *Sie sind [nur] knapp davongekommen. A narrow escape from sth.* is mostly expressed by *nur knapp entgehen* + dat. *Sie sind dem Tod nur knapp entgangen.* For alternatives see below. Stronger syns. are **mit knapper Not**, which suggests a serious situation, and **mit knapper Mühe und Not**, which suggests effort as well as a narrow escape. All are applied to something someone only just manages to do successfully. *Ich habe die Prüfung mit knapper [Mühe und] Not geschafft/bestanden*, just scraped through, got a bare pass only with difficulty.

Er war nur knapp davongekommen. Die Kugel hatte seine Stirn gestreift.
Sie sind dem Tod [nur] knapp entronnen (formal style). *Sie sind mit knapper Not davongekommen* (everyday language).
Nur knapp konnte sie vor dem Ertrinken gerettet werden is more usual than *Nur knapp war sie dem Ertrinken entronnen/dem Tod durch Ertrinken entkommen/entgangen.*
Nur knapp/mit knapper Not entgimg er der Verhaftung.
Nur mit knapper Not entgingen/entkamen sie dem Blutbad.

Related expressions are **um Haaresbreite**, by a hair's breadth, *Wir sind um Haaresbreite einem Zusammensstoß entgangen*, and **um ein Haar**, which is mostly at the beginning, *Um ein Haar, und wir wären alle erstickt.*

ii. With *to miss* and *to escape*, **narrowly** means 'only just' and is mostly followed by a gerund, *He narrowly escaped being arrested* or *He narrowly missed being injured/run over*, though a n. is sometimes possible, *They narrowly escaped arrest.* These sents. can be translated by *nur knapp* as explained in the previous section. A simple alternative is **fast** or **beinahe** + subjunctive with the gerund or n. expressed as a v. *Er wäre fast überfahren worden. Sie wäre beinahe ertrunken*, narrowly/just escaped drowning. Cf. NEARLY. A further alternative with some ns. is **gerade noch**, 'only just', + *entgehen*, 'to ESCAPE', + n. *Er ist gerade noch der Verhaftung entgangen.* Cf. JUST 2.

nature *n.*

1. Nature refers to the material world, often the features and products of the earth as contrasted with those of human civilization. **Die Natur** denotes the natural world, all organic and inorganic things existing outside human consciousness. *Die belebte und unbelebte Natur. Wieviele Elemente kommen in der Natur vor? Der Mensch verändert die Natur/macht sich die Natur untertan. Die Schönheiten der Natur.* Like the E. word, *Natur* can denote the creative and regulative power which is conceived of as operative in the material world, the force which has brought this forth. *Die Kräfte/Gesetze der Natur. Dieser Kristall ist ein Meisterstück der Natur. Die Natur* is applied to the totality of natural phenomena, particularly as they exist in a certain area which is largely untouched by human beings. *Hinaus in die Natur. Sie suchten ein Stück einsame Natur. Diese Pflanzen/Tiere gedeihen nur in der freien Natur.* Hence its use in sents. like *Die Industrieanlage verunstaltet die Natur* or *Ohne schwerwiegende Eingriffe* *in die Natur kann die Fabrik nicht gebaut werden.* Natur is also applied to the physical nature of human beings, the power or force by which their bodily and mental activities are sustained, and is found mostly in sents. like *Jmd. hat eine robuste/kräftige/gesunde/schwächliche Natur* or *Die Natur (des Kranken) wird sich selbst helfen.*

2. Nature also denotes what something or someone is like, the combination of qualities and properties giving the thing or person its fundamental character. Here G. has two words, *die Natur* and *das Wesen*.

i. In philosophical language, *das Wesen* means 'essence', but although it retains a philosophical tone, it is also common in non-philosophical discourse where **nature** is usual in E. There is hardly any difference in meaning between *Wesen* and *Natur* in this sense. **Das Wesen** may suggest the peculiar or special nature while **die Natur** refers to the general character, but the main difference lies in the use. *Das Wesen* is mostly used without an adj. when talking of the nature of a thing, especially of abstracts. *Das Wesen der Kunst/der Mathematik. Das Wesen eines Rechtsverhältnisses/einer Kontroverse/der Liebe.* Besides *Es liegt im Wesen einer Sache* or *gehört zum Wesen einer Sache,* there is the equally common *Es liegt in der Natur der Sache. Das liegt in der Natur der Dinge* is a fixed phr. *Natur* is used with adjs., *die demokratische Natur des Staates* and *Fragen allgemeiner Natur. Diese Krankheitserscheinungen sind nervöser Natur. Natur* is the more common word.

ii. For **nature** in the sense 'the innate disposition of a human being or animal', both **das Wesen** and **die Natur** are also used. They express the same meaning, but in certain expressions only one is normal. *Das Wesen* refers more to character, all the mental qualities which are seen as determining an individual's attitudes, behaviour, and the manner in which his or her life is led. *Die Natur* is more comprehensive and includes bodily characteristics as well as mental ones. *Jmds. Natur* is often regarded as being given by nature and therefore unchangeable. *Man kann seine Natur nicht ändern.* By nature is *von Natur aus. Sie ist von Natur aus schüchtern. Etw. wird jmdm. zur zweiten Natur. Jmd. zeigt sein wahres Wesen* is a fixed expression. (More usual is *Jmd. zeigt sein wahres Gesicht.*) Both are used with *haben* and *sein. Jmd. ist eine heitere/schöpferische/liebenswürdige Natur* or *Jmd. ist ein gutmütiges/schöpferisches Wesen. Jmd. hat eine gutmütige/kindliche/gesellige/friedfertige Natur. Jmd. hat ein freundliches/ angenehmes* or *ein gerades/sensibles/einnehmendes Wesen.* In *ein Mensch von heftigem/ liebenswürdigem Wesen, Natur* can be substituted for *Wesen.*

> *Mein Vetter und sein Vater verstanden einander nicht, ihre Naturen waren zu gründlich verschieden.*
> *Heucheln war seiner innersten Natur zuwider.*
> *Sie sah ein, daß er eine unaufrichtige Handlung nicht begehen konnte. Sie würde seiner Natur widersprechen.*   *Das Wesen seiner Frau hat er nie richtig verstanden.*
> *Sein rücksichtloses/aufdringliches/unhöfliches Wesen wirkte abstoßend.*
> *Sie legten ein lebhaftes/lustiges Wesen an den Tag.*

iii. In reference to the nature or disposition of a person, **die Art** is possibly more common than *Natur* or *Wesen. Es lag nicht in seiner Art, so was zu machen. Das ist nun einmal meine Art,* that is my nature, that's what I'm like, that's my way. *(S.o.'s)* way is a common transl. of *Art* in this sense.

> *Es war nicht ihre Art, mit Kollegen so unfreundlich umzugehen.*
> *Seine Kinder schlecht zu behandeln entsprach nicht seiner Art.*
> *Ich fürchtete, sie sei schon abgereist. Wer konnte das wissen bei ihrer unbegreiflichen Art?*

iv. Das Naturell also means 'nature' as a syn. of *disposition.* It is often translated as *temperament,* which in one sense denotes a person's disposition or nature, particularly as this affects the way of thinking, feeling, and behaving. *She has an artis-*

tic temperament. Das liegt in jmds. Naturell. Das widerspricht seinem Naturell. Jmd. hat ein lebensfrohes/fröhliches/sorgloses Naturell.

v. Die Natur designates human nature in general, i.e. the disposition of all of mankind, *Das liegt in der menschlichen Natur,* and a characteristic common to all human beings, *die tierische Natur des Menschen,* as well as the nature of men and women in general, *die männliche/weibliche Natur.*

3. Die Beschaffenheit denotes the way something is constituted or made up, its physical structure, qualities, or composition, and translates **nature** in more technical language. *Die Beschaffenheit des Bodens. Von der Beschaffenheit/Art der Wolken schließt man auf das Wetter.* (In some contexts, such as *Er überprüft die Beschaffenheit des Materials,* it means 'state or condition'.)

4. i. In one sense, **nature** means 'kind or sort'. *Things of this/that nature do not interest me.* The usual equivalent is **die Art**. **Die Natur** is also possible, especially with a preceding adj. *Fragen allgemeiner Natur. Of this nature* can be *[von] dieser Art.*

Verbrechen dieser Art kommen immer häufiger vor.   Dinge dieser Art interessieren mich nicht.
Zuerst befasse ich mich mit einigen Fragen grundsätzlicher Natur/Art.
Bemerkungen geistreicher Natur verstand dieses Publikum nicht.

ii. The two adjs. **beschaffen** and **geartet** mean 'of a nature or kind' and are used with words like *so, derartig,* or *anders. Derartig beschaffene/geartete Strukturen. Irgendwie geartet* means 'of some kind'. Both belong to learned style. *Sein Charakter war so beschaffen, daß man ihn leicht kränken konnte* does not belong to everyday speech in which *beschaffen* would simply be omitted. It is usually included in the written language. The expression *wie auch immer beschaffen/geartet,* 'of whatever nature/kind', is not restricted to learned language, but is nevertheless more learned than *welcher Art auch immer* or *ganz gleich welcher Art.*

Das Metall war so beschaffen, daß es sich leicht formen ließ.
Wie die beiden Fälle auch immer beschaffen sein mögen, wir müssen hier eine Ausnahme machen.

near, nearby *adjs.* close[ly] *adj. and adv.*

1. In their basic sense 'not far away in space', these words are synonymous, though not always interchangeable.

i. The main equivalent of all three is **nahe**. While **near** and **close** are only used predicatively in this sense, *The town is quite close* or *The Post Office is quite near,* **nearby** is used both attributively, *Nottingham and nearby towns,* and predicatively, *There is a river nearby. Nahe* is used in both ways. *Die Stadt/Die Post ist ganz nahe. Wir gehen im nahen Wald spazieren.* A variant for the attributive use is **nahegelegen,** nearby. *Die Kinder gehen im nahegelegenen Dorf zur Schule.* An alternative for the predicative use is **in der Nähe.** *Die Stadt/Das Postamt ist ganz in der Nähe. In der Nähe* tends to be less precise and less close than *nahe,* although there is often little difference. To give an approximate idea of where something is, someone might say, '*Das Geschäft liegt in der Nähe des Bahnhofs',* but to stress that it is close to or near the station, i.e. only a short distance from the station, *Das Haus liegt nahe am/beim Bahnhof* is more likely. *Sie kam in unsere Nähe* implies a less close approach than *Sie kam nahe an uns heran.* **Close to** or **near** + a n. is thus either **nahe bei/an** or **in der Nähe** + gen. or von. *Das Museum ist/liegt nahe beim Rathaus/liegt in der Nähe des Rathauses. Das Haus liegt nahe am/beim Park/in der Nähe vom Park.* **Nearby** used predicatively is either *In der Nähe ist ein Fluß* or *Nahe dabei ist ein Fluß. Nahe* + dat. is now mostly fig. *Allem Anschein nach sind wir einer Lösung nahe. Dem Ziel nahe* is 'close to our objective', while *nahe am Ziel* is 'close to/near our destination'. Cf. 3. *Von nah und fern* and *von nahem* are fixed expressions. *Die Leute kamen von nah und fern. Man* *betrachtet ein Bild von nahem/aus nächster Nähe.* (Note that besides meaning 'next', **nächst** means 'nearest or closest', *Das nächste Dorf ist zehn Kilometer entfernt,* and also 'shortest', *der nächste Weg zum Schloß.*)

> *Du kannst ganz nahe an das Pferd herangehen.*   *Bitte kommen Sie näher!*
> *Er sucht Arbeit in Nottingham oder in einer nahegelegenen Stadt.*
> *Der Stuhl steht zu nahe am Ofen.*   *Nahe dabei steht eine alte Eiche.*
> *Sie saßen in unserer Nähe/standen ganz nahe bei uns.*   *Wir wohnen nahe bei der Kirche.*
> *Nahe bei unserem Haus hat der Blitz in einen Baum eingeschlagen.*

ii. Dicht also means 'close' and suggests closer than *nahe.* In this sense it is always followed by a prep., as it would otherwise have its other meaning 'dense'. Cf. THICK. *Ein Haus, das nahe am Waldrand steht,* could be a hundred or more metres away, while *ein Haus, das dicht am Waldrand steht,* adjoins the wood. *Ein Schrank, der dicht an der Wand steht,* is right up against it. With regard to people *dicht* can describe something desired or pleasant, *Ich ging dicht hinter ihm her, Er zog sie dicht an sich,* but it may suggest an action which is threatening in some way, *Sie traten dicht vor ihn hin, Er trat dicht an mich heran. Zu dicht auffahren* is 'to get too close to the car ahead'. *Dicht* translates *close* in *I keep/stick close to s.o./sth.* when space is meant. *Ich halte mich dicht bei dir.* (Cf. 4. iii.) With *sitzen* or *stehen, dicht* implies squashed up; *nahe* means 'close' or 'near' in the normal sense.

> *Dicht neben mir im Nebel tauchte ein anderer Wagen auf.*
> *Die Polizei ist den Verbrechern dicht auf den Fersen.*   *Die Bauernhöfe liegen dicht beieinander.*

iii. *I always have the reference books* **near at hand** is *Ich habe die Nachschlagewerke* **immer zur Hand** or **in greifbarer Nähe** or **in Griffnähe.**

2. Near or **close** in time is **nahe.** *Der Sonnenuntergang/Der Frühling ist nahe. Niemand zweifelte am nahen Konkurs des Unternehmens. In naher Zukunft.* An alternative is **bevorstehen,** which means that something will happen in the immediate future. *Die bevorstehenden Prüfungen. Nahe* is often added. *Die Prüfung/Weihnachten stand nahe bevor.*

3. Close to a state, as in *close to tears,* is **nahe** + dat. *Sie war den Tränen/der Verzweiflung/einer Ohnmacht nahe.* If **close** is followed by a gerund, as in *close to giving up,* the usual equivalent is **nahe daran** + infin., but **dicht daran** is also used. *Ich war nahe daran, das Geheimnis auszuplaudern. Er war nahe daran, aufzustehen und zu gehen. Wir waren dicht daran, umzukehren, als der Regen plötzlich aufhörte.* This construction presupposes the carrying out of an intention or decision and cannot be used to translate *He came close to being sacked* where **close to** = 'NEARLY'. This sent. becomes *Er wäre beinahe entlassen.*

4. Other senses of **close.**

i. A **close** relative, a **close** friend. For relatives, **nahe** is used. *Sie sind nahe Verwandte* or *nahe verwandt.* The comparative *näher* is often preferred. *Nur die näheren Verwandten wurden eingeladen.* For friends, **eng** is the usual word; *nahe* implies a less close relationship than *eng. Sie sind eng miteinander befreundet.*

ii. Close contact, a **close** connection, etc. **Eng** is used with words like *Beziehung, Kontakt, zusammenarbeiten, verbinden,* or *berühren. Zwischen den beiden bestanden enge Beziehungen. Eng verwandt* is 'closely related' when *related* means 'connected'. *Eng verwandte Begriffe/Gebiete.*

> *Ich habe mit diesen Studenten eng zusammengearbeitet.*
> *Er stand in engem Kontakt mit Forschern in mehreren Ländern.*

iii. Close, in *to stick/keep close to* something like a text, is *sich* **eng** *halten an* or *eng folgen.* With *übersetzen, eng* is usual, but *nahe* is possible. *Sie übersetzt sehr nahe/zu eng am Original.*

> *Bei der Verfilmung dieses Romans hat man sich eng an den Text gehalten.*
> *Er hielt sich eng an das Thema und schweifte nicht ab.*

iv. Close meaning 'thorough', as in *a close examination* or *to examine sth. closely*, can be expressed by **genau**, CAREFUL. **Closely** can also be translated by **genauestens**. *After close consideration* is *nach genauer Überlegung. Ich habe genau hingehört*, listened closely. *Wir haben alles genauestens geprüft*, examined very closely. **Näher** can translate **closer** or **more closely**. *Bei näherer Betrachtung. Ich werde mir die Sache näher ansehen. Bei näherem Hinsehen*, 'if/when one looks more closely', is a fixed expression, but *wenn man sich die Sache genau ansieht* is also used. *This deserves close attention* could be *Es verdient unsere volle Aufmerksamkeit. Pay close attention!* would usually be *Achte genau auf das, was er sagt!*

v. In *A close resemblance*, **close** is **groß**. *Eine große Ähnlichkeit. Es besteht eine große Ähnlichkeit zwischen den beiden Erzählungen.*

vi. Nahekommen expresses the idea that one thing comes close to another in an abstract sense. *Die Schätzung kam dem Ergebnis sehr nahe. Was er Ihnen da erzählt hat, kommt der Wahrheit sehr nahe.* A **close** equivalent (in meaning) can be paraphrased as *Dieses deutsche Wort ist eine fast genaue Entsprechung des englischen [Wortes]*. An alternative is *Die Bedeutung dieses deutschen Wortes kommt der des englischen sehr nahe.*

nearly, almost *advs.*

1. The everyday equivalents are **beinahe** and **fast**. *Ich bin fast/beinahe fertig.* They do not differ in meaning, but in cases in which an emotion such as surprise, relief, or satisfaction is expressed, *fast* tends to be used. *Das ist fast ein Wunder. Das ist fast zum Verzweifeln.* The third syn. **nahezu** belongs to the written language and is the preferred bureaucratic term. *Das betrifft nahezu alle, die daran teilgenommen haben.* **So gut wie** is used in everyday speech as a syn. of **nearly** or **almost**. *So gut wie alle haben die Änderung gutgeheißen.*

Der Graben ist fast/beinahe fünf Meter breit.   *Wir haben uns beinahe täglich getroffen.*
Es ist beinahe sechs Uhr, ich warte seit fast einer Stunde.
Dieser Zustand dauerte nahezu fünf Jahre an.
Nahezu die Hälfte aller Angestellten beherrschen zwei Fremdsprachen.
So gut wie achtzig Prozent der Anträge sind schon bearbeitet worden.

2. In stating that something almost happened, *I almost fell over*, **fast** and **beinahe** are used, and in educated speech usually with the subjunctive. *Er hätte mich fast umgerannt. Ich wäre fast überfahren. Ich hätte den Schirm beinahe vergessen. Ich wäre beinahe hingefallen. Ich hätte mich beinahe verletzt.* Although the non-native speaker is best advised to observe this rule, some native speakers use the indicative.

3. Not nearly is an emphatic way of stating that something is not the case. *She is not nearly as old as her husband. I haven't worked nearly long enough on the case. I have saved £5,000, but that is not nearly enough.* The equivalents are **bei weitem nicht** and **[noch] lange nicht**, both = 'not by a long way', which are interchangeable except in a sent. which already contains *lange. Ich habe mich bei weitem nicht lange genug mit dem Fall beschäftigt.*

Sie ist bei weitem nicht so alt wie ihr Mann.   *Ich verdiene bei weitem nicht so viel wie er.*
Ich habe 5 000 Pfund gespart, aber das ist bei weitem nicht genug/noch lange nicht genug.
Er ist bei weitem/[noch] lange nicht so intelligent wie du.
Das ist noch lange/bei weitem nicht alles, was ich darüber weiß.

Ich bin noch lange nicht fertig is the usual expression, but *bei weitem noch nicht fertig* is also possible.

necessary, requisite, unnecessary *adjs.*

i. Both **nötig** and **notwendig** are usually translated as **necessary** and are very close in meaning. The difference lies only in the fact that *nötig* is the everyday word and may suggest a less compelling necessity than *notwendig*. The latter belongs to a stylistically higher level, as well as suggesting a more compelling reason. Although the distinction as to the degree of necessity is not always closely observed, *notwendig* tends to be used when the sense is 'essential from the nature or logic of the situation', and when it is implied that someone had no other choice but to do something. *Die für die Ausbildung notwendige Zeit. Die notwendigen Unterlagen. Es war notwendig, ihn zu benachrichtigen—wir brauchen seine Hilfe. Ein notwendiges Übel* is a fixed expression. Only *notwendig* is used as an adv. and means 'necessarily' or 'of necessity'; there is the alternative form **notwendigerweise**. *Diese Aussagen widersprechen sich—eine muß notwendig[erweise] falsch sein. Der Hirte muß notwendigerweise Tag und Nacht bei seiner Herde bleiben.* Cf. NEED 5. ii. (*Nötig* is used colloquially as an adv. with *brauchen*, meaning 'badly, urgently'. *Wir brauchen nötig Regen.*) For *nötig haben*, see NEED 2.

Wir haben die nötigen Kleider gepackt. *Wir müssen mit der nötigen Vorsicht vorgehen.*
Die Regierung hat die nötigen finanziellen Mittel bereitgestellt.
Vorbereitungen sind im Augenblick nicht nötig. *Es ist noch nicht nötig, Licht zu machen.*
Es ist nötig, daß du einen Beruf ergreifst. *Es mußte notwendig zum Krieg kommen.*
Gewisse Anschaffungen sind notwendig und lassen sich nicht länger aufschieben.
Die Bundesrepublik muß alle notwendigen Rohstoffe einführen.
Dieser Konkurs ist die notwendige Folge der kurzsichtigen Finanzplanung.

ii. Erforderlich has the same sense as *nötig* but is an official, commercial, and bureaucratic word which resembles **requisite**. It tends, however, to be used on all stylistic levels for something which is necessary because it is prescribed or required by law, a regulation, a decision of those in authority, and so on.

Die Regierung hat die erforderlichen Mittel für den Bau der Brücke bereitgestellt.
Bei der Abstimmung im Parlament wurde die erforderliche Zweidrittelmehrheit nicht erreicht.
Eine Vorbildung ist für diese Stelle nicht unbedingt erforderlich.

iii. Etw. ist vonnöten, 'necessary', is only used in the written language. *Ordnung und Disziplin waren dringend vonnöten.* The syn. **etw. tut not** also belongs to elevated diction. *Vorsicht tut hier not.*

iv. Unnecessary. Only *nötig* forms a compound with *un-*, **unnötig**. *Du machst dir unnötige Sorgen. Diese Ausgabe ist völlig unnötig.* *Unnötig* is also an adv. *Das hat die Sache unnötig kompliziert.* An alternative to the adv. is **unnötigerweise**. *Er hat sich unnötigerweise aufgeregt.* Both **nicht nötig** and **nicht notwendig** are used as adjs. *Es ist nicht nötig, daß du hingehst. Weitere Erkundigungen sind nicht notwendig.*

need, necessity *ns.* need *v.*

1. In its basic sense 'necessity arising from facts or circumstances in which sth. is necessary or action is required', **need** now only occurs in the phrs. *if need[s] be* and *there is need* qualified by *no, any, what,* or *little*. *If need be, you can show them the letter. There is no need for alarm. Is there any need for all this rush? There was no need for you to tell them that.*

i. As these expressions have no direct equivalents, the sense is mostly expressed by **nötig** and **notwendig**, NECESSARY. **If need be** is thus *wenn es nötig/notwendig ist. Sollte* makes the possibility more remote: *Wenn/Falls es nötig sein sollte.* **Little/No great need** can be *kaum nötig. Es ist kaum nötig, sie zu benachrichtigen.* The infin. in *There is* **no need** *[for you] to ring up* can be translated as an infin. if *for you* is not stated, only implied. *Es ist nicht nötig anzurufen. Es war nicht nötig, ihnen das zu erzählen. Es ist nicht nötig, heute zu zahlen.* The sense can also be expressed by a *daß*-clause the subj. of which is the person carrying out the action of the infin. *Es ist* *nicht nötig, daß wir uns so beeilen.* This construction is necessary when *for s.o.* precedes the infin. *Es ist nicht nötig, daß er hingeht,* no need for him to go. A common alternative is **brauchen** with the person as subj. *Du brauchst nicht hinzugehen/dich nicht so zu beeilen.* The impersonal, but very formal construction **es bedarf** + gen. means 'there is need of or for sth.' *Es bedurfte der Vorsicht. Das bedarf keiner weiteren Erklärung.* Cf. 2. ii.

ii. Die Notwendigkeit, 'need, necessity', can be used in a word-for-word transl. of the E. expressions, but as it suggests a strong necessity and is fairly formal, it is less frequently encountered than **need**. *Besteht für uns denn überhaupt die Notwendigkeit, weitere Maßnahmen zu ergreifen? Es besteht keinerlei Notwendigkeit zur Beunruhigung.* Words close in sense which might translate **need** are *Grund* and *Veranlassung* discussed under CAUSE n. Cf. also *nottun* under NECESSARY iii and *nötig haben* under 2. ii below.

2. Need, used with *for* + a n. or *for* + an infin. or gerund, denotes a requirement or an imperative demand for something. *I do not see the need for harsh measures. Everyone acknowledges the need to pay taxes/for paying taxes.* **Necessity,** meaning 'the fact of being indispensable', is a syn. *Point out to them the necessity of/for adopting some measures to assist the sugar industry! An understanding of these facts is a necessity.* (For *a necessity* = 'sth. indispensable' see 4. iii.)

i. This sense of **need** and **necessity** is expressed by **die Notwendigkeit.** It is, however, not as common as the E. words and is confined to fairly formal language. In speech the meaning would mostly be expressed by **nötig** or **notwendig.** *Das Verständnis dieser Tatsachen ist [absolut] nötig/notwendig,* is a necessity.

> *Führen Sie ihnen die Notwendigkeit vor Augen, Maßnahmen zur Unterstützung der Zuckerindustrie zu ergreifen!   Jeder erkennt die Notwendigkeit an, Steuern zu zahlen.*
> *Die Notwendigkeit eines strengen Vorgehens gegen die Demonstranten sehen wir nicht ein.*

ii. Need has a similar sense in the expressions **have [no] need of** and **be in need of.** The simplest way to translate these expressions is to use **brauchen,** which covers needs felt subjectively as well as ones arising from external circumstances. *Sie brauchen unsere Unterstützung nicht.* There are several syns. **Nötig haben** is stylistically somewhat higher than *brauchen. Ich habe sein Geld/diesen Rat nicht nötig. Es nötig haben* is used with an infin. *Er hat es nicht nötig, mit seinem Können zu prahlen; wir kennen seine Fähigkeiten und wissen ihn auch so zu schätzen.* **Benötigen** is a refined variant on *brauchen.* In reference to people, it sounds impersonal and unemotional. *Die Kinder benötigen [dringend] warme Kleidung.* **Bedürfen** + gen. is very formal, usually occurs with abstract ns., but is little used. *Dann bedürfen Sie meines Rates nicht mehr,* you have no further need of . . .

> *Brauchen Sie Hilfe?   Wir brauchen keine weitere Hilfe/keinen weiteren Rat.*
> *Sie hat das Geld/neue Schuhe/Nachhilfestunden/Ruhe dringend nötig.*
> *Ein paar Punkte bedürfen noch der Klärung.*
> *Der Betrieb benötigt dringend erfahrene Fachkräfte.*

iii. Bedürftig, applied to people, means 'poor, needy', *Wir sollten den Bedürftigen helfen,* but in compounds it means 'in need of'. *Pflegebedürftig, schutzbedürftig, reformbedürftig, korrekturbedürftig, hilfsbedürftig. Meine Arbeitsweise ist verbesserungsbedürftig,* is in need of improvement.

3. Need also denotes a condition of affairs placing someone in difficulty or distress, a time of adversity or trouble. It mostly occurs in the phrs. *in need* or *in times of/one's hour of need.* It is applied specifically to a state of destitution or lack of the means of subsistence.

i. Die Not is applied both to a mental state of distress or trouble and to extreme poverty, distress, or lack of things which sustain life as a result of a natural disaster etc. The former sense may need to be made clear by the addition of an adj., as in *die seelische Not des Patienten*. *Not leiden* usually means 'to be in need' in the sense 'lacking material goods'. *Man verrsorgte die notleidende Bevölkerung der betroffenen Gebiete mit Nahrungsmitteln.*

> *Sie hielt ihre Not/ihre Bedrängnis (cf. 3. ii) geheim.*   *Man tat alles, um die Not zu lindern.*
> *Ein Freund in der Not ist ein wahrer Freund.*   *Sie half mir in der Stunde der Not.*
> *Er schrie mit allen Kräften in höchster Not* (this could imply grave danger).
> *Der Staat sorgt für diejenigen, die in Not sind.*
> *In den von der Dürre heimgesuchten Dörfern herrschte die bitterste Not.*

ii. Alternatives. *Die Not* is a strong word denoting an extreme situation and is often avoided. *Die Familie war oft in Not/in großer Not* is used if 'extreme distress' is meant. More frequent would be *Es fehlte ihr am Notwendigsten* or *Sie war finanziell in einer sehr bedrängten Lage*. Other related expressions are **eine ausweglose Lage**, 'a hopeless situation', and **die Notlage**, 'plight, difficult position'. *Sie befanden sich in einer finanziellen Notlage. Jmd. nutzt die Notlage eines anderen aus*. **Die Bedrängnis** is a stylistically higher term, translated as *affliction, tribulation*, or *distress*, but **eine bedrängte Lage** is stylistically not as elevated. *Sie befanden sich in Bedrängnis/in einer bedrängten Lage.*

iii. Der Notfall, lit. 'case of need', can refer to an emergency, but it also suggests a situation in which everything else has failed and one thing is the last resort. *Dieses Telefon ist nur im Notfall/in Notfällen zu benutzen. Das Geld habe ich für den Notfall zurückgelegt. Das Geld will ich nur im Notfall angreifen. Im Notfall können wir ihn um Hilfe bitten.* **Notfalls** is weaker and means 'if necessary'. *Notfalls können wir uns mit dem alten Gerät behelfen.*

iv. Necessity can also denote poverty or the state of being in difficulties, especially through lack of means. In this sense it is now usually found with *sheer* or *dire*. *Only sheer/dire necessity would force me to sell this ring*. It is translated by the words discussed in 3. i–iii. *Nur die äußerste Not/Notlage könnte mich dazu zwingen, diesen Ring zu verkaufen. Aus purer Not* is 'from dire/sheer necessity'.

> *Die Witwe mußte die schlecht bezahlte Arbeit aus purer Not annehmen.*

v. Die Not in some fixed proverbial expressions can be translated as **need** or **necessity**. *Aus der Not eine Tugend machen. Not macht erfinderisch. Not kennt kein Gebot.*

4. Need also refers to something requisite, desirable, or useful, a thing which is felt to be necessary. The need can be mental or physical and relate to a person or an organization. *The farm supplied their daily needs. We require a building adequate for the company's needs. There is a growing need for qualified computer operators.*

i. Der Bedarf denotes something concrete which is needed in a particular situation. Most frequently it refers to goods or energy needed in everyday life or by industry. *Der Bedarf an Lebensmitteln/Strom, der Bürobedarf*, the thgs. needed in an office. It is translated by DEMAND as well as by **need**. It can also refer to a need for room or space or for people to do work. *Es besteht/gibt Bedarf an Fachkräften. Bedarf* can be applied to animals' needs, *Bedarf an Nahrung/Brutstätten*, and is found with ns. which refer only indirectly to something concrete, *Es gibt Bedarf an einer Erweiterung des Lehrkörpers*. It does not have a pl. Cf. *Bedürfnis. Je nach Bedarf* means 'according to need'. *Jeder kann Pfeffer und Salz je nach Bedarf nehmen.* (*Notwendigkeit*, by comparison, denotes an abstract need or necessity. *Er betonte die dringende Notwendigkeit weiterer Verhandlungen.*)

> *Der Bauernhof sorgt selbst für den täglichen Bedarf der Familie.*
> *Es besteht ein wachsender Bedarf an qualifizierten Datenverarbeitern.*
> *Die Firma sucht ein Gebäude, das ihrem Raumbedarf angemessen ist.*

Wenn Sie die Notrufnummer wählen, verlangen Sie je nach Bedarf Polizei, Krankenwagendienst oder Feuerwehr. Die Liste (der zu behandelnden Romane) kann bei Bedarf ergänzt werden.

ii. Das Bedürfnis, which is followed by *nach* + n. or by an infin., means firstly 'a mental need or desire' and can be a syn. of *das Verlangen,* desire. It covers both **need** and **want**, may or may not be justified, and in some cases is not felt to be very pressing. *Wir haben das natürliche Bedürfnis nach Schlaf/Ruhe. Ihm ist es ein Bedürfnis, drei Autos zu besitzen. Jmd. hat viele Bedürfnisse* usually suggests wants. There are compounds like *das Geltungsbedürfnis,* a psychological term denoting a need for recognition and approbation, *das Abwechslungsbedürfnis,* 'need for variety', *Sensationsbedürfnis, Sicherheitsbedürfnis, Liebesbedürfnis,* etc. The pl. **Bedürfnisse** also refers in an unspecified way to material things which are necessary for life. *Bedürfnisse* thus often functions as the pl. of *Bedarf* which does not form a pl. *Lebensnotwendigkeiten* and *Lebensbedürfnisse* both mean 'necessities of life'. *Nahrung, Kleidung und eine warme Unterkunft sind Lebensnotwendigkeiten. Meine Lebensbedürfnisse sind gering.*
   Er hatte das Bedürfnis, ihr die volle Wahrheit zu sagen.
   Sie spürt anscheinend das Bedürfnis, bewundert zu werden.
   Er scheint ein ständiges Bedürfnis nach Aufregung zu haben.
   Welche Bedürfnisse treiben die Leute dazu, sich solchen Schund anzusehen?
   Wir haben alle die gleichen Bedürfnisse, wir wollen essen, trinken, schlafen.
   Wir sollten zufrieden sein, wenn wir so viel haben, daß es unseren Bedürfnissen entspricht.
   Dieser Lohn reichte nicht aus, um die Bedürfnisse der Familie zu befriedigen.

iii. Necessity, in the sense of 'sth. indispensable', can be expressed by **die Notwendigkeit,** which is mostly modified by an adv. or adj. *Ein Auto ist heutzutage eine nicht mehr diskutierte Notwendigkeit* or *ist zweifellos eine Notwendigkeit.* If this does not fit, the sense can be conveyed by **lebensnotwendig.** *Bäume und frische Luft sind für mich lebensnotwendig.*
   Sie verfügten nur über das Lebensnotwendigste (the bare necessities).

5. Mostly with adjs. like *logical* and *absolute,* **necessity** denotes constraint or compulsion having its basis in the natural order of things. *It is a mathematical necessity that the sum of the lengths of two sides of a triangle should be greater than the length of the third.* In **of necessity,** the meaning is extended to the constraining power of circumstances, a state compelling someone to a course of action. *The account given here is of necessity simplified.*

i. The usual equivalent of the n. **necessity** in this sense is **die Notwendigkeit.** Related expressions are **eine notwendige/logische Folge** and **die Gesetzmäßigkeit,** the fact of being in conformity with a law of nature or logic.
   Es gibt keine zwingende Notwendigkeit in der Schlußfolgerung, zu der Sie gekommen sind.
   Es ist eine mathematische Notwendigkeit/Gesetzmäßigkeit, daß zwei Seiten eines Dreiecks länger sind als die dritte.
   Es ist eine notwendige/logische Folge, daß die Lebenshaltungskosten steigen, wenn Löhne und Gehälter angehoben werden.

ii. Of necessity is mostly **notwendigerweise** or **zwangsläufig.** The former is an adv. which can also be translated as *necessarily. Aus dieser Zeugenaussage folgt notwendigerweise, daß Schmidt lügt.* The latter is an adj. meaning 'unavoidable' or 'necessary', 'arising of necessity from the circumstances of the case', as well as an adv. *Eine zwangsläufige Folge dieser Politik. In dieser Position wird er zwangsläufig dieselben Schwierigkeiten haben wie seine Vorgänger. Zwangsläufig* is often applied to a logical necessity. *Aus diesen Prämissen ergibt sich zwangsläufig nur ein Schluß.* **Notgedrungen** means 'out of necessity', 'compelled by circumstances'. *Er hat notgedrungen einen Teil des Hofes verkauft, um seine Schulden zu tilgen.*
   Wenn die Regierung die finanziellen Zuwendungen für die Universitäten kürzt, müssen diese notwendigerweise Stellen abbauen.

Unsere Lösungen stimmen nicht überein. Eine muß notwendigerweise falsch sein.

Wenn du so veraltete Anschauungen hast, wirst du zwangsläufig umlernen müssen.

Diese Darstellung der historischen Vorgänge ist notwendigerweise/zwangsläufig stark vereinfacht.

Notgedrungen mußte ich den Arbeitsraum wechseln. Der Lärm im alten war nämlich unerträglich geworden.

negotiate *v*. One sense. try/hear a (court) case *v. phr.*

1. negotiate can be either intr., *They have been negotiating for weeks*, or trans., *They have negotiated a settlement*. **Verhandeln** is intr. only. *Sie verhandeln hinter verschlossenen Türen. A verhandelt mit B. About* is *über. Die Gewerkschaften verhandeln mit den Unternehmern über eine Lohnerhöhung. Verhandeln* cannot be used when **negotiate** is trans. and means 'to achieve a result through negotiations'. *The union negotiated a 3 per cent wage rise*. The equivalent is **aushandeln**, which needs an obj. *Wir haben mit dem Mieter einen Preis für die Wohnung ausgehandelt.*

> *Die Verhandlungen wurden gestern unterbrochen, aber beide Seiten wollen nächste Woche weiter verhandeln.*
>
> *Man verhandelt mit der Gegenseite über einen Waffenstillstand.*
>
> *In Verhandlungen, die drei Wochen dauerten, hat die Gewerkschaft neue Tarife für die Metallarbeiter ausgehandelt.* *Wir haben einen Kompromiß ausgehandelt.*
>
> *Die Firma hat einen langfristigen Vertrag mit dem Rohstofflieferanten ausgehandelt.*

2. Verhandeln is also applied to law courts and means 'to try a criminal case' or 'to hear a civil case or an appeal'. It is used with *gegen* + a person, *Das Gericht verhandelt gegen einen Rauschgifthändler*, and with *über* when the case or its nature is stated, *Das Gericht verhandelt über einen Fall von Erpressung* or *verhandelt über schwere Körperverletzung*. In legal parlance, however, *verhandeln* can take *Fall* as obj. *Das Gericht hat diesen Fall vor zwei Monaten verhandelt*. Thus the pass. *Der Fall wird nächste Woche in zweiter Instanz verhandelt* instead of *Über den Fall wird nächste Woche verhandelt.*

note *n*. Some equivalents.

1. Note is 'a short record of what is said to help the memory', as in *to make a note of sth., take notes*, or *lecture notes*.

i. The general term is **die Notiz**, which is found mainly in the pl. and suggests a written summary or outline as an aid to remembering.

> *Ich habe mir eine knappe Notiz über das Gespräch/die Rede gemacht.*
>
> *Er machte sich über die Ereignisse/die Vorlesung/die Stunde ausführliche Notizen.*

ii. Mitschreiben and **nachschreiben** express the sense 'to take notes'. Both imply writing something down as it is being said. *Der Chef diktierte, und die Sekretärin schrieb mit. Ich schrieb den Vortrag nach*. They are also applied to taking down only the essential features. *Ich habe nur das mitgeschrieben, was mir wichtig erschien*. Both are used only in reference to something spoken, not for events observed. *Nachschreiben* forms the n. **die Nachschrift**, which often means 'lecture notes'. Although not included in the monolingual dictionaries, **die Mitschrift** also exists. *Ihre Nachschrift/Mitschrift enthält alles, was gesagt wurde*. (*Eine Nachschrift* is also 'a PS' in a letter.)

> *Alle Studenten schreiben die Vorlesung mit/nach.*
>
> *Stefan hat mir seine Nachschrift der Vorlesung geliehen, aber ich kann sie kaum entziffern.*

iii. The best equivalents of **make a note of** sth. are often **sich notieren**, 'to note down', and **[sich/jmdm.] aufschreiben**, 'to WRITE DOWN'. *Ich notiere mir die Nummer. Ich schreibe die Ankunftszeit auf.*

> *Ich habe mir die Telefonnummer im Terminkalender/die Bestellung auf einem Blatt notiert.*

Ich habe dir die Adresse aufgeschrieben. Der Polizist schrieb [sich] die Nummer des Autos auf.
2. Note = 'a short letter', as in *I wrote her a note.* **Die Note** is used only for diplomatic notes exchanged by governments. *Die Regierungen von Kanada und Japan wechselten Noten über den Zwischenfall.* In everyday circumstances, a **note** is mostly **ein paar Zeilen** or **ein kurzer Brief**. *Ich habe ihnen ein paar Zeilen zum Dank/zur Entschuldigung geschrieben. Heute morgen habe ich diesen kurzen Brief von ihm bekommen.* **Eine [kurze] Nachricht** *für jmdn.* hinterlassen could be 'to leave a note for s.o.', but it could also imply an oral message that someone is asked to pass on. *Da sie nicht zur Verabredung kommen konnte, hinterließ sie eine Nachricht.* **Der Zettel** is 'a small piece of paper' with various functions. *Ich habe mir die Adresse/das Kennzeichen des Autos auf einem Zettel notiert.* It is not used as the obj. of *schreiben*, but in *Ich habe einen Zettel für sie hingelegt/hinterlassen*, and in *Würden Sie ihr bitte diesen Zettel geben?*, it would imply a note.

3. Note = 'an explanation of a word or passage in a book' or 'a short handwritten comment on sth.' *A new edition of* Hamlet *with copious notes/annotations. She had made a few notes in the margin in pencil.*
i. An explanatory note in a text is is **eine Anmerkung**. *Eine neue Ausgabe von* Hamlet *mit zahlreichen Anmerkungen. Die Anmerkungen in dieser Ausgabe sind sehr ausführlich und besonders nützlich.* A footnote is either *eine Anmerkung* or **eine Fußnote**. *Die Anmerkungen/Fußnoten in jedem Kapitel sind durchnumeriert.*
ii. *Eine Anmerkung* is part of the printed text, not what is added in handwriting. A handwritten note is either **die Randbemerkung** or **die Notiz**. In one sense *bemerken* means 'to remark', and *eine Bemerkung* is 'a remark'. *Eine Randbemerkung* is usually 'a written marginal note', but it can sometimes be spoken. Someone might say in a discussion, *'Dazu/Zu diesem Punkt möchte ich eine Randbemerkung machen.'* (The E. equivalent here is *comment* or *remark*.)
Auf jeder Seite der Akte hatte sie witzige Randbemerkungen geschrieben.
Der Rand [von] fast jeder Seite seines Lehrbuchs war mit Notizen voll.
iii. Der Vermerk is a bureaucratic term and can refer to an official addition e.g. in a passport, *ein Vermerk in einem Paß*, or a note made on a document, such as a date, a stamp, or a remark. *Der Beamte versah jedes Aktenstück mit einem Vermerk/mit Vermerken.*
4. Note = 'a quality, especially of the voice, pointing to the influence of a concealed emotion etc.' *There was a note of self-satisfaction in the speech/a note of irritation in his voice.* The specific term is **der Unterton**, an undertone or a veiled, but still perceptible, tone in the voice. **Der Beiklang** is 'a sound which can be heard beside the main one in music or speech and is often felt to be irritating'. *Das Klavier hatte einen klirrenden Beiklang.* **Der Anflug** means 'just a little of, a mere suggestion or hint of, a touch or tinge of' an emotion etc. *Ein Anflug von Lächeln/Röte.*
In der Rede war ein Unterton/Beiklang von Selbstgenügsamkeit.
Ein Unterton mühsam niedergehaltenen Zornes war in seiner Stimme zu hören.
Aus ihrem Gespräch war ein Unterton von Vertraulichkeit zu hören.
Man hörte ihrer Stimme einen Anflug von Spott/Selbstironie an.
Ein Anflug von Ärger machte sich in seiner Stimme bemerkbar.
(Note that *die Note* can mean 'a special quality or touch' or 'the hallmark of a pers.' *Die Blumen verleihen dem Ganzen eine heitere Note. Diese ausgefallenen Hüte sind ihre persönliche Note.*)

5. Take note means 'to pay attention' or 'take heed'. *Take good note of what he tells you!* One near equivalent is **sich merken**, to note, retain in the mind, REMEMBER. *Nun merk' dir gut, was er sagt!* **Berherzigen** means 'to take to heart and follow words of warning or advice'. *Ich werde Ihren Rat beherzigen.* Cf. also *beachten* under NOTICE *n.* 4. **Worthy of note** is beachtenswert.

> *Ich werde mir alles merken, was sie sagt.*   *Diese Warnung solltest du gründlich beherzigen.*

6. Equivalents in reference to music. **Der Ton** is 'a musical note of a certain pitch'. *Sie schlug den Ton C auf dem Klavier an. Wie unterscheidet sich der Ton A des Klaviers von dem der Klarinette?* **Die Note** is 'the sign representing *einen Ton* in printed music'. Hence *Sie singt/spielt nach Noten*, from music.

7. Der Geldschein or **die Banknote** is 'a bank note'.

8. *A singer* **of note** is *ein Sänger* **von Rang**.

notice *v.*

1. i. Both *merken* and one sense of *bemerken* are translated as *to notice.* **Bemerken** denotes a sense perception, usually by the sight, but sometimes by smell or hearing. *Sie hat das Auto noch rechtzeitig bemerkt. Ich habe keine Veränderung an ihr bemerkt.* Only *bemerken* is used with a person as obj. *Ich habe ihn im Theater bemerkt.* **Merken** presupposes not just seeing with the eyes but also drawing a conclusion, however brief, from what is seen or from the way people behave. It suggests becoming aware of what is not immediately clear or is the hidden motive behind some action. It is often close to *realize* and frequently suggests intuition rather than a distinct sense perception. Thus *Ich merke es sofort, wenn jmd. mich belügt,* or *Ich merkte, daß sie mir mit dieser Frage eine Falle stellen wollte. Merkst du was?* implies: Do you notice that something is not as it should be, for example, that there is some concealed intention? Both *merken* and *bemerken* are used with human beings or animals as subj. and with *an* = 'from, in, about'. While *merken* is a common everyday term, *bemerken* belongs more to the educated language. It is thus a word which some people do not use at all in speech. Instead they use *sehen, hören,* or *riechen.*

> *Ich bemerkte sofort, daß sich etw. verändert hatte.*   *Sie hofft, daß man ihre neue Frisur bemerkt.*
> *Plötzlich merkten Hänsel und Gretel, daß sie sich verlaufen hatten.*
> *Er schien nicht zu merken, daß er beobachtet wurde.*
> *An seinem Benehmen konnte man merken, daß etw. vorgefallen war.*
> *Man merkt an ihrer Verlegenheit, daß da etw. nicht stimmt.*
> *An dem Haus waren einige Veränderungen zu bemerken.*
> *Ich habe überhaupt nichts [von irgendwelchen Unstimmigkeiten] gemerkt.*

ii. Merken lassen with people as subj. and obj. states that one person lets or does not let another person notice or become aware of something relating to the first person. *Sie ließ mich ihre Enttäuschung nicht merken* or *Sie ließ mich nichts von ihrer Enttäuschung merken.* A clause can also follow. *Er ließ mich nicht merken, daß er gekränkt war.*

> *Sie ließ mich ohne Worte deutlich merken, daß sie mich verachtete.*

iii. Anmerken + dat. and acc. or clause means 'to notice, see, or tell sth. or that sth. has happened by looking at a pers.' *Ich merkte ihr die Enttäuschung an,* noticed her disappointment, could tell she was disappointed. *Man merkt ihm seine Sorgen an,* can notice/tell by looking at him that he is worried.

> *Man merkt es dir an, daß du gestern Nacht nicht geschlafen hast.*
> *Niemand soll mir anmerken, daß ich nicht immer Kellner gewesen bin.*

iv. Sich (dat.) *etw.* **nicht anmerken lassen** means 'not to let sth. be noticed in one's behaviour or appearance'. *Ich lasse mir meine Enttäuschung nicht anmerken,* I do not let other unspecified people notice that I am disappointed. When you are advised not to let anyone notice something relating to yourself, the construction is *Du darfst dir nicht anmerken lassen, daß du dich so geärgert hast.* Thus *Ich ließ mir [äußerlich] nichts anmerken.*

Lassen Sie sich nicht anmerken, daß Sie schon von der Sache gehört haben!

2. Auffallen, which means 'to attract s.o.'s attention' or 'to strike s.o. as strange, remarkable, unusual, etc.', is often used where **notice** would be the normal E. word.

Es fiel mir auf, daß er den ganzen Abend fast nichts sagte.

Ist Ihnen etw. Ungewöhnliches an den Leuten/an der Sache aufgefallen?

notice *n.* Although the equivalents in some senses are ns., the sense carried by **notice** in combination with some vs. such as *to give* or *take notice* is often expressed by a single v. in G. The original meaning of **notice** was 'information, intimation, or warning'.

1. Notice = 'a written or printed announcement giving information which is placed where it can be read by everyone or in a newspaper'.

i. Die Bekanntmachung is a notice which is in some way official. It can be a notice attached to a notice-board or put in a newspaper by any branch of government, from a ministry of the central government down to the local council, or it can originate from a private firm when it concerns something which has to be made public by law.

Während ich im Rathaus wartete, habe ich sämtliche Bekanntmachungen gelesen.

Die Gemeindeverwaltung muß diese Bekanntmachungen in der Presse veröffentlichen.

ii. A non-official notice on a notice-board is called either **der Anschlag** or **der Aushang**. The two words do not differ in sense, but one or the other may be preferred in different parts of the country. A **notice** in a newspaper of a non-official nature is called **die Anzeige**. Cf. ADVERTISE. **Ein (das) Plakat** is 'a poster or placard' meant for *eine Litfaßsäule*, advertising pillar, or for *eine Plakatwand*, hoarding, billboard. A *notice-board* is usually *das Anschlagbrett*, but in universities it is called *das Schwarze Brett*.

Die Ergebnisse der Verhandlungen werden im Betrieb per Anschlag bekanntgegeben.

Die große Heiratsanzeige, die sie in die Zeitung gesetzt haben, muß sehr viel gekostet haben.

2. Phrs. like **at short notice**, **24 hours' notice**, and **without notice** are expressed in G. in different ways.

i. At short notice. Die Frist is 'a period of time within which or by the expiry of which sth. has to be done'. *Jmd. hat eine Frist von zwei Wochen zur Begleichung einer Rechnung* or *zur Erledigung einer Arbeit*. **Kurzfristig** can mean 'short-term', *ein kurzfristiges Darlehen*, but also 'at short notice', *Die Sitzung wurde kurzfristig einberufen* or *kurzfristig abgesagt*. *Waren, die kurzfristig lieferbar sind*, can be delivered a short time after the order is received.

ii. A period of time + **notice. Kündigen** means 'to give [s.o.] notice'. *Man kündigt jmdm./etw. mit achttägiger/dreimonatiger Frist* or *Man muß eine Wohnung/einem Angestellten drei Monate vorher kündigen*. **Die Kündigungsfrist** is 'period of notice'. *Als er die Stelle annahm, hat er mit der Firmenleitung eine dreimonatige Kündigungsfrist vereinbart*. Cf. 3. *Man hat ihnen fristgerecht gekündigt*, given them due/proper notice. **At 24 hours' notice.** *Die Sitzung wurde [erst] 24 Stunden vorher einberufen/angesetzt.* **At a day's notice.** *Bücher werden mit eintägiger Vorherbestellung geliefert.* **At a moment's notice. Jederzeit/Zu jeder Zeit** *einsatzbereit*, ready for action at any time, can be used in some situations. **Auf Abruf** means that someone is ready to do something as soon as called upon. *Ich stehe dir auf Abruf zur Verfügung* means that I am ready to help you (or do whatever is involved) whenever you call on me and could translate *at a moment's notice*. *Er hält sich auf Abruf bereit loszufahren*. **Der Abruf** in commercial language is a request for delivery of goods. *Waren sind lieferbar auf Abruf* is translated as *on call*.

iii. Without notice. *Preise werden* **unangekündigt/ohne [Vor]ankündigung** *geändert*. **Fristlos**, 'without notice', is used with *entlassen*, 'to dismiss', *Sie wurden fristlos entlassen*, and with *kündigen* (cf. 3), which can mean 'to give notice that employment is being terminated', *Ihm wurde fristlos gekündigt*.

iv. Till further notice is **bis auf weiteres**. *Wir bleiben bis auf weiteres hier*.

3. i. Give s.o. **notice of** sth. means 'to inform or notify s.o.' and corresponds to **jmdn. von etw. in Kenntnis setzen** and **jmdm. von etw. Bescheid geben**. *Wir haben unsere Partner von dem Plan in Kenntnis gesetzt. Wenn Sie mir rechtzeitig Bescheid geben, werde ich es so einrichten, daß ich dabei bin.*

ii. Give notice denotes an intimation by one of the parties to an agreement that it is to be terminated at a specified time, especially with reference to quitting a house, lodgings, or employment. **Kündigen** means 'to notify the other party to a contract that one intends to terminate this'. The contract can relate to employment, rent of a house, a loan or credit, or other agreements. With employment, either the employee or employer can be subj. When an employee is the subj., *kündigen* often has no obj., *Er hat zum Quartalsende gekündigt*, but *die Stelle* can be added, *Sie hat ihre Stelle gekündigt*. When an employer is the subj., the person given notice is usually in the dat. *Der Betrieb hat einem Angestellten und drei Arbeitern gekündigt*. *I have been given notice* is thus *Mir ist gekündigt worden*. However *Man hat mich gekündigt* and *Ich bin gekündigt worden* are also heard. In other fields the thing to which the notice relates is acc., and a person, if included, dat. Thus *Die Wirtin hat dem Untermieter das Zimmer gekündigt* or *Die Bank hat mir das Darlehen gekündigt*. *Wir haben die Wohnung zum Monatsende gekündigt*. **Die Kündigung** is 'notice to leave or quit' in the same contexts. *Die Firma/Der Hausbesitzr hat die Kündigung zurückgenommen*.

4. Notice also means 'attention', particularly in *to take [no] notice*. Again various expressions convey the idea.

i. The main equivalent is **beachten**, which can mean 'to pay attention to', 'to take note or notice of'. *Nicht beachten* is 'to take no notice of' or 'to disregard' with a person or thing as obj. *Er hat die Warnung [nicht] beachtet*. *Beachten* is here a syn. of **achten auf**. The latter can mean 'to pay attention to', but it also suggests willingness to follow or react, and thus means 'to take notice of or heed'. *Er achtete [nicht] auf die Warnung*. With certain words *beachten* implies observing or complying with rules or regulations. *Wir müssen die Schutzbestimmungen/die Regeln/die Gebrauchsanweisungen/diese Hinweise genau beachten*. With a neg. in these contexts it could mean 'to take no notice of'. *Etw. ist keiner Beachtung wert*, not worthy of attention/notice or beneath someone's notice.

> *Sie haben nicht auf meinen Rat/die Zurechtweisung/den Warnruf/die Gefahr/die Anweisungen geachtet.*
> *Er sprach weiter, ohne auf die Zwischenrufe zu achten.*
> *Sie hat ihn überhaupt nicht/kaum/wenig beachtet.*   *Beachte nicht, was sie über dich sagen!*
> *Wenn du seine Ratschläge beachtet hättest, wärst du jetzt nicht in dieser mißlichen Lage.*
> *Ich habe ein paar Einwände gemacht, aber man hat sie nicht beachtet.*
> *Wir haben beim Experiment die Begleiterscheinungen genau/gut/nicht weiter beachtet.*
> *Achte nicht auf den Hund! Er bellt nur und wird dich nicht beißen.*

ii. Hören auf, 'to heed, LISTEN TO', implies acting on advice etc. as well as listening to it. **Take notice** *of what s.o. says* could be translated by any of the vs. in i and ii. *Was sie sagte, habe ich beachtet. Achte/Höre auf das, was er sagt!*

iii. Sich kümmern um means 'to BOTHER, trouble, or concern oneself about' and can translate in particular *to take no notice of. Laß sie reden, kümmere dich nicht darum!* *Kümmere dich nicht um das, was sie sagen!*

iv. Notiz nehmen von etw. means 'to take notice of', but is now not common and may be dropping out of use. *Die Presse hat von den Ereignissen nicht die geringste Notiz genommen.*

v. *Die Kenntnis* means 'knowledge' and, in phrs., 'attention' or 'notice'. These phrs. are all formal in tone. *To bring sth. to s.o.'s* **notice** is **jmdm. etw. zur Kenntnis bringen.** *Sth. has come to my* **notice** is **Es ist mir zur Kenntnis gekommen** or **Ich erhielt/bekam Kenntnis davon** or less formally **Es ist mir zu Ohren gekommen.** **Etw. zur Kenntnis nehmen** is 'to take note of sth.' *Sie nahm es nicht zur Kenntnis,* didn't take any notice of it.

now *adv.*

1. i. In the sense 'at the present time or moment', **jetzt** and **nun** are interchangeable, the only difference being that *nun* is stylistically slightly higher.

Jetzt muß ich gehen.   *Ich muß nun gehen.*

Jetzt/Nun bin ich diese Sorge endlich los.   *Jetzt sind Sie an der Reihe, dann wir.*

Ich habe vorige Woche geschrieben, nun bist du an der Reihe.

ii. Nunmehr belongs more to the written language and to formal speech. It has the same sense as *nun* and *jetzt* but is more emphatic.

Anfangs war mir vieles unklar, nunmehr weiß ich über alles Bescheid.

Nach all dem bleibt uns nunmehr keine andere Wahl.

2. Both **jetzt** and **nun** are also used like **now** to express a connection between the pres. and what has preceded it. The meaning is 'in view of what has happened (recently)', 'under these circumstances'. *I was hoping to see you tomorrow—that won't be possible now.*

Nun darf ich nicht länger zögern.   *Jetzt ist aber Schluß damit!*

Ihr habt die Arbeit angefangen, jetzt müßt ihr sie zu Ende führen.

Ich hatte gehofft, dich morgen zu besuchen—das wird nun/jetzt nicht möglich sein.

Es ist der schönste Ort, den ich jemals gesehen habe. Jetzt/Nun verstehe ich, warum ihr so oft hierher
   kommt.   *Was ist da nun/jetzt wieder los?*

3. From now on is either **von nun an** or **von jetzt an.** **Now or never** is **jetzt oder nie. And now** *for the next question* is **Und jetzt zur nächsten Frage. Now that** or **now** introducing a clause is **jetzt, wo. Nun, wo** belongs to the literary language.

Von jetzt an werden wir eng zusammenarbeiten.   *Von nun an wird alles anders sein.*

Jetzt, wo ich pensioniert bin, kann ich all die Bücher lesen, die ich immer lesen wollte.

Jetzt, wo er älter ist, mag ich ihn viel mehr.

Nun, wo ich das lang ersehnte Ziel erreicht habe, kommen mir Bedenken, ob sich die Mühe gelohnt
   hat.

4. i. By now = 'by this time'. *She will be in Tasmania by now* can be expressed simply as *Sie wird* **nun/jetzt schon** *in T. sein,* or **inzwischen** or **mittlerweile,** 'in the mean time', can be used with the future perf. and an appropriate v., *Inzwischen/ Mittlerweile wird sie in T. angekommen sein. Inzwischen hatte sich die Landschaft völlig verändert. Die Lage hatte sich nun/inzwischen stabilisiert.* (Mittlerweile is stylistically higher than the everyday *inzwischen.*) (Bis jetzt means 'up to now/the present'. *Bis jetzt sind nur zwei solche Fälle bekannt. Bis jetzt ist alles reibungslos verlaufen.*)

ii. Now or **by now** refers to a particular time in the past that someone is talking or writing about and which is opposed to an earlier time. *It was 10 o'clock now. By now it was 10 o'clock.* **Inzwischen** and **mittlerweile** can be used here, but **nun** and **jetzt** are also possible. *Es war inzwischen 10 Uhr geworden. Es war nun zehn Uhr. They were walking more slowly now. Inzwischen gingen sie langsamer. Jetzt gingen sie langsamer.*

5. Other expressions. **Now** *is the time to find that out* is **Es ist jetzt die Zeit, das herauszubekommen.** One transl. of *How long have you been living here* **now**? is **Seit wann**

wohnen Sie hier? An alternative is *Wie lange wohnen Sie jetzt [schon] hier?* The answer *For three years* **now** would be *Seit drei Jahren [schon].* *It's* **now** *a fortnight since I wrote to her* or *It's* **now** *a fortnight ago that I wrote* would have to be *Es ist nun/jetzt zwei Wochen her, daß ich ihr geschrieben habe* (her = 'AGO'). *They should arrive anytime* **now** is *Sie müssen jeden Augenblick ankommen. Sie können jetzt jeden Tag ankommen,* any day now.

6. Now is also used in many ways in which the temporal sense is weakened or effaced. Mostly without reference to time, it can indicate the mood of the speaker, explain, warn, or comfort. In G. *nun* has this function in several cases. (*Nun,* it should be noted, also has some of the functions of WELL, particularly at the beginning of a sent. *Nun, wie steht's?*)

i. **Nun** is added, like **now**, to questions to make them sound more emphatic and make the person addressed answer either yes or no. A question with *nun* and without an interrogative or *oder nicht* suggests a neg. answer. *Ich habe da geholfen—war das nun schlecht?* would expect the answer *nein. Hältst du das nun für richtig?* implies that the person addressed should not consider it right. When such questions are not meant to suggest an answer, *oder nicht* is added, as this makes either yes or no possible. The last question could be formulated neutrally as *War das nun richtig oder nicht?* In questions with an interrogative, *nun* simply calls for a clear answer. *Was soll ich nun sagen?* Unlike **now**, *nun* in this use is usually in the body of the sent., but can be at the beginning. *War das nun ein gelungenes Fest oder nicht?* Or *Nun, war das ein gelungenes Fest oder nicht?*

> *Was ist denn nun?* (Now what are you/we doing?)   *Hat sich das nun gelohnt?*
> *Fahren wir nun am Wochenende nach Trier oder nicht?*
> *Ist das nun deine endgültige Meinung?*
> *Wie wollen wir uns nun in dieser Angelegenheit entscheiden?*

ii. **Nun** gives a statement a special emphasis. In response to the question '*Hat er das Studium ernst genommen?*', someone could answer, '*Das muß man nun wirklich sagen*', which can be translated as *Now you have to admit/you can't dispute that.*

> *Das stimmt nun wirklich.*   *Das geht nun [aber] wirklich zu weit!*
> *Man kann nun nicht gerade behaupten, daß er einen guten Geschmack hat.*

iii. **Now** introduces a point in an argument or narrative. **Nun** also has this function, but unlike **now**, it is often not at the beginning of the sent. Thus *Now this was bad enough* would usually be *Das war nun schon schlimm genug, was aber als nächstes geschah, übertraf unsere schlimmsten Befürchtungen.* If *nun* is used for this purpose at the beginning of the sent., it changes the word order, unlike *nun* = 'well'.

> *Als man nun erfuhr, wofür das Geld ausgegeben worden war, gab es einen Riesenkrach.*
> *Dieser König hatte nun drei Töchter.*
> *Unser Kamel, Daisy, hatte nur die eine gefährliche Schwäche. Sie schlug gern aus. Nun kann ein Kamel in jede Richtung in einem Umkreis von zwei Metern ausschlagen.*

iv. In *Now, let me see!* **now** is *nun. Die Adresse habe ich irgendwo. Nun, ich muß mal nachsehen. Nun, ich muß mal überlegen/nachdenken.*

v. **Now** can introduce a contrast, *I don't know anything about car engines. Now, if Richard were here, he'd be able to help you.* This would be **aber**, but *nun* may be added.

> *Von Automotoren verstehe ich gar nichts. Wenn [nun] aber Richard hier wäre, könnte er euch helfen.*

vi. **Now** and **well now** are used at the beginning of a sent. as an introduction or simply as something to say while the speaker thinks of what to say next. **Also** is the usual equivalent. In this use it is meant to attract attention and has almost no meaning.

> *Also, was dann passierte, war folgendes.*   *Also, ich habe die folgenden Vorschläge.*

vii. **Now** gives emphasis to commands or requests. *Be very careful now!* could be

Nehmt euch ja in acht! Nun macht ja/bloß keine Dummheiten! is a transl. of *No nonsense now!* Both **ja** and **bloß** express a warning. *Bloß* is usual in speech.

viii. So sums up what has happened and suggests something like *as that is done* or *finished* or *has happened*.It is often combined with *jetzt* or *nun*. A transl. of *Now that's the end!* is *So, jetzt/nun ist Schluß!* This could imply *Ihr habt lange genug gespielt. So, Peter, nun komm mal her, wir wollen was Ernstes besprechen* implies that something has happened. *Now stop quarrelling and come here!* could thus be *So, hört doch auf, euch zu streiten und kommt mal her!*

    So, jetzt können wir was trinken.   *So, Peter, benimm dich mal!*

ix. Now [then] introduces a protest. **Na** can express impatience or annoyance. *Now then, what's the trouble/what's going on here?* could be *Na, was ist denn hier los? Na, was soll denn das?* is like *Now then, what do you think you're doing? Now, look here!* can be *Na, hören Sie mal, das geht doch nicht!* Na also expresses doubt. An expression meaning something like *Come now, you don't expect me to believe that!* is *Na, wer das glaubt!* Implied is *der glaubt auch alles. Na, was du mir da alles erzählst! Na, stimmt das denn wirklich?*

x. Na is also used like **now** to calm or soothe in a friendly way. *Na, weine nur nicht gleich!* can translate *There now/Now come on, don't cry! Na, na, so schlimm wird es ja nicht sein.*

number *n.*

1. i. In the sense 'a unit in a numerical series', *Seven is his lucky number*, or *a number divisible by two*, **number** is **die Zahl**. *Fünf ist eine ungerade Zahl. Addieren Sie diese Zahlen!* Note that the pl. *die Zahlen* can mean 'figures', i.e.'numerical data to support sth.' *Sie müssen diese Behauptung durch Zahlen belegen.*

    Tausend ist eine vierstellige Zahl.   *Dreizehn gilt als Unglückszahl.*
    Gerade Zahlen sind durch zwei teilbar, ungerade nicht.

ii. Die Ziffer is a written sign by which *eine Zahl* is represented, i.e. a digit. Thus *Die Zahl 15 wird mit den Ziffern 1 und 5 geschrieben. Die Ziffer 6 stellt die Zahl sechs dar.* *516 ist eine Zahl*, but each figure is *eine Ziffer*. Hence *arabische und römische Ziffern* and *das Zifferblatt*, face of a clock. (*Arabische und römische Zahlen* is also used.)

    Die Zahl XL setzt sich aus den Ziffern X und L zusammen.
    Der Code benutzt Ziffern sowie Buchstaben.

2. Number means 'the total or sum of the units involved'. *The number of desks in the room. The number of people in the hall.*

i. Die Zahl is the usual equivalent. Like **number** it is mostly used with the definite article in this sense. *Die Zahl der Pulte im Klassenzimmer. Die Zahl der Schüler in der Klasse.* Hence compounds like *die Abonnentenzahl, die Bandzahl, die Stückzahl*, or *die Gesamtzahl*.

    Die Zahl der Mitglieder war inzwischen auf 200 angewachsen.
    Er berechnete die Zahl der Ziegelsteine in der Mauer.
    Es kommt mir nicht auf die Zahl der Aufnahmen an, sondern auf deren Qualität.
    Die Mannschaften waren in ungleicher Zahl angetreten.
    Solche Bäume wachsen dort in großer Zahl.   *Wir waren sieben an der Zahl* (in number).

ii. A difficulty arises because, in formal and bureaucratic style, **die Anzahl**, the specific meaning of which is discussed in 3, can refer to the total number and thus be a syn. of *Zahl* in 2. i. A speaker at a meeting might say, '*Ich freue mich, Sie hier in so großer Anzahl begrüßen zu können.*' Likewise *Das Publikum ist in beträchtlicher Anzahl erschienen.* Except in such formal circumstances, *Zahl* is the normal word in both these cases. Thus *Anzahl der Stücke* can be *Stückzahl* or *Zahl der Stücke*. Only *Zahl* forms compounds.

Die beiden Parteien sind in gleicher Zahl/Anzahl/in der gleichen Zahl/Anzahl/mit gleicher Sitzzahl im Parlament vertreten.   Die Zahl/Anzahl der Mitglieder hat sich erhöht.

3. When an unspecified number or total is involved, **number** is preceded by the indefinite article. *A number of the members abstained.* Here, both *eine Zahl* and *eine Anzahl* are found. **Eine Zahl** again denotes the total and needs an adj., *Eine große Zahl von Besuchern war gekommen,* while **eine Anzahl** denotes a certain number which represents a part of a whole, *Eine Anzahl der Teilnehmer war gegen den Vorschlag. Anzahl* is followed by the gen. or *von.* The same distinction holds when an adj. precedes *number. Nur eine unbedeutende Zahl von Studenten war erschienen. Leider können wir nur eine begrenzte Anzahl der Bewerber einstellen.*

Eine Anzahl der Mitglieder enthielten sich der Stimme.
Eine Anzahl der Studenten versuchten, den Redner niederzubrüllen.
Nur eine geringe Anzahl der alten Häuser ist erhalten geblieben.
Wir haben genug Geld, um eine beträchtliche Anzahl der gewünschten Bücher zu kaufen.

4. Eine Anzahl also means 'a small number, a few'. *Eine Anzahl Kinder/von Kindern kam auf uns zu* (up to about 10). *Man hat eine Anzahl von Lösungen vorgeschlagen.*

5. Number when it means 'a digit or group of digits used as a means of identification' is **die Nummer.** Hence *die Hausnummer, die Kontonummer, die Schecknummer, die Zimmernummer, die Bestellnummer, die Bandnummer, Telefonnummer.* It is used for things in a list or series, *Symphonie Nr. 5 von Beethoven,* and often also for the registration number of a car (although this may contain letters) instead of the formal term, **das Kennzeichen.** In some cases there is a choice of word. *He marked each ball with a number* could be *Er markierte jeden Ball mit einer Nummer,* but *mit einer Zahl* is also possible and, if there were fewer than ten, *mit einer Ziffer.*

Unter welcher Nummer sind Sie zu erreichen? (Telefonnummer)
Wählen Sie bitte die Nummer 692 3146!   Ich bin Nummer vier auf der Liste.
Jeder muß eine Nummer ziehen und nach der Reihenfolge der Nummern eintreten.

6. Other expressions. **A number of** *times* can only be *mehrere Male.* **A number of** *examples* could be *einige/mehrere Beispiele* as well as *eine Anzahl von Beispielen.* **Numbers of** *students* when it means 'a fairly large number of' is *eine ziemlich große Zahl von Studenten.* **Large numbers of** *people* is *sehr viele Leute* or *eine große Zahl von Leuten. Eine Menge* means 'an unspecified large number (or amount) of'. *Ich habe dort eine Menge Kollegen getroffen. Eine Menge Leute hat zugesehen. In rauhen Mengen* is like *any number of. Er hat Bücher in rauhen Mengen. Dieses Jahr gibt es Kirschen in rauhen Mengen.*

O

object, protest *vs.*

1. Object to s.o. or sth. means 'to express opposition to or dislike or disapproval of him/her/it'. **Protest about/against** s.o. or sth. is 'to say or show publicly that one objects to that pers. or thg.'

i. I object/protest! when nothing follows can sometimes be **Ich muß doch sehr bitten!** which expresses indignation and a protest against, for example, an unjust accusation or unacceptable behaviour. *Bitten* has this sense only in this expression. Nothing can be added. When what is objected to is stated, **I object to** *such a tone of voice/to people smoking in my office*, **sich etw. verbitten**, 'to demand emphatically that something cease or not happen', is the usual v. *Ich verbitte mir solche Beschuldigungen/dieses Benehmen. Ich verbitte mir einen solchen Ton.* It needs an obj. and is not restricted to the first person. *Sie verbat sich jede Einmischung in ihre persönlichen Angelegenheiten. Ich verbitte es mir, daß in meinem Büro geraucht wird.*

ii. Sich gegen etw. verwahren is a more elevated and less common expression. It is found with *ich* as subj., but more often in the third person, and is mostly refers to objections to criticism or accusations.

Ich verwahre mich gegen diese Verdächtigung.   *'Das stimmt nicht', verwahrte sie sich.*

iii. Protestieren is 'to make a protest in words or other ways' and 'to reject an assertion, demand, suggestion, etc. as unsuitable, unwise, untrue, etc.' It is used with and without *gegen*. *Die Schüler haben nur schwach protestiert. Sie protestierten gegen diese Behauptung. Ich protestiere*, 'I protest/object', is often used when nothing follows. *Protestieren* can translate *to object to [doing] sth.* if some kind of protest is involved. *Ich protestiere dagegen, so geringschätzig behandelt zu werden/daß man mir die Arbeit anderer Kollegen aufbürdet.* **Widerspruch erheben** is a syn. *Sie erhoben Widerspruch/protestierten gegen diese Behandlung.* Another syn., **Einspruch erheben**, can stand alone or take a phr. with *gegen*. *Ich erhebe Einspruch. Der Verteidiger erhob Einspruch gegen die Vorgehensweise des Staatsanwalts.* Cf. OBJECTION 2. i and 2. iii.

iv. Widersprechen means 'to declare what s.o. says to be incorrect'. It can mean 'to contradict', *'Widersprich mir nicht immer!', sagte die Mutter*, but in other situations, it means 'to oppose or object to'. It takes a dat.

Dem Redner/Dieser Behauptung wurde von vielen Seiten widersprochen.

Der Betriebsrat hat der von der Firmenleitung beschlossenen Entlassung von fünfzig Arbeitern widersprochen.   *'Das ist nicht so', widersprach sie.*

(*Widersprechen* also means 'to contradict' in the sense 'to be logically inconsistent with'. *Mit dieser Behauptung widersprichst du dem, was du vorhin gesagt hast.*)

v. Sich wehren gegen, the basic meaning of which is 'to defend oneself or to put up resistance or a fight against', also means 'to oppose strongly' something asserted such as an accusation, an insinuation, or the casting of suspicion on someone. In such contexts it can translate **object to** and **protest against**. *Er wehrte sich gegen diese Beschuldigung. Ich wehre mich gegen die Verdächtigung, ich hätte wichtige Tatsachen verschwiegen.*

Ich wehre mich gegen die Stigmatisierung der ganzen Jugend in der Ex-DDR als Rechtsradikale.

2. i. In *I object to getting up early*, **object** denotes a temperamental dislike and expresses the same meaning as *I have an objection to getting up early*. This sense is conveyed by **die Abneigung**, aversion. Cf. OBJECTION 3. *Ich habe eine [starke/tiefe] Abneigung gegen frühes Aufstehen*. Or *Ich habe eine starke Abneigung dagegen, früh aufzustehen*.

ii. In *I [do not] object to s.o./sth./doing sth.*, **object** means 'to dislike or disapprove of it'. The equivalent is **etw./nichts gegen jmdn./etw. haben**. *Haben Sie etw. gegen diesen Mitarbeiter? Possible answers are Ja, ich habe etw. gegen ihn* or *Nein, ich habe nichts gegen ihn. Ich habe nichts gegen diese Arbeitsweise*. An E. gerund becomes an infin. *Would you object to helping her?* is *Hätten Sie etw. dagegen, ihr zu helfen/die Arbeit des erkrankten Kollegen zu übernehmen?* Cf. OBJECTION 4.

3. Object means 'to offer in opposition or by way of counter-argument to a statement, accusation, etc.' and is followed by a clause or direct speech. *He objected that the report was misleading. 'That will cost too much', she objected*.

i. Einwenden [gegen] means 'to advance a contrary reason, argument, or reservation against sth.' *Ich habe etw. gegen den Plan einzuwenden* is usually translated as *I have an objection to*. The neg. is *Ich habe nichts gegen den Plan einzuwenden*, no objection to.

> *'Das können wir uns gar nicht leisten', wandte sie ein.*
>
> *Er wandte gegen diese vorschnelle Verurteilung ein, daß man nicht genug über die Umstände wisse, um ein Urteil zu fällen.*

ii. *Beanstanden* as a commercial term means 'to make a complaint about or to object to the state or quality of goods'. *Sie beanstandeten den Zustand der gelieferten Waren. Die beanstandeten Mängel am Auto wurden schnell wieder behoben*. In other situations **etw. [an etw.] beanstanden** means 'to take exception to, criticize, or object to'. *Ich habe nichts daran zu beanstanden*, I find nothing wrong with it or don't object to anything about it. *Ich habe etw. zu beanstanden*. Sents. with *einwenden gegen* can often be formulated with *beanstanden an. Er wandte gegen den Plan ein, daß er viel zu kostspielig war. Sie beanstandete an dem Plan, daß er viel zu kostspielig war*. *Beanstanden* is stronger, suggesting serious objections or criticism which might make reconsideration necessary, while *einwenden* implies misgivings or reservations.

> *Der Lehrer beanstandete die Schrift des Schülers, die er beinahe unleserlich fand.*
>
> *An dem Film beanstandeten zahlreiche Zuschauer die vielen Nacktszenen.*

objection, protest *ns*. Senses: (i) The basic sense of **objection** is 'sth. stated in opposition to a pers. or thg.' It can refer to a specific reason that is advanced or may be presented in opposition to something. *He presented his objections in a formal report. Your objection will be considered. The objection was not taken seriously*. (ii) A weaker and vaguer sense is 'disapproval or disagreement', especially in the expression *to take objection to* and in the neg. *There was no objection to the plan* or *The motion was carried without [any] objection*. In the last two sents. it is a syn. of *opposition*. While **objection** implies nothing about the manner and may exist only in the mind of the person concerned, **protest** is always 'an uttered objection which may be delivered either with due formality or with spontaneous emotion'. *The bill was passed despite the protests of several senators*.

1. *Der Einwand* is the main equivalent of sense i of **objection**.

i. Der Einwand refers to a specific reason advanced against something, a counter-argument or misgiving. *Einwände [gegen etw.] machen/erheben* suggests putting forward reasons or arguments against what has been proposed. *Den/Einen Einwand machen/erheben/geltend machen* means 'to raise the/an objection'. The definite article *den* is mostly followed by a *daß*-clause. *Sie erhob den Einwand, daß Schmidt nur* *wenig Erfahrung hatte, aber man beachtete ihn nicht. Er erhob einen Einwand, den ich sehr vernünftig fand. Ich habe keinen Einwand/keine Einwände* is often a more formal syn. of *Ich habe nichts dagegen.* Cf. 4.

Gegen diese Hypothese/Theorie wurden keine Einwände erhoben.

Er machte sofort den Einwand, daß wir mit diesem Vorgehen auf beträchtlichen Widerstand stoßen würden.

Alle Einwände gegen den Plan werden berücksichtigt.

Sie machte den Einwand, daß die Kosten unsere Mittel übersteigen würden.

Sie machte ein paar freundliche Einwände gegen den Vorschlag, und er versuchte, sie zu widerlegen.

ii. Die Einwendung has the same sense as *Einwand* but is more formal and less frequently used. It is found mostly in the pl. and in the expressions *Einwendungen/keine Einwendungen machen.*

Wir haben wohlüberlegte und berechtigte Einwendungen/Einwände vorgebracht/gemacht.

Ich habe ihre Einwendungen/Einwände angehört.

Wir bitten Sie höflich, die nachstehende Aufstellung (list) *Ihrer bei uns gebuchten Wertpapiere zu prüfen. Diese Aufstellung gilt als genehmigt, wenn Sie nicht innerhalb einer Frist von einem Monat seit ihrem Zugang schriftliche Einwendungen dagegen an uns abgesandt haben* (commercial style).

2. The words discussed in this section are the equivalents of **objection** and **protest** when they are more or less synonymous and refer to the expression of opposition without stating specifically what objections are raised.

i. Der Widerspruch is 'an utterance with which one objects to s.o.'s remark or expression of opinion'. Depending on the circumstances, it can be either 'contradiction', *Der Vater duldet keinen Widerspruch*, or 'a protest' or 'opposition'. In the latter meaning it can express sense ii of **objection**, when it can be replaced by *opposition. Widerspruch gegen etw. erheben* means 'to dispute the justification of a claim or of sth. said', 'to protest against it', and can translate *to take objection to.* Although it necessarily implies either condemning what was said, stating the opposite of it, or making a counter-assertion, it stresses more the action of expressing disapproval or disagreement than stating an argument. It is used alone or with *gegen;* a clause is not added.

Gegen diese Behauptung muß ich Widerspruch erheben.

Der Vorschlag wurde ohne Widerspruch angenommen (without objection or opposition).

Gegen diese Ansicht erhob sich allgemeiner Widerspruch.

Vor vollendete Tatsachen gestellt, erhob die Regierung keinen Widerspruch.

ii. Der Protest is usually 'a spontaneous and vigorous expression of disapproval or disagreement'. Hence *ein formeller Protest. Sie blieben aus Protest der Sitzung fern,* stayed away by way of protest; *sie verließen unter Protest den Sitzungssaal,* left it, protesting as they did so.

Obwohl einige Senatoren energischen Protest gegen den Gesetzentwurf erhoben, wurde er dennoch ver-abschiedet.   Die Proteste drangen nicht durch/nutzten nichts.

Die Zahl derer, die einen öffentlichen Protest gegen das Naziregime wagten, war sehr klein.

iii. Der Einspruch is 'an emphatic written or spoken expression of disagreement or disapproval'. Although it is like *Widerspruch* in stressing the action of raising an objection or of protesting rather than putting forward arguments, it suggests something having greater consequences than *Widerspruch.* If, for example, the defence counsel objects to something the prosecution does, he/she says, '*Ich erhebe Einspruch.*' This makes a decision necessary. In non-legal spheres, *Jmd. erhebt gegen eine Forderung Einspruch* suggests a serious objection. (With *das Urteil,* verdict, *Einspruch erheben gegen* can imply an appeal as well as a protest, although there are the specific terms for an appeal, *Berufung/Revision einlegen.*)

Die Angestellten erhoben Einspruch gegen die Art und Weise, wie der neue Abteilungsleiter sie behandelte.

Gegen das Urteil, das sich nur auf Indizien stützte, erhob der Verteidiger Einspruch und beantragte Revision in der nächsten Instanz.

3. Particularly in the expression *to have an objection to,* **objection** denotes a feeling of disinclination or dislike. *I have a strong objection to having to start work at 6 a.m.* The equivalent is **die Abneigung,** dislike, aversion. *Ich habe eine starke Abneigung dagegen, schon um sechs Uhr früh mit der Arbeit anfangen zu müssen.* Cf. OBJECT 2. i.

4. **Etw./nichts gegen etw. haben** or **etw./nichts dagegen haben** + infin. or clause often translate *have any* or *no objection to sth.* or *doing sth.* It expresses not only an emotional objection in the form of dislike, but may refer to considered mental reservations. *Etw.* is used in questions or pos. sents. *Habt ihr etw. dagegen, daß er Mitglied unserer Mannschaft wird?* The answer could be *Ja, ich habe etw. dagegen* or *Nein, ich habe nichts dagegen.* To emphasize that the objection is a reasoned one, **einzuwenden** is often added. *Sie hatten nichts gegen den Vorschlag einzuwenden.* It could be added to the first three examples. *Viel* or *vieles* or *einiges* can replace *etw.* A question with *was* asks for the objection to be specified. *Was haben Sie gegen den Plan [einzuwenden]?* Cf. OBJECT 3. i.

Ich habe nichts dagegen, mit ihnen ein Glas Bier zu trinken.
Ich habe sehr viel/vieles gegen die vorgeschlagene Reform einzuwenden.

occur, happen, take place *vs.*

1. One meaning of **occur** is 'exist', 'to be met with or found in some place'. *Misprints occur on every page. These commonly occurring weeds grow anywhere.* The usual word in this sense is **vorkommen.** An alternative is **sich finden.** Cf. FIND.

Wasserstoff kommt in freier Form nur in geringen Mengen vor. Er kommt meist in Verbindungen vor.
Das Kängeruh kommt nur in Australien vor.   *Diese Pflanzen kommen nur in den Tropen vor.*
Druckfehler kommen auf jeder Seite vor.   *Dieses Wort kommt oft bei Lessing vor.*

2. One meaning of **happen** is 'to come about without plan or apparent cause'. *The accident happened at midnight.* It also means 'to take place as a result or effect of a situation or a course of action'. *What will happen if the police find out? They said that these measures would produce an upturn in the economy—this has not happened.* **Occur** is a syn. of **happen** and frequently interchangeable with it. **Occur** may suggest an event which commands attention and may be preferred in certain contexts. A number of vs., including those discussed in 3 and 4, express the meaning 'to happen' and translate **occur** and **happen.**

i. Vorkommen expresses this sense, but only to a limited extent as it implies happening as one of a series. *Auseinandersetzungen dieser Art kommen hier oft vor.* It cannot refer in the pos. to a single event, as in *When did the accident occur?* On the other hand, the series need consist of only two. *Dieser Fall kam schon einmal vor.* In the neg., such as a warning that something should not occur again, this condition is fulfilled as a repetition is seen as a possibility. *Dieser Fehler darf nicht wieder vorkommen. Solche Widersetzlichkeit soll nicht wieder vorkommen.* With the dat. and *noch nicht* or *noch nie,* vorkommen means that something has not previously occurred in someone's experience. *Eine solche Ungerechtigkeit/Gemeinheit ist uns noch nie/nicht vorgekommen.*

Eine solche Gelegenheit kommt nur selten vor.   *Es kam öfters vor, daß er sich verspätete.*

ii. The main equivalent is **geschehen.** *Der Unfall geschah an dieser Stelle/kurz vor Mitternacht. Was wird geschehen, wenn die Polizei erfährt, was wir planen?* A less formal v. commonly used in everyday language is **passieren.** *Wie konnte das nur* *passieren/geschehen?* **Sich ereignen** belongs to the neutral level which can be used both in speech and writing. In precise usage, which is not always observed, it is restricted to something remarkable which attracts special attention. *Wenn sich das jemals ereignet, benachrichtigen Sie mich sofort. Am dritten Tag ereignete sich ein ungewöhnlicher/kleiner Zwischenfall.* All three vs. are used either with *das, was, etw., nichts,* or ns. like *der Unfall* or *das Unglück* as subj. (Note that *geschehen* can mean 'to be done'. *Dein Wille geschehe! Was Sie befohlen haben, ist schon geschehen.*)

> *Etw. Schreckliches/Außerordentliches ist gestern abend passiert/geschehen/hat sich gestern ereignet.*
> *Es ist nun einmal geschehen, und wir können es nicht ungeschehen machen.*
> *Wenn sie ihren Willen nicht hätten durchsetzen wollen, wäre das ganze Unglück nicht passiert/geschehen.*   *Wann/Wo hat sich der Unfall ereignet?*
> *Es hat sich heute nichts Besonderes ereignet.*

iii. Sich zutragen belongs to written and formal language and often stresses how something happened.

> *Der Vorfall hat sich folgendermaßen zugetragen.*   *Wie hat sich das zugetragen?*

iv. Vorgehen is often used as a question in the pres. *Was geht hier vor?* This can be no more than a request for information, but it can expresses suspicion or surprise, like *What's going on here? Passieren, geschehen, sich ereignen,* and *sich zutragen* are used in questions, but without the implication of suspicion. *Was passiert hier? Was ist denn passiert/geschehen? Was hat sich denn ereignet/zugetragen?* Vorgehen can convey the same meaning as *sich ereignen,* but it is often used when what is happening is mysterious, extraordinary, or unfathomable, or when someone suspects that something is happening, without knowing exactly what it is. *Sie ahnte, daß etw. Ungeheuerliches vorging.* It is often used for what is going on in someone's mind. *Was geht in diesem Menschen/hinter seiner Stirn vor?*

> *Er kümmerte sich nicht um das, was draußen vorging.*
> *Es sind einige Veränderungen vorgegangen.*
> *Aus der Zeitung erfährt man, was in der Welt vorgeht.*
> *Was geht eigentlich vor, wenn ich diese Taste drücke?*
> *Niemand weiß, was da eigentlich vorgeht.*
> *Ich möchte mal wissen, was in deinem Gehirn so vorgeht.*

v. Sich begeben would now be used, if at all, only in elevated and solemn diction. *Es begab sich* is used in the G. Bible where the AV has *It came to pass* and resembles this E. expression stylistically.

> *Es begab sich aber zu der Zeit, daß ein Gebot von dem Kaiser Augustus ausging, daß alle Welt geschätzt würde.* (Luke 2: 1.)

vi. Vorfallen suggests that something suddenly occurs which is mostly unpleasant or disruptive for the people involved. *Sobald ich sie sah, war es klar, daß irgendetwas vorgefallen war.*

> *An dem Abend war nichts Ungewöhnliches/Unangenehmes vorgefallen.*

vii. Sich abspielen is often used when someone describes one or a series of occurrences. *Das ganze hat sich so abgespielt* introduces a description. However, it is also used as a syn. of *passieren* and *geschehen.*

> *Er sagte mir, es habe sich ganz anders abgespielt, als wir glaubten.*
> *Sie erzählte uns den Vorgang, der sich kurz vor Mitternacht abgespielt hatte.*

viii. Es kam zu can express a meaning like 'to happen or occur'. *In Seoul ist es gestern zu heftigen Auseinandersetzungen zwischen der Polizei und Studenten gekommen.* Another transl. is *there was,* etc.

3. i. Applied to difficulties, problems, dangers, or differences of opinion, etc., **auftreten** means 'to occur'. It suggests that during a complicated process or procedure, one or more problems suddenly arise.

Bei der Benutzung des neuen, komplizierten Apparats traten Probleme auf, aber wir konnten sie alle beseitigen.

Im Laufe der Verhandlungen traten unerwartete Meinungsverschiedenheiten auf.

In reference to diseases, *auftreten* means 'to occur' without any implications.

Die Ärzte bekämpften die Krankheiten, die unter den Soldaten aufgetreten waren.

Die Diphtherie tritt zur Zeit kaum noch als Epidemie auf.

ii. Eintreten in one sense means 'to occur in a way which produces a change in the existing situation'. *Es ist etw. eingetreten, was vieles ändert. Plötzlich trat Stille ein* suggests that up to that point there had been anything but *Stille,* and *Eine Finanzkrise trat ein* implies that the finances had previously been in order. A change in the existing situation is also implied when *unerwartete Ereignisse* is the subj. *Wenn der Fall eintritt/eintreten sollte, daß* . . . , if the case occurs/should it happen that . . .

Während der Nacht ist eine Besserung im Befinden/Zustand der Kranken eingetreten.

Kurze Zeit danach ist eine günstige Wendung eingetreten. (A change for the better occurred.)

Der Minister sagte vor achtzehn Monaten, die neuen Maßnahmen würden einen wirtschaftlichen Aufschwung herbeiführen. Dies (or *Dieser versprochene Aufschwung) ist nicht eingetreten.*

iii. Eintreten means 'to occur or take place' without any implication with regard to natural phenomena, *Ein Wetterumschwung/Eine Mondfinsternis/Die Ebbe trat ein,* and in contexts like *Es kann der Fall/der Umstand eintreten, daß niemand Ihnen helfen kann.*

iv. Eintreten, applied to *Vermutungen* and *Befürchtungen,* means that what was conjectured or feared actually happened. *Genau das, was wir befürchtet hatten, trat ein.* **Eintreffen** has the same meaning but is mostly restricted to prophecies and forecasts. *Alles, was sie vorausgesagt hatte, traf ein.*

Was er vermutet hatte, trat auch ein. *Was sie vorausgesagt hatte, traf/trat Punkt für Punkt ein.*

Nichts von dem, was wir befürchtet hatten, war eingetreten.

4. Take place can refer to a chance occurrence, *Our first encounter took place by chance,* but often implies a plan, *Elections take place every four years.* It is used with historical events, either ones of short duration, *The battle took place on the last day of October,* or ones which stretch over a long period. *The transition from an agricultural economy to an industrial one took place in the last century.*

i. The main equivalent of **take place** is **stattfinden**. Although it sometimes refers to an occurrence which is not planned, *Meine erste Begegnung mit ihr fand rein zufällig statt, als ich an einer Bushaltestelle wartete,* it is mostly applied to events which are arranged and planned. *Die Hochzeit findet morgen abend statt. Bundestagswahlen finden alle vier Jahre statt.* It is used for historical events, but mostly for those of short duration. *Die Schlacht bei Waterloo fand am 18. Juni 1815 statt.*

ii. A syn. is **vor sich gehen**. Rather than stating that something takes place at a particular time, it stresses the whole course of an action in all its phases from beginning to end. *Diese Rangelei* (wrangling) *war im Stillen vor sich gegangen, hinter den Kulissen.* It also means 'to be taking place' in the sense 'to be going on'. *Obwohl die Abstimmung noch vor sich geht, ist das Ergebnis in Kürze zu erwarten.* Abstracts are often the subj. *Diese Neubesinnung/Eine Neuorientierung/Diese Gewissenserforschung ging in dieser Zeit vor sich.*

Eine Pressekonferenz wurde schon einberufen, während die Beratungen noch vor sich gingen.

Die Tarifverhandlungen gehen noch vor sich, ohne daß ein Ende abzusehen ist.

Die Immatrikulation—wie geht das vor sich?

iii. Sich vollziehen is applied either to events, processes, or changes which occur gradually or to ones which take place in a certain way, i.e. it needs an adv. or phr.

Im letzten Drittel des 19. Jahrhundert vollzog sich der Übergang Deutschlands vom Agrar- zum Industriestaat. *Diese Wandlung vollzog sich unbewußt/unerwartet schnell/zögernd.*

5. Happen to s.o./sth. **Passieren** and **geschehen** both take a dat. and express this meaning. *Was ist Ihnen passiert/geschehen?* They are usually interchangeable, but in the idiom *Das geschieht dir recht*, that serves you right, *geschehen* only is possible. **Zustoßen** + dat. implies that something bad, usually an accident, happens to someone. *Sie müßten schon längst da sein. Hoffentlich ist ihnen nichts zugestoßen*, I hope nothing has happened to them or they haven't had/met with an accident. *Ihm ist ein Unfall zugestoßen.*

6. Occur to in the sense 'to present itself to the thought or to come into one's mind', is **einfallen** + dat. *Einfallen* can be applied to a new thought, *Es ist mir gerade eingefallen, wie man das machen kann*, or to something remembered, *Erst später fiel mir ein, daß ich Briefmarken kaufen wollte.* A n. can be subj. *Der Name fällt mir im Augenblick nicht ein.* In the last two sents. *einfallen* could be translated as REMEMBER. *Was fällt dir ein?* is also a protest like *What do you think you're doing?* or even *You're mad to do such a thg.* An alternative to *einfallen* when something not previously known occurs to someone is **jmdm. kam der Gedanke**. *Mir kam plötzlich der Gedanke, daß man die Aufgabe auf andere Weise lösen könnte.*

7. Happen + infin., as in *to happen to do sth./to be somewhere*, means 'to do it or be there as a result of chance'. *If you happen so see Jane, ask her to ring me. There happened to be a policeman on the corner.* In most constructions the meaning of **happen to** is expressed by **zufällig[erweise]**, by chance. *Wenn du Jane zufällig siehst, kannst du sie mal bitten, mich anzurufen? An der Ecke stand zufällig[erweise] ein Polizist, und ich fragte ihn nach dem Weg.* *Zufällig* is used in *Ich weiß zufällig, daß er nicht zu Hause ist*, 'I happen to know', and in *Wissen Sie zufällig* (or *vielleicht*), *wo sie wohnt?* But note **wie kommt es, daß**: *How do they happen to know that already?* becomes *Wie kommt es, daß sie das schon wissen? Wie kommt es, daß die beiden hier sind?*, how do these two happen to be here.

offer v. Some senses of **present** v.
1. The chief sense of **offer** is 'invite s.o. to have sth. or hold out sth. to a pers. to take or reject as he/she wishes' or 'to indicate willingness to do sth. if the pers. addressed agrees'. *He offered me a cup of tea/an apple/his help.* An organization, country, etc. which offers something possesses something valuable or provides an opportunity which people may wish to take advantage of. *The car plant offers the prospect of 2,000 new jobs. The natural world offers much of interest/has . . . to offer.* If s.o./sth. has something to offer, he/she/it has a quality which may be found attractive or useful. *Switzerland has much to offer winter sports enthusiasts.*
i. The equivalent of the chief sense of **offer** is **anbieten**, which describes a situation in which the person addressed has to answer yes or no to an offer. *Der Schüler bot der alten Dame seinen Platz an, weil alle anderen Plätze im Bus besetzt waren.* **Bieten** is now mostly confined to situations which state that something is present or available, so that the idea of acceptance or rejection does not directly arise. *Das Autowerk bietet die Aussicht auf 2 000 neue Arbeitsplätze. Der Nachbar bot mir seine Hilfe sofort an* implies that in the original situation in which he would have said something like '*Kann ich Ihnen helfen?*', I had to give him an answer, whereas *Die Schweiz bietet Wintersportlern viele Betätigungsmöglichkeiten* simply states that these opportunities exist for those who wish to avail themselves of them. *Anbieten* is used when one person invites another to have something to eat or drink or holds out food or drink, for someone to take if desired, and when a position, university place, scholarship, etc. is offered to someone. However, an advertisement for a vacant position will often state what will be *geboten* or available to the successful

applicant. *Bieten* has as obj. words like *Schutz, ein Ausweg, Unterschlupf, eine Garantie, Platz* (= 'room, space', but not *Platz* = 'seat, place').

Der Gastgeber bot seinen Gästen einen Aperitif oder Saft an.

Kann ich Ihnen etw. zu essen anbieten?

Die Natur bietet viel, was von großem Interesse ist. Or *Die Natur hat viel zu bieten, was ...*

Dem erfolgreichen Bewerber werden ein hohes Gehalt und gute Aufstiegsmöglichkeiten geboten.

Eine Firma hat ihr eine Stelle als zweisprachige Sekretärin angeboten.

Die Universität hat zwanzig Abiturienten Stipendien angeboten.

Eine Hütte bot uns Schutz vor dem Gewitter.

Dieser Plan bot einen Ausweg aus der schwierigen Lage.

Ich kann Ihnen natürlich keine Garantie dafür bieten, daß alles reibungslos abläuft.

Das Sprachlabor ist erweitert worden und bietet jetzt allen Schülern einer Klasse Platz.

Die Lösung solcher mathematischen Probleme bietet keine Schwierigkeiten (presents no difficulties).

ii. In the sense 'to offer sth. for acceptance or rejection', **bieten** mainly occurs with *Arm* or *Hand*. *Er bot der Dame den Arm. Ich biete Ihnen die Hand zur Versöhnung.* With money as obj. *bieten* and **anbieten** are found. *Was/Wieviel hat er Dir für den Wagen geboten/angeboten? Bieten* is usual in announcements offering *eine Belohnung*, but *anbieten* also occurs. With *Chance, Gelegenheit,* and *Möglichkeit, bieten* states that they are available, *anbieten* that someone is actively offering them to an individual. *Der Betrieb bietet zahlreiche Fortbildungsmöglichkeiten* or *bietet jedem Mitarbeiter Fortbildungsmöglichkeiten an.*

Er bot mir Geld an, damit ich ihm helfen würde.

Er bot mir Geld, wenn ich bereit wäre, ihm zu helfen. (Could mean 'promised'.)

Hoffentlich bekommt sie ihre Uhr zurück. Sie hat eine Zeitungsannonce aufgegeben und dem Finder eine hohe Belohnung geboten.   Sein Vorgesetzter bot ihm eine letzte Chance [an].

2. i. Offer for sale is always **anbieten**. *Diese Woche bietet der Supermarkt Fleisch und Käse zu besonders günstigen Preisen an.* Hence *das Sonderangebot. Zum Verkauf* can be added. *Das Haus wurde zum Verkauf angeboten.*

ii. Only **anbieten** is used for courses and subjects offered in schools or universities.

Latein wird heutzutage nur noch an einigen wenigen Gymnasien angeboten.

Ein Anfängerkurs in Russisch wird in jedem Semester angeboten.

iii. Anbieten is used in a sent. like *X bot Y an, in seinem Haus zu wohnen,* or *X bot Y an, daß er in seinem Haus wohnen konnte,* where *to let* must be added in E. *Ich bot ihr an, mein Auto zu benutzen.*

3. i. Sich bieten means that an opportunity, chance, possibility, etc. offers or presents itself.

Bei der nächsten Gelegenheit, die sich bietet, werde ich es ihm sagen.

Bei der ersten sich bietenden Gelegenheit werden wir die ganze Angelegenheit besprechen.

Hier bietet sich dir eine Chance/eine günstige Gelegenheit.

ii. Sich bieten also means that some kind of sight becomes visible or presents itself. *Ein schrecklicher Anblick bot sich unseren Augen, als wir in die von dem Erdbeben verwüstete Stadt hineinfuhren.* If *Stadt* is made the subj. and *Anblick* the obj. of the main clause of this sent., it reads *Die Stadt bot einen schrecklichen Anblick. Dar* could be added in this sent. and in the previous one, but **darbieten** is now an elevated v. *Vom Gipfel des Berges bot sich uns ein herrlicher Anblick dar.*

4. Darbieten also means 'to present' in the sense 'to perform' songs, dances, etc. Hence *die Darbietung* is 'an item' in a musical etc. programme. *Alle Darbietungen hatten hohen künstlerischen Wert.*

Im Laufe des Abends wurden Lieder und Szenen aus Dramen dargeboten.

5. i. With a personal subj. **sich anbieten** means 'to express willingness to do sth. if the pers. addressed assents'. It translates **offer** in *He offered himself as intermedi-*

ary or in *They offered to help us*. With *als* the refl. is necessary, but it may be omitted when an infin. follows.

Er hat sich als Vermittler in dem Streit angeboten. Er bot [sich] an, in dem Streit zu vermitteln.

Sie bot [sich] an, mich zum Bahnhof zu fahren/uns zu helfen.

ii. Sich erbieten is a syn. of *sich anbieten* in the sense defined in 5. i, but it is very formal or elevated. *Die Frau des Oberbürgermeisters erbot sich, den Delegationsmitgliedern die Sehenswürdigkeiten der Stadt zu zeigen.*

iii. With a non-personal subj. **sich anbieten** means 'to offer itself' in the sense 'to present itself as obvious'. *Diese Lösung bot sich an. Die folgende Möglichkeit bietet sich an.*

6. Other uses of *bieten* and **offer**.

i. Auf etw. bieten means 'to bid for sth. at auction'.

Das Museum hat auf das Bild eine Million Pfund geboten, wurde aber überboten.

Als der herrenlose Acker versteigert wurde, waren zwei Bauern die einzigen, die auf ihn boten.

Bei Versteigerungen/Auktionen werden die versteigerten Waren dem meistbietenden zugeschlagen.

ii. Sich etw. bieten lassen means 'to submit to', 'to put up with'.

Eine so schlechte Behandlung hätte ich mir von den Leuten nicht bieten lassen sollen.

Wenn du dir alles bieten läßt, kann dir niemand helfen.

iii. S.o. offers or *puts up resistance* is *Jmd. leistet Widerstand.* May I **offer** *a suggestion?* becomes *Darf ich einen Vorschlag machen? I* would like to **offer**/*make a few remarks: Ich möchte ein paar Worte sagen/ein paar Bemerkungen machen.*

only *adv.* **not until** *prep.* or *conj.* with neg. The following discusses the equivalents of **only** used as an adv. with expressions of number, quantity, and time.

1. In contexts expressing a number, quantity, amount, distance, etc. **only** emphasizes how small the number, amount, etc. is or how short the distance is. *Only half the class is here. It only cost £5. We've only done five kilometres/written two letters.* For something which is expressed as a number or could conceivably be expressed as one, such as *a short distance,* both *nur* and *erst* translate *only* and mean 'no more than the small number stated'. **Nur** denotes a total which in the situation described is complete. **Erst** implies that more is to follow, that in the stated situation or time the number given represents only a part which will be completed. *Nur die Hälfte der Klasse ist da,* for some reason at that time the rest are absent. *Erst die Hälfte der Klasse ist da,* the rest will turn up soon. *Ich bin in dem Buch nur bis [auf] Seite 20 gekommen,* for some reason I couldn't get further than that and won't go on. *Ich habe erst bis Seite 20 gelesen,* that's as far as I've read, but I intend to go on. *Ich habe gestern nur 20 Seiten gelesen,* that is my total for yesterday. *Wir sind heute nur 100 Kilometer gefahren,* we haven't managed to do more than that today. If only part of the distance to be covered has been completed, someone could say, '*Wir sind erst 100 Kilometer gefahren und müssen noch weitere 250 zurücklegen.*' Thus *Wir haben heute nur eine kurze Strecke geschafft* and *Wir haben erst eine kurze Strecke geschafft und müssen gleich weiter.* Although this distinction always holds good, it makes no great difference in some contexts which one is used.

Nur die Hälfte der Arbeit ist fertig.   *Erst die Hälfte der Arbeit ist fertig.*

Das können die Kinder nicht wissen. Sie sind ja erst/nur neun Jahre alt.

2. Expressions of time.

i. Period of time. **Only** is used with a period of time. *They only stayed two weeks* or *They have only been here for a short time/for two weeks.* The distinction between **nur** and **erst** given in 1 applies in such cases. If the action is complete in the past or seen as a complete period in the future, **nur** is necessary. *Ich bin nur drei Tage da geblieben/will nur zwei Tage da bleiben. Ich habe nur zwei Stunden gebraucht,* it took only two hours to do something, and now it is finished. If the action of the v. is not complete, i.e. if it continues into the present or was still going on at the time referred to in the past, **erst** is used. *Ich bin erst seit zwei Tagen hier* (and will stay longer). *Ich war erst seit zwei Tagen da, als das geschah. Ich habe erst zwei Stunden gearbeitet*, I started working only two hours ago and intend to work longer.

> *Ich will heute nur vier Stunden arbeiten.*
> *Sie sind erst seit kurzer Zeit hier. Sie wollen sich nur kurze Zeit hier aufhalten.*
> *Sie wohnten erst zwei Monate in Berlin, als der Krieg ausbrach.*

ii. A point of time. Many sents. containing **only** + a point of time can be formulated with **not until**. *I only got up at ten o'clock* or *didn't get up until ten o'clock*. Both mean that something does/did not happen before the time or point mentioned but that it does/did happen then. *Women did not gain the vote until after the First World War*. With a point of time **erst** translates *only* and *not until*. *Frauen wurden erst nach dem ersten Weltkrieg wahlberechtigt. Erst* also translates *only* used with a precise time. *It's only nine o'clock* becomes *Es ist erst neun Uhr.*

> *Ich bin erst um zehn Uhr aufgestanden.*   *Das habe ich erst vor kurzem erfahren.*
> *Sie ist seit einer Woche hier, aber ich habe sie erst gestern gesehen.*

iii. When an **until**-clause follows a neg. main clause, *I won't go home until the work is finished*, **erst** appears in the main clause, and the neg. drops out. The following clause begins with *wenn* or *als. Dann* is often added after *erst. Ich gehe erst dann nach Hause, wenn die Arbeit fertig ist. Sie haben das andere Auto erst [dann] bemerkt, als es beinahe zu spät war.* This construction also translates *I'll only go home, when . . .* In a more literary style, this meaning can be expressed as **nicht eher . . . als bis**. *Ich gehe nicht eher nach Hause, als bis die ganze Arbeit fertig ist.*

iv. Only is also used with a point of time in the past and means 'as late as' or 'as recently as'. It can express surprise because there is only a short time between two occurrences, *Only last year he was the office-boy, and now he's the boss*, or it expresses certainty because the speaker has been informed of or seen something only a very short time ago, *Only yesterday he told me he was leaving—I can't believe he's changed his mind overnight*. **Only** in *Only yesterday he told me he was leaving* is **noch**. *Noch* is placed either before or after the expression of time, *noch gestern* or *gestern noch. Noch gestern/Gestern noch hat er gesagt, daß er weggeht*. When *noch* follows the time expression, **erst** may precede it, **erst gestern noch**. This strengthens the meaning without changing it. *Erst gestern noch waren sie hier.* (In order to recognize this meaning, it should be noted that, unlike other senses of **only**, it does not, if at the beginning, reverse the order of subj. and v. *Only yesterday he told me what he intended to do* as against *Only two days before he left did he tell us what he intended to do*. (Or *Not until two days before he left did he tell us . . .*) The last two sents. become *Erst zwei Tage bevor er wegging, hat er uns gesagt, was er vorhatte.*)

> *Noch gestern hat er mir gesagt, er wollte die Stelle bei Siemens annehmen. Ich kann mir nicht denken, daß er es sich inzwischen anders überlegt hat.*
> *Noch vor drei Tagen waren sie bei uns zu Besuch, und heute haben sie aus Deutschland angerufen.*

open v.

1. Open can be trans. *S.o. opens sth*. **Aufmachen** is the usual trans. v. in everyday lang. **Öffnen** is a common syn. which may be felt to be stylistically somewhat higher, but there is little difference. Either can be used with objs. like *eine Tür, ein Fenster, ein Koffer, ein Brief, ein Paket, eine Flasche, eine Dose* or *Büchse, ein Schrank, eine Schublade*, with *die Augen, die Hand*, and *der Mund*, and in a context like *Man muß die Kiste mit einem Hammer aufmachen* or *Ich habe die Kiste mit der Brechstange geöffnet*. *Öffnen* only is used with *die Grenze. 1853 öffneten die Japaner ihre Grenzen für Waren aus* *dem Westen.* An alternative to *den Mund aufmachen* when this implies beginning to speak is *den Mund* **auftun**.

Mach' doch die Tür auf! Es hat geklingelt.
Sobald ich den Mund auftue, unterbricht er mich.

Ich kann das Fenster nicht öffnen.
Er hatte Angst, den Mund aufzutun.

2. Open is also intr. Sth. opens.

i. Both **aufmachen** and **öffnen** are used intr. only in reference to shops etc. in the sense 'to open daily for business'. *Die Geschäfte machen um 8.30 Uhr auf. Die Banken öffnen um 9.30 Uhr. Die Post macht um 9 Uhr auf.* However, in statements that something is open from one time to another, **geöffnet sein/haben** is often used. *Das Konsulat ist/hat nur von 9 bis 13 Uhr geöffnet. Opening times* are *Öffnungszeiten.* In speech, **aufhaben** and **aufsein** are common. *Die Geschäfte haben/sind bis 21 Uhr auf.* These vs. also mean 'to have or be open' in other contexts. *Ich hatte die Augen auf. Das Fenster ist auf.*

Einige Lebensmittelgeschäfte machen um 8 Uhr auf.
Die Geschäfte sind von 9 bis 17.30 Uhr geöffnet. *Wann öffnet die Bibliothek?*
Viele Leute standen vor der Tür und warteten, bis das Geschäft aufmachte/öffnete.
Das Museum ist jeden Tag/sonntags nur von 14 bis 17 Uhr geöffnet.

ii. Aufgehen is the usual equivalent of other intr. uses such as *The door opened/came open.* Applied to a door or window, *aufgehen* means 'to come open or undone or to open (as it were) by itself'. *Das Fenster ist durch den Windstoß aufgegangen. Die Tür ging auf, und Aschenputtel trat herein. Aufgehen* is a syn. of **sich öffnen** although they are not always interchangeable. *Blüten gehen auf* or *öffnen sich.* Only *sich öffnen* is used for a parachute, *Der Fallschirm hat sich zum vorgesehenen Zeitpunkt geöffnet,* and in the fairly rare imp., *Sesam, öffne dich! Sich öffnen* is used for doors which open automatically. *Die Tür öffnet sich automatisch/selbsttätig. Die Tür öffnet sich nicht* suggests that the mechanism is not working, something is stopping the door from opening. How something opens is expressed by *aufgehen* + adv. or *sich öffnen lassen* + adv. *Das Fenster geht leicht auf/läßt sich leicht öffnen.* If something is jammed so that effort is required to [try to] open it, either *Das Fenster geht schwer auf/geht nicht auf* or *läßt sich schwer/nicht öffnen* is used. **Aufkriegen** and **aufbekommen** mean 'to get sth. [to] open'. *Ich bekomme/kriege das Fenster nicht auf.*

3. i. Eröffnen means 'to open' when this is a syn. of *to begin.* It is applied to activities which begin with a ceremony, *Die Königin hat die Parlamentssitzung eröffnet,* and to meetings which the chairman declares open, *Ich erkläre die Sitzung für eröffnet,* but can be applied to a large range of activities. *Der Premierminister eröffnete die Debatte mit einer glänzenden Rede. Die Premiere eines neuen Stückes eröffnet die neue Spielzeit des Stadttheaters.* **Einweihen** is also often used in reference to the ceremonial opening of new buildings etc. Although originally a religious term meaning 'to consecrate', *Die neue Kirche wurde eingeweiht,* it is now also used for purely secular structures, *Das neue Stadion/Die Schule/Die Brücke wird morgen eingeweiht.*

ii. Like **open**, **eröffnen** is used with *das Feuer, eine Offensive,* and *die Feindseligkeiten* as obj.

Sobald das feindliche Schiff in Schußweite kam, eröffnete der Kreuzer das Feuer.

iii. Eröffnen is used for opening a bank account. *Gleich nach meiner Ankunft in Deutschland muß ich ein Bankkonto eröffnen.* An alternative is *ein Bankkonto* **einrichten**. *Ein Testament eröffnen* means that at a formal meeting of those concerned the authorized person opens the will and reads it aloud. Under less formal circumstances *öffnen* can be used.

iv. Another meaning of **eröffnen** is 'to open sth. to the public' or 'to open sth. for use for the first time'. The obj. can be an exhibition or new businesses, branches, etc. *Man wird das Geschäft/die neue Bahnlinie nächste Woche eröffnen. Eröffnen* is trans. only, and to translate *A new supermarket has opened,* it would have to be used in the pass. *Ein neuer Supermarkt wurde eröffnet.* **Aufmachen** is used colloquially in this context and is both trans. and intr. *Die Bank hat vor kurzem eine Filiale hier eröffnet/aufgemacht* and *Ein neuer Supermarkt hat aufgemacht.*

Die Ausstellung wurde vom Wirtschaftsminister eröffnet.

Der neue Laden soll nächste Woche eröffnet werden.

Die neue Fluglinie wurde letzte Woche eröffnet.

Die Firma hat im vorigen Jahr zwei neue Fabriken eröffnet.

Der Parteivorsitzende eröffnete den Parteitag mit einer kurzen Rede.

v. With *Möglichkeiten, Aussichten,* 'prospects', *eine Chance,* etc. as obj. **eröffnen** means 'to open up' used as a trans. v. *Der Abbau der Zollschranken in Japan würde der australischen Landwirtschaft neue Möglichkieten eröffnen.* The intr. use of **open up** with *prospects, possibilities,* etc. as subj. is expressed by **sich eröffnen.** *In dieser Stelle eröffneten sich ihr gute Aussichten für die Zukunft.*

Die neue Stellung hat dem jungen Ingenieur in beruflicher Hinsicht gute Aussichten eröffnet.

In diesem Betrieb haben sich mir gute Entwicklungsmöglichkeiten/die besten Aufstiegschancen eröffnet.

4. Other equivalents.

i. Freigeben means 'to open (a thoroughfare) to traffic'. *Die Straße/Die neue Autobahnstrecke wird für den Verkehr freigegeben.*

ii. Open *a book.* **Aufschlagen** is the usual v. and has either *Buch* etc. or a page as obj. The constructions for the latter are either *Schlagen Sie Seite 20 [in Ihren Büchern] auf!* or *Schlagen Sie Ihre Bücher auf Seite 20 auf! Öffnen* and *aufmachen* are also possible, but only with *Buch, Zeitung,* etc. as obj.

iii. *The crowd* **opened** *and let us pass: Die Menge* **teilte sich** (= 'DIVIDED') *und ließ uns durch.*

iv. *The door* **opens on to** . . . : *Die Tür* **geht auf** *den Garten/die Terrasse* **hinaus.**

v. Erschließen means 'to open up' or 'to make accessible to commercial development or exploitation'. *Man erschließt ein neues Gebiet für die Landwirtschaft/für den Fremdenverkehr. Man will die neu entdeckten Bodenschätze erschließen.*

vi. Aufklappen means 'to open sth. which is fixed on one side'. *Ich klappte den Koffer/das Fotoalbum auf. Aufklappen* can always be replaced by *aufmachen.*

opinion, view, concept, conception ns. **Opinion** ranges from purely personal prejudice to a relatively authoritative judgement, *She sought the opinion of several experts.* In an expression like *public opinion,* it is also a collective term for the ideas many people hold in common. **View** can be a personal opinion about something. *Her views on politics have changed. In my view the conference was a success.* It is also applied to the way someone understands and thinks of things that are happening around him/her, or considers how something happens or is or should be done. *His view of life/of the world/of how to look after a car/of how children should be treated.* In this sense it is similar to *conception.* The relevant senses of **concept** and **conception** are defined as follows: 'Concept also refers to a widely held idea of what sth. is or should be: *The concept of government of many small nations has been influenced by the parliamentary model of Westminster.* The meaning of *conception* is much like this . . . sense of *concept,* but differs in that the idea of what a thg. is or should be is here held by an individual or small group and is often coloured by imagination or feeling: *A child's conception of the universe is formed by his limited experience and his own fancies.*' (Hayakawa and Fletcher 1987: 277–8). For **concept** when it means 'the idea of a class of objects' and for **conception** when it means 'an image in the mind', see IDEA. Also cf. ATTITUDE for related words.

1. Opinion.

i. Die Meinung is 'what s.o. thinks about a matter or pers.' *Eine Meinung* is personal and subject to change and is an equivalent of **opinion** in all senses except that of 'an expert judgement'. *In my opinion* is *meiner Meinung nach. I am of the opinion that* . . . is *Ich bin der Meinung, daß Umfragen dieser Art sehr wertvoll sind. Zwei Menschen sind derselben Meinung* or *teilen eine/dieselbe Meinung. Die Meinungsverschiedenheit* is 'difference of opinion'. *Wie ist Ihre Meinung über diese Sache?* asks for someone's opinion on a matter, but more common are *Was denken Sie über diesen Fall?* or *Was halten Sie von den jüngsten Ereignissen?* Cf. CONSIDER 1. i and 8. Also common is *Wie stellt er sich zu dieserFrage?* Weightier is *Wie beurteilen Sie seine Chancen?* Cf. JUDGE.

> *Die Studenten wollten unbedingt ihre Meinungen zu dieser Frage äußern.*
> *Wenn Sie meine ehrliche Meinung hören wollen, so glaube ich nicht, daß wir das durchsetzen können.*
> *Die freie Meinungsäußerung gehört zu den Grundrechten der Menschen.*

ii. In reference to what people think about s.o./sth., **opinion** is used with *high, low,* and *good.* In G. the possibilities are **eine hohe Meinung** or *keine hohe Meinung* or **eine gute/schlechte Meinung von jmdm. haben.** *Ich habe eine hohe/schlechte Meinung von Braun/von Brauns Fähigkeiten. My opinion of Mr Smith rose sharply because of this* can be translated as *Dadurch habe ich eine bessere Meinung von Herrn Smith bekommen* or *Dadurch ist Herr Smith in meiner Achtung/Wertschätzung gestiegen.* (*Die Achtung* and *die Wertschätzung* mean 'esteem or estimation'.) Close in meaning to *have a high/low opinion of* is *jmdn.* or *jmds. Fähigkeiten* or *Leistung* **hoch/niedrig/richtig einschätzen,** to have a high/low/correct opinion or assessment of s.o./of his or her abilities or performance. *Ich habe sie/ihre Fähigkeiten immer hoch eingeschätzt.*

iii. Die öffentliche Meinung is 'public opinion'. Apart from this expression, the E. collective use must be translated by the pl. **Meinungen.** Thus *A broad range of interest and opinion should be represented* becomes *Eine breite Skala von Interessen und Meinungen sollte vertreten sein.*

iv. Die Ansicht denotes a personal way of looking at a matter and is a close syn. of *Meinung* defined in 1. i. *Ich kann Ihre Ansicht nicht teilen. Das ist eine weit verbreitete Ansicht.* It is not used for an estimate of people nor for public opinion but, apart from this, *Meinung* and *Ansicht* occur in the same constructions. *That's a matter of opinion* is, however, always *Das ist Ansichtssache. Ansicht* is often translated as *view,* but is not used for *a view of life,* etc. Cf. 2. The pl. *Ansichten* tends to be used when someone's total views in a particular field or about things in general are meant. *Jmds. politische/philosophische/künstlerische Ansichten.*

> *Wir sind also derselben Ansicht.*   *Ich schließe mich dieser Ansicht an.*
> *Nach seiner Ansicht hatten wir alles erreicht, was zu erreichen war.*
> *Dieser Lehrer hatte altmodische/außergewöhnliche/fortschrittliche Ansichten.*

v. Meines Erachtens is a formal equivalent of **in my opinion.** It belongs to educated speech and is often heard in discussions, seminars, and formal situations. *Meines Erachtens sind diese Maßnahmen überfällig.*

vi. The sense of **die Auffassung** and **die Anschauung** (cf. 2) has been weakened so that they are now often merely weightier syns. of *Meinung* and *Ansicht. Jmd. vertrat die Auffassung* could in many cases be *Er/Sie vertrat die Ansicht.* In precise use they are reserved for comprehensive views on matters of fundamental importance. *Das ist meine Anschauung* suggests a considered judgement on an important matter. *Die Anschauungen* is used like *Ansichten* for the totality of a person's opinions either on a topic or on broader areas of experience. *Er hat fortschrittliche/gesunde/ naive/rückständige Anschauungen.*

vii. When an expert opinion is meant, **das Gutachten** is possible if the opinion is in writing and carefully sets out all the reasons. It is often translated as *report* and is discussed under ANNOUNCE 4. If a doctor says to a patient, 'Perhaps you would like to get a second opinion', this would be expressed as *'Vielleicht möchten Sie einen anderen Arzt dazu hören.'* **Hören** can suggest getting an expert opinion in any field. *Dazu müssen wir einen Fachmann hören. In the opinion of my doctor, I can travel next week,* would usually be expressed as *Mein Arzt meint, daß ich nächste Woche reisen kann.* The only n. that could be used is **das Urteil,** as *Meinung* suggests a personal view. *Nach Urteil meines Arztes kann ich nächste Woche reisen.*

2. The equivalents of **concept** and **conception** as well as of **view** in *view of life/the world* or *view of how sth. is or should be done* are **die Anschauung** and **die Auffassung.** Both occur in compounds such as *Lebensanschauung, Weltanschauung, Kunstanschauung, Lebensauffassung, Geschichtsauffassung, Rechtsauffassung,* etc. When the area to which the conception or view relates is given in the gen., *Auffassung* is usual. *Ihre Auffassung der Pflicht/der Gesellschaft/der Ehe.* Only *Auffassung* is used for someone's view of how something should be carried out. *Bei deiner Auffassung von Pflege werden deine [Zimmer]pflanzen bald eingehen.* The compounds of *Anschauung* and *Auffassung* presuppose a mature and considered view, although it need not be deeply philosophical. **Das Weltbild** means 'view/concept of the world' and can be applied to anyone's view, whether mature, considered, philosophical, or not. The sent. about a child's conception of the universe in the introduction is best translated as *Das Weltbild eines Kindes wird geprägt von seiner begrenzten Erfahrung und seiner Phantasiewelt.*

> *Ihre Auffassung von Beruf/Ehre/Moral/Liebe ist anders als meine.*
> *In vielen Ländern ist die Auffassung davon, wie ein Staat regiert werden soll, vom Westminstermodell stark beeinflußt.*
> *Die praktische Weltanschauung und die poetische vertragen sich wie Hund und Katze.*
> *Der Sturm und Drang hatte noch keine Weltanschaung im Sinne einer zusammenhängenden und ausgebildeten Philosophie.*
> *Das Weltbild/Die Weltanschauung des Mittelalters unterscheidet sich stark von dem/der der Gegenwart.*
> *Menschen tragen die verschiedensten Weltbilder und gewöhnlich auch die verschiedensten Neigungen in sich.*

oppose *v.* Some uses.

1. When **oppose** sth. or **be opposed to** sth. mean no more than 'to be against', as in *He opposes everything/is opposed to everything I suggest,* the equivalent can be **gegen etw. sein.** *Sie sind gegen jede Änderung. Er ist gegen alles, was ich vorschlage. Opposed to* + gerund as in *They are opposed to building more nuclear power stations* or *I am opposed to you[r] studying abroad* is *dagegen sein* + *daß*-clause. *Sie sind dagegen, daß man weitere Atomkraftwerke baut. Ich bin dagegen, daß du im Ausland studierst.* (*Dagegen sein* is also one equivalent recommended for OBJECT TO.)

> *Mehrere Minister sind gegen die Erhöhung der Mehrwertsteuer.*
> *Mehrere Minister sind dagegen, daß man die Zuwendungen für Universitäten weiter kürzt.*

2. There are several expressions meaning 'to set oneself against' or 'to fight against'. *Ankämpfen gegen,* which is often translated as **oppose,** is discussed under FIGHT 3, as are the progressively stronger *kämpfen gegen* and *bekämpfen.*
i. The general equivalent which, like **oppose,** suggests resistance on an intellectual plane relating to a disputed issue is **entgegentreten** + dat. It implies opposition to what one considers harmful or bad, without suggesting that there is universal agreement about its badness. *Eine Gruppe tritt den Maßnahmen entgegen,*

die eine andere befürwortet.

> *Der Vorredner hat zu diesem Punkt eine Meinung vertreten, der ich entgegentreten muß.*
>
> *Der in letzter Zeit wieder enormen Aufschwung erfahrende Okkultismus ist eine Bewegung, der man mit allen Mitteln entgegentreten muß.*
>
> *Die Oppositionspartei war den Regierungsplänen zur Sanierung des Gesundheitswesens entschieden entgegengetreten.*
>
> *Sie traten der Regierung in praktisch jedem Punkt entgegen, der auf der Tagesordnung stand.*

ii. Angehen gegen means 'to attempt to prevent or overcome sth. which one considers undesirable'. It can refer to opposition in words or in action. *Man geht gegen Vorurteile/Mißstände/einen Beschluß/Kriminelle an.* **Vorgehen gegen**, which implies the taking of action or active measures against something considered harmful, is stronger. Cf. ACT 2. ii. *Sie gingen energisch gegen den Rassismus vor.*

> *Gegen die Vorverurteilung bestimmter Personen in diesem Skandal möchte ich entschieden angehen.*
>
> *Der Betriebsrat gab bekannt, daß er gegen die geplanten Entlassungen angehen werde.*
>
> *Wir müssen gegen die Korruption/gegen bestechliche Beamte entschieden/mit allen Mitteln vorgehen.*

iii. Zu Felde ziehen suggests a broadly based campaign against something considered misguided or harmful using every means at one's disposal. *Man zieht gegen die Trunksucht/Tierversuche/die Diskriminierung von Ausländern am Arbeitsplatz etc. zu Felde.*

> *Der Verein hatte es sich zur Aufgabe gemacht, gegen die verführerische Zigarettenwerbung zu Felde zu ziehen.*

iv. Sich widersetzen suggests resistance to s.o./sth. It can mean 'not to obey the directions or wishes of s.o. in authority when obedience is expected' (*die Widersetzlichkeit* is 'insubordination'), as well as 'to put up resistance, in the form of arguments, against sth. planned'. In the latter use it means 'to oppose'.

> *Sollten sie sich der Dienstanweisung/meinen Wünschen widersetzen, so ist mit erheblichen Konsequenzen zu rechnen.*
>
> *Die Mehrzahl der Demonstrationsteilnehmer widersetzten sich der Aufforderung der Polizei, den Versammlungsort zu verlassen.*   *Die Opposition widersetzte sich der geplanten Steuerreform.*
>
> *Viele Ratsmitglieder widersetzten sich dem Plan zum Bau eines neuen Konferenzgebäudes.*

opposite *n.* Both **der Gegensatz** and **das Gegenteil** can mean 'the opposite'. While the former has a pl., the latter does not. It is therefore necessary to say *Mut und Feigheit sind Gegensätze* and *Gegensätze ziehen sich an*. After a sing. subj. and *sein*, *Gegenteil* is the main equivalent of the n. **opposite**. *Haß ist das Gegenteil von Liebe. Gut ist das Gegenteil von böse.* In some contexts *Gegensatz* is also possible: *Im Temperament war er das Gegenteil von* or *der Gegensatz zu seiner Frau*; these tend to be cases in which *direct contrast* or *antithesis* are also possible in E. If nothing follows **opposite**, *Gegenteil* only is used. *Sie ist meistens freundlich, gelegentlich aber das Gegenteil. Bilden* is used with *Gegensatz* only. In translating *Eine Sache bildet den Gegensatz zu einer anderen* words like *direct contrast* or *antithesis* could be used, or *bilden* could be translated as a form of *to be*. *Ihre Arbeitsweise bildet den genauen Gegensatz zu dem, was ich unter rationellem Arbeiten verstehe. Gegensatz* can imply opposition and antagonism because of differing views. *Die Gleichnisse Jesu spiegeln seinen Gegensatz gegen den Pharasäismus mit besonderer Klarheit wieder.* **Im Gegensatz zu** is a fixed expression meaning 'in contrast to' or 'unlike'. *Im Gegensatz zu seinem Bruder ist er groß und schlank.* **Im Gegenteil** is used without anything being added and means 'on the contrary'. *A. Sie haben sich bestimmt gelangweilt. B. Im Gegenteil, ich fand es sehr interessant.*

> *Was du eben gesagt hast, ist das genaue Gegenteil von dem, was du gestern sagtest.*
>
> *Sie wollte eine Versöhnung herbeiführen, hat aber das Gegenteil bewirkt.*
>
> *Was man Ihnen sagte, ist nicht wahr. Das Gegenteil ist der Fall.*

Zwischen den beiden Parteien bestand ein unversöhnlicher/scharfer Gegensatz.
Das ist einer der wichtigsten Gegensätze zwischen dem Kommunismus und dem Kapitalismus.

opposite *adj.* For each of the three meanings of **opposite** there is a different G. word. One of these, *entgegengesetzt*, can, however, be used in certain combinations in the other two senses.

1. Opposite = 'on the other side in space'. *On the opposite side of the road.* The equivalent is **gegenüberliegend**. *Auf der gegenüberliegenden Straßenseite. Sie trat durch die gegenüberliegende Tür ein. Gegenüberliegend* implies more or less directly opposite; otherwise **entgegengesetzt** is used. *Der Sportplatz befindet sich am entgegengesetzten Ende der Stadt.*

2. Opposite = 'turned or moving the other way'. *They were going in the opposite direction.* For directions, only **entgegengesetzt** is used.
Sie standen nahe beieinander, sahen aber in entgegengesetzte Richtungen.
Zwei Züge, die aus entgegengesetzten Richtungen kamen, sind zusammengestoßen.

3. Opposite = 'contrary in nature or character'. *The opposite point of view.* **Gegenteilig** means 'the opposite of what was mentioned' and is used with ns. like *die Aussage, die Antwort, die Ansicht, die Wirkung, die Annahme,* etc. **Gegensätzlich** means 'opposite' in the sense 'opposing or contrasting' and is also applied to opinions. *Die beiden Regierungen nahmen in dieser Frage gegensätzliche Positionen ein. Gegensätzliche Begriffe* are 'two concepts which express the opposite of each other'. *Gegenteilig* and *gegensätzlich* are only used attributively and can also be translated as *opposing, opposed,* or *contrary.* **Entgegengesetzt** also describes opposing opinions. It is used attributively, *Fritze vertrat die entgegengesetzte Auffassung,* and predicatively after *sein, Die zweite Feststellung ist [genau] entgegengesetzt zu der ersten.*
Ich möchte Ihnen eine gegenteilige Zeugenaussage vorlegen.
Unser Reporter hat uns gegenteilige Beobachtungen berichtet.
Beide Kinder sind gegensätzlich veranlagt/von gegensätzlicher Natur.
Beide Parteien haben gegenteilige/gegensätzliche/entgegengesetzte Standpunkte vertreten.
Sherlock Holmes nahm den entgegengesetzten Standpunkt ein.
Die Meinungen waren so entgegengesetzt, daß ein Kompromiß kaum möglich erschien.
Das ist genau entgegengesetzt zu dem, was Sie vorhin so kühn behauptet haben.

order, command *vs.* **direct or instruct s.o. to do sth.** *vs.* **expel, prescribe** *vs.*

1. Order an action or **order/command/direct/instruct** s.o. to do sth.
i. Anordnen and **anweisen** mean 'to order, instruct, or direct'. They are weaker than *befehlen,* although *anordnen* may be used in a military context or one presupposing official authority. They differ from each other in that *anordnen* requires a n. denoting an action as obj. or a *daß*-clause, while *anweisen* needs a person or something standing for people, such as *die Bank,* as obj. and takes an infin. Thus *Der Richter ordnete die Räumung des Gerichtssaales an* or *Er ordnete an, daß der Gerichtssaal geräumt werden sollte,* and *Er wies die Anwesenden an, den Gerichtssaal zu räumen.*
Der Geschäftsführer ordnete an, daß die Waren sofort verladen werden sollten. Or . . . ordnete die sofortige Verladung der Waren an.
Der Direktor wies seine Sekretärin an, allen Anrufern zu sagen, daß er sie im Laufe des Nachmittags zurückrufen würde.
Man wies die Arbeiter an, pünktlich um 7 Uhr an der Baustelle zu erscheinen.
Er wies die Bank an, die Zahlungen an seine geschiedene Frau einzustellen.
ii. Befehlen presupposes strong authority such as that possessed by an army

officer or by a judge in a court, although it can be used in private life when people take such authority upon themselves. *Er sprach in befehlendem Ton. Von Ihnen lasse ich mir nicht befehlen.* It takes a dat. and is used with an obj., an infin., or a clause. *Der Oberst befahl den Soldaten, langsam vorzurücken.*

Der Richter befahl Ruhe im Saal/befahl die Räumung des Gerichtssaales.

Der Richter befahl, daß die im Gerichtssaal Anwesenden sich ruhig verhalten sollten. Or Er befahl den Anwesenden, sich ruhig zu verhalten.   *Den Soldaten wurde befohlen, die Brücke zu sprengen.*

Der General befahl den Rückzug/ordnete den Rückzug an.

Er befahl mir strenges Stillschweigen. Or Er wies mich an, strenges Stillschweigen zu bewahren.

iii. Verfügen also presupposes authority. It can refer to directions given by courts, governmental authorities, or private industry. *Der Richter verfügte die Räumung des Saales. Verfügen* is also used in wills in the sense of 'direct', as are *anordnen* and *bestimmen*. Cf. 4.

Der Vorstand hat die Auszahlung einer Jahresgratifikation verfügt.

Das Gericht verfügte die Beschlagnahme der geschmuggelten Waren/die Vertagung des Prozesses.

Das Ministerium hat den Ausbau der Straße verfügt.

iv. Beordern is always used with an expression stating where someone is to go and implies that the person would be expected to comply. It is used of the military, government officials, employees of private firms, and something under human control. *Der Zerstörer wurde nach dem persischen Golf beordert.*

Ohne vorherige Ankündigung hat das Verteidigungsministerium den Major an das NATO-Hauptquartier in Brüssel beordert.

Ein Experte wurde nach Oldenburg beordert, um den Fall zu untersuchen.

v. Auferlegen, 'to impose on', sometimes translates *to order to pay. Das Gericht hat mir eine Geldstrafe auferlegt. Dem Kläger/Dem Beklagten wurden die Kosten (des Gerichtsverfahrens) auferlegt*, was ordered to pay the costs of a court case

2. Order from/out of a room, country, **off** the field, etc. Two possible transls. of *The judge ordered me out of the room* are *Der Richter wies mich an, den Saal zu verlassen* and *Der Richter ordnete an, daß ich den Saal verlassen sollte*, but more usual would be *weisen* which, with two of its derivatives *ausweisen* and *verweisen*, means 'to order from' or 'to expel'. **Weisen** is used with *aus* or *von* in reference to a room or small area. *Der Wirt wies die Jugendlichen aus dem Lokal.* If the sent. does not contain a phr. with *aus*, **hinausweisen** must be used. *Der Wirt wies die Jugendlichen hinaus.* **Ausweisen** means 'to expel from a country' and can be used either alone, *Die illegalen Einwanderer wurden ausgewiesen*, or with *aus, Die illegalen Einwanderer wurden aus Australien ausgewiesen.* **Verweisen** is used either with *aus* or *von, Der General verwies alle Journalisten aus dem eroberten Gebiet*, or with the gen. in fixed phrs. like *des Landes verweisen.* While the name of the country follows *ausweisen aus, des Landes verweisen* is used when the country is clear from the context. *Weisen* is weaker than *verweisen. Der Lehrer hat den Schüler aus dem Klassenzimmer gewiesen* suggests that the pupil would only stay away for a limited period; he could well come back at the end of the lesson. *Der Direktor hat den Schüler von der Schule verwiesen* means that he has been expelled. In formal language the construction is *Er wurde der Schule verwiesen.* In formal style *verweisen* is used in sport for ordering someone off the field. *Wegen eines groben Fouls verwies der Schiedsrichter den Spieler vom Feld* (sometimes *des Feldes*). **Vom Feld stellen** is the usual expression in everyday language.

Der Richter drohte, einige der Anwesenden, die sich Zwischenbemerkungen erlaubten, aus dem Saal zu weisen.   *Man wies die Zigeuner aus der Stadt.*

Die britische Regierung hat in diesem Jahr acht Diplomaten wegen schwerer Verkehrsdelikte in Verbindung mit Trunkenheit am Steuer des Landes verwiesen. Die Ausweisung von Botschaftsangehörigen ist trotz Immunität unter bestimmten Umständen möglich.

Wegen seiner ungenügenden Leistungen hat man den Schüler [von] der Schule verwiesen.

3. Prescribe.

i. Vorschreiben means 'to prescribe' in the sense 'to lay sth. down as a rule'. The subj. is either a law, regulation, custom, etc. or a person. It is often translated as *lay down*.

Die Straßenverkehrsordnung schreibt vor, wie sich die Verkehrsteilnehmer zu verhalten haben.

Es ist vorgeschrieben, welche Kleidung Arbeiter und Angestellte am Arbeitsplatz tragen müssen.

Der Leiter des Fortbildungskurses beschloß, bestimmte Vorkenntnisse bei den Teilnehmern vorzuschreiben.

Ich brauche mir von ihm nichts vorschreiben zu lassen.

ii. In connection with doctors, **verschreiben** means 'to prescribe'. **Verordnen** is a formal syn. The obj. of *verordnen* need not be a medicine but something like *Bettruhe*. **Anordnen** also occurs with the latter type of obj. *Der Arzt hat dem Kranken Bettruhe verordnet/hat strenge Bettruhe angeordnet.*

Der Arzt sagte: 'Ich verordne Ihnen ein Medikament/Tabletten/eine Diät/eine Brille.'

Der Arzt hat dem Patienten ein Medikament gegen den Husten verschrieben.

4. Command = 'to be in charge of, have the command of, have the right to say what is to happen'.

i. In everyday situations the usual word would be **bestimmen**, which implies having the authority or right to decide what is to be done. Cf. DETERMINE 2. i. It is intr. and trans. When intr., as in *Hier bestimme ich*, the equivalents can be *to be the boss* or *to be in charge* as well as *to be in command*. When trans., as in *Der Lehrplan bestimmt die Reihenfolge der zu behandelnden Texte*, and when a clause follows, *Der Chef bestimmt, was hier zu geschehen hat/wer versetzt wird*, the equivalent is *to lay down, give orders*, or *determine*, sometimes **order**. *Das Schicksal hatte es anders bestimmt.*

In dieser Angelegenheit werde ich alles allein bestimmen.   Hier hat er nichts zu bestimmen.

ii. The military terms are **kommandieren** and **befehligen**, to be in command of a fleet, army, etc.

Die Flotte wurde vom Admiral von Prittwitz befehligt.

Wer kommandiert diese Truppen?   Der kommandierende General heißt Bühler.

Colloquially, *kommandieren* and **herumkommandieren** mean 'to order or boss others around'.

Er versucht, uns immer zu kommandieren.

Ich lasse mich nicht so [von ihr] herumkommandieren.

5. Order in a shop, restaurant, etc. is **bestellen**. It can be trans. *Ich habe die Ersatzteile bestellt* or intr. *Haben Sie schon bestellt?* The n. is *die Bestellung*, which can be used for a small or large order. *Der Auftrag* is also 'an order for goods or for work to be done'. It tends to be used for larger orders. **Etw. in Auftrag geben** is a syn. of *bestellen*, but it is usually restricted to fairly large orders for goods or work. *Wir haben den Umbau des Hauses bei einer kleinen Baufirma in Auftrag gegeben.*

Für welche Zeit soll ich das Taxi bestellen?

Bestellungen laufen ständig ein.

Der Betrieb hat einen Auftrag über die Lieferung von 400 Stühlen erhalten.

order, sequence, succession, series *ns.*

1. The sense of **order** discussed here is 'the way a set of thgs. is arranged or done when one thg. is placed or done first, another second, etc.' *We must decide in which order the rooms will be cleaned*. In one sense **sequence** means 'the particular order or pattern in which thgs. or events follow one another'. *I have done the calculations in the correct sequence/order. The paintings are exhibited more or less in chronological sequence/order.*

i. The usual equivalent of both words in these senses is **die Reihenfolge**, the way things follow one another according to some criterion. *You must do the exercises in order* and *. . . in the right/correct/proper order* express the same meaning. *Reihenfolge* needs an adj., gen., or clause. *Die Übungen hast du nicht in der richtigen Reihenfolge gemacht.*

Wir haben entschieden, in welcher Reihenfolge wir die Zimmer putzen werden.
Ich habe die Berechnungen in der richtigen Reihenfolge gemacht.
Die Reihenfolge der Reden, wie sie im Programm steht, muß strikt eingehalten werden.
Die Gemälde sind mehr oder weniger in der Reihenfolge ihrer Entstehung ausgestellt.
Erst wenn man die Bilder in die richtige Reihenfolge bringt, ergeben sie einen Sinn.
Beschreiben Sie die Ereignisse in der richtigen Reihenfolge!
Sie müssen die Anträge in der Reihenfolge ihres Eingangs bearbeiten.
Die Startnummern wurden in umgekehrter Reihenfolge aufgerufen.

ii. While *die Reihenfolge* refers to a concrete arrangement, **die Ordnung** denotes a system or principle according to which things are arranged. *Ordnung* is often used to state that something lacks order. *Die Anordnung der Ausstellungsstücke* (arrangement of the exhibits) *läßt keine Ordnung erkennen. In dem Aufsatz fehlt einfach die Ordnung.* In some pos. sents. both *Ordnung* and *Reihenfolge* are possible. *Bringen Sie Ihre Argumente in die logische Reihenfolge/Ordnung. In alphabetischer/chronologischer Reihenfolge* seems to be the preferred expression, but *Ordnung* is not uncommon.
iii. Arrange thgs. **in order of** size etc. can often be most easily expressed as *sie* **nach** *Größe* etc. **ordnen.** Cf. ARRANGE 1. *Ich habe die Angelegenheiten nach ihrer Wichtigkeit geordnet.*

2. Sequence also denotes a number of things or events that come one after the other in a certain order or pattern and usually move towards a particular result. *They were discussing the sequence of events which led to the fall of the government.* A **succession** *of thgs.* of the same kind is also 'a number of them coming one after the other'. *The holiday was spoiled by a succession of rainy days* or *by several rainy days in succession.* A **series** *of thgs.* or *events* has a meaning similar to those of *sequence* and *succession. The region has suffered a series of natural disasters.* **Series** is the usual word in relation to books, lectures, etc.
i. Die Folge denotes a number of similar events or things which follow one another or form a group. It may, but need not, suggest a closer link between the constituent parts than that they are of the same kind. *Eine Folge von Bildern* implies a connected cycle, while *Die Mannschaft errang eine Folge von glänzenden Siegen* does not. If **series** means 'several or a [small] number', **eine Anzahl** (cf. NUMBER 4) could be used. *Das Land wurde von einer Anzahl von Naturkatastrophen getroffen.* **Eine Reihe** *von Bildern* is similar in meaning to *eine Anzahl von Bildern*, but may suggest a larger number. *Reihe* sometimes suggests that the things are related, but need not. *Eine Reihe von Frauen hat protestiert* simply implies several. *Es gibt eine Reihe von Fragen, die beantwortet werden müssen.* **Die Serie** usually implies a connection between the components. While *eine Anzahl von Versuchen*, 'experiments', need not be connected in any way and *eine Reihe von Versuchen* need not be linked nor even on the same subject, *eine Serie von Versuchen* would be connected.

Eine Folge/Reihe von Mißernten brachten viele bäuerliche Familien an den Rand des Hungers.
Eine Folge von seltsamen Ereignissen führte zum Sturz der Regierung.
Es kam zu einer ganzen Folge/Reihe von Unfällen.
Er zählte eine Reihe von typischen Merkmalen auf.
Das Buch enthält eine Serie von sorgfältig zusammengestellten Unterrichtseinheiten.
Eine Serie von Verbrechen versetzte die Bevölkerung in Angst und Schrecken.
Die Post gibt zu Weihnachten eine neue Briefmarkenserie heraus.

Die Reihe is used for a series of books and lectures. *Eine Vortragsreihe. Sie gibt eine soziologische Reihe für einen Taschenbuchverlag heraus. Die Serie* can refer to a radio or

television series. *Eine Folge is 'an episode'. Die Einschaltquote für diese Serie soll sehr hoch sein, aber die Folgen, die ich gesehen habe, waren schlecht.*
ii. In succession can be **in Folge**. *Zwölf Siege in Folge ist eine großartige Leistung. In schneller/rascher Folge* means 'in rapid succession'. *Nach diesem Erfolg erschienen mehrere Romane des Autors in rascher Folge.* Often heard is **hintereinander**. *Die Mannschaft gewann achtmal hintereinander. Das Stück wurde an hundert Abenden hintereinander gegeben.*
  Berühmte Persönlichkeiten fuhren in schneller Folge vorbei.
  Der Urlaub wurde dadurch verdorben, daß es an fünf Tagen hintereinander regnete.
iii. Die Aufeinanderfolge suggests a fairly rapid succession of things or events. *Die rasche Aufeinanderfolge dieser tragischen Ereignisse nahm ihm den Lebensmut.* **Die Abfolge** is either a syn. of *Reihenfolge, in chronologischer Abfolge*, or a syn. of *Folge* and *Aufeinanderfolge* referring to things that follow one another in time. *Der Polizist beschrieb die Abfolge der Ereignisse. (Abfolge* = 'sequence' may be used instead of *Folge* to avoid a clash of meaning with *Folge* = 'consequence'. *Die Inflation war die Folge dieser Ereignisse.)*
  Das Leben ist eine Aufeinanderfolge/Folge von Freuden und Enttäuschungen.
  Die Abfolge der Programmpunkte bei der Feier ist noch nicht festgelegt worden.
  Die rasche Abfolge der Beleidigungen ließ den Streit ausufern.

other, another *adjs.*

1. In one sense **another** means 'one or some more in addition to one or a number of the same kind'.
i. In reference to things which are eaten or drunk, as in *Have another piece of cake!*, the equivalent is **noch ein, zwei**, etc. *Nehmen Sie noch ein Stück Kuchen! Er bestellte noch ein [Glas] Bier. Wir bestellten noch zwei Stück Kuchen. Would you like another cup/drink/sth. else to drink?* is *Möchten Sie noch eine Tasse/noch etw. trinken?* or *Kann ich Ihnen noch etw. zu trinken geben?* Also often encountered is *Ich habe noch eine Bitte*, but *eine weitere Bitte* is common too.
ii. Ander refers to things which are not consumed. **Weiter** also denotes a further person or thing of the same kind. *Nehmen wir ein anderes/weiteres Beispiel! Das andere Beispiel ist leichter zu verstehen.*
  Dieses Tuch ist nicht groß genug. Gib mir mal ein anderes! Or Gib mir mal das andere!
  Bevor ich ausgehe, muß ich ein anderes Kleid anziehen.
  Sie verließen ihre Heimat und siedelten in ein anderes Land über.
  Ein weiterer Flüchtling schloß sich unserer Gruppe an.   *Ich habe eine andere/weitere Frage.*
iii. Another + an expression of time or distance is **noch** or **weiter**. *Another three hours/kilometres. Er mußte noch drei Stunden/weitere drei Stunden warten. Ich fuhr noch/weitere fünfzig Kilometer.*

2. i. Ander translates **other** relating to food and drink when it means 'different'. *Wenn Ihnen dieser Saft nicht schmeckt, nehmen Sie einen anderen!*, take another or a different sort, or if there are only two, *Nehmen Sie den anderen! Möchten Sie noch ein Glas Saft?* refers to another glass of the same juice. *Probieren Sie eine andere Birne!* is one of a different sort from the one you have just had, but *Ich esse noch eine Birne*, I'll have another one of the same kind.
ii. *I became* **another** *man/woman* meaning 'my character changed' is *Ich wurde ein anderer Mensch.*
iii. Zweit is the equivalent of **another** in some contexts. *Das möchte ich kein zweites Mal erleben. He thought he was another Napoleon: Er glaubte, ein zweiter Napoleon zu sein.*

ought, should *vs.* Some uses.

1. Should or **ought** mean that something is probably true or is likely to happen in the way mentioned. *That shouldn't be difficult. We should be there by six.*

i. One equivalent is the pres. of **müssen**. It expresses an expectation which the speaker feels will be realized. Someone who feels that a bus should arrive soon says, '*Der Bus muß jeden Augenblick kommen.*' Of a person who is expected to arrive soon, people say, '*Er muß gleich/jeden Augenblick da sein.*' *Müssen* indicates a high degree of certainty in the speaker's mind. A more qualified sense of certainty is expressed by the subjunctive **müßte**. If a bus had not appeared ten minutes after the due time, I might say, '*Er müßte gleich kommen.*' This suggests that I still think it will turn up soon, but have some doubts. If I ask for a book I have ordered, the shop assistant might say, '*Das Buch muß da sein.*' This might mean that because orders always arrive within a certain time, it could be expected to be there. If he or she were not so certain but considered it likely to be there, the answer might be, '*Es müßte schon da sein.*' *Das müßte reichen* expresses a fair degree of certainty that an amount will be sufficient.

> *Das müßte [doch eigentlich] nicht so schwierig sein. Versuchen wir es mal!*
> *Sie müßten bis ein Uhr hier sein, denk' ich.*

ii. Dürfte indicates a high degree of probability but belongs more to the written language. *Es dürfte nicht schwer sein, das zu beweisen.* Although *dürfte* can often be translated as **should**, *probably* or *likely* is needed in many cases. *Diese Darstellung der Ereignisse dürfte den Tatsachen entsprechen*, probably corresponds to the facts. **Werden** + **wohl** also expresses probability and is more common than *dürfte* in speech. *Wir werden wohl bis Freitag fertig sein.* **Wahrscheinlich** can also be used. *Es wird wahrscheinlich klappen.* (*Wir sollten bis Freitag fertig sein* implies that this is expected or planned but that the expectation is unlikely to be met.)

> *Es wird wohl/dürfte keine Schwierigkeiten geben.*   *Wir werden wohl bis sechs da sein.*
> *Morgen dürfte das Wetter besser sein als heute.*   *Der Regen dürfte bald aufhören.*
> *Die Kickers werden wohl gewinnen.*   *Das wird wohl reichen.*
> *Bis ein Uhr werden sie wohl hier sein.*   *Der Regen wird wohl bald aufhören.*

2. i. Someone who has every reason to believe that e.g. a map is in a certain place but cannot find it says, 'The map should be here.' **Müßte** expresses this sense. *Die Karte müßte hier sein.* It may imply that if things were done properly or carried out as planned, a certain result could be expected.

> *In der Bibliothek: 'Das Buch müßte an diesem Platz stehen, da es nicht ausgeliehen ist. Jmd. muß es verstellt haben.'*

ii. Müßte and **hätte . . . müssen** express a feeling that something would be the right and proper thing to have happened. *Sie müßten schon längst hier sein* or *Sie hätten schon längst hier sein müssen*, 'they should have been here long ago', could be said if the time of someone's expected arrival had long since past. If a bus had not arrived half an hour after the due time, someone might say, '*Der Bus hätte vor einer halben Stunde hier sein müssen*', should have been here.

iii. *Das müßte sie wissen* means 'she could be expected to know it', and *Das hätte er wissen müssen*, 'he could have been expected to know it, he should have known it'.

> *Wenn er nur halbwegs gebildet wäre, müßte er wissen, wer Goethe ist.*
> *Du hättest wissen müssen, daß dieses Buch nicht unter die Nachschlagewerke gehört.*

3. Ought/Should and *ought not/should not* state that in the speaker's view an action or someone's behaviour is morally right or wrong. *We ought to help those in need. You ought not to have insulted him.* They also state that the speaker thinks it is a good idea, advisable, or important for him, her, or someone else to do something, and that it would be wrong not to do it. *We should develop an alternative to petrol.*

Shouldn't you switch it off first? The government should create more jobs.

i. To understand the use of *müssen* it helps to distinguish two senses of *must*. *Must* can mean that someone is compelled by physical, social, or legal necessity to do something, *We must eat to live* and *In Australia you must drive on the left*, or that something is absolutely necessary to carry out a purpose, *We must hurry if we want to catch the bus*. It also presents an action not as a necessity, but as important or highly desirable, and can be paraphrased as **certainly should** or **ought**. It can be applied to oneself. *I don't know how they're getting on—I must go over and ask* or *I mustn't stay gossiping any longer*. It is also used when someone urges others to do something. *You must see that film*. **Müssen** denotes a necessity, but also expresses a feeling that something is or would be proper or desirable. It is translated by **ought to** or **should** as well as by *must*. This use is confined to contexts in which *müssen* is not taken to mean 'have to'. *Ich weiß nicht, wie es ihnen geht—ich muß mal hingehen und mich erkundigen.*

> *Wenn dir jmd. einen Ratschlag gibt, mußt du das nicht immer gleich als Kritik auffassen und ärger- lich reagieren.* (*Darfst nicht* is stronger. *Mußt nicht* is fairly weak like *should*.)
>
> *Der Roman hat mich gefesselt. Du mußt ihn unbedingt auch lesen* (stronger than *solltest*).
>
> *Ich habe meine Tante seit einiger Zeit nicht mehr gesehen. Ich muß sie mal wieder besuchen.*

ii. Müßte also expresses a feeling that something is proper or desirable. It is often heard in everyday speech. **Sollte** is frequently interchangeable with *müßte* but tends to be used for more abstract moral obligations and to express advisability. While *müßte und sollte* refer to the present, *Eigentlich sollte/müßte ich hingehen, aber ich bin so müde*, the pluperfect subjunctive states what should have happened in the past, *Das hätte er sich eher überlegen müssen/sollen—nun ist es zu spät. Müßtest du den Strom nicht vorher abschalten?* is stronger than *solltest. Dieses Wörterbuch solltest du haben* is weaker than *Dieses Wörterbuch müßtest du haben. Sollte* is used when someone thinks it advisable or a good thing that something be done. *Die Regierung sollte mehr Arbeitsplätze schaffen. Die Regierung müßte mehr Arbeitsplätze schaffen* is also used but suggests criticism or a reproach because this has not been done.

> *Du solltest/müßtest einmal so richtig ausspannen.*   *Alle Bürger sollten den Bedürftigen helfen.*
>
> *Diese Arbeit hätten wir schon längst erledigen sollen/müssen.*
>
> *In Zukunft solltest du vorsichtiger sein.*   *Du hättest auf seinen Rat hören sollen.*
>
> *Du solltest sie nicht länger im Unklaren über deine Pläne lassen.*
>
> *Du solltest den Wagen nie unverschlossen stehen lassen.*
>
> *Du hättest pünktlicher sein müssen.*   *Man hätte früher daran denken sollen.*

iii. The strongest moral condemnation is expressed by the neg. of **dürfen**. The neg. pres. means that someone is not justified in doing something either for ethical reasons or because of circumstances, and is translated as *must not* or *should certainly not. So etw. darf man nicht sagen. Ich darf nicht länger mit euch quatschen—ich habe nämlich viel zu tun.* (In such sents. *sollte* leaves it open as to whether the person will actually do what is stated.) The neg. pluperfect subjunctive of *dürfen* suggests that someone has either broken a law, *Du hättest nicht bei Rot über die Kreuzung fahren dürfen*, or offended against a moral or social standard, *Du hättest ihn nicht kränken dürfen.* It is often used with *tun* to state that someone should not have done something. *Du hast ihn schwer beleidigt—das hättest du nicht tun dürfen. Das hättest du nicht tun sollen* is weaker, suggesting that it would have been better if the person had not done it or that it is not advisable to act in this way.

4. Some other uses of *sollen.*

i. The main use of the pres. of **sollen** is to convey what one person wants another to do. In the commandment *Du sollst nicht stehlen*, it is translated as *shalt*. In everyday situations the usual equivalent is *to be* + infin. *S.o. is to do sth. Was soll ich in*

Hamburg machen? Der Ausschuß soll Vorschläge ausarbeiten. My boss might say to me, *'Sagen Sie bitte Frau Lange, sie soll sofort zu mir kommen.'* In delivering the message, I would say, *'Du sollst sofort zum Chef gehen.' Ich soll das Rauchen aufgeben,* someone has told me to do so. (*Ich sollte das Rauchen aufgeben* means that it would be advisable for me to do so, and leaves it unclear whether the advice will be followed.)

ii. *I don't know what to do/what I* **should** *do* both become *Ich weiß nicht, was ich machen soll.* When the main v. is in the past, the past of *sollen* is used. *Ich wußte nicht, wen ich um Rat bitten sollte.*

iii. Different tenses of *sollen* translate certain expressions containing **should**. A. *Warum ist sie nicht hier?* B. *Woher soll ich das wissen?* The answer to *'Hast du Angst?'* can be *'Warum sollte ich Angst haben.* I might protest against an order I considered unjustified by saying, *'Warum soll ich das machen?—das ist nicht meine Aufgabe.'* However, in talking to a third person I would say, *'Ich seh' nicht ein, warum ich das machen sollte'* or *'Warum sollte ich [das machen]? Meine Aufgabe ist es nicht.'*

iv. The preterite subjunctive is usual in indirect commands, though the pres. subjunctive is possible. *Sie sagten, daß ich mir keine Sorgen darüber machen sollte/solle. Sollte* is used in conditional clauses. *Wenn du meine Hilfe brauchen solltest, bin ich zu Hause zu erreichen.* Or *Solltest du meine Hilfe brauchen, . . .*

5. Idioms. *Geld müßte man haben* or *Reich müßte man sein* suggest *That's what we could do if we were rich* or *It would be nice to be rich.* So *müßte es immer sein* means that it would be nice or good if things were always like that, but unfortunately they are not. *Jeder müßte einmal auf einem Bauernhof gearbeitet haben,* everybody should have . . . *Den hättest du sehen sollen/müssen,* you should have seen him (he was surprising, unusual, amusing, magnificent, etc.). Also *Das hättest du sehen sollen/müssen.*

overtake, catch up [with/on] *vs.* Two senses of **pass** *v.*

1. The equivalent of **catch up with** s.o. or sth. meaning 'to draw level with or reach' is **einholen**. *Sie war 100 Meter vor mir, da ich aber schneller ging als sie, holte ich sie ein. Er lief so schnell, daß ich ihn nicht einholen konnte.* It is applied fig. to other fields of activity. *Die Firma bemüht sich, ihren Hauptkonkurrenten einzuholen.*

2. Catch up means 'to reduce the distance or gap between oneself, a vehicle, etc. and the next pers., vehicle, etc.' *Can't you drive faster?—they're catching up.* This sense is expressed by **aufholen**. *Der deutsche Läufer konnte in der letzten Runde [um ein paar Meter] aufholen.* It is also applied to school and other work. *Sie hat eine Zeitlang gefehlt und muß jetzt tüchtig aufholen,* has to work hard to catch up, has considerable leeway/a considerable backlog to make up. *Aufholen* is also trans., mostly with *der Rückstand,* the distance one person etc. is behind another, or *der Vorsprung,* the distance one person etc. is ahead of another, as obj. In these contexts it is a syn. of *einholen. Es ist fraglich, ob die deutsche Läuferin in den verbleibenden zehn Minuten diesen Rückstand/diesen Vorsprung aufholen kann.* The E. equivalent can be *to make up* (the distance) as well as **catch up**. This sense also occurs in relation to work. *Ihr Sohn ist zwar im (Lern)stoff etwas zurück, aber mit ein wenig Fleiß wird er das wieder aufholen.* The usual trans. v. when something that one has missed or failed to do is the obj. is **nachholen**, to catch up on work not done, make up for lost working time. *Wegen der Krankheit muß das Kind viel Unterrichtsstoff nachholen.* Or *Das Kind muß jetzt das Versäumte/den Stoff von drei Monaten nachholen. Ich habe viel nachzuholen,* have a large backlog to deal with, a lot of work/leeway to make up.

Kannst du nicht schneller fahren?—sie holen auf.

Auf weite Strecken des Rennens hatte Mey zurückgelegen, aber auf den letzten Metern holte er stark auf.

Alles, was sie versäumt hatte, hat sie in sehr kurzer Zeit nachgeholt.

3. Overtake and **pass** mean 'to draw level with and move ahead of' a person vehicle, or animal. The equivalent is **überholen**. It implies a person or thing moving in the same direction. Like both E. vs. it is both trans., *Alle westdeutschen Autos überholten den langsamen Trabi,* and intr., *Man darf nur links überholen.*

4. An jmdm./etw. vorbeifahren/vorbeigehen mean 'to pass or go past'. In most situations they imply that the other person/thing is stationary or going in the opposite direction. *Ich fahre an dem Bahnhof vorbei und setze dich dort ab. Ich bin an ihm vorbeigegangen, aber er hat mich nicht erkannt. Wir sind an euch auf der Autobahn vorbeigefahren* suggests that the others had stopped or were going in the opposite direction; otherwise *überholen* would be used. In spite of this the person or thing passed can sometimes be going in the same direction. *Ich bin an ihr vorbeigegangen, als wir die Bahnhofsstraße entlang gingen, aber sie hat in die entgegengesetzte Richtung gesehen.* **An etw. vorbeikommen** means 'to go past'. *Kommt der Bus hier vorbei? Sie verteilte Flugblätter an die Vorbeikommenden.* In everyday speech *vorbeikommen* suggests that someone goes past something by chance while going somewhere else, *Auf dem Weg zur Arbeit komme ich an der Post vorbei und kann den Brief einwerfen,* or *Wenn wir nicht bald an einer Tankstelle vorbeikommen, geht uns das Benzin aus,* while *vorbeigehen* and *vorbeifahren* imply an intention, *Wenn du willst, kann ich an der Post vorbeigehen und das Paket für dich abholen. Vorbeikommen* also means 'to get past' an obstruction etc. *Die Einfahrt war mit Bauschutt versperrt—deshalb konnten wir mit dem Wagen nicht vorbeikommen. Niemand kommt an dem Posten vorbei.*

5. In one trans. sense **pass** means 'to proceed across or through'. *We passed the frontier/the barrier.* When intr., it means 'to go or make one's way through'. *The guard permitted no one to pass.* **Passieren,** 'to go over or through', translates both uses. With an obj.: *Das Auto passierte die Brücke/den Fluß/die Grenze. Wir passierten die Gefahrenstelle.* Hence *Der Gebirgspaß ist wegen des schweren Schneefalls unpassierbar.* Without an obj.: *Der Posten ließ uns ungehindert passieren/ließ niemand passieren.*

owe v. Cf. THANK.

i. Owe *s.o. money* can be expressed by the v. **schulden** or by **jmdm. etw. schuldig sein**. *Ich schulde ihr noch 100 Mark* or *Ich bin ihr noch eine kleine Summe schuldig. Was bin ich [Ihnen] schuldig? Wieviel bin ich dir schuldig? Was schulde ich Ihnen? (Schuldig* without a dat. means 'guilty'. *Der Angeklagte wurde für schuldig befunden.)*

ii. The expressions in i can also be used to express the idea of owing someone an apology, an explanation, etc. *Ich schulde ihm Rechenschaft* or *Ich bin Ihnen eine/keine Erklärung schuldig. Ich bin ihr eine Entschuldigung für mein Fehlen bei der gestrigen Sitzung schuldig.*

iii. Schulden is used in formal language with *Dank* as obj. *Dank schulden wir auch den Reformbewegungen in Mittel-, Ost- und Südosteuropa* (from a speech by the German Chancellor on 3 Oct. 1990). In less formal circumstances the expression used is **jmdm. zu Dank verpflichtet sein,** to owe someone a debt of gratitude. *Der Verfasser dieser Dissertation ist Prof. Dr. Paul Hartmann für langjährige Förderung zu Dank verpflichtet.*

p

packet *n.* For **packet** meaning 'a container in which goods are sold and/or its contents', G. has three main words, *das Päckchen, die Packung,* and *das Paket.* **Das Päckchen** suggests a small packet; **die Packung** is bigger, but the dividing line is not clear, and there is some overlapping with *Päckchen.* **Das Paket** is a fairly large container. Hence *ein Päckchen/eine Packung Rasierklingen, ein Päckchen Kaugummi, ein Päckchen Papiertaschentücher* (ten *Päckchen* together are called *eine Packung*), *eine Packung Streichhölzer* (contains several *Schachteln,* boxes), *eine Packung Kekse/Gebäck, eine Packung Müsli* (depending on the size, *Päckchen* and *Paket* are also found), *eine Packung Reis, eine Packung Eier* (also *ein Karton Eier*), *eine Packung Tee/Kaffee, ein Paket Waschpulver.* Some packets are called **eine Tüte** which usually denotes a bag (cf. box) made of paper or plastic. *Eine Tüte Mehl/Zucker. Die Packung* also refers to the material in which something is packaged. *Ich nehme den Kaffee in der braunen Packung. Die Packung ist gerissen.* (*Das Paket* is also 'a parcel'. *Das Päckchen* is also 'a small parcel up to two kilogrammes' for which the G. Post Office charges special rates.)

painful[ly], laborious[ly], arduous[ly], onerous[ly], painstaking[ly]
adjs. and advs.

1. In reference to something which is not a part of the body, such as *The wound was painful* or *It was painful to admit I was wrong,* **painful** has two equivalents *schmerzhaft* and *schmerzlich.* The general distinction is that **schmerzhaft** refers to bodily pain and **schmerzlich** to mental pain, grief, sadness, anxiety, regret, etc. Thus *eine schmerzhafte Wunde, ein schmerzhafter Sonnenbrand,* and *eine schmerzliche Erinnerung. Sie erlitten einen schmerzlichen Verlust.* If followed, this distinction will always produce correct G. However, *schmerzhaft* is sometimes used for mental pain. *Ich habe mich von meinem Mann getrennt—es war sehr schmerzhaft.* Hence *eine schmerzhafte Trennung.* Some people consider this wrong; others feel it to be stronger than *schmerzlich. Schmerzlich* would be just as good and more common. With *Erlebnis* and *Erfahrung,* both = 'experience', *schmerzhaft* and *schmerzlich* occur with different implications. If a child burns its hand on a hotplate, this experience is called *ein schmerzhaftes Erlebnis. Das schmerzhafte Erlebnis mit der Herdplatte blieb mir monatelang im Gedächtnis.* Thus also *Das Kind machte die schmerzhafte Erfahrung, daß Herdplatten Verbrennungen verursachen.* A painful experience which is purely mental is described as *schmerzlich. Die schmerzliche Erfahrung, daß allen Menschen nicht zu trauen ist.* For me after **painful** is either the dat. or *für mich. Es war mir/für mich sehr schmerzlich.* An infin. can follow. *Es war mir schmerzlich, den Leuten sagen zu müssen, daß die Firma ihre Stellen gestrichen hatte.* An alternative is *Ich empfand es als sehr schmerzlich.*

Die Operation/Die Behandlung war sehr schmerzhaft.
Die Flüchtlinge waren sich der Tatsache schmerzlich bewußt, daß sie nie wieder in ihre Heimat zurückkehren könnten.   Am Körper spürte er mehrere schmerzhafte Stellen.
Es war mir sehr schmerzlich, zugeben zu müssen, daß ich einen so schweren Fehler gemacht hatte.

In its full sense **qualvoll** is a strong word often translated as *agonizing* but in some contexts as **painful.** *Er starb einen qualvollen Tod/an einem qualvollen Leiden.* It is applied to what causes mental pain or agony and to time. *Wie lange müssen wir diese qualvoll Ungewißheit noch ertragen? Er verbrachte qualvolle Stunden/Tage an ihrem Krankenbett.*

Sie wurde von qualvollen Erinnerungen verfolgt.   *Der Abschied war qualvoll.*

Es war qualvoll, mitansehen zu müssen, wie das Pferd verendete.

2. Painful is applied to parts of the body. *My arm is so painful that I cannot move it.* This is expressed by vs. meaning 'to hurt', **schmerzen** or **weh tun.** Cf. DAMAGE 5. The question *Is it painful?* would mostly be *Tut es weh?*

Der Arm schmerzte mir so sehr, daß ich ihn nicht bewegen konnte. Or Mein Arm schmerzte so sehr
. . .
Er konnte nicht gehen, weil ihm das Bein sehr schmerzte, sobald er es belastete.

Die Stelle tut weh, wenn man sie berührt (is painful to touch/to the touch).

3. Painful describing a performance or entertainment means 'so bad that it is distressing to watch or listen to'. G. expresses this idea in various ways. *Eine denkbar schlechte Liebeskomödie* could be a transl. of a *painful romantic comedy,* although the lit. sense is 'as bad as can possibly be imagined'. Other transls. are *Das Theaterstück/Die Aufführung war so schlecht, daß es wehtat* or *Die Leistung der Schauspieler/Die Aufführung war mehr als peinlich.* **Peinlich** means 'embarrassing' (cf. EMBARRASS). In *Ich war von dieser Bemerkung peinlich berührt* it is strong enough to translate *painfully embarrassed.* **Qualvoll** is used in an exaggerated way. *Es was direkt/geradezu qualvoll, die beiden singen zu hören.* If **painful** means 'boring', it could be **totlangweilig** or **sterbenslangweilig,** deadly dull. *Die Konferenz war totlangweilig—die meisten Redner haben das Naheliegende ausführlich erörtert.*

4. Painful is also applied to something which is done slowly and with a lot of effort. *Progress is rather painful/was painfully slow. Although he could scarcely write, he had painfully scrawled out a statement.* The closest equivalents are words which mean 'laborious, arduous, or onerous'. Three are derived from *die Mühe,* trouble or effort.

i. Mühevoll is applied to activities which demand much patience, perseverance, and effort. **Mühsam** or **mit großer Mühe** mean 'necessitating great effort or exertion'. While *mühsam* in strict use points to the personal effort required and *mühevoll* to the difficult nature of a task, the difference is very slight. *Mühsam* is the more usual word. *Nur mühsam* means 'only with effort or difficulty'. *Nur mühsam konnte er seine Wut beherrschen.* **Painfully** *slow[ly]* could be *langsam und mühsam,* but, because of the two *sam* sounds, would probably be *langsam und mühevoll* or *langsam und mit großer Mühe.*

Nach diesen mühevollen Vorbereitungen können wir jetzt anfangen.

Es wird sehr mühevoll/mühsam sein, in diesem Durcheinander die richtigen Papiere zu finden.

Es ist eine mühevolle/mühsame Aufgabe, diese Klasse zu unterrichten. Man muß alles vier- oder fünfmal erklären, bevor die meisten Schüler es kapieren.

Sie bahnten sich mühsam einen Weg durch den dichten Urwald.

Die kleine schlechte Schrift konnte ich nur sehr langsam und mit großer Mühe entziffern.

Mühselig expresses the sense of *mühevoll* and *mühsam* in a strengthened form. It suggests that the work is intricate and fiddly, that much effort and many difficulties are involved, that it is a trial of one's patience and a burden. It can express sympathy and admiration when used about another person.

Du kannst dir gar nicht denken, wie mühselig es war, diese Kartei anzulegen.

Er hatte das Beweismaterial mühselig zusammengebracht.

ii. Beschwerlich is applied to something that presents difficulties and requires great effort and exertion. *Nach dem beschwerlichen Fußmarsch waren alle erschöpft.*

Das Steigen durch den hohen Schnee wurde immer beschwerlicher.

Die Fahrt war lang und beschwerlich.

iii. *The bus went/travelled painfully slowly* could be *Der Bus fuhr denkbar langsam*. One sense of **sich quälen**, 'to move forward with great effort or exertion' or 'to struggle to get somewhere', can express the meaning of **painfully**. *Mühsam* may be added. *Das alte Vehikel quälte sich [mühsam] über den steilen Berg* or *quälte sich [mühsam] den steilen Hügel hinauf,* crawled painfully and slowly. Another sense of *sich quälen* is 'to do work with great effort', 'to struggle with or slave away at a task'. This can express a meaning similar to *to make painful progress*. *Ich quäle mich schon stundenlang mit dieser Übersetzung.*

Er quälte sich mit der schweren Schubkarre über den Hof.
Der Schüler quälte sich mit den Hausaufgaben.
Wir quälten uns mühsam durch den hohen Schnee.

5. Another sense of **peinlich** is 'meticulous or painstaking'. *Die Arbeit haben sie mit peinlicher Sorgfalt ausgeführt.* **Penibel** expresses the same meaning but has a neg. or critical overtone suggesting that the care and precision are exaggerated. *Jmd. ist mit seiner Arbeit/seiner Kleidung/mit allem sehr penibel.*

paint *v.*

i. The normal word for painting a house, room, fence, etc. is **streichen**, although **malen** is occasionally found. The notice *Wet Paint* is *Vorsicht! Frisch gestrichen! Der Maler* can denote either an artist who paints pictures or a tradesman who paints houses etc. So that no misunderstanding arises, the tradesman is often called *ein Malermeister*, while a well-known artist is referred to as *ein Maler* and a not so well-known artist as *ein Kunstmaler*. The business of a *Malermeister* is called *ein Malerbetrieb,*

Ich muß das Haus/das Zimmer/die Wand/den Gartenzaun streichen [lassen].
Eine Decke zu streichen ist eine recht anstrengende Angelegenheit.
Die Fensterläden sind weiß gestrichen. Soll ich sie rot streichen?
Im Hafen wurde das Schiff neu gestrichen.   *Rubens war ein großer Maler.*
Der Maler hat die Türen und Fenster im Haus gestrichen.

ii. Anstreichen is a syn. of *streichen. Ich lasse das Zimmer anstreichen. Ich streiche den Tisch mit Lack* (varnish) *an. Anstreichen* is often used when the colour is mentioned, but *streichen* is just as common. *Er hat die Tür gelb angestrichen/gestrichen. Ich finde, es ist eine entsetzliche Farbe, um ein ganzes Haus damit anzustreichen.* The tradesman is also called *der Anstreicher,* but a n. with this meaning is not formed from *streichen*.
iii. Malen means 'to paint a picture'. The obj. can either be the result of the activity, *Er malte ein Bild/ein Porträt/ein Gemälde,* etc., or the thing represented, *Sie hat ihre Mutter/den Fluß gemalt. Zeichnen* means 'to draw with a pencil, crayon, etc.' but has further connotations. It implies care and accuracy, as in *technische Zeichnung,* or artistic ability in drawing. For children, *malen* is used for both painting with a brush and drawing with a pencil etc. In the latter case it may sometimes be necessary to add *mit dem Bleistift* or *mit Farbstiften. Das Kind malt ein Bild. Malen* is the usual v. when someone carefully paints or draws words, letters, numbers, etc., e.g. on a placard. *Malen* is also used fig. *Sie malten die Lage in düsteren Farben.*

Dieses Bild malte van Gogh, als er zwanzig Jahre alt war.
Im großen, weithin sichtbaren Buchstaben malte sie die Parole auf das Pappschild.

iv. Bemalen means either 'to apply paint to a mostly fairly small object' or 'to paint a decorative picture or pattern on sth.' It implies skill and care. *Sie bemalt die Vasen, die sie anfertigt. Die Teller sind mit Blumen/mit einem Muster bemalt.* It is used for painting the body. *Die Indianer bemalen sich den Körper und das Gesicht. Bei Naturvölkern ist die Körperbemalung häufig anzutreffen.*
v. Anmalen also means 'to apply a coat of paint to' but suggests less skill than

bemalen. It is usual to say *Die Kinder malen Ostereier an*. If this were done with considerable skill *bemalen* would be used. *Das Mädchen malt einen Löwen an* implies that the outline is already present and that she colours it. (An alternative implying greater care is *ausmalen*.) *Das Mädchen malt einen Löwen* implies drawing the outline as well. **Sich anmalen** means 'to put on make-up' in a way which is both inexpert and overdone.

> *Das Schaukelpferd ist fertig und muß nur noch angemalt werden.*
> *Ich habe nichts dagegen, wenn du die Fensterläden blau anmalst, aber lila geht doch ein bißchen zu*
> *weit.   'Mußt du dich immer so anmalen, wenn du mit mir ausgehst', murrte ihr Bruder.*

pattern *n*. **model** *n*. and *adj*. **sample** *n*. The equivalents of some meanings of the first word carry senses of the second.

1. i. Pattern means 'instructions for knitting or a diagram or shape that is used as a guide in making a piece of clothing'. The equivalent is **das Muster**. *A knitting pattern* is *ein Strickmuster*.

> *Sie häkelt/strickt nach Muster.   Das Kostüm ist nach einem Muster geschneidert.*

ii. The meaning of **Muster** is extended to things which serve as a guide for the way something is to be done, a concept for which E. uses **model**. *Schreiben Sie Ihren Lebenslauf nach diesem Muster!* A related word is **die Vorlage**, something which is to be copied. It may, but need not, imply that it is copied exactly. *Das diente mir als Vorlage* may mean no more than that the general plan was followed. **Das Modell** can be a syn.

> *Nehmen Sie diesen Lebenslauf als Vorlage/Muster, um den eigenen zu schreiben!*
> *Ich schlage vor, nach folgendem Muster vorzugehen.*
> *Eine Schule nach demselben Muster wird geplant.*
> *Die Rede war nach einem bestimmten/bekannten Muster angelegt.*
> *Verschiedene afrikanische Länder haben diese Regierungsform zum Modell genommen.*
> *Das Schloß war nach dem Modell von Versailles gebaut.*
> *Diese Wohnform soll als Modell für weitere Rehabilitierungsversuche dienen.*

2. Pattern means 'an arrangement of lines, shapes, etc. repeated at regular intervals over a surface, a design on a carpet, wallpaper, etc.', a sense also carried by **das Muster**.

> *Das Muster dieser Tapete/dieser Decke/dieses Teppichs gefällt mir.*
> *Sie kaufte ein Kleid mit einem Muster von kleinen, roten Äpfeln. Also Das Kleid war mit kleinen, roten*
> *Äpfeln gemustert.   Er wählte ein gewürfeltes Muster für seinen Anzug.*
> *Der Junge saß am Strand und malte mit dem Finger ein Muster von Kreuzen in den Sand.*

3. Pattern is also applied to a particular, recognizable way in which something is done, organized, or happens, or to constantly recurring features in action or behaviour. **Das Muster** has also become usual in this sense. *Behaviour patterns* are *Verhaltensmuster*. **Die Struktur** refers to the way in which the elements of a system are built up and connected with each other, but it is extended to groups of people, a family, an organization, or a society, and means 'the pattern of their relationships with each other and the way various roles and powers are arranged'. *Patterns of family life* are *die Strukturen des Familienlebens*. Also *Die wirtschaftlichen Strukturen*.

> *Ihre Untersuchungen weisen ein stets wiederkehrendes Muster in der Wirtschaftsgeschichte des*
> *Landes nach.   Die Diebstahlserie weist ein gängiges Muster auf.*

4. Das Muster can also be 'a sample, a specimen offered as an example of the whole'. *Der Vertreter hat ihnen verschiedene Muster dagelassen.* Here *Muster* is a shortened form of **das Warenmuster**.

5. Model in the sense of 'a representation in three dimensions of some projected or existing structure or of some natural or artifical object' is **das Modell**. *Das Modell eines Flugzeugs/eines Schiffes.*

Roland hat eine Modelleisenbahn als Weihnachtsgeschenk bekommen.

Im Städtischen Museum ist ein Modell der Stadt im 18. Jahrhundert.

6. Das Modell is used for an artist's model and for someone on whom a character in a play etc. is modelled.

Sie verdiente ihren Unterhalt als Modell bekannter Maler.

Eine Bekannte stand dem Maler Modell.

Ein Lehrer an seiner Schule diente dem Schriftsteller als Modell für die Hauptperson des Romans.

7. Das Modell is used for a dress etc. designed by someone. *Die Mannequins führten die neuen Modelle der Herbstkollektion vor.* The people who model such clothes are called **das Modell, das Mannequin**, or occasionally **die Vorführdame**. *Die Modelle betraten den Laufsteg.*

8. Model meaning 'a type of industrial product produced in large numbers' also corresponds to **das Modell**. *Er fährt immer das neueste Modell.* **Der Typ** is a common syn. *Zehn Autos desselben Typs.*

Dieses Modell läuft aus und ist deshalb billiger.

Dies ist das am meisten gekaufte/beliebteste Modell.

Dieser Typ hat sich zwar gut verkauft, aber man hat beschlossen, die Produktion einzustellen, und ihn durch ein neues Modell zu ersetzen.

9. A model is also 'a pers. worthy of imitation'. **Das Vorbild** is now used only in reference to people or qualities people display. *Dieser Sportler ist für viele junge Menschen ein Vorbild* or *ist ihnen [ein] Vorbild.* It usually refers to pos. qualities, but someone can be *ein schlechtes* as well as *ein gutes Vorbild.*

Sein Großvater galt ihm als nachahmenswertes Vorbild. Or Er sah/hatte in ihm ein . . . Vorbild.

Nimm dir diese Hilfsbereitschaft/diesen Mut ruhig zum Vorbild!

Sie fragte sich, ob sie dieses Vorbild jemals erreichen könnte.

Er hatte sich einen namhaften Künstler zum Vorbild gewählt.

10. As a n. and adj., **model** also denotes a perfect example of some quality. *The essay was a model of clarity.*

i. Das Muster is applied to something which is a perfect example of its kind and often has the connotation that it is worthy of imitation. *Jmd. ist ein Muster an Ausdauer/an Tapferkeit/an gutem Benehmen. Diese Übersetzung ist ein Muster an Genauigkeit.* Another word, which is often used ironically, is **das Musterbild**. *Er war ein Musterbild an Fleiß. Sie war ein Musterbild weiblicher Tugenden.* The [very] model of (a modern major-general) could be **das Musterbeispiel** or **das Musterexemplar**. *Er war ein Musterbeispiel für Treue/das Musterexemplar eines Bürokraten/eines modernen Generalmajors.*

ii. The adj., e.g. *a model student*, can be expressed by **musterhaft, vorbildlich**, or **mustergültig**, corresponding exactly to the (ideal) model, therefore perfect, exemplary, impeccable. *Sie ist eine musterhafte Hausfrau. Das ist eine musterhafte/ mustergültige Übersetzung. Dort herrschte musterhafte/vorbildliche/mustergültige Ordnung. Sein Verhalten ist vorbildlich.* There are a few compounds with *Muster* like *die Musterehe, der Musterschüler*, but they can be used with an undertone of irony. *A model farm* etc., one serving as a model of how it should be, is *der Musterhof.* Hence *der Musterbetrieb.*

pay *v.*

1. *Zahlen* and derivatives.

i. There is no difference in meaning between **zahlen** and **bezahlen**. Since G. vs.

beginning with *be-* are usually trans., it might be expected that *bezahlen* is trans. and *zahlen* intr., but this helps only to a limited extent. Although *bezahlen* often has an obj. and *zahlen* often occurs without one, both can be either trans. or intr. In restaurants it is usual to say, '[*Ich möchte*] *zahlen*' or '*Zahlen bitte!*', but both *Der Verlag zahlt nicht im voraus*, and *Jmd. zahlt/bezahlt immer regelmäßig/pünktlich* are possible.

> *Unverzüglich stand er auf, zahlte und verließ das Lokal.*
> *Sie zahlte/bezahlte in fremder Währung.*   *Sie zahlte/bezahlte bar/mit einem Scheck.*

ii. Bezahlen means 'to bring sth. into one's possession by paying the amount asked', 'to pay the price for goods, services, and work done'. *Man muß die Waren bei Ablieferung bezahlen.* It is also used for discharging an obligation such as a bill, instalment, the rent, or a debt. *Ich habe diese Rechnung/die Miete schon bezahlt.* It is usual in connection with shopping. *Mein Einkaufswagen ist voll—ich gehe jetzt zur Kasse, um zu bezahlen* (*zahlen* possible). It tends to be used with *Preis* as obj., *Er hat einen unverhältnismäßig hohen Preis bezahlt*, but *Einen so hohen Preis hätte ich nicht zahlen können* also occurs.

> *Nachdem ich meine Schulden bezahlt hatte, blieb mir vom Lohn sehr wenig übrig.*

iii. Zahlen originally denoted the action of handing over money. Although *zahlen* and *bezahlen* are often interchangeable, *zahlen* is preferred when the payment is voluntary without anything being given in return. In this sense, it is used mostly for (regular) payments to help others. It tends to be used with *die Gebühr, die Geldbuße, die* [*Geld*]*strafe, Steuern, ein* [*Jahres*]*beitrag,* 'membership fee', and *Zinsen* as obj. A dat. is used with either v. *Ich muß der Hauswirtin die Miete zahlen/bezahlen.*

> *Er zahlte seinen Eltern 200 Mark im Monat.*   *Auf Spareinlagen zahlt die Bank 3,5% Zinsen.*
> *Für Radfahren in der Fußgängerzone mußte er 10 Mark Strafe zahlen.*
> *Er zahlte dem Sohn 900 Mark im Monat, während er studierte.*

iv. With wages, **bezahlen** is often used. *Wir müssen ihn für seine Arbeit bezahlen. Ihre Tätigkeit wurde gut bezahlt.* However, *Die Firma zahlt gut, Dort werden hohe Löhne gezahlt*, and *Die Firma zahlt hohe Gehälter* are also common.

v. When the sent. states no more than what is being paid for, **pay for** is usually **bezahlen** + acc. *Ich habe das Essen/die Fahrkarte schon bezahlt. Für* is possible. *Ich habe für die Waren bar bezahlt* instead of *Ich habe die Waren bar bezahlt. Für* is only necessary when there is another obj., e.g. *viel, wenig, was,* an amount, or a person. *Ich habe 5 000 Mark für das Auto bezahlt. Ich habe nur sehr wenig dafür bezahlt. Was hast du dafür bezahlt? Wofür bezahle ich Sie denn?*

vi. Pay sth. **for** s.o. or **on** s.o.'s **behalf** is usually **bezahlen**. The person paid for can be dat. or be expressed by the gen. *Sie bezahlte der Tochter die Reise, damit sie nicht per Autostop zu fahren brauchte. Es fiel der Witwe schwer, die Ausbildung ihres Sohnes zu bezahlen.*

vii. *Die Löhne werden mittwochs gezahlt,* 'paid or handed out', is possible, but the normal v. for paying [out] wages etc. is **auszahlen**. *Man zahlt die Gehälter am letzten Tag des Monats aus. Löhne werden freitags ausgezahlt. Die Renten werden jeden zweiten Donnerstag ausgezahlt.*

2. Formal syns. of [*be*]*zahlen.* **Begleichen**, a formal word meaning 'to meet a financial obligation in full', is applied to bills, debts, and to what one owes. **Entrichten** is a bureaucratic word used for the payment of fees, contributions, tolls, etc. **Entlohnen**, a more formal and general term denoting payment for work, could in its stylistic level be compared to *to remunerate.* **Besolden** is used for the payment of civil servants and members of the armed forces. **Vergüten** is a bureaucratic term for payment of wages or salary. All these words can be replaced by *bezahlen.*

> *Er hat seine Schulden/die Rechnung beglichen.*

Anbei finden Sie einen Scheck zur Begleichung der Rechnung vom vorigen Quartal.
Diese Arbeiter werden nach Lohngruppe drei entlohnt.
Wir bitten Sie, diese Gebühr/den monatlichen Beitrag sofort zu entrichten.
Die staatlichen Behörden besolden ihre Angestellten nicht gut.
Der Direktor versicherte ihm, daß man seine Tätigkeit im Betrieb angemessen vergüten würde.

3. Colloquial words like *to cough up* or *fork out* are **blechen,** 'to pay usually more than one wants to', and **berappen,** 'to pay unwillingly'. While *blechen* suggests annoyance about unjustified expenses, *berappen* stresses the regret with which one hands over a sum of money. *Ich mußte 500 Mark für die Reparatur* **hinblättern** is also often heard in colloquial speech. It suggests having to pay a considerable amount.

Ich habe ganz schön viel dafür blechen müssen/100 Mark dafür blechen müssen.
Man muß tüchtig blechen, wenn man Mitglied in diesem Klub werden will.
Für diese Reparatur mußte ich 800 Mark berappen.
Dafür mußte ich eine große Summe hinblättern.

4. Pay for in the fig. sense, 'to endure the penalty for', can be translated by either **zahlen** or **bezahlen**. *Für ihre Unvorsichtigkeit zahlte sie mit einem Beinbruch* or *Sie bezahlte ihre Unvorsichtigkeit mit einem Beinbruch.* The specific word is **büßen** which is only used with *müssen, Für diesen Fehler mußte sie schwer büßen,* or in threats with *sollen. Das sollst du mir büßen* means 'you shall pay for that'. Such a threat could also be expressed by *Das werde ich dir heimzahlen,* I'll get my own back on you or I'll make you pay for that. Cf. also COSTLY 5.

Er mußte diesen Leichtsinn mit großen Schmerzen büßen.

people *n.*

1. People = 'the body of persons composing a tribe, community, race, or nation'. *The people of Scotland. The Ethiopian people.* **Das Volk** covers the same groups as the E. word, although it is now mostly used in reference to a nation. The pl. translates *peoples. Die englisch-sprechenden Völker.*

Nomadisierende Völker bewohnten damals das Küstengebiet.
Zur Zeit der ersten englischen Besiedlung des Landes waren die australischen Ureinwohner ein Volk von Jägern und Sammlern.   Die Schotten sind ein tapferes/seefahrendes Volk.
Ein friedliches Zusammenleben der europäischen Völker sollte doch möglich sein.

2. *Das Volk* also translates **people** in other senses.
i. 'People in relation to a superior'. In *Der König und sein Volk,* **Volk** means 'the population over which he rules'. (If only the people attending or accompanying him are meant, this is **das Gefolge.** *Der König und sein Gefolge verließen den Saal.*)
ii. Like *the common people,* **Volk** also means 'the mass of the (working) community as distinguished from the aristocracy or the ruling or official classes'.

Das arbeitende/einfache Volk.   Er stammt aus dem Volk.
Das Volk erhob sich gegen die Gewaltherrschaft.

iii. Like **people, Volk** denotes the electorate in a democratic state, the whole body of enfranchised citizens considered as the source of power. *Die Parlamentsabgeordneten sind die gewählten Vertreter des Volkes.* The constitutional principle is expressed as *Die Staatsgewalt* (or *Die Macht*) *geht vom Volk aus. Die Volksbefragung* is 'a plebiscite or referendum'. *Urteilsverkündungen* (pronouncements of judgment) in G. courts begin with the words *Im Namen des Volkes. To go to the people* means 'to call an election'. G. sents. expressing a similar meaning are *Die Regierung will vom Volk bestätigt werden* or *will ihr Mandat vom Volk neu bestätigen lassen* or *Die Regierung sucht vom Volk ein neues Mandat* .

3. Other senses of **people.** *a.* 'Those belonging to a place or constituting a particular company, class, or group'. *The people living near the river were evacuated. There* *were 120 people at the lecture/three people at the bus stop. There are some people who like that kind of music.* b. 'Men and women indefinitely'. *Crowds of people. There has been a complete change in people's ideas on the subject recently.* The G. equivalents are *die Leute* and *die Menschen*. Their uses spread over the two E. senses. Except in very general statements, the difference between *Menschen* and *Leute* is only slight, and often either is possible.

i. When a group of whatever kind, or people who can be regarded as belonging together in some way are meant, **die Leute** is used.

Zu dem Vortrag waren 123 Leute gekommen.
Ein paar Leute standen an der Bushaltestelle.
Ich habe fünf Leute eingeladen.
Heute habe ich nur wenig[e] Leute hier gesehen.　　*Viele Leute sind dagegen.*
Er hat die Sache zu ausführlich erklärt. Verschiedenen Leuten wurde die Erklärung zu lang.
Die Leute in den Großstädten sind anders als die Leute auf dem Lande.

Note, however, that when an adj. is present, **people** often need not be translated. *He spoke with the people affected* is *Er sprach mit den Betroffenen. Mit den betroffenen Leuten* would not be wrong, but unusual.

ii. Die Menschen means 'human beings'. It corresponds to **people** in the sense 'men and women indefinitely', when they are not thought of as forming a group, or in general statements about what people do/should [not] do, or about their characteristics. *Crowds of people* are *große Menschenmengen* or *Massen von Menschen*. Someone might say, *'Der Platz war voll von Menschen',* but in a different situation see them as a group and use *die Leute auf dem Platz. Die Menschen sollten freundlich zueinander sein* is the only possibility, as human beings in general are meant. Only *Mensch* forms compounds: *die Renaissancemenschen, Durchschnittsmenschen, Großstadtmenschen,* or *Gewaltmenschen. Land und Leute kennenlernen* is a fixed expression.

Alte und Junge/Arme und reiche Leute/Menschen haben verschiedene Interessen.
Viele Leute/Menschen glauben jeden Unsinn.　　*Tausende von Menschen strömten zum Festplatz.*
Den meisten Leuten/Menschen fällt es schwer, eine zehnminütige Rede zu halten.

Mensch is often used to state what kind of man or woman someone is (cf. MAN, WOMAN), and the pl. is used in the same way. *Alle drei sind liebenswürdige Menschen. Es sind zuverlässige/kluge Menschen.*

Von Leuten/Menschen dieses Schlages kann man nichts anderes erwarten.

iii. When **people** means 'the population of a village etc.', it is often best to use **die Bevölkerung**.

Die Bevölkerung von Kleinkleckersdorf mußte evakuiert werden.

4. People means 'the public (in a certain locality)'.

i. Where E. has **people**, G. uses **die Leute**. Hence expressions like *Die Leute sagen/behaupten, daß es alles Betrug sei,* and *Die Leute reden über uns*. The idiom *vor allen Leuten* means 'in public, in view of everyone'. *Sie zeigte sich vor allen Leuten. Er hat mich vor allen Leuten einen Idioten genannt.*

Die Verhältnisse liegen anders, als die Leute allgemein annehmen/als man allgemein annimmt.
Was die Leute über diese Frage denken, hat sich in letzter Zeit erheblich geändert.

ii. Man can express the meaning of *die Leute* but does not suggest a specific group. *People tell me I should be an actor* is *Man sagt mir, ich sollte Schauspieler werden. Man sagt, es sei alles Betrug. Über diese Frage denkt man anders als vor zehn Jahren.*

5. Leute like **people** can mean 'employees or subordinates' and 'relatives or family'.

Der Meister rief seine Leute zusammen.　　*Der Hauptmann kommt mit seinen Leuten gut aus.*
Meine Leute leben alle auf dem Lande und freuen sich, wenn ich sie besuche.

persistent, stubborn, dogged *adjs.* **Persistent** means 'continuing firmly in some action'. Whether it expresses praise or criticism depends on what follows. In *his persistent efforts* or *She is persistent in her efforts*, it expresses praise, but not in *a persistent trouble-maker*. While **dogged** connotes great and unwavering determination, **stubborn** in one sense means 'unreasonably or perversely obstinate', and in another the point of view expressed depends on the context. *Stubborn resistance to oppression* is praiseworthy, but *stubborn resistance to reason* is not.

i. Applied to people, **beharrlich** means 'pursuing an aim or sticking to one's efforts, opinion, etc. firmly and steadily'. It suggests a positive attitude on the part of the speaker to the person spoken about and to what he or she is doing. It is also applied to qualities like diligence, or to work and efforts, and means 'constant, unceasing, dogged, or persistent'.

Sie setzten den Kampf gegen die Korruption beharrlich fort.
Er weigerte sich beharrlich, diese Kosten zu übernehmen, da er sie für ungerechtfertigt hielt.
Sie fuhren fort, mit beharrlichem Fleiß zu arbeiten.
Ihre beharrlichen Bemühungen führten schließlich zum Erfolg.

ii. While *beharrlich* expresses a pos. attitude, **hartnäckig** varies according to the context and can have a neg. colouring. It can thus translate **stubborn** both in pos. and neg. contexts. It also translates **persistent** describing objectionable qualities and applied to illnesses. *Ein hartnäckiger Schnupfen.*

Ich wunderte mich über ihre hartnäckige Weigerung, diesen Menschen zu helfen.
Die Verteidiger leisteten hartnäckigen Widerstand.
Nachdem er einen Monat lang seine Schuld hartnäckig geleugnet hatte, gestand er plötzlich.

iii. Verbissen means 'sticking tenaciously to sth.' which can be either good or bad.
Mit verbissener Energie arbeitete sie an ihrer Erfindung.
Mit verbissenem Trotz starrte er vor sich hin.   *Die Mannschaft kämpfte verbissen um den Sieg.*

iv. Verstockt suggests sticking to unreasonable behaviour or attitudes and unwillingness to see or be touched by reason. *Ein verstockter Sünder*, unrepentant. *Er blieb verstockt und wollte nicht gestehen.*

v. Stur is colloquial and mildly pejorative. It means 'sticking unyieldingly to sth.' and often suggests mental inflexibility. *Diese Beamten handeln stur nach Vorschrift.*
Wenn er nicht will, kann er furchtbar stur sein.
Wir wollten ihn davon abbringen, aber er blieb stur.

vi. Stubborn meaning 'unreasonably obstinate' has several equivalents. **Eigensinnig, starrköpfig**, and **halsstarrig** belong to the standard language and mean 'insisting on one's own will or opinion', 'unwilling to yield to reason'. **Dickköpfig** and **dickschädelig** are colloquial.
Sie bestand eigensinnig auf ihrer Meinung.   *Die beiden waren zu dickköpfig, um nachzugeben.*
Es war ihm unmöglich, diesen starrköpfigen Alten umzustimmen.
Trotz aller Warnungen bestand der Kapitän halsstarrig auf Einhaltung des Kurses.

---

persuade, convince *vs.* Senses: (i) **persuade** means 'to prevail on a pers. by advice, urging, reasons, inducements, etc. to do sth.' It usually takes an infin., *She persuaded me to go to the concert*, but is occasionally found with *into* + gerund, *He is the sort of man who can be persuaded into doing anything.* (ii) **Persuade** also means 'to induce s.o. to believe sth., to convince or cause s.o. to accept sth. as true'. *We worked hard to persuade them of the benefits of co-operation/that we were genuinely interested in the project. I had persuaded myself that I could continue indefinitely like this.* Hence the use in formal language of the past part. *I am persuaded that this is useful work.* (iii) **Convince** s.o. is 'to cause him or her to admit as true what is advanced as argument' or 'to persuade s.o. by argument or evidence that sth. is true or should be done'. It either takes a clause or *of. He convinced us of his innocence/that he was innocent. It is never difficult to convince oneself of what one wants to believe.* (iv) In reference to actions, **convince** is a syn. of sense i of **persuade** and is used either with a clause containing *should, We convinced her that she should go to a lawyer,* or sometimes with an infin., *Powerful advertising can convince/persuade people to buy almost anything.*

1. When **persuade** has sense i and **convince** sense iv, the chief equivalent is **überreden**. It is used with *zu* and a n. denoting an action or an infin. *Sie hat mich zum Mitkommen überredet/hat mich überredet mitzukommen.* To persuade s.o. into doing sth. has to be turned into one of these constructions, usually an infin. *Gewisse Menschen kann man überreden, alles zu machen.*

> Ich möchte Sie doch nicht zum Kauf einer Waschmaschine überreden, sondern Ihnen lediglich die Vorzüge unseres Produkts darlegen.   Er ließ sich überreden, mit ins Theater zu kommen.
> Mit allen Tricks versuchten sie, mich zu überreden, doch mitzukommen.

2. Überzeugen means 'convince' in sense iii and 'persuade' in sense ii, i.e. 'to induce s.o. by arguments to acknowledge sth. as true or necessary'. It is used with an obj. only, *Wir konnten sie nur schwer überzeugen,* with *von, Er überzeugte uns von seiner Unschuld,* or with *davon, daß, Es muß gelingen, die Raucher davon zu überzeugen, daß ihre Sucht ihre Arbeitskollegen gefährdet.* The *davon, daß* construction means 'to convince s.o. of a fact' and can only be adapted to persuading someone to do something by adding *daß es notwendig/ratsam ist. Sie hat mich davon überzeugt, daß es notwendig war, zu einem Rechtsanwalt zu gehen.* This meaning could also be expressed as *Sie hat mich von der Notwendigkeit weiterer Schritte überzeugt. Ich bin [davon] überzeugt* means 'I am convinced/persuaded'. Note that *sich von etw. überzeugen* also means 'to SATISFY oneself about sth. which is real or factual'. Cf. *sich etw. einreden* under 5.

> Es war schwierig, ihn von der Durchführbarkeit des Projekts zu überzeugen.
> Die Regierung wollte die Wähler davon überzeugen, daß ihre Wirtschaftspolitik die einzig richtige war.
> Ich bin [davon] überzeugt, daß du recht hast.

3. Zureden means 'to talk to s.o. with the aim of getting him or her to react in a certain way'. The word suggests that the aim has a pos. value, but does not imply success in attaining it. When persuasion is implied, it means 'to try to persuade'. Thus *Er redete mir zu, das Auto zu kaufen,* tried to persuade me to buy or talk me into buying the car. *Zureden* often means 'to encourage' or 'to speak words of comfort to'. *Sie redete mir gut/aufmunternd zu,* encouraged me.

> Alles Zureden nutzte nichts. (All persuasion was to/of no avail.)
> Sie war eine gute Krankenschwester: Immer nahm sie sich Zeit, den Patienten zuzureden, nicht den Kopf hängen zu lassen.   Auf Zureden seiner Freunde nahm er das Stipendium an.
> Nach dem Unfall redete er ihr gut zu, und sie überwand den Schock.

4. Bequatschen, beschwatzen, and **bereden** are colloquial words suggesting that someone persistently tries to talk another into doing something that the other would be well advised not to do. *Beschwatzen* may imply trickery. **Herumkriegen** means 'to talk around'. **Breitschlagen** means 'to overcome s.o.'s opposition to a plan or request by continuous persuasion' but belongs to familiar language used only among friends.

> Wie hast du es nur wieder geschafft, ihn zu bequatschen, mit ins Kino zu gehen?
> Ich bequatschte meinen Vater einfach so lange, bis er mir den Mantel kaufte.
> Sie konnte einen jeden beschwatzen, ihr behilflich zu sein.
> Er war leicht zu bereden, wenn es darum ging, einen Ausflug zu machen.
> Ich werde Mutter schon herumkriegen, daß sie uns erlaubt, bis zwei Uhr wegzubleiben.
> Er hat seinen Vater breitgeschlagen, ihm das Auto fürs Wochenende zu überlassen.

5. Auf jmdn. einreden means 'to talk persistently to s.o.' The aim may be persuasion, but it could be to get one's views etc. over. Out of context *Sie redete eine* *halbe Stunde auf mich ein* leaves the purpose open, whereas *Er redete derart auf mich ein, daß ich am Ende nicht wußte, wo mir der Kopf stand, und den Wagen kaufte* suggests persuasion. **Jmdm. etw. einreden** is 'to make s.o. believe sth. which is false'. *So einen Unsinn lasse ich mir doch nicht einreden.* **Sich** (dat.) **etw. einreden** therefore means 'to make oneself believe sth. wrong' or 'to convince or persuade oneself of sth. false'. *Es geschah immer wieder, daß er sich einredete, etw. zu können, und sich dabei maßlos überschätzte. Das hast du dir selbst eingeredet.* **Jmdm. einreden** + infin. or clause means 'to induce or persuade s.o. to believe sth. or to act in a certain way', but here, too, the implication is that what is urged is false or not in the person's best interest. *Sie hatte ihm eingeredet, sich zunächst ruhig zu verhalten* suggests at least that this proved to be unwise.

> *Durch Werbekampagnen kann man den Leuten einreden, alle möglichen Waren zu kaufen/ . . . den Leuten einreden, daß sie alle möglichen Waren besitzen müssen.*
> *Hitler redete einer ganzen Generation ein, daß Deutschland unbesiegbar wäre.*
> *Immer wieder redete er sich ein, daß das Blatt sich doch noch einmal wenden würde.*
> *Er redete ihr ein, nur Vertrauen zu ihm zu haben; danach hat er sie bitter enttäuscht.*
> *Etw., was man gern glauben möchte, redet man sich leicht ein.*

6. Jmdn. bewegen zu, 'to induce s.o. to do sth.', is a formal syn. of *überreden* when a person is the subj. *Wir konnten sie nicht zur Teilnahme an der Veranstaltung bewegen/sie nicht [dazu] bewegen, an der Veranstaltung teilzunehmen. Alle versuchten, ihn zum Bleiben zu bewegen.* It is often used with a non-personal subj. and could be translated as *induce*, *lead*, or **convince**. *Der Erfolg des ersten Films bewog den Produzenten, einen zweiten drehen zu lassen.*

place *n.*

1. For the concept 'a particular part of space where a pers. or thg. is or where sth. happens', G. has two words, *der Ort* and *die Stelle*, which have some specific senses, but overlap in others.

i. **Der Ort** denotes a place or location in a broad and general way, somewhere where s.o./sth. is, or somewhere where something has happened or is to happen. **Die Stelle** is more precise, suggesting a fairly exactly known and usually relatively small place within a larger space or area. It corresponds to *spot* as well as to **place**. Unlike *Ort*, *Stelle* indicates a place or spot in relation to its surroundings and suggests that the special nature of the locality is known, but in this sense it often makes little difference which is used. *An diesem Ort* means 'in this place' and expresses the same meaning as *an dieser Stelle*, although it is less precise. *An diesem Ort/An dieser Stelle haben wir uns zum erstenmal getroffen.* In stating where something happened, *Stelle* would be used when *Ort* could be understood as a town etc. Cf. 1. ii. When there is no danger of misinterpretation, either is possible, but *Stelle* remains more precise. *Das ist der Ort, wo das Verbrechen geschah. Dies ist die Stelle, wo das Verbrechen verübt wurde.* Only *Ort* is followed by a gen. *Die Polizei gibt keine Auskunft über den Ort des Verbrechens.* There is only one compound, *der Tatort*, the scene of the crime.

> *Man sucht die Stelle, wo das Flugzeug abstürzte.*
> *An windgeschützten Orten/Stellen blühen schon die Apfelbäume.*
> *An der Stelle, wo wir eben noch gestanden hatten, schlug der Blitz ein.*
> *Ich kann nicht zur gleichen Zeit an zwei Orten/Stellen sein.*
> *An dieser Stelle geschah der Unfall. Er wurde an dieser Stelle überfallen.*
> *X kennzeichnet die Stelle, wo der Schatz vergraben ist.*

ii. Like **place**, *Ort* refers to a larger area like a city, town, or village. *Seine Familie und meine stammen aus demselben Ort. In diesem Ort* normally suggests a town. **Eine**

Ortschaft means 'a settlement, village, or small town' and sometimes translates **place**. *Eine große/größere/kleine Ortschaft. Die Geschwindigkeits-begrenzung gilt in geschlossenen Ortschaften. Die Ganze Ortschaft weiß es schon.*

iii. Der Ort is used with a precise sense for arranging a place for a meeting or for meeting someone. *Die nächste Sitzung findet in vier Wochen statt; Ort und genaue Zeit teilen wir Ihnen später mit. Wir treffen uns morgen um neun am vereinbarten Ort. Wir müssen einen Ort ausmachen, wo wir uns treffen. Die Stelle* is also possible in the last two sents. *Ich wartete an der ausgemachten/vereinbarten Stelle.* (Also *Wir machen einen Treffpunkt aus,* this being the usual word for a place where people arrange to meet.)

iv. *Ort* does not denote a (precise) place in or on something else, for which in E. both **place** and *spot* are possible. *A place/spot in the forest.* This can only be **eine Stelle** *im Wald.* Thus *An zwei Stellen ist der Bergpfad gefährlich. Die Stelle* is also a particular place on a surface either of the body or of some other object.

> *An meinem Bein ist noch eine schmerzhafte Stelle.*
> *An dem Teppich sind einige schadhafte/abgenutzte Stellen.*

2. i. Die Stelle denotes a place in a book etc. where someone has left off reading, playing music, etc. *To mark a place in a book* where one has got to is usually *die Seite markieren.*

> *Ich kann die Stelle nicht finden, wo ich aufgehört habe zu lesen.*

ii. Die Stelle also means 'a place or part' in the sense of 'a passage or section in a book, piece of music, etc.'

> *An anderer Stelle schildert der Autor diese Erscheinung ausführlicher.*
> *Diese Stelle der Symphonie höre ich besonders gern.*   *An den traurigen Stellen weint sie immer.*
> *Ich mußte ein paar Stellen der Sonate immer wieder üben.*
> *An zahlreichen Stellen der Rede haben die Zuhörer gelacht.*

3. When **place** means 'a position or space which is or appears suitable for a pers. to pursue some activity in or for a thg. to be put', 'a space occupied by or reserved for a pers. or thg.', it corresponds to **der Platz**. *Wir suchten uns einen [freien] Platz am Strand. Das ist der geeignete Platz für den großen Schrank/für das Haus/für den Komposthaufen.* (In *Hier ist noch Platz für den Schrank, Platz* means 'ROOM'.) When *Platz* has the sense 'an area for carrying on an activity', the E. equivalent is not always *place.* While *der Marktplatz* is 'the market-place', *Spielplätze* are 'playgrounds', and *Sportplätze* are 'sportsgrounds'. *Platz* can refer to a seat in a hall, theatre, classroom, etc. or to a place assigned to someone whether to sit, stand, or whatever. *Der Schüler ging zu seinem Platz zurück. Dieser Platz ist belegt. Die Anwesenden erhoben sich von ihren Plätzen. Sind hier Plätze frei? My place in a queue is mein Platz in einer Schlange. Nehmen Sie Platz!* means 'take a seat', while *Nehmen Sie Ihre Plätze ein!* is 'take up your positions' whether these are seats or positions to stand in. Hence *Die Spieler nahmen ihre Plätze auf dem Spielfeld ein* and *Auf Ihre Plätze! Fertig! Los!*

> *Der Schüler überließ der alten Dame seinen Platz.*
> *In der Mailänder Oper gibt es Sitz- und Stehplätze.*
> *Für die Vorstellung heute abend gibt es nur noch teure Plätze.*

When the idea of purpose is not important, **die Stelle** can also be used. *Die Stelle, wo wir am Strand gesessen haben, ist nur bei Ebbe frei.*

4. i. Place and **der Platz** both express the meaning 'the proper, normal, or natural position for a pers. or thg.' *Jmd. findet seinen Platz im Leben. Dein Platz ist hier bei uns. Das Buch steht nicht an seinem Platz.* In reference to things. *Platz* is often qualified by adjs. like *richtig* or *recht. Stelle die Vase an ihren/den richtigen Platz [zurück]! Ich stelle das Buch an den rechten Platz.* There are some alternatives. **Der Ort** can denote the proper place if the sense is clear from the context. *Der ordentliche Mensch hat für alles einen Ort. Stelle das Geschirr wieder an seinen Ort!* **Die Stelle** can be used with a possessive, *Stell' das Buch an seine Stelle zurück!*, but *Platz* is more common in this use than either *Stelle* or *Ort*. *Stelle* is usually found with an adj. *Stell' das Buch an die richtige Stelle zurück! Die Vase stand gestern an einer anderen Stelle. Er hat die Sachen an die falsche Stelle gelegt.* In one sense **an Ort und Stelle** means 'in the right/proper place or in place/position'. *Alles ist an Ort und Stelle. Stell' die Sachen wieder an Ort und Stelle! Alle Ordner sind wieder an ihren Plätzen* and *sind wieder an Ort und Stelle* express the same meaning. (In *etw. an Ort und Stelle untersuchen* the phr. means 'on the spot, in the place where it has happened/is happening'. *Schon fünf Minuten nach dem Unfall war die Polizei an Ort und Stelle*.)

ii. Platz translates s.o.'s **place** in literature etc. *Diesen Dramen gebührt ein bedeutender Platz in der Literaturgeschichte.* S.o.'s **place** or POSITION *in society* is, however, **jmds. Stellung** *in der Gesellschaft*.

iii. In their fig. senses **not in place** and **out of place** mean 'unsuitable or inappropriate', or for people, 'not fitting comfortably into a situation'. The equivalents are **nicht am Platz[e]** or **fehl am Platz[e]**. *Diese Bemerkung war nicht/fehl am Platze. Er fühlte sich in dieser Gesellschaft fehl am Platze.* The pos. is occasionally found, but only in reply to the contrary statement. If one person says, *'Dieser Vorschlag war fehl am Platze'*, another could answer, *'Er war doch am Platze'* or *'Er war sehr wohl am Platze.'*

5. Der Platz is applied to the order in which contestants or competitors complete a race etc. *Jmd. belegte den ersten/zweiten Platz*, took first/second place, was first/second. **Die Stelle** is used when the position at a certain time during the competition is given, when the idea of winning is not involved. *Unsere Ruderer waren [zu der Zeit] an zweiter Stelle. Von den Bewerbern steht einer an erster Stelle.* This construction is also used to state in what order competitors passed the post or crossed the line. *Er ging an zweiter Stelle/als zweiter durchs Ziel.*

6. Place = 'house'. *Come round to our place!* is usually *Kommen Sie mal zu uns!* I'm *going to Jim's [place]* is *Ich gehe zu Jim.* At *Jim's [place]* is *bei Jim.*

7. Place can mean 'duty or responsibility' in a sent. like *It's your place to see that junior members of staff arrive on time.* This meaning can be conveyed by **die Aufgabe** or **die Sache**. *Es ist Ihre Aufgabe/Ihre Sache, dafür zu sorgen, daß die jüngeren Mitarbeiter rechtzeitig zur Arbeit kommen. Es ist Ihre Sache, sich um Ihre Gäste zu kümmern.*

8. Die Stätte is an elevated term for a place which has a special significance because some important event happened there, *historische Stätten in Deutschland*, or because an important ceremony takes place there, or because it serves a purpose which is in some way out of the ordinary. Compounds are e.g. *die Kultstätte* and *die Gedenkstätte*. What the Australian Aborigines call sacred sites are in G. *heilige Stätten*. **Der Ort** is also applied to a place which has some unusual significance, but it concentrates attention more on what it stands for than on the place. *Eilends verließ er diesen Ort des Grauens.*

> *Die Kirche war die heilige Stätte, um die sich die kleine Gemeinde scharte.*
> *Der Aufstand verwandelte die Stadt in eine Stätte des Entsetzens.*
> *Er kehrte in Gedanken noch einmal an den Ort seiner glücklichsten Kinderjahre zurück.*

9. Take the place of. If the meaning is 'displace', it is expressed by **verdrängen** or **ersetzen**. *Plastik hat viele andere Stoffe verdrängt/ersetzt.* If *to take s.o.'s place in an organization* means 'to be s.o.'s successor', **übernehmen** or **bekommen** can be used. *Wer wird seine Stelle im Betrieb übernehmen/bekommen?* **An die Stelle von etw. treten** means 'to take the place of sth., be substituted for it.' *Die UNO trat an die Stelle des früheren Völkerbundes. Plastik ist an die Stelle von vielen anderen Stoffen getreten.*

10. Some other expressions. *In your place* = 'if I were you'. *An deiner Stelle würde ich das Angebot annehmen. People in high places: Hochgestellte/Einflußreiche Personen.* The right man in the right place is in colloquial speech *Der rechte Mann am rechten Fleck*, and more formally *. . . am rechten Platz. Put yourself in my place/position!: Versetzen Sie sich in meine Lage! His thgs.* were lying/scattered all over the place is *Seine Sachen lagen überall herum [wie Kraut und Rüben].* This/That is the best place to buy G. books in Sydney could be *In Sydney kauft man deutsche Bücher am besten hier/dort/in diesem Geschäft.*

pool, puddle, pond *ns.* A public swimming pool is **das Schwimmbad**. An open air pool is called **ein Freibad**, an enclosed one **ein Hallenbad**. Each pool in such a complex is called **ein Becken**, *das Kinderbecken, das Planschbecken.* Signs say *Nicht vom Beckenrand springen!* A private swimming pool can be called *ein Schwimmbad*, but the E. term is often found, *eine Villa mit* **Swimming-pool**.
Der Teich can be an artifically constructed pond, *ein Fischteich im Garten*, or a natural one, i.e. a small lake. It implies fresh, clear water, being fed by a stream, possibly with fish. **Der Tümpel**, which is only found in certain types of terrain, suggests stagnant and dirty water, often reeds, sometimes mouldering vegetation, and little life except frogs. **Der Pfuhl** is smaller than a *Tümpel* but often consists more of mud than of water. It may be a spot which rain turns to mud, or it may be a water-hole which is drying out. **Die Pfütze** is a puddle, an accumulation of water in a small depression. *Alle Pfützen sind während der Nacht zugefroren.* **Die Lache** is an accumulation of liquid on a flat surface. *Die Blutlache* is 'a pool of blood', but *Lache* is also used for rain-water. It suggests a small stretch or sheet of water on a fairly even surface.
> Der einzig[e] erhaltengebliebene Teil des alten Wassergrabens ist jetzt ein Schwanenteich.
> Der Urwald bestand aus absterbenden Riesenbäumen, sumpfigen Tümpeln und undurchdringlichem Gestrüpp. Vor mir lag ein schwarzer, morastiger Pfuhl.
> Der Verwundete lag in einer Lache von Blut. Ich bin mitten in eine Pfütze getreten.
> Das Wasser stand in Lachen auf der Straße. Ich mußte über die Wasserlachen springen.

popular *adj.*
1. Something that is popular is enjoyed or liked by most people, and a person who is popular is liked by most people or by most people in a group.
i. There are two main equivalents, **beliebt** and **populär**. In reference to people who are popular with those belonging to a group, *beliebt* tends to be used. *Der Lehrer ist bei seinen Schülern sehr beliebt. Populär* on the other hand means 'liked by the majority of the population'. *Herbert Wehner war ein populärer Politiker.* In reference to films, books, songs, games, etc. *populär* tends to be used when something is new and catches on, while *beliebt* tends to be used for things which have maintained their popularity over a period of time. Thus *populär* is often found with *werden.*
> Onkel Herbert ist der beliebteste Mann in der Familie.
> Claudia ist unter ihren Bekannten sehr beliebt.
> Monopoly ist ein in vielen Kreisen beliebtes Spiel.
> Dieser Schauspieler ist durch eine Fernsehserie populär geworden.
> Nach den Verkaufszahlen zu urteilen, ist Der Name der Rose schnell populär geworden.
> Die Lorelei ist ein bekanntes und bei vielen Menschen beliebtes Lied.
> Das Werk des vor einigen Jahren verstorbenen Künstlers Joseph Beuys ist zur Zeit sehr populär.
ii. **Volkstümlich** means 'corresponding in sentiments, thinking, manner, and behaviour to that of the general run of people'. It is applied to highly placed people who think and act like the majority of the population, *ein volkstümlicher Herrscher*, to *Dichter*, and to *Lieder, Balladen, Tänze*, etc. In the last two contexts the

word has declined in use and now often suggests something popular in a peasant or rural culture. *Die volkstümlichen Bezeichnungen für Pflanzen* are the terms used in everyday language.

2. The other senses of **popular** must be expressed in different ways.

i. Popular *ideas* or *attitudes* meaning 'those approved of or held by most people', could be **weit verbreitete** *Ansichten. Contrary to* **popular** *belief* could be *im Gegensatz zur weitverbreiteten Ansicht/Meinung/Annahme.* **Allgemein**, 'general', would be an alternative. *The* **popular** *cry for a scapegoat* could be *der allgemeine Schrei nach einem Sünderbock.*

ii. Popular also means 'involving all the people'. *Popular government* is *die Regierung durch das Volk, die Volksherrschaft,* or simply *die Demokratie. This issue deserves wide popular debate* could be *Diese Frage verdient, in der breiten Öffentlichkeit/unter allen Schichten der Bevölkerung diskutiert zu werden.* Note *die Basisdemokratie*, grass-roots democracy.

iii. In *a popular presentation of a topic* **popular** means 'aimed at the needs of the general public rather than specialists'. The general term is **allgemeinverständlich.** A syn. is **populärwissenschaftlich.**

> *Diesen Herbst kamen wieder viele populärwissenschaftliche Bücher auf den Markt.*
> *Oft werden im Fernsehen populärwissenschaftliche Sendungen, z. B. über die Gefährdung der Ozonschicht, gezeigt.*
> *Die Universität veranstaltet allgemeinverständliche Vorträge über verschiedene Themen.*
> *Das Buch beschreibt die neuesten Entwicklungen in der Physik in allgemeinverständlicher Sprache.*

position, situation *ns.*

1. E. **position** means 'the exact place where sth. or s.o. is or stands', either permanently or at a particular time.

i. The **position** of a building or the (geographical) **position** of a town, area, etc., i.e. 'its exact and permanent location', is **die Lage.**

> *Das Geschäft/Die Gaststätte hat eine verkehrsgünstige Lage.*
> *Das Haus hat eine schöne Lage am Waldrand.*   *In höheren Lagen ist mit Frost zu rechnen.*

ii. In reference to people in a sent. like *We had a good* **position** *from which we could see the whole procession,* the usual equivalent is **der Platz** or **die Stelle**, which are discussed under PLACE 1, 3, and 4. There is often little difference between them. *Stelle* denotes a position in a neutral way while *Platz* may suggest a purpose. *Wir hatten einen guten Platz, von dem aus wir den ganzen Umzug sehen konnten,* or . . . *eine gute Stelle . . . They took up their positions* becomes *Sie nahmen ihre Plätze ein. In position* is *am richtigen Platz* or *an ihren richtigen Plätzen,* and **out of position** is *nicht am richtigen Platz* or the other expressions given under PLACE 4. *Slightly out of position* could be *leicht verschoben.* (*Verschieben* = 'to displace', 'put out of position'.)

2. Other words meaning 'the place where s.o./sth. is or stands' belong more to specialist language.

i. As a military term, **der Standort** denotes the place or barracks where a unit is permanently stationed. *Der Standort der Garnison liegt an einem See.* In a military context **die Stellung** denotes a defensive position at or near the front line where dugouts or trenches are made and gun-posts set up in order to stop an enemy's advance. *Der Stellungskrieg* is a war waged by armies in such *Stellungen.*

> *Die Soldaten hoben eine Stellung aus und tarnten sie.*
> *Die Truppen bezogen neue Stellungen/verteidigten ihre Stellung/belegten die gegnerischen Stellungen mit Feuer.*

Die Position is also a military term but suggests the place where someone is, rather than a fortified position. *Die Truppen haben ihre vorgeschriebene Position eingenommen.*

ii. In one sense, **der Posten** is 'the post or position of a sentry or guard'. *Die Wachen bezogen ihre Posten.*

iii. Die Position is now frequently used for the position of a ship, aircraft, etc. at a particular time, *die Position eines Schiffes/eines Satelliten/eines Flugzeugs*, but **Standort** still occurs.

> *Der Pilot ließ sich vom Kontrollturm seine Position/seinen Standort geben.*
> *Der Kapitän berechnete den Standort/die Position des Schiffes.*

iv. Die Stellung is used for the position of stars and planets, but **Position** is also possible. *Die Stellung der Planeten zur Sonne/der Gestirne am Himmel.*

v. Der Standort is used on maps displayed in public to give the position of the person looking at them. It also means 'the site for a building etc.' *Man sucht einen Standort für die geplante Fabrik/für das Denkmal.* It can also refer to people. In *jmd. nahm seinen Standort ein*, the formal term *Standort* replaces the everyday *Platz*. It might be found in a document setting out someone's duties. *Nur im Notfall darf der Kranführer seinen Standort verlassen.* (*Die Position* is a *Fremdwort* for the same idea. *Er bezog seine Position am Eingang.*) *Standort* is used, again in specialist language, for the position of a tree etc. *Die Pflanze braucht einen sonnigen Standort* and *Die Lichtung ist ein guter Standort für Eichen* might occur in formal style, but someone considering positions in a garden for a shrub or tree would be more likely to use *die Stelle* or to rephrase the idea completely.

vi. In one sense **der Stand** denotes where someone or something stands, but it is confined to a few expressions, *der Stand des Beobachters/des Jägers,* and *der Stand der Sonne.* **Position** is also used. *Das ist eine ungünstige Position für einen Beobachter. Ein Stand für Taxis* is 'a stand or rank'.

3. E. **position** also denotes the way someone or something is placed or arranged. It can refer to the position of the body, *to sit/lie in a comfortable position*, or the way a technical device or a word is placed, *the position of the lever/signal.* **Die Lage** can only refer to things which have a more or less horizontal position or to the way a person lies. *Wir müssen den Balken in die waagerechte Lage bringen. Der Kranke wurde in eine bequeme Lage gebracht.* For other positions of the body or for that of a technical device, **die Stellung** is used. Thus *Jmd. ist in kniender/gekrümmter/gebückter/unbequemer Stellung, nimmt eine andere Stellung ein,* or *[ver]ändert die Stellung.* Also *die Stellung einer Weiche/eines Signals. Die Wortstellung* is 'the position of a word in a sent.' (*Die Wortfolge* is 'the sequence of words'. *Die Wortfolge im Englischen ist meist Subjekt, Verb, Objekt.*) For the bearing or position of the body, cf. also *Haltung* under ATTITUDE.

> *Die Hebel müssen alle in gleicher Stellung sein.*
> *Die Stellungen der Uhrzeiger ändern sich ständig.*
> *An der Stellung des Schalters sieht man, ob die Maschine unter Strom steht.*

4. E. **position** is also applied to the degree of respect someone enjoys, someone's rank or place in relation to others in employment or society. The usual G. word for this sense is **die Stellung**, though **die Position** is also possible. Thus *jmds. gesellschaftliche Stellung, die Stellung der Frau in der Gesellschaft, jmds. Stellung im Betrieb/in der Partei,* or *die Stellung der Bundesrepublik innerhalb der Europäischen Union.* An alternative is **der Rang**, which can refer to someone's position in a hierarchical organization, *Er hat einen niedrigen/hohen Rang im diplomatischen Dienst,* and also in society, *Alle wurden ohne Rücksicht auf ihren gesellschaftlichen Rang behandelt.* When E. **position** implies a high position, *hoch* must be added. A transl. of *people of wealth and position* can be *wohlhabende Leute von hohem Rang* or *wohlhabende/reiche und hochgestellte Personen.*

> *Der beste Maßstab für die Kultur eines Volks ist die Stellung der Frau in dem Land.*

Er hat auf seine Stellung in der Gesellschaft zu achten.
Unter den Wissenschaftlern dieses Fachgebiets nimmt sie eine hervorragende Stellung ein.
Alle wurden in der gleichen Weise behandelt ohne Rücksicht auf ihren gesellschaftlichen Rang.

5. E. **position** also means 'a state of being advantageously placed with respect to others in war or in any kind of struggle or contest'. It is used alone, but *good* or *bad* can be added. *They were manœuvring for position (in war/at chess). We were in a good/bad position to attack.* In this sense **die Position** is used, but it always needs an adj. like *gut* or *schlecht* or a gen. like *Position der Stärke.*

Sie versuchten, sich in eine möglichst günstige Position zu bringen.
Er befindet sich seinem Hauptkonkurrenten gegenüber in einer starken/schwachen/aussichtslosen Position.   Wir befanden uns in keiner guten Position, um einen Angriff zu beginnen.
Bei den Verhandlungen hatten die Arbeitgeber eine starke Position.

6. Be in a position to do sth. is **in der Lage sein, etw. zu tun.** *Er ist durchaus in der Lage, einen wertvollen Beitrag zu leisten. I am not in a position to do sth.* is thus *Ich würde Ihnen gerne helfen, bin aber im Augenblick nicht dazu in der Lage.*

7. For *in your* **position** and *to put oneself in s.o.'s* **position** see PLACE 10.

8. For **position** meaning 'attitude or opinion' as in *The government's position on this issue has not changed,* the usual word would be **der Standpunkt.** Cf. ATTITUDE 2. iii. **Die Position** is also used. *Welche Position nimmt sie in dieser Sache ein?*

9. Both E. words **position** and **situation** refer to a state of affairs or circumstances, especially at a certain time. *That puts me in a difficult position. She felt pleased with herself at having coped with the situation so well. The economic situation. The position/situation is that our legal advisers are happy. After the Napoleonic wars, the position/situation of farm labourers worsened further.* There are two G. words, **die Lage** and **die Situation**, which are practically synonymous. Some people prefer *Situation* for the situation or position of one or more person and *Lage* for a broad non-personal state of affairs, but this is not a firm rule, and in most cases either is possible. *Was würden Sie in meiner Situation tun? Die finanzielle Lage des Unternehmens hat sich verbessert.* In certain contexts other words are used. In a question like *What is the position with her application?,* the usual expression would be **Wie steht es mit** *ihrer Bewerbung?* This would expect a simple answer. *Wie verhält es sich damit?* has the same sense, but **sich verhalten mit** is a formal v. and suggests a more detailed answer. *Wie verhält es sich eigentlich mit seiner Scheidung?*

Das bringt mich in eine schwierige/peinliche/schlimme/unangenehme Situation/Lage.
Sie freute sich, daß sie mit der Situation so schnell fertig geworden war.
Die wirtschaftliche Lage des Landes hat sich in letzter Zeit kaum geändert.
In dieser Situation/Lage hätte er gar nicht anders handeln können.
Nach den Napoleonischen Kriegen verschlechterte sich die Lage der Landarbeiter noch mehr.
Die Situation ist die, daß unsere Rechtsberater zufrieden sind.
Die politische Lage/Situation hat sich zugespitzt/sich grundlegend geändert.
Mit einem Scherzwort rettete sie die Situation.

10. E. **position** also denotes a job or employment. *She has a good position with a bank.* The commonest word in the spoken language is **die Stelle.** It simply suggests that this is how someone earns his or her living and says nothing about the type of position. *Sie sucht eine Stelle. Wir haben eine offene Stelle in unserer Buchhaltung.* The heading *Situations vacant* in newspapers is *Stellenangebote.* **Der Arbeitsplatz** is a general term for a position or employment and also says nothing about the kind of position. *Die Schulabgänger suchen Arbeitsplätze.* (*Arbeitsplatz* also means 'the place of work'. *Sie wohnt ganz in der Nähe ihres Arbeitsplatzes.*) Unless qualified by an adj.

der Posten suggests a modest job. *Er hat einen Posten als Nachtwächter.* It can, however, be modified by words which imply a high position. *Er hat einen hohen/verantwortlichen Posten* or *ist in den Posten des Generaldirektors aufgerückt.* **Die Stellung** and **die Anstellung** both imply a permanent and fairly good position. *Ich habe eine Anstellung in der Handelsbank angenommen. Er hat eine feste Stellung bei der Bundesbahn.* **Die Position** is always an elevated position which commands respect. *Sie hat jetzt eine verantwortungsvolle Position im Betrieb.* **Das Amt** is usually a fairly high position in the government, the civil service, or local governments. *Das Amt des Innenministers/eines Staatssekretärs/des Burgermeisters. Sie hat ein wichtiges Amt in der Regierung inne.* It is also the usual word for a position or office held in a club or society, although *Posten* is possible. *Er bekleidet das Amt des Schatzmeisters im Fußballclub.*

> *Er hat häufig die Stelle/den Arbeitsplatz gewechselt.*   *Sie tritt morgen ihre neue Stelle an.*
>
> *In Gebieten, wo hohe Arbeitslosigkeit herrscht, melden sich immer viele Bewerber für jeden ausgeschriebenen Posten/für jede ausgeschriebene Stelle.*
>
> *Die wichtigsten Positionen in der Staatsverwaltung sind von Konservativen besetzt.*
>
> *Er hat/sucht eine Stellung/Anstellung (bei dieser Firma) als Architekt.*

possibly, perhaps *advs.*

1. Possibly and **perhaps** are synonymous in one sense. Both mean that something may or may not be true. *The threat was perhaps/possibly not very great. Television is possibly/perhaps to blame for this.* The main equivalent is *vielleicht. Etwa* is a syn. with an emotional overtone, and *möglicherweise* is fairly formal.

i. Vielleicht is quite neutral and can be used in all situations and constructions. *Sie haben vielleicht recht. Sie ist vielleicht zu Hause.* **Etwa** always expresses an emotion and is more restricted in use than *vielleicht.* Unless preceded by *nicht,* it is mainly found in questions. *Kennen Sie ihn etwa?* expresses surprise that the person addressed knows the person referred to. *Ist das etwa verboten?* also expresses surprise and could be paraphrased as *You don't really mean to say that it's not allowed. Glaubt das etwa jmd.?* implies that it is hard to imagine anyone believing it, and *Zweifelt etwa jmd. daran?* suggests that no one could possibly doubt it. *Das glaubst du doch nicht etwa?* suggests that the speaker finds it hard to believe that the other person could possibly believe it. In saying, '*Denken Sie nicht etwa, daß Sie mich täuschen konnen!*', the speaker is suggesting that the other cannot be so naïve as to believe this. A pos. question can have the same implication. *Meinen Sie etwa, Sie könnten mich hinters Licht führen? Bilde dir nicht etwa ein, daß ich dir das Geld leihen werde!* could also be formulated as *Du bildest dir doch nicht etwa ein, daß* . . . If two people arrive at the theatre and one starts searching everywhere for the tickets, the other might say, '*Hast du etwa die Karten vergessen?*' This expresses a strong reproach if the person spoken to has actually forgotten them. In a sent. in which it seems neutral, e.g. *Kann ich etwa Montag nach drei kommen ?— das würde mir nämlich sehr gut passen,* it is more tentative and deferential than *vielleicht.* If I say, '*Störe ich etwa?*', I have the feeling that I am interrupting, partly excuse myself by using *etwa,* and suggest that I would be quite prepared for the other person to answer yes.

> *Ich habe mich vielleicht geirrt.*   *Das nimmst du doch nicht etwa ernst?*
>
> *Wollen Sie etwa behaupten, ich hätte gelogen?*   *Du willst doch nicht etwa sagen, daß ich lüge?*

ii. Möglicherweise suggests a more careful weighing up of the possibilities and is more tentative than *vielleicht,* but it belongs more to formal language. *Sie werden die Arbeit möglicherweise morgen abschließen.*

> *Möglicherweise stellen wir ungebührlich hohe Anforderungen an unsere Studenten.*

Wenn Sie morgen anrufen, werde ich möglicherweise nicht da sein.
Das Fernsehen ist möglicherweise am Verhalten dieser Kinder schuld.

iii. Like **perhaps**, **vielleicht** is common in polite requests. *Sind Sie vielleicht so nett und helfen mir, den Kinderwagen hinaufzutragen? Würdest du vielleicht für mich zum Supermarkt gehen?* It can also give a command an angry, but ironic, undertone. *Vielleicht paßt du in Zukunft ein bißchen besser auf! Vielleicht benimmst du dich jetzt anständig!* (*Vielleicht* also expresess surprise in an exclamatory sent. *Der hat vielleicht einen Unsinn geredet!* implies *What nonsense he talked!* or *What a load of rubbish his remarks were! Das Restaurant war vielleicht teuer!*, to your surprise it was terribly expensive.)

2. Possibly, mostly combined with *can*, emphasizes that someone tries his or her hardest to do something or does it as well as can be expected in a particular situation. *He will do everything he possibly can to help you. I made myself as comfortable as I possibly could. I will help you if I possibly can.* It is also used in questions to emphasize that the speaker is surprised, puzzled, or shocked by something he or she has seen, heard, or been asked to do. *How could you possibly think that? What could the police possibly want with me?*
i. The equivalent in all constructions is **nur**. *Er wird alles tun, was er nur kann, um euch zu helfen.* **Bloß** is much used in speech, but only in questions. *Wie kannst du das nur/bloß glauben?* **Überhaupt** is stronger. *Wie kannst du überhaupt so was glauben?* (All three also translate an interrogative + *on earth* or *ever*. *How on earth do you know that?* or *Whatever do the police want with me?*)

> *Er kaufte ihr das schönste Kleid, das er nur/bloß finden konnte.*
> *Alles, was wir nur tun können, sollten wir versuchen.*   *Woher weiß sie das nur?*
> *Er ist der beste Freund, den ich mir überhaupt vorstellen kann.*
> *Was will die Polizei bloß mit mir?*
> *Wie kann er nur hoffen, daß sie ihm noch einmal vergibt?*
> *Womit haben wir das nur verdient?*
> *Wie kannst du bloß/überhaupt so was denken/behaupten?*   *Wie kann das nur/bloß wahr sein?*

ii. Possibly in *as soon as I possibly can* is translated by **nur**. *Ich machte es mir so bequem, wie ich [es] nur konnte. Ich erledige es, so bald [wie] ich es nur kann.*
iii. In *If I possibly can*, **possibly** can be expressed by **nur**. *Ich werde dir helfen, wenn ich es nur kann.* An alternative in formal style is **irgend möglich** in a clause introduced by *wenn. Wenn irgend möglich, schreibe ich den Brief heute noch.* In everyday language this is expressed as *wenn es überhaupt möglich ist.* Both clauses could be translated as *if I possibly can* or *if at all possible.*

3. Possibly is used with a neg. and emphasizes that someone is unable or unwilling to do something or that something cannot happen or be done by anyone. *I can't possibly stay here until Sunday. No one can possibly tell the difference.* **Unmöglich** conveys this sense. As *unmöglich* is neg., the E. negation drops out. *I can't possibly stay longer* becomes *Ich kann unmöglich länger bleiben. No one* or *nobody* becomes *man. Man kann die beiden unmöglich unterscheiden.* An alternative is **unter keinen Umstanden**.

> *Das kannst du unmöglich von ihm verlangen.*   *Die Rechnung kann unmöglich stimmen.*
> *Sie konnen sich unmöglich ein weiteres Auto leisten.*   *Das kann unmöglich so gewesen sein.*
> *Ich kann unter keinen Umständen/unmöglich bis Sonntag hier bleiben.*

4. Eventuell refers to a possibility which may eventuate in the future if certain circumstances occur. It is both an adj. and adv. *Wir müssen eventuelle Schwierigkeiten einkalkulieren. Sie kommen eventuell erst morgen an.* **Etwaig**, that may or may not occur, is only an adj. In expressions like *etwaige negative Folgen, etwaige Terminänderungen, etwaige Probleme, bei eventuellen Schwierigkeiten,* and *eventuelle*

Beschwerden, etwaig and *eventuell* are interchangeable.

Ich fahre Montag, eventuell Dienstag.

Wir bekommen eine Gehaltserhöhung von 4%, eventuell 5%.

post, stake, pole, stick, rod, bar *ns.*

1. For **sticks** in the sense 'small pieces of dead wood from a tree', G. uses the collective n. **das Reisig.** One such stick would be called *ein trockener Zweig*, 'a dry twig', or if bigger *ein trockener Ast*.

Wir sammelten Reisig und machten ein Feuer.

2. The branch of a tree used for a particular purpose, e.g. as an aid in walking or to drive cattle, is called **der Stecken** in the south and **der Stock** in the north. These words suggest a stick up to about a metre and a half in length and, if not completely in its natural state, simply cut to size and roughly shaped. Apart from this use, *der Stock* is used throughout Germany to denote a not very long, carefully shaped object of wood used for a special purpose. Thus *der Spazierstock, der Taktstock eines Dirigenten*, and *der Schlagstock der Polizei. Der Junge bekam den Stock zu spüren* suggests a beating. **Der Stab** is a smooth, carefully formed, straight piece of wood or metal or sometimes glass of varying lengths. It is mostly translated as **rod** or **bar**. The upright parts of a lattice are called *[Gitter]stäbe. Ein Geländer*, 'railing, banister', may contain *Stäbe. Der Zauberstab is* 'a wand'. *Stäbchen* are 'chopsticks'. *Stab* can be used for a conductor's baton but, unlike *Stock*, not as a compound. *Der Dirigent hob seinen Stab/den Taktstock. Der Stabhochsprung is* 'pole-vault'. (One would expect *Stange*.) **Die Stange** is a straight, smooth length of wood or metal more than about two metres long and thus longer than most *Stäbe. Mit der Stange holten wir das Tuch aus dem Wasser*. Typical compounds are *die Bohnenstange* and *die Telegraphenstange. Eine Hühnerstange is* 'a perch'.

3. Der Pfosten is a carefully made round or square piece of timber or metal which either supports another structure, *die Türpfosten, die Pfosten des Bettgestells*, or stands by itself. In the latter case, it usually implies that it is carefully set in the ground. *A goalpost is ein Torpfosten. Der Ball prallte gegen den Torpfosten*. (The piece joining the two posts is called *die Latte*.) *A signpost is ein Wegweiser*. **Der Pfahl**, if of wood, may be less well constructed than *ein Pfosten*, but it can be made of other material. One end is pointed and driven into the ground. *Pfahl* is usually translated as **stake**, but *ein Laternenpfahl is* 'a lamppost'. *Ein Pfahlbau ist ein Steinzeitwohnhaus, das im Wasser oder am Ufer eines Gewässers auf eingerammten Pfählen steht.*

postpone, defer, put off *vs.* Verschieben, aufschieben, and *hinausschieben* all express the sense of the E. vs. **Verschieben** is used when a time is stated. *Die Sitzung wurde auf den nächsten Tag/auf Freitag/um eine Woche verschoben.* The new time may be indefinite. *Wir verschoben die Abstimmung auf später. Die Reise wurde auf unbestimmte Zeit verschoben.* Even when *verschieben* is used without a new time being specified, the implication is that the action will take place at a later date. **Aufschieben** means 'to put sth. off' without the time at which it will be done being stated or in any way clear. *An deiner Stelle würde ich die Antwort aufschieben.* The reasons for delay are usually of a subjective nature; the matter in question may be something unpleasant. **Hinausschieben** also says nothing about when what is put off will be done; it may contain a note of criticism about the way someone [always] puts things off. *Er schiebt alles bis zur letzten Minute hinaus.*

Die Zusammenkunft wurde auf einen späteren Zeitpunkt verschoben.

Man verschob die Gerichtsverhandlung um zwei Wochen.

Diese Arbeit läßt sich nicht länger verschieben/aufschieben.
Sie haben ihre Abreise nun zum zweiten Mal aufgeschoben.
Er schiebt wichtige Entscheidungen immer wieder hinaus.

Vertagen means 'to defer to a later, sometimes an indefinite, date', 'to adjourn', and is mainly used in the legal and official spheres. *Man beschloß, die Sitzung auf morgen/auf später zu vertagen. Die Debatte/Verhandlung wurde einstweilen vertagt.* (Note that *sich vertagen* means 'to adjourn' used intr. *Das Gericht hat sich vertagt.*)

pour, spill *vs.*

1. Trans. use. **pour** is used both for liquids and for granular solids such as sugar, sand, or salt. **Gießen** is only used for liquids. *Sie goß den Kaffee in die Tassen.* **Schütten** is used for solids but can be used for liquids as well, although some people use it only for the former. *Er schüttete Salz/Zucker/Mehl aus der Tüte in den Behälter. Ich schüttete Wasser in die Schüssel/aus dem Eimer.* In reference to larger quantities where a truck is involved, *schütten* is also translated as tip. *Wir haben den Sand auf einen Haufen vor dem Haus geschüttet.* **Gießen** expresses the sense 'to pour in[to]' when a phr. with *in* follows as in the example above. When there is no *in*-phr., **eingießen** is used. *Er goß dem Gast Kognak ein. Meine Mutter goß mir immer wieder ein.* To make the meaning clear E. could use more or other words than **pour**. In refined language people use **einschenken** instead of the everyday *eingießen. Sie goß/schenkte mir eine Tasse Tee ein.*

2. When intr., **pour** means 'to move or issue from or into sth. with a continuous flow'. The main equivalent is **strömen**, which is applied to liquids, *Tränen strömten ihr aus den Augen,* to people, *Tausende von Menschen strömten aus der U-Bahn-Station* or *Die Fans strömten ins Stadion,* and sometimes to gas, *Kalte Luft strömte durch das offene Fenster in den Saal.* It's pouring (with rain) is *Es gießt* or *Es regnet in Strömen. Im strömenden Regen reisten wir ab,* in [the] pouring rain. **Dringen** is used for smoke. *Rauch drang aus allen Fenstern.*

Der Schweiß strömte mir übers Gesicht.   *Wasser strömte aus dem geplatzten Rohr.*
Tausende von jungen Menschen strömten zur Halle, wo der Popstar auftreten sollte.
Die Menschen strömten durch das Messegelände.   *Es regnet nicht, sondern es gießt.*

3. Spill a liquid is **vergießen** or **danebengießen**, **spill** a solid or a liquid **verschütten**. *Ich habe etwas Milch vergossen/danebengegossen. Ich habe leider etwas Tee/Zucker/Salz verschüttet.*
(*Verschütten* also means 'to bury under a mass of rubble, snow, etc.' *Der Erdrutsch hat den Hohlweg verschüttet. Die Lawine hat die Straße verschüttet.*)

power, strength, force *ns.*

1. Power means 'the possession of control or command over others' in a community, country, the world, or an industry, etc.
i. Die Macht is used in a general way for this power over others and over the way things are run or done. It refers specifically to governmental control of a country, especially in expressions like *an die Macht kommen* and *an der Macht sein,* but also to power in other spheres such as *wirtschaftliche Macht.* It suggests a position from which authority may be exercised, but not specific powers or rights. (Cf. 2.) Some compounds are *der Machtkampf, die Machtstellung, die Machtergreifung,* and *das Machtstreben* (usually *das Streben nach Macht*). A country which is powerful is called *eine Macht;* hence *die Großmächte, eine Mittelmacht.*
Durch diese Wahl kam die konservative Partei wieder an die Macht.
Die neue Verfassung gibt dem Präsidenten zu viel Macht. Er könnte sie leicht mißbrauchen.

Die Macht Roms reichte von Britannien bis nach Kleinasien.
Alle Macht war in einer Hand vereinigt. *Damals war Spanien auf der Höhe seiner Macht.*
Alle Macht wirkt korrumpierend, und die absolute Macht neigt dazu, total zu korrumpieren.
Dieses Kartell übte große Macht im Wirtschaftsleben des Landes aus.
Die Größe Elisabeths I. lag in der Macht, die sie über das Volk hatte.
Es ist für einen Politiker gefährlich, die Macht der öffentlichen Meinung zu unterschätzen.
Das Militärregime kam durch einen Staatsstreich an die Macht.
Das kleine Land lag an der Grenze zwischen den Machtbereichen der beiden Machtblöcke.

To go **out of power** is *die Macht verlieren.* To be *returned* **to power** is often *wiedergewählt werden.* That someone was returned to power can be expressed as *Er wurde in seinem Amt bestätigt.*

ii. Die Macht also refers to the power or hold one person has over another. *Sie gewann/hatte Macht über ihn. Er übte eine unwiderstehliche Macht auf/über sie aus.*

iii. In a few expressions in which it is usually translated as **power**, **Macht** implies mental ability or power arising from someone's position or influence. *Sie tat alles, was in ihrer Macht stand, um uns zu helfen. Ich will [das] tun, was in meiner Kraft/in meinen Kräften steht,* and *Ich will ihnen nach Kräften helfen* suggest 'everything I am able to do' and 'as far as I am able'. For *Kraft* cf. 4.

> *Wir sollten alles tun, was in unserer Macht steht, um ein Auto zu entwickeln, das die Atmosphäre mit Abgasen nicht belastet.* *Er stemmte sich mit aller Macht gegen jede Reform.*

iv. Die Macht is also used for mysterious powers. *Dunkle, böse Mächte. Die Mächte der Finsternis.*

v. Die Macht translates **force** in *force of habit. Die Macht der Gewohnheit.* By *force of habit* could be *Aus alter Gewohnheit steht er immer um sechs Uhr auf:*

2. Power also denotes authority given or the right delegated or assigned by the constitution, parliament, etc. to act or decide questions at one's discretion. *The police have the power to fine speeding motorists. Are the powers of the Prime Minister defined by law? The President has exceeded his power[s].*

i. The specific term is **die Befugnis. Die Machtbefugnis** is a commonly used syn. **Die Macht** is also used, but now mostly in more or less fixed expressions, such as *Etw. liegt [nicht] in meiner Macht.* An alternative is **das Recht**, right. The idea can also be expressed by the parts. **befugt** and **ermächtigt**, authorized. Both are used in the public domain, but *ermächtigen* is also used in the private sphere when one person authorizes another to do something. **Jmdm. Vollmacht geben** is 'to give s.o. power of attorney, the authority to act on one's behalf'. Thus *Jmd. hat die Vollmacht/ist ermächtigt, etw. zu tun.*

> *Der Präsident hat seine Befugnisse/seine Machtbefugnisse überschritten.*
> *1910 hat das englische Unterhaus die Befugnisse/die Macht des Oberhauses stark eingeschränkt.*
> *Er hat die Macht/ist befugt, das zu tun, was er für richtig hält.*
> *Sind die Befugnisse des Premierministers in Gesetzen festgelegt?*
> *Im Mittelalter hatten die Bischöfe die Befugnis/die Macht, Ketzer verhaften zu lassen.*
> *Es lag in ihrer Macht, mir vieles, was ich für meine Arbeit brauchte, zu verweigern.*
> *Anfang 1948 hatte Ludwig Erhard die Vollmacht/war L. E. ermächtigt, das Geldwesen der Bizone zu reformieren.*
> *Die Polizei ist ermächtigt, Kraftfahrer, die die Geschwindigkeitsbegrenzung überschreiten, mit einer Geldbuße zu belegen.*

ii. Die Gewalt refers to legal or constitutional power or authority and combines the meanings of *Macht* in sense 1 and *Befugnis* in 2. i. *Die Staatsgewalt* denotes the power of the state in general. *In absoluten Monarchien übte der König die gesamte Staatsgewalt aus.* The G. *Grundgesetz* states: *Die Staatsgewalt geht von dem Volk aus.* Although mostly confined to legal and learned language, it is the same as *Macht* when referring to government, but in this sense it implies legal power, while

Macht can be illegal. *Die Machtübernahme* can be legal or illegal, but *die Gewaltübernahme* is always legal. *Die Teilung der Gewalten* is '(the theory of) the separation of powers'. *Die gesetzgebende, ausführende und richterliche Gewalten* are 'the legislature, executive, and judiciary'. *Widerstand gegen die Staatsgewalt* or *Jmd. widersetzt sich der Staatsgewalt* implies resistance to the police or a branch of the executive. *Das Parlament, die Beamten in den Ministerien und die Gerichte üben in einem modernen demokratischen Staat die Staatsgewalt aus.*

Nach der bedingungslosen Kapitulation des Deutschen Reiches im Mai 1945 übernahmen die vier alliierten Militärbefehlshaber die oberste Gewalt in Deutschland.

iii. *Jmd. hat Gewalt uber Leben und Tod* (occasionally *Macht*) is a fixed expression, likewise *die elterliche Gewalt. Höhere Gewalt* is what in insurance parlance is called *an act of God.* (In *Den Korper/Die Zunge/Ein Fahrzeug in der Gewalt haben, Gewalt* means 'CONTROL'.)

3. Other uses of *Gewalt.*

i. Force meaning 'the use of physical strength to constrain the actions of others' is **die Gewalt.** *Rohe* or *brutale Gewalt anwenden* is 'to use brute force'. *Sie öffneten die Tür mit Gewalt,* by force. The meaning 'by force' is also expressed by **gewaltsam.** *Gewaltsam verschafften sie sich Eintritt in das Haus. Die Gewalt der Wellen/des Windes* suggests particular strength and is usually translated as *violence.* Cf. VIOLENT.

Nichts wird die Anwendung von Gewalt rechtfertigen, solange andere Mittel unversucht bleiben.

Der Junge, der eine Ohrfeige bekommen hatte, sagte, 'Gewalt ist kein Argument'.

ii. In *to have s.o. in one's power* **power** expresses the definition of *force* in 3. i. The equivalent is **die Gewalt.** *In jmds. Gewalt sein, jmdn. in seine Gewalt bekommen, jmdn. in seiner Gewalt haben,* and *Gewalt über jmdn. gewinnen* suggest power in a bad sense, i.e. power that is illegal or at least undesirable.

Obwohl die Kaufleute sich tapfer wehrten, bekamen die Raubritter sie doch endlich in ihre Gewalt.

Die Geiselnehmer hatten zwanzig Geiseln in ihrer Gewalt.

4. Strength.

i. The general sense of **die Kraft** is 'the ability to act and to bring sth. about'. It refers first to the physical strength of a human being or an animal. *Die Kraft eines Mannes/eines Pferdes. Die körperliche Kraft. Die Kraft der Muskeln.* It also denotes mental and moral strength or power. *Die Kraft des Geistes. Sittliche/Moralische Kraft.* It is applied to things for which E. uses **force** and **power** as well as **strength.** *Die Kraft des Sturms. Die militärische/wirtschaftliche Kraft eines Landes. Der Wind nahm an Kraft zu. Die Kraft des Windes riß den Baum um. Wir unterschätzten die Kraft der Explosion.* In reference to people, *Kraft* is often used in the pl. where E. uses the sing. *Das übersteigt meine Kraft/Kräfte.* The pl. sometimes has to be translated as *energies. In der neuen Stelle konnte sie ihre Kräfte richtig entfalten. Seine Kräfte lassen nach* can be translated as *His strength is failing,* but an alternative is *His powers are failing. Jmd. kommt wieder zu Kräften,* regains strength (after an illness). There are numerous compounds such as *die Anziehungskraft der Erde, die Kampfkraft, die Kaufkraft, die Widerstandskraft. Die Ausdruckskraft seiner Worte wirkte stark auf die Leser.*

Die Kraft eines Mannes reicht nicht aus, um diese Kiste zu heben.

Seine Kraft nahm zu/hat sich verdoppelt/wurde durch Krankheit untergraben.

Seine Kräfte verließen ihn im entscheidenden Moment.

Sorgen haben seine Kraft gebrochen.   *Der Bursche versuchte seine Kraft an dem Baumast.*

Ich fühle neue Kraft in mir.

Unter Aufbietung aller seiner Kräfte erreichte er den Gipfel.

Mit letzter Kraft schleppte sich der Verletzte zur Telefonzelle.

Die Kraft dieses Gedankens wird stärker sein als jeder Versuch, ihn zu unterdrücken.

ii. Die Stärke can also denote physical strength, but, at least in the spoken language, it seems to have given way to **die Kraft** in this sense. Although *Muskelkraft* and *Muskelstärke* are both possible, *Kraft* is more usual, as it would be in the following sents., especially when a particular activity is referred to.

Seine Kraft/Stärke reichte aus, um das Auto aus dem Schlamm zu schieben.

Obwohl er klein ist, zeugt das Heben von drei Zentnern von erstaunlicher Kraft/Stärke.

iii. Both **die Stärke** and **die Kraft** are used for mental strength, strength of character and will, but *Stärke* seems to be preferred. *Willenskraft* and *-stärke*, *Geisteskraft* and *-stärke*, and *Nervenkraft* and *-stärke* do not differ in meaning. However, in certain combinations, such as *Charakterstärke* and *Glaubensstärke*, one or the other tends to be preferred.

Daß sie jahrelang gegen das Regime Widerstand geleistet haben, zeugt von außergewöhnlicher Stärke.

In diesem Verhalten zeigt sich seine moralische Stärke.

5. Other uses of *die Kraft*.

i. In physics, **die Kraft** means 'force'.

Jeder Körper verharrt in einem Zustand der Ruhe oder der gleichförmig geradlinigen Bewegung, wenn er nicht durch einwirkende Kräfte gezwungen wird, seinen Zustand zu ändern.

ii. **Die Kraft** also corresponds to **power** when it means 'energy or force that can be used to do work'. *Steam power* is *Dampfkraft*. Thus *Wasserkraft* and *Antriebskraft*. **Power** when it means 'electricity' is **die Elektrizität** or **der Strom**. *Turn the power on!* is *Schalte mal den Strom ein!*

Das neue Kraftwerk wird 300 Megawatt Strom erzeugen.   Im Sturm fiel der Strom aus.

iii. A law, regulation, etc. can be **in Kraft**, 'in force', or **außer Kraft**, 'not in force'.

Die neuen Bestimmungen treten am 1. Januar in Kraft.

iv. The **strength** or **power** of s.o.'s logic or of an argument is **die Beweiskraft** *seiner Logik/dieser Argumente*. Also **die Schlagkraft** *eines Arguments*.

v. *Die heilende Kraft eines Medikaments* is its 'healing power'.

vi. **Die Kraft** also refers to a person or a factor which exerts influence in a specified direction. Thus *die fortschrittlichen/reaktionären Kräfte im Lande. Das freie Spiel der Kräfte in einem demokratischen Staat. Jmd. ist die treibende Kraft in einem Unternehmen*, the driving force.

vii. **Die Kraft** is also applied to employees and soldiers or troops. *Die Post sucht weibliche und männliche Kräfte* and *Der Betrieb stellt jederzeit erfahrene Kräfte ein*. For *Kräfte* in *Die Armee warf die gegnerischen Kräfte zurück*, E. uses *forces*.

viii. **Die Streitkräfte** is the collective term for 'armed forces'. *US-Streitkräfte sind noch in Deutschland stationiert. An armed force* (= 'body') *of men* is **eine Streitmacht**. *Er landete an der Küste mit einer Streitmacht von 5 000 Mann. The police force* as a whole is **die Polizei**, but *a force of police*, i.e. 'a certain number brought into action for a special purpose', is **das Polizeiaufgebot**. *Ein großes Polizeiaufgebot riegelte die Innenstadt ab.*

6. Other uses of *die Stärke*.

i. **Die Stärke** is a n. corresponding to (the G. adj.) *stark*. Thus the n. from *eine starke Gewerkschaft* is *die Stärke der Gewerkschaft*. *Ein starkes Herz—die Stärke des Herzens*. Similarly *starke Taue, starkes Papier, starker Bindfaden, eine starke Strömung* and *die Stärke der Taue/der Strömung. Die Stärke des Papiers/des Bindfadens reicht für diesen Zweck aus.*

ii. **Die Stärke** is 'strength' meaning 'intensity' or 'degree' and often suggests a position on a scale. *Böen erreichten Windstärke acht.* (Here E. uses *force*.) *Der Sturm/Der Regen nahm an Stärke zu.* It is used for the strength of coffee, wine, a drug, etc. *Die Stärke des Lichts/eines Gefühls/einer Arznei/des Tees/des Alkohols/eines Gifts. Kaffee normaler Stärke. Eine Brille mittlerer Stärke. Die Stärke eines Motors* is 'power' and suggests a scale. Hence the old *Pferdestärke*.

iii. Die Stärke corresponds to **strength** in the sense 'a particular quality or ability which those possessing it display in a high degree and so gain an advantage'. *Geduld ist ihre Stärke.* For *Mathematik war nie meine Stärke*, E. uses *strong point*.

Arbeiten Sie klar heraus, was Sie für die Schwächen und Stärken des Buches halten!

Die Stärke dieser Mannschaft liegt in ihrem guten Zusammenspiel.

iv. Like **strength** in a context such as *a regiment with a strength of 3,000 men*, **die Stärke** also means 'number'. *Ein Regiment mit einer Stärke von 3 000 Mann hat seinen Standort hier.*

Die Stärke der Handelsflotte hat sich im letzten Jahrzehnt beträchtlich erhöht.

Fans appeared in strength could be *Die Fans sind in großer Zahl erschienen.*

7. Die Wucht is 'the force or impact produced when one thg. hits another'. *Die Wucht des Schlages ließ ihn gegen die Wand stürzen. Der Schnellzug fuhr mit voller Wucht auf den stehenden Güterzug auf.*

Die Äste hatten die Wucht des Aufpralls vermindert.

Wucht is applied to the force of a gale etc. which strikes something. *Das Schiff bekam die volle Wucht des Sturms zu spüren.* Without the idea of an impact, **die Kraft** is used. *The force of the wind uprooted the trees* would be *Die Kraft des Windes entwurzelte die Bäume* or *Der Wind war so stark, daß er die Bäume entwurzelte. The force of the water drives the wheel* is *Die Kraft des Wassers treibt das Rad.*

8. Power occasionally denotes a specific ability in living beings. *The power of sight* is **die Sehkraft**, which is applied to people only, or **das Sehvermögen**, which is also used for animals. Otherwise **die Fähigkeit**, 'ability', can be used or the formal syn. **das Vermögen**, 'capacity'. *Das Chamäleon hat die Fähigkeit/das Vermögen, die Färbung seiner Haut zu wechseln.* The meaning can be expressed as a v. by *können* + infin. or *vermögen* + *zu* + infin. *Die Chamäleons können die Färbung ihrer Haut wechseln* or *vermögen . . . zu wechseln. Das Vermögen* is often found in compounds; the meaning is the same as that of the compound with *Fähigkeit. Das Konzentrationsvermögen* or *die Konzentrationsfähigkeit. Das Denkvermögen/-fähigkeit.*

practise, exercise, exert *vs.*

I. i. Practise in the meaning 'to do sth. repeatedly in order to gain proficiency or improve one's skill' is **üben**. It can be intr., *Ich übe jeden Tag mehrere Stunden*, or trans., *Die Kinder übten das Einmaleins.* With regard to music, the obj. can be as in E. either the instrument, *Sie übte täglich eine Stunde Violine*, or the piece of music, *Er übte die Sonate. Üben* is used for sport, *Der Turner übte am Barren*, but in intr. use relating to sport, **trainieren** is probably more usual. *Die Turner trainieren täglich für den Wettkampf.* Schoolchildren use *üben* when they practise skills for a test or examination. *Die Schuler üben fleißig für die Mathematikarbeit.* Cf. STUDY. A variant is **sich üben**. This implies, on the one hand, that a certain skill has already been acquired—*üben* leaves this point open—and, on the other, that the aim is the attainment of the greatest possible proficiency. *Jmd. übt sich im Tanzen/im Reden/im Schießen* etc. *Das Kind übt sich in Rechtschreiben.*

Obwohl sie ihre Kür so gut geübt hatten und jeden Schritt perfekt beherrschten, machten sie im entscheidenden Moment einen Fehler. *In der Fahrstunde haben wir das Einparken geübt.*

Er übte auf dem Klavier fleißig Tonleitern, Akkorde und Kadenzen.

Die Schwimmerin übte sich täglich in verschiedenen [Schwimm]stilen.

ii. Einüben implies practising something until it can be carried out with a certain mastery. It often refers to a theatrical or musical performance. The subj. can be either the performers, *Das Orchester/Der Chor übte mehrere (Musik)stücke ein*, or someone in charge of the performance such as a director, *Der Regisseur übte das neue Theaterstück zunächst einmal mit den Hauptdarstellern alleine ein.* In some cases, *eingeübt* can imply that a speech etc. is learned off by heart, lacks spontaneity. *Die Rede/Diese Antwort klang eingeübt.* *Proben* means 'to rehearse', but unlike *einüben*, it says nothing about quality.

> *Die Klasse führt ein Theaterstück auf, und der Lehrer übt gewisse Teile mit einzelnen Schülern ein. Also Er übt das Stück mit der Klasse ein.*
>
> *Der Chorleiter brachte uns zur Besinnung: Wir hätten genug herumgealbert; uns blieben nur noch zwei Wochen, um den Choral einzuüben.*

2. Practise is used with *profession* as obj. The word related to *üben* in this sense is **ausüben**. *Einen Beruf ausüben* is 'to carry on a profession or occupation'. Cf. BUSINESS 3. *Ausüben* is commonly used with *Tätigkeit*. *Welche Tätigkeit üben Sie aus?*, what is your work/occupation. **Praktizieren** is used as an intr. v. in reference to *Ärzte* and *Rechtsanwälte*. *Er praktiziert als Arzt/als Rechtsanwalt auf dem Lande.* An alternative is *Er führt eine Arztpraxis/Rechtsanwaltspraxis.*

> *Infolge des Unfalls konnte er eine Zeitlang seinen Beruf nicht ausüben.*
>
> *Sein eigentlicher Beruf ist Lehrer, aber die Tätigkeit, die er momentan ausübt, ist Taxifahren.*

3. Some uses of **exercise** and **exert**.

i. Ausüben with *Macht* as obj. is 'to exercise power'. It is also used with *die Herrschaft*, 'rule, power, control', and *ein Recht*, 'right'. With objs. like *der Druck* and *der Einfluß*, it means 'to exert'. With *Wirkung*, it means 'to have an effect'. *Die Rede übte eine starke Wirkung auf die Zuhörer aus.*

> *Eine kleine Gruppe von reichen Großgrundbesitzern übte die Macht im Land aus.*
>
> *Jmd. übt einen guten/schlechten Einfluß auf andere aus.*　　　*Das Bild übt einen gewissen Reiz aus.*
>
> *Der Lehrer übte einen guten und nachhaltigen Einfluß auf die Schüler aus.*

ii. Üben is used with a few ns. denoting mainly good qualities in the meaning 'to manifest them in one's behaviour'. *Man übt Geduld/Gerechtigkeit/Nachsicht/ Zurückhaltung einem anderen gegenüber.* The usual transl. is *to display patience* etc. or simply *to be patient* etc.; with *Zurückhaltung*, the equivalent is *to exercise restraint*. The common expression *Kritik üben an* is translated as *to criticize*. Cf. BLAME 5.

iii. Exercise meaning 'to do physical exercises' is **Leibesubungen machen**.

4. Less common meanings of **practise**.

i. In one sense *a practice* is a syn. of CUSTOM, a meaning expressed by either *die Sitte* or *der Brauch*. These ns. can be used to translate **practise** meaning 'observe a particular custom'. *This tribe practises monogamy* etc.: *Bei diesem Stamm ist die Einehe Sitte.*

ii. Practise also means 'to inflict sth. unpleasant on people'. Here the idea needs to be expressed. *They practise torture* could be *Sie wenden Folter an*, and *They practised cruelty on their helpless victims* could become *Sie mißhandelten ihre hilflosen Opfer.* (*Mißhandeln*, to maltreat.) An alternative is *Sie gingen mit großer/beispielloser Grausamkeit gegen ihre hilflosen Opfer vor.*

praise, commend *vs.*

1. Praise = 'to express appreciation of' with people and things as obj. The main equivalent is **loben**. *Der Lehrer lobte die Schülerin* or *lobte ihren Fleiß/ihre Arbeit.* The usual preps. are *wegen* and *für* and in formal language *um . . . willen*. The construction corresponding to *I praise s.o. for doing/having done sth.* is *Ich lobe jmdn. dafür, daß er etw. tut/getan hat.* *Ich muß sie dafür loben, daß sie bestellte Arbeit immer zum versprochenen Termin abliefert.*

> *Die Mutter lobte den Jungen wegen seiner/für seine Hilfsbereitschaft der Nachbarin gegenüber.*
>
> *Vater wird dich auch für ein mittelmäßiges Zeugnis loben.*
>
> *Man hat ihn um seiner Leistung/dieses Opfers willen gelobt.*
>
> *Ich muß dich sehr dafür loben, daß du ausgeharrt hast.*

Loben implies that the praise is justified. If the praise is exaggerated, advs. like *übermäßig* or *überschwenglich* are added. The colloquial expression *jmdn./etw. über den grünen Klee loben* always implies exaggerated praise, even though it may be to some extent deserved. *Jmdn. in den Himmel heben* has the same sense.

Wenn du deine Mitarbeiter so übermäßig/überschwenglich lobst, wird dich niemand ernst nehmen.
Er lobt seinen Freund so über den grünen Klee, der muß ja ein einmaliges Genie sein.

2. Beloben is an elevated and uncommon word meaning that a higher authority acknowledges officially in front of others what someone has done. *Der Burgermeister belobte in seiner Rede mehrere Beamte.* **Belobigen** is the equivalent of **commend** in e.g. to *commend a soldier for bravery. Der Soldat wurde wegen seiner Tapferkeit belobigt.*

3. Preisen means 'to extol enthusiastically the good qualities of a pers. or thg.' Like **praise** meaning 'to express respect, honour, and thanks to God', it is used in religious language (*loben* is also possible), but it is not confined to this. **Rühmen** is similar to *preisen*, meaning 'to draw people's attention emphatically to the outstanding qualities of a pers. or thg.'

Ihr preist den Schöpfer, der das alles erschaffen hat.
Er pries ihre Geschicklichkeit in den höchsten Tönen/pries sie als vorzügliche Köchin.
Die Bergleute rühmten den Mut der Männer, die sie gerettet hatten.
Sie war früher eine sehr gepriesene/viel gerühmte Schönheit.

4. Anpreisen means 'to recommend or praise sth. enthusiastically' but now has the implication that the person is praising the thing in order to sell it.

Die Händler auf dem orientalischen Markt preisen ihre Waren an.
In der Werbung/Auf der Messe werden die unterschiedlichsten Waren angepriesen.

prepare, get ready *vs.* prepared *part.*

1. The usual equivalent of **prepare** with an obj. denoting a thing, *to prepare a lesson/meal/speech*, etc., is **vorbereiten**. *Sie bereitet ihre Rede/die [Unterrichts]stunde/die Predigt/eine Mahlzeit etc. vor. Vorbereiten* + obj. also translates **to prepare for** when the n. following *for* is not a person or *everything. They are preparing for a party* is *Sie bereiten eine Fete vor.* When *everything* or a person is the obj. of *prepare*, the construction is as in E. *Sie bereiten alles für das Fest vor* and *Der Lehrer bereitet die Schüler auf/für die Prüfung vor.* [*Sich*] *vorbereiten* suggests that a certain amount of time is taken and that some effort is expended. **Prepare [oneself]** [for sth./to do sth.] or **get ready** [for sth. or to do sth.] is expressed by **sich vorbereiten**. *Die Sportler bereiten sich auf den Wettkampf vor.* When an infin. follows, the construction is *Ich bereite mich darauf vor, Dias zu zeigen.*

Der Abgeordnete bereitete die Rede, die er im Bundestag halten wollte, sorgfältig vor.
Sie bereitet die Abschiedsfeier vor, zu der sie etwa 20 Freunde und Bekannte eingeladen hat.
Die Studenten bereiten sich auf das Seminar vor.   Wir bereiten uns auf die Reise vor.
Offensichtlich bereitete sich der Feind darauf vor, uns anzugreifen.

2. While *vorbereiten* is the everyday word for preparing food, the more technical term, e.g. in recipe books, is **zubereiten**. *Sie bereitete ein chinesisches Essen für ihre Gäste zu.* The cooking instructions in recipe books and on ready-cooked food which only has to be heated are headed *Zubereitung.* **Bereiten** is occasionally found in the same sense, but only in very elevated language. *Erfahrene Köche hatten ein fürstliches Essen für den Staatsgast bereitet.*

3. While *vorbereiten* belongs to the standard language, the everyday word resembling **get s.o./sth. ready** is **fertigmachen**. *Ich mache das Mittagessen fertig. Die Mutter machte die Kinder für den Ausflug fertig.* The refl. **sich fertigmachen** translates *to get ready for sth., to go somewhere*, or *to do sth.* with a person as subj. *Wir machen uns für* *den Theaterbesuch/zum Aufbruch fertig. Die Sportler machten sich für den Wettkampf fertig.* With an infin.: *Ich mache mich fertig, um auszugehen. Sie machten sich fertig, nach London zu fahren.* The sense of the infin. can be expressed as a n. *Sie machten sich zur Fahrt nach London fertig.* (Note *eine Arbeit* etc. *fertigmachen*, to finish it off.)

Die Schüler machten sich zum Schwimmen fertig und stellten sich auf die Startblöcke.

4. Prepare s.o. mentally **for** bad news etc. **Jmdn. auf etw. vorbereiten** is used. *Ich muß ihn auf diese schlechte Nachricht schonend vorbereiten.* The pass. *to be prepared for* is *auf etw. vorbereitet sein. Auf diesen schweren Schlag war sie nicht vorbereitet.* A syn. is **auf etw. gefaßt sein.** *Ich bin auf das Schlimmste gefaßt. Gefaßt* means 'calm, composed'. It is combined with *machen* to form a verbal expression with the same meaning as *sich auf etw. vorbereiten. Bereiten Sie sich auf eine schlechte Nachricht vor! Machen Sie sich auf eine schlechte Nachricht gefaßt!*

Auf diese Enttäuschung war ich schon gefaßt/vorbereitet.
Machen Sie sich darauf gefaßt, daß einiges schiefgehen kann!

5. Prepared meaning 'willing', as in *I am prepared to take on the job*, is **bereit sein** + infin.

Ich bin nicht bereit, das zuzugeben.   Sind Sie bereit, Stillschweigen zu bewahren?
Ich bin bereit, Ihnen unter gewissen Bedingungen zu helfen.
Sie sind nicht bereit, die Sache weiter zu besprechen.   Ich bin bereit, die Arbeit zu übernehmen.

6. Less common G. words.
i. Sich für/zu etw. rüsten is a formal syn. of *sich vorbereiten. Sie rüsteten sich zum Aufbruch. Sie haben sich für ihre Ferienreise/für die Prüfung gut gerüstet.*
ii. *Er schickte sich an zu arbeiten* means that he was preparing to start work. **Sich anschicken,** *etw. zu tun* means 'to be preparing or about to do sth. or on the point of doing sth.' *She was just preparing to go out* is *Sie schickte sich zum Ausgehen an.* It also takes an infin. *Sie schickten sich an, in die Oper zu gehen, als das Telefon klingelte. Sich anschicken* is not an everyday expression.

press, squeeze, squash, depress, oppress, suppress, urge *vs.* The distinction between the two basic vs. *drücken* and *pressen* is fairly subtle. In many cases they are interchangeable, but in others one tends to be the preferred word. The following gives the common uses.

1. Press a button, knob, doorbell, etc. and **press** [lightly] **on** sth. Here **drücken** is used, mostly with *auf, Um Das Radio einzuschalten, drückt man auf diesen Knopf,* but it can take an acc., *Drück' bitte mal den Knopf! Drücken* is the sign on doors where E. has *push* or *press.* Also *Sie drückte die Türklinke herunter. Drück' mit dem Finger auf den Knoten!,* put your finger . . .

Weil das Auto vor ihm sich nicht bewegte, drückte er auf die Hupe.
Sie drückte [auf] die Stoptaste des Kassettenrecorders und spulte zurück.
Ich drückte gegen die Tür, und sie ging auf.
Der Postbeamte drückte den Stempel auf das Stempelkissen und dann auf die Bescheinigung.

2. Press = 'to hold firmly against' in reference to people and parts of the body. *He pressed his hand to his heart. She held the receiver pressed against her ear.* Here either **drücken** or **pressen** is possible. The difference is slight, but *pressen* suggests a somewhat higher degree of intensity. Fixed expressions are *Das Kind drückte sich an der Scheibe die Nase platt* and *Das Kind preßte die Nase an die Scheibe.*

Er preßte die Hand aufs Herz.   Sie preßte beide Hände stark zusammen.
Der Junge preßte das Ohr an die Tür, um zu hören, was gesagt wurde.
Sie drückte/preßte das Gesicht in die Kissen.
Er drückte/preßte sie an seine Brust.   Die Mutter drückte/preßte das Kind an sich.

Jmdm. die Hand drücken is 'to shake s.o.'s hand firmly'. (*Jmdm. die Hand geben,* to shake hands.) *Jmds. Hand pressen* is 'to press on s.o.'s hand so that it hurts at least slightly'.

3. Press is used trans., intr., and in the refl. with expressions of direction. Trans.: *The crowd pressed them [back] against the wall.* In the pass.: *They were pressed back against the wall.* Intr.: *They pressed back against the wall.* Refl.: *He pressed himself to the ground.*

i. Here too both **drücken** and **pressen** are possible, the difference being that *pressen* suggests greater force. The E. intr. and refl. forms are refl. in G. *Er drückte sich in die Ecke/auf die Erde. Sie preßten sich gegen die Mauer.*

> *Die Menge drückte/preßte ihn an die Wand* and *Er wurde von der Menge an die Wand gedrückt/gepreßt.*
>
> *Als der Demonstrationszug vorbeikam, drückte er sich an die Wand.*
>
> *Ich wurde durch den Demonstrationszug an die Hauswand gepreßt.*
>
> *Die Menschen standen zusammengedrückt am Straßenrand und wartet auf den Karnevalszug.*

ii. **Drücken** and **pressen** are followed by *in*. *Drücken* implies care. *Sie drückten die kleinen Pflanzen [sorgfältig] in die Erde.* *Pressen* again suggests greater force. *Druckluft wird in den Behälter gepreßt. Preßluft* is 'compressed air', and *ein Preßlufthammer* 'a pneumatic drill'.

4. Press fruit etc. and **press** or **squeeze** juice etc. **out of** sth. For fruit **pressen** is usual in both senses. *Trauben werden gepreßt. Sie preßte den Saft aus der Zitrone/Orange.* *Pressen* suggests a certain effort. **Drücken** is not wrong, only less common. It is usual when little effort is required. *Sie drückte Zahnpasta aus der Tube auf die Zahnbürste.* Here too, *pressen* could be appropriate under certain circumstances. *Die Zahnpastatube war fast leer, so daß er den letzten Rest mit beiden Händen herauspressen mußte.* Likewise, *Sie drückte das Wasser aus dem Schwamm* and *preßte den letzten Rest Wasser aus dem Schwamm.* (Pressed flowers are *gepreßte Blumen*.)

5. Squash also means 'to press or crush sth., often with great force, so that it becomes flat or loses its shape'. **Zerdrucken** and **zerquetschen** mean 'to squash flat', 'to crush'. *Er zerdrückte/zerquetschte die Mücke, die ihn gestochen hatte, zwischen den Fingern. Das Kleid wurde im Koffer zerdrückt. Paß auf, daß der Kuchen nicht zerdrückt wird!* **Zerquetschen** can mean 'to mash'. **Quetschen** and **klemmen** mean 'to jam' a hand or finger. *Ich habe mir/ihm aus Versehen die Finger an der Tür gequetscht/geklemmt.* Without a phr. with *an*, **einklemmen** or **einquetschen** are used. *Ich habe mir den Daumen eingeklemmt/eingequetscht.*

> *Die Ratte ist unter dem Rad des Autos zerdrückt worden.*
>
> *Der Fuß wurde ihm von dem umstürzenden Wagen zerquetscht.* (The injury is called *eine Quetschung*. The part. used as an adj. is *gequetscht. Er hat einen gequetschten Fuß.*)

6. Squeeze or **squash** [s.o./sth.] **into** sth. **Pressen** is used with things and people as obj. *Er preßte die Kleider in den Koffer. Ein letzter Passagier wurde in das überfüllte Abteil gepreßt.* **Zwängen** means 'to squeeze one thg. into another'. It implies skill in taking advantage of a small space and putting something or oneself into it even though the space is really too small. *Er hat alle Kleider in den Koffer gezwängt.* **squash** s.o./sth. **into** sth. is **quetschen**. *Er quetschte die Hemden in die Tasche.* For the E. intr. use *They squeezed/squashed into the bus*, the refl. forms **sich pressen, sich zwängen**, and **sich quetschen** are necessary. *Sie zwängte sich in das überfüllte Abteil*, squeezed into it. *Sie quetschten sich in den schon vollen Bus.* **Sich drücken** is also used like **squeeze** with crowded buses, trams, compartments, etc. *Sie drückte sich in das überfüllte Abteil.*

7. Press for sth. or to **press** or **urge** s.o. to do sth. mean 'to advise or request strongly that it be granted or that s.o. do sth.' The two equivalents *drängen* and *dringen* differ only syntactically. **Drängen** takes a person as obj. and an infin. *Sie drängt mich schon lange, sie zu besuchen.* It is also used with *auf. Alle drängten auf eine friedliche Lösung des Konflikts.* It is therefore found with *darauf* + a *daß* clause. *Er drängt darauf, daß sie den Aufsatz so bald wie möglich abgibt.* **Dringen** is also used with *auf. Sie dringen auf eine schnelle Erledigung der Angelegenheit. Er hat darauf gedrungen, daß wir weitere Schritte unternehmen sollten.* It can be used with *in* + a person and an infin. *Sie drang in mich, den Mann zu entlassen.* In many contexts they are interchangeable. *Die Gläubiger drängten/drangen auf Zahlung.*

8. Oppress means 'treat people unfairly and cruelly and prevent them from having the same opportunities, rights, freedoms, etc. as others'. *The minority felt oppressed.* In one sense, **suppress** means 'prevent an activity from continuing or a group etc. from pursuing its interests or aims by using force'. *The dictator suppressed all dissent/the protest movement.* **Unterdrücken** has both these meanings.

> *Die Männer haben die Frauen jahrhundertelang unterdrückt.*
> *Die Armee hat den Aufstand schnell unterdrückt.*   *Die Minderheit fühlte sich unterdrückt.*
> *Die Polizei hat jeden Protest/die Unabhängigkeitsbewegung brutal/rücksichtslos unterdrückt.*
> *Die herrschenden Klassen im Staat unterdrückten die Arbeiterklasse.*

9. Depress s.o. means 'make s.o. feel sad or hopeless'. *The bad news depressed us all.* **Oppress** s.o. can mean 'cause s.o. to feel anxious, troubled, or depressed', 'weigh heavily on the mind'. *He was oppressed by cares/anxiety.*

i. Bedrücken means 'to have a depressing effect on s.o.'s mental state'. *Was bedrückt dich?*, what is troubling or worrying you?

> *Den Schüler bedrückten seine wiederholten Mißerfolge.*
> *Ihr schlechtes Verhältnis zu ihren Schwiegereltern bedrückt sie sehr.*
> *Ihn bedrückte das Gefühl der Einsamkeit/die Sorge um seine Zukunft sehr.*

ii. The past parts. **niedergeschlagen** and **niedergedrückt** both mean 'mentally depressed'. *Niederdrücken* is also used as a v. Both suggest a state not as serious as that denoted by *bedrücken.*

> *Die Spieler hatten verloren und waren sehr niedergedrückt/niedergeschlagen.*
> *Sie macht einen sehr niedergeschlagenen Eindruck.*
> *Die schlechte Nachricht hat uns sehr niedergedrückt.*

10. Drücken means 'to depress' or 'to oppress' in a few cases.

i. It denotes a depressed mood or state of mind. *Nach diesem Streit mit meiner Freundin kehrte ich in gedrückter Stimmung nach Hause.*

ii. In reference to the conscience it means 'to oppress'. *Man sah ihm an, daß sein schlechtes Gewissen ihn drückte.*

iii. It is applied to prices. *Gedrückte Preise* are 'depressed'. *The market is depressed* is *Der Markt ist flau.*

iv. The pres. part. means 'oppressive' in relation to the weather, an atmosphere, etc.

> *An jedem Tag herrschte eine drückende Hitze/Schwüle.*
> *Es herrschte ein drückendes Schweigen/eine drückende Stille/Atmosphäre.*

pretend, make out, affect (indifference etc.) *vs.*

Pretend can be used alone, *You're not hurt—you're only pretending,* with an infin., *She pretended not to have heard this remark,* and a clause, *He tried to pretend that nothing had happened.* **Make out** in the sense discussed here means 'pretend or make s.o. believe'. It is used alone, *It's not as important as they make out,* or with a clause, *They made out that they were experts* or *He opened a drawer and made out that he was looking for sth.* One sense of **affect** is 'pretend one has a certain feeling or characteristic'. *He affected interest.* It is also found with an infin. *He affected to despise all his colleagues.* Several G. words express similar ideas. The following discusses some of the more important ones.

1. Sich stellen and **sich verstellen** both mean 'to pretend or make out [to be sth.]' but differ syntactically. *Sich stellen* is used with an adj. *Er stellt sich nur unwissend.* If it is clear what is meant, *so* can take the place of the adj. *Er ist nicht verletzt, er stellt sich nur so.* Sich verstellen is used without an adj. *Du schläfst doch nicht, du verstellst dich nur.* It is thus the equivalent of **pretend** used without an infin. or clause. The meaning of *sich verstellen* can be expressed by *sich so stellen* if it is clear what adj. is referred to. *Du bist nicht krank—du verstellst dich nur* or *Du bist nicht krank—du stellst dich nur so.*

> Auf der Polizeiwache stellte er sich dümmer, als er war.
> Um nicht in die Schule gehen zu müssen, stellte sich das Mädchen krank.
> 'Du brauchst gar nicht zu versuchen, dich zu verstellen', sagte die Mutter. 'Ich habe genau gesehen, daß du die Schokolade genommen hast.'

2. Jmdn./Etw. als/für jmdn./etw. ausgeben means 'to pass off as'. *Er gab das gefälschte Bild als echt aus.* The refl. means 'to pass oneself off as, pretend to be' or 'to make oneself out to be or make out that one is sth.'. *Er gab sich für einen Millionär aus.* **Vorgeben** means 'to pretend to be' and is mostly used with an infin. It implies a false claim in words, not actions. *Sie gab vor, krank gewesen zu sein.* It is occasionally found with a n. *Er gab Verpflichtungen gegenüber seinen Eltern vor,* pretended he had obligations to his parents.

> Er gab diese Bekannte für/als seine Schwester aus.   Sie gab das Gedicht als ihr Werk aus.
> Die beiden gaben sich für Experten auf diesem Gebiet aus/ . . . gaben vor, Experten zu sein.
> Sie gab sich für älter aus, als sie wirklich war.   Er gab sich für deinen Bruder aus.
> Fritz gab vor, von der Sache gar nichts zu wissen.
> Da er nicht Fußball spielen wollte, gab er vor, sich das Bein verletzt zu haben.

3. Sich (dat.) **den Anschein geben** means 'to create the false impression that sth. is the case'. It is followed either by an infin. or an *als ob*-clause (often shortened to *als*) and occasionally by the gen. Cf. APPEARANCE 3. **So tun, als ob** is an equivalent in everyday language.

> Er gab sich den Anschein, ein guter Maler zu sein, doch niemand hatte jemals ein Bild von ihm zu Gesicht bekommen.   Gib dir doch nicht den Anschein, als ob du etw. davon verstündest!
> Christine konnte sich nicht erinnern, jemals mit der ehemaligen Klassenkameradin so nahe befreundet gewesen zu sein, wie sich diese den Anschein gab.
> Sie tat so, als ob sie ihn nicht gesehen hätte.   Sie tat so, als wäre gar nichts geschehen.
> Er tat so, als wäre er Weltreisender, hatte aber sein Wissen meist aus Büchern.
> Er machte die Schublade auf und tat so, als ob er etw. suchte.

4. Vortäuschen means 'to pretend, feign, or simulate', and suggests that this is done for one's own advantage, either to get out of doing something one does not want to do or to avoid an embarrassing situation. It suggests action rather than, or as well as, words and is used with an obj. or an infin.

> Weil sie nicht zur Ausschußsitzung gehen wollte, täuschte sie starke Kopfschmerzen vor.
> Er täuschte eine Beinverletzung vor. Or Er täuschte vor, verletzt zu sein.

5. Vorschützen means 'to use sth. falsely as an excuse or pretext'. It suggests a claim rather than action.

> Um die Klassenarbeit nicht mitschreiben zu müssen, schützte der Schüler starkes Zahnweh vor.

6. Heucheln is stronger than the other words discussed. As it implies hypocrisy, it involves an adverse judgement, whereas *vortäuschen* need not express disapproval. *Heucheln* either has no obj. or has qualities like *die Liebe, die Reue, die Fröhlichkeit,* etc. as obj. The past part. of *erheucheln* **erheuchelt** is occasionally found in the same sense, but *geheuchelt* is also used. *Seine Zufriedenheit war nur erheuchelt/geheuchelt.*

Er heuchelt nur, in Wirklichkeit denkt er gar nicht so.
Um Interesse zu heucheln, betrachtete Marion das Bild aufmerksam.

prevent, stop s.o. [from] doing sth., keep s.o. from doing sth., hinder

vs. The meaning of the first three *vs.* is 'to ensure that s.o. does not do sth. or that sth. does not happen'. **Prevent** takes either an obj., *This prevented an accident, loss, war*, etc., or a gerund with and without *from, They prevented s.o. [from] doing sth.*

1. In its main meaning 'to prevent s.o. [from] doing sth.' **hindern** is a syn. of *verhindern* and differs from it only syntactically. *Hindern* is used with a personal obj. and *an* with a verbal n. or a n. denoting an action. An infin. may follow with *an* appearing as *daran*. Although optional, *daran* is usually included.

Der Knebel hinderte ihn am Sprechen.   *Der Knebel hinderte ihn daran, zu sprechen.*
Der Polizist hinderte den Betrunkenen an der Weiterfahrt.
Der Polizist hinderte den Betrunkenen daran, weiterzufahren.
Die iranischen Behörden hinderten viele Franzosen an der Ausreise or hinderten sie daran, auszureisen.

(*Hindern an* is occasionally found with a non-personal obj., *Der Streik hinderte die Zeitung am Erscheinen*, but non-native speakers are best advised to avoid this use as such sents. can always be formulated with *verhindern. Der Streik verhinderte das Erscheinen der Zeitung.* Likewise *Die Hose, die er trug, war viel zu groß, aber ein breiter Gürtel hinderte sie am Herunterrutschen*, can just as well be . . . *ein breiter Gürtel verhinderte, daß sie herunterrutschte.*)

2. Verhindern, 'to prevent', is used most frequently:
i. With a non-personal obj. *Durch einen anonymen Telefonanruf alarmiert, konnte die Polizei einen Banküberfall verhindern. Dieser Kompromiß verhinderte einen Krieg.*
ii. With *es* and *das* as obj. *Wenn du in dein Unglück rennen willst,—ich kann es nicht verhindern. Das müssen wir um jeden Preis verhindern.*
iii. With a *daß*-clause. *Durch härtere Strafen will man verhindern, daß die Kriminalität noch weiter ansteigt.*

The meaning of many sents. can often be expressed by more than one construction. The last sent. could be recast as *Durch härtere Strafen will man einen weiteren Anstieg der Kriminalität verhindern.* Since *hindern* and *verhindern* differ only in the constructions in which they are used, certain statements can be formulated with either. For some sents. there are four possibilities: (i) *Nichts soll uns daran hindern, den Plan durchzuführen*; or (ii) *Nichts soll uns an der Durchführung des Planes hindern*; or (iii) *Nichts soll verhindern, daß wir den Plan durchführen*; or (iv) *Nichts soll die Durchführung des Planes verhindern.* The first sent. in 2. ii could be *Wenn du in dein Unglück rennen willst,—ich kann dich nicht daran hindern.* Although all four transformations are not always possible, two often are.

3. Formerly *verhindern* was used with an infin. in act. forms, but this has gone out of use. It survives, however, in the pass. with *sein*. **Verhindert sein** means 'to be prevented from attending/doing sth. as planned'. In this pass. use, it is a fixed expression. Although most frequently encountered alone, it may be followed by an infin. or *an.*

Der Minister ist leider verhindert. Er muß an einer kurzfristig einberufenen Kabinettssitzung teilnehmen.
Ich bin dienstlich verhindert [zu kommen/an der Veranstaltung teilzunehmen].
Ich war umständehalber/durch eine Erkrankung am Erscheinen verhindert.
Er war wegen eines Todesfalles in der Familie an der Teilnahme verhindert.
Ich wollte dich schon besuchen, war aber verhindert.

4. Syns. of *hindern* and *verhindern.*

i. In one of its several senses **abhalten** means 'to keep or stop s.o. from doing sth.' or 'to restrain s.o. from some action' and is thus closely related to *hindern* and *verhindern*. It needs a personal obj. which can be followed by *von* + n., or by *davon* alone, or by an optional *davon* + infin. Cf. KEEP 11.

Er hielt den Freund von der unüberlegten Handlung/von einem dummen Streich ab.

Dringende Geschäfte haben mich leider [davon] abgehalten, an der Sitzung teilzunehmen.

Nichts kann uns davon abhalten, unseren Plan durchzuführen.

Er wollte unbedingt hingehen. Ich konnte ihn leider nicht davon abhalten.

ii. Verhüten means 'to prevent sth. not desired' and is a formal syn. of *verhindern*. It now occurs only in a few fixed expressions. *Es gelang mir, das Schlimmste zu verhüten. Das verhüte Gott!* It is found with *ein Unglück, ein Unfall, ein Brand,* and *Schaden* as objs., but *verhindern* is also commonly used with these ns.

iii. Vorbeugen implies foreseeing the possibility of an undesirable occurrence and taking steps to prevent it in good time. *Man beugt einem Konflikt/einem möglichen Angriff/einer Krankheit/einer Seuche vor.*

Durch Verhandlungen wollte man der Möglichkeit einer militärischen Auseinandersetzung vorbeugen.

Um Mißverständnissen/einer Fehlinterpretation/Fehlern vorzubeugen, möchte ich zuerst einiges erklären.

5. Hinder, hamper, impede. Behindern, which means 'to cause an activity or s.o. doing sth. to be interrrupted, delayed, or slowed down', is the main equivalent. It takes *bei* when the obj. is a person. *Der Lärm/Das Kind behinderte mich bei der Arbeit.*

Die Verletzung/Die schweren Gepäckstücke behinderte[n] ihn beim Gehen.

Das Gestrüpp behinderte unsere Schritte.

Dieser eine langsame Traktor behindert den ganzen Verkehr.

Ich glaube, sie stellen alle diese unnötigen Fragen, um die Verhandlungen zu behindern.

Hemmen suggests causing an action or development which has already begun to be delayed or slowed down. It is stylistically higher than *behindern*, and what it refers to is more abstract in nature. *Etw. hemmt die Entwicklung/den Fortschritt von etw.*

Organisationsfehler hemmten die Produktion.

Durch die mangelnde Düngung wurden die Pflanzen in ihrem Wachstum gehemmt.

Er war in seiner Entwicklung/fühlte sich in seiner Tätigkeit gehemmt.

Die unvermeidliche finanzielle Aufwand war ein hemmender Faktor.

process *n.* One sense. **Der Vorgang** can denote a single occurrence (cf. EVENT) or a series of occurrences which thus become a process, either a historical one or a natural, biological, or chemical one. *Ein historischer/biologischer Vorgang. Wachstumsvorgänge.* In the sense of 'a process', *der Vorgang* refers to a process that happens naturally or by itself. *Der Vorgang der Verdauung ist ziemlich kompliziert.* It is not applied to a process, technique, or method by which something is made to happen. One sense of **das Verfahren** conveys this meaning. An industrial process is always *ein Verfahren. Ammoniak wird durch das Haber-Bosch-Verfahren hergestellt. Sie entwickelten ein Verfahren, mit dem man minderwertige Eisenerze zu hochwertigem Eisen verhütten kann.*

produce, manufacture, mine. *vs.* **Produce** has two main meanings, 'bring into existence', i.e. 'to grow, manufacture, cause, or create', *to produce potatoes/cars/an effect,* and 'to bring forward to be examined', *to produce evidence.* It is a broad term whose meanings are divided among a number of G. vs. Section A discusses vs. relating to agricultural production and natural effects. Section B deals with vs. denoting industrial production, Section C lists vs. meaning 'to mine', and section D treats the equivalents of **produce** used with emotions, people, profit, results, and effects as obj. Section E discusses **produce** used with evidence, a ticket, etc. as obj.

A. Vs. referring to nature and to agricultural production. The area **produce** covers can be divided into several categories: (i) 'To bring into existence by a natural process'. *This soil/field produces a good crop. The earth produces trees and grass/an abundance of food. Friction produces heat. The power station produces electricity.* (ii) For plants and animals: 'To bring forth, yield offspring, seed, fruit'. *The trees produce fruit. The goat only produces two young at a time.* (iii) Of an area: 'To supply'. *A region produces wool and wheat.* (iv) With a sound as obj.: 'To cause to come about'. *How is the ch-sound produced?*

1. Erzeugen implies that something arises, apparently from nothing, often by a natural process. It refers to:
i. Agricultural products.
> Die Genossenschaft erzeugt in diesem Jahr mehr Milch, Eier und andere landwirtschaftliche Produkte als im vorigen Jahr.
> Der Boden erzeugt alles, was die Bewohner der Insel brauchen.

Produzieren sometimes occurs in this sense. *Gummi wurde ursprünglich nur in Brasilien produziert.*

ii. Effects in nature, including electricity and energy, *Reibung erzeugt Wärme*, and the whole process by which a sound is produced, *Wie werden die verschiedenen Laute erzeugt?* Cf. D. 4. iii.
> Das Kraftwerk erzeugt so viel Strom, daß ganz Berlin damit versorgt werden kann.
> Die Anziehungskraft der Sonne und des Mondes erzeugt die Gezeiten.

iii. It can translate *An area/A country produces cotton. Ägypten erzeugt sehr viel hochwertige Baumwolle.* **Anbauen**, 'to grow on a commercial scale', is an alternative. Cf. GROW 5. ii and iii. *In diesem Gebiet wird viel Weizen angebaut.* Only *erzeugen* states how much of an agricultural product is produced. *200 000 Tonnen Zucker werden jährlich erzeugt.* The adj. *wheat-producing* followed by *areas* becomes *Weizenanbaugebiete.*
> In Deutschland wird nicht so viel Wein erzeugt wie in Frankreich. Or Deutschland erzeugt nicht . . .

2. i. Bringen is used in reference to trees and land, as is **tragen**, which sometimes means 'to bear'.
> Diese Felder bringen immer einen guten Ertrag.   Der schlechte Boden bringt wenig.
> Der Baum/Acker trägt gut/schlecht/wenig.   Dieser Baum bringt immer eine gute Ernte.
> Der Apfelbaum trägt zum ersten Mal in diesem Jahr.

ii. In formal language **hervorbringen** can have trees, soil, and the earth as subj., but it is less commonly used than *erzeugen*. *Die Erde bringt alles hervor, was die Menschen brauchen. Der Baum bringt unzählige Früchte/Blüten hervor.* More usually *trägt Früchte* etc.

3. Produce offspring. *Whales only produce young every two years* can be *Wale* **haben/zeugen Nachwuchs** *nur alle zwei Jahre* or *Sie* **haben ein Junges** *nur alle zwei Jahre.* **Gebären**, 'to bear [young]', is another possibility. *Eine Ziegin gebiert nur zwei Junge auf einmal.*

B. Vs. denoting industrial production. (i) **Produce** means 'to work up from raw material or manufacture'. *To produce cars, textiles, steel, etc.* (ii) In relation to mines it means 'to supply'. *The mine produces silver.*

1. In everyday language **herstellen** is the usual v. expressing the meaning 'to manufacture or make'. It is used when things are produced as a trade, not as a hobby, and continuously, either by hand or more frequently by machines; hence *die Massenherstellung.*

Der Betrieb stellt Stahlmöbel her.   *Die Fabrik/Das Werk stellt täglich 2 000 Autos her.*

Die Herstellung dieses Produktes wurde eingestellt, weil man nur 500 Stück im Monat absetzen konnte.

Das Fernsehgerät wird in Serie hergestellt.

(*Herstellen* also means 'to establish or bring about' in combination with abstract ns. like *eine Verbindung, ein Verhältnis,* 'relationship', or *Beziehungen,* relations. *Die Lehrer sind bemüht, ein gutes Verhältnis zu den Eltern der Schüler herzustellen.*)

2. Produzieren is also used, particularly in the language of economists, in the sense 'to manufacture'.

In dem Werk werden Chemikalien produziert.

Die Industrie produziert mehr als sie absetzen kann.

3. Fertigen, being the technical term for *herstellen,* is not usual in everyday language but occurs often in writing or discourse about manufacturing. It refers most frequently to industrial production but can also be applied to hand-made goods. *Das Gerät wird am Fließband gefertigt.*

Die Einzelteile der Airbus-Flugzeuge wurden bisher in den Fabriken der Partnerfirmen gefertigt und anschließend in Toulouse zusammenmontiert.

4. Anfertigen is often translated by *make* as well as by **produce**. It implies making with care, and it is the appropriate word when things are made singly or in small numbers for a special purpose or order.

Die schönen Kleider, die Großvater von Schneiderinnen für Großmutter hatte anfertigen lassen, hingen noch im Schrank.

Es gibt noch Handwerker, die auf Bestellung, nach Maß, und nach persönlichem Geschmack Möbelstücke aus hochwertigem Rohstoff anfertigen.

The obj. is frequently something produced by mental effort.

Man fertigt ein Gutachten/eine Zeichnung/ein Verzeichnis/eine Liste/ein Protokoll/eine Übersetzung an.

5. Gewinnen means 'to obtain, extract, or produce one thg. from another, often from a natural product'.

Zucker wird in Europa aus Rüben, in tropischen Ländern aus Zuckerrohr gewonnen.

Roheisen wird aus Eisenerz gewonnen.   *Der Saft wird aus reifen Früchten gewonnen.*

The *mine produces silver* is expressed as *In diesem Bergwerk wird Silber abgebaut/gefördert/gewonnen.* Cf. C.

C. Vs. relating to mining.

1. One sense of **abbauen** is the chief equivalent of **mine**. It does not specify the method.

Erze und Kohle werden in dieser Gegend abgebaut.   *Die Braunkohle wird im Tagebau abgebaut.*

2. In relation to mining **fördern** means 'to bring material from under the earth to the surface along horizontal or up vertical shafts'. *Öl, Erdgas, Kohle und Erze werden gefördert.* It is often used with *zutage,* to bring to daylight or to the surface.

In der Berichtzeit wurden 100 000 Tonnen Kohle gefördert.

Im Erzgebirge wurde eine reiche Ausbeute von Uran zutage gefördert.

3. Besides meaning 'to win and to gain', **gewinnen** expresses the sense 'to mine' mineral resources. In the case of precious metals it usually covers both the process of removal from the earth and that of refining. *Gold wird noch in Westaustralien gewonnen.*

D. Meanings of **produce** discussed here. (i) 'To cause, give rise to, bring about an emotion, condition, effect, or action'. *Sth. produces a feeling of contentment/a desire for* *change/tension/a reaction. Certain bacteria produce fermentation. Sth. produces an effect/a result.* (ii) Of countries, families, and periods: 'To bring forth'. *The family has produced several great mathematicians. The country has produced some outstanding sportsmen of late.* (iii) 'To compose a work of literature or art'. *From 1878 until his death Fontane produced a new work each year.*

1. Hervorrufen means 'to cause, bring about, give rise to'. In combination with certain ns. it translates **produce**. The obj. can be *Gelächter, Heiterkeit, Erstaunen, Kritik, ein Eindruck, eine Reaktion, Diskussion, Protest, Beifall, eine Änderung, Spannungen, Verwirrung, Verwunderung, Interesse.*

> *Der Krieg in Vietnam hat auch in den Ländern, deren Truppen dort kämpften, Protest hervorgerufen.*
> *Gewisse Zustände rufen bestimmte Krankheiten hervor.*
> *Die Rede rief bei allen Heiterkeit/ein Lächeln/einen tiefen Eindruck hervor.*
> *Der Brand hat eine Panik/allgemeine Verwirrung hervorgerufen.*
> *Die endlosen Diskussionen haben bei der Öffentlichkeit Gleichgültigkeit diesem Thema gegenüber hervorgerufen.* *Diese Bakterien rufen Gärung hervor.*

2. Erzeugen is sometimes used with intangibles and emotions as obj. *Hervorrufen* is more usual.

> *Der erste Teil des Vortrags war interessant, aber der Rest hat bei den Zuhörern nur Langeweile erzeugt. Also . . . hervorgerufen.* *Hunger erzeugt Unzufriedenheit.*
> *Statt zu beruhigen, hat die Anwesenheit der Polizei Spannung erzeugt/hervorgerufen.*

3. Entstehen means 'to come into existence' and can express the meaning 'to be formed or produced'. *Bei dieser Reaktion entsteht ein giftiges Gas,* a poisonous gas is produced in/by this reaction. Sents. of the type *A produces B* can sometimes be translated by *entstehen* if formulated in the form *Through* or *As a result of A, B is produced. Durch diese unklaren Worte entstand ein völlig falscher Eindruck.*

> *In diesen Jahren entstanden die bedeutendsten Werke des Künstlers.*
> *Erkrankungen, die durch Vitaminmangel entstanden sind, sind leicht zu behandeln.*
> *Es dauerte einige Zeit, bis man die schlechten Lebensbedingungen, die durch den Krieg entstanden waren, beseitigt hatte.*

4. Hervorbringen expresses the meaning 'to produce' in the following contexts.
i. The subj. is a country, region, family, race, or some aspect of civilization, and the obj. artists, great men and women, or their works. In this context *hervorbringen* is not considered formal.

> *Die Familie hat mehrere bedeutende Mathematiker hervorgebracht.*
> *Die Stadt hat bedeutende Musiker hervorgebracht.*
> *In dieser Zeit brachte Italien seine bedeutendsten Kunstwerke hervor.*
> *In vieler Hinsicht ist Charles Dickens der größte Romancier, den England bisher hervorgebracht hat.*

ii. The subj. is a creative person, the obj. his or her works.

> *Trotz der ständigen Überwachung durch die Geheimpolizei brachte der Dichter bedeutende Werke hervor.*

iii. The obj. is a sound, either of speech or of musical instruments. It refers to the manner in which an individual produces a sound. In contrast, *wie ein Laut erzeugt wird* refers to everything that is involved in the production of a sound.

> *Keine Worte schildern, wie wunderbar dieser Mann den Nasallaut hervorbrachte.*
> *Holger konnte nicht Trompete spielen. Er versuchte es aber und brachte nur einen kläglichen Ton hervor.*

(With *Töne* and *Worte* as obj. and frequently neg., *hervorbringen* is translated as [*not to*] *utter* or [*not to*] *say* or *to be speechless with surprise*, etc. This idea is expressed more commonly by **von sich geben** and **herausbringen.** *Der Verletzte gab nur Schmerzenslaute von sich. Vor Angst/Aufregung brachte das Kind kein Wort/keinen Ton hervor/heraus.*)

5. Bringen is used with *Ergebnis* or *Resultat* as obj. *Die Versuchsreihe brachte aufschlußreiche/negative Ergebnisse. Seine Bemühungen brachten keine positiven Ergebnisse/Resultate.* **Erbringen** also means 'to produce sth. of the nature of a result' but is more formal than *bringen. Die Versuche erbrachten neue Erkenntnisse/gar nichts.* **Erzielen**, 'to ACHIEVE', can be used with *man* or a person as subj., or in the pass. to translate *produce a result*, etc. *Mit dieser Methode hat man/wurden gute Ergebnisse erzielt* is a transl. of *This method produced . . . Man hat mit dieser Methode der Bodenbearbeitung hohe Erträge erzielt*, produced high yields. With *Wirkung*, *erzielen* implies that the effect was aimed at. *Die Maßnahmen zur Förderung der Industrie haben nicht die gewünschte Wirkung erzielt.* **Hervorrufen** states that an effect occurred. *Diese Antwort rief bei verschiedenen Zuhörern verschiedene Wirkungen hervor.* The usual v. with *Wirkung* is **haben**. *Die Rede hatte eine völlig unerwartete Wirkung.* **Hervorbringen** is used in all these contexts, but only in elevated language. *Die Reformen brachten gute Resultate hervor. Diese Arznei bringt eine Wirkung auf das Gehirn hervor.*

6. The obj. of **bringen** and **tragen** can also be monetary profit and interest, but the E. equivalent is not always **produce**. *Mein Guthaben bei der Sparkasse bringt zur Zeit hohe Zinsen. Die Spareinlagen tragen Zinsen. Das Geschäft brachte einen guten Gewinn.* An alternative is **abwerfen**. *Das Geschäft wirft einen guten Gewinn ab/wirft nichts ab.*

7. Bringen and **erbringen** are used with *Gewinn* = 'benefit' and the syn. *der Nutzen. Diese Reformen brachten einen dauernden Gewinn. Diese Erfindung/Verbesserung hat großen Nutzen/Gewinn erbracht.*

E. Produce also means 'to bring forth or out of sth. so that it can be looked at or examined'. *After some searching she produced an old photograph from the drawer. To be accepted as evidence, the documents must be produced. The defence produced conclusive evidence during the trial. He failed to produce his ticket/passport.*

1. Sometimes this meaning can be translated by **hervorbringen**, which means 'to take or produce a thg. from a place of concealment'. In the spoken language, **hervorholen** is usual.

Er brachte/holte einen Korkenzieher aus seiner Hosentasche hervor.

Nach einigem Suchen brachte sie eine alte Photographie aus der Schublade hervor.

2. Produce *proof* or *evidence: Beweise* **liefern/vorlegen/erbringen**. **Produce** *a witness: Einen Zeugen* **beibringen**. *Beibringen* is a formal word also used for documents, evidence, etc.

Die Verteidigung legte dem Gericht neues Beweismaterial vor.

Für seine Behauptungen muß er noch den Beweis erbringen/Beweise beibringen.

Der Wissenschaftler hat überzeugende Beweise für seine Theorie geliefert.

Der Staatsanwalt konnte schlüssige Beweise für die Schuld des Angeklagten beibringen/erbringen.

Er konnte ein Alibi erbringen.   *Bringen Sie ein ärztliches Attest/die nötigen Papiere bei!*

3. With *Fahrkarte/Paß/Führerschein* etc. **vorzeigen** is the normal word, **vorweisen** the official one. With *Ausweis, Zeugnisse*, and *Referenzen*, **vorlegen** is also used.

Wer eine Sendung von der Post abholt, muß den Paß oder Personalausweis vorweisen.

Man muß die Benutzerkarte vorzeigen, wenn man Bücher ausleiht. Ich habe meine vergessen.

protect *v.*

1. Schützen, meaning 'to offer or provide protection against a danger or sth. unpleasant or threatening', is the general term. It is used with people, animals, and things as subj. and obj., with *vor* or sometimes *gegen*, and can also be refl.

Die Familie hatte den Greis vor Verfolgungen geschützt.

Es ist die Pflicht der Armee, das Land vor Feinden zu schützen/die Landesgrenzen zu schützen.

Isolierungen sollen Wand und Dach vor Wärmeverlust schützen.

Wir müssen die Landschaft vor/gegen Umweltverschmutzung schützen.
Du solltest deine Augen vor der grellen Sonne schützen.
Die Sonnebrille schützt die Augen vor der grellen Sonne.
Er tat alles, um sich vor Eindringlingen zu schützen.   *Diese Zahnpasta schützt gegen Karies.*
Die Dunkelheit schützte den Dieb vor Entdeckung.   *Vögel und Tiere schützen ihre Jungen.*
Unkenntnis der Gesetze schützt nicht vor Strafe.
Du mußt dich vor Sonnenbrand schützen.

2. Beschützen is only used with people and animals as subj. and obj., not with things. It presupposes an imminent danger which the protector wards off with courage and energy from someone who is helpless or at least weaker.

Sie können sich ihm anvertrauen. Er wird Sie beschützen.
Der Junge beschützte seine kleine Schwester vor dem großen Hund.

3. Less common words. **Behüten** is 'to watch over lovingly and to protect or shield from harm'. It occurs in religious language, *Der Herr behüte dich vor allem Übel!* (Psalm 121: 7), and the past part. means 'protected' or 'sheltered' in the expression *ein behütetes Kind* or *eine behütete Kindheit.* In *Gott behüte uns vor solchem Unglück!* it is an elevated syn. of **bewahren vor**, to preserve or keep from harm etc. Cf. KEEP 8. *Man muß Kinder vor Unfällen bewahren. Bewahre mich, Herr, vor der Hand der Gottlosen; behüte mich vor den Gewalttätigen, die mich zu Fall bringen wollen* (Psalm 140: 4). **Beschirmen** means 'to shield in the moment of danger', but it belongs to the written language. *Er beschirmte sie vor allen Gefahren.*

Behüte mich wie einen Augapfel im Auge, beschirme mich unter dem Schatten deiner Flügel . . . vor meinen Feinden, die mir von allen Seiten nach dem Leben trachten. (Psalm 17: 8, 9)

provide *v.*

1. Provide for means 'to supply what is needed for sustenance and support'. *He provides for a large family* or *has a large family to provide for.* **Provide** sth. [**for** s.o.] or **provide** s.o. **with** sth. means 'to supply or furnish it' so that the person has it when needed. *Most animals provide food for their young. The government cannot provide all young people with jobs.*
i. With reference to the necessities of life, food, clothing, shelter, money, etc., **jmdn. versorgen** and **für jmdn. sorgen** both mean 'to provide for s.o.', 'to provide financially for s.o.'s upkeep'. *Er hat fünf Kinder zu versorgen* expresses the same meaning as *Er muß für fünf Kinder sorgen.* The past part. *versorgt* is often found, mostly with an adv. like *gut* or *reichlich, Die Witwe ist gut versorgt,* but *gesorgt* is not uncommon, *Für die Witwe ist gesorgt.* Only *versorgen* is used with *mit.* **Jmdn. versorgen mit** translates both *to provide sth. for s.o.* and *to provide s.o. with sth.* *Man versorgte die Flüchtlinge mit Nahrung und Kleidung.*

Er sorgt immer gut für seine alte Mutter/seine Familie.
Der Witwer konnte seine vier Kinder nur notdürftig versorgen.
Wer wird für die Familie sorgen, da der Vater nicht arbeiten kann?
Der alte Mann wurde von seiner Tochter mit Essen versorgt.

ii. Sorgen für and **versorgen mit** cover a wider range of contexts than those given in i. *Für etw. sorgen* means 'to see to it that sth. is done, obtained, or made available', i.e. 'to provide it'. Cf. SEE TO S.O./STH. 2. *Bei dem Picknick sorge ich für das Essen,* I am providing the food. The obj. of *versorgen* can be a person, a thing, or the refl. pronoun, and many kinds of ns. can follow *mit.*

Im Zirkus sorgt der Clown für Unterhaltung.
Während er im Krankenhaus war, versorgten ihn die Freunde mit Lesestoff.
Das Gehirn wird normalerweise sehr reichlich mit Blut versorgt.
Sie versorgten sich mit Trinkwasser, bevor sie zu ihrer Fahrt durch die Wüste aufbrachen.
Die Gemeinde wird mit Wasser aus dem Stausee versorgt.

iii. When **provide** means 'procure or get for s.o.', **beschaffen** may be the appropriate v. Cf. GET 6.

Die Regierung kann nicht allen Jugendlichen Arbeitsplätze beschaffen.

iv. In one of its senses **versehen mit** means 'to equip, supply, or fit [out] with' and translates **provide with** when it is synonymous with these words. *Das kleine Krankenhaus ist mit allem versehen, was zur Krankenpflege nötig ist. Versehen* is also refl. *Sie hatten sich für ihre Indienreise mit genügend Geld versehen.* In formal language *versehen* occurs where a simple v. would be used in E. *Man versieht einen Brief mit einer Unterschrift,* signs it; *man versieht ein Dokument mit einem Amtssiegel/Flaschen mit Etiketten/einen Text mit Anmerkungen.*

Bevor er nach London fuhr, versahen ihn Bekannte der Familie mit einigen Empfehlungsschreiben.
Für die lange Fahrt haben sie sich mit Proviant/mit allem Nötigen versehen.
Man hat das neue Theater mit sehr bequemen Polstersesseln versehen.

v. Ausrüsten means 'to equip'. It refers to the provision of special technical equipment for a particular purpose. *Alle Klassenzimmer sind mit modernen Unterrichtsmitteln ausgerüstet.* **Ausstatten** has a similar basic sense but is used in less technical contexts and is more like **provide** or *fit [out] with. Die Schule ist mit zwei Sprachlabors ausgestattet.* (*Ausstatten* can also mean 'to furnish' = 'to put furniture in', *ein geschmackvoll ausgestattetes Zimmer,* occasionally 'to endow with natural gifts', *ein mit vielen Talenten ausgestatter Mensch,* and 'to produce' (a book), *Der Verlag hat das Buch gut ausgestattet.*)

Die Nato-Streitkräfte sind mit den modernsten Waffen ausgerüstet.
Der Betrieb ist mit einem Computer/mit Spezialmaschinen für den Brückenbau ausgerüstet.
Man hat die Antarktisexpedition mit den neuesten Maschinen ausgerüstet.
Das Auto ist mit allem Komfort ausgestattet.
Sie haben ihre Wohnung mit antiken Möbeln ausgestattet.

vi. When two or more persons, towns, firms, etc. each make a contribution or provide something for an undertaking they support in common, the v. is **stellen**. If someone says, *'Ich stelle die Getränke',* it is implied that other people are providing something else. *Stellen* is often used to state what proportion of a total one component provides or makes up. *Lehrer stellen zur Zeit in der Bundesrepublik ein Drittel aller arbeitslosen Akademiker.*

Das kleinste Dorf stellte zehn Mann zur Bekämpfung des Waldbrandes, die größeren mehr.
Die Studenten haben die Getränke bezahlt, aber die Lehrkräfte stellten das Essen.

Stellen can be a shortened form of **jmdm. etw. zur Verfügung stellen**, to make available, to provide. This is often the appropriate expression when money or other things are provided for some purpose. **Bereitstellen** also means 'to provide or make money and other thgs. available'.

Die Stadt hat genügend Mittel für die Sanierung der Altstadt zur Verfügung gestellt.
Man stellte den Forschern alles zur Verfügung, was sie für die Untersuchung brauchten.
Die Bundesregierung hat die Mittel zum Ausbau der Autobahn bereitgestellt.

Zur Verfügung is understood in *Die Firma stellt den leitenden Angestellten einen Wagen* and *Für die Schüleraufführung stellte das Stadttheater die Kostüme. Hier werden die Lehrbücher, die die Schüler brauchen, von der Schule gestellt.*

vii. Aufkommen für means 'to accept responsibility for the cost of sth.' and may sometimes translate **provide**. *Solange meine Kinder studieren, muß ich für ihren Unterhalt aufkommen.*

Der reiche Bankier kam für die Schulden seines armen Bruders auf.
Die Versicherung wird für den Schaden an ihrem Auto aufkommen.

2. In another sense, **provide** means 'to have or give' a desirable or useful feature or quality. Common objs. are *satisfaction, an answer, an opportunity, an example, a solution, proof,* etc. In these cases, it is necessary to use the G. v. which customarily goes with the corresponding G. n. **Liefern**, the basic sense of which is 'to deliver', is used with *der Beweis, der Gesprächsstoff,* and *der Vorwand.* **Erbringen**, 'to yield', is used with *der Beweis, der Nachweis, der Nutzen,* and *die Aufklärung,* but is formal in tone. **Bieten** is used with *die Gelegenheit, eine Antwort,* and *eine Lösung.* Cf. OFFER 1. **Bereiten** is used with mental states, such as *die Genugtuung* and *das Vernügen.* Cf. GIVE 9. **Leisten** is used with *die Entschädigung,* 'compensation', and **spenden** with *Schatten, Wärme,* and *Trost.*

> Der Rechtswanwalt hat den Beweis erbracht, daß sein Mandant unschuldig war.
> Die Rationalisierung soll wirtschaftlichen Nutzen erbringen (provide/produce economic benefit).
> Die Untersuchung hat keine Aufklärung des Falles erbracht.
> Der Korruptionsfall lieferte der Stadt wochenlang Gesprächsstoff.
> Diese Ausstellung bietet die Gelegenheit, sich über Picassos Gesamtwerk zu informieren.
> Dieser Vorschlag bietet uns eine leichte Lösung, auf die wir selbst nie gekommen wären.
> Die Transportfirma leistet Entschädigung für alle Sendungen, die verloren gehen.
> Der Ofen spendet Wärme für zwei Zimmer.   Der Baum/Der Felsen spendete Schatten.

3. If a law, agreement, etc. provides for something, it states that this is to happen. **Provide** meaning 'to order or lay down' can be expressed by **bestimmen** and **festlegen**, discussed under DETERMINE 2, or **verfügen**, discussed under ORDER 1. iii. A syn. is **vorsehen**, 'to provide for', with a law, regulation, contract, plan, etc. as subj. (Its primary sense is 'to intend'. *Das Geld ist für die Anschaffung von Büchern vorgesehen.*)

> Das Testament verfügt/bestimmt, daß seine Frau und Kinder sein Vermögen erben sollen. Also In seinem Testament bestimmte/verfügte er, daß . . .
> Das Gesetz legt fest, daß alle Kinder die Schule vom sechsten bis zum sechzehnten Lebensjahr besuchen müssen.   Dieser Fall ist in den Vorschriften nicht vorgesehen.
> In dem Abkommen ist eine Erweiterung des Handels vorgesehen.
> Die Vereinbarung zwischen dem Bund und den Ländern sieht eine Erhöhung der Zahlungen an die Universitäten vor.

public *n.* The n. **public** has two senses. One is 'all the people or the community as a whole in a particular area or country, but not in any organized capacity'. *The general public hardly understood what was happening. The public is calling for sweeping reforms.* Another meaning is 'a particular section or group of a community who share a common interest, activity, or characteristic'. *The sporting public. The reading public. This author/film director has a large public in France.* For the first sense G. uses *die Öffentlichkeit,* for the second *das Publikum.*

1. Die Öffentlichkeit means 'all the community'. *The general public is die breite Öffentlichkeit.* The phrs. *in der Öffentlichkeit* and *in aller Öffentlichkeit* mean 'in public', *aller* expressing some surprise. An alternative is *vor allen Leuten.* Cf. PEOPLE 4.

> Die Öffentlichkeit fordert einschneidende Änderungen.
> Diese Politiker haben die Öffentlichkeit absichtlich irregeführt.
> Der Skandal war allmählich an die Öffentlichkeit gesickert.
> Er hat über Privatangelegenheiten in aller Öffentlichkeit geredet.
> Der Untersuchungsausschuß tagte unter Ausschluß der Öffentlichkeit.

(Note that *die Öffentlichkeit* is also the n. from *öffentlich* and means 'publicness or accessibility to the public'. *1848 forderten die Revolutionäre die Einführung von Schwurgerichten und die Öffentlichkeit aller Gerichtsverhandlungen.*)

2. i. Das Publikum can mean 'the audience', *Als der Vorhang fiel, klatschte das Publikum lange Beifall,* but it also means 'groups who are interested in some activity or who have sth. in common'. There are compounds like *das Sportpublikum, das Lesepublikum, das Musikpublikum.*

> Er muß immer ein Publikum haben.   Solche Romane finden immer ihr Publikum.
> Dieser Autor hat ein großes Publikum in Frankreich.
> In dieser Gaststätte verkehrt ein vornehmes Publikum (clientele).

ii. In another sense **das Publikum** denotes a large section of population. It is often, though not always, combined with *breit*. It is not used in relation to politics or public opinion and usually implies interest in a particular thing. *Er wollte seine Bildersammlung dem breiten Publikum zugänglich machen,* open it/make it accessible to the general public. *Sie wendet sich mit ihren Filmen/mit ihren Reden an ein breites Publikum. Solche Musik gefällt dem Publikum immer* suggests that it is popular with a wide section of the public. *Der Publikumserfolg* means 'success with a broad section of the community' and *der Publikumsgeschmack* 'the taste of the general community' or 'popular taste'.

Der Schauspieler/Der Sänger ist beim Publikum beliebt/ein Liebling des Publikums.

pull, draw, drag, tug, tear *vs.* Some senses.

1. The sense of **pull** dealt with here is 'to use force so that a pers. or thg. is drawn towards or after s.o./sth. or removed from somewhere'. *Pull your chair up to the table! The baby pulled its father's hair. Can you pull the cork out? The tractor pulled the car out of the mud. They pulled him out of the water.* **Draw** is used in similar contexts but suggests a gentler action. *He drew me aside/her into the conversation. An animal draws a cart or other vehicle. She drew the document out of its folder.* **Tug** suggests pulling quickly and intermittently on or at something, but the intensity varies, so that a tug can vary from gentle to hard. *She tugged at my sleeve.*
i. The equivalent of both **pull** and **draw** when normal intensity is involved is **ziehen**. It can be used in translating all the examples above. *Ziehen Sie den Stuhl an den Tisch [heran]! Man zieht einen Vorhang in die Höhe/zieht den Vorhang zu. Sie zogen das Boot ans Land. Sie zog den Schleier vors Gesicht. Man zieht einen Korken aus einer Flasche* or *zieht den Korken heraus.* Someone might say to a child, '*Zieh deine Socken hoch!*' The sign *Pull!* on doors is *Ziehen! Ziehen* is used for animals and carts etc. *Ein Esel zog den Wagen. Das Pferd konnte die schwere Last nicht ziehen. Wie viele Waggons kann diese Lokomotive ziehen? Die Hunde zogen den Schlitten mit großer Geschwindigkeit.* People can be the obj. *Er zog mich beiseite/ins Zimmer. Er zog sie zärtlich an sich. Sie zog alle ins Gespräch. Sie zog ihn neben sich aufs Sofa. Der Junge zog sich die Mütze über die Ohren. Ziehen* is used with *aus. Der erschöpfte Schwimmer wurde aus dem Wasser/an Bord gezogen.* (Another transl. is hauled.) *Wir zogen das Unkraut aus der Erde.* Refl.: *Sie zog sich ans Ufer/aus dem Wasser.*
ii. Ziehen an corresponds to **pull by** or **pull on** but is sometimes needed where E. has no prep. *Das Baby zog den Vater an den Haaren. Sie zog mich am Ärmel.* (Also *zupfte.*) *Der Lehrer zog den Jungen am Ohr. Wir zogen alle an dem Seil. Der Hund zog an der Leine.*
iii. Ziehen is also used for drawing a watch out of a pocket, *Er zog seine Uhr aus der Tasche* or *zog die Uhr [heraus],* as well as for drawing a sword, gun, etc. *Der Ritter zog sein Schwert. Er zog einen Revolver/ein Messer und bedrohte uns.*
iv. Zupfen is 'to pull gently and carefully at' something and is similar to **tug** implying a gentle action. If another person is involved, *zupfen* implies the wish to attract that person's attention. It is also used for removing a loose thread etc. gently. *Sie zupfte [sich] einen losen Faden vom Mantel.*

Er zupfte nervös an seiner Krawatte.   *Er zupfte sich ein Haar vom Bart.*
Sie zupfte ihn so verdeckt am Ärmel, daß es niemand sonst bemerkte.

2. Drag sth. means 'to pull it along the ground slowly and with difficulty, usually because it is too heavy to carry'. In *I drag s.o./sth. into or out of a place,* **drag** suggests pulling roughly and using force. *They turned the car over and dragged the driver out.* **Tug** too can imply pulling hard or violently [at sth.] *We tugged so hard that the rope broke.*

i. Zerren implies greater force, effort, and difficulty than *ziehen*, a jerking or uneven motion, and often resistance on the part of the person or thing moved. With people as obj. it may suggest violence. It is close in meaning to **drag**. *Er zerrte den Sack über den Hof* suggests that it was very heavy and that considerable effort was needed. *Zerren an* means 'to pull violently at or to tug at'. *Der Hund zerrte an der Kette/Leine. Eine Sehne/Muskel zerren* is 'to pull a muscle'.

> *Die Entführer zerrten den Industriellen aus seinem Wagen.*
> *Die Räuber zerrten ihn in den Wald.*   *Wir haben so heftig am Seil gezerrt, daß es gerissen ist.*
> *Der Hund zerrte so lange an der Tischdecke, bis sie samt Geschirr und Besteck auf dem Boden lag.*

ii. The primary sense of **schleppen** is 'to tow'. *Der Dampfer schleppt die Lastkähne. Der beschädigte Schiff wurde in den Hafen geschleppt. Widerrechtlich abgestellte Fahrzeuge werden kostenpflichtig abgeschleppt.* With a person as obj. it means 'to drag or pull roughly and with effort'. *Passanten schleppten den Taumelnden in ein Haus.* With a thing as obj. *schleppen* can mean 'to drag' but frequently means 'to carry with difficulty' because of the weight. *Sie schleppte zwei große Koffer mit. Ich muß das Paket zur Post schleppen.* To convey the meaning 'drag', *hinter sich her* is normally added. *Er schleppte den schweren Sack hinter sich her in die Scheune. Er zog den Sack hinter sich her* suggests less effort.

> *Der Löwe schleppte das Beutetier ins Gebüsch* (carried or dragged).
> *Die Männer schleppten den schweren Ast hinter sich her.*

3. Schleppen expresses two other senses of **drag**. One is 'to take s.o. where the pers. does not want to go'. *Sie haben mich durch die ganze Stadt/mit ins Kino geschleppt.* The other, **sich schleppen**, is 'to drag oneself' meaning 'to move with great difficulty'. *Er konnte sich kaum noch zur Arbeit schleppen. Der Verletzte schleppte sich mit letzter Kraft an den Straßenrand. Sie konnte sich gerade noch ins Bett schleppen.* (*Sie schleppt sich mit dem schweren Gepäck*, she has a lot of trouble/difficulty in carrying it.)

4. The degree of force implied by **pull** varies. Where strong force is implied, E. can use **tear**. *The wind tore branches from many trees.* **Tear** is the usual v. when one thing is pulled or detached sharply from another. *She tore several pages out of the book.* The G. word in these situations is **reißen**. It translates **pull** when it implies a sudden and forceful pulling from or off something, or detachment of one thing from another. It translates **drag** in a more fig. context. *Der Diktator hat das ganze Land ins Verderben gerissen.*

> *Der starke Wind hat Äste von vielen Bäumen gerissen.*
> *Sie hat mehrere Blätter aus dem Buch gerissen.*
> *Er versuchte, mir die Zeitung aus der Hand zu reißen.*
> *Irgendjemand hat während der Nacht die Pflanzen aus der Erde gerissen. Or . . . hat sie ausgerissen.*
> *Die Strömung hat den Schwimmer weit weg vom Strand gerissen.*
> *Zuerst müssen wir die alte Tapete von der Wand reißen.*
> *Der Hund riß an der Leine/Kette. Or Der Hund zerrte an der Leine.*

5. Draw a picture, line, etc. The usual equivalent of **draw** with a picture or figure as obj. is **zeichnen**. *Jmd. zeichnet ein Bild/eine Landschaft/ein Kind/einen Grundriß/ein Dreieck.* Cf. PAINT iii. When *die Linie*, 'LINE', is the obj., the usual v. is **ziehen**. *Er zog eine Linie mit dem Lineal unter der Aufgabe. Zeichnen* is occasionally found, but it suggests special care and often that the line drawn is in addition to others. *Man muß auch hier eine Linie zeichnen.* With *der Strich*, *ziehen* and **machen** are used. *Ich kann nicht besonders gut zeichnen—ich kann ja nicht einmal aus freier Hand einen geraden Strich ziehen. Er machte einen Strich durch die falschen Zahlen. Sie machte einen Strich unter jeder Aufgabe.*

punish v.

i. The normal equivalent is **bestrafen**, which needs an obj. *Bestrafen* takes *für* and *wegen* meaning 'for', and sometimes *mit*.

> *Die Mutter bestrafte den Jungen für seinen Ungehorsam, indem sie ihm nicht erlaubte, schwimmen zu gehen.* *Er wurde mit zehn Jahren Gefängnis bestraft.*
> *Bei dem geringsten Vergehen bestrafte er seine Kinder mit Stockhieben.*
> *Der Verbrecher wurde streng/schwer/hart bestraft.* *Zuwiderhandlungen werden bestraft.*

ii. Strafen is now not common, being used in the act. only with *das Schicksal* or *Gott* as subj. *Das Schicksal hat ihn schwer gestraft. Gott strafe mich, wenn ich lüge!* Some idiomatic expressions survive. *Ich bin mit etw. gestraft* means that I consider it a punishment that I have to do something or I am condemned to do something. *Ich bin mit dieser sinnlosen, langweiligen Arbeit gestraft. Mit dem Leben in diesem Ort ist er gestraft genug. Jmdn. mit Verachtung strafen* is 'to completely ignore him or her'. *Jmdn. strafend ansehen* and *jmdm. einen strafenden Blick zuwerfen* mean 'to look at s.o. with disapproval or cast s.o. a disapproving glance'.

iii. Ahnden is a legal term meaning 'to punish', but the obj. is a crime or a violation of the law, not a person.

> *Die Gerichte ahndeten streng jeden Verstoß gegen die Gesetze/jede Übertretung der Gesetze/alle Verbrechen.*

push v.

Push means 'cause s.o./sth. to move or fall by pressing against him/her/it with some force'. *Boys were pushing each other into the water.* **Push** also means 'cause sth. to move by walking along behind it'. *We pushed our bicycles up the steep hills.* It is also used fig.

1. The first sense of **push** is divided between *stoßen* and *drängen*.

i. Stoßen implies a sudden, forceful, or violent action which sets s.o./sth. in motion. The typical action is pushing someone deliberately with the hands. (In other senses *stoßen* need not imply a resulting change of position. *Er hat mich in die Rippen gestoßen.*)

> *Jeder, der am Rand des Schwimmbeckens stand, wurde ins Wasser gestoßen.*
> *Er wurde an die Wand gestoßen/zur Tür hinausgestoßen.* *Er stieß sie mit der Hand zur Seite.*

ii. Drängen is not as violent, forceful, or quick as *stoßen*, and can, but need not, be unintentional. *Die Menschen in einer [Menschen]menge drängen jmdn. irgendwohin.* If an action is suggested, it is using the lower part of the arm to move someone away. It is the usual v. for pushing someone away or from his/her place when violent action is not implied. *Man hat das Kind in die Ecke gedrängt. Ich wurde aus der Tür gedrängt.* **Abdrängen** implies that someone is moving in a certain direction and is pushed off his or her direct course. *Sie haben mich vom Bürgersteig abgedrängt.*

2. Drängen is used fig. *Eine Nachricht/Sache wird durch eine andere in den Hintergrund gedrängt.*

3. The equivalent of the second sense of **push** 'to move by walking behind' is **schieben**. It implies a fairly calm, even, and steady motion. *Sie schob den Kinderwagen auf den Balkon.*

> *Wir schoben die Fahrräder die steilen Hänge hoch.* Or in more formal language *Wir schoben sie . . . hinauf.*
> *Wir haben versucht, den Wagen zu schieben, aber er war im Schlamm festgefahren.*
> *Wenn du schiebst und ich ziehe, können wir die Karre vielleicht aus dem Schlamm kriegen.*
> *Er schob ein paar Kisten aus dem Weg, damit wir hindurchkönnten.*

Jmdm. etw. **zuschieben** is 'to push sth. over to s.o.' *Er schob mir das Buch zu.*

4. Push *a button* is *[auf] einen Knopf* **drücken**. Cf. PRESS. **Push** *the door open,* if no great effort is required, is *die Tür* **aufdrücken**; if more effort is needed **aufstoßen** is used. *Sie drückte die angelehnte Tür auf und ging hinein. Er stieß die Tür mit dem Fuß auf.*

5. Push one's way *through a crowd.* Ich **bahnte mir** *einen Weg durch die Menge* means that I made or worked my way through the crowd and says nothing about the manner. **Sich drängen** implies more force and usually lack of consideration for others. *Rücksichtslos drängte er sich durch die Menge.*

put *v.* **Put** has several meanings and is used with a wide variety of objs. The main meanings are 1. **Put** = 'to move or place sth. or s.o. somewhere'. *I put the book on the table. She put the child to bed.* 2. **Put** = 'to express'. *How can I put it?* 3. **Put** = 'to write somewhere'. *I'll put a cross here.* 4. **Put** = 'to propound, express'. *I'll put my views/point of view.* 5. **Put** = 'to submit'. *I put a proposal.* 6. **Put** = 'suggest'. *I put it to you that this evidence is invented.* 7. **Put** = 'to invest'. *She put her money into shares.* 8. **Put** = 'to bet'. *He put £10 on that horse.* 9. **Put** = 'estimate'. *I put the distance at five kilometres.* 10. **Put** = 'to expend'. *I put time/effort into sth.* 11. **Put** = 'to classify'. *I wouldn't put X in the same category/class as Y.* 12. **Put** = 'to cause people and thgs. to be in a particular state or condition'. *That puts me in a difficult position.* 13. **Put** = 'to make s.o. bear sth.' *This/They put additional responsibility/pressure on a pers.* 14. **Put** + abstract n. + prep. + n. *I put my trust in s.o./sth.* 15. Some idioms. The sections below follow these numbers. Cf. *hineingeben* under ADD 10.

1. Put means 'to place, move into a place'. In extended use, there are expressions like *to put a satellite into orbit* and *We put an advertisement in a newspaper/power into s.o.'s hands/sth. on the market.* People can be the obj. *They put the sick man to bed. He was put in hospital. We have put a man on the moon. They put s.o. out of the house.* **Put** is a broad term which denotes a number of actions. Although **tun** has a similar range of meaning, it is more usual to divide up the action according to the resulting position of the object or person moved. Thus when something is placed in a vertical or upright position **stellen**, 'to stand sth. somewhere', is used. Cf. STAND. When someone puts something in a horizontal, lying position, **legen** is the normal v., and when s.o./sth. is put in a sitting position, **setzen**. **Stecken** is 'to put one thg. into another which usually covers or encloses it', not e.g. for putting something in a cupboard. *Er steckte die Hände in die Taschen.* **Stecken** is also used when **put** and *stick* are syns. *Er steckte den Kopf durch die Tür/aus dem Fenster.* **Hängen** is used when a hanging position results. As Eggeling (1961b: 278) points out, it is imperative that the appropriate word be used. Sents. containing the wrong v., such as *Die Mutter stellte das Kind ins Bett* or *Sie legte das Glas auf den Tisch,* sound absurd.

i. One sense of **tun** is a general equivalent of **put**. It tends to be used when none of the other vs. fits exactly or when the resulting position is not clear. As explained under ADD, it is used for adding a liquid or granular solid to something else, but it has a wider range than this.

Wohin hast du die Schere getan?   *Ich muß noch die Abfälle in den Mülleimer tun.*
Tu' den Deckel auf die Dose/die Schachtel!   *Ich tue gerade die Wäsche in die Waschmaschine.*

ii. Stellen means 'to put or stand in an upright position'.
With things as obj. *Ich stelle die Bücher in das Regal zurück.*

Man stellt die Blumen ins Wasser/in eine Vase/einen Topf auf den Herd/ein Fahrrad in den Keller/den Ellbogen auf den Tisch. Das Auto habe ich gerade in die Garage gestellt.
Wenn du den Tisch deckst, stell' bitte zu jedem Teller ein Glas!
Stell' bitte die Flasche in den Kühlschrank!

With reference to people. Sometimes it means 'to put so that they stand'.

Sie stellte den kleinen Jungen zum Anziehen auf den Stuhl.

Das gestürzte Kind wurde wieder auf die Füße gestellt.

Fig. expressions. *Die Soldaten wurden vor ein Kriegsgericht gestellt.*

Er stellt mit seinem Tennisspiel die anderen Spieler in den Schatten.

iii. Legen is 'to put in a horizontal position' so that the object lies.

Sie legte das Buch/die Teller auf den Tisch/die Gabeln neben die Teller.

Lege deine Anzüge sorgfältig in den Koffer!   *Er legte ihr ein Kissen unter den Kopf.*

Er legte ihr die Hand auf den Arm/legte den Arm um sie.

Ich lege die Handtücher zu den anderen in den Schrank.

Man legt [lose] Seiten in ein Ringbuch/einen Brief zu den Akten.

Leg' bitte den Deckel auf den Topf!   *Legst du denn immer die Füße auf den Tisch?*

Legen is also used for putting one thing over another. *Er zog die Jacke aus und legte sie sich über die Schulter. Man legt die Hände auf die Ohren. Man legt einen Verband auf eine Wunde/um das verletzte Bein*, puts a bandage on/round it.

With reference to people. Only in reference to a baby who has to be placed in a bed is *legen* used for *to put to bed. Die Mutter legte das Kind ins Bett/in den Kinderwagen.* Otherwise the expression is *ins Bett bringen. Es ist spät—wir müssen die Kinder ins Bett bringen.*

Legen is used in connection with *die Kette*, chain. *Man legt einen Hund an die Kette/einen Menschen in Ketten. Er legte ihr eine Kette um den Hals.* Also *Er hängte ihr eine Kette . . . (Die [Hals]kette*, necklace.)

Etw. aus der Hand legen is 'to put it down'.

Fig. expressions. *Man legt jmdm. Hindernisse in den Weg. Jmdm. Steine in den Weg legen* is 'to put difficulties in s.o.'s way'. *Man legt die Karten [offen] an/auf den Tisch.* (Also *Man deckt sie auf.*) *Man legt jmdm. Knüppel zwischen die Beine. Wollen Sie die Sache in meine Hände legen? Man legt sein Schicksal/die Macht in jmds. Hände.*

iv. Setzen means 'to put in a sitting position'. With people as obj. it means 'to sit s.o. somewhere'.

Sie setzte ihm das Kind auf den Schoß.   *Der Vater setzte den Jungen aufs Pferd.*

In reference to things *setzen* has largely given way to *stellen.* Although *setzen* is possible, *stellen* is now the usual v. in *Man stellt Tassen auf den Tisch/einen Topf auf den Herd/den Eimer/einen Koffer auf den Boden.* Either can be used in *Ich setze/stelle mal den Koffer ab, er ist sehr schwer,* but *Ich setze [Tee]wasser auf* is the only possibility. *Setzen* is the normal v. with *Fuß* as obj. and means 'to put or set foot on'. *Sie waren froh, als sie ihren Fuß wieder an Land setzten. Nie wieder setze ich meinen Fuß über die Schwelle dieses Hauses.* But *Er stellte/setzte einen Fuß auf die Treppe und blieb stehen. Setzen* is used for putting something near, on, or to a part of the body. It is not used for clothes, with the exception of hats, nor for a bandage.

Sie wollte gerade das Glas an den Mund setzen; da mußte sie lachen und stellte es wieder auf den Tisch.

Er setzte ihm ein Messer an die Kehle/eine Pistole auf die Brust.

Er setzte den Hut auf den Kopf.   *Er setzte den Hut auf.*

With reference to people *setzen* is used for putting someone on a diet, rations, etc. *Man setzte die Expeditionsteilnehmer auf halbe Ration/jmdn. auf Krankenkost/einen Häftling auf Brot und Wasser.* Also *Man setzt jmdn. an die Stelle eines anderen. Man setzt jmdm. einen Verfolger auf die Spur/Fährte* but *setzt Hunde auf eine Spur an. Man setzt jmdn. vor die Tür/auf die Straße/an die frische Luft,* puts/turns s.o. out of the room/house. **Versetzen** is used for putting oneself in another's position. *Versetzen sie sich in meine Lage!*

v. Stecken, to put an object wholly or partly in a hollow space. *Sie versuchte, den Schlüssel in das Schloß zu stecken, aber er paßte nicht.*

Nachdem er den Knopf angenäht hatte, steckte er den Nadel ins Nadelkissen zurück.
Ich steckte meine Wäsche der letzten drei Wochen in einen großen Plastiksack und ging zum Waschsalon.
Sie steckte sich eine Brosche an das Kleid/einen Ring an den Finger/den Brief in den (Brief)kasten.
Er steckte sich eine Blume ins Knopfloch/eine Feder in den Hut/Watte in die Ohren.

With reference to people. *Man steckt Kinder in neue Kleider. Man steckt jmdn. ins Gefängnis. Er steckt immer die Nase in Sachen, die ihn nichts angehen.*

vi. Hängen. *Sie hängte den Mantel in den Schrank.* For other examples see HANG.

vii. Bringen is used when the movement is not made with the hand. *Der Satellit wurde in eine neue Umlaufbahn gebracht. Man hat einen Menschen auf den Mond gebracht.*

viii. The formal equivalent of **put** s.o. in hospital is **einweisen.** *Die geretteten Seeleute wurden in ein Krankenhaus eingewiesen. Bringen* could also be used.

ix. More specific terms. **Put** *string round a parcel* is *Bindfaden um ein Paket binden.* **Put** *a patch on sth.: Einen Flicken auf etw. nähen.* **Put** *a new handle on sth.: Einen neuen Griff anbringen.* **Put** *a stamp on a letter: Eine Briefmarke auf einen Brief kleben.*

2. If I put an idea or remark in a certain way, I express or state it in that way. *The speaker put his arguments well/clearly/plainly. You have put it bluntly/mildly/elegantly.* The mode of expression can be words or a certain form. *They cannot put their feelings into words. He put his feelings into a song.* **Formulieren** denotes the way something is expressed in words. Thus *Wie kann man den Satz/den Gedanken anders formulieren?* or *Er hat den Hauptunterschied kurz und bündig formuliert.* **Ausdrücken,** 'to EXPRESS', can be a syn of *formulieren, Der Redner hat seine Argumente klar ausgedrückt/formuliert,* but it is needed when a specific form of expression is meant. *Er drückte seine Gefühle in einem Lied aus.* **Put** *in[to] words* is **in Worte fassen.** *Ihre Gefühle können sie nicht in Worte fassen.*

> *Deine Meinung hast du direkt/unverblümt/sehr gewählt/geschmackvoll formuliert/ausgedrückt.*
> *Formulieren Sie die Absage so, daß die Leute nicht gekränkt werden!*

Put is also applied to features of language. *Put the v. into the past tense!* Here **setzen** is used. *Setzt das Verb in die Vergangenheit!* **Sagen** is often used when stating how something is put or expressed. **Put** *it plainly/bluntly* could be *um es ungeschminkt/unverblümt zu sagen. Gelinde gesagt/ausgedrückt* means 'to put it mildly'. *How do you put that in French?* can be *Wie drückt man das auf Französisch aus?* or *Wie würde man das auf Französisch sagen?*

(Note: **Put** *or set to music. Jmd. setzt ein Gedicht in Musik/Noten* or *vertont ein Gedicht.*)

3. Put *a word or sent. somewhere* means 'write or type it there'. *He put his signature to the document. I've put a mark against her name. Put a comma here! Put this on paper!* For writing, the general word is **setzen.** *Ich habe ein Kreuz vor ihren Namen gesetzt.* **Put** *sth. in writing* is **aufschreiben,** to WRITE DOWN. *Gedanken etc. auf Papier bringen* is also used. For *What address did he put?* see *angeben* under GIVE.

> *Ich werde diesen Punkt auf die Tagesordnung setzen.*
> *Jmd. hat seinen Namen/seine Unterschrift auf den Brief/unter ein Dokument gesetzt.*
> *Sie beschlossen, mehrere neue Gerichte auf die Speisekarte zu setzen.*
> *Setzen Sie bitte diese Telefongespräche auf die Rechnung!*

4. Whoever puts a case or point of view states his or her reasons for it in some detail. *Jmd.* **stellt** *seine Ansichten/seinen Standpunkt [klar/genau/gut]* **dar,** 'presents them/it', or in formal style **legt** *seine Gründe/Ansichten* **dar,** 'explains, expounds them'. Another possibility is *Jmd.* **führt** *Argumente für/gegen etw.* **an,** puts a case or arguments for or against sth. *Sie führten überzeugende Argumente für den Plan an.*

5. Put also means 'to submit'. *I put a proposal to s.o. I put an amendment. The chairman put the motion to the meeting.* **Put** *a proposal/suggestion,* if done orally, is *einen*

Vorschlag **machen**. *Sie machte einen Vorschlag, den alle sehr vernünftig fanden.* **Einreichen**, 'to hand in', suggests in writing. **Unterbreiten** is 'to put sth. in spoken or written words before other people'. *Sie hat uns ihre Gedanken zur Weiterentwicklung des Projekts unterbreitet. Er hat der Versammlung eine Resolution/einen Antrag unterbreitet.* [*Anderen*] *einen Plan* **vorlegen** means 'to put a plan forward for consideration'. *A motion is put to a meeting*, i.e. it is put to the vote, is *Man* **stimmt** *über den Antrag* **ab**, or in the pass., *Über den Antrag wird jetzt abgestimmt*. **Put**/move an amendment is *einen Änderungsantrag* **stellen**. **Put** a question [*to s.o.*]: *Jmdm. eine Frage stellen*.

6. In *I put it to you that your evidence is invented*, **put** means 'to suggest', but it implies that the person addressed will in all likelihood be unwilling to admit that what is stated is true. This can be expressed in several ways. *Ich habe den Eindruck, daß ihre Aussage erfunden ist*, is an indirect way of suggesting it is untrue. *Was Sie da gesagt haben, ist doch wohl frei erfunden* tones down a direct statement slightly. *Warum geben Sie nicht zu, daß Ihre Aussage frei erfunden ist?* says bluntly that the person is lying. **Nahelegen**, 'to SUGGEST', implies putting or suggesting something to someone in a way that can hardly be rejected, even though it runs counter to the person's wishes. It is mostly used when one person describes what someone else suggested to a third person. *Es wurde dem Minister nahegelegt, daß er zurücktreten sollte*, it was put to him.

7. Put money **into** property, government bonds, etc. is 'to invest' it. **Anlegen** means 'to invest'. *Er hat sein Geld in Immobilien angelegt. Sie hat ihre Ersparnissen in Bundesanleihen/Aktien angelegt.* Colloquially [**hinein**]**stecken** is used like **put** in this sense. *Hinein* is optional if the sent. contains a phr. with *in. Die Regierung hat sehr viel Geld in das Projekt [hinein]gesteckt* but *hat zwanzig Millionen hineingesteckt.* **Put** money in a bank (account) = 'to pay it in' is **einzahlen**. *Ich habe 1 000 Mark auf mein Konto eingezahlt.*

8. Put also means 'to bet, stake, or wager' money. *He put his last penny on that horse.* **Setzen** is used for betting. *Er hat seinen letzten Pfennig auf dieses Pferd gesetzt.* (In one sense, *der Einsatz* denotes the amount of the bet, the sum staked or wagered. *Bei dem Rennen gab es hohe Einsätze.*)

9. In *I put the distance at ten miles/s.o.'s age at 50/the fur coat at £2,000*, **put** means 'to ESTIMATE'. The main equivalent is **schätzen**. *Ich schätze die Entfernung auf zwanzig Meilen. Der Wert das Gemäldes wird auf zehn Millionen Dollar geschätzt.*

10. If I put time, effort, or strength into something, I expend, use, or apply these in carrying out that task. The vs. expressing this concept are not discussed here but will be found under SPEND 3. In colloquial speech, people say, '*Sie hat viel Arbeit/Mühe/Zeit in diese Sache gesteckt* or *hat viel Arbeit hineingesteckt.*'

11. Put people/thgs. **in** a particular class or group means 'to classify' them that way. *I would put it among his early works. I wouldn't put him in the same class as Verdi.* With *before, over, above*, and *below*, **put** expresses someone's comparative estimate of the worth of s.o./sth. *She puts Keats above Byron.* **Stellen** is used for putting one person or thing above or below s.o./sth. else in a scale of values.

Sie stellt Keats über Byron/Byron unter Keats.   *Er scheint Gelderwerb vor Grundsätze zu stellen.* When **put** means 'to regard sth. as belonging to a particular group or style', or 'to assign it to or put it in a particular period, style, etc.', the equivalent is **zuordnen** or **zurechnen**. Cf. CALCULATE 2. iii.

Dieses Bild ist der mittleren Schaffensperiode des Künstlers zuzurechnen/zuzuordnen.
Ich würde ihn nicht derselben Klasse zurechnen wie Verdi.

Einstufen implies a scale of some kind in which people are assigned a place.

Sie ist in die Gehaltsstufe drei eingestuft worden.

Ich habe diesen Studenten unter die Fortgeschrittenen eingestuft.

12. Put people or thgs. in a particular state or condition is 'to cause them to be in that state'. *It puts me in a difficult position. The factory closed a month ago putting 120 people out of work. That puts the matter beyond all doubt.* Also *We put thgs. in order/s.o. in possession of the facts/s.o. on trial/one's knowledge to practical use* and *we put s.o. at his ease/in a good humour/in a state of anxiety/in danger/in charge of sth.* Although the syntactic pattern is always *put s.o./sth. + prep. + n.*, the various expressions have very little in common. **Put** does not have a distinct meaning in these expressions but states that something brings about what the rest of the construction denotes. For this reason there are a wide variety of equivalents. Often a v. expressing the same meaning is the best transl. even though there is an expression like the E. one. **Put** *names in alphabetical order* could be *die Namen alphabetisch ordnen*, although *die Namen in alphabetische Reihenfolge bringen* is quite possible.

The following are some typical examples. **Put** *sth. at s.o.'s disposal* is *jmdm. etw. zur Verfügung stellen.* **Put** *a plan into operation* can be *einen Plan ausführen/durchführen*, to carry out. **Put** *s.o. in possession of the facts* or **put** *s.o. in the picture* is *jmdm. über die Gegebenheiten ins Bild setzen. Ich weiß nicht genau, was passiert ist—können Sie mich bitte mal ins Bild setzen?* **Put** *a ship out of action: Ein Schiff außer Gefecht setzen.* **Put** *to flight: Jmdn. in die Flucht schlagen.* **Put** *to death: Hinrichten.* **Put** *s.o. to great expense: Jmdm. hohe Unkosten verursachen.* **Put** *s.o. to great inconvenience* is either *jmdm. Unannehmlichkeiten bereiten* or *jmdn. in Ungelegenheiten bringen.* **Put** *sth. into practice/to practical use: Kenntnisse etc. in die Praxis umsetzen* or *von Kenntnissen Gebrauch machen.* **Put** *[in]to use: Von etw. Gebrauch machen.* **Put** *to good use: Gib mir das alte Fahrrad! Ich kann es gut gebrauchen.* Cf. USE 1. ii. **Put** *sth. into production: Mit der Produktion von etw. beginnen.* **Put** *s.o. to the test: Jmdn. auf die Probe stellen.* **Put** *s.o. on trial: Jmdn. vor Gericht bringen/stellen.* **Put** *sth. on the market* is *auf den Markt bringen* if it is a newly introduced product: *Die Firma hat ein angeblich verbessertes Waschmittel auf den Markt gebracht;* if **put** *on the market* means 'to offer' a house etc. 'for sale', it is *zum Verkauf anbieten.* **Put** *s.o. in charge of sth.: Jmdm. die Aufsicht über etw. geben* or *jmdm. die Leitung [eines Betriebs] übertragen.* **Put** *s.o. in danger: Jmdn. in Gefahr bringen.* **Put** *s.o. in a difficult etc. position: Jmdn. in eine schwierige/gefährliche Lage bringen.* **Put** *in power: An die Macht bringen. Diese Wahl brachte die Labourpartei wieder an die Macht.* **Put** *s.o. on the right/wrong track* (fig. use): *Jmdn. auf den rechten/falschen Weg bringen, jmdn. auf die richtige/falsche Spur/Fährte bringen.* **Put** *s.o. through a severe examination: Jmdn. einer strengen Prüfung/einem strengen Verhör unterziehen.* **Put** *the idea out of your head!: Schlag dir den Gedanken aus dem Kopf!* **Put** *s.o. in a state of anxiety: Jmdn. in Angst [und Schrecken] versetzen* in more formal style, or colloquially, *jmdm. Angst einjagen.* **Put** *s.o. in a good/bad humour/mood: Jmdn. in gute/schlechte Laune bringen* or *versetzen.* **Put** *workers out of work: Arbeiter arbeitslos machen.* **Put** *a line through sth.: Etw. durchstreichen.* Cf. CROSS 4.

13. Put a burden etc. **on** s.o. means 'to make s.o. bear sth.' **Auferlegen** means 'to impose on' and **aufbürden** 'to burden with'. *Wir sollten ihm diese zusätzliche Last nicht auferlegen/aufbürden.* **Put** *additional responsibility on s.o.* can be translated by *jmdm. zusätzliche Verantwortung auferlegen/aufbürden* or colloquially by **aufhalsen**, to saddle s.o. with sth. An alternative is **belasten**. *Man belastet jmdn. mit zusätzlicher Arbeit/immer mehr Verantwortung*, burdens with. **Put** *pressure on s.o.* is **jmdn. unter Druck setzen**.

Er hat mir die ganze Last der Verantwortung für die Planung der Konferenz aufgebürdet.

Man wollte mir noch mehr Arbeit aufhalsen, aber ich kann unmöglich so viel schaffen.

14. The syntactic pattern is here **put** + abstract n. + prep. + n. *They put the blame on the butler.* Again the simple v. is often the best equivalent. **Put** [*special etc.*] *emphasis on* is often best translated by [*besonders*] *hervorheben* or *betonen*, 'to emphasize', although the expression [*besonderen*] *Nachdruck auf etw. legen* exists. *Gewicht auf etw. legen* also means 'to emphasize or put emphasis on'.

> *Diese Tatsache hat er in seinem Aufsatz besonders hervorgehoben.*
> *Er hat sich allzu sehr auf diesen Mitarbeiter verlassen* (he put too much reliance on).
> *Sie legten besonderen Nachdruck auf den steigenden Absatz.*

Put *a false interpretation on events* can be *die Ereignisse falsch deuten.* Cf. INTERPRET. **Put** *one's mind to a task: Sich auf die Aufgabe konzentrieren.* **Put** *new life into sth.: Etw. neu/wieder beleben.* With *das Vertrauen*, trust, confidence, and *die Hoffnung, setzen* is used. For **put** *the blame on s.o.,* there is *jmdm. die Schuld zuschieben/in die Schuhe schieben* or *die Schuld auf jmdn. abwälzen* as well as *jmdm. die Schuld geben. Sie gaben dem Butler die Schuld/schoben ihm die Schuld zu.* Cf. BLAME 2. **Put** *an idea into s.o.'s head* is *jmdn. auf einen Gedanken bringen.* **Put** *an end to sth.* is *etw. (dat.) ein Ende setzen* or *machen. Der Vorsitzende mußte der Diskussion ein Ende setzen.* Cf. END 5.

15. A few idioms. **Put** occurs in numerous idiomatic expressions in which it hardly has a meaning of its own.
i. One group is formed with parts of the body, **put** your back into sth., **put** your heads together, **put** a bold face on sth., etc. In such cases, the idea has to be expressed. The equivalents are usually found in the dictionary under the n., not under **put**. **Put** *one's back into sth.: Sich bei etw. Mühe geben/anstrengen,* to exert oneself. Colloquially: *Er kniete sich mit ganzer Kraft in die Arbeit* [*hinein*]. If *in die Arbeit* is not included, *Er kniete sich hinein* is used. A meaning like that of *if you put your heads together* is expressed by *Wenn ihr drei die Köpfe zusammensteckt, kommt ihr bestimmt auf eine Lösung.* A transl. of *if he puts a foot wrong* is *Wenn er auch nur den kleinsten Fehler macht, weist man ihn zurecht.* If I put a bold or brave face on something, I try not to show how unhappy I am about it. This could be *Ich war schwer enttäuscht, ließ es mir aber nicht anmerken.* Cf. NOTICE v. 1. iv.
ii. *I was* **hard put** [**to it**] *to raise the money: Ich hatte große Mühe/Es fiel mir schwer, das Geld zusammenzubringen.* **Not to put it past** s.o. [to do sth.] is expressed by the pos. of *zutrauen. Ich traue es ihm zu/würde es ihm zutrauen, seine eigene Familie zu betrügen.* Cf. TRUST v. To **put** *pen to paper* is *zur Feder greifen.* **Put** *to sea* is *in See stechen. Auslaufen* is usual in the sense 'to leave a harbour, set out'. *Das Schiff läuft heute aus.* The ship *puts into a harbour: Das Schiff läuft einen Hafen an.*

quality

1. i. Quality means 'the degree of goodness or worth'. *We check the quality of the products.* A further meaning 'a high degree of goodness, i.e. excellence' can be expressed by adding *high*, but **quality** can have this sense without *high* being stated. *Merchandise of quality.* The equivalent, **die Qualität**, tends to be neutral, and the different degrees are expressed by adjs. such as *die hohe, ausgezeichnete,* or *minderwertige Qualität eines Produktes.* It sometimes suggests excellence. *Qualitätserzeugnisse* means 'products of high quality'. However, to translate *a quality TV/radio programme* or *a programme of quality* it is best to use *eine Sendung von hoher Qualität.* *Qualität* is applied to commercial products and to the standard of workmanship of man-made things including artistic works. *Wir waren von der Qualität der Arbeit/derAufführung beeindruckt. Die Qualität des Fernsehbildes/des Empfangs. Das Bild ist von hoher künstlerischer Qualität.*

> *Dieser Stoff ist von hervorragender/erstklassiger Qualität.*
> *Wir können die gleiche Qualität liefern wie unsere Konkurrenten.*
> *Die Qualität unserer Produkte wird ständig überwacht/kontrolliert/geprüft.*
> *Die Firma ist stets auf Qualität bedacht/ . . ist stets bemüht, die Qualität ihrer Produkte zu verbessern.*

ii. Die Güte is used for degrees of quality, or relative goodness, of commercial goods as determined by some standard. There are recognized *Gütegrade*, and products can be *von verschiedenen Güteklassen.* Used alone, it can imply high quality. *Diese Marke bürgt für Güte.* Otherwise an adj. is necessary to denote the degree of goodness. *Waren erster/zweiter/letzter Güte.*

> *Das Geschäft führt Stoffe verschiedener Güte.*   *Das ist ein Wein mittlerer Güte.*

iii. *Qualität* is not used for people. *There does not seem to have been a decline in the **quality** of the applicants this year* has, therefore, to be expressed differently. One possibility is to use *gut. Die diesjährigen Bewerber sind ebenso gut wie die vorjährigen. He's always proclaiming the quality of his staff: Er sagt jedem, der es hören will, wie gut seine Leute sind. Nicht nachstehen,* 'not to be inferior to', can also express this sense. *Die diesjährigen Bewerber scheinen den vorjährigen nicht nachzustehen.*

2. A **quality** means 'a characteristic or attribute, such as kindness, patience, or honesty, that is part of a pers.'s nature'. *What qualities characterize a good teacher?* **Quality** also denotes a characteristic of a substance or thing. *One quality of pinewood is that it can be sawn easily.*

i. The general term is **die Eigenschaft**, characteristic, property. It is neutral, and someone or a thing can have *gute* or *schlechte Eigenschaften.* Cf. iii. (In relation to things *Eigenschaft* is often translated as *property. Wasser hat die Eigenschaft, bei 0° zu gefrieren.*) **Der Vorzug** is a valuable characteristic which distinguishes a person or thing.

> *Diese beiden Männer hatten viele Eigenschaften gemeinsam, darunter Fleiß, Bescheidenheit und Großzügigkeit.*   *Welche Eigenschaften kennzeichnen einen guten Lehrer?*
> *Einer ihrer besonderen Vorzüge ist ihre unbedingte Ehrlichkeit.*
> *Eine Eigenschaft/Ein Vorzug des Tannenholzes besteht darin, daß es sich leicht sägen läßt.*

ii. Die Qualität is often used in the pl. to denote good personal qualities and abili-

ties. *Seine Qualitäten erkenne ich vorbehaltlos an. Ich schätze sie wegen ihrer mensch-lichen/moralischen Qualitäten.*
iii. *Eine Eigenschaft* is a static quality. When **quality** refers to a more dynamic abil-ity, **die Fähigkeit,** 'ability', or **die Begabung,** 'gift', are more appropriate. A syn. is **das Vermögen.** Cf. POWER. *Er hat die Fähigkeit/die Begabung/das Vermögen, Vertrauen zu erwecken.*

quite

1. Quite can mean either 'completely', *He has quite recovered, I quite agree* [*with you*], and *I stood quite still,* or 'to some extent, to a fairly great extent, or to a greater extent than average', *He was quite young* or *It is quite likely that she will pass.*
i. The adj. **ganz** means 'whole'. *Ich habe das ganze Wochenende daran gearbeitet. Sie hat mir die ganze Geschichte erzählt.* The adv. means 'wholly, completely' and is a syn. of *völlig,* COMPLETELY. The E. equivalent varies. *Wir müssen das Zimmer ganz/völlig räumen. Sie haben den Kuchen ganz aufgegessen.* The adv. *ganz* translates **quite** in the sense of 'completely' in the neg. with adjs., advs., and vs. *Das ist nicht ganz dasselbe. Das Gerät funktioniert nicht ganz einwandfrei. Das habe ich nicht ganz verstanden.* It is also used with vs. with a neg. implication and is stressed. *Das habe ich ganz vergessen. Er hat seine Pflichten ganz vernachlässigt.* **Völlig** is just as common, and is necessary with a v. like *verstehen* which does not have a neg. implication. *Ich verstehe völlig, warum er sich die Sache anders überlegt hat.* *Ganz* also occurs in pos. sents. with certain adjs. and advs. and is stressed. When the adj. involves a value judgement which expresses the highest degree of a pos. or neg. quality, *völlig* cannot be used. *Das Buch ist ganz hervorragend/ganz schlecht. Sie hat sich ganz großartig benommen. Es ist ein ganz herrliches Bild. Die Arbeit ist leider ganz fehlerhaft.* (Here *völlig* is possible, but unusual.) When the adj. or adv. does not imply a judgement, both *ganz* and *völlig* can be used. *Ich will ganz offen/völlig offen mit dir reden. Sie lebt da ganz allein/völlig allein.*

Ich bin nicht ganz sicher.	*Das ist nicht ganz sechs Wochen her.*
Meine Uhr geht nicht ganz richtig.	*Er hat sich ganz unvernünftig gebärdet.*
Ich bin noch nicht ganz fertig.	*Ich habe ganz still gestanden.*
Ich habe den Fahrer ganz deutlich gesehen.	*Das weiß ich ganz genau.*
Das ist etw. ganz anderes. Also etw. völlig anderes.	*Das ist ganz/völlig unmöglich.*
Du hast ganz/völlig recht.	*Sie hat sich von der Erkrankung völlig erholt.*
Ich stimme völlig mit dir überein. Or Ich stimme dir völlig zu.	

ii. In the second sense, 'to some extent', **ganz** is used only with a small number of adjs. and advs. which express approval or praise, and indicates a moderate degree. It is not stressed. *Das Essen hat ganz gut geschmeckt. Das ist eine ganz gute Arbeit. Er hat ganz gut abgeschnitten. Ich finde sie ganz nett/ganz hübsch. Der Film hat mir ganz gut gefallen.* The main equivalent is **ziemlich,** rather. (Cf. FAIRLY.)
Sie hat ihn zwar ganz gern, heiraten möchte sie ihn aber nicht.
Beide sind noch ziemlich jung.   *Es ist heute ziemlich warm.*
Sie weiß ziemlich viel, aber nicht alles.
Es ist ziemlich wahrscheinlich, daß sie die Prüfung besteht.
iii. Quite + *n. Quite a distance.* For the use of **ziemlich** with a n. as in *ein ziemlicher Erfolg,* 'quite a success', and *Sie ist eine ziemliche Schönheit,* cf. FAIRLY 2. In *ein ziemlicher Erfolg, ziemlich* means 'fairly great'. *Das eine ziemliche Strecke,* quite a distance/long way from here. If in *quite a success,* **quite** is taken to mean 'REAL' or 'COMPLETE', **richtig** or **vollkommen** express the sense. *Ein richtiger* or *vollkommener Erfolg.* For *eine ganze Menge,* 'quite a lot', cf. AMOUNT 1. ii.
2. Quite and **quite so** are used to express agreement with what has just been said.

The equivalent is **eben**. Variants are **ja eben** and **na eben**, which are often like *That's just what I mean/was saying/think/[have always] said.*

    A. Wir wollen ja schließlich keinen Streit. B. Eben.

    A. Kati habe ich in der Vorlesung gar nicht gesehen. B. Na eben. (Refers to something said before and implies e.g. *I told you sth. was wrong.*)

    A. Ich könnte es wohl selbst machen. B. Ja eben. (Implied: That is what I have advised you to do.)

3. As **durchaus** can be stressed on either syllable, the following offers suggestions.

i. Quite often follows an assertion to the contrary. *A. That's not true. B. It's quite/perfectly true.* **Durchaus** can assert the direct opposite of what has been said. In pos. sents. it is usually stressed on the second syllable, *durch<u>aus</u>*, but in neg. ones, *nicht* or a similar word carries the stress. It corresponds to *quite* in pos. sents. and in neg. ones to [*not*] *at all.*

    A. Das ist nicht möglich. B. Das ist durch<u>aus</u> möglich.

    A. Das geht nicht. B. Das geht durch<u>aus</u>.

    A. Sie hat unrecht. B. Sie hat durch<u>aus</u> recht.

    A. Das ist der Fall. B. Das ist durchaus <u>nicht</u> der Fall.

    Was Sie getan haben, genügt durch<u>aus</u>. Beruhigen Sie sich! (Answer to a doubt.)

ii. Like **quite**, **durchaus** expresses affirmation in a response. It can be used as an answer to a question and is stressed on the first syllable. *A. Halten Sie das für möglich? B. <u>Durch</u>aus.* It often implies a reservation which could be introduced by *aber* (as explained in 3. iii). In other situations *durchaus* may express opposition (as explained in 3. i), but the view being disputed may not be expressed explicitly. *Ich bin durchaus zufrieden mit dem Ergebnis* may anticipate or ward off an unexpressed objection. If these conditions do not apply, *durchaus* can still be used, but *völlig* is more usual. *Ich bin völlig zufrieden.* In this use, when an adj. or adv. follows, *durchaus* is usually stressed on the first syllable.

    A. Wird es heute sonnig bleiben? B. Das ist <u>durch</u>aus möglich.

    Sie hat sich in der Sache <u>durch</u>aus korrekt verhalten.

    Er hat <u>durch</u>aus alles gemacht, was in seinen Kräften stand.

    Ich bin mit der Sache <u>durch</u>aus zufrieden/ . . <u>durch</u>aus damit einverstanden, daß sie mitkommt.

iii. Durchaus is also used to concede a point as correct, but then to qualify it in some way. It thus presupposes a following clause with *aber*, or a sent. expressing reservations. If someone says, *'Das Stück hat mir durchaus gefallen'*, this expresses praise on the one hand but implies some reservations. In this use *durchaus* is like *zwar.* Cf. CONFESS 1. iii. It is usually stressed on the first syllable.

    Was Sie sagen, ist <u>durch</u>aus richtig, aber gehört nicht zur Sache.

    A. Hätten Sie Interesse an einer Schiffsreise? B. Wir hätten <u>durch</u>aus Interesse daran, aber es fehlt uns an Geld.

    Ich bin <u>durch</u>aus nicht abgeneigt mitzukommen, habe aber keine Zeit.

    Ich sehe <u>durch</u>aus ein, warum das so sein muß, finde es aber trotzdem bedauerlich.

iv. Note: *Durchaus* also means 'absolutely' and is a syn. of *unbedingt. Er will durchaus dabei sein,* insists absolutely on being there.

r

raise, lift, pick up *vs.* Some uses.

1. Raise means 'to move from a low[er] to a high[er] level'. It is used for parts of the body, *I raise my hand/head/eyes,* and things, *S.o. raises a glass/a barrier/a lid/his hat/a sunken ship/the curtain.* **Lift** means 'to move to a higher level or position', usually with the hands and arms, and often from the ground or floor. *The crane lifts ten tons. He lifted the child out of a cot. I lifted the bag on to the lorry.* **Pick up** means 'to lift from the floor or ground' something that either has its normal position there or has fallen. *She picked up the bucket/the coin.* **Lift** expresses the ability or inability to take something up. *I can/can't lift it. It's very heavy—can you lift it?*

i. The equivalent of **lift**, **pick up**, and **raise** in most of the senses just defined is **heben**. *Heben* is used with a person or a thing as subj., with a person, thing, or part of the body as obj., and with preps. *Die Mutter hob das Kind aus dem Wagen. Der Kran hob die schweren Träger vom Lastwagen. Bei einer Abstimmung heben die Mitglieder des Vereins die Hand.* *Heben* is also used when something partly attached to something else is raised. *Sobald der Zug durch ist, hebt man die [Bahn]schranke.* **Anheben** is 'to raise slightly', possibly to test the weight. *Ich hob die Kiste an.* **Hochheben** means 'to raise to a level roughly above the knee'. *Er hob das Kind hoch.* When the subj. is a person and the obj. is neither part of the body nor something partly attached to something else, *heben* is found only when an adv. and/or a phr. is present. *Er hob den schweren Sack mühelos auf die Schulter.* When there is no adv. or phr., one of the derivatives, usually *hochheben*, is used, as **lift up** or **pick up** are in E. *Er hob den Sack hoch—dann trug er ihn in den Keller.* Only *heben* is used when it is a question of being able to lift something or not, whatever the resulting height. *Der Sack ist schwer— kannst du ihn heben?*

> *Der Kran hebt 5 000 Kilogramm auf 10 Meter Höhe.*   *Beim Gehen hebt er kaum die Füße.*
> *Der Stein ist zu schwer, als daß ich ihn heben könnte.*   *Man hebt den Vorhang im Theater.*
> *Er hob den Eimer mit der einen Hand und das Kind mit der anderen [hoch].* (*Hoch* possible, but not necessary.)
> *Wir hoben die Säcke vom Lastwagen.*   *Sie hob den Deckel der Truhe.*
> *Mehrere Spieler der siegreichen Mannschaft wurden von den Zuschauern auf die Schultern gehoben.*
> *Es ist endlich gelungen, das Wrack/das gesunkene Schiff zu heben.*
> *Sie hoben den Schrank an und trugen ihn hinaus.*
> *Hebe mal den Koffer an! Du wirst sehen, wie schwer er ist.*
> *Er hob den schweren Koffer hoch und legte ihn ins Gepäcknetz.*

ii. Aufheben is 'to pick up from the ground or floor sth. which is not in its normal position there', i.e. it has fallen or been dropped. *Aufheben* thus implies bending or stooping. *Man hebt einen Ball/ein Stück Papier/eine Stricknadel/eine Münze auf.* It also means 'to help s.o. to his/her feet'. *Das kleine Kind, das hingefallen war, hob die Mutter wieder auf.* **Hochnehmen** means 'to take or pick up' something which has not fallen, a book from a table etc. *Sie nahm den Koffer/den Telefonhörer/das Buch vom Tisch hoch.* An alternative is **in die Hand nehmen**. *Er nahm die Zeitung in die Hand und fing an zu lesen.* **Aufnehmen** is now used only when someone takes up something with an instrument. *Sie nahm das kleine Stück Tuch mit der Pinzette auf.*

iii. Erheben is used in solemn or ceremonious situations or in elevated language with parts of the body or *Glas* as obj. In everyday language **heben** is the usual v. *Auf die Frage des Lehrers erhoben mehrere Schüler die Hand* is formal style. Schoolchildren would say of one of their number, *'Er/Sie hat die Hand gehoben.'* To everyday style belong *Schüler heben die Hand, wenn sie etw. sagen möchten,* and *Die Gäste hoben ihre Gläser und tranken auf das Wohl des Brautpaares.* In a more ceremonious atmosphere, someone might say, *'Erheben wir unsere Gläser, und trinken wir auf das Wohl des Brautpaares!'* Only the past. part. of *erheben,* not of *heben,* is used as an adj. in this sense. *Mit erhobenen Händen traten die verhafteten Räuber aus der Bank.*

2. Raise means 'to improve in a general way'. *The government tried to raise the standard of living.* This sense is also carried by **heben.** *Man hebt den Lebensstandard/den Wohlstand/den Handel/den Umsatz/das allgemeine Bildungsniveau/das geistige oder künstlerische Niveau* etc. It is sometimes applied to people. *Dieser Erfolg hob sein Selbstbewußtsein. Heben* is not used with a prep. meaning 'to raise to a higher level'. This must be **auf ein höheres Niveau bringen.** *Diese Lehrer bemühten sich, den Bildungsstand des Volkes auf ein höheres Niveau zu bringen.*

3. i. Among other senses, **erheben** means 'to raise to a higher degree or status'. *Die Pädagogische Hochschule* (Teachers' Training College) *wurde erweitert und zur Universität erhoben. Im Kaiserreich wurden viele Großindustrielle in den Adelstand erhoben,* they were raised into the aristocracy, ennobled, knighted. If **raise** means 'to promote' a person, the equivalent is **befördern.** *Er wurde zum Major befördert,* raised to the rank of major.

Der Fürst wollte seiner Hauptstadt einen Glanz geben, der sie über alle anderen Städte erhob.

ii. Erheben translates **raise** when this means 'to levy or impose' taxes, a toll, charge, etc. *Die Regierung beschloß, eine ganz neue Steuer zu erheben. Eine kleine Gebühr wird für die Benutzung des Parkplatzes erhoben.* (*To raise taxes,* if it means 'to increase them', is *die Steuern erhöhen/heraufsetzen.*)

iii. Erheben is also used with certain ns., as **raise** is with *objection, accusation,* etc. *Man erhebt gegen jmdn./etw. Vorwürfe/Protest/einen Einwand/Beanstandungen/eine Beschwerde/eine Anklage/eine Beschuldigung/Einspruch,* etc. *Sie erhoben Protest gegen etw.* can translate *They raised an outcry.* Cf. OBJECTION. *Die Zuschauer erhoben Protest gegen die Entscheidung des Schiedsrichters.*

iv. *Die Stimme erheben* is an elevated expression meaning 'to begin to speak'. *Die Stimme heben* means 'to speak more loudly', i.e. 'to raise one's voice!' *Jmdn./den Geist erheben* means 'to elevate, uplift, or edify s.o./the mind'. *Ihre Liebe hat ihn erhoben. Seine Predigten/Diese Romane haben viele gerührt und erhoben. Alle gingen erhoben aus der Feier.*

4. Raise is used in other contexts, each of which needs a different v. It is best to look up the n. in the dictionary to find the appropriate v. Here are a few examples. **Raise** *a question/issue: Eine Frage aufwerfen,* to put forward in or for discussion anywhere, *eine Frage vorbringen,* put forward in a meeting or under similar formal circumstances. **Raise** *a mortgage: Eine Hypothek aufnehmen.* **Raise,** *procure,* or *get money/funds* is *eine Summe/Geld aufbringen* or *zusammenbringen. This result* **raised** *our hopes* can be expressed as *Dieses Ergebnis gab uns neue Hoffnung* or *Aus diesem Ergebnis schöpften wir neue Hoffnung. Dieses Ergebnis bestärkte uns in der Hoffnung, daß wir schließlich Erfolg haben würden,* is another possibility. For **raise** children and animals cf. EDUCATE; for **raise** crops cf. GROW.

Wir haben das nötige Geld/die erforderlichen Mittel für den Anbau aufgebracht.
Für die Hilfsaktion wurde aus der Tombola 1 000 Mark aufgebracht.
Er wußte nicht, wie er das Geld zusammenbringen sollte.
Es fiel mir schwer, die Mittel für den teuren Flug zusammenzubringen.

5. Raise prices etc. = 'to increase'. For most equivalents see INCREASE. The derivative of *heben* expressing this sense is **anheben**. *Man hebt den Preis/eine Gebühr/die Löhne an. Die Mehrwertssteuer wurde von 14 auf 15% angehoben.*

rate *n.* Main equivalents. **at any rate** phr. used as *adv.*

1. The **rate** of exchange, taxation, interest, etc. or the **rates** of postage etc. mean 'their level at a particular time'.

i. **The exchange rate** is der **[Wechsel]kurs**. *Der Kurs des australischen Dollars gegenüber der D-Mark ist in den letzten Wochen um etwa 15 Pfennig gestiegen/gefallen.*

ii. **Der Kurs** is also used for prices of shares, bonds, and securities. *Die Aktienkurse. Die Kurse der Wertpapiere.* **Der Preis** is an alternative. *Der Preis dieser Aktien hat sich in den letzten sechs Monaten kaum geändert.*

iii. **Der Satz** translates **rate** meaning 'an amount or level that is paid or has to be paid for some purpose, especially interest and taxation'. Thus *Die Zinssätze sind in letzter Zeit gefallen. Der höchste Steuersatz beträgt 60%.* G. students who receive financial assistance from the State (the Federal Government) get, according to the income of their parents, *einen hohen/niedrigen Bafögsatz. (Bafög:* Bundesausbildungsförderungsgesetz.)

iv. **Rates** charged for letters, telephone calls, etc. are called **eine Gebühr**. *Die Postgebühren in der Bundesrepublik sind sehr hoch.* (In other areas, *die Gebühr* is 'a fee'. *Der Makler erhebt für die Vermittlung eine Gebühr. Die Bank erhebt für die Einlösung von Reiseschecks eine kleine Gebühr.)*

> *Man hat die Gebühren für Auslandsgespräche herabgesetzt* (rates/charges for telephone calls abroad).   *Drucksache zu ermäßigter Gebühr.*

v. **Der Tarif** denotes officially fixed rates or charges for certain services, particularly transport and water, gas, and electricity. *Der Stromtarif ist sehr niedrig. Die Tarife der Bahn/der Müllabfuhr haben sich erhöht.* Freight rates are *Frachttarife* or *Frachtsätze. Tarif* is applied to telephone charges as a collective term. *Nachts gilt der Billigtarif, der zwei Drittel des Normaltarifs beträgt. Tarif* is used in more formal language for the rates in hotels. *Es gibt unterschiedliche Tarife in der Haupt- und in der Nebensaison.* (The usual word is *der Preis.)*

vi. Something is sold **at the rate** *of £50 per metre* is *zum Preis von . . .* **At special rates** is *zu Sonderpreisen.* **At reduced rates** is *zu herabgesetzten Preisen.* **At cut rates** can be *zu Schleuderpreisen.*

2. Rate of pay. **Der Tarif** implies wage rates which have been the subject of negotiations between organizations of employees and employers, and whose results are then agreed to in a contract. *Tarifverhandlungen* are negotiations about wage rates for at least one group of employees in a specific area. If someone is paid *unter Tarif* or *über Tarif* or *untertariflich* or *übertariflich*, he or she is paid less or more than the going or award rate. *Die Gewerkschaft hat die Tarife gekündigt* means that the union has given notice that it wants to negotiate new rates. The general equivalent of *pay* = 'the amount s.o. gets', **die Bezahlung**, can also translate *rate of pay. Die Bezahlung war gut/schlecht/zu niedrig.* **Die Entlohnung** in one sense is a formal and official syn. *Eine niedrige/hohe Entlohnung/Bezahlung. Gute Entlohnung wird geboten.* Someone might say, *'Die Bezahlung für Schreibarbeiten hat sich im letzten Jahr nicht geändert.'* The question 'What is the rate for typing?' would, however, be formulated differently, possibly as *Was kostet eine [Schreibmaschinen]seite?* or *Wieviel verlangen Sie pro Seite?* Cf. ASK 5. **Das Honorar** is 'a fee for work done' and suggests professional work of some importance, e.g. *das Honorar eines Rechtanwalts/eines Arztes* and *das Honorar für eine Übersetzung/einen Vortrag/einen Zeitungsartikel. S.o.'s* *hourly rate of pay* can be *Jmds. Stundenlohn beträgt DM 20. Double rates apply on Sundays: Sonntags wird doppelt bezahlt.*

Die Gewerkschaften streben eine höhere/gerechte Bezahlung/Entlohnung an.

Das Honorar/Die Bezahlung für eine Übersetzung richtet sich nach dem Schwierigkeitsgrad des Textes.

3. The **rate** of a particular phenomenon is the 'number of times it occurs in a certain period or on a particular occasion'. *The birth rate is decreasing. The failure rate was high.* When **rate** means 'the ratio between at least two quantities, one of which is taken as a base', **die Rate** is now common and is mostly expressed as a percentage. There are compounds such as *die Geburtenrate, die Wachstumsrate,* 'rate of growth', and *die Zuwachsrate,* 'rate of increase', *die Preissteigerungsrate. Die steigende Rate der Produktivität. (Die Rate* also means 'instalment'. *Wir kaufen die Möbel auf Raten. Die sechste Rate für den Fernseher ist am Montag fällig.)* **Die Ziffer** has a related sense and suggests a statistically established figure. *Nach der Statistik steigt die Geburtenziffer noch.* **Die Quote** means 'proportion (as a percentage)', *die Arbeitslosenquote.* It sometimes translates **rate**. *Die Durchfallquote liegt bei etwa 20%.*

Die Inflationsrate ist im vorigen Jahr noch weiter zurückgegangen.

In Indien ist die Sterblichkeitsrate bei Säuglingen gesunken.

Die Unfallziffer steigt/geht zurück.   Die Quote der Verkehrsunfälle ist leicht zurückgegangen.

4. The **rate** at which something happens is 'the speed at which it happens'.

i. Die Geschwindigkeit is the usual equivalent of *speed* or *velocity*. **Das Tempo** also denotes the speed of a human being or vehicle. Both can translate **rate**. *Geschwindigkeit* is used with a number or an adj. *Der Zug fuhr mit einer Geschwindigkeit von 120 Stundenkilometern. Er fuhr mit großer Geschwindigkeit weg.* Although *Tempo* is used in bureaucratic language with a number, *Hier gilt Tempo vierzig*, it is used elsewhere only with an adj. or alone. *Er fuhr mit atemberaubendem Tempo durch die engen Straßen. Das Tempo der Schritte änderte sich. Das Tempo* is used for the rate or speed of more abstract things. *Das Tempo der wirtschaftlichen Entwicklung. Die Produktion steigerte sich in raschem Tempo.* Our *rate of advance/progress* or *our speed* in the concrete sense becomes *Unsere Geschwindigkeit (betrug 15 Kilometer pro Stunde).* In the discussion about introducing a speed limit on *Autobahnen, das Tempolimit* often occurs. *Viele Deutsche befürworten ein Tempolimit auf Autobahnen.*

ii. Rate often need not be translated. *The rate of progress in the last century* could be simply *der [schnelle] Fortschritt im letzten Jahrhundert. The rate of acceleration* of a car is *Die Beschleunigung von Null auf 100 beträgt 14 Sekunden. The machine copies at a rate of one per second: Das Kopiergerät macht eine Kopie pro Sekunde. S.o. works at a rapid rate: Jmd. arbeitet schnell/zügig.*

iii. At this rate, meaning 'if the present rate of progress or state of affairs continues', can be *bei diesem Tempo. Bei diesem Tempo wirst du erst um Mitternacht fertig sein.* Alternatives are *wenn du so weiter machst* and *wenn das so weiter geht.*

Es ist unsinnig, jeden Pfennig deines Gehalts sofort auszugeben. Wenn du so weiter machst, wirst du nie Geld für größere Anschaffungen haben.

5. At any rate.

i. This phr. indicates that a statement is too general and that it should be more precise or limited to part of what was said. *We must do sth. for the family,* or **at any rate** *for the children.* **Jedenfalls** confirms that what was said holds for at least a part of what was previously asserted, and in this sense it is a syn. of *wenigstens* or *zumindest*, at LEAST.

Wir müssen etw. für die Familie tun, jedenfalls für die Kinder.

Er hat sehr umfangreiche Kenntnisse, jedenfalls auf seinem Gebiet.

ii. At any rate also indicates that the important thing is what is about to be said, not what has just been said, which may not necessarily be completely true or relevant. *I don't know what he does exactly—sth. in industry—but at any rate, a chauffeur collects him every morning.* In one of its uses *in any case* also limits an opinion or statement to what is definitely known to be true. *I don't think there's been an edition since 1977; in any case/at any rate that's the one I've been using.* **Jedenfalls** translates both of these.

> *Ich weiß nicht genau, was er macht—etw. in der Industrie—jedenfalls wird er jeden Morgen von einem Chauffeur abgeholt.*   *Ob er Millionär ist, weiß ich nicht, jedenfalls ist er sehr reich.*
> *Wir treffen uns jedenfalls um halb acht vor dem Kino.* (Regardless of whatever else has changed in the mean time.)
> *Seit 1977 hat es, soweit ich weiß, keine neue Ausgabe mehr gegeben. Ich benutze jedenfalls diese Ausgabe.*

iii. With the imp. and *müssen*, **jedenfalls** means that someone should do something in any case or at any rate, but it is fairly weak and may mean no more than 'just to be on the safe side'. *Kann sein, daß es regnet. Nimm jedenfalls einen Schirm mit! Bei schönem Wetter gehen wir baden—bring jedenfalls dein Badezeug mit!* **Auf jeden Fall** is stronger and means that what is said must definitely be done. *Kann sein, daß es regnet. Nimm auf jeden Fall deinen Schirm mit!* is stronger than *jedenfalls* in the same sent. *Schreib' ihm auf jeden Fall so bald wie möglich! Auf jeden Fall mußt du zum Rechtsanwalt gehen.* **Auf alle Fälle** is a further syn. which is stronger again and could be used in the last two sents. *Wir wissen nicht, wie das Wetter sein wird, wir müssen auf alle Fälle einen Schirm mitnehmen.*

reach, range, scope *ns.*

1. The primary meaning of **reach**, 'the extent to which the hand or arm can be stretched out', now occurs mainly in the expressions *within reach* and *out of reach*.
i. Die Reichweite has the same sense and also occurs in this meaning only in the phrs. *in/außer Reichweite. I like to have reference books within reach* is thus *Ich möchte Nachschlagewerke in Reichweite haben.* Alternative expressions are *in Griffnähe* or *griffbereit*.
ii. E. expressions with a related, but extended, sense of **reach** have to be put differently. *The hotel is within easy reach of the beach* or *The flat is within easy reach of shops/station* can be translated by compounds or expressions containing **die Nähe**. Cf. NEAR 1. *Das Hotel ist/liegt in Strandnähe. Die Wohnung ist [ganz] in der Nähe des Bahnhofs/der Geschäfte.* An alternative is *Der Strand etc. ist vom Hotel aus bequem zu Fuß zu erreichen. To keep* poisons etc. *out of [the] reach of children* is *vor Kindern sicher aufbewahren.* Cf. KEEP 7. vii.
iii. The fig. uses *A video recorder is **within the reach** of most families* or *Overseas trips are **out of the reach** of most people* can be expressed by **[un]erschwinglich**, [not] affordable, or by **sich leisten**, to afford. *Ein Videogerät ist für die meisten Familien erschwinglich* or *Die meisten Familien können sich ein Videogerät leisten. Auslandsreisen sind für die meisten unerschwinglich. Die meisten können sich Auslandsreisen nicht leisten.*

2. i. Range denotes the distance to which a gun etc. is capable of sending a bullet, or the eye, a telescope, or a transmitter is capable of seeing or reaching. **Die Reichweite** also has this sense and means 'the greatest distance sth. can cover'. For ships and aircraft both words denote the distance which can be covered without refuelling. **Der Aktionsradius** is a syn. in military language. *Die Weite* is combined with some vs. as in *Hörweite, Schußweite, Rufweite.*

> *Das Geschoß/Der Sender hat eine große/geringe Reichweite.*
> *Die Reichweite eines Teleskops ist größer als die eines gewöhnlichen Feldstechers.*

Das Schiff geriet/Die Panzer blieben außer Reichweite der Geschütze.
Bei Nebel verringert sich die Sicht[weite] bis auf 20 Meter.
Sie lagen außer Schußweite der Kanonen.

ii. Range also means 'the distance away of the object aimed at'. *At this range you can hardly hope to hit it.* The equivalent of this sense is **die Entfernung**, DISTANCE. *Aus dieser Entfernung wirst du kaum treffen können.* At close range is *aus nächster Nähe.*

3. The upper and lower **reaches** of a river are **der Oberlauf** and **der Unterlauf eines Flusses.**

4. A range of thgs. means 'a number or series of thgs. of the same general kind'. *S.o.'s views on a wide range of subjects. A wide range of possibilities. A narrow range of options.*

i. Die Skala means 'the scale of a thermometer etc.' and can also denote a full series of related phenomena. *Die ganze Skala der Gefühle. Jmd. hat eine breite Interessenskala* or *hat vielseitige Interessen. Das enthält/erschöpft nicht die volle Skala der Möglichkeiten.* Without *full*, as in *the range of possibilities open to us, range of* need not be translated. *Die Möglichkeiten, die uns offenstehen, sind sehr begrenzt.* A possible transl. of *a range of proposals* is *einige/mehrere Vorschläge.* **Das Spektrum** is also used in more learned language. *Man besprach ein breites Spektrum von Fragen.*

Man hat ihm Fragen über eine breite Skala von Themen gestellt.
Die Mitglieder der Forschungsgruppe verfügten über ein breites Spektrum von Spezialkenntnissen.

ii. A range of products means 'the number produced by a company or sold by a shop'. For the number of products a shop etc. has, **die Auswahl**, 'selection' (cf. CHOICE 4), is the simplest equivalent. **Das Angebot**, 'range or selection of things on offer or sale', is also common. Both can be used with *an. Dieser Händler hat ein gutes Angebot/eine gute Auswahl an Gebrauchtwagen.* **Das Sortiment** is a more technical term for the range of goods offered by a retailer. **Die Palette**, originally 'a palette', has spread from advertising and commercial language and suggests a wide selection or diverse range of things. *Die Palette von Produkten. Eine bunte Palette von Farben. Eine breite Palette von Möglichkeiten.* It frequently has an adj., but can be used without one. *Eine Palette (or Ein Spektrum) von Meinungen.*

Das Kaufhaus hat immer ein vielseitiges Angebot an Kostümen/eine große Auswahl an Hosen.
Das Kaufhaus führt ein gutes/breites Sortiment an Anzügen/. . . hat ein reichhaltiges Sortiment an
    Sommerkleidern.   *Wir möchten uns die ganze Angebotspalette ansehen.*

iii. A/The whole range of. When *a whole range of* means 'many', equivalents are *viele* or *eine Vielzahl von. Im Urlaub haben wir viele interessante Leute/eine Vielzahl von interessanten Leuten kennengelernt.* Related words are *eine Vielfalt an*, 'a multiplicity', *eine Fülle*, 'an abundance', and *breit gefächert*, 'varied'. *Eine Vielfalt an Pflanzen. Eine Fülle interessanter Gedanken.* We cater for *a whole range of* customers could be *Wir haben eine breit gefächerte Kundschaft.* (*Fächern* means 'to divide up into subject areas'.) *Diese Partei bleibt an der Macht, weil sie eine breit gefächerte Wählerschaft anspricht.* When the meaning is 'all those available', *the whole/full range of* can often be translated by *all* or *sämtlich. Sie können sich bei uns alle/sämtliche Modelle ansehen.*

5. Range also denotes the limits within which a thing varies in amount or degree. *The temperature/price range.* Here **range** means 'the complete group that is included between two fixed points on a scale of measurement'. In reference to the voice or a musical instrument, **der Umfang** is used. *Die Sängerin hat einen großen Stimmumfang.* Elsewhere **der Bereich**, 'AREA', is the normal term. Teachers talk of marks *im zweier Bereich*, the range between 2– and 2+. *Die meisten Noten in der Prüfung lagen im Bereich zwischen 60% und 80%. Schiffe im Bereich von 8 000 bis 10 000 Tonnen. Der Bereich der Temperaturschwankungen ist nur gering.* **Die Bandbreite**, a term taken from radio frequencies, was applied to the range within which exchange rates or share prices fluctuate and has spread to other fields. *Der Aktienkurs schwankt in der Bandbreite zwischen 230 und 270. Bereich* is also possible. In reference to prices, **die Preislage** suggests only a small variation. *In the medium price range* is *in der mittleren Preislage*. Thus *ein Haus in der Preislage um 100 000 Dollar* and *An welche Preislage haben Sie gedacht?* Sometimes **range** need not be translated. *Das Alter der Teilnehmer ist unterschiedlich,* the age range.

6. Range is also applied to the area covered by or included in something. *The range of influence. The range and diversity of research activities in universities. He said it was outside the range of his responsibility.* **Der Umfang** denotes the area covered by something but implies considerable size. Cf. EXTENT 5. *Der Bericht vermittelt einen Eindruck vom Umfang und von der Vielseitigkeit der Forschungsvorhaben.* For *range of influence* or *responsibility,* **der Bereich** + gen. can be used, or compounds like *der Einflußbereich* or *der Zuständigkeitsbereich. Diese Frage liegt nicht in meinem Zuständigkeitsbereich* can also be expressed as *liegt außerhalb meiner Zuständigkeit,* or more simply as *Für diese Frage bin ich nicht zuständig.* Cf. RESPONSIBLE 2. ii and AREA 6.

7. i. The **scope** of an activity, topic, or piece of work is 'the whole area it deals with or includes'. *That question is beyond the scope of this essay. The scope of a course.* **Der Rahmen** is lit. 'the frame' and is used fig. for the limits which are set for a piece of work, an investigation, etc. *Den Rahmen einer Untersuchung festlegen* or *stecken,* to lay down or fix the scope of an investigation. Otherwise **der Umfang,** 'EXTENT', could be used. *Die zur Verfügung stehende Zeit bestimmt den Umfang des in dem Kurs zu behandelnden Stoffes.*

    Die Behandlung einer solchen Frage geht über den Rahmen dieses Aufsatzes hinaus.
    Der Unterschied liegt darin, daß das erste Programm einen anderen Umfang hat (the difference is one of scope).   *Man hat den Rahmen der Untersuchung sehr weit gesteckt.*

ii. With regard to people **scope** means 'the opportunity for unhampered action or thought or the opportunity to use one's abilities'. *There is no scope for originality. You have scope for developing your own ideas.* The equivalent is **der Spielraum** which, in its fig. sense, means 'the area in which sth. is free to move'. It occurs mostly in the phrs. *genug/keinen Spielraum für die Phantasie/für eigene Ideen/für Eigeninitiative haben. S.o. has [the] scope to do/for doing sth.* is often best expressed as a v. *Jmd. kann seine Fähigkeiten/Talente voll entwickeln/voll entfalten* or *kann seine eigenen Gedanken ungehindert in die Tat umsetzen.*

read *v.*

1. Read and **read aloud.**

i. Lesen means 'to read with the eyes and take in the sense mentally'. *Ich lese einen Roman von Tolstoi. Lesen* does not mean 'to read aloud'. When reading aloud is meant, **vorlesen** is used. It is trans. and intr. *Der Vater liest den Kindern eine Geschichte vor. Der Vater liest den Kindern vor.* An exception to this rule is reading aloud to an audience on a formal organized occasion for which *lesen* is used. *Der Schriftsteller las aus seinem neuen Roman.* Under less formal circumstances the v. is *vorlesen. Der Schriftsteller las seiner Frau seine neue Erzählung vor.* (*Lesen* also means 'to lecture'. *Professor Wolf liest in diesem Semester über Bismarck.*)

    Alle Kinder lernen lesen, schreiben und rechnen.   *Lies mal vor, was auf dem Zettel steht!*
    Zwei Studenten haben heute ihre Referate im Seminar vorgelesen.

ii. Verlesen implies making something important known by reading it out. It also implies that at least a few people are listening, not just one. It is used for official communications. *Der Regierungssprecher verlas die Regierungserklärung/das*

Schlußkommuniqué. Man verlas die Anklage, read the charge or indictment. Elsewhere it means 'to announce by reading'. *Die Vorsitzende des Vereins verliest die Namen der Gewinner in einer Tombola. Der Präsident verlas die Liste der Preisträger.*

2. Ablesen is 'to read a meter' or 'to read sth. off from a gauge'. *Man liest den Stromzähler/die Gasuhr/die Wasseruhr ab.* It also means 'to read a speech, etc. [off] from a manuscript' and in this case has a slightly neg. tone. *Er sprach nicht frei, er las [die Rede] ab.* **Herunterlesen** expresses more criticism of the expressionless way something is read than *ablesen.*

> *Jede Stunde muß die Temperatur/der Dampfdruck abgelesen werden.*
> *Es hinterläßt keinen guten Eindruck, wenn ein Minister seine Reden nur abliest.*
> *Was auf dem Papier stand, las er monoton und anscheinend ohne Verständnis herunter.*

3. Nachlesen means 'to read again what one has only an unclear recollection of'. *Ich glaube, daß die Sache sich so verhält, aber ich lese es schnell im Bürgerlichen Gesetzbuch nach.* It also means 'to read [up] details for oneself at a later time'. A lecturer might say, '*Ich habe Ihnen die Sache in groben Zügen dargestellt. Die Einzelheiten können Sie in der einschlägigen Literatur nachlesen.*'

4. Read *thoughts,* or *s.o.'s mind,* is usually *jmds. Gedanken* **lesen,** though **ablesen** can express a similar meaning.

> *Auf/Aus ihrem Gesicht war deutlich zu lesen, was sie dachte.*
> *Die Meinung der Anwesenden war an ihren Gesichtern deutlich abzulesen.*

5. Other senses. *The passage* **reads** *[as follows]* when a quotation follows is *Die Stelle* **lautet** *[wie folgt].* *Sth.* **reads well** is *Etw.* **liest sich** *gut. Der Roman liest sich leicht/wie eine Übersetzung. The news* **is read** *by s.o.* on the radio or television. *Es folgen Nachrichten* **gesprochen** *von . . .* Thus *Der Nachrichtensprecher. The thermometer* **reads** *35°* is *Das Thermometer* **zeigt** *35°* **an.**

real, actual, true, genuine *adjs.* really, actually *advs.*

1. Real = 'actually existing', 'having a foundation in fact', the opposite of *imagined. Real pain/hardship.* **Really** also states that what is said corresponds to reality, is not imagined or invented. *I really saw her. We really had to work hard.* **Really** also emphasizes the exact truth or facts of a situation. *I want to find out what really happened. He's not really going to work—he's going to lie in the sun.* In neg. contexts **real** and **really** state that something cannot be correctly described as existing or being fully present, although it may be present to a limited extent. *They have no real understanding of the problem/don't really understand what's happening.*

i. The main equivalent of the adj. and adv. is **wirklich.** *Die Darstellung entspricht nicht den wirklichen Ereignissen. Ist das wirklich wahr? Wirklich* is used in countering a doubt and is stressed. *Das ist wirklich geschehen* can be an answer to the view that something has not happened. *Das hat sie wirklich gesagt. Das ist wirklich so..*

> *Sie litten wirkliche Not/befanden sich in einer wirklich mißlichen Lage.*
> *Er ging wirklich hin und entschuldigte sich.*   *Ich möchte erfahren, was wirklich passiert ist.*
> *Alles hat sich wirklich so zugetragen, wie der Autor es darstellt.*
> *Hat König Artur wirklich gelebt?* (Best transl. of *Was he a real person?*)
> *Ich weiß nicht, ob das, was ich gesehen habe, wirklich war oder nur Einbildung.*
> *Er hat die wirkliche Welt kennengelernt.*
> *Das wirkliche Leben sieht anders aus, als er dachte.*
> *Er geht nicht wirklich arbeiten, er will bloß in der Sonne liegen.*
> *Das Stück beruht auf einer wirklichen Begebenheit.*
> *Ich zweifle daran, ob er Goethe wirklich versteht.*
> *Er hat wirklich alles allein gemacht.* (Reply to a doubt.)

Really is also often used for emphasis. *I'm really sorry. We had to work really hard.*

The smoke of these cigars is really obnoxious. **Wirklich** can give emphasis, but it is less commonly used than **really**. *Da bin ich wirklich neugierig. Es tut mir wirklich leid. Das ist wirklich liebenswürdig von Ihnen.* If **really** means 'very', **sehr** is more appropriate. *Es tut mir sehr leid. Sie arbeiten sehr schwer.*

Der Qualm dieser Zigarren ist wirklich widerlich.   *Wir mußten wirklich schwer arbeiten.*

ii. Wahrhaftig is occasionally found as an adv. meaning 'really, in reality'. *Das hat sich wahrhaftig so zugetragen. Wirklich und wahrhaftig*, 'really and truly', is sometimes met with. *Wirklich und wahrhaftig, so ist es gewesen! Das habe ich wirklich und wahrhaftig nicht getan.* It also gives force or assurance to a statement. *Es hat wahrhaftig keinen Zweck, länger auf sie zu warten. Wirklich* is the normal word in everyday speech. (Applied to people, *wahrhaftig* means 'telling the truth, truthful'. *Sie ist ein wahrhaftiger Mensch. Sei wahrhaftig!*)

iii. G. **real** is a *Fremdwort* for *wirklich*, encountered more in learned language but restricted in use. It can mean 'existing in reality, not merely as an idea', *die reale Welt*, and can also mean 'realistic', *reale Werte, ein real denkender Politiker. Der real existierende Sozialismus*, socialism as it actually was in practice, not as an idea. (Note: *Reele Preise* are realistic, fair, or reasonable. *Jmd. hat eine reele Chance*, a reasonable prospect of success.)

iv. *a.* In its basic sense, **eigentlich** also states what exists in fact or reality, but implies a contrast with what seems to be the case or what people mistakenly take to be true. It is translated as *actual[ly], real[ly]*, or *in actual fact. Die Sache ist eigentlich anders* suggests 'different from what is believed'. *Die Sängerin Tripelli hieß eigentlich Trippel* implies 'contrary to what might be believed'. In *Dieser Mantel gehört eigentlich meiner Tante—sie hat ihn mir geliehen, wirklich* could be substituted for *eigentlich* only if the ownership or right of use had been questioned.

Sie wurde als Sekretärin angestellt, aber ihre eigentliche Arbeit besteht in der Durchsicht der Zeitschriften.   *Das ist der eigentliche Grund für den Schlamassel.*

Er spielt gut Klavier, aber seine eigentliche Begabung liegt auf zeichnerischem Gebiet.

Was ist sein eigentlicher Beruf?   *Was ist der eigentliche Zweck der Sache?*

Er hat wirklich alles allein gemacht. (Reply to a doubt.)

b. As an answer to *Gibt es andere Probleme?*, **eigentlich nicht** means 'not really'. *Wirklich nicht* or *Ich habe wirklich keine* is a strong assurance of the contrary in reply to e.g. *Haben Sie andere Probleme?* when this assumes that there are some.

c. The adv. **eigentlich** can translate **real** used with *no. There was no real cause for alarm. Es besteht eigentlich kein Grund, uns zu beunruhigen*, i.e. although there might seem to be.

Eigentlich besteht keine Aussicht, daß er als Kandidat aufgestellt wird. (He has no real chance/prospect . . .)

d. **Eigentlich** also corresponds to **actual** used attributively to refer to the most important part of what is being talked about, i.e. in contrast to what may seem important but is only secondary. *Die eigentliche Bedeutung eines Wortes* is 'the primary meaning' in contrast to fig. ones.

Die eigentliche Hochzeitsprozession fängt erst um 11.55 an.

Wir kommen nun zum eigentlichen Problem.

Die eigentliche Wahlkampagne dauert nur drei Wochen.

v. Tatsächlich means 'actual' or 'real' in the sense of 'corresponding to the facts'. *Ich schilderte ihnen die tatsächliche Situation.* It is somewhat stronger than *wirklich*. It is also used as an adv. when stating the real facts. *Die Sache hat sich tatsächlich so zugetragen. Sie ist es tatsächlich. Das ist tatsächlich besser so. Wirklich* could be used in all three sents. In the first, *tatsächlich* is only slightly stronger. In the other two the speaker would use *tatsächlich* to express surprise and suggest that what is stated had originally not been believed. *Das ist wirklich sehr schwierig* is a general fact, but

Das ist tatsächlich sehr schwierig implies that it had not been thought that it would be difficult. *Tatsächlich* is stronger than *wirklich* in a question such as *Gibt es wirklich etw. Neues, was man darüber sagen kann?* and suggests that the speaker finds it extremely hard to believe that there could be anything new to say and would expect 'no' as an answer.

Sie hat tatsächlich/wirklich vor, allein um die Welt zu fahren.

2. Another meaning of E. **real** is 'actually or truly such as its name implies, possessing all the qualities such a thg. should (ideally) have', 'free from pretence, genuine, not artificial'. *A real friend/patriot.* **True** is a syn. and is used to describe people or things which possess all the characteristics of a thing or of a particular kind of person or animal. *A true friend. A true democracy. True love.* **Genuine** means 'not a fake or imitation'. *The painting was genuine. A genuine democracy.* Applied to feelings and reactions, **genuine** means 'really and truly felt and not displayed in order to deceive'. *She looked at him with genuine astonishment. I was genuinely angry with him.* **Wirklich** is also used here. *Ein wirklicher Freund/Künstler.* **Echt** means 'not a fake or imitation', i.e. 'genuine'. *Das Bild ist echt, keine Fälschung. Der Schmuck ist echt, keine Imitation.* *Echt* is very common in everyday language as both an adv. and adj. *Das war eine echte Enttäuschung* is used in speech instead of *wirklich. Echte Liebe* is more common than *wahre Liebe.* **Wahr** is 'true' in the sense described. *Ein wahrer Freund. Etw. ist eine wahre Wohltat/ein wahrer Segen. Wahr* is stylistically higher in this sense and tends to be preferred for loftier abstracts. *Wahre Freundschaft.* As in E., there is considerable overlapping between the syns.

Er ist ein wirklicher/wahrer/echter Freund, und sie sind selten.

Darin sehe ich ein echtes/wirkliches Problem.   *Das war für mich eine wirkliche Hilfe.*

Er interessiert sich wirklich dafür, nicht bloß zum Schein.

Dort herrschte eine echte/wahre Mißwirtschaft.   *Sie sah ihn mit echtem/wahrem Erstaunen an.*

Es ist ein wahres Wunder, daß dir nichts dabei passiert ist.

Wahrhaft is an elevated syn. of *wahr* and *echt*. Although *ihre wahrhafte Liebe* or *seine wahrhafte Bescheidenheit* occur, *wahrhaft* is used mainly as an adv. *Ein wahrhaft demokratisches Land.* (But *eine echte Demokratie.*) *Das ist eine wahrhaft vorbildliche Haltung.* Here *wirklich* could be used. *Wahr* is not an adv.

3. E. **real** also emphasizes the speaker's description of something and states that the following n. is exactly as it is stated to be. This is the same meaning as that given in 2, but at a stylistically lower level. *It's a real mess. That was a real stroke of luck.* In spoken E. *proper* is sometimes a syn. *He was a real/proper miser.* **Wirklich** and **echt** are possible. As mentioned in 2, *echt* is frequently heard in everyday speech. *Mein erster Auftritt war ein echter Reinfall. Ich war echt böse mit ihm.* **Wahr** is mostly too lofty for this sense. Words common in speech are **richtig**, which is used for good and bad qualities, and **regelrecht**, which is mostly confined, both as an adj. and adv., to things which are bad. *Im Büro gab es ein richtiges/regelrechtes Durcheinander. Das ist eine regelrechte Unverschämtheit. Er war regelrecht unverschämt.* A real shame or pity is *wirklich schade*, as *schade* is not a n. In a few cases, **recht** is used, but *richtig* is more common. *Es war eine rechte Schande/ein rechtes Elend/ein rechter Jammer* and sometimes *eine rechte Freude.*

Das war ein wirklicher/echter/richtiger Glücksfall.

Du bist ein wirklicher/echter/richtiger Phantast.

Im vorigen Jahr hatten wir keinen richtigen Sommer.

Er hat wirklich/echt Pech gehabt.   *Das [Theater]stück war ein richtiger/regelrechter Reinfall.*

Das Zimmer, das dem Studenten angeboten wurde, war ein regelrechtes Kellerloch.

Das kleine Kind war über den Anblick der Giraffe regelrecht erstaunt.

4. Both **wirklich** and **tatsächlich** express surprise or doubt at what has been said, as does **really** used alone. *A. No one was allowed into the area unless he had police permission. B. Really! A. Niemand durfte das Gelände ohne polizeiliche Genehmigung betreten. B. Wirklich!* *Tatsächlich* is stronger.

5. Really expresses annoyance in *Really, that's the limit/the last straw* or *I've really had enough.* There is no exact equivalent, but *wirklich* can be added to the expression. *Das ist doch wirklich die Höhe!* **Aber** can express annoyance and impatience, and in commands or virtual commands it suggests that something has gone far enough or gone on long enough. *Jetzt reicht's mir aber [wirklich]* or *Jetzt ist aber [wirklich] Schluß!*

6. Other senses of **true**.

i. Wahr is 'true' meaning 'corresponding to the facts or the real situation'. *Das ist eine wahre Geschichte. An dem, was er sagte, ist kein wahres Wort* or *ist kein Wort wahr. Ich erkannte die wahren Beweggründe meines Kollegen. Der wahre Wert einer Freundschaft* suggests value in an abstract sense whereas *der wirkliche Wert von etw.* suggests a monetary value.

ii. Treu is 'true' meaning 'faithful'. *Er blieb ihr treu. Ein treuer Bundesgenosse.*

iii. Getreu is applied to representations, translations, etc. which are faithful or true to the facts or an original. *Eine getreue Widergabe der Tatsachen. Eine getreue Übersetzung des Textes.*

7. Some equivalents of **actually**.

i. Eigentlich is often used in answers as a way of saying 'No' which is more polite than a blunt *nein.* At the same time it may show a readiness to make a concession.

    A. Möchtest du etw. essen? B. Ich habe eigentlich keinen Hunger (aber ich esse noch ein bißchen).

    A. Hast du Lust ins Theater zu gehen? B. Ich habe eigentlich nicht viel Geld, aber ich komme trotzdem mit.

ii. Eigentlich is also used like **actually** to give in a polite way a new piece of information which may not be known to the person spoken to and which gives him/her the opportunity to react accordingly. *A. Kommst du mit ins Kino? B. Eigentlich bin ich gerade dabei, einen Aufsatz zu schreiben (und will deshalb nicht mitkommen).*

    A. Können Sie am Donnerstag Überstunden machen? B. Ich wollte eigentlich Tennis spielen.

iii. Eigentlich means 'actually' in the sense 'by rights'. It states what someone is expected to do but is often followed by, or implies, an *aber* which shows willingness to compromise. *Eigentlich müßte ich jetzt gehen, aber ich bleibe noch ein bißchen. Eigentlich hätte sie das nicht sagen dürfen* suggests that the speaker considers the remark regrettable but understands why she said it, sympathizes with her position, etc. **Eigentlich** can imply: If I consider the situation properly. *Ich will zwar ins Kino, aber eigentlich habe ich keine Zeit.*

iv. Actually also introduces a totally new topic into the conversation. Someone might say, 'Actually, Tom (or Herr Maier), I didn't come here just to help you with the party. I wanted to borrow your drill.' *'Du, Thomas, eigentlich bin ich nicht gekommen, um dir bei den Vorbereitungen für die Fete zu helfen. Ich wollte fragen, ob du mir deine Bohrmaschine leihen kannst.'* Or *'Wissen Sie, Herr Maier, ich bin eigentlich nicht gekommen, um Ihnen . . .*

v. Eigentlich is used like **[well,] actually**, when someone is nervous or anxious about what he or she is saying.

    Vater: Sag mal, Daniel, hat man dir einen Studienplatz angeboten?

    Sohn: Tja, eigentlich, Vater, habe ich mich noch nicht entschlossen, zur Uni. zu gehen. Or *Weißt du, Vater, eigentlich . . .'*

vi. When **actually** introduces information which contrasts with what has been said, i.e. makes a polite objection, **allerdings** is used. *Wir haben allerdings ganz* *andere/nicht die gleichen Erfahrungen gemacht,* actually, our experience was quite different.

vii. Übrigens is used to correct a statement. *A. David Smith could help us. He's a teacher. B. Actually he's a university lecturer, not a teacher. Übrigens, er ist nicht Lehrer, sondern Dozent.*

viii. When **actually** indicates something surprising, as in *You may actually be doing the right thg. by walking out,* the equivalent is **sogar**, EVEN. *Vielleicht machst du sogar das Richtige, wenn du weggehst.*

ix. If **actually** introduces an instruction or advice which the speaker will certainly carry out, as in *Actually it might be a good idea if we left now,* this would be *Wir sollten jetzt lieber/besser gehen.*

realize, recognize, acknowledge *vs.* One sense of see *v.*

1. Realize a fact or that something is true, false, wrong, etc. means 'to become aware or gain an understanding that this is so'. *She realized the significance of what he was trying to do. I later realized that I had been wrong.* **Recognize** means 'to have a clear awareness and understanding of sth.' *He was one of the few people to recognize the problem and foresee the dangers. They recognized that the success of the scheme was by no means certain.* **See** also denotes more than perception with the eyes and can suggest a conclusion drawn from something seen. *I can see that you're interested in the idea. I see that your sense of humour hasn't changed. As you can see, there's still a lot to be done here.* **See** what someone means or why something happens, how it happens, or what it is, means 'to understand or realize'. *I can see why he's worried. Can't you see that there is no alternative? It took him a long time to see that he had made a mistake. Money has disappeared from the safe over the weekend, and I don't see how.*

i. When the understanding or realization is gained by thought or deduction from the information available, either *erkennen* or *einsehen* is used. **Erkennen** means 'to gain an exact understanding or knowledge of sth. which was hitherto unknown or not fully known'. It is translated as **realize, recognize**, and sometimes **see**. It suggests, however, that someone comes to this understanding or realization by a process of thought alone. This understanding or realization may arise from something observed, but the assumption is that the person gains it without the intervention of others. The actual insight may be separated in time from what it concerns and may occur suddenly and unexpectedly. It is often used with *plötzlich*. *Plötzlich erkannte ich, was wir falsch gemacht hatten.* **Einsehen**, on the other hand, presupposes remarks by one person, or occasionally the effect of circumstances, to get the person who is the subj. of *einsehen* to understand or acknowledge something. What is to be recognized is often something the person is reluctant to admit about his or her own actions or beliefs. In certain sents., both *erkennen* and *einsehen* are possible, but the implication is different. *Erst später habe ich erkannt, daß ich mich geirrt hatte* suggests a sudden recognition or realization, either a flash of inspiration or the result of something seen or heard. *Eingesehen* in the same sent. suggests that someone pointed out the mistake, that the other person was initially unwilling to concede this, but later realized he/she was wrong and admitted it. Likewise *Am Ende erkannte ich/sah ich ein, daß wir keine andere Wahl hatten.* Because of its implication, *erkennen* can be used dishonestly to suggest that the speaker arrived at the understanding alone and unaided. In the neg. and in questions both vs. can have the meanings just defined for pos. sents. *Das hatte ich damals noch nicht erkannt,* the realization had not come to me at that stage. *Das hat er lange nicht eingesehen. Hat sie das noch nicht eingesehen?* Only *einsehen* is used with *nicht wollen. Das wollte er nicht einsehen,* understand and acknowledge it. The often heard *Ich sehe nicht ein (warum das notwendig ist),* which is translated as *I don't see* or *understand,* suggests that the speaker is not convinced by the point of view put by someone else.

Er gehörte zu den wenigen, die das Problem/die Gefahr/den Ernst der Lage erkannt hatten.

Sie sahen ein/erkannten, daß der Erfolg des Unternehmens keineswegs sicher war.

Erst als sie anfing zu weinen, sah ich ein, daß ich etw. falsch gemacht hatte.

Erst nach Jahren sah sie die Bedeutung seiner Arbeit ein. Also erkannte.

Siehst du nicht ein, daß wir nichts anderes tun können?

ii. Erkennen only is used with **an** and means 'to recognize a fact by the way s.o. does sth.' It suggests an immediate realization and translates **see** as well as **recognize.** *An der Art und Weise, wie er die Maschine bediente, erkannte ich, daß er neu war.*

iii. Sehen is used only when the conclusion is based directly on sense perception. It does not suggest a conclusion arrived at only by a process of thought. If two people had disagreed about how far it is from one place to another and had then later seen a sign giving the distance, the one who was right might say, '*Siehst du jetzt, daß ich recht hatte?*' or '*Siehst du jetzt, daß du unrecht hattest?*'

Sie sah, daß er nicht richtig zuhörte.   *Wie Sie sehen können, bleibt hier noch viel zu tun.*

Ich sehe, daß Ihr Sinn für Humor sich nicht verändert hat. (Implies behaviour justifying this conclusion.)

iv. When **see** does not refer to a conclusion drawn from a sense perception and carries the second sense of **see** defined above, 'to understand or realize', it is best translated by **verstehen.** Cf. SEE 1.

Eine Geldsumme ist aus dem Tresor verschwunden, aber ich verstehe nicht wie.

Ich verstehe den Sinn dieses Satzes nicht.

Jetzt verstehe ich, was sie meint. But *Ich erkannte plötzlich, was gemeint war.*

I see when it means no more than 'I understand' can be *Ich verstehe schon* or simply *verstehe.* Alternatives are *Das sehe ich schon ein* and **Das ist mir klar. Ach so!** is an exclamation expressing surprise when something suddenly becomes clear to the speaker and may correspond to *I see. Ach so! Er war gar nicht dabei—das habe ich nicht gewußt.*

2. i. Realize also means 'to know' and is translated by **wissen.** *I didn't realize you lived so close: Ich wußte nicht, daß Sie so nahe bei uns wohnen. Wissen Sie, daß Sie das erste Mädchen sind, daß ich ausgeführt habe?* do you realize/know? *He is more conscientious than many people realize: Er ist ein viel gewissenhafterer Mensch, als viele Leute wissen.* Alternatives to the last clause: *. . . als vielen Leuten bewußt/bekannt ist.*

ii. In *If you realize what a desperate position we were in,* **realize** suggests an effort to picture something to oneself. The equivalent is **sich vergegenwärtigen,** to visualize, IMAGINE. *Wenn Sie sich die verzweifelte Lage vergegenwärtigen, in der wir uns befanden, werden Sie verstehen, warum wir so gehandelt haben.*

3. Other uses of **erkennen.**

i. 'To recognize' in the sense 'to know who or what people or thgs. once encountered are, when one sees them again'. In talking of a person one knows but has not seen for some time or who has changed, *wieder* is usually added. *Ich habe sie sofort wieder erkannt.* By is an. *Man kann ihn an seiner Haarfarbe erkennen.* As is als. *Augenzeugen erkannten ihn als den Bankräuber.*

Obwohl ich sie seit Jahren nicht mehr gesehen hatte, habe ich sie gleich wieder erkannt.

Er hat sich so sehr verändert, daß ich ihn auf der Straße wahrscheinlich nicht wieder erkannt hätte.

Erkennst du die Stadt auf dem Bild nicht?

ii. Erkennen also corresponds to **recognize** in the sense 'to identify sth. because of previous experience and/or knowledge of the distinguishing features'.

Der Arzt hatte die Krankheit sofort erkannt.   *Er hat das Getreide sofort als Gerste erkannt.*

iii. Erkennen also means 'to recognize s.o./sth. for what he/she/it really is' and is applied both to good and bad qualities. *Sie hatten den Betrug/die egoistische Absicht schnell erkannt.*

> *Man hat ihr musikalisches Talent früh erkannt.*   *Sie hatte ihn bald als Lügner erkannt.*

iv. Applied to things seen, **erkennen** means 'to make out, distinguish, or discern'.

> *Aus dieser Entfernung kann ich nur die Großbuchstaben erkennen.*
> *In der Dunkelheit konnte man nur die Umrisse erkennen.*
> *Radspuren sind an aufgeweichten Stellen des Weges noch zu erkennen.*

4. Acknowledge, recognize.

i. Anerkennen in its primary sense is the equivalent of **acknowledge** meaning 'admit as genuine, legally binding, valid, or justified', and **recognize** meaning 'treat as valid or genuine'. The difference between the E. words is that **recognize** suggests an authority, *officially recognized* being the usual expression. The one G. v. covers both ideas. *Man erkennt ein Testament/eine Unterschrift/eine Schuld/eine Verpflichtung/einen Anspruch/die Vaterschaft eines Kindes an. Das Verfahren wurde staatlich geprüft und anerkannt. Anerkennen* is used for the diplomatic recognition of countries. *Die meisten Regierungen haben den neuen Staat/das neue Regime anerkannt.*

> *Der Kanzler war eine autoritäre Persönlichkeit, der die Berechtigung einer Opposition kaum anerkannte.*
> *Er wurde als rechtmäßiger Erbe anerkannt.*
> *Ich erkenne an, daß deine Forderungen berechtigt sind.*

ii. Anerkennen has another sense which varies between acknowledging and appreciating the worth of someone's work etc. and expressing praise for someone in the presence of others, often officially. It is like **recognize** when it means 'to show official recognition for', *They recognized her work by making her house a museum*, but it is also translated as *appreciate* and **acknowledge** or *praise*. *Anerkennend* is 'appreciative'. *Der Chef sprach einige anerkennende Worte über die Arbeit unserer Gruppe.*

> *Ich erkenne das Werk meiner Kollegen voll an.*
> *Alle haben ihn als tüchtigen Menschen anerkannt.*
> *Man erkennt die Verdienste/die Leistung/die Bemühungen eines anderen an.*

People, achievements, or qualities that are acknowledged by others are widely known and appreciated. This sense is conveyed by the past part. **anerkannt**. *Er ist ein anerkannter Fachmann auf seinem Gebiet. Sie ist eine international anerkannte Schriftstellerin.*

5. Other equivalents of acknowledge.

i. Acknowledge can mean 'to admit'. *They refused to acknowledge that they had made a wrong decision.* This could be **zugeben**, but for variants see ADMIT under CONFESS 1. *Sie wollten nicht zugeben, daß sie eine Fehlentscheidung getroffen hatten. They refused to recognize in the same sent.* would be *Sie wollten nicht einsehen.*

ii. Another sense of **acknowledge** is 'to express gratitude'. *They acknowledged the applause of the crowd/s.o.'s kindness.* This sense is expressed by **sich dankbar/erkenntlich zeigen für**. Both adjs. mean 'grateful'. *Sie zeigten sich für den Beifall/ihre Freundlichkeit erkenntlich/dankbar.*

iii. Bestätigen, 'to confirm', translates **acknowledge** in *I acknowledge the receipt of your letter. Ich bestätige hiermit den Empfang Ihres Briefes.*

iv. Acknowledge *a greeting* is *einen Gruß erwidern.* For **erwidern** cf. ANSWER 3.

6. Other senses of **realize**.

i. Realize *a plan* etc. meaning 'to carry it out, make it reality' is **verwirklichen**. *Man verwirklicht einen Plan/eine Idee/einen Wunsch/einen Traum.* The refl. is used where E. has the pass. *Ihre Hoffnungen/Wünsche haben/Ihr Traum hat sich verwirklicht.* An alternative is [sich] **erfüllen**. Cf. ꜰɪʟʟ 4. *Er hat seine Hoffnungen erfüllt. Seine Hoffnungen haben sich erfüllt. Meine schlimmsten Befürchtungen haben sich erfüllt/verwirklicht.* Cf. also *eintreffen* under ᴏᴄᴄᴜʀ 3.

ii. Realize oneself or *one's potential* is *seine Möglichkeiten entfalten* or *sich richtig entfalten. Entfalten* is lit. 'to unfold'.

iii. Realize an amount of money. *Der Erlös* is the sum received from the sale of something or raised by a collection, etc. Combined with *erbringen* or *erhalten*, it can express this sense of **realize**. *Die Sammlung erbrachte einen Erlös von DM 5 500.* With a personal subj.: *Jmd. erhielt einen Erlös von 300 000 Mark vom Verkauf des Hauses.*

reasonable, rational *adjs.*

1. Rational meaning 'possessing or endowed with the power of reasoning' is **vernunftbegabt**. *Der Mensch ist ein vernunftbegabtes Wesen.*

> *Man hat Obelisken auf dem Mond entdeckt, die so aussehen, als ob vernunftbegabte Wesen sie errichtet hätten.*

2. Rational describing a person means 'able to think clearly and make decisions based on reason rather than emotion'. *Let's discuss this rationally/talk about it like two rational people!* **Reasonable** means 'possessing good sound judgement' and is a syn. of *sensible* and *rational* in this sense. *You should consider carefully the advice of such a reasonable/sensible man.*

i. Vernünftig is the normal equivalent. It is applied to people as both an adj. and adv. *Sie ist eine vernünftige junge Frau. Sie handelt/urteilt/spricht sehr vernünftig. Er besitzt die Fähigkeit, vernünftig/logisch zu denken,* the ability to think rationally. **Verständig** is applied to people and to what they say. It means 'sensible and moderate, intelligent'. It may also suggest an understanding of others' positions, but it is now not much used. *Eine verständige junge Frau. Sie handelten verständig.*

> *Wir wollen die ganze Sache vernünftig besprechen.* Or . . . *wie zwei vernünftige Menschen besprechen.*
> *Über den Rat eines so vernünftigen Mannes solltest du sorgfältig/ernsthaft nachdenken.*
> *Sie ist ein verständiger/vernünftiger Mensch.*   *Sie hat sehr verständig geantwortet.*

ii. Be reasonable! can be *Sei doch vernünftig! Was du da vorhast, ist verrückt—sei doch vernünftig!* Alternatives are *Nimm doch Vernunft an!* and *Habe doch Einsicht!* An alternative expressing the same meaning is *Du mußt doch einsehen, daß das, was du da vorhast, verrückt ist.*

3. Reasonable, applied to a conclusion, opinion, argument, etc. and to what people do, means 'understandable, in agreement with right thinking, not absurd or ridiculous'. *A reasonable argument/objection/point of view. Reasonable principles.* **Rational**, applied to people's ideas and actions, expresses the same sense. *Rational behaviour.*

i. Vernünftig means 'in conformity with reason, sensible, reasonable, rational' and describes such things as *eine Rede, eine Meinung, ein Plan, ein Vorschlag, ein Argument, ein Einwand,* etc. *The debate soon lost all semblance of a rational exchange of opinions* can be expressed as *Mit dem Austausch vernünftiger Argumente hatte die Debatte immer weniger zu tun/bald nichts mehr zu tun/kaum noch etw. zu tun.*

> *Das ist eine vernünftige Antwort/Frage/Ansicht.*   *Das sind vernünftige Grundsätze.*
> *Sie hat einige Einwände erhoben, die ich sehr vernünftig gefunden habe.*
> *Man kann kein vernünftiges Wort mit ihm reden.*
> *Dich vernünftig verhalten nenne ich es nicht, wenn du jmd[n]., der deine Meinung nicht teilt, beschimpfst.*

ii. Vertretbar means 'of such a nature that it can be approved of', 'justifiable', and is often used like **reasonable** in this sense. *Ein vertretbarer Standpunkt.*

> *Jeder sollte seinen Alkoholgenuß auf ein vertretbares/vernünftiges Maß beschränken.*

iii. Rational is found in learned discourse. *Rationales Verhalten.*

iv. *It is [quite]* **reasonable** *to suppose/claim/conclude that . . .* A transl. expressing this meaning is *Man kann mit einigem Recht/mit einiger Berechtigung annehmen/behaupten, daß die meisten uns unterstützen werden.* (Both ns. mean 'justification'.) Or *Die Annahme erscheint berechtigt, daß . . .* **Naheliegen,** 'to be obvious', can also express this sense. *Der Schluß liegt nahe, daß andere dabei im Spiele waren* or *Es ist naheliegend, daß . . . Eine naheliegende Vermutung/Schlußfolgerung,* a reasonable or obvious conjecture/conclusion.

4. Reasonable applied to a person can also mean 'not demanding too much', 'fair, just', a meaning conveyed by **gerecht.** *A reasonable boss. Our mother was always very reasonable. Er ist ein gerechter Chef. Unsere Mutter war immer sehr gerecht.*

5. Reasonable means 'within the bounds of reason, not extreme, not excessive'. *A reasonable request/demand. A reasonable risk. Reasonable conditions. Reasonable prices/costs.*

i. Annehmbar, 'acceptable', can translate *reasonable* in relation to *ein Vorschlag, eine Bedingung, eine Forderung, der Preis, ein Angebot, eine Entschuldigung,* etc.

> *Diese Bedingungen erscheinen uns annehmbar. Der Unterzeichnung des Vertrages steht also nichts im Wege.*

ii. Vertretbar is used in this meaning in the sense defined in 3. ii. *Vertretbare Kosten. Ein vertretbares Risiko.*

iii. Berechtigt means 'justified' and can translate **reasonable.** *Ein berechtigter Wunsch. Eine berechtigte Bitte/Forderung. Ein berechtigter Einwand.*

iv. Mäßig, 'moderate', can express this sense of **reasonable.** *Mäßige Forderungen/Ansprüche. Die Arbeit ging in mäßigem Tempo voran.*

v. *Man kann ihm diese Arbeit zumuten* means that it is reasonable to expect him to do this work or that he can reasonably be expected to do it. Cf. WAIT 3. v. *Eine für jmdn. zumutbare Aufgabe* is 'a reasonable task for s.o.' or 'a task s.o. can reasonably be expected to do'. A dat. is also possible after *sein. Diese Aufgabe ist ihr/für sie zumutbar.*

vi. Reasonable *prices.* **Angemessen** means 'appropriate to what is being offered'. *Das ist ein angemessener Preis für drei Tage Vollpension.* If **reasonable** means 'cheap', **mäßig,** 'moderate', or **günstig,** 'favourable', can be used, as well as **billig,** 'cheap', or **preiswert,** 'inexpensive'. *Fresh vegetables are now very reasonable* can be *Frisches Gemüse ist jetzt sehr preiswert.* In everyday speech **vernünftig** is used with *Preis.*

> *Diese Preise sind mäßig/sehr günstig.*   *Ich habe den Wagen günstig gekauft.*
> *Der Wochentarif ist besonders günstig/wirklich sehr mäßig.*
> *Er hat für den alten Wagen einen vernünftigen Preis bekommen/verlangt/bezahlt.*

6. Something that is reasonable or reasonably good is fairly, but not very, good. *He has reasonable prospects of success. They were reasonably satisfied. She plays reasonably/reasonably well.*

i. Reasonable or **reasonably** meaning 'fairly or moderately good/well' and *reasonably good/well* can be expressed by **ziemlich,** 'rather, FAIRLY', + *gut. Sie spielt ziemlich gut. Er hat ziemlich gute Erfolgsaussichten.* **Einigermaßen** has a similar sense, but it suggests a lower degree than *ziemlich.* Without a following adj. or adv. it means 'to a certain extent, just adequate'. *Jetzt ist es einigermaßen in Ordnung.* It is not used with *gut* but implies this. *Es geht ihr einigermaßen. Es ist ihm einigermaßen gelungen,* he has been reasonably successful. *Ziemlich* and *einigermaßen* are used with other adjs. and advs. besides *gut. Wir sind mit dem Ergebnis ziemlich/einigermaßen zufrieden.*

> *Du hast ziemlich gut/einigermaßen befriedigend abgeschnitten* (done reasonably satisfactorily).

Unsere Erfolgschancen sind ziemlich gut.
Wir haben heute eine ziemlich weite Strecke geschafft (covered a reasonable/fair distance).
Wir haben heute ziemlich viel Arbeit geschafft (managed to do a reasonable amount). Also *Wir haben . . . einiges an Arbeit geschafft.*   *Das Hotelzimmer war einigermaßen sauber.*

ii. Leidlich means 'moderately or reasonably good', 'better than average and of acceptable standard, though not especially good'. It is used with and without *gut.* *Er ist ein leidlicher* or *ein leidlich guter Tennisspieler. Das Wetter war leidlich/leidlich gut.* **Passabel** is a syn. *Das Essen war ganz leidlich/passabel. Sie spricht leidlich/passabel Französisch. Er ist ein leidlich guter/passabler Koch.* Another syn., **halbwegs**, is an adv. only. *Bin ich halbwegs anständig angezogen? Das ist ein halbwegs brauchbares Buch.*

Das Hotel war leidlich sauber.   *Das Geschäft geht leidlich.*
Während Herr Schmitz seine Rolle passabel spielte, versagten die anderen Laiendarsteller kläglich.
Seine Vermutung war halbwegs richtig.   *Ich habe mich halbwegs zurechtgefunden.*

iii. In everyday speech **vernünftig** often means 'reasonably good, reasonable, decent, proper'. *Nimm dir doch eine vernünftige Portion! Das war ein vernünftiges Buch. Ich habe seit einiger Zeit keinen vernünftigen Film mehr gesehen.* When an aesthetic judgement is involved there are alternatives. *Das Niveau* can refer to the intellectual or artistic level of a film, novel, etc. *Der Film hat Niveau* means that it has (artistic) merit, is reasonable. **Anspruchsvoll** could also be used but suggests a higher standard. It means 'satisfying high intellectual or aesthetic expectations'. *Das ist ein anspruchsvoller Roman und wird dir gefallen.* **Erträglich** means 'not absolutely bad, even though not particularly good', 'passable, fair to middling'. *Ich fand diesen Roman/Film erträglich.*

7. Beyond reasonable doubt. There is no corresponding expression, so that the sense has to be reproduced. The legal expression *hinreichend erwiesen*, adequately proven, is not as strong. Some other possibilities are: *Es kann nicht ernsthaft angezweifelt werden, daß X der Täter ist. Es steht außer Zweifel/darf als erwiesen gelten, daß der Beamte bestochen worden war. Man darf mit an Sicherheit grenzender Wahrscheinlichkeit behaupten, daß die Mafia dahinter steckt.*

receive *v.*

1. Receive in its primary sense means 'to get or take sth. given, offered, or sent'.
i. When **receive** means that something has arrived or been given to someone, the sense is expressed by **bekommen**, 'to GET', or at a stylistically higher level by **erhalten**. Being more formal, *erhalten* is used in business and official style. *Wir haben Ihren Brief/Ihren Auftrag erhalten.* In everyday language and situations *bekommen* and *erhalten* are interchangeable. *Jmd. erhält/bekommt ein Geschenk/ein Paket/einen Brief/eine Antwort/eine Anweisung/einen Auftrag/eine Verwarnung*, etc.
ii. In certain formal contexts **receive** and *accept* are interchangeable. *Applications/Orders are received/accepted at any time.* The formal v. **entgegennehmen** expresses this sense. Cf. ACCEPT 1. ii. *Jmd. nimmt Auskunft/eine Bestellung entgegen. Er nahm den Auftrag/die Bewerbung/die (schriftliche) Beschwerde entgegen. Entgegennehmen* suggests taking something which is handed over or lodged or noting information given. It cannot be used when asking whether something has been received, in which case *erhalten* or *bekommen* is needed. *Haben Sie meine Bewerbung erhalten? Entgegennehmen* is the usual v. when stating that someone is handed a prize etc. at a ceremony, *Der Preisträger nahm den Preis entgegen und dankte in einer kurzen Rede für die Auszeichnung*, and when speaking of highly placed personages receiving expressions of gratitude, homage, etc., *Der Kaiser nahm die Huldigung des Adels in Paderborn entgegen.*
iii. Empfangen is stylistically higher again, and in connection with everyday

things like *ein Brief, ein Befehl, ein Auftrag,* or *eine Strafe,* sounds pompous and would only be found in bureaucratic language. It can be used like *erhalten* for something mental, *Man empfängt/erhält neue Anregungen/neue Impulse/einen bestimmten Eindruck,* and instead of *entgegennehmen* when someone receives something in a ceremony, *Er empfing den Orden/den Preis in einer Zeremonie im Palast.*

iv. In Empfang nehmen is a bureaucratic term meaning 'to receive'. *Eine Empfangsbescheinigung,* stating that someone has received or collected something, could be worded: *Ich bestätige hiermit, den Paß/den Einschreibebrief in Empfang genommen zu haben. Erhalten* would be the normal word.

2. The obj. of **erhalten** can be punishment, *Jmd. hat eine Freiheitsstrafe erhalten,* but *Man bekommt/kriegt Schläge* etc. is more usual. *Erhalten* and *bekommen* are used for receiving an idea or impresssion. *Ich habe eine neue Vorstellung von etw./einen anderen Eindruck erhalten/bekommen.*

3. Receive means 'to receive or welcome visitors'.

i. When no adj. or phr. describing the manner follows, **empfangen** usually suggests a fairly formal and official reception of one or more people, by highly placed persons, diplomatic personnel, cabinet ministers, etc. *Heute empfing der Bundespräsident in seiner Berliner Residenz, Schloß Bellevue, Prinz Rainier von Monako. Der Minister/Der Bürgermeister empfängt heute abend die Teilnehmer an der internationalen Konferenz. Der Botschafter empfing Gäste in seiner Residenz.* Words stating how someone was received can be added, *Jmd. wurde herzlich/kühl/frostig empfangen,* and with such advs. **empfangen** is not restricted to the higher echelons of society. *Empfangen* normally suggests only the actual reception on arrival which may last only a short time. *Ich wurde vom Staatssekretär herzlich empfangen, bekam aber keine Gelegenheit, mich mit ihm zu unterhalten.*

ii. If more than the initial reception is meant, the v. is **aufnehmen**, which makes a judgement on the whole of the time spent with people. *Ich wurde von diesen Leuten sehr herzlich/mit großer Freundlichkeit aufgenommen. Aufnehmen* is confined to receptions which are friendly and welcoming. **Empfangen** can be used for both a friendly and an unfriendly reception and is the only v. possible in *Die Polizei empfing die Demonstranten mit Wasserwerfern/mit Gummiknüppeln.*

iii. Aufnehmen also means 'to put a pers. up, to receive as a guest in one's house'. *Viele Familien sind bereit, Schüler der Partnerschule in Deutschland [bei sich] aufzunehmen. Ein Hotel* etc. can also be the subj. *Das völlig renovierte Hotel nimmt Gäste wieder auf.*

4. Aufnehmen means 'to accept, admit s.o. into a club or organization'. Cf. ACCEPT 5. It also translates **receive** when it has this sense. *Einen Monat vorher wurde sie in die katholische Kirche aufgenommen.*

5. Empfangen is usual in relation to radio and television reception. *Kann man hier das holländische Fernsehen empfangen? Diesen Kurzwellensender empfängt man jeden Abend ohne Störung.* Colloquially **kriegen** and **hereinbekommen** are also used, as get is in E. *Diese Sendung kriegt man hier nur auf Mittelwelle. Die Deutsche Welle und den BBC-Kurzwellendienst bekommt man hier gut herein.* The question asked when trying to make contact by radio, 'Are you receiving me?' is *'Hören Sie mich?'*

6. Aufnehmen means 'to receive or take news, s.o.'s remarks in a certain way', i.e. 'to react to'. It also describes the way a book, play, performance, etc. is received by the audience or public.

Wie hat sie die Nachricht aufgenommen?   *Er hat diese Erklärung mit Skepsis aufgenommen.*

Meine Bemerkung war als Scherz gemeint, aber er hat sie ziemlich übel aufgenommen.

Das Publikum nahm das Stück mit Beifall/mit Begeisterung auf.

Der neueste Roman des Autors ist von der Kritik und dem Lesepublikum gut aufgenommen worden.

Entgegennehmen is a more formal word for receiving a command in a certain way. *Er nahm den Befehl mit Bestürzung entgegen. Der Offizier nahm den Befehl schweigend/mit Protest entgegen.* (Note: *Er erhielt den Befehl* means he received the order in the sense that it was given to him. This sense is also expressed by *entgegennehmen* without an adv. or phr. *Er nahm den Befehl entgegen.*)

7. In some contexts **receive** means 'to experience or meet with'. *They received very harsh treatment/criticism.* Here it can be translated by **zuteilwerden** or **widerfahren** discussed under MEET 9. ii. *Ihr ist eine rücksichtsvolle Behandlung zuteilgeworden. Ihnen widerfuhr eine sehr harte Kritik.* **Finden**, used with a few ns., means 'to meet with or receive'. *Seine Arbeit fand Anerkennung bei seinen Vorgesetzten. Der Plan fand unerwartete Unterstützung. Das Buch fand eine freundliche Aufnahme/keinerlei Beachtung. Der Vorschlag fand seine Zustimmung/seine Billigung.*

recent *adj.* **recently** *adv.* **the other day** *phr.* used as *adv.*

1. i. The most commonly used equivalent of **recently** referring to a point of time is **vor kurzem**. With *vor kurzem* the time that has elapsed must be at least a few hours but is usually a few days or weeks. *Vor kurzem hat mir Christian erzählt, was sich da alles ereignet hatte. Bis vor kurzem* is 'until recently'. Closely related to *vor kurzem* are *kürzlich* and *neulich*. **Kürzlich**, 'not long ago', suggests that at least a few days or weeks have passed. *Kürzlich ist eine Taschenbuchausgabe seiner Werke erschienen.* **Neulich**, which suggests a strong association of the earlier time with the time of speaking and a clear recollection of what had been said or had happened, is like **the other day**. *Renate sagte, sie könne das Kleid nicht tragen, weil sie es neulich angehabt habe.*

> *Schmidt wurde vor kurzem zum Hauptmann befördert.*
> *Mir ist kürzlich eine merkwürdige Sache passiert.*
> *Ich habe sie erst vor kurzem in der Stadt getroffen.*
> *Bis vor kurzem haben sie auf dem Lande gewohnt.*
> *Erinnern Sie sich an unser Gespräch von neulich?*
> *Wir wollen heute die Diskussion von neulich fortsetzen.*
> *Neulich, als ich in Braunschweig war, habe ich sie besucht.*
> *Das war neulich,—bei der zweiten Sitzung des Ausschusses.*

ii. Other expressions. Both **jüngst** and **unlängst** belong for speakers in the north to the written language only, although they are commonly used in some areas. *Sie war jüngst in Wien. Ich habe ihn jüngst gesehen. Auf den Gangsterboß ist unlängst ein Attentat verübt worden. Das Buch ist erst unlängst erschienen.* **Letztens** is often used when something that happened recently relates to the present. *Letztens las ich einen Bericht darüber in der Zeitung. Letztens hat mich jmd. nach dir gefragt.* **[Erst] vor ein paar Tagen** may express the meaning 'recently'. *Ich habe sie erst vor ein paar Tagen wieder gesehen.* **Dieser Tage** can mean 'in the last few days'. *Ich habe dieser Tage gehört, daß sie wieder nach Göttingen kommt.* (Note that *dieser Tage* also means 'in the next few days'. *Er wird dieser Tage abreisen.*) Colloquially, **die Tage** is used like *the other day, a few days ago. Ich bin die Tage in Frankfurt gewesen.*

iii. Neuerdings is an adv. referring to actions which begin in the recent past and continue into the present. It presupposes a change or innovation. In reference to people, it means that recently someone began to do something different from what he or she had been accustomed to doing. *Neuerdings steht er um sechs Uhr auf und geht joggen.* It often needs to be translated as *Recently s.o. began/started to do sth.* **Seit kurzem** means that someone began to do something a short time ago or recently. *Seit kurzem kürzt die Regierung die Ausgaben, wo sie nur kann.*

> *Neuerdings kann man Geld zu jeder Tageszeit von Geldautomaten abheben.*

Das Wort 'unterschiedlich' erfreut sich neuerdings besonderer Beliebtheit.

2. In letzter Zeit denotes not a point of time but a span or period of time beginning a short time before the moment of speaking or the time spoken about. It is like *in recent weeks/months*.

In letzter Zeit ist es öfter zu Zwischenfällen dieser Art gekommen.

Ich habe ihn in letzter Zeit ein paar Mal/kein einziges Mal gesehen.

3. Recent is difficult to express in G. Only **kürzlich** can be an adj., but it does not occur very frequently. *Eine kürzliche Entscheidung des Obersten Gerichts. Der kürzliche Zwischenfall an der Grenze.* **Jüngst** is also an adj. *Die jüngsten Landtagswahlen. Deutsche Geschichte in jüngster Vergangenheit. Die jüngsten Ereignisse in Kambodscha.* Sometimes **recent** + n. can be translated as one of the advs. discussed in 1 + a past part. *Das jüngst erschienene Buch von X, X's recent book. Ein vor kurzem verabschiedetes Gesetz. Die kürzlich erfolgte Stillegung der Eisenbahnlinie. Die jüngst getroffene Entscheidung. Die unlängst/kürzlich beschlossene Gebührenerhöhung.* **Recent** + n. can be turned into a clause. *At our recent meeting: Als wir uns kürzlich trafen. Rainer is a recent acquaintance: Ich habe Rainer erst vor kurzem kennengelernt.* **Neu** can translate **recent** in some contexts. *Eine neue Erfindung. Eine neue Entwicklung.* **Neuer** is 'more or fairly recent', and **neuest** 'most recent'. *Eine neuere Untersuchung. Die neuesten Ereignisse/Nachrichten. Our most recent meeting: Unsere letzte Begegnung.*

record *v.*

1. The basic sense of the v. **record** is 'to put or set down in writing'. This sense is connected with the original meaning of the n. *record* which, according to the *OED*, is 'the fact of having been committed to writing as authentic evidence of a matter having legal importance, specifically as evidence of the proceedings or verdict of a court', and is used chiefly in the phr. *to be on record*. The meaning of the E. v. has been extended in recent times as instruments were developed for taking down information, sound, etc. so that a general definition of **record** is 'to set down in some permanent form'.

i. The main v. meaning 'to commit to writing and thereby retain permanently' is **festhalten**. *Ich habe die Diskussion in Stichworten festgehalten.* The sense has been extended to include giving something a permanent form by a drawing, painting, etc. or in a photograph, film, or on tape. In the latter cases it is not the technical term for the process, but states that something is not lost but given a permanent form. In *Es liegt mir daran, hier festzuhalten, daß der Film meinen Intentionen entspricht, festhalten* is like *to put on record* or *to state for the record*. It is used with a person as subj., *Eckermann hat seine Gespräche mit Goethe für die Nachwelt festgehalten*, but the subj. can be the medium by means of which something is recorded. *Eine versteckte Kamera hat alles, was geschehen ist, festgehalten.*

Die Schulzeitschrift hält eine interessante Debatte fest.

Das Protokoll hält fest, daß eine erhitzte Debatte erfolgte.

Die Antwort meines Vaters verdient, festgehalten zu werden.

ii. Aufzeichnen is 'to write or note down, usually carefully'. It is often used for writing down what one has experienced or observed, but can be used for information one has been told by others. It suggests, however, an endeavour to write down only what is accurate.

Sein Leben lang führte er Tagebuch und zeichnete alle Ereignisse auf.

Jmd. hat seine Erinnerungen/seine Gedanken/diese wahre Begebenheit/Volkslieder aufgezeichnet.

iii. Aufnehmen can mean 'to take down in writing' and translates some uses of **record**. *Jmds. Personalien aufnehmen* is 'to record or take down' someone's name, address, etc. *Man nimmt über einen Unfall/Diebstahl,* etc. *ein Protokoll auf*, records or writes down the details. The G. word for *a court record* is **das Protokoll**, which is also used for the minutes of a meeting or conference and for the record or report, e.g. by the police, of something that happened or of statements made.

iv. If I record my opinion or objection, I express it publicly so that it can be included in a report or in the minutes or be given some permanent form. A person keeping the record records my opinion etc. *I'd like to record my reservations about this plan* is *Ich möchte meine Vorbehalte gegen diesen Plan* **zu Protokoll geben**. The person keeping the record **nimmt** *den Einwand* **zu Protokoll**, or **nimmt** *ihn* **ins Protokoll auf**. *Alle vertretenen Standpunkte wurden ins Protokoll aufgenommen*, were recorded or included in the minutes/record. *Die Einwände wurden im Protokoll festgehalten* is also possible. **Record** *a vote*, if it means 'to cast one', is *eine Stimme abgeben*. To tell someone how I wish to vote and have it recorded is *zu Protokoll geben*. *The jury recorded a verdict of not guilty* is *Die Geschworenen erklärten den Angeklagten für nicht schuldig*.

2. In reference to historical events, someone's words, etc., **aufzeichnen** and **festhalten** are possible, but **überliefern**, 'to hand down (in writing)', is common. *Diese Geschichte wurde zuerst von Plutarch überliefert/aufgezeichnet. Nur wenige seiner Worte sind überliefert. Throughout recorded history* is *solange es eine schriftliche Geschichtsüberlieferung gibt. When did mankind begin to record its history?* is *Wann hat die Menschheit angefangen, ihre Geschichte niederzuschreiben/schriftlich festzuhalten? The earliest recorded use* of a word etc. is *der erste* **Beleg**, written record or evidence. *Der erste Beleg für diese Bedeutung ist aus dem 15. Jahrhundert.*

3. Verzeichnen means 'to enter, write down, or record sth. in a list'. *Alle Waren sind auf der Versandanzeige verzeichnet.* **Registrieren** has a similar sense but mostly implies that the list has some official character. *Alle Stücke der wertvollen Sammlung waren genau verzeichnet/registriert.*

> *Alle Namen sind/stehen in der Liste verzeichnet.*
> *Die Personalien/Die Straftaten wurden registriert.*

In commercial language *verzeichnen* means 'to record' a profit etc. *Die Firma hat einen Gewinn von DM 20 000 000 verzeichnet.* Also *Man verzeichnet einen Überschuß/ein Defizit. Verzeichnen* is used with some ns. to state that the action described by the n. took place or was achieved by someone. *Einige Änderungen sind zu verzeichnen*, some changes have occurred. *Jmd. hat einen Erfolg/einen Gewinn zu verzeichnen*, achieved a success or gain. *Fortschritte sind nicht zu verzeichnen* or *wurden nicht verzeichnet*, there was not any progress.

4. Beurkunden is 'to record and issue an official certificate or copy'. *Auf dem Standesamt werden alle Geburten, Eheschließungen und Todesfälle beurkundet.* **Registrieren** is also used.

5. Record music, films, etc. **Aufzeichnen** has become the technical term for recording on audio and video-tape. It implies high quality and is used for professional work of this kind. It is also often used if a non-professional records something from radio or television. *Ich habe alle dreizehn Folgen aufgezeichnet.* In one of its senses **aufnehmen** means 'to take down in a permanent form' and was applied first to gramophone records and then to tape and video recordings. (*Ihre Stimme läßt sich gut aufnehmen*, records well.) *Aufnehmen* is an alternative to *aufzeichnen* particularly for non-professional recording, but also for professional. *Ich habe das Gespräch/die Symphonie/die Sendung [auf Tonband/Kassette] aufgenommen.* On G. radio it is often stated that music which is played is *eine Aufnahme der Schallplattenindustrie.* Hence *die Aufnahme einer Oper, eine Aufnahme aus dem Jahr 1950. Die Aufzeichnung* could also be used. A third possibility for private recording is **mitschneiden**. The

n. is *der Mitschnitt. Sein Vortrag wurde auf Tonband mitgeschnitten.* (*Aufnehmen* is also used for photographing and filming so that *die Aufnahme* is also 'a photograph', a syn. of *das Foto. Er hat mir seine Aufnahmen von Griechenland gezeigt.*)

6. Record (of instruments).

i. In E. we can say that the thermometer recorded 31° when **recorded** means 'showed'. The v. here is **anzeigen**. Cf. SHOW 5. ii. *Das Thermometer zeigte 31° an.* If the instrument produces a permanent record, e.g. by drawing a line on paper, **aufzeichnen** is used. *Das Gerät zeichnet den Luftdruck auf.* An alternative is *registrieren.* **Registrieren**, which implies automatically registering and recording, is now the usual v. for instruments, although **verzeichnen** is sometimes found. *Das Gerät registriert/verzeichnet auch die geringsten Erderschütterungen.*

    Meßgeräte registrieren die Luftfeuchtigkeit/die Niederschlagsmenge.

    Die Seismographen registrierten ein schweres Erdbeben in der Nähe von Neuseeland.

    Die Kasse registriert alle eingehenden Beträge.

ii. Speichern, 'to store', translates **record** in relation to a computer. *Ein Computer könnte alle diese Daten/Einzelheiten speichern*, record all these data/details.

reduce, lessen *vs.* One sense of decline *v.*

1. Reduce means 'to bring down to a smaller number, amount, or extent, or to a single thg.', or 'to make smaller in size'. It is mostly trans., *We must reduce our expenses*, but in the sense 'to lose weight' it is intr., *She has been reducing for the last two weeks.* **Decline** is intr. only. If something declines, it becomes less in quantity, number, importance, or strength. *The number of members declined from 500 to 450. Their influence has declined.* **Lessen** can be trans. and intr. It means much the same as **reduce**, but it is mostly used with abstracts. *Hard work lessens the risk of failure. Their financial hardship has lessened.* A number of G. vs. carry these senses.

i. Verkleinern refers primarily to a reduction in size. *Eine Photographie wird verkleinert.* (The opposite is *Die Photographie wird vergrößert.*) *Verkleinern* can be followed by *um,* 'by', and *auf,* 'to'. *Durch den Anbau wurde der Garten um die Hälfte verkleinert. Der Garten wurde auf ein Viertel seiner ursprünglichen Größe verkleinert. Verkleinern* occasionally has numbers and quantities as obj., but *verringern* is the normal v. in these contexts. Cf. ii. *Der Betrieb hat die Zahl der Beschäftigten verkleinert. Verkleinern* is also sometimes intr. *Eine Linse verkleinert stark.* The refl. **sich verkleinern** can have the meaning of the E. pass. 'to be reduced', or can mean 'to become smaller'. *Durch den Anbau hat sich der Garten verkleinert.*

    Diese Verluste haben sein Vermögen beträchtlich verkleinert.

    Der Betrieb soll verkleinert werden.

    Durch diese Verluste hat sich sein Vermögen beträchtlich verkleinert.

    Dadurch, daß die beiden Sessel nun hier stehen, verkleinert sich der Platz um die Hälfte.

ii. Verringern is the main v. meaning 'to reduce in quantity, amount, number, and occasionally quality'. *Man verringert die Kosten/die Lautstärke/die Zahl der Teilnehmer/den Druck,* etc. **Vermindern** means, in strict use, 'to weaken the intensity of sth.' and is thus found primarily with abstracts. *Etw. vermindert die Gefahr/das Risiko/die Qualität. Diese Ereignisse verminderten jmds. Einfluß/meine Bewunderung für jmdn./die Spannungen.* Despite this special sense, it is now also used with ns. denoting a measurable quantity where *verringern* would be the usual word. *Es ist ratsam, bei regnerischem Wetter die Geschwindigkeit zu verringern/zu vermindern.* A third alternative is **herabsetzen**, to reduce numerically. It is not used in relation to intensity, but is usual with prices and numbers. *Wir haben den Preis um 25% herabgesetzt,* reduced or cut it. Both *herabsetzen* and *verringern* are used with *auf* and *um. Die Zahl der Kinder in einer Klasse sollte auf 25 herabgesetzt/verringert werden. Für* *zwei Personen verringert man die angegebenen Mengen um die Hälfte.* Both *verringern* and *vermindern* have refl. forms which differ in the same way as the base vs. and are translated by the E. pass. or by **lessen** used intr. *Die Aussichten auf Erfolg haben sich verringert. Dadurch, daß ich etw. über seine Vergangenheit weiß, vermindert sich die Achtung nicht, die ich für ihn empfinde. The pain was reduced can be Die Schmerzen verringerten sich* or *ließen nach.* **Nachlassen**, 'to decline, to become less in strength or intensity', is intr. Only the past part. of *vermindern* is used as an adj. *Sie fuhren mit verminderter Geschwindigkeit weiter. Der Kranke war nur vermindert zurechnungsfähig.* Hence also *unvermindert*, undiminished. *Sie arbeiteten mit unvermindertem Eifer weiter.*

Die moderne Technik hat die Zahl der Arbeiter verringert, die benötigt werden, um eine Fabrik zu betreiben.

Wenn wir unsere Ausgaben nicht verringern, wird uns das Geld bald ausgehen.

Er tat alles, um die Spannungen zwischen den Mitarbeitern zu vermindern.

Wird durch die Fahrlässigkeit eines Untergebenen die Verantwortung eines Vorgesetzten vermindert?

Im Sommerschlußverkauf werden viele Sachen zu stark herabgesetzten Preisen angeboten.

Die Regierung hat beschlossen, den höchsten Steuersatz herabzusetzen.

Die Hoffnung, daß es eines Tages wieder ein vereinigtes Deutschland geben könnte, hatte sich Anfang der achtziger Jahre erheblich verringert/vermindert. Niemand sah den Umbruch in Osteuropa voraus.

Sein Interesse für das Mädchen hat merklich nachgelassen.

Die Leistungen des Schülers lassen nach.

Die Kämpfe um die Hauptstadt setzen sich mit unverminderter Heftigkeit fort.

iii. Words related in meaning to *verringern* are **kürzen**, 'to cut expenditure etc.', cf. SHORTEN, and **einschränken**, 'to LIMIT'. *Die Zuwendungen für Universitäten wurden drastisch gekürzt. Wir müssen unsere Ausgaben einschränken.* **Reduzieren** is also used like *herabsetzen* and *verringern. Wir müssen die Kosten auf ein Minimum reduzieren.* It occurs frequently in relation to prices. *Alle Geschäfte haben die Preise vieler Waren stark reduziert.* It is also used in the refl. *Die Zahl der Unfälle hat sich reduziert* or *ist zurückgegangen* (cf. 1. vii) or *hat sich verringert.*

iv. In one sense **senken** also means 'to lower or reduce' and is a syn. of *verringern.*

Sie haben die Produktionskosten gesenkt.   *Man hat das Fieber [des Kranken] gesenkt.*

v. **Ermäßigen** is 'to reduce a price because of special circumstances'. *Kinder, Jugendliche und Rentner zahlen ermäßigte Preise. Drucksache zu ermäßigter Gebühr.*

vi. **Mindern** is still occasionally found instead of *vermindern*, but with a restricted number of ns. with which it forms more or less fixed expressions. Still heard is *Sein Ansehen ist durch diesen Fehler nicht gemindert worden. Minderung der Kräfte/der Leistungsfähigkeit* and *Wertminderung* are also possible, as well as *Der Wert der Maschine wird durch Abnutzung gemindert. Vermindern* and *verringern* are, however, not wrong in all the examples just given. *Der Alkoholgenuß minderte die Reaktionsfähigkeit des Autofahrers* is possible, but *verringern* and *herabsetzen* would be more usual.

vii. **Zurückgehen** is intr. and means 'to become less', 'to fall or decline in number'.

Die Zahl der Mitglieder ist auf 300 zurückgegangen.

Die Produktion/Das Hochwasser ging zurück.

viii. Reduce [weight] referring to people is **abnehmen**. *Er hält sich für zu dick und will abnehmen.* A weight can be added. *Sie hat fünf Kilogramm/zehn Pfund abgenommen.*

ix. Schmälern is a formal syn. of *verringern.* The obj. can denote something concrete, *Das hat meinen Anteil am gemeinschaftlichen Vermögen nicht geschmälert,* and is often an abstract, *Etw. schmälerte meinen Genuß/mein Vergnügen/meine Verehrung für jmdn.* The meaning of *jmds. Rechte schmälern*, 'to reduce or curtail someone's rights', can also be expressed as *jmdn. in seinen Rechten schmälern.* With an obj. like

jmds. Verdienste, Fähigkeiten, or *Leistungen, schmälern,* **herabsetzen,** and **verkleinern**
all mean 'to belittle or disparage'. The sense is 'to present sth. falsely as less than
it is'. The main v. in this sense is *herabsetzen. Herabsetzende Bemerkungen.*

> *Bäume schmälern den Ertrag einer Wiese.*
>
> *Er versuchte, die Verdienste seines Gegners zu schmälern/zu verkleinern/herabzusetzen.*
>
> *Der Versuch, den Gegenkandidaten in den Augen der Wähler herabzusetzen, schlug fehl.*
>
> *Diese kritischen Worte sollen den Wert des Buches nicht schmälern.*

2. Reduce also means 'to bring into a different form'. It implies a less complicated form that simply states the key propositions. *This kind of analysis reduces the
problem to a few simple questions/its simplest form.*
i. The word of G. origin for reducing something to one or more simple[r] propositions is **zurückführen. Reduzieren** is also used, but neither is common in combination with *die Form. Wir wollen das komplizierte Problem auf ein paar einfache Fragen
zurückführen/reduzieren.* In combination with either v. *Maß* means 'level'. *Man darf
nicht mit übertriebenem Idealismus an diese Aufgabe herangehen—man muß den
Idealismus auf ein vernünftiges Maß zurückführen,* reduce it to a reasonable level. Only
reduzieren can be refl. *Diese (mathematische) Aufgabe reduziert sich auf eine einfache
Gleichung.*

> *Diese Lehre läßt sich auf ein paar Grundgedanken zurückführen/reduzieren.*
>
> *Um diese Aufgabe zu lösen, muß man sie auf eine einfache Gleichung zurückführen.*

ii. With *die Form* or *das System,* **bringen** is usual. *Durch diese Art von Analyse bringt
man das Problem auf seine einfachste Form/auf eine einfachere Form. Wir versuchen, diese
Gedanken in ein System zu bringen. Man bringt Brüche* (= 'fractions') *auf einen gemeinsamen Nenner* (= 'denominator').

3. Reduce means 'to convert sth. into a different physical state or form'.
i. For **reduce** to powder etc. the appropriate v. is used, i.e. **zermahlen, zerkleinern,** etc. *Die Kaffeemühle zermahlt die Kaffeebohnen,* grinds them up. *Hier werden die
Steine zerkleinert,* crushed, reduced to small pieces. When there is no specific term,
a general v. is **verwandeln,** to CHANGE, convert. Both *Das Erdbeben verwandelte die
Stadt in einen Trümmerhaufen* and *Das Gebäude wurde durch die Explosion in einen
Schutthaufen verwandelt* are possible transls. of *reduced to rubble.*
ii. This meaning also occurs with a person as obj. *Sth. reduced me to a nervous wreck.*
A transl. is *Die anhaltende Angst hatte mich zu einem Nervenbündel gemacht.* The prison-
ers of war were reduced to skeletons: *Die Kriegsgefangenen magerten zum Skelett ab.* Or
Man ließ die Kriegsgefangenen zum Skelett abmagern.

4. Reduce to means 'to bring down to a bad or disagreeable condition'. *They were
reduced to penury. She was reduced to tears.*
i. The only G. v. which has a similar sense is **bringen.** While **reduce** implies being
in an undesirable state as a result of an unpleasant action or process, *bringen* is
used for good or bad results. Expressions in which it corresponds to **reduce** are
jmdn. ins Elend/in Not/an den Bettelstab/auf den Hund bringen, and *jmdn. zur
Verzweiflung/zum Weinen bringen.* Otherwise, the underlying idea needs to be
expressed. *Never before had the government been reduced to such desperate
measures/straits* could be *Nie zuvor hatten derartige widrige Umstände die Regierung
gezwungen, solch verzweifelte Maßnahmen zu ergreifen* (cf. 4. ii) or more simply *Nie zuvor
war die Regierung in einer so verzweifelten Lage gewesen.*
ii. Reduce to is also used with a gerund. Whoever is reduced to working or behaving in a particular way is compelled by circumstances to work or behave in that
way, even though it is unpleasant or humiliating. *We were reduced to selling the car
to pay the phone bill. He was reduced to eating dog food.* The sense can be expressed by

using **zwingen** in the pass. with the person as subj. or by making *widrige Umstände*, 'adverse circumstances', the subj. and the person the obj. Thus *Wir wurden gezwungen, das Auto zu verkaufen, um die Telefonrechnung zu bezahlen* and *Widrige Umstände zwangen uns, das Auto zu verkaufen, um* . . . or *Widrige Umstände hatten ihn gezwungen, Hundefutter zu essen.*

5. Reduce to also means 'to bring down to a lower rank, dignity, or position'. The military term for *to reduce to the ranks/to the rank of* . . . is **degradieren**. *Der Unteroffizier wurde zum Soldaten degradiert.* **Reduce to** is used in other spheres in the same sense. *When the emperor became head of the church, the Pope was reduced to the role of chief bishop of his realm.* The meaning can be expressed by **beschränken**, to LIMIT. *Als der Kaiser Kirchenoberhaupt wurde, wurde die Rolle des Papstes auf die des Hauptbischofs in seinem Reich beschränkt.* Alternatives. *Seine Rolle wurde begrenzt/ beschränkte sich auf* . . . *Schmidts Einfluß beschränkte sich von dieser Zeit an auf einige wenige Gebiete.*

refer *v.*

1. Someone who refers to particular things wishes what is said to be understood as concerning them. *I refer to one of the previous speaker's remarks.* If a remark etc. refers to s.o./sth., it concerns this person or thing. *Does this remark/criticism refer to me?*

i. Sich beziehen auf expresses the meaning just defined and can have either a person or thing as subj. *Ich beziehe mich auf unser gestriges Gespräch. Auf wen bezieht sich diese Bemerkung/diese Kritik?* It also translates *to relate to* when this means 'to concern or be connected with'. *Diese Frage bezieht sich nicht auf die besprochene Angelegenheit.*

> *Ich beziehe mich auf eine Äußerung des Vorredners/auf die schon zitierte Stelle im Vertrag/auf das soeben erwähnte Buch/auf die Aussage des ersten Zeugen* etc.
> *Dieser Vorwurf bezieht sich auf alle.*   *Diese Bemerkung bezieht sich nicht auf dich.*

Sich beziehen auf is used in business letters like **refer**. An alternative is **Bezug nehmen auf.**

> *Ich beziehe mich auf Ihr Schreiben vom 2. Mai und teile Ihnen mit, daß die bestellten Waren schon abgeschickt worden sind.* Or *Ich nehme Bezug auf Ihr Schreiben vom 31. d. M.*

ii. Whereas *sich beziehen auf* with a person as subj. presupposes a linking up with or the taking up of something previously talked about or written, **refer to** often means 'to talk about' or 'to mention' without this implication. *In his letters he rarely refers to political events. Her story appeared in several papers—I am referring, of course, to Anne Russell.* The general equivalents are **sagen, schreiben**, or **erwähnen**, to mention. **Reden von** and **meinen**, 'to MEAN', can also be used. *In seinen Briefen schreibt er kaum/oft über die politischen Ereignisse/* . . . *sagt er nichts/wenig über die politischen Ereignisse. Er erwähnt die politischen Ereignisse nicht. Ihre Geschichte ist in einigen Zeitungen erschienen—ich rede natürlich von A.R.* or *Ich meine natürlich A.R. To refer to s.o. by name* is *jmdn. namentlich erwähnen* or *jmds. Namen nennen.*

2. Refer to people or thgs. **as** sth. means 'to give them that name or call them that'. *The subject of the lecture was the decline of what he referred to as the industrial working class.* An equivalent is **bezeichnen als**, to denote as, CALL, or DESCRIBE. *Das Thema des Vortrags war der Rückgang vom dem, was er als die industrielle Arbeiterklasse bezeichnete.*

3. If a name, symbol, or number refers to a particular thing, it denotes this. *The first figure in the serial number refers to the country of origin.* Here the v. **bezeichnen** or the n. **die Bezeichnung** can be used. *Die erste Ziffer bezeichnet das Herkunftsland des*

Buches. Das Kürzel/Wort ist die Bezeichnung für ein Herstellungsverfahren. Alternatives. *Die erste Ziffer steht für . . . /gibt . . . an. Angeben,* to GIVE.

4. Refer to a source of information such as a reference book means 'to look at it in order to find sth. out'. To consult or to **refer to** a dictionary, encyclopaedia, etc. is **zu Rate ziehen** and **zu Hilfe nehmen**. *Wenn Sie ein Wort nicht kennen, müssen Sie das Wörterbuch zu Rate ziehen. Dieses Gericht kann ich zubereiten, ohne das Kochbuch zu Hilfe zu nehmen.* **Nachsehen in** *and* **nachschlagen in**, 'to look up in', can also express this sense of **refer**. *Sehen Sie in Ihren Grammatiken nach! Ich habe [es] im Lexikon nachgeschlagen. Er sah in der Akte nach, bevor er antwortete.* For *nachsehen* and *nachschlagen* cf. LOOK 6. To *refer to information* stored in a computer is **abrufen** or **abfragen**, to call up. *Die gespeicherten Daten kann man jederzeit abrufen.*

5. Refer people to a source of information meaning to 'tell them where they are likely to discover it' is **verweisen auf**. The general sense is 'to direct s.o. to sth.' or 'to point sth. out to s.o.' When act., it normally has a personal obj., *Sie verwies mich auf die gesetzliche Bestimmung,* but it can be intr., *Er verwies auf die betreffende Stelle im Buch.* The impersonal pass. is often found. *Es wird auf die Abbildung auf Seite 50 verwiesen,* you are referred to.

> *Bei der dritten Bedeutung des Wortes wird auf ein anderes Stichwort/ein Synonym verwiesen.*
> *Ich verweise Sie auf das Gesetz zum Schutz der Jugend/auf den Artikel von H. Schmidt.*

6. Verweisen an is the usual expression for referring a matter to another person (in whose field of responsibility it lies), to an organization, or to another or a higher court.

> *Ich kann Ihnen leider nicht helfen und muß Sie an meinen Kollegen Baumann verweisen.*
> *Man hat mich an die für solche Angelegenheiten zuständige Stelle verwiesen.*
> *Sie beschloß, die [Rechts]sache an den Europäischen Gerichtshof zu verweisen.*

For doctors, **überweisen** is the usual v. *Der Arzt überwies den Patienten an einen Facharzt.* For other fields of work, **übertragen**, 'to transfer', or **jmdn. mit etw. beauftragen**, 'to commission s.o. to do sth.', can be used. *Bauunternehmer haben ihm gewisse Arbeiten übertragen/ihn mit gewissen Arbeiten beauftragt.*

refuse, reject, decline, turn down *vs.* These words are close syns. in several, though not all, meanings. Order of treatment: 1. **Refuse** a request, wish, etc. 2. **Refuse** an offer or sth. offered. 3. **Reject** a proposal. 4. **Refuse/reject** a pers. 5. **Reject** sth. said or an accusation. 6. **Refuse** to do sth. 7. **Reject** products, ones that are not up to standard.

1. Refuse = 'to be unwilling to give sth. asked for, to grant a request, a wish, an application, etc.' **Reject** is a syn. **Turn down** is a colloquial syn. *My application was refused/rejected/turned down.*

i. Abschlagen is mostly confined to not granting requests and wishes for everyday things in the personal sphere. It needs an acc. to which a dat. can be added. The acc. can be *Wunsch* or *Bitte, es,* or sometimes the thing requested. *Sie haben unsere Bitte um ein Darlehen abgeschlagen.* When *es* is the obj., as in *Er hat es mir abgeschlagen,* it does not refer to a specific n., but implies that a request is refused.

> *Ich habe meine Schwester gebeten, mir mit den Hausaufgaben zu helfen, aber sie schlug es mir ab/schlug mir die Bitte ab.*   *Er konnte seinen Kindern keinen Wunsch abschlagen.*
> *Ein bißchen Milch werdet ihr mir doch nicht abschlagen* (implies a request for it).
> *Der Junge bat um ein neues Fahrrad, aber der Vater hat es ihm abgeschlagen.*
> *Zum ersten Mal nehmen deutsche Truppen an 'Blauhelm-Aktionen' teil. Alle Parteien in Bonn hatten diesmal wohl gespürt, daß die Deutschen die Bitte der UN nicht wieder abschlagen konnten.*

ii. Ablehnen is unemotional, neutral, and polite in tone. It is used in the official and legal domains (cf. 1. v) or in reference to schools, universities, businesses, etc., as well as in the personal sphere. It takes an acc. only, not a dat. of the person who is refused something. The person refused in *He refused me the request* can only be expressed as a possessive. *Er hat meine Bitte abgelehnt.* Despite this limitation in use, *ablehnen* is probably the commonest of the vs. treated in this article, having all senses except 7.

> *Mein Antrag auf ein Stipendium ist abgelehnt worden. Or Man hat meinen Antrag abgelehnt.*
> *Die Unternehmen haben die Forderung der Gewerkschaft um eine zehnprozentige Lohnerhöhung abgelehnt.*   *Das Ministerium lehnte die Zahlung weiterer Zuschüsse ab.*

iii. Jmdm. etw. verweigern is usually confined to weighty matters, often of an official nature. It is the only word used with *die Erlaubnis* as obj. in both the official and private spheres. *Der Vater verweigerte dem Sohn die Erlaubnis, sein Dienstauto zu benutzen. Verweigern* needs an obj. *We asked for permission, but they refused/but were refused* becomes *Wir baten um Erlaubnis, aber man verweigerte sie uns.*

> *Die Behörden haben dem Journalisten jede Auskunft über die verhafteten Rebellen verweigert.*
> *Früher hatte man ihm die Einreise in die Tschechoslowakei verweigert.*
> *Die Polizei verweigerte uns die Erlaubnis, in diesem Teil des Landes zu filmen.*

iv. Abweisen suggests a firm and decisive rejection, usually by someone in a superior position or by a higher authority. It takes an acc. only.

> *Was können wir dagegen unternehmen, wenn die Behörde den Antrag zum zweiten Mal ohne Prüfung abweist?*   *Das Gericht wies die Klage nach nur einem Verhandlungstag ab.*

v. Zurückweisen is the strongest term, suggesting a flat and decisive rejection without any willingness to compromise. It takes an acc. only. *Er wies die Bitte/die Forderung [entrüstet] zurück.* In some cases, it may mean 'not to be willing to take or receive sth.' *Die Behörde wies den Antrag zurück, weil ich die richtigen Formulare nicht benutzt hatte. Zurückweisen* is not uncommon in legal language. *Ein höheres Gericht wies die Berufung zurück. Ablehnen* is also frequently encountered in legal language. *Das Landgericht Stade hat den Antrag auf Erlaß einer einstweiligen Verfügung abgelehnt.* With *die Klage,* '[legal] action or [law]suit', *ablehnen, abweisen,* and *zurückweisen* are all found.

> *Den Wunsch der Schüler, von Hausaufgaben befreit zu werden, wies das Lehrerkollegium mit Entschiedenheit zurück.*

2. The sense 'to be unwilling to accept sth. offered or given' is expressed by several vs. *We* **refuse/reject/decline/turn down** *an offer, invitation, gift,* etc.

i. Ablehnen is again completely neutral in tone, stating nothing about the person's feelings nor about the way the offer is refused. Though it often needs to be translated by words other than *decline,* it resembles it in being mild and courteous in tone and not having the idea of active repulse often present in **refuse**.

> *Ich bedauere sehr, Ihre Einladung ablehnen zu müssen.*
> *Man bot ihm das Amt des Bürgermeisters an, aber er lehnte es ab.*
> *[Ein Angebot von] 3 000 Dollar für das Auto würde ich nicht ablehnen.*
> *Ich nehme an, daß sie seinen Heiratsantrag abgelehnt hat.*

ii. Ausschlagen usually carries a note of surprise that the offer is not being accepted, and expresses regret or criticism on the part of the speaker. Sometimes a speaker uses it about an offer he or she has refused when it is to be expected that the refusal will surprise others.

> *Ich habe ihm meine Hilfe angeboten, aber er hat sie doch [tatsächlich] ausgeschlagen.*
> *Sie überlegte sich, ob sie die Erbschaft ausschlagen sollte.*
> *Sollte ich die mir angebotene Beförderung ausschlagen, so könnte ich lange auf eine andere warten.*
> *Eine Einladung zum Abendessen bei meinen reichen Verwandten würde ich nie ausschlagen.*

iii. Abweisen and **zurückweisen** are used with offers with the implications described in 1. iv and 1. v.

> *Er hatte sich um eine Stelle bei einer Chemiefirma beworben. Als er aber das Angebot bekam, wies er es ab, weil das Gehalt viel zu niedrig war.*

3. Reject = 'to refuse to agree to a proposal, suggestion, plan, motion, etc.' **Verwerfen, ablehnen, ab-** and **zurückweisen** all convey this sense. *Verwerfen* is mostly found in formal language and contexts but is necessary in one case. When someone makes plans and then rejects them in his or her own mind, the v. used is *verwerfen. Ich hatte einen Einfall, den ich zuerst für sehr gut hielt, aber später habe ich ihn doch verworfen. Ablehnen* suggests that a plan put forward by one person is rejected by another or others.

> *Das Unterhaus hat den Gesetzentwurf mit großer Mehrheit abgelehnt.*
> *Viele haben für den Antrag gestimmt, aber er wurde trotzdem abgelehnt.*
> *Sie weisen jeden Gedanken an einen Kompromiß zurück.*
> *Das Gericht hat die Berufung abgewiesen/verworfen* (dismissed, rejected the appeal).
> *Man hat den Plan geprüft, ihn aber als zu kostspielig verworfen/abgelehnt.*

4. Ablehnen, abweisen, and **zurückweisen** occur with a person as obj. and translate **reject** or **refuse** with a personal obj. *S.o. rejects an applicant/candidate* or *S.o. rejects/refuses a suitor.* When *abweisen* has as its obj. people who want to see someone, it need not imply brusqueness or unfriendliness, so that *einen Besucher* (caller) *abweisen [müssen]* can mean 'to decline to see' as well as 'to refuse to see' or 'not to receive' or '[to have] to turn away'. *Zurückweisen* can also mean 'to turn back or away'. *Man wies mich an der Grenze zurück, weil ich keinen gültigen Paß hatte.*

> *Die Wähler haben die radikalen Kandidaten entschieden abgelehnt.*
> *Der Verteidiger lehnte zwei Geschworene als befangen ab.*
> *Der Chef bat die Sekretärin, alle Besucher abzuweisen, bis die Konferenz zu Ende war.*
> *Weil wichtige Gespräche im Gange waren, mußte er Besucher abweisen.*
> *'Sie weisen mich zurück', sagte Grünlich tonlos, als Toni Buddenbrook seinen Heiratsantrag ablehnte.*
>   (adapted from Thomas Mann)
> *Viele, die den Vortrag hören wollten, mußte man zurückweisen, weil der Saal überfüllt war.*

5. Reject = 'to be unwilling to recognize as true or applicable'. **Ablehnen** is used with ns. such as *ein Argument, eine Theorie, eine Ansicht, eine Interpretation, ein Einwand, die Verantwortung*, etc. and can be applied also to thinkers and artists whose work one rejects, or to political systems etc. one is not in agreement with. **Zurückweisen**, which means 'to protest against and declare to be false', is often found with words expressing criticism or an accusation. *Er wies die Beschuldigung/ den Verdacht/die Kritik zurück.* Cf. *verneinen* under DENY 2.

> *Einige Wissenschaftler lehnen die Theorie ab, andere lassen sie gelten.*
> *Dieses Argument erscheint mir nicht stichhaltig. Ich lehne es ab.*
> *Die moderne Malerei lehne ich ab.*   *Ich lehne Nietzsche als Philosophen ab.*
> *Ich lehne jede Verantwortung für den Unfall ab.*
> *Sie wies sämtliche Vorwürfe entschieden zurück.*
> *Der Minister wies die Beschuldigung der Opposition, er habe Aufträge an seine Freunde erteilt, entrüstet zurück.*
> *Der Lehrer wies die Kritik an seinem Unterricht zurück und war zu keinem klärenden Gespräch bereit.*

6. Refuse to do sth. = 'to express determination not to do sth.'
i. The weakest term **ablehnen** is used with an infin. usually preceded by *es*, or with a verbal n. which has the same meaning as an infin. *Er lehnte es ab, den Befehl auszuführen* or *Er lehnte die Ausführung des Befehls ab.* It needs a personal subj.

> *Der Pressesprecher des Unternehmens lehnte es ab, weitere Auskunft zu erteilen.*
> *Sie lehnten es ab, einen so hohen Preis für das Haus zu bezahlen.*
> *Die Lehrerin lehnte es ab, den fadenscheinigen Entschuldigungen des Schülers Glauben zu schenken.*

ii. Sich weigern and **verweigern**, which suggest a more forceful refusal than *ablehnen*, differ only in the way they are used. *Sich weigern* is used either with an infin. or alone, and *verweigern* needs an obj. *Sie weigerte sich, uns zu helfen. Ich hatte gehofft, er würde mir helfen, aber er hat sich geweigert. Sie verweigerte uns ihre Hilfe.*

Verweigern + n. often needs to be translated as an infin. *Der Soldat weigerte sich, seinem Vorgesetzten zu gehorchen,* and *Er verweigerte seinem Vorgesetzten den Gehorsam* both become *He refused to obey his superior officer. Verweigern* is formal in tone. The subj. of both vs. is either a person or an animate being. *Das Pferd weigerte sich beharrlich, auch nur einen Schritt nach vorn zu machen.*

> *Sie hat sich geweigert, vor Gericht auszusagen.* Or *Sie hat die Aussage vor Gericht verweigert.*
>
> *Die Bundesregierung weigerte sich, die Staatsbürgerschaft von DDR-Bürgern anzuerkennen.* Or *Die Bundesrepublik verweigerte die Anerkennung der Staatsbürgerschaft von DDR-Bürgern.*
>
> *Die Spieler weigerten sich, im strömenden Regen weiterzuspielen.*
>
> *Man erwartete von den Spielern, daß sie trotz des Regens weiter spielen würden, aber sie weigerten sich.*

iii. When **refuse** in this sense has a non-personal subj. **nicht wollen** may express the sense.

> *Meine Haare wollen gar nicht flach liegen.*   *Die Tür will nicht offen bleiben.*

iv. When a part of the body is the subj. of **refuse**, the sense can be expressed by **versagen**, to fail. *Meine Beine versagten mir den Dienst,* refused to move or support me.

7. Reject products because they are not up to standard is expressed by **aussondern**. *Die Waren mit Mängeln werden ausgesondert.* **Aussortieren** also denotes the removal of substandard products. *Die schlechten Kartoffeln/Die Waren mit Fehlern werden aussortiert. Rejects* are *der Ausschuß* or *die zweite Wahl.*

relation, relationship, connection, ratio, proportion *ns.* Some uses.

1. A **ratio** expresses in figures how two things relate to each other. *The ratio between attackers and defenders was approximately 5 to 1.*
i. The equivalent is **das Verhältnis**, which also translates **proportion** when it denotes a similar numerical relation between two things. *Mix the flour and fat in the proportion of 2 to 1: Man mische das Mehl und das Fett im Verhältnis von 2 zu 1! In inverse proportion* is *in umgekehrtem Verhältnis.*

> *Das Verhältnis zwischen Angreifern und Verteidigern betrug etwa 5 : 1.*
>
> *Lehrkörper und Schülerschaft stehen in einem Verhältnis von 1 : 15.*
>
> *Die für gewisse Angelegenheiten benötigte Zeit steht in umgekehrtem Verhältnis zu deren Wichtigkeit.*

ii. Im Verhältnis zu is 'in proportion to' or 'in comparison with'. *Kleinkinder haben große Köpfe im Verhältnis zu ihrer Körpergröße. Eine Sache wächst in gleichem Verhältnis wie eine andere.* **In proportion as** + a clause is **in dem Maße wie** or **in dem Verhältnis wie**. *In dem Maße/Verhältnis wie sich ihr Wortschatz erweitert, können die Schüler schwierigere Texte lesen.* Both can be translated as *as,* i.e. *in proportion* need not be expressed.

> *Im Verhältnis zu den Städten schritt die Industrie doppelt so schnell voran.*
>
> *Die Städte wuchsen im gleichen Verhältnis wie die Industrie.*
>
> *In dem Maße wie die Industrie sich entwickelte, wuchsen auch die Städte.*
>
> *In dem Verhältnis wie die Infrastruktur dieses Entwicklungslandes ausgebaut wurde, konnte man größere Industrieprojekte durchführen.*

iii. *To be* **out of all proportion to** and *to bear* **no relation to** mean that something is greater or more serious than is necessary or appropriate. *The fine was out of all proportion/bore no relation to the seriousness of the offence.* **In keinem Verhältnis stehen zu** translates *proportion* and *relation* in the expressions. *Die aufgewandte Mühe steht in keinem Verhältnis zu dem Ergebnis,* the effort expended is out of all proportion to the result, or the result bears no relation to the effort expended. In some contexts **unverhältnismäßig** means 'out of proportion'. *Er wurde unverhältnismäßig hoch or gering bezahlt,* paid too much or too little, out of proportion to the normal wage.

> *Die Geldstrafe steht in keinem Verhältnis zu der Geringfügigkeit des Vergehens.*
>
> *Seine Ausgaben stehen in keinem Verhältnis zu seinen Einnahmen.*

2. A sense of proportion means 'a feeling that a certain reaction is right for or appropriate to the circumstances'. The equivalent is **der Sinn für das rechte Maß**, a sense of what is moderate. *Der Sinn für das rechte Maß ist unbedingt notwendig, wenn Sport Vergnügen bereiten soll. Hasn't this got out of all proportion?* could be *Haben wir bei dieser Sache nicht das rechte Maß verloren?*

3. A proportion of a whole means 'part' of it and indicates the relative size of the part and the whole. When a sing. n. follows, *part* and *proportion* are interchangeable. *A large part/proportion of the earth's surface is covered by water.* Only **proportion** is used with a pl. n. *A small proportion of the electors. The proportion of matriculants who go to university has increased.* Some adjs. are combined only with one of these ns. *A vast proportion of our revenue. A large part/proportion of my income.* Only **proportion** is followed by *in. The proportion of one kind of thg. in a group.* The equivalents are **der Teil** and **der Anteil**, which also translate *part* and SHARE. With a sing. n. either can be used. *Ein großer Teil/Anteil der Erdoberfläche ist von Wasser bedeckt.* When *Teil* is also possible, *Anteil* is stylistically higher. Only *Anteil* is used when a precise portion is suggested. *Welcher Anteil des Familieneinkommens wird für Lebensmittel ausgegeben? Wie groß ist der Anteil der Industrie, der sich in Privathand befindet? Anteil* is used when a pl. n. follows. *Der Anteil der Abiturienten, die studieren wollen, ist gestiegen.* There must be an adj. between *ein* and *Anteil. Ein gewisser Anteil der Studenten. Ein bestimmter Anteil der Bevölkerung.* (In the last sent. also *Teil*, which could be translated as *part* or *section*.) If there is no adj., *Teil* is used whether the following n. is sing. or pl. *Bei jedem Fußballspiel will immer ein Teil der Fans, daß es zu einer Schlägerei kommt.* Only *Anteil* is followed by *in. Der Anteil der Gastarbeiter in der deutschen Bevölkerung.* Some adjs. form fixed expressions. *Ein großer Teil* but *ein hoher Anteil*, and *ein kleiner Teil* but *ein geringer Anteil*. An alternative, but one suggesting greater precision, is **der Prozentsatz**, percentage.

> *Der Teil/Anteil der Bevölkerung, der eine Fremdsprache beherrscht, ist ziemlich klein.*
> *Ein Teil der Industrie ist verstaatlicht worden.*
> *Der Anteil der Frauen in leitenden Stellen ist noch weiter gestiegen.*
> *Der Anteil der Ureinwohner in der australischen Bevölkerung wächst ständig.*

4. i. The **relation** or **relations** between countries, peoples, groups of people, and individuals and **relationship** in the sense 'the way two people or groups of people, including countries, think and feel about each other'.

i. Two G. words express this sense, **die Beziehung** and **das Verhältnis**. For countries and relations of an economic nature, e.g. between firms, *die Beziehung* is used, mostly in the pl. While in reference to countries *Beziehungen* is mainly confined to relations at government or commercial level, the expression *das deutsch–französische Verhältnis* suggests what the general population of the one country thinks about the general population of the other. *Beziehung* is also used for relations between individuals, and differs in degree and depth from *Verhältnis. Beziehung* is 'the way people relate to each other'. If there are *gute Beziehungen* between two people, they understand one another, see each other often, take part in activities together, and so on. *Verhältnis* suggests a deeper emotional attachment as well. *Verhältnis* is therefore the normal word for people with whom someone can be expected to have a close relationship, e.g. one's parents or family, even in a neg. context. *Sein Verhältnis zu seinen Eltern war gestört/schlecht. Ein freundschaftliches Verhältnis* is deeper than *freundschaftliche Beziehungen*. Race **relations** are *die Beziehungen zwischen den Rassen*. When the relationship is to something nonpersonal such as a town, *Verhältnis* is the usual word but *Beziehung* is possible. *Adenauers Verhältnis zu Berlin war kein herzliches.* Only *Verhältnis* is used in *Zwischen* *uns bestand nur ein dienstliches Verhältnis,* a relationship between employer and employee or between two employees. *Beziehung* is used like **relationship** meaning 'a close friendship between two people involving romantic feelings'. *Er hat eine Beziehung zu ihr. Ein Verhältnis* stresses the sexual side and is usually translated as *an affair.* For *Beziehung* to have this meaning it is necessary to say *intime Beziehungen.* While *ein Verhältnis,* 'affair', lasts for some time, **eine Affäre**, in the same sense, is of relatively short duration.

> *Ein Land unterhält diplomatische/wirtschaftliche Beziehungen zu einem anderen. Also . . . nimmt die diplomatischen Beziehungen auf/ . . . bricht die diplomatischen Beziehungen ab.*
> *Die Beziehungen zwischen den beiden Ländern sind gut/gespannt/schlecht,* etc.
> *Es bestehen besonders enge/gute Beziehungen zwischen den beiden Firmen.*
> *Der Lehrer pflegt gute Beziehungen zu allen Schülern.*
> *In was für einem Verhältnis stehen Sie zu Ihm?*
> *Es bestand ein gutes Verhältnis zwischen den Geschwistern.*
> *Das Verhältnis zwischen ihr und ihrem Bruder war nie besonders eng.*

ii. Die Verbindung suggests a close association between people or groups and is usually translated as *contact. Politische/Geschäftliche/Internationale Verbindungen. Ich habe die Verbindung zu ihnen verloren/abgebrochen. Ich will die Verbindung zu ihr nicht abreißen lassen.*

iii. Jmds. Beziehungen also means 's.o.'s connections', i.e. 'the people he/she knows who are in a position to help'. *Er hat diese Stelle durch seine Beziehungen bekommen.*

5. Relationship, meaning 'being linked with s.o. by being a member of the same family', is expressed by **die Verwandtschaft** or by the adj. **verwandt**. *Sie mußte ihre Verwandtschaft mit dem Verstorbenen nachweisen.* The question *What is your relationship with the patient?* is *Wie sind Sie mit dem Patienten verwandt?*

6. The **relation of** one thg. **to** another or **between** two thgs. There is a relation or connection between two things when one causes the other to happen, one leads to or on to the other, or they refer to the same matter or topic. The G. words in ascending order of closeness of connection are **die Beziehung, die Verbindung,** and **der Zusammenhang.** *Die Beziehung* is the vaguest and most general term and would be used if nothing is known precisely about the nature of the relation or connection. *Der Zusammenhang* suggests a close connection and is often used with *direkt.* It often implies a causal connection; *ursächlich,* 'causal', can be added to stress the idea. *Die Verbindung* lies between these. In some cases all three could be used with the distinction just given. *Die politische Krise steht im direkten Zusammenhang mit der Rezession. In Verbindung* would be less close, and *in Beziehung* even less so. *Die Krise steht nur in indirekter Beziehung mit der Rezession* or *hat nur eine indirekte Beziehung dazu.* In the neg. the distinction tends to be lost, and *Beziehung* is normally used. *Etw. steht in keiner Beziehung zu etw. anderem,* it is not connected with it.

> *Zuerst erkläre ich die Beziehung zwischen Angebot und Nachfrage.*
> *Zwischen diesen Ereignissen besteht keine Beziehung. Or . . . besteht nur eine lose Beziehung.*
> *Die Antwort steht in keiner Beziehung zur Frage. Also Zwischen der Antwort und der Frage besteht kein Zusammenhang.*
> *Der Rücktritt des Ministers steht in keiner Beziehung zu dem aufgedeckten Korruptionsfall.*
> *Der Detektiv vermutete eine Verbindung zwischen diesen Vorkommnissen.*
> *Meine Frage steht im Zusammenhang mit unserer gestrigen Diskussion.*
> *Zwischen dieser Krankheit und seiner Arbeit wird wohl ein Zusammenhang bestehen.*

In this connection is *in dieser Beziehung* or *in diesem Zusammenhang. The police want to ask him some questions in connection with the murder* becomes *Die Polizei will ihm einige Fragen im Zusammenhang mit dem Mord stellen. To connect certain events* is *gewisse*

Ereignisse miteinander in Beziehung/in Verbindung/in Zusammenhang bringen. Die Polizei brachte sein Verschwinden mit dem Verbrechen in Verbindung.

remember *v.*

1. Remember = 'to recollect or recall to mind'. *I remember her. I remember seeing him there.*

i. An important equivalent is **sich erinnern**, which implies being able to remember s.o./sth. It is now used with *an* but may occasionally be found with the gen. in literary or elevated language.

> *Ich kann mich noch gut an Dinge erinnern, die in meiner frühesten Kindheit geschehen sind.*
> *An diesen Tag erinnere ich mich genau.   Erinnern Sie sich an mich?*
> *Wenn ich mich recht erinnere, haben wir uns vor einigen Monaten kennengelernt.*

Sich erinnern an also translates the E. construction *to remember doing sth.* or **remember** + a clause. Note that whereas both pres. and perf. gerundial constructions are possible in E., *I remember seeing her/having seen her*, G. needs a perf. infin. *Ich erinnere mich daran, sie gesehen zu haben.* Thus *Ich erinnere mich daran, ihn bezahlt zu haben*, translates . . . *paying him* as well as *having paid him*.

> *Ich erinnere mich [daran], davon gelesen zu haben.*
> *Ich erinnere mich daran, daß wir zweimal über den Fluß gefahren sind.*

ii. *Sich erinnern* suggests that someone can or cannot remember something, rather than a conscious effort to recall something, and is thus not used in the imp. When an attempt to remember is implied, **zurückdenken** and **sich** (dat.) **ins Gedächtnis zurückrufen** can be used. *So weit ich zurückdenken kann, hat er nie einen Fehler gemacht. Er bemühte sich, sich die Vorgänge an dem Abend/das Aussehen des Mädchens ins Gedächtnis zurückzurufen.* The imp. *Remember what she said then!* is expressed by **denken an**. *Denken Sie an das, was sie uns damals sagte! Denk' daran, wie er sich vor ein paar Wochen benommen hat!*

iii. When someone remembers something suddenly, **einfallen**, 'to occur to s.o.', is often used. It is common in the neg. where E. uses *I* etc. *can't remember*. The obj. of *remember* becomes the subj. of *einfallen. Der Titel des Buches fällt mir nicht ein.*

> *Plötzlich fiel ihr ein, daß sie eine Verabredung hatte.*
> *Sein Name fällt mir im Augenblick nicht ein.*

iv. Sich entsinnen has now mostly given way to *sich erinnern* but is still occasionally heard.

> *Ich entsinne mich.   Ich entsinne mich dessen nicht mehr.*
> *Wenn ich mich recht entsinne, war er ungefähr 1,80 groß.*

v. Sich besinnen is no longer used in the lit. sense 'to remember'. It is still found, however, in a context like *Er besann sich endlich auf sich selbst*, which means that after behaving in a way which was not his normal way of acting, he remembered what kind of person he really was and began to act accordingly. One transl. is *He remembered what he owed [to] himself.* If words are referred to, *sich besinnen* means that they are immediately put into practice, not just recalled to mind.

> *Nach hektischem Beginn und anfänglichem Foulspiel besann sich die Mannschaft auf ihre spielerischen Fertigkeiten.*
> *Er besann sich auf die mahnenden Worte des Schiedsrichters/auf die Worte der heiligen Schrift.*

vi. Gedenken + gen. is an elevated v. meaning 'to remember' and usually refers to ceremonies at which events and people are commemorated. *Wir gedenken der Gefallenen zweier Weltkriege.* It is sometimes applied to individuals who remember the dead. *Sie gedachte ihres Vaters/der Toten mit Dankbarkeit.*

2. Remember, meaning 'not to forget', as in *Remember your promise!* or *Did you remember to pay the telephone bill?*, is translated by **denken an**. It is followed either by a n., *Denk an das Geburtstagsgeschenk!*, or by an infin. construction after *daran*. It must be used to translate **remember** + infin. Thus *Did you remember to post the letters?* is *Hast du daran gedacht, die Briefe einzuwerfen? Denk' daran, die Telefonrechnung zu bezahlen!*

> *Hast du an die Theaterkarten gedacht?* (remember [to get] the tickets)
> *Denk' daran, die Pflanzen jeden Tag zu gießen!*   *Denk' an dein Versprechen!*

3. Remember meaning 'to retain sth. deliberately in the memory', as in *I don't think I can remember all that—I'll have to write it down*, is either **behalten** or **sich merken**. The latter implies some effort not to forget something, and it alone is used in the imp. *Merkt euch diese Definition! Behalten* suggests a retentive memory rather than effort to remember. (Note: In the imp. *behalten* means 'to KEEP'.)

> *Diese Telefonnummer kann man sich gut merken.* Or . . . *kann man gut behalten.*
> *Ist dein Gedächtnis so gut, daß du die Adresse behalten kannst, ohne sie aufzuschreiben?*

4. Remember + as, as in *I remember her as a slim young girl*, is translated by **in [der] Erinnerung haben als**. *Ich habe sie in [der] Erinnerung als junges, schlankes Mädchen.* The *als*-phr. can be replaced by *so*. *So habe ich das Dorf in Erinnerung*, that's how/the way I remember the village.

> *Ich habe ihn als hochaufgeschossenen Burschen in Erinnerung.*

5. Remember in *Remember me to s.o.!* is usually **grüßen**. *Grüße deine Mutter von mir!*

responsible *adj.* One sense of **liable** *adj.* **responsibility** *n.*

1. If people or things are responsible for a bad event or situation, they are the cause of it, to blame for it. For this use of **verantwortlich** cf. BLAME 1 and 2.

2. To be **responsible for** sth. or s.o. means 'to have control or authority over them and to have the obligation to make sure that all necessary work is carried out'.

i. One sense of **verantwortlich** expresses this meaning. It can be applied to people in charge of an organization or to someone who is responsible for carrying out a task or for looking after others.

> *Der für den Bau der Brücke verantwortliche Ingenieur heißt Richter.*
> *Als Gastgeberin fühlte sie sich für das Wohl ihrer Gäste verantwortlich.*
> *Er ist der verantwortliche Redakteur des Lokalteils der Zeitung.*
> *Eltern sind für ihre Kinder verantwortlich.*
> *Er ist für die Vorbereitung der Konferenz verantwortlich.*

ii. Zuständig für means that it is a person's or an organization's normal duty to carry out certain work or deal with certain matters, or that certain work or matters belong properly in that person's or organization's area of responsibility. '*Ich bin für solche Fragen zuständig*', *sagte der Beamte. Die zuständige Behörde muß den Fall bearbeiten*, i.e. the authority whose task it is to deal with such cases.

> *Der zuständige Minister muß über den Fall entscheiden.*
> *Das Luftfahrtministerium ist auch für die Flughäfen zuständig.*
> *Sie müssen den Antrag bei der zuständigen Stelle einreichen.*

3. Responsible to is also applied to people who are controlled by others and have to report to them to explain what they have done. *I am responsible only to the chairman.* This sense is also carried by **verantwortlich** + dat. or **gegenüber** + dat.

> *Abgeordnete sind dem Volk verantwortlich, und Minister sind dem Parlament gegenüber verantwortlich.*
> *Ich bin nur dem Chef verantwortlich/ . . . nur dem Chef gegenüber verantwortlich.*

4. The v. **haften** is a legal term meaning 'to be liable or responsible for'. It implies that in case of injury, damage, or loss, *der Haftende* is obliged to make restitution or provide some form of compensation. Common notices in restaurants are *Wir* *haften nicht für Garderobe* or *Für Garderobe wird nicht gehaftet*, and in playgrounds and escalators *Eltern haften für ihre Kinder*. In the first two it means 'responsible or liable for any losses', in the third 'responsible for their safety' or sometimes 'liable for any damage they may cause'. *Eine Gesellschaft mit beschränkter Haftung* is 'a company with limited liability'. *Haftpflichtversicherung* is 'third party (liability) insurance'. *Jmd. haftet für den Schaden/den Verlust* means that that person is liable for the loss or damage. *Jmdm. haften für* expresses the same meaning as *jmdm. verantwortlich sein für*. *Du haftest mir persönlich dafür, daß der Termin eingehalten wird*, is somewhat stronger than *Du bist mir persönlich verantwortlich*, and stresses the consequences of non-compliance.

5. Responsible is a legal term meaning 'able to answer for one's actions and to discriminate between right and wrong', 'capable of rational conduct'. The equivalent is **zurechnungsfähig**.

> *Der Kranke war voll/nur vermindert zurechnungsfähig.*
> *Nach dem Gutachten des Psychiaters war der Angeklagte unzurechnungsfähig.*

6. In non-legal use, a responsible person works properly and makes the right decisions without having to be controlled or watched by others. This meaning can be expressed by **verantwortungsvoll** or **verantwortungsbewußt**, 'aware of one's responsibilities and carrying them out faithfully', or by **zuverlässig** or **verläßlich**, both = 'reliable', or **vertrauenswürdig**, trustworthy.

> *Sie ist ein verantwortungsbewußter/verantwortungsvoller/zuverlässiger/vertrauenswürdiger Mensch.*
> *Er macht seine Arbeit in gewissenhafter und verantwortungsvoller Weise.*

7. Duties, work, activities, decisions, etc. can be described as **responsible**. *Isn't he too young for such a responsible task?* Both **verantwortlich** and the slightly stronger **verantwortungsvoll** mean 'involving responsibility'. *Sie hat eine verantwortliche Stellung inne. Er bekleidet ein verantwortungsvolles Amt. Ist er nicht zu jung, um eine so verantwortungsvolle Aufgabe zu übernehmen?* With *Entscheidung* only **verantwortungsvoll** is used. *Eine verantwortungsvolle Entscheidung.*

8. Responsibility. The main equivalent, **die Verantwortung**, is only rarely used in the pl.

i. One meaning is 'the obligation and willingness to be held accountable for doing sth., s.o.'s safety, etc.'

> *Er übernahm die Verantwortung für die Durchführung des Projekts.*
> *Auf ihr lastet eine große/schwere Verantwortung.*
> *Die Eltern haben/tragen die Verantwortung für ihre Kinder.*
> *Ich bin mir meiner Verantwortung Ihnen gegenüber voll bewußt.*
> *Dieser Verantwortung kann dich niemand entheben . Or Diese Verantwortung nimmt uns keiner ab.*
> *Ich tue es auf deine Verantwortung.* (I'll do it, but you must take responsibility.)

ii. Verantwortung also means 'blame', 'the obligation to bear the consequences of an action, such as a failure, mistake, etc.' For **die Verantwortung übernehmen** and **auf sich nehmen** cf. ACCEPT 4. ii.

> *Sie lehnte die Verantwortung für den Mißerfolg ab/versuchte die Verantwortung für den Mißerfolg von sich [auf einen anderen] abzuwälzen.*
> *Für den Unfall/Vorfall trage ich die volle Verantwortung.*
> *Er versuchte, sich der Verantwortung durch die Flucht zu entziehen.*

iii. Sense of responsibility is either **das Verantwortungsbewußtsein, das Verantwortungsgefühl, die Verantwortlichkeit**, or **die Verantwortung**. *An seinem Verantwortungsbewußtsein/-gefühl besteht nicht der geringste Zweifel. Durch die Übertragung von Aufgaben, die sie selbst erledigen müssen, erzieht man Kinder zur Verantwortlichkeit. Er kennt keinerlei Verantwortung.*

iv. Die Verantwortlichkeit means 'the state of being responsible' but is more abstract and more formal than *Verantwortung*. *Der Betrieb trägt die Verantwortung für die termingerichte Lieferung der Waren. Diese Verantwortlichkeit bedeutet, daß Kunden für die Nichteinhaltung der Lieferbedingungen entschädigt werden müssen.*

v. Die Verantwortlichkeit also means 'the area for which s.o. is responsible' and can be pl.

Diese Sache stelle ich unter Ihre Verantwortlichkeit.

Wir müssen die Verantwortlichkeiten festlegen und verteilen.

Der Vertrag muß die Rechte und Verantwortlichkeiten der Vertragspartner klar regeln.

vi. When **responsibility** means 'a task one is obliged to do', the equivalent is **die Verpflichtung**, obligation. *Sie hat alle Verpflichtungen gewissenhaft erfüllt. Ich bin nicht bereit, eine weitere dienstliche Verpflichtung zu übernehmen.* Dienstpflichten means 'responsibilities of office', and *die Pflichten eines Amtes* 'the obligations of office'.

rest, remainder *ns.*

i. Der Rest means 'remainder' like E. **the rest**, but it suggests more strongly what is left over or remains, so that it is not always an equivalent of the E. word. In relation to what is eaten or consumed, G. *Rest* means 'what is left over'. In relation to things which can be seen as consisting of parts, it is often 'the smaller part, less than half'. This implication holds for number, food, and place, and in part for time. The alternatives are **übrig**, 'remaining', **restlich**, which also means 'remaining' but is stylistically higher, and often **andere**. All of these do not have any implications. These are all adjs., so that *the rest of the class* becomes *die übrige Klasse*. This section discusses the use of *Rest* and the alternatives in different contexts.

Number. If five of a group of twenty pupils go away, we refer to the remaining fifteen as **the rest**. *The rest of you stay here!* This becomes *Die anderen/übrigen bleiben hier. Der Rest der Schüler/Klasse* is correct G. but, as explained above, it suggests less than half. Thus *He left the room with the rest of the students* must be *Er verließ das Zimmer mit den anderen/übrigen Studenten. Der Rest* can be used for the larger part only if modified. *Die intelligenten Schüler hatten die Lösung schnell verstanden, der große Rest blieb noch im ungewissen.*

Food. For food, *der Rest* is 'what is left over'. *Er aß den Rest der Suppe. Die Reste* are 'leftovers'. *Heute gibt es zum Essen nur Reste. Wir gaben die Speisereste den Hunden.*

Place. *In the south, it will be sunny, but in the rest of the country, it will rain.* The phr. with **rest** becomes *im übrigen/restlichen Land* or *in den übrigen/anderen Landesteilen*. **Rest** would only be used for the smaller part. *Ich gehe den Rest des Weges zu Fuß.* It is not uncommon at football matches and on other similar occasions in villages or small towns to see banners, *Spruchbänder*, proclaiming something like *Soltau grüßt den Rest der Welt!* As *Rest* usually implies that the rest of the world is less big and important, the choice of word is possibly meant as a joke which points ironically to the insignificance of Soltau. The usual expression is *die übrige Welt.* (This usage may be changing, so that *der Rest der Welt* could soon have the same meaning as *die übrige Welt.*)

Time. *Der Rest seines Lebens* should mean 'the shorter part'. A 65-year old might say what he intends to do *mit dem Rest seines Lebens*. It could be expected that *Rest* is not applied to a much younger person, but *Für den Rest seines Lebens war er davon kuriert* and *Den Rest ihres Lebens vergißt sie das nicht* are used without implying a shorter or longer part. Occasionally in a biography one reads *Er zog mit 25 Jahren nach Wien und blieb für den Rest seines Lebens dort.* This might suggest that he did not live for another twenty-five years, but this is not necessarily meant. *Der Rest des Tages* usually suggests the shorter part, while *der übrige Tag* does not specify the proportion. With seasons and *die Saison* '(tourist etc.) season', *der Rest* does not always denote the smaller part; *der Rest des Winters/der Saison* can be more than half.

Money. For money, the distinction does not always hold. *Wenn Sie eine Anzahlung von 10% machen, können Sie den Rest nächste Woche zahlen.* More in accord with the implication is *Von dem Geld war nur noch ein kleiner Rest übrig. Übrig* is often found with *Geld. Das übrige Geld ist für neue Gardinen bestimmt.*

> *Der Rest der Strafe wurde ihm erlassen.*   *Ich erließ ihm den Rest der Schuld.*
> *Im Dezember und Januar hat es viermal geschneit, aber der Rest des Winters war sehr mild.*
> *Es war ein Haus wie alle anderen auch* (like all the rest).
> *Ich dachte, Sie wüßten etw., was uns anderen unbekannt war* (the rest of us).
> *Zehn Fensterläden waren rot, die übrigen/restlichen grün.*
> *Die restlichen Ferientage verbrachten wir zu Hause.*
> *Mit dem übrigen/restlichen Geld kaufte sie ein Kleid.*

ii. The main equivalent of **the rest of** sth. is **übrig** + a sing. or pl. n.

> *Ich brauche nur zwei Zimmer für mich selbst, das übrige Haus steht Ihnen zur Verfügung.*
> *Den übrigen Tag verbrachten wir zu Hause.*
> *Ungefähr fünf Bilder waren gut, die übrigen waren nicht besonders interessant.*
> *Von neun bis zehn bin ich in der Bibliothek, die übrige Zeit arbeite ich in meinem Zimmer.*

When a specific n. is not referred to, i.e. when **the rest** is used without *of*, **das übrige** or **alles übrige**, 'the rest', are used.

> *Ich habe einen Teil der Arbeit gemacht, das übrige mache ich morgen.*
> *Den ersten Punkt erledigen wir jetzt. Alles übrige besprechen wir später.*

iii. Other uses of *der Rest*. *Der Rest*, unlike **rest**, is used with the indefinite article and in the pl., but in such uses it is translated by words other than **rest**. *Du findest einen Rest Brot im Schrank*, a little bit. *Der Rest der Erbschaft*, the residue. *Von der Farbe ist nur noch ein Rest da.* **Die Reste** are 'remnants' or 'remainders' of various things, for things sold 'oddments'. *Die Hunde fraßen die Reste. Auf der Insel gibt es Reste eines antiken Tempels. Können die Reste des Stammes überleben? Reste werden zu ermäßigten Preisen/billig verkauft.* (An alternative for book remainders is **Restbestände**. *Man verkauft Restbestände zu stark herabgesetzten Preisen.*)

iv. Two expressions. *a.* **As for the rest**. *As for the rest, it's not very important: Was die anderen Punkte angeht—sie sind nicht besonders wichtig. b.* **All the rest of it**. *Method, theory, and all the rest of it you can read [up] for yourselves: Ich habe Ihnen das Wichtigste erklärt. Über Methode, Theorie und alles übrige/alles, was noch dazu gehört, können Sie selbst nachlesen.*

rest *v.* and *n.* **quiet, calm** *ns.* and *adjs.* **still** *adj.* **stillness** *n.*

A. Vs.

1. Sich ausruhen is 'to recover one's strength after a period of possibly strenuous activity'. It does not suggest sleep, but rather taking a break or having a spell in order to gain new strength for further activity, and it usually refers to physical rather than to mental exertion. It need last only a few minutes, but can be longer depending on the circumstances. *Ich schlage vor, wir ruhen uns ein wenig aus, bevor wir mit der neuen Arbeit anfangen.*

> *Nachdem wir den Paß geschafft hatten, mußten sich alle erst mal ausruhen.*
> *Nach der Pause waren wir ausgeruht.*
> *Man ruht sich von einer Anstrengung/von den Strapazen/nach der Arbeit aus.*
> *Der alte Mann blieb auf dem ersten [Treppen]absatz stehen, um sich auszuruhen.*

2. Ausspannen is 'to stop an activity for a time in order to rest and relax and so regain one's strength'. It usually refers to mental exertion or to general strain and

stress, and suggests more than a short break. It can imply ceasing work for a few hours, often for a day or more, or for a longer period. *Ich habe wochenlang angestrengt gearbeitet—ich muß ein bißchen ausspannen.*
Nach einer so anstrengenden Woche braucht man einfach das Wochenende, um auszuspannen.

3. Sich erholen is 'to regain or recover one's strength after an illness or activity' and can be used for recovering from both mental and physical exertion over a longer or shorter period. *Sie haben sich im Urlaub gut erholt* implies that they had a good rest. In *Sie kehrten gut erholt aus ihrem Urlaub zurück, gut erholt* can therefore be translated as *well-rested.*

4. Sich entspannen is 'to relax mind and body'. It can suggest detaching oneself from what is happening around one for a short time to free oneself from mental and physical strain and to get new strength. *Den ganzen Tag arbeite ich intensiv und entspanne mich am Abend.* It can be used for a relaxing activity. *Sie entspannen sich beim Sport.* (*Entspannen* can take an obj. *Man entspannt die Muskeln.*) *Ich höre mir Barockmusik an, um mich zu entspannen.*

5. Ruhen means 'to be lying down in order to rest'. It does not necessarily imply that the person is asleep, but this is always a possibility. It is much the same as *sich ausruhen,* but the latter stresses regaining strength after exertion. *Ich will auf dem Sofa/im Schatten ein wenig ruhen* or *mich ein wenig ausruhen. Ich lasse die müden Glieder ruhen* is a fixed expression. *Ruhen* can mean 'to sleep' in formal style. *Sie hat gut geruht,* slept well. *Ich wünsche wohl zu ruhen,* 'I hope you sleep well', is very formal.
Ich muß nach dem Mittagessen einfach ein halbes Stündchen ruhen.   *Sie ruhte in seinen Armen.*
Laß Großvater noch ein wenig ruhen, bevor du zu üben anfängst, auch wenn er nicht mehr schläft.

6. Other senses of *ruhen.*
i. A fig. use is *Ich werde nicht eher ruhen, als bis ihnen Gerechtigkeit zuteilgeworden ist,* will not rest until . . .
ii. *Hier ruht . . .* is used on gravestones.
iii. Ruhen can also mean 'to be stationary, to have come to a standstill, not to be working, or to be suspended'. *Ein ruhender Körper,* a stationary object, body. *Die Arbeit/Die Produktion/Die Maschine ruht. Der Prozeß ruht. Ein Ruhetag* is 'a day on which sth. is not operating or working'.
iv. Ruhen auf can mean 'to be supported by'. *Das Dach ruht auf Säulen.* It is also used with *die Verantwortung* as subj. *Die ganze Verantwortung ruht auf ihm.*

7. Beruhen auf means 'to rest on' in the sense 'to be based on or caused by'. *Das ganze beruht auf einem Mißverständnis. Die Überlegenheit dieser Maschine beruht darauf, daß sie wenig Strom verbraucht und sehr schnell arbeitet.*

8. Ruhenlassen means 'to let (sth.) rest' in the sense 'not to stir (it) up again'. *Kannst du diese alte Geschichte/diese Sache nicht endlich ruhenlassen? Laß das Vergangene ruhen!* **Auf sich beruhen lassen** means 'not to pursue (sth.) any further', 'to let (sth.) rest', 'not to take (sth.) any further'. *Wir wollen diese Angelegenheit auf sich beruhen lassen.*

B. Ns.

1. Die Ruhe means 'rest' in the sense 'cessation of movement'. *Der Pendel ist in Ruhe,* stationary. *In bleierner Ruhe lag der spiegelglatte See unter dem weißlichen Himmel. Die Maschine befindet sich in Ruhe* and *Die Räder kamen zur Ruhe* occur, but **stillstehen, zum Stillstand/zum Stehen kommen** are more usual in everyday language. *Warten Sie, bis der Zeiger stillsteht/zur Ruhe kommt/zum Stillstand kommt!*

2. *Ruhe* and *Stille* overlap in some senses.
i. Quiet or *peace* meaning 'the absence of noise in nature' is expressed by

die Stille. *Die tiefe Stille der Winternacht/des Waldes.* **Die Ruhe** is often used synony-mously. *Die nächtliche Ruhe im windstillen Wald wurde nur selten von dem Knacken eines Zweiges oder vom Schrei eines Tieres unterbrochen.*

Die abendliche Stille über den Gärten wurde durch einen Windstoß gestört.

ii. Die Ruhe means 'quiet, calm, peace among people, the state of not being dis-turbed while either working or relaxing'. *Ich brauche Ruhe [bei der Arbeit/zum Nachdenken].* It can also mean 'the normal or expected state of peace and quiet' in a certain place or in someone's life. *Die Rocker störten mit ihren Motorrädern die Ruhe im Dorf. Er läßt mir gar keine Ruhe,* he doesn't give me any peace. *Ruhe [bitte]!* is the request or command for quiet or silence. Although *Ruhe* is the normal word for quiet among people, **die Stille** is also possible. *Im Saal herrschte absolute Ruhe/Stille.*

Ich möchte jetzt meine Ruhe haben.   *Eine wunderbare Ruhe herrschte im Garten.*

Sie sehnt sich nach Ruhe/findet Ruhe in der Natur.

Als der letzte Bus weggefahren war, kehrte die Ruhe im Dorf wieder ein.

Beglückt über die ungewohnte Stille im Klassenzimmer, fuhr der Lehrer fort.

iii. Die Ruhe also means 'inner or mental calm' and 'balance or equanimity'. Common expressions are *Jmd. behält/bewahrt/verliert die Ruhe* and *Etw. schreckt jmdn. aus der Ruhe auf, nimmt jmdm. die Ruhe,* or *gibt jmdm. die Ruhe [wieder].* **Die Stille** also means 'mental calm or stillness' but is stylistically higher, even poetical. *Von dem Augenblick an, in dem er sich entschieden hatte, war eine wohltuende Stille in seinem Herzen eingekehrt.*

Sie ließ sich dadurch nicht aus der Ruhe bringen.   *Er strahlt eine erstaunliche Ruhe aus.*

3. Die Ruhe also denotes the state in which a society, town, country, etc. normally functions without any disturbance of the public order. *Nach dem Putschversuch herrscht in der Hauptstadt wieder Ruhe. Die Ruhestörung* is 'a breach or disturbance of the peace'. Hence *die Ruhestörer. Ruhe und Ordnung* (occasionally *Ruhe und Frieden*) *wiederherstellen* is 'to restore [law and] order'.

Nach den schweren Unruhen braucht das Land eine Zeit der Ruhe.

4. Die Ruhe is the n. from *ausruhen* and *ruhen* and can mean either 'rest' in the sense of 'relaxation after exertion' or 'sleep'. In *Der Arzt hat ihm Ruhe verordnet,* it means 'rest' in the sense of 'no exertion'. If a patient has to stay in bed, *Bettruhe* is used. *Eine Ruhepause einlegen* or *machen* is 'to take a break'. *Angenehme Ruhe!* is the polite wish that someone may sleep well. *Sich zur Ruhe legen/begeben* is an elevated syn. of *ins Bett gehen* or *schlafen gehen. Sich zur Ruhe setzen* is 'to retire', i.e. 'give up one's work'. *Jmdn. zur letzten Ruhe tragen* means 'to bury'. *Der arme Mann hat jetzt Ruhe* implies that he is dead.

Was ich brauche, ist Ruhe. (This could imply peace and quiet (sense 2. ii) or relaxation.)

Nachdem er das Unternehmen zwanzig Jahre lang geleitet hatte, entschloß er sich, sich zur Ruhe zu setzen.

C. Quiet[ly], calm[ly], still. There are three main equivalents of the adj. **quiet:** *ruhig, still,* and *leise.*

1. i. If a place is still or quiet, there is little noise. For this concept both **ruhig** and **still** are used. *Still* tends to be used when the quiet belongs to nature, *ruhig* when people are quiet, but this distinction is not a hard and fast rule. *Im Wald war es still, man hörte nur die Vögel zwitschern. Im Klassenzimmer war es ruhig. Die Kinder waren ganz ruhig/still. Ein ruhiges Dorf/Haus. Eine ruhige Straße/Familie. Sei ruhig!* is an order to be quiet, not to speak.

ii. Ruhig means 'without disturbance', 'quiet, calm'. *Sie führten ein ruhiges Leben. Das Kind schläft ruhig. Die Nacht/Sitzung verlief ruhig. Man kann da ruhig arbeiten.* With a few expressions of time **still** is also used. *Sie wird in einem ruhigen/stillen Augenblick darüber nachdenken. In einer stillen Stunde* is a fixed expression.

2. Other senses of *ruhig*.

i. Ruhig also means 'uniformly', 'without disturbance in action'. *Die Maschine läuft ruhig. Ihr Herz schlägt ruhig.*

ii. Ruhig is applied to the air and sea. *Die Luft war ruhig*, 'still', and *Der See war ruhig*, 'calm'. *A still day*, one on which there is no wind, is *ein windstiller Tag*.

iii. In reference to towns, countries, etc., it means that the normal state of public calm and order prevails. *Nach den Krawallen war es in der Stadt wieder ruhig.*

iv. Ruhig, applied to people, means 'mentally calm'. *Er ist ein ruhiger Mensch. Bleiben Sie nur ruhig! Sie reagierte/antwortete ganz ruhig. Ein ruhiges Gewissen*, a clear conscience.

v. Ruhig is used as an adv. to assure people that they can do something without any worries or concern.

    Du kannst ruhig mitkommen.   *Sie können sich ruhig an ihn wenden.*

3. Other senses of G. *still*.

i. One meaning is 'without movement'. *Er stand ganz still und rührte kein Glied. Wir mußten vier Minuten lang absolut still bleiben/liegen. Ein stilles Gewässer. Jmd. lag still und ruhig da*, lay there quietly and without moving.

ii. G. **still** also means 'having little or nothing to say, either as a permanent characteristic or on a particular occasion'. *Er ist ein stiller Mensch* implies 'quiet by nature', but *Du bist heute sehr still* suggests quietness that is different from normal. *To keep quiet* can be translated by **schweigen**, to be silent. Cf. SILENCE. *Da es nichts zu sagen gab, schwieg sie/sagte sie nichts.*

4. Quiet and *soft* mean 'making no or only a small amount of noise'.

i. The equivalent is **leise**. *Wir hörten leise Musik/Schritte. Schließen Sie die Türen bitte etwas leiser! 'Ich gehe jetzt', sagte sie leise.*

    Mit leiser Stimme und voll Würde sagte er: 'Ich habe mein Amt niedergelegt.'

ii. An alternative in relation to machinery, motors, etc. is **wenig geräuschvoll** or, in more technical language, **geräuscharm**. *Dieses Modell ist einer der weniger geräuschvollen Flugzeugtypen, die den Flughafen benutzen. Ein geräuscharmer Motor. Das Gerät läuft geräuscharm. Leise* is used after *sein. Dieser Flugzeugtyp ist leiser als alle anderen.*

rock, totter, sway, stagger, reel, lurch, wobble *vs*. The meaning common to all these vs. is 'to move from side to side or backwards and forwards either steadily or unsteadily'. **Rock** when intr. means 'to sway or swing backwards or forwards or from side to side in a range of motion which extends from gentle to violent'. *The boat rocked.* When trans., it means 'to cause s.o./sth. to make such a movement'. *The waves rocked the boat.* **Totter** means 'to walk or move with unsteady steps', **reel** expresses the sense 'to move unsteadily from side to side when walking', and **stagger** is defined as 'to move unsteadily as a consequence of weakness, drunkenness, a heavy load, or a blow'.

i. Schaukeln suggests a regular and, unless modified by an adv. like *heftig*, gentle motion from side to side. It is both trans. and intr. *Die Wellen schaukeln das Boot. Die Boote schaukelten hilflos im Sturm/heftig auf den Wellen.* Common compounds are *das Schaukelpferd* and *der Schaukelstuhl. Die Schaukel* is 'a swing', and *schaukeln* also means 'to swing'. *Kinder schaukeln gern. Laß den Klaus auch mal schaukeln!*

    Der Dreijährige kletterte auf das Schaukelpferd und schaukelte wild drauflos.

    Das Wirtshausschild schaukelte im Wind.   *Du sollst den Kahn nicht schaukeln.*

    Sie schaukelte das Baby in der Wiege in den Schlaf.   *Der Wind schaukelte die Lampions.*

ii. The specific term for rocking a baby (to sleep) is **wiegen**. *Eine Wiege* is 'a cradle'.

    Kaum hatte sie das Kind ein wenig gewiegt, dann hörte es auf zu schreien.

Er hatte erstaunliches Talent, das Baby in den Schlaf zu wiegen.
Wiegen is used for waves which gently rock a boat, but is rather poetical in tone, as is the intr. form **sich wiegen**. *Sanft wiegten die Wellen das Boot auf und ab. Das Boot wiegte sich langsam auf den Wellen.*

iii. Schwanken is 'to rock or swing backwards and forwards, from side to side, or up and down'. It is intr. only and not applied to deliberate action. A stronger motion than *schaukeln* is implied, but *schwanken* can be modified by advs. like *sanft*. *Die Brücke schwankte unter ihren Füßen.* The action can continue for some time. Unlike *wanken*, *schwanken* does not suggest an imminent collapse. *Während der Überfahrt hatte das Boot unaufhörlich geschwankt*, rocked or rolled. *Zweige, Bäume,* or *ein Mast* which sway or move to and fro can be the subj. *Mir wird schwindelig, wenn ich dem schwankenden Mast zusehe.* It is applied to people both when they stand unsteadily, i.e. they sway or totter, and when in walking they move irregularly from side to side. In the latter sense it translates **totter, reel**, and **stagger** as defined above. *Er war ein baumlanger Kerl, und keiner dachte, daß er schon nach den ersten Schlägen schwanken würde.* In relation to a vehicle *schwanken* means 'to lurch, to make a movement to the side'. *Als ich den Gang entlang ging, schwankte der Zug plötzlich, so daß ich beinahe hingefallen wäre.*

> *Die Spitze des Fernsehturms kann bis zu einigen Metern hin und her schwanken, ohne daß Gefahr besteht.*
> *Er konnte sich nur mühsam erheben und schwankte bedenklich, als er den Trinkspruch sprach/ausbrachte.*   *Trotz der Ermahnung schwankte der Betrunkene zu seinem Wagen.*

iv. Wanken denotes the same motion as *schwanken*, but with things it implies their imminent collapse. It corresponds to **totter** meaning 'to rock or shake to and fro on its base as if about to collapse'. This definition also holds for people who are standing still. *Dieser Schlag ließ den Boxer kurz wanken, dann brach er zusammen.* With regard to a moving person *wanken* may imply the same motion as *schwanken*, but often suggests greater effort to remain standing and the possibility of collapse. In *Der Boden wankte* (instead of the usual *bebte*), *wankte* would be translated as *shook* or *quaked. Jmds. Beine wankten*, sagged.

> *Der Steg war nicht mehr passierbar; schon nach den ersten Schritten wankte er, und die morschen Planken gaben nach.*   *Der Turm wankte bedenklich.*
> *Er nahm den schweren Sack auf die Schultern und wankte die Treppe hinauf.*

v. Schlingern is used for ships which roll from side to side in heavy sea, when either stationary or moving. It also translates *lurch* when this is a repeated action, not a single one. For a single movement, *plötzlich* can be added. *Das Schiff schlingerte plötzlich. Schlingern* is applied as well to vehicles to describe movement from side to side, e.g. in violent skidding. *Der Wagen schlingerte gegen die Leitplanke.*

> *Die Böen ließen die Schiffe in unstetem Kurs schlingern.*
> *Das Kind schlingerte mit dem Fahrrad von einer Straßenseite zur anderen.*

vi. Taumeln can refer to a person who is standing or to one who is moving. It means 'to be no longer steady on one's feet and to seem likely to fall over'. The cause is usually weakness, hunger, exhaustion, or a blow. It is translated as **stagger, reel**, and **lurch**. It is used with and without a prepositional phr. *Jmd. taumelte gegen den Zaun. Er taumelte nach Hause/zum Fenster.*

> *Der Rekonvaleszent taumelte sofort, als er zum ersten Mal das Bett verließ.*
> *Schon in der dritten Runde ließen ihn die Schläge des Gegners taumeln.*
> *Er war von ihrem Tod so niedergeschlagen, daß er wie im Traum durch die Straßen taumelte.*

vii. Torkeln means 'to be unsteady on one's feet' or 'to move unsteadily', thus 'to stagger, totter, or reel'. It is mostly applied to people who are intoxicated, *Der Betrunkene torkelte durch die Straßen*, but the cause may also be weakness. It is used with and without a prepositional phr.

Im Sitzen fühlten wir uns noch recht klar im Kopf, aber nachdem wir aufgestanden waren, torkelten
wir doch.   Von weitem sahen wir einen Mann über die Straße torkeln.
Dieser Schlag ließ ihn in die Ecke torkeln, und der Schiedsrichter mußte ihn anzählen.

viii. Wackeln is 'to wobble' in the sense 'not to sit firmly on the floor and to move
up and down when used'. *Der Tisch/Der Stuhl wackelt.*

roll *v.*

1. Trans. use. S.o. **rolls** sth. [somewhere].

i. Rollen suggests an even, smooth motion, that the object moved is of such a
shape that it moves fairly easily. **Wälzen** implies slowness and difficulty in movement, that the object is heavy, of an awkward shape, and if round, then long and
not easy to move. If round and easy to move, or if something has wheels, only
rollen is possible. *Das Bett der Kranken wurde auf die Veranda gerollt.*

> *Die Bierkutscher ließen die Fässer vom Wagen auf Säcke fallen und rollten sie dann scheppernd zum*
> *Keller.   Nun rollt jeder den Medizinball zehnmal um sich herum.*
> *Elefanten wälzen schwere Holzstämme, indem sie immer wieder mit ihrer Stirn dagegen stoßen.*
> *Um den Hohlweg passieren zu können, mußten wir zuerst einen herabgestürzten Felsbrocken beiseite*
> *wälzen.* (If it is round and easy to move, *rollen.*)

Fig. uses are *die Schuld auf andere wälzen* or *abwälzen*, 'to push the blame on to others', and *Lexika/Akten/Bücher wälzen*, 'to look through a large number of them to
find sth. out'.

ii. Roll sth. **flat** or **roll** sth. **out** in order to make its surface smooth. **Rollen** and
the syn. **ausrollen** are used in cooking. *Man rollt den Teig* or *rollt den Teig aus.*
Walzen and **auswalzen** are used for rolling metal. *Eisen/Blech wird gewalzt. Stahl*
wird ausgewalzt. Aluminium wird zu Folien ausgewalzt. **Walzen** is used for rolling
ground or a surface. *Man walzt einen Acker/den Rasen/den Tennisplatz/eine Straße.*

iii. Roll sth. **up** is **zusammenrollen.** *Wir müssen das Zelt/den Teppich zusammenrollen.*
> *Um das Bild zu tragen, rolle ich es zusammen.*
> *Anstatt den Perserteppich zusammenzurollen, legten sie ihn wie ein Tischtuch zusammen.*

2. Intr. use. Sth. **rolls** [somewhere].

i. Rollen again suggests an even and easy motion. It is used alone or with an
expression of place and can be applied to things which are spherical or round, to
drops of liquid like tears, to waves which roll up the beach, and to vehicles on
wheels. *Das Auto rollt. Der Zug rollt.* Sometimes the sense is 'to begin to move'. *Rollen*
is used for turning on to one's back or side if the movement is smooth and easy.
Im Schlaf war er auf die andere Seite gerollt.

> *Dem Torwart fiel der Ball aus der Hand, und er rollte über die Torlinie.*
> *Die Münze rollte unter den Schrank.   Dicke Regentropfen rollten die Scheibe herunter.*
> *Schäumend rollte eine Welle nach der anderen an den Strand.*
> *In diesem Werk rollen täglich ein paar hundert Wagen vom Fließband.*
> *Der schrille Pfiff war in der Bahnhofshalle noch nicht verklungen, da rollte der Zug schon.*

ii. Sich wälzen means 'to turn over awkwardly, not smoothly nor evenly, usually
with a series of movements'. It can refer to one turn, *Er wälzte sich auf die andere*
Seite, or to several in the one direction, *Jmd. wälzte sich über den Boden.* It also means
'to roll around, to turn backwards and forwards more or less in the one spot'.
Manchmal wälze ich mich stundenlang ruhelos im Bett. **Sich wälzen** can also be applied
to a body of people slowly pushing their way through streets, and to masses of
earth moving down an incline. *Eine große Menschenmenge wälzte sich durch die Straße.*

> *Ferkel balgen und wälzen sich mit Vorliebe in Schlamm und Dreck.*
> *Man befürchtet, daß bei erneuten Regenfällen der Schuttdamm brechen und Millionen von*
> *Kubikmetern Geröll und Wasser sich durch das Tal wälzen werden.*

iii. With paper, carpets, etc. as subj., **sich rollen** means 'to curl or roll up at the corners or edges'. *Mehr als einmal versuchte ich, das Papier glatt zu streichen, aber es rollte sich immer wieder an den Ecken.*

3. Colloquially **kullern** is used trans. and intr. in the sense 'to roll'. It means 'to roll slowly and often noisily'. The action is not as even nor as smooth as with *rollen*.

Die Tüte ist geplatzt, und die Äpfel sind auf den Boden/unter den Tisch gekullert.

Die Kinder kullerten Murmeln über den Boden.

4. Roll up *one's sleeves* or *trousers* is *die Ärmel/die Hosenbeine* **aufkrempeln** or **hochkrempeln**.

room *n.*

1. Das Zimmer is now the normal word for a **room** in a house, flat, or hotel. Thus *eine Vier- oder Fünfzimmerwohnung. Ein Einzelzimmer oder Doppelzimmer im Hotel.* **Der Raum** can be used for a room in a private dwelling, but it is unusual. When the room is not in a private house, both occur. *A classroom* can be *ein Klassenzimmer* or *ein Klassenraum.* Although the two are not sharply divided, *Zimmer* is mainly associated with living and sleeping or someone's special domain, and *Raum* more with a room used for a specific purpose. Both are used in reference to rooms in an office area. *Wir arbeiten zu dritt in diesem Raum* or *in diesem Zimmer.* In combination with a possessive or a gen., *Zimmer* is normal. *Das ist mein Zimmer* could be an office as well as a room in a private dwelling. *Das Zimmer des Direktors. Raum* tends to be used for rooms in public institutions, *der Seminarraum, der Warteraum,* and when an activity or purpose is paramount. It is somewhat more official in tone than *Zimmer. Arbeitsraum, Ausstellungsraum, Dienstraum, Empfangsraum, Aufenthaltsraum, Duschraum, die Geschäftsräume, der Zuschauerraum,* etc.

Er ging in sein Zimmer und schloß sich ein.   *Haben Sie ein Zimmer frei?*

Ich betrat einen großen, mit Licht erfüllten Raum.

Die Tagung fand in den Räumen der Universität statt.

2. A room is called **ein Saal** when it has a greater floor area and usually a higher ceiling than a room used for living purposes. Although *ein Sitzungssaal eines Gerichts* and *der Operationsaal eines Krankenhauses* need not be very big, *ein Saal* is roughly about 20 × 30 × 5 metres in size and above. It is often the equivalent of *a hall.* Outside universities (where *Saal* often denotes a lecture room) *ein Saal* is used for cultural activities, ceremonies, or meetings. Common compounds are *der Hörsaal, der Lesesaal einer Bibliothek, der Ballsaal, der Konferenzsaal, der Konzertsaal, der Plenarsaal.*

Um fünf vor acht betrat der Premierminister den festlich geschmückten Saal.

Im großen Saal wurde getanzt.

Der Saal war überfüllt.

3. Die Kammer is now applied only to rooms used for storage. Compounds are *Speisekammer, Abstellkammer, Besenkammer, Rumpelkammer, Kleiderkammer. Kammer* has gone out of use in the sense 'a fairly small, simply furnished bedroom, usually separate from the main house'. *Die Kammer des Dienstmädchen.*

4. Die Stube has now gone out of use in the north, except to denote a room in which several people sleep, e.g. in the *Bundeswehr, Internaten,* and *Jugendherbergen.* (In some parts of the country *Stube* means 'living room'. *Wir traten in eine helle, geräumige Stube. Die gute Stube* is or was the best-furnished room in a house or flat used only on special occasions. *Großmutters gute Stube.*)

Wir schliefen zu sechst in einer Stube.   *Die Soldaten sind auf ihren Stuben.*

5. Das Gemach is only used for the important and imposing rooms of *Paläste* and *Schlösser. Das Schlafgemach Ludwigs XIV.*

room, space *ns.*

1. Both **der Platz** and **der Raum** express the sense 'area available for a pers. or thg.'. *Der Platz* is, like **room**, the everyday word. *Hier haben wir/gibt es genug Platz. Für vier Koffer reicht der Platz nicht. Der Raum* is stylistically somewhat higher and tends to mean 'space'. *Die Möbel nehmen zu viel Raum ein.* When **room** means 'the space left over by others', as in *Is there any room at your table for me?*, only *Platz* is used. *Ist bei euch am Tisch Platz für mich?* When adequate space for something to be put permanently is meant, *Raum* can be used, but *Platz* is the everyday term. *Auf dieser Wand ist noch genug Platz/Raum für das Bild. Wir sind räumlich sehr beschränkt* means 'limited in space'. The same sense is conveyed by *Sie leben auf engstem Raum, Raum* being in this context the only word possible. *Platz* is usual in *Bitte den Platz vor dieser Tür freihalten!*, but *Raum* is also possible. *Platz* is used in talking about a surface area outside. Hence *Da hast du Platz für dein Auto* and *Hier wäre Platz für einen Tennisplatz.* *[Jmdm.] Platz machen* is a fixed phr. meaning 'to make room or way for a pers.' It is also used fig. *Durch seinen Rücktritt hat er Platz gemacht für einen jüngeren Kollegen.* In the examples below the usual word is given first.

In der neuen Wohnung haben wir mehr Platz/Raum.   *Das Klavier nimmt viel Platz/Raum ein.*
Für einen so großen Schrank ist nicht genug Platz/Raum vorhanden.
In diesem Koffer ist noch Platz.   *Das Klavier nimmt viel Platz weg.*
Der Saal bietet fünfzig Personen Platz/Raum.   *Der Wagen bietet fünf Personen bequem Platz.*
Auf dem Videoband ist noch Platz für eine halbstündige Sendung.

2. Space meaning 'the area beyond the earth's atmosphere, what lies between the stars and planets' is **der Weltraum**. In compounds it is usually shortened to *Raum. Die Raumfahrt. Das Raumschiff.*

ruin *n.* Der Ruin means 'the economic or financial collapse' of a person or firm.

Jmd./Die Firma steht vor dem Ruin/wurde vor dem Ruin bewahrt. It is also applied to someone's health, *Diese schlechten Arbeitsbedingungen führten zum Ruin seiner Gesundheit,* as well as to someone's moral downfall, *Das ausschweifende Leben brachte ihn an den Rand des [moralischen] Ruins.* **Die Ruine** is 'what is left of a building which has been destroyed or fallen into decay'. *Die Burg ist nur noch eine malerische Ruine.*

Diese Fehlspekulation bedeutete für ihn/das Geschäft den [finanziellen] Ruin.
Wegen dieser Verluste schien der Ruin der Firma unabwendbar zu sein.
Nach dem schweren Erdbeben bestand die Stadt nur noch aus Ruinen.
Der Alkohol/Diese Frau war sein Ruin.   *Das wäre mein Ruin.*

run, walk *vs.* A few uses.

1. i. The usual equivalent of **run** meaning 'to move faster than when walking' is **laufen**. *Der Hund/Dieb lief weg.* **Rennen** suggests very rapid running, faster than *laufen,* but mostly only for a short distance. *He ran for his life* is *Er rannte/lief um sein Leben. Sie rannten/liefen, so schnell sie nur konnten* or *Sie liefen, was sie nur konnten* or *was die Beine hergaben* are like *They ran for all they were worth.*

Ich mußte zur Haltestelle laufen, um den Bus in die Stadt noch zu erreichen.
Weil ihr kalt war, lief sie eine Runde um den Sportplatz.
Ich bin zur Bushaltestelle gerannt und habe den Bus gerade noch erwischt.
Sie rannte über die Straße, um von einem Auto, das mit großer Geschwindigkeit auf sie zukam, nicht überfahren zu werden.   *Mehrere Spieler rannten hinter dem Ball her.*

Laufen is trans. with a distance as obj., *Sie läuft jeden Tag zwei Kilometer,* and in relation to sport, *Er hat die Strecke in Rekordzeit gelaufen/hat/ist einen neuen Rekord gelaufen. Sie ist hundert Meter in zehn Sekunden gelaufen.*

ii. A difficulty arises because **laufen** also means 'to walk' and can thus be ambiguous. While in *Kann das Kind schon laufen?* and *Ich laufe heute, statt mit dem Auto zu fahren,* and *Er läuft im Augenblick zur Schule, weil sein Fahrrad kaputt ist,* the meaning 'to walk' seems clear, in a sent. like *Ich bin gestern mit zwei Freunden durch den Wald gelaufen, laufen* is ambiguous as it could mean 'walk' or 'run'. To make the sense clear it is often better to use the normal vs. meaning 'to walk', **gehen** or **zu Fuß gehen**, which are unambiguous. *Er geht so schnell, daß ich Mühe habe, mit ihm Schritt zu halten. Den letzten Kilometer gehe ich zu Fuß.* For a long walk or hike, **wandern** is usual, sometimes **marschieren**.

A. *Willst du mit dem Auto fahren?* B. *Nein, ich laufe lieber* or *Ich gehe lieber zu Fuß.*

Um zur Schule zu kommen, muß sie zwanzig Minuten/zwei Kilometer gehen. Also laufen.

Er geht den langen Weg zur Schule zu Fuß. *Wir sind gestern etwa zwölf Kilometer gewandert.*

Usually with *schnell,* or *rasch, laufen* implies going quickly but without running. *Ich laufe noch schnell zu Post.*

2. Laufen can be used for liquids. *Mir lief der Schweiß über die Stirn/in die Augen.* Hence *Das Öl ist aus dem Behälter ausgelaufen.* **Rinnen** is applied to liquids which run or flow evenly, uniformly, and gently. *Der Schweiß rinnt mir von der Stirn.* Rinnen can also be used for granular solids, like sand or sugar, which run in the same way, and fig. for money. *Das Geld rinnt einem nur so durch die Finger.*

Dem Verletzten lief das Blut über das Gesicht. *Der alten Frau liefen die Tränen über das Gesicht.*

Regentropfen rannen über die Fensterscheiben.

Blut rann aus der Wunde und tropfte auf seine Hand.

Das Kind ließ den feinen gelben Sand durch die Finger rinnen.

3. When a road, border, river, or line is the subj. of **run**, the appropriate v. is **verlaufen.**

Die Eisenbahnlinie/Die Straße verläuft hundert Kilometer schnurgerade.

Die Grenze verläuft mitten durch den See/auf dem Kamm des Gebirges/in der Mitte des Flusses.

Die zweite Linie verläuft parallel zur ersten.

4. i. With a shop, business, organization, etc. as obj. **run** is trans. and means 'to be in charge of'. The simplest transl. of *He runs a business/hotel/kiosk* is *Er hat ein Hotel/Geschäft/einen Kiosk. Er betreibt ein Geschäft* is more formal. **Führen** and **leiten** mean 'to conduct or manage' a business etc. and are discussed under LEAD. *Ein gut geführtes Hotel. Er leitet das Projekt/die Abteilung.* To run a town is *eine Stadt verwalten,* i.e. to administer it. **Veranstalten,** cf. ARRANGE 5. iii, takes ns. such as *ein Wettbewerb, ein Wettrenner, ein Lehrgang, eine Konferenz,* etc. as object. *Botengänge machen* is 'to run messages/errands'. **Bewirtschaften** is used for running a farm or something like a restaurant. *Jmd. bewirtschaftet einen Bauernhof/ein Gut [gut/rentabel/schlecht]. Ein ehemaliger Kellner bewirtschaftet die Kantine/die Gaststätte im Bahnhof. Das Ehepaar hat das Restaurant musterhaft bewirtschaftet.*

ii. To run one's hand or fingers **over** or **through** sth. is expressed by **mit etw. fahren.** *Er fuhr sich mit der Hand/mit den Fingern/mit dem Kamm durch die Haare. Sie fuhr mit dem Staubtuch über die Möbel.*

S

sacrifice, give [up] *vs.* Sich **aufopfern** means 'to sacrifice oneself' in the sense of making sacrifices, putting the interests and wishes of others before one's own. *Er hat sich sein Leben lang für seine Familie aufgeopfert. Aufopfern* is usually refl. but is occasionally found with an obj. The meaning is exactly the same as that of *opfern* in the same construction. *Ich habe alles für dieses Projekt [auf]geopfert.* Like **sacrifice**, **opfern** originally meant 'to offer sth. to a deity', *Im Altertum opferte man den Göttern Tiere.* It is now applied fig. to things one forgoes for the sake of s.o./sth. else and is used with an acc. alone or with an acc. + *für* or a dat. *Sie hat ihre Feierabende geopfert. Er hat viel Geld für dieses Projekt geopfert.* The refl. **sich opfern** means 'to give one's life for s.o./sth.' *Er hat sich für das Vaterland geopfert.* In one of its meanings **hingeben** has the same sense as *opfern*, but it is more elevated, solemn, and emotional, and stresses the nobility of the deed. *Sie sind bereit, für ihre Ideen ihr Leben hinzugeben.* It is the usual equivalent of **give** when this means 'to sacrifice or give [up] sth.' *Er würde die Hälfte seines Vermögens hingeben, wenn er in seine Heimat zurückkehren könnte. Ich würde mein Letztes hingeben, um ihr zu helfen.* If these words sound too serious and formal, **verzichten auf**, 'to forgo', may be an appropriate equivalent of **sacrifice**. *Sie verzichtete auf ihre Freizeit, um für das Rote Kreuz zu arbeiten.*

    Er opferte sich für die Befreiung seines Landes auf. Or Er opferte sein ganzes Leben für die . . .
    Er opferte sich, um das Kind vor dem Ertrinken zu retten.
    Sie gab ihre Ersparnisse hin, um der armen Familie zu helfen.
    Sie waren bereit, alles, auch ihr Leben, für ihren Glauben zu opfern/hinzugeben.
    Ich bin nicht bereit, auf meine Wahlfreiheit zu verzichten.

safe, secure *adjs.*

1. Safe = 'free or protected from danger'. *They felt safe in the cave.* It is also applied to things, *Your job is safe*, and is used with *from*, *We are now safe from attack.* **Secure** is a syn. in some contexts. *Is sth. secure/safe from harm?* or *Are we safe/secure from attack? S.o. has a safe/secure position. Sth. is safe/secure in s.o.'s keeping* or *in safe custody.* The equivalent in all these cases is **sicher**. *From* is *vor. Jetzt sind wir vor Gefahr/Verfolgung sicher. Ich fühle mich sicher* means 'I feel safe' not 'I feel sure'. (With *sein* the context makes it clear whether *sicher* means 'safe', or 'sure' (cf. SURE). *Jetzt bist du sicher*, safe. *Ich bin sicher* (sure), *daß er sein Wort halten wird.*)

    Die Verfolgten fühlten sich sicher in der Höhle/in ihrem Versteck.
    Wir sind nun vor Angriffen/vor einem Angriff/vor Unterbrechungen sicher.
    Im Luftschutzkeller waren sie vor Bomben sicher.
    Deine Stelle/Dein Arbeitsplatz ist sicher. Also gesichert.
    Sie hat eine sichere Stelle/einen sicheren Arbeitsplatz in der Stadtverwaltung.

Expressions meaning 'in safe custody/keeping' are *in sicherem Gewahrsam* or *in sicheren Händen. Die Wertsachen waren in sicherem Gewahrsam*, in safe keeping/custody. Alternatives are *gut aufgehoben* or *sicher aufbewahrt* (for the vs. see KEEP 7), or the sense can be expressed as *vor Diebstahl/vor Verlust sicher. Gut aufgehoben*, applied to people, means 'in good/safe hands, well looked after'. *Die Kinder sind bei der Großmutter sicher/gut aufgehoben.*

Er glaubte, daß sein Geld in einer Bank sicher [aufbewahrt] sei.
Das Geld war in sicheren Händen.

Sicher is used for safe parliamentary seats. *Das ist ein sicherer Sitz für die Labour Partei.*
Sicher can also translate *a secure place/position in history. Er nimmt einen sicheren/festen/gesicherten Platz in der Geschichte der englischen Lyrik ein.*

2. Safe, meaning 'unhurt, no longer threatened by danger or injury', occurs as an adj., adv., and in the phr. *safe and sound. They arrived home safe after a rough crossing. They arrived back safe and sound. He returned safely from the perilous expedition.* **Heil** expresses this sense. *Sie sind heil am Ziel angekommen. Ich werde froh sein, wenn wir hier nur heil herauskommen.* Alternatives are **unverletzt,** 'uninjured', **unversehrt,** 'unscathed', and **wohlbehalten,** 'safe and well'. *Sind sie unverletzt? Man barg den Schifahrer unversehrt aus der Lawine. Wir sind wohlbehalten angekommen.* For situations where no great danger is involved, **gut** is used. *Kommen Sie gut nach Hause!* A phr. similar to *safe and sound* is **gesund und munter,** but it is not used in reference to anything particularly dangerous, such as a war. *Die Kinder kamen nach ihrer langen Reise gesund und munter zu Hause an.* In contexts relating to escaping harm or injury *heil* may need to be translated by *unhurt* or *unharmed* as **safe** does not suit the context. *Er hat den Unfall heil überstanden. Sie waren in einen Unfall verwickelt, sind aber heil davongekommen.* A synonymous phr. is *Sie sind mit heiler Haut davongekommen. Heil, wohlbehalten,* and *unversehrt* can refer to things as well as to people and mean 'undamaged'. *Nach dem Bombenangriff gab es kaum ein heiles Gebäude mehr in der Stadt. Die Waren sind wohlbehalten angekommen. Das Gebäude hat den Krieg unversehrt überstanden.*

Nach der stürmischen Überfahrt sind alle heil nach Hause gekommen .
Sie kehrten wohlbehalten/unverletzt/unversehrt von der gefährlichen Expedition zurück.
Obwohl der Soldat an zahlreichen Schlachten teilgenommen hatte, kehrte er unverletzt/unversehrt aus
dem Krieg zurück.   Er hat sie gut nach Hause gebracht.

3. Safe = 'not causing or likely to cause harm or danger'. *Is 120 kilometres an hour safe on this road? Are these toys safe for children?* It is applied to places in the sense 'not dangerous'. *Is this beach safe for swimming? Children can swim here safely.* **Ungefährlich** is used only after *sein.* Otherwise, **gefahrlos, ungefährdet,** and **ohne Gefahr** express the meaning, the first two mainly as advs.

Ist dieses Spielzeug/Sind diese Spielsachen für kleine Kinder ungefährlich? Ist es ungefährlich, wenn
Kinder mit diesen Spielsachen spielen?
Kann man hier gefahrlos/ohne Gefahr [mit] 120 Kilometer[n] pro Stunde fahren? Ist es ungefährlich,
wenn man [mit] 120 Stundenkilometer[n] fährt?
Kann man gefahrlos/ohne Gefahr bei so starker Brandung baden gehen? Ist es ungefährlich, an
diesem Strand/hier baden zu gehen?
Kinder können ungefährdet hier baden. Also . . . gefahrlos/ohne Gefahr baden.

For motor vehicles, *sicher* is used alone or in the compound *verkehrssicher. Ist dieses Fahrzeug [verkehrs]sicher?*

4. Applied to assumptions and statements, **safe** means 'probably correct, unlikely to produce controversy or contradiction'. *It is a safe assumption* or *safe to assume* can be *Man geht wohl nicht fehl in der Annahme/wenn man annimmt, daß sie uns unterstützen wird. You can safely say that the price is not too high: Man kann mit [ziemlicher/einiger] Sicherheit/ohne Bedenken* (misgivings) *sagen, daß der Preis nicht zu hoch ist.* (Note: *Mit Sicherheit,* 'with certainty', but *in Sicherheit,* 'in safety'.)

5. To be on the safe side is **um sicher zu gehen** or **zur Sicherheit.**

Obwohl die Sonne schien, nahm er, um [ganz] sicherzugehen, seinen Regenschirm mit.
Zur Sicherheit nehme ich etwas mehr Geld mit. (Cf. *Vorsichtshalber,* as a/by way of precaution.)

6. Secure = 'free from anxiety'. *Most people like to feel secure. I think you can feel secure about your future.* A transl. of the first sent. is *Die meisten Leute fühlen sich gern* **geborgen/sicher.** When a phr. is added to *secure*, different words are needed. *Ich glaube, daß du deine Zukunft als gesichert betrachten kannst/daß du deiner Zukunft beruhigt entgegensehen kannst/daß du einer gesicherten Zukunft entgegensehen kannst.*

7. Secure in the belief. *Im sicheren/festen Glauben, daß alles gut ausgehen würde, ließ er sich von keiner Enttäuschung unterkriegen.* In the last example and in *eine sichere Überzeugung* or *sichere Zuversicht, sicher* means 'unshakeable, certain, untroubled'. *Fest* is 'firm'.

8. Applied to material, a support, the manner of fastening, etc., **secure** means 'not liable to yield under strain or be displaced', hence 'firm or firmly fixed and unlikely to involve risk'. *Is that ladder secure? Don't go any higher [up] unless you find secure footholds!* **Sicher** stresses safety, but where the meaning is 'firm', **fest** is the appropriate equivalent. *Ist diese Leiter sicher? Or Steht diese Leiter fest?*

   Die Brücke scheint nicht [einsturz]sicher zu sein.

   Das Kälbchen war noch nicht ganz sicher auf den Beinen.

   Klettere nicht weiter hinauf/nach oben, bis du festen Halt gefunden hast!

   Glaubst du, daß der Bolzen richtig fest sitzt/richtig befestigt ist/fest verschraubt ist?

9. For **secure** = 'guaranteed certain', as in *Our victory seemed secure,* see SURE.

satisfy *v.* satisfaction *n.*

1. Satisfy means 'to meet or fulfil a wish, desire, or expectation, or a mental or bodily need', *This satisfied s.o.'s curiosity/appetite,* or 'to give a pers. enough of what is wanted so that he or she is pleased or contented', *This explanation satisfied everyone.*

i. Befriedigen can be used in these senses, but, because it also means 'to satisfy s.o.'s sexual desire' and *sich befriedigen* means 'to masturbate', it tends to be avoided with a personal subj. and obj. when there is any chance of ambiguity. *Diese Erklärung hat alle befriedigt* is unambiguous as are *Diese Arbeit/Dieser Beruf befriedigt jmdn.* **Zufriedenstellen** is a syn. of *befriedigen* which does not have its secondary senses. *Der Chef ist nicht leicht zufriedenzustellen—man muß alles genau nach seinen Wünschen machen. Befriedigen* is used with objs. like *jmds. Ansprüche, Wünsche, Neugier, Hunger, Ehrgeiz, ein Bedürfnis,* or *die Nachfrage,* (economic) DEMAND. *Befriedigen* is also used with *Gläubiger,* 'creditor', as obj. *Die Firma hat ihre Gläubiger befriedigt.* The pres. parts. of both vs. are equally common. *Ein Ergebnis ist befriedigend* or *zufriedenstellend.*

   Diese Antworten schienen seine Neugier voll befriedigt zu haben.

   Die Firma war nicht in der Lage, die Nachfrage nach ihrem neuen Kleinwagen zu befriedigen.

   Diese Antwort befriedigte ihn nicht.   Diese Lösung befriedigte alle.

   Es ist ein Glück, daß ich so leicht zufriedenzustellen bin.

   Die Leistungen dieses Schülers sind befriedigend/zufriedenstellend.

ii. The pass. **to be satisfied with** sth. is *mit etw.* **zufrieden sein.**

   Sind Sie mit Ihrem neuen Auto zufrieden?

2. Satisfy or *meet* requirements, demands, or conditions is **genügen** + dat. or **erfüllen** + acc. Cf. FILL 4. i and MEET 7. *Sie konnte den wachsenden Anforderungen genügen. Er hat allen Bedingungen genügt. Sie hat alle Bedingungen erfüllt.* (Note that the v. in *Das genügt uns/für uns/für diesen Zweck* means 'it's enough or will suffice'.) *Anforderungen,* 'demands', means 'sth. required in a job etc.' or 'a standard which has to be reached'. *Demand* also means 'a firm request' and is *die Forderung.* To satisfy *a demand* in this sense is expressed by **nachkommen** + dat. or *erfüllen. Sie sind* *unseren Forderungen nachgekommen* or *Sie haben unsere Forderungen erfüllt.* For *Nachfrage*, '(economic) demand', cf. 1. i.

3. Satisfy s.o. of the truth etc. of a claim means 'furnish with sufficient proof or information, to free from doubt, or convince'. The equivalent is **überzeugen**, to convince. Cf. PERSUADE 2. *Er überzeugte die Polizei von seiner Identität,* satisfied the police regarding his identity. **Satisfy oneself about** sth. or + clause is **sich [von etw.] überzeugen**. *Die Polizei überzeugte sich von der Richtigkeit seines Alibis. Sie überzeugte sich an Ort und Stelle, daß alles in Ordnung war. Ich sah mich um, überzeugte mich, daß der letzte Gast gegangen war und knipste die Lichter aus.* I am satisfied in this sense is *Ich habe mich davon überzeugt, daß alles, was möglich gewesen wäre, auch getan worden ist,* or *Ich bin [davon] überzeugt, daß er sein Bestes getan hat.* The court is satisfied that the accused is innocent is usually expressed as *Die Unschuld des Angeklagten wurde zur Zufriedenheit des Gerichts bewiesen.*

4. Satisfaction.
i. Die Zufriedenheit expresses the meaning 'the state of being satisfied or content'. *Sie verbrachten ihr Leben in Glück und Zufriedenheit. Sie hat alle Aufgaben zu meiner Zufriedenheit erledigt. Sein Gesichtsausdruck zeigte deutlich seine Zufriedenheit mit diesem Ergebnis.*
ii. Die Befriedigung means either 'the action of satisfying wishes, desires, etc.', *die Befriedigung solcher Bedürfnisse/aller Gläubiger*, or 'satisfaction' = 'the pleasure felt when sth. has been accomplished or when sth. happens which was desired or needed'. *Das gute Ergebnis erfüllte alle Mitarbeiter mit Befriedigung. Ich stelle etw. mit Befriedigung fest* or *nehme etw. mit Befriedigung zur Kenntnis*, note it with satisfaction.
  Diese Arbeit gewährte ihm nicht die erwartete/gewünschte Befriedigung.
  Sie fand volle Befriedigung/die erhoffte Befriedigung in dem neuen Beruf.
iii. Die Genugtuung was originally 'satisfaction' in the sense of 'an opportunity for satisfying one's honour by a duel'. It is now applied to something offered as recompense for an injustice or wrong. *Jmd. fordert/erhält Genugtuung.* In a sent. like *Customers who have been unable to get satisfaction from the local branch should write direct to the chairman of the board*, it could only be used if a considerable injustice is involved. If this condition is not met, it could be translated as *Kunden, deren Ansprüche von der Ortsvertretung nicht befriedigt worden sind, sollten sich direkt an den Vorsitzenden wenden.*
iv. Die Genugtuung is also a syn. of the second sense of *Befriedigung*, i.e. 'pleasure felt when sth. is accomplished or happens'. *Diese Entwicklung/Ihre Beförderung sehe ich mit großer Genugtuung. Dieses unerwartet gute Ergebnis bereitete allen Genugtuung.*
  Der Abschluß dieser schwierigen Aufgabe erfüllt mich mit großer Befriedigung/Genugtuung.

save, rescue *vs.*

1. A person rescues or saves someone or saves someone from drowning etc. or saves someone's life.
i. The equivalent of both **save** and **rescue** in this sense is **retten**. It is used with an obj., *Er hat mich gerettet*, with a dat. of the person and an obj., *Sie rettete mir das Leben*, or with an obj. and *vor*, *Er hat das Kind vorm Ertrinken gerettet. Retten* implies saving people from immediate danger and thus preserving them from injury or death. With things as obj. it means 'to save from destruction'. *Dem alten Haus droht der Abbruch, aber der Verein will es retten. Jmd. aus Lebensgefahr retten* is a fixed expression, as is *die Situation retten. Diese witzige Bemerkung hat die Situation gerettet.* Cf. *sich retten* under ESCAPE 1. iv.
  Diese Spenden retteten viele vor dem Verhungern.   *Rette sich, wer kann!*

Bei dem Brand seines Hauses konnte er gerade noch rechtzeitig einige wertvolle Möbelstücke retten.

ii. Bergen, 'to bring to safety', is a syn. which can be used for people and things. The people are in peril but not in the same immediate danger as with *retten. Bergen* also means 'to get or take s.o./sth. from a place where an accident or disaster has occurred'. If the people concerned are alive, it is translated as **rescue**.

Der Rettungskutter lief sofort aus, um die Schiffbrüchigen zu bergen.

Zwei der Verschütteten wurden geborgen. Der dritte konnte nur noch tot geborgen werden.

Die Familie barg ihren Hausrat aus den Trümmern ihres von einer Bombe getroffenen Hauses.

2. Save s.o. **from** sth. is also used when the grave situation implied in 1 does not exist, but when s.o. prevents a potentially harmful situation from arising. *S.o. was saved from disgrace/from his enemies/from injury.* This is translated by **bewahren vor**, to keep or preserve from. Cf. KEEP 8. *Der Freund bewahrte mich vor einer Verletzung/vor Schande/vor einer Demütigung/vor einem Sturz/vor meinen Feinden/vor der Gefahr. Retten* in contrast implies that the person is already in acute danger.

3. Save money.

i. Sparen means 'to accumulate money by not spending it'. It is used alone, *Du mußt bald anfangen zu sparen* or *Sie hatte eifrig gespart*, with *auf* or *für* meaning 'for', *Er spart auf/für ein Auto*, or with an amount as obj., *Sie hatte im letzten Jahr 4 000 Mark gespart.* (A bank savings account is *das Sparkonto. Die Spareinlagen* are 'customers' deposits or savings with a bank'. *Die Spareinlagen der Kunden werden verzinst.*) Although *die Ersparnisse* are 's.o.'s savings', **ersparen** is now uncommon in the sense of saving money, but it is occasionally found meaning 'to save an amount with difficulty'. *Mühsam hatte sie das Geld für den teuren Photoapparat erspart und überlegte sich, ob sie es dafür tatsächlich ausgeben sollte.*

ii. Ansparen means 'to succeed in saving up a sum of money'. *Er hatte schon 30% des Kaufpreises angespart und konnte die Anzahlung leisten.*

4. i. Like **save** sparen also carries the sense 'not to spend or use'. *Ich spare 10 Mark, wenn ich etw. für 15 Mark kaufe statt für 25. Wir gingen zu Fuß hin, um die Kosten für die Fahrt zu sparen.* Other objs. are *Zeit, Energie, Strom*, or a distance.

Sie sparte, wo sie nur konnte, was von vielen Leuten schon als Geiz angesehen wurde.

Wir versuchen, Strom zu sparen.

Durch sorgfältige Planung sparen wir später viel Zeit und Geld.

Dadurch, daß du die Abkürzung nimmst, sparst du fünf Kilometer.

ii. Einsparen implies a comparison with what was hitherto spent or used. If last winter I spent 2,000 marks on heating, but through more economical and efficient use of fuel only 1,500 this winter, I have saved 500 marks. In G.: *Ich habe 500 Mark eingespart. Einsparen* thus means 'to reduce expenditure' or 'to get by with less than was previously required'. The obj. can be *Kosten, Zeit, Arbeit, Material* as well as *Arbeitskräfte* or *Arbeitsstellen.*

Durch drastische Kürzungen im sozialen Bereich hoffte die Regierung, viel Geld einzusparen.

Die Wegabkürzung war zwar steiler und anstrengender, aber sie konnten dadurch viel Zeit einsparen.

Durch die Einführung von Robotern hat man viele Arbeitsplätze eingespart. Die eingesparten Arbeitskräfte wurden anderswo eingesetzt.

5. i. Aufsparen means 'to save sth. [up] for a later time' or 'to reserve sth. for a particular time or purpose'. *Wir sparen uns den Kuchen für später auf. Diesen Witz spare ich mir bis zum Schluß auf.*

ii. Save sth. that might be used or useful at a later time or **save** sth. **for** s.o. is **aufheben** or **aufbewahren**. Cf. KEEP 7. vi and vii. *Ich habe diese Kirschen für dich aufgehoben. Ich bewahre die Briefmarken für meine Sammlung auf.*

6. Whoever saves me the trouble of doing something, or saves me doing something, makes a particular task unnecessary, especially one that involves effort or difficulty. *He resigned immediately to save them the trouble of sacking him. That will save [us] a trip into town.* It is often refl. *You'd save yourself a lot of work if you used a computer.* The equivalent in the standard language is **jmdm./sich etw. ersparen**, which, depending on the context, is translated as **save** or SPARE. In *Ein Computer würde dir viel Arbeit ersparen*, the equivalent is **save**, but in *Ich wollte Ihnen den Kummer/die Kränkung/den Ärger ersparen*, either *spare* or **save**. *Wir wollten ihnen diese Demütigung ersparen. Das kannst du dir ersparen*, you can save yourself the trouble of doing that, is used like an imp., which does not exist. **Sich etw. sparen [können]** is a syn. of the refl. which is common in speech and can be used in the imp. *Spar' dir die Mühe!*, save yourself the effort/trouble. *Du kannst dir die Mühe sparen* has virtually the same meaning. A colloquial syn. is **Das kannst du dir schenken**. *Er hätte sich die Reise schenken können*. An alternative to *Du kannst dir den Weg [zur Post] sparen*, 'save yourself the trouble of going there', is *Ich nehme dir den Weg zur Post ab, wenn ich den Brief für dich einwerfe*.

> *Die meisten Leute sind froh, wenn ihnen die Mühe erspart bleibt, selbst zu denken.*
> *Er kündigte sofort, um ihnen die Mühe zu ersparen, ihn zu entlassen.*
> *Das erspart uns eine Fahrt in die Stadt.*　　　　*Spar' dir deine Erklärungen!*
> *Die Ratschläge kannst du dir sparen.*　　　　　*Spar' dir die Worte!*
> *Du sparst/ersparst uns viel Ärger, wenn du das unterläßt.*
> *Deiner Mutter kannst du diese Arbeit abnehmen.*
> *Die weitere Erklärung kannst du dir schenken.*
> *Den Theaterbesuch kannst du dir schenken—das Stück ist miserabel.*

7. Other expressions.

i. For **save** one's eyes and **save** one's strength = 'go easy on', cf. **schonen** under SPARE 1.

ii. *Machines* **save** *labour* is *Maschinen machen mühselige Arbeit überflüssig*.

iii. *God* **save** *the queen!* is *Gott erhalte die Königin! Erhalten*, to preserve. Cf. KEEP 8.

say *v.* This article discusses only a few special uses.

1. Say is used to state one example out of a number of possible ones. *If we consider an African country, let us say Ghana . . . Compare, say, a Michelangelo painting with a van Gogh!* Both **say** and **let us say** could be translated by **zum Beispiel** or **etwa**, both = 'for example, for instance', but **sagen wir einmal** is also common. *Einmal* is often shortened in speech to *mal*.

> *Wenn wir ein afrikanisches Land betrachten, sagen wir [ein]mal Ghana . . . /zum Beispiel/etwa Ghana!*
> *Vergleichen Sie, sagen wir [ein]mal, ein Gemälde von Michel Angelo mit einem von van Gogh!*
> *Kommen Sie heute nachmittag vorbei, sagen wir mal um 16.30!*

2. In *What would you say to a trip to Paris?* **say** asks for someone's reaction. In putting a proposal directly **gefallen** is the usual word, *Wie würde dir eine Reise nach Paris gefallen?*, but **sagen** can be used with **zu**. *Was sagst du dazu?* is a common way of asking someone's response to a suggestion or plan. *Ich schlage vor, wir fahren zu Ostern nach Paris—was sagst du dazu?* Thus also *Ich weiß nicht, was ich dazu sagen soll*.

> *Wie würde dir eine Woche in der Schweiz gefallen?*
> *Was sagst du zu meinem neuen Anzug/Haarschnitt?*

3. Although *to say* is superfluous in *She wrote to me to say that she wanted to meet me*, it is commonly used in some E.-speaking countries. In G. the clause follows *schreiben* directly and *to say* is not translated. *Sie schrieb mir, daß sie mich kennen lernen wollte*.

4. *Let us say you won $10 000! What would you do with it? Just say you found a buried trea-sure in your garden! Say the car breaks down on the journey!* **Say** here assumes some-thing which might happen and could be replaced by *suppose*. The equivalent in everyday language is *annehmen* in the form **nehmen wir an** or **angenommen**. **Gesetzt den Fall, daß** . . . has the same sense but, being restricted to more learned language, it is more like *assuming* or *let us assume*.

> *Nehmen wir an, du hättest einen vergrabenen Schatz im Garten gefunden!*
> *Angenommen, du hättest 10 000 Dollar gewonnen. Was würdest du damit machen?*
> *Nehmen wir an, du hast eine Panne!*

5. Say words, lines, a poem, etc. learnt **by heart**. For a poem, etc. **vortragen** is the neutral word and is used for children and others who recite poems. **Rezitieren** is used in educated speech, but suggests a speaker trained to recite or a skilled actor. **Aufsagen** is to say something, mostly a poem, learnt by heart without mistakes but also usually without much art or skill. It is mostly used for (school-)children. **Hersagen** is to repeat a poem etc. without any expression or feeling and in a monotonous voice.

> *Sie rezitierte ein paar Gedichte von Goethe und Heine.*
> *Wolfgang trug eine Ballade vor, von der er wußte, daß sie seiner Schwester gefallen würde.*
> *Sie schwankte gleichmäßig hin und zurück wie ein Schulkind, das ein Gedicht aufsagt.*
> *Es genügt nicht, daß du die Verse fehlerfrei hersagst. Trag' sie mit Ausdruck vor!*

6. Say or repeat words **after** s.o. One equivalent is **nachsprechen**, which is used either with a dat., *Sprechen Sie mir die folgenden Wörter nach!*, 'say or repeat them after me', or without one, *Er sprach den Eid nach*. When there is no dat., **wieder-holen**, 'to repeat', can also be used. *Wiederholen Sie die folgenden Sätze/Wörter!* *Wiederholen* also translates **say** or *repeat to oneself*. *Sie wiederholte die Vokabeln so lange, bis sie sie konnte*. *To say again* something which has not been understood is expressed by *wiederholen*. *Wiederholen Sie die Nummer bitte!*

7. In those parts of the G.-speaking area in which *sprechen* is not used, **nachsagen** carries the meaning of *nachsprechen* given in 6. *Das Kind sagte [mir] den Satz nach*. The main meaning of **jmdm. etw. nachsagen** is 'to say sth. about s.o. behind his/her back'. *Man sagt ihm Geiz nach* or *Ihm wird Geiz nachgesagt*, he is said to be a miser. The meaning of the n. can be expressed as a clause. *Man sagt ihm nach, er sei geizig. Ihr wird nachgesagt, sie lese jeden Abend einen Krimi. Man sagt der Firma nach, sie sei tief verschuldet.*

8. If a notice, sign, poster, badge, newspaper, etc. says something, it expresses it in written words.
i. Common is **stehen** discussed under BE 5. *What does the letter say?* is *Was steht im Brief? Was steht auf dem Schild/auf dem Wegweiser/darüber in der Zeitung/auf dem Aufkleber/auf dem Abzeichen?* In reference to a clock the possibilities are *Die Uhr zeigt 10 Uhr an*, or . . . *steht auf 10 Uhr*, or colloquially . . . *sagt 10 Uhr*.
ii. *The road was not exactly where the map* **said** *it was/should be* could be expressed as *Die Straße war nicht da, wo sie nach der Karte hätte sein sollen* or . . . , *wo sie auf der Karte verzeichnet war*.

9. With a passage, law, document, etc. as subj., **say** means 'to have as its content', 'to state'. There are several equivalents.
i. *What does the law say?* can be *Was* **steht** *im Gesetz?* The impersonal expression **es heißt** means in one sense that something is (written) in a text. *In der Bibel heißt es* . . . *Bei Goethe/In dem bekannten Lied heißt es* . . . *Wie heißt es im Gesetz? Es heißt* intro-duces the content of a passage in a more or less accurate form. (*Es heißt* also means 'people say/are saying', 'a rumour is going round'. *Es heißt, daß eine neue Fabrik hier gebaut wird.*)

ii. Sagen, used in the act. and pass., states in a very general way what a passage says. It may reproduce the wording or give its sense, and it usually has, or implies, a clause giving the content of the passage.

Diese Verordnung sagt eindeutig, daß die bisherigen Vorschriften nicht mehr gelten.

Diese Erklärung sagt nichts anderes, als daß immer noch Zweifel an der Durchführbarkeit des Unternehmens bestehen.

iii. Besagen is also used to state the content of something, but it suggests that someone is reproducing the general sense accurately in his or her own words, possibly with an explanation which the situation may require. *Faradays erstes Gesetz besagt* . . . implies someone's version of it, not the exact wording. The exact text would be introduced as *Fs. erstes Gesetz lautet*. Cf. READ 5. Thus *Diese Stelle im Vertrag/Die Verordnung besagt* introduces a statement giving its general meaning. Because of its implication *besagen* is also translated as MEAN, but it states the general significance rather than a specific meaning. Common are *Das besagt doch gar nichts*, 'says or means nothing', and *Was soll das denn besagen? Es besagt gar nichts, daß er heute nicht dabei ist. Wahrscheinlich ist etw. Unerwartetes dazwischengekommen.*

Die amtlichen Informationen über die berufliche Gliederung der Bundestagabgeordneten besagen wenig, zumal die Angaben oft keinen genauen Aufschluß über die Berufsausübung geben.

iv. Aussagen is occasionally used with a word, concept, passage, etc. as subj. Unlike *besagen*, it does not imply giving the general sense, but clearly stating the specific meaning. Cf. 10.

Noch Goethe hat Bildung als das verstanden, was das Wort wirklich aussagt, nämlich plastische Formung des Menschen.

10. Say applied to artists, writers, works of art, etc. The general term is **sagen**. *Was versucht er in dem Stück zu sagen?* would refer to someone's general first impression of the ideas a writer is trying to communicate. *Der Autor hat in dem Stück nicht viel zu sagen.* **Aussagen** refers to the themes of a work, the ideas that a writer or artist develops or puts over, and suggests a careful analysis rather than a general first impression. *Was sagt das Werk aus?* or *Was hat der Autor auszusagen?* therefore calls for a more detailed and reasoned answer. *Was sagt dieses Gleichnis aus? Was will der Karikaturist mit dieser Zeichnung aussagen?*

seal v.

1. The original sense of **seal** is 'to place a seal on a document' as a sign of authoritative ratification or approval, or as evidence of its genuineness. This was formerly the way of signifying official approval and of concluding contracts, and it survives in the seals of companies and institutions. *Das Siegel* is the equivalent of the n., and **siegeln** of the v. *Siegeln* is still used in the official sphere for placing a symbolic mark on something to show that it is genuine, although the seal has mostly given way to a stamp.

Eine Urkunde/Ein Dokument/Ein amtliches Schriftstück wird [von einer Behörde] gesiegelt.

2. From the original sense has developed the meaning 'to conclude or make an agreement binding by affixing the seals of the parties' and, in extended use, 'to ratify or clinch a deal by some ceremonial act'.

i. Besiegeln is 'to make binding', now usually only by one's signature. *Sie besiegelten den Vertrag mit ihren Unterschriften.* It is also used for ceremonial acts which follow or celebrate an agreement. *Der Trainer pflegte eine Vertragsverlängerung per Handsschlag zu besiegeln.* The lit. transl. of the expression *signed, sealed, and delivered* is *unterschrieben, besiegelt* (or *gesiegelt*) *und vollzogen.*

Die Geschäftsfreunde besiegelten mit ihren Unterschriften die Zusammenarbeit für weitere fünf Jahre.

Ihre Liebe schien durch diesen Kuß besiegelt zu sein.

ii. Besiegeln also translates **seal** meaning 'to decide irrevocably the fate of a pers. or thg.' or 'to place a victory or defeat beyond dispute or reversal'.

Obwohl das Schicksal des Unternehmers bereits besiegelt erschien, konnte er aus eigener Kraft den Konkurs abwenden.

Er mußte der Partei beitreten, oder sein wirtschaftlicher Untergang war besiegelt.

Die Niederlage der Mannschaft schien besiegelt zu sein, als ein entscheidender Spieler wegen Verletzungen ausscheiden mußte.

Eine gelungene Mischung aus erfahrenen und jüngeren Spielern besiegelte letztendlich den Sieg/den Erfolg.

3. Seal, which originally meant and still means 'to fasten with a seal', has acquired the sense 'to stick up' a letter, envelope, etc.

i. Versiegeln meant originally 'to seal with sealing wax and the imprint of a personal or institutional seal'. This procedure is still occasionally used as a means of showing by the seal being intact that a package has not been opened. *Die Post versiegelt oft Wertbriefe, um zu garantieren, daß kein Unbefugter sie öffnet. Ein versiegelter Befehl* or *eine versiegelte Order* is 'sealed orders'. Like **seal**, *versiegeln* also means 'to place a seal' on the opening of a door, chest, etc. *Um allen Spuren nachgehen zu können, ließ die Polizei das Zimmer, in dem der Mord geschah, versiegeln.* **Plombieren** is a technical term used by customs officials for sealing shipments etc. to show that they have not been opened. *Man plombiert einen Container/einen Güterwagen. Da die Ladung plombiert ist, kann der Lastwagen die Grenze zügig passieren.*

ii. The usual words for sealing a letter or envelope are **zukleben, schließen**, and colloquially **zumachen. Verschließen** is an elevated syn. *Zukleben, zumachen*, and sometimes *verschließen* are used for sealing or sticking something up with sticky tape, *der Klebestreifen.*

Sie las den Brief noch einmal, steckte ihn in den Umschlag und klebte ihn zu/machte ihn zu.

Die junge Frau verschloß sehr nachdenklich den Brief an ihren Freund/klebte den Brief an ihn zu.

Ich wollte gerade den Brief einwerfen, als ich sah, daß ich den Umschlag nicht geschlossen hatte.

4. Seal also means 'to close completely by a lid, coating, or other fastening that prevents access or leakage'.

i. In reference to sealing fruit and vegetables preserved in jars, tins, or cans, the usual word is **verschließen**. It is also used for the sealing of bottles. (*To put the lid back on* an already opened bottle is *zumachen* or *schließen.*) Although the usual expression for foodstuffs sealed in a packet is *vakuumverpackt, vakuum* or *luftdicht verschlossen* or *versiegelt* are also found.

Die Flaschen werden sofort verschlossen, damit die Kohlensäure erhalten bleibt.

Der Quark in der Packung war luftdicht verschlossen.

Erdnüsse werden vakuum verschlossen, um ihre Frische zu erhalten.

ii. Verschließen means 'to seal [off]' in other spheres. *Während der Aufnahme war das Studio schalldicht verschlossen.* It is used with *hermetisch*, as is **abriegeln** when an area is sealed off, i.e. no one is allowed in. *Die Polizei hat das Gelände hermetisch abgeriegelt.*

5. A crack, crevice, break, or something that is leaking is sealed.

i. The standard term is **abdichten**, the everyday one **dicht machen**. *Man dichtet eine Fuge/eine Ritze/ein Fenster ab.*

Nach starkem Regen stand immer Wasser auf der Fensterbank, weil das Fenster nicht richtig abgedichtet war. Also versiegelt.   Wir müssen die lecke Stelle dicht machen/abdichten.

ii. Seal up a door, window, or large opening means 'to fill up with bricks or masonry'. **Zumauern** is 'to fill in an opening' such as a door or window. *Die Tür und die Fenster an einer Seite des Hauses wurden zugemauert.* **Vermauern** also means in one sense 'to block up permanently'.

Infolge einer Explosion brach im Bergwerk ein Brand aus. Man mauerte den Stollen zu und leitete Stickstoff ein, um das Feuer zu ersticken.
Er hat den hinteren Eingang zu seinem Haus vermauert.

secret *adj.* **Secret** has several shades of meaning which arise from the context: (i) 'Kept from public knowledge or from the people specified'. *The documents are top secret.* (ii) With organizations, ceremonies, etc. it means 'known only to the initiated', 'kept from the knowledge of the general public'. *A secret society. A secret drawer, door, passage,* etc. (iii) Of a committee, hearing, etc., it means 'conducted without the public being informed'. *A secret investigation.* (iv) In reference to people it means 'working without the purpose being known'. *A secret agent.* (v) In reference to actions it means 'done with the intention of being concealed'. *Secret negotiations. A secret meeting.* (vi) Secret feelings or thoughts are not openly admitted or expressed. *A secret wish. I felt secret joy at this news.*

i. Geheim expresses the above senses i–iv either as an adj. or in compounds like *der Geheimbund,* secret society. Senses v and vi above are usually expressed by **heimlich**. There are certain constructions in which only one of these words can be used. *Geheim* only is used with *halten,* to keep. Cf. ii. *Man hielt seine Abreise geheim. Heimlich* is an attributive adj. or an adv. only. *Ich hatte eine heimliche Zuneigung zu ihr. Sie steckte ihm heimlich Geld zu.* It is not used predicatively. Unlike *heimlich, geheim* is not an adv., but the phrs. discussed under *in secret* (cf. iii) can be used. *Sie trafen sich heimlich/im geheimen.* Only *geheim* is a predicative adj. *Es lag in ihrem Interesse wie in dem meinen, daß die ganze Sache geheim blieb.* When both are syntactically possible, the distinction, which is fairly slight, is that *geheim* is used for things of an official nature and for those concerning a country or a wider public or the initiated, whereas *heimlich* refers more to one or only a few individuals, and to something of a private nature. *Streng geheim* is 'top secret'. The overlap occurs with words like *die Verschwörung,* 'conspiracy', *die Zusammenkunft,* 'meeting', *der Plan, die Verabredung,* 'agreement'. Common compounds are *das Geheimabkommen, die Geheimnummer, der Geheimgang, die Geheimtür, der Geheimagent, die Geheimtreppe, das Geheimfach, der Geheimauftrag.* Secret ballot is *die geheime Wahl. Heimlich* means 'not openly admitted' with regard to feelings, *heimliches Mißtrauen, heimliche Liebe,* and actions, *Sie trafen sich heimlich. Heimlich, still und leise* strengthens the idea of secrecy and is used with actions. *Heimlich, still und leise schlich er sich davon.*

Die Untersuchung des Mordes an den Terroristen sollte geheim sein.
Der Botschafter handelte im geheimen Auftrag seiner Regierung.
Die Akte/Der Urlaubsort des Brautpaares war streng geheim.
Ich empfand eine heimliche Freude/heimliche Angst über diese Nachricht.
Sie hatte den heimlichen Wunsch, Schauspielerin zu werden.
Er ist heimlicher Anhänger einer radikalen Partei.
Er jubelte/triumphierte heimlich über den von seinem Konkurrenten erlittenen Rückschlag.

ii. A v. with the same meaning as *geheimhalten* is **verheimlichen**. *Man verheimlichte seine Abreise.* With a dat. *verheimlichen* means 'to keep secret or HIDE from others'. *Der Junge verheimlichte seiner Mutter, was passiert war.* This can also be expressed as *Er hielt das, was passiert war, vor seiner Mutter geheim.*

iii. In secret. Im geheimen means firstly 'so that others do not notice'. *Im geheimen wurde ein Fest vorbereitet.* It also means 'not revealed to others, in one's heart', and is a syn. of **insgeheim**. *Insgeheim bewunderte er sie. Im geheimen/Insgeheim bedauerte sie den Vorfall, wollte es aber nicht zugeben.*

see *v.* Although **see** and *sehen* often correspond, there are cases in G. in which different vs. or prefixed forms are needed. An important instance in which a different v. is required is **see** meaning 'to understand'. This article discusses the senses in which **see** does not correspond, or only sometimes corresponds, to *sehen*. 1–7 treat senses of **see** which mostly require a v. other than *sehen*, and 7–11 derivatives of *sehen* for whose meanings E. can use *see*.

1. See = 'understand'.

i. The general equivalent is **verstehen**. *Ich verstehe nicht, was Sie meinen*, I don't see/fail to see. *Ich verstehe nicht, warum wir uns darüber streiten*, I don't see why we are quarrelling. *Den Sinn seiner Bemerkung verstehe ich nicht*, I don't see the point of it or see what he's getting at. Also *Ich verstehe die Bedeutung dieses Satzes nicht* and *Ich verstehe nicht, was der Satz bedeutet*. To see a joke: *Einen Witz verstehen*.

ii. Es ist mir klar is common, particularly in speech, in the sense of 'understand'. *Es ist mir jetzt klar, warum er so handeln mußte*, I now see/understand. *Mir ist noch nicht klar, wie man zu diesem Ergebnis kommt.*

iii. In a pos. statement **einsehen** (cf. REALIZE) implies coming to a realization about something often relating to one's own behaviour as a result of another's remarks. **See** would not be the equivalent in *Sie werden wohl einsehen, daß ich nichts versprechen kann*, but could well be in *Das sehe ich nun/jetzt ein*, or in pos. and neg. questions *Siehst du jetzt ein, daß das nicht geht?* and *Siehst du nicht ein, daß das eine Illusion ist?* and in neg. statements. *Ich sehe nicht ein, warum ich das alles alleine soll. Ich sehe jetzt ein, daß du dich unter den gegebenen Umständen nicht anders hättest entscheiden können.*

Often any of the expressions in i–iii can be used. *I don't see why we should go there again/should arrive so early* is *Ich verstehe nicht, warum wir noch einmal hingehen müssen/warum wir so früh ankommen müssen*, or *Es ist mir nicht klar, warum . . .* or *Ich sehe nicht ein, warum . . . Now, do you see?* is *Verstehst du nun/jetzt?* or *Ist dir das nun klar?* or *Siehst du das nun ein? Yes, I see* is *Ja, ich verstehe* or *Das ist mir klar* or *Das sehe ich nun ein.*

iv. Sehen is used when only sense perception is involved. *I can't see where the wire is attached to the motor* is *Ich sehe nicht, wo der Draht an den Motor angeschlossen ist.* But *I can't see how to do it/how it works* becomes, if more than sight is required, *Ich verstehe nicht/Es ist mir nicht klar, wie man es macht/wie es funktioniert*. Cf. REALIZE 1. iii and iv. *Go and see for yourself!* is *Geh' hin und sieh' es dir selbst an!*

v. See *the point/sense/use/good of an action* or *doing sth. Point* or *sense of* + a n. becomes *der Zweck* or *der Sinn* + gen. *Den Sinn dieses Protestes verstehe ich nicht. Der Zweck seines Vorgehens ist mir nicht klar. Den Sinn dieses Schrittes seh' ich nicht ein.* The gerundial construction *the use/good/sense/point of doing sth.* is turned into a clause or infin. *I don't see the use of going there again* or *the good of being so early* can be formulated as *I don't see what good it does/what use it is to go there again/to be so early*. These constructions can be translated either as *Ich verstehe nicht, daß es was nutzt/nützt, so früh anzukommen*, or *Ich verstehe nicht, welchen Zweck es hat, daß wir wieder hinfahren*, or *Ich verstehe nicht, was es soll, daß wir nochmal hinfahren*. An alternative is *Ich sehe nicht ein, daß es was bringen wird, wenn wir uns darüber streiten*, I don't see the sense/point/use/good of quarrelling.

> *Ich verstehe nicht, daß es was nutzt, es noch einmal zu versuchen.*
> *Ich verstehe nicht, welchen Zweck es hat, das zu machen.*
> *Ich sehe nicht ein, daß es was bringen wird, wenn wir die Sache anders machen.*

2. See a person = 'to meet, visit, receive or consult'.

i. Sehen is used like *meet* but is ambiguous, as is **see**. *I see her every day* and *Ich sehe* *sie jeden Tag* leave open whether we do more than just catch sight of each other. *Wir sehen uns morgen bei der Sitzung/heute abend bei mir. Sie sehen sich jeden Tag. I'll see you* etc. *later* is expressed as the refl. *Wir sehen uns später.*

ii. **Go and see** s.o. privately is **besuchen.** *Jochen besuche ich morgen abend.*

iii. **See** = 'to receive'. It expresses a request that someone go into an office etc. *Mr X will see you now* is in polite and formal language *Herr X läßt bitten. I'll see him/her now* is *Ich lasse bitten.*

iv. **See** = 'to consult'. *I must see the dentist, doctor,* etc. is expressed by **gehen zu.** *Ich muß zum Zahnarzt gehen.* **Sprechen** + acc. is used for seeing someone on a business or professional matter. *Ich möchte den Direktor sprechen. Wen möchten Sie sprechen? Schließlich konnte er den Botschafter doch sprechen. Ich muß sie dringend sprechen. Ich möchte den Kreditleiter noch heute sprechen, wenn [es] irgend möglich [ist].*

v. When the purpose is not consultation, as in *The committee will see all the applicants today,* **sprechen mit** is used. *Der Ausschuß spricht heute mit allen Bewerbern. Ich muß dringend mit ihr/Ihnen sprechen.*

3. See s.o. somewhere. *I'll see you home/to the station* is **begleiten,** to accompany, *Ich begleite Sie nach Hause/zum Bahnhof,* or in everyday language **mitkommen,** *Ich komme mit zum Bahnhof.*

4. See means 'to imagine' in *I can't see him as an actor.* The equivalent is **sich vorstellen.** *Als Schauspieler kann ich ihn mir nicht vorstellen. Ich kann mir gut vorstellen, daß dieser Zwischenfall zu einer Verschlechterung unserer Beziehungen führen wird, see it leading to.*

5. See ='to experience'.

i. The general equivalent is **erleben,** to EXPERIENCE. *I have never seen such rudeness: Solche Unhöflichkeit/So was Unfreundliches/Unhöfliches habe ich noch nie erlebt.*

ii. S.o. has **seen** 20 years' service: *Jmd. hat eine zwanzigjährige Dienstzeit hinter sich.*

iii. With a non-personal subj., such as *The nineteenth century* **saw** *the foundation/rise of the second German empire,* the meaning needs to be expressed. *Im 19. Jahrhundert wurde das . . . Reich gegründet* or *. . . entstand das . . . Reich* or *. . . stieg das Reich zu einer bedeutenden Macht auf. In jedem der letzten Jahre hat eine bedeutende Zeitschrift das Erscheinen eingestellt,* could be a transl. of *saw the disappearance of.*

6. See also means 'to regard sth. in a certain way'. *I see the matter differently.* **Sehen** conveys this sense in some expressions. *Ich sehe die Sache anders. I've come to see the problem in a different light* would be *Seit einiger Zeit sehe ich das Problem in einem anderen Licht.* **Ansehen** is the main equivalent of *regard* in this sense and is used with *als* and in some contexts where E. has *see. Ich sehe es als meine Pflicht an, ihnen zu helfen,* see or regard. *Ich sehe ihn als guten Freund an. Ich sehe die Sache von einem anderen Standpunkt aus an.*

7. In one sense **zusehen** means 'to watch s.o. doing sth. or watch sth. happening'. *Die Eltern sahen den Kindern beim Spiel zu.* It is advisable to use *zusehen* when **see** means 'to watch sth. undesirable going on'. *Ich verstehe einfach nicht, wie er bei so etw. zusehen konnte, ohne einzugreifen.* Or *. . . wie er dem zusehen konnte.*

8. See = 'to find out'.

i. **Nachsehen,** discussed under LOOK 5, translates *see, look and see,* or *go and see. See how much milk is left!* is *Sieh' mal nach, wieviel Milch wir noch haben!* If going and seeing involves asking rather than looking, the expression used is *Geh' mal hin und frag' ihn, was er möchte!* go and see what he wants. *Nachsehen* implies actual looking. For more abstract seeing cf. next section.

ii. **See,** meaning 'to find out' and often followed by *if* or *whether,* as in *Let's see/I'll*

dog to get or catch a person. With a personal obj. **anfassen** means 'to take by the hand'. A parent might say to a child, *'Faß mich an, wenn wir über die Straße gehen!'* With *fassen*, *'Faß mich bei der Hand!'*

> *Als der Lastwagen nur ein paar Meter weg war, faßte er das Kind beim Arm und zerrte es von der Straße zurück.*   *Sie faßte den Blinden am Arm und führte ihn über die Straße.*

Fassen also means 'to arrest' and frequently suggests catching in the act or in flight.

> *Es gelang der Polizei, alle Mitglieder der Bande bei einem Überfall zu fassen.*
> *Erst nach einer langen Untersuchung hat die Polizei den Mörder gefaßt.*

ii. With things as obj. **fassen** is now usual only in a few cases. In most contexts it has given way to **anfassen** and **zufassen**. *Fassen* means 'to get a firm hold or grip on' with ns. like *das Seil, der Rettungsring,* or *die Zügel* as obj. With other ns. as obj. *anfassen* or *zufassen*, which express the same meaning, are usually preferred. If two people were preparing to lift a heavy object, one might ask *'Wo können wir am besten fassen?'* (also *anfassen*) or *'Hast du gut gefaßt?'* (or *zugefaßt*). *Fassen* can also have an obj. *'Hast du ihn (den Tisch) gut gefaßt?'* Also *'Hast du ihn richtig angefaßt?'*

> *Wir fassen den Tisch unter der Kante, nicht oben, weil die Platte lose ist.*

Fassen and *anfassen* are used for an instrument. *Er faßte den Draht mit der Zange [an].* *Der Kran faßte den Baumstamm.* For an animal. *Der Vogel faßte die Beute mit dem Schnabel/den Klauen. Packen* is, however, usual in relation to claws. Cf. 1. iv.

> *Faß ein bißchen weiter rechts an!*   *Jetzt faßt mal an!*
> *Wenn du das Bett am Kopf anfaßt, fasse ich es am Fuß an.*   *Ich fasse hier an, du dort.*
> *Die Kanne war schon so heiß geworden, daß man sie nicht ohne Topflappen anfassen konnte.*

While *anfassen* is used with and without an obj., *zufassen* does not take an obj. What someone takes hold of or seizes is only implied. *Ehe ich zufassen konnte, hatte er sich zur Seite gewandt und war weggerannt* implies before I could grab/seize/ take hold of him. *Jmd. hat blitzschnell/kräftig zugefaßt* means 'seized/grabbed s.o. or sth.' which must be clear from the context.

> *Wir gruppierten uns um die Kiste und wollten schon zufassen/anfassen.*

In *Faß mal bitte mit an!* and *Faß bitte mal zu!* both vs. mean 'to lend a hand', 'help with some work'.

iii. Ergreifen also means 'to reach for, take in one's hand, and retain one's grip', but is stylistically somewhat higher than *fassen* and its derivatives. It also says nothing about the way the action is carried out. It needs an obj., but it is used without restriction for both things and people, and with the latter it may also imply taking into lawful custody. *Er ergriff das Tauende/ihre Hand. Die Polizei ergriff den Verbrecher.* As *anfassen* also means 'to TOUCH', *ergreifen* can avoid ambiguity. *Ergreifen* is frequently found in learned or scientific prose, but it is not restricted to it. *Viele Einzelbewegungen werden benötigt, um einen Gegenstand sicher mit der Hand zu ergreifen.* To seize power is *die Macht ergreifen*, more poetically *die Macht an sich reißen.* Like *zufassen*, **zugreifen** is used without an obj. and is also higher stylistically than it. *Ehe sie zugreifen konnte, war die Vase heruntergefallen.* To seize an opportunity can be *eine Gelegenheit ergreifen.* *Zugreifen,* used without an obj., also means 'to seize an opportunity'. *Der Wagen war in gutem Zustand und so preiswert, daß ich sofort zugriff.* **Greifen**, used with *nach* and *zu*, means 'to reach for' and may imply taking hold of. *Greifen nach* implies moving the hand in the direction of something, but it leaves the question open as to whether the person gets a grip on the thing. *Er griff nach dem Seil, hat es aber verfehlt. Er griff nach seinem Hut. Er griff nach ihrer Hand.* *Greifen zu* implies taking the thing into one's hand with the intention of using it for some purpose. *Als er das Geräusch hörte, griff er zum Gewehr. Er griff zum Spaten and fing an zu graben.*

> *Sie ergriff den Ertrinkenden beim Schopf und zog ihn aus dem Wasser.*

Er ergriff sein Glas und trank auf ihr Wohl.

Im Fallen ergriff er einen Ast.   Zwanzig Fäuste ergriffen den Übeltäter.

Ich schlage vor, du ergreifst die Initiative, statt alles nur treiben zu lassen.

Ich an deiner Stelle würde zugreifen und nicht zögern.

Greifen Sie zu!, said at meals, means 'help yourself'. Like *zufassen, zugreifen* also means 'to lend a hand'. *Wenn alle zugreifen, ist die Arbeit schnell erledigt.*

iv. Packen implies taking hold of s.o./sth. with a firm grip and with an action which is quick and often violent. With people as obj. it suggests grabbing or taking roughly and suddenly, and may imply arrest. It is similar in meaning to **seize** or **grab**. It is much used colloquially, particularly by children, without the nuances being strictly observed. It is the normal term when animals are the subj. and can be used when seizing with the teeth is meant. When the part of the body or clothing grabbed is not stated, **anpacken** is also found. *Der Polizist packte den Jungen heftig an* but *packte ihn am Kragen/am Arm. Er packte mich von hinten an.* **Zupacken** carries the same implication of quickness and firmness, but what is seized is not stated. *Du mußt mit beiden Händen/kräftiger zupacken*, get a firmer grip or hold. *Die Ringer gingen aufeinander los und packten zu.* Zupacken is more colloquial in tone than *zufassen* and *zugreifen*.

Der Wirt packte den Burschen an den Schultern und warf ihn hinaus.

Blitzschnell packte er Meckels Haarschopf.   Das Raubtier packte die Beute mit den Zähnen.

Er packte/ergriff den erstbesten Gegenstand und schleuderte ihn gegen die Wand.

Wenn wir gemeinsam zupacken, sind wir schnell fertig.

Es ist der Polizei gelungen, eine Bande von Autodieben zu packen.

Like *zugreifen*, *zupacken* can mean 'to seize and make full use of an opportunity', *Er packte zu, wo immer er einen Vorteil erkannte*, and 'to help with work', *Er redet nur, statt zuzupacken.*

2. When **seize**, **grab**, or **snatch** imply taking something from someone, **reißen** is used. The basic sense is 'to TEAR'. *Er riß mir das Buch aus der Hand/den Händen.* **Entreißen** + dat. is a more formal syn.

Der Dieb entriß ihr die Handtasche und verschwand in die U-Bahn-Station.

Der Polizist hat dem Jugendlichen den Revolver/das Messer entrissen.

3. Other vs. meaning 'grab, snatch, and seize'.

Raffen can mean 'to grab hastily a number of thgs. at a time (and put them somewhere)'. *Ich raffte die Kleider aus dem Schrank und warf sie in den Koffer.* In another sense it means 'to get into one's possession as many thgs. as one can', i.e. 'to grab', as in *They grabbed everything they could get their hands on. Sie haben alles an sich gerafft, was sie nur kriegen konnten.* It is pejorative, but does not necessarily imply anything criminal. *Raffgierig* means 'grasping'.

Grapschen is colloquial and implies unbridled greed in taking or grabbing something. *Er grapschte das Geld und rannte hinaus.* With *nach*, it means 'to reach quickly and greedily for sth.' *Er grapschte nach ihrer Hand.*

Erbeuten is 'to take as booty'. *Die Truppen haben Waffen und Munition des Feindes erbeutet.* It is also used for thieves, pirates, etc. where E. would use *to get away with* or sometimes **seize**. *Die Diebe haben/Die Diebesbande hat Juwelen und Geld erbeutet.*

Sich bemächtigen + gen. means 'to use force to bring s.o./sth. into one's power or control' and often corresponds to **seize**. *Der Polizist bemächtigte sich des Messers, das der Mann in der Tasche trug.*

Die Bankräuber bemächtigten sich mehrerer Geiseln.

Das eindringende feindliche Heer bemächtigte sich der beiden Flughäfen im Grenzgebiet.

4. **Seize** meaning 'to take possession of sth. by law' is **beschlagnahmen**, to confiscate, but only if the seizure is by a government body. *Diese Waren wurden von* *der Zollbehörde beschlagnahmt.* For *ein Gerichtsvollzieher*, 'bailiff', and seizure of property to settle a private debt, **pfänden** is used. *Ihre Möbel wurden gepfändet. Er wurde gepfändet*, his property was seized to pay a debt.

Die Schmuggelwaren wurden beschlagnahmt.   *Die Polizei hat das Diebesgut beschlagnahmt.*

5. Seize can also have a mental state as subj. *Panic seized the crowd.* In the pass.: *She was seized by fear/by the sudden desire to leave.* The normal vs. are **erfassen** and **ergreifen**. *Ergreifen* may suggest that the mind is completely filled by the feeling, but the difference is slight.

Ich wurde von großer Sehnsucht nach meiner Heimat ergriffen.
Eine Unruhe/Panische Angst erfaßte ihn.   *Zorn/Erregung/Grauen hatte alle ergriffen.*
Ein Verlangen nach frischer Luft erfaßte sie plötzlich.
Von Abscheu/Ekel erfaßt/ergriffen, wandte sie sich ab.
Eine Welle der Empörung hatte die Weltöffentlichkeit erfaßt.

Packen suggests greater violence of emotion. *Jmd. wird von Entsetzen/Leidenschaft/Zorn/Abenteuerlust gepackt. Beim Anblick der Flammen wurden die Zuschauer von Panik ergriffen/gepackt/erfaßt.* (*Packen* is also applied to an illness. *Fieber hatte ihn gepackt.*) *Packen* also means 'to grip', i.e. 'to claim a pers.'s total interest, rivet the attention'. A syn. is **fesseln**, whose basic meaning is 'to bind, fetter, shackle, or handcuff'. *Das Theaterstück/Der Film packte/fesselte die Zuschauer. Man sieht, daß er gerade einen packenden/fesselnden Roman liest.*

---

self-conscious, self-assured *adjs.* **Self-conscious** meaning 'shy and easily embarrassed' is **befangen**. *Das Kind ist Fremden gegenüber sehr befangen.* **Sich genieren** means 'to feel unsure, awkward, inhibited'. *Sie genierte sich, ihre Meinung offen auszusprechen.* The non-refl. form means that s.o./sth. has this effect on another. *Ihre Blicke genierten ihn.* Cf. EMBARRASS. **Selbstbewußt** means 'self-confident or self-assured'. A syn. is **selbstsicher**, sure of oneself or self-assured. *Jmds. selbstsicheres/selbstbewußtes Auftreten.*

Seine Gegenwart machte sie befangen.   *Du brauchst dich nicht zu genieren.*
Ein selbstsicherer/selbstbewußter Mensch.   *Sie genierte sich, den Fehler einzugestehen.*
Ich weiß nicht, ob diese selbstsichere Haltung alle für ihn einnimmt.

---

selfish *adj.* The usual equivalent is **egoistisch**, or the idea can be expressed as **Jmd. denkt nur an sich selbst**. **Selbstisch** is no longer commonly used; **selbstsüchtig** may be found occasionally, but is not in general use. **Eigennützig** means that someone is unduly concerned with his or her own advantage, and is still used. It is mostly applied to actions and motives, not directly to people. **Uneigennützig** is the usual equivalent of *unselfish*.

Mußt du denn immer so egoistisch sein/handeln?   *Sein egoistisches Verhalten stieß alle ab.*
Sie hatte nicht gedacht, daß die Freundin so eigennützig handeln würde.
Das hat er aus eigennützigen Motiven/aus reinem Eigennutz/aus Egoismus getan.
In der ganzen Angelegenheit hat er völlig uneigennützig gehandelt.

---

send, dispatch, transmit *vs.*

1. i. The everyday equivalent of **send** meaning 'to cause s.o./sth. to go or be taken somewhere without going oneself' is **schicken**. It needs an acc., *Er schickte einen Vertreter/ein Telegramm*, and can also have a dat. of the person, *Sie schickte mir die Zeitung*, or a phr. of direction, *Der Lehrer schickte das Kind nach Hause* or *Er schickte einen Boten zur Bank*. **Send for** s.o. can be **nach jmdm. schicken**, which implies sending one person to get another, *Sie schickte nach einem Arzt*, but **jmdn. kommen**

lassen is probably more usual. *Der Polizist ließ einen Krankenwagen kommen.* In *Ich lasse mir ein Taxi kommen,* mir can be omitted.

> *Ich habe ihm das Geld schon geschickt.*
> *Er rechnet jeden Tag damit, aufs Land geschickt zu werden.*
> *An welche Adresse soll ich das Buch schicken?*   *Um acht Uhr schicke ich die Kinder ins Bett.*
> *Der Chef brauchte Auskunft in dieser Angelegenheit und schickte nach der Sachbearbeiterin.*
> *Er ließ sich jede Stunde eine Tasse Kaffee kommen.*

ii. Senden is a formal word for the same idea. In the private sphere it sounds slightly pretentious, but it does occur. *Er sandte ihr einen großen Blumenstrauß/ein Glückwunschtelegramm.* It is, however, common in business language. *Die Waren senden wir an Ihre Adresse mit der Bahn.* With people as subj. and obj., it is restricted to those of some importance. Cf. 2. iii. *Der Vatikan sandte sofort einen Legaten nach München, der die Angelegenheit in Ordnung bringen sollte.*

> *Ich werde Ihnen den Betrag sofort senden.*   *Anbei senden wir Ihnen unseren Prospekt.*

2. Derivatives of *schicken* and *senden.*

i. When **send** means 'to send off', it is necessary to use **abschicken** or in formal language **absenden**. *Ich habe das Paket/den Brief gestern abgeschickt. Er telegraphierte, daß er das Warenpaket gerade abgesandt habe.*

ii. Versenden and **verschicken** are interchangeable terms in commercial language which are similar to **dispatch**. The everyday v. is *abschicken. Die Waren wurden vor zwei Tagen mit der Post/mit der Bahn versandt/verschickt. Verschicken* is occasionally found in the sense of sending people somewhere for health or safety reasons. *Die Kinder wurden aufs Land verschickt.*

iii. Entsenden is a formal and elevated word used mostly for sending important people somewhere.

> *Der Premierminister entsandte einen Bevollmächtigten, um die Verhandlungen zu führen.*

iv. Zuschicken + dat. means 'to send sth. to s.o.' and stresses that something is specially sent to an individual. **Zusenden** and **übersenden** have a similar meaning and are common in written commercial language.

> *Sobald ich mit dem Buch fertig bin, bringe ich es dir, oder ich schicke es dir zu.*
> *Der neue Katalog wird gleich nach Fertigstellung allen Kunden zugesandt.*
> *In der Anlage übersenden wir Ihnen das Merkblatt und die Bewerbungsformulare.*

v. Aussenden and **ausschicken** mean 'to send out', but the former is more formal in tone. *Der Major schickte einen Spähtrupp aus* is everyday language, while *Der Major sandte eine Patrouille zur Erkundung des Geländes aus* is stylistically higher.

3. Send s.o. word or a message is simply expressed by **[jmdm.] [durch jmdn.] ausrichten lassen** + clause. *Ausrichten* means here 'to give s.o. a message'. *Er ließ [uns] durch sie ausrichten, daß er erst eine Stunde nach der vereinbarten Zeit ankommen würde.* **Jmdm. sagen lassen** + clause is also used. *Ich ließ ihm ausrichten/sagen, daß er nicht auf mich warten solle/sollte.*

4. Transmit, broadcast, emit. From being used for phenomena of nature, *Die Sonne sendet ihre Strahlen zur Erde,* senden is now used for radio. *Es gelang Marconi, ein Funksignal über den Atlantik zu senden.* **Senden** means 'to transmit or broadcast' and is used when stating what programmes a station is broadcasting. *Der Sender/NDR III sendet* (or *bringt*) *um 10 Uhr Nachrichten/ein Musikprogramm.* An announcer would say *Wir senden/bringen . . . Eine Sendung* is 'a radio or television programme' as well as 'a parcel' sent by post etc., or 'a consignment of goods', and *der Sender* is 'a radio station or a transmitter'. (*Das Programm* is either 'a television channel', *das erste/zweite Programm,* or a collective n. for all the programmes (*Sendungen*) of a radio or television station in a particular time, *Das Fernsehprogramm am Wochenende ist gut/schlecht.*) **Ausstrahlen** is also used for broadcasting radio and television programmes. *Ein interessanter Film wird heute abend im ersten Programm ausgestrahlt.* Its basic sense is 'to emit or radiate'. *Die Lampe strahlt ein mildes Licht aus.* **Aussenden** means 'to emit'. *Uran sendet radioaktive Strahlen aus.*

sense *n.* The meanings of **sense** carried by *der Sinn* are explained in sections 1 to 4 with alternatives.

1. Der Sinn denotes the five physical senses of man and animals. These are *der Gehörsinn, der Geruchssinn, der Geschmackssinn, der Gesichtssinn,* and *der Tastsinn. Die Wahrnehmungen der Sinne* are 'the perceptions of the senses', but there is also the compound *die Sinneswahrnehmung.*

> *Hunde haben einen sehr scharfen Geruchssinn.*
> *Der Alkohol/Die Erschöpfung hatte seine Sinne getrübt.*

2. People who have a sense of duty or justice consider these important and seek to show them in the way they act. A **sense** is also 'a natural ability or talent for sth. like humour or business'. **Der Sinn** is the general equivalent in both these cases, but there are exceptions.

> *Diese Handlungsweise zeugt von ihrem ausgeprägten Gerechtigkeitssinn.*
> *Der Sinn für Ordnung und Pünktlichkeit geht ihm völlig ab.*
> *Alle Mitglieder der Familie hatten einen ausgeprägten Geschäftssinn.*
> *Sie hatten [keinen] Sinn für die Schönheiten der Natur.*

'Sense of humour' is *Sinn für Humor. Sense of duty* is either *das Pflichtgefühl* or *das Pflichtbewußtsein. Er hat ein ausgeprägtes/starkes Pflichtgefühl* Cf. 6. **Sense** in *They have an exaggerated sense of their own importance* must be expressed differently. The only possible n. is *die Meinung: Sie haben eine übertriebene Meinung von sich selbst/von ihrer eigenen Wichtigkeit.* Cf. OPINION 1. *Sie nehmen sich selbst sehr wichtig* and *Sie kommen sich selbst sehr wichtig vor* are alternatives.

> *Sie war von hohem Pflichtbewußtsein erfüllt.*   *Das habe ich nur aus Pflichtgefühl getan.*

3. *There is* **no/little sense** in *doing sth.* means that nothing useful is to be gained by doing it. A syn. is *There is no point in going there again.* One equivalent is **es hat keinen/wenig Sinn** + infin. This sense of *Sinn* is mostly neg., *Es hat keinen/wenig Sinn, länger zu bleiben,* but it occurs in the pos. both in questions and statements. *Welchen Sinn hat es denn, weiter zu machen? Hat es überhaupt [einen] Sinn, es noch einmal zu versuchen? Es hat doch Sinn, wieder anzufragen.* A syn. of this sense of *Sinn* is **der Zweck,** lit. 'purpose', which can be substituted for it, as can point for **sense.** *Es hat keinen Zweck hinzugehen. Welchen Zweck hat das denn überhaupt? (Es ist/erscheint)* **sinnlos/zwecklos** + infin. mean 'pointless' and are alternatives to the neg. *Es ist sinnlos/zwecklos, wieder anzurufen. Es ist* **sinnvoll** + infin. is an alternative to the pos. *Es wäre sinnvoll, um weitere Auskunft zu bitten. Sinn* and *Zweck* occur without an infin., *Seine Bemühungen hatten überhaupt keinen Sinn/Zweck,* and with *in, In dem, was sie jetzt machen/In diesen Maßnahmen sehe/erkenne ich gar keinen Sinn.* Cf. SEE 1. iv.

> *Es hat keinen Sinn/keinen Zweck, sich darüber zu ärgern/darüber zu streiten.*
> *Ob es Zweck hat, noch länger zu warten?* (This form of question is often encountered.)

4. The **sense** of sth. written or spoken is 'its general meaning', and the **sense** of a word or expression is 'one of its possible meanings'. **Der Sinn** expresses both these meanings. *Ich verstehe den Sinn seiner Worte/dieser Passage nicht. Im wahrsten/strengen/vollen/engen Sinne des Wortes,* the true or real, strict, full, and narrow sense of the word.

> *Ich habe nicht jedes Wort verstanden, mir war aber der allgemeine Sinn klar.*
> *Sie redeten so schnell, daß es ihr schwer fiel, den Sinn von dem, was sie sagten, zu verstehen.*
> *Vielleicht lügt er nicht im strengen Sinne des Wortes, aber er verbirgt uns ganz bestimmt etw. Wichtiges.*

Sinn is used in contexts in which it would mostly be translated as *meaning. Das Gleichnis hat einen tiefen Sinn. Die Frage nach dem Sinn des Lebens.*

> *Diese Aufgabe hat ihrem Leben einen neuen Sinn gegeben.*
>
> *Nach dem Tod seiner Frau schien sein Leben seinen Sinn verloren zu haben.*

5. Make [no] sense.

i. The equivalent is **einen/keinen Sinn ergeben/haben** if the subj. is a word, a sent., statement, etc. *Diese Textstelle ergibt keinen Sinn. Was er sagt, hat keinen Sinn. Diese Worte sind sinnvoll* and *Das ist ein sinnloser Satz* are also used. When a person is the subj., as in *I eventually made sense of it* or *I can't make any sense of it,* **verstehen** is the usual equivalent. *Diese Textstelle kann ich einfach nicht verstehen.* **Den Sinn erfassen**, 'to grasp the sense', or **einen Sinn in etw. erkennen**, 'to see some/any sense/meaning in sth.', can also be used. **Sich keinen Reim auf etw. machen können** means 'to be able to make no sense or head nor tail of sth.' *Das Buch ist vor drei Wochen erschienen, doch in keiner Buchhandlung zu bekommen—daraus kann ich mir keinen Reim machen.*

> *Ich las die Worte, die da gedruckt standen, aber sie ergaben keinen Sinn.*
>
> *Du mußt den Text mehrere Male lesen, um ihn zu verstehen/um den Sinn zu erfassen/um einen Sinn in den Wörtern zu erkennen.*
>
> *Alle Kinder empfinden das Bedürfnis, die Welt zu verstehen* (make sense of it).
>
> *Vorhin war er noch so lieb zu ihr gewesen, und jetzt diese Grobheit. Sie konnte sich keinen Reim darauf machen.*

ii. Einen Sinn ergeben can be applied to an action which makes sense, but **sinnvoll** is more usual. *Under these conditions, it makes sense to adopt labour-saving methods* is *Unter diesen Umständen ergibt es einen Sinn/ist es sinnvoll, Arbeitsmethoden einzuführen, die Arbeitskräfte einsparen. Sth. makes economic sense* is *Etw. ist wirtschaftlich sinnvoll* or *vom wirtschaftlichen Standpunkt aus gesehen sinnvoll.*

iii. *On defence matters he talked a great deal of sense* or *What he said/had to say about defence makes a great deal of sense* can be translated as *Was er über die Verteidigung sagte, klingt sehr vernünftig,* or as *Über die Verteidigung hat er [viel] Vernünftiges/ Gescheites geredet/gesagt.*

6. Someone can have a sense of something, such as freedom or independence, and can have a sense that something is happening or that something is true. The equivalent is **das Gefühl**. It corresponds to both *feeling* and **sense**. *A sense of security* etc. is *ein Gefühl der Sicherheit/der Geborgenheit/der Dankbarkeit/der Leere.*

> *Dadurch, daß sie schon mit sechzehn nicht mehr zu Hause wohnte, hatte sie ein Gefühl der Selbständigkeit bekommen.*
>
> *Ich wurde vom Gefühl überwältigt, daß ich gescheitert sei. Also . . . vom Bewußtsein . . .*

For *This left me with the sense/feeling that sth. was wrong* cf. *zurücklassen* and *hinterlassen* under LEAVE 5. *Diese Bemerkungen ließen mich mit dem Gefühl zurück, daß irgendetw. nicht in Ordnung war.*

7. Sense is 'the ability to make good judgements and to behave in a practical and reasonable way'. The equivalent is **der Verstand**. *Jmd. hat viel/wenig/keinen Verstand. To have the sense to do sth.* is often best expressed as **vernünftig/verständig genug sein**. Cf. REASONABLE. *Er war vernünftig genug, um sich Rat bei einem erfahrenen Kollegen zu holen.* **Der gesunde Menschenverstand** is 'common sense'. *Das sagt einem doch der gesunde Menschenverstand.*

> *Sie war vernünftig genug, um zu erkennen, daß der Plan sich nie verwirklichen lassen würde. Also*
>> *Sie hatte genug Verstand, um die Sinnlosigkeit eines solchen Plans zu erkennen.*
>
> *Deine Freunde scheinen mehr Geld als Verstand zu haben.*
>
> *Ich dachte, er hätte mehr Verstand, als so was Dummes/eine solche Dummheit zu machen.*
>
> *Ich hätte dir mehr Verstand zugetraut, als solchen Unsinn zu glauben.*

8. In phrs. **senses** means 'the normal and right state of mind'. There are several
equivalents of *to take leave of one's senses. Er ist nicht bei Sinnen* and *Sie hat den Verstand
verloren* belong to the standard language, as does *Du bist wohl nicht recht bei Verstand.
Nicht ganz bei Trost sein* is colloquial. *This brought me to my senses is Dies brachte mich
zur Vernunft. I came to my senses: Ich kam zur Vernunft. The explosion frightened me out
of my senses/wits: Die Explosion hat mich zu Tode erschreckt.*

> *Sie warteten darauf, daß ich zur Vernunft kam und einsah, daß ich Unrecht hatte.*
> *Diese Verwarnung wird ihn hoffentlich zur Vernunft bringen.*

9. In a sense means 'to a certain extent' or 'if the statement etc. is taken in a particular way'. *What you say is true in a sense.* The main equivalent is **in einer Hinsicht**
or **in gewisser Hinsicht**, in one or a certain respect. *Was sie sagten, ist in gewisser
Hinsicht wahr.* **In what sense** is **inwiefern**, to what extent. *Inwiefern gilt das für uns?*
(*In einem Sinn[e]* exists, but it means 'in one sense or meaning'.)

> *In einer Hinsicht sind wir nicht ganz ehrlich gewesen.*
> *In gewisser Hinsicht ist das ganze Buch ein Kommentar zu dem Roman.*

In no sense can be **keineswegs**. *In no sense do they have the right to speak for the
nation: Sie haben keineswegs das Recht, für die ganze Nation zu sprechen.* **In a very real
sense**, used to emphasize that something is true, could be **tatsächlich** (cf. REAL) or
im wahren/wahrsten Sinne des Wortes. *Das war das Ziel, das wir uns steckten, und
wir haben es tatsächlich/im wahren Sinne des Wortes erreicht.*

sensitive *adj.*

1. Sensitive is applied to photographic film, paper, etc. and to instruments and
institutions thought of as measuring things.

i. Both **sensitive** and **empfindlich** mean 'reacting to or affected by' a physical
force, substance, or stimulus coming from the outside. *Photographic film is sensitive
to light. Der Film/Die Netzhaut des Auges ist empfindlich für Licht* or *reagiert empfindlich
auf Licht.* For *sensitive to light* there is the compound *lichtempfindlich. Die Zunge ist ein
sehr empfindliches Organ.*

> *Die photographische Lösung ist nicht für Rotlicht empfindlich.*

ii. Sensitive and **empfindlich** are applied to measuring instruments which register very small changes or react to something which is difficult to detect. *Ein
empfindliches Thermometer. Eine empfindliche Waage.*

> *Das Gerät reagiert empfindlich auf die leiseste Erschütterung der Erdoberfläche.*

In fig. use they are applied to people and institutions which are thought of as
measuring or registering things. *Der Aktienmarkt ist empfindlich für politische
Änderungen.*

> *Diese Partei reagiert empfindlich auf jede Änderung in der öffentlichen Meinung.*

iii. An alternative for the last sent. is *Die Partei ist empfänglich für jede Änderung . . .*
Empfänglich means 'particularly able to take in impressions and influences',
'receptive'.

> *Von einem Maler erwartet man, daß er für Schönheit empfänglich ist.*
> *Ihr empfängliches Gemüt war von diesen Erlebnissen erfüllt.*
> *Dieser Politiker zeigte sich empfänglich für jeden Stimmungsumschwung unter den Wählern.*

(Only in a few contexts is *empfänglich* translated as **sensitive** as that could convey
the wrong meaning. *In seinem Zustand (d. h. Krankheit) war er für Zuspruch und
Anteilnahme sehr empfänglich.*)

2. Applied to people and parts of the body, plants, etc., **empfindlich** and often
sensitive also mean that exposure to, or contact with, the agent will result in
pain or some other untoward effect.

> *Empfindliche Haut wird durch zu starke Sonneneinwirkung verletzt.*

Sie ist sehr empfindlich gegen Kälte/gegen Zugluft.

Die Pflanze ist sehr empfindlich und geht in einer ungünstigen Lage bald ein.

3. Sensitive and its G. equivalents vary between or combine two meanings; one is 'easily hurt in the mind' and the other 'receiving impressions easily and quickly', often about another's state of mind.

i. Applied to people, both **sensitive** and **empfindlich** mean 'easily hurt in the mind, easily offended'. *Sei doch nicht so empfindlich! Kinder sind gewöhnlich empfindlich für Beschuldigungen.*

Er ist gegen Kritik sehr empfindlich. Or Ein Autor muß nicht überempfindlich für Kritik sein.

People are said to be sensitive about something relating to themselves when this does not please them and they worry about it. *He is sensitive about his accent.* **Sich etw. sehr zu Herzen nehmen**, 'to take something to heart or to be upset about it', may be an appropriate transl. *Er nimmt sich seine wenig anziehende Erscheinung/seinen Akzent sehr zu Herzen.*

Die Krankenschwester nahm sich den Mißerfolg bei der Prüfung so [sehr] zu Herzen, daß sie beschloß, ihren Beruf aufzugeben.

ii. People who are sensitive to other people's feelings, attitudes, and problems, or to ideas, show a deep understanding of them. *Her remarks show she is sensitive to the problems of the unemployed. A sensitive story about growing up.* In a special sense **sensitive** means 'possessing a fine awareness of the subtleties of a work of art'. *A sensitive interpretation of a piece of music/of a literary work.* Several G. words stress different aspects of this definition. **Feinfühlig** suggests, on the one hand, being able to put oneself in the position of others, in particular to understand their worries, on the other, interest in and responsiveness to art, literature, etc. It always expresses praise. *Er/Sie ist ein sehr feinfühliger Mensch.* **Sensibel** means 'reacting strongly to impressions' and may imply that the person finds it difficult to cope with such impressions. It is usually felt to express a higher degree of the meaning of *feinfühlig*. It also usually expresses praise. *Sie wirkt sehr sensibel.* Only with *zu* and *über-* does it clearly express criticism, but even without these disapproval is sometimes implied. *Der ist aber sensibel!* suggests over-sensitive. *Ein sensibler Mensch* or *ein sensibles Kind* may also suggest that he or she is too easily hurt or offended, or unable to handle situations which arouse emotions. Another related word is **empfindsam**, which also usually expresses praise, but is now confined to educated speech. It implies a strong emotional life, responsiveness to subtle influences, and the ability to feel with others and appreciate their position. *Er/Sie ist [nicht] empfindsam für andere Menschen.* It may, however, express criticism by suggesting that the emotions are more important than the reason, thus excessive. *Dein Freund hat aber eine empfindsame Seele.* The expression *eine empfindsame Geschichte*, though now not common, mostly expresses criticism and implies sentimentality. The idea of feeling with others or with a work of art is most clearly expressed by **einfühlsam**. *Jmd. hat ein Musikstück/einen Text/eine Rolle einfühlsam interpretiert.* **Zartbesaitet**, 'highly sensitive', and **mimosenhaft**, 'over-sensitive', express a note of criticism. *Jmd. hat/ist ein zartbesaitetes Gemut. Bei einem Menschen mit einer solchen mimosenhaften Natur muß man vorsichtig vorgehen.*

Der Junge darf nicht geschlagen werden, er ist doch zu sensibel.

König David war talentiert als Dichter, Musiker und Sänger. Er war ein Mann mit empfindsamer Seele; weich und gutmütig aber war er nicht. Grausamkeit war ihm keineswegs fremd.

Er hat das Musikstück empfindsam/einfühlsam gespielt.

Ich wußte nicht, daß er so zartbesaitet war.

iii. Aufgeschlossen means 'open or receptive to' influences, new ideas, the situation of other people, etc. *Diese heutige Jugend steht dem Problem der Minderheiten*

aufgeschlossener gegenüber als frühere Generationen. Politisch aufgeschlossen is 'interested in politics'. *Aufgeschlossen* can be used to translate *to make people sensitive to*, as the words in 3. ii denote a permanent state. It also suggests a more robust state than the other terms. *Wir wollen erreichen, daß die Leser den Problemen der Arbeitslosen aufgeschlossener gegenüberstehen.* A v. expressing the same meaning is **sensibilisieren**. *Durch dieses Erlebnis ist sie für das Leid der Flüchtlinge sensibilisiert worden.*
iv. In a second sense **feinfühlig** is a syn. of **feinsinnig**. They refer to the way something is put in words and imply that what is said or written combines feeling with brilliance of expression and intellect. One transl. is *sensitive and subtle. Eine feinsinnige Bemerkung. Ein feinsinniger Schriftsteller.*

> *Sie hat die Unterschiede zwischen den verschiedenen Auffassungen feinfühlig charakterisiert.*
> *Er hat ein feinsinniges Kunstwerk/feinsinnige Aphorismen geschrieben.*

4. A **sensitive** subject or issue involves difficult problems and is likely to cause disagreement or strong feeling. **Heikel** means that something can easily cause difficulties or have unpleasant consequences and therefore needs to be treated with great care and tact. **Kitzlig**, lit. 'ticklish' when applied to people, is also used to describe situations and issues. *Das ist eine heikle/kitzlige Sache/Frage, die ein großes Maß an Takt erfordert.*

> *Das Parlament befaßte sich mit der heiklen Frage der Beziehungen zwischen den Rassen.*

separate[ly] *adj.* and *adv.*

1. In the sense 'detached in space, set or kept apart from, or not connected to sth. else', **getrennt** is the general word. It means 'separated' and stresses that two or more things are not joined or combined with something else. Thus *Bewahre das Fleisch getrennt vom Fisch auf!* or *Die Kinder schliefen in getrennten Zimmern.* **Gesondert** is a more formal syn. *Diese Summe bewahre ich gesondert vom übrigen Haushaltsgeld auf.* **Eigen** would probably be preferred to express the meaning of **separate** in *Each child has a separate room*, as 'separate from sth.' is not the paramount idea. *Of his/her own* could equally well be used in E. *Jedes Kind hat ein eigenes Zimmer.* Also *Die Kinder haben eigene/getrennte Zimmer.*

> *Er teilte das Gut in drei gesonderte/getrennte Bauernhöfe auf.*
> *Herr Braun und seine Frau leben getrennt.*   *Jedes Fach benötigt eigene Seminarräume.*
> *Die Bücher über Fontane stehen in einem eigenen Regal.*

2. In the sense 'dealing with or treating sth. separately', both **getrennt** and **gesondert** are used. *Man muß diese Texte getrennt voneinander betrachten. Die spätere Entwicklung wollen wir gesondert behandeln.* **Eigen** can sometimes be used in this context, but it is not an adv. An alternative to *Ich empfehle Ihnen, diesen Themenkreis in einem gesonderten Kapitel zu behandeln* is *in einem eigenen Kapitel.* **Extra** is also used for paying for something separately. *Das Frühstück wird extra bezahlt/berechnet.*

> *Spesen sind bei der Reisekostenabrechnung gesondert aufzuführen.*
> *Ausgaben für Porto und Bürobedarf gehören in getrennte Spalten.*
> *Die Getränke habe ich extra berechnet. Sie sind nicht im Pauschalpreis inbegriffen.*

3. Getrennt and **gesondert** are used for packing, wrapping, or sending things separately. *Bettlaken und Kissenbezüge sollen getrennt verpackt werden. Die Weihnachtsgeschenke gehen heute ab—weil die Uhr zerbrechlich ist, schicke ich sie gesondert.* **Extra**, which means that one item or set of items is packed separately from the rest, is also common; it cannot be used to state that several things are to be packed individually. *Die Kissenbezüge nehme ich auch, aber verpacken Sie sie bitte extra!*

> *Soll ich die Bücher zusammen oder getrennt einpacken?*
> *Die Bücher habe ich in diesen Karton verpackt/gepackt und ich werde die Zeitschriften extra schicken.*
> But *Ich werde Bücher und Zeitschriften getrennt schicken.*

4. Separate also means 'divided from sth. else so as to have an independent existence of its own or by itself'. *That is a separate question* could be *Das ist eine Frage* **für sich**, for/in itself, but for the pl., *Those are separate questions*, **getrennt** is used. *Das sind [zwei] getrennte Fragen.* An alternative to the latter is **verschiedene**, DIFFERENT. *Das sind [zwei] verschiedene Fragen.* **Eigen** also expresses the idea sometimes. *Das ist ein eigener Fragenkomplex, den zu diskutieren hier zu weit führen würde.*

> *Die beiden Großmächte hatten verschiedene/getrennte Einflußgebiete.*
> *Dieser Roman weist zwei verschiedene Handlungsstränge auf.*
> *Über die Beratungen des Auschusses wurde ein eigenes Protokoll angefertigt.*

5. A **separate** entrance is *ein separater Eingang.* **Separat** forms a few compounds. *Das Separatabkommen. Das Separatzimmer.*

6. *To enter* **separately** is **einzeln** *eintreten.* Cf. SINGLE 1.

serious, grave, earnest *adjs.* **Serious** can mean 'grave and thoughtful in disposition, appearance or manner' and can refer to a permanent characteristic. *She looks very serious. He's a very serious pers.* It is also applied to the attitudes displayed by people in particular situations. If behaviour, intentions, and attitude are serious, the people are sincere and are not joking, pretending, or deceiving, and give due care and attention to what they are dealing with. *At first I thought he was continuing the joke, but he was serious. Please be serious! You can't be serious. I've given it a lot of serious thought.* A serious matter, decision, etc. requires much deep thought or thorough consideration. *I think this is a serious matter which deserves serious consideration.* **Grave** and **earnest** differ from **serious** in expressing different degrees of the quality concerned. A person whose appearance is grave looks very serious. Someone who is earnest is extremely serious and sincere, but may be unable to see when something is funny or ridiculous. These distinctions cannot be expressed in G. by single words. The three equivalents, *ernst, ernsthaft,* and less commonly *ernstlich,* can, depending on the situation, translate or be translated by all three E. words.

1. There is considerable overlapping between the three G. words in connection with people, their appearance, and behaviour. The following attempts to give the common uses of each. Both **ernst** and **ernsthaft** suggest as their basic meaning 'not jesting, trifling, or laughing'. In reference to appearance which is permanent, *ernst* is used. *Jmd. hat ein ernstes Gesicht* or *Eine Frau mit ernster Miene saß am Schreibtisch.* For people, *ernst* refers also to the disposition. *Er ist ein ernster Mensch. Er war der ernsteste von allen. Durch diese Enttäuschungen war sie ernster geworden.* Depending on the speaker's views, these statements can be meant as praise or criticism. *Ernst* often has a slightly neg. colouring, just as **serious** or **earnest** may suggest a lack of humour. *Ernsthaft* suggests that someone takes seriously or treats with due earnestness whatever requires such treatment, so that *ein ernsthafter Mensch* is conscientious, careful, correct, and exact in whatever he or she does, i.e. serious when this is called for, but not necessarily all the time. Thus *ernsthaft* refers to the way someone behaves or to what he or she says on a particular occasion. Because of this connotation one would expect *Jmd. machte ein ernsthaftes Gesicht* or *setzte eine ernsthafte Miene auf,* but the distinction is not always clearly observed, and *ernst* also occurs. In addition, *ernsthaft* is not used predicatively (hence *Die Diskussion war sehr ernst*) and is preferred as an adv. except with *nehmen* and *meinen.* Cf. 2. Although *ernste* and *ernsthafte Überlegungen* are both used, the adv. is *ernsthaft. Ich überlege mir ernsthaft, ob ich das nicht tun soll.* Also *Ich habe mich nie ernsthaft mit der Frage beschäftigt.* There also seem to be standard combinations.

Jmd. redet in ernstem Ton is a more or less fixed phr. *Ich möchte ein paar ernste Worte mit dir reden* and *Ich muß ernsthaft mit dir reden/sprechen* seem to be standard expressions. *Eine ernste Angelegenheit* is the normal expression. With *Ermahnungen* and *eine Auseinandersetzung, ernst* is usual. Often either is possible. *Eine ernste Diskussion* is found alongside *eine ernsthafte Diskussion/Aussprache* and *etw. ernsthaft diskutieren/besprechen*. *Ein ernstes [Theater]stück* exists besides *eine ernsthafte Lektüre. Jmd. wurde plötzlich ernsthaft* is used as well as *Jmd. wurde plötzlich ernst und nachdenklich*. With *die Entscheidung*, both *ernst* and *ernsthaft* occur.

> *Er sah sehr ernst aus/war ernst gestimmt.   In ernstem Nachdenken versunken kehrte er heim.*
> *Er dachte lange nach, denn es kam selten vor, daß so ernsthaft zu ihm gesprochen wurde.*
> *Ich habe lange und ernsthaft über die Sache nachgedacht.*
> *Sie stand neben ihm und betrachtete ihn ernsthaft.*
> *Das ist kein Scherz, sondern eine ernsthafte Frage/ein ernsthafter Einwand.*

Ernsthaft also suggests that someone has a firm and sincere purpose and a definite aim and is applied to what people do or intend. Ns. often combined with it are *das Angebot, der Wunsch*, and *die Absicht*. Although *ernsthaft* is the usual word, *ernst* is also found with these ns. and, as explained in 2, is used with *meinen* and *nehmen*. *Ernsthaft* is also used with *der Versuch, die Anstrengungen*, and *die Arbeit*. **Ernstlich** is occasionally found with *Wunsch, Absicht*, and *Anstrengungen* and other actions and, in strict use, stresses more the underlying attitude than the way something is done.

> *Ernsthafte Arbeit kann man das nicht nennen.*
> *Er unternahm den ernsthaften Versuch, die Beziehungen zu seinem Chef zu verbessern.*
> *Sie hatte den ernsthaften/ernstlichen Wunsch, uns zu helfen.*
> *Geblendet von der primitiven Gleichung, daß die Höhe des Lebensstandards gleich Höhe der Menschlichkeit sei, haben wir gar nicht ernsthaft/ernstlich begonnen, den Fortschritt unter dem Gesichtspunkt der erhöhten oder erniedrigten Menschlichkeit zu betrachten.*
> *Sie sind ernsthaft/ernstlich bemüht, den Fall aufzuklären.*

2. i. Be serious or **in earnest about** sth. The everyday expression is **es ernst meinen**. *Hast du es ernst gemeint mit dem Vorschlag?* Somewhat more formal are *War es dir ernst mit dem Vorschlag? Vollkommen* can be added to the first two sents. as an adv.: *Hast du es vollkommen ernst gemeint?* and *War es dir vollkommen ernst mit der Antwort? Das war mein Ernst* means 'I was serious when I said that.' Here *Ernst* is the n. *der Ernst*. A dat., an adj., and phr. with *mit* can be added to *der Ernst. Mir ist es vollkommener Ernst mit dem Versprechen.* The n. occurs in phrs. which correspond to **serious[ly]**, but are mostly formal, such as *Ich meine es im Ernst*. However, *Ich sage es dir im Ernst* is a common expression. *Nun sag mir nochmal im Ernst, ob du, ein eingefleischter Junggeselle, tatsächlich heiraten willst? Etw. in vollem Ernst/allen Ernstes sagen* mean 'to say sth. in all seriousness or seriously'. The first is more usual. *Be serious!* is either *Nun aber im Ernst!* or *Spaß beiseite! (Mit etw. Ernst machen*, to carry out what one has said one would do. *Niemand glaubte, daß sie mit der Drohung, die Firma zu verlassen, Ernst machen würde.)*

ii. Take sth. **seriously** is **ernst nehmen**. *Können wir seine Bemerkungen überhaupt ernst nehmen?*

3. A serious situation, illness, or condition is one which is attended with danger or gives cause for anxiety. *The situation is serious enough to warrant special action. A serious illness.* **Ernst, ernsthaft**, and **ernstlich** all express this meaning. In this sense *ernst* is used with *die Lage* and *der Zustand*. While *Jmd. ist ernstlich krank* is normal, so is *eine ernste Krankheit. Jmd. ist ernstlich erkrankt* and *eine ernsthafte Erkrankung/Verletzung* are found. *Ernsthaft krank* is also possible. *Eine ernste Krise, eine ernsthafte Krise*, and *eine ernstliche Krise* all occur. *Ernstlich* is used only as an attributive adj. or an adv. *Etw. hat ernsthafte/ernstliche Folgen,* but *Die Folgen waren ernst.* A **grave** situation is more worrying or likely to produce more harm than a serious one. It is mostly translated by the same words as **serious**, but they could be strengthened by *äußerst,* if it is possible to add it.

Die Lage ist ernst genug, um besondere Maßnahmen zu rechtfertigen.

Die Wunde hielten wir nicht für ernsthaft/ernst.   Sie haben sich ernsthaft/ernstlich gestritten.

Das hat den Erfolg des Unternehmens ernstlich gefährdet/bedroht.

4. Serious also means 'considerable in quantity or degree'. *I have serious doubts about the plan. Serious losses. Serious damage.* **Ernst** and **ernsthaft** are used with *Mißstände, Mängel,* and *Sorgen,* and with *Zweifel* and *Bedenken. Ich habe ernste/ernsthafte Zweifel an seinen Fähigkeiten. Drei Mitglieder äußerten ernste/ernsthafte Bedenken.* **Ernstlich** is also used with *Sorgen, Mißstände, Zweifel,* and *Gefahr. Jmd./Etw. ist in ernster* or *ernstlicher Gefahr.* In cases in which *schwer* and *schlimm* (cf. BAD) would express the lowest degree, *ernsthaft* is applied to a higher one. Thus *ein ernsthafter Verlust, ein ernsthafter Fehler, ernsthafter Schaden, ein ernsthafter Unfall, eine ernsthafte Niederlage.* (In some contexts this sense and the one defined in 3 run together.) In some contexts **gravierend** translates **serious** and suggests a higher degree of seriousness than *ernst* etc. *Gravierende Verluste. Ein gravierender Fehler. Der Fehler ist nicht gravierend.*

Ich zweifle ernsthaft daran, ob er das schafft.   Sie wurde ernstlich/ernsthaft böse.

Ich habe ihn ernstlich im Verdacht, gelogen zu haben.   Er hat sie ernstlich beleidigt.

I didn't take any serious part in the discussion is *Ich habe mich nicht ernsthaft daran beteiligt.*

5. Seriös implies trustworthy, reliable, morally sound. It is used for people and for things which stand for people, such as *eine seriöse Firma. Ein seriöser Geschäftsmann* is honest and reliable. *Ein seriöser Student* suggests reliability.

serve *v.*

1. *Dienen* + dat. has several meanings most of which are also expressed by **serve**.

i. One meaning of **dienen** is 'to work for or carry out certain duties to benefit a pers. or organization, usually over a fairly long period and for a salary or wages'.

Er hat seinem Land/dem König/der Firma treu/loyal gedient.

Niemand kann zwei Herren dienen.

Er hat seiner Heimatstadt lange Jahre als Stadtdirektor/Bürgermeister gedient.

ii. **Dienen** can refer to service in the armed forces.

Er hat 12 Jahre bei der Bundeswehr/bei der Marine/bei der Luftwaffe gedient.

iii. With people as subj., **dienen** also means 'to work for a cause or some worthwhile aim'.

Mit ihrer freiwilligen Arbeit glaubt sie, einer guten Sache/der sozialen Gerechtigkeit/der Gemeinschaft zu dienen.

iv. With things as subj., **dienen** means 'to help achieve some purpose', *Diese Maßnahmen dienen der Erhaltung des Friedens,* or 'to be used for or fulfil a certain purpose', *Die Spendensammlung dient einem guten Zweck.* In the latter sense *dienen* is commonly found with *zu* + verbal n. meaning 'to be used for', *Ein Messer dient zum Schneiden,* and appears in the form *dazu dienen* + infin., *Ihre Bemerkungen dienten dazu, Mißverständnisse auszuräumen.* While **serve as** suggests that something is used for a purpose because nothing more satisfactory is available, *dienen als* can have this connotation, *Der alte Schuppen diente als Kantine,* but need not, *Edelsteine dienen als Schmuck.*

Das Schloß dient jetzt als Museum/Schule.

Das laß dir als Warnung dienen! Or Das möge dir zur Warnung dienen!

v. Dienen also means 'to help' in some situations. *Womit kann ich dienen?* may still be heard in shops or elsewhere. *Mit dieser Auskunft/Damit war mir wenig/nicht gedient*, it didn't help me or was of no use.

2. Bedienen means 'to serve' in a shop or restaurant or hotel. The obj. in the act. or the subj. in the pass. can only be a person. *Wer hat Sie bedient? Ich werde schon bedient.*

> *Der Kellner/Die Verkäuferin hat die Gäste/die Kunden schnell bedient.*

3. Servieren means 'to serve' in the sense 'to bring to the table' when [a course of] a meal or [a kind of] food or drink is the obj. *Das Abendessen wird um 18.30 h serviert. Man serviert Getränke in den Pausen zwischen den Vorträgen. Die Nachspeise wird gleich serviert.* A dat. can be added. *Sie servierte ihren Gästen Erfrischungen/Kaffee. Wir servieren Ihnen das Abendessen in einer Viertelstunde.* The syn. of G. origin **auftragen** now occurs only in elevated language in relation to formal occasions or ironically. *Das Essen ist aufgetragen. Am Abend trug man den Staatsgästen ein fürstliches Essen auf.*

service *n.* and *v.*

1. Service is applied to an organization or system that provides something the public needs, especially to an official organization or a government department that does a particular job, and to transport and communication facilities. **Services** can refer to what is provided by a local, state, or federal government.

i. In some cases this idea is expressed by **der Dienst** in compounds. *The postal service is der Postdienst.* Also *Der Telefondienst. Der Zolldienst. Der Seenotdienst. Der Gesundheitsdienst. Der diplomatische Dienst. Der Spionageabwehrdienst. Der Krankenwagendienst.* Also *ein Informationsdienst [für Bürger/Touristen].* **Dienste** is used in compounds like *Wohlfahrtsdienste* or *Sozialdienste. Der öffentliche Dienst* is 'the public sector'. *Jmd. ist im mittleren/gehobenen Dienst* suggests a grade or rank in an organization run by some branch of government.

> *Die Beschäftigten im öffentlichen Dienst bekommen eine dreiprozentige Lohn- und Gehaltserhöhung.*
> *Die Sozialdienste in vielen Entwicklungsländern sind verbesserungsbedürftig.*

ii. Bus/train **service**, etc. To state that there is a bus etc. service between two places, **[regelmäßig] fahren/verkehren** can be used. *Busse/Züge fahren [regelmäßig] zwischen Adorf und Kassel.* Pl. ns. expressing the sense are **die [öffentlichen] Verkehrsmittel**, '[public] transport service', and a syn. **die Verkehrsverbindungen**. (The latter can also refer to roads.) *Die öffentlichen Verkehrsmittel sind hier gut und billig. In diesem Teil des Landes waren die Verkehrsverbindungen äußerst schlecht. Verbindung* is also combined with *Bus, die Busverbindung*, and other ns. denoting transport. *Die Flugverbindung. Eine gute/schlechte Zugverbindung. Es gibt eine gute Busverbindung zwischen Duderstadt und Göttingen.* If **service** refers to one train, bus, etc., it is necessary to say e.g. *Dieser Zug/Bus wird in einer Viertelstunde in Manchester ankommen.*

2. Jmdm. einen guten Dienst erweisen is 'to do s.o. a service, a good turn, or favour'. *Er hat mir damit einen guten/schlechten Dienst erwiesen. Ein Dienst ist des anderen wert*, one good turn deserves another. **Gute Dienste leisten** or *tun* is 'to do good service'. *Der Mantel hat mir gute Dienste geleistet.*

3. Bring/put into service or *operation* is **in Dienst stellen** or **in Betrieb nehmen**. The opposite, if permanent, is **außer Dienst stellen**. For temporary withdrawal from service, **vorübergehend stilllegen** is used. *Außer Betrieb* is 'out of service, not working'.

> *Das neue Kraftwerk wird nächste Woche in Betrieb genommen.*
> *Die neue Fähre wurde erst vor zwei Wochen in Dienst gestellt.*
> *Wegen der Mängel, die aufgetreten sind, wurden alle Flugzeuge dieses Typs vorübergehend stillgelegt.*

4. A **church service** is **ein Gottesdienst**. *The wedding service* or *ceremony* is *die [kirchliche] Trauung. A funeral service* is *eine Trauerfeier*.

5. *Jmd. war vierzig Jahre lang im Dienst der Öffentlichkeit/Gemeinschaft tätig* is a neutral statement that someone has worked for the benefit of the community. *Seine/Ihre* **Verdienste** *um die Gemeinschaft* mean that the person has made a considerable contribution and this deserves public recognition. Although *Verdienste* in *jmds. Verdienste als Historiker* is translated as *achievements*, it is also used where E. has **service**. In *In Anerkennung ihrer Verdienste [um die Ureinwohner] wollte das Land sie ehren, Verdienste* would be translated as *her services [to the aborigines]*.

6. Das Service, pronounced as in French, is 'a dinner service, a set of crockery'. *Ein einfaches/geschmackvolles Service für sechs Personen.*

7. i. Service also denotes the state of working for a particular person or organization. *His service with our company ended last week. I would like to participate in service to the community. He was too young for military service in the Second World War.* **Der Dienst** expresses this sense in a few cases, but may sound old-fashioned. *Er steht seit zwanzig Jahren im Dienst der Firma Siemens. Jmd. reist im Dienste seiner Firma* or *im Dienste Gottes/Allahs/des Friedens.* With reference to military service, *Wehrdienst* or *Kriegsdienst* are used. *Jeder taugliche Zwanzigjährige muß zwölf Monate Wehrdienst ableisten. Im zweiten Weltkrieg war er zu jung für den Wehrdienst/Kriegsdienst.* To say that someone has seen service in various parts of the world, the v. *dienen* would be usual. *Er hat überall in der Welt gedient. Dienen* would also translate *participate in service to. Ich möchte der Gemeinschaft dienen. Außer Dienst* means 'retired'.

ii. People's **services** are 'the work done by them, either as part of their employment or voluntarily'. In general statements **Dienste** can be used. *They gave their services free of charge: Sie stellten ihre Dienste kostenlos zur Verfügung. S.o.'s services are no longer required* is *Jmds. Dienste werden nicht mehr gebraucht. Skilled workers are well paid for their services* is more likely to be *Fachkräfte/Gelernte Arbeiter werden für ihre Arbeit gut bezahlt. Ich stehe zu Ihren Diensten* or *Ich stehe Ihnen zu Diensten,* 'I am at your service', are now very formal expressions.

iii. Der Dienst has a broader meaning than the sense of **service** discussed in 7. i and often has to be translated by *work* or *duty. Dienst* is now used mostly in reference to the work of *Beamte,* thus to the *Polizei, Post, Bundesbahn, Bundeswehr,* and *Krankenhäuser.* It is not normally used for work at any level of private industry. Thus *Der Dienst eines Verkehrspolizisten/einer Krankenschwester ist leicht/schwer* etc. *Er hat Dienst,* he is on duty. *Sie tritt heute den Dienst bei einer Behörde an,* 'starts work[ing] there today', but *Sie tritt den Dienst um 20 Uhr an,* 'goes on duty'. *Der Genuß von Alkohol im Dienst ist verboten. Ich gehe zum Dienst* is still heard in the meaning 'I'm going to work', but has mostly given way to *Ich gehe zur Arbeit. Gleich nach dem Dienst/nach Dienstschluß gehen sie schwimmen* could refer to people in the categories listed above or to others, but for both groups *nach der Arbeit* is now usual. *Den Dienst quittieren* means either 'to leave s.o.'s employment' or 'to quit military service'. In compounds *Dienst* denotes any kind of work. *Dienstjahre, Nachtdienst, Sonntagsdienst,* and *Schalterdienst* are not confined to particular occupations. *Ärzte haben Wochenenddienst.*

8. Service also denotes the period during which someone has worked. *She has ten years' service with this firm.* This is **die Dienstzeit** or **die Dienstjahre.**

> *Wenn der Absatz stockt und Personal abgebaut wird, werden diejenigen mit der kürzesten Dienstzeit zuerst entlassen. Sie hatte dreißig Dienstjahre hinter sich.*

9. Die Bedienung is the equivalent of **service** when it describes the process of being served in a shop, restaurant, etc. *Die Bedienung in diesem Restaurant ist gut/schlecht/mittelmäßig/miserabel.*

10. Service also denotes a type of work that a person or organization can provide if wanted or required. *They provide a twenty-four-service. The Post Office can forward your letters; the fee for this service is £6.*
i. In a general statement that a firm offers its services to the public **der Dienst** is used. *Eine Firma bietet ihren Dienst rund um die Uhr an.* When a specific service is meant, the equivalent is **die Dienstleistung**. *Die Post schickt Briefe und Pakete nach; für diese Dienstleistung beträgt die Gebühr 15 Mark. Das Dienstleistungsangebot ist sehr umfangreich*, the range of services offered.
  Viele Bürger wissen nicht, wie viele Dienstleistungen die Bibliothek [an]bietet.
Dienstleistungen is also used like **services** for those jobs in which people are paid to do something for others rather than to produce goods. *Dienstleistungsbetriebe* are 'service industries'.
  Durch die Mehrwertsteuer erhöht sich der Preis von Waren und Dienstleistungen um etwa 15%.
ii. Der Kundendienst can refer to a service made available for use of customers, possibly free of charge, in order to make it easier for them to avail themselves of what the firm, shop, etc. has to offer.
  Als Kundendienst bietet das Kaufhaus eine große Parkfläche und einen Kindergarten.
  Die Lieferung der Waren frei Haus gehört zum Kundendienst.
iii. Der Kundendienst is also the name of that section of a firm which services and repairs cars, appliances, etc.
  Reparaturen und Wartung werden von unserem Kundendienst fachmännisch durchgeführt.
  Die Firma hat Kundendienste in allen größeren Städten. Alternative: *Serviceabteilungen.*
Der Service, pronounced as in E., is often used instead of both senses of *Kundendienst*, and often occurs in judgements about the quality of such service. *Die Lieferung der Waren frei Haus gehört zum Service. Der Service dieser Autowerkstatt ist vorbildlich. Der Kundendienst/Service ist gut/schlecht. Service* can also be used instead of *die Bedienung.* In connection with hotels etc. *Service* suggests more than service at table, rather everything that is offered for the convenience of guests. *Ein altes Hotel mit ausgezeichnetem Service.* Also possible is *Die Dienstleistungen sind hervorragend.*
11. Service *a car* is *ein Auto warten.* Hence the n. *service* in this sense is **die Wartung. Die Inspektion** is also used, but may involve only checking and not any work or repair. *Ich muß das Auto warten lassen*, have the car serviced. *Ich muß das Auto zur Wartung anmelden*, book it in for service.

settle *v.*

1. In relation to people who make their homes in a certain place **settle** can be trans. or intr. The trans. v. means either 'to establish one or more people as residents somewhere', *The king settled peasants on the newly cleared land*, or 'to plant a colony in an area', *The Portuguese settled the newly discovered island.* When intr. **settle** means 'to make one's home permanently' or 'to start living or working' somewhere. *They settled in Tasmania.* In this intr. use **settle** expresses a sense similar to that of **settle down**, meaning 'to begin to live a life which requires permanent residence in one place'. *You must get a job and settle down. He got a job in Wagga and settled [down] there.*
i. The trans. v. when people are obj. is **ansiedeln.** *Der König siedelte Bauern auf dem neu gerodeten Land an.* **Besiedeln** is used when a country or other place is the obj. *Kolonisten haben diese Insel/dieses Land früh besiedelt.* Cf. 1. iii.
ii. One equivalent of the E. intr. use is **sich niederlassen**, to make one's home in a place after having lived somewhere else or having had no permanent place of residence. It also translates **settle down**, but the place must be stated or be replaced by *dort* or a similar expression. *Er wollte sich irgendwo auf dem Lande niederlassen.*

Die Familie verließ nach dem Staatsstreich ihre Heimat und ließ sich in England/in Birmingham nieder.

Er versprach, daß er, sobald der Arbeitsvertrag mit der afrikanischen Firma ausgelaufen sei, sich irgendwo niederlassen und sie heiraten würde. (Here it could be translated as *settle down.*)

Er fand einen Arbeitsplatz in einer Kleinstadt und ließ sich dort nieder.

A special meaning of *sich niederlassen* is 'to start a business' or 'set up practice' as a lawyer or doctor. *Er ließ sich als Rechtsanwalt/als Arzt in Oldenburg nieder.*

iii. A syn. of *sich niederlassen* is **sich ansiedeln**. It is used for individuals or groups. *Jmd./Die Gruppe von Flüchtlingen siedelte sich auf dem Lande/in der Stadt an.* With a changed construction it expresses the meaning of *besiedeln*. *Kolonisten haben sich auf der Insel früh angesiedelt.*

iv. If **settle down** expresses a contrast with someone's previous unsettled life, **seßhaft werden** can be used. *Jmd. wurde in einem Ort seßhaft.* The place need not be stated. *Ich würde gern seßhaft werden. Seßhaft* translates the part. *settled. Du mußt dich nun an ein seßhaftes Leben/an eine seßhafte Lebensweise gewöhnen. Seßhafte und nomadisierende Stämme.*

v. Siedeln, which is always intr., means 'to settle in a hitherto unsettled area and begin to build dwellings and cultivate the land'. It is not used for people in present-day Western society.

Nach einer langen Wanderschaft siedelte der Stamm in einem fruchtbaren Tal.

Kelten siedelten am Oberlauf des Flusses.

2. Sich niederlassen also translates **settle down** when it means 'to sit down and make oneself comfortable' in an armchair etc., usually in anticipation of remaining there for some time. It is a somewhat formal syn. of *sich setzen. Sie schaltete den Fernseher ein und ließ sich in einem Sessel nieder.* Also *Sie machte es sich in einem Sessel bequem.* Cf. COMFORTABLE 1. **Settle back** in an armchair is *sich im Sessel zurücklehnen. Sich niederlassen* also translates **settle** in relation to birds. *Ein Schwarm Vögel ließ sich auf den Ästen des Baumes nieder.*

3. Settle an argument, dispute, strike, etc. means 'to bring to a conclusion acceptable to both sides'.

i. Beilegen means 'to bring a quarrel, argument, dispute, etc. amicably to an end'. The subj. can only be the people involved in the quarrel etc. *Friedlich, gütlich,* or *im guten* are often added.

Zwei oder mehr Menschen legen Streitigkeiten/Differenzen/einen Konflikt/einen Streit bei.

Die Meinungsverschiedenheiten konnten von den Fraktionsmitgliedern glücklicherweise beigelegt werden.

ii. Bereinigen means 'to conclude or settle amicably, bring back to the proper state'. The subj. is also those involved.

Es wird einige Zeit dauern, bis wir alle diese Konfliktpunkte/diese Mißverständnisse/alle Meinungsverschiedenheiten bereinigt haben.

Die meisten Länder verzichten auf die Anwendung von Gewalt, um Streitigkeiten zu bereinigen.

iii. Schlichten implies the intervention of an impartial third person to get people involved in a dispute or quarrel to settle their differences. It translates *settle* and *arbitrate*. It takes an obj., *Er schlichtete den Streit*, or a prep., *Jmd. schlichtete in einem Konflikt* and *Jmd. schlichtete zwischen den Parteien in einem Konflikt. Eine Schlichtungskommission* arbitrates in industrial disputes.

Ich hoffe, daß die Sache geschlichtet werden kann, bevor es zu einem Prozeß kommt.

Es ist mir nicht gelungen, den Streit zu schlichten.

iv. Settle *a strike* can be translated in several ways. *The strike has been settled* can be *Der Arbeitskonflikt (in der Stahlindustrie) ist beendet worden* (cf. END 2) if bringing it to an end is meant. An alternative expression in E. is *Strikers and management have* *reached a settlement.* This could be *Unternehmensleitung und Streikende haben den Arbeitskonflikt beigelegt.* If someone has mediated or arbitrated, the sense could be expressed as *Es ist [der Schlichtungskommission] gelungen, zwischen der Unternehmensleitung und den Streikenden zu schlichten [und den Arbeitskonflikt zu beenden].*

4. Settle a question, meaning 'to decide it one way or the other', is **entscheiden**, to DECIDE. *Um die Frage endgültig zu entscheiden, müssen wir uns alle Dokumente ansehen. Es ist noch nichts entschieden worden,* nothing has been settled yet, none of the questions has been settled/resolved/decided. **Den Ausschlag geben** meant originally 'to tip the scales one way or the other', thus fig. 'to decide or settle the issue, determine the outcome'. *Die Aussage dieses Zeugen gab den Ausschlag zugunsten des Angeklagten.*

> *Haben sie sich entschieden, wo sie ihren Urlaub verbringen wollen?*
> *Wir haben lange darüber diskutiert, ob wir im Urlaub an die See oder ins Gebirge fahren sollten. Den Ausschlag für die Berge gab schließlich das kühle Wetter.*

5. Settle a matter when no conflict is involved is 'to bring it to a conclusion' or 'to come to an agreement about it'. *We still have to settle two matters/this point. When we next meet is still to be settled.*

i. Erledigen implies carrying out a task or dealing with a matter and stresses its completion so that there is no need to bother about it any more. *Erledigt* is the appropriate equivalent when **settled** means 'dealt, finished with'. It translates *settled* with ns. such as *eine Sache* or *Angelegenheit*, 'matter', *ein Fall*, 'case', *der Einwand*, 'objection', and *der Zweifel*, 'doubt'. *Der Fall ist erledigt. Die neue Auskunft erledigt jeden Zweifel. Dieser Einwand läßt sich nicht mit einem Witz erledigen.* The subjunctive may be used in a sent. stating that something is settled. *Damit ist/wäre die Angelegenheit erledigt. Die Sache wäre also erledigt. Sich erledigen* means 'to settle itself' or 'to be settled'. *Der Fall/die Frage hat sich erledigt. Die Angelegenheit hat sich von selbst erledigt.*

ii. The basic sense of **regeln** is 'to bring order to a matter', sometimes by establishing a rule or procedure. It suggests coming to an agreement rather than just dealing with a matter. A matter affecting two parties to a contract, how something is to be carried out, or what is to happen should a certain eventuality arise can be *vertraglich geregelt,* settled or laid down in a contract. Cf. CONTROL 4. *Regeln* is used for settling, dealing with, or arranging a single matter, and, particularly in colloquial speech, it is a syn. of *erledigen. Diesen Punkt müssen wir jetzt regeln. Diese Sache muß geregelt werden. Ich werde das schon mit ihm regeln.* Of a certain task A might ask, *'Machst du das denn?',* to which B would reply, *'Ja. Das regle ich.'* One person might ask another, *'Mensch, (or Du, Jochen), du wolltest ein neues Auto kaufen und dein altes in Zahlung geben. Hast du das geregelt?'* In sloppy language: *'Hast du das geregelt gekriegt?' Sich regeln* is a syn. of *sich erledigen. Die Sache wird sich regeln,* will resolve or settle itself, sort itself out.

> *Ich habe noch einiges zu regeln.   Wir haben die Sache auf gütlichem Wege geregelt.*
> *Wir müssen Zeit und Ort der nächsten Sitzung noch regeln.*
> *Wir müssen diese Angelegenheit noch regeln/erledigen.*
> *Wie die Zahlung zu erfolgen hat, wird vertraglich/durch Gesetz/vernünftig geregelt.*

Settle one's affairs, i.e. 'to put them in order before undertaking a long journey etc.', is *seine Angelegenheiten regeln* or *ordnen.*

iii. When **settle** implies an arrangement or agreement, **ausmachen** or **abmachen**, 'to arrange', or **sich einigen** and its syns. may be appropriate. Cf. ARRANGE 2 and AGREE 1. In the following sents. **settle** could be the equivalent. *Das muß er mit sich/ mußt du mit dir allein abmachen/ausmachen* and *Das muß sie für sich abmachen* all imply settling or deciding something for oneself. *Macht das unter euch aus!,* settle it among yourselves. *Wir müssen noch ausmachen, wann wir uns wieder treffen. Wir* *müssen den Termin für die nächste Sitzung noch ausmachen.* So that's settled [then] is *Das ist also abgemacht.* It's all settled is *Wir haben alles abgemacht/ausgemacht* or *Wir haben uns über alles geeinigt.*

> *Habt ihr euch über den Preis geeinigt?* (settled the question of price)
>
> *Der Minister überließ es den Botschaftern, sich über die Einzelheiten zu einigen/verständigen* (left it to the ambassadors to settle the details).

iv. Settle as a legal term, meaning 'to reach an amicable agreement with s.o. as a result of mutual compromise', is **sich mit jmdm. vergleichen.** *Die streitenden Parteien haben sich verglichen.* They settled out of court is *Sie haben sich außergerichtlich/ außerhalb des Gerichtes/auf nicht-gerichtlichem Wege verglichen.* That two people reach a settlement or agreement in a non-legal situation can be expressed by **sich arrangieren.** *Er verstand es, sich mit seinem Gegner zu arrangieren. Die beiden Kontrahenten haben sich arrangiert.*

6. Settle a bill or account is **bezahlen** or **begleichen.** Cf. PAY. **Settle up** with s.o. is **mit jmdm. abrechnen.** The fig. sense means 'to settle a score with s.o.' or 'to settle accounts with s.o.' For examples see CALCULATE 3. vi.

7. Settle money/property on a person. The general term is **überschreiben** or **übereignen,** to transfer. *Er überschrieb/übereignete das Haus seiner Tochter.* If a will is implied, the technical term is **vermachen,** to bequeath. Cf. INHERIT. Also used is **jmdn. bedenken mit,** to remember or include in a will. *Der Onkel hatte sie in seinem Testament mit einer größeren Summe bedacht.*

8. Dust, sediment, mud, etc. **settles** is expressed by **sich absetzen.** *Der Schlamm setzt sich am Boden ab.*

> *Wir müssen warten, bis der Staub sich absetzt, bevor wir anfangen zu streichen.*

9. Settle s.o. **down** means 'make s.o. become calm' and **settle down** 'become calm'. These two senses can be expressed by **beruhigen** and **sich beruhigen.** *Der Lehrer bemühte sich, die Klasse zu beruhigen. Die Mutter beruhigte das weinende Kind. Warte, bis die Kinder sich beruhigt haben, bevor du mit der Stunde anfängst.*

10. *A feeling* **settles** *on a person or place.* Sich bemächtigen + gen. is 'to take possession of'. *Eine düstere Stimmung bemächtigte sich der Partei nach dieser Wahlniederlage.* Alternatives are *Ein Gefühl überkommt jmdn.* or *kommt über jmdn.*—these two expressions are synonymous. *A peculiar hardness settled on his face: Sein Gesicht nahm einen seltsam harten Ausdruck an.* Of things: *Stille kam über den Wald* or *Im Wald wurde es wieder still. Im Dorf trat Stille wieder ein* suggests it had not been quiet before. For *eintreten* cf. OCCUR 3. ii. *Dunkelheit/Nebel senkte sich/legte sich über das Tal.*

severe, strict, stern *adjs.*

1. The primary sense of **severe** is 'rigorous in punishment or condemnation, liable to treat people harshly, and unwilling to forgive their offences or weaknesses'. Thus in reference to the treatment of offenders, it means 'unsparing in the exaction of a penalty, not given to leniency', and can be applied to people, *a severe judge, He punished them severely,* and to such things as a (prison) sentence, punishment, penalty, or a law, *Martial law is very severe on such offenders.* Whether **severe** expresses criticism depends on the circumstances. If a severe punishment is meted out for a trifling offence, **severe** expresses condemnation, but people say that certain criminals need to be severely dealt with without expressing disapproval. In other situations **severe** suggests harshness and lack of leniency resulting from a rigid observance of standards and regulations. *A severe taskmaster. A severe disciplinarian.* To be **severe on** s.o. is 'to treat him or her harshly either as punishment or in general'. In reference to a critic or to criticism, censure, reproof, etc., **severe** means 'passing harsh or sarcastic judgement on'. *I was his severest critic.* **Strict**, applied to people, means 'not tolerating behaviour which is considered improper, impolite, disobedient, or not in accordance with the rules'. *Formerly parents were much stricter than they are now. A strict upbringing. They were strict with their children.* **Stern** means 'very serious and expecting to be obeyed'. *She had a stern father who never praised her.* **Streng** can express all these meanings. Its primary sense is 'not given to leniency, indulgence, or mercy, insisting rigorously that regulations, standards, and discipline be maintained'. The meaning it expresses varies between 'severe' and 'strict'.

i. In reference to punishment, penalties, judgements, and reprimands, **streng** is the main equivalent of **severe**. *Der Lehrer hat den Jungen streng bestraft/verwarnt/ zurechtgewiesen. Das Gericht fällte ein strenges Urteil/verhängte eine strenge Strafe. Ein strenger Richter. Strenge Vorwürfe.* If we put the adjs. often associated with *die Strafe* in ascending order of severity, we get *mild, gerecht, streng, hart, schwer.* If we imagine a scale of punishment from the minimum to the maximum, *eine strenge Strafe* suggests more than half the permitted penalty, but it does not normally express disapproval. If **severe** implies an adverse judgement on the severity of the punishment, it is best to use **hart** or **schwer**, harsh. *Eine harte/schwere Strafe. Er wurde hart/schwer bestraft. Hart gegen* translates **severe on**. *Der Lehrer war hart gegen diesen Schüler.*

> *Das Gericht hat für dieses Verbrechen eine strenge Strafe verhängt.*
> *Die beiden wurden streng bestraft.*

ii. In relation to criticism and critical judgements, **streng** also translates **severe**. Although it means 'not mild', *streng* does not suggest that the judgement is unjust. *Er ist ein strenger Kritiker/übt strenge Kritik. Sie hat die Arbeit streng beurteilt. Ich war sein strengster Kritiker. Bei seiner Beurteilung des Stückes hat er strenge Maßstäbe angewandt/angelegt.* **Hart** and **scharf** express an adverse judgement on the severity of the criticism. *Sie urteilen hart/üben harte/scharfe Kritik.*

iii. **Streng** is frequently understood as 'strict' and mostly implies no criticism of what it is applied to. People say, *'Der Lehrer ist streng, aber gerecht.'* Although the judgement implied depends on the speaker's attitude, *streng* usually expresses criticism only when used with *zu* or sometimes *sehr*. Common expressions are *ein strenger Lehrer, ein strenger Aufseher, eine strenge Erziehung, strenge Aufsicht, strenge Kontrolle.*

> *Die Eltern sind zu streng mit/zu den Kindern/ . . . haben die Kinder streng erzogen.*
> *Er ist gegen sich selbst und gegen andere sehr streng.*
> *Hoffentlich war man nicht zu streng mit ihm/ . . . hat man ihn nicht mit übergroßer Strenge behandelt.*

2. A person whose appearance is severe looks unfriendly and lacking in kindness or humour. *She wore a habitually severe expression.* **Stern** is also applied to the way people speak, *'Give that to me!' he said sternly,* to what they say, *He gave them a stern warning,* and to someone's looks or expression, *He looked very stern all the time. The teacher looked at him sternly.* In reference to appearance and tone of voice, **streng** translates **severe** or **stern**. *Der neue Lehrer sah streng aus/sah den Jungen streng an. 'Wo wart ihr so lange?' fragte der Vater streng.*

> *Er ging auf den Jungen zu und sagte streng/mit strenger Stimme, 'Her damit!'*
> *Sie sah ihn mit strengem Blick/mit strengen Augen/mit strenger Miene an.*
> *Mir gegenüber hat er einen sehr strengen Ton angeschlagen.*
> *Sie macht immer einen sehr strengen Eindruck.*   *Mach' nicht so ein strenges Gesicht!*

3. Another sense of **stern** is 'very severe and strictly enforced'. *People are beginning* *to call for sterner measures.* **Streng** can translate this sense. *Die Leute fordern/Die Öffentlichkeit fordert strengere Maßnahmen.* **Scharf** is applied to measures and actions taken against people. It usually suggests that the strong measures taken are necessary or deserved, but sometimes implies misgivings about their severity. *Man forderte scharfe Maßnahmen. Die Polizei griff scharf durch,* took strong action. *Gegen Plünderer wurde scharf vorgegangen.* An alternative is **hart**, *harte Maßnahmen,* but this would normally suggest an adverse judgement on their severity (except perhaps if the speaker considered harsh measures necessary). In *Er hat uns hart behandelt, hart* means 'harshly', 'very severely'.

4. Strict means 'firmly maintained and to be obeyed absolutely' in reference to rules, orders, obligations, etc. Here **streng** is also used, but **strikt** is not unusual. Both mean that a rule, order, etc. has to be followed exactly and that no exception is tolerated. Hence *strenge* or *strikte Disziplin, ein strenger/strikter Befehl, die strenge/ strikte Einhaltung der Vorschriften, strenge/strikte Geheimhaltung,* but only *streng geheim,* top-secret. The adv. *streng* means 'not deviating in any way from the regulation, order, etc.' *Ich halte mich streng an die Anweisung/die Vorschriften. Sie haben die vereinbarten Bedingungen streng eingehalten.* The superlative is often used for emphasis.

> *Wir haben die strenge/strikte Anweisung erhalten, nichts darüber zu sagen.*
> *Diese Sache ist streng vertraulich. Ich bitte dich um strenge Verschwiegenheit.*
> *Werden strengere Gesetze über den Besitz von Waffen zu einer Verringerung der Gewalttätigkeit führen?*
> *Diese Leute hatten eine strenge Moral/strenge Anstandsregeln/strenge Ansichten.*
> *Die Soldaten achteten darauf, daß das über die Stadt verhängte nächtliche Ausgangsverbot streng befolgt wurde.   Rauchen ist streng/aufs strengste verboten/untersagt.*

5. Strict is applied to people who follow carefully and exactly the principles, rules, and conventions of a particular group. This meaning can be conveyed by **streng**. A strict vegetarian is *ein strenger Vegetarier* or, as an adv., *Jmd. lebt streng vegetarisch. Ein strenger Katholik* is also found. In everyday speech, one sense of **stramm** is used with the same meaning and is mostly slightly pejorative. *Ein strammer Katholik/Sozialdemokrat/Marxist.*

6. Strict and sometimes **severe** are applied to thought and intellectual operations and mean 'conforming to an exact standard of mental effort, rigorously accurate and exact'. *Severe/Strict standards of scholarship. Strict logic.* **Streng** also carries this sense. *Eine strenge Logik. Sie wandten eine streng wissenschaftliche Methode an/sind streng methodisch vorgegangen.*

7. Strict, used with the n. **sense**, refers to the basic and precise meaning of a word. *He may not be lying in the strict sense of the word, but he's certainly not telling us the whole truth. That is not strictly true.* This is also **streng**, but for the adv. it is necessary to use **strenggenommen**, strictly speaking.

> *Vielleicht lügt er nicht im strengen/strengsten Sinne des Wortes, aber die volle Wahrheit sagt er uns auch nicht.   Strenggenommen ist das nicht wahr/falsch.*

8. In reference to works of art or architecture, **strict** means 'conforming exactly to a certain style or principle'. *The author adheres to the strict form/structure of a classical drama.* **Streng** has this sense. *Der strenge Aufbau des Dramas/des Chorals/der Fuge* or *strenge Symmetrie* or *der klassisch strenge Stil des Bauwerks.*

9. In reference to architecture **severe** means 'shunning ornamentation, austere, or plain', a sense also conveyed by **streng**. *Der strenge Stil der romanischen Kirche.* In reference to clothes, *streng* is sometimes applied to the simple way something is made. *Der strenge Schnitt eines Kostüms.* When **severe** means 'SIMPLE', it is best expressed by **schlicht**. *Das Bild eines Mannes in der schlichten Kleidung eines Puritaners.*

10. Severe means 'making great demands on one's powers or resources' in expressions like *to subject s.o. to a severe test* or *a competitive examination of the severest kind.* **Streng** is used with *Prüfung, Untersuchung,* and *Verhör,* 'interrogation'. *Ich wurde einer strengen Prüfung/einem strengen Verhör unterzogen.* **Auf eine harte Probe stellen**, 'to put to a severe test or through a severe ordeal', may be appropriate in some circumstances. *Diese weitschweifigen Antworten stellten meine Geduld auf eine harte Probe.*

11. Applied to impersonal conditions such as the weather, **severe** means 'inflicting physical hardship'. **Streng** is restricted to winter, *ein strenger Winter,* and cold, *strenge Kälte.* In *rauhes Wetter* and *ein rauher Winter,* **rauh** means 'unpleasantly or bitterly cold'. **Hart** also expresses this sense. *Ein harter Winter. Severe alpine conditions* could be *die harten Wetterverhältnisse im Gebirge. Severe heat* is **starke** or **große Hitze.** *The conditions were too severe to effect a rescue by boat* has to be expressed by other words. *Der Seegang war zu heftig, als daß man die Schiffbrüchigen mit einem Boot hätte retten können;* or *Bei so starkem Seegang konnte man die Schiffbrüchigen . . . nicht retten.*

12. Severe denotes an increased degree of something bad or serious and is often translated by **schwer** and **schlimm.** Both mean 'BAD'. The idea of a higher degree expressed by **severe** cannot be shown. *Schwere Verluste. Schwerer Schaden. Jmd. wurde [sehr] schwer verwundet. Eine schwere Krankheit. Ein schwerer Anfall. Severe economic conditions* can only be *schlimme/schlechte wirtschaftliche Zustände. Schwer behindert,* applied to people, means 'severely handicapped'. **Stark** or **heftig** translate *severe pain, starke/heftige Schmerzen,* and *severe pressure, Jmd./Etw. setzt jmdn. unter starken Druck. Severely hamper* can be *stark behindern* or *sehr/besonders erschweren. Der hohe/starke/rauhe Seegang hatte die Rettung stark behindert/besonders/sehr erschwert. A severe shortage* is *eine große Knappheit.*

Der Brand hatte die Schule schwer beschädigt.
Das Schiff wurde bei dem Zusammenstoß stark beschädigt.
Die kleinen Länder wurden vom Preisrückgang für Rohstoffe schwer getroffen (hard/severely hit).
Der Absatz von Waren der heimischen Industrie wurde durch die billigen Importe stark beeinträchtigt.

shake *v.*

1. Trans. use. S.o./Sth. **shook** a person/thing.
i. Schütteln is the general term for making something move vigorously backwards and forwards or up and down. It is applied to people, to parts of the body, and things, and ranges from a mild action in *Er schüttelte den Kopf* or *schüttelte mit dem Kopf* to a relatively strong one. With people as subj. and obj. it usually suggests anger and an attempt to bring the person to his or her senses, but it may occasionally imply shaking someone out of an indecisive state or a condition of inertia, for which *rütteln* is the usual v. Cf. 1. ii. *Schütteln* is also used for shaking something e.g. from a tree or out of a bottle etc. It can also be refl. *Der Hund schüttelte sich. Er schüttelte sich vor Ekel.*

Schüttle mal die Milch! Die ganze Sahne ist oben.   *Der Löwe schüttelte die Mähne.*
Im Zorn über die unverschämten Bemerkungen des Jungen faßte ihn der Lehrer an den Schultern und
*   schüttelte ihn.*   *Schüttle mal den Staub aus/von dem Teppich!*
Du kannst die Pflaumen von den Bäumen schütteln.   *Das Schluchzen schüttelte ihren Körper.*
Um die Frage zu verneinen, schüttelte er den Kopf.   *Vor Gebrauch schütteln!*

Derivatives. **Abschütteln** means 'to shake off'. *Ab* is optional if a phr. with *von* is present, *Ich schüttelte den Schnee vom Mantel [ab],* but *Ich schüttelte den Staub ab.* The obj. can be a person. *Es gelang ihr schließlich, ihren Verfolger abzuschütteln.*

Ausschütteln is 'to shake out'. *Man schüttelt die Tischdecke/einen Sack aus* or *den Sand [aus dem Sack] aus.* **Aufschütteln** is 'to shake sth. consisting of solid particles up so that the contents are evenly distributed'. *Man schüttelt das Federbett/die Kissen auf.* **Durchschütteln** is 'to shake a liquid thoroughly'. *Man muß die Medizin gut durchschütteln.*

ii. When it is trans., **rütteln** mostly refers to situations in which one person rouses another from sleep or takes someone by the arm or shoulders in order to arouse him or her from a particular state, lethargy, melancholy, irresolution, etc. It denotes the same motion as *schütteln* but suggests a stronger action. The derivatives **wachrütteln** and **aufrütteln** mean 'to rouse from sleep', but *rütteln* is used without a prefix with the phr. *aus dem Schlaf.* Both derivatives are used for arousing someone's moral sense etc. *Man rüttelt jmds. Gewissen wach* or *Er versuchte, die anderen aus ihrer Gleichgültigkeit aufzurütteln.*

> *Er packte den Jugendlichen an den Schultern und rüttelte ihn, um ihn von seiner Grübelei abzubringen.*
> *Mein Vater kam ins Schlafzimmer und rüttelte mich aus dem Schlaf/rüttelte mich wach/auf.*

iii. Applied to a thing which cannot move, **rütteln an** means 'to take hold of or apply force to' and 'to move strongly or try to do so'. The intention may be to get a door etc. open. The subj. can be a person or an impersonal agent, such as the wind or storm. *Der Wind rüttelte an den Fensterläden,* it shook the shutters. *Der Wind rüttelte an den Bäumen* is the usual constr. but an acc. is possible: *Der Sturm rüttelte die Bäume.*

> *Sie rüttelte an der Türklinke, aber die ließ sich nicht öffnen.*

iv. Erschüttern means 'to cause to shift with a strong movement' and is used with large objects.

> *Ein Erdbeben hat die Stadt erschüttert. Die Stadt wurde durch einen Erdstoß erschüttert.*
> *Die Explosion erschütterte das Gebäude.*

v. Shake one's hand/fist at s.o. is **jmdm. mit der Hand/Faust drohen**. *Den Jungen, die der Bauer in Verdacht hatte, Äpfel stehlen zu wollen, drohte er mit der Hand/Faust/mit dem Stock.*

2. Intr. use. A pers./thg. **shook**.

i. Rütteln is used with things and vehicles as subj. *Die Fenster rüttelten. Der uralte Zug hat furchtbar gerüttelt.* It is often combined with *schütteln. Der Wagen rüttelte und schüttelte auf dem holprigen Pflaster.*

ii. For parts of the body **zittern**, 'to tremble or shake', is used.

> *Ihr zitterte die Hand so sehr, daß sie die Tassen beinahe fallengelassen hätte.*
> *Er zitterte vor Schreck am ganzen Körper.*   *Ihre Stimme/Hand zitterte vor Aufregung.*

iii. Beben is a stronger movement. *Die Erde bebte,* quaked. For people: *Jmds. Knie bebten. Er bebte am ganzen Körper. Ihre Stimme bebte vor Empörung. Er bebte vor Lachen,* his sides shook with laughter.

3. Fig. uses of **shake**.

i. An etw. rütteln expresses the fig. sense 'to change, affect'. *Die neue Zeit rüttelte an den alten Vorstellungen. Die Entscheidung ist gefallen—es läßt sich nicht daran rütteln.*

> *Die Antwort ist eindeutig. Es ist daran nicht zu rütteln.*

ii. Erschüttern is used for civil disturbances. *Das Land wurde von Hungerrevolten/ schweren Unruhen erschüttert.*

iii. Like **shake** with someone's faith, convictions, courage, reputation, etc., or evidence as obj., **erschüttern** means 'to affect strongly', 'to make less strong than it was'.

> *Dieser Vorfall erschütterte unser Vertrauen in seine Fähigkeiten.*
> *Ihr Mut/Ihr Glaube/Ihre Überzeugung war durch nichts zu erschüttern.*

Die Verteidigung versuchte, die von dem Staatsanwalt beigebrachten Beweise zu erschüttern.

iv. Erschüttern is the equivalent when **shake** means that something unexpected or frightening makes someone feel upset or frightened or unable to think clearly and calmly. *Der plötzliche Tod des Freundes hatte ihn tief erschüttert. Er war durch/über das Scheitern aller seiner Pläne tief erschüttert.*

v. Vs. related to the last sense of *erschüttern* are **schockieren** and **schocken**. The former means 'to shock' applied to things which people find offensive or morally wrong. *Die Nacktphotos hatten sie schockiert. Schocken* is stronger and akin to *erschüttern*. It is a *Fremdwort* which is much used by some native speakers, but avoided by others. *Der Schock* is 'mental upset caused by severe misfortune or sth. unexpected'. The sense conveyed by *der Schock* can be expressed by *erschüttern. Durch die Todesnachricht bekam sie einen schweren Schock/war sie tief erschüttert.*

> *Er war tief geschockt/erschüttert, als er sah, wie völlig unvorhersehbare Ereignisse den Familienbetrieb an den Rand des Bankrotts brachten.*

4. Shake hands with s.o. or s.o.'s hand is either **jmdm. die Hand geben** or **jmdm. die Hand schütteln**. *Als er mich sah, kam er auf mich zu und gab mir die Hand.* They shook hands is *Sie gaben sich die Hand.* When an adv. is included, only *schütteln* is possible. *Er schüttelte mir herzlich die Hand.*

> *Geben/Schütteln wir uns die Hand, und vertragen wir uns wieder!*

shame, disgrace *ns.*

1. Shame is 'a distressed feeling, a painful loss of self-respect, caused by wrong, dishonourable, or foolish behaviour or a by a failure by oneself or one's family, etc.' *He felt deep shame at having told a lie/at having failed the examination. I lowered my face/hung my head in shame.* A second sense is 'the capacity to feel shame'. *He has no shame. They are quite without shame.* **Die Scham** has both these meanings. In the second sense **das Schamgefühl**, 'sense of shame', is often preferred.

> *Er empfand/fühlte eine tiefe Scham, daß er gelogen hatte/daß/weil er die Prüfung nicht bestanden hatte. Voll Scham dachte sie an ihre Fehler/Mißerfolge. Nur keine falsche Scham!*
> *Alle Gäste erröteten vor Scham wegen dieser geschmacklosen Bemerkungen.*
> *Er hätte sich am liebsten vor Scham in ein Mauseloch verkrochen.*
> *Jmd. hat keine Scham/besitzt kein Schamgefühl.*   *Sie sind ohne jegliches Schamgefühl.*
> *Sein Schamgefühl verbot [es] ihm, zu einer solchen Veranstaltung zu gehen.*

2. Shame also means 'the state of having lost the good opinion of others, being scorned by them, dishonour'. *He brought shame upon his family.* **Disgrace** means 'loss of respect or reputation in the eyes of others' and is a syn. *A man who is sent to prison for a crime brings disgrace [up]on himself and his family. There is no disgrace in being poor.*

i. The equivalent of both these senses is **die Schande**, a state in which one's good name, reputation, or honour has been greatly harmed so that one is looked down on by others. When a thing is subj., the v. used is *bringen, Etw. bringt jmdm. Schande;* when a person is subj., the v. is *machen, Jmd. hat seinem Namen/seiner Familie Schande gemacht. Schande* is not always used in its strict sense. *Mach' uns keine Schande!* may mean that the person addressed should behave properly or acquit him/herself well in some competition and has a meaning like 'Don't disgrace us!' *Zu meiner Schande* is 'to my shame' but may not always be meant very seriously. *Mit Schimpf und Schande* means 'in complete/utter disgrace'.

> *Sein Benehmen war eine Schande für die ganze Familie.*
> *Konnte man der alten Frau nicht diese Schande ersparen?*   *Es ist keine Schande, arm zu sein.*
> *Der Kanzler sagte, Ausländerfeindlichkeit und Antisemitismus seien eine Schande für Deutschland.*
> *Zu meiner Schande muß ich gestehen, daß ich nicht zu ihm gegangen bin, wie ich versprochen hatte.*

Nachdem das ganze Ausmaß seiner Untat bekannt geworden war, wurde er mit Schimpf und Schande davongejagt.

ii. Be in disgrace when this means 'to no longer enjoy the favour of one or a few people whose favour one previously enjoyed' or 'to have incurred s.o.'s displeasure' is **bei jmdm. in Ungnade sein. Bei jmdm. in Ungnade fallen** denotes the action which results in such a state.

3. i. *It's a* **disgrace/shame** *that* . . . If something is a disgrace, it is a cause of shame or discredit. *It's a disgrace to the city authorities that these slums are still standing.* **Schande** also expresses this sense. Common expressions are *Es ist eine Schande* or *Ich finde es eine Schande, daß* . . . *Es ist eine Schande für die Stadtverwaltung, daß diese Slums noch stehen.*

> *Die Anwendung von Waffengewalt, um Streitigkeiten zu beseitigen, ist eine Schande für die Regierungen aller Länder.   Der schlechte Zustand der Straßen ist eine Schande.*
> *Es ist eine Schande, daß einige Palästinenser immer noch in Flüchtlingslagern leben.*

Used with *real,* or *crying,* **shame** is a syn. of **disgrace** and is translated as **eine wahre Schande.** *Es ist eine wahre Schande, daß so viele Menschen obdachlos sind,* it's a crying shame that so many people are homeless.

ii. In a much weaker sense *it's a* **shame** means 'it is regrettable' and is a syn. of *pity. It's a shame/pity that the rain spoilt your holiday. It's a shame* or *pity* is **es ist schade** or the stronger **jammerschade.** *Es ist schade, daß der Regen euch den Urlaub verdorben hat. Schade, daß du nicht dabei warst. Es ist jammerschade, daß ihr schon gehen müßt.* Sth. *is a real shame* can fit definition i or ii. Which transl. is used depends on the seriousness of the situation described. *Es ist eine wahre Schande, daß diese armen Kinder kein Zuhause haben. Es ist wirklich schade, daß so wenig Studenten dabei waren.*

iii. Der Schandfleck refers to something which is aesthetically offensive and at the same time a disgrace. *Diese Slums sind ein Schandfleck in der Stadt. Die Mülldeponie ist ein Schandfleck in der Landschaft.*

shame, be ashamed *vs.*

1. Sich schämen means 'to feel ashamed', mostly about one's own actions, but sometimes about the actions of someone with whom one is associated. It is used alone, *Nach seinen Wutausbrüchen mußte er sich immer schämen,* with a gen., *Später schämte er sich seiner Feigheit,* or with an infin., *Ich schämte mich, einen so schweren Fehler gemacht zu haben,* or *Ich würde mich schämen, so zu handeln.* In everyday speech the gen. is often replaced by *wegen, Ich schämte mich wegen dieser dummen Bemerkung,* or *für, Er schämte sich für sein Versagen* and *Ich schäme mich für dich* (instead of *Ich schäme mich deiner*). The imp. *Schäm' dich!* to which an infin. may be added, *Schäm dich, so zu lügen!,* means that you ought to be ashamed of yourself for doing such a thing. A lit. transl. of the E. words is also used: *Du solltest dich schämen, so mit deiner Mutter zu sprechen.*

> *Alle Mitarbeiter schämten sich für das Verhalten ihres Vorgesetzten.*
> *Vor diesem Mann schämte ich mich wegen meiner schmutzigen Kleidung.*
> *Ich schämte mich lange einzugestehen, daß ich gelogen hatte.*

2. Beschämen means 'to shame s.o., to cause s.o. to experience shame, or put s.o. to shame'. *Das dumme Verhalten des Chefs hat alle Mitarbeiter beschämt.* It is often found in this primary sense as a pres. part., *Dein Verhalten ist beschämend,* or as a past part., *Ich schlug beschämt die Augen nieder. Ich war tief beschämt* expresses the same meaning as *ich schämte mich sehr.* **Beschämen** often occurs in contexts which suggest that the good qualities shown by one person put others to shame because they contrast with their own behaviour. *Sie beschämt alle durch ihre Güte* or *Sein Großmut hat uns alle beschämt.* Like *She put the others to shame, Sie hat alle anderen*

beschämt can mean that she was much better than the others at some activity.
Sein rücksichtsloses Verhalten während der letzten Zeit ist zutiefst beschämend/hat uns alle beschämt.
*Und als Rut sich aufmachte zu lesen, gebot Boas seinen Knechten und sprach: Laßt sie auch zwischen
den Garben lesen und beschämt sie nicht!* (Ruth 2: 15. *Lesen* here = 'to glean'.)
Durch ihre Großzügigkeit beschämten die Kinder alle Erwachsenen.

shameful, shameless, brazen, barefaced *adjs.* Schändlich means 'shame-
ful, disgraceful, of such a nature that it is felt to bring disgrace'. It describes
morally reprehensible behaviour as an adj., *schändliche Taten, eine schändliche
Absicht*, or as an adv., *Er hat uns schändlich hintergangen.* An alternative to the adv.
is the phr. *in schändlicher Weise. Sie haben uns in schändlicher Weise im Stich gelassen.* It
also has the looser sense 'very bad'. *Wir mußten für einen schändlichen Lohn arbeiten.*
Schamlos means 'shameless, brazen', i.e. 'not trying to hide behaviour which is
offensive to others', 'without any sense of decency'. *Eine schamlose Person.
Schamloses Benehmen. Schamlose Ausdrücke/Gebärden.* In another sense it means
'unscrupulous, shameless, barefaced', 'not caring how wrongly one is behaving'
and is a syn. of *unverschämt.* It is used as an adj. or an adv. *Eine schamlose
Beleidigung/Beschuldigung/Frechheit. Er hat uns schamlos belogen.* **Unverschämt** is a
much-used word which suggests effrontery, the lack of all sense of shame or
decency in the way someone acts, or takes or demands things from others. It is
translated as **shameless, brazen, barefaced**, *blatant*, or *impudent. Ein unverschämter Lügner. Eine unverschämte Lüge. Ein unverschämter, zudringlicher Kerl. Uns
gegenüber benahmen sie sich unverschämt. (Ein unverschämter Preis,* outrageous.)
Verschämt means 'bashful'. *Er sah sie verschämt an.*)
Für diese schändlichen Verbrechen wurde die Bande hart bestraft.
Er hat uns in schändlicher Weise betrogen.
Durch seine schamlosen Forderungen brüskierte er seine Verhandlungspartner.
Diese Firma beutet die Arbeiterinnen in schamloser Weise aus.
Ihr unverschämtes Benehmen verschlug allen die Sprache.
Die Schüler gaben von Tag zu Tag unverschämtere Antworten.
Nachdem sie ein paar Gläser getrunken hatten, wurden sie unverschämt.

shape, form *ns.* Some uses of **figure** *n.* The two G. ns. *die Form* and *die Gestalt*
correspond to some senses of the E. words, but they are used in different contexts
and have special meanings.

1. Shape is 'the outer form, the total effect produced by the outline of sth.' *The
building has a strange shape/has the shape of a ship. The garden is in the shape of a triangle. The shape of s.o.'s head. Clouds of different shapes.* **Form** also denotes the outward or visible appearance. *The form/shape of a crystal. The arena is in the form/shape
of a U. The human form.*
i. The general distinction in current usage is that **die Gestalt** is used in this sense
when talking of human beings or animals, and *die Form* elsewhere. Although this
will never be wrong, there is some overlapping. *Die menschliche Gestalt* is 'the
human form'. *Gestalt* in other contexts can mean 'figure' or 'stature'. *Sie hat eine
schöne Gestalt* (now usually *Figur*). *Er ist von hoher Gestalt. Jmd. erscheint in seiner wahren
Gestalt* means 'in his true nature or colours'.
Jmd. hat eine kräftige/schlanke/schmächtige/stämmige/gedrungene Gestalt.
Viele hielten den Diktator für den Teufel in menschlicher Gestalt.
Er ist von untersetzter Gestalt (or *Figur*). *Sie ist klein von Gestalt.*
Der griechische Gott Proteus konnte in jeder beliebigen Gestalt erscheinen. Or *Er konnte die Gestalt
jedes Tieres annehmen.*   *Eine lange, hagere Gestalt kam auf mich zu.*
Der Teufel erscheint Faust in Gestalt eines Hundes.

ii. Die Form is now the usual equivalent of **shape** or **form** when they do not refer to people or animals. *Die Form eines Kristalls. Die Schädelform.*

> *Die Form der Vase erinnert an eine Kirsche.*   *Der Garten hat die Form eines Dreiecks.*
> *Die Schale hat eine schöne/zierliche/elegante Form.*
> *Das Gebäude hat eine sonderbare Form/die Form eines Schiffes.*

iii. Förmig is often found in compounds. *Das Stadion ist hufeisenförmig. Etw. ist kreisförmig/trichterförmig.*

2. Shape, referring to a dimly perceived, indistinctly seen, or not clearly recognizable human or animal figure, is **die Gestalt**. *In der Ferne/Im Nebel tauchten zwei Gestalten auf.*

> *Vermummte Gestalten liefen durch die Straßen.*   *Zwielichtige Gestalten lungerten herum.*

3. Both **shape** and **form** denote the shape given to something. *A paperweight in the shape/form of a lizard.* An extended use is *a reward in the form/shape of an extra week's holiday.* **Die Form** is now usual, but **die Gestalt** is still possible. *Der Briefbeschwerer hat die Form/Gestalt einer Eidechse.* Both are used in the phr. *in Form/Gestalt* + gen or von, but *Form* is probably more usual. *Eine Belohnung in Form/Gestalt einer zusätzlichen Woche Urlaub.*

> *Sie machte einen Ring in Form einer Schlange.*
> *Die Nachricht erschien in Form/Gestalt einer dicken Schlagzeile.*
> *Dieser heidnische Brauch hat sich in veränderter Form bis heute erhalten.*

4. Take shape is either **Gestalt annehmen/gewinnen** or **Form[en] annehmen**. Adjs. are often combined with *Formen. Etw. nimmt feste Formen an. Der Streit nahm häßliche Formen an.*

> *Der Gedanke gewann allmählich Gestalt.*   *Das Projekt nimmt greifbare Gestalt an.*
> *Die Idee/Der Plan nimmt Form an/nimmt Gestalt an/nimmt feste Formen an.*
> *Die Unruhen nahmen eine bürgerkriegsähnliche Form an.*

5. Shape, meaning 'proper shape' as in *The hat has lost its shape*, is **die Form**. Common expressions are *Der Hut hat seine Form verloren* or *ist aus der Form gekommen/geraten. Der Hut wird wieder in seine Form gebracht. Das Kleidungsstück hat nach dem Waschen seine Form behalten.*

6. i. In reference to a literary composition or other work of art, **form** denotes the general arrangement or structure, the way things are put together to form a whole, the manner of presentation contrasted with the subject-matter. **Die Form** also carries this meaning. Thus *die Form und der Inhalt eines Romans.*

> *Die Form dieses Gedichts ist ein Sonnett.*
> *Für diesen Teil der [Roman-]Handlung hat der Autor die Form eines Zwiegesprächs gewählt.*

ii. In connection with literary works **eine Gestalt** means 'a character or figure'. *Diese Frau ist die Hauptgestalt der Novelle. In seinen 74 Romanen hat Balzac eine eigene Welt mit zweitausend Gestalten geschaffen.* **Die Figur** is also used. *Die Figuren dieses Romans sind alle Karikaturen. Die Gestalt* also denotes a historical figure or personality. *Die Gestalt Wallensteins hat viele Autoren fasziniert.*

7. E. **form** also means 'the manner in which sth. exists, the kind, variety, or type'. *Forms of government. Ice, snow, and steam are forms of water.* Here too **die Form** is common. *Verschiedene Regierungsformen. Formen des tierischen und pflanzlichen Lebens. Die einfachsten Lebensformen. Eine Arznei in Pulverform. Eis, Schnee und Dampf sind Formen des Wassers.* The normal expression is *(Malaria tritt) in verschiedenen Formen (auf)*, but *in verschiedener Gestalt* is occasionally found and may be a personification. Where **form** is an exact syn. of *kind*, **die Art** might be more appropriate. *Eine Art der Gottesverehrung. Die Steuerhinterziehung ist eine Art von Unehrlichkeit.*

Der Zeuge benutzte die religiöse Form der Eidesformel.

Mit örtlichen Niederschlägen in Form von Regen oder Schnee ist zu rechnen.

In *etw. in höflicher/scharfer Form ablehnen, Form* refers to the language in which the refusal is couched.

8. i. In the expressions *good/bad form* and *It's polite form to shake hands when you are introduced to a person,* **form** means 'customary, proper behaviour'. **Die Form** or **die Formen** can denote the etiquette observed in polite society. The idea is, however, often expressed by the compound **die Umgangsformen**. *Ein Mensch ohne Formen* is possible, but more usual is *Jmd. hat keine Umgangsformen. Es gehört zu den guten Umgangsformen, jmdm., dem man vorgestellt wird, die Hand zu geben.* Someone can do something *um der Form willen* and *die Form wahren* or *verletzen. Die Form* can be used as criticism. *Das ist alles nur Form,* empty formality or ceremony.

ii. Form also denotes the proper way of doing something legally in a phr. like *in due* or *proper form.* **Die Form** denotes the prescribed legal way of writing or presenting something. *Man wird den Antrag zurückweisen, wenn er nicht in der richtigen Form ist. In aller Form* means 'formally, in conformity with all the rules'. *Ich habe in aller Form meine Versetzung beantragt.*

Auf Grund eines Formfehlers wurde der Antrag nicht angenommen.

Die gesetzliche Form der Eheschließung.   *Die festgelegte Form des Testaments.*

9. When it refers to the state of repair, health or fitness, **shape** is a syn. of *condition.* In reference to the state of repair the equivalent is **der Zustand**, condition. *Das alte Haus war in gutem/schlechtem Zustand,* in good/poor/bad shape/condition. Cf. STATE 2, especially *in/im Schuß.* When **shape** refers to health as in *He was sick last year but is in good shape again now,* the equivalent is **die Gesundheit**. *Er war letztes Jahr krank, ist aber wieder bei guter/bester Gesundheit.* Swimming keeps you in good shape could be *Schwimmen hält einen bei guter Gesundheit.* **Shape** and **form** in *to be in [good] form* mean 'condition of fitness and training'. **Die Form** has taken on this sense. *Die Spieler wollten ihre Form verbessern.* **Die Kondition** is a syn. *Ich habe keine Kondition.* **Fit** and **topfit** are also common. **In Spitzenform** is the expression of G. origin of the latter.

Die Mannschaft war in Form/in guter Form/in guter Kondition/fit.

Sie waren in schlechter Form/schlechter Kondition/außer Form.

10. Fill in *a form* is **ein Formular ausfüllen**. *Ich muß acht Formulare ausfüllen und morgen abgeben.*

share *n.* E. senses treated: (i) **Share** denotes the amount of something someone is entitled to receive or the amount someone is expected or ought to contribute to something. *He tried to rob her of her share of her father's estate. You have to pay your share of the costs.* (ii) **Share** also means 'part' and implies a division among a group. When there is no adj. *share* and *part* are interchangeable. *We have done our share/part of the work. What share/part of the work is being done by computer?* With certain adjs. only one or the other is possible. *We must do our fair share of the work. An increasing share of the work is being done by computers. We have already done the greater part of the work.*

1. Share in the first sense is **der Anteil**. It is often used with a possessive adj., *mein Anteil an der Verantwortung,* or a gen., *der Anteil jedes Piraten an der Beute,* but also occurs without this when the sense is clear, *Ein Anteil steht jmdm. zu* or *[ent]fällt auf jmdn.* It can refer either to an entitlement or to a contribution. It normally implies that the division is fair or proper, and these adjs. may not need to be translated. *Er versuchte, sie um ihren Anteil am Vermögen ihres Vaters zu bringen. Jeder hat seinen Anteil an der Arbeit zu leisten.* The lion's share is **der Löwenanteil**.

Sie ließ sich ihren Anteil am Gewinn auszahlen. Also . . . ihren Gewinnanteil.
Der reiche Bruder verzichtete auf seinen Anteil am väterlichen Vermögen, wodurch sich der Anteil erhöhte, den seine Geschwister bekamen.
Mein Anteil an den Kosten beträgt 85 Mark.
Jeder muß seinen Anteil an den Kosten übernehmen.

2. Anteil also means 'share' or 'part' when used with *nehmen* and *haben* and an adj. referring to the extent. Thus *Jmd. hat großen Anteil* or *nur geringen Anteil an einer Arbeit*, did a large or small part or share of it. Likewise *Sie nahm keinen Anteil an dem Gespräch* or *nahm tätigen Anteil an der Aufführung des Theaterstücks. Sie hatte großen Anteil daran, daß dieses ausgezeichnete Ergebnis zustandekam.*

3. i. In the sents. illustrating E. meaning ii, the normal equivalent of **share** and *part* is **der Teil**. *Anteil* expresses the same meaning but is stylistically higher and is regarded as the equivalent of *proportion*. Cf. RELATION 3. *Let me take a share in the expenses!* is *Erlauben Sie mir, einen Teil der Ausgaben zu übernehmen! Ich möchte meinen Teil der Rechnung bezahlen*, pay my share. *Fair* is often not translated. *Ich habe mehr als meinen Teil der Arbeit getan*, my fair share. *Zu gleichen Teilen* means 'in equal parts or shares'. *Die Kinder erbten zu gleichen Teilen. Beide Länder finanzieren das Stahlwerk zu gleichen Teilen.*

Ein zunehmender/wachsender Teil der Arbeit wird vom Computer erledigt.
Du mußt deinen Teil der Schuld auf dich nehmen. Jeder bekam seinen Teil von der Torte ab.
Wir haben den größeren Teil der Arbeit schon geschafft.

A complication arises from the fact that *Teil* is also a syn. of *Anteil* in sense i. In this sense *Teil* is mainly found in fixed expressions and is translated as **share** or *part*. Common expressions are *Jeder bekommt seinen [gebührenden] Teil. Sie hatte ihren Teil getan. Er hat seinen Teil zum Erfolg beigetragen. Du hast deinen Teil schon weg/ab*, you've had your share. (Most speakers now make *Teil* in this sense masculine. It used to be neuter, and forms such as *sein gebührendes Teil* may still occasionally be found alongside *sein gebührender Teil*. In older literary G., the former neuter sing. adj. form may still be encountered. *Ein gut Teil der Schuld trifft dich* instead of *ein guter* or *gutes Teil*.)

ii. In *Sie hatte ihren Teil zu tragen*, **Teil** means 'share of troubles and difficulties in life'.

4. Der Anteil also expresses the sense 'a share in a business'. *Er hat einen Anteil an dem Geschäft gekauft. Sie hat ihren Anteil an der Firma verkauft.* The pl. *jmds. Anteile* implies 'shares' = 'the number of equal parts into which the capital of a company is divided'. *Die Anteile der Landesregierung betragen 10% des Kapitals.* **Share** in the sense just defined is mostly **die Aktie**. *Sie legte ihr Geld in Aktien an.*

5. Go shares with s.o. is translated by the v. **teilen**. *Teilen wir die Kosten!*

shoot, fire a gun/shot *vs.*

1. i. Schießen is mostly intr. *Er schoß zweimal. Er schießt gut/schlecht. Er hat daneben geschossen* means 'he missed'. *Es wurde geschossen* means that shots were fired. *Es wurde vom Dach her geschossen. Die Soldaten schoßen in die Luft. Schießen auf* means 'to shoot at'. *Er schoß auf den Hasen.* The weapon used is expressed by *mit: Er schoß mit dem Revolver [auf den Polizisten]. Die Soldaten schossen mit Geschützen [auf den Feind].*

Hände hoch, oder ich schieße! Er hat auf die Zielscheibe geschossen und ins Schwarze getroffen.
Gestern hat ein Unbekannter auf das Auto geschossen, in dem zwei Minister saßen.

The part of the body hit can be stated by a prep. *Der Räuber hatte ihm in den Arm/in die Wade/ins Herz/in den Kopf geschossen.*

ii. Schießen is trans. when animals which are hunted are the obj. *Bei der Jagd hat* *man 10 Rehe geschossen.* It takes the projectile shot as obj. only if the sent. contains a phr. of direction. E. uses **shoot** or **fire**. *Er schoß den Pfeil in die Luft. Die Polizei schoß Gummikugeln in die Menge. Man schoß die Weltraumstation auf eine Umlaufbahn.*

2. When there is no phr. of direction and either a firearm or the projectile is the obj., E. uses **fire**. *He fired the gun/an arrow.* One equivalent is **abschießen**. *Er schoß die Pistole/die Kanone ab. Er schoß die Patrone/das Geschoß/eine Rakete/einen Pfeil ab.* An alternative is **abfeuern**. *Die Soldaten feuerten eine Ehrensalve/ein Geschütz/einen Schuß ab.* In more formal language **einen Schuß abgeben** is often found. *Die Truppe nahm das Dorf ein, ohne einen Schuß abzugeben. Er gab mehrere Schüsse hintereinander ab.* (Note that *ein Flugzeug abschießen* means 'to shoot it down', *einen Panzer abschießen* 'to knock it out'.) **Feuern** is intr. *Sie feuerten weiter, bis die ganze Munition verschossen war.*

3. Erschießen is 'to shoot a pers. dead', whether deliberately or accidentally. As Leisi (1961: 67) points out, someone might say, '*Er glaubte, einen Hirsch geschossen zu haben, hatte aber einen Menschen erschossen.*' The refl. therefore means 'to shoot oneself'.
> *Der Bankräuber hat einen Passanten erschossen, als dieser ihn aufhalten wollte.*
> *Der Bankier erschoß sich, weil er den Bankrott nicht erleben wollte.*

Erschießen is also used for destroying sick or injured animals by shooting them.
> *Er mußte das verletzte Pferd/den alten Hund erschießen.*

The colloquial v. **totschießen** takes people and animals as obj. and can be refl. *Er hat seinen Gegner/den alten Hund/sich totgeschossen.*

4. Anschießen is 'to wound by a shot'. It suggests that the wound is only superficial.
> *Der Einbrecher hat den Polizisten angeschossen, es war jedoch nur ein Streifschuß.*

5. Niederschießen means 'to shoot s.o. [without mercy] so that he or she collapses'. It leaves the question open as to whether the person shot is wounded or killed.
> *Ein Polizist, den der Bankräuber niedergeschossen hatte, liegt schwer verwundet im Krankenhaus.*

shorten v. **cut short** v. + *adj.* Some senses of **reduce** v. *Kürzen, verkürzen,* and *abkürzen,* which are discussed in 1, 2, and 3 respectively, all express the meaning 'to make shorter'.

1. i. Kürzen means 'to shorten an object in length', e.g. a dress, piece of timber, cord, etc., but in speech **kürzer machen** is frequently preferred.
> *Der Rock muß [um fünf cm] gekürzt werden/kürzer gemacht werden.*
> *Ich habe die Ärmel um zwei cm kürzen lassen.*   *Die Schnur muß gekürzt werden.*

ii. Kürzen is used for shortening or abridging something in writing, a text, speech, letter, etc. *Verkürzen* is sometimes found in this sense, mainly in the phr. *in verkürzter Form,* but *kürzen* is now the usual v. and *gekürzt* the usual equivalent of *shortened* or *abridged.*
> *Ich war gezwungen, meinen Vortrag zu kürzen, weil mir statt einer Stunde nur 45 Minuten zur Verfügung standen.*   *Wir benutzen eine gekürzte Fassung des Romans.*

iii. Kürzen occurs frequently in the sense 'to reduce or cut' expenses, wages, income, rations, etc. It usually suggests a reduction, which is unwelcome to those affected by it.
> *Angesichts der schlechten wirtschaftlichen Lage muß die australische Bundesregierung die Staatsausgaben um mehrere Milliarden Dollar kürzen.*
> *Weil die Vorräte knapp waren, sah sich der Expeditionsleiter gezwungen, die Rationen zu kürzen.*
> *Die Unternehmer wollten die Löhne kürzen, aber die Gewerkschaften waren nicht bereit, Lohnkürzungen hinzunehmen.*

iv. With regard to time, *verkürzen* (cf. 2. i) is the usual word, but **kürzen** may be used when the reduction is unfavourable to those concerned and is imposed on them. It is used with *von/auf/um*, like *verkürzen*.

> *Wegen Absatzschwierigkeiten mußte der Betrieb die Zahl der Wochenstunden von 40 auf 30 kürzen.*
> *Die Pause wurde um fünf Minuten gekürzt.*

2. i. Verkürzen now most commonly means 'to reduce or make shorter in respect to time'. A phr. with a prep., usually *von*, *um*, or *auf*, may follow the obj. The reduction can be neutral, or welcome or unwelcome to those affected. Cf. 1. iv. *Viele deutsche Politiker wollen die Schulzeit [von derzeit dreizehn auf zwölf Jahre] verkürzen.* Only *verkürzen* is possible in *Durch übermäßiges Rauchen hat er sich das Leben verkürzt* because the result is not imposed by someone else. **Sich verkürzen** means 'to be reduced in time'. *Durch das neue System verkürzt sich die Wartezeit für den Patienten auf ein Minimum.*

> *Im Laufe der letzten dreißig Jahre wurde die durchschnittliche wöchentliche Arbeitszeit von 48 auf 38 Stunden verkürzt.   Wir haben Ihnen die Wartezeit verkürzt.*
> *Durch den Erlaß des Königs wurden allen Häftlingen die Gefängnisstrafen verkürzt.*
> *Die Firma hat den Urlaub für alle Beschäftigten verkürzt. Also . . . um zwei Tage gekürzt oder verkürzt.*
> *Man bäckt die gefrorene Pizza ohne Deckel ca. 20 Minuten auf der untersten Schiene des vorher auf 250° erhitzten Backofens. War sie schon aufgetaut, verkürzt sich die Backzeit.*

ii. Sich die Zeit verkürzen. *Ich verkürze mir die Zeit* means that I occupy myself with something so that an unpleasantly long period of time, spent, for example, in waiting, does not appear so unpleasant.

> *Ich habe mir die Zeit mit Briefeschreiben/Stricken/Lesen verkürzt.*
> *Sie verkürzten sich die langen Winterabende mit Kartenspielen.*

iii. In formal language **verkürzen** sometimes has the sense 'to shorten an object in length'. *Die Schnur mußte verkürzt werden. Durch die Operation wurde das Bein um ein paar Zentimeter verkürzt. Verkürzen* is also a technical term in art, meaning 'to foreshorten'. *Im Bild ist der Arm perspektivisch verkürzt.* **Sich verkürzen** is found in formal language in the sense 'to become shorter' instead of *kürzer werden*, which is common in speech. *Ein Schatten verkürzt sich oder wird länger je nach der Entfernung des Gegenstandes, der ihn wirft, von der Lichtquelle.*

3. Abkürzen has three meanings.

i. 'To abbreviate'. *Dieses Wort kann man abkürzen.* To in *I abbreviate a name etc. to sth.* is *mit*. *Die Vereinigten Staaten von Amerika wird auch im Deutschen gewöhnlich mit USA abgekürzt.*

ii. 'To shorten a distance'. *Wir kürzen uns den Weg ab, wenn wir durch den Wald gehen,* or *Wir kürzen ab, wenn wir durch den Wald gehen.* Hence *die Wegabkürzung*, short cut.

iii. 'To reduce in time'. It implies that something is made shorter than was originally intended and often corresponds to *to cut short*. Some possible objs. are *ein Besuch/eine Reise/ein Aufenthalt/ein Gespräch/eine Konferenz/ein Verfahren/eine Behandlung.*

> *Die Konferenz war für drei Stunden angesetzt. Da man sich aber nach anderthalb Stunden über alle wichtigen Punkte geeinigt hatte, wurde sie abgekürzt.*
> *Die Unmutsäußerungen des Publikums zwangen ihn dazu, seine Rede abzukürzen.* (= 'cut short'. *Kürzen* would imply shortening it before it began.)

show, display *vs.* Many senses of *to* **show** are carried by *zeigen*. In each section *zeigen* is dealt with first if it also expresses the sense being discussed. Note that *zeigen auf* means 'to point to'.

1. Show s.o. the way or **show** s.o. where sth. *is* mean either 'to point to' or 'to explain how to get to'. **Zeigen** is now the normal equivalent. Although *der*

Wegweiser is 'a signpost' and *jmdm. den richtigen Weg weisen* or *jmdm. die Richtung weisen* are heard, **weisen** is not as common as *zeigen*.

> *Da ich die Straße nicht finden konnte, fragte ich einen Passanten, und er zeigte mir den Weg/zeigte mir, wie ich hinkomme.*   *Ich zeige Ihnen den Weg zum Bahnhof.*

2. Show s.o. **to** a room, seat, table, etc. can mean 'to take s.o. there'. In *Der Portier nahm den Schlüssel vom Haken und zeigte mir den Weg zu meinem Zimmer,* **zeigen** normally only suggests pointing out or explaining the way to it. If *show* implies accompanying someone or leading the way, **führen** or the everyday term **bringen** are used. *Er führte/brachte mich zu meinem Zimmer. Wir wurden in das Wohnzimmer geführt/gebracht.*

3. Show s.o. **out** can be **jmdn. hinausbegleiten** or **jmdn. zum Ausgang führen/bringen.** *Ich begleite Sie hinaus—man verläuft sich leicht. Bringen Sie diesen Herrn bitte zum Ausgang!* With *aus,* **weisen** means 'to order out'. Cf. ORDER *v*. 2. *Er wurde aus dem Zimmer gewiesen.* **Jmdm. die Tür weisen** means 'to tell s.o. to leave', i.e. 'to show s.o. the door', as does **jmdn. hinausweisen.** *Sie wiesen die ungebetenen Gäste hinaus.* **Jmdm. den Ausgang zeigen** usually means 'to point out where the exit is'. In certain contexts, it may, however, imply telling the person to leave.

4. Show s.o. sth. or **show** sth. **to** s.o. when these mean 'to allow s.o. to see sth.' or 'to explain how to do sth.' or 'to do sth. oneself so that s.o. else sees how it is done' are expressed by **zeigen.** The E. infin. after **show** + interrogative, *Can you show me how to operate the machine?,* must be expressed in G. as a finite *v. Können Sie mir zeigen, wie man die Maschine bedient? Zeigen Sie mir, was ich machen soll!*

> *Der Makler hat uns das Haus gezeigt.*   *Ich zeige dir den Brief.*
> *Der Führer zeigte uns das Schloß. Also . . . führte uns durch das Schloß.*
> *Er zeigte uns den Garten/die Dias von seiner Reise nach Zentralaustralien.*
> *Können Sie mir das nochmal zeigen?*   *Wir zeigen den Film zweimal.*
> *Er zeigte mir, wie man die Reparatur ausführt.*

5. i. With a picture, diagram, table, etc. as subj., **zeigen** means 'to represent or express information'.

> *Die Aufnahme zeigt die drei Kinder mit ihren Eltern/zeigt ihn an seinem Schreibtisch sitzend.*
> *Die Tabelle zeigt, wieviel Kohle wir in den letzten Jahren ausgeführt haben.*

ii. For an instrument which shows a level of measurement, **anzeigen** is usual.

> *Der Zähler zeigt den Stromverbrauch an.*
> *Das Barometer zeigt schönes Wetter an.*
> *Das Thermometer zeigte 35° an.*
> *Die Uhr zeigte halb acht an.*

6. As explained in section E. 3 of PRODUCE, **vorzeigen** is the everyday word for showing or producing a ticket, passport, licence, etc., **vorweisen** the official one. *Ich habe meine Karte nur einmal während der Fahrt vorgezeigt. An der Grenze muß man den Paß vorweisen/vorzeigen.*

7. With a person or thing as subj. **sich zeigen** can mean 'to allow oneself/itself to be seen, to appear'. *Das Mädchen zeigte sich am Fenster. Am Horizont zeigte sich ein roter Schein.*

> *Er schämte sich, sich auf der Straße zu zeigen.*   *Kein Käufer hat sich bisher gezeigt.*
> *In diesem Aufzug kann ich mich unmöglich vor den Leuten zeigen.*
> *Seine Verärgerung zeigte sich am Ton seiner Stimme.*   *Erst viel später zeigten sich die Folgen.*

Don't **show** *yourself/your face here again!* is *Laß dich hier nie wieder blicken/sehen!* With a person as subj. *sich zeigen* means 'to show oneself [to be]' + adj. *Jmd. zeigte sich dankbar. Jmd. zeigte sich großzügig/ein wenig erstaunt.* When a n. follows, *als* is needed. *Er zeigte sich als Feigling.* When a n. not denoting a person is the subj. and an adj. follows, *sich zeigen* also needs *als.* In this use it is interchangeable with **sich**

erweisen als, which can be translated as *to prove* or *turn out to be. Der Plan zeigte sich als/erwies sich als undurchführbar. Es zeigt sich* + clause means 'it becomes apparent or obvious'. *Es zeigte sich bald, daß sie der Aufgabe durchaus gewachsen war.* Only *sich erweisen* is used with impersonal *es* and *als* + adj. or n. *Es erwies sich als wünschenswert, neue Stellen zu schaffen. Es erwies sich als Fehler, so teure Maschinen gekauft zu haben.*

> *Es zeigte sich bald, daß wir uns verrechnet hatten.*
> *Erst viel später zeigte [es] sich, daß die Entscheidung falsch war.*
> *Er hat sich wieder als guter Freund gezeigt/erwiesen.*　　*Seine Behauptung erwies sich als wahr.*
> *Es hat sich leider als notwendig erwiesen, Stellen abzubauen.*
> *Der Plan erwies sich als Mißerfolg.*

8. S.o./Sth. that shows that a state of affairs exists gives evidence which proves this. *The pupils' answers show whether/that they have understood.* **Zeigen** also has this sense and is used with an obj. or a clause. *Die Antworten der Schüler auf diese Fragen zeigen, ob sie die Erzählung verstanden haben.* Syns. are **nachweisen** and **beweisen.** Both mean 'to prove or demonstrate', but *beweisen* is stronger, suggesting a straightforward and clear proof, whereas *nachweisen* often implies a proof by a series of steps. The E. constructions *They showed sth. to be false* or *proved sth. [to be] correct* must be translated by *nachweisen* as it alone takes *als* = 'to be'. Thus *Wir haben die Unrichtigkeit der Geschichte gezeigt/nachgewiesen/bewiesen,* or *Wir haben gezeigt/nachgewiesen/bewiesen, daß die Geschichte falsch ist,* but only *Wir haben die Geschichte als falsch nachgewiesen.* Formerly it was possible to say *Die Forschung hat die Theorie als richtig erwiesen,* but now, apart from the refl. use mentioned in 6 and the use given in 9. ix, *erweisen* is found only as the past part., *erwiesen* meaning 'proved or proven'. *Eine erwiesene Tatsache. Das ist schon erwiesen.*

> *Sein neuester Roman zeigt/beweist, daß er ein erstklassiger Romancier ist.*
> *Die Erfahrung zeigt, daß man sich leicht überschätzen kann.*
> *Diese Antwort zeigt mir Ihr Verständnis der behandelten Fragen.*

9. Show is used with people or things as subj. and with qualities, characteristics, or feelings as obj. and, in some cases, with a dat. stating to whom these are directed. *Can't you show [us] a bit more consideration? The sketch shows a lot of talent.* **Display** is also used with characteristics, qualities, or emotions as obj. *He displayed/showed great courage.*

i. Zeigen is usual with similar ns. *Man zeigt seinen Ärger/seine Freude/seine Ungeduld/seine Unruhe. Jmd. zeigt [kein] Bedauern/[keine] Reue/[gar kein] Interesse/[kein] Mitleid* or *zeigt jmdm. seine Verärgerung/seine Liebe/seine Verachtung.* Other ns. often found as obj. are qualities like *die Ausdauer, der Fleiß, die Geschicklichkeit, die Zuverlässigkeit,* or *die Rücksicht.*

> *Es ist nicht immer ratsam, seine Gefühle zu zeigen.*
> *Ihr Verhalten zeigt einen Mangel an Rücksicht anderen gegenüber.*
> *Der letzte Auftritt zeigt das große Talent der Schauspielerin.*
> *Durch diese Bemerkung zeigst du nur deine Unwissenheit.*
> *Jetzt kannst du dein Können zeigen/ . . . zeigen, was du kannst* (show your skill/what you can do).

ii. Beweisen means 'to show or display' qualities in the sense 'to prove that one possesses them'.

> *Bei der Planung des neuen Stadtviertels bewiesen die Architekten eine große Weitsicht.*
> *Mit dem Kauf dieser Luxuslimousine hat er nur seine Eitelkeit bewiesen.*
> *Tag für Tag mußten die Piloten ihren Mut und ihr Können beweisen.*

iii. An den Tag legen can be used with the same qualities as *beweisen.* It suggests that what is shown comes about in an unexpected or surprising way and may even imply that there is something suspicious about it.

> *In der letzten Zeit legt er eine auffallende Geschäftigkeit an den Tag.*

In manchen Situationen legt er einen großen Ehrgeiz an den Tag.

iv. Zur Schau stellen has a neg. colouring. It suggests a lack of the due or expected restraint in displaying feelings or moods and is often best translated as *to make a display of.*

Sie stellte ihre schlechte Laune unverhohlen zur Schau.

Es gelang ihm oft, die Situation zu seinen Gunsten zu beeinflussen, indem er seine Gefühle zur Schau stellte.

v. Entfalten means lit. 'to unfold', but with objs. like *Talente, Fähigkeiten,* and *Eigenschaften,* its sense is 'to display or reveal'. *In dieser Stelle konnte er seine Fähigkeiten nicht entfalten.*

Bei der neuen Aufgabe konnte sie ihre ganzen Talente entfalten.

Ausnahmsweise entfaltete er eine hektische Betriebsamkeit an seinem Arbeitsplatz.

vi. From its derivation **bezeugen** means 'to give evidence of' something. It expresses the same meaning as the more usual *zeigen,* but it is more formal. (It is also a legal term meaning 'to bear witness to'.)

Durch einen riesigen Blumenstrauß bezeugte er seine Verehrung für seine Kollegin.

Um ihr Interesse zu bezeugen, traf die Gruppe eine Stunde vor Eröffnung der Ausstellung ein.

vii. Bekunden is a formal term meaning 'to display'.

Das Publikum bekundete lautstark sein Mißfallen an der Aufführung.

Sympathie gegenüber diesem Angeklagten zu bekunden war eine mutige Tat.

viii. Bezeigen occurs in expressions like *jmdm. Ehre/Achtung/Respekt bezeigen,* but it is elevated and unusual. *Das Publikum bezeigte dem Staatsmann seine Hochachtung.*

ix. Erweisen, which needs a dat., is a more common equivalent of **display** than the three preceding vs.

Den Schülern wird beigebracht, ihren Eltern Achtung zu erweisen.

Jmd. erweist einem anderen Liebe/Güte/Barmherzigkeit/Geduld.

(*Erweisen* is used in *jmdm. einen guten/schlechten Dienst erweisen,* to do s.o. a good/bad turn or service.)

x. Erzeigen has become rare. While earlier versions of the Bible had *Welch eine Liebe hat uns der Vater erzeiget, daß wir Gottes Kinder sollen heißen!,* the latest has *erwiesen.*

10. Aufweisen means 'to show, display or exhibit' deficiencies, faults, etc., i.e. 'to have' these. *Der Teppich weist Schmutzflecken auf. Der Plan weist gewisse Mängel auf.* **Jmd./Etw. hat etw. aufzuweisen** means the person/thing has something to offer or show. *Er hatte große Erfolge aufzuweisen. Die Stadt hat viele Sehenswürdigkeiten aufzuweisen.* *Aufweisen* can be used to translate *We had nothing to show for our efforts: Trotz unserer Bemühungen hatten wir nichts/kein Ergebnis aufzuweisen.* (*Vorzeigen* and *vorweisen* (cf. 6) are also possible in this sense but suggest showing the result to someone else.)

11. Display or *exhibit* goods is **ausstellen.** *Das Geschäft stellt Waren in geschickter und wirksamer Weise aus.*

Die Waren, die in den Schaufenstern dieses Geschäfts ausgestellt sind, sind meist sehr teuer.

sign, indication *ns.*

1. Das Zeichen is the general word for something concrete which stands for or indicates something else, and means 'mark or sign'. *Den Rindern wird ein Zeichen eingebrannt. Er machte sich ein Zeichen auf die betreffende Seite.* It can denote a sign or symbol, *ein chemisches/mathematisches Zeichen,* or a sign given by the hand, or in the form of a gesture or sound. *Der Trainer gab den Spielern ein Zeichen. Sie gaben sich die Hand zum Zeichen der Versöhnung.*

Sie nickte zum/als Zeichen, daß sie verstanden hatte.

Der Dirigent gibt das Zeichen zum Einsatz.

Ein kurzer Pfiff war das Zeichen zum Stehenbleiben.
Da sie keine gemeinsame Sprache hatten, verständigten sie sich durch Zeichen.

2. Sign also refers to an occurrence which leads someone to believe that something is developing or will happen, or which suggests a conclusion about something unclear in the present or past. An **indication** is 'any piece of evidence from which a whole situation can be inferred' and tends to be less definite than a sign. **i. Das Zeichen** is used when a speaker considers the significance of an occurrence to be clear. The conclusion drawn can relate to present, past, or future. **Das Anzeichen** differs mainly in the degree of probability expressed. While *Zeichen* implies a high degree of likelihood, *Anzeichen* suggests only a possible outcome or significance of certain occurrences and may or may not be correct. In many contexts either is possible. When *Anzeichen* replaces *Zeichen* in *In Bonn zeigen sich die ersten Zeichen einer Regierungskrise*, the statement becomes more tentative. In *Im Rückgang der Produktion sehen viele die ersten Anzeichen einer Rezession*, *Anzeichen* could be translated as **indications** if this is understood as being less definite than **signs**. *Wenn er nachgibt, wird man es als Zeichen der Schwäche bewerten* is a fixed expression, as are *Im Dorf gab es kein Zeichen von Leben* and *Die Wahl dieses Mannes ist [k]ein gutes Zeichen* or *ein schlechtes Zeichen*. Both *Zeichen* and *Anzeichen* are used with *für*, and when a clause follows with *dafür, daß* . . . *Drückende Hitze ist oft ein Zeichen/Anzeichen für ein kommendes Gewitter*, or . . . *dafür, daß ein Gewitter sich nähert. Sie zeigten Zeichen der Ermüdung* is the usual expression, but *Anzeichen* occurs in neg. sents. *Es gab/Sie zeigten nicht das geringste Anzeichen von/für etw. Wenn nicht alle Zeichen täuschen* (or *trügen*) is now the normal expression, although *Anzeichen* is also possible. (In medical language *die Anzeichen* is a syn. of *Symptome. Die ersten Anzeichen einer Krankheit.*)

> *Das Ehepaar, das das alte Bauernhaus kaufen wollte, schreckte von dem Kauf zurück, als es am Haus Zeichen des Verfalls sah.*
> *Das ist ein Zeichen dafür, daß mehr als einer an dem Verbrechen beteiligt waren.*
> *Es gibt Anzeichen für einen Wetterumschwung/ . . . [dafür], daß das Wetter bald umschlägt.*
> *Es gibt Anzeichen dafür/keine/keinerlei Anzeichen dafür, daß sie sich bald einigen werden.*
> *Bei dem geringsten Anzeichen von Widerstand muß das Polizeiaufgebot verstärkt werden.*

ii. Both **das Zeichen** and **das Anzeichen** refer to signs which show that someone is experiencing an emotion. They take the gen. or *von. Er gab deutliche Zeichen der Ungeduld. Ohne das geringste Anzeichen von Trauer. Jmd. zeigte Zeichen der Reue* can be made neg. with *kein.* Stronger than *keine Zeichen von Reue* is *kein[e] Anzeichen* which means 'not the slightest sign or not even a trace of regret'. *Keinerlei Anzeichen* is even stronger. *Anzeichen* is also used in contexts which are neg. in sense, although *Zeichen* is possible. *Jmd. ließ jegliches Anzeichen von Bedauern vermissen.*

iii. In one sense **der Hinweis** means 'indication of a development'. It is a syn. of *Anzeichen* but suggests less concrete evidence and implies that the conclusion drawn is the speaker's interpretation of what is happening or has happened. It is often found with *[be]werten als*, to judge as. *Die Entlassung weiterer Arbeiter durch zwei große Firmen [be]wertet er als Hinweis dafür/darauf, daß die Rezession die Talsohle* (bottom) *noch nicht erreicht hat. Es gibt nicht den geringsten Hinweis für/auf etw.* is often found, but *nicht das geringste Anzeichen* is also common. *That gives some indication of how serious the situation is* can be expressed as *Das mag als Hinweis darauf gelten, wie ernst die Lage ist.*

> *Es gibt nicht den geringsten Hinweis darauf/dafür, daß wir es hier mit einem Verbrechen zu tun haben.*
> *Hier finden wir den ersten Hinweis auf einen Wandel in seiner Lebensauffassung.*

iv. Other equivalents of **indication**.
a. All the indications are that . . . and *There is every indication that* . . . can be translated

by *Alle Anzeichen sprechen dafür, daß. . .*, but *Alles deutet darauf hin, daß . . .* is a common alternative. *Alles deutet darauf hin, daß die beiden Seiten demnächst eine Einigung erzielen werden.* Cf. SUGGEST 2. i.

b. There is no **indication** that . . . is *Nichts deutet darauf hin, daß Rohstoffpreise demnächst steigen werden.*

c. The President gave a clear **indication** of his willingness to meet the delegation can be translated in several ways. *Der Präsident ließ deutlich erkennen, daß er bereit ist, mit der Delegation zusammenzutreffen* suggests he made it unmistakably clear, although he did not say it directly. Alternatives are *Er brachte seine Bereitschaft zum Ausdruck* or *Er bekundete seine Bereitschaft. Er ließ durchblicken, daß er bereit ist . . .* suggests that his intention was implied in what he said, though not stated clearly. Cf. SUGGEST 3. ii.

d. That gives some **indication** of his feelings in the matter can be *Das zeigt in etwa seine Einstellung/Haltung in dieser Sache. In etwa* = 'to some extent or degree'.

3. Das Vorzeichen is 'the plus or minus sign'. *Wenn man x auf die andere Seite der Gleichung versetzt, muß man das Vorzeichen verändern. Vorzeichen* also means 'omen'. *Etw. ist ein gutes/ungünstiges Vorzeichen. Das erschien mir als ein schlimmes/böses Vorzeichen.*

4. No sign of. There is no sign of s.o. in a place is *Jmd. ist nirgendwo zu sehen.* There is no sign of the book: *Das Buch ist nirgendwo zu finden.* When There is no sign of s.o. means that he/she has not arrived or turned up, it becomes *Jmd. hat sich noch nicht gezeigt.* Cf. SHOW 7.

5. Show signs/no sign of doing sth., as in They showed no signs of going, is **[keine] Anstalten machen, etw. zu tun.** The meaning is 'to show that one intends to do sth.' *Sie machten keine Anstalten, mit dem Lärm aufzuhören/zu gehen.*

> *Wenn du nicht bald Anstalten machst zu arbeiten, werden wir heute nicht fertig.*

6. A **street sign** is *ein Straßenschild. (Das Schild).* A **signpost** is **ein Wegweiser.**

silence *n.* quiet *n.* and *adj.* be silent/quiet *v.* + *adj.* silent, tacit *adjs.*

A. Ns.

1. Quiet or **silence** = 'the absence of disturbing sounds, especially in nature'.

i. The main equivalent is **die Stille.** *Die Stille des Waldes. Die Stille des Abends. Stille* can also refer to people, *Der Redner wartete, bis Stille eingetreten war,* but here *Ruhe* is the usual word. Cf. REST *v.* and *n.* B. 2.

> *Die abendliche Stille im Wald wurde durch ein Flugzeug gestört.*

ii. Das Schweigen means 'the silence which occurs when people are not talking', or 'a particular individual's not saying anything'. (In poetical language *Schweigen* is also applied to nature.) *Jmd./Etw. unterbrach das Schweigen,* broke the silence among people.

> *In dem Klassenzimmer herrschte tiefes Schweigen.* Also . . . *absolute Stille.*

> *Als sie während des Essens sein Schweigen nicht mehr ertragen konnte, fragte sie ihn rundheraus, warum er so schweigsam wäre.*

> *Ihr Schweigen während der Diskussion war nicht aufgefallen.*

iii. Das Stillschweigen is an emphatic variant on *Schweigen*, meaning 'complete silence among people'. *Nach einem Augenblick des Stillschweigens nahm sie das Gespräch wieder auf.*

2. Silence = 'not saying anything about a matter'.

i. Jmds. Schweigen means that the person says nothing about a particular matter. *Er hat sein Schweigen über etw. gebrochen,* broke his silence, i.e. revealed what he knows about it.

Statt sich zu der Frage zu äußern, wie alle erwarteten, hüllte sie sich in Schweigen.
Über ihr Schweigen über diese wichtige Angelegenheit haben sich alle gewundert.

ii. Das Stillschweigen also has the sense 'unwillingness to mention a matter'. A common expression is *etw. mit Stillschweigen übergehen*, to pass over sth. in silence. *Gewisse Worte, die während der Auseinandersetzung gefallen waren, beschloß sie mit Stillschweigen zu übergehen.*

iii. Das Stillschweigen also means 'silence enjoined on s.o.' or 'the undertaking to keep certain information to oneself'. Thus *jmdm. Stillschweigen auferlegen*, 'to impose on s.o. the obligation not to reveal sth.', and *Stillschweigen [über etw.] bewahren*, 'to keep silent about'.

Er beschwor den Freund, Stillschweigen über das ihm anvertraute Geheimnis zu bewahren.

iv. Die Verschwiegenheit denotes the quality some people possess of being able to keep something to themselves. *Unter dem Siegel der Verschwiegenheit erzählte er dem Freund, was vorgefallen war.*

Ich verließ mich früher auf ihre Verschwiegenheit und wurde nicht enttäuscht.

B. Vs. The v. **schweigen** has three nuances.

1. It means 'not to speak or say anything on a particular occasion'. *Um einen Streit zu vermeiden, hat er die ganze Zeit geschwiegen. Sie wechselten ein paar Worte, aber dann schwiegen sie wieder.*

Alternatives. **Stillschweigen** is more emphatic. The imp. *Schweig still!* is sometimes used, for example, when talking to children. The pres. part. *stillschweigend* is used like **in silence**, although *schweigend* also occurs. *Die beiden Schachspieler saßen sich schweigend/stillschweigend gegenüber.*

Sie verließen stillschweigend das Restaurant.
Er nahm die Vorwürfe stillschweigend hin, weil er wußte, daß sie berechtigt waren.

Verstummen means 'to fall silent suddenly'. *Als sie die Explosion hörten, verstummten alle vor Schreck.*

Als sie sah, daß sie ihn doch nicht überzeugen konnte, verstummte sie plötzlich.

Ruhig/still sein also mean 'to be quiet' and are often used as a command. *Seid still/ruhig!* **Den Mund halten** has the same sense. *Halt doch endlich den Mund!*

2. Schweigen also means 'not to say anything about sth. when one is asked about it or when it is expected that one will say sth.' It is used with *auf eine Frage, Der Politiker schwieg auf die Frage des Journalisten, ob seine Partei Schmiergelder angenommen hätte*, and with *über ein Thema* etc., *Obwohl alle eine Erklärung erwarteten, schwieg der Kanzler über dieses Thema.*

Alternatives. **Sich über etw. ausschweigen** means 'to say absolutely nothing about sth. when a statement or explanation is expected'. *Über den Vorfall, an dem er ja beteiligt war, schwieg er sich aus.*

Obwohl alle erwarteten, daß sie in der Diskussion ihren Standpunkt erklären würde, schwieg sie sich aus.

Die Schüler hatten die Gelegenheit, dem Lehrer zu sagen, was sie an seinem Unterricht schlecht fanden, aber sie schwiegen sich aus.

3. Schweigen is a syn. of *Stillschweigen bewahren*, to keep sth. to oneself. *Ich möchte Ihnen etw. anvertrauen, können Sie schweigen?*

Alternatives. **Reinen Mund halten** is a colloquial equivalent of *Stillschweigen bewahren*. *Du kannst ganz offen mit uns reden, wir werden reinen Mund halten.*

Verschwiegen is said of people who can be relied on not to divulge something. *Instetten glaubte nicht, daß Wüllersdorf das Versprechen, verschwiegen wie ein Grab zu sein, halten könnte.* The v. *verschweigen* means 'not to reveal sth.' and is discussed under HIDE.

Dieser Mann war wegen seiner verschwiegenen Natur bekannt.
Ihm kannst du die Sache anvertrauen. Er ist ein verschwiegener Mensch.

C. Adjs.

1. Silent. As already mentioned, **schweigend** and **stillschweigend** mean 'in silence' or 'silent on a particular occasion'. *Der Angeklagte hörte sich das Urteil schweigend/stillschweigend an.* **Schweigsam** normally means 'quiet or silent as a permanent characteristic', *Er ist ein schweigsamer Mensch,* but if the context makes it clear it can mean 'silent on one occasion', *Warum bist du auf einmal so schweigsam?* Cf. G. *still* under REST *v.* and *n.* C. 3. ii. *Florian ist ein stiller Mensch,* a quiet man. **Wortkarg** means 'having little to say at all times'. **Einsilbig** means 'having little to say either on a particular occasion or always'. *Warum bist du heute so einsilbig?* In *Auf diese Frage antwortete sie einsilbig,* it suggests a minimal reply.

2. Tacit. **Stillschweigend** means 'tacit' = 'understood or implied without actually being spoken'. *Eine stillschweigende Übereinkunft. Jmds. stillschweigendes Einverständnis.*
    Der Unterhändler hatte die Bedingungen des Verhandlungspartners stillschweigend angenommen.

simple *adj.* The general term is *einfach.*

1. i. Both **simple** and **einfach** mean 'not complicated in nature', therefore 'easy to solve, do, carry out, use, or understand'. Combinations often encountered are *eine einfache Regel, eine einfache Anweisung, eine einfache Maschine, eine einfache Angelegenheit, ein einfacher Apparat, ein einfaches Gesetz, eine einfache Lösung, eine einfache Aufgabe, einfache Arbeit. Der Fall ist ganz einfach. Ich tue das aus dem einfachen Grunde, weil ich nicht sehr viel Geld habe.* An infin. can follow *einfach, Die Aufgabe ist einfach zu lösen,* but *Man kann sie leicht lösen* is more usual.
    Das einfachste Mittel, Lebensmittel vor dem Verderben zu bewahren, ist das Einfrieren.
ii. Simpel is a syn. but presents the simplicity in a neg. light. In reference to things requiring mental effort, it means 'making no or the barest demands on the intelligence'. *Eine ganz simple Rechenaufgabe. Die Lösung ist ganz simpel.*

2. i. Simple is applied to the way people express themselves, *I've expressed it as simply as I could,* to things made by human beings, *a simple dress, a simple building,* and to food, *a simple meal.* The concept underlying this use is that the manner of expression or the thing made contains only those elements which are necessary without any additional features. Applied to the manner of expression and to things made, **schlicht** means 'natural and without artificiality', while **einfach** means 'free from rhetorical and emotional trappings or ornamentation'. In relation to the way something is expressed *einfach* suggests natural feeling expressing itself directly in sincere and unemotional words, whereas *schlicht* suggests that someone carefully avoids rhetorical effects to give the impression of simplicity. Both are possible in *Diese einfache/schlichte Rede hat alle tief bewegt,* but the word chosen would say something about the person speaking. This distinction belongs, however, more to the written language. Only *einfach* is likely to be met with in everyday language. *Ich bemühte mich, mich klar und einfach auszudrücken.* With reference to things made by people, *einfach* means offering no more than what is necessary to fulfil its purpose, while *schlicht* implies that what is made has no resplendent decoration where this could easily be present, and produces an impression of beauty without such ornamentation. *Einfach* and *schlicht* register an impression of simplicity made by words or by something designed or made. *Einfach* says that the intention and the resulting words or objects are uncomplicated in nature, while *schlicht* implies the will to create deliberately something pleasing yet simple. Although *schlicht* suggests an impression intentionally created, it does not imply disapproval. The aim may be to create beauty in simplicity or, more often, not to be ostentatious. *Ein einfaches Kleid* simply fulfils its purpose.

To say that a designer created a simple dress, only *schlicht* would be used, as this implies an effort to be simple. *Die Prinzessin trug ein schlichtes Kleid [eines bekannten Modeschöpfers].* While *schlicht* is usually combined with *Schönheit*, both *schlicht* and *einfach* are possible in other contexts. *Ein einfacher/schlichter Stil. Einfache/schlichte Architektur.*

> *Die echte Gläubigkeit der alten Frau sprach aus diesen einfachen Zeilen.*
> *Ihre schlichten Worte machten großen Eindruck auf sie. Er hielt eine kurze Predigt in einfachen Worten.*
> *Er erzählte mit schlichten überzeugenden Worten.   Sie trug ein Kostüm von schlichter Eleganz.*
> *Das Haus war schlicht eingerichtet. Also Das Haus war ganz einfach eingerichtet.*

ii. In reference to things made, **simpel** means 'consisting of no more than is absolutely necessary to fulfil its purpose, unassumingly simple', and is often pejorative. *Das Haus war sehr simpel eingerichtet. Sogar ein simples Kleid kostet dort sehr viel.* With reference to the way something is expressed, *sich simpel ausdrücken* often means 'in an unduly simple way'. *Wenn ich mich so simpel ausdrücke, halten mich alle für dumm.*

iii. In reference to food, **einfach** suggests that it satisfies the hunger but has no refinements, **schlicht** that it is simply prepared but nourishing. The difference is very slight. *Einfach* is now the usual word.

> *Wir verzehrten genußvoll die schlichte dörfliche Mahlzeit.*
> *Sie hatte inzwischen das einfache Abendbrot auf den Tisch gestellt.*

3. Simple is applied to people with three nuances. Firstly, if someone talks e.g. of simple farmers or people, this usually implies approval of their uncomplicated way of life. Secondly, **simple**, applied to a person or behaviour, suggests natural, honest, and straightforward, without pretence, exaggeration, or artificiality. *She found him level-headed, simple, and sincere. How simple and unselfish her action seemed when he reflected for a moment.* Thirdly, it means 'simple-minded or mentally backward'.

i. In expressions like *ein einfacher Bauer, ein einfacher Arbeiter,* or *ein einfacher Mann,* **einfach** suggests an uncomplicated, unassuming, modest, or plain person. It is used like *ordinary* or *average* and is a syn. of *gewöhnlich.* Cf. COMMON 6. *Der einfache Mann von/auf der Straße.* **Schlicht** implies on the one hand an unaffected and modest nature, on the other uncritical and naïve views, someone who accepts what happens at face value and is unable to see what lies behind it. *Ein schlichter Mensch* and *ein schlichtes Gemüt* are not condemnatory, and *schlicht* can express the first two nuances of **simple**. Another possibility is **treuherzig**, which means 'good-natured, trusting, and credulous in a childlike way, ingenuous'. Whereas *naiv* always contains a note of criticism, *treuherzig* expresses approval of a disposition which is guileless, open, and trusting, though also somewhat naïve. *Ein junges, unerfahrenes, treuherziges Geschöpf. Ein treuherziger Charakter.* When **simple** means 'sincere and straightforward', the equivalent is **ehrlich** or **aufrichtig**. *Eine freimütige, aufrichtige/ehrliche Antwort,* a frank, simple answer.

> *Ihr schlichtes Wesen machte auf ihn einen großen Eindruck.*
> *Wie aufrichtig und uneigennützig erschien ihm diese Handlung, als er einen Augenblick darüber nachdachte.   Er war, wie ihr bald klar wurde, besonnen, schlicht und aufrichtig.*
> *Er antwortete mir so offen und treuherzig, daß ich jeden Zweifel beiseite schob.*
> *Zu einer deutschen Delegation in New York gehörten ein aus Leipzig stammender Politiker und seine Frau. Treuherzig fragte ein städtischer Beamter die Dame: 'Sind Sie zum ersten Mal in New York?', worauf die Ex-DDR-Bürgerin antwortete: 'Wir sind überall zum ersten Mal.'*

ii. Einfältig now mostly means 'simple-minded' and is a syn. of *dumm* and *beschränkt. Er macht einen sehr einfältigen Eindruck.* However, at least in literary use, *einfältig* and the n. *die Einfalt* can suggest guilelessness and describe people who know no cunning and are uncorrupted by the world. *Es war eine Frau, gottesfürchtig, fleißig, und einfältigen Gemüts. Kindliche Einfalt.* Applied to people **simpel** means 'having a limited outlook, simple-minded'. *Der Wächter hatte einen simplen Gesichtsausdruck.*

single, singly, sole[ly], individual[ly] *adjs.* and *advs.* Some uses of **only** *adj.* and *adv.*

1. In one sense **single** means that things or people belonging to a group are considered or seen on their own and separately from the others. *Please enter singly! We are not only dealing with single cells but with groups of cells.* **Individual** also indicates that each member of a group is being dealt with separately. *The individual steps are explained here. We must deal with each case individually.*

i. The equivalent of both these meanings is **einzeln**, by himself/herself/itself, not together with others. *Bitte einzeln eintreten! Ein einzelner kann da wenig ausrichten.* In this sense it is mostly found in the pl., *Wir müssen uns mit den einzelnen Fällen befassen*, or as an adv., *Die Bände dieser Ausgabe sind einzeln erhältlich*, available separately, singly.

> *Wir befassen uns nicht nur mit einzelnen Zellen, sondern auch mit Gruppen von Zellen.*
> *Ich habe einen einzelnen Handschuh gefunden.*   *Wir müssen jedes Stück einzeln verpacken.*
> *Jeder Posten muß einzeln aufgeführt werden.*   *Sie werden einzeln aufgerufen.*
> *Wir müssen diese Fälle einzeln betrachten.*   *Wir haben jeden Fall einzeln behandelt.*
> *Einzeln kann ich Ihnen die Dosen nicht verkaufen, nur im Sechserpack.*

In the pl. with the definite article *einzeln* means 'individual'. *Die einzelnen Schritte werden in der Gebrauchsanweisung erklärt.* Without the article, the pl. means 'a FEW', a syn. of *einige wenige. Selbst bei starkem Wind kann man einzelne Surfer auf dem Wasser beobachten. Einzelne Fragen gingen glatt am Thema vorbei.* In expressions like *einzelne Regenschauer* the E. equivalent is *isolated*.

ii. In *Ein einzelner Spaziergänger ging am Flußufer entlang*, **einzeln** means 'lone, solitary'. *Am Waldrand steht ein einzelnes Haus.* (Note: *Ein einziges Haus* means 'only one'. Cf. 2.)

iii. Single is used for emphasis after *every*, as in *every single pupil* or *every single day. Jeder einzelne* is used for people. *Der Direktor kannte jeden einzelnen Schüler. Er schüttelte jedem einzelnen Teilnehmer die Hand.* This combination is less common than in E., and if *einzeln* is omitted, the difference in meaning is only slight. *Sie hat jedem Teilnehmer einen Brief geschrieben*, every [single] one. With things *einzeln* does occur, but not often. *Jeder einzelne Fall wurde untersucht* is possible, but *Wir sind jeden Tag hingefahren* is normal.

iv. Single need not be translated in e.g. *This is the most important single invention since printing* where its meaning is very vague. *Das ist die wichtigste Erfindung seit der Einführung der Buchdruckerkunst.*

v. Einzel is used in a number of compounds meaning 'for or with one pers. or thg.' and is translated as **single** or **individual**. *Das Einzelzimmer, das Einzelbett, der Einzelfall, die Einzelerscheinung, die Einzelhaft, der Einzelunterricht*, etc.

2. A single. Not a single. The only or **sole.**
i. In *We heard a single shot*, **single** means 'only one'. **Einzig** expresses this sense. *Ein* + *einzig* means that only one thing or person of the type specified exists and is sometimes translated as **single**, sometimes as *only one. Wir hörten einen einzigen Schuß. Dies gilt für alle Novellen mit einer einzigen Ausnahme. Einzig* is often strengthened by *nur. Ich sehe nur einen einzigen Ausweg. Ich habe es nur ein einziges Mal versucht.*

> *Wenn man einen einzigen Fehler dieser Art macht, dann ist alles vorbei.*

Wir haben nur ein einziges Modell dieser Art.

Gibt es einen einzigen Menschen dieser Art in unserer Organisation?

ii. Single preceded by *not a*, as in *not a single word*, is expressed by **kein + einzig**. *Von dem, was er sagte, war kein einziges Wort wahr. Kein einziger Student wußte, was das Wort bedeutet.*

iii. Not a single thg. in *I couldn't think of a single thg. to say* is a strengthened form of *nothing* and must be translated by an intensified variant on *nichts* such as *Mir fiel* **absolut/rein gar nichts ein,** *was ich hätte sagen können.*

iv. Only in contexts like *the only guest[s]* or *The only E. city I enjoyed working in was Birmingham,* and the more emphatic **sole** in *the only/sole survivor[s],* is translated by **einzig.** *The only one is der/die einzige. She was the only one to volunteer* becomes *Sie war die einzige, die sich meldete,* or *Sie hat sich als einzige gemeldet. The only thg. is das einzige. Das wäre das einzige, was ich für ihn tun könnte.*

Ich war der einzige Gast. Wir waren die einzigen Gäste.

Dübeln (dowelling) ist die einzige Möglichkeit, die ich sehe, das Regal fest zu bekommen.

Diese fünf Matrosen waren die einzigen Überlebenden des Schiffbruchs.

Sie war die einzige, die die Frage beantworten konnte.

Das ist das einzige, was sich beweisen läßt.

Das einzige, was ich weiß, habe ich dir schon erzählt.

v. Only used as an adv., as in *the only possible solution* or *the only surviving manuscript,* is the adv. **einzig** followed by an adj. *Die einzig mögliche Lösung. Der einzig durchführbare Plan. Die einzig zuverlässige Quelle. Das wäre das einzig Vernünftige, the only sensible thg. Das ist das einzig Glaubwürdige an dem ganzen Bericht. Die einzig erhaltene Handschrift.* (The adj. *einzig* is possible before a part. like *erhalten,* but uncommon. *Der einzig[e] erhaltene Teil des früheren Stadtgrabens ist jetzt ein Schwanenteich.*)

vi. Einzig appears in the strengthened form **einzig und allein,** which is a variant on *nur. Er denkt einzig und allein an sich selbst,* only of himself, of himself alone. *Ich verdanke das alles einzig und allein ihr. Einzig und allein* can be used to translate *sole[ly]* in e.g. *They went for the sole purpose/solely for the purpose of making a nuisance of themselves. Sie gingen einzig und allein zu dem Zwecke hin, um den anderen lästig zu werden.* Or more simply *Sie sind nur deshalb hingegangen, um . . .*

vii. *Christa is an only child* is *Christa ist ein Einzelkind.* When *the only child of s.o.* is meant, *einzig* is used. *Sie/Er ist das einzige Kind [ihrer/seiner Eltern]. Sie hatten nur die einzige Tochter/den einzigen Sohn.*

viii. Alleinig is a stronger syn. of *einzig,* as **sole** is of **only.** *Er war der alleinige Erbe.* Like **sole,** it is often used when the meaning is 'not shared'. *Jmd. ist der alleinige Besitzer.*

Die Mutter hat die alleinige Verantwortung für die Erziehung der Kinder.

Er brachte die Firma unter seine alleinige Kontrolle.

3. In the sense 'not double or multiple', **single** is **einfach.** *A single* or *one-way ticket* is *eine einfache Fahrkarte.* Someone asking for a single to Kassel says, '*Kassel einfach, bitte!*' *Two singles to Kassel* is '*Zweimal Kassel einfach, bitte!*' *Eine zweifache* or *dreifache Schicht* is 'a double or triple layer'. *A single layer* is *eine einfache Schicht. Nur eine einzige Schicht* stresses that there is only one.

4. Single meaning 'unmarried' is **ledig,** particularly in official forms. Alternatives are **unverheiratet** and **alleinstehend. Der/Die Alleinerziehende** is 'a parent who is bringing up a child alone'.

sink *v.* One equivalent of **lower** *v.* 1 and 2 discuss the E. intr. uses, 3 the trans. use. 4 deals with other meanings of *sinken,* 5 with *[sich] senken,* and 6 with derivatives of *sacken.*

1. i. In the basic intr. sense 'to become submerged in water and go to the bottom', the equivalent of **sink** in reference to things is **sinken**. *Sinken* implies the whole process of settling in the water, going under the surface and then to the bottom, and is the usual word for the sinking of ships. It is used with *auf den Grund/Boden*. *Das Wasser war so klar, daß ich sehen konnte, wie der Stein auf den Grund sank. Die Teeblätter sinken bald auf den Boden der Kanne.*

> *Das Schiff war in wenigen Minuten gesunken, so daß alle Rettungsversuche scheiterten.*
> *Das Schiff wird sinken, wenn es uns nicht gelingt, das eingedrungene Wasser abzupumpen.*

ii. **Versinken** denotes the moment in the sinking of a vessel etc. when it disappears from sight under the surface of the water or becomes completely covered by water. It is often found with *vor jmds. Augen*. *Der Dampfer versank vor ihren Augen, und viele konnten noch nicht glauben, daß sie gerettet worden waren.* A syn. is **untergehen**. *Das Schiff war in wenigen Minuten untergegangen/ging mit Mann und Maus unter.* The past parts. of *sinken* and *versinken* are used without distinction. *Das gesunkene/versunkene Schiff konnte wieder gehoben werden.*

> *Die Schiffe, die kollidiert waren, sanken sehr schnell und waren bereits versunken, als die Rettungsboote ankamen.   Das Floß ging in der reißenden Strömung unter.*

iii. Because it refers to disappearance beneath the surface, **versinken**, and not *sinken*, is used for people. **Untergehen** is also possible.

> *Als er das Kind in etwa zehn Meter Entfernung versinken sah, sprang er ins Wasser.*
> *Man befürchtete, daß er in der reißenden Strömung untergehen würde.*

2. Another intr. sense of **sink** is 'to become partly or completely submerged' in quicksand, marshy ground, mud, snow, etc. *We sank up to our hips in the snow.* It is applied fig. to absorption in mental states. *He was sunk in thought/melancholy.*

i. **Versinken**, used without a phr. stating how far someone sinks, means 'to be completely submerged'. *Die Armee des Generals Pantopidan ist im Sumpf versunken.* It is used for towns etc. submerged in the sea. *Veneta ist eine im Meer versunkene Stadt.* It is also found with a phr. stating to what extent someone sinks. *Sie versanken bis zu den Knöcheln im Morast/im Schnee/im Schlamm.* A syn. in the latter sense is **einsinken**, which can only mean 'to sink to a certain extent'. *Man sinkt im Schnee/im nassen Sand ein.* A phr. stating how far can be added. It is also used for things which partly sink into the ground. *Die Säulen waren im Boden eingesunken.*

> *Der Mann, der in das Moor geraten war, sank immer tiefer, und niemand hörte seine Hilferufe. Es dauerte keine halbe Stunde, dann war er versunken.*
> *Auf unserer tagelangen Wanderung regnete es so heftig, daß wir selbst auf den Wegen bis an die Knie im Schlamm einsanken.*
> *Venedig sinkt immer mehr in den weichen Untergrund ein, bis es eines Tages ganz im Meer versunken sein wird.*

ii. In fig. use **versinken** means 'to become so absorbed in sth. as to be oblivious to everything else'. What the person is absorbed in can be an undesirable state like *Trauer* or *Schwermut* but also something pos. like *die Arbeit* or *jmds. Anblick*.

> *Sie war so tief in die Musik versunken, daß sie nicht bemerkte, daß jmd. zur Tür hereinkam und sie ansprach.*
> *Weil seine Gedanken sich mit etw. anderem beschäftigten, versank er nach und nach in Schweigen und nahm nicht mehr am Gespräch teil.   Die Bevölkerung versank in Angst und Schrecken.*
> *Sie war in ihre Arbeit so versunken, daß sie nicht merkte, was um sie herum vorging.*

iii. **Versinken** is the v. used in the context of sinking into the earth for shame. *Aus Scham über sein dummes Verhalten wäre er am liebsten in den Erdboden versunken.*

3. i. The equivalent of the trans. v. **sink** meaning 'to cause a vessel etc. to go down beneath the surface of the water' is **versenken**. *Die Piraten kaperten das Handelsschiff und versenkten es. Das Schiff wurde von einem U-Boot versenkt. Die Mannschaft versenkte das Schiff selbst.*

ii. The refl. **sich versenken** is applied to people who concentrate on something so intensely that they become completely absorbed in it. *Sie versenkte sich in das Buch/in die Arbeit/ins Gebet.*

4. Other meanings of *sinken* and two derivatives.

i. Sinken often means 'to fall' in the sense 'to become lower in level or standard'. **Absinken** expresses the same meaning. *Der Wasserspiegel sinkt* and *sinkt ab* do not differ in meaning. *Absinken* tends to be used when the new lower level reached is stated, but *ab* is optional. Thus *Die Temperatur sinkt*, is falling, but *ist um 10°/auf 5° abgesunken*. Either can be used for a fall in standard. *Jmds. Leistungen sind beträchtlich [ab]gesunken. Das Interesse ist auf Null gesunken* is a fixed expression. *Sinken* is the usual v. in relation to prices.

> *Im Vergleich zum Vorjahr sank die Zahl der Besucher um 7% [ab]/ist auf 10 000 [ab]gesunken.*
> *In der Nacht war die Außentemperatur auf –5 °C [ab]gesunken.*
> *Der Kurs des Dollars ist in letzter Zeit erheblich gesunken.*
> *Das Niveau der Fernsehfilme ist meiner Meinung nach in den letzten Jahren gesunken.*

ii. Sinken also means 'to sink morally'. *Moralisch* or *sittlich* can be added. *Ich hätte nie gedacht, daß er so tief hätte sinken können.*

iii. Sinken is also used intr. with *der Mut, die Hoffnung* and *das Vertrauen* as subj. *Mein Mut sank.* It is also used with *lassen. Den Mut nur nicht sinken lassen!*

> *Der unerwartete Erfolg hob ihren gesunkenen Mut.*
> *Ihnen sank jede Hoffnung auf ein Wiedersehen.*   *Mein Vertrauen sank immer mehr.*

iv. With a phr. of direction **sinken** means 'to fall down or sink'. *Sie sank ohnmächtig auf den Boden. Er sank auf/in die Knie.*

> *Er sank erschöpft in den Sessel.*   *Sie sanken einander in die Arme.*

v. Zusammensinken means 'to collapse' or 'to sink down'.

> *Sie ist unter der Last plötzlich ohnmächtig zusammengesunken.*
> *Er sank vor Müdigkeit auf dem Sessel zusammen.*

5. i. Senken means 'to lower' in three senses. *Er senkte den Angelhaken ins Wasser. Sie senkte den Kopf/den Blick/die Augen.* Another is 'to lower one's voice'. *Dann sagte er mit gesenkter Stimme . . .* It is also used with prices, costs, etc. as obj. *Man senkt die Preise/die Steuern/die Produktionskosten/eine Quote.*

> *Die Ärzte versuchten alles Mögliche, um das Fieber zu senken.*

ii. Sich senken means 'to become lower' in two senses. *Der Boden hat sich gesenkt* implies subsiding, but *Die Straße/Das Gelände senkt sich* means that it gradually falls away. Unlike *abfallen*, a syn. of the second sense, it is not used with *steil. Das Gelände fällt steil zum Fluß ab*, but *Das Gelände senkt sich zum Fluß hin.*

6. Colloquially, *sacken* and its derivatives express meanings of *sinken* and its prefixed forms. The main meaning of **sacken** is 'to fall or sink'. *Er sackte in die Knie/auf den Boden/zur Seite.* **Absacken** corresponds to *sinken*, **versacken** to *versinken*, and **einsacken** and **zusammensacken** to *einsinken* and *zusammensinken.*.

> *Das Schiff sackt ab. Also Der Schüler ist in seinen Leistungen abgesackt.*
> *Der Wagen sackte auf dem aufgeweichten Weg ein.*   *Die Räder versackten im Morast.*
> *In einer plötzlich aufkommenden Bö kenterte das hilflose Boot und versackte wie ein Stein.*
> *Plötzlich sackte er zusammen.*
> *Das Gebäude sackte zusammen.*

slip, slide, creep, glide *vs.* A few equivalents.

1. Schlüpfen implies moving quickly and skilfully out of or into something through a narrow opening. *Die Eidechse/Die Maus schlüpfte in/durch die Mauerspalte. Ein kleines Tier schlüpft aus einem Loch* or *schlüpft in ein Versteck. Der Hund schlüpfte unauffällig durch die Tür* suggests that the door is only slightly open. For a human being *schlüpfen* can suggest reaching a hiding place or a refuge, or evading danger, or only just getting through a door before it shuts. *Als er Schritte hörte, schlüpfte er in sein Versteck/ins nächste Zimmer. Der Dieb ist der Polizei durch die Finger geschlüpft.* It is also used for putting clothes on quickly. *Sie schlüpfte in das Kleid/in die Schuhe/in den Mantel.*

2. Schleichen means 'to move [away] cautiously, slowly, and with as little noise as possible in order not to be noticed'. The refl. **sich schleichen** does not differ in meaning. Used with *aus* they are translated as **slip**, *Sie schlich [sich] unbemerkt aus dem Zimmer,* and with most other preps. as **creep** or *sneak, Wir schlichen die Mauer/den Gang entlang.* In *Der Dieb muß sich unbemerkt ins Haus geschlichen haben,* it could be translated by all these vs. *[Sich] schleichen* may imply shyness or moving quietly out of consideration for others, but often it suggests some nefarious purpose or a bad conscience. *Jmd. schlich sich in das Vertrauen eines anderen* is a fig. use.
   Er schlich langsam und lautlos durch die Büsche.
   Sie schlich [sich] auf Zehenspitzen über den Gang.

3. Gleiten means 'to glide'. *Man gleitet mit Schlittschuhen über das Eis or mit Schiern über den Schnee. Tänzer gleiten über das Parkett. Ein Boot gleitet durchs Wasser.*

4. The derivative **ausgleiten** is one equivalent of **slip [over]** and belongs more to formal language. The everyday term is **ausrutschen**. *Ich glitt aus/rutschte aus und landete in einer Pfütze.*
   Ich bin auf dem Glatteis ausgeglitten/ausgerutscht.
   Er rutschte auf einer Bananenschale aus und fiel hin.

5. Rutschen is 'to move by sliding over a surface', usually unintentionally. *Ich bin auf dem gefrorenen Schnee gerutscht.* Sometimes the action can be deliberate. *Die Kinder rutschten auf dem Eis. Eine Rutschbahn* is 'a slide'. In reference to the feet *rutschen* is translated as **slide** or **slip** provided that the latter does not imply slipping over, in which case the vs. in 4 are used. In the example with a car below, the v. would be translated as *slid* or *skidded*. In *Er rutschte aus dem Sattel, rutschte* would be translated as *slipped*. As with the E. v. the action could be intentional or unintentional.
   Beim scharfen Bremsen auf der nassen Fahrbahn ist das Auto gegen die Leitplanke gerutscht.

6. Rutschen carries the meaning 'to slip out of position'. *Das Messer ist mir aus der Hand gerutscht. Die Brille rutscht mir dauernd auf die Nase. Das Hemd ist dir aus der Hose gerutscht.*

7. Slip over *to the shop!* meaning 'Go there quickly!' can be *Lauf' mal schnell zu dem Geschäft rüber!* or more colloquially *Flitz' mal schnell zum Geschäft rüber und hol mir ein Pfund Butter!*

soft, gentle, tender, delicate, mild *adjs.* Only some equivalents are discussed here. Order of meanings: 1. *Weich* = 'soft'. 2. *Leise* = 'soft'. 3. *Sanft* = 'gentle'. 4. *Zart* = 'tender'. 5. *Zart* = 'delicate'. 6. **Delicate** applied to food, situations, and instruments. 7. *Zärtlich*. 8. E. **mild**. 9. *Sachte*. 10. Three other E. uses. Some alternatives are given in each section.

1. *Weich* corresponds to four senses of **soft**.
i. Soft and **weich** are applied to things which change shape easily when pressed. *Weicher Teig. Ein weiches Bett/Kopfkissen. Jmd. liegt or sitzt weich.*
   Die Butter ist in der Wärme ganz weich geworden.   Durch den Regen war die Erde sehr weich.
   Die Nudeln müssen etwa 10 Minuten sprudelnd kochen, bis sie weich sind.
ii. Weich is the equivalent of **soft** when it means 'smooth and pleasant to the

touch'. Hence *weiches Haar. Weiches Fell. Ein weicher Pelz. Weiche Haut. Weiche Wolle. Weiches Leder. Etw. ist weich wie Samt* or *wie Seide*. One sense of **geschmeidig** is a syn. *Geschmeidige Haut* or *geschmeidiges Leder* is 'supple' meaning 'soft and bending easily without breaking'. (*Ein geschmeidiger Körper* is 'supple' = 'bending easily'.)

iii. Weich translates **soft** in *a soft landing. Eine weiche Landung. Das Raumschiff ist auf dem Mond weich gelandet*. An alternative is **sanft** *landen*. Cf. 3. iv. *Das Flugzeug landete mit einem sanften Aufprall.*

iv. Applied to people, **weich** means 'easily moved emotionally' and/or 'inclined to give way to others'. It can translate **soft** in the sense 'easily upset'. *I was in tears by the end of the film—I'm awfully soft* can be *Am Ende des Films war ich in Tränen aufgelöst— ich habe ein weiches Herz/Gemüt/Wesen* or *ich bin sehr weich. Waldemar ist ein weicher Mensch.* The second part of the definition often becomes the dominant idea, as in *Nur nicht weich werden!* In *Die Lehrer/Polizisten sind heutzutage zu weich*, it implies softhearted and giving in too easily (in G. *zu nachgiebig*). For *to be too* **soft** *on s.o.* see *sanft*, 3. iv.

2. Soft when it is the opposite of *loud* is **leise**. *'Hör' mal!' sagte sie leise*, softly, quietly. *Sie murmelte leise vor sich hin. Er trat leise auf. Seien Sie bitte leise! Türen leise schließen! Stell das Radio bitte leiser!*

3. *Sanft* expresses some senses of **gentle**.

i. A gentle person is kind, mild, and pleasantly calm in character and behaviour. **Sanft** suggests kind, friendly, balanced, peaceable, calm. *Sie ist sanft/ein sanfter Mensch.*

Die junge Frau war sanft und religiös veranlagt.	*Er/Sie war eine sanfte, sensible Natur.*
Sie lächelte ihn sanft an.	*Ihre sanfte Art wirkte beruhigend.*
'Machen Sie sich keine Sorgen!' sagte sie sanft.	*Das Pferd ist ganz sanft.*

ii. Applied to eyes and voice, **sanft** means 'expressing *eine sanfte Natur*', and thus translates **gentle** = 'calm, friendly, and kind'. *Sie hatte sanfte blaue Augen/sprach mit sanfter Stimme.*

iii. Sanft also means 'not strong or harsh, but moderate and pleasant' in relation to light and colours, for which E. uses **soft** or sometimes **gentle**. *Ein sanfter Glanz. Sanfte Beleuchtung. Das sanfte Licht des Mondes. Eine sanfte Melodie*, gentle.

iv. Gentle applied to movements or actions or to the way people are treated means 'even and calm, not causing pain or damage'. **Sanft** suggests without intensity, not causing harm or disturbance. Thus *ein sanfter Wind/Regen. Sanfter Druck. Ein sanfter Händedruck. Er berührte sanft ihre Hand.* **Leise** is a syn., but it occurs only in poetical language. *Ein leiser Händedruck. Er strich ihr leise über das Haar.* **Sanft** is applied to the way people are treated. *Du hast ihn nicht gerade sanft behandelt.* To be too **soft** *on s.o.* can be *zu sanft mit jmdm. umgehen. Du gehst zu sanft mit diesen Schülern um.*

Sie schob das Kind sanft beiseite.	*Er drückte sanft auf die wunde Stelle.*
Er hat ihre Hand sanft gestreichelt.	*Sie schaukelte das Kind sanft in den Armen.*

v. Sanft also corresponds to **gentle** in *sanfte Vorwürfe/Ermahnungen*, 'gentle reproaches/criticism and exhortations', and *eine sanft ansteigende Höhe* or *ein sanfter Anstieg*, 'a gentle slope'.

4. *Zart* is the equivalent of **tender** in several senses.

i. Used of people, **tender** means 'displaying gentle and caring feelings'. **Zart** means in one sense 'considerate and loving'. *Jmdn. mit zarter Fürsorge behandeln*, to treat s.o. with tender care. *Zarte Aufmerksamkeit, zarte Zuneigung*, and *zarte Rücksichtnahme* also occur. *Jmdm. gegenüber zarte Gefühle haben* suggests tender or loving feelings.

Du hast den Jungen nicht gerade zart angefaßt. (Also *sanft* in sense 3. iv, which is more common than *zart* in this context.)

Wie zart eine Löwenmutter ihr Junges mit den Zähnen am Nacken doch packen kann!

ii. Zart is used with *das Alter*, as is **tender** with *age*. *Im zarten Alter von fünf Jahren spielte er schon Klavier in der Öffentlichkeit.* Both E. and G. words are applied to crops and trees which are at an easily harmed stage of development. *Die zarten Pflanzen müssen vor Frost geschützt werden.*

iii. Zart means 'tender' in relation to meat and food. *Der Schnitzel war sehr zart. Der Kranke ißt nur zartes Gemüse.*

5. Zart expresses some senses of **delicate**.

i. Delicate means 'small, graceful, and attractive' and is applied among other things to the body and parts of it. *She had long delicate fingers.* Zart means 'of slim or slender structure' and is used for the body or parts of it. *Sie hatte zarte Glieder/lange zarte Finger. Jmd. ist von zarter Gestalt/von zartem Wuchs/hat ein zartes Gesicht.* An alternative is one sense of **fein**. *Jmd. hat feine Glieder/Hände/eine feine Gestalt. Feine/Zarte Gesichtszüge.* Only *fein* translates *a delicate floral pattern*: *Ein feines Blumenmuster.*

ii. In reference to colour, taste, and smell, **delicate** means 'pleasant, not strong or intense'. Zart means 'not intense', but is applied mostly to colours and light. *Zarte Farben. Ein Stoff von zartem Rosa. Ihr blasses Gesicht überzog sich mit einer zarten Röte.*

iii. Delicate meaning 'fragile' suggests the object needs to be handled carefully. It is applied mostly to fabrics and china. Zart means 'thin in structure, soft to the touch, and liable to be harmed by rough handling'. *Zarte Haut/Wangen. Blumen sind zarte Gebilde. Der zarte Flaum (eines Pfirsichs). Eine Bluse aus zarter Seide.* Fein means 'of thin texture', *ein feines Gewebe*, but suggests less fragility than *zart*, just as *fine* suggests less fragility than **delicate**. *Feines Garn. Feines Haar. Feine Wolle.* Both *zart* and *fein* are combined with words meaning 'line'. *Zarte Linien/Striche. Ein feiner Strich.*

iv. Like **delicate**, zart can be applied to *health. Ein zartes Kind* is delicate in the sense of 'having little resistance to illness'. *Jmd. hat zarte Gesundheit/ist von zarter Gesundheit.* (Related is **anfällig**, 'susceptible', which is used alone or with *für* or *gegen. Das Kind war sehr anfällig [für Erkältungen].*)

6. Other senses of **delicate**.

i. While **delicate**, applied to food, means 'pleasing to the taste and not strongly flavoured', *delikat* means 'delicious, exquisite'. *Die Soße ist/schmeckt ganz delikat. Ein delikates Aroma.* **Leicht** or **mild** convey the meaning 'delicate' just defined. Thus *a delicate (mushroom) sauce* becomes *eine leicht gewürzte/mild gewürzte Champignon Soße.*

ii. A situation described as **delicate** needs care and tactful treatment. **Heikel** means that a situation, topic, etc. can cause great difficulties and needs to be treated with care and tact. **Delikat** means 'requiring discretion and sensitivity' or, applied to a person's action, 'displaying discretion etc.' *Ein heikles/delikates Thema/Problem. Eine heikle/delikate Angelegenheit/Situation.* In *Er hat die Angelegenheit in sehr delikater Weise behandelt, delikat* suggests tactfulness.

Sie berührten die heikle Frage/das heikle Thema der Beziehungen zwischen den Rassen.

iii. A **delicate** *instrument*, i.e. 'one registering the slightest changes', is *ein* **empfindliches** *Meßgerät.* Cf. SENSITIVE. **Fein** is also used. *Feine Instrumente.* Both are applied to the senses. *Bienen haben einen empfindlichen/feinen Geruchssinn.*

7. **Zärtlich** means 'tender' in the sense 'loving and affectionate' and is applied only to human beings. *Ein Mensch empfindet zärtliche Gefühle für einen anderen* and *Er hat sie zärtlich angelächelt/geküßt.*

8. i. E. **mild** means 'gentle, kind, and warm-hearted'. It describes someone's nature, *She has a mild nature,* or actions, *a mild answer,* but is only rarely applied directly to people, *I'm the mildest man imaginable.* For people, *gentle* or *mild-mannered* are more common. G. **mild** means 'lenient, not strict' and is used in contexts such as *ein mildes Urteil, eine milde Zurechtweisung/Strafe,* or *Seine Augen waren nicht mehr mild, sondern funkelten vor Zorn.* The adv. in *jmdn. mild beurteilen* is translated as *mildly,* but in *jmdn. mild behandeln* or *mit jmdm. mild umgehen* as *gently.* When E. **mild** or *mild-mannered* mean 'gentle', the best transl. is **sanft.** *'Du brauchst nicht zu schreien', sagte sie sanft,* mildly, gently. *Eine sanfte Antwort. Ich bin der sanfteste Mensch, den man sich vorstellen kann. Sie hat eine sanfte Natur.*
ii. Like E. **mild**, G. **mild** means 'not strong and not hard on the eyes' in reference to light. *Ein milder Glanz. Das milde Licht/Der milde Schein des Mondes/einer Lampe.*
iii. Like E. **mild**, G. **mild** is applied to the weather, food, soap, etc. *Ein mildes Klima. Mildes Wetter. Ein milder Curry. Ein milder Käse. Eine milde Seife.*
iv. Leicht means 'light or slight' and translates some senses of **mild**. *A mild illness/infection* is *eine leichte Erkrankung/Entzündung. We looked at each other in mild astonishment: Wir sahen uns leicht erstaunt an. They protested mildly: Sie haben leicht protestiert/erhoben leichten Widerspruch. Sanft protestieren,* to protest gently. *A gentle or mild satire: Eine leichte Satire. Mild anger* can be *leichter Zorn.* **Mäßig,** 'moderate', can also be used. *The film was mildly amusing: Der Film war nur mäßig unterhaltsam. They made a mild attempt to break open the door* could be *Sie machten einen halbherzigen Versuch, die Tür aufzubrechen.*

9. Sachte now suggests being careful and cautious so as not to break something, upset people, or spoil things. *Sachte, sachte!* is used as a warning not to rush things, to take them gently and easily. *Man geht sachte mit jmdm. um/behandelt jmdn. sachte/ermahnt jmdn. sachte.*

10. Other E. uses.
i. *The government is* **soft** *on tax evasion. Sie geht nicht streng genug gegen die Steuerhinterziehung vor.* For *streng* see SEVERE.
ii. *A* **gentle** *hint: Ein leiser Hinweis.*
iii. Tender describing a part of the body means 'sensitive and painful' and could be translated by *empfindlich,* SENSITIVE. *Er berührte die empfindliche Stelle am Bein.*

some *adj.* Main equivalents. **Some** refers to a quantity of something or a number of people or things without stating the quantity or number precisely. It is used with a certain variation in meaning: (i) **Some** does not state whether the amount or number is small or large. The quantity or number may be unknown or not important. **Some** in this sense is unstressed. *She had some coffee and a piece of cake. Some friends are coming over tonight. I've got́ some important thgs. to discuss with you. Margot bought some paper/some stamps yesterday.* **Some** in this sense is common in invitations and requests. *Please have some cake!* (ii) In interrogative sents. **some** suggests an affirmative answer. *Aren't there some stamps in that drawer?* or *There are some stamps in that drawer, aren't there? He gave you some money, didn't he?* (iii) **Some** or *any* are used in *if-*clauses. *If we had some/any money, we could buy it. If we find some/any mushrooms, we'll share them with you.*

1. Some in senses i, ii, and iii above, in which it refers to an unspecified amount or number, is frequently not expressed in G. Someone might ask '*Möchten Sie Kuchen?*' which in E. can only be *some cake.* The meaning 'some' is implied in *Er hat dir [doch] Geld gegeben, nicht wahr?* and in *Wenn wir Geld hätten, könnten wir es kaufen.* The main equivalents of **some** are *etwas* and *einige.* **Etwas** and **einige** emphasize the meanings 'not none' and 'not all'. Someone might say, *'Nehmen Sie doch etwas Kuchen!' Etwas* can be added to *In der Kanne ist noch Tee.* It is often unnecessary to use *einige* with a pl. n. where E. has **some**. *Ich hatte Schwierigkeiten, mich im Nebel zurechtzufinden. Sind [da] Briefmarken in der Schublade? If you have some/any questions* is *wenn Sie Fragen haben. Einige* can emphasize the meaning 'not none'. *Es waren einige Studenten da, obwohl bei weitem nicht alle.*

Sie nahm ein Stück Kuchen und Kaffee.	*[Einige] Freunde besuchen uns heute abend.*
Wenn wir Pilze finden, teilen wir sie mit euch.	*Margot kaufte Briefmarken/Papier gestern.*

2. Some can also indicate that the quantity or number is fairly small, but nevertheless greater than none, and can be stressed or unstressed. It is applied to something concrete, *I have got some money left, but not much* or *Some people understand what's going on, though they're few and far between,* and to abstracts, *We haven't achieved everything we set out to do, but we have had some success.*

i. With sing. ns. referring to something concrete only **etwas** is used. In this sense it means 'a small amount of, a little'. *A. Du hast wohl kein Geld mehr. B. Etwas Geld habe ich noch, aber nicht sehr viel. Gib mir bitte etwas Milch! Ich brauche etwas Zucker. Man löse etwas Salz im Wasser auf! Sie spricht etwas Russisch.*

Es gab etwas Gelächter, als der Vorsitzende sagte, er habe das Manuskript seiner Rede verloren.

Noch etwas is 'some more' when a n. follows. *Möchten Sie noch etwas Käse?* (Without a n., *noch etwas* means 'sth. else'. *Ich möchte noch etwas sagen.*) *Ich hätte gern etwas mehr* also means 'some or a little more'. The difference between *noch etwas* and **etwas mehr** is that the former implies some more of what the person has already used up, e.g. eaten, while the latter implies some more in addition to what one already has. A person who had finished one cup or helping could be asked, *'Möchten Sie noch etwas Tee/Suppe?'* If someone had already taken some cream, but not yet eaten it, and was being urged to take some more, the hostess might say, *'Nehmen Sie [doch] etwas mehr [Sahne]!'*

ii. Only **einige** is used with pl. ns. and denotes an unspecified, fairly small number. It translates both *some* and *a* FEW. In this sense it is usually unstressed.

Ich kenne noch einige ähnliche Fälle.   Einige Kinder kamen vorbei.
Einige Kollegen von uns wollen an der Tagung teilnehmen, und wir fahren mit.
Einige Leute verstehen, was sich da abspielt, aber deren Zahl ist sehr klein.

iii. With sing. ns. not denoting something concrete, both **etwas** and **einige** express the meaning 'some'. Both mean 'a little, not very much'. *Etwas* is more common. *Mit etwas gutem Willen. Mit einigem gutem Willen. Dazu ist etwas Geduld nötig. Mit einiger Geduld wäre das zu erreichen. Etwas* does not differ appreciably in meaning from *ein wenig; einige* can be a syn., but it may differ in meaning as explained in the next section.

Er hat immer noch etwas/einige Hoffnung.
Ich betrachte diese Vorgänge mit etwas/einiger Besorgnis.
Wir haben nicht alles erreicht, was wir uns vorgenommen hatten, aber wir haben doch etwas/einigen Erfolg gehabt.   Jmd. hat etwas/einige Erfahrung auf diesem Gebiet.

3. Some also indicates that the quantity or number is fairly large. It means 'a fair amount or number' or 'considerable' and is always stressed. *I didn't meet her again for some years. It took some doing* or *some effort. I shall be away for some time. She was sitting on a bench some distance away. The railway station is some distance from the house. He spoke at some length.*

i. *Du brauchst Übung* does not specify the amount of practice needed. In *Du brauchst noch etwas Übung, etwas* means 'not very much'. *Mit dem Autofahren klappt es schon ganz gut—du brauchst aber noch etwas Übung.* When **einige** is stressed in *Du brauchst noch einige Übung,* it means 'a fair bit, quite a bit'. (Underlining denotes stress.) This is also its sense in *Ich habe es mit einiger Mühe geschafft*. If *Mühe* were stressed instead of *einige*, *einige* would mean the same as *etwas*, but in such a case *etwas* would usually be preferred. *Mit etwas Mühe/Fleiß könnte er es schaffen*. There are some fixed expressions such as *nach einigem Nachdenken*. *Nach einiger Überlegung*. *Nach einigem Hin und Her*. *In einiger Entfernung*. *Eine Stadt von einiger Bedeutung*. In *Nach einiger Zeit* and *Es wird noch einige Zeit dauern*, *einige* means 'some' = 'quite a bit'. *Wir haben noch etwas Zeit* and *Gib mir noch etwas Zeit!* imply only a small amount. The pronoun **einiges** can also mean 'quite a bit'. *Die Reparatur wird sicher einiges kosten*.

> *Ich sah sie erst nach einigen Jahren wieder.*   *Dafür habe ich einige Zeit gebraucht.*
> *Mit einigem Aufwand (an Energie) schafft er es schon.*   *Es wird einigen Ärger geben.*
> *Der Fall hat einiges Aufsehen erregt.*   *Das bringt noch einige Überlegung mit sich.*
> *Es wird einige Mühe kosten, ihn zu überzeugen.* (He'll take some convincing.)

ii. Mancher and the pl. **manche** mean 'quite a few among many'. Whether used in the sing. or pl., they denote an unspecified number of people or things seen as individuals, not as a group, one here and there in a number, and correspond to stressed **some** in meaning 3. Hammer (1991: 111) defines the meaning as 'a fair number, but by no means all'. *Manche Senatoren sprachen sich gegen die Ratifizierung des Vertrags aus* suggests that the number was not particularly large. *Einige Senatoren* may be a few more, but it is much the same. *An manchen Tagen fühlte er sich miserabel* suggests on a small number of days, seen individually, one here and there, but *an einigen Tagen des Monats* suggests several, forming a group. **Manches** has the same meaning as *einiges*, some things. *Manches/Einiges hat sich gebessert*.

> *In mancher Beziehung hat er recht.* (In some/quite a few respects. *In vieler Beziehung*, in many respects.)   *Manche Kinder lernen Sprachen schneller als andere.*
> *Manche Schüler werden es wohl nie begreifen*, meinte der resignierende Lehrer.
> *In manchen Fällen muß man einfach eine Ausnahme machen.*

iii. Although **at some distance** is *in einiger Entfernung*, to be **some distance from** sth. is usually translated by *ziemlich weit von etw. entfernt sein*. *Das Haus ist ziemlich weit vom Bahnhof entfernt*. He spoke **at some length** becomes *Er hat ziemlich lange gesprochen*.

4. Stressed **some** also means 'a certain degree of'. *That is some help towards understanding the issue. There is some chance that it will work. That is still true to some extent.* This sense is expressed by the adj. **gewiß**. *Das ist eine gewisse Hilfe beim Verständnis der Frage. Das ist ein gewisser Trost*, some consolation. *Eine gewisse Chance gibt es schon, daß es klappen wird.* To some extent is *bis zu einem gewissen Grade*. *Ich bin bis zu einem gewissen Grade selbst daran schuld. Unsere Meinungen stimmen bis zu einem gewissen Grade überein. Bis zu einem gewissen Grade ist das noch wahr. In gewisser Hinsicht hat sie recht*, in some/certain respects.

5. Some also refers to a part of a quantity or of a group of persons or things. *I've spent some of the money. The marchers divided, and some went north.* **Etwas** is used when a sing. n. is referred to, and **einige** when more than one person or thing is meant. *Das Geld habe ich heute früh abgehoben und etwas schon ausgegeben. Nimm dir etwas von dem Geld! Die Marschierenden teilten sich, und einige gingen nach Norden.*

6. When **some** or *any* replace a n., both are **welcher**. *I haven't any sugar. Could you lend me some?/Have you any? Ich habe keinen Zucker. Kannst du mir welchen borgen? Hast du welchen?*

> A. *Brauchst du Geld?* B. *Danke, ich habe noch welches.*
> *Man muß Zentimeterpapier mitnehmen. Hast du welches? Ich gebe dir welches.*

7. Some refers to a particular person, thing, place, etc. when it is not stated which one is meant. *Or other* is often added. *I read it in some newspaper [or other].* **Some** + a n. in this sense is **irgendein**. *Irgendein Junge hat es gebracht. Ich habe es in irgendeiner Zeitung gelesen. Sie muß irgendeinen Grund dafür haben. Some man at the door wants to* *speak to you is*, however, *An der Tür ist ein Mann, der dich sprechen möchte. He's living at some place [or other] in Scotland is Er wohnt* **irgendwo** *in Schottland. At some time or other is* **irgendwann***. Sie hat es mir irgendwann erzählt, ich weiß aber nicht mehr genau wann.*

8. Some *150 miles* is expressed by **ungefähr** or **etwa**, both of which mean 'approximately'. *Ungefähr/Etwa 150 Meilen weiter nach Süden. Some ten years ago is vor ungefähr zehn Jahren.* There were *some thirty people there* can be *Es waren etwa dreißig Leute da* or *Es waren einige dreißig Leute da.*

sound, noise *ns.*

1. In one sense a **noise** denotes a sound that someone or something makes. *A sudden noise made Brody jump. The branch snapped with a loud noise.* In this sense it is a syn. of **sound** defined as 'sth. that s.o. hears', although they are not always interchangeable. *She heard a sound/a noise in the hall. He opened the door without a sound/without making a noise.* The equivalent of both words in this sense is **das Geräusch**, an unspecified sound or noise, often one that arises when something moves or is moved. *Was man hört, wenn z. B. Papier knistert, nennt man ein Geräusch.* Someone who hears a sound or noise might ask, '*Was ist denn das für ein Geräusch?*' Thus *das Geräusch einer Handsäge/eines Bohrers/eines Motors*, etc. and *Die Heizung macht Geräusche.* In itself it does not suggest that the noise is disturbing or irritating, but adjs. indicating this may be added. *Ein störendes/monotones Geräusch. Der Geräuschpegel* is 'noise level' and *geräuschvoll* 'noisy/noisily'. *Die Kinder traten geräuschvoll ins Klassenzimmer.*

Sie hörte ein Geräusch im Gang/Stimmengeräusch im Garten/das Geräusch von Schritten.
Die Geräusche des Waldes wirken auf viele Menschen unheimlich.
Ein plötzliches Geräusch ließ ihn aufspringen.　　　*Er trat geräuschlos ein.*
Plötzlich brach der Ast mit einem lauten Geräusch.　　*Die Tür öffnete sich ohne Geräusch.*

2. Noise also denotes loud or unpleasant sounds which continue for some time and are disturbing to those hearing them. The equivalent in the standard language is **der Lärm** and in the spoken language **der Krach**. *Kannst du bei solchem Lärm/Krach arbeiten?* The dividing line between *Lärm* and *Geräusch* is not always clear. *Das Motorengeräusch* is 'the sound of the motors' and does not suggest a disturbance. If it becomes very loud and unpleasant, *der Motorenlärm* is used. Unlike *Geräusch*, both *Lärm* and *Krach* are collective ns. used only in the sing.

Es erhob sich ein unbeschreiblicher/schrecklicher/unerträglicher/ohrenbetäubender Lärm.
Der Lärm der Maschinen war zu stark, als daß wir uns hätten unterhalten können.
Der Lärm, der von der Straße ins Zimmer hereindrang, war so stark, daß die Fenster geschlossen bleiben mußten.　　*Ich kann diesen Krach nicht mehr aushalten.*
Die Mutter rief den spielenden Kindern zu, 'Macht nicht so viel Krach!' Also: Lärm.

Der Krach also denotes a sudden, very loud noise, often caused by the impact of one thing on another. *Die Tür schlug mit lautem Krach/Geräusch zu.*

Plötzlich gab es einen furchtbaren Krach.　　*Das Gebäude stürzte mit lautem Krach zusammen.*

3. Der Schall denotes sound as a physical phenomenon and is the equivalent of **sound** in physics or scientific contexts. It does not occur frequently in everyday speech, except in compounds which have become common, such as *Das Flugzeug hat die Schallmauer durchbrochen*, and *schalldicht*, soundproof.

Die Geschwindigkeit des Schalls in der Luft beträgt etwa 330 Meter pro Sekunde.
Der Schall pflanzt sich im Wasser schneller fort als in der Luft.

Schall is used instead of *Geräusch* and *Klang* in formal language and often suggests a fairly loud and echoing sound. *In dem menschenleeren Tunnel klang der Schall der Schritte unheimlich.*

Der Schall von Stimmen dröhnte aus der Schlucht.   *Der Schall der Glocken war weithin zu hören.*

4. Der Klang is 'a resonant sound, often that of music'. Unless otherwise stated, the sound is pleasant. *Klang* is applied to music and the human voice and is the usual term for the sound of prose or verse. *Ein heller/schriller/leiser/tiefer/reiner/ melodischer/harmonischer Klang.* In reference to music it is often pl. *Sie lauschte den Klängen des Orchesters.* It is also applied to the particular way someone's voice or words sound. *Seine Stimme hatte/Seine Worte hatten einen bitteren/spöttischen Klang.*

> *Der Klang der Stimme des Redners war so angenehm, daß man ihm lange mühelos zuhören konnte.*
> *Der Klang der Glocken war weit über das Dorf hinaus zu hören.*
> *Dem Klang seiner Stimme nach hat er Gesangsunterricht genommen.*
> *Unter den Klängen eines Marsches zogen die Sportler in das Stadion ein.*

5. Der Laut denotes the smallest acoustic unit of human speech which is represented by one or more letters of the alphabet. *Ich konnte nicht erkennen, ob es ein ch- oder ein sch-Laut war. Sprechen Sie mir die folgenden Laute nach!* It is also applied to sounds people make to express an emotional state, such as surprise, *Er stieß einen Laut der Überraschung aus,* and to speech-like sounds which animals make, *Man hat zwanzig verschiedene Laute identifiziert, die Delphine erzeugen können.*

6. Ein Ton means 'a NOTE (in music)', *ein hoher Ton,* and often corresponds to *tone, Der Ton des Briefes gefällt mir nicht,* and to *tone of voice, Sie sprach in freundlichem Ton.* In some expressions it is translated as **sound** or *word. Er gab keinen Ton von sich* is *He didn't say a word* or *There was not a sound from him. Laut* is a syn. here. *Er gab keinen Laut von sich/ließ keinen Laut hören. Laß keinen Ton darüber verlauten!* can be rendered as *Don't say a word* or *breathe a sound about it. Sie hätte nur einen Ton zu sagen brauchen, und wir hätten ihr geholfen. Nur ein Wort* is an alternative.

> *Vor Aufregung brachte sie keinen Ton heraus.*   *Wir hörten keinen Ton/nur wimmernde Töne.*

7. In some cases it is better to use a specific term where E. has the general words **sound** or **noise**. Some examples are: *Das Rauschen des Baches wirkte beruhigend. Das Klingeln des Telefons. Das Läuten der Kirchenglocken.* (*Klingeln* denotes a continuous ringing, while *läuten* denotes ringing in separate strokes like a church bell.) *Das Dröhnen der Kanonen. Das Tosen des Sturmes/der Brandung. Das Brausen der Wellen.* (Both *tosen* and *brausen* mean 'to roar', mostly in reference to water, but *tosen* suggests a stronger and louder sound.) *The sound of laughter* can be translated as *das Gelächter. Ich hörte Gelächter im Nachbarzimmer.* The meaning of *I don't like the sound of it* can be expressed as *Die Sache gefällt mir nicht.*

spare *v.*

1. This section discusses the equivalents of four closely related senses of **spare**. (i) The basic meaning is 'to leave unhurt, not to destroy, punish, or harm', or, seen pos., 'to show mercy to'. *Many ships were sunk, but a few were spared. Was he spared by fate earlier only to be ruined now?* (ii) Another meaning is 'to refrain from attacking, criticizing, reprimanding, or speaking too severely'. *In his sermons he spared neither high nor low, rich nor poor.* (iii) In *to spare s.o.'s feelings,* **spare** means 'to refrain from hurting'. *She spared his feelings and did not criticize him.* (iv) In the refl. or with a person as obj. **spare** means 'to refrain from making great demands on'. *He spares neither himself nor his employees. Verschonen* is the main equivalent of senses i and ii, and *schonen* of senses iii and iv.

i. In one sense **verschonen** means 'to save people or thgs. from sth. harmful' or 'to refrain from inflicting harm on or attacking s.o.' It implies that the subj. is in a position to cause damage, destruction, or harm, but does not do so. *Hat ihn das Schicksal früher verschont, damit es ihn nun zugrunderichten könnte?*

Nur wenige Gebäude wurden vom Luftangriff verschont.

Er verschonte niemand mit seiner Kritik.

Viele Schiffe wurden versenkt, aber einige blieben verschont.

Der moderne Krieg ist äußerst zerstörerisch und verschont niemand und nichts.

Es sah so aus, als ob der wütende Mann den kleinen Werner verprügeln wollte. Aber dann verschonte
er ihn, vermutlich aus einer besseren Einsicht heraus.

In seinen Predigten verschonte er weder Reiche noch Arme, weder Hohe noch Niedrige.

ii. The base v. **schonen** means 'to show consideration for, to treat carefully, not to put too great a strain on'. It translates the uses given in E. sense iv above, *Er schont sich nicht bei der Arbeit*, and **spare** with *feelings* and *s.o.'s life* as obj., *Du mußt ihre Gefühle schonen* and *Die Regierung beschloß, das Leben des zum Tode verurteilten Generals zu schonen. Schone deine Augen!* could be translated as *Spare your eyes!*, the meaning being 'to treat them properly'. *Um die Pferde zu schonen, ritten sie Schritt.* (With a thing as obj., as in *Das Kind schont seine Sachen [nicht], schonen* has the related sense 'to take care of, look after'.)

Sie schonte seine Gefühle und hat ihn nicht kritisiert.

Er schont seine Untergebenen nicht, ist aber immer bereit, ihre Leistung anzuerkennen.

Sich schonen often implies refraining from exertion because of one's state of health and suggests that the person is ill or recovering from illness. *Es geht ihr schon besser, aber sie muß sich noch schonen. Du mußt deine Kräfte schonen* can imply not exerting oneself because of one's state of health, but it is also applied to sportspeople who save their strength for a later event. *Die Sportler schonten ihre Kräfte für das Endspiel.*

2. Spare = 'to save s.o. from sth. unpleasant' or 'to save s.o. the trouble or effort of doing sth.'

i. In its second weakened sense **verschonen** means 'not to bother s.o. with sth., not to inflict sth. annoying or troublesome on a pers.' It corresponds to **spare** used with two objs., meaning 'to save s.o. from sth. disagreeable'. *Spare us the gory details!* With *verschonen*, the second E. obj. follows *mit. Verschone uns mit den widerlichen Einzelheiten! Verschone mich bitte mit diesen Lappalien/solchen Klatschgeschichten! Verschone mich mit deinen Ratschlägen!*

ii. In *We wanted to spare him the embarrassment*, *save* could replace **spare**. This sense of SAVE or **spare** in *to save/spare s.o. the cost/trouble*, etc. *of sth.* or *of doing sth.* is carried by **ersparen**. *Sie wollte ihren Eltern Kosten ersparen, deshalb ging sie nicht zur Universität*, save or spare them the expense. The pass. can be expressed by *bleiben* as well as *werden. Mir wurde/blieb diese Demütigung erspart.*

Wir wollten ihm die peinliche Situation ersparen.   *Ihm blieb nichts erspart.*

Diese Scherereien wurden mir erspart.   *Möge Ihnen das erspart bleiben!*

iii. Often both *verschonen* and *ersparen* are possible as equivalents of **spare**. Thus *Verschone mich mit diesen albernen Witzen!* or *Erspare mir diese albernen Witze!* Also *Erspare uns die widerlichen Einzelheiten!* and *Erspare mir deine Ratschläge!* instead of the transls. given in 2. i. *Verschonen* stresses that someone finds something unwelcome, while *ersparen* emphasizes that something is superfluous or that one person does not allow something to happen which might distress another person.

3. Spare also means 'to consume economically, refrain from using freely'. It is mostly used as a pres. part. *Be sparing with the butter!* The idea can be expressed both pos. and neg. by **sparsam mit etw. umgehen**. *Geh sparsam mit der Butter um, wir haben fast keine mehr! Du brauchst nicht so sparsam mit der Sahne umzugehen!* **Sparen an**, 'to save on', can also express the sense. *Spart nicht am Wein/an der Sahne!*

4. Another sense of **spare** is 'to give away without inconvenience', *Could you spare me a cup of sugar?*, or 'to part with as not being needed at the time', *Could you spare*

[*me*] *two of your workmen for a couple of days?*, or 'to make time available without inconvenience', *Could you spare me ten minutes today?*

i. The general term is **entbehren**, to do without. *Wir können diesen Mitarbeiter nicht entbehren.* **Erübrigen** means 'to make available' by saving time, expenses, etc., but it is not a common word. *Ich kann die Zeit dazu nicht erübrigen.* Neither word is used in reference to trivial things. For these, words expressing the meaning of the E. v. are used. *Hast du genug Zucker, um mir eine Tasse voll zu leihen? We can't spare the car tonight* could be *Wir brauchen das Auto heute abend* or *Wir können heute abend nicht auf das Auto verzichten. I can spare you tomorrow* could be *Ich brauche Sie nicht unbedingt morgen* or *Ich komme morgen ohne Sie aus.*

> *Der Oberst konnte keine Soldaten entbehren, schickte aber einen Offizier.*
> *Während der Stoßzeit können wir keinen einzigen Mitarbeiter entbehren.*
> *Könnten Sie ein paar Dollar für die Heilsarmee entbehren/erübrigen?* Or *Hätten Sie ein paar Dollar*
> *für die Heilsarmee?* Colloquially: *Ein paar Mark kannst du doch bestimmt loseisen.*

ii. *Could you* **spare** *the time to help me?* is usually *Hättest du etwas Zeit, um mir zu helfen? Could you* **spare** *me half an hour some time this week?* is *Hättest du im Laufe der Woche eine halbe Stunde Zeit für mich?* In **Zeit [für jmdn.] haben**, *Zeit* is not omitted as *time* is in E. *Hätten Sie zehn Minuten Zeit für uns?*

5. If people spare no expense in doing something or spare no effort to bring something about, they do it without any attempt to reduce the amount spent or the effort expended. *Nothing was spared in making/to make them comfortable. He spared neither time nor effort in attaining/to attain his end.* This sense is expressed by **scheuen** + a neg., 'to shy away from or avoid', thus to refrain from incurring costs, making an effort, etc.

> *Sie scheuten keine Kosten, um es ihren Gästen bequem zu machen.*
> *Sie scheuten weder Geld noch Mühe, um ihren Kindern eine gute Schulbildung zu geben.*

6. To spare can mean 'left over as a surplus'. *We have enough and to spare. We caught the train with five minutes to spare.* As there is no fixed equivalent, the sense has to be translated and can often be expressed by **übrig**. *Die Regale paßten genau, ohne daß ein Millimeter Platz übrig blieb,* with no room to spare. *Wir sind gerade rechtzeitig angekommen und hatten keine Minute übrig,* with no time/not a minute to spare. In a pos. sent. relating to time *Zeit* is used. *Wir hatten fünf Minuten Zeit. We have enough and to spare* could be *Wir haben mehr als genug.* Where the AV has *How many hired servants of my father's have bread enough and to spare?*, the modernized *Lutherbibel* has *Wie viele Tagelöhner hat mein Vater, die Brot in Fülle haben?*

> *Sie hatten zwei Tage übrig, bevor sie Rom verlassen mußten.*
> *Wir waren um elf am Bahnsteig und hatten noch zehn Minuten Zeit [vor Abfahrt des Zuges].*

spend *v.*

1. In everyday language **spend money** is **Geld ausgeben**. *So viel [Geld] will ich für ein Kleid nicht ausgeben.* **Aufwenden** is used in formal language for the expenditure of money, mostly with a government, council, etc. as subj. *Für den Bau der neuen Brücke hat man/das Land Nordrhein-Westfalen/die Gemeinde zwanzig Millionen Mark aufgewendet.*

> *Für Lebensmittel habe ich diese Woche nur 150 Mark ausgegeben.*
> *Für den Umbau ist eine halbe Million bereits aufgewendet worden.*

2. Spend time. Three words express a slightly different perspective on the way time is spent.

i. Verbringen is neutral, i.e. it does not imply anything about the speaker's feelings with regard to the time spent. It is used with *mit* + a person or an activity, or *damit* + infin.

Wir verbringen den Urlaub entweder an der See oder in den Bergen.
Ich habe das Wochenende mit Freunden verbracht.
Ich habe den ganzen Tag mit Aufräumen verbracht.
Den Vormittag habe ich damit verbracht, die Wohnung wieder sauber zu machen.

ii. In neutral contexts **zubringen** is interchangeable with *verbringen*. *Sie haben einige Tage bei mir zugebracht/verbracht.* It is, however, preferred in contexts with neg. force, i.e. ones which suggest that the time was spent under unfavourable circumstances or that one is glad that the time is over. The unfavourable circumstances must be clear from the context. Like *verbringen*, it is used with *mit* + a n. or an infin. which mostly suggest a not completely agreeable or useful activity. *Ich habe drei Stunden mit diesen Formalitäten zugebracht. Um ein bißchen Geld zu verdienen, habe ich den Sommer damit zugebracht, in der Fabrik zu arbeiten.* (Or vs. expressing an unfavourable judgement like *schuften* or *malochen*.)

> *Wir haben uns im Wald verlaufen und mußten eine Nacht bei niedrigen Temperaturen im Freien zubringen.*   *Sie mußte einige Wochen im Bett zubringen.*
>
> *Im Paßamt habe ich lange gewartet. Ich habe mehr als zwei Stunden auf dem zugigen Flur zugebracht.*

iii. Verleben implies that the time spent was an enjoyable and pos. experience. *Wir haben schöne Tage/Wochen hier verlebt.*

> *Sie hat ihre Kindheit auf dem Lande verlebt, und es waren schöne und erfreuliche Jahre.*
>
> *Er hat seine Kindheit bei den Großeltern im Dorf verlebt.* (Implied: *Sie war angenehm, reich an Erfahrungen.*)

3. Spend effort, energy, time, etc. **on** sth. = 'to expend'.

i. The most common word is **verwenden auf**, but **aufwenden für** is also used. The general sense of both is 'to use or employ strength, effort, etc.' *Sie hat viel Mühe/Kraft/Fleiß auf diese Arbeit verwandt/verwendet. Er wandte viel Mühe für das Projekt auf.* They are not always translated as *spend. Aufwenden* is more common without a prep. so that it is usually found as a past part. used as an adj. *Die aufgewandte Mühe hatte sich doch gelohnt.*

> *Man sieht diesem selbstgebastelten Spielzeug an, wieviel Sorgfalt darauf verwandt/verwendet wurde.*
>
> *Er wandte alle Kräfte auf, um den Freund zu überreden, an dem Projekt teilzunehmen.*
>
> *Die aufgewandte Mühe/Zeit steht in keinem Verhältnis zum Ergebnis.*

ii. Verbringen is the usual v. when a specific period of time is spent on something. *Ich habe zwei Wochen damit verbracht*, and is often found with *viel Zeit, Ich habe viel Zeit damit verbracht.* **Verwenden** suggests a large but unspecified amount of time. *Ich habe sehr viel Zeit darauf verwandt.* When *Zeit* is coupled with *Mühe*, only *verwenden* is possible. *Ich habe sehr viel Zeit und Mühe auf diese Arbeit verwandt.*

4. Spend may still be found in literary language meaning 'to use up or exhaust its strength', particularly with *force* or *fury* as obj. *The storm has spent its force.* It can be refl. *The storm gradually spent itself. Austoben* means 'to work off' anger etc. *Er hat seinen Ärger/seine Wut ausgetobt.* The refl. **sich austoben**, applied to a force, means 'to spend itself or become exhausted'. *Der Sturm/Der Brand/Das Unwetter hatte sich ausgetobt.* A spent force is *eine verbrauchte Kraft.* Cf. USE 4.

> *Das Fieber hatte sich nach drei Tagen ausgetobt.*

(Applied to people, *sich austoben* means 'to let off steam, have their fling'. *Jugend will sich austoben.*)

spread, extend, expand, stretch, distribute, scatter, sprinkle *vs.*

1. The concept underlying the sense of **spread** and its syns. discussed in this section is that, if a person spreads something or something spreads, the thing spread covers a larger area than it originally did. **Spread** is applied to concrete objects like a map or rug, things packed together, arms and wings, or intangibles like news, fear, control, or power. **Spread** is trans., *She spread the rug [out] on the ground and sat down on it,* and intr., *A liquid, smoke, gas, fire, a rumour,* or *a disease spreads.* Applied to power, influence, and territory, **extend** is both trans. and intr., while **spread** is intr. only. *He extended his power over the whole country* and *His power soon extended/spread over the whole country.* **Expand** is mostly intr., *Metals expand with heat and contract with cold, The business has expanded in the last few years,* but is sometimes trans., *The government decided to expand the air force.* The E. intr. forms are refl. in G. *The rumour spread* becomes *Das Gerücht verbreitete sich,* but *He spread the rumour* is *Er verbreitete das Gerücht. Ausbreiten, verbreiten,* and *ausdehnen* are the main equivalents. Although there is some overlapping in everyday use, a clear distinction, which is always correct, is that *ausbreiten* is applied to concrete objects, *verbreiten* to non-concrete things such as news or feelings, while *ausdehnen* refers to an expansion of power, influence, and territory.

i. Ausbreiten is used for spreading [out] something folded, such as *eine Landkarte, ein Stadtplan, eine Zeitung, eine Tischdecke, ein Teppich,* etc. *Arme* or *Flügel* can also be the obj. (for *Arme* cf. iv), as well as a number of single objects packed together which are then placed at a distance from each other over an area, i.e. spread out, *Die Händler breiten ihre Waren aus.* The subj. of **sich ausbreiten** can be *ein Feuer, eine Seuche, eine ansteckende Krankheit, Nebel, Rauch[schwaden],* or people, animals, or plants which spread over an area. *Angehörige des Stammes hatten sich/Diese Baumart hatte sich über das ganze Gebiet ausgebreitet.* With something static as subj. *sich ausbreiten* means 'to stretch [out], spread out'. *Vor uns/unseren Augen,* is often added. *Wiesen und Felder breiteten sich vor unseren Augen aus. Eine breite Ebene breitete sich vor uns aus, als wir den Gipfel des Berges erreichten. Sich ausbreiten* is sometimes found with emotions as subj., *Angst and Schrecken breiteten sich in der Stadt aus,* but *sich verbreiten* is the normal v. in this context.

Sie breiteten die Karte auf dem Tisch aus und beugten sich über sie.
Der Photograph breitete die Bilder vor ihnen aus, damit sie sich die besten aussuchen könnten.
Mit ausgebreiteten Armen lief er auf sie zu.
Der Architekt breitete die Pläne vor dem Auftraggeber aus.
Der Hautausschlag breitete sich über seinen ganzen Körper aus.
Das Feuer/Die Seuche breitete sich schnell aus.

ii. When the obj. is a n. like *eine Nachricht, ein Gerücht, eine Neuigkeit,* etc., **verbreiten** expresses the meaning 'to spread'. *Wie kommst du dazu, solche Lügen über mich zu verbreiten?* Such ns. become the subj. of the refl. *Die Nachricht verbreitete sich schnell.* Thus *Eine weitverbreitete Ansicht,* a widespread view/opinion. Applied to states of mind, *verbreiten* also means 'to cause s.o. to feel them', the subj. being either a person who spreads or radiates something like calm or cheerfulness (*Ruhe or Heiterkeit*), or news or a state of affairs which spreads joy, fear, etc. *Wo er auch hinkommt, er verbreitet Fröhlichkeit/eine hektische Stimmung. Die Erfolgsmeldung verbreitete große Freude unter den Anwesenden.* The obj. can also be a disease or something concrete which is spread around unevenly over a fairly large area. *Welche Insekten verbreiten Infektionskrankheiten? Der Wind verbreitet die Samen der Bäume. Schriften verbreiten* means 'to distribute' them by sale or gift. Only *verbreiten* has *der Geruch* and *der Duft* as obj. *Die Flüssigkeit verbreitet einen unangenehmen Geruch. Die Blumen verbreiteten einen schönen Duft im ganzen Haus.* However, both *sich ausbreiten* and *sich verbreiten* are possible with these ns. as subj. *Der Gasgeruch breitete sich im ganzen Haus aus. Der Duft verbreitete sich schnell und erfüllte bald das Haus.*

Ich würde gern wissen, in wessen Interesse es liegt, dieses Gerücht zu verbreiten.
Die Nachricht über die Siege des Feindes verbreitete Angst und Schrecken unter der Bevölkerung.

Die Pollen werden von Insekten verbreitet.   *Ratten können Krankheiten verbreiten.*

Die Krankheit hat sich schnell verbreitet/ausgebreitet.

iii. The base v. **breiten** is occasionally found in the sense of *ausbreiten*, but it has a poetical or biblical ring. *Schützend breitete sie die Hände über die Kinder.* Still used is *Wir wollen den Mantel des Schweigens über diese Sache breiten.*

iv. Spreizen means 'to spread [apart]' and is mainly used with parts of the body like *Finger, Arme*, and *Beine*. Unlike *ausbreiten*, which is used for spreading the arms as a gesture of welcome, *spreizen* suggests no emotion but states a fact. Animals can be the subj. *Ein Vogel spreizt die Federn.*

Der Junge spreizt die Beine weit/stand mit gespreizten Beinen da.

Die Zehen spreizen sich im nassen Sand.   *Ein Raubvogel spreizt die Fänge/die Klauen.*

v. Ausdehnen means 'to extend' in reference to an area under one's control, one's sphere of influence, etc. *Alexander der Große dehnte sein Reich immer weiter aus.* The refl. **sich ausdehnen** means 'to spread or extend [to or over]'. *Sein Reich dehnte sich immer weiter aus/dehnte sich über immer mehr Länder aus.* The refl. is sometimes used without referring to power, control, or influence with the same meaning as *sich ausbreiten. Eine Kältewelle hat sich über ganz Deutschland ausgedehnt/ausgebreitet. Ein See dehnte sich/breitete sich vor uns aus. Ausdehnen* corresponds to **extend** in relation to time. *Sie dehnte ihren Aufenthalt aus. Die Besprechung dehnte sich über mehrere Stunden aus. Ausdehnen* is also used for extending laws, regulations, etc. to others than those to whom they initially applied. *Bei der Vereinigung der beiden deutschen Staaten wurde das westdeutsche Rechtssystem auf die neuen Bundesländer ausgedehnt.* In reference to material objects *sich ausdehnen* means 'to expand', the opposite of *contract. Die meisten Stoffe dehnen sich bei Erwärmung aus und ziehen sich bei Abkühlung zusammen.*

Der Diktator versuchte, seinen Einfluß auf die kleinen Nachbarländer auszudehnen.

Im zweiten Weltkrieg versuchte Hitler, seine Macht auf ganz Europa auszudehnen.

Mein Kollege will seinen Aufgabenbereich weiter ausdehnen.

Später dehnte der Autor diese Novelle zu einem Roman aus.

Sie mußten den Besuch über die vorgesehene Zeit hinaus ausdehnen.

Die Suche nach geeignetem Textmaterial dehnte sich aus, und sie blieb länger, als sie eigentlich vorhatte.

Diese Bestimmung, die zuerst nur für Studenten der philosophischen Fakultät galt, hat man auf alle Studenten ausgedehnt.

vi. Ausweiten means 'to expand or make larger'. *Man weitet die Produktion/den Export/den Umsatz aus.* In relation to strikes, disputes, etc., the refl. **sich ausweiten** means that something small becomes of greater significance, begins to affect other organizations, i.e. it spreads. *Der Streik weitete sich aus/ . . . weitete sich auf andere Betriebe aus.*

Der Grenzzwischenfall weitete sich zu einem bewaffneten Konflikt aus.

vii. Erweitern means 'to widen', *Man erweitert eine Durchfahrt*, and 'to expand or extend', *Man erweitert seine Kenntnisse/seinen Einflußbereich/die Produktionskapazität*, etc. The refl. means 'to expand' in the sense 'to become larger'. *Die Pupillen erweitern sich im Dunkel. Ihr Einflußbereich hat sich erweitert.*

Die Regierung beschloß, die Luftwaffe/die Streitkräfte zu erweitern. Also . . . zu vergrößern.

viii. Übergreifen auf means 'to spread quickly from one thg. to another'.

Unversehens griff das Feuer auf das Nachbarhaus über.

Der Streik in den Stahlhütten griff auf die Zechen über.

ix. Um sich greifen is a syn. of *sich ausbreiten* and expresses the sense of intr. **spread**. It suggests that something pernicious such as a fire, disease, famine, or trouble spreads out as from a centre and affects other places and people.

Das Feuer griff [immer weiter] um sich, und bald sah man sich einem Flammenmeer gegenüber.

Die Kaninchenplage griff rasch um sich.

2. With an obj. like *Probleme, Leben, Forschungsergebnisse,* **ausbreiten** means 'to describe fully'. *Sie breitete ihr ganzes Leben vor uns aus.* This is a fig. use of the v. which sees the obj. as a map etc. What the person says is seen in a favourable light. By contrast the more common **sich über ein Thema ausbreiten** (sometimes **verbreiten**), to spread oneself on a subject, presents the action in a neg. light, suggesting that the person talks on the subject at inordinate length or in a long-winded way. *Wenn er von Politik anfängt, breitet er sich stundenlang darüber aus. Sie hat sich lange über Kochrezepte/die neueste Mode/ihre Kinder ausgebreitet/verbreitet.*

3. Spread or **distribute** are trans. and mean 'to put the individual parts of a set of thgs. in different places over an area or period of time'. Both are mostly used with an adv. like *evenly* but also imply an even dispersement without it. *The weight/load must be evenly spread/distributed. We will spread/distribute the costs equally among all the participants. The payments are spread over two years.* The equivalent is **verteilen**. For an alternative to one use of the pass cf. 4. For other uses of **distribute** cf. DIVIDE 3.

> *Das Gewicht der Ladung muß beim Transport auf alle vier Räder verteilt werden.*
> *Wir werden die Kosten auf alle gleichmäßig verteilen.*
> *Man verteilt die Rückzahlungen auf fünf Jahre.*
> *Der Lehrer hat seine Sympathien gleichmäßig unter seine Schüler verteilt.*

4. Sich erstrecken means 'to stretch or extend from one point to another' or 'to stretch, extend, or be spread or distributed' over an area, a period of time, group of people, etc.

> *Das Römische Reich erstreckte sich von Britannien bis Kleinasien.*
> *Weizenfelder erstreckten sich, so weit das Auge sehen konnte.*
> *Die Rückzahlungsraten erstrecken sich über [einen Zeitraum von] 18 Monaten.*
> *Großbritannien geht zu metrischen Maßen über, aber die Umstellung soll sich über zwanzig Jahre erstrecken.* *Die Ausbildung erstreckt sich über/auf drei Jahre.*
> *Der Amnestieerlaß erstreckte sich auf alle politischen Häftlinge.*

5. Spread *butter/jam* **on** bread or ointment **on** a wound is expressed by **schmieren** and **streichen**. *Schmieren* may be more usual in the spoken language, but both are common. The constructions are *Ich habe Butter und Marmelade auf ein Stück Brot geschmiert* or *Ich habe ein Brötchen mit Butter geschmiert. Jmd. schmiert Salbe auf eine Wunde.* Similarly *Er streicht Honig aufs Brot/Salbe auf eine Wunde,* and *Sie streicht ein Brötchen mit Leberwurst.* **Bestreichen** is less common. *Jmd. bestreicht Brot mit Marmelade.*

6. In contexts such as *He spread sand on the blood/fertilizer on a field,* **spread** means 'to cause a relatively large amount of sth. to fall on an area'. **Sprinkle** means 'to distribute a small amount over an area in small pieces or droplets'. **Scatter** means 'to distribute widely at irregular intervals'.

i. The equivalent of **spread** and **sprinkle** is **streuen**, to let something consisting of pieces, grains, or powder fall gradually and in a controlled way on a certain area so that they are distributed as evenly as possible. *Man streut Salz und Pfeffer auf ein Ei/Dünger auf den Garten/Sand auf eine Blutlache. Streuen* or *die Straße/den Bürgersteig streuen* is 'to scatter or spread sand or loose chippings (*Rollsplitt*) on the street or footpath when there is black ice (*Glatteis*)'. A fig. expression: *Man streut Salz in eine Wunde.*

ii. Verstreuen means 'to scatter or spread around without any order or plan' things which belong together. *Er hat seine Papiere über den ganzen Tisch verstreut. Der Junge hat seine Kleidung im ganzen Zimmer verstreut. Die Häuser liegen im ganzen Tal verstreut,* are scattered all over the valley. (*Zucker verstreuen* means 'to spill sugar'.) In one sense **zerstreuen** is a syn., but it now either has a natural force as subj., *Der Wind hatte die Blätter zerstreut*, or implies that the action is brought about by fate or circumstances, *Ihre ehemaligen Klassenkameraden waren nun in alle Teile des Landes zerstreut. Meine Studienfreunde sind in alle Welt zerstreut.*

7. Equivalents of other senses of **stretch**.

i. Strecken means 'to stretch' arms and legs. A phr. can be added. *Er streckte die Beine [unter den Tisch]. Sie streckt den Arm in die Höhe/den Kopf durchs Fenster.* **Sich strecken** means 'to stretch oneself'. *Er gähnte und streckte sich.* **Recken** is a syn.; both are often combined in the refl. *Er reckte und streckte sich.* **Dehnen** is also possible and can be combined with *strecken* or *recken. Er streckte und dehnte die Glieder. Er streckte/reckte und dehnte sich.* **Sich rekeln** is 'to stretch oneself with pleasure'. *Er/Die Katze rekelte sich in der Sonne.* **Stretch** one's legs, meaning 'to go for a short walk after sitting for some time', is **sich die Beine vertreten**.

ii. Dehnen means 'to stretch' e.g. elastic, a rubber band. *Er dehnte das Gummiband, bis es riß. Dehnen* is a formal term in this sense, **auseinanderziehen** being the everyday word. *Sie zog das Gummiband auseinander. Dieses Material läßt sich gut auseinanderziehen.*

iii. Sich dehnen, used for articles of clothing, means 'to stretch or become bigger'. *Die Handschuhe dehnen sich mit der Zeit. Bei der ersten Wäsche wird sich der Pullover dehnen. Sich dehnen* is occasionally used instead of *sich ausbreiten* or *sich erstrecken* in the sense of stretching over an area. *Die Wiesen dehnten sich weithin.* (**Sich in die Länge dehnen** or **ziehen** means 'to last or take longer than anticipated', 'to be prolonged'. *Die Diskussion dehnte/zog sich in die Länge, aber keiner dachte ans Nachhausegehen.*)

iv. Stretch *a rope* (across a space etc.) is *ein Seil* **spannen**.

staff *n.* To ask how many people there are on the staff it is usual to say, 'Wieviele sind hier beschäftigt?' or 'Wieviele **Beschäftigte** hat die Firma?' We have a staff of forty could be *Der Betrieb beschäftigt 40 Leute, Hier arbeiten 40 Leute*, or if one of them is speaking, *Wir sind vierzig Leute. The staff are demanding better conditions* is likely to be expressed as *Die Beschäftigten des Betriebs fordern bessere Arbeitsbedingungen. The staff of the airline* is *die Beschäftigen der Fluggesellschaft. This error of judgement by a member of staff* can be expressed as *diese Fehleinschätzung durch einen* **Mitarbeiter/ Angestellten** *der Firma.* To take on staff is *neue* **Arbeitskräfte einstellen**. To lay off staff is *Arbeitskräfte abbauen* although *Personal abbauen* is possible. For *beschäftigen* and *einstellen* cf. APPOINT 1 and 2. Although **das Personal** is the equivalent of **staff**, it is restricted in use. *Das Personal*, like *personnel*, is more used in special contexts and specialized language. It can refer to all the employees, *das gesamte Personal des Hotels*, but is also used for the people in a particular section, *das technische Personal, das Bodenpersonal. Der Personalmangel* is 'staff shortage' (alternative *Mangel an Fachkräften/an ausgebildeten Kräften); ein Personalleiter* or *-chef* is in charge of *die Personalabteilung.* An entrance may be marked as *Personaleingang* or carry a sign *Nur für Personal.* **Die Belegschaft** denotes the total work-force of an industrial enterprise, i.e. workers and clerical and managerial staff. *Die Belegschaft beträgt 3 000 Personen. Der Betriebsrat* (works committee, workers' council) *vertritt die Belegschaft seiner Firma.* **Der Stab** is a group of people brought together to deal with a special problem. They may be called in for a particular purpose, *der Krisenstab*, or be permanent employees, *der redaktionelle Stab einer Zeitung.* For educational institutions, **die Lehrkräfte** is the usual word. *Nur Lehrkräfte dürfen diesen Parkplatz benutzen.* **Das Kollegium** is a collective term for the staff of a school. *Das Kollegium war vollzählig* *im Lehrerzimmer zu einer Sitzung versammelt.* **Der Lehrkörper** is a more bureaucratic and administrative term denoting the teaching body or the whole staff. *Der feierliche Einzug des Lehrkörpers in die Aula beginnt um 15 Uhr.* Cf. *employees* under APPOINT.

> *An dieser Universität beträgt das Verhältnis von Lehrkräften zu Studenten 1 : 10.*
> *Als jüngstes Mitglied des Lehrerkollegiums muß ich bei allen Sitzungen Protokoll führen.*
> *Der Direktor und der Lehrkörper begrüßten die Delegation aus China, die die Schule besichtigen wollte.*

stand *v.* **Stehen** denotes a static condition, the action of standing somewhere or being in a particular position. E. **stand** describes both a position and a movement to a position. The command 'Go and stand at the window!' clearly implies a movement, but *go and* is often omitted, so that *Stand at the window!* has the same sense as *go and stand.* When motion is involved, G. uses **sich stellen.** *Sie stellte sich ans Fenster* means 'she [went and] stood at the window', while *Sie stand am Fenster* is best translated as *She was standing at the window.* If the place is not stated, it is necessary to use **sich hinstellen.** *Hin* corresponds to *there. Ich werde mich hinstellen und auf ihn warten.*

> *Der Zug war so voll, daß wir stehen mußten.*
> *Stell' dich ja nicht mitten auf die Straße! Wir sind doch nicht auf dem Lande.*
> *Sie stellten sich ans Ende der Schlange.*   *Stell' dich einen Augenblick zu ihnen hin!*

Stand a thg. somewhere can only be **stellen.** *Er stellte das Gewehr in die Ecke.* Cf. PUT. When the place is not stated as a prep. + n., **hinstellen** is used, even if the sent. contains *da* or *dort. In der Ecke ist genug Platz. Wir können den Schrank da hinstellen.* The question can be either *'Wohin soll ich die Vase stellen?'* or *'Wo soll ich die Vase hinstellen?'*

start, begin, commence *vs.* A few uses.

1. Anfangen and **beginnen** both mean 'to begin', but *anfangen* is the everyday word, while *beginnen* is more formal and more often encountered in the written language. Both are intr., *Wir müssen jetzt anfangen/beginnen,* and trans., *Ich habe den Brief angefangen/begonnen.* Both take an infin., *Es fing an/begann zu regnen,* and are used with *mit, Wir fangen mit dem dritten Punkt der Tagesordnung an/beginnen mit . . .* With a person as subj., *anfangen* and *beginnen* are used with *ein Gespräch, eine Diskussion,* etc. as obj. *I started a conversation* becomes *Ich fing ein Gespräch mit dem Mann an, der mir gegenüber im Abteil saß.*

> *Wir haben die Übersetzung/die Arbeit gestern angefangen.*
> *Danach fing er an, laut zu lachen.*   *Wir fangen mit dem zweiten Kapitel an.*
> *Die Schule fängt um 10 vor 8 an.*   *Der Wald fängt einen Kilometer von hier an.*
> *Er mußte wieder ganz von vorn anfangen/beginnen.*
> *Die Vorstellung/Das Spiel hat schon begonnen.*

2. Losgehen is an equivalent of **start** which is common in speech. It is intr. and does not take an infin. Only an activity can be subj. *Jetzt geht es los* refers to an activity which would be clear in the situation.

> *Wann geht das Spiel los?*   *Das Feuerwerk ist erst sehr spät losgegangen.*

3. Start *a motor* or *a car* is *den Motor/den Wagen/das Auto* **anlassen.** Also *einen Motor anstellen* or *starten.* Cf. 5. The E. intr. use *The car engine started at once* is expressed by **anspringen.** *Der Motor ist sofort angesprungen. Der Wagen springt nicht an/springt nur schwer an.* **Anlaufen** is used for a machine which takes time to gain momentum. *Die Turbine ist langsam angelaufen.*

4. Anlaufen is also used for the start of production, a campaign, or plan. *Die Produktion des neuen Modells ist vor zwei Wochen angelaufen. Die Werbekampagne ist bereits angelaufen.*

5. In relation to cars **starten** is trans., *Sie startete den Motor,* and intr., *Er stieg ins Auto und startete.* For aircraft it means 'to take off'. *Wegen des Nebels konnte das Flugzeug nicht starten.* In reference to competitive races, it means either 'to take part', *Zwanzig Läufer starten im Marathonlauf,* or 'to give the signal for starting', *Der Starter hob die Pistole und startete das Rennen,* or 'to get a good/bad start', *Er ist gut gestartet.*

6. In E. we say that an event or remark started a heated debate/a discussion on a topic/a controversy/a new round of talks, etc. The equivalent is **auslösen,** to cause, produce, set going, give rise to. *Dieser Unfall löste heftige Diskussionen über die Atomkraft aus.*

> *Diese Entscheidung des höchsten Gerichts löste eine heftige Kontroverse/eine neue Verhandlungsrunde aus.*

state, condition *ns.*

1. The **state** of a person or thing is 'what that pers. of thg. is generally like' or 'what he/she/it is like at a particular time'. *The state of the roads. S.o.'s state of health. They returned to the negotiating table in a cheerful state. The building is in its original state. The state of the negotiations.* The **condition** of a pers. or thg. is 'the particular state he/she/it is in'. *You can't go home in that condition. Congress is to consider the unfavourable financial condition of the country.* The two words are often interchangeable. Although *der Zustand* mostly translates both words, one sense of *der Stand* is the equivalent of one sense of **state.**

i. Der Zustand denotes what something is generally like and also refers to the state of something at a particular time, without the idea of development. The state usually continues for some time, but this does not mean that it will not change. *Der Zustand der Straßen/eines Gebäudes/der Bücher,* etc. It is used with adjs., *Jmd. befand sich in einem elenden/betrunkenen/verzweifelten/erschöpften Zustand,* or a gen., *in einem Zustand der Erschöpfung.* In relation to people, *Zustand* refers both to the bodily and mental state. *Sie wurde in kritischem Zustand ins Krankenhaus eingeliefert. Ihr Zustand hat sich gebessert. Der Gemütszustand* is 'the emotional or mental state'. There are several compounds such as *der Dauerzustand, der Ausnahmezustand, der Endzustand, der Idealzustand, der Naturzustand, der Kriegszustand, der Gleichgewichtszustand,* etc.

> *Der Zustand der Brücke ließ befürchten, daß sie bald einstürzen würde.*
> *Ihr allgemeiner Gesundheitszustand ist zufriedenstellend.*
> *Der Zeuge ist nicht in vernehmungsfähigem Zustand.*
> *Diese Nachricht versetzte alle in einen Zustand der Erregung.*

ii. One sense of **der Stand** refers to things which in the course of time undergo a development. The development may be towards a conclusion, as in *der Stand der Verhandlungen,* or it may be a continuous process of change, *der Stand der Forschung, der Stand der Entwicklung der Biologie. Stand* denotes a stage which has been reached in this process and implies that things have developed to this point and will continue to develop after it. In this sense, it is only found with a restricted number of ns. and does not refer to people. It is also used in the expressions *etw. auf den neuesten Stand bringen,* 'to bring up to date', and *etw. auf den internationalen Stand bringen,* 'to bring up to the standard reached internationally'. *Der gegenwärtige Stand der Dinge* means 'the state of affairs prevailing at the moment with regard to a matter' and implies further development. In sport *Stand* is the shortened form of *Spielstand,* state of play. *Beim Stand von 3 : 2 mußte das Fußballspiel abgebrochen werden.*

> *Der Professor erkundigte sich nach dem Stand meiner Arbeit.*
> *Der Minister informierte sich über den Stand der Elektrifizierung des Eisenbahnnetzes.*

2. The **condition** of sth. is 'its physical quality which depends on its age and on how well it has been looked after'.

i. The usual term is **der Zustand**. *Der Wagen/Die Wohnung befindet sich in gutem Zustand/in einem tadellosen Zustand. Das Haus war in einem baufälligen Zustand.* In this sense, *Stand* survives only in the expressions *etw.* **instandhalten** or **instandsetzen**, to keep or put in good condition. (An alternative spelling is *in Stand*.) 'Good' is implied in these expressions and need not be stated as with *Zustand*. A colloquial equivalent is *Etw. ist [gut]* **in/im Schuß**. *Gut* can be omitted as *Schuß* implies 'good condition', 'well-cared for state'. Also *Man hält etw. in Schuß* and *bringt* or *bekommt es in Schuß* .

> *Das Schloß wurde in seinen ursprünglichen Zustand versetzt.*
> *Wir müssen den Motor wieder in betriebsfähigen Zustand bringen.*
> *Man hat das alte Haus/das Auto instandgesetzt/instandgehalten.*   *Der Wagen ist gut im Schuß.*
> *Er hat den Wagen wieder in Schuß gebracht.*   *Er hält seine Sachen/den Garten in Schuß.*

ii. The **condition** of a group of people is expressed by **die Lage**. *Die Lage der Indianer in Kanada*. *Zustand* is not used in relation to finances. The *financial condition* is *die finanzielle Lage*, position. *Das Parlament debatiert morgen die ungünstige finanzielle Lage des Landes.*

(*Jmdn. in den Stand setzen*, to put s.o. in a position to do sth., is now rare. More common is *jmdn. in die Lage versetzen*. *Imstande sein* or *in der Lage sein, etw. zu tun* is 'to be in a position or able'. *Durch sein Vermögen ist er imstande/in der Lage, ausgedehnte Reisen zu unternehmen*.)

3. State of affairs means 'the general situation or circumstances relating to a pers. or thg.' and can be translated by **die Lage** or **die Umstände**. *Die gegenwärtige Lage erfordert/Die jetzigen Umstände erfordern strenge Maßnahmen. Alle würden es begrüßen, wenn man versuchte, diese ungerechte Lage zu ändern.*

4. Condition, meaning 'a stipulation or part of a contract or agreement which s.o. insists be fulfilled before he or she will do sth. else', is **die Bedingung**. *To make a condition* is *eine Bedingung stellen* or *etw. zur Bedingung machen. On condition that . . .* is *unter der Bedingung, daß . . . Die Verkaufsbedingungen*, conditions of sale.

> *Die Firma stellte Bedingungen, die die Lieferanten nicht erfüllen konnten.*
> *Man bot ihm ein Darlehen zu günstigen Bedingungen an. Er nahm die Bedingungen an.*
> *Sie können sechs Monate lang umsonst im Haus wohnen, unter der Bedingung, daß sie alle Zimmer neu streichen.*

Die Kondition is used in commercial language for the conditions of payment and/or supply of goods.

> *Wir haben die Waren zu günstigen Konditionen gekauft/verkauft.*

5. Condition is also 'sth. that must occur, happen, be true, or be done first before it is possible for sth. else to happen'. *Our people's independence is a condition for stability and peace in this area. One of the necessary conditions for producing chemicals which are free of impurities is clean apparatus.* The equivalent is **die Voraussetzung**, sth. which must be present so that sth. else can happen. While *Bedingung* refers to conditions laid down by people, *Voraussetzung* suggests a basic or essential requirement which lies more in the nature of things. The dividing line is, however, not always clear. *Voraussetzung* can also be 'a prerequisite', i.e. 'a requirement which must be fulfilled before s.o. can do sth.' *Ein abgeschlossenes Studium ist die Voraussetzung für diese Stelle.* (*Bedingung* is also possible.) *Unter der Voraussetzung, daß . . .* is translated as *on condition that . . .*

> *Kohle in der Nähe eines Eisenerzvorkommens ist die Voraussetzung für die Entstehung einer Stahlindustrie.*
> *Vorher muß man die notwendigen technischen Voraussetzungen für ein solches Projekt schaffen.*

Eine saubere Apparatur ist eine der notwendigen Voraussetzungen dafür, Chemikalien herzustellen, die von Verunreinigungen frei sind.

Die unerläßliche Voraussetzung dafür, ein Erfolgsschriftsteller zu werden, bleibt also die, daß man Romane oder Theaterstücke schreibt, die ein breites Publikum ansprechen.

Voraussetzung für die Zulassung eines Ausländers zum Studium an einer deutschen Hochschule ist der Nachweis einer der deutschen Hochschulreife entsprechenden Vorbildung.

6. Conditions are 'all the factors and circumstances affecting sth.' *The experiments were carried out under primitive working conditions. We saw some appalling living conditions. They protested about the conditions in the jail.* Although each word occurs in certain fixed expressions, **die Verhältnisse** and **die Bedingungen** are sometimes interchangeable in this sense. *Arbeitsverhältnisse* and *Arbeitsbedingungen* are synonymous. **Die Zustände** is a syn., although it is often reserved for bad conditions. *Es herrschen dort chaotische/unerträgliche Zustände.* The colloquial expression *Das sind hier Zustände!* implies objectionable ones, and *Das ist doch kein Zustand!* suggests a bad state that should not be allowed to continue. *Zustände* thus tends to be used when badness is implied but not stated. *Sie protestierten gegen die Zustände im Gefängnis.* Hence, *die politischen Verhältnisse* is more neutral than *die politischen Zustände.* With reference, for example, to the working atmosphere (*Arbeitsklima*) in some organization, someone might say, '*Die Verhältnisse/Bedingungen haben sich verändert.*' *Die Zustände dort haben sich verbessert* suggests that they were particularly bad. *Die gesellschaftlichen Verhältnisse*, 'social conditions, conditions in society', is the standard expression, as is *wie die Verhältnisse sind*, 'as conditions are'. *Die klimatischen Verhältnisse* are 'conditions' meaning 'circumstances or what exists', and are the same as *die klimatischen Bedingungen. Die klimatischen Voraussetzungen zum Anbau von Reis sind hier gegeben* are 'conditions' in sense 5. (*Bedingungen* is also possible.)

Bergleute arbeiten unter Tage unter sehr ungünstigen Verhältnissen/Bedingungen.

Röntgen führte seine Versuche unter primitiven technischen Arbeitsbedingungen aus.

Wir haben schreckliche Wohnverhältnisse gesehen.

7. On any condition in *I won't do that on any condition* is synonymous with *under any circumstances.* The equivalent is **unter keinen Umständen.** *Das mache ich unter [gar] keinen Umständen.*

8. Apart from the sense already mentioned in 4 , **die Kondition** means 'a pers.'s physical condition'. It is mostly used in reference to sport and implies good condition or fitness. *Ich habe keine Kondition. Sie treiben Konditionssport/Konditionstraining.* **Die Verfassung** denotes in one sense someone's physical and mental state without any implications. *Seine körperliche und geistige Verfassung ist ausgezeichnet.*

steer *v.* Grimm defines the original meaning of **steuern** as 'den Lauf des Schiffes mit Hilfe des Steuers lenken', whereas **lenken** was used for land vehicles as well as boats. *Steuern* is now the usual word for both, as well as for aircraft. *Er steuerte das Schiff/das Auto. Lenken* is still used in formal language for steering a car. *Bei Glatteis muß man vorsichtig lenken.* Both are used with a phr. of direction. *Sie lenkte/steuerte den Wagen nach rechts/links. Er steuerte das Boot in den Hafen. Die Lenkung* is 'the steering of a car etc.', but *die Steuerung* is also used. *Das Steuerrad* is 'the wheel' of a ship, and *das Lenkrad* that of a vehicle, but *das Steuerrad* is used in everyday speech for the steering-wheel of a car. *Das Steuer* means 'the steering-wheel or controls of a vehicle, ship, or aircraft' or fig. 'control'. *Wer saß am Steuer?* means 'who was driving?' *Er übernahm das Steuer*, 'took the wheel', or fig., 'took control'. *Steuern* is also intr. *Die Jacht ist in den Hafen gesteuert.* Applied to people, it suggests endeavouring with some determination to avoid obstacles and reach a destination. *Der Kellner steuerte durch die Tischreihen.* (*Steuern* + dat., as in *Wir müssen diesem Mißbrauch steuern*, means 'to check or curb'. Cf. CONTROL.)

> *Ich lasse die Lenkung in der Werkstatt überprüfen.*   *Er lenkte das Auto in eine Nebenstraße.*
> *Ein Auto kann man nicht richtig steuern, wenn man telefoniert.*

step *n.*

1. In its basic sense 'an advance or movement made by raising the foot and putting it down at another place' **step** has two equivalents, *der Schritt* and *der Tritt*. **Der Schritt** is now the usual word. *Man macht/tut einen Schritt*, takes a step. *Er kam mit raschen Schritten auf mich zu. Seine Schritte beschleunigten/verlangsamten sich. Das Kind hat die ersten Schritte getan. Schritt* also means 'the sound produced by the feet in walking or running', *Ich hörte Schritte*, and 'the distance covered by a step, a pace', *Ich ging ein paar Schritte hinter ihr her. Er trat einen Schritt zurück.* Two idiomatic expressions are *mit jmdm. Schritt halten*, which in the lit. sense means 'to keep up with' or 'to keep pace with s.o.' and is also used fig., and *einen Schritt zulegen*, to walk more quickly. **Der Tritt** survives in the first two senses only in a few expressions. *Noch einen Tritt, und du fällst herunter.* It still occurs with adjs., in particular *leicht* and *leise. Er ging mit leisen Tritten die Treppe hinab. Schritte* is just as common. *Man hörte Tritte* is now literary. *Tritt* now usually means 'a kick', a shortened form of *der Fußtritt. Tritt fassen* means 'to get into a rhythm of working or doing sth.', 'to get into one's stride'.

> *Die Dielen knarrten unter seinen schweren Schritten.*   *Ich habe [leise] Schritte gehört.*
> *Sie brauchten nicht lange, um die Tanzschritte zu beherrschen.*
> *Obwohl Bernt einige Zeit krank gewesen ist, kann er mit seinen Klassenkameraden Schritt halten.*
> *Das trockene Herbstlaub raschelte bei jedem Schritt.* Also sometimes . . . *bei jedem Tritt.*
> *Einen falschen Tritt, und du stürzt in die Tiefe.*
> *Er versetzte dem Hund einen Tritt.*   *Er gab mir einen Fußtritt.*
> *Unsere Fußballmannschaft hat endlich Tritt gefaßt und die ersten Spiele gewonnen.*

Jmd. auf Schritt und Tritt beobachten/folgen/verfolgen is 'to observe, follow, or pursue s.o. constantly'. *Unbemerkt folgte der Detektiv dem Verdächtigen auf Schritt und Tritt.*

2. In a sense without a pl. s.o.'s **step** describes the manner in which that person walks or puts his or her feet down. *Tread* in the sense 'the way of walking' is a syn. The usual equivalent is **der Schritt**, but occasionally **der Tritt** occurs. *Ich habe ihn sofort an seinem [forschen] Schritt erkannt. Er hat einen schwerfälligen Schritt. Sie hat einen leichten, federnden Schritt/Tritt. Er kam mit festem Tritt die Treppe herunter.*

3. To be **in step** or **out of step**. The usual term is **der Gleichschritt**. *Sie gingen im Gleichschritt nebeneinander her.* *Man kommt in Gleichschritt* or *aus dem Gleichschritt*. An alternative here is *in den Tritt/aus dem Tritt kommen*. To change step is, however, only *den Schritt wechseln. Im Gleichschritt marsch!* is the military command *Quick march!* The fig. use of *to be* **in/out of step with** s.o. is carried by **[nicht] im Einklang/in Harmonie mit jmdm. sein**. *Er ist nie/nur selten im Einklang mit den anderen Mitarbeitern.*

4. The **step** of a staircase is **die Stufe**, and the **step** or rung of a ladder **die Sprosse**. *A flight of steps* is **eine Treppe**. *Eine Treppe, die zehn Stufen hat, führt zur Haustür.* (*Stufe* also has the fig. meaning 'stage' or 'level'. *Ihre Bildung steht/ist auf einer hohen/niedrigen Stufe.* Thus *die Unterstufe, die Mittelstufe*, and *die Oberstufe eines Gymnasiums*.)

> *Er nimmt immer drei Stufen auf einmal.*   *Die steinernen Stufen sind etwas ausgetreten.*
> *Ich hielt mich am Geländer fest und stieg die Stufen der steilen Treppe vorsichtig hinauf.*
> *Schon auf der frühesten Stufe seiner Entwicklung ahmt ein Kind seine Eltern nach.*

Ich stand auf der untersten/letzten/obersten Sprosse der Leiter.
Ich stieg die Leiter langsam Sprosse für Sprosse hinauf.

5. Other senses of **step**.
i. Der Schritt denotes a step in a process, explanation, or method. *Wir bringen Ihnen das in 100 einfachen Schritten bei. Wir können die beiden nächsten Schritte überspringen. Sie war mir um ein paar Schritte voraus* can have the lit. or a fig. sense. In *der erste Schritt auf dem Weg zum Erfolg* and *ein Schritt in die richtige Richtung*, the sense is fig.
ii. Der Schritt means 'step' as a syn. of *action*. Cf. ACT 2. iii. Note that *to take steps* in this sense is *Schritte unternehmen*.

stop *v.*

1. Stop meaning 'to come to or bring to a stationary position' can be either intr. or trans. The previous state can be movement of a person or vehicle, or the operation of a machine. Intr.: *The car stopped. The motor stopped.* Trans.: *He stopped the car.*
i. Halten is intr. only. For trains, trams, and buses it implies a regular, prescribed stop. *Alle Züge halten in Göttingen. Hier hält alle fünf Minuten ein Bus.* Hence the announcement in a railway station: *'Der nächste Haltebahnhof ist Bebra.'* For people and private motor vehicles it denotes a stop of unspecified duration. *Sie hielt vor jedem Schaufenster. Das Auto hielt vor der Schule. Halten* is usual in statements about where vehicles may or may not stop. *Hier darf man nicht halten.* Although HALT has given way to STOP on G. street signs, *ein Halteverbot* means that nobody is allowed to stop. *Halten* may mean 'to stop just for a short time', *Ich kann hier nicht lange halten* or *Ich kann hier nur so lange halten, bis wir das Gepäck aus dem Kofferraum genommen haben*, but normally suggests stopping for a longer period, *Weil die Parkplätze voll waren, hielten sie am Straßenrand. Halten* also translates the intr. v. *to halt* used in military and other contexts. *Abteilung, halt!* A sentry calls, *'Halt, wer da?'* or perhaps, *'Halt, oder ich schieße!'* (Although *Haltet den Dieb!* translates *Stop thief!*, *halten* here means 'to hold'.)
  Der Bummelzug hielt in jedem Dorf, und es dauerte lange, bis sie ihr Ziel erreicht hatten.
  Er hielt vor dem Gasthaus, um die anderen aussteigen zu lassen.
  Die Ausflügler hielten in der Nähe des Sees und packten ihre Proviantkörbe aus.
ii. When intr., **anhalten** means 'to stop for a short time'. It thus expresses the same meaning as one sense of *halten*, but it is often preferred in order to make the meaning 'for a short time' clear, although either is often possible. *Sie bat den Fahrer, beim Briefkasten kurz zu halten/anzuhalten.* For buses etc. *anhalten* implies a stop that is not prescribed.
  Wir hielten an, um Erfrischungen zu kaufen.   *Halt doch mal eben an!*
  Würden Sie bitte hinter der nächsten Kreuzung anhalten?
  Der Fahrer hielt plötzlich/abrupt an.
iii. Anhalten is also trans. and again suggests stopping s.o./sth. only temporarily. *Als sie die Dorfstraße entlang ging, hielten sie Bekannte immer wieder an, um ihr zu gratulieren. Der Reiter hielt das Pferd an. Der Polizist hielt den Wagen/den Verkehr an. Er hielt die Maschine/die Uhr an.*
  Sie wurde von der Polizei angehalten, da sie die Geschwindigkeitsbegrenzung nicht beachtet hatte.
iv. Aufhalten means 'to prevent s.o./sth. proceeding', but mostly only for a limited time. It thus corresponds to *stop* in some contexts but more frequently to *hold up* or *detain*. It means 'to stop' in the following three examples. *Die Armee hielt den anrückenden Feind/den Vormarsch der feindlichen Truppen auf. Er hielt den Fliehenden/das durchgehende Pferd auf. Der Staatsmann ließ nichts unversucht, um die verhängnisvolle Entwicklung/die drohende Katastrophe aufzuhalten.* In *Der Unfall hielt den Verkehr auf*, the

v. suggests slowing it either by stopping it for a time, making a detour necessary, or causing vehicles to travel more slowly. *The policeman stopped the traffic* is *Der Polizist hielt den Verkehr an* (i.e. brought it to a standstill).

v. In one sense **stehen** and **stillstehen** mean 'not to be in operation or in motion'. *Er wartete, bis die Maschine [still]stand. Der D-Zug ist auf einen stehenden Güterzug aufgefahren.* **Etw. zum Stehen bringen** is thus 'to stop sth. moving or operating'. The context may suggest that it is getting out of control. *Es gelang ihm, das Pferd/das Auto zum Stehen zu bringen. Man brachte die Blutung schnell zum Stehen.* **Zum Stillstand bringen** is a syn. *Er brachte das Fließband/die Maschine zum Stillstand. Nur mit Mühe gelang es ihr, das Fahrrad zum Stillstand zu bringen, denn die Räder griffen bei der Nässe auf der abschüssigen Straße nur schlecht.* **Zum Stehen/Stillstand kommen** mean 'to come to a stop'. *Er bremste scharf, und schon nach wenigen Metern kam der Wagen zum Stehen. Die Blutung kam schnell zum Stillstand.* If *to stop a machine or motor* means 'to turn it off', the v. is **abstellen.** Cf. TURN 7.

vi. Stoppen is frequently heard as both a trans. and intr. v., although some native speakers do [or did] not regard it as good G. and avoid(ed) it. *Sie stoppte an der Ampel. Der Polizist stoppte den Bus. Er stoppte mitten im Lauf.* (*Löhne/Preise stoppen* is 'to freeze wages or prices'; hence *der Lohnstopp, der Preisstopp. Die Zeit eines Schwimmers* etc. *stoppen* is 'to measure it with a stop-watch (*eine Stoppuhr*)'.)

vii. Haltmachen is intr. and means 'to stop temporarily during a journey for a particular purpose'. It suggests a break in a journey which will be resumed. *Machen wir für einen Kaffee halt!* The break can be a short stop for a rest or a meal, or it may be an overnight stop if the journey is to be continued the next day. *Irgendwo* **Station machen** also means 'to break a journey or make a temporary stop somewhere'. *Wir machen am nächsten Rastplatz Station/halt.* In an idiomatic use with *erst*, *haltmachen* refers to the end of a journey. *Die Kinder liefen so schnell sie nur konnten und machten erst vor ihrem Haus halt! Die Kompanie machte erst vor dem Kasernentor halt.* Cf. 7 for another sense of *haltmachen*.

> *Der Fahrer sagte, sie müßten bald haltmachen, sonst würde er einschlafen.*
>
> *Beim nächsten Gasthof machen wir halt und essen zu Mittag/und verbringen dort die Nacht.*
>
> *Auf der Fahrt von Hamburg nach Wien haben wir mehrere Male Station gemacht.*

viii. Stehenbleiben is intr. and, applied to people, means 'to stop walking for a short time', *Sie blieb vor jedem Schaufenster stehen.* There are other uses. *Wo sind wir stehengeblieben?* asks the point or place we reached or stopped at in reading, discussing something, etc. and is a transl. of *Where did we get to? Gestern sind wir (bei der Lektüre) auf Seite 37 stehengeblieben. Jmd. ist in seiner Entwicklung stehengeblieben,* stopped at a certain point of development. *Stehenbleiben* is also applied to mechanical devices and vehicles which stop functioning, possibly because of a defect. *Der Motor bleibt dauernd stehen.* In reference to a vehicle it may be a syn. of *anhalten* if it is clear from the context that the stop was intentional rather than the result of a breakdown. *Das Auto blieb vor der Bahnschranke stehen.* Without such a phr. as *vor der Bahnschranke* this sent. would usually be understood as implying a breakdown. *Das Auto war ihr mitten auf der Kreuzung stehengeblieben, und sie mußte Passanten bitten, ihr beim Wegschieben zu helfen.*

> *Sie bat die anderen, für einen Augenblick stehenzubleiben, damit sie auf die Karte sehen könnte.*
>
> *Das Dorf war so unberührt, daß man das Gefühl hatte, hier sei das Leben vor 50 Jahren stehengeblieben.*
>
> *Er begegnete einem Bekannten in der Stadt, doch, da er keine Zeit hatte, um stehenzubleiben, grüßte er nur kurz.*   *Die Uhr/Der Apparat ist stehengeblieben.*

ix. In one sense **aussetzen** conveys the idea that something suddenly stops, often only for a short time. *Plötzlich setzte der Motor/die Maschine/der Atem aus.* A partial syn. is **stocken**, which can be used for things which move regularly, *Der Atem/Der Motor stockte*, or for things which have a flowing movement, *Der Verkehr/Die Produktion/Das Gespräch stockte. Beim Lesen/Beim Erzählen stocken* implies stopping involuntarily.

x. In reference to an engine **ausgehen** means that it ceases working either because someone turns it off or because of a defect. *Wenn man die Zündung ausschaltet, geht der Motor aus. Der Motor ging plötzlich aus.* **Ausfallen** implies that it stops because of a defect. *Ein Triebwerk ist plötzlich ausgefallen. Ausfallen* is also used with subjs. for which E. does not use *stop: Die Ampel/Der Strom ist ausgefallen.*

2. Stop is intr. meaning 'not to continue an action'. *She started work at three o'clock and didn't stop until midnight.* A gerund may follow. *Stop crying!* It is also trans. meaning 'to cause an action not to continue'. *Stop that noise!*
i. The main equivalent is **aufhören**. It is intr. but can translate the E. trans. use. It is used with people and things as subj. *Sie fing um drei an zu arbeiten und hörte erst um Mitternacht auf. Der Sturm hörte plötzlich auf.* It is also used with an infin. which corresponds to the E. gerund, *Sie hörten auf zu lärmen*, and with *mit* + a n. denoting an action, *Sie hörten mit dem Lärmen auf.* The E. obj. can be expressed by *mit* or turned into an infin. *Stop that nonsense!* becomes *Hört doch auf mit dem Blödsinn! We stopped work at six* can be *Wir hörten um sechs mit der Arbeit auf* or *Wir hörten um sechs auf zu arbeiten!* An alternative for the imp. is **lassen**, which has a meaning like *to leave off. Laßt doch den Blödsinn! Laß das!*, stop it! Although common in the imp. *lassen* = 'stop' is now unusual elsewhere. Still possible are *Jmd. kann das Rauchen nicht lassen* and *Sie konnte es nicht lassen, sich in alles einzumischen.* Another alternative for the imp. is **Schluß mit**. *Schluß jetzt mit dem Krach!* expresses the same meaning as *Hört doch auf mit dem Krach!* Thus *Und jetzt Schluß [damit]!* is a command to stop doing something. It may suggest that the speaker's patience is at an end. **Schluß machen mit** conveys the meaning of a v. *Wir machen jetzt [für heute] [mit etw.] Schluß. Er machte Schluß mit dem Rauchen.*

> *Seit Tagen regnete es nun schon, und alle fragten sich, wann es/der Regen aufhören würde.*
> *Sie hörte auf, weiter darüber nachzugrübeln.*
> *Hör' doch auf zu meckern! Or Laß das Meckern doch! Or Schluß jetzt mit dem Meckern!*
> *Laß doch die Albernheiten! Ich habe ein ernstes Wort mit dir zu reden.*

ii. Einstellen means 'not to continue with sth.' or 'not to let sth. continue' and needs an obj. It is not used for trivial actions and can be translated as *suspend*.

> *Die beiden Armeen haben das Feuer/die Kriegshandlungen/die Feindseligkeiten eingestellt.*
> *Wegen des anhaltend schlechten Wetters mußten die Bauarbeiten eingestellt werden.*
> *Er stellte die Zahlungen an seine geschiedene Frau ein.*
> *Die Polizei hat die Suchaktion eingestellt.*

iii. Einhalt gebieten/tun + dat. is 'to stop' in the sense 'to put an end to' something harmful or disturbing. It is a formal expression. Cf. *ein Ende machen* under END 5. *Wir müssen diesem Mißbrauch/diesen Umtrieben/diesem Übel Einhalt gebieten. Die Behandlung scheint der Krankheit Einhalt getan zu haben.*
iv. Unterbinden means 'to take firm action to stop sth. considered undesirable'. *Man sollte den Verkauf von Schußwaffen an Privatpersonen unterbinden. Die Lehrer sollten diese Disziplinlosigkeit unter den Schülern unterbinden.*

3. Stop = 'to pause while doing sth.' **Innehalten** and **einhalten** are only used in formal style. In a speech or a sermon someone might say, 'Halten wir einen Augenblick inne, um uns die Folgen einer solchen Handlungsweise zu vergegenwärtigen!' *Jmd. hält im Lesen/im Spiel/in einer Beschäftigung ein.* **Kurz/Einen Augenblick aufhören** is more usual and appropriate to all activities. *Sie hörte einen Augenblick auf, wischte sich die Tränen aus den Augen und fuhr dann fort.* **Pause machen** is 'to stop or take a break while working'. *Machen wir jetzt Pause!—wir haben uns alle sehr angestrengt.*

4. Stop s.o. doing sth. and **stop** sth. happening have two meanings.

i. Stop can be a syn. of *prevent* in the sense 'to ensure that an action, though possibly planned, does not take place'. *Nothing will stop me going.* The vs. discussed under PREVENT express this sense, the main ones being **hindern, verhindern,** and **jmdn. von etw. abhalten.** *Er hinderte mich daran, an der Sitzung teilzunehmen. Er wollte verhindern, daß ich das Auto kaufte. Ich lasse mich durch nichts abhalten hinzugehen.*

ii. The second sense is 'to cause an action that is going on to cease' or 'to get a pers. who is already doing sth. to desist'. *How can I stop the tap dripping? Wie kann man verhindern, daß der Wasserhahn tropft?* is the lit. transl. An alternative in speech is *Was kann ich tun, damit der Hahn nicht mehr tropft?* Likewise *Tu' doch was, damit die Tür nicht immer quietscht!* With a person as obj. **stop** in this sense is often, but need not be, combined with *get: How can we stop him being so foolhardy?* or *We finally got them to stop making so much noise.* Both E. versions become *Wie können wir ihn dazu bringen, daß er aufhört, so leichtsinnig zu sein? Schließlich haben wir sie dazu gebracht aufzuhören, so viel Krach zu machen.*

5. Stop meaning 'to prevent sth. reaching s.o./sth.' corresponds to **abhalten.** *The sandbags stop the bullets: Die Sandsäcke halten die Kugeln ab.*

> *Die Mauer ist so dick, daß sie den Lärm abhält.*   *Die Hecke hält den Wind ab.*

6. Stop in a hotel, town, etc. means 'to stay'. **Wohnen** is used for being temporarily accommodated in a hotel or at someone's place. *In welchem Hotel wohnen Sie? Ich verbringe drei Tage in Trier und wohne bei Verwandten/Freunden.* **Übernachten,** 'to spend the night', is also common. *Wir übernachteten in einem Dorf.* **Bleiben** and **sich aufhalten** mean 'to stop or stay' in the sense 'to spend [a short] time in a place'. *Wir sind ein paar Tage dort geblieben,* stayed/stopped there a few days. *A. Wollen sie ablegen? B. Danke. Ich kann leider nicht bleiben. Wie lange halten wir uns hier auf? Wir konnten uns nur fünf Tage in Rom aufhalten.*

7. Stop at nothing means 'to take any risks and even use dishonest means to gain one's ends'. The equivalents are **vor nichts zurückschrecken/ zurückscheuen.** *Er schrickt/scheut vor nichts zurück, um seine Ziele zu erreichen.* **Vor nichts haltmachen** implies that the person is unscrupulous and will stop at nothing. *Er machts vor nichts [und niemandem] halt, wenn er etw. erreichen will.*

8. For the use of **abbrechen** and **unterbrechen** which sometimes means 'to stop' see BREAK 4. iv.

9. For **stop up,** e.g. *a crack* or *Leaves stopped up the drain,* see BLOCK 1. v and vi.

strange *adj.* **Strange** has three meanings.

1. A strange place is one someone has never visited previously, and a strange person is one someone has never met before, i.e. a stranger. *How does being in a strange land affect you? I don't like strange people coming into my house.* The main equivalent is **fremd,** which has a broader range of meaning than 'strange' in this sense. It means 'completely unknown or not familiar' to the person concerned. *Die Gegend ist mir fremd. Ich bin in dieser Stadt fremd,* I'm a stranger here. *Ein fremder Mann sprach sie an. Meine Freundin fühlt sich nicht wohl unter den vielen fremden Menschen/Gesichtern. Eine Stadt/Ein Ausdruck/Ein Begriff ist mir fremd,* not familiar to me. *Das ist ein fremder Zug an ihm,* an unaccustomed trait not hitherto shown. *Jmds. Stimme klingt fremd. Sie sieht in der Perrücke fremd aus.* A strengthened form for people and places is **wild-**

fremd. *Eine wildfremde Gegend. Wildfremde Menschen.* (Another senses of *fremd* is 'foreign', 'not one's own'. *Fremde Länder, fremde Völker, fremde Sprachen.* It also means 'other people's' or 'another person's'. *Du sollst dich nicht in fremde Angelegenheiten mischen. Ohne fremde Hilfe kann ich den Schrank nicht bewegen. Er reist unter einem fremden Namen.*)

Das Kind schlief nicht gern in einem fremden Haus.
In dieser Gesellschaft fühle ich mich ganz fremd.
Ich bin oft in Spanien gewesen, aber es bleibt mir fremd.

2. Strange = 'out of the ordinary, strikingly unfamiliar, causing surprise, and possibly producing a feeling of uneasiness'. *He behaved in a very strange way. It's strange you should come today. Truth may well be stranger than fiction.*

i. The basic equivalent is **seltsam**, which is applied to things which someone finds unusual, hard to explain or understand, or surprising, including a person's behaviour and character.

Das sind seltsame Dinge, die du mir da erzählt hast.   *Das war ein seltsamer Anblick.*
Ein seltsamer Vorgang ereignete sich gestern im Dorf.
Ich wunderte mich über sein seltsames Verhalten.

ii. Sonderbar is stronger than *seltsam*, although in everyday speech they are used more or less interchangeably. *Ich habe gestern ein sehr sonderbares/seltsames Erlebnis gehabt.*

Es ist sonderbar, daß er den Vorfall gar nicht erwähnt hat.
Die beiden sind sehr sonderbare Menschen.   *Er ist ein sonderbarer Mensch.*

iii. Merkwürdig is a weak term comparable to *peculiar*. It expresses a vague feeling of strangeness and is mostly applied to something not expected and not quite usual. *Mir ist gestern etw. Merkwürdiges passiert.*

Nun geschah ein Vorfall, der uns damals sehr merkwürdig vorkam.
Das ist eine merkwürdige Geschichte, die Sie mir da erzählt haben.

iv. Eigenartig is also a weak term, suggesting something not immediately comprehensible.

Ich gebe zu, daß seine Methoden etwas eigenartig sind.   *Er verhält sich so eigenartig.*

v. Komisch is often used in speech when someone finds something unusual or unexpected. Cf. FUNNY.

Er hat manchmal ein wirklich komisches Benehmen an sich.
Sie hat einen komischen Geschmack.

vi. Fremdartig means 'belonging to a country which is not one's own', i.e. 'exotic' and suggests this confers a special or striking quality. *Gewisse Dinge besitzen einen fremdartigen Reiz. Das Fremdartige der weiten Welt regte meine kindliche Phantasie an.* It also means 'foreign'. *Jmd. hat eine fremdartige Aussprache/ein fremdartiges Aussehen.* A further use combines the meaning of *fremd*, 'not familiar', with *seltsam*. *In der Dunkelheit kam mir die Gegend fremdartig vor. Der Bahnhof, in dem nur ein Licht brannte, erschien mir fremdartig und ein wenig beunruhigend.*

vii. The v. **befremden** is a strong word which combines the sense of *seltsam* with that of 'unpleasant'. It implies a feeling not only of unfamiliarity but also of surprise or shock and disappointment. *Etw., was jmd[n.] befremdet,* strikes him or her as strange, odd, or queer. *Sein Verhalten hat sie befremdet. Es befremdet mich, daß . . . ,* I find it strange that. *Es ist seltsam/sonderbar, daß . . .* can also be used.

Der Ton seines Briefes hat sie befremdet/wirkte befremdend auf sie.
Es befremdet mich, diese Menschen hier zu sehen.

3. Strange, applied to the way someone feels, means 'to have uncomfortable or unpleasant feelings, either physical or emotional'. *Can I sit down? I feel a bit strange.* **Mir ist komisch** is used when someone feels unwell but does not know why. **Mir ist nicht wohl/unwohl/nicht gut** all refer to a feeling of nausea. **Mir ist seltsam**

zu Mute refers to someone's mood. It often suggests that the person feels melancholy or depressed, but it can refer to a feeling of elation which the person finds unusual.

street, road, path, track *ns.*

1. The original distinction between **street** and **road** was that **street** designated a town or village thoroughfare with buildings on one or both sides, while **road** suggested a connection between two places through open country. The distinction has been blurred in the names of streets through the expansion of towns in the last two hundred years or so, but we still expect, for example, Oxford Road to lead eventually to Oxford, whereas Oxford Street need not do so, and we speak of a country road, not of a country street. With the preps. *across*, *down*, and *on*, and with the v. *to cross*, **road** and **street** are now interchangeable. *Across the road/street. The children were playing on the road/street.* G. does not make the distinction made in E., **die Straße** being used for both. *Eine Straße* is paved or sealed and can be used by vehicles. It is immaterial whether it is in a built-up area or in the open country. G. roads are divided according to size into *Landstraßen*, *Bundesstraßen*, and *Autobahnen*. Note that *in/on* [to] the street/road is *auf die/der Straße. Sie trat auf die Straße*, stepped on to the road. *Die Kinder spielten auf der Straße.*

> *Bundesstraßen sind oft sehr stark befahren, und häufig wird dort ebenso gerast wie auf den Autobahnen.*   *Die Straßen im Gebirge sind oft sehr schmal.*

A G. word which partly fulfils the original condition of **street** is **die Gasse**, which must have a paved or sealed surface and be between buildings built side by side. It is usually very narrow. However, the word is not in common use in the north, although it survives in a few street names. *Die Pandektengasse ist eine enge Straße an der westlichen Seite von Karstadt.*

2. Der Weg is the main equivalent of **path** and **track**. It is used for properly built paths in a private garden or park and for the worn and not properly constructed tracks used by people, tractors, etc. between fields or through woods. It may be covered with gravel or loose road metal. Tracks for walkers or hikers are called *ein Weg, ein Fußweg*, or *ein Wanderweg*. **Der Pfad** is a narrow track, not as wide as *ein Weg*. Common compounds are *der Waldpfad* and *der Wiesenpfad*. *Ein Waldweg* is wider. (*Weg* also occurs in street names. *Der Nikolausbergerweg führt nach dem Dorf Nikolausberg.*)

> *Durch den anhaltenden Regen sind die Wege im Park stark aufgeweicht.*
>
> *Auf einem schmalen Pfad, dessen Verlauf manchmal nur schwer zu erkennen war, gelangten wir zum Gipfel.*   *Nach etwa 100 Metern zweigt ein Weg ab, der durch den Wald führt.*

strengthen, reinforce *vs.*

i. Both *kräftig* and *stark* mean 'strong' and form the vs. **kräftigen** and **stärken**. Applied to people, *kräftig* refers only to bodily strength, while *stark* is used both for physical and mental strength. *Kräftigen* and *stärken* are syns. in reference to the body. *Frische Luft und sportliche Betätigung kräftigen/stärken den Körper* or *Die Kinder bekamen kräftigende/stärkende Nahrung. Menschen werden gestärkt, indem sie essen oder schlafen.* The refl. of both vs. means 'to become stronger'. *Durch diese Übungen kräftigen/stärken sich die Muskeln.* The refl. often refers to the effect of eating or drinking. *Wir wollen uns erst einmal stärken, bevor wir anfangen zu arbeiten.* Only *stärken* is applied to mental phenomena, and in relation to a person it means 'to give s.o. inner or mental strength' or 'to make a quality of mind stronger'. *Ihr Glaube hat sie in diesen schweren Tagen gestärkt. Man stärkt jmdm. den Willen/den Mut. Jmd./Etw.*

stärkt jmds. Hoffnung/jmds. [Selbst]vertrauen. Etw. stärkt die Moral der Truppe/der Soldaten. (With *Moral*, 'morale', also *heben*, 'RAISE', and *verbessern*, 'IMPROVE'.) *Stärken* implies that s.o./sth. has lost, or does not have, the strength that could be expected, and needs to gain or regain this. A variety of ns. can be the obj. *Diese Bündnisse stärkten seine Macht. Dieser Wahlausgang stärkte das demokratische Bewußtsein/eine Partei.*

> *Die Gymnastik stärkt/kräftigt den Körper. Durch tägliche Gymnastik kräftigt/stärkt sich ihr Körper.*
> *Die Hungernden im Katastrophengebiet wurden erst einmal durch eine warme Mahlzeit gestärkt.*
> *Das Gespräch mit dem Pfarrer hat mich [seelisch] gestärkt.*

ii. Verstärken means 'to strengthen' in the sense 'to make sth. stronger than it already is'. It is translated as *to strengthen* or *reinforce* when a construction of some kind is made stronger. *Das Fundament muß verstärkt werden, wenn der Bau erweitert wird. Man verstärkt eine Brücke/eine Mauer/ein Gerüst/eine Befestigung* etc. It can be translated as *strengthen* when this means 'to increase numerically', i.e. 'to reinforce'. *Man verstärkt eine Polizeieinheit/Truppen/die Wachen/den rechten Flügel/einen Chor um mehrere Stimmen* etc. In reference to sound, it means to 'amplify'. *Die Stimme wurde durch Lautsprecher verstärkt.* Applied to efforts, resistance, opposition, an impression, belief, etc., it means 'to intensify'. *Wir müssen unsere Anstrengungen/ Bemühungen verstärken. Etw. verstärkt die Spannungen.* The refl. means 'to be intensified or strengthened'. *Statt nachzulassen, verstärkte sich der Widerstand. Der Sturm hat sich von Stunde zu Stunde verstärkt.* In some cases both *stärken* and *verstärken* are possible depending on the speaker's assessment as to whether the initial situation is one of weakness or strength. If the situation suggests weakness, *stärken* is used *Dieser Erfolg stärkte seine Macht.* Otherwise *verstärken* can be used. *Sein mutiges Auftreten stärkte/verstärkte seine Autorität.*

> *Die an der Grenze stationierten Truppen wurden durch neue Einheiten verstärkt.*
> *Sein dubioses Verhalten verstärkte unsere Zweifel an seiner Aufrichtigkeit.*
> *Ihr Eindruck, daß etw. nicht in Ordnung sei, verstärkte sich immer mehr.*

iii. Bestärken is now only used with a person as obj. + *in* followed by an attitude of mind, and means 'to strengthen s.o. in a belief, purpose, etc.' *Bestärken* used to be found with a n. denoting a belief, view, etc. as obj., but this is now rare, and in such contexts **verstärken** is the normal v. The typical uses of the two vs. are *Sein Verhalten hat mich in meinem Verdacht bestärkt* and *Sein Verhalten hat meinen Verdacht verstärkt. Bestärken* can also take an infin., *darin* being optional. *Die ermutigenden Worte des Freundes bestärkten mich [darin], das Vorhaben fortzusetzen.*

> *Dieser Politiker bestärkt die Leute nur in ihren Vorurteilen/verstärkt die Vorurteile der Leute.*
> *Ihre ablehnende Haltung bestärkte ihn in seiner Meinung, daß eine konstruktive Zusammenarbeit zwischen ihnen unmöglich wäre.*
> *Das Gespräch mit dem Dozenten bestärkte sie in ihrem Vorsatz, die Zwischenprüfung so bald wie möglich zu versuchen.*

iv. Bekräftigen can be a syn. of *bestärken*, but it is not the usual word in that sense. It now mostly means 'to confirm or reaffirm emphatically what has been agreed to or previously stated'.

> *Diese Ereignisse bekräftigen mich in der Überzeugung, daß wir richtig gehandelt haben.*
> *Der amerikanische Präsident bekräftigte seine Bereitschaft, über die Abschaffung von Atomwaffen zu verhandeln. 'Wir wollen euch helfen', bekräftigte er.*

strike *v.* One sense. The equivalent of the intr. v. **strike** meaning 'to refuse to go on working' is **streiken**. *Die Arbeiter streiken [für höhere Löhne].* The pass. can only be impersonal. *Es wird hier gestreikt. Hier wird gestreikt.* A related v. **bestreiken**, 'to take strike action against', needs an obj. *Die Arbeiter bestreiken den Betrieb.* Hence the pass.: *Die Fabrik/Die Firma wird bestreikt.*

student, pupil *ns.* study *v.*

i. Ein Student or **eine Studentin** can only be applied to someone enrolled at a tertiary institution of some kind. Those attending a primary or secondary school are called **Schüler** (*der Schüler, die Schülerin*). *Sie ist Studentin der Philosophie/ Naturwissenschaften. Er ist ein guter/eifriger/schlechter/fauler Schüler. In der Klasse sind 31 Schüler.* Schüler is also the equivalent of **pupil** in the sense 'one who has been taught or influenced by a teacher of distinction'. *Renate Beyer ist Schülerin Albrecht Schönes. Die Schüler verbreiteten die Lehren ihres Meisters.*

ii. In some cases the v. **studieren** expresses the meaning that someone is a student or attends a post-secondary educational establishment. *Mein Bruder studiert/wollte gern studieren. Meine Schwester studiert im ersten Semester/Studienjahr.* Studieren also takes an academic subject as obj. *Sie studiert Jura/Germanistik.* It also means 'to study' in the sense 'to occupy oneself intensively with', 'to investigate'. *Jmd. studiert ein Lehrbuch/die Lebensgewohnheiten und Sprache eines Bergstammes/die Verhältnisse in einem Gebiet/die Akten über einen Fall/die Speisekarte/den Fahrplan/die Inserate.* **Study**, as in *I'm studying for a test or examination*, is **lernen** when memorizing knowledge is implied, or **üben** when practice of skills is involved. *Ich lerne für die Französischarbeit. Ich übe für die Mathearbeit.* Cf. PRACTISE. Colloquial words used among *Schüler* are **pauken**, **büffeln**, and **ochsen**. All suggest a great effort to learn, but imply that the learning is superficial and only done to pass an examination or test. All three can be trans. or intr. *Ich habe Vokabeln gepaukt/Grammatik gebüffelt/physikalische Lehrsätze geochst. Ich habe vor jeder Prüfung gepaukt/für die Prüfung gebüffelt/den ganzen Nachmittag geochst.*

succeed, manage [to do] sth., be successful *vs.*

1. Gelingen means 'to succeed', but it is only used with something attempted or *es* as subj., not with a person as subj. Thus *Ein Versuch/Ein Plan/Ein Vorhaben/Ein Projekt/Ein Unternehmen/Ein Angriff,* etc. *ist gelungen. Unsere Bemühungen sind gelungen.* The impersonal form can be used without a dat. *Es gelang, den Waldbrand zu löschen.* (This can be translated as *It has been possible to put out the bushfire*; if *succeed* or *manage* are used, a subj. has to be added. *S.o. succeeded in putting out the bushfire.*) With a dat. *gelingen* means 'to succeed in doing sth.' or 'to manage to do sth.' *Es gelang dem Torwart, den Angriff abzuwehren. Es ist dem Löschtrupp gelungen, den Brand unter Kontrolle zu bringen.* A syn. is **glücken**, which often has the connotation that, through fortunate or favourable circumstances, the desired result was achieved. Like *gelingen* it is used with a n. subj., *Der Plan ist geglückt,* or with *es* + infin., *Es ist mir geglückt, sie zu finden.* A syn. in a few contexts is **geraten**. *Der Kuchen ist dir wieder gut geraten/geglückt.* Both mean 'to turn out well'. Sometimes they are translated as *succeed. Ihr scheint alles zu glücken/geraten/gelingen. Ihm glückt/gerät alles, was er anfängt.*

2. Schaffen is much used in the spoken language with a personal subj. in the sense 'to manage [to do] sth.' It means both 'to get through [an amount of] work', *Ich habe heute sehr viel geschafft,* and 'to be successful in doing sth.', *Ich habe es geschafft, ihn zu überzeugen,* I have managed to convince/succeeded in convincing him.

> *Wenn mir keiner hilft, schaffe ich es nie.*   *Er schaffte es endlich, Bürgermeister zu werden.*
> *Von der Übersetzung habe ich heute vier Seiten geschafft.*
> *Wenn wir uns beeilen, schaffen wir es vielleicht noch, [den Zug zu erwischen].*

3. Applied to people, *erfolgreich* means that they achieve good results in what they set out to do. *Er war ein erfolgreicher Geschäftsmann. Sie ist in ihrem Beruf erfolgreich* *gewesen.* It also means that a particular activity has a positive result. *Der Raketenstart ist erfolgreich verlaufen. Alle sind erfreut über den erfolgreichen Abschluß der Verhandlungen.* **Erfolg haben** expresses a similar meaning. The neg. is *keinen Erfolg haben.* [*Keinen*] *Erfolg haben* is used alone or with *mit,* and with people or things as subj.

Ich bemühe mich seit einiger Zeit darum, habe aber erst jetzt Erfolg gehabt. Or . . . *habe aber keinen Erfolg gehabt.* *Ich habe mit meinen Vorschlägen Erfolg gehabt.*

Meine Bemühungen hatten keinen Erfolg. Also . . . blieben ohne Erfolg.

4. Klappen means 'to turn out as planned' or 'to be successful' and is common in informal speech. It is used with a non-personal n. as subj., *Hat die Reparatur geklappt?* or in an impersonal construction with and without *mit. Hat es mit der Reparatur geklappt? Hat es geklappt?*

Die Generalprobe hat ausgezeichnet geklappt. Wir wollen hoffen, daß die Premiere auch klappt.

Mit der Verlängerung seines Arbeitsvertrags hat es geklappt. *Die Sache muß klappen.*

5. Erreichen + **daß**-clause means 'to succeed in bringing sth about'. It can be applied to a result of any kind, but it is often found when one person gets another to agree to, change, or implement something.

Durch die Impfaktion erreichte man, daß die Seuche sich nicht mehr ausbreitete.

Durch viele Protestkundgebungen erreichte man, daß die Regierung von der Verabschiedung der Gesetzesvorlage absah.

Wir haben endlich bei der Firmenleitung erreicht, daß wir samstags freihaben.

suffer, tolerate *vs.* **Suffer**, the basic sense of which is 'undergo or endure', is both intr. and trans. *With the new drug you won't suffer at all. They suffered heavy losses.*

A. Intr. uses. (i) When intr. **suffer** means 'to undergo or submit to pain, discomfort, etc.', but what is endured is not stated. *A brave man suffers in silence. He suffered terribly during the voyage.* (ii) It takes *from* + a disease or ailment. *She was suffering from a cold/what she called a fit of depression.* (iii) It is also intr. in the sense 'to sustain, injury, damage, or loss'. *From* or *through* state the cause of the damage, harm, etc. *Your health is likely to suffer from/through overwork. The business suffers from lack of capital.* The impairment undergone and its cause may only be implied. *Your reputation will suffer.*

i. Leiden is now mainly intr. Without a prep. it corresponds to E. sense i above. *Der Verletzte litt sehr/schwer. Ein tapferer Mensch leidet schweigend.*

Der Besitzer beschloß, das verletzte Pferd zu erschießen, damit es nicht unnötig leiden müßte.

ii. With the preps. **an** or **unter**, leiden corresponds to E. uses ii and iii above. *Leiden an* is now used for physical illnesses. *Jmd. leidet an einer Erkältung/an Zahnschmerzen/an einer schweren Krankheit.* The same meaning can be expressed by *haben. Sie hat eine Erkältung.* With mental illnesses and disturbances, both preps. are found. *Jmd. leidet an/unter Klaustrophobie/Verfolgungsangst/Depressionen.* In such contexts, *an* states the fact, *unter* either stresses the adverse effects or suggests that the condition continues for some time. *Leiden unter* often states that someone suffers adverse effects because of something. *Alle litten unter dem frostigen Arbeitsklima/der Hitze.* Only *unter* is used for adverse effects which are not connected with bodily ailments. *Die Firma leidet unter Kapitalmangel. Unter* also appears in the form *darunter, daß. Das Buch leidet darunter, daß die Hauptthesen nicht bewiesen werden. Your reputation will suffer* is *Ihr Ruf wird darunter leiden. Darunter* may be omitted. *Durch,* which can be replaced by *unter,* states a cause. *Durch die Kreditverknappung hat die Industrie sehr gelitten.* Cf. B. 2. ii for another use of *leiden unter.*

Er leidet an Rheuma/an Asthma/an Zwangsvorstellungen.

Sie leidet noch an den Folgen des Sturzes.
Der Junge litt sehr unter der strengen Hand des Vaters.
Der Mais hatte sehr unter der Trockenheit der vergangenen Wochen gelitten.
Ihre Gesundheit wird wahrscheinlich unter der fortgesetzten Überanstrengung sehr leiden.
Die Uhr hatte durch die unsanfte Behandlung während der Reise sehr gelitten.

B. Trans. uses of **suffer**. (i) When **suffer** is trans., the painful, distressing, or injurious condition undergone or endured is the obj. *S.o. suffers pain/grief/distress/a humiliation/hardship/wrong.* (ii) A further trans. sense is 'to be subjected to or undergo sth. evil or painful'. *Three more suffered the same fate. They will have to suffer the consequences.* (iii) With a thing as well as a person as subj. it means 'to sustain injury, damage, or loss'. *The house suffered some damage in the recent floods. The regiment suffered severe losses.*

1. Erleiden needs an obj. and is the main equivalent of the E. senses just defined. *Man wollte das Unrecht, das sie erlitten hatte, wiedergutmachen. Andere erlitten ein ähnliches Schicksal.* Ns. often found as its obj. are *eine Enttäuschung, eine Niederlage, eine Schlappe, eine Demütigung, der Spott, der Verlust, ein Nervenzusammenbruch, Verbrennungen, Verletzungen. Das Schiff erlitt Schiffbruch* means lit. 'the ship was wrecked', but the expression is used fig. with a person, enterprise, etc. as subj. and means 'failed or came to grief'. In elevated style, *Das Schiff* (but not a person) *litt Schiffbruch* is found, as is *leiden* with *Schaden* as obj., but *erleiden* is the usual v.

Die Mannschaft erlitt im Spiel gegen England eine weitere Niederlage.
Beim Unfall erlitten sowohl der Fahrer als auch der Beifahrer Verletzungen.
Der Marktplatz erlitt keinen großen Schaden, als die Stadt beschossen wurde.
Diese Männer waren erbittert über die Kränkungen und Beleidigungen, die sie durch die Regierung erlitten hatten.   *Dieses zweifelhafte Unternehmen wird bald Schiffbruch erleiden.*
Er erlitt Schiffbruch bei der Ausbeutung des Patentes, weil er nicht genug Kapital hatte.

2. i. Leiden + obj. is now restricted in use. *Not leiden*, 'to suffer distress or hardship', is still common. *Viele Bauern leiden Not, weil die Dürre die Ernte vernichtet hat. Hunger, Durst, [große] Angst, Qualen,* and *Mangel leiden* are also possible. *Jmd. leidet Schmerzen* is possible in elevated language. *Unter Schmerzen leiden* is more usual, and *Schmerzen haben* is the normal expression.
ii. Leiden unter can translate *suffer* + obj. *Jmd. leidet sehr unter Traurigkeit/Langeweile,* suffers great sadness/boredom. *S.o. suffered pangs of conscience* can be expressed as *Jmd. litt unter Gewissensbissen;* an alternative is *jmd. hatte Gewissensbisse. They suffered great discomfort but didn't complain* could be *Sie litten sehr darunter, daß Sie so unbequem lagen/saßen, klagten aber nicht. She suffered great grief because of the death of her husband* could be *Sie litt sehr unter dem Tod ihres Mannes.* If *grief* is translated, a different v. is needed, such as *Der Tod ihres Mannes bereitete ihr großen Kummer/schweres Leid.*

3. Suffer *the consequences: Du mußt die Folgen/die Konsequenzen deiner Handlungen tragen.* Cf. BEAR 3.

4. For *jmdn./etw. nicht leiden können/mögen* cf. LIKE 2. iii.

C. Other equivalents. **Dulden** is intr. and belongs to a fairly elevated level of style. *Sie hat tapfer geduldet* implies that someone is badly affected by an unfavourable, unpleasant, or harmful situation, but bears it with patience and composure and without complaint. The situation is usually confined to trying external circumstances, not bodily pain. It can be translated as *suffer. Man behandelt sie schlecht, aber sie duldet still und lehnt sich nicht auf.* **Erdulden** is trans. and means 'to bear or put up with'. *Sie hat viel erduldet. Sie mußten diese rohe Behandlung lange erdulden.* It is an emotional and not very common word which may be slightly old-fashioned.

Ertragen and *aushalten*, discussed under BEAR, are more usual.

> *Er mußte die Beschimpfungen und Beleidigungen erdulden, die auf ihn niederprasselten, als er zum Gerichtssaal geführt wurde.*

D. Tolerate. Both **suffer** and *leiden* used to mean 'to tolerate'. This is now the main sense of **dulden**, which in this sense is trans. *Jmd. duldet keinen Widerspruch/keine Kritik/keinen Ungehorsam*. It is also used with *es* + *daß*-clause. *Ich dulde es nicht länger, daß gewisse Mitarbeiter bevorzugt behandelt werden*. A person can be the obj. *Jmd. duldet einen anderen nicht in seinem Haus.*

> *Dieses ungehörige Benehmen den Nachbarn gegenüber kann ich nicht dulden.*
> *Bei ihren Spielen bleiben die Jungen lieber unter sich. Mädchen werden nicht geduldet.*

suggest, imply, indicate, insinuate *vs.*

1. Suggest means 'to put sth. to s.o. as a possible course of action for his or her acceptance' and takes an obj., a clause, or a gerund. *We are to suggest seminar topics for next year. No one would dream of suggesting retirement to him/that he [should] retire. She suggested selling the house*. It is also used with *for* or *as*. *He suggested John for the job. Colin has been suggested as the next president of the society. We have suggested Hobart [as a suitable place] for the next convention.*

i. Vorschlagen is the main equivalent of **suggest** in these uses and of the more formal syn. *to propose*. It needs a person as subj. It takes *für* or *als* or an infin. which translates the E. gerund. With a person as obj. it also means 'to nominate'. (*Nominieren* also exists.)

> *Wir sollen Seminarthemen fürs nächste Jahr vorschlagen.*
> *Ich schlage vor, daß du jetzt schlafen gehst. Du siehst müde aus.*
> *Ich habe vorgeschlagen, das Haus zu kaufen.*
> *Es würde niemand[em] einfallen vorzuschlagen, daß er sich zur Ruhe setzen sollte/sich pensionieren lassen sollte.   Wir haben Hobart als Tagungsort vorgeschlagen.*
> *Ich schlage Andreas für das Amt des Vorsitzenden/für die Stelle vor.*
> *Während der Sitzung wurde Herr Schöken als neuer Kassenwart vorgeschlagen.*

ii. One sense of **anregen** is also often translated as *suggest*, but it does not imply as direct a proposal as *vorschlagen*. The meaning is more 'to give an indication that sth. would be advisable, desirable, or worthwhile'. It takes an obj., a clause, or an infin. (With *zu* + n. or infin. it means 'to stimulate or prompt'. *Durch den Vorfall wurde ich zum Nachdenken angeregt*.)

> *Der Professor regte das Forschungsprojekt an. Er regt oft die Erforschung gewisser Themen an.*
> *In seiner Rede regte der Politiker an, den benachteiligten Menschen mehr zu helfen.*
> *Ich werde anregen, daß wir demnächst den ganzen Fragenkomplex gründlich diskutieren.*

iii. With a person as subj. and another person in the dat. **nahelegen** means 'to suggest, recommend, or advise s.o. strongly to do sth.' It is not used when the suggestion is put directly to the person concerned, but when someone describes what one person suggests another do. *Es wurde ihm nahegelegt, das Haus zu verlassen/sich bei der Kollegin zu entschuldigen*. Depending on the relationship between the people involved, it can often imply strong urging, *Ich habe meinem Bruder nahegelegt, lieber nach Athen zu fliegen als mit dem Auto zu fahren*, or if the relationship is between superior and subordinate, it implies not just that the superior puts something to the subordinate for acceptance or rejection, but that the superior virtually tells the other person to do something. *Der Kanzler legte dem Minister den Rücktritt nahe* implies that compliance is expected.

> *Nachdem sie mehrere Male zu spät zur Arbeit gekommen war, legte ihr der Chef nahe, pünktlich zu erscheinen.*
> *Wegen der fortgesetzten Disziplinschwierigkeiten legte der Direktor dem Schüler nahe, die Schule zu verlassen.*

Von einem Dozenten wurde ihm nahegelegt, seine Aufsätze in Zukunft mehr zu straffen und Allgemeinplätze zu vermeiden.

iv. Both **Jmdn. auf den Gedanken/die Idee bringen** and **jmdn. darauf bringen +** infin. either stated or implied mean 'to put sth., or the idea of doing sth., into s.o.'s head' and can sometimes be used to translate **suggest** in this sense. Both *Idee* and *Gedanke* are used when the idea leads to action, but *Gedanke* tends to be preferred when the result is purely mental. *Diese Bemerkung/Diese Reaktion brachte den Detektiv auf den Gedanken, daß der Zeuge etw. verheimlichte.* When a thing is the subj., the implication is that from what is said or observed someone draws a conclusion about something he or she could do. *Der schöne Pullover ihrer Freundin brachte sie auf die Idee, auch einmal wieder zu stricken.* When a person is the subj., these expressions may imply a direct proposal on that person's part, but often the action is an indirect consequence of something that person says or does. *Weil sie beide gut tanzen konnten, brachten Freunde sie auf den Gedanken, sich beim nächsten Turnier anzumelden.* (*Seine jetzigen Freunde bringen den Jungen ständig auf dumme Gedanken*, 'put foolish ideas into his head', is a fixed expression.)

> *Das Gespräch mit den Freunden brachte mich auf die Idee, es noch einmal, aber auf andere Weise, zu versuchen.* *Er brachte mich darauf, mich sofort zu beschweren.*
> *Die ständig steigenden Gemüsepreise brachten sie auf den Gedanken, Gemüse im Garten selbst zu ziehen.*

v. Suggerieren means 'to influence s.o. so that he or she believes sth. false or does sth. which the other pers. wants, but which is unreasonable'.

> *Durch die Werbung wird suggeriert, daß man durch den Kauf eines Autos nicht bloß ein Beförderungsmittel bekommt, sondern auch glücklich wird.*
> *Sie suggerieren mir ständig, daß ich mich ihrer maoistischen Splittergruppe anschließen soll.*

2. If one thing suggests another, the first makes someone think that the second is so, or the first makes the second seem likely. *His expression suggested that he was pleased to see us. It is stupid to raise public expenditure at a time when everything suggests it should be cut.* In one sense **indicate** is a syn. and means 'to show or point to with a fair degree of certainty', 'to be a fairly certain sign of'. *These figures indicate/suggest a turn-around in the economy. The fever indicates severe inflammation.*

i. Both **deuten auf** and **hindeuten auf** mean 'to give evidence of [the existence of] sth. not fully revealed', 'to indicate, suggest, or point to'. *Hindeuten* is the everyday and more usual word; *deuten* is stylistically higher. *Alles deutet auf einen baldigen Umschwung in der Wirtschaft hin. Der Abschiedsbrief deutet auf Selbstmord.* (The basic sense of *deuten* is 'to point with the hand or finger'. *Sie deutete mit dem Finger auf ein Haus, das ihr gefiel.*)

> *Nichts in ihrem Verhalten deutet darauf hin, daß sie eine Berühmtheit ist.*
> *Es ist kaum vernünftig, die Staatsausgaben zu einer Zeit zu erhöhen, wo alles darauf hindeutet, daß man sie kürzen muß.*

ii. With a thing as subj. **nahelegen** means that one thing makes another appear to be the natural or obvious conclusion or reaction. *Der Erfolg der ersten Versuche legte die Fortsetzung der Arbeit nahe.*

iii. Schließen lassen auf means 'to allow a conclusion to be drawn about sth.' *Sein Gesichtsausdruck läßt darauf schließen, daß er sich über unseren Besuch freute* implies a justified conclusion and is more definite than . . . *deutete darauf hin, daß* . . .

> *Eine unparteiische Nachprüfung des Beweismaterials läßt darauf schließen, daß der Urteilsspruch durch Vorurteile beeinflußt wurde.* *Alle Beweise lassen auf Mord schließen.*
> *Das Fieber läßt auf eine schwere Entzündung schließen/deutet auf eine schwere Entzündung hin.*

A syn. of *schließen lassen* is **den Schluß nahelegen**, to make the conclusion appear obvious. *Sein Verhalten legt den Schluß nahe, daß er an der Sachlage nicht ganz unschuldig ist.* Related expressions which suggest a less certain conclusion are **die**

Vermutung nahelegen and **den Verdacht nahelegen**. *Seine Antwort legt die Vermutumg nahe, daß er mehr wußte, als er zugab. Das Verhalten der Zeugen legte den Verdacht nahe, sie wären bestochen worden.*

iv. A further related expression is **vermuten lassen**. As *vermuten* means 'to conjecture or surmise' (cf. GUESS), this expression implies a less definite and conclusive deduction than *schließen lassen*. *Vermuten lassen* is, however, the only possibility in a clause with *wie* = 'as'. *Amerika wurde nicht—wie der Name vermuten läßt—von Amerigo Vespucci endeckt.*

> *Die Ergebnisse unserer Untersuchungen lassen vermuten, daß Erdöl in dieser Gegend vorhanden ist.*

3. With a person as subj. **imply** means 'to express indirectly that sth. is the case without actually saying so'. *Somehow he implied that he was the one who had done all the work. I don't want to imply that you have made no effort.* **Suggest** can be a syn. *Are you suggesting/trying to suggest that I am lying?* As a syn. of these vs., **indicate** means 'to state or mention briefly without going into details'. *They indicated that they were willing to negotiate.*

i. Andeuten means 'to refer to sth. cautiously and briefly, as a hint rather than stating it clearly' and is translated as *imply*, *indicate*, or **suggest** depending on the context. A clause follows or objs. such as *die Hauptpunkte, die wichtigsten Argumente*, or something planned. The means of giving an impression of the shape of something without details can be a sketch. *Auf einem Blatt Papier deutete sie die Umrisse der Gestalt an.*

> *Im Laufe des Gesprächs deutete der Minister seinen baldigen Rücktritt an.*
> *Sie deutete an, daß sie demnächst verreisen werde.*
> *Damit wollte er andeuten, daß er mit unserer Arbeit zufrieden ist.*
> *Sie hat die Hauptpunkte nur angedeutet; auf die Gründe dafür ist sie nicht näher eingegangen.*
> *Sie deuteten an, daß sie bereit wären, über einige Punkte in Verhandlungen mit uns zu treten.*

ii. Etw. durchblicken lassen means 'to let sth. be seen or realized from what is said without stating it openly'. It suggests a less clear statement than *andeuten. Der Abgeordnete ließ durchblicken, daß er bei der nächsten Wahl nicht kandidieren würde. Der Junge ließ durchblicken, daß er mehr Taschengeld haben will.*

iii. In a question or a neg. sent., **sagen** can express the sense 'imply or suggest'. *Are you suggesting/trying to suggest that they are dishonest?* can be *Wollen Sie damit sagen, daß sie unehrlich seien? Damit will ich nicht sagen, daß sie sich keine Mühe gegeben haben*, I'm not suggesting that you haven't taken any trouble.

> *Wollen Sie damit sagen, daß Sie unser Vorgehen mißbilligen?*
> *Niemand sagt/behauptet, daß sie unehrlich seien* (no one suggests/is suggesting).

iv. In some cases, such as the second E. example, **unterstellen** could be used. It needs a dat. *Ich unterstelle euch nicht, euch keine Mühe gegeben zu haben.* Cf. 6.

4. With a statement, word, name, etc. as subj. **imply** means 'to contain a meaning not expressed directly'. *These remarks imply a certain disdain for his colleagues. Do her words/Does what she said imply that she doesn't want to continue?*

i. Etw. schwingt in etw. mit means that one thing, such as *Spott* or *Ironie*, is perceptible in what someone says. *In dem, was er sagte, schwingt eine Verachtung seiner Vorgesetzten mit*, his words imply contempt for his superiors. *In seinem Lob schwingt eine gewisse Kritik an seinen Kollegen mit.* **Heraushören** means 'to perceive in a remark sth. not expressly stated' and can translate *s.o.'s remarks imply sth. Aus ihren Bemerkungen konnte man Verbitterung/einen Vorwurf heraushören. Eine gewisse Unzufriedenheit war aus seinen Äußerungen herauszuhören.* **Implizieren** is used in learned language. *Die Wörter, die er für seine Antwort gewählt hat, implizieren eine kaum überhörbare Drohung. Was er da sagt, impliziert eine Wertung, die ich für nicht berechtigt halte.* In a question **Soll das besagen, daß** or **Soll das heißen/bedeuten, daß** can be used. Cf. SAY and MEAN. The following clause states what the unexpressed meaning is understood to be. *Soll das besagen, daß Sie nicht weitermachen wollen? Soll das heißen, daß ich das Geld nicht hätte ausgeben dürfen?*

ii. In relation to words **imply** means 'to signify in addition to the exact meaning'. *What does this word imply?* **In etw. mitschwingen** and **implizieren** can also be used for words, as well as **[mit] in etw. enthalten sein**, to be included in. *In dem Wort schwingt die Vorstellung einer freien Entscheidung mit*, the word implies a free decision. *In* Sei ein Mann! *impliziert* Mann Mut. *In diesem Satz ist in dem Wort* Mann *die Vorstellung von Mut mit enthalten.*

5. Imply means 'to involve or comprise logically'. If one situation or condition implies another, it suggests that the second is the natural and necessary consequence of the first. **Implizieren** expresses this sense. *Die Durchführung des Plans impliziert hohe Anforderungen an alle Mitarbeiter.* Alternatives are **zur Folge haben**, 'to result in', and **sich aus etw. ergeben**, 'to result from'. *Der Auftrag wird eine Menge Arbeit zur Folge haben. Aus dem Auftrag wird sich eine Menge Arbeit ergeben.*

6. Insinuate means 'to imply in an unpleasant way that sth. bad about a pers. is true'. Although **suggest** does not in itself imply anything bad, it can be used in similar contexts. *Are you insinuating/suggesting that I am lying? He destroyed the witness's character by insinuating/suggesting base and selfish motives for his actions.* **Unterstellen** means 'to state sth. bad about a pers. without any real evidence for it'. It needs a dat. and takes either an obj. or a clause. *Are you suggesting/insinuating that I am not telling the truth?* becomes *Unterstellen Sie mir, daß ich die Unwahrheit gesagt habe?* **Unterstellen** translates both **suggest** and **insinuate**. **Unterschieben** is 'to ascribe or impute knowingly and with malicious intent sth. false to a pers.' and can translate some uses of **insinuate**. It takes a dat. and an obj. only, not a clause. *Die anderen haben ihm eigennützige und niedrige Beweggründe/Absichten unterschoben.*

Wie kannst du mir unterstellen, daß ich so was getan haben könnte?/ daß ich dich belogen habe?
Du hast mir unterstellt, daß ich etw. behauptet hätte, was ich nie gesagt habe.
Die Äußerungen, die man mir unterschoben hat, sind völlig aus der Luft gegriffen.

7. In *It would be misleading to suggest that all Germans are rich*, **suggest** means 'to create the impression'. This sense is conveyed by **den Eindruck erwecken**. *Es wäre irreführend, wenn ich den Eindruck erwecken wollte, als wären alle Deutschen reich.*

8. I suggest is used in parentheses to introduce a personal opinion which is offered for consideration. *He was a dignified man with, I suggest, an obscure past.* The simplest rendering is **meiner Ansicht/Meinung nach** or **wie ich glaube**. *Er ist ein sehr würdevoller Mensch mit, meiner Ansicht nach, einer dunklen Vergangenheit.* A stylistically more elevated transl. is **ich wage zu behaupten**. *Alles hatte sich, so wage ich zu behaupten, so abgespielt*, this, I venture to suggest, was how it all happened.

suit, fit, match vs. **suitable** *adj.* A few uses. In different syntactic patterns *passen* covers senses of all three E. vs.

1. i. Fit. **Passen** means that an article of clothing is the right size, shape, and cut for the person who is wearing or is to wear it. It is used alone or with a dat. *Der Anzug paßt* and *Paßt dir der Anzug?* thus refer to size. *Die Hose paßt [ihm]. Die Jeans passen ihr gut/genau/nicht/schlecht. Ein Kleidungsstück passend machen* is 'to make it fit'. With an adv. **sitzen** has the same sense and usually means that something fits very well. *Ich muß wirklich sagen, das Kostüm/das Kleid/der Rock/die Hose/die Bluse sitzt ausgezeichnet.* (Note that *sitzen* means 'to be firmly in place, to sit firmly or properly', but usually refers to things other than clothes. *Die Schrauben müssen ganz genau sitzen.*)

ii. With preps., mostly *auf* and *in*, **passen** means 'to be of the right size or shape to fit on or into sth., including a space'. It can be used without a prep. if this meaning is clear from the context. *Der Deckel paßt genau* could imply *Er paßt genau auf den Topf.* If the sent. does not include an *in*-phr., *hinein* is used. *Etw. paßt nicht hinein*, doesn't fit in. If the sent. contains *in, hinein* is optional as it only strengthens a meaning which is clear without it. *In den Koffer paßt nichts mehr [hinein].*

Das kleine Auto paßt in diese Parklücke.   *Der Schlüssel paßt nicht in das Schloß.*
Der Karton paßt nicht in diese Tragetasche.

iii. [Hinein] **passen** + **in** is used when a person fits in with a group of people or when something fits in with its surroundings. *Die beiden passen gut in euren Kreis [hinein]. Das Bild paßt nicht in das Zimmer [hinein].*

2. Suit and **match**.

i. Passen + **zu** means that one thing or person suits, matches, or goes with another. *Der Hut paßt zu dem Mantel. Die Farbe der Gardinen paßt zu der Tapete. Ich finde, Kathrin paßt gut zu Florian.* With a pl. subj.: *Ich finde, die Farben/die beiden jungen Leute passen zueinander* or *passen zusammen. Passend* in this sense means 'matching'. *Ein zum Kleid passender Schal/Hut.*

ii. Suit means 'to be convenient or the best thg. for the pers. under the circumstances'. *Does ten o'clock suit you?* **Passen** + dat. expresses this sense. The subj. can be a time, place, position, etc. *Paßt dir der 21.? Passen* is also used impersonally as in E. *Paßt es dir, wenn ich heute abend vorbei komme?* A common alternative is **jmdm. recht sein**, which can also be used impersonally. *Das ist mir recht*, it suits me well/fine or it's all right with me.

Paßt Ihnen vier Uhr? Paßt es Ihnen, wenn ich um vier vorbeikomme? Ja, das paßt mir gut/Das paßt
  mir leider nicht.   *Eine solche Stelle würde mir ausgezeichnet passen.*
Ist es dir recht, wenn ich statt morgen übermorgen komme?

Suit yourself! is *Wie du willst. He suits himself* becomes *Er tut nur das, was ihm paßt/was er will.*

iii. Suit s.o. in the sense 'to make s.o. look attractive' is in everyday language **stehen**. *Das Kleid steht dir [gut]. Gut* is optional as the meaning is the same whether it is included or not. The neg. is *Der Hut steht dir nicht* or *steht dir schlecht.* A stylistically higher syn. is one sense of **kleiden**. *Das Kostüm kleidet sie*, it suits her. *Kleidsam*, used with articles of clothing, means 'becoming or flattering'. *Ein kleidsamer Mantel/Rock. Der Mantel/Die Frisur ist kleidsam.*

3. Suitable.

i. The idea that s.o./sth. is suitable for or suited to a particular purpose can be expressed by **sich eignen** or the past part. **geeignet**. Both take *für*, which is always implied, if not stated. *Er eignet sich nicht für diese Aufgabe. Das Papier eignet sich gut für diesen Druck. Es kann [für diese Stelle] keinen geeigneteren Bewerber geben als Künert.* (Note that *geeignet* also occurs in contexts in which **suitable** is not used in E. *Diese Maßnahmen sind nicht dazu geeignet, die Spannungen abzubauen.*)

Er ist der geeignete Mann für diese Arbeit.
Sie eignet sich gut/nicht für diese Aufgabe/diese Rolle.
Nur wer schon einige Erfahrung hat, eignet sich für die Stellung.
Der Stoff eignet sich gut für die Verwendung in Flugzeugen.
Dieser Roman ist kein geeigneter Text für Studenten im ersten Jahr des Studiums.
Diese Wohnungen sind für Familien mit mehr als zwei Kindern nicht geeignet.

ii. The equivalent of **suitable** meaning 'appropriate from the viewpoint of propriety, convenience, or fitness, proper, right' is **passend**. It is only used attributively. *Bei einer passenden Gelegenheit sage ich es ihm. Hältst du diese Bemerkung für passend? Ich fand sein Benehmen [un]passend. Ein für eine solche Feier [un]passendes Kleid.*

Die passende Beschäftigung für zehnjährige Kinder. Ein passendes Thema. Das passende Wort. It also translates *convenient. Ein passender Zeitpunkt.* Colloquially, it is applied to people instead of *geeignet. Er ist der passende Mann für diese Stelle.*

iii. Angemessen means 'suitable' or 'appropriate' in the sense 'adapted to or in proportion to the circumstances'. *Eine angemessene Strafe* is one that is in the correct relation to or fits the crime. *Etw. ist den Umständen angemessen.* It belongs more to the written language.

> *Das ist ein angemessener Lohn für solch anstrengende Arbeit.*

iv. Angebracht means 'suitable, appropriate, or proper in a particular situation or in particular circumstances, fitting or opportune'. *Diese Bemerkung ist schlecht angebracht,* ill-timed, uncalled for, out of place.

> *Ich halte es für angebracht, ihr schon jetzt zu gratulieren. Obwohl es noch nicht amtlich bestätigt ist, wird sie die Stelle bekommen.*
>
> *Die Veröffentlichung dieser Tatsachen wäre jetzt angebracht.*

4. In the now not very common use as a trans. v., *to suit sth. to the circumstances,* **suit** can only be **anpassen,** to adapt. *Er paßte seine Bemerkungen der Situation/der Zuhörerschaft an.*

support, prop up *vs.*

1. i. If something supports a structure, it holds it firmly from below so that it does not drop downwards. *Columns support the roof/the dome.* The usual equivalent is **tragen,** to carry or bear the weight of. *Zwei Säulen tragen das Dach.* A person's legs or feet can be the subj. of *tragen. Meine Füße/Beine wollten mich nicht mehr tragen.* **Stützen** occasionally has the meaning of *tragen. Säulen stützen das Gewölbe.*

ii. Support and **prop up** mean 'to prevent from falling, collapsing, sagging, or slipping by placing sth. against or under'. *The wall had to be supported/propped up by steel girders.* **Stützen** means 'to prop up or support sth. that could well collapse, fall over, or break'. *Man stützt einen Zaun/ein baufälliges Haus/einen Ast.* It is used for things other than buildings. *In Regalen, die nicht voll sind, wird das letzte Buch von einem Halter gestützt, damit alle nicht umkippen.* In reference to a building, fence, pile, etc. which might collapse, **abstützen** is a syn. of *stützen. Eine Wand wird abgestützt. Abstützen* is unambiguous whereas *stützen* could have sense 1. i. *Der Stollen wurde mit Balken abgestützt. Sie hatten die Holzscheite falsch gestapelt und nicht richtig abgestützt, so daß alles zusammenfiel. Stützen* is used fig. *Ein Regime stützen* is 'to shore or prop it up'.

iii. Stützen is the usual v. when a part of the body is supported by another or on something *Er stützte den Kopf in die Hände/die Ellbogen auf den Tisch.* (Here *stützen* does not imply weakness as it does in 2.)

2. Applied to people, **stützen** implies that someone is so weak as to be unable to stand alone and is supported by someone else. *Er war so schwach, daß sie ihn beim Gehen stützen mußte. S.o. was supported by . . .* can be translated by the pass. or past part. *An den ersten Tagen nach der Operation konnte sie zwar gehen, aber nur auf den Arm der Schwester gestützt.* As in E. there is also the refl. *Der Verletzte mußte sich beim Gehen auf ihren Arm stützen.*

> *Stütz' dich auf mich!*   *Beim Gehen stützte er sich auf einen Stock.*

3. If **support oneself** means 'to prevent oneself from falling by holding on to s.o./sth. for reasons other than weakness', **sich an jmdm./etw. festhalten** is used. *Um nicht zu fallen, hielt ich mich in der Dunkelheit am Geländer/an jmds. Arm fest.*

4. Whatever supports a statement, claim, or theory helps to show that it is true or correct. **Stützen** is used in this sense with a person or thing as subj. *Er konnte* *seine Behauptung/seine Theorie durch Beweise stützen. Sie hat ihren Anspruch auf die Erbschaft durch Urkunden gestützt. Die neue Entdeckung stützt die Theorie.* The pass. is possible, *Die Beschuldigung wird nicht durch Beweise gestützt,* but the refl. is also common, *Die Theorie stützt sich auf seine Beobachtungen/auf die Ergebnisse seiner Versuche. Seine Behauptungen stützen sich nicht auf Tatsachen, sondern nur auf Vermutungen.* An expression related in meaning is **sprechen für**, to speak or argue in favour of something in a fig. sense. *Einiges spricht für die Theorie.* **Untermauern** is stronger, meaning 'to back up'. *Jmd. hat seine Interpretation durch zahlreiche Belege untermauert.* Stronger too is **erhärten**, to substantiate. *Die Angaben eines vorbeifahrenden Motorradfahrers erhärteten die Aussage des Zeugen. Die neuesten Forschungsergebnisse haben die Theorie erhärtet.*

5. i. Support s.o., especially members of one's family, means 'to earn or provide the money that is needed to buy food, clothing, etc.' *He has a wife and five children to support.* The main equivalent is **unterhalten**, discussed under KEEP 2. *Er hat eine große Familie/eine Frau und fünf Kinder zu unterhalten.* Another possibility is **sorgen für**. Cf. PROVIDE 1. *Er sorgt noch für seine Kinder aus erster Ehe.* Cf. also **ernähren** under FEED 1. *Er hat eine sechsköpfige Familie zu kleiden und ernähren.* Unterhalten also translates **support** in *This charity now supports three orphanages,* where it means 'to maintain'. *Dieser karitative/wohltätige Verein unterhält drei Waisenhäuser in Lateinamerika.*

ii. If the land in a place supports the people who live there, it is fertile enough to provide the food they need. **Ernähren** carries this sense. *Der Boden im Tal war sehr fruchtbar und ernährte an die 200 Familien.* The idea that a place cannot support people or animals can be formulated with the neg. of *ernähren,* but it is often expressed by other words. Two such possibilities are: *In Wüstengebieten ist nicht genug Nahrung vorhanden, um viele Tiere am Leben zu halten,* and *Auf dieser Insel gibt es/ist so wenig Nahrung, daß ein Mensch nur kurze Zeit dort leben könnte,* there is not enough food to support a man/human being for long.

6. Whoever supports people who are in difficulties or trying to do something, or supports what they are trying to do, helps them in a practical way, often financially. *He supported his friend in the crisis/emotionally. She supported me in my work.* It also means 'to speak in favour of' and 'to vote for'. *His colleagues refused to support him/the plan. People support a politician/a political party/a policy.*

i. In one sense **unterstützen** means 'to assist people in a special, often difficult, situation'. *Man unterstützte die Bevölkerung des Katastrophengebiets mit Hilfssendungen. Jmd. unterstützt einen anderen emotional.* In reference to financial support, it does not mean 'to provide for permanently' (cf. 5) but rather 'to assist in time of need or in special circumstances which may extend over a short or a longer period'. *Finanziell* is added if this is not clear from the context. *Während des Studiums wurden alle drei Kinder von den Eltern [finanziell] unterstützt.* Although this sent. would in many situations be understood as meaning that all their costs were met, *unterstützte* could also mean 'assisted'. An unambiguous sent. is *Wie viele Eltern kommen für den Unterhalt ihrer Kinder während des Studiums auf?*

ii. In *Man unterstützt jmdn. bei/in seiner Arbeit/seinen Bemühungen* the v. implies helping actively.

iii. Unterstützen also means 'to encourage actively', 'to approve of and speak in favour of', sometimes 'to vote for'. *Jmd. unterstützt einen Plan/einen Vorschlag/jmds. Bewerbung/eine Bitte/ein Projekt usw. Man unterstützt eine Partei mit seiner Stimme.*

Der Pfarrer unterstützte die Jugendlichen bei ihrem Plan, den Obdachlosen zu helfen.

Der Bürgermeister hofft, daß die Wähler seinen Plan unterstützen werden, ein neues Schwimmbad zu bauen.

Acht Abgeordnete unterstützten die Koalition nicht, die ihre Partei eingegangen war, und traten aus ihr aus.

iv. Fördern can mean 'to assist people in their development of special abilities'. *Man fördert Talente/den Nachwuchs/junge Musiker*, etc. It also translates *support* when this means 'to provide financial assistance for', e.g. for research, special projects, etc. *Das Ministerium fördert viele Forschungsprojekte.*

v. Für jmdn./etw. eintreten means 'to give one's support to' a person, cause, resolution, etc., i.e. 'to declare oneself in favour of him/her/it'. With a person as obj. it can be like *to stand up for. Er ist öffentlich und mutig für den Freund eingetreten, obwohl viele diesen für schuldig hielten.* **Sich für jmdn./etw. einsetzen** has the same meaning, but it is much stronger. It suggests making a great effort, doing one's utmost to help or achieve something. Unlike *eintreten, sich einsetzen* can be intensified by *sehr. Sie setzte sich sehr für diese Sache ein.* Both take *für* or *dafür, daß. Er trat für eine gerechte Verteilung der Lasten ein* or *Er trat dafür ein, daß die Lasten gerecht verteilt werden [sollten].* **Sich für/gegen etw. aussprechen**, 'to speak in favour of/against', is close in meaning to **[not] support**. *Er sprach sich für die Reformpläne aus. Sie sprach sich gegen die geplante Steuersenkung aus.*

Sie traten für die sofortige Durchführung der Beschlüsse ein/ . . . für den Bau einer neuen Schule ein.
Der Priester setzte sich mit ganzer Energie für die armen Landarbeiter ein.

sure, certain *adjs.* surely, certainly *advs.*

1. Sure is used predicatively about people only in the meaning 'free from doubt, having, or believing one has, good reason for considering sth. correct'. *I'm sure I saw her. I'm not sure whether I have a copy.* **Certain** has the same meaning, but the subj. of the clause can be *it* as well as a person. *I'm certain/sure he saw me. It is certain that they were there.*

i. Sicher is the usual equivalent. **Gewiß** is a less commonly used alternative. Both occur in clauses which have a person or *es* as subj. Both *to be sure* and *to feel sure* are *sicher sein. Ich bin sicher, daß er sein Wort halten wird. Ich bin mir sicher* is often heard, but the refl. dat. is optional.

Ich bin [mir] sicher, daß er mich gesehen hat.   *Ich bin [mir] nicht sicher, ob ich eine Kopie habe.*
Ich bin [mir] nicht [ganz] sicher, wer sie ist/wohin sie gegangen ist.
Es ist sicher, daß sie dort waren.   *Soviel ist sicher/gewiß, er konnte nichts dafür.*

ii. Be sure/certain about/of. *Dessen*, 'of/about it/this/that', can be added to *sicher* but is optional. A transl. of *I think the answer's correct, but I'm not sure [about it]* becomes *Ich halte die Antwort für richtig, aber ich bin mir [dessen] nicht ganz sicher.* The last clause also translates *I don't know for certain. Schmidt scheint mir ein geeigneter Mann für diese Stelle zu sein, aber ich bin [mir] nicht sicher, ob Maier es auch ist* could be a transl. of *I'm not sure about Maier. Are you sure of your facts?* is *Sind Sie sicher, daß Ihre Angaben stimmen?*

iii. Sich vergewissern means 'to make sure/certain of a fact'. *Ich glaube, daß ein Zug um 8.20 Uhr fährt, aber vergewissere dich lieber noch einmal!* A clause can follow. *Hast du dich vergewissert, daß die Tür abgeschlossen ist/ob das Gas abgestellt ist?* A n. in the gen. is also possible. *Ich habe mich ihrer Zustimmung vergewissert.*

iv. For *Make/Be* **sure** *you're on time!* cf. SEE TO S.O./STH.

2. Certain and **secure** = 'assured, guaranteed, very likely to occur'. Both can refer to an anticipated result. *The younger player had such a good lead that his victory seemed certain/secure.* **Sure** and **certain** + **of** or an infin. also refer to a person. *You're sure of a welcome there. He is sure of their support. She's sure/certain to win.*

i. Sicher can be used with the outcome as subj. of the clause. *Der/Sein Erfolg war [nicht] sicher.* Alternatively *gewiß* and *sicher* can be used with a dat. of the person.

Der Erfolg/Der Sieg/Die Strafe ist ihr gewiß/sicher, 'she is sure/certain to succeed/win/be punished', or the person can be the subj. of the clause and the result in the gen. *Heinz war/fühlte sich seines Erfolges sicher/gewiß.*

> *Der jüngere Spieler hatte eine so klare/deutliche Führung, daß sein Sieg sicher erschien.*
> *Nächste Woche wählt die SPD einen neuen Vorsitzenden; die Wahl des rheinland-pfälzischen Ministerpräsidenten gilt aber als sicher.*
> *Nach dieser Kür war die Goldmedaille sicher.*   *Dort ist dir ein freundlicher Empfang gewiß.*
> *Sie ist ihrer Sache/unserer Zustimmung/unserer Unterstützung gewiß.*

ii. Sure or **certain** + infin., as in *She is sure/certain to win*, is translated by the adv. **sicher**, certainly. *Sie wird sicher gewinnen.* (Cf. 9. i, which is a variant on this construction.) **Bestimmt**, 'definitely', is also possible. *Er wird bestimmt Erfolg haben.*

iii. The sents. in 2. ii express someone else's opinion. *She is* **sure of** *winning* expresses her opinion about herself. The usual construction is **sicher** + *daß*-clause. *Sie ist sicher, daß sie gewinnen wird. Er ist sicher, daß man ihn wählen wird.* With a double infin. containing *können*, an infin. construction is possible, but a *daß*-clause is more usual. *Sie ist sicher, die Prüfung bestehen zu können/daß sie die Prüfung bestehen kann.*

3. Sure enough. *I said it would happen, and sure enough it did.* **Auch** and **dann auch** confirm that something occurred as predicted, expected, etc. *Ich sagte, daß es geschehen würde, und so ist es dann auch [tatsächlich] eingetroffen.* Or more colloquially *. . . und es ist [dann] auch tatsächlich passiert.*

4. Both **sure** and **certain** mean 'proved or tested', 'reliable, trustworthy'. *There is no sure/certain remedy for colds.* **Sicher** also carries this sense. *Absolut* is often added.

> *Es gibt kein [absolut] sicheres Mittel gegen Erkältungen.*
> *Ich habe keinen sicheren Beweis, daß sie etw. damit zu tun haben.*
> *Das ist eine absolut sichere Methode, das Alter eines Baumes zu bestimmen.*

5. Certain = 'inevitable' is also **sicher**. *Die eingeschlossenen Bergleute sahen sich dem sicheren Tod gegenüber, wenn es nicht gelänge, sie innerhalb von 48 Stunden zu retten.*

6. Certain = 'not named, stated, or described, although it is possible to do so'. *He is prepared to help under certain conditions. For a certain reason they won't start till next week.* **Gewiß** fits the definition. *Gewisse Leute verfolgen nur ihre eigenen Ziele. A certain Mrs Blumenthal is eine gewisse Frau Blumenthal.* **Bestimmt** is often translated as **certain** but suggests more definiteness than *gewiß*.

> *Er ist bereit, unter gewissen/bestimmten Bedingungen zu helfen.*
> *Aus einem bestimmten Grunde wollen sie erst nächste Woche anfangen.*

7. Certain means 'some but not much', 'an unspecified amount of'. *There is a certain similarity between them.* **Gewiß** expresses this sense. *Es besteht eine gewisse Ähnlichkeit zwischen den beiden.*

> *In ihrem Verhalten mir gegenüber zeigte sie eine gewisse Kälte.*

8. Surely.

i. In its chief current sense **surely** expresses a strong belief in the correctness of a statement on the basis of experience or probability, but without absolute proof. It is used to emphasize that a speaker thinks something true but is surprised and begins to doubt when, for example, others do not agree. *We've surely met before. Surely there's no truth in it. A. He won't ring us. B. Surely he'll ring us.* There are several ways of conveying the sense. In one of its many functions **doch** turns a statement into a question, in the same way as an E. question tag. **Oder** may be added. *Sie fahren doch Sonntag ab, [oder]?*, you're leaving on Sunday, aren't you? *Doch* thus introduces a note of uncertainty by making a statement into a question. *Wir kennen uns doch, [oder]? Sie kommen doch mit?* These sents. need the intonation of a question. *Doch* is sometimes combined with *bestimmt* or *sicher* and again makes the sent. a question. *Sie werden dich doch bestimmt daran teilnehmen lassen, oder? Du wolltest sie doch bestimmt/sicher nicht beleidigen? Sie ist doch bestimmt angekommen, oder? Er wird uns doch bestimmt anrufen?* **Ja wohl** expresses a high degree of probability or confidence but admits some doubts. *Der Brief wird ja wohl rechtzeitig ankommen. Der Regen wird ja wohl bald aufhören. Es ist ja wohl allgemein bekannt, daß* . . . **Doch wohl** expresses confidence in the accuracy of the statement but with a little more doubt than *ja wohl*. *Du hast doch wohl einen zweiten Schlüssel. Zweihundert Mark werden doch wohl reichen. Es steckt doch wohl mehr dahinter als das.*

ii. Surely not is used when a speaker asks a question about something that has just been said in the endeavour to get the other person to agree with what is stated. A question tag may be added. *You're surely not suggesting they did it on purpose, [are you]? You surely don't believe that, [do you]?* **Doch wohl nicht** has this function. *Das ist doch wohl nicht dein Ernst?*, you're surely not serious. *Sie können doch wohl nicht erwarten, daß ich das glaube?* **Doch wohl nicht** and the next expression are questions in the form of a statement. **Doch nicht etwa** is a stronger and blunter expression which implies that the person addressed could not possibly do what is stated. *Du willst doch nicht etwa sagen, sie hätten es mit Absicht getan? Diesen Unsinn nimmst du doch nicht etwa ernst.*

> *Du glaubst doch nicht etwa, daß ich dieses Verhalten billige.*
> *Du bildest dir doch nicht etwa ein, ich werde dir das Geld leihen.*

iii. In literary language **surely** can mean 'definitely' and is translated by **bestimmt.** *Der Plan wird bestimmt scheitern,* the plan will surely/definitely fail. *So sicher wie ich hier stehe,* as surely as I am standing here.

iv. Langsam, aber sicher means 'slowly but surely'. *Die Polizei deckte langsam, aber sicher, immer mehr Einzelheiten auf,* were slowly but surely uncovering the facts. *Diese Neuerungen setzten sich langsam, aber sicher durch.*

9. i. There are several equivalents of **certainly** and **for certain** = 'definitely, without doubt'. *He will certainly fail if he doesn't make more effort. Er wird* **[ganz] sicher/[ganz] bestimmt/[ganz] gewiß** *durchfallen, wenn er sich nicht mehr anstrengt.* A further alternative is **[ganz] sicherlich.** *Er wird [ganz] sicherlich durchfallen.* In *Ich weiß ganz bestimmt, daß er hier war,* **bestimmt** means 'for certain, definitely'. (An alternative here is *Ich weiß ganz genau.*) *Ich kann nicht bestimmt sagen, wann sie abfährt,* say for certain.

> *Das ist sicher sehr schwierig.*   *Er wird dich sicherlich nicht im Stich lassen.*
> *Ihre Aufgabe ist gewiß nicht leicht.*   *Das ist bestimmt wahr/nicht richtig.*
> *Das habe ich bestimmt nie gesagt.*   *Er hat es bestimmt nicht mit Absicht getan.*

ii. Certainly as an answer to a question is **sicher** or **gewiß.** They are often preceded by *aber*. *Aber sicher* and *aber gewiß* strengthen, but do not change, the meaning. (*Gewiß doch* is a syn. but is old-fashioned.) (*Bestimmt* used as an answer means 'definitely'. *A. Wird sie gewinnen? B. Bestimmt.*)

> *A. Würden Sie mir Ihr Wörterbuch leihen? B. Aber sicher!*
> *A. Schreibst du mir? B. Aber ganz gewiß!*

iii. Certainly not is **auf [gar] keinen Fall, bestimmt nicht,** or **unter [gar] keinen Umständen.**

> *A. Würden Sie mir Ihr Auto leihen? B. Ganz bestimmt nicht/Auf [gar] keinen Fall.*

surprise *v.*

1. The first main meaning of **surprise** is 'to attack unexpectedly, and without warning'. *They surprised the little garrison and captured the fort. At dawn the household was surprised by a sudden Indian attack.* Closely related to this is the meaning 'to come upon s.o. unexpectedly, to take unawares in an act or by an unexpected visit'. *The police surprised the burglars leaving the store. My uncle and aunt surprised us at lunch.* **Überraschen** implies taking someone by surprise. It can refer to an attack or to something natural like a storm, rain, or earthquake. *Die Indianer überraschten die kleine Truppe und nahmen die Festung ein. Der Regen hat mich überrascht—ich hatte keinen Regenschirm mit.* It also means 'to catch s.o. in the act or doing sth.' *Die Polizei überraschte die Bande/die Einbrecher beim Verladen des Diebesguts.* A further sense is 'to surprise s.o. with sth.' thereby giving unexpected pleasure or the opposite. *Er wollte sie mit dem Geschenk überraschen.* It can be used with *angenehm* and *unangenehm. Ich war von seiner Hilfsbereitschaft angenehm überrascht.* In relation to news, information, etc. *überraschen* suggests that this takes someone by surprise or comes as a surprise. *Sie hat mich mit dieser Nachricht überrascht. Die Nachricht hat mich sehr überrascht/nicht überrascht. Überraschend* means 'coming as a surprise'. *Ein überraschender Erfolg.*

Onkel und Tante hatten sich nicht angemeldet und überraschten uns beim Mittagessen.
Sie überraschten das Lager des feindlichen Heeres und trieben die Soldaten in die Flucht.
Die Schnelligkeit, mit der das Gesetz verabschiedet wurde, überraschte alle.
Er überraschte seine Frau mit einem Blumenstrauß. *Ihr Angebot kommt überraschend.*
Das Erdbeben hat die Bewohner der Stadt im Schlaf überrascht.

2. The second main sense of **surprise** is 'to affect with a sudden feeling of wonder or amazement because something is different from what has been anticipated and cannot readily be understood or explained'. *His conduct surprised me. I'm surprised you didn't think of that before. Don't be surprised if she refuses! I'm surprised at you!* Three syns. express a high degree of surprise. **Astonish** means 'to surprise so greatly as to seem incredible'. **Astound** denotes a strong emotional reaction resulting from the difference between what is anticipated and what actually happens. **Amaze** suggests great surprise mixed with perplexity.

i. Wundern is used with a thing as subj. and impersonally in *es wundert mich*, which means 'I'm surprised'. These two uses express a fairly weak degree of surprise and suggest that someone finds something unusual because it does not correspond to his/her ideas or expectations. *Seine Unpünktlichkeit/Diese Unordnung wundert mich. Es wundert mich, daß dir das nicht schon vorher eingefallen ist. Das/Es sollte/würde mich [doch] [sehr] wundern, wenn sie durchfällt* (or *durchfiele/durchfallen würde*) translates *I'd be [very much] surprised if . . . Es wunderte mich, ihn dort zu sehen* means that his being there was unexpected and that I could not understand it, whereas *Es überraschte mich, ihn dort zu sehen* means that seeing him took me completely by surprise. *Wundern* does not form a n. in *-ung*, and its past part. is not used as an adj. Cf. 2. iv.

Die gute Note wunderte sie, denn sie hatte eigentlich mit einer schlechteren gerechnet.
Es hat uns alle gewundert, daß die Rechnung so niedrig war.
Es würde mich wundern, wenn er es tatsächlich schafft.
Es sollte mich wundern, wenn sie noch erschienen.

ii. Sich wundern means 'to be unable to understand or explain', e.g. what is seen or heard or what has happened. In cases in which both *wundern* and *sich wundern* could easily be used, the refl. is stronger. *Ich wundere mich über dein Verhalten* expresses a higher degree of surprise than *Dein Verhalten wundert mich.*

Wundere dich nicht, wenn sie das Angebot ausschlagen!
Er hat sich über den neuen Gartenzaun gewundert.
Meine Mutter wunderte sich, als ich schon so früh nach Hause kam.

iii. Staunen means 'to be amazed or astonished'. While the surprise expressed by *sich wundern* is not outwardly visible, *staunen* suggests that the surprise is apparent in the way someone acts or in his or her facial expression. *Ich staunte über seine Größe. Da staunst du aber!* It may, but need not, imply that the surprise is accompanied by admiration. *Ich staunte über seine Leistungen.*

Die Kinder staunten über die exotischen Tiere, die im Zoo zu sehen waren.

Sie werden staunen, wie sehr er sich verändert hat.

Sie staunte über die Kenntnisse der Schüler und drückte ihre Bewunderung aus.

iv. Verwundern is somewhat stronger than *wundern* but is mostly confined to the written language. The past part. is, however, still found, as is *Es ist nicht zu verwundern,* it is not surprising. The past part. of *wundern* is not used as an adj., nor does *wundern* form a n. in *-ung*. The past part. of *verwundern* and the n. *die Verwunderung* have taken on the missing functions of *wundern. Er sah sie verwundert/mit tiefer Verwunderung an. Jmdn. in Verwunderung setzen* is occasionally found, but it does not differ in meaning from the v.

Daß sie sich jetzt benachteiligt fühlen, wird niemand verwundern/in Verwunderung setzen.

Ohne Erklärung verließ sie den Saal, und alle sahen ihr verwundert nach.

Zu ihrer Verwunderung kam es nicht zu der erwarteten Auseinandersetzung.

Es ist nicht zu verwundern, daß er durch die Prüfung gefallen ist. (In speech: *Es wundert mich nicht . . .*)

v. Sich verwundern is a stronger syn. of *sich wundern*. The older transl. of Luke 7: 9, where the AV has *marvelled,* is *Da das Jesus hörte, verwunderte er sich.* The newest version has *wunderte er sich,* but it retains *sich verwundern* in *Alle, die ihm zuhörten, verwunderten sich über seinen Verstand und seine Antworten,* where the AV has *were astonished at. Sich verwundern* is now little used. *Über ihre plötzliche Sinnesänderung haben wir uns sehr verwundert.*

vi. Erstaunen is also stronger then *wundern,* but it is a stylistically higher term like *astonish* or *astound.* It is both trans. and intr. Trans.: *Sie erstaunte mich durch ihre Kenntnisse.* Intr.: *Ich erstaunte sehr über diesen weisen Ratschlag.* It is mostly found as a past part. *Ich bin über seinen Rücktritt erstaunt. Sie sah mich mit erstaunter Miene an. 'Wie bitte?' fragte er erstaunt. Das Erstaunen* is a syn. of *die Verwunderung. Ich höre mit Erstaunen/Verwunderung, daß du dich für diese Sache sehr interessierst. Jmdn. in Erstaunen versetzen/setzen* is also used and is more emphatic than the v. *erstaunen.*

Die Leichtigkeit, mit der ihm alles anscheinend mühelos von der Hand ging, erstaunte sie.

Er war erstaunt darüber, wie schnell die Kinder die fremde Sprache gelernt hatten.

Seine Schlagfertigkeit versetzte alle in Erstaunen.

vii. Verblüffen means 'to surprise s.o. to such an extent that he or she cannot assess the situation adequately, becomes confused, and does not immediately know what to say or do'. Equivalents are **surprise**, *baffle, amaze, bewilder, flabbergast, dumbfound,* and *perplex. Viele Käufer verblüffen die niedrigen Preise, so daß sie nicht auf die Qualität der Ware achten. Er war so verblüfft, daß er alles zugab.*

Ihn konnte nichts verblüffen; immer wußte er eine Antwort.

Sie sah verblüfft aus/sah mich verblüfft an. Die Frage hatte ihn verblüfft.

3. The third less common meaning of **surprise** is 'to lead, drive, or cause s.o. to do sth., usually to betray or say sth. not intended'. *The detective tried to surprise the facts from the man/to surprise him into a confession.* One transl. close to the first E. example is *Der Detektiv wollte den Mann so überraschen, daß er die gewünschte Auskunft preisgab/verriet.* Another possibility is *Der Detektiv wollte ihn so verblüffen, daß er alles gestand/zugab.*

suspicion *n.* **suspicious** *adj.* **suspect** *v.* **suspect** *n.* and *adj.*

1. One sense of **suspicion** is 'the conjecture of the existence of sth. evil or wrong on slight grounds or without clear proof'. *My suspicion that Perkins was the culprit proved to be correct.* The equivalent is **der Verdacht**, which is defined as 'a justified conjecture or a surmise based on reasons and indications' and may suggest more evidence than **suspicion** does. *Verdacht* refers both to suspected wrongdoing and to something in some way undesirable of which someone has no direct knowledge but some inkling.

Der Verdacht fiel auf sie, da ihre Aussage mit denen der anderen Zeugen nicht übereinstimmte.

Der Verdacht, daß er gelogen hatte, bestätigte sich/erwies sich als unbegründet.

Mein Verdacht, daß Perkins der Täter war, stellte sich als richtig heraus.

Durch ein geschicktes Manöver gelang es ihm, den Verdacht von sich abzulenken.

2. To **suspect** is 'to imagine sth., especially sth. bad, about a pers. or thg. with slight or no proof'. *I suspect him of lying. I suspect that he's a liar. You're crazy to suspect her.*

i. Verbal expressions often express this meaning of **suspect**, especially when what someone is suspected of is not particularly bad. **Den Verdacht haben** (in elevated style **hegen**) is used with a clause, *Ich habe den Verdacht, daß er lügt*, and **jmdn. im/in Verdacht haben** is mostly followed by an infin., *Ich habe sie im Verdacht, uns belogen zu haben.* The equivalent of the E. pass. **be suspected [of]** is **im Verdacht stehen**. *Der jüngste Sohn steht im Verdacht, das Geld gestohlen zu haben. Im Verdacht haben/stehen* can be used without an infin. *Ich habe ihn im Verdacht. Sie steht im Verdacht*, is suspected, under suspicion. **Den Verdacht fassen** is 'to begin to suspect sth. suddenly'. *Er faßte den Verdacht, man wolle ihm mit diesen Fragen eine Falle legen.*

Ich habe den Verdacht, daß du mir nicht die volle Wahrheit gesagt hast. Or Ich habe dich in Verdacht, mir nicht die volle Wahrheit gesagt zu haben.

Er hegt schon längere Zeit den Verdacht, daß man ihn betrügt.

Ich habe diesen Kollegen im Verdacht, unsere Pläne hintertreiben zu wollen.

ii. Verdächtigen means 'to suspect s.o. of having done wrong, mostly of committing a crime' and suggests that there are reasonable grounds for this conclusion. It is used for more serious wrongdoing than *im Verdacht haben*. *Verdächtigen* takes either an acc. only, *Alle verdächtigen mich*, or an acc. + a gen., *Ich verdächtige ihn einer Falschaussage*, or an acc. + an infin., *Ich verdächtige ihn, gelogen zu haben.*

Warum verdächtigst du mich? Ich habe mit der ganzen Sache nichts zu tun.

Die Polizei verdächtigte ihn, den Diebstahl begangen zu haben.

Solange der Fall nicht geklärt ist, werden alle verdächtigt/sind alle verdächtig.

iii. Verdächtig means 'arousing suspicion' and is translated as *suspicious[-looking]* or **suspect**. It is applied to people, *Ein paar verdächtige Individuen standen da herum*, and to actions or situations which give rise to suspicion, *Sein Verhalten war verdächtig* or *Diese ausweichende Antwort kam uns verdächtig vor. Es war verdächtig still.* Unlike **suspicious**, *verdächtig* is applied to people who are believed to be guilty, for which E. uses **suspect**, *suspected*, or *subject to/under suspicion. Wir sind alle verdächtig. Der junge Mann war des Diebstahls verdächtig. Durch dieses seltsame Verhalten hatte er sich verdächtig gemacht.*

iv. The **suspect** is either **der Verdächtige**, 's.o. who has aroused suspicion in some way', or **der Verdächtigte**, 's.o. on whom suspicions fall'. *Ein Polizist ist dem Verdächtigen/dem Verdächtigten unauffällig gefolgt.*

3. In another sense to **suspect** means 'to feel doubt about'. *I suspect his honesty/their good intentions/the accuracy of the report.*

i. This sense is expressed by **zweifeln an**, to DOUBT. *Ich zweifle an ihrer Ehrlichkeit/an ihren guten Absichten. Wir zweifelten alle an der Genauigkeit der Meldung.*

ii. The corresponding E. n. is used in the pl. *I have my **suspicions** about the accuracy of this report* becomes *Ich habe Zweifel an der Richtigkeit dieser Meldung. Ich nehme dir deine Zweifel an der Aufrichtigkeit meiner Beweggründe sehr übel. Ich habe Zweifel, ob das alles mit rechten Dingen zugegangen ist.*

4. i. To **suspect** also means 'to distrust or mistrust'. It is used with a person as obj. but without *of sth.* being stated or implied. *The people suspected the nobles, and the nobles feared the people.* The equivalent is **mißtrauen** + dat., to mistrust or distrust, to feel that behind a façade there is a dishonest or hostile intent. *Mißtrauen* is used with a person or ns. like *die Absicht* or *jmds. freundliche Worte* in the dat.

> *Das Volk mißtraute dem Adel, und der Adel fürchtete sich vor dem Volk.*
> *Sie mißtraute den freundlichen Worten und war auf der Hut.*
> *Ich mißtraue ihren Absichten.*

ii. The corresponding n. is **das Mißtrauen**. *Alle haben mich mit Mißtrauen gesehen. To arouse suspicion* in this sense is *jmds. Mißtrauen erregen* or *[er]wecken.*

> *Sie blickte den Mann mit unverhohlenem Mißtrauen an.*
> *Das Arbeitsklima hier ist schlecht—es herrscht eine Atmosphäre des Mißtrauens.*

iii. Mißtrauisch means 'suspicious' in its main sense 'distrustful' when applied to people. *Sein Verhalten machte mich mißtrauisch. Ich wurde plötzlich mißtrauisch gegen diesen Mann. Sie sahen uns mit mißtrauischen Blicken an.* **Stutzig** werden or *jmdn.* stutzig machen mean 'to become or be made suddenly suspicious or distrustful'. *Diese Antwort machte sie stutzig, denn bisher hatte er stets das genaue Gegenteil behauptet.*

5. Der Argwohn is a word now not very often encountered which combines the senses of *Verdacht* and *Mißtrauen*. In contrast to *Verdacht*, it suggests a feeling, rather than evidence, that things are not what they seem. In comparison with *Mißtrauen*, it denotes more a permanent disposition to believe that others are acting from hostile or dishonest motives. **Argwöhnen** has the same sense as *den Verdacht haben* or *jmdn. im Verdacht haben* but is now fairly unusual.

> *Er hegte den Argwohn, man wolle seine Pläne durch allerlei Intrigen durchkreuzen.*
> *Sie argwöhnte, daß man ihr etw. verheimlichte.*

6. To **suspect** also means 'to imagine sth. to be possible', 'to have a faint notion or inkling of'. *I suspect the boy is in love.*

i. Three G. vs. cover different parts of the definition. Similar in meaning are **vermuten**, 'to draw a probable conclusion on the basis of indications' (cf. GUESS), and **annehmen**, 'to assume'. *Ich vermute/nehme an, daß der Junge verliebt ist. Vermuten* is used when the police etc. suspect a certain kind of crime (not a person). *Die Polizei vermutet Brandstiftung.* **Ahnen** denotes a purely instinctive feeling or presentiment or a faint notion. *Ich habe es geahnt,* suspected, guessed by intuition. *Sie ist viel intelligenter, als wir ahnten. Jmd. ahnte nichts,* 'suspected nothing', e.g. of someone's hostile or dishonest intentions or of what was happening, had happened, or was to happen.

> *Man vermutet einen Fehler in der Konstruktion.   Es war so, wie er [es] vermutet hatte.*
> *Wir haben Grund anzunhmen, daß der Verstorbene gestern zwischen 18 Uhr und 18.30 ermordet wurde.*
> *Da er nicht am ausgemachten Treffpunkt erschienen war, vermuteten wir, daß er sich in der Zeit geirrt hatte.   Er ahnte nichts von dem, was ihm bevorstand.*
> *Wenn sie etw. von der Gefährlichkeit der Wanderung geahnt hätte, wäre sie auf keinen Fall mitgekommen.*

ii. A **suspicion** is 'a feeling that sth. is probably true or likely to happen'. The equivalent is **die Vermutung** when there are reasonable grounds for drawing this conclusion or **die Ahnung** when the feeling is only intuitive. *Meine Vermutung war richtig—er hat das alles angezettelt. Meine Ahnung hat mich nicht getrogen.* Only *Ahnung* is used with *haben* and in the neg. *Ich hatte nicht die geringste Ahnung, daß ich dort auf die beiden treffen würde.*

swallow, devour *vs.*

1. Swallow = 'to cause sth. to pass from the mouth to the stomach'.

i. Schlucken is the general equivalent and is trans. and intr. In the intr. use it may, like **swallow**, suggest letting food or drink pass the throat, or it may imply making a movement of the throat as if swallowing in order to suppress emotion.

Man muß die Tabletten unzerkaut schlucken. Sie schmecken nämlich sehr bitter.

Ich habe beim Schwimmen etwas Wasser geschluckt.

Es fällt mir schwer zu schlucken, weil ich Halsschmerzen habe.

Bei so viel Frechheit mußte sie erst ein paarmal schlucken, bevor sie antworten konnte.

ii. The chief meaning of **verschlucken** is 'to swallow sth. by mistake'. *Ich habe einen Kirschkern verschluckt.* It is occasionally found when deliberate swallowing is meant, but whereas *schlucken* emphasizes the process, *verschlucken* stresses the result. *Sie hat endlich die Tablette/den Bissen verschluckt.*

Der Junge hat beim Spielen versehentlich eine Murmel verschluckt.

Es ist gefährlich, eine Gräte zu verschlucken.

Ich habe mich verschluckt means that something I have swallowed has gone down the wrong way. *Sie hat sich beim Trinken an der Cola verschluckt und fing an zu husten. Jmdm. ist diese Bemerkung in die falsche Kehle gekommen* or *Jmd. hat die Bemerkung in die falsche Kehle bekommen* now only have the fig. sense 'to misunderstand and take amiss' or 'to take offence at'. *Heinz scheint etwas verschnupft (peeved) zu sein. Meine kritischen Bemerkungen müssen ihm in die falsche Kehle gekommen sein, aber ich habe ihn gar nicht gemeint.*

iii. Herunterschlucken and **hinunterschlucken**, which both become *runterschlucken* in colloquial speech, suggest a certain degree of difficulty or unwillingness in swallowing or eating something.

Sie kaute jeden Bissen lange und schluckte ihn dann herunter/hinunter.

Die Suppe war sehr scharf und brannte ihm im Mund, aber er schluckte sie tapfer herunter/hinunter.

iv. Herunterwürgen implies that someone has great difficulty in getting something down, mostly because the food is so unpalatable.

Der Kuchen war sehr trocken, aber ich habe ihn trotzdem heruntergewürgt.

Den Fraß habe ich nur mit Mühe heruntergewürgt, obwohl ich einen Mordshunger hatte.

v. Schlingen means 'to eat hastily or greedily'. While *schlucken* refers only to the process of swallowing, *schlingen* includes putting food into one's mouth and is like *to gulp* or *to bolt one's food*. It is trans. and intr. *Hungrig schlangen sie das Mittagessen. Iß langsam und schling' nicht so!—dann bekommt es dir besser.*

vi. Verschlingen means that an animal devours food without chewing it. This may be its normal way of eating. *Der Hund verschlang ein großes Stück Fleisch.* Applied to people, *verschlingen* means 'to eat hastily or greedily' and is usually pejorative.

Der Frosch verschlang eine Fliege nach der anderen, fast ohne Pause.

Er hatte seit zwei Tagen nichts gegessen und verschlang alles mit Heißhunger, was ihm vorgesetzt wurde.   *Das Kind verschlang eine große Portion Eis.*

2. Fig. uses.

i. *The earthquake had* **swallowed** *the village. This area was* **swallowed [up] by** *the sea. They were soon* **swallowed up in/by** *the mist.* **Schlucken** is possible, *Er war spurlos verschwunden, als ob ihn die Erde geschluckt hätte,* but **verschlucken** is more usual as it denotes the completed process. *Es ist, als wäre der Junge/die Halskette vom Erdboden verschluckt.* With *die Dunkelheit* or *der Nebel*, both *schlucken* and *verschlucken* are found. *Bald waren sie von der Dunkelheit/von dem Nebel geschluckt/verschluckt.* Also used in such contexts is **verschlingen**, which suggests suddenness, rapidity, and complete wiping out. *Es war, als hätte ihn die Erde verschlungen. Verschlingen* is also used with a fire as subj. like *devour*. *Das Feuer hatte das alte Haus bald verschlungen.*

Die U-Bahn schluckt täglich ungeheure Menschenmassen.
Die große Sturmflut hatte einen Teil der Küste verschlungen.

ii. When one organization or country swallows another up, i.e. takes possession of it or takes it over and absorbs it, the equivalent is **schlucken**.

Die kleinen Betriebe konnten nicht mit den großen konkurrieren und wurden von den Großunternehmen geschluckt.

iii. Swallow means 'to put up with without protest, to submit to patiently'. *I swallowed the insult and went on with my work.* **Schlucken** also has this sense, but it is fairly colloquial. *Ich mußte diese Kränkung schlucken. Jmd. mußte die bittere Pille/den harten Brocken schlucken,* had to accept something unpleasant. **Herunter-** and **hinunterschlucken** also express this sense.

Er hatte viele Vorwürfe/Beleidigungen von ihr geschluckt.
Sie schluckte alle diese Beleidigungen hinunter und fuhr mit ihrer Arbeit fort.

iv. In colloquial use **swallow** can mean 'to believe'. *Do you think he'll swallow that story?* **Schlucken** expresses this sense too and is also fairly colloquial. The neutral v. is *glauben*.

Der Verkäufer hat die angeblichen Vorzüge des Staubsaugers gepriesen, und er hat es geschluckt.
Ich glaube nicht, daß sie diese Ausrede schlucken wird.
Ich hatte damals solches Vertrauen zu ihr, daß ich jede Geschichte geschluckt hätte, die sie mir auftischte.

v. Swallow, meaning 'to refrain from expressing or uttering' or 'to repress an emotion', is **verschlucken**. *Sie verschluckte ihre Tränen/ihren Ärger/ihre Enttäuschung.* **Hinunterschlucken** and **herunterschlucken** are syns. *Ich schluckte meinen Ärger hinunter/herunter.*

vi. Swallow means 'not to pronounce sounds clearly' or 'not to complete a sent.' **Verschlucken** expresses this sense. *Viele junge Norddeutsche verschlucken die Endsilben, wenn sie schnell sprechen. Sie verschluckte den Rest des Satzes/das letzte Wort/was sie sagen wollte.*

vii. Swallow [up] money. **Schlucken** is often used. *Die europäische Landwirtschaft schluckt jedes Jahr Subventionen in Milliardenhöhe. Die Anschaffungen haben viel Geld geschluckt.* **Verschlingen** is also common, and perhaps stronger. *Die Instandhaltung der Straßen verschlingt jedes Jahr Millionen.* **Verschlucken** is possible, but unusual. *Der Bau hat viel Geld verschluckt.* These vs. do not mean that there is nothing to show for the expenditure, but that the project etc. cost an enormous amount.

Das neue Haus hat unser ganzes Geld geschluckt.
Der Bau der neuen Universitätsbibliothek hat eine Unmenge Geld verschlungen.

viii. Devour means 'to take in greedily with the eyes or ears' and is applied to novels etc. or to what people say. **Verschlingen** carries this sense. *Pro Nacht verschlingt er einen Krimi. Die Zuhörer hatten seine Worte förmlich verschlungen.*

take *v.* **Take** has a wide range of meaning. The *OED* lists i–vi as the main senses: (i) The oldest is 'to get hold of or capture'. *They took two prisoners. The army has taken the town.* It is applied fig. also to diseases and feelings. *She was taken ill. He bought a vase that had taken his fancy.* (ii) In its principal sense **take** denotes the action by which people take something into their hands, *He took the money and left,* but it has developed uses in which this meaning is hardly apparent, *They took the house for six months.* A train, bus, road, or course can be the obj. *I'll take a taxi.* (iii) It also means 'to use, use up, or consume' mostly time, but also material, energy, and space. *It took a year to build the bridge.* (iv) It means 'to receive sth. given or offered' and is the opposite of *give. He didn't want to take any payment.* (v) The acceptance or receiving can be mental. *Don't take that too literally/seriously! She took my advice.* (vi) **Take** also means 'to convey s.o./sth. from one place to another'. *I'll take her to the airport. I'll take these things with me.* (vii) The most frequent use of **take** is in expressions in which it does not have a distinct meaning of its own, but where most of the meaning is in the n. which follows it. *He took a step backwards/a deep breath/no risks. The government took no action.*

The equivalents are arranged in the following way: 1. Senses of **take** carried by *nehmen.* Related expressions are also given. 2. **Take** referring to mental action. *I take another example/sth. seriously. I don't know how to take this remark.* 3. Equivalents of **take** in sense vi meaning 'to convey', mainly *bringen.* 4. Equivalents of iii, **take** time etc., mainly *brauchen* and *dauern.* 5. Senses carried by derivatives of *nehmen.* 6. Senses requiring other vs. than *nehmen* and equivalents of **take** in sense vii, when it is used as a *Funktionsverb,* i.e. one deriving its meaning from the following n.

1. Senses of **take** carried by nehmen, and related expressions. *Nehmen* is the chief equivalent of **take** in meanings ii and iv.
i. The concept underlying **nehmen** is using one's hand to take hold of a thing or person. *Er nahm den Hammer und schlug den Nagel ein. Sie nahm das Kind bei der Hand. Nehmen* does not contain the idea of an extended movement so that one of the main differences between it and **take** is that the G. v. is not used for taking s.o./sth. to a place, i.e. E. sense vi. With the appropriate prep. *nehmen* means 'to take from, off, on to, in, etc.' *Nimm die Ellbogen vom Tisch! Er nahm das Kind auf den Schoß. Etw. in die Hand nehmen* means 'to take sth. into one's hand' and is used like *to pick up* or *take sth. up.* (*Nehmen* alone could imply that the thing was given or stolen.) *Etw. in die Hand nehmen* is also used fig. like *to take in hand. Als er die Organisation in die Hand genommen hatte, lief alles bestens. Jmdn. unter seine Fittiche nehmen* is 'to take s.o. under one's wing'. The refl. dat. can be added to *nehmen. Sich etw. nehmen* can be translated as *to help oneself to sth. Er nimmt sich immer das Beste. Er nahm sich das größte Stück.*

Ich ging zum Tisch und nahm ein Stück Kuchen.   *Darf ich Ihren Mantel nehmen?*
Sie nahm seine Hand.   *Er nahm seinen Hut und ging.*
Sie machte das Buch zu und legte es wieder an die Stelle, von der sie es genommen hatte.
Man nehme ein Pfund Mehl/Krabben! (Construction still used in cookery books.)
Er nahm die Rechnung aus der Schublade/das Bild von der Wand/die Münzen aus dem Portemonnaie.

Wenn ich mir den Sack auf die Schultern nehme, kann ich ihn leichter tragen.
Er nahm sie in den Arm/in die Arme/bei der Hand.   *Nimm die Hände aus den Hosentaschen!*
Sie nahm mich zur/auf die Seite, um mir etw. zu sagen, was sie gerade erfahren hatte.

ii. Take means 'to receive into one's body by one's own act, to eat or drink'. *She took an aspirin/a meal. I take milk.*The technical term for taking medicine, tablets, etc. is **einnehmen**, but in everyday language **nehmen** is used. The instruction on a bottle of tablets might read, *Die Tabletten sind dreimal täglich einzunehmen,* but people say, *'Ich muß diese Tabletten nehmen'* or *'Ich nehme zwei Aspirin'.* Hence *Jmd. nahm eine Überdosis eines Schlafmittels/nahm Gift.* Also *Sie nahm nur einen Schluck Wein.* **Zu sich nehmen** means 'to eat' in formal language. Thus *Sie haben nur eine Kleinigkeit zu sich genommen, bevor sie losgefahren sind,* and *Der Patient hat heute noch nichts zu sich genommen.* Nehmen means 'to take' milk or sugar, *Nimmst du Milch/Zucker [im Tee]?,* but *I take my coffee black with no sugar* is *Ich trinke Kaffee schwarz und ohne Zucker.* In formal language *nehmen* is used for taking a meal. *Einnehmen* is even more formal. *Wir nehmen das Frühstück um 8.30 auf dem Balkon [ein].*

iii. Take also means 'to bring by one's own action into one's possession'. *I'll take the green coat.* **Nehmen** means 'to buy or to pick out from a number of thgs., often with the intention of buying'. *Ich nehme den grünen Mantel, obwohl der blaue mir auch gut steht.*

Er hat es sich lange überlegt, dann nahm er den kleinen Wagen.
Ich nehme auch eine Packung Eier/ein Pfund Äpfel.

Like **take** *nehmen* means 'to secure sth. by payment or contract'. *Wir haben das Haus für sechs Monate genommen* or *Sie nahmen eine kleine Wohnung in Brüssel.* People can also be the obj. of *nehmen* in the related sense 'to make use of for a purpose'. *You must take whoever is available: Sie müssen diejenigen [Arbeiter] nehmen, die im Moment/gerade da sind.*

iv. Nehmen is used for taking a taxi, car, bus, train, and a road, path, or course. It suggests on one occasion. *Wenn wir das Auto nehmen, sind wir in ungefähr 10 Minuten da.* If regular use is meant, as in *I take the bus to work every day,* **fahren** is used. *Ich fahre jeden Tag mit dem Bus zur Arbeit.* Fig. use: *Etw. nimmt eine unerwartete Wendung.* Cf. COURSE for the use of *nehmen* with *der Lauf* and *Verlauf.*

Für diese kurze Strecke brauchen wir kein Taxi zu nehmen. Es ist billiger, wenn wir den Bus nehmen.
Das Schiff nahm Kurs auf Auckland.   *Sie nahmen die falsche Richtung.*
Wenn Sie zur Weggabelung kommen, nehmen Sie die rechte Abzweigung!
Wissen Sie, welchen Weg wir nehmen müssen, um zur Plesseburg zu kommen?
Wenn ich noch einen Platz bekommen kann, nehme ich das nächste Flugzeug.

v. Nehmen corresponds to **take** in the basic sense of meaning iv, 'to receive sth. given or offered'. In this sense it is very close to *annehmen,* to ACCEPT.

Wären Sie bereit, 2 000 Mark zu nehmen/anzunehmen?
Für die Arbeit hat er keine Bezahlung genommen.
Sie will keine Belohnung nehmen/annehmen.
Nehmen Sie noch ein Stück Kuchen!
Ich werde das angebotene Darlehen nehmen.

vi. While **take** is the counter-action to *give,* things can be taken which are not given. *The thieves took everything they possessed.* This also holds for *nehmen. Er wollte das Geld nicht von mir nehmen* (or *annehmen*) means 'he did not want to take (or accept) the money from me'. In *Ein Dieb hatte ihr das ganze Geld genommen,* **jmdm. etw. nehmen** means 'to steal or take sth. away from s.o.' When *nehmen* is used, the implication that something is being stolen must be clear from the context; otherwise, it is better to use the everyday *stehlen* or the more formal *entwenden* or *wegnehmen.* In one sense **wegnehmen** means 'to take away', but as in E., it does not always imply that the action is illegal. *'Wenn du unartig bist, nehme ich dir das Fahrrad wieder weg', drohte die Mutter.* In cases of theft, *an sich* may be used with *nehmen,* or *mit Gewalt* or *heimlich* can be added to *nehmen* or *wegnehmen.*

> *Die Einbrecher hatten alles genommen, was ihnen wertvoll erschien.*
> *Die Flüchtlinge besaßen nichts. Man hatte ihnen alles [weg]genommen.*
> *Jmd. hat meinen Kugelschreiber genommen.* (Could be by mistake. *An sich* and *weg* imply an intention.)   *Mit vorgehaltener Pistole nahm ihm der Bandit die Brieftasche weg.*

Only *nehmen* is found in the sense 'to take away from' with the dat. and abstract ns. The meaning is sometimes 'to free s.o. from' worries, anxiety, etc. *Diese Nachricht hat mir die Angst und Ungewißheit genommen.* In formal and elevated language **benehmen** is found in this sense in the same contexts. *Das hat mir die Lust weiterzumachen/den Atem benommen.* In *Jmd. nahm sich das Leben,* 'took his life', only *nehmen* is possible.

> *Etw. nimmt jmdm. die Hoffnung/seine Illusionen/die Freude/den Appetit,* etc.
> *Dadurch war ihm der finanzielle Druck der letzten Wochen genommen.*
> *Mit seiner ständigen Kritik hat er mir das Interesse an meiner Arbeit genommen.*

vii. Take, used with an adv. or phr., means 'to clear an obstacle', *The horse took the fence effortlessly,* but is often found without the idea of an obstacle being prominent, *The car took the corner at high speed.* **Nehmen** is used when overcoming an obstacle is implied and is followed by an adv. or phr. describing the manner. *Das Pferd nahm die Hürden/das Hindernis mühelos. Er nimmt immer zwei Stufen auf einmal. Die Kurve* can be the obj. of *nehmen,* but not *die Ecke. Dieser Rennfahrer nahm auch außerhalb der Rennbahn alle Kurven in halsbrecherischem Tempo.* When *nehmen* is not used, *springen* or *fahren* can express the meaning. *Das Pferd sprang über den Graben. Das Auto fuhr mit hoher Geschwindigkeit um die Ecke.*

viii. Take sth. **upon oneself** is *etw.* **auf sich nehmen.** Its use and that of **übernehmen** is discussed in ACCEPT 4. *Er nahm diese undankbare Aufgabe auf sich. Er übernahm die Aufgabe. Ich nahm es auf mich, nach Leeds zu fahren.* **Take** the consequences is *die Folgen/Konsequenzen auf sich nehmen. Wenn du so leichtsinnig handeln willst, mußt du die Konsquenzen auf dich nehmen.*

ix. Nehmen is used for taking school and university subjects. *Ich nehme Französisch/Geschichte/Biologie.*

x. Take a sent./quotation, etc. **from** a (written) source is usually **aus etw. nehmen.** *Diese Erklärung habe ich aus einem Artikel von X genommen.* **Entnehmen** + dat. belongs to a higher stylistic level. *Diesen Satz habe ich dem Buch von Y entnommen.*

xi. Nehmen, but not **take,** is used with *das Ende. Die Schwierigkeiten schienen kein Ende nehmen zu wollen,* seemed never-ending. *Etw. nimmt ein böses/jähes Ende,* comes to a bad/sudden end. *Die Sache nimmt kein gutes Ende.*

xii. Some expressions using **take** whose equivalents contain *nehmen.* **Take** a holiday is *Urlaub nehmen,* colloquially *machen.* **Take** a day off: *Sich einen Tag frei nehmen.* **Take** or *exact one's revenge* is *Rache an jmdm. nehmen. Ein Fisch nimmt den Köder. Abschied nehmen von jmdm.* is 'to take one's leave'. **Take** a bath is *ein Bad nehmen.* **Take** *a piece* in chess or other games is *nehmen* or *schlagen. Sie hat meine Königin genommen. Er schlug die Dame mit dem Turm.*

2. Take referring to mental action.

i. In an extended use of meaning i, **take** means 'to deal with mentally, consider, imagine'. *Let us take another example!* **Nehmen** is not as widely used as **take,** but *nehmen* expresses the sense in some contexts. *Nehmen wir ein anderes Beispiel!* Words which can convey this meaning of **take** are **betrachten,** 'to CONSIDER', or **behandeln,** 'to deal with or treat'. *Let us take one point at a time!* is *Behandeln/Betrachten wir diese Punkte einzeln/der Reihe nach! Diese Ereignisse dürfen Sie nicht losgelöst von einander* *betrachten,* take in isolation. *If we take wage-earners as a whole: Wenn wir die Arbeitnehmergruppe als Ganzes betrachten . . .*

> *Die Armut in Afrika hat erschreckende Ausmaße angenommen. Nehmen wir als Beispiel Namibia!*
> *Nehmen wir einen konservativen Politiker wie etwa Bismarck!*
> *Betrachten wir jetzt einen Fall, der voriges Jahr viel Aufmerksamkeit auf sich gezogen hat!*
> *Wir müssen diese Abschnitte in der richtigen Reihenfolge behandeln.*

Take *into account/consideration* or **take** *account of* is *berücksichtigen.* Cf. CONSIDER 6.

ii. Sense v of **take**, 'to receive intellectually or mentally', has two meanings. One is 'to regard as or react to in a stated way', *Don't take that too seriously!*, and the other is 'to ascribe a meaning to, to interpret or understand in a certain way', *I don't know whether to take this remark as praise or criticism. Nehmen* is used for the first and in certain expressions for the second.

a. **Nehmen** takes an adv. like *ernst* or *wörtlich.* It is occasionally used with *für* or *als. Diese Behauptung kann ich nicht ernst nehmen* or *Er nimmt alles leicht. Sie nahm diese Äußerung für Wahrheit.* The main equivalent of **take for** is **halten für.** *Do you take me for a fool?* is *Halten Sie mich für einen Dummkopf?* Cf. CONSIDER 8. Cf. also some uses of *annehmen* under 5. i and *aufnehmen* under 5. ii.

> *Sie hatten die Bemerkung wörtlich genommen, obwohl sie spaßig gemeint war.*
> *Du nimmst die Sache viel zu ernst.*   *Diese Kritik darfst du nicht persönlich nehmen.*
> *Er nimmt alles auf die leichte Schulter* (takes it lightly, in a happy-go-lucky fashion).
> *Du mußt die Dinge so nehmen wie sie sind.*   *Ich nahm sein Schweigen als Zustimmung.*
> *Diese Bemerkung nahm er für Wahrheit, sie war aber eine glatte Lüge.*

b. The second sense, 'to ascribe a meaning to', is generally expressed by **auffassen,** 'to INTERPRET', and **verstehen.** Cf. UNDERSTAND 7. In *Ich weiß nicht, wie ich diese Bemerkung auffassen/verstehen soll,* either v. could be translated as **take.** Similarly *Sie haben meine Worte als Vorwurf/als Lob aufgefaßt. So hat man die Textstelle aufgefaßt* could translate *That was the way the passage was taken. The law was taken to mean this* could be translated as *Das Gesetz wurde so aufgefaßt* or as *Das Gesetz wurde so ausgelegt.*

iii. Other equivalents of sense v of **take.** *S.o. takes sth. at face value* could be *Er urteilt nach dem ersten Eindruck* or *schätzt etw. nach dem ersten Eindruck ein.* Cf. JUDGE 1 and ESTIMATE 4. The idiom *etw. für bare Münze nehmen* means 'to take (words) at their face value'. *Mit dem darfst du keinen Spaß machen, der nimmt jedes auch noch so scherzhafte Wort für bare Münze. Jmdn. beim Wort nehmen* means 'to expect s.o. to carry out what has been said or promised', 'to take s.o. at his or her word'. *Du hast versprochen, mir den Ring nach der nächsten Gehaltszulage zu schenken—jetzt nehme ich dich beim Wort. Take my word, it's a good car,* can be *Glauben Sie mir, der Wagen ist in Ordnung!* or stylistically higher, *Seien Sie versichert! You can take it from me* is thus either *Sie können mir glauben* or *Ich versichere Ihnen.* **Take** *offence at* or *exception to sth.* is *Anstoß nehmen an: Der Chef nahm Anstoß am saloppen Benehmen des Angestellten.*

3. Equivalents of **take** in sense vi when it means 'to convey s.o./sth. somewhere'. **Take** is used in a variety of contexts in the sense 'to convey, carry, lead, or escort a pers., animal, or thg. to a place'. *I'll take you to the station.* The subj. can be a person, a vehicle, and a road or journey.

i. The commonest equivalent is **bringen,** which means 'to take or bring a pers. or thg. to a place and then leave him, her, or it there'. *Ich bringe dich zur Post. Der Bus bringt die Kinder zur Schule.* If I am at point A and X is at point B, **take** describes my action in conveying something to X, and *bring* X's action in conveying something to me. If C and D are two points at a distance from me, I use **take** to describe the action by which someone or something is conveyed from C to D or from D to C. In all these situations G. uses *bringen* only. Someone at the scene of an accident could say, *'Der Krankenwagen wird den Verletzen ins Krankenhaus bringen',* where E.

uses **take**. If I am with the children, and intend to take them to their grand-mother, I say, '*Ich bringe die Kinder zur Großmutter'*, and the grandmother also says, '*Helmut bringt die Kinder hierher.' Bringen* is used for taking people or things to a place only if the person taking them simply sets them down there and then goes away. *Ich bringe dich zum Bahnhof.* It is not used if I take, e.g. to a place of enter-tainment, someone whom I have invited to go with me, e.g. *He took her to the opera.* Cf. 3. v. *Bringen* suggests that taking a person or thing somewhere is a special trip. **Mitnehmen** means 'to take s.o./sth. with one when going somewhere on foot or in a vehicle' or 'to take a pers. or thg. to a place which is on one's way to some-where else'. *Kannst du mich nicht zum Bahnhof mitnehmen, wenn du sowieso vorbeifährst? Mitnehmen* is also used like *to take with me/us*, etc., when taking someone along with one to a place of entertainment etc. is meant. *Wir gehen ins Kino und nehmen Paul mit.* **Mitbringen** means 'to bring with one' and 'to take with one when going somewhere'. It often means 'to take a gift to a place one is going to'. *Wir müssen den Kindern etw. mitbringen.*

> *Bringst du mich noch rasch zur Bank, bevor du die Kinder von der Schule abholst?*
> *Du bist heute dran, die Kinder zur Schule zu bringen.*
> *Draußen wartet ein Auto, das mich zum Flughafen bringen soll.*
> *Schließlich beschlossen sie, die Sache vor Gericht zu bringen* (to take it to court).
> *Vergiß nicht, deinen Schirm mitzunehmen!*   *Ich nehme das Paket mit und gebe es bei ihm ab.*
> *Wenn du mit dem Auto zum Supermarkt fährst, kannst du ein paar Sachen für mich mitbringen?*
> *Was können wir der Dame des Hauses/der Gastgeberin mitbringen? Wir müssen ihr Blumen oder*
>   *Pralinen mitbringen.*   *Wir haben so viele Pflaumen, wir bringen der Tante einige mit.*
> *Natürlich kannst du deinen Freund in unser Ferienhaus mitbringen.*

ii. When commercial transport is referred to, **bringen** is the everyday word. **Befördern** is the technical term meaning 'to transport'. *Die Bahn bringt diese Pakete schnell nach Edinburg. Die Bahn befördert Waren/Güter in kurzer Zeit in alle Teile des Landes.*

iii. Tragen, 'to carry', is often used for taking things from one place to another when only a short distance is involved, e.g. about the house. **Bringen** is an alter-native. Cf. *schaffen* under MOVE 2. ii.

> *Ich trage/bringe Ihr Gepäck in Ihr Zimmer.*
> *Er trug/brachte das Tablett mit den leeren Gläsern in die Küche zurück.*

iv. Führen, 'to lead', is used for taking or leading an animal somewhere, *Er führte das Pferd in den Stall*, and for taking or showing someone into a room, *Die Sekretärin führte den Besucher ins Büro des Direktors. Der Portier führte mich in mein Zimmer.* It translates *take* when this means 'to guide'. *Sie führte uns durch die Ausstellung.* Cf. LEAD 1. It is also used with a n. such as *der Beruf* or *eine Untersuchung* as subj. *Sein Beruf führt ihn sehr viel in der Welt herum* or *Die Untersuchung führte ihn in viele Länder der Welt.* A road etc. can be the subj. *Diese Straße führt direkt zum Dorf/nach Paris*, leads or takes you there. **Take** = 'to intend to construct', as in *They're taking the road through the valley*, is also *führen. Man will die neue Autobahnstrecke durch dieses schöne Tal führen.*

v. Ausführen means 'to take out' mostly a girl, woman, or visitor. It is a some-what formal word which suggests polite and correct behaviour. *Er führte seine neue Freundin letzte Woche zweimal aus.* A phr. like *ins Theater* is not added (except as an addition, as in the first sent. below). With phrs. **mitnehmen** is the usual v. *Er nahm seine Freundin in die Oper/ins Theater mit. Einen Hund ausführen* is 'to take it for a walk'.

> *Er hat sie ganz groß ausgeführt, erst zum Essen und dann in die Oper.*
> *Du mußt deine Frau mal wieder ausführen, sie langweilt sich.*

vi. Special cases. *Andrew said he always* **took his problems to** *his mother: Er geht immer mit seinen Problemen zu seiner Mutter. They wanted to* **take** *the matter* **further**: *Sie wollten die Sache weiter verfolgen. Verfolgen*, to pursue. Cf. FOLLOW 12. v.

4. Equivalents of sense iii of **take**, **take** time, money, effort, etc. **Take**, which is often used impersonally, means 'to require or use up' when it is combined with an obj. denoting time, energy, skill, etc. *It took a lot of time and effort to translate that text. I took/It took me two weeks to write that essay.*

i. If I take time doing something or take my time to do something, I do not hurry but allow myself as much time as I need. A period of time implies that this is sufficient to carry out the action without haste. *Take a day or two to think about it!* This sense is expressed both by **sich** (dat.) **Zeit nehmen** and **sich** (dat.) **Zeit lassen**. *Nimm/Laß dir Zeit mit der Übersetzung!* A phr. giving a length of time may be added, *Laß dir ein oder zwei Tage Zeit/Nimm dir ein oder zwei Tage Zeit, um darüber nachzudenken! Zeit* cannot be omitted. Both imply not hurrying, and the statement of time suggests that this is sufficient to do what has to be done unhurriedly. The ironic use *You certainly took your time!* is *Das hat aber lange gedauert!* Cf. 4. ii. *Sich Zeit nehmen* has a second sense, 'to find or make time'. *Ich nahm mir Zeit, meine alten Tanten zu besuchen. Der Lehrer mußte sich Zeit nehmen, um einigen Kindern die Regeln ein zweites und drittes Mal zu erklären.*

ii. For **take** a specified amount of time or **take** a lot/very little time to do sth., there are two main equivalents. With a personal subj. **brauchen** is used. *Ich habe zwei Wochen gebraucht, um den Text zu übersetzen.* This translates *I took* and *It took me.* A vehicle, a means of transport, or a machine can also be the subj. of *brauchen. Der Zug braucht 70 Minuten für diese Strecke. Die Raumsonde brauchte sechs Jahre, um Jupiter zu erreichen. Das Gerät braucht nur ein paar Minuten, um die Berechnungen durchzuführen/um diese Seiten auszudrucken.* The alternative is **dauern**, which needs as subj. either a n. denoting an action that takes a certain amount of time, or *es* or *das.* Such ns. could be *Die Bearbeitung des Antrags/Die Untersuchung des Falles/Die Beantwortung aller Fragen dauerte ziemlich lange/länger als erwartet. Der Bau der Brücke dauerte zwei Jahre.* The same meaning can be expressed by using *es dauert* either with an infin. or with a clause introduced by *bis. Es dauerte länger als zwei Stunden, [um] alle Fragen zu beantworten. Es dauerte länger als zwei Stunden, bis wir alle Fragen beantwortet hatten.* An infin. is only possible when in E. the infin. directly follows the expression of time without a phr. with *for*, but the *bis* construction can always be used. Thus *It took two years to build the bridge* could be *Es dauerte zwei Jahre, die Brücke zu bauen* or *bis man die Brücke gebaut hatte.* If a phr. with *for* follows the expression of time, *It took about two weeks for the wound to heal*, the *bis* construction must be used. *Es dauerte ungefähr zwei Wochen, bis die Wunde verheilt war.* When it is clear what is being referred to, *es* or *das* can be the subj. of *dauern*, and only an expression of time need be added. *Wie lange wird es wohl dauern?*, I wonder how long it will take. *Das wird mindestens eine Stunde dauern.* (A further possibility for the bridge sent. is to use *man* as the subj. of *brauchen. Man brauchte zwei Jahre, um die Brücke fertigzustellen.*)

Impersonal statements without a personal obj. like *It takes a long time to become a good tennis player* are best translated by **erfordern**, 'to require', or *es dauert. Es erfordert viel Zeit, ein guter Tennisspieler zu werden.* (Colloquially: *Es braucht.*) *Es dauert immer einige Zeit, bis man eine andere Sprache fließend sprechen kann.*

> *Es dauerte nur ein paar Sekunden, bis ihre Augen sich an die Dunkelheit gewöhnt hatten.*
>
> *Es kann zehn Jahre dauern, einen neuen Flugzeugtyp zu entwickeln/bis man einen neuen Flugzeugtyp entwickelt hat.*

Another possibility for saying or asking how long it takes to get to a place by car etc. is to use **fahren**. *Man fährt drei Stunden nach Düsseldorf. Wie lange fährt man nach Eschwege?*

iii. **In Anspruch nehmen** with an activity as subj. means 'to take or require time' and is a syn. of *dauern*. *Die Übersetzung des schwierigen Textes hat ungefähr drei Wochen in Anspruch genommen/hat längere Zeit in Anspruch genommen, als wir erwarteten*. These sents. can also be formulated with *es* as subj. and an infin. *Es hat sehr viel Zeit in Anspruch genommen, alles vorzubereiten/den Text zu übersetzen*.

iv. Take used impersonally with materials, energy, money, people, etc. as obj. is best translated by words related to NECESSARY, *need*, and *require*. *Anyone can make a road, but it takes an experienced engineer to build a bridge: Ein erfahrener Ingenieur ist nötig, um eine Brücke zu bauen. Man braucht einen . . . Ingenieur, um . . . One movement of the wrist was all it took: Eine Drehung der Hand war alles, was nötig war. It took a lot of effort to . . . : Wir brauchten eine Menge Mühe, um . . . Sehr viel Mühe war nötig . . . Es erforderte sehr viel Mühe, um . . . It takes a lot of money to fight a general election: Man braucht/Es erfordert sehr viel Geld, um eine Wahlkampagne durchzuführen. Sehr viel Geld ist nötig . . . Eine Wahlkampagne, die das ganze Land erfassen soll, erfordert sehr viel Geld. It took a lot of money to get the car in order: Wir haben sehr viel Geld gebraucht, um das Auto in Ordnung zu bringen. Eine Menge Geld war nötig, um . . . The garden paths took two tonnes of cement: Wir haben zwei Tonnen Zement beim Bau der Gartenwege verbraucht.* (*Verbrauchen* = 'to consume, use up'. Cf. USE 4.) *It took a lot of courage to admit his mistake: Es gehörte sehr viel Mut dazu, den Fehler einzugestehen.* Cf. BELONG.

5. Derivatives of *nehmen* expressing senses of **take** together with alternatives. Many of these vs. also express meanings of ACCEPT.

i. The basic senses of *annehmen* are 'to accept (sth. given or offered)' and 'to assume'.

a. **Annehmen** is the usual v. for taking or accepting a job, although *nehmen* is possible. *Sie hat eine Stelle bei einem Verlag angenommen.* **Take** advice, a hint, or a warning can only be *Rat, einen Wink*, and *eine Warnung annehmen*. For **take** [*no*] *notice of*, cf. NOTICE *n.* 4.

b. **I take it** + clause, as in *I take it then* [*that*] *you don't agree* or *I take it* [*that*] *you're being quite candid with us*, can be translated by **annehmen** meaning 'to assume'. *Ich nehme an, daß Sie anderer Meinung sind. Ich nehme an, daß Sie ganz aufrichtig gewesen sind und uns nichts verbergen.* **Take** sth. for granted can be translated by *annehmen*, but it is not as strong as the E. expression. *Ich nehme an, daß alle mit einem Computer umgehen können.* A stronger alternative is **voraussetzen**, which means 'to assume sth. to be true, known, etc.' and can take *als* + an adj. *Etw. als selbstverständlich voraussetzen* is a word-for-word transl. of *take for granted. Es wird als selbstverständlich vorausgesetzt, daß jedes Kind Rechnen lernen soll. Voraussetzen* can, however, express the meaning without the *als* phr. *Wir setzen voraus, daß Ihnen unsere Bedingungen bekannt sind*, we presume/take it [for granted] that you are acquainted with our terms. *Man setzt voraus, daß wir mit einem Computer umgehen können. Wir setzten die Kenntnis der Grammatik voraus. Ich setze diese Tatsache als bekannt voraus*, take the knowledge of these facts for granted.

Ich nehme an/setze voraus, daß Sie wissen, was ein Stethoskop ist.

c. **Annehmen** translates *to take on a certain form* and *to take shape*. Cf. SHAPE 4. *Die Unruhen nahmen eine bürgerkriegsähnliche Form an. Die Krankheit nimmt zwei verschiedene Formen an.* Sth. is beginning to take shape can be *Etw. nimmt konkrete Form/Gestalt an.* A gen. after *form* needs to be rephrased. Thus *Such aggressiveness often takes the form of bad lang.* is *Diese Art von Aggressivität äußert sich oft im Gebrauch vieler Kraftausdrücke.* Cf. EXPRESS.

ii. *a.* As explained under ACCEPT 5 and INCLUDE 4 **aufnehmen** means in one sense 'to accept or admit people into a place or group' or 'to make a thg. part of a larger whole'. **Take**, *accept*, or *admit refugees* is *Flüchtlinge aufnehmen. Aufnehmen* can be used for taking someone into a firm etc., but *nehmen* is not uncommon. *Die beiden*

Partner nahmen den jungen Rechtsanwalt in ihre Praxis auf. The school takes all children can be *Die Schule nimmt alle Kinder auf*, but *annehmen* and *nehmen* are also possible.

Da er seine Fähigkeiten unter Beweis gestellt hat, können wir ihn in die Firma nehmen/aufnehmen.
Die Schule nimmt nur Schüler [an/auf], die sich für einen praktischen Beruf vorbereiten wollen.
Einige Ärzte nehmen nur Privatpatienten [an].

b. **Aufnehmen** is the equivalent of **take** meaning 'to hold or provide room for'. *Der Saal nimmt 200 Personen auf. Wie viel Weizen nimmt das Silo auf?* A syn. and the main v. expressing this sense is **fassen**. *Das Stadion faßt ungefähr 20 000 Zuschauer*, takes, holds about . . . The case won't take any more can be *Der Koffer faßt nichts mehr* or *Der Koffer nimmt nichts mehr auf* or *In den Koffer geht/paßt nichts mehr rein.*

Es hat lange geregnet, so daß das Erdreich keine Feuchtigkeit mehr aufnehmen kann.

c. **Aufnehmen** also translates **take** or RECEIVE meaning 'to react to sth. in a certain way'. *S.o. took the [bad] news well/badly: Jmd. hat die Nachricht gut/schlecht aufgenommen. Wie hat er die Nachricht aufgenommen?* **Take** *a joke etc. badly* is expressed by **übelnehmen**, to take amiss, hold against someone. *Den Witz hat er mir sehr übelgenommen.* **Take** *a joke etc. in good part* is usually expressed neg. *Er hat mir den Scherz nicht übelgenommen (und hat mitgelacht).* How did he take it? in this context could be *Wie hat er reagiert, als er merkte, daß du ihn hochgenommen hattest?*

iii. *a.* **Einnehmen** is used for taking or capturing a town, fort, territory, etc. *Sie nahmen die Stadt ein, ohne daß ein Schuß abgegeben würde.*

b. **Einnehmen** is used when a shop or business takes a certain amount of money. *Jeden Abend nimmt das Restaurant etwa 1 000 Mark ein. Wir haben heute zweimal so viel eingenommen wie an normalen Tagen.*

c. **Einnehmen** is used for taking [up] an attitude or point of view. *Man nimmt in einer Frage eine bestimmte Einstellung/Haltung ein. That's a foolish attitude to take* can be *Das ist ein sehr dummer Standpunkt, den du da eingenommen hast. Was für eine Haltung hat er denn eingenommen?*

d. **Einnehmen** is also used for taking [up] or occupying space. *Der Schreibtisch nimmt sehr viel Platz ein. Etw. nimmt sehr viel Platz weg* suggests little is left over.

e. With people as subj. *Platz nehmen* is 'to take a seat', *Nehmen Sie doch Platz!*, while *seinen/ihren Platz/ihre Plätze einnehmen* is 'to take one's seat'. *Die Vorstellung beginnt um acht Uhr. Nehmen Sie Ihre Plätze bitte deshalb bis fünf vor acht ein!*

iv. **Festnehmen** is 'to arrest or take into custody'. *Die Polizei hat mehrere Randalierer festgenommen.* The lit. transl. of *take into custody* is **in Gewahrsam nehmen**. *Der auf frischer Tat ertappte Dieb wurde in [polizeilichen] Gewahrsam genommen.* For *gefangennehmen*, 'to take prisoner', cf. CATCH 1. i. **Take** *prisoners (of war)* is **Gefangene machen**. *Sie haben zehn Gefangene gemacht.*

v. **Herausnehmen** means 'to take one thg. out of another'. *Sie machte die Schublade auf und nahm einen Brief heraus. Heraus* is optional if a phr. with *aus* is present. *Er nahm ein Buch aus dem Regal [heraus].* **Sich etw. herausnehmen** means 'to presume, to take sth. to which one does not have a right'. *Sie nimmt sich viel/allerhand heraus. Sich jmdm. gegenüber zu viel herausnehmen* means 'to take too many liberties'. **Sich die Freiheit herausnehmen** suggests that this goes too far. *Jmd. nahm sich die Freiheit heraus, mich allerlei über das Privatleben meiner Freunde zu fragen.* **Sich die Freiheit nehmen**, 'to take the liberty', is neutral. *Ich nehme mir die Freiheit, Sie an unsere Vereinbarung zu erinnern.*

vi. **Hinnehmen**, which is also discussed under ACCEPT 3, means 'to put up with sth. disadvantageous without protest'. It is necessary in certain contexts where E. has **take** in this sense. *Workers have to take a pay cut* is *Die Arbeiter müssen eine Lohnkürzung hinnehmen. I just used to listen and take it: Ich habe früher bloß zugehört und habe alles hingenommen.* One transl. of *The regiment took heavy losses* is *Das Regiment*

hatte schwere Verluste erlitten (cf. SUFFER), but *Das Regiment mußte schwere Verluste hin-nehmen* is also used. *(The camp was heavily shelled but took no casualties* is, however, *Das Lager wurde schwer beschossen, aber das forderte keine Toten und Verwundeten. Or . . . niemand wurde verwundet oder getötet.) I can't take any more* would usually be *Ich kann es nicht länger aushalten/ertragen.* Cf. BEAR 4. **Take** in *Some people can take hostility more easily than others* can be interpreted in two ways. *Aggressives/Feindseliges Verhalten hinnehmen* means 'to put up with it without protest'. If **take** is construed as mean-ing 'to cope with', the v. is **fertigwerden mit.** *Einigen Leuten fällt es schwer, mit Aggressionen/feindseligem Verhalten fertigzuwerden.*
    Der Verlust seines Arbeitsplatzes war ein schwerer Schlag, aber er hat ihn mutig hingenommen.

vii. In one sense **mitnehmen** means 'to exhaust, to wear out, to have a bad effect on'. It can sometimes be used to translate *Sth. takes a lot out of you. Die schwere Arbeit bei der sengenden Hitze hat uns alle sehr mitgenommen. Er sah sehr strapaziert/mitgenom-men aus.* Words expressing the sense 'to take a lot out of s.o.' are *sein + anstrengend* or *strapazierend*, strenuous. *Talking in a foreign language all day takes a lot out of you* could become *Es ist sehr anstrengend, den ganzen Tag eine Fremdsprache zu sprechen.*

viii. Übernehmen, which can only be trans., translates *to take (responsibility)* and *to take on (a task).* Cf. ACCEPT 4. It also means 'to take sth. over' either permanently, *Jmd. übernimmt die Leitung des Betriebs,* or on one occasion or temporarily, *Herr X übernimmt die Stunde um 10 Uhr.* (Also *Herr X vertritt einen anderen Lehrer.*) *Übernehmen* can sometimes translate *to take [charge of]. Sie bat mich, die Klasse/das Geschäft solange zu übernehmen, bis sie zurückkehrte.* (It is not used in a sent. like *Y takes us for maths*, which is *Wir haben Herrn Y in Mathe* or *Herr Y unterrichtet uns in Mathe. I take/teach two French classes* is *Ich habe/unterrichte zwei Französischklassen. Mrs Z takes history and geography* is *Frau Z unterrichtet/gibt Geschichte und Erdkunde.)To* **take the chair** at a meeting is *den Vorsitz übernehmen.* **Take office** [*as sth.*] is *ein Amt übernehmen* or *antreten. Morgen übernimmt Herr N das Amt des Bürgermeisters. Der US-Präsident tritt sein Amt erst dreieinhalb Monate nach der Wahl an. Er übernahm die Macht/die Regierung* means 'he took power' or 'took over government'. *Nach diesem Wahlsieg übernahm die SPD die Macht.* The takeover need not be legal. If illegal, e.g. by a coup, *die Macht übernehmen* has the same meaning as the unambiguous *die Macht ergreifen,* to seize power.

6. Expressions containing **take** which require words other than *nehmen.* **Take** often has no meaning of its own but derives its meaning from the following n.
i. Illnesses. **Be taken ill** is the v. *erkranken. Er war plötzlich erkrankt und mußte nach Hause. S.o. was taken by the plague/cholera: Jmd. ist an der Cholera gestorben/durch die Cholera ums Leben gekommen.* A stylistically higher syn., which may, but need not, suggest considerable numbers, is *dahinraffen. Viele wurden von der Seuche dahinge-rafft.*
ii. Emotions and the mind. **Take** *s.o.'s* **fancy** can be translated by *gefallen* (cf. LIKE 2) or by the somewhat old-fashioned *Gefallen finden an. Er kaufte eine Vase, die ihm gefallen hatte* or . . . , *an der er Gefallen gefunden hatte.* **Take heart** is *Mut fassen* or *sich ein Herz fassen.* **Take a liking/dislike** to *s.o.* is *eine Neigung zu jmdm./Abneigung gegen jmdn. fassen.* **Take** *one's* **mind off** *sth.: Jmd. von etw. ablenken. Der Besuch lenkte ihn von seinen Sorgen ab.* **Take pains** or **trouble** with *sth./to do sth.* is *sich Mühe geben.* Cf. TROU-BLE 1. In a clause the idea would be expressed by *mühevoll: Sie trug das Kleid, das sie so mühevoll genäht hatte,* she had taken so much effort/trouble/such pains to make. Cf. PAINFUL 5. **Take pity** on *s.o.* is *Mitleid mit jmdm. haben.* **Take pleasure** in *sth.* is *Vergnügen an etw. finden* or [*seine*] *Freude an etw. haben.* **Take pride** in *sth.: Stolz auf etw. sein.* **Take by surprise** is *überraschen.* Cf. SURPRISE. *Da sie mit seinem Besuch rech-nete, war sie nicht überrascht, als er plötzlich in der Tür stand.*

iii. *The ducks took to the water when the dog appeared* could be *Sie nahmen im Wasser Zuflucht* or *Sie rannten ins Wasser. The dancers took the floor: Sie begaben sich auf die Tanzfläche.*

iv. Take *sth.* **down** *in writing* is *etw. aufschreiben,* cf. WRITE DOWN, or *etw. schriftlich festhalten,* cf. RECORD. **Take down** *in shorthand* is *stenographieren.*

v. Take *£3.50* **off** *the price: Einen Betrag (z. B. zehn Mark) vom Preis abziehen.*

vi. Take ACTION or **steps**: *Schritte unternehmen.* **Take advantage** *of s.o.: Man nutzt jmdn./jmds.Gutmütigkeit aus.* **Take** *a deep* **breath**: *Tief Atem holen.* **Take**/make *a* **decision**: *Eine Entscheidung treffen/fällen* or *einen Beschluß/Entschluß fassen.* **Take** *an* **examination**: *Eine Prüfung machen* or *ablegen.* **Take** *a* **leap**: *Einen Sprung/Satz machen.* **Take measures** (= 'action'): *Maßnahmen ergreifen.* **Take** *the* **minutes** *(of a meeting)* is *das Protokoll führen.* **Take** *its* **name** *from sth.: Nach etw. benannt sein.* Cf. CALL 4. ii. **Take a nap** *after lunch: Ein Mittagsschläfchen machen.* **Take** *an* **oath** is *einen Eid leisten.* **Take** *the* **opportunity** is usually *die Gelegenheit nutzen* (cf. USE) or, *in formal language, eine Gelegenheit wahrnehmen.* **Take** *a* **periodical** is usually *abonnieren, to subscribe to. Die Bibliothek abonniert an die 2 000 Zeitschriften.* **Take photographs**: *Aufnahmen machen.* **Take** *the* **point**. *The audience took the point that anything nuclear is potentially dangerous: Die Zuhörer zeigten Verständnis für den (vom Redner vertretenen) Standpunkt, daß alles, was mit der Atomkraft zu tun hat, gefährlich ist.* Or *Sie ließen den Standpunkt, daß . . . , erst mal gelten.* Cf ACCEPT 6. **Take** *the* **position** *of a ship, etc.* is *die Position bestimmen.* Cf. DETERMINE 4. **Take precedence** [*over s.o./sth.*]: [*Vor jmdm./etw.*] *Vorrang haben. Familien mit Kindern haben Vorrang. Die Bewahrung von Arbeitsplätzen hat Vorrang vor Lohnerhöhungen.* **Take** *s.o.'s* **pulse/temperature** is *jmds. Puls/Temperatur messen.* **Take** *a* **risk**: *Ein Risiko eingehen* or *auf sich nehmen.* **Take** *a* **shower**: [*Sich*] *duschen.* **Take** *s.o.'s* **side** is *jmds. Partei ergreifen, Partei nehmen für jmdn.,* or more strongly, *sich auf jmds. Seite schlagen. He* **took** *a step towards me: Er trat einen Schritt auf mich zu.* **Take turns**. *Michael and I took turns driving/I took turns with Michael: Michael und ich wechselten uns im Fahren ab* or *Ich wechselte mich im Fahren mit Michael ab.* **Take** *a different etc.* **view** *of. We do not take the same view of the matter as you: Wir denken nicht wie du darüber* or *Wir sind anderer Meinung darüber als du.* **Take** *a* **vow** is *ein Gelübte ablegen.* **Take**/go *for a* **walk**: *Einen Spaziergang machen.*

taste *v.*

1. Taste can be trans. meaning 'to have or exercise the sense of taste', *If you have a bad cold, you can't taste anything,* and 'to experience or to distinguish flavours', *Can you taste the garlic in this soup?* **Schmecken** used trans. expresses these meanings. It can take an indefinite obj., *Wegen der Erkältung kann ich nichts schmecken,* and is also found with a substance as obj. when it means 'to perceive or experience a particular flavour by the sense of taste', *Kannst du den Zimt in dem Kuchen schmecken?* **Herausschmecken**, which implies that a flavour emerges clearly from, or can be tasted in, something eaten, can be used to emphasize the second meaning, but *schmecken* is usually sufficient. *Kannst du den Wein in der Soße schmecken?/den Wein aus der Soße herausschmecken?*

> *Ich konnte das Meersalz noch auf den Lippen schmecken.*

> *Ich kann den Pfeffer in dem Eintopf schmecken.*   *Kannst du schmecken, was du ißt?*
> *Schmeckt man die ranzige Butter im Kuchen?*   *Kannst du den Knoblauch herausschmecken?*

2. Schmecken is also intr. and corresponds to **taste** used intr. with a substance, usually food or drink, as subj. and meaning 'to have a taste of a specific kind'. *It tastes sour/sweet. Die Milch schmeckt sauer.* **Taste of** is **schmecken nach**. *Die Milch schmeckt nach Fisch.*

Etw. schmeckt gut/schlecht/süß/herb/bitter/angebrannt usw.   *Das Getränk schmeckt nach Anis.*
Das Essen schmeckt nach gar nichts.   *Die Torte schmeckt stark nach Rum.*

Schmecken + dat., *Etw. schmeckt jmdm.*, means that sth. is pleasant to someone's taste, i.e. someone LIKES something.

3. Taste also means 'to test the flavour or quality by the sense of taste', 'to put a small quantity into the mouth or eat a small amount in order to ascertain whether one likes it or not'. The main equivalent is **probieren**. It also translates TRY when it is a syn. of this sense of **taste**. *Sie probierte ein Stück Wurst/den Wein.* **Versuchen** is also used, but it belongs to a higher stylistic level. It is often heard when people are offered samples of a new food to try in a shop. *Probieren* could also be used but sounds less refined. *Probier'/Versuch' mal etwas von diesem Käse!* Where E. uses *taste sth. to see whether*, an *ob*-clause follows *probieren* and *versuchen* directly. *Probier' die Suppe, ob genug Salz drin ist!* **Kosten** is the technical term for tasting food and drink professionally. *Er kostete den Wein.* It is less used than *probieren* in everyday language, but does occur. *Sie gab ihm ein Stück zum Kosten.* *Kosten von* means 'to taste a sample of' and suggests giving an opinion based on experience. *Der Chefkoch des Feinschmeckerlokals kostete von jeder Speise, bevor er sie den Gästen servieren ließ.* **Abschmecken** also means 'to taste' in the sense 'to try or test'. It implies that someone has prepared food and tries it to see whether it is properly seasoned or asks another person to do this. He/she may suggest adding salt, pepper, or spices if necessary. *Sie schmeckte das Essen ab.* Like *versuchen* and *probieren*, it can be followed by an *ob*-clause. *Schmeck' mal ab, ob genug Salz in der Suppe ist!*

> *Jede Schokolade schmeckte gleich für mich, bis ich diese Sorte probierte.*
> *In Supermärkten werden einem oft kleine Stücke von neuen Produkten zum Probieren/Kosten angeboten.*
> *Probiere/Koste von der Soße, bevor du Salz dazu gibst!*
> *Probiere diesen Kaffee, ob er dir schmeckt!*
> *Probiere den Eintopf/Schmeck' den Eintopf ab, ob noch mehr Gewürze hineinmüssen!*

4. *I've never tasted caviar* can be *Ich habe Kaviar nie probiert. Probiert* here could be understood as 'tried'. *Gegessen* is an alternative. **Essen** alone is possible in translating a sent. like *They had not tasted food for three days. Sie hatten seit drei Tagen nichts/keinen Bissen gegessen.*

5. Taste is also used fig. *Whoever has tasted victory, tries to avoid defeat.* **Kosten** is used in elevated style. *Wer einmal den Sieg gekostet hat, meidet die Niederlage.* Somewhat more usual are **zu kosten bekommen** and **zu schmecken bekommen**.

> *Jetzt hat er die Bitternis des Kummers/die Bitternis der Enttäuschung/den Ernst des Lebens/die Süße des Lebens gekostet/zu kosten bekommen/zu schmecken bekommen.*

teach *v.*

1. i. The general term is **lehren**. It takes two objs. in the acc. as in E. *Sie hat mich Deutsch gelehrt. Er lehrte uns die Grundbegriffe des Faches. Wer hat dich das gelehrt?* It also takes an infin. If the infin. precedes or follows closely, *zu* is usually omitted, but when the infin. construction consists of several words, *zu* is mostly included. Thus *Mein Vater lehrt mich schwimmen/hat mich schwimmen gelehrt* as against *Der Meister lehrte mich, mit dem Werkzeug richtig umzugehen.* **Lehren** is used when the subj. is *die Erfahrung*, experience. *Die Erfahrung lehrt, daß viele Unfälle aus Unachtsamkeit geschehen.*

> *Die älteren Geschwister haben die jüngeren lesen und schreiben gelehrt.*

ii. A syn. of *lehren* commonly used in everyday speech is **jmdm. etw. beibringen**. It is mostly confined to activities of everyday life, but can be used for school subjects. It always needs a dat. and acc. *Mein Vater brachte mir das Fahren bei.* An E. infin. consisting of *to* + v. only is mostly translated as a verbal n. *Er brachte mir [das] Schwimmen bei.* An infin. construction is used with an extended infin. *Sie brachte den Kindern bei, höflich zu sein.* A *wie*-clause may also follow. *Er brachte mir bei, wie man den Computer bedient.* The obj. can be a way of behaving. *Der Lehrer brachte den Schülern Disziplin bei.* *Dir werde ich's schon beibringen!* is used like *I'll teach you!* as a threat.

> *Sie hat den Kindern gutes Benehmen beigebracht/ . . . den Kindern beigebracht, wie man sich be-*
> *nimmt.*
> *Er hat uns das Schachspielen/das Lesen/das Tanzen/Rechnen beigebracht.*
> *Die Jungen haben dem Kleinen nur schlechte Gewohnheiten beigebracht.*
> *Wer hat dir diesen Unsinn beigebracht?*

2. i. Unterrichten is the usual word for teaching at a school or for teaching certain subjects. *Sie unterrichtet Englisch/Physik/Erdkunde/Deutsch/Mathematik.* The E. double acc. *She teaches us French* is *Sie unterricht uns in Französisch.* It refers to a permanent arrangement. A sent. like *I'm only teaching three lessons today* is *Heute gebe/habe ich nur drei Stunden.*

> *Herr Kohl unterrichtet die Klasse in Geschichte.*
> *Ich unterrichte seit zehn Jahren an einem der Gymnasien im Ort.*

ii. Lehren is the usual word for teaching at a tertiary institution. *Er/Sie lehrt Geschichte/Chemie an der Universität Aberdeen. Gelehrt* is 'learned', and *der Gelehrte* 'a scholar'.

3. *Sth. has taught me a great deal/a lot: Ich habe sehr viel daraus gelernt.* Thus *Working with them has taught me a lot* is *Durch die Zusammenarbeit mit ihnen habe ich sehr viel gelernt.*

4. If a person is the subj of **teach** *s.o. a lesson,* it means that the first person punishes or scolds the second for something the second has done as a warning that the same mistake or behaviour should not occur again. *His father gave him a smack to teach him a lesson.* Where a reprimand is involved, G. uses one sense of *die Lektion,* but not with a v. meaning 'to teach'. *Laß dir das eine Lektion sein!* could translate *That will teach you a lesson. Weil er gelogen hatte, gab ihm sein Vater ein paar Schläge— das sollte ihm eine Lektion sein. Sth. taught me a lesson* can also refer to an experience which acts as a warning or as an example from which I should learn. This is expressed by one sense of *die Lehre,* but again not with a v. meaning 'to teach'. *Laß dir das eine Lehre sein!*, let that be a lesson to you/teach you a lesson. *Du sollst fremde Hunde nicht streicheln—laß dir das eine Lehre sein! Welche Lehren können wir aus der Geschichte ziehen?*, what lessons can we learn from history? or what does history teach us?

> *Das war für mich eine heilsame/nützliche Lehre/Lektion.* Also . . . *eine bittere Lehre.*

tear *v.* A few equivalents.

1. The use of *reißen* and *zerreißen* when they refer to something solid but flexible, like rope or thread, is discussed under BREAK 1. iv. In reference to *Stoff* or *Papier* they mean 'to tear' and can be intr. and trans.

i. When intr. **reißen** suggests an unspecified tear. *Das Papier ist gerissen.* **Zerreißen** implies that the thing that tears becomes ruined and useless. *Die Tüte ist zerrissen.* Only *zerrissen* is used as a past part. *So eine schmutzige und zerrissene Hose trag ich nicht. In zerrissenen Strümpfen kann ich nicht zur Arbeit gehen.*

ii. When trans. with *Papier* or *Stoff* as obj., **reißen** needs a word or phr. stating the result. *Er riß das Blatt in Stücke. Sie hat den Stoff in Fetzen gerissen. Er riß den Vertrag* *entzwei*. **Zerreißen** does not take a phr. In some contexts it is like **tear** sth. **up**. *Sie hat den Brief zerrissen.* In reference to articles of clothing *zerreißen* means 'to tear a hole in'. *Ich habe mir die Hose/das Kleid/die Strümpfe zerrissen.* Here *zerreißen* expresses the same meaning as *ein Loch in etw. reißen*. *Reißen* is used with the result of the tearing as obj., usually *ein Loch*. *Der Junge ist im Stacheldraht hängengeblieben und hat sich ein Loch in die Hose gerissen.* *Reißen* is also used for tearing one thing out of or off another. *Sie riß eine Seite aus dem Heft. Er riß den Knopf von der Jacke.* (Without a phr. with *von* it is necessary to use *Er riß den Knopf ab.*)

2. If people tear somewhere, they move very quickly, usually in an uncontrolled and dangerous way. For a short distance, **stürzen**, 'to rush', can be used. *Er stürzte in das Zimmer/aus dem Zimmer.* **Rasen** is used for greater distances, but is now mostly restricted to motor vehicles. *Es wird auf den Bundesstraßen ebenso sehr gerast wie auf den Autobahnen.* (The usual transl. is *speed.*) *Rasen* can sometimes imply on foot. *Ich bin den ganzen Tag herumgerast. Wir sind zum Bahnhof gerast, aber der Zug war schon weg.* In the last sent. *Wir sind gerannt* would be more usual. Cf. RUN.

tease, banter, make fun of, mock, have s.o. on *vs.*

1. Tease = 'make fun of s.o., sometimes playfully, but mostly in an unkind, slightly cruel, or irritating way by causing embarrassment or by making him or her believe sth. that is not true'. *They teased him for using such inflated language.* **Banter** = 'to tease good-naturedly or speak with s.o. in a witty, friendly manner. *We just stood and bantered for half an hour.*

i. Necken covers both implications of **tease**. It can describe a playful action, in which case it can be translated as **banter**, or it can be unkind and meant to annoy. When playful, it generally refers to people between whom there is a close relationship or close ties. It suggests good-natured joking about or making fun of someone a little in remarks which are not really meant seriously. According to the proverb *Was sich liebt, das neckt sich*, it is a sign of affection. It needs an obj., which can be the refl. pronoun or *einander*. *Er neckte das Mädchen. Sie neckten sich/einander gern.* A phr. with *wegen* = 'about' can follow. *Er wurde immer wegen seiner roten Haare geneckt.* When unkind, it suggests that one person persists in pointing to and making fun of another's supposed fault or weakness so that the second person becomes annoyed or feels hurt. In this sense it is usually followed by *mit* = 'about'. *Die anderen neckten ihn immer mit dieser merkwürdigen Eigenart.* The vs. discussed in ii suggest a more hostile intent than is implied by *necken*.

> *Wir standen vor dem Haus und neckten uns eine halbe Stunde lang.*
> *Sie neckte ihn wegen seiner seltsamen Aussprache mancher Silben/wegen seiner geschwollenen Ausdrucksweise.*   *Neckt sie doch nicht immer mit ihrem heimlichen Freund!*

ii. Hänseln always suggests an unfriendly intention. *Der Hänselnde* acts from *Schadenfreude*, 'malicious pleasure', or a motive which is *hämisch*, 'spiteful'. It implies that the teaser makes fun of another's weaknesses, shows no consideration for the other's feelings, does not stop when it is clear that the other is hurt, and that *der Gehänselte* is defenceless. While *hänseln* suggests motives which tend towards malice, **aufziehen** suggests that the subj. considers what is said to be funny, although its recipient may be of a different opinion. It can suggest a joke at another's expense or mild derision, or pointing out a weakness or a personal feature often indirectly by presenting it as valuable, or making untrue assertions. It also suggests that the perpetrator does not stop when his action clearly becomes too much for the other. It corresponds to **tease** implying unpleasantness and to **make fun of**. It is used with *mit* or *wegen*. *Es ist gemein, ihn ständig wegen* *seines Sprachfehlers aufzuziehen. Hänseln* would be stronger in such a sent. and express greater condemnation.

Er lispelte stark und wurde deshalb oft gehänselt.

Kotzenrother, der inzwischen die Arbeit in der Landwirtschaft mit einem Arbeitsplatz im Kölner Raum vertauscht hatte, wurde immer wieder wegen des anrüchigen Namens gehänselt.

Die anderen haben ihn mächtig aufgezogen, als sie merkten, daß er in das junge Mädchen verliebt war.

Wenn sie ihn noch weiter mit seinen langen Haaren aufziehen, wird er bald die Geduld verlieren und sie sich abschneiden lassen.

2. i. Sich über jmdn./etw. lustig machen means 'to make fun of'. It usually suggests unpleasantness and expresses condemnation of the action because of its arrogance, stupidity, or ignorance, but may sometimes be gentle and harmless and not meant to hurt. *Die beiden machten sich lustig über die Unbeholfenheit des neuen Schülers. Nie wäre ich auf den Gedanken gekommen, mich über ihre Sprechweise lustig zu machen.*

ii. There are several vs. related in meaning to *sich lustig machen*. The mildest is **sich über jmdn./etw. amüsieren**. It suggests laughing at or making fun of something or someone, but not in the person's presence, in a mild and unhurtful way. *Die Leute amüsierten sich über ihn/über sein ungewöhnliches Hobby. Sie amüsierten sich darüber, daß die Kleidungsstücke, die er trug, nie zusammenpaßten.* **Auslachen** suggests laughing as a spontaneous reaction to what someone says or does or to something about the person in the presence of the person concerned. As the laughter can vary in nature from kind to malicious and derisive, it can mean 'to laugh at' or 'to make fun of' or 'to jeer at'. *Wenn Sie mir diese Geschichte aufbinden wollten—ich würde Sie auslachen. Die anderen hatten ihn wegen seiner schlecht sitzenden Kleidung oft ausgelacht.* **Verlachen** means 'to ridicule, deride, hold up to ridicule'. It can be to the person's face or behind his or her back. It usually implies that the scorn is unjustified and expresses an adverse judgement on the scorner's action and attitude of mind. *Er wurde verlacht und verhöhnt.* It takes *als* = 'because of'. *Alle anderen fanden seine sanften Augen fad und affektiert; die Art und Weise, wie er beim Sprechen langsam mit den Fingern spielte, verlachten sie als weibisch* (Musil). *Die anderen haben seine Vorschläge als unrealistisch verlacht.* **Spotten** suggests expressing one's disdain in a refined, witty, or veiled manner. The remarks are not directed in an offensive way to the person concerned, but to a third person. It is used alone, *Er spottet gern* and *Du hast gut spotten*, or with *über*, *Sie spottete oft über die altmodischen Ansichten ihrer Lehrer.* **Verspotten** means 'to mock, jeer at, or deride' and needs an obj. It does not suggest a spontaneous reaction as *auslachen* does, but well-thought-out ridicule. *Der Autor der Posse verspottete die Unschlüssigkeit des Kanzlers.* **Höhnen** means 'to mock or jeer' and is intr. *'Das hast du nun davon', höhnte er.* **Verhöhnen**, 'to mock, deride, jeer at', suggests spiteful derision and is trans. *Das Lachen machte den anderen mißtrauisch, und er sprang gereizt auf: 'Willst du mich verhöhnen?'* (Broch).

3. i. A group of expressions mean 'to mislead s.o. deliberately as a joke', i.e. 'to have s.o. on' or 'to pull s.o.'s leg'. **Anführen** denotes harmless deceit or a good-natured trick which causes amusement. It is often heard with reference to children and is used when someone, without being in any way angry, admits that he/she has been tricked. *Kinder! Da habt ihr mich aber ganz schön/gründlich angeführt.* Alternative: *an der Nase [he]rumgeführt.* **Foppen** means 'to tell s.o. sth. untrue' or 'to arouse false expectations and to find it funny when the other pers. believes it', but it is now rare except in the past part. *Ich war der Gefoppte,* I'd been had, tricked. *Jmd. kam sich als der Gefoppte vor. Du willst mich wohl foppen.* **Jmdn. zum Besten halten** or **haben** means 'to tell s.o. sth. false as a joke, but without wanting to do anyone any harm'. *Die Geschichte klang sehr unglaubwürdig, und er nahm an, daß man ihn zum Besten halten wollte. Das Ganze entpuppte sich als ein geschickt eingefädelter Schwindel* (lie or trick), *und sie mußte erkennen, daß man sie zum Besten gehalten hatte.* **Veräppeln, verkohlen,** and **jmdm. einen Bären aufbinden** also suggest telling someone something untrue and being amused if it is believed. *Je weiter ich ging, desto klarer wurde es mir, daß man mich veräppelt hatte. Denke nur nicht, daß du mich verkohlen kannst! Du willst mich wohl verkohlen/veräppeln? Glaubt nicht, daß er im Lotto gewonnen hat, er wollte euch nur einen Bären aufbinden.* **Nasführen,** translated as to *lead up the garden path,* is now only literary. *Er fühlte sich von ihr genasführt.*

ii. **Jmdn. auf die Schippe nehmen** and **jmdn. auf den Arm nehmen** can mean 'to tell s.o. sth. untrue as if it were true'. They can therefore be syns. of the expressions in 3. i, but they may also mean 'to make fun of'. They normally suggest a good-natured intention. *Auf den Arm nehmen* is stylistically neutral and higher than the slangy *auf die Schippe nehmen. Sie hatte ihn nur auf den Arm nehmen wollen und war nun entsetzt darüber, daß er das Gesagte glaubte und ernste Konsequenzen daraus zog.* **Hochnehmen** is also colloquial. *Glaubt nicht alles, was er sagt!—es macht ihm Spaß, andere hochzunehmen.* Further syns. in both senses are **veräppeln** and **veralbern.** *Willst du mich veräppeln/veralbern? Die anderen wollten ihn veralbern, aber er verstand es, sich zu wehren.* An often heard syn. in the current *Jugendsprache* is **verarschen.** *Du willst mich wohl verarschen. Laß dich nicht von so einem Idioten wie diesem Politiker verarschen!* **Verulken** means 'to pull s.o.'s leg', *Du willst mich wohl verulken,* and 'to make fun of', but in the latter sense need not imply a malicious intent. *Seine Mitschüler haben ihn verulkt, weil er Gedichte schreib.*

> *Du willst mich wohl veräppeln/auf den Arm nehmen, aber gib dir keine Mühe! Ich weiß, daß es nicht stimmt.*
> A. *Manfred hat mir gesagt, der Termin für die Anmeldung ist schon vorbei.* B. *Ach was, der hat dich doch nur auf die Schippe genommen.*

tempt, entice *vs.*

1. i. In the basic religious sense of 'put to the proof or test, usually in a presumptuous way' which is now found only in the expressions to *tempt God, fate,* or *providence,* **tempt** is **versuchen.** *Man sollte Gott/die Vorsehung/das Schicksal nicht versuchen.*
ii. **Versuchen** also expresses the other religious sense of **tempt**, i.e. 'to try to attract or to entice a pers. to do evil, to allure or incite to evil with the prospect of some pleasure or advantage'. *Die Versuchung* is 'temptation'.

> *Niemand sage, wenn er versucht wird, daß er von Gott versucht werde. Denn Gott kann nicht versucht werden zum Bösen, und er selbst versucht niemand.* (James 1: 13)
> *Die Versuchung, wieder zu rauchen, war sehr stark, aber er widerstand ihr.*

2. Tempt means 'to attract or induce to an action or to do sth.' and is a syn. of **entice.** It does not imply anything evil, but something one feels a strong inclination to do even though it may be inadvisable. *The fine weather had tempted many people into the open. One is tempted to think that it had all been pre-arranged.*
i. **Versucht sein** or **sich versucht fühlen,** *etw. zu tun* mean that a person feels a strong inclination to do something. **In Versuchung sein,** *etw. zu tun* and **in Versuchung kommen,** *etw. zu tun* also mean 'to be tempted' and may be more usual in ordinary language.

> *Ich fühlte mich versucht, ihm zu sagen, was ich dachte.*
> *Ich war versucht, in den Streit einzugreifen.*
> *Ich bin versucht anzunehmen, die beiden hätten alles miteinander abgesprochen.*
> *Ich war schon in Versuchung, ihm eine strenge Lektion zu erteilen, besann mich aber eines Besseren.*
> *Jedesmal wenn ich hier bin, komme ich in Versuchung, für immer hier zu bleiben.*

ii. Because the above expressions are not widely used, other vs. usually translate this sense of **tempt**. The basic sense of **locken** is 'to lure' an animal. *Die Maus ließ sich in die Falle locken. Der Jäger lockte den Fuchs aus dem Bau.* Applied to people, it is translated as *attract* or **entice**. It normally needs an obj. and a phr. of direction. *Die Sonne lockte viele ins Freie.* The obj. or phr. may, however, be understood. *Die Bahn lockt mit herabgesetzten Preisen.* When a phr. is not added, *anlocken* is used. *Er wollte Kunden in sein Geschäft locken. Er wollte Kunden anlocken. Locken* also means 'to attract s.o. to do sth.' and can be used with an infin., but this use is now old-fashioned, having mostly given way to *reizen*, 'ATTRACT', and *verlocken*. Cf. 2. iii. *Die Arbeit lockt/reizt mich*, tempts or attracts me. *Es lockt/verlockt mich, ihm nach Italien zu folgen*, I am tempted. *Ein lockendes Angebot*, tempting.

> *Er hat ihn in einen Hinterhalt gelockt, um ihn dort zu überfallen.*
> *Die Tanzmusik lockte viele in die Kneipe. Die Tanzmusik lockte viele an/herein.*

iii. Verlocken means 'to be so appealing that it cannot be resisted'. The prefix *ver-* also suggests that the appeal is to do something bad or to neglect what ought to be done. Though this connotation has largely been lost, it may still sometimes be apparent, when *verlocken* implies that the consequences are bad or a disappointment. *Die hohen Gewinnaussichten hatten ihn dazu verlockt, seine gesamten Ersparnisse zu riskieren, und er verlor alles. Verlocken* is now used with an infin. instead of *locken*. *Die Sonne verlockt direkt dazu, schwimmen zu gehen.* The pres. part. is often found and now does not differ from *lockend. Ein verlockendes Angebot. Verlockende Aussichten. Die Verlockung* is close in meaning to *temptation. Der Politiker konnte den Verlockungen des großen Geldes nicht widerstehen und nahm Schmiergelder an.*

> *Der Sonnenschein und das Meer verlocken geradezu zum Baden.*
> *Das Wetter ist zwar verlockend, aber ich habe viel zu tun.*
> *Das schöne Wetter verlockte ihn, ein paar Tage Urlaub zu nehmen. Jetzt muß er eine Menge nachholen.*
> *Der Fußballstar erlag den Verlockungen des süßen Lebens und ließ sich feiern, statt zu trainieren.*

iv. Verleiten has a neg. connotation and means 'to induce s.o. to do sth. unwise or wrong'. It suggests that a person or thing causes someone to do what is foolish or misleads him or her in some way. *Das schöne Wetter verleitete sie zum Baden* suggests that this was at best a waste of time or that something important was neglected. The context could be: *Eigentlich wollte sie an ihrer Examensarbeit weiter arbeiten, aber das schöne Wetter verleitete sie dazu, ins Schwimmbad to gehen.* With *zu* + n. or infin. it is translated as *lead* or *encourage. Jmd./Etw. hat ihn zum Lügen/zum Diebstahl verleitet. Der Erfolg verleitete sie dazu, sich zu überschätzen.* **Verführen**, which can mean 'to seduce', also means 'to entice to do sth. which is known to be stupid or wrong and which would not be done without another pers.'s influence'.

> *Seine Kameraden haben ihn wieder zum Spiel/zum Trinken verleitet/verführt.*
> *Ich ließ mich zu einer unvorsichtigen Äußerung verleiten.*
> *Das günstige Angebot verführte/verleitete viele dazu, die Ware zu kaufen.*

3. If **be tempted** to do sth. simply expresses a wish relating to a fairly trivial matter, **große Lust haben** or **nicht übel Lust haben** can be used. *Ich hätte große Lust/nicht übel Lust, wieder hinzugehen.*

thank *v.* One sense of **owe** *v.*

1. For the sense 'to express one's gratitude to someone in speech or writing' G. has **danken** and **sich bedanken**, which differ only syntactically. *Danken* takes a dat. and *für: Ich danke dir für deine Hilfe. Sich bedanken* is used with *bei* + a person and *für. Ich bedankte mich bei ihm für seine Hilfe.* Thus *Ich muß ihr noch [für das Geschenk] danken* or *Ich muß mich noch bei ihr [für das Geschenk] bedanken.* Another usage survives in the idiom *Niemand wird dir die Arbeit/die Mühe danken. Danke!* is the usual word for *Thank you!* Slightly stronger are *Danke schön/sehr!* and *Besten/Vielen/Schönen Dank!* or *Ich danke Ihnen sehr [für Ihre Hilfe]*.

2. If someone or something owes a condition or quality to someone or something else, they have it only because of the other person or thing. *The plains of the Ganges owe their fertility to the minerals deposited there by the river. I owe my life to him.* To **have** s.o. **to thank for** sth. often has a neg. connotation meaning that someone has caused something undesirable (cf. 3), but it also occurs when the result is of pos. value. *We have her to thank for our success/for the fact that everything went off smoothly.* These senses are now expressed by **verdanken**. *Ich verdanke ihm mein Leben/meine Rettung. Diesen/Unseren Erfolg verdanken wir ihr.* When a following *daß*-clause is the obj. of *verdanken*, *es* is inserted into the main clause. *Wir verdanken es ihr/ihrer Arbeit, daß alles reibungslos abgelaufen ist.*

> *Seinen Erfolg verdankt er diesen günstigen Umständen.*
> *Die Ebene des Ganges verdankt ihre Fruchtbarkeit den Mineralien, die der Fluß dort abgelagert hat.*
> *Seine Einstellung verdankt er dem Umstand, daß er Deutsch kann. Also Er hat seine Einstellung dem Umstand zu verdanken, daß er Deutsch kann.*
> *Das gute Ergebnis ist seinem Fleiß/seiner Arbeit zu verdanken.*

3. Jmdm. [für etw.] verdanken also expresses the neg. sense of *You have s.o. to thank for sth.* meaning that he or she is responsible or to blame for it. *Daß ich jetzt in einer so mißlichen Lage bin, habe ich allein dir zu verdanken.* **Sich bei jmdm. für etw. bedanken** is heard in the spoken language, but it is much harder in tone than *verdanken. Für dieses Schlamassel kannst du dich bei ihm bedanken. You have only yourself to thank for that* could be translated by **verschulden**. *Das hast du selbst verschuldet.* Cf. CAUSE *n.* An alternative is *Diesen Mißerfolg kannst du dir selbst zuschreiben.* **Zuschreiben**, 'to ascribe sth. to a cause or a pers.', occurs in other contexts. *Es ist seinem Ungeschick zuzuschreiben, daß alles schief gegangen ist.* **Jmdm./sich etw. einbrocken** means 'to cause oneself/others to get into difficulties because of one's foolish behaviour'. *Diese Strafe hast du dir selbst eingebrockt. Da hast du uns was Schönes eingebrockt,* we have you to thank for this mess we're in.

then *adv.* and *adj.*

1. Then = 'at a particular time either in the past or in the future'.

i. For the past G. uses **damals**, *Damals gab es noch keine Autos,* or for the very or fairly recent past **da** (only at the beginning), *Wo ich um fünf Uhr war?—da war ich noch im Büro.* The dividing-line between *damals* and *da* is not clear so that both are found in the same context. In answering the question, *'Waren Sie vor zwei Jahren an der Uni.?'* someone might say, *'Nein, da/damals war ich noch Schüler.'* Likewise *Vor zwei Monaten habe ich drei Tage in Hamburg verbracht. Da/Damals hat es die ganze Zeit geregnet.* In both cases many people might prefer *damals*, but *da* would not be regarded as wrong. Sometimes both are found in the same sent. *Da wohnte ich damals noch zu Hause.*

> *Damals ging es uns bei weitem nicht so gut wie jetzt.*   *Gestern—da war es noch sonnig.*
> *Früher, da/damals ging es uns besser.*   *Ich war vorgestern hier. Da regnete es noch.*

ii. The equivalent of **then** referring to the future is **dann**. *Nur noch eine Woche—dann fangen die Ferien an.*

> *Nächstes Jahr geht sie nicht mehr zur Schule, dann steht sie schon im Beruf.*
> *Ich möchte, daß du zu mir kommst. Dann werde ich dir alles erklären.*
> *In zehn Tagen sind wir mit dieser Arbeit fertig. Dann brauchen wir uns nicht mehr so zu hetzen wie jetzt.*

Dann is often found at the beginning of a main clause when the initial *wenn*-clause refers to the future, although it is really optional. *Wenn dieser Teil der Arbeit fertig ist, dann können wir nach Hause gehen.*

iii. Then used as an adj., *the then Chancellor*, is **damalig**. *Der damalige Kanzler.*

iv. Da often introduces the second of two main clauses which form a sent. but are not joined by a conj. It is translated as *then, and then, and so,* or *so then*.

> *Sie schimpfte mit dem Kind, da fing es an zu weinen.*   *Sie beleidigte ihn, da ging er weg.*
> *Ich stand vorne im Bus, mit dem meine Klasse zum Museum fahren sollte, und zählte die Schüler, da kam eine Kollegin in aller Eile angerannt.*
> *Eben ertönte der Startschuß, da waren alle Schwimmer schon im Wasser.*

v. Neither *dann* nor *damals* is used with a prep. **Since then** is **seitdem** or **seither**. *Seitdem habe ich sie nicht mehr gesehen. Seither hat sich vieles geändert.* **Bis dahin** translates both *till then* and *by then*. *Er kommt am 26. zurück—ich bleibe bis dahin hier. Kommen Sie um sieben!—bis dahin bin ich fertig.* **Von da an** means 'from then on'. *Von da an ging alles besser. Von da an herrschte Ruhe im Dorf.* A syn. in elevated language is **von Stund an**. *Von Stund an wollte er nichts mehr mit uns zu tun haben.*

2. The equivalent of **then** introducing the items in a sequence is **dann**. The sequence can be in time, space, or rank. It often follows *erst* or *zuerst*. *Zuerst kamen die Oldtimer, dann folgten die Motorräder.*

> *Erst gehe ich für zwei Stunden in die Bibliothek, dann komme ich zu dir.*
> *Dann zieht man die Quadratwurzel aus dieser Zahl.*   *Erst überlegen, dann handeln.*
> *Zuerst hatte ich keine Ahnung, wer er sein könnte, dann fiel es mir aber ein.*
> *Sie ging zuerst zur Dorfschule, dann zum Gymnasium, und dann zur Universität.*

Just then, i.e. after something else had happened, is **gerade dann**. *Gerade dann trat sie ein.*

3. Then and **dann** often introduce the main clause of a sent. which begins with a conditional clause. *If we say that $y = ax^2$, then we get a curve like this. Wenn wir sagen, daß $y = ax^2$ ist, dann erhalten wir eine Kurve, die so aussieht.* Both the E. and G. words are optional. **So** is found in formal style instead of *dann. Wenn du es mir rechtzeitig gesagt hättest, so/dann hätte ich dir helfen können. Dann* is used at the beginning of a sent. with the condition implied. *Ich denke darüber nach. Dann wird es mir bestimmt einfallen. Dann* implies 'if what has just been said (or you have said) is the position or the case'. *Na, dann ist es ja gut.* The construction *dann* + imp. + *doch* also presents an action as the logical thing to do. *A. Kurt wird es mir bestimmt sagen können. B. Dann frag' ihn doch!* Transls. are *Then ask him!* or *Why don't you ask him then?*

> *Das ist dann genug.* (If you've done that amount.)
> *Wenn du unbedingt hingehen willst, dann geh doch!*
> *A. Hier ist sehr kalt. B. Dann mach doch die Heizung an!*

4. Then is added at the end of a question when your first assumption has proved to be wrong and you ask for an explanation which you expect to be willingly given. *A. I take it you are a student? B. No, I'm not. A. What are you then?* Many questions in spoken G. contain **denn**. If someone says, *'Du wirst am Telefon verlangt,'* the usual response would be, *'Wer ist es denn?' Wer ist es?* is not wrong but sounds somewhat abrupt. In such questions *denn* is not stressed. It is frequently heard as it gives a question a milder tone. *Was machst du denn? Wo kann sie denn sein? Warum denn? Sind Sie denn Student?* For the E. situation given above in which *then* is used after the initial assumption has proved to be incorrect, either stressed *denn* or **denn dann** with *dann* stressed is needed. *Was sind Sie <u>denn</u>? Was sind Sie denn <u>dann</u>?*

> *A. Arbeiten Sie noch als Schlosser? B. Nein. A. Als was <u>denn</u>? Or Als was denn <u>dann</u>?*
> *A. Elmar war gar nicht in Hamburg. B. Wo war er <u>denn</u>? Or Wo war er denn <u>dann</u>?*

5. If someone is offered something, more or less refuses, but, on being pressed, relents, the words exchanged might be: *A. Do have some more cake! B. Oh, all right* *then*. Responses expressing a reluctant acquiescence are **Also gut!** and **Na gut!** or **Also gut denn!** and **Na gut denn!** and on a higher stylistic level **Nun gut!** and **Nun gut denn!** *A. Nimm doch noch ein Stück Kuchen! B. Also gut [denn].*

6. Then is also used to draw a conclusion or to sum up what has been said. *That, then, is my idea of how we should work together.* This is expressed by **also**. *Das sind also meine Gedanken darüber, wie wir zusammenarbeiten sollten.* **Then** is also used at the end of a statement or when there is nothing more to be said on a topic, to draw a conclusion, or to confirm something that has been arranged. *You have a different opinion then. We'll meet tomorrow then. We have no alternative then.* It is often combined with *well*. *Well, that's settled then. Well then, we'll meet next Thursday at eight. Also* expresses this sense, but has a different position in the sent. from **then.**

> *Die Bedeutung der Bildung ist also im 20. Jahrhundert ungleich größer gewesen als in früheren Zeiten.*
> *Sie sind also anderer Meinung.*　　　*Das ist/wäre also erledigt/abgemacht.*
> *Wir gehen uns also morgen wieder hin.*　　*Wir haben also keine andere Wahl.*
> *Also, wir treffen uns am nächsten Donnerstag um acht. Or Wir treffen uns also am nächsten . . .*

7. Then is also often added when someone says goodbye. *Goodbye then!* is *Tschüß denn! Denn* is not used with *Auf Wiedersehen.* Possible is *Auf Wiedersehen also!* or *Also dann, auf Wiedersehen! Bis morgen also!* is another possibility. *Bis dann!* is used when leaving someone and means something like 'until our next meeting'.

8. And then is used at the beginning of a sent. to add another piece of information. This can be **außerdem**, besides, in addition. *Außerdem gibt es einige Sachen, die wir mit dem Finanzamt regeln müssen* could translate *And then there are a few matters we have to settle with the Tax Office.*

9. i. But then introduces a point to be considered which slightly contradicts what has just been said. *Iron would be better. But then you can't bend iron so easily.* The sense can be expressed by **aber** or **allerdings**. For the difference cf. HOWEVER 5. *Eisen wäre besser. Es läßt sich aber nicht so leicht biegen.* Or *Allerdings läßt es sich nicht so leicht biegen/Es läßt sich allerdings . . . I've always thought that. But then I could be wrong. Das habe ich mir immer gedacht. Ich könnte mich allerdings irren.*

ii. But then also introduces a remark which explains what has just been said and suggests that the first statement should not be regarded as surprising. *They're very close. But then they've known each other for years.* **Ja auch** inserted in one statement indicates that this gives an explanation of the preceding remark. *Sie sind eng miteinander befreundet. Sie kennen sich ja auch seit Jahren.*

> *Es ist erstaunlich, wie stark Karola ist—sie treibt ja auch viel Sport.*

there *adv.* The sense discussed here is 'in that place', for which there are two G. words, **da** and **dort**. In strict use *da* means 'fairly close at hand', while *dort* designates a place further away. However, in most situations they seem to be used interchangeably. Only in one circumstance is it necessary to adhere to the distinction. If in pointing out positions *there* is used twice, *He lives there, and I live there, da* must be the closer of the two. Pointing to places on a map which are progressively further away, someone might say, *'Ulrich wohnt hier, Dirk wohnt da, und ich wohne dort'.* Both *da* and *dort* can be combined with a part of *sein.* Again *da* is best used for something relatively close, and *dort* for something further away, but the distinction is not always made. *Da ist das Geschäft, das Sie suchen,* if it is close by, *Dort finden Sie das Geschäft,* when it is at some distance (possibly not visible). *Bis da und nicht weiter* means 'as far as that and no further'.

> *Er fährt jeden Tag nach Hannover, denn er wohnt hier und arbeitet da/dort.*
> *Sie schlug im Lexikon nach und fand da/dort die folgende Erklärung.*

Wo ist denn die Haltestelle? Da/Dort vor der Post.   Wer ist der Mann da/dort?
Wo ist das Buch? Da liegt es. Es liegt da auf dem Tisch or *Es liegt dort in der Ecke.*

Both form compounds with *hin* and *her.* **Dahin** and **dorthin** are interchangeable.
Dein Fahrrad steht im Schuppen—ich habe es dahin geschoben, weil es hier im Wege ist. In
talking of a town, someone might ask, '*Wie kommt man am schnellsten dorthin?*'
Daher and **dorther** are also interchangeable and are often combined with an
optional *von.* A. *Ich muß zur Post.* B. *Daher/Von daher komme ich gerade.* Or *Ich komme*
gerade dorther/von dorther. Vater war im Studierzimmer; von daher/dorther hörte man
laute Stimmen. **Von dort** is also used. *Ich komme gerade von dort.*

therefore, thus, hence, so *advs.* on that account *phr.* used as *adv.*

i. Four G. words have the same sense as **therefore, hence,** or **thus.** Of these
deshalb is probably the most frequently used, but **darum, daher,** and **deswegen**
are by no means uncommon. All four express a logical connection, result, or
explanation.

Die Straßen sind vereist. Du mußt deshalb langsam fahren.
Sie war krank; deshalb/deswegen konnte sie nicht zur Arbeit kommen.
Es hat vier Monate lang nicht geregnet. Daher/Deshalb muß das Wasser rationiert werden.
Das Kleid war zu lang. Darum/Deshalb hat sie es kürzen lassen.
Er hat gute Arbeit geleistet, aber darum/deshalb ist er noch kein Meister.

ii. Also expresses the same meaning as the words in i. While *deshalb* gives an
explanation or reason, *also* implies that the other person will understand and
accept what is said. It is thus like **so** in *She's ill—so she won't be here.* Both E. **so** and
G. *also* expect this explanation to be accepted without question. *Sie ist krank. Sie*
wird also nicht dabei sein.

Er hat nicht angerufen. Wir wissen also nicht, ob er kommt oder nicht.
Es ist schon spät, wir müssen also gehen.

thick, dense, fat *adjs.*

1. *Dick* = 'thick'.

i. Dick corresponds to **thick** when it means 'having a larger distance between its
two opposite surfaces than most other objects of the same kind'. *A thick slice of*
bread. A thick concrete wall. Thick material. Sie schnitt sich eine dicke Scheibe Brot ab. Eine
dicke Betonmauer. Der Stoff ist ziemlich dick. Ein dicker Ast. Das Papier ist zu dick.

ii. Thick and **dick** are applied to a layer of something such as paint, or to something not spread thinly like butter.

Er verlangte von seiner Mutter, daß sie ihm seine Schulbrote dick mit Wurst und Käse belegte.
Damit die Farbe auf diesem grellen Untergrund deckt, muß man sie besonders dick auftragen.

iii. Thick and **dick** are used when stating the width or distance between opposite
surfaces. *The branch that had broken was about four inches thick: Der abgebrochene Ast*
was ungefähr zehn Zentimeter dick. Die Pappe ist drei Millimeter dick. Die Schloßmauer ist
einen Meter dick.

2. *Dicht* = 'thick, dense'.

i. Thick also means 'growing or being grouped very closely together or in large
quantities or numbers'. *The trees were so thick that it was as dark as night on the forest*
floor. She had thick black hair. They were on the edge of a thick forest. Hence *Trees grew*
thickly on both sides of the river. The area is thickly populated. **Dense** is a syn. of **thick**
in this sense, but they are not always interchangeable. The equivalent of both is
dicht.

Die Bäume stehen so dicht, daß der Waldboden kein Licht bekommt.
Java ist der am dichtesten bevölkerte/besiedelte Teil Indonesiens.

In Städten ist der Verkehr dichter als auf dem Lande.
Beide Seiten des Flusses sind dicht bewaldet.
Eine dichte Menschenmenge jubelte den Siegern zu.   *Der Flieder war dicht mit Blüten besetzt.*
Nicht nur seine Beine sind dicht behaart, sondern auch Brust und Rücken.

ii. Like **thick** and **dense** dicht is applied to smoke, fog, or clouds which are difficult or impossible to see through. *Eine dichte Wolkendecke. Der Schnee fiel so dicht vom Himmel, daß man den Vordermann nicht mehr sah* refers to the way the snow falls; if the snow forms a layer ten centimetres thick on the ground, this is *eine zehn Zentimeter dicke Schneeschicht.*

> *Oft ist der Nebel so dicht, daß man die Häuser der gegenüberliegenden Straßenseite nicht mehr sieht.*
> *Gleich nach der Explosion begann dichter Rauch von dem Gebäude aufzusteigen.*

Although *dicht* is the usual word in senses 2. i and ii, **dick** is also found. *Dicke Rauchschwaden. Dick* in this sense also occurs in *dicker Verkehr* and *im dicksten Gewühl.* While these uses may not be incorrect, the non-native speaker is best advised to use *dicht,* which is never wrong.

3. The technical term *viscous,* applied to certain types of liquids, is **dickflüssig**. *Öl ist dickflüssig.* In everyday language **dick** is used, like **thick**, for liquids which are thicker than usual. *Eine dicke Soße/Suppe.*

> *Häufig gab es samstags in der Kaserne so eine dicke Brühe, daß der Löffel darin stehen blieb.*

4. Fat. *Fatty.*

i. Applied to people, parts of the body, or animals, **dick** is the normal equivalent of **fat**. *Sie will nicht dick werden. Ein dickes Schwein. Der Hund ist zu dick.* For people **fett** is stronger, meaning 'excessively fat'. *Ein fetter Mann. Er hat einen fetten Bauch.* For animals, *fett* means 'very fat'. *Ein fettes Schwein.* **Fleischig** means 'considerably fatter than normal' and suggests flabbiness. *Fleischige Arme/Waden.* **Feist** is stronger again and means 'grossly fat' or 'fat in an unpleasant or repulsive way', but it is now somewhat old-fashioned. It refers either to the whole body, *Ein feister Mensch watschelte an meinem Fenster vorbei,* or to parts of it, *Jmd. hat feiste Hände/ein feistes Gesicht.*

ii. In reference to food **fett** means 'containing a large amount of fat'. *Fettes Fleisch. Fettes Essen.* **Fettig** means 'extremely fatty', *ein fettiges Essen,* or 'covered with fat', *Die Hände sind mir ganz fettig.*

5. Other uses of **thick**.

i. *A* **thick** *accent* is *ein starker Akzent.*

ii. One transl of *Graduates are* **thick** *on the ground* is *Hochschulabsolventen gibt es in rauhen Mengen,* in large numbers.

iii. Thick meaning 'stupid' is *dumm* or *blöd.*

iv. *That's a bit* **thick!** meaning 'unfair or unreasonable' is *Das ist doch allerhand!* or *Das ist doch ein starkes Stück! Er will, daß wir jeden Tag Überstunden machen und auch samstags arbeiten. Das ist doch allerhand/ein starkes Stück!*

v. *Things happened* **thick** *and fast* could be *Die Ereignisse folgten dicht aufeinander.*

6. Other uses of *dick* and *dicht.*

i. With parts of the body, *dick* can mean 'swollen'. *Eine dicke Backe. Sein Fuß war infolge der Verstauchung so dick angeschwollen, daß er in keinen Schuh mehr paßte.*

ii. *Jmd. hat einen dicken Kopf* refers to a hangover.

iii. In *Sie sind dicke Freunde* and *Zwischen den beiden bestand eine dicke Freundschaft, dick* means 'close, intimate'. The normal word is *eng.* Cf. NEAR 4. i.

iv. *Dicht* also means 'impervious, impenetrable, not leaking'. *Das Rohr ist nicht ganz dicht.* Hence *undicht,* leaking.

thin, lean, sparse, meagre, scanty *adjs.*

1. Dünn expresses several senses of **thin**.

i. Both words describe things like paper, cloth, or a board which have relatively little extension between opposite surfaces.

Dünnes Papier. Ein dünnes Brett. Ein dünner Ast.   *Ein dünner Faden/Vorhang.*
Der Mantel ist zu dünn/aus zu dünnem Stoff für den Winter.   *Die Wand ist sehr dünn.*
Das Rohr ist zu groß. Es muß um einen Zentimeter dünner sein.

ii. Applied to a liquid both mean 'of slight consistency'. *Eine dünne Suppe. Zu dünne Soßen kann man mit Mehl eindicken. Du hast den Kaffee zu dünn gemacht* (= too watery, weak).

iii. Describing the way something is spread, both mean 'not thick'. *Man muß die Farbe dünn auftragen.*

iv. Both describe a voice which is high-pitched and not loud. *Eine dünne Stimme.*

2. Applied to people, animals, or a part of the body, both **dünn** and **thin** mean 'having little flesh'. *Sein Arm war so dünn, daß kein Uhrenarmband passen wollte. Dünne Beine.* Applied to people, *dünn* means 'not fat enough'. *Ein langer, dünner Junge. Infolge der Krankheit ist sie sehr dünn geworden.*

Alternatives. **Schlank**, 'slim', suggests well-proportioned, neither too fat nor too thin. *Eine schlanke Gestalt. Eine schlanke Taille.* **Mager** means 'having little flesh and fat on one's bones', hence 'lean', defined as 'wanting in flesh, not plump'. *Infolge der Erkrankung ist sie sehr mager.* **Hager** means 'bony, sinewy, and very tall', hence 'gaunt'. *Ein hagerer Mann. Jmds. hagere Gestalt.* **Dürr** is 'thin in an unattractive way', 'skinny'. *Ein langer, dürrer Kerl.*

Sie ißt wenig, um die schlanke Linie zu bewahren.   *Er ist schlank wie eine Tanne.*
Die häßlichen und mageren Kühe fraßen die sieben schönen, fetten Kühe.
Nach der langen Dürre waren viele Tiere mager und schwach.
Ein derber Khakianzug umhüllte eine lange, hagere Figur.
Unsere Vorräte nehmen ab, und die Gesichter werden allmählich hager.
Sie hatte die Krankheit zwar überwunden, war aber immer noch dürr wie ein Skelett.

3. Other senses of *mager*. **Mager** is 'lean' in the sense 'containing little or no fat'. *Mageres Fleisch. Magere Kost* can be low in fat, but *die magere Kost im Internat* means 'the frugal fare'. *Ein magerer Boden* is not very fertile. *Magere Jahre*, lean years.

4. In reference to smoke, vegetation, growth, and population, **thin** means 'not dense'. **Sparse** means 'small in number or amount', 'thinly scattered'. *A sparse population.* **Meagre** means 'very small in quantity or amount', 'only just enough'. *A meagre income/meal.* **Scanty** means 'smaller in size or amount than one thinks it should be'. *A scanty but enthusiastic audience. Scanty information/knowledge about a subject. A scanty crop/harvest.*

i. Dünn means 'consisting of individual parts placed at relatively large intervals', i.e. 'thin or sparse'. *Das Gebiet ist dünn besiedelt/bevölkert. Ich habe dünnes Haar. Die Insel ist nur dünn bewaldet. Ausländische Besucher sind dieses Jahr dünn gesät*, few and far between, there's only a sprinkling of them.

Je höher man steigt, desto dünner wird die Luft.   *Der Wald/Das Gras ist hier sehr dünn.*
Sonnentage waren in diesem Sommer dünn gesät.   *Der Hügel ist nur dünn bewachsen.*

ii. Spärlich is applied to vegetation and the growth of hair and implies a fairly meagre amount. *Spärliche Vegetation. Spärlicher Haarwuchs. In großer Höhe ist der Pflanzenwuchs spärlich.*

Wenn man den spärlichen Baumbestand noch weiter abholzt, wird man das schon trockene Gebiet in
    eine Wüste verwandeln.

iii. Spärlich is applied to other spheres in the sense 'not large in number or extent', 'meagre, poor, or scanty'. *Der Vortrag war nur spärlich besucht. Spärlicher*

Beifall. Der spärliche Lohn. Diese Tiere sind nur noch in spärlichen Resten vorhanden. Der Landstrich ist spärlich besiedelt. Ein spärlicher Ertrag. Eine spärliche Ausbeute. Die Ernte fiel nur spärlich aus. Sie waren spärlich bekleidet.

iv. Dürftig can refer to the effects of poverty and means 'poor, wretched, or miserable', *dürftige Kleidung, eine dürftige Unterkunft,* and in reference to food, 'meagre', *dürftige Nahrung, eine dürftige Mahlzeit.*

v. Dürftig and **mager** also describe something which is inadequate or insufficient in quality or quantity, i.e. meagre, scanty, thin, or, to use a stronger word, miserable. *Ein dürftiges Ergebnis,* a poor or thin one. Both are applied to something concrete. *Die mageren/dürftigen Erträge in der Landwirtschaft. Eine magere/dürftige Ausbeute.*

> *Trocken trug er die mageren Ergebnisse vor, die keinen beeindrucken konnten.*
> *Das Angebot an guten Fernsehsendungen ist im Sommer ziemlich mager.*
> *Den ganzen Tag streunte der Wolf durch die Wälder und brachte am Abend nur die magere Beute von zwei Hasen zum Bau.   Das Warenangebot in diesem Land ist äußerst dürftig.*
> *Bei deutschen Autos ist leider allzuoft die magere Ausstattung zu beklagen.*

5. Thin meaning 'not very convincing or having little to offer' is applied to something like an explanation or what someone has to say.

i. Dünn also has this sense. *Was er in der Prüfung geschrieben hat, war sehr dünn.*

> *Mit so dünnen Argumenten können Sie mich aber nicht überzeugen.*
> *Die Aussage des Romans ist sehr dünn.*

ii. Dürftig is applied to products of the mind which have little to say. *Der Vortrag war ziemlich dürftig.* **Mager** is a syn. *Der Aufsatz ist ein bißchen mager/dürftig,* a bit thin.

> *Verzweifelt suchte er sich mit dürftigen Argumenten zu verteidigen.*
> *Der Inspektor sagte ihm, daß er mit einem so dürftigen Alibi nicht durchkommen würde.*

thing *n.*

1. Thing = 'a physical object'.

i. Das Ding refers to a specific concrete object, *Ein Messer ist ein nützliches Ding,* and is used in a general way, *Man nennt die Dinge beim rechten Namen. Die tausend kleinen Dinge des täglichen Bedarfs.*

> *Er hob die seltsame Maschine vorsichtig auf—so ein Ding hatte er noch nie in Händen gehalten.*
> *Das müssen Sie schon von Hand machen. Ein Ding, das Ihnen diese Arbeit abnimmt, muß man erst noch erfinden.*
> *Die kleine Gruppe sah erwartungsvoll zum Himmel, um ja den Kometen nicht zu übersehen. 'Wer das Ding zuerst sieht, dem geb ich einen aus', rief Lutz ungeduldig.*

ii. In this sense *die Sache* is only used in the pl. **die Sachen** and thus resembles the use of *your things, my things,* etc. when this denotes possessions and belongings, particularly clothes, and articles which are used for an activity or ones which the situation makes clear. *Sachen* thus refers to implements, tools, clothes, what someone makes, things to eat, and much more. *Ein Kind, das aufhört zu spielen, räumt seine Sachen/die Spielsachen auf. Wer seine Hausaufgaben gemacht hat oder sich für die Schule fertig macht, packt seine Sachen zusammen. Ein Elektriker packt seine Sachen aus* or *zusammen. Bring' deine Badesachen mit!,* your swimming things (also *Badezeug*). *Die zweite Schublade rührst du nicht an—da sind nur persönliche Sachen drin.* In reference to a few letters or parcels, someone might say, *'Ich muß diese Sachen zur Post bringen'.* To find out where someone had put my things I might ask, *'Wo hast du meine Sachen hingelegt?'* Likewise *Ich habe meine Sachen am Bahnhof zurückgelassen.* A pianist might play only *alte, bekannte Sachen,* and what an architect designs might be all ultramodern, i.e. *hochmoderne Sachen.* Of the furniture in a house, someone might say, *'Sie haben schöne Sachen in ihrem Haus.'* For *I washed up the breakfast things, das Frühstücksgeschirr* is probably preferred, but *Ich muß diese Sachen abwaschen* is possible. *Hast du deine Sachen schon gepackt?* can refer to clothes, as do *Sie trägt immer* *auffällige Sachen, Er trägt die Sachen seines Bruders auf, Du mußt warme Sachen mit-nehmen*, and *Zieh' deine nassen Sachen aus! Sie hält ihre Sachen in Ordnung* could refer to clothes or to other belongings. *Es gab gute/leckere Sachen zum Essen* refers to food, as does *Ich habe sehr viele süße Sachen gegessen* (also *Süßigkeiten*). **Das Zeug** is a collective n. used colloquially as a syn. of *Sachen*. When neutral, it refers to tools or clothing. *Der Klempner holt sein Zeug. Er fror in dem dünnen Zeug. Das Arbeitszeug* can be either tools or clothes. It is also applied to several objects in a pejorative sense suggesting they are worthless and is translated as *stuff* or **things**. *Du könntest endlich dein Zeug aufräumen. Ist das dein Zeug hier? Nimm das Zeug da weg!*

iii. Thing is applied to a specific concrete object when the speaker wants to express contempt, dislike, irritation, or surprise. *Do you know how to drive this thing?* Only **das Ding** conveys such emotions. *Hast du denn überhaupt eine Ahnung, wie man so ein Ding fährt? Was willst du mit dem alten Ding?* The question is *Was ist denn das für ein Ding? Was kostet das Ding?* also expresses neg. feelings. The emotion can, however, be pleasant surprise. *Das Ding gefällt mir. Das Ding will ich haben.* A related sense is 'sth. which is striking in its goodness or badness'. *Ein großes/tolles/ verfluchtes Ding. What's that thing he's carrying?* would, if quite neutral, be *Was trägt er eigentlich in der Hand?* or *Was trägt er denn da? Was ist denn das für ein Ding, das er in der Hand trägt?* expresses surprise or another emotion.

> *Sie zeigte unschlüssig auf den Rasenmäher und erklärte, daß sie sich nicht vorstellen könnte, wie sie so ein Ding in Gang bringen sollte.*

The pl. in this sense is *Dinger* as well as *Dinge*. Of nails (*Nägel*) someone might say, '*Die Dinger taugen nichts. Das ist der sechste, der sich verbogen hat.*' *Diese paar Dinger kannst du mitmehmen. Wirf doch die alten Dinger weg!* (*Das ist ja ein Ding!* is used colloquially to express surprise or indignation. '*Das ist ja ein Ding!*' *rief er erstaunt, 'und keiner weiß, wie die Millionen verschwunden sind.*')

iv. The pl. *Dinge* and **Sachen** are both often possible, sometimes with the difference in implication explained in iii. *What are those things on the table?* could be *Was sind das denn für Sachen auf dem Tisch? Was sind das für Dinge?* would express surprise. Neutral are *Sie kauft gern schöne Dinge/Sachen* and *Ihr gehören diese Sachen/Dinge.*

2. Things also refers to the situation or the circumstances at a particular time, especially in relation to the way this situation or these circumstances are changing or affecting someone. *Things are going well. He takes things too seriously.* The equivalent is **die Dinge**, although certain expressions are translated by other words. *Die Dinge scheinen oft anders zu sein, als sie in Wirklichkeit sind. As things stand: So wie die Dinge liegen/stehen* or *nach Lage der Dinge. So wie es jetzt aussieht* is an alternative in everyday language. *How are things in the office?* becomes *Wie sieht es im Büro aus? I must think things over* can be *Ich muß mir die Sache überlegen.* Here *die Sache* has its primary meaning of 'matter'. Alternatives are *Ich muß mir alles überlegen* or *über die Lage nachdenken. I hope I haven't spoilt things* could be *Hoffentlich habe ich nicht alles verdorben.*

> *Die Dinge werden immer besser.*   *Die Dinge sehen immer besser aus.*
> *Du nimmst die Dinge viel zu ernst.*   *Man muß die Dinge nehmen, wie sie sind.*
> *Nach Lage der Dinge hatten sie keine Chance mehr, den Rückstand aufzuholen.*
> *So sind die Dinge nun einmal, und wir können sie nicht ändern.*
> *Du mußt die Dinge klar und in Zusammenhang sehen.*

3. *Er fragte mich nach mehreren Dingen* is colloquially *Er hat mich nach mehreren Sachen gefragt.* Both **Dinge** and **Sachen** mean 'matters', a sense **things** can also have. *Sie hatte vor der Reise noch mehrere Dinge zu erledigen.* Like **things**, *Dinge* tends to be vague in its reference, whereas *Sachen* suggests specific matters. *Wir haben über diese Sachen lange genug gesprochen. Verschone mich bitte mit solchen belanglosen Sachen!*

Also . . . *mit derlei Dingen.* For other meanings of *Sache* see BUSINESS 6, CAUSE *n.* 4, and
PLACE 7.

Das sind persönliche Dinge, die niemand[en] etwas angehen.

Sie sprachen über praktische Dinge.   In technischen Dingen weiß er Bescheid.

Wir haben Kaffee zusammen getrunken und sprachen über unsere Arbeit und andere Dinge (Sachen
more specific).   *Viele Dinge gingen ihm im Kopf herum.*

4. Things can also refer to actions and events. **Dinge** is in this sense quite neutral. *Der Lauf/Gang der Dinge* is 'the course of events', 'the way things are developing'. *Er kehrte unverrichteter Dinge zurück*, returned without having achieved
anything, or having done what he hoped to.

Er konnte sich nicht erklären, wie sich solche Dinge in seiner Firma zugetragen hatten.

Wir können nichts am Gang der Dinge ändern.

Wir müssen den Dingen ihren freien Lauf lassen.

Sie mischt sich immer in Dinge ein, die sie nicht angehen.

Sachen also refers to actions and is mostly slightly pejorative. *Was machst du denn
da für Sachen?* suggests things that are out of the ordinary, if not illegal, as does
the exclamation *Was sind das denn für Sachen! Sie machten alle neumodischen Sachen
mit* expresses a certain disapproval.

Ich hatte sie im Verdacht, irgendwelche schiefe/krumme Sachen zu machen.

Things = 'events' may be translated by **Ereignisse**. *Things were happening thick and
fast. Die Ereignisse überstürzten sich.*

5. *I've heard* **things** *about them* refers to facts or stories and usually suggests that
these are too nasty to describe in detail. **Einiges** in *Ich habe einiges über sie gehört* is
neutral, suggesting neither good nor bad. In *Ich habe Sachen/Dinge über sie gehört,*
both ns. mainly express surprise but need not imply anything bad. If something
unfavourable is meant, *Dinge* is worse than *Sachen*. Clearly bad are *schlimme Sachen*
and *Schlimmes. Er hat mir schlimme Sachen über die beiden erzählt.*

6. Only **Sachen** refers to things said or remarks. *Solche Sachen sagt man nicht!* or *So
etw. sagt man nicht.*

7. A person or animal is called a thing to emphasize the speaker's feelings
towards him/her/it. *She was trembling all over, the poor little* **thing**. *Das Ding* is used
for children, particularly for small girls. *Ein kleines/hübsches/lebhaftes/freches Ding. Sie
war ein niedliches, kleines Ding.* **Das Geschöpf**, 'creature', is stylistically higher. *You
lucky thing!* could be *Du Glücklicher!* or *Du Glückspilz!*

Sie zitterte am ganzen Körper, das arme Ding/das arme Geschöpf.

8. *Not + a thing* is used instead of *nothing* or *not + anything* to emphasize what is
said, *I haven't done a thing today*, and is translated by **nichts**. *Ich habe heute [gar] nichts
getan.* In *I just couldn't think of a single thing to say, not + a single thing* is a stronger form
of *nothing* and is translated by a strengthened form of *nichts. Mir fiel überhaupt/gar
nichts ein, was ich sagen könnte.* Also *absolut nichts* and colloquially *rein gar nichts.*

Sie haben [absolut/gar] nichts getan, um uns zu helfen.

Im Haus war gar nichts zu essen (there was not a thing to eat).

9. *Such a thing* is *so etwas* or *etwas Derartiges. So etwas ist völlig unmöglich. I said
no such thing/didn't say any such thing* is *So etwas habe ich nicht/nie gesagt*, or in more
formal style *Etwas Derartiges habe ich nie gesagt. Such a thing as* and *no such thing as*
are often used in statements about whether something exists or not. *Is there such
a thing as perfection?* The lit. transl. is *so etwas wie*, but these words are often best
omitted. *Gibt es [so etwas wie] die Vollkommenheit?*

10. Thing preceded by an adj. can be translated by *das* + adj. used as a n., or the
neuter of the adj. used as a n. *Das Bedauerliche ist, daß nur wenige dabei waren*, the

regrettable thing. *Er sagt ihr nur Gutes/Schlechtes nach*, says only good/bad things about her. *The good thing about it* is *das Gute daran/dabei*. Hence *Das Bemerkenswerte an diesem Ergebnis*. *Das erste, was sie tat, war, ihn anzurufen*, can be expressed as *Als erstes rief sie ihn an*. *What's the next thing to be done?* is *Was tun wir als Nächstes?* *I'll do that first thing tomorrow*: *Das mache ich morgen als erstes*. *One thing* is **eines**. *Eines muß ich dir noch sagen* (also *Eine Sache*). *Das eine* means lit. 'the one thing'. *Das eine blieb ungeklärt*. *Überlegen und Handeln sind zweierlei*, two different things.

> *Das Eigenartige an ihren Romanen ist, daß die Hauptgestalt immer ein Mann ist.*
> *Ein paar Wochen Urlaub im Gebirge wären das Beste für Sie.*
> *Sie wollte auf ihrem Gebiet Großes leisten.*   *Er scheint immer das Falsche zu sagen.*
> *Das eine möchte ich noch wissen.* (There's one thing I'd still like to know.)

In some cases **thing** is not translated. *It's a good thing you said that* is *Gut, daß du mir das gesagt hast*. *That was not a kind thing to say*: *Was Sie gesagt haben, war nicht sehr freundlich*. *The proper thing to do is to apologize*: *Eine Entschuldigung wäre jetzt angebracht*. *The thing to do in this case is to cancel the cheque*: *Was du jetzt tun mußt, ist, den Scheck sperren zu lassen*. An adj. + **thing** referring to an occurrence, as in *A terrible thing happened to me*, is usually expressed by *etwas* + adj. *Etwas Schreckliches/ Ungewöhnliches ist mir geschehen*, although *eine schreckliche Sache* is possible. An adj. + **thing** referring to a concrete object can be translated either by *Ding* or *etwas*. *Wo bekommt man so ein ausgefallenes Ding in einer Kleinstadt wie Duderstadt?* could be . . . *etwas so Ausgefallenes*.

11. Other uses of **thing**.

i. *There's **another thing** I'd like to discuss*: *Ich möchte etwas anderes* (= 'sth. different') *besprechen* or *Ich möchte noch etwas* (= 'sth. additional') *besprechen*. Also *Es gibt noch eine Sache, die ich besprechen möchte*.

ii. *She sobbed all night, **a thing** [that] she rarely does* is *Sie hat die ganze Nacht hindurch geweint, [etwas], was sie nur selten tut*. *Etw.* is optional. **The thing** *[that] I like about the plan is its simplicity*: *Was mir an dem Plan gefällt, ist seine Einfachheit*.

iii. *When you are young you dream of all sorts of **things*** can be *Man träumt über alles mögliche/allerlei/alle möglichen Sachen*.

iv. *The unfortunate **thing** is that I'm going away tomorrow* can be *Leider fahre ich übermorgen weg*.

v. The thing is introduces an explanation, objection, or opinion relating to something just said. *Thursday doesn't suit me. The thing is I've already arranged sth. else*. *Weil* can express the meaning. *Donnerstag paßt mir nicht, weil ich eine andere Verabredung habe*. An alternative is *nämlich* in the second main clause. *Donnerstag paßt mit nicht. Ich habe nämlich eine andere Verabredung*.

vi. *The done **thing*** can be translated by *üblich*, usual, customary. *Damals war es üblich, mit den Fingern zu essen*.

vii. *It's **one thing** to know the theory, but another to apply it to a particular case*. In speech: *Es ist eine Sache, einen Computer zu benutzen, aber eine andere zu verstehen, wie er funktioniert*. In the written language: *Es ist eines, die Theorie zu verstehen, aber ein anderes, sie in einem bestimmten Fall anzuwenden*.

viii. *I prefer badminton to squash—**for one thing**, it's less strenuous, and then it's also. . .* can be *erstens . . . zweitens*, or *zum einen . . . zum anderen. Ich komme nicht mit—zum einen/erstens habe ich kein Geld, zum anderen/zweitens habe ich zu viel zu tun*.

think *v.*

1. The basic meaning of **denken** is 'to use one's ability to reason, form judgements, consider issues, etc.' It is used alone, or with an adv. stating how someone thinks, and states what someone is thinking. *Ein Ereignis/Buch*, etc. *gibt jmdm. zu* *denken*, it makes someone think. *Sie denkt logisch. Ich saß da und dachte, wie lächerlich das Ganze war. 'Wie läßt sich das vermeiden?' dachte er.*

Erst denken, dann handeln!   *Können Tiere denken?*

Ich bin so müde, daß ich nicht mehr klar denken kann.   *Seine Worte gaben mir zu denken.*

Jmd. denkt schnell/nüchtern/praktisch/gründlich/scharf/konservativ/liberal, etc.

Sie denken sehr kleinlich/großherzig—das spiegelt sich in allen ihren Urteilen wieder.

Er denkt wie ein Naturwissenschaftler/Geschäftsmann.

Vor zwanzig Jahren hätte kein Student so gedacht.

2. Think = 'to be of the opinion'. *I think you should go.* If I think that something is so or will happen, I have the impression that this is likely to be the case without being sure. *I think she is right. I think Smith will win.*

i. The vs. **glauben**, **meinen**, and **denken** as well as **der Meinung/Ansicht sein** express these senses. The three vs. are used with *was* as obj. or with a clause. *Was glaubst/denkst/meinst du? Ich glaube/denke/meine, daß sie recht hat. Denken* is used with *über* and *von*, and *meinen* with *zu*. *Glauben* is not used with a prep. corresponding to *about*. *Was meinst du dazu? Was denkst du davon/darüber?* Also *Wie denken Sie darüber?* Cf. 10 for other uses and CONSIDER 1.

Ich glaube/meine/denke, du solltest an der Sitzung teilnehmen/ . . . daß Schmidt gewinnen wird.

Glaubst/Denkst/Meinst du, daß es regnen wird? Ich denke/glaube schon.

Ich glaube/denke/meine, daß eine Fahrradtour jetzt gerade das Richtige wäre.

Wir meinen, daß wir im Recht sind.   *Meinst du, du könntest was ändern?*

Es wird am besten sein, wenn wir früh losfahren, glaubst/meinst du nicht?

Ich glaube, die Entfernung beträgt ungefähr sechzig Kilometer. Or Die Entfernung beträgt, glaube
   ich, sechzig Kilometer.   *Wer hätte je gedacht, daß er Mönch werden würde?*

Seine Aufgabe war es, mich zu schützen—so dachte ich wenigstens.

Ich bin der Meinung/der Ansicht, daß alles in bester Ordnung ist. Wir brauchen uns nicht zu beun-
   ruhigen.

ii. When I realize that something I thought correct is wrong, or have doubts about what I think I heard etc., I express this by the past of **denken** or **glauben** + the past or pluperfect subjunctive. *Ich dachte, du wärst verreist* (but obviously you are not). *Ich dachte/glaubte, ich hätte Schritte gehört, aber es war nur ein Vogel draußen.*

Ich glaubte, ich hätte Stimmen gehört, aber ich muß mich getäuscht haben.

Sie dachte zuerst, sie hätte sich verrechnet, aber das Ergebnis stellte sich doch als richtig heraus.

iii. The E. acc. and infin. construction, as in *I think Smith to be the best candidate* and *I think this point to be the most important one*, cannot be translated word for word. If *glauben/denken/meinen* are used, the infin. must be turned into a clause: *Ich glaube/meine, daß Schmidt der beste Kandidat ist. Ich denke/glaube, daß dieser Punkt der wichtigste ist.* **Think**, used in the act. with acc. and infin. or in the pass. with *to be*, as in *The conservatives thought him to be a dangerous radical* or *He was thought to be a dangerous radical*, is often best translated by **halten für** or **betrachten als**. Cf. CONSIDER 8. *Die Konservativen hielten ihn für einen gefährlichen Radikalen. Er wurde für einen gefährlichen Radikalen gehalten* or *Man hielt ihn für eine gefährlichen Radikalen. Halten* and *betrachten* are also often the best transl. of **think** when it is used without *to be*, as in *I think Smith the best candidate* or *I think this an interesting question.* They also translate *to think of s.o. as sth.*, as in *She thought of him as a good friend*, and **think** in sents. like *I think you are brave* or *I think that [is] likely. Sie hielt ihn für einen guten Freund. Ich halte dich für sehr tapfer. Das halte ich für wahrscheinlich.*

Ich halte Schmidt für den besten Kandidaten. Ich betrachte diesen Punkt als den wichtigsten.

Das halte ich für eine sehr interessante Frage.

iv. **Glauben** and **meinen** can be used with an infin., but only when the subj. and the (unexpressed) person carrying out the action of the infin. are identical. *Ich* *meinte, mich verhört zu haben.* This construction has to be translated into E. by a clause. *Ich glaubte, einen Schrei gehört zu haben,* I thought I heard a cry.

3. Sich denken means 'to form an idea or picture of sth. in one's mind' and is used when **think [of]** means 'to IMAGINE' or 'to picture to oneself'. It is translated as **think of** or *imagine* depending on the context. *Ich kann mir keinen Grund denken, warum sie hingefahren sind,* I can't think of/imagine any reason. *Denk' dir mal, was sich uns da für eine Gelegenheit bietet!,* just think. (Or *Stell' dir vor.*) Cf. IMAGINE 1.

> *Ich kann mir denken, daß alles reibungslos verlaufen ist. Man hat es nämlich so gründlich vorbereitet.*
> *Ich denke ihn mir als einen alten und sehr weisen Mann.*
> *Ich kann mir denken, daß sie sich die Stadt ansehen wollen.*
> *Ich kann mir nicht denken, wie ich ihn dazu bringen kann, seine Zustimmung zu geben.*

4. *Denken an* expresses some, but not all, senses of **think of**.

i. Denken an and **think of** mean 'to direct one's thoughts towards'. *Ich dachte gerade an meine Großmutter. Woran denkst du?* (If more intense reflection is suggested, for which E. is likely to use *think about, nachdenken über* is used. *Worüber denkst du nach?* Cf. 8.) *An die Folgen hat sie gar nicht gedacht. Ich denke oft an die alten Freunde/an meine Kindheit.*

ii. Denken an means 'to think of' in the sense 'to consider people's interests, needs, etc.' *Sie denkt immer an ihre Familie.* Hence *Er denkt nur an sich selbst. Ich muß an meine eigene Zukunft denken.*

iii. Denken an is used for thinking of a particular instance or example. *Ich denke insbesondere an Lehrer. Denken Sie an Ägypten! Sie denkt an das Gesetz, das die Ehescheidung regelt.*

iv. *Denken an* does not translate *to think of sth.* when it means that something [readily] occurs to someone. For such contexts **einfallen,** 'to OCCUR', can be used. *I can think of two examples of the government's stupidity: Mir fallen sofort zwei Beispiele ein, die die Dummheit der Regierung zeigen. If you think of anything else becomes Wenn euch etw. anderes einfällt, sagt mir Bescheid. I can't think of the name is either Der Name fällt mir nicht ein or Ich komme nicht auf den Namen.*

v. Think of means 'to conceive the idea of sth. new'. **Denken an** + n. means 'to hit upon sth. new' only in a few contexts in which it cannot have sense 5 or mean 'to REMEMBER'. *An diese Möglichkeit haben wir nicht gedacht.* An alternative is **auf etw. kommen,** or **auf den Gedanken/die Idee kommen,** [*etw. zu tun*], to get the idea of [doing] sth. *I could kick myself for not having thought of it before could be Ich könnte mich ins Bein beißen, weil ich bisher nicht darauf gekommen bin. Also . . . weil ich bisher nicht auf den Gedanken/die Idee gekommen bin, [das zu machen].*

> *Er fand die Lösung, die viele gesucht hatten, auf die aber bisher niemand gekommen war/an die aber niemand gedacht hatte.*

The main equivalent of **think of** meaning 'to work or think out, devise' in everyday language is **sich** (dat.) **ausdenken. Ersinnen** is a formal syn.

> *Er dachte [sich] einen Plan/eine Antwort/eine Ausrede/einen Scherz aus.*
> *Sie hatte sich rasch ein paar Witze ausgedacht.*
> *Da dachte er eine List aus und bestrich den Boden mit Pech.* (Märchen)
> *Er hatte eine Ausrede/einen Vorwand ersonnen, um eine peinliche Szene zu vermeiden.*
> *Sie ersann einen Plan/ein neues System/etw. Lustiges/etw. Nützliches.*

vi. Idioms. *Daran ist gar nicht zu denken,* it is out of the question. *Ich denke [gar] nicht daran hinzugehen,* I have no intention of going. *Sie dachte nicht daran, dieses Angebot anzunehmen.*

5. Think about buying sth. means 'to debate with oneself whether to buy it'. **Think of** buying sth. can be a syn., but it may suggest an almost formed intention to buy. *We think we'll buy it* implies an at least half-formed intention. **Sich über-legen** and **nachdenken**, which can only take an *ob*-clause, mean 'to turn sth. over in one's mind'. *Ich überlege mir, ob ich eine Wohnung kaufen soll*, I've been thinking about/of buying a flat. *Ich denke darüber nach, ob ich Sportreporter werden soll.* **Denken daran** + infin. suggests serious consideration of something as a possibility. *Sie denken daran, sich ein Haus zu kaufen. Wir denken daran, im Sommer nach Italien zu fahren. Ich dachte daran, Sportreporter zu werden.* The half-formed intention in *I think I'll go for a swim* is expressed by **glauben**. *Ich glaube, ich gehe schwimmen/baden.* **Ich denke** + infin. expresses an intention and suggests that it will be carried out. *Wir denken, im Herbst nach Neuseeland zu fliegen.* In one sense **gedenken** also means 'to intend', but it is now a fairly elevated word which is appropriate only in serious contexts. *Ich gedenke, meine Stellung aufzugeben. Was gedenken Sie zu unternehmen?*

6. I think + clause is used as a polite way of suggesting something. *I think we ought to go.* **Ich denke** and **ich glaube** have this function. *Ich denke, wir sollten gehen* or *Es ist, glaube ich, Zeit, daß wir gehen.* A suggestion relating to the future is made even more polite and tentative by the subjunctive. *Ich dachte, wir könnten morgen schwimmen gehen.* Both are used to correct someone politely, as *I think* can be. *Ich denke, Sie meinen das 18., nicht das 19. Jahrhundert.* A polite refusal like *Thank you, I don't think I will [have any more]* could be *Vielen Dank, ich möchte nichts mehr.*

Ich denke, Sie werden herausfinden, daß die Zahlen, die ich genannt habe, richtig sind.

Das wäre, glaube/denke ich, der geeignete Zeitpunkt, die Sitzung zu schließen.

7. Think is used in questions to express anger or make a protest. *What do you think you're doing?* could be **Was fällt dir ein?** or **Was soll das?** The first could also translate *Who do you think you are?* **Hindenken** is used in the question *Wo denkst du nur bloß hin?* as a protest against an impossible suggestion or a mistaken idea, and is like *What[ever] are you thinking of?* or *What an idea!*

A. *Hast du das Buch gestern gelesen?* B. *Wo denkst du bloß hin? An einem Tag kann ich unmöglich 500 Seiten schaffen.*

8. Think about = 'to reflect on' or 'to make a mental effort to consider'. The equivalents are **nachdenken** and **überlegen**, discussed under CONSIDER 1. These vs. must be used when **think** and **think about** mean 'to reflect on'. *Wir müssen darüber nachdenken, wie wir ein besseres Produkt auf den Markt bringen können,* think about how . . . *She thought for a moment* is *Sie dachte einen Augenblick nach* or *uberlegte einen Augenblick. Lassen Sie mich einen Augenblick nachdenken/überlegen!* (In *Einen Augenblick lang dachte er, daß* . . . the v. means that he was of a certain opinion or under a certain impression. *Was denkst du [darüber]?* asks for an opinion.) *I'm try-ing to think what other companies I could try* is *Ich überlege mir, an welche Firmen ich mich noch wenden kann.* (Also *nachdenken.*) These vs. also translate *to think twice* or *to think again* about something. *Man muß es sich genau/gut überlegen, bevor man vierzig Mark für ein Buch ausgibt. Er wird es sich wohl nochmal überlegen, wenn er erfährt, wieviel es kostet.*

9. Various E. expressions.

i. Think *a lot of s.o.* is *viel von jmdm. halten* or *eine hohe Meinung von jmdm. haben.* Cf. OPINION 1. ii. *I don't think much of that film*: *Von dem Film halte ich nicht viel. Was halten Sie davon/von jmdm.?* is used to ask someone's estimation of something or a person.

ii. Think *the best of s.o.* is *das Beste von jmdm. denken.* Hence *das Schlimmste/nur Schlimmes von jmdm. denken.*

iii. Think *better of sth.*: *Sich eines Besseren besinnen. Der Fahrer leugnete zunächst hart-näckig, den Unfall verschuldet zu haben; dann aber besann er sich eines Besseren und gab seine Schuld zu.*

iv. Think *nothing of doing sth.* is translated by *jmdm. nichts ausmachen*, not to matter to someone. *Es machte uns nichts aus, sechs Kilometer zu Fuß zu gehen, bloß um einen Brief einzuwerfen*, we would think nothing of walking . . .

v. Think is used to make a comment on something one has done in the past. *To think that I trusted him!: Wenn ich mir nur vorstelle/nur daran denke, daß ich ihm traute! When I think how he behaved then . . . : Wenn ich bedenke/daran denke, wie er sich damals benahm, verstehe ich, warum du jetzt so mißtrauisch bist.*

10. Transl. of E. constructions containing **think**.

i. For relative clauses which include an interpolated *I think/thought, it was thought*, etc. G. uses a different construction from E. *This is the picture which I think deserves the first prize* becomes *Dies ist das Bild, von dem ich glaube, daß es den ersten Preis verdient. The climbers, who it was thought had been killed in an avalanche, had taken refuge in a hut: Die Bergsteiger, von denen man glaubte/dachte, daß sie in einer Lawine ums Leben gekommen wären, hatten tatsächlich Zuflucht in einer Berghütte gefunden.* Alternatively, the interpolated v. can be put in a *wie*-clause. *Die Maßnahmen, die, wie man glaubte/meinte, die Wirtschaft ankurbeln würden, erwiesen sich als wirkungslos.* Or *Die Maßnahmen, von denen man glaubte/meinte, daß sie die Wirtschaft ankurbeln würden, erwiesen sich als wirkungslos.*

ii. *Do you think* is also interpolated into a question, as in *Who do you think I met?* or *What do you think it will cost?* There are two G. equivalents. When an opinion or an estimate is requested, the construction is as in E. *Was, glaubst du, wird das kosten? Wer/Welche Partei, glaubst du, wird gewinnen?* When the interpolated *do you think* expresses surprise or asks someone to guess something when the speaker knows the answer, *Was glaubst/meinst du* followed by the question in the word order of a subordinate clause is used. *Was meinst du, wen ich heute getroffen habe?* The second question can begin with *was. Was glaubst du, was er gesagt hat?* In speech the distinction between the constructions is not always made, and *was glaubst du . . .* is used in all circumstances.

> *Was glaubst/meinst du, wo ich gewesen bin?*
> *Was glaubst du, wieviel es gekostet hat?*

iii. The pass. of **think** with a person/thing as subj. + infin., as in *They were thought to be lost*, or *it is/was* **thought** + a clause, e.g. *It was thought that they were lost*, can be translated by *man glaubt* or *es wird/wurde geglaubt*. Both E. sents. become either *Man glaubte* or *Es wurde geglaubt, daß sie verloren wären. They are thought to be staying in the south of France* becomes *Man glaubt, daß sie sich in Südfrankreich aufhalten.* If the person/thing is to be stressed, the following variant can be used: *Von Käubler wurde geglaubt/glaubte man, daß er Geld gefälscht hätte. The ship was thought to have sunk* becomes *Von dem Schiff wurde geglaubt/glaubte man, daß es gesunken sei.*

thought *n.*

1. Thought meaning a 'single idea that occupies the mind' is **der Gedanke**. Cf. IDEA 1. ii. *Ein neuer/kluger/vernünftiger/ernster/kritischer/gefährlicher Gedanke. Ein Gedanke ging mir durch den Kopf. Ein Gedanke* can be important or trivial. Like **thought**, it is applied to someone's immediate reaction. *Was war Ihr erster Gedanke, als Sie die Nachricht hörten?* In expressions like *der rettende/erlösende Gedanke* or *ein guter Gedanke*, it is a syn. of *der Einfall*, a sudden idea which changes a situation, discussed in 2. *Gedanke* can imply an intention or plan, as can **thought**. *Als ich das hörte, war mein einziger Gedanke, möglichst schnell wegzukommen. I had vague thoughts of changing my job* could be *Ich spielte mit dem Gedanken, meine Stelle zu wechseln*, or *Ich trug mich mit dem Gedanken, meine Stelle zu wechseln*, which suggests more serious consideration. *Sie tauschten ihre Gedanken über das Buch/ihre Arbeit aus*, exhanged ideas, views. *Ein Gedankenaustausch* is 'an exchange of ideas'.

Der Gedanke, daß ich wieder hingehen müßte, war mir unerträglich.
Ich würde Ihnen raten, diesen Gedanken weiter zu verfolgen/zu Ende zu denken.
Der Gedanke der Toleranz entwickelte sich stark im 18. Jahrhundert.

The pl. **die Gedanken** refers to the ideas in or what occupies a person's mind. This concept is expressed in E. by both the sing. and pl. of **thought**. The E. sing. must be translated by the G. pl. Thus *They walked back in silence, each deep in thought/deep in their own thoughts* both become *Sie gingen schweigend zurück, in Gedanken versunken/vertieft/verloren.* (Or *jeder in seinen eigenen Gedanken versunken/vertieft.*) A not very common alternative is *Sie waren ins Nachdenken versunken.* Cf. 3.

Mehrere Schüler waren mit ihren Gedanken weit weg/nicht bei der Sache.
Meine Gedanken schweiften immer wieder ab.   *Sie war oft in seinen Gedanken.*

2. Der Einfall is a thought or idea which occurs suddenly and brings about a turn in events, offers a solution, or overcomes a difficulty, etc., or gives rise to an amusing remark or to a plan or intention of no great moment. *Sie hatte den [plötzlichen] Einfall/Ihr kam der Einfall, übers Wochenende zu verreisen.*

Schon sah ich mich niedergetrampelt, als ich in letzter Menschennot den rettenden Einfall bekam.
Aus einem plötzlichen Einfall heraus rief er seine Freundin an und erzählte ihr, was passiert war.
Alle lachten über diesen witzigen/lustigen/skurrilen (droll, comical)/*merkwürdigen Einfall.*

3. Thought also means 'the action of thinking carefully about sth., especially deeply and with concentration'. *After some thought I decided to accept.* The equivalent is **das Nachdenken** or **die Überlegung**. *Wir brauchen eine Pause zum Nachdenken/eine Nachdenkpause. Er scheint immer ohne Überlegung zu handeln. Nach einiger Überlegung entschloß ich mich, das Angebot anzunehmen. Nach nochmaliger Überlegung,* 'on second thoughts', is used when the conclusion follows the thinking. *Nach nochmaliger Überlegung beschloß sie, zu Hause zu bleiben. Bei nochmaliger Überlegung* suggests that the conclusion and the thinking take place together. *Bei nochmaliger Überlegung fiel mir ein, daß wir einen wichtigen Faktor übersehen hatten.*

Nach viel/reiflicher Überlegung habe ich mich entschlossen, nun doch mitzufahren.
Dieser Vorschlag scheint mir der Überlegung wert zu sein.
Er suchte durch angestrengtes Nachdenken eine Lösung für die aufgetretenen Schwierigkeiten.

4. Eine Überlegung also denotes what emerges as a result of thinking and thus means 'a thought or reflection'. It is usually in the pl. and implies a series of thoughts, often ones leading to a decision. *Dieses Ereignis war der Ausgangspunkt für seine Überlegungen.*

Die Überlegungen, die sie zu diesem Thema angestellt hat, finde ich sehr interessant.
Es gibt ein paar andere Punkte, die du in deine Überlegungen einbeziehen solltest.

5. Das Denken corresponds to **thought** in two senses.
i. It means 'a pers.'s way of thinking' or 'thought or thinking of a particular kind'. *Sie ist langsam im Denken. Sein Denken ist unstrukturiert/wirr.*

Logisches/Abstraktes Denken kennzeichnet seine Werke.

ii. The second sense is 'the group of ideas or the way of thinking which belongs to a particular religion, philosopher, political party, period of history, academic subject, etc.'

Das Denken des Mittelalters unterscheidet sich stark von dem späterer Jahrhunderte.
Das naturwissenschaftliche Denken beeinflußt viele Bereiche unseres Lebens.

6. Some E. expressions are best translated by a v. *He gave our predicament some* **thought**: *Er dachte eine Zeitlang über unsere mißliche Lage nach. They gave* **no thought** whatsoever to the subject: *Über das Thema haben sie überhaupt nicht nachgedacht. The*

thought *never crossed my mind* could be *An so etw. habe ich nie gedacht* or *Ein solcher Gedanke ist/wäre mir nie in den Sinn gekommen.* Someone might say, 'That was a very kind thought' when acknowledging a considerate action. A similar expression is *Das war sehr rücksichtsvoll [von Ihnen].* Cf. THOUGHTFUL 3.

thoughtful, considered, contemplative, considerate *adjs.*

1. If people are thoughtful, they are quiet and serious because they are thinking about something. *He looked thoughtful for a moment.* **Thoughtful** is also applied to moods, *That put us in a thoughtful mood,* and, as an adv., can describe actions, *She looked at him thoughtfully.* In relation to people **thoughtful** refers not only to temporary thought, but also to a permanent state of mind which is disposed to think about matters, i.e. is reflective or contemplative. *She is a thoughtful person who enjoys analysing what she reads and hears.*

i. The usual equivalent of E. senses just defined is **nachdenklich**, which can denote either a temporary or a permanent state and is applied to people, the way they look, what they say, and to moods.

> Du siehst heute so nachdenklich aus. Ist etw. geschehen?   Er/Sie ist ein nachdenklicher Mensch.
> Sie machte ein nachdenkliches Gesicht/setzte eine nachdenkliche Miene auf/saß nachdenklich
> da/antwortete nachdenklich.   Diese Worte stimmten uns nachdenklich.
> Der Vorfall machte uns nachdenklich/versetzte uns in eine nachdenkliche Stimmung.
> Sie ist eine nachdenkliche Frau, die gern analysiert, was sie liest und hört.

ii. Related words. **Beschaulich**, which denotes a permanent state, means 'contemplative' and can suggest introspection. *Ein beschaulicher Mensch. Sie ist eine beschauliche Natur.* **Besinnlich** also means 'thoughtful' as a characteristic, i.e. 'given to deep thought' or 'contemplative'. *Dieser Autor schreibt nur für besinnliche Leser.* It is also used for something which gives rise to contemplation, *eine besinnliche Erzählung,* and to time in which people feel contemplative. *Besinnliche Stunden. Es war ein besinnlicher Abend, weil er das Ende unserer Studienzeit bedeutete.* **Gedankenvoll** is a syn. of *nachdenklich* when a temporary state is meant, but it is now literary. It describes people or their actions and appearance. *Der Jüngling ging gedankenvoll nach Hause* (Schiller). **Besonnen** means 'calm and level-headed'. *Durch ihr besonnenes Verhalten hat sie Schlimmeres verhütet.* **[Wohl/Gut] überlegt**, '[well] considered', is used for actions, judgements, plans, etc. *Eine überlegte Handlung. Jmd. handelt überlegt. Ein wohl überlegter Plan/Einwand.*

> Er saß gedankenvoll am Schreibtisch und überlegte, wie er die Aufgabe lösen sollte
> Auch in gefährlichen Situationen bleibt er immer ruhig und besonnen.
> Sie ist äußerst besonnen und macht nie etw. Unüberlegtes.
> Das ist ein überlegtes Urteil, das sehr überzeugend wirkt.

2. Things written are described as thoughtful if they have been well thought out and are characterized by reflection or original thought. **Gedankenreich** means 'displaying an abundance of ideas' and can be applied to people as well as to products of their minds. *Seine gedankenreiche Rede hat alle sehr beeindruckt.* An alternative in some cases is **gut durchdacht**, well thought out or considered. *Ein gut durchdachter Einwand.*

> Seine Aufsätze sind immer gedankenreich/gut durchdacht.

3. A thoughtful or considerate person remembers what others want, need, or feel, and tries not to upset them. *That is very thoughtful of you. I thanked him for his thoughtful gesture.* **Rücksichtsvoll** means 'considerate' and thus expresses this sense of **thoughtful**. Related are **zuvorkommend**, which suggests that someone is kind and helpful and does small favours for others and is often translated as *obliging,* and **aufmerksam**, which, in this sense, means 'attentive to others' needs or wishes'.

Das war sehr rücksichtsvoll von Ihnen.   *Sie ist eine sehr aufmerksame Gastgeberin.*

Ich dankte ihm für die zuvorkommende Art und Weise, in der er mir geholfen hat.

threaten, menace *vs.* The three vs. translated as **threaten**, *drohen, bedrohen,* and *androhen,* differ syntactically and partly in meaning.

1. i. Threaten means 'to proclaim that one is going to do sth., usually unpleasant, if the pers. addressed does not comply with demands or do what is expected, etc.' It can imply an attempt to intimidate others. *He threatened me with dismissal. He threatened to sack me.* The equivalent is **drohen**, which can take a dat. and a phr. with *mit,* or an infin. *Er drohte mir mit Entlassung. Er drohte, mich zu entlassen.* Of the three vs. only *drohen* is used with an infin. Cf. 2. i and 3.

Die Geschäftsleitung drohte den Streikenden mit der Aussperrung.

Der Minister drohte mit seinem Rücktritt/ . . . drohte zurückzutreten.

Er drohte [mir], mich niederzuschlagen.   *'Ich werde es dir heimzahlen', drohte er.*

ii. If someone or something threatens to do something undesirable or to have an unfavourable result, this seems likely to happen. *The riots threatened to get out of hand.* **Drohen** in this context is used with an infin.

Die Krawalle drohten, in einen blutigen Aufstand auszuarten/ . . . außer Kontrolle zu geraten.

Das Haus war so vernachlässigt, daß das Dach einzustürzen drohte.

Nach dem Gewaltmarsch drohten viele Soldaten, vor Erschöpfung zusammenzubrechen.

iii. If something unpleasant threatens, or threatens someone or something (e.g. a place), it seems likely that this will happen. **Drohen** is used either alone, *Eine Überschwemmung droht,* or with a dat., *Eine Überschwemmung droht der Stadt* or *Ihm drohen üble Folgen.* Cf. 2. ii. Senses ii and iii of *drohen* differ only syntactically—ii has an infin., and iii can have a dat.

Dem kleinen Land droht eine Wirtschaftskrise, wenn der Kupferpreis demnächst nicht steigt.

Das gleiche Schicksal drohte den Bewohnern anderer Städte.

Von dorther droht [euch] keine Gefahr.

iv. Drohend means 'threatening' in all senses of *drohen:* (i) *Drohende Worte. Eine drohende Gebärde* (ii and iii). *Der drohende Zusammenbruch/Konkurs. Eine drohende Krise. Eine drohende Gefahr.*

2. If one person threatens someone, it is likely that the latter will be harmed or destroyed. *He threatened me with a gun.* **Menace** means 'to make a show of intention to harm', 'to make threatening gestures against'. *They were menaced by a soldier with a sub-machine gun.* An animal is sometimes the subj.

i. With a person as subj. **bedrohen** means that one person threatens another with violence. It suggests that there is danger to life and limb and translates **menace** as well as **threaten**. It needs an obj., but is not used with an infin. A *mit*-phr. states the weapon with which the person is threatened. *Er bedrohte mich mit einem Messer.* When the result, should the threat be carried out, is stated, the v. used is **drohen**. *Er drohte, sie zu erschießen* or *Er drohte ihnen mit der Erschießung,* but *Er bedrohte sie mit einem Gewehr.*

Mit erhobenen Händen bedrohte er uns.   *Er bedrohte mich mit einer Axt/einer Waffe.*

Die Geiselnehmer drohten den Geiseln mit dem Tod/ . . . bedrohten sie mit ihren Maschinenpistolen.

Das Kind wurde von einem großen Schäferhund bedroht.

ii. Threaten is also applied to an event, condition, etc. which indicates that something dire or disturbing is about to or likely to happen. *Famine threatens the town. The war threatened the peace of the whole region.* **Menace** means 'imperil, pose a threat to'. *These devastating weapons menace the whole world.* With a non-personal subj. **bedrohen** means 'to be a grave danger for or to endanger'. **Drohen** + dat. in sense 1. iii is possible in such sents., but it suggests a less grave danger. *Eine Über-schwemmung bedroht die Stadt* suggests a greater danger than *Eine Überschwemmung droht [der Stadt]*. The past part. *bedroht* translates **threatened** = 'in danger [of sth.]' in contexts like *She felt threatened* or *These animals are threatened with extinction. Aus unerklärlichen Gründen fühlten sie sich ständig bedroht. Viele Tierarten sind vom Aussterben bedroht.*

> *Der Damm war gebrochen, und die Wassermassen bedrohten die im Unterlauf gelegenen Siedlungen.*
> *Das steigende Wasser bedrohte viele Dörfer.   Sein Leben ist bedroht.*
> *Eine Hungersnot drohte dem Land/bedrohte das Land.*
> *Diese äußerst zerstörerischen Waffen bedrohen jeden Teil der Welt.*
> *Die Seuche bedrohte die Bevölkerung dieses Landstrichs.*
> *Die Flammen bedrohten das Nachbarhaus.*
> *Der Krieg bedrohte den Frieden des ganzen Gebiets.*

3. Androhen has the same sense as *drohen* in 1. i but differs syntactically. *Der Chef drohte dem Arbeiter mit der Entlassung* can be expressed as *Der Chef drohte dem Arbeiter die Entlassung an. Androhen* always needs an obj. but may be used without a dat. *Sie drohten Vergeltungsmaßnahmen an. Die [uns] angedrohte Strafe. Androhen* belongs to more formal or bureaucratic language and occurs with objs. like *eine Strafe, eine hohe Geldstrafe, die Verhaftung*, etc. *Übertretern dieses Gesetzes droht man eine hohe Geldstrafe an.* **Threatened**, as in *a threatened strike/punishment/fine*, etc., is **ange-droht**. *Der angedrohte Streik fand nun doch nicht statt.*

> *Sie drohten ihren Nachbarn ein Gerichtsverfahren an, falls sie nicht aufhörten, nachts so viel Krach zu machen.*
> *Das Kriegsrecht droht jedem, der nicht unverzüglich dem Befehl eines Militärs folgt, die sofortige Verhaftung an.*
> *Als nach einigem Zögern die angedrohte Blockade verhängt wurde, lenkte der Diktator ein.*

time, times (including **double** *n.* and *adj.*), **date** *ns.*

A. Date.

1. In its primary sense **date** refers to a particular day in the calendar.
i. There are several ways of asking the day's date: *Der wievielte ist heute?, Den wieviel-ten haben wir heute?, Welches Datum haben wir heute?*, or more formally *Was ist das heutige Datum? Was ist heute für ein Tag?* suggests the day of the week. **Das Datum** refers to a specific day, but is more restricted in use than **date**. Common uses are *Wie bestimmt man das Datum für Ostern?* and *Welches Datum ist/steht auf dem Brief?* and *Was ist das Datum des Poststempels ? On what date does school begin next year?* is, how-ever, likely to be *Wann fängt die Schule an? An welchem Tag* would usually be under-stood as referring to the date, although it could be taken to mean the day of the week. *An welchem Datum* is possible, but unusual.
ii. When **date** refers to a day on which something is to take place, as in *Has the date of the examination been fixed?* or *We had to change the date of the meeting, Datum* is possible, but **der Termin** is usual. *Der Termin* is a date, day, or time set down for something to take place. (It also means 'APPOINTMENT'.) It mostly implies a day and the time of day. *Den Termin für die Prüfung müssen wir noch festlegen. Man hat den Termin der nächsten Sitzung geändert. Man hat die Zeit der Sitzung geändert* refers to the hour of day, e.g. 2.30, and not the day itself. (Note: *Der Abgabetermin für den Aufsatz ist der 30. August.* Cf. B. 5. i.)

> *Wir mußten den Termin für das Treffen ändern.*
> *Hat man sich schon für einen Termin für die Wiedereröffnung des Theaters entschieden?/ . . . über den Termin/das Datum für die Vollversammlung schon geeinigt?*

2. Date can also refer to a year. *Most people know the date of the discovery of America. The important dates in G. history. If you want to study history, you must be prepared to learn some dates.* For the first sent. **das Jahr** would be used, as a specific year is meant. *Die meisten Leute kennen das Jahr, in dem Columbus Amerika entdeckte,* or . . . *wissen, in welchem Jahr Amerika entdeckt wurde.* In reference to the dates in the history of a country, **Datum** is used. Particularly with the pl., *die Daten,* it must be clear from the context, or be made clear by the addition of *historisch,* that 'dates' are meant; otherwise *Daten* could be taken to mean 'DATA'. *Das ist ein wichtiges Datum der englischen Geschichte. Er kennt alle wichtigen Daten der deutschen Geschichte. Ich muß mir die wichtigsten historischen Daten einprägen.* In general statements about learning dates **Jahreszahlen** is the usual equivalent. **Geschichtszahlen** also occurs occasionally. *Einige Schüler können sich Jahreszahlen gut merken, während andere sie nur mit Mühe lernen.*

> *Wenn du Geschichte studieren willst, mußt du darauf vorbereitet sein, Jahreszahlen/historische Daten auswendig zu lernen.*

If **date** does not refer to a specific year but rather to a period, **die Zeit** is used. *What date is this church?* is *Aus welcher Zeit stammt diese Kirche?* Cf. B. 1. v.

3. A **date** meaning 'an arrangement to meet' is **die Verabredung**. Cf. *sich verabreden* under ARRANGE 2.

B. Time.

1. *Die Zeit* carries many of the meanings of **time**, but there are often alternative expressions.

i. Die Zeit denotes what is measured in minutes, hours, years, etc. *Die Zeit vergeht schnell/langsam.* Hence *Die Zeit wird zeigen, wer Recht hat,* time will tell. *In time* when it means 'with the passage of time' is **mit der Zeit**. *Mit der Zeit wird es schon klarwerden/wirst du dich daran gewöhnen.* This phr. also translates *as time went on. Mit der Zeit wurde er immer ängstlicher.*

ii. Die Zeit also refers to a specific point in time which is measured by an hour and minute. The specific term is **die Uhrzeit**. *Können Sie mir die Uhrzeit sagen? What's the time?* is mostly *Wie spät ist es?,* but also heard is *Welche Zeit haben wir jetzt?,* and someone can ask, '*Haben Sie die genaue Zeit?' Zeit* is combined with *Ort.* Man *setzt Zeit und Ort einer Versammlung fest.* [At] *what time did you get here?* is usually **Wann sind sie hier angekommen?,** but *Um welche Zeit sind sie angekommen?* is also possible. *To tell the time: Das Kind kann schon* **die Uhr lesen** or *schon sagen, wieviel Uhr es ist. At the same time* is *zur selben/gleichen Zeit.*

iii. Die Zeit also denotes the appropriate point in the development of something for an action, i.e. the time for something to happen. *Die Zeit ist noch nicht reif für solche Reformen. It's time to do sth.* and *It's time that we did sth.* are **Es ist Zeit** + infin. or *daß*-clause. *Es ist Zeit zu gehen,* or *Es ist Zeit, daß wir gehen.* The n. or pronoun after *for* in *It's time for us to start work* becomes the subj. of the clause: *Es ist Zeit, daß wir mit der Arbeit anfangen.* An alternative is **Es ist höchste Zeit**, *diesem Mißbrauch ein Ende zu machen/daß wir hier eingreifen.* A further, stylistically higher alternative is **Es ist an der Zeit** + infin. or *daß*-clause. *Es ist an der Zeit, einiges zu ändern/daß wir einiges ändern.* **Es wird Zeit** or **Es wird allmählich/langsam Zeit** + clause or infin. mean that the time either has arrived or is (gradually) approaching. *Es wird Zeit, daß wir mit der Arbeit ernsthaft anfangen. Es wird allmählich/langsam Zeit, daß wir uns über den Preis einigen.* In more solemn style *Die Zeit ist gekommen* is found. Another less formal alternative is *Die Zeit ist da, wo wir handeln müssen.* The equivalent of the E. neg. **no time**, as in *This is no time to argue about trifles,* is **Es ist nicht die richtige/passende Zeit**, *uns über Bagatellfragen zu streiten.*

iv. A specific word meaning 'point of time' is **der Zeitpunkt**. It often occurs in contexts in which E. would use **time**. *Man wählt den günstigen Zeitpunkt,* chooses/picks one's time. *Der Zeitpunkt unserer Abreise steht noch nicht fest. Wir müssen den geeigneten/richtigen Zeitpunkt abwarten. Ich halte den Zeitpunkt für noch nicht gekommen, da einzugreifen. Zu diesem Zeitpunkt der Woche/des Monats,* at this time of the week/month. (But *at this time of day/year* is *zu dieser Tages-/Jahreszeit.*)

v. Die Zeit also denotes a period of time, either a historical one or one in the life of an individual. As in E., it is often in the pl. *In früheren/alten Zeiten. In vorgeschichtlichen Zeiten.* At the time of is *zur Zeit der ersten Königin Elisabeth.* That's a long time ago is *Das ist schon lange her* or *Das ist schon geraume/längere Zeit her* (cf. AGO). *Vor geraumer/langer Zeit,* a long time ago (something happened).

> *Viele Leute nennen die Zeit vor dem ersten Weltkrieg die gute alte Zeit.*
> *Zu der Zeit, von der Sie sprechen, war ich in Kanada.*
> *Es waren gute/schlechte/schwere Zeiten.   Nach kurzer Zeit kehrte er zurück.*
> *Ich habe das ganze Haus nach dem Brief abgesucht, und er war die ganze Zeit in meiner Tasche.*

vi. Die Zeit also means 'the length of time available for sth.' or 'the time spent somewhere or doing sth.' *Wir haben genug Zeit, um alles ohne Hetze zu erledigen. Wir haben eine herrliche Zeit miteinander verbracht.* A long time is often **lange**. *Du bist aber lange weggewesen!* For *to take one's time* see TAKE 4. *Die Zeit ist um,* [the] time is up. *Eine Zeitlang,* for a time. *Sie dachte eine Zeitlang nach, bevor sie antwortete.*

> *Diese Übersetzung erforderte sehr viel Zeit.   Wir dürfen keine Zeit verlieren.*
> *Ich habe nur wenig/nicht viel Zeit für Sport.   Ich brauche noch etwas Zeit für die Arbeit.*
> *Er hat diese Arbeit in vier Stunden gemacht. Ich hätte sie in der Hälfte der Zeit/in der halben Zeit geschafft.*
> *Sie schwamm die Strecke in Rekordzeit.   Er wird eine Zeitlang bei uns bleiben.*

vii. It is usual to include **Zeit** when asking people if they can give or spare a specified amount of time or some of their time, or when stating that someone has a certain length of time to do something.

> *Hast du heute oder morgen etwa eine Viertelstunde Zeit/zehn Minuten Zeit/ein bißchen Zeit für mich?*
> *Für diese Arbeit hast du vierzehn Tage Zeit.*

5. i. Time means 'a period of time within which sth. has to be done or obligations met'. *The time within which we have to pay runs out at the end of the quarter.* **Die Frist** is used with regard to applications, work, results, payments, etc. which have to be made or handed in by a specific date. *Wir müssen die Arbeit innerhalb der festgesetzten Frist abschließen. Frist* is a formal and bureaucratic word. **Die Zeit** is the everyday word which stresses more that a certain amount of time is available rather than that an obligation has to be met within a certain period. *Wir haben für diese Arbeit eine Frist von drei Monaten. Wir haben für diese Arbeit drei Monate Zeit.* **Der Termin** is 'the last day by which sth. has to be done', the end of a *Frist. Wir hatten die Arbeit schon vor dem festgelegten Termin beendet. Die Frist/Den Termin einhalten* is 'to keep to/observe a time limit' or 'to meet a deadline'. The v. **befristen** means 'to set a time limit to'. *Das Visum ist befristet. Eine befristete Stelle* is 'a position which runs only for a specified time'. *Eine Stelle auf Zeit* expresses the same meaning. (*Die Frist* can be a syn. of *Termin. Zu dieser Frist muß er bezahlen.*)

> *Sie müssen die auf dem Formular angegebene Frist zur Einreichung Ihres Antrages unbedingt einhalten.*
> *Die Zeit, in der man Bücher aus der Bibliothek behalten darf, wurde von drei auf vier Wochen verlängert. But Die Leihfrist beträgt vier Wochen.*
> *Die Zeit/Frist für die Abgabe der Aufsätze läuft am Freitag ab. Der Termin für die Abgabe . . . ist Freitag.*
> *Der allerletzte Gnadentermin für die Abgabe der Seminararbeiten ist der 30. Juni.*

ii. Die Frist has a further sense. Someone who has not met an obligation, frequently a financial one, by the due date (*Termin*) can be allowed an extension of time, *eine Frist*, to comply with it, i.e. a period of grace or a respite. *Man gewährte/ließ ihm noch eine Frist [zur Begleichung der Rechnung]*. Related words for payments of debts are **der Aufschub** and **die Stundung**, 'time to pay', but they are vaguer with regard to the period of time allowed than *Frist*. *Jmdm. eine Schuld/Zahlung* **stunden** is 'to give s.o. time to pay'.

> *Als wir seinen guten Willen zur Begleichung der Schulden sahen, gewährten wir ihm eine Frist von zwei Monaten.*
>
> *Obwohl er fleißig arbeitete, mußte er doch schließlich um Stundung seiner Schulden/um Aufschub bitten.*

6. Der Zeitraum is 'an unspecified period of time', whether short or long, and is the general term. **Die Zeitspanne** is occasionally used in the sense 'a relatively short period'. The dividing line is unclear. *Diese Entwicklung umfaßt einen Zeitraum von mehreren Jahren.* Also: *Ein Zeitraum von mehreren Monaten. Eine Zeitspanne von vier Monaten. In der Zeitspanne vom Schulanfang bis zu den Herbstferien. In der Zeitspanne zwischen den Gerichtsterminen/Terminen.*

7. Equivalents of some E. expressions. *Pressed for* **time** is *unter Zeitdruck*. *The train is ten minutes* **behind time**: *Der Zug hat zehn Minuten Verspätung. To be* **behind [time]** (with payments) is *mit Zahlungen im Verzug* or *im Rückstand sein*. **On time** or **in time for** *sth.* or *to do sth.* can often be expressed by *rechtzeitig*. Equivalents of the E. constructions are *Der Zug ist rechtzeitig angekommen, Wir sind noch rechtzeitig zum Abendessen angekommen,* and *Wir sind noch rechtzeitig angekommen, um den Zug zu erreichen. By the time* is *bis. Bis du wieder hier bist, bin ich mit der Arbeit fertig.* The conj. *bis* is not much used in colloquial speech. More common than *Bis wir das Haus erreichten, hatte es schon angefangen zu regnen,* is *Bevor wir das Haus erreichten . . .*

C. The first **time**. The number of **times**. Three **times** the/that quantity.

1. The **time** or **times** when sth. happens means 'the occasion or number of occasions on which it occurs'. *I rang four times.* **-mal** is joined to cardinal numbers. *Einmal, zweimal, dreimal,* etc., once, twice, three times, etc. When combined with an ordinal number or an adj., it appears in the form **das Mal**, *das dritte Mal, das letzte Mal, das einzige Mal,* or in the pl. *mehrere Male.* A following clause is introduced by *daß. Das war das erste Mal, daß ich sie gesehen habe. Next time* is *beim nächsten Mal* when people expect to meet regularly, otherwise *das nächste Mal. Ich erkläre es Ihnen beim nächsten Mal. Das nächste Mal, daß ich sie sah, war zwei Monate später. Jedesmal* means 'every time', and *mehrmals* 'several times'. *Er hat jedesmal eine andere Ausrede. Ich habe es mehrmals versucht, aber es hat kein einziges Mal geklappt. How many times* is usually *Wie oft hast du ihn gesehen? Reich' mir zwei Ziegelsteine auf einmal!,* two at a time.

2. For E. speakers it is necessary to distinguish between compounds with *mal* and those with *fach,* since the E. compound *-fold* in *threefold, fourfold,* etc. is not much used, its meanings having been taken over by **times**.

i. Compounds with **-fach** denote multiples of a quantity or sum of money. I have a tonne of gravel but require three times that amount, i.e. 1 tonne × 3, *Ich brauche die dreifache Menge. Das ist das Vierfache der geforderten Summe. I was expecting to pay $20, but had to pay three times that* (also *three times as much/that amount*) becomes *Ich hatte mit 20 Dollar gerechnet, mußte aber das Dreifache zahlen* or *den dreifachen Betrag zahlen.* The *-fach* compounds belong to educated or written style. An alternative for the last sent. more usual in the spoken language is *Ich mußte dreimal so viel zahlen.* The **-mal** compounds + **so viel** express in everyday language the meaning of a number + *-fach. Wir brauchen die fünffache Menge* can be expressed as *Wir brauchen fünfmal so viel.*

ii. The *-fach* compounds occur on all stylistic levels with the preps. *auf* and *um*. In *Man hat die Produktion um das Dreifache erhöht* and *Der Ertrag ist auf das Dreifache gestiegen*, the phrs. mean 'threefold' or 'three times over'. The meaning 'to increase by the specified number of times' is also conveyed by a v. formed with *ver-* + *-fach*. The non-refl. form. e.g. **vervierfachen**, is trans. *Man hat die Produktion vervierfacht*, while the refl. v. **sich vervierfachen** expresses the intr. meaning, *Der Ertrag hat sich vervierfacht*.

iii. A cardinal number + *-fach* also means 'repeated that number of times'. *Ein dreifacher Sieg. Ein dreifaches Hoch. Ein vierfacher Olympiasieger. In dreifacher/vierfacher Ausfertigung* is 'in triplicate/quadruplicate'.

iv. For **zweifach** there is the more usual alternative **doppelt**. *Die Maschine fliegt mit zweifacher/doppelter Schallgeschwindigkeit. Doppelt* is both an adj. and adv. *Wir brauchen die doppelte Menge. Das ist doppelt so viel/lang wie nötig. Die Fenster sind doppelt verglast.* Where **double** is a n. or where E. has *double that*, meaning 'double an already mentioned amount', **das Doppelte** is used. *Maschinen leisten das Doppelte, wenn man sie gut pflegt. Ich habe mit hundert Mark gerechnet, mußte aber das Doppelte zahlen.* **Zweimal so viel** and **doppelt so viel** are also used. *Es hat mich nur sechs Mark gekostet, aber er hat das Doppelte/den doppelten Betrag/zweimal so viel/doppelt so viel bezahlt. Das Doppelte* is used with *auf* and *um* as described in C. 2. ii. *Die Produktion ist auf das Doppelte gestiegen. Die Preise sind in kurzer Zeit ums Doppelte gestiegen. Verdoppeln* and **sich verdoppeln** also exist. *Wir müssen unsere Anstrengungen verdoppeln. Die Zahl der Mitglieder hat sich verdoppelt.*

timid, anxious, fearful *adjs*. Applied to people, **timid** means 'lacking in courage or self-confidence, easily frightened or overawed, shy'. *He was a tall, timid man. A timid driver is reluctant to overtake trucks and buses.* **Timid** suggests a feeling of fear without any real foundation that is a habitual state of mind, at least for a period. Such a period may be a stage in someone's development. **Anxious** and **fearful** imply that there is some basis for the fear and that it lasts a relatively short time. **Anxious** means 'characterized by extreme uneasiness of mind about some contingency'. *He was wounded by the disapproval of his friends and anxious for the future. I am anxious for/about their safety. He peered around anxiously.* **Fearful** means 'full or fear, alarm, or concern, afraid of sth. or of doing sth.' *The boys looked at each other fearfully. He was fearful of offending his superiors.* Applied to what people do, **timid** means 'marked by a lack of boldness or determination'. *A timid policy/look/smile. I got out of the car and timidly rang the doorbell.*

1. Timid.

i. Describing a person, **furchtsam** suggests that experiencing fear or being overawed is a permanent characteristic or one that lasts for some time. It is mostly applied to shy people, especially children, and to animals. *Ein furchtsames Kind. Ein furchtsames Reh.* When it describes an action, *furchtsam* differs from *ängstlich* only in being stylistically higher. *Das Kind wich furchtsam zurück/kam furchtsam näher. Ein furchtsamer Blick. Das kleine Mädchen sah uns furchtsam an.* In neither context is *furchtsam* a commonly used word; *ängstlich* is the everyday equivalent of **timid**.

ii. Applied to people, **ängstlich** suggests that the person has a tendency to become fearful easily and that while such fears may have some basis, the person's reaction is exaggerated. *Er/Sie ist ein ängstlicher Mensch* implies a person who reacts with exaggerated fear to danger. *Sei doch nicht so ängstlich!* In relation to actions or facial expression it means 'displaying fear' and carries the same implication. *Er sah* *ängstlich um sich. Die Kinder schrieen ängstlich. Sie drehte sich ängstlich um. Das Kind machte ein ängstliches Gesicht.*

> *Ein ängstlicher Autofahrer überholt Lastwagen und Busse nur ungern.*

iii. Schreckhaft means 'easily frightened'. *Das Kind ist schreckhaft wie ein Hase. Du bist aber heute sehr schreckhaft.*

iv. Although *furchtsam* and *ängstlich* describe some actions, mostly looks, the main equivalent of **timid** applied to actions is **zaghaft**. It means 'lacking in determination, without confidence in the success of what one undertakes' and mostly describes how people do or attempt to do something or how they approach others. *Wenn sie nur solche zaghaften Schritte unternehmen, wird sich gar nichts ändern.*

> *Seine zaghaften Versuche waren/Dieser zaghafte Annäherungsversuch war/Diese zaghafte Politik war von vornherein zum Scheitern verurteilt.*
>
> *Er wagte nur einen zaghaften Einwand.*
>
> *Ich stieg aus dem Auto und klingelte zaghaft an der Tür.*

2. When **anxious** and **fearful [about sth.]** imply fear that has some justification and that lasts only a limited time, there are several equivalents.

i. Angstvoll suggests genuine and not exaggerated fear, but is restricted to the context of looking at someone. *Die Jungen sahen sich angstvoll an/wechselten angstvolle Blicke.*

ii. Bange is used alone, *Mir ist bange*, or in the combination *Ihm/Ihr war/wurde [es] angst und bange*. Both these expressions mean either 'frightened, scared' or 'anxious, worried'. *Mir ist bange um ihn* expresses the same meaning as the less common *Ich bange um ihn*, i.e. 'I am anxious, uneasy, worried about him'. **Bangen um** is often used in reference to the future. *Sie bangten um ihre Zukunft. Wegen der Rationalisierungspläne der Mineralölgesellschaften bangen die deutschen Tankstellenpächter um ihre Existenz.*

iii. Anxious can mean 'worried'. *It's time to be going home—your mother will be getting anxious.* One equivalent is **sich Sorgen machen [um]**. *Es ist Zeit, nach Hause zu gehen—eure Mutter wird sich Sorgen machen. Ich mache mir Sorgen um meinen Mann/um diese Sache.* An alternative is **besorgt**, worried, concerned. *Warum bist du denn so besorgt?—hier wird dir nichts zustoßen.* In this sense *besorgt* takes *wegen*. *Sie war wegen des Gesundheitszustandes ihres Mannes besorgt.* (**Besorgt um** means 'concerned with s.o.'s well-being'. *Sie war um ihre Gäste besorgt.*)

iv. Be **fearful [of]** can be a syn. of *to fear*. *The playwright was fearful that the opening night of his new play would be a failure. They were fearful (or afraid) of losing their way.* This sense is expressed by **befürchten** or **Angst haben** discussed in FEAR 1. iii. *Der Dramatiker befürchtete/hatte Angst, daß sein neues Stück bei der Erstaufführung durchfallen würde. Sie hatten Angst, sie würden sich verlaufen.*

4. Anxious is also applied to a period of time in which people experience anxiety. *It was an anxious time for us all. We spent a few anxious hours.* The sense is expressed by **bange** and **angsterfüllt**.

> *Sie erlebten ein paar bange Minuten, bevor das defekte Flugzeug auf der Landebahn aufsetzte.*
>
> *Sie hatten bange/angsterfüllte Tage hinter sich, in denen sie um das Leben des verletzten Kindes fürchteten.*

5. Fearful is still sometimes found as a syn. of *terrible* in the sense 'very unpleasant or bad'. *This led to all sorts of fearful consequences. I've just had a fearful row with my parents. They were making a fearful row/racket.* Both **furchtbar** und **fürchterlich** mean 'extremely unpleasant', but **schrecklich** is probably the commonest equivalent. *Für mich hatte diese Fehlentscheidung allerlei furchtbare/fürchterliche/ schreckliche Folgen. Die Nachbarn machen einen schrecklichen/fürchterlichen Krach. Ich hatte [einen] furchtbaren Krach mit meinen Eltern.* (Like *row*, *der Krach* means both 'a loud noise' and 'a quarrel'.) *Die Leute nebenan machten gestern abend einen furchtbaren/fürchterlichen/ schrecklichen Spektakel. Die Kinder machen einen fürchterlichen Radau auf dem Hof.* (*Der Spektakel* is 'a loud noise', and *der Radau* 'a loud noise or commotion made by people, usually children'.)

touch *v.*

1. The primary sense when **touch** is a trans. v. is 'to make voluntary or involuntary contact with s.o. or sth. with the hand, another part of the body, or with an object or instrument'. *The baby stretched out its hand to touch the balloon. The wood is so rotten that it crumbles when you touch it. My arm must have touched the wet paint.* A second, related meaning is the use in the neg. **Not to touch** something means 'to avoid picking it up, damaging it, or interfering with the way it is arranged'. *Put it down!— you mustn't touch anything.* The two main equivalents are *berühren* and *anfassen*.

i. Etw./Jmdn. berühren is 'to make, either intentionally or unintentionally, gentle and often barely perceptible contact with s.o. or sth., either with the hand, in particular with the tips of the fingers, or with sth. held in the hand'. Other parts of the body or one object which touches another can also be the subj. *Das Baby streckte die Hand aus, um den Luftballon zu berühren.* The third E. example above becomes *Ich muß mit dem Arm die frisch gestrichene Wand berührt haben* as only *berühren* denotes accidental contact.

> *Er berührte ihren Arm mit der Hand.*   *Der Arzt berührte die Wunde vorsichtig mit der Pinzette.*
> *Ich war bei ihm in der Wohnung. Der Typ is so penibel, daß man seine Sachen nicht einmal berühren*
>   *kann.*   *Die Zweige der Eiche berühren die Fensterscheiben.*

ii. Etw. anfassen is 'to put one's hand firmly on or around sth. or to take it in one's hand'. It also means 'to take hold of' (cf. SEIZE) and presupposes the intention to make direct contact so as to be able to take the object up. It means 'to touch' when this contact is established without the object being moved. *Anfassen* is restricted to contact with the hand and cannot refer to an action which is accidental. If we disregard this semantic difference between *anfassen* and *berühren*, the main distinction is that *anfassen* is the usual word in everyday language when a person is the subj. Only *anfassen* is appropriate for the second E. meaning, i.e. not to touch something. The last E. example in the first paragraph becomes *Stell' das [bloß] wieder hin!—du darfst nichts anfassen.* The sign in museums is usually *Nicht anfassen!*, but *berühren* is also found. Either v. could be used in translating the second E. example. *Das Holz ist so morsch, daß es zerfällt, wenn man es berührt/anfaßt*, but *anfaßt* would be expected as it suggests a firmer contact.

> *Er ist ein schrecklicher Junge, er muß immer alles anfassen.*

iii. Touch is also intr. With at least two things as subj. it means 'to be in contact'. *The wires mustn't touch. Our shoulders were touching.* The equivalent is **sich berühren**.

> *Zwei nicht isolierte elektrische Leitungen dürfen sich nicht berühren.*
> *Die Menschen standen so dicht beieinander, daß ihre Schultern sich berührten.*

iv. Fig. uses. *Ihre Interessen berühren sich mit meinen* or *Unsere Interessen berühren sich*, our interests are close or similar. *Jmd. berührt ein Thema* or *streift ein Thema*, touches on it.

v. Etw./Jmdn. anrühren is now uncommon in the primary sense 'to make contact with the hand' except in a few fixed, mostly neg. expressions. *Rühr' meine Sachen nicht dauernd an!* or *Rühr' meine Werkzeuge nicht an!* mean that the person addressed should leave them alone, neither fiddle with nor touch them. If someone is advised to use something belonging to someone else, he/she might answer, *'Ich weiß nicht, ob ich das anrühren darf'. Jmd. hat das Essen nicht berührt* is used, but *nicht angerührt* is also frequently heard. *Anrühren* seems to be the normal v. in *Jmd. rührt*

den Alkohol nicht an or *hat nie wieder eine Spielkarte angerührt.* A person can be the obj. *Keiner wagte, den Verletzten anzurühren.*
  Rühr' mich nicht an!   *Ich habe nichts angerührt.*

vi. Rühren an in *an jmds. Arm/Schulter rühren* means 'to touch gently', but it is now used only in literary prose. Still used is *Rühre nicht an diese Sache!*, don't mention or bring up this matter. It implies an unpleasant matter.

vii. A child might say, 'I didn't touch him'. The sense could be conveyed by *Ich habe ihm nichts getan.* Cf. DO 7. *Angefaßt* is possible, but not clear.

2. Touch s.o. means 'affect with a feeling', especially a tender one such as pity or gratitude. **Rühren** is always 'to move s.o. to pity, tears, or gratitude'. *Das Schicksal der Waisenkinder hat uns alle tief gerührt. Eine rührende Geschichte*, a touching story. Cf. MOVE 5. For *berühren*, relating to the mind, cf. AFFECT 3.

3. Unberührt means 'untouched, unmoved, unaffected' in three senses: (i) 'Physically untouched'. *Diese Speisen ließ sie unberührt. Eine unberührte Landschaft.* (ii) 'Emotionally untouched or unmoved'. *Unberührt von diesen Klagen/Bitten, ging er weiter.* (iii) 'Unaffected by an influence'. *Von diesen schädlichen Einflüssen blieben die Kinder unberührt.*

4. *No one can* **touch** *this actress in the role of Ophelia* means that her standard is so high that it cannot be equalled. Possible transls. are *Niemand reicht* or *kommt an sie heran.* Cf. APPROACH 7.

trouble *n.*

1. Trouble, used with *take*, means 'effort, care, or exertion in doing or attempting sth.' *She takes a lot of trouble with her work. He'd be a good worker, if only he'd take the trouble to get to work on time. You can see that they haven't taken a lot of trouble with the translation.* With other vs. the sense is 'inconvenience, extra work, difficulties, or problems'. *Did the work give you much trouble? Did you have any trouble finding your way? This would save everyone a lot of trouble.*
i. Die Mühe means both 'effort or exertion' and 'difficult or additional work or inconvenience', and, as with **trouble**, the senses are hard to separate. **Sich Mühe geben** means 'to take trouble' or 'to make an effort'. *Du mußt dir Mühe geben*, make an effort, try hard. *Du mußt dir mehr Mühe geben*, take more trouble. An infin. can follow, *Er gab sich [viel] Mühe, die in ihn gesetzten Erwartungen zu erfüllen*, 'he took a lot of trouble, was at pains', or a phr. with *mit*, *Der Lehrer gab sich viel Mühe mit den schlechten Schülern*, 'took/went to a lot of trouble'. *Geben Sie sich keine Mühe!*, don't go to/put yourself to any trouble. **Sich [viel] Mühe machen**, to take or go to a lot of trouble, also suggests effort. *Man sieht der Übersetzung an, daß Sie sich viel Mühe gemacht haben. Sie machte sich sehr viel Mühe mit der Arbeit.* A stylistically higher variant is **Mühe auf etw. verwenden.** *Sie verwendete sehr viel Mühe auf die Arbeit.* **Sich die Mühe machen, etw. zu tun**, means 'to take the trouble to do sth.' *Er machte sich die Mühe, dem neuen Mitarbeiter alles genau zu erklären.* **Mühe haben mit**, as in *Ich hatte mit der Übersetzung sehr viel Mühe*, implies difficulty, as does **Mühe kosten**, *Die Arbeit macht/kostet [sehr viel] Mühe*, it causes trouble. *Die täglichen Mühen* suggests the thgs. that have to be done each day requiring effort. **Jmdm. Mühe machen**, to cause someone trouble. *Ich möchte Ihnen keine Mühe machen*, I wouldn't like to cause/put you to any trouble. Thus *Es macht mir keine Mühe*, causes no trouble. *Save yourself the trouble/effort!* is *Spar dir die Mühe! Ich wollte ihr diese Mühe sparen/ersparen.* Cf. SPARE. *Ich habe mit jmdm./etw. meine Mühe gehabt*, have had a lot of trouble with him/her/it. *Sth. is more trouble than it's worth* could be *Es ist nicht der (or die) Mühe wert*, which also translates *not worth the effort.*

Er wäre ein guter Arbeiter, wenn er sich die Mühe geben wollte, pünktlich zur Arbeit zu kommen.

Es ist sehr enttäuschend, daß man das Projekt fallengelassen hat, nachdem wir uns so viel Mühe damit gegeben haben.   Sie gibt sich sehr viel Mühe mit ihrer Arbeit.

Ich danke Ihnen sehr für die Mühe, die Sie sich gegeben haben, um meiner Tochter zu helfen.

Das Ergebnis zeigt, daß unsere Mühe nicht umsonst gewesen ist/sich gelohnt hat.

Niemand hatte sich die Mühe gemacht, in die Akten hineinzusehen.

Diese Arbeit habe ich ohne große Mühe bewältigt/erledigt.

ii. Certain contexts require other words to convey the sense 'inconvenience and difficulty'. **Die Schwierigkeit[en]** can often translate **trouble**. Thus *Das macht [uns] keine Schwierigkeiten/nicht die geringste Schwierigkeit*, causes us no/not the slightest trouble. *Jmd. hat private/berufliche/finanzielle Schwierigkeiten*, trouble at home, at work, and financial troubles.

Die Lösung des Problems machte mehr Schwierigkeiten, als wir angenommen hatten.

Wir sind bei der Arbeit auf unerwartete Schwierigkeiten gestoßen.

Mit ihm hat es oft/nie Schwierigkeiten gegeben. Or Er hat uns oft/nie Schwierigkeiten gemacht.

Die Firma befindet sich in erheblichen Schwierigkeiten/hat mit wachsenden, finanziellen Schwierigkeiten zu kämpfen.   Haben Sie Schwierigkeiten gehabt, sich zurechtzufinden?

iii. Die Umstände suggests time-consuming preparations and exertions. It is frequently used in the private sphere, where people acknowledge that others have gone to a lot of trouble for their sakes, or in the neg., when they ask someone not to go to any trouble on their behalf. *Bitte, nur keine Umstände!* or *Machen Sie sich meinetwegen keine [großen] Umstände!*, don't go to any trouble on my account. (*Umstände machen* can also imply being formal and ceremonious. *Machen Sie keine Umstände!*, don't stand on ceremony.)

Wenn sie Gäste erwartet, macht sie mit dem Abendessen immer viele/große Umstände.

iv. Die Unannehmlichkeiten usually arise from a troublesome matter, often with officialdom, which causes difficulties and unpleasantness and consequently a feeling of annoyance. **Die Scherereien** is a colloquial syn.

Diese Behördengänge haben uns sehr viel Unannehmlichkeiten gemacht/bereitet.

Wir haben mit den Nachbarn wegen ihrer Hunde Unannehmlichkeiten bekommen.

Die Behörden haben uns sehr viel Scherereien gemacht.

Ich habe mit einigen Kollegen Scherereien gehabt.

v. If there is trouble between people, there is unpleasant or strongly felt disagreement between them. **Der Ärger** is a frequently used word referring to unpleasant experiences which cause one to feel annoyance, the basic sense of *Ärger. Ärger* usually refers to trouble with other people, but the cause may be a difficult matter which makes one person feel another is causing trouble, so that *Ärger* can be used like *Unannehmlichkeiten* or *Scherereien. Ich habe viel Ärger/nichts als Ärger mit diesem Mann/dieser Sache gehabt. Mach' keinen Ärger!* is like *Don't cause us any trouble/annoyance!*

In letzter Zeit habe ich sehr viel Ärger mit meinem Chef gehabt.

Wo <u>der</u> Mann ist, da gibt's immer Ärger. (<u>Der</u> stressed = 'that'.)

To *ask for* **trouble** can be *sich* (dat.) **Ärger einhandeln.** *Sich Ärger einhandeln* means 'to bring unpleasant consequences on oneself as a result of one's behaviour'. *Wenn du so viele Pausen machst, handelst du dir nur Ärger ein. Jmd. hat Ärger mit der Polizei* suggests that the annoyance is justified and that the police are being unreasonable. *Er hat sich Ärger mit der Polizei eingehandelt* suggests that the police are justified in their actions against him. To *get into trouble with the police* is mostly **mit dem Gesetz in Konflikt geraten.**

2. i. *What's the* **trouble**? *Was fehlt dir?* and *Was hast du denn?* are used if the trouble concerns one person. They refer either to a bodily ailment or to something causing mental distress, e.g. sadness. *Was ist [hier] los?*, what's wrong/the trouble/the matter/going on [here]?, refers to difficulties between a number of people or to an unpleasant event.

ii. Sth. is the **trouble** means that a particular aspect is causing problems or difficulties. *We have spent all the money available—that's the trouble. The trouble with you is [that] you don't try.* The first example could be *Wir haben das ganze Geld ausgegeben, das uns zur Verfügung steht,—darin liegt die Schwierigkeit/das Problem,* and the second could become *Die Schwierigkeit liegt darin, daß du dir keine Mühe gibst.* Also possible for people is *Dein Fehler ist, daß du . . . His greatest trouble is oversensitivity: Seine größte Schwäche/Sein größter Fehler ist die übermässige Empfindlichkeit.*

3. Particularly in the pl. **trouble** means 'cares and worries'. *She shares her husband's troubles. A secret trouble weighed on his mind.* This is **die Sorge** or **der Kummer**, discussed under CARE 1. i and ii. *Er hat viele Sorgen. Sie teilt die Sorgen ihres Mannes. Eine heimliche Sorge lastete auf ihm. The boy has been a trouble to his parents* could be *Der Junge hat seinen Eltern ständig Sorgen bereitet* or *viel Kummer bereitet.* A similar meaning is expressed by *Der älteste Sohn war das Sorgenkind der Familie,* the problem child.

4. If there is **trouble** somewhere, there is fighting, rioting, etc., usually in a public place. *The police will intervene immediately if there's any trouble.* This meaning is expressed by **die Unruhen.** *Die Polizei wird sofort eingreifen, wenn Unruhen ausbrechen sollten. Wir hören täglich von Unruhen in verschiedenen Teilen der Welt. The police rushed to the scene of the trouble* could be *Die Polizei fuhr sofort zum Ort des Geschehens,* i.e. the place where something undesirable was happening. *Labour trouble* denotes some kind of industrial dispute and could be **der Arbeitskampf,** which mostly implies a strike. *In der Metallindustrie ist ein Arbeitskampf ausgebrochen.*

5. Trouble can refer to a physical ailment. *S.o. has liver/stomach trouble.* **Das Leiden** is a general term. *Jmd. hat ein Magenleiden/ein Leberleiden.* **Die Beschwerde** is a syn. and is often found in compounds. *Nierenbeschwerden. Atembeschwerden. Verdauungsbeschwerden.*

    Sie hat verschiedene organische Leiden.   *Seine rheumatischen Beschwerden nahmen zu.*

6. Trouble also means 'a breakdown or fault in sth. mechanical'. *Our plane was delayed because of engine trouble.* The G. word is **die Störung,** the *Fremdwort* **der Defekt.**

Wir mußten mehrere Stunden in Colombo warten, bis die Störung/der Defekt in einem der Triebwerke beseitigt wurde.

trust, entrust, confide *vs.*

1. Trust a person. Whoever trusts someone is convinced of that person's honesty and sincerity and believes that he or she will not deliberately do any harm. For this concept there are two G. vs., *trauen* and *vertrauen,* which both make a judgement about whether a person is by nature trustworthy or reliable, but they present different aspects of the situation. **Trauen** has a neg. colouring and suggests no more than that nothing dishonest or treacherous is to be expected from the person. The often used neg., *Ich traue ihm nicht,* thus states that dishonesty is to be expected. **Vertrauen** views the situation positively, suggesting that only good is to be expected from the person, that he or she will act correctly or honestly in any situation and do what the circumstances require. Because it denotes something pos., *vertrauen* often implies that someone will do what he or she says, promises, etc., or what can be expected. Both take the dat.

    Einem Freund muß man vorbehaltlos trauen können.

    Nach diesen Enttäuschungen traut er niemand mehr.

> *Ihm ist nicht [über den Weg] zu trauen, er betrügt, wo er nur kann.* Also *Ich traue ihm nicht über den Weg.*
>
> *Es ist schwer, einem Menschen zu trauen, den man nicht achtet.*
>
> *Du kannst ihm vertrauen. Er ist zuverlässig und macht seine Arbeit gut.*
>
> *Sie vertraute ihm blindlings, und seine Ratschläge erwiesen sich immer als richtig.*

2. Trust a thg.

i. Trauen is found in neg. sents. with ns. like *jmds. Worte/Freundlichkeit* or *eine Sache*, a matter or business in which someone is involved or in which someone is trying to get another person involved. *Ich traue jmds. Worten nicht* suggests that I suspect a hidden, bad, or selfish intention behind his words or that I do not take what appears on the surface to be the reality of the situation. This also holds for *Ich traue der Sache nicht. Trauen* is also used with *Augen* and *Ohren*.

> *Ich traue ihrer Freundlichkeit nicht. Ich glaube, sie planen etw. hinter unseren Rücken.*
>
> *Sie trauten dem Frieden nicht und befürchteten, der Feind bereitete einen neuen Angriff vor.*
>
> *Der Held (im Märchen) konnte seinen Augen kaum trauen, als hinter einem Baum eine Fee hervortrat und sagte, er habe drei Wünsche frei. Er vertraute der schönen Frau sofort und begann sich zu überlegen, was er sich wünschen könnte.*

ii. Trust also means 'to rely on the veracity of, or believe, an account, report, or story'. *I'm not sure I trust their story/account.* Provided that the reference to a person is clear, **trauen** can be used in the neg. *Ich traue seinem Bericht nicht.* Another construction is *Ich traue dem nicht, was sie uns da erzählt hat/was hier steht.* When there is no clear reference to a person, **sich verlassen auf**, 'to rely on', can be used in either a pos. or neg. sent. *Auf die Berichte in dieser Zeitung kann man sich [nicht] immer verlassen*, or the meaning can be expressed by different words, *Diese Meldung halte ich [nicht] für richtig [in jeder Einzelheit].*

3. Vertrauen auf means 'to be certain that another pers., a protective power like God or fortune, or sth. like one's skill or abilities will not disappoint, fail, or let one down'. Depending on the context, it corresponds to **trust** + obj., **trust in**, and **trust to**. To trust [in] God is *auf Gott vertrauen.* To trust one's luck or to trust to luck is *auf sein/das Glück vertrauen.* With abilities the dat. is sometimes found, *Er vertraute seiner Kraft*, but *auf* is now usual, *Er vertraute auf seine Kraft/Geschicklichkeit.* The construction *We can only trust that everything will turn out all right* becomes *Wir können nur darauf vertrauen, daß alles gut ausgeht*; i.e. we are relying on whatever benign force we regard as determining human destiny. *Vertrauen darauf, daß* translates *You can trust s.o. to do sth.* where this means 'to rely on'. The person becomes the subj. of the *daß*-clause. *Du kannst darauf vertrauen, daß er die Arbeit gut macht.* A close syn. of *vertrauen auf* is **sich verlassen auf**. *Sie verließ sich auf sein Versprechen. Du kannst dich darauf verlassen, daß er die Arbeit gut macht.*

> *Du solltest nicht auf ihn vertrauen. Er ist völlig unzuverlässig.*
>
> *Ich vertraue auf ihre Ehrlichkeit/auf ihren gesunden Menschenverstand.*
>
> *Er hatte sich für die Prüfung kaum vorbereitet und vertraute auf sein gutes Gedächtnis und auf seine Kenntnisse.* *Wir vertrauen darauf, daß das gute Wetter noch ein paar Tage anhält.*

4. The imp. of **trust**, *Trust them to be late!* and *You can trust him to do sth. stupid!*, imply that this is typical of the person. The meaning can be conveyed by **Man kann sich darauf verlassen**, *daß sie zu spät kommen/daß er etw. Dummes macht.* An alternative is **Man kann [sich] sicher sein**, *daß er sich blöd anstellt.*

5. i. Jmdm. etw. anvertrauen expresses the meanings 'to trust s.o. with sth.' and 'to entrust sth. to s.o.' Thus *Du kannst ihr das Auto anvertrauen—sie wird es nicht kaputtfahren*, 'trust her with it', and *Man vertraut jmdm. Wertsachen/eine Geldsumme an*, 'entrusts them to someone'. *Größere Geldbeträge würde ich ihm nicht anvertrauen.* People can be the obj. *Sie vertraute die Kinder für die Zeit der Reise einer Nachbarin an.*

ii. Jmdm. etw. anvertrauen also means 'to confide sth. to s.o.' *Er vertraute dem Freund seinen Liebeskummer/das Geheimnis an.* **Sich jmdm. anvertrauen** is 'to tell s.o. one's troubles etc.', 'to confide in s.o.' *Sie vertraute sich der Mutter rückhaltlos an.*

6. If I trust someone to do something, I believe that person capable of doing it properly, *She didn't trust anyone to look after her child properly.* **Jmdm. etw. zutrauen** means 'to think s.o. capable of sth.' which can be both good and bad. *Ich traue ihm nichts Böses, nur Gutes zu. Traust du mir eine solche Gemeinheit zu? To think s.o. capable of* is often a more appropriate transl. than *to trust.* When *jmdm. etw. zutrauen* is used in connection with something bad, it can be translated as not to *put it past s.o. to do sth. Ich traue es ihm zu, uns zu betrügen. Ich traue ihm einen solchen Betrug zu. Ich traue [es] mir/jmdm. [nicht] zu, etw. zu tun,* 'I [don't] think myself/s.o. capable of doing sth.', can also translate *I don't trust myself/s.o. to do the job properly. Ich traue [es] mir/ihm nicht zu, die Arbeit richtig zu machen.* (This is not the same as *You can trust him to do the work well.* Cf. 3.)

> *Sie traute es niemand[em] zu, richtig auf das Kind aufzupassen.*
> *Ich hätte ihr nicht zugetraut, eine so gute Rede zu halten.*
> *So viel Verstand hätte ich ihm nicht zugetraut.*
> *Ich traue [es] ihm zu, sie im Stich zu lassen/uns zu belügen.*
> *Ich traue [es] mir nicht zu, alle diese Fachausdrücke richtig zu übersetzen.*
> *Er traut sich nichts zu* (lacks [self-]confidence).

7. If I say that I trust that something is true, I mean that I hope or expect it to be true. *I trust you all drink coffee.* This sense can be conveyed by **ich hoffe** or **hoffentlich.** *Ich hoffe, daß Sie sich jetzt wieder wohl fühlen. Ihr trinkt alle hoffentlich Kaffee. Ich hoffe, daß diese Meldung wahr ist. Diese Meldung ist hoffentlich wahr.*

trust, confidence, faith *ns.*

1. Trust denotes a feeling of certainty that someone or something will not fail in any situation in which protection, discretion, fairness, honesty, and sincerity are essential. *They put their trust in us, and we will defend them if they are attacked. She placed/put her trust in him to keep secret what she had told him.* **Faith** suggests an intensified feeling of trust, an even deeper conviction of fidelity and integrity, sometimes in spite of no or contrary evidence. *I've got faith in human nature. You're destroying all my faith in the medical profession.* (For **faith** in the religious sense, cf. BELIEF 1. ii.) **Confidence** is also a feeling that people can be trusted to do what they are supposed to do and that they will not disappoint or let you down. While **trust** might be an intuitive reaction on brief acquaintance, **confidence** suggests a conviction based on the proven reliance of a person or thing or on long-term familiarity with him/her/it. *His confidence in his ability to survive the crisis was based on his many narrow escapes in the past. I have every confidence in her/in her abilities.* The equivalent of all three words is mostly *das Vertrauen.* The distinctions made in E. are not expressed. In some cases, *das Zutrauen* is an alternative.

i. Das Vertrauen is 'a conviction that one can rely completely on a pers. or thg.' The things can be one's own abilities or strength. *Ich habe volles Vertrauen zu ihr/auf/in ihre Fähigkeiten/zur Güte im Menschen. Sein Vertrauen auf/in jmdn./etw. setzen ,* to put one's trust, faith, or confidence in. *Ich habe mein Vertrauen öfters auf ihn gesetzt, und er hat mich nie im Stich gelassen.* An E. infin. construction as in the second example in the first paragraph can be turned into a *daß*-clause with the person as subj. *Sie hat ihr Vertrauen darin gesetzt, daß er über das, was sie ihm erzählt hatte, Stillschweigen bewahrt.* It would, however, be more usual to say *Sie vertraute darauf, daß er . . . Das Vertrauen* is used in parliamentary language. *Ein Vertrauensvotum* is 'a vote of confidence'. The opposite is *ein Mißtrauensvotum,* a vote of no confidence.

Jmd. hatte [ein] festes/unbegrenztes/unbedingtes/blindes Vertrauen zu einem anderen.

Ihr Vertrauen auf Gott war unerschütterlich.   *Er hat/besitzt mein volles/vollstes Vertrauen.*

Dieser Fall hat meinem Vertrauen auf die Ärzteschaft einen starken Schlag versetzt.

Dieser Vorfall hat mein Vertrauen [zu ihm] erschüttert/zerstört.

Wir haben unser Vertrauen zu diesem Politiker verloren.

Er hat das in ihn gesetzte Vertrauen mißbraucht/nicht gerechtfertigt.

Sein Vertrauen in seine Fähigkeit, die Krise durchzustehen, kommt daher, daß er in der Vergangenheit in ähnlichen Situationen immer glimpflich davongekommen ist.

ii. Das Zutrauen can only exist between two or more people. It suggests a stronger and deeper feeling of trust in one person by another than *Vertrauen* and may arise from the person's nature. It is often seen as typical of children and sometimes even as dangerous. *Allmählich gewann das Kind Zutrauen zu ihr.*

Ihr Verhalten erweckt Zutrauen.   *Ich habe kein/viel Zutrauen zu ihm.*

Nachdem wir uns besser kennengelernt hatte, schenkte er mir sein Zutrauen.

Ich habe kein Zutrauen mehr zu ihm/das Zutrauen zu ihm verloren— er verdient es nicht.

2. Have [complete] confidence, **faith**, or **trust** in the future or that some event will turn out well. Although *Vertrauen* is possible in this context, *Jmd. blickt/schaut voll Vertrauen in die Zukunft*, the usual word is **die Zuversicht**, a firm confidence that certain expectations of good will be fulfilled or that everything will develop favourably in the way one desires. *Jmd. blickt/schaut voll[er] Zuversicht in die Zukunft.* **Zuversichtlich** is 'confident' in the sense 'expecting good' and is similar to *optimistisch*.

Sie haben die Arbeit voll Zuversicht begonnen.

Obwohl alle Zahlen, die dem Wirtschaftsministerium vorlagen, zu tiefstem Pessimismus berechtigten, ließ sich die Bundesregierung ihre gewohnte Zuversicht nicht nehmen.

3. Confidence is also 'a belief that one can deal with a situation successfully by using one's own abilities'. It is a syn. of *self-confidence*. *Working in a group gives you a bit more [self-]confidence. I've lost my confidence.* This sense is usually best translated by **das Selbstvertrauen**. *Das Arbeiten in einer Gruppe stärkt das Selbstvertrauen. Er scheint sein Selbstvertrauen verloren zu haben.* The addition of certain words to *das Vertrauen* can express the same meaning. *Du mußt mehr Vertrauen zu dir selbst haben/bekommen.*

4. i. In confidence is applied to a situation in which one person tells another a secret and trusts that it will not be revealed to others. *I'm telling you that in confidence.* The equivalent is **im Vertrauen**. *Das sage ich Ihnen im Vertrauen.* Common expressions are: *im Vertrauen gesagt* and *ein Wort im Vertrauen*. *Jmd. ins Vertrauen ziehen* is 'to take s.o. into one's confidence'. *Im Vertrauen auf ihre Verschwiegenheit erzählte ich ihr, was ich herausbekommen hatte* could be a transl. of *Trusting in her discretion . . .*

Ziehe sie so viel wie möglich in dein Vertrauen!

Ganz im Vertrauen gesagt, ich kann Michael Meyer gar nicht leiden.

ii. Vertraulich in one sense means 'confidential', *eine vertrauliche Information/Unterredung, ein vertraulicher Bericht*, and is used as an adv. to translate *in strict confidence*. *Ich habe ihr streng vertraulich mitgeteilt, daß man ihr die Stelle anbieten wird. Ich habe die Sache vertraulich behandelt.* (*Streng* = 'strict' is not added to *im Vertrauen*.) (*Vertraulich* also means 'familiar'. *Er hat sehr vertraulich mit uns geredet.*)

iii. A confidence is 'a piece of secret and often personal information that one pers. confides to another', a meaning expressed by **eine vertrauliche Mitteilung** or **ein Geheimnis**.

Der Brief enthält einige vertrauliche Mitteilungen.   *Die beiden tauschten Geheimnisse aus.*

iv. Das Vertrauen also corresponds to **trust** meaning 'responsibility to carry out properly tasks entrusted to one and/or to keep secret information that is important'. Hence *ein Vertrauensposten* means 'a position of trust', and *ein Vertrauensbruch* is 'a breach of confidence' or 'a breach of trust'.

5. A further sense of **confidence** is 'a feeling of certainty that what one is saying is correct'. *I can say with complete confidence that what I have told you is correct.* This is **die Sicherheit**, certainty.

> Ich kann mit absoluter Sicherheit sagen, daß das, was ich Ihnen gerade erzählt habe, sich wirklich zugetragen hat.

try, attempt, try out, test *vs.*

1. i. Try combines two concepts. One is 'to make an attempt', 'to begin sth. to ascertain whether one can do it or what can be achieved', and the second is 'to endeavour or make an effort'. There are two equivalents, *versuchen* and *sich bemühen*. Although **versuchen** does not exclude making an effort, the sense it conveys is more 'to begin sth. which may be difficult and carry it out to the extent that one is able', while **sich bemühen** suggests considerable and, often, repeated effort. Thus *I tried* can be either *Ich habe es versucht* or *Ich habe mich bemüht*, depending on which part of the E. definition is stressed. *Versuchen* is not used with any advs. denoting intensity except *angestrengt*. *Sie hat es angestrengt versucht, und es hat geklappt.* *Sich bemühen* is therefore used to translate expressions like *S.o. tried hard [to do sth.].* *Er hat sich wirklich sehr bemüht und hat es schließlich geschafft.* *Versuchen* is used with an infin., *Ich versuche, die Schrift zu entziffern*, and (in this sense) with a few objs., *Jmd. hat das Unmögliche/das Äußerste/sein Bestes/die Flucht versucht* and *Er versuchte ein Lächeln.* *Sich bemühen* is used with an infin., *Er hat sich bemüht, pünktlich zu sein*, or alone, *Sie hat sich bemüht.* While *sich bemühen* is used alone, *versuchen* always needs *es* if nothing follows. Therefore *I'll try* becomes either *Ich werde mich bemühen* or *Ich werde es versuchen.* Thus *Ich habe es versucht, aber es hat nicht geklappt.*

> Versuchen Sie bitte, sich präziser auszudrücken!   Ich werde es einmal versuchen.
> Sie versuchte, den Kanal zu durchschwimmen/ihre Tränen zurückzuhalten.
> Wenn es dir das erste Mal nicht gelingt, versuch' es immer wieder!
> Nachdem er sich ausgeschlossen hatte, versuchte er, die Tür mit verschiedenen Werkzeugen aufzubekommen.
> Die Dame von der Touristeninformation bemühte sich, ein Hotelzimmer für uns ausfindig zu machen.
> So sehr ich mich auch bemühte, es mißlang mir immer wieder.

ii. Try one's hardest. Several expressions have a similar meaning. *Ich habe mich wirklich sehr bemüht* or *Ich habe mir wirklich sehr viel Mühe gegeben* or *Ich habe mein Bestes getan* are possible transls. Stronger are *Ich habe mir jede [nur] erdenkliche Mühe gegeben* and *Ich habe es auf jede nur erdenkliche Weise versucht.* *Ich habe mich sehr angestrengt*, made a great effort, and *Ich habe mein möglichstes getan*, done my utmost, are other possibilities.

2. Try a particular place to see if it can provide something needed and **try** an implement, quantity, means of approach, etc. to see if a certain result can be achieved are translated by **es versuchen**. *I've tried everywhere/several shops and can't get the book: Ich habe es überall versucht* or *Ich habe es in verschiedenen Buchhandlungen versucht, aber ohne Erfolg.* *Versuch' es doch mit der größeren Zange, wenn es mit der kleinen nicht geht! Er versuchte es mit dem Jungen im Guten/mit Strenge.*

> Ich habe es bei allen Kaufhäusern vergeblich versucht.
> Versuch' es mal mit der doppelten Menge!   Versuchen Sie es mit Güte statt mit Strenge!
> Der erste Schlüssel paßte nicht. Als er es aber mit einem anderen versuchte, ging es.

3. Try means 'to attempt to find out what can be done, whether sth. is possible, or whether s.o. can do sth.' *Try how far you can jump/whether you can jump across the* *stream!* **Versuchen** and the syn. **probieren** mean 'to see whether sth. is possible' or 'to see whether it is in s.o.'s power to do sth.' Both take an obj. or a clause often introduced by *ob, wieviel, was,* etc. *Wollen Sie Ihr Glück versuchen?,* try your luck. *Versuch'/Probier' doch mal, wie weit du springen kannst/ob du über den Bach springen kannst!* (For the use of both in relation to food, cf. TASTE.)

> *Versuche doch wenigstens, ob du die Aufgabe nicht alleine lösen kannst!*
>
> *Versucht doch mal, wie lange ihr die Luft anhalten könnt!/ . . . wie weit ihr tauchen könnt!*
>
> *Laß mich mal versuchen/probieren, ob dieser Schlüssel paßt!*
>
> *Ich will probieren/versuchen, ob ich ihn jetzt zu Hause erreichen kann.*
>
> *Als er das Kunststück probierte/versuchte, ist er auf die Nase gefallen.*
>
> *Probieren Sie, wie sanft dieser Füller (Füllfederhalter) gleitet!* Also *Probieren Sie diesen Füller, wie sanft er gleitet!   Probiere, ob es gelingt, wenn du eine andere Methode benutzt!*
>
> *Er versuchte einen Sprung vom Zehnmeter-Brett.   Ich habe alles probiert, aber nichts hilft.*
>
> *Wir haben alle möglichen Mittel versucht.   Ich habe alles versucht, was in meiner Macht steht.*

Sich versuchen means 'to try one's hand at sth.' or 'to try some activity in which one has no experience'. *Er versucht sich nun in der Malerei. Versuchen Sie sich auf einem anderen Gebiet!*

4. Try all the doors and windows before leaving could be expressed by **überprüfen**, to check. *Überprüfe, ob alle Türen und Fenster abgeschlossen/verschlossen sind!* Cf. INVESTIGATE 2. iii. An alternative is *Sieh' mal nach, ob alle Türen . . . abgeschlossen sind!* Cf. LOOK 5.

5. Try s.o.'s *courage/honesty,* etc. is *jmds. Mut/Ehrlichkeit* **auf die Probe stellen**, to put it to the test. *S.o./sth.* tried my patience meaning 'put it to a severe test' is *Dieser Junge hat meine Geduld auf eine harte Probe gestellt. This small print tries the eyes* could be *Dieser kleine Druck ermüdet die Augen.*

6. Try s.o./a case in court. With a court as subj. **verhandeln** is used. *Das Gericht verhandelt gegen jmdn. wegen Diebstahls.* Cf. NEGOTIATE. When a person is the subj. of the pass. *He is being tried for theft,* a common expression is **sich verantworten mussen**. Cf. ANSWER 4. *Er muß sich vor Gericht wegen Diebstahls verantworten.* Also common is **vor Gericht stehen**. *Er steht wegen Diebstahls vor Gericht.* With a judge as subj., as in *Judge N. will try the case,* **führen** is the usual v. *Richter N. führt die Verhandlung.*

7. Ausprobieren is 'to try sth. out in order to find out whether it is what is wanted, is suitable for a purpose, it works, etc.' *Morgen will ich das neue Rezept/eine andere Arbeitsweise ausprobieren.* It is the appropriate v. when **try** a *new method/approach/thg.* means 'to try out or test'. *Ich habe die Bremsen ausprobiert* (tried the brakes); *sie funktionieren einwandfrei.* (Note that *prüfen* is 'to check'. *Eine Probefahrt,* 'a test drive', and *probefahren* are used for cars.)

> *Ich will nur schnell ausprobieren, ob auch alles an dem Gerät funktioniert.*
>
> *Wir wollen mit der Lasagne den Mikrowellenherd ausprobieren.*
>
> *Da die ersten Experimente fehlgeschlagen waren, probierte sie eine andere Methode aus.*

8. Test = 'to carry out trials on a product'.

i. Erproben means 'to carry out extensive tests or trials to establish how well a new product or device works, how it performs, etc.' *Ein Gerät auf seine Funktionstüchtigkeit erproben* is 'to test it to see if it works'. *Die Erprobung* is usually carried out by the manufacturer. If a prospective customer wishes to try out a product that is on the market before buying it, the appropriate v. is *ausprobieren*.

> *Unsere sämtlichen Produkte sind unter härtesten Bedingungen erprobt.*
>
> *Die Wagen wurden auf einer Strecke von je 100 000 Kilometern erprobt.*

ii. Testen is now often used in the sense of conducting tests to see what a product is like. The subj. is usually someone other than the manufacturer.

> *Unabhängige Sachverständige haben das neue Material unter extremen Bedingungen getestet.*

Das Gesundheitsministerium testet neue Arzneimittel, bevor sie zugelassen werden.

Getestet wurden 25 Staubsauger von fünf Herstellern im Preis zwischen 140 und 400 Mark.

Testen Sie unverbindlich vierzehn Tage lang diese neuartige Pfanne!—Sie werden begeistert sein.

9. Erproben is also applied to people and their qualities. *Jmds. Zuverlässigkeit wird erprobt.* The past. part. **erprobt** is applied to things and people that have proven their worth, i.e. have been tried and tested. Thus *ein erprobtes Mittel gegen Sonnenbrand,* well-tried, proven. *Ein erprobter Freund,* a proven, staunch, or long-standing friend. *Ein Mann von erprobter Zuverlässigkeit oder Ehrlichkeit,* of proven reliability or honesty. *Diese Neuerung hat sich bewährt* means that the innovation has been tried and proved its worth, proved to be suitable, valuable, etc. **Sich bewähren** is also used for people. *Sie hat sich in der Stelle/in dieser Arbeit [gut] bewährt,* proved herself. The past part. **bewährt** is a syn. of *erprobt. Ein bewährter Freund. Eine bewährte Methode. Dieser Stoff ist ein erprobtes/bewährtes Material für Regenmäntel,* a tried and tested material, one that has proved reliable.

Wir bieten unseren erprobten/bewährten Wagenheber in einer Sonderaktion zum halben Preis an.

turn v. Main uses. The three main equivalents are *drehen, kehren,* and *wenden.*

1. Turn, whose primary meaning is 'to rotate or revolve', is both trans. and intr. *I turn the wheel. The wheel turns.*

i. Drehen is trans., meaning 'to cause to move round either completely or partially on an axis or about a centre'. *Er drehte das Rad/den Türgriff.* With a key as obj. *drehen, umdrehen,* and *herumdrehen* are used without distinction. *Ich steckte den Schlüssel in das Schloß und drehte ihn [um/herum].* **Sich drehen** expresses the sense of the E. intr. v., 'to move round an axis or about a centre'. *Ein Plattenteller* (turntable) *dreht sich 33-mal in der Minute. Sich drehen* is also used for people who turn round several times on the same spot. *Sie drehte sich mehrere Male, damit wir das neue Kleid bewundern könnten.* It can be fig. *Als ich auf die Rechnung sah, drehte sich mir alles im Kopf,* my head spun. Intr. **turn** in *The screw won't turn* means 'can[not] be turned', which is **sich [nicht] drehen lassen.** *Die Schraube läßt sich nicht drehen—der Schlitz ist ausgeleiert.*

Um die Lautstärke zu regeln, mußt du den großen Knopf drehen. Also . . . an dem Knopf drehen.

Ich habe die Antenne in die stärkste Empfangsrichtung gedreht.

Jupiter dreht sich alle zehn Stunden um seine Achse.

Alle Planeten drehen sich um die Sonne.

Wenn die Achse nicht geschmiert wird, wird sich das Rad bald nicht mehr drehen.

Die Mannequins drehten sich bei jedem Gang auf dem Laufsteg mindestens zehnmal.

Bei seinen Nachforschungen hatte der Kommissar das Gefühl, sich im Kreis zu drehen.

Die Tür drehte sich quietschend in den rostigen Angeln.   *Der Schlüssel läßt sich nicht drehen.*

ii. Fig. use. If a debate, election, dispute, etc. turns on a certain matter, it has this matter as its central issue. **Sich drehen um** is used in this sense and is often impersonal. *Das Gespräch drehte sich um/Bei dem Gespräch drehte es sich um Familienangelegenheiten.* The impers. **es geht bei einem Gespräch** etc. **um,** 'to be about, to concern', can express a similar sense. *Bei dem Gespräch ging es um Geld/Politik.*

Der Wahlkampf drehte sich im wesentlichen darum, ob die Reichen höhere Steuern zahlen sollten.

Bei der Vernehmung drehte es sich/ging es darum, wo er sich am Abend, an dem das Verbrechen geschah, aufgehalten hatte.

iii. Turn also means 'to form or shape by rotation'. The machine is called *eine Drehbank.* **Drehen** is used for metals, **drechseln** for timber. *Man dreht Schrauben. Die Schüler drechselten Leuchter. Das Drechseln runder Tischbeine auf der Drehbank ist verhältnismäßig einfach.* Also *Er drehte sich eine Zigarette.*

iv. Turn over, meaning 'to somersault through the air', as in *The car turned over*, is **sich überschlagen**. *Das Auto durchbrach die Leitplanke und überschlug sich [mehrmals].* For people, it means 'to turn head over heels'. *Der kleine Junge fiel hin und überschlug sich. To turn a somersault* is normally *einen Purzelbaum schlagen.*

2. Turn also means 'to change or reverse position by a rotary motion through 180° so as to change the position of an object or a pers.'s lying or standing position'. When there is no phr. of direction, E. adds *over* for something in a lying position and *round* for something standing. *She turned the letter over/the chair round. He turned on to his back/turned over.*

i. The most common words are **drehen** and **umdrehen**, which means 'to put sth. on the opposite side or in another, usually the opposite, position', i.e. 'to turn over or round'. The refl. of both is needed when **turn** is intr. *Drehen* is used like **turn** with a phr. of direction, *umdrehen* when this is missing. *Man drehte den Bewußtlosen vorsichtig auf den Rücken. Man dreht eine Münze/ein Blatt Papier um. Dreh' deine Hand um!* (or *herum*). *Sie drehte sich auf die andere Seite*, but *Er drehte sich im Schlaf um. Umdrehen* also means 'to turn upside down'. *Er drehte das Glas um.* (Also *Er stellte das Glas auf den Kopf.*) *Einen Stuhl umdrehen* means both 'to turn it upside down' and 'to turn it so that it faces the other way', i.e. 'to turn it round'. **Kehren** has the general sense discussed here but is now very restricted in use. *Sie kehrte das Gesicht zur Sonne.* It occurs in fixed idiomatic expressions such as *das unterste zu oberst kehren*, to turn everthing upside down. *To turn sth. inside out* can be *die Innenseite nach außen kehren*, but *wenden* is probably more usual. *Inside out* is *links herum*, *links* also meaning 'the inside'. *Verkehrt herum* is 'the wrong way round' and can translate *inside out* or *back to front* or *upside down*. **Wenden** is the technical term in cooking and other fields meaning 'to turn over on to the other side', *Man wendet den Braten/das Omelett*, but *umdrehen* is heard in speech. In more formal language. *Man wendet die Unterseite des Geräts nach oben* is found. **Sich wenden** is also not uncommon when people who are standing turn in a certain direction, *Sie wendete/wandte sich zur Seite*, but *sich drehen* is also used. In general, *[sich] wenden* is more formal and technical than *[sich] drehen* and its derivatives. *Als er sie kommen sah, kehrte er sich und ging in sein Zimmer* is possible but uncommon. *Er drehte sich um* is the normal expression.

> *Er hob das Messer auf und drehte es hin und her.*   *Langsam drehte er den Kopf.*
> *Sie drehte/wendete das Gesicht zur Tür, als sie ein Geräusch hörte.*
> *Beim Umdrehen der Schallplatte beschädigte er die Plattennadel.*
> *Dein Großvater würde sich im Grab umdrehen, wenn er das wüßte.*
> *Heute kehrt er seine beste Seite nach außen/seine rauhe Seite nach außen.*
> *Sie war sehr geschickt beim Pfannkuchenwenden.*
> *Das Gras muß, nachdem man es gemäht hat, alle zwei Tage gewendet werden.*
> *Nachdem ein Vogel Eier gelegt hat, wendet er sie häufig. Or . . . dreht er die Eier . . . um.*
> *Beim Schreiten durch die Menge blieb die Königin oft stehen und wendete sich nach rechts und links, um ein kurzes Gespräch mit den Anwesenden zu führen.*

ii. Derivatives.

a. As explained in 2. i, **turn round** referring to people is usually **sich umdrehen**. *Dreh' dich um! Er drehte sich zu mir um*, turned [round] towards me. *Er drehte sich nach ihr um*, turned [his head] to look at her. **Sich umwenden** is also used. **Sich umkehren** is less common.

> *Als er ein Geräusch hinter sich hörte, drehte er sich um, um zu sehen, was es war.*
> *Erst als sie sich umdrehte und ich ihr Gesicht sah, erkannte ich sie.*
> *In der Tür wendete/wandte er sich nochmal um und winkte zum Abschied.*
> *Als ein Zuschauer plötzlich aufschrie, wendeten/wandten sich alle nach ihm um.*
> *Als sie mich erblickte, drehte/wandte sie sich nach mir um.*

b. **Turn towards** is **sich zudrehen** + dat. if the whole body is meant; otherwise the part is stated. *Er drehte sich ihr zu* or *drehte ihr das Gesicht zu.* **[Sich] zuwenden** is also fairly common. *Sie wandte mir den Rücken zu. Er wandte sich seinem Nebenmann zu.*

Als er sich erhob, wendeten sich ihm alle Gesichter zu. (Usual v. *drehen* is also possible.)

c. **Turn** sth. **away** is **abwenden** or **wegdrehen**, occasionally **abkehren**. *Sie wandte den Kopf ab/drehte das Gesicht weg.* The refl. forms render the E. intr. uses. *S.o. turned away: Jmd. drehte sich weg/wendete sich ab/kehrte sich ab. Er wandte sich von mir ab.*

Die der Sonne abgewandte/abgekehrte Seite der Erde liegt in Dunkelheit.

Sie kehrte die Augen ab.

iii. Turn = 'to reverse a leaf in a book in order to read or write on the other side'. **Wenden** is used for a single detached sheet or page. *Bitte wenden!* at the bottom of a page means 'turn over/to the back'. For a printed book etc. **umblättern** is the usual v. *Man blättert eine Seite um* or *blättert zur nächsten Seite um.* **Weiterblättern** normally means 'to turn over several pages' but may be used for one. *Wenn du ein paar Seiten weiterblätterst/umblätterst, findest du das Diagramm.* Also *Eine Seite weiterblättern.* Less common words are **umwenden** and **umschlagen**. *Ich wende die Notenblätter für dich um. Sie schlug die Seiten in der Zeitung um, bis sie die Kinoanzeigen fand.* (In some contexts *umschlagen* means 'to turn up', e.g. *Er schlug den Kragen um. Wenn die Ärmel zu lang sind, schlag sie doch einfach um!*) **Turn to** a certain page etc. means 'to open to it'. One equivalent is **aufschlagen**. *Sie griff zur Lokalzeitung und schlug die Seiten mit den Kinoanzeigen auf.* Cf. OPEN 4. ii.

iv. Special cases.

a. The military command *Right/Left* **turn** is *Rechtsum/linksum kehrt.* The refl. is omitted. *'Ganze Abteilung, rechtsum kehrt!' rief der Feldwebel, und wir drehten uns alle nach rechts.*

b. *The soil has just been* **turned** is *umgegraben* if by hand, or *gepflügt* or *umgepflügt*, by a plough.

c. *My stomach* **turned** *at the sight* can be *Bei diesem Anblick hat sich mir der Magen umgedreht.* An alternative expressing the meaning is *Der Anblick widerte mich an.*

3. Turn or **turn round** also mean 'to reverse course or direction'. Vehicles which turn in this sense or turn round face ultimately, and proceed, in the opposite direction. **Turn** is both intr., *You can turn at the end of the street,* and trans., *Can you turn the car in this narrow street?* (To turn into/out of a street is discussed in 4.)

i. The usual equivalents are **wenden** and **drehen** and their derivatives with **um**. In the situations referred to here, movement is implied so that a change of course results. For vehicles *wenden* is used in official language and often in everyday speech, but *drehen* is common in the everyday language. *Wo können wir wenden/drehen?* Both are intr. in this use, *Der Autofahrer drehte/wendete und fuhr zurück,* but only *wenden* is trans., *Es war schwer, den Lastwagen in dem begrenzten Platz zu wenden.* In this sense *wenden* is weak only. *Ich wendete das Boot.* For vehicles **umdrehen** and **umwenden** are used intr. with the same meaning as the base vs., as **turn round** is. *An der Einfahrt ist das Auto umgedreht/umgewendet.*

Die Busse wenden am Ende der Straße.

Hast du genug Platz, um [das Auto] in dieser engen Straße zu wenden?

Das Schiff kann allein auf verhältnismäßig kleinem Raum ohne Hilfe eines Bugsierers wenden.

ii. An animal can be the obj. of **turn**. If a 180° turn is meant, **umwenden** is used. *Der Reiter wendete das Pferd um und galoppierte weg.* **Wenden** + phr. of direction is used for a partial turn. *Durch das Zaumzeug kann man ein Pferd nach links oder rechts wenden.*

iii. Applied to people **turn** is intr. and denotes either a complete turn, *They turned and fled,* or a partial one, *She turned towards the exit/left.* The E. and G. vs. do not necessarily imply continuous motion, but rather a turn followed by movement. G. requires refl. vs. and, for a complete turn, the derivatives with *um*. **Sich umwenden** suggests a fairly dignified and slow movement, **sich umdrehen** usually a quick one. *They turned and fled* becomes *Sie drehten sich um und flohen* as this is not dignified and slow, but *Er wandte/wendete sich um und ging weg* would be appropriate under other circumstances. *Sich umdrehen* is the usual v. when an animal is the subj. *Als wir uns ihm bis auf fünf Meter genähert hatten, drehte sich das Reh um und lief weg.* **Sich wenden** + phr. of direction is used for a partial turn. *Sie wandte sich zum Ausgang/zur Tür und ging hinaus.* (*Sie wandten sich zur Flucht*, 'turned and fled', is now purely literary.) **Umkehren**, used intr. for people, means 'to retrace one's steps, to turn round and go back the way one has come'. *Als es anfing zu regnen, mußten wir umkehren.*

Sie drehte/wendete sich nach der Stelle um, wo ihr Bruder stand, und ging auf ihn zu.

iv. Special cases.

a. The military command *About* **turn** is *Kehrt! Ganze Abteilung kehrt! Erster Zug kehrt!*

b. Kehrtmachen is 'to turn or turn around', particularly when an immediate reaction is suggested. It translates *to turn on one's heel. Als sie das hörte, machte sie auf dem Absatz kehrt und verließ den Saal.*

c. Wenden means 'to turn' in swimming. *Der führende Schwimmer hat schon gewendet.*

d. Sich drehen is used of the wind. *Gegen Mittag drehte sich der Wind, und es fing an zu regnen.*

e. Umleiten, 'to change the course of, divert', applied to something flowing or moving. *Die Polizei leitete den Verkehr in eine Nebenstraße um. Man leitete den Fluß in einen Stausee um*, turned the river into a dam.

4. Turn, used intr., means 'to change course so as to proceed in a different direction'. *They turned out of/into the High Street. The road turns sharply to the left a kilometre from here.* It can also be trans. *The car turned the corner.*

i. Here G. does not use any of the main vs. so far discussed. The main equivalents are **biegen** and its derivatives which imply turning in an arc (*ein Bogen*). They are used both for vehicles and for people on foot. *Der Wagen bog in die Toreinfahrt [ein].* (*Ein* is optional with a phr. with *in*.) **Turn into** is **einbiegen**, *Sie bogen in eine Nebenstraße ein*, and **turn off** is **abbiegen**, *Das Auto bog von der Hauptstraße/nach rechts ab.* The E. trans. form, *He turned the car into a side-street*, becomes *Er bog mit dem Auto in eine Seitenstraße ein*, and *The car turned the corner* becomes *Das Auto bog um die Ecke.* *Abbiegen* is also used with a road, path, line, etc. as subj. *Einen Kilometer von hier biegt die Straße nach links ab.* Alternatives are *Die Straße macht einen Bogen* or *eine Kurve*, more specifically *eine Rechtskurve* or *eine Linkskurve.* Alternatives for vehicles are *fahren, Der Lastwagen fuhr in die Hauptstraße*, and *abfahren, Wir fahren bald von dieser Straße ab.*

Als sie ein paar Minuten später von der Hauptstraße in eine schmale Gasse eingebogen sind, habe ich sie aus den Augen verloren.   *Biege links ab, wenn du zum Wegweiser kommst!*
Siehst du die Straße am Ende des nächsten Feldes? Wir müssen dort abbiegen/einbiegen.
Ungefähr zwei Kilometer von hier biegt die Straße nach rechts zum Fluß hin ab.

ii. The military term *Left/Right wheel!* is *Links/Rechts schwenkt!* **Einschwenken** is used with people marching as subj. in the sense 'to turn into'. *Die Marschkolonne schwenkte in die Hauptstraße ein.* It is sometimes applied to vehicles. *Das Fahrzeug schwenkte in den Hof ein.*

5. Turn into or **turn** + adj. = 'to change into or become'. The E. v. is trans. meaning 'to change or transform', *They turned the abandoned monastery into a school*, and intr. meaning 'to become', *Caterpillars turn into butterflies.*

i. **Verwandeln** and **umwandeln**, 'to change, transform', discussed under CHANGE 3, translate the trans. use, and **sich verwandeln/umwandeln** express the intr. sense. In the following sents. the vs. could be translated as *turn*. *Man hat das verlassene Kloster in eine Schule umgewandelt. Raupen wandeln sich in Schmetterlinge um.*

> *Die schweren Regenfälle verwandeln die träge dahinfließenden Bäche in reißende Ströme.*
> *Sein Neid verwandelte sich in Zorn, und sein Zorn in Haß.*
> *Siedendes/Kochendes Wasser verwandelt sich in Dampf.*

ii. *One thg.* **turns [in]to** *another* indicates a change of state. Here **werden zu** is used, as well as the refl. vs in i. *Water turns to ice below 0 °C: Unter 0 °C wird Wasser zu Eis. Bei 100° wird Wasser zu Dampf* or *Bei 100° verwandelt sich Wasser in Dampf. Werden zu* is also used for people. *Ich habe es erlebt, daß Sozialisten zu Konservativen geworden sind, or . . . , daß aus Konservativen Sozialisten geworden sind.*

> *Er wurde zum Verräter.* (He turned [into a] traitor.)

iii. **Turn**, followed by an adj., is expressed by **werden**. *Die Lösung wurde blau,* turned blue.

> *Die anfänglich grauen Schwanjungen werden bald weiß.*   *Seine Haare werden grau.*
> *Durch die Erwärmung wird der Teer flüssig.*
> *Wenn die Halme gelb werden, sind die Pflanzen reif, geerntet zu werden.*
> *'Meine Mutter!' sagte Lucie und wurde weiß wie die Wand.*

iv. **Werden** also translates **turn** in *He has just turned fourteen. Er ist gerade vierzehn geworden.*

6. Turn into can mean 'to change from one lang. into another', which would normally be **übersetzen**. *Es ist schwer, diese lustigen Reime ins Deutsche zu übersetzen.* In reference to language **turn into** also means 'to change from one form of expression into another', as in *Can you turn that legal jargon into plain E.? Kannst du den juristischen Jargon in einfaches Englisch umformulieren?* **Umformulieren** means 'to reformulate'. The base v. **formulieren** can be used with an adv. *Wir müssen diesen Absatz einfacher formulieren* could translate *turn it into simpler lang.* An alternative is **ausdrücken**, to EXPRESS. *Drück' es einfacher aus!*

> *Diese englische Konstruktion muß anders formuliert werden, weil im Deutschen eine solche Infinitivkonstruktion fehlt.*

Umschreiben in one sense means 'to rewrite in a different literary form'.

> *Das Stück hat er zuerst in Prosa geschrieben, aber dann in Verse umgeschrieben.*

7. Turn on/off, to switch on/off. G. has more words than E. that express this sense, and individual speakers will have preferences. For a light, an electrical appliance, radio, and television, **einschalten** and **anschalten** are the standard words for *turn/switch on*, and **ausschalten** and **abschalten** for the opposite. Colloquially, **anmachen** and **ausmachen** are often used. **Anknipsen** and **ausknipsen** are less common. **Anstellen** and **abstellen** are used with *die Heizung* as obj. For a tap, when *der Hahn,* i.e. *Wasserhahn* or *Gashahn,* is the obj., the standard terms are **aufdrehen** and **zudrehen**. When *Wasser* and *Gas* are the obj., i.e. when *der Hahn* is not mentioned, *anstellen* and *abstellen* are usual. **Abdrehen** is often heard in speech for *zudrehen* and *abstellen*. *To turn a car engine off* is *abstellen*. (The opposite *anlassen*.) *To turn on* an electric motor is expressed by *einschalten, anschalten, anmachen,* and *anstellen*. **Anschmeißen** is common in colloquial speech. Vs. meaning to turn an electric motor off are *ausschalten, abschalten, ausmachen,* and *abstellen*.

> *Wie schaltet man den Staubsauger ein?*   *Schalte das Licht mal an!*
> *Mach' das Radio mal an!*   *Hast du den Fernseher ausgemacht/ausgeschaltet?*
> *Schalte den Strom bitte mal ab!*   *Stell' mal eben den Herd an!*
> *Stell'/Mach' doch die Heizung an, wenn dir kalt ist.*

8. Fig. and extended uses of senses of **turn**.

i. *I turned the conversation to sth. else*: *Ich brachte das Gespräch auf ein anderes Thema.* The intr. use *The conversation turned to another topic* can be *Ohne daß wir es merkten, kamen wir auf ein anderes Thema.* Or *Das Gespräch kam auf etw. anderes/ein anderes Thema.*

ii. *Thousands of dollars were being turned over every hour*: *Tausende von Dollar wurden in jeder Stunde umgesetzt. Der Umsatz* is 'turnover'.

iii. *The tide has turned* is, depending on whether it is coming in or going out, *Die Ebbe/Flut hat eingesetzt.*

iv. With regard to luck. *Jmds. Glück hat sich gewendet*, it has become the opposite of what it was. *Hoffentlich wird sich das Blatt bald wenden* expresses the wish for a change from bad to good.

v. Turn a gun, one's eyes **on** sth. means 'to aim, point, or direct at', a sense expressed by **richten**, to AIM. *Er entriß seinem Bruder das Gewehr und richtete es auf/gegen sich selbst. Er richtete die Geschütze auf den Palast und drohte, ihn in Stücke zu schießen. Sie richtete ihre Augen auf ihn.* The pass. *The eyes of all Europe were turned on this army* becomes *Die Augen ganz Europas richteten sich auf diese Armee.* Richten also translates *She could turn the whole force of her mind at a moment's notice to any subject*: *In kürzester Zeit konnte sie die ganze Kraft ihres Geistes auf ein beliebiges Thema richten.*

vi. Sich jmdm./einem Thema **zuwenden** means 'to turn to' or 'turn one's attention to'. *Wir wandten uns dem armen Thomas zu* is ambiguous as it can mean either 'turned towards him' or 'turned our attention to him'. **Meine** etc. **Aufmersamkeit auf etw. richten** expresses the latter unambiguously. *Wir richteten unsere Aufmerksamkeit nun auf den armen Thomas/auf Punkt vier.*

> *Nach dieser Betrachtung der Gedichte wenden wir uns nun dem Leben des Dichters zu.*
> *Um genaue Auskunft zu erhalten, müssen Sie sich den parlamentarischen Berichten zuwenden.* Also
> ... *die parlamentarischen Berichte heranziehen* (to consult).
> *Die Zeit drängt. Wir müssen uns den anderen Punkten auf der Tagesordnung zuwenden.*
> *Mit einem Gefühl der Erleichterung wandten wir uns einem angenehmeren Thema zu.*

Sich zuwenden also translates *What will he turn to next?— he seems to have tried most hobbies/sports. Welchem Hobby/Welcher Sportart wird er sich nun zuwenden?—er scheint die meisten schon ausprobiert zu haben.*

vii. Turn to s.o. for help, advice, etc. is **sich wenden an.** *Um Hilfe/Rat* can, but need not, be added. *Sie wußte nicht, an wen sie sich [um Hilfe] wenden sollte.* Cf. APPROACH 4. ii.

viii. There are several expressions similar to **not to know which way to turn**. *Jmd. ist ratlos/weiß weder aus noch ein.* Also possible are *Er weiß nicht, an wen er sich wenden soll/wohin er sich wenden soll/was er machen/tun soll.* We were at our wits' end and didn't know which way to turn: *Wir waren mit unserer Weisheit am Ende und wußten nicht, wohin wir uns wenden sollten.*

ix. There are several expressions like **turn s.o. out** or **away** or **from one's door**. Similar to **turn** s.o. **out** are **hinauswerfen, vor die Tür setzen, auf die Straße setzen,** or the more refined **hinausweisen.** Cf. ORDER *v.* 2. **Abweisen** means 'to turn away or turn from one's door'. Cf. REFUSE 4.

> *Wenn ihm danach zu Mute wäre, würde er mich hinauswerfen/vor die Tür setzen, ohne auch nur mit*
> *der Wimper zu zucken.*   *Sie wollen mich doch nicht etwa abweisen?*

x. Turn against. In E. this can be intr. *His followers began to turn against him*, or trans. *She tried to turn him against his parents.* **Sich wenden gegen** corresponds to the intr. use. *Seine Anhänger fingen an, sich gegen ihn zu wenden.* A transl. of the trans. use needs to express the meaning. Two versions of the second sent. are *Sie versuchte, ihm Haß/Verachtung gegen seine Eltern einzuimpfen*; and *Sie wirkte so auf ihn ein, daß er seine Eltern zu hassen/verachten begann.*

> *Die Leute, die dir jetzt nachlaufen, werden sich als Erste gegen dich wenden.*

Die Schmeichler von gestern haben keine Bedenken, sich gegen ihn zu wenden und ihn zu zerreißen.
Transls. of *Thgs. may suddenly turn against you* are *Du weißt nicht, wann sich für dich das Blatt wenden kann,* and *Du weißt nicht, wann sich das Glück sich von dir abwenden wird.*

xi. Turn s.o.'s **head**. *Success has turned his head*: *Ihm ist der Erfolg zu Kopf gestiegen*. A more general expression is *jmdm. die Gedanken/Sinne verwirren*. *Jmdm. den Kopf verdrehen* is 'to make s.o. fall in love with you'.

> *Diese Erlebnisse haben seine Gedanken so verwirrt, daß er zwischen Wirklichkeit und Phantasie nicht unterscheiden kann.*
>
> *Der Jochem ist jetzt oft bei Hoffmanns. Die Enkelin, die seit ein paar Wochen da wohnt, hat ihm gehörig den Kopf verdreht.*

u

understand *v.* The main equivalent is *verstehen*. A common syn. in several senses is *begreifen*. In general *begreifen* is stronger and more emphatic and emotional than *verstehen*. It can always be replaced by *verstehen*, but the nuance it conveys is then lost. **Understand**, *verstehen*, and *begreifen* can be trans. and intr.

1. Understand means 'to grasp the meaning of sth. spoken or written'. *Did you understand that explanation?* This sense can always be expressed by **verstehen**. *Ich verstehe, was du sagen willst.* **Begreifen** often refers not only to a particular instance but to someone's ability to understand explanations etc. in general. *Das Kind begreift schnell/leicht/langsam/schwer.* If A is talking to B who does not understand, *begreifen* suggests that, in A's opinion, B ought to understand or is slow to understand. It occurs in questions like *Hast du das endlich begriffen?* or *Hast du das immer noch nicht begriffen?* Such a question could easily cause offence and would be used only by a superior, e.g. teacher to pupil. *Begreifen* is more offensive than *verstehen*. *Begreifen* can be used of oneself. *Das habe ich nun endlich begriffen*. *Begreifen* is also often used for the process of becoming aware of a meaning etc. *Sie begriff den Sinn sofort. Ich habe allmählich/plötzlich begriffen, was gemeint war.*

> *Ich verstehe/begreife nicht, was du meinst.* *Sie hat die Erklärung nicht verstanden/begriffen.*
> *Ich verstehe den Sinn dieser Bemerkung/die Bedeutung dieses Wortes nicht.*
> *Er erklärte es ihnen in einfachen Worten, in der Hoffnung, daß sie ihn verstehen/begreifen würden.*
> Or . . . *es verstehen/begreifen würden.* *Kein Mensch begreift, was das bedeuten soll.*
> *So oft ich es dir auch erklärt habe, du begreifst/verstehst es immer noch nicht.*

2. Syns. of *verstehen* in sense 1.

i. Auffassen in one sense means 'to grasp fully sth. presented as an explanation'. It is both trans., *Die Kinder haben die Erklärung schnell aufgefaßt*, and intr., *Es sind Kinder, die schnell auffassen.*

> *Die Pädagogik ist ständig bemüht, Methoden zu entwickeln, durch die Lernende einfacher und schneller auffassen.*

ii. Erfassen is a more formal term for understanding intellectually. It needs an obj. *Sie hat den Unterschied zwischen den beiden Theorien sofort erfaßt.*

> *Obwohl er zwanzig Minuten zu spät gekommen war, erfaßte er schnell, worum es in der Vorlesung ging.*
> *Die genaue Bedeutung dieses dehnbaren Begriffes läßt sich nur schwer, wenn überhaupt, erfassen.*

iii. Kapieren is a colloquial word meaning 'to take in or understand an explanation etc.' It is similar to *get*, when this means 'to understand'.

> *Sagen Sie es noch einmal? Ich habe es immer noch nicht kapiert/verstanden/begriffen.*
> *Ich war froh, daß ich die Formel kapiert hatte und anwenden konnte.*

iv. Klar is often heard in situations in which **understand** might be used in E. *Es ist mir noch nicht ganz klar, wie man zu diesem Ergebnis kommt. Es* is mostly omitted when a clause follows unless it is the first word. *Es ist mir noch nicht ganz klar, wie* . . . but *Mir ist noch nicht ganz klar, wie* . . . The synonymous expressions **Ich bin mir darüber klar** and **Ich bin mir darüber im klaren** are slightly more emphatic.

> *Ist dir jetzt klar, worum es geht?*
> *Wir sind uns jetzt darüber im klaren, wie der Fehler entstanden ist.*

v. The questions 'You understand?' and 'Is that understood?' are asked to make sure that the person spoken to realizes what he or she must do. *Haben Sie das verstanden?* or *Ist dir das klar?* are neutral in tone. *Verstanden?* or *Kapiert?* or *Hast du das kapiert/begriffen?* are also used, especially when the tone of voice suggests a warning or threat.

3. Three senses of **understand** are carried only by **verstehen**. One is 'to hear properly'. *The noise made it impossible for me to understand the telephone operator. Wegen des Lärms war es unmöglich, die Telefonistin zu verstehen.* Only *verstehen* has the sense 'to make out the meaning of s.o.'s speech'. *Er sprach mit so starkem Akzent, daß niemand ihn verstehen konnte.* Only *verstehen* means 'to apprehend the meaning by knowing what is conveyed by the words'. In both languages the obj. can be a language or code. *Versteht hier jmd. Japanisch?*

> *Das brauchen Sie nicht zu wiederholen, ich habe Sie das erste Mal verstanden.* Or *Ich habe das erste Mal schon verstanden.*
>
> *Nur er verstand die verschlüsselte Nachricht.*   *Ich verstehe ein bißchen Russisch.*

4. Understand and **verstehen** both mean 'to apprehend clearly the nature or character of a pers. or why people behave in the way they do'. *No one understands me. I cannot understand how anyone can be so foolish.* Again **verstehen** is the main equivalent. Applied to people and their conduct, **begreifen** is more emotional than *verstehen* and is usually neg. *Ich kann dich einfach nicht begreifen.*

> *Ich begreife/verstehe nicht, wie man so leichtsinnig sein kann.*
>
> *Er verstand/begriff sich selbst nicht mehr. Er hatte sich so schlecht benommen und brachte es nicht übers Herz, sich zu entschuldigen.*   *Keiner versteht mich.*
>
> *Je besser ich ihn verstand, desto mehr mochte ich ihn.*   *Sie ist die einzige, die mich versteht.*
>
> *Ich verstehe Ihre Reaktion/diesen Wunsch sehr gut.*
>
> *Ich verstehe/begreife nicht, wie man so etw. tun kann.*
>
> *Solches Benehmen ist schwer zu begreifen/verstehen.*

5. Mostly with a clause as obj. **understand** means 'to be aware of the reason' or 'to be able to explain why sth. is happening or has happened'. *I don't understand why the engine isn't working. It's easy to understand how it happened.*

i. Verstehen also has this sense. **Begreifen** may suggest that the situation is difficult to understand, e.g. a sudden change in someone's life which that person cannot take in or get used to. *Begreifen* is often neg., is used with *nur schwer*, or is found in questions. *Noch nach Wochen konnte er nicht begreifen, daß sie ihn verlassen hatte.* In pos. sents. it has the same meaning as *verstehen*. *Du wirst gleich begreifen/verstehen, warum ich das gemacht habe. Begreifen* is often used when someone [suddenly] becomes aware of something. *Ich teilte dem Kapitän mit, was ich gesehen hatte. Nach kurzer Überlegung begriff er blitzartig, welche Gefahr uns bedrohte.*

> *Es tut mir leid, aber ich verstehe/begreife ebensowenig wie Sie, was sich dort abspielt.*
>
> *Ich verstehe/begreife nicht, warum der Motor nicht anspringt.*
>
> *Man kann leicht verstehen/begreifen, warum er weggegangen ist.*
>
> *Was eigentlich geschehen war, hatte sie noch nicht ganz begriffen.*
>
> *Sie hatte schnell begriffen/verstanden, worum es ging, und daß alles für sie auf dem Spiel stand.*
>
> *Ich verstehe/begreife den Zweck dieser Maßnahmen/dieser Änderungen nicht/den Grund nicht.*
>
> *Sie scheinen nicht zu verstehen/begreifen, was es heißt, Verantwortung zu tragen.*
>
> *Um die Funktion heutiger Institutionen zu verstehen/begreifen, muß man etw. von ihrer Entstehung und Entwicklung wissen.*

ii. Einsehen is discussed under REALIZE 1. i. It implies being able to understand something as a result of what someone says by way of explanation or justification. *Die Notwendigkeit dieser Maßnahmen sehe ich [nicht] ein.*

> *Ich sehe ein, daß du unter diesen Umständen dich nicht anders entscheiden konntest.*
>
> *Ich sehe nicht ein, warum das nötig ist/warum wir uns so beeilen müssen.*

iii. Fassen in two closely related senses means 'to grasp, comprehend' and 'to believe' in the sense 'to consider possible or real'. It is neg. in these senses and only occurs in the constructions *Etw. ist nicht zu fassen* and *Jmd. kann etw. nicht fassen*. A word which is neg. in sense like *kaum* can replace *nicht*.

Sie hatte gewonnen, und man sah es ihr an, daß sie es kaum fassen konnte.

Ich habe viel gelernt und kann es nicht fassen, daß ich bei der Prüfung durchgefallen bin.

iv. When **understand** means 'to show a sympathetic insight into or attitude towards another's actions or position', it is often most clearly expressed by **Verständnis für jmdn./etw. haben**, which implies goodwill, putting oneself into the other's place, and finding his/her action justified. Cf. UNDERSTANDING 4. iii. and APPRECIATE 2. ii. *Wenn du nicht hingehen kannst, wird er bestimmt Verständnis dafür haben.*

6. Verstehen means 'to understand' a theory or work of art, 'to understand or know about' machinery such as cars, boats, etc., and 'to know' his/her trade etc. *Jmd. versteht eine Theorie/ein Kunstwerk/eine Epoche* as well as *sein Handwerk/sein Fach.* For fields of study, mechanical devices, practical activities, plants, etc., it is more usual to say *Jmd. versteht etw./viel/nur wenig von. Jmd. versteht etw./viel von Chemie/Autos/Rosen,* etc. To this sense belongs also *verstehen* + infin., meaning 'to know or understand how to do sth.' With an extended infin., *es* is usually added. *Sie versteht es, zwischen verfeindeten Parteien diplomatisch zu vermitteln.*

Er versteht zu schreiben, und seine Bücher verkaufen sich gut.

Es war bewundernswert, wie gut er es verstand, mit wenig Geld auszukommen.

The infin. construction could translate *She [thoroughly] understands children* when 'how to handle them' is meant. *Sie versteht es ausgezeichnet, mit Kindern umzugehen.* Also possible is *Sie versteht etw. von kleinen Kindern.* **Sich verstehen auf** means 'to understand intellectually and to be expert in doing sth.' *Er versteht sich auf die Behandlung schwieriger Kunden.*

Er versteht sich auf Fahrräder und kann immer helfen, wenn man ihn bei Reparaturen um Rat fragt.

7. Understand and **verstehen** both mean 'to take or interpret in a certain way'. A syn. is **auffassen**, to INTERPRET. *What did you understand this remark to mean?* becomes *Wie hast du diese Bemerkung verstanden/aufgefaßt? How does she intend these words to be understood?: Wie sollen wir diese/ihre Worte verstehen/auffassen?* Only *verstehen* takes a personal obj. *What do you understand her/her words to mean?: Wie hast du sie verstanden? Wie haben Sie ihre Worte verstanden/aufgefaßt?* To *mean* need not be translated as it is implied in *verstehen* and *auffassen.*

Wie soll ich das verstehen?   Wie haben Sie denn seine Worte verstanden?

Sie haben meine Bemerkungen falsch aufgefaßt. Sie sind nicht als Drohung zu verstehen.

Verstehe ich Sie richtig/recht, daß sie dem Vertrag zum Ende des Quartals kündigen wollen?

Verstehe ich Sie etwa recht, wenn ich annehme, daß Ihre Ablehnung endgültig ist? (am I to understand)

Here belong E. sents. like *I understand the message to mean they aren't coming: Ich habe die Worte so verstanden/aufgefaßt, daß sie nicht kommen werden. Verstehe ich dich recht, daß du diese giftige Lösung in die Milchkanne getan hast?* could be a transl. of *Do I understand you to mean . . . ? Wenn Sie meine Worte so aufgefaßt haben, dann haben Sie mich völlig falsch verstanden* is a transl. of *No one could understand that from my words.* **Understand by** a word etc. is **verstehen unter.** *Sie müssen mir erklären, was sie unter multikulturell verstehen.*

8. With a pl. subj. or a sing. subj. + *mit* **sich verstehen** means 'to understand or get on [well] with each other or s.o.' *Wir haben uns immer gut verstanden.* Or *Ich habe mich immer gut mit ihm/ihr verstanden.*

Je älter die Kinder wurden, desto besser verstanden sie sich mit den Eltern.

9. Understand means 'to regard as settled or implied without specific mention'. If it is understood that a particular rule, condition, etc. applies in a particular situation, everyone concerned has agreed or is aware that it will operate. *It is understood that the firm will refund all our expenses.* This meaning is expressed by **sich verstehen**. *Das versteht sich,* that's understood, taken for granted. *Es versteht sich, daß alle dazu beisteuern werden.* A phr. can follow. *Der Preis versteht sich einschließlich Mehrwertsteuer. Von selbst* is often added. *Etw. versteht sich von selbst.* means 'it goes without saying' or 'it is taken for granted.'

> *Daß ich dir helfen würde, versteht sich [von selbst]. Du bist mir auch immer entgegengekommen.*
> *Es versteht sich von selbst, daß die Firma alle Unkosten erstattet.*
> *Es verstand sich von selbst, daß sie pünktlich ankamen, denn sie wußten, daß er jedes Zuspätkommen als Unhöflichkeit empfand.*   *Die Bettenpreise verstehen sich einschließlich Frühstück.*

10. Give s.o. **to understand** is **jmdm. zu verstehen geben.** *Er gab der Gruppe zu verstehen, er sei nicht länger bereit, solches Benehmen zu dulden.* In the pass.: *Uns wurde zu verstehen gegeben, daß wir sofort verschwinden mußten.*

> *Man hat mir unmißverständlich zu verstehen gegeben, daß man mich nicht mehr braucht.*

11. I understand that means 'I believe or assume on the basis of information received'. *I understand that we have got the contract.* The meaning has to be expressed. Some possibilities are *soweit ich weiß, ich habe gehört,* or *ich habe mir sagen lassen,* was told on enquiring. *Soweit ich weiß/Ich habe gehört/Ich habe mir sagen lassen, daß wir den Zuschlag bekommen haben.*

> *Ich habe gehört/habe mir sagen lassen, daß Sie aufs Land ziehen wollen.*
> *Soweit ich weiß, ist der Fremde, der sich seit vorgestern bei Meyers aufhält, ein Vetter von Frau Meyer.*

12. Understand, mostly + **from,** means 'to infer from information received'. *I understand from what he said that he's in favour.* Here **entnehmen** + dat. or *aus,* or **schließen** + *aus,* 'to deduce or conclude from', can be used. Cf. GATHER 9. *Aus dem, was er sagte, habe ich entnommen/geschlossen, daß er dafür ist.*

> *Wir entnehmen aus ihrem Brief, daß sie in drei Wochen hierher kommt.*
> *Seinen Ausführungen entnehme ich, daß er noch viele ungelöste Probleme gibt.*

13. In one sense **sich verständigen** means 'to make oneself understood when the people do not speak the same lang.' *Sie verständigten sich durch Zeichen/auf Russisch.*

> *Ich kann ein bißchen Italienisch und kann mich mit den Leuten verständigen.*

understanding *n.* Some uses of **agreement** *n.*

1. In its basic sense, which is still readily understood but no longer belongs to the active vocabulary, **(the) understanding** refers to the power or ability to comprehend and reason, and thus means 'intelligence' or 'intellect'. A quotation in the *OED* reads: *Understanding is a power of the soul, by which we perceive, know, remember, and judge* (written in 1621). Expressions such as *a man of understanding* or *of some/no/little understanding* may sometimes be heard. The still commonly used G. equivalent is **der Verstand,** which is also discussed under BRAIN, MIND, and SENSE. It denotes the faculty by which we think, judge, and understand reality, i.e. the mind or intelligence, and may be contrasted to the emotions. *Jmd. hat viel/wenig/keinen Verstand* or *einen klaren/praktischen/scharfen Verstand. Ein Mensch mit Verstand.*

> *Er war gewitzter, als sie zunächst annahm. So viel Verstand hätte sie bei einem Mann seiner Herkunft nicht erwartet.*
> *Es war Liebe auf den ersten Blick: Sein Verstand war ausgeschaltet. Es regierten nur die Gefühle.*

2. Another sense of **understanding** is 'the power to make experience intelligible, the capacity to formulate and apply to experience concepts and categories, to judge and draw logical conclusions'. The equivalent is **die Einsicht**. *Der zweite Teil der Autobiographie handelt von der Suche des Autors als junger Mann nach Einsicht und Weisheit. Ich hatte mehr Einsicht als alle meine Lehrer* (Psalm 119: 99). (The AV has *understanding*.) *Einsicht* is also translated as *insight, discernment, judgement, good sense, reason. Er zeigte wenig Einsicht. Ist sie nun endlich zur Einsicht gekommen? Haben Sie doch Einsicht!*, do show some understanding/be reasonable.

Die Einsicht kommt mit den Jahren.   *Er ist ein Mann von großer Einsicht.*

Wohl dem Menschen, der Weisheit erlangt, und dem Menschen, der Einsicht gewinnt! (Proverbs 3: 13)

3. Whoever has an understanding of something has a good knowledge of it, knows what it means or how it works. *I have some understanding of the matter. I doubt whether he has any real understanding of Shakespeare.* This idea is best expressed by the v. **verstehen**. *Von dieser Sache/Angelegenheit verstehe/weiß ich etw. Ich zweifle daran, ob er S. wirklich versteht.* A good understanding of G. history is gute **Kenntnisse** *der deutschen Geschichte.* Cf. KNOWLEDGE ii. *The job requires an understanding of Spanish: Für diese Stelle sind Spanischkenntnisse erforderlich* or *muß man etwas Spanisch verstehen können*, depending on what is meant.

4. Das Verständnis, which is followed by a gen. or prep., has three senses.

i. 'The ability to comprehend a text or a fact', 'the process of understanding sth.'
Der Lehrer versucht den Schülern das Verständnis der Gedichte zu erleichtern.
Die Kenntnis dieser Tatsache ist für das Verständnis der späteren Entwicklung unentbehrlich.

ii. 'S.o.'s understanding of sth.' i.e. 'the meaning s.o. attributes to a particular statement or passage', 'the way s.o. understands or interprets sth. written or spoken'. An alternative is *die Auffassung*. Cf. *auffassen* under INTERPRET 1 and UNDERSTAND 7. *My understanding of the passage is obviously different from yours: Mein Verständnis dieser Textstelle ist offenbar anders als deines.* Or *Meine Auffassung . . . ist anders als deine. Die Tagebucheintragungen des Dichters geben uns den Schlüssel zum Verständnis einiger Szenen im Roman.*

iii. A further meaning is 'the ability and willingness to put oneself in s.o. else's position, to feel with the endeavours of artists etc., or to feel one's way into a work of art'. It thus includes appreciation, and is more than intellectual understanding. In *Sie hat Verständnis für jmdn./für die Jugend*, it suggests sympathy or sympathetic understanding. *Er hatte für ihre Lage viel Verständnis.* Cf. APPRECIATE 2. ii and UNDERSTAND 5. iv. *Für diesen Passus* (passage of text, law, etc.) *geht mir jegliches Verständnis ab* does not mean that I do not understand the words, but that I cannot comprehend how anyone could express such views.

Er brachte großes Verständnis für ihre Schwierigkeiten auf und versprach zu helfen.

Ich habe überhaupt kein Verständnis dafür, wenn sich jmd. so gehen läßt. Or *. . . für solche Schlampereien.*   *Sie hat kein/ein feines Verständnis für Malerei.*

Mir fehlt einfach das Verständnis für expressionistische Gedichte.

5. (A good) **understanding between** people means that amicable or friendly relations exist between them. *What is needed is greater understanding between workers and management. Raleigh strove to bring about a good understanding between Essex and Cecil.* When an existing relationship, rather than one which is to be brought about, is referred to, the idea is often best expressed by **sich mit jmdm. verstehen**, to get along well with. Cf. UNDERSTAND 8. *A versteht sich gut mit B*, or *A und B verstehen sich gut* [*miteinander*]. The only n. is **das Einvernehmen**, but it is restricted in use. *A lebt mit B in gutem Einvernehmen* or *Zwischen A und B herrscht Einvernehmen.* **Ein gutes Verhältnis**, 'a good RELATIONSHIP', can also express the meaning. *Ein gutes Verhältnis besteht zwischen verschiedenen Menschen.* It is the only possiblity when the context refers to establishing or bringing about an understanding between two or more people and when *bestehen*, 'to exist', is used. *Er bemühte sich, ein gutes Verhältnis zwischen den beiden herzustellen/herbeizuführen. Was wir dringend nötig haben, ist ein besseres Verhältnis zwischen der Belegschaft und der Betriebsleitung/Unternehmensleitung.* (Note that *Verständnis für jmdn./etw. haben* has the sense defined in 4. iii. Although *Die Betriebsleitung hat Verständnis für die Arbeiter* or *muß mehr Verständnis für die Arbeiter haben* is quite acceptable G., *Verständnis* is not the subj. of vs. meaning 'to exist'.)

6. An **understanding** is 'an informal agreement about sth., e.g. between firms or countries'. *The two firms have reached an understanding about further cooperation. Sich verständigen*, discussed under AGREE 1. iv, means 'to come to an agreement or understanding with s.o.' Although the main equivalent of **agreement**, *die Einigung*, and **die Verständigung** are sometimes used interchangeably, one distinction between them is that whereas *eine Einigung* denotes a complete and formal agreement, *eine Verständigung* suggests an initial or informal agreement, or a readiness to make concessions from which *eine Einigung* may result. *Verständigung* is thus close to the E. definition above. *Die Unterhändler haben schon eine Verständigung erzielt. Verständigung* takes the gen., referring to people, *mit* + one person or group, *zwischen* + at least two people, and *über* + a matter. *Die schnelle Verständigung der Tarifpartner [über die Lohnerhöhung] überraschte alle. Über diesen Punkt ist mit X keine Verständigung möglich. Es kam zu keiner Verständigung zwischen X und Y [über die ausstehenden Fragen].*

> *Der US-Außenminister reist in mehrere Hauptstädte im Nahen Osten und bemüht sich um Verständigung zwischen den Gegnern.*
> *Firma A hat eine Verständigung mit Firma B über weitere Zusammenarbeit erzielt.*
> *Die Verständigung der zerstrittenen Parteien kam erstaunlich rasch und reibungslos zustande.*

7. Die Verständigung also has the other sense of *sich verständigen*, 'to make oneself understood when people do not speak the same lang.' *Ohne eine gemeinsame Sprache ist die Verständigung schwierig.* Cf. UNDERSTAND 13.

8. To do sth. **on the understanding that** sth. will be done means 'to do it in the belief or after having been told that this thg. will be done'. *I signed the contract on the understanding that the goods would be delivered next Monday.* The closest equivalents are **unter der Bedingung, daß** or **unter der Voraussetzung, daß.** Both ns. mean 'condition' (cf. STATE 4 and 5), but they suggest more formality than **understanding** does. *Ich habe den Vertrag unter der Bedingung/Voraussetzung unterschrieben, daß man die Waren am kommenden Montag liefern würde.* An alternative in less formal style is *Als ich den Vortrag unterschrieb, habe ich damit gerechnet/hat man mir gesagt/nahm ich an, daß* . . .

9. Agreement = 'approval'. **Das Einverständnis** has two meanings.

i. 'Agreement' meaning 'approval or consent'. *Wird euch die geplante Wanderung zu sehr ermüden, oder können wir mit eurem Einverständnis rechnen?*

> *Die Partei stellte sie als Kandidatin auf, ohne vorher ihr Einverständnis eingeholt zu haben.*

ii. *Ich tue etw.* **im Einverständnis mit** *einem anderen* means that the other person has no objection to what I am doing or approves of or agrees to it. A more formal alternative is **im Einvernehmen mit.** *In Übereinstimmung mit* and *mit Zustimmung* + gen. express a similar sense. Cf. AGREE.

> *Eine solche Anschaffung würde sie nur im Einverständnis mit ihrem Mann machen.*
> *Ich habe den Entschluß im Einverständnis/Einvernehmen mit meinen Eltern gefaßt.*
> *Ich handle natürlich im Einvernehmen/in Übereinstimmung mit dem Firmenleiter.*
> *Einen solchen Plan kannst du nur mit ausdrücklicher Zustimmung des Chefs durchführen.*

undo *v.* **Undo** is a general word applied to a number of actions. G. also has general terms, but specific terms are often preferred.

1. General terms.

i. Aufmachen and **öffnen**, which also mean 'to OPEN', take buttons (*Knöpfe*) as obj. as well as garments, a belt (*ein Gürtel*), string, and something tied. *Routiniert öffnete der Zöllner das Paket. Man öffnet einen Reißverschluß* (zip) or *macht ihn auf. Öffnen* and *aufmachen* can also have *eine Dose* and *eine Flasche* as obj.

    Das Kleid hatte viele Knöpfe, so daß sie einige Zeit brauchte, es aufzumachen.
    Kannst du mir die Knöpfe auf dem Rücken aufmachen?
    Da sie es sehr eilig hatte, machte sie den Bindfaden nicht auf, sondern schnitt ihn durch.
    Der Junge war schon alt genug, um sich die Schnürsenkel aufzumachen.
    Als Ines ein Paket zum Geburtstag bekam, freute sie sich sehr und machte es schnell auf.

ii. Aufhaben means 'to have managed to get sth. open or undone'. *Hast du den Koffer noch nicht auf?* The first sent. in 1. i could be formulated as *Das Kleid hatte viele Knöpfe, so daß es einige Zeit dauerte, bis sie es aufhatte.*

iii. Aufbekommen or **aufkriegen** mean 'to get open or undone'. *Ich kann die Schublade nicht aufbekommen—sie klemmt.*

2. Specific terms. **Aufbinden** can translate **undo** in the sense 'to untie'. *Sie band die Schürze auf. Er band den Blumenstrauß auf. Schnürsenkel* or *Schuhbänder*, 'shoelaces', or *Bindfaden*, 'string', can be the obj. Other words are **aufknüpfen** and **aufknoten**, to undo a knot. *Mit geschickten Fingern knüpfte er den Knoten im Bindfaden auf.* One sense of **lösen** is also possible, but it is rather poetical in tone. *Die Mutter löste dem Kind die Schnürsenkel.* **Aufknöpfen** is the specific term for undoing buttons, i.e. 'to unbutton', but only takes a garment as obj. *Sie knöpfte den Mantel auf.* **Aufziehen** can be used with *ein Reißverschluß* as obj. and is the usual v. with *der Vorhang. Man zieht einen Vorhang auf*, draws or pulls it open. *Aufziehen* and **aufräufeln** mean 'to undo sth. knitted or crocheted'. *Sie hat den alten Pullover aufgezogen/aufgeräufelt.* To **undo** a seam or hem is *eine Naht* **auftrennen.**

3. Offen sein states that a shoelace is undone. *Bleib' doch eben mal stehen! Mein Schnürsenkel/Schuhband ist offen.* **Aufgehen** means 'to come undone'. Cf. OPEN 2. ii. *Mein Schnürsenkel ist gerade aufgegangen.*

4. In fig. use **undo** means 'to destroy the effect of what has been done'. *It will take years to undo what the dictator did to this country.* A general expression is **etw. ungeschehen machen.** *Was einmal geschehen ist, kann man nicht ungeschehen machen.* **Etw. vergessen machen** may correspond to the meaning in some cases. The vs. used when *Schaden/Schäden*, 'harm, damage', are the obj. are **beseitigen** and **beheben.** *Schaden* refers primarily to damage to a concrete obj., but with appropriate adjs. it can also denote adverse mental effects. *Alle trugen seelische Schäden davon, die sich nur schwer beseitigen ließen.*

    Man braucht Jahre, um das, was der Diktator diesem Land angetan hat, ungeschehen/vergessen zu machen.
    Eine Sünde, die man begangen hat, läßt sich nicht ungeschehen machen. Sie kann nur vergeben werden.
    Kein auch noch so kleiner psychologischer Schaden kann durch ein Gerichtsurteil und Schmerzensgeld vergessen gemacht werden.

unify, unite *vs.* There are four vs. derived from *ein-, einen, einigen, vereinen,* and *vereinigen.*

i. Einen means 'to bring separate groups or organizations together into one unit'. *Bismarck hat Deutschland/die deutschen Staaten geeint.* Such a sent. is, however, now felt to be old-fashioned or appropriate only for elevated style. The usual word would now be *vereinigen*. *Einen* is still used for bringing together again an only outwardly united group which threatens to break up because of divisions in its ranks. *Ihm wurde das Verdienst zugesprochen, die zersplitterte Partei erneut geeint zu haben.*

ii. Einigen also means 'to bring together into a unit' people, parties, groups, organizations, etc. *Es gelang nicht, die verschiedenen Stämme zu einigen.* **Vereinigen** is however more usual. The prefix *ver-* does not alter the meaning, but strengthens it. *Einigen* often means 'to unite mentally'. *Ein geeinigtes Land* means one in which the various groups are not at odds with each other and live together harmoniously. Likewise *Die alle Menschen einigende christliche Wahrheit war der Standpunkt, der sein Handeln bestimmte.* The n. is often encountered. *Die politische/wirtschaftliche Einigung von mehreren Staaten. Der europäische Einigungsprozeß.*

iii. While **unify** is only trans., *Bismarck unified Germany,* **unite** is trans. and intr. *Common interests unite our countries. England and Scotland united in 1707.* The refl. of all three above verbs translates **unite** used intr. *Die verschiedenen Stämme haben sich geeint/geeinigt,* have united. *England und Schottland haben sich 1707 vereinigt.*

iv. Both **vereinen** and **vereinigen** mean 'to bring together into a larger unit'. *Vereinen* implies that two or more groups or organizations work together for a common purpose while otherwise maintaining their independence. *Am 4. September 1946 vereinbarten die britische und die amerikanische Militärregierung (in Deutschland), ihre beiden Zonen wirtschaftlich zu vereinen.* Abstracts are often the subj. *Gemeinsame Interessen/Ziele/Werte vereinen unsere Länder. Vereinigen* implies that two organizations etc. forgo some or all of their independence and form a new and greater whole. Thus *die Vereinten Nationen* work together to attain certain goals, while each state *der Vereinigten Staaten von Amerika* loses at least some of its independence to the federal body. *Diese Unternehmen* (business enterprises) *sind unter einem Dachverband vereint* implies that they work together, but remain separate, whereas *Diese Unternehmen sind vereinigt* means that they have become parts of one new organization. Such a company could be called *Die Vereinigten Eisenhüttenwerke.* The E. vs. used for businesses are CONSOLIDATE and *amalgamate*. The fact that *ein vereintes Europa* and *ein vereinigtes Europa* both occur may suggest uncertainty about the nature of a united Europe. (Another explanation is that few people understand the distinction between the two vs.) In relation to people *vereinen* is most frequently found as a past part. *Sie hoffen, mit vereinten Kräften die Aufgabe zu lösen. Wir gehen vereint gegen etw. vor* or *treten vereint auf.* A syn. is here **gemeinsam**, together. *Wenn wir gemeinsam/vereint Schritte unternähmen, hätten wir mehr Aussicht auf Erfolg.*

When people are the obj., *vereinen* means 'to bring together'. *Die Hochzeit hat die Familie wieder vereint. Vereinigen* and especially *sich vereinigen* suggest that people come together or unite to form a new group for a purpose. *Sie vereinigten sich zu einer Arbeitsgruppe. Proletarier aller Länder, vereinigt euch!* thus suggests joining together to work for common ends. When qualities such as beauty and utility are the obj., *[sich] vereinen* is the usual v., though *[sich] vereinigen* also occurs. *Die Sportlerin vereint Kraft und Anmut in sich. Schönheit und Zweckmäßigkeit vereinen/vereinigen sich in diesem Bauwerk.*

Die beiden Firmeninhaber vereinigten ihre Unternehmen zu einer neuen Gesellschaft.

Der Zirkus X mußte sich mit dem Zirkus Y vereinigen, denn allein hätten sie wirtschaftlich nicht mehr existieren können.   Nach langer Zeit waren alle Familienmitglieder wieder vereint.

Alles vereinigte sich, um die Standhaftigkeit dieses großen Mannes zu erschüttern. (Schiller)

Sein Kunstverständnis vereinte sich mit einem nüchternen Geschäftssinn.

v. Sich zusammenschließen means 'to join together to form a larger unit'.

Am 1. Januar 1901 schlossen sich die sechs australischen Kolonien zum australischen Bund zusammen.
Die beiden Betriebe haben sich zusammengeschlossen/vereinigt.

urge, impulse, incentive, stimulus *ns*. The concept common to these words is 'that which gives rise to action'. An **urge** is 'a strong desire, an impelling force or pressure entirely from within'. It can, but need not, arise suddenly. *She felt a [sudden] urge to leave everything and to run away.* An **incentive** is 'that which rouses or encourages s.o. to do sth.' *They have every/little/no incentive to work hard.* In its non-specialized senses **stimulus** means (i) 'An influence that leads to action or that quickens an activity or process'. *There is no greater stimulus to improvement than fair competition.* (ii) 'Sth. which causes people to feel energetic and enthusiastic'. *This success became a source of stimulus for all.* In the senses we are concerned with here **impulse** means (i) 'A force or influence exerted on the mind by some external stimulus', especially one giving new impetus. *From America he received fresh artistic impulses. This movement gave religious life a new impulse.* (ii) 'A spontaneous inclination to act which arises either directly from feeling or from an external influence and which prompts s.o. to act without premeditation or reflection'. *He always acts on impulse. Some uncontrollable impulse may have driven the defendant to commit this crime.* (iii) 'A propensity or natural tendency, usually other than rational'. *The basic impulse of self-expression. The sexual impulse. The systematizing impulse, the passion for order of the Greeks.*

1. Der Antrieb is the general term meaning 'that which gives rise to action'. The equivalents are **impulse, urge, incentive,** *inducement,* and **stimulus.** *Der Antrieb seines Handelns* is quite neutral and does not suggest suddenness or make a judgement as to goodness etc. *Ein Antrieb* can arise from a lack which needs to be met or from basic needs such as hunger, thirst, or desire, or from the cultural situation of the individual. *Sie spürte den Antrieb zu flüchten.* The phr. in *Ich handle aus eigenem Antrieb* means 'of my own accord' or 'of my own free will or volition'. A related word is **die Triebfeder,** 'driving or motivating force, motive', but it is mostly used in combination with *das Handeln* or *die Handlung. Hemmungsloser Ehrgeiz war die Triebfeder seines Handelns/von seinem Handeln. Eifersucht war die Triebfeder seiner Handlung.*

> *Es fehlt heute jeder Antrieb zum Sparen.*   *Für diese Handlung gab es wichtige Antriebe.*
> *Sie haben keinen/nur wenig Antrieb, fleißiger zu arbeiten.*
> *Einem inneren Antrieb folgend, erklärte sie sich bereit mitzumachen.*

2. Der Antrieb also translates **stimulus** in sense ii, 'sth. causing people to feel energetic and enthusiastic', and in sense i in so far as it refers to something which quickens a human activity. The more usual word in both senses is **der Auftrieb.** *Der Erfolg gab mir Auftrieb/[neuen] Antrieb. Das gab dem Handel Auftrieb/neuen Antrieb.*

3. The general sense of **der Trieb** is 'an inner driving force'. The original meaning was 'inclination', but the use of the original sense in *Der Junge hatte nicht den geringsten Trieb zum Lernen* is now unusual or confined to writing. In the eighteenth century *Trieb* began to be used in the sense of 'instinct' and has retained this meaning in psychological language. The current uses have developed from this, although influenced by the original meaning. One definition of *Trieb* is 'an innate or acquired, strong inner striving for action which is necessary for the preservation of life or for the satisfaction of fundamental needs'. As a psychological term, it corresponds to *drive,* which is defined as either 'an urgent basic or instinctual need pressing for satisfaction or impelling to activity, such as hunger, thirst, or sexual desire', or 'a culturally acquired interest or longing that incites s.o. to unremitting action'. *He was possessed with a drive for perfection.* Ein Trieb can be good, even noble, but the chief current use equates *Trieb* with *Geschlechtstrieb. Jmd. folgt seinen Trieben* is now unlikely to be taken as implying noble urges. *Ein Triebtäter* commits sexual crimes. Despite this *Trieb* is still found, at least in writing, in the sense 'a strong urge to sth. good'. It is usually seen as a permanent part of a person's nature and is contrasted with reason. Some adjs. used with *Trieb* are *ein edler/höherer/mütterlicher Trieb* or *ein dunkler/böser/roher/tierischer/sinnlicher/sexueller/verdrängter Trieb.* Compounds are *der Selbsterhaltungstrieb, Herdentrieb, Nachahmungstrieb, Fortpflanzungstrieb, Bildungstrieb, Zerstreuungstrieb, Tätigkeitstrieb* or *Trieb zur Tätigkeit.*

> *Hille (a man's name) erkannte die Begabung und den Trieb zu großen Taten des jungen Friedrich (des Großen) an, kritisierte aber seine Unwissenheit.*
> *Ein unwiderstehlicher Trieb zog sie immer wieder zu den Orten ihrer Kindheit zurück.*
> *Nur sadistische Triebe können zu einer solchen grausamen Tat führen.*

4. **Der Drang** is 'a particularly strong inner impulsion to do sth.' It can be both for physical action, *der Drang nach körperlicher Bewegung,* or for something mental, *der Wissensdrang.* In itself it does not say whether the feeling is good or bad, and the results can be either. It is often translated as **urge**. *Impulse* in sense iii, 'a propensity not arising from reason', is either *Trieb, der Sexualtrieb,* or *Drang. Der grundlegende Trieb/Drang, sich selbst auszudrücken.* Another word with a similar sense is *das menschliche Grundbedürfnis,* cf. NEED 4. ii.

> *Der Wissensdrang dieser jungen Menschen versetzte mich in Erstaunen.*
> *Sie fühlte den starken Drang, alles stehen und liegen zu lassen und wegzulaufen.*
> *Ich gab dem Drang nach mitzusingen/laut aufzuschreien.*

5. i. **Der Impuls** expresses sense i of **impulse**, 'an influence exerted by an external stimulus'. *In Amerika bekam er neue künstlerische Impulse.* The words of G. origin are **die Anregung**, something which stimulates to action (cf. *anregen* under SUGGEST 1. ii), and **der Anstoß**, cf. 8, or **der Antrieb**.

> *Diejenigen, die dem religiösen Leben neue Impulse/Anstöße geben, brauchen Anhänger, die den Anstoß/Impuls verwirklichen, bevor er sich erschöpft.*
> *Der Gedanke an seine Zukunft gab ihm einen neuen Impuls, die Arbeit fortzusetzen.*
> *Seine erfolgreichen Erzählungen entstammen demselben Impuls/Antrieb wie seine Gedichte.* (Could refer to an inner force as well as to an external one.)

ii. **Der Impuls** also carries sense ii of **impulse**, 'a spontaneous inclination to act', and is close to *der Drang,* although *Drang* lacks the idea of spontaneity. A related expression is *die [innere] Regung.* Cf. EMOTION 1. *S.o. acts on impulse,* referring to a permanent feature of someone's behaviour, can be expressed by the adv. **impulsiv**. *Handelt er denn immer impulsiv?* If I *acted on impulse* refers to one action, *Ich bin einem Impuls gefolgt* conveys the sense.

> *Mein erster Impuls war wegzulaufen, aber dann bin ich doch geblieben.*
> *Sie war von Natur aus geneigt, Impulsen/inneren Regungen zu widerstehen.*
> *Unkontrollierbare Impulse dürften den Angeklagten dazu gebracht haben, das Verbrechen zu begehen.*

6. **Der Ansporn** is applied to what encourages or stimulates someone to achieve something, thus 'an incentive' or 'stimulus' in sense i, 'an influence that leads to action'. (*Ein Pferd anspornen* is 'to set the spurs to a horse' and *jmdn. anspornen* 'to spur or urge s.o. on'. A related expression is *jmdn. zum Handeln anfeuern,* to kindle someone's enthusiasm, to rouse someone to enthusiasm for a task.)

> *Die lobenden Worte des Lehrers waren dem Schüler ein Ansporn zu noch besseren Leistungen.*
> *Durch diesen Roman erhielt er den Ansporn, sein Verhalten neu zu überdenken.*

7. **Der Anreiz** stresses the reward to be gained. *Der Anreiz für diese Handlung* suggests the material gain to be received if the action is carried out and therefore means 'incentive, stimulus, inducement'.

Hohe Zinsen bieten einen Anreiz zum Sparen.
Auch ein starker materieller Anreiz konnte ihn nicht dazu bringen, das Angebot anzunehmen.

8. Den Anstoß zu etw. geben means that the person or thing that is the subj. is the indirect cause of what resulted. *Neue Anstöße* can also translate *new impulses* or *a new impetus.*

Er hat den Anstoß zur Gründung des Forschungsinstituts gegeben.
Die Ablehnung dieser Bitten, die alle für berechtigt hielten, gab den Anstoß zum Streik.

use *v.* Order of treatment: 1. **Use** something meaning 'to employ for a purpose'. 2. G. vs. related in sense to those dealt with in 1. 3. **Use** = 'to know how to handle'. 4. **Use** = 'consume' and 'to exhaust a supply of sth.' 5. **Use** = 'to treat a pers. in a certain way'.

1. Use means 'to employ deliberately for a purpose or to achieve a result'. The obj. can be a tool or instrument, a skill, quality, or advantage, a kind or brand of product, or a word or expression. The main equivalents are the syns. *benutzen, gebrauchen,* and *verwenden.*

i. Benutzen is the main equivalent. (*Nutzen* and its derivatives can also be spelt with an *Umlaut.*) The objs. which are as varied as those used with the E. v. can be instruments, tools, machines, a conveyance like *die Straßenbahn* or *ein Auto,* a room, a street or path, products (e.g. *diese Zahnpasta, dieses Waschmittel, eine Marke,* 'brand'), clothes, words, a name, people, an ability or skill (including mental endowments like *der Verstand* or *die Vernunft*), or time. *Benutzen* suggests a purpose and can be followed by *als, zu,* or an infin. construction. *Wir benutzen dieses Zimmer normalerweise nur als Gästezimmer. Sie benutzten die Pause zu einem privaten Gespräch. Sie benutzten den Aufenthalt dazu, alte Freunde wiederzusehen.* Only *benutzen* (not *verwenden* and *gebrauchen*) expresses **use** = 'to take advantage of'. Thus *Man benutzt eine gute Gelegenheit/das schöne Wetter/jmds. Abwesenheit/einen Vorteil.* In *Das Geschirrtuch ist doch erst einmal benutzt worden, du brauchst es also nicht zu waschen, gebraucht* is also possible but less usual.

Wir benutzen diese Werkzeuge/diese Maschine.
Der Zahnarzt benutzte verschiedenene Bohrer.
Benutzen Sie besser den Hinterausgang/den Aufzug!
Benutzen Sie doch das Auto, wenn es zum Radfahren zu kalt ist!
Nur Anlieger dürfen diese Straße benutzen.   *Benutz' doch deinen Verstand!*
Er benutzte anderweitige Verpflichtungen als Entschuldigung für sein Zuspätkommen.
Er wollte mich zu unlauteren Zwecken benutzen.   *Zum Braten benutzt sie nur Olivenöl.*
Sie hat das Geld dazu benutzt, sich einen Pelzmantel zu kaufen.
Ich habe schon gesehen, wie sich das benutzte/gebrauchte Geschirr sich seit Tagen in der Küche stapelt.

ii. Gebrauchen can, like *benutzen,* take instruments or implements as obj. as well as mental endowments, but it is less common. *Wir gebrauchen die kleine Zange/den großen Schraubenzieher. Gebrauche deinen Verstand!* The obj. cannot be a means of transport nor a street. *Gebrauchen* is the v. usually chosen in *Ich kann den verletzten Arm wieder gebrauchen* and *Man gebraucht dieses Arzneimittel nur äußerlich.*

Der Klempner gebraucht verschiedene Werkzeuge, wenn er die Heizung installiert.
Zum Anziehen der Mutter (nut) sollten Sie einen Drehmomentschlüssel gebrauchen.

The main use of *gebrauchen* is to state whether someone can find a use for s.o./sth. or put s.o./sth. to use. It often occurs in the constructions **Jmd. kann etw. gut [zu etw.] gebrauchen** or **Etw./Jmd. ist [zu etw.] zu gebrauchen.** Except in these expressions the prep. in relation to people is *für. Man kann sie für diese Aufgabe gebrauchen.* (Note also: *Er ist sehr anstellig. Man kann ihn überall einsetzen.* Cf. ACT 5.)

Gib mir bitte das alte Fahrrad! Ich kann es gut gebrauchen.
Der Schirm lag zwar im Mülleimer, ist aber noch einwandfrei zu gebrauchen.

Ein bißchen mehr Geld/Einen neuen Regenmantel kann ich gut gebrauchen.

Danke, Ratschläge von einem älteren und erfahrenen Kollegen kann ich immer gut gebrauchen.

Er stellt dauernd etw. an und ist zu nichts zu gebrauchen.

With words and aspects of language as obj., *gebrauchen* is the usual word, particularly when talking of the correct usage, but *benutzen* and *verwenden* are also found. *Ich weiß nicht, ob ich das Wort richtig gebraucht habe. Benutzen/Gebrauchen Sie häufig Fremdwörter/solche Ausdrücke? Gebrauchen Sie doch die gelernten Vokabeln!* **Gebraucht** is the equivalent of **used** = 'second-hand'. *Wir haben den Kinderwagen gebraucht gekauft.* It also forms compounds. *Beim Kauf eines Gebrauchtwagens muß man vorsichtig sein.*

iii. Verwenden means 'to use sth. for a purpose' and stresses the purpose. The obj. is usually a thing (but not a street, conveyance, nor *ein Aufzug*, lift, elevator) and can be abstract, like knowledge. *Verwenden* is more formal than *benutzen* and is often preferred in more learned discourse. It is interchangeable with *benutzen* when the sense is 'to employ to achieve a result'. *Man benutzt/verwendet Maschinen bei der Feldarbeit. Ich benutze/verwende das Brett als Unterlage.* (In these two sents. *gebrauchen* is also possible.) *Wir benutzen/verwenden das Geld zu einer Reise. Den übrig gebliebenen Stoff können wir für ein Kinderkleid verwenden.* (*Benutzen* is also possible.) Either can be used in *Wir können den Stoff verwenden/benutzen, um ein Kleid zu machen* or *Wir können den Stoff zur Herstellung eines Kleides verwenden/benutzen. Verwenden* is the v. mostly employed when something is used for a purpose other than its intended one. *Ich verwende den Hammer, um die Tür offen zu halten, indem ich ihn in den Türspalt klemme. Verwenden* is often used when someone makes a judgement on how well, sensibly, etc. someone uses something, but *benutzen* is equally common. *Jmd. verwendet etw. sinnvoll/richtig/falsch/gut/schlecht/zweckmäßig. Jmd. verwendet seine Zeit nutzbringend* is the usual expression, probably to avoid two *nutz-* sounds.

Zum Kochen verwendet/benutzt sie nur Butter und Vollkornmehl.

Alle Lehrer verwenden/benutzen im Unterricht das gleiche Lehrbuch.

Die Prüfer verwenden in den Texten immer dieselben Fangfragen.

Bei dieser Stelle kannst du deine Französischkenntnisse verwenden.

Was an Beton übrig bleibt, können wir zur Fixierung der losen Treppenstufen verwenden.

Er verwendet alle seine Einkünfte, um an der Börse zu spekulieren.

Sie verwendet/benutzt in ihren Vorträgen stets das gleiche Vokabular.

iv. For uses of *anwenden* and *verwenden*, cf. APPLY 2. *Verwenden auf* with ns. like *die Mühe, die Energie, der Fleiß*, etc. as obj., *Sie hat viel Mühe auf die Arbeit verwandt*, is translated with SPEND or *expend*.

v. Sich bedienen + gen. is now an elevated syn. of the vs. in 1. i–iii. *Ich werde mich der erstbesten Gelegenheit bedienen. Sie bediente sich stets gepflegter Redewendungen.*

2. Vs. related in sense to those discussed in 1.

i. One of the special senses of **use** is 'to make use of (land) by working or tilling it'. The equivalent is **nutzen**, which states in a general way that something is utilized or put to use. It is not restricted to land. Although the meaning necessarily implies a purpose, the fact that something is used, rather than the purpose, is of primary importance. Common are *Man nutzt die Gelegenheit/einen Umstand/die Zeit/die Gunst der Stunde*. Schiller wrote: *Nütze den Augenblick, der einmal nur sich bietet!* In a general statement *nutzen* is usual, *Die Wasserkraft der Flüsse wird zur Stromerzeugung genutzt*, but in a specific case *benutzen* is likely, *Man will das Wasser dieses Flusses benutzen, um ein Kraftwerk zu betreiben.* In reference to a room s.o. might say as a general remark, '*Jetzt ist alles so schön renoviert worden, und kaum einer nutzt den Raum*', but in a specific case, '*Wenn Sie den Konferenzraum benutzen wollen, sollten Sie sich rechtzeitig anmelden.*' *Die Gelegenheit nutzen*, which is used both when no purpose is stated and when a purpose follows, is usually translated as *to take the opportunity. Wenn sich dir eine Gelegenheit bietet, nutze sie doch!* When a purpose follows *benutzen* is also possible.

Nach der Rodung wurde der Boden landwirtschaftlich genutzt.

Land, das sich zur Landwirtschaft nicht eignet, kann man forstwirtschaftlich nutzen.

Er nutzt jeden Vorteil, der sich ihm bietet.   *An deiner Stelle würde ich alle Möglichkeiten nutzen.*

ii. With people or their traits of character as obj. **ausnutzen** means 'to exploit, to use in a selfish and inconsiderate way for one's own ends, to take advantage of', and often implies criticism of what the person who is the subj. does. *Man nutzt jmdn./jmds. Gutmütigkeit/jmds. Schwäche/die Notlage eines Landes aus.* With *die Situation, der Vorteil,* or *seine Stellung* as obj. it is often pejorative, implying 'to use so as to derive personal advantage'. *Ausnutzen* translates **use** in sents. like *I felt used. I'd just been used. Ich fühlte mich ausgenutzt. Man hatte mich bloß ausgenutzt.*

Sogar seine nächsten Verwandten nutzte er immer aus.

Wie leicht könnte man seine Zerstreutheit ausnutzen, ihn zu hintergehen.

Die Vereinigten Staaten könnten die Situation ausnutzen, um ihre europäischen Verbündeten unter Druck zu setzen.   *Sie nutzte ihre Beziehungen aus, um Karriere zu machen.*

Er nutzte seine Stellung aus, um seine Kinder und Freunde zu fördern.

In keinem Land ist es wünschenswert, daß Militärbehörden ihre offizielle Position zur Verbreitung umstrittener Ansichten ausnutzen.

In another sense *ausnutzen* means 'to use to the full' and expresses no judgement. The obj. is mostly a n. like *Raum* or *Zeit* which does not permit a pejorative sense. *Wir haben die uns zur Verfügung stehende Zeit [voll] ausgenutzt.*

Sie haben die ihnen zur Verfügung stehenden Geldmittel gut/optimal ausgenutzt.

Wird die moderne Technik zum Wohl der ganzen Menschheit ausgenutzt?

Sie benutzten jede Gelegenheit zum Ankauf weiterer Antiquitäten. (Ausnutzen also takes *Gelegenheit* as obj.)

iii. Verwerten is 'to utilize sth. which has not been put to any useful purpose in a new way', *Man verwertet Reste/Altpapier/Abfälle,* and 'to put to use', *Man verwertet Anregungen/Ideen/Erfahrungen/eine Erfindung.*

Sie hat die Stoffreste zu einem Kinderkleid verwertet.

Essensreste braucht man doch nicht wegzuwerfen; sie lassen sich doch meist noch verwerten.

Er hat nicht bloß diese Maschine erfunden, sondern verstand es auch, sie kommerziell zu verwerten.

Ihre Anregung werde ich sicher in meinem nächsten Aufsatz verwerten können.

3. The meaning of **use** 'to know how to handle or operate sth.' as in *Do you know how to use the computer?* is conveyed by **umgehen mit** and **bedienen**. *Umgehen mit* is the everyday word and is used at all stylistic levels for simpler things. *Kleine Kinder müssen lernen, mit Messer und Gabel umzugehen.* In informal speech it is also used for any kind of apparatus, however complicated. *Kannst du mit dieser riesigen Computeranlage umgehen? Bedienen* means 'to use or operate' and is applied to relatively complicated machines whose operation requires at least a brief training. Without *können* it means 'to operate'. *Der Arbeiter bedient die Maschine.* With *können* it means 'to know how to use or operate'. *Kannst du den Projektor/die neue Schreibmaschine/einen Personalcomputer bedienen?* The dividing line between *umgehen mit* and *bedienen* is fairly subjective. For a camera or pocket calculator etc. *eine Bedienungsanleitung* is supplied, as no n. is formed from *umgehen mit,* but in less formal style *die Gebrauchsanweisung* is the usual word. *Benutzen* with a clause or question with *wie* sometimes expresses the sense discussed in this section. *Weißt du, wie man diesen Projektor benutzt?*

Am Anfang der Lehre wußte er kaum, wie man eine Feile benutzt. Am Ende der Ausbildung aber konnte er die kompliziertesten Maschinen bedienen.

Weißt du, wie man mit diesem Fotoapparat/Taschenrechner umgeht?

4. Use is the normal v. for stating what amount of something s.o./sth. consumes. *How much electricity do we use/consume each month? The car doesn't use much petrol.* **Use all of** sth. and **use** sth. **up** mean 'to exhaust a [limited] supply of sth. by consuming it completely'. **Verbrauchen** has both senses and is the equivalent when **use** means 'consume'. The objs. can be *Strom, Gas, Wasser, Benzin, Kraftstoff, Treibstoff* as well as *Lebensmittel* and *Vorräte. Wieviel Strom verbrauchen wir jeden Monat? Das Auto verbraucht sieben Liter auf hundert Kilometer. Alle Vorräte waren verbraucht.* If the material is burnt, the v. is **verbrennen**. *Wir verbrennen jede Woche eine halbe Tonne Kohle.* Cf. BURN B. 1. ii. A syn. in the sense 'to use up' is **aufbrauchen**. *Die Vorräte waren aufgebraucht.* If I notice that someone has been using my shampoo, I might ask (if some were still left), *'Wer hat denn mein Haarshampoo benutzt?'* If none were left, the appropriate v. would be *aufbrauchen* or *verbrauchen. 'Wer hat denn mein Haarshampoo verbraucht/aufgebraucht?'*

Wir verbrauchen zuviel Lebensmittel.   Wir haben alle unsere Lebensmittel aufgebraucht.
Mit den neuen Glühbirnen verbrauchen Sie nur ein Drittel soviel Strom wie früher.
Das Auto verbraucht ziemlich viel Benzin/Kraftstoff/Sprit.
Ich hatte meine ganze Kraft verbraucht.
Schon nach einigen Tagen war die Notration verbraucht/aufgebraucht.
Wenn Sie so wirtschaften, werden Sie Ihre Ersparnisse in wenigen Monaten verbrauchen/aufbrauchen.

5. Use also means 'to treat or deal with a pers. in a specified way'. *He considers himself unfairly used.* The equivalent of this somewhat old-fashioned use is **behandeln**, to treat. For **use** = 'exploit' cf. 2. ii.

Er glaubt, daß man ihn ungerecht behandelt hat.
Seine Angestellten behandelt er ziemlich rücksichtslos.

V

[in] vain, for nothing phrs. used as *advs.* **vain (attempts, etc.), free** *adj.*
gratis *adv.*

1. In vain, for nothing, vain. Three G. words, *umsonst, vergebens,* and *vergeblich,*
express the sense 'to no effect or purpose'. **Umsonst** is probably the most common and means 'without achieving the result which was expected'. *Ich bin zweimal
umsonst hingegangen—es war niemand zu Hause.* While *umsonst* states that there was
no result, **vergebens** expresses in addition regret about the wasted or fruitless
effort and is like *[all] for nothing* or *to no purpose at all.* It is found in a sent., *Ich habe
mich vergebens bemüht,* or is combined with *aber* or *allerdings, Ich habe versucht, ihn
von seinem Vorhaben abzubringen, aber vergebens,* or follows the v. *sein, Es ist alles
vergebens, ich gebe es auf. Ich habe mich bemüht, aber es war vergebens.* Both *umsonst* and
vergebens are used as an exclamation. *Alles umsonst!* or *Alles vergebens!* Like *vergebens,*
vergeblich expresses regret about the lack of success, but it is more formal than
the other words. It is used as an adv., *Ich habe mich vergeblich bemüht,* and after *sein,
Unser Protest war vergeblich/vergebens.* Only *vergeblich* can be an attributive adj. *Ein
vergeblicher Versuch* is 'a vain attempt'. *Vergebliche Bemühungen* or *vergebliche
Nachforschungen/Anstrengungen* lead to no result. A synonymous, but very colloquial, expression is **Es war für die Katz.** *Ich habe tagelang an dem Vortrag gearbeitet,
aber das war für die Katz—er fällt ins Wasser.*

 Ich habe mich mit der Sache lange herumgeplagt, aber alle Mühe war umsonst.
 Sie hatten sich redlich bemüht, das Spiel zu gewinnen, allerdings vergebens.
 Vergebens hielt er schon zwanzig Minuten an dem verabredeten Platz nach ihr Ausschau.
 *Die Beteuerungen des Angeklagten, er hätte den Diebstahl nicht begangen, waren vergebens. Das
  Gericht glaubte ihm nicht. Versuch' es nochmal! Es wird nur vergebliche Mühe sein.*
 *Da sie wieder einmal vergeblich auf dem Arbeitsamt gewesen war, beschloß sie, sich umschulen zu
  lassen.*
 Man suchte tagelang vergeblich im Dschungel nach dem abgestürzten Flugzeug.
 *Solange es noch schneit, hat es keinen Sinn, den Bürgersteig zu räumen. Das wäre ja doch alles für
  die Katz.*

2. Take s.o.'s **name in vain.** The G. Bible has *Du sollst den Namen deines Herrn nicht
mißbrauchen.*

3. For nothing, free, gratis. Umsonst also means 'for nothing' or 'at no cost,
although payment is normally expected'. *Er hat die Arbeit umsonst gemacht, er hat
nichts dafür verlangt.* The chief word in this sense is **kostenlos,** free of charge. *Einige
Patienten behandelt der Arzt kostenlos.* Alternatives are **gratis** and **frei.** *Prospekte und
Kataloge sind gratis zum Mitnehmen. Jeder Fluggast/Passagier hat zwanzig Kilogramm
Gepäck frei.* **Unentgeltlich,** which is stylistically higher, is applied to work which is
carried out without any payment being expected. *Alle Auskünfte sind unentgeltlich.*

 Wir können morgen umsonst ins Kino gehen. *Sie hat mir das Buch umsonst überlassen.*
 Die Teilnahme an den Lehrgängen ist kostenlos. *Kostenlose Verpflegung wird geboten.*
 Die Unterricht ist für die Schüler unentgeltlich. *Der Eintritt ist frei.*
 Da das Auto noch unter Garantie steht, machen wir die Reparatur natürlich gratis.
 Wenn Sie ein Probeexemplar bestellen, erhalten Sie gratis ein schönes Poster.

4. Nicht umsonst means 'not without good reason or cause'.

Das hat er nicht umsonst gesagt/getan.   *Sie hat uns nicht umsonst vor diesem Mann gewarnt.*

very *adv.* and *adj.*

1. The normal equivalent of **very** = 'to a high degree' used as an intensifier before adjs. and advs. is **sehr**. *Die Aussicht finde ich sehr schön. Es regnet sehr stark.* **Überaus** is a formal synonym which may be stronger. *Das Theaterstück hat mir überaus gut gefallen. Sie befanden sich in einer überaus schwierigen Lage.* **Ausgesprochen** is more colloquial than *sehr* and stronger, like *decidedly, extremely,* or *especially. Jmd. hat einen ausgesprochen festen Character. Den Roman fand ich ausgesprochen komisch.* **Äußerst** means 'extremely', 'not to be surpassed'. *Er ist äußerst unglücklich. Die Photosynthese ist ein äußerst komplizierter Vorgang.* **Höchst** means 'in a very high degree'. *Es ist höchst unwahrscheinlich, daß sie kandidiert. Er war höchst leichtsinnig.*

2. Very used with a superlative, *one of his very best plays* or *the very latest model,* is translated either not at all, *eines seiner besten Stücke* and *das neueste Modell,* or by the compound with **aller**, *eines seiner allerbesten Stücke* and *das allerneueste Modell.*

3. The adjective **very** still survives in a few expressions. The equivalents express the meaning carried by **very**, but they may not be as emphatic.
i. Very is used with a few ns. as an intensifier, either to denote the inclusion of something regarded as extreme or exceptional or to emphasize the exceptional prominence of some ordinary thing or feature. *The room was crammed to the very door* could be *Der Saal war gerammelt voll* or *war voll bis zur Tür. We do not see what is happening before/under our very eyes: Das, was sich direkt vor unseren Augen abspielt, sehen wir nicht. His very defects were the cause of his popularity: Gerade seine Schwächen machten ihn beliebt.*
ii. With certain ns. **very** indicates an extreme position in space or time. *For from the very beginning/outset,* there are *von vornherein* and *schon von Anfang an. Es war mir von vornherein klar, daß wir einen schweren Stand haben würden. At the very beginning/outset is gleich am Anfang. We climbed to the very top/to the very highest point: Wir sind zum allerhöchsten Punkt gestiegen. Zum höchsten Gipfel is also used. At the very back of the auditorium: Ganz hinten im Zuschauerraum. We stayed to the very end: Wir sind bis zum absoluten Schlußpunkt geblieben. We must reduce these variations to the very minimum: Wir müssen diese Schwankungen auf ein absolutes Minimum/Mindestmaß beschränken.*
iii. In reference to someone's words **very** means 'exactly corresponding to those used' and can be translated by **genau, eben,** or **gerade**. *Those are the very words I used/my very words: Das sind genau die Wörter, die ich gebraucht habe,* or *Das waren genau meine Worte.* An alternative is *Das sind meine eigenen Worte.*
iv. The idea of exact correspondence or identity occurs in other contexts and is also conveyed by **genau, gerade,** or **eben**. *Genau das weiß ich nicht* could translate *That's **the very thg**. I don't know.* (It is also the equivalent of *That's just/precisely the thg. I don't know.*) Alternatives are *Eben/Gerade das wollte ich fragen.* Also *Genau das/Eben das/Gerade das wollte ich sagen. Eben/Gerade darum/deshalb/deswegen* could be *for that very reason.* An alternative is *aus eben/gerade dem Grund.* **Ebendarum** and **ebendeshalb** are often written as one word. *Er hat uns allen oft geholfen—ebendarum müssen wir ihm jetzt helfen. That's the very thg. I was looking for: Genau/Gerade das suche ich* or *Genau/Gerade das ist es, was ich suche. I think it's the very thg. for you: Ich denke, es ist genau/gerade das richtige für dich. They take for granted the very question at issue: Genau/Gerade die Frage, um die es hier geht, scheint für sie schon beantwortet zu sein.*
v. Genau or **gerade** translates *the **very*** opposite. *Das gerade/genaue Gegenteil* or *Gerade/Genau das Gegenteil ist geschehen.*

vi. Very relating to people can also be expressed by **gerade** or **genau**. *You're the very pers. I'm looking for: Sie sind gerade der Mann/die Frau, den/die ich suche. Sie sind es gerade, den/die ich suche.* He's the very man for the job could be *Genau dieser Mann ist für diese Aufgabe der richtige.*

> *Von genau dem Mann, der sie in Rechtsfragen hätte beraten sollen, haben sie über den Inhalt des Briefes falsche Auskunft bekommen* (from the very man who . . .).

vii. Very also expresses exact correspondence after *the, this, that,* and with *the same* relating to time. **Gerade** and **genau** are used with stressed *der, die, das,* but only *genau* with *derselbe. An gerade/genau dem Tag* or *gerade/genau an dem Tag,* on that very day. On the very day of our departure: *Genau/Gerade an dem Tag unserer Abreise.* That very day or the very same day: *An genau demselben Tag mußte auch etwas anderes schiefgehen.* The very same afternoon is *An genau demselben Nachmittag (ist etw. anderes geschehen).*

viii. Very is also used with a limiting sense meaning that the thing mentioned, without anything else, was sufficient to produce a certain result. *The very thought of such a possibility made me tremble.* This idea can be expressed by **bloß** as an adj. or by **schon, allein,** or **bloß** as advs. *Der bloße Gedanke an eine solche Möglichkeit ließ mich zittern,* the very or mere thought . . . Or *Schon/Allein/Bloß der Gedanke an eine solche Möglichkeit . . .*

> *Allein die Nennung dieses Names reichte aus, um ihn wütend zu machen* (the very/mere mention).
> *Schon die Bitte um Änderungen betrachtete man als Verrat.*
> *Schon die Tatsache, daß er dabei war, ließ sie nicht entmutigen.*

view, sight *ns.*

1. View = 'natural scenery or landscape which can be seen from a particular position'. **Der Blick,** which is followed by *von* = 'from' and/or *auf* or *über* but not by a gen., is the normal word for any view, whether good or bad. It is used for the restricted view from a window but can be applied to a broader view from a mountain peak etc. *Vom Turm hat man einen schönen Blick über die ganze Stadt.* The specific term for a vista or all-round panoramic view is **die Aussicht.** *Von dort aus hat man eine herrliche Aussicht aufs Meer/weit übers Land.* **Der Ausblick** is 'the broad or distant view from a particular point' and is always good. *Vom Gipfel hat man einen weiten/herrlichen Ausblick auf die Küste.* **Die Sicht** is also sometimes used, with what can be seen specified. *Ein Garten mit Sicht auf Fluß und Berge.* It is often found when a view is blocked. *Das neue Haus versperrt uns die Sicht auf das Tal.* In one sense **die Ansicht** is 'a picture or photograph showing a view of sth.' *Das Buch enthält viele Alpenansichten. Einige Ansichten von Berlin. Eine Ansichtskarte.*

> *Ich hätte gern ein Zimmer mit Blick auf den Fluß/mit Blick auf etw. anderes als Dächer.*
> *Der Blick/Die Aussicht vom Balkon ist atemberaubend.*
> *Du hast einen guten Blick auf die Bergspitze/eine gute Aussicht über das Tal.*
> *Vom Gipfel hat man einen besonders schönen Ausblick.*

2. i. The words discussed in 1 denote something static. When *to have a good view of something* refers to something moving, like a procession, **gut sehen können** is used. *Von hier aus konnte ich den Umzug gut sehen.*

ii. *The latest fashions are* **on view** could be *Die neueste Mode ist nun in den großen Geschäften zu sehen.*

3. One sense of **sight** is 'the state of seeing or being seen'. *At the sight of the accident she began to cry. At the sight of the police they ran away. At first sight, the problem seemed insoluble. I can't bear the sight of blood. After the earthquake, the city was a terrible sight.* **View** can be a syn., but it occurs mostly in fixed expressions. *Clouds obscured our view of the climbers/peaks. Another runner came into sight/view. He was standing in full view of the crowd.*

i. Der Anblick is 'sth. which presents itself to the sight or is seen'. *Ein seltsamer Anblick bot sich unseren Augen.* The phr. *beim Anblick* + gen. or *von* means 'when sth. is/was seen' or 'at the sight of sth.' *Beim Anblick des Unfalls fing sie an zu weinen. At the first sight of sth.* is *Beim ersten Anblick des Meeres jauchzten die Kinder auf.*

Die durch das Erdbeben verwüstete Stadt bot einen schrecklichen Anblick [dar].
Sie lachten alle beim Anblick des alten Percy, der mit einem Mädchen von sechzehn tanzte.
Der Wächter hatte die Anweisung, beim Anblick eines illegalen Eindringlings zu schießen.
Sie konnte den Anblick des gequälten Tieres nicht ertragen.
Den Anblick von Blut kann ich nicht vertragen.   *Beim Anblick der Polizei rannten sie weg/davon.*

ii. Der Blick in the sense we are concerned with in this section is 'the action of directing the sight at s.o./sth.', thus 'a glance or look'. (The difference between *glance* and *look* depends on the duration; this distinction is not made in G.) *Ich habe nur einen flüchtigen Blick auf den Brief geworfen. Blick* is not used with a gen. denoting the thing seen, but can be used with one stating what the glance or look expresses. *Sie tauschte einen Blick des Einverständnisses mit mir. Blick* is often translated by *eyes. Sie verfolgte ihn mit dem Blick. Die ganze Zeit wandte er den Blick nicht von ihr.* Although *at the first sight of s.o./sth.* is *beim ersten Anblick* + gen., *at first sight* is **auf den ersten Blick**, lit. 'at first glance'. *Er hat sich auf den ersten Blick in sie verliebt. Auf den ersten Blick erschien das Problem unlösbar.*

iii. Die Sicht means 'the distance within which seeing is possible', i.e. 'sight', 'range of vision'. It is translated as **sight** and **view** in *in Sicht kommen/bleiben/sein. Außer Sicht geraten* and *aus der Sicht verschwinden* mean 'to disappear from sight or view', and *jmdn./etw. aus der Sicht verlieren* 'to lose sight of'. *Der Zug war noch in Sicht/nicht mehr in Sicht. The ship is out of sight* can be translated as *Das Schiff ist außer Sicht* or *Man kann das Schiff nicht mehr sehen*, and *to lose sight of* as *aus den Augen* or *aus dem Blick verlieren. In Sicht* is used fig. e.g. for the approaching end of a task. *Das Ende dieser langwierigen Arbeit ist nun in Sicht.* (*Die Sicht* can mean 'visibility'. *Gute/Schlechte Sicht.*) A formal term like *range of vision* is **die Sichtweite**. *Das Flugzeug war außer Sichtweite.*

Als Land in Sicht kam, nachdem sie sieben Wochen auf hoher See gewesen waren, stießen sie einen Seufzer der Erleichterung aus. Or *Beim Anblick des Landes . . .*
Wolken kamen herunter, und die Bergspitzen verschwanden uns aus der Sicht.
Die Segler wollten das Land in Sicht behalten/nicht aus der Sicht verlieren.
Ich habe sie aus den Augen/aus dem Blick verloren, als sie in eine Seitenstraße gebogen sind.

iv. The formal term **das Blickfeld** is 'the area one can see by moving one's eyes but without moving one's head', 'field of vision'. *Jmd./Etw. kommt/gerät in jmds. Blickfeld. In full view of . . .* could be *Er stand im Blickfeld der Menge* or **vor den Augen** *der Menge. Das geschah vor den Augen aller Passanten.*

v. *Know s.o.* **by sight** is *jmdn.* **von/vom Ansehen** *kennen.*

4. Sight is also 'sth. to be seen', especially something remarkable, a sense conveyed by **die Sehenswürdigkeit**. *Der Grand Canyon ist eine der bedeutendsten Sehenswürdigkeiten der Welt*, one of the great sights. *Komm' mit und sieh' dir die Sehenswürdigkeiten Londons an!* For something less remarkable **der Anblick** is used. *Die Tulpen sind dieses Jahr ein wunderbarer Anblick* or *sind wunderbar anzusehen.* Cf. LOOK 2. i.

5. Sight meaning 'the ability to see' is **die Sehkraft** or **das Sehvermögen**. They do not differ in sense, but the second is more formal. Cf. POWER 8. For *to lose one's sight*, see BLIND B. 2.

Ohne Brille ist er nicht mehr in der Lage, die Buchstaben zu erkennen. Sein Sehvermögen ist zu schwach/Seine Sehkraft läßt nach.

6. Sight also means 's.o.'s mental view, judgement or way of looking at s.o./sth.' *All men/people are equal in God's sight: Alle Menschen sind gleich vor Gott.* (Note: *Alle*

Menschen sind vor dem Gesetz gleich, equal in the eyes of the law.) *Do what is right in your sight/view!*: *Tue, was deiner Meinung nach/deines Erachtens richtig ist!* For **view** = 'opinion' and 'conception' cf. OPINION.

7. A **sight** is also 's.o. or sth. that is surprising in appearance and excites unfavourable comment'. *What a sight you are!* is *Wie siehst du denn aus!* which here has a neg. sense. *He does look a sight: Er sieht aber komisch aus!* or *Er ist ein komischer Anblick.* *She does look a sight in that old dress: In dem alten Kleid sieht sie aber furchtbar aus/ist sie ein furchtbarer Anblick/ist sie furchtbar anzusehen.* But *You're a sight for sore eyes* could be *Es ist eine Freude/ein Vergnügen, dich mir anzusehen.*

8. Catch sight of. Erblicken means 'to perceive by the sight, usually suddenly and unexpectedly'. It is a formal word. In speech the sense is mostly expressed by *sehen. Als ich aufsah, erblickte/sah ich einen Freund auf der anderen Straßenseite.*

violent *adj.* **violence** *n.* **Violent** has two main meanings. One is 'marked by abnormal intensity', *violent pain, violent grief/hatred/emotion, violent words, a violent storm*, and the other 'using physical force to injure or destroy', *a violent man*. These are dealt with in 1 and 2 + 3 respectively.

1. Violent = 'exhibiting an unusually marked or powerful effect', 'intense, very strong'. It is applied to a variety of effects.
i. In relation to pain, an attack of a disease, a blow, and emotions, the equivalent is **heftig**, the general meaning of which is 'of great intensity, very strong (in effect)'. In different contexts it is translated as **violent**, *fierce, severe, vehement*, and *passionate*. It is also applied to strong heat of the sun. *Die Sonne brannte heftig auf die Erde.*

> *Plötzlich verspürte er heftige Schmerzen im linken Bein.*   *Er bekam einen heftigen Schlag.*
> *Sie litt an heftigen Kopfschmerzen.*   *Der Arm schmerzte sie heftig.*
> *Das Kind hatte einen heftigen Fieberanfall.* But . . . *hatte starkes Fieber.*
> *Ich habe ihre heftigen Wutausbrüche erlebt.*   *Heftiger Zorn packte ihn.*
> *Die beiden wurden von einer heftigen Liebe ergriffen.*
> *Ein heftiges Verlangen, sie wiederzusehen, packte ihn.*

With *Kummer*, both *heftig* and **schwer** are used, with *Leid* only *schwer*, and with *Haß* and *Wut* only **groß**. Neither *schwer* nor *groß* suggests as strong an effect as *heftig* or **violent**.
ii. In reference to natural forces **violent** means 'of great force and strength', a sense also carried by **heftig**. *Ein heftiger Sturm.* *Heftig* is also applied to phenomena which are characterised by the exercise of great physical force or strength. Hence *eine heftige Explosion/Bewegung* and *Das kleine Boot schaukelte heftig.*

> *Ein heftiges Unwetter tobte über der Stadt.*   *Ein heftiger Sturm brach los.*

iii. Applied to people or their dispositions, **violent** in one sense means 'displaying excessive emotion or lack of moderation in lang., action, or conduct'. In reference to the language people use and to behaviour **heftig** mean 'immoderate', 'resulting from strong or excessive emotion'. *Heftig* refers to the intensity of the emotion and may, but need not, express disapproval. *Er fluchte heftig. Das Kind weinte heftig.* Both *heftig* and **violent** refer to the way something is expressed in words, mostly in speech, but also in writing. Typical uses are *heftige Worte, heftige Kritik*, or *heftige Schmähartikel, heftig schimpfen* or *jmdn. heftig beschimpfen, heftige Kontroversen/ Auseinandersetzungen. Man protestiert, debattiert,* or *widerspricht heftig. Er wies mich heftig zurecht.*

> *Du hast wieder viel zu heftig reagiert.*   *Er umarmte und küßte sie heftig.*
> *Warum so heftig?*   *Du wirst immer gleich so heftig/zu heftig.*
> *Er legte heftigen Protest ein* (strong, vehement).   *Es gab eine heftige Auseinandersetzung.*

A syn. possible in some contexts, but belonging to more elevated style, is **ungestüm**, unrestrained or violent. *Er hat sie ungestüm geküßt/umarmt. Ein ungestümer Bursche.*

iv. Heftig has the specific meaning of 'uncontrolled, inclined to [outbursts of] anger'. It does not suggest physical violence. *Er wurde heftig* means that he flared up or lost his temper. *Mit dem muß man vorsichtig umgehen—er wird leicht heftig.* **Jähzornig**, 'violent-tempered', implies more intense anger than this sense of *heftig*, and may include physical violence. *Jmd. ist ein jähzorniger Mensch/Charakter. Er hat seine Frau jähzornig beschimpft/geschlagen.*

> *Jähzornig warf er dem anderen ein Bierglas an den Kopf.*

v. Violent describing a colour means 'extremely bright' and is translated by **grell**, glaring or bright. *Ein grelles Rot/Blau.*

vi. Besides meaning 'powerful', *ein gewaltiger König*, and 'huge', *gewaltige Felsen/Berge/Bäume*, **gewaltig** means' very strong or great'. Hence with regard to sound **violent** and *gewaltig* mean 'extremely loud'. *Gewaltiger Donner. Ein gewaltiger Krach. Die Bombe explodierte mit einem gewaltigen Knall.* It also means 'very great' in *gewaltige Hitze* and *gewaltige Kälte.* It can be applied to *Schmerzen*, but *heftig* is more usual.

vii. Violent referring to physical exercise could be **sehr anstrengend**. *Sehr/Äußerst anstrengende Leibesübungen.*

2. Violence = 'exertion of physical force so as to injure or destroy'. *The police were unable to prevent further [acts of] violence.* To use force to do something means 'to employ physical strength'. *Force* does not necessarily suggest that harm is done to people or things. **Violence**, on the other hand, is 'the exercise of physical force so as to inflict injury on or cause damage to pers. or property'. For both concepts G. has the one word, **die Gewalt**, which means 'brute physical strength'. Whether it leads to injury or damage must emerge from the context. In *Sie haben die Tür mit Gewalt geöffnet* or *jmdn. mit Gewalt hinausbefördert, mit Gewalt* means 'by force'. But in *Als unter dem Gejohle von 3 000 Motorradfahrern eine Bande von 300 die Fernsehleute umzingelten und Kameras und Aufnahmegeräte in die Flammen warfen, kamen die Polizeieinheiten gegen diesen Ausbruch von Gewalt nicht an, Gewalt* means 'violence'. *Rohe Gewalt*, which means 'brute force' and implies violence, can be used to make the difference clear. Cf. *Gewalttätigkeiten* in 3. i. *Unter Gewaltanwendung* is 'using force or violence'. *Eine Gewalttat* is 'an act of violence', *ein Gewaltverbrechen* 'a violent crime', and *ein Gewaltverbrecher* 'a violent criminal'.

> *Nur mit Gewalt/unter Anwendung von Gewalt konnte man weitere Ausschreitungen unterbinden.*

3. Violent = 'acting with physical force and causing harm or destruction'.

i. From *Gewalt* two adjs., *gewalttätig* and *gewaltsam*, are derived. **Gewalttätig** means 'characterized by destructive or brutal behaviour'. It is applied to people, and describes actions both as an adj., *eine gewalttätige Handlung*, and as an adv., *gewalttätig handeln* or *sich gewalttätig verhalten*. **Gewalttätigkeiten**, lit. 'violent actions', is often used like **violence**. *In der Nähe des Hauptbahnhofs kam es nach dem Fußballspiel zu Gewalttätigkeiten.*

> *Ein solches gewalttätiges Verhalten läßt auf geistige Instabilität schließen.*
> *Die aufgewiegelte Masse ließ sich zu Gewalttaten/Gewalttätigkeiten hinreißen.*

ii. *Gewalttätig* tends to be used to describe a permanent dispostion. *Er ist ein gewalttätiger Mensch.* Two adjs. referring to violent action on a specific occasion are **handgreiflich** and **tätlich**. *Jmd. wird gegen einen anderen handgreiflich/tätlich*, he becomes violent or uses his fists. *Eine heftige Auseinandersetzung* is one marked by violence of language or strong feeling. *Zwei Menschen setzen sich handgreiflich auseinander* implies coming to blows. *Jmd. mißhandelt/bedroht einen anderen tätlich*, uses or threatens to use violence. *Jmd. greift einen anderen an*, need imply only an attack with words, but *A greift B tätlich an* implies blows. Cf. *handgemein werden* under FIGHT 4. vi.

> *Der Dieb versuchte einer Frau die Handtasche zu entreißen. Als aber Herumstehende ihn daran hindern wollten, wurde er handgreiflich.*

> *Als der Prediger Sydow, der die gefallenen Barrikadenkämpfer vom 18. März 1848 warm gefeiert hatte, später gegen die Anerkennung der Revolution auftrat, erregte er durch diese Doppelzüngigkeit besonderen Zorn und wurde tätlich angegriffen.*

iii. Gewaltsam means 'characterized by the use of force or violence' and is applied as an adj. or adv. to actions. *Der gewaltsame Sturz der Regierung* means 'the violent overthrow', i.e. 'one brought about by the use of force or violence'. Likewise *ein gewaltsamer Tod* or *gewaltsam sterben. Ein gewaltsamer Diebstahl* is 'theft with violence'. In some contexts, however, *gewaltsam* means 'by force' (as opposed to violence) and expresses the same meaning as *mit Gewalt. Der Lehrer mußte die beiden Jungen, die sich prügelten, gewaltsam/mit Gewalt auseinanderbringen.* Similarly *Man hielt ihn gewaltsam/mit Gewalt fest.* Both *gewaltsam* and *mit Gewalt* are used when someone has to force him/herself to do something. *Ich habe mich gewaltsam/mit Gewalt zurückgehalten. Heftiger Widerstand* is 'strong resistance'; *gewaltsamer Widerstand* is 'resistance which uses force or violence'. E. could use **violent** in both contexts.

> *Er ist eines gewaltsamen Todes gestorben. Mitglieder einer rivalisierenden Gangsterbande haben ihn erschossen.   Die Polizei hat die Protestdemonstration gewaltsam unterdrückt.*

> *Obwohl ihr gar nicht danach zu Mute war, bemühte sie sich mit Gewalt, fröhlich zu sein.*

wait, await, expect *vs.*

1. Warten denotes a state of waiting. It is used without a prep., *Ich habe drei Stunden gewartet*, and with *auf* = 'for'. *Ich warte auf den Bus. Ich warte vor dem Kino auf dich.* The n. following *auf* can denote something of a non-concrete nature. *Ich warte auf eine Erklärung von dir. Warten* also takes a clause with *bis. Er wartete, bis sie fertig war.* Followed by an infin., as in *I'm waiting to hear what has happened* or *I'm waiting to be served*, **wait** becomes *darauf warten* + act. or pass. infin. *Ich warte darauf zu hören, was passiert ist*, and *Ich warte darauf, bedient zu werden.* When a phr. with *for* precedes the infin., as in *I'm waiting for the library to open* , the G. construction is *darauf warten* + *daß*-clause which has as its subj. the n. after *for. Ich warte darauf, daß die Bibliothek öffnet.*

  Ich warte schon seit drei Wochen auf eine Antwort.   *Warte mal!*
  Ich konnte nicht länger [auf dich] warten, denn dann wäre ich selbst zu spät gekommen.
  Viele Leute standen vor der Tür und warteten darauf, hineingelassen zu werden.
  Er wartet darauf, dem Chef zu sagen, was er erfahren hat.
  Ich warte darauf, daß der Chef mir sagt, was ich machen soll.
  Sie wartet darauf, daß man ihr einen Studienplatz zuweist.

Jmdn. warten lassen is 'to keep s.o. waiting'. *Er entschuldigte sich dafür, daß er uns eine Viertelstunde hatte warten lassen.* A phr. with *auf* can be added. *Sie hat mich nie lange auf eine Antwort warten lassen.*

2. *Abwarten* is used in four ways. *Erwarten* is interchangeable with *abwarten* in one use and can mean 'to wait for'.
i. Used alone, **abwarten** means 'to wait patiently', 'to bide one's time'.
  Warten wir ab!   *Nicht abwarten, sondern handeln!*
  Als eine Bresche in die nördliche Stadtbefestigung geschlagen worden war, da wartete Pompejus noch
    ab, ehe er das Signal zum Angriff geben ließ.
  Es war klar, daß der alte Kaiser unfähig war, weiter zu regieren, und daß er bald abdanken müßte.
    Die Hofpartei wünschte aber den unvermeidlichen Akt noch hinauszuschieben. Feldmarschall
    Windischgrätz wartete mit wohlberechneter Ruhe ab.

Abwarten is also used with a *bis*-clause, but in the spoken language *warten* is the usual v.
  Ich warte noch ab, bis das Gewitter vorbei ist or *Ich warte noch ein bißchen, bis . . .*
  Ich warte noch/warte ab, bis der Kuchen fertig ist.

ii. With an obj. **abwarten** means 'to wait until sth. happens or arrives'. *Ich warte auf eine Antwort auf meinen Brief* indicates general waiting and is translated as *I am waiting for . . .* In *Ich warte die Antwort auf meinen Brief ab, bevor ich weitere Schritte unternehme*, the second action is made dependent on the first, so that it means *I'll wait for the answer to arrive, before . . .* or *I won't take further action till the answer arrives. Ich warte auf eine günstige Gelegenheit*, I'm waiting for an opportunity to arise. *Ich warte eine günstige Gelegenheit ab, um es ihm zu erzählen* is very similar but suggests the person will not say anything until a favourable opportunity arises or will wait until one does present itself. Some pedestrian traffic lights carry the notice: *Knopf drücken und Fußgängergrün abwarten.* As someone might well say, *'Ich bin zur Ampel gelaufen, mußte aber auf Grün warten und verpaßte den Bus'*, the difference here lies only in the fact that *abwarten* is more formal. *Abwarten* is found at all stylistic levels with an obj. denoting an answer or information of some kind; *warten* is not possible. *Warte den Ausgang (der Wahl) ab! Ich warte das Ergebnis ab* could be translated as *I'm waiting for the result* or *I'm waiting to see what the result is*. In this use *abwarten* is affected by the meaning treated in 2. iii.

> *Wir haben zwei Tage lang in einer kleinen Hütte besseres Wetter abgewartet, mußten aber dann aufbrechen.* Also . . . *auf* . . . *gewartet.*
> *Man soll erst das Ende abwarten, bevor man ein Urteil fällt.*
> *Er wartete ihre Antwort nicht ab, sondern fügte gleich hinzu, daß er dabei sein würde.*
> *Da sie annahm, daß ihre Freundin den ersten Zug nicht erreicht hatte, wartete sie den nächsten ab.*

iii. Abwarten also means 'to wait and see' or 'await further developments etc.' It takes an obj. and is often used with a clause with *ob, wie,* or *was. Let's wait and see!* is *Warten wir es ab!* Without *es*, it has sense 2. i. *Es bleibt abzuwarten, wie sich alles entwickeln wird*, it remains to be seen.

> *Wir müssen den weiteren Verlauf der Dinge abwarten.*
> *Wir wollen abwarten, ob alles gut geht/wie die Abstimmung ausfällt.*
> *Warten wir ab, was morgen beschlossen wird!*

iv. Both **abwarten** and **erwarten**, used with *können* + *nicht* or *kaum*, mean that someone can hardly wait for something [to happen]. When a clause follows, *es* is often inserted before the infin., but it is optional. The clause corresponds to (*I can hardly wait*) *for sth. to occur.*

> *Die Schulkinder können die Ferien kaum erwarten.*
> *Nach der langen Trennung konnte er [es] kaum abwarten/erwarten, sie in seinen Armen zu halten.*
> *Der kleine Peter konnte es kaum abwarten, daß man ihn zum Essen rief.*
> *Ich kann es kaum abwarten, daß man mir das Ergebnis bringt.*

v. In two further situations **erwarten** means 'to wait for'. In *Er erwartete sie ungeduldig am Bahnhof, erwartete* is translated as *waited for*. It is more formal and emotional than the normal *warten auf* and suggests longing for the person. *Erwarten* is used on all stylistic levels for events that await one in the future. *Das Schicksal, das ihn [dort] erwartete, hatte niemand vorhergesehen. Sie ahnten nicht, was sie in Indien erwartete.*

3. i. Erwarten means 'to expect s.o./sth.' or 'to expect or anticipate that sth. will happen'. *Wir erwarten euch also um vier. Wir erwarten Besuch/einen wichtigen Brief/Gäste zum Essen. Alle erwarten einen Wahlsieg der SPD. Alle erwarten, daß die SPD gewinnen wird. Ein besseres Ergebnis war nicht zu erwarten.*

ii. Expect also means 'to anticipate that s.o. will act in a certain way or that sth. will have a certain result'. It takes an acc. and infin. construction, *I expect him to say sth. stupid*, or a clause, *I expect that he'll say sth. stupid*. It also takes *from, I only expect stupid remarks from him*, and *of, The party was expecting a lot of the new leader*. These senses are expressed by **erwarten** + clause or **erwarten von** + n. *Ich erwarte, daß er etw. Dummes sagen wird. Von ihm erwarte ich nur dumme Bemerkungen. Solche Rücksichtslosigkeit hätte ich von dir nicht erwartet*, I wouldn't have expected such inconsiderateness from you.

> *Was erwartest du denn von so einem Mann?*   *Von dir habe ich gescheiteres Benehmen erwartet.*
> *Viel Gutes war von ihm nicht zu erwarten.*   *Die Partei erwartete viel von dieser Initiative.*

iii. Expect sth. **from** s.o./sth. also means 'to regard it as one's right to get this or have it done'. *We expect honesty from our politicians. Expect* + an acc. and infin. construction expresses the same meaning. *We expect our politicians to be honest. I expect he'll be at the meeting* states one person's anticipation that another will be there and is *Ich erwarte, daß er an der Sitzung teilnimmt*, but the acc. and infin. construction in *I expect you to be at the meeting* implies that I feel you are obliged to be there, that I have a right to expect your attendance. This latter sense is expressed by **von jmdm. erwarten** usually + clause. *Ich erwarte von dir, daß du an der Sitzung teil-*

nimmst. Von preußischen Soldaten erwartete man blinden Gehorsam. Mehr kann er von uns nicht erwarten. This meaning can be formulated with a clause as *Von uns kann er nicht erwarten, daß wir [noch] mehr machen.* This construction translates **expect** in this sense regardless of whether an obj. or clause follows. *Wir erwarten von unseren Politikern, daß sie ehrlich sind/daß sie immer die Wahrheit sagen,* is thus not only a transl. of *We expect them to be honest/to tell the truth,* but the best way to express *We expect honesty/the truth from our politicians.* In the pass. the construction is *Es wird von einem Soldaten erwartet, daß er alle Befehle sofort ausführt.*

> *Der König erwartete von seinen Untertanen, daß sie ihm gehorchten.*
> *England erwartet von jedem Mann, daß er seine Pflicht tut.*
> *Von einer so teuren Uhr erwartet man, daß sie lange hält.*

iv. *Ich erwarte, daß mein Sohn mich vom Flughafen abholt* is ambiguous, as it could imply an obligation (with *von* discussed in 3. iii being omitted) as well as the anticipation of what will happen. When only anticipation is to be expressed, a syn. of *erwarten*, **rechnen mit**, is often preferred as it does not suggest an obligation. *Ich rechne damit, daß mein Sohn mich vom Bahnhof abholt.*

> *Ich rechne damit, daß alle bis Freitag fertig sind.* (*Erwarten* would sound like a command.)

v. Jmdm. etw. zumuten means 'to expect sth. of s.o.' It stresses reservations about whether the expectation is reasonable or not. *Man kann ihr diese Aufgabe [durchaus] zumuten* means that it is [quite] reasonable to expect her to do it. However, a statement like *Er mutet uns zu, den langen Weg zu Fuß zu gehen* presents the expectation as unreasonable. *Sie erwartet von uns, daß wir diese Arbeit in zwei Wochen erledigen* is neutral and makes no judgement about the reasonableness of the expectation, whereas *Sie mutet uns zu, eine solche Arbeit in zwei Wochen zu erledigen* implies that the expectation is unreasonable. The question *Kann man das von ihnen erwarten?* does not express a judgement, while *Kann man ihnen das zumuten?* expresses considerable doubt about whether the expectation is justifiable. Thus the use in neg. sents.: *Das kannst du uns nicht zumuten* and *Das ist keinem Menschen zuzumuten. Das mute ich Ihnen zu* implies that the speaker has anticipated and considered the question of reasonableness and reached a decision. *Zumuten* can also be applied to what one expects of oneself. *Ich habe mir/meinen Kräften zuviel zugemutet. Jmdm. etw. zumuten* also means 'to expect s.o. to put up with sth.' *Kann man den Nachbarn diesen Krach zumuten?*

vi. I expect can introduce a statement that the speaker considers likely to be correct. *I expect the map's in the drawer.* This sense is expressed by **glauben**, 'to believe', or **annehmen**, 'to assume'. *Ich nehme an, du hast Hunger,* I expect you're hungry. *Ich glaube/nehme an, der Hut gehört Frau Schmidt. Ich nehme an, daß die Karte in der Schublade ist. Ich glaube schon,* or *Ich nehme [es] an,* I expect so.

4. *A matter* **can wait** is *Die Sache* **eilt nicht** or *Mit der Sache* **hat es keine Eile**. Colloquially: *Die Arbeit kann warten.*

5. The usual v. for **wait on** people at table is **bedienen**. Cf. SERVE. *Der Kellner bedient die Gäste.* (*Den Gästen bei Tisch aufwarten* used to have this sense but has become uncommon. It now means 'to have to offer (to the public)'. *Das Warenhaus konnte mit einem großen Warenangebot aufwarten. Er kann immer mit ein paar Neuigkeiten/ Witzen aufwarten.*)

wake [up], waken, awaken, arouse *vs.* awake *adj.* Wecken and its derivatives are trans., while *wachen* and its prefixed forms are intr.

1. Trans. vs.

i. Wecken means 'to cause a pers. to become awake, to rouse s.o. from sleep'. *Wann möchten Sie geweckt werden? Wecken Sie mich bitte um sieben!* **Aufwecken**

stresses becoming fully conscious or awake, often getting up. As the difference
between *wecken* and *aufwecken* is slight, both are often possible.

Ich lasse mich morgens um 5.30 telefonisch [auf]wecken.   *Dein Schnarchen hat mich geweckt.*
Ich wurde durch das Gewitter in den frühen Morgenstunden geweckt.
Sei leise and weck das Kind nicht [auf]!   *Das Klingeln hat mich aufgeweckt.*

ii. Erwecken is no longer usual in the lit. sense 'to rouse s.o. from sleep'. It is used
fig. meaning 'to revive a custom etc.', *Man versucht, diese alten Bräuche wieder zum
Leben zu erwecken*, but is mostly found in the sense 'to call forth, waken, or arouse
a state of mind or an emotion' such as interest or pity. *Der Anblick der Opfer des
Unfalls erweckte Mitleid bei den Umstehenden.* **Wecken** expresses the same meaning.
*Ich studiere Germanistik hauptsächlich deshalb, weil eine Lehrerin an der höheren Schule
mein Interesse für die Literatur geweckt hat. Wecken* may be regarded as resembling
rouse, **arouse**, or *stir* in the sense 'to make a dormant quality active', while
erwecken suggests bringing it about or to life for the first time, but they are mostly
interchangeable, and individual speakers may prefer one or the other. As a guide,
wecken can be used with *Begeisterung, Vertrauen, Neugier, ein Gefühl*, and *Widerstand*,
and *erwecken* with *Liebe, Bedürfnisse, Furcht, Haß, Verdacht*, and *Zweifel*. Both are possible with *Hoffnungen* and *Illusionen. Etw. weckt/erweckt bestimmte Vorstellungen/alte
Erinnerungen. Ein Wunsch wird geweckt* or *erweckt.*

Man versucht, in den Kindern den Sinn für die Schönheiten der Natur zu wecken.
Sie wollte immer das Gute im Menschen wecken.   *Dieser Vorfall [er]weckte unser Mißtrauen.*
Der anfängliche Erfolg weckte/erweckte übertriebene Hoffnungen in dem Geschäftsmann.

2. Intr. vs. The everyday equivalent of **wake [up]** used intr. is **wach werden.** *Ich bin
erst um acht wach geworden.* It does not necessarily imply full wakefulness. *Ich bin in
der Nacht zweimal wach geworden*, I woke up twice. **Wachen** now means 'to stay
awake in order to watch', *Er wachte die ganze Nacht*, mostly with the connotation
of caring for someone, *Die Mutter wachte am Bett des Kindes.* With *über*, it means 'to
watch over', *Die Vogeleltern wachen über ihre Jungen*, or 'to watch in order to ensure
that sth. happens', *Sie wachen darüber, daß überall Ordnung herrscht.* **Aufwachen**
implies becoming completely awake, fully conscious. *Ich bin mitten in der Nacht plötzlich aus einem Traum/aus tiefem Schlaf aufgewacht.* In the lit. sense 'to awake from
sleep' **erwachen** now belongs to more elevated style, but it is still found referring
to states other than normal sleep, *Jmd. erwachte aus der Narkose/aus einer Ohnmacht/
aus seiner Gleichgültigkeit*, in fig. uses in relation to nature, *Der Winter ist vorbei, die
Erde/Natur erwacht*, and when feelings, memories, someone's senses, etc. are the
subj., *Der Wunsch hinzugehen erwachte in mir.*

Als alter Gewohnheit werde ich jeden Morgen um sechs wach/wache ich jeden Morgen um sechs auf.
Ich bin heute früh/spät aufgewacht.
Durch diese Vorgänge ist ihr Interesse/ihre Neugier erwacht.
Als man ihm den weiteren Plan erklärte, ist sein Gewissen erwacht.

3. Wake up to [the existence of] a danger, threat, etc. means 'to become aware of
it' and is **sich etw. (gen.) bewußt werden.** *Jmd. wurde sich der Gefahr bewußt*, woke
up to it, became aware of it. The trans. form *This incident woke them [up] to the threat*
can be expressed by *durch: Durch diesen Vorfall wurden sie sich der Bedrohung bewußt*,
this incident awoke them to the threat.

4. The adj. **wach** means 'awake'. *Ich schlafe nicht, ich bin schon wach. Ein wacher Geist*
is 'wide-awake, lively'. **Aufgeweckt** means 'bright, intelligent'. *Ein aufgewecktes
Kind. Wach* is also a prefix. *Sie hat mich wachgerüttelt.* Cf. SHAKE 1. ii.

wall *n.* A **wall** can be a free-standing structure of stone or masonry which is built
on the perimeter and encloses a town, castle, prison, factory, or a garden, as well

as the side of a room or building. The equivalent of the first sense is **die Mauer**. *Eine zwei Meter hohe Mauer umgibt den Garten.* The main equivalent of the second sense is **die Wand**. *Die Wand zwischen den Zimmern ist sehr dünn.* Compounds are *die Außen-* and *Innenwand. Mauer* may, but need not, be used for the exterior wall of a house which is clearly made of stone or masonry. **Der Wall** is 'a rampart'. *Die Burg war mit Wall und Graben umgeben. Der Wall* is also used for an earth-wall constructed as protection against water, *Man baute Wälle auf beiden Seiten des Flusses, um zu verhindern, daß er über die Ufer tritt,* and can be used fig., *ein Wall gegen schädliche Einflüsse.* While in fig. use *Wall* suggests protection, *Mauer* and *Wand* imply obstruction. *Sie sahen sich einer Wand von Mißtrauen gegenüber.*

> *Die erste Stadtmauer stammt aus dem 12. Jahrhundert.*
> *Der Häftling warf eine Strickleiter über die Gefängnismauer und kletterte hinüber.*
> *Wir streichen die Decke und tapezieren die Wände.*
> *Am Kriegsende standen in vielen deutschen Städten nur noch die Wände/Mauern vieler Häuser.*
> *Der größte Teil des alten Walls um die Stadt ist noch erhalten.*
> *Ein Wall aus Schnee umgab das Haus.*
> *Sie stießen auf eine Mauer von Verständnislosigkeit/Vorurteilen.*

want, wish *vs.*

1. The dominant sense of **want** is 'to desire or wish for'.

i. This meaning is mainly conveyed by **wollen**. *Wollen* is used with an obj., an infin., or alone where E. has *want* [to]. *Willst du noch eine Tasse Tee? Sie will Geschichte studieren. Du kannst mitkommen, wenn du willst.* A common alternative in the last sent. is *wenn du Lust hast.* Although **Lust haben** is translated as *to feel inclined*, it is more frequently used than the E. expression and occurs in contexts in which E. has **want [to]**. *Haben Sie Lust mitzugehen?*

> *Ich will wissen, was geschehen ist.*   *Sie können essen, soviel Sie wollen.*
> *Wir haben sie zum Mitspielen aufgefordert, aber sie wollten nicht/hatten keine Lust, [Tennis zu spielen].*
> *Er muß es tun, er mag wollen oder nicht.*   *Was wollen Sie jetzt tun?*
> *A. Kommst du mit? B. Nein (or Nee). A. Warum denn nicht? B. Hab' keine Lust.*

The infins. *gehen, fahren,* and *kommen* are frequently omitted in speech after *wollen* when the sentence contains a phr. of direction. *Er will in die Stadt. Sie wollte nach Hause. Zu wem will er denn?* When these infins. have a prefix indicating direction, the infin. is also often omitted, and the prefix is added to *wollen. Wo will er denn hin? Sie wollten unbedingt hinein. Mehrere Kinder wollten hinaus. Willst du nicht mit? Wir wollen pünktlich weg. Wir wollen noch heute zurück.*

ii. With an obj. **wollen** means 'to desire to get or possess sth. or to see the existence of a thg. or the performance of an action'. *Die Arbeiter wollen höhere Löhne. Max will mehr Taschengeld. Wir wollen nur dein Glück/dein Bestes. Hitler wollte den Krieg um jeden Preis. Alle Völker wollen den Frieden. Das habe ich nicht gewollt. Was wollen Sie eigentlich?* It is also used with *von. Was willst du denn von mir?*

iii. **Wollen** is often used with **haben** and an obj. *Welches Fahrrad willst du denn haben? Sie wollen mehr Taschengeld haben. Haben* is not really necessary, but is often added, particularly in questions. *Er will seine Ruhe [haben]. Sie will ihre Kinder immer um sich [haben]. Wollen Sie das Auto für die Ferien [haben]? Haben* may be used with the first person pres., *Ich will einen Apfel haben,* to make it sound less peremptory. In such a sent. it would be more usual to use **möchte** as this sounds more polite. *Möchten Sie Tee oder Kaffee?* Children are taught to use *möchte* instead of *wollen* when saying what they want or asking what others would like. *To want sth. back* can be **zurückwollen**. *Ich will das Geld zurück,* but **zurückhaben** or **wiederhaben wollen** are probably more used. *Er will seinen Fußball wiederhaben. Sie will ihr Wörterbuch zurückhaben.*

iv. Verlangen nach means 'to desire' in formal language. *Jmd. verlangt nach Ruhe. Der Patient verlangte nach dem Arzt.* Less commonly it is used impersonally. *Es verlangte mich nach Abwechselung.*

v. Transl. of constructions with **want**.

a. One difference between **wollen** and **want** is that an acc. and infin. construction is not possible in G. The E. acc. must become the subj. of a *daß*-clause. *I want you to help me* becomes *Ich will, daß du mir hilfst. What do you want me to do?* is *Was willst du, daß ich tue? I've only done what they wanted [me to]* is *Ich habe nur das getan, was sie wollten.*

> *Ich will nicht, daß davon gesprochen wird.*   *Ich will, daß du mir erzählst, was geschehen ist.*
> *Wollen Sie, daß ich länger bleibe?*
> *Er wollte, daß wir die Arbeit so schnell wie möglich erledigten.*

b. A *daß*-clause is also necessary with **ich möchte**. *Ich möchte, daß alle an der Sitzung teilnehmen.*

c. The pass. of **want** is rendered by **man will** + clause. *Am I wanted for anything else? Will man, daß ich jetzt etw. anderes tue? Man will, daß ihr alle mit anpackt,* all are wanted to lend a hand.

2. i. Want also means 'to desire to see or speak to a pers.' or 'to desire the presence or assistance of s.o. in a place'. *You are wanted on the phone.* One equivalent is **verlangen**, to ask for. Cf. ASK 5. *Du wirst am Telefon verlangt. Du wirst an der Tür verlangt* is also possible, although *An der Tür ist jmd., der dich sprechen will* is probably more common. *You are wanted in Room 20* can be *Man möchte Sie im Zimmer 20 sprechen. I know when I'm not wanted: Ich weiß, wann meine Gegenwart nicht erwünscht ist.*

ii. *What does he want with such people?* The sense is expressed by **[anfangen] wollen mit**. *Was will er denn überhaupt mit solchen Leuten [anfangen]? Er hat ein Darlehen von 10 000 Mark aufgenommen. Was will er denn überhaupt mit dieser Menge Geld [anfangen]?* An alternative here is *Was hat er denn mit einer solchen Summe vor?*

3. Want in its original sense 'to be without' or 'to lack' may still be found in literary style. *Mullgrave, though he lacked experience, wanted neither intelligence nor courage.* The equivalent is **mangeln**, to LACK. The first verse of Psalm 23 which in the AV is *The Lord is my shepherd; I shall not want,* is *Der Herr ist mein Hirte, mir wird nichts mangeln* in the current G. version. *They want for nothing* is *Es mangelt ihnen an nichts* or *Sie haben alles, was sie brauchen.*

> *Mullgrave hatte zwar noch wenig Erfahrung, aber es mangelte ihm weder an Intelligenz noch an Mut.*

4. i. Want also means 'to stand in need of sth. salutary'. *What you want is a good rest.* This meaning can be expressed by **brauchen** or **nötig haben**. Cf. NEED 2. ii. *Du brauchst Ruhe* or *Was du brauchst, ist Ruhe. Du hast Ruhe dringend nötig.*

ii. Want + gerund or infin. is best translated by **sollte**, which means 'should' or 'is advisable'. *There are a couple of jobs that want doing in the garden: Es gibt einiges, was man im Garten tun sollte. Your hair wants/needs cutting: Du solltest dir das Haar schneiden lassen. You want to be more careful: Du solltest vorsichtiger sein. You want to book as soon as possible: Ihr solltet so bald wie möglich buchen.*

5. Wish can be a formal syn. of **want**.

i. When it is followed by an infin., it is often translated by **wollen** or **möchte**. *Sie lieben sich und wollen heiraten.* This also applies to expressions like *if he wishes* and *as you wish* and *I don't wish to interrupt. Er kann mitkommen, wenn er will/möchte.*

> *Sie könnte, wenn sie wollte, den größten Teil der Arbeit zu Hause machen.*
> *Ich will nicht stören, sondern Ihnen nur diesen Brief geben.*
> *A. Er soll sofort hierher kommen. B. Wie Sie wollen.*

ii. *Wie Sie wünschen* could also be used in the last sent. In such a clause, or with an infin., such as *Die Damen wünschen zu speisen*, **wünschen** is more formal than **wish** and may sound somewhat stilted. When it is used with an obj. and a *daß*-clause, an appropriate transl. is either of the formal vs. **wish** or *desire*. *Was wünschen Sie?* is a more polite question than *Was wollen Sie?*

> *Die Eltern wünschen, daß die Kinder das Abitur machen.*
> *Wünschen Sie noch eine Tasse Tee?* (Very polite question by e.g. *ein Kellner.*)
> *Sehnlichst wünschte der Detektiv die völlige Aufklärung des Falles.*

6. Wish = 'to have or express the hope that sth. will happen'.

i. Wünschen expresses a wish that something will happen, *Wir können nur hoffen und wünschen, daß alles gut geht,* and that someone will experience something, *Ich wünsche Ihnen viel Erfolg/alles Gute zum Geburtstag. Sie wünschte uns eine glückliche Reise/einen guten Morgen.* Wünschen is also used for wishing someone somewhere. *Ich wünschte mich weit weg von hier. Er wünschte diesen Gast zum Teufel.* **Jmdm. wohlwollen** means 'to wish s.o. well' or 'to be well-disposed towards s.o.'. *Jeder wollte ihr wohl.* **Jmdm. übelwollen** means 'to wish s.o. ill', 'to be unkindly disposed towards'. *Er hat dem jüngeren Kollegen übelgewollt. I don't wish her any harm/ill* or *I don't wish harm/ill on her* is *Ich wünsche ihr nichts Böses.*

ii. The refl. **sich** (dat.) **wünschen** means 'to wish [for]' or 'wish to receive'. *Wenn du drei Wünsche frei hättest, was würdest du dir wünschen?* It is used for wishing for or wanting something for one's birthday or Christmas. *Was wünschst du dir zum Geburtstag/zu Weihnachten?*

iii. Sich wünschen is also used in the indicative with an infin. if there is a reasonable possibility that the wish can be fulfilled. *Früher hat sie sich oft gewünscht, woanders zu leben, aber jetzt ist sie zufrieden in Deutschland.*

iv. When the wish is a vague desire which cannot or is unlikely to be fulfilled, the subjunctive form **ich wünschte** is used with a clause whose v. is also in the subjunctive. The syn. *ich wollte* + subjunctive belongs more to everyday speech. *Ich wünschte, ich hätte ihn nie kennengelernt. Ich wollte, ich hätte genug Geld. Ich wünschte/wollte, ich wäre nicht bei Rot über die Kreuzung gefahren/die Ferien wären schon da.*

warm *v.*

1. Warm [up] trans. = 'to make warm or warmer'.

i. The general term **wärmen** is mostly trans., *Der Ofen wärmt das Zimmer,* but can be intr. with the obj. implied, *Im März wärmt die Sonne schon.* The subj. is usually the thing giving warmth; it is a person only in two circumstances—firstly, when one person warms another with the heat of his or her own body, *Sie nahm das Kind zu sich ins Bett, um es zu wärmen,* and secondly, when *wärmen* has a refl. dat., *Ich wärme mir die Hände am Ofen.*

ii. The usual expression for warming [up] food or drink is **warm machen**. *Soll ich dir etwas Milch warm machen?* It is also used for warming a room. *Ich stelle die Heizung auf sechs, um das Zimmer schnell warm zu machen.* Otherwise **einheizen**, 'to HEAT', can be used. *Wir müssen das Zimmer einheizen. Das Essen* **warm stellen** means 'to keep warm', 'to prevent from becoming cold'. **Aufwärmen** is used for warming up food etc. which was once warm but has become cold. *Ich wärme das Essen von Mittag/den Kaffee auf.*

iii. Sich aufwärmen means 'to go into a warm room etc. or drink a warm or an alcoholic drink in order to overcome a feeling of cold', 'to warm oneself or warm up'. *Wir unterbrachen die Wanderung und gingen in ein Restaurant, um uns aufzuwärmen. Um uns zu wärmen* is also possible, but less common.

iv. Anwärmen is 'to warm slightly'. *Ich habe das Wasser [etwas] angewärmt.*

v. While *wärmen* suggests making something warmer by an unspecified amount and keeping it at that heat, **erwärmen** stresses the process of raising the temperature. It alone is used when a temperature is given. *Wir haben die Lösung auf 60° erwärmt.* It is often used without a temperature, but the sense is still 'to warm sth. up', 'to make warmer by a fairly definite amount'. *Die Zentralheizung hat das Zimmer schnell erwärmt* suggests warming it up on a particular occasion while *Der Ofen wärmt das Zimmer* implies keeping it warm all the time. *Erwärmen* is the usual v. in scientific contexts. *Die Sonne erwärmt das Meerwasser nur langsam.*

2. Warm up intr. = 'to become warm or warmer'.

i. With **Sich erwärmen** expresses the intr. sense 'to warm up'. *Das Meerwasser erwärmt sich langsamer als das Land,* the ocean [water] warms up more slowly than the land. *Gegenüber vorgestern hat sich die Luft um 15° erwärmt.*

ii. Sich aufwärmen is used for athletes who warm up before an event. *Der Sprinter wärmt sich vor dem Start auf.*

iii. For an engine or machine the usual expression is **sich warm laufen**. *Bei dieser Kälte braucht der Motor einige Zeit, um sich warm zu laufen. Es dauert fünf Minuten, bis das Kopiergerät sich warm gelaufen hat.*

3. Fig. uses.

i. With *Herz* as obj. **erwärmen** is the usual v. *Dieser Anblick hat mir das Herz erwärmt,* although in the pres. tense *wärmt mir das Herz* is also found. *Ihr Lächeln erwärmte ihm das Herz.*

ii. Erwärmen is used with a person as obj. meaning 'to rouse s.o.'s interest in or enthusiasm for sth.'. *Er versuchte, die Partei für den Plan zu erwärmen.* **Sich für etw. erwärmen** means 'to become interested in or enthusiastic about sth.' and can translate *to warm to a task/one's work,* etc. *Sie haben sich für das Theaterstück sehr erwärmt. Allmählich erwärmte sie sich für die Arbeit/die Aufgabe.* With *nicht können* it means 'not to be able to work up any enthusiasm for'. *Ich kann mich für diesen Plan/diese Idee nicht erwärmen. Für solche abgedroschenen Phrasen kann ich mich nicht erwärmen. The speaker warmed to his subject* can be *Er steigerte sich in sein Thema hinein.*

iii. Warm to a pers. can be *Ich fand ihn/sie immer sympathischer* or *Er/Sie wurde mir immer sympathischer.*

iv. In fig. use **aufwärmen** means either 'to drag up a scandal, old story, etc.' or 'to rehash a literary style'. *Warum mußt du diese alte Geschichte wieder aufwärmen? Diese Erzählung ist kaum originell—sie ist nur aufgewärmter Kafka.*

warn, caution *vs.*

1. Warn [of/about] = 'to make aware or to put on one's guard by giving timely notice of impending danger'. The equivalent is **warnen**, which means 'to put a pers. on his/her guard'. It is used with an obj., *Ich habe euch gewarnt,* or with an obj. + *vor* = 'of', 'about', or 'against', *Ich habe sie vor der Gefahr/vor diesem Mann gewarnt.* Cf. 2 for *warn* + infin. and 4.

> *Wir haben sie rechtzeitig gewarnt, aber sie ließen sich nicht [von uns] warnen.*
>
> *Die Wissenschaftler warnten die Öffentlichkeit vor den Folgen der Luftverschmutzung.*
>
> *Wegen der Einbruchgefahr warnt die Polizei vor dem Betreten des Eises. Also Vor dem Betreten des Eises wird gewarnt.* *Vor Taschendieben wird gewarnt.*
>
> *Der Seewetterdienst warnte alle Schiffe vor dem herannahenden Orkan.*

2. i. Warn + neg. infin. *I warned you not to go.* **Warn against** + gerund. *I warned you against going.* **Jmdn. davor warnen** can be followed by a pos. infin. construction. This construction corresponds either to **warn** + neg. infin., *Man hat mich davor* *gewarnt, mich auf ihn zu verlassen,* they warned me not to rely on him, or to *warn against* + gerund, *They warned me against relying on him. Ich habe dich davor gewarnt, nochmal hinzugehen,* warned you not to go again or against going again. (*Davor* may be omitted. *Nicht* is sometimes added to the infin. *Ich habe ihn gewarnt, diesen Weg [nicht] zu gehen.* Educated speakers regard this use of *nicht* as substandard, and non-native speakers should avoid it.)

> *Der Polizist warnte die Kinder davor, auf das Eis zu gehen.*
> *Ich warnte ihn davor, unvorsichtig zu sein.*
> *Ich habe sie mehrmals davor gewarnt, diesem Mann zu trauen.*

Warn s.o. **not** to do sth. may be a way of expressing a neg. command. This can be translated by *sagen* + *daß* + neg. *I warned you not to make a noise* could therefore become *Ich habe euch doch gesagt, ihr solltet keinen Krach machen* or . . . *gesagt, ihr solltet leise sein.*

ii. When a pos. infin. follows **warn**, *I warned you to leave it alone, warnen* cannot be used. *I warned you to drive slowly* must become something like *Ich habe dir gesagt, daß du langsam fahren solltest. Ich habe dich [davor] gewarnt, langsam zu fahren* is a perfectly correct sent., but means 'warned you *not* to drive slowly'. *Ich habe dir gesagt, du solltest es nicht anfassen.*

3. Warn also means 'to inform or advise s.o. of sth. requiring attention'. Although the idea of avoiding danger or punishment is sometimes present, in many cases it is only a remote possibility. *I need some sleep—warn me when they arrive! The clock warned them that it was time to get ready. Warnen* is only possible when the information given represents a threat or danger. *Sie haben uns gewarnt, daß der Hund bissig/gefährlich ist. Die Kundschafter warnten uns, daß der Feind sich näherte.* Both sents. could be recast with *vor: Sie warnten uns vor dem bissigen Hund/vor dem Herannahen des Feindes/vor dem herannahenden Feind.* Where the information given does not represent a threat or danger, an expression meaning 'to inform' is used. **Sagen** or **Bescheid sagen** can be used when the meaning is 'to inform'. *Ich brauche etwas Schlaf. Sag' es mir/Sag' mir Bescheid, wenn sie ankommen! Die Uhr sagte ihnen, daß es an der Zeit sei, sich fertig zu machen.* When **warn** means 'to advise to do sth.', **[dringend] raten** or **empfehlen** express the sense. *The marine meteorological service warned that all ships should head for port* or *It warned all ships to head for port* is best translated as *Der Seewetterdienst hat allen Schiffen [dringend] geraten/empfohlen, sobald wie möglich einen Hafen anzulaufen. Der Seewetterdienst hat allen Schiffen gesagt, sie sollten . . . anlaufen* is also possible.

4. Warnen is used to conclude remarks pointing to a danger and to express a threat. *I've warned you!* or *I'm warning you! Ich habe dich gewarnt. Du wirst es bereuen— ich warne dich!* **Warn** s.o. **off** is 'to tell s.o. to keep away because of danger or punishment'. The meaning needs to be expressed. *Der Wächter sagte den Jungen, sie sollten verschwinden/nicht näher [he]rankommen.* In direct speech: *Er sagte, 'Verschwindet!'* or *'Macht, daß ihr wegkommt!'*

> *'Ich warne dich! Wenn das noch einmal vorkommt, werde ich nicht da sein, um dir aus der Patsche zu helfen.'*

5. Another meaning of **warn** is 'to give a pers. cautionary notice or advice with regard to his/her actions or conduct' or 'to caution against neglect of duty or against wrong or mistaken behaviour'. **Caution** means 'to charge s.o. to take heed not to do sth. again'. **Warnen** is used when the bad consequences are stated in a clause. *Er warnte mich, daß ich durch die Prüfung fallen würde, wenn ich so weiter machte, wie bisher.* **Verwarnen** means 'to caution or to give s.o. a warning'. It implies that in a situation which could well merit a penalty, the person is cautioned or severely reprimanded instead of being punished, and made to understand that, in the event of a repetition, the full penalty will be imposed. Thus *Der Schiedsrichter verwarnte den Spieler* or *Der Spieler erhielt eine Verwarnung.* (This reports what happened. The umpire's words would be something like, '*Wenn du noch einmal foulst, wirst du vom Feld gestellt.*') In school: *Bei Halbjahrszeugnissen wird man verwarnt, wenn man zwei Fünfen im Zeugnis hat. Wenn die Leistungen sich nicht verbessern, bleibt man sitzen.*

> *Ich habe ihn gewarnt, daß er die Prüfung nicht bestehen wird, wenn er nicht fleißiger lernt.*
> *Das Gericht verwarnte die jugendlichen Straftäter, aber sah von einer härteren Strafe ab, um ihnen mit einer Vorstrafe nicht die Zukunft zu verbauen.*
> *Der Polizist verwarnte einen Fahrer, der die Geschwindigkeitsbegrenzung überschritten hatte.*

6. In the sense 'to warn' **mahnen** is used only for a reminder that a bill or debt has not been paid. *Das Kaufhaus hat mich gemahnt. Ich hatte vergessen, die Rechnung vom vorletzten Monat zu bezahlen.*

waste, squander *vs.* The main sense of **waste** dealt with here is 'to spend or use needlessly', 'to consume or employ to no purpose'. The obj. is most frequently money, time, or effort, but sometimes also sympathy, affection, etc. **Squander** money or resources is 'to use it or them in a foolish and wasteful way'. Another meaning of **waste** is 'to allow to be used inefficiently' or 'to become dissipated or lost'. In this use it is a syn. of **lose** meaning 'not to utilize properly'. *The heat was wasted/lost in the process. He lost no time in telling everyone.* **Waste** a chance/opportunity is 'to let one pass without taking advantage of it'.

1. Verschwenden is 'to use or spend in too great an amount without receiving the proper advantage'. The obj. can be concrete, *Geld, Öl, Kohle, Wasser,* etc. or nontangible, *Zeit, seine/ihre Energie,* or *Mühe. Verschwenden* usually refers not to a single wasteful action but to an improvident use of resources over a period of time. *Viele Menschen, die im Wohlstand leben, verschwenden Lebensmittel.* It is translated as **waste** or **squander**. From *verschwenden* are derived the adj. *verschwenderisch,* 'spendthrift, wasteful', and the n. *der Verschwender,* 'a spendthrift or wasteful person'. **Vergeuden** is 'to use sth. which is, or is regarded as, valuable to no purpose'. It emphasizes the pointless way it has been used and expresses regret about an irreparable loss or waste. It does not suggest repetition nor that someone is temperamentally inclined to waste things, but rather an occasion which the speaker regrets. *Vergeudet kein Material!* In reference to time *Vergeudet keine Zeit!* and *Verschwendet keine Zeit!* are both used. The first implies that time is a valuable commodity that the people addressed should strive to use sensibly, while the second implies that the people spoken to are inclined to use time in a foolish way. *Er verschwendet immer sehr viel Zeit,* but *Wir haben sehr viel Zeit mit Warten/mit unnötigen Vorarbeiten vergeudet.* Both vs. form compound ns., *die Zeitverschwendung* and *die Zeitvergeudung.* The above distinction also holds when the objs. are ns. like *Geld, Lebensmittel, Wasser, Strom,* etc., although it sometimes does not make much difference which is used, particularly in the neg. For material things **verschwenderisch mit etw. umgehen** can be used instead of *verschwenden.*

> *Er verschwendet sein Leben mit Kleinigkeiten, ohne ein Ziel vor Augen zu haben.*
> *Ihre Blätter waren stets eng beschrieben. Sie wollte kein Papier verschwenden.*
> *Bei seinen Malerarbeiten verschwendet er immer viel Farbe.* Cf. *Da ich sehr unerfahren war, habe ich viel Farbe vergeudet.   Du verschwendest dein Mitleid an einen Unwürdigen.*
> *Er verschwendet/vergeudet all seine Energie an eine Aufgabe, die man wahrscheinlich nie zu einem befriedigenden Abschluß bringen kann.*
> *Vergeudet eure Kräfte nicht, sondern spart sie euch lieber für den Nachmittag auf, wenn wir den schwierigsten Teil des Weges zu bewältigen haben.*

Er glaubte, seine Jugend durch zu viel Arbeit vergeudet zu haben.
Du verdienst zwar nicht sehr viel, aber wenn du nicht verschwenderisch mit deinem Geld umgehst, wirst du nie in Geldschwierigkeiten geraten.

2. Vertun, which is common in speech, refers to a single wasteful action. It is not as serious nor as strongly neg. in tone as the vs. discussed in 1. *Jmd. vertut Geld/Zeit/eine Chance/den Augenblick/die einmalige Chance/eine Gelegenheit.* (Neg. syns. are *Man nutzt die Gelegenheit nicht/läßt sie ungenutzt.* Cf. USE 2. i.) No n. is formed from *vertun.* **A waste of time** etc. is expressed by the past part.: *Das ist/wäre nur vertane Zeit.* In a sent. like *Der Tennisspieler hatte wegen einer momentanen Unkonzentriertheit den sicheren Sieg vertan,* it suggests spoiling or wasting the opportunity by not doing the right thing. (Note that *sich vertun* means 'to make a mistake'. *Er hat sich in der Zeit/in der Abrechnung vertan.*)
Sie vertut viel Zeit mit Nebensächlichkeiten, anstatt sich auf die wesentlichen Punkte zu beschränken.
Er erwies sich als unzuverlässig und hat somit seine Chancen vertan.
Geben Sie sich keine Mühe, mich zu überreden! Sie vertun nur ihre Zeit damit.

3. Verlieren means 'to lose' in the sense 'not to utilize properly' and is found in expressions in which **waste** would be usual in E. *Das war verlorene Mühe,* a waste of effort, wasted effort.
Über diese Sache möchte ich kein weiteres Wort verlieren.   Wir haben zu viel Zeit verloren.
Wir dürfen keine Sekunde verlieren, sondern müssen sofort aufbrechen.
Die Wärme, die bei dem Prozeß verloren geht, will man nutzen.

4. Vertrödeln is 'to use time foolishly, to no purpose, not as could be expected', 'to dawdle away'.
Ich darf keine Zeit mehr verlieren. Den größten Teil des Vormittags habe ich bereits vertrödelt.

5. Other vs. meaning 'to waste money'. **Verschleudern** means 'to fling around or away' when these imply being wasteful, as well as 'to sell at a ridiculously low price'. It always expresses condemnation.
Man hat Millionen für dieses sinnlose Projekt verschleudert.
Da sie möglichst schnell viel Geld brauchte, verschleuderte sie ihren Schmuck zu Preisen, die weit unter dem eigentlichen Wert lagen.   Er hatte sein väterliches Erbe verschleudert.
Hinauswerfen means 'to throw out'. In *Das ist nur hinausgeworfenes Geld* it also implies waste. Cf. *Jmd. wirft/schmeißt mit Geld um sich,* throws or chucks money around. **Durchbringen** is 'to spend uselessly or get through money'. *Durch seine Leidenschaft zum Kartenspiel hatte er das Vermögen bald durchgebracht.* **Prassen** means 'to live extravagantly' or 'to live it up'. *Er hat Monate lang geschlemmt und gepraßt, bis sein Geld alle war.* Geld **verprassen** is 'to spend money ostentatiously in extravagant living'. *Sie haben ihr Geld/ihr Hab und Gut verpraßt.* Some sents. from two translations of the Prodigal Son (*der verlorene Sohn*) illustrate the use of these words: (i) *Nach wenigen Tagen packte der jüngere Sohn alles zusammen und zog in ein fernes Land. Dort führte er ein zügelloses Leben und verschleuderte sein Vermögen. Als er alles durchgebracht hatte, kam eine große Hungersnot über das Land, und es ging ihm sehr schlecht.* (ii) *Dort vergeudete er sein Vermögen durch ein zügelloses Leben.* (*Der ältere Bruder sagte:*) *'Kaum aber ist der hier gekommen, der dein Vermögen mit Dirnen verpraßt hat, da hast du für ihn das Mastkalb geschlachtet.'*

way *n.* Order of meanings: 1.'A thoroughfare used for travelling on'. *The new highway.* 2. 'Place to go along'. *He made his way through the crowd. The way in/out.* 3. 'Route to be taken'. *The way to the station. We go this way.* 4. 'Space for passing'. *You're in my way.* 5. 'Distance'. *We've got a long way to go.* 6. 'Direction'. *You're going the wrong way.* 7. 'Manner of behaving or living'. *That's my way.* 8. 'A method to attain an end or do sth.' *A way to earn a living. A simple way of learning.* 9. 'Manner in which sth. is done'. *That's the simplest way to repair it. We did it this way/[in] another way.* 10. Transls. of E. idiomatic expressions.

1. The original sense of **way** as defined by the *OED* is 'a track prepared or available for travelling along, a road, lane, or path'. This sense of *way* survives only in a few expressions such as *across/over the way* and in the compounds *footway, highway, expressway,* and *motorway.*

i. Der Weg still means 'track or path'. Cf. STREET. *Benutze diesen Weg nicht!—er ist aufgeweicht. The houses across/over the way* is *Die Häuser auf der anderen/gegenüberliegenden Straßenseite.* An alternative for *S.o. lives across the way* is *Jmd. wohnt gegenüber. The Milky Way* is *die Milchstraße.* Lit. equivalents of *highway* are *die Landstraße* or *der Hauptverkehrsweg. Die Landstraße, die die Städte X und Y verbindet, wird ausgebaut* (is being improved). *Der Hauptverkehrsweg zwischen den beiden Orten ist stark befahren.* A *highway, motorway,* or *expressway* would now, however, usually be *eine Autobahn.* A *pedestrian way* or *footway* is *der Fußgängerweg.*

ii. Way and **der Weg** are used fig. *Du bist auf dem richtigen Weg,* on the right track. *Das ist nicht der richtige Weg zum Erfolg. They went their separate ways: Jeder ging seinen eigenen Weg. You go your way, I'll go mine: Geh' du deinen Weg! Ich gehe den meinen. Hier trennen sich unsere Wege* is used fig. to suggest that people's opinions etc. are so divergent that they can no longer work or live together.

> *Es war ein schwerer Weg, den sie zurücklegen mußte, um dieses Ziel zu erreichen.*
>
> *Wir waren Jahrelang zusammen in derselben Klasse, aber seitdem gehen wir verschiedene Wege.*

2. i. A **way** is 'a place to go along'. In this sense **way** does not suggest a made path or road but an opening through a crowd or through something which obstructs one's passage. **Der Weg** also expresses this sense. *Sie bahnte* (made, worked, pushed) *sich einen Weg durch die Menge* or *Er bahnte sich einen Weg durch das dichte Unterholz/durch den Schlamm. Sie schlugen sich den Weg durch den Dschungel,* hacked their way.

ii. In some cases the meaning of an E. v. + *way* is expressed by a G. v. *Ich muß mich durch diese Stapel Papiere durcharbeiten,* work my way through. *Jmd. drängte sich hinein,* pushed/forced his way in. **Make one's way** somewhere means 'to go there' and can be **sich begeben.** *Ich begab mich nach vorn. Der D-Zug 201 nach Paderborn, Abfahrt 9.20, fährt heute ausnahmsweise von Gleis 11 ab. Passagiere werden gebeten, sich dorthin zu begeben. Jmd. macht seinen Weg* suggests steady success and progress in a career. **Feel one's way** is **sich tasten,** to FEEL. *Ich tastete mich zur Tür/die Mauer entlang.*

iii. The way in/out meaning 'the actual place where one goes in or out', i.e. 'the entrance and exit', is **der Eingang** and **der Ausgang.** *Which/Where is the way in?* is either *Wo ist der Eingang?* or *Wo geht man hinein?* (colloquially *rein*) or impersonally *Wo geht's hinein?* The opposite is *Wo ist der Ausgang?* or *Wo geht man hinaus? I went out the back way: Ich bin durch die Hintertür/den Hinterausgang/hinten hinausgegangen.* (**Der Ausweg** is 'a means of escape from difficulty'. *Es gab nur einen Ausweg aus dieser hoffnungslosen Lage.*)

3. Way + **to** either stated or implied means 'the line or course, whether direct or circuitous, by which a place may be reached'. *Can you show me the way to the university?*

i. Der Weg also expresses this sense. While sense 1 suggests a road or path, this one implies a route to be taken to get somewhere. Thus *der Weg nach Hause, der direkte/schnellste/kürzeste Weg nach Hameln. She asked the way to the station* is *Sie fragte nach dem Weg zum Bahnhof. I'm going your way* can be *Wir haben denselben Weg* or *Wir gehen denselben Weg.*

Könnten Sie mir bitte den Weg zur Universität zeigen?
Ich bin ihr auf dem Weg zur Arbeit begegnet.
Es gibt mehr als einen Weg dorthin.   *Sie hat mir den Weg zur Schule gezeigt.*
Im dichten Nebel sind wir vom richtigen Weg abgekommen.
Wir sind denselben Weg zurückgekehrt, den wir gekommen waren.

ii. *Einen* **Umweg** *machen* is 'to take a round-about way', sometimes 'to make a detour'. Common expressions are *Man macht einen großen/kleinen Umweg. Ich bin auf einem Umweg nach Hause gefahren.* It is also used fig. *Man erreicht ein Ziel auf Umwegen.*

iii. Expressions in which **way** in this sense is combined with a v. are sometimes translated by **der Weg** + v., sometimes by a v. alone. **Miss one's way** is *den Weg verfehlen* or *verpassen. Sie können den Weg gar nicht verfehlen.* **Lose one's way** can be *den rechten Weg verlieren*, but more usually **sich verlaufen** or **sich verirren**, or if in a car **sich verfahren**. *Wir haben uns im Wald verlaufen / verirrt. Wir hatten uns im Nebel verfahren.* **Know the way** is *den Weg kennen.* **Know one's way around/about a place** is *sich irgendwo* **auskennen.** Cf. KNOW 8. **Take the wrong way** is *den falschen Weg nehmen.* For *Food goes [down] the wrong way* see SWALLOW 1. ii. **Find one's way** is **sich zurechtfinden,** and **lead the way** is **vorangehen,** to go ahead.

4. In various phrs. **way** means 'space for passing' or 'the absence of obstruction to forward movement'. *You're in my way. Please get out of the/my way! Which car has right of way?*

i. In many cases **der Weg** also carries this sense. *Du bist/stehst mir* **im Weg[e],** you are [standing] in my way. *Ich bekomme die Tür nicht auf—etw. steht im Wege. Jmd. kommt einem anderen in den Weg,* gets in the other person's way. Also fig.: *Diese Verpflichtungen standen seinem Ehrgeiz im Weg.* **Not to be in the way** or **be out of the way** in this sense is **niemand[em] im Weg[e] sein.** *Ich stelle den Karton in die Ecke. Er wird da niemand[em] im Wege sein.*

ii. Get out of the way/make way [for]. The command *Out of my way!* or *[Please] make way!* can be **Aus dem Weg!,** but **jmdm. Platz machen** is more usual and more polite. *Machen Sie bitte mal Platz!* Children on sleds *(Schlitten)* or billy-carts *(Seifenkisten)* say, '**Bahn frei!**' when they want someone to get out of their way. **Jmdm. aus dem Weg gehen** has, in the lit. sense, no overtones. *Als er mit dem Tablett auf mich zukam, ging ich ihm aus dem Weg/machte ich ihm Platz.* It also means 'to avoid s.o. intentionally'. *Wenn es geht, gehe ich ihr aus dem Weg[e].* Platz machen is used fig. *Er beschloß, einem jüngeren Mann Platz zu machen.*

iii. Jmdm. in die Quere kommen means 'to get in s.o.'s way' in the lit. sense or 'to disturb or interfere with s.o.'s plans and intentions'. *Unsere Wohnung ist so klein daß man sich selbst zu zweit dauernd in die Quere kommt. Wir wollten nach Spanien fahren, aber eine dringende geschäftliche Angelegenheit ist mir in die Quere gekommen.*

iv. *The* **way** *is now clear for us to take over the company* could be **Nichts steht** *der Über-nahme dieses Unternehmens [durch unsere Firma] mehr* **im Wege** or **Der Weg ist nun frei** *für die Fusion der beiden Unternehmen.*

v. For motor vehicles **die Vorfahrt** is 'right of way'. *Man läßt,* or in more formal language *gewährt einem anderen Auto die Vorfahrt. Welches Auto hat Vorfahrt?*

5. Way also means 'the distance travelled or to be travelled along a particular route'. *We've already come a good way.*

i. Der Weg occurs mainly in fixed expressions. *You've got a long way to go* is *Du hast einen weiten/langen Weg vor dir. We've come half-way* or *covered half the distance* is *Wir haben die Hälfte des Weges zurückgelegt.* Exactly how far can be stated: *Bis dorthin ist es ein Weg von 15 Kilometern;* in this context *Weg* would be translated as *distance.*
Es ist ein weiter Weg nach Muckelsberg.   *Ich habe einen langen Weg zum Arbeitsplatz.*

ii. *Ich habe jmdn. ein Stück/eine Strecke Weg* (formerly *Weges*) *begleitet*, 'accompanied [for] part of the way', may occur in formal language. In everyday language the expression is *Ich gehe ein Stück Weg mit*, but *Weg* is almost always omitted. **Das Stück** or **ein Stück** thus means 'a little way, an unspecified short distance'. *Das Stück bis zur Post macht mir nichts aus. Sie stand ein Stück entfernt von der Tür*, a little way off/from. An alternative is *etwas entfernt*. *Ein Stückchen mitgehen* is also used for going with someone for a short distance. *You still have a way/some/quite a way to go* can be *Sie müssen noch ein Stück gehen* or *noch eine ziemliche Strecke fahren*. **Die Strecke** is used for a longer distance. *We've come a good/long way today* is *Wir haben heute eine gute/lange/große Strecke geschafft* or *sind eine gute Strecke gefahren*. A stylistically higher variant is *Wir haben eine große Entfernung zurückgelegt*. For *Strecke* and *Entfernung*, cf. DISTANCE.

iii. Weit can often express the lit. and fig. uses of **a long way**. *Sie sind weit gefahren, bevor sie einen anderen Menschen sahen. Sie sind uns weit voraus* can have the lit. or fig. meaning.

Other fig. uses of *a long way*. *The work is a long way off completion* is *Die Arbeit ist noch weit vom Abschluß entfernt*. *That is still a long way from the truth* can be translated as *Das ist noch weit von der Wahrheit entfernt*. *They are still a long way from trusting him: Sie sind noch weit davon entfernt, ihm zu vertrauen*. *S.o. has gone a long way* can be *Jmd. hat es weit gebracht* or *hat es in der Geschäftswelt zu etw. gebracht*. *Goodwill can go a long way to overcoming these difficulties: Guter Wille kann viel dazu beitragen, diese Schwierigkeiten zu überwinden. Dieser Aufsatz ist weit unter dem Niveau, das wir erwarten. Ich bin weit über dreißig.*

iv. A good way = 'quite a distance' can be **ziemlich weit**. *The tree is a good way off/away: Der Baum ist ziemlich weit weg. Ich war ziemlich weit weg, als der Unfall geschah.*

v. By a long way is **bei weitem** or **weitaus**. *Er ist bei weitem der beste Fußballspieler in der Mannschaft*, he's the best player by a long way, or *Er spielt weitaus besser als die anderen*, plays better than the others by a long way. *Das ist bei weitem mein Lieblingsbild. Dieses Mädchen ist weitaus begabter als die anderen Schüler. Weit verfehlen* means 'to miss a target or fig. sth. by a long way'. *Du hast die Zielscheibe weit verfehlt.* Cf. MISS 1.

6. Way also means 'direction'. *You're going the same/wrong way. I looked the other way.*

i. The main equivalent is **die Richtung**. In *Wie stellt man fest, in welche Richtung das Wasser fließt/aus welcher Richtung der Wind weht?*, *Richtung* could be translated as *way* or *direction*. *A car going our way: Ein Auto, das in dieselbe Richtung fährt wie wir.* For *I don't know which way to turn*, see TURN 8. viii.

    Ich bin in die falsche Richtung gefahren (went the wrong way). Or *Ich schlug die falsche Richtung ein.*

    Als sie anfing zu weinen, habe ich in die andere Richtung gesehen/geguckt (the other way).

    Wenn wir Briefe einwerfen, müssen wir fünf Meilen gehen/fahren—in jeder Richtung (each way).

ii. *We have to* **go this way/that way**. In speech **hier lang** and **da lang** convey this meaning, although the full form is **hier/da entlang**. *Wir müssen da lang. Hier/Da geht es lang*, this is/that's the way. The prefixes **hin-**, **her-**, and **zu-** sometimes express the sense. *Which way did she go?* is *Wohin ist sie gegangen? Everyone look this way!: Alle mal hersehen!* or *Seht mal alle her! Everyone face this way!: Wendet euch mir zu!* or *Wendet euch alle zu mir!* Cf. TURN 8. vi.

iii. Richtig/falsch herum is 'the right/wrong way up or [a]round'. *Liegt das richtig herum? Das Buch hast du falsch herum.* **Anders herum** is 'the other way round'. *Du muß das Bild anders herum halten.* **The other way round** meaning 'conversely or vice versa' is **umgekehrt**. *Du hast ihn eingeladen, nicht umgekehrt. Ich habe es umgekehrt gemeint.*

iv. One way or the other. *You must make up your mind one way or the other* can be *Du mußt dich für das eine oder das andere entscheiden.* Also . . . *dich für den einen oder den anderen Weg entscheiden*, where *Weg* is used fig. *They seem to have no opinion about it, one way or the other*: *Sie scheinen weder dafür noch dagegen zu sein. It doesn't matter to me one way or the other*: *Du kannst machen, was du willst/Du kannst dich entscheiden, wie du willst—es ist mir eigentlich gleich.*

Either way. *I should be glad to be convinced either way/one way or the other* can be *Ich würde mich freuen, wenn jmd. mich überzeugen könnte, daß der eine oder der andere Standpunkt richtig ist. I can't lose either way* (= 'whatever the outcome'): *Ich werde nichts verlieren, was auch immer passiert/wie die Sache auch immer ausgeht. Auf ein paar Mark [mehr oder weniger] kommt es mir nicht an*, a few marks don't matter either way. **So oder so** means 'one way or the other, either way'. *Das kannst du so oder so betrachten. Du kannst dich so oder so entscheiden. Was wir auch tun, es ist so oder so ein Risiko dabei.*

The other way. *The vote could easily have gone the other way*: *Die Abstimmung hätte leicht anders ausfallen können.*

7. Way also means 'manner of behaving or living'. *It's not his way to be unfriendly. Each country has its own ways.*

i. In the sing. **way** means 'a habitual or characteristic manner of acting or behaving'. *Don't take offence—it's his way.* The closest n. is **die Art**, which means 'NATURE' or 'manner'. *Nun [ein]mal* or *eben* is often added, suggesting that the characteristic referred to cannot be changed. Cf. JUST 4. *Nimm es ihm nicht übel!—es ist nun einmal seine Art.* An alternative is *So ist er nun [ein]mal. John, as is his way, tipped the waiter generously* could be *John, nach seiner Art/wie es seine Art ist, gab dem Keller ein reichliches Trinkgeld. It's/That's her way* or *always the way with her* can be *Das ist nun einmal ihre Art* or *Sie ist nun einmal so.* For *That's the way of the world* there is *Das ist der Lauf der Welt* or *So ist es nun einmal auf der Welt.*

> *Es ist sonst nicht seine Art, so unfreundlich zu sein. Solche Unfreundlichkeit ist sonst nicht seine Art.*
> *Es ist ihre Art, immer zu spät zu kommen. Man muß sich eben damit abfinden.*

ii. The pl. **ways** means 'habits of life' and can refer to moral conduct. *It is difficult to change one's ways* could be *Es ist schwierig, sein Verhalten/Benehmen zu ändern.* Both ns. = 'behaviour'. Cf. BEHAVE. A transl. of *s.o.'s awkward ways* is *jmds. schwerfälliges Verhalten/Benehmen.* **Der Lebenswandel** refers to a person's moral conduct. *S.o. considered his ways* could be *Jmd. dachte über seinen Lebenswandel nach*, although *Verhalten* is equally applicable. (*Lebenswandel* is found in expressions like *Jmd. hat/führt einen ruhigen/stetigen/liederlichen Lebenswandel.*) *S.o. saw/realized the error of his ways* could be, if the error is not particularly grave, *Jmd. sah ein, was er falsch gemacht hatte* or, if more serious, *Er sah ein, wie ungerecht er gehandelt hatte.*

iii. The **ways** of a country are **die Sitten**, customs. Cf. HABIT 2. *Jedes Land hat seine eigenen Sitten.*

8. Way also means 'a course of action', 'a method or means by which some end may be attained', 'a procedure or technique for doing sth.' *Where there's a will there's a way. A simple way of learning French. A way of arriving at the truth. A way to make a living/of making a living. A way he could win the game* (or *of winning the game*) *suddenly occurred to him.* In this sense **way** is a syn. of *means*, 'a method or process by which a result may be obtained'. *There is no way/means of learning what is happening.* The sense discussed in 9, **way** = 'manner', is not far removed from this sense. In particular *this/that way*, as in *He thought he could win the game that way*, would be *auf diese Weise. Er glaubte, er könnte das Spiel auf diese Weise gewinnen. Möglichkeit* expresses senses 8 and 9. Cf. 8. iv and 9. i. The suggestions how to avoid translating **way** discussed in 9. iv–vii also apply to this sense.

i. Der Weg can refer to the method by which someone proceeds, but it retains something of the image of a path or track. It is common as the obj. of *finden*, *suchen, sehen*, and *kennen* and as the subj. of *führen*, but it is not used with *haben* or *verstehen*.

> Ich suche einen anderen/besseren Weg, ihnen zu helfen.   *Dieser Weg steht uns noch offen.*
>
> Es gibt einen einfacheren Weg, die Reparatur zu machen.   *Wo ein Wille ist, ist auch ein Weg.*
>
> Ich sehe keinen Weg, unsere Produktionskosten zu senken. Or . . . *wie wir unsere Produktionskosten*
>   *senken können.*   Ich kenne keinen anderen Weg. *diese Aufgabe zu lösen.*
>
> Die Lehrerin suchte einen einfacheren Weg, die Grammatikregel zu erklären.
>
> Das ist der einzige Weg, der zur Einigkeit führt/um dieses Ziel zu erreichen.

Weg is also used with some adjs., as in the phr. *auf friedlichem Wege*. This can be translated as *in a peaceful way*, but such expressions are often translated as an adv. *peacefully*. Other examples are *auf direktem Wege, auf diplomatischem Wege, auf gesetzlichem/legalem Wege. Sie haben sich auf gütlichem Wege geeinigt*, they have reached an amicable agreement. *Du sollst auf dem schnellsten Wege nach Hause gehen*, as quickly as possible.

ii. Mittel und Wege means 'ways and means' or 'a procedure which is likely to lead to success', and can translate **way** or **ways**. *Er sann auf Mittel und Wege, wie er schnell reich werden könnte.*

> Wir müssen Mittel und Wege finden, wie wir aus dieser mißlichen finanziellen Lage wieder herauskommen.

iii. When **way** means 'method', **die Methode** is often the appropriate equivalent.
Sie entwickelten eine neue Methode, Kohle abzubauen/Französisch zu unterrichten.

> Man hat eine Methode entwickelt, aus Zuckerrohr Treibstoff zu machen.
>
> Eine Methode, durch die man Fremdsprachen mühelos lernen kann, gibt es nicht.

iv. Die Möglichkeit means 'a possible procedure', 'a feasible way or means'.

> Ihm fiel plötzlich eine Möglichkeit ein, wie er das Spiel gewinnen könnte.
>
> Es gibt andere Möglichkeiten, Senioren/alten Menschen zu helfen.
>
> Es gibt eine/keine Möglichkeit, die Schwierigkeiten zu überwinden.
>
> Es bleiben keine anderen Möglichkeiten offen, den Plan durchzuführen.

v. Other expressions related in sense. *Du hast die Sache falsch angepackt*, gone the wrong way about it. *The best way is to say nothing* is best translated as *Das Beste ist, gar nichts zu sagen.*

9. Way also means 'the manner in which sth. is done or takes place'. It forms a phr. with *in, in this way*, and is used with an infin. *Is this the [right] way to express the idea?*, with *of* + a n., *The way of life of these societies is very different from our own*, with *of* + gerund, *Her way of doing her hair*, and with a relative clause. When a clause follows, the relative pronouns *in which* and *that* are usually omitted. *I don't like the way [in which/that] they expressed it.* The equivalents are *die Weise*, which is restricted in use, *die Art*, and *die Art and Weise*. *Die Möglichkeit* also expresses this sense. Often the meaning of *way* can be expressed without using one of these equivalents. iv–vii give examples. Cf. 8.

i. Die Art is used with an infin. which translates the E. infin. and gerund. *Ihre Art, mit den Kindern umzugehen, ist sehr eindrucksvoll. Sie hat eine angenehme Art, sich auszudrücken.* It is also followed by a *wie*-clause which corresponds to *that* and *in which. Die Art, wie sie mit den Kindern umgeht, ist sehr eindrucksvoll.* A relative clause, as in *Die Art [und Weise], auf die/in der etw. geschieht*, can be used instead of a *wie*-clause. *Wie* or *auf die/in der* + a relative clause must be added in translating a clause without a relative pronoun. *Die Art, wie/in der er schreibt*, the way he writes.
Die Art und Weise is more common, at least in speech, in the same constructions. The difference in sense is very slight, *Art* being like *manner*, while *Art und Weise* may suggest more aspects of the way something is done. *Seine Art/Art und*

Weise, sich auszudrücken, gefällt mir sehr. Die Art/Art und Weise, wie sie sich ausdrückt, gefällt mir nicht. A lobte die Art und Weise, auf die/in der B spielte. Sie hat eine angenehme Art, sich auszudrücken. Art und Weise lacks a pl. The pl. of *Art* is possible, but not common. *Dieses Kapitel beschreibt zwei Arten, die Untersuchung durchzuführen.* Both are sometimes found with a gen. *Die Art/Art und Weise seines Klavierspiels.* (Note that *Art* can also mean 'NATURE'.) Both can take an adj. *Die beste/einfachste/billigste Art, den Schaden zu beseitigen. Das ist die richtige/rechte Art und Weise, die Sache anzupacken. Die phantasievolle Art/Art und Weise, wie sie die Sonate spielte, hat uns alle sehr beeindruckt.* **Die Möglichkeit**, which suggests a possible way of doing something, is used with and without an infin. and with a *wie*-clause. It is often found with *eine, keine, einzige,* and in the pl. *Es gibt eine Möglichkeit, schneller voranzukommen. Das ist die einzige Möglichkeit, den Umsatz zu erhöhen. Es gibt eine andere Möglichkeit, wie wir das Geld zusammenbringen können.* **Die Weise** is now found alone only with preps. (cf. ii) but occurs in a number of compounds like *Denkweise, Lebensweise, Bauweise, Arbeitsweise, Ausdrucksweise, Produktionsweise,* etc. *Ihre Arbeitsweise* expressed as an infin. is *ihre Art [und Weise] zu arbeiten,* and as a clause, *die Art [und Weise], wie sie arbeitet,* or *die Art [und Weise], auf die/in der sie die Aufgabe anfaßte.*

> *Es gibt mehrere Arten, Fisch zuzubereiten.* Or *Möglichkeiten.* (Having no pl., *Art und Weise* cannot be used, but the sent. could be formulated as *Man kann Fisch auf verschiedene Art und Weise zubereiten.*)
>
> *Seine Art zu sprechen läßt darauf schließen, daß er diese Arbeit für unter seiner Würde hält.*
>
> *Sie hat eine ungenierte Art, sich zu allen möglichen Fragen zu äußern.*
>
> *Ihre Art, mit den Kindern umzugehen, ist sehr eindrucksvoll.*
>
> *Er billigte die Art/Art und Weise nicht, wie die Verhandlungen geführt wurden.*
>
> *Die Art/Art und Weise, wie er die Symphonie dirigierte, haut einen vom Hocker.*
>
> *Die Art/Art und Weise, wie die Armee organisiert wird, trägt den neuesten Methoden der Kriegsführung Rechnung.*
>
> *Die Art/Art und Weise, wie er antwortete, ließ Zweifel an seiner Aufrichtigkeit aufkommen.*
>
> *Die Art und Weise, in der die einzelnen Abgeordneten ihr Mandat wahrnehmen, ist sehr verschieden.*
>
> *Zunächst einmal möchte ich ein paar Worte zu der Art und Weise sagen, wie wir vorgegangen sind.*
>
> *Es gibt zwei Möglichkeiten, ein Stipendium zu bekommen/ . . . viele Möglichkeiten, Energie zu sparen.*
>
> *Die Lebensweise dieser Gesellschaften und die unsere sind grundverschieden.*

ii. [In] this way, in the same way, etc. *Die Weise* is used with *auf* and *in,* **auf diese Weise, in dieser Weise. Auf diese Art und Weise** has the same sense. The preps. cannot be omitted in G. In many cases all three are possible. *Handeln Sie in der Weise/auf die Weise/auf die Art und Weise, die Sie für richtig halten! Auf diese Weise* is the most common, then *auf diese Art und Weise. Auf diese Weise* serves as an introduction to a following description or details. *Es spielte sich auf diese Weise ab,* begins an account of what happened. (Cf. archaic E.: *Now the birth of Jesus Christ was on this wise.*) *Auf,* not *in,* is used with possessives. *Das erledige ich auf meine Weise. In* is often followed by an adj., *Sie handelte in der ihr eigenen Weise* and *Sie unterstützten uns in großzügiger Weise,* but *auf* also occurs, *Jeder sucht sein Glück auf [seine] eigene Weise. Das Bild verschwand auf geheimnisvolle Weise. Das machen wir auf die gleiche Weise. Auf ähnliche Weise* and *in ähnlicher Weise* are both found. *In* is also used with *Art und Weise. Er handelte in einer Art und Weise, die ich nicht billigen kann. Auf* only is used with the pl. of *Weise. Ich habe es auf alle möglichen Weisen versucht. Auf alle/jede mögliche Art und Weise* and *auf verschiedene Weise* (= 'various') and *in zweierlei Weise* are pl. in sense, although sing. in form. Another less common possibility is **Art** with *auf* or *in* + adj. *Er lachte auf eine seltsame, wilde Art. Das hast du auf die richtige Art angefangen. Er hat es in der gewohnten Art getan.*

> *Er verschwindet immer auf seltsame Weise/Art und Weise, wenn er arbeiten soll.*

Sie benahm sich in so seltsamer Weise, daß wir uns alle fragten, was los war. Or *auf so seltsame Weise.*

In dieser Weise können wir nicht weitermachen. Or *Auf diese Art und Weise . . .*

Machen Sie es auf die Weise/in der Weise/auf die Art und Weise, die Ihnen paßt!

Auf diese Weise/Art und Weise kann ich Arbeit und Vergnügen verbinden.

Man hat ihm auf die übelste Weise/in der übelsten Weise/auf die übelste Art und Weise/auf die übelste Art mitgespielt.   *Die Tür des Tresors wird auf diese Weise geöffnet.*

Sie brachte die Argumente in logischer Weise vor.   *Sie redete in unzusammenhängender Weise.*

Auf diese Art/Art und Weise/Weise werden wir alles verlieren.

Wir müssen die Arbeit auf die eine oder die andere Art und Weise abschließen.

Die Ermordung des Staatsmannes beeinflußte das politische Geschehen in einer Art und Weise, mit der niemand gerechnet hatte.   *Er wurde in mehr als einer Weise gekränkt.*

Man kann den Versuch in zweierlei Weise durchführen.

iii. Some E. expressions. *She is convinced that* **her way is the only way** can be *Sie ist davon überzeugt, daß ihr Weg der einzig richtige ist,* or *. . ., daß die Art und Weise, wie sie die Arbeit macht, die einzig richtige ist. He's a nice fellow* **in his [own] way**: *Auf seine Art und Weise ist er ein netter Kerl.*

iv. Wie translates *in what way* and can express the meaning of 'way or manner' in other contexts.

Wie kann ich Ihnen helfen? (how/in what way)

Ich weiß nicht, wie ich stimmen soll (which way to vote).

Wie er lächelt, gefällt mir nicht. Es gefällt mir nicht, wie er lächelt (the way he smiles).

Es ist sehr beunruhigend, wie die Preise dauernd steigen (the way prices keep on rising).

Ich möchte ein paar Vorschläge machen, wie man Studenten helfen kann (about the way you can help).   *Erinnerst du dich daran, wie er lacht?* (the way he laughs)

Wie can also translate *what's the* + adj. + **way** *of doing/to do sth.? Wie löst man diese Aufgabe am leichtesten? Wie übersetzt man diesen Satz am besten?*

v. G. **so** means 'in this way' and translates **way** in *This/that is the way* and elsewhere. It can be used when someone demonstrates how to do something. *So wird es gemacht* or *So macht man es,* that's the way it's done/you do it/to do it. *So* also introduces and concludes a description. *Das hat sich so abgespielt* introduces a description. *So hat sich das abgespielt* is used as a conclusion: That's how/the way it happened. It also translates *That's the* + adj. + *way. That's the best/easiest way to solve this problem* can be *So löst man diese Aufgabe am besten/einfachsten. That's the most comfortable way to travel* can be *Das ist die bequemste Art zu reisen* or *So reist man am bequemsten. Do you still feel the same way about it?* could be *Denkst du noch so darüber wie früher?* or *Bist du noch derselben Meinung wie früher? Things won't ever be the way they used to be: Die Dinge/Die Verhältnisse werden nie wieder so sein, wie sie [es] früher waren. Es ist kindisch, so zu reden,* a childish way of talking. *You're doing it the wrong way* or *The way you're doing it is wrong* is in speech *So, wie du das hier machst, ist es verkehrt* or *Es ist falsch, die Sache so zu machen, wie du es tust* or *So, wie du es da machst, ist es falsch.*

vi. When **way** + infin. or gerund is used with an adj., it can often be omitted. In *a* + adj. + *way of doing/to do sth.* the adj. can be turned into an adv. and **way** omitted. The question *Is there another/a simpler way of doing it?* could become *Kann man das anders/einfacher machen?* (Alternatives here and in a statement are *Gibt es einen anderen Weg/eine andere Möglichkeit, das zu machen?*) *She has a different way of dressing: Sie kleidet sich anders.* In a statement like *That's a complicated way of repairing the motor, Art und Weise* would be usual because an infin. follows: *Das ist eine sehr umständliche Art und Weise, den Motor zu reparieren.* With an infin. *Weg* is also used. *Du hast aber einen umständlichen Weg gewählt, den Motor zu reparieren!* When nothing follows, it is sufficient to say, '*Du machst es aber sehr umständlich!*'

vii. Sometimes **way** is used to form an adv. in E. when the adj. does not take *-ly.*

Condescending and *superior* do not form advs., but the corresponding G. words can be used as advs. *He smiled in a condescending/superior way* becomes simply *Er lächelte herablassend/überlegen*.

10. E. idiomatic phrs.

i. Clear the way in a fig. sense is **den Weg** *für Reformen* etc. **bereiten**. (*Den Weg räumen* has the lit. sense, 'to clear or free a path etc. from obstructions'.) **Pave the way** used fig. is **jmdm./einer Sache den Weg ebnen**. *The business pays its way: Das Geschäft* **ist rentabel** or **rentiert sich**, is profitable. *Die neue Anlage wird sich schon innerhalb eines Jahres rentieren.*

ii. See one's way clear to doing sth. can be **sich entschließen zu**. Cf. DECIDE 1. i. *Wir können uns nicht dazu entschließen, im Augenblick so viel Geld auszugeben.* An alternative is *Ich halte es [nicht] für ratsam, so viel Geld auszugeben.*

iii. Have/get one's [own] way is **seinen Willen durchsetzen**. *Er ist ein Mensch, der immer seinen Willen durchsetzen will.* With *if I had my way* it is less a question of insisting on one's own will than on arranging things according to one's insights. *If I had my way, lots of thgs. would be done differently* could be **Wenn es nach mir ginge**, *würde man vieles anders machen.*

iv. Get into the way of doing sth. is **sich daran gewöhnen**. Cf. ACCUSTOM. *Wenn man sich daran gewöhnt hat, in Luxus zu leben, kann man es sich nur schwer wieder abgewöhnen. Die Arbeit wird dir nicht schwer fallen, wenn du dich einmal daran gewöhnt hast.* An alternative in this context is *wenn du dich eingearbeitet hast.*

v. By the way as a syn. of *incidentally* is mostly **übrigens**. *Übrigens* can be at the beginning or in the sent. *Übrigens, kannst du mir einen Gefallen tun? Kannst du mir übrigens einen Gefallen tun?* A stylistically higher alternative is **nebenbei bemerkt/gesagt**. *Nebenbei bemerkt, das Geld, das ich ihm geliehen habe, hat er noch nicht zurückgezahlt.* Or . . . *hat er, nebenbei bemerkt, noch nicht zurückgezahlt.*

Übrigens, wo wir gerade über Briefe reden, hast du einen Brief vom Deutschen Seminar bekommen? Dieser Besuch vom Generaldirektor ist übrigens streng geheim.

By the way, used when someone is suddenly reminded of something, is **ach ja**. *Ach ja, wo wir gerade über Briefe reden, da fällt mir ein, daß ich vorgestern einen sehr seltsamen bekommen habe.*

vi. By way of meaning 'via' is **über**. *Wir sind über Rom nach Cairo geflogen.*

vii. By way of meaning 'with the function of' is often **als**, but the idea can be expressed by **zu** and a verbal n. or by **um** . . . **zu**. *By way of introduction I'd like to explain how . . .* is *Als Einleitung möchte ich erklären, wie . . . Als/Zur Entschuldigung streckte er die Hand aus, by way of apology. Als Zahlung gab sie mir einen Sack Kartoffeln. Ich stelle diese Fragen, um mich über den wahren Sachverhalt zu informieren, by way of finding out the real circumstances/facts.*

viii. Sth. is **on my way**. *Das Geschäft liegt an/auf meinem Weg* or *Ich gehe in die Stadt und komme an dem Geschäft vorbei.*

ix. Sth. happened **on the way to** N is *Etw. ist auf dem Weg nach N passiert. Etw. Merkwürdiges ist mir passiert, [als ich] auf dem Weg nach Hause [war]. Wir hatten eine Panne auf dem Weg nach T.*

x. Under way can be **unterwegs**. *Das Schiff ist schon unterwegs. Unterwegs* or **auf dem Weg** translate *on my/their*, etc. *way. They are already [well] on their way* is *Sie sind schon [lange] unterwegs/auf dem Weg. Das Paket ist schon unterwegs/auf dem Weg.* Fig. use: *Jmd. ist schon auf dem Weg der Besserung. The negotiations/preparations are already under way* could be *Die Verhandlungen/Die Vorbereitungen sind schon im Gange. Better weather is on the way: Besseres Wetter nähert sich.* Cf. APPROACH 1.

xi. An **out of the way** place is **abgelegen** or **entlegen**. *Sie wohnen in einem abgelegenen Dorf.* In reply to 'Would you like a lift?', someone might say, 'Yes, if it's not out of your way.' *'Kann ich Sie mitnehmen?' 'Ja, wenn Sie keinen Umweg machen müssen/wenn es auf Ihrem Weg liegt.'* For the usual equivalent of *Keep poisons where they are out of the way of children!* cf. REACH 1. Another transl. is *Man muß Giftstoffe dort aufbewahren, wo Kinder nicht dran kommen. I'm happy now that the matter is out of the way* could be *Ich bin froh, daß diese Sache nun [endgültig] erledigt ist.* Cf. SETTLE 5. *When this meeting is out of the way: Wenn diese Sitzung vorbei ist.* **Go out of one's way** to do sth. **Ein übriges tun** is 'to do more than would normally be expected'. *Sie tat ein übriges, um uns zu helfen.* Also *Sie bemühte sich, möglichst viel für uns zu tun.*

xii. In one way, in every way, in some/many/all ways. In these phrs. **way** means 'respect' and is **die Hinsicht**. As *Hinsicht* is only used in the sing., *in jeder Hinsicht* has to be used for *in all ways*, *in mancher Hinsicht* for *in some ways*, and *in vieler Hinsicht* for *in many ways*. *Als Abgeordneter ist er in jeder Hinsicht geeigneter als ich. Der Plan ist in mancher Hinsicht mangelhaft. In vieler Hinsicht waren die alten Methoden besser als die neuen.*

xiii. In no way is **keineswegs** or **in keiner Weise, auf keine Weise**, or more emphatically **in keinerlei Weise**. *Sie ist keineswegs/in keiner Weise/in keinerlei Weise für den Mißerfolg verantwortlich. Dazu war er in keiner Weise/in keinerlei Weise/auf keine Weise bereit.*

xiv. For **in a big/small way**, there are several possibilities. *To start a business* etc. *in a big* or *small way* could be **groß** or **bescheiden/klein/unten** *anfangen. Du kannst nicht erwarten, groß anzufangen.* An alternative is *Man exportiert/produziert bestimmte Waren* **in großem/kleinem Ausmaß**. Cf. EXTENT 5. *Sie stiegen ins Waffengeschäft groß/in großem Ausmaß ein.*

xv. A **way** *of looking at* or *of seeing sth.* refers to a point of view or attitude that leads to a particular interpretation of things. *There are two ways of looking at this: Das kann man* **auf zweierlei Weise** *sehen* or *Das kann man* **von verschiedenen Standpunkten aus** *betrachten. Try to see it my way!* could be *Versuche, die Sache von meinem Standpunkt aus zu sehen! Als Konservativer sieht man die Sachen von einem Standpunkt an, als Sozialist von einem anderen.*

xvi. Both ways. *Do you want a party or a holiday?—you can't have it both ways: Willst du eine Fete haben oder in Urlaub fahren?—beides kannst du nicht haben.*

xvii. No two ways. *He's not on board. There are no two ways about it: Er ist nicht an Bord.* **Daran gibt es gar keinen Zweifel.**

xviii. There's no way or **isn't any way** *that we can leave tomorrow* means that it is impossible and can be translated by **es ist völlig unmöglich** or **es ist ausgeschlossen**, or the idea can be expressed by **unter [gar] keinen Umständen.** *Es ist völlig unmöglich, morgen abzufahren. Es ist ausgeschlossen, daß wir morgen abfahren. Ich werde ihm unter gar keinen Umständen einen weiteren Gefallen tun.*

Es ist völlig unmöglich, so weiter zu machen wie bisher.

Es ist ausgeschlossen, daß das Ministerium mehr als 50 000 Mark für dieses Projekt bewilligt.

Diesem Plan werde ich unter gar keinen Umständen zustimmen.

weaken *v.*

1. Trans. uses.

i. If something weakens a person, it brings about the loss of some or most of his or her physical strength. If someone or something weakens a political group, a social institution, someone's position, a military force, currency, etc., the group etc. becomes less powerful, effective, or strong. **Weaken** in these contexts is **schwächen**, which is always trans. and means 'to make weak or weaker'. A partial and more formal syn. is **entkräften**, to deprive of strength.

Die Krankheit/Der Hunger/Das Fieber hat ihn sehr geschwächt/entkräftet.

Durch den Ausfall gerade des besten Stürmers sah sich die Mannschaft hoffnungslos geschwächt.
Mit einem im Ansehen stark geminderten Kanzler muß die Partei nun geschwächt in den Wahlkampf ziehen.
Die wiederholten Handelsdefizite haben die Währung des Landes erheblich geschwächt.
Die Anstrengungen der langen Reise haben das ältere Ehepaar entkräftet.

ii. Abschwächen is 'to make a thg. weaker than it was before without depriving it completely of strength'. It is now mostly confined to what people say and to the way something is expressed, i.e to ns. like *eine Äußerung, Behauptung,* or *Aussage,* and means 'to tone down or reduce in intensity'. *Später schwächte er seine Äußerung/Aussagen ab.* Other common objs. are *die Wirkung* and *der Eindruck.* A syn. is **abmildern.** *Bald bedauerte er diese scharfe Äußerung und wollte sie abmildern.*

Die Polemik vom Vortag wagte der Botschafter vor den Parlamentariern nur in abgeschwächter Form zu wiederholen (repeat it in a weakened/toned down form).
Die Wirkung einer Säure wird durch Verdünnung abgeschwächt.
Muß er denn immer den guten Eindruck, den alle zunächst von ihm bekommen, durch solche frechen Bemerkungen abschwächen?   *Die langatmigen Dialoge schwächen die Wirkung des Films ab.*
Er versuchte, den von seinem Verhalten hervorgerufenen schlechten Eindruck abzumildern.

iii. If I weaken someone's arguments etc., I make them less effective by showing that they are incorrect or illogical. **Entkräften** is used with ns. like *Argumente, ein Beweis,* or *ein Verdacht* and ranges in meaning from weakening to completely invalidating. It usually means 'to deprive sth. of some of its force', but it can be close to *widerlegen,* to refute.

Es gelang ihm, die gegen ihn erhobenen Beschuldigungen/die Behauptungen seines Gegners/diese bösartigen Gerüchte zu entkräften.
Der Verteidiger bemühte sich, die von dem Staatsanwalt erbrachten Beweise zu entkräften.

2. Intr. uses.

i. *A pers.* **weakened** [*in his/her resolve*] or *A pers.'s resolve* **weakened. Nachlassen,** to decline in intensity, is not used with a person as subj., so that both E. sents. are translated as *Jmds. Entschlossenheit ließ nach.* **Nachgeben,** 'to relent or give in' to someone's insistence, requests, demands, etc., takes a person as subj. *Jmd. gab nach* could translate *S.o. weakened in his resolve,* but *resolve* is only implied. *Er hielt den Plan für schwachsinnig und stellte sich ihm zuerst entschieden entgegen, aber dann gab er nach.*

ii. Sich abschwächen is 'to lose strength or effectiveness'. It is often heard in weather forecasts. *Das Tief[druckgebiet] über Spanien schwächt sich ab.* Die Wirkung and *der Eindruck* are sometimes found as subj. as well as a mental state or emotion. *Das Interesse schwächt sich allmählich ab.* (An alternative here is *nachlassen. Das Interesse ließ nach.*) When a thing is subj., **schwächer werden** is often used. *Der Widerstand gegen den neuen Herrscher schwächte sich schnell ab/wurde mit der Zeit schwächer.*

Ein Hochdruckgebiet über den britischen Inseln schwächt sich ab und verlagert sich nach Osten.

weigh *v.*

1. When trans., **weigh** means 'to determine the weight of a pers. or thg.' and when intr., 'to be of a particular weight'. **Wiegen** expresses both senses. *Bei der ärztlichen Untersuchung werden alle Kinder gewogen. Der Koffer wiegt 22 Kilo.*

Der Postbeamte wog das Paket. Es wog etwas weniger als zehn Kilo.

In fig. use, mainly with the advs. *schwer* and *wenig, wiegen* means 'to be of importance'. *Dieses Argument wiegt bei mir schwer/wenig.* Hence *schwerwiegende Gründe/Einwände.*

2. Abwiegen in one sense means 'to weigh out', i.e 'to take from a larger amount of sth. as much as is required to give a particular quantity'. *Man wiegt 20 Gramm. ab. Sie wog die Zutaten für den Kuchen ab.* It is, however, often used like *wiegen* meaning 'to determine the weight of', but only for fairly small quantities and mainly for food in shops. *'Wiegen Sie diese Äpfel bitte mal ab!'* could be a request to a shop assistant. (*Wiegen* is also possible.) **Auswiegen** has both senses of *abwiegen*. It too is used only for small amounts in shops.

> *Wiegen Sie mir bitte mal zwei Kilo Äpfel ab/aus!*
> *Die Kirschen wurden kiloweise abgewogen/ausgewogen.*

Ausgewogen means 'balanced'. *Eine ausgewogene Darstellung einer verzwickten politischen Frage.*

3. Wägen is now only used fig. meaning 'to consider carefully the value or importance of sth.' and is confined to elevated prose. *Wir werden diese Worte/jmds. Handlungen wägen.*

4. Abwägen is 'to weigh up one thg. against another'. *Man wägt das Für und das Wider ab* or *wägt das Pro und Kontra einer Sache ab* or *wägt verschiedene Faktoren gegeneinander ab.* It is also used with an obj. denoting a single thing. *Jmd. wägt sein Urteil/seine Worte genau/sorgfältig/kühl ab.* More common would be *Sie überlegte sich ihre Worte genau.* Cf. CONSIDER 1.

> *Erst wägen, dann wagen.* (*Sprichwort.* In everyday language, *Erst überlegen, dann handeln.*)
> *Um zu entscheiden, ob ein Ausbau des Flughafens wünschenswert ist, muß man die wirtschaftlichen Vorteile gegen die ökologischen Nachteile abwägen.*

5. Used fig., as in *The responsibility/guilt weighed heavily on a pers.*, **weigh on** means 'to be a burden on'. The equivalent is **lasten auf**. *Die Verantwortung/Die Sorge/Die viele Arbeit lastet schwer auf ihr. Die Schuld lastete schwer auf seinem Gewissen.*

well *adv.* and *adj.* Order of treatment: 1. Adv. of *good* and special meanings of **well**. 2. *Wohl* = 'well' and [*sehr*] *wohl* in an answer disputing a statement. 3. *To know very/perfectly/only too well.* 4. *Well enough.* 5. **Well** expressing probability. 6. **Well** = 'sound in health'. 7. *All is well with. Thgs. are well somewhere.* 8. **Well** + adjs. *Well able/aware/worth.* 9. *Well before/after/away from/over.* 10. *It's as well you said that. Just as well.* 11. *I couldn't well refuse him. You may well laugh.* 12. *That is all well and good/all very well.* 13. *To do well.* 14. *As well he might.* 15. *As well [as]. I might as well do sth.* 16. *Well and good. Well rid of. Well out of sth. Speak well of. You may well ask.* 17. Idiomatic uses of **well**.

1. i. As an adv. corresponding to *good*, **well** is now mostly **gut**. *To do sth. well* means in general 'to do it to a high standard', but in certain contexts, **well** means 'satisfactorily, expertly, skilfully, thoroughly, or completely'. *Gut* also expresses these senses.

> *Jmd. spricht gut französisch/schwimmt gut/tanzt gut/kocht gut/singt gut.*
> *Diese Pflanzen wachsen hier gut.*   *Sie haben gut gearbeitet.*
> *Die Mannschaft hat gut gespielt.*   *Man muß die Kleider gut trocknen.*
> *Die Schuhe haben gut gehalten.*   *Ich komme gut mit ihnen aus.*
> *Das Fleisch muß gut durchgekocht werden.*   *Diese Zeit paßt mir gut.*

ii. Other special meanings of **well** are also carried by **gut**.

a. 'Closely, intimately'.
> *Ich kenne ihn zu gut, um zu glauben, daß er sich jemals entschuldigen wird.*

b. 'In a kindly or friendly way'. *Man hat uns gut behandelt. Sie hat den Scherz gut aufgenommen.*

c. 'Carefully, attentively'. *Der Garten ist gut gepflegt. Du hast dich um sie gut gekümmert.*
> *Ich habe mir die Sache gut überlegt.*   *Du hast ihn gut beobachtet.*

d. 'Fittingly'. *Das hast du gut gesagt. Das war gut ausgedrückt/gut formuliert.*

e. 'In a state of plenty or comfort'. *Von dem Einkommen kann die Familie gut leben.*
f. 'Successfully'. *Ich komme mit der Arbeit gut voran.*

2. Wohl also means 'well', but it is now restricted in use.

i. Still common is the use of **wohl** with *sich fühlen*, although *gut* is not unusual. *Jmd. fühlt sich [nicht] wohl. Er fühlt sich in seiner Haut nicht wohl* or *Ihm ist in seiner Haut nicht wohl*, he doesn't feel at ease/comfortable in the position he is in. Fixed expressions are *Wohl bekomm's!*, either 'enjoy your food' or, with a drink, 'your health', and *Lebe wohl!*, 'farewell', and *das kann man wohl sagen*, 'you can certainly say that'.
   Am wohlsten fühlte sie sich zu Hause.   *Er hatte es wohl verdient, bestraft zu werden.*

ii. Well, used with past parts. as the adv. of *good*, is now mostly **gut**, but **wohl** is still sometimes possible. *Well-considered* is *gut/wohl überlegt; well-thought-out* is *gut/wohl durchdacht. Wohl* sounds more formal. *Wohlbehalten*, 'in good condition, not damaged', is still used. With most parts. *gut* is the equivalent of **well**. *Ein gut ausgestattetes Labor. Eine gut erhaltene Kirche aus dem elften Jahrhundert. Well-advised* is *gut beraten. Er wäre gut beraten, sofort hinzufahren.* Some expressions require neither. *Well-educated* is simply *gebildet. Well-satisfied* is *ganz, sehr,* or colloquially *rundum, zufrieden. Well-kept: Ein gepflegter Garten. Belesen* means 'well-read'. *Eine erprobte* or *bewährte Methode*, a well-tried method.

iii. In one circumstance **wohl** or **sehr wohl** still occurs. It is used as a response to a negative statement in the same way as *perfectly well* is in E. A. *You won't remember that.* B. *I remember it perfectly well.* In talking of some event someone might say, *'Ich kann mich noch gut daran erinnern.'* This refers to the vividness of the memory and does not presuppose any remark about the state of the person's recollections. If someone said, *'Du erinnerst dich [bestimmt] nicht mehr an den Vorfall'*, an answer disputing this statement might be, *'Ich erinnere mich sehr wohl daran.' Wohl* is an emphatic assertion of the contrary of what was stated. It is fairly formal. (*Doch* is more usual when someone contradicts the previous statement. *Ich erinnere mich doch daran*, I do remember it. Cf. AFTER 2. Cf. QUITE 3. i.) *Du hast es nicht gesehen.—Ich habe es wohl gesehen. Du hast seine Absicht nicht gemerkt.—Ich habe sie sehr wohl gemerkt. Es lohnt sich nicht.—Es lohnt sich wohl. Wohl* is much used only when an assertion is disputed. Otherwise the adv. is *gut*.

3. *Know +* **well. Wohl** in *Cäsar wußte wohl, was auf dem Spiele stand* is now confined to literary prose. With *wissen*, **genau** is the usual equivalent of *very/perfectly/only too well. Warum hast du dieses Brot gekauft? Du weißt ganz genau, welche Sorte ich immer kaufe*, you know very/perfectly well. **Gut** is used with *kennen. Ich kenne sie [nicht] gut.*
   Ich wußte [ganz] genau, daß er ablehnen würde/daß etw. schief gehen würde (only too well).
   Du weißt ganz genau, worum es geht—mir machst du nichts vor.

4. Well enough. Whoever likes something well enough or knows someone well enough likes or knows them quite or fairly well. *I like it here well enough* becomes when no infin. construction follows *Es gefällt mir hier* **ganz/ziemlich gut.** Cf. QUITE and FAIRLY. When an infin. follows, the E. expression can be translated word for word. *Es hat ihnen dort gut genug gefallen, um eine weitere Woche bleiben zu wollen*, they liked it well enough to want to stay another week. *Ich kenne sie gut genug, um zu beurteilen, ob sie so etw. im Ernst sagen würde.*

5. Well used with *may* indicates a possibility or likelihood. *We may well never find out. That may well be.*

i. While this use in E. is extremely restricted, **wohl** is widely used to indicate probability. Although it is used with all tenses, it is particularly common with the future, which can translate *may. Das werden wir wohl nie erfahren.* It is also used in more formal language with *mögen* and in everyday language with *können*, both of which are equivalents of *may*. *Es mag wohl schon zu spät sein. That may well be* is *Das kann/mag wohl sein* or *Das ist gut möglich*. (Note that *wohl* also means 'I suppose'. *Du hast wohl heute keine Zeit für uns*.)

> *Die Regierung wagte nicht, einen Gesetzentwurf zu verabschieden, dessen Verfassungsgemäßheit wohl angefochten werden mochte* (whose constitutional validity might well be challenged).

ii. When a clause with *aber* follows, **wohl** has a concessive sense like *zwar*. Cf. 12. ii. *Die hier vertretenen Gedanken mögen euch wohl zuerst in Erstaunen versetzen, aber nach reiflicher Überlegung werdet ihr sie keineswegs ungewöhnlich finden.*

6. Well = 'sound in health, free or recovered from illness'. The usual expression is **Es geht jmdm. gut**. As this covers several areas of life, *gesundheitlich* may be added to avoid ambiguity. The attributive use of **well**, as in *He's not a well man*, could be *Es geht ihm gesundheitlich nicht gut*. The only possible adj. is **gesund**. *Gesund* must be used to translate *well*, whether predicative or attributive, where *es geht gut* is syntactically impossible. *Um gesund zu bleiben, muß man sich gut ernähren und sich regelmäßige Bewegung verschaffen. Jmd. sieht gesund aus*, looks 'well, healthy'. (*Sie sieht gut aus*, 'she looks good', i.e. 'is of pleasing appearance'.) To state that someone is well again, *wieder* is added both to *es geht* and *gesund sein*. *Ich mußte ein paar Tage im Bett bleiben, aber es geht mir wieder gut/ich bin wieder gesund*. **Be doing well** when it refers to health is *es geht gut. Dem Verletzten geht es den Umständen entsprechend gut*. **Wohlauf sein/bleiben** means 'to be or remain well'. It is used for newly born babies and their mothers, *Mutter und Kind sind wohlauf*, but apart from this is not very common. *Er ist wieder wohlauf* sounds old-fashioned, although *Bleib' wohlauf!* is occasionally heard. **Wohl** occurs in *Ist dir nicht wohl?* a question which might be asked if someone shows signs of being or feeling unwell, but **gut** is just as common in everyday speech.

> *Er wurde am Bein verwundet, aber es geht ihm wieder gut.*
> *Sie hatte eine leichte Lungenentzündung, ist aber wieder gesund.*

7. Referring to the state of things, **well** means 'in such a condition as to meet with approval'. It is used in the expression *All is [not] well with a pers. or thg.* or *Thgs. are not well somewhere*.

i. A general equivalent is **es ist in Ordnung** to which a phr. with *mit* or one denoting a place can be added. *Sie erkannte sofort, daß mit ihm nicht alles in Ordnung war. Alles ist nicht in Ordnung im Büro.*

ii. Related idioms. *Es wird schon werden* and *Alles wird gut werden*, everything will be/turn out all right, all will be well. *Es wird gut sein* suggests that something like a mistake will have no bad or irreparable consequences.

8. Well is used with a few adjs. and varies in sense from 'completely' to 'considerably'.

i. *He is* **well able** *to help: Er ist* **gut imstande** or **wohl in der Lage**, *euch zu helfen. Well aware: Ich bin mir der Gefahr* **wohl** (or *durchaus*) **bewußt**. In these fixed phrs. *wohl* has its original sense, not that of 4.

ii. The meaning of **well worth** + gerund has to be expressed. *Das Schloß ist durchaus/bestimmt/gewiß einen Besuch wert*, well worth visiting. *Es lohnt sich bestimmt/durchaus hinzugehen*, it's well worth going. *The film is well worth seeing* could be *Der Film ist wirklich/durchaus sehenswert* or *Es lohnt sich wirklich, sich den Film anzusehen*. The idiom *Er läßt sich sehen*, it is quite reasonable, is another possibility.

iii. *It's* **well worth it** can be *Es lohnt sich bestimmt/durchaus* or *Es ist bestimmt/durchaus der Mühe wert*. **Well worth** + a numerical value: *Sie glaubte, daß das Haus bestimmt 200 000 Dollar wert war*, was well worth $200,000.

9. Well is used with phrs. to state that something happened a long time before or after a particular point, or is a long way from a place, or is much greater or less than the figure mentioned. *It was well past midnight/well into the second half. They stood well back from the fire. There are well over 100.* For time [schon] **lange** or [schon] **längst** can express the idea. *Es war schon lange Mitternacht vorbei. Die zweite Halbzeit hatte schon längst angefangen.* Or *Es war mitten in der zweiten Halbzeit.* For number and place **weit** is the usual equivalent. *Es waren weit mehr als 100. Sie standen weit weg vom Feuer. Halte dich weit rechts!,* keep well to the right. But *Halte dich so weit rechts wie möglich!,* keep as far to the right as possible.

Ich war [schon] lange vor dir da. Or *. . . geraume Zeit vor dir da* (well before you).
Man muß das Zimmer lange im voraus bestellen.
Weit weniger als hundert Studenten haben sich beworben (well under a hundred).
Sie waren weit außer der Reichweite feindlicher Granaten.

10. i. *It's* **as well** *you said that* means 'it's a good thg.' or 'advisable, desirable, or fortunate'. The sense is expressed by **es ist gut** or **es ist ein Glück**, it is fortunate. *Es ist gut, daß du das gesagt hast. Es ist ein Glück, daß ich so viel Geld bei mir habe. It would be as well for you to follow this advice* is usually *Es wäre gut, wenn du diesem Rat folgen würdest.* Cf. **gut daran tun** under **13. vi.**

Es ist gut/ein Glück, daß du zu der Sitzung gekommen bist.
Es ist gut, daß du nicht mehr da bist.

ii. *It is* **just as well** followed by *that/if* or *Sth. is just as well* is a variant on **as well** in i and is also translated by **gut** or **ein Glück**. *Es ist gut, daß du schon hier bist,* it's [just] as well that . . . *In that case it would be just as well if you stayed here: Wenn das so ist, wäre es gut, wenn ihr hier bleiben würdet.*

Vielleicht war es gut, daß er nicht hingegangen ist (It was just as well).
Er braucht nicht oft Reden zu halten, was an sich ein Glück für ihn ist, da er nur sehr ungern vor vielen Leuten redet (which is just as well).

iii. Just as well can also express or imply a comparison. *The small car serves our purposes just as well [as the big one].* This sense is conveyed by **ebenso gut** or **genau so gut**. *Das kleine Auto dient unseren Zwecken genau so gut [wie das große]. Die Botschafter blieben drei Monate weg, obwohl sie genau so gut nach einem Monat hätten zurückkehren können.*

Wir können ebenso gut/genau so gut gleich aufbrechen, und nicht erst um zwei Uhr.

11. Gut translates **well** meaning approximately 'easily'.
i. *I can't well refuse him* is *Ich kann ihm diese Bitte nicht gut abschlagen.* Hence *Ich kann ihr das doch nicht gut sagen,* can't very well tell her that.
ii. *You may well laugh* or *It's all very well for you to laugh* is *Du hast gut lachen.* Hence *Du hast gut reden.*

12. That's **all well and good, but** and That's **all very well, but** mean that something is right, proper, and satisfactory in itself or under certain circumstances, but are followed by an objection or contrary view either expressed or implied.
i. A similar expression is **Etw. ist ja [ganz] schön und gut, aber** . . . *Das ist ja alles schön und gut, aber es hilft uns nicht weiter.* The function of these expressions is that of a concessive clause. It is conceded that something is true, but this is then modified or qualified.
ii. The same sense can be expressed by **zwar** or **schon**. *Ein Vertrag ist schon/zwar sehr sinnvoll, aber er nutzt nichts, wenn der Vertragspartner pleite macht. Schon/zwar* mean 'admittedly'. They also translate *all very well [in its way]. Mr C. is all very well in his way, but he's not the right man for this job: Herr C. ist auf seine Art und Weise schon/zwar in Ordnung, aber für diese Stelle ist er nicht der richtige Mann.*

13. Do well. For *to be doing* **well** relating to health see 6.
i. For **do well** at school, cf. **sich machen** and syns. under DO 6. vii. *Der Junge macht sich jetzt [in der Schule] gut.*

ii. Abschneiden means 'to gain a certain result in an examination or competition', i.e. 'to do well, badly, etc.' *Sie hat bei der Prüfung gut/schlecht abgeschnitten. Er hat im Wettbewerb ganz ordentlich abgeschnitten.*

iii. Es zu etw. bringen and **es weit bringen** mean 'to do well in business etc.' *Er hat es [in der Geschäftswelt] zu etw. gebracht. Alle glauben, daß sie es weit bringen wird.*

iv. *He sold it* **well/did well out of it** is *Er hat es mit einem guten Gewinn verkauft.*

v. *She is not satisfied with what she has written, but I think it will* **do very well** can be *Sie ist nicht zufrieden mit dem, was sie geschrieben hat, ich dagegen bin der Meinung, daß es schon gut ist/es durchaus den Zweck erfüllt.*

vi. S.o. would **do well to do** sth. A possibility in formal style is **gut daran tun**. *Du tätest gut daran, diesem Rat zu folgen,* you would do well to. In everyday language: **Es wäre gut,** *wenn du diesem Rat folgen würdest.* Cf. 10. i.

vii. Well done! is, when speaking to children, *Das hast du fein gemacht,* otherwise *Das hast du gut gemacht. Bravo!* is an exclamation. *Kind: 'Ich habe eine Eins im Rechnen gekriegt.' Mutter: 'Bravo!' Bravo* is also used to express enthusiasm after a concert or other performance. *Toll, wie du das kannst/machst!* is used in speech by some people.

14. As well he/she/it might (or **may**). *She took pride in her appearance, as well she might* can be *Sie war stolz auf ihr Aussehen, was durchaus berechtigt/verständlich war. Mr B. looked astonished, as well he might* can be *Er war erstaunt, was nicht verwunderlich/zu verwundern war* or . . . , *Grund dazu hatte er schon* or . . . *und zwar mit gutem Grund.*

15. As well [as].

i. *They excused their absence as* **well as** *they could: Sie entschuldigten ihre Abwesenheit* **so gut** *es ging* or **so gut** *[wie] sie [es] konnten.*

ii. *The women* **as well as** *the men: Die Frauen* **sowie** *die Männer.*

iii. As well can be **auch**. *He wanted to go as well* is thus *Er wollte auch mitkommen/mitfahren.* **Auch noch** is similar but is more emotional. *Du bist schon zu spät zum Frühstuck gekommen. Wenn du nicht schnell ißt, wirst du auch noch zu spät in die Schule kommen.*

iv. I might as well do sth. If I say I might as well do something, I mean that I will do it even though I feel no particular inclination to do so. The meaning has to be expressed. *I might as well admit: Ich sollte gleich zugeben, daß ich die Antwort schon kenne.* (**Sollte** suggests that something is advisable.) *I thought I might as well go: Eigentlich hatte ich keine Lust hinzugehen, aber man kann nicht immer nein sagen, wenn die Leute einen einladen.*

> *Eigentlich habe ich keine Lust dazu, aber gemacht muß es werden, und wohl am besten gleich.* (I might as well do it now.)

16. Some E. expressions.

i. One transl. of *If you want to bow and scrape to the rich,* **well and good** is *Wenn du um die Reichen scharwenzeln willst, ist das deine Sache.* Alternatives: *Wenn du hier ganz alleine bleiben willst, warum denn nicht?/dann habe ich nichts dagegen,* as well as *ist das deine Sache.*

ii. Be well rid of s.o./sth. *Es ist ein Glück, daß wir das/ihn los sind.* Cf. 10.

iii. However, I'm **well out of it** can be *Ich freue mich, daß ich nichts mehr damit zu tun habe,* or *Ich bin nun seit einiger Zeit aus der Sache heraus.*

iv. Speak well of s.o. is *Sie hat immer nur Gutes von Dir gesprochen.* **Think well of** s.o. can be *eine hohe Meinung von jmdm. haben.* Cf. OPINION 1. ii.

v. You **may well ask**. *Wie hat man überhaupt das ganze Baumaterial auf den Gipfel der Zugspitze gebracht? Das kann man mit gutem Grund fragen/Das ist eine gute/berechtigte Frage.*

17. Well is much used in spoken E. with a variety of functions. It often indicates that someone is about to say something. The following is a brief guide to G. expressions with a similar purpose.

i. Well introduces a remark which can be someone's opinion or a reply to a question.The most frequent equivalents are *also, nun, na,* and *tja.* Sometimes **well** may not need to be translated. **Also** at the beginning of a sent. is used both with and without a clear reference to what has gone before. It may just attract attention and/or indicate that the speaker intends to say something. *Also, ich wohnte damals noch auf dem Lande. Also, warten wir es ab!* It is used, even in formal circumstances, with little or no connection to the preceding remarks. *Also, meine Damen und Herren, die Tagesordnung wurde gestern verteilt, und Sie wissen ja, daß wir in der heutigen Sitzung sehr viel zu erledigen haben.*

> A. *Du redest, als wäre er schon (des Verbrechens) überführt.* B. *Also, ich bin der Meinung, er war's.*
> C. *Ich bin der Meinung, er ist der Dieb. Was meinst du dazu?* D. *Also, es gibt vieles, was dafür spricht, aber auch einiges, was dagegen spricht, aber es scheint mir, daß . . .*
> *Also, wenn Sie mich fragen—ich würde ihn nicht befördern.*
> *Also, damit habe ich nicht gerechnet.*   *Also, das werde ich mir gut überlegen.*

Nun is used in formal and serious situations particularly when people are speaking slowly and considering carefully what they say and thus may introduce an important remark, conclusion, or summing up. *Nun, die Frage ist leicht zu beantworten. Nun, ich werde mal sehen, was sich machen läßt.*

> *Nun, da läßt sich nichts machen.*   *Nun, darüber läßt sich reden.*
> *'Warum dürfen wir nicht hineingehen?' 'Nun, solange es nicht geläutet hat, dürfen wir nicht hineingehen.'* (Kafka)

Na is frequently used in ordinary rapid speech in several situations. One is to express a mild objection to what someone says or does, *Na, so schlimm wird es doch nicht sein,* or relief or pleasure about a piece of news, *Na, da können wir aufatmen.*

> *Na, da mußt du doch nicht gleich weinen!*   *Na, wir wollen es mal abwarten.*
> *Na, der wird sich freuen.*   *Na, das wird eine Freude für sie sein.*

Tja expresses hesitation, reservations, *Tja, kann schon sein* or *Tja, das wäre möglich,* or thought or consideration. *Tja, was soll man da machen?*

Well introducing an answer may convey a note of doubt. A. *Is that right?* B. *Well, I think so.* This need not be translated. *Ich glaube schon* would be enough, or *Soweit ich weiß, stimmt es.* An alternative is *Nun, ich glaube schon.* Instead of *nun, Also, ich glaube schon* could be used.

ii. Also is used at the beginning of a sent. to indicate that the speaker intends to carry on speaking about a subject which has been under discussion or talked about but which, because of an interruption, he or she has strayed from. It may also indicate that someone is taking up a subject again after a break. *Also, wo waren wir stehengeblieben?* is like *Well, where did we get to?* (Similar in a different situation is *Und nun zurück zum eigentlichen Thema!*)

> *Also, nachdem ich diese Frage, wie ich glaube, erschöpfend beantwortet habe, kann ich wohl mit der Vorlesung fortfahren.*

iii. Also is used like **well** in *Well, that's finished/done,* to sum up with pleasure what has been accomplished. In this use it has something of the meaning of 'THEREFORE'. *Also* is not placed at the beginning of the sent. It is often used with the subjunctive to indicate satisfaction that something has been accomplished. *Das wäre also erledigt. Wir wären also fertig.*

> *Wir sind auf dem Gipfel. Das hätten wir also geschafft.*
> *Drei Seiten (des Hauses) wären also gestrichen. Jetzt bleibt nur noch der Rest.*
> *Die Reparatur hätten wir also hingekriegt; jetzt muß der Wagen nur noch laufen.*

At the beginning of a sent. only **so** is used in this way. It is found in the same situations as *also.*

> *So, jetzt bin ich fertig.*   *So, das wäre nun erledigt.*
> *So, nun können wir gehen.*   *So, das hätten wir geschafft.*

iv. Na expresses relief e.g. that someone has arrived or completed something. *Na, da wären wir endlich.*

Also sums up the result of a discussion which may be an agreement. *Also, wir bleiben dabei*, well, we'll stick to what we originally agreed on. *Also, darüber sind wir uns nun einig.* *Also* and *na* are used in threats or to point to potential bad consequences.

> *Also, ich warne euch, wenn mir das nochmal zu Ohren kommt, dann gnade euch Gott!*
> *Na, wenn das der Chef erfährt!*

v. Also is used like **well** to introduce a question. If I knew that someone had to make a decision, I might ask on meeting the person again, '*Also, wie hast du dich entschieden?*' One person whom another wishes to talk to could ask, '*Also, was gibt's?*' **Nun** is also used. *Nun, wie steht's? Nun?* is used like **Well?** and implies a question, e.g. 'What has happened?' or 'What do you want?' **Na?** is used in familiar speech and is usually friendly. *Na, wie geht's denn? Na, was hast du auf dem Herzen? Na, bist du schon fertig?* In *Na, wird's bald?*, however, it expresses impatience or insistence that the action be completed soon, and is a call to hurry up.

> *Welches Fahrrad willst du haben? Also?*   *Also, hilfst du mir jetzt oder nicht?*
> *Ich habe das Fragen jetzt langsam satt. Also, zum letzten Mal: Kommst du jetzt mit oder nicht?*
> *Na, und wie geht es Achim?* (directed to someone who had just seen him)

vi. Also can be used like **well** in commands or virtual commands, but it is less direct than *doch* discussed in vii. *b* and sums up the situation. *Also, gehen wir, das Taxi wartet schon unten! Also, los!* means that someone should start working or get on his/her way and is translated as [Well,] *Get on with it!, Get cracking! Off you go!*, or *Let's go! Also Na, los! Na* can express a certain impatience. *Na, komm schon!*

> *Also, fahren wir, sonst kommen wir noch zu spät!*   *Na, fangt doch endlich mal an damit!*
> *Also, gehen Sie schon, wenn Sie unbedingt hingehen wollen!*

The command can take the form of a statement. *Also, Jungs, wir fangen mal an, wir haben genug Zeit vertan* or *Also, jetzt müssen wir an die Arbeit.* Also possible is *Also, laßt uns mal anfangen!*

vii. *a.* If **well then** denotes a consequence, it can be translated by **also**. The sense is 'therefore, thus'. A. *Ich möchte Herrn Häfner sprechen.* B. *Er ist nicht da.* A. *Ich werde also warten* [*müssen*], well then, I'll wait, or well, I'll [have to] wait then. *Du mußt also tun, was du für richtig hältst!* or *Tu' also, was du für richtig hältst*, well, you must do what you think right then! or well then, do what . . .

b. **Well** and **well then** are used to make a suggestion. They present the advice as the obvious thing to do and may express a note of criticism because the person addressed has not already done it. *Well, ask him!* or *Well, ask him then!* This is expressed by **doch** alone or by **dann** . . . **doch**. A. *Ich habe Appetit auf Eis.* B. *Dann kauf dir doch eins!* Thus *Frag' ihn doch!* or *Dann frag ihn doch!* This construction also translates *Why don't you ask him then?* If there were a dispute about what was said on a tape, someone might say, 'Well, let's play the tape back [then]!' *Laßt uns doch zurückspulen und uns die Stelle nochmal anhören!* Less direct and suggesting more reflection is *Also, hören wir uns die Stelle nochmal an, dann wissen wir genau, was er sagte.* Cf. vi.

viii. Well often introduces thanks. *Well, thank you very much for your invitation!* Here nothing is used. The E. sent. becomes *Vielen Dank für Ihre Einladung!* If I had already thanked someone once for the hospitality I had received, I could say, '*Also, nochmals besten Dank für die ausgezeichnete Bewirtung!*'

ix. Well is used when the speaker is looking for the precise expression. *It was, well,* *a bit tactless.* This could be **sagen wir mal**. *Es war, sagen wir mal, ein bißchen taktlos. Er war, sagen wir mal, nicht absolut unfreundlich.* **Well** is also used to gain time to think of what to say. *I told her that you are—well—helping me.* This is best not translated. A clear and direct word like *helfen* would not be used with *sagen wir mal*.

x. Well also modifies or corrects what has been said. *We walked along in silence for a while; well, not really in silence, because she was singing to herself: Wir gingen eine zeitlang schweigend nebeneinander her—***eigentlich** *nicht ganz schweigend, da sie vor sich hin sang.* **Genaugenommen**, 'strictly speaking', is an alternative. With regard to time, **doch** could be used or *well* not translated. *It took me ages, well months at least, to realize he'd lied to me: Es hat ewig gedauert, oder zumindest [doch] mehrere Monate, bis mir klar wurde, daß er mich belogen hatte.*

xi. Well expresses doubt about what has been said. *A. He also has a great love for his father. B. Well, do you really think so?* Colloquially **was** is used, and in more polite language **wie bitte**. *Was, glaubst du das wirklich?* More politely: *Wie bitte? Das meinst du doch nicht ernst.*

xii. Well really! *That's the limit! Das ist* **doch wirklich** *die Höhe! Das ist* **ja** *unerhört.* **Na** can express disapproval and annoyance. *Na, da hört [sich] doch alles auf!* suggests something has gone on long enough and must stop. *Na, du bist gut!*, well really, you're a fine one.

xiii. Oh well! means that the speaker accepts that a situation cannot be changed, although he or she is not pleased with it. **Tja** expresses resignation. **Eben** or **nun [ein]mal** are usually added to the sent. Cf. JUST 4. *Tja, wir können es eben nicht ändern. Tja, nun ist es passiert.* **Na ja** also suggests that people resign themselves to a situation. *Na ja, damit müssen wir uns eben abfinden. Na ja, dann mach', was du willst!*

> *Tja, so ist das eben.*   *Na ja, es hat wohl so kommen müssen.*
> *Na ja, man sollte derartige Ausrutscher nicht überbewerten.*

xiv. Also gut and **nun gut** express approval or acquiescence even if with some reluctance. **Gut** can have the same sense. They correspond to **very well [then]** or **oh well [then]** meaning 'all right then'.

> *A. Sie müssen den Wagen unbedingt bis morgen fertig haben. B. Also gut, ich will sehen, was sich machen läßt.   Nun gut, ich sage nichts mehr darüber.*
> *Nun gut/Gut, dann komme ich gleich nach dem Mittagessen vorbei.*

xv. Nun ja is used when people admit a disadvantageous feature but then state a pos. or advantageous factor. *Nun ja, wir haben viel Zeit gebraucht, aber es hat sich doch gelohnt*, well, it did take a long time, but . . .

xvi. Well, well! or **Well!** denote surprise. **Na** expresses surprise. *Na, das ist aber eine Überraschung! Well, well, what are you doing here?* Colloquially this could be *Mensch, was machst du denn hier?* or *Du hier! Das ist aber eine Überraschung!*

whenever *conj.*

1. In one sense **whenever** means that the event described in the clause it introduces happens as frequently as that stated in the main clause. It can be replaced by *every time that* or *as often as. Whenever he went out, he took his umbrella with him. Whenever she made an effort, she succeeded.* With vs. in the pres. **wenn** can mean 'when', 'whenever', or 'if'. *Wenn ich Zeit habe, gehe ich schwimmen.* With vs. in the past indicative it means 'whenever' or 'when' referring to repeated action, or 'if'. In *Wenn sie sich anstrengte, schaffte sie es*, wenn can be translated as *whenever*, or *when* = 'every time that', or *if*. To make the meaning 'every time that' clear, *jedesmal* or *immer* is often added in both tenses. *Jedesmal wenn wir uns begegnen, grüßt sie freundlich. Immer wenn er uns besuchte, brachte er Blumen mit. Jedesmal wenn es klingelte, erschrak er.* An unambiguous, but stylistically higher syn. of *wenn* = 'every time that' is **sooft**. *Sooft er uns besuchte, brachte er Blumen mit. Sooft wir uns begegnen, grüßt sie freundlich.*

2. i. In *You can ring me, whenever you need help,* **whenever** can be understood as meaning 'as often as you want to', i.e. 'irrespective of the frequency'. In *Come and see me, whenever you need help/whenever you want to/whenever you like!,* **whenever** can also be construed as 'at whatever time, no matter when', i.e. 'irrespective of the time'. Frequency is expressed by **jedesmal wenn**. *Jedesmal wenn du Hilfe brauchst, ruf mich an!* or *Du kannst mich jedesmal anrufen, wenn du Hilfe brauchst.* The meaning 'no matter what time it is' is expressed by **wann**, to which either or both **auch** and **immer** may be added. *Du kannst vorbeikommen, wann du willst/wann immer du Hilfe brauchst, wann es dir paßt. Du bist bei mir jederzeit willkommen/wann es auch ist/sei.* The distinction sometimes seems to be lost. *Du kannst vorbeikommen, wann immer du Lust hast,* and *Wir werden helfen, wann immer es nötig ist,* could refer either to frequency or to time. *Ich fahre hin, wann immer ich Zeit habe* and *Jedesmal wenn ich Zeit habe, fahre ich hin,* seem to have the same meaning.

> *Komm mich besuchen, wann [immer] du möchtest! Du weißt ja, du bist bei mir jederzeit willkommen.*
> *Der Strand war ganz in der Nähe, und sie konnten schwimmen gehen, wann immer sie Lust dazu hatten.   Bei ihm kannst du anrufen, wann du willst—er ist nie zu Hause.*
> *Hier ist meine Telefonnummer. Ruf mich an, wann immer du willst, sei es Tag oder Nacht!*

ii. A further sense of **whenever** is 'in any or every case in which sth. may happen'. *The army is ready to repulse an attack, whenever one occurs.* This does not mean that an attack will take place; it is merely a possibility. *If ever one occurs* is much the same, though the possibility is somewhat more remote. *When the official report is published—whenever that may be—some details in my book may need to be altered* suggests at an unspecifiable time in the future, if at all. **Wann [auch] immer** can state a condition which may or may not be fulfilled and is often like *if ever*. *Sie können sich an mich wenden, wann immer es nötig ist,* can have the sense discussed in 2. i, but can be more tentative like *if ever the need arises*. It is therefore used in polite requests. *Wann immer Sie bei uns in der Gegend sind, kommen Sie mal vorbei! Jedesmal wenn* would sound like an order.

> *Die Armee ist bereit, einen Angriff zurückzuschlagen, wann immer einer erfolgen sollte.*
> *Mit der Veröffentlichung des amtlichen Berichts—wann immer das geschehen mag—müssen vielleicht einige Einzelheiten in meinem Buch geändert werden.*

Note that **wann auch immer** introduces a concessive clause. When such clauses begin a sent., v. and subj. of the main clause are usually not inverted. *Wann es auch immer sein mag, ich bin bereit, Ihnen zu helfen.* This can be translated as *no matter when* or *whenever it may be*.

iii. Wann [auch] immer is used elliptically like *whenever* in *Komm' doch morgen vorbei oder wann [auch] immer,* and means 'at any other time'.

3. Whenever also expresses surprise and bewilderment and may be broken into two parts. *Whenever did I make such a promise?* or *When did I ever . . . ?* This is expressed in speech by **bloß**. **Nur** is more formal. *Wann habe ich bloß ein solches Versprechen gegeben? Wann habe ich nur so was gesagt?*

4. Whenever possible is so oft wie möglich. *Ich besuche sie so oft wie möglich.*

while, whereas, as long as *conjs.*

1. While means 'during the time that' or 'during the same time' and can indicate either that two things happen at the same time or that one happens at some point during the duration of the other. *While their parents were away, the grandmother looked after the children. While he was doing his homework, he fell asleep.*

In both these cases G. uses **während**. *Er las, während er aß. Während sie beim Essen waren, klingelte das Telefon.* A pres. part. can follow *while*. This construction can be regarded as a *while*-clause with subj. and v. omitted. *He was arrested while [he was] committing a burglary.* A *während*-clause needs a subj. and v. *Er wurde verhaftet, während er einen Einbruch verübte.* (**Indem** can be a syn. of *während* used as a temporal conjunction, e.g. *Indem er dies sagte, klingelte es*, but this use has become unusual. *Indem* is now mostly a syn. of *dadurch daß* and translates the E. construction *by* + gerund, *by doing sth. Man setzt die Maschine in Betrieb, indem man den Hebel herunterdrückt. Man setzt die Maschine dadurch in Betrieb, daß man den Hebel herunterdrückt.*)

> *Während die Eltern verreist waren, sorgte die Oma für die Kinder.*
> *Während er Kartoffeln schälte, hatte sie die Wohnung schnell durchgesaugt.*
> *Michael ist eingeschlafen, während er seine Hausaufgaben machte.*

2. While also means 'during the whole duration of' or 'until the end of a specified time'. *While there is life, there is hope. While I've got a tongue in my head, he won't get away with that unchallenged.* It is a syn. of **as long as** when it refers to time, as in *As long as the machine is operating, it produces heat.* **Solange** expresses this sense. *Solange die Maschine in Betrieb ist, erzeugt sie Wärme.*

> *Solange du hier bist, habe ich keine Angst.*   *Der Mensch hofft, solange er lebt.*
> *Solange ich noch reden kann, wird er so etw. nicht unwidersprochen tun können.*

3. While also introduces a contrast and is a syn. of **whereas**. *While Fred gambles his money away, Julia saves hers.* The equivalent is **während** or on a stylistically higher level **wohingegen**. The latter follows the main clause. *Er hat studiert, wohingegen seine Geschwister alle ein Handwerk erlernt haben.*

> *Während Fred seinen Lohn verwettet, spart Julia so viel sie nur kann.* Or *Fred verwettet seinen Lohn, wohingegen Julia so viel spart, wie sie nur kann.*
> *Ich halte den ersten Vorschlag für vernünftig, wohingegen der zweite mir schwachsinnig erscheint.*

In some sents. the contrast is virtually lost, so that **while** joins two facts and means 'and'. *The walls are panelled, while the ceiling is of plaster.* The simplest transl. here is **und**. *Die Wände sind getäfelt, und die Decke ist verputzt.*

4. While also means 'despite the fact that' or 'although' and must be translated by **obwohl** or **obgleich**. *While I have sympathy for his aims, I think his proposals too extreme: Obwohl ich volles Verständnis für seine Ziele habe, halte ich seine Vorschläge für zu radikal. Obwohl die Beweise, die sie anführt, die Theorie stützen, hat sie wichtige Gegenargumente nicht berücksichtigt*, and *Obgleich er die Spionage in musterhafter Weise organisierte, war er selbst ein schlechter Beobachter*, the conjunctions could be translated as **while** or [al]though.

5. As long as also means 'on condition that, provided that'. *You may borrow the book as long as you don't lend it to anyone else.* The equivalents are **vorausgesetzt, daß**, 'provided that', or **wenn**, 'if'.

> *Du kannst dir das Buch ausleihen, vorausgesetzt daß du es nicht weiter verleihst.*
> *Wenn der Chef mit deiner Arbeit zufrieden ist, brauchst du dir keine Sorgen zu machen.*

When a *solange*-clause contains a neg., it acquires the meaning of a conditional clause introduced by **as long as**. *Solange du deine Hausaufgaben nicht gemacht hast, darfst du nicht spielen gehen.*

willing[ly], unwilling[ly] *adjs. and advs.*

1. i. The usual equivalent of **willing** + infin. is **bereit** + infin. *Sie sind bereit, uns zu helfen.* The sense of an infin. can also be expressed by a n.: *Sie ist bereit, die Aufgabe zu übernehmen*, or *Sie ist zur Übernahme der Aufgabe bereit.* *Bereit* also translates

PREPARED. **Unwilling** + infin. is mostly expressed by **nicht bereit** + infin. *Er ist nicht bereit, uns weitere Auskunft zu geben.*

ii. Willens, which is confined to formal and elevated language, needs an infin. *Sie waren willens, auf den Vorschlag einzugehen. Wir sind nicht willens, den Vertrag zu unterzeichnen.*

iii. Gewillt is also used with an infin. It is stylistically much higher than *bereit. Sind Sie gewillt, sich für unsere Ziele einzusetzen? Ich bin nicht gewillt, solches Verhalten zu dulden.* In some contexts it is stronger than *willing*, meaning 'determined'. *Er war ernsthaft gewillt, sein Leben zu ändern.*

2. Willing is also applied as an adj. and adv. to people who do something enthusiastically because they want to, not because they are forced to. *He was a willing worker/helper. They willingly gave us the information desired.*

i. The usual equivalent is **bereitwillig**, which suggests that someone is happy to do something, but it presupposes a definite situation in which one person makes a request and another gladly complies. It is used as an adj. and adv., but not with an infin.

Sie haben uns bereitwillig die gewünschte Auskunft gegeben.
Bei den Vorbereitungen für das Sportfest war sie eine bereitwillige Helferin.

ii. Willig has the sense of **willing** defined in 2, but suggests willingness to do what is expected in a general way, not on a specific occasion. It is an adj. only and is not used with an infin.

Sie sind willige Arbeiter.   Die Kinder der Klasse waren willig und gelehrig.
Der Geist ist willig, aber das Fleisch ist schwach. (Matthew 26: 41)

3. Unwilling[ly]. The lit. equivalent is **widerwillig**. It is only rarely used as a adj. and is not applied directly to people. *Sie unternahmen ein paar widerwillige Schritte, die uns nur wenig halfen,* is possible, but not common. E. sents. like *They were unwilling helpers/workers* are best translated by the adv. *Sie haben nur widerwillig geholfen/mitgearbeitet.* In speech **ungern** is probably more commonly found as an adv., but *widerwillig* does occur. *Er hat es getan, aber nur widerwillig/sehr ungern.* **Unwillig**, which can also mean 'angry', is occasionally found in the sense of 'unwilling'. *Er hat seine Pflicht unwillig erfüllt.* Two vs. express a related sense. The impersonal expression **es widerstrebt mir, etw. zu tun** means that I am unwilling or reluctant to do something because of moral scruples. *Es widerstrebt mir, ihn zu belügen/ihr Mißtrauen zu mißbrauchen.* (The pres. part. and the phr. in *Sie ging nur* **widerstrebend**/*nur* **mit Widerstreben** *mit* mean 'unwillingly or reluctantly'. **Ohne Widerstreben** means 'willingly' *Er kam ohne Widerstreben mit.*) **Sich gegen etw. sträuben** means 'not only to be unwilling to do sth. but also to put up considerable resistance against it'. *Er sträubte sich [dagegen], irgendetw. in dem Text zu ändern.*

Das Kind gehorchte nur widerwillig.   Ich stimmte dem Vorschlag ungern zu (reluctantly).
Sie nimmt nur widerwillig/ungern Bücher in die Hand, wenn es darum geht, für die Schule zu lernen.
Es widerstrebt mir, mit meinen Untergebenen in einem so verächtlichen Ton zu reden.
Er sträubte sich mit Händen und Füßen gegen den Dienst in der Armee.
Anfangs sträubten wir uns dagegen, doch später gefiel uns die Arbeit.

woman, lady *ns.* Some remarks on **gentleman** *n.*

1. i. The general equivalent of **woman** meaning 'an adult female human being' is now **die Frau**. It also means 'wife' and is a form of address before a name.

Mit den Frauen und Kindern sind wir 27 Personen.
Im Parteivorstand sitzen sechs Männer und vier Frauen.
Er fragte sie, ob sie seine Frau werden wollte.   Er hat eine zwei Jahre ältere Frau geheiratet.
Ich möchte unsere neue Mitarbeiterin, Frau Immermann, vorstellen.

ii. Das Weib was once the normal word for **woman** and *wife*, but is now mostly pejorative. The neutral sense survives only in religious and literary language, but here it is mostly felt to be a relic of an older usage. The latest revision of the *Lutherbibel* (1984) has for Genesis 1: 27: *Und Gott schuf den Menschen zu seinem Bilde, zum Bilde Gottes schuf er ihn; und schuf sie als Mann und Weib.* The *Einheitsbibel* (joint Catholic and Protestant transl.) of 1980 had: *Gott schuf also den Menschen als sein Abbild; als Abbild Gottes schuf er ihn. Als Mann und Frau schuf er sie.* Elsewhere *Weib* is almost always linked with adjs. expressing disapproval. *Ein albernes/zänkisches/klatschsüchtiges/ falsches/gehässiges Weib. Ein tolles* or *prächtiges Weib* may seem to contradict this, as the adjs. express pos. qualities. Such expressions as the latter, which are used mostly by certain young men, acknowledge the attractiveness of the woman referred to, but have a strongly erotic overtone which is not always complimentary.

Laß dich von diesen hysterischen Weibern nicht aus der Ruhe bringen!

iii. She was an outstanding etc. *woman.* In a description of the character of a man or woman in G. **der Mensch** is often found. *Sie war ein ausgezeichneter/netter/sympa- thischer/verständnisvoller Mensch.* In some cases, especially with characteristics regarded as particularly feminine, *Frau* is also used. *Sie ist eine mütterliche Frau/eine intelligente/karrieresüchtige/liebenswürdige/mildtätige Frau.*

2. Die Dame, 'lady', has two main uses.

i. It is firstly a polite way of referring to women in general, *Die Damen haben den Vortritt* or *Die Damen des Betriebes werden gebeten, um ein Uhr in die Halle zu kommen,* and the customary form of address when a woman's name is not known or used. A shop assistant might ask one woman, *'Was darf es sein, meine Dame?'* (E.: Madam). Two or more women are addressed as *meine Damen. Meine Damen, bewahren Sie doch Ruhe! Dame* is used in this sense irrespective of the social status or the personal qualities of the woman or women concerned. The corresponding appropriate word for a man is *der Herr.* Hence the form of address at meetings etc.: *Meine Damen und Herren!* The form of address in a letter whose exact recipient is not known is now *Sehr geehrte Damen und Herren! Damen* is used in the language of sport where *women* is usual in E., though *ladies* is possible. *Brustschwimmen der Damen. Bei den Damen siegte die polnische Staffel. Kür der Damen beim Eiskunstlauf.*

ii. In the second use **Die Dame** denotes a female person who according to the *Wörterbuch der deutschen Gegenwartssprache* has refined manners, education, and a well-groomed appearance. It corresponds to **lady** defined as 'a woman of refinement whose conduct conforms to a certain standard of propriety and correct behaviour'. *Ein vollendete/feine/junge/ältere Dame. Sie sieht wie eine Dame aus.* The usual equivalent for a man in this sense in *der Kavalier.* It suggests a tactful and polite man with an obliging nature and chivalrous behaviour. It always expresses praise. *Er benahm sich wie ein echter/vollkommener Kavalier. Es gibt also noch Kavaliere.* Alternatives are *der Weltmann* and *der Gentleman. Er hatte Aussehen und Auftreten eines Weltmannes, war aber im Innern ein rechter Spießbürger geblieben. Er ist durch und durch ein Gentleman.*

iii. We might say when talking of a woman whose acquaintance we have never made, 'I've never even met the woman.' In this context **die Dame** is usual in G. *Ich kenne die Dame nicht. Ich bin der Dame nie begegnet.*

wonder *v. Wundern* means 'to SURPRISE', a sense **wonder [at]** retains. *Wundern* does not mean 'to want to know', which is the main meaning of **wonder**.

1. The usual meaning of **wonder** is 'to feel curiosity', 'to ask oneself, or wish to know', *I wonder what will happen now/how they got on,* but it is used idiomatically in contexts in which the meaning is fairly vague. *I wonder if you'd care to join me/drop in some time.*

i. When no particular emphasis is placed on *wonder*, i.e. in sents. in which it is a way of asking a question, the particle **wohl** in a question expresses the idea simply. *Wohl* occurs frequently with the future, but also with other tenses. *Werden sie uns wohl helfen?*, I wonder if they will help us. *Was wird jetzt wohl geschehen?* Direct questions without an interrogative are also commonly introduced by *ob*, and *wohl* is added to them. *Ob sie uns wohl helfen werden?* (Note that in statements *wohl* often means 'I suppose'. *Du hast wohl viel zu tun. Es gibt wohl keinen anderen Ausweg. A. Jmd. hat angerufen. B. Das wird wohl Detlef gewesen sein.*)

> *Haben wir wohl noch genug Zeit, um den Dom zu besichtigen?*
> *Ob wir wohl genug Zeit haben?*   *Ob er es wohl geschafft hat?*
> *Wird es wohl klappen?*   *Ob es wohl klappen wird?*

Wohl is also the simplest transl. when *I wonder* follows a question in E. *Is he telling the truth, I wonder? Sagt er wohl die Wahrheit? Or Ob er wohl die Wahrheit sagt?*

ii. Sich fragen expresses the meaning of **wonder** defined in 1 and is more emphatic than *wohl*. It could be used instead of *wohl* in the above sents. *Ich frage mich, wie sie in der Prüfung abgeschnitten hat. Sich fragen* is essential only where *wohl* is syntactically impossible, e.g. where a clause does not follow *wonder*. *I wonder too* is *Das frag ich mich auch.* Without a clause *I wonder* expresses reservations about the preceding statement. Explanatory words need to be added to *ich frage mich* when translating *I wonder* in this use. *'It was entirely his own idea,' said Tom. Mr Mason looked at him in surprise. 'I wonder,' he said. 'Er ist ganz von selbst auf den Gedanken gekommen', sagte Tom. Mr Mason sah ihn verwundert an und sagte, 'Ich frage mich, ob das stimmt/ob das wahr ist.' Or 'Ob das wohl stimmt?' He said he had found it, but I (or you) can't help wondering* can be *Er sagte, er hätte es gefunden, aber ich frage mich, ob das stimmt/ob das wahr ist.*

> *Ich frage mich nur, ob das überhaupt noch Sinn/Zweck hat.* (*Hat das wohl noch Sinn/Zweck?* is perfectly acceptable, but *nur*, 'just', cannot be added.)
> *Ich frage mich nach dem Grund seiner Absage.*

iii. Ich möchte wissen also expresses the same meaning as *sich fragen*.

> *Ich frage mich/Ich möchte wissen, wie so etw. hätte passieren können.*

2. Sich wundern, which means 'to feel SURPRISE', is found in a construction which resembles the E. use, but it differs by expressing a strong element of surprise. *Deine Freunde werden sich gewundert haben, daß ich so einsilbig war* can be paraphrased as *Sie werden sich erstaunt gefragt haben, warum ich so einsilbig war.* The surprise is combined with the desire to know why. Thus *Er wunderte sich, daß ich gar nichts unternommen hatte.* In north Germany *sich wundern* in this sense can only be followed by a *daß*-clause. (According to *Duden: Das große Wörterbuch* and *Brockhaus-Wahrig*, Swiss G. uses *es wundert mich* and *sich wundern* as syns. of *sich fragen* in the sense 'to desire to know'. *Es wundert mich, woher er das weiß/wann sie ankommen werden. Ich wundere mich, ob sie damit einverstanden sind. Er wunderte sich, warum sie so einsilbig war.* Unless they take Swiss G. as their standard, E. speakers should avoid these uses as they sound like E. translated word for word.)

3. In **wonder at** + n. and *I wonder [at the fact that] he wasn't run over*, and *not to wonder* + *if*, **wonder** means 'to be surprised' and needs to be translated by equivalents of SURPRISE. **Es wundert mich** is the most common one. **Ich wundere mich darüber** is stronger. *Es wundert mich, daß er nicht überfahren wurde. Ich wundere mich nicht darüber, daß er gekündigt hat—die Bezahlung war doch miserabel.*

> *Es wundert mich, daß sie dort ganz alleine lebt, meilenweit vom nächsten Haus entfernt* (I wonder at her living there quite/all alone).

Es sollte/würde mich nicht wundern, wenn sie ihn verläßt, behandelt er sie doch wie eine Sklavin (shouldn't/wouldn't wonder if . . .). Also *Ich würde mich nicht wundern, wenn . . .*

4. Wonder at also means 'to be in a state of rapt attention towards sth. extraordinary', 'to feel or become struck with wonder'. (The n. *wonder* is defined as 'a state of fascinated attention before what strikes one as strange' and/or 'a feeling of amazed admiration'.) *She wondered at his skill/at the beauty of the picture.* If the emotion is predominantly a feeling of strangeness, **sich verwundern**, which is stronger than *sich wundern*, expresses the sense. *Sie verwunderte sich über seine Geschicklichkeit.* **Staunen** can express a feeling of strangeness, but also one of admiration. *Wir staunten über diesen einfältigen Menschen. Die Kinder staunten über die Größe des Elefanten. Sie staunte, wie schön das Gemälde war. Sie staunte über die Schönheit des Gemäldes.* **Erstaunen über** is somewhat stronger than *staunen. Alle erstaunten über/verwunderten sich über diese weise Antwort.* Cf. SURPRISE. *Staunen* is a word in everyday use; the others are stylistically higher and more akin to this sense of **wonder at**.

5. Wonder is also used frequently in polite expressions. Instead of asking directly whether someone would like to visit us, we often say, 'I wonder/was just wondering if you'd like to visit us.' Such a question can be expressed by **vielleicht**. It is even more polite with the subjunctive. *Vielleicht hätten Sie Lust, uns einmal zu besuchen? Möchten Sie sich vielleicht zu uns setzen?* Polite requests are also introduced in E. by *I wonder if you'd mind . . . Vielleicht* is also used in requests. *Vielleicht helfen Sie mir, den Kinderwagen die Treppe hinaufzutragen?* **Wohl** and **wohl mal** added to a request make it sound polite. *Wohl mal* is more direct and colloquial. *Könnten Sie wohl [mal] einen Platz weiter rücken?*

> *Vielleicht bist du so freundlich, das für mich zu erledigen/die Briefe für mich einzuwerfen?*
> *Vielleicht bist du so gut und hilfst mir dabei?*   *Würden Sie mir wohl eine Frage erlauben?*
> *Würden Sie wohl mal einen Platz weiter rücken? Also . . . wohl bitte mal . . .*
> *Würde es Ihnen wohl etw. ausmachen, wenn ich das Fenster aufmachte?*

work *v.* Some equivalents.

1. Work means 'to do sth. involving effort or exertion of body or mind for a purpose, either to produce sth., to bring about a result, to gain one's livelihood, or to pursue an occupation'.

i. Arbeiten is the main equivalent of this sense. *Er arbeitet zehn Stunden am Tag/den ganzen Tag hier/bei einer Computerfirma. Jmd. arbeitet fleißig/intensiv/sorgfältig/fieberhaft/ schnell/ruhig* or *schwer/nachlässig/langsam.* In the former DDR the part of the population in employment was called *die werktätige Bevölkerung.* In the old *Bundesrepublik, die arbeitende Bevölkerung* was more usual.

ii. A formal syn. of *arbeiten* in the sense 'to pursue an occupation' is **tätig sein**. *Als Arzt/Lehrer*, etc. or *an einer Universität/Schule*, etc. *tätig sein. Ich bin bei dieser Firma schon seit zwanzig Jahren tätig.* Women who work are said to be **berufstätig**. *Da alle Kinder zur Schule gehen, ist sie wieder [halbtags] berufstätig. Berufstätige Frauen.*

iii. Wirken means 'to work' in the sense defined above, but is confined to formal language. It implies that the work is of some importance and that the person exerts a beneficial influence on those among or for whom he or she works.

> *Die beiden haben längere Zeit als Missionare in Neuguinea gewirkt/gearbeitet.*
> *Während seines Wirkens als Leiter der Schule haben die Schüler gelernt, was Arbeiten heißt.*

2. In the special sense, 'to bring about or produce an effect', **wirken** is used with *Wunder*, to work wonders. *Die neue Wirtschaftspolitik wirkte Wunder—die Produktion stieg schnell auf das Dreifache.* **Wirken** corresponds to **work** in reference to medicines etc. *Die Spritze scheint schon zu wirken. Das Gift begann zu wirken. Diese Arznei wirkt gut/schnell [gegen Erkältungen].* For other uses cf. AFFECT 1. For a complete therapy **anschlagen** means 'to be successful'. *Die Behandlung hatte gut angeschlagen.*

3. Work means 'to bestow labour or effort on' in various contexts. *S.o. works a mine, land,* or *timber.*

i. Work *a mine* is *eine Mine/eine Grube* **ausbeuten.** *Das Erzvorkommen/Die Grube wird seit vierzig Jahren ausgebeutet.* **Work** or *run a farm* etc. is *einen Bauernhof* **bewirtschaften.**

> *Die Familie bewirtschaftet ein Landgut.*
> *Das Ertrag pro Hektar bewirtschafteter Fläche ist gestiegen.*

ii. The basic sense of **bearbeiten** is 'to apply labour to sth.' *Der Boden wird bearbeitet.* (Syns. like *till* or *cultivate* are *bebauen* and *bestellen.*) *Jmd. bearbeitet Holz/Leder/Metall/Rohstoffe.* In relation to mental work *bearbeiten* means 'to work on or deal with'. *Jmd. bearbeitet ein Thema/eine Frage.* Close in meaning is *Sie arbeitet über ein Thema.* (*Sie arbeitet an einem Referat,* she is working on it in the sense of being occupied with it.) *Zwei Beamte bearbeiten den Fall/die Anträge. Ein Buch bearbeiten,* to revise it. *Sie bearbeitete das Theaterstück für das Fernsehen,* adapts it.

iii. Verarbeiten means that the material worked on is made into a new product, is changed by being worked on. The result is often stated after *zu. Holz wird zu Papier verarbeitet. Sie verarbeiten das Leder zu Handtaschen. Der Autor hat seinen Roman zu einem Drehbuch für eine Fernsehserie verarbeitet. Sie verarbeitete ihre Notizen zu einem Artikel. Verarbeiten* also means 'to turn a basic material to use by mental or other work', hence 'to utilize' or 'to process'. Thus *Daten verarbeiten,* 'to process data', or *Der Verfasser hat dieses Zahlenmaterial in seinem Buch verarbeitet,* 'utilized', or *Wir verarbeiten nur hochwertige Stoffe/Metall,* 'use, utilize'. What the starting material is made into need not be stated.

4. Further uses of *be-* and *verarbeiten.* **Bearbeiten** also means 'to work on' in the sense of influencing or persuading, but it has a neg. connotation suggesting against the will of the other[s]. *Sie haben ihn so lange bearbeitet, bis er einwilligte. Die Parteien bearbeiten die Wähler durch Fernsehen und Presse.* Another meaning of **verarbeiten** is 'to digest mentally or work on' things seen, heard, or experienced. *Jeder braucht Zeit, um neue Erkenntnisse/Eindrücke zu verarbeiten.*

5. Work one's way through sth. means 'to make one's way, usually slowly and laboriously and by surmounting difficulties'. **Sich arbeiten** means 'to make one's way with effort and by overcoming obstructions to an objective'. It is only used for natural conditions, *Wir haben uns durch das dichte Unterholz gearbeitet,* or for working one's way up in an organization, *Sie hat sich nach oben gearbeitet* or *sich hochgearbeitet.* **Work one's way** mentally through a report, a pile of letters, etc. is **sich durcharbeiten.** *Ich muß mich durch diesen Stapel Anträge/dieses dicke Lehrbuch durcharbeiten.*

6. In reference to a machine, or apparatus, or organs of the body, **work** means 'to function properly', 'to operate or run in a certain way' and 'to be in operation'. Several G. vs. express these senses. The general one is *funktionieren.*

i. Funktionieren can always be used to state whether something is capable of working or not, or functions properly. *Funktioniert Ihre Waschmaschine/der Schalter jetzt?*

> *Der Fahrstuhl/Der Reißverschluß/Das Telefon funktioniert nicht/funktioniert wieder.*
> *Er nahm die Leuchtpistole in die Hand und dachte, 'Hoffentlich funktioniert sie.'*

Gehen is only used for simpler and smaller mechanisms. *Großvaters Taschenuhr ist mehr als 100 Jahre alt und geht noch. Die Bremse geht nicht. Ich nehme den alten*

Rasierapparat mit—er geht noch. Colloquially **es tun** is used mostly for household appliances. *Solange der alte Staubsauger es noch tut, brauchen wir keinen neuen.* (*Laufen* has this sense only with an adv. *Die Maschine läuft,* 'is in operation', cf. 6. v.)

ii. Work + adv. **Funktionieren** is used with advs. like *gut, richtig, einwandfrei,* etc. *Der alte Fernseher funktioniert noch gut.* **Gehen** is used with an adv. or phr. stating how something operates, runs, or works. *Die Uhr geht [nicht/wieder] richtig.* **Laufen** is used for larger machines and apparatus. *Der Apparat läuft endlich wieder. Der Dieselmotor des Generators läuft nicht richtig.* **Arbeiten** belongs more to technical language. It presupposes a certain complexity in the machine and is applied to larger mechanisms, to production plants, or to something complicated like a large computer. It is found with general advs. like *einwandfrei, Alle vier Triebwerke arbeiten einwandfrei,* but mostly states specific properties. Only *arbeiten* would be used in sents. like *Die Anlage arbeitet vollautomatisch* or *Der Absorberkühlschrank arbeitet ohne Kompressor.*

Trotz der Kriegshandlungen funktioniert die Nachrichtenübermittlung noch normal.
Die Maschine läuft ruhig/einwandfrei.   *Der Motor läuft seit einiger Zeit unrund.*
Die Schiffsmotoren arbeiten wieder, als wenn nichts gewesen wäre.

iii. Arbeiten is the specific term for organs of the body, but in everyday speech **funktionieren** is used.

Das Herz des Patienten arbeitet normal.
Trotz seines hohen Alters funktionert sein Gedächtnis noch gut.

iv. Funktionieren is the v. used when asking for an explanation of how something works. *Wie funktioniert das?*

v. Be working = 'to be in operation at a particular time'. The usual expression is **in Betrieb sein.** *Wieviele Maschinen sind hier in Betrieb?* **Laufen** can mean 'to be going or running'. *Der Motor läuft.* **Arbeiten** also means 'to be going, in operation'. *Unsere Maschinen arbeiten Tag und Nacht.*

Die Telefonzentrale der Universität ist an gesetzlichen Feiertagen nicht in Betrieb.
Alle Maschinen laufen auf vollen Touren.   *Der Computer arbeitet jetzt.*

Note that *außer Betrieb sein* means 'not to be working' either because it is turned off or because something is wrong or defective—it is *kaputt. Der Aufzug ist schon wieder außer Betrieb.*

7. A plan or arrangement that works acts in the desired way or proves effective. Other subjs. are a method, something attempted, and systems of various kinds. *The plan worked. The free market economy seems to work.*

i. Funktionieren is used for governmental and other systems. *Ein gut funktionierendes Regierungssystem. Die freie Marktwirtschaft scheint zu funktionieren.* It is also used for the organization of activities, *Die Organisation funktionierte einwandfrei/reibungslos,* or for a way of doing something, *Die Durchführung der Versuche/Experimente funktionierte problemlos.*

ii. For plans etc. the v. depends on the context. **Gelingen** and **klappen** are possibilities. *Ein Plan gelingt* or *klappt.* **Erfolg haben mit etw.**, and **schaffen,** 'to SUCCEED', can also be used, but need a personal subj. Sents. with a thing as subj. can be rephrased. *Mit dem anderen Plan hatten wir Erfolg/haben wir es geschafft. Als die ersten Versuche fehlgeschlagen waren, versuchte er es mit einer anderen Methode, und damit hat er Erfolg gehabt* or *. . . damit hat er es geschafft.*

Wir haben uns eine neue Arbeitsweise ausgedacht und hoffen, daß sie gelingt.

iii. For **It works/doesn't work**, referring to what someone tries, **es geht** can be used, especially in the neg. *Ich habe es versucht, aber es ging nicht.* **Klappen** also occurs. *Du brauchst es nicht erst lange zu versuchen—es klappt nicht.* **Das/Es läßt sich machen** is used in pos. and neg. sents. *So wie du das hier angefangen hast, läßt es sich* *nicht machen/geht es nicht. Ich glaube, es läßt sich machen, wenn wir es auf andere Weise versuchen.* **Bringen** in the sense 'to achieve a result' can express the meaning. *It was a good idea, but it didn't work* could be in speech *Es war ein guter Gedanke, er hat aber nichts gebracht,* brought no result; . . . *aber er hat nicht funktioniert* is also possible.

iv. With a trick, flattery, etc. as subj. **work** means 'to have the desired effect'. *Flattery won't work with her* can be *Bei ihr verfängt die Schmeichelei nicht.* **Verfangen** means here 'to allow oneself to be caught or deceived', is usually neg., but is now not very common. *Dieser Trick verfängt bei mir nicht.* An alternative is *Mit Schmeichelei wirst du bei ihr nichts erreichen/ausrichten.* Cf. ACHIEVE 1. In speech **ziehen** is used. *Dieser Trick zieht nicht mehr bei ihm. Solche Ausreden ziehen nicht mehr.*

work *n.* Some equivalents. The n. **work** has several meanings. One is 'the expending of sustained physical or mental effort to achieve a result'. *It was hard work getting to the top of the mountain.* Another is 'a task or job to be done'. *There's always plenty of work around the house. I have some work for you to do.* Another is 'the activities that provide one's accustomed means of livelihood'. *It is difficult to find work during a depression.* A further sense is 'the result produced by effort'. *Her work is always of a high standard. The work of three famous sculptors can be seen in the art gallery this month.*

1. Work is applied to an activity which is difficult to do and requires sustained mental or physical effort. It frequently has an adj. like *hard. Rowing against the current was hard work.* **Die Arbeit** expresses this sense, usually with an adj. like *schwer* or *viel. Gegen den Strom zu rudern war schwere Arbeit.* Sometimes the adj. is only implied. *Das war aber eine Arbeit! Ein großes Stück Arbeit lag noch vor mir.*

    In einem solchen Buch steckt viel Arbeit.   *Die Übersetzung hat mir sehr viel Arbeit gemacht.*
    Du hast dir mit dieser Sache unnötige Arbeit gemacht.
    Sie hat sehr viel Arbeit mit diesen Kindern.
    Es war schwere Arbeit, den Gipfel des Berges zu erreichen.
    Sie scheuten keine Mühe und Arbeit und erreichten, was sie sich vorgenommen hatten.

2. Work = 'a task or job to be done' and 'employment'.

i. Die Arbeit can denote a single task or an occupation. *Jmd. geht an die Arbeit* or *macht sich an die Arbeit,* 'gets down to work', which can be a particular task or one's job. *Zur Arbeit gehen/fahren* is 'to go to one's place of employment'. In *Jmd. sucht Arbeit, ist ohne Arbeit* or *ist arbeitslos,* and *geht seiner Arbeit nach, Arbeit* usually refers to employment, and in *Ich habe eine interessante Arbeit für dich* to a task.

    Die Arbeit an der Brücke wurde unterbrochen/kommt gut voran/wird nächste Woche fortgesetzt.
    Diese Arbeit geht mir leicht von der Hand/sagt mir zu/fällt mir schwer.
    Durch die Mechanisierung wurden den Menschen viele Arbeiten abgenommen.
    Die Gastarbeiter führen die schmutzigen Arbeiten/die schmutzige Arbeit in den Fabriken aus.
    Er verdient seinen Lebensunterhalt durch geistige/handwerkliche Arbeit.
    Sie hat eine gut bezahlte/interessante/leichte Arbeit.   *Sie haben die Arbeit gut gemacht.*
    Diese Arbeit erfordert ein hohes Maß an Konzentration.
    Er macht/tut seine Arbeit gewissenhaft.

ii. In a few expressions **das Werk** means 'the activity of working', but it usually suggests important work and is not an everyday word. *Sie machten sich/begaben sich ans Werk. Er mußte sein Werk abbrechen. Sie durfte an dem Werk ihres Mannes mitarbeiten.*

3. In the sense 'the result produced by labour', **die Arbeit** is the general term. In *Jmd. macht/tut/leistet gute Arbeit* it can refer to work done by any person, whether a worker or tradesman, a pupil in school (but cf. 4), a student at a university, a researcher, writer, teacher, or something else. While **das Werk**, referring to literary or artistic products, often contains a value judgement, *die Arbeit* is quite neutral. *Das Werk* now mostly denotes the result of creative work and implies high quality. *Die jungen Künstler stellen ihre Arbeiten aus. Die Werke des bekannten Künstlers werden ausgestellt.* However, *die neuesten Arbeiten eines renommierten Künstlers* is also possible. *Werk* is used for important scholarly work, *Er hat ein bedeutendes Werk über die Reformation/ein wichtiges medizinisches Werk geschrieben,* but *eine bahnbrechende Arbeit auf einem Gebiet* is also used. *Er hat eine historische Arbeit über den siebenjährigen Krieg verfaßt. Ein Nachschlagewerk* is 'a reference book'. *Ein Machwerk* is 'a poor piece of work'. *Arbeit* is used for an essay, paper, or composition written by students. *Die Studenten müssen ihre Arbeiten für das Kleistseminar morgen abgeben.* In schools *eine Arbeit* is often a shortened form of *die Klassenarbeit,* a written test or examination. *Die Klasse schreibt morgen eine Englischarbeit. Der Lehrer korrigiert/benotet/zensiert die Arbeiten.* Hausaufgaben is the usual equivalent of *homework* done by those attending school. *Die Hausarbeit* means in one sense 'housework'. It also denotes a fairly long piece of work secondary pupils or students do at home. In connection with students it is often used as a syn. of *Examensarbeit,* a thesis written for an examination.

> *Sie hat eine sorgfältige/ausgezeichnete/tadellose/solide/gründliche Arbeit abgeliefert.*
> *Die Arbeit ist mißlungen/schwach/zeigt viele Ungenauigkeiten.*
> *Mit dieser Arbeit bewies er sein Können.*
> *Die Bücherei besitzt alle bedeutenden Werke der Weltliteratur.*
> *Sie hat alle Werke Beethovens, die auf Schallplatten zu haben sind.*

Die Werke der Natur is a fixed, fairly literary expression.

4. Work is also applied to what a schoolboy or schoolgirl does, his or her performance. *This pupil's work has to improve/is very good.* The equivalent is **die Leistung** or **die Leistungen**, what is achieved.

> *Die Leistungen des Schülers haben sich in letzter Zeit verbessert/haben nachgelassen.*
> *Du mußt deine Leistungen verbessern, wenn du einen Studienplatz bekommen willst.*

5. Work or **works** also refer to a person's actions or deeds. Except in a few expressions, it has a somewhat old-fashioned ring. *Their works are the works of iniquity. Works of charity. Sth. was the work of a moment.* The equivalent is **das Werk**, which is also confined to a few expressions. *Gute Werke tun* is 'to do good works'. *Diese Unordnung—das ist dein Werk* is possible in literary prose instead of e.g. *Das hast du verschuldet.*

> *Die Zerstörung der Stadt war das Werk von ein paar Sekunden.*
> *Sie haben viele Werke der Nächstenliebe/der Barmherzigkeit/der Mildtätigkeit getan.*
> *Die Stiftung des Waisenhauses war ein gemeinnütziges Werk.*

write down *v.* Three derivatives of *schreiben* mean 'to write down', *hinschreiben, aufschreiben,* and *niederschreiben.* **Hinschreiben** means 'to write down quickly, often carelessly and without thinking much about it'. It implies jotting down one or a few unconnected words in order not to forget something. **Aufschreiben**, which implies writing down carefully, is the main equivalent and is the appropriate v. in most contexts. *Ich muß die Nummer aufschreiben. Ich schreibe es mir auf* also translates *I shall note it down.* **Niederschreiben** is a formal syn. The prefix *nieder* is now little used, and words containing it are felt to belong to a stylistically high level. *Niederschreiben,* therefore, sounds solemn or weighty, and is used only for things which are of particular importance. As it suggests that the writer has thought and worked out what he or she wants to say before committing it to paper, it is appropriate for literary composition. It is not used for writing down something more or less at the same time as one hears it, nor for noting something [down]. **Mitschreiben** means 'to write or take down what is being said'. *Sie schrieb die Vorlesung mit.* Cf. NOTE *n.* 1. ii. For related words see RECORD.

> *Die Gliederung ist noch nicht fertig. Ich habe erst einmal ein paar Gedanken nur so hingeschrieben.*
> *In ihrem Tagebuch hat sie alles aufgeschrieben, was sie in Afrika erlebt und gesehen hatte.*
> *Dieses Ereignis verdient aufgeschrieben zu werden.*   *Ich habe mir den Titel aufgeschrieben.*
> *Hast du dir aufgeschrieben, wann das nächste Treffen des Literaturkreises stattfindet?*
> *Den Text des Liedes schreibe ich für dich auf.*   *Ich diktiere. Schreiben Sie bitte mit!*
> *Mit achtzig Jahren hat er seine aufregende Lebensgeschichte niedergeschrieben.*
> *Nachdem der Schriftsteller lange über den Satz nachgedacht hatte, schrieb er ihn nieder.*

Works Used and Consulted

Brockhaus-Wahrig. Deutsches Wörterbuch in Sechs Bänden, ed. G. Wahrig (Wiesbaden, 1980–4).
Collins Cobuild English Language Dictionary, ed. J. M. Sinclair *et al.* (London and Glasgow, 1987).
Collins German–English English–German Dictionary, ed. P. Terrell *et al.*, 1st edn. (Glasgow, 1980); 2nd edn. (Glasgow, 1991).
Deutsches Wörterbuch, ed. G. Wahrig (Gütersloh, 1965).
Deutsches Wörterbuch, ed. H. Paul, rev. W. Betz (Tübingen, 1966).
Duden: Das große Wörterbuch der deutschen Sprache (6 vols.; Mannheim, 1976–81).
Harrap's Standard German and English Dictionary, ed. T. Jones (London, 1963–).
Langenscheidts Enzyklopädisches Wörterbuch der englishen und deutschen Sprach, ed. O. Springer *et al.*, 3rd edn. (Berlin, 1969).
Langenscheidts Großwörterbuch: Deutsch als Fremdsprache, ed. D. Götz, G. Haentsch, and H. Wellmann (Berlin, 1993).
Langenscheidts Handwörterbuch Englisch–Deutsch Deutsch–Englisch, ed. H. Messinger (Berlin, 1988).
Oxford Advanced Learner's Dictionary of Current English, ed. A. S. Hornby (Oxford, 1980).
The Oxford–Duden German–English Pictorial Dictionary, ed. J. Phelby *et al.* (Oxford, 1980).
The Oxford English Dictionary: A New English Dictionary on Historical Principles, ed. J. Murray *et al.*, 1st edn. (Oxford, 1884–1928).
A Supplement to the Oxford English Dictionary, ed. R. W. Burchfield (Oxford, 1972–86).
The Oxford English Dictionary, ed. J. A. Simpson and E. S. C. Weiner, 2nd edn. (Oxford, 1989).
Webster's Third New International Dictionary, ed. P. B. Gore *et al.* (Springfield, Mass., 1961).
Webster's New Dictionary of Synonyms (Springfield, Mass., 1978).
Wörterbuch der deutschen Gegenwartssprache, ed. R. Klappenbach and W. Steinitz (Berlin/GDR, 1964–77).

ASBACH-SCHNITKER, B. (1979), 'Die adversativen Konnektoren *aber, sondern* und *but* nach negierten Sätzen'. In: H. Weydt (ed.): *Die Partikeln der deutschen Sprache* (Berlin), 457–67.
BASTERT, U. (1985), *Modalpartikel und Lexikographie: Eine exemplarische Studie zur Darstellbarkeit von DOCH in einsprachigen Wörterbüchern* (Tübingen).
BENWARE, W. A. (1986), 'The Acquisition of Verb Synonyms and a Difficult Case', *Unterrichtspraxis*, 19: 185–92.
—— (1989), 'German Synonyms: A Bibliography of Works Explaining their Usage'. *Unterrichtspraxis*, 22: 69–81.
BUSCHA, A., and BUSCHA, J. (1981), *Deutsches Übungsbuch* (Leipzig).
COX, J. E. (1970a), '*Sehr* oder *sehr viel*', *Unterrichtspraxis*, 3: 82–6.
—— (1970b), '*Aber* oder *sondern*', *Unterrichtspraxis*, 3: 86–8.
DUDEN (1972), *Zweifelsfälle der deutschen Sprache*, 2nd edn., rev. D. Berger (Mannheim). (First edn. under the title *Hauptschwierigkeiten der deutschen Sprache*.)
DURRELL, M. (1992), *Using German: A Guide to Contemporary Usage* (Cambridge).
EGGELING, H. F. (1961a), *Advanced German Prose Composition* (Oxford; 1st edn. 1933).
—— (1961b), *A Dictionary of Modern German Prose Usage* (Oxford).
ERDMANN, P. (1974), 'Die Strukturierung von Synonymen: Zur Übersetzung von dt. *Rand* ins Englische', *Neophilologus*, 58: 305–20.
FARRELL, R. B. (1953), *Dictionary of German Synonyms*, 1st edn. (Cambridge); 2nd edn. with additions (otherwise unchanged), 1971.
FLEISCHER, H., HERZOG, A., and RIEDEL, W. (1979), *Starke und unregelmäßige Verben im Deutschen* (Leipzig).
FRIEDRICH, W. (1966), *Moderne deutsche Idiomatik* (Munich).
—— (1981), *Technik des Übersetzens: Englisch und Deutsch* (Munich).

FRIEDRICH, W., and CANAVAN, J. (1979), *Dictionary of English Words in Context* (Dortmund).

GÖRNER, H. (1979), *Redensarten: Kleine Idiomatik der deutschen Sprache* (Leipzig).

GREBE, P., and MÜLLER, W. (1964), *Vergleichendes Synonymwörterbuch* (Mannheim).

GRIESBACH, H., and SCHULZ, D. (1962), *Grammatik der deutschen Sprache*, 2nd edn. (Munich).

HAMMER, A. E. (1991), *German Grammar and Usage*, 2nd edn. rev. M. Durrell (London).

HAYAKAWA, S. I., and FLETCHER, P. J. (1987), *The Penguin Modern Guide to Synonyms* (London). (First UK edn. Cassell, 1971.)

HELBIG, G. (1988), *Lexikon deutscher Partikeln* (Leipzig).

—— and BUSCHA, J. (1977), *Deutsche Grammatik: Ein Handbuch für den Ausländerunterricht* (Leipzig).

KEMPKE, G. (1984), *Handwörterbuch der deutschen Gegenwartssprache* (Berlin/GDR).

KÖHLER, C., HERZOG, A., and KURSITZA, W. (1976), *Deutsche Verbale Wendungen für Ausländer* (Leipzig).

LEISI, E. (1961), *Der Wortinhalt: Seine Struktur im Deutschen und Englischen* (Heidelberg).

MEHLDAU, R., and WHITLING, R. B. (1972), *Synonymik der englischen Sprache* (Frankfurt am Main).

MIEL, K., and ARNDT, M. (1973), *ABC der starken Verben*, 7th edn. (Munich).

—— —— (1978), *ABC der schwachen Verben*, 3rd edn. (Munich).

PARKES, G., and CORNELL, A. (1991–2), *German–English False Friends* (Southampton: Book 1, 2nd edn., 1992; Book 2, 1991).

RÜDENBERG, W., and PEARL, K. (1955), *4,000 German Idioms—Redensarten—and Colloquialisms and their English Equivalents* (London).

SCHMITZ, W. (1973), *Übungen zu synonymen Verben*, 5th edn. (Munich).

SPALDING, K., and BROOKE, K. (1959–), *An Historical Dictionary of German Figurative Usage* (Oxford).

TAYLOR, R., and GOTTSCHALK, W. (1960), *A German–English Dictionary of Idioms* (Munich).

WEYDT, H., HARDEN, TH., HENTSCHEL, E., and RÖSLER, D. (1983), *Kleine deutsche Partikellehre* (Stuttgart).

WHITE, D. V. (1958), 'Der Gebrauch der Konjunktionen *indem* und *während* in der deutschen Prosa der Gegenwart', *Deutschunterricht für Ausländer*, 8: 1–5.

ZINDLER, H., and BARRY, W. (1984), *Fehler ABC English–German*, 2nd edn. (Stuttgart).

Index of English Terms

All the major English terms discussed in the *Dictionary* are included in the following index. The inclusion of minor words and of idiomatic phrases is selective, and many more of these may be found in the appropriate sections of the text. A similar index of German terms begins on page 858.

Page-numbers not in bold type denote minor references. Where parts of speech have been noted to prevent ambiguity, the following abbreviations have been used: *adj* = *adjective*; *adv*= *adverb*; *conj* = *conjunction*; *n* = *noun*; *prep* = *preposition*; *pron* = *pronoun*.

abandon
  abandon to one's fate **400**
  desert 397
abbreviate 634
ability, power 519
able, well able 792
abolish, cancel 129
about
  about turn 744
  approximately 653
  concerned with 79–80, 175
abridge 633
absent (*adj*) 388–9
absolute, complete 172–3
absorb, absorbed 362
accelerate, speed something up 342
accent [way of speaking]
  broad accent 111–12
  thick accent 713
accept 1–3, 27
  accept as true 176
  admit to an organization 564
  receive 563
  take 694
accepted (*adj*) 3
accident 3–5
  meet with an accident 435
accidental 5
accompany, see 602
accomplish 8–9
accord (*n*), of one's own accord 756
accordance, act in accordance with 300
account (*n*)
  on that account 712
  report 36–8
  take into account 124, 696
accumulate 310, 312
accuse 5–6
  blame 94
accustom 6–7
  accustom [someone] to 6–7
accustomed (*adj*) 7
achieve 8–9
  do 232, 233
achievement 8, 9

acknowledge 3, 558–60
  accept as genuine 560
  acknowledge receipt 560
  admit 176, 560
  appreciate 52
  grant 321–2
  show thanks 560
acknowledged (*adj*) 560
acquit, acquit oneself 292–3
act (*n*) 10–13
  act of violence 767
  catch in the act 140
  in the act 11
act (*v*)
  act contrary to 11
  act on 18–19
  act upon [instructions] 300
  perform, appear 44
  take action 11
action (*n*) 10–13
  action of a play/novel 13
  answer for someone's actions 41
  be in action 13
  be killed in action 379
  bring an action 13
  legal action 13
  man of action 11
  military action 13
  out of action 13
  put/bring into action 11, 13
  ready for action 13
  take action 11, 12
  take action against 11
active, busy 120, 121
activity, bustle 121
actual 554, 555–6
actually 554, 557–8
  [contradictory] 557–8
  in reality 555
adapt, change 151
add 13–16
  add on 14
  add on [building] 16
  add something solid/liquid 15–16
  add something written/spoken 14–15
  add together 13–14

add up 13–14
  add up to [clarify a situation] 14
  add up to [mean] 14
  add up to [reach a large amount] 14
  add . . . to 14
  be added as a further element 15–16
  contribute in addition 14
  increase 16
  make complete by adding 14–15
  mix 16
  reckon 122
addition, in addition 15
adjoin 364, 365
adjourn 515
administer
  apply 47
  control 185
  run 590
admit 176
  acknowledge 560
  allow to enter 178
  grant 321–2
admittedly 176
adulterate 279, 280
advantage
  take advantage of 702, 760
  take full advantage of 760
advertise 16–18
advertisement 16–18
  answer an advertisement 40
  notice 465
advertising (*n*) 17–18
advice, take advice 699
advisable 235
  ought 491–3
  should 491–3
advise
  suggest 677–8
  well-advised 791
affect (*v*) 18–21
  afflict 21
  cause emotional reaction 18, 21
  change 19, 21

cardboard, boxes 105
care (n) 131–6
  attention 131–2, 133–6
  care and protection 133
  caution 132, 133–6
  handle with care 132, 136
  protection 132–3
  supervision 133
  take care [be careful] 133–6
  take care [beware] 134–5
  take care of 103, 132–3
  take care to 603–4
care (v), care for 131
careful 136–7
  attentive 133–4
  be careful 133–4
  cautious 132, 136
  considerate 137
  gentle 137
  meticulous 136
careless, slovenly 138
carry
  bear 82
  carry out [perform] 231,
    294
  take 696–7
carton 105
case (n) [1] [container] 105–6
case (n) [2] [instance]
  in any case 551
  in that case 710
casual 137–9
  casual clothes 139
  casual work 137–8
  chance 137
  inconsequent 137
  informal 138–9
  unconcerned 138–9
casualty, take casualties
  700–1
catch, catch red-handed 140
catch (v) 11, 139–43
  capture 139–40
  capture artistically 143
  catch attention 143
  catch fire 141
  catch hold of 141–2
  catch an illness 142
  catch sight of 142–3
  catch up 493–4
  catch up on work 493
  'catch your death' 142
  caught up [involved] 142
  collect 142
  entangle 141–2
  entrap 140
  get 314
  get an illness 314, 315
  hear 142
  hit 141, 142
  intercept 140–1
  intercept a projectile 142

perceive 142–3
reach in time 140
receive from another 142
seize 141–2
take by surprise 140
category, kind 381–2
cater, cater for 285
cause (n) 143–4
  cause and effect 143
  good cause 144
  make common cause 144
  motive 143–4
  not without good cause
    763
  principle to defend 144
  responsibility 143
cause (v) 144–6
  bring about 144–5
  cause some one to do
    something 145–6
  contribute to 185
  make 421–4
  start 663
caution (n) 131, 132
caution (v) 776, 777–8
cautious 132, 136–7
celebrate, mark 427
censure (v) 92
ceremony 11
  etiquette 631
  stand on ceremony 734
certain 684–5
  be certain of 217
  a certain Herr Bauer 685
  certainly 684, 686
  certainly not 686
  for certain 686
  in certain respects 652
  make certain 684
  reliable 685
  secure 684–5
  some 685
  unspecified 685
certainty, confidence 739
chair, take the chair 701
challenge (v)
  'dare' 206–7
  sentry/police call 125–6
chance (adj), casual 137
chance (n) 5
  by chance 5, 477
change (v) 146–51
  alternate 148
  become different 146–7
  change location 148
  change money 148–9, 150
  change over 150, 151
  change time 150
  change TV channels 19
  exchange 148–9
  have an effect 19
  make different 146–8

replace 148
shake up 626–7
substitute 148–9
transform 149
turn into 744–5
channel, television channel
  19, 608
chap, man 288
character
  literary character 630
  nature 454–5
characteristic 427
characterize, mark 427
charge (n) [1] [accusation],
  answer a charge 41
charge (n) [2] [fee], free of
  charge 762
charge (n) [3] [care]
  be in charge of 488
  supervision 133, 185
charge (v) [1] [accuse] 5
  [legal uses] 6
charge (v) [2] [ask fee] 124
cheat (v) 208, 209
  copy to cheat 189
check (v)
  control 185
  examine 358, 359–60, 417
  try 740
cheek (body-part) 151–2
cheeky 418
cheerful 319, 320
  lively 412
cheerfulness 320
cheque, cancel cheque 130
child
  only child 644
  problem child 735
childhood, sheltered
  childhood 532
chit, paper communication
  463
choice (adj), select 154
choice (n) 152–3
  alternative 153
  by choice 152, 277–8
  have no choice 153
  take your choice 152
  varied collection 153
choke, 'swallow the wrong
  way' 691
choose 153–5
  cannot choose but 154
  decide to do 155
  identify 155
  little to choose between
    154
  so many to choose from
    154
  think fit 155
chop 203
chopstick 514

declare
  assert 155–6
  declare one's love 176
decline (v)
  lessen 568
  refuse 572
  refuse an offer 573–4
decorating, house-painting
  497
decrease
  disappear 225
  reduce 568–70
deduce
  conclude 248
  gather 312
deed 10, 11
deep, heartfelt 241
defeat (n), concede defeat 177
defeat (v), beat 84, 85
defective, low quality 73–4
defend, defend oneself
  against a charge 41
defer 514–15
deficient, be deficient in 388
definitely 685, 686
degree 268–9
  academic qualification
    268–9
  by degrees 268
  a certain degree of 652
  extent 268–9
  intensity 518
  relative extent 268
  to a high degree 763
  to some degree 639
  unit of measurement
    268–9
delay, without delay 349
delete, cancel 129
deliberate (v) 179
delicate 647, 649
  delicate situation 649
  delicately-flavoured 649
  fragile 649
  sensitive 649
  slender 649
  of weak health 649
delicious 649
deliver (v), signed, sealed and
  delivered 598
delude 208
demand (n) 213–14
  desire to buy 214
  in demand 214
  make demands on 213, 214
  need 460
  request 593–4
  requirement 593
  satisfy demand 593–4
demand (v) 63, 65, 212–13
  demand a lot of 213
  require 213

demanding (adj), severe 625
demeanour, appearance 44–5
democracy, grass-roots
  democracy 509
denial (n), issue a denial 215
denote, name 128
denounce 37
dense 712
deny 214–16
  disown 215–16
  there is no denying 214
  withhold 216
depart 396–7
depend 216–18
  be sure 217
  depending on 217
  that depends 218
dependent 216
  dependent/conditional on
    145
deposit (n), safe deposit 376
deposit (v), be deposited 312
depraved 75–6
depress 522
  depressed market 524
  depressed prices 524
  sadden 524
depth, out of one's depth 104
deride 706
describe 218
  characterize 218
  define 128
description
  answer a description 41
  kind 380
desert (v) 397
deserted (adj) 397
designate, name 128
desirable, fitting 492
desire (n), need 461
desire (v)
  burn for 113
  want 773–5
desirous, keen 239–40
despite, despite the fact that
  799
destiny 281–2
destroy 203, 219
detachment, distance 228
detail (n), go into details 253
detain, stop 667
determine 219–21
  ascertain 220–1
  be the cause of 220
  be determined 221, 432
  resolve 221
determined (adj) 800
detonate 403
detour 781
develop
  grow 327–8
  there developed 80

devote
  devote oneself, apply one's
    efforts 48
  give 319
devour
  devour with the senses 692
  swallow whole 691
dexterity 162
dial, misdial 443
die 221–2
  be dying for 221
  die away 222
  die of 221
  die out 221, 222
diet 303
dietetics 302
difference
  make a difference 428, 429
  what difference does it
    make 429
different 222–3
difficult 224–5
difficulty
  only with difficulty 224,
    496
  with great difficulty 496–7
dig, dig up [an old story] 776
digest, digest mentally 804
digit, number 469
direct (v)
  be directed at 30
  command 486–7
  direct a weapon 29
  direct remarks etc. 29–30
  refer 572
direction
  change direction 743–4
  reverse direction 743–4
directly, immediately 348–9
disadvantageous 74–5
disappear 225–6
disapproving (adj), a
  disapproving look 537
disarm 59
disaster 3–5
disastrous, fatal 281
disbelieve 236
discern 560
discharge, discharge one's
  duties 295
discover 226–7
discretion, judgement 366
disgrace (n) 627–8
  blot on the landscape 628
  a disgrace 628
  in disgrace 628
  shame and disgrace 627–8
disgrace (v) 304
disgraceful 629
disguise (v), hide 336
dislike (n), objection 474
disorder, trouble 735

else, something else 651
elude 255
avoid 71-2
embarrass 243-4, 304
embarrassing 243
embarrassment 243
financial embarrassment
243
embroil 360, 361
emit 608, 609
emotion 244-5
emotional 245-6
an emotional issue 246
emotional state 245
emphasize 543
employ
be employed 118
have in one's employment
49
take on an employee 48-51
use 758-60
employee 49
class of employed persons
49
engage an employee 48-9
workforce of an industrial
plant 49
employment
paid work 48-51
established employment 49
work 806
emulate 190, 191
enclose, add to a communication 16
encounter (v), meet 433-5
encourage
persuade 504
support 683-4
end (n)
at the end 392-3
come to an end 695
in the end 391
put an end to 248, 669
end (v) 9, 246-9
endanger, menace 726
endeavour (v), try 739-40
endow 306
endure 82-4
last 391
engage, engage for work 48
engagement
agreement to meet 51
military action 13
of performer 51-2
engross, be engrossed 362
enjoy 249-50
appreciate 52
enjoy oneself 250
enjoy your food 791
have the benefit of 250
enough, enough and to spare
656

enquire 62-3
apply for information 48
enrol 252-3
ensnare 140, 141
ensue 299, 301
ensure, see that 603-4
entail, suggest 680
entangle 360, 361
catch 141-2
enter 250-3
burst into 115
enrol for 252-3
enter a competition 251,
252-3
enter employment 252
enter in writing 252
enter a vehicle 252
enterprise, business 118
enthusiasm, arouse
enthusiasm 776
enthusiastic, keen 239
entice 707-8
entire, complete 171, 172
entrance
appearance on stage 45
way in 780
entrap 140, 141
entrust 735, 736-7
environs 57
equal (v), touch 733
equalize, cancel out 131
equip 533
erode, [figurative uses] 20
err, make a mistake 443
errand, run errands 590
error 442-3
error of thought 443
escape (n), a narrow escape
453
escape (v) 253-5
escape notice 255
escape one's lips 255
leak out 255
slip through fingers 254
especially, very 763
essence, nature 454
essential, necessary 458
establish 305-6
estate, bequeathed property
355
estimate (n) 256
at a rough estimate 256
tradesman's estimate 256
estimate (v) 255-7
estimate incorrectly 443
guess 330
judge size 367
put 541
reckon 123
etiquette, form 631
evade 254
avoid 71-2

evaluate 365, 366
even (adv) 257-8
even as little as 257
even if 258
even though 258
not even 257
still [more] 258
evenly, without disturbance
585
event 258-9
course of events 259, 717
happy event [birth] 259
in the event of 259
eventual 391, 392
eventually 391, 392
ever, if ever 798
every
every single 643
every time 729
every time that 797-8
every (adj) 31, 32
every five minutes 32
every kind of 32
every reason to believe 32
have every confidence 32
everyday (adj), common 168
evict, turn out 746
evidence 259-61
be in evidence 260-1
for lack of evidence 260
indication 203
produce evidence 531
evil (adj) 73, 75-6
evil (n) 75
deliver us from evil 75
exactly, just 367-8
examination [test]
answer examination
questions 40
take an examination 702
examine 358-60
give school examination
359
inspect visually 46
make scientific analysis
358
example
for example 596
take an example 695-6
exceed 261
exceedingly, most 445
excellent 173
exchange (n), rate of
exchange 549
exchange (v)
exchange bought goods
150
exchange rings 148
replace 146, 148-50
excite 261-2
exclaim, call out 126
exclude, ostracize 77-8

immerse, immerse/devote
    oneself 116
immigrate, enter 251
imminent, happening in the
    near future 456
immobilize, spellbind 78
immoral
    loose 418
    wicked 75–6
impact 337
    force 519
impassioned 246
impede 527
imperil, menace 725–6
impersonate 191
implore 64, 202
imply 677, 679–80
import (v) 251
importance, be of importance
    429–30
impose 542
    impose a tax 548
impression [visual/perceptual]
    appearance 44
    give a false impression 46
    give the impression 43–4
    have the wrong impression
        209
    idea 345
improve 349–50
    improve on/upon 349–50
    improve one's knowledge
        350
    raise 350
impulse 756–8
in, way in 780
inattentive, casual 138–9
incensed 35
incentive 756–8
incident (n) 258–9
incidental, casual 137
incidentally, by the way 787
incite 207, 262
    cause 146
incline, be inclined to 773
include 350–2
    apply to 352
    count among 123
    include in a category 352
    include in something else
        351–2
    included in a cost 351
    including 351
    involve 361
    take into account 124
incompetent, painful 496
inconsistent, be inconsistent
    with 471
inconvenience, trouble 733–4
incorrect 73
increase (v) 16, 352–4
    increase in number 353

increase in value 52
increase production 353–4
increase three/fourfold 730
    raise 548
indelicate, broad 111
indicate 677
    make clear 639
    suggest 678–9
indication 637, 638–9
    all the indications are
        638–9
    evidence 260
    give an indication 639
indict 6
indifferent, casual 138–9
indispensability, necessity
    459
individual 643
individually 643
indolent 164, 165
induce 708
    cause to decide 212
    persuade 505
inducement, incentive 757–8
inevitable, necessary 461
inexact, loose 418
infect 142
infer, understand 751
inferior, low quality 73–4
inflict, cause 146
influence (n)
    area of influence 553
    reactionary influences 518
influence (v) 18, 19
inform
    give notice 466
    name 127
    report 37–8
    warn 777
informal, casual 138–9
information
    data 207–8
    seek information 62–6
ingenious, skilful 163
inhabitant 354
inherit 354
inheritance 355
injury 205
inside, inside out 742
insight, knowledge 387
insinuate 677, 680
insist, demand 212
inspect 46, 416
    control 185
instalment 550
instance, for instance 596
instead, rather 278
instinct, drive 756–7
instruct, command 486–7
instruction
    education 242–3
    [written] instructions 760

insult, swallow an insult 692
insure
    amount insured 33
    cover 198
intellect 438
    understanding 751
intelligence
    brain 107
    limited intelligence 406
    understanding 751
intelligent
    bright 772
    clever 160
intend
    mean 431–2
    think of 721
intense, violent 766–7
intensify 673
intent (adj), intent on 239
intention 438
    mean well 432
inter (v) 115–16
intercept, catch 140–1, 142
interest (n) 355–6
    community of interests 170
    have a financial interest in
        356
    take an interest in 300
interest (v) 355
    become interested in 776
interfere 444–5
interpret 356–7
    explain 356
    interpret law 356
    interpret literature 356
    interpret music 357
    interpret parable 356
    interpret a role 357
    translate 357
interpretation, understand-
    ing 752
intersect 199, 200
interval, at intervals of 228
intervene 12
introduce 357–8
introduction 357
invade 251
invalid, cancelled 129
invariable, constant 182
invest, put 541
investigate 358–60
invite 66
involve 360–3
    absorb 362
    affect 361–2
    be involved [active] 362–3
    be a matter of, 80, 362
    entail 361
    include 361
    involve in relationship 362
    involve the reader 362
ire 35

long-lasting **183**
see us through **603**
suffice for a time **390**
lasting (*adj*), permanent **183**
late
dead **221**
lately **565–6**
latest [most recent] **566**
trust them to be late! **735**
Latin 312
laugh
burst out laughing **115**
laugh at **706**
laughter 320
law
annul a law **129**
in the eyes of the law **766**
law and order **584**
promulgate a law **37**
lay (*v*)
lay about oneself [beat] **84**
lay [direct] artillery on **29**
lay down [determine] **220**
lay down [promulgate] a
rule **488**
lay off [dismiss] **661**
put **539**
lead (*n*), be in the lead **393–4**
lead (*v*) **393–4**
induce **708**
lead by the nose **707**
lead to **145**
lead up the garden path
707
lead the way **781**
leaking 713
lean
lean meat **714**
lean years **714**
thin **714**
learn 394–5
discover **226–7**
learn about **227**
learn of **227**
learn a trade **394**
study **674**
least
at least **23, 395–6**
least one can do **395–6**
leave (*n*) **338–9**
annual leave **338**
take one's leave [say
goodbye] **695**
leave (*v*) **396–401**
abandon **397**
abandon to one's fate **400**
be left over **400–1**
entrust **400**
keep unchanged **397–8**
leave alone **398**
leave behind **398–9**
leave for safe keeping **399**

leave home **397**
leave in the lurch **397**
leave off **669**
leave over **400–1**
leave a place **397**
leave school **397**
leave a surplus **400–1**
leave undisturbed **400**
leave undone **399–400**
outpace **399**
stop **400**
lecture (*v*) **553**
left [direction]
left turn **743**
left wheel! **744**
left-hand bend **744**
leftovers 581
leg
pull someone's leg **706–7**
stretch one's legs **661**
legacy 355
lend 401–2
lend a hand **605, 606**
length, at some length **652**
lenient, mild **650**
lessen 568–71
lesson
let that be a lesson to you
704
teach someone a lesson
704
let
allow **421, 423**
let know [inform] **423**
let off steam **657**
letter [epistle], answer a letter
40
letter-box 105
level (*adj*)
draw level with **493, 494**
flat **298**
level (*n*)
noise level **653**
stage [of progress] **666**
levy (*v*), impose a tax **548**
liability, limited liability **580**
liable 579–80
liberty
take liberties **700**
take the liberty of **322, 700**
lie (*n*)
falsehood **402**
tell a lie **402**
lie (*v*) [1] [be at rest]
be located **79**
consist in **79**
here lies **583**
lie (*v*) [2] [speak falsehood]
209, 402
life
lead a life **411**
meaning of life **610**

power of life and death **517**
put new life into **543**
lift (*v*) **547**
lift up one's voice [to speak]
548
remove [a ban] **129**
light (*n*)
bring to light **226, 636–7**
light-sensitive **611**
throw light on **403**
light (*v*) **403**
catch fire **403**
ignite **403**
illuminate **403**
light the way **403**
lighting, soft lighting **648**
lightly, casually **137**
lightning, lightning strikes
337
like (*prep*), look like **417**
like (*v*) **404–5**
appreciate **52**
be keen on **240**
not like the sound of it **654**
should/would like **404, 405,
773–4**
likely
more likely **278**
ought/should **491**
liking, take a liking **701**
limit (*n*)
meet a time-limit **728**
set a time-limit to **728**
speed limit **550**
limit (*v*) **406**
limited **406**
limited liability **580**
line 406–7
draw a line **536**
write a few lines **407**
link (*v*) **364**
lion, lion's share **631**
listen 407–9
listen! **409**
listen closely **408**
literal 410
literal-minded **410**
word for word **410**
literally 410
take literally **410**
little, a little **651**
live (*v*) **410–11**
be alive **411**
dwell **410–11**
lead a life **411**
live for **411**
live it up **779**
'live to see . . . ' **265**
make a living **411**
lively 411–12
wide-awake **772**
liver, liver trouble **735**

turn to page . . . 743
turn to [try an activity] 746
turn to [turn one's
  attention to] 746
turn towards 743
turn up [be found] 296
turn up [sleeves etc.] 743
turn upside down 742
turn . . . on [direct] 746
wind turns 744
turnover, financial movement
  746
twice 729
  twice as long 730
twig 514
two, two at a time 729
twofold 730
type (n)
  exemplar 382
  kind 380, 381–2
typify, mark 427

ultimate, final 392
unacceptable, low quality
  73–4
unadorned, simple 641–2
unaffected, simple 642
unanimous 25
unassuming, simple 642
unavoidable, necessary 461
unbutton, undo 754
unchanging, constant 182
uncomplicated, simple 641–2
unconfined, loose 418–19
uncontrolled, violent 767
unconventional 187–8
  casual 138–9
  unusual 188
uncover 197
under
  go under 645
  under way 787
undergo 266
underline 426
underside 103–4
understand 748–51
  accept an explanation 749
  appreciate 53
  get on well together 750
  give one to understand 751
  have some expertise in 750
  he understands quickly 748
  hear clearly 749
  I understand that . . . 751
  infer 751
  interpret as 356
  interpret meaning 750
  is that understood 749
  know one's trade 750
  know a reason or cause 749
  make oneself understood
    751

realize 558–60
regard as previously
  established 751
see 601
show sympathy 750
take for granted 751
take something in 750
understand from [some-
  one's words] 750
understand a language 749
understand a person's
  behaviour 749
understanding (n) 751–3
  agreement 753
  come to an understanding
    25–7
  comprehension 752
  condition 753
  harmony 752–3
  have an understanding
    of/appreciate 53
  intellect 751
  interpretation 752
  judgement 751–2
  knowledge 752
  mind 438
  on the understanding that
    753
  pass one's understanding
    752
  sympathetic relationship
    752–3
undertaking (n), business 118
undertone 463
undesirable 73
undiminished 569
undo 754
  be undone 754
  come undone 754
  destroy 754
  get open 754
  get undone 754
uneasy, anxious 730
unfaithful, be unfaithful 209
unfamiliar 671
unfasten, undo 754
unfavourable 74–5
unfounded 104
unharmed, safe 592
unify 754–6
unimaginative, literal-minded
  410
uninterested, casual 138–9
unite 754–6
  consolidate 181
  United Nations 755
  United States of America
    755
united, common 166
unknown, strange 670–1
unlace, undo 754
unlike 222–3

unlimited 406
unmarried 644
unmitigated, complete 173
unmoved 245
  unmoved emotionally 733
unnecessary 457, 458
unpick, undo stitching 754
unpleasant 73, 74–5
  stupid 304
unravel, undo knitting 754
unrefined, common 168
unreliable, casual 138–9
unreserved, unrestricted 406
unrest, trouble 735
unrestrained
  loose 418–19
  violent 767
unrestricted 406
unsuitable, out of place 507
unterbrechen, stop 670
untie, undo 754
until, not until 298, 479,
  480
untouched 733
unusual
  strange 671
  unconventional 188
unwell
  bad 77
  feeling unwell 671
unwilling 799, 800
unwillingly 800
unyielding, persistent 503
unzip, undo 754
up
  get up to [do] 233
  right way up 782
  time is up 728
  use up 761
uphill, go uphill 164
uphold 374
uplift (v), edify 548
upper, 'upper school' 666
upset (adj), distressed 262
upset (v)
  bother 100–2
  excite unfavourably 262
upside
  turn everything upside
    down 742
  turn upside down 742
upstairs, go upstairs 163
urge (n) 756–8
urge (v) 207, 522, 523–4
  suggest 677–8
urgent 343
use (n)
  find a use for 758–9
  make full use of 760
  make use of 758–60
  make use of [apply] 47
  put to use 542, 758–9

Index of German Terms

All the major German terms discussed in the *Dictionary* are included in the following index. The inclusion of minor words and of idiomatic phrases is selective, and many more of these may be found in the appropriate sections of the text. A similar index of English terms begins on page 811.

Page-numbers *not* in bold type denote minor references. Where parts of speech have been noted to prevent ambiguity, the following abbreviations have been used: *adj = adjective*; *adv= adverb*; *conj = conjunction*; *n = noun*; *prep = preposition*; *pron = pronoun*.

anstecken
  infect 142
  light 403
  sich anstecken 142
ansteigen
  climb 164
  increase 352
  rise 352
  slope upwards 353
anstellen
  do/get up to 233
  employ someone for a
    specific purpose 49
  engage for employment
    48-9
  start 662
  turn on 745
Anstellung, job 512
anstiften
  cause 146
  incite 146
Anstoß
  Anstoß nehmen 696
  den Anstoß geben 758
  impetus 758
  impulse 757
anstreben, strive for 30
anstreichen
  mark 426
  paint 497
Anstreicher, house-painter
  497
anstrengen
  legal action 13
  sich anstrengen 739
anstrengend
  busy 121
  violent 767
Anteil
  commercial interest 356
  part 632
  proportion 576
  share 631-2
  share in a business 632
Antrag, den Antrag stellen
  451
antreffen, meet 434
antreiben, zur Eile antreiben
  342
antreten
  enter [employment] 252
  take 701
Antrieb
  impetus 756
  impulse 757
antun, do to 234
antworten
  answer 39-40
  answer an advertisement
    40
anvertrauen
  confide 737

entrust 736-7
anvisieren, aim for 29, 30
anwachsen, increase 327, 352
anwärmen, warm slightly
  776
anweisen, command 486
anwenden, apply 47
Anzahl
  a few 470
  a number of 470
  series 489
  total counted 469-70
Anzeichen
  alle Anzeichen sprechen
    dafür 639
  indication 638
  keinerlei Anzeichen 638
  symptom 638
Anzeige
  advertisement 16-17
  notice 17, 465
anzeigen
  advertise 16-17
  denounce 37
  notify police 37
  record 568
  represent 635
Anzeigenabteilung,
  advertisement section 17
Anzeigenteil, advertisement
  section 16-17
anziehen
  angezogen sein 237
  attract 70
  dress 237
  put on 237
  sich anziehen 70, 237
anziehend, attractive 70
Anzugsjacke, suit jacket 164
anzünden, light 403
anzweifeln, doubt 236
Appel
  appeal 41-2
  einem Appel folgen 41
appellieren (v), call on 126
Arbeit
  business 118
  an die Arbeit! 121
  student's essay 807
  viel Arbeit machen 120
  work 806-7
arbeiten
  be in operation 805
  function 805
  sich arbeiten 804
  work 803
Arbeitgeber, class of
  employers 49
Arbeitnehmer, employed
  person 49
Arbeitskamerad, workmate
  289

Arbeitskampf, labour
  troubles 735
Arbeitsklima, working
  atmosphere 665
Arbeitskollege, workmate
  289
Arbeitskraft, neue
  Arbeitskräfte einstellen 661
Arbeitsplatz
  job 511-12
  workplace 511
arbeitsreich, busy 121
arg
  bad 76
  severely 77
Ärger
  mach' keinen rger 734
  sich rger einhandeln 734
  trouble 734
Ärgerlich
  annoyed 34
  ein ärgerliches Gesicht 34
Ärgern
  annoy 34
  sich ärgern 34
Argwohn, suspicion 690
argwöhnen, suspect 690
Arm, auf den Arm nehmen
  707
arrangieren
  arrange 61
  sich arrangieren 622
Art
  aller/jeder Art 32
  auf eine wilde Art 785
  die Art und Weise 784, 785
  form 630
  kind 380-1, 382
  nature 454, 455
  nun einmal seine Art 783
  way 783, 784-6
Arztpraxis, medical practice
  520
aßen, die Innenseite nach
  außen wenden 742
association, community
  168-70
Ast, trockener Ast 514
Atembeschwerde, breathing
  trouble 735
attackieren, attack 66
auch
  as well 794
  auch nicht 257
  auch noch 794
  auch nur 257
  auch wenn 258
  dann auch 685
  even 257
  ja auch 711
  sure enough 685
  wann auch immer 798

aufschlagen
add on a cost 14
hit the ground 337
open a book 482
turn to page . . . 743
aufschneiden, boast 99
aufschreiben
make a note 462-3, 807
sich aufschreiben 462-3
take down in writing 702
write down 540, 807-8
Aufschub, extension of time 729
aufschütteln, shake 625
aufsein, open 481
aufsetzen, put on 237
Aufsicht, supervision 133
aufsitzen, be duped 210
aufsparen
keep 376
leave 400
save up 595
aufstauen, sich aufstauen 312
aufstoßen, push open 538
aufsuchen, visit 127
auftanken, take on fuel 294
aufteilen, share out 230
Auftrag
Aufträge, business check 119
in Auftrag geben 488
order 488
auftragen
serve a meal 617
spread on a surface 47
auftreiben, get 316
auftrennen, undo 754
auftreten
appear in play/film 44
appearance 45
enter 253
occur 475-6
Auftrieb, stimulus 756
Auftritt
appearance in play/film 45
entrance (in play/film) 45
auftun, open 481
aufwachen, wake up 772
aufwachsen, grow up 326-7
Aufwand
Aufwand treiben 195
expenditure 194-5
aufwärmen
dig up [an old story] 776
rehash 776
reheat 775, 776
sich aufwärmen 775, 776
warm . . . up 775
aufwarten
bei Tisch aufwarten 771
have on offer 771

aufwecken
augeweckt 772
wake up 771-2
aufweisen
display 637
etwas aufzuweisen haben 637
aufwenden
expend 194, 657
spend 656
aufwendig, expensive 192
Aufwendung, expenditure 194-5
aufwerfen, eine Frage aufwerfen 548
aufwiegeln, incite 262
aufzeichen, record [by instrumentation] 568
aufzeichnen
record 566, 567
record electronically 567
aufziehen
bring up 241
tease 705-6
undo 754
Auge, vor den Augen 765
Augenblick
Augenblick mal 368
einen Augenblick aufhören 669
im Augenblick 368
Augenlicht
das Augenlicht nehmen 97
das Augenlicht verlieren 97
Augenschein
appearance 46
dem Augenschein nach 46
in Augenschein nehmen 46
sich vom Augenschein überzeugen 46
Augenwinkel, corner of one's eye 191
aus, von mir aus 175
ausbeuten
eine Grube ausbeuten 804
eine Mine ausbeuten 804
ausbilden, train 243
Ausbildung, training 243
ausbitten, sich ausbitten 63
ausbleiben, fail 274
Ausblick, view 764
ausbrechen
ausbrechen aus 110
burst into expression of emotion 115
escape 253
ausbreiten
describe 660
expand 658
sich ausbreiten 658, 659, 660, 661
spread out 658

ausbrennen, burn out 113-14
ausdehnen
expand 658, 659
extend 659
extend in time 659
sich ausdehnen 659
Ausdehnung, extent 269
ausdenken, sich ausdenken 720
Ausdruck, zum Ausdruck bringen 267
ausdrücken
express 266-7, 745
put 540
sich ausdrücken 267, 268
auseinanderziehen, stretch 661
ausfallen
ausfallen lassen 130
be cancelled 130-1
fail 274
stop 668-9
Ausfertigung
in dreifacher Ausfertigung 730
in vierfacher Ausfertigung 730
ausfindig, ausfindig machen 226
Ausflucht
Ausflüchte 264
excuse 264
ausforschen, acquire information 65
ausfragen, question 65
ausführen
attend to a matter 68
carry out 9
take out 697
ausfüllen
bring fulfilment 294-5
fill a position 295
fill the mind 294
fill time 294
fill up 293
fill up a form 294
Ausgabe, expenditure 194
Ausgang
time off 339
way out 780
zum Ausgang bringen 635
ausgeben
pass off 525
sich ausgeben 525
spend 656
ausgehen
end 246-7
go out [fire/light] 271
stop 668-9
ausgelassen, boisterous 320
ausgemacht, complete 173
ausgesprochen, very 763

ausgewachsen, fully grown
327
ausgewählt (adj), selected 154
ausgewogen, balanced 790
ausgfallen, unconventional
188
ausgleiten
 miss one's footing 440
 slip [and fall] 647
aushalten
 endure 83
 persevere 84
aushandeln, negotiate 462
aushändigen, give 317
Aushang, notice 465
auskennen, sich auskennen
386, 781
ausknipsen, turn off 745
auskommen
 auskommen mit 390
 get by/make do 235, 390
 gut mit jemandem
  auskommen 28–9
auslachen, tease 706
Auslagen, expenses 194
auslassen, miss 442
auslegen, interpret 356
ausleihen, lend/borrow 401–2
auslernen, finish learning
394
Auslese
 choice 153
 natürliche Auslese 153
auslesen, select 155
ausleuchten, light up 403
auslöschen, extinguish
 completely 270
auslösen
 move 450
 start 663
ausmachen
 arrange 27, 60–1
 extinguish 270
 matter 428–9
 nichts ausmachen 101, 722
 settle 621–2
 turn off 745
ausmalen
 colour with paint 498
 sich ausmalen 348
Ausmaß, extent 269–70
ausnutzen/ausnützen
 exploit 760
 Gutmütigkeit ausnutzen
  702
 make full use of 760
 take advantage of 760
 take full advantage of 760
ausprobieren, try out 740
ausrechnen, work out 122–3,
124
Ausrede, excuse 264

ausreichen, last 390
ausrichten
 achieve 8–9, 234
 ausrichten lassen 608
 give a message 608
ausrollen, roll out 587
ausrotten, exterminate 219
ausrufen
 announce 126
 exclaim 126
 proclaim 126
ausruhen, sich ausruhen
582, 583
ausrüsten
 arm 59
 equip 533
ausrutschen, slip [and fall] 647
Aussage, evidence 259
aussagen
 give evidence 259
 work of art says 598
 written communication
  says 598
ausschalten, turn off 745
Ausschau, Ausschau halten
417
ausschicken, send out 608
ausschimpfen, scold 95
Ausschlag, den Ausschlag
 geben 621
ausschlagen, decline 573
ausschreiben, advertise 17
Ausschuß, reject 575
ausschütteln, shake out 625
ausschweigen, sich auss-
 chweigen 640
Aussehen
 appearance 44, 45
 aussehen nach 417
 es sieht so aus 417
 look [appear] 417
 seem 44, 45
außen, die Innenseite nach
 außen kehren 742
aussenden
 emit 609
 send out 608
außer
 außer Betrieb sein 805
 außer Kraft 518
 äußerst 445
außerdem, then 711
Äußere, appearance 44, 45
Äußeres, appearance 44
äußern
 express 268
 sich äußern 268
äußerst
 most 445
 very 763
aussetzen
 criticize 95

fail 274
 sich aussetzen, to risk 206
 stop 668–9
Aussicht, view 764
ausspannen, rest 582–3
Aussprache, breite
 Aussprache 111
aussprechen
 ausgesprochen 763
 express 267–8
 sich aussprechen 267–8,
  684
ausstatten
 equip 59, 533
 furnish 533
 produce 533
ausstehen, endure 83–4
aussteigen, get out of 316–17
ausstellen, display 637
aussterben, die out 221, 222
ausstrahlen
 broadcast [electronically]
  608–9
 floodlight 403
 radiate 608–9
ausstreichen, cross out 200
ausströmen, escape 255
aussuchen, choose 154
austauschen, exchange 150
austeilen, distribute 230–1
austilgen, exterminate 219
austoben
 sich austoben 657
 spend 657
ausüben
 carry on business 117–18
 carry on profession 520
 Macht ausüben 520
 Recht ausüben 520
auswachsen
 develop 328
 grow up 327
Auswahl
 choice 152
 range 552
 zur Auswahl 152, 154
auswählen, choose 153–4
auswalzen, roll flat 587
auswechseln, change 149
Ausweg, way of escape 780
ausweglos, ausweglose Lage
460
ausweichen, avoid 71–2
ausweisen, deport 487
ausweiten
 expand 659
 sich ausweiten 659
auswiegen
 ausgewogen 790
 weigh 789–90
auswirken, sich auswirken
18–19

auszahlen, pay 500
auszeichnen
  mark 426
  mark with price 426
ausziehen
  leave home 397
  move out 450

Babykost, baby food 303
Backe, cheek 151–2
Bademantel, dressing-gown
  164
Bafögsatz, student grant 549
Bahn, Bahn frei 158, 781
bahnen, sich einen Weg
  bahnen 538
balgen, sich balgen 292
Bandbreite, range 552–3
bändigen, sich bändigen 187
bange
  anxious 731
  mir ist bange 731
  scared 731
bangen
  be scared 731
  be worried 731
Banknote, banknote 464
bankrott, bankrupt 110
Bann
  exclusion 77–8
  in Acht und Bann 77
  spell 78
bannen
  exclude 77–8
  fix 78
  spellbind 78
Bär, einen Bären aufbinden
  707
Basisdemokratie 509
  grass-roots democracy 509
Bauer
  farmer 280
  peasant 280
bäuerlich, bäuerlicher Betrieb
  280
Bauernhof
  einen Bauernhof
    bewirtschaften 804
  farm 280
beabsichtigen, aim 30
beachten
  mark 427
  take note 464
  take notice 466
beachtenswert, noteworthy
  464
Beachtung, keiner Beachtung
  wert 466
beängstigen, cause to fear
  307–8
beanspruchen
  claim 156, 213

demand 214
beanstanden
  complain 472
  object 472
beantragen
  apply formally 48
  propose a motion 451
  submit for approval 48
beantworten
  answer 39, 40
  react to 42
bearbeiten
  arrange music 62
  revise 804
  work 804
  work on someone 804
beaufsichtigen, control 185
beauftragen, refer 572
bebauen, till 804
beben
  quake 626
  vor Lachen beben 626
Becken, swimming-pool 508
bedacht, keen 239–40
bedanken, sich bedanken
  708, 709
bedarf
  es bedarf 459
  demand 214, 460, 461
  need 460–1
bedauern, ich bedaure 283
bedecken, cover 196–7
bedenken
  consider 179, 180
  settle 622
  wenn ich bedenke 722
bedeuten
  add up to 14
  imply 679–80
  matter a lot 430, 432
  mean 430–1, 432
bedienen
  deal with customers 68
  operate [machine] 760
  serve a client 617
  sich bedienen 759
  wait on 771
Bedienung, serving of clients
  618, 619
Bedienungsanleitung,
  instructions 760
bedingen, cause 145
Bedingung
  Bedingungen 665
  condition 145, 664
  unter der Bedingung 753
  unter der Bedingung, daß
    664
bedrängen, eine bedrängte
  Lage 460
Bedrängnis, affliction 460
bedrohen

menace 725–6
  threaten 725, 726
bedrücken, depress 524
bedürfen
  be needful 459
  es bedarf 459
Bedürfnis
  Bedürfnisse 461
  desire 461
  need 461
bedürftig
  in need of . . . 459
  needy 459
beeiden, take the oath 201–2
beeidigen, take the oath
  201–2
beeilen, sich beeilen 342
beeinflussen, influence 19
beeinträchtigen
  harm 205
  have a bad effect 19
beenden, end 247, 248
beendigen, end 247
beerben, become an heir 354
beerdigen, bury 115–16
Beerdigung, burial 116
befahren, stark befahren 121
Befall, attack 67
befallen, attack 20, 67
befangen
  catch 142
  self-conscious 607
befassen, sich befassen 175,
  180
Befehl
  command 129
  versiegelter Befehl 599
befehlen, command 486–7
befehligen, be in command
  488
befestigen, consolidate 181
befinden
  adjudge 296
  sich befinden 79, 295
befolgen, follow 300
befördern
  promote 50, 548
  take 697
befragen
  das Volk befragen 64
  question 64–5
befreien, sich befreien 254–5
befremden, impress as
  strange 671
befreundet, friendly 383
befriedigen
  satisfy 593
  sich befriedigen 593
Befriedigung, satisfaction
  594
befristen, set a time-limit to
  728

Bewegung
  emotion 244
  exercise 447
  in Bewegung setzen 447
  keine Bewegung 447
  movement/motion 447
  sich Bewegung machen 447
Beweis
  Beweise erbringen 531
  die Beweise 260
  evidence 259–60
  mangels Beweis/Beweises
    260
beweisen
  evince personal quality
    636–7
  show 635
Beweiskraft, power 518
Beweismaterial, evidence 260
Beweisstück, piece of
  evidence 260
bewerben, sich bewerben 48
bewerten
  judge 366
  mark schoolwork 427
bewilligen, grant [a request]
  323
bewirken, cause 144–5
bewirten, feed 285
bewirtschaften
  einen Bauernhof
    bewirtschaften 804
  run 590
Bewohner, dweller/inhabitant
  354
bewußt
  sich . . . bewußt werden
    772
  wohl bewußt sein 792
bezahlen
  pay 499–500
  pay the penalty 501
  settle 622
Bezahlung, pay 549–50
bezähmen, sich bezähmen
  187
bezeichnen
  bezeichnend 427
  call [characterize] 128
  describe 218
  mark 426
  refer 571–2
  sign 426
Bezeichnung, reference 571–2
bezeigen, display 637
bezeugen
  bear witness 260
  show 637
Bezichtigen, accuse 6
beziehen
  refer 47
  sich beziehen 571

Beziehung
  connection 577–8
  eine Beziehung haben zu
    53
  relationship 576–7
  romantic friendship 577
Bezirk
  administrative area 56
Bezug
  Bezug nehmen 571
  reference 571
bezüglich, bezüglich [. . .]
  ansprechen 55
bezwecken, aim at 431
bezweifeln, doubt 236
bezwingen, climb 163
biegen
  bend 90, 744, 991
  sich biegen 90
  sich biegen lassen 90
  sich vor Lachen biegen 90
  turn 744
bieten
  bid at auction 479
  offer 477–8, 479
  provide 534
  sich bieten 478
  sich bieten lassen 479
Bild, mental image 345
bilden
  educate 242
  gebildet 791
Bildung, education 242
Bildungsniveau, level of
  education 242
Bildungswesen, educational
  system 242, 243
billig
  cheap/unworthy 264
  reasonable 562
billigen
  approve officially 323
  have a favourable opinion
    323–4
Billion, million million 437
bis
  bis auf weiteres 466
  bis da 711
  bis dahin 710
  by the time 729
bißchen, ein bißchen 277
bitten
  ask 62–3
  bitten lassen 602
  hereinzukommen bitten 66
  invite 66
  object 471
  protest 471
  trouble 103
blamieren
  disgrace 304
  embarrass 304

  sich blamieren 304
blank, broke 110
blaß, keine blaße Ahnung
  346
Blatt, das Blatt kann wenden
  746, 747
blechen, pay up 501
bleiben
  become of 316
  bleib' wohlauf 792
  bleiben bei 156
  continue 185
  keep 375
  sich gleich bleiben 430
  stop 670
bleibend, lasting 183
bleibenlassen, leave 400
bleibten, es bleibt
  abzuwarten 770
blenden, dazzle 96–7
blendend, dazzling 97
Blick
  auf den ersten Blick 765
  Blicke ziehen 71
  böser Blick 33–4
  look 765
  view 764
Blickfeld, field of vision 765
blind
  blind 96–7
  heedless 96
blindlings, blindly 96
blockieren, block 98–9
blöd
  foolish 303, 304
  thick 713
blödsinnig, stupid 304
bloß
  just 369
  now then 469
  possibly 513
  very 764
  wann . . . bloß 798
Blut, böses Blut 34
Blutlache, pool of blood 508
Bluttat, bloody deed 10
Boden
  an Boden gewinnen 325
  bottom 103–4
  ground 325
  Grund und Boden 326
  land 325
  property 326
  soil 325–6
bodenlos, bottomless 104
Bodenstreitkräfte, ground
  forces 325
Bogen
  arc 744
  bow 744
  einen Bogen machen 744
Bord, Mann über Bord 425

empfindsam, sensitive 612
Empfindung, feeling 244–5
empfühlsam, sensitive 612
emsig, busy 120
Ende
  am Ende 392–3
  bottom of street/garden
    104
  ein Ende nehmen 695
  end 246
  Ende bereiten 248
  Ende machen 248
  Ende setzen 248
  final 392
  zu Ende 246, 248
  zu Ende sein 246, 247
enden, end 246–7
endgültig, final 392
endigen, finish 246
endlich
  finally 391–2
  finite 392
Endsumme, final total 33
energy, strength 517
eng
  close 456
  engere Wahl 152
  narrow 452
  tight 452
Engagement, engagement of
  performer 51–2
engagieren, sich engagieren
  362
engstirnig, narrow-minded
  452
entbehren
  go without 389
  spare 655–6
entdecken, discover 226
entfahren, escape 254, 255
entfallen, escape 255
entfalten
  realize 561
  reveal 637
entfernt
  distant 229
  weit entfernt 111
Entfernung
  distance 227–8
  in einiger Entferning 652
  range 552
entfliegen, escape 254
entfliehen, escape 254
entgegenfahren, meet 434
entgegengehen, meet 434
entgegengesetzt, opposite
  486
entgegenkommen
  meet 434
  meet wishes 435
entgegennehmen
  receive 1, 563

  receive a command 565
entgegentreten, oppose
  484–5
entgegnen, answer in
  opposed mode 40–1
entgehen
  be missed 442
  entgehen lassen 441
  escape 255
  evade 254
enthalten
  enthalten sein 350–1
  include 350–1
  involve 361
entkommen
  escape 253, 255
  evade 254
entkräften, weaken 788–9
entlang
  da entlang 782
  hier entlang 782
entlaufen, escape 254
entlegen, out of the way
  787–8
entlehnen, borrow 402
entleihen, borrow 401, 402
entlohnen, pay 500–1
Entlohnung, pay 549–50
entnehmen
  deduce 312
  see [from a letter] 603
  take from a book 695
  understand 751
entreißen, seize 606
entrichten, pay 500–1
entrinnen, escape 254
entscheiden
  decide 211, 212
  determine 219–20
  judge 366
  settle 621
  sich entscheiden 211, 212
Entscheidung, aus freier
  Entscheidung 152
entschließen
  entschlossen sein 221
  kurz entschlossen 210
  sich entschließen 210, 211,
    221
  sich entschließen zu 787
entschlüpfen, escape 254
entschuldigen
  entschuldigen Sie 263
  excuse 263
  sich entschuldigen 263
Entschuldigung
  apology 263–4
  Entschuldigung! 263
  pardon 263
  sorry! 263
entschwinden, fade from
  sight 225

entsenden, send 608
entsinnen, sich entsinnen
  578
entspannen, sich entspannen
  583
entsprechen
  der Beschreibung
    entsprechen 41
  meet 434–5
entspringen, escape 253
entstehen
  be produced 530
  develop 327
enttäuschen, disappoint 208
entwaffnen, disarm 59
entweichen, escape 254, 255
entwenden, steal 694
entwischen, escape 253
entziehen
  sich entziehen 254
  withdraw 129
entzünden
  light 403
  sich entzünden 403
entzweischneiden, cut in two
  202
erachten
  judge 367
  deines Erachtens 766
  meines Erachtens 483
Erbe [1] [heir] 50
Erbe [2] [inheritance] 355
erben
  geerbt 354
  inherit 354
erbeuten, seize as booty 606
erbieten, sich erbieten 479
erbitten, request 63
erblicken, catch sight of
  142–3, 766
erblinden, go blind 97
erbringen
  Beweise erbringen 531
  produce 531
  provide 534
  yield 534
Erbschaft, inheritance 355
Erbteil, share of inheritance
  355
Erdboden, ground 325
Erde
  Earth [planet] 325
  ground 325
  land 325
  soil 325
Erdreich, soil 325–6
erdrosseln, kill 379
erdulden, bear 676–7
ereignen, sich ereignen 475
Ereignis
  event 258–9
  thing 717

ererben
  ererbt 354
  inherit 354
erfahren
  discover 227, 266
  experience 265–6
Erfahrung, experience 264
erfassen
  collide 337
  den Sinn erfassen 610
  run into [hit] 337
  seize 607
  understand 748
Erfolg
  Erfolg haben 675
  Erfolg haben mit 805
  keinen Erfolg haben 276
  success 675
erfolgen, ensue 301
erfolgreich, successful 674–5
erforderlich, requisite 458
erfordern
  involve 361
  require 213
  take 698
erforschen
  explore 360
  research 360
erfreuen
  please 319
  sich erfreuen 250
erfrieren
  be frostbitten 307
  freeze to death 307
erfüllen
  answer a need 41
  fill 294
  fill [the mind] 294
  fulfil 294
  grant wish 323
  meet 434–5
  satisfy 593–4
  sich erfüllen 294
Erfüllung
  fulfilment 295
  in Erfüllung gehen 294
ergänzen, complete 15
ergeben
  add up to 14
  sich ergeben 68, 301, 680
  yield 301
Ergebnis, Ergebnisse bringen
  531
ergreifen
  affect emotionally 451
  Gelegenheit ergreifen 605
  Partei ergreifen 702
  seize 605–6, 607
  take [an action] 12
Ergriffenheit, emotion 244
ergründen, get to the bottom
  of 104

erhalten
  Gott erhalte die Königin 596
  keep 372, 377
  receive 563, 564
  save 596
  sich erhalten 377
erhängen
  execute by hanging 334
  sich erhängen 334
erhärten, support 683
erheben
  den Geist erheben 548
  die Stimme heben 548
  Einspruch erheben 471,
    473–4
  levy a tax 548
  raise 548
  raise an objection 548
  raise to higher status 548
  Widerspruch erheben 471,
    473
erheiternd, amusing 309
erheucheln, erheuchelt 525
erhitzen
  apply heat 47
  heat 335
  sich erhitzen 335
erhöhen
  improve 350
  increase 548
  raise 353
  sich erhöhen 352–3
erholen, sich erholen 317,
  583
erinnern, sich erinnern 578
Erinnerung
  in Erinnerung haben 579
  memento 437
  memory 436, 437
Erinnerungsstück, memento
  437
Erinnerungsvermögen,
  memory 435–6
erkennen
  appreciate 53
  discern 560
  einen Sinn erkennen 610
  erkennen lassen 639
  know 386
  realize 558–9
  recognize 559–60
  wieder erkennen 559
erkenntlich, grateful 560
Erkenntnis, knowledge 387
erklären
  sich bereit erklären zu 27
  sich einverstanden erklären
    27
erkranken, be taken ill 701
erlauben
  allow 322, 423
  sich erlauben 322

Erlaubnis
  Erlaubnis entziehen 129
  permission 573
erleben
  experience 265–6
  'live to see . . . ' 265
  see 602
  experience 265
Erlebnis, experience 264–5
erledigen
  attend to 68
  settle 621
erleiden
  Schiffbruch erleiden 676
  suffer 676
erlernen, learn 394
erleuchten, light 403
erlogen
  erstunken und erlogen 402
  lied 402
Erlös, einen Erlös erbringen
  561
erlöschen, go out [fire/light]
  271
erlügen, lie 402
ermächtigt, authorized 516
ermangeln, be lacking 389
Ermangelung, in
  Ermangelung 389
ermäßigen, reduce 569
ermessen
  judge 366
  discretion 366
  judgement 366
ermitteln
  discover 226
  investigate 359
ermöglichen, make possible
  322
ermorden, kill 380
ernähren
  feed 284
  sich ernähren 284
  support 683
Ernährung
  feeding 302
  nutrition 284, 302
Ernährungslage, nutritional
  level 302
Ernährungswissenschaft,
  dietetics 302
ernennen, appoint 49–50,
  129
Ernst
  das war mein Ernst 615
  Ernst machen 615
  ernst nehmen 615, 696
  ernster Mensch 614
  es ernst meinen 615
  im Ernst 615
  in ernstem Ton reden 615
  serious 614–16

Gefühlsregung, emotion 244
Gefühlswärme, emotional
 warmth 245
Gegebenheit, fact 273
gegen
 gegen sein 484
 nichts gegen haben 472,
 474
Gegend
 area 57
 body-part 58
Gegensatz
 im Gegensatz zu 485
 opposite 485–6
gegensätzlich, opposite 486
Gegenteil
 im Gegenteil 485
 opposite 485
gegenteilig, opposite 486
gegenüber, responsible to
 579
geheim
 geheim halten 600
 im geheimen 600
 secret 600
 streng geheim 600, 624
Geheimagent, secret agent
 600
Geheimbund, secret society
 600
geheimhalten, keep secret
 600
Geheimnis, confidence 738
gehen
 bei etwas gehen um 741
 es geht ihm gut 792
 es geht nicht 805
 es geht um/darum 175,
 362
 gehen auf 163
 gehen in 250
 gehen zu 67, 602
 gehen . . . ab 388
 go 320, 321
 gut gehen 233
 leave 321, 396
 seinen eigenen Weg gehen
 780
 vor sich gehen 476
 walk 590
 work 804, 805
 zu Fuß gehen 590
Gehirn, brain 107
gehören
 be included 351
 belong 89–90
 have proper location 89
 involve 361
Gehörsinn, [sense of] hearing
 609
Gehsteig, pavement 304
Gehweg, pavement 304

Geist
 brains 107
 den Geist erheben 548
 Mann von Geist 438
 mind 438
 spirit 438
Geistesarbeit, brain-work 107
Geistesgegenwart, presence
 of mind 438
Geisteskrankheit, mental
 illness 438
geistreich
 clever 161
 witty 309
Gelände
 area 57
 terrain 326
Geld
 Geld aufbringen 548
 Geld um sich werfen 779
Geldbetrag, sum of money 33
Geldbeutel, purse 106
Geldbörse, purse 106
Geldschein, banknote 464
Gelegenheit, Gelegenheit
 ergreifen 605
Gelegenheitsarbeit, casual
 work 137–8
gelernt (adj), skilled 394
gelingen
 der Plan ist gelungen 674
 es gelang dem Löschtrupp
 . . . 674
 es gelingt ihm nicht 275
 succeed 674
 work 805
geloben
 sich geloben 201
 swear 201
gelten
 be valid for 47–8
 gelten als/für 180
 gelten lassen 3
 include 352
geltend (adj), accepted 3
Geltungsbedürfnis, need for
 approbation 461
Gelübte, eine Gelübte ablegen
 702
Gemach, room 588
gemächlich, leisurely 165
gemein
 common 166, 168
 general 167
 low 420
 nasty 168
 vulgar 168
Gemeinde
 community 169, 170
 congregation 170
 local authority 133, 170
 parish 170

Gemeindebeamte, local
 government officer 170
gemeingefährlich, of public
 danger 167
Gemeinwohl, common good
 167
gemeinhin, commonly 167
gemeinnützig, for public
 interest 167
gemeinsam
 common 166
 united 755
Gemeinsamkeit, common
 ground 170
Gemeinschaft
 community 166, 168–70
 europäische Gemeinschaft
 169
 fellowship 170
gemeinschaftlich, common
 166
Gemeinschaftsgefühl, sense
 of community 169
Gemeinschaftsgeist,
 community spirit 169
Gemeinschaftskonto, joint
 account 166
Gemeinschaftsraum,
 common room 166
Gemeinwesen, community
 169
Gemüt
 die Gemüter 439
 feeling 244, 245, 246
 mind 438–9
gemütlich
 comfortable 165
 leisurely 165
Gemütsbewegung, emotion
 244–5
Gemütslage, emotional state
 245
Gemütsverfassung, emotional
 state 245, 439
Gemütszustand, emotional
 state 245
genau
 close 457
 genau die Wörter 763
 genau hören 408
 genau so gut 793
 just 367
 meticulous 136
 very 763–4
 well 791
genauestens, closely 457
genaugenommen, well 797
genehmigen, grant approval
 323
genieren
 make self-conscious 607
 sich genieren 243–4, 607

Idee
  auf die Idee bringen 678
  auf die Idee kommen 720
  die Idee bringen 678
  idea 344–5
identifizieren, sich identifizieren 362
Idiot, fool 304
idiotisch, stupid 304
ihretwegen, as far as [you're]
  concerned 175
Imitation, replica 190
imitieren
  copy [artefact etc.] 190
  imitate [person etc.] 191
  impersonate 191
immer
  immer wenn 797
  immer wieder 24
  so müßte es immer sein
    493
  wann auch immer 798
  wann immer 798
immerhin
  all the same 23
  at least 396
implizieren
  entail 680
  imply 679, 680
importieren, import 251
Impuls, impulse 757
impulsiv, on impulse 757
imstande
  gut imstande sein 792
  imstande sein 664
inbegriffen, included 351
inbrünstig, fervent 241
indem
  by 799
  while 799
innehalten, stop 669
Innenseite
  die Innenseite nach außen
    kehren 742
  die Innenseite nach außen
    wenden 742
innere
  ein[e] innere
    Beziehung/Verhältnis
    haben 53
  innere Regung 757
innig, fervent 241
Inserat, advertisement 16–17
Inseratenteil, advertisement
  section 16
inserieren
  advertise 17
  inserieren wegen 17
insgeheim, in secret 600
Inspektion, service [for a car]
  619
instandhalten

keep in good condition 664
  maintain 372
instandsetzen, put in good
  condition 664
Instinkthandlung 10
intelligent, clever 160
Interesse
  Interesse erregen 71
  material interest 356
  mental interest 355–6
interessieren
  interessiert an 355
  interessiert sein 240
  interest 355
  sich interessieren 240, 355
interpretieren
  interpret literature 356
  interpret music 357
inwiefern
  in what sense 611
  to what extent 270
inwieweit, to what extent
  270
inzwischen, in the mean time
  467
irgend, irgend möglich 513
irgendein, some [or other]
  652–3
irgendwann, some time [or
  other] 653
irgendwo, some place [or
  other] 653
irren, sich irren 208
Irrtum, error 443

ja
  ach ja 787
  bejahen 40
  ja auch 711
  ja eben 546
  jawohl 686
  just 369
  na ja 797
  now then 469
  nun ja 797
  well really 797
Jacke, coat 164
Jackett, jacket 164
Jahr
  date 727
  es dauerte zwei Jahre 698
  magere Jahre 714
Jahreszahl, Jahreszahlen 727
Jahreszeit, time of year 728
Jähzorn, violent temper 35
jähzornig, violent-tempered
  767
jammern, complain 171
jammerschade, es ist schade
  628
je
  each 32

je nach 217
je nachdem 217–18
jedenfalls, at any rate 550–1
jeder
  every 32
  jede Menge 33
  jeder Art 32
  jeder dritter Tag 32
  ohne jeden Grund 32
  über jeden Zweifel 32
jederzeit, at a moment's
  notice 465
jedesmal
  every time 729
  jedesmal wenn 797, 798
jedoch, however 340
jetzt
  bis jetzt 467
  jetzt oder nie 467
  jetzt, wo … 467
  now 467–9
  von jetzt an 467
Job
  job 138
  temporary position 138
jobben, do casual work 138
Junge
  boy 107
  Jungs 107
jüngst
  recent 566
  recently 565

Kadaver, carcass 192
Kamerad, fellow/-fellow 289
Kammer, room 588
Kämpf, fight 291
kämpfen
  fight 291
  oppose 484
Kampfhandlungen, action
  13
Kanone, artillery 330
Kante, edge 241
kapieren, understand 748–9
kaputt
  broken down 110
  inoperative 805
kaputtgehen, get broken 110
kaputtmachen, make 110
Karneval, carnival 304
Karton, cardboard box 105
Kästchen, box 106
Kasten, storage-box 105
Katastrophe, disaster 4–5
Katz, für die Katz 762
Kaufkraft, purchasing power
  517
kaum
  es kaum abwarten 770
  es kaum erwarten 770
Kavalier, gentleman 801

kehren
    das unterste zu oberst
        kehren 742
    die Innenseite nach außen
        kehren 742
    kehrt! 744
    linksum kehrt 743
    rechtsum kehrt 743
    sich kehren 742
    turn 741
    turn over 742
    turn round 742
kehrtmachen
    turn on one's heel 744
    turn round 744
kein
    kein einzig 644
    no amount of 33
    not a single 644
keinerlei
    in keinerlei Weise 788
    no sort of [no . . . whatso-
        ever] 381
keineswegs
    in no sense 611
    in no way 788
kennen, know 383-4, 385,
    386
kennenlernen, meet 434
Kenntnis
    in Kenntnis setzen 466
    Kenntnisse 387
    Kentnisse 752
    knowledge 386-7
    notice 467
    zur Kenntnis bringen 467
kennzeichnen
    characterize 427
    identify 426
    kennzeichnend 427
    mark 426
    registration number 470
    sich kennzeichnen 427
Kerl
    das war ein Kerl 289
    man 288-9
Kilometer, ein Weg von
    fünfzehn Kilometern 781
Kind, das einzige Kind . . .
    644
Kinderbecken, children's
    swimming-pool 508
Kindheit, behütete Kindheit
    532
Kintrolle, strenge Kontrolle
    623
Kiste, crate 105
Kittel, overall coat 164
kitzlig, sensitive 613
Klage, legal action 13
klagen
    complain 170-1

sich beklagen 170, 171
    sue 6
Kläger, plaintiff 6
Klang
    Klang seiner Stimme 654
    Klängen des Orchesters 654
    sound 653, 654
klappen
    be successful 675
    es klappt nicht 805
    work 805
klar
    clear 157-8, 748
    das ist mir klar 559
    ich bin mir darüber im
        klaren 748
    ich bin mir darüber klar
        748
    klar sein 601
    klar und deutlich 157
    klarer Wink/Hinweis 111
    klipp und klar 157
Klassenarbeit, school test 807
Klassenkamerad, schoolfel-
    low/-friend/classmate 289
Klausel, clause 129
kleben, am Buchstaben
    kleben 410
Klebestreifen, sticky tape 599
Klee, über den grünen Klee
    loben 521
kleid, becoming 681
kleiden
    dress/clothe 236-7
    suit 237, 681
kleinlich, petty 112
klemmen
    catch 142
    jam [crush] 523
klettern, climb 163-4
Klingeln, ringing 654
klipp, klipp und klar 157
klopfen
    beat clean 85
    knock 85
    pat/tap 85
kloppen, sich kloppen 292
klug, clever 159-60, 161
Knabe, boy 106
Knabenchor 106
Knabenstimme 106
Knall, report [sound] 39
knapp
    just under 370
    low 420
    mit knapper Not 453
    narrow 452-3
Knappheit, große Knappheit
    625
knicken, bend/crease 91
Knopf, einen Knopf drücken
    538

knoten, zusammen knoten
    364
kochen
    boil 188-9
    cook 188
    zum Kochen bringen 188
Koffer, suitcase 106
Kollegium, teaching staff
    661-2
Kolonie, community 170
Komfort, amenity 165
Komfortabel, well-appointed
    165
komisch
    feeling strange 671
    funny 309
    strange 309, 671
Komma, decimal point 122
kommandieren
    command 488
    order about 488
kommen
    auf den Gedanken kommen
        720
    auf die Idee kommen 720
    auf etwas kommen 720
    get to 316
    hinter . . . kommen 227
    in die Quere kommen 781
    kommen in 250
    kommen lassen 607-8
    kommen zu 475
    ums Leben kommen 379
    wie kommt es, daß 477
Kommilitone, fellow student
    290
Kommune, commune 170
Kondition
    condition of transaction
        664
    keine Kondition haben 665
    physical fitness 665
    sporting fitness 631
Konflikt, mit dem Gesetz in
    Konflikt geraten 734
Königin, Gott erhalte die
    Königin 596
Konjunktur, business 118-19
Konkurs, in Konkurs gehen
    110, 276
können
    gut leiden können 405
    know 385-6
Konservendose, tin 106
konstant, constant 182
kontinuierlich, steady 183
Kontrolle
    control 186
    unter Kontrolle halten/brin-
        gen 186
kontrollieren
    check 186, 358

mangeln
   be lacking 388
   es mangelt 388
   lack 774
   mangelnd 388
mangels
   for lack of 274
   mangels Beweis/Beweises
      260
Maniküreetui, manicure-case
   106
Mann
   alle Mann 425
   einfacher Mann 168
   husband 425
   man 288, 425
   Mann über Bord 425
   seinen Mann stehen 425
Mannequin, model 499
Mantel, overcoat 164
Mappe, folder 106
markieren
   mark 426
   Seite markieren 506
marsch, im Gleichschritt
   marsch 666
marschieren, walk 590
Maschinengewehr, machine-
   gun 330
Maschinenpistole, subma-
   chine-gun 330
Maß
   amount 33, 269
   extent 269
   in dem Maße wie 575
   in steigendem Maße 353
   in zunehmendem Maße
      352
   level 570
   measurement 269
   moderation 269
   Sinn für das rechte Maß
      576
massakrieren, kill 380
Massenherstellung, mass
   production 529
mäßig
   mild 650
   reasonable 562
mäßigen
   control 187
   sich mäßigen 187
Maßnahme 12
   scharfe Maßnahmen 624
maßregeln
   penalize 94
   reprimand 94
Maßstab, einen Maßstab
   anlegen 46
Mauer, wall 773
meckern, grouse 95
Meeresboden, sea-bed 104

Meeresgrund, sea-bed 104
mehr
   etwas mehr 651
   mehr als genug 656
   nicht mehr 414
mehren
   increase 353
   sich mehren 353
mehrere, a number of 470
mehrmals, several times 729
meiden
   avoid 71
   keep clear 159
meinen
   be of opinion 719
   believe 719–20
   es ernst meinen 615
   es gut meinen 432
   mean 431–2
   reckon 125
   refer 571
meinesgleichen, of my kind
   381
meinetwegen
   as far as I'm concerned 175
   meinetwegen keine
      Umstände 734
Meinung 69, 70
   belief 88
   deiner Meinung nach 766
   der Meinung sein 719
   der/derselben Meinung sein
      28, 483
   jemands Meinung teilen 28
   meiner Meinung nach 483,
      680
   opinion 438, 483
Meinungsverschiedenheit,
   difference of opinion 483
meist
   am meisten 445
   das meiste 446
   die meiste Zeit 446
   most 445–6
   mostly 446
meistens, mostly 446
melden
   register 37
   report 37–8
   report for press/broadcast-
      ing 38–9
   sich melden 38, 252–3
   answer advertisement 40
   answer on telephone 40
   ask leave to speak 38
   ich melde mich 38
   make situation reports 38
   'put one's hand up' [in
      school] 38
   volunteer 38, 253
Meldung, announcement 38,
   39

Menge
   a large number 470
   amount 32, 33
   die dreifache Menge 729
   diese Menge Brot 32
   eine (ganze) Menge kosten
      32
   in rauhen Mengen 470,
      713
   jede Menge 33
mengen, mix 444
Mensch
   human 425
   man 288, 425
   Menschen 502
   person 502
   woman 801
Menschengedenken, memory
   436
Menschenmenge, crowd of
   people 502
Menschenschlag, kind 381
Menschenverstand, gesunde
   Menschenverstand 610
Menschheit, mankind 425
menschlich, menschliche
   Regung 244
merken
   merken lassen 464
   notice 464
   realize 464
   sich merken 463, 579
merkwürdig, strange 671
messen, measure 269
Methode, way 784
mies
   rotten 73–4
   wicked 75
Milchstraße, Milky Way 780
mild
   delicately-flavoured 649
   lenient 650
   mildes Wetter 650
Milliarde, thousand million
   437
Million, million 437
mimosenhaft, sensitive 612
mindern, reduce 569
mindestens, at least 395
Mine, eine Mine ausbeuten
   804
mischen
   mix 443–5
   sich mischen 444–5
mißbrauchen, den Namen
   mißbrauchen 762
missen, miss 442
Mißerfolg, failure 4
Mißgeschick, mishap 4
mißglücken, fail 275–6
Mißgriff, mistake 443
mißlingen, fail 275–6

sich regen 448
Regenmantel, raincoat 164
Region, region 57
registrieren
    record 567
    record [by instrumentation]
        568
Regler, control knob 186
regnen, in Strömen regnen
    515
regulieren, control 186, 187
Regung
    emotion 244
    impulse 757
    innere Regung 757
    menschliche Regung 244
reichen 58
    last 235, 390-1
    pass [give] 317
    see through [last] 603
    sich die Hände reichen 364
    touch 733
Reichweite
    range 551-2
    reach 551
reif, die Zeit ist reif 727
Reihenfolge, order 488-9
Reim, keinen Reim machen
    610
rein
    clear 158
    Luft ist rein 158
    reinen Mund halten 640
Reinfall, failure 276
reinigen
    clean 157
    dry-clean 157
Reinigung, cleaning 157
reisen, leave 396
Reisig, sticks 514
reißen 108
    snatch 606
    tear 704-5
    tear off 536
reiten, go on horseback 321
reizen, attract 70
rekeln, sich rekeln 661
Reklame 16, 17-18
    Reklame machen für 17
Reklamesendung 18
Reklamewand 18
rennen, run 589
Rest
    little bit 582
    relic 582
    remainder 581-2
    residue 582
    Reste 581, 582
    smaller part 581
Restbestände, book remain-
    ders 582
Restbetrag, balance

[remaining sum] 33
restlich, remaining 581
restlos, complete 173
retten
    rescue 594-5
    sich retten 254
Rettungsaktion, rescue
    operation 13
Revier
    district 56
    police station 56
    policeman's beat 56
Revolver, revolver 330
rezitieren, recite 597
richten 29
    judge 365
    point 198
    seine Aufmerksamkeit
        richten auf 746
    sich richten an 30
    sich richten gegen 30
    sich richten nach 300
    turn . . . on [direct] 746
Richter, judge 365
richtig
    proper 556
    quite a . . . 545
    richtig herum 782
Richtkanonier 29
Richtschütze 29
Richtung, way 782
riechen, notice 464
rinnen, flow 590
riskieren, risk 206
Rock, coat/skirt 164
roh, rohe Gewalt 517, 767
Rolle, eine Rolle spielen 429
rollen
    roll 587
    sich rollen 587-8
rübergehen, cross 199
rücken
    auf den Leib rücken 100
    auf den Pelz rücken 101
    auf die Pelle rücken 101
    move 448-9
    move in game 450
rückgängig machen, cancel
    129, 130
Rückruf, return call
    [telephone] 126
Rucksack, rucksack 106
Rücksicht, Rücksicht nehmen
    181
rücksichtsvoll, considerate
    724-5
Rückstand, mit Zahlungen im
    Rückstand sein 729
rudern, go by rowing-boat
    321
Ruf, einen Ruf
    erhalten/bekommen 50

rufen
    call 125
    ring up/telephone 126
rügen, rebuke 94
Racheakt, act of vengeance
    11
Radau, loud noise 732
Rädelsführer, ringleader 393
Radio
    ansagen 36
    durchsagen 36
raffen, grab 606
raffgierig, grasping 606
raffiniert, clever 162
Rahmen, scope 553
ramponieren, damage 204
Rand, edge 241
Randbemerkung, annotation
    463
Rang
    note 464
    position in society 510-11
ranhalten, sich ranhalten
    342
ranken, sich ranken 164
rasch, in rascher Folge 490
rasen
    speed 705
    tear 705
Rasse, Beziehungen zwischen
    den Rassen 576
Rat, zu Rate ziehen 572
Rate
    instalment 33, 550
    rate 550
raten
    dringend raten 777
    guess 329, 330
    warn 777
rational, reasonable 562
ratsam, advisable 235
Rätsel
    puzzle 329
    riddle 329
raufen, sich raufen 292
rauh
    in rauhen Mengen 713
    rauher Winter 625
    severe 625
Raum
    room [chamber] 588
    room [space] 589
Raumfahrt, space-travel/-
    flight 589
räumlich, räumlich
    beschränkt 589
reagieren
    greet 325
    reagieren auf 42
real
    real 555
    realistic 555

schneiden
  cut 202–3
  klein schneiden 203
schnell, schnell machen 342
schocken, shock 627
schockieren, shock 627
schon
  admittedly 793
  drei Jahre schon 468
  mach schon 342
  now 468
  schon einmal 86
  schon lange 793
  schon längst 793
  schon von Anfang an 763
  schon wieder 24
  very 764
schön
  ganz schön 77, 277
  ganz schön und gut aber
    793
schonen 654, 655
  save 596
  sich schonen 655
  treat with consideration
    655
schonend, careful 137
schrauben, zusammen
  schrauben 364
Schreck, fright 307
Schrecken, fright 307
schreckhaft, timid 731
schrecklich, fearful 731–2
schreiben
  refer 571
  write to say 596
Schreibfehler, spelling
  mistake 442–3
Schritt
  action 12, 667
  auf Schritt und Tritt
    [beobachten] 666
  division in progress 667
  einen Schritt zulegen 666
  footstep [sound] 666
  legal action 13
  pace [distance] 666
  Schritt halten 666
  Schritt wechseln 666
  Schritte unternehmen 667
  step 268, 666
  way of walking 666
schrittweise, by degrees 268
Schuhkarton, shoebox 105
Schuhschachtel, shoebox
  105
Schulbildung, education 242
schuld
  cause of 143
  schuld haben 92
  schuld sein 92, 143
  Schuld geben 92–3

schulden
  Dank schulden wir 494
  owe 494
schuldig
  guilty 494
  schuldig befunden 494
  schuldig sein 494
  sich schuldig bekennen 177
  was bin ich schuldig 494
schulen, train 243
Schüler, school pupil 674
Schülerin, school pupil 674
Schulmappe, school-bag 106
Schulranzen, school satchel
  106
Schultasche, school-bag 106
schummeln, cheat 209
Schuß
  einen Schuß abgeben 633
  good condition 664
Schußwaffe, handgun 330
schütteln
  die Hand schütteln 627
  shake 625
schütten
  pour 515
  tip 515
schützen, protect 531–2
schwach, of poor achievement
  73
schwächen, weaken 788–9
schwachsinnig, stupid 304
schwanken
  lurch 586
  rock 586
  roll [boat] 586
  stagger 586
  swing 586
schweigen
  be silent 585, 640
  das Schweigen unter-
    brechen 639
  say nothing 640
  sein Schweigen brechen
    639
  silence 639–40
schweigend, silent 640, 641
schweigsam, quiet 641
Schwein, Sparschwein 106
schwenken
  links schwenkt 744
  rechts schwenkt 744
schwer
  bad 73, 74
  badly 73, 77
  das schwerste 224
  difficult 224–5
  harsh 623
  nur schwer 224
  schweren Stand haben 224
  severe 625
  violent 766–7

schwerfallen, be difficult
  224–5
schwierig, difficult 224–5
Schwierigkeit
  die Schwierigkeit liegt
    darin, daß 735
  private Schwierigkeiten
    734
  trouble 734
Schwimmbad, swimming-
  pool 508
schwindeln, lie 402
schwinden
  disappear 225
  waning 225
schwingen, schwingen . . . mit
  679
schwören
  schwören auf 201
  schwören lassen 201
  swear 201
Seele
  Leib und Seele 100
  mind 439
  soul 100
seelisch, psychological 245
segeln, go by sailing-boat 321
sehen
  flüchtig zu sehen bekom-
    men 142–3
  look 414–15
  meet 601–2
  nirgendwo zu sehen sein
    639
  notic 464
  realize 559
  regard a matter 602
  see 601
  sehen nach 603
Sehenswürdigkeit, sight 765
Sehkraft
  power of sight 519
  sight 765
sehr
  badly 77
  fairly 276–7
  much 451
  really 555
  sehr viel 451
  very 763
  very much 451
  well 791
Sehvermögen
  power of sight 519
  sight 765
seicht, shallow 298–9
sein
  be 78–82
  mehr Schein als Sein 45
seinetwegen, as far as [he's]
  concerned 175
seit, seit kurzem 565

streiken
hier wird gestreikt **673**
strike [refuse to work] **673**
streiten
quarrel **293**
sich streiten **293**
Streitkräfte
armed forces **518**
konventionelle Streitkräfte
188
Streitmacht, armed force **518**
streng
im strengsten Sinne des
Wortes **624**
severe **623–4, 625**
severely simple **624**
stern **623–4**
streng geheim **600, 624**
strenge Kälte **625**
strenge Kontrolle **623**
strenge Logik **624**
strenger Vegetarier **624**
strict **623, 624**
strenggenommen, strictly
speaking **624**
streuen
Salz in einer Wunde
streuen **660**
scatter **660**
Strich, line **407, 536**
Strickmuster, knitting
pattern **498**
strikt
strict **624**
strikte Disziplin **624**
Strom
electricity **518**
in Strömen regnen **515**
strömen
im strömendem Regen **515**
stream out **515**
Struktur, pattern **498**
Stube
die 'gute Stube' **588**
room **588**
Stück
ein starkes Stück **713**
fünfzig Pf. das/pro Stück
32
little way **782**
Student, student **674**
Studentin, student **674**
studieren
be a student **674**
study **674**
Stufe
rung/tread **268**
stage **666**
step of staircase **666**
stufenweise, by degrees **268**
Stund, von Stund an **710**
Stunde, eine stille Stunde **584**

Stundung, extension of time
729
stur, persistent **503**
stürzen
fall **278**
tear **705**
stützen
prop up **682**
sich stützen **682**
support **682–3**
stutzig, suspicious **690**
substantiate **305, 306**
Suchaktion, search operation
13
suchen
find/try to find **295**
nichts zu suchen **119**
zu suchen haben **236**
Suff, drink **238**
suggerieren, suggest **678**
Summe, amount **33**
summieren, sich summieren
14
Sünde, Sünden beichten **176**
Sündenbekenntnis,
confession [religious] **176**
Sundenbock, scapegoat **509**
Supermarkt, supermarket
303
Swimming-pool, swimming-
pool **508**
sympatisch, likeable **405**

Tadel, reproof **94**
tadellos, perfect **94**
tadeln, rebuke **93–4**
Tag
an den Tag legen **636–7**
die Tage **565**
dieser Tage **565**
erst vor ein paar Tagen **565**
Tageszeit, time of day **728**
Taktstock, baton **514**
tanken, fill up with petrol
294
Tarif
tariff **549**
über Tarif **549**
utilities charges **549**
wage-rate **549**
Tasche, bag **106**
tasten
feel for [search] **288**
sich tasten **288, 780**
Tastsinn, [sense of] touch **609**
Tat
auf frischer Tat **11**
deed **10–11**
in die Tat umsetzen **11**
Mann der Tat **11**
mit Wort und Tat **11**
Tatbestand, facts **273**

Täter, culprit **11**
tätig, tätig sein **118, 803**
tätlich, violent **767–8**
Tatort, scene of the
crime/incident **11**
Tatsache
erwiesene Tatsache **636**
fact **272**
Tatsache ist **272**
tatsächlich
actual **555–6**
in a very real sense **611**
is that so **272**
really? **556–7**
tauchen, dive **229**
taumeln, stagger **586**
tauschen, change **148–50**
täuschen
deceive **208**
sich täuschen **209**
Taxi, Stand für Taxis **510**
taxieren, assess **256**
Teich, pond **508**
Teil
der größte Teil **445–6**
ein gut Teil **632**
proportion **576**
seinen Teil tun **632**
seinen Teil zu tragen haben
632
share **632**
teilen
divide **229–30**
share **230**
sich teilen **230, 482**
teilhaben, share **230**
teilnehmen, teilnehmen an
67
Telefon
abnehmen **40**
ich gehe mal ran **40**
sich melden **40**
telefonisch, sich melden
telefonisch **40**
Telegraphenstange,
telegraph-pole **514**
Tempo
bei diesem Tempo **550**
rate **550**
Tempolimit, speed limit **550**
Termin **51**
appointed date **726**
deadline **728**
den Termin einhalten **108**
due date **728–9**
Termin haben [legal uses]
51
Terrorakt, terrorist act **11**
testen, test **740–1**
teuer
expensive **192, 193**
held in affection **193**

Wasser, mit allen Wassern
    gewaschen 162
wechselhaft, changeable 148
Wechselkurs, exchange-rate
    549
wechseln
    change 148–9, 151
    exchange 150
    replace 148
    Schritt wechseln 666
wecken
    arouse 772
    wake 771–2
weg
    away 321
    distant 229
    gone 321
Weg
    auf friedlichem Wege 783
    aus dem Weg 781
    den rechten Weg verlieren
        781
    den Weg ebnen 787
    den Weg verfehlen 781
    den Weg verpassen 781
    ein Weg von fünfzehn
        Kilometern 781
    ein weiter Weg 781
    im Weg stehen 781
    Mittel und Wege 784
    path 672, 780
    route 780–1
    seinen eigenen Weg gehen
        780
    sich einen Weg bahnen 780
    track 672
wegdrehen
    sich wegdrehen 743
    turn away 743
wegen, meinet-/seinetwegen
    175
wegfahren, leave 396
weggeben, give away 318
weggehen, leave 396
weglaufen, run away 254
wegnehmen
    steal 694–5
    take away 448, 694–5
wegschaffen, move away 448
Wegweiser, signpost 514,
    635, 639
wegziehen, leave home 397
weh
    painful 77
    weh tun 205, 496
Wehrdienst, military service
    618
wehren, sich wehren 471
Weib
    wife 801
    woman 801
weich

emotionally weak 648
soft 647–8
weiches Herz 648
weigern, sich weigern 574–5
Weihnachten
    frohe Weihnachten 320
    fröhliche Weihnachten 320
Weile, vor einer Weile 368
Weinachten, sich zu
    Weinachten wünschen 775
Weinen, zum Weinen bringen
    570
Weise
    auf diese Weise 785
    auf keine Weise 788
    die Art und Weise 784, 785
    in dieser Weise 785
    in keiner Weise 788
    in keinerlei Weise 788
    way 783, 784–6
weisen
    aus . . . weisen 635
    die Tür weisen 635
    order out of 487
    show the way 635
weit 111–12
    a long way 782
    bei weitem 782
    bei weitem nicht 457
    ein weiter Weg 781
    es weit bringen 794
    far 111
    loose (clothes) 111
    von weitem 227
    weit entfernt 111
    weit mehr als hundert 793
    weit rechts 793
    weit verbreitet 167
    well 793
    ziemlich weit 782
weitaus 782
weiter
    another 490
    bis auf weiteres 466
    especially 429
    further 184
    weiter gehen 185, 448
    wenn das so weiter geht
        550
weiterblättern, turn over
    pages 743
weitergeben, pass on 38
weitergehen, continue 184–5
weiterhin, further 184
weitermachen, continue 184
weitherzig, broadminded
    112
Weizenanbaugebiet, wheat-
    producing area 528
welcher
    any [of a named substance]
        652

some [of a named
    substance] 652
Welt, übrige Welt 581
Weltanschauung, view of the
    world 484
Weltbild, view of the world
    484
Weltmann, gentleman 801
Weltraum, [extraterrestrial]
    space 589
wenden
    bitte wenden 743
    die Innenseite nach außen
        wenden 742
    die Unterseite nach oben
        wenden 742
    sein Glück hat sich
        gewendet 746
    sich wenden 742, 744, 746
    sich wenden an 48, 55
    sich wenden gegen 746–7
    sich zur Flucht wenden 744
    turn 741, 742
    turn a page/sheet of paper
        743
    turn over 742
    turn round 743
    wann das Blatt wenden
        kann 747
wenig
    ein wenig 651
    einige wenige 290
    mindeste 395
    small amount 33
    wenige 290
    wenigste 395
wenigstens, at least 395
wenn
    as long as [provided that]
        799
    auch/sogar/selbst wenn 258
    immer wenn 797
    jedesmal wenn 797, 798
    wenn auch . . . so doch 258
    wenn . . ., dann . . . 710
    wenn . . ., so . . . 710
    whenever 797
wer, halt, wer da 667
Werbefirma, advertising
    agency 18
Werbefläche, hoarding 18
werben
    seek to gain 17
    werben für 17–18
Werbespot, radio/TV
    'commercial' 17–18
Werbung, advertising 16,
    17–18
werden
    become 745
    get 317
    grow into 327